OFFICIAL
NBA REGISTER
2006-2007 EDITION

W9-BNT-198

Editors/Official NBA Register
ZACH BODENDIECK
ROB REHEUSER

Contributing Editors/Official NBA Register
JED TAI

ON THE COVER: Dirk Nowitzki by Bob Leverone / SN

COVER DESIGN AND BOOK LAYOUT BY: Chad Painter / SN.

Certain statistical data have been selected, compiled and exclusively supplied by NBA Properties, Inc. Elias Sports Bureau, New York, is the official statistician of the NBA.

Published by the Sporting News, a division of Vulcan Sports Media. 14500 S. Outer 40, Suite 300, Chesterfield, MO 63017. Printed in the U.S.A.

ISBN: 0-89204-856-5

10 9 8 7 6 5 4 3 2 1

CONTENTS

Veteran players..**4**

This section includes veteran NBA players who appeared in at least one NBA game during the 2005-06 season or appeared on a roster as of August 28, 2006.

Promising newcomers..**264**

Head coaches..**281**

All-time great players...**308**

This section includes nonactive players who reached one or more of the following plateaus: 17,000 NBA or NBA/ABA points; 10,000 rebounds; 5,000 assists and 10,000 points; named to either the 25th, 35th or 50th NBA Anniversary All-Time Teams; NBA or ABA Most Valuable Player; four-time first-, second- or third-team All-NBA selection or All-NBA plus All-ABA or All-NBL; six NBA All-Star Games or NBA All-Defensive first-team selections; career scoring average of 23 points per game.

All-time great coaches...**446**

This section includes nonactive coaches who compiled 400 or more regular-season NBA victories.

National Basketball Association statistical leaders...**478**

EXPLANATION OF FOOTNOTES AND ABBREVIATIONS

*   Led league.

†   Tied for league lead.

‡   College freshman or junior varsity statistics; not counted toward totals.

... Statistic unavailable, unofficial or mathematically impossible to calculate.

   Statistic inapplicable.

POSITIONS: C: center. **F:** forward. **G:** guard.

STATISTICS: APG: Assists per game. **Ast.:** Assists. **Blk.:** Blocked shots. **Def.:** Defensive rebounds. **Dq.:** Disqualifications. **FGA:** Field goals attempted. **FGM:** Field goals made. **FTA:** Free throws attempted. **FTM:** Free throws made. **G:** Games. **L:** Losses. **Min.:** Minutes. **Off.:** Offensive rebounds. **Pct.:** Percentage. **PF:** Personal fouls. **PPG:** Points per game. **Pts.:** Points. **Reb.:** Rebounds. **RPG:** Rebounds per game. **Stl.:** Steals. **TO:** Turnovers. **Tot.:** Total. **W:** Wins.

LEAGUES/ORGANIZATIONS: AABA: All-America Basketball Alliance. **ABA:** American Basketball Association. **ABL:** American Basketball League. **BAA:** Basketball Association of America. **CBA:** Continental Basketball Association. **EBL:** Eastern Basketball League. **IL:** Inter-State League. **MBL:** Metropolitan Basketball League. **NAIA:** National Association of Intercollegiate Athletics. **NBA:** National Basketball Association. **NBDL:** National Basketball Developmental League. **NBL:** National Basketball League or National League. **NCAA:** National Collegiate Athletic Association. **NIT:** National Invitation Tournament. **NYSL:** New York State League. **PBLA:** Professional Basketball League of America. **WBA:** Western Basketball Association.

TEAMS: Ala.: Alabama. **Al.:** Albany. **Amw. Zaragoza:** Amway Zaragoza. **And.:** Anderson. **Ark.:** Arkansas. **Atl.:** Atlanta. **Bakers.:** Bakersfield. **Balt.:** Baltimore. **Bay St.:** Bay State. **B., Bos.:** Boston. **Buck. Beer Bolo.:** Buckler Beer Bologna. **Buff.:** Buffalo. **Cha., Char.:** Charlotte. **Ch., Chi.:** Chicago. **Chip. Panionios:** Chipita Panionios. **Cin.:** Cincinnati. **Cl., Clev.:** Cleveland. **Col.:** Columbus. **Dal., Dall.:** Dallas. **Den.:** Denver. **Det.:** Detroit. **Fargo/Moor., F./M.:** Fargo-Moorhead. **Ft. Wayne, F.W.:** Fort Wayne. **Frank. & Marsh.:** Franklin & Marshall. **George Wash.:** George Washington. **Gold. St., G.S.:** Golden State. **G.R., Gr. Rap.:** Grand Rapids. **Grupo Ifa Espa.:** Grupo Ifa Espanol's. **Hfrd.:** Hartford. **Hou.:** Houston. **Ind.:** Indiana. **K.C.:** Kansas City. **K.C./O., K.C./Omaha:** Kansas City/Omaha. **L.A.:** Los Angeles. **L.A.C., LA Clip.:** Los Angeles Clippers. **La Cr.:** La Crosse. **L.A.L., LA Lak.:** Los Angeles Lakers. **Il Mess. Roma:** Il Messaggero Roma. **Mil.:** Milwaukee. **Min., Minn.:** Minnesota. **Neptunas Klaib.:** Neptunas Klaibeda. **N.J.:** New Jersey. **N.O.:** New Orleans. **N.Y.:** New York. **N.C.:** North Carolina. **Okla. C., O.C.:** Oklahoma City. **Or., Orl.:** Orlando. **Penn.:** Pennsylvania. **Pens.:** Pensacola. **Pfizer R. Calabria:** Pfizer Reggio Calabria. **Phi., Phil.:** Philadelphia. **Phoe.:** Phoenix. **Pitt.:** Pittsburgh. **Port.:** Portland. **Quad C., Q.C.:** Quad City. **Rancho San.:** Rancho Santiago. **Rap. C., R.C.:** Rapid City. **Roch.:** Rochester. **Rock.:** Rockford. **S.A., San Ant.:** San Antonio. **Sac.:** Sacramento. **S.F., San Fran.:** San Francisco. **Sav.:** Savannah. **Sea.:** Seattle. **Shamp. C. Cantu:** Shampoo Clear Cantu. **Shb.:** Sheboygan. **Sioux F.:** Sioux Falls. **St.L.:** St. Louis. **Syr., Syrac.:** Syracuse. **Team. Fabriano:** Teamsystem Fabriano. **Tele. Brescia:** Telemarket Brescia. **Teore. Milan:** Teorematur Milan. **Top.:** Topeka. **Tri C.:** Tri-Cities. **Tul.:** Tulsa. **Va.:** Virginia. **W.:** Warren. **Wash.:** Washington. **Wash. & Jeff.:** Washington & Jefferson. **Wis., Wisc.:** Wisconsin. **Yak.:** Yakima.

BASEBALL STATISTICS: A.A.: American Association. **A:** Assists. **AB:** At-bats. **A.L.:** American League. **Avg.:** Average. **BB:** Bases on balls. **E:** Errors. **East.:** Eastern League. **ER:** Earned runs. **ERA:** Earned-run average. **G:** Games. **H:** Hits. **HR:** Home runs. **Int'l.:** International. **IP:** Innings pitched. **L:** Losses. **N.L.:** National League. **NYP:** New York-Pennsylvania. **OF:** Outfield. **Pct.:** Winning percentage. **PO:** Putouts. **Pos.:** Position. **R:** Runs. **RBI:** Runs batted in. **SB:** Stolen bases. **SO:** Strikeouts. **South.:** Southern Association. **SS:** Shortstop. **Sv.:** Saves. **W:** Wins. **1B:** First base. **2B:** Doubles or second base. **3B:** Triples or third base.

A

ABDUR-RAHIM, SHAREEF   F   KINGS

PERSONAL: Born December 11, 1976, in Marietta, Ga. ... 6-9/230. (2.06/104.3). ... Name pronounced shah-REEF ab-DOOR-Rah-heem.
HIGH SCHOOL: Wheeler (Marietta, Ga.).
COLLEGE: California.
TRANSACTIONS/CAREER NOTES: Selected after freshman season by Vancouver Grizzlies in first round (third pick overall) of 1996 NBA Draft. ... Grizzlies franchise moved to Memphis for 2001-02 season. ... Traded by Grizzlies with draft rights to G Jamaal Tinsley to Atlanta Hawks for F/C Lorenzen Wright, G Brevin Knight and draft rights to F Pau Gasol (July 19, 2001). ... Traded by Hawks with C Theo Ratliff and G Dan Dickau to Portland Trail Blazers for F Rasheed Wallace and G Wesley Person (February 9, 2004). ... Traded by Trail Blazers to New Jersey Nets for 2006 first-round pick and Nets' trade exception (August 2, 2005). ... New Jersey rescinds trade with Portland (August 9, 2005). ... Signed as free agent by Sacramento Kings (August 12, 2005).
MISCELLANEOUS: Member of gold-medal-winning U.S. Olympic team (2000). ... Memphis Grizzlies franchise all-time scoring leader (7,801 points; 1996-97 through 2000-01).

COLLEGIATE RECORD

Season Team	G	Min.	FGM	FGA	Pct.	FTM	FTA	Pct.	Reb.	Ast.	Pts.	RPG	APG	PPG
95-96—California	28	972	206	398	.518	170	249	.683	236	29	590	8.4	1.0	21.1

Three-point field goals: 1995-96, 8-for-21 (.381). Totals, 8-for-21 (.381).

NBA REGULAR-SEASON RECORD

HONORS: NBA All-Rookie first team (1997).

Season Team	G	Min.	FGM	FGA	Pct.	FTM	FTA	Pct.	Off.	Def.	Tot.	Ast.	St.	Blk.	TO	Pts.	RPG	APG	PPG
96-97—Vancouver	80	2802	550	1214	.453	387	519	.746	216	339	555	175	79	79	225	1494	6.9	2.2	18.7
97-98—Vancouver	82	2950	653	1347	.485	502	640	.784	227	354	581	213	89	76	257	1829	7.1	2.6	22.3
98-99—Vancouver	50	2021	386	893	.432	369	439	.841	114	260	374	172	69	55	*186	1152	7.5	3.4	23.0
99-00—Vancouver	82	3223	594	1277	.465	446	551	.809	218	607	825	271	89	87	249	1663	10.1	3.3	20.3
00-01—Vancouver	81	3241	604	1280	.472	443	531	.834	175	560	735	250	90	77	231	1663	9.1	3.1	20.5
01-02—Atlanta	77	2980	598	1297	.461	419	523	.801	198	498	696	239	98	81	250	1636	9.0	3.1	21.2
02-03—Atlanta	81	3087	566	1183	.478	455	541	.841	175	502	677	242	87	38	212	1608	8.4	3.0	19.9
03-04—Atlanta-Portland	85	2684	501	1054	.475	373	429	.869	189	450	639	174	68	37	184	1384	7.5	2.0	16.3
04-05—Portland	54	1867	337	670	.503	220	254	.866	123	269	392	111	49	26	117	909	7.3	2.1	16.8
05-06—Sacramento	72	1961	332	632	.525	218	278	.784	106	251	357	149	48	42	108	887	5.0	2.1	12.3
Totals	744	26816	5121	10847	.472	3832	4705	.814	1741	4090	5831	1996	766	598	2019	14225	7.8	2.7	19.1

Three-point field goals: 1996-97, 7-for-27 (.259). 1997-98, 21-for-51 (.412). 1998-99, 11-for-36 (.306). 1999-00, 29-for-96 (.302). 2000-01, 12-for-64 (.188). 2001-02, 21-for-70 (.300). 2002-03, 21-for-60 (.350). 2003-04, 9-for-34 (.265). 2004-05, 15-for-39 (.385). 2005-06, 5-for-22 (.227). Totals, 151-for-499 (.303).
Personal fouls/disqualifications: 1996-97, 199/0. 1997-98, 201/0. 1998-99, 137/1. 1999-00, 244/3. 2000-01, 238/1. 2001-02, 214/2. 2002-03, 240/2. 2003-04, 222/1. 2004-05, 150/3. 2005-06, 227/1. Totals, 2072/14.

NBA PLAYOFF RECORD

Season Team	G	Min.	FGM	FGA	Pct.	FTM	FTA	Pct.	Off.	Def.	Tot.	Ast.	St.	Blk.	TO	Pts.	RPG	APG	PPG
05-06—Sacramento	6	129	23	43	.535	9	15	.600	8	21	29	7	2	0	13	55	4.8	1.2	9.2

Three-point field goals: 2005-06, 0-for-3. Totals, 0-for-3 (.000).
Personal fouls/disqualifications: 2005-06, 27/0. Totals, 27/0.

NBA ALL-STAR GAME RECORD

Season Team	Min.	FGM	FGA	Pct.	FTM	FTA	Pct.	Off.	Def.	Tot.	Ast.	PF	Dq.	St.	Blk.	TO	Pts.
2002—Atlanta	21	4	4	1.000	0	0	...	1	5	6	0	2	0	0	0	0	9

Three-point field goals: 2002, 1-for-1 (1.000). Totals, 1-for-1 (1.000).

ACKER, ALEX   G

PERSONAL: Born January 21, 1983, in Compton, Calif. ... 6-5/185. (1.96/83.9).
HIGH SCHOOL: Cajon (San Bernardino, Calif.), then Eisenhower (Rialto, Calif.).
COLLEGE: Pepperdine.
TRANSACTIONS/CAREER NOTES: Selected after junior season by Detroit Pistons in second round (60th pick overall) of 2005 NBA Draft. ... Signed with Olympiakos of Greek League for 2006-07 season.

COLLEGIATE RECORD

Season Team	G	Min.	FGM	FGA	Pct.	FTM	FTA	Pct.	Reb.	Ast.	Pts.	RPG	APG	PPG
01-02—Pepperdine						Did Not Play - Ineligible								
02-03—Pepperdine	28	931	128	269	.476	79	97	.814	139	24	364	5.0	0.9	13.0
03-04—Pepperdine	29	940	138	307	.450	85	107	.794	155	111	393	5.3	3.8	13.6
04-05—Pepperdine	31	1152	183	407	.450	91	106	.858	201	114	516	6.5	3.7	16.6
Totals	88	3023	449	983	.457	255	310	.823	495	249	1273	5.6	2.8	14.5

Three-point field goals: 2002-03, 29-for-68 (.426). 2003-04, 32-for-87 (.368). 2004-05, 59-for-137 (.431). Totals, 120-for-292 (.411).

NBA REGULAR-SEASON RECORD

Season Team	G	Min.	FGM	FGA	Pct.	FTM	FTA	Pct.	Off.	Def.	Tot.	Ast.	St.	Blk.	TO	Pts.	RPG	APG	PPG
05-06—Detroit	5	35	4	16	.250	0	0	...	1	4	5	4	1	0	4	9	1.0	0.8	1.8

Three-point field goals: 2005-06, 1-for-5 (.200). Totals, 1-for-5 (.200).

Personal fouls/disqualifications: 2005-06, 4/0. Totals, 4/0.

NBA DEVELOPMENT LEAGUE RECORD

Season Team	G	Min.	FGM	FGA	Pct.	FTM	FTA	Pct.	Reb.	Ast.	Pts.	RPG	APG	PPG
05-06—Fayetteville....................	17	603	111	254	.437	63	77	.818	82	81	306	4.8	4.8	18.0

Three-point field goals: 2005-06, 21-for-57 (.368). Totals, 21-for-57 (.368).

ALLEN, MALIK   F   BULLS

PERSONAL: Born June 27, 1978, in Willingboro, N.J. ... 6-10/255. (2.08/115.7).
HIGH SCHOOL: Shawnee (Medford, N.J.).
COLLEGE: Villanova.
TRANSACTIONS/CAREER NOTES: Not drafted by an NBA franchise. ... Played in American Basketball Association 2000 with San Diego Wild Fire (2000-01). ... Played in International Basketball Association with Trenton Stars (2000-01). ... Signed as free agent by Miami Heat (July 20, 2001). ... Traded by Heat to Charlotte Bobcats for G Steve Smith (February 24, 2005). ... Signed as free agent by Chicago Bulls (September 2, 2005).

COLLEGIATE RECORD

Season Team	G	Min.	FGM	FGA	Pct.	FTM	FTA	Pct.	Reb.	Ast.	Pts.	RPG	APG	PPG
96-97—Villanova......................	33	357	24	51	.471	19	45	.422	96	13	67	2.9	0.4	2.0
97-98—Villanova......................	29	715	91	194	.469	58	80	.725	168	22	240	5.8	0.8	8.3
98-99—Villanova......................	32	887	136	241	.564	85	107	.794	201	31	357	6.3	1.0	11.2
99-00—Villanova......................	33	1103	184	360	.511	99	143	.692	243	32	467	7.4	1.0	14.2
Totals	127	3062	435	846	.514	261	375	.696	708	98	1131	5.6	0.8	8.9

AMERICAN BASKETBALL ASSOCIATION RECORD

Season Team	G	Min.	FGM	FGA	Pct.	FTM	FTA	Pct.	Reb.	Ast.	Pts.	RPG	APG	PPG
00-01—San Diego......................	31	1066	208	424	.491	85	112	.759	242	50	506	7.8	1.6	16.3

Three-point field goals: 2000-01, 4-for-8 (.500). Totals, 4-for-8 (.500).

INTERNATIONAL BASKETBALL LEAGUE RECORD

Season Team	G	Min.	FGM	FGA	Pct.	FTM	FTA	Pct.	Reb.	Ast.	Pts.	RPG	APG	PPG
00-01—Trenton...........................	5	93	16	32	.500	3	4	./60	24	5	37	4.8	1.0	7.4

Three-point field goals: 2000-01, 16-for-42 (.381). Totals, 16-for-42 (.381).
Personal fouls/disqualifications: 2000-01, 17/0. Totals, 17/0.

NBA REGULAR-SEASON RECORD

Season Team	G	Min.	FGM	FGA	Pct.	FTM	FTA	Pct.	Off.	Def.	Tot.	Ast.	St.	Blk.	TO	Pts.	RPG	APG	PPG
01-02—Miami	12	161	22	51	.431	8	10	.800	18	13	30	6	3	8	7	52	3.2	0.4	4.3
02-03—Miami	80	2318	335	790	.424	97	121	.802	134	291	425	54	37	78	128	767	5.3	0.7	9.6
03-04—Miami	45	616	83	198	.419	25	33	.758	42	77	119	16	12	28	27	191	2.6	0.4	4.2
04-05—Mia-Cha..........	36	519	84	177	.475	26	28	.929	40	59	99	18	9	22	18	194	2.8	0.5	5.4
05-06—Chicago	54	701	121	247	.490	23	38	.605	44	96	140	20	14	16	34	266	2.6	0.4	4.9
Totals	227	4315	645	1463	.441	179	230	.778	275	546	821	113	75	152	209	1470	3.6	0.5	6.5

Three-point field goals: 2001-02, 0-for-1. 2002-03, 0-for-4. 2005-06, 1-for-1 (1.000). Totals, 1-for-6 (.167).
Personal fouls/disqualifications: 2001-02, 16/0. 2002-03, 234/1. 2003-04, 81/0. 2004-05, 53/0. 2005-06, 92/0. Totals, 476/1.

NBA PLAYOFF RECORD

Season Team	G	Min.	FGM	FGA	Pct.	FTM	FTA	Pct.	Off.	Def.	Tot.	Ast.	St.	Blk.	TO	Pts.	RPG	APG	PPG
03-04—Miami	10	138	22	49	.449	6	9	.667	12	18	30	4	2	9	4	50	3.0	0.4	5.0
05-06—Chicago	6	116	14	30	.467	0	1	.000	5	13	18	7	2	6	10	28	3.0	1.2	4.7
Totals	16	254	36	79	.456	6	10	.600	17	31	48	11	4	15	14	78	3.0	0.7	4.9

Personal fouls/disqualifications: 2003-04, 21/0. 2005-06, 16/0. Totals, 37/0.

ALLEN, RAY   G   SUPERSONICS

PERSONAL: Born July 20, 1975, in Merced, Calif. ... 6-5/205. (1.96/93.0). ... Full name: Walter Ray Allen.
HIGH SCHOOL: Hillcrest (Dalzell, S.C.).
COLLEGE: Connecticut.
TRANSACTIONS/CAREER NOTES: Selected after junior season by Minnesota Timberwolves in first round (fifth pick overall) of 1996 NBA Draft. ... Draft rights traded by Timberwolves with future first-round draft choice to Milwaukee Bucks for draft rights to G Stephon Marbury (June 26, 1996). ... Traded by Bucks with G Kevin Ollie, G Ronald Murray and conditional first-round draft choice to Seattle SuperSonics for G Gary Payton and G Desmond Mason (February 20, 2003).
MISCELLANEOUS: Member of gold-medal-winning U.S. Olympic team (2000).

COLLEGIATE RECORD

NOTES: THE SPORTING NEWS All-America first team (1996).

Season Team	G	Min.	FGM	FGA	Pct.	FTM	FTA	Pct.	Reb.	Ast.	Pts.	RPG	APG	PPG
93-94—Connecticut	34	735	158	310	.510	80	101	.792	155	53	429	4.6	1.6	12.6
94-95—Connecticut	32	1051	255	521	.489	80	110	.727	218	75	675	6.8	2.3	21.1
95-96—Connecticut	35	1098	292	618	.472	119	147	.810	228	117	818	6.5	3.3	23.4
Totals	101	2884	705	1449	.487	279	358	.779	601	245	1922	6.0	2.4	19.0

Three-point field goals: 1993-94, 33-for-82 (.402). 1994-95, 85-for-191 (.445). 1995-96, 115-for-247 (.466). Totals, 233-for-520 (.448).

NBA REGULAR-SEASON RECORD

RECORDS: Shares single-game record for most three-point field goals made in one half—8 (April 14, 2002, vs. Charlotte). ... Shares NBA record for most seasons leading league in three-point field goals made—2.
HONORS: All-NBA third team (2001). ... NBA All-Rookie second team (1997). ... Long Distance Shootout winner (2001). ... NBA Sportsmanship Award (2003). ... All-NBA second team (2005).
NOTES: Led NBA with 229 three-point field goals made (2002). ... Led NBA with 201 three-point field goals made (2003). ... Led NBA with 269 three-point field goals made and 653 three-point field goals attempted (2005).

Season Team	G	Min.	FGM	FGA	Pct.	FTM	FTA	Pct.	Off.	Def.	Tot.	Ast.	St.	Blk.	TO	Pts.	RPG	APG	PPG
96-97—Milwaukee	82	2532	390	908	.430	205	249	.823	97	229	326	210	75	10	149	1102	4.0	2.6	13.4
97-98—Milwaukee	82	3287	563	1315	.428	342	391	.875	127	278	405	356	111	12	263	1602	4.9	4.3	19.5
98-99—Milwaukee	50	1719	303	673	.450	176	195	.903	57	155	212	178	53	7	122	856	4.2	3.6	17.1
99-00—Milwaukee	82	3070	642	1411	.455	353	398	.887	83	276	359	308	110	19	183	1809	4.4	3.8	22.1
00-01—Milwaukee	82	3129	628	1309	.480	348	392	.888	101	327	428	374	124	20	204	1806	5.2	4.6	22.0
01-02—Milwaukee	69	2525	530	1148	.462	214	245	.873	81	231	312	271	88	18	159	1503	4.5	3.9	21.8
02-03—Mil.-Seattle	76	2880	598	1363	.439	316	345	.916	94	287	381	334	103	14	198	1713	5.0	4.4	22.5
03-04—Seattle	56	2152	447	1017	.440	245	271	.904	69	217	286	268	71	11	156	1287	5.1	4.8	23.0
04-05—Seattle	78	3064	640	1494	.428	378	428	.883	79	268	347	289	84	5	171	1867	4.4	3.7	23.9
05-06—Seattle	78	3022	681	1500	.454	324	359	.903	71	261	332	286	105	16	188	1955	4.3	3.7	25.1
Totals	**735**	**27380**	**5422**	**12138**	**.447**	**2901**	**3273**	**.886**	**859**	**2529**	**3388**	**2874**	**924**	**132**	**1793**	**15500**	**4.6**	**3.9**	**21.1**

Three-point field goals: 1996-97, 117-for-298 (.393). 1997-98, 134-for-368 (.364). 1998-99, 74-for-208 (.356). 1999-00, 172-for-407 (.423). 2000-01, 202-for-467 (.433). 2001-02, 229-for-528 (.434). 2002-03, 201-for-533 (.377). 2003-04, 148-for-378 (.392). 2004-05, 209-for-556 (.376). 2005-06, 269-for-653 (.412). Totals, 1755-for-4396 (.399).
Personal fouls/disqualifications: 1996-97, 218/0. 1997-98, 244/2. 1998-99, 117/0. 1999-00, 187/1. 2000-01, 192/2. 2001-02, 157/0. 2002-03, 220/4. 2003-04, 132/2. 2004-05, 167/2. 2005-06, 151/2. Totals, 1785/15.

NBA PLAYOFF RECORD

Season Team	G	Min.	FGM	FGA	Pct.	FTM	FTA	Pct.	Off.	Def.	Tot.	Ast.	St.	Blk.	TO	Pts.	RPG	APG	PPG
98-99—Milwaukee	3	120	25	47	.532	8	13	.615	8	14	22	13	3	1	11	67	7.3	4.3	22.3
99-00—Milwaukee	5	186	40	90	.444	20	22	.909	10	23	33	18	8	0	9	110	6.6	2.6	22.0
00-01—Milwaukee	18	768	158	331	.477	79	86	.919	19	55	74	108	24	10	43	452	4.1	6.0	25.1
04-05—Seattle	11	436	102	215	.474	56	63	.889	12	35	47	43	14	4	34	291	4.3	3.9	26.5
Totals	**37**	**1510**	**325**	**683**	**.476**	**163**	**184**	**.886**	**49**	**127**	**176**	**177**	**49**	**15**	**97**	**920**	**4.8**	**4.8**	**24.9**

Three-point field goals: 1998-99, 9-for-19 (.474). 1999-00, 10-for-26 (.385). 2000-01, 57-for-119 (.479). 2004-05, 31-for-82 (.378). Totals, 107-for-246 (.435).
Personal fouls/disqualifications: 1998-99, 9/0. 1999-00, 10/0. 2000-01, 44/0. 2004-05, 22/0. Totals, 85/0.

NBA ALL-STAR GAME RECORD

NOTES: Shares record for most career three-point field goals made (11) and holds career record for most three-point field goals attempted (45).

Season Team	Min.	FGM	FGA	Pct.	FTM	FTA	Pct.	Off.	Def.	Tot.	Ast.	PF	Dq.	St.	Blk.	TO	Pts.
2000—Milwaukee............	17	4	13	.308	5	6	.833	1	0	1	2	2	0	3	1	3	14
2001—Milwaukee............	19	7	15	.467	0	0	...	1	2	3	2	0	0	1	1	1	15
2002—Milwaukee............	25	6	17	.353	0	0	...	1	2	3	5	3	0	3	0	1	15
2004—Seattle.................	23	6	13	.462	3	4	.750	2	1	3	4	2	0	1	0	3	16
2005—Seattle.................	23	6	16	.375	0	0	...	0	4	4	1	2	0	0	0	1	17
2006—Seattle.................	18	4	13	.308	0	0	...	0	2	2	1	2	0	0	0	1	8
Totals........................	**125**	**33**	**87**	**.379**	**8**	**10**	**.800**	**5**	**11**	**16**	**15**	**11**	**0**	**8**	**2**	**10**	**85**

Three-point field goals: 2000, 1-for-6 (.167). 2001, 1-for-7 (.143). 2002, 3-for-10 (.300). 2004, 1-for-4 (.250). 2005, 5-for-11 (.455). 2006, 0-for-7. Totals, 11-for-45 (.244).

ALLEN, TONY   G   CELTICS

PERSONAL: Born January 11, 1982, in Chicago. ... 6-4/213. (1.93/96.6).
HIGH SCHOOL: Crane (Chicago).
JUNIOR COLLEGE: Butler County Community (Kansas), then Wabash Valley.
COLLEGE: Oklahoma State.
TRANSACTIONS/CAREER NOTES: Selected by Boston Celtics in first round (25th pick overall) of 2004 NBA Draft.

COLLEGIATE RECORD

Season Team	G	Min.	FGM	FGA	Pct.	FTM	FTA	Pct.	Reb.	Ast.	Pts.	RPG	APG	PPG
00-01—Butler County C.C...........	32	967	207	406	.510	101	166	.608	194	105	527	6.1	3.3	16.5
01-02—Wabash Valley College ...	38	...	219	398	.550	82	129	.636	202	100	551	5.3	2.6	14.5
02-03—Oklahoma State	32	998	163	365	.447	105	152	.691	173	87	461	5.4	2.7	14.4
03-04—Oklahoma State	35	1107	204	405	.504	236	346	.682	193	109	561	5.5	3.1	16.0
Junior College Totals.............	**70**	**...**	**426**	**804**	**.530**	**183**	**295**	**.620**	**396**	**205**	**1078**	**5.7**	**2.9**	**15.4**
4-Year-College Totals	**67**	**1022**	**367**	**770**	**.477**	**341**	**498**	**.685**	**366**	**196**	**1022**	**5.5**	**2.9**	**15.3**

Three-point field goals: 2000-01, 12-for-32 (.375). 2001-02, 31-for-92 (.337). 2002-03, 30-for-76 (.395). 2003-04, 22-for-74 (.297). 4-year Totals, 52-for-150 (.347).

NBA REGULAR-SEASON RECORD

Season Team	G	Min.	FGM	FGA	Pct.	FTM	FTA	Pct.	Off.	Def.	Tot.	Ast.	St.	Blk.	TO	Pts.	RPG	APG	PPG
04-05—Boston	77	1262	184	387	.475	112	152	.737	85	136	221	64	76	24	77	492	2.9	0.8	6.4
05-06—Boston	51	978	129	274	.471	100	134	.746	32	79	111	67	51	18	67	369	2.2	1.3	7.2
Totals	**128**	**2240**	**313**	**661**	**.474**	**212**	**286**	**.741**	**117**	**215**	**332**	**131**	**127**	**42**	**144**	**861**	**2.6**	**1.0**	**6.7**

Three-point field goals: 2004-05, 12-for-31 (.387). 2005-06, 11-for-34 (.324). Totals, 23-for-65 (.354).
Personal fouls/disqualifications: 2004-05, 156/2. 2005-06, 126/0. Totals, 282/2.

NBA PLAYOFF RECORD

Season Team	G	Min.	FGM	FGA	Pct.	FTM	FTA	Pct.	REBOUNDS Off.	Def.	Tot.	Ast.	St.	Blk.	TO	Pts.	RPG	APG	PPG
04-05—Boston	7	90	8	18	.444	3	7	.429	4	8	12	2	3	2	5	19	1.7	0.3	2.7

Personal fouls/disqualifications: 2004-05, 17/1. Totals, 17/1.

ALSTON, RAFER   G   ROCKETS

PERSONAL: Born July 24, 1976, in New York. ... 6-2/173. (1.88/78.5).
HIGH SCHOOL: Cardozo (Queens, N.Y.).
JUNIOR COLLEGE: Ventura College (Calif.), then Fresno (Calif.) C.C.
COLLEGE: Fresno State.
TRANSACTIONS/CAREER NOTES: Selected after junior season by Milwaukee Bucks in second round (39th pick overall) of 1998 NBA Draft. ... Played in Continental Basketball Association with Idaho Stampede (1998-99). ... Signed as free agent by Golden State Warriors (September 6, 2002). ... Waived by Warriors (October 23, 2002). ... Played in National Basketball Development League with Mobile Revelers (2002-03). ... Signed as free agent by Toronto Raptors (January 17, 2003). ... Signed as free agent by Miami Heat (September 4, 2003). ... Signed as free agent by Raptors (July 14, 2004). ... Traded by Raptors to Houston Rockets for G Mike James (October 4, 2005).

COLLEGIATE RECORD

Season Team	G	Min.	FGM	FGA	Pct.	FTM	FTA	Pct.	Reb.	Ast.	Pts.	RPG	APG	PPG
94-95—Ventura College						Statistics unavailable.								
95-96—Fresno C.C.						Did not play.								
96-97—Fresno C.C.	32	...	197	395	.499	69	85	.812	64	275	554	2.0	8.6	17.3
97-98—Fresno State	33	1030	124	309	.401	50	66	.758	71	240	364	2.2	7.3	11.0
Junior College Totals.............	32	...	197	395	.499	69	85	.812	64	275	554	2.0	8.6	17.3
4-Year-College Totals.............	33	1030	124	309	.401	50	66	.758	71	240	364	2.2	7.3	11.0

Three-point field goals: 1996-97, 91-for-223 (.408). 1997-98, 66-for-196 (.337). Totals, 157-for-419 (.375).

CBA RECORD

Season Team	G	Min.	FGM	FGA	Pct.	FTM	FTA	Pct.	Reb.	Ast.	Pts.	RPG	APG	PPG
98-99—Idaho	17	427	45	116	.388	13	19	.684	33	106	111	1.9	6.2	6.5

Three-point field goals: 1998-99, 8-for-28 (.286). Totals, 8-for-28 (.286).
Personal fouls/disqualifications: 1998-99, 38/0. Totals, 38/0.

NBA REGULAR-SEASON RECORD

Season Team	G	Min.	FGM	FGA	Pct.	FTM	FTA	Pct.	REBOUNDS Off.	Def.	Tot.	Ast.	St.	Blk.	TO	Pts.	RPG	APG	PPG
99-00—Milwaukee	27	361	27	95	.284	3	4	.750	5	18	23	70	12	0	29	60	0.9	2.6	2.2
00-01—Milwaukee	37	288	30	84	.357	9	13	.692	4	27	31	68	13	0	20	77	0.8	1.8	2.1
01-02—Milwaukee	50	600	66	191	.346	18	29	.621	10	62	72	143	32	2	40	177	1.4	2.9	3.5
02-03—Toronto	47	1000	118	305	.416	27	54	.685	21	86	107	192	38	15	86	366	2.3	4.1	7.8
03-04—Miami	82	2581	287	764	.376	103	134	.769	26	200	226	512	114	18	188	000	0.0	0.0	10.1
04-05—Toronto	80	2717	403	974	.414	191	258	.740	42	237	279	514	118	7	170	1136	3.5	6.4	14.2
05-06—Houston	63	2431	280	738	.379	99	143	.692	36	219	255	425	101	15	157	761	4.0	6.7	12.1
Totals	386	9958	1232	3181	.387	460	635	.724	144	849	993	1784	428	57	630	3415	2.6	4.6	8.8

Three-point field goals: 1999-00, 3-for-14 (.214). 2000-01, 8-for-30 (.267). 2001-02, 27-for-71 (.380). 2002-03, 51-for-130 (.392). 2003-04, 161-for-434 (.371). 2004-05, 139-for-389 (.357). 2005-06, 102-for-312 (.327). Totals, 491-for-1380 (.356).
Personal fouls/disqualifications: 1999-00, 29/0. 2000-01, 27/0. 2001-02, 42/0. 2002-03, 120/0. 2003-04, 212/1. 2004-05, 212/0. 2005-06, 194/3. Totals, 836/4.

NBA PLAYOFF RECORD

Season Team	G	Min.	FGM	FGA	Pct.	FTM	FTA	Pct.	REBOUNDS Off.	Def.	Tot.	Ast.	St.	Blk.	TO	Pts.	RPG	APG	PPG
99-00—Milwaukee	4	16	0	3	.000	0	2	.000	0	0	0	1	0	0	1	0	0.0	0.3	0.0
00-01—Milwaukee	5	8	0	1	.000	0	0	...	0	0	0	1	0	0	2	0	0.0	0.2	0.0
03-04—Miami	13	295	29	91	.319	21	25	.840	4	25	29	22	5	1	10	91	2.2	1.7	7.0
Totals	22	319	29	95	.305	21	27	.778	4	25	29	24	5	1	13	91	1.3	1.1	4.1

Three-point field goals: 1999-00, 0-for-1. 2003-04, 12-for-52 (.231). Totals, 12-for-53 (.226).
Personal fouls/disqualifications: 2003-04, 22/0. Totals, 22/0.

NBA DEVELOPMENT LEAGUE RECORD

Season Team	G	Min.	FGM	FGA	Pct.	FTM	FTA	Pct.	Reb.	Ast.	Pts.	RPG	APG	PPG
02-03—Mobile	6	217	38	84	.452	13	17	.765	23	58	95	3.8	9.7	15.8

Three-point field goals: 2002-03, 6-for-13 (.462). Totals, 6-for-13 (.462).
Personal fouls/disqualifications: 2002-03, 17/0. Totals, 17/0.

ANDERSEN, CHRIS   F/C

PERSONAL: Born July 7, 1978, in Iola, Texas. ... 6-10/230. (2.08/104.3).
HIGH SCHOOL: Iola (Texas).
JUNIOR COLLEGE: Blinn Community College (Texas).
TRANSACTIONS/CAREER NOTES: Not drafted by an NBA franchise. ... Played in China (1999-2000). ... Played in International Basketball League with New Mexico Slam (1999-2000). ... Played in International Basketball Association with Fargo-Moorhead Beez (2000-01). ... Played in NBA Development League with Fayetteville Patriots (2001-02). ... Signed as free agent by Denver Nuggets (November 21, 2001). ... Signed as free agent by New Orleans Hornets (July 19, 2004).

COLLEGIATE RECORD

Season Team	G	Min.	FGM	FGA	Pct.	FTM	FTA	Pct.	Reb.	Ast.	Pts.	AVERAGES RPG	APG	PPG
97-98—Blinn C.C.	29	618	108	214	.505	70	133	.526	224	20	292	7.7	0.7	10.1
98-99—Blinn C.C.							Did not play.							
Totals	29	618	108	214	.505	70	133	.526	224	20	292	7.7	0.7	10.1

Three-point field goals: 1997-98, 6-for-25 (.240). Totals, 6-for-25 (.240).

INTERNATIONAL BASKETBALL LEAGUE RECORD

Season Team	G	Min.	FGM	FGA	Pct.	FTM	FTA	Pct.	Reb.	Ast.	Pts.	AVERAGES RPG	APG	PPG
99-00—New Mexico..................	10	55	4	15	.267	3	4	.750	16	1	11	1.6	0.1	1.1

NBA REGULAR-SEASON RECORD

Season Team	G	Min.	FGM	FGA	Pct.	FTM	FTA	Pct.	REBOUNDS Off.	Def.	Tot.	Ast.	St.	Blk.	TO	Pts.	AVERAGES RPG	APG	PPG
01-02—Denver	24	262	25	74	.338	22	28	.786	38	38	76	7	7	28	13	72	3.2	0.3	3.0
02-03—Denver	59	907	114	285	.400	77	140	.550	109	165	274	32	30	60	60	305	4.6	0.5	5.2
03-04—Denver	71	1029	90	203	.443	63	107	.589	89	209	298	35	34	114	48	243	4.2	0.5	3.4
04-05—New Orleans ...	67	1430	191	358	.534	131	190	.689	137	273	410	71	14	100	64	513	6.1	1.1	7.7
05-06—NO/Okla. City ..	32	570	56	98	.571	49	103	.476	61	94	155	6	8	41	26	161	4.8	0.2	5.0
Totals	253	4198	476	1018	.468	342	568	.602	434	779	1213	151	93	343	211	1294	4.8	0.6	5.1

Three-point field goals: 2001-02, 0-for-4. 2002-03, 0-for-1. 2003-04, 0-for-1. 2004-05, 0-for-3. Totals, 0-for-9 (.000).
Personal fouls/disqualifications: 2001-02, 35/0. 2002-03, 90/1. 2003-04, 119/0. 2004-05, 144/0. 2005-06, 84/0. Totals, 472/1.

NBA PLAYOFF RECORD

Season Team	G	Min.	FGM	FGA	Pct.	FTM	FTA	Pct.	REBOUNDS Off.	Def.	Tot.	Ast.	St.	Blk.	TO	Pts.	AVERAGES RPG	APG	PPG
03-04—Denver	5	34	3	9	.333	0	0	...	6	8	14	2	1	2	2	6	2.8	0.4	1.2

Personal fouls/disqualifications: 2003-04, 3/0. Totals, 3/0.

NBA DEVELOPMENT LEAGUE RECORD

Season Team	G	Min.	FGM	FGA	Pct.	FTM	FTA	Pct.	Reb.	Ast.	Pts.	AVERAGES RPG	APG	PPG
01-02—Fayetteville....................	3	42	4	9	.444	6	8	.750	11	1	14	3.7	0.3	4.7

Three-point field goals: 2001-02, 0-for-1. Totals, 0-for-1 (.000).
Personal fouls/disqualifications: 2001-02, 6/0. Totals, 6/0.

ANDERSON, ALAN — G/F — BOBCATS

PERSONAL: Born October 16, 1982, in Minneapolis. ... 6-6/220. (1.98/99.8).
HIGH SCHOOL: DeLaSalle (Minneapolis).
COLLEGE: Michigan State.
TRANSACTIONS/CAREER NOTES: Not drafted by an NBA franchise. ... Signed as free agent by Charlotte Bobcats (August 9, 2005).

COLLEGIATE RECORD

Season Team	G	Min.	FGM	FGA	Pct.	FTM	FTA	Pct.	Reb.	Ast.	Pts.	AVERAGES RPG	APG	PPG
01-02—Michigan State	31	759	67	149	.450	67	87	.770	130	51	203	4.2	1.6	6.5
02-03—Michigan State	32	883	90	179	.503	128	152	.842	117	104	312	3.7	3.3	9.8
03-04—Michigan State	30	861	78	167	.467	70	87	.805	93	96	243	3.1	3.2	8.1
04-05—Michigan State	33	877	149	268	.556	114	130	.877	184	56	437	5.6	1.7	13.2
Totals	126	3380	384	763	.503	379	456	.831	524	307	1195	4.2	2.4	9.5

Three-point field goals: 2001-02, 2-for-5 (.400). 2002-03, 4-for-13 (.308). 2003-04, 17-for-48 (.354). 2004-05, 25-for-65 (.385). Totals, 48-for-131 (.366).

NBA REGULAR-SEASON RECORD

Season Team	G	Min.	FGM	FGA	Pct.	FTM	FTA	Pct.	REBOUNDS Off.	Def.	Tot.	Ast.	St.	Blk.	TO	Pts.	AVERAGES RPG	APG	PPG
05-06—Charlotte	36	564	75	181	.414	33	41	.805	23	47	70	32	11	4	32	207	1.9	0.9	5.8

Three-point field goals: 2005-06, 24-for-58 (.414). Totals, 24-for-58 (.414).
Personal fouls/disqualifications: 2005-06, 48/0. Totals, 48/0.

ANDERSON, DEREK — G — HEAT

PERSONAL: Born July 18, 1974, in Louisville, Ky. ... 6-5/195. (1.96/88.5). ... Full name: Derek Lamont Anderson
HIGH SCHOOL: Doss (Louisville, Ky.).
COLLEGE: Ohio State, then Kentucky.
TRANSACTIONS/CAREER NOTES: Selected by Cleveland Cavaliers in first round (13th pick overall) of 1997 NBA Draft. ... Traded by Cavaliers with F Johnny Newman to Los Angeles Clippers for F Lamond Murray (August 4, 1999). ... Signed as free agent by San Antonio Spurs (August 4, 2000). ... Traded by Spurs with G Steve Kerr and 2003 second-round draft choice to Portland Trail Blazers for G Steve Smith (July 25, 2001). ... Waived by Trail Blazers (August 3, 2005). ... Signed as free agent by Houston Rockets (August 22, 2005). ... Traded by Rockets to Miami Heat for G Gerald Fitch (February 23, 2006).

COLLEGIATE RECORD

NOTES: Member of NCAA Division I championship team (1996).

Season Team	G	Min.	FGM	FGA	Pct.	FTM	FTA	Pct.	Reb.	Ast.	Pts.	AVERAGES		
												RPG	APG	PPG
92-93—Ohio State	22	587	72	158	.456	72	89	.809	72	59	225	3.3	2.7	10.2
93-94—Ohio State	22	695	108	232	.466	92	113	.814	108	107	329	4.9	4.9	15.0
94-95—Kentucky						Did not play—transfer student.								
95-96—Kentucky	36	700	117	230	.509	80	102	.784	122	88	337	3.4	2.4	9.4
96-97—Kentucky	19	481	111	226	.491	77	95	.811	77	67	337	4.1	3.5	17.7
Totals	99	2463	408	846	.482	321	399	.805	379	321	1228	3.8	3.2	12.4

Three-point field goals: 1992-93, 9-for-35 (.257). 1993-94, 21-for-62 (.339). 1995-96, 23-for-59 (.390). 1996-97, 38-for-94 (.404). Totals, 91-for-250 (.364).

Personal fouls/disqualifications: 1995-96, 82/0. Totals, 82/0.

NBA REGULAR-SEASON RECORD

HONORS: NBA All-Rookie second team (1998).

Season Team	G	Min.	FGM	FGA	Pct.	FTM	FTA	Pct.	REBOUNDS			Ast.	St.	Blk.	TO	Pts.	AVERAGES		
									Off.	Def.	Tot.						RPG	APG	PPG
97-98—Cleveland	66	1839	239	586	.408	275	315	.873	55	132	187	227	86	13	128	770	2.8	3.4	11.7
98-99—Cleveland	38	978	125	314	.398	138	165	.836	20	89	109	145	48	4	82	409	2.9	3.8	10.8
99-00—L.A. Clippers	64	2201	377	860	.438	271	309	.877	80	178	258	220	90	11	167	1080	4.0	3.4	16.9
00-01—San Antonio	82	2859	413	993	.416	342	402	.851	75	288	363	301	120	14	165	1269	4.4	3.7	15.5
01-02—Portland	70	1860	247	612	.404	178	208	.856	47	142	189	216	68	8	87	757	2.7	3.1	10.8
02-03—Portland	76	2556	355	832	.427	231	269	.859	53	211	264	325	90	16	128	1057	3.5	4.3	13.9
03-04—Portland	51	1810	230	612	.376	155	188	.824	26	156	182	228	66	3	90	694	3.6	4.5	13.6
04-05—Portland	47	1239	152	391	.389	70	87	.805	25	103	128	143	36	4	70	432	2.7	3.0	9.2
05-06—Houston-Miami	43	1047	108	303	.356	93	111	.838	21	122	143	101	23	6	54	349	3.3	2.3	8.1
Totals	537	16389	2246	5503	.408	1753	2054	.853	402	1421	1823	1906	627	79	971	6817	3.4	3.5	12.7

Three-point field goals: 1997-98, 17-for-84 (.202). 1998-99, 21-for-69 (.304). 1999-00, 55-for-178 (.309). 2000-01, 101-for-253 (.399). 2001-02, 85-for-228 (.373). 2002-03, 116-for-331 (.350). 2003-04, 79-for-259 (.305). 2004-05, 58-for-151 (.384). 2005-06, 40-for-134 (.299). Totals, 572-for-1687 (.339).

Personal fouls/disqualifications: 1997-98, 136/0. 1998-99, 73/0. 1999-00, 149/2. 2000-01, 188/1. 2001-02, 113/1. 2002-03, 141/1. 2003-04, 79/0. 2004-05, 89/0. 2005-06, 98/1. Totals, 1066/6.

NBA PLAYOFF RECORD

Season Team	G	Min.	FGM	FGA	Pct.	FTM	FTA	Pct.	REBOUNDS			Ast.	St.	Blk.	TO	Pts.	AVERAGES		
									Off.	Def.	Tot.						RPG	APG	PPG
97-98—Cleveland	4	103	10	22	.455	23	26	.885	0	9	9	11	5	1	12	43	2.3	2.8	10.8
00-01—San Antonio	7	194	16	61	.262	16	21	.762	3	16	19	17	3	0	15	54	2.7	2.4	7.7
01-02—Portland	3	76	13	30	.433	16	18	.889	3	4	7	7	2	0	6	44	2.3	2.3	14.7
02-03—Portland	2	22	1	4	.250	0	1	1.000	1	0	1	0	0	0	1	2	0.5	0.0	1.0
05-06—Miami	8	66	6	20	.300	7	8	.875	0	9	9	5	2	0	3	24	1.1	0.6	3.0
Totals	24	461	46	137	.336	62	74	.838	7	38	45	40	12	1	37	167	1.9	1.7	7.0

Three-point field goals: 2000-01, 6-for-22 (.273). 2001-02, 2-for-6 (.333). 2002-03, 0-for-1. 2005-06, 5-for-14 (.357). Totals, 13-for-43 (.302).
Personal fouls/disqualifications: 1997-98, 10/0. 2000-01, 10/0. 2001-02, 1/0. 2002-03, 1/0. 2005-06, 13/0. Totals, 35/0.

ANDERSON, SHANDON   F   HEAT

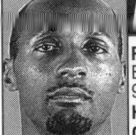

PERSONAL: Born December 31, 1973, in Atlanta. ... 6-6/210. (1.98/95.3). ... Full name: Shandon Rodriguez Anderson in Brother of Willie Anderson, guard/forward with San Antonio Spurs (1988-89 through 1994-95), Toronto Raptors (1995-96), New York Knicks (1995-96) and Miami Heat (1996-97).
HIGH SCHOOL: Crim (Atlanta).
COLLEGE: Georgia.
TRANSACTIONS/CAREER NOTES: Selected by Utah Jazz in second round (54th pick overall) of 1996 NBA Draft. ... Signed as free agent by Houston Rockets (September 29, 1999). ... Traded by Rockets to New York Knicks as part of three-team trade in which Knicks acquired G Howard Eisley from Mavericks, Mavericks acquired G Muggsy Bogues from Knicks and Rockets acquired F Glen Rice from Knicks and draft rights to G Kyle Hill from Mavericks (August 10, 2001). ... Signed as free agent by Miami Heat (November 14, 2004).
MISCELLANEOUS: Member of NBA championship team (2006).

COLLEGIATE RECORD

Season Team	G	Min.	FGM	FGA	Pct.	FTM	FTA	Pct.	Reb.	Ast.	Pts.	AVERAGES		
												RPG	APG	PPG
92-93—Georgia	29	554	99	201	.493	64	105	.610	103	44	271	3.6	1.5	9.3
93-94—Georgia	30	859	157	324	.485	93	141	.660	168	114	413	5.6	3.8	13.8
94-95—Georgia	28	827	149	315	.473	59	95	.621	145	83	371	5.2	3.0	13.3
95-96—Georgia	31	891	176	327	.538	94	143	.657	171	83	462	5.5	2.7	14.9
Totals	118	3131	581	1167	.498	310	484	.640	587	324	1517	5.0	2.7	12.9

Three-point field goals: 1992-93, 9-for-26 (.346). 1993-94, 6-for-34 (.176). 1994-95, 17-for-53 (.321). 1995-96, 16-for-52 (.308). Totals, 48-for-165 (.291).

NBA REGULAR-SEASON RECORD

Season Team	G	Min.	FGM	FGA	Pct.	FTM	FTA	Pct.	REBOUNDS			Ast.	St.	Blk.	TO	Pts.	AVERAGES		
									Off.	Def.	Tot.						RPG	APG	PPG
96-97—Utah	65	1066	147	318	.462	68	99	.687	52	127	179	49	27	8	73	386	2.8	0.8	5.9
97-98—Utah	82	1602	269	500	.538	136	185	.735	86	141	227	89	66	18	92	681	2.8	1.1	8.3
98-99—Utah	50	1072	162	363	.446	89	125	.712	49	83	132	56	39	10	66	427	2.6	1.1	8.5
99-00—Houston	82	2700	368	778	.473	194	253	.767	91	293	384	239	96	32	194	1009	4.7	2.9	12.3
00-01—Houston	82	2396	263	590	.446	138	188	.734	72	261	333	189	82	40	131	710	4.1	2.3	8.7
01-02—New York	82	1596	149	373	.399	74	107	.692	57	192	249	76	48	15	97	411	3.0	0.9	5.0
02-03—New York	82	1731	248	537	.462	139	190	.732	64	190	254	87	73	20	114	687	3.1	1.1	8.4
03-04—New York	80	1974	238	564	.422	123	161	.764	53	169	222	122	68	17	118	635	2.8	1.5	7.9
04-05—New York-Miami	66	1171	98	217	.452	54	66	.818	41	150	191	70	40	14	50	255	2.9	1.1	3.9
05-06—Miami	48	638	54	126	.429	13	18	.722	18	63	81	30	17	6	24	126	1.7	0.6	2.6
Totals	719	15946	1996	4366	.457	1028	1392	.739	583	1669	2252	1007	556	180	959	5327	3.1	1.4	7.4

Three-point field goals: 1996-97, 24-for-47 (.511). 1997-98, 7-for-32 (.219). 1998-99, 14-for-41 (.341). 1999-00, 79-for-225 (.351). 2000-01, 46-for-170 (.271). 2001-02, 39-for-141 (.277). 2002-03, 52-for-140 (.371). 2003-04, 36-for-128 (.281). 2004-05, 5-for-29 (.172). 2005-06, 5-for-19 (.263). Totals, 307-for-972 (.316).

Personal fouls/disqualifications: 1996-97, 113/0. 1997-98, 145/0. 1998-99, 89/0. 1999-00, 182/0. 2000-01, 202/0. 2001-02, 134/1. 2002-03, 177/1. 2003-04, 182/1. 2004-05, 138/1. 2005-06, 75/1. Totals, 1437/5.

NBA PLAYOFF RECORD

Season Team	G	Min.	FGM	FGA	Pct.	FTM	FTA	Pct.	Off.	Def.	Tot.	Ast.	St.	Blk.	TO	Pts.	RPG	APG	PPG
96-97—Utah	18	296	29	66	.439	20	28	.714	20	28	48	13	11	1	13	83	2.7	0.7	4.6
97-98—Utah	20	378	53	103	.515	25	37	.676	26	37	63	19	5	1	30	134	3.2	1.0	6.7
98-99—Utah	11	297	37	77	.481	24	34	.706	8	33	41	13	6	3	14	104	3.7	1.2	9.5
03-04—New York	4	117	7	27	.259	1	2	.500	5	4	9	11	4	1	8	17	2.3	2.8	4.3
04-05—Miami	8	97	3	12	.250	2	2	1.000	3	16	19	8	5	0	6	8	2.4	1.0	1.0
05-06—Miami	13	90	4	13	.308	4	6	.667	3	9	12	4	0	1	6	13	0.9	0.3	1.0
Totals	74	1275	133	298	.446	76	109	.697	65	127	192	68	31	7	77	359	2.6	0.9	4.9

Three-point field goals: 1996-97, 5-for-12 (.417). 1997-98, 3-for-11 (.273). 1998-99, 6-for-14 (.429). 2003-04, 2-for-7 (.286). 2004-05, 0-for-1. 2005-06, 1-for-3 (.333). Totals, 17-for-48 (.354).

Personal fouls/disqualifications: 1996-97, 28/0. 1997-98, 30/0. 1998-99, 34/2. 2003-04, 19/0. 2004-05, 10/0. 2005-06, 8/0. Totals, 129/2.

ANDRIUSKEVICIUS, MARTYNAS   C   BULLS

PERSONAL: Born March 12, 1986, in Kaunas, Lithuania. ... 7-2/240. (2.18/108.9).
COLLEGE: Did not attend.
TRANSACTIONS/CAREER NOTES: Played in Lithuania (2004-05). ... Selected by Orlando Magic in second round (44th pick overall) of 2005 NBA Draft. ... Draft rights traded by Magic to Cleveland Cavaliers for 2006 second-round pick and future considerations (June 28, 2005). ... Traded by Cavaliers to Chicago Bulls for G Eddie Basden (August 18, 2006).

LITHUANIAN LEAGUE RECORD

Season Team	G	Min.	FGM	FGA	Pct.	FTM	FTA	Pct.	Reb.	Ast.	Pts.	RPG	APG	PPG
04-05—Zalgiris Kaunas	21	202	30	60	.500	29	46	.630	53	4	93	2.5	0.2	4.4

Three-point field goals: 2004-05, 4-for-8 (.500). Totals, 4-for-8 (.500).

NBA DEVELOPMENT LEAGUE RECORD

Season Team	G	Min.	FGM	FGA	Pct.	FTM	FTA	Pct.	Reb.	Ast.	Pts.	RPG	APG	PPG
05-06—Arkansas	15	286	37	74	.500	30	45	.667	63	7	105	4.2	0.5	7.0

Three-point field goals: 2005-06, 1-for-9 (.111).

NBA REGULAR-SEASON RECORD

Season Team	G	Min.	FGM	FGA	Pct.	FTM	FTA	Pct.	Off.	Def.	Tot.	Ast.	St.	Blk.	TO	Pts.	RPG	APG	PPG
05-06—Cleveland	6	9	0	1	.000	0	0	...	1	3	4	0	2	0	0	0	0.7	0.0	0.0

Personal fouls/disqualifications: 2005-06, 1/0. Totals, 1/0.

ANTHONY, CARMELO   F   NUGGETS

PERSONAL: Born May 29, 1984, in New York, N.Y. ... 6-8/220. (2.03/99.8). ... Full name: Carmelo K. Anthony
HIGH SCHOOL: Towson Catholic (Towson, Md.), then Oak Hill Academy (Mouth of Wilson, Va.).
COLLEGE: Syracuse.
TRANSACTIONS/CAREER NOTES: Selected after freshman season by Denver Nuggets in first round (third pick overall) of 2003 NBA Draft.
MISCELLANEOUS: Member of bronze-medal-winning U.S. Olympic Team (2004).

COLLEGIATE RECORD

NOTES: Member of NCAA Division I championship team (2003). ... The SPORTING NEWS All-America first team (2003). ... The SPORTING NEWS Freshman of the Year (2003). ... NCAA Division I Tournament Most Outstanding Player (2003).

Season Team	G	Min.	FGM	FGA	Pct.	FTM	FTA	Pct.	Reb.	Ast.	Pts.	RPG	APG	PPG
02-03—Syracuse	35	1274	277	612	.453	168	238	.706	349	77	778	10.0	2.2	22.2

Three-point field goals: 2002-03, 56-for-166 (.337). Totals, 56-for-166 (.337).

NBA REGULAR-SEASON RECORD

HONORS: NBA All-Rookie first team (2004). ... All-NBA third team (2006).

Season Team	G	Min.	FGM	FGA	Pct.	FTM	FTA	Pct.	Off.	Def.	Tot.	Ast.	St.	Blk.	TO	Pts.	RPG	APG	PPG
03-04—Denver	82	2995	624	1465	.426	408	525	.777	183	315	498	227	97	41	247	1725	6.1	2.8	21.0
04-05—Denver	75	2608	530	1230	.431	456	573	.796	141	285	426	194	68	30	224	1558	5.7	2.6	20.8
05-06—Denver	80	2941	756	1572	.481	573	709	.808	122	272	394	216	88	42	218	2122	4.9	2.7	26.5
Totals	237	8544	1910	4267	.448	1437	1807	.795	446	872	1318	637	253	113	689	5405	5.6	2.7	22.8

Three-point field goals: 2003-04, 69-for-214 (.322). 2004-05, 42-for-158 (.266). 2005-06, 37-for-152 (.243). Totals, 148-for-524 (.282).
Personal fouls/disqualifications: 2003-04, 225/1. 2004-05, 229/1. 2005-06, 229/3. Totals, 683/5.

NBA PLAYOFF RECORD

Season Team	G	Min.	FGM	FGA	Pct.	FTM	FTA	Pct.	Off.	Def.	Tot.	Ast.	St.	Blk.	TO	Pts.	RPG	APG	PPG
03-04—Denver	4	143	21	64	.328	16	20	.800	7	26	33	11	5	0	17	60	8.3	2.8	15.0
04-05—Denver	5	180	35	83	.422	26	32	.813	14	13	27	10	3	1	13	96	5.4	2.0	19.2
05-06—Denver	5	193	33	99	.333	39	52	.750	12	21	33	14	4	1	15	105	6.6	2.8	21.0
Totals	14	516	89	246	.362	81	104	.779	33	60	93	35	12	2	45	261	6.6	2.5	18.6

Three-point field goals: 2003-04, 2-for-11 (.182). 2004-05, 0-for-1. 2005-06, 0-for-4. Totals, 2-for-16 (.125).
Personal fouls/disqualifications: 2003-04, 11/1. 2004-05, 20/0. 2005-06, 20/1. Totals, 51/2.

ARAUJO, RAFAEL　　　　　C　　　　　JAZZ

PERSONAL: Born August 12, 1980, in Curitiba, Brazil. ... 6-11/290. (2.11/131.5). ... Full name: Rafael Paulo Araujo
HIGH SCHOOL: Padre Anacleto (Sau Paulo, Brazil).
JUNIOR COLLEGE: Arizona Western.
COLLEGE: Brigham Young.
TRANSACTIONS/CAREER NOTES: Selected by Toronto Raptors in first round (eighth pick overall) of 2004 NBA Draft. ... Traded by Raptors to Utah Jazz for F Kris Humphries and F Robert Whaley (June 8, 2006).

COLLEGIATE RECORD

Season Team	G	Min.	FGM	FGA	Pct.	FTM	FTA	Pct.	Reb.	Ast.	Pts.	RPG	APG	PPG
00-01—Arizona Western College	32	624	150	232	.647	84	143	.587	269	22	306	8.4	0.7	12.1
01-02—Arizona Western College	31	697	220	386	.570	101	149	.678	331	29	555	10.7	0.9	17.9
02-03—Brigham Young	32	802	155	278	.558	70	109	.642	286	38	383	8.9	1.2	12.0
03-04—Brigham Young	30	895	211	368	.573	122	169	.722	303	37	552	10.1	1.2	18.4
Junior College Totals	63	1321	370	618	.599	185	292	.634	600	51	941	9.5	0.8	14.9
4-Year-College Totals	62	1697	366	646	.567	192	278	.691	589	75	935	9.5	1.2	15.1

Three-point field goals: 2000-01, 2-for-5 (.400). 2001-02, 14-for-49 (.286). 2002-03, 3-for-11 (.273). 2003-04, 8-for-30 (.267). Totals, 27-for-95 (.284).

NBA REGULAR-SEASON RECORD

									REBOUNDS							AVERAGES		
Season Team	G	Min.	FGM	FGA	Pct.	FTM	FTA	Pct.	Off.	Def.	Tot.	Ast.	St.	Blk.	TO	Pts.	RPG	APG	PPG
04-05—Toronto	59	736	76	175	.434	43	55	.782	59	126	185	16	21	8	52	196	3.1	0.3	3.3
05-06—Toronto	52	601	53	145	.366	15	28	.536	43	101	144	15	24	6	42	121	2.8	0.3	2.3
Totals	111	1337	129	320	.403	58	83	.699	102	227	329	31	45	14	94	317	3.0	0.3	2.9

Three-point field goals: 2004-05, 1-for-3 (.333). 2005-06, 0-for-1. Totals, 1-for-4 (.250).
Personal fouls/disqualifications: 2004-05, 157/0. 2005-06, 104/0. Totals, 261/0.

ARENAS, GILBERT　　　　　G　　　　　WIZARDS

PERSONAL: Born January 6, 1982, in Los Angeles. ... 6-3/191. (1.91/86.6). ... Full name: Gilbert Jay Arenas
HIGH SCHOOL: Grant (Van Nuys, Calif.).
COLLEGE: Arizona.
TRANSACTIONS/CAREER NOTES: Selected after sophomore season by Golden State Warriors in second round (31st pick overall) of 2001 NBA Draft. ... Signed as free agent by Washington Wizards (August 8, 2003).

COLLEGIATE RECORD

Season Team	G	Min.	FGM	FGA	Pct.	FTM	FTA	Pct.	Reb.	Ast.	Pts.	RPG	APG	PPG
99-00—Arizona	34	1093	187	410	.456	111	148	.750	138	71	523	4.1	2.1	15.4
00-01—Arizona	36	1044	208	434	.479	97	134	.724	131	84	502	3.6	2.3	16.1
Totals	70	2137	395	847	.466	208	282	.738	269	155	1105	3.8	2.2	15.8

Three-point field goals: 1999-00, 38-for-130 (.292). 2000-01, 69-for-166 (.416). Totals, 107-for-296 (.361).
Personal fouls/disqualifications: 1999-00, 83/0. 2000-01, 82/0. Totals, 165/0.

NBA REGULAR-SEASON RECORD

HONORS: NBA Most Improved Player award (2003). ... All-NBA third team (2005, 2006).

									REBOUNDS							AVERAGES		
Season Team	G	Min.	FGM	FGA	Pct.	FTM	FTA	Pct.	Off.	Def.	Tot.	Ast.	St.	Blk.	TO	Pts.	RPG	APG	PPG
01-02—Golden State	47	1155	174	384	.453	124	160	.775	41	91	132	174	69	11	97	511	2.8	3.7	10.9
02-03—Golden State	82	2866	509	1180	.431	370	468	.791	97	289	386	514	124	17	290	1497	4.7	6.3	18.3
03-04—Washington	55	2066	358	914	.392	237	317	.748	55	199	254	275	103	12	226	1078	4.6	5.0	19.6
04-05—Washington	80	3274	655	1523	.431	521	640	.814	83	295	378	411	139	23	242	2038	4.7	5.1	25.5
05-06—Washington	80	3384	746	1668	.447	655	799	.820	59	221	280	484	161	25	*297	2346	3.5	6.1	29.3
Totals	344	12745	2443	5669	.431	1907	2384	.800	335	1095	1430	1858	596	88	1152	7470	4.2	5.4	21.7

Three-point field goals: 2001-02, 39-for-113 (.345). 2002-03, 109-for-313 (.348). 2003-04, 125-for-333 (.375). 2004-05, 205-for-562 (.365). 2005-06, 199-for-540 (.369). Totals, 677-for-1861 (.364).
Personal fouls/disqualifications: 2001-02, 115/3. 2002-03, 260/3. 2003-04, 176/2. 2004-05, 245/1. 2005-06, 286/4. Totals, 1082/13.

NBA PLAYOFF RECORD

									REBOUNDS							AVERAGES		
Season Team	G	Min.	FGM	FGA	Pct.	FTM	FTA	Pct.	Off.	Def.	Tot.	Ast.	St.	Blk.	TO	Pts.	RPG	APG	PPG
04-05—Washington	10	450	73	194	.376	72	94	.766	8	44	52	62	21	6	39	236	5.2	6.2	23.6
05-06—Washington	6	284	65	140	.464	54	70	.771	7	26	33	32	13	4	20	204	5.5	5.3	34.0
Totals	16	734	138	334	.413	126	164	.768	15	70	85	94	34	10	59	440	5.3	5.9	27.5

Three-point field goals: 2004-05, 18-for-77 (.234). 2005-06, 20-for-46 (.435). Totals, 38-for-123 (.309).
Personal fouls/disqualifications: 2004-05, 34/1. 2005-06, 21/1. Totals, 55/2.

NBA ALL-STAR GAME RECORD

								REBOUNDS								
Season Team	Min.	FGM	FGA	Pct.	FTM	FTA	Pct.	Off.	Def.	Tot.	Ast.	PF	Dq.	St.	Blk.	TO	Pts.
2005—Washington	15	3	11	.273	0	0	...	1	1	2	2	1	0	0	0	0	7
2006—Washington	10	0	4	.000	1	2	.500	0	0	0	1	1	0	1	0	1	1
Totals	25	3	15	.200	1	2	.500	1	1	2	3	2	0	1	0	1	8

Three-point field goals: 2005, 1-for-3 (.333). 2006, 0-for-2. Totals, 1-for-5 (.200).

ARIZA, TREVOR F MAGIC

PERSONAL: Born June 30, 1985, in Miami, Fla. ... 6-7/194. (2.01/88.0). ... Full name: Trevor Anthony Ariza
HIGH SCHOOL: Westchester (Los Angeles).
COLLEGE: UCLA.
TRANSACTIONS/CAREER NOTES: Selected after freshman season by New York Knicks in second round (43rd pick overall) of 2004 NBA Draft. ... Traded by Knicks with G/F Anfernee Hardaway to Orlando Magic for G Steve Francis (February 22, 2006).

COLLEGIATE RECORD

Season Team	G	Min.	FGM	FGA	Pct.	FTM	FTA	Pct.	Reb.	Ast.	Pts.	RPG	APG	PPG
03-04—UCLA	25	789	107	251	.426	57	113	.504	162	52	289	6.5	2.1	11.6

Three-point field goals: 2003-04, 18-for-76 (.237). Totals, 18-for-76 (.237).

NBA REGULAR-SEASON RECORD

Season Team	G	Min.	FGM	FGA	Pct.	FTM	FTA	Pct.	Off.	Def.	Tot.	Ast.	St.	Blk.	TO	Pts.	RPG	APG	PPG
04-05—New York	80	1382	172	389	.442	121	174	.695	89	153	242	85	70	18	73	468	3.0	1.1	5.9
05-06—N.Y.-Orlando	57	999	93	226	.412	77	127	.606	78	140	218	61	57	11	62	264	3.8	1.1	4.6
Totals	137	2381	265	615	.431	198	301	.658	167	293	460	146	127	29	135	732	3.4	1.1	5.3

Three-point field goals: 2004-05, 3-for-13 (.231). 2005-06, 1-for-5 (.200). Totals, 4-for-18 (.222).
Personal fouls/disqualifications: 2004-05, 150/0. 2005-06, 100/1. Totals, 250/1.

ARMSTRONG, DARRELL G PACERS

PERSONAL: Born June 22, 1968, in Gastonia, N.C. ... 6-1/180. (1.85/81.6).
HIGH SCHOOL: Ashbrook (Gastonia, N.C.).
COLLEGE: Fayetteville State.
TRANSACTIONS/CAREER NOTES: Not drafted by an NBA franchise. ... Played in Global Basketball Association with South Georgia (1991-93). ... Played in United States Basketball League with Atlanta Trojans (1992-94). ... Played in Continental Basketball Association with Capital Region Pontiacs (1992-93). ... Played in Cyprus (1993-94). ... Signed as free agent by Orlando Magic (April 8, 1995). ... Signed as free agent by New Orleans Hornets (July 29, 2003) ... Traded by Hornets to Dallas Mavericks for G Dan Dickau and a second-round draft choice (December 3, 2004). ... Traded by Mavericks with G/F Rawle Marshall and F Josh Powell to Indiana Pacers for G Anthony Johnson (July 24, 2006).

COLLEGIATE RECORD

Season Team	G	Min.	FGM	FGA	Pct.	FTM	FTA	Pct.	Reb.	Ast.	Pts.	RPG	APG	PPG
87-88—Fayetteville State							Did not play.							
88-89—Fayetteville State	27	662	131	255	.514	93	116	.802	80	58	369	3.0	2.1	13.7
89-90—Fayetteville State	27	800	125	235	.532	83	106	.783	140	125	350	5.2	4.6	13.0
90-91—Fayetteville State	24	643	117	233	.502	115	152	.757	86	113	393	3.6	4.7	16.4
Totals	78	2105	373	723	.516	291	374	.778	306	296	1112	3.9	3.8	14.3

Three-point field goals: 1988-89, 14-for-40 (.350). 1989-90, 17-for-40 (.425). 1990-91, 44-for-107 (.411). Totals, 75-for-187 (.401).

CBA RECORD

Season Team	G	Min.	FGM	FGA	Pct.	FTM	FTA	Pct.	Reb.	Ast.	Pts.	RPG	APG	PPG
92-93—Capital Region	2	13	1	3	.333	0	0	...	1	1	2	0.5	0.5	1.0

Three-point field goals: 1992-93, 0-for-2. Totals, 0-for-2 (.000).

NBA REGULAR-SEASON RECORD

HONORS: NBA Sixth Man Award (1999). ... NBA Most Improved Player (1999).

Season Team	G	Min.	FGM	FGA	Pct.	FTM	FTA	Pct.	Off.	Def.	Tot.	Ast.	St.	Blk.	TO	Pts.	RPG	APG	PPG
94-95—Orlando	3	8	3	8	.375	2	2	1.000	1	0	1	3	1	0	1	10	0.3	1.0	3.3
95-96—Orlando	13	41	16	32	.500	4	4	1.000	0	2	2	5	6	0	6	42	0.2	0.4	3.2
96-97—Orlando	67	1010	132	345	.383	92	106	.868	35	41	76	175	61	9	99	411	1.1	2.6	6.1
97-98—Orlando	48	1236	156	380	.411	105	123	.854	65	94	159	236	58	5	112	442	3.3	4.9	9.2
98-99—Orlando	50	1502	230	522	.441	161	178	.904	53	127	180	335	108	4	158	690	3.6	6.7	13.8
99-00—Orlando	82	2590	484	1119	.433	225	247	.911	65	205	270	501	169	9	248	1330	3.3	6.1	16.2
00-01—Orlando	75	2767	413	1002	.412	220	249	.884	94	249	343	524	135	13	200	1189	4.6	7.0	15.9
01-02—Orlando	82	2730	347	828	.419	182	205	.888	83	236	319	453	157	10	175	1015	3.9	5.5	12.4
02-03—Orlando	82	2350	263	643	.409	165	188	.878	91	204	295	323	135	13	160	769	3.6	3.9	9.4
03-04—New Orleans	79	2247	291	736	.395	123	144	.854	63	163	226	311	133	16	155	840	2.9	3.9	10.6
04-05—N.O.-Dallas	66	988	89	277	.321	58	68	.853	35	80	115	178	45	8	67	264	1.7	2.7	4.0
05-06—Dallas	63	622	43	128	.336	33	42	.786	18	63	81	86	27	3	58	130	1.3	1.4	2.1
Totals	709	18091	2467	6020	.410	1370	1556	.880	603	1464	2067	3130	1035	90	1439	7132	2.9	4.4	10.1

Three-point field goals: 1994-95, 2-for-6 (.333). 1995-96, 6-for-12 (.500). 1996-97, 55-for-181 (.304). 1997-98, 25-for-68 (.368). 1998-99, 69-for-189 (.365). 1999-00, 137-for-403 (.340). 2000-01, 143-for-403 (.355). 2001-02, 139-for-398 (.349). 2002-03, 78-for-232 (.336). 2003-04, 135-for-429 (.315). 2004-05, 28-for-111 (.252). 2005-06, 11-for-48 (.229). Totals, 828-for-2480 (.334).
Personal fouls/disqualifications: 1994-95, 3/0. 1995-96, 4/0. 1996-97, 114/1. 1997-98, 96/1. 1998-99, 90/0. 1999-00, 137/0. 2000-01, 155/2. 2001-02, 166/2. 2002-03, 167/1. 2003-04, 148/1. 2004-05, 92/6. 2005-06, 71/0. Totals, 1243/10.

NBA PLAYOFF RECORD

Season Team	G	Min.	FGM	FGA	Pct.	FTM	FTA	Pct.	Off.	Def.	Tot.	Ast.	St.	Blk.	TO	Pts.	RPG	APG	PPG
96-97—Orlando	5	143	20	42	.476	11	13	.846	3	18	21	17	8	1	7	57	4.2	3.4	11.4
98-99—Orlando	4	163	17	46	.370	16	16	1.000	6	14	20	25	9	0	25	59	5.0	6.3	14.8

Season Team	G	Min.	FGM	FGA	Pct.	FTM	FTA	Pct.	Off.	Def.	Tot.	Ast.	St.	Blk.	TO	Pts.	RPG	APG	PPG
00-01—Orlando............	4	167	17	45	.378	12	13	.923	5	17	22	19	8	2	11	53	5.5	4.8	13.3
01-02—Orlando............	4	158	20	42	.476	17	21	.810	3	8	11	13	5	0	7	61	2.8	3.3	15.3
02-03—Orlando............	7	226	20	44	.455	20	22	.909	7	10	17	26	6	0	17	66	2.4	3.7	9.4
03-04—New Orleans ...	7	150	8	34	.235	3	3	1.000	6	9	15	16	6	0	13	24	2.1	2.3	3.4
04-05—Dallas.............	9	66	8	16	.500	0	0	...	3	1	4	9	3	2	2	18	0.4	1.0	2.0
05-06—Dallas.............	11	47	3	15	.200	2	2	1.000	1	6	7	2	3	1	1	8	0.6	0.2	0.7
Totals	51	1120	113	284	.398	81	90	.900	34	83	117	127	48	6	83	346	2.3	2.5	6.8

Three-point field goals: 1996-97, 6-for-18 (.333). 1998-99, 9-for-24 (.375). 2000-01, 7-for-19 (.368). 2001-02, 4-for-17 (.235). 2002-03, 6-for-18 (.333). 2003-04, 5-for-25 (.200). 2004-05, 2-for-8 (.250). 2005-06, 0-for-7. Totals, 39-for-136 (.287).

Personal fouls/disqualifications: 1996-97, 6/0. 1998-99, 16/1. 2000-01, 10/0. 2001-02, 14/0. 2002-03, 22/0. 2003-04, 10/0. 2004-05, 9/0. 2005-06, 9/0. Totals, 96/1.

SPANISH LEAGUE RECORD

Season Team	G	Min.	FGM	FGA	Pct.	FTM	FTA	Pct.	Reb.	Ast.	Pts.	RPG	APG	PPG
94-95—Coren Orense	38	1481	309	631	.490	176	293	.601	170	94	936	4.5	2.5	24.6

Three-point field goals: 1994-95, 142-for-338 (.420). Totals, 142-for-338 (.420).

Personal fouls/disqualifications: 1994-95, 99/0. Totals, 99/0.

ARROYO, CARLOS　　　　　G　　　　　MAGIC

PERSONAL: Born July 30, 1979, in Fajardo, Puerto Rico. ... 6-2/202. (1.88/91.6).
HIGH SCHOOL: Brookwood (Thomasville, Ga.), then Fajardo (Puerto Rico).
COLLEGE: Florida International.
TRANSACTIONS/CAREER NOTES: Not drafted by an NBA franchise. ... Played in Spain (2001-02). ... Signed as free agent by Toronto Raptors (September 28, 2001). ... Waived by Raptors (January 8, 2002). ... Signed by Denver Nuggets to 10-day contract (March 7, 2002). ... Signed by Nuggets for remainder of season (March 26, 2002). ... Signed as free agent by Utah Jazz (September 10, 2002). ... Traded by Jazz to Detroit Pistons for C Elden Campbell and a future first-round draft choice (January 21, 2005). ... Traded by Pistons with F/C Darko Milicic to Orlando Magic for C Kelvin Cato and a future first-round draft choice (February 15, 2006).
MISCELLANEOUS: Member of Puerto Rican Olympic Team (2004).

COLLEGIATE RECORD

Season Team	G	Min.	FGM	FGA	Pct.	FTM	FTA	Pct.	Reb.	Ast.	Pts.	RPG	APG	PPG
97-98—Florida International	29	773	128	276	.464	56	92	.609	87	135	347	3.0	4.7	12.0
98-99—Florida International	20	596	83	190	.437	50	72	.694	57	93	249	2.9	4.7	12.5
99-00—Florida International	22	792	136	299	.455	63	87	.724	57	114	389	2.6	5.2	17.7
00-01—Florida International	29	1113	215	499	.431	134	180	.744	100	117	616	3.4	4.0	21.2
Totals	100	3274	562	1264	.445	303	431	.703	301	459	1601	3.0	4.6	16.0

Three-point field goals: 1997-98, 35-for-94 (.372). 1998-99, 33-for-88 (.375). 1999-00, 63-for-87 (.724). 2000-01, 52-for-176 (.295). Totals, 183-for-445 (.411).

NBA REGULAR-SEASON RECORD

Season Team	G	Min.	FGM	FGA	Pct.	FTM	FTA	Pct.	Off.	Def.	Tot.	Ast.	St.	Blk.	TO	Pts.	RPG	APG	PPG
01-02—Tor.-Denver	37	371	49	111	.441	13	18	.722	12	28	40	70	11	1	23	111	1.1	1.9	3.0
02-03—Utah	44	287	50	109	.459	18	22	.818	11	15	26	53	12	1	30	121	0.6	1.2	2.8
03-04—Utah	71	2008	339	768	.441	181	225	.804	41	144	185	355	63	5	156	897	2.6	5.0	12.6
04-05—Utah-Detroit....	70	1448	167	429	.389	119	149	.799	26	78	104	280	44	4	107	461	1.5	4.0	6.6
05-06—Det.-Orlando ...	77	1194	168	378	.444	106	137	.774	33	97	130	232	38	4	83	449	1.7	3.0	5.8
Totals	299	5308	773	1795	.431	437	551	.793	123	362	485	990	168	15	399	2039	1.6	3.3	6.8

Three-point field goals: 2001-02, 0-for-2. 2002-03, 3-for-7 (.429). 2003-04, 38-for-117 (.325). 2004-05, 8-for-30 (.267). 2005-06, 7-for-20 (.350). Totals, 56-for-176 (.318).

Personal fouls/disqualifications: 2001-02, 30/0. 2002-03, 28/0. 2003-04, 165/0. 2004-05, 143/0. 2005-06, 119/1. Totals, 485/1.

NBA PLAYOFF RECORD

Season Team	G	Min.	FGM	FGA	Pct.	FTM	FTA	Pct.	Off.	Def.	Tot.	Ast.	St.	Blk.	TO	Pts.	RPG	APG	PPG
02-03—Utah	3	27	3	9	.333	3	4	.750	2	0	2	5	0	0	0	9	0.7	1.7	3.0
04-05—Detroit	19	150	16	45	.356	8	12	.667	1	9	10	39	4	2	10	40	0.5	2.1	2.1
Totals	22	177	19	54	.352	11	16	.688	3	9	12	44	4	2	10	49	0.5	2.0	2.2

Three-point field goals: 2004-05, 0-for-1. Totals, 0-for-1 (.000).

Personal fouls/disqualifications: 2002-03, 2/0. 2004-05, 19/0. Totals, 21/0.

SPANISH LEAGUE RECORD

Season Team	G	Min.	FGM	FGA	Pct.	FTM	FTA	Pct.	Reb.	Ast.	Pts.	RPG	APG	PPG
01-02—Tau Ceramica................	4	32	3	9	.333	10	11	.909	2	4	17	0.5	1.0	4.3

Three-point field goals: 2001-02, 1-for-3 (.333). Totals, 1-for-3 (.333).

ARTEST, RON　　　　　G/F　　　　　KINGS

PERSONAL: Born November 13, 1979, in Queensbridge, N.Y. ... 6-7/246. (2.01/111.6). ... Full name: Ronald William Artest
HIGH SCHOOL: La Salle Academy (New York, N.Y.).
COLLEGE: St. John's.
TRANSACTIONS/CAREER NOTES: Selected after sophomore season by Chicago Bulls in first round (16th pick overall) of 1999 NBA Draft. ... Traded by Bulls with C Brad Miller, G Ron Mercer and G Kevin Ollie to Indiana Pacers for G Jalen Rose,

G Travis Best, G Norman Richardson and conditional second-round draft choice (February 19, 2002). ... Traded by Pacers to Sacramento Kings for F/G Peja Stojakovic (January 25, 2006).

COLLEGIATE RECORD

Season Team	G	Min.	FGM	FGA	Pct.	FTM	FTA	Pct.	Reb.	Ast.	Pts.	RPG	APG	PPG
97-98—St. John's	32	870	139	335	.415	60	114	.526	201	62	372	6.3	1.9	11.6
98-99—St. John's	37	1265	196	418	.469	85	132	.644	232	156	535	6.3	4.2	14.5
Totals	69	2135	335	753	.445	145	246	.589	433	218	907	6.3	3.2	13.1

Three-point field goals: 1997-98, 34-for-104 (.327). 1998-99, 58-for-155 (.374). Totals, 92-for-259 (.355).

NBA REGULAR-SEASON RECORD

HONORS: NBA Defensive Player of the Year (2004). ... All-NBA third team (2004). ... NBA All-Defensive first team (2004 and 2006). ... NBA All-Defensive second team (2003). ... NBA All-Rookie second team (2000).

Season Team	G	Min.	FGM	FGA	Pct.	FTM	FTA	Pct.	Off.	Def.	Tot.	Ast.	St.	Blk.	TO	Pts.	RPG	APG	PPG
99-00—Chicago	72	2238	309	759	.407	188	279	.674	62	246	308	202	119	39	166	866	4.3	2.8	12.0
00-01—Chicago	76	2363	327	815	.401	210	280	.750	59	235	294	228	152	45	159	907	3.9	3.0	11.9
01-02—Chi.-Indiana	55	1642	269	636	.423	136	204	.667	73	198	271	127	141	39	118	727	4.9	2.3	13.2
02-03—Indiana	69	2317	362	846	.428	273	371	.736	101	261	362	198	159	50	145	1068	5.2	2.9	15.5
03-04—Indiana	73	2714	468	1112	.421	322	439	.733	100	285	385	272	152	50	202	1333	5.3	3.7	18.3
04-05—Indiana	7	291	59	119	.496	47	51	.922	8	37	45	22	12	6	17	172	6.4	3.1	24.6
05-06—Indiana-Sac.	56	2207	350	867	.404	206	305	.675	75	211	286	203	122	41	131	984	5.1	3.6	17.6
Totals	408	13772	2144	5154	.416	1382	1929	.716	478	1473	1951	1252	857	270	938	6057	4.8	3.1	14.8

Three-point field goals: 1999-00, 60-for-191 (.314). 2000-01, 43-for-148 (.291). 2001-02, 53-for-170 (.312). 2002-03, 71-for-211 (.336). 2003-04, 75-for-242 (.310). 2004-05, 7-for-17 (.412). 2005-06, 78-for-253 (.308). Totals, 387-for-1232 (.314).

Personal fouls/disqualifications: 1999-00, 159/0. 2000-01, 254/7. 2001-02, 217/10. 2002-03, 242/7. 2003-04, 194/2. 2004-05, 27/0. 2005-06, 164/1. Totals, 1257/27.

NBA PLAYOFF RECORD

Season Team	G	Min.	FGM	FGA	Pct.	FTM	FTA	Pct.	Off.	Def.	Tot.	Ast.	St.	Blk.	TO	Pts.	RPG	APG	PPG
01-02—Indiana	5	167	22	54	.407	9	13	.692	6	24	30	16	13	3	9	59	6.0	3.2	11.8
02-03—Indiana	6	252	35	90	.389	32	40	.800	11	24	35	13	15	6	16	114	5.8	2.2	19.0
03-04—Indiana	15	584	98	259	.378	61	85	.718	24	74	98	48	21	16	37	276	6.5	3.2	18.4
05-06—Sacramento	5	198	31	81	.383	16	23	.696	8	17	25	15	8	4	5	87	5.0	3.0	17.4
Totals	31	1201	186	484	.384	118	161	.733	49	139	188	92	57	29	67	536	6.1	3.0	17.3

Three-point field goals: 2001-02, 6-for-13 (.462). 2002-03, 12-for-31 (.387). 2003-04, 19-for-66 (.288). 2005-06, 9-for-27 (.333). Totals, 46-for-137 (.336).

Personal fouls/disqualifications: 2001-02, 19/1. 2002-03, 25/2. 2003-04, 45/2. 2005-06, 15/0. Totals, 104/5.

NBA ALL-STAR GAME RECORD

Season Team	Min.	FGM	FGA	Pct.	FTM	FTA	Pct.	Off.	Def.	Tot.	Ast.	PF	Dq.	St.	Blk.	TO	Pts.
2004—Indiana	17	3	5	.600	1	2	.500	1	2	3	3	2	0	1	0	1	7

Three-point field goals: 2004, 0-for-1. Totals, 0-for-1 (.000).

ATKINS, CHUCKY   G   GRIZZLIES

PERSONAL: Born August 14, 1974, in Orlando, Fla. ... 5-11/160. (1.80/72.6). ... Full name: Kenneth Lavon Atkins
HIGH SCHOOL: Evans (Orlando, Fla.).
COLLEGE: South Florida.
TRANSACTIONS/CAREER NOTES: Not drafted by an NBA franchise. ... Played in Continental Basketball Association with LaCrosse Catbirds (1996-97). ... Played in Croatia (1997-99). ... Signed as free agent by Orlando Magic (September 20, 1999). ... Traded by Magic with F Ben Wallace to Detroit Pistons for F Grant Hill (August 3, 2000). ... Traded by Pistons to Boston Celtics as part of three-team deal in which Celtics also received G Lindsey Hunter and a 2004 first-round draft choice from Pistons. Atlanta Hawks received F Zeljko Rebraca, G Bob Sura and a future first-round draft choice from Pistons and F Chris Mills from Celtics. Pistons received F/C Rasheed Wallace from Hawks and G Mike James from Celtics (February 19, 2004). ... Traded by Celtics with F/C Chris Mihm and F Jumaine Jones to Los Angeles Lakers for G Gary Payton, F Rick Fox and a first-round draft choice (August 6, 2004). ... Traded by Lakers with F Caron Butler to Washington Wizards for C Kwame Brown and F Laron Profit (August 2, 2005). ... Waived by Wizards (January 17, 2006). ... Signed by Memphis Grizzlies (January 23, 2006).

COLLEGIATE RECORD

Season Team	G	Min.	FGM	FGA	Pct.	FTM	FTA	Pct.	Reb.	Ast.	Pts.	RPG	APG	PPG
92-93—South Florida	27	867	94	221	.425	46	72	.639	93	108	275	3.4	4.0	10.2
93-94—South Florida	26	787	96	269	.357	70	94	.745	62	105	299	2.4	4.0	11.5
94-95—South Florida	30	1067	161	389	.414	98	131	.748	96	196	504	3.2	6.5	16.8
95-96—South Florida	28	1064	175	405	.432	109	141	.773	85	111	541	3.0	4.0	19.3
Totals	111	3785	526	1284	.410	323	438	.737	336	520	1619	3.0	4.7	14.6

Three-point field goals: 1992-93, 41-for-101 (.406). 1993-94, 37-for-134 (.276). 1994-95, 84-for-219 (.384). 1995-96, 82-for-220 (.373). Totals, 244-for-674 (.362).

Personal fouls/disqualifications: 1992-93, 51/0. 1993-94, 48/0. 1994-95, 55/0. 1995-96, 54/0. Totals, 208/0.

CBA RECORD

NOTES: CBA All-Rookie first team (1997).

Season Team	G	Min.	FGM	FGA	Pct.	FTM	FTA	Pct.	Reb.	Ast.	Pts.	RPG	APG	PPG
96-97—La Crosse	50	1907	288	644	.447	148	189	.783	139	375	812	2.8	7.5	16.2

Three-point field goals: 1996-97, 88-for-240 (.367). Totals, 88-for-240 (.367).
Personal fouls/disqualifications: 1996-97, 128/0. Totals, 128/0.

CROATIAN LEAGUE RECORD

Season Team	G	Min.	FGM	FGA	Pct.	FTM	FTA	Pct.	Reb.	Ast.	Pts.	AVERAGES RPG	APG	PPG
97-98—Cibona Zagreb	26	603	108	190	.568	76	98	.776	98	97	318	3.8	3.7	12.2
98-99—Cibona Zagreb	20	512	84	145	.579	40	56	.714	24	49	225	1.2	2.5	11.3
Totals	46	1115	192	335	.573	116	154	.753	122	146	543	2.7	3.2	11.8

Three-point field goals: 1997-98, 26-for-59 (.441). 1998-99, 17-for-48 (.354). Totals, 43-for-107 (.402).
Personal fouls/disqualifications: 1997-98, 24/0. 1998-99, 38/0. Totals, 62/0.

NBA REGULAR-SEASON RECORD

HONORS: NBA All-Rookie second team (2000).

Season Team	G	Min.	FGM	FGA	Pct.	FTM	FTA	Pct.	Off.	Def.	Tot.	Ast.	St.	Blk.	TO	Pts.	RPG	APG	PPG
99-00—Orlando	82	1626	314	741	.424	97	133	.729	20	106	126	306	52	3	142	782	1.5	3.7	9.5
00-01—Detroit	81	2363	380	952	.399	90	130	.692	28	145	173	330	67	5	149	971	2.1	4.1	12.0
01-02—Detroit	79	2285	368	790	.466	83	120	.692	31	127	158	263	72	11	128	957	2.0	3.3	12.1
02-03—Detroit	65	1398	168	465	.361	40	49	.816	21	75	96	175	27	4	77	462	1.5	2.7	7.1
03-04—Detroit-Boston	64	1544	192	484	.397	73	97	.753	9	84	93	223	45	2	92	538	1.5	3.5	8.4
04-05—L.A. Lakers	82	2903	388	910	.426	163	203	.803	31	166	197	358	73	2	151	1115	2.4	4.4	13.6
05-06—Wash.Mem.	71	1713	226	573	.394	129	163	.791	23	97	120	198	43	2	87	678	1.7	2.8	9.5
Totals	524	13832	2036	4915	.414	675	895	.754	163	800	963	1853	379	29	826	5503	1.8	3.5	10.5

Three-point field goals: 1999-00, 57-for-163 (.350). 2000-01, 121-for-339 (.357). 2001-02, 138-for-336 (.411). 2002-03, 86-for-242 (.355). 2003-04, 81-for-241 (.336). 2004-05, 176-for-455 (.387). 2005-06, 97-for-274 (.354). Totals, 756-for-2050 (.369).
Personal fouls/disqualifications: 1999-00, 137/1. 2000-01, 184/2. 2001-02, 177/1. 2002-03, 108/0. 2003-04, 102/0. 2004-05, 181/0. 2005-06, 152/4. Totals, 1041/8.

NBA PLAYOFF RECORD

Season Team	G	Min.	FGM	FGA	Pct.	FTM	FTA	Pct.	Off.	Def.	Tot.	Ast.	St.	Blk.	TO	Pts.	RPG	APG	PPG
01-02—Detroit	10	294	43	118	.364	13	17	.765	5	19	24	34	6	1	14	113	2.4	3.4	11.3
02 03—Detroit	17	312	32	91	.352	21	26	.808	2	18	20	26	17	0	18	103	1.2	1.5	6.1
03-04—Boston	4	133	17	39	.436	17	19	.895	3	11	14	15	3	0	10	54	3.5	3.8	13.5
05-06—Memphis	4	103	15	37	.405	5	8	.625	0	3	3	12	2	0	4	39	0.8	3.0	9.8
Totals	35	842	107	285	.375	56	70	.800	10	51	61	87	28	1	46	309	1.7	2.5	8.8

Three-point field goals: 2001-02, 14-for-39 (.359). 2002-03, 18-for-49 (.367). 2003-04, 3-for-10 (.300). 2005-06, 4-for-11 (.364). Totals, 39-for-109 (.358).
Personal fouls/disqualifications: 2001-02, 25/0. 2002-03, 39/0. 2003-04, 2/0. 2005-06, 15/1. Totals, 81/1.

AUGMON, STACEY — F — MAGIC

PERSONAL: Born August 1, 1968, in Pasadena, Calif. ... 6-8/213. (2.03/96.6). ... Full name: Stacey Orlando Augmon ... Name pronounced AWG-men.
HIGH SCHOOL: John Muir (Pasadena, Calif.).
COLLEGE: UNLV.
TRANSACTIONS/CAREER NOTES: Selected by Atlanta Hawks in first round (ninth pick overall) of 1991 NBA Draft. ... Traded by Hawks with F Grant Long to Detroit Pistons for three conditional draft choices (July 15, 1996). ... Traded by Pistons to Portland Trail Blazers for G Aaron McKie, G Randolph Childress and G Reggie Jordan (January 24, 1997). ... Traded by Trail Blazers with C Kelvin Cato, G/F Walt Williams, G Brian Shaw, G Ed Gray and F/C Carlos Rogers to Houston Rockets for F Scottie Pippen (October 2, 1999). ... Waived by Rockets (October 12, 1999). ... Signed as free agent by Trail Blazers (October 18, 1999). ... Signed as free agent by Charlotte Hornets (July 25, 2001). ... Hornets franchise moved to New Orleans for 2002-03 season. ... Signed as free agent by Orlando Magic (August 2, 2004).
MISCELLANEOUS: Member of bronze-medal-winning U.S. Olympic team (1988).

COLLEGIATE RECORD

NOTES: THE SPORTING NEWS All-America first team (1991). ... Member of NCAA Division I championship team (1990).

Season Team	G	Min.	FGM	FGA	Pct.	FTM	FTA	Pct.	Reb.	Ast.	Pts.	AVERAGES RPG	APG	PPG
86-87—UNLV						Did not play—ineligible.								
87-88—UNLV	34	884	117	204	.574	75	116	.647	206	64	311	6.1	1.9	9.1
88-89—UNLV	37	1091	210	405	.519	106	160	.663	274	101	567	7.4	2.7	15.3
89-90—UNLV	39	1246	210	380	.553	118	176	.670	270	143	554	6.9	3.7	14.2
90-91—UNLV	35	1062	220	375	.587	101	139	.727	255	125	579	7.3	3.6	16.5
Totals	145	4283	757	1364	.555	400	591	.677	1005	433	2011	6.9	3.0	13.9

Three-point field goals: 1987-88, 2-for-2 (1.000). 1988-89, 41-for-98 (.418). 1989-90, 16-for-50 (.320). 1990-91, 38-for-81 (.469). Totals, 97-for-231 (.420).

NBA REGULAR-SEASON RECORD

HONORS: NBA All-Rookie first team (1992).

Season Team	G	Min.	FGM	FGA	Pct.	FTM	FTA	Pct.	Off.	Def.	Tot.	Ast.	St.	Blk.	TO	Pts.	RPG	APG	PPG
91-92—Atlanta	82	2505	440	899	.489	213	320	.666	191	229	420	201	124	27	181	1094	5.1	2.5	13.3
92-93—Atlanta	73	2112	397	792	.501	227	307	.739	141	146	287	170	91	18	157	1021	3.9	2.3	14.0
93-94—Atlanta	82	2605	439	861	.510	333	436	.764	178	216	394	187	149	45	147	1212	4.8	2.3	14.8
94-95—Atlanta	76	2362	397	876	.453	252	346	.728	157	211	368	197	100	47	152	1053	4.8	2.6	13.9
95-96—Atlanta	77	2294	362	738	.491	251	317	.792	137	167	304	137	106	31	138	976	3.9	1.8	12.7
96-97—Atlanta	60	942	105	220	.477	69	97	.711	47	91	138	56	42	17	64	279	2.3	0.9	4.7
97-98—Portland	71	1445	154	372	.414	94	156	.603	104	131	235	88	57	32	81	403	3.3	1.2	5.7
98-99—Portland	48	874	78	174	.448	52	76	.684	47	78	125	58	57	18	30	208	2.6	1.2	4.3
99-00—Portland	59	642	83	175	.474	37	55	.673	42	74	116	53	27	11	38	203	2.0	0.9	3.4
00-01—Portland	66	1182	127	266	.477	57	87	.655	60	99	159	98	48	21	48	311	2.4	1.5	4.7
01-02—Charlotte	77	1319	140	328	.427	77	101	.762	59	166	225	103	56	12	54	357	2.9	1.3	4.6

Season Team	G	Min.	FGM	FGA	Pct.	FTM	FTA	Pct.	Off.	Def.	Tot.	Ast.	St.	Blk.	TO	Pts.	RPG	APG	PPG
									REBOUNDS								AVERAGES		
02-03—New Orleans ...	70	862	79	192	.411	54	72	.750	26	93	119	69	27	9	40	212	1.7	1.0	3.0
03-04—New Orleans ...	69	1416	143	347	.412	110	139	.791	52	122	174	85	55	15	76	397	2.5	1.2	5.8
04-05—Orlando..........	55	663	68	167	.407	57	77	.740	45	54	99	36	23	8	31	193	1.8	0.7	3.5
05-06—Orlando..........	36	385	25	73	.342	21	30	.700	18	35	53	23	12	6	11	71	1.5	0.6	2.0
Totals	1001	21658	3037	6480	.469	1904	2616	.728	1304	1912	3216	1561	974	317	1248	7990	3.2	1.6	8.0

Three-point field goals: 1991-92, 1-for-6 (.167). 1992-93, 0-for-4. 1993-94, 1-for-7 (.143). 1994-95, 7-for-26 (.269). 1995-96, 1-for-4 (.250). 1997-98, 1-for-7 (.143). 1998-99, 0-for-2. 1999-00, 0-for-2. 2000-01, 0-for-4. 2001-02, 0-for-3. 2002-03, 0-for-7. 2003-04, 1-for-7 (.143). Totals, 12-for-79 (.152).

Personal fouls/disqualifications: 1991-92, 161/0. 1992-93, 141/1. 1993-94, 179/0. 1994-95, 163/0. 1995-96, 188/1. 1996-97, 87/0. 1997-98, 144/0. 1998-99, 81/0. 1999-00, 69/0. 2000-01, 105/0. 2001-02, 115/0. 2002-03, 80/0. 2003-04, 114/2. 2004-05, 83/0. 2005-06, 40/0. Totals, 1750/4.

NBA PLAYOFF RECORD

Season Team	G	Min.	FGM	FGA	Pct.	FTM	FTA	Pct.	Off.	Def.	Tot.	Ast.	St.	Blk.	TO	Pts.	RPG	APG	PPG
									REBOUNDS								AVERAGES		
92-93—Atlanta	3	93	14	31	.452	8	12	.667	3	5	8	5	4	0	4	36	2.7	1.7	12.0
93-94—Atlanta	11	324	46	89	.517	27	38	.711	13	16	29	28	7	2	15	119	2.6	2.5	10.8
94-95—Atlanta	3	52	6	14	.429	9	12	.750	3	4	7	5	3	0	2	21	2.3	1.7	7.0
95-96—Atlanta	10	314	35	72	.486	33	40	.825	9	27	36	27	11	6	17	103	3.6	2.7	10.3
96-97—Portland	4	35	2	6	.333	3	4	.750	1	0	1	3	1	0	1	7	0.3	0.8	1.8
97-98—Portland	4	28	2	4	.500	1	2	.500	1	2	3	1	2	1	2	5	0.8	0.3	1.3
98-99—Portland	13	176	10	28	.357	15	18	.833	10	23	33	5	8	3	3	35	2.5	0.4	2.7
99-00—Portland	7	34	4	12	.333	1	2	.500	0	2	2	0	0	0	0	9	0.3	0.0	1.3
00-01—Portland	2	28	4	10	.400	2	2	1.000	1	3	4	4	1	0	1	10	2.0	2.0	5.0
01-02—Charlotte	9	152	16	41	.390	16	21	.762	7	20	27	13	10	1	12	48	3.0	1.4	5.3
02-03—New Orleans ...	4	69	5	15	.333	7	8	.875	1	9	10	3	3	0	3	17	2.5	0.8	4.3
03-04—New Orleans ...	7	168	18	48	.375	16	18	.889	4	15	19	7	6	1	13	52	2.7	1.0	7.4
Totals	77	1473	162	370	.438	138	177	.780	53	126	179	101	56	14	73	462	2.3	1.3	6.0

Three-point field goals: 1995-96, 0-for-1. 1998-99, 0-for-1. 2003-04, 0-for-1. Totals, 0-for-3 (.000).

Personal fouls/disqualifications: 1992-93, 7/0. 1993-94, 26/0. 1994-95, 8/0. 1995-96, 26/0. 1996-97, 6/0. 1997-98, 2/0. 1998-99, 15/0. 1999-00, 6/0. 2000-01, 3/0. 2001-02, 21/1. 2002-03, 8/0. 2003-04, 13/0. Totals, 141/1.

BAKER, VIN   F   CLIPPERS

PERSONAL: Born November 23, 1971, in Lake Wales, Fla. ... 6-11/250. (2.11/113.4). ... Full name: Vincent Lamont Baker.
HIGH SCHOOL: Old Saybrook (Conn.).
COLLEGE: Hartford.
TRANSACTIONS/CAREER NOTES: Selected by Milwaukee Bucks in first round (eighth pick overall) of 1993 NBA Draft. ... Traded by Bucks to Seattle SuperSonics in three-way deal in which SuperSonics sent F Shawn Kemp to Cavaliers and Bucks sent G Sherman Douglas to Cleveland Cavaliers for G Terrell Brandon and F Tyrone Hill (September 25, 1997); Bucks also received 1998 conditional first-round draft choice from Cavaliers. ... Traded by SuperSonics with G Shammond Williams to Boston Celtics for G Kenny Anderson, F/C Vitaly Potapenko and G Joseph Forte (July 22, 2002). ... Released by Celtics (February 18, 2004). ... Signed as free agent by New York Knicks (March 12, 2004). ... Traded by Knicks with G Moochie Norris and second-round pick in 2006 draft to Houston Rockets for F Maurice Taylor (February 24, 2005). ... Waived by Rockets (October 7, 2005). ... Signed by Los Angeles Clippers (February 20, 2006).
MISCELLANEOUS: Member of gold-medal-winning U.S. Olympic team (2000).

COLLEGIATE RECORD

Season Team	G	Min.	FGM	FGA	Pct.	FTM	FTA	Pct.	Reb.	Ast.	Pts.	RPG	APG	PPG
												AVERAGES		
89-90—Hartford.....................	28	374	58	94	.617	16	41	.390	82	7	132	2.9	0.3	4.7
90-91—Hartford.....................	29	899	216	440	.491	137	202	.678	302	18	569	10.4	0.6	19.6
91-92—Hartford.....................	27	997	281	638	.440	142	216	.657	267	36	745	9.9	1.3	27.6
92-93—Hartford.....................	28	1019	305	639	.477	150	240	.625	300	54	792	10.7	1.9	28.3
Totals	112	3289	860	1811	.475	445	699	.637	951	115	2238	8.5	1.0	20.0

Three-point field goals: 1991-92, 41-for-214 (.192). 1992-93, 32-for-119 (.269). Totals, 73-for-333 (.219).

NBA REGULAR-SEASON RECORD

HONORS: All-NBA second team (1998). ... All-NBA third team (1997). ... NBA All-Rookie first team (1994).

Season Team	G	Min.	FGM	FGA	Pct.	FTM	FTA	Pct.	Off.	Def.	Tot.	Ast.	St.	Blk.	TO	Pts.	RPG	APG	PPG
									REBOUNDS								AVERAGES		
93-94—Milwaukee.....	82	2560	435	869	.501	234	411	.569	277	344	621	163	60	114	162	1105	7.6	2.0	13.5
94-95—Milwaukee.....	82	*3361	594	1229	.483	256	432	.593	289	557	846	296	86	116	221	1451	10.3	3.6	17.7
95-96—Milwaukee.....	82	3319	699	1429	.489	321	479	.670	263	545	808	212	68	91	216	1729	9.9	2.6	21.1
96-97—Milwaukee.....	78	3159	632	1251	.505	358	521	.687	267	537	804	211	81	112	245	1637	10.3	2.7	21.0
97-98—Seattle..........	82	2944	631	1164	.542	311	526	.591	286	370	656	152	91	86	174	1574	8.0	1.9	19.2
98-99—Seattle..........	34	1162	198	437	.453	72	160	.450	86	125	211	56	32	34	76	468	6.2	1.6	13.8
99-00—Seattle..........	79	2849	514	1129	.455	281	412	.682	227	378	605	148	47	66	213	1311	7.7	1.9	16.6
00-01—Seattle..........	76	2129	347	822	.422	232	321	.723	179	251	430	90	38	73	158	927	5.7	1.2	12.2
01-02—Seattle..........	55	1710	315	649	.485	143	226	.633	168	182	350	72	22	36	127	774	6.4	1.3	14.1
02-03—Boston	52	942	99	207	.478	72	107	.673	90	108	198	29	22	30	61	270	3.8	0.6	5.2
03-04—Boston-N.Y. ...	54	1313	208	432	.481	114	157	.726	112	168	280	66	29	32	77	531	5.2	1.2	9.8
04-05—N.Y.-Houston.	27	204	13	42	.310	9	17	.529	17	22	39	10	2	4	17	35	1.4	0.4	1.3
05-06—L.A. Clippers .	8	85	7	15	.467	13	18	.722	7	19	7	4	4	4	9	27	2.4	0.5	3.4
Totals	791	25737	4692	9675	.485	2416	3787	.638	2263	3604	5867	1509	582	798	1756	11839	7.4	1.9	15.0

Three-point field goals: 1993-94, 1-for-5 (.200). 1994-95, 7-for-24 (.292). 1995-96, 10-for-48 (.208). 1996-97, 15-for-54 (.278). 1997-98, 1-for-7 (.143). 1998-99, 0-for-3. 1999-00, 2-for-8 (.250). 2000-01, 1-for-16 (.063). 2001-02, 1-for-8 (.125). 2002-03, 0-for-4. 2003-04, 1-for-3 (.333). 2004-05, 0-for-1. Totals, 39-for-181 (.215).

Personal fouls/disqualifications: 1993-94, 231/3. 1994-95, 277/5. 1995-96, 272/3. 1996-97, 275/8. 1997-98, 278/7. 1998-99, 121/2. 1999-00, 288/6. 2000-01, 264/2. 2001-02, 197/4. 2002-03, 146/1. 2003-04, 160/3. 2004-05, 38/0. 2005-06, 13/1. Totals, 2560/45.

NBA PLAYOFF RECORD

Season Team	G	Min.	FGM	FGA	Pct.	FTM	FTA	Pct.	REBOUNDS Off.	Def.	Tot.	Ast.	St.	Blk.	TO	Pts.	AVERAGES RPG	APG	PPG
97-98—Seattle..........	10	371	71	134	.530	16	38	.421	41	53	94	18	18	15	22	158	9.4	1.8	15.8
99-00—Seattle..........	5	177	30	75	.400	10	17	.588	16	22	38	10	5	2	16	70	7.6	2.0	14.0
01-02—Seattle..........	5	144	29	58	.500	7	9	.778	11	14	25	4	3	6	4	66	5.0	0.8	13.2
03-04—New York	4	57	8	14	.571	6	9	.667	6	6	12	1	3	2	2	22	3.0	0.3	5.5
Totals	24	749	138	281	.491	39	73	.534	74	95	169	33	29	25	44	316	7.0	1.4	13.2

Three-point field goals: 1999-00, 0-for-1. 2001-02, 1-for-1 (1.000). Totals, 1-for-2 (.500).
Personal fouls/disqualifications: 1997-98, 38/1. 1999-00, 19/0. 2001-02, 23/1. 2003-04, 8/1. Totals, 88/3.

NBA ALL-STAR GAME RECORD

Season Team	Min.	FGM	FGA	Pct.	FTM	FTA	Pct.	REBOUNDS Off.	Def.	Tot.	Ast.	PF	Dq.	St.	Blk.	TO	Pts.
1995—Milwaukee..........	11	0	2	.000	2	4	.500	2	0	2	0	1	0	0	1	1	2
1996—Milwaukee..........	14	2	5	.400	2	2	1.000	1	1	2	2	4	0	1	0	0	6
1997—Milwaukee..........	24	8	12	.667	3	4	.750	7	5	12	1	2	0	0	0	0	19
1998—Seattle.................	21	3	12	.250	2	2	1.000	6	2	8	0	1	0	1	0	0	8
Totals	70	13	31	.419	9	12	.750	16	8	24	3	8	0	2	1	1	35

BANKS, MARCUS   G   SUNS

PERSONAL: Born November 19, 1981, in in Las Vegas, Nev. ... 6-2/220. (1.88/99.8). ... Full name: Arthur Lemarcus Banks
HIGH SCHOOL: Cimarron-Memorial (Las Vegas, Nev.).
JUNIOR COLLEGE: Dixie College
COLLEGE: UNLV.
TRANSACTIONS/CAREER NOTES: Selected by Memphis Grizzlies in first round (13th pick overall) of 2003 NBA Draft. ... Draft rights traded by Grizzlies with draft rights to C Kendrick Perkins to Boston Celtics for draft rights to G Troy Bell and G/F Dahntay Jones (June 26, 2003). ... Traded by Celtics with G Ricky Davis, C Mark Blount, SF Justin Reed and two second-round draft choices to Minnesota Timberwolves for F Wally Szczerbiak, C Michael Olowokandi, F/C Dwayne Jones and a future first-round draft choice (January 26, 2006) ... Signed as free agent by Phoenix Suns (July 20, 2006).

COLLEGIATE RECORD

Season Team	G	Min.	FGM	FGA	Pct.	FTM	FTA	Pct.	Reb.	Ast.	Pts.	AVERAGES RPG	APG	PPG
99-00—Dixie College	33	...	234	471	.497	87	140	.621	120	111	592	3.6	3.4	17.9
00-01—Dixie College	37	...	193	371	.520	216	288	.750	205	137	622	5.5	3.7	16.8
01-02—UNLV	31	1006	158	336	.470	150	213	.704	103	94	490	3.3	3.0	15.8
02-03—UNLV	32	1154	223	434	.514	162	214	.757	107	175	649	3.3	5.5	20.3
Junior College Totals.............	70	...	427	842	.507	303	428	.708	325	248	1214	4.6	3.5	17.3
4-Year College Totals.............	63	2160	381	770	.495	312	427	.731	210	269	1139	3.3	4.3	18.1

Three-point field goals: 2001-02, 24-for-75 (.320). 2002-03, 41-for-122 (.336). Totals, 65-for-197 (.330).

NBA REGULAR-SEASON RECORD

Season Team	G	Min.	FGM	FGA	Pct.	FTM	FTA	Pct.	REBOUNDS Off.	Def.	Tot.	Ast.	St.	Blk.	TO	Pts.	AVERAGES RPG	APG	PPG
03-04—Boston	81	1385	177	442	.400	99	131	.756	30	103	133	175	88	13	125	480	1.6	2.2	5.9
04-05—Boston	81	1145	115	286	.402	121	163	.742	29	97	126	155	63	13	79	372	1.6	1.9	4.6
05-06—Boston-Minn...	58	1496	219	468	.468	118	147	.803	23	112	135	220	54	11	119	578	2.3	3.8	10.0
Totals	220	4026	511	1196	.427	338	441	.766	82	312	394	550	205	37	323	1430	1.8	2.5	6.5

Three-point field goals: 2003-04, 27-for-86 (.314). 2004-05, 21-for-59 (.356). 2005-06, 22-for-63 (.349). Totals, 70-for-208 (.337).
Personal fouls/disqualifications: 2003-04, 171/2. 2004-05, 146/2. 2005-06, 162/0. Totals, 479/4.

NBA PLAYOFF RECORD

Season Team	G	Min.	FGM	FGA	Pct.	FTM	FTA	Pct.	REBOUNDS Off.	Def.	Tot.	Ast.	St.	Blk.	TO	Pts.	AVERAGES RPG	APG	PPG
03-04—Boston	4	60	7	16	.438	4	4	1.000	1	6	7	7	2	1	3	20	1.8	1.8	5.0
04-05—Boston	7	106	13	29	.448	3	6	.500	1	10	11	7	4	0	6	32	1.6	1.0	4.6
Totals	11	166	20	45	.444	7	10	.700	2	16	18	14	6	1	9	52	1.6	1.3	4.7

Three-point field goals: 2003-04, 2-for-5 (.400). 2004-05, 3-for-6 (.500). Totals, 5-for-11 (.455).
Personal fouls/disqualifications: 2003-04, 9/0. 2004-05, 16/0. Totals, 25/0.

BARBOSA, LEANDRO   G   SUNS

PERSONAL: Born November 28, 1982, in Sao Paulo, Brazil. ... 6-3/176. (1.91/79.8). ... Full name: Leandrinho Mateus Barbosa
TRANSACTIONS/CAREER NOTES: Played in Brazil (1999-2003). ... Selected by San Antonio Spurs in first round (28th pick overall) of 2003 NBA Draft. ... Draft rights traded by Spurs to Phoenix Suns for future first-round pick (June 26, 2003).

BRAZILIAN LEAGUE RECORD

Season Team	G	Min.	FGM	FGA	Pct.	FTM	FTA	Pct.	Reb.	Ast.	Pts.	AVERAGES RPG	APG	PPG
01-02—Bauru Tilibra..................	43	...	253	464	.545	103	142	.725	155	275	678	3.6	6.4	15.8
02-03—Bauru Tilibra..................	20	...	190	378	.503	100	120	.833	80	140	564	4.0	7.0	28.2
Totals	63	...	443	842	.526	203	262	.775	235	415	1242	3.7	6.6	19.7

Three-point field goals: 2001-02, 64-for-150 (.427). 2002-03, 68-for-152 (.447). Totals, 132-for-302 (.437).

NBA REGULAR-SEASON RECORD

Season Team	G	Min.	FGM	FGA	Pct.	FTM	FTA	Pct.	REBOUNDS Off.	Def.	Tot.	Ast.	St.	Blk.	TO	Pts.	AVERAGES RPG	APG	PPG
03-04—Phoenix	70	1500	210	470	.447	47	61	.770	23	100	123	165	93	7	120	550	1.8	2.4	7.9
04-05—Phoenix	63	1087	168	354	.475	55	69	.797	32	98	130	126	30	7	87	442	2.1	2.0	7.0
05-06—Phoenix	57	1592	273	567	.481	111	147	.755	31	119	150	158	48	6	89	744	2.6	2.8	13.1
Totals	190	4179	651	1391	.468	213	277	.769	86	317	403	449	171	20	296	1736	2.1	2.4	9.1

Three-point field goals: 2003-04, 83-for-210 (.395). 2004-05, 51-for-139 (.367). 2005-06, 87-for-196 (.444). Totals, 221-for-545 (.406).
Personal fouls/disqualifications: 2003-04, 184/6. 2004-05, 127/0. 2005-06, 145/3. Totals, 456/9.

NBA PLAYOFF RECORD

Season Team	G	Min.	FGM	FGA	Pct.	FTM	FTA	Pct.	REBOUNDS Off.	Def.	Tot.	Ast.	St.	Blk.	TO	Pts.	AVERAGES RPG	APG	PPG
04-05—Phoenix	12	116	12	35	.343	2	4	.500	5	12	17	12	3	0	5	30	1.4	1.0	2.5
05-06—Phoenix	20	632	103	219	.470	50	58	.862	5	27	32	54	15	4	29	283	1.6	2.7	14.2
Totals	32	748	115	254	.453	52	62	.839	10	39	49	66	18	4	34	313	1.5	2.1	9.8

Three-point field goals: 2004-05, 4-for-10 (.400). 2005-06, 27-for-69 (.391). Totals, 31-for-79 (.392).
Personal fouls/disqualifications: 2004-05, 8/0. 2005-06, 66/1. Totals, 74/1.

BARNES, MATT   F

PERSONAL: Born March 9, 1980, in Santa Clara, Calif. ... 6-7/226. (2.01/102.5). ... Full name: Matt Kelly Barnes
HIGH SCHOOL: Del Campo (Sacramento).
COLLEGE: UCLA.
TRANSACTIONS/CAREER NOTES: Selected by Memphis Grizzlies in second round (46th pick overall) of NBA Draft. ... Draft rights traded by Grizzlies with G/F Nick Anderson to Cleveland Cavaliers for G/F Wesley Person (June 26, 2002). ... Played in NBA Development League (2002-03). ... Waived by Cavaliers (October 18, 2002). ... Signed as free agent by Seattle SuperSonics (September 27, 2003). ... Waived by SuperSonics (October 13, 2003). ... Played in ABA (2003-04). ... Signed by Los Angeles Clippers to first of two consecutive 10-day contracts (January 18, 2004). ... Signed by Clippers for remainder of season (February 8, 2004). ... Signed as free agent by Sacramento Kings (October 1, 2004). ... Traded by Kings with Fs Michael Bradley and Chris Webber to Philadelphia 76ers for Fs Kenny Thomas and Corliss Williamson and C Brian Skinner (February 23, 2005). ... Signed as a free agent by New York Knicks (October 6, 2005). ... Waived by Knicks (December 3, 2005). ... Signed by Philadelphia 76ers (December 9, 2005).

COLLEGIATE RECORD

Season Team	G	Min.	FGM	FGA	Pct.	FTM	FTA	Pct.	Reb.	Ast.	Pts.	AVERAGES RPG	APG	PPG
98-99—UCLA	30	394	43	99	.434	22	46	.478	86	23	118	2.9	0.8	3.9
99-00—UCLA	28	413	65	138	.471	21	43	.488	74	29	156	2.6	1.0	5.6
00-01—UCLA	32	971	142	297	.478	85	148	.574	232	85	372	7.3	2.7	11.6
01-02—UCLA	31	953	152	323	.471	73	118	.619	192	108	420	6.2	3.5	13.5
Totals	121	2731	402	857	.469	201	355	.566	584	245	1066	4.8	2.0	8.8

Three-point field goals: 1998-99, 10-for-34 (.294). 1999-00, 5-for-32 (.156). 2000-01, 3-for-25 (.120). 2001-02, 43-for-103 (.417). Totals, 61-for-194 (.314).

NBA DEVELOPMENT LEAGUE RECORD

Season Team	G	Min.	FGM	FGA	Pct.	FTM	FTA	Pct.	Reb.	Ast.	Pts.	AVERAGES RPG	APG	PPG
02-03—Fayetteville	50	932	172	442	.389	79	113	.699	164	56	484	3.3	1.1	9.7

Three-point field goals: 2002-03, 61-for-175 (.349). Totals, 61-for-175 (.349).

AMERICAN BASKETBALL ASSOCIATION RECORD

Season Team	G	Min.	FGM	FGA	Pct.	FTM	FTA	Pct.	Reb.	Ast.	Pts.	AVERAGES RPG	APG	PPG
03-04—Long Beach	17	...	122	240	.508	46	60	.767	116	81	328	6.8	4.8	19.3

Three-point field goals: 2003-04, 38-for-104 (.365). Totals, 38-for-104 (.365).

NBA REGULAR-SEASON RECORD

Season Team	G	Min.	FGM	FGA	Pct.	FTM	FTA	Pct.	REBOUNDS Off.	Def.	Tot.	Ast.	St.	Blk.	TO	Pts.	AVERAGES RPG	APG	PPG
03-04—L.A. Clippers	38	724	63	138	.457	43	61	.705	53	98	151	48	27	3	44	171	4.0	1.3	4.5
04-05—Sac.-Phila.	43	715	62	151	.411	35	58	.603	49	84	133	57	30	7	45	164	3.1	1.3	3.8
05-06—N.Y.-Phila.	56	631	70	140	.500	32	47	.681	48	73	121	28	20	7	30	175	2.2	0.5	3.1
Totals	137	2070	195	429	.455	110	166	.663	150	255	405	133	77	17	119	510	3.0	1.0	3.7

Three-point field goals: 2003-04, 2-for-13 (.154). 2004-05, 5-for-22 (.227). 2005-06, 3-for-15 (.200). Totals, 10-for-50 (.200).
Personal fouls/disqualifications: 2003-04, 76/0. 2004-05, 80/0. 2005-06, 100/2. Totals, 256/2.

BARRETT, ANDRE   G

PERSONAL: Born February 21, 1982, in Bronx, N.Y. ... 5-10/173. (1.78/78.5). ... Full name: Andre Rashawd Barrett
HIGH SCHOOL: Rice (New York, N.Y.).
COLLEGE: Seton Hall.
TRANSACTIONS/CAREER NOTES: Not drafted by an NBA franchise. ... Signed as free agent by Houston Rockets (October 28, 2004). ... Waived by Rockets (March 19, 2005). ... Signed to 10-day contract by Orlando Magic (March 31, 2005). ... Signed for remainder of season by Magic (April 10, 2005). ... Signed as free agent by Milwaukee Bucks (September 27, 2005). ... Waived by Bucks (October 27, 2005). ... Signed by Phoenix Suns to 10-day contract (March 1, 2006). ... Signed by Toronto Raptors to 10-day contract (March 15, 2006). ... Signed by Raptors for remainder of season and the 2006-07 season (April 4, 2006). ... Waived by Raptors (July 13, 2006).

COLLEGIATE RECORD
NOTES: The SPORTING NEWS All-America third team (2004).

Season Team	G	Min.	FGM	FGA	Pct.	FTM	FTA	Pct.	Reb.	Ast.	Pts.	RPG	APG	PPG
00-01—Seton Hall	31	1005	113	311	.363	44	63	.698	103	169	317	3.3	5.5	10.2
01-02—Seton Hall	30	1035	164	414	.396	110	146	.753	108	151	506	3.6	5.0	16.9
02-03—Seton Hall	30	1137	162	374	.433	122	146	.836	115	159	502	3.8	5.3	16.7
03-04—Seton Hall	31	1119	187	411	.455	89	117	.761	120	183	536	3.9	5.9	17.3
Totals	122	4296	626	1510	.415	365	472	.773	446	662	1861	3.7	5.4	15.3

Three-point field goals: 2000-01, 47-for-156 (.301). 2001-02, 68-for-198 (.343). 2002-03, 56-for-152 (.368). 2003-04, 73-for-190 (.384). Totals, 244-for-696 (.351).

NBA REGULAR-SEASON RECORD

Season Team	G	Min.	FGM	FGA	Pct.	FTM	FTA	Pct.	REBOUNDS Off.	Def.	Tot.	Ast.	St.	Blk.	TO	Pts.	RPG	APG	PPG
04-05—Houston-Orl.	38	483	45	124	.363	14	19	.737	11	29	40	69	19	1	27	118	1.1	1.8	3.1
05-06—Phoenix-Tor.	19	282	38	104	.365	9	12	.750	9	16	25	52	10	0	15	87	1.3	2.7	4.6
Totals	57	765	83	228	.364	23	31	.742	20	45	65	121	29	1	42	205	1.1	2.1	3.6

Three-point field goals: 2004-05, 14-for-52 (.269). 2005-06, 2-for-14 (.143). Totals, 16-for-66 (.242).
Personal fouls/disqualifications: 2004-05, 51/0. 2005-06, 13/0. Totals, 64/0.

NBA DEVELOPMENT LEAGUE RECORD

Season Team	G	Min.	FGM	FGA	Pct.	FTM	FTA	Pct.	Reb.	Ast.	Pts.	RPG	APG	PPG
05-06—Florida	33	1175	217	457	.475	111	148	.750	117	217	561	3.5	6.6	17.0

Three-point field goals: 2005-06, 16-for-46 (.348). Totals, 16-for-46 (.348).

BARRON, EARL   C   HEAT

PERSONAL: Born August 14, 1981, in Clarksdale, Miss. ... 7-0/245. (2.13/111.1).
HIGH SCHOOL: Clarksdale (Miss.).
COLLEGE: Memphis.
TRANSACTIONS/CAREER NOTES: Not drafted by an NBA franchise ... Played in Turkey (2003-04) ... Played in NBA Development League (2003-06). ... Signed as free agent by Orlando Magic (October 4, 2004). ... Waived by Magic (October 14, 2004). ... Signed as free agent by Miami Heat (August 8, 2005).

COLLEGIATE RECORD

Season Team	G	Min.	FGM	FGA	Pct.	FTM	FTA	Pct.	Reb.	Ast.	Pts.	RPG	APG	PPG
99-00—Memphis	30	508	64	149	.430	40	73	.548	117	23	168	3.9	0.8	5.6
00-01—Memphis	36	690	112	207	.541	74	127	.583	170	16	298	4.7	0.4	8.3
01-02—Memphis	36	781	119	229	.520	90	115	.783	193	31	331	5.4	0.9	9.2
02-03—Memphis	26	555	65	166	.392	74	91	.813	142	22	205	5.5	0.8	7.9
Totals	128	2534	360	751	.479	278	406	.685	622	92	1002	4.9	0.7	7.8

Three-point field goals: 1999-00, 0-for-4. 2001-02, 3-for-9 (.333). 2002-03, 10-for-1 (.100). Totals, 13-for-14 (.929).

NBA DEVELOPMENT LEAGUE RECORD

Season Team	G	Min.	FGM	FGA	Pct.	FTM	FTA	Pct.	Reb.	Ast.	Pts.	RPG	APG	PPG
03-04—Huntsville	10	227	32	59	.542	16	21	.762	61	6	80	6.1	0.6	8.0
04-05—Huntsville	45	1159	209	419	.499	133	164	.811	256	36	551	5.7	0.8	12.2
05-06—Florida	6	175	43	84	.512	16	21	.762	58	13	102	9.7	2.2	17.0
Totals	61	1561	284	562	.505	165	206	.801	375	55	733	6.1	0.9	12.0

Three-point field goals: 2005-06, 0-for-1. Totals, 0-for-1 (.000).

TURKISH LEAGUE RECORD

Season Team	G	Min.	FGM	FGA	Pct.	FTM	FTA	Pct.	Reb.	Ast.	Pts.	RPG	APG	PPG
03-04—Tuborg Pilsener	17	417	59	149	.396	20	28	.714	90	8	161	5.3	0.5	9.5

Three-point field goals: 2003-04, 23-for-70 (.329). Totals, 23-for-70 (.329).

NBA REGULAR-SEASON RECORD

Season Team	G	Min.	FGM	FGA	Pct.	FTM	FTA	Pct.	REBOUNDS Off.	Def.	Tot.	Ast.	St.	Blk.	TO	Pts.	RPG	APG	PPG
05-06—Miami	8	45	5	16	.313	3	4	.750	2	8	10	0	0	0	5	13	1.3	0.0	1.6

Personal fouls/disqualifications: 2005-06, 10/0. Totals, 10/0.

BARRY, BRENT   G   SPURS

PERSONAL: Born December 31, 1971, in Hempstead, N.Y. ... 6-6/215. (1.98/97.5). ... Full name: Brent Robert Barry ... Son of Rick Barry, forward with San Francisco/Golden State Warriors (1965-66, 1966-67 and 1972-73 through 1977-78) and Houston Rockets of NBA (1978-79 and 1979-80) and three American Basketball Association teams (1968-69 through 1971-72) and member of Naismith Memorial Basketball Hall of Fame; brother of Jon Barry, guard with seven NBA teams (1992-2006); brother of Drew Barry, guard with Atlanta Hawks (1997-98 and 2000-01), Seattle SuperSonics (1998-99) and Golden State Warriors (2000-01).
HIGH SCHOOL: De La Salle Catholic (Concord, Calif.).
COLLEGE: Oregon State.
TRANSACTIONS/CAREER NOTES: Selected by Denver Nuggets in first round (15th pick overall) of 1995 NBA Draft. ... Draft rights traded by Nuggets with F Rodney Rogers to Los Angeles Clippers for G Randy Woods and draft rights to F Antonio McDyess (June 28, 1995). ... Traded by Clippers to Miami Heat for C Isaac Austin, G Charles Smith and 1998 first-round draft choice (February 19, 1998). ... Signed as free agent by Chicago Bulls (January 25, 1999). ... Traded by Bulls to Seattle SuperSonics for G Hersey Hawkins and G James Cotton (August 12, 1999). ... Signed as free agent by San Antonio Spurs (July 15, 2004).

MISCELLANEOUS: Member of NBA championship team (2005).

COLLEGIATE RECORD

Season Team	G	Min.	FGM	FGA	Pct.	FTM	FTA	Pct.	Reb.	Ast.	Pts.	AVERAGES		
												RPG	APG	PPG
90-91—Oregon State						Did not play—redshirted.								
91-92—Oregon State	31	545	57	136	.419	22	33	.667	47	70	161	1.5	2.3	5.2
92-93—Oregon State	23	607	55	134	.410	40	47	.851	49	83	165	2.1	3.6	7.2
93-94—Oregon State	27	959	144	289	.498	85	112	.759	141	94	411	5.2	3.5	15.2
94-95—Oregon State	27	1012	181	352	.514	153	186	.823	159	104	567	5.9	3.9	21.0
Totals	108	3123	437	911	.480	300	378	.794	396	351	1304	3.7	3.3	12.1

Three-point field goals: 1991-92, 25-for-77 (.325). 1992-93, 15-for-64 (.234). 1993-94, 38-for-104 (.365). 1994-95, 52-for-132 (.394). Totals, 130-for-377 (.345).

NBA REGULAR-SEASON RECORD

HONORS: Slam Dunk championship winner (1996). ... NBA All-Rookie second team (1996).
NOTES: Led NBA with .476 three-point field goal percentage (2001).

Season Team	G	Min.	FGM	FGA	Pct.	FTM	FTA	Pct.	REBOUNDS			Ast.	St.	Blk.	TO	Pts.	AVERAGES		
									Off.	Def.	Tot.						RPG	APG	PPG
95-96—L.A. Clippers ...	79	1898	283	597	.474	111	137	.810	38	130	168	230	95	22	120	800	2.1	2.9	10.1
96-97—L.A. Clippers ..	59	1094	155	379	.409	76	93	.817	30	80	110	154	51	15	76	442	1.9	2.6	7.5
97-98—L.A.C.-Miami...	58	1600	213	506	.421	115	134	.858	29	142	171	153	64	27	104	631	2.9	2.6	10.9
98-99—Chicago	37	1181	141	356	.396	78	101	.772	39	105	144	116	42	11	72	412	3.9	3.1	11.1
99-00—Seattle	80	2726	327	707	.463	127	157	.809	50	322	372	291	103	31	142	945	4.7	3.6	11.8
00-01—Seattle	67	1778	198	401	.494	84	103	.816	33	178	211	225	80	14	86	589	3.1	3.4	8.8
01-02—Seattle	81	3040	401	790	.508	198	234	.846	58	383	441	426	147	37	165	1164	5.4	5.3	14.4
02-03—Seattle	75	2480	264	577	.458	128	161	.795	48	253	301	384	113	15	142	774	4.0	5.1	10.3
03-04—Seattle	59	1803	215	427	.504	91	110	.827	21	183	204	342	85	16	139	635	3.5	5.8	10.8
04-05—San Antonio	81	1742	194	459	.423	113	135	.837	29	161	190	178	39	20	64	601	2.3	2.2	7.4
05-06—San Antonio	74	1259	156	345	.452	39	59	.661	29	130	159	123	39	27	52	431	2.1	1.7	5.8
Totals	750	20601	2547	5544	.459	1160	1424	.815	404	2067	2471	2622	858	235	1162	7424	3.3	3.5	9.9

Three-point field goals: 1995-96, 123-for-296 (.416). 1996-97, 56-for-173 (.324). 1997-98, 90-for-229 (.393). 1998-99, 52-for-172 (.302). 1999-00, 164-for-399 (.411). 2000-01, 109-for-229 (.476). 2001-02, 164-for-387 (.424). 2002-03, 118-for-293 (.403). 2003-04, 114-for-252 (.452). 2004-05, 100-for-280 (.357). 2005-06, 80-for-202 (.396). Totals, 1170-for-2912 (.402).

Personal fouls/disqualifications: 1995-96, 196/2. 1996-97, 88/1. 1997-98, 118/0. 1998-99, 98/2. 1999-00, 228/4. 2000-01, 126/1. 2001-02, 182/3. 2002-03, 199/1. 2003-04, 121/0. 2004-05, 123/0. 2005-06, 99/1. Totals, 1578/15.

NBA PLAYOFF RECORD

Season Team	G	Min.	FGM	FGA	Pct.	FTM	FTA	Pct.	REBOUNDS			Ast.	St.	Blk.	TO	Pts.	AVERAGES		
									Off.	Def.	Tot.						RPG	APG	PPG
96-97—L.A. Clippers ...	3	84	11	27	.407	8	9	.889	1	6	7	10	4	0	4	35	2.3	3.3	11.7
99-00—Seattle	5	155	12	33	.364	10	14	.714	3	10	13	15	3	3	7	42	2.6	3.0	8.4
01-02—Seattle	5	149	14	34	.412	4	4	1.000	6	17	23	14	3	4	9	39	4.6	2.8	7.8
04-05—San Antonio	23	555	48	105	.457	17	21	.810	13	43	56	44	15	4	27	141	2.4	1.9	6.1
05-06—San Antonio	13	301	34	61	.557	16	21	.762	3	29	32	22	9	3	9	101	2.5	1.7	7.8
Totals	49	1244	119	260	.458	55	69	.797	26	105	131	105	34	14	56	358	2.7	2.1	7.3

Three-point field goals: 1996-97, 5-for-11 (.455). 1999-00, 8-for-20 (.400). 2001-02, 7-for-16 (.438). 2004-05, 28-for-66 (.424). 2005-06, 17-for-34 (.500). Totals, 65-for-147 (.442).

Personal fouls/disqualifications: 1996-97, 10/0. 1999-00, 20/2. 2001-02, 12/0. 2004-05, 44/1. 2005-06, 29/0. Totals, 115/3.

BARRY, JON   G

PERSONAL: Born July 25, 1969, in Oakland. ... 6-5/210. (1.96/95.3). ... Full name: Jon Alan Barry ... Son of Rick Barry, forward with San Francisco/Golden State Warriors (1965-66, 1966-67 and 1972-73 through 1977-78) and Houston Rockets of NBA (1978-79 and 1979-80) and three American Basketball Association teams (1968-69 through 1971-72), and member of Naismith Memorial Basketball Hall of Fame; brother of Brent Barry, guard, San Antonio Spurs; and brother of Drew Barry, guard with Atlanta Hawks (1997-98 and 2000-01), Seattle SuperSonics (1998-99) and Golden State Warriors (2000-01).
HIGH SCHOOL: De La Salle Catholic (Concord, Calif.).
JUNIOR COLLEGE: Paris (Texas) Junior College.
COLLEGE: Pacific, then Georgia Tech.
TRANSACTIONS/CAREER NOTES: Selected by Boston Celtics in first round (21st pick overall) of 1992 NBA Draft. ... Traded by Celtics to Milwaukee Bucks for F Alaa Abdelnaby (December 4, 1992). ... Signed as unrestricted free agent by Golden State Warriors (October 4, 1995). ... Signed as free agent by Atlanta Hawks (August 13, 1996). ... Signed as free agent by Los Angeles Lakers (August 27, 1997). ... Signed as free agent by Sacramento Kings (January 22, 1999). ... Traded by Kings with future first-round draft choice to Detroit Pistons for G Mateen Cleaves (September 7, 2001). ... Signed as free agent by Denver Nuggets (August 19, 2003). ... Signed as free agent by Atlanta Hawks (September 16, 2004). ... Traded by Hawks to Houston Rockets for G Tyronn Lue (December 23, 2004). ... Waived by Rockets (March 1, 2006).

COLLEGIATE RECORD

Season Team	G	Min.	FGM	FGA	Pct.	FTM	FTA	Pct.	Reb.	Ast.	Pts.	AVERAGES		
												RPG	APG	PPG
87-88—Pacific	29	809	100	269	.372	53	71	.746	74	108	275	2.6	3.7	9.5
88-89—Paris J.C.						Did not play.								
89-90—Paris J.C.	30	...	204	358	.570	58	73	.795	108	90	513	3.6	3.0	17.1
90-91—Georgia Tech	30	1088	180	405	.444	41	56	.732	110	110	478	3.7	3.7	15.9
91-92—Georgia Tech	35	1231	201	468	.429	101	145	.697	152	207	602	4.3	5.9	17.2
Junior College Totals............	30	...	204	358	.570	58	73	.795	108	90	513	3.6	3.0	17.1
4-Year-College Totals	94	3128	481	1142	.421	195	272	.717	336	425	1355	3.6	4.5	14.4

Three-point field goals: 1987-88, 22-for-59 (.373). 1990-91, 77-for-209 (.368). 1991-92, 99-for-265 (.374). Totals, 245-for-533 (.460).

NBA REGULAR-SEASON RECORD

| | | | | | | | | REBOUNDS | | | | | | | AVERAGES | | |
Season Team	G	Min.	FGM	FGA	Pct.	FTM	FTA	Pct.	Off.	Def.	Tot.	Ast.	St.	Blk.	TO	Pts.	RPG	APG	PPG
92-93—Milwaukee	47	552	76	206	.369	33	49	.673	10	33	43	68	35	3	42	206	0.9	1.4	4.4
93-94—Milwaukee	72	1242	158	382	.414	97	122	.795	36	110	146	168	102	17	83	445	2.0	2.3	6.2
94-95—Milwaukee	52	602	57	134	.425	61	80	.763	15	34	49	85	30	4	41	191	0.9	1.6	3.7
95-96—Golden State...	68	712	91	185	.492	31	37	.838	17	46	63	85	33	11	42	257	0.9	1.3	3.8
96-97—Atlanta	58	965	100	246	.407	37	46	.804	26	73	99	115	55	3	59	285	1.7	2.0	4.9
97-98—L.A. Lakers	49	374	38	104	.365	27	29	.931	8	29	37	51	24	3	22	121	0.8	1.0	2.5
98-99—Sacramento	43	736	59	138	.428	71	84	.845	25	71	96	112	53	5	47	213	2.2	2.6	5.0
99-00—Sacramento	62	1281	161	346	.465	107	116	.922	38	121	159	150	75	7	85	495	2.6	2.4	8.0
00-01—Sacramento	62	1010	103	255	.404	64	73	.877	16	78	94	130	28	6	53	316	1.5	2.1	5.1
01-02—Detroit	82	1985	255	522	.489	108	116	.931	42	192	234	274	94	20	111	739	2.9	3.3	9.0
02-03—Detroit	80	1473	191	424	.450	86	100	.860	33	147	180	206	63	14	81	555	2.3	2.6	6.9
03-04—Denver...........	57	1101	120	297	.404	60	71	.845	25	98	123	147	57	8	53	351	2.2	2.6	6.2
04-05—Atl.-Houston ...	69	1505	161	368	.438	62	71	.873	26	133	159	167	60	9	67	455	2.3	2.4	6.6
05-06—Houston..........	20	342	25	65	.385	24	29	.828	1	30	31	26	13	1	22	86	1.6	1.3	4.3
Totals	821	13880	1595	3672	.434	868	1023	.848	318	1195	1513	1784	722	111	808	4715	1.8	2.2	5.7

Three-point field goals: 1992-93, 21-for-63 (.333). 1993-94, 32-for-115 (.278). 1994-95, 16-for-48 (.333). 1995-96, 44-for-93 (.473). 1996-97, 48-for-124 (.387). 1997-98, 18-for-61 (.295). 1998-99, 24-for-79 (.304). 1999-00, 66-for-154 (.429). 2000-01, 46-for-132 (.348). 2001-02, 121-for-258 (.469). 2002-03, 87-for-214 (.407). 2003-04, 51-for-138 (.370). 2004-05, 71-for-165 (.430). 2005-06, 12-for-32 (.375). Totals, 657-for-1676 (.392).

Personal fouls/disqualifications: 1992-93, 57/0. 1993-94, 110/0. 1994-95, 54/0. 1995-96, 51/1. 1996-97, 56/0. 1997-98, 33/0. 1998-99, 61/1. 1999-00, 104/1. 2000-01, 66/0. 2001-02, 134/0. 2002-03, 104/0. 2003-04, 66/0. 2004-05, 95/0. 2005-06, 25/0. Totals, 1016/3.

NBA PLAYOFF RECORD

| | | | | | | | | REBOUNDS | | | | | | | AVERAGES | | |
Season Team	G	Min.	FGM	FGA	Pct.	FTM	FTA	Pct.	Off.	Def.	Tot.	Ast.	St.	Blk.	TO	Pts.	RPG	APG	PPG
96-97—Atlanta	2	9	0	3	.000	0	0	...	0	0	0	0	0	0	0	0	0.0	0.0	0.0
97-98—L.A. Lakers	7	18	0	8	.000	0	0	...	0	2	2	0	1	0	0	0	0.3	0.0	0.0
98-99—Sacramento	5	112	12	34	.353	11	12	.917	3	7	10	9	6	1	9	40	2.0	1.8	8.0
99-00—Sacramento	5	102	9	21	.429	14	16	.875	2	10	12	12	3	0	4	39	2.4	2.4	7.8
00-01—Sacramento	7	55	7	17	.412	0	0	...	3	0	3	4	1	0	3	16	0.4	0.6	2.3
01-02—Detroit	10	177	29	61	.475	5	8	.625	4	16	20	21	5	1	19	80	2.0	2.1	8.0
02-03—Detroit	14	172	23	54	.426	9	9	1.000	5	19	24	20	8	1	7	70	1.7	1.4	5.0
03-04—Denver...........	5	100	8	24	.333	2	3	.667	4	14	18	10	3	0	4	21	3.6	2.0	4.2
04-05—Houston..........	7	183	21	48	.438	7	8	.875	1	28	29	9	5	0	6	60	4.1	1.3	8.6
Totals	62	928	109	270	.404	48	56	.857	22	96	118	85	32	3	52	326	1.9	1.4	5.3

Three-point field goals: 1997-98, 0-for-5. 1998-99, 5-for-19 (.263). 1999-00, 7-for-12 (.583). 2000-01, 2-for-7 (.286). 2001-02, 17-for-38 (.447). 2002-03, 15-for-33 (.455). 2003-04, 3-for-9 (.333). 2004-05, 11-for-23 (.478). Totals, 60-for-146 (.411).

Personal fouls/disqualifications: 1997-98, 1/0. 1998-99, 9/0. 1999-00, 7/0. 2000-01, 7/0. 2001-02, 14/0. 2002-03, 14/0. 2003-04, 4/0. 2004-05, 13/0. Totals, 69/0.

BASDEN, EDDIE   G   CAVALIERS

PERSONAL: Born February 15, 1983, in New York, N.Y. ... 6-5/215. (1.96/97.5).
HIGH SCHOOL: Eleanor Roosevelt (Greenbelt, Md.).
COLLEGE: Charlotte.
TRANSACTIONS/CAREER NOTES: Not drafted by an NBA franchise. ... Signed as free agent by Chicago Bulls (August 9, 2005). ... Traded by Bulls to Cleveland Cavaliers for C Martynas Andriuskevicius (August 18, 2006).

COLLEGIATE RECORD

| | | | | | | | | | | | AVERAGES | | |
Season Team	G	Min.	FGM	FGA	Pct.	FTM	FTA	Pct.	Reb.	Ast.	Pts.	RPG	APG	PPG
01-02—Charlotte..................	30	566	45	96	.469	37	58	.638	128	39	128	4.3	1.3	4.3
02-03—Charlotte..................	29	742	60	133	.451	60	83	.723	200	74	183	6.9	2.6	6.3
03-04—Charlotte..................	30	850	105	196	.536	87	135	.644	192	93	313	6.4	3.1	10.4
04-05—Charlotte..................	29	1049	155	318	.487	110	152	.724	245	108	442	8.4	3.7	15.2
Totals	118	3207	365	743	.491	294	428	.687	765	314	1066	6.5	2.7	9.0

Three-point field goals: 2001-02, 1-for-8 (.125). 2002-03, 3-for-12 (.250). 2003-04, 16-for-42 (.381). 2004-05, 22-for-57 (.386). Totals, 42-for-119 (.353).

NBA REGULAR-SEASON RECORD

| | | | | | | | | REBOUNDS | | | | | | | AVERAGES | | |
Season Team	G	Min.	FGM	FGA	Pct.	FTM	FTA	Pct.	Off.	Def.	Tot.	Ast.	St.	Blk.	TO	Pts.	RPG	APG	PPG
05-06—Chicago	19	141	15	37	.405	8	10	.800	7	21	28	8	9	2	9	39	1.5	0.4	2.1

Three-point field goals: 2005-06, 1-for-7 (.143). Totals, 1-for-7 (.143).
Personal fouls/disqualifications: 2005-06, 17/0. Totals, 17/0.

NBA DEVELOPMENT LEAGUE RECORD

| | | | | | | | | | | | AVERAGES | | |
Season Team	G	Min.	FGM	FGA	Pct.	FTM	FTA	Pct.	Reb.	Ast.	Pts.	RPG	APG	PPG
05-06—Tulsa..................	14	356	63	130	.485	14	30	.467	63	39	147	4.5	2.8	10.5

Three-point field goals: 2005-06, 7-for-23 (.304). Totals, 7-for-23 (.304).

BASS, BRANDON   F   HORNETS

PERSONAL: Born April 30, 1985, in Baton Rouge, La. ... 6-8/240. (2.03/108.9). ... Full name: Brandon Sam Bass
HIGH SCHOOL: Capitol (Baton Rouge, La.).
COLLEGE: LSU.
TRANSACTIONS/CAREER NOTES: Selected after sophomore season by New Orleans Hornets in second round (33rd overall pick) of 2005 NBA Draft.

COLLEGIATE RECORD

Season Team	G	Min.	FGM	FGA	Pct.	FTM	FTA	Pct.	Reb.	Ast.	Pts.	AVERAGES RPG	APG	PPG
03-04—LSU	29	1013	121	240	.504	123	157	.783	214	17	370	7.4	0.6	12.8
04-05—LSU	30	1007	181	319	.567	146	188	.777	272	25	520	9.1	0.8	17.3
Totals	59	2020	302	559	.540	269	345	.780	486	42	890	8.2	0.7	15.1

Three-point field goals: 2003-04, 5-for-19 (.263). 2004-05, 12-for-26 (.462). Totals, 17-for-45 (.378).

NBA REGULAR-SEASON RECORD

Season Team	G	Min.	FGM	FGA	Pct.	FTM	FTA	Pct.	REBOUNDS Off.	Def.	Tot.	Ast.	St.	Blk.	TO	Pts.	AVERAGES RPG	APG	PPG
05-06—NO/Okla. City ..	29	268	28	70	.400	12	19	.632	18	50	68	3	3	7	11	68	2.3	0.1	2.3

Personal fouls/disqualifications: 2005-06, 18/0. Totals, 18/0.

NBA DEVELOPMENT LEAGUE RECORD

Season Team	G	Min.	FGM	FGA	Pct.	FTM	FTA	Pct.	Reb.	Ast.	Pts.	AVERAGES RPG	APG	PPG
05-06—Tulsa	1	26	7	13	.538	2	4	.500	5	0	16	5.0	0.0	16.0

BATISTA, ESTEBAN F/C HAWKS

PERSONAL: Born March 3, 1983 ... 6-10/270. (2.08/122.5). ... Full name: Esteban Damian Batista
TRANSACTIONS/CAREER NOTES: Not drafted by an NBA franchise ... Played in Spain (2004-05). ... Signed as free agent by Atlanta Hawks (September 12, 2005).

SPANISH LEAGUE RECORD

Season Team	G	Min.	FGM	FGA	Pct.	FTM	FTA	Pct.	Reb.	Ast.	Pts.	AVERAGES RPG	APG	PPG
04-05—San Jose dos Pinhais	8	192	33	62	.532	19	29	.655	44	8	85	5.5	1.0	10.6

Three-point field goals: 2004-05, 0-for-2. Totals, 0-for-2 (.000).

NBA REGULAR-SEASON RECORD

Season Team	G	Min.	FGM	FGA	Pct.	FTM	FTA	Pct.	REBOUNDS Off.	Def.	Tot.	Ast.	St.	Blk.	TO	Pts.	AVERAGES RPG	APG	PPG
05-06—Atlanta	57	495	34	80	.425	33	53	.623	61	83	144	7	15	11	38	101	2.5	0.1	1.8

Three-point field goals: 2005-06, 0-for-1. Totals, 0-for-1 (.000).
Personal fouls/disqualifications: 2005-06, 111/2. Totals, 111/2.

BATTIE, TONY F/C MAGIC

PERSONAL: Born February 11, 1976, in Dallas. ... 6-11/240. (2.11/108.9). ... Full name: Demetrius Antonio Battie
HIGH SCHOOL: South Oak Cliff (Dallas).
COLLEGE: Texas Tech.
TRANSACTIONS/CAREER NOTES: Selected after junior season by Denver Nuggets in first round (fifth pick overall) of 1997 NBA Draft. ... Traded by Nuggets with draft rights to G Tyronn Lue to Los Angeles Lakers for G Nick Van Exel (June 24, 1998). ... Traded by Lakers to Boston Celtics for C Travis Knight (January 21, 1999). ... Traded by Celtics with F Kedrick Brown and F Eric Williams to Cleveland Cavaliers for G Ricky Davis, F/C Chris Mihm, C Michael Stewart and a second-round draft choice (December 15, 2003). ... Traded by Cavaliers with two future second-round draft choices to Orlando Magic for F Drew Gooden, C Steven Hunter and the draft rights to F Anderson Varejao (July 23, 2004).

COLLEGIATE RECORD

Season Team	G	Min.	FGM	FGA	Pct.	FTM	FTA	Pct.	Reb.	Ast.	Pts.	AVERAGES RPG	APG	PPG
94-95—Texas Tech	29	368	47	96	.490	18	27	.667	129	17	112	4.4	0.6	3.9
95-96—Texas Tech	30	806	114	221	.516	60	95	.632	266	32	292	8.9	1.1	9.7
96-97—Texas Tech	28	978	206	356	.579	107	163	.656	329	23	525	11.8	0.8	18.8
Totals	87	2152	367	673	.545	185	285	.649	724	72	929	8.3	0.8	10.7

Three-point field goals: 1994-95, 0-for-6. 1995-96, 4-for-14 (.286). 1996-97, 6-for-16 (.375). Totals, 10-for-36 (.278).
Personal fouls/disqualifications: 1994-95, 50/1. 1995-96, 88/3. Totals, 138/4.

NBA REGULAR-SEASON RECORD

Season Team	G	Min.	FGM	FGA	Pct.	FTM	FTA	Pct.	REBOUNDS Off.	Def.	Tot.	Ast.	St.	Blk.	TO	Pts.	AVERAGES RPG	APG	PPG
97-98—Denver	65	1506	234	525	.446	73	104	.702	138	213	351	60	54	69	98	544	5.4	0.9	8.4
98-99—Boston	50	1121	147	283	.519	41	61	.672	96	204	300	53	29	71	45	335	6.0	1.1	6.7
99-00—Boston	82	1505	219	459	.477	102	151	.675	152	258	410	63	47	70	67	541	5.0	0.8	6.6
00-01—Boston	40	845	108	201	.537	44	69	.638	73	160	233	16	27	60	37	260	5.8	0.4	6.5
01-02—Boston	74	1819	211	390	.541	88	130	.677	184	297	481	35	60	67	51	510	6.5	0.5	6.9
02-03—Boston	67	1683	199	369	.539	88	118	.746	148	285	433	49	33	81	48	487	6.5	0.7	7.3
03-04—Boston-Cleve..	73	1478	170	384	.443	66	89	.742	118	241	359	58	26	67	63	408	4.9	0.8	5.6
04-05—Orlando	81	1894	163	354	.460	68	94	.723	109	343	452	42	30	81	81	394	5.6	0.5	4.9
05-06—Orlando	82	2215	280	552	.507	89	134	.664	145	312	457	49	46	69	88	649	5.6	0.6	7.9
Totals	614	14066	1731	3517	.492	659	950	.694	1163	2313	3476	425	352	635	578	4128	5.7	0.7	6.7

Three-point field goals: 1997-98, 3-for-14 (.214). 1998-99, 0-for-3. 1999-00, 1-for-8 (.125). 2000-01, 0-for-3. 2001-02, 0-for-2. 2002-03, 1-for-5 (.200). 2003-04, 2-for-9 (.222). 2004-05, 0-for-6. 2005-06, 0-for-6. Totals, 7-for-56 (.125).
Personal fouls/disqualifications: 1997-98, 199/6. 1998-99, 159/1. 1999-00, 249/4. 2000-01, 126/3. 2001-02, 219/3. 2002-03, 197/2. 2003-04, 159/0. 2004-05, 244/3. 2005-06, 250/4. Totals, 1802/26.

NBA PLAYOFF RECORD

								REBOUNDS								AVERAGES		
Season Team	G	Min.	FGM	FGA	Pct.	FTM	FTA	Pct.	Off.	Def.	Tot.	Ast.	St.	Blk.	TO	Pts.	RPG	APG	PPG
01-02—Boston	16	443	42	86	.488	13	21	.619	39	82	121	13	10	30	11	97	7.6	0.8	6.1
02-03—Boston	10	213	31	55	.564	4	8	.500	13	36	49	5	4	14	7	66	4.9	0.5	6.6
Totals	26	656	73	141	.518	17	29	.586	52	118	170	18	14	44	18	163	6.5	0.7	6.3

Three-point field goals: 2002-03, 0-for-3. Totals, 0-for-3 (.000).
Personal fouls/disqualifications: 2001-02, 51/1. 2002-03, 42/1. Totals, 93/2.

BATTIER, SHANE — F — ROCKETS

B

PERSONAL: Born September 9, 1978, in Birmingham, Mich. ... 6-8/220. (2.03/99.8). ... Full name: Shane Courtney Battier
HIGH SCHOOL: Detroit Country Day (Birmingham, Mich.).
COLLEGE: Duke.
TRANSACTIONS/CAREER NOTES: Selected by Vancover Grizzlies in first round (sixth pick overall) of 2001 NBA Draft. ... Grizzlies franchise moved to Memphis for 2001-02 season. ... Traded by Grizzlies to Houston Rockets for draft rights to F Rudy Gay and F Stromile Swift (July 12, 2006).
MISCELLANEOUS: Memphis Grizzlies franchise all-time steals leader (507).

COLLEGIATE RECORD

NOTES: Member of NCAA Division I championship team (2001). ... The SPORTING NEWS All-America first team (2001). ... The SPORTING NEWS College Player of the Year (2001). ... Naismith Award winner (2001). ... Wooden Award winner (2001). ... NCAA Division I Tournament Most Outstanding Player (2001). ... The SPORTING NEWS All-America second team (2000).

											AVERAGES		
Season Team	G	Min.	FGM	FGA	Pct.	FTM	FTA	Pct.	Reb.	Ast.	Pts.	RPG	APG	PPG
97-98—Duke	36	887	96	178	.539	79	108	.731	230	40	275	6.4	1.1	7.6
98-99—Duke	37	881	114	209	.545	71	98	.724	180	55	338	4.9	1.5	9.1
99-00—Duke	34	1206	190	383	.496	134	164	.817	192	72	593	5.6	2.1	17.4
00-01—Duke	39	1363	251	533	.471	152	191	.796	285	72	778	7.3	1.8	19.9
Totals	146	4337	651	1303	.500	436	561	.777	887	239	1984	6.1	1.6	13.6

Three-point field goals: 1997-98, 4-for-24 (.167). 1998-99, 39-for-94 (.415). 1999-00, 79-for-178 (.444). 2000-01, 124-for-296 (.419). Totals, 246-for-592 (.416).
Personal fouls/disqualifications: 1997-98, 67/0. 1998-99, 78/0. 1999-00, 71/0. 2000-01, 80/0. Totals, 296/0.

NBA REGULAR-SEASON RECORD

HONORS: NBA All-Rookie first team (2002).

									REBOUNDS								AVERAGES		
Season Team	G	Min.	FGM	FGA	Pct.	FTM	FTA	Pct.	Off.	Def.	Tot.	Ast.	St.	Blk.	TO	Pts.	RPG	APG	PPG
01-02—Memphis	78	3097	412	961	.429	198	283	.700	180	238	418	216	121	81	155	1125	5.4	2.8	14.4
02-03—Memphis	78	2383	275	569	.483	120	145	.828	128	217	345	105	102	88	68	756	4.4	1.3	9.7
03-04—Memphis	79	1947	242	543	.446	120	164	.732	102	201	303	101	101	58	56	669	3.8	1.3	8.5
04-05—Memphis	80	2516	271	613	.442	180	228	.789	158	255	413	126	91	77	75	792	5.2	1.6	9.9
05-06—Memphis	81	1939	303	621	.488	117	999	.797	164	265	429	136	92	114	90	818	5.3	1.7	10.1
Totals	396	12782	1503	3307	.454	765	1028	.744	732	1176	1908	684	507	418	444	4160	4.8	1.7	10.5

Three-point field goals: 2001-02, 103-for-276 (.373). 2002-03, 86-for-216 (.398). 2003-04, 65-for-186 (.349). 2004-05, 70-for-177 (.395). 2005-06, 65-for-165 (.394). Totals, 389-for-1020 (.381).
Personal fouls/disqualifications: 2001-02, 215/2. 2002-03, 207/0. 2003-04, 187/1. 2004-05, 201/2. 2005-06, 223/3. Totals, 1033/8.·

NBA PLAYOFF RECORD

									REBOUNDS								AVERAGES		
Season Team	G	Min.	FGM	FGA	Pct.	FTM	FTA	Pct.	Off.	Def.	Tot.	Ast.	St.	Blk.	TO	Pts.	RPG	APG	PPG
03-04—Memphis	4	69	6	15	.400	4	6	.667	6	6	12	1	0	1	4	19	3.0	0.3	4.8
04-05—Memphis	4	119	13	31	.419	2	5	.400	10	17	27	6	2	4	4	29	6.8	1.5	7.3
05-06—Memphis	4	129	10	20	.500	2	6	.333	7	16	23	2	4	2	8	24	5.8	0.5	6.0
Totals	12	317	29	66	.439	8	17	.471	23	39	62	9	6	7	16	72	5.2	0.8	6.0

Three-point field goals: 2003-04, 3-for-7 (.429). 2004-05, 1-for-7 (.143). 2005-06, 2-for-7 (.286). Totals, 6-for-21 (.286).
Personal fouls/disqualifications: 2003-04, 17/0. 2004-05, 14/0. 2005-06, 16/0. Totals, 47/0.

BAXTER, LONNY — F

PERSONAL: Born July 27, 1979, in Silver Spring, Md. ... 6-8/264. (2.03/119.7). ... Full name: Lonny Leroy Baxter
HIGH SCHOOL: Richard Montgomery (Rockville, Md.), then Anacostia (Washington, D.C.), then Hargrave Military Academy.
COLLEGE: Maryland.
TRANSACTIONS/CAREER NOTES: Selected by Chicago Bulls in second round (44th pick overall) of 2002 NBA Draft. ... Traded by Bulls with F Donyell Marshall and G Jalen Rose to Toronto Raptors for F/C Antonio Davis, F Chris Jefferies and F Jerome Williams (December 1, 2003). ... Waived by Raptors (February 29, 2004). ... Claimed off waivers by Washington Wizards (March 3, 2004). ... Selected by Charlotte Bobcats from Wizards in NBA Expansion Draft (June 22, 2004). ... Signed as free agent by Atlanta Hawks (October 4, 2004). ... Released by Hawks (October 28, 2004). ... Played in Continental Basketball Association (2004). ... Signed as free agent by New Orleans Hornets (December 12, 2004). ... Waived by Hornets (December 27, 2004). ... Signed as free agent by Houston Rockets (September 8, 2005). ... Traded by Rockets to Charlotte Bobcats for F/G Keith Bogans (February 9, 2006).

COLLEGIATE RECORD

NOTES: Member of NCAA Division I championship team (2002).

											AVERAGES		
Season Team	G	Min.	FGM	FGA	Pct.	FTM	FTA	Pct.	Reb.	Ast.	Pts.	RPG	APG	PPG
98-99—Maryland	32	463	82	137	.599	51	89	.573	116	18	217	3.6	0.6	6.8
99-00—Maryland	35	970	218	409	.533	111	187	.594	308	31	547	8.8	0.9	15.6

Season Team	G	Min.	FGM	FGA	Pct.	FTM	FTA	Pct.	Reb.	Ast.	Pts.	AVERAGES RPG	APG	PPG
00-01—Maryland	36	935	219	387	.566	122	206	.592	286	19	561	7.9	0.5	15.6
01-02—Maryland	35	1005	193	354	.545	147	236	.623	288	28	533	8.2	0.8	15.2
Totals	138	3373	712	1287	.553	431	718	.600	998	96	1858	7.2	0.7	13.5

Three-point field goals: 1998-99, 2-for-2 (1.000). 2000-01, 1-for-2 (.500). 2001-02, 0-for-1. Totals, 3-for-5 (.600).

NBA REGULAR-SEASON RECORD

Season Team	G	Min.	FGM	FGA	Pct.	FTM	FTA	Pct.	REBOUNDS Off.	Def.	Tot.	Ast.	St.	Blk.	TO	Pts.	AVERAGES RPG	APG	PPG
02-03—Chicago	55	682	96	206	.466	70	103	.680	65	100	165	16	9	22	46	262	3.0	0.3	4.8
03-04—Chi.-Tor.-Wash.	62	766	103	209	.493	44	76	.579	64	123	187	20	17	29	38	251	3.0	0.3	4.0
04-05—New Orleans ...	4	36	3	11	.273	0	2	.000	4	4	8	0	0	0	4	6	2.0	0.0	1.5
05-06—Houston-Char.	41	401	45	104	.433	28	35	.800	45	72	117	4	11	8	20	118	2.9	0.1	2.9
Totals	162	1885	247	530	.466	142	216	.657	178	299	477	40	37	59	108	637	2.9	0.2	3.9

Three-point field goals: 2002-03, 0-for-2. 2003-04, 1-for-3 (.333). Totals, 1-for-5 (.200).
Personal fouls/disqualifications: 2002-03, 135/1. 2003-04, 123/3. 2004-05, 10/0. 2005-06, 56/1. Totals, 324/5.

CBA RECORD

Season Team	G	Min.	FGM	FGA	Pct.	FTM	FTA	Pct.	Reb.	Ast.	Pts.	AVERAGES RPG	APG	PPG
04-05—Yakima	6	180	38	85	.447	22	33	.667	222	45	98	37.0	7.5	16.3

GREEK LEAGUE RECORD

Season Team	G	Min.	FGM	FGA	Pct.	FTM	FTA	Pct.	Reb.	Ast.	Pts.	AVERAGES RPG	APG	PPG
04-05—Panathinaikos.................	12	174	37	57	.649	12	60	.200	59	2	86	4.9	0.2	7.2

BELL, CHARLIE   G   BUCKS

PERSONAL: Born March 12, 1979, in Flint, Mich. ... 6-3/200. (1.91/90.7).
HIGH SCHOOL: Southwestern Academy (Flint, Mich.).
COLLEGE: Michigan State.
TRANSACTIONS/CAREER NOTES: Not drafted by an NBA franchise. ... Signed as free agent by Phoenix Suns (August 1, 2001). ... Released by Suns (December 11, 2001). ... Played in American Basketball Association 2000 with Phoenix Eclipse (2001-02). ... Played in Italy (2001-04). ... Played in Spain (2004-05). ... Signed by Dallas Mavericks to 10-day contract (January 13, 2002). ... Signed by Mavericks for remainder of season (January 15, 2002). ... Signed as free agent by Milwaukee Bucks (August 18, 2005).

COLLEGIATE RECORD

NOTES: Member of NCAA Division I championship team (2000).

Season Team	G	Min.	FGM	FGA	Pct.	FTM	FTA	Pct.	Reb.	Ast.	Pts.	AVERAGES RPG	APG	PPG
97-98—Michigan State	30	725	94	216	.435	69	87	.793	133	40	276	4.4	1.3	9.2
98-99—Michigan State	38	861	116	243	.477	49	65	.754	146	39	297	3.8	1.0	7.8
99-00—Michigan State	39	1078	159	351	.453	93	116	.802	190	123	449	4.9	3.2	11.5
00-01—Michigan State	33	1034	150	373	.402	94	122	.770	155	169	446	4.7	5.1	13.5
Totals	140	3698	519	1183	.439	305	390	.782	624	371	1468	4.5	2.7	10.5

Three-point field goals: 1997-98, 19-for-56 (.339). 1998-99, 16-for-45 (.356). 1999-00, 38-for-111 (.342). 2000-01, 52-for-152 (.342). Totals, 125-for-364 (.343).
Personal fouls/disqualifications: 1997-98, 53/0. 1998-99, 85/2. 1999-00, 94/3. 2000-01, 53/0. Totals, 285/5.

AMERICAN BASKETBALL ASSOCIATION 2000 RECORD

Season Team	G	Min.	FGM	FGA	Pct.	FTM	FTA	Pct.	Reb.	Ast.	Pts.	AVERAGES RPG	APG	PPG
01-02—Phoenix	4	137	28	65	.431	11	14	.786	16	25	76	4.0	6.3	19.0

Three-point field goals: 2001-02, 9-for-24 (.375). Totals, 9-for-24 (.375).

ITALIAN LEAGUE RECORD

Season Team	G	Min.	FGM	FGA	Pct.	FTM	FTA	Pct.	Reb.	Ast.	Pts.	AVERAGES RPG	APG	PPG
01-02—Benetton Treviso	7	152	30	65	.462	6	6	1.000	24	11	79	3.4	1.6	11.3
02-03—Virtus Bologna	23	721	114	306	.373	54	62	.871	78	41	329	3.4	1.8	14.3
03-04—Mabo..............................	34	1275	290	687	.422	145	187	.775	116	82	868	3.4	2.4	25.5
Totals	64	2148	434	1058	.410	205	255	.804	218	134	1276	3.4	2.1	19.9

Three-point field goals: 2001-02, 13-for-28 (.464). 2002-03, 47-for-130 (.362). 2003-04, 143-for-384 (.372). Totals, 203-for-542 (.375).

NBA REGULAR-SEASON RECORD

Season Team	G	Min.	FGM	FGA	Pct.	FTM	FTA	Pct.	REBOUNDS Off.	Def.	Tot.	Ast.	St.	Blk.	TO	Pts.	AVERAGES RPG	APG	PPG
01-02—Pho.-Dal.	7	44	3	11	.273	2	2	1.000	2	3	5	2	0	0	5	8	0.7	0.3	1.1
05-06—Milwaukee	59	1283	180	410	.439	63	89	.708	21	99	120	130	59	5	41	494	2.0	2.2	8.4
Totals	66	1327	183	421	.435	65	91	.714	23	102	125	132	59	5	46	502	1.9	2.0	7.6

Three-point field goals: 2001-02, 0-for-6. 2005-06, 71-for-168 (.423). Totals, 71-for-174 (.408).
Personal fouls/disqualifications: 2001-02, 3/0. 2005-06, 126/1. Totals, 129/1.

NBA PLAYOFF RECORD

Season Team	G	Min.	FGM	FGA	Pct.	FTM	FTA	Pct.	REBOUNDS Off.	Def.	Tot.	Ast.	St.	Blk.	TO	Pts.	AVERAGES RPG	APG	PPG
05-06—Milwaukee	5	108	17	43	.395	7	7	1.000	2	1	3	7	3	2	4	46	0.6	1.4	9.2

Three-point field goals: 2005-06, 5-for-11 (.455). Totals, 5-for-11 (.455).
Personal fouls/disqualifications: 2005-06, 15/0. Totals, 15/0.

SPANISH LEAGUE RECORD

Season Team	G	Min.	FGM	FGA	Pct.	FTM	FTA	Pct.	Reb.	Ast.	Pts.	RPG	APG	PPG
04-05—Leche Rio	28	936	252	530	.475	135	162	.833	91	53	756	3.3	1.9	27.0

Three-point field goals: 2004-05, 117-for-263 (.445). Totals, 117-for-263 (.445).

BELL, RAJA — G — SUNS

PERSONAL: Born September 19, 1976, in St. Croix, Virgin Islands. ... 6-5/215. (1.96/97.5).
HIGH SCHOOL: Killian (Miami).
COLLEGE: Boston University, then Florida International.
TRANSACTIONS/CAREER NOTES: Not drafted by an NBA franchise. ... Played in Continental Basketball Association with Yakima Sun Kings (1999-2001). ... Signed as free agent by San Antonio Spurs (August 2, 2000). ... Waived by Spurs (October 30, 2000). ... Signed by Philadelphia 76ers to 10-day contract (April 6, 2001). ... Re-signed by 76ers for remainder of season (April 16, 2001). ... Signed as free agent by Dallas Mavericks (October 1, 2002). ... Signed as free agent by Utah Jazz (September 26, 2003). ... Signed as free agent by Phoenix Suns (August 3, 2005).

B

COLLEGIATE RECORD

Season Team	G	Min.	FGM	FGA	Pct.	FTM	FTA	Pct.	Reb.	Ast.	Pts.	RPG	APG	PPG
94-95—Boston University	30	866	119	291	.409	59	81	.728	127	37	330	4.2	1.2	11.0
95-96—Boston University	28	932	155	360	.431	74	112	.661	114	52	421	4.1	1.9	15.0
96-97—Florida International						Did not play—transfer student.								
97-98—Florida International	29	855	165	373	.442	112	146	.767	118	65	481	4.1	2.2	16.6
98-99—Florida International	29	1011	167	366	.456	102	137	.745	124	79	484	4.3	2.7	16.7
Totals	116	3664	606	1390	.436	347	476	.729	483	233	1716	4.2	2.0	14.8

Three-point field goals: 1994-95, 33-for-77 (.429). 1995-96, 37-for-112 (.330). 1997-98, 39-for-121 (.322). 1998-99, 48-for-138 (.348). Totals, 157-for-448 (.350).
Personal fouls/disqualifications: 1994-95, 92/0. 1995-96, 73/0. 1997-98, 75/0. 1998-99, 87/0. Totals, 327/0.

CBA RECORD

Season Team	G	Min.	FGM	FGA	Pct.	FTM	FTA	Pct.	Reb.	Ast.	Pts.	RPG	APG	PPG
99-00—Yakima	52	1494	238	464	.513	104	137	.759	146	142	597	2.8	2.7	11.5
00-01—Yakima	9	293	58	124	.468	44	57	.772	39	37	172	4.3	4.1	19.1
Totals	61	1787	296	588	.503	148	194	.763	185	179	769	3.0	2.9	12.6

Three-point field goals: 1999-00, 17-for-46 (.370). 2000-01, 12-for-36 (.333). Totals, 29-for-82 (.354).
Personal fouls/disqualifications: 1999-00, 137/0. 2000-01, 22/0. Totals, 159/0.

NBA REGULAR-SEASON RECORD

Season Team	G	Min.	FGM	FGA	Pct.	FTM	FTA	Pct.	Off.	Def.	Tot.	Ast.	St.	Blk.	TO	Pts.	RPG	APG	PPG
00-01—Philadelphia	5	70	2	7	.200	0	0	...	0	1	1	0	1	0	2	5	0.2	0.0	1.0
01-02—Philadelphia	74	890	103	240	.429	36	48	.750	31	80	111	71	21	4	48	254	1.5	1.0	3.4
02-03—Dallas	75	1173	93	211	.441	23	34	.676	47	98	145	57	52	8	43	230	1.9	0.8	3.1
03-04—Utah	82	2020	329	805	.409	195	248	.786	60	181	241	107	63	13	111	915	2.9	1.3	11.2
04-05—Utah	63	1790	303	667	.454	112	150	.747	48	153	201	91	44	8	79	772	3.2	1.4	12.3
05-06—Phoenix	79	2959	425	930	.457	115	146	.788	44	209	253	207	76	22	89	1162	3.2	2.6	14.7
Totals	378	8862	1255	2860	.439	481	626	.768	230	722	952	533	257	55	372	3338	2.5	1.4	8.8

Three-point field goals: 2000-01, 1-for-3 (.333). 2001-02, 12-for-44 (.273). 2002-03, 21-for-51 (.412). 2003-04, 62-for-166 (.373). 2004-05, 54-for-134 (.403). 2005-06, 197-for-446 (.442). Totals, 347-for-844 (.411).
Personal fouls/disqualifications: 2000-01, 1/0. 2001-02, 109/0. 2002-03, 134/1. 2003-04, 262/6. 2004-05, 205/4. 2005-06, 248/5. Totals, 959/16.

NBA PLAYOFF RECORD

Season Team	G	Min.	FGM	FGA	Pct.	FTM	FTA	Pct.	Off.	Def.	Tot.	Ast.	St.	Blk.	TO	Pts.	RPG	APG	PPG
00-01—Philadelphia	15	124	12	27	.444	8	14	.571	4	9	13	7	15	0	5	34	0.9	0.5	2.3
01-02—Philadelphia	3	8	1	3	.333	0	0	...	1	0	1	0	0	0	0	2	0.3	0.0	0.7
02-03—Dallas	17	305	40	73	.548	11	20	.550	13	38	51	27	5	0	6	97	3.0	1.6	5.7
05-06—Phoenix	17	673	79	165	.479	34	41	.829	8	40	48	37	11	4	10	232	2.8	2.2	13.6
Totals	52	1110	132	268	.493	53	75	.707	26	87	113	71	31	4	21	365	2.2	1.4	7.0

Three-point field goals: 2000-01, 2-for-8 (.250). 2001-02, 0-for-2. 2002-03, 6-for-13 (.462). 2005-06, 40-for-86 (.465). Totals, 48-for-109 (.440).
Personal fouls/disqualifications: 2000-01, 20/0. 2002-03, 41/0. 2005-06, 70/2. Totals, 131/2.

BENDER, JONATHAN — F

PERSONAL: Born January 30, 1981, in Picayune, Miss. ... 6-11/220. (2.11/99.8). ... Full name: Jonathan Rene Bender
HIGH SCHOOL: Picayune (Miss.) Memorial.
COLLEGE: Did not attend college.
TRANSACTIONS/CAREER NOTES: Selected out of high school by Toronto Raptors in first round (fifth pick overall) of 1999 NBA Draft. ... Draft rights traded by Raptors to Indiana Pacers for F/C Antonio Davis (August 1, 1999). ... Waived by Pacers (June 8, 2006).

NBA REGULAR-SEASON RECORD

Season Team	G	Min.	FGM	FGA	Pct.	FTM	FTA	Pct.	Off.	Def.	Tot.	Ast.	St.	Blk.	TO	Pts.	RPG	APG	PPG
99-00—Indiana	24	130	23	70	.329	16	24	.667	4	17	21	3	1	5	7	64	0.9	0.1	2.7
00-01—Indiana	59	574	66	186	.355	50	68	.735	14	60	74	32	7	28	42	193	1.3	0.5	3.3
01-02—Indiana	78	1647	198	460	.430	140	181	.773	64	180	244	62	19	49	96	581	3.1	0.8	7.4

Season Team	G	Min.	FGM	FGA	Pct.	FTM	FTA	Pct.	REBOUNDS Off.	Def.	Tot.	Ast.	St.	Blk.	TO	Pts.	AVERAGES RPG	APG	PPG
02-03—Indiana	46	819	112	254	.441	60	84	.714	42	91	133	42	8	56	42	303	2.9	0.9	6.6
03-04—Indiana	21	271	50	106	.472	39	47	.830	9	31	40	9	5	11	33	148	1.9	0.4	7.0
04-05—Indiana	7	93	16	40	.400	3	6	.500	5	9	14	4	1	2	10	36	2.0	0.6	5.1
05-06—Indiana	2	21	4	5	.800	2	2	1.000	0	4	4	2	0	1	0	10	2.0	1.0	5.0
Totals	237	3555	469	1121	.418	310	412	.752	138	392	530	154	41	152	230	1335	2.2	0.6	5.6

Three-point field goals: 1999-00, 2-for-12 (.167). 2000-01, 11-for-41 (.268). 2001-02, 45-for-125 (.360). 2002-03, 19-for-53 (.358). 2003-04, 9-for-22 (.409). 2004-05, 1-for-5 (.200). Totals, 87-for-258 (.337).

Personal fouls/disqualifications: 1999-00, 18/0. 2000-01, 73/0. 2001-02, 147/1. 2002-03, 86/0. 2003-04, 23/0. 2004-05, 9/0. 2005-06, 2/0. Totals, 358/1.

NBA PLAYOFF RECORD

Season Team	G	Min.	FGM	FGA	Pct.	FTM	FTA	Pct.	REBOUNDS Off.	Def.	Tot.	Ast.	St.	Blk.	TO	Pts.	AVERAGES RPG	APG	PPG
99-00—Indiana	9	21	4	6	.667	3	6	.500	0	3	3	0	1	0	0	12	0.3	0.0	1.3
00-01—Indiana	1	4	0	1	.000	0	0	...	0	0	0	0	0	0	0	0	0.0	0.0	0.0
01-02—Indiana	5	45	3	6	.500	0	0	...	0	4	4	2	2	3	5	6	0.8	0.4	1.2
02-03—Indiana	3	34	5	15	.333	4	6	.667	3	4	7	0	0	2	0	17	2.3	0.0	5.7
03-04—Indiana	16	200	28	69	.406	12	16	.750	10	18	28	7	2	14	12	77	1.8	0.4	4.8
Totals	34	304	40	97	.412	19	28	.679	13	29	42	9	5	19	17	112	1.2	0.3	3.3

Three-point field goals: 1999-00, 1-for-1 (1.000). 2001-02, 0-for-1. 2002-03, 3-for-9 (.333). 2003-04, 9-for-25 (.360). Totals, 13-for-36 (.361).

Personal fouls/disqualifications: 1999-00, 2/0. 2000-01, 1/0. 2001-02, 6/0. 2002-03, 2/0. 2003-04, 19/0. Totals, 30/0.

BIBBY, MIKE   G   KINGS

PERSONAL: Born May 13, 1978, in Cherry Hill, N.J. ... 6-1/190. (1.85/86.2). ... Son of Henry Bibby, guard with New York Knicks (1972-73 through 1974-75), New Orleans Jazz (1974-75 and 1975-76), Philadelphia 76ers (1976-77 through 1979-80) and San Diego Clippers (1980-81); brother-in-law of Eddie House, guard, New Jersey Nets.
HIGH SCHOOL: Shadow Mountain (Phoenix).
COLLEGE: Arizona.
TRANSACTIONS/CAREER NOTES: Selected after sophomore season by Vancouver Grizzlies in first round (second pick overall) of 1998 NBA Draft. ... Traded by Grizzlies with G Brent Price to Sacramento Kings for G Jason Williams and G/F Nick Anderson (June 27, 2001).

COLLEGIATE RECORD

NOTES: Member of NCAA Division I championship team (1997). ... The SPORTING NEWS All-America first team (1998).

Season Team	G	Min.	FGM	FGA	Pct.	FTM	FTA	Pct.	Reb.	Ast.	Pts.	AVERAGES RPG	APG	PPG
96-97—Arizona	34	1110	151	339	.445	89	127	.701	109	176	458	3.2	5.2	13.5
97-98—Arizona	35	1124	209	450	.464	108	143	.755	106	199	603	3.0	5.7	17.2
Totals	69	2234	360	789	.456	197	270	.730	215	375	1061	3.1	5.4	15.4

Three-point field goals: 1996-97, 67-for-170 (.394). 1997-98, 77-for-199 (.387). Totals, 144-for-369 (.390).

NBA REGULAR-SEASON RECORD

HONORS: NBA All-Rookie first team (1999).

Season Team	G	Min.	FGM	FGA	Pct.	FTM	FTA	Pct.	REBOUNDS Off.	Def.	Tot.	Ast.	St.	Blk.	TO	Pts.	AVERAGES RPG	APG	PPG
98-99—Vancouver	50	1758	260	605	.430	127	169	.751	30	106	136	325	78	5	146	662	2.7	6.5	13.2
99-00—Vancouver	82	3155	459	1031	.445	195	250	.780	73	233	306	665	132	15	247	1190	3.7	8.1	14.5
00-01—Vancouver	82	3190	525	1157	.454	143	188	.761	47	257	304	685	107	12	248	1301	3.7	8.4	15.9
01-02—Sacramento	80	2659	446	985	.453	155	193	.803	37	185	222	403	87	15	134	1098	2.8	5.0	13.7
02-03—Sacramento	55	1835	329	700	.470	161	187	.861	34	113	147	285	72	8	127	875	2.7	5.2	15.9
03-04—Sacramento	82	2980	527	1170	.450	304	373	.815	67	210	277	444	112	18	175	1506	3.4	5.4	18.4
04-05—Sacramento	80	3084	560	1264	.443	320	413	.775	77	255	332	541	124	30	203	1571	4.2	6.8	19.6
05-06—Sacramento	82	3167	597	1382	.432	342	403	.849	29	211	240	444	82	10	199	1728	2.9	5.4	21.1
Totals	593	21828	3703	8294	.446	1747	2176	.803	394	1570	1964	3792	794	113	1479	9931	3.3	6.4	16.7

Three-point field goals: 1998-99, 15-for-74 (.203). 1999-00, 77-for-212 (.363). 2000-01, 108-for-285 (.379). 2001-02, 51-for-138 (.370). 2002-03, 56-for-137 (.409). 2003-04, 148-for-378 (.392). 2004-05, 131-for-364 (.360). 2005-06, 192-for-497 (.386). Totals, 778-for-2085 (.373).

Personal fouls/disqualifications: 1998-99, 122/0. 1999-00, 171/1. 2000-01, 148/1. 2001-02, 133/0. 2002-03, 93/0. 2003-04, 146/0. 2004-05, 191/0. 2005-06, 169/0. Totals, 1173/2.

NBA PLAYOFF RECORD

Season Team	G	Min.	FGM	FGA	Pct.	FTM	FTA	Pct.	REBOUNDS Off.	Def.	Tot.	Ast.	St.	Blk.	TO	Pts.	AVERAGES RPG	APG	PPG
01-02—Sacramento	16	661	114	257	.444	71	86	.826	14	46	60	80	23	3	37	324	3.8	5.0	20.3
02-03—Sacramento	12	404	57	135	.422	27	34	.794	8	23	31	60	14	5	18	152	2.6	5.0	12.7
03-04—Sacramento	12	497	84	196	.429	48	55	.873	9	41	50	84	23	5	35	240	4.2	7.0	20.0
04-05—Sacramento	5	200	36	92	.391	21	27	.778	5	17	22	33	7	2	13	98	4.4	6.6	19.6
05-06—Sacramento	6	255	32	92	.348	27	30	.900	6	17	23	31	9	0	18	100	3.8	5.2	16.7
Totals	51	2017	323	772	.418	194	232	.836	42	144	186	288	76	15	121	914	3.6	5.6	17.9

Three-point field goals: 2001-02, 25-for-59 (.424). 2002-03, 11-for-39 (.282). 2003-04, 24-for-55 (.436). 2004-05, 5-for-23 (.217). 2005-06, 9-for-26 (.346). Totals, 74-for-202 (.366).

Personal fouls/disqualifications: 2001-02, 30/0. 2002-03, 31/1. 2003-04, 40/1. 2004-05, 11/0. 2005-06, 17/0. Totals, 129/2.

BIEDRINS, ANDRIS   F   WARRIORS

PERSONAL: Born April 2, 1986, in Riga, Latvia. ... 6-11/240. (2.11/108.9).
HIGH SCHOOL: Valters Basketball School (Latvia).
TRANSACTIONS/CAREER NOTES: Played in Latvia (2002-04). ... Selected by Golden State Warriors in first round (11th pick overall) of 2004 NBA Draft.

Season Team	G	Min.	FGM	FGA	Pct.	FTM	FTA	Pct.	Reb.	Ast.	Pts.	RPG	APG	PPG
												AVERAGES		
02-03—Skonto Riga..................	41	541	55	92	.598	14	43	.326	190	22	124	4.6	0.5	3.0
03-04—Skonto Riga..................	30	835	209	350	.597	105	187	.561	262	35	524	8.7	1.2	17.5
Totals	71	1376	264	442	.597	119	230	.517	452	57	648	6.4	0.8	9.1

Three-point field goals: 2003-04, 1-for-2 (.500). Totals, 1-for-2 (.500).

NBA REGULAR-SEASON RECORD

Season Team	G	Min.	FGM	FGA	Pct.	FTM	FTA	Pct.	REBOUNDS			Ast.	St.	Blk.	TO	Pts.	AVERAGES		
									Off.	Def.	Tot.						RPG	APG	PPG
04-05—Golden State...	30	384	45	78	.577	19	40	.475	47	71	118	12	12	24	12	109	3.9	0.4	3.6
05-06—Golden State...	68	1000	118	185	.638	22	72	.306	124	159	283	24	23	47	34	258	4.2	0.4	3.8
Totals	98	1384	163	263	.620	41	112	.366	171	230	401	36	35	71	46	367	4.1	0.4	3.7

Three-point field goals: 2004-05, 0-for-1. Totals, 0-for-1 (.000).
Personal fouls/disqualifications: 2004-05, 87/2. 2005-06, 190/2. Totals, 277/4.

BILLUPS, CHAUNCEY　　　　　　G　　　　　　PISTONS

PERSONAL: Born September 25, 1976, in Denver. ... 6-3/202. (1.91/91.6). ... Full name: Chauncey Ray Billups
HIGH SCHOOL: George Washington (Denver).
COLLEGE: Colorado.
TRANSACTIONS/CAREER NOTES: Selected after sophomore season by Boston Celtics in first round (third pick overall) of 1997 NBA Draft. ... Traded by Celtics with G Dee Brown, F John Thomas and F Roy Rogers to Toronto Raptors for G Kenny Anderson, C Zan Tabak and F Popeye Jones (February 18, 1998). ... Traded by Raptors with draft rights to G Tyson Wheeler to Denver Nuggets in three-way deal in which Raptors received 1999 first-round draft choice from Nuggets and draft rights to F Zeljko Rebraca, G Micheal Williams and 1999 or 2000 first-round draft choice from Minnesota Timberwolves and Timberwolves received C Dean Garrett and G Bobby Jackson from Nuggets (January 21, 1999). ... Traded by Nuggets with G/F Ron Mercer, F Johnny Taylor and draft considerations to Orlando Magic for F/C Chris Gatling, F Tariq Abdul-Wahad, a future first-round draft pick and cash considerations (February 1, 2000). ... Signed as free agent by Timberwolves (August 8, 2000). ... Signed as free agent by Detroit Pistons (July 17, 2002).
MISCELLANEOUS: Member of NBA championship team (2004).

COLLEGIATE RECORD

NOTES: THE SPORTING NEWS All-America second team (1997).

Season Team	G	Min.	FGM	FGA	Pct.	FTM	FTA	Pct.	Reb.	Ast.	Pts.	AVERAGES		
												RPG	APG	PPG
95-96—Colorado.......................	26	919	145	351	.413	130	151	.861	165	143	465	6.3	5.5	17.9
96-97—Colorado.......................	29	947	152	368	.413	176	206	.854	141	139	555	4.9	4.8	19.1
Totals	55	1866	297	719	.413	306	357	.857	306	282	1020	5.6	5.1	18.5

Three-point field goals: 1995-96, 45-for-127 (.354). 1996-97, 75-for-187 (.401). Totals, 120-for-314 (.382).
Personal fouls/disqualifications: 1995-96, 75/3. Totals, 75/3.

NBA REGULAR-SEASON RECORD

HONORS: NBA All-Defensive second team (2005, 2006). All-NBA second team (2006).

Season Team	G	Min.	FGM	FGA	Pct.	FTM	FTA	Pct.	REBOUNDS			Ast.	St.	Blk.	TO	Pts.	AVERAGES		
									Off.	Def.	Tot.						RPG	APG	PPG
97-98—Bos.-Tor.	80	2216	280	749	.374	226	266	.850	62	128	190	314	107	4	174	893	2.4	3.9	11.2
98-99—Denver............	45	1488	191	495	.386	157	172	.913	24	72	96	173	58	14	98	624	2.1	3.8	13.9
99-00—Den.-Orl.	13	305	34	101	.337	37	44	.841	8	26	34	39	10	2	24	112	2.6	3.0	8.6
00-01—Minnesota........	77	1790	248	587	.422	144	171	.842	32	126	158	260	51	11	111	713	2.1	3.4	9.3
01-02—Minnesota........	82	2355	348	823	.423	207	234	.885	35	191	226	450	66	17	138	1027	2.8	5.5	12.5
02-03—Detroit	74	2327	366	870	.421	318	362	.878	38	235	273	287	63	15	134	1199	3.7	3.9	16.2
03-04—Detroit	78	2758	392	996	.394	404	460	.878	35	241	276	446	84	8	189	1318	3.5	5.7	16.9
04-05—Detroit	80	2866	404	913	.442	343	382	.898	48	223	271	464	81	9	180	1316	3.4	5.8	16.5
05-06—Detroit	81	2925	423	1012	.418	465	520	.894	41	211	252	699	71	8	170	1495	3.1	8.6	18.5
Totals	610	19030	2686	6546	.410	2301	2611	.881	323	1453	1776	3132	591	88	1218	8697	2.9	5.1	14.3

Three-point field goals: 1997-98, 107-for-325 (.329). 1998-99, 85-for-235 (.362). 1999-00, 7-for-41 (.171). 2000-01, 73-for-194 (.376). 2001-02, 124-for-315 (.394). 2002-03, 149-for-380 (.392). 2003-04, 130-for-335 (.388). 2004-05, 165-for-387 (.426). 2005-06, 184-for-425 (.433). Totals, 1024-for-2637 (.388).
Personal fouls/disqualifications: 1997-98, 172/2. 1998-99, 115/0. 1999-00, 27/0. 2000-01, 178/2. 2001-02, 169/1. 2002-03, 136/0. 2003-04, 177/2. 2004-05, 194/1. 2005-06, 160/2. Totals, 1328/10.

NBA PLAYOFF RECORD

NOTES: NBA Finals Most Valuable Player (2004).

Season Team	G	Min.	FGM	FGA	Pct.	FTM	FTA	Pct.	REBOUNDS			Ast.	St.	Blk.	TO	Pts.	AVERAGES		
									Off.	Def.	Tot.						RPG	APG	PPG
00-01—Minnesota......	3	26	1	6	.167	1	1	1.000	1	4	5	2	0	0	1	3	1.7	0.7	1.0
01-02—Minnesota......	3	134	23	51	.451	14	20	.700	1	14	15	17	3	1	9	66	5.0	5.7	22.0
02-03—Detroit	14	485	71	190	.374	84	90	.933	4	43	47	66	9	2	34	252	3.4	4.7	18.0
03-04—Detroit	23	881	110	286	.385	121	136	.890	14	56	70	136	31	2	60	378	3.0	5.9	16.4
04-05—Detroit	25	985	145	339	.428	133	149	.893	23	85	108	162	25	5	49	467	4.3	6.5	18.7
05-06—Detroit	18	705	93	229	.406	105	116	.905	7	54	61	117	22	2	43	323	3.4	6.5	17.9
Totals	86	3216	443	1101	.402	458	512	.895	50	256	306	500	90	12	196	1489	3.6	5.8	17.3

Three-point field goals: 2000-01, 0-for-1. 2001-02, 6-for-15 (.400). 2002-03, 26-for-84 (.310). 2003-04, 37-for-107 (.346). 2004-05, 44-for-126 (.349). 2005-06, 32-for-94 (.340). Totals, 145-for-427 (.340).
Personal fouls/disqualifications: 2000-01, 5/0. 2001-02, 14/1. 2002-03, 38/0. 2003-04, 57/1. 2004-05, 71/1. 2005-06, 43/1. Totals, 228/4.

NBA ALL-STAR GAME RECORD

Season Team	Min.	FGM	FGA	Pct.	FTM	FTA	Pct.	REBOUNDS			Ast.	PF	Dq.	St.	Blk.	TO	Pts.
								Off.	Def.	Tot.							
2006—Detroit..................	16	6	10	.600	1	1	1.000	0	4	4	7	1	0	0	0	2	15

Three-point field goals: 2006, 2-for-5 (.400). Totals, 2-for-5 (.400).

B

BLAKE, STEVE   G   BUCKS

PERSONAL: Born February 26, 1980, in Hollywood, Fla. ... 6-3/172. (1.91/78.0). ... Full name: Steven Hanson Blake
HIGH SCHOOL: Miami Killian and Miami Senior (Miami, Fla.), then Oak Hill Academy (Mouth of Wilson, Va.).
COLLEGE: Maryland.
TRANSACTIONS/CAREER NOTES: Selected by Washington Wizards in second round (38th pick overall) of 2003 NBA Draft. ... Signed by Portland Trail Blazers after Wizards declined to match offer sheet (September 28, 2005). ... Traded by Trail Blazers with F Brian Skinner and C Ha Seung-Jin to Milwaukee Bucks for C Jamaal Magloire (July 31, 2006).

COLLEGIATE RECORD

NOTES: Member of NCAA Division I championship team (2002).

Season Team	G	Min.	FGM	FGA	Pct.	FTM	FTA	Pct.	Reb.	Ast.	Pts.	RPG	APG	PPG
99-00—Maryland	35	1115	86	211	.408	35	51	.686	106	217	244	3.0	6.2	7.0
00-01—Maryland	36	1036	83	208	.399	45	63	.714	108	248	248	3.0	6.9	6.9
01-02—Maryland	36	1153	91	238	.382	61	74	.824	137	286	287	3.8	7.9	8.0
02-03—Maryland	31	1009	114	275	.415	68	83	.819	114	221	360	3.7	7.1	11.6
Totals	138	4313	374	932	.401	209	271	.771	465	972	1139	3.4	7.0	8.3

Three-point field goals: 1999-00, 37-for-102 (.363). 2000-01, 37-for-94 (.394). 2001-02, 44-for-128 (.344). 2002-03, 64-for-154 (.416). Totals, 182-for-478 (.381).

NBA REGULAR-SEASON RECORD

Season Team	G	Min.	FGM	FGA	Pct.	FTM	FTA	Pct.	REBOUNDS Off.	Def.	Tot.	Ast.	St.	Blk.	TO	Pts.	RPG	APG	PPG
03-04—Washington	75	1392	157	407	.386	55	67	.821	18	99	117	209	57	7	128	444	1.6	2.8	5.9
04-05—Washington	44	648	61	186	.328	33	41	.805	18	53	71	69	13	0	39	191	1.6	1.6	4.3
05-06—Portland	68	1781	206	470	.438	72	91	.791	26	120	146	306	42	5	83	560	2.1	4.5	8.2
Totals	187	3821	424	1063	.399	160	199	.804	62	272	334	584	112	12	250	1195	1.8	3.1	6.4

Three-point field goals: 2003-04, 75-for-202 (.371). 2004-05, 36-for-93 (.387). 2005-06, 76-for-184 (.413). Totals, 187-for-479 (.390).
Personal fouls/disqualifications: 2003-04, 100/0. 2004-05, 47/0. 2005-06, 107/0. Totals, 254/0.

NBA PLAYOFF RECORD

Season Team	G	Min.	FGM	FGA	Pct.	FTM	FTA	Pct.	REBOUNDS Off.	Def.	Tot.	Ast.	St.	Blk.	TO	Pts.	RPG	APG	PPG
04-05—Washington	4	17	1	4	.250	0	0	...	0	3	3	2	0	0	1	2	0.8	0.5	0.5

Three-point field goals: 2004-05, 0-for-1. Totals, 0-for-1 (.000).
Personal fouls/disqualifications: 2004-05, 3/0. Totals, 3/0.

BLATCHE, ANDRAY   F   WIZARDS

PERSONAL: Born August 22, 1986, in Syracuse, N.Y. ... 6-11/235. (2.11/106.6).
HIGH SCHOOL: Henninger (Syracuse, N.Y.) then South Kent Prep (Conn.).
COLLEGE: Did not attend college.
TRANSACTIONS/CAREER NOTES: Selected out of high school by Washington Wizards in second round (49th pick overall) of 2005 NBA Draft.

NBA REGULAR-SEASON RECORD

Season Team	G	Min.	FGM	FGA	Pct.	FTM	FTA	Pct.	REBOUNDS Off.	Def.	Tot.	Ast.	St.	Blk.	TO	Pts.	RPG	APG	PPG
05-06—Washington	29	175	26	67	.388	10	12	.833	12	26	38	10	5	7	12	65	1.3	0.3	2.2

Three-point field goals: 2005-06, 3-for-13 (.231). Totals, 3-for-13 (.231).
Personal fouls/disqualifications: 2005-06, 36/0. Totals, 36/0.

NBA DEVELOPMENT LEAGUE RECORD

Season Team	G	Min.	FGM	FGA	Pct.	FTM	FTA	Pct.	Reb.	Ast.	Pts.	RPG	APG	PPG
05-06—Roanoke	6	148	25	49	.510	16	19	.842	41	8	67	6.8	1.3	11.2

Three-point field goals: 2005-06, 1-for-5 (.200). Totals, 1-for-5 (.200).

BLOUNT, MARK   C   TIMBERWOLVES

PERSONAL: Born November 30, 1975, in Dobbs Ferry, N.Y. ... 7-0/230. (2.13/104.3). ... Full name: Mark D. Blount
HIGH SCHOOL: Oak Hill Academy (Mouth of Wilson, Va.), then Sacred Heart and Dobbs Ferry (N.Y.).
COLLEGE: Pittsburgh.
TRANSACTIONS/CAREER NOTES: Selected after sophomore season by Seattle SuperSonics in second round (55th pick overall) of 1997 NBA Draft. ... Waived by SuperSonics (October 7, 1997). ... Played in Continental Basketball Association with Yakima Sun Kings (1997-98). ... Signed as free agent by Los Angeles Clippers (January 22, 1999). ... Waived by Clippers (January 31, 1999). ... Played in International Basketball League with Baltimore Bayrunners (1999-2000). ... Signed as free agent by Boston Celtics (August 1, 2000). ... Signed as free agent by Denver Nuggets (August 8, 2002). ... Traded by Nuggets with F/C Mark Bryant to Celtics for G Shammond Williams, 2003 second-round draft choice and cash (February 20, 2003). ... Traded by Celtics with G Ricky Davis, G Marcus Banks, SF Justin Reed and two second-round draft choices to Minnesota Timberwolves for F Wally Szczerbiak, C Michael Olowokandi, F/C Dwayne Jones and a future first-round draft choice (January 24, 2006).

COLLEGIATE RECORD

Season Team	G	Min.	FGM	FGA	Pct.	FTM	FTA	Pct.	Reb.	Ast.	Pts.	RPG	APG	PPG
95-96—Pittsburgh	27	389	35	85	.412	26	48	.542	80	9	96	3.0	0.3	3.6
96-97—Pittsburgh	29	760	101	207	.488	61	120	.508	198	30	264	6.8	1.0	9.1
Totals	56	1149	136	292	.466	87	168	.518	278	39	360	5.0	0.7	6.4

Three-point field goals: 1996-97, 1-for-2 (.500). Totals, 1-for-2 (.500).
Personal fouls/disqualifications: 1995-96, 79/0. 1996-97, 94/0. Totals, 173/0.

CBA RECORD

Season Team	G	Min.	FGM	FGA	Pct.	FTM	FTA	Pct.	Reb.	Ast.	Pts.	AVERAGES RPG	APG	PPG
97-98—Yakima	5	64	8	22	.364	2	2	1.000	9	0	18	1.8	0.0	3.6

INTERNATIONAL BASKETBALL LEAGUE RECORD

Season Team	G	Min.	FGM	FGA	Pct.	FTM	FTA	Pct.	Reb.	Ast.	Pts.	AVERAGES RPG	APG	PPG
99-00—Baltimore.....................	54	1077	189	352	.537	98	152	.645	274	44	471	5.1	0.8	8.7

Three-point field goals: 1999-00, 0-for-1. Totals, 0-for-1 (.000).
Personal fouls/disqualifications: 1999-00, 122/0. Totals, 122/0.

NBA REGULAR-SEASON RECORD

Season Team	G	Min.	FGM	FGA	Pct.	FTM	FTA	Pct.	REBOUNDS Off.	Def.	Tot.	Ast.	St.	Blk.	TO	Pts.	AVERAGES RPG	APG	PPG
00-01—Boston	64	1098	101	200	.505	46	66	.697	97	134	231	32	39	76	62	248	3.6	0.5	3.9
01-02—Boston	44	415	32	76	.421	30	37	.811	26	59	85	10	16	19	23	94	1.9	0.2	2.1
02-03—Den-Bos...	81	1403	150	347	.432	101	139	.727	111	197	308	56	42	68	103	401	3.8	0.7	5.0
03-04—Boston	82	2402	342	604	.566	159	221	.719	207	382	589	75	80	106	150	843	7.2	0.9	10.3
04-05—Boston	82	2130	327	618	.529	117	164	.713	143	254	397	129	33	64	158	771	4.8	1.6	9.4
05-06—Boston-Minn...	81	2240	373	734	.508	168	222	.757	96	269	365	99	40	76	194	914	4.5	1.2	11.3
Totals..................	434	9688	1325	2579	.514	621	849	.731	680	1295	1975	401	250	409	690	3271	4.6	0.9	7.5

Three-point field goals: 2004-05, 0-for-1. Totals, 0-for-1 (.000).
Personal fouls/disqualifications: 2000-01, 183/0. 2001-02, 59/0. 2002-03, 187/2. 2003-04, 253/4. 2004-05, 229/4. 2005-06, 254/6. Totals, 1165/16.

NBA PLAYOFF RECORD

Season Team	G	Min.	FGM	FGA	Pct.	FTM	FTA	Pct.	REBOUNDS Off.	Def.	Tot.	Ast.	St.	Blk.	TO	Pts.	AVERAGES RPG	APG	PPG
01-02—Boston	4	39	2	4	.500	2	2	1.000	3	4	7	1	2	2	1	6	1.8	0.3	1.5
02-03—Boston	10	144	12	22	.545	7	10	.700	12	24	36	2	11	8	8	31	3.6	0.2	3.1
03-04—Boston	4	145	17	35	.486	14	19	.737	10	27	37	4	6	8	9	48	9.3	1.0	12.0
04-05—Boston	4	43	4	14	.286	0	2	.000	3	3	6	1	0	0	5	8	1.5	0.3	2.0
Totals..................	22	371	35	75	.467	23	33	.697	28	58	86	8	19	18	23	93	3.9	0.4	4.2

Personal fouls/disqualifications: 2001-02, 7/0. 2002-03, 20/0. 2003-04, 17/0. 2004-05, 6/0. Totals, 50/0.

BOGANS, KEITH　　　　G　　　　MAGIC

PERSONAL: Born May 12, 1980, in Washington, D.C. ... 6-5/215. (1.96/97.5). ... Full name: Keith Ramon Bogans
HIGH SCHOOL: DaMatha Catholic (Hyattsville, Md.).
COLLEGE: Kentucky.
TRANSACTIONS/CAREER NOTES: Selected by Milwaukee Bucks in second round (43rd pick overall) of 2003 NBA Draft. ... Draft rights traded to Orlando Magic for cash considerations (June 26, 2003). ... Traded by Magic to Charlotte Bobcats for F Brandon Hunter (November 1, 2004). ... Traded by Bobcats to Houston Rockets for F Lonny Baxter (February 9, 2006). ... Signed as free agent by Orlando Magic (July 13, 2006).

COLLEGIATE RECORD

NOTES: The SPORTING NEWS All-America third team (2003).

Season Team	G	Min.	FGM	FGA	Pct.	FTM	FTA	Pct.	Reb.	Ast.	Pts.	AVERAGES RPG	APG	PPG
99-00—Kentucky	33	917	138	339	.407	87	135	.644	119	57	411	3.6	1.7	12.5
00-01—Kentucky	34	1050	210	444	.473	83	119	.697	158	80	577	4.6	2.4	17.0
01-02—Kentucky	32	878	129	327	.394	61	91	.670	137	79	371	4.3	2.5	11.6
02-03—Kentucky	36	1068	194	425	.456	96	130	.738	138	98	564	3.8	2.7	15.7
Totals..................	135	3913	671	1535	.437	327	475	.688	552	314	1923	4.1	2.3	14.2

Three-point field goals: 1999-00, 48-for-164 (.293). 2000-01, 74-for-205 (.361). 2001-02, 52-for-165 (.315). 2002-03, 80-for-209 (.383). Totals, 254-for-743 (.342).

NBA REGULAR-SEASON RECORD

Season Team	G	Min.	FGM	FGA	Pct.	FTM	FTA	Pct.	REBOUNDS Off.	Def.	Tot.	Ast.	St.	Blk.	TO	Pts.	AVERAGES RPG	APG	PPG
03-04—Orlando..........	73	1787	183	454	.403	65	103	.631	106	211	317	98	46	10	75	498	4.3	1.3	6.8
04-05—Charlotte........	74	1791	262	688	.381	133	183	.727	76	150	226	135	68	8	122	714	3.1	1.8	9.6
05-06—Char.-Houston	72	1912	215	544	.395	127	186	.683	55	200	255	128	71	9	90	622	3.5	1.8	8.6
Totals..................	219	5490	660	1686	.391	325	472	.689	237	561	798	361	185	27	287	1834	3.6	1.6	8.4

Three-point field goals: 2003-04, 67-for-187 (.358). 2004-05, 57-for-173 (.329). 2005-06, 65-for-200 (.325). Totals, 189-for-560 (.338).
Personal fouls/disqualifications: 2003-04, 128/2. 2004-05, 167/1. 2005-06, 167/1. Totals, 462/4.

BOGUT, ANDREW　　　　C　　　　BUCKS

PERSONAL: Born November 28, 1984, in Melbourne, Australia. ... 7-0/245. (2.13/111.1). ... Full name: Andrew Michael Bogut
HIGH SCHOOL: Australian Institute of Sport (Melbourne, Australia).
COLLEGE: Utah.
TRANSACTIONS/CAREER NOTES: Selected after sophmore season by Milwaukee Bucks in first round (first pick overall) of 2005 NBA Draft.
MISCELLANEOUS: Member of Australian Olympic Team (2004).

COLLEGIATE RECORD

NOTES: National player of the year (2005). ... The SPORTING NEWS All-America first team (2005).

Season Team	G	Min.	FGM	FGA	Pct.	FTM	FTA	Pct.	Reb.	Ast.	Pts.	RPG	APG	PPG
												AVERAGES		
03-04—Utah	33	1002	168	291	.577	71	111	.640	326	73	411	9.9	2.2	12.5
04-05—Utah	35	1224	281	453	.620	144	208	.692	427	82	715	12.2	2.3	20.4
Totals	68	2226	449	744	.603	215	319	.674	753	155	1126	11.1	2.3	16.6

Three-point field goals: 2003-04, 4-for-11 (.364). 2004-05, 9-for-25 (.360). Totals, 13-for-36 (.361).

NBA REGULAR-SEASON RECORD

HONORS: NBA All-Rookie first team (2006).

Season Team	G	Min.	FGM	FGA	Pct.	FTM	FTA	Pct.	REBOUNDS Off.	Def.	Tot.	Ast.	St.	Blk.	TO	Pts.	AVERAGES RPG	APG	PPG
05-06—Milwaukee	82	2348	323	606	.533	122	194	.629	189	384	573	192	49	68	125	768	7.0	2.3	9.4

Three-point field goals: 2005-06, 0-for-3. Totals, 0-for-3 (.000).
Personal fouls/disqualifications: 2005-06, 259/3. Totals, 259/3.

NBA PLAYOFF RECORD

Season Team	G	Min.	FGM	FGA	Pct.	FTM	FTA	Pct.	REBOUNDS Off.	Def.	Tot.	Ast.	St.	Blk.	TO	Pts.	AVERAGES RPG	APG	PPG
05-06—Milwaukee	5	172	20	46	.435	3	8	.375	9	22	31	17	3	0	8	43	6.2	3.4	8.6

Personal fouls/disqualifications: 2005-06, 21/1. Totals, 21/1.

BONNER, MATT　　　　　　　F　　　　　　　SPURS

PERSONAL: Born April 5, 1980, in Concord, N.H. ... 6-10/240. (2.08/108.9). ... Full name: Matthew Robert Bonner
HIGH SCHOOL: Concord (N.H.).
COLLEGE: Florida.
TRANSACTIONS/CAREER NOTES: Selected by Chicago Bulls in second round (45th pick overall) of 2003 NBA Draft. ... Draft rights traded by Bulls to Toronto Raptors for future second-round draft pick (June 26, 2003). ... Traded by Raptors with Eric Williams and a 2009 second-round draft choice to San Antonio Spurs for C Rasho Nesterovic (June 21, 2006).

COLLEGIATE RECORD

Season Team	G	Min.	FGM	FGA	Pct.	FTM	FTA	Pct.	Reb.	Ast.	Pts.	AVERAGES RPG	APG	PPG
99-00—Florida	36	485	66	150	.440	26	30	.867	115	15	174	3.2	0.4	4.8
00-01—Florida	31	883	150	292	.514	71	107	.664	238	46	411	7.7	1.5	13.3
01-02—Florida	31	876	182	355	.513	74	93	.796	224	48	484	7.2	1.5	15.6
02-03—Florida	33	1037	182	357	.510	74	101	.733	201	49	501	6.1	1.5	15.2
Totals	131	3281	580	1154	.503	245	331	.740	778	158	1570	5.9	1.2	12.0

Three-point field goals: 1999-00, 16-for-56 (.286). 2000-01, 40-for-105 (.381). 2001-02, 46-for-124 (.371). 2002-03, 63-for-133 (.474). Totals, 165-for-418 (.395).

ITALIAN LEAGUE RECORD

Season Team	G	Min.	FGM	FGA	Pct.	FTM	FTA	Pct.	Reb.	Ast.	Pts.	AVERAGES RPG	APG	PPG
03-04—Sicilia Messina	33	1215	230	423	.544	136	167	.814	308	26	634	9.3	0.8	19.2

Three-point field goals: 2003-04, 38-for-105 (.362). Totals, 38-for-105 (.362).

NBA REGULAR-SEASON RECORD

Season Team	G	Min.	FGM	FGA	Pct.	FTM	FTA	Pct.	REBOUNDS Off.	Def.	Tot.	Ast.	St.	Blk.	TO	Pts.	AVERAGES RPG	APG	PPG
04-05—Toronto	82	1553	247	463	.533	56	71	.789	108	177	285	48	39	19	40	589	3.5	0.6	7.2
05-06—Toronto	78	1710	209	467	.448	63	76	.829	86	198	284	56	49	31	32	583	3.6	0.7	7.5
Totals	160	3263	456	930	.490	119	147	.810	194	375	569	104	88	50	72	1172	3.6	0.7	7.3

Three-point field goals: 2004-05, 39-for-92 (.424). 2005-06, 102-for-243 (.420). Totals, 141-for-335 (.421).
Personal fouls/disqualifications: 2004-05, 220/1. 2005-06, 216/2. Totals, 436/3.

BOOTH, CALVIN　　　　　　　C

PERSONAL: Born May 7, 1976, in Reynoldsburg, Ohio. ... 6-11/241. (2.11/109.3). ... Full name: Calvin L. Booth
HIGH SCHOOL: Groveport Madison (Reynoldsburg, Ohio).
COLLEGE: Penn State.
TRANSACTIONS/CAREER NOTES: Selected by Washington Wizards in second round (35th pick overall) of 1999 NBA Draft. ... Traded by Wizards with F Juwan Howard and F Obinna Ekezie to Dallas Mavericks for F/C Christian Laettner, G Courtney Alexander, F Loy Vaught, G Hubert Davis, F/C Etan Thomas and cash considerations (February 22, 2001). ... Signed as free agent by Seattle SuperSonics (July 31, 2001). ... Traded by SuperSonics to Dallas Mavericks for F Danny Fortson (July 26, 2004). ... Traded by Mavericks with F Alan Henderson to Milwaukee Bucks for F Keith Van Horn (February 24, 2005). ... Waived by Bucks (August 15, 2005). ... Signed as free agent by Washington Wizards (September 7, 2005).

COLLEGIATE RECORD

Season Team	G	Min.	FGM	FGA	Pct.	FTM	FTA	Pct.	Reb.	Ast.	Pts.	AVERAGES RPG	APG	PPG
94-95—Penn State					Did not play—redshirted.									
95-96—Penn State	28	670	100	182	.549	61	96	.635	150	35	261	5.4	1.3	9.3
96-97—Penn State	27	706	87	204	.426	61	84	.726	134	15	236	5.0	0.6	8.7
97-98—Penn State	32	955	156	294	.531	65	97	.670	208	8	377	6.5	0.3	11.8
98-99—Penn State	27	942	157	306	.513	100	129	.775	236	24	414	8.7	0.9	15.3
Totals	114	3273	500	986	.507	287	406	.707	728	82	1288	6.4	0.7	11.3

Three-point field goals: 1996-97, 1-for-3 (.333). 1997-98, 0-for-1. 1998-99, 0-for-6. Totals, 1-for-10 (.100).

NBA REGULAR-SEASON RECORD

Season Team	G	Min.	FGM	FGA	Pct.	FTM	FTA	Pct.	REBOUNDS Off.	Def.	Tot.	Ast.	St.	Blk.	TO	Pts.	AVERAGES RPG	APG	PPG
99-00—Washington	11	143	16	46	.348	10	14	.714	15	17	32	7	3	14	6	42	2.9	0.6	3.8
00-01—Wash.-Dallas ..	55	933	120	252	.476	53	78	.679	77	169	246	42	29	111	53	293	4.5	0.8	5.3
01-02—Seattle	15	279	35	82	.427	23	24	.958	20	34	54	16	6	13	16	93	3.6	1.1	6.2
02-03—Seattle	47	575	52	119	.437	34	47	.723	32	77	109	12	11	33	22	138	2.3	0.3	2.9
03-04—Seattle	71	1206	135	290	.466	75	94	.798	86	194	280	28	17	101	45	345	3.9	0.4	4.9
04-05—Dallas-Mil.	51	451	49	108	.454	26	32	.813	29	78	107	8	15	28	16	124	2.1	0.2	2.4
05-06—Washington	33	250	20	47	.426	5	9	.556	19	33	52	12	9	9	8	46	1.6	0.4	1.4
Totals	283	3837	427	944	.452	226	298	.758	278	602	880	125	90	309	166	1081	3.1	0.4	3.8

Three-point field goals: 2002-03, 0-for-2. 2003-04, 0-for-2. 2004-05, 0-for-1. 2005-06, 1-for-2 (.500). Totals, 1-for-7 (.143).
Personal fouls/disqualifications: 1999-00, 23/0. 2000-01, 146/1. 2001-02, 47/1. 2002-03, 74/0. 2003-04, 150/2. 2004-05, 78/0. 2005-06, 44/0. Totals, 562/4.

NBA PLAYOFF RECORD

Season Team	G	Min.	FGM	FGA	Pct.	FTM	FTA	Pct.	REBOUNDS Off.	Def.	Tot.	Ast.	St.	Blk.	TO	Pts.	AVERAGES RPG	APG	PPG
00-01—Dallas..............	10	137	15	37	.405	8	9	.889	16	12	28	2	7	6	4	38	2.8	0.2	3.8

Personal fouls/disqualifications: 2000-01, 29/0. Totals, 29/0.

BOOZER, CARLOS — F/C — JAZZ

PERSONAL: Born November 20, 1981, in Juneau, Alaska. ... 6-8/258. (2.03/117.0).
HIGH SCHOOL: Juneau-Douglas (Juneau, Alaska).
COLLEGE: Duke.
TRANSACTIONS/CAREER NOTES: Selected after junior season by Cleveland Cavaliers in second round (35th pick overall) of 2002 NBA Draft. ... Signed as free agent by Utah Jazz (July 30, 2004).
MISCELLANEOUS: Member of bronze-medal-winning U.S. Olympic Team (2004).

COLLEGIATE RECORD

NOTES: Member of NCAA Division I championship team (2001).

Season Team	G	Min.	FGM	FGA	Pct.	FTM	FTA	Pct.	Reb.	Ast.	Pts.	AVERAGES RPG	APG	PPG
99-00—Duke.............................	34	807	164	267	.614	115	155	.742	213	37	443	6.3	1.1	13.0
00-01—Duke.............................	32	820	160	265	.604	105	146	.719	208	40	425	6.5	1.3	13.3
01-02—Duke.............................	35	993	230	346	.665	178	236	.754	303	38	638	8.7	1.1	18.2
Totals	101	2620	554	878	.631	398	537	.741	724	115	1506	7.2	1.1	14.9

Three-point field goals: 2001-02, 0-for-1. Totals, 0-for-1 (.000).

NBA REGULAR-SEASON RECORD

HONORS: NBA All-Rookie second team (2003).

Season Team	G	Min.	FGM	FGA	Pct.	FTM	FTA	Pct.	REBOUNDS Off.	Def.	Tot.	Ast.	St.	Blk.	TO	Pts.	AVERAGES RPG	APG	PPG
02-03—Cleveland	81	2018	331	610	.543	170	252	.774	262	497	559	103	49	188	135	818	7.5	1.0	10.0
03-04—Cleveland	75	2592	471	900	.523	219	285	.768	230	627	857	148	74	55	134	1162	11.4	2.0	15.5
04-05—Utah	51	1772	361	693	.521	187	268	.698	141	316	457	144	41	24	137	909	9.0	2.8	17.8
05-06—Utah	33	1025	219	399	.549	99	137	.723	73	212	285	88	30	8	69	537	8.6	2.7	16.3
Totals	240	7438	1382	2610	.530	653	882	.740	646	1562	2208	486	204	137	443	3418	9.2	2.0	14.2

Three-point field goals: 2002-03, 0-for-1. 2003-04, 1-for-6 (.167). 2004-05, 0-for-1. Totals, 1-for-8 (.125).
Personal fouls/disqualifications: 2002-03, 224/2. 2003-04, 199/0. 2004-05, 179/3. 2005-06, 105/2. Totals, 707/7.

BOSH, CHRIS — F — RAPTORS

PERSONAL: Born March 2, 1984, in Dallas. ... 6-10/210. (2.08/95.3). ... Full name: Christopher Wesson Bosh
HIGH SCHOOL: Lincoln (Dallas).
COLLEGE: Georgia Tech.
TRANSACTIONS/CAREER NOTES: Selected after freshman season by Toronto Raptors in first round (fourth pick overall) of 2003 NBA Draft.

COLLEGIATE RECORD

Season Team	G	Min.	FGM	FGA	Pct.	FTM	FTA	Pct.	Reb.	Ast.	Pts.	AVERAGES RPG	APG	PPG
02-03—Georgia Tech	31	960	168	300	.560	127	174	.730	278	38	485	9.0	1.2	15.6

Three-point field goals: 2002-03, 22-for-46 (.478). Totals, 22-for-46 (.478).

NBA REGULAR-SEASON RECORD

HONORS: NBA All-Rookie first team (2004).

Season Team	G	Min.	FGM	FGA	Pct.	FTM	FTA	Pct.	REBOUNDS Off.	Def.	Tot.	Ast.	St.	Blk.	TO	Pts.	AVERAGES RPG	APG	PPG
03-04—Toronto	75	2510	327	712	.459	202	288	.701	191	366	557	78	59	106	107	861	7.4	1.0	11.5
04-05—Toronto	81	3017	473	1005	.471	412	542	.760	194	524	718	153	76	113	187	1361	8.9	1.9	16.8
05-06—Toronto	70	2751	549	1087	.505	474	581	.816	204	443	647	181	50	79	157	1572	9.2	2.6	22.5
Totals	226	8278	1349	2804	.481	1088	1411	.771	589	1333	1922	412	185	298	451	3794	8.5	1.8	16.8

Three-point field goals: 2003-04, 5-for-14 (.357). 2004-05, 3-for-10 (.300). 2005-06, 0-for-13. Totals, 8-for-37 (.216).
Personal fouls/disqualifications: 2003-04, 215/2. 2004-05, 226/3. 2005-06, 209/3. Totals, 650/8.

NBA ALL-STAR GAME RECORD

Season Team	Min.	FGM	FGA	Pct.	FTM	FTA	Pct.	REBOUNDS Off.	Def.	Tot.	Ast.	PF	Dq.	St.	Blk.	TO	Pts.
2006—Toronto	17	3	7	.429	2	3	.667	2	6	8	2	1	0	0	1	1	8

PERSONAL: Born June 14, 1971, in Merced, Calif. ... 6-7/200. (2.01/90.7).
HIGH SCHOOL: Edison (Fresno, Calif.).
COLLEGE: Cal State Fullerton.
TRANSACTIONS/CAREER NOTES: Not drafted by an NBA franchise. ... Played in France (1994-95; 1996-97). ... Signed as free agent by Miami Heat (October 5, 1995). ... Waived by Heat (October 13, 1995). ... Played in Continental Basketball Association with Fort Wayne Fury (1995-96) and Rockford Lightning (1995-97). ... Signed by Heat to 10-day contract (March 15, 1997). ... Signed by Heat for remainder of season (March 25, 1997). ... Signed as free agent by Boston Celtics (July 28, 1997). ... Signed as free agent by Philadelphia 76ers (September 16, 1999). ... Traded by 76ers to Chicago Bulls for F Toni Kukoc in three-way deal in which 76ers sent G Larry Hughes and F/G Billy Owens to Golden State Warriors and Warriors sent G John Starks and future first-round draft choice to Bulls (February 16, 2000). ... Waived by Bulls (February 18, 2000). ... Signed as free agent by Heat (February 23, 2000). ... Signed as free agent by San Antonio Spurs (July 31, 2001).
MISCELLANEOUS: Member of NBA championship team (2003, 2005).

COLLEGIATE RECORD

												AVERAGES		
Season Team	G	Min.	FGM	FGA	Pct.	FTM	FTA	Pct.	Reb.	Ast.	Pts.	RPG	APG	PPG
89-90—Cal State Fullerton	18	98	9	22	.409	10	13	.769	18	4	31	1.0	0.2	1.7
90-91—Cal State Fullerton	28	849	89	236	.377	83	120	.692	196	75	275	7.0	2.7	9.8
91-92—Cal State Fullerton	28	969	138	311	.444	120	161	.745	196	75	408	7.0	2.7	14.6
92-93—Cal State Fullerton	27	987	148	318	.465	131	201	.652	176	62	441	6.5	2.3	16.3
Totals	101	2903	384	887	.433	344	495	.695	586	216	1155	5.8	2.1	11.4

Three-point field goals: 1989-90, 3-for-5 (.600). 1990-91, 14-for-60 (.233). 1991-92, 12-for-44 (.273). 1992-93, 14-for-43 (.326). Totals, 43-for-152 (.283).

FRENCH LEAGUE RECORD

												AVERAGES		
Season Team	G	Min.	FGM	FGA	Pct.	FTM	FTA	Pct.	Reb.	Ast.	Pts.	RPG	APG	PPG
94-95—Evreux	21	...	...	...	...	...	...	...	79	21	642	3.8	1.0	30.6
96-97—Bescanson	20	768	173	333	.520	97	142	.683	70	55	509	3.5	2.8	25.5
Totals	41	768	173	333	.520	97	142	.683	149	76	1151	3.6	1.9	28.1

Three-point field goals: 1996-97, 25-for-67 (.373). Totals, 25-for-67 (.373).

CBA RECORD

												AVERAGES		
Season Team	G	Min.	FGM	FGA	Pct.	FTM	FTA	Pct.	Reb.	Ast.	Pts.	RPG	APG	PPG
95-96—Fort Wayne-Rockford	46	1228	182	404	.450	133	191	.696	160	59	510	3.5	1.3	11.1
96-97—Rockford	16	619	94	206	.456	75	98	.765	70	45	277	4.4	2.8	17.3
Totals	62	1847	276	610	.452	208	289	.720	230	104	787	3.7	1.7	12.7

Three-point field goals: 1996-97, 14-for-43 (.326). Totals, 14-for-43 (.326).
Personal fouls/disqualifications: 1996-97, 46/0. Totals, 46/0.

NBA REGULAR-SEASON RECORD

HONORS: NBA All-Defensive first team (2004, 2005 and 2006). ... NBA All-Defensive second team (2001, 2002, 2003).
NOTES: Led NBA with .441 three-point shooting percentage (2002-03).

									REBOUNDS								AVERAGES		
Season Team	G	Min.	FGM	FGA	Pct.	FTM	FTA	Pct.	Off.	Def.	Tot.	Ast.	St.	Blk.	TO	Pts.	RPG	APG	PPG
96-97—Miami	1	1	0	0	...	0	0	...	0	0	0	0	0	1	0	0	0.0	0.0	0.0
97-98—Boston	61	1305	122	298	.409	76	122	.623	79	95	174	81	87	29	52	340	2.9	1.3	5.6
98-99—Boston	30	494	26	93	.280	11	24	.458	15	37	52	28	21	9	13	70	1.7	0.9	2.3
99-00—Phila.-Miami	69	878	72	194	.371	25	43	.581	27	69	96	34	23	15	19	196	1.4	0.5	2.8
00-01—Miami	82	2685	211	581	.363	98	161	.609	45	200	245	132	83	53	74	623	3.0	1.6	7.6
01-02—San Antonio	59	1699	155	398	.389	46	96	.479	42	120	162	88	62	25	66	412	2.7	1.5	7.0
02-03—San Antonio	82	2566	223	479	.466	36	89	.404	59	180	239	113	66	42	72	583	2.9	1.4	7.1
03-04—San Antonio	82	2624	211	502	.420	66	114	.579	45	208	253	113	84	33	90	565	3.1	1.4	6.9
04-05—San Antonio	82	2627	251	598	.420	71	112	.634	50	235	285	126	55	39	57	675	3.5	1.5	8.2
05-06—San Antonio	82	2755	232	536	.433	51	84	.607	35	285	320	126	79	30	67	619	3.9	1.5	7.5
Totals	630	17634	1503	3679	.409	480	845	.568	397	1429	1826	841	560	276	510	4083	2.9	1.3	6.5

Three-point field goals: 1997-98, 20-for-59 (.339). 1998-99, 7-for-26 (.269). 1999-00, 27-for-58 (.466). 2000-01, 103-for-307 (.336). 2001-02, 56-for-148 (.378). 2002-03, 101-for-229 (.441). 2003-04, 77-for-212 (.363). 2004-05, 102-for-253 (.403). 2005-06, 104-for-245 (.424). Totals, 597-for-1537 (.388).

Personal fouls/disqualifications: 1997-98, 174/0. 1998-99, 51/2. 1999-00, 118/0. 2000-01, 269/8. 2001-02, 116/0. 2002-03, 195/0. 2003-04, 166/1. 2004-05, 175/0. 2005-06, 191/0. Totals, 1455/11.

NBA PLAYOFF RECORD

									REBOUNDS								AVERAGES		
Season Team	G	Min.	FGM	FGA	Pct.	FTM	FTA	Pct.	Off.	Def.	Tot.	Ast.	St.	Blk.	TO	Pts.	RPG	APG	PPG
99-00—Miami	10	157	10	27	.370	10	16	.625	1	9	10	8	7	4	6	35	1.0	0.8	3.5
00-01—Miami	3	58	5	16	.313	0	0	...	1	1	2	2	2	2	2	12	0.7	0.7	4.0
01-02—San Antonio	10	345	25	61	.410	7	14	.500	9	24	33	14	11	7	7	68	3.3	1.4	6.8
02-03—San Antonio	24	750	54	145	.372	23	42	.548	14	55	69	39	20	17	15	166	2.9	1.6	6.9
03-04—San Antonio	10	298	23	63	.365	3	13	.231	6	23	29	10	4	3	4	60	2.9	1.0	6.0
04-05—San Antonio	23	814	46	128	.359	11	17	.647	9	57	66	36	11	13	15	132	2.9	1.6	5.7
05-06—San Antonio	13	442	32	61	.525	1	2	.500	6	22	28	16	11	8	9	80	2.2	1.2	6.2
Totals	93	2864	195	501	.389	55	104	.529	46	191	237	125	66	54	58	553	2.5	1.3	5.9

Three-point field goals: 1999-00, 5-for-22 (.227). 2000-01, 2-for-8 (.250). 2001-02, 11-for-25 (.440). 2002-03, 35-for-80 (.438). 2003-04, 11-for-29 (.379). 2004-05, 29-for-67 (.433). 2005-06, 15-for-30 (.500). Totals, 108-for-261 (.414).
Personal fouls/disqualifications: 1999-00, 27/1. 2000-01, 8/0. 2001-02, 28/0. 2002-03, 52/0. 2003-04, 24/0. 2004-05, 77/0. 2005-06, 42/0. Totals, 258/1.

BOWEN, RYAN   F   ROCKETS

PERSONAL: Born November 20, 1975, in Fort Madison, Iowa. ... 6-7/220. (2.01/99.8). ... Full name: Ryan Cleo Bowen
HIGH SCHOOL: Fort Madison (Iowa).
COLLEGE: Iowa.
TRANSACTIONS/CAREER NOTES: Selected by Denver Nuggets in second round (55th pick overall) of 1998 NBA Draft. ... Played in Turkey (1998-99). ... Signed as free agent by Houston Rockets (September 30, 2004).

COLLEGIATE RECORD

Season Team	G	Min.	FGM	FGA	Pct.	FTM	FTA	Pct.	Reb.	Ast.	Pts.	RPG	APG	PPG
94-95—Iowa	33	647	58	110	.527	35	59	.593	148	16	151	4.5	0.5	4.6
95-96—Iowa	27	554	55	91	.604	39	58	.672	121	16	149	4.5	0.6	5.5
96-97—Iowa	29	827	120	217	.553	93	135	.689	264	35	343	9.1	1.2	11.8
97-98—Iowa	31	852	164	272	.603	111	161	.689	271	48	447	8.7	1.5	14.4
Totals	120	2880	397	690	.575	278	413	.673	804	115	1090	6.7	1.0	9.1

Three-point field goals: 1994-95, 0-for-1. 1996-97, 10-for-32 (.313). 1997-98, 8-for-15 (.533). Totals, 18-for-48 (.375).

TURKISH LEAGUE RECORD

Season Team	G	Min.	FGM	FGA	Pct.	FTM	FTA	Pct.	Reb.	Ast.	Pts.	RPG	APG	PPG
98-99—Oyak Renau	23	873	139	271	.513	64	80	.800	189	39	370	8.2	1.7	16.1

Three-point field goals: 1998-99, 28-for-84 (.333). Totals, 28-for-84 (.333).

NBA REGULAR-SEASON RECORD

Season Team	G	Min.	FGM	FGA	Pct.	FTM	FTA	Pct.	Off.	Def.	Tot.	Ast.	St.	Blk.	TO	Pts.	RPG	APG	PPG
99-00—Denver	52	589	46	117	.393	38	53	.717	75	39	114	20	39	13	14	131	2.2	0.4	2.5
00-01—Denver	57	696	80	144	.556	27	44	.614	62	51	113	30	37	12	24	191	2.0	0.5	3.4
01-02—Denver	75	1686	147	307	.479	69	92	.750	134	165	299	52	75	41	41	364	4.0	0.7	4.9
02-03—Denver	62	996	97	197	.492	27	41	.659	78	79	157	54	65	29	43	223	2.5	0.9	3.6
03-04—Denver	52	392	18	53	.340	10	12	.833	39	48	87	18	18	16	6	46	1.7	0.3	0.9
04-05—Houston	66	604	47	111	.423	14	21	.667	21	55	76	18	23	5	7	111	1.2	0.3	1.7
05-06—Houston	68	652	37	124	.298	11	14	.786	31	57	88	24	21	6	13	88	1.3	0.4	1.3
Totals	432	5615	472	1053	.448	196	277	.708	440	494	934	216	278	122	148	1154	2.2	0.5	2.7

Three-point field goals: 1999-00, 1-for-9 (.111). 2000-01, 4-for-11 (.364). 2001-02, 1-for-12 (.083). 2002-03, 2-for-7 (.286). 2004-05, 3-for-6 (.500). 2005-06, 3-for-22 (.136). Totals, 14-for-67 (.209).
Personal fouls/disqualifications: 1999-00, 95/0. 2000-01, 95/0. 2001-02, 171/1. 2002-03, 82/0. 2003-04, 47/0. 2004-05, 61/0. 2005-06, 85/0. Totals, 636/1.

NBA PLAYOFF RECORD

Season Team	G	Min.	FGM	FGA	Pct.	FTM	FTA	Pct.	Off.	Def.	Tot.	Ast.	St.	Blk.	TO	Pts.	RPG	APG	PPG
03-04—Denver	4	6	1	1	1.000	0	0	...	0	0	0	0	0	0	0	2	0.0	0.0	0.5
04-05—Houston	7	125	8	25	.320	2	3	.667	7	7	14	6	6	0	6	18	2.0	0.9	2.6
Totals	11	131	9	26	.346	2	3	.667	7	7	14	6	6	0	6	20	1.3	0.5	1.8

Personal fouls/disqualifications: 2004-05, 23/2. Totals, 23/2.

BOYKINS, EARL   G   NUGGETS

PERSONAL: Born June 2, 1976, in Cleveland. ... 5-5/133. (1.65/60.3). ... Full name: Earl Antoine Boykins
HIGH SCHOOL: Central Catholic (Cleveland).
COLLEGE: Eastern Michigan.
TRANSACTIONS/CAREER NOTES: Not drafted by an NBA franchise. ... Played in Continental Basketball Association with Rockford Lightning (1998-2000). ... Signed as free agent by New Jersey Nets (January 21, 1999). ... Waived by Nets (February 19, 1999). ... Signed by Cleveland Cavaliers to 10-day contract (March 10, 1999). ... Waived by Cavaliers (March 19, 1999). ... Re-signed by Cavaliers to 10-day contract (March 23, 1999). ... Signed by Cavaliers for remainder of the season (April 2, 1999). ... Waived by Cavaliers (October 28, 1999). ... Signed as free agent by Orlando Magic (November 15, 1999). ... Waived by Magic (December 20, 1999). ... Signed by Cavaliers to first of two consecutive 10-day contracts (February 8, 2000). ... Re-signed by Cavaliers for remainder of season (February 24, 2000). ... Signed as free agent by Los Angeles Clippers (September 29, 2000). ... Waived by Clippers (June 28, 2002). ... Signed as free agent by Golden State Warriors (November 27, 2002). ... Signed as free agent by Denver Nuggets (August 18, 2003).

COLLEGIATE RECORD

NOTES: Naismith Award winner (1998).

Season Team	G	Min.	FGM	FGA	Pct.	FTM	FTA	Pct.	Reb.	Ast.	Pts.	RPG	APG	PPG
94-95—Eastern Michigan	30	976	129	312	.413	83	118	.703	73	136	375	2.4	4.5	12.5
95-96—Eastern Michigan	31	1029	156	361	.432	144	179	.804	71	181	479	2.3	5.8	15.5
96-97—Eastern Michigan	32	1163	208	492	.423	156	183	.852	67	147	611	2.1	4.6	19.1
97-98—Eastern Michigan	29	1070	266	563	.472	129	158	.816	66	160	746	2.3	5.5	25.7
Totals	122	4238	759	1728	.439	512	638	.803	277	624	2211	2.3	5.1	18.1

Three-point field goals: 1994-95, 34-for-99 (.343). 1995-96, 23-for-75 (.307). 1996-97, 39-for-130 (.300). 1997-98, 85-for-209 (.407). Totals, 181-for-513 (.353).

CBA RECORD

Season Team	G	Min.	FGM	FGA	Pct.	FTM	FTA	Pct.	Reb.	Ast.	Pts.	RPG	APG	PPG
98-99—Rockford	29	503	85	209	.407	32	37	.865	40	106	215	1.4	3.7	7.4
99-00—Rockford	18	681	147	302	.487	74	88	.841	64	167	389	3.6	9.3	21.6
Totals	47	1184	232	511	.454	106	125	.848	104	273	604	2.2	5.8	12.9

Three-point field goals: 1998-99, 13-for-47 (.277). 1999-00, 21-for-59 (.356). Totals, 34-for-106 (.321).
Personal fouls/disqualifications: 1998-99, 36/0. 1999-00, 46/0. Totals, 82/0.

NBA REGULAR-SEASON RECORD

Season Team	G	Min.	FGM	FGA	Pct.	FTM	FTA	Pct.	REBOUNDS Off.	Def.	Tot.	Ast.	St.	Blk.	TO	Pts.	AVERAGES RPG	APG	PPG
98-99—N.J.-Cleve.	22	221	30	79	.380	2	3	.667	7	10	17	33	6	0	20	65	0.8	1.5	3.0
99-00—Orlando-Cleve.	26	261	56	116	.483	18	23	.783	12	14	26	48	12	1	17	138	1.0	1.8	5.3
00-01—L.A. Clippers...	10	149	25	63	.397	14	17	.824	4	7	11	32	5	0	9	65	1.1	3.2	6.5
01-02—L.A. Clippers...	68	761	110	275	.400	47	61	.770	27	27	54	145	20	2	44	280	0.8	2.1	4.1
02-03—Golden State ...	68	1321	199	464	.429	173	200	.865	35	53	88	221	38	4	73	600	1.3	3.3	8.8
03-04—Denver	82	1849	321	766	.419	142	162	.877	42	101	143	295	51	3	100	839	1.7	3.6	10.2
04-05—Denver	82	2162	340	824	.413	279	303	.921	37	106	143	372	78	12	121	1015	1.7	4.5	12.4
05-06—Denver	60	1542	271	661	.410	152	174	.874	21	60	81	230	48	4	83	756	1.4	3.8	12.6
Totals	418	8266	1352	3248	.416	827	943	.877	185	378	563	1376	258	26	467	3758	1.3	3.3	9.0

Three-point field goals: 1998-99, 3-for-18 (.167). 1999-00, 8-for-20 (.400). 2000-01, 1-for-8 (.125). 2001-02, 13-for-42 (.310). 2002-03, 29-for-77 (.377). 2003-04, 55-for-171 (.322). 2004-05, 56-for-166 (.337). 2005-06, 62-for-179 (.346). Totals, 227-for-681 (.333).
Personal fouls/disqualifications: 1998-99, 20/0. 1999-00, 23/0. 2000-01, 9/0. 2001-02, 44/0. 2002-03, 75/0. 2003-04, 84/0. 2004-05, 122/0. 2005-06, 73/0. Totals, 450/0.

NBA PLAYOFF RECORD

Season Team	G	Min.	FGM	FGA	Pct.	FTM	FTA	Pct.	REBOUNDS Off.	Def.	Tot.	Ast.	St.	Blk.	TO	Pts.	AVERAGES RPG	APG	PPG
03-04—Denver	5	121	28	63	.444	6	7	.857	6	6	12	19	5	1	6	67	2.4	3.8	13.4
04-05—Denver	5	152	27	68	.397	17	19	.895	2	3	5	19	4	1	9	71	1.0	3.8	14.2
05-06—Denver	5	140	19	59	.322	13	17	.765	3	4	7	20	4	0	3	55	1.4	4.0	11.0
Totals	15	413	74	190	.389	36	43	.837	11	13	24	58	13	2	18	193	1.6	3.9	12.9

Three-point field goals: 2003-04, 5-for-14 (.357). 2004-05, 0-for-7. 2005-06, 4-for-19 (.211). Totals, 9-for-40 (.225).
Personal fouls/disqualifications: 2003-04, 6/0. 2004-05, 13/0. 2005-06, 6/0. Totals, 25/0.

BRADLEY, MICHAEL   F

PERSONAL: Born April 18, 1979, in Worcester, Mass. ... 6-10/225. (2.08/102.1). ... Full name: Michael Thomas Bradley
HIGH SCHOOL: Burncoat (Worcester, Mass.).
COLLEGE: Kentucky, then Villanova.
TRANSACTIONS/CAREER NOTES: Selected after junior season by Toronto Raptors in first round (17th pick overall) of 2001 NBA Draft. ... Waived by Raptors (March 12, 2004). ... Signed by Atlanta Hawks for remainder of season (March 18, 2004). ... Signed as free agent by Orlando Magic (July 29, 2004). ... Traded by Magic with G Cuttino Mobley to Sacramento Kings for G/F Doug Christie (January 10, 2005). ... Traded by Kings with Fs Chris Webber and Matt Barnes to Philadelphia 76ers for Fs Kenny Thomas and Corliss Williamson and C Brian Skinner (February 23, 2005).

COLLEGIATE RECORD

NOTES: Member of NCAA Division I championship team (1998). ... The SPORTING NEWS All-America second team (2001).

Season Team	G	Min.	FGM	FGA	Pct.	FTM	FTA	Pct.	Reb.	Ast.	Pts.	AVERAGES RPG	APG	PPG
97-98—Kentucky	32	221	30	45	.667	18	35	.514	55	15	78	1.7	0.5	2.4
98-99—Kentucky	37	811	157	239	.657	50	110	.455	182	37	364	4.9	1.0	9.8
99-00—Villanova.........................						Did not play—transfer student.								
00-01—Villanova.........................	31	1053	254	367	.692	125	212	.590	303	81	645	9.8	2.6	20.8
Totals	100	2085	441	651	.677	193	357	.541	540	133	1087	5.4	1.3	10.9

Three-point field goals: 2000-01, 12-for-34 (.353). Totals, 12-for-34 (.353).
Personal fouls/disqualifications: 1997-98, 26/0. 1998-99, 72/0. 2000-01, 89/0. Totals, 187/0.

NBA REGULAR-SEASON RECORD

Season Team	G	Min.	FGM	FGA	Pct.	FTM	FTA	Pct.	REBOUNDS Off.	Def.	Tot.	Ast.	St.	Blk.	TO	Pts.	AVERAGES RPG	APG	PPG
01-02—Toronto	26	118	13	25	.520	4	8	.500	7	17	24	3	0	6	6	30	0.9	0.1	1.2
02-03—Toronto	67	1314	151	314	.481	35	67	.522	162	247	409	67	16	32	76	338	6.1	1.0	5.0
03-04—Tor.-Atl...........	16	98	7	15	.467	1	2	.500	6	17	23	1	3	0	7	15	1.4	0.1	0.9
04-05—Orl.-Sac.-Phi...	18	119	15	24	.625	3	8	.375	8	20	28	5	1	2	5	33	1.6	0.3	1.8
05-06—Philadelphia	46	367	32	79	.405	2	3	.667	40	67	107	17	5	7	19	67	2.3	0.4	1.5
Totals	173	2016	218	457	.477	45	88	.511	223	368	591	93	25	47	113	483	3.4	0.5	2.8

Three-point field goals: 2001-02, 0-for-2. 2002-03, 1-for-6 (.167). 2004-05, 0-for-1. 2005-06, 1-for-5 (.200). Totals, 2-for-14 (.143).
Personal fouls/disqualifications: 2001-02, 10/0. 2002-03, 125/0. 2003-04, 14/0. 2004-05, 12/0. 2005-06, 39/0. Totals, 200/0.

NBA PLAYOFF RECORD

Season Team	G	Min.	FGM	FGA	Pct.	FTM	FTA	Pct.	REBOUNDS Off.	Def.	Tot.	Ast.	St.	Blk.	TO	Pts.	AVERAGES RPG	APG	PPG
01-02—Toronto	1	3	0	0	...	0	0	...	0	1	1	1	0	0	0	0	1.0	1.0	0.0

Personal fouls/disqualifications: 2001-02, 1/0. Totals, 1/0.

BRAND, ELTON   F   CLIPPERS

PERSONAL: Born March 11, 1979, in Cortland, N.Y. ... 6-8/265. (2.03/120.2). ... Full name: Elton Tyron Brand
HIGH SCHOOL: Peekskill (N.Y.).
COLLEGE: Duke.
TRANSACTIONS/CAREER NOTES: Selected after sophomore season by Chicago Bulls in first round (first pick overall) of 1999 NBA Draft. ... Traded by Bulls to Los Angeles Clippers for F Brian Skinner and draft rights to C Tyson Chandler (June 27, 2001).

COLLEGIATE RECORD

NOTES: The SPORTING NEWS College Player of the Year (1999). ... Wooden Award winner (1999). ... Naismith Award winner (1999). ... The SPORTING NEWS All-America first team (1999).

Season Team	G	Min.	FGM	FGA	Pct.	FTM	FTA	Pct.	Reb.	Ast.	Pts.	RPG	APG	PPG
												AVERAGES		
97-98—Duke..................	21	493	100	169	.592	81	134	.604	154	10	281	7.3	0.5	13.4
98-99—Duke..................	39	1141	255	411	.620	181	256	.707	382	41	691	9.8	1.1	17.7
Totals	60	1634	355	580	.612	262	390	.672	536	51	972	8.9	0.9	16.2

NBA REGULAR-SEASON RECORD

HONORS: NBA Co-Rookie of the Year (2000). ... NBA All-Rookie first team (2000). ... MVP of Rookie Challenge (2000). ... NBA Sportsmanship Award winner (2006). ... All-NBA second team (2006).

Season Team	G	Min.	FGM	FGA	Pct.	FTM	FTA	Pct.	REBOUNDS Off.	Def.	Tot.	Ast.	St.	Blk.	TO	Pts.	AVERAGES RPG	APG	PPG
99-00—Chicago	81	2999	630	1306	.482	367	536	.685	348	462	*810	155	66	132	228	1627	10.0	1.9	20.1
00-01—Chicago	74	2906	578	1215	.476	334	472	.708	285	461	746	240	71	118	219	1490	10.1	3.2	20.1
01-02—L.A. Clippers...	80	3020	532	1010	.527	389	524	.742	396	529	*925	191	80	163	173	1453	11.6	2.4	18.2
02-03—L.A. Clippers...	62	2454	451	899	.502	244	356	.685	283	420	703	157	71	158	161	1146	11.3	2.5	18.5
03-04—L.A. Clippers...	69	2670	484	982	.493	411	532	.773	269	445	714	227	64	154	193	1379	10.3	3.3	20.0
04-05—L.A. Clippers...	81	3001	629	1251	.503	364	484	.752	296	474	770	208	62	169	183	1622	9.5	2.6	20.0
05-06—L.A. Clippers...	79	3099	756	1435	.527	440	568	.775	236	554	790	208	81	201	173	1953	10.0	2.6	24.7
Totals	526	20149	4060	8098	.501	2549	3472	.734	2113	3345	5458	1386	495	1095	1330	10670	10.4	2.6	20.3

Three-point field goals: 1999-00, 0-for-2. 2000-01, 0-for-2. 2002-03, 0-for-1. 2003-04, 0-for-1. 2004-05, 0-for-3. 2005-06, 1-for-3 (.333). Totals, 1-for-12 (.083).

Personal fouls/disqualifications: 1999-00, 259/3. 2000-01, 243/4. 2001-02, 254/3. 2002-03, 204/3. 2003-04, 229/1. 2004-05, 240/2. 2005-06, 227/0. Totals, 1656/16.

NBA PLAYOFF RECORD

Season Team	G	Min.	FGM	FGA	Pct.	FTM	FTA	Pct.	REBOUNDS Off.	Def.	Tot.	Ast.	St.	Blk.	TO	Pts.	AVERAGES RPG	APG	PPG
05-06—L.A. Clippers...	12	517	124	225	.551	57	76	.750	51	72	123	48	11	31	29	305	10.3	4.0	25.4

Three-point field goals: 2005-06, 0-for-1. Totals, 0-for-1 (.000).
Personal fouls/disqualifications: 2005-06, 34/1. Totals, 34/1.

NBA ALL-STAR GAME RECORD

Season Team	Min.	FGM	FGA	Pct.	FTM	FTA	Pct.	REBOUNDS Off.	Def.	Tot.	Ast.	PF	Dq.	St.	Blk.	TO	Pts.
2002—L.A. Clippers	19	3	5	.600	0	0	...	5	5	10	1	2	0	0	1	2	6
2006—L.A. Clippers	17	6	11	.545	0	0	...	3	4	7	0	2	0	1	0	3	12
Totals..........................	36	9	16	.563	0	0	...	8	9	17	1	4	0	1	1	5	18

BREZEC, PRIMOZ   F   BOBCATS

PERSONAL: Born October 2, 1979, in Postojna, Slovenia. ... 7-1/243. (2.16/110.2).
TRANSACTIONS/CAREER NOTES: Played in Slovenia (1997-2001). ... Selected by Indiana Pacers in first round (27th pick overall) of 2000 NBA Draft. ... Selected by Charlotte Bobcats from Pacers in NBA Expansion Draft (June 22, 2004).

SLOVENIAN LEAGUE RECORD

Season Team	G	Min.	FGM	FGA	Pct.	FTM	FTA	Pct.	Reb.	Ast.	Pts.	AVERAGES RPG	APG	PPG
96-97—Kraski	30	...	164	283	.580	201	258	.779	207	12	577	6.9	0.4	19.2
97-98—Kraski	12	...	36	47	.766	28	41	.683	38	4	100	3.2	0.3	8.3
98-99—Olimpija Ljubljana..........	23	203	40	52	.769	31	45	.689	40	4	111	1.7	0.2	4.8
99-00—Olimpija Ljubljana..........	30	609	111	150	.740	76	105	.724	155	5	298	5.2	0.2	9.9
00-01—Olimpija Ljubljana..........	30	618	132	190	.695	78	122	.639	127	19	342	4.2	0.6	11.4
Totals	125	1430	483	722	.669	414	571	.725	567	44	1428	4.5	0.4	11.4

Three-point field goals: 1996-97, 16-for-52 (.308). Totals, 16-for-52 (.308).
Personal fouls/disqualifications: 2000-01, 84/0. Totals, 84/0.

NBA REGULAR-SEASON RECORD

Season Team	G	Min.	FGM	FGA	Pct.	FTM	FTA	Pct.	REBOUNDS Off.	Def.	Tot.	Ast.	St.	Blk.	TO	Pts.	AVERAGES RPG	APG	PPG
01-02—Indiana............	22	160	14	29	.483	15	25	.600	16	12	28	6	0	7	6	43	1.3	0.3	2.0
02-03—Indiana............	22	111	15	38	.395	12	20	.600	13	10	23	4	2	4	7	42	1.0	0.2	1.9
03-04—Indiana............	18	72	12	26	.462	4	6	.667	5	10	15	3	0	3	6	28	0.8	0.2	1.6
04-05—Charlotte	72	2276	387	756	.512	164	220	.745	226	305	531	86	33	55	106	938	7.4	1.2	13.0
05-06—Charlotte	79	2165	409	791	.517	164	224	.732	181	259	440	45	19	32	85	982	5.6	0.6	12.4
Totals	213	4784	837	1640	.510	359	495	.725	441	596	1037	144	54	101	210	2033	4.9	0.7	9.5

Three-point field goals: 2002-03, 0-for-1. 2005-06, 0-for-2. Totals, 0-for-3 (.000).
Personal fouls/disqualifications: 2001-02, 28/0. 2002-03, 16/0. 2003-04, 13/0. 2004-05, 183/2. 2005-06, 227/2. Totals, 467/4.

BROWN, P.J.   F   BULLS

PERSONAL: Born October 14, 1969, in Detroit. ... 6-11/239. (2.11/108.4).
HIGH SCHOOL: Winnfield (La.) Senior.
COLLEGE: Louisiana Tech.
TRANSACTIONS/CAREER NOTES: Selected by New Jersey Nets in second round (29th pick overall) of 1992 NBA Draft. ... Played in Greece (1992-93). ... Signed as free agent by Miami Heat (July 18, 1996). ... Traded by Heat with F Jamal Mashburn, F/C Otis Thorpe, F Tim James and G/F Rodney Buford to Charlotte Hornets for G Eddie Jones, F Anthony Mason, G Ricky Davis and G/F Dale Ellis (August 1, 2000). ... Hornets franchise moved to New Orleans for 2002-03 season. ... Traded by Hornets with G J.R. Smith to Chicago Bulls for F Tyson Chandler (July 14, 2006).

COLLEGIATE RECORD

Season Team	G	Min.	FGM	FGA	Pct.	FTM	FTA	Pct.	Reb.	Ast.	Pts.	AVERAGES		
												RPG	APG	PPG
88-89—Louisiana Tech	32	569	61	147	.415	25	44	.568	178	36	149	5.6	1.1	4.7
89-90—Louisiana Tech	27	672	94	204	.461	48	81	.593	230	29	239	8.5	1.1	8.9
90-91—Louisiana Tech	31	936	170	315	.540	98	150	.653	301	58	445	9.7	1.9	14.4
91-92—Louisiana Tech	31	931	151	309	.489	84	115	.730	308	53	395	9.9	1.7	12.7
Totals	121	3108	476	975	.488	255	390	.654	1017	176	1228	8.4	1.5	10.1

Three-point field goals: 1988-89, 2-for-3 (.667). 1989-90, 3-for-5 (.600). 1990-91, 7-for-20 (.350). 1991-92, 9-for-25 (.360). Totals, 21-for-53 (.396).
Personal fouls/disqualifications: 1988-89, 87/4. 1989-90, 80/3. 1990-91, 90/7. 1991-92, 97/4. Totals, 354/18.

GREEK LEAGUE RECORD

Season Team	G	Min.	FGM	FGA	Pct.	FTM	FTA	Pct.	Reb.	Ast.	Pts.	AVERAGES		
												RPG	APG	PPG
92-93—Panionios	26	...	164	299	.548	107	151	.709	357	...	441	13.7	...	17.0

NBA REGULAR-SEASON RECORD

HONORS: NBA Sportsmanship Award (2004). ... J. Walter Kennedy Citizenship Award (1997). ... NBA All-Defensive second team (1997, 1999, 2001).

Season Team	G	Min.	FGM	FGA	Pct.	FTM	FTA	Pct.	REBOUNDS			Ast.	St.	Blk.	TO	Pts.	AVERAGES		
									Off.	Def.	Tot.						RPG	APG	PPG
93-94—New Jersey	79	1950	167	402	.415	115	152	.757	188	305	493	93	71	93	72	450	6.2	1.2	5.7
94-95—New Jersey	80	2466	254	570	.446	139	207	.671	178	309	487	135	69	135	80	651	6.1	1.7	8.1
95-96—New Jersey	81	2942	354	798	.444	204	265	.770	215	345	560	165	79	100	133	915	6.9	2.0	11.3
96-97—Miami	80	2592	300	656	.457	161	220	.732	239	431	670	92	85	98	113	761	8.4	1.2	9.5
97-98—Miami	74	2362	278	590	.471	151	197	.766	235	400	635	103	66	98	97	707	8.6	1.4	9.6
98-99—Miami	50	1611	229	477	.480	113	146	.774	115	231	346	66	46	48	69	571	6.9	1.3	11.4
99-00—Miami	80	2302	322	671	.480	120	159	.755	216	384	600	145	65	61	100	764	7.5	1.8	9.6
00-01—Charlotte	80	2811	249	561	.444	178	209	.852	257	485	742	127	78	92	108	676	9.3	1.6	8.5
01-02—Charlotte	80	2563	250	527	.474	169	197	.858	273	513	786	107	59	78	85	669	9.8	1.3	8.4
02-03—New Orleans ...	78	2609	319	601	.531	194	232	.836	243	458	701	147	67	80	98	832	9.0	1.9	10.7
03-04—New Orleans ...	80	2753	339	712	.476	158	185	.854	237	453	690	155	78	73	101	836	8.6	1.9	10.5
04-05—New Orleans ...	82	2817	338	758	.446	210	243	.864	266	471	737	178	74	50	101	886	9.0	2.2	10.8
05-06—NO/Okla. City ..	75	2380	269	583	.461	139	168	.827	182	365	547	90	46	50	90	677	7.3	1.2	9.0
Totals	999	32158	3668	7906	.464	2051	2580	.795	2844	5150	7994	1603	883	1056	1247	9395	8.0	1.6	9.4

Three-point field goals: 1993-94, 1-for-6 (.167). 1994-95, 4-for-24 (.167). 1995-96, 3-for-15 (.200). 1996-97, 0-for-2. 1999-00, 0-for-1. 2000-01, 0-for-1. 2002-03, 0-for-3. 2003-04, 0-for-1. Totals, 8-for-56 (.143).
Personal fouls/disqualifications: 1993-94, 177/1. 1994-95, 262/8. 1995-96, 249/5. 1996-97, 283/7. 1997-98, 264/9. 1998-99, 166/2. 1999-00, 264/4. 2000-01, 260/6. 2001-02, 222/1. 2002-03, 203/3. 2003-04, 203/2. 2004-05, 233/3. 2005-06, 216/2. Totals, 3002/53.

NBA PLAYOFF RECORD

Season Team	G	Min.	FGM	FGA	Pct.	FTM	FTA	Pct.	REBOUNDS			Ast.	St.	Blk.	TO	Pts.	AVERAGES		
									Off.	Def.	Tot.						RPG	APG	PPG
93-94—New Jersey	4	56	2	9	.222	8	8	1.000	4	4	8	3	0	2	3	12	2.0	0.8	3.0
96-97—Miami	15	451	42	103	.408	38	53	.717	48	81	129	10	9	20	16	122	8.6	0.7	8.1
97-98—Miami	5	190	19	37	.514	8	22	.364	15	29	44	4	7	3	6	46	8.8	0.8	9.2
98-99—Miami	5	144	21	45	.467	9	10	.900	14	17	31	5	2	2	3	51	6.2	1.0	10.2
99-00—Miami	10	308	35	82	.427	5	6	.833	26	56	82	11	8	4	11	75	8.2	1.1	7.5
00-01—Charlotte	10	385	28	67	.418	24	29	.828	41	59	100	11	12	14	12	80	10.0	1.1	8.0
01-02—Charlotte	9	331	32	75	.427	28	37	.757	29	57	86	14	6	12	8	92	9.6	1.6	10.2
02-03—New Orleans ...	6	193	21	44	.477	19	25	.760	20	26	46	6	7	3	5	61	7.7	1.0	10.2
03-04—New Orleans ...	7	256	26	71	.366	10	11	.909	29	39	68	15	3	11	13	62	9.7	2.1	8.9
Totals	71	2314	226	533	.424	149	201	.741	226	368	594	79	54	71	77	601	8.4	1.1	8.5

Three-point field goals: 1998-99, 0-for-1. Totals, 0-for-1 (.000).
Personal fouls/disqualifications: 1993-94, 13/0. 1996-97, 40/0. 1997-98, 22/1. 1998-99, 42/3. 2000-01, 31/1. 2001-02, 37/3. 2002-03, 22/0. 2003-04, 16/0. Totals, 240/8.

BROWN, DEVIN   G   WARRIORS

PERSONAL: Born December 30, 1978, in Salt Lake City. ... 6-5/210. (1.96/95.3).
HIGH SCHOOL: South San West Campus (San Antonio).
COLLEGE: University of Texas at San Antonio.
TRANSACTIONS/CAREER NOTES: Not drafted by an NBA franchise ... Played in NBA Development League with Fayetteville Patriots (2002-03). ... Signed by San Antonio Spurs (July 31, 2003) ... Signed as free agent by Utah Jazz (September 14, 2005). ... Traded by Jazz with Gs Keith McLeod and Andre Owens to Golden State Warriors for G Derek Fisher (July 12, 2006).
MISCELLANEOUS: Member of NBA championship team (2005).

COLLEGIATE RECORD

Season Team	G	Min.	FGM	FGA	Pct.	FTM	FTA	Pct.	Reb.	Ast.	Pts.	AVERAGES		
												RPG	APG	PPG
98-99—Texas-San Antonio	29	896	160	380	.421	112	148	.757	177	65	483	6.1	2.2	16.7
99-00—Texas-San Antonio	20	657	129	330	.391	83	113	.735	129	69	370	6.5	3.5	18.5
00-01—Texas-San Antonio	28	906	186	436	.427	139	193	.720	212	71	556	7.6	2.5	19.9
01-02—Texas-San Antonio	28	905	162	402	.403	144	198	.727	233	78	513	8.3	2.8	18.3
Totals	105	3364	637	1548	.411	478	652	.733	751	283	1922	7.2	2.7	18.3

Three-point field goals: 1998-99, 51-for-156 (.327). 1999-00, 29-for-115 (.252). 2000-01, 45-for-157 (.287). 2001-02, 45-for-123 (.366). Totals, 170-for-551 (.309).

NBA REGULAR-SEASON RECORD

									REBOUNDS								AVERAGES		
Season Team	G	Min.	FGM	FGA	Pct.	FTM	FTA	Pct.	Off.	Def.	Tot.	Ast.	St.	Blk.	TO	Pts.	RPG	APG	PPG
02-03—S.A.-Denver	10	93	12	35	.343	6	8	.750	8	10	18	7	4	1	9	30	1.8	0.7	3.0
03-04—San Antonio....	58	627	85	196	.434	60	74	.811	38	92	130	33	15	4	38	234	2.2	0.6	4.0
04-05—San Antonio....	67	1238	173	409	.423	103	130	.792	37	139	176	92	39	12	53	494	2.6	1.4	7.4
05-06—Utah..............	81	1711	207	527	.393	158	212	.745	73	134	207	104	44	14	99	611	2.6	1.3	7.5
Totals	216	3669	477	1167	.409	327	424	.771	156	375	531	236	102	31	199	1369	2.5	1.1	6.3

Three-point field goals: 2002-03, 0-for-1. 2003-04, 4-for-14 (.286). 2004-05, 45-for-121 (.372). 2005-06, 39-for-118 (.331). Totals, 88-for-254 (.346).
Personal fouls/disqualifications: 2002-03, 14/0. 2003-04, 61/0. 2004-05, 83/0. 2005-06, 153/0. Totals, 311/0.

NBA PLAYOFF RECORD

									REBOUNDS								AVERAGES		
Season Team	G	Min.	FGM	FGA	Pct.	FTM	FTA	Pct.	Off.	Def.	Tot.	Ast.	St.	Blk.	TO	Pts.	RPG	APG	PPG
03-04—San Antonio....	9	130	18	37	.486	10	17	.588	4	14	18	9	3	1	7	52	2.0	1.0	5.8
04-05—San Antonio....	12	60	7	20	.350	4	7	.571	1	6	7	3	1	0	1	21	0.6	0.3	1.8
Totals	21	190	25	57	.439	14	24	.583	5	20	25	12	4	1	8	73	1.2	0.6	3.5

Three-point field goals: 2003-04, 6-for-10 (.600). 2004-05, 3-for-7 (.429). Totals, 9-for-17 (.529).
Personal fouls/disqualifications: 2003-04, 18/1. 2004-05, 3/0. Totals, 21/1.

NBA DEVELOPMENT LEAGUE RECORD

											AVERAGES		
Season Team	G	Min.	FGM	FGA	Pct.	FTM	FTA	Pct.	Reb.	Ast.	Pts.	RPG	APG	PPG
02-03—Fayetteville....................	44	1086	270	540	.500	185	225	.822	182	88	742	4.1	2.0	16.9

Three-point field goals: 2002-03, 17-for-46 (.370). Totals, 17-for-46 (.370).
Personal fouls/disqualifications: 2002-03, 108/0. Totals, 108/0.

BROWN, KWAME   C/F   LAKERS

PERSONAL: Born March 10, 1982, in Charleston, S.C. ... 6-11/243. (2.11/110.2). ... Cousin of Jabari Smith, center, Sacramento Kings (2000-02) and Philadelphia 76ers (2001-02 and 2003-04).
HIGH SCHOOL: Glynn Academy (Brunswick, Ga.).
COLLEGE: Did not attend college.
TRANSACTIONS/CAREER NOTES: Selected out of high school by Washington Wizards in first round (first pick overall) of 2001 NBA Draft. ... Traded by Wizards with F Laron Profit to Los Angeles Lakers for F Caron Butler and G Chucky Atkins (August 2, 2005).

NBA REGULAR-SEASON RECORD

									REBOUNDS								AVERAGES		
Season Team	G	Min.	FGM	FGA	Pct.	FTM	FTA	Pct.	Off.	Def.	Tot.	Ast.	St.	Blk.	TO	Pts.	RPG	APG	PPG
01-02—Washington	57	817	94	243	.387	70	99	.707	63	135	198	43	16	26	43	258	3.5	0.8	4.5
02-03—Washington	80	1773	224	502	.446	145	217	.668	128	298	426	58	50	80	110	593	5.3	0.7	7.4
03-04—Washington	74	2239	288	589	.489	228	334	.683	178	372	550	112	66	52	140	805	7.4	1.5	10.9
04-05—Washington	42	908	109	237	.460	74	129	.574	72	134	206	39	25	15	67	292	4.9	0.9	7.0
05-06—L.A. Lakers	72	1978	204	388	.526	128	235	.545	182	291	473	72	27	46	100	536	6.6	1.0	7.4
Totals	325	7715	919	1959	.469	645	1014	.636	623	1230	1853	324	184	219	460	2484	5.7	1.0	7.6

Three-point field goals: 2001-02, 0-for-1. 2002-03, 0-for-3. 2003-04, 1-for-2 (.500). 2005-06, 0-for-1. Totals, 1-for-7 (.143).
Personal fouls/disqualifications: 2001-02, 105/2. 2002-03, 159/1. 2003-04, 144/0. 2004-05, 112/0. 2005-06, 196/3. Totals, 716/6.

NBA PLAYOFF RECORD

									REBOUNDS								AVERAGES		
Season Team	G	Min.	FGM	FGA	Pct.	FTM	FTA	Pct.	Off.	Def.	Tot.	Ast.	St.	Blk.	TO	Pts.	RPG	APG	PPG
04-05—Washington	3	60	5	13	.385	5	9	.556	4	11	15	3	0	2	2	15	5.0	1.0	5.0
05-06—L.A. Lakers	7	225	34	65	.523	22	31	.710	17	29	46	7	2	6	12	90	6.6	1.0	12.9
Totals	10	285	39	78	.500	27	40	.675	21	40	61	10	2	8	14	105	6.1	1.0	10.5

Personal fouls/disqualifications: 2004-05, 5/0. 2005-06, 21/0. Totals, 26/0.

BRUNSON, RICK   G

PERSONAL: Born June 14, 1972, in Syracuse, N.Y. ... 6-4/190. (1.93/86.2). ... Full name: Rick Daniel Brunson
HIGH SCHOOL: Salem (Mass.).
COLLEGE: Temple.
TRANSACTIONS/CAREER NOTES: Not drafted by an NBA franchise. ... Played in Australia (1995-96). ... Played in Continental Basketball Association with Quad City Thunder (1996-97) and Connecticut Pride (1997-99). ... Signed as free agent by Orlando Magic (September 30, 1997). ... Waived by Magic (October 20, 1997). ... Signed as free agent by New York Knicks (October 23, 1997). ... Waived by Knicks (October 30, 1997). ... Signed as free agent by Portland Trail Blazers (December 2, 1997). ... Signed as free agent by Knicks (January 21, 1999). ... Signed as free agent by Miami Heat (September 28, 2000). ... Waived by Heat (October 20, 2000). ... Signed as free agent by Boston Celtics (November 6, 2000). ... Claimed on waivers by Knicks (November 27, 2000). ... Signed as free agent by Trail Blazers (September 21, 2001). ... Signed as free agent by Chicago Bulls (September 18, 2002). ... Signed as free agent by Toronto Raptors (August 13, 2003). ... Traded by Raptors to Chicago Bulls for G Roger Mason Jr. (December 16, 2003). ... Waived by Bulls (March 15, 2004). ... Signed as free agent by Los Angeles Clippers (September 30, 2004). ... Waived by Clippers (August 3, 2005). ... Signed as free agent by Seattle SuperSonics (August 5, 2005). ... Claimed on waivers by Houston Rockets (March 2, 2006).

COLLEGIATE RECORD

											AVERAGES		
Season Team	G	Min.	FGM	FGA	Pct.	FTM	FTA	Pct.	Reb.	Ast.	Pts.	RPG	APG	PPG
91-92—Temple..........................	30	537	41	128	.320	53	87	.609	79	56	147	2.6	1.9	4.9
92-93—Temple..........................	33	1205	147	371	.396	112	171	.655	98	149	463	3.0	4.5	14.0
93-94—Temple..........................	31	1221	128	346	.370	77	119	.647	127	142	383	4.1	4.6	12.4
94-95—Temple..........................	30	1149	164	448	.366	100	143	.699	177	123	500	5.9	4.1	16.7
Totals	124	4112	480	1293	.371	342	520	.658	481	470	1493	3.9	3.8	12.0

Three-point field goals: 1991-92, 12-for-53 (.226). 1992-93, 57-for-177 (.322). 1993-94, 50-for-167 (.299). 1994-95, 72-for-252 (.286). Totals, 191-for-649 (.294).

CBA RECORD

Season Team	G	Min.	FGM	FGA	Pct.	FTM	FTA	Pct.	Reb.	Ast.	Pts.	RPG	APG	PPG
96-97—Quad City	56	1953	231	567	.407	148	198	.747	218	380	652	3.9	6.8	11.6
97-98—Connecticut	8	333	66	133	.496	45	54	.833	29	53	191	3.6	6.6	23.9
98-99—Connecticut	21	817	134	332	.404	73	101	.723	48	154	367	2.3	7.3	17.5
Totals	85	3103	431	1032	.418	266	353	.754	295	587	1210	3.5	6.9	14.2

Three-point field goals: 1996-97, 42-for-154 (.273). 1997-98, 14-for-40 (.350). 1998-99, 26-for-82 (.317). Totals, 82-for-276 (.297).
Personal fouls/disqualifications: 1996-97, 134/0. 1997-98, 27/0. 1998-99, 50/0. Totals, 211/0.

NBA REGULAR-SEASON RECORD

Season Team	G	Min.	FGM	FGA	Pct.	FTM	FTA	Pct.	Off.	Def.	Tot.	Ast.	St.	Blk.	TO	Pts.	RPG	APG	PPG
97-98—Portland	38	622	49	141	.348	42	62	.677	14	42	56	100	25	3	52	162	1.5	2.6	4.3
98-99—New York	17	95	6	21	.286	5	18	.278	3	7	10	19	9	0	12	17	0.6	1.1	1.0
99-00—New York	37	289	29	70	.414	11	18	.611	3	24	27	49	9	1	31	71	0.7	1.3	1.9
00-01—Boston-N.Y.	22	208	18	54	.333	8	15	.533	5	16	21	31	8	1	17	46	1.0	1.4	2.1
01-02—Portland	59	520	45	113	.398	29	41	.707	23	45	68	114	25	2	47	125	1.2	1.9	2.1
02-03—Chicago	17	196	23	50	.460	10	12	.833	4	15	19	36	10	3	17	60	1.1	2.1	3.5
03-04—Tor.-Chi.	40	412	40	105	.381	27	31	.871	9	28	37	82	25	3	33	118	0.9	2.1	3.0
04-05—L.A. Clippers	80	1945	166	442	.376	57	74	.770	23	164	187	410	82	7	125	437	2.3	5.1	5.5
05-06—Seattle-Hous.	27	247	21	54	.389	7	12	.583	1	21	22	35	8	1	22	54	0.8	1.3	2.0
Totals	337	4534	397	1050	.378	196	283	.693	85	362	447	876	201	21	356	1090	1.3	2.6	3.2

Three-point field goals: 1997-98, 22-for-61 (.361). 1998-99, 0-for-5. 1999-00, 2-for-13 (.154). 2000-01, 2-for-14 (.143). 2001-02, 6-for-11 (.545). 2002-03, 4-for-6 (.667). 2003-04, 11-for-23 (.478). 2004-05, 48-for-130 (.369). 2005-06, 5-for-13 (.385). Totals, 100-for-276 (.362).
Personal fouls/disqualifications: 1997-98, 55/0. 1998-99, 8/0. 1999-00, 35/0. 2000-01, 21/0. 2001-02, 51/0. 2002-03, 20/0. 2003-04, 44/0. 2004-05, 106/0. 2005-06, 22/0. Totals, 362/0.

NBA PLAYOFF RECORD

Season Team	G	Min.	FGM	FGA	Pct.	FTM	FTA	Pct.	Off.	Def.	Tot.	Ast.	St.	Blk.	TO	Pts.	RPG	APG	PPG
98-99—New York	9	18	2	5	.400	2	2	1.000	1	0	1	2	0	0	4	6	0.1	0.2	0.7
99-00—New York	3	4	0	1	.000	0	0	...	0	0	0	1	1	0	0	0	0.0	0.3	0.0
00-01—New York	2	4	0	1	.000	3	4	.750	0	0	0	0	0	0	1	3	0.0	0.0	1.5
01-02—Portland	2	2	0	0	...	0	0	...	0	0	0	0	0	0	0	0	0.0	0.0	0.0
Totals	16	28	2	7	.286	5	6	.833	1	0	1	3	1	0	5	9	0.1	0.2	0.6

Personal fouls/disqualifications: 1998-99, 3/0. 1999-00, 2/0. Totals, 5/0.

BRYANT, KOBE   G   LAKERS

PERSONAL: Born August 23, 1978, in Philadelphia. ... 6-7/210. (2.01/95.3). ... Full name: Kobe B. Bryant ... Son of Joe "Jelly Bean" Bryant, forward with Philadelphia 76ers (1975-75 through 1978-79), San Diego Clippers (1980-81 through 1981-82) and Houston Rockets (1982-83). ... Name pronounced Co-bee.
HIGH SCHOOL: Lower Merion (Pa.).
COLLEGE: Did not attend college.
TRANSACTIONS/CAREER NOTES: Selected out of high school by Charlotte Hornets in first round (13th pick overall) of 1996 NBA Draft. ... Draft rights traded by Hornets to Los Angeles Lakers for C Vlade Divac (July 11, 1996).
MISCELLANEOUS: Member of NBA championship team (2000, 2001, 2002).

NBA REGULAR-SEASON RECORD
RECORDS: Shares NBA record for most three-point field goals made in one game—12 (January 7, 2003). ... Shares NBA record for most three-point field goals made in one half—8 (March 28, 2003).
HONORS: Slam Dunk championship winner (1997). ... All-NBA first team (2002, 2003, 2006). ... All-NBA second team (2000, 2001). ... All-NBA third team (1999, 2005). ... NBA All-Defensive first team (2000, 2003, 2004 and 2006). ... NBA All-Defensive second team (2001, 2002). ... NBA All-Rookie second team (1997).

Season Team	G	Min.	FGM	FGA	Pct.	FTM	FTA	Pct.	Off.	Def.	Tot.	Ast.	St.	Blk.	TO	Pts.	RPG	APG	PPG
96-97—L.A. Lakers	71	1103	176	422	.417	136	166	.819	47	85	132	91	49	23	112	539	1.9	1.3	7.6
97-98—L.A. Lakers	79	2056	391	913	.428	363	457	.794	79	163	242	199	74	40	157	1220	3.1	2.5	15.4
98-99—L.A. Lakers	50	1896	362	779	.465	245	292	.839	53	211	264	190	72	50	157	996	5.3	3.8	19.9
99-00—L.A. Lakers	66	2524	554	1183	.468	331	403	.821	108	308	416	323	106	62	182	1485	6.3	4.9	22.5
00-01—L.A. Lakers	68	2783	701	1510	.464	475	557	.853	104	295	399	338	114	43	220	1938	5.9	5.0	28.5
01-02—L.A. Lakers	80	3063	749	1597	.469	488	589	.829	112	329	441	438	118	35	223	2019	5.5	5.5	25.2
02-03—L.A. Lakers	82	3401	*868	1924	.451	601	713	.843	106	458	564	481	181	67	288	*2461	6.9	5.9	30.0
03-04—L.A. Lakers	65	2447	516	1178	.438	454	533	.852	103	256	359	330	112	28	171	1557	5.5	5.1	24.0
04-05—L.A. Lakers	66	2689	573	1324	.433	542	664	.816	95	297	392	398	86	53	270	1819	5.9	6.0	27.6
05-06—L.A. Lakers	80	3277	*978	*2173	.450	*696	819	.850	71	354	425	360	147	30	250	*2832	5.3	4.5	*35.4
Totals	707	25239	5868	13003	.451	4331	5193	.834	878	2756	3634	3148	1059	431	2030	16866	5.1	4.5	23.9

Three-point field goals: 1996-97, 51-for-136 (.375). 1997-98, 75-for-220 (.341). 1998-99, 27-for-101 (.267). 1999-00, 46-for-144 (.319). 2000-01, 61-for-200 (.305). 2001-02, 33-for-132 (.250). 2002-03, 124-for-324 (.383). 2003-04, 71-for-217 (.327). 2004-05, 131-for-387 (.339). 2005-06, 180-for-518 (.347). Totals, 799-for-2379 (.336).
Personal fouls/disqualifications: 1996-97, 102/0. 1997-98, 180/1. 1998-99, 153/3. 1999-00, 220/4. 2000-01, 222/3. 2001-02, 228/1. 2002-03, 218/0. 2003-04, 176/0. 2004-05, 174/1. 2005-06, 233/1. Totals, 1906/14.

NBA PLAYOFF RECORD
NOTES: Shares single-game playoff record for most three-point field goal attempts in one half—11 (May 13, 2003).

Season Team	G	Min.	FGM	FGA	Pct.	FTM	FTA	Pct.	Off.	Def.	Tot.	Ast.	St.	Blk.	TO	Pts.	RPG	APG	PPG
96-97—L.A. Lakers	9	133	21	55	.382	26	30	.867	1	10	11	11	3	2	14	74	1.2	1.2	8.2
97-98—L.A. Lakers	11	220	31	76	.408	31	45	.689	7	14	21	16	3	8	11	96	1.9	1.5	8.7

Season Team	G	Min.	FGM	FGA	Pct.	FTM	FTA	Pct.	Off.	Def.	Tot.	Ast.	St.	Blk.	TO	Pts.	RPG	APG	PPG
										REBOUNDS								AVERAGES	
98-99—L.A. Lakers	8	315	61	142	.430	28	35	.800	13	42	55	37	15	10	31	158	6.9	4.6	19.8
99-00—L.A. Lakers	22	857	174	394	.442	95	126	.754	26	72	98	97	32	32	55	465	4.5	4.4	21.1
00-01—L.A. Lakers	16	694	168	358	.469	124	151	.821	29	87	116	97	25	12	51	471	7.3	6.1	29.4
01-02—L.A. Lakers	19	833	187	431	.434	110	145	.759	28	83	111	87	27	17	54	506	5.8	4.6	26.6
02-03—L.A. Lakers	12	531	137	317	.432	86	104	.827	16	45	61	62	14	1	42	385	5.1	5.2	32.1
03-04—L.A. Lakers	22	973	190	460	.413	135	166	.813	18	86	104	121	42	7	61	539	4.7	5.5	24.5
05-06—L.A. Lakers	7	314	72	145	.497	37	48	.771	4	40	44	36	8	3	33	195	6.3	5.1	27.9
Totals	126	4870	1041	2378	.438	672	850	.791	142	479	621	564	169	92	352	2889	4.9	4.5	22.9

Three-point field goals: 1996-97, 6-for-23 (.261). 1997-98, 3-for-14 (.214). 1998-99, 8-for-23 (.348). 1999-00, 22-for-64 (.344). 2000-01, 11-for-34 (.324). 2001-02, 22-for-58 (.379). 2002-03, 25-for-62 (.403). 2003-04, 24-for-97 (.247). 2005-06, 14-for-35 (.400). Totals, 135-for-410 (.329).

Personal fouls/disqualifications: 1996-97, 23/0. 1997-98, 28/0. 1998-99, 24/1. 1999-00, 89/1. 2000-01, 53/0. 2001-02, 65/1. 2002-03, 35/0. 2003-04, 59/0. 2005-06, 25/0. Totals, 401/3.

NBA ALL-STAR GAME RECORD

NOTES: NBA All-Star Game Most Valuable Player (2002). Shares career record for most three-point field goals made—11.

Season Team	Min.	FGM	FGA	Pct.	FTM	FTA	Pct.	Off.	Def.	Tot.	Ast.	PF	Dq.	St.	Blk.	TO	Pts.
									REBOUNDS								
1998—L.A. Lakers...........	22	7	16	.438	2	2	1.000	2	4	6	1	1	...	2	0	1	18
2000—L.A. Lakers...........	28	7	16	.438	0	0	...	1	0	1	3	3	0	2	0	1	15
2001—L.A. Lakers...........	30	9	17	.529	0	0	...	2	2	4	7	3	0	1	0	3	19
2002—L.A. Lakers...........	30	12	25	.480	7	7	1.000	2	3	5	5	2	0	1	0	0	31
2003—L.A. Lakers...........	36	8	17	.471	3	6	.500	2	5	7	6	5	0	3	2	5	22
2004—L.A. Lakers...........	36	9	12	.750	0	1	.000	1	3	4	4	3	0	5	1	6	20
2005—L.A. Lakers...........	29	7	14	.500	0	0	...	3	3	6	7	5	0	3	1	4	16
2006—L.A. Lakers...........	26	4	11	.364	0	0	...	0	7	7	8	5	0	3	0	3	8
Totals...........................	237	63	128	.492	12	16	.750	13	27	40	41	27	0	20	4	23	149

Three-point field goals: 1998, 2-for-3 (.667). 2000, 1-for-4 (.250). 2001, 1-for-2 (.500). 2002, 0-for-4. 2003, 3-for-5 (.600). 2004, 2-for-3 (.667). 2005, 2-for-5 (.400). 2006, 0-for-5. Totals, 11-for-31 (.355).

BUCKNER, GREG   G   MAVERICKS

PERSONAL: Born September 16, 1976, in Hopkinsville, Ky. ... 6-4/210. (1.93/95.3). ... Full name: Gregory Derayle Buckner.
HIGH SCHOOL: University Heights Academy (Hopkinsville, Ky.).
COLLEGE: Clemson.
TRANSACTIONS/CAREER NOTES: Selected by Dallas Mavericks in second round (53rd pick overall) of 1998 NBA Draft. ... Played in Continental Basketball Association with Grand Rapids Hoops (1998-99). ... Waived by Mavericks (February 2, 1999). ... Re-signed as free agent by Mavericks (August 3, 1999). ... Waived by Mavericks (November 1, 1999). ... Signed by Mavericks to the first of two consecutive 10-day contracts (January 6, 2000). ... Re-signed by Mavericks for remainder of season (January 26, 2000). ... Signed as free agent by Philadelphia 76ers (July 25, 2002). ... Waived by 76ers (September 8, 2004). ... Signed as free agent by Denver Nuggets (October 4, 2004). ... Signed as free agent by Mavericks (July 13, 2006).

COLLEGIATE RECORD

Season Team	G	Min.	FGM	FGA	Pct.	FTM	FTA	Pct.	Reb.	Ast.	Pts.	RPG	APG	PPG
													AVERAGES	
94-95—Clemson	28	911	141	268	.526	41	80	.513	165	58	336	5.9	2.1	12.0
95-96—Clemson	29	950	144	305	.472	92	137	.672	147	48	381	5.1	1.7	13.1
96-97—Clemson	33	1071	190	393	.483	119	168	.708	150	63	516	4.5	1.9	15.6
97-98—Clemson	32	1022	204	380	.537	94	135	.696	130	83	521	4.1	2.6	16.3
Totals	122	3954	679	1346	.504	346	520	.665	592	252	1754	4.9	2.1	14.4

Three-point field goals: 1994-95, 13-for-44 (.295). 1995-96, 1-for-25 (.040). 1996-97, 17-for-54 (.315). 1997-98, 19-for-58 (.328). Totals, 50-for-181 (.276).

CBA RECORD

Season Team	G	Min.	FGM	FGA	Pct.	FTM	FTA	Pct.	Reb.	Ast.	Pts.	RPG	APG	PPG
													AVERAGES	
98-99—Grand Rapids	47	1064	161	365	.441	64	81	.790	182	96	406	3.9	2.0	8.6

Three-point field goals: 1998-99, 20-for-87 (.230). Totals, 20-for-87 (.230).
Personal fouls/disqualifications: 1998-99, 144/0. Totals, 144/0.

NBA REGULAR-SEASON RECORD

Season Team	G	Min.	FGM	FGA	Pct.	FTM	FTA	Pct.	Off.	Def.	Tot.	Ast.	St.	Blk.	TO	Pts.	RPG	APG	PPG
										REBOUNDS								AVERAGES	
99-00—Dallas..............	48	923	111	233	.476	43	63	.683	56	118	174	55	38	20	36	275	3.6	1.1	5.7
00-01—Dallas..............	37	820	84	192	.438	59	81	.728	60	97	157	49	33	9	27	229	4.2	1.3	6.2
01-02—Dallas..............	44	885	104	198	.525	40	58	.690	67	106	173	48	31	19	27	253	3.9	1.1	5.8
02-03—Philadelphia ...	75	1514	185	398	.465	65	81	.802	72	144	216	96	72	16	62	450	2.9	1.3	6.0
03-04—Philadelphia	53	703	66	175	.377	20	27	.741	28	75	103	45	21	4	34	164	1.9	0.8	3.1
04-05—Denver	70	1522	160	303	.528	63	81	.778	66	142	208	133	75	6	49	432	3.0	1.9	6.2
05-06—Denver	73	1758	181	417	.434	43	55	.782	31	178	209	127	87	20	52	491	2.9	1.7	6.7
Totals	400	8125	891	1916	.465	333	446	.747	380	860	1240	553	357	94	287	2294	3.1	1.4	5.7

Three-point field goals: 1999-00, 10-for-26 (.385). 2000-01, 2-for-7 (.286). 2001-02, 5-for-16 (.313). 2002-03, 15-for-55 (.273). 2003-04, 12-for-44 (.273). 2004-05, 49-for-121 (.405). 2005-06, 86-for-243 (.354). Totals, 179-for-512 (.350).
Personal fouls/disqualifications: 1999-00, 148/1. 2000-01, 118/2. 2001-02, 124/1. 2002-03, 203/0. 2003-04, 77/0. 2004-05, 169/0. 2005-06, 180/0. Totals, 1019/4.

NBA PLAYOFF RECORD

Season Team	G	Min.	FGM	FGA	Pct.	FTM	FTA	Pct.	Off.	Def.	Tot.	Ast.	St.	Blk.	TO	Pts.	RPG	APG	PPG
										REBOUNDS								AVERAGES	
00-01—Dallas..............	5	75	11	23	.478	7	10	.700	8	13	21	3	5	0	2	30	4.2	0.6	6.0
01-02—Dallas..............	7	105	12	25	.480	3	4	.750	13	13	26	4	3	1	3	27	3.7	0.6	3.9

B

Season Team	G	Min.	FGM	FGA	Pct.	FTM	FTA	Pct.	REBOUNDS Off.	Def.	Tot.	Ast.	St.	Blk.	TO	Pts.	AVERAGES RPG	APG	PPG
02-03—Philadelphia	10	112	10	31	.323	4	4	1.000	3	14	17	3	1	2	3	26	1.7	0.3	2.6
04-05—Denver	5	100	4	18	.222	0	0	...	1	15	16	5	2	1	3	10	3.2	1.0	2.0
05-06—Denver	5	137	23	55	.418	7	8	.875	3	11	14	6	3	1	1	63	2.8	1.2	12.6
Totals	32	529	60	152	.395	21	26	.808	28	66	94	21	14	5	12	156	2.9	0.7	4.9

Three-point field goals: 2000-01, 1-for-3 (.333). 2001-02, 0-for-1. 2002-03, 2-for-9 (.222). 2004-05, 2-for-9 (.222). 2005-06, 10-for-32 (.313). Totals, 15-for-54 (.278).

Personal fouls/disqualifications: 2000-01, 12/0. 2001-02, 15/0. 2002-03, 18/0. 2004-05, 14/0. 2005-06, 12/0. Totals, 71/0.

BURKE, PAT   C   SUNS

PERSONAL: Born December 14, 1973, in Dublin, Ireland. ... 6-11/250. (2.11/113.4).
HIGH SCHOOL: Mariner (Cape Coral, Fla.).
COLLEGE: Auburn.
TRANSACTIONS/CAREER NOTES: Not drafted by an NBA franchise. ... Played in Spain (1997-98; 2003-05) ... Played in Greece (1998-2002). ... Signed as free agent by Orlando Magic (September 25, 2002). ... Signed as free agent by Phoenix Suns (August 18, 2005).

COLLEGIATE RECORD

Season Team	G	Min.	FGM	FGA	Pct.	FTM	FTA	Pct.	Reb.	Ast.	Pts.	AVERAGES RPG	APG	PPG
93-94—Auburn	28	390	48	100	.480	16	32	.500	82	14	112	2.9	0.5	4.0
94-95—Auburn	29	640	107	201	.532	43	67	.642	139	29	260	4.8	1.0	9.0
95-96—Auburn	32	898	138	287	.481	63	97	.649	278	28	352	8.7	0.9	11.0
96-97—Auburn	31	794	128	270	.474	80	124	.645	216	23	340	7.0	0.7	11.0
Totals	120	2722	421	858	.491	202	320	.631	715	94	1064	6.0	0.8	8.9

Three-point field goals: 1993-94, 0-for-1. 1994-95, 3-for-9 (.333). 1995-96, 13-for-54 (.241). 1996-97, 4-for-26 (.154). Totals, 20-for-90 (.222).

SPANISH LEAGUE RECORD

Season Team	G	Min.	FGM	FGA	Pct.	FTM	FTA	Pct.	Reb.	Ast.	Pts.	AVERAGES RPG	APG	PPG
97-98—Tau Ceramica.................	34	848	143	232	.616	42	60	.700	218	15	328	6.4	0.4	9.6
03-04—Auna Gran Canaria	33	705	131	254	.516	36	54	.667	174	11	315	5.3	0.3	9.5
04-05—Real Madrid....................	31	589	102	198	.515	29	43	.674	136	17	236	4.4	0.5	7.6
Totals	98	2142	376	684	.550	107	157	.682	528	43	879	5.4	0.4	9.0

Three-point field goals: 2003-04, 17-for-42 (.405). 2004-05, 3-for-5 (.600). Totals, 20-for-47 (.426).

GREEK LEAGUE RECORD

Season Team	G	Min.	FGM	FGA	Pct.	FTM	FTA	Pct.	Reb.	Ast.	Pts.	AVERAGES RPG	APG	PPG
98-99—Panathinaikos.................	24	299	31	61	.508	15	32	.469	40	5	77	1.7	0.2	3.2
99-00—Panathinaikos.................	24	350	48	86	.558	23	72	.319	94	12	119	3.9	0.5	5.0
00-01—Panathinaikos.................	20	300	53	99	.535	34	46	.739	93	11	140	4.7	0.6	7.0
01-02—Marousi..........................	26	805	153	265	.577	69	98	.704	255	31	375	9.8	1.2	14.4
Totals	94	1754	285	511	.558	141	248	.569	482	59	711	5.1	0.6	7.6

Three-point field goals: 2000-01, 0-for-1. 2001-02, 0-for-5. Totals, 0-for-6 (.000).

NBA REGULAR-SEASON RECORD

Season Team	G	Min.	FGM	FGA	Pct.	FTM	FTA	Pct.	REBOUNDS Off.	Def.	Tot.	Ast.	St.	Blk.	TO	Pts.	AVERAGES RPG	APG	PPG
02-03—Orlando..........	62	783	113	296	.382	40	58	.690	57	89	146	23	19	25	47	267	2.4	0.4	4.3
05-06—Phoenix	42	346	63	127	.496	13	21	.619	21	52	73	16	6	13	33	141	1.7	0.4	3.4
Totals	104	1129	176	423	.416	53	79	.671	78	141	219	39	25	38	80	408	2.1	0.4	3.9

Three-point field goals: 2002-03, 1-for-7 (.143). 2005-06, 2-for-7 (.286). Totals, 3-for-14 (.214).
Personal fouls/disqualifications: 2002-03, 99/1. 2005-06, 62/2. Totals, 161/3.

NBA PLAYOFF RECORD

Season Team	G	Min.	FGM	FGA	Pct.	FTM	FTA	Pct.	REBOUNDS Off.	Def.	Tot.	Ast.	St.	Blk.	TO	Pts.	AVERAGES RPG	APG	PPG
02-03—Orlando..........	6	43	6	10	.600	5	6	.833	1	10	11	1	1	0	4	17	1.8	0.2	2.8
05-06—Phoenix	3	7	2	4	.500	0	1	.000	1	2	3	0	0	1	0	5	1.0	0.0	1.7
Totals	9	50	8	14	.571	5	7	.714	2	12	14	1	1	1	4	22	1.6	0.1	2.4

Three-point field goals: 2005-06, 1-for-2 (.500). Totals, 1-for-2 (.500).
Personal fouls/disqualifications: 2002-03, 9/0. Totals, 9/0.

BURKS, ANTONIO   G

PERSONAL: Born February 25, 1980, in Memphis, Tenn. ... 6-0/195. (1.83/88.5). ... Full name: Antonio Cornell Burks.
HIGH SCHOOL: Booker T. Washington (Memphis, Tenn.).
JUNIOR COLLEGE: Hiwassee College (Tenn.).
COLLEGE: Memphis.
TRANSACTIONS/CAREER NOTES: Selected by Orlando Magic in second round (36th pick overall) of 2004 NBA Draft. ... Draft rights traded by Magic to Memphis Grizzlies (June 24, 2004).

COLLEGIATE RECORD

Season Team	G	Min.	FGM	FGA	Pct.	FTM	FTA	Pct.	Reb.	Ast.	Pts.	AVERAGES RPG	APG	PPG
99-00—Hiwassee College						Statistics unavailable								
00-01—Memphis						Did not play								

Season Team	G	Min.	FGM	FGA	Pct.	FTM	FTA	Pct.	Reb.	Ast.	Pts.	RPG	APG	PPG
												AVERAGES		
01-02—Memphis	36	1086	117	258	.453	66	95	.695	86	182	304	2.4	5.1	8.4
02-03—Memphis	25	670	98	205	.478	45	63	.714	51	140	243	2.0	5.6	9.7
03-04—Memphis	30	1030	176	371	.474	72	114	.632	96	165	481	3.2	5.5	16.0
Totals	91	2786	391	834	.469	183	272	.673	233	487	1028	2.6	5.4	11.3

Three-point field goals: 2001-02, 4-for-12 (.333). 2002-03, 2-for-7 (.286). 2003-04, 57-for-138 (.413). Totals, 63-for-157 (.401).

NBA REGULAR-SEASON RECORD

Season Team	G	Min.	FGM	FGA	Pct.	FTM	FTA	Pct.	Off.	Def.	Tot.	Ast.	St.	Blk.	TO	Pts.	RPG	APG	PPG
									REBOUNDS								AVERAGES		
04-05—Memphis	24	219	28	60	.467	14	19	.737	1	11	12	28	13	1	12	73	0.5	1.2	3.0
05-06—Memphis	57	570	51	144	.354	10	23	.435	4	33	37	76	20	0	36	113	0.6	1.3	2.0
Totals	81	789	79	204	.387	24	42	.571	5	44	49	104	33	1	48	186	0.6	1.3	2.3

Three-point field goals: 2004-05, 3-for-11 (.273). 2005-06, 1-for-6 (.167). Totals, 4-for-17 (.235).
Personal fouls/disqualifications: 2004-05, 25/0. 2005-06, 45/0. Totals, 70/0.

NBA PLAYOFF RECORD

Season Team	G	Min.	FGM	FGA	Pct.	FTM	FTA	Pct.	Off.	Def.	Tot.	Ast.	St.	Blk.	TO	Pts.	RPG	APG	PPG
									REBOUNDS								AVERAGES		
04-05—Memphis	1	3	0	0	...	0	0	...	0	0	0	1	0	0	0	0	0.0	1.0	0.0
05-06—Memphis	2	13	1	1	1.000	1	2	.500	0	1	1	2	1	0	0	3	0.5	1.0	1.5
Totals	3	16	1	1	1.000	1	2	.500	0	1	1	3	1	0	0	3	0.3	1.0	1.0

Personal fouls/disqualifications: 2005-06, 2/0. Totals, 2/0.

BURLESON, KEVIN   G   BOBCATS

PERSONAL: Born April 9, 1979, in Seattle. ... 6-3/205. (1.91/93.0).
HIGH SCHOOL: O'Dea (Seattle).
COLLEGE: Minnesota.
TRANSACTIONS/CAREER NOTES: Not drafted by an NBA franchise ... Played in Germany (2003-05). ... Signed as free agent by Charlotte Bobcats (August 31, 2005).

COLLEGIATE RECORD

Season Team	G	Min.	FGM	FGA	Pct.	FTM	FTA	Pct.	Reb.	Ast.	Pts.	RPG	APG	PPG
												AVERAGES		
98-99—Minnesota						Did Not Play - Redshirted								
99-00—Minnesota	28	696	81	222	.365	40	46	.870	74	57	246	2.6	2.0	8.8
00-01—Minnesota	31	655	62	164	.378	31	47	.660	54	77	196	1.7	2.5	6.3
01-02—Minnesota	31	787	64	174	.368	49	64	.766	67	146	203	2.2	4.7	6.5
02-03—Minnesota	33	979	65	173	.376	55	76	.724	101	160	222	3.1	4.8	6.7
Totals	123	3117	272	733	.371	175	233	.751	296	440	867	2.4	3.6	7.0

Three-point field goals: 1999-00, 44-for-136 (.324). 2000-01, 41-for-108 (.380). 2001-02, 26-for-92 (.283). 2002-03, 37-for-111 (.333). Totals, 148-for-447 (.331).

GERMAN LEAGUE RECORD

Season Team	G	Min.	FGM	FGA	Pct.	FTM	FTA	Pct.	Reb.	Ast.	Pts.	RPG	APG	PPG
												AVERAGES		
04-05—Walter	30	880	126	338	.373	92	115	.800	113	56	428	3.8	1.9	14.3

Three-point field goals: 2004-05, 84-for-234 (.359). Totals, 84-for-234 (.359).

NBA REGULAR-SEASON RECORD

Season Team	G	Min.	FGM	FGA	Pct.	FTM	FTA	Pct.	Off.	Def.	Tot.	Ast.	St.	Blk.	TO	Pts.	RPG	APG	PPG
									REBOUNDS								AVERAGES		
05-06—Charlotte	39	340	22	88	.250	16	17	.941	4	22	26	48	26	2	25	70	0.7	1.2	1.8

Three-point field goals: 2005-06, 10-for-54 (.185). Totals, 10-for-54 (.185).
Personal fouls/disqualifications: 2005-06, 63/2. Totals, 63/2.

BUTLER, JACKIE   C   SPURS

PERSONAL: Born March 10, 1985, in McComb, Miss. ... 6-10/250. (2.08/113.4).
HIGH SCHOOL: McComb (Miss.), then Laurinburg Institute (N.C.).
COLLEGE: Did not attend college.
TRANSACTIONS/CAREER NOTES: Not drafted by an NBA franchise. ... Played for Great Lakes Storm of Continental Basketball Association (2004-05). ... Signed as free agent by New York Knicks (February 27, 2005). ... Signed as free agent by San Antonio Spurs (July 21, 2006).

CBA RECORD

Season Team	G	Min.	FGM	FGA	Pct.	FTM	FTA	Pct.	Reb.	Ast.	Pts.	RPG	APG	PPG
												AVERAGES		
04-05—Great Lakes	41	1419	300	588	.510	138	193	.715	439	72	738	10.7	1.8	18.0

Three-point field goals: 2004-05, 0-for-6. Totals, 0-for-6 (.000).

NBA REGULAR-SEASON RECORD

Season Team	G	Min.	FGM	FGA	Pct.	FTM	FTA	Pct.	Off.	Def.	Tot.	Ast.	St.	Blk.	TO	Pts.	RPG	APG	PPG
									REBOUNDS								AVERAGES		
04-05—New York	3	5	4	4	1.000	2	2	1.000	0	0	0	0	1	0	1	10	0.0	0.0	3.3
05-06—New York	55	740	117	215	.544	58	77	.753	67	116	183	25	17	31	62	292	3.3	0.5	5.3
Totals	58	745	121	219	.553	60	79	.759	67	116	183	25	18	31	63	302	3.2	0.4	5.2

Personal fouls/disqualifications: 2005-06, 127/0. Totals, 127/0.

B

BUTLER, CARON   F   WIZARDS

PERSONAL: Born March 13, 1980, in Racine, Wis. ... 6-7/235. (2.01/106.6). ... Full name: James Caron Butler
HIGH SCHOOL: Park (Racine, Wis.), then Maine Central Institute.
COLLEGE: Connecticut.
TRANSACTIONS/CAREER NOTES: Selected after sophomore season by Miami Heat in first round (10th pick overall) of 2002 NBA Draft. ... Traded by Heat with F Lamar Odom, F Brian Grant, a first-round draft choice and a second-round draft choice to Los Angeles Lakers for C Shaquille O'Neal (July 14, 2004). ... Traded by Lakers with G Chucky Atkins to Washington Wizards for C Kwame Brown and F Laron Profit (August 2, 2005).

COLLEGIATE RECORD

NOTES: THE SPORTING NEWS All-America second team (2002).

Season Team	G	Min.	FGM	FGA	Pct.	FTM	FTA	Pct.	Reb.	Ast.	Pts.	RPG	APG	PPG
00-01—Connecticut	29	950	151	347	.435	129	171	.754	221	89	445	7.6	3.1	15.3
01-02—Connecticut	34	1223	253	521	.486	155	199	.779	256	101	691	7.5	3.0	20.3
Totals	63	2173	404	868	.465	284	370	.768	477	190	1136	7.6	3.0	18.0

Three-point field goals: 2000-01, 14-for-46 (.304). 2001-02, 30-for-75 (.400). Totals, 44-for-121 (.364).

NBA REGULAR-SEASON RECORD

HONORS: NBA All-Rookie first team (2003).

Season Team	G	Min.	FGM	FGA	Pct.	FTM	FTA	Pct.	Off.	Def.	Tot.	Ast.	St.	Blk.	TO	Pts.	RPG	APG	PPG
02-03—Miami	78	2858	429	1032	.416	309	375	.824	135	262	397	213	137	31	192	1201	5.1	2.7	15.4
03-04—Miami	68	2030	240	631	.380	143	176	.756	92	234	326	126	75	13	91	623	4.8	1.9	9.2
04-05—L.A. Lakers	77	2746	441	991	.445	275	319	.862	146	304	450	146	110	23	125	1195	5.8	1.9	15.5
05-06—Washington	75	2708	494	1086	.455	289	332	.870	114	352	466	186	127	18	175	1318	6.2	2.5	17.6
Totals	298	10342	1604	3740	.429	1006	1202	.837	487	1152	1639	671	449	85	583	4337	5.5	2.3	14.6

Three-point field goals: 2002-03, 34-for-107 (.318). 2003-04, 10-for-42 (.238). 2004-05, 38-for-125 (.304). 2005-06, 41-for-120 (.342). Totals, 123-for-394 (.312).

Personal fouls/disqualifications: 2002-03, 230/3. 2003-04, 162/0. 2004-05, 213/2. 2005-06, 238/4. Totals, 843/9.

NBA PLAYOFF RECORD

Season Team	G	Min.	FGM	FGA	Pct.	FTM	FTA	Pct.	Off.	Def.	Tot.	Ast.	St.	Blk.	TO	Pts.	RPG	APG	PPG
03-04—Miami	13	511	59	153	.386	47	57	.825	18	92	110	31	28	7	23	167	8.5	2.4	12.8
05-06—Washington	6	262	42	101	.416	24	29	.828	16	47	63	16	12	4	14	111	10.5	2.7	18.5
Totals	19	773	101	254	.398	71	86	.826	34	139	173	47	40	11	37	278	9.1	2.5	14.6

Three-point field goals: 2003-04, 2-for-11 (.182). 2005-06, 3-for-14 (.214). Totals, 5-for-25 (.200).
Personal fouls/disqualifications: 2003-04, 45/0. 2005-06, 31/2. Totals, 76/2.

BUTLER, RASUAL   F   HORNETS

PERSONAL: Born May 23, 1979, in Philadelphia. ... 6-7/205. (2.01/93.0).
HIGH SCHOOL: Roman Catholic (Philadelphia).
COLLEGE: La Salle.
TRANSACTIONS/CAREER NOTES: Selected by Miami Heat in second round (53rd pick overall) of 2002 NBA Draft. ... Traded by Heat to New Orleans Hornets in five-team trade (August 2, 2005).

COLLEGIATE RECORD

Season Team	G	Min.	FGM	FGA	Pct.	FTM	FTA	Pct.	Reb.	Ast.	Pts.	RPG	APG	PPG
98-99—La Salle	21	773	105	276	.380	43	58	.741	83	31	298	4.0	1.5	14.2
99-00—La Salle	28	1072	183	450	.407	67	82	.817	148	45	516	5.3	1.6	18.4
00-01—La Salle	29	1114	231	574	.402	82	97	.845	136	57	641	4.7	2.0	22.1
01-02—La Salle	32	1252	233	537	.434	147	172	.855	283	44	670	8.8	1.4	20.9
Totals	110	4211	752	1837	.409	339	409	.829	650	177	2125	5.9	1.6	19.3

Three-point field goals: 1998-99, 45-for-137 (.328). 1999-00, 83-for-218 (.381). 2000-01, 91-for-272 (.335). 2001-02, 57-for-158 (.361). Totals, 276-for-785 (.352).

NBA REGULAR-SEASON RECORD

Season Team	G	Min.	FGM	FGA	Pct.	FTM	FTA	Pct.	Off.	Def.	Tot.	Ast.	St.	Blk.	TO	Pts.	RPG	APG	PPG
02-03—Miami	72	1514	207	572	.362	76	104	.731	29	157	186	93	21	43	77	540	2.6	1.3	7.5
03-04—Miami	45	675	119	250	.476	16	21	.762	4	57	61	23	10	13	28	304	1.4	0.5	6.8
04-05—Miami	65	1203	163	409	.399	37	48	.771	15	136	151	62	18	29	37	420	2.3	1.0	6.5
05-06—NO/Okla. City	79	1875	257	633	.406	79	114	.693	51	181	232	40	33	45	65	685	2.9	0.5	8.7
Totals	261	5267	746	1864	.400	208	287	.725	99	531	630	218	82	130	207	1949	2.4	0.8	7.5

Three-point field goals: 2002-03, 50-for-171 (.292). 2003-04, 50-for-108 (.463). 2004-05, 57-for-153 (.373). 2005-06, 92-for-242 (.380). Totals, 249-for-674 (.369).

Personal fouls/disqualifications: 2002-03, 105/0. 2003-04, 72/0. 2004-05, 104/0. 2005-06, 142/0. Totals, 423/0.

NBA PLAYOFF RECORD

Season Team	G	Min.	FGM	FGA	Pct.	FTM	FTA	Pct.	Off.	Def.	Tot.	Ast.	St.	Blk.	TO	Pts.	RPG	APG	PPG
03-04—Miami	10	58	9	22	.409	0	0	...	0	11	11	2	1	0	1	21	1.1	0.2	2.1
04-05—Miami	12	182	22	59	.373	1	3	.333	1	17	18	7	1	1	2	56	1.5	0.6	4.7
Totals	22	240	31	81	.383	1	3	.333	1	28	29	9	2	1	3	77	1.3	0.4	3.5

Three-point field goals: 2003-04, 3-for-9 (.333). 2004-05, 11-for-30 (.367). Totals, 14-for-39 (.359).
Personal fouls/disqualifications: 2003-04, 12/0. 2004-05, 21/0. Totals, 33/0.

B

BYNUM, ANDREW   C   LAKERS

PERSONAL: Born October 27, 1987, in Plainsboro, N.J. ... 7-0/285. (2.13/129.3).
HIGH SCHOOL: Solebury Prep (New Hope, Pa.), then St. Joseph's (Metuchen, N.J.).
COLLEGE: Did not attend college.
TRANSACTIONS/CAREER NOTES: Selected out of high school by Los Angeles Lakers in first round (10th pick overall) of 2005 NBA Draft.

NBA REGULAR-SEASON RECORD

Season Team	G	Min.	FGM	FGA	Pct.	FTM	FTA	Pct.	Off.	Def.	Tot.	Ast.	St.	Blk.	TO	Pts.	RPG	APG	PPG
05-06—L.A. Lakers	46	338	33	82	.402	8	27	.296	34	46	80	9	4	22	17	74	1.7	0.2	1.6

Personal fouls/disqualifications: 2005-06, 56/0. Totals, 56/0.

NBA PLAYOFF RECORD

Season Team	G	Min.	FGM	FGA	Pct.	FTM	FTA	Pct.	Off.	Def.	Tot.	Ast.	St.	Blk.	TO	Pts.	RPG	APG	PPG
05-06—L.A. Lakers	1	2	0	1	.000	0	0	...	0	0	0	0	0	0	0	0	0.0	0.0	0.0

BYNUM, WILL   G

PERSONAL: Born January 4, 1983 ... 6-0/185. (1.83/83.9).
HIGH SCHOOL: Crane Tech (Chicago).
COLLEGE: Arizona, then Georgia Tech.
TRANSACTIONS/CAREER NOTES: Not drafted by an NBA franchise. ... Signed as free agent by Boston Celtics (August 19, 2005). ... Waived by Celtics (October 25, 2005). ... Signed by Golden State Warriors to 10-day contract (March 17, 2006). ... Signed by Warriors for remainder of season (April 7, 2006). ... Waived by Warriors (July 14, 2006).

COLLEGIATE RECORD

Season Team	G	Min.	FGM	FGA	Pct.	FTM	FTA	Pct.	Reb.	Ast.	Pts.	RPG	APG	PPG
01-02—Arizona	31	584	73	212	.344	26	40	.650	48	44	197	1.5	1.4	6.4
02-03—Arizona	8	133	21	59	.356	7	12	.583	22	12	62	2.8	1.5	7.8
03-04—Georgia Tech	30	616	92	223	.413	69	90	.767	65	75	287	2.2	2.5	9.6
04-05—Georgia Tech	32	873	128	322	.398	96	126	.762	80	79	401	2.5	2.5	12.5
Totals	101	2206	314	810	.385	198	200	.739	215	210	947	2.1	2.1	9.4

Three-point field goals: 2001-02, 25-for-98 (.255). 2002-03, 13-for-37 (.351). 2003-04, 34-for-97 (.351). 2004-05, 49-for-158 (.310). Totals, 121-for-390 (.310).

NBA REGULAR-SEASON RECORD

Season Team	G	Min.	FGM	FGA	Pct.	FTM	FTA	Pct.	Off.	Def.	Tot.	Ast.	St.	Blk.	TO	Pts.	RPG	APG	PPG
05-06—Golden State ...	15	162	21	52	.404	10	16	.625	3	9	12	19	7	0	14	54	0.8	1.3	3.6

Three-point field goals: 2005-06, 2-for-9 (.222). Totals, 2-for-9 (.222).
Personal fouls/disqualifications: 2005-06, 10/0. Totals, 10/0.

NBA DEVELOPMENT LEAGUE RECORD

Season Team	G	Min.	FGM	FGA	Pct.	FTM	FTA	Pct.	Reb.	Ast.	Pts.	RPG	APG	PPG
05-06—Roanoke	29	1094	206	440	.468	260	305	.852	83	193	697	2.9	6.7	24.0

Three-point field goals: 2005-06, 25-for-83 (.301). Totals, 25-for-83 (.301).

CABARKAPA, ZARKO   F/C   WARRIORS

PERSONAL: Born May 21, 1981, in Zrenjanin, Serbia & Montenegro. ... 6-11/235. (2.11/106.6).
TRANSACTIONS/CAREER NOTES: Selected by Phoenix Suns in first round (17th pick overall) of 2003 NBA Draft. ... Traded by Suns to Golden State Warriors for two future second-round draft choices (January 3, 2005).

YUGOSLAVIAN LEAGUE RECORD

Season Team	G	Min.	FGM	FGA	Pct.	FTM	FTA	Pct.	Reb.	Ast.	Pts.	RPG	APG	PPG
97-98—Beopetrol	9	47	4	12	.333	0	1	.000	3	3	8	0.3	0.3	0.9
98-99—Beopetrol	4	30	3	9	.333	1	2	.500	8	4	7	2.0	1.0	1.8
99-00—Beopetrol	21	445	55	107	.514	33	51	.647	56	13	152	2.7	0.6	7.2
00-01—Beopetrol	22	640	112	224	.500	54	76	.711	121	48	297	5.5	2.2	13.5
01-02—Buducnost	14	271	50	82	.610	24	37	.649	57	11	132	4.1	0.8	9.4
02-03—Buducnost	19	302	102	167	.611	57	75	.760	89	28	277	4.7	1.5	14.6
Totals	89	1735	326	601	.542	169	242	.698	334	107	873	3.8	1.2	9.8

Three-point field goals: 1997-98, 0-for-2. 1998-99, 0-for-2. 1999-00, 9-for-25 (.360). 2000-01, 19-for-54 (.352). 2001-02, 8-for-19 (.421). 2002-03, 16-for-41 (.390). Totals, 52-for-143 (.364).

NBA REGULAR-SEASON RECORD

Season Team	G	Min.	FGM	FGA	Pct.	FTM	FTA	Pct.	Off.	Def.	Tot.	Ast.	St.	Blk.	TO	Pts.	RPG	APG	PPG
03-04—Phoenix	49	570	81	197	.411	35	53	.660	26	73	99	40	10	13	54	203	2.0	0.8	4.1
04-05—Phoenix-G.S..	40	475	86	177	.486	53	65	.815	35	67	102	25	10	5	30	238	2.6	0.6	6.0
05-06—Golden State .	61	505	67	174	.385	60	84	.714	37	74	111	20	13	7	35	199	1.8	0.3	3.3
Totals	150	1550	234	548	.427	148	202	.733	98	214	312	85	33	25	119	640	2.1	0.6	4.3

Three-point field goals: 2003-04, 6-for-32 (.188). 2004-05, 13-for-36 (.361). 2005-06, 5-for-20 (.250). Totals, 24-for-88 (.273).
Personal fouls/disqualifications: 2003-04, 75/0. 2004-05, 59/0. 2005-06, 87/0. Totals, 221/0.

CALDERON, JOSE   G   RAPTORS

PERSONAL: Born September 28, 1981, in Villanueva de la Serena, Spain. ... 6-3/210 (1,91/95,3). ... Full name: Jose Manuel Claderon Borrallo.
TRANSACTIONS/CAREER NOTES: Played in Spain (2000-05). ... Not drafted by an NBA franchise. ... Signed as free agent by Toronto Raptors (August 3, 2005).
MISCELLANEOUS: Member of Spanish Olympic team (2004).

SPANISH LEAGUE RECORD

Season Team	G	Min.	FGM	FGA	Pct.	FTM	FTA	Pct.	Reb.	Ast.	Pts.	RPG	APG	PPG
00-01—Lucentum Alicante.........	34	861	111	238	.466	48	74	.649	78	48	294	2.3	1.4	8.6
01-02—Fuenlabrada...............	32	587	94	224	.420	87	104	.837	49	51	306	1.5	1.6	9.6
02-03—Tau Ceramica................	32	623	58	134	.433	58	67	.866	59	56	193	1.8	1.8	6.0
03-04—Tau Ceramica................	33	678	89	168	.530	52	63	.825	93	72	251	2.8	2.2	7.6
04-05—Tau Ceramica................	31	926	140	261	.536	90	111	.811	83	97	411	2.7	3.1	13.3
Totals	162	3675	492	1025	.480	335	419	.800	362	324	1455	2.2	2.0	9.0

Three-point field goals: 2000-01, 24-for-67 (.358). 2001-02, 31-for-89 (.348). 2002-03, 19-for-52 (.365). 2003-04, 21-for-58 (.362). 2004-05, 41-for-89 (.461). Totals, 136-for-355 (.383).

NBA REGULAR-SEASON RECORD

Season Team	G	Min.	FGM	FGA	Pct.	FTM	FTA	Pct.	Off.	Def.	Tot.	Ast.	St.	Blk.	TO	Pts.	RPG	APG	PPG
05-06—Toronto..........	64	1487	132	312	.423	78	92	.848	30	111	141	288	42	4	101	349	2.2	4.5	5.5

Three-point field goals: 2005-06, 7-for-43 (.163). Totals, 7-for-43 (.163).
Personal fouls/disqualifications: 2005-06, 93/0. Totals, 93/0.

CAMBY, MARCUS   C   NUGGETS

PERSONAL: Born March 22, 1974, in Hartford. ... 6-11/235. (2.11/106.6). ... Full name: Marcus D. Camby
HIGH SCHOOL: Hartford Public (Conn.).
COLLEGE: Massachusetts.
TRANSACTIONS/CAREER NOTES: Selected after junior season by Toronto Raptors in first round (second pick overall) of 1996 NBA Draft. ... Traded by Raptors to New York Knicks for F Charles Oakley, draft rights to F/C Sean Marks and cash (June 25, 1998). ... Traded by Knicks with G Mark Jackson and draft rights to F/C Nene Hilario to Denver Nuggets for F Antonio McDyess, draft rights to G Frank Williams and 2003 second-round draft choice (June 26, 2002).

COLLEGIATE RECORD

NOTES: THE SPORTING NEWS College Player of the Year (1996). ... Naismith Award winner (1996). ... Wooden Award winner (1996). ... THE SPORTING NEWS All-America first team (1996).

Season Team	G	Min.	FGM	FGA	Pct.	FTM	FTA	Pct.	Reb.	Ast.	Pts.	RPG	APG	PPG
93-94—Massachusetts	29	634	117	237	.494	62	104	.596	185	36	296	6.4	1.2	10.2
94-95—Massachusetts	30	679	166	302	.550	83	129	.643	186	37	416	6.2	1.2	13.9
95-96—Massachusetts	33	1011	256	537	.477	163	233	.700	271	58	675	8.2	1.8	20.5
Totals	92	2324	539	1076	.501	308	466	.661	642	131	1387	7.0	1.4	15.1

Three-point field goals: 1993-94, 0-for-4. 1994-95, 1-for-1 (1.000). 1995-96, 0-for-6. Totals, 1-for-13 (.077).

NBA REGULAR-SEASON RECORD

HONORS: NBA All-Rookie first team (1997). ... NBA All-Defensive second team (2005, 2006).
NOTES: Led NBA with 3.65 blocked shots per game (1998). ... Led NBA with 3.29 blocked shots per game (2005-06).

Season Team	G	Min.	FGM	FGA	Pct.	FTM	FTA	Pct.	Off.	Def.	Tot.	Ast.	St.	Blk.	TO	Pts.	RPG	APG	PPG
96-97—Toronto	63	1897	375	778	.482	183	264	.693	131	263	394	97	66	130	134	935	6.3	1.5	14.8
97-98—Toronto	63	2002	308	747	.412	149	244	.611	203	263	466	111	68	230	134	765	7.4	1.8	12.1
98-99—New York	46	945	136	261	.521	57	103	.553	102	151	253	12	29	74	39	329	5.5	0.3	7.2
99-00—New York	59	1548	226	471	.480	148	221	.670	174	287	461	49	43	116	72	601	7.8	0.8	10.2
00-01—New York	63	2127	304	580	.524	150	225	.667	196	527	723	52	66	136	63	759	11.5	0.8	12.0
01-02—New York	29	1007	130	290	.448	62	99	.626	89	233	322	33	34	50	42	322	11.1	1.1	11.1
02-03—Denver	29	616	93	227	.410	33	50	.660	75	133	208	47	20	40	27	221	7.2	1.6	7.6
03-04—Denver	72	2162	262	549	.477	98	136	.721	211	516	727	132	86	187	98	622	10.1	1.8	8.6
04-05—Denver	66	2015	279	600	.465	125	173	.723	131	530	661	152	61	*199	103	683	10.0	2.3	10.3
05-06—Denver	56	1857	302	649	.465	111	156	.712	132	536	668	115	79	184	92	716	11.9	2.1	12.8
Totals	546	16176	2415	5152	.469	1116	1671	.668	1444	3439	4883	800	552	1346	804	5953	8.9	1.5	10.9

Three-point field goals: 1996-97, 2-for-14 (.143). 1997-98, 3-for-10 (.300). 1998-99, 0-for-1. 2000-01, 1-for-8 (.125). 2001-02, 0-for-1. 2002-03, 2-for-5 (.400). 2003-04, 0-for-2. 2004-05, 0-for-4. 2005-06, 1-for-11 (.091). Totals, 7-for-49 (.143).
Personal fouls/disqualifications: 1996-97, 214/7. 1997-98, 200/1. 1998-99, 131/2. 1999-00, 204/5. 2000-01, 205/4. 2001-02, 107/3. 2002-03, 69/1. 2003-04, 239/4. 2004-05, 177/0. 2005-06, 158/1. Totals, 1704/28.

NBA PLAYOFF RECORD

Season Team	G	Min.	FGM	FGA	Pct.	FTM	FTA	Pct.	Off.	Def.	Tot.	Ast.	St.	Blk.	TO	Pts.	RPG	APG	PPG
98-99—New York	20	509	81	143	.566	45	73	.616	51	102	153	6	24	38	15	207	7.7	0.3	10.4
99-00—New York	16	386	29	86	.337	19	31	.613	35	77	112	6	8	23	12	77	7.0	0.4	4.8
00-01—New York	4	141	10	26	.385	5	13	.385	4	28	32	7	2	9	2	25	8.0	1.8	6.3
03-04—Denver	5	194	27	55	.491	8	14	.571	14	43	57	12	4	7	6	63	11.4	2.4	12.6
04-05—Denver	5	184	17	41	.415	17	27	.630	4	52	56	9	3	16	11	51	11.2	1.8	10.2
05-06—Denver	5	175	26	62	.419	5	9	.556	13	42	55	11	4	14	4	57	11.0	2.2	11.4
Totals	55	1589	190	413	.460	99	167	.593	121	344	465	51	45	107	50	480	8.5	0.9	8.7

Three-point field goals: 1998-99, 0-for-1. 1999-00, 0-for-1. 2003-04, 1-for-2 (.500). Totals, 1-for-4 (.250).
Personal fouls/disqualifications: 1998-99, 76/2. 1999-00, 51/1. 2000-01, 18/1. 2003-04, 21/0. 2004-05, 18/0. 2005-06, 14/0. Totals, 198/4.

CARDINAL, BRIAN — F — GRIZZLIES

PERSONAL: Born May 2, 1977, in Tolono, Ill. ... 6-8/245. (2.03/111.1). ... Full name: Brian Lee Cardinal
HIGH SCHOOL: Unity (Tolono, Ill.).
COLLEGE: Purdue.
TRANSACTIONS/CAREER NOTES: Selected by Detroit Pistons in second round (44th pick overall) of 2000 NBA Draft. ... Traded by Pistons with G/F Jerry Stackhouse and C Ratko Varda to Washington Wizards for G/F Richard Hamilton, G/F Bobby Simmons and G Hubert Davis (September 11, 2002). ... Waived by Wizards (March 1, 2003). ... Played in Spain (2002-03). ... Signed as free agent by Memphis Grizzlies (July 14, 2004).

COLLEGIATE RECORD

Season Team	G	Min.	FGM	FGA	Pct.	FTM	FTA	Pct.	Reb.	Ast.	Pts.	RPG	APG	PPG
95-96—Purdue					Did not play—redshirted.									
96-97—Purdue	30	865	100	220	.455	98	139	.705	182	58	319	6.1	1.9	10.6
97-98—Purdue	36	925	140	275	.509	122	155	.787	178	66	432	4.9	1.8	12.0
98-99—Purdue	34	960	118	246	.480	114	147	.776	186	82	387	5.5	2.4	11.4
99-00—Purdue	32	943	137	333	.411	130	169	.769	203	71	446	6.3	2.2	13.9
Totals	132	3693	495	1074	.461	464	610	.761	749	277	1584	5.7	2.1	12.0

Three-point field goals: 1996-97, 21-for-63 (.333). 1997-98, 30-for-70 (.429). 1998-99, 37-for-99 (.374). 1999-00, 42-for-124 (.339). Totals, 130-for-356 (.365).

NBA REGULAR-SEASON RECORD

Season Team	G	Min.	FGM	FGA	Pct.	FTM	FTA	Pct.	Off.	Def.	Tot.	Ast.	St.	Blk.	TO	Pts.	RPG	APG	PPG
00-01—Detroit	15	126	10	31	.323	11	18	.611	8	15	23	3	7	2	9	31	1.5	0.2	2.1
01-02—Detroit	8	43	6	13	.462	2	2	1.000	2	4	6	2	1	0	0	17	0.8	0.3	2.1
02-03—Washington	5	15	1	4	.250	2	2	1.000	3	2	5	1	0	0	1	4	1.0	0.2	0.8
03-04—Golden State	76	1634	220	466	.472	238	271	.878	100	217	317	103	66	20	84	733	4.2	1.4	9.6
04-05—Memphis	58	1433	160	432	.370	158	181	.873	63	162	225	114	88	19	83	522	3.9	2.0	9.0
05-06—Memphis	36	402	46	111	.414	19	27	.704	11	44	55	33	23	0	27	124	1.5	0.9	3.4
Totals	198	3653	443	1057	.419	430	501	.858	187	444	631	256	185	41	204	1431	3.2	1.3	7.2

Three-point field goals: 2000-01, 0-for-5. 2001-02, 3-for-7 (.429). 2002-03, 0-for-1. 2003-04, 55-for-124 (.444). 2004-05, 44-for-125 (.352). 2005-06, 13-for-29 (.448). Totals, 115-for-291 (.395).
Personal fouls/disqualifications: 2000-01, 27/0. 2001-02, 5/0. 2003-04, 206/0. 2004-05, 172/3. 2005-06, 65/0. Totals, 475/3.

NBA PLAYOFF RECORD

Season Team	G	Min.	FGM	FGA	Pct.	FTM	FTA	Pct.	Off.	Def.	Tot.	Ast.	St.	Blk.	TO	Pts.	RPG	APG	PPG
04-05—Memphis	4	78	9	23	.391	8	11	.727	2	10	12	2	3	0	1	26	3.0	0.5	6.5
05-06—Memphis	3	22	1	2	.500	0	0	...	1	3	4	1	1	0	0	3	1.3	0.3	1.0
Totals	7	100	10	25	.400	8	11	.727	3	13	16	3	4	0	1	29	2.3	0.4	4.1

Three-point field goals: 2004-05, 0-for-4. 2005-06, 1-for-2 (.500). Totals, 1-for-6 (.167).
Personal fouls/disqualifications: 2004-05, 11/0. 2005-06, 2/0. Totals, 13/0.

SPANISH LEAGUE RECORD

Season Team	G	Min.	FGM	FGA	Pct.	FTM	FTA	Pct.	Reb.	Ast.	Pts.	RPG	APG	PPG
02-03—Pamesa Valencia	4	80	8	25	.320	2	4	.500	16	3	22	4.0	0.8	5.5

Three-point field goals: 2002-03, 4-for-11 (.364). Totals, 4-for-11 (.364).
Personal fouls/disqualifications: 2002-03, 18/0. Totals, 18/0.

CARROLL, MATT — G — BOBCATS

PERSONAL: Born August 28, 1980, in Pittsburgh. ... 6-6/212. (1.98/96.2).
HIGH SCHOOL: Hatboro-Horsham (Horsham, Pa.).
COLLEGE: Notre Dame.
TRANSACTIONS/CAREER NOTES: Not drafted by an NBA franchise. ... Signed as free agent by New York Knicks (September 29, 2003). ... Waived by Knicks (October 27, 2003). ... Signed as free agent by Portland Trail Blazers (November 7, 2003). ... Waived by Trail Blazers (January 7, 2004). ... Played in NBA Development League with Roanoke Dazzle (2004). ... Signed by San Antonio Spurs (March 8, 2004). ... Signed as free agent by Golden State Warriors (October 4, 2004). ... Signed as free agent by Charlotte Bobcats (February 23, 2005).

COLLEGIATE RECORD

Season Team	G	Min.	FGM	FGA	Pct.	FTM	FTA	Pct.	Reb.	Ast.	Pts.	RPG	APG	PPG
99-00—Notre Dame	37	968	125	310	.403	50	65	.769	98	78	364	2.6	2.1	9.8
00-01—Notre Dame	30	991	128	274	.467	51	61	.836	150	114	372	5.0	3.8	12.4
01-02—Notre Dame	32	1034	160	341	.469	57	69	.826	153	67	450	4.8	2.1	14.1
02-03—Notre Dame	34	1154	215	487	.441	135	160	.844	169	55	664	5.0	1.6	19.5
Totals	133	4147	628	1412	.445	293	355	.825	570	314	1850	4.3	2.4	13.9

Three-point field goals: 1999-00, 64-for-183 (.350). 2000-01, 65-for-159 (.409). 2001-02, 73-for-177 (.412). 2002-03, 99-for-243 (.407). Totals, 301-for-762 (.395).

NBA REGULAR-SEASON RECORD

Season Team	G	Min.	FGM	FGA	Pct.	FTM	FTA	Pct.	Off.	Def.	Tot.	Ast.	St.	Blk.	TO	Pts.	RPG	APG	PPG
03-04—Portland-S.A.	16	70	7	16	.438	4	6	.667	1	5	6	2	1	0	6	19	0.4	0.1	1.2
04-05—Charlotte	25	430	70	180	.389	71	83	.855	13	47	60	17	17	2	25	224	2.4	0.7	9.0

Season Team	G	Min.	FGM	FGA	Pct.	FTM	FTA	Pct.	Off.	Def.	Tot.	Ast.	St.	Blk.	TO	Pts.	RPG	APG	PPG
05-06—Charlotte........	78	1275	192	476	.403	138	168	.821	34	123	157	35	47	11	48	594	2.0	0.4	7.6
Totals...................	119	1775	269	672	.400	213	257	.829	48	175	223	54	65	13	79	837	1.9	0.5	7.0

Three-point field goals: 2003-04, 1-for-3 (.333). 2004-05, 13-for-39 (.333). 2005-06, 72-for-185 (.389). Totals, 86-for-227 (.379).
Personal fouls/disqualifications: 2003-04, 8/0. 2004-05, 37/0. 2005-06, 120/0. Totals, 165/0.

NBA DEVELOPMENT LEAGUE RECORD

Season Team	G	Min.	FGM	FGA	Pct.	FTM	FTA	Pct.	Reb.	Ast.	Pts.	RPG	APG	PPG
03-04—Roanoke......................	11	956	62	146	.425	35	39	.897	31	25	171	2.8	2.3	15.5
04-05—Roanoke......................	24	761	177	352	.503	106	123	.862	67	38	483	2.8	1.6	20.1
Totals.....................................	35	1717	239	498	.480	141	162	.870	98	63	654	2.8	1.8	18.7

Three-point field goals: 2003-04, 12-for-33 (.364). 2004-05, 23-for-38 (.605). Totals, 35-for-71 (.493).

CARTER, ANTHONY   G   TIMBERWOLVES

PERSONAL: Born June 16, 1975, in Atlanta. ... 6-1/190. (1.85/86.2). ... Full name: Anthony Bernard Carter
HIGH SCHOOL: Alonzo A. Crim (Atlanta).
JUNIOR COLLEGE: Saddleback Community College (Calif.).
COLLEGE: Hawaii.
TRANSACTIONS/CAREER NOTES: Not drafted by an NBA franchise. ... Played in Continental Basketball Association with Yakima Sun Kings (1998-99). ... Signed as free agent by Miami Heat (August 6, 1999). ... Signed as free agent by San Antonio Spurs (July 30, 2003) ... Signed as free agent by Minnesota Timberwolves (October 4, 2004).

COLLEGIATE RECORD

Season Team	G	Min.	FGM	FGA	Pct.	FTM	FTA	Pct.	Reb.	Ast.	Pts.	RPG	APG	PPG
94-95—Saddleback C.C.	33	...	261	508	.514	100	146	.685	203	116	641	6.2	3.5	19.4
95-96—Saddleback C.C.	33	...	324	668	.485	209	278	.752	216	178	889	6.5	5.4	26.9
96-97—Hawaii	29	1005	211	426	.495	89	138	.645	107	191	543	3.7	6.6	18.7
97-98—Hawaii	29	1041	191	422	.453	111	142	.782	152	212	527	5.2	7.3	18.2
Junior College Totals.............	66	...	585	1176	.497	309	424	.729	419	294	1530	6.3	4.5	23.2
4-Year-College Totals.............	58	2046	402	848	.474	200	280	.714	259	403	1070	4.5	6.9	18.4

Three-point field goals: 1994-95, 19-for-81 (.235). 1995-96, 32-for-110 (.291). 1996-97, 32-for-90 (.356). 1997-98, 34-for-110 (.309). Totals, 117-for-391 (.299).
Personal fouls/disqualifications: 1994-95, 77/0. 1995-96, 82/0. 1996-97, 86/0. 1997-98, 73/0. Totals, 318/0.

CBA RECORD

Season Team	G	Min.	FGM	FGA	Pct.	FTM	FTA	Pct.	Reb.	Ast.	Pts.	RPG	APG	PPG
98-99—Yakima	48	1202	220	502	.438	101	141	.716	130	209	555	2.7	4.4	11.6

Three-point field goals: 1998-99, 14-for-63 (.222). Totals, 14-for-63 (.222).
Personal fouls/disqualifications: 1998-99, 104/0. Totals, 104/0.

NBA REGULAR-SEASON RECORD

Season Team	G	Min.	FGM	FGA	Pct.	FTM	FTA	Pct.	Off.	Def.	Tot.	Ast.	St.	Blk.	TO	Pts.	RPG	APG	PPG
99-00—Miami	79	1859	201	509	.395	93	124	.750	48	151	199	378	93	5	173	498	2.5	4.8	6.3
00-01—Miami	72	1630	195	480	.406	65	103	.631	46	134	180	268	73	10	119	461	2.5	3.7	6.4
01-02—Miami	46	1050	89	260	.342	19	36	.528	19	98	117	214	50	3	72	198	2.5	4.7	4.3
02-03—Miami	49	912	83	233	.356	33	50	.660	12	71	83	203	45	5	81	199	1.7	4.1	4.1
03-04—San Antonio...	5	87	11	37	.297	0	0	...	2	9	11	12	4	0	12	22	2.2	2.4	4.4
04-05—Minnesota......	66	742	72	177	.407	35	51	.686	12	57	69	161	35	18	62	181	1.0	2.4	2.7
05-06—Minnesota......	45	589	53	137	.387	40	55	.727	9	53	62	101	24	9	40	150	1.4	2.2	3.3
Totals....................	362	6869	704	1833	.384	285	419	.680	148	573	721	1337	324	50	559	1709	2.0	3.7	4.7

Three-point field goals: 1999-00, 3-for-23 (.130). 2000-01, 6-for-40 (.150). 2001-02, 1-for-19 (.053). 2002-03, 0-for-8. 2003-04, 0-for-3. 2004-05, 2-for-17 (.118). 2005-06, 4-for-15 (.267). Totals, 16-for-125 (.128).
Personal fouls/disqualifications: 1999-00, 167/0. 2000-01, 154/1. 2001-02, 85/2. 2002-03, 70/0. 2003-04, 9/0. 2004-05, 88/2. 2005-06, 71/0. Totals, 644/5.

NBA PLAYOFF RECORD

Season Team	G	Min.	FGM	FGA	Pct.	FTM	FTA	Pct.	Off.	Def.	Tot.	Ast.	St.	Blk.	TO	Pts.	RPG	APG	PPG
99-00—Miami	10	275	32	77	.416	12	16	.750	8	32	40	56	12	2	23	77	4.0	5.6	7.7
00-01—Miami	3	69	9	19	.474	0	0	...	0	6	6	11	2	1	10	18	2.0	3.7	6.0
Totals....................	13	344	41	96	.427	12	16	.750	8	38	46	67	14	3	33	95	3.5	5.2	7.3

Three-point field goals: 1999-00, 1-for-6 (.167). 2000-01, 0-for-1. Totals, 1-for-7 (.143).
Personal fouls/disqualifications: 1999-00, 22/0. 2000-01, 9/0. Totals, 31/0.

CARTER, VINCE   G/F   NETS

PERSONAL: Born January 26, 1977, in Daytona Beach, Fla. ... 6-6/225. (1.98/102.1). ... Full name: Vincent Lamar Carter
HIGH SCHOOL: Daytona Beach (Fla.) Mainland.
COLLEGE: North Carolina.
TRANSACTIONS/CAREER NOTES: Selected after junior season by Golden State Warriors in first round (fifth pick overall) of 1998 NBA Draft. ... Draft rights traded by Warriors with cash to Toronto Raptors for draft rights to F Antawn Jamison (June 24, 1998). ... Traded by Raptors to New Jersey Nets for C Alonzo Mourning, F Aaron Williams, F Eric Williams and two first-round draft picks (December 17, 2004).

MISCELLANEOUS: Member of gold-medal-winning U.S. Olympic team (2000). ... Toronto Raptors all-time points leader with 9,420 and all-time blocks leader with 415 (1998-99 through 2004).

COLLEGIATE RECORD

NOTES: The SPORTING NEWS All-America second team (1998).

Season Team	G	Min.	FGM	FGA	Pct.	FTM	FTA	Pct.	Reb.	Ast.	Pts.	RPG	APG	PPG
												AVERAGES		
95-96—North Carolina	31	555	91	185	.492	31	45	.689	119	40	232	3.8	1.3	7.5
96-97—North Carolina	34	937	166	316	.525	75	100	.750	152	83	443	4.5	2.4	13.0
97-98—North Carolina	38	1185	224	379	.591	100	147	.680	195	74	592	5.1	1.9	15.6
Totals	103	2677	481	880	.547	206	292	.705	466	197	1267	4.5	1.9	12.3

Three-point field goals: 1995-96, 19-for-55 (.345). 1996-97, 38-for-107 (.355). 1997-98, 44-for-107 (.411). Totals, 101-for-269 (.375).

NBA REGULAR-SEASON RECORD

HONORS: NBA Rookie of the Year (1999). ... All-NBA second team (2001). ... All-NBA third team (2000). ... NBA All-Rookie first team (1999). ... Slam Dunk championship winner (2000).

Season Team	G	Min.	FGM	FGA	Pct.	FTM	FTA	Pct.	Off.	Def.	Tot.	Ast.	St.	Blk.	TO	Pts.	RPG	APG	PPG
									REBOUNDS								AVERAGES		
98-99—Toronto	50	1760	345	766	.450	204	268	.761	94	189	283	149	55	77	110	913	5.7	3.0	18.3
99-00—Toronto	82	3126	788	1696	.465	436	551	.791	150	326	476	322	110	92	178	2107	5.8	3.9	25.7
00-01—Toronto	75	2979	762	1656	.460	384	502	.765	176	240	416	291	114	82	167	2070	5.5	3.9	27.6
01-02—Toronto	60	2385	559	1307	.428	245	307	.798	138	175	313	239	94	43	154	1484	5.2	4.0	24.7
02-03—Toronto	43	1471	355	760	.467	129	160	.806	59	129	188	143	48	41	74	884	4.4	3.3	20.6
03-04—Toronto	73	2785	608	1457	.417	336	417	.806	95	254	349	348	88	65	223	1645	4.8	4.8	22.5
04-05—Toronto-N.J.	77	2828	696	1541	.452	367	460	.798	106	295	401	327	109	48	168	1886	5.2	4.2	24.5
05-06—New Jersey	79	2906	653	1518	.430	480	601	.799	135	327	462	338	94	53	213	1911	5.8	4.3	24.2
Totals	539	20240	4766	10701	.445	2581	3266	.790	953	1935	2888	2157	712	501	1287	12900	5.4	4.0	23.9

Three-point field goals: 1998-99, 19-for-66 (.288). 1999-00, 95-for-236 (.403). 2000-01, 162-for-397 (.408). 2001-02, 121-for-313 (.387). 2002-03, 45-for-131 (.344). 2003-04, 103-for-243 (.383). 2004-05, 127-for-313 (.406). 2005-06, 125-for-367 (.341). Totals, 787-for-2066 (.381).

Personal fouls/disqualifications: 1998-99, 140/2. 1999-00, 263/2. 2000-01, 205/1. 2001-02, 191/4. 2002-03, 121/2. 2003-04, 212/1. 2004-05, 243/3. 2005-06, 235/1. Totals, 1610/16.

NBA PLAYOFF RECORD

NOTES: Holds single-game record for most three-point field goals made in one half—8 (May 11, 2001, vs. Philadelphia).

Season Team	G	Min.	FGM	FGA	Pct.	FTM	FTA	Pct.	Off.	Def.	Tot.	Ast.	St.	Blk.	TO	Pts.	RPG	APG	PPG
									REBOUNDS								AVERAGES		
99-00—Toronto	3	119	15	50	.300	27	31	.871	9	9	18	19	3	4	8	58	6.0	6.3	19.3
00-01—Toronto	12	539	122	280	.436	58	74	.784	37	41	78	56	20	20	27	327	6.5	4.7	27.3
04 05 New Jersey	4	179	35	96	.365	31	36	.861	9	25	34	23	9	0	15	107	8.5	5.8	26.8
05-06—New Jersey	11	450	113	244	.463	86	108	.796	16	61	77	58	20	6	26	326	7.0	5.3	29.6
Totals	30	1287	285	670	.425	202	249	.811	71	136	207	156	52	30	76	818	6.9	5.2	27.3

Three-point field goals: 1999-00, 1-for-10 (.100). 2000-01, 25-for-61 (.410). 2004-05, 16-for-39 (.316). 2005-06, 14-for-58 (.241). Totals, 46-for-148 (.311).

Personal fouls/disqualifications: 1999-00, 12/0. 2000-01, 45/1. 2004-05, 17/0. 2005-06, 34/0. Totals, 108/1.

NBA ALL-STAR GAME RECORD

Season Team	Min.	FGM	FGA	Pct.	FTM	FTA	Pct.	Off.	Def.	Tot.	Ast.	PF	Dq.	St.	Blk.	TO	Pts.
2000—Toronto	28	6	11	.545	0	0	...	2	2	4	2	0	0	2	0	2	12
2001—Toronto	24	7	18	.389	1	1	1.000	1	2	3	4	1	0	1	1	3	16
2002—Toronto							Selected, did not play—injured										
2003—Toronto	25	4	9	.444	0	0	...	1	0	1	2	1	0	0	0	1	9
2004—Toronto	16	5	7	.714	0	0	...	1	1	2	0	1	0	2	0	2	11
2005—New Jersey	18	4	8	.500	0	0	...	0	3	3	1	0	0	0	0	2	11
2006—New Jersey	18	2	5	.400	1	2	.500	1	3	4	2	3	0	1	0	2	5
Totals	129	28	58	.483	2	3	.667	6	11	17	11	6	0	6	1	12	64

Three-point field goals: 2000, 0-for-2. 2001, 1-for-4 (.250). 2003, 1-for-1 (1.000). 2004, 1-for-3 (.333). 2005, 3-for-5 (.600). Totals, 6-for-15 (.400).

CASSELL, SAM   G   CLIPPERS

PERSONAL: Born November 18, 1969, in Baltimore. ... 6-3/185. (1.91/83.9). ... Full name: Samuel James Cassell ... Name pronounced KUH-sell.

HIGH SCHOOL: Dunbar (Baltimore).

JUNIOR COLLEGE: San Jacinto College (Texas).

COLLEGE: Florida State.

TRANSACTIONS/CAREER NOTES: Selected by Houston Rockets in first round (24th pick overall) of 1993 NBA Draft. ... Traded by Rockets with F Chucky Brown, F Robert Horry and F Mark Bryant to Phoenix Suns for F Charles Barkley and 1999 second-round draft choice (August 19, 1996). ... Traded by Suns with F A.C. Green, F Michael Finley and 1997 or 1998 conditional second-round draft choice to Dallas Mavericks for G Jason Kidd, F Tony Dumas and C Loren Meyer (December 26, 1996). ... Traded by Mavericks with C Eric Montross, G Jim Jackson, F/C Chris Gatling and F/G George McCloud to New Jersey Nets for G Shawn Bradley, F Ed O'Bannon, G Khalid Reeves and G Robert Pack (February 17, 1997). ... Traded by Nets with F Chris Gatling to Milwaukee Bucks in three-way deal in which Bucks also received C Paul Grant from Minnesota Timberwolves, Timberwolves received F Brian Evans, 1999 first-round draft choice and an undisclosed draft choice from Nets, Bucks sent G Terrell Brandon to Timberwolves and Timberwolves sent G Stephon Marbury, G Chris Carr and F Bill Curley to Nets and Nets received G Elliot Perry from Bucks (March 11, 1999). ... Traded by Bucks with C Ervin Johnson to Minnesota Timberwolves for F Joe Smith and G Anthony Peeler (June 27, 2003). ... Traded by Timberwolves with a first-round pick to Los Angeles Clippers for Gs Marko Jaric and Lionel Chalmers (August 12, 2005).

MISCELLANEOUS: Member of NBA championship team (1994, 1995).

COLLEGIATE RECORD

Season Team	G	Min.	FGM	FGA	Pct.	FTM	FTA	Pct.	Reb.	Ast.	Pts.	RPG	APG	PPG
												AVERAGES		
89-90—San Jacinto College	38	1061	296	597	.496	136	170	.800	208	200	810	5.5	5.3	21.3

Season Team	G	Min.	FGM	FGA	Pct.	FTM	FTA	Pct.	Reb.	Ast.	Pts.	RPG	APG	PPG
90-91—San Jacinto College........	31	864	233	471	.495	198	246	.805	157	237	727	5.1	7.6	23.5
91-92—Florida State	31	1046	206	454	.454	100	142	.704	141	119	570	4.5	3.8	18.4
92-93—Florida State	35	1298	234	466	.502	123	162	.759	152	170	641	4.3	4.9	18.3
Junior College Totals.............	69	1925	529	1068	.495	334	416	.803	365	437	1537	5.3	6.3	22.3
4-Year-College Totals	66	2344	440	920	.478	223	304	.734	293	289	1211	4.4	4.4	18.3

Three-point field goals: 1989-90, 82-for-184 (.446). 1990-91, 63-for-160 (.394). 1991-92, 58-for-164 (.354). 1992-93, 50-for-131 (.382). Totals, 253-for-639 (.396).

NBA REGULAR-SEASON RECORD

HONORS: All-NBA second team (2004).

Season Team	G	Min.	FGM	FGA	Pct.	FTM	FTA	Pct.	REBOUNDS Off.	Def.	Tot.	Ast.	St.	Blk.	TO	Pts.	RPG	APG	PPG
93-94—Houston.........	66	1122	162	388	.418	90	107	.841	25	109	134	192	59	7	94	440	2.0	2.9	6.7
94-95—Houston.........	82	1882	253	593	.427	214	254	.843	38	173	211	405	94	14	167	783	2.6	4.9	9.5
95-96—Houston.........	61	1682	289	658	.439	235	285	.825	51	137	188	278	53	4	157	886	3.1	4.6	14.5
96-97—Pho.-Dal.-N.J..	61	1714	337	783	.430	212	251	.845	47	135	182	305	77	19	168	967	3.0	5.0	15.9
97-98—New Jersey	75	2606	510	1156	.441	436	507	.860	73	155	228	603	121	20	269	1471	3.0	8.0	19.6
98-99—N.J.-Mil..........	8	199	39	93	.419	47	50	.940	5	10	15	36	9	0	20	127	1.9	4.5	15.9
99-00—Milwaukee	81	2899	545	1170	.466	390	445	.876	69	232	301	729	102	8	267	1506	3.7	9.0	18.6
00-01—Milwaukee	76	2709	537	1132	.474	277	323	.858	46	244	290	580	88	8	220	1381	3.8	7.6	18.2
01-02—Milwaukee	74	2605	554	1197	.463	282	328	.860	54	258	312	493	90	12	177	1461	4.2	6.7	19.7
02-03—Milwaukee	78	2700	546	1162	.470	385	447	.861	57	285	342	450	88	14	177	1536	4.4	5.8	19.7
03-04—Minnesota	81	2838	620	1270	.488	289	331	.873	44	227	271	592	102	18	220	1603	3.3	7.3	19.8
04-05—Minnesota	59	1522	319	687	.464	134	155	.865	25	132	157	301	36	14	109	799	2.7	5.1	13.5
05-06—L.A. Clippers ...	78	2653	493	1112	.443	289	335	.863	40	247	287	491	74	11	175	1345	3.7	6.3	17.2
Totals	880	27131	5204	11401	.456	3280	3818	.859	574	2344	2918	5455	993	149	2220	14305	3.3	6.2	16.3

Three-point field goals: 1993-94, 26-for-88 (.295). 1994-95, 63-for-191 (.330). 1995-96, 73-for-210 (.348). 1996-97, 81-for-231 (.351). 1997-98, 15-for-80 (.188). 1998-99, 2-for-10 (.200). 1999-00, 26-for-90 (.289). 2000-01, 30-for-98 (.306). 2001-02, 71-for-204 (.348). 2002-03, 59-for-163 (.362). 2003-04, 74-for-186 (.398). 2004-05, 27-for-103 (.262). 2005-06, 70-for-190 (.368). Totals, 617-for-1844 (.335).

Personal fouls/disqualifications: 1993-94, 136/1. 1994-95, 209/3. 1995-96, 166/2. 1996-97, 200/9. 1997-98, 262/5. 1998-99, 22/1. 1999-00, 255/5. 2000-01, 214/5. 2001-02, 208/3. 2002-03, 216/1. 2003-04, 247/2. 2004-05, 160/2. 2005-06, 225/1. Totals, 2520/40.

NBA PLAYOFF RECORD

Season Team	G	Min.	FGM	FGA	Pct.	FTM	FTA	Pct.	REBOUNDS Off.	Def.	Tot.	Ast.	St.	Blk.	TO	Pts.	RPG	APG	PPG
93-94—Houston.........	22	478	63	160	.394	64	74	.865	19	40	59	93	21	5	47	207	2.7	4.2	9.4
94-95—Houston.........	22	485	74	169	.438	71	85	.835	8	34	42	89	21	2	33	243	1.9	4.0	11.0
95-96—Houston.........	8	206	26	81	.321	23	29	.793	1	16	17	34	6	1	18	83	2.1	4.3	10.4
97-98—New Jersey	3	26	3	9	.333	0	0	...	1	2	3	5	0	1	2	6	1.0	1.7	2.0
98-99—Milwaukee	3	102	16	32	.500	14	16	.875	0	6	6	26	3	0	7	46	2.0	8.7	15.3
99-00—Milwaukee	5	178	30	72	.417	18	21	.857	0	17	17	45	4	0	9	79	3.4	9.0	15.8
00-01—Milwaukee	18	682	110	278	.396	84	97	.866	12	71	83	120	19	3	52	314	4.6	6.7	17.4
02-03—Milwaukee	6	217	39	83	.470	14	15	.933	3	16	19	16	3	1	17	103	3.2	2.7	17.2
03-04—Minnesota	16	497	94	202	.465	52	61	.852	3	37	40	70	12	3	43	265	2.5	4.4	16.6
05-06—L.A. Clippers ...	12	404	73	167	.437	55	68	.809	9	39	48	69	8	2	28	216	4.0	5.8	18.0
Totals	115	3275	528	1253	.421	395	466	.848	56	278	334	567	97	18	256	1562	2.9	4.9	13.6

Three-point field goals: 1993-94, 17-for-45 (.378). 1994-95, 24-for-60 (.400). 1995-96, 8-for-29 (.276). 1998-99, 0-for-1. 1999-00, 1-for-5 (.200). 2000-01, 10-for-30 (.333). 2002-03, 11-for-21 (.524). 2003-04, 25-for-60 (.417). 2005-06, 15-for-43 (.349). Totals, 111-for-294 (.378).

Personal fouls/disqualifications: 1993-94, 62/1. 1994-95, 66/1. 1995-96, 20/0. 1997-98, 7/0. 1998-99, 14/1. 1999-00, 19/1. 2000-01, 76/2. 2002-03, 20/0. 2003-04, 53/2. 2005-06, 35/0. Totals, 372/8.

NBA ALL-STAR GAME RECORD

Season Team	Min.	FGM	FGA	Pct.	FTM	FTA	Pct.	REBOUNDS Off.	Def.	Tot.	Ast.	PF	Dq.	St.	Blk.	TO	Pts.
2004—Minnesota	13	2	3	.667	0	0	...	0	1	1	7	0	0	1	0	1	4

CATO, KELVIN   C

PERSONAL: Born August 26, 1974, in Atlanta. ... 6-11/275. (2.11/124.7). ... Full name: Kelvin T. Cato

HIGH SCHOOL: Lithonia (Decatur, Ga.).

COLLEGE: South Alabama, then Iowa State.

TRANSACTIONS/CAREER NOTES: Selected by Dallas Mavericks in first round (15th pick overall) of 1997 NBA Draft. ... Draft rights traded by Mavericks to Portland Trail Blazers for draft rights to C Chris Anstey and cash (June 25, 1997). ... Traded by Trail Blazers with F Stacy Augmon, G/F Walt Williams, G Brian Shaw, G Ed Gray and F/C Carlos Rogers to Houston Rockets for F Scottie Pippen (October 2, 1999). ... Traded by Rockets with G Steve Francis and G Cuttino Mobley to Orlando Magic for G Tracy McGrady, F Juwan Howard, G Tyronn Lue and G Reece Gaines (June 29, 2004). ... Traded by Magic with future first-round draft choice to Detroit Pistons for G Carlos Arroyo and F/C Darko Milicic (February 15, 2006).

COLLEGIATE RECORD

Season Team	G	Min.	FGM	FGA	Pct.	FTM	FTA	Pct.	Reb.	Ast.	Pts.	RPG	APG	PPG
92-93—South Alabama...............						Did not play—ineligible.								
93-94—South Alabama...............	24	433	49	123	.398	45	79	.570	138	17	143	5.8	0.7	6.0
94-95—Iowa State						Did not play—transfer student.								
95-96—Iowa State	27	697	94	187	.503	71	111	.640	209	17	259	7.7	0.6	9.6
96-97—Iowa State	28	801	128	234	.547	61	113	.540	235	15	317	8.4	0.5	11.3
Totals	79	1931	271	544	.498	177	303	.584	582	49	719	7.4	0.6	9.1

Three-point field goals: 1996-97, 0-for-1. Totals, 0-for-1 (.000).

Personal fouls/disqualifications: 1993-94, 60/0. 1995-96, 87/4. Totals, 147/4.

NBA REGULAR-SEASON RECORD

								REBOUNDS								AVERAGES		
Season Team	G	Min.	FGM	FGA	Pct.	FTM	FTA	Pct.	Off.	Def.	Tot.	Ast.	St.	Blk.	TO	Pts.	RPG	APG	PPG
97-98—Portland	74	1007	98	229	.428	86	125	.688	91	161	252	23	29	94	44	282	3.4	0.3	3.8
98-99—Portland	43	545	58	129	.450	34	67	.507	49	101	150	19	23	56	27	151	3.5	0.4	3.5
99-00—Houston	65	1581	216	402	.537	135	208	.649	102	287	389	26	33	124	71	567	6.0	0.4	8.7
00-01—Houston	35	624	64	111	.577	37	57	.649	47	94	141	11	13	31	25	165	4.0	0.3	4.7
01-02—Houston	75	1917	190	326	.583	113	194	.582	176	349	525	29	40	95	53	493	7.0	0.4	6.6
02-03—Houston	73	1247	133	256	.520	66	124	.532	132	296	428	20	38	85	56	332	5.9	0.3	4.5
03-04—Houston	69	1743	161	360	.447	96	142	.676	153	319	472	72	52	96	84	418	6.8	1.0	6.1
04-05—Orlando	62	1525	160	297	.539	112	143	.783	102	314	416	40	55	82	64	432	6.7	0.6	7.0
05-06—Orl.-Detroit	27	333	36	84	.429	26	35	.743	20	50	70	4	6	12	18	98	2.6	0.1	3.6
Totals	523	10522	1116	2194	.509	705	1095	.644	872	1971	2843	244	289	675	442	2938	5.4	0.5	5.6

Three-point field goals: 1997-98, 0-for-3. 1998-99, 1-for-1 (1.000). 1999-00, 0-for-4. 2001-02, 0-for-1. 2002-03, 0-for-4. Totals, 1-for-13 (.077).
Personal fouls/disqualifications: 1997-98, 164/3. 1998-99, 100/3. 1999-00, 175/1. 2000-01, 89/1. 2001-02, 208/5. 2002-03, 176/0. 2003-04, 203/0. 2004-05, 170/1. 2005-06, 52/0. Totals, 1337/14.

NBA PLAYOFF RECORD

								REBOUNDS								AVERAGES		
Season Team	G	Min.	FGM	FGA	Pct.	FTM	FTA	Pct.	Off.	Def.	Tot.	Ast.	St.	Blk.	TO	Pts.	RPG	APG	PPG
97-98—Portland	4	58	9	17	.529	8	11	.727	3	9	12	1	1	7	4	26	3.0	0.3	6.5
98-99—Portland	8	43	1	9	.111	4	10	.400	6	1	7	2	1	1	2	6	0.9	0.3	0.8
03-04—Houston	5	148	13	22	.591	3	7	.429	14	20	34	2	5	4	5	29	6.8	0.4	5.8
05-06—Detroit	4	15	3	5	.600	0	0	...	3	4	7	0	0	0	0	6	1.8	0.0	1.5
Totals	21	264	26	53	.491	15	28	.536	26	34	60	5	7	12	11	67	2.9	0.2	3.2

Three-point field goals: 1997-98, 0-for-1. Totals, 0-for-1 (.000).
Personal fouls/disqualifications: 1997-98, 12/0. 1998-99, 13/0. 2003-04, 18/1. 2005-06, 2/0. Totals, 45/1.

C

CHANDLER, TYSON   F   HORNETS

PERSONAL: Born October 2, 1982, in Hanford, Calif. ... 7-1/235. (2.16/106.6). ... Full name: Tyson Cleotis Chandler
HIGH SCHOOL: Dominguez (Compton, Calif.).
COLLEGE: Did not attend college.
TRANSACTIONS/CAREER NOTES: Selected out of high school by Los Angeles Clippers in first round (second pick overall) of 2001 NBA Draft. ... Draft rights traded by Clippers with F Brian Skinner to Chicago Bulls for F Elton Brand (June 27, 2001). ... Traded by Bulls to New Orleans/Oklahoma City Hornets for F P.J. Brown and G J.R. Smith (July 14, 2006).

NBA REGULAR-SEASON RECORD

								REBOUNDS								AVERAGES		
Season Team	G	Min.	FGM	FGA	Pct.	FTM	FTA	Pct.	Off.	Def.	Tot.	Ast.	St.	Blk.	TO	Pts.	RPG	APG	PPG
01-02—Chicago	71	1389	151	304	.497	134	222	.604	114	229	343	54	28	93	99	436	4.8	0.8	6.1
02-03—Chicago	75	1827	257	484	.531	177	291	.608	169	345	514	76	37	106	135	691	6.9	1.0	9.2
03-04—Chicago	35	782	67	158	.424	79	118	.669	82	188	270	23	17	43	38	213	7.7	0.7	6.1
04-05—Chicago	80	5189	567	413	.434	559	900	.673	314	773	711	81	89	141	118	040	8.7	0.9	8.8
05-06—Chicago	79	2121	160	283	.565	97	193	.503	265	449	714	81	41	104	123	417	9.0	1.0	5.3
Totals	340	8308	842	1648	.511	713	1160	.615	891	1725	2616	299	192	487	513	2397	7.7	0.9	7.1

Three-point field goals: 2003-04, 0-for-1. 2004-05, 0-for-2. 2005-06, 0-for-1. Totals, 0-for-4 (.000).
Personal fouls/disqualifications: 2001-02, 179/1. 2002-03, 220/3. 2003-04, 87/2. 2004-05, 268/4. 2005-06, 298/14. Totals, 1052/24.

NBA PLAYOFF RECORD

								REBOUNDS								AVERAGES		
Season Team	G	Min.	FGM	FGA	Pct.	FTM	FTA	Pct.	Off.	Def.	Tot.	Ast.	St.	Blk.	TO	Pts.	RPG	APG	PPG
04-05—Chicago	6	172	19	40	.475	32	46	.696	29	29	58	8	1	13	8	70	9.7	1.3	11.7
05-06—Chicago	6	104	4	6	.667	3	10	.300	8	19	27	3	2	2	6	11	4.5	0.5	1.8
Totals	12	276	23	46	.500	35	56	.625	37	48	85	11	3	15	14	81	7.1	0.9	6.8

Personal fouls/disqualifications: 2004-05, 27/2. 2005-06, 29/1. Totals, 56/3.

CHEANEY, CALBERT   G/F   WARRIORS

PERSONAL: Born July 17, 1971, in Evansville, Ind. ... 6-7/217. (2.01/98.4). ... Full name: Calbert N. Cheaney ... Name pronounced CHAIN-ee.
HIGH SCHOOL: Harrison (Evansville, Ind.).
COLLEGE: Indiana.
TRANSACTIONS/CAREER NOTES: Selected by Washington Bullets in first round (sixth pick overall) of 1993 NBA Draft. ... Bullets franchise renamed Washington Wizards for 1997-98 season. ... Signed as free agent by Boston Celtics (August 5, 1999). ... Traded by Celtics with G Robert Pack to Denver Nuggets for G Chris Herren and G Bryant Stith (October 16, 2000). ... Signed as free agent by Utah Jazz (July 25, 2002). ... Signed as free agent by Golden State Warriors (August 27, 2003).

COLLEGIATE RECORD

NOTES: THE SPORTING NEWS College Player of the Year (1993). ... Naismith Award winner (1993). ... Wooden Award winner (1993). ... THE SPORTING NEWS All-America first team (1993). ... THE SPORTING NEWS All-America third team (1991).

											AVERAGES		
Season Team	G	Min.	FGM	FGA	Pct.	FTM	FTA	Pct.	Reb.	Ast.	Pts.	RPG	APG	PPG
89-90—Indiana	29	928	199	348	.572	72	96	.750	133	48	495	4.6	1.7	17.1
90-91—Indiana	34	1029	289	485	.596	113	141	.801	188	47	734	5.5	1.4	21.6
91-92—Indiana	34	991	227	435	.522	112	140	.800	166	48	599	4.9	1.4	17.6
92-93—Indiana	35	1181	303	552	.549	132	166	.795	223	84	785	6.4	2.4	22.4
Totals	132	4129	1018	1820	.559	429	543	.790	710	227	2613	5.4	1.7	19.8

Three-point field goals: 1989-90, 25-for-51 (.490). 1990-91, 43-for-91 (.473). 1991-92, 33-for-86 (.384). 1992-93, 47-for-110 (.427). Totals, 148-for-338 (.438).

NBA REGULAR-SEASON RECORD

Season Team	G	Min.	FGM	FGA	Pct.	FTM	FTA	Pct.	REBOUNDS Off.	Def.	Tot.	Ast.	St.	Blk.	TO	Pts.	AVERAGES RPG	APG	PPG
93-94—Washington	65	1604	327	696	.470	124	161	.770	88	102	190	126	63	10	108	779	2.9	1.9	12.0
94-95—Washington	78	2651	512	1129	.453	173	213	.812	105	216	321	177	80	21	151	1293	4.1	2.3	16.6
95-96—Washington	70	2324	426	905	.471	151	214	.706	67	172	239	154	67	18	129	1055	3.4	2.2	15.1
96-97—Washington	79	2411	369	730	.505	95	137	.693	70	198	268	114	77	18	94	837	3.4	1.4	10.6
97-98—Washington	82	2841	448	981	.457	139	215	.647	82	242	324	173	96	36	104	1050	4.0	2.1	12.8
98-99—Washington	50	1266	172	415	.414	33	67	.493	33	108	141	73	39	16	42	385	2.8	1.5	7.7
99-00—Boston	67	1309	120	273	.440	9	21	.429	23	115	138	80	44	14	46	267	2.1	1.2	4.0
00-01—Denver	9	153	10	30	.333	1	2	.500	5	15	20	9	4	2	5	21	2.2	1.0	2.3
01-02—Denver	68	1631	224	466	.481	46	67	.687	57	183	240	110	34	21	70	494	3.5	1.6	7.3
02-03—Utah	81	2351	325	651	.499	40	69	.580	73	211	284	163	65	13	108	700	3.5	2.0	8.6
03-04—Golden State ...	79	2067	278	578	.481	47	77	.610	77	183	260	136	60	12	85	603	3.3	1.7	7.6
04-05—Golden State ...	55	951	113	265	.426	24	37	.649	32	92	124	64	17	15	35	250	2.3	1.2	4.5
05-06—Golden State ...	42	448	42	108	.389	8	8	1.000	20	41	61	19	13	2	17	92	1.5	0.5	2.2
Totals	825	22007	3366	7227	.466	890	1288	.691	732	1878	2610	1398	659	198	994	7826	3.2	1.7	9.5

Three-point field goals: 1993-94, 1-for-23 (.043). 1994-95, 96-for-283 (.339). 1995-96, 52-for-154 (.338). 1996-97, 4-for-30 (.133). 1997-98, 15-for-53 (.283). 1998-99, 8-for-37 (.216). 1999-00, 18-for-54 (.333). 2001-02, 0-for-4. 2002-03, 10-for-25 (.400). 2003-04, 0-for-10. 2004-05, 0-for-3. 2005-06, 0-for-8. Totals, 204-for-684 (.298).

Personal fouls/disqualifications: 1993-94, 148/0. 1994-95, 215/0. 1995-96, 205/1. 1996-97, 226/3. 1997-98, 264/4. 1998-99, 146/0. 1999-00, 158/3. 2000-01, 14/0. 2001-02, 156/1. 2002-03, 225/1. 2003-04, 184/1. 2004-05, 95/0. 2005-06, 38/0. Totals, 2074/14.

NBA PLAYOFF RECORD

Season Team	G	Min.	FGM	FGA	Pct.	FTM	FTA	Pct.	REBOUNDS Off.	Def.	Tot.	Ast.	St.	Blk.	TO	Pts.	AVERAGES RPG	APG	PPG
96-97—Washington	3	120	18	41	.439	9	12	.750	6	5	11	4	3	2	5	45	3.7	1.3	15.0
02-03—Utah	5	122	10	27	.370	2	4	.500	3	4	7	8	2	1	7	22	1.4	1.6	4.4
Totals	8	242	28	68	.412	11	16	.688	9	9	18	12	5	3	12	67	2.3	1.5	8.4

Three-point field goals: 1996-97, 0-for-2. Totals, 0-for-2 (.000).
Personal fouls/disqualifications: 1996-97, 10/0. 2002-03, 15/0. Totals, 25/0.

CHILDRESS, JOSH   F   HAWKS

PERSONAL: Born June 20, 1983, in Harbor City, Calif. ... 6-8/210. (2.03/95.3). ... Full name: Joshua Malik Childress
HIGH SCHOOL: Mayfair (Lakewood, Calif.).
COLLEGE: Stanford.
TRANSACTIONS/CAREER NOTES: Selected after junior season by Atlanta Hawks in first round (sixth pick overall) of 2004 NBA Draft.

COLLEGIATE RECORD

NOTES: The SPORTING NEWS All-America third team (2004).

Season Team	G	Min.	FGM	FGA	Pct.	FTM	FTA	Pct.	Reb.	Ast.	Pts.	AVERAGES RPG	APG	PPG
01-02—Stanford	30	645	94	234	.402	25	36	.694	144	24	235	4.8	0.8	7.8
02-03—Stanford	33	1128	168	393	.427	82	114	.719	266	70	466	8.1	2.1	14.1
03-04—Stanford	23	685	124	254	.488	78	95	.821	173	61	360	7.5	2.7	15.7
Totals	86	2458	386	881	.438	185	245	.755	583	155	1061	6.8	1.8	12.3

Three-point field goals: 2001-02, 22-for-80 (.275). 2002-03, 48-for-144 (.333). 2003-04, 34-for-86 (.395). Totals, 104-for-310 (.335).

NBA REGULAR-SEASON RECORD

HONORS: NBA All-Rookie second team (2005).

Season Team	G	Min.	FGM	FGA	Pct.	FTM	FTA	Pct.	REBOUNDS Off.	Def.	Tot.	Ast.	St.	Blk.	TO	Pts.	AVERAGES RPG	APG	PPG
04-05—Atlanta	80	2376	302	642	.470	190	231	.823	195	287	482	151	74	35	106	807	6.0	1.9	10.1
05-06—Atlanta	74	2249	278	504	.552	154	201	.766	134	253	387	131	86	39	101	742	5.2	1.8	10.0
Totals	154	4625	580	1146	.506	344	432	.796	329	540	869	282	160	74	207	1549	5.6	1.8	10.1

Three-point field goals: 2004-05, 13-for-56 (.232). 2005-06, 32-for-65 (.492). Totals, 45-for-121 (.372).
Personal fouls/disqualifications: 2004-05, 184/1. 2005-06, 184/1. Totals, 368/2.

CHRISTIE, DOUG   G/F

PERSONAL: Born May 9, 1970, in Seattle. ... 6-6/205. (1.98/93.0). ... Full name: Douglas Dale Christie ... Name pronounced CHRIS-tee.
HIGH SCHOOL: Rainier Beach (Seattle).
COLLEGE: Pepperdine.
TRANSACTIONS/CAREER NOTES: Selected by Seattle SuperSonics in first round (17th pick overall) of 1992 NBA Draft. ... Traded by SuperSonics with C Benoit Benjamin to Los Angeles Lakers for F/C Sam Perkins (February 22, 1993). ... Traded by Lakers to New York Knicks for two future second-round draft choices (October 13, 1994). ... Traded by Knicks with C/F Herb Williams and cash to Toronto Raptors for G Willie Anderson and F/C Victor Alexander (February 18, 1996). ... Traded by Raptors to Sacramento Kings for F Corliss Williamson (September 29, 2000). ... Traded by Kings to Orlando Magic for G Cuttino Mobley and F Michael Bradley (January 10, 2005). ... Waived by Magic (August 11, 2005). ... Signed as free agent by Dallas Mavericks (August 19, 2005). ... Waived by Mavericks (November 25, 2005).
MISCELLANEOUS: Toronto Raptors all-time steals leader with 664 (1995-96 through 1999-2000).

COLLEGIATE RECORD

Season Team	G	Min.	FGM	FGA	Pct.	FTM	FTA	Pct.	Reb.	Ast.	Pts.	AVERAGES RPG	APG	PPG
88-89—Pepperdine						Did not play—ineligible.								
89-90—Pepperdine	28	687	84	167	.503	70	98	.714	115	112	250	4.1	4.0	8.9

Season Team	G	Min.	FGM	FGA	Pct.	FTM	FTA	Pct.	Reb.	Ast.	Pts.	AVERAGES RPG	APG	PPG
90-91—Pepperdine	28	913	188	401	.469	143	187	.765	145	134	536	5.2	4.8	19.1
91-92—Pepperdine	31	1058	211	453	.466	144	193	.746	183	149	606	5.9	4.8	19.5
Totals	87	2658	483	1021	.473	357	478	.747	443	395	1392	5.1	4.5	16.0

Three-point field goals: 1989-90, 12-for-47 (.255). 1990-91, 17-for-65 (.262). 1991-92, 40-for-120 (.333). Totals, 69-for-232 (.297).

NBA REGULAR-SEASON RECORD

RECORDS: Shares single-game record for most steals in one half—8 (April 2, 1997, at Philadelphia).
HONORS: NBA All-Defensive first team (2003). ... NBA All-Defensive second team (2001, 2002, 2004).

Season Team	G	Min.	FGM	FGA	Pct.	FTM	FTA	Pct.	REBOUNDS Off.	Def.	Tot.	Ast.	St.	Blk.	TO	Pts.	AVERAGES RPG	APG	PPG
92-93—L.A. Lakers	23	332	45	106	.425	50	66	.758	24	27	51	53	22	5	50	142	2.2	2.3	6.2
93-94—L.A. Lakers	65	1515	244	562	.434	145	208	.697	93	142	235	136	89	28	140	672	3.6	2.1	10.3
94-95—New York	12	79	5	22	.227	4	5	.800	3	10	13	8	2	1	13	15	1.1	0.7	1.3
95-96—N.Y.-Tor.	55	1036	150	337	.445	69	93	.742	34	120	154	117	70	19	95	415	2.8	2.1	7.5
96-97—Toronto	81	3127	396	949	.417	237	306	.775	85	347	432	315	201	45	200	1176	5.3	3.9	14.5
97-98—Toronto	78	2939	458	1071	.428	271	327	.829	94	310	404	282	190	57	228	1287	5.2	3.6	16.5
98-99—Toronto	50	1768	252	650	.388	207	246	.841	59	148	207	187	113	26	119	760	4.1	3.7	15.2
99-00—Toronto	73	2264	311	764	.407	182	216	.843	63	222	285	321	102	43	144	903	3.9	4.4	12.4
00-01—Sacramento	81	2939	311	788	.395	280	312	.897	95	260	355	289	*183	45	154	996	4.4	3.6	12.3
01-02—Sacramento	81	2798	338	735	.460	206	242	.851	74	300	374	340	160	25	164	972	4.6	4.2	12.0
02-03—Sacramento	80	2710	267	557	.479	141	174	.810	61	281	342	376	180	37	144	748	4.3	4.7	9.4
03-04—Sacramento	82	2780	317	688	.461	148	172	.860	69	260	329	347	151	41	155	831	4.0	4.2	10.1
04-05—Sac.-Orlando...	52	1525	130	332	.392	70	78	.897	38	139	177	199	80	18	104	345	3.4	3.8	6.6
05-06—Dallas.............	7	185	9	26	.346	8	12	.667	2	11	13	14	9	1	6	26	1.9	2.0	3.7
Totals	820	25997	3233	7587	.426	2018	2457	.821	794	2577	3371	2984	1552	391	1716	9288	4.1	3.6	11.3

Three-point field goals: 1992-93, 2-for-12 (.167). 1993-94, 39-for-119 (.328). 1994-95, 1-for-7 (.143). 1995-96, 46-for-106 (.434). 1996-97, 147-for-383 (.384). 1997-98, 100-for-307 (.326). 1998-99, 49-for-161 (.304). 1999-00, 99-for-275 (.360). 2000-01, 94-for-250 (.376). 2001-02, 90-for-256 (.352). 2002-03, 73-for-185 (.395). 2003-04, 49-for-142 (.345). 2004-05, 15-for-62 (.242). 2005-06, 0-for-1. Totals, 804-for-2266 (.355).

Personal fouls/disqualifications: 1992-93, 53/0. 1993-94, 186/2. 1994-95, 18/1. 1995-96, 141/5. 1996-97, 245/6. 1997-98, 198/3. 1998-99, 111/1. 1999-00, 167/1. 2000-01, 224/2. 2001-02, 200/3. 2002-03, 186/1. 2003-04, 186/0. 2004-05, 106/0. 2005-06, 10/0. Totals, 2040/25.

NBA PLAYOFF RECORD

Season Team	G	Min.	FGM	FGA	Pct.	FTM	FTA	Pct.	REBOUNDS Off.	Def.	Tot.	Ast.	St.	Blk.	TO	Pts.	AVERAGES RPG	APG	PPG
92-93—L.A. Lakers	5	39	4	11	.364	0	0	...	1	3	4	6	2	2	4	9	0.8	1.2	1.8
94-95—New York	2	6	0	4	.000	0	0	...	0	0	0	0	0	1	0	0	0.0	0.0	0.0
99-00—Toronto	3	61	3	13	.231	3	6	.500	1	4	5	6	4	1	4	12	1.7	2.0	4.0
00-01—Sacramento	8	304	25	68	.368	24	29	.828	7	28	35	26	20	9	19	79	4.4	3.3	9.9
01-02—Sacramento	16	644	54	132	.409	52	65	.800	19	73	92	79	33	9	44	177	5.8	4.9	11.1
02-03—Sacramento	12	381	37	99	.374	29	31	.935	15	59	74	55	12	3	22	109	6.2	4.6	9.1
03-04—Sacramento	12	461	56	141	.397	41	48	.854	17	57	74	47	22	5	22	166	6.2	3.9	13.8
Totals	58	1896	179	468	.382	149	179	.832	60	224	284	219	93	29	116	552	4.9	3.8	9.5

Three-point field goals: 1992-93, 1-for-3 (.333). 1999-00, 3-for-8 (.375). 2000-01, 5-for-17 (.294). 2001-02, 17-for-64 (.266). 2002-03, 6-for-24 (.250). 2003-04, 13-for-33 (.391). Totals, 15-for-119 (.202).

Personal fouls/disqualifications: 1992-93, 5/0. 1994-95, 3/0. 1999-00, 10/0. 2000-01, 31/1. 2001-02, 64/3. 2002-03, 22/0. 2003-04, 35/0. Totals, 170/4.

CLAXTON, SPEEDY   G   HAWKS

PERSONAL: Born May 8, 1978, in Hempstead, N.Y. ... 5-11/166. (1.80/75.3).
HIGH SCHOOL: Christ the King (Middle Village, N.Y.).
COLLEGE: Hofstra.
TRANSACTIONS/CAREER NOTES: Selected by Philadelphia 76ers in first round (20th pick overall) of 2000 NBA Draft. ... Traded by 76ers to San Antonio Spurs for F/C Mark Bryant, draft rights to G/F John Salmons and draft rights to F Randy Holcomb (June 26, 2002). ... Signed as free agent by Golden State Warriors (July 23, 2003) ... Traded by Warriors with F Dale Davis to New Orleans Hornets for G Baron Davis (February 24, 2005). ... Signed as free agent by Atlanta Hawks (July 12, 2006).
MISCELLANEOUS: Member of NBA championship team (2003).

COLLEGIATE RECORD

Season Team	G	Min.	FGM	FGA	Pct.	FTM	FTA	Pct.	Reb.	Ast.	Pts.	AVERAGES RPG	APG	PPG
96-97—Hofstra	27	916	134	310	.432	132	187	.706	123	91	406	4.6	3.4	15.0
97-98—Hofstra	31	1081	182	375	.485	138	189	.730	144	224	504	4.6	7.2	16.3
98-99—Hofstra	30	970	136	282	.482	121	151	.801	131	159	399	4.4	5.3	13.3
99-00—Hofstra	31	1089	253	538	.470	149	195	.764	168	186	706	5.4	6.0	22.8
Totals	119	4056	705	1505	.468	540	722	.748	566	660	2015	4.8	5.5	16.9

Three-point field goals: 1996-97, 6-for-38 (.158). 1997-98, 2-for-11 (.182). 1998-99, 6-for-19 (.316). 1999-00, 51-for-134 (.381). Totals, 65-for-202 (.322).

NBA REGULAR-SEASON RECORD

Season Team	G	Min.	FGM	FGA	Pct.	FTM	FTA	Pct.	REBOUNDS Off.	Def.	Tot.	Ast.	St.	Blk.	TO	Pts.	AVERAGES RPG	APG	PPG
00-01—Philadelphia						Did not play—injured.													
01-02—Philadelphia	67	1528	181	452	.400	114	136	.838	46	114	160	198	95	6	95	480	2.4	3.0	7.2
02-03—San Antonio	30	471	67	145	.462	39	57	.684	22	34	56	75	22	7	35	173	1.9	2.5	5.8
03-04—Golden State ...	60	1595	224	524	.427	182	224	.813	38	118	156	267	97	9	102	634	2.6	4.5	10.6
04-05—G.S.-N.O.	62	1866	257	611	.421	187	254	.736	37	147	184	374	109	8	119	712	3.0	6.0	11.5
05-06—NO/Okla. City ..	71	2019	304	736	.413	246	320	.769	39	154	193	339	108	6	154	871	2.7	4.8	12.3
Totals	290	7479	1033	2468	.419	768	991	.775	182	567	749	1253	431	36	505	2870	2.6	4.3	9.9

Three-point field goals: 2001-02, 4-for-33 (.121). 2002-03, 0-for-11. 2003-04, 4-for-22 (.182). 2004-05, 11-for-61 (.180). 2005-06, 17-for-63 (.270). Totals, 36-for-190 (.189).

Personal fouls/disqualifications: 2001-02, 145/1. 2002-03, 43/0. 2003-04, 146/2. 2004-05, 184/7. 2005-06, 177/1. Totals, 695/11.

NBA PLAYOFF RECORD

Season Team	G	Min.	FGM	FGA	Pct.	FTM	FTA	Pct.	REBOUNDS Off.	Def.	Tot.	Ast.	St.	Blk.	TO	Pts.	AVERAGES RPG	APG	PPG
01-02—Philadelphia	5	49	4	12	.333	4	6	.667	1	0	1	14	5	0	3	12	0.2	2.8	2.4
02-03—San Antonio	24	326	46	105	.438	33	44	.750	7	38	45	45	16	5	24	125	1.9	1.9	5.2
Totals	29	375	50	117	.427	37	50	.740	8	38	46	59	21	5	27	137	1.6	2.0	4.7

Three-point field goals: 2001-02, 0-for-1. Totals, 0-for-1 (.000).
Personal fouls/disqualifications: 2001-02, 8/0. 2002-03, 38/0. Totals, 46/0.

CLEAVES, MATEEN   G

PERSONAL: Born September 7, 1977, in Flint, Mich. ... 6-3/210. (1.91/95.3).
HIGH SCHOOL: Northern (Flint, Mich.).
COLLEGE: Michigan State.
TRANSACTIONS/CAREER NOTES: Selected by Detroit Pistons in first round (14th pick overall) of 2000 NBA Draft. ... Traded by Pistons to Sacramento Kings for G Jon Barry and future first-round draft choice (September 7, 2001). ... Traded by Kings to Cleveland Cavaliers for G Jumaine Jones (September 10, 2002); trade voided because Cleaves failed physical (September 17, 2002). ... Played in NBA Development League with Huntsville Flight (2003-04). ... Signed by Cavaliers to 10-day contract (March 29, 2004). ... Waived by Cavaliers (April 6, 2004). ... Signed by Seattle SuperSonics (October 4, 2004). ... Waived by SuperSonics (October 28, 2004). ... Re-signed by SuperSonics (November 5, 2004). ... Waived by SuperSonics (January 4, 2006). ... Re-signed by SuperSonics to first of consecutive 10-day contracts (January 28, 2006).
MISCELLANEOUS: Member of bronze-medal-winning U.S. World Championship team (1998).

COLLEGIATE RECORD
NOTES: Member of NCAA Division I championship team (2000). ... NCAA Division I Tournament Most Outstanding Player (2000). ... The SPORTING NEWS All-America first team (2000). ... The SPORTING NEWS All-America second team (1999).

Season Team	G	Min.	FGM	FGA	Pct.	FTM	FTA	Pct.	Reb.	Ast.	Pts.	AVERAGES RPG	APG	PPG
96-97—Michigan State	29	750	111	277	.401	57	79	.722	73	146	297	2.5	5.0	10.2
97-98—Michigan State	30	1005	161	403	.400	111	158	.703	75	217	484	2.5	7.2	16.1
98-99—Michigan State	38	1185	159	392	.406	85	108	.787	62	274	445	1.6	7.2	11.7
99-00—Michigan State	26	820	109	259	.421	65	86	.756	46	179	315	1.8	6.9	12.1
Totals	123	3760	540	1331	.406	318	431	.738	256	816	1541	2.1	6.6	12.5

Three-point field goals: 1996-97, 18-for-76 (.237). 1997-98, 51-for-152 (.336). 1998-99, 42-for-144 (.292). 1999-00, 32-for-85 (.376). Totals, 143-for-457 (.313).

NBA REGULAR-SEASON RECORD

Season Team	G	Min.	FGM	FGA	Pct.	FTM	FTA	Pct.	REBOUNDS Off.	Def.	Tot.	Ast.	St.	Blk.	TO	Pts.	AVERAGES RPG	APG	PPG
00-01—Detroit	78	1268	160	400	.400	97	137	.708	26	106	132	207	49	1	139	422	1.7	2.7	5.4
01-02—Sacramento	32	153	30	68	.441	8	9	.889	1	7	8	25	7	0	27	70	0.3	0.8	2.2
02-03—Sacramento	12	55	6	23	.261	3	4	.750	1	7	8	10	2	0	14	16	0.7	0.8	1.3
03-04—Cleveland	4	92	7	23	.304	1	2	.500	1	6	7	19	4	2	5	15	1.8	4.8	3.8
04-05—Seattle	14	65	5	14	.357	3	4	.750	2	4	6	7	2	0	13	13	0.4	0.5	0.9
05-06—Seattle	27	230	25	71	.352	19	24	.792	2	12	14	42	3	2	14	73	0.5	1.6	2.7
Totals	167	1863	233	599	.389	131	180	.728	33	142	175	310	67	5	201	609	1.0	1.9	3.6

Three-point field goals: 2000-01, 5-for-17 (.294). 2001-02, 2-for-8 (.250). 2002-03, 1-for-1 (1.000). 2003-04, 0-for-1. 2004-05, 0-for-2. 2005-06, 4-for-16 (.250). Totals, 12-for-45 (.267).
Personal fouls/disqualifications: 2000-01, 153/1. 2001-02, 9/0. 2002-03, 6/0. 2003-04, 13/0. 2004-05, 2/0. 2005-06, 30/0. Totals, 213/1.

NBA DEVELOPMENT LEAGUE RECORD

Season Team	G	Min.	FGM	FGA	Pct.	FTM	FTA	Pct.	Reb.	Ast.	Pts.	AVERAGES RPG	APG	PPG
03-04—Huntsville	42	1235	209	459	.455	145	186	.780	216	121	615	5.1	2.9	14.6
05-06—Fayetteville....................	11	360	71	145	.490	47	63	.746	33	76	206	3.0	6.9	18.7
Totals	53	1595	280	604	.464	192	249	.771	249	197	821	4.7	3.7	15.5

Three-point field goals: 2003-04, 13-for-26 (.500). 2005-06, 17-for-37 (.459). Totals, 30-for-63 (.476).

COLLINS, JARRON   F   JAZZ

PERSONAL: Born December 2, 1978, in Northridge, Calif. ... 6-11/255. (2.11/115.7). ... Full name: Jarron Thomas Collins ... Twin brother of Jason Collins, center, New Jersey Nets.
HIGH SCHOOL: Harvard-Westlake (North Hollywood, Calif.).
COLLEGE: Stanford.
TRANSACTIONS/CAREER NOTES: Selected by Utah Jazz in second round (53rd pick overall) of 2001 NBA Draft.

COLLEGIATE RECORD

Season Team	G	Min.	FGM	FGA	Pct.	FTM	FTA	Pct.	Reb.	Ast.	Pts.	AVERAGES RPG	APG	PPG
97-98—Stanford	34	460	44	83	.530	39	64	.609	119	18	128	3.5	0.5	3.8
98-99—Stanford	30	516	58	117	.496	60	101	.594	157	53	176	5.2	1.8	5.9
99-00—Stanford	31	850	114	235	.485	113	157	.720	201	53	342	6.5	1.7	11.0
00-01—Stanford	34	963	154	276	.558	125	182	.687	229	47	435	6.7	1.4	12.8
Totals	129	2789	370	711	.520	337	504	.669	706	171	1081	5.5	1.3	8.4

Three-point field goals: 1997-98, 1-for-5 (.200). 1998-99, 0-for-1. 1999-00, 1-for-4 (.250). 2000-01, 2-for-6 (.333). Totals, 4-for-16 (.250).
Personal fouls/disqualifications: 1997-98, 69/0. 1998-99, 70/0. 1999-00, 76/0. 2000-01, 69/0. Totals, 284/0.

NBA REGULAR-SEASON RECORD

Season Team	G	Min.	FGM	FGA	Pct.	FTM	FTA	Pct.	Off.	Def.	Tot.	Ast.	St.	Blk.	TO	Pts.	RPG	APG	PPG
									REBOUNDS								AVERAGES		
01-02—Utah	70	1440	158	343	.461	134	181	.740	138	158	296	58	29	22	56	450	4.2	0.8	6.4
02-03—Utah	22	421	38	86	.442	44	62	.710	32	28	60	14	5	6	19	120	2.7	0.6	5.5
03-04—Utah	81	1732	147	295	.498	188	262	.718	117	199	316	77	26	18	79	482	3.9	1.0	6.0
04-05—Utah	50	961	65	157	.414	83	119	.697	57	107	164	61	11	6	34	213	3.3	1.2	4.3
05-06—Utah	79	1730	129	280	.461	157	219	.717	134	199	333	97	36	27	61	415	4.2	1.2	5.3
Totals	302	6284	537	1161	.463	606	843	.719	478	691	1169	307	107	79	249	1680	3.9	1.0	5.6

Three-point field goals: 2001-02, 0-for-1. 2002-03, 0-for-1. 2003-04, 0-for-1. 2004-05, 0-for-1. Totals, 0-for-4 (.000).
Personal fouls/disqualifications: 2001-02, 234/4. 2002-03, 70/2. 2003-04, 255/3. 2004-05, 146/1. 2005-06, 252/7. Totals, 957/17.

NBA PLAYOFF RECORD

Season Team	G	Min.	FGM	FGA	Pct.	FTM	FTA	Pct.	Off.	Def.	Tot.	Ast.	St.	Blk.	TO	Pts.	RPG	APG	PPG
									REBOUNDS								AVERAGES		
01-02—Utah	4	47	10	18	.556	2	2	1.000	4	3	7	0	0	0	4	22	1.8	0.0	5.5

Personal fouls/disqualifications: 2001-02, 11/0. Totals, 11/0.

COLLINS, JASON   C   NETS

PERSONAL: Born December 2, 1978, in Northridge, Calif. ... 7-0/260. (2.13/117.9). ... Full name: Jason Paul Collins ... Twin brother of Jarron Collins, forward, Utah Jazz.
HIGH SCHOOL: Harvard-Westlake (North Hollywood, Calif.).
COLLEGE: Stanford.
TRANSACTIONS/CAREER NOTES: Selected by Houston Rockets in first round (18th pick overall) of 2001 NBA Draft. ... Draft rights traded by Rockets with draft rights to F Richard Jefferson and G Brandon Armstrong to New Jersey Nets for draft rights to F Eddie Griffin (June 27, 2001).

COLLEGIATE RECORD

NOTES: Granted medical redshirt (1997-98 and 1998-99).

Season Team	G	Min.	FGM	FGA	Pct.	FTM	FTA	Pct.	Reb.	Ast.	Pts.	RPG	APG	PPG
												AVERAGES		
97-98—Stanford	1	15	1	4	.250	5	7	.714	6	0	7	6.0	0.0	7.0
98-99—Stanford	7	89	9	18	.500	11	23	.478	23	2	29	3.3	0.3	4.1
99-00—Stanford	31	607	84	135	.622	88	133	.662	190	20	256	6.1	0.6	8.3
00-01—Stanford	34	895	168	271	.620	145	185	.784	265	51	493	7.8	1.5	14.5
Totals	73	1606	262	428	.612	249	348	.716	484	73	785	6.6	1.0	10.8

Three-point field goals: 1999-00, 0-for-1. 2000-01, 12-for-26 (.462). Totals, 12-for-27 (.444).
Personal fouls/disqualifications: 1997-98, 4/0. 1998-99, 7/0. 1999-00, 71/0. 2000-01, 79/0. Totals, 166/0.

NBA REGULAR-SEASON RECORD

Season Team	G	Min.	FGM	FGA	Pct.	FTM	FTA	Pct.	Off.	Def.	Tot.	Ast.	St.	Blk.	TO	Pts.	RPG	APG	PPG
									REBOUNDS								AVERAGES		
01-02—New Jersey	77	1407	117	278	.421	115	164	.701	132	169	301	31	29	47	72	350	3.9	1.1	4.5
02-03—New Jersey	81	1900	140	338	.414	180	236	.763	136	232	368	87	47	44	85	460	4.5	1.1	5.7
03-04—New Jersey	78	2220	163	384	.424	136	184	.739	143	257	400	153	67	56	97	462	5.1	2.0	5.9
04-05—New Jersey	80	2542	186	451	.412	137	209	.656	153	335	488	105	71	71	91	511	6.1	1.3	6.4
05-06—New Jersey	71	1895	104	262	.397	44	86	.512	93	249	342	70	46	40	61	255	4.8	1.0	3.6
Totals	387	9964	710	1713	.414	612	879	.696	657	1242	1899	496	260	258	406	2038	4.9	1.3	5.3

Three-point field goals: 2001-02, 1-for-2 (.500). 2002-03, 0-for-4. 2003-04, 0-for-2. 2004-05, 2-for-6 (.333). 2005-06, 3-for-12 (.250). Totals, 6-for-26 (.231).
Personal fouls/disqualifications: 2001-02, 173/1. 2002-03, 252/4. 2003-04, 251/2. 2004-05, 322/14. 2005-06, 251/7. Totals, 1249/28.

NBA PLAYOFF RECORD

Season Team	G	Min.	FGM	FGA	Pct.	FTM	FTA	Pct.	Off.	Def.	Tot.	Ast.	St.	Blk.	TO	Pts.	RPG	APG	PPG
									REBOUNDS								AVERAGES		
01-02—New Jersey	17	227	12	33	.364	25	38	.658	24	17	41	7	5	6	12	49	2.4	0.4	2.9
02-03—New Jersey	20	529	33	91	.363	51	61	.836	51	74	125	17	13	12	18	117	6.3	0.9	5.9
03-04—New Jersey	11	266	14	38	.368	12	16	.750	18	26	44	17	3	10	15	40	4.0	1.5	3.6
04-05—New Jersey	4	128	4	17	.235	3	8	.375	9	17	26	1	2	0	5	11	6.5	0.3	2.8
05-06—New Jersey	11	302	9	25	.360	13	22	.591	20	35	55	3	5	2	9	31	5.0	0.3	2.8
Totals	63	1452	72	204	.353	104	145	.717	122	169	291	45	28	30	59	248	4.6	0.7	3.9

Three-point field goals: 2002-03, 0-for-2. Totals, 0-for-2 (.000).
Personal fouls/disqualifications: 2001-02, 48/2. 2002-03, 74/2. 2003-04, 49/2. 2004-05, 19/0. 2005-06, 55/3. Totals, 245/9.

COLLISON, NICK   F   SUPERSONICS

PERSONAL: Born October 26, 1980, in Orange City, Iowa. ... 6-9/255. (2.06/115.7). ... Full name: Nicholas John Collison
HIGH SCHOOL: Iowa Falls (Iowa Falls, Iowa).
COLLEGE: Kansas.
TRANSACTIONS/CAREER NOTES: Selected by Seattle SuperSonics in first round (12th pick overall) of 2003 NBA Draft.

COLLEGIATE RECORD

NOTES: The SPORTING NEWS All-America second team (2003).

Season Team	G	Min.	FGM	FGA	Pct.	FTM	FTA	Pct.	Reb.	Ast.	Pts.	RPG	APG	PPG
												AVERAGES		
99-00—Kansas	34	774	145	292	.497	62	92	.674	234	38	357	6.9	1.1	10.5
00-01—Kansas	33	892	187	313	.597	85	136	.625	222	71	461	6.7	2.2	14.0

Season Team	G	Min.	FGM	FGA	Pct.	FTM	FTA	Pct.	Reb.	Ast.	Pts.	RPG	APG	PPG
01-02—Kansas	37	990	245	414	.592	84	146	.575	307	64	577	8.3	1.7	15.6
02-03—Kansas	38	1232	281	507	.554	127	200	.635	380	84	702	10.0	2.2	18.5
Totals	142	3888	858	1526	.562	358	574	.624	1143	257	2097	8.0	1.8	14.8

Three-point field goals: 1999-00, 5-for-13 (.385). 2000-01, 2-for-5 (.400). 2001-02, 3-for-8 (.375). 2002-03, 13-for-38 (.342). Totals, 23-for-64 (.359).

NBA REGULAR-SEASON RECORD

Season Team	G	Min.	FGM	FGA	Pct.	FTM	FTA	Pct.	REBOUNDS Off.	Def.	Tot.	Ast.	St.	Blk.	TO	Pts.	RPG	APG	PPG
03-04—Seattle									Did not play—injured										
04-05—Seattle	82	1396	190	354	.537	83	118	.703	156	220	376	32	34	50	62	463	4.6	0.4	5.6
05-06—Seattle	66	1448	207	394	.525	79	113	.699	143	225	368	74	21	35	77	493	5.6	1.1	7.5
Totals	148	2844	397	748	.531	162	231	.701	299	445	744	106	55	85	139	956	5.0	0.7	6.5

Three-point field goals: 2004-05, 0-for-3. 2005-06, 0-for-3. Totals, 0-for-6 (.000).
Personal fouls/disqualifications: 2004-05, 252/4. 2005-06, 213/4. Totals, 465/8.

NBA PLAYOFF RECORD

Season Team	G	Min.	FGM	FGA	Pct.	FTM	FTA	Pct.	REBOUNDS Off.	Def.	Tot.	Ast.	St.	Blk.	TO	Pts.	RPG	APG	PPG
04-05—Seattle	11	218	37	61	.607	17	27	.630	22	33	55	5	3	5	6	92	5.0	0.5	8.4

Three-point field goals: 2004-05, 1-for-1 (1.000). Totals, 1-for-1 (1.000).
Personal fouls/disqualifications: 2004-05, 40/0. Totals, 40/0.

C

COOK, BRIAN   F   LAKERS

PERSONAL: Born December 4, 1980, in Lincoln, Ill. ... 6-10/240. (2.08/108.9). ... Full name: Brian Joshua Cook
HIGH SCHOOL: Lincoln (Lincoln, Ill.).
COLLEGE: Illinois.
TRANSACTIONS/CAREER NOTES: Selected by Los Angeles Lakers in first round (24th pick overall) of 2003 NBA Draft.

COLLEGIATE RECORD

NOTES: The SPORTING NEWS All-America second team (2003).

Season Team	G	Min.	FGM	FGA	Pct.	FTM	FTA	Pct.	Reb.	Ast.	Pts.	RPG	APG	PPG
99-00—Illinois	32	595	112	213	.526	51	83	.614	143	24	287	4.5	0.8	9.0
00-01—Illinois	35	846	147	269	.546	69	86	.802	212	43	391	6.1	1.2	11.2
01-02—Illinois	35	1008	174	342	.509	96	110	.873	233	44	471	6.7	1.3	13.5
02-03—Illinois	30	940	202	422	.479	168	205	.820	227	60	599	7.6	2.0	20.0
Totals	132	3389	635	1246	.510	384	484	.793	815	171	1748	6.2	1.3	13.2

Three-point field goals: 1999-00, 12-for-38 (.316). 2000-01, 28-for-76 (.368). 2001-02, 27-for-74 (.365). 2002-03, 27-for-89 (.303). Totals, 94-for-277 (.339).

NBA REGULAR-SEASON RECORD

Season Team	G	Min.	FGM	FGA	Pct.	FTM	FTA	Pct.	REBOUNDS Off.	Def.	Tot.	Ast.	St.	Blk.	TO	Pts.	RPG	APG	PPG
03-04—L.A. Lakers	35	442	67	141	.475	21	28	.750	31	70	101	20	16	16	17	155	2.9	0.6	4.4
04-05—L.A. Lakers	72	1087	176	422	.417	28	37	.757	63	153	216	35	23	26	29	458	3.0	0.5	6.4
05-06—L.A. Lakers	81	1535	261	511	.511	84	101	.832	88	186	274	74	37	32	61	642	3.4	0.9	7.9
Totals	188	3064	504	1074	.469	133	166	.801	182	409	591	129	76	74	107	1255	3.1	0.7	6.7

Three-point field goals: 2003-04, 0-for-5. 2004-05, 78-for-199 (.392). 2005-06, 36-for-84 (.429). Totals, 114-for-288 (.396).
Personal fouls/disqualifications: 2003-04, 64/0. 2004-05, 139/3. 2005-06, 205/3. Totals, 408/6.

NBA PLAYOFF RECORD

Season Team	G	Min.	FGM	FGA	Pct.	FTM	FTA	Pct.	REBOUNDS Off.	Def.	Tot.	Ast.	St.	Blk.	TO	Pts.	RPG	APG	PPG
03-04—L.A. Lakers	13	46	5	15	.333	2	2	1.000	3	9	12	1	1	0	3	12	0.9	0.1	0.9
05-06—L.A. Lakers	7	78	18	46	.391	4	4	1.000	11	11	22	8	1	0	3	44	3.1	1.1	6.3
Totals	20	124	23	61	.377	6	6	1.000	14	20	34	9	2	0	6	56	1.7	0.5	2.8

Three-point field goals: 2005-06, 4-for-11 (.364). Totals, 4-for-11 (.364).
Personal fouls/disqualifications: 2003-04, 7/0. 2005-06, 15/0. Totals, 22/0.

CRAWFORD, JAMAL   G   KNICKS

PERSONAL: Born March 20, 1980, in Seattle. ... 6-5/175. (1.96/79.4).
HIGH SCHOOL: Rainier Beach (Seattle).
COLLEGE: Michigan.
TRANSACTIONS/CAREER NOTES: Selected after freshman season by Cleveland Cavaliers in first round (eighth pick overall) of 2000 NBA Draft. ... Draft rights traded by Cavaliers with cash to Chicago Bulls for draft rights to F/C Chris Mihm (June 28, 2000). ... Traded by Bulls with F Jerome Williams to New York Knicks for F Othella Harrington, C Dikembe Mutombo, C Cezary Trybanski and G Frank Williams (August 5, 2004).

COLLEGIATE RECORD

Season Team	G	Min.	FGM	FGA	Pct.	FTM	FTA	Pct.	Reb.	Ast.	Pts.	RPG	APG	PPG
99-00—Michigan	17	577	105	255	.412	40	51	.784	47	76	283	2.8	4.5	16.6

Three-point field goals: 1999-00, 33-for-101 (.327). Totals, 33-for-101 (.327).

NBA REGULAR-SEASON RECORD

								REBOUNDS									AVERAGES		
Season Team	G	Min.	FGM	FGA	Pct.	FTM	FTA	Pct.	Off.	Def.	Tot.	Ast.	St.	Blk.	TO	Pts.	RPG	APG	PPG
00-01—Chicago	61	1050	107	304	.352	27	34	.794	9	80	89	141	43	14	85	282	1.5	2.3	4.6
01-02—Chicago	23	481	89	187	.476	10	13	.769	5	29	34	55	18	5	32	214	1.5	2.4	9.3
02-03—Chicago	80	1992	334	808	.413	104	129	.806	21	164	185	334	77	25	134	858	2.3	4.2	10.7
03-04—Chicago	80	2811	509	1318	.386	200	240	.833	46	237	283	405	111	29	193	1383	3.5	5.1	17.3
04-05—New York	70	2688	437	1097	.398	182	216	.843	33	170	203	302	92	19	148	1241	2.9	4.3	17.7
05-06—New York	79	2555	366	879	.416	295	357	.826	36	212	248	301	87	15	175	1128	3.1	3.8	14.3
Totals	393	11577	1842	4593	.401	818	989	.827	150	892	1042	1538	428	107	767	5106	2.7	3.9	13.0

Three-point field goals: 2000-01, 41-for-117 (.350). 2001-02, 26-for-58 (.448). 2002-03, 86-for-242 (.355). 2003-04, 165-for-521 (.317). 2004-05, 185-for-512 (.361). 2005-06, 101-for-293 (.345). Totals, 604-for-1743 (.347).

Personal fouls/disqualifications: 2000-01, 68/0. 2001-02, 18/0. 2002-03, 126/0. 2003-04, 161/0. 2004-05, 135/0. 2005-06, 150/0. Totals, 658/0.

CROSHERE, AUSTIN F MAVERICKS

PERSONAL: Born May 1, 1975, in Los Angeles. ... 6-9/242. (2.06/109.8). ... Full name: Austin Nathan Croshere.
HIGH SCHOOL: Crossroads (Los Angeles).
COLLEGE: Providence.
TRANSACTIONS/CAREER NOTES: Selected by Indiana Pacers in first round (12th pick overall) of 1997 NBA Draft. ... Traded by Pacers to Dallas Mavericks for F Marquis Daniels (July 12, 2006).

COLLEGIATE RECORD

											AVERAGES		
Season Team	G	Min.	FGM	FGA	Pct.	FTM	FTA	Pct.	Reb.	Ast.	Pts.	RPG	APG	PPG
93-94—Providence	25	233	38	95	.400	29	40	.725	55	3	115	2.2	0.1	4.6
94-95—Providence	30	570	106	231	.459	66	85	.776	147	33	307	4.9	1.1	10.2
95-96—Providence	30	863	151	359	.421	109	128	.852	173	33	458	5.8	1.1	15.3
96-97—Providence	36	1192	200	440	.455	182	205	.888	270	54	643	7.5	1.5	17.9
Totals	121	2858	495	1125	.440	386	458	.843	645	123	1523	5.3	1.0	12.6

Three-point field goals: 1993-94, 10-for-31 (.323). 1994-95, 29-for-85 (.341). 1995-96, 47-for-141 (.333). 1996-97, 61-for-175 (.349). Totals, 147-for-432 (.340).

NBA REGULAR-SEASON RECORD

								REBOUNDS									AVERAGES		
Season Team	G	Min.	FGM	FGA	Pct.	FTM	FTA	Pct.	Off.	Def.	Tot.	Ast.	St.	Blk.	TO	Pts.	RPG	APG	PPG
97-98—Indiana...........	26	243	32	86	.372	8	14	.571	10	35	45	8	9	5	13	76	1.7	0.3	2.9
98-99—Indiana...........	27	249	32	75	.427	20	23	.870	16	29	45	10	7	8	23	92	1.7	0.4	3.4
99-00—Indiana...........	81	1885	288	653	.441	196	231	.848	135	381	516	89	44	60	121	835	6.4	1.1	10.3
00-01—Indiana...........	81	1874	276	701	.394	200	231	.866	123	264	387	92	36	50	136	822	4.8	1.1	10.1
01-02—Indiana...........	76	1286	185	448	.413	97	114	.851	74	220	294	77	26	29	67	516	3.9	1.0	6.8
02-03—Indiana...........	49	633	86	209	.411	53	65	.815	40	115	155	56	6	13	28	252	3.2	1.1	5.1
03-04—Indiana...........	77	1001	113	307	.368	81	100	.810	79	181	260	91	31	11	55	307	3.2	1.2	4.0
04-05—Indiana...........	73	1827	188	497	.378	226	256	.883	103	272	375	98	48	17	104	647	5.1	1.3	8.9
05-06—Indiana...........	50	1148	132	285	.463	90	102	.882	62	203	265	62	22	7	48	408	5.3	1.2	8.2
Totals	540	10196	1338	3261	.410	983	1140	.862	623	1702	2325	544	222	203	595	4035	4.3	1.0	7.5

Three-point field goals: 1997-98, 4-for-13 (.308). 1998-99, 8-for-29 (.276). 1999-00, 63-for-174 (.362). 2000-01, 70-for-207 (.338). 2001-02, 49-for-145 (.338). 2002-03, 27-for-69 (.391). 2003-04, 56-for-144 (.389). 2004-05, 45-for-174 (.259). 2005-06, 54-for-140 (.386). Totals, 376-for-1095 (.343).

Personal fouls/disqualifications: 1997-98, 32/1. 1998-99, 32/0. 1999-00, 203/2. 2000-01, 180/1. 2001-02, 106/0. 2002-03, 48/0. 2003-04, 101/0. 2004-05, 154/1. 2005-06, 105/2. Totals, 961/7.

NBA PLAYOFF RECORD

NOTES: Shares NBA Finals single-game record for most free throws made in one quarter—9 (June 16, 2000, vs. Los Angeles Lakers).

								REBOUNDS									AVERAGES		
Season Team	G	Min.	FGM	FGA	Pct.	FTM	FTA	Pct.	Off.	Def.	Tot.	Ast.	St.	Blk.	TO	Pts.	RPG	APG	PPG
98-99—Indiana...........	1	1	0	1	.000	2	2	1.000	1	0	1	0	0	0	0	2	1.0	0.0	2.0
99-00—Indiana...........	23	490	64	153	.418	73	87	.839	31	78	109	19	9	16	25	216	4.7	0.8	9.4
00-01—Indiana...........	4	129	14	35	.400	13	15	.867	5	15	20	6	4	2	9	43	5.0	1.5	10.8
01-02—Indiana...........	4	59	8	20	.400	6	8	.750	4	10	14	2	1	1	6	24	3.5	0.5	6.0
02-03—Indiana...........	4	46	5	19	.263	6	7	.857	8	9	17	3	0	1	3	16	4.3	0.8	4.0
03-04—Indiana...........	13	214	19	55	.345	17	21	.810	13	27	40	12	4	3	6	63	3.1	0.9	4.8
04-05—Indiana...........	10	88	4	10	.400	15	18	.833	7	10	17	0	4	1	6	25	1.7	0.0	2.5
05-06—Indiana...........	6	175	12	38	.316	16	18	.889	5	17	22	7	5	0	6	49	3.7	1.2	8.2
Totals	65	1202	126	331	.381	148	176	.841	74	166	240	49	27	24	61	438	3.7	0.8	6.7

Three-point field goals: 1999-00, 15-for-37 (.405). 2000-01, 2-for-10 (.200). 2001-02, 2-for-6 (.333). 2002-03, 0-for-6. 2003-04, 8-for-24 (.333). 2004-05, 2-for-4 (.500). 2005-06, 9-for-23 (.391). Totals, 38-for-110 (.345).

Personal fouls/disqualifications: 1999-00, 51/0. 2000-01, 15/1. 2001-02, 7/1. 2002-03, 5/0. 2003-04, 17/1. 2004-05, 10/0. 2005-06, 11/0. Totals, 116/3.

CURRY, EDDY F/C BULLS

PERSONAL: Born December 5, 1982, in Harvey, Ill. ... 6-11/285. (2.11/129.3).
HIGH SCHOOL: Thornwood (South Holland, Ill.).
COLLEGE: Did not attend college.
TRANSACTIONS/CAREER NOTES: Selected out of high school by Chicago Bulls in first round (fourth pick overall) of 2001 NBA Draft. ... Traded by Bulls with F/C Antonio Davis to New York Knicks for F Tim Thomas, F Michael Sweetney and G Jermaine Jackson and 2007 and 2009 second-round draft picks, a conditional 2006 first-round pick and a conditional right to swap 2007 first-round picks (October 4, 2005).

C

NBA REGULAR-SEASON RECORD

Season Team	G	Min.	FGM	FGA	Pct.	FTM	FTA	Pct.	Off.	Def.	Tot.	Ast.	St.	Blk.	TO	Pts.	RPG	APG	PPG
01-02—Chicago	72	1150	189	377	.501	105	160	.656	111	161	272	25	16	53	69	483	3.8	0.3	6.7
02-03—Chicago	81	1571	335	573	*.585	179	287	.624	116	237	353	37	18	62	137	849	4.4	0.5	10.5
03-04—Chicago	73	2154	417	840	.496	235	350	.671	143	308	451	68	24	83	177	1070	6.2	0.9	14.7
04-05—Chicago	63	1808	393	730	.538	226	314	.720	116	222	338	37	21	58	163	1012	5.4	0.6	16.1
05-06—New York	72	1865	336	597	.563	307	486	.632	145	287	432	19	28	56	179	979	6.0	0.3	13.6
Totals	361	8548	1670	3117	.536	1052	1597	.659	631	1215	1846	186	107	312	725	4393	5.1	0.5	12.2

Three-point field goals: 2003-04, 1-for-1 (1.000). Totals, 1-for-1 (1.000).
Personal fouls/disqualifications: 2001-02, 173/0. 2002-03, 226/3. 2003-04, 258/11. 2004-05, 202/4. 2005-06, 239/4. Totals, 1098/22.

DALEMBERT, SAMUEL　　　　　C　　　　　76ERS

PERSONAL: Born May 10, 1981, in Port-Au-Prince, Haiti. ... 6-11/250. (2.11/113.4). ... Full name: Samuel Davis Dalembert
HIGH SCHOOL: Surenpagge (Montreal), then St. Patrick's (Elizabeth, N.J.).
COLLEGE: Seton Hall.
TRANSACTIONS/CAREER NOTES: Selected after sophomore season by Philadelphia 76ers in first round (26th pick overall) of 2001 NBA Draft.

COLLEGIATE RECORD

Season Team	G	Min.	FGM	FGA	Pct.	FTM	FTA	Pct.	Reb.	Ast.	Pts.	RPG	APG	PPG
99-00—Seton Hall...................	30	643	75	149	.503	29	56	.518	179	10	179	6.0	0.3	6.0
00-01—Seton Hall...................	29	622	100	177	.565	40	72	.556	166	9	240	5.7	0.3	8.3
Totals	59	1265	175	326	.537	69	128	.539	345	19	419	5.8	0.3	7.1

Personal fouls/disqualifications: 1999-00, 92/0. 2000-01, 95/0. Totals, 187/0.

NBA REGULAR-SEASON RECORD

Season Team	G	Min.	FGM	FGA	Pct.	FTM	FTA	Pct.	Off.	Def.	Tot.	Ast.	St.	Blk.	TO	Pts.	RPG	APG	PPG
01-02—Philadelphia ..	34	177	22	50	.440	7	18	.389	25	43	68	5	6	13	14	51	2.0	0.1	1.5
02-03—Philadelphia...								Did not play—injured											
03-04—Philadelphia ..	82	2198	270	499	.541	112	174	.644	194	432	626	21	44	189	86	652	7.6	0.3	8.0
04-05—Philadelphia ..	72	1785	250	477	.524	89	148	.601	187	355	542	35	46	121	114	589	7.5	0.5	8.2
05-06—Philadelphia ..	66	1761	196	369	.531	93	132	.705	159	382	541	25	34	160	107	485	8.2	0.4	7.3
Totals	254	5921	738	1395	.529	301	472	.638	565	1212	1777	86	130	483	321	1777	7.0	0.3	7.0

Three-point field goals: 2003-04, 0-for-1. 2005-06, 0-for-1. Totals, 0-for-2 (.000).
Personal fouls/disqualifications: 2001-02, 30/0. 2003-04, 273/4. 2004-05, 241/4. 2005-06, 244/9. Totals, 788/17.

NBA PLAYOFF RECORD

Season Team	G	Min.	FGM	FGA	Pct.	FTM	FTA	Pct.	Off.	Def.	Tot.	Ast.	St.	Blk.	TO	Pts.	RPG	APG	PPG
04-05—Philadelphia ..	5	192	26	47	.553	6	15	.400	18	46	64	2	2	7	9	58	12.8	0.4	11.6

Personal fouls/disqualifications: 2004-05, 19/0. Totals, 19/0.

DAMPIER, ERICK　　　　　C　　　　　MAVERICKS

PERSONAL: Born July 14, 1974, in Jackson, Miss. ... 6-11/265. (2.11/120.2). ... Full name: Erick Trevez Dampier
HIGH SCHOOL: Lawrence County (Monticello, Miss.).
COLLEGE: Mississippi State.
TRANSACTIONS/CAREER NOTES: Selected after junior season by Indiana Pacers in first round (10th pick overall) of 1996 NBA Draft. ... Traded by Pacers with F Duane Ferrell to Golden State Warriors for F Chris Mullin (August 12, 1997). ... Traded by Warriors with G Dan Dickau, C Evan Eschmeyer and draft rights to G Steve Logan to Dallas Mavericks for F/C Christian Laettner, F Eduardo Najera, draft rights to G Luis Flores and G/F Mladen Sekularac, two future first-round draft choices and cash (August 24, 2004).

COLLEGIATE RECORD

Season Team	G	Min.	FGM	FGA	Pct.	FTM	FTA	Pct.	Reb.	Ast.	Pts.	RPG	APG	PPG
93-94—Mississippi State............	29	678	133	226	.588	78	159	.491	251	23	344	8.7	0.8	11.9
94-95—Mississippi State............	30	853	153	239	.640	87	146	.596	291	28	393	9.7	0.9	13.1
95-96—Mississippi State............	34	1112	195	354	.551	104	170	.612	317	77	494	9.3	2.3	14.5
Totals	93	2643	481	819	.587	269	475	.566	859	128	1231	9.2	1.4	13.2

NBA REGULAR-SEASON RECORD

Season Team	G	Min.	FGM	FGA	Pct.	FTM	FTA	Pct.	Off.	Def.	Tot.	Ast.	St.	Blk.	TO	Pts.	RPG	APG	PPG
96-97—Indiana...........	72	1052	131	336	.390	107	168	.637	96	198	294	43	19	73	84	370	4.1	0.6	5.1
97-98—Golden State ...	82	2656	352	791	.445	267	399	.669	272	443	715	94	39	139	175	971	8.7	1.1	11.8
98-99—Golden State ...	50	1414	161	414	.389	120	204	.588	164	218	382	54	26	58	92	442	7.6	1.1	8.8
99-00—Golden State ...	21	495	70	173	.405	27	51	.529	48	86	134	19	8	15	29	167	6.4	0.9	8.0
00-01—Golden State ...	43	1038	126	314	.401	67	126	.532	97	153	250	59	17	58	82	319	5.8	1.4	7.4
01-02—Golden State ...	73	1740	209	480	.435	136	211	.645	167	220	387	87	17	167	156	554	5.3	1.2	7.6
02-03—Golden State ...	82	1978	259	522	.496	155	222	.698	248	295	543	58	27	154	112	673	6.6	0.7	8.2
03-04—Golden State ...	74	2403	348	650	.535	217	332	.654	*344	543	887	60	33	137	131	913	12.0	0.8	12.3
04-05—Dallas.............	59	1609	202	367	.550	138	228	.605	183	318	501	51	15	80	102	542	8.5	0.9	9.2
05-06—Dallas.............	82	1934	171	347	.493	127	215	.591	273	367	640	51	27	106	115	469	7.8	0.6	5.7
Totals	638	16319	2029	4394	.462	1361	2156	.631	1892	2841	4733	576	228	987	1078	5420	7.4	0.9	8.5

Three-point field goals: 1996-97, 1-for-1 (1.000). 1997-98, 0-for-2. 2000-01, 0-for-2. 2002-03, 0-for-2. 2003-04, 0-for-2. 2004-05, 0-for-3. Totals, 1-for-12 (.083).

Personal fouls/disqualifications: 1996-97, 153/1. 1997-98, 281/6. 1998-99, 165/2. 1999-00, 75/1. 2000-01, 123/3. 2001-02, 235/4. 2002-03, 242/3. 2003-04, 227/3. 2004-05, 205/2. 2005-06, 263/3. Totals, 1969/28.

NBA PLAYOFF RECORD

								REBOUNDS							AVERAGES		
Season Team	G	Min.	FGM	FGA	Pct.	FTM	FTA	Pct.	Off.	Def.	Tot.	Ast.	St.	Blk.	TO	Pts.	RPG	APG	PPG
04-05—Dallas	13	308	40	67	.597	11	28	.393	51	46	97	7	7	18	12	91	7.5	0.5	7.0
05-06—Dallas	19	454	34	63	.540	27	44	.614	55	72	127	6	11	24	12	95	6.7	0.3	5.0
Totals	32	762	74	130	.569	38	72	.528	106	118	224	13	18	42	24	186	7.0	0.4	5.8

Three-point field goals: 2004-05, 0-for-1. 2005-06, 0-for-1. Totals, 0-for-2 (.000).
Personal fouls/disqualifications: 2004-05, 54/2. 2005-06, 75/2. Totals, 129/4.

DANIELS, ANTONIO G WIZARDS

PERSONAL: Born March 19, 1975, in Columbus, Ohio. ... 6-4/205. (1.93/93.0). ... Full name: Antonio Robert Daniels
HIGH SCHOOL: St. Francis DeSales (Columbus, Ohio).
COLLEGE: Bowling Green.
TRANSACTIONS/CAREER NOTES: Selected by Vancouver Grizzlies in first round (fourth pick overall) of 1997 NBA Draft. ... Traded by Grizzlies to San Antonio Spurs for F Carl Herrera and draft rights to G Felipe Lopez (June 24, 1998). ... Traded by Spurs with G Charles Smith and F/C Amal McCaskill to Portland Trail Blazers for G Erick Barkley and G Steve Kerr (August 5, 2002). ... Signed as free agent by Seattle SuperSonics (July 19, 2003). ... Signed as free agent by Washington Wizards (August 2, 2005).
MISCELLANEOUS: Member of NBA championship team (1999).

COLLEGIATE RECORD

											AVERAGES		
Season Team	G	Min.	FGM	FGA	Pct.	FTM	FTA	Pct.	Reb.	Ast.	Pts.	RPG	APG	PPG
93-94—Bowling Green State	28	864	132	258	.512	84	103	.816	81	110	354	2.9	3.9	12.6
94-95—Bowling Green State	26	753	97	196	.495	58	83	.699	73	100	268	2.8	3.8	10.3
95-96—Bowling Green State	25	922	142	297	.478	99	137	.723	77	147	400	3.1	5.9	16.0
96-97—Bowling Green State	32	1181	279	510	.547	164	211	.777	90	216	767	2.8	6.8	24.0
Totals	111	3700	650	1261	.515	405	534	.758	321	573	1789	2.9	5.2	16.1

Three-point field goals: 1993-94, 4-for-17 (.235). 1994-95, 16-for-38 (.421). 1995-96, 17-for-37 (.459). 1996-97, 45-for-104 (.433). Totals, 82-for-196 (.418).

NBA REGULAR-SEASON RECORD

								REBOUNDS							AVERAGES		
Season Team	G	Min.	FGM	FGA	Pct.	FTM	FTA	Pct.	Off.	Def.	Tot.	Ast.	St.	Blk.	TO	Pts.	RPG	APG	PPG
97-98—Vancouver	74	1956	228	548	.416	112	170	.659	22	121	143	334	55	10	164	579	1.9	4.5	7.8
98-99—San Antonio	47	614	83	183	.454	49	65	.754	13	41	54	106	30	6	44	220	1.1	2.3	4.7
99-00—San Antonio	68	1195	163	344	.474	72	101	.713	16	70	86	177	55	5	58	420	1.3	2.6	6.2
00-01—San Antonio	79	2060	275	588	.468	121	156	.776	26	137	163	304	61	14	109	745	2.1	3.8	9.4
01-02—San Antonio	82	2175	269	612	.440	158	210	.752	23	153	176	228	48	12	70	753	2.1	2.8	9.2
02-03—Portland	67	872	84	186	.452	65	76	.855	11	61	72	85	33	9	32	251	1.1	1.3	3.7
03-04—Seattle	71	1810	187	500	.374	166	191	.812	28	115	142	236	43	0	61	571	2.0	4.2	8.0
04-05—Seattle	75	2026	273	623	.438	248	304	.816	20	149	169	309	51	3	78	843	2.3	4.1	11.2
05-06—Washington	80	2283	230	550	.418	284	336	.845	19	153	172	284	52	8	89	767	2.2	3.6	9.6
Totals	643	14693	1792	4032	.444	1264	1602	.789	173	1004	1177	2125	430	73	705	5149	1.8	3.3	8.0

Three-point field goals: 1997-98, 11-for-52 (.212). 1998-99, 5-for-17 (.294). 1999-00, 22-for-66 (.333). 2000-01, 74-for-183 (.404). 2001-02, 57-for-196 (.291). 2002-03, 18-for-59 (.305). 2003-04, 42-for-116 (.362). 2004-05, 49-for-165 (.297). 2005-06, 23-for-101 (.228). Totals, 301-for-955 (.315).
Personal fouls/disqualifications: 1997-98, 88/0. 1998-99, 39/0. 1999-00, 73/0. 2000-01, 120/0. 2001-02, 104/0. 2002-03, 43/0. 2003-04, 64/0. 2004-05, 78/0. 2005-06, 96/0. Totals, 705/0.

NBA PLAYOFF RECORD

								REBOUNDS							AVERAGES		
Season Team	G	Min.	FGM	FGA	Pct.	FTM	FTA	Pct.	Off.	Def.	Tot.	Ast.	St.	Blk.	TO	Pts.	RPG	APG	PPG
98-99—San Antonio	15	106	9	21	.429	5	6	.833	1	9	10	16	4	0	10	27	0.7	1.1	1.8
99-00—San Antonio	4	82	9	23	.391	9	13	.692	2	8	10	6	7	0	6	29	2.5	1.5	7.3
00-01—San Antonio	13	406	63	131	.481	33	35	.943	4	22	26	38	7	1	13	176	2.0	2.9	13.5
01-02—San Antonio	10	224	35	77	.455	19	22	.864	3	24	27	15	7	3	5	95	2.7	1.5	9.5
02-03—Portland	6	98	9	19	.474	1	2	.500	3	5	8	12	1	1	2	22	1.3	2.0	3.7
04-05—Seattle	11	331	44	94	.468	60	70	.857	4	27	31	49	11	0	11	152	2.8	4.5	13.8
05-06—Washington	6	216	28	52	.538	20	22	.909	2	15	17	20	3	1	10	79	2.8	3.3	13.2
Totals	65	1463	197	417	.472	147	170	.865	19	110	129	156	40	6	57	580	2.0	2.4	8.9

Three-point field goals: 1998-99, 4-for-6 (.667). 1999-00, 2-for-8 (.250). 2000-01, 17-for-46 (.370). 2001-02, 6-for-16 (.375). 2002-03, 3-for-5 (.600). 2004-05, 4-for-14 (.286). 2005-06, 3-for-11 (.273). Totals, 39-for-106 (.368).
Personal fouls/disqualifications: 1998-99, 7/0. 1999-00, 5/0. 2000-01, 22/0. 2001-02, 13/0. 2002-03, 5/0. 2004-05, 13/0. 2005-06, 4/0. Totals, 69/0.

DANIELS, MARQUIS F PACERS

PERSONAL: Born January 7, 1981, in Orlando, Fla. ... 6-6/200. (1.98/90.7). ... Full name: Marquis Antwane Daniels
HIGH SCHOOL: Mount Zion Christian Academy (Durham, N.C.).
COLLEGE: Auburn.
TRANSACTIONS/CAREER NOTES: Not drafted by an NBA franchise. ... Signed as free agent by Dallas Mavericks (July 29, 2003) ... Traded by Mavericks to Indiana Pacers for F Austin Croshere (July 12, 2006).

COLLEGIATE RECORD

											AVERAGES		
Season Team	G	Min.	FGM	FGA	Pct.	FTM	FTA	Pct.	Reb.	Ast.	Pts.	RPG	APG	PPG
99-00—Auburn	17	216	32	72	.444	10	20	.500	45	8	77	2.6	0.5	4.5

Season Team	G	Min.	FGM	FGA	Pct.	FTM	FTA	Pct.	Reb.	Ast.	Pts.	RPG	APG	PPG
00-01—Auburn	32	974	206	395	.522	80	124	.645	223	50	503	7.0	1.6	15.7
01-02—Auburn	28	807	115	260	.442	73	115	.635	148	116	325	5.3	4.1	11.6
02-03—Auburn	34	1187	244	476	.513	107	159	.673	210	113	625	6.2	3.3	18.4
Totals	111	3184	597	1203	.496	270	418	.646	626	287	1530	5.6	2.6	13.8

Three-point field goals: 1999-00, 3-for-15 (.200). 2000-01, 11-for-48 (.229). 2001-02, 22-for-62 (.355). 2002-03, 30-for-98 (.306). Totals, 66-for-223 (.296).

NBA REGULAR-SEASON RECORD

HONORS: NBA All-Rookie second team (2004).

Season Team	G	Min.	FGM	FGA	Pct.	FTM	FTA	Pct.	Off.	Def.	Tot.	Ast.	St.	Blk.	TO	Pts.	RPG	APG	PPG
03-04—Dallas	56	1039	203	411	.494	60	78	.769	66	80	146	116	53	12	44	477	2.6	2.1	8.5
04-05—Dallas	60	1412	220	504	.437	98	133	.737	87	129	216	128	83	14	86	545	3.6	2.1	9.1
05-06—Dallas	62	1766	246	512	.480	138	183	.754	81	143	224	172	67	13	100	634	3.6	2.8	10.2
Totals	178	4217	669	1427	.469	296	394	.751	234	352	586	416	203	39	230	1656	3.3	2.3	9.3

Three-point field goals: 2003-04, 11-for-36 (.306). 2004-05, 7-for-35 (.200). 2005-06, 4-for-19 (.211). Totals, 22-for-90 (.244).
Personal fouls/disqualifications: 2003-04, 51/0. 2004-05, 124/0. 2005-06, 143/2. Totals, 318/2.

NBA PLAYOFF RECORD

Season Team	G	Min.	FGM	FGA	Pct.	FTM	FTA	Pct.	Off.	Def.	Tot.	Ast.	St.	Blk.	TO	Pts.	RPG	APG	PPG
03-04—Dallas	5	184	32	75	.427	14	22	.636	10	21	31	15	10	3	15	79	6.2	3.0	15.8
04-05—Dallas	11	165	26	60	.433	19	27	.704	15	19	34	14	6	3	13	72	3.1	1.3	6.5
05-06—Dallas	20	222	25	56	.446	16	21	.762	10	11	21	26	5	1	12	68	1.1	1.3	3.4
Totals	36	571	83	191	.435	49	70	.700	35	51	86	55	21	7	40	219	2.4	1.5	6.1

Three-point field goals: 2003-04, 1-for-7 (.143). 2004-05, 1-for-6 (.167). 2005-06, 2-for-5 (.400). Totals, 4-for-18 (.222).
Personal fouls/disqualifications: 2003-04, 14/0. 2004-05, 15/0. 2005-06, 26/0. Totals, 55/0.

DAVIS, ANTONIO   F/C

PERSONAL: Born October 31, 1968, in Oakland. ... 6-9/230. (2.06/104.3). ... Full name: Antonio Lee Davis
HIGH SCHOOL: McClymonds (Oakland).
COLLEGE: Texas-El Paso.
TRANSACTIONS/CAREER NOTES: Selected by Indiana Pacers in second round (45th pick overall) of 1990 NBA Draft. ... Played in Greece (1990-92). ... Played in Italy (1992-93). ... Traded by Pacers to Toronto Raptors for draft rights to F Jonathan Bender (August 1, 1999). ... Traded by Raptors with F Chris Jefferies and F Jerome Williams to Chicago Bulls for F Lonny Baxter, F Donyell Marshall and G Jalen Rose (December 1, 2003). ... Traded by Bulls with C Eddy Curry to New York Knicks for F Tim Thomas, F Michael Sweetney and G Jermaine Jackson and 2007 and 2009 second-round draft picks, a conditional 2006 first-round pick and a conditional right to swap 2007 first-round picks (October 4, 2005). ... Traded by Knicks to Toronto Raptors for G/F Jalen Rose and a first-round draft choice (February 3, 2006). ... Waived by Raptors (March 23, 2006).
MISCELLANEOUS: Toronto Raptors all-time leading rebounder with 2,839 (1999-2000 through 2003).

COLLEGIATE RECORD

Season Team	G	Min.	FGM	FGA	Pct.	FTM	FTA	Pct.	Reb.	Ast.	Pts.	RPG	APG	PPG
86-87—Texas-El Paso	28	240	11	32	.344	13	30	.433	51	4	35	1.8	0.1	1.3
87-88—Texas-El Paso	30	907	108	183	.590	63	115	.548	195	20	279	6.5	0.7	9.3
88-89—Texas-El Paso	32	1014	162	298	.544	135	218	.619	255	14	459	8.0	0.4	14.3
89-90—Texas-El Paso	32	991	119	228	.522	106	165	.642	243	21	344	7.6	0.7	10.8
Totals	122	3152	400	741	.540	317	528	.600	744	59	1117	6.1	0.5	9.2

Three-point field goals: 1988-89, 0-for-1. 1989-90, 0-for-1. Totals, 0-for-2 (.000).

ITALIAN LEAGUE RECORD

Season Team	G	Min.	FGM	FGA	Pct.	FTM	FTA	Pct.	Reb.	Ast.	Pts.	RPG	APG	PPG
92-93—Philips Milano	29	892	121	195	.621	81	130	.623	286	5	323	9.9	0.2	11.1

Three-point field goals: 1992-93, 0-for-1. Totals, 0-for-1 (.000).
Personal fouls/disqualifications: 1992-93, 0/7. Totals, 0/7.

NBA REGULAR-SEASON RECORD

Season Team	G	Min.	FGM	FGA	Pct.	FTM	FTA	Pct.	Off.	Def.	Tot.	Ast.	St.	Blk.	TO	Pts.	RPG	APG	PPG
93-94—Indiana	81	1732	216	425	.508	194	302	.642	190	315	505	55	45	84	107	626	6.2	0.7	7.7
94-95—Indiana	44	1030	109	245	.445	117	174	.672	105	175	280	25	19	29	64	335	6.4	0.6	7.6
95-96—Indiana	82	2092	236	482	.490	246	345	.713	188	313	501	43	33	66	87	719	6.1	0.5	8.8
96-97—Indiana	82	2335	308	641	.480	241	362	.666	190	408	598	65	42	84	141	858	7.3	0.8	10.5
97-98—Indiana	82	2191	254	528	.481	277	398	.696	192	368	560	61	45	72	103	785	6.8	0.7	9.6
98-99—Indiana	49	1271	164	348	.471	135	192	.703	116	228	344	33	22	42	50	463	7.0	0.7	9.4
99-00—Toronto	79	2479	313	712	.440	284	371	.765	235	461	696	105	38	100	121	910	8.8	1.3	11.5
00-01—Toronto	78	2729	375	866	.433	319	423	.754	274	513	787	106	22	151	135	1069	10.1	1.4	13.7
01-02—Toronto	77	2978	410	963	.426	293	358	.818	254	486	740	155	54	83	159	1113	9.6	2.0	14.5
02-03—Toronto	53	1894	261	641	.407	216	280	.771	130	307	437	131	23	62	118	738	8.2	2.5	13.9
03-04—Tor.-Chi.	80	2570	266	660	.403	176	230	.765	207	464	671	137	37	65	114	708	8.4	1.7	8.9
04-05—Chicago	72	1843	193	419	.461	115	152	.757	152	276	428	80	27	41	96	501	5.9	1.1	7.0
05-06—N.Y.-Tor.	44	940	82	190	.432	52	81	.642	90	118	208	21	23	10	51	216	4.7	0.5	4.9
Totals	903	26084	3187	7120	.448	2665	3668	.727	2323	4432	6755	1017	430	889	1346	9041	7.5	1.1	10.0

Three-point field goals: 1993-94, 0-for-1. 1995-96, 1-for-2 (.500). 1996-97, 1-for-14 (.071). 1997-98, 0-for-3. 2000-01, 0-for-1. 2001-02, 0-for-1. 2005-06, 0-for-1. Totals, 2-for-23 (.087).
Personal fouls/disqualifications: 1993-94, 189/1. 1994-95, 134/2. 1995-96, 248/6. 1996-97, 260/4. 1997-98, 234/6. 1998-99, 136/3. 1999-00, 267/2. 2000-01, 230/4. 2001-02, 225/3. 2002-03, 150/0. 2003-04, 206/1. 2004-05, 147/0. 2005-06, 125/0. Totals, 2551/32.

Season Team	G	Min.	FGM	FGA	Pct.	FTM	FTA	Pct.	REBOUNDS Off.	Def.	Tot.	Ast.	St.	Blk.	TO	Pts.	AVERAGES RPG	APG	PPG
93-94—Indiana...........	16	401	48	89	.539	37	66	.561	37	69	106	7	11	18	22	134	6.6	0.4	8.4
94-95—Indiana...........	17	367	32	71	.451	37	59	.627	38	59	97	7	9	11	23	101	5.7	0.4	5.9
95-96—Indiana...........	5	127	13	25	.520	13	15	.867	12	19	31	3	3	6	10	39	6.2	0.6	7.8
97-98—Indiana...........	16	459	42	91	.462	63	94	.670	37	71	108	14	12	18	25	147	6.8	0.9	9.2
98-99—Indiana...........	13	326	31	75	.413	41	62	.661	23	69	92	8	5	14	20	103	7.1	0.6	7.9
99-00—Toronto..........	3	105	14	24	.583	11	14	.786	7	18	25	3	1	4	4	39	8.3	1.0	13.0
00-01—Toronto..........	12	485	77	154	.500	43	53	.811	41	92	133	23	10	22	21	197	11.1	1.9	16.4
01-02—Toronto..........	5	202	34	75	.453	17	28	.607	16	37	53	7	2	5	10	85	10.6	1.4	17.0
04-05—Chicago	6	175	20	46	.435	17	23	.739	17	24	41	11	4	4	9	57	6.8	1.8	9.5
Totals	93	2647	311	650	.478	279	414	.674	228	458	686	83	57	102	144	902	7.4	0.9	9.7

Three-point field goals: 1993-94, 1-for-1 (1.000). Totals, 1-for-1 (1.000).

Personal fouls/disqualifications: 1993-94, 47/0. 1994-95, 61/0. 1995-96, 12/0. 1997-98, 65/5. 1998-99, 39/0. 1999-00, 9/0. 2000-01, 35/0. 2001-02, 17/0. 2004-05, 25/1. Totals, 310/6.

NBA ALL-STAR GAME RECORD

Season Team	Min.	FGM	FGA	Pct.	FTM	FTA	Pct.	REBOUNDS Off.	Def.	Tot.	Ast.	PF	Dq.	St.	Blk.	TO	Pts.
2001—Toronto	20	4	11	.364	0	0	...	7	2	9	0	0	0	1	1	0	8

DAVIS, BARON — G — WARRIORS

PERSONAL: Born April 13, 1979, in Los Angeles. ... 6-3/223. (1.91/101.2).
HIGH SCHOOL: Crossroads (Santa Monica, Calif.).
COLLEGE: UCLA.
TRANSACTIONS/CAREER NOTES: Selected after sophomore season by Charlotte Hornets in first round (third pick overall) of 1999 NBA Draft. ... Hornets franchise moved to New Orleans for 2002-03 season. ... Traded by Hornets to Golden State Warriors for G Speedy Claxton and F Dale Davis (February 24, 2005).

D

COLLEGIATE RECORD

Season Team	G	Min.	FGM	FGA	Pct.	FTM	FTA	Pct.	Reb.	Ast.	Pts.	AVERAGES RPG	APG	PPG
97-98—UCLA............................	32	1003	137	259	.529	75	111	.676	129	161	373	4.0	5.0	11.7
98-99—UCLA............................	27	828	150	312	.481	94	157	.599	97	97	429	3.6	3.6	15.9
Totals	59	1831	287	571	.503	169	268	.631	226	258	802	3.8	4.4	13.6

Three-point field goals: 1997-98, 24-for-78 (.308). 1998-99, 59-for-180 (.328). Totals, 83-for-258 (.322).

Personal fouls/disqualifications: 1997-98, 111/9. Totals, 111/9.

NBA REGULAR-SEASON RECORD

HONORS: All-NBA third team (2004).

Season Team	G	Min.	FGM	FGA	Pct.	FTM	FTA	Pct.	REBOUNDS Off.	Def.	Tot.	Ast.	St.	Blk.	TO	Pts.	AVERAGES RPG	APG	PPG
99-00—Charlotte........	82	1523	182	433	.420	97	153	.634	48	117	165	309	97	19	140	486	2.0	3.8	5.9
00-01—Charlotte........	82	3192	409	957	.427	228	337	.677	129	279	408	598	170	36	226	1131	5.0	7.3	13.8
01-02—Charlotte........	82	3318	559	1341	.417	196	338	.580	93	256	349	698	172	47	246	1484	4.3	8.5	18.1
02-03—New Orleans ...	50	1889	332	798	.416	93	131	.710	56	130	186	320	91	22	140	856	3.7	6.4	17.1
03-04—New Orleans ...	67	2686	554	1402	.395	237	352	.673	66	221	287	501	158	27	215	1532	4.3	7.5	22.9
04-05—N.O.-G.S........	46	1581	291	752	.387	185	243	.761	32	143	175	362	81	14	131	885	3.8	7.9	19.2
05-06—Golden State ...	54	1971	335	861	.389	195	289	.675	45	191	236	480	89	14	159	967	4.4	8.9	17.9
Totals	463	16160	2662	6544	.407	1231	1843	.668	469	1337	1806	3268	858	179	1257	7341	3.9	7.1	15.9

Three-point field goals: 1999-00, 25-for-111 (.225). 2000-01, 85-for-274 (.310). 2001-02, 170-for-478 (.356). 2002-03, 99-for-283 (.350). 2003-04, 187-for-582 (.321). 2004-05, 118-for-354 (.333). 2005-06, 102-for-324 (.315). Totals, 786-for-2406 (.327).

Personal fouls/disqualifications: 1999-00, 201/1. 2000-01, 267/1. 2001-02, 241/0. 2002-03, 148/3. 2003-04, 178/2. 2004-05, 126/1. 2005-06, 165/3. Totals, 1326/11.

NBA PLAYOFF RECORD

Season Team	G	Min.	FGM	FGA	Pct.	FTM	FTA	Pct.	REBOUNDS Off.	Def.	Tot.	Ast.	St.	Blk.	TO	Pts.	AVERAGES RPG	APG	PPG
99-00—Charlotte........	4	57	10	23	.435	2	4	.500	3	3	6	4	0	3	23	1.5	1.5	5.8
00-01—Charlotte........	10	397	59	123	.480	40	56	.714	9	35	44	58	28	5	22	178	4.4	5.8	17.8
01-02—Charlotte........	9	401	71	188	.378	40	67	.597	16	47	63	71	32	5	27	203	7.0	7.9	22.6
02-03—New Orleans ...	5	194	37	83	.446	16	22	.727	4	14	18	42	7	2	15	102	3.6	8.4	20.4
03-04—New Orleans ...	7	260	43	114	.377	25	33	.758	6	23	29	49	11	5	19	127	4.1	7.0	18.1
Totals	35	1309	220	531	.414	123	182	.676	38	122	160	226	82	17	86	633	4.6	6.5	18.1

Three-point field goals: 1999-00, 1-for-6 (.167). 2000-01, 20-for-50 (.400). 2001-02, 21-for-62 (.339). 2002-03, 12-for-35 (.343). 2003-04, 16-for-49 (.327). Totals, 70-for-202 (.347).

Personal fouls/disqualifications: 1999-00, 6/0. 2000-01, 33/0. 2001-02, 36/2. 2002-03, 20/0. 2003-04, 21/0. Totals, 116/2.

NBA ALL-STAR GAME RECORD

NOTES: Won NBA All-Star Sports Skills Challenge (2004).

Season Team	Min.	FGM	FGA	Pct.	FTM	FTA	Pct.	REBOUNDS Off.	Def.	Tot.	Ast.	PF	Dq.	St.	Blk.	TO	Pts.
2002—Charlotte	13	1	5	.200	0	0	...	0	1	1	5	1	0	0	0	3	2
2004—New Orleans.........	16	3	9	.333	0	0	...	0	0	0	7	0	0	1	0	1	7
Totals.........................	29	4	14	.286	0	0	...	0	1	1	12	1	0	1	0	4	9

Three-point field goals: 2002, 0-for-3. 2004, 1-for-6 (.167). Totals, 1-for-9 (.111).

DAVIS, DALE   F

PERSONAL: Born March 25, 1969, in Toccoa, Ga. ... 6-11/252. (2.11/114.3). ... Full name: Elliott Lydell Davis
HIGH SCHOOL: Stephens County (Toccoa, Ga.).
COLLEGE: Clemson.
TRANSACTIONS/CAREER NOTES: Selected by Indiana Pacers in first round (13th pick overall) of 1991 NBA Draft. ... Traded by Pacers to Portland Trail Blazers for F Jermaine O'Neal and C Joe Kleine (August 31, 2000). ... Traded by Trail Blazers with G Dan Dickau to Golden State Warriors for G Nick Van Exel (July 20, 2004). ... Traded by Warriors with G Speedy Claxton to New Orleans Hornets for G Baron Davis (February 24, 2005). ... Waived by Hornets (March 1, 2005). ... Signed by Detroit Pistons (August 26, 2005).

COLLEGIATE RECORD

Season Team	G	Min.	FGM	FGA	Pct.	FTM	FTA	Pct.	Reb.	Ast.	Pts.	RPG	APG	PPG
87-88—Clemson	29	714	91	171	.532	45	89	.506	223	10	227	7.7	0.3	7.8
88-89—Clemson	29	736	146	218	.670	93	144	.646	258	16	385	8.9	0.6	13.3
89-90—Clemson	35	1077	205	328	.625	127	213	.596	395	21	537	11.3	0.6	15.3
90-91—Clemson	28	971	191	359	.532	119	205	.580	340	37	501	12.1	1.3	17.9
Totals	121	3498	633	1076	.588	384	651	.590	1216	84	1650	10.0	0.7	13.6

Three-point field goals: 1989-90, 0-for-1. 1990-91, 0-for-2. Totals, 0-for-3 (.000).

NBA REGULAR-SEASON RECORD

Season Team	G	Min.	FGM	FGA	Pct.	FTM	FTA	Pct.	Off.	Def.	Tot.	Ast.	St.	Blk.	TO	Pts.	RPG	APG	PPG
91-92—Indiana	64	1301	154	279	.552	87	152	.572	158	252	410	30	27	74	49	395	6.4	0.5	6.2
92-93—Indiana	82	2264	304	535	.568	119	225	.529	291	432	723	69	63	148	79	727	8.8	0.8	8.9
93-94—Indiana	66	2292	308	582	.529	155	294	.527	280	438	718	100	48	106	102	771	10.9	1.5	11.7
94-95—Indiana	74	2346	324	576	.563	138	259	.533	259	437	696	58	72	116	124	786	9.4	0.8	10.6
95-96—Indiana	78	2617	334	599	.558	135	289	.467	252	457	709	76	56	112	119	803	9.1	1.0	10.3
96-97—Indiana	80	2589	370	688	.538	92	215	.428	301	471	772	59	60	77	108	832	9.7	0.7	10.4
97-98—Indiana	78	2174	273	498	.548	80	172	.465	233	378	611	70	51	87	73	626	7.8	0.9	8.0
98-99—Indiana	50	1374	161	302	.533	76	123	.618	155	261	416	22	20	57	43	398	8.3	0.4	8.0
99-00—Indiana	74	2127	302	602	.502	139	203	.685	256	473	729	64	52	94	91	743	9.9	0.9	10.0
00-01—Portland	81	2162	242	487	.497	96	152	.632	233	373	606	103	44	76	67	580	7.5	1.3	7.2
01-02—Portland	78	2447	296	580	.510	150	212	.708	262	426	688	96	62	83	62	742	8.8	1.2	9.5
02-03—Portland	78	2282	237	438	.541	105	166	.633	233	331	564	94	51	70	71	579	7.2	1.2	7.4
03-04—Portland	76	1682	133	281	.473	65	106	.613	158	240	398	72	43	62	40	331	5.2	0.9	4.4
04-05—G.S.-N.O.-Ind.	61	1307	112	234	.479	60	99	.606	152	223	375	47	32	65	43	284	6.1	0.8	4.7
05-06—Detroit	28	178	9	24	.375	8	15	.533	21	32	53	6	0	9	4	26	1.9	0.2	0.9
Totals	1048	29142	3559	6705	.531	1505	2682	.561	3244	5224	8468	966	681	1236	1075	8623	8.1	0.9	8.2

Three-point field goals: 1991-92, 0-for-1. 1993-94, 0-for-1. 1994-95, 0-for-1. 2000-01, 0-for-4. 2005-06, 0-for-1. Totals, 0-for-8 (.000).
Personal fouls/disqualifications: 1991-92, 191/2. 1992-93, 274/5. 1993-94, 214/1. 1994-95, 222/2. 1995-96, 238/0. 1996-97, 233/3. 1997-98, 209/1. 1998-99, 115/0. 1999-00, 203/1. 2000-01, 199/0. 2001-02, 193/1. 2002-03, 189/1. 2003-04, 154/1. 2004-05, 162/1. 2005-06, 23/0. Totals, 2819/19.

NBA PLAYOFF RECORD

Season Team	G	Min.	FGM	FGA	Pct.	FTM	FTA	Pct.	Off.	Def.	Tot.	Ast.	St.	Blk.	TO	Pts.	RPG	APG	PPG
91-92—Indiana	3	69	4	10	.400	0	0	...	5	14	19	2	0	5	1	8	6.3	0.7	2.7
92-93—Indiana	4	117	8	12	.667	1	4	.250	4	28	32	4	4	4	3	17	8.0	1.0	4.3
93-94—Indiana	16	578	56	106	.528	11	36	.306	63	96	159	11	18	17	30	123	9.9	0.7	7.7
94-95—Indiana	17	490	56	105	.533	23	47	.489	53	83	136	6	7	14	22	135	8.0	0.4	7.9
95-96—Indiana	5	184	16	31	.516	4	11	.364	20	36	56	4	3	6	10	36	11.2	0.8	7.2
97-98—Indiana	16	466	56	86	.651	29	64	.453	44	76	120	12	5	18	21	141	7.5	0.8	8.8
98-99—Indiana	13	394	45	77	.584	28	50	.560	45	87	132	11	10	18	21	118	10.2	0.8	9.1
99-00—Indiana	23	714	79	151	.523	32	59	.542	83	180	263	17	11	31	18	190	11.4	0.7	8.3
00-01—Portland	2	20	0	2	.000	1	2	.500	3	1	4	0	1	0	1	1	2.0	0.0	0.5
01-02—Portland	3	70	3	11	.273	1	2	.500	6	14	20	4	4	3	2	7	6.7	1.3	2.3
02-03—Portland	6	162	14	24	.583	17	26	.654	20	28	48	9	5	2	10	45	8.0	1.5	7.5
04-05—Indiana	13	311	26	58	.448	17	25	.680	37	44	81	5	9	6	9	69	6.2	0.4	5.3
05-06—Detroit	8	36	0	6	.000	2	4	.500	1	8	9	1	0	0	3	2	1.1	0.1	0.3
Totals	129	3611	363	679	.535	166	330	.503	384	695	1079	86	77	124	151	892	8.4	0.7	6.9

Three-point field goals: 1993-94, 0-for-1. 2000-01, 0-for-1. Totals, 0-for-2 (.000).
Personal fouls/disqualifications: 1991-92, 8/0. 1992-93, 15/0. 1993-94, 52/0. 1994-95, 56/0. 1995-96, 16/0. 1997-98, 42/0. 1998-99, 42/0. 1999-00, 83/4. 2000-01, 7/1. 2001-02, 16/2. 2002-03, 11/0. 2004-05, 35/0. 2005-06, 11/0. Totals, 394/7.

NBA ALL-STAR GAME RECORD

Season Team	Min.	FGM	FGA	Pct.	FTM	FTA	Pct.	Off.	Def.	Tot.	Ast.	PF	Dq.	St.	Blk.	TO	Pts.
2000—Indiana	14	2	3	.667	0	0	...	3	5	8	1	0	...	0	0	0	4

DAVIS, JOSH   F

PERSONAL: Born August 10, 1980 ... 6-8/240. (2.03/108.9).
HIGH SCHOOL: Salem Academy (Oregon).
COLLEGE: Wyoming.
TRANSACTIONS/CAREER NOTES: Not drafted by an NBA franchise. ... Played in Italy (2002-03). ... Signed as free agent by Chicago Bulls (September 29, 2003). ... Waived by Bulls (October 20, 2003). ... Played in Continental Basketball Association (2003-04). ... Signed by Atlanta Hawks to 10-day contract (March 9, 2004). ... Signed as free agent by Milwaukee Bucks (October 2, 2005). ... Waived by Bucks (November 24, 2005). ... Signed by Houston Rockets (December 29, 2005). ... Waived by Rockets (January 4, 2006). ... Signed by Phoenix Suns to 10-day contract (January 9, 2006).

Season Team	G	Min.	FGM	FGA	Pct.	FTM	FTA	Pct.	Reb.	Ast.	Pts.	AVERAGES		
												RPG	APG	PPG
98-99—Wyoming	27	590	93	198	.470	30	53	.566	161	28	231	6.0	1.0	8.6
99-00—Wyoming	31	842	175	351	.499	67	104	.644	270	39	442	8.7	1.3	14.3
00-01—Wyoming	30	851	150	309	.485	88	120	.733	281	53	404	9.4	1.8	13.5
01-02—Wyoming	31	848	142	268	.530	70	120	.583	244	47	362	7.9	1.5	11.7
Totals	119	3131	560	1126	.497	255	397	.642	956	167	1439	8.0	1.4	12.1

Three-point field goals: 1998-99, 15-for-53 (.283). 1999-00, 25-for-55 (.455). 2000-01, 16-for-79 (.203). 2001-02, 8-for-43 (.186). Totals, 64-for-230 (.278).

ITALIAN LEAGUE RECORD

Season Team	G	Min.	FGM	FGA	Pct.	FTM	FTA	Pct.	Reb.	Ast.	Pts.	AVERAGES		
												RPG	APG	PPG
02-03—Sicc Cucine Jesi	20	449	78	142	.549	30	45	.667	145	10	200	7.3	0.5	10.0

Three-point field goals: 2002-03, 14-for-31 (.452). Totals, 14-for-31 (.452).

CBA RECORD

Season Team	G	Min.	FGM	FGA	Pct.	FTM	FTA	Pct.	Reb.	Ast.	Pts.	AVERAGES		
												RPG	APG	PPG
03-04—Idaho	40	1340	299	507	.590	89	108	.824	385	96	747	9.6	2.4	18.7
05-06—Idaho	14	465	105	212	.495	50	55	.909	125	34	292	8.9	2.4	20.9
Totals	54	1805	404	719	.562	139	163	.853	510	130	1039	9.4	2.4	19.2

Three-point field goals: 2003-04, 60-for-146 (.411). 2005-06, 32-for-77 (.416). Totals, 92-for-223 (.413).

NBA REGULAR-SEASON RECORD

Season Team	G	Min.	FGM	FGA	Pct.	FTM	FTA	Pct.	REBOUNDS			Ast.	St.	Blk.	TO	Pts.	AVERAGES		
									Off.	Def.	Tot.						RPG	APG	PPG
03-04—Atlanta	4	23	2	5	.400	1	1	1.000	1	4	5	0	0	0	2	5	1.3	0.0	1.3
04-05—Philadelphia	42	328	42	111	.378	14	17	.824	29	50	79	12	8	4	15	117	1.9	0.3	2.8
05-06—Mil.-Hou.-Pho.	6	17	2	7	.286	2	3	.667	3	1	4	1	2	0	1	6	0.7	0.2	1.0
Totals	52	368	46	123	.374	17	21	.810	33	55	88	13	10	4	18	128	1.7	0.3	2.5

Three-point field goals: 2003-04, 0-for-2. 2004-05, 19-for-53 (.358). 2005-06, 0-for-2. Totals, 19-for-57 (.333).
Personal fouls/disqualifications: 2003-04, 3/0. 2004-05, 45/0. 2005-06, 3/0. Totals, 51/0.

NBA PLAYOFF RECORD

Season Team	G	Min.	FGM	FGA	Pct.	FTM	FTA	Pct.	REBOUNDS			Ast.	St.	Blk.	TO	Pts.	AVERAGES		
									Off.	Def.	Tot.						RPG	APG	PPG
04-05—Philadelphia	2	4	0	1	.000	0	0		0	1	1	0	0	0	0	0	0.5	0.0	0.0

Three-point field goals: 2004-05, 0 for-1. Totals, 0-for-1 (.000).
Personal fouls/disqualifications: 2004-05, 1/0. Totals, 1/0.

D

DAVIS, RICKY   G   TIMBERWOLVES

PERSONAL: Born September 23, 1979, in Las Vegas. ... 6-7/197. (2.01/89.4). ... Full name: Tyree Ricardo Davis
HIGH SCHOOL: North (Davenport, Iowa).
COLLEGE: Iowa.
TRANSACTIONS/CAREER NOTES: Selected after freshman season by Charlotte Hornets in first round (21st pick overall) of 1998 NBA Draft. ... Traded by Hornets with G Eddie Jones, F Anthony Mason and G/F Dale Ellis to Miami Heat for F P.J. Brown, F Jamal Mashburn, F/C Otis Thorpe, F Tim James and G/F Rodney Buford (August 1, 2000). ... Traded by Heat to Cleveland Cavaliers as part of three-way deal in which Toronto Raptors sent F/C Brian Skinner to Cavaliers, Cavaliers sent F/C Chris Gatling to Cavaliers and Heat sent F Don MacLean and cash considerations to Raptors (October 26, 2001). ... Traded by Cavaliers with F/C Chris Mihm, C Michael Stewart and a second-round draft choice to Boston Celtics for F/C Tony Battie, F Kedrick Brown and F Eric Williams (December 15, 2003). ... Traded by Celtics with C Mark Blount, G Marcus Banks, SF Justin Reed and two second-round draft choices to Minnesota Timberwolves for F Wally Szczerbiak, C Michael Olowokandi, F/C Dwayne Jones and a future first-round draft choice (January 26, 2006).

COLLEGIATE RECORD

Season Team	G	Min.	FGM	FGA	Pct.	FTM	FTA	Pct.	Reb.	Ast.	Pts.	AVERAGES		
												RPG	APG	PPG
97-98—Iowa	31	825	173	371	.466	90	129	.698	148	74	464	4.8	2.4	15.0

Three-point field goals: 1997-98, 28-for-91 (.308). Totals, 28-for-91 (.308).

NBA REGULAR-SEASON RECORD

Season Team	G	Min.	FGM	FGA	Pct.	FTM	FTA	Pct.	REBOUNDS			Ast.	St.	Blk.	TO	Pts.	AVERAGES		
									Off.	Def.	Tot.						RPG	APG	PPG
98-99—Charlotte	46	557	81	200	.405	45	59	.763	40	44	84	58	30	7	54	209	1.8	1.3	4.5
99-00—Charlotte	48	570	94	187	.503	39	51	.765	29	54	83	62	30	8	46	227	1.7	1.3	4.7
00-01—Miami	7	70	12	29	.414	7	8	.875	1	6	7	11	5	2	5	32	1.0	1.6	4.6
01-02—Cleveland	82	1954	376	781	.481	196	248	.790	63	180	243	178	69	23	148	959	3.0	2.2	11.7
02-03—Cleveland	79	3131	602	1470	.410	348	465	.748	97	293	390	436	125	36	277	1626	4.9	5.5	20.6
03-04—Cleve.-Bos.	79	2474	446	950	.469	196	273	.718	77	281	358	259	96	22	189	1140	4.5	3.3	14.4
04-05—Boston	82	2696	481	1041	.462	286	351	.815	66	183	249	246	89	27	205	1309	3.0	3.0	16.0
05-06—Boston-Minn.	78	3207	584	1304	.448	275	345	.797	65	286	351	394	91	17	213	1516	4.5	5.1	19.4
Totals	501	14659	2676	5962	.449	1392	1800	.773	438	1327	1765	1644	535	142	1137	7018	3.5	3.3	14.0

Three-point field goals: 1998-99, 2-for-12 (.167). 1999-00, 0-for-4. 2000-01, 1-for-1 (1.000). 2001-02, 11-for-35 (.314). 2002-03, 74-for-204 (.363). 2003-04, 52-for-140 (.371). 2004-05, 61-for-180 (.339). 2005-06, 73-for-242 (.302). Totals, 274-for-818 (.335).
Personal fouls/disqualifications: 1998-99, 46/0. 1999-00, 39/0. 2000-01, 7/0. 2001-02, 145/0. 2002-03, 180/0. 2003-04, 171/1. 2004-05, 174/1. 2005-06, 190/2. Totals, 952/4.

NBA PLAYOFF RECORD

								REBOUNDS							AVERAGES		
Season Team	G	Min.	FGM	FGA	Pct.	FTM	FTA	Pct.	Off.	Def.	Tot.	Ast.	St.	Blk.	TO	Pts.	RPG	APG	PPG
03-04—Boston	4	123	16	40	.400	11	16	.688	3	9	12	14	2	0	12	47	3.0	3.5	11.8
04-05—Boston	7	240	32	74	.432	20	26	.769	5	20	25	14	9	2	21	87	3.6	2.0	12.4
Totals	11	363	48	114	.421	31	42	.738	8	29	37	28	11	2	33	134	3.4	2.5	12.2

Three-point field goals: 2003-04, 4-for-10 (.400). 2004-05, 3-for-9 (.333). Totals, 7-for-19 (.368).
Personal fouls/disqualifications: 2003-04, 7/0. 2004-05, 23/1. Totals, 30/1.

DELFINO, CARLOS   G/F   PISTONS

PERSONAL: Born August 29, 1982, in Santa Fe, Argentina. ... 6-6/230. (1.98/104.3). ... Full name: Carlos Francisco Delfino
TRANSACTIONS/CAREER NOTES: Played in Argentina (1998-2000). ... Played in Italy (2000-04). ... Selected by Detroit Pistons in first round (25th pick overall) of 2003 NBA Draft.
MISCELLANEOUS: Member of gold-medal-winning Argentinian Olympic team (2004).

ITALIAN LEAGUE RECORD

											AVERAGES		
Season Team	G	Min.	FGM	FGA	Pct.	FTM	FTA	Pct.	Reb.	Ast.	Pts.	RPG	APG	PPG
00-01—Reggio Calabria	24	495	71	154	.461	36	56	.643	61	23	211	2.5	1.0	8.8
01-02—Reggio Calabria	31	955	143	315	.454	94	119	.790	157	52	420	5.1	1.7	13.5
02-03—Skipper Bologna	26	670	92	213	.432	40	54	.741	145	27	255	5.6	1.0	9.8
03-04—Skipper Bologna	34	861	124	295	.420	54	76	.711	161	41	343	4.7	1.2	10.1
Totals	115	2981	430	977	.440	224	305	.734	524	143	1229	4.6	1.2	10.7

Three-point field goals: 2000-01, 33-for-95 (.347). 2001-02, 40-for-139 (.288). 2002-03, 31-for-89 (.348). 2003-04, 42-for-128 (.320). Totals, 104-for-323 (.322).

NBA REGULAR-SEASON RECORD

								REBOUNDS							AVERAGES		
Season Team	G	Min.	FGM	FGA	Pct.	FTM	FTA	Pct.	Off.	Def.	Tot.	Ast.	St.	Blk.	TO	Pts.	RPG	APG	PPG
04-05—Detroit	30	459	42	117	.359	23	40	.575	13	42	55	38	22	6	23	116	1.8	1.3	3.9
05-06—Detroit	68	726	91	226	.403	45	67	.672	28	85	113	44	21	15	36	247	1.7	0.6	3.6
Totals	98	1185	133	343	.388	68	107	.636	41	127	168	82	43	21	59	363	1.7	0.8	3.7

Three-point field goals: 2004-05, 9-for-35 (.257). 2005-06, 20-for-60 (.333). Totals, 29-for-95 (.305).
Personal fouls/disqualifications: 2004-05, 44/0. 2005-06, 86/0. Totals, 130/0.

NBA PLAYOFF RECORD

								REBOUNDS							AVERAGES		
Season Team	G	Min.	FGM	FGA	Pct.	FTM	FTA	Pct.	Off.	Def.	Tot.	Ast.	St.	Blk.	TO	Pts.	RPG	APG	PPG
05-06—Detroit	8	32	1	6	.167	2	2	1.000	0	4	4	2	1	0	6	5	0.5	0.3	0.6

Three-point field goals: 2005-06, 1-for-2 (.500). Totals, 1-for-2 (.500).
Personal fouls/disqualifications: 2005-06, 4/0. Totals, 4/0.

DELK, TONY   G

PERSONAL: Born January 28, 1974, in Covington, Tenn. ... 6-2/189. (1.88/85.7). ... Full name: Tony Lorenzo Delk
HIGH SCHOOL: Haywood (Brownsville, Tenn.).
COLLEGE: Kentucky.
TRANSACTIONS/CAREER NOTES: Selected by Charlotte Hornets in first round (16th pick overall) of 1996 NBA Draft. ... Traded by Hornets with G Muggsy Bogues to Golden State Warriors for G B.J. Armstrong (November 7, 1997). ... Signed as free agent by Sacramento Kings (August 16, 1999). ... Signed as free agent by Phoenix Suns (August 1, 2000). ... Traded by Suns with F Rodney Rogers to Boston Celtics for G/F Joe Johnson, G Milt Palacio, G Randy Brown and 2002 first-round draft choice (February 20, 2002). ... Traded by Celtics with F Antoine Walker to Dallas Mavericks for F/C Raef LaFrentz, F Chris Mills, G Jiri Welsch and 2004 first-round draft choice (October 20, 2003). ... Traded by Mavericks with F Antoine Walker to Atlanta Hawks for G Jason Terry, F Alan Henderson and a future first-round draft choice (August 4, 2004). ... Waived by Hawks (February 24, 2006). ... Signed by Detriot Pistons (March 1, 2006). ... Signed with Panathinaikos of Greek League for 2006-07 season.

COLLEGIATE RECORD
NOTES: Member of NCAA Division I championship team (1996). ... THE SPORTING NEWS All-America second team (1996). ... NCAA Division I Tournament Most Outstanding Player (1996).

											AVERAGES		
Season Team	G	Min.	FGM	FGA	Pct.	FTM	FTA	Pct.	Reb.	Ast.	Pts.	RPG	APG	PPG
92-93—Kentucky	30	287	47	104	.452	24	33	.727	57	22	136	1.9	0.7	4.5
93-94—Kentucky	34	957	200	440	.455	69	108	.639	153	59	564	4.5	1.7	16.6
94-95—Kentucky	33	960	207	433	.478	60	89	.674	110	65	551	3.3	2.0	16.7
95-96—Kentucky	36	947	229	464	.494	88	110	.800	150	64	639	4.2	1.8	17.8
Totals	133	3151	683	1441	.474	241	340	.709	470	210	1890	3.5	1.6	14.2

Three-point field goals: 1992-93, 18-for-51 (.353). 1993-94, 95-for-254 (.374). 1994-95, 77-for-197 (.391). 1995-96, 93-for-210 (.443). Totals, 283-for-712 (.397).

NBA REGULAR-SEASON RECORD

								REBOUNDS							AVERAGES		
Season Team	G	Min.	FGM	FGA	Pct.	FTM	FTA	Pct.	Off.	Def.	Tot.	Ast.	St.	Blk.	TO	Pts.	RPG	APG	PPG
96-97—Charlotte	61	867	119	256	.465	42	51	.824	31	68	99	99	36	6	68	332	1.6	1.6	5.4
97-98—Char.-G.S.	77	1681	314	798	.393	111	151	.735	38	134	172	172	73	12	109	781	2.2	2.2	10.1
98-99—Golden State	36	630	92	253	.364	46	71	.648	11	43	54	95	16	6	45	246	1.5	2.6	6.8
99-00—Sacramento	46	682	120	279	.430	47	59	.797	36	52	88	55	35	5	32	296	1.9	1.2	6.4
00-01—Phoenix	82	2288	383	923	.415	185	235	.787	76	185	261	160	75	17	101	1005	3.2	2.0	12.3
01-02—Pho.-Boston	63	1447	226	588	.384	78	97	.804	58	145	203	132	53	10	59	597	3.2	2.1	9.5
02-03—Boston	67	1873	233	560	.416	68	87	.782	41	191	232	146	72	10	69	654	3.5	2.2	9.8
03-04—Dallas	33	509	70	184	.380	37	44	.841	16	43	59	28	27	7	17	197	1.8	0.8	6.0
04-05—Atlanta	56	1340	246	591	.416	103	136	.757	28	102	130	104	47	3	54	667	2.3	1.9	11.9
05-06—Atlanta-Detroit	24	385	71	161	.441	20	27	.741	14	39	53	33	13	1	19	182	2.2	1.4	7.6
Totals	545	11702	1874	4593	.408	737	958	.769	349	1002	1351	1024	447	77	573	4957	2.5	1.9	9.1

D

Three-point field goals: 1996-97, 52-for-112 (.464). 1997-98, 42-for-157 (.268). 1998-99, 16-for-66 (.242). 1999-00, 9-for-40 (.225). 2000-01, 54-for-168 (.321). 2001-02, 67-for-214 (.313). 2002-03, 120-for-304 (.395). 2003-04, 20-for-66 (.303). 2004-05, 72-for-202 (.356). 2005-06, 20-for-47 (.426). Totals, 472-for-1376 (.343).

Personal fouls/disqualifications: 1996-97, 71/1. 1997-98, 96/0. 1998-99, 47/0. 1999-00, 58/0. 2000-01, 171/1. 2001-02, 98/0. 2002-03, 124/0. 2003-04, 46/0. 2004-05, 123/3. 2005-06, 28/0. Totals, 862/5.

NBA PLAYOFF RECORD

Season Team	G	Min.	FGM	FGA	Pct.	FTM	FTA	Pct.	REBOUNDS Off.	Def.	Tot.	Ast.	St.	Blk.	TO	Pts.	AVERAGES RPG	APG	PPG
96-97—Charlotte	3	85	13	31	.419	0	0	...	5	5	10	6	2	0	2	31	3.3	2.0	10.3
99-00—Sacramento	5	101	18	41	.439	17	23	.739	11	7	18	7	3	0	8	56	3.6	1.4	11.2
00-01—Phoenix	4	114	18	43	.419	7	11	.636	5	11	16	4	3	0	5	47	4.0	1.0	11.8
01-02—Boston	14	227	23	65	.354	7	12	.583	8	26	34	16	8	5	15	66	2.4	1.1	4.7
02-03—Boston	10	368	54	114	.474	28	32	.875	5	42	47	36	12	4	13	158	4.7	3.6	15.8
03-04—Dallas	1	5	0	0	...	0	0	...	0	1	1	2	1	0	0	0	1.0	2.0	0.0
05-06—Detroit	16	138	19	47	.404	7	10	.700	4	14	18	8	6	0	4	48	1.1	0.5	3.0
Totals	53	1038	145	341	.425	66	88	.750	38	106	144	79	35	9	47	406	2.7	1.5	7.7

Three-point field goals: 1996-97, 5-for-13 (.385). 1999-00, 3-for-5 (.600). 2000-01, 4-for-10 (.400). 2001-02, 13-for-33 (.394). 2002-03, 22-for-49 (.449). 2005-06, 3-for-15 (.200). Totals, 50-for-125 (.400).

Personal fouls/disqualifications: 1996-97, 10/0. 1999-00, 11/0. 2000-01, 7/0. 2001-02, 13/0. 2002-03, 24/0. 2005-06, 14/0. Totals, 79/0.

DENG, LUOL   F   BULLS

PERSONAL: Born April 16, 1985, in The Sudan. ... 6-8/220. (2.03/99.8).
HIGH SCHOOL: Blair Academy (Blairstown, N.J.).
COLLEGE: Duke.
TRANSACTIONS/CAREER NOTES: Selected after freshman season by Phoenix Suns in first round (seventh pick overall) of 2004 NBA Draft. ... Draft rights traded by Suns to Chicago Bulls for draft rights to F/C Jackson Vroman and future first-round draft choice (June 24, 2004).

COLLEGIATE RECORD

Season Team	G	Min.	FGM	FGA	Pct.	FTM	FTA	Pct.	Reb.	Ast.	Pts.	AVERAGES RPG	APG	PPG
03-04—Duke	37	1149	210	442	.475	98	138	.710	255	68	558	6.9	1.8	15.1

Three-point field goals: 2003-04, 40-for-111 (.360). Totals, 40-for-111 (.360).

NBA REGULAR-SEASON RECORD

HONORS: NBA All-Rookie first team (2005).

Season Team	G	Min.	FGM	FGA	Pct.	FTM	FTA	Pct.	REBOUNDS Off.	Def.	Tot.	Ast.	St.	Blk.	TO	Pts.	AVERAGES RPG	APG	PPG
04-05—Chicago	61	1663	280	645	.434	120	162	.741	92	230	322	135	48	27	118	711	5.3	2.2	11.7
05-06—Chicago	78	2604	442	954	.463	207	276	.750	127	389	516	147	72	50	105	1112	6.6	1.9	14.3
Totals	139	4267	722	1599	.452	327	438	.747	219	619	838	282	120	77	223	1823	6.0	2.0	13.1

Three-point field goals: 2004-05, 31-for-111 (.279). 2005-06, 21-for-93 (.226). Totals, 52-for-204 (.255).

Personal fouls/disqualifications: 2004-05, 98/0. 2005-06, 128/1. Totals, 226/1.

NBA PLAYOFF RECORD

Season Team	G	Min.	FGM	FGA	Pct.	FTM	FTA	Pct.	REBOUNDS Off.	Def.	Tot.	Ast.	St.	Blk.	TO	Pts.	AVERAGES RPG	APG	PPG
05-06—Chicago	6	180	24	56	.429	12	21	.571	8	21	29	3	5	4	5	61	4.8	0.5	10.2

Three-point field goals: 2005-06, 1-for-5 (.200). Totals, 1-for-5 (.200).
Personal fouls/disqualifications: 2005-06, 13/0. Totals, 13/0.

DIAW, BORIS   G/F   SUNS

PERSONAL: Born April 16, 1982, in Cormeille-en-Parisis, France. ... 6-8/203. (2.03/92.1).
TRANSACTIONS/CAREER NOTES: Played in France (1998-2003). ... Selected by Atlanta Hawks in first round (21st pick overall) of 2003 NBA Draft. ... Traded by Hawks with two first-round draft picks to Phoenix Suns for G/F Joe Johnson (August 15, 2005).

FRENCH LEAGUE RECORD

Season Team	G	Min.	FGM	FGA	Pct.	FTM	FTA	Pct.	Reb.	Ast.	Pts.	AVERAGES RPG	APG	PPG
98-99—Centre Federal	25	...	70	130	.538	25	43	.581	90	63	178	3.6	2.5	7.1
99-00—Centre Federal	25	884	163	296	.551	66	109	.606	231	126	420	9.2	5.0	16.8
00-01—Pau Orthez	27	390	39	69	.565	20	27	.741	72	42	107	2.7	1.6	4.0
01-02—Pau Orthez	29	610	89	155	.574	41	63	.651	135	57	226	4.7	2.0	7.8
02-03—Pau Orthez	27	677	77	142	.542	24	43	.558	140	110	194	5.2	4.1	7.2
Totals	133	2561	438	792	.553	176	285	.618	668	398	1125	5.0	3.0	8.5

Three-point field goals: 1998-99, 13-for-39 (.333). 1999-00, 28-for-80 (.350). 2000-01, 9-for-22 (.409). 2001-02, 7-for-30 (.233). 2002-03, 16-for-38 (.421). Totals, 73-for-209 (.349).

NBA REGULAR-SEASON RECORD

HONORS: NBA Most Improved Player (2006).

Season Team	G	Min.	FGM	FGA	Pct.	FTM	FTA	Pct.	REBOUNDS Off.	Def.	Tot.	Ast.	St.	Blk.	TO	Pts.	AVERAGES RPG	APG	PPG
03-04—Atlanta	76	1919	140	313	.447	56	93	.602	111	231	342	182	59	37	126	342	4.5	2.4	4.5
04-05—Atlanta	66	1201	124	294	.422	57	77	.740	54	116	170	149	37	18	87	314	2.6	2.3	4.8
05-06—Phoenix	81	2874	449	853	.526	174	238	.731	159	399	558	503	58	85	189	1080	6.9	6.2	13.3
Totals	223	5994	713	1460	.488	287	408	.703	324	746	1070	834	154	140	402	1736	4.8	3.7	7.8

Three-point field goals: 2003-04, 6-for-26 (.231). 2004-05, 9-for-50 (.180). 2005-06, 8-for-30 (.267). Totals, 23-for-106 (.217).
Personal fouls/disqualifications: 2003-04, 191/2. 2004-05, 123/0. 2005-06, 260/5. Totals, 574/7.

NBA PLAYOFF RECORD

Season Team	G	Min.	FGM	FGA	Pct.	FTM	FTA	Pct.	REBOUNDS Off.	Def.	Tot.	Ast.	St.	Blk.	TO	Pts.	AVERAGES RPG	APG	PPG
05-06—Phoenix	20	796	152	289	.526	67	88	.761	39	94	133	104	18	22	55	374	6.7	5.2	18.7

Three-point field goals: 2005-06, 3-for-7 (.429). Totals, 3-for-7 (.429).
Personal fouls/disqualifications: 2005-06, 64/0. Totals, 64/0.

DICKAU, DAN   G   TRAIL BLAZERS

PERSONAL: Born September 16, 1978, in Portland. ... 6-0/190. (1.83/86.2). ... Full name: Daniel David Dickau
HIGH SCHOOL: Prairie (Vancouver, Wash.).
COLLEGE: Washington, then Gonzaga.
TRANSACTIONS/CAREER NOTES: Selected by Sacramento Kings in first round (28th pick overall) of 2002 NBA Draft. ... Draft rights traded by Kings to Atlanta Hawks for future first-round draft choice (June 26, 2002). ... Traded by Hawks with F Shareef Abdur-Rahim and C Theo Ratliff to Portland Trail Blazers for F Rasheed Wallace and G Wesley Person (February 9, 2004). ... Traded by Trail Blazers with F Dale Davis to Golden State Warriors for G Nick Van Exel (July 20, 2004). ... Traded by Warriors with C Erick Dampier, C Evan Eschmeyer and draft rights to G Steve Logan to Dallas Mavericks for F/C Christian Laettner, F Eduardo Najera, draft rights to G Luis Flores and G/F Mladen Sekularac, two future first-round draft choices and cash (August 24, 2004). ... Traded by Mavericks with a second-round draft choice to New Orleans Hornets for G Darrell Armstrong (December 3, 2004). ... Traded by Hornets to Boston Celtics for 2006 second-round pick (September 30, 2005). ... Traded by Celtics with F/C Raef LaFrentz and a first-round pick (G Randy Foye) in 2006 draft to Portland Trail Blazers for G Sebastian Telfair, F/C Theo Ratliff and a second-round pick in 2008 draft (June 28, 2006).

COLLEGIATE RECORD

NOTES: THE SPORTING NEWS All-America first team (2002).

Season Team	G	Min.	FGM	FGA	Pct.	FTM	FTA	Pct.	Reb.	Ast.	Pts.	AVERAGES RPG	APG	PPG
97-98—Washington	28	262	26	69	.377	31	39	.795	24	29	105	0.9	1.0	3.8
98-99—Washington	13	296	22	56	.393	5	7	.714	38	34	60	2.9	2.6	4.6
99-00—Gonzaga						Did not play—transfer student.								
00-01—Gonzaga	24	809	133	274	.485	116	134	.866	79	150	453	3.3	6.3	18.9
01-02—Gonzaga	32	1110	195	442	.441	165	191	.864	95	149	672	3.0	4.7	21.0
Totals	97	2477	376	841	.447	317	371	.854	236	362	1290	2.4	3.7	13.3

Three-point field goals: 1997-98, 16-for-30 (.533). 1998-99, 11-for-31 (.355). 2000-01, 71-for-148 (.480). 2001-02, 117-for-256 (.457). Totals, 215-for-465 (.462).

NBA REGULAR-SEASON RECORD

Season Team	G	Min.	FGM	FGA	Pct.	FTM	FTA	Pct.	REBOUNDS Off.	Def.	Tot.	Ast.	St.	Blk.	TO	Pts.	AVERAGES RPG	APG	PPG
02-03—Atlanta	50	515	70	170	.412	21	26	.808	9	34	43	85	14	2	53	183	0.9	1.7	3.7
03-04—Atlanta-Portland	43	294	37	98	.378	11	14	.786	7	19	26	38	17	0	26	95	0.6	0.9	2.2
04-05—Dallas-N.O.	71	2090	306	756	.405	190	228	.833	34	146	180	347	76	4	145	887	2.5	4.9	12.5
05-06—Boston	19	234	17	46	.370	18	18	1.000	5	11	16	40	11	1	18	62	0.8	2.1	3.3
Totals	183	3133	430	1070	.402	240	286	.839	55	210	265	510	118	7	242	1227	1.4	2.8	6.7

Three-point field goals: 2002-03, 22-for-61 (.361). 2003-04, 10-for-30 (.333). 2004-05, 85-for-245 (.347). 2005-06, 10-for-20 (.500). Totals, 127-for-356 (.357).
Personal fouls/disqualifications: 2002-03, 66/0. 2003-04, 44/0. 2004-05, 201/3. 2005-06, 40/1. Totals, 351/4.

DIENER, TRAVIS   G   MAGIC

PERSONAL: Born March 1, 1982, in Fond du Lac, Wisc. ... 6-1/175. (1.85/79.4). ... Full name: Travis Lyle Diener
HIGH SCHOOL: Goodrich (Fond du Lac, Wisc.).
COLLEGE: Marquette.
TRANSACTIONS/CAREER NOTES: Selected by Orlando Magic in second round (38th pick overall) of 2005 NBA Draft.

COLLEGIATE RECORD

Season Team	G	Min.	FGM	FGA	Pct.	FTM	FTA	Pct.	Reb.	Ast.	Pts.	AVERAGES RPG	APG	PPG
01-02—Marquette.....................	33	781	77	179	.430	51	67	.761	81	86	262	2.5	2.6	7.9
02-03—Marquette.....................	33	1146	124	313	.396	74	91	.813	105	184	391	3.2	5.6	11.8
03-04—Marquette.....................	31	1060	179	424	.422	136	154	.883	97	187	584	3.1	6.0	18.8
04-05—Marquette.....................	23	783	131	312	.420	124	148	.838	90	160	454	3.9	7.0	19.7
Totals	120	3770	511	1228	.416	385	460	.837	373	617	1691	3.1	5.1	14.1

Three-point field goals: 2001-02, 57-for-129 (.442). 2002-03, 69-for-190 (.363). 2003-04, 90-for-200 (.450). 2004-05, 68-for-168 (.405). Totals, 284-for-687 (.413).

NBA REGULAR-SEASON RECORD

Season Team	G	Min.	FGM	FGA	Pct.	FTM	FTA	Pct.	REBOUNDS Off.	Def.	Tot.	Ast.	St.	Blk.	TO	Pts.	AVERAGES RPG	APG	PPG
05-06—Orlando...........	23	246	29	69	.420	5	6	.833	4	17	21	16	7	0	10	88	0.9	0.7	3.8

Three-point field goals: 2005-06, 25-for-57 (.439). Totals, 25-for-57 (.439).
Personal fouls/disqualifications: 2005-06, 22/0. Totals, 22/0.

DIOGU, IKE   F   WARRIORS

PERSONAL: Born September 11, 1983, in Buffalo, N.Y. ... 6-8/250. (2.03/113.4). ... Full name: Ikechukwu Somotochukwa Diogu
HIGH SCHOOL: Garland (Texas).
COLLEGE: Arizona State.
TRANSACTIONS/CAREER NOTES: Selected after junior season by Golden State Warriors in first round (ninth pick overall) of 2005 NBA Draft.

COLLEGIATE RECORD

NOTES: The SPORTING NEWS All-America second team (2005).

												AVERAGES		
Season Team	G	Min.	FGM	FGA	Pct.	FTM	FTA	Pct.	Reb.	Ast.	Pts.	RPG	APG	PPG
02-03—Arizona State	32	1030	209	344	.608	180	245	.735	249	26	607	7.8	0.8	19.0
03-04—Arizona State	27	996	179	338	.530	243	298	.815	241	44	615	8.9	1.6	22.8
04-05—Arizona State	32	164	229	398	.575	248	311	.797	312	43	724	9.8	1.3	22.6
Totals	91	2190	617	1080	.571	671	854	.786	802	113	1946	8.8	1.2	21.4

Three-point field goals: 2002-03, 9-for-24 (.375). 2003-04, 14-for-37 (.378). 2004-05, 18-for-45 (.400). Totals, 41-for-106 (.387).

NBA REGULAR-SEASON RECORD

									REBOUNDS								AVERAGES		
Season Team	G	Min.	FGM	FGA	Pct.	FTM	FTA	Pct.	Off.	Def.	Tot.	Ast.	St.	Blk.	TO	Pts.	RPG	APG	PPG
05-06—Golden State ...	69	1031	175	334	.524	136	168	.810	95	134	229	29	15	30	78	486	3.3	0.4	7.0

Personal fouls/disqualifications: 2005-06, 164/4. Totals, 164/4.

DIOP, DESAGANA   C   MAVERICKS

PERSONAL: Born January 30, 1982, in Dakar, Senegal. ... 7-0/300. (2.13/136.1). ... Full name: DeSagana Ngagne Diop
HIGH SCHOOL: Oak Hill Academy (Mouth of Wilson, Va.).
COLLEGE: Did not attend college.
TRANSACTIONS/CAREER NOTES: Selected out of high school by Cleveland Cavaliers in first round (eighth pick overall) of 2001 NBA Draft. ... Signed as free agent by Dallas Mavericks (August 19, 2005).

NBA REGULAR-SEASON RECORD

									REBOUNDS								AVERAGES		
Season Team	G	Min.	FGM	FGA	Pct.	FTM	FTA	Pct.	Off.	Def.	Tot.	Ast.	St.	Blk.	TO	Pts.	RPG	APG	PPG
01-02—Cleveland	18	109	12	29	.414	1	5	.200	5	12	17	5	1	10	12	25	0.9	0.3	1.4
02-03—Cleveland	80	943	54	154	.351	11	30	.367	63	152	215	43	33	81	56	119	2.7	0.5	1.5
03-04—Cleveland	56	730	57	147	.388	12	20	.600	72	127	199	34	26	51	29	126	3.6	0.6	2.3
04-05—Cleveland	39	306	20	69	.290	0	5	.000	30	40	70	15	8	27	12	40	1.8	0.4	1.0
05-06—Dallas..............	81	1510	75	154	.487	39	72	.542	145	229	374	23	44	146	36	190	4.6	0.3	2.3
Totals	274	3598	218	553	.394	63	132	.477	315	560	875	120	112	315	145	500	3.2	0.4	1.8

Three-point field goals: 2004-05, 0-for-2. 2005-06, 1-for-2 (.500). Totals, 1-for-4 (.250).
Personal fouls/disqualifications: 2001-02, 19/0. 2002-03, 148/4. 2003-04, 116/1. 2004-05, 53/0. 2005-06, 253/3. Totals, 589/8.

NBA PLAYOFF RECORD

									REBOUNDS								AVERAGES		
Season Team	G	Min.	FGM	FGA	Pct.	FTM	FTA	Pct.	Off.	Def.	Tot.	Ast.	St.	Blk.	TO	Pts.	RPG	APG	PPG
05-06—Dallas..............	22	407	24	39	.615	11	18	.611	40	69	109	2	14	28	11	59	5.0	0.1	2.7

Personal fouls/disqualifications: 2005 06, 81/2. Totals, 81/2.

DIXON, JUAN   G   TRAIL BLAZERS

PERSONAL: Born October 9, 1978, in Baltimore. ... 6-3/164. (1.91/74.4).
HIGH SCHOOL: Calvert Hall (Baltimore).
COLLEGE: Maryland.
TRANSACTIONS/CAREER NOTES: Selected by Washington Wizards in first round (17th pick overall) of 2002 NBA Draft. ... Signed as free agent by Portland Trail Blazers (August 4, 2005).

COLLEGIATE RECORD

NOTES: THE SPORTING NEWS All-America first team (2002). ... Member of NCAA Division I championship team (2002) ... NCAA Division I Tournament Most Outstanding Player (2002).

												AVERAGES		
Season Team	G	Min.	FGM	FGA	Pct.	FTM	FTA	Pct.	Reb.	Ast.	Pts.	RPG	APG	PPG
97-98—Maryland					Did not play—redshirted.									
98-99—Maryland	34	505	85	192	.443	44	53	.830	88	47	250	2.6	1.4	7.4
99-00—Maryland	35	1190	234	506	.462	113	143	.790	192	127	630	5.5	3.6	18.0
00-01—Maryland	36	1098	232	480	.483	128	148	.865	153	93	654	4.3	2.6	18.2
01-02—Maryland	36	1209	251	535	.469	141	157	.898	166	104	735	4.6	2.9	20.4
Totals	141	4002	802	1713	.468	426	501	.850	599	371	2269	4.2	2.6	16.1

Three-point field goals: 1998-99, 36-for-97 (.371). 1999-00, 49-for-135 (.363). 2000-01, 62-for-151 (.411). 2001-02, 92-for-232 (.397). Totals, 239-for-615 (.389).

NBA REGULAR-SEASON RECORD

									REBOUNDS								AVERAGES		
Season Team	G	Min.	FGM	FGA	Pct.	FTM	FTA	Pct.	Off.	Def.	Tot.	Ast.	St.	Blk.	TO	Pts.	RPG	APG	PPG
02-03—Washington	42	647	104	271	.384	37	46	.804	13	59	72	40	26	3	42	270	1.7	1.0	6.4
03-04—Washington	71	1478	247	637	.388	111	139	.799	30	118	148	137	82	4	104	664	2.1	1.9	9.4
04-05—Washington	63	1054	186	447	.416	87	97	.897	32	87	119	111	43	4	68	507	1.9	1.8	8.0
05-06—Portland..........	76	1920	357	821	.435	156	194	.804	30	147	177	149	58	6	113	935	2.3	2.0	12.3
Totals	252	5099	894	2176	.411	391	476	.821	105	411	516	437	209	17	327	2376	2.0	1.7	9.4

Three-point field goals: 2002-03, 25-for-84 (.298). 2003-04, 59-for-198 (.298). 2004-05, 48-for-147 (.327). 2005-06, 65-for-170 (.382). Totals, 197-for-599 (.329).
Personal fouls/disqualifications: 2002-03, 54/0. 2003-04, 111/1. 2004-05, 98/0. 2005-06, 157/0. Totals, 420/1.

NBA PLAYOFF RECORD

									REBOUNDS								AVERAGES		
Season Team	G	Min.	FGM	FGA	Pct.	FTM	FTA	Pct.	Off.	Def.	Tot.	Ast.	St.	Blk.	TO	Pts.	RPG	APG	PPG
04-05—Washington	10	219	41	101	.406	21	25	.840	3	23	26	13	7	0	12	114	2.6	1.3	11.4

Three-point field goals: 2004-05, 11-for-34 (.324). Totals, 11-for-34 (.324).
Personal fouls/disqualifications: 2004-05, 19/0. Totals, 19/0.

DOLEAC, MICHAEL   C   HEAT

PERSONAL: Born June 15, 1977, in San Antonio. ... 6-11/262. (2.11/118.8). ... Full name: Michael Scott Doleac
HIGH SCHOOL: Central Catholic (Portland, Ore.).
COLLEGE: Utah.
TRANSACTIONS/CAREER NOTES: Selected by Orlando Magic in first round (12th pick overall) of 1998 NBA Draft. ... Traded by Magic to Cleveland Cavaliers for draft rights to C Brendan Haywood (June 27, 2001). ... Signed as free agent by New York Knicks (August 7, 2002). ... Traded by Knicks to Atlanta Hawks in three-team deal in which Knicks also traded 2005 second-round draft choice to Hawks and F Keith Van Horn to Milwaukee Bucks. Hawks also acquired C Joel Przybilla from Bucks. Knicks acquired F Nazr Mohammed from Hawks and F Tim Thomas from Bucks (February 15, 2004). ... Waived by Hawks (February 18, 2004). ... Signed as free agent by Denver Nuggets (February 20, 2004). ... Signed as free agent by Miami Heat (July 15, 2004).
MISCELLANEOUS: Member of NBA championship team (2006).

COLLEGIATE RECORD

												AVERAGES		
Season Team	G	Min.	FGM	FGA	Pct.	FTM	FTA	Pct.	Reb.	Ast.	Pts.	RPG	APG	PPG
94-95—Utah	32	547	81	179	.453	72	97	.742	144	6	234	4.5	0.2	7.3
95-96—Utah	34	819	101	218	.463	92	116	.793	261	26	294	7.7	0.8	8.6
96-97—Utah	33	876	166	309	.537	135	174	.776	253	25	475	7.7	0.8	14.4
97-98—Utah	32	876	165	338	.488	173	215	.805	228	17	516	7.1	0.5	16.1
Totals	**131**	**3118**	**513**	**1044**	**.491**	**472**	**602**	**.784**	**886**	**74**	**1519**	**6.8**	**0.6**	**11.6**

Three-point field goals: 1994-95, 0-for-1. 1995-96, 0-for-1. 1996-97, 8-for-18 (.444). 1997-98, 13-for-32 (.406). Totals, 21-for-52 (.404).

NBA REGULAR-SEASON RECORD

HONORS: NBA All-Rookie second team (1999).

									REBOUNDS								AVERAGES		
Season Team	G	Min.	FGM	FGA	Pct.	FTM	FTA	Pct.	Off.	Def.	Tot.	Ast.	St.	Blk.	TO	Pts.	RPG	APG	PPG
98-99—Orlando	49	780	125	267	.468	54	80	.675	66	82	148	20	19	17	26	304	3.0	0.4	6.2
99-00—Orlando	81	1335	242	535	.452	80	95	.842	89	245	334	63	29	34	65	565	4.1	0.8	7.0
00-01—Orlando	77	1398	220	527	.417	50	59	.847	70	203	273	65	37	41	59	490	3.5	0.8	6.4
01-02—Cleveland	42	705	78	187	.417	38	46	.826	47	121	168	25	15	11	37	194	4.0	0.6	4.6
02-03—New York	75	1041	146	343	.426	36	46	.783	65	154	219	42	16	16	49	328	2.9	0.6	4.4
04-05—Miami	80	1175	148	331	.447	25	41	.610	74	185	259	47	23	22	36	321	3.2	0.6	4.0
05-06—Miami	31	371	37	88	.420	24	30	.800	23	62	85	8	10	7	14	98	2.7	0.3	3.2
Totals	**435**	**6805**	**996**	**2278**	**.437**	**307**	**397**	**.773**	**434**	**1052**	**1486**	**270**	**149**	**148**	**286**	**2300**	**3.4**	**0.6**	**5.3**

Three-point field goals: 1999-00, 1-for-2 (.500). 2000-01, 0-for-3. 2004-05, 0-for-2. Totals, 1-for-7 (.143).
Personal fouls/disqualifications: 1998-99, 117/1. 1999-00, 224/3. 2000-01, 239/10. 2001-02, 98/4. 2002-03, 150/1. 2004-05, 160/0. 2005-06, 45/0. Totals, 1033/19.

NBA PLAYOFF RECORD

									REBOUNDS								AVERAGES		
Season Team	G	Min.	FGM	FGA	Pct.	FTM	FTA	Pct.	Off.	Def.	Tot.	Ast.	St.	Blk.	TO	Pts.	RPG	APG	PPG
98-99—Orlando	4	43	5	18	.278	7	9	.778	5	7	12	0	0	1	3	17	3.0	0.0	4.3
00-01—Orlando	4	45	6	16	.375	0	0	...	4	10	14	1	3	0	2	12	3.5	0.3	3.0
03-04—Denver	5	49	5	10	.500	0	0	...	2	5	7	3	0	0	1	10	1.4	0.6	2.0
04-05—Miami	9	65	7	16	.438	2	2	1.000	2	12	14	0	1	1	3	16	1.6	0.0	1.8
05-06—Miami	8	72	7	13	.538	2	2	1.000	6	16	22	0	1	0	3	16	2.8	0.0	2.0
Totals	**30**	**274**	**30**	**73**	**.411**	**11**	**13**	**.846**	**19**	**50**	**69**	**4**	**5**	**2**	**12**	**71**	**2.3**	**0.1**	**2.4**

Three-point field goals: 1998-99, 0-for-1. Totals, 0-for-1 (.000).
Personal fouls/disqualifications: 1998-99, 6/0. 2000-01, 10/0. 2003-04, 8/0. 2004-05, 13/0. 2005-06, 12/0. Totals, 49/0.

DOOLING, KEYON   G   MAGIC

PERSONAL: Born May 8, 1980, in Fort Lauderdale, Fla. ... 6-3/196. (1.91/88.9). ... Full name: Keyon Latwae Dooling
HIGH SCHOOL: Dillard (Fort Lauderdale, Fla.).
COLLEGE: Missouri.
TRANSACTIONS/CAREER NOTES: Selected after sophomore season by Orlando Magic in first round (10th pick overall) of 2000 NBA Draft. ... Draft rights traded by Magic with F Corey Maggette and F Derek Strong to Los Angeles Clippers for a future first-round draft choice (June 28, 2000). ... Signed as free agent by Miami Heat (July 22, 2004). ... Signed as free agent by Orlando Magic (August 3, 2005).

COLLEGIATE RECORD

												AVERAGES		
Season Team	G	Min.	FGM	FGA	Pct.	FTM	FTA	Pct.	Reb.	Ast.	Pts.	RPG	APG	PPG
98-99—Missouri	28	676	78	170	.459	79	110	.718	58	85	243	2.1	3.0	8.7
99-00—Missouri	31	983	145	373	.389	124	167	.743	84	113	473	2.7	3.6	15.3
Totals	**59**	**1659**	**223**	**543**	**.411**	**203**	**277**	**.733**	**142**	**198**	**716**	**2.4**	**3.4**	**12.1**

Three-point field goals: 1998-99, 8-for-28 (.286). 1999-00, 59-for-170 (.347). Totals, 67-for-198 (.338).

NBA REGULAR-SEASON RECORD

									REBOUNDS								AVERAGES		
Season Team	G	Min.	FGM	FGA	Pct.	FTM	FTA	Pct.	Off.	Def.	Tot.	Ast.	St.	Blk.	TO	Pts.	RPG	APG	PPG
00-01—L.A. Clippers	76	1237	148	362	.409	125	179	.698	8	81	89	177	41	11	94	449	1.2	2.3	5.9
01-02—L.A. Clippers	14	155	22	57	.386	10	12	.833	0	3	3	12	4	3	10	58	0.2	0.9	4.1
02-03—L.A. Clippers	55	969	128	329	.389	44	57	.772	9	63	72	89	24	6	60	350	1.3	1.6	6.4
03-04—L.A. Clippers	58	1137	137	352	.389	78	94	.830	17	62	79	130	45	6	65	360	1.4	2.2	6.2
04-05—Miami	74	1184	139	345	.403	85	109	.780	11	79	90	132	39	11	65	382	1.2	1.8	5.2
05-06—Orlando	50	1137	178	405	.440	101	121	.835	11	67	78	109	49	4	82	470	1.6	2.2	9.4
Totals	**327**	**5819**	**752**	**1850**	**.406**	**443**	**572**	**.774**	**56**	**355**	**411**	**649**	**202**	**41**	**376**	**2069**	**1.3**	**2.0**	**6.3**

Three-point field goals: 2000-01, 28-for-80 (.350). 2001-02, 4-for-14 (.286). 2002-03, 50-for-139 (.360). 2003-04, 8-for-46 (.174). 2004-05, 19-for-75 (.253). 2005-06, 13-for-43 (.302). Totals, 122-for-397 (.307).
Personal fouls/disqualifications: 2000-01, 107/0. 2001-02, 20/0. 2002-03, 93/0. 2003-04, 108/2. 2004-05, 120/0. 2005-06, 116/1. Totals, 564/3.

NBA PLAYOFF RECORD

| | | | | | | | | REBOUNDS | | | | | | | | AVERAGES | | |
Season Team	G	Min.	FGM	FGA	Pct.	FTM	FTA	Pct.	Off.	Def.	Tot.	Ast.	St.	Blk.	TO	Pts.	RPG	APG	PPG
04-05—Miami	15	264	43	87	.494	17	21	.810	1	15	16	25	6	1	14	110	1.1	1.7	7.3

Three-point field goals: 2004-05, 7-for-19 (.368). Totals, 7-for-19 (.368).
Personal fouls/disqualifications: 2004-05, 34/0. Totals, 34/0.

DUHON, CHRIS — G — BULLS

PERSONAL: Born August 31, 1982, in Mamou, La. ... 6-1/185. (1.85/83.9). ... Full name: Chris Nicholas Duhon
HIGH SCHOOL: Salmen (Slidell, La.).
COLLEGE: Duke.
TRANSACTIONS/CAREER NOTES: Selected by Chicago Bulls in second round (38th pick overall) of 2004 NBA Draft.

NOTES: Member of NCAA Division I championship team (2001).

COLLEGIATE RECORD

| | | | | | | | | | | | | AVERAGES | | |
Season Team	G	Min.	FGM	FGA	Pct.	FTM	FTA	Pct.	Reb.	Ast.	Pts.	RPG	APG	PPG
00-01—Duke	39	1085	92	217	.424	52	80	.650	124	174	280	3.2	4.5	7.2
01-02—Duke	35	1229	100	244	.410	59	83	.711	109	208	313	3.1	5.9	8.9
02-03—Duke	33	1188	102	264	.386	66	96	.688	106	212	305	3.2	6.4	9.2
03-04—Duke	37	1311	138	308	.448	65	90	.722	150	225	370	4.1	6.1	10.0
Totals	144	4813	432	1033	.418	242	349	.693	489	819	1268	3.4	5.7	8.8

NBA REGULAR-SEASON RECORD

| | | | | | | | | REBOUNDS | | | | | | | | AVERAGES | | |
Season Team	G	Min.	FGM	FGA	Pct.	FTM	FTA	Pct.	Off.	Def.	Tot.	Ast.	St.	Blk.	TO	Pts.	RPG	APG	PPG
04-05—Chicago	82	2177	172	488	.352	49	67	.731	23	190	213	398	82	3	119	487	2.6	4.9	5.9
05-06—Chicago	74	2155	215	538	.400	117	143	.818	28	192	220	373	70	3	117	647	3.0	5.0	8.7
Totals	156	4332	387	1026	.377	166	210	.790	51	382	433	771	152	6	236	1134	2.8	4.9	7.3

Three-point field goals: 2004-05, 94-for-265 (.355). 2005-06, 100-for-278 (.360). Totals, 194-for-543 (.357).
Personal fouls/disqualifications: 2004-05, 205/1. 2005-06, 152/0. Totals, 357/1.

NBA PLAYOFF RECORD

| | | | | | | | | REBOUNDS | | | | | | | | AVERAGES | | |
Season Team	G	Min.	FGM	FGA	Pct.	FTM	FTA	Pct.	Off.	Def.	Tot.	Ast.	St.	Blk.	TO	Pts.	RPG	APG	PPG
04-05—Chicago	6	159	11	37	.297	9	11	.818	6	20	26	21	2	0	12	37	4.3	3.5	6.2
05-06—Chicago	6	131	9	25	.360	5	6	.833	1	15	16	13	2	0	5	30	2.7	2.2	5.0
Totals	10	290	20	62	.323	14	17	.824	7	35	42	34	4	0	17	67	3.5	3.4	5.6

Three-point field goals: 2004-05, 6-for-22 (.273). 2005-06, 7-for-16 (.438). Totals, 13-for-38 (.342).
Personal fouls/disqualifications: 2004-05, 6/0. 2005-06, 13/0. Totals, 19/0.

DUNCAN, TIM — F/C — SPURS

PERSONAL: Born April 25, 1976, in St. Croix, Virgin Islands. ... 7-0/260. (2.13/117.9). ... Full name: Timothy Theodore Duncan
HIGH SCHOOL: St. Dunstan's Episcopal High (Virgin Islands).
COLLEGE: Wake Forest.
TRANSACTIONS/CAREER NOTES: Selected by San Antonio Spurs in first round (first pick overall) of 1997 NBA Draft.
MISCELLANEOUS: Member of NBA championship team (1999, 2003, 2005). ... Member of bronze-medal-winning U.S. Olympic Team (2004).

COLLEGIATE RECORD

NOTES: The SPORTING NEWS College Player of the Year (1997). ... Naismith Award winner (1997). ... Wooden Award winner (1997). ... The SPORTING NEWS All-America first team (1996 and 1997). ... Holds NCAA Division I career record for most career rebounds (since 1973)—1,570. ... Led NCAA Division I with 14.7 rebounds per game (1997).

| | | | | | | | | | | | | AVERAGES | | |
Season Team	G	Min.	FGM	FGA	Pct.	FTM	FTA	Pct.	Reb.	Ast.	Pts.	RPG	APG	PPG
93-94—Wake Forest	33	997	120	220	.545	82	110	.745	317	30	323	9.6	0.9	9.8
94-95—Wake Forest	32	1168	208	352	.591	118	159	.742	401	67	537	12.5	2.1	16.8
95-96—Wake Forest	32	1190	228	411	.555	149	217	.687	395	93	612	12.3	2.9	19.1
96-97—Wake Forest	31	1137	234	385	.608	171	269	.636	457	98	645	14.7	3.2	20.8
Totals	128	4492	790	1368	.577	520	755	.689	1570	288	2117	12.3	2.3	16.5

Three-point field goals: 1993-94, 1-for-1 (1.000). 1994-95, 3-for-7 (.429). 1995-96, 7-for-23 (.304). 1996-97, 6-for-22 (.273). Totals, 17-for-53 (.321).
Personal fouls/disqualifications: 1993-94, 82/2. 1994-95, 79/3. 1995-96, 74/0. Totals, 235/5.

NBA REGULAR-SEASON RECORD

HONORS: NBA Most Valuable Player (2002, 2003). ... NBA Rookie of the Year (1998). ... IBM Award, for all-around contributions to team's success (2002). ... All-NBA first team (1998, 1999, 2000, 2001, 2002, 2003, 2004, 2005). ... NBA All-Defensive first team (1999, 2000, 2001, 2002, 2003, 2005). ... NBA All-Defensive second team (1998, 2004, 2006). ... NBA All-Rookie first team (1998). ... All-NBA second team (2006).

| | | | | | | | | REBOUNDS | | | | | | | | AVERAGES | | |
Season Team	G	Min.	FGM	FGA	Pct.	FTM	FTA	Pct.	Off.	Def.	Tot.	Ast.	St.	Blk.	TO	Pts.	RPG	APG	PPG
97-98—San Antonio	82	3204	706	1287	.549	319	482	.662	274	703	977	224	55	206	279	1731	11.9	2.7	21.1
98-99—San Antonio	50	1963	418	845	.495	247	358	.690	159	412	571	121	45	126	146	1084	11.4	2.4	21.7
99-00—San Antonio	74	2875	628	1281	.490	459	603	.761	262	656	918	234	66	165	242	1716	12.4	3.2	23.2

Season Team	G	Min.	FGM	FGA	Pct.	FTM	FTA	Pct.	REBOUNDS Off.	Def.	Tot.	Ast.	St.	Blk.	TO	Pts.	AVERAGES RPG	APG	PPG
00-01—San Antonio....	82	3174	702	1406	.499	409	662	.618	259	738	997	245	70	192	242	1820	12.2	3.0	22.2
01-02—San Antonio....	82	3329	*764	*1504	.508	*560	701	.799	268	*774	*1042	307	61	203	263	2089	12.7	3.7	25.5
02-03—San Antonio....	81	3181	714	1392	.513	450	634	.710	259	784	1043	316	55	237	248	1884	12.9	3.9	23.3
03-04—San Antonio....	69	2527	592	1181	.501	352	588	.599	227	632	859	213	62	185	183	1538	12.4	3.1	22.3
04-05—San Antonio....	66	2203	517	1042	.496	305	455	.670	202	530	732	179	45	174	127	1342	11.1	2.7	20.3
05-06—San Antonio....	80	2784	574	1185	.484	335	533	.629	231	650	881	253	70	162	198	1485	11.0	3.2	18.6
Totals	666	25240	5615	11123	.505	3436	5016	.685	2141	5879	8020	2092	529	1650	1928	14689	12.0	3.1	22.1

Three-point field goals: 1997-98, 0-for-10. 1998-99, 1-for-7 (.143). 1999-00, 1-for-11 (.091). 2000-01, 7-for-27 (.259). 2001-02, 1-for-10 (.100). 2002-03, 6-for-22 (.273). 2003-04, 2-for-12 (.167). 2004-05, 3-for-9 (.333). 2005-06, 2-for-5 (.400). Totals, 23-for-113 (.204).

Personal fouls/disqualifications: 1997-98, 254/1. 1998-99, 147/2. 1999-00, 210/1. 2000-01, 247/0. 2001-02, 217/2. 2002-03, 231/2. 2003-04, 164/1. 2004-05, 144/0. 2005-06, 219/2. Totals, 1833/11.

NBA PLAYOFF RECORD

NOTES: NBA Finals Most Valuable Player (1999, 2003, 2005). ... Holds NBA Finals record for most blocked shots—32 (2003). ... Shares NBA Finals single-game record for blocked shots—8 (June 15, 2003, vs. New Jersey).

Season Team	G	Min.	FGM	FGA	Pct.	FTM	FTA	Pct.	REBOUNDS Off.	Def.	Tot.	Ast.	St.	Blk.	TO	Pts.	AVERAGES RPG	APG	PPG
97-98—San Antonio....	9	374	73	140	.521	40	60	.667	20	61	81	17	5	23	25	186	9.0	1.9	20.7
98-99—San Antonio....	17	733	144	282	.511	107	143	.748	55	140	195	48	13	45	52	395	11.5	2.8	23.2
00-01—San Antonio....	13	526	120	246	.488	76	119	.639	54	134	188	49	14	35	50	317	14.5	3.8	24.4
01-02—San Antonio....	9	380	82	181	.453	83	101	.822	28	102	130	45	6	39	37	248	14.4	5.0	27.6
02-03—San Antonio....	24	1021	218	412	.529	157	232	.677	96	273	369	127	15	79	76	593	15.4	5.3	24.7
03-04—San Antonio....	10	405	83	159	.522	55	87	.632	33	80	113	32	8	20	42	221	11.3	3.2	22.1
04-05—San Antonio....	23	869	197	425	.464	147	205	.717	87	199	286	63	8	52	62	542	12.4	2.7	23.6
05-06—San Antonio....	13	493	121	211	.573	94	131	.718	33	104	137	43	11	25	34	336	10.5	3.3	25.8
Totals	118	4801	1038	2056	.505	759	1078	.704	406	1093	1499	424	80	318	378	2838	12.7	3.6	24.1

Three-point field goals: 1997-98, 0-for-1. 1998-99, 0-for-3. 2000-01, 1-for-1 (1.000). 2001-02, 1-for-3 (.333). 2002-03, 0-for-7. 2003-04, 0-for-1. 2004-05, 1-for-5 (.200). 2005-06, 0-for-2. Totals, 3-for-23 (.130).

Personal fouls/disqualifications: 1997-98, 24/1. 1998-99, 50/1. 2000-01, 43/0. 2001-02, 22/0. 2002-03, 78/0. 2003-04, 34/0. 2004-05, 66/1. 2005-06, 50/1. Totals, 367/4.

NBA ALL-STAR GAME RECORD

NOTES: NBA All-Star Game co-Most Valuable Player (2000).

Season Team	Min.	FGM	FGA	Pct.	FTM	FTA	Pct.	REBOUNDS Off.	Def.	Tot.	Ast.	PF	Dq.	St.	Blk.	TO	Pts.
1998—San Antonio	14	1	4	.250	0	0	...	1	10	11	1	0	0	0	0	2	2
2000—San Antonio	33	12	14	.857	0	0	...	7	7	14	4	3	0	1	1	2	24
2001—San Antonio	28	5	11	.455	4	4	1.000	4	10	14	1	1	0	2	1	2	14
2002—San Antonio	29	7	11	.636	0	0	...	3	11	14	2	1	0	0	2	3	14
2003—San Antonio	40	8	18	.444	3	3	1.000	5	10	15	4	2	0	1	0	3	19
2004—San Antonio	26	6	11	.545	2	4	.500	2	11	13	5	2	0	1	0	2	14
2005—San Antonio	16	7	10	.700	0	1	.000	2	7	9	2	0	0	0	0	2	15
2006—San Antonio	21	6	7	.857	3	3	1.000	6	4	10	1	2	0	1	1	5	15
Totals	207	52	86	.605	12	15	.800	30	70	100	20	11	0	6	5	21	117

Three-point field goals: 1998, 0-for-1. 2005, 1-for-1 (1.000). Totals, 1-for-2 (.500).

DUNLEAVY, MIKE — G/F — WARRIORS

PERSONAL: Born September 15, 1980, in Fort Worth, Texas. ... 6-9/221. (2.06/100.2). ... Full name: Michael Joseph Dunleavy ... Son of Mike Dunleavy, guard with four NBA teams (1976-77 through 1983-84, 1988-89 and 1989-90) and head coach with Los Angeles Lakers (1990-91 through 1995-96), Portland Trail Blazers (1997-98 through 2000-01) and Los Angeles Clippers (2003-present).

HIGH SCHOOL: Jesuit (Portland).

COLLEGE: Duke.

TRANSACTIONS/CAREER NOTES: Selected after junior season by Golden State Warriors in first round (third pick overall) of 2002 NBA Draft.

COLLEGIATE RECORD

NOTES: THE SPORTING NEWS All-America second team (2002). ... Member of NCAA Division I championship team (2001).

Season Team	G	Min.	FGM	FGA	Pct.	FTM	FTA	Pct.	Reb.	Ast.	Pts.	AVERAGES RPG	APG	PPG
99-00—Duke..............................	30	724	97	211	.460	45	61	.738	128	50	273	4.3	1.7	9.1
00-01—Duke..............................	39	1137	184	388	.474	68	98	.694	222	103	493	5.7	2.6	12.6
01-02—Duke..............................	35	1133	218	451	.483	81	119	.681	251	72	605	7.2	2.1	17.3
Totals	104	2994	499	1050	.475	194	278	.698	601	225	1371	5.8	2.2	13.2

Three-point field goals: 1999-00, 34-for-97 (.351). 2000-01, 57-for-153 (.373). 2001-02, 88-for-233 (.378). Totals, 179-for-483 (.371).

NBA REGULAR-SEASON RECORD

Season Team	G	Min.	FGM	FGA	Pct.	FTM	FTA	Pct.	REBOUNDS Off.	Def.	Tot.	Ast.	St.	Blk.	TO	Pts.	AVERAGES RPG	APG	PPG
02-03—Golden State ...	82	1305	168	417	.403	78	100	.780	66	148	214	106	53	19	86	466	2.6	1.3	5.7
03-04—Golden State ...	75	2336	323	720	.449	137	185	.741	87	355	442	220	68	13	143	877	5.9	2.9	11.7
04-05—Golden State ...	79	2570	408	905	.451	134	172	.779	97	338	435	203	79	26	132	1057	5.5	2.6	13.4
05-06—Golden State ...	81	2578	331	816	.406	196	252	.778	78	321	399	237	60	32	120	932	4.9	2.9	11.5
Totals	317	8789	1230	2858	.430	545	709	.769	328	1162	1490	766	260	90	481	3332	4.7	2.4	10.5

Three-point field goals: 2002-03, 52-for-150 (.347). 2003-04, 94-for-254 (.370). 2004-05, 107-for-276 (.388). 2005-06, 74-for-260 (.285). Totals, 327-for-940 (.348).

Personal fouls/disqualifications: 2002-03, 120/0. 2003-04, 169/2. 2004-05, 198/3. 2005-06, 199/1. Totals, 686/6.

DUPREE, RONALD   F   PISTONS

PERSONAL: Born January 26, 1981, in Biloxi, Miss. ... 6-7/209. (2.01/94.8). ... Full name: Ronald Edmund Dupree
HIGH SCHOOL: Biloxi (Miss.).
COLLEGE: Louisiana State.
TRANSACTIONS/CAREER NOTES: Not drafted by an NBA franchise. ... Signed as free agent by Detroit Pistons (September 29, 2003). ... Waived by Pistons (October 23, 2003). ... Played in NBA Development League with Huntsville Flight (2003-04). ... Signed by Chicago Bulls to 10-day contract (January 7, 2004). ... Signed by Bulls for remainder of season (January 28, 2004). ... Signed as free agent by Detroit Pistons (July 2004). ... Traded by Pistons to Minnesota Timberwolves for a second-round draft pick (October 31, 2005). ... Signed as free agent by Pistons (July 17, 2006).

COLLEGIATE RECORD

Season Team	G	Min.	FGM	FGA	Pct.	FTM	FTA	Pct.	Reb.	Ast.	Pts.	RPG	APG	PPG
99-00—Louisiana State	34	433	63	136	.463	39	68	.574	112	14	167	3.3	0.4	4.9
00-01—Louisiana State	29	1012	183	377	.485	116	166	.699	256	41	503	8.8	1.4	17.3
01-02—Louisiana State	34	1203	220	487	.452	81	145	.559	290	73	552	8.5	2.1	16.2
02-03—Louisiana State	32	1063	199	376	.529	93	137	.679	249	77	504	7.8	2.4	15.8
Totals	129	3711	665	1376	.483	329	516	.638	907	205	1726	7.0	1.6	13.4

Three-point field goals: 1999-00, 2-for-14 (.143). 2000-01, 21-for-64 (.328). 2001-02, 31-for-108 (.287). 2002-03, 13-for-37 (.351). Totals, 67-for-223 (.300).

NBA REGULAR-SEASON RECORD

									REBOUNDS								AVERAGES		
Season Team	G	Min.	FGM	FGA	Pct.	FTM	FTA	Pct.	Off.	Def.	Tot.	Ast.	St.	Blk.	TO	Pts.	RPG	APG	PPG
03-04—Chicago	47	893	111	282	.394	66	105	.629	55	112	167	55	32	18	51	292	3.6	1.2	6.2
04-05—Detroit	47	472	61	127	.480	29	47	.617	34	61	95	24	7	10	22	152	2.0	0.5	3.2
05-06—Minnesota	36	265	33	63	.524	14	41	.341	21	28	49	14	12	0	14	80	1.4	0.4	2.2
Totals	130	1630	205	472	.434	109	193	.565	110	201	311	93	51	28	87	524	2.4	0.7	4.0

Three-point field goals: 2003-04, 4-for-9 (.444). 2004-05, 1-for-2 (.500). 2005-06, 0-for-1. Totals, 5-for-12 (.417).
Personal fouls/disqualifications: 2003-04, 134/4. 2004-05, 60/0. 2005-06, 44/1. Totals, 238/5.

NBA PLAYOFF RECORD

									REBOUNDS								AVERAGES		
Season Team	G	Min.	FGM	FGA	Pct.	FTM	FTA	Pct.	Off.	Def.	Tot.	Ast.	St.	Blk.	TO	Pts.	RPG	APG	PPG
04-05—Detroit	14	38	2	7	.286	0	0	...	2	4	6	0	0	0	1	4	0.4	0.0	0.3

Personal fouls/disqualifications: 2004-05, 6/0. Totals, 6/0.

NBA DEVELOPMENT LEAGUE RECORD

Season Team	G	Min.	FGM	FGA	Pct.	FTM	FTA	Pct.	Reb.	Ast.	Pts.	RPG	APG	PPG
03-04—Huntsville	15	483	104	187	.556	45	59	.763	69	22	254	4.6	1.5	16.9

EDWARDS, JOHN   C   PACERS

PERSONAL: Born July 31, 1981 ... 7-0/275. (2.13/124.7).
HIGH SCHOOL: Hudson (Ohio).
COLLEGE: Kent State.
TRANSACTIONS/CAREER NOTES: Not drafted by an NBA franchise. ... Signed as free agent by Indiana Pacers (September 14, 2004). ... Signed as free agent by Atlanta Hawks (August 30, 2005). ... Traded by Hawks with F Al Harrington to Indiana Pacers for a first-round draft choice (August 22, 2006).

COLLEGIATE RECORD

Season Team	G	Min.	FGM	FGA	Pct.	FTM	FTA	Pct.	Reb.	Ast.	Pts.	RPG	APG	PPG
99-00—Kent St						Did Not Play - Redshirted								
00-01—Kent St	32	218	25	58	.431	14	30	.467	54	3	64	1.7	0.1	2.0
01-02—Kent St	35	422	49	81	.605	24	37	.649	72	2	122	2.1	0.1	3.5
02-03—Kent St	31	521	93	147	.633	37	52	.712	106	10	223	3.4	0.3	7.2
03-04—Kent St	30	775	157	297	.529	81	120	.675	197	12	395	6.6	0.4	13.2
Totals	128	1936	324	583	.556	156	239	.653	429	27	804	3.4	0.2	6.3

NBA REGULAR-SEASON RECORD

									REBOUNDS								AVERAGES		
Season Team	G	Min.	FGM	FGA	Pct.	FTM	FTA	Pct.	Off.	Def.	Tot.	Ast.	St.	Blk.	TO	Pts.	RPG	APG	PPG
04-05—Indiana	25	139	11	30	.367	7	14	.500	8	11	19	3	3	4	8	29	0.8	0.1	1.2
05-06—Atlanta	40	296	31	64	.484	8	11	.727	18	30	48	5	3	15	12	70	1.2	0.1	1.8
Totals	65	435	42	94	.447	15	25	.600	26	41	67	8	6	19	20	99	1.0	0.1	1.5

Personal fouls/disqualifications: 2004-05, 12/0. 2005-06, 76/1. Totals, 88/1.

EISLEY, HOWARD   G

PERSONAL: Born December 4, 1972, in Detroit. ... 6-2/180. (1.88/81.6). ... Full name: Howard Jonathan Eisley
HIGH SCHOOL: Southwestern (Detroit).
COLLEGE: Boston College.
TRANSACTIONS/CAREER NOTES: Selected by Minnesota Timberwolves in second round (30th pick overall) of 1994 NBA Draft. ... Waived by Timberwolves (February 13, 1995). ... Signed by San Antonio Spurs to first of two consecutive 10-day

contracts (February 26, 1995). ... Signed by Spurs for remainder of season (March 18, 1995). ... Waived by Spurs (April 17, 1995). ... Signed as free agent by Utah Jazz (October 5, 1995). ... Waived by Jazz (October 30, 1995). ... Played in Continental Basketball Association with Rockford Lightning (1995-96). ... Signed as free agent by Jazz (December 7, 1995). ... Traded by Jazz to Dallas Mavericks as part of four-team deal in which Boston Celtics received G Robert Pack, C John Williams and cash considerations from Mavericks and a conditional first-round draft choice from Jazz, Mavericks received G Dana Barros from Celtics, F Bill Curley from Golden State Warriors, Jazz received F Donyell Marshall from Warriors and C Bruno Sundov from Mavericks and Warriors received F Danny Fortson from Celtics and F Adam Keefe from Jazz (August 16, 2000). ... Traded by Mavericks to New York Knicks as part of three-team trade in which Knicks acquired F Shandon Anderson from Houston Rockets, Mavericks acquired G Muggsy Bogues from Knicks and Rockets acquired F Glen Rice from Knicks and draft rights to G Kyle Hill from Mavericks (August 10, 2001). ... Traded by Knicks with F Maciej Lampe, F Antonio McDyess, G Charlie Ward, draft rights to G Milos Vujanic, 2004 first-round draft choice and future first-round draft choice to Phoenix Suns for G Stephon Marbury, F/G Anfernee Hardaway and C Cezary Trybanski (January 5, 2004). ... Waived by Suns (October 29, 2004). ... Signed by Los Angeles Clippers (November 17, 2005). ... Waived by Clippers (January 3, 2006). ... Signed by Denver Nuggets to 10-day contract (March 3, 2006). ... Signed by Nuggets for remainder of season (March 23, 2006). ... Traded by Nuggets with two second-round picks in 2007 draft to Chicago Bulls for G J.R. Smith (July 20, 2006).

COLLEGIATE RECORD

Season Team	G	Min.	FGM	FGA	Pct.	FTM	FTA	Pct.	Reb.	Ast.	Pts.	AVERAGES RPG	APG	PPG
90-91—Boston College	30	1011	95	264	.360	81	108	.750	79	100	297	2.6	3.3	9.9
91-92—Boston College	31	1071	118	242	.488	88	118	.746	111	135	361	3.6	4.4	11.6
92-93—Boston College	31	1162	131	296	.443	121	145	.834	107	153	426	3.5	4.9	13.7
93-94—Boston College	34	1203	529	1191	.444	373	476	.784	116	156	544	3.4	4.6	16.0
Totals	126	4447	873	1993	.438	663	847	.783	413	544	1628	3.3	4.3	12.9

Three-point field goals: 1990-91, 26-for-74 (.351). 1991-92, 37-for-75 (.493). 1992-93, 43-for-104 (.413). 1993-94, 91-for-188 (.484). Totals, 197-for-441 (.447).

NBA REGULAR-SEASON RECORD

Season Team	G	Min.	FGM	FGA	Pct.	FTM	FTA	Pct.	REBOUNDS Off.	Def.	Tot.	Ast.	St.	Blk.	TO	Pts.	AVERAGES RPG	APG	PPG
94-95—Minn.-S.A.	49	552	40	122	.328	31	40	.775	12	36	48	95	18	6	50	120	1.0	1.9	2.4
95-96—Utah	65	961	104	242	.430	65	77	.844	22	56	78	146	29	3	77	287	1.2	2.2	4.4
96-97—Utah	82	1083	139	308	.451	70	89	.787	20	64	84	198	44	10	110	368	1.0	2.4	4.5
97-98—Utah	82	1726	229	519	.441	127	149	.852	25	141	166	346	54	13	160	633	2.0	4.2	7.7
98-99—Utah	50	1038	140	314	.446	67	80	.838	12	82	94	185	30	2	109	368	1.9	3.7	7.4
99-00—Utah	82	2096	282	675	.418	84	102	.824	23	147	170	347	59	9	132	708	2.1	4.2	8.6
00-01—Dallas	82	2426	265	675	.393	104	126	.825	23	174	197	295	99	12	102	741	2.4	3.6	9.0
01-02—New York	39	609	59	175	.337	39	49	.796	9	40	49	100	24	3	53	171	1.3	2.6	4.4
02-03—New York	82	2243	262	628	.417	89	105	.848	24	162	186	444	71	9	149	744	2.3	5.4	9.1
03-04—New York-Pho.	67	1457	166	451	.368	76	89	.854	20	109	129	273	56	5	98	460	1.9	4.1	6.9
04-05—Utah	74	1428	161	405	.398	66	83	.795	15	75	90	250	45	9	111	415	1.2	3.4	5.6
05-06—L.A. Clip-Den.	32	394	34	103	.330	20	24	.833	3	30	33	69	11	2	21	101	1.0	2.2	3.2
Totals	786	16013	1881	4617	.407	838	1013	.827	208	1116	1324	2748	540	83	1172	5116	1.7	3.5	6.5

Three-point field goals: 1994-95, 9-for-37 (.243). 1995-96, 14-for-62 (.226). 1996-97, 20-for-72 (.278). 1997-98, 48-for-118 (.407). 1998-99, 21-for-50 (.420). 1999-00, 60-for-163 (.368). 2000-01, 107-for-269 (.398). 2001-02, 14-for-58 (.241). 2002-03, 131-for-337 (.389). 2003-04, 52-for-163 (.319). 2004-05, 27-for-103 (.262). 2005-06, 13-for-42 (.310). Totals, 516-for-1474 (.350).

Personal fouls/disqualifications: 1994-95, 81/0. 1995-96, 130/0. 1996-97, 141/0. 1997-98, 182/3. 1998-99, 122/0. 1999-00, 223/2. 2000-01, 218/3. 2001-02, 55/0. 2002-03, 222/1. 2003-04, 137/1. 2004-05, 156/1. 2005-06, 34/0. Totals, 1701/11.

NBA PLAYOFF RECORD

Season Team	G	Min.	FGM	FGA	Pct.	FTM	FTA	Pct.	REBOUNDS Off.	Def.	Tot.	Ast.	St.	Blk.	TO	Pts.	AVERAGES RPG	APG	PPG
95-96—Utah	18	202	16	42	.381	18	22	.818	4	14	18	22	44	3	2	11	53	1.2	2.4	2.9
96-97—Utah	20	217	38	76	.500	27	28	.964	4	14	18	40	3	0	17	112	0.9	2.0	5.6
97-98—Utah	20	366	46	125	.368	12	13	.923	4	36	40	81	12	5	31	112	2.0	4.1	5.6
98-99—Utah	11	241	26	71	.366	24	29	.828	3	17	20	32	7	3	20	81	1.8	2.9	7.4
99-00—Utah	10	200	17	55	.309	8	9	.889	1	17	18	19	6	1	13	51	1.8	1.9	5.1
00-01—Dallas	9	194	19	53	.358	4	4	1.000	1	11	12	17	5	1	13	52	1.3	1.9	5.8
Totals	88	1420	162	422	.384	93	105	.886	17	113	130	233	36	12	105	461	1.5	2.6	5.2

Three-point field goals: 1995-96, 3-for-9 (.333). 1996-97, 9-for-19 (.474). 1997-98, 8-for-27 (.296). 1998-99, 5-for-24 (.208). 1999-00, 9-for-19 (.474). 2000-01, 10-for-26 (.385). Totals, 44-for-124 (.355).

Personal fouls/disqualifications: 1995-96, 29/0. 1996-97, 27/1. 1997-98, 42/0. 1998-99, 27/0. 1999-00, 24/0. 2000-01, 18/0. Totals, 167/1.

CBA RECORD

Season Team	G	Min.	FGM	FGA	Pct.	FTM	FTA	Pct.	Reb.	Ast.	Pts.	AVERAGES RPG	APG	PPG
95-96—Rockford	7	168	32	58	.552	17	17	1.000	16	23	87	2.3	3.3	12.4

Three-point field goals: 1995-96, 6-for-15 (.400). Totals, 6-for-15 (.400).
Personal fouls/disqualifications: 1995-96, 21/0. Totals, 21/0.

ELLIS, MONTA   G   WARRIORS

PERSONAL: Born October 26, 1985 ... 6-3/175. (1.91/79.4).
HIGH SCHOOL: Lanier (Jackson, Miss.).
COLLEGE: Did not attend college.
TRANSACTIONS/CAREER NOTES: Selected out of high school by Golden State Warriors in second round (40th pick overall) of 2005 NBA Draft.

NBA REGULAR-SEASON RECORD

Season Team	G	Min.	FGM	FGA	Pct.	FTM	FTA	Pct.	REBOUNDS Off.	Def.	Tot.	Ast.	St.	Blk.	TO	Pts.	AVERAGES RPG	APG	PPG
05-06—Golden State	49	886	132	318	.415	42	59	.712	22	83	105	78	32	11	58	334	2.1	1.6	6.8

Three-point field goals: 2005-06, 28-for-82 (.341). Totals, 28-for-82 (.341).
Personal fouls/disqualifications: 2005-06, 69/0. Totals, 69/0.

ELSON, FRANCISCO   C   SPURS

PERSONAL: Born February 28, 1976, in Rotterdam, the Netherlands. ... 6-11/230. (2.11/104.3). ... Full name: Francisco Marinho Robby Elson
HIGH SCHOOL: Maria Regina M.A.V.O. (Rotterdam, the Netherlands).
JUNIOR COLLEGE: Kilgore Junior College (Texas).
COLLEGE: California.
TRANSACTIONS/CAREER NOTES: Selected by Denver Nuggets in second round (41st pick overall) of 1999 NBA Draft. ... Played in Spain (1999-2003). ... Signed as free agent by San Antonio Spurs (August 2, 2006).

COLLEGIATE RECORD

Season Team	G	Min.	FGM	FGA	Pct.	FTM	FTA	Pct.	Reb.	Ast.	Pts.	RPG	APG	PPG
95-96—Kilgore College	18	...	...	...	...	...	...	...	68	...	52	3.8	...	2.9
96-97—Kilgore College	22	...	145	285	.509	88	127	.693	257	31	378	11.7	1.4	17.2
97-98—California	27	497	53	123	.431	30	49	.612	126	14	136	4.7	0.5	5.0
98-99—California	32	632	80	156	.513	21	51	.412	162	16	181	5.1	0.5	5.7
Junior College Totals	40	...	...	...	...	...	...	...	325	...	430	8.1	...	10.8
4-year College Totals	59	1129	133	279	.477	51	100	.510	288	30	317	4.9	0.5	5.4

Three-point field goals: 1996-97, 0-for-3. Totals, 0-for-3 (.000).
Personal fouls/disqualifications: 1997-98, 83/5. Totals, 83/5.

SPANISH LEAGUE RECORD

Season Team	G	Min.	FGM	FGA	Pct.	FTM	FTA	Pct.	Reb.	Ast.	Pts.	RPG	APG	PPG
99-00—FC Barcelona	32	473	47	73	.644	14	27	.519	124	6	109	3.9	0.2	3.4
00-01—FC Barcelona	34	703	98	152	.645	37	63	.587	152	13	233	4.5	0.4	6.9
01-02—Pamesa Valencia	34	542	140	235	.596	26	50	.520	148	18	140	4.4	0.5	4.1
02-03—Caja San Fernando	34	932	140	235	.596	50	91	.549	281	33	330	8.3	1.0	9.7
Totals	134	2650	425	695	.612	127	231	.550	705	70	812	5.3	0.5	6.1

Three-point field goals: 1999-00, 1-for-1 (1.000). 2000-01, 0-for-1. 2001-02, 0-for-2. 2002-03, 0-for-1. Totals, 1-for-5 (.200).

NBA REGULAR-SEASON RECORD

Season Team	G	Min.	FGM	FGA	Pct.	FTM	FTA	Pct.	Off.	Def.	Tot.	Ast.	St.	Blk.	TO	Pts.	RPG	APG	PPG
03-04—Denver	62	875	94	199	.472	30	45	.667	65	138	203	32	35	39	35	218	3.3	0.5	3.5
04-05—Denver	67	939	101	216	.468	45	79	.570	61	140	201	34	34	41	40	248	3.0	0.5	3.7
05-06—Denver	72	1579	151	284	.532	49	74	.662	99	240	339	47	54	45	65	352	4.7	0.7	4.9
Totals	201	3393	346	699	.495	124	198	.626	225	518	743	113	123	125	140	818	3.7	0.6	4.1

Three-point field goals: 2003-04, 0-for-1. 2004-05, 1-for-3 (.333). 2005-06, 1-for-5 (.200). Totals, 2-for-9 (.222).
Personal fouls/disqualifications: 2003-04, 145/2. 2004-05, 129/1. 2005-06, 211/0. Totals, 485/3.

NBA PLAYOFF RECORD

Season Team	G	Min.	FGM	FGA	Pct.	FTM	FTA	Pct.	Off.	Def.	Tot.	Ast.	St.	Blk.	TO	Pts.	RPG	APG	PPG
03-04—Denver	4	60	7	12	.583	1	2	.500	1	8	9	2	2	1	3	15	2.3	0.5	3.8
04-05—Denver	1	6	0	1	.000	0	0	...	0	3	3	0	0	0	0	0	3.0	0.0	0.0
05-06—Denver	5	75	3	5	.600	0	0	...	5	6	11	2	4	0	3	6	2.2	0.4	1.2
Totals	10	141	10	18	.556	1	2	.500	6	17	23	4	6	1	6	21	2.3	0.4	2.1

Personal fouls/disqualifications: 2003-04, 14/0. 2005-06, 13/1. Totals, 27/1.

ELY, MELVIN   F/C   BOBCATS

PERSONAL: Born May 2, 1978, in Harvey, Ill. ... 6-10/260. (2.08/117.9).
HIGH SCHOOL: Thornton Township (Harvey, Ill.).
COLLEGE: Fresno State.
TRANSACTIONS/CAREER NOTES: Selected by Los Angeles Clippers in first round (12th pick overall) of 2002 NBA Draft. ... Traded by Clippers with G Eddie House to Charlotte Bobcats for second-round draft choices in 2005 and 2006 (July 14, 2004).

COLLEGIATE RECORD

Season Team	G	Min.	FGM	FGA	Pct.	FTM	FTA	Pct.	Reb.	Ast.	Pts.	RPG	APG	PPG
97-98—Fresno State						Did not play—ineligible.								
98-99—Fresno State	32	988	155	276	.562	48	111	.432	207	17	359	6.5	0.5	11.2
99-00—Fresno State	31	1035	180	297	.606	51	77	.662	216	27	411	7.0	0.9	13.3
00-01—Fresno State	33	1009	208	357	.583	112	167	.671	247	45	528	7.5	1.4	16.0
01-02—Fresno State	28	999	246	437	.563	161	219	.735	254	50	653	9.1	1.8	23.3
Totals	124	4031	789	1367	.577	372	574	.648	924	139	1951	7.5	1.1	15.7

Three-point field goals: 1998-99, 1-for-2 (.500). 2001-02, 1-for-2 (.500). Totals, 2-for-4 (.500).

NBA REGULAR-SEASON RECORD

Season Team	G	Min.	FGM	FGA	Pct.	FTM	FTA	Pct.	Off.	Def.	Tot.	Ast.	St.	Blk.	TO	Pts.	RPG	APG	PPG
02-03—L.A. Clippers	52	802	92	186	.495	52	74	.703	64	110	174	15	10	32	50	236	3.3	0.3	4.5
03-04—L.A. Clippers	42	510	66	153	.431	25	42	.595	48	53	101	22	9	17	20	157	2.4	0.5	3.7
04-05—Charlotte	79	1649	227	526	.432	122	212	.575	142	184	326	76	32	69	115	576	4.1	1.0	7.3
05-06—Charlotte	57	1348	216	425	.508	128	192	.667	94	183	277	76	29	44	100	560	4.9	1.3	9.8
Totals	230	4309	601	1290	.466	327	520	.629	348	530	878	189	80	162	285	1529	3.8	0.8	6.6

Three-point field goals: 2003-04, 0-for-1. 2005-06, 0-for-2. Totals, 0-for-3 (.000).
Personal fouls/disqualifications: 2002-03, 95/0. 2003-04, 68/0. 2004-05, 199/1. 2005-06, 160/1. Totals, 522/2.

EVANS, MAURICE — G — LAKERS

PERSONAL: Born November 8, 1978, in Wichita, Kan. ... 6-5/220. (1.96/99.8). ... Full name: Maurice Eugene Evans
HIGH SCHOOL: Wichita Collegiate (Wichita, Kan.).
COLLEGE: Wichita State, then Texas.
TRANSACTIONS/CAREER NOTES: Not drafted by an NBA franchise. ... Signed as free agent by Minnesota Timberwolves (July 23, 2001). ... Waived by Timberwolves (October 24, 2002). ... Played in Italy (2003-04). ... Signed as free agent by Sacramento Kings (2004). ... Signed as free agent by Detroit Pistons (September 3, 2005). ... Traded by Pistons to Los Angeles Lakers for draft rights to C Cheick Samb (June 28, 2006).

COLLEGIATE RECORD

Season Team	G	Min.	FGM	FGA	Pct.	FTM	FTA	Pct.	Reb.	Ast.	Pts.	RPG	APG	PPG
97-98—Wichita State	31	761	130	339	.383	66	98	.673	141	27	375	4.5	0.9	12.1
98-99—Wichita State	28	903	211	458	.461	141	178	.792	130	57	632	4.6	2.0	22.6
99-00—Texas						Did not play—transfer student								
00-01—Texas	34	1122	181	411	.440	84	111	.757	179	56	532	5.3	1.6	15.6
Totals	93	2786	522	1208	.432	291	387	.752	450	140	1539	4.8	1.5	16.5

Three-point field goals: 1997-98, 49-for-149 (.329). 1998-99, 69-for-164 (.421). 2000-01, 86-for-221 (.389). Totals, 204-for-534 (.382).
Personal fouls/disqualifications: 1997-98, 88/0. 1998-99, 81/0. 2000-01, 101/0. Totals, 270/0.

NBA REGULAR-SEASON RECORD

Season Team	G	Min.	FGM	FGA	Pct.	FTM	FTA	Pct.	Off.	Def.	Tot.	Ast.	St.	Blk.	TO	Pts.	RPG	APG	PPG
01-02—Minnesota	10	45	9	19	.474	3	4	.750	3	1	4	4	0	0	2	21	0.4	0.4	2.1
04-05—Sacramento	65	1233	165	373	.442	59	78	.756	88	113	201	45	37	8	34	416	3.1	0.7	6.4
05-06—Detroit	80	1139	154	341	.452	52	65	.800	76	87	163	60	41	15	39	403	2.0	0.8	5.0
Totals	155	2417	328	733	.447	114	147	.776	167	201	368	109	78	23	75	840	2.4	0.7	5.4

Three-point field goals: 2001-02, 0-for-3. 2004-05, 27-for-82 (.329). 2005-06, 43-for-116 (.371). Totals, 70-for-201 (.348).
Personal fouls/disqualifications: 2001-02, 9/0. 2004-05, 104/1. 2005-06, 122/0. Totals, 235/1.

NBA PLAYOFF RECORD

Season Team	G	Min.	FGM	FGA	Pct.	FTM	FTA	Pct.	Off.	Def.	Tot.	Ast.	St.	Blk.	TO	Pts.	RPG	APG	PPG
04-05—Sacramento	3	56	6	10	.600	4	5	.800	2	5	7	3	2	0	0	18	2.3	1.0	6.0
05-06—Detroit	16	101	16	30	.533	14	16	.875	6	8	14	3	1	1	2	53	0.9	0.2	3.3
Totals	19	157	22	40	.550	18	21	.857	8	13	21	6	3	1	2	71	1.1	0.3	3.7

Three-point field goals: 2004-05, 2-for-4 (.500). 2005-06, 7-for-11 (.636). Totals, 9-for-15 (.600).
Personal fouls/disqualifications: 2004-05, 6/0. 2005-06, 10/0. Totals, 16/0.

ITALIAN LEAGUE RECORD

Season Team	G	Min.	FGM	FGA	Pct.	FTM	FTA	Pct.	Reb.	Ast.	Pts.	RPG	APG	PPG
03-04—Benetton Treviso	27	854	191	358	.534	69	90	.767	123	39	520	4.6	1.4	19.3

Three-point field goals: 2003-04, 69-for-143 (.483). Totals, 69-for-143 (.483).

EVANS, REGGIE — F — NUGGETS

PERSONAL: Born May 18, 1980, in Pensacola, Fla. ... 6-8/245. (2.03/111.1).
HIGH SCHOOL: Woodham (Pensacola, Fla.).
JUNIOR COLLEGE: Coffeyville (Kan.)
COLLEGE: Iowa.
TRANSACTIONS/CAREER NOTES: Not drafted by an NBA franchise ... Signed as free agent with Seattle SuperSonics (September 30, 2002). ... Traded by SuperSonics to Denver Nuggets as part of four-way deal (February 23, 2006).

COLLEGIATE RECORD

Season Team	G	Min.	FGM	FGA	Pct.	FTM	FTA	Pct.	Reb.	Ast.	Pts.	RPG	APG	PPG
98-99—Coffeyville	27	...	140	277	.505	146	250	.584	285	37	426	10.6	1.4	15.8
99-00—Coffeyville	26	900	186	361	.515	204	332	.614	310	48	584	11.9	1.8	22.5
00-01—Iowa	35	1220	155	326	.475	218	346	.630	416	55	529	11.9	1.6	15.1
01-02—Iowa	34	1156	169	341	.496	187	302	.619	378	44	525	11.1	1.3	15.4
Junior College Totals	53	900	326	638	.511	350	582	.601	595	85	1010	11.2	1.6	19.1
4-Year-College Totals	69	2376	324	667	.486	405	648	.625	794	99	1054	11.5	1.4	15.3

Three-point field goals: 1998-99, 0-for-2. 1999-00, 8-for-20 (.400). 2000-01, 1-for-1 (1.000). 2001-02, 0-for-1. Totals, 9-for-24 (.375).

NBA REGULAR-SEASON RECORD

Season Team	G	Min.	FGM	FGA	Pct.	FTM	FTA	Pct.	Off.	Def.	Tot.	Ast.	St.	Blk.	TO	Pts.	RPG	APG	PPG
02-03—Seattle	67	1365	66	140	.471	80	154	.519	167	278	445	34	38	11	52	212	6.6	0.5	3.2
03-04—Seattle	75	1280	67	165	.406	83	148	.561	156	252	408	33	54	10	65	217	5.4	0.4	2.9
04-05—Seattle	79	1881	131	275	.476	125	234	.534	254	482	736	58	58	15	104	387	9.3	0.7	4.9
05-06—Seattle-Denver	67	1393	131	268	.489	115	217	.530	171	331	502	38	40	10	85	377	7.5	0.6	5.6
Totals	288	5919	395	848	.466	403	753	.535	748	1343	2091	163	190	46	306	1193	7.3	0.6	4.1

Three-point field goals: 2003-04, 0-for-3. 2004-05, 0-for-2. 2005-06, 0-for-1. Totals, 0-for-6 (.000).
Personal fouls/disqualifications: 2002-03, 173/2. 2003-04, 176/0. 2004-05, 202/0. 2005-06, 166/0. Totals, 717/2.

Season Team	G	Min.	FGM	FGA	Pct.	FTM	FTA	Pct.	Off.	Def.	Tot.	Ast.	St.	Blk.	TO	Pts.	RPG	APG	PPG
									REBOUNDS								AVERAGES		
04-05—Seattle	11	208	15	37	.405	11	21	.524	27	54	81	5	5	3	11	41	7.4	0.5	3.7
05-06—Denver...........	5	69	3	7	.429	13	18	.722	8	15	23	0	2	1	6	19	4.6	0.0	3.8
Totals	16	277	18	44	.409	24	39	.615	35	69	104	5	7	4	17	60	6.5	0.3	3.8

Three-point field goals: 2005-06, 0-for-2. Totals, 0-for-2 (.000).
Personal fouls/disqualifications: 2004-05, 32/0. 2005-06, 11/0. Totals, 43/0.

EWING, DANIEL — G — CLIPPERS

PERSONAL: Born March 26, 1983, in Milton, Fla. ... 6-3/185. (1.91/83.9). ... Full name: Daniel George Ewing
HIGH SCHOOL: Willowridge (Missouri City, Texas).
COLLEGE: Duke.
TRANSACTIONS/CAREER NOTES: Selected by Los Angeles Clippers in second round (32nd overall pick) of 2005 NBA Draft.

COLLEGIATE RECORD

Season Team	G	Min.	FGM	FGA	Pct.	FTM	FTA	Pct.	Reb.	Ast.	Pts.	RPG	APG	PPG
												AVERAGES		
01-02—Duke..............................	35	638	80	167	.479	35	51	.686	78	47	227	2.2	1.3	6.5
02-03—Duke..............................	33	920	126	293	.430	101	123	.821	104	45	395	3.2	1.4	12.0
03-04—Duke..............................	37	1131	151	362	.417	92	124	.742	96	69	468	2.6	1.9	12.6
04-05—Duke..............................	33	1138	181	424	.427	74	107	.692	104	132	505	3.2	4.0	15.3
Totals	138	3827	538	1246	.432	302	405	.746	382	293	1595	2.8	2.1	11.6

Three-point field goals: 2001-02, 32-for-70 (.457). 2002-03, 42-for-105 (.400). 2003-04, 74-for-180 (.411). 2004-05, 69-for-199 (.347). Totals, 217-for-554 (.392).

NBA REGULAR-SEASON RECORD

Season Team	G	Min.	FGM	FGA	Pct.	FTM	FTA	Pct.	Off.	Def.	Tot.	Ast.	St.	Blk.	TO	Pts.	RPG	APG	PPG
									REBOUNDS								AVERAGES		
05-06—L.A. Clippers...	66	971	97	255	.380	36	46	.783	23	62	85	84	37	6	57	252	1.3	1.3	3.8

Three-point field goals: 2005-06, 22-for-78 (.282). Totals, 22-for-78 (.282).
Personal fouls/disqualifications: 2005-06, 86/0. Totals, 86/0.

NBA PLAYOFF RECORD

Season Team	G	Min.	FGM	FGA	Pct.	FTM	FTA	Pct.	Off.	Def.	Tot.	Ast.	St.	Blk.	TO	Pts.	RPG	APG	PPG
									REBOUNDS								AVERAGES		
05-06—L.A. Clippers...	6	5	1	1	1.000	0	0	...	0	0	0	0	0	0	0	2	0.0	0.0	0.3

FELIX, NOEL — F/C — SUPERSONICS

PERSONAL: Born October 1, 1981, in Los Angeles. ... 6-9/225. (2.06/102.1).
HIGH SCHOOL: Inglewood (Calif.).
COLLEGE: Fresno State.
TRANSACTIONS/CAREER NOTES: Not drafted by an NBA franchise ... Played in China (2003-04) ... Played in Italy (2004-05) ... Played in Philippines (2004-05) ... Played in CBA (2003-06). ... Signed as free agent by Seattle SuperSonics (September 30, 2005). ... Waived by SuperSonics (October 29, 2005). ... Signed to 10-day contract by SuperSonics (March 2, 2006). ... Signed for rest of season by SuperSonics (March 22, 2006).

COLLEGIATE RECORD

Season Team	G	Min.	FGM	FGA	Pct.	FTM	FTA	Pct.	Reb.	Ast.	Pts.	RPG	APG	PPG
												AVERAGES		
99-00—Fresno St....................	33	350	34	62	.548	19	37	.514	71	3	87	2.2	0.1	2.6
00-01—Fresno St....................	33	413	43	93	.462	14	23	.609	93	6	100	2.8	0.2	3.0
01-02—Fresno St....................	34	811	115	232	.496	32	61	.525	172	18	269	5.1	0.5	7.9
02-03—Fresno St....................	28	640	99	194	.510	40	59	.678	135	25	238	4.8	0.9	8.5
Totals	128	2214	291	581	.501	105	180	.583	471	52	694	3.7	0.4	5.4

Three-point field goals: 2000-01, 0-for-5. 2001-02, 7-for-23 (.304). 2002-03, 0-for-5. Totals, 7-for-33 (.212).

CBA RECORD

Season Team	G	Min.	FGM	FGA	Pct.	FTM	FTA	Pct.	Reb.	Ast.	Pts.	RPG	APG	PPG
												AVERAGES		
03-04—Idaho..........................	37	611	123	204	.603	81	97	.835	141	25	327	3.8	0.7	8.8
04-05—Yakima.......................	30	1032	178	360	.494	113	137	.825	222	45	471	7.4	1.5	15.7
05-06—Sioux Falls.................	41	1322	259	476	.544	126	154	.818	287	69	644	7.0	1.7	15.7
Totals	108	2965	560	1040	.538	320	388	.825	650	139	1442	6.0	1.3	13.4

Three-point field goals: 2004-05, 2-for-7 (.286). 2005-06, 0-for-2. Totals, 2-for-9 (.222).

ITALIAN LEAGUE RECORD

Season Team	G	Min.	FGM	FGA	Pct.	FTM	FTA	Pct.	Reb.	Ast.	Pts.	RPG	APG	PPG
												AVERAGES		
04-05—Carife Ferrara..............	14	325	47	116	.405	10	17	.588	59	9	118	4.2	0.6	8.4

Three-point field goals: 2004-05, 14-for-42 (.333). Totals, 14-for-42 (.333).

NBA REGULAR-SEASON RECORD

Season Team	G	Min.	FGM	FGA	Pct.	FTM	FTA	Pct.	Off.	Def.	Tot.	Ast.	St.	Blk.	TO	Pts.	RPG	APG	PPG
									REBOUNDS								AVERAGES		
05-06—Seattle...........	12	82	6	25	.240	5	8	.625	3	10	13	2	2	3	8	18	1.1	0.2	1.5

Three-point field goals: 2005-06, 1-for-3 (.333). Totals, 1-for-3 (.333).
Personal fouls/disqualifications: 2005-06, 13/0. Totals, 13/0.

F

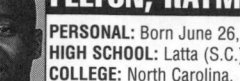

FELTON, RAYMOND — G — BOBCATS

PERSONAL: Born June 26, 1984, in Marion, S.C. ... 6-1/198. (1.85/89.8). ... Full name: Raymond Bernard Felton
HIGH SCHOOL: Latta (S.C.).
COLLEGE: North Carolina.
TRANSACTIONS/CAREER NOTES: Selected after junior season by Charlotte Bobcats in first round (fifth pick overall) of 2005 NBA Draft.

COLLEGIATE RECORD

NOTES: Member of NCAA Division I championship team (2005).

Season Team	G	Min.	FGM	FGA	Pct.	FTM	FTA	Pct.	Reb.	Ast.	Pts.	AVERAGES RPG	APG	PPG
02-03—North Carolina	35	1240	151	379	.398	79	114	.693	143	236	450	4.1	6.7	12.9
03-04—North Carolina	30	1039	113	269	.420	85	105	.810	119	213	346	4.0	7.1	11.5
04-05—North Carolina	36	1142	150	330	.455	94	134	.701	155	249	464	4.3	6.9	12.9
Totals	101	3421	414	978	.423	258	353	.731	417	698	1260	4.1	6.9	12.5

Three-point field goals: 2002-03, 69-for-193 (.358). 2003-04, 35-for-112 (.313). 2004-05, 70-for-159 (.440). Totals, 174-for-464 (.375).

NBA REGULAR-SEASON RECORD

HONORS: NBA All-Rookie second team (2006).

Season Team	G	Min.	FGM	FGA	Pct.	FTM	FTA	Pct.	REBOUNDS Off.	Def.	Tot.	Ast.	St.	Blk.	TO	Pts.	AVERAGES RPG	APG	PPG
05-06—Charlotte	80	2406	345	883	.391	161	222	.725	77	188	265	446	102	8	182	948	3.3	5.6	11.9

Three-point field goals: 2005-06, 97-for-271 (.358). Totals, 97-for-271 (.358).
Personal fouls/disqualifications: 2005-06, 181/0. Totals, 181/0.

FINLEY, MICHAEL — G/F — SPURS

PERSONAL: Born March 6, 1973, in Melrose Park, Ill. ... 6-7/215. (2.01/97.5). ... Full name: Michael H. Finley
HIGH SCHOOL: Proviso East (Maywood, Ill.).
COLLEGE: Wisconsin.
TRANSACTIONS/CAREER NOTES: Selected by Phoenix Suns in first round (21st pick overall) of 1995 NBA Draft. ... Traded by Suns with G Sam Cassell, F A.C. Green and 1997 or 1998 conditional second-round draft choice to Dallas Mavericks for G Jason Kidd, F Tony Dumas and C Loren Meyer (December 26, 1996). ... Signed as free agent by San Antonio Spurs (September 2, 2005).

COLLEGIATE RECORD

Season Team	G	Min.	FGM	FGA	Pct.	FTM	FTA	Pct.	Reb.	Ast.	Pts.	AVERAGES RPG	APG	PPG
91-92—Wisconsin	31	920	130	287	.453	95	128	.742	152	85	381	4.9	2.7	12.3
92-93—Wisconsin	28	979	223	478	.467	111	144	.771	161	86	620	5.8	3.1	22.1
93-94—Wisconsin	29	1046	208	446	.466	110	140	.786	194	92	592	6.7	3.2	20.4
94-95—Wisconsin	27	1000	178	470	.379	140	181	.773	141	108	554	5.2	4.0	20.5
Totals	115	3945	739	1681	.440	456	593	.769	648	371	2147	5.6	3.2	18.7

Three-point field goals: 1991-92, 26-for-72 (.361). 1992-93, 63-for-173 (.364). 1993-94, 66-for-182 (.363). 1994-95, 58-for-204 (.284). Totals, 213-for-631 (.338).

NBA REGULAR-SEASON RECORD

HONORS: NBA All-Rookie first team (1996).

Season Team	G	Min.	FGM	FGA	Pct.	FTM	FTA	Pct.	REBOUNDS Off.	Def.	Tot.	Ast.	St.	Blk.	TO	Pts.	AVERAGES RPG	APG	PPG
95-96—Phoenix	82	3212	465	976	.476	242	323	.749	139	235	374	289	85	31	133	1233	4.6	3.5	15.0
96-97—Pho.-Dal.	83	2790	475	1071	.444	198	245	.808	88	284	372	224	68	24	164	1249	4.5	2.7	15.0
97-98—Dallas	82	*3394	675	1505	.449	326	416	.784	149	289	438	405	132	30	219	1763	5.3	4.9	21.5
98-99—Dallas	50	2051	389	876	.444	186	226	.823	69	194	263	218	66	15	107	1009	5.3	4.4	20.2
99-00—Dallas	82	3464	748	1636	.457	260	317	.820	122	396	518	438	109	32	196	1855	6.3	5.3	22.6
00-01—Dallas	82	*3443	711	1552	.458	252	325	.775	109	316	425	360	118	32	190	1765	5.2	4.4	21.5
01-02—Dallas	69	2754	569	1228	.463	210	251	.837	90	270	360	230	65	25	117	1424	5.2	3.3	20.6
02-03—Dallas	69	2642	507	1193	.425	198	230	.861	107	295	402	205	76	21	114	1331	5.8	3.0	19.3
03-04—Dallas	72	2778	514	1159	.443	164	193	.850	78	247	325	212	84	39	83	1342	4.5	2.9	18.6
04-05—Dallas	64	2358	387	907	.427	113	136	.831	45	217	262	169	48	18	60	1003	4.1	2.6	15.7
05-06—San Antonio	77	2038	286	695	.412	98	115	.852	31	216	247	116	37	7	62	780	3.2	1.5	10.1
Totals	812	30924	5726	12798	.447	2247	2777	.809	1027	2959	3986	2866	888	274	1445	14754	4.9	3.5	18.2

Three-point field goals: 1995-96, 61-for-186 (.328). 1996-97, 101-for-280 (.361). 1997-98, 87-for-244 (.357). 1998-99, 45-for-136 (.331). 1999-00, 99-for-247 (.401). 2000-01, 91-for-263 (.346). 2001-02, 76-for-224 (.339). 2002-03, 119-for-322 (.370). 2003-04, 150-for-370 (.405). 2004-05, 116-for-285 (.407). 2005-06, 110-for-279 (.394). Totals, 1055-for-2836 (.372).

Personal fouls/disqualifications: 1995-96, 199/1. 1996-97, 138/0. 1997-98, 163/0. 1998-99, 96/1. 1999-00, 171/1. 2000-01, 174/2. 2001-02, 144/1. 2002-03, 105/0. 2003-04, 118/0. 2004-05, 123/0. 2005-06, 97/0. Totals, 1528/6.

NBA PLAYOFF RECORD

Season Team	G	Min.	FGM	FGA	Pct.	FTM	FTA	Pct.	REBOUNDS Off.	Def.	Tot.	Ast.	St.	Blk.	TO	Pts.	AVERAGES RPG	APG	PPG
00-01—Dallas	10	434	72	200	.360	36	44	.818	13	40	53	44	12	2	24	197	5.3	4.4	19.7
01-02—Dallas	8	373	69	148	.466	45	50	.900	13	37	50	18	12	4	15	197	6.3	2.3	24.6
02-03—Dallas	20	822	131	301	.435	57	66	.864	25	90	115	60	26	12	31	366	5.8	3.0	18.3
03-04—Dallas	5	196	26	68	.382	6	10	.600	6	10	16	13	4	3	9	65	3.2	2.6	13.0
04-05—Dallas	13	491	65	153	.425	16	18	.889	13	43	56	28	17	0	13	170	4.3	2.2	13.1
05-06—San Antonio	13	411	50	105	.476	18	20	.900	1	48	49	18	8	3	9	136	3.8	1.4	10.5
Totals	69	2727	413	975	.424	178	208	.856	71	268	339	181	79	24	101	1131	4.9	2.6	16.4

Three-point field goals: 2000-01, 17-for-47 (.362). 2001-02, 14-for-37 (.378). 2002-03, 47-for-114 (.412). 2003-04, 7-for-26 (.269). 2004-05, 24-for-61

F

(.393). 2005-06, 18-for-47 (.383). Totals, 127-for-332 (.383).
Personal fouls/disqualifications: 2000-01, 23/0. 2001-02, 24/0. 2002-03, 46/0. 2003-04, 8/0. 2004-05, 32/0. 2005-06, 19/0. Totals, 152/0.

NBA ALL-STAR GAME RECORD

Season Team	Min.	FGM	FGA	Pct.	FTM	FTA	Pct.	Off.	Def.	Tot.	Ast.	PF	Dq.	St.	Blk.	TO	Pts.
2000—Dallas...................	10	5	6	.833	0	0	...	0	1	1	0	0	0	0	0	1	11
2001—Dallas...................	19	5	15	.333	2	2	1.000	2	1	3	5	0	0	0	0	1	12
Totals...........................	29	10	21	.476	2	2	1.000	2	2	4	5	0	0	0	0	2	23

Three-point field goals: 2000, 1-for-2 (.500). 2001, 0-for-2. Totals, 1-for-4 (.250).

FISHER, DEREK   G   JAZZ

PERSONAL: Born August 9, 1974, in Little Rock, Ark. ... 6-1/200. (1.85/90.7). ... Brother of Duane Washington, guard with New Jersey Nets (1987-88) and Los Angeles Clippers (1992-93).
HIGH SCHOOL: Parkview (Little Rock, Ark.).
COLLEGE: Arkansas-Little Rock.
TRANSACTIONS/CAREER NOTES: Selected by Los Angeles Lakers in first round (24th pick overall) of 1996 NBA Draft. ... Signed as free agent by Golden State Warriors (July 16, 2004). ... Traded by Warriors to Utah Jazz for Gs Keith McLeod, Devin Brown and Andre Owens (July 12, 2006).
MISCELLANEOUS: Member of NBA championship team (2000, 2001, 2002).

COLLEGIATE RECORD

												AVERAGES		
Season Team	G	Min.	FGM	FGA	Pct.	FTM	FTA	Pct.	Reb.	Ast.	Pts.	RPG	APG	PPG
92-93—Arkansas-Little Rock......	27	749	57	138	.413	71	92	.772	89	92	194	3.3	3.4	7.2
93-94—Arkansas-Little Rock......	28	888	94	212	.443	72	93	.774	109	102	283	3.9	3.6	10.1
94-95—Arkansas-Little Rock......	27	938	153	386	.396	130	180	.722	135	124	479	5.0	4.6	17.7
95-96—Arkansas-Little Rock......	30	1041	128	313	.409	126	169	.746	155	154	437	5.2	5.1	14.6
Totals	112	3616	432	1049	.412	399	534	.747	488	472	1393	4.4	4.2	12.4

Three-point field goals: 1992-93, 9-for-31 (.290). 1993-94, 23-for-55 (.418). 1994-95, 43-for-113 (.381). 1995-96, 50-for-130 (.385). Totals, 125-for-329 (.380).

NBA REGULAR-SEASON RECORD

								REBOUNDS								AVERAGES		
Season Team	G	Min.	FGM	FGA	Pct.	FTM	FTA	Pct.	Off.	Def.	Tot.	Ast.	St.	Blk.	TO	Pts.	RPG	APG	PPG
96-97—L.A. Lakers	80	921	104	262	.397	79	120	.658	25	72	97	119	41	5	71	309	1.2	1.5	3.9
97-98—L.A. Lakers	82	1760	164	378	.434	115	152	.757	38	155	193	333	75	5	119	474	2.4	4.1	5.8
98-99—L.A. Lakers	50	1131	99	263	.376	60	79	.759	21	70	91	197	61	1	77	296	1.8	3.9	5.9
99-00—L.A. Lakers	78	1803	167	483	.346	105	145	.724	22	121	143	216	80	3	75	491	1.8	2.8	6.3
00-01 L.A. Lakers	20	709	77	187	.412	50	62	.806	5	54	59	87	39	2	29	229	3.0	4.4	11.5
01-02—L.A. Lakers	70	1974	274	666	.411	94	111	.847	15	131	146	181	66	9	62	786	2.1	2.6	11.2
02-03—L.A. Lakers	82	2829	339	775	.437	100	125	.800	40	199	239	298	93	15	94	863	2.9	3.6	10.5
03-04—L.A. Lakers	82	1769	203	576	.352	122	153	.797	30	122	152	187	103	4	70	590	1.9	2.3	7.1
04-05 Golden State ...	81	2222	237	700	.339	173	203	.862	38	180	218	301	76	4	129	877	2.9	4.1	11.9
05-06—Golden State ...	82	2589	364	887	.410	244	293	.833	36	175	211	352	125	8	156	1089	2.6	4.3	13.3
Totals	700	17707	2088	5232	.399	1144	1443	.793	270	1279	1549	2271	759	56	891	5994	2.2	3.2	8.6

Three-point field goals: 1996-97, 22-for-73 (.301). 1997-98, 31-for-81 (.383). 1998-99, 38-for-97 (.392). 1999-00, 52-for-166 (.313). 2000-01, 25-for-63 (.397). 2001-02, 144-for-349 (.413). 2002-03, 85-for-212 (.401). 2003-04, 52-for-179 (.291). 2004-05, 108-for-291 (.371). 2005-06, 117-for-295 (.397). Totals, 674-for-1806 (.373).
Personal fouls/disqualifications: 1996-97, 87/0. 1997-98, 126/1. 1998-99, 95/0. 1999-00, 150/1. 2000-01, 50/0. 2001-02, 121/0. 2002-03, 195/4. 2003-04, 115/0. 2004-05, 176/1. 2005-06, 237/3. Totals, 1352/10.

NBA PLAYOFF RECORD

								REBOUNDS								AVERAGES		
Season Team	G	Min.	FGM	FGA	Pct.	FTM	FTA	Pct.	Off.	Def.	Tot.	Ast.	St.	Blk.	TO	Pts.	RPG	APG	PPG
96-97—L.A. Lakers	6	34	3	11	.273	2	3	.667	0	3	3	6	1	0	6	8	0.5	1.0	1.3
97-98—L.A. Lakers	13	278	27	68	.397	18	29	.621	2	23	25	49	17	0	15	78	1.9	3.8	6.0
98-99—L.A. Lakers	8	238	28	67	.418	12	15	.800	6	23	29	39	8	0	11	78	3.6	4.9	9.8
99-00—L.A. Lakers	21	322	34	79	.430	19	25	.760	4	18	22	41	11	1	9	99	1.0	2.0	4.7
00-01—L.A. Lakers	16	576	77	159	.484	26	34	.765	5	56	61	48	21	1	12	215	3.8	3.0	13.4
01-02—L.A. Lakers	19	649	60	168	.357	44	56	.786	10	52	62	52	19	1	20	193	3.3	2.7	10.2
02-03—L.A. Lakers	12	424	53	102	.520	18	22	.818	5	31	36	22	18	1	18	153	3.0	1.8	12.8
03-04—L.A. Lakers	22	507	60	148	.405	23	35	.657	10	46	56	49	18	0	19	166	2.5	2.2	7.5
Totals	117	3028	342	802	.426	162	219	.740	42	252	294	306	113	4	110	990	2.5	2.6	8.5

Three-point field goals: 1996-97, 0-for-5. 1997-98, 6-for-20 (.300). 1998-99, 10-for-29 (.345). 1999-00, 12-for-29 (.414). 2000-01, 35-for-68 (.515). 2001-02, 29-for-81 (.358). 2002-03, 29-for-47 (.617). 2003-04, 23-for-55 (.418). Totals, 144-for-334 (.431).
Personal fouls/disqualifications: 1996-97, 4/0. 1997-98, 33/0. 1998-99, 20/1. 1999-00, 30/0. 2000-01, 44/1. 2001-02, 49/0. 2002-03, 39/1. 2003-04, 47/0. Totals, 266/3.

FITCH, GERALD   G

PERSONAL: Born August 12, 1982, in Columbus, Ga. ... 6-3/188. (1.91/85.3). ... Full name: Gerald Edwind Fitch
HIGH SCHOOL: Westside (Macon, Ga.).
COLLEGE: Kentucky.
TRANSACTIONS/CAREER NOTES: Not drafted by an NBA franchise ... Played in Adriatic League (2004-05) ... Played in Ukraine (2004-05) ... Played in NBA Development League (2005-06). ... Signed as free agent by Washington Wizards (October 1, 2004). ... Waived by Wizards (October 30, 2004). ... Signed with KK Cibona VIP Zagreb of the Euroleague (December, 2004). ... Signed by Khimik-OPZ Yuzny of the Ukraine Superleague (March, 2005). ... Signed as free agent by Miami Heat (August 12, 2005). ... Traded by Heat to Houston Rockets for G Derek Anderson (February 23, 2006).

F

COLLEGIATE RECORD

Season Team	G	Min.	FGM	FGA	Pct.	FTM	FTA	Pct.	Reb.	Ast.	Pts.	AVERAGES RPG	APG	PPG
00-01—Kentucky	34	673	76	167	.455	49	71	.690	150	63	230	4.4	1.9	6.8
01-02—Kentucky	28	760	85	187	.455	48	69	.696	151	44	248	5.4	1.6	8.9
02-03—Kentucky	36	1041	152	322	.472	78	102	.765	108	85	443	3.0	2.4	12.3
03-04—Kentucky	29	864	148	343	.431	95	125	.760	119	40	470	4.1	1.4	16.2
Totals	127	3338	461	1019	.452	270	367	.736	528	232	1391	4.2	1.8	11.0

Three-point field goals: 2000-01, 29-for-71 (.408). 2001-02, 30-for-87 (.345). 2002-03, 61-for-147 (.415). 2003-04, 79-for-197 (.401). Totals, 199-for-502 (.396).

ADRIATIC LEAGUE RECORD

Season Team	G	Min.	FGM	FGA	Pct.	FTM	FTA	Pct.	Reb.	Ast.	Pts.	AVERAGES RPG	APG	PPG
04-05—Cibona Zagreb	5	122	28	47	.596	15	22	.682	17	4	83	3.4	0.8	16.6

Three-point field goals: 2004-05, 12-for-18 (.667). Totals, 12-for-18 (.667).

NBA REGULAR-SEASON RECORD

Season Team	G	Min.	FGM	FGA	Pct.	FTM	FTA	Pct.	REBOUNDS Off.	Def.	Tot.	Ast.	St.	Blk.	TO	Pts.	AVERAGES RPG	APG	PPG
05-06—Mia.-Hou.	18	239	30	89	.337	17	23	.739	7	23	30	33	7	5	15	84	1.7	1.8	4.7

Three-point field goals: 2005-06, 7-for-26 (.269). Totals, 7-for-26 (.269).
Personal fouls/disqualifications: 2005-06, 28/0.

NBA DEVELOPMENT LEAGUE RECORD

Season Team	G	Min.	FGM	FGA	Pct.	FTM	FTA	Pct.	Reb.	Ast.	Pts.	AVERAGES RPG	APG	PPG
05-06—Austin	3	69	11	39	.282	11	11	1.000	13	6	35	4.3	2.0	11.7

Three-point field goals: 2005-06, 2-for-11 (.182). Totals, 2-for-11 (.182).

FIZER, MARCUS　　　　　　F

PERSONAL: Born August 10, 1978, in Detroit. ... 6-8/260. (2.03/117.9). ... Full name: Darnell Marcus Lamar Fizer
HIGH SCHOOL: Arcadia (La.).
COLLEGE: Iowa State.
TRANSACTIONS/CAREER NOTES: Selected after junior season by Chicago Bulls in first round (fourth pick overall) of 2000 NBA Draft. ... Selected by Charlotte Bobcats from Bulls in NBA Expansion Draft (June 22, 2004). ... Signed as free agent by Milwaukee Bucks (November 4, 2004). ... Signed by Seattle SuperSonics to 10-day contract (March 8, 2006). ... Signed by New Orleans Hornets to 10-day contract (March 31, 2006). ... Signed by Hornets for remainder of season (April 10, 2006).

COLLEGIATE RECORD

NOTES: The SPORTING NEWS All-America second team (2000).

Season Team	G	Min.	FGM	FGA	Pct.	FTM	FTA	Pct.	Reb.	Ast.	Pts.	AVERAGES RPG	APG	PPG
97-98—Iowa State	30	784	173	365	.474	101	164	.616	202	19	447	6.7	0.6	14.9
98-99—Iowa State	30	961	190	422	.450	153	208	.736	229	34	539	7.6	1.1	18.0
99-00—Iowa State	37	1243	327	562	.582	175	239	.732	285	41	844	7.7	1.1	22.8
Totals	97	2988	690	1349	.511	429	611	.702	716	94	1830	7.4	1.0	18.9

Three-point field goals: 1997-98, 0-for-2. 1998-99, 6-for-28 (.214). 1999-00, 15-for-42 (.357). Totals, 21-for-72 (.292).

NBA REGULAR-SEASON RECORD

HONORS: NBA All-Rookie second team (2001).

Season Team	G	Min.	FGM	FGA	Pct.	FTM	FTA	Pct.	REBOUNDS Off.	Def.	Tot.	Ast.	St.	Blk.	TO	Pts.	AVERAGES RPG	APG	PPG
00-01—Chicago	72	1580	278	646	.430	117	161	.727	76	237	313	76	30	19	124	683	4.3	1.1	9.5
01-02—Chicago	76	1963	371	848	.438	189	283	.668	128	299	427	120	49	24	131	938	5.6	1.6	12.3
02-03—Chicago	38	809	178	383	.465	88	134	.657	80	136	216	48	14	17	57	445	5.7	1.3	11.7
03-04—Chicago	46	738	134	350	.383	90	120	.750	61	141	202	43	16	8	51	360	4.4	0.9	7.8
04-05—Milwaukee	54	903	133	292	.455	70	103	.680	29	146	175	64	25	13	63	336	3.2	1.2	6.2
05-06—Sea.-N.O.	3	39	9	17	.529	1	2	.500	1	6	7	1	0	0	2	20	2.3	0.3	6.7
Totals	289	6032	1103	2536	.435	555	803	.691	375	965	1340	352	134	81	428	2782	4.6	1.2	9.6

Three-point field goals: 2000-01, 10-for-39 (.256). 2001-02, 7-for-41 (.171). 2002-03, 1-for-6 (.167). 2003-04, 2-for-17 (.118). 2004-05, 0-for-6. 2005-06, 1-for-1 (1.000). Totals, 21-for-110 (.191).
Personal fouls/disqualifications: 2000-01, 175/0. 2001-02, 186/1. 2002-03, 89/0. 2003-04, 97/0. 2004-05, 96/0. 2005-06, 5/0. Totals, 648/1.

NBA DEVELOPMENT LEAGUE RECORD

Season Team	G	Min.	FGM	FGA	Pct.	FTM	FTA	Pct.	Reb.	Ast.	Pts.	AVERAGES RPG	APG	PPG
05-06—Austin	35	1210	286	557	.513	207	279	.742	272	116	796	7.8	3.3	22.7

Three-point field goals: 2005-06, 17-for-53 (.321). Totals, 17-for-53 (.321).

FORD, SHARROD　　　　　　F

PERSONAL: Born January 9, 1982, in Washington, D.C. ... 6-9/225. (2.06/102.1).
HIGH SCHOOL: Gwynn Park (Brandywine, Md.), then Hargrave Military Academy.
COLLEGE: Clemson.
TRANSACTIONS/CAREER NOTES: Not drafted by an NBA franchise ... Played in NBA Development League (2005-06) ... Played in Germany (2005-06). ... Signed as free agent by Phoenix Suns (November 2, 2005). ... Waived by Suns (December 24, 2005).

COLLEGIATE RECORD

												AVERAGES		
Season Team	G	Min.	FGM	FGA	Pct.	FTM	FTA	Pct.	Reb.	Ast.	Pts.	RPG	APG	PPG
01-02—Clemson	30	423	60	99	.606	16	35	.457	108	2	136	3.6	0.1	4.5
02-03—Clemson	28	675	88	156	.564	33	72	.458	191	17	209	6.8	0.6	7.5
03-04—Clemson	28	803	116	216	.537	100	159	.629	202	16	332	7.2	0.6	11.9
04-05—Clemson	32	922	185	361	.512	107	183	.585	261	36	477	8.2	1.1	14.9
Totals	118	2823	449	832	.540	256	449	.570	762	71	1154	6.5	0.6	9.8

Three-point field goals: 2003-04, 0-for-2. 2004-05, 0-for-3. Totals, 0-for-5 (.000).

GERMAN LEAGUE RECORD

												AVERAGES		
Season Team	G	Min.	FGM	FGA	Pct.	FTM	FTA	Pct.	Reb.	Ast.	Pts.	RPG	APG	PPG
05-06—Alba Berlin	8	126	20	33	.606	17	23	.739	39	2	57	4.9	0.3	7.1

Three-point field goals: 2005-06, 0-for-1. Totals, 0-for-1 (.000).

NBA REGULAR-SEASON RECORD

									REBOUNDS							AVERAGES		
Season Team	G	Min.	FGM	FGA	Pct.	FTM	FTA	Pct.	Off.	Def.	Tot.	Ast.	St.	Blk.	TO	Pts.	RPG	APG	PPG
05-06—Phoenix	3	13	2	3	.667	0	0	...	1	2	3	0	0	1	2	4	1.0	0.0	1.3

Personal fouls/disqualifications: 2005-06, 7/0. Totals, 7/0.

NBA DEVELOPMENT LEAGUE RECORD

												AVERAGES		
Season Team	G	Min.	FGM	FGA	Pct.	FTM	FTA	Pct.	Reb.	Ast.	Pts.	RPG	APG	PPG
05-06—Fayetteville	15	411	73	139	.525	49	75	.653	126	16	195	8.4	1.1	13.0

Three-point field goals: 2005-06, 0-for-3. Totals, 0-for-3 (.000).

FORD, T.J.   G   RAPTORS

PERSONAL: Born March 24, 1983, in Baytown, Texas. ... 5-10/165. (1.78/74.8). ... Full name: Terrance Jerod Ford
HIGH SCHOOL: Willowridge (Sugar Land, Texas.).
COLLEGE: Texas.
TRANSACTIONS/CAREER NOTES: Selected after sophomore season by Milwaukee Bucks in first round (eighth pick overall) of 2003 NBA Draft. ... Traded by Bucks to Toronto Raptors for F Charlie Villanueva and cash (June 30, 2006).

COLLEGIATE RECORD

NOTES: The SPORTING NEWS College Player of the Year (2003). ... The SPORTING NEWS All-America first team (2003). ... Naismith Award winner (2003). ... Wooden Award winner (2003).

												AVERAGES		
Season Team	G	Min.	FGM	FGA	Pct.	FTM	FTA	Pct.	Reb.	Ast.	Pts.	RPG	APG	PPG
01-02—Texas	33	1068	123	298	.413	107	138	.775	125	273	358	3.8	8.3	10.8
02-03—Texas	33	1110	159	397	.401	159	194	.819	128	254	495	3.9	7.7	15.0
Totals	66	2178	282	695	.406	266	332	.801	253	527	853	3.8	8.0	12.9

Three-point field goals: 2001-02, 5-for-33 (.152). 2002-03, 18-for-68 (.265). Totals, 23-for-101 (.228).

NBA REGULAR-SEASON RECORD

HONORS: NBA All-Rookie second team (2004).

									REBOUNDS							AVERAGES		
Season Team	G	Min.	FGM	FGA	Pct.	FTM	FTA	Pct.	Off.	Def.	Tot.	Ast.	St.	Blk.	TO	Pts.	RPG	APG	PPG
03-04—Milwaukee	55	1472	153	398	.384	80	98	.816	37	140	177	356	60	3	139	391	3.2	6.5	7.1
04-05—Milwaukee								Did not play—Injured											
05-06—Milwaukee	72	2557	328	789	.416	187	248	.754	63	248	311	473	104	7	219	878	4.3	6.6	12.2
Totals	127	4029	481	1187	.405	267	346	.772	100	388	488	829	164	10	358	1269	3.8	6.5	10.0

Three-point field goals: 2003-04, 5-for-21 (.238). 2005-06, 35-for-104 (.337). Totals, 40-for-125 (.320).
Personal fouls/disqualifications: 2003-04, 123/0. 2005-06, 196/3. Totals, 319/3.

NBA PLAYOFF RECORD

									REBOUNDS							AVERAGES		
Season Team	G	Min.	FGM	FGA	Pct.	FTM	FTA	Pct.	Off.	Def.	Tot.	Ast.	St.	Blk.	TO	Pts.	RPG	APG	PPG
05-06—Milwaukee	5	162	25	51	.490	11	12	.917	3	17	20	32	3	0	16	63	4.0	6.4	12.6

Three-point field goals: 2005-06, 2-for-5 (.400). Totals, 2-for-5 (.400).
Personal fouls/disqualifications: 2005-06, 20/0. Totals, 20/0.

FORTSON, DANNY   F   SUPERSONICS

PERSONAL: Born March 27, 1976, in Philadelphia. ... 6-8/260. (2.03/117.9). ... Full name: Daniel Anthony Fortson
HIGH SCHOOL: Altoona (Pa.), then Shaler (Pittsburgh).
COLLEGE: Cincinnati.
TRANSACTIONS/CAREER NOTES: Selected after junior season by Milwaukee Bucks in first round (10th pick overall) of 1997 NBA Draft. ... Draft rights traded by Bucks with F Johnny Newman and F/C Joe Wolf to Denver Nuggets for C Ervin Johnson (June 25, 1997). ... Traded by Nuggets with F Eric Williams, G Eric Washington and first-round draft choice within the next three years to Boston Celtics for G/F Ron Mercer, F Popeye Jones and C Dwayne Schintzius (August 3, 1999). ... Traded by Celtics with a future draft choice to Toronto Raptors for G Alvin Williams, F/C Sean Marks and cash considerations (February 9, 2000); trade later voided because Williams failed physical. ... Traded by Celtics to Golden State Warriors as part of four-team deal in which Celtics received G Robert Pack, C John Williams and cash considerations from Dallas Mavericks and a conditional first-round draft choice from Utah Jazz, Mavericks received G Dana Barros from Celtics, F Bill Curley from Warriors and G Howard Eisley from Jazz, Jazz received F Donyell Marshall from Warriors and C Bruno Sundov from Mavericks and Warriors received F Adam Keefe from Jazz (August 16, 2000). ... Traded by Warriors with F Antawn

F

Jamison, F Chris Mills and G Jiri Welsch to Dallas Mavericks for G Nick Van Exel, G Avery Johnson, F Popeye Jones, F Antoine Rigaudeau and C Evan Eschmeyer (August 18, 2003). ... Traded by Mavericks to Seattle SuperSonics for C Calvin Booth (July 26, 2004).

COLLEGIATE RECORD

NOTES: THE SPORTING NEWS All-America second team (1996). ... THE SPORTING NEWS All-America first team (1997).

Season Team	G	Min.	FGM	FGA	Pct.	FTM	FTA	Pct.	Reb.	Ast.	Pts.	RPG	APG	PPG
94-95—Cincinnati	34	797	190	355	.535	134	196	.684	258	38	514	7.6	1.1	15.1
95-96—Cincinnati	33	909	222	413	.538	220	292	.753	316	45	664	9.6	1.4	20.1
96-97—Cincinnati	33	986	243	392	.620	217	281	.772	299	36	703	9.1	1.1	21.3
Totals	100	2692	655	1160	.565	571	769	.743	873	119	1881	8.7	1.2	18.8

Three-point field goals: 1994-95, 0-for-1. 1995-96, 0-for-1. 1996-97, 0-for-1. Totals, 0-for-3 (.000).
Personal fouls/disqualifications: 1994-95, 119/5. 1995-96, 118/4. Totals, 237/9.

NBA REGULAR-SEASON RECORD

NOTES: Led NBA with 212 personal fouls (1998-99) and tied for NBA lead with nine disqualifications (1998-99).

Season Team	G	Min.	FGM	FGA	Pct.	FTM	FTA	Pct.	REBOUNDS Off.	Def.	Tot.	Ast.	St.	Blk.	TO	Pts.	RPG	APG	PPG
97-98—Denver	80	1811	276	611	.452	263	339	.776	182	266	448	76	44	30	157	816	5.6	1.0	10.2
98-99—Denver	50	1417	191	386	.495	168	231	.727	210	371	*581	32	31	22	77	550	11.6	0.6	11.0
99-00—Boston	55	856	140	265	.528	139	189	.735	141	225	366	29	20	5	67	419	6.7	0.5	7.6
00-01—Golden State	6	203	29	50	.580	42	54	.778	29	69	98	5	2	0	10	100	16.3	0.8	16.7
01-02—Golden State	77	2216	309	722	.428	245	308	.795	290	609	899	127	44	17	160	864	11.7	1.6	11.2
02-03—Golden State	17	223	20	54	.370	19	29	.655	28	45	73	12	9	0	15	59	4.3	0.7	3.5
03-04—Dallas	56	625	71	139	.511	75	92	.815	114	136	250	9	12	11	37	217	4.5	0.2	3.9
04-05—Seattle	62	1047	118	226	.522	227	258	.880	157	191	348	8	15	7	91	463	5.6	0.1	7.5
05-06—Seattle	23	276	27	51	.529	33	43	.767	31	47	78	2	4	2	26	87	3.4	0.1	3.8
Totals	426	8674	1181	2504	.472	1211	1543	.785	1182	1959	3141	300	181	94	640	3575	7.4	0.7	8.4

Three-point field goals: 1997-98, 1-for-3 (.333). 1998-99, 0-for-3. 2001-02, 1-for-4 (.250). 2002-03, 0-for-1. Totals, 2-for-11 (.182).
Personal fouls/disqualifications: 1997-98, 314/7. 1998-99, 212/9. 1999-00, 180/4. 2000-01, 22/1. 2001-02, 255/5. 2002-03, 43/0. 2003-04, 148/0. 2004-05, 265/12. 2005-06, 76/2. Totals, 1515/40.

NBA PLAYOFF RECORD

Season Team	G	Min.	FGM	FGA	Pct.	FTM	FTA	Pct.	REBOUNDS Off.	Def.	Tot.	Ast.	St.	Blk.	TO	Pts.	RPG	APG	PPG
04-05—Seattle	11	105	12	21	.571	12	15	.800	5	21	26	0	3	1	13	36	2.4	0.0	3.3

Personal fouls/disqualifications: 2004-05, 42/0. Totals, 42/0.

FOSTER, JEFF — F — PACERS

PERSONAL: Born January 16, 1977, in San Antonio. ... 6-11/242. (2.11/109.8). ... Full name: Jeffrey Douglas Foster
HIGH SCHOOL: James Madison (San Antonio).
COLLEGE: Southwest Texas State.
TRANSACTIONS/CAREER NOTES: Selected by Golden State Warriors in first round (21st pick overall) of 1999 NBA Draft. ... Draft rights traded by Warriors to Indiana Pacers for draft rights to G Vonteego Cummings and future first-round draft choice (June 30, 1999).

COLLEGIATE RECORD

Season Team	G	Min.	FGM	FGA	Pct.	FTM	FTA	Pct.	Reb.	Ast.	Pts.	RPG	APG	PPG
95-96—Southwest Texas State	26	340	31	70	.443	19	39	.487	108	19	82	4.2	0.7	3.2
96-97—Southwest Texas State	29	637	87	170	.512	71	110	.645	222	25	248	7.7	0.9	8.6
97-98—Southwest Texas State	28	816	140	263	.532	77	126	.611	285	44	357	10.2	1.6	12.8
98-99—Southwest Texas State	28	787	142	285	.498	113	163	.693	316	43	397	11.3	1.5	14.2
Totals	111	2580	400	788	.508	280	438	.639	931	131	1084	8.4	1.2	9.8

Three-point field goals: 1995-96, 1-for-1 (1.000). 1996-97, 3-for-3 (1.000). Totals, 4-for-4 (1.000).

NBA REGULAR-SEASON RECORD

Season Team	G	Min.	FGM	FGA	Pct.	FTM	FTA	Pct.	REBOUNDS Off.	Def.	Tot.	Ast.	St.	Blk.	TO	Pts.	RPG	APG	PPG
99-00—Indiana	19	86	13	23	.565	17	25	.680	12	20	32	5	5	1	2	43	1.7	0.3	2.3
00-01—Indiana	71	1152	100	213	.469	47	91	.516	144	245	389	33	39	28	52	249	5.5	0.5	3.5
01-02—Indiana	82	1786	177	394	.449	111	182	.610	206	350	556	70	71	38	79	467	6.8	0.9	5.7
02-03—Indiana	77	802	64	178	.360	34	63	.540	118	161	279	51	28	21	34	162	3.6	0.7	2.1
03-04—Indiana	82	1961	197	362	.544	103	154	.669	248	362	610	64	71	27	60	497	7.4	0.8	6.1
04-05—Indiana	61	1594	168	324	.519	90	142	.634	205	345	550	43	46	12	55	426	9.0	0.7	7.0
05-06—Indiana	63	1581	138	250	.552	96	159	.604	224	350	574	50	41	27	64	372	9.1	0.8	5.9
Totals	455	8962	857	1744	.491	498	816	.610	1157	1833	2990	316	301	154	346	2216	6.6	0.7	4.9

Three-point field goals: 1999-00, 0-for-1. 2000-01, 2-for-7 (.286). 2001-02, 2-for-15 (.133). 2002-03, 0-for-2. 2003-04, 0-for-4. 2004-05, 0-for-5. 2005-06, 0-for-4. Totals, 4-for-38 (.105).
Personal fouls/disqualifications: 1999-00, 18/0. 2000-01, 152/3. 2001-02, 232/4. 2002-03, 103/0. 2003-04, 189/1. 2004-05, 186/3. 2005-06, 191/2. Totals, 1071/13.

NBA PLAYOFF RECORD

Season Team	G	Min.	FGM	FGA	Pct.	FTM	FTA	Pct.	REBOUNDS Off.	Def.	Tot.	Ast.	St.	Blk.	TO	Pts.	RPG	APG	PPG
00-01—Indiana	4	52	4	9	.444	2	2	1.000	3	9	12	2	0	3	4	10	3.0	0.5	2.5
01-02—Indiana	5	78	7	13	.538	4	9	.444	5	19	24	7	3	1	9	20	4.8	1.4	4.0
02-03—Indiana	6	38	6	11	.545	2	2	1.000	4	4	8	2	0	3	0	14	1.3	0.3	2.3
03-04—Indiana	16	307	25	43	.581	8	10	.800	44	61	105	12	13	5	13	58	6.6	0.8	3.6
04-05—Indiana	13	245	31	52	.596	15	21	.714	46	50	96	5	6	12	8	77	7.4	0.4	5.9
05-06—Indiana	4	80	4	11	.364	3	4	.750	11	13	24	3	4	1	0	11	6.0	0.8	2.8
Totals	48	800	77	139	.554	34	48	.708	113	156	269	31	26	25	34	190	5.6	0.6	4.0

Three-point field goals: 2001-02, 2-for-4 (.500). 2003-04, 0-for-1. Totals, 2-for-5 (.400).
Personal fouls/disqualifications: 2000-01, 8/0. 2001-02, 13/0. 2002-03, 3/0. 2003-04, 37/0. 2004-05, 27/0. 2005-06, 9/0. Totals, 97/0.

FOYLE, ADONAL   C   WARRIORS

PERSONAL: Born March 9, 1975, in Island of Canouan, Grenadines. ... 6-10/250. (2.08/113.4). ... Full name: Adonal David Foyle
HIGH SCHOOL: Hamilton (N.Y.).
COLLEGE: Colgate.
TRANSACTIONS/CAREER NOTES: Selected after junior season by Golden State Warriors in first round (eighth pick overall) of 1997 NBA Draft.

COLLEGIATE RECORD

NOTES: Holds NCAA Division I single-season record for highest blocked-shots-per-game average-6.4 (1997). ... Led NCAA Division I with 6.4 blocked shots per game (1997).

Season Team	G	Min.	FGM	FGA	Pct.	FTM	FTA	Pct.	Reb.	Ast.	Pts.	RPG	APG	PPG
												AVERAGES		
94-95—Colgate	30	1063	207	370	.559	95	190	.500	371	36	682	12.4	1.2	22.7
95-96—Colgate	29	1060	228	441	.517	129	264	.489	364	44	585	12.6	1.5	20.2
96-97—Colgate	28	1055	277	490	.565	127	261	.487	368	54	682	13.1	1.9	24.4
Totals	87	3178	712	1301	.547	351	715	.491	1103	134	1949	12.7	1.5	22.4

Three-point field goals: 1995-96, 0-for-3. 1996-97, 1-for-10 (.100). Totals, 1-for-13 (.077).

NBA REGULAR-SEASON RECORD

Season Team	G	Min.	FGM	FGA	Pct.	FTM	FTA	Pct.	Off.	Def.	Tot.	Ast.	St.	Blk.	TO	Pts.	RPG	APG	PPG
									REBOUNDS								AVERAGES		
97-98—Golden State	55	656	69	170	.406	27	62	.435	73	111	184	14	13	52	50	165	3.3	0.3	3.0
98-99—Golden State	44	614	52	121	.430	25	51	.490	79	115	194	18	15	43	31	129	4.4	0.4	2.9
99-00—Golden State	76	1654	193	380	.508	34	90	.378	174	250	424	42	26	136	71	420	5.6	0.6	5.5
00-01—Golden State	58	1457	156	375	.416	30	68	.441	156	249	405	48	31	156	79	342	7.0	0.8	5.9
01-02—Golden State	79	1485	171	385	.444	37	93	.398	150	234	384	41	36	168	76	379	4.9	0.5	4.8
02-03—Golden State	82	1787	185	345	.536	70	104	.673	176	314	490	37	40	205	73	440	6.0	0.5	5.4
03-04—Golden State	44	572	59	130	.454	19	35	.543	54	113	167	17	6	46	21	137	3.8	0.4	3.1
04-05—Golden State	78	1700	156	311	.502	40	72	.556	165	264	429	56	26	159	58	352	5.5	0.7	4.5
05-06—Golden State	77	1824	152	300	.507	41	67	.612	143	281	424	33	44	125	80	345	5.5	0.4	4.5
Totals	593	11749	1193	2517	.474	323	642	.503	1170	1931	3101	306	237	1090	539	2709	5.2	0.5	4.6

Three-point field goals: 1997-98, 0-for-1. 2002-03, 0-for-1. Totals, 0-for-2 (.000).
Personal fouls/disqualifications: 1997-98, 94/0. 1998-99, 90/0. 1999-00, 218/2. 2000-01, 136/0. 2001-02, 179/2. 2002-03, 214/3. 2003-04, 68/1. 2004-05, 201/5. 2005-06, 215/1. Totals, 1415/14.

FRAHM, RICHIE   G

PERSONAL: Born August 14, 1977 ... 6-5/210. (1.96/95.3).
HIGH SCHOOL: Battle Ground (Wash.).
COLLEGE: Gonzaga.
TRANSACTIONS/CAREER NOTES: Not drafted by an NBA franchise. ... Played in Philippines (2001-02). ... Played in American Basketball Association (2001-02). ... Played in Turkey (2002-03). ... Signed as free agent by Seattle SuperSonics (September 27, 2003). ... Selected by Charlotte Bobcats from SuperSonics in NBA Expansion Draft (June 22, 2004). ... Signed as free agent by Minnesota Timberwolves (September 26, 2005). ... Claimed on waivers by Houston Rockets (March 20, 2006).

COLLEGIATE RECORD

Season Team	G	Min.	FGM	FGA	Pct.	FTM	FTA	Pct.	Reb.	Ast.	Pts.	RPG	APG	PPG
												AVERAGES		
96-97—Gonzaga	27	381	44	107	.411	17	23	.739	57	25	125	2.1	0.9	4.6
97-98—Gonzaga	33	899	132	292	.452	58	70	.829	127	60	399	3.8	1.8	12.1
98-99—Gonzaga	35	980	165	378	.437	81	100	.810	149	70	504	4.3	2.0	14.4
99-00—Gonzaga	35	1165	194	414	.469	115	146	.788	153	88	593	4.4	2.5	16.9
Totals	130	3425	535	1191	.449	271	339	.799	486	243	1621	3.7	1.9	12.5

Three-point field goals: 1996-97, 20-for-48 (.417). 1997-98, 77-for-173 (.445). 1998-99, 93-for-217 (.429). 1999-00, 90-for-224 (.402). Totals, 280-for-662 (.423).

NBA REGULAR-SEASON RECORD

Season Team	G	Min.	FGM	FGA	Pct.	FTM	FTA	Pct.	Off.	Def.	Tot.	Ast.	St.	Blk.	TO	Pts.	RPG	APG	PPG
									REBOUNDS								AVERAGES		
03-04—Seattle	54	469	63	139	.453	23	26	.885	12	44	56	24	16	4	7	183	1.0	0.4	3.4
04-05—Portland	43	499	56	140	.400	21	25	.840	17	44	61	30	15	4	14	164	1.4	0.7	3.8
05-06—Minn.-Hous.	33	342	39	100	.390	7	10	.700	3	30	33	21	4	2	8	108	1.0	0.6	3.3
Totals	130	1310	158	379	.417	51	61	.836	32	118	150	75	35	10	29	455	1.2	0.6	3.5

Three-point field goals: 2003-04, 34-for-92 (.370). 2004-05, 31-for-80 (.388). 2005-06, 23-for-70 (.329). Totals, 88-for-242 (.364).
Personal fouls/disqualifications: 2003-04, 50/0. 2004-05, 35/0. 2005-06, 30/0. Totals, 115/0.

F

FRANCIS, STEVE   G   KNICKS

PERSONAL: Born February 21, 1977, in Silver Spring, Md. ... 6-3/195. (1.91/88.5). ... Full name: Steve D'Shawn Francis
HIGH SCHOOL: Montgomery Blair (Silver Spring, Md.).
JUNIOR COLLEGE: San Jacinto College (Texas), then Allegany (Md.) C.C.
COLLEGE: Maryland.
TRANSACTIONS/CAREER NOTES: Selected after junior season by Vancouver Grizzlies in first round (second pick overall)

of 1999 NBA Draft. ... Draft rights traded by Grizzlies with F Tony Massenburg to Houston Rockets as part of three-way deal in which Grizzlies received G Michael Dickerson, F/C Othella Harrington, G Brent Price, F/C Antoine Carr and future first-round draft choice from Rockets, Rockets received F Don MacLean and future first-round draft choice from Orlando Magic, and Magic received G Michael Smith, G/F Rodrick Rhodes, G Lee Mayberry and F Makhtar Ndiaye from Grizzles (August 27, 1999). ... Traded by Rockets with G Cuttino Mobley and C Kelvin Cato to Orlando Magic for G Tracy McGrady, F Juwan Howard, G Tyronn Lue and G Reece Gaines (June 29, 2004). ... Traded by Magic to New York Knicks for G/F Anfernee Hardaway and F Trevor Ariza (February 22, 2006).

COLLEGIATE RECORD

NOTES: The SPORTING NEWS All-America second team (1999).

Season Team	G	Min.	FGM	FGA	Pct.	FTM	FTA	Pct.	Reb.	Ast.	Pts.	RPG	APG	PPG
96-97—San Jacinto College........	35	971	138	248	.556	146	184	.793	263	264	437	7.5	7.5	12.5
97-98—Allegany C.C.	35	...	295	561	.526	204	248	.823	248	304	885	7.1	8.7	25.3
98-99—Maryland	34	1044	205	392	.523	124	157	.790	154	152	579	4.5	4.5	17.0
Junior College Totals.............	70	971	433	809	.535	350	432	.810	511	568	1322	7.3	8.1	18.9
4-Year-College Totals............	34	1044	205	392	.523	124	157	.790	154	152	579	4.5	4.5	17.0

Three-point field goals: 1996-97, 15-for-39 (.385). 1997-98, 91-for-241 (.378). 1998-99, 45-for-116 (.388). Totals, 151-for-396 (.381).

NBA REGULAR-SEASON RECORD

HONORS: NBA Co-Rookie of the Year (2000). ... NBA All-Rookie first team (2000).

Season Team	G	Min.	FGM	FGA	Pct.	FTM	FTA	Pct.	REBOUNDS Off.	Def.	Tot.	Ast.	St.	Blk.	TO	Pts.	RPG	APG	PPG
99-00—Houston.........	77	2776	497	1117	.445	287	365	.786	152	257	409	507	118	29	306	1388	5.3	6.6	18.0
00-01—Houston.........	80	3194	550	1219	.451	358	438	.817	190	363	553	517	141	31	265	1591	6.9	6.5	19.9
01-02—Houston.........	57	2343	420	1007	.417	326	422	.773	102	299	401	362	71	25	221	1234	7.0	6.4	21.6
02-03—Houston.........	81	3318	571	1312	.435	476	595	.800	159	340	499	502	141	41	299	1703	6.2	6.2	21.0
03-04—Houston.........	79	3194	450	1117	.403	337	435	.775	116	317	433	493	139	35	294	1310	5.5	6.2	16.6
04-05—Orlando..........	78	2978	563	1330	.423	499	606	.823	126	324	450	547	112	28	317	1663	5.8	7.0	21.3
05-06—Orlando-N.Y. ...	70	2393	333	765	.435	314	399	.787	74	216	290	345	74	17	214	1005	4.1	4.9	14.4
Totals	522	20196	3384	7867	.430	2597	3260	.797	919	2116	3035	3273	796	206	1916	9894	5.8	6.3	19.0

Three-point field goals: 1999-00, 107-for-310 (.345). 2000-01, 133-for-336 (.396). 2001-02, 68-for-210 (.324). 2002-03, 85-for-240 (.354). 2003-04, 73-for-250 (.292). 2004-05, 38-for-127 (.299). 2005-06, 25-for-83 (.301). Totals, 529-for-1556 (.340).

Personal fouls/disqualifications: 1999-00, 231/2. 2000-01, 274/7. 2001-02, 172/2. 2002-03, 251/2. 2003-04, 257/3. 2004-05, 273/5. 2005-06, 204/3. Totals, 1662/24.

NBA PLAYOFF RECORD

Season Team	G	Min.	FGM	FGA	Pct.	FTM	FTA	Pct.	REBOUNDS Off.	Def.	Tot.	Ast.	St.	Blk.	TO	Pts.	RPG	APG	PPG
03-04—Houston.........	5	222	30	70	.429	29	40	.725	6	36	42	38	7	1	21	96	8.4	7.6	19.2

Three-point field goals: 2003-04, 7-for-17 (.412). Totals, 7-for-17 (.412).

Personal fouls/disqualifications: 2003-04, 18/1. Totals, 18/1.

NBA ALL-STAR GAME RECORD

Season Team	Min.	FGM	FGA	Pct.	FTM	FTA	Pct.	REBOUNDS Off.	Def.	Tot.	Ast.	PF	Dq.	St.	Blk.	TO	Pts.
2002—Houston	18	1	8	.125	1	2	.500	1	1	2	3	1	0	2	0	2	3
2003—Houston	32	9	12	.750	0	0	...	1	1	2	9	1	0	0	0	3	20
2004—Houston	23	6	9	.667	0	0	...	1	3	4	4	1	0	0	0	1	13
Totals............................	73	16	29	.552	1	2	.500	3	5	8	16	3	0	2	0	6	36

Three-point field goals: 2002, 0-for-1. 2003, 2-for-3 (.667). 2004, 1-for-2 (.500). Totals, 3-for-6 (.500).

FRYE, CHANNING   C   KNICKS

PERSONAL: Born May 17, 1983, in White Plains, N.Y. ... 6-11/248. (2.11/112.5). ... Full name: Channing Thomas Frye.
HIGH SCHOOL: St. Mary's (Phoenix.).
COLLEGE: Arizona.
TRANSACTIONS/CAREER NOTES: Selected by New York Knicks in first round (eighth pick overall) of 2005 NBA Draft.

COLLEGIATE RECORD

Season Team	G	Min.	FGM	FGA	Pct.	FTM	FTA	Pct.	Reb.	Ast.	Pts.	RPG	APG	PPG
01-02—Arizona..................	34	814	122	205	.595	80	110	.727	214	25	324	6.3	0.7	9.5
02-03—Arizona..................	32	814	165	290	.569	73	110	.664	257	23	403	8.0	0.7	12.6
03-04—Arizona..................	30	910	193	352	.548	89	113	.788	222	56	478	7.4	1.9	15.9
04-05—Arizona..................	37	1148	227	410	.554	127	153	.830	282	71	584	7.6	1.9	15.8
Totals	133	3686	707	1257	.562	369	486	.759	975	175	1789	7.3	1.3	13.5

Three-point field goals: 2001-02, 0-for-0. 2002-03, 0-for-1. 2003-04, 3-for-5 (.600). 2004-05, 3-for-17 (.176). Totals, 6-for-23 (.261).

NBA REGULAR-SEASON RECORD

HONORS: NBA All-Rookie first team (2006).

Season Team	G	Min.	FGM	FGA	Pct.	FTM	FTA	Pct.	REBOUNDS Off.	Def.	Tot.	Ast.	St.	Blk.	TO	Pts.	RPG	APG	PPG
05-06—New York........	65	1572	305	640	.477	189	229	.825	138	236	374	53	30	47	97	802	5.8	0.8	12.3

Three-point field goals: 2005-06, 3-for-9 (.333). Totals, 3-for-9 (.333).

Personal fouls/disqualifications: 2005-06, 200/3. Totals, 200/3.

PERSONAL: Born August 2, 1978, in Den Haag, Holland. ... 6-11/240. (2.11/108.9).
HIGH SCHOOL: Gov. Drummer Academy (Byfield, Mass.).
COLLEGE: UCLA.
TRANSACTIONS/CAREER NOTES: Selected by Milwaukee Bucks in second round (34th pick overall) of 2002 NBA Draft.

COLLEGIATE RECORD

Season Team	G	Min.	FGM	FGA	Pct.	FTM	FTA	Pct.	Reb.	Ast.	Pts.	RPG	APG	PPG
98-99—UCLA	24	480	88	163	.540	31	62	.500	136	17	207	5.7	0.7	8.6
99-00—UCLA	33	740	140	248	.565	39	101	.386	136	17	319	4.1	0.5	9.7
00-01—UCLA	32	861	156	292	.534	63	139	.453	275	18	375	8.6	0.6	11.7
01-02—UCLA	33	865	164	296	.554	58	123	.472	255	23	386	7.7	0.7	11.7
Totals	122	2946	548	999	.549	191	425	.449	802	75	1287	6.6	0.6	10.5

Three-point field goals: 2001-02, 0-for-1. Totals, 0-for-1 (.000).

NBA REGULAR-SEASON RECORD

Season Team	G	Min.	FGM	FGA	Pct.	FTM	FTA	Pct.	REBOUNDS Off.	Def.	Tot.	Ast.	St.	Blk.	TO	Pts.	RPG	APG	PPG
02-03—Milwaukee	49	760	70	145	.483	29	56	.518	66	131	197	9	22	52	27	169	4.0	0.2	3.4
03-04—Milwaukee	75	1260	183	349	.524	58	118	.492	126	220	346	28	51	105	45	424	4.6	0.4	5.7
04-05—Milwaukee	81	1783	243	451	.539	107	199	.538	261	413	674	30	47	106	81	593	8.3	0.4	7.3
05-06—Milwaukee	74	885	171	309	.553	41	89	.461	91	141	232	24	25	43	35	383	3.1	0.3	5.2
Totals	279	4688	667	1254	.532	235	462	.509	544	905	1449	91	145	306	188	1569	5.2	0.3	5.6

Three-point field goals: 2002-03, 0-for-1. 2003-04, 0-for-1. 2005-06, 0-for-1. Totals, 0-for-3 (.000).
Personal fouls/disqualifications: 2002-03, 125/3. 2003-04, 186/0. 2004-05, 224/1. 2005-06, 171/2. Totals, 706/6.

NBA PLAYOFF RECORD

Season Team	G	Min.	FGM	FGA	Pct.	FTM	FTA	Pct.	REBOUNDS Off.	Def.	Tot.	Ast.	St.	Blk.	TO	Pts.	RPG	APG	PPG
03-04—Milwaukee	1	9	2	4	.500	0	1	.000	0	1	1	2	1	0	0	4	1.0	2.0	4.0
05-06—Milwaukee	4	16	8	9	.889	1	2	.500	2	2	4	0	0	1	0	17	1.0	0.0	4.3
Totals	5	25	10	13	.769	1	3	.333	2	3	5	2	1	1	0	21	1.0	0.4	4.2

Personal fouls/disqualifications: 2003-04, 1/0. 2005-06, 3/0. Totals, 4/0.

GAI, DENG   F

PERSONAL: Born March 22, 1982, in Sudan. ... 6-9/250. (2.06/113.4).
HIGH SCHOOL: Milford Academy (Conn.).
COLLEGE: Fairfield.
TRANSACTIONS/CAREER NOTES: Not drafted by an NBA franchise. ... Signed as free agent by Philadelphia 76ers (August 5, 2005). ... Waived by 76ers (December 8, 2005).

COLLEGIATE RECORD

NOTES: Led NCAA Division I with 5.5 blocked shots per game (2004-05).

Season Team	G	Min.	FGM	FGA	Pct.	FTM	FTA	Pct.	Reb.	Ast.	Pts.	RPG	APG	PPG
01-02—Fairfield	29	743	114	247	.462	68	86	.791	137	21	320	4.7	0.7	11.0
02-03—Fairfield	25	726	111	205	.541	79	110	.718	171	23	319	6.8	0.9	12.8
03-04—Fairfield	16	539	80	194	.412	41	57	.719	137	11	213	8.6	0.7	13.3
04-05—Fairfield	30	1040	157	331	.474	83	115	.722	254	40	416	8.5	1.3	13.9
Totals	100	3048	462	977	.473	271	368	.736	699	95	1268	7.0	1.0	12.7

Three-point field goals: 2001-02, 24-for-73 (.329). 2002-03, 18-for-48 (.375). 2003-04, 12-for-40 (.300). 2004-05, 19-for-57 (.333). Totals, 73-for-218 (.335).

NBA REGULAR-SEASON RECORD

Season Team	G	Min.	FGM	FGA	Pct.	FTM	FTA	Pct.	REBOUNDS Off.	Def.	Tot.	Ast.	St.	Blk.	TO	Pts.	RPG	APG	PPG
05-06—Philadelphia	2	5	0	0	...	0	0	...	0	0	0	0	0	0	0	0	0.0	0.0	0.0

GAINES, REECE   G

PERSONAL: Born January 7, 1981, in Madison, Wis. ... 6-6/205. (1.98/93.0). ... Full name: Clifton Reece Gaines
HIGH SCHOOL: Madison West (Madison, Wis.).
COLLEGE: Louisville.
TRANSACTIONS/CAREER NOTES: Selected by Orlando Magic in first round (15th overall pick) of 2003 NBA Draft. ... Traded by Magic with G Tracy McGrady, F Juwan Howard and G Tyronn Lue to Houston Rockets for G Steve Francis, G Cuttino Mobley and C Kelvin Cato (June 29, 2004). ... Traded by Rockets with second-round picks in 2006 and 2007 NBA drafts to Milwaukee Bucks for G Mike James and C Zendon Hamilton (February 24, 2005).

COLLEGIATE RECORD

NOTES: The SPORTING NEWS All-America third team (2003).

Season Team	G	Min.	FGM	FGA	Pct.	FTM	FTA	Pct.	Reb.	Ast.	Pts.	RPG	APG	PPG
99-00—Louisville	31	921	98	220	.445	66	86	.767	101	104	281	3.3	3.4	9.1
00-01—Louisville	30	946	148	337	.439	81	120	.675	105	98	417	3.5	3.3	13.9
01-02—Louisville	32	1049	209	458	.456	164	205	.800	124	114	673	3.9	3.6	21.0
02-03—Louisville	32	1030	177	383	.462	145	197	.736	94	159	574	2.9	5.0	17.9
Totals	125	3946	632	1398	.452	456	608	.750	424	475	1945	3.4	3.8	15.6

Three-point field goals: 1999-00, 19-for-61 (.311). 2000-01, 40-for-94 (.426). 2001-02, 91-for-241 (.378). 2002-03, 75-for-192 (.391). Totals, 225-for-588 (.383).

NBA REGULAR-SEASON RECORD

Season Team	G	Min.	FGM	FGA	Pct.	FTM	FTA	Pct.	Off.	Def.	Tot.	Ast.	St.	Blk.	TO	Pts.	RPG	APG	PPG
03-04—Orlando..........	38	364	25	86	.291	16	25	.640	8	31	39	40	11	2	18	69	1.0	1.1	1.8
04-05—Houston-Mil....	21	187	17	50	.340	3	4	.750	1	13	14	7	5	1	7	41	0.7	0.3	2.0
05-06—Milwaukee	12	54	6	12	.500	1	4	.250	0	0	0	3	1	0	1	13	0.0	0.3	1.1
Totals	71	605	48	148	.324	20	33	.606	9	44	53	50	17	3	26	123	0.7	0.7	1.7

Three-point field goals: 2003-04, 3-for-10 (.300). 2004-05, 4-for-14 (.286). 2005-06, 0-for-2. Totals, 7-for-26 (.269).
Personal fouls/disqualifications: 2003-04, 22/0. 2004-05, 17/0. 2005-06, 1/0. Totals, 40/0.

GARCIA, FRANCISCO　　　　F/G　　　　KINGS

PERSONAL: Born December 31, 1981, in Santo Domingo, Dominican Republic. ... 6-7/195. (2.01/88.5). ... Full name: Francisco Alberto Garcia
HIGH SCHOOL: Winchendon School (Mass.).
COLLEGE: Louisville.
TRANSACTIONS/CAREER NOTES: Selected after junior season by Sacramento Kings in first round (23rd pick overall) of 2005 NBA Draft.

COLLEGIATE RECORD

Season Team	G	Min.	FGM	FGA	Pct.	FTM	FTA	Pct.	Reb.	Ast.	Pts.	RPG	APG	PPG
02-03—Louisville	32	696	126	258	.488	49	55	.891	94	67	358	2.9	2.1	11.2
03-04—Louisville	28	850	149	345	.432	110	138	.797	127	131	460	4.5	4.7	16.4
04-05—Louisville	38	1211	187	428	.437	150	171	.877	158	148	595	4.2	3.9	15.7
Totals	98	2757	462	1031	.448	309	364	.849	379	346	1413	3.9	3.5	14.4

Three-point field goals: 2002-03, 57-for-134 (.425). 2003-04, 52-for-160 (.325). 2004-05, 71-for-194 (.366). Totals, 180-for-488 (.369).

NBA REGULAR-SEASON RECORD

Season Team	G	Min.	FGM	FGA	Pct.	FTM	FTA	Pct.	Off.	Def.	Tot.	Ast.	St.	Blk.	TO	Pts.	RPG	APG	PPG
05-06—Sacramento	67	1301	130	325	.400	78	101	.772	39	146	185	94	41	47	75	377	2.8	1.4	5.6

Three-point field goals: 2005-06, 39-for-137 (.285). Totals, 39-for-137 (.285).
Personal fouls/disqualifications: 2005-06, 135/0. Totals, 135/0.

NBA PLAYOFF RECORD

Season Team	G	Min.	FGM	FGA	Pct.	FTM	FTA	Pct.	Off.	Def.	Tot.	Ast.	St.	Blk.	TO	Pts.	RPG	APG	PPG
05-06—Sacramento	6	41	5	11	.455	2	2	1.000	0	2	2	1	2	2	0	13	0.3	0.2	2.2

Three-point field goals: 2005-06, 1-for-4 (.250). Totals, 1-for-4 (.250).
Personal fouls/disqualifications: 2005-06, 5/0. Totals, 5/0.

GARNETT, KEVIN　　　　F　　　　TIMBERWOLVES

PERSONAL: Born May 19, 1976, in Mauldin, S.C. ... 6-11/220. (2.11/99.8).
HIGH SCHOOL: Mauldin (S.C.), then Farragut Academy (Chicago).
COLLEGE: Did not attend college.
TRANSACTIONS/CAREER NOTES: Selected out of high school by Minnesota Timberwolves in first round (fifth pick overall) of 1995 NBA Draft.
MISCELLANEOUS: Member of gold-medal-winning U.S. Olympic team (2000). ... Minnesota Timberwolves all-time points leader with 17,337, all-time steals leader with 1,193, all-time leading rebounder with 9,567, all-time assists leader with 3,833 and all-time blocked shots leader with 1,450 (1995-96 through 2005-06).

NBA REGULAR-SEASON RECORD

HONORS: NBA Most Valuable Player (2004). ... All-NBA first team (2000, 2003, 2004). ... All-NBA second team (2001, 2002, 2005). ... All-NBA third team (1999). ... NBA All-Defensive first team (2000, 2001, 2002, 2003, 2004, 2005). ... NBA All-Rookie second team (1996). ... NBA All-Defensive second team (2006). ... NBA J. Walter Kennedy Citizenship Award winner (2006).

Season Team	G	Min.	FGM	FGA	Pct.	FTM	FTA	Pct.	Off.	Def.	Tot.	Ast.	St.	Blk.	TO	Pts.	RPG	APG	PPG
95-96—Minnesota.......	80	2293	361	735	.491	105	149	.705	175	326	501	145	86	131	110	835	6.3	1.8	10.4
96-97—Minnesota.......	77	2995	549	1100	.499	205	272	.754	190	428	618	236	105	163	175	1309	8.0	3.1	17.0
97-98—Minnesota.......	82	3222	635	1293	.491	245	332	.738	222	564	786	348	139	150	192	1518	9.6	4.2	18.5
98-99—Minnesota.......	47	1780	414	900	.460	145	206	.704	166	323	489	202	78	83	135	977	10.4	4.3	20.8
99-00—Minnesota.......	81	3243	759	1526	.497	309	404	.765	223	733	956	401	120	126	268	1857	11.8	5.0	22.9
00-01—Minnesota.......	81	3202	704	1475	.477	357	467	.764	219	702	921	401	111	145	230	1784	11.4	5.0	22.0
01-02—Minnesota.......	81	3175	659	1401	.470	359	448	.801	243	738	981	422	96	126	229	1714	12.1	5.2	21.2
02-03—Minnesota.......	82	3321	743	1481	.502	377	502	.751	244	*858	1102	495	113	129	229	1883	13.4	6.0	23.0
03-04—Minnesota.......	82	3231	*804	*1611	.499	368	465	.791	245	*894	*1139	409	120	178	212	*1987	*13.9	5.0	24.2
04-05—Minnesota.......	82	3121	683	1360	.502	445	549	.811	247	*861	*1108	466	121	112	222	1817	*13.5	5.7	22.2
05-06—Minnesota.......	76	2957	626	1191	.526	396	489	.810	214	*752	966	308	104	107	180	1656	*12.7	4.1	21.8
Totals	851	32540	6937	14073	.493	3311	4283	.773	2388	7179	9567	3833	1193	1450	2182	17337	11.2	4.5	20.4

Three-point field goals: 1995-96, 8-for-28 (.286). 1996-97, 6-for-21 (.286). 1997-98, 3-for-16 (.188). 1998-99, 4-for-14 (.286). 1999-00, 30-for-81 (.370). 2000-01, 19-for-66 (.288). 2001-02, 37-for-116 (.319). 2002-03, 20-for-71 (.282). 2003-04, 11-for-43 (.256). 2004-05, 6-for-25 (.240). 2005-06, 8-for-30 (.267). Totals, 152-for-511 (.297).
Personal fouls/disqualifications: 1995-96, 189/2. 1996-97, 199/2. 1997-98, 224/1. 1998-99, 152/5. 1999-00, 205/1. 2000-01, 204/0. 2001-02, 184/0. 2002-03, 199/0. 2003-04, 202/1. 2004-05, 207/0. 2005-06, 206/3. Totals, 2171/15.

G

NBA PLAYOFF RECORD

Season Team	G	Min.	FGM	FGA	Pct.	FTM	FTA	Pct.	REBOUNDS Off.	Def.	Tot.	Ast.	St.	Blk.	TO	Pts.	AVERAGES RPG	APG	PPG
96-97—Minnesota	3	125	24	51	.471	3	3	1.000	14	14	28	11	4	3	4	52	9.3	3.7	17.3
97-98—Minnesota	5	194	36	75	.480	7	9	.778	17	31	48	20	4	12	22	79	9.6	4.0	15.8
98-99—Minnesota	4	170	35	79	.443	17	23	.739	16	32	48	15	7	8	13	87	12.0	3.8	21.8
99-00—Minnesota	4	171	30	78	.385	13	16	.813	13	30	43	35	5	3	11	75	10.8	8.8	18.8
00-01—Minnesota	4	165	27	58	.466	30	36	.833	10	38	48	17	4	6	6	84	12.0	4.3	21.0
01-02—Minnesota	3	130	24	56	.429	23	32	.719	16	40	56	15	5	5	12	72	18.7	5.0	24.0
02-03—Minnesota	6	265	71	138	.514	17	28	.607	11	83	94	31	10	10	18	162	15.7	5.2	27.0
03-04—Minnesota	18	783	168	372	.452	97	125	.776	39	224	263	92	24	41	75	438	14.6	5.1	24.3
Totals	47	2003	415	907	.458	207	272	.761	136	492	628	236	63	88	161	1049	13.4	5.0	22.3

Three-point field goals: 1996-97, 1-for-1 (1.000). 1998-99, 0-for-2. 1999-00, 2-for-3 (.667). 2000-01, 0-for-3. 2001-02, 1-for-2 (.500). 2002-03, 3-for-9 (.333). 2003-04, 5-for-16 (.313). Totals, 12-for-36 (.333).

Personal fouls/disqualifications: 1996-97, 6/0. 1997-98, 17/0. 1998-99, 10/0. 1999-00, 12/0. 2000-01, 13/0. 2001-02, 11/0. 2002-03, 23/1. 2003-04, 57/2. Totals, 149/3.

NBA ALL-STAR GAME RECORD

NOTES: Shares record for most field goals in one game—17 (2003). ... NBA All-Star Game Most Valuable Player (2003).

Season Team	Min.	FGM	FGA	Pct.	FTM	FTA	Pct.	REBOUNDS Off.	Def.	Tot.	Ast.	PF	Dq.	St.	Blk.	TO	Pts.
1997—Minnesota	18	1	7	.143	4	4	1.000	1	8	9	1	2	0	1	0	0	6
1998—Minnesota	21	6	11	.545	0	0	...	1	3	4	2	0	...	2	1	3	12
2000—Minnesota	35	10	19	.526	4	4	1.000	3	7	10	5	1	0	1	1	0	24
2001—Minnesota	27	7	12	.583	0	0	...	1	3	4	4	0	0	1	3	2	14
2002—Minnesota	24	7	15	.467	0	0	...	6	6	12	2	1	0	2	0	0	14
2003—Minnesota	41	17	24	.708	3	3	1.000	1	8	9	3	3	0	5	1	4	37
2004—Minnesota	29	6	14	.429	0	0	...	3	4	7	6	0	0	2	1	1	12
2005—Minnesota	16	5	8	.625	0	1	.000	0	3	3	2	2	0	0	0	2	10
2006—Minnesota	16	1	9	.111	0	0	...	2	7	9	4	1	0	1	0	2	2
Totals	227	60	119	.504	11	12	.917	18	49	67	29	10	0	14	8	14	131

Three-point field goals: 1998, 0-for-1. 2000, 0-for-1. 2002, 0-for-1. 2004, 0-for-1. Totals, 0-for-4 (.000).

GARRITY, PAT   F   MAGIC

PERSONAL: Born August 23, 1976, in Las Vegas. ... 6-9/238. (2.06/108.0). ... Full name: Patrick Joseph Garrity.
HIGH SCHOOL: Lewis Palmer (Monument, Colo.).
COLLEGE: Notre Dame.
TRANSACTIONS/CAREER NOTES: Selected by Milwaukee Bucks in first round (19th pick overall) of 1998 NBA Draft. ... Draft rights traded by Bucks with draft rights to C Dirk Nowitzki to Dallas Mavericks for draft rights to F Robert Traylor (June 24, 1998). ... Draft rights traded by Mavericks with F Martin Muursepp, G/F Bubba Wells and 1999 first-round draft choice to Phoenix Suns for G Steve Nash (June 24, 1998). ... Traded by Suns with F/C Danny Manning and two future first-round draft choices to Orlando Magic for G Anfernee Hardaway (August 5, 1999).

COLLEGIATE RECORD

NOTES: The SPORTING NEWS All-America second team (1998).

Season Team	G	Min.	FGM	FGA	Pct.	FTM	FTA	Pct.	Reb.	Ast.	Pts.	AVERAGES RPG	APG	PPG
94-95—Notre Dame	27	744	136	260	.523	82	107	.766	137	34	361	5.1	1.3	13.4
95-96—Notre Dame	27	893	177	372	.476	96	140	.686	193	38	464	7.1	1.4	17.2
96-97—Notre Dame	30	1056	221	457	.484	152	196	.776	221	84	633	7.4	2.8	21.1
97-98—Notre Dame	27	956	214	445	.481	159	212	.750	225	66	627	8.3	2.4	23.2
Totals	111	3649	748	1534	.488	489	655	.747	776	222	2085	7.0	2.0	18.8

Three-point field goals: 1994-95, 7-for-18 (.389). 1995-96, 14-for-51 (.275). 1996-97, 39-for-102 (.382). 1997-98, 40-for-108 (.370). Totals, 100-for-279 (.358).

NBA REGULAR-SEASON RECORD

Season Team	G	Min.	FGM	FGA	Pct.	FTM	FTA	Pct.	REBOUNDS Off.	Def.	Tot.	Ast.	St.	Blk.	TO	Pts.	AVERAGES RPG	APG	PPG
98-99—Phoenix	39	538	85	170	.500	40	56	.714	26	49	75	18	8	3	20	217	1.9	0.5	5.6
99-00—Orlando	82	1479	258	585	.441	80	111	.721	44	166	210	58	31	19	85	675	2.6	0.7	8.2
00-01—Orlando	76	1579	223	576	.387	85	98	.867	51	159	210	51	40	15	68	628	2.8	0.7	8.3
01-02—Orlando	80	2406	327	767	.426	61	73	.836	77	261	338	99	61	28	68	884	4.2	1.2	11.1
02-03—Orlando	81	2584	312	744	.419	83	100	.830	72	234	306	121	62	20	77	868	3.8	1.5	10.7
03-04—Orlando	2	22	1	3	.333	0	0	...	0	0	0	1	0	0	0	2	0.0	0.5	1.0
04-05—Orlando	71	955	123	306	.402	29	33	.879	21	103	124	30	19	9	30	324	1.7	0.4	4.6
05-06—Orlando	57	938	101	242	.417	30	37	.811	31	77	108	38	12	9	38	282	1.9	0.7	4.9
Totals	488	10501	1430	3393	.421	408	508	.803	322	1049	1371	416	233	103	386	3880	2.8	0.9	8.0

Three-point field goals: 1998-99, 7-for-18 (.389). 1999-00, 79-for-197 (.401). 2000-01, 97-for-224 (.433). 2001-02, 169-for-396 (.427). 2002-03, 161-for-407 (.396). 2004-05, 49-for-147 (.333). 2005-06, 50-for-129 (.388). Totals, 612-for-1518 (.403).

Personal fouls/disqualifications: 1998-99, 62/0. 1999-00, 197/1. 2000-01, 241/3. 2001-02, 230/1. 2002-03, 255/1. 2003-04, 2/0. 2004-05, 107/0. 2005-06, 108/0. Totals, 1202/6.

NBA PLAYOFF RECORD

Season Team	G	Min.	FGM	FGA	Pct.	FTM	FTA	Pct.	REBOUNDS Off.	Def.	Tot.	Ast.	St.	Blk.	TO	Pts.	AVERAGES RPG	APG	PPG
98-99—Phoenix	3	52	9	17	.529	6	6	1.000	6	3	9	1	1	1	3	27	3.0	0.3	9.0
00-01—Orlando	4	117	17	36	.472	4	5	.800	1	4	5	2	0	1	2	48	1.3	0.5	12.0
01-02—Orlando	4	147	12	32	.375	3	4	.750	4	26	30	9	2	1	3	34	7.5	2.3	8.5
02-03—Orlando	7	163	10	35	.286	4	4	1.000	4	14	18	5	2	3	5	28	2.6	0.7	4.0
Totals	18	479	48	120	.400	17	19	.895	15	47	62	17	5	6	13	137	3.4	0.9	7.6

G

Three-point field goals: 1998-99, 3-for-3 (1.000). 2000-01, 10-for-20 (.500). 2001-02, 7-for-18 (.389). 2002-03, 4-for-17 (.235). Totals, 24-for-58 (.414). Personal fouls/disqualifications: 1998-99, 9/0. 2000-01, 11/0. 2001-02, 18/0. 2002-03, 24/0. Totals, 62/0.

GASOL, PAU   F   GRIZZLIES

PERSONAL: Born July 6, 1980, in Barcelona, Spain. ... 7-0/227. (2.13/103.0).
COLLEGE: Did not attend college.
TRANSACTIONS/CAREER NOTES: Played in Spain (1998-2001). ... Selected by Atlanta Hawks in first round (third pick overall) of 2001 NBA Draft. ... Draft rights traded by Hawks with F/C Lorenzen Wright and G Brevin Knight to Memphis Grizzlies for F Shareef Abdur-Rahim and draft rights to G Jamaal Tinsley (July 19, 2001).
MISCELLANEOUS: Member of Spanish Olympic team (2004).... Memphis Grizzlies franchise all-time leading rebounder (3,173) and all-time blocked shots leader (695).

SPANISH LEAGUE RECORD

Season Team	G	Min.	FGM	FGA	Pct.	FTM	FTA	Pct.	Reb.	Ast.	Pts.	AVERAGES RPG	APG	PPG
98-99—FC Barcelona	2	11	2	4	.500	1	3	.333	2	1	6	1.0	0.5	3.0
99-00—FC Barcelona	26	385	40	79	.506	23	44	.523	68	12	109	2.6	0.5	4.2
00-01—FC Barcelona	30	716	129	235	.549	70	119	.588	156	23	328	5.2	0.8	10.9
Totals	58	1112	171	318	.538	94	166	.566	226	36	443	3.9	0.6	7.6

Three-point field goals: 1998-99, 1-for-3 (.333). 1999-00, 6-for-20 (.300). 2000-01, 15-for-43 (.349). Totals, 22-for-66 (.333).
Personal fouls/disqualifications: 1998-99, 1/0. 1999-00, 27/0. 2000-01, 58/0. Totals, 86/0.

NBA REGULAR-SEASON RECORD

HONORS: NBA Rookie of the Year (2002). ... NBA All-Rookie first team (2002).

Season Team	G	Min.	FGM	FGA	Pct.	FTM	FTA	Pct.	REBOUNDS Off.	Def.	Tot.	Ast.	St.	Blk.	TO	Pts.	AVERAGES RPG	APG	PPG
01-02—Memphis	82	3007	551	1064	.518	338	477	.709	238	492	730	223	41	169	224	1441	8.9	2.7	17.6
02-03—Memphis	82	2948	569	1116	.510	416	565	.736	192	528	720	229	34	148	213	1555	8.8	2.8	19.0
03-04—Memphis	78	2458	506	1049	.482	365	511	.714	206	394	600	198	44	132	187	1381	7.7	2.5	17.7
04-05—Memphis	56	1790	357	695	.514	282	367	.768	130	280	410	135	37	93	137	997	7.3	2.4	17.8
05-06—Memphis	80	3135	600	1194	.503	425	617	.689	191	522	713	371	46	153	235	1628	8.9	4.6	20.4
Totals	378	13338	2583	5118	.505	1826	2537	.720	957	2216	3173	1156	202	695	996	7002	8.4	3.1	18.5

Three-point field goals: 2001-02, 1-for-5 (.200). 2002-03, 1-for-10 (.100). 2003-04, 4-for-15 (.267). 2004-05, 1-for-6 (.167). 2005-06, 3-for-12 (.250). Totals, 10-for-48 (.208).
Personal fouls/disqualifications: 2001-02, 195/2. 2002-03, 220/3. 2003-04, 185/1. 2004-05, 146/1. 2005-06, 184/1. Totals, 930/8.

NBA PLAYOFF RECORD

Season Team	G	Min.	FGM	FGA	Pct.	FTM	FTA	Pct.	REBOUNDS Off.	Def.	Tot.	Ast.	St.	Blk.	TO	Pts.	AVERAGES RPG	APG	PPG
03-04—Memphis	4	134	28	49	.571	18	20	.900	4	16	20	10	4	6	5	74	5.0	2.5	18.5
04-05—Memphis	4	133	39	80	.488	6	12	.500	15	15	30	10	2	7	7	85	7.5	2.5	21.3
05-06—Memphis	4	158	29	67	.433	23	30	.767	4	23	27	12	2	5	11	81	6.8	3.0	20.3
Totals	12	425	96	196	.490	47	62	.758	23	54	77	32	8	18	23	240	6.4	2.7	20.0

Three-point field goals: 2004-05, 1-for-1 (1.000). 2005-06, 0-for-1. Totals, 1-for-2 (.500).
Personal fouls/disqualifications: 2003-04, 10/0. 2004-05, 12/0. 2005-06, 11/0. Totals, 33/0.

NBA ALL-STAR GAME RECORD

Season Team	Min.	FGM	FGA	Pct.	FTM	FTA	Pct.	REBOUNDS Off.	Def.	Tot.	Ast.	PF	Dq.	St.	Blk.	TO	Pts.
2006—Memphis	14	0	3	.000	0	0	...	6	6	12	1	1	0	0	0	1	0

GEORGE, DEVEAN   G/F   MAVERICKS

PERSONAL: Born August 29, 1977, in Minneapolis. ... 6-8/220. (2.03/99.8). ... Full name: Devean Jamar George
HIGH SCHOOL: Benilde-St. Margaret (St. Louis Park, Minn.).
COLLEGE: Augsburg (Minn.).
TRANSACTIONS/CAREER NOTES: Selected by Los Angeles Lakers in first round (23rd pick overall) of 1999 NBA Draft. ... Signed as free agent by Dallas Mavericks (August 1, 2006).
MISCELLANEOUS: Member of NBA championship team (2000, 2001, 2002).

COLLEGIATE RECORD

Season Team	G	Min.	FGM	FGA	Pct.	FTM	FTA	Pct.	Reb.	Ast.	Pts.	AVERAGES RPG	APG	PPG
95-96—Augsburg (Minn.)	17	500	93	185	.503	55	78	.705	111	28	258	6.5	1.6	15.2
96-97—Augsburg (Minn.)	25	766	207	419	.494	109	152	.717	178	39	566	7.1	1.6	22.6
97-98—Augsburg (Minn.)	26	751	218	433	.503	185	246	.752	262	31	664	10.1	1.2	25.5
98-99—Augsburg (Minn.)	28	969	281	542	.518	163	213	.765	317	58	770	11.3	2.1	27.5
Totals	96	2986	799	1579	.506	512	689	.743	868	156	2258	9.0	1.6	23.5

Three-point field goals: 1995-96, 17-for-40 (.425). 1996-97, 43-for-129 (.333). 1997-98, 43-for-134 (.321). 1998-99, 45-for-138 (.326). Totals, 148-for-441 (.336).

NBA REGULAR-SEASON RECORD

Season Team	G	Min.	FGM	FGA	Pct.	FTM	FTA	Pct.	REBOUNDS Off.	Def.	Tot.	Ast.	St.	Blk.	TO	Pts.	AVERAGES RPG	APG	PPG
99-00—L.A. Lakers	49	345	56	144	.389	27	41	.659	29	46	75	12	10	4	21	155	1.5	0.2	3.2
00-01—L.A. Lakers	59	593	64	207	.309	39	55	.709	35	75	110	19	15	15	34	182	1.9	0.3	3.1
01-02—L.A. Lakers	82	1759	215	523	.411	85	126	.675	78	225	303	111	71	42	66	581	3.7	1.4	7.1
02-03—L.A. Lakers	71	1613	180	461	.390	83	105	.790	91	195	286	92	56	38	65	492	4.0	1.3	6.9

G

Season Team	G	Min.	FGM	FGA	Pct.	FTM	FTA	Pct.	REBOUNDS Off.	Def.	Tot.	Ast.	St.	Blk.	TO	Pts.	AVERAGES RPG	APG	PPG
03-04—L.A. Lakers	82	1951	233	571	.408	73	96	.760	87	245	332	112	81	38	88	604	4.0	1.4	7.4
04-05—L.A. Lakers	15	306	37	104	.356	15	20	.750	13	40	53	14	8	2	12	110	3.5	0.9	7.3
05-06—L.A. Lakers	71	1542	170	425	.400	58	86	.674	82	192	274	68	66	34	54	448	3.9	1.0	6.3
Totals	429	8109	955	2435	.392	380	529	.718	415	1018	1433	428	307	173	340	2572	3.3	1.0	6.0

Three-point field goals: 1999-00, 16-for-47 (.340). 2000-01, 15-for-68 (.221). 2001-02, 66-for-178 (.371). 2002-03, 49-for-132 (.371). 2003-04, 65-for-186 (.349). 2004-05, 21-for-58 (.362). 2005-06, 50-for-160 (.313). Totals, 282-for-829 (.340).

Personal fouls/disqualifications: 1999-00, 54/0. 2000-01, 87/1. 2001-02, 190/3. 2002-03, 180/2. 2003-04, 189/4. 2004-05, 32/1. 2005-06, 159/1. Totals, 891/12.

NBA PLAYOFF RECORD

Season Team	G	Min.	FGM	FGA	Pct.	FTM	FTA	Pct.	REBOUNDS Off.	Def.	Tot.	Ast.	St.	Blk.	TO	Pts.	AVERAGES RPG	APG	PPG
99-00—L.A. Lakers	9	45	7	19	.368	6	11	.545	4	6	10	2	1	0	3	22	1.1	0.2	2.4
00-01—L.A. Lakers	7	27	6	12	.500	1	2	.500	3	2	5	1	0	0	3	14	0.7	0.1	2.0
01-02—L.A. Lakers	19	327	38	104	.365	11	15	.733	24	44	68	11	11	10	12	95	3.6	0.6	5.0
02-03—L.A. Lakers	11	318	35	78	.449	8	9	.889	11	38	49	24	11	4	12	88	4.5	2.2	8.0
03-04—L.A. Lakers	22	470	43	100	.430	13	20	.650	11	39	50	11	21	8	11	121	2.3	0.5	5.5
05-06—L.A. Lakers	7	121	13	34	.382	2	5	.400	2	14	16	4	4	1	0	37	2.3	0.6	5.3
Totals	75	1308	142	347	.409	41	62	.661	55	143	198	53	48	23	41	377	2.6	0.7	5.0

Three-point field goals: 1999-00, 2-for-10 (.200). 2000-01, 1-for-2 (.500). 2001-02, 8-for-35 (.229). 2002-03, 10-for-30 (.333). 2003-04, 22-for-59 (.373). 2005-06, 9-for-21 (.429). Totals, 52-for-157 (.331).

Personal fouls/disqualifications: 1999-00, 5/0. 2000-01, 6/0. 2001-02, 51/0. 2002-03, 29/0. 2003-04, 45/0. 2005-06, 13/0. Totals, 149/0.

GILL, EDDIE   G   PACERS

PERSONAL: Born August 16, 1978, in Aurora, Colo. ... 6-0/190. (1.83/86.2).
HIGH SCHOOL: Overland (Colo.).
JUNIOR COLLEGE: Eastern Utah, then Salt Lake Community College.
COLLEGE: Weber State.
TRANSACTIONS/CAREER NOTES: Not drafted by an NBA franchise. ... Played in Italy (2000-01). ... Played in International Basketball League with Las Vegas Bandits (2000-01). ... Played in American Basketball Association 2000 with Kansas City Knights (2000-02). ... Signed by New Jersey Nets to the first of two consecutive 10-day contracts (March 29, 2001). ... Signed to 10-day contract by Memphis Grizzlies (February 23, 2002). ... Signed by Grizzlies for remainder of season (March 4, 2002). ... Waived by Grizzlies (October 24, 2002). ... Played in Continental Basketball Association (2003-04). ... Signed as free agent by Portland Trail Blazers (February 5, 2004). ... Traded by Trail Blazers to New Jersey Nets for draft rights to F Viktor Khryapa (June 24, 2004). ... Waived by Nets (July 6, 2004). ... Signed as free agent by Indiana Pacers (July 28, 2004).

COLLEGIATE RECORD

Season Team	G	Min.	FGM	FGA	Pct.	FTM	FTA	Pct.	Reb.	Ast.	Pts.	AVERAGES RPG	APG	PPG
96-97—College of Eastern Utah..	33	...	70	165	.424	32	55	.582	62	79	200	1.9	2.4	6.1
97-98—Salt Lake C.C.	31	...	148	325	.455	144	184	.783	131	197	507	4.2	6.4	16.4
98-99—Weber State	33	1145	141	331	.426	97	111	.874	129	150	462	3.9	4.5	14.0
99-00—Weber State	28	1009	128	325	.394	149	173	.861	179	194	457	6.4	6.9	16.3
Junior College Totals............	64	...	218	490	.445	176	239	.736	193	276	707	3.0	4.3	11.0
4-Year-College Totals............	61	2154	269	656	.410	246	284	.866	308	344	919	5.0	5.6	15.1

Three-point field goals: 1996-97, 28-for-73 (.384). 1997-98, 67-for-159 (.421). 1998-99, 83-for-203 (.409). 1999-00, 52-for-142 (.366). Totals, 230-for-577 (.399).

Personal fouls/disqualifications: 1998-99, 73/0. 1999-00, 74/0. Totals, 147/0.

AMERICAN BASKETBALL ASSOCIATION 2000 RECORD

Season Team	G	Min.	FGM	FGA	Pct.	FTM	FTA	Pct.	Reb.	Ast.	Pts.	AVERAGES RPG	APG	PPG
00-01—Kansas City	1	28	4	8	.500	1	2	.500	1	9	10	1.0	9.0	10.0
01-02—Kansas City	18	606	67	173	.387	50	57	.877	88	120	214	4.9	6.7	11.9
Totals	19	634	71	181	.392	51	59	.864	89	129	224	4.7	6.8	11.8

Three-point field goals: 2000-01, 1-for-3 (.333). 2001-02, 30-for-82 (.366). Totals, 31-for-85 (.365).

ITALIAN LEAGUE RECORD

Season Team	G	Min.	FGM	FGA	Pct.	FTM	FTA	Pct.	Reb.	Ast.	Pts.	AVERAGES RPG	APG	PPG
00-01—Fortitudo Bologna...........	1	29	2	8	.250	7	8	.875	4	4	12	4.0	4.0	12.0

Three-point field goals: 2000-01, 1-for-5 (.200). Totals, 1-for-5 (.200).

Personal fouls/disqualifications: 2000-01, 1/0. Totals, 1/0.

INTERNATIONAL BASKETBALL LEAGUE RECORD

Season Team	G	Min.	FGM	FGA	Pct.	FTM	FTA	Pct.	Reb.	Ast.	Pts.	AVERAGES RPG	APG	PPG
00-01—Las Vegas	31	1169	134	324	.414	113	156	.724	129	213	436	4.2	6.9	14.1

Three-point field goals: 2000-01, 55-for-139 (.396). Totals, 55-for-139 (.396).

Personal fouls/disqualifications: 2000-01, 104/0. Totals, 104/0.

NBA REGULAR-SEASON RECORD

Season Team	G	Min.	FGM	FGA	Pct.	FTM	FTA	Pct.	REBOUNDS Off.	Def.	Tot.	Ast.	St.	Blk.	TO	Pts.	AVERAGES RPG	APG	PPG
00-01—New Jersey	8	152	16	41	.390	4	5	.800	0	9	9	24	4	1	10	39	1.1	3.0	4.9
01-02—Memphis	23	384	39	92	.424	31	39	.795	7	21	28	49	11	3	34	116	1.2	2.1	5.0
03-04—Portland..........	22	157	15	36	.417	17	20	.850	4	13	17	16	9	1	12	50	0.8	0.7	2.3

Season Team	G	Min.	FGM	FGA	Pct.	FTM	FTA	Pct.	REBOUNDS Off.	Def.	Tot.	Ast.	St.	Blk.	TO	Pts.	AVERAGES RPG	APG	PPG
04-05—Indiana............	73	1021	81	242	.335	71	81	.877	16	96	112	83	59	5	60	269	1.5	1.1	3.7
05-06—Indiana............	41	122	10	45	.222	18	23	.783	0	15	15	12	11	1	9	45	0.4	0.3	1.1
Totals	167	1836	161	456	.353	141	168	.839	27	154	181	184	94	11	125	519	1.1	1.1	3.1

Three-point field goals: 2000-01, 3-for-9 (.333). 2001-02, 7-for-22 (.318). 2003-04, 3-for-8 (.375). 2004-05, 36-for-117 (.308). 2005-06, 7-for-23 (.304). Totals, 56-for-179 (.313).

Personal fouls/disqualifications: 2000-01, 9/0. 2001-02, 38/0. 2003-04, 16/0. 2004-05, 105/0. 2005-06, 13/0. Totals, 181/0.

NBA PLAYOFF RECORD

Season Team	G	Min.	FGM	FGA	Pct.	FTM	FTA	Pct.	REBOUNDS Off.	Def.	Tot.	Ast.	St.	Blk.	TO	Pts.	AVERAGES RPG	APG	PPG
04-05—Indiana............	7	45	5	16	.313	13	15	.867	0	4	4	5	1	0	3	24	0.6	0.7	3.4
05-06—Indiana............	2	1	0	0	...	0	0	...	0	0	0	0	0	0	1	0	0.0	0.0	0.0
Totals	9	46	5	16	.313	13	15	.867	0	4	4	5	1	0	4	24	0.4	0.6	2.7

Three-point field goals: 2004-05, 1-for-6 (.167). Totals, 1-for-6 (.167).

CBA RECORD

Season Team	G	Min.	FGM	FGA	Pct.	FTM	FTA	Pct.	Reb.	Ast.	Pts.	AVERAGES RPG	APG	PPG
03-04—Dakota Wizards	25	913	136	307	.443	152	171	.889	121	200	452	4.8	8.0	18.1

Three-point field goals: 2003-04, 28-for-73 (.384). Totals, 28-for-73 (.384).

GINOBILI, MANU   G   SPURS

PERSONAL: Born July 28, 1977 in Argentina. ... 6-6/210. (1.98/95.3).
TRANSACTIONS/CAREER NOTES: Played in Argentina (1997-98). ... Played in Italy (1998-2002). ... Selected by San Antonio Spurs in second round (57th pick overall) of 1999 NBA Draft.
MISCELLANEOUS: Member of NBA championship team (2003, 2005). ... Member of gold-medal-winning Argentinian Olympic team (2004).

ARGENTINIAN LEAGUE RECORD

Season Team	G	Min.	FGM	FGA	Pct.	FTM	FTA	Pct.	Reb.	Ast.	Pts.	AVERAGES RPG	APG	PPG
97-98—Estudiante	49	1666	370	807	.458	303	428	.708	195	114	1155	4.0	2.3	23.6

Three-point field goals: 1997-98, 111-for-371 (.299). Totals, 111-for-371 (.299).

ITALIAN LEAGUE RECORD

Season Team	G	Min.	FGM	FGA	Pct.	FTM	FTA	Pct.	Reb.	Ast.	Pts.	AVERAGES RPG	APG	PPG
98-99—Reggio Calabria..............	29	802	159	329	.483	122	161	.758	81	44	490	2.8	1.5	16.9
99-00—Reggio Calabria..............	30	917	168	362	.464	115	163	.706	93	73	509	3.1	2.4	17.0
00-01—Kinder Bologna...............	34	981	199	387	.514	116	155	.748	150	86	580	4.4	2.5	17.1
01-02—Kinder Bologna...............	36	1163	236	445	.530	175	250	.700	158	79	715	4.4	2.2	19.9
Totals	129	3863	762	1523	.500	528	729	.724	482	282	2294	3.7	2.2	17.8

Three-point field goals: 1998-99, 49-for-146 (.336). 1999-00, 58-for-164 (.354). 2000-01, 66-for-173 (.382). 2001-02, 68-for-171 (.398). Totals, 241-for-654 (.369).

NBA REGULAR-SEASON RECORD

HONORS: NBA All-Rookie second team (2003)

Season Team	G	Min.	FGM	FGA	Pct.	FTM	FTA	Pct.	REBOUNDS Off.	Def.	Tot.	Ast.	St.	Blk.	TO	Pts.	AVERAGES RPG	APG	PPG
02-03—San Antonio....	69	1431	174	397	.438	126	171	.737	47	114	161	138	96	17	100	525	2.3	2.0	7.6
03-04—San Antonio....	77	2260	330	789	.418	239	298	.802	86	258	344	291	136	16	161	987	4.5	3.8	12.8
04-05—San Antonio....	74	2193	367	780	.471	355	442	.803	75	254	329	288	119	27	172	1186	4.4	3.9	16.0
05-06—San Antonio....	65	1813	309	669	.462	280	360	.778	42	188	230	235	101	26	121	981	3.5	3.6	15.1
Totals	285	7697	1180	2635	.448	1000	1271	.787	250	814	1064	952	452	86	554	3679	3.7	3.3	12.9

Three-point field goals: 2002-03, 51-for-148 (.345). 2003-04, 88-for-245 (.359). 2004-05, 97-for-258 (.376). 2005-06, 83-for-217 (.382). Totals, 319-for-868 (.368).

Personal fouls/disqualifications: 2002-03, 170/3. 2003-04, 181/0. 2004-05, 190/1. 2005-06, 156/0. Totals, 697/4.

NBA PLAYOFF RECORD

Season Team	G	Min.	FGM	FGA	Pct.	FTM	FTA	Pct.	REBOUNDS Off.	Def.	Tot.	Ast.	St.	Blk.	TO	Pts.	AVERAGES RPG	APG	PPG
02-03—San Antonio....	24	660	71	184	.386	56	74	.757	29	63	92	70	41	9	36	226	3.8	2.9	9.4
03-04—San Antonio....	10	280	42	94	.447	36	44	.818	15	38	53	31	17	1	21	130	5.3	3.1	13.0
04-05—San Antonio....	23	772	145	286	.507	147	185	.795	19	114	133	97	28	6	66	479	5.8	4.2	20.8
05-06—San Antonio....	13	426	76	157	.484	73	87	.839	9	50	59	39	19	7	33	239	4.5	3.0	18.4
Totals	70	2138	334	721	.463	312	390	.800	72	265	337	237	105	23	156	1074	4.8	3.4	15.3

Three-point field goals: 2002-03, 28-for-73 (.384). 2003-04, 10-for-35 (.286). 2004-05, 42-for-96 (.438). 2005-06, 14-for-42 (.333). Totals, 94-for-246 (.382).

Personal fouls/disqualifications: 2002-03, 62/1. 2003-04, 30/0. 2004-05, 69/0. 2005-06, 43/1. Totals, 204/2.

NBA ALL-STAR GAME RECORD

Season Team	Min.	FGM	FGA	Pct.	FTM	FTA	Pct.	REBOUNDS Off.	Def.	Tot.	Ast.	PF	Dq.	St.	Blk.	TO	Pts.
2005—San Antonio	22	3	6	.500	2	2	1.000	2	1	3	1	3	0	1	1	3	8

Three-point field goals: 2005, 0-for-2. Totals, 0-for-2 (.000).

G

GIRICEK, GORDAN F JAZZ

PERSONAL: Born June 20, 1977, in Zagreb, Croatia. ... 6-5/210. (1.96/95.3).
TRANSACTIONS/CAREER NOTES: Played in Croatia (1996-2001). ... Played in Russia (2001-02). ... Selected by Dallas Mavericks in second round (40th pick overall) of 1999 NBA Draft. ... Draft rights traded by Mavericks with future second-round draft choice to San Antonio Spurs for draft rights to F Leon Smith (June 30, 1999). ... Draft rights traded by Spurs to Memphis Grizzlies for 2004 second-round draft choice and cash (June 28, 2002). ... Traded by Grizzlies with F Drew Gooden to Orlando Magic for F Mike Miller, F Ryan Humphrey, 2003 first-round draft choice and 2004 second-round draft choice (February 19, 2003). ... Traded by Magic to Utah Jazz for G DeShawn Stevenson and conditional second-round draft choice (February 19, 2004).

CROATIAN LEAGUE RECORD

												AVERAGES		
Season Team	G	Min.	FGM	FGA	Pct.	FTM	FTA	Pct.	Reb.	Ast.	Pts.	RPG	APG	PPG
96-97—Cibona Zagreb	12		22	42	.524	10	16	.625	15	6	59	1.3	0.5	4.9
97-98—Cibona	22	480	105	173	.607	53	60	.883	48	24	290	2.2	1.1	13.2
98-99—Cibona	20	542	112	187	.599	69	91	.758	64	34	324	3.2	1.7	16.2
99-00—Cibona	21	588	156	265	.589	79	104	.760	82	55	428	3.9	2.6	20.4
00-01—Cibona Zagreb	16	475	103	222	.464	34	43	.791	62	22	268	3.9	1.4	16.8
Totals	91	2085	498	889	.560	245	314	.780	271	141	1369	3.0	1.5	15.0

Three-point field goals: 1996-97, 5-for-15 (.333). 1997-98, 27-for-65 (.415). 1998-99, 31-for-64 (.484). 1999-00, 38-for-81 (.469). 2000-01, 28-for-76 (.368). Totals, 129-for-301 (.429).

RUSSIAN LEAGUE RECORD

												AVERAGES		
Season Team	G	Min.	FGM	FGA	Pct.	FTM	FTA	Pct.	Reb.	Ast.	Pts.	RPG	APG	PPG
01-02—CSKA	33	865	224	402	.557	147	178	.826	102	56	646	3.1	1.7	19.6

Three-point field goals: 2001-02, 51-for-115 (.443). Totals, 51-for-115 (.443).

NBA REGULAR-SEASON RECORD

HONORS: NBA All-Rookie second team (2003).

									REBOUNDS								AVERAGES		
Season Team	G	Min.	FGM	FGA	Pct.	FTM	FTA	Pct.	Off.	Def.	Tot.	Ast.	St.	Blk.	TO	Pts.	RPG	APG	PPG
02-03—Mem-Orl	76	2148	350	803	.436	150	183	.820	36	202	238	137	52	8	145	935	3.1	1.8	12.3
03-04—Orlando-Utah	73	2041	316	724	.436	135	158	.854	51	175	226	122	56	15	103	827	3.1	1.7	11.3
04-05—Utah	81	1660	283	632	.448	111	137	.810	25	157	182	137	46	11	90	715	2.2	1.7	8.8
05-06—Utah	37	956	166	383	.433	43	57	.754	15	55	70	63	16	4	63	393	1.9	1.7	10.6
Totals	267	6805	1115	2542	.439	439	535	.821	127	589	716	459	170	38	401	2870	2.7	1.7	10.7

Three-point field goals: 2002-03, 85-for-249 (.341). 2003-04, 60-for-152 (.395). 2004-05, 38-for-105 (.362). 2005-06, 18-for-59 (.305). Totals, 201-for-565 (.356).
Personal fouls/disqualifications: 2002-03, 159/0. 2003-04, 144/0. 2004-05, 155/1. 2005-06, 87/0. Totals, 545/1.

NBA PLAYOFF RECORD

									REBOUNDS								AVERAGES		
Season Team	G	Min.	FGM	FGA	Pct.	FTM	FTA	Pct.	Off.	Def.	Tot.	Ast.	St.	Blk.	TO	Pts.	RPG	APG	PPG
02-03—Orlando	7	202	20	70	.001	0	11	.000	1	18	22	7	2	1	13	66	3.1	1.0	9.4

Three-point field goals: 2002-03, 5-for-15 (.333). Totals, 5-for-15 (.333).
Personal fouls/disqualifications: 2002-03, 27/0. Totals, 27/0.

GOLDWIRE, ANTHONY G

PERSONAL: Born September 6, 1971, in West Palm Beach, Fla. ... 6-2/182. (1.88/82.6).
HIGH SCHOOL: Suncoast (Riviera Beach, Fla.).
JUNIOR COLLEGE: Pensacola Junior College (Fla.).
COLLEGE: Houston.
TRANSACTIONS/CAREER NOTES: Selected by Phoenix Suns in second round (52nd pick overall) of 1994 NBA Draft. ... Waived by Suns (November 1, 1994). ... Played in Continental Basketball Association with Yakima Sun Kings (1994-96). ... Signed by Charlotte Hornets to 10-day contract (January 22, 1996). ... Re-signed by Hornets for remainder of season (January 31, 1996). ... Traded by Hornets with C George Zidek to Denver Nuggets for G Ricky Pierce (February 20, 1997). ... Played in Greece (1998-99). ... Played in Spain (1999-2000). ... Signed as free agent by Nuggets (October 2, 2000). ... Waived by Nuggets (October 25, 2000). ... Played in American Basketball Association 2000 with Kansas City Knights (2000-01). ... Signed by Nuggets to first of two consecutive 10-day contracts (January 29, 2001). ... Signed by Nuggets for remainder of season (February 18, 2001). ... Signed as free agent by Cleveland Cavaliers (October 1, 2001). ... Waived by Cavaliers (October 23, 2001). ... Signed as free agent by Suns (September 30, 2002). ... Waived by Suns (October 23, 2002). ... Played in Italy (2001-02) ... Signed as free agent by San Antonio Spurs (November 20, 2002). ... Waived by Spurs (December 28, 2002). ... Signed by Washington Wizards to first of two consecutive 10-day contracts (March 1, 2003). ... Waived by Wizards (March 13, 2003). ... Played in CBA (2003-04). ... Signed by Minnesota Timberwolves to 10-day contract (January 7, 2004). ... Released by Timberwolves (January 27, 2004). ... Signed by Milwaukee Bucks to 10-day contract (February 28, 2004). ... Released by Bucks (March 5, 2004). ... Signed by New Jersey Nets to first of two consecutive 10-day contracts (March 22, 2004). ... Waived by Nets (April 6, 2004). ... Signed as free agent by Minnesota Timberwolves (October 4, 2004). ... Waived by Timberwolves (October 28, 2004). ... Signed by Milwaukee Bucks for remainder of season (March 7, 2005). ... Signed as a free agent by Los Angeles Clippers (October 23, 2005). ... Waived by Clippers (November 16, 2005).

COLLEGIATE RECORD

												AVERAGES		
Season Team	G	Min.	FGM	FGA	Pct.	FTM	FTA	Pct.	Reb.	Ast.	Pts.	RPG	APG	PPG
90-91—Pensacola J.C.	30	...	105	234	.449	84	104	.808	91	169	305	3.0	5.6	10.2
91-92—Pensacola J.C.	31	939	155	360	.431	128	168	.762	128	241	477	4.1	7.8	15.4
92-93—Houston	30	1110	139	313	.444	124	158	.785	92	170	427	3.1	5.7	14.2
93-94—Houston	27	995	144	366	.393	138	171	.807	100	164	463	3.7	6.1	17.1
Junior College Totals	61	939	260	594	.438	212	272	.779	219	410	782	3.6	6.7	12.8
4-Year-College Totals	57	2105	283	679	.417	262	329	.796	192	334	890	3.4	5.9	15.6

Three-point field goals: 1990-91, 11-for-39 (.282). 1991-92, 39-for-95 (.411). 1992-93, 25-for-88 (.284). 1993-94, 37-for-123 (.301). Totals, 112-for-345 (.325).

G

CBA RECORD

NOTES: Member of CBA championship team (1995). ... CBA All-Rookie second team (1995).

Season Team	G	Min.	FGM	FGA	Pct.	FTM	FTA	Pct.	Reb.	Ast.	Pts.	RPG	APG	PPG
94-95—Yakima	55	1121	150	312	.481	119	160	.744	83	217	439	1.5	3.9	8.0
95-96—Yakima	27	977	71	373	.190	139	163	.853	96	189	319	3.6	7.0	11.8
02-03—Yakima	17	523	108	212	.509	62	72	.861	42	81	307	2.5	4.8	18.1
03-04—Yakima	37	1600	277	619	.447	219	252	.869	114	221	861	3.1	6.0	23.3
05-06—Yakima	40	1431	236	510	.463	164	189	.868	105	341	707	2.6	8.5	17.7
Totals	176	5652	842	2026	.416	703	836	.841	440	1049	2633	2.5	6.0	15.0

Three-point field goals: 1994-95, 20-for-60 (.333). 1995-96, 38-for-99 (.384). 2002-03, 29-for-58 (.500). 2003-04, 88-for-186 (.473). 2005-06, 71-for-160 (.444). Totals, 246-for-563 (.437).

Personal fouls/disqualifications: 1994-95, 107/0. 1995-96, 72/0. 2002-03, 19/0. Totals, 198/0.

NBA REGULAR-SEASON RECORD

Season Team	G	Min.	FGM	FGA	Pct.	FTM	FTA	Pct.	Off.	Def.	Tot.	Ast.	St.	Blk.	TO	Pts.	RPG	APG	PPG
95-96—Charlotte	42	621	76	189	.402	46	60	.767	8	35	43	112	16	0	63	231	1.0	2.7	5.5
96-97—Char.-Denver	60	1188	131	330	.397	61	78	.782	12	72	84	219	33	2	76	387	1.4	3.7	6.5
97-98—Denver	82	2212	269	636	.423	150	186	.806	40	107	147	277	86	7	85	751	1.8	3.4	9.2
00-01—Denver	20	201	30	80	.375	13	17	.765	1	11	12	34	9	0	15	82	0.6	1.7	4.1
02-03—S.A.-Wash.	15	85	9	25	.360	4	7	.571	0	6	6	4	3	0	6	25	0.4	0.3	1.7
03-04—Minn.-Mil.-N.J.	11	85	7	22	.318	1	1	1.000	1	6	7	11	5	0	3	17	0.6	1.0	1.5
04-05—Detroit-Mil.	33	537	57	136	.419	26	31	.839	10	49	59	78	15	0	15	172	1.8	2.4	5.2
05-06—L.A. Clippers	3	22	1	7	.143	0	0	...	0	1	1	2	0	0	1	2	0.3	0.7	0.7
Totals	266	4951	580	1425	.407	301	380	.792	72	287	359	737	167	9	264	1667	1.3	2.8	6.3

Three-point field goals: 1995-96, 33-for-83 (.398). 1996-97, 64-for-153 (.418). 1997-98, 63-for-164 (.384). 2000-01, 9-for-34 (.265). 2002-03, 3-for-9 (.333). 2003-04, 2-for-8 (.250). 2004-05, 32-for-80 (.400). 2005-06, 0-for-2. Totals, 206-for-533 (.386).

Personal fouls/disqualifications: 1995-96, 79/0. 1996-97, 104/1. 1997-98, 149/0. 2000-01, 13/0. 2002-03, 6/0. 2003-04, 5/0. 2004-05, 32/0. Totals, 388/1.

GREEK LEAGUE RECORD

Season Team	G	Min.	FGM	FGA	Pct.	FTM	FTA	Pct.	Reb.	Ast.	Pts.	RPG	APG	PPG
98-99—Olympiakos S.F.P.	25	784	95	227	.419	58	80	.725	38	60	295	1.5	2.4	11.8

Three-point field goals: 1998-99, 47-for-108 (.435). Totals, 47-for-108 (.435).

SPANISH LEAGUE RECORD

Season Team	G	Min.	FGM	FGA	Pct.	FTM	FTA	Pct.	Reb.	Ast.	Pts.	RPG	APG	PPG
99-00—FC Barcelona	33	750	114	266	.429	80	97	.825	56	60	363	1.7	1.8	11.0

Three-point field goals: 1999-00, 55-for-144 (.382). Totals, 55-for-144 (.382).

Personal fouls/disqualifications: 1999-00, 59/0. Totals, 59/0.

AMERICAN BASKETBALL ASSOCIATION 2000 RECORD

Season Team	G	Min.	FGM	FGA	Pct.	FTM	FTA	Pct.	Reb.	Ast.	Pts.	RPG	APG	PPG
00-01—Kansas City	14	504	98	216	.454	47	49	.959	44	68	290	3.1	4.9	20.7

Three-point field goals: 2000-01, 41-for-98 (.418). Totals, 41-for-98 (.418).

ITALIAN LEAGUE RECORD

Season Team	G	Min.	FGM	FGA	Pct.	FTM	FTA	Pct.	Reb.	Ast.	Pts.	RPG	APG	PPG
01-02—Skipper Bologna	23	236	73	194	.376	53	63	.841	58	47	236	2.5	2.0	10.3

Three-point field goals: 2001-02, 37-for-104 (.356). Totals, 37-for-104 (.356).

Personal fouls/disqualifications: 2001-02, 54/0. Totals, 54/0.

GOMES, RYAN   F   CELTICS

PERSONAL: Born September 1, 1982, in Waterbury, Conn. ... 6-7/250. (2.01/113.4). ... Full name: Ryan Anthony Gomes
HIGH SCHOOL: Wilby (Waterbury, Conn.).
COLLEGE: Providence.
TRANSACTIONS/CAREER NOTES: Selected by Boston Celtics in second round (50th pick overall) of 2005 NBA Draft.

COLLEGIATE RECORD

NOTES: The SPORTING NEWS All-America first team (2004).

Season Team	G	Min.	FGM	FGA	Pct.	FTM	FTA	Pct.	Reb.	Ast.	Pts.	RPG	APG	PPG
01-02—Providence	24	756	132	236	.559	68	111	.613	188	37	332	7.8	1.5	13.8
02-03—Providence	32	1152	213	397	.537	163	194	.840	311	66	589	9.7	2.1	18.4
03-04—Providence	29	1008	192	379	.507	134	154	.870	274	67	547	9.4	2.3	18.9
04-05—Providence	31	1161	247	498	.496	124	161	.770	255	100	670	8.2	3.2	21.6
Totals	116	4077	784	1510	.519	489	620	.789	1028	270	2138	8.9	2.3	18.4

Three-point field goals: 2001-02, 0-for-3. 2002-03, 0-for-3. 2003-04, 29-for-87 (.333). 2004-05, 52-for-137 (.380). Totals, 81-for-230 (.352).

HONORS: NBA All-Rookie second team (2006).

NBA REGULAR-SEASON RECORD

Season Team	G	Min.	FGM	FGA	Pct.	FTM	FTA	Pct.	Off.	Def.	Tot.	Ast.	St.	Blk.	TO	Pts.	RPG	APG	PPG
05-06—Boston	61	1376	173	355	.487	112	149	.752	102	196	298	58	35	5	55	461	4.9	1.0	7.6

Three-point field goals: 2005-06, 3-for-9 (.333). Totals, 3-for-9 (.333).
Personal fouls/disqualifications: 2005-06, 83/1. Totals, 83/1.

GOODEN, DREW   F   CAVALIERS

PERSONAL: Born September 24, 1981, in Oakland. ... 6-10/230. (2.08/104.3). ... Full name: Andrew Melvin Gooden
HIGH SCHOOL: El Cerrito (Calif.).
COLLEGE: Kansas.
TRANSACTIONS/CAREER NOTES: Selected after junior season by Memphis Grizzlies in first round (fourth pick overall) of 2002 NBA Draft. ... Traded by Grizzlies with F Gordan Giricek to Orlando Magic for F Mike Miller, F Ryan Humphrey, 2003 first-round draft choice and 2004 second-round draft choice (February 19, 2003). ... Traded by Magic with C Steven Hunter and the draft rights to F Anderson Varejao to Cleveland Cavaliers for F/C Tony Battie and two future second-round draft choices (July 23, 2004).

COLLEGIATE RECORD

NOTES: THE SPORTING NEWS All-America first team (2002).

Season Team	G	Min.	FGM	FGA	Pct.	FTM	FTA	Pct.	Reb.	Ast.	Pts.	RPG	APG	PPG
99-00—Kansas	33	686	143	317	.451	60	91	.659	248	36	351	7.5	1.1	10.6
00-01—Kansas	28	761	166	322	.516	105	162	.648	234	47	441	8.4	1.7	15.8
01-02—Kansas	37	1119	285	566	.504	154	204	.755	423	73	734	11.4	2.0	19.8
Totals	98	2566	594	1205	.493	319	457	.698	905	156	1526	9.2	1.6	15.6

Three-point field goals: 1999-00, 5-for-16 (.313). 2000-01, 4-for-10 (.400). 2001-02, 10-for-36 (.278). Totals, 19-for-62 (.306).

NBA REGULAR-SEASON RECORD

HONORS: NBA All-Rookie first team (2003).

Season Team	G	Min.	FGM	FGA	Pct.	FTM	FTA	Pct.	Off.	Def.	Tot.	Ast.	St.	Blk.	TO	Pts.	RPG	APG	PPG
02-03—Mem-Orl	70	1873	355	777	.457	151	212	.712	163	292	455	83	53	35	150	875	6.5	1.2	12.5
03-04—Orlando	79	2134	369	829	.445	167	262	.637	160	356	516	89	62	72	126	914	6.5	1.1	11.6
04-05—Cleveland	82	2523	464	943	.492	251	310	.810	207	546	753	130	77	76	133	1184	9.2	1.6	14.4
05-06—Cleveland	79	2174	334	652	.512	176	258	.682	237	428	665	56	52	49	106	845	8.4	0.7	10.7
Totals	310	8704	1522	3201	.475	745	1042	.715	767	1622	2389	358	244	232	515	3818	7.7	1.2	12.3

Three-point field goals: 2002-03, 14-for-48 (.292). 2003-04, 9-for-42 (.214). 2004-05, 5-for-28 (.179). 2005-06, 1-for-3 (.333). Totals, 29-for-121 (.240).
Personal fouls/disqualifications: 2002-03, 172/2. 2003-04, 196/2. 2004-05, 233/2. 2005-06, 190/2. Totals, 791/8.

NBA PLAYOFF RECORD

Season Team	G	Min.	FGM	FGA	Pct.	FTM	FTA	Pct.	Off.	Def.	Tot.	Ast.	St.	Blk.	TO	Pts.	RPG	APG	PPG
02-03—Orlando	7	234	36	90	.400	26	36	.722	28	61	89	4	3	6	12	98	12.7	0.6	14.0
05-06—Cleveland	13	282	45	85	.529	17	18	.944	31	67	98	8	3	2	18	107	7.5	0.6	8.2
Totals	20	516	81	175	.463	43	54	.796	59	128	187	12	6	8	30	205	9.4	0.6	10.3

Three-point field goals: 2002-03, 0-for-3. Totals, 0-for-3 (.000).
Personal fouls/disqualifications: 2002-03, 23/1. 2005-06, 40/1. Totals, 63/2.

GORDON, BEN   G   BULLS

PERSONAL: Born April 4, 1983, in London, England. ... 6-3/200. (1.91/90.7).
HIGH SCHOOL: Mount Vernon (N.Y.).
COLLEGE: Connecticut.
TRANSACTIONS/CAREER NOTES: Selected after junior season by Chicago Bulls in first round (third pick overall) of 2004 NBA Draft.

COLLEGIATE RECORD

NOTES: Member of NCAA Division I championship team (2003).

Season Team	G	Min.	FGM	FGA	Pct.	FTM	FTA	Pct.	Reb.	Ast.	Pts.	RPG	APG	PPG
01-02—Connecticut	34	844	140	315	.444	85	117	.726	93	105	427	2.7	3.1	12.6
02-03—Connecticut	33	1101	211	476	.443	143	177	.808	138	156	645	4.2	4.7	19.5
03-04—Connecticut	39	1346	239	551	.434	141	170	.829	184	176	723	4.7	4.5	18.5
Totals	106	3291	590	1342	.440	369	464	.795	415	437	1795	3.9	4.1	16.9

Three-point field goals: 2001-02, 62-for-150 (.413). 2002-03, 80-for-191 (.419). 2003-04, 104-for-240 (.433). Totals, 246-for-581 (.423).

NBA REGULAR-SEASON RECORD

HONORS: NBA Sixth Man Award (2005). ... NBA All-Rookie first team (2005).

Season Team	G	Min.	FGM	FGA	Pct.	FTM	FTA	Pct.	Off.	Def.	Tot.	Ast.	St.	Blk.	TO	Pts.	RPG	APG	PPG
04-05—Chicago	82	2002	434	1056	.411	233	270	.863	55	160	215	164	53	10	186	1235	2.6	2.0	15.1
05-06—Chicago	80	2482	486	1152	.422	211	268	.787	43	176	219	240	75	5	180	1349	2.7	3.0	16.9
Totals	162	4484	920	2208	.417	444	538	.825	98	336	434	404	128	15	366	2584	2.7	2.5	16.0

Three-point field goals: 2004-05, 134-for-331 (.405). 2005-06, 166-for-382 (.435). Totals, 300-for-713 (.421).
Personal fouls/disqualifications: 2004-05, 224/1. 2005-06, 238/2. Totals, 462/3.

NBA PLAYOFF RECORD

Season Team	G	Min.	FGM	FGA	Pct.	FTM	FTA	Pct.	Off.	Def.	Tot.	Ast.	St.	Blk.	TO	Pts.	RPG	APG	PPG
04-05—Chicago	6	153	30	74	.405	20	25	.800	6	10	16	15	5	2	13	87	2.7	2.5	14.5
05-06—Chicago	6	245	43	106	.406	25	37	.676	5	15	20	18	6	0	17	126	3.3	3.0	21.0
Totals	12	398	73	180	.406	45	62	.726	11	25	36	33	11	2	30	213	3.0	2.8	17.8

Three-point field goals: 2004-05, 7-for-22 (.318). 2005-06, 15-for-41 (.366). Totals, 22-for-63 (.349).
Personal fouls/disqualifications: 2004-05, 18/0. 2005-06, 12/0. Totals, 30/0.

G

GRAHAM, JOEY F RAPTORS

PERSONAL: Born June 11, 1982, in Wilmington, Del. ... 6-7/225. (2.01/102.1). ... Full name: Joey Joseph Graham ... Twin brother of Stephen Graham, G, Cleveland Cavaliers.
HIGH SCHOOL: Brandon (Fla.).
COLLEGE: Central Florida, then Oklahoma State.
TRANSACTIONS/CAREER NOTES: Selected by Toronto Raptors in first round (16th pick overall) of 2005 NBA Draft.

COLLEGIATE RECORD

Season Team	G	Min.	FGM	FGA	Pct.	FTM	FTA	Pct.	Reb.	Ast.	Pts.	RPG	APG	PPG
00-01—Central Florida	31	632	91	192	.474	69	82	.841	117	33	262	3.8	1.1	8.5
01-02—Central Florida	29	832	134	263	.510	98	128	.766	163	70	386	5.6	2.4	13.3
02-03—Oklahoma State					Did Not Play—Transfer Student									
03-04—Oklahoma State	35	864	171	297	.576	78	110	.709	183	40	434	5.2	1.1	12.4
04-05—Oklahoma State	33	1009	201	380	.529	157	177	.887	204	67	585	6.2	2.0	17.7
Totals	128	3337	597	1132	.527	402	497	.809	667	210	1667	5.2	1.6	13.0

Three-point field goals: 2000-01, 11-for-52 (.212). 2001-02, 20-for-52 (.385). 2003-04, 14-for-29 (.483). 2004-05, 26-for-55 (.473). Totals, 71-for-188 (.378).

NBA REGULAR-SEASON RECORD

Season Team	G	Min.	FGM	FGA	Pct.	FTM	FTA	Pct.	Off.	Def.	Tot.	Ast.	St.	Blk.	TO	Pts.	RPG	APG	PPG
05-06—Toronto	80	1581	198	414	.478	108	133	.812	57	187	244	60	37	13	92	533	3.1	0.8	6.7

Three-point field goals: 2005-06, 29-for-87 (.333). Totals, 29-for-87 (.333).
Personal fouls/disqualifications: 2005-06, 228/4. Totals, 228/4.

GRAHAM, STEPHEN G CAVALIERS

PERSONAL: Born June 11, 1982, in Wilmington, Del. ... 6-6/215. (1.98/97.5). ... Twin brother of Joey Graham, F, Toronto Raptors.
HIGH SCHOOL: Brandon (Fla.).
COLLEGE: Central Florida, then Oklahoma State.
TRANSACTIONS/CAREER NOTES: Not drafted by an NBA franchise ... Played in CBA (2005-06). ... Signed as free agent by San Antonio Spurs (September 29, 2005). ... Released by Spurs (October 26, 2005). ... Signed by Houston Rockets (December 11, 2005). ... Released by Rockets (December 29, 2005). ... Signed by Chicago Bulls to 10-day contract (January 17, 2006). ... Signed by Cleveland Cavaliers to first of two consecutive 10-day contracts (February 6, 2006). ... Signed by Cavaliers for remainder of season (February 24, 2006).

COLLEGIATE RECORD

Season Team	G	Min.	FGM	FGA	Pct.	FTM	FTA	Pct.	Reb.	Ast.	Pts.	RPG	APG	PPG
00-01—Central Florida	23	212	26	64	.406	18	27	.667	30	6	83	1.3	0.3	3.6
01-02—Central Florida	29	786	118	265	.445	82	102	.804	112	80	348	3.9	2.8	12.0
02-03—Oklahoma St.					Did not play—Transfer student									
03-04—Oklahoma St.	34	272	38	76	.500	16	24	.667	47	25	94	1.4	0.7	2.8
04-05—Oklahoma St.	33	592	71	147	.483	58	80	.725	105	36	215	3.2	1.1	6.5
Totals	119	1862	253	552	.458	174	233	.747	294	147	740	2.5	1.2	6.2

Three-point field goals: 2000-01, 13-for-29 (.448). 2001-02, 30-for-82 (.366). 2003-04, 2-for-12 (.167). 2004-05, 15-for-33 (.455). Totals, 60-for-156 (.385).

CBA RECORD

Season Team	G	Min.	FGM	FGA	Pct.	FTM	FTA	Pct.	Reb.	Ast.	Pts.	RPG	APG	PPG
05-06—Sioux Falls	16	554	118	204	.578	87	101	.861	88	69	336	5.5	4.3	21.0

Three-point field goals: 2005-06, 13-for-21 (.619). Totals, 13-for-21 (.619).

NBA REGULAR-SEASON RECORD

Season Team	G	Min.	FGM	FGA	Pct.	FTM	FTA	Pct.	Off.	Def.	Tot.	Ast.	St.	Blk.	TO	Pts.	RPG	APG	PPG
05-06—Hous.Chi.-Cleve.	22	175	21	54	.389	14	15	.933	5	22	27	7	5	2	13	58	1.2	0.3	2.6

Three-point field goals: 2005-06, 2-for-10 (.200). Totals, 2-for-10 (.200).
Personal fouls/disqualifications: 2005-06, 31/0. Totals, 31/0.

G

GRANGER, DANNY F PACERS

PERSONAL: Born April 20, 1983, in New Orleans, La. ... 6-8/225. (2.03/102.1).
HIGH SCHOOL: Grace King (Metairie, La.) .
COLLEGE: Bradley, then New Mexico.
TRANSACTIONS/CAREER NOTES: Selected by Indiana Pacers in first round (17th pick overall) of 2005 NBA Draft.

COLLEGIATE RECORD

Season Team	G	Min.	FGM	FGA	Pct.	FTM	FTA	Pct.	Reb.	Ast.	Pts.	RPG	APG	PPG
01-02—New Mexico	29	712	111	249	.446	98	124	.790	207	21	323	7.1	0.7	11.1
02-03—New Mexico	14	380	99	191	.518	65	95	.684	111	16	269	7.9	1.1	19.2
03-04—New Mexico	22	703	136	277	.491	133	175	.760	197	46	429	9.0	2.1	19.5
04-05—New Mexico	30	900	183	349	.524	154	204	.755	266	71	565	8.9	2.4	18.8
Totals	95	2695	529	1066	.496	450	598	.753	781	154	1586	8.2	1.6	16.7

Three-point field goals: 2001-02, 3-for-17 (.176). 2002-03, 6-for-20 (.300). 2003-04, 24-for-72 (.333). 2004-05, 45-for-104 (.433). Totals, 78-for-213 (.366).

NBA REGULAR-SEASON RECORD

HONORS: NBA All-Rookie second team (2006).

Season Team	G	Min.	FGM	FGA	Pct.	FTM	FTA	Pct.	REBOUNDS Off.	Def.	Tot.	Ast.	St.	Blk.	TO	Pts.	AVERAGES RPG	APG	PPG
05-06—Indiana............	78	1765	221	478	.462	115	148	.777	131	253	384	90	58	62	80	587	4.9	1.2	7.5

Three-point field goals: 2005-06, 30-for-93 (.323). Totals, 30-for-93 (.323).
Personal fouls/disqualifications: 2005-06, 211/1. Totals, 211/1.

NBA PLAYOFF RECORD

Season Team	G	Min.	FGM	FGA	Pct.	FTM	FTA	Pct.	REBOUNDS Off.	Def.	Tot.	Ast.	St.	Blk.	TO	Pts.	AVERAGES RPG	APG	PPG
05-06—Indiana............	6	162	18	34	.529	4	4	1.000	7	24	31	10	4	7	7	49	5.2	1.7	8.2

Three-point field goals: 2005-06, 9-for-16 (.563). Totals, 9-for-16 (.563).
Personal fouls/disqualifications: 2005-06, 20/0. Totals, 20/0.

GRANT, BRIAN   F   CELTICS

PERSONAL: Born March 5, 1972, in Columbus, Ohio. ... 6-9/254. (2.06/115.2). ... Full name: Brian Wade Grant
HIGH SCHOOL: Georgetown (Ohio).
COLLEGE: Xavier.
TRANSACTIONS/CAREER NOTES: Selected by Sacramento Kings in first round (eighth pick overall) of 1994 NBA Draft. ... Signed as free agent by Portland Trail Blazers (August 23, 1997). ... Traded by Trail Blazers to Miami Heat as part of three-way deal in which Heat sent F/C Chris Gatling, F Clarence Weatherspoon, future first-round draft choice and cash to Cleveland Cavaliers, Cavaliers sent F Shawn Kemp to Trail Blazers and Trail Blazers sent G Gary Grant to Cavaliers (August 30, 2000). ... Traded by Heat with F Lamar Odom, F Caron Butler, a first-round draft choice and a second-round draft choice to Los Angeles Lakers for C Shaquille O'Neal (July 14, 2004). ... Waived by Lakers (August 10, 2005). ... Signed by Phoenix Suns (August 18, 2005). ... Traded by Suns with draft rights to G Rajon Rondo to Boston Celtics for a first-round pick in 2007 draft (June 28, 2006).

COLLEGIATE RECORD

Season Team	G	Min.	FGM	FGA	Pct.	FTM	FTA	Pct.	Reb.	Ast.	Pts.	AVERAGES RPG	APG	PPG
90-91—Xavier	32	932	135	236	.572	100	144	.694	273	20	370	8.5	0.6	11.6
91-92—Xavier	26	729	117	203	.576	74	127	.583	237	23	308	9.1	0.9	11.8
92-93—Xavier	30	944	223	341	.654	110	159	.692	283	46	556	9.4	1.5	18.5
93-94—Xavier	29	894	181	324	.559	122	171	.713	287	47	485	9.9	1.6	16.7
Totals	117	3499	656	1104	.594	406	601	.676	1080	136	1719	9.2	1.2	14.7

Three-point field goals: 1993-94, 1-for-3 (.333). Totals, 1-for-3 (.333).

NBA REGULAR-SEASON RECORD

HONORS: J. Walter Kennedy Citizenship Award (1999). ... NBA All-Rookie first team (1995).

Season Team	G	Min.	FGM	FGA	Pct.	FTM	FTA	Pct.	REBOUNDS Off.	Def.	Tot.	Ast.	St.	Blk.	TO	Pts.	AVERAGES RPG	APG	PPG
94-95—Sacramento	80	2289	413	809	.511	231	363	.636	207	391	598	99	49	116	163	1058	7.5	1.2	13.2
95-96—Sacramento	78	2000	417	811	.500	170	300	.500	210	610	810	127	48	105	165	1120	7.0	1.6	14.4
96-97—Sacramento	24	607	91	207	.440	70	90	.778	49	93	142	28	19	25	44	252	5.9	1.2	10.5
97-98—Portland..........	61	1921	283	557	.508	171	228	.750	197	358	555	86	44	45	110	737	9.1	1.4	12.1
98-99—Portland..........	48	1525	183	382	.479	184	226	.814	173	297	470	67	21	34	96	550	9.8	1.4	11.5
99-00—Portland..........	63	1322	173	352	.491	112	166	.675	121	223	344	64	32	28	84	459	5.5	1.0	7.3
00-01—Miami	82	2771	484	1010	.479	282	354	.797	217	501	718	101	60	71	170	1250	8.8	1.2	15.2
01-02—Miami	72	2256	286	610	.469	101	119	.849	168	407	575	137	48	31	122	673	8.0	1.9	9.3
02-03—Miami	82	2641	344	676	.509	158	205	.771	241	596	837	104	63	47	129	846	10.2	1.3	10.3
03-04—Miami	76	2303	289	613	.471	86	110	.782	174	350	524	69	51	35	82	664	6.9	0.9	8.7
04-05—L.A. Lakers	69	1136	103	209	.493	57	79	.722	101	156	257	34	23	23	43	263	3.7	0.5	3.8
05-06—Phoenix	21	248	27	65	.415	7	8	.875	11	46	57	7	5	3	7	61	2.7	0.3	2.9
Totals	756	21417	3103	6332	.490	1721	2306	.746	1834	3788	5622	923	455	561	1235	7933	7.4	1.2	10.5

Three-point field goals: 1994-95, 1-for-4 (.250). 1995-96, 4-for-17 (.235). 1997-98, 0-for-1. 1999-00, 1-for-2 (.500). 2000-01, 0-for-1. 2001-02, 0-for-2. 2003-04, 0-for-1. Totals, 6-for-28 (.214).
Personal fouls/disqualifications: 1994-95, 276/4. 1995-96, 269/9. 1996-97, 75/0. 1997-98, 184/3. 1998-99, 136/1. 1999-00, 166/2. 2000-01, 293/5. 2001-02, 236/6. 2002-03, 300/8. 2003-04, 254/4. 2004-05, 175/2. 2005-06, 45/0. Totals, 2409/44.

NBA PLAYOFF RECORD

Season Team	G	Min.	FGM	FGA	Pct.	FTM	FTA	Pct.	REBOUNDS Off.	Def.	Tot.	Ast.	St.	Blk.	TO	Pts.	AVERAGES RPG	APG	PPG
95-96—Sacramento	4	124	16	42	.381	7	14	.500	7	13	20	4	2	7	13	39	5.0	1.0	9.8
97-98—Portland..........	4	135	19	36	.528	15	18	.833	18	25	43	6	4	3	5	53	10.8	1.5	13.3
98-99—Portland..........	13	482	63	119	.529	45	72	.625	34	85	119	14	10	16	21	171	9.2	1.1	13.2
99-00—Portland..........	16	320	29	65	.446	29	39	.744	37	55	92	8	6	6	17	87	5.8	0.5	5.4
00-01—Miami	3	84	10	24	.417	10	14	.714	6	18	24	1	0	5	6	30	8.0	0.3	10.0
03-04—Miami	13	399	42	98	.429	8	14	.571	45	67	112	10	7	8	18	92	8.6	0.8	7.1
05-06—Phoenix	5	12	1	3	.333	0	2	.000	2	0	2	0	0	0	0	2	0.4	0.0	0.4
Totals	58	1556	180	387	.465	114	173	.659	149	263	412	43	29	45	80	474	7.1	0.7	8.2

Three-point field goals: 2003-04, 0-for-1. Totals, 0-for-1 (.000).
Personal fouls/disqualifications: 1995-96, 14/1. 1997-98, 20/0. 1998-99, 48/1. 1999-00, 53/1. 2000-01, 9/0. 2003-04, 52/1. 2005-06, 7/0. Totals, 203/4.

GREEN, DEVIN   G   LAKERS

PERSONAL: Born October 25, 1982 ... 6-7/210. (2.01/95.3).
HIGH SCHOOL: Beechcroft (Columbus, Ohio).
COLLEGE: Hampton.
TRANSACTIONS/CAREER NOTES: Not drafted by an NBA franchise. ... Signed as free agent by Los Angeles Lakers (September 7, 2005).

G

COLLEGIATE RECORD

Season Team	G	Min.	FGM	FGA	Pct.	FTM	FTA	Pct.	Reb.	Ast.	Pts.	RPG	APG	PPG
												AVERAGES		
01-02—Hampton	33	973	154	336	.458	78	104	.750	152	68	432	4.6	2.1	13.1
02-03—Hampton	30	890	155	347	.447	99	134	.739	159	72	447	5.3	2.4	14.9
03-04—Hampton	30	998	154	345	.446	109	147	.741	228	70	456	7.6	2.3	15.2
04-05—Hampton	30	974	149	327	.456	99	138	.717	228	65	422	7.6	2.2	14.1
Totals	123	3835	612	1355	.452	385	523	.736	767	275	1757	6.2	2.2	14.3

Three-point field goals: 2001-02, 46-for-124 (.371). 2002-03, 38-for-124 (.306). 2003-04, 39-for-111 (.351). 2004-05, 25-for-68 (.368). Totals, 148-for-427 (.347).

NBA REGULAR-SEASON RECORD

Season Team	G	Min.	FGM	FGA	Pct.	FTM	FTA	Pct.	Off.	Def.	Tot.	Ast.	St.	Blk.	TO	Pts.	RPG	APG	PPG
									REBOUNDS								AVERAGES		
05-06—L.A. Lakers	27	135	6	28	.214	13	21	.619	10	14	24	7	3	0	5	25	0.9	0.3	0.9

Three-point field goals: 2005-06, 0-for-2. Totals, 0-for-2 (.000).
Personal fouls/disqualifications: 2005-06, 13/0. Totals, 13/0.

GREEN, GERALD — F — CELTICS

PERSONAL: Born January 26, 1986, in Houston, Texas. ... 6-8/200. (2.03/90.7).
HIGH SCHOOL: Gulf Shores Academy (Texas).
COLLEGE: Did not attend college.
TRANSACTIONS/CAREER NOTES: Selected out of high school by Boston Celtics in first round (18th pick overall) of 2005 NBA Draft.

NBA REGULAR-SEASON RECORD

Season Team	G	Min.	FGM	FGA	Pct.	FTM	FTA	Pct.	Off.	Def.	Tot.	Ast.	St.	Blk.	TO	Pts.	RPG	APG	PPG
									REBOUNDS								AVERAGES		
05-06—Boston	32	374	66	138	.478	29	37	.784	10	31	41	18	13	4	22	167	1.3	0.6	5.2

Three-point field goals: 2005-06, 6-for-20 (.300). Totals, 6-for-20 (.300).
Personal fouls/disqualifications: 2005-06, 41/1. Totals, 41/1.

NBA DEVELOPMENT LEAGUE RECORD

Season Team	G	Min.	FGM	FGA	Pct.	FTM	FTA	Pct.	Reb.	Ast.	Pts.	RPG	APG	PPG
												AVERAGES		
05-06—Fayetteville	8	211	40	93	.430	16	20	.800	43	14	101	5.4	1.8	12.6

Three-point field goals: 2005-06, 5-for-11 (.455). Totals, 5-for-11 (.455).

GREEN, WILLIE — G — 76ERS

PERSONAL: Born July 28, 1981, in Detroit. ... 6-4/200. (1.93/90.7). ... Full name: Willie J. Green
HIGH SCHOOL: Cooley (Detroit).
COLLEGE: Detroit Mercy.
TRANSACTIONS/CAREER NOTES: Selected by Seattle SuperSonics in second round (41st pick overall) of 2003 NBA Draft. ... Draft rights traded by SuperSonics to Philadelphia 76ers for draft rights to G Paccelis Morlende (June 26, 2003).

COLLEGIATE RECORD

Season Team	G	Min.	FGM	FGA	Pct.	FTM	FTA	Pct.	Reb.	Ast.	Pts.	RPG	APG	PPG
												AVERAGES		
99-00—Detroit Mercy	32	800	91	218	.417	61	75	.813	83	60	269	2.6	1.9	8.4
00-01—Detroit Mercy	33	1012	167	352	.474	70	97	.722	166	80	436	5.0	2.4	13.2
01-02—Detroit Mercy	29	888	147	341	.431	77	115	.670	122	55	396	4.2	1.9	13.7
02-03—Detroit Mercy	30	1021	244	498	.490	153	190	.805	148	75	678	4.9	2.5	22.6
Totals	124	3721	649	1409	.461	361	477	.757	519	270	1779	4.2	2.2	14.3

Three-point field goals: 1999-00, 26-for-68 (.382). 2000-01, 32-for-86 (.372). 2001-02, 25-for-88 (.284). 2002-03, 37-for-99 (.374). Totals, 120-for-341 (.352).

NBA REGULAR-SEASON RECORD

Season Team	G	Min.	FGM	FGA	Pct.	FTM	FTA	Pct.	Off.	Def.	Tot.	Ast.	St.	Blk.	TO	Pts.	RPG	APG	PPG
									REBOUNDS								AVERAGES		
03-04—Philadelphia	53	767	143	357	.401	59	81	.728	16	49	65	53	26	5	59	364	1.2	1.0	6.9
04-05—Philadelphia	57	1066	155	423	.366	97	125	.776	22	111	133	100	34	6	75	437	2.3	1.8	7.7
05-06—Philadelphia	10	153	28	66	.424	4	5	.800	1	14	15	5	2	0	12	70	1.5	0.5	7.0
Totals	120	1986	326	846	.385	160	211	.758	39	174	213	158	62	11	146	871	1.8	1.3	7.3

Three-point field goals: 2003-04, 19-for-61 (.311). 2004-05, 30-for-105 (.286). 2005-06, 10-for-19 (.526). Totals, 59-for-185 (.319).
Personal fouls/disqualifications: 2003-04, 83/0. 2004-05, 121/0. 2005-06, 13/0. Totals, 217/0.

NBA PLAYOFF RECORD

Season Team	G	Min.	FGM	FGA	Pct.	FTM	FTA	Pct.	Off.	Def.	Tot.	Ast.	St.	Blk.	TO	Pts.	RPG	APG	PPG
									REBOUNDS								AVERAGES		
04-05—Philadelphia	5	63	8	18	.444	9	10	.900	3	6	9	3	1	0	2	27	1.8	0.6	5.4

Three-point field goals: 2004-05, 2-for-9 (.222). Totals, 2-for-9 (.222).
Personal fouls/disqualifications: 2004-05, 5/0. Totals, 5/0.

GREENE, ORIEN — G — PACERS

PERSONAL: Born February 4, 1982, in Gainesville, Fla. ... 6-4/208. (1.93/94.3). ... Full name: Orien Randolph Greene
COLLEGE: Florida, then La.-Lafayette.
TRANSACTIONS/CAREER NOTES: Selected by Boston Celtics in second round (53rd pick overall) of 2005 NBA Draft. ... Waived by Celtics (June 30, 2006). ... Signed as free agent by Indiana Pacers (July 12, 2006).

G

COLLEGIATE RECORD

												AVERAGES		
Season Team	G	Min.	FGM	FGA	Pct.	FTM	FTA	Pct.	Reb.	Ast.	Pts.	RPG	APG	PPG
00-01—Florida	31	591	35	99	.354	21	28	.750	72	85	104	2.3	2.7	3.4
01-02—Florida	31	737	63	145	.434	14	22	.636	88	89	160	2.8	2.9	5.2
02-03—La-Lafayette...................						Did Not Play - Transfer Student								
03-04—La-Lafayette...................	18	464	68	150	.453	22	32	.688	82	54	188	4.6	3.0	10.4
04-05—La-Lafayette...................	24	775	92	237	.388	62	82	.756	113	98	280	4.7	4.1	11.7
Totals	104	2567	258	631	.409	119	164	.726	355	326	732	3.4	3.1	7.0

Three-point field goals: 2000-01, 13-for-52 (.250). 2001-02, 20-for-66 (.303). 2003-04, 30-for-83 (.361). 2004-05, 34-for-106 (.321). Totals, 97-for-307 (.316).

NBA REGULAR-SEASON RECORD

									REBOUNDS								AVERAGES		
Season Team	G	Min.	FGM	FGA	Pct.	FTM	FTA	Pct.	Off.	Def.	Tot.	Ast.	St.	Blk.	TO	Pts.	RPG	APG	PPG
05-06—Boston	80	1235	100	253	.395	45	68	.662	37	108	145	129	77	10	109	254	1.8	1.6	3.2

Three-point field goals: 2005-06, 9-for-40 (.225). Totals, 9-for-40 (.225).
Personal fouls/disqualifications: 2005-06, 181/1. Totals, 181/1.

GRIFFIN, ADRIAN — G/F — BULLS

PERSONAL: Born July 4, 1974, in Wichita, Kan. ... 6-5/215. (1.96/97.5).
HIGH SCHOOL: Wichita East (Kansas).
COLLEGE: Seton Hall.
TRANSACTIONS/CAREER NOTES: Not drafted by an NBA franchise. ... Played in Continental Basketball Association with Connecticut Pride (1996-99). ... Played in Italy (1998-99). ... Signed by Miami Heat (January 21, 1999). ... Waived by Heat (February 1, 1999). ... Signed by Boston Celtics (August 1, 1999). ... Signed as free agent by Dallas Mavericks (July 27, 2001). ... Signed as free agent by Houston Rockets (August 7, 2003) ... Traded by Rockets with G Mike Wilks and G/F Eric Piatkowski to Chicago Bulls for C Dikembe Mutombo (September 8, 2004). ... Signed as free agent by Mavericks (November 28, 2005). ... Signed as free agent by Chicago Bulls (July 31, 2006).

COLLEGIATE RECORD

												AVERAGES		
Season Team	G	Min.	FGM	FGA	Pct.	FTM	FTA	Pct.	Reb.	Ast.	Pts.	RPG	APG	PPG
92-93—Seton Hall......................	35	465	44	87	.506	31	53	.585	123	29	29	3.5	0.8	0.8
93-94—Seton Hall......................	30	893	106	224	.473	76	126	.603	233	66	290	7.8	2.2	9.7
94-95—Seton Hall......................	30	949	184	332	.554	86	119	.723	216	85	460	7.2	2.8	15.3
95-96—Seton Hall......................	28	983	213	438	.486	107	161	.665	231	86	454	8.3	3.1	16.2
Totals	123	3290	547	1081	.506	300	459	.654	803	266	1233	6.5	2.2	10.0

Three-point field goals: 1992-93, 0-for-2. 1993-94, 2-for-6 (.333). 1994-95, 6-for-20 (.300). 1995-96, 12-for-44 (.273). Totals, 20-for-72 (.278).
Personal fouls/disqualifications: 1992-93, 41/0. 1993-94, 75/0. 1994-95, 71/0. 1995-96, 82/0. Totals, 275/0.

CBA RECORD

NOTES: Member of CBA championship team (1999). ... CBA Most Valuable Player (1999). ... CBA Finals MVP (1999). ... CBA All-League first team (1998, 1999). ... CBA All-Defensive team (1998, 1999). ... CBA All-Rookie first team (1997).

												AVERAGES		
Season Team	G	Min.	FGM	FGA	Pct.	FTM	FTA	Pct.	Reb.	Ast.	Pts.	RPG	APG	PPG
96-97—Connecticut	54	1894	312	621	.502	127	169	.751	361	116	751	6.7	2.1	13.9
97-98—Connecticut	56	2157	391	798	.490	165	213	.775	376	188	961	6.7	3.4	17.2
98-99—Connecticut	47	1758	319	699	.456	*222	261	.851	358	159	888	7.6	3.4	18.9
Totals	157	5809	1022	2118	.483	514	643	.799	1095	463	2600	7.0	2.9	16.6

Three-point field goals: 1996-97, 0-for-9. 1997-98, 14-for-52 (.269). 1998-99, 28-for-84 (.333). Totals, 42-for-145 (.290).
Personal fouls/disqualifications: 1996-97, 178/0. 1997-98, 186/0. 1998-99, 138/0. Totals, 502/0.

ITALIAN LEAGUE RECORD

												AVERAGES		
Season Team	G	Min.	FGM	FGA	Pct.	FTM	FTA	Pct.	Reb.	Ast.	Pts.	RPG	APG	PPG
98-99—Cordivari.........................	8	226	41	71	.577	19	30	.633	48	7	103	6.0	0.9	12.9

Three-point field goals: 1998-99, 2-for-6 (.333). Totals, 2-for-6 (.333).
Personal fouls/disqualifications: 1998-99, 26/0. Totals, 26/0.

NBA REGULAR-SEASON RECORD

									REBOUNDS								AVERAGES		
Season Team	G	Min.	FGM	FGA	Pct.	FTM	FTA	Pct.	Off.	Def.	Tot.	Ast.	St.	Blk.	TO	Pts.	RPG	APG	PPG
99-00—Boston	72	1927	175	413	.424	119	158	.753	128	244	372	177	116	15	93	485	5.2	2.5	6.7
00-01—Boston	44	377	33	97	.340	18	24	.750	27	60	87	27	18	5	18	93	2.0	0.6	2.1
01-02—Dallas	58	1383	179	359	.499	41	49	.837	68	161	229	106	75	12	42	415	3.9	1.8	7.2
02-03—Dallas	74	1373	146	337	.433	27	32	.844	88	176	264	105	77	6	47	325	3.6	1.4	4.4
03-04—Houston	19	133	5	18	.278	0	4	.000	1	18	19	10	7	2	3	11	1.0	0.5	0.6
04-05—Chicago	69	667	58	161	.360	33	44	.750	52	94	146	53	43	4	30	151	2.1	0.8	2.2
05-06—Dallas	52	1245	98	204	.480	41	53	.774	75	152	227	89	51	9	39	237	4.4	1.7	4.6
Totals	388	7105	694	1589	.437	279	364	.766	439	905	1344	567	387	53	272	1717	3.5	1.5	4.4

Three-point field goals: 1999-00, 16-for-57 (.281). 2000-01, 9-for-26 (.346). 2001-02, 16-for-54 (.296). 2002-03, 6-for-24 (.250). 2003-04, 1-for-2 (.500). 2004-05, 2-for-9 (.222). 2005-06, 0-for-2. Totals, 50-for-174 (.287).
Personal fouls/disqualifications: 1999-00, 222/3. 2000-01, 45/0. 2001-02, 142/2. 2002-03, 157/0. 2003-04, 17/0. 2004-05, 78/0. 2005-06, 113/1. Totals, 774/6.

NBA PLAYOFF RECORD

									REBOUNDS								AVERAGES		
Season Team	G	Min.	FGM	FGA	Pct.	FTM	FTA	Pct.	Off.	Def.	Tot.	Ast.	St.	Blk.	TO	Pts.	RPG	APG	PPG
01-02—Dallas.............	4	57	10	17	.588	0	2	.000	2	7	9	4	2	1	3	20	2.3	1.0	5.0
02-03—Dallas.............	15	131	17	41	.415	2	2	1.000	17	27	44	8	4	0	9	37	2.9	0.5	2.5
04-05—Chicago	5	86	15	29	.517	4	5	.800	5	15	20	9	5	0	3	34	4.0	1.8	6.8

G

Season Team	G	Min.	FGM	FGA	Pct.	FTM	FTA	Pct.	REBOUNDS Off.	Def.	Tot.	Ast.	St.	Blk.	TO	Pts.	AVERAGES RPG	APG	PPG
05-06—Dallas..............	20	349	32	59	.542	7	8	.875	28	43	71	24	15	2	11	71	3.6	1.2	3.6
Totals	44	623	74	146	.507	13	17	.765	52	92	144	45	26	3	26	162	3.3	1.0	3.7

Three-point field goals: 2001-02, 0-for-2. 2002-03, 1-for-3 (.333). Totals, 1-for-5 (.200).
Personal fouls/disqualifications: 2001-02, 6/0. 2002-03, 24/0. 2004-05, 14/1. 2005-06, 42/0. Totals, 86/1.

GRIFFIN, EDDIE   F   TIMBERWOLVES

PERSONAL: Born May 30, 1982, in Philadelphia. ... 6-10/222. (2.08/100.7). ... Full name: Eddie J. Griffin
HIGH SCHOOL: Roman Catholic (Philadelphia).
COLLEGE: Seton Hall.
TRANSACTIONS/CAREER NOTES: Selected after freshman season by New Jersey Nets in first round (seventh pick overall) of 2001 NBA Draft. ... Draft rights traded by Nets to Houston Rockets for draft rights to F Richard Jefferson, C Jason Collins and G Brandon Armstrong (June 27, 2001). ... Released by Rockets (December 19, 2003). ... Signed as free agent by Nets (January 8, 2004). ... Waived by Nets (February 27, 2004). ... Signed as free agent by Minnesota Timberwolves (October 4, 2004).

COLLEGIATE RECORD

NOTES: The SPORTING NEWS Freshman of the Year (2001).

Season Team	G	Min.	FGM	FGA	Pct.	FTM	FTA	Pct.	Reb.	Ast.	Pts.	AVERAGES RPG	APG	PPG
00-01—Seton Hall.....................	30	979	206	480	.429	80	109	.734	323	49	533	10.8	1.6	17.8

Three-point field goals: 2000-01, 41-for-128 (.320). Totals, 41-for-128 (.320).
Personal fouls/disqualifications: 2000-01, 71/0. Totals, 71/0.

NBA REGULAR-SEASON RECORD

HONORS: NBA All-Rookie second team (2002).

Season Team	G	Min.	FGM	FGA	Pct.	FTM	FTA	Pct.	REBOUNDS Off.	Def.	Tot.	Ast.	St.	Blk.	TO	Pts.	AVERAGES RPG	APG	PPG
01-02—Houston.........	73	1896	244	666	.366	64	86	.744	117	299	416	53	17	134	47	642	5.7	0.7	8.8
02-03—Houston.........	77	1890	271	678	.400	58	94	.617	138	323	461	86	52	111	76	664	6.0	1.1	8.6
04-05—Minnesota.......	70	1492	202	522	.387	56	78	.718	128	325	453	53	23	118	55	527	6.5	0.8	7.5
05-06—Minnesota.......	70	1359	130	370	.351	44	74	.595	107	282	389	40	13	148	43	320	5.6	0.6	4.6
Totals	290	6637	847	2236	.379	222	332	.669	490	1229	1719	232	105	511	221	2153	5.9	0.8	7.4

Three-point field goals: 2001-02, 90-for-273 (.330). 2002-03, 64-for-192 (.333). 2004-05, 67-for-204 (.328). 2005-06, 16-for-82 (.195). Totals, 237-for-751 (.316).
Personal fouls/disqualifications: 2001-02, 117/1. 2002-03, 136/1. 2004-05, 120/1. 2005-06, 125/0. Totals, 498/3.

GRUNDY, ANTHONY   G

PERSONAL: Born April 15, 1979, in Louisville, Ky. ... 6-3/185. (1.91/83.9). ... Full name: Anthony Montreace Grundy
HIGH SCHOOL: Warren Central (Bowling Green, Ky.).
COLLEGE: North Carolina State.
TRANSACTIONS/CAREER NOTES: Not drafted by an NBA franchise. ... Played in Germany (2002-04). ... Played in Sweden (2004-05) ... Played in Israel (2004-05) ... Played in Dominican Republic (2004-05) ... Played in Venezuela (2004-05) ... Played in NBA Development League (2005-06). ... Signed by Atlanta Hawks to 10-day contract (March 27, 2006). ... Signed with Treamo of Italian League for 2006-07 season.

COLLEGIATE RECORD

Season Team	G	Min.	FGM	FGA	Pct.	FTM	FTA	Pct.	Reb.	Ast.	Pts.	AVERAGES RPG	APG	PPG
98-99—NC State	25	535	73	180	.406	30	47	.638	75	50	200	3.0	2.0	8.0
99-00—NC State	33	1012	152	380	.400	60	102	.588	152	91	412	4.6	2.8	12.5
00-01—NC State	29	907	145	351	.413	88	115	.765	125	95	423	4.3	3.3	14.6
01-02—NC State	34	1102	219	451	.486	121	158	.766	186	120	606	5.5	3.5	17.8
Totals	121	3556	589	1362	.432	299	422	.709	538	356	1641	4.4	2.9	13.6

Three-point field goals: 1998-99, 24-for-69 (.348). 1999-00, 48-for-153 (.314). 2000-01, 45-for-135 (.333). 2001-02, 47-for-136 (.346). Totals, 164-for-493 (.333).

GERMAN LEAGUE RECORD

Season Team	G	Min.	FGM	FGA	Pct.	FTM	FTA	Pct.	Reb.	Ast.	Pts.	AVERAGES RPG	APG	PPG
02-03—Oldenburg	21	537	89	248	.359	50	70	.714	61	49	253	2.9	2.3	12.0

Three-point field goals: 2002-03, 25-for-96 (.260). Totals, 25-for-96 (.260).

ISRAELI LEAGUE RECORD

Season Team	G	Min.	FGM	FGA	Pct.	FTM	FTA	Pct.	Reb.	Ast.	Pts.	AVERAGES RPG	APG	PPG
04-05—Klal Bituah	19	660	119	295	.403	57	86	.663	109	50	336	5.7	2.6	17.7

Three-point field goals: 2004-05, 41-for-125 (.328). Totals, 41-for-125 (.328).

SWEDISH LEAGUE RECORD

Season Team	G	Min.	FGM	FGA	Pct.	FTM	FTA	Pct.	Reb.	Ast.	Pts.	AVERAGES RPG	APG	PPG
04-05—Ockelbo	9	361	102	229	.445	75	99	.758	75	24	301	8.3	2.7	33.4

Three-point field goals: 2004-05, 22-for-76 (.290). Totals, 22-for-76 (.289).

VENEZUELAN LEAGUE RECORD

Season Team	G	Min.	FGM	FGA	Pct.	FTM	FTA	Pct.	Reb.	Ast.	Pts.	AVERAGES RPG	APG	PPG
04-05—Panteras	12	426	99	209	.474	39	50	.780	37	54	286	3.1	4.5	23.8

G

Three-point field goals: 2004-05, 49-for-123 (.398). Totals, 49-for-123 (.398).

NBA REGULAR-SEASON RECORD

								REBOUNDS								AVERAGES		
Season Team	G	Min.	FGM	FGA	Pct.	FTM	FTA	Pct.	Off.	Def.	Tot.	Ast.	St.	Blk.	TO	Pts.	RPG	APG	PPG
05-06—Atlanta	12	108	19	38	.500	9	14	.643	1	16	17	9	7	0	9	52	1.4	0.8	4.3

Three-point field goals: 2005-06, 5-for-15 (.333). Totals, 5-for-15 (.333).
Personal fouls/disqualifications: 2005-06, 14/0. Totals, 14/0.

NBA DEVELOPMENT LEAGUE RECORD

											AVERAGES		
Season Team	G	Min.	FGM	FGA	Pct.	FTM	FTA	Pct.	Reb.	Ast.	Pts.	RPG	APG	PPG
05-06—Roanoke	44	1753	340	787	.432	231	292	.791	237	193	1012	5.4	4.4	23.0

Three-point field goals: 2005-06, 101-for-256 (.395). Totals, 101-for-256 (.395).

HA, SEUNG-JIN — C — BUCKS

PERSONAL: Born August 4, 1985, in Seoul, Korea. ... 7-3/305. (2.21/138.3).
HIGH SCHOOL: Samil Commercial (Korea).
COLLEGE: Yonsei University (Korea).
TRANSACTIONS/CAREER NOTES: Selected by Portland Trail Blazers in second round (46th pick overall) of 2004 NBA Draft. ... Played in American Basketball Association (2004-05). ... Traded by Trail Blazers with F Brian Skinner and G Steve Blake to Milwaukee Bucks for C Jamaal Magloire (July 31, 2006).

AMERICAN BASKETBALL ASSOCIATION RECORD

											AVERAGES		
Season Team	G	Min.	FGM	FGA	Pct.	FTM	FTA	Pct.	Reb.	Ast.	Pts.	RPG	APG	PPG
04-05—Portland	6	...	10	14	.714	8	19	.421	43	7	28	7.2	1.2	4.7

NBA REGULAR-SEASON RECORD

								REBOUNDS								AVERAGES		
Season Team	G	Min.	FGM	FGA	Pct.	FTM	FTA	Pct.	Off.	Def.	Tot.	Ast.	St.	Blk.	TO	Pts.	RPG	APG	PPG
04-05—Portland	19	104	10	23	.435	6	11	.545	6	12	18	2	1	5	12	26	0.9	0.1	1.4
05-06—Portland	27	212	18	31	.581	8	17	.471	14	35	49	1	3	8	14	44	1.8	0.0	1.6
Totals	46	316	28	54	.519	14	28	.500	20	47	67	3	4	13	26	70	1.5	0.1	1.5

Personal fouls/disqualifications: 2004-05, 21/0. 2005-06, 41/0. Totals, 62/0.

NBA DEVELOPMENT LEAGUE RECORD

											AVERAGES		
Season Team	G	Min.	FGM	FGA	Pct.	FTM	FTA	Pct.	Reb.	Ast.	Pts.	RPG	APG	PPG
05-06—Fort Worth......................	5	72	5	14	.357	0	4	.000	19	1	10	3.8	0.2	2.0

HAMILTON, RICHARD — G/F — PISTONS

PERSONAL: Born February 14, 1978, in Coatesville, Pa. ... 6-6/185. (1.98/83.9). ... Full name: Richard Clay Hamilton
HIGH SCHOOL: Coatesville (Pa.) Area.
COLLEGE: Connecticut.
TRANSACTIONS/CAREER NOTES: Selected after junior season by Washington Wizards in first round (seventh pick overall) of 1999 NBA Draft. ... Traded by Wizards with G/F Bobby Simmons and G Hubert Davis to Detroit Pistons for G/F Jerry Stackhouse, F Brian Cardinal and G Hubert Davis (September 11, 2002).
MISCELLANEOUS: Member of NBA championship team (2004).

COLLEGIATE RECORD

NOTES: Member of NCAA Division I championship team (1999). ... NCAA Division I Tournament Most Outstanding Player (1999). ... The SPORTING NEWS All-America first team (1999). ... The SPORTING NEWS All-America second team (1998).

											AVERAGES		
Season Team	G	Min.	FGM	FGA	Pct.	FTM	FTA	Pct.	Reb.	Ast.	Pts.	RPG	APG	PPG
96-97—Connecticut	32	980	174	451	.386	91	116	.784	138	88	509	4.3	2.8	15.9
97-98—Connecticut	37	1203	270	614	.440	156	185	.843	163	87	795	4.4	2.4	21.5
98-99—Connecticut	34	1091	247	557	.443	170	204	.833	163	91	732	4.8	2.7	21.5
Totals	103	3274	691	1622	.426	417	505	.826	464	266	2036	4.5	2.6	19.8

Three-point field goals: 1996-97, 70-for-186 (.376). 1997-98, 99-for-245 (.404). 1998-99, 68-for-196 (.347). Totals, 237-for-627 (.378).

NBA REGULAR-SEASON RECORD

NOTES: Led NBA with .458 three-point shooting percentage (2005-06).

								REBOUNDS								AVERAGES		
Season Team	G	Min.	FGM	FGA	Pct.	FTM	FTA	Pct.	Off.	Def.	Tot.	Ast.	St.	Blk.	TO	Pts.	RPG	APG	PPG
99-00—Washington...	71	1373	254	605	.420	103	133	.774	38	91	129	108	28	6	84	639	1.8	1.5	9.0
00-01—Washington...	78	2519	547	1249	.438	277	319	.868	75	163	238	224	75	10	201	1411	3.1	2.9	18.1
01-02—Washington...	63	2203	472	1084	.435	300	337	.890	73	143	216	171	38	14	132	1260	3.4	2.7	20.0
02-03—Detroit..........	82	2640	570	1286	.443	440	528	.833	88	230	318	208	64	13	200	1612	3.9	2.5	19.7
03-04—Detroit..........	78	2772	530	1166	.455	297	342	.868	78	201	279	310	103	17	210	1375	3.6	4.0	17.6
04-05—Detroit..........	76	2926	510	1160	.440	368	429	.858	74	221	295	372	77	13	217	1424	3.9	4.9	18.7
05-06—Detroit..........	80	2825	649	1322	.491	256	303	.845	84	172	256	275	52	16	173	1609	3.2	3.4	20.1
Totals	528	17258	3532	7872	.449	2041	2391	.854	510	1221	1731	1668	437	89	1217	9330	3.3	3.2	17.7

Three-point field goals: 1999-00, 28-for-77 (.364). 2000-01, 40-for-146 (.274). 2001-02, 16-for-42 (.381). 2002-03, 32-for-119 (.269). 2003-04, 18-for-68 (.265). 2004-05, 36-for-118 (.305). 2005-06, 55-for-120 (.458). Totals, 225-for-690 (.326).
Personal fouls/disqualifications: 1999-00, 142/2. 2000-01, 203/2. 2001-02, 136/0. 2002-03, 249/2. 2003-04, 222/3. 2004-05, 232/8. 2005-06, 207/1. Totals, 1391/18.

H

NBA PLAYOFF RECORD

Season Team	G	Min.	FGM	FGA	Pct.	FTM	FTA	Pct.	REBOUNDS Off.	Def.	Tot.	Ast.	St.	Blk.	TO	Pts.	AVERAGES RPG	APG	PPG
02-03—Detroit..........	17	659	134	303	.442	106	117	.906	18	48	66	45	13	1	57	383	3.9	2.6	22.5
03-04—Detroit..........	23	924	181	405	.447	117	138	.848	32	74	106	97	27	1	72	494	4.6	4.2	21.5
04-05—Detroit..........	25	1079	198	437	.453	95	119	.798	30	78	108	107	21	3	78	501	4.3	4.3	20.0
05-06—Detroit..........	18	690	128	310	.413	97	114	.851	16	36	52	48	17	5	39	367	2.9	2.7	20.4
Totals	83	3352	641	1455	.441	415	488	.850	96	236	332	297	78	10	246	1745	4.0	3.6	21.0

Three-point field goals: 2002-03, 9-for-27 (.333). 2003-04, 15-for-39 (.385). 2004-05, 10-for-34 (.294). 2005-06, 14-for-40 (.350). Totals, 48-for-140 (.343).

Personal fouls/disqualifications: 2002-03, 51/0. 2003-04, 72/2. 2004-05, 79/1. 2005-06, 59/1. Totals, 261/4.

NBA ALL-STAR GAME RECORD

Season Team	Min.	FGM	FGA	Pct.	FTM	FTA	Pct.	REBOUNDS Off.	Def.	Tot.	Ast.	PF	Dq.	St.	Blk.	TO	Pts.
2006—Detroit................	13	3	7	.429	0	0	...	0	0	0	1	1	0	0	0	1	6

HAMILTON, ZENDON   C

PERSONAL: Born April 29, 1975, in Queens, N.Y. ... 6-11/240. (2.11/108.9).
HIGH SCHOOL: Sewanhaka (Floral Park, N.Y.).
COLLEGE: St. John's.
TRANSACTIONS/CAREER NOTES: Not drafted by an NBA franchise. ... Played in Spain (1998-99). ... Signed as free agent by Dallas Mavericks (October 4, 1999). ... Waived by Mavericks (October 15, 1999). ... Played in Greece (1999-2000). ... Signed as free agent by Los Angeles Clippers (September 29, 2000). ... Signed as free agent by Denver Nuggets (September 29, 2001). ... Signed by Toronto Raptors to 10-day contract (January 27, 2003). ... Signed by Philadelphia 76ers (December 10, 2003). ... Waived by 76ers (January 6, 2004). ... Played in Continental Basketball Association (2003-04). ... Signed by 76ers to first of two consecutive 10-day contracts (January 9, 2004). ... Signed by 76ers for remainder of season (January 30, 2004). ... Signed as free agent by Milwaukee Bucks (August 5, 2004). ... Traded by Bucks with G Mike James to Houston Rockets for G Reece Gaines and second-round picks in 2006 and 2007 NBA drafts (February 24, 2005). ... Waived by Rockets (February 24, 2005). ... Signed by Cleveland Cavaliers (September 27, 2005). ... Waived by Cavaliers (January 5, 2006). ... Signed by 76ers to 10-day contract (February 1, 2006).

COLLEGIATE RECORD

Season Team	G	Min.	FGM	FGA	Pct.	FTM	FTA	Pct.	Reb.	Ast.	Pts.	AVERAGES RPG	APG	PPG
94-95—St. John's	28	693	112	214	.523	95	154	.617	141	18	319	5.0	0.6	11.4
95-96—St. John's	27	958	179	368	.486	204	256	.797	277	21	542	10.3	0.8	20.1
96-97—St. John's	27	882	132	306	.431	173	242	.715	254	11	437	9.4	0.4	16.2
97-98—St. John's	32	1038	161	341	.472	170	260	.654	277	12	492	8.7	0.4	15.4
Totals	114	3571	584	1229	.475	642	912	.704	949	62	1790	8.3	0.5	15.7

Three-point field goals: 1994-95, 0-for-1. 1995-96, 0-for-4. 1996-97, 0-for-1. Totals, 0-for-6 (.000).

SPANISH LEAGUE RECORD

Season Team	G	Min.	FGM	FGA	Pct.	FTM	FTA	Pct.	Reb.	Ast.	Pts.	AVERAGES RPG	APG	PPG
98-99—Forum Valladolid	18	443	84	175	.480	67	100	.670	111	6	235	6.2	0.3	13.1

Three-point field goals: 1998-99, 0-for-2. Totals, 0-for-2 (.000).
Personal fouls/disqualifications: 1998-99, 35/0. Totals, 35/0.

GREEK LEAGUE RECORD

Season Team	G	Min.	FGM	FGA	Pct.	FTM	FTA	Pct.	Reb.	Ast.	Pts.	AVERAGES RPG	APG	PPG
99-00—Dafni................	21	620	109	245	.445	88	119	.739	143	13	310	6.8	0.6	14.8

Three-point field goals: 1999-00, 4-for-15 (.267). Totals, 4-for-15 (.267).

NBA REGULAR-SEASON RECORD

Season Team	G	Min.	FGM	FGA	Pct.	FTM	FTA	Pct.	REBOUNDS Off.	Def.	Tot.	Ast.	St.	Blk.	TO	Pts.	AVERAGES RPG	APG	PPG
00-01—L.A. Clippers...	3	19	2	9	.222	5	8	.625	3	5	8	0	0	0	2	9	2.7	0.0	3.0
01-02—Denver............	54	848	103	245	.420	118	181	.652	110	143	253	14	21	18	60	324	4.7	0.3	6.0
02-03—Toronto	3	12	2	5	.400	2	2	1.000	1	3	4	0	1	0	1	6	1.3	0.0	2.0
03-04—Philadelphia ...	45	472	51	95	.537	67	96	.698	49	97	146	13	8	8	27	169	3.2	0.3	3.8
04-05—Mil.-Hou..........	16	159	11	32	.344	29	48	.604	18	24	42	6	5	2	12	51	2.6	0.4	3.2
05-06—Clev-Phil	12	48	7	14	.500	12	18	.667	3	8	11	0	4	0	6	26	0.9	0.0	2.2
Totals	133	1558	176	400	.440	233	353	.660	184	280	464	33	39	28	108	585	3.5	0.2	4.4

Personal fouls/disqualifications: 2000-01, 4/0. 2001-02, 104/0. 2002-03, 2/0. 2003-04, 74/0. 2004-05, 26/0. 2005-06, 5/0. Totals, 215/0.

CBA RECORD

Season Team	G	Min.	FGM	FGA	Pct.	FTM	FTA	Pct.	Reb.	Ast.	Pts.	AVERAGES RPG	APG	PPG
03-04—Yakima	11	371	63	116	.543	94	118	.797	154	26	220	14.0	2.4	20.0

H

HARDAWAY, ANFERNEE   G/F

PERSONAL: Born July 18, 1971, in Memphis. ... 6-7/215. (2.01/97.5). ... Full name: Anfernee Deon Hardaway ... Nickname: Penny. ... Name pronounced ANN-fur-nee.
HIGH SCHOOL: Treadwell (Memphis).
COLLEGE: Memphis.
TRANSACTIONS/CAREER NOTES: Selected after junior season by Golden State Warriors in first round (third pick overall)

of 1993 NBA Draft. ... Draft rights traded by Warriors with 1996, 1998 and 2000 first-round draft choices to Orlando Magic for draft rights F/C Chris Webber (June 30, 1993). ... Traded by Magic to Phoenix Suns for F/C Danny Manning, F Pat Garrity and two future first-round draft choices (August 5, 1999). ... Traded by Suns with G Stephon Marbury and C Cezary Trybanski to New York Knicks for G Howard Eisley, F Maciej Lampe, F Antonio McDyess, G Charlie Ward, draft rights to G Milos Vujanic, 2004 first-round draft choice and future first-round draft choice (January 5, 2004). ... Traded by Knicks with F Trevor Ariza to Orlando Magic for G Steve Francis (February 22, 2006). ... Waived by Magic (February 24, 2006).

MISCELLANEOUS: Member of gold-medal-winning U.S. Olympic team (1996).

COLLEGIATE RECORD

NOTES: THE SPORTING NEWS All-America first team (1993).

Season Team	G	Min.	FGM	FGA	Pct.	FTM	FTA	Pct.	Reb.	Ast.	Pts.	RPG	APG	PPG
90-91—Memphis						Did not play—ineligible.								
91-92—Memphis	34	1224	209	483	.433	103	158	.652	237	188	590	7.0	5.5	17.4
92-93—Memphis	32	1196	249	522	.477	158	206	.767	273	204	729	8.5	6.4	22.8
Totals	66	2420	458	1005	.456	261	364	.717	510	392	1319	7.7	5.9	20.0

Three-point field goals: 1991-92, 69-for-190 (.363). 1992-93, 73-for-220 (.332). Totals, 142-for-410 (.346).

NBA REGULAR-SEASON RECORD

HONORS: All-NBA first team (1995, 1996). ... All-NBA third team (1997). ... NBA All-Rookie first team (1994). ... MVP of Rookie Game (1994).

									REBOUNDS							AVERAGES		
Season Team	G	Min.	FGM	FGA	Pct.	FTM	FTA	Pct.	Off.	Def.	Tot.	Ast.	St.	Blk.	TO	Pts.	RPG	APG	PPG
93-94—Orlando	82	3015	509	1092	.466	245	330	.742	192	247	439	544	190	51	292	1313	5.4	6.6	16.0
94-95—Orlando	77	2901	585	1142	.512	356	463	.769	139	197	336	551	130	26	258	1613	4.4	7.2	20.9
95-96—Orlando	82	3015	623	1215	.513	445	580	.767	129	225	354	582	166	41	229	1780	4.3	7.1	21.7
96-97—Orlando	59	2221	421	941	.447	283	345	.820	82	181	263	332	93	35	145	1210	4.5	5.6	20.5
97-98—Orlando	19	625	103	273	.377	90	118	.763	8	68	76	68	28	15	46	311	4.0	3.6	16.4
98-99—Orlando	50	1944	301	717	.420	149	211	.706	74	210	284	266	111	23	150	791	5.7	5.3	15.8
99-00—Phoenix	60	2253	378	798	.474	226	286	.790	91	256	347	315	94	38	153	1015	5.8	5.3	16.9
00-01—Phoenix	4	112	15	36	.417	7	11	.636	5	13	18	15	6	1	3	39	4.5	3.8	9.8
01-02—Phoenix	80	2462	389	931	.418	158	195	.810	98	252	350	324	122	32	189	959	4.4	4.1	12.0
02-03—Phoenix	58	1777	256	573	.447	77	97	.794	66	192	258	235	66	26	145	615	4.4	4.1	10.6
03-04—Phoenix-N.Y.	76	2095	279	678	.411	111	138	.804	69	218	287	176	70	20	107	699	3.8	2.3	9.2
04-05—New York	37	894	110	260	.423	34	46	.739	19	70	89	74	28	3	50	269	2.4	2.0	7.3
05-06—New York-Orl.	4	72	4	14	.286	2	2	1.000	0	10	10	8	2	0	6	10	2.5	2.0	2.5
Totals	688	23386	3973	8671	.458	2183	2822	.774	972	2139	3111	3490	1106	311	1773	10624	4.5	5.1	15.4

Three-point field goals: 1993-94, 50-for-187 (.267). 1994-95, 87-for-249 (.349). 1995-96, 89-for-283 (.314). 1996-97, 85-for-267 (.318). 1997-98, 15-for-50 (.300). 1998-99, 40-for-140 (.286). 1999-00, 33-for-102 (.324). 2000-01, 2-for-8 (.250). 2001-02, 23-for-83 (.277). 2002-03, 26-for-73 (.356). 2003-04, 30-for-79 (.380). 2004-05, 15-for-50 (.300). 2005-06, 0-for-1. Totals, 495-for-1572 (.315).

Personal fouls/disqualifications: 1993-94, 205/2. 1994-95, 158/1. 1995-96, 160/0. 1996-97, 123/1. 1997-98, 45/0. 1998-99, 111/0. 1999-00, 164/1. 2000-01, 6/0. 2001-02, 184/0. 2002-03, 150/1. 2003-04, 146/1. 2004-05, 79/0. 2005-06, 7/0. Totals, 1538/7.

NBA PLAYOFF RECORD

									REBOUNDS							AVERAGES		
Season Team	G	Min.	FGM	FGA	Pct.	FTM	FTA	Pct.	Off.	Def.	Tot.	Ast.	St.	Blk.	TO	Pts.	RPG	APG	PPG
93-94—Orlando	3	133	22	50	.440	7	10	.700	8	13	20	21	5	6	9	59	6.7	7.0	19.7
94-95—Orlando	11	440	111	206	.172	64	111	.751	30	49	79	162	40	15	73	412	3.8	7.7	19.6
95-96—Orlando	12	473	101	217	.465	58	78	.744	20	36	56	72	20	4	26	280	4.7	6.0	23.3
96-97—Orlando	5	220	52	111	.468	40	54	.741	7	23	30	17	12	7	9	155	6.0	3.4	31.0
98-99—Orlando	4	167	20	57	.351	30	39	.769	9	11	20	22	9	1	12	76	5.0	5.5	19.0
99-00—Phoenix	9	386	67	145	.462	44	62	.710	14	30	44	51	14	9	25	183	4.9	5.7	20.3
02-03—Phoenix	6	244	27	70	.386	13	18	.722	9	27	36	26	13	5	13	76	6.0	4.3	12.7
03-04—New York	4	168	23	63	.365	15	18	.833	4	14	18	23	6	1	10	66	4.5	5.8	16.5
Totals	64	2640	456	1018	.448	291	390	.746	101	202	303	394	119	48	188	1304	4.7	6.2	20.4

Three-point field goals: 1993-94, 5-for-11 (.455). 1994-95, 40-for-99 (.404). 1995-96, 20-for-55 (.364). 1996-97, 11-for-30 (.367). 1998-99, 6-for-13 (.462). 1999-00, 5-for-19 (.263). 2002-03, 9-for-25 (.360). 2003-04, 5-for-14 (.357). Totals, 101-for-266 (.380).

Personal fouls/disqualifications: 1993-94, 10/0. 1994-95, 70/0. 1995-96, 27/1. 1996-97, 14/0. 1998-99, 13/0. 1999-00, 29/0. 2002-03, 26/2. 2003-04, 8/0. Totals, 197/3.

NBA ALL-STAR GAME RECORD

								REBOUNDS								
Season Team	Min.	FGM	FGA	Pct.	FTM	FTA	Pct.	Off.	Def.	Tot.	Ast.	PF	Dq.	St.	Blk.	TO	Pts.
1995—Orlando	31	4	9	.444	4	6	.667	4	1	5	11	1	0	0	0	3	12
1996—Orlando	31	6	8	.750	4	4	1.000	0	0	3	7	0	0	2	0	3	18
1997—Orlando	24	7	10	.700	2	2	1.000	4	3	7	3	2	0	2	0	1	19
1998—Orlando	12	3	5	.600	0	0	...	0	0	0	3	0	0	0	0	1	6
Totals	98	20	32	.625	10	12	.833	8	4	15	24	3	0	4	0	8	55

Three-point field goals: 1995, 0-for-2. 1996, 2-for-4 (.500). 1997, 3-for-5 (.600). 1998, 0-for-1. Totals, 5-for-12 (.417).

HARPRING, MATT   F   JAZZ

PERSONAL: Born May 31, 1976, in Cincinnati. ... 6-7/231. (2.01/104.8). ... Full name: Matthew Joseph Harpring
HIGH SCHOOL: Marist (Atlanta).
COLLEGE: Georgia Tech.
TRANSACTIONS/CAREER NOTES: Selected by Orlando Magic in first round (15th pick overall) of 1998 NBA Draft. ... Traded by Magic to Cleveland Cavaliers for F/C Andrew DeClercq (August 3, 2000). ... Traded by Cavaliers with F Cedric Henderson and F/C Robert Traylor to Philadelphia 76ers for F Tyrone Hill and F Jumaine Jones (August 3, 2001). ... Signed as free agent by Utah Jazz (August 15, 2003).

COLLEGIATE RECORD

Season Team	G	Min.	FGM	FGA	Pct.	FTM	FTA	Pct.	Reb.	Ast.	Pts.	RPG	APG	PPG
94-95—Georgia Tech	29	966	121	250	.484	81	110	.736	180	68	351	6.2	2.3	12.1
95-96—Georgia Tech	36	1328	233	457	.510	138	181	.762	293	79	670	8.1	2.2	18.6

Season Team	G	Min.	FGM	FGA	Pct.	FTM	FTA	Pct.	Reb.	Ast.	Pts.	AVERAGES RPG	APG	PPG
96-97—Georgia Tech	27	1015	169	410	.412	110	163	.675	222	60	513	8.2	2.2	19.0
97-98—Georgia Tech	32	1163	230	504	.456	179	221	.810	302	82	691	9.4	2.6	21.6
Totals	124	4472	753	1621	.465	508	675	.753	997	289	2225	8.0	2.3	17.9

Three-point field goals: 1994-95, 28-for-73 (.384). 1995-96, 66-for-154 (.429). 1996-97, 65-for-190 (.342). 1997-98, 52-for-168 (.310). Totals, 211-for-585 (.361).

HONORS: NBA All-Rookie first team (1999).

NBA REGULAR-SEASON RECORD

Season Team	G	Min.	FGM	FGA	Pct.	FTM	FTA	Pct.	REBOUNDS Off.	Def.	Tot.	Ast.	St.	Blk.	TO	Pts.	AVERAGES RPG	APG	PPG
98-99—Orlando	50	1114	148	320	.463	102	143	.713	88	126	214	45	30	6	73	408	4.3	0.9	8.2
99-00—Orlando	4	63	4	17	.235	6	7	.857	5	7	12	8	5	1	1	16	3.0	2.0	4.0
00-01—Cleveland	56	1615	238	524	.454	134	165	.812	90	152	242	102	42	17	90	623	4.3	1.8	11.1
01-02—Philadelphia	81	2541	386	838	.461	165	222	.743	203	370	573	107	70	5	127	958	7.1	1.3	11.8
02-03—Utah	78	2557	521	1020	.511	262	331	.792	190	324	514	133	73	17	160	1370	6.6	1.7	17.6
03-04—Utah	31	1134	193	410	.471	108	157	.688	91	156	247	63	22	2	65	502	8.0	2.0	16.2
04-05—Utah	78	2584	418	855	.489	245	315	.778	196	284	480	142	70	16	133	1090	6.2	1.8	14.0
05-06—Utah	71	1944	322	678	.475	227	313	.725	158	210	368	98	59	14	109	885	5.2	1.4	12.5
Totals	449	13552	2230	4662	.478	1249	1653	.756	1021	1629	2650	698	371	78	758	5852	5.9	1.6	13.0

Three-point field goals: 1998-99, 10-for-25 (.400). 1999-00, 2-for-2 (1.000). 2000-01, 13-for-52 (.250). 2001-02, 21-for-69 (.304). 2002-03, 66-for-160 (.413). 2003-04, 8-for-33 (.242). 2004-05, 9-for-43 (.209). 2005-06, 14-for-39 (.359). Totals, 143-for-423 (.338).
Personal fouls/disqualifications: 1998-99, 112/0. 1999-00, 7/0. 2000-01, 161/1. 2001-02, 201/1. 2002-03, 217/4. 2003-04, 102/1. 2004-05, 250/2. 2005-06, 202/2. Totals, 1252/11.

NBA PLAYOFF RECORD

Season Team	G	Min.	FGM	FGA	Pct.	FTM	FTA	Pct.	REBOUNDS Off.	Def.	Tot.	Ast.	St.	Blk.	TO	Pts.	AVERAGES RPG	APG	PPG
98-99—Orlando	4	82	12	26	.462	8	11	.727	7	13	20	7	1	0	5	33	5.0	1.8	8.3
01-02—Philadelphia	5	119	22	44	.500	7	9	.778	13	13	26	7	5	0	5	51	5.2	1.4	10.2
02-03—Utah	5	156	30	62	.484	13	16	.813	9	18	27	5	5	1	8	74	5.4	1.0	14.8
Totals	14	357	64	132	.485	28	36	.778	29	44	73	19	11	1	18	158	5.2	1.4	11.3

Three-point field goals: 1998-99, 1-for-5 (.200). 2002-03, 1-for-7 (.143). Totals, 2-for-12 (.167).
Personal fouls/disqualifications: 1998-99, 9/0. 2001-02, 12/0. 2002-03, 23/1. Totals, 44/1.

HARRINGTON, AL   F   PACERS

PERSONAL: Born February 17, 1980, in Los Angeles. ... 6-9/250. (2.06/113.4).
HIGH SCHOOL: Roselle (N.J.), then St. Patrick's (Elizabeth, N.J.)
COLLEGE: Did not attend college.
TRANSACTIONS/CAREER NOTES: Selected out of high school by Indiana Pacers in first round (25th pick overall) of 1998 NBA Draft. ... Traded by Pacers to Atlanta Hawks for G Stephen Jackson (July 15, 2004). ... Traded by Hawks with C John Edwards to Indiana Pacers for a first-round draft choice (August 22, 2006).

NBA REGULAR-SEASON RECORD

Season Team	G	Min.	FGM	FGA	Pct.	FTM	FTA	Pct.	REBOUNDS Off.	Def.	Tot.	Ast.	St.	Blk.	TO	Pts.	AVERAGES RPG	APG	PPG
98-99—Indiana	21	160	18	56	.321	9	15	.600	20	19	39	5	4	2	11	45	1.9	0.2	2.1
99-00—Indiana	50	854	121	264	.458	78	111	.703	47	112	159	38	25	9	65	328	3.2	0.8	6.6
00-01—Indiana	78	1892	241	543	.444	103	157	.656	119	262	381	130	63	18	148	586	4.9	1.7	7.5
01-02—Indiana	44	1313	230	484	.475	115	144	.799	96	180	276	54	41	21	78	576	6.3	1.2	13.1
02-03—Indiana	82	2467	389	896	.434	211	274	.770	159	352	511	125	71	33	163	1002	6.2	1.5	12.2
03-04—Indiana	79	2441	421	909	.463	185	252	.734	163	345	508	131	80	22	163	1048	6.4	1.7	13.3
04-05—Atlanta	66	2550	453	986	.459	236	351	.672	145	316	461	208	85	16	204	1158	7.0	3.2	17.5
05-06—Atlanta	76	2782	551	1220	.452	243	350	.694	132	391	523	238	85	14	195	1411	6.9	3.1	18.6
Totals	496	14459	2424	5358	.452	1180	1654	.713	881	1977	2858	929	454	135	1027	6154	5.8	1.9	12.4

Three-point field goals: 1998-99, 0-for-5. 1999-00, 8-for-34 (.235). 2000-01, 1-for-7 (.143). 2001-02, 1-for-3 (.333). 2002-03, 13-for-46 (.283). 2003-04, 21-for-77 (.273). 2004-05, 16-for-74 (.216). 2005-06, 66-for-191 (.346). Totals, 126-for-437 (.288).
Personal fouls/disqualifications: 1998-99, 26/0. 1999-00, 130/0. 2000-01, 223/2. 2001-02, 166/4. 2002-03, 280/3. 2003-04, 250/1. 2004-05, 249/2. 2005-06, 301/5. Totals, 1625/17.

NBA PLAYOFF RECORD

Season Team	G	Min.	FGM	FGA	Pct.	FTM	FTA	Pct.	REBOUNDS Off.	Def.	Tot.	Ast.	St.	Blk.	TO	Pts.	AVERAGES RPG	APG	PPG
00-01—Indiana	3	40	2	13	.154	1	2	.500	3	1	4	3	0	0	1	5	1.3	1.0	1.7
02-03—Indiana	6	103	7	33	.212	4	6	.667	7	15	22	5	6	3	10	18	3.7	0.8	3.0
03-04—Indiana	16	427	60	140	.429	30	55	.545	33	69	102	12	23	9	28	152	6.4	0.8	9.5
Totals	25	570	69	186	.371	35	63	.556	43	85	128	20	29	12	39	175	5.1	0.8	7.0

Three-point field goals: 2000-01, 0-for-2. 2002-03, 0-for-4. 2003-04, 2-for-5 (.400). Totals, 2-for-11 (.182).
Personal fouls/disqualifications: 2000-01, 8/0. 2002-03, 21/0. 2003-04, 56/1. Totals, 85/1.

HARRINGTON, OTHELLA   F   BOBCATS

H

PERSONAL: Born January 31, 1974, in Jackson, Miss. ... 6-9/235. (2.06/106.6).
HIGH SCHOOL: Murrah (Jackson, Miss.).
COLLEGE: Georgetown.
TRANSACTIONS/CAREER NOTES: Selected by Houston Rockets in second round (30th pick overall) of 1996 NBA Draft. ... Traded by Rockets with G Michael Dickerson, G Brent Price, F/C Antoine Carr and future first-round draft choice to Vancouver Grizzlies as part of three-way deal in which Rockets received draft rights to G Steve Francis and F Tony Massenburg from Grizzlies

and F Don MacLean and future first-round draft choice from Orlando Magic, and Magic received F Michael Smith, G/F Rodrick Rhodes, G Lee Mayberry and F Makhtar Ndiaye from Grizzles (August 27, 1999). ... Traded by Grizzlies to New York Knicks for G Erick Strickland, 2001 first-round draft choice and 2001 second-round draft choice (January 30, 2001). ... Traded by Knicks with C Dikembe Mutombo, C Cezary Trybanski and G Frank Williams to Chicago Bulls for G Jamal Crawford and F Jerome Williams (August 5, 2004). ... Waived by Bulls (July 7, 2006). ... Signed by Charlotte Bobcats (July 19, 2006).

COLLEGIATE RECORD

Season Team	G	Min.	FGM	FGA	Pct.	FTM	FTA	Pct.	Reb.	Ast.	Pts.	RPG	APG	PPG
												AVERAGES		
92-93—Georgetown	33	1075	205	358	.573	144	193	.746	291	32	554	8.8	1.0	16.8
93-94—Georgetown	31	897	152	276	.551	151	206	.733	248	36	455	8.0	1.2	14.7
94-95—Georgetown	31	767	132	236	.559	115	163	.706	187	25	379	6.0	0.8	12.2
95-96—Georgetown	37	983	161	288	.559	129	174	.741	257	44	451	6.9	1.2	12.2
Totals	132	3722	650	1158	.561	539	736	.732	983	137	1839	7.4	1.0	13.9

NBA REGULAR-SEASON RECORD

Season Team	G	Min.	FGM	FGA	Pct.	FTM	FTA	Pct.	Off.	Def.	Tot.	Ast.	St.	Blk.	TO	Pts.	RPG	APG	PPG
									REBOUNDS								AVERAGES		
96-97—Houston	57	860	112	204	.549	49	81	.605	75	123	198	18	12	22	57	273	3.5	0.3	4.8
97-98—Houston	58	903	129	266	.485	92	122	.754	73	134	207	24	10	27	47	350	3.6	0.4	6.0
98-99—Houston	41	903	156	304	.513	88	122	.721	72	174	246	15	6	25	61	400	6.0	0.4	9.8
99-00—Vancouver	82	2677	420	830	.506	236	298	.792	196	367	563	97	36	58	217	1076	6.9	1.2	13.1
00-01—Van.-New York	74	1815	247	507	.487	171	224	.763	139	249	388	56	34	45	145	665	5.2	0.8	9.0
01-02—New York	77	1563	237	450	.527	122	172	.709	125	224	349	37	30	36	95	596	4.5	0.5	7.7
02-03—New York	74	1850	225	443	.508	123	150	.820	165	311	476	62	12	23	90	573	6.4	0.8	7.7
03-04—New York	56	872	100	202	.495	58	78	.744	58	119	177	29	12	14	65	258	3.2	0.5	4.6
04-05—Chicago	70	1271	217	424	.512	127	177	.718	106	186	292	56	24	18	84	561	4.2	0.8	8.0
05-06—Chicago	72	824	135	273	.495	77	123	.626	54	100	154	39	7	13	61	347	2.1	0.5	4.8
Totals	661	13538	1978	3903	.507	1143	1547	.739	1063	1987	3050	433	183	281	922	5099	4.6	0.7	7.7

Three-point field goals: 1996-97, 0-for-3. 1997-98, 0-for-1. 1999-00, 0-for-2. 2000-01, 0-for-3. 2001-02, 0-for-2. Totals, 0-for-11 (.000).
Personal fouls/disqualifications: 1996-97, 112/2. 1997-98, 112/1. 1998-99, 103/0. 1999-00, 287/3. 2000-01, 237/4. 2001-02, 250/5. 2002-03, 231/2. 2003-04, 134/3. 2004-05, 188/2. 2005-06, 131/1. Totals, 1785/23.

NBA PLAYOFF RECORD

Season Team	G	Min.	FGM	FGA	Pct.	FTM	FTA	Pct.	Off.	Def.	Tot.	Ast.	St.	Blk.	TO	Pts.	RPG	APG	PPG
									REBOUNDS								AVERAGES		
96-97—Houston	7	15	1	2	.500	7	10	.700	1	3	4	0	0	0	2	9	0.6	0.0	1.3
97-98—Houston	3	23	6	12	.500	4	5	.800	3	4	7	0	0	1	0	16	2.3	0.0	5.3
98-99—Houston	4	42	9	14	.643	4	6	.667	5	9	14	1	0	1	3	22	3.5	0.3	5.5
00-01—New York	5	77	7	14	.500	4	5	.800	7	8	15	2	4	2	3	18	3.0	0.4	3.6
04-05—Chicago	6	103	21	42	.500	6	11	.545	6	9	15	3	1	0	8	48	2.5	0.5	8.0
05-06—Chicago	3	15	0	3	.000	0	0	—	0	2	2	0	1	0	0	0	0.7	0.0	0.0
Totals	28	275	44	87	.506	25	37	.676	22	35	57	6	6	4	16	113	2.0	0.2	4.0

Three-point field goals: 1997-98, 0-for-1. Totals, 0-for-1 (.000).
Personal fouls/disqualifications: 1996-97, 1/0. 1997-98, 1/0. 1998-99, 2/0. 2000-01, 16/1. 2004-05, 19/0. 2005-06, 2/0. Totals, 41/1.

HARRIS, DEVIN   G   MAVERICKS

PERSONAL: Born February 27, 1983, in Milwaukee. ... 6-3/185. (1.91/83.9). ... Full name: Devin Lamar Harris.
HIGH SCHOOL: Wauwatosa East (Milwaukee).
COLLEGE: Wisconsin.
TRANSACTIONS/CAREER NOTES: Selected after junior season by Washington Wizards in first round (fifth pick overall) of 2004 NBA Draft. ... Draft rights traded by Wizards with G Jerry Stackhouse and F/C Christian Laettner to Dallas Mavericks for F Antawn Jamison (June 24, 2004).

COLLEGIATE RECORD

NOTES: The SPORTING NEWS All-America second team (2004).

Season Team	G	Min.	FGM	FGA	Pct.	FTM	FTA	Pct.	Reb.	Ast.	Pts.	RPG	APG	PPG
												AVERAGES		
01-02—Wisconsin	32	1094	117	283	.413	101	130	.777	105	56	394	3.3	1.8	12.3
02-03—Wisconsin	32	1100	132	285	.463	90	119	.756	147	98	407	4.6	3.1	12.7
03-04—Wisconsin	32	1162	189	412	.459	171	216	.792	139	141	624	4.3	4.4	19.5
Totals	96	3356	438	980	.447	362	465	.778	391	295	1425	4.1	3.1	14.8

Three-point field goals: 2001-02, 59-for-161 (.366). 2002-03, 53-for-137 (.387). 2003-04, 75-for-201 (.373). Totals, 187-for-499 (.375).

NBA REGULAR-SEASON RECORD

Season Team	G	Min.	FGM	FGA	Pct.	FTM	FTA	Pct.	Off.	Def.	Tot.	Ast.	St.	Blk.	TO	Pts.	RPG	APG	PPG
									REBOUNDS								AVERAGES		
04-05—Dallas	76	1173	157	366	.429	78	103	.757	28	74	102	169	77	19	82	436	1.3	2.2	5.7
05-06—Dallas	56	1275	190	405	.469	169	236	.716	26	99	125	177	53	16	84	554	2.2	3.2	9.9
Totals	132	2448	347	771	.450	247	339	.729	54	173	227	346	130	35	166	990	1.7	2.6	7.5

Three-point field goals: 2004-05, 44-for-131 (.336). 2005-06, 5-for-21 (.238). Totals, 49-for-152 (.322).
Personal fouls/disqualifications: 2004-05, 139/0. 2005-06, 121/2. Totals, 260/2.

NBA PLAYOFF RECORD

Season Team	G	Min.	FGM	FGA	Pct.	FTM	FTA	Pct.	Off.	Def.	Tot.	Ast.	St.	Blk.	TO	Pts.	RPG	APG	PPG
									REBOUNDS								AVERAGES		
04-05—Dallas	9	80	7	16	.438	6	9	.667	0	11	11	11	4	1	10	22	1.2	1.2	2.4
05-06—Dallas	23	558	82	171	.480	52	74	.703	15	24	39	50	18	3	42	216	1.7	2.2	9.4
Totals	32	638	89	187	.476	58	83	.699	15	35	50	61	22	4	52	238	1.6	1.9	7.4

Three-point field goals: 2004-05, 2-for-6 (.333). 2005-06, 0-for-8. Totals, 2-for-14 (.143).
Personal fouls/disqualifications: 2004-05, 5/0. 2005-06, 69/0. Totals, 74/0.

H

HARRISON, DAVID   C   PACERS

PERSONAL: Born August 15, 1982, in Nashville, Tenn. ... 7-0/250. (2.13/113.4). ... Full name: David Joshua Harrison
HIGH SCHOOL: Brentwood Academy (Nashville, Tenn.).
COLLEGE: Colorado.
TRANSACTIONS/CAREER NOTES: Selected after junior season by Indiana Pacers in first round (29th pick overall) of 2004 NBA Draft.

COLLEGIATE RECORD

Season Team	G	Min.	FGM	FGA	Pct.	FTM	FTA	Pct.	Reb.	Ast.	Pts.	RPG	APG	PPG
01-02—Colorado	27	656	139	218	.638	97	173	.561	188	11	375	7.0	0.4	13.9
02-03—Colorado	32	908	164	300	.547	117	208	.563	265	16	445	8.3	0.5	13.9
03-04—Colorado	29	916	186	295	.631	125	232	.539	254	25	497	8.8	0.9	17.1
Totals	88	2480	489	813	.601	339	613	.553	707	52	1317	8.0	0.6	15.0

Three-point field goals: 2003-04, 0-for-1. Totals, 0-for-1 (.000).

NBA REGULAR-SEASON RECORD

Season Team	G	Min.	FGM	FGA	Pct.	FTM	FTA	Pct.	Off.	Def.	Tot.	Ast.	St.	Blk.	TO	Pts.	RPG	APG	PPG
04-05—Indiana	43	760	106	184	.576	52	91	.571	48	87	135	13	16	55	53	264	3.1	0.3	6.1
05-06—Indiana	67	1034	148	294	.503	89	174	.511	84	170	254	14	23	59	79	385	3.8	0.2	5.7
Totals	110	1794	254	478	.531	141	265	.532	132	257	389	27	39	114	132	649	3.5	0.2	5.9

Personal fouls/disqualifications: 2004-05, 134/6. 2005-06, 193/3. Totals, 327/9.

NBA PLAYOFF RECORD

Season Team	G	Min.	FGM	FGA	Pct.	FTM	FTA	Pct.	Off.	Def.	Tot.	Ast.	St.	Blk.	TO	Pts.	RPG	APG	PPG
05-06—Indiana	6	31	3	9	.333	7	12	.583	1	4	5	0	1	1	4	13	0.8	0.0	2.2

Personal fouls/disqualifications: 2005-06, 11/0. Totals, 11/0.

HART, JASON   G   KINGS

PERSONAL: Born April 29, 1978, in Los Angeles. ... 6-3/185. (1.91/83.9). ... Full name: Jason Keema Hart
HIGH SCHOOL: Inglewood (Calif.).
COLLEGE: Syracuse.
TRANSACTIONS/CAREER NOTES: Selected by Milwaukee Bucks in second round (49th pick overall) of 2000 NBA Draft. ... Waived by Bucks (October 29, 2001). ... Played in National Basketball Development League with Asheville Altitude (2001-02). ... Signed as free agent by San Antonio Spurs (December 19, 2001). ... Played in Greece (2002-03). ... Signed as free agent by Seattle SuperSonics (September 27, 2003). ... Waived by SuperSonics (October 23, 2003). ... Signed as free agent by Spurs (October 31, 2003). ... Signed as free agent by Charlotte Bobcats (July 14, 2004). ... Traded by Bobcats to Sacramento Kings for future second-round draft pick (August 2, 2005).

COLLEGIATE RECORD

Season Team	G	Min.	FGM	FGA	Pct.	FTM	FTA	Pct.	Reb.	Ast.	Pts.	RPG	APG	PPG
96-97—Syracuse	32	1142	113	298	.379	58	84	.690	113	184	307	3.5	5.8	9.6
97-98—Syracuse	35	1198	120	328	.366	91	133	.684	126	174	356	3.6	5.0	10.2
98-99—Syracuse	33	1068	167	407	.410	71	96	.740	98	143	458	3.0	4.3	13.9
99-00—Syracuse	32	1083	125	304	.411	94	128	.734	96	208	382	3.0	6.5	11.9
Totals	132	4491	525	1337	.393	314	441	.712	433	709	1503	3.3	5.4	11.4

Three-point field goals: 1996-97, 23-for-70 (.329). 1997-98, 25-for-96 (.260). 1998-99, 53-for-145 (.366). Totals, 101-for-311 (.325).

NBA REGULAR-SEASON RECORD

Season Team	G	Min.	FGM	FGA	Pct.	FTM	FTA	Pct.	Off.	Def.	Tot.	Ast.	St.	Blk.	TO	Pts.	RPG	APG	PPG
00-01—Milwaukee	1	10	1	1	1.000	0	0	...	0	0	0	1	0	0	2	2	0.0	1.0	2.0
01-02—San Antonio	10	92	10	19	.526	6	6	1.000	4	9	13	12	7	1	8	26	1.3	1.2	2.6
03-04—San Antonio	53	660	79	159	.447	33	43	.767	10	69	79	81	28	5	29	177	1.5	1.5	3.3
04-05—Charlotte	74	1887	257	573	.449	157	200	.785	18	185	203	367	99	14	102	706	2.7	5.0	9.5
05-06—Sacramento	66	818	86	221	.389	37	56	.661	12	59	71	70	31	5	43	218	1.1	1.1	3.3
Totals	204	3467	425	973	.437	233	305	.764	44	322	366	531	165	25	184	1129	1.8	2.6	5.5

Three-point field goals: 2001-02, 0-for-2. 2003-04, 2-for-9 (.222). 2004-05, 35-for-95 (.368). 2005-06, 9-for-31 (.290). Totals, 46-for-137 (.336).
Personal fouls/disqualifications: 2001-02, 16/0. 2003-04, 59/0. 2004-05, 167/1. 2005-06, 85/0. Totals, 327/1.

NBA PLAYOFF RECORD

Season Team	G	Min.	FGM	FGA	Pct.	FTM	FTA	Pct.	Off.	Def.	Tot.	Ast.	St.	Blk.	TO	Pts.	RPG	APG	PPG
03-04—San Antonio	7	62	11	20	.550	0	0	...	0	3	3	1	5	0	1	22	0.4	0.1	3.1
05-06—Sacramento	5	52	4	13	.308	2	2	1.000	1	1	2	3	3	0	4	10	0.4	0.6	2.0
Totals	12	114	15	33	.455	2	2	1.000	1	4	5	4	8	0	5	32	0.4	0.7	2.7

Personal fouls/disqualifications: 2003-04, 5/0. 2005-06, 8/0. Totals, 13/0.

NBA DEVELOPMENT LEAGUE RECORD

Season Team	G	Min.	FGM	FGA	Pct.	FTM	FTA	Pct.	Reb.	Ast.	Pts.	RPG	APG	PPG
01-02—Asheville	12	304	58	130	.446	31	39	.795	52	47	152	4.3	3.9	12.7

Three-point field goals: 2001-02, 5-for-14 (.357). Totals, 5-for-14 (.357).
Personal fouls/disqualifications: 2001-02, 32/0. Totals, 32/0.

H

Season Team	G	Min.	FGM	FGA	Pct.	FTM	FTA	Pct.	Reb.	Ast.	Pts.	AVERAGES RPG	APG	PPG
02-03—Makedonikos	23	745	113	250	.452	86	109	.789	72	101	344	3.1	4.4	15.0

Three-point field goals: 2002-03, 32-for-74 (.432). Totals, 32-for-74 (.432).

HASLEM, UDONIS — C — HEAT

PERSONAL: Born June 9, 1980, in Miami, Fla. ... 6-9/246. (2.06/111.6).
HIGH SCHOOL: Miami Senior (Miami, Fla.).
COLLEGE: Florida.
TRANSACTIONS/CAREER NOTES: Not drafted by an NBA franchise ... Played in France (2002-03). ... Signed as free agent by Miami Heat (August 6, 2003).
MISCELLANEOUS: Member of NBA championship team (2006).

COLLEGIATE RECORD

Season Team	G	Min.	FGM	FGA	Pct.	FTM	FTA	Pct.	Reb.	Ast.	Pts.	AVERAGES RPG	APG	PPG
98-99—Florida	31	660	117	194	.603	93	157	.592	154	24	327	5.0	0.8	10.5
99-00—Florida	37	830	169	292	.579	99	155	.639	189	33	437	5.1	0.9	11.8
00-01—Florida	31	870	188	315	.597	146	206	.709	232	31	522	7.5	1.0	16.8
01-02—Florida	31	876	159	283	.562	177	255	.694	256	51	495	8.3	1.6	16.0
Totals	130	3236	633	1084	.584	515	773	.666	831	139	1781	6.4	1.1	13.7

Three-point field goals: 1998-99, 0-for-2. 2001-02, 0-for-1. Totals, 0-for-3 (.000).

FRENCH LEAGUE RECORD

Season Team	G	Min.	FGM	FGA	Pct.	FTM	FTA	Pct.	Reb.	Ast.	Pts.	AVERAGES RPG	APG	PPG
02-03—Chalon	30	924	181	315	.575	120	167	.719	282	43	482	9.4	1.4	16.1

Three-point field goals: 2002-03, 0-for-3. Totals, 0-for-3 (.000).

NBA REGULAR-SEASON RECORD

HONORS: NBA All-Rookie second team (2004).

Season Team	G	Min.	FGM	FGA	Pct.	FTM	FTA	Pct.	REBOUNDS Off.	Def.	Tot.	Ast.	St.	Blk.	TO	Pts.	AVERAGES RPG	APG	PPG
03-04—Miami	75	1795	205	447	.459	140	183	.765	189	284	473	51	33	24	74	550	6.3	0.7	7.3
04-05—Miami	80	2675	346	641	.540	178	225	.791	239	487	726	108	63	41	113	870	9.1	1.4	10.9
05-06—Miami	81	2491	300	591	.508	157	199	.789	167	467	634	95	50	17	80	757	7.8	1.2	9.3
Totals	236	6961	851	1679	.507	475	607	.783	595	1238	1833	254	146	82	267	2177	7.8	1.1	9.2

Three-point field goals: 2003-04, 0-for-3. 2004-05, 0-for-4. 2005-06, 0-for-2. Totals, 0-for-9 (.000).
Personal fouls/disqualifications: 2003-04, 197/2. 2004-05, 260/5. 2005-06, 216/2. Totals, 673/9.

NBA PLAYOFF RECORD

Season Team	G	Min.	FGM	FGA	Pct.	FTM	FTA	Pct.	REBOUNDS Off.	Def.	Tot.	Ast.	St.	Blk.	TO	Pts.	AVERAGES RPG	APG	PPG
03-04—Miami	13	199	13	33	.394	21	31	.677	18	26	44	3	5	3	3	47	3.4	0.2	3.6
04-05—Miami	15	543	52	106	.491	34	46	.739	38	112	150	15	8	6	18	138	10.0	1.0	9.2
05-06—Miami	22	650	74	150	.493	41	60	.683	49	113	162	17	13	7	31	189	7.4	0.8	8.6
Totals	50	1392	139	289	.481	96	137	.701	105	251	356	35	26	16	52	374	7.1	0.7	7.5

Three-point field goals: 2005-06, 0-for-1. Totals, 0-for-1 (.000).
Personal fouls/disqualifications: 2003-04, 22/0. 2004-05, 48/0. 2005-06, 79/2. Totals, 149/2.

HASSELL, TRENTON — G — TIMBERWOLVES

PERSONAL: Born March 4, 1979, in Clarksville, Tenn. ... 6-5/200. (1.96/90.7). ... Full name: Trenton Lavar Hassell
HIGH SCHOOL: Clarksville (Tenn.).
COLLEGE: Austin Peay.
TRANSACTIONS/CAREER NOTES: Selected after junior season by Chicago Bulls in second round (30th pick overall) of 2001 NBA Draft. ... Waived by Bulls (October 23, 2003). ... Signed as free agent by Minnesota Timberwolves (October 29, 2003).

COLLEGIATE RECORD

Season Team	G	Min.	FGM	FGA	Pct.	FTM	FTA	Pct.	Reb.	Ast.	Pts.	AVERAGES RPG	APG	PPG
97-98—Austin Peay						Did not play—ineligible.									
98-99—Austin Peay	25	963	166	369	.450	107	140	.764	251	102	481	10.0	4.1	19.2
99-00—Austin Peay	25	868	167	352	.474	91	118	.771	185	129	452	7.4	5.2	18.1
00-01—Austin Peay	32	1213	246	507	.485	148	186	.796	249	144	693	7.8	4.5	21.7
Totals	82	3044	579	1228	.471	346	444	.779	685	375	1626	8.4	4.6	19.8

Three-point field goals: 1998-99, 42-for-136 (.309). 1999-00, 27-for-82 (.329). 2000-01, 53-for-136 (.390). Totals, 122-for-354 (.345).
Personal fouls/disqualifications: 1998-99, 53/0. 1999-00, 34/0. 2000-01, 67/0. Totals, 154/0.

NBA REGULAR-SEASON RECORD

Season Team	G	Min.	FGM	FGA	Pct.	FTM	FTA	Pct.	REBOUNDS Off.	Def.	Tot.	Ast.	St.	Blk.	TO	Pts.	AVERAGES RPG	APG	PPG
01-02—Chicago	78	2237	267	628	.425	87	114	.763	65	190	255	172	55	44	101	681	3.3	2.2	8.7
02-03—Chicago	82	1999	144	392	.367	41	55	.745	37	218	255	151	45	61	83	342	3.1	1.8	4.2
03-04—Minnesota	81	2264	177	381	.465	48	61	.787	68	189	257	133	36	54	46	406	3.2	1.6	5.0

H

Season Team	G	Min.	FGM	FGA	Pct.	FTM	FTA	Pct.	REBOUNDS Off.	Def.	Tot.	Ast.	St.	Blk.	TO	Pts.	AVERAGES RPG	APG	PPG
04-05—Minnesota......	82	2068	225	475	.474	90	114	.789	80	139	219	128	30	30	64	541	2.7	1.6	6.6
05-06—Minnesota......	77	2514	286	616	.464	131	176	.744	82	134	216	203	43	29	124	710	2.8	2.6	9.2
Totals	400	11082	1099	2492	.441	397	520	.763	332	870	1202	787	209	218	418	2680	3.0	2.0	6.7

Three-point field goals: 2001-02, 60-for-165 (.364). 2002-03, 13-for-40 (.325). 2003-04, 4-for-13 (.308). 2004-05, 1-for-11 (.091). 2005-06, 7-for-23 (.304). Totals, 85-for-252 (.337).
Personal fouls/disqualifications: 2001-02, 184/2. 2002-03, 197/2. 2003-04, 200/1. 2004-05, 200/1. 2005-06, 201/3. Totals, 982/9.

NBA PLAYOFF RECORD

Season Team	G	Min.	FGM	FGA	Pct.	FTM	FTA	Pct.	REBOUNDS Off.	Def.	Tot.	Ast.	St.	Blk.	TO	Pts.	AVERAGES RPG	APG	PPG
03-04—Minnesota......	18	472	62	119	.521	13	16	.813	21	23	44	27	10	7	16	138	2.4	1.5	7.7

Three-point field goals: 2003-04, 1-for-2 (.500). Totals, 1-for-2 (.500).
Personal fouls/disqualifications: 2003-04, 42/0. Totals, 42/0.

HAYES, CHUCK   F   ROCKETS

PERSONAL: Born June 11, 1983, in San Leandro, Calif. ... 6-6/242. (1.98/109.8). ... Full name: Chuck Edwards Hayes
HIGH SCHOOL: Modesto Christian (Calif.).
COLLEGE: Kentucky.
TRANSACTIONS/CAREER NOTES: Not drafted by an NBA franchise ... Played in NBA Development League (2005-06). ... Signed as free agent by Houston Rockets (October 5, 2005). ... Waived by Rockets (October 25, 2005). ... Signed to 10-day contract by Houston Rockets (January 18, 2006). ... Signed by Rockets for remainder of season (January 28, 2006).

COLLEGIATE RECORD

Season Team	G	Min.	FGM	FGA	Pct.	FTM	FTA	Pct.	Reb.	Ast.	Pts.	AVERAGES RPG	APG	PPG
01-02—Kentucky	32	534	67	145	.462	48	65	.738	143	34	188	4.5	1.1	5.9
02-03—Kentucky	36	996	110	225	.489	82	104	.788	244	84	310	6.8	2.3	8.6
03-04—Kentucky	32	991	131	246	.533	77	113	.681	260	97	342	8.1	3.0	10.7
04-05—Kentucky	34	995	144	83	1.735	81	111	.730	263	77	371	7.7	2.3	10.9
Totals	134	3516	452	699	.647	288	393	.733	910	292	1211	6.8	2.2	9.0

Three-point field goals: 2001-02, 6-for-22 (.273). 2002-03, 8-for-33 (.242). 2003-04, 3-for-12 (.250). 2004-05, 2-for-11 (.182). Totals, 19-for-78 (.244).

NBA REGULAR-SEASON RECORD

Season Team	G	Min.	FGM	FGA	Pct.	FTM	FTA	Pct.	REBOUNDS Off.	Def.	Tot.	Ast.	St.	Blk.	TO	Pts.	AVERAGES RPG	APG	PPG
05-06—Houston.........	40	535	59	105	.562	29	45	.644	67	112	179	14	26	14	12	147	4.5	0.4	3.7

Three-point field goals: 2005-06, 0-for-1. Totals, 0-for-1 (.000).
Personal fouls/disqualifications: 2005-06, 76/2. Totals, 76/2.

NBA DEVELOPMENT LEAGUE RECORD

Season Team	G	Min.	FGM	FGA	Pct.	FTM	FTA	Pct.	Reb.	Ast.	Pts.	AVERAGES RPG	APG	PPG
05-06—Albuquerque..................	15	483	65	120	.542	32	47	.681	171	36	162	11.4	2.4	10.8

HAYES, JARVIS   G/F   WIZARDS

PERSONAL: Born August 9, 1981, in Atlanta, Ga. ... 6-7/220. (2.01/99.8). ... Full name: Jarvis James Hayes
HIGH SCHOOL: Frederick Douglass (Atlanta, Ga.).
COLLEGE: Western Carolina, then Georgia.
TRANSACTIONS/CAREER NOTES: Selected after junior season by Washington Wizards (10th pick overall) in 2003 NBA Draft.

COLLEGIATE RECORD

Season Team	G	Min.	FGM	FGA	Pct.	FTM	FTA	Pct.	Reb.	Ast.	Pts.	AVERAGES RPG	APG	PPG
99-00—Western Carolina............	28	784	178	420	.424	69	90	.767	151	28	479	5.4	1.0	17.1
00-01—Georgia...........................						Did not play—transfer student								
01-02—Georgia...........................	29	980	212	470	.451	65	85	.765	152	45	538	5.2	1.6	18.6
02-03—Georgia...........................	27	872	185	368	.503	69	88	.784	119	54	493	4.4	2.0	18.3
Totals	84	2636	575	1258	.457	203	263	.772	422	127	1510	5.0	1.5	18.0

Three-point field goals: 1999-00, 54-for-149 (.362). 2001-02, 49-for-150 (.327). 2002-03, 54-for-127 (.425). Totals, 157-for-426 (.369).

HONORS: NBA All-Rookie second team (2004).

NBA REGULAR-SEASON RECORD

Season Team	G	Min.	FGM	FGA	Pct.	FTM	FTA	Pct.	REBOUNDS Off.	Def.	Tot.	Ast.	St.	Blk.	TO	Pts.	AVERAGES RPG	APG	PPG
03-04—Washington	70	2044	278	695	.400	77	98	.786	71	193	264	106	71	11	110	673	3.8	1.5	9.6
04-05—Washington	54	1560	206	530	.389	99	118	.839	41	186	227	90	49	9	62	553	4.2	1.7	10.2
05-06—Washington	21	516	77	183	.421	25	30	.833	19	57	76	27	16	1	22	196	3.6	1.3	9.3
Totals	145	4120	561	1408	.398	201	246	.817	131	436	567	223	136	21	194	1422	3.9	1.5	9.8

Three-point field goals: 2003-04, 40-for-131 (.305). 2004-05, 42-for-123 (.341). 2005-06, 17-for-47 (.362). Totals, 99-for-301 (.329).
Personal fouls/disqualifications: 2003-04, 157/1. 2004-05, 107/1. 2005-06, 38/0. Totals, 302/2.

H

HAYWOOD, BRENDAN   C   WIZARDS

PERSONAL: Born November 11, 1979, in New York. ... 7-0/268. (2.13/121.6). ... Full name: Brendan Todd Haywood
HIGH SCHOOL: Dudley (Greensboro, N.C.).
COLLEGE: North Carolina.
TRANSACTIONS/CAREER NOTES: Selected by Cleveland Cavaliers in first round (20th pick overall) of 2001 NBA Draft. ... Draft rights traded by Cavaliers to Orlando Magic for C Michael Doleac (June 27, 2001). ... Draft rights traded by Magic to Washington Wizards for G/F Laron Profit and future first-round draft choice (August 1, 2001).

COLLEGIATE RECORD

NOTES: The SPORTING NEWS All-America second team (2001).

Season Team	G	Min.	FGM	FGA	Pct.	FTM	FTA	Pct.	Reb.	Ast.	Pts.	RPG	APG	PPG
97-98—North Carolina	38	308	35	66	.530	40	63	.635	91	6	110	2.4	0.2	2.9
98-99—North Carolina	34	1035	160	247	.648	88	131	.672	235	33	408	6.9	1.0	12.0
99-00—North Carolina	36	1071	191	274	.697	106	179	.592	271	37	488	7.5	1.0	13.6
00-01—North Carolina	33	901	155	262	.592	95	184	.516	242	42	405	7.3	1.3	12.3
Totals	141	3315	541	849	.637	329	557	.591	839	118	1411	6.0	0.8	10.0

Personal fouls/disqualifications: 1997-98, 44/0. 1998-99, 96/0. 1999-00, 108/0. 2000-01, 97/0. Totals, 345/0.

NBA REGULAR-SEASON RECORD

Season Team	G	Min.	FGM	FGA	Pct.	FTM	FTA	Pct.	Off.	Def.	Tot.	Ast.	St.	Blk.	TO	Pts.	RPG	APG	PPG
01-02—Washington	62	1266	109	221	.493	97	160	.606	143	179	322	29	21	91	50	315	5.2	0.5	5.1
02-03—Washington	81	1930	173	339	.510	155	245	.633	192	212	404	29	32	119	65	501	5.0	0.4	6.2
03-04—Washington	77	1484	200	388	.515	137	234	.585	186	201	387	43	32	100	80	537	5.0	0.6	7.0
04-05—Washington	68	1865	239	427	.560	159	261	.609	202	262	464	57	52	114	96	637	6.8	0.8	9.4
05-06—Washington	79	1879	222	432	.514	131	224	.585	200	267	467	46	30	104	97	575	5.9	0.6	7.3
Totals	367	8424	943	1807	.522	679	1124	.604	923	1121	2044	204	167	528	388	2565	5.6	0.6	7.0

Three-point field goals: 2003-04, 0-for-1. Totals, 0-for-1 (.000).
Personal fouls/disqualifications: 2001-02, 158/1. 2002-03, 225/3. 2003-04, 154/0. 2004-05, 218/6. 2005-06, 232/2. Totals, 987/12.

NBA PLAYOFF RECORD

Season Team	G	Min.	FGM	FGA	Pct.	FTM	FTA	Pct.	Off.	Def.	Tot.	Ast.	St.	Blk.	TO	Pts.	RPG	APG	PPG
04-05—Washington	10	296	39	72	.542	28	44	.636	35	41	76	10	14	20	10	106	7.6	1.0	10.6
05-06—Washington	6	155	15	22	.682	13	25	.520	7	12	19	5	2	11	7	43	3.2	0.8	7.2
Totals	16	451	54	94	.574	41	69	.594	42	53	95	15	16	31	17	149	5.9	0.9	9.3

Personal fouls/disqualifications: 2004-05, 40/1. 2005-06, 22/0. Totals, 62/1.

HEAD, LUTHER   G   ROCKETS

PERSONAL: Born November 26, 1982, in Chicago, Ill. ... 6-3/185. (1.91/83.9). ... Full name: Luther D. Head
HIGH SCHOOL: Manley Career Academy (Chicago).
COLLEGE: Illinois.
TRANSACTIONS/CAREER NOTES: Selected by Houston Rockets in first round (24th pick overall) of 2005 NBA Draft.

COLLEGIATE RECORD

Season Team	G	Min.	FGM	FGA	Pct.	FTM	FTA	Pct.	Reb.	Ast.	Pts.	RPG	APG	PPG
01-02—Illinois	35	581	63	124	.508	14	25	.560	67	59	156	1.9	1.7	4.5
02-03—Illinois	25	509	68	131	.519	34	46	.739	71	42	198	2.8	1.7	7.9
03-04—Illinois	29	863	107	239	.448	56	72	.778	110	75	319	3.8	2.6	11.0
04-05—Illinois	39	1297	214	462	.463	78	99	.788	155	150	622	4.0	3.8	15.9
Totals	128	3250	452	956	.473	182	242	.752	403	326	1295	3.1	2.5	10.1

Three-point field goals: 2001-02, 16-for-55 (.291). 2002-03, 28-for-66 (.424). 2003-04, 49-for-143 (.343). 2004-05, 116-for-283 (.410). Totals, 209-for-547 (.382).

NBA REGULAR-SEASON RECORD

HONORS: NBA All-Rookie second team (2006).

Season Team	G	Min.	FGM	FGA	Pct.	FTM	FTA	Pct.	Off.	Def.	Tot.	Ast.	St.	Blk.	TO	Pts.	RPG	APG	PPG
05-06—Houston	80	2310	254	630	.403	86	123	.699	33	233	266	215	89	9	119	707	3.3	2.7	8.8

Three-point field goals: 2005-06, 113-for-313 (.361). Totals, 113-for-313 (.361).
Personal fouls/disqualifications: 2005-06, 169/2. Totals, 169/2.

HENDERSON, ALAN   F   CAVALIERS

PERSONAL: Born December 2, 1972, in Indianapolis. ... 6-9/240. (2.06/108.9). ... Full name: Alan Lybrooks Henderson
HIGH SCHOOL: Brebeuf Prep (Indianapolis).
COLLEGE: Indiana.
TRANSACTIONS/CAREER NOTES: Selected by Atlanta Hawks in first round (16th pick overall) of 1995 NBA Draft. ... Traded by Hawks with G Jason Terry and a future first-round draft choice to Dallas Mavericks for F Antoine Walker and G Tony Delk (August 4, 2004). ... Traded by Mavericks with C Calvin Booth to Milwaukee Bucks for F Keith Van Horn (February 24, 2005). ... Waived by Bucks (February 25, 2005). ... Signed as free agent by Dallas Mavericks (March 1, 2005). ... Signed as free agent by Cleveland Cavaliers (September 17, 2005).

H

Season Team	G	Min.	FGM	FGA	Pct.	FTM	FTA	Pct.	Reb.	Ast.	Pts.	AVERAGES		
												RPG	APG	PPG
91-92—Indiana	33	783	151	297	.508	80	121	.661	238	17	383	7.2	0.5	11.6
92-93—Indiana	30	737	130	267	.487	72	113	.637	243	27	333	8.1	0.9	11.1
93-94—Indiana	30	983	198	373	.531	136	207	.657	308	36	534	10.3	1.2	17.8
94-95—Indiana	31	1093	284	476	.597	159	251	.633	302	54	729	9.7	1.7	23.5
Totals	124	3596	763	1413	.540	447	692	.646	1091	134	1979	8.8	1.1	16.0

Three-point field goals: 1991-92, 1-for-4 (.250). 1992-93, 1-for-6 (.167). 1993-94, 2-for-6 (.333). 1994-95, 2-for-10 (.200). Totals, 6-for-26 (.231).

HONORS: NBA Most Improved Player (1998).

NBA REGULAR-SEASON RECORD

Season Team	G	Min.	FGM	FGA	Pct.	FTM	FTA	Pct.	REBOUNDS			Ast.	St.	Blk.	TO	Pts.	AVERAGES		
									Off.	Def.	Tot.						RPG	APG	PPG
95-96—Atlanta	79	1416	192	434	.442	119	200	.595	164	192	356	51	44	43	87	503	4.5	0.6	6.4
96-97—Atlanta	30	501	77	162	.475	45	75	.600	47	69	116	23	21	6	29	199	3.9	0.8	6.6
97-98—Atlanta	69	2000	365	753	.485	253	388	.652	199	243	442	73	42	36	110	986	6.4	1.1	14.3
98-99—Atlanta	38	1142	187	423	.442	100	149	.671	100	150	250	28	33	19	58	474	6.6	0.7	12.5
99-00—Atlanta	82	2775	429	930	.461	224	334	.671	265	306	571	77	81	54	139	1083	7.0	0.9	13.2
00-01—Atlanta	73	1810	298	671	.444	173	271	.638	180	226	406	50	51	29	126	769	5.6	0.7	10.5
01-02—Atlanta	26	422	59	116	.509	24	45	.533	31	66	97	11	11	15	21	143	3.7	0.4	5.5
02-03—Atlanta	82	1494	153	327	.468	88	138	.638	156	242	398	41	33	32	61	394	4.9	0.5	4.8
03-04—Atlanta	6	68	10	21	.476	4	6	.667	11	10	21	2	1	2	3	24	3.5	0.3	4.0
04-05—Dallas	78	1203	116	220	.527	41	76	.539	164	184	348	21	29	37	49	273	4.5	0.3	3.5
05-06—Cleveland	51	531	47	91	.516	33	49	.673	60	77	137	10	9	12	22	127	2.7	0.2	2.5
Totals	614	13362	1933	4148	.466	1104	1731	.638	1377	1765	3142	387	355	285	705	4975	5.1	0.6	8.1

Three-point field goals: 1995-96, 0-for-3. 1997-98, 3-for-6 (.500). 1998-99, 0-for-1. 1999-00, 1-for-10 (.100). 2000-01, 0-for-1. 2001-02, 1-for-1 (1.000). 2002-03, 0-for-2. 2004-05, 0-for-2. 2005-06, 5-for-26 (.192).

Personal fouls/disqualifications: 1995-96, 217/5. 1996-97, 73/1. 1997-98, 175/1. 1998-99, 96/1. 1999-00, 233/3. 2000-01, 164/2. 2001-02, 40/0. 2002-03, 168/1. 2003-04, 1/0. 2004-05, 149/1. 2005-06, 58/0. Totals, 1374/15.

NBA PLAYOFF RECORD

Season Team	G	Min.	FGM	FGA	Pct.	FTM	FTA	Pct.	REBOUNDS			Ast.	St.	Blk.	TO	Pts.	AVERAGES		
									Off.	Def.	Tot.						RPG	APG	PPG
95-96—Atlanta	10	145	23	40	.575	7	10	.700	17	10	27	7	1	4	9	53	2.7	0.7	5.3
96-97—Atlanta	10	136	19	34	.559	20	26	.769	11	22	33	0	1	3	7	58	3.3	0.0	5.8
97-98—Atlanta	4	126	20	38	.526	11	18	.611	10	12	22	4	3	1	6	51	5.5	1.0	12.8
98-99—Atlanta	1	4	0	0	...	0	0	...	0	0	0	0	0	0	0	0	0.0	0.0	0.0
04-05—Dallas	9	92	8	14	.571	2	2	1.000	11	6	17	0	2	2	2	18	1.9	0.0	2.0
05-06—Cleveland	2	9	0	2	.000	0	0	...	1	1	2	0	0	0	0	0	1.0	0.0	0.0
Totals	36	512	70	128	.547	40	56	.714	50	51	101	11	7	10	24	180	2.8	0.3	5.0

Three-point field goals: 1997-98, 0-for-1. Totals, 0-for-1 (.000).

Personal fouls/disqualifications: 1995-96, 20/0. 1996-97, 26/0. 1997-98, 13/0. 1998-99, 1/0. 2004-05, 15/0. 2005-06, 1/0. Totals, 76/0.

HILL, GRANT   F   MAGIC

PERSONAL: Born October 5, 1972, in Dallas. ... 6-8/225. (2.03/102.1). ... Full name: Grant Henry Hill ... Son of Calvin Hill, running back with three NFL teams (1969-74 and 1976-81) and the Hawaii Hawaiians of the World Football League (1975). **HIGH SCHOOL:** South Lakes (Reston, Va.). **COLLEGE:** Duke. **TRANSACTIONS/CAREER NOTES:** Selected by Detroit Pistons in first round (third pick overall) of 1994 NBA Draft. ... Traded by Pistons to Orlando Magic for G Chucky Atkins and F Ben Wallace (August 3, 2000). **MISCELLANEOUS:** Member of gold-medal-winning U.S. Olympic team (1996).

COLLEGIATE RECORD

NOTES: THE SPORTING NEWS All-America first team (1994). ... Member of NCAA Division I championship team (1991, 1992).

Season Team	G	Min.	FGM	FGA	Pct.	FTM	FTA	Pct.	Reb.	Ast.	Pts.	AVERAGES		
												RPG	APG	PPG
90-91—Duke	36	887	160	310	.516	81	133	.609	185	79	402	5.1	2.2	11.2
91-92—Duke	33	1000	182	298	.611	99	135	.733	187	134	463	5.7	4.1	14.0
92-93—Duke	26	822	185	320	.578	94	126	.746	166	72	468	6.4	2.8	18.0
93-94—Duke	34	1213	218	472	.462	116	165	.703	233	176	591	6.9	5.2	17.4
Totals	129	3922	745	1400	.532	390	559	.698	771	461	1924	6.0	3.6	14.9

Three-point field goals: 1990-91, 1-for-2 (.500). 1991-92, 0-for-1. 1992-93, 4-for-14 (.286). 1993-94, 39-for-100 (.390). Totals, 44-for-117 (.376).

NBA REGULAR-SEASON RECORD

HONORS: NBA Co-Rookie of the Year (1995). ... IBM Award, for all-around contributions to team's success (1997). ... All-NBA first team (1997). ... All-NBA second team (1996, 1998, 1999, 2000). ... NBA All-Rookie first team (1995).

Season Team	G	Min.	FGM	FGA	Pct.	FTM	FTA	Pct.	REBOUNDS			Ast.	St.	Blk.	TO	Pts.	AVERAGES		
									Off.	Def.	Tot.						RPG	APG	PPG
94-95—Detroit	70	2678	508	1064	.477	374	511	.732	125	320	445	353	124	62	202	1394	6.4	5.0	19.9
95-96—Detroit	80	3260	564	1221	.462	485	646	.751	127	656	783	548	100	48	263	1618	9.8	6.9	20.2
96-97—Detroit	80	3147	625	1259	.496	450	633	.711	123	598	721	583	144	48	259	1710	9.0	7.3	21.4
97-98—Detroit	81	3294	615	1361	.452	479	647	.740	93	530	623	551	143	53	285	1712	7.7	6.8	21.1
98-99—Detroit	50	1852	384	802	.479	285	379	.752	65	290	355	300	80	27	184	1053	7.1	6.0	21.1
99-00—Detroit	74	2776	696	1422	.489	480	604	.795	97	393	490	385	103	43	240	1906	6.6	5.2	25.8
00-01—Orlando	4	133	19	43	.442	16	26	.615	8	17	25	25	5	2	11	55	6.3	6.3	13.8
01-02—Orlando	14	512	83	195	.426	69	80	.863	29	96	125	64	8	4	37	235	8.9	4.6	16.8
02-03—Orlando	29	843	151	307	.492	118	144	.819	40	166	206	122	28	13	84	421	7.1	4.2	14.5
03-04—Orlando							Did not play—injured												

H

Season Team	G	Min.	FGM	FGA	Pct.	FTM	FTA	Pct.	REBOUNDS Off.	Def.	Tot.	Ast.	St.	Blk.	TO	Pts.	AVERAGES RPG	APG	PPG
04-05—Orlando	67	2338	517	1015	.509	280	341	.821	77	241	318	220	97	28	161	1317	4.7	3.3	19.7
05-06—Orlando	21	613	119	243	.490	78	102	.765	15	65	80	48	24	6	35	318	3.8	2.3	15.1
Totals	570	21446	4281	8932	.479	3114	4113	.757	799	3372	4171	3199	856	334	1761	11739	7.3	5.6	20.6

Three-point field goals: 1994-95, 4-for-27 (.148). 1995-96, 5-for-26 (.192). 1996-97, 10-for-33 (.303). 1997-98, 3-for-21 (.143). 1998-99, 0-for-14. 1999-00, 34-for-98 (.347). 2000-01, 1-for-1 (1.000). 2001-02, 0-for-2. 2002-03, 1-for-4 (.250). 2004-05, 3-for-13 (.231). 2005-06, 2-for-8 (.250). Totals, 63-for-247 (.255).

Personal fouls/disqualifications: 1994-95, 203/1. 1995-96, 242/1. 1996-97, 186/0. 1997-98, 196/1. 1998-99, 114/0. 1999-00, 190/0. 2000-01, 9/0. 2001-02, 40/2. 2002-03, 46/0. 2004-05, 144/1. 2005-06, 50/0. Totals, 1420/6.

NBA PLAYOFF RECORD

Season Team	G	Min.	FGM	FGA	Pct.	FTM	FTA	Pct.	REBOUNDS Off.	Def.	Tot.	Ast.	St.	Blk.	TO	Pts.	AVERAGES RPG	APG	PPG
95-96—Detroit	3	115	22	39	.564	12	14	.857	4	18	22	11	3	0	8	57	7.3	3.7	19.0
96-97—Detroit	5	203	45	103	.437	28	39	.718	13	21	34	27	4	5	19	118	6.8	5.4	23.6
98-99—Detroit	5	176	42	92	.457	13	16	.813	7	29	36	37	10	2	12	97	7.2	7.4	19.4
99-00—Detroit	2	55	6	16	.375	9	10	.900	0	11	11	9	1	0	10	22	5.5	4.5	11.0
Totals	15	549	115	250	.460	62	79	.785	24	79	103	84	18	7	49	294	6.9	5.6	19.6

Three-point field goals: 1995-96, 1-for-2 (.500). 1998-99, 0-for-1. 1999-00, 1-for-2 (.500). Totals, 2-for-5 (.400).

Personal fouls/disqualifications: 1995-96, 13/0. 1996-97, 14/0. 1998-99, 12/0. 1999-00, 7/0. Totals, 46/0.

NBA ALL-STAR GAME RECORD

Season Team	Min.	FGM	FGA	Pct.	FTM	FTA	Pct.	REBOUNDS Off.	Def.	Tot.	Ast.	PF	Dq.	St.	Blk.	TO	Pts.
1995—Detroit	20	5	8	.625	0	4	.000	0	0	0	3	2	0	2	0	1	10
1996—Detroit	26	6	10	.600	2	2	1.000	1	2	3	2	1	0	1	0	2	14
1997—Detroit	22	4	7	.571	3	4	.750	2	1	3	2	2	0	1	1	3	11
1998—Detroit	28	7	11	.636	0	0	...	0	3	3	5	1	0	1	0	0	15
2000—Detroit	19	3	7	.429	1	1	1.000	0	3	3	5	0	0	1	0	3	7
2001—Orlando							Selected, did not play—injured										
2005—Orlando	18	3	6	.500	0	0	...	1	2	3	2	1	0	1	0	1	6
Totals	133	28	49	.571	6	11	.545	4	11	15	19	7	0	7	1	10	63

Three-point field goals: 1998, 1-for-1 (1.000). 2000, 0-for-1. Totals, 1-for-2 (.500).

HINRICH, KIRK   G   BULLS

PERSONAL: Born January 2, 1981, in Sioux City, Iowa. ... 6-3/190. (1.91/86.2). ... Full name: Kirk James Hinrich
HIGH SCHOOL: Sioux City West (Sioux City, Iowa).
COLLEGE: Kansas.
TRANSACTIONS/CAREER NOTES: Selected by Chicago Bulls in first round (seventh pick overall) of 2003 NBA Draft.

COLLEGIATE RECORD

NOTES: The SPORTING NEWS All-America third team (2002, 2003).

Season Team	G	Min.	FGM	FGA	Pct.	FTM	FTA	Pct.	Reb.	Ast.	Pts.	AVERAGES RPG	APG	PPG
99-00—Kansas	34	726	69	161	.429	25	34	.735	82	123	188	2.4	3.6	5.5
00-01—Kansas	33	1079	116	232	.500	91	108	.843	134	229	378	4.1	6.9	11.5
01-02—Kansas	37	1142	198	366	.541	84	104	.808	177	186	546	4.8	5.0	14.8
02-03—Kansas	37	1241	232	488	.475	88	125	.704	139	130	641	3.8	3.5	17.3
Totals	141	4188	615	1247	.493	288	371	.776	532	668	1753	3.8	4.7	12.4

Three-point field goals: 1999-00, 25-for-80 (.313). 2000-01, 55-for-109 (.505). 2001-02, 66-for-138 (.478). 2002-03, 89-for-219 (.406). Totals, 235-for-546 (.430).

NBA REGULAR-SEASON RECORD

HONORS: NBA All-Rookie first team (2004).

Season Team	G	Min.	FGM	FGA	Pct.	FTM	FTA	Pct.	REBOUNDS Off.	Def.	Tot.	Ast.	St.	Blk.	TO	Pts.	AVERAGES RPG	APG	PPG
03-04—Chicago	76	2706	318	823	.386	135	168	.804	42	217	259	517	101	21	204	915	3.4	6.8	12.0
04-05—Chicago	77	2800	445	1122	.397	171	216	.792	32	272	304	494	122	21	176	1206	3.9	6.4	15.7
05-06—Chicago	81	2955	451	1078	.418	256	314	.815	29	259	288	514	94	21	188	1284	3.6	6.3	15.9
Totals	234	8461	1214	3023	.402	562	698	.805	103	748	851	1525	317	63	568	3405	3.6	6.5	14.6

Three-point field goals: 2003-04, 144-for-369 (.390). 2004-05, 145-for-408 (.355). 2005-06, 126-for-341 (.370). Totals, 415-for-1118 (.371).
Personal fouls/disqualifications: 2003-04, 276/9. 2004-05, 254/5. 2005-06, 251/4. Totals, 771/22.

NBA PLAYOFF RECORD

Season Team	G	Min.	FGM	FGA	Pct.	FTM	FTA	Pct.	REBOUNDS Off.	Def.	Tot.	Ast.	St.	Blk.	TO	Pts.	AVERAGES RPG	APG	PPG
04-05—Chicago	6	213	45	100	.450	20	29	.690	4	18	22	35	12	4	14	127	3.7	5.8	21.2
05-06—Chicago	6	234	39	94	.415	36	42	.857	0	20	20	46	8	2	24	123	3.3	7.7	20.5
Totals	12	447	84	194	.433	56	71	.789	4	38	42	81	20	6	38	250	3.5	6.8	20.8

Three-point field goals: 2004-05, 17-for-33 (.515). 2005-06, 9-for-26 (.346). Totals, 26-for-59 (.441).
Personal fouls/disqualifications: 2004-05, 18/0. 2005-06, 22/1. Totals, 40/1.

HODGE, JULIUS   G   NUGGETS

PERSONAL: Born November 18, 1983, in New York. ... 6-7/210. (2.01/95.3). ... Full name: Julius Melvin Hodge
HIGH SCHOOL: St. Raymond's (Bronx, N.Y.).
COLLEGE: North Carolina State.
TRANSACTIONS/CAREER NOTES: Selected by Denver Nuggets in first round (20th pick overall) of 2005 NBA Draft.

H

COLLEGIATE RECORD

NOTES: The SPORTING NEWS All-America first team (2004).

Season Team	G	Min.	FGM	FGA	Pct.	FTM	FTA	Pct.	Reb.	Ast.	Pts.	RPG	APG	PPG
												AVERAGES		
01-02—North Carolina State.......	33	907	115	260	.442	89	120	.742	160	71	352	4.8	2.2	10.7
02-03—North Carolina State.......	31	1093	164	374	.439	179	219	.817	190	109	548	6.1	3.5	17.7
03-04—North Carolina State.......	31	1081	189	373	.507	159	192	.828	198	112	563	6.4	3.6	18.2
04-05—North Carolina State.......	34	1177	197	400	.493	169	53	3.189	225	162	577	6.6	4.8	17.0
Totals	129	4258	665	1407	.473	596	584	1.021	773	454	2040	6.0	3.5	15.8

Three-point field goals: 2001-02, 33-for-95 (.347). 2002-03, 41-for-125 (.328). 2003-04, 26-for-72 (.361). 2004-05, 14-for-55 (.255). Totals, 114-for-347 (.329).

NBA REGULAR-SEASON RECORD

Season Team	G	Min.	FGM	FGA	Pct.	FTM	FTA	Pct.	REBOUNDS			Ast.	St.	Blk.	TO	Pts.	AVERAGES		
									Off.	Def.	Tot.						RPG	APG	PPG
05-06—Denver	14	33	5	13	.385	3	8	.375	5	2	7	6	2	0	8	13	0.5	0.4	0.9

Personal fouls/disqualifications: 2005-06, 7/0. Totals, 7/0.

NBA DEVELOPMENT LEAGUE RECORD

Season Team	G	Min.	FGM	FGA	Pct.	FTM	FTA	Pct.	Reb.	Ast.	Pts.	RPG	APG	PPG
												AVERAGES		
05-06—Austin............................	11	331	66	134	.493	58	78	.744	61	30	195	5.5	2.7	17.7

Three-point field goals: 2005-06, 5-for-11 (.455). Totals, 5-for-11 (.455).

HOLCOMB, RANDY   F

PERSONAL: Born August 8, 1979, in Chicago. ... 6-9/220. (2.06/99.8). ... Full name: Randy Alfred Holcomb.
HIGH SCHOOL: Lincoln Park (Chicago).
JUNIOR COLLEGE: Los Angeles City College.
COLLEGE: Fresno State, then San Diego State.
TRANSACTIONS/CAREER NOTES: Selected by San Antonio Spurs in second round (57th pick overall) of 2002 NBA Draft. ... Draft rights traded by Spurs with F/C Mark Bryant and draft rights to G/F John Salmons to Philadelphia 76ers for G Craig Claxton (June 26, 2002). ... Played in Poland (2002-03). ... Traded by 76ers with first-round draft pick and cash considerations to Atlanta Hawks in three-team deal in which 76ers also dealt F Keith Van Horn to New York Knicks and acquired F Glenn Robinson and a 2006 second-round pick from Atlanta Hawks and F/C Marc Jackson from Minnesota Timberwolves. Timberwolves acquired G Latrell Sprewell from Knicks and traded G Terrell Brandon to Hawks (July 23, 2003) ... Waived by Hawks (October 27, 2003). ... Played in Greece and Venezuela (2004-05). ... Played in CBA (2005-06). ... Played in Spain (2005-06). ... Signed to 10-day contract by Chicago Bulls (January 6, 2006).

COLLEGIATE RECORD

Season Team	G	Min.	FGM	FGA	Pct.	FTM	FTA	Pct.	Reb.	Ast.	Pts.	RPG	APG	PPG
												AVERAGES		
97-98—Fresno State						Did not play—ineligible.								
98-99—Fresno State	31	429	63	128	.492	30	53	.566	93	18	164	3.0	0.6	5.3
99-00—Los Angeles City College						Statistics unavailable								
00-01—San Diego State.............	28	863	163	386	.422	99	145	.683	185	40	444	6.6	1.4	15.9
01-02—San Diego State.............	33	1067	220	426	.516	106	167	.635	296	57	558	9.0	1.7	16.9
Junior College Totals.............	...	...	...	...	...	...	...	...	...	...	...	...	...	...
4-Year-College Totals	92	2359	446	940	.474	235	365	.644	574	115	1166	6.2	1.3	12.7

Three-point field goals: 1998-99, 8-for-19 (.421). 2000-01, 19-for-65 (.292). 2001-02, 12-for-40 (.300). Totals, 39-for-124 (.315).

POLISH LEAGUE RECORD

Season Team	G	Min.	FGM	FGA	Pct.	FTM	FTA	Pct.	Reb.	Ast.	Pts.	RPG	APG	PPG
												AVERAGES		
02-03—Wroclaw	11	270	58	103	.563	39	51	.765	58	7	161	5.3	0.6	14.6

Three-point field goals: 2002-03, 6-for-19 (.316). Totals, 6-for-19 (.316).

GREEK LEAGUE RECORD

Season Team	G	Min.	FGM	FGA	Pct.	FTM	FTA	Pct.	Reb.	Ast.	Pts.	RPG	APG	PPG
												AVERAGES		
04-05—Apollon Patras...............	3	88	10	23	.435	4	8	.500	13	3	27	4.3	1.0	9.0

Three-point field goals: 2004-05, 3-for-6 (.500). Totals, 3-for-6 (.500).

VENEZUELAN LEAGUE RECORD

Season Team	G	Min.	FGM	FGA	Pct.	FTM	FTA	Pct.	Reb.	Ast.	Pts.	RPG	APG	PPG
												AVERAGES		
04-05—Caracas	41	1356	261	487	.536	216	316	.684	275	96	757	6.7	2.3	18.5

Three-point field goals: 2004-05, 19-for-54 (.352). Totals, 19-for-54 (.352).

CBA RECORD

Season Team	G	Min.	FGM	FGA	Pct.	FTM	FTA	Pct.	Reb.	Ast.	Pts.	RPG	APG	PPG
												AVERAGES		
05-06—Gary	34	1256	243	495	.491	159	234	.679	247	104	652	7.3	3.1	19.2

Three-point field goals: 2005-06, 7-for-30 (.233). Totals, 7-for-30 (.233).

NBA REGULAR-SEASON RECORD

Season Team	G	Min.	FGM	FGA	Pct.	FTM	FTA	Pct.	REBOUNDS			Ast.	St.	Blk.	TO	Pts.	AVERAGES		
									Off.	Def.	Tot.						RPG	APG	PPG
05-06—Chicago	4	11	1	1	1.000	0	0	...	1	0	1	0	0	0	0	2	0.3	0.0	0.5

Personal fouls/disqualifications: 2005-06, 2/0. Totals, 2/0.

H

Season Team	G	Min.	FGM	FGA	Pct.	FTM	FTA	Pct.	Reb.	Ast.	Pts.	AVERAGES		
												RPG	APG	PPG
05-06—Joventut	8	167	30	53	.566	19	31	.613	27	5	81	3.4	0.6	10.1

Three-point field goals: 2005-06, 2-for-12 (.167). Totals, 2-for-12 (.167).

HORRY, ROBERT — F — SPURS

PERSONAL: Born August 25, 1970, in Hartford, Md. ... 6-10/235. (2.08/106.6). ... Full name: Robert Keith Horry ... Name pronounced OR-ee.
HIGH SCHOOL: Andalusia (Ala.).
COLLEGE: Alabama.
TRANSACTIONS/CAREER NOTES: Selected by Houston Rockets in first round (11th pick overall) of 1992 NBA Draft. ... Traded by Rockets with F Matt Bullard and two future second-round draft choices to Detroit Pistons for F Sean Elliott (February 4, 1994); trade voided when Elliott failed physical (February 7, 1994). ... Traded by Rockets with G Sam Cassell, F Chucky Brown and F Mark Bryant to Phoenix Suns for F Charles Barkley and 1999 second-round draft choice (August 19, 1996). ... Traded by Suns with C Joe Kleine to Los Angeles Lakers for F Cedric Ceballos and G Rumeal Robinson (January 10, 1997). ... Signed as free agent by San Antonio Spurs (July 24, 2003).
MISCELLANEOUS: Member of NBA championship team (1994, 1995, 2000, 2001, 2002, 2005).

COLLEGIATE RECORD

Season Team	G	Min.	FGM	FGA	Pct.	FTM	FTA	Pct.	Reb.	Ast.	Pts.	AVERAGES		
												RPG	APG	PPG
88-89—Alabama	31	590	79	185	.427	38	59	.644	156	35	200	5.0	1.1	6.5
89-90—Alabama	35	1022	164	351	.467	79	104	.760	217	9	457	6.2	0.3	13.1
90-91—Alabama	32	959	133	296	.449	82	102	.804	260	56	381	8.1	1.8	11.9
91-92—Alabama	35	1185	196	417	.470	120	165	.727	296	88	554	8.5	2.5	15.8
Totals	133	3756	572	1249	.458	319	430	.742	929	188	1592	7.0	1.4	12.0

Three-point field goals: 1988-89, 4-for-13 (.308). 1989-90, 50-for-117 (.427). 1990-91, 33-for-98 (.337). 1991-92, 42-for-120 (.350). Totals, 129-for-348 (.371).

NBA REGULAR-SEASON RECORD

HONORS: NBA All-Rookie second team (1993).

Season Team	G	Min.	FGM	FGA	Pct.	FTM	FTA	Pct.	REBOUNDS			Ast.	St.	Blk.	TO	Pts.	AVERAGES		
									Off.	Def.	Tot.						RPG	APG	PPG
92-93—Houston..........	79	2330	323	682	.474	143	200	.715	113	279	392	191	80	83	156	801	5.0	2.4	10.1
93-94—Houston..........	81	2370	322	702	.459	115	157	.732	128	312	440	231	119	75	137	803	5.4	2.9	9.9
94-95—Houston..........	64	2074	240	537	.447	86	113	.761	81	243	324	216	94	76	122	652	5.1	3.4	10.2
95-96—Houston..........	71	2634	300	732	.410	111	143	.776	97	315	412	281	116	109	160	853	5.8	4.0	12.0
96-97—Phoe.-L.A.L.	54	1395	157	360	.436	60	90	.667	68	169	237	110	66	55	72	423	4.4	2.0	7.8
97-98—L.A. Lakers	72	2192	200	420	.476	117	169	.692	186	356	542	163	112	94	99	536	7.5	2.3	7.4
98-99—L.A. Lakers	38	744	67	146	.459	34	46	.739	56	96	152	56	36	39	49	188	4.0	1.5	4.9
99-00—L.A. Lakers	76	1685	159	363	.438	89	113	.788	133	228	361	118	84	80	73	436	4.8	1.6	5.7
00-01—L.A. Lakers	80	1881	161	410	.393	81	111	.730	117	300	417	218	90	70	107	462	5.2	2.7	5.8
01-02—L.A. Lakers	81	2140	183	460	.398	108	138	.783	130	349	479	232	77	89	88	550	5.9	2.9	6.8
02-03—L.A. Lakers	80	2343	184	476	.387	103	134	.769	181	333	514	233	96	61	112	522	6.4	2.9	6.5
03-04—San Antonio....	81	1290	141	348	.405	69	107	.645	108	164	272	101	48	49	55	392	3.4	1.2	4.8
04-05—San Antonio....	75	1396	157	375	.419	86	109	.789	91	177	268	80	67	60	69	451	3.6	1.1	6.0
05-06—San Antonio....	63	1182	112	292	.384	44	68	.647	71	171	242	79	43	51	41	321	3.8	1.3	5.1
Totals	994	25362	2692	6273	.429	1224	1670	.733	1536	3395	4931	2219	1092	975	1312	7335	5.0	2.2	7.4

Three-point field goals: 1992-93, 12-for-47 (.255). 1993-94, 44-for-136 (.324). 1994-95, 86-for-227 (.379). 1995-96, 142-for-388 (.366). 1996-97, 49-for-154 (.318). 1997-98, 19-for-93 (.204). 1998-99, 20-for-45 (.444). 1999-00, 29-for-94 (.309). 2000-01, 54-for-156 (.346). 2001-02, 76-for-203 (.374). 2002-03, 51-for-177 (.288). 2003-04, 41-for-108 (.380). 2004-05, 51-for-138 (.370). 2005-06, 53-for-144 (.368). Totals, 727-for-2110 (.345).

Personal fouls/disqualifications: 1992-93, 210/1. 1993-94, 186/0. 1994-95, 161/0. 1995-96, 197/3. 1996-97, 153/2. 1997-98, 238/5. 1998-99, 103/2. 1999-00, 189/0. 2000-01, 210/3. 2001-02, 208/1. 2002-03, 247/2. 2003-04, 165/0. 2004-05, 138/1. 2005-06, 115/2. Totals, 2520/22.

NBA PLAYOFF RECORD

NOTES: Holds NBA Finals single-game record for most steals—7 (June 9, 1995, at Orlando). ... Holds single-game playoff records for most three-point field goals, none missed—7 (May 6, 1997, vs. Utah).

Season Team	G	Min.	FGM	FGA	Pct.	FTM	FTA	Pct.	REBOUNDS			Ast.	St.	Blk.	TO	Pts.	AVERAGES		
									Off.	Def.	Tot.						RPG	APG	PPG
92-93—Houston..........	12	374	47	101	.465	20	27	.741	14	48	62	38	18	16	28	123	5.2	3.2	10.3
93-94—Houston..........	23	778	98	226	.434	39	51	.765	40	101	141	82	35	20	27	269	6.1	3.6	11.7
94-95—Houston..........	22	841	93	209	.445	58	78	.744	40	115	155	76	32	26	25	288	7.0	3.5	13.1
95-96—Houston..........	8	308	37	91	.407	10	23	.435	15	42	57	24	21	13	15	105	7.1	3.0	13.1
96-97—L.A. Lakers	9	279	17	38	.447	14	18	.778	12	36	48	13	10	7	11	60	5.3	1.4	6.7
97-98—L.A. Lakers	13	422	39	70	.557	28	41	.683	34	50	84	40	14	14	18	112	6.5	3.1	8.6
98-99—L.A. Lakers	8	177	12	26	.462	11	14	.786	10	26	36	11	6	6	7	40	4.5	1.4	5.0
99-00—L.A. Lakers	23	618	59	145	.407	40	57	.702	38	85	123	58	20	19	30	175	5.3	2.5	7.6
00-01—L.A. Lakers	16	382	32	87	.368	13	22	.591	30	53	83	31	22	16	18	94	5.2	1.9	5.9
01-02—L.A. Lakers	19	703	61	136	.449	30	38	.789	36	118	154	61	33	16	30	176	8.1	3.2	9.3
02-03—L.A. Lakers	12	373	30	94	.319	5	9	.556	23	57	80	37	15	12	17	67	6.7	3.1	5.6
03-04—San Antonio....	10	211	20	43	.465	13	14	.929	25	38	63	9	8	2	10	61	6.3	0.9	6.1
04-05—San Antonio....	23	618	73	163	.448	30	41	.732	46	79	125	47	21	20	20	214	5.4	2.0	9.3
05-06—San Antonio....	13	224	15	37	.405	19	26	.731	19	29	48	11	5	9	10	55	3.7	0.8	4.2
Totals	211	6308	633	1466	.432	330	459	.719	382	877	1259	538	260	196	266	1839	6.0	2.5	8.7

Three-point field goals: 1992-93, 9-for-30 (.300). 1993-94, 34-for-89 (.382). 1994-95, 44-for-110 (.400). 1995-96, 21-for-53 (.396). 1996-97, 12-for-28 (.429). 1997-98, 6-for-17 (.353). 1998-99, 5-for-12 (.417). 1999-00, 17-for-59 (.288). 2000-01, 17-for-47 (.362). 2001-02, 24-for-62 (.387). 2002-03, 2-for-38 (.053). 2003-04, 8-for-22 (.364). 2004-05, 38-for-85 (.447). 2005-06, 6-for-17 (.353). Totals, 243-for-669 (.363).

Personal fouls/disqualifications: 1992-93, 30/1. 1993-94, 68/0. 1994-95, 69/2. 1995-96, 29/1. 1996-97, 27/0. 1997-98, 45/0. 1998-99, 29/1. 1999-00, 88/3. 2000-01, 50/0. 2001-02, 66/1. 2002-03, 37/0. 2003-04, 31/0. 2004-05, 53/0. 2005-06, 31/0. Totals, 653/9.

H

HOUSE, EDDIE   G   NETS

PERSONAL: Born May 14, 1978, in Berkeley, Calif. ... 6-0/176. (1.83/79.8). ... Full name: Edward L. House ... Son-in-law of Henry Bibby, guard with New York Knicks (1972-73 through 1974-75), New Orleans Jazz (1974-75 and 1975-76), Philadelphia 76ers (1976-77 through 1979-80) and San Diego Clippers (1980-81); brother-in-law of Mike Bibby, guard, Sacramento Kings.
HIGH SCHOOL: Hayward (Union City, Calif.).
COLLEGE: Arizona State.
TRANSACTIONS/CAREER NOTES: Selected by Miami Heat in second round (37th pick overall) of 2000 NBA Draft. ... Signed as free agent by Los Angeles Clippers (August 13, 2003). ... Traded by Clippers with F/C Melvin Ely to Charlotte Bobcats for second-round draft choices in 2005 and 2006 (July 14, 2004). ... Waived by Bobcats (December 4, 2004). ... Signed by Milwaukee Bucks (December 18, 2004). ... Claimed on waivers by Sacramento Kings (January 7, 2005). ... Signed as free agent by Phoenix Suns (September 12, 2005). ... Signed as free agent by New Jersey Nets (August 17, 2006).

COLLEGIATE RECORD

Season Team	G	Min.	FGM	FGA	Pct.	FTM	FTA	Pct.	Reb.	Ast.	Pts.	RPG	APG	PPG
96-97—Arizona State	30	886	151	363	.416	18	28	.643	84	108	377	2.8	3.6	12.6
97-98—Arizona State	32	983	143	331	.432	22	29	.759	96	93	363	3.0	2.9	11.3
98-99—Arizona State	30	1106	206	477	.432	91	115	.791	147	93	568	4.9	3.1	18.9
99-00—Arizona State	32	1189	263	623	.422	137	164	.835	175	111	736	5.5	3.5	23.0
Totals	124	4164	763	1794	.425	268	336	.798	502	405	2044	4.0	3.3	16.5

Three-point field goals: 1996-97, 57-for-179 (.318). 1997-98, 55-for-137 (.401). 1998-99, 65-for-167 (.389). 1999-00, 73-for-200 (.365). Totals, 250-for-683 (.366).

NBA REGULAR-SEASON RECORD

Season Team	G	Min.	FGM	FGA	Pct.	FTM	FTA	Pct.	Off.	Def.	Tot.	Ast.	St.	Blk.	TO	Pts.	RPG	APG	PPG
00-01—Miami	50	550	104	247	.421	24	35	.686	5	37	42	52	13	0	35	251	0.8	1.0	5.0
01-02—Miami	64	1230	209	524	.399	42	49	.857	17	93	110	123	43	5	80	514	1.7	1.9	8.0
02-03—Miami	55	1025	172	444	.387	31	36	.861	17	84	101	87	44	1	46	411	1.8	1.6	7.5
03-04—L.A. Clippers	60	1188	161	449	.359	36	45	.800	28	110	138	148	65	4	63	409	2.3	2.5	6.8
04-05—Char.-Mil.-Sac.	68	891	165	366	.451	23	27	.852	16	67	83	96	44	6	35	397	1.2	1.4	5.8
05-06—Phoenix	81	1421	320	759	.422	33	41	.805	15	117	132	148	42	12	76	796	1.6	1.8	9.8
Totals	378	6305	1131	2789	.406	189	233	.811	98	508	606	654	251	28	335	2778	1.6	1.7	7.3

Three-point field goals: 2000-01, 19-for-55 (.345). 2001-02, 54-for-157 (.344). 2002-03, 36-for-120 (.300). 2003-04, 51-for-136 (.375). 2004-05, 44-for-97 (.454). 2005-06, 123-for-316 (.389). Totals, 327-for-881 (.371).
Personal fouls/disqualifications: 2000-01, 58/0. 2001-02, 98/1. 2002-03, 73/0. 2003-04, 92/1. 2004-05, 65/0. 2005-06, 96/0. Totals, 482/2.

NBA PLAYOFF RECORD

Season Team	G	Min.	FGM	FGA	Pct.	FTM	FTA	Pct.	Off.	Def.	Tot.	Ast.	St.	Blk.	TO	Pts.	RPG	APG	PPG
00-01—Miami	3	64	16	40	.400	4	5	.800	1	4	5	5	3	1	5	38	1.7	1.7	12.7
04-05—Sacramento	3	23	3	8	.375	2	2	1.000	1	1	2	4	0	0	1	9	0.7	1.3	3.0
05-06—Phoenix	14	130	19	52	.365	3	4	.750	0	9	9	6	1	2	5	44	0.6	0.4	3.1
Totals	20	217	38	100	.380	9	11	.818	2	14	16	15	4	3	11	91	0.8	0.8	4.6

Three-point field goals: 2000-01, 2-for-7 (.286). 2004-05, 1-for-1 (1.000). 2005-06, 3-for-14 (.214). Totals, 6-for-22 (.273).
Personal fouls/disqualifications: 2000-01, 7/0. 2004-05, 2/0. 2005-06, 10/0. Totals, 19/0.

HOWARD, DWIGHT   F   MAGIC

PERSONAL: Born December 8, 1985, in Atlanta. ... 6-11/240. (2.11/108.9). ... Full name: Dwight David Howard
HIGH SCHOOL: Southwest Atlanta Christian Academy (Atlanta).
COLLEGE: Did not attend college.
TRANSACTIONS/CAREER NOTES: Selected out of high school by Orlando Magic in first round (first pick overall) of 2004 NBA Draft.

NBA REGULAR-SEASON RECORD

HONORS: NBA All-Rookie first team (2005).

Season Team	G	Min.	FGM	FGA	Pct.	FTM	FTA	Pct.	Off.	Def.	Tot.	Ast.	St.	Blk.	TO	Pts.	RPG	APG	PPG
04-05—Orlando	82	2670	352	677	.520	277	413	.671	287	536	823	75	77	136	165	981	10.0	0.9	12.0
05-06—Orlando	82	3021	468	881	.531	356	598	.595	288	734	*1022	125	65	115	217	1292	12.5	1.5	15.8
Totals	164	5691	820	1558	.526	633	1011	.626	575	1270	1845	200	142	251	382	2273	11.3	1.2	13.9

Three-point field goals: 2004-05, 0-for-2. 2005-06, 0-for-2. Totals, 0-for-4 (.000).
Personal fouls/disqualifications: 2004-05, 232/3. 2005-06, 277/1. Totals, 509/4.

HOWARD, JOSH   F   MAVERICKS

PERSONAL: Born April 28, 1980, in Winston-Salem, N.C. ... 6-6/203. (1.98/92.1). ... Full name: Joshua Jay Howard
HIGH SCHOOL: Glenn (Winston-Salem, N.C.), then Hargrave Military Academy.
COLLEGE: Wake Forest.
TRANSACTIONS/CAREER NOTES: Selected by Dallas Mavericks in first round (29th pick overall) of 2003 NBA Draft.

COLLEGIATE RECORD

NOTES: The SPORTING NEWS All-America first team (2003).

H

Season Team	G	Min.	FGM	FGA	Pct.	FTM	FTA	Pct.	Reb.	Ast.	Pts.	RPG	APG	PPG
99-00—Wake Forest	36	896	128	278	.460	63	108	.583	168	64	331	4.7	1.8	9.2
00-01—Wake Forest	29	790	143	292	.490	89	130	.685	171	52	393	5.9	1.8	13.6
01-02—Wake Forest	31	848	170	337	.504	65	99	.657	240	64	431	7.7	2.1	13.9
02-03—Wake Forest	31	1002	204	428	.477	145	174	.833	257	59	606	8.3	1.9	19.5
Totals	127	3536	645	1335	.483	362	511	.708	836	239	1761	6.6	1.9	13.9

Three-point field goals: 1999-00, 12-for-42 (.286). 2000-01, 18-for-46 (.391). 2001-02, 26-for-79 (.329). 2002-03, 53-for-142 (.373). Totals, 109-for-309 (.353).

NBA REGULAR-SEASON RECORD

HONORS: NBA All-Rookie second team (2004).

Season Team	G	Min.	FGM	FGA	Pct.	FTM	FTA	Pct.	Off.	Def.	Tot.	Ast.	St.	Blk.	TO	Pts.	RPG	APG	PPG
03-04—Dallas	67	1589	229	532	.430	97	138	.703	149	219	368	97	69	54	67	575	5.5	1.4	8.6
04-05—Dallas	76	2446	377	793	.475	170	232	.733	169	315	484	109	116	49	122	958	6.4	1.4	12.6
05-06—Dallas	59	1915	350	743	.471	196	267	.734	123	248	371	111	68	26	79	923	6.3	1.9	15.6
Totals	202	5950	956	2068	.462	463	637	.727	441	782	1223	317	253	129	268	2456	6.1	1.6	12.2

Three-point field goals: 2003-04, 20-for-66 (.303). 2004-05, 34-for-115 (.296). 2005-06, 27-for-63 (.429). Totals, 81-for-244 (.332).
Personal fouls/disqualifications: 2003-04, 168/6. 2004-05, 211/3. 2005-06, 167/2. Totals, 546/11.

NBA PLAYOFF RECORD

Season Team	G	Min.	FGM	FGA	Pct.	FTM	FTA	Pct.	Off.	Def.	Tot.	Ast.	St.	Blk.	TO	Pts.	RPG	APG	PPG
03-04—Dallas	5	86	8	36	.222	10	11	.909	17	15	32	4	6	6	7	27	6.4	0.8	5.4
04-05—Dallas	13	428	78	155	.503	41	55	.745	33	63	96	24	11	7	28	201	7.4	1.8	15.5
05-06—Dallas	23	824	140	309	.453	80	99	.808	41	130	171	32	23	14	52	384	7.4	1.4	16.7
Totals	41	1338	226	500	.452	131	165	.794	91	208	299	60	40	27	87	612	7.3	1.5	14.9

Three-point field goals: 2003-04, 1-for-5 (.200). 2004-05, 4-for-16 (.250). 2005-06, 24-for-65 (.369). Totals, 29-for-86 (.337).
Personal fouls/disqualifications: 2003-04, 12/0. 2004-05, 60/3. 2005-06, 85/1. Totals, 157/4.

HOWARD, JUWAN   F   ROCKETS

PERSONAL: Born February 7, 1973, in Chicago. ... 6-9/250. (2.06/113.4). ... Full name: Juwan Antonio Howard
HIGH SCHOOL: Vocational (Chicago).
COLLEGE: Michigan.
TRANSACTIONS/CAREER NOTES: Selected after junior season by Washington Bullets in first round (fifth pick overall) of 1994 NBA Draft. ... Signed as free agent by Miami Heat (July 15, 1996). ... Contract disallowed by NBA (July 31, 1996). ... Re-signed as free agent by Bullets (August 5, 1996). ... Bullets franchise renamed Washington Wizards for 1997-98 season. ... Traded by Wizards with C Calvin Booth and F Obinna Ekezie to Dallas Mavericks for F/C Christian Laettner, G Courtney Alexander, F Loy Vaught, G Hubert Davis, F/C Etan Thomas and cash considerations (February 22, 2001). ... Traded by Mavericks with G Tim Hardaway, F Donnell Harvey, cash considerations and first-round draft choice to Denver Nuggets for G Nick Van Exel, F/C Raef LaFrentz, G Avery Johnson and G/F Tariq Abdul-Wahad (February 21, 2002). ... Signed as free agent by Orlando Magic (July 16, 2003) ... Traded by Magic with G Tracy McGrady, G Tyronn Lue and C Reece Gaines to Houston Rockets for G Steve Francis, G Cuttino Mobley and C Kelvin Cato (June 29, 2004).

COLLEGIATE RECORD

Season Team	G	Min.	FGM	FGA	Pct.	FTM	FTA	Pct.	Reb.	Ast.	Pts.	RPG	APG	PPG
91-92—Michigan	34	956	150	333	.450	77	112	.688	212	62	377	6.2	1.8	11.1
92-93—Michigan	36	1095	206	407	.506	112	160	.700	267	69	524	7.4	1.9	14.6
93-94—Michigan	30	1020	261	469	.557	102	151	.675	266	71	625	8.9	2.4	20.8
Totals	100	3071	617	1209	.510	291	423	.688	745	202	1526	7.5	2.0	15.3

Three-point field goals: 1991-92, 0-for-2. 1992-93, 0-for-2. 1993-94, 1-for-7 (.143). Totals, 1-for-11 (.091).

NBA REGULAR-SEASON RECORD

HONORS: All-NBA third team (1996). ... NBA All-Rookie second team (1995).

Season Team	G	Min.	FGM	FGA	Pct.	FTM	FTA	Pct.	Off.	Def.	Tot.	Ast.	St.	Blk.	TO	Pts.	RPG	APG	PPG
94-95—Washington	65	2348	455	931	.489	194	292	.664	184	361	545	165	52	15	166	1104	8.4	2.5	17.0
95-96—Washington	81	3294	733	1500	.489	319	426	.749	188	472	660	360	67	39	303	1789	8.1	4.4	22.1
96-97—Washington	82	3324	638	1313	.486	294	389	.756	202	450	652	311	93	23	246	1570	8.0	3.8	19.1
97-98—Washington	64	2559	463	991	.467	258	358	.721	161	288	449	208	82	23	185	1184	7.0	3.3	18.5
98-99—Washington	36	1430	286	604	.474	110	146	.753	90	203	293	107	42	14	95	682	8.1	3.0	18.9
99-00—Washington	82	2909	509	1108	.459	202	275	.735	132	338	470	247	67	21	225	1220	5.7	3.0	14.9
00-01—Wash.-Dallas	81	2974	583	1218	.479	296	383	.773	171	401	572	224	75	37	242	1462	7.1	2.8	18.0
01-02—Dallas-Denver	81	2635	462	1005	.460	261	343	.761	223	389	612	169	46	47	152	1185	7.6	2.1	14.6
02-03—Denver	77	2730	567	1261	.450	282	351	.803	181	404	585	234	77	27	189	1418	7.6	3.0	18.4
03-04—Orlando	81	2877	529	1169	.453	318	393	.809	171	399	570	158	54	22	178	1376	7.0	2.0	17.0
04-05—Houston	61	1624	244	541	.451	97	115	.843	126	220	346	94	32	5	79	585	5.7	1.5	9.6
05-06—Houston	80	2537	394	859	.459	154	191	.806	168	367	535	112	49	8	133	942	6.7	1.4	11.8
Totals	871	31241	5863	12500	.469	2785	3662	.761	1997	4292	6289	2389	736	281	2193	14517	7.2	2.7	16.7

Three-point field goals: 1994-95, 0-for-7. 1995-96, 4-for-13 (.308). 1996-97, 0-for-2. 1997-98, 0-for-2. 1998-99, 0-for-3. 1999-00, 0-for-7. 2000-01, 0-for-3. 2001-02, 0-for-2. 2002-03, 2-for-4 (.500). 2003-04, 0-for-1. 2004-05, 0-for-1. 2005-06, 0-for-4. Totals, 6-for-49 (.122).
Personal fouls/disqualifications: 1994-95, 236/2. 1995-96, 269/3. 1996-97, 259/3. 1997-98, 225/3. 1998-99, 130/1. 1999-00, 299/2. 2000-01, 292/2. 2001-02, 265/4. 2002-03, 239/2. 2003-04, 284/1. 2004-05, 0/0. 2005-06, 253/2. Totals, 2876/25.

NBA PLAYOFF RECORD

Season Team	G	Min.	FGM	FGA	Pct.	FTM	FTA	Pct.	Off.	Def.	Tot.	Ast.	St.	Blk.	TO	Pts.	RPG	APG	PPG
96-97—Washington	3	129	20	43	.465	16	18	.889	10	8	18	5	2	2	3	56	6.0	1.7	18.7
00-01—Dallas	10	391	49	136	.360	36	45	.800	29	54	83	14	6	5	14	134	8.3	1.4	13.4
Totals	13	520	69	179	.385	52	63	.825	39	62	101	19	8	7	17	190	7.8	1.5	14.6

Personal fouls/disqualifications: 1996-97, 9/0. 2000-01, 38/0. Totals, 47/0.

H

								REBOUNDS									
Season Team	Min.	FGM	FGA	Pct.	FTM	FTA	Pct.	Off.	Def.	Tot.	Ast.	PF	Dq.	St.	Blk.	TO	Pts.
1996—Washington..........	16	1	5	.200	0	0	...	4	2	6	2	3	0	1	0	0	2

HUDSON, TROY　　　　　　　G　　　　　　TIMBERWOLVES

PERSONAL: Born March 13, 1976, in Carbondale, Ill. ... 6-1/170. (1.85/77.1).
HIGH SCHOOL: Carbondale (Ill.).
COLLEGE: Missouri, then Southern Illinois.
TRANSACTIONS/CAREER NOTES: Not drafted by an NBA franchise. ... Signed as free agent by Utah Jazz (October 3, 1997). ... Waived by Jazz (December 28, 1997). ... Played in Continental Basketball Association with Yakima Sun Kings (1997-98) and Sioux Falls Skyforce (1997-98 and 1998-99). ... Signed as free agent by Minnesota Timberwolves (January 22, 1999). ... Waived by Timberwolves (February 3, 1999). ... Signed by Los Angeles Clippers to first of two consecutive 10-day contracts (March 23, 1999). ... Re-signed by Clippers for remainder of season (April 13, 1999). ... Waived by Clippers (March 27, 2000). ... Signed as free agent by Orlando Magic (August 10, 2000). ... Signed as free agent by Timberwolves (August 26, 2002).

COLLEGIATE RECORD

Season Team	G	Min.	FGM	FGA	Pct.	FTM	FTA	Pct.	Reb.	Ast.	Pts.	AVERAGES		
												RPG	APG	PPG
94-95—Missouri........................	2	20	4	10	.400	1	2	.500	2	4	10	1.0	2.0	5.0
95-96—Southern Illinois............	25	812	179	459	.390	82	103	.796	110	38	533	4.4	1.5	21.3
96-97—Southern Illinois............	30	1075	209	534	.391	79	96	.823	107	83	631	3.6	2.8	21.0
Totals	57	1907	392	1003	.391	162	201	.806	219	125	1174	3.8	2.2	20.6

Three-point field goals: 1994-95, 1-for-6 (.167). 1995-96, 82-for-103 (.796). 1996-97, 134-for-362 (.370). Totals, 217-for-471 (.461).
Personal fouls/disqualifications: 1994-95, 1/0. 1995-96, 39/0. 1996-97, 50/0. Totals, 90/0.

CBA RECORD

Season Team	G	Min.	FGM	FGA	Pct.	FTM	FTA	Pct.	Reb.	Ast.	Pts.	AVERAGES		
												RPG	APG	PPG
97-98—Yakima-Sioux Falls........	22	399	71	163	.436	25	31	.806	46	38	199	2.1	1.7	9.0
98-99—Sioux Falls.....................	37	1213	173	449	.385	52	60	.867	113	170	461	3.1	4.6	12.5
Totals	59	1612	244	612	.399	77	91	.846	159	208	660	2.7	3.5	11.2

Three-point field goals: 1997-98, 32-for-78 (.410). 1998-99, 63-for-205 (.307). Totals, 95-for-283 (.336).
Personal fouls/disqualifications: 1998-99, 48/0. Totals, 48/0.

NBA REGULAR-SEASON RECORD

Season Team	G	Min.	FGM	FGA	Pct.	FTM	FTA	Pct.	REBOUNDS			Ast.	St.	Blk.	TO	Pts.	AVERAGES		
									Off.	Def.	Tot.						RPG	APG	PPG
97-98—Utah...............	8	23	6	14	.429	0	0	...	1	1	2	4	2	0	1	12	0.3	0.5	1.5
98-99—L.A. Clippers...	25	524	60	150	.400	34	38	.895	15	40	55	92	11	2	38	169	2.2	3.7	6.8
99-00—L.A. Clippers...	62	1592	204	541	.377	77	95	.811	28	120	148	242	43	0	108	545	2.4	3.9	8.8
00-01—Orlando..........	75	1008	125	372	.336	85	104	.817	38	67	105	162	37	3	92	357	1.4	2.2	4.8
01-02—Orlando..........	81	1854	354	815	.434	176	201	.876	30	115	145	255	57	6	163	950	1.8	3.1	11.7
02-03—Minnesota......	79	2600	409	956	.428	208	231	.900	42	141	183	452	60	7	182	1123	2.3	5.7	14.2
03-04—Minnesota......	29	503	80	207	.386	27	33	.818	4	31	35	70	7	0	34	218	1.2	2.4	7.5
04-05—Minnesota......	79	1729	266	664	.401	70	90	.778	19	86	105	283	27	6	113	691	1.3	3.6	8.7
05-06—Minnesota......	36	800	127	333	.381	48	52	.923	8	36	44	106	12	4	40	342	1.2	2.9	9.5
Totals	474	10633	1631	4052	.403	725	844	.859	185	637	822	1666	256	28	771	4407	1.7	3.5	9.3

Three-point field goals: 1997-98, 0-for-3. 1998-99, 15-for-47 (.319). 1999-00, 60-for-193 (.311). 2000-01, 22-for-109 (.202). 2001-02, 66-for-187 (.353). 2002-03, 97-for-266 (.365). 2003-04, 31-for-77 (.403). 2004-05, 89-for-258 (.345). 2005-06, 40-for-101 (.396). Totals, 420-for-1241 (.338).
Personal fouls/disqualifications: 1997-98, 1/0. 1998-99, 28/1. 1999-00, 65/0. 2000-01, 82/0. 2001-02, 119/0. 2002-03, 160/1. 2003-04, 32/0. 2004-05, 121/0. 2005-06, 55/0. Totals, 663/2.

NBA PLAYOFF RECORD

Season Team	G	Min.	FGM	FGA	Pct.	FTM	FTA	Pct.	REBOUNDS			Ast.	St.	Blk.	TO	Pts.	AVERAGES		
									Off.	Def.	Tot.						RPG	APG	PPG
00-01—Orlando..........	4	56	6	21	.286	5	6	.833	5	4	9	9	1	0	3	17	2.3	2.3	4.3
01-02—Orlando..........	4	106	18	48	.375	15	16	.938	0	4	4	6	0	0	8	51	1.0	1.5	12.8
02-03—Minnesota......	6	221	44	106	.415	36	38	.947	1	11	12	33	8	0	16	141	2.0	5.5	23.5
Totals	14	383	68	175	.389	56	60	.933	6	19	25	48	9	0	27	209	1.8	3.4	14.9

Three-point field goals: 2000-01, 0-for-3. 2001-02, 0-for-5. 2002-03, 17-for-39 (.436). Totals, 17-for-47 (.362).
Personal fouls/disqualifications: 2000-01, 3/0. 2001-02, 4/0. 2002-03, 5/0. Totals, 12/0.

HUGHES, LARRY　　　　　　　G　　　　　　CAVALIERS

PERSONAL: Born January 23, 1979, in St. Louis. ... 6-5/184. (1.96/83.5). ... Full name: Larry Darnell Hughes
HIGH SCHOOL: Christian Brothers (St. Louis).
COLLEGE: Saint Louis.
TRANSACTIONS/CAREER NOTES: Selected after freshman season by Philadelphia 76ers in first round (eighth pick overall) of 1998 NBA Draft. ... Traded by 76ers with F/G Billy Owens to Golden State Warriors in three-way deal in which Warriors sent G John Starks and a future first-round draft choice to Chicago Bulls and 76ers sent F Bruce Bowen to Bulls for F Toni Kukoc (February 16, 2000). ... Signed as free agent by Washington Wizards (July 18, 2002). ... Signed as free agent by Cleveland Cavaliers (August 2, 2005).

COLLEGIATE RECORD

NOTES: The SPORTING NEWS Freshman of the Year (1998).

Season Team	G	Min.	FGM	FGA	Pct.	FTM	FTA	Pct.	Reb.	Ast.	Pts.	AVERAGES		
												RPG	APG	PPG
97-98—St. Louis......................	32	1038	224	540	.415	180	260	.692	162	77	670	5.1	2.4	20.9

Three-point field goals: 1997-98, 42-for-145 (.290). Totals, 42-for-145 (.290).

NBA REGULAR-SEASON RECORD

HONORS: NBA All-Defensive first team (2005).

								REBOUNDS								AVERAGES		
Season Team	G	Min.	FGM	FGA	Pct.	FTM	FTA	Pct.	Off.	Def.	Tot.	Ast.	St.	Blk.	TO	Pts.	RPG	APG	PPG
98-99—Philadelphia	50	988	170	414	.411	107	151	.709	83	106	189	77	44	14	68	455	3.8	1.5	9.1
99-00—Phila.-G.S.	82	2324	459	1147	.400	279	377	.740	113	236	349	205	115	28	195	1226	4.3	2.5	15.0
00-01—Golden State ..	50	1846	308	805	.383	193	252	.766	76	200	276	223	96	29	152	823	5.5	4.5	16.5
01-02—Golden State ..	73	2049	343	810	.423	191	259	.737	83	162	245	316	113	23	171	895	3.4	4.3	12.3
02-03—Washington ...	67	2137	346	741	.467	136	186	.731	67	241	308	205	86	24	136	857	4.6	3.1	12.8
03-04—Washington ..	61	2061	401	1009	.397	267	335	.797	96	230	326	148	95	26	152	1148	5.3	2.4	18.8
04-05—Washington ...	61	2358	467	1086	.430	352	453	.777	74	308	382	285	176	18	153	1345	6.3	4.7	22.0
05-06—Cleveland	36	1281	192	469	.409	146	193	.756	26	135	161	131	53	21	99	558	4.5	3.6	15.5
Totals	480	15044	2686	6481	.414	1671	2206	.757	618	1618	2236	1590	778	183	1126	7307	4.7	3.3	15.2

Three-point field goals: 1998-99, 8-for-52 (.154). 1999-00, 29-for-125 (.232). 2000-01, 14-for-75 (.187). 2001-02, 18-for-93 (.194). 2002-03, 29-for-79 (.367). 2003-04, 79-for-232 (.341). 2004-05, 59-for-209 (.282). 2005-06, 28-for-76 (.368). Totals, 264-for-941 (.281).

Personal fouls/disqualifications: 1998-99, 97/0. 1999-00, 191/2. 2000-01, 147/2. 2001-02, 150/0. 2002-03, 149/1. 2003-04, 147/2. 2004-05, 168/0. 2005-06, 117/0. Totals, 1166/7.

NBA PLAYOFF RECORD

								REBOUNDS								AVERAGES		
Season Team	G	Min.	FGM	FGA	Pct.	FTM	FTA	Pct.	Off.	Def.	Tot.	Ast.	St.	Blk.	TO	Pts.	RPG	APG	PPG
98-99—Philadelphia	8	198	31	77	.403	20	24	.833	17	20	37	16	15	9	12	82	4.6	2.0	10.3
04-05—Washington	10	401	68	181	.376	64	77	.831	17	54	71	37	20	7	25	207	7.1	3.7	20.7
05-06—Cleveland	9	336	36	113	.319	23	31	.742	9	18	27	36	20	1	16	100	3.0	4.0	11.1
Totals	27	935	135	371	.364	107	132	.811	43	92	135	89	55	17	53	389	5.0	3.3	14.4

Three-point field goals: 1998-99, 0-for-7. 2004-05, 7-for-33 (.212). 2005-06, 5-for-18 (.278). Totals, 12-for-58 (.207).

Personal fouls/disqualifications: 1998-99, 21/0. 2004-05, 35/1. 2005-06, 34/2. Totals, 90/3.

HUMPHRIES, KRIS   F   RAPTORS

PERSONAL: Born February 6, 1985, in Minneapolis. ... 6-9/235. (2.06/106.6). ... Full name: Kris Nathan Humphries
HIGH SCHOOL: Hopkins (Minneapolis).
COLLEGE: Minnesota.
TRANSACTIONS/CAREER NOTES: Selected after freshman season by Utah Jazz in first round (14th pick overall) of 2004 NBA Draft. ... Traded by Utah with F Robert Whaley to Toronto Raptors for C Rafael Araujo (June 8, 2006).

COLLEGIATE RECORD

											AVERAGES		
Season Team	G	Min.	FGM	FGA	Pct.	FTM	FTA	Pct.	Reb.	Ast.	Pts.	RPG	APG	PPG
03-04—Minnesota	29	990	221	498	.444	170	229	.742	293	20	629	10.1	0.7	21.7

Three-point field goals: 2003-04, 17-for-50 (.340). Totals, 17-for-50 (.340).

NBA REGULAR SEASON RECORD

								REBOUNDS								AVERAGES		
Season Team	G	Min.	FGM	FGA	Pct.	FTM	FTA	Pct.	Off.	Def.	Tot.	Ast.	St.	Blk.	TO	Pts.	RPG	APG	PPG
04-05—Utah	67	873	116	287	.404	44	101	.436	73	124	197	43	25	18	52	278	2.9	0.6	4.1
05-06—Utah	62	619	77	203	.379	34	65	.523	56	101	157	30	23	16	31	188	2.5	0.5	3.0
Totals	129	1492	193	490	.394	78	166	.470	129	225	354	73	48	34	83	466	2.7	0.6	3.6

Three-point field goals: 2004-05, 2-for-6 (.333). 2005-06, 0-for-5. Totals, 2-for-11 (.182).

Personal fouls/disqualifications: 2004-05, 96/0. 2005-06, 82/0. Totals, 178/0.

HUNTER, LINDSEY   G   PISTONS

PERSONAL: Born December 3, 1970, in Utica, Miss. ... 6-2/195. (1.88/88.5). ... Full name: Lindsey Benson Hunter
HIGH SCHOOL: Murrah (Jackson, Miss.).
COLLEGE: Alcorn State, then Jackson State.
TRANSACTIONS/CAREER NOTES: Selected by Detroit Pistons in first round (10th pick overall) of 1993 NBA Draft. ... Traded by Pistons to Milwaukee Bucks for F Billy Owens (August 22, 2000). ... Traded by Bucks to Los Angeles Lakers for C Greg Foster (June 28, 2001). ... Traded by Lakers with draft rights to F Chris Jeffries to Toronto Raptors for F Tracy Murray and draft rights to G Kareem Rush (June 26, 2002). ... Traded by Raptors to Detroit Pistons for G Michael Curry (August 28, 2003). ... Traded by Pistons to Boston Celtics as part of three-team trade in which Celtics also received G Chucky Atkins and a 2004 first-round draft choice from Pistons. Atlanta Hawks received F Zeljko Rebraca, G Bob Sura and a first-round draft choice from Pistons and F Chris Mills from Celtics. Pistons received F/C Rasheed Wallace from Hawks and G Mike James from Celtics (February 19, 2004). ... Waived by Celtics (February 25, 2004). ... Signed as free agent by Pistons (February 26, 2004).
MISCELLANEOUS: Member of NBA championship team (2002, 2004).

COLLEGIATE RECORD

NOTES: Holds NCAA Division I single-game record for most three-point field goals attempted—26 (December 27, 1992, vs. Kansas, 11 made).

											AVERAGES		
Season Team	G	Min.	FGM	FGA	Pct.	FTM	FTA	Pct.	Reb.	Ast.	Pts.	RPG	APG	PPG
88-89—Alcorn State..................	27	624	70	178	.393	23	32	.719	67	99	167	2.5	3.7	6.2
89-90—Jackson State................	Did not play—transfer student.													
90-91—Jackson State...............	30	1042	229	560	.409	82	118	.695	100	105	626	3.3	3.5	20.9
91-92—Jackson State...............	28	960	249	605	.412	100	157	.637	96	121	693	3.4	4.3	24.8
92-93—Jackson State...............	34	1152	320	777	.412	155	201	.771	115	115	907	3.4	3.4	26.7
Totals	119	3778	868	2120	.409	360	508	.709	378	440	2393	3.2	3.7	20.1

Three-point field goals: 1988-89, 4-for-21 (.190). 1990-91, 86-for-235 (.366). 1991-92, 95-for-257 (.370). 1992-93, 112-for-328 (.341). Totals, 297-for-841 (.353).

H

HONORS: NBA All-Rookie second team (1994).

Season Team	G	Min.	FGM	FGA	Pct.	FTM	FTA	Pct.	REBOUNDS			Ast.	St.	Blk.	TO	Pts.	AVERAGES		
									Off.	Def.	Tot.						RPG	APG	PPG
93-94—Detroit	82	2172	335	893	.375	104	142	.732	47	142	189	390	121	10	184	843	2.3	4.8	10.3
94-95—Detroit	42	944	119	318	.374	40	55	.727	24	51	75	159	51	7	79	314	1.8	3.8	7.5
95-96—Detroit	80	2138	239	628	.381	84	120	.700	44	150	194	188	84	18	80	679	2.4	2.4	8.5
96-97—Detroit	82	3023	421	1042	.404	158	203	.778	59	174	233	154	129	24	96	1166	2.8	1.9	14.2
97-98—Detroit	71	2505	316	826	.383	145	196	.740	61	186	247	224	123	10	110	862	3.5	3.2	12.1
98-99—Detroit	49	1755	228	524	.435	67	89	.753	26	142	168	193	86	8	92	582	3.4	3.9	11.9
99-00—Detroit	82	2919	379	892	.425	117	154	.760	35	215	250	327	129	22	145	1043	3.0	4.0	12.7
00-01—Milwaukee	82	2002	298	783	.381	77	96	.802	32	137	169	222	102	12	68	825	2.1	2.7	10.1
01-02—L.A. Lakers	82	1616	187	490	.382	20	40	.500	18	103	121	129	66	19	55	473	1.5	1.6	5.8
02-03—Toronto	29	673	106	302	.351	34	47	.723	15	44	59	71	35	5	57	280	2.0	2.4	9.7
03-04—Detroit	33	661	49	143	.343	5	8	.625	13	54	67	85	39	6	34	117	2.0	2.6	3.5
04-05—Detroit	76	1144	108	302	.358	46	58	.793	38	85	123	130	68	13	68	285	1.6	1.7	3.8
05-06—Detroit	30	353	37	100	.370	2	4	.500	10	30	40	62	19	1	20	87	1.3	2.1	2.9
Totals	820	21905	2822	7243	.390	899	1212	.742	422	1513	1935	2334	1052	155	1088	7556	2.4	2.8	9.2

Three-point field goals: 1993-94, 69-for-207 (.333). 1994-95, 36-for-108 (.333). 1995-96, 117-for-289 (.405). 1996-97, 166-for-468 (.355). 1997-98, 85-for-265 (.321). 1998-99, 59-for-153 (.386). 1999-00, 168-for-389 (.432). 2000-01, 152-for-407 (.373). 2001-02, 79-for-208 (.380). 2002-03, 34-for-107 (.318). 2003-04, 14-for-50 (.280). 2004-05, 23-for-84 (.274). 2005-06, 11-for-43 (.256). Totals, 1013-for-2778 (.365).

Personal fouls/disqualifications: 1993-94, 174/1. 1994-95, 94/1. 1995-96, 185/0. 1996-97, 206/1. 1997-98, 174/3. 1998-99, 126/2. 1999-00, 216/2. 2000-01, 172/1. 2001-02, 120/0. 2002-03, 50/1. 2003-04, 45/0. 2004-05, 125/0. 2005-06, 44/0. Totals, 1731/12.

NBA PLAYOFF RECORD

Season Team	G	Min.	FGM	FGA	Pct.	FTM	FTA	Pct.	REBOUNDS			Ast.	St.	Blk.	TO	Pts.	AVERAGES		
									Off.	Def.	Tot.						RPG	APG	PPG
95-96—Detroit	2	36	2	8	.250	1	2	.500	1	1	2	1	1	0	0	6	1.0	0.5	3.0
96-97—Detroit	5	201	29	66	.439	5	7	.714	4	14	18	6	6	1	1	75	3.6	1.2	15.0
98-99—Detroit	5	180	14	53	.264	5	5	1.000	5	10	15	12	7	0	7	36	3.0	2.4	7.2
99-00—Detroit	3	93	10	32	.313	4	6	.667	0	7	7	5	5	1	5	25	2.3	1.7	8.3
00-01—Milwaukee	18	289	24	99	.242	8	11	.727	2	29	31	34	14	3	13	64	1.7	1.9	3.6
01-02—L.A. Lakers	18	132	14	45	.311	0	0	...	2	5	7	10	2	0	5	36	0.4	0.6	2.0
03-04—Detroit	23	273	19	65	.292	11	12	.917	5	28	33	21	18	4	13	56	1.4	0.9	2.4
04-05—Detroit	25	374	36	113	.319	16	22	.727	10	30	40	39	22	7	15	96	1.6	1.6	3.8
05-06—Detroit	18	217	26	78	.333	10	10	1.000	8	11	19	29	15	1	14	76	1.1	1.6	4.2
Totals	117	1795	174	559	.311	60	75	.800	37	135	172	157	90	17	73	470	1.5	1.3	4.0

Three-point field goals: 1995-96, 1-for-4 (.250). 1996-97, 12-for-29 (.414). 1998-99, 3-for-11 (.273). 1999-00, 1-for-9 (.111). 2000-01, 8-for-53 (.151). 2001-02, 8-for-29 (.276). 2003-04, 7-for-30 (.233). 2004-05, 8-for-36 (.222). 2005-06, 14-for-44 (.318). Totals, 62-for-245 (.253).

Personal fouls/disqualifications: 1995-96, 2/0. 1996-97, 9/0. 1998-99, 11/0. 1999-00, 4/0. 2000-01, 24/0. 2001-02, 19/0. 2003-04, 42/0. 2004-05, 45/0. 2005-06, 41/0. Totals, 197/0.

HUNTER, STEVEN   C   76ERS

PERSONAL: Born October 31, 1981, in Chicago. ... 7-0/220. (2.13/99.8). ... Full name: Steven D. Hunter.
HIGH SCHOOL: Proviso East (Maywood, Ill.).
COLLEGE: DePaul.
TRANSACTIONS/CAREER NOTES: Selected after sophomore season by Orlando Magic in first round (15th pick overall) of 2001 NBA Draft. ... Traded by Magic with F Drew Gooden and the draft rights to F Anderson Varejao to Cleveland Cavaliers for F/C Tony Battie and two future second-round draft choices (July 23, 2004). ... Waived by Cavaliers (August 10, 2004). ... Signed as free agent by Phoenix Suns (August 20, 2004). ... Signed by Philadelphia 76ers (August 12, 2005). ... Traded by 76ers to New Orleans Hornets for two second-round draft choices in 2006 and 2007 (February 1, 2006); Hornets rescind trade (February 8, 2006).

COLLEGIATE RECORD

Season Team	G	Min.	FGM	FGA	Pct.	FTM	FTA	Pct.	Reb.	Ast.	Pts.	AVERAGES		
												RPG	APG	PPG
99-00—DePaul	33	744	114	197	.579	53	75	.707	128	9	281	3.9	0.3	8.5
00-01—DePaul	30	808	138	233	.592	67	125	.536	169	15	343	5.6	0.5	11.4
Totals	63	1552	252	430	.586	120	200	.600	297	24	624	4.7	0.4	9.9

Three-point field goals: 1999-00, 0-for-2. Totals, 0-for-2 (.000).
Personal fouls/disqualifications: 1999-00, 71/0. 2000-01, 70/0. Totals, 141/0.

NBA REGULAR-SEASON RECORD

Season Team	G	Min.	FGM	FGA	Pct.	FTM	FTA	Pct.	REBOUNDS			Ast.	St.	Blk.	TO	Pts.	AVERAGES		
									Off.	Def.	Tot.						RPG	APG	PPG
01-02—Orlando	53	516	67	147	.456	55	94	.585	40	57	97	5	5	43	16	189	1.8	0.1	3.6
02-03—Orlando	33	447	56	103	.544	18	44	.409	38	55	93	6	9	36	15	130	2.8	0.2	3.9
03-04—Orlando	59	789	82	155	.529	23	69	.333	54	116	170	12	5	73	29	187	2.9	0.2	3.2
04-05—Phoenix	76	1046	135	220	.614	78	163	.479	98	129	227	13	4	102	44	348	3.0	0.2	4.6
05-06—NO/Ok. City-Phila.	69	1312	175	291	.601	71	138	.514	110	161	271	17	12	76	64	421	3.9	0.2	6.1
Totals	290	4110	515	916	.562	245	508	.482	340	518	858	53	35	330	168	1275	3.0	0.2	4.4

Three-point field goals: 2004-05, 0-for-1. Totals, 0-for-1 (.000).
Personal fouls/disqualifications: 2001-02, 81/0. 2002-03, 56/0. 2003-04, 101/0. 2004-05, 131/1. 2005-06, 120/0. Totals, 489/1.

NBA PLAYOFF RECORD

Season Team	G	Min.	FGM	FGA	Pct.	FTM	FTA	Pct.	REBOUNDS			Ast.	St.	Blk.	TO	Pts.	AVERAGES		
									Off.	Def.	Tot.						RPG	APG	PPG
02-03—Orlando	7	40	3	10	.300	0	3	.000	1	2	3	1	0	3	1	6	0.4	0.1	0.9
04-05—Phoenix	15	213	24	43	.558	12	20	.600	17	21	38	3	1	18	8	60	2.5	0.2	4.0
Totals	22	253	27	53	.509	12	23	.522	18	23	41	4	1	21	9	66	1.9	0.2	3.0

Personal fouls/disqualifications: 2002-03, 10/0. 2004-05, 25/0. Totals, 35/0.

H

IGUODALA, ANDRE   F   76ERS

PERSONAL: Born January 28, 1984, in Springfield, Ill. ... 6-6/207. (1.98/93.9). ... Full name: Andre Tyler Iguodala
HIGH SCHOOL: Lanphier (Springfield, Ill.).
COLLEGE: Arizona.
TRANSACTIONS/CAREER NOTES: Selected after sophomore season by Philadelphia 76ers in first round (ninth pick overall) of 2004 NBA Draft.

COLLEGIATE RECORD

Season Team	G	Min.	FGM	FGA	Pct.	FTM	FTA	Pct.	Reb.	Ast.	Pts.	RPG	APG	PPG
02-03—Arizona	32	614	69	181	.381	59	88	.670	156	66	206	4.9	2.1	6.4
03-04—Arizona	30	962	136	302	.450	93	118	.788	253	147	388	8.4	4.9	12.9
Totals	62	1576	205	483	.424	152	206	.738	409	213	594	6.6	3.4	9.6

Three-point field goals: 2002-03, 9-for-44 (.205). 2003-04, 23-for-73 (.315). Totals, 32-for-117 (.274).

HONORS: NBA All-Rookie first team (2005).

NBA REGULAR-SEASON RECORD

Season Team	G	Min.	FGM	FGA	Pct.	FTM	FTA	Pct.	Off.	Def.	Tot.	Ast.	St.	Blk.	TO	Pts.	RPG	APG	PPG
04-05—Philadelphia	82	2686	269	546	.493	156	210	.743	89	375	464	246	138	48	139	741	5.7	3.0	9.0
05-06—Philadelphia	82	3086	344	688	.500	263	349	.754	117	364	481	255	135	21	153	1007	5.9	3.1	12.3
Totals	164	5772	613	1234	.497	419	559	.750	206	739	945	501	273	69	292	1748	5.8	3.1	10.7

Three-point field goals: 2004-05, 47-for-142 (.331). 2005-06, 56-for-158 (.354). Totals, 103-for-300 (.343).
Personal fouls/disqualifications: 2004-05, 204/2. 2005-06, 198/4. Totals, 402/6.

NBA PLAYOFF RECORD

Season Team	G	Min.	FGM	FGA	Pct.	FTM	FTA	Pct.	Off.	Def.	Tot.	Ast.	St.	Blk.	TO	Pts.	RPG	APG	PPG
04-05—Philadelphia	5	192	20	43	.465	6	12	.500	8	15	23	15	14	5	5	49	4.6	3.0	9.8

Three-point field goals: 2004-05, 3-for-9 (.333). Totals, 3-for-9 (.333).
Personal fouls/disqualifications: 2004-05, 12/0. Totals, 12/0.

ILGAUSKAS, ZYDRUNAS   C   CAVALIERS

PERSONAL: Born June 5, 1975, in Kaunas, Lithuania. ... 7-3/260. (2.21/117.9). ... Name pronounced ZHEE-drew-nus ill-GAUS-kus.
TRANSACTIONS/CAREER NOTES: Played in Lithuania (1994-96). ... Selected by Cleveland Cavaliers in first round (20th pick overall) of 1996 NBA Draft.

LITHUANIAN LEAGUE RECORD

Season Team	G	Min.	FGM	FGA	Pct.	FTM	FTA	Pct.	Reb.	Ast.	Pts.	RPG	APG	PPG
94-95—Atletas	36	1091	303	504	.601	123	180	.683	460	26	731	12.8	0.7	20.3
95-96—Atletas						Did not play—injured.								
Totals	36	1091	303	504	.601	123	180	.683	460	26	731	12.8	0.7	20.3

Three-point field goals: 1994-95, 2-for-9 (.222). Totals, 2-for-9 (.222).

NBA REGULAR-SEASON RECORD

HONORS: NBA All-Rookie first team (1998). ... MVP of Rookie game (1998).

Season Team	G	Min.	FGM	FGA	Pct.	FTM	FTA	Pct.	Off.	Def.	Tot.	Ast.	St.	Blk.	TO	Pts.	RPG	APG	PPG
96-97—Cleveland							Did not play—injured.												
97-98—Cleveland	82	2379	454	876	.518	230	302	.762	279	444	723	71	52	135	146	1139	8.8	0.9	13.9
98-99—Cleveland	5	171	29	57	.509	18	30	.600	17	27	44	4	4	7	9	76	8.8	0.8	15.2
99-00—Cleveland							Did not play—injured.												
00-01—Cleveland	24	616	114	234	.487	53	78	.679	65	95	160	18	15	37	60	281	6.7	0.8	11.7
01-02—Cleveland	62	1329	241	567	.425	208	276	.754	136	198	334	70	17	84	94	690	5.4	1.1	11.1
02-03—Cleveland	81	2432	495	1122	.441	400	512	.781	240	371	611	127	56	152	210	1390	7.5	1.6	17.2
03-04—Cleveland	81	2539	466	965	.483	303	406	.746	279	374	653	109	39	201	163	1237	8.1	1.3	15.3
04-05—Cleveland	78	2615	458	979	.468	402	503	.799	*299	373	672	100	53	165	191	1320	8.6	1.3	16.9
05-06—Cleveland	78	2283	450	889	.506	317	380	.834	245	346	591	91	38	136	155	1217	7.6	1.2	15.6
Totals	491	14364	2707	5689	.476	1931	2487	.776	1560	2228	3788	590	274	917	1028	7350	7.7	1.2	15.0

Three-point field goals: 1997-98, 1-for-4 (.250). 2000-01, 0-for-2. 2001-02, 0-for-5. 2002-03, 0-for-5. 2003-04, 2-for-7 (.286). 2004-05, 2-for-7 (.286). 2005-06, 0-for-5. Totals, 5-for-35 (.143).
Personal fouls/disqualifications: 1997-98, 288/4. 1998-99, 24/1. 2000-01, 78/0. 2001-02, 187/4. 2002-03, 274/4. 2003-04, 277/2. 2004-05, 313/7. 2005-06, 280/5. Totals, 1721/27.

NBA PLAYOFF RECORD

Season Team	G	Min.	FGM	FGA	Pct.	FTM	FTA	Pct.	Off.	Def.	Tot.	Ast.	St.	Blk.	TO	Pts.	RPG	APG	PPG
97-98—Cleveland	4	147	28	49	.571	13	25	.520	14	16	30	2	2	5	10	69	7.5	0.5	17.3
05-06—Cleveland	13	354	54	119	.454	27	36	.750	33	49	82	10	5	27	24	135	6.3	0.8	10.4
Totals	17	501	82	168	.488	40	61	.656	47	65	112	12	7	32	34	204	6.6	0.7	12.0

Personal fouls/disqualifications: 1997-98, 22/2. 2005-06, 46/3. Totals, 68/5.

NBA ALL-STAR GAME RECORD

Season Team	Min.	FGM	FGA	Pct.	FTM	FTA	Pct.	Off.	Def.	Tot.	Ast.	PF	Dq.	St.	Blk.	TO	Pts.
2003—Cleveland	4	0	1	.000	0	0	...	0	0	0	0	1	0	0	0	1	0
2005—Cleveland	17	5	8	.625	2	2	1.000	3	4	7	1	2	0	0	2	1	12
Totals	21	5	9	.556	2	2	1.000	3	4	7	1	3	0	0	2	2	12

IVERSON, ALLEN   G   76ERS

PERSONAL: Born June 7, 1975, in Hampton, Va. ... 6-0/165. (1.83/74.8).
HIGH SCHOOL: Bethel (Hampton, Va.).
COLLEGE: Georgetown.
TRANSACTIONS/CAREER NOTES: Selected after sophomore season by Philadelphia 76ers in first round (first pick overall) of 1996 NBA Draft.
MISCELLANEOUS: Member of bronze-medal-winning U.S. Olympic team (2004).

COLLEGIATE RECORD

NOTES: The SPORTING NEWS All-America first team (1996).

Season Team	G	Min.	FGM	FGA	Pct.	FTM	FTA	Pct.	Reb.	Ast.	Pts.	RPG	APG	PPG
94-95—Georgetown	30	966	203	520	.390	172	250	.688	99	134	613	3.3	4.5	20.4
95-96—Georgetown	37	1213	312	650	.480	215	317	.678	141	173	926	3.8	4.7	25.0
Totals	67	2179	515	1170	.440	387	567	.683	240	307	1539	3.6	4.6	23.0

Three-point field goals: 1994-95, 35-for-151 (.232). 1995-96, 87-for-238 (.366). Totals, 122-for-389 (.314).

NBA REGULAR-SEASON RECORD

RECORDS: Shares NBA record for most seasons leading league in steals per game—3 (2000-01, 2001-02, 2002-03). ... Holds career record for most consecutive seasons leading league in steals per game—3 (2000-01 through 2002-03).
HONORS: NBA Most Valuable Player (2001). ... NBA Rookie of the Year (1997). ... All-NBA first team (1999, 2001, 2005). ... All-NBA second team (2000, 2002, 2003). ... NBA All-Rookie first team (1997). ... MVP of Rookie Game (1997). ... All-NBA third team (2006).
NOTES: Led NBA with 2.51 steals per game (2001), 2.80 steals per game (2002) and 2.74 steals per game (2003).

Season Team	G	Min.	FGM	FGA	Pct.	FTM	FTA	Pct.	Off.	Def.	Tot.	Ast.	St.	Blk.	TO	Pts.	RPG	APG	PPG
96-97—Philadelphia	76	3045	625	1504	.416	382	544	.702	115	197	312	567	157	24	*337	1787	4.1	7.5	23.5
97-98—Philadelphia	80	3150	649	1407	.461	390	535	.729	86	210	296	494	176	25	244	1758	3.7	6.2	22.0
98-99—Philadelphia	48	1990	435	*1056	.412	356	474	.751	66	170	236	223	110	7	167	1284	4.9	4.6	*26.8
99-00—Philadelphia	70	2853	729	1733	.421	442	620	.713	71	196	267	328	144	5	230	1989	3.8	4.7	28.4
00-01—Philadelphia	71	2979	762	1813	.420	585	719	.814	50	223	273	325	178	20	237	*2207	3.8	4.6	*31.1
01-02—Philadelphia	60	2622	665	1669	.398	475	585	.812	44	225	269	331	168	13	237	1883	4.5	5.5	*31.4
02-03—Philadelphia	82	3485	804	1940	.414	570	736	.774	68	276	344	454	*225	13	286	2262	4.2	5.5	27.6
03-04—Philadelphia	48	2040	435	1125	.387	339	455	.745	34	144	178	324	115	5	209	1266	3.7	6.8	26.4
04-05—Philadelphia	75	3174	771	*1818	.424	*656	786	.835	51	248	299	596	*180	9	*344	*2302	4.0	7.9	*30.7
05-06—Philadelphia	72	3103	815	1822	.447	675	*829	.814	44	188	232	532	140	10	248	2377	3.2	7.4	33.0
Totals	682	28441	6690	15887	.421	4870	6283	.775	629	2077	2706	4174	1593	131	2539	19115	4.0	6.1	28.0

Three-point field goals: 1996-97, 155-for-455 (.341). 1997-98, 70-for-235 (.298). 1998-99, 58-for-199 (.291). 1999-00, 89-for-261 (.341). 2000-01, 98-for-306 (.320). 2001-02, 78-for-268 (.291). 2002-03, 84-for-303 (.277). 2003-04, 57-for-199 (.286). 2004-05, 104-for-338 (.308). 2005-06, 72-for-223 (.323). Totals, 865-for-2787 (.310).

Personal fouls/disqualifications: 1996-97, 233/5. 1997-98, 200/2. 1998-99, 98/0. 1999-00, 162/1. 2000-01, 147/0. 2001-02, 102/0. 2002-03, 149/2. 2003-04, 87/0. 2004-05, 140/1. 2005-06, 121/0. Totals, 1439/11.

NBA PLAYOFF RECORD

NOTES: Holds single-game playoff record for most steals—10 (May 13, 1999, vs. Orlando). ... Shares NBA Finals single-game record for most free throws made in one quarter—9 (June 10, 2001, vs. Los Angeles Lakers).

Season Team	G	Min.	FGM	FGA	Pct.	FTM	FTA	Pct.	Off.	Def.	Tot.	Ast.	St.	Blk.	TO	Pts.	RPG	APG	PPG
98-99—Philadelphia	8	358	88	214	.411	37	52	.712	14	19	33	39	20	2	24	228	4.1	4.9	28.5
99-00—Philadelphia	10	444	91	237	.384	68	92	.739	14	26	40	45	12	1	32	262	4.0	4.5	26.2
00-01—Philadelphia	22	1016	257	661	.389	161	208	.774	15	89	104	134	52	7	63	723	4.7	6.1	32.9
01-02—Philadelphia	5	209	45	118	.381	51	63	.810	1	17	18	21	13	0	12	150	3.6	4.2	30.0
02-03—Philadelphia	12	557	137	329	.416	87	118	.737	11	41	52	89	29	1	47	380	4.3	7.4	31.7
04-05—Philadelphia	5	238	59	126	.468	26	29	.897	0	11	11	50	10	2	21	156	2.2	10.0	31.2
Totals	62	2822	677	1685	.402	430	562	.765	55	203	258	378	136	13	199	1899	4.2	6.1	30.6

Three-point field goals: 1998-99, 15-for-53 (.283). 1999-00, 12-for-39 (.308). 2000-01, 48-for-142 (.338). 2001-02, 9-for-27 (.333). 2002-03, 19-for-55 (.345). 2004-05, 12-for-29 (.414). Totals, 115-for-345 (.333).

Personal fouls/disqualifications: 1998-99, 19/0. 1999-00, 24/0. 2000-01, 55/0. 2001-02, 8/0. 2002-03, 25/0. 2004-05, 12/0. Totals, 143/0.

NBA ALL-STAR GAME RECORD

NOTES: NBA All-Star Game Most Valuable Player (2001). ... Holds career record for highest points per game average—22.8.

Season Team	Min.	FGM	FGA	Pct.	FTM	FTA	Pct.	Off.	Def.	Tot.	Ast.	PF	Dq.	St.	Blk.	TO	Pts.
2000—Philadelphia	28	10	18	.556	4	5	.800	0	2	2	9	0	0	2	0	5	26
2001—Philadelphia	27	9	21	.429	6	6	1.000	0	2	2	5	0	0	4	0	4	25
2002—Philadelphia	25	2	9	.222	1	2	.500	1	3	4	3	0	0	0	0	2	5
2003—Philadelphia	41	13	23	.565	8	9	.889	3	2	5	7	2	0	5	0	6	35
2004—Philadelphia	23	1	6	.167	1	4	.250	0	1	1	11	3	0	0	0	4	3
2005—Philadelphia	32	4	14	.286	7	7	1.000	0	4	4	10	0	0	5	0	7	15
2006—Philadelphia	26	5	14	.357	2	4	.500	0	2	2	2	0	0	0	0	3	12
Totals	202	44	105	.419	29	37	.784	6	14	20	47	5	0	16	0	31	121

Three-point field goals: 2000, 2-for-2 (1.000). 2001, 1-for-1 (1.000). 2003, 1-for-3 (.333). Totals, 4-for-6 (.667).

IVEY, ROYAL   G   HAWKS

PERSONAL: Born December 20, 1981, in Harlem, N.Y. ... 6-3/200. (1.91/90.7). ... Full name: Royal Terence Ivey
HIGH SCHOOL: Cardozo (Brooklyn, N.Y.), then Blair Academy (Blairstown, N.J.).
COLLEGE: Texas.
TRANSACTIONS/CAREER NOTES: Selected by Atlanta Hawks in second round (37th pick overall) of 2004 NBA Draft.

COLLEGIATE RECORD

Season Team	G	Min.	FGM	FGA	Pct.	FTM	FTA	Pct.	Reb.	Ast.	Pts.	RPG	APG	PPG
												AVERAGES		
00-01—Texas	33	520	31	85	.365	29	44	.659	54	57	94	1.6	1.7	2.8
01-02—Texas	34	962	133	280	.475	78	100	.780	120	48	370	3.5	1.4	10.9
02-03—Texas	33	826	92	194	.474	65	84	.774	99	54	261	3.0	1.6	7.9
03-04—Texas	33	979	111	248	.448	77	123	.626	133	141	311	4.0	4.3	9.4
Totals	133	3287	367	807	.455	249	351	.709	406	300	1036	3.1	2.3	7.8

Three-point field goals: 2000-01, 3-for-12 (.250). 2001-02, 26-for-69 (.377). 2002-03, 12-for-45 (.267). 2003-04, 12-for-31 (.387). Totals, 53-for-157 (.338).

NBA REGULAR-SEASON RECORD

Season Team	G	Min.	FGM	FGA	Pct.	FTM	FTA	Pct.	Off.	Def.	Tot.	Ast.	St.	Blk.	TO	Pts.	RPG	APG	PPG
									REBOUNDS								AVERAGES		
04-05—Atlanta	62	809	85	198	.429	47	67	.701	19	65	84	103	39	7	58	220	1.4	1.7	3.5
05-06—Atlanta	73	978	116	264	.439	24	33	.727	31	65	96	74	24	7	23	260	1.3	1.0	3.6
Totals	135	1787	201	462	.435	71	100	.710	50	130	180	177	63	14	81	480	1.3	1.3	3.6

Three-point field goals: 2004-05, 3-for-9 (.333). 2005-06, 4-for-10 (.400). Totals, 7-for-19 (.368).
Personal fouls/disqualifications: 2004-05, 140/1. 2005-06, 147/1. Totals, 287/2.

JACK, JARRETT   G   TRAIL BLAZERS

PERSONAL: Born October 28, 1983, in Fort Washington, Md. ... 6-3/202. (1.91/91.6). ... Full name: Jarrett Matthew Jack
HIGH SCHOOL: Worcester Academy (Worcester, Mass.).
COLLEGE: Georgia Tech.
TRANSACTIONS/CAREER NOTES: Selected after junior season by Denver Nuggets in first round (22nd pick overall) of 2005 NBA Draft. ... Draft rights traded by Nuggets to Portland Trail Blazers for draft rights to Fs Linas Kleiza and Ricky Sanchez (June 28, 2005).

COLLEGIATE RECORD

Season Team	G	Min.	FGM	FGA	Pct.	FTM	FTA	Pct.	Reb.	Ast.	Pts.	RPG	APG	PPG
												AVERAGES		
02-03—Georgia Tech	31	984	97	213	.455	83	118	.703	110	185	294	3.5	6.0	9.5
03-04—Georgia Tech	38	1185	145	318	.456	154	192	.802	185	213	474	4.9	5.6	12.5
04-05—Georgia Tech	32	1091	164	319	.514	123	142	.866	155	145	497	4.8	4.5	15.5
Totals	101	3260	406	850	.478	360	452	.796	450	543	1265	4.5	5.4	12.5

Three-point field goals: 2002-03, 17-for-60 (.283). 2003-04, 30-for-95 (.316). 2004-05, 46-for-104 (.442). Totals, 93-for-259 (.359).

NBA REGULAR-SEASON RECORD

Season Team	G	Min.	FGM	FGA	Pct.	FTM	FTA	Pct.	Off.	Def.	Tot.	Ast.	St.	Blk.	TO	Pts.	RPG	APG	PPG
									REBOUNDS								AVERAGES		
05-06—Portland	79	1599	189	428	.442	128	160	.800	18	142	160	219	41	2	102	526	2.0	2.8	6.7

Three-point field goals: 2005-06, 20-for-76 (.263). Totals, 20-for-76 (.263).
Personal fouls/disqualifications: 2005-06, 138/0. Totals, 138/0.

JACKSON, BOBBY   G   HORNETS

PERSONAL: Born March 13, 1973, in East Spencer, N.C. ... 6-1/185. (1.85/83.9).
HIGH SCHOOL: Salisbury (N.C.).
JUNIOR COLLEGE: Western Nebraska Community College.
COLLEGE: Minnesota.
TRANSACTIONS/CAREER NOTES: Selected by Seattle SuperSonics in first round (23rd pick overall) of 1997 NBA Draft. ... Draft rights traded by SuperSonics to Denver Nuggets for draft rights to G James Cotton and 1998 second-round draft choice (June 25, 1997). ... Traded by Nuggets with C Dean Garrett to Minnesota Timberwolves in three-way deal in which Nuggets received G Chauncey Billups and draft rights to G Tyson Wheeler from Toronto Raptors and Raptors received 1999 first-round draft choice from Nuggets and draft rights to F Zeljko Rebraca, G Michael Williams and 1999 or 2000 first-round draft choice from Timberwolves (January 21, 1999). ... Signed as free agent by Sacramento Kings (August 1, 2000). ... Traded by Kings with C Greg Ostertag to Memphis Grizzlies for F Bonzi Wells (August 2, 2005). ... Signed as free agent by New Orleans/Oklahoma City Hornets (July 26, 2006).

COLLEGIATE RECORD

Season Team	G	Min.	FGM	FGA	Pct.	FTM	FTA	Pct.	Reb.	Ast.	Pts.	RPG	APG	PPG
												AVERAGES		
93-94—Western Nebraska C.C.	39	...	155	298	.520	98	136	.721	158	105	413	4.1	2.7	10.6
94-95—Western Nebraska C.C.	32	...	166	302	.550	52	79	.658	161	143	406	5.0	4.5	12.7
95-96—Minnesota	25	683	115	283	.406	74	94	.787	119	68	332	4.8	2.7	13.3
96-97—Minnesota	35	1101	191	433	.441	121	154	.786	213	139	534	6.1	4.0	15.3
Junior College Totals	71	...	321	600	.535	150	215	.698	319	248	819	4.5	3.5	11.5
4-Year-College Totals	60	1784	306	716	.427	195	248	.786	332	207	866	5.5	3.5	14.4

Three-point field goals: 1993-94, 5-for-28 (.179). 1994-95, 22-for-67 (.328). 1995-96, 28-for-95 (.295). 1996-97, 31-for-97 (.320). Totals, 86-for-287 (.300).
Personal fouls/disqualifications: 1995-96, 63/1. Totals, 63/1.

NBA REGULAR-SEASON RECORD

HONORS: NBA All-Rookie second team (1998). ... NBA Sixth Man Award (2003).

Season Team	G	Min.	FGM	FGA	Pct.	FTM	FTA	Pct.	Off.	Def.	Tot.	Ast.	St.	Blk.	TO	Pts.	RPG	APG	PPG
									REBOUNDS								AVERAGES		
97-98—Denver	68	2042	310	791	.392	149	183	.814	78	224	302	317	105	11	184	790	4.4	4.7	11.6
98-99—Minnesota	50	941	141	348	.405	61	79	.772	43	92	135	167	39	3	75	353	2.7	3.3	7.1

J

Season Team	G	Min.	FGM	FGA	Pct.	FTM	FTA	Pct.	REBOUNDS Off.	Def.	Tot.	Ast.	St.	Blk.	TO	Pts.	AVERAGES RPG	APG	PPG
99-00—Minnesota	73	1034	140	346	.405	76	98	.776	50	103	153	172	48	7	58	369	2.1	2.4	5.1
00-01—Sacramento	79	1648	231	526	.439	65	88	.739	74	172	246	161	87	7	103	566	3.1	2.0	7.2
01-02—Sacramento	81	1750	334	754	.443	149	184	.810	82	169	251	164	73	11	93	896	3.1	2.0	11.1
02-03—Sacramento	59	1676	340	732	.464	126	149	.846	57	162	219	182	71	3	106	895	3.7	3.1	15.2
03-04—Sacramento	50	1185	263	592	.444	82	109	.752	55	119	174	105	49	8	63	689	3.5	2.1	13.8
04-05—Sacramento	25	536	109	255	.427	50	58	.862	23	62	85	59	14	2	28	301	3.4	2.4	12.0
05-06—Memphis	71	1775	286	748	.382	107	146	.733	44	179	223	195	61	1	101	808	3.1	2.7	11.4
Totals	556	12587	2154	5092	.423	865	1094	.791	506	1282	1788	1522	547	53	811	5667	3.2	2.7	10.2

Three-point field goals: 1997-98, 21-for-81 (.259). 1998-99, 10-for-27 (.370). 1999-00, 13-for-46 (.283). 2000-01, 39-for-104 (.375). 2001-02, 79-for-219 (.361). 2002-03, 89-for-235 (.379). 2003-04, 81-for-219 (.370). 2004-05, 33-for-96 (.344). 2005-06, 129-for-332 (.389). Totals, 494-for-1359 (.364).

Personal fouls/disqualifications: 1997-98, 160/0. 1998-99, 75/1. 1999-00, 114/0. 2000-01, 139/0. 2001-02, 145/1. 2002-03, 126/0. 2003-04, 106/1. 2004-05, 58/1. 2005-06, 155/2. Totals, 1078/6.

NBA PLAYOFF RECORD

Season Team	G	Min.	FGM	FGA	Pct.	FTM	FTA	Pct.	REBOUNDS Off.	Def.	Tot.	Ast.	St.	Blk.	TO	Pts.	AVERAGES RPG	APG	PPG
98-99—Minnesota	4	27	2	10	.200	0	0	...	1	3	4	2	0	0	1	4	1.0	0.5	1.0
99-00—Minnesota	3	30	4	8	.500	6	6	1.000	0	5	5	4	2	1	2	15	1.7	1.3	5.0
00-01—Sacramento	8	182	21	48	.438	10	14	.714	6	20	26	18	8	0	7	56	3.3	2.3	7.0
01-02—Sacramento	16	374	65	146	.445	34	43	.791	15	37	52	32	14	3	18	175	3.3	2.0	10.9
02-03—Sacramento	12	331	63	138	.457	31	35	.886	11	43	54	40	12	1	17	172	4.5	3.3	14.3
04-05—Sacramento	5	79	10	37	.270	3	3	1.000	2	4	6	9	1	1	3	26	1.2	1.8	5.2
05-06—Memphis	4	100	12	29	.414	5	7	.714	0	8	8	5	1	0	14	33	2.0	1.3	8.3
Totals	52	1123	177	416	.425	89	108	.824	35	120	155	110	38	6	62	481	3.0	2.1	9.3

Three-point field goals: 1998-99, 0-for-3. 1999-00, 1-for-3 (.333). 2000-01, 4-for-14 (.286). 2001-02, 11-for-43 (.256). 2002-03, 15-for-43 (.349). 2004-05, 3-for-18 (.167). 2005-06, 4-for-11 (.364). Totals, 38-for-135 (.281).

Personal fouls/disqualifications: 1998-99, 3/0. 1999-00, 4/0. 2000-01, 18/0. 2001-02, 31/0. 2002-03, 22/1. 2004-05, 5/0. 2005-06, 7/0. Totals, 90/1.

JACKSON, JIM   G   LAKERS

PERSONAL: Born October 14, 1970, in Toledo, Ohio. ... 6-6/220. (1.98/99.8). ... Full name: James Arthur Jackson
HIGH SCHOOL: Macomber-Whitney (Toledo, Ohio).
COLLEGE: Ohio State.
TRANSACTIONS/CAREER NOTES: Selected after junior season by Dallas Mavericks in first round (fourth pick overall) of 1992 NBA Draft. ... Traded by Mavericks with C Eric Montross, F/C Chris Gatling, F/G George McCloud and G Sam Cassell to New Jersey Nets for C Shawn Bradley, F Ed O'Bannon, G Khalid Reeves and G Robert Pack (February 17, 1997). ... Traded by Nets with draft rights to F Tim Thomas, draft rights to G Anthony Parker and C Eric Montross to Philadelphia 76ers for C Michael Cage, G Lucious Harris, F Don MacLean and draft rights to F Keith Van Horn (June 27, 1997). ... Traded by 76ers with F Clarence Weatherspoon to Golden State Warriors for F Joe Smith and G Brian Shaw (February 17, 1998). ... Signed as free agent by Portland Trail Blazers (February 2, 1999). ... Traded by Trail Blazers with G Isaiah Rider to Atlanta Hawks for G Steve Smith and G Ed Gray (August 2, 1999). ... Traded by Hawks with G Anthony Johnson and F/G Larry Robinson to Cleveland Cavaliers for G Brevin Knight (January 2, 2001). ... Signed as free agent by Miami Heat (December 2, 2001). ... Signed as free agent by Sacramento Kings (November 30, 2002). ... Signed as free agent by Houston Rockets (September 30, 2003). ... Traded with F Bostjan Nachbar to New Orleans Hornets for G David Wesley (December 27, 2004). ... Traded by Hornets with a 2005 second-round draft choice to Phoenix Suns for G/F Casey Jacobsen, F Maciej Lampe and F/C Jackson Vroman (January 21, 2005). ... Waived by Suns (March 1, 2006). ... Signed by Los Angeles Lakers (March 6, 2006).

COLLEGIATE RECORD

NOTES: THE SPORTING NEWS All-America first team (1992). ... THE SPORTING NEWS All-America third team (1991).

Season Team	G	Min.	FGM	FGA	Pct.	FTM	FTA	Pct.	Reb.	Ast.	Pts.	AVERAGES RPG	APG	PPG
89-90—Ohio State	30	1035	194	389	.499	73	93	.785	166	110	482	5.5	3.7	16.1
90-91—Ohio State	31	997	228	441	.517	112	149	.752	169	133	585	5.5	4.3	18.9
91-92—Ohio State	32	1133	264	535	.493	146	180	.811	217	129	718	6.8	4.0	22.4
Totals	93	3165	686	1365	.503	331	422	.784	552	372	1785	5.9	4.0	19.2

Three-point field goals: 1989-90, 21-for-59 (.356). 1990-91, 17-for-51 (.333). 1991-92, 44-for-108 (.407). Totals, 82-for-218 (.376).

NBA REGULAR-SEASON RECORD

Season Team	G	Min.	FGM	FGA	Pct.	FTM	FTA	Pct.	REBOUNDS Off.	Def.	Tot.	Ast.	St.	Blk.	TO	Pts.	AVERAGES RPG	APG	PPG
92-93—Dallas	28	938	184	466	.395	68	92	.739	42	80	122	131	40	11	115	457	4.4	4.7	16.3
93-94—Dallas	82	3066	637	1432	.445	285	347	.821	169	219	388	374	87	25	*334	1576	4.7	4.6	19.2
94-95—Dallas	51	1982	484	1026	.472	306	380	.805	120	140	260	191	28	12	160	1309	5.1	3.7	25.7
95-96—Dallas	82	2820	569	1308	.435	345	418	.825	173	237	410	235	47	22	191	1604	5.0	2.9	19.6
96-97—Dal.-N.J.	77	2831	444	1029	.431	252	310	.813	132	279	411	316	86	32	208	1226	5.3	4.1	15.9
97-98—Phila.-G.S.	79	3046	476	1107	.430	229	282	.812	130	270	400	381	79	8	263	1242	5.1	4.8	15.7
98-99—Portland	49	1175	152	370	.411	85	101	.842	36	123	159	128	43	6	82	414	3.2	2.6	8.4
99-00—Atlanta	79	2767	507	1235	.411	186	212	.877	101	293	394	230	57	10	185	1317	5.0	2.9	16.7
00-01—Atl.-Cleve.	56	1690	239	632	.378	139	169	.822	53	171	224	163	53	10	130	643	4.0	2.9	11.5
01-02—Miami	55	1825	238	538	.442	75	87	.862	54	236	290	140	42	14	106	589	5.3	2.5	10.7
02-03—Sacramento	63	1309	204	462	.442	47	55	.855	84	178	262	118	31	4	80	487	4.2	1.9	7.7
03-04—Houston	80	3119	380	900	.424	107	127	.843	52	435	487	226	86	23	175	1033	6.1	2.8	12.9
04-05—Hous.-N.O.-Pho.	64	1987	248	582	.426	54	58	.931	33	236	269	183	35	5	115	672	4.2	2.9	10.5
05-06—Phoe.-L.A.L.	40	512	47	160	.294	9	13	.692	11	65	76	35	12	6	35	121	1.9	0.9	3.0
Totals	885	29067	4811	11247	.428	2187	2651	.825	1190	2962	4152	2851	726	188	2179	12690	4.7	3.2	14.3

Three-point field goals: 1992-93, 21-for-73 (.288). 1993-94, 17-for-60 (.283). 1994-95, 35-for-110 (.318). 1995-96, 121-for-333 (.363). 1996-97, 86-for-247 (.348). 1997-98, 61-for-191 (.319). 1998-99, 25-for-90 (.278). 1999-00, 117-for-303 (.386). 2000-01, 26-for-80 (.325). 2001-02, 38-for-81 (.469). 2002-03, 32-for-71 (.451). 2003-04, 162-for-405 (.400). 2004-05, 122-for-295 (.414). 2005-06, 18-for-74 (.243). Totals, 881-for-2413 (.365).

Personal fouls/disqualifications: 1992-93, 80/0. 1993-94, 161/0. 1994-95, 92/0. 1995-96, 165/0. 1996-97, 194/0. 1997-98, 186/0. 1998-99, 80/0. 1999-00, 167/0. 2000-01, 139/0. 2001-02, 145/0. 2002-03, 132/0. 2003-04, 227/1. 2004-05, 153/1. 2005-06, 51/0. Totals, 1972/2.

NBA PLAYOFF RECORD

								REBOUNDS								AVERAGES		
Season Team	G	Min.	FGM	FGA	Pct.	FTM	FTA	Pct.	Off.	Def.	Tot.	Ast.	St.	Blk.	TO	Pts.	RPG	APG	PPG
98-99—Portland	13	265	26	72	.361	38	42	.905	8	22	30	19	7	1	18	95	2.3	1.5	7.3
02-03—Sacramento	12	296	49	98	.500	24	31	.774	16	31	47	14	8	3	17	135	3.9	1.2	11.3
03-04—Houston	5	221	29	73	.397	8	12	.667	3	49	52	10	5	1	9	74	10.4	2.0	14.8
04-05—Phoenix	15	474	63	129	.488	7	8	.875	13	48	61	22	10	8	10	165	4.1	1.5	11.0
05-06—L.A. Lakers	3	21	2	6	.333	0	0	...	2	1	3	2	1	1	2	4	1.0	0.7	1.3
Totals	48	1277	169	378	.447	77	93	.828	42	151	193	67	31	14	56	473	4.0	1.4	9.9

Three-point field goals: 1998-99, 5-for-18 (.278). 2002-03, 13-for-28 (.464). 2003-04, 8-for-29 (.276). 2004-05, 32-for-62 (.516). 2005-06, 0-for-1. Totals, 58-for-138 (.420).

Personal fouls/disqualifications: 1998-99, 26/0. 2002-03, 34/1. 2003-04, 9/0. 2004-05, 42/1. 2005-06, 4/0. Totals, 115/2.

JACKSON, JERMAINE   G

PERSONAL: Born June 7, 1976, in Detroit. ... 6-5/204. (1.96/92.5).
HIGH SCHOOL: Finney (Detroit).
COLLEGE: Detroit Mercy.
TRANSACTIONS/CAREER NOTES: Not drafted by an NBA franchise. ... Signed as free agent by Detroit Pistons (October 4, 1999). ... Signed as free agent by Philadelphia 76ers (August 17, 2000). ... Waived by 76ers (October 30, 2000). ... Played in Italy (2000-01). ... Played in Continental Basketball Association with Quad City Thunder (2000-01) and Flint Fuze (2001-02). ... Signed by Toronto Raptors to first of two consecutive 10-day contracts (January 10, 2002). ... Signed by Raptors for remainder of season (January 30, 2002). ... Waived by Raptors (October 25, 2002). ... Re-signed as free agent by Raptors (November 20, 2002). ... Waived by Raptors (January 7, 2003). ... Signed by Atlanta Hawks to first of consecutive 10-day contracts (January 30, 2003). ... Re-signed by Hawks for remainder of season (February 21, 2003). ... Signed by New York Knicks to 10-day contract (February 28, 2005). ... Traded by Knicks with F Michael Sweetney and F Tim Thomas and 2007 and 2009 second-round draft picks, a conditional 2006 first-round pick and a conditional right to swap 2007 first-round picks to Chicago Bulls for C Eddy Curry and F/C Antonio Davis (October 4, 2005). ... Waived by Bulls (October 18, 2005). ... Signed by Milwaukee Bucks (December 15, 2005).

COLLEGIATE RECORD

												AVERAGES		
Season Team	G	Min.	FGM	FGA	Pct.	FTM	FTA	Pct.	Reb.	Ast.	Pts.	RPG	APG	PPG
95-96—Detroit	27	955	83	200	.415	53	82	.646	106	100	240	3.9	3.7	8.9
96-97—Detroit	29	1003	90	218	.413	76	108	.704	106	120	295	3.7	4.1	10.2
97-98—Detroit	31	993	124	275	.451	110	157	.701	143	149	374	4.6	4.8	12.1
98-99—Detroit	31	1081	131	305	.430	146	194	.753	198	140	432	6.4	4.5	13.9
Totals	118	4032	428	998	.429	385	541	.712	553	509	1341	4.7	4.3	11.4

Three-point field goals: 1995-96, 21-for-58 (.362). 1996-97, 39-for-97 (.402). 1997-98, 16-for-50 (.320). 1998-99, 24-for-75 (.320). Totals, 100-for-280 (.357).

Personal fouls/disqualifications: 1995-96, 47/0. 1996-97, 54/0. 1997-98, 58/0. 1998-99, 56/1. Totals, 215/1.

NBA REGULAR-SEASON RECORD

								REBOUNDS								AVERAGES		
Season Team	G	Min.	FGM	FGA	Pct.	FTM	FTA	Pct.	Off.	Def.	Tot.	Ast.	St.	Blk.	TO	Pts.	RPG	APG	PPG
99-00—Detroit	7	73	1	11	.091	5	8	.625	1	10	11	4	3	0	7	7	1.6	0.6	1.0
01-02—Toronto	24	280	20	42	.476	16	24	.667	3	24	27	57	9	1	14	57	1.1	2.4	2.4
02-03—Toronto-Atlanta	53	559	40	110	.364	40	55	.727	19	38	57	74	19	6	34	121	1.1	1.4	2.3
04-05—New York	21	230	17	33	.515	8	13	.615	3	20	23	24	7	1	10	42	1.1	1.1	2.0
05-06—Milwaukee	30	202	11	26	.423	12	14	.857	8	19	27	25	4	1	13	35	0.9	0.8	1.2
Totals	135	1344	89	222	.401	81	114	.711	34	111	145	184	42	9	78	262	1.1	1.4	1.9

Three-point field goals: 1999-00, 0-for-1. 2001-02, 1-for-2 (.500). 2002-03, 1-for-10 (.100). 2004-05, 0-for-2. 2005-06, 1-for-4 (.250). Totals, 3-for-19 (.158).

Personal fouls/disqualifications: 1999-00, 7/0. 2001-02, 24/0. 2002-03, 51/0. 2004-05, 26/0. 2005-06, 19/0. Totals, 127/0.

NBA PLAYOFF RECORD

								REBOUNDS								AVERAGES		
Season Team	G	Min.	FGM	FGA	Pct.	FTM	FTA	Pct.	Off.	Def.	Tot.	Ast.	St.	Blk.	TO	Pts.	RPG	APG	PPG
01-02—Toronto	4	12	2	3	.667	2	6	.333	0	1	1	0	0	0	3	6	0.3	0.0	1.5
05-06—Milwaukee	2	4	0	2	.000	0	0	...	0	0	0	2	0	0	0	0	0.0	1.0	0.0
Totals	6	16	2	5	.400	2	6	.333	0	1	1	2	0	0	3	6	0.2	0.3	1.0

Personal fouls/disqualifications: 2001-02, 2/0. 2005-06, 1/0. Totals, 3/0.

CBA RECORD

												AVERAGES		
Season Team	G	Min.	FGM	FGA	Pct.	FTM	FTA	Pct.	Reb.	Ast.	Pts.	RPG	APG	PPG
00-01—Quad City	50	1794	288	693	.416	186	230	.809	206	306	827	4.1	6.1	16.5
01-02—Flint	32	1107	174	405	.430	154	186	.828	114	267	525	3.6	8.3	16.4
02-03—Great Lakes	8	319	53	102	.520	46	58	.793	42	68	160	5.3	8.5	20.0
03-04—Great Lakes	6	279	49	88	.557	41	54	.759	42	61	143	7.0	10.2	23.8
04-05—Great Lakes	15	685	101	188	.537	83	101	.822	85	176	304	5.7	11.7	20.3
Totals	111	4184	665	1476	.451	510	629	.811	489	878	1959	4.4	7.9	17.6

Three-point field goals: 2000-01, 65-for-208 (.313). 2001-02, 23-for-60 (.383). 2002-03, 8-for-17 (.471). 2003-04, 4-for-11 (.364). 2004-05, 19-for-40 (.475). Totals, 119-for-336 (.354).

Personal fouls/disqualifications: 2000-01, 28/0. 2002-03, 19/0. Totals, 47/0.

ITALIAN LEAGUE RECORD

												AVERAGES		
Season Team	G	Min.	FGM	FGA	Pct.	FTM	FTA	Pct.	Reb.	Ast.	Pts.	RPG	APG	PPG
00-01—Muller Verona	4	145	27	57	.474	9	16	.563	12	11	65	3.0	2.8	16.3
03-04—Benetton Treviso	17	466	47	100	.470	39	55	.709	43	36	145	2.5	2.1	8.5
Totals	21	611	74	157	.471	48	71	.676	55	47	210	2.6	2.2	10.0

Three-point field goals: 2000-01, 2-for-11 (.182). 2003-04, 12-for-32 (.375). Totals, 14-for-43 (.326).

Season Team	G	Min.	FGM	FGA	Pct.	FTM	FTA	Pct.	Reb.	Ast.	Pts.	AVERAGES RPG	APG	PPG
03-04—Aris Castrol	5	176	15	41	.366	19	28	.679	10	31	49	2.0	6.2	9.8

Three-point field goals: 2003-04, 0-for-6. Totals, 0-for-6 (.000).

SPANISH LEAGUE RECORD

Season Team	G	Min.	FGM	FGA	Pct.	FTM	FTA	Pct.	Reb.	Ast.	Pts.	AVERAGES RPG	APG	PPG
04-05—Pamesa Valencia	10	319	37	73	.507	29	38	.763	22	38	112	2.2	3.8	11.2

Three-point field goals: 2004-05, 9-for-25 (.360). Totals, 9-for-25 (.360).

JACKSON, LUKE   F   CAVALIERS

PERSONAL: Born November 6, 1981, in Eugene, Ore. ... 6-7/215. (2.01/97.5). ... Full name: Luke Ryan Jackson
HIGH SCHOOL: Creswell (Ore.).
COLLEGE: Oregon.
TRANSACTIONS/CAREER NOTES: Selected by Cleveland Cavaliers in first round (10th pick overall) of 2004 NBA Draft.

COLLEGIATE RECORD

NOTES: The SPORTING NEWS All-America first team (2004).

Season Team	G	Min.	FGM	FGA	Pct.	FTM	FTA	Pct.	Reb.	Ast.	Pts.	AVERAGES RPG	APG	PPG
00-01—Oregon	28	506	73	172	.424	54	73	.740	114	55	218	4.1	2.0	7.8
01-02—Oregon	35	1069	189	413	.458	159	184	.864	188	115	583	5.4	3.3	16.7
02-03—Oregon	32	1018	173	383	.452	130	150	.867	221	115	513	6.9	3.6	16.0
03-04—Oregon	31	1072	210	430	.488	163	189	.862	223	139	656	7.2	4.5	21.2
Totals	126	3665	645	1398	.461	506	596	.849	746	424	1970	5.9	3.4	15.6

Three-point field goals: 2000-01, 18-for-50 (.360). 2001-02, 46-for-115 (.400). 2002-03, 37-for-102 (.363). 2003-04, 73-for-166 (.440). Totals, 174-for-433 (.402).

NBA REGULAR-SEASON RECORD

Season Team	G	Min.	FGM	FGA	Pct.	FTM	FTA	Pct.	REBOUNDS Off.	Def.	Tot.	Ast.	St.	Blk.	TO	Pts.	AVERAGES RPG	APG	PPG
04-05—Cleveland	10	43	10	27	.370	5	6	.833	2	4	6	3	0	0	2	29	0.6	0.3	2.9
05-06—Cleveland	36	315	29	85	.341	26	33	.788	16	24	40	25	11	2	31	96	1.1	0.7	2.7
Totals	46	358	39	112	.348	31	39	.795	18	28	46	28	11	2	33	125	1.0	0.6	2.7

Three-point field goals: 2004-05, 4-for-6 (.667). 2005-06, 12-for-36 (.333). Totals, 16-for-42 (.381).
Personal fouls/disqualifications: 2004-05, 4/0. 2005-06, 30/0. Totals, 34/0.

JACKSON, MARC   F/C   HORNETS

PERSONAL: Born January 16, 1975, in Philadelphia. ... 6-10/270. (2.08/122.5). ... Full name: Marc Anthony Jackson
HIGH SCHOOL: Roman Catholic (Philadelphia).
COLLEGE: Virginia Commonwealth, then Temple.
TRANSACTIONS/CAREER NOTES: Selected after junior season by Golden State Warriors in second round (38th pick overall) of 1997 NBA Draft. ... Played in Turkey (1997-98). ... Played in Spain (1998-2000). ... Traded by Warriors to Minnesota Timberwolves for C Dean Garrett and 2007 second-round draft choice (February 21, 2002). ... Traded by Timberwolves to Philadelphia 76ers in three-team deal in which Timberwolves also dealt G Terrell Brandon to Atlanta Hawks and acquired G Latrell Sprewell from New York Knicks. Knicks acquired F Keith Van Horn from 76ers, Hawks acquired F Randy Holcomb, a first-round draft pick and cash considerations from 76ers and 76ers acquired F Glenn Robinson and 2006 second-round pick from Hawks (July 23, 2003) ... Traded by 76ers to New Jersey Nets for a conditional second-round pick (August 9, 2005). ... Traded by Nets with F Linton Johnson and cash to New Orleans Hornets for F Bostjan Nachbar (February 23, 2006).

COLLEGIATE RECORD

Season Team	G	Min.	FGM	FGA	Pct.	FTM	FTA	Pct.	Reb.	Ast.	Pts.	AVERAGES RPG	APG	PPG
93-94—Virginia Commonwealth .	22	277	23	52	.442	12	21	.571	67	9	58	3.0	0.4	2.6
94-95—Temple............................						Did not play—transfer student.								
95-96—Temple..........................	32	1117	183	384	.477	133	199	.668	287	24	501	9.0	0.8	15.7
96-97—Temple..........................	31	1201	175	366	.478	148	193	.767	278	38	500	9.0	1.2	16.1
Totals	85	2595	381	802	.475	293	413	.709	632	71	1059	7.4	0.8	12.5

Three-point field goals: 1995-96, 2-for-4 (.500). 1996-97, 2-for-6 (.333). Totals, 4-for-10 (.400).
Personal fouls/disqualifications: 1993-94, 35/0. 1995-96, 62/0. Totals, 97/0.

TURKISH LEAGUE RECORD

Season Team	G	Min.	FGM	FGA	Pct.	FTM	FTA	Pct.	Reb.	Ast.	Pts.	AVERAGES RPG	APG	PPG
97-98—Tofas Bursa	27	...	179	316	.566	155	206	.752	293	39	518	10.9	1.4	19.2

Three-point field goals: 1997-98, 7-for-15 (.467). Totals, 7-for-15 (.467).

SPANISH LEAGUE RECORD

Season Team	G	Min.	FGM	FGA	Pct.	FTM	FTA	Pct.	Reb.	Ast.	Pts.	AVERAGES RPG	APG	PPG
98-99—Lobos Caja Cantabria	14	505	119	254	.469	60	79	.759	130	27	298	9.3	1.9	21.3
99-00—Cantabria Lobos	23	852	156	315	.495	108	168	.643	192	27	427	8.3	1.2	18.6
Totals	37	1357	275	569	.483	168	247	.680	322	54	725	8.7	1.5	19.6

Three-point field goals: 1998-99, 0-for-9. 1999-00, 7-for-17 (.412). Totals, 7-for-26 (.269).
Personal fouls/disqualifications: 1998-99, 34/0. 1999-00, 66/0. Totals, 100/0.

HONORS: NBA All-Rookie first team (2001).

Season Team	G	Min.	FGM	FGA	Pct.	FTM	FTA	Pct.	REBOUNDS Off.	Def.	Tot.	Ast.	St.	Blk.	TO	Pts.	AVERAGES RPG	APG	PPG
00-01—Golden State...	48	1410	237	508	.467	154	192	.802	119	242	361	59	34	27	93	633	7.5	1.2	13.2
01-02—G.S.-Minn.	39	495	60	164	.366	66	80	.825	48	80	128	14	11	6	30	186	3.3	0.4	4.8
02-03—Minnesota.......	77	1041	153	349	.438	114	149	.765	86	139	225	37	24	30	59	421	2.9	0.5	5.5
03-04—Philadelphia	22	598	71	171	.415	64	81	.790	45	81	126	18	12	6	24	206	5.7	0.8	9.4
04-05—Philadelphia	81	1976	340	731	.465	289	349	.828	184	222	406	81	32	18	131	969	5.0	1.0	12.0
05-06—N.J.-NO/Okla. City	64	1027	174	369	.472	66	82	.805	86	131	217	44	13	8	65	415	3.4	0.7	6.5
Totals	331	6547	1035	2292	.452	753	933	.807	568	895	1463	253	126	95	402	2830	4.4	0.8	8.5

Three-point field goals: 2000-01, 5-for-23 (.217). 2001-02, 0-for-1. 2002-03, 1-for-1 (1.000). 2003-04, 0-for-1. 2004-05, 0-for-2. 2005-06, 1-for-2 (.500). Totals, 7-for-30 (.233).

Personal fouls/disqualifications: 2000-01, 138/1. 2001-02, 69/0. 2002-03, 137/0. 2003-04, 45/0. 2004-05, 171/0. 2005-06, 126/1. Totals, 686/2.

NBA PLAYOFF RECORD

Season Team	G	Min.	FGM	FGA	Pct.	FTM	FTA	Pct.	REBOUNDS Off.	Def.	Tot.	Ast.	St.	Blk.	TO	Pts.	AVERAGES RPG	APG	PPG
01-02—Minnesota.......	1	1	0	0	...	0	0	...	0	0	0	0	0	0	0	0	0.0	0.0	0.0
02-03—Minnesota.......	6	110	17	32	.531	16	19	.842	10	23	33	8	2	1	9	50	5.5	1.3	8.3
04-05—Philadelphia	5	65	5	20	.250	7	11	.636	3	5	8	0	2	2	6	17	1.6	0.0	3.4
Totals	12	176	22	52	.423	23	30	.767	13	28	41	8	4	3	15	67	3.4	0.7	5.6

Three-point field goals: 2002-03, 0-for-1. Totals, 0-for-1 (.000).
Personal fouls/disqualifications: 2001-02, 1/0. 2002-03, 19/0. 2004-05, 9/0. Totals, 29/0.

JACKSON, STEPHEN   G/F   PACERS

PERSONAL: Born April 5, 1978, in Houston. ... 6-8/218. (2.03/98.9). ... Full name: Stephen Jesse Jackson
HIGH SCHOOL: Lincoln (Port Arthur, Texas), then Oak Hill Academy (Mouth of Wilson, Va.).
JUNIOR COLLEGE: Butler County (Kan.) C.C. (did not play basketball).
TRANSACTIONS/CAREER NOTES: Selected after freshman season by Phoenix Suns in second round (43rd pick overall) of 1997 NBA Draft. ... Waived by Suns (October 30, 1997). ... Played in Continental Basketball Association with La Crosse Bobcats (1997-98) and Fort Wayne Fury (1999-2000). ... Played in Venezuela (1999-2000). ... Signed as free agent by Vancouver Grizzlies (October 4, 1999). ... Waived by Grizzlies (October 28, 1999). ... Signed by New Jersey Nets (October 2, 2000). ... Signed as free agent by San Antonio Spurs (August 2, 2001). ... Signed as free agent by Atlanta Hawks (October 3, 2003). ... Traded by Hawks to Indiana Pacers for F Al Harrington (July 15, 2004).
MISCELLANEOUS: Member of NBA championship team (2003).

CBA RECORD

Season Team	G	Min.	FGM	FGA	Pct.	FTM	FTA	Pct.	Reb.	Ast.	Pts.	AVERAGES RPG	APG	PPG
97-98—La Crosse	6	76	8	20	.400	0	0	...	2	4	16	0.3	0.7	2.7
99-00—Fort Wayne	5	84	12	31	.387	2	3	.667	8	5	26	1.6	1.0	5.2
Totals	11	160	20	51	.392	2	3	.667	10	9	42	0.9	0.8	3.8

Three-point field goals: 1997-98, 0-for-1. 1999-00, 0-for-2. Totals, 0-for-3 (.000).
Personal fouls/disqualifications: 1999-00, 16/0. Totals, 16/0.

VENEZUELAN LEAGUE RECORD

Season Team	G	Min.	FGM	FGA	Pct.	FTM	FTA	Pct.	Reb.	Ast.	Pts.	AVERAGES RPG	APG	PPG
99-00—Marinos	50	1776	437	756	.578	191	265	.721	143	197	1153	2.9	3.9	23.1

Three-point field goals: 1999-00, 88-for-199 (.442). Totals, 88-for-199 (.442).
Personal fouls/disqualifications: 1999-00, 136/0. Totals, 136/0.

NBA REGULAR-SEASON RECORD

Season Team	G	Min.	FGM	FGA	Pct.	FTM	FTA	Pct.	REBOUNDS Off.	Def.	Tot.	Ast.	St.	Blk.	TO	Pts.	AVERAGES RPG	APG	PPG
00-01—New Jersey	77	1660	243	572	.425	97	135	.719	41	167	208	140	86	14	130	635	2.7	1.8	8.2
01-02—San Antonio	23	227	34	91	.374	12	17	.706	3	23	26	11	15	3	23	89	1.1	0.5	3.9
02-03—San Antonio	80	2254	356	818	.435	139	183	.760	66	220	286	183	125	30	176	946	3.6	2.3	11.8
03-04—Atlanta	80	2940	536	1261	.425	233	297	.785	97	273	370	244	142	20	223	1450	4.6	3.1	18.1
04-05—Indiana..........	51	1806	330	819	.403	190	229	.830	44	206	250	119	64	14	123	953	4.9	2.3	18.7
05-06—Indiana..........	81	2910	472	1148	.411	268	341	.786	48	264	312	225	104	43	203	1329	3.9	2.8	16.4
Totals	392	11797	1971	4709	.419	939	1202	.781	299	1153	1452	922	536	124	878	5402	3.7	2.4	13.8

Three-point field goals: 2000-01, 52-for-155 (.335). 2001-02, 9-for-36 (.250). 2002-03, 95-for-297 (.320). 2003-04, 145-for-427 (.340). 2004-05, 103-for-286 (.360). 2005-06, 117-for-339 (.345). Totals, 521-for-1540 (.338).

Personal fouls/disqualifications: 2000-01, 166/2. 2001-02, 29/0. 2002-03, 202/1. 2003-04, 216/3. 2004-05, 154/4. 2005-06, 195/0. Totals, 962/10.

NBA PLAYOFF RECORD

Season Team	G	Min.	FGM	FGA	Pct.	FTM	FTA	Pct.	REBOUNDS Off.	Def.	Tot.	Ast.	St.	Blk.	TO	Pts.	AVERAGES RPG	APG	PPG
02-03—San Antonio	24	811	108	261	.414	53	66	.803	19	79	98	65	33	9	68	307	4.1	2.7	12.8
04-05—Indiana...........	13	472	70	178	.393	49	60	.817	7	43	50	29	25	6	34	209	3.8	2.2	16.1
05-06—Indiana...........	6	227	30	82	.366	14	18	.778	5	22	27	20	4	1	15	80	4.5	3.3	13.3
Totals	43	1510	208	521	.399	116	144	.806	31	144	175	114	62	16	117	596	4.1	2.7	13.9

Three-point field goals: 2002-03, 38-for-113 (.336). 2004-05, 20-for-63 (.317). 2005-06, 6-for-26 (.231). Totals, 64-for-202 (.317).
Personal fouls/disqualifications: 2002-03, 53/0. 2004-05, 39/0. 2005-06, 23/1. Totals, 115/1.

JAMES, JEROME   C   KNICKS

PERSONAL: Born November 17, 1975, in Tampa. ... 7-1/300. (2.16/136.1). ... Full name: Jerome Keith James
HIGH SCHOOL: Pentacostal Christian Academy (Tampa).
COLLEGE: Florida A&M.
TRANSACTIONS/CAREER NOTES: Selected by Sacramento Kings in second round (36th pick overall) of 1998 NBA Draft. ... Waived by Kings (October 20, 2000). ... Played in Yugoslavia (2000-01). ... Signed as free agent by Seattle SuperSonics (September 5, 2001). ... Signed as free agent by New York Knicks (August 2, 2005).

COLLEGIATE RECORD

NOTES: Led NCAA Division I with 4.6 blocked shots per game (1998).

Season Team	G	Min.	FGM	FGA	Pct.	FTM	FTA	Pct.	Reb.	Ast.	Pts.	RPG	APG	PPG
94-95—Florida A&M						Did not play—ineligible.								
95-96—Florida A&M	27	685	129	288	.448	62	137	.453	219	8	320	8.1	0.3	11.9
96-97—Florida A&M	27	706	177	334	.530	82	147	.558	242	16	436	9.0	0.6	16.1
97-98—Florida A&M	27	799	208	416	.500	120	217	.553	282	30	536	10.4	1.1	19.9
Totals	81	2190	514	1038	.495	264	501	.527	743	54	1292	9.2	0.7	16.0

Three-point field goals: 1995-96, 0-for-1. 1996-97, 0-for-1. Totals, 0-for-2 (.000).

NBA REGULAR-SEASON RECORD

Season Team	G	Min.	FGM	FGA	Pct.	FTM	FTA	Pct.	Off.	Def.	Tot.	Ast.	St.	Blk.	TO	Pts.	RPG	APG	PPG
98-99—Sacramento	16	42	9	24	.375	6	12	.500	11	17	1	2	6	9	24	1.1	0.1	1.5	
99-00—Sacramento						Did not play—injured.													
01-02—Seattle	56	949	134	273	.491	30	60	.500	89	143	232	24	25	86	74	298	4.1	0.4	5.3
02-03—Seattle	51	766	111	232	.478	54	92	.587	78	138	216	27	12	82	75	276	4.2	0.5	5.4
03-04—Seattle	65	990	129	259	.498	66	100	.660	78	152	230	32	20	60	82	324	3.5	0.5	5.0
04-05—Seattle	80	1330	174	342	.509	47	65	.723	81	160	241	19	23	111	88	395	3.0	0.2	4.9
05-06—New York	45	406	56	121	.463	25	40	.625	39	52	91	12	3	23	51	137	2.0	0.3	3.0
Totals	313	4483	613	1251	.490	228	369	.618	371	656	1027	115	85	368	379	1454	3.3	0.4	4.6

Three-point field goals: 2004-05, 0-for-2. Totals, 0-for-2 (.000).
Personal fouls/disqualifications: 1998-99, 11/0. 2001-02, 174/0. 2002-03, 166/3. 2003-04, 180/1. 2004-05, 279/5. 2005-06, 104/0. Totals, 914/9.

NBA PLAYOFF RECORD

Season Team	G	Min.	FGM	FGA	Pct.	FTM	FTA	Pct.	Off.	Def.	Tot.	Ast.	St.	Blk.	TO	Pts.	RPG	APG	PPG
98-99—Sacramento	1	4	1	2	.500	3	4	.750	1	1	2	0	0	0	1	5	2.0	0.0	5.0
01-02—Seattle	5	70	9	23	.391	0	2	.000	4	8	12	4	0	5	4	18	2.4	0.8	3.6
04-05—Seattle	11	295	57	111	.514	23	30	.767	33	42	75	5	6	20	14	137	6.8	0.5	12.5
Totals	17	369	67	136	.493	26	36	.722	38	51	89	9	6	25	19	160	5.2	0.5	9.4

Personal fouls/disqualifications: 1998-99, 1/0. 2001-02, 18/1. 2004-05, 48/3. Totals, 67/4.

YUGOSLAVIAN LEAGUE RECORD

Season Team	G	Min.	FGM	FGA	Pct.	FTM	FTA	Pct.	Reb.	Ast.	Pts.	RPG	APG	PPG
00-01—Buducnost	10	154	47	76	.618	27	42	.643	67	6	121	6.7	0.6	12.1

Three-point field goals: 2000-01, 0-for-1. Totals, 0-for-1 (.000).

JAMES, LEBRON   F   CAVALIERS

PERSONAL: Born December 30, 1984, in Akron, Ohio. ... 6-8/240. (2.03/108.9).
HIGH SCHOOL: St. Vincent-St. Mary (Akron, Ohio).
COLLEGE: Did not attend college.
TRANSACTIONS/CAREER NOTES: Selected out of high school by Cleveland Cavaliers in first round (first pick overall) of 2003 NBA Draft.
MISCELLANEOUS: Member of bronze-medal-winning U.S. Olympic Team (2004).

NBA REGULAR-SEASON RECORD

HONORS: NBA Rookie of the Year (2004). ... NBA All-Rookie first team (2004). ... All-NBA second team (2005). ... All-NBA first team (2006).

Season Team	G	Min.	FGM	FGA	Pct.	FTM	FTA	Pct.	Off.	Def.	Tot.	Ast.	St.	Blk.	TO	Pts.	RPG	APG	PPG
03-04—Cleveland	79	3122	622	1492	.417	347	460	.754	99	333	432	465	130	58	273	1654	5.5	5.9	20.9
04-05—Cleveland	80	3388	*795	1684	.472	477	636	.750	111	477	588	577	177	52	262	2175	7.4	7.2	27.2
05-06—Cleveland	79	3361	875	1823	.480	601	814	.738	75	481	556	521	123	66	260	2478	7.0	6.6	31.4
Totals	238	9871	2292	4999	.458	1425	1910	.746	285	1291	1576	1563	430	176	795	6307	6.6	6.6	26.5

Three-point field goals: 2003-04, 63-for-217 (.290). 2004-05, 108-for-308 (.351). 2005-06, 127-for-379 (.335). Totals, 298-for-904 (.330).
Personal fouls/disqualifications: 2003-04, 149/0. 2004-05, 146/1. 2005-06, 181/0. Totals, 476/1.

NBA PLAYOFF RECORD

Season Team	G	Min.	FGM	FGA	Pct.	FTM	FTA	Pct.	Off.	Def.	Tot.	Ast.	St.	Blk.	TO	Pts.	RPG	APG	PPG
05-06—Cleveland	13	604	146	307	.476	87	118	.737	22	83	105	76	18	9	65	400	8.1	5.8	30.8

Three-point field goals: 2005-06, 21-for-63 (.333). Totals, 21-for-63 (.333).
Personal fouls/disqualifications: 2005-06, 44/0. Totals, 44/0.

NBA ALL-STAR GAME RECORD

NOTES: Named Most Valuable Player (2006).

Season Team	Min.	FGM	FGA	Pct.	FTM	FTA	Pct.	Off.	Def.	Tot.	Ast.	PF	Dq.	St.	Blk.	TO	Pts.
2005—Cleveland	31	6	13	.462	0	1	.000	1	7	8	6	0	0	2	0	3	13
2006—Cleveland	31	12	21	.571	1	5	.200	2	4	6	2	2	0	2	0	1	29
Totals	62	18	34	.529	1	6	.167	3	11	14	8	2	0	4	0	4	42

Three-point field goals: 2005, 1-for-4 (.250). 2006, 4-for-10 (.400). Totals, 5-for-14 (.357).

JAMES, MIKE   G   TIMBERWOLVES

PERSONAL: Born June 23, 1975, in Amityville, N.Y. ... 6-2/188. (1.88/85.3). ... Full name: Michael Lamont James
HIGH SCHOOL: Amityville (N.Y.).
COLLEGE: Duquesne.
TRANSACTIONS/CAREER NOTES: Not drafted by an NBA franchise. ... Played in Austria (1998-99). ... Played in France (1999-2001). ... Signed as free agent by Miami Heat (July 20, 2001). ... Waived by Heat (October 25, 2001). ... Played in Continental Basketball Association with Rockford Lightning (2001-02). ... Re-signed as free agent by Heat (December 18, 2001). ... Signed as free agent by Boston Celtics (July 25, 2003). ... Traded by Celtics to Detroit Pistons in three-team deal in which Pistons also received F/C Rasheed Wallace from Atlanta Hawks. Celtics received G Chucky Atkins, G Lindsey Hunter and a 2004 first-round draft choice from Pistons. Hawks received F Zeljko Rebraca, G Bob Sura and a future first-round draft choice from Pistons and F Chris Mills from Celtics (February 19, 2004). ... Signed as free agent by Milwaukee Bucks (August 5, 2004). ... Traded by Bucks with C Zendon Hamilton to Houston Rockets for Reece Gaines and second-round picks in 2006 and 2007 NBA drafts (February 24, 2005). ... Traded by Rockets to Toronto Raptors for G Rafer Alston (October 4, 2005). ... Signed as free agent by Minnesota Timberwolves (July 13, 2006).
MISCELLANEOUS: Member of NBA championship team (2004).

COLLEGIATE RECORD

Season Team	G	Min.	FGM	FGA	Pct.	FTM	FTA	Pct.	Reb.	Ast.	Pts.	RPG	APG	PPG
94-95—Duquesne	27	381	55	123	.447	24	35	.686	36	27	135	1.3	1.0	5.0
95-96—Duquesne	27	843	151	318	.475	79	108	.731	94	106	384	3.5	3.9	14.2
96-97—Duquesne	27	862	141	325	.434	60	84	.714	93	76	366	3.4	2.8	13.6
97-98—Duquesne	30	1029	190	443	.429	81	109	.743	106	104	526	3.5	3.5	17.5
Totals	111	3115	537	1209	.444	244	336	.726	329	313	1411	3.0	2.8	12.7

Three-point field goals: 1994-95, 1-for-13 (.077). 1995-96, 3-for-19 (.158). 1996-97, 24-for-67 (.358). 1997-98, 65-for-184 (.353). Totals, 93-for-283 (.329).

AUSTRIAN LEAGUE RECORD

Season Team	G	Min.	FGM	FGA	Pct.	FTM	FTA	Pct.	Reb.	Ast.	Pts.	RPG	APG	PPG
98-99—St. Polten	15	556	103	217	.475	61	80	.763	83	110	282	5.5	7.3	18.8

Three-point field goals: 1998-99, 15-for-56 (.268). Totals, 15-for-56 (.268).

FRENCH LEAGUE RECORD

Season Team	G	Min.	FGM	FGA	Pct.	FTM	FTA	Pct.	Reb.	Ast.	Pts.	RPG	APG	PPG
99-00—ESPE	30	1061	196	422	.464	104	124	.839	91	144	536	3.0	4.8	17.9
00-01—ELAN	30	1028	169	360	.469	60	90	.667	109	154	451	3.6	5.1	15.0
Totals	60	2089	365	782	.467	171	214	.799	200	298	987	3.3	5.0	16.5

Three-point field goals: 1999-00, 40-for-99 (.404). 2000-01, 46-for-125 (.368). Totals, 86-for-224 (.384).

CBA RECORD

Season Team	G	Min.	FGM	FGA	Pct.	FTM	FTA	Pct.	Reb.	Ast.	Pts.	RPG	APG	PPG
01-02—Rockford	14	620	124	259	.479	40	49	.816	92	88	326	6.6	6.3	23.3

Three-point field goals: 2001-02, 38-for-91 (.418). Totals, 38-for-91 (.418).

NBA REGULAR-SEASON RECORD

Season Team	G	Min.	FGM	FGA	Pct.	FTM	FTA	Pct.	Off.	Def.	Tot.	Ast.	St.	Blk.	TO	Pts.	RPG	APG	PPG
01-02—Miami	15	119	15	43	.349	4	7	.571	2	12	14	19	6	1	13	42	0.9	1.3	2.8
02-03—Miami	78	1722	218	585	.373	104	142	.732	26	123	149	246	64	5	108	607	1.9	3.2	7.8
03-04—Boston-Detroit	81	2196	272	657	.414	103	127	.811	28	206	234	339	96	3	124	753	2.9	4.2	9.3
04-05—Mil.-Houston...	74	1859	331	751	.441	109	145	.752	35	173	208	263	65	6	106	871	2.8	3.6	11.8
05-06—Toronto	79	2925	576	1228	.469	283	338	.837	45	217	262	460	72	3	206	1604	3.3	5.8	20.3
Totals	327	8821	1412	3264	.433	603	759	.794	136	731	867	1327	303	18	557	3877	2.7	4.1	11.9

Three-point field goals: 2001-02, 8-for-21 (.381). 2002-03, 67-for-228 (.294). 2003-04, 106-for-281 (.377). 2004-05, 100-for-259 (.386). 2005-06, 169-for-382 (.442). Totals, 450-for-1171 (.384).
Personal fouls/disqualifications: 2001-02, 17/0. 2002-03, 176/1. 2003-04, 156/0. 2004-05, 174/2. 2005-06, 214/1. Totals, 737/4.

NBA PLAYOFF RECORD

Season Team	G	Min.	FGM	FGA	Pct.	FTM	FTA	Pct.	Off.	Def.	Tot.	Ast.	St.	Blk.	TO	Pts.	RPG	APG	PPG
03-04—Detroit	22	195	21	53	.396	9	16	.563	7	19	26	24	5	0	15	57	1.2	1.1	2.6
04-05—Houston	7	171	29	62	.468	23	24	.958	2	11	13	16	6	2	10	81	1.9	2.3	11.6
Totals	29	366	50	115	.435	32	40	.800	9	30	39	40	11	2	25	138	1.3	1.4	4.8

Three-point field goals: 2003-04, 6-for-14 (.429). 2004-05, 0-for-9. Totals, 6-for-23 (.261).
Personal fouls/disqualifications: 2003-04, 23/0. 2004-05, 17/0. Totals, 40/0.

JAMISON, ANTAWN   F   WIZARDS

PERSONAL: Born June 12, 1976, in Shreveport, La. ... 6-9/223. (2.06/101.2). ... Full name: Antawn Cortez Jamison
HIGH SCHOOL: Providence (Charlotte).
COLLEGE: North Carolina.
TRANSACTIONS/CAREER NOTES: Selected after junior season by Toronto Raptors in first round (fourth pick overall) of 1998 NBA Draft. ... Draft rights traded by Raptors to Golden State Warriors for draft rights to G Vince Carter and cash (June

24, 1998). ... Traded by Warriors with F Danny Fortson, F Chris Mills and G Jiri Welsch to Dallas Mavericks for G Nick Van Exel, G Avery Johnson, F Popeye Jones, F Antoine Rigaudeau and C Evan Eschmeyer (August 18, 2003). ... Traded by Mavericks to Washington Wizards for G Jerry Stackhouse, F/C Christian Laettner and draft rights to G Devin Harris (June 24, 2004).

COLLEGIATE RECORD

NOTES: The SPORTING NEWS College Player of the Year (1998). ... Naismith Award winner (1998). ... Wooden Award winner (1998). ... The SPORTING NEWS All-America first team (1998). ... The SPORTING NEWS All-America second team (1997).

Season Team	G	Min.	FGM	FGA	Pct.	FTM	FTA	Pct.	Reb.	Ast.	Pts.	RPG	APG	PPG
95-96—North Carolina	32	1052	201	322	.624	82	156	.526	309	33	484	9.7	1.0	15.1
96-97—North Carolina	35	1199	270	496	.544	126	203	.621	329	30	668	9.4	0.9	19.1
97-98—North Carolina	37	1227	316	546	.579	184	276	.667	389	30	822	10.5	0.8	22.2
Totals	104	3478	787	1364	.577	392	635	.617	1027	93	1974	9.9	0.9	19.0

Three-point field goals: 1995-96, 0-for-1. 1996-97, 2-for-11 (.182). 1997-98, 6-for-15 (.400). Totals, 8-for-27 (.296).

NBA REGULAR-SEASON RECORD

HONORS: NBA Sixth Man Award (2004). ... NBA All-Rookie second team (1999).

Season Team	G	Min.	FGM	FGA	Pct.	FTM	FTA	Pct.	Off.	Def.	Tot.	Ast.	St.	Blk.	TO	Pts.	RPG	APG	PPG
98-99—Golden State	47	1058	178	394	.452	90	153	.588	131	170	301	34	38	16	68	449	6.4	0.7	9.6
99-00—Golden State	43	1556	356	756	.471	127	208	.611	172	187	359	90	30	15	113	841	8.3	2.1	19.6
00-01—Golden State	82	3394	800	1812	.442	382	534	.715	280	435	715	164	114	28	199	2044	8.7	2.0	24.9
01-02—Golden State	82	3033	614	1375	.447	323	440	.734	211	345	556	161	70	45	161	1619	6.8	2.0	19.7
02-03—Golden State	82	3226	691	1471	.470	375	475	.789	195	383	578	156	76	45	177	1822	7.0	1.9	22.2
03-04—Dallas	82	2376	488	913	.535	220	294	.748	233	287	520	70	83	30	81	1212	6.3	0.9	14.8
04-05—Washington	68	2605	519	1189	.437	225	296	.760	160	359	519	154	55	16	118	1334	7.6	2.3	19.6
05-06—Washington	82	3288	660	1494	.442	217	297	.731	167	598	765	158	90	12	137	1684	9.3	1.9	20.5
Totals	568	20536	4306	9404	.458	1959	2697	.726	1549	2764	4313	987	556	207	1054	11005	7.6	1.7	19.4

Three-point field goals: 1998-99, 3-for-10 (.300). 1999-00, 2-for-7 (.286). 2000-01, 62-for-205 (.302). 2001-02, 68-for-210 (.324). 2002-03, 65-for-209 (.311). 2003-04, 16-for-40 (.400). 2004-05, 71-for-208 (.341). 2005-06, 147-for-373 (.394). Totals, 434-for-1262 (.344).
Personal fouls/disqualifications: 1998-99, 102/1. 1999-00, 115/0. 2000-01, 225/2. 2001-02, 187/0. 2002-03, 197/1. 2003-04, 174/2. 2004-05, 151/1. 2005-06, 189/1. Totals, 1340/8.

NBA PLAYOFF RECORD

Season Team	G	Min.	FGM	FGA	Pct.	FTM	FTA	Pct.	Off.	Def.	Tot.	Ast.	St.	Blk.	TO	Pts.	RPG	APG	PPG
03-04—Dallas	5	109	26	57	.456	11	15	.733	15	10	25	2	5	2	5	65	5.0	0.4	13.0
04-05—Washington	10	380	73	162	.451	22	32	.688	16	47	63	12	7	4	16	185	6.3	1.2	18.5
05-06—Washington	6	253	42	99	.424	21	27	.778	9	34	43	18	6	2	11	115	7.2	3.0	19.2
Totals	21	742	141	318	.443	54	74	.730	40	91	131	32	18	8	32	365	6.2	1.5	17.4

Three-point field goals: 2003-04, 2-for-8 (.250). 2004-05, 17-for-34 (.500). 2005-06, 10-for-32 (.313). Totals, 29-for-74 (.392).
Personal fouls/disqualifications: 2003-04, 15/0. 2004-05, 24/0. 2005-06, 23/0. Totals, 62/0.

NBA ALL-STAR GAME RECORD

Season Team	Min.	FGM	FGA	Pct.	FTM	FTA	Pct.	Off.	Def.	Tot.	Ast.	PF	Dq.	St.	Blk.	TO	Pts.
2005—Washington	13	2	5	.400	0	0	...	1	3	4	1	0	0	0	0	0	5

Three-point field goals: 2005, 1-for-1 (1.000). Totals, 1-for-1 (1.000).

JARIC, MARKO — G — TIMBERWOLVES

PERSONAL: Born December 10, 1978, in Belgrade, Yugoslavia. ... 6-8/210. (2.03/95.3).
TRANSACTIONS/CAREER NOTES: Played in Greece (1996-98). ... Played in Italy (1998-2002). ... Selected by Los Angeles Clippers in second round (30th pick overall) of 2000 NBA Draft. ... Traded by Clippers with G Lionel Chalmers to Minnesota Timberwolves for G Sam Cassell and a first-round draft pick (August 12, 2005).

GREEK LEAGUE RECORD

Season Team	G	Min.	FGM	FGA	Pct.	FTM	FTA	Pct.	Reb.	Ast.	Pts.	RPG	APG	PPG
96-97—Peristeri Nikas	30	247	27	52	.519	22	33	.667	36	15	76	1.2	0.5	2.5
97-98—Peristeri Nikas	29	554	50	98	.510	38	49	.776	73	35	165	2.5	1.2	5.7
Totals	59	801	77	150	.513	60	82	.732	109	50	241	1.8	0.8	4.1

Three-point field goals: 1996-97, 0-for-3. 1997-98, 9-for-24 (.375). Totals, 9-for-27 (.333).

ITALIAN LEAGUE RECORD

Season Team	G	Min.	FGM	FGA	Pct.	FTM	FTA	Pct.	Reb.	Ast.	Pts.	RPG	APG	PPG
98-99—Fortitudo Bologna	25	587	42	73	.575	43	49	.878	73	34	196	2.9	1.4	7.8
99-00—Fortitudo Bologna	26	627	72	126	.571	57	77	.740	74	36	258	2.8	1.4	9.9
00-01—Virtus Kinder Bologna	33	971	152	327	.465	71	104	.683	127	81	406	3.8	2.5	12.3
01-02—Virtus Kinder Bologna	33	987	171	374	.457	107	142	.754	162	87	503	4.9	2.6	15.2
Totals	117	3172	437	900	.486	278	372	.747	436	238	1363	3.7	2.0	11.6

Three-point field goals: 1998-99, 23-for-59 (.390). 1999-00, 42-for-117 (.359). 2000-01, 31-for-98 (.316). 2001-02, 54-for-139 (.388). Totals, 150-for-413 (.363).

NBA REGULAR-SEASON RECORD

Season Team	G	Min.	FGM	FGA	Pct.	FTM	FTA	Pct.	Off.	Def.	Tot.	Ast.	St.	Blk.	TO	Pts.	RPG	APG	PPG
02-03—L.A. Clippers	66	1379	179	446	.401	79	105	.752	35	125	160	193	97	11	103	490	2.4	2.9	7.4
03-04—L.A. Clippers	58	1760	185	477	.388	74	101	.733	44	131	175	281	93	20	115	495	3.0	4.8	8.5
04-05—L.A. Clippers	50	1656	189	457	.414	59	82	.720	20	141	161	303	84	17	98	493	3.2	6.1	9.9
05-06—Minnesota	75	2102	226	566	.399	95	138	.688	60	173	233	293	108	21	127	587	3.1	3.9	7.8
Totals	249	6897	779	1946	.400	307	426	.721	159	570	729	1070	382	69	443	2065	2.9	4.3	8.3

Three-point field goals: 2002-03, 53-for-166 (.319). 2003-04, 51-for-150 (.340). 2004-05, 56-for-151 (.371). 2005-06, 40-for-133 (.301). Totals, 200-for-600 (.333).
Personal fouls/disqualifications: 2002-03, 125/0. 2003-04, 132/1. 2004-05, 107/0. 2005-06, 189/3. Totals, 553/4.

JASIKEVICIUS, SARUNAS   G   PACERS

PERSONAL: Born March 5, 1976 ... 6-4/195. (1.93/88.5).
COLLEGE: Maryland.
TRANSACTIONS/CAREER NOTES: Not drafted by an NBA franchise. ... Played in Lithuania (1998-99). ... Played in Slovenia (1999-00). ... Played in Spain (2000-03). ... Played in Israel (2003-05). ... Signed as free agent by Indiana Pacers (August 11, 2005).
MISCELLANEOUS: Member of bronze-medal-winning Lithuanian Olympic team (2000). ... Member of Lithuanian Olympic team (2004).

COLLEGIATE RECORD

Season Team	G	Min.	FGM	FGA	Pct.	FTM	FTA	Pct.	Reb.	Ast.	Pts.	RPG	APG	PPG
94-95—Maryland	29	177	29	65	.446	17	21	.810	19	16	89	0.7	0.6	3.1
95-96—Maryland	27	261	38	89	.427	10	20	.500	31	21	106	1.1	0.8	3.9
96-97—Maryland	32	928	115	275	.418	66	89	.742	80	78	338	2.5	2.4	10.6
97-98—Maryland	32	937	135	296	.456	66	87	.759	104	80	396	3.3	2.5	12.4
Totals	120	2303	317	725	.437	159	217	.733	234	195	929	2.0	1.6	7.7

Three-point field goals: 1994-95, 14-for-37 (.378). 1995-96, 20-for-44 (.455). 1996-97, 42-for-131 (.321). 1997-98, 60-for-151 (.397). Totals, 136-for-363 (.375).

LITHUANIAN LEAGUE RECORD

Season Team	G	Min.	FGM	FGA	Pct.	FTM	FTA	Pct.	Reb.	Ast.	Pts.	RPG	APG	PPG
98-99—Lietuvos	30	945	180	353	.510	89	110	.809	103	151	526	3.4	5.0	17.5

Three-point field goals: 1998-99, 77-for-166 (.464). Totals, 77-for-166 (.464).

SLOVENIAN LEAGUE RECORD

Season Team	G	Min.	FGM	FGA	Pct.	FTM	FTA	Pct.	Reb.	Ast.	Pts.	RPG	APG	PPG
99-00—Olimpija Ljubljana	30	945	180	353	.510	89	110	.809	103	151	526	3.4	5.0	17.5

Three-point field goals: 1998-99, 77-for-166 (.464). Totals, 77-for-166 (.464).

SPANISH LEAGUE RECORD

Season Team	G	Min.	FGM	FGA	Pct.	FTM	FTA	Pct.	Reb.	Ast.	Pts.	RPG	APG	PPG
00-01—FC Barcelona	28	753	135	265	.509	56	69	.812	60	140	388	2.1	5.0	13.9
01-02—FC Barcelona	30	730	138	286	.483	102	121	.843	77	131	444	2.6	4.4	14.8
02-03—FC Barcelona	34	832	129	272	.474	74	83	.892	43	113	402	1.3	3.3	11.8
Totals	92	2315	402	823	.488	232	273	.850	180	384	1234	2.0	4.2	13.4

Three-point field goals: 2000-01, 62-for-142 (.437). 2001-02, 66-for-158 (.418). 2002-03, 70-for 150 (.467). Totals, 198-for-450 (.440).

ISRAELI LEAGUE RECORD

Season Team	G	Min.	FGM	FGA	Pct.	FTM	FTA	Pct.	Reb.	Ast.	Pts.	RPG	APG	PPG
03-04—Maccabi Tel-Aviv	21	547	88	162	.543	19	29	.655	35	110	251	1.7	5.2	12.0
04-05—Maccabi Tel-Aviv	17	411	69	131	.527	29	34	.853	36	85	211	2.1	5.0	12.4
Totals	38	958	157	293	.536	48	63	.762	71	195	462	1.9	5.1	12.2

Three-point field goals: 2003-04, 56-for-99 (.566). 2004-05, 44-for-86 (.512). Totals, 100-for-185 (.541).

NBA REGULAR-SEASON RECORD

									REBOUNDS							AVERAGES		
Season Team	G	Min.	FGM	FGA	Pct.	FTM	FTA	Pct.	Off.	Def.	Tot.	Ast.	St.	Blk.	TO	Pts.	RPG	APG	PPG
05-06—Indiana	75	1557	170	429	.396	121	133	.910	19	134	153	227	40	4	116	547	2.0	3.0	7.3

Three-point field goals: 2005-06, 86-for-236 (.364). Totals, 86-for-236 (.364).
Personal fouls/disqualifications: 2005-06, 108/0. Totals, 108/0.

NBA PLAYOFF RECORD

									REBOUNDS							AVERAGES		
Season Team	G	Min.	FGM	FGA	Pct.	FTM	FTA	Pct.	Off.	Def.	Tot.	Ast.	St.	Blk.	TO	Pts.	RPG	APG	PPG
05-06—Indiana	6	66	7	19	.368	1	2	.500	1	5	6	6	0	1	5	17	1.0	1.0	2.8

Three-point field goals: 2005-06, 2-for-9 (.222). Totals, 2-for-9 (.222).
Personal fouls/disqualifications: 2005-06, 7/0. Totals, 7/0.

JEFFERSON, AL   F   CELTICS

PERSONAL: Born January 4, 1985, in Monticello, Miss. ... 6-10/265. (2.08/120.2).
HIGH SCHOOL: Prentiss (Miss.).
COLLEGE: Did not attend college.
TRANSACTIONS/CAREER NOTES: Selected out of high school by Boston Celtics in first round (15th pick overall) of 2004 NBA Draft.

HONORS: NBA All-Rookie second team (2005).

NBA REGULAR-SEASON RECORD

									REBOUNDS							AVERAGES		
Season Team	G	Min.	FGM	FGA	Pct.	FTM	FTA	Pct.	Off.	Def.	Tot.	Ast.	St.	Blk.	TO	Pts.	RPG	APG	PPG
04-05—Boston	71	1051	195	369	.528	85	135	.630	119	193	312	24	22	55	66	475	4.4	0.3	6.7
05-06—Boston	59	1062	189	379	.499	86	134	.642	97	202	299	30	30	46	62	464	5.1	0.5	7.9
Totals	130	2113	384	748	.513	171	269	.636	216	395	611	54	52	101	128	939	4.7	0.4	7.2

Three-point field goals: 2004-05, 0-for-3. 2005-06, 0-for-4. Totals, 0-for-7 (.000).
Personal fouls/disqualifications: 2004-05, 195/4. 2005-06, 166/1. Totals, 361/5.

NBA PLAYOFF RECORD

Season Team	G	Min.	FGM	FGA	Pct.	FTM	FTA	Pct.	Off.	Def.	Tot.	Ast.	St.	Blk.	TO	Pts.	RPG	APG	PPG
									REBOUNDS								**AVERAGES**		
04-05—Boston	7	136	17	41	.415	9	12	.750	17	28	45	2	4	8	4	43	6.4	0.3	6.1

Personal fouls/disqualifications: 2004-05, 16/0. Totals, 16/0.

JEFFERSON, RICHARD　　　　F　　　　NETS

PERSONAL: Born June 21, 1980, in Los Angeles. ... 6-7/222. (2.01/100.7). ... Full name: Richard Allen Jefferson
HIGH SCHOOL: Moon Valley (Phoenix).
COLLEGE: Arizona.
TRANSACTIONS/CAREER NOTES: Selected after junior season by Houston Rockets in first round (13th pick overall) of 2001 NBA Draft. ... Draft rights traded by Rockets with draft rights to C Jason Collins and G Brandon Armstrong to New Jersey Nets for draft rights to F Eddie Griffin (June 27, 2001).
MISCELLANEOUS: Member of bronze-medal-winning U.S. Olympic team (2004).

COLLEGIATE RECORD

Season Team	G	Min.	FGM	FGA	Pct.	FTM	FTA	Pct.	Reb.	Ast.	Pts.	RPG	APG	PPG
												AVERAGES		
98-99—Arizona	28	755	104	210	.495	97	125	.776	134	80	317	4.8	2.9	11.3
99-00—Arizona	21	495	84	167	.503	45	63	.714	92	58	230	4.4	2.8	11.0
00-01—Arizona	35	961	147	307	.479	72	110	.655	190	94	397	5.4	2.7	11.3
Totals	84	2211	335	684	.490	214	298	.718	416	232	944	5.0	2.8	11.2

Three-point field goals: 1998-99, 12-for-33 (.364). 1999-00, 17-for-40 (.425). 2000-01, 31-for-90 (.344). Totals, 60-for-163 (.368).
Personal fouls/disqualifications: 1998-99, 68/0. 1999-00, 53/0. 2000-01, 98/0. Totals, 219/0.

NBA REGULAR-SEASON RECORD

HONORS: NBA All-Rookie second team (2002).

Season Team	G	Min.	FGM	FGA	Pct.	FTM	FTA	Pct.	Off.	Def.	Tot.	Ast.	St.	Blk.	TO	Pts.	RPG	APG	PPG
									REBOUNDS								**AVERAGES**		
01-02—New Jersey	79	1917	270	591	.457	189	265	.713	85	208	293	140	64	48	107	742	3.7	1.8	9.4
02-03—New Jersey	80	2879	456	911	.501	324	436	.743	150	364	514	201	80	44	156	1242	6.4	2.5	15.5
03-04—New Jersey	82	3133	555	1115	.498	357	468	.763	109	355	464	315	92	28	198	1515	5.7	3.8	18.5
04-05—New Jersey	33	1355	238	564	.422	227	269	.844	49	191	240	133	33	17	132	733	7.3	4.0	22.2
05-06—New Jersey	78	3059	495	1005	.493	471	580	.812	95	439	534	297	59	17	174	1521	6.8	3.8	19.5
Totals	352	12343	2014	4186	.481	1568	2018	.777	488	1557	2045	1086	328	154	767	5753	5.8	3.1	16.3

Three-point field goals: 2001-02, 13-for-56 (.232). 2002-03, 6-for-24 (.250). 2003-04, 48-for-132 (.364). 2004-05, 30-for-89 (.337). 2005-06, 60-for-188 (.319). Totals, 157-for-489 (.321).
Personal fouls/disqualifications: 2001-02, 211/5. 2002-03, 216/1. 2003-04, 224/1. 2004-05, 109/1. 2005-06, 193/1. Totals, 953/9.

NBA PLAYOFF RECORD

Season Team	G	Min.	FGM	FGA	Pct.	FTM	FTA	Pct.	Off.	Def.	Tot.	Ast.	St.	Blk.	TO	Pts.	RPG	APG	PPG
									REBOUNDS								**AVERAGES**		
01-02—New Jersey	20	441	53	114	.465	33	60	.550	16	76	92	25	11	9	26	139	4.6	1.3	7.0
02-03—New Jersey	20	711	110	231	.476	61	85	.718	29	98	127	47	16	4	46	281	6.4	2.4	14.1
03-04—New Jersey	11	460	66	158	.418	77	108	.713	14	55	69	42	14	8	43	218	6.3	3.8	19.8
04-05—New Jersey	4	140	20	50	.400	21	31	.677	8	14	22	9	3	0	8	63	5.5	2.3	15.8
05-06—New Jersey	11	437	90	165	.545	52	63	.825	7	38	45	45	10	4	30	244	4.1	4.1	22.2
Totals	66	2189	339	718	.472	244	347	.703	74	281	355	168	54	25	153	945	5.4	2.5	14.3

Three-point field goals: 2001-02, 0-for-2. 2002-03, 0-for-3. 2003-04, 9-for-33 (.273). 2004-05, 2-for-10 (.200). 2005-06, 12-for-29 (.414). Totals, 23-for-77 (.299).
Personal fouls/disqualifications: 2001-02, 40/0. 2002-03, 67/0. 2003-04, 35/0. 2004-05, 14/0. 2005-06, 32/0. Totals, 188/0.

JEFFRIES, JARED　　　　F　　　　KNICKS

PERSONAL: Born November 25, 1981, in Bloomington, Ind. ... 6-10/215. (2.08/97.5). ... Full name: Jared Scott Carter Jeffries
HIGH SCHOOL: Bloomington North (Bloomington, Ind.).
COLLEGE: Indiana.
TRANSACTIONS/CAREER NOTES: Selected after sophomore season by Washington Wizards in first round (11th pick overall) of 2002 NBA Draft. ... Signed as free agent by New York Knicks (August 7, 2006).

COLLEGIATE RECORD

NOTES: The SPORTING NEWS All-America third team (2002).

Season Team	G	Min.	FGM	FGA	Pct.	FTM	FTA	Pct.	Reb.	Ast.	Pts.	RPG	APG	PPG
												AVERAGES		
00-01—Indiana	34	1108	164	971	.169	129	208	.620	234	82	469	6.9	2.4	13.8
01-02—Indiana	36	1175	189	414	.457	134	201	.667	273	74	539	7.6	2.1	15.0
Totals	70	2283	353	1385	.255	263	409	.643	507	156	1008	7.2	2.2	14.4

Three-point field goals: 2000-01, 12-for-49 (.245). 2001-02, 27-for-71 (.380). Totals, 39-for-120 (.325).

NBA REGULAR-SEASON RECORD

Season Team	G	Min.	FGM	FGA	Pct.	FTM	FTA	Pct.	Off.	Def.	Tot.	Ast.	St.	Blk.	TO	Pts.	RPG	APG	PPG
									REBOUNDS								**AVERAGES**		
02-03—Washington	20	292	30	63	.476	16	29	.552	26	32	58	16	8	5	21	79	2.9	0.8	4.0
03-04—Washington	82	1913	177	469	.377	105	171	.614	180	244	424	93	48	28	107	464	5.2	1.1	5.7
04-05—Washington	77	2007	203	434	.468	101	173	.584	152	222	374	151	66	35	114	523	4.9	2.0	6.8
05-06—Washington	77	1951	187	415	.451	99	168	.589	164	215	379	148	58	50	99	489	4.9	1.9	6.4
Totals	256	6163	597	1381	.432	321	541	.593	522	713	1235	408	180	118	341	1555	4.8	1.6	6.1

Three-point field goals: 2002-03, 3-for-6 (.500). 2003-04, 5-for-30 (.167). 2004-05, 16-for-51 (.314). 2005-06, 16-for-50 (.320). Totals, 40-for-137 (.292).
Personal fouls/disqualifications: 2002-03, 28/0. 2003-04, 212/3. 2004-05, 206/1. 2005-06, 223/3. Totals, 669/7.

NBA PLAYOFF RECORD

Season Team	G	Min.	FGM	FGA	Pct.	FTM	FTA	Pct.	Off.	Def.	Tot.	Ast.	St.	Blk.	TO	Pts.	RPG	APG	PPG
										REBOUNDS								AVERAGES	
04-05—Washington	10	247	24	49	.490	13	17	.765	19	22	41	18	9	9	13	64	4.1	1.8	6.4
05-06—Washington	6	215	17	43	.395	13	17	.765	20	17	37	9	1	7	11	48	6.2	1.5	8.0
Totals	16	462	41	92	.446	26	34	.765	39	39	78	27	10	16	24	112	4.9	1.7	7.0

Three-point field goals: 2004-05, 3-for-6 (.500). 2005-06, 1-for-7 (.143). Totals, 4-for-13 (.308).
Personal fouls/disqualifications: 2004-05, 34/0. 2005-06, 19/1. Totals, 53/1.

JOHNSON, AMIR   F   PISTONS

PERSONAL: Born May 1, 1987, in Los Angeles. ... 6-9/210. (2.06/95.3).
HIGH SCHOOL: Verbum Dei (Los Angeles), then Westchester (Los Angeles).
COLLEGE: Did not attend college.
TRANSACTIONS/CAREER NOTES: Selected out of high school by Detroit Pistons in second round (56th pick overall) of 2005 NBA Draft.

NBA REGULAR-SEASON RECORD

Season Team	G	Min.	FGM	FGA	Pct.	FTM	FTA	Pct.	Off.	Def.	Tot.	Ast.	St.	Blk.	TO	Pts.	RPG	APG	PPG
										REBOUNDS								AVERAGES	
05-06—Detroit	3	39	7	10	.700	4	4	1.000	3	1	4	3	0	2	4	20	1.3	1.0	6.7

Three-point field goals: 2005-06, 2-for-3 (.667). Totals, 2-for-3 (.667).
Personal fouls/disqualifications: 2005-06, 7/0. Totals, 7/0.

NBA DEVELOPMENT LEAGUE RECORD

Season Team	G	Min.	FGM	FGA	Pct.	FTM	FTA	Pct.	Reb.	Ast.	Pts.	RPG	APG	PPG
													AVERAGES	
05-06—Fayetteville.....................	18	508	119	178	.669	70	97	.722	128	21	309	7.1	1.2	17.2

Three-point field goals: 2005-06, 1-for-1 (1.000). Totals, 1-for-1 (1.000).

JOHNSON, ANTHONY   G   MAVERICKS

PERSONAL: Born October 10, 1974, in Charleston, S.C. ... 6-3/190. (1.91/86.2). ... Full name: Anthony Mark Johnson
HIGH SCHOOL: Stall (Charleston, S.C.).
COLLEGE: College of Charleston.
TRANSACTIONS/CAREER NOTES: Selected by Sacramento Kings in second round (40th pick overall) of 1997 NBA Draft. ... Signed as free agent by Atlanta Hawks (January 21, 1999). ... Traded by Hawks to Orlando Magic for conditional second-round draft choice (February 24, 2000). ... Signed as free agent by Hawks (August 21, 2000). ... Traded by Hawks with G Jim Jackson and F/G Larry Robinson to Cleveland Cavaliers for G Brevin Knight (January 2, 2001). ... Played in National Basketball Development League with Mobile Revelers (2001-02). ... Signed by New Jersey Nets to first of two consecutive 10-day contracts (January 7, 2002). ... Re-signed by Nets for remainder of season (January 28, 2002). ... Signed as free agent by Cleveland Cavaliers (~~~~~~~~~ ~~, ~~~~). ... Waived by Cavaliers (~~~~~~~ ~~, ~~~~). ... Signed as free agent by Nets (October 25, 2002). ... Signed as free agent by Indiana Pacers (July 24, 2003) ... Traded by Pacers to Dallas Mavericks for G Darrell Armstrong, G/F Rawle Marshall and F Josh Powell (July 24, 2006).

COLLEGIATE RECORD

Season Team	G	Min.	FGM	FGA	Pct.	FTM	FTA	Pct.	Reb.	Ast.	Pts.	RPG	APG	PPG
													AVERAGES	
92-93—College of Charleston	27	273	23	58	.397	37	52	.712	44	30	84	1.6	1.1	3.1
93-94—College of Charleston						Did not play—redshirted.								
94-95—College of Charleston	29	490	34	87	.391	22	34	.647	53	68	100	1.8	2.3	3.4
95-96—College of Charleston	29	946	119	259	.459	65	97	.670	92	193	329	3.2	6.7	11.3
96-97—College of Charleston	32	1138	158	313	.505	100	126	.794	113	229	446	3.5	7.2	13.9
Totals	117	2847	334	717	.466	224	309	.725	302	520	959	2.6	4.4	8.2

Three-point field goals: 1992-93, 1-for-3 (.333). 1994-95, 10-for-25 (.400). 1995-96, 26-for-64 (.406). 1996-97, 30-for-74 (.405). Totals, 67-for-166 (.404).

NBA REGULAR-SEASON RECORD

Season Team	G	Min.	FGM	FGA	Pct.	FTM	FTA	Pct.	Off.	Def.	Tot.	Ast.	St.	Blk.	TO	Pts.	RPG	APG	PPG
										REBOUNDS								AVERAGES	
97-98—Sacramento	77	2266	226	609	.371	80	110	.727	51	120	171	329	64	6	120	574	2.2	4.3	7.5
98-99—Atlanta	49	885	91	225	.404	57	82	.695	16	59	75	107	35	7	65	244	1.5	2.2	5.0
99-00—Atlanta-Orl.	56	637	62	164	.378	28	39	.718	21	30	51	72	33	4	32	154	0.9	1.3	2.8
00-01—Atl.-Cleve.	53	511	53	152	.349	23	33	.697	10	34	44	78	23	6	34	130	0.8	1.5	2.5
01-02—New Jersey	34	366	37	90	.411	16	25	.640	10	19	29	48	31	1	20	94	0.9	1.4	2.8
02-03—New Jersey	66	842	103	231	.446	51	74	.689	13	65	78	86	37	5	41	270	1.2	1.3	4.1
03-04—Indiana...........	73	1598	167	411	.406	75	94	.798	28	102	130	202	64	8	75	450	1.8	2.8	6.2
04-05—Indiana...........	63	1747	203	456	.445	85	113	.752	32	147	179	302	59	15	96	532	2.8	4.8	8.4
05-06—Indiana...........	75	1981	267	603	.443	106	141	.752	31	137	168	324	63	22	115	691	2.2	4.3	9.2
Totals	546	10833	1209	2941	.411	521	711	.733	212	713	925	1548	409	74	598	3139	1.7	2.8	5.7

Three-point field goals: 1997-98, 42-for-128 (.328). 1998-99, 5-for-19 (.263). 1999-00, 2-for-11 (.182). 2000-01, 1-for-5 (.200). 2001-02, 4-for-12 (.333). 2002-03, 13-for-35 (.371). 2003-04, 41-for-122 (.336). 2004-05, 41-for-108 (.380). 2005-06, 51-for-155 (.329). Totals, 200-for-595 (.336).
Personal fouls/disqualifications: 1997-98, 188/1. 1998-99, 67/0. 1999-00, 58/0. 2000-01, 62/0. 2001-02, 30/0. 2002-03, 93/1. 2003-04, 138/0. 2004-05, 144/0. 2005-06, 132/0. Totals, 912/2.

NBA PLAYOFF RECORD

Season Team	G	Min.	FGM	FGA	Pct.	FTM	FTA	Pct.	Off.	Def.	Tot.	Ast.	St.	Blk.	TO	Pts.	RPG	APG	PPG
										REBOUNDS								AVERAGES	
98-99—Atlanta	9	111	8	29	.276	7	10	.700	3	6	9	10	1	1	5	24	1.0	1.1	2.7
01-02—New Jersey	19	161	20	53	.377	9	11	.818	2	12	14	21	6	0	8	50	0.7	1.1	2.6

Season Team	G	Min.	FGM	FGA	Pct.	FTM	FTA	Pct.	REBOUNDS Off.	Def.	Tot.	Ast.	St.	Blk.	TO	Pts.	AVERAGES RPG	APG	PPG
02-03—New Jersey	17	122	17	31	.548	5	6	.833	3	9	12	19	2	0	8	42	0.7	1.1	2.5
03-04—Indiana...........	16	332	25	69	.362	17	22	.773	7	27	34	34	13	4	11	73	2.1	2.1	4.6
04-05—Indiana...........	13	316	27	77	.351	29	36	.806	4	34	38	66	13	5	25	91	2.9	5.1	7.0
05-06—Indiana...........	6	242	45	87	.517	22	33	.667	8	22	30	31	6	0	14	120	5.0	5.2	20.0
Totals	80	1284	142	346	.410	89	118	.754	27	110	137	181	41	10	71	400	1.7	2.3	5.0

Three-point field goals: 1998-99, 1-for-2 (.500). 2001-02, 1-for-10 (.100). 2002-03, 3-for-6 (.500). 2003-04, 6-for-20 (.300). 2004-05, 8-for-23 (.348). 2005-06, 8-for-20 (.400). Totals, 27-for-81 (.333).

Personal fouls/disqualifications: 1998-99, 9/0. 2001-02, 24/0. 2002-03, 15/0. 2003-04, 34/0. 2004-05, 28/0. 2005-06, 17/0. Totals, 127/0.

NBA DEVELOPMENT LEAGUE RECORD

Season Team	G	Min.	FGM	FGA	Pct.	FTM	FTA	Pct.	Reb.	Ast.	Pts.	AVERAGES RPG	APG	PPG
01-02—Mobile	15	394	72	156	.462	32	43	.744	46	44	179	3.1	2.9	11.9

Three-point field goals: 2001-02, 3-for-12 (.250). Totals, 3-for-12 (.250).

Personal fouls/disqualifications: 2001-02, 40/0. Totals, 40/0.

JOHNSON, DERMARR   G   NUGGETS

PERSONAL: Born May 5, 1980, in Washington, D.C. ... 6-9/201. (2.06/91.2). ... Full name: DerMarr Miles Johnson
HIGH SCHOOL: Bladensburg (Md.), then Parkdale (Riverdale, Md.).
COLLEGE: Cincinnati.
TRANSACTIONS/CAREER NOTES: Selected after freshman season by Atlanta Hawks in first round (sixth pick overall) of 2000 NBA Draft. ... Signed as free agent by Phoenix Suns (October 1, 2003). ... Waived by Suns (October 16, 2003). ... Played in ABA (2003-04). ... Signed as free agent by Denver Nuggets (October 18, 2004).

COLLEGIATE RECORD

Season Team	G	Min.	FGM	FGA	Pct.	FTM	FTA	Pct.	Reb.	Ast.	Pts.	AVERAGES RPG	APG	PPG
99-00—Cincinnati	32	879	140	293	.478	70	95	.737	123	45	402	3.8	1.4	12.6

Three-point field goals: 1999-00, 52-for-140 (.371). Totals, 52-for-140 (.371).

NBA REGULAR-SEASON RECORD

Season Team	G	Min.	FGM	FGA	Pct.	FTM	FTA	Pct.	REBOUNDS Off.	Def.	Tot.	Ast.	St.	Blk.	TO	Pts.	AVERAGES RPG	APG	PPG
00-01—Atlanta	78	1313	146	390	.374	64	87	.736	56	122	178	64	43	30	93	397	2.3	0.8	5.1
01-02—Atlanta	72	1727	214	540	.396	85	105	.810	59	188	247	81	62	56	102	602	3.4	1.1	8.4
02-03—Atlanta............								Did not play—injured											
03-04—New York	21	287	36	97	.371	28	31	.903	5	34	39	11	8	7	16	113	1.9	0.5	5.4
04-05—Denver	71	1232	185	371	.499	80	101	.792	43	108	151	75	43	18	65	503	2.1	1.1	7.1
05-06—Denver	58	924	132	306	.431	34	42	.810	19	77	96	55	25	26	46	354	1.7	0.9	6.1
Totals	300	5483	713	1704	.418	291	366	.795	182	529	711	286	181	137	322	1969	2.4	1.0	6.6

Three-point field goals: 2000-01, 41-for-127 (.323). 2001-02, 89-for-247 (.360). 2003-04, 13-for-36 (.361). 2004-05, 53-for-148 (.358). 2005-06, 56-for-160 (.350). Totals, 252-for-718 (.351).

Personal fouls/disqualifications: 2000-01, 134/0. 2001-02, 163/1. 2003-04, 32/0. 2004-05, 140/0. 2005-06, 86/0. Totals, 555/1.

NBA PLAYOFF RECORD

Season Team	G	Min.	FGM	FGA	Pct.	FTM	FTA	Pct.	REBOUNDS Off.	Def.	Tot.	Ast.	St.	Blk.	TO	Pts.	AVERAGES RPG	APG	PPG
03-04—New York	3	17	0	5	.000	0	0	...	0	2	2	2	0	1	0	0	0.7	0.7	0.0
04-05—Denver	4	78	11	20	.550	3	3	1.000	3	5	8	3	2	2	0	29	2.0	0.8	7.3
05-06—Denver	3	34	3	13	.231	0	0	...	2	8	10	2	0	1	1	7	3.3	0.7	2.3
Totals	10	129	14	38	.368	3	3	1.000	5	15	20	7	2	4	1	36	2.0	0.7	3.6

Three-point field goals: 2003-04, 0-for-3. 2004-05, 4-for-11 (.364). 2005-06, 1-for-10 (.100). Totals, 5-for-24 (.208).

Personal fouls/disqualifications: 2003-04, 2/0. 2004-05, 9/0. 2005-06, 1/0. Totals, 12/0.

AMERICAN BASKETBALL ASSOCIATION RECORD

Season Team	G	Min.	FGM	FGA	Pct.	FTM	FTA	Pct.	Reb.	Ast.	Pts.	AVERAGES RPG	APG	PPG
03-04—Long Beach	20	...	152	321	.474	87	102	.853	135	63	441	6.8	3.2	22.1

Three-point field goals: 2003-04, 50-for-132 (.379). Totals, 50-for-132 (.379).

JOHNSON, ERVIN   C

PERSONAL: Born December 21, 1967, in New Orleans. ... 6-11/255. (2.11/115.7).
HIGH SCHOOL: Block (Jonesville, La.).
COLLEGE: New Orleans.
TRANSACTIONS/CAREER NOTES: Selected by Seattle SuperSonics in first round (23rd pick overall) of 1993 NBA Draft. ... Signed as free agent by Denver Nuggets (July 17, 1996). ... Traded by Nuggets to Milwaukee Bucks for F Johnny Newman, F/C Joe Wolf and draft rights to F Danny Fortson (June 25, 1997). ... Traded by Bucks with G Sam Cassell to Minnesota Timberwolves for F Joe Smith and G Anthony Peeler (June 27, 2003) ... Signed as free agent by Milwaukee Bucks (August 29, 2005).

COLLEGIATE RECORD

Season Team	G	Min.	FGM	FGA	Pct.	FTM	FTA	Pct.	Reb.	Ast.	Pts.	AVERAGES RPG	APG	PPG
88-89—New Orleans..................						Did not play—redshirted.								
89-90—New Orleans.................	32	757	84	145	.579	32	57	.561	218	29	200	6.8	0.9	6.3
90-91—New Orleans.................	30	899	162	283	.572	58	108	.537	367	34	382	12.2	1.1	12.7

Season Team	G	Min.	FGM	FGA	Pct.	FTM	FTA	Pct.	Reb.	Ast.	Pts.		AVERAGES	
												RPG	APG	PPG
91-92—New Orleans..................	32	1073	185	317	.584	122	171	.713	356	56	492	11.1	1.8	15.4
92-93—New Orleans..................	29	965	208	336	.619	118	175	.674	346	16	534	11.9	0.6	18.4
Totals	123	3694	639	1081	.591	330	511	.646	1287	135	1608	10.5	1.1	13.1

NBA REGULAR-SEASON RECORD

NOTES: Led NBA with 321 personal fouls (1998).

Season Team	G	Min.	FGM	FGA	Pct.	FTM	FTA	Pct.	REBOUNDS			Ast.	St.	Blk.	TO	Pts.	AVERAGES		
									Off.	Def.	Tot.						RPG	APG	PPG
93-94—Seattle	45	280	44	106	.415	29	46	.630	48	70	118	7	10	22	24	117	2.6	0.2	2.6
94-95—Seattle	64	907	85	192	.443	29	46	.630	101	188	289	16	17	67	54	199	4.5	0.3	3.1
95-96—Seattle	81	1519	180	352	.511	85	127	.669	129	304	433	48	40	129	98	446	5.3	0.6	5.5
96-97—Denver	82	2599	243	467	.520	96	156	.615	*231	682	913	71	65	227	118	582	11.1	0.9	7.1
97-98—Milwaukee	81	2261	253	471	.537	143	238	.601	242	443	685	59	79	158	117	649	8.5	0.7	8.0
98-99—Milwaukee	50	1027	96	189	.508	64	105	.610	120	200	320	19	29	57	47	256	6.4	0.4	5.1
99-00—Milwaukee	80	2129	144	279	.516	95	157	.605	233	415	648	44	81	127	80	383	8.1	0.6	4.8
00-01—Milwaukee	82	1981	108	198	.545	50	93	.538	205	408	613	40	44	97	47	266	7.5	0.5	3.2
01-02—Milwaukee	81	1660	89	193	.461	30	66	.455	142	324	466	27	37	82	52	208	5.8	0.3	2.6
02-03—Milwaukee	69	1170	61	135	.452	30	44	.682	117	177	294	24	34	63	34	152	4.3	0.3	2.2
03-04—Minnesota.......	66	965	55	103	.534	17	28	.607	61	171	232	24	27	43	30	127	3.5	0.4	1.9
04-05—Minnesota.......	46	410	28	54	.519	16	25	.640	43	70	113	6	7	13	18	73	2.5	0.1	1.6
05-06—Milwaukee	18	81	7	17	.412	1	2	.500	5	19	24	2	1	2	5	15	1.3	0.1	0.8
Totals	845	16989	1393	2756	.505	685	1133	.605	1677	3471	5148	387	471	1087	724	3473	6.1	0.5	4.1

Three-point field goals: 1994-95, 0-for-1. 1995-96, 1-for-3 (.333). 1996-97, 0-for-2. 1999-00, 0-for-1. 2001-02, 0-for-1. 2003-04, 0-for-1. 2004-05, 1-for-1 (1.000). Totals, 2-for-10 (.200).

Personal fouls/disqualifications: 1993-94, 45/0. 1994-95, 163/1. 1995-96, 245/3. 1996-97, 288/5. 1997-98, 321/7. 1998-99, 151/1. 1999-00, 298/6. 2000-01, 257/4. 2001-02, 219/4. 2002-03, 178/3. 2003-04, 132/0. 2004-05, 86/0. 2005-06, 23/0. Totals, 2430/35.

NBA PLAYOFF RECORD

Season Team	G	Min.	FGM	FGA	Pct.	FTM	FTA	Pct.	REBOUNDS			Ast.	St.	Blk.	TO	Pts.	AVERAGES		
									Off.	Def.	Tot.						RPG	APG	PPG
93-94—Seattle	2	8	0	1	.000	0	0	...	0	4	4	0	0	0	1	0	2.0	0.0	0.0
94-95—Seattle	4	54	4	14	.286	6	6	1.000	8	13	21	0	1	4	1	14	5.3	0.0	3.5
95-96—Seattle	18	253	23	62	.371	9	11	.818	28	42	70	7	6	15	14	55	3.9	0.4	3.1
98-99—Milwaukee	3	92	6	13	.462	1	2	.500	8	10	18	1	2	5	0	13	6.0	0.3	4.3
99-00—Milwaukee	5	155	10	20	.500	11	18	.611	14	35	49	2	6	6	3	31	9.8	0.4	6.2
00-01—Milwaukee	18	577	39	68	.574	20	32	.625	59	135	194	10	9	37	12	98	10.8	0.6	5.4
02-03—Milwaukee	6	76	3	8	.375	0	0	...	6	18	24	3	3	5	3	6	4.0	0.5	1.0
03-04—Minnesota.......	18	356	19	38	.500	10	16	.625	27	57	84	13	11	10	6	48	4.7	0.7	2.7
05-06—Milwaukee	3	11	0	1	.000	2	2	1.000	0	4	4	0	1	0	1	2	1.3	0.0	0.7
Totals	77	1582	104	225	.462	59	87	.678	150	318	468	36	39	82	41	267	6.1	0.5	3.5

Personal fouls/disqualifications: 1993-94, 1/0. 1994-95, 10/0. 1995-96, 43/0. 1998-99, 10/0. 1999-00, 0/0. 2000-01, 76/1. 2002-03, 8/0. 2003-04, 56/0.
2005-06, 1/0. Totals, 219/1.

JOHNSON, JOE   G/F   HAWKS

PERSONAL: Born July 29, 1981, in Little Rock, Ark. ... 6-7/225. (2.01/102.1). ... Full name: Joe Marcus Johnson
HIGH SCHOOL: Little Rock Central (Little Rock, Ark.).
COLLEGE: Arkansas.
TRANSACTIONS/CAREER NOTES: Selected after sophomore season by Boston Celtics in first round (10th pick overall) of 2001 NBA Draft. ... Traded by Celtics with G Milt Palacio, G Randy Brown and 2002 first-round draft choice to Phoenix Suns for G Tony Delk and F Rodney Rogers (February 20, 2002). ... Traded by Suns to Atlanta Hawks for G/F Boris Diaw and two future first-round draft picks (August 19, 2005).

COLLEGIATE RECORD

Season Team	G	Min.	FGM	FGA	Pct.	FTM	FTA	Pct.	Reb.	Ast.	Pts.		AVERAGES	
												RPG	APG	PPG
99-00—Arkansas	23	732	140	302	.464	60	79	.759	132	50	368	5.7	2.2	16.0
00-01—Arkansas	30	873	162	346	.468	68	91	.747	193	77	427	6.4	2.6	14.2
Totals	53	1605	302	648	.466	128	170	.753	325	127	795	6.1	2.4	15.0

Three-point field goals: 1999-00, 28-for-76 (.368). 2000-01, 35-for-79 (.443). Totals, 63-for-155 (.406).
Personal fouls/disqualifications: 1999-00, 44/0. 2000-01, 46/0. Totals, 90/0.

NBA REGULAR-SEASON RECORD

HONORS: NBA All-Rookie second team (2002).

Season Team	G	Min.	FGM	FGA	Pct.	FTM	FTA	Pct.	REBOUNDS			Ast.	St.	Blk.	TO	Pts.	AVERAGES		
									Off.	Def.	Tot.						RPG	APG	PPG
01-02—Bos.-Phoenix ..	77	1916	251	584	.430	41	53	.774	75	182	257	179	59	20	71	581	3.3	2.3	7.5
02-03—Phoenix	82	2255	316	796	.397	96	124	.774	57	207	264	210	62	19	108	803	3.2	2.6	9.8
03-04—Phoenix	82	3331	555	1291	.430	174	232	.750	80	305	385	362	93	26	199	1367	4.7	4.4	16.7
04-05—Phoenix	82	3240	544	1179	.461	135	180	.750	120	302	422	291	79	24	148	1400	5.1	3.5	17.1
05-06—Atlanta	82	3340	632	1395	.453	261	330	.791	98	237	335	536	103	31	267	1653	4.1	6.5	20.2
Totals	405	14082	2298	5245	.438	707	919	.769	430	1233	1663	1578	396	120	793	5804	4.1	3.9	14.3

Three-point field goals: 2001-02, 38-for-130 (.292). 2002-03, 75-for-205 (.366). 2003-04, 83-for-272 (.305). 2004-05, 177-for-370 (.478). 2005-06, 128-for-360 (.356). Totals, 501-for-1337 (.375).
Personal fouls/disqualifications: 2001-02, 114/0. 2002-03, 143/0. 2003-04, 177/1. 2004-05, 167/0. 2005-06, 187/0. Totals, 788/1.

NBA PLAYOFF RECORD

Season Team	G	Min.	FGM	FGA	Pct.	FTM	FTA	Pct.	REBOUNDS Off.	Def.	Tot.	Ast.	St.	Blk.	TO	Pts.	AVERAGES RPG	APG	PPG
02-03—Phoenix	6	164	14	51	.275	2	5	.400	6	20	26	8	4	2	12	32	4.3	1.3	5.3
04-05—Phoenix	9	355	63	125	.504	23	33	.697	7	32	39	30	10	4	10	169	4.3	3.3	18.8
Totals	15	519	77	176	.438	25	38	.658	13	52	65	38	14	6	22	201	4.3	2.5	13.4

Three-point field goals: 2002-03, 2-for-13 (.154). 2004-05, 20-for-36 (.556). Totals, 22-for-49 (.449).
Personal fouls/disqualifications: 2002-03, 15/0. 2004-05, 18/0. Totals, 33/0.

JOHNSON, LINTON   F

PERSONAL: Born June 13, 1980, in Chicago. ... 6-8/205. (2.03/93.0).
HIGH SCHOOL: Providence St. Mel (Chicago).
COLLEGE: Tulane.
TRANSACTIONS/CAREER NOTES: Not drafted by an NBA franchise. ... Signed as free agent by Chicago Bulls (September 29, 2003). ... Waived by Bulls (January 6, 2004). ... Played in Continental Basketball Association (2004). ... Signed by Bulls to first of two consecutive 10-day contracts (February 28, 2004). ... Signed by Bulls for remainder of season (March 19, 2004). ... Signed as free agent by San Antonio Spurs (August 25, 2004). ... Signed as free agent by New Jersey Nets (September 1, 2005). ... Traded by Nets with F/C Marc Jackson and cash to New Orleans Hornets for F Bostjan Nachbar (February 23, 2006).

COLLEGIATE RECORD

Season Team	G	Min.	FGM	FGA	Pct.	FTM	FTA	Pct.	Reb.	Ast.	Pts.	AVERAGES RPG	APG	PPG
98-99—Tulane............................	25	205	16	46	.348	9	20	.450	47	8	42	1.9	0.3	1.7
99-00—Tulane............................	31	350	33	68	.485	20	31	.645	98	13	87	3.2	0.4	2.8
00-01—Tulane............................	30	1018	153	300	.510	59	87	.678	242	73	394	8.1	2.4	13.1
01-02—Tulane............................	21	500	77	179	.430	19	25	.760	136	24	189	6.5	1.1	9.0
Totals	107	2073	279	593	.470	107	163	.656	523	118	712	4.9	1.1	6.7

Three-point field goals: 1998-99, 1-for-8 (.125). 1999-00, 1-for-5 (.200). 2000-01, 29-for-80 (.363). 2001-02, 16-for-56 (.286). Totals, 47-for-149 (.315).

CBA RECORD

Season Team	G	Min.	FGM	FGA	Pct.	FTM	FTA	Pct.	Reb.	Ast.	Pts.	AVERAGES RPG	APG	PPG
03-04—Rockford	22	715	136	285	.477	39	55	.709	183	39	332	8.3	1.8	15.1

Three-point field goals: 2003-04, 21-for-57 (.368). Totals, 21-for-57 (.368).

NBA REGULAR-SEASON RECORD

Season Team	G	Min.	FGM	FGA	Pct.	FTM	FTA	Pct.	REBOUNDS Off.	Def.	Tot.	Ast.	St.	Blk.	TO	Pts.	AVERAGES RPG	APG	PPG
03-04—Chicago	41	734	72	203	.355	22	37	.595	59	124	183	27	37	32	37	173	4.5	0.7	4.2
04-05—San Antonio....	2	15	0	2	.000	0	0	...	0	3	3	0	1	0	1	0	1.5	0.0	0.0
05-06—N.J.-NO/OK. City	36	524	61	149	.409	18	27	.667	40	82	122	14	12	12	28	153	3.4	0.4	4.3
Totals	79	1273	133	354	.376	40	64	.625	99	209	308	41	50	44	66	326	3.9	0.5	4.1

Three-point field goals: 2003-04, 7-for-33 (.212). 2004-05, 0-for-1. 2005-06, 13-for-36 (.361). Totals, 20-for-70 (.286).
Personal fouls/disqualifications: 2003-04, 90/2. 2004-05, 1/0. 2005-06, 61/2. Totals, 152/4.

JONES, DAHNTAY   G/F   GRIZZLIES

PERSONAL: Born December 27, 1980, in Trenton, N.J. ... 6-6/210. (1.98/95.3). ... Full name: Dahntay Lavall Jones
HIGH SCHOOL: Steinert (Hamilton, N.J.).
COLLEGE: Rutgers, then Duke.
TRANSACTIONS/CAREER NOTES: Selected by Boston Celtics in first round (20th pick overall) of 2003 NBA Draft. ... Draft rights traded by Celtics with draft rights to G Troy Bell to Memphis Grizzlies for draft rights to G Marcus Banks and C Kendrick Perkins (June 26, 2003).

COLLEGIATE RECORD

Season Team	G	Min.	FGM	FGA	Pct.	FTM	FTA	Pct.	Reb.	Ast.	Pts.	AVERAGES RPG	APG	PPG
98-99—Rutgers	32	841	119	281	.423	92	113	.814	130	49	341	4.1	1.5	10.7
99-00—Rutgers	31	1041	166	401	.414	124	175	.709	142	63	495	4.6	2.0	16.0
00-01—Duke..............................						Did not play—transfer student								
01-02—Duke..............................	35	1011	153	303	.505	74	102	.725	146	40	392	4.2	1.1	11.2
02-03—Duke..............................	33	1014	198	421	.470	140	187	.749	180	29	583	5.5	0.9	17.7
Totals	131	3907	636	1406	.452	430	577	.745	598	181	1811	4.6	1.4	13.8

Three-point field goals: 1998-99, 11-for-34 (.324). 1999-00, 39-for-113 (.345). 2001-02, 12-for-52 (.231). 2002-03, 47-for-118 (.398). Totals, 109-for-317 (.344).

NBA REGULAR-SEASON RECORD

Season Team	G	Min.	FGM	FGA	Pct.	FTM	FTA	Pct.	REBOUNDS Off.	Def.	Tot.	Ast.	St.	Blk.	TO	Pts.	AVERAGES RPG	APG	PPG
03-04—Memphis	20	154	15	53	.283	5	11	.455	7	16	23	12	5	6	12	36	1.2	0.6	1.8
04-05—Memphis	52	649	83	190	.437	44	64	.688	11	58	69	21	13	11	29	233	1.3	0.4	4.5
05-06—Memphis	71	967	109	263	.414	60	93	.645	20	84	104	39	38	15	50	281	1.5	0.5	4.0
Totals	143	1770	207	506	.409	109	168	.649	38	158	196	72	56	32	91	550	1.4	0.5	3.8

Three-point field goals: 2003-04, 1-for-4 (.250). 2004-05, 23-for-60 (.383). 2005-06, 3-for-21 (.143). Totals, 27-for-85 (.318).
Personal fouls/disqualifications: 2003-04, 23/0. 2004-05, 81/0. 2005-06, 108/1. Totals, 212/1.

NBA PLAYOFF RECORD

								REBOUNDS								AVERAGES		
Season Team	G	Min.	FGM	FGA	Pct.	FTM	FTA	Pct.	Off.	Def.	Tot.	Ast.	St.	Blk.	TO	Pts.	RPG	APG	PPG
04-05—Memphis	3	71	8	21	.381	3	4	.750	2	7	9	1	1	0	2	22	3.0	0.3	7.3
05-06—Memphis	4	46	5	7	.714	7	10	.700	1	6	7	0	1	0	2	17	1.8	0.0	4.3
Totals	7	117	13	28	.464	10	14	.714	3	13	16	1	2	0	4	39	2.3	0.1	5.6

Three-point field goals: 2004-05, 3-for-5 (.600). Totals, 3-for-5 (.600).
Personal fouls/disqualifications: 2004-05, 8/0. 2005-06, 7/0. Totals, 15/0.

JONES, DAMON G CAVALIERS

J

PERSONAL: Born August 25, 1976, in Galveston, Texas. ... 6-3/185. (1.91/83.9).
HIGH SCHOOL: Ball (Galveston, Texas).
COLLEGE: Houston.
TRANSACTIONS/CAREER NOTES: Not drafted by an NBA franchise. ... Played in International Basketball Association with Black Hills Posse (1997-98). ... Played in Continental Basketball Association with Idaho Stampede (1998-99). ... Signed as free agent by Orlando Magic (January 21, 1999). ... Waived by Magic (February 2, 1999). ... Signed as free agent by New Jersey Nets (February 16, 1999). ... Waived by Nets (March 8, 1999). ... Signed by Boston Celtics to first of two consecutive 10-day contracts (April 14, 1999). ... Re-signed by Celtics for remainder of season (May 4, 1999). ... Signed as free agent by Golden State Warriors (October 4, 1999). ... Waived by Warriors (November 30, 1999). ... Signed as free agent by Dallas Mavericks (December 2, 1999). ... Waived by Mavericks (January 5, 2000). ... Signed by Mavericks to first of two consecutive 10-day contracts (January 8, 2000). ... Re-signed by Mavericks for remainder of season (January 28, 2000). ... Signed as free agent by Vancouver Grizzlies (August 8, 2000). ... Signed as free agent by Houston Rockets (October 1, 2001). ... Waived by Rockets (October 25, 2001). ... Signed as free agent by Detroit Pistons (October 29, 2001). ... Signed as free agent by Sacramento Kings (October 18, 2002). ... Signed as free agent by Milwaukee Bucks (July 23, 2003). ... Signed as free agent by Miami Heat (August 6, 2004). ... Signed as free agent by Cleveland Cavaliers (September 8, 2005).

COLLEGIATE RECORD

												AVERAGES		
Season Team	G	Min.	FGM	FGA	Pct.	FTM	FTA	Pct.	Reb.	Ast.	Pts.	RPG	APG	PPG
94-95—Houston	27	781	91	262	.347	40	64	.625	92	77	277	3.4	2.9	10.3
95-96—Houston	27	857	115	266	.432	34	51	.667	111	105	321	4.1	3.9	11.9
96-97—Houston	27	968	159	341	.466	55	78	.705	120	132	443	4.4	4.9	16.4
Totals	81	2606	365	869	.420	129	193	.668	323	314	1041	4.0	3.9	12.9

Three-point field goals: 1994-95, 55-for-168 (.327). 1995-96, 57-for-167 (.341). 1996-97, 70-for-186 (.376). Totals, 182-for-521 (.349).
Personal fouls/disqualifications: 1994-95, 40/0. 1995-96, 37/0. 1996-97, 49/0. Totals, 126/0.

IBA RECORD

												AVERAGES		
Season Team	G	Min.	FGM	FGA	Pct.	FTM	FTA	Pct.	Reb.	Ast.	Pts.	RPG	APG	PPG
97-98—Black Hills	34	726	148	330	.448	53	75	.707	84	115	423	2.5	3.4	12.4

Three-point field goals: 1997-98, 74-for-200 (.370). Totals, 74-for-200 (.370).

CBA RECORD

NOTES: CBA Newcomer of the Year (1999). ... CBA All-League first team (1999). ... Led CBA with 120 three-point field goals made and 336 three-point field goals attempted (1999).

												AVERAGES		
Season Team	G	Min.	FGM	FGA	Pct.	FTM	FTA	Pct.	Reb.	Ast.	Pts.	RPG	APG	PPG
98-99—Idaho............................	35	1400	269	645	.417	100	130	.769	137	222	758	3.9	6.3	*21.7

Three-point field goals: 1998-99, 120-for-336 (.357). Totals, 120-for-336 (.357).
Personal fouls/disqualifications: 1998-99, 68/0. Totals, 68/0.

NBA REGULAR-SEASON RECORD

								REBOUNDS								AVERAGES		
Season Team	G	Min.	FGM	FGA	Pct.	FTM	FTA	Pct.	Off.	Def.	Tot.	Ast.	St.	Blk.	TO	Pts.	RPG	APG	PPG
98-99—N.J.-Boston	24	344	43	119	.361	14	17	.824	6	38	44	42	13	0	17	125	1.8	1.8	5.2
99-00—G.S.-Dallas......	55	612	80	208	.385	32	48	.667	12	43	55	96	18	1	40	233	1.0	1.7	4.2
00-01—Vancouver.......	71	1415	170	416	.409	37	52	.712	16	108	124	224	36	1	76	461	1.7	3.2	6.5
01-02—Detroit	67	1083	114	284	.401	43	59	.729	13	90	103	140	23	1	61	340	1.5	2.1	5.1
02-03—Sacramento ...	49	709	80	210	.381	20	27	.741	11	59	70	80	18	4	23	224	1.4	1.6	4.6
03-04—Milwaukee	82	2016	210	524	.401	55	72	.764	15	155	170	478	30	4	103	573	2.1	5.8	7.0
04-05—Miami	82	2576	331	726	.456	68	86	.791	14	217	231	350	44	5	98	955	2.8	4.3	11.6
05-06—Cleveland	82	2089	190	491	.387	32	50	.640	14	119	133	169	37	1	55	552	1.6	2.1	6.7
Totals	512	10844	1218	2978	.409	301	411	.732	101	829	930	1579	219	17	473	3463	1.8	3.1	6.8

Three-point field goals: 1998-99, 25-for-62 (.403). 1999-00, 41-for-114 (.360). 2000-01, 84-for-231 (.364). 2001-02, 69-for-186 (.371). 2002-03, 44-for-121 (.364). 2003-04, 98-for-273 (.359). 2004-05, 225-for-521 (.432). 2005-06, 140-for-371 (.377). Totals, 726-for-1879 (.386).
Personal fouls/disqualifications: 1998-99, 23/0. 1999-00, 34/0. 2000-01, 58/0. 2001-02, 83/0. 2002-03, 42/0. 2003-04, 92/0. 2004-05, 121/0. 2005-06, 112/0. Totals, 565/0.

NBA PLAYOFF RECORD

								REBOUNDS								AVERAGES		
Season Team	G	Min.	FGM	FGA	Pct.	FTM	FTA	Pct.	Off.	Def.	Tot.	Ast.	St.	Blk.	TO	Pts.	RPG	APG	PPG
01-02—Detroit	10	181	16	42	.381	3	4	.750	1	20	21	25	5	0	6	43	2.1	2.5	4.3
03-04—Milwaukee	5	144	18	34	.529	4	6	.667	2	18	20	37	5	0	9	50	4.0	7.4	10.0
04-05—Miami	15	498	62	129	.481	18	30	.600	3	38	41	60	7	0	17	181	2.7	4.0	12.1
05-06—Cleveland	13	181	8	26	.308	3	4	.750	2	14	16	12	2	0	3	24	1.2	0.9	1.8
Totals	43	1004	104	231	.450	28	44	.636	8	90	98	134	19	0	35	298	2.3	3.1	6.9

Three-point field goals: 2001-02, 8-for-27 (.296). 2003-04, 10-for-21 (.476). 2004-05, 39-for-91 (.429). 2005-06, 5-for-18 (.278). Totals, 62-for-157 (.395).
Personal fouls/disqualifications: 2001-02, 14/0. 2003-04, 14/0. 2004-05, 24/0. 2005-06, 17/0. Totals, 69/0.

JONES, DWAYNE — F/C — CELTICS

PERSONAL: Born June 9, 1983, in Morgantown, W.Va. ... 6-11/250 (2,11/113,4).
HIGH SCHOOL: American Christian (Aston, Pa.).
COLLEGE: St. Joseph's.
TRANSACTIONS/CAREER NOTES: Not drafted by an NBA franchise ... Played in NBA Development League (2005-06). ... Signed as free agent by Minnesota Timberwolves (August 26, 2005). ... Traded by Timberwolves with F Wally Szczerbiak, C Michael Olowokandi and a future first-round draft choice to Boston Celtics for G Ricky Davis, C Mark Blount, G Marcus Banks, SF Justin Reed and two second-round draft choices (January 26, 2006).

COLLEGIATE RECORD

Season Team	G	Min.	FGM	FGA	Pct.	FTM	FTA	Pct.	Reb.	Ast.	Pts.	RPG	APG	PPG
01-02—St. Joseph's					Did not play—ineligible									
02-03—St. Joseph's	30	631	50	95	.526	26	74	.351	189	8	126	6.3	0.3	4.2
03-04—St. Joseph's	32	868	79	145	.545	47	104	.452	224	29	205	7.0	0.9	6.4
04-05—St. Joseph's	36	1254	115	227	.507	133	248	.536	418	31	363	11.6	0.9	10.1
Totals	98	2753	244	467	.522	206	426	.484	831	68	694	8.5	0.7	7.1

NBA REGULAR-SEASON RECORD

Season Team	G	Min.	FGM	FGA	Pct.	FTM	FTA	Pct.	Off.	Def.	Tot.	Ast.	St.	Blk.	TO	Pts.	RPG	APG	PPG
05-06—Minn.Boston	14	87	4	10	.400	6	13	.462	10	21	31	2	1	3	3	14	2.2	0.1	1.0

Personal fouls/disqualifications: 2005-06, 14/0. Totals, 14/0.

NBA DEVELOPMENT LEAGUE RECORD

Season Team	G	Min.	FGM	FGA	Pct.	FTM	FTA	Pct.	Reb.	Ast.	Pts.	RPG	APG	PPG
05-06—Florida	26	808	76	163	.466	80	124	.645	304	32	232	11.7	1.2	8.9

JONES, EDDIE — G — GRIZZLIES

PERSONAL: Born October 20, 1971, in Pompano Beach, Fla. ... 6-7/194. (2.01/88.0). ... Full name: Eddie Charles Jones
HIGH SCHOOL: Ely (Pompano Beach, Fla.).
COLLEGE: Temple.
TRANSACTIONS/CAREER NOTES: Selected by Los Angeles Lakers in first round (10th pick overall) of 1994 NBA Draft. ... Traded by Lakers with F/C Elden Campbell to Charlotte Hornets for F Glen Rice, F/C J.R. Reid and G B.J. Armstrong (March 10, 1999). ... Traded by Hornets with F Anthony Mason, G Ricky Davis and G/F Dale Ellis to Miami Heat for F P.J. Brown, F Jamal Mashburn, F/C Otis Thorpe, F Tim James and G/F Rodney Buford (August 1, 2000). ... Traded by Heat to Memphis Grizzlies in five-team trade (August 2, 2005).

COLLEGIATE RECORD

Season Team	G	Min.	FGM	FGA	Pct.	FTM	FTA	Pct.	Reb.	Ast.	Pts.	RPG	APG	PPG
90-91—Temple					Did not play—ineligible.									
91-92—Temple	29	764	122	279	.437	41	75	.547	122	30	332	4.2	1.0	11.4
92-93—Temple	32	1169	212	463	.458	70	116	.603	225	56	543	7.0	1.8	17.0
93-94—Temple	31	1184	231	491	.470	88	133	.662	210	58	595	6.8	1.9	19.2
Totals	92	3117	565	1233	.458	199	324	.614	557	144	1470	6.1	1.6	16.0

Three-point field goals: 1991-92, 47-for-134 (.351). 1992-93, 49-for-141 (.348). 1993-94, 45-for-128 (.352). Totals, 141-for-403 (.350).

NBA REGULAR-SEASON RECORD

HONORS: All-NBA third team (2000). ... NBA All-Defensive second team (1998, 1999, 2000). ... NBA All-Rookie first team (1995). ... MVP of Rookie Game (1995).
NOTES: Led NBA with 2.7 steals per game (2000).

Season Team	G	Min.	FGM	FGA	Pct.	FTM	FTA	Pct.	Off.	Def.	Tot.	Ast.	St.	Blk.	TO	Pts.	RPG	APG	PPG
94-95—L.A. Lakers	64	1981	342	744	.460	122	169	.722	79	170	249	128	131	41	75	897	3.9	2.0	14.0
95-96—L.A. Lakers	70	2184	337	685	.492	136	184	.739	45	188	233	246	129	45	99	893	3.3	3.5	12.8
96-97—L.A. Lakers	80	2998	473	1081	.438	276	337	.819	90	236	326	270	189	49	169	1374	4.1	3.4	17.2
97-98—L.A. Lakers	80	2910	486	1005	.484	234	306	.765	85	217	302	246	160	55	146	1349	3.8	3.1	16.9
98-99—L.A.L.-Char.	50	1881	260	595	.437	212	271	.782	50	144	194	186	125	58	93	780	3.9	3.7	15.6
99-00—Charlotte	72	2807	478	1119	.427	362	419	.864	81	262	343	305	*192	49	160	1446	4.8	4.2	20.1
00-01—Miami	63	2282	388	871	.445	228	270	.844	75	217	292	171	110	58	135	1094	4.6	2.7	17.4
01-02—Miami	81	3156	517	1198	.432	297	355	.837	61	317	378	262	117	77	148	1480	4.7	3.2	18.3
02-03—Miami	47	1789	291	688	.423	189	230	.822	35	191	226	173	64	31	85	869	4.8	3.7	18.5
03-04—Miami	81	2998	473	1156	.409	278	333	.835	38	270	308	258	92	34	129	1401	3.8	3.2	17.3
04-05—Miami	80	2839	351	820	.428	174	216	.806	38	367	405	212	86	38	99	1018	5.1	2.7	12.7
05-06—Memphis	75	2437	292	722	.404	168	215	.781	35	244	279	177	131	27	93	885	3.7	2.4	11.8
Totals	843	30262	4688	10684	.439	2676	3305	.810	712	2823	3535	2634	1526	562	1431	13486	4.2	3.1	16.0

Three-point field goals: 1994-95, 91-for-246 (.370). 1995-96, 83-for-227 (.366). 1996-97, 152-for-389 (.391). 1997-98, 143-for-368 (.389). 1998-99, 48-for-142 (.338). 1999-00, 128-for-341 (.375). 2000-01, 90-for-238 (.378). 2001-02, 149-for-382 (.390). 2002-03, 98-for-241 (.407). 2003-04, 177-for-479 (.370). 2004-05, 142-for-382 (.372). 2005-06, 133-for-374 (.356). Totals, 1434-for-3809 (.376).
Personal fouls/disqualifications: 1994-95, 175/1. 1995-96, 162/0. 1996-97, 226/3. 1997-98, 164/0. 1998-99, 128/1. 1999-00, 176/1. 2000-01, 183/5. 2001-02, 258/2. 2002-03, 137/1. 2003-04, 226/2. 2004-05, 251/4. 2005-06, 201/2. Totals, 2287/22.

NBA PLAYOFF RECORD

Season Team	G	Min.	FGM	FGA	Pct.	FTM	FTA	Pct.	Off.	Def.	Tot.	Ast.	St.	Blk.	TO	Pts.	RPG	APG	PPG
94-95—L.A. Lakers	10	286	30	80	.375	15	21	.714	7	25	32	20	8	9	17	87	3.2	2.0	8.7
95-96—L.A. Lakers	4	155	27	49	.551	5	8	.625	7	14	21	6	8	1	4	69	5.3	1.5	17.3

Season Team	G	Min.	FGM	FGA	Pct.	FTM	FTA	Pct.	Off.	Def.	Tot.	Ast.	St.	Blk.	TO	Pts.	RPG	APG	PPG
									REBOUNDS								AVERAGES		
96-97—L.A. Lakers	9	283	33	72	.458	26	35	.743	8	23	31	29	9	4	13	101	3.4	3.2	11.2
97-98—L.A. Lakers	13	476	69	148	.466	63	76	.829	12	39	51	32	26	21	17	221	3.9	2.5	17.0
99-00—Charlotte	4	171	22	58	.379	15	16	.938	4	16	20	19	10	3	5	68	5.0	4.8	17.0
00-01—Miami	3	108	22	44	.500	6	7	.857	2	16	18	7	3	1	7	57	6.0	2.3	19.0
03-04—Miami	13	478	56	153	.366	40	50	.800	3	44	47	29	18	11	19	172	3.6	2.2	13.2
04-05—Miami	15	601	71	156	.455	31	42	.738	10	77	87	39	18	9	22	205	5.8	2.6	13.7
05-06—Memphis	4	119	14	29	.483	10	15	.667	3	8	11	10	3	1	1	41	2.8	2.5	10.3
Totals	75	2677	344	789	.436	211	270	.781	56	262	318	191	103	60	105	1021	4.2	2.5	13.6

Three-point field goals: 1994-95, 12-for-27 (.444). 1995-96, 10-for-19 (.526). 1996-97, 9-for-24 (.375). 1997-98, 20-for-48 (.417). 1999-00, 9-for-26 (.346). 2000-01, 7-for-16 (.438). 2003-04, 20-for-67 (.299). 2004-05, 32-for-80 (.400). 2005-06, 3-for-7 (.429). Totals, 122-for-314 (.389).

Personal fouls/disqualifications: 1994-95, 27/0. 1995-96, 16/0. 1996-97, 24/0. 1997-98, 37/0. 1999-00, 12/0. 2000-01, 9/0. 2003-04, 37/0. 2004-05, 57/1. 2005-06, 10/0. Totals, 229/1.

NBA ALL-STAR GAME RECORD

Season Team	Min.	FGM	FGA	Pct.	FTM	FTA	Pct.	Off.	Def.	Tot.	Ast.	PF	Dq.	St.	Blk.	TO	Pts.
								REBOUNDS									
1997—L.A. Lakers...........	17	3	4	.750	4	7	.571	1	0	1	1	1	0	1	2	3	10
1998—L.A. Lakers...........	25	7	19	.368	1	2	.500	7	4	11	1	1	0	2	0	0	15
2000—Charlotte	21	4	7	.571	0	0	...	1	3	4	3	1	0	1	0	1	10
Totals...........................	63	14	30	.467	5	9	.556	9	7	16	5	3	0	4	2	4	35

Three-point field goals: 1997, 0-for-1. 1998, 0-for-7. 2000, 2-for-3 (.667). Totals, 2-for-11 (.182).

JONES, FRED   G   RAPTORS

PERSONAL: Born March 11, 1979, in Malvern, Ark. ... 6-4/210. (1.93/95.3). ... Full name: Frederick Terrell Jones
HIGH SCHOOL: Barlow (Gresham, Ore.).
COLLEGE: Oregon.
TRANSACTIONS/CAREER NOTES: Selected by Indiana Pacers in first round (14th pick overall) of 2002 NBA Draft. ... Signed as free agent by Toronto Raptors (July 25, 2006).

COLLEGIATE RECORD

Season Team	G	Min.	FGM	FGA	Pct.	FTM	FTA	Pct.	Reb.	Ast.	Pts.	RPG	APG	PPG
												AVERAGES		
98-99—Oregon	32	675	103	201	.512	50	74	.676	108	62	290	3.4	1.9	9.1
99-00—Oregon	30	857	100	249	.402	62	81	.765	177	99	291	5.9	3.3	9.7
00-01—Oregon	28	892	136	288	.472	108	134	.806	157	95	413	5.6	3.4	14.8
01-02—Oregon	35	1103	215	413	.521	169	194	.871	189	111	650	5.4	3.2	18.6
Totals	125	3527	554	1151	.481	389	483	.805	631	367	1644	5.0	2.9	13.2

Three-point field goals: 1998-99, 34-for-83 (.410). 1999-00, 29-for-107 (.271). 2000-01, 33-for-108 (.306). 2001-02, 51-for-137 (.372). Totals, 147-for-435 (.338).

NBA REGULAR-SEASON RECORD

Season Team	G	Min.	FGM	FGA	Pct.	FTM	FTA	Pct.	Off.	Def.	Tot.	Ast.	St.	Blk.	TO	Pts.	RPG	APG	PPG
									REBOUNDS								AVERAGES		
02-03—Indiana...........	19	115	9	24	.375	3	4	.750	4	5	9	5	6	1	6	23	0.5	0.3	1.2
03-04—Indiana...........	81	1508	123	311	.395	124	149	.832	25	101	126	173	65	18	73	397	1.6	2.1	4.9
04-05—Indiana...........	77	2268	275	647	.425	176	207	.850	34	208	242	196	61	31	114	813	3.1	2.5	10.6
05-06—Indiana...........	68	1837	233	559	.417	122	160	.763	18	152	170	154	55	20	107	651	2.5	2.3	9.6
Totals	245	5728	640	1541	.415	425	520	.817	81	466	547	528	187	70	300	1884	2.2	2.2	7.7

Three-point field goals: 2002-03, 2-for-7 (.286). 2003-04, 27-for-89 (.303). 2004-05, 87-for-229 (.380). 2005-06, 63-for-187 (.337). Totals, 179-for-512 (.350).

Personal fouls/disqualifications: 2002-03, 13/0. 2003-04, 132/0. 2004-05, 171/1. 2005-06, 142/3. Totals, 458/4.

NBA PLAYOFF RECORD

Season Team	G	Min.	FGM	FGA	Pct.	FTM	FTA	Pct.	Off.	Def.	Tot.	Ast.	St.	Blk.	TO	Pts.	RPG	APG	PPG
									REBOUNDS								AVERAGES		
03-04—Indiana...........	14	263	25	51	.490	5	7	.714	3	30	33	16	7	7	9	66	2.4	1.1	4.7
04-05—Indiana...........	13	234	16	54	.296	12	13	.923	1	22	23	13	8	2	15	53	1.8	1.0	4.1
05-06—Indiana...........	6	167	15	36	.417	11	12	.917	2	18	20	15	6	1	8	47	3.3	2.5	7.8
Totals	33	664	56	141	.397	28	32	.875	6	70	76	44	21	10	32	166	2.3	1.3	5.0

Three-point field goals: 2003-04, 11-for-22 (.500). 2004-05, 9-for-23 (.391). 2005-06, 6-for-16 (.375). Totals, 26-for-61 (.426).
Personal fouls/disqualifications: 2003-04, 31/0. 2004-05, 13/0. 2005-06, 13/0. Totals, 57/0.

JONES, JAMES   F   SUNS

PERSONAL: Born October 4, 1980, in Miami, Fla. ... 6-8/215. (2.03/97.5). ... Full name: James Andrew Jones
HIGH SCHOOL: American Senior (Miami, Fla.).
COLLEGE: Miami (Fla.).
TRANSACTIONS/CAREER NOTES: Selected by Indiana Pacers in second round (49th pick overall) of 2003 NBA Draft. ... Traded by Pacers to Phoenix Suns for a second-round draft choice (August 25, 2005).

COLLEGIATE RECORD

Season Team	G	Min.	FGM	FGA	Pct.	FTM	FTA	Pct.	Reb.	Ast.	Pts.	RPG	APG	PPG
												AVERAGES		
99-00—Miami (Fla.)....................	33	424	52	122	.426	15	18	.833	64	11	129	1.9	0.3	3.9
00-01—Miami (Fla.)....................	29	922	122	285	.428	60	74	.811	170	34	345	5.9	1.2	11.9
01-02—Miami (Fla.)....................	32	1048	133	332	.401	111	132	.841	203	48	410	6.3	1.5	12.8
02-03—Miami (Fla.)....................	28	957	157	351	.447	118	142	.831	169	49	472	6.0	1.8	16.9
Totals	122	3351	464	1090	.426	304	366	.831	606	142	1356	5.0	1.2	11.1

Three-point field goals: 1999-00, 10-for-32 (.313). 2000-01, 41-for-87 (.471). 2001-02, 33-for-105 (.314). 2002-03, 40-for-100 (.400). Totals, 124-for-324 (.383).

NBA REGULAR-SEASON RECORD

Season Team	G	Min.	FGM	FGA	Pct.	FTM	FTA	Pct.	Off.	Def.	Tot.	Ast.	St.	Blk.	TO	Pts.	RPG	APG	PPG
03-04—Indiana	6	26	2	9	.222	2	2	1.000	0	2	2	0	1	0	0	7	0.3	0.0	1.2
04-05—Indiana	75	1330	126	318	.396	53	62	.855	39	135	174	57	31	28	43	371	2.3	0.8	4.9
05-06—Phoenix	75	1772	243	581	.418	103	121	.851	44	209	253	57	38	49	35	699	3.4	0.8	9.3
Totals	156	3128	371	908	.409	158	185	.854	83	346	429	114	70	77	78	1077	2.8	0.7	6.9

Three-point field goals: 2003-04, 1-for-4 (.250). 2004-05, 66-for-166 (.398). 2005-06, 110-for-285 (.386). Totals, 177-for-455 (.389).
Personal fouls/disqualifications: 2003-04, 1/0. 2004-05, 123/1. 2005-06, 142/0. Totals, 266/1.

NBA PLAYOFF RECORD

Season Team	G	Min.	FGM	FGA	Pct.	FTM	FTA	Pct.	Off.	Def.	Tot.	Ast.	St.	Blk.	TO	Pts.	RPG	APG	PPG
04-05—Indiana	13	214	19	46	.413	4	9	.444	5	22	27	10	7	7	4	52	2.1	0.8	4.0
05-06—Phoenix	20	353	28	82	.341	22	26	.846	16	56	72	5	5	18	9	86	3.6	0.3	4.3
Totals	33	567	47	128	.367	26	35	.743	21	78	99	15	12	25	13	138	3.0	0.5	4.2

Three-point field goals: 2004-05, 10-for-25 (.400). 2005-06, 8-for-26 (.308). Totals, 18-for-51 (.353).
Personal fouls/disqualifications: 2004-05, 18/0. 2005-06, 25/0. Totals, 43/0.

JONES, JUMAINE   F   SUNS

PERSONAL: Born February 10, 1979, in Cocoa, Fla. ... 6-8/218. (2.03/98.9). ... Full name: Jumaine Lanard Jones
HIGH SCHOOL: Mitchell-Baker (Camilla, Ga.).
COLLEGE: Georgia.
TRANSACTIONS/CAREER NOTES: Selected after sophomore season by Atlanta Hawks in first round (27th pick overall) of 1999 NBA Draft. ... Draft rights traded by Hawks to Philadelphia 76ers for future first-round draft choice (June 30, 1999). ... Traded by 76ers with F Tyrone Hill to Cleveland Cavaliers for F Matt Harpring, F Cedric Henderson and F/C Robert Traylor (August 3, 2001). ... Traded by Cavaliers to Sacramento Kings for G Mateen Cleaves (September 10, 2002); trade voided because Cleaves failed physical (September 17, 2002). ... Traded by Cavaliers to Boston Celtics for G J.R. Bremer, C Bruno Sundov and conditional second-round draft pick (July 29, 2003) ... Traded by Celtics with F/C Chris Mihm and G Chucky Atkins to Los Angeles Lakers for G Gary Payton, F Rick Fox and a first-round draft choice (August 13, 2004). ... Traded by Lakers to Charlotte Bobcats for a second-round draft pick (October 26, 2005). ... Signed as free agent by Phoenix Suns (August 31, 2006).

COLLEGIATE RECORD

Season Team	G	Min.	FGM	FGA	Pct.	FTM	FTA	Pct.	Reb.	Ast.	Pts.	RPG	APG	PPG
97-98—Georgia	35	1031	188	415	.453	95	121	.785	299	30	515	8.5	0.9	14.7
98-99—Georgia	30	1032	197	443	.445	122	168	.726	284	30	564	9.5	1.0	18.8
Totals	65	2063	385	858	.449	217	289	.751	583	60	1079	9.0	0.9	16.6

Three-point field goals: 1997-98, 44-for-124 (.355). 1998-99, 48-for-138 (.348). Totals, 92-for-262 (.351).

NBA REGULAR-SEASON RECORD

Season Team	G	Min.	FGM	FGA	Pct.	FTM	FTA	Pct.	Off.	Def.	Tot.	Ast.	St.	Blk.	TO	Pts.	RPG	APG	PPG
99-00—Philadelphia	33	138	22	58	.379	11	18	.611	16	22	38	5	6	5	14	57	1.2	0.2	1.7
00-01—Philadelphia	65	866	122	275	.444	40	53	.755	63	126	189	32	30	15	39	304	2.9	0.5	4.7
01-02—Cleveland	81	2142	287	640	.448	45	68	.662	125	365	490	116	75	46	79	671	6.0	1.4	8.3
02-03—Cleveland	80	2204	308	710	.434	57	83	.687	106	299	405	112	67	22	107	784	5.1	1.4	9.8
03-04—Boston	42	373	33	96	.344	14	23	.609	24	44	68	14	12	9	19	93	1.6	0.3	2.2
04-05—L.A. Lakers	76	1830	210	486	.432	55	75	.733	107	291	398	65	44	24	49	577	5.2	0.9	7.6
05-06—Charlotte	76	2089	298	736	.405	88	121	.727	105	271	376	63	68	22	74	799	4.9	0.8	10.5
Totals	453	9642	1280	3001	.427	310	441	.703	546	1418	1964	407	302	143	381	3285	4.3	0.9	7.3

Three-point field goals: 1999-00, 2-for-4 (.500). 2000-01, 20-for-60 (.333). 2001-02, 52-for-168 (.310). 2002-03, 111-for-314 (.354). 2003-04, 13-for-44 (.295). 2004-05, 102-for-261 (.391). 2005-06, 115-for-335 (.343). Totals, 415-for-1186 (.350).
Personal fouls/disqualifications: 1999-00, 10/0. 2000-01, 68/0. 2001-02, 184/3. 2002-03, 176/1. 2003-04, 48/0. 2004-05, 165/1. 2005-06, 200/4. Totals, 851/9.

NBA PLAYOFF RECORD

Season Team	G	Min.	FGM	FGA	Pct.	FTM	FTA	Pct.	Off.	Def.	Tot.	Ast.	St.	Blk.	TO	Pts.	RPG	APG	PPG
99-00—Philadelphia	4	8	1	3	.333	0	0	...	0	0	0	0	0	0	0	2	0.0	0.0	0.5
00-01—Philadelphia	23	447	52	125	.416	15	21	.714	35	49	84	17	10	11	14	127	3.7	0.7	5.5
03-04—Boston	2	28	2	6	.333	0	0	...	1	4	5	2	0	0	0	4	2.5	1.0	2.0
Totals	29	483	55	134	.410	15	21	.714	36	53	89	19	10	11	14	133	3.1	0.7	4.6

Three-point field goals: 1999-00, 0-for-2. 2000-01, 8-for-32 (.250). 2003-04, 0-for-2. Totals, 8-for-36 (.222).
Personal fouls/disqualifications: 2000-01, 33/0. 2003-04, 4/0. Totals, 37/0.

KAMAN, CHRIS   C   CLIPPERS

PERSONAL: Born April 28, 1982, in Grand Rapids, Mich. ... 7-0/255. (2.13/115.7). ... Full name: Christopher Zane Kaman
HIGH SCHOOL: Tri-unity Christian (Wyoming, Mich.).
COLLEGE: Central Michigan.
TRANSACTIONS/CAREER NOTES: Selected after junior season by Los Angeles Clippers in first round (sixth pick overall) of 2003 NBA Draft.

COLLEGIATE RECORD

Season Team	G	Min.	FGM	FGA	Pct.	FTM	FTA	Pct.	Reb.	Ast.	Pts.	RPG	APG	PPG
00-01—Central Michigan	28	520	105	183	.574	63	90	.700	135	6	273	4.8	0.2	9.8

Season Team	G	Min.	FGM	FGA	Pct.	FTM	FTA	Pct.	Reb.	Ast.	Pts.	AVERAGES		
												RPG	APG	PPG
01-02—Central Michigan	24	604	97	158	.614	89	137	.650	199	22	283	8.3	0.9	11.8
02-03—Central Michigan	31	1055	244	392	.622	206	275	.749	373	37	694	12.0	1.2	22.4
Totals	83	2179	446	733	.608	358	502	.713	707	65	1250	8.5	0.8	15.1

NBA REGULAR-SEASON RECORD

Season Team	G	Min.	FGM	FGA	Pct.	FTM	FTA	Pct.	REBOUNDS			Ast.	St.	Blk.	TO	Pts.	AVERAGES		
									Off.	Def.	Tot.						RPG	APG	PPG
03-04—L.A. Clippers	82	1843	200	435	.460	99	142	.697	126	335	461	85	23	73	155	499	5.6	1.0	6.1
04-05—L.A. Clippers	63	1632	246	495	.497	80	121	.661	135	288	423	73	26	68	115	572	6.7	1.2	9.1
05-06—L.A. Clippers	78	2560	369	706	.523	194	252	.770	187	563	750	79	45	108	176	932	9.6	1.0	11.9
Totals	223	6035	815	1636	.498	373	515	.724	448	1186	1634	237	94	249	446	2003	7.3	1.1	9.0

Three-point field goals: 2003-04, 0-for-2. 2004-05, 0-for-1. 2005-06, 0-for-2. Totals, 0-for-5 (.000).
Personal fouls/disqualifications: 2003-04, 211/1. 2004-05, 182/2. 2005-06, 269/5. Totals, 662/8.

NBA PLAYOFF RECORD

Season Team	G	Min.	FGM	FGA	Pct.	FTM	FTA	Pct.	REBOUNDS			Ast.	St.	Blk.	TO	Pts.	AVERAGES		
									Off.	Def.	Tot.						RPG	APG	PPG
05-06—L.A. Clippers	11	324	51	86	.593	16	21	.762	21	67	88	10	5	9	33	118	8.0	0.9	10.7

Personal fouls/disqualifications: 2005-06, 38/1. Totals, 38/1.

KAPONO, JASON   F   HEAT

PERSONAL: Born February 2, 1981, in Long Beach, Calif. ... 6-8/213. (2.03/96.6). ... Full name: Jason Alan Kapono.
HIGH SCHOOL: Artesia (Los Angeles, Calif.).
COLLEGE: UCLA.
TRANSACTIONS/CAREER NOTES: Selected by Cleveland Cavaliers in second round (31st pick overall) of 2003 NBA Draft. ... Selected by Charlotte Bobcats from Cavaliers in NBA Expansion Draft (June 22, 2004). ... Signed as free agent by Miami Heat (October 3, 2005).
MISCELLANEOUS: Member of NBA championship team (2006).

COLLEGIATE RECORD

Season Team	G	Min.	FGM	FGA	Pct.	FTM	FTA	Pct.	Reb.	Ast.	Pts.	AVERAGES		
												RPG	APG	PPG
99-00—UCLA	33	1080	191	368	.519	65	95	.684	144	64	529	4.4	1.9	16.0
00-01—UCLA	32	1122	167	379	.441	133	153	.869	183	72	551	5.7	2.3	17.2
01-02—UCLA	33	1142	170	370	.459	101	118	.856	169	70	528	5.1	2.1	16.0
02-03—UCLA	29	969	171	374	.457	81	92	.880	151	59	487	5.2	2.0	16.8
Totals	127	4313	699	1491	.469	380	458	.830	647	265	2095	5.1	2.1	16.5

Three-point field goals: 1999-00, 82-for-173 (.474). 2000-01, 84-for-184 (.457). 2001-02, 87-for-192 (.453). 2002-03, 64-for-161 (.398). Totals, 317-for-710 (.446).

NBA REGULAR-SEASON RECORD

Season Team	G	Min.	FGM	FGA	Pct.	FTM	FTA	Pct.	REBOUNDS			Ast.	St.	Blk.	TO	Pts.	AVERAGES		
									Off.	Def.	Tot.						RPG	APG	PPG
03-04—Cleveland	41	427	52	129	.403	20	24	.833	19	36	55	14	13	2	21	145	1.3	0.3	3.5
04-05—Charlotte	81	1491	269	671	.401	70	85	.824	32	132	164	61	40	6	46	688	2.0	0.8	8.5
05-06—Miami	51	665	79	177	.446	28	33	.848	12	59	71	37	7	3	20	207	1.4	0.7	4.1
Totals	173	2583	400	977	.409	118	142	.831	63	227	290	112	60	11	87	1040	1.7	0.6	6.0

Three-point field goals: 2003-04, 21-for-44 (.477). 2004-05, 80-for-194 (.412). 2005-06, 21-for-53 (.396). Totals, 122-for-291 (.419).
Personal fouls/disqualifications: 2003-04, 41/0. 2004-05, 132/1. 2005-06, 89/0. Totals, 262/1.

NBA PLAYOFF RECORD

Season Team	G	Min.	FGM	FGA	Pct.	FTM	FTA	Pct.	REBOUNDS			Ast.	St.	Blk.	TO	Pts.	AVERAGES		
									Off.	Def.	Tot.						RPG	APG	PPG
05-06—Miami	1	2	0	0	...	0	0	...	0	0	0	0	0	0	0	0	0.0	0.0	0.0

KASUN, MARIO   C

PERSONAL: Born April 5, 1980, in Croatia. ... 7-1/260. (2.16/117.9).
TRANSACTIONS/CAREER NOTES: Played in Croatia (1998-99 and 1999-2000). ... Played in Germany (2001-03). ... Selected by Los Angeles Clippers in second round (41st pick overall) of 2002 NBA Draft. ... Draft rights traded by Clippers to Orlando Magic for future considerations (June 26, 2002). ... Signed as free agent by Orlando Magic (August 16, 2004). ... Signed with FC Barcelona of Spanish League for 2006-07 season.

CROATIAN LEAGUE RECORD

Season Team	G	Min.	FGM	FGA	Pct.	FTM	FTA	Pct.	Reb.	Ast.	Pts.	AVERAGES		
												RPG	APG	PPG
98-99—Zagreb	11	94	14	19	.737	10	16	.625	19	3	38	1.7	0.3	3.5
99-00—Zagreb	19	266	43	85	.506	18	31	.581	55	4	104	2.9	0.2	5.5
Totals	30	360	57	104	.548	28	47	.596	74	7	142	2.5	0.2	4.7

Three-point field goals: 1999-00, 0-for-1. Totals, 0-for-1 (.000).

COLLEGIATE RECORD

Season Team	G	Min.	FGM	FGA	Pct.	FTM	FTA	Pct.	Reb.	Ast.	Pts.	AVERAGES		
												RPG	APG	PPG
00-01—Gonzaga							Did Not Play							

K

NBA REGULAR-SEASON RECORD

									REBOUNDS								AVERAGES		
Season Team	G	Min.	FGM	FGA	Pct.	FTM	FTA	Pct.	Off.	Def.	Tot.	Ast.	St.	Blk.	TO	Pts.	RPG	APG	PPG
04-05—Orlando..........	45	356	47	98	.480	24	43	.558	52	76	128	8	8	13	26	118	2.8	0.2	2.6
05-06—Orlando..........	28	213	31	69	.449	18	23	.783	24	36	60	3	2	3	15	80	2.1	0.1	2.9
Totals	73	569	78	167	.467	42	66	.636	76	112	188	11	10	16	41	198	2.6	0.2	2.7

Three-point field goals: 2004-05, 0-for-1. Totals, 0-for-1 (.000).
Personal fouls/disqualifications: 2004-05, 86/1. 2005-06, 69/0. Totals, 155/1.

GERMAN LEAGUE RECORD

												AVERAGES		
Season Team	G	Min.	FGM	FGA	Pct.	FTM	FTA	Pct.	Reb.	Ast.	Pts.	RPG	APG	PPG
01-02—Cologne.........................	1	1	0	0	...	0	0	...	0	0	0	0.0	0.0	0.0
02-03—Frankfurt.......................	20	383	74	136	.544	58	96	.604	109	12	206	5.5	0.6	10.3
03-04—Frankfurt.......................	27	553	105	185	.568	42	85	.494	193	15	252	7.1	0.6	9.3
Totals	48	937	179	321	.558	100	181	.552	302	27	458	6.3	0.6	9.5

Three-point field goals: 2003-04, 0-for-1. Totals, 0-for-1 (.000).

KHRYAPA, VIKTOR   F   BULLS

PERSONAL: Born August 3, 1982, in Kiev, Ukraine. ... 6-9/210. (2.06/95.3).
TRANSACTIONS/CAREER NOTES: Played in Russia (1999-04). ... Selected by New Jersey Nets in first round (22nd pick overall) of 2004 NBA Draft. ... Draft rights traded by Nets to Portland Trail Blazers for G Eddie Gill (June 24, 2004). ... Traded by Trail Blazers with draft rights to F Tyrus Thomas to Chicago Bulls for draft rights to LaMarcus Aldridge and a conditional second-round draft pick (June 28, 2006).

RUSSIAN LEAGUE RECORD

												AVERAGES		
Season Team	G	Min.	FGM	FGA	Pct.	FTM	FTA	Pct.	Reb.	Ast.	Pts.	RPG	APG	PPG
99-00—Avtodor Saratov	13	137	17	32	.531	10	13	.769	33	12	46	2.5	0.9	3.5
00-01—Avtodor Saratov	34	445	157	310	.506	116	192	.604	193	87	445	5.7	2.6	13.1
01-02—Avtodor Saratov	32	1036	150	262	.573	104	139	.748	234	155	419	7.3	4.8	13.1
02-03—CSKA.............................	30	652	107	189	.566	62	73	.849	178	75	312	5.9	2.5	10.4
03-04—CSKA.............................	32	584	69	129	.535	62	73	.849	126	56	219	3.9	1.8	6.8
Totals	141	2854	500	922	.542	354	490	.722	764	385	1441	5.4	2.7	10.2

Three-point field goals: 1999-00, 2-for-7 (.286). 2000-01, 15-for-55 (.273). 2001-02, 15-for-49 (.306). 2002-03, 36-for-58 (.621). 2003-04, 26-for-57 (.456). Totals, 94-for-226 (.416).

NBA REGULAR-SEASON RECORD

									REBOUNDS								AVERAGES		
Season Team	G	Min.	FGM	FGA	Pct.	FTM	FTA	Pct.	Off.	Def.	Tot.	Ast.	St.	Blk.	TO	Pts.	RPG	APG	PPG
04-05—Portland.........	32	523	54	124	.435	23	42	.548	28	80	108	25	20	18	33	135	3.4	0.8	4.2
05-06—Portland.........	69	1492	158	342	.462	77	111	.694	114	193	307	88	50	29	84	403	4.4	1.3	5.8
Totals	101	2015	212	466	.455	100	153	.654	142	273	415	113	70	47	117	538	4.1	1.1	5.3

Three-point field goals: 2004-05, 4-for-11 (.364). 2005-06, 10-for-30 (.333). Totals, 14-for-41 (.341).
Personal fouls/disqualifications: 2004-05, 80/0. 2005-06, 209/7. Totals, 289/7.

KIDD, JASON   G   NETS

PERSONAL: Born March 23, 1973, in San Francisco. ... 6-4/212. (1.93/96.2). ... Full name: Jason Frederick Kidd
HIGH SCHOOL: St. Joseph of Notre Dame (Alameda, Calif.).
COLLEGE: California.
TRANSACTIONS/CAREER NOTES: Selected after sophomore season by Dallas Mavericks in first round (second pick overall) of 1994 NBA Draft. ... Traded by Mavericks with G Tony Dumas and C Loren Meyer to Phoenix Suns for G Sam Cassell, F A.C. Green, F Michael Finley and 1997 or 1998 conditional second-round draft choice (December 26, 1996). ... Traded by Suns with C Chris Dudley to New Jersey Nets for G Stephon Marbury, F Johnny Newman and C Soumaila Samake (July 18, 2001).
MISCELLANEOUS: Member of gold-medal-winning U.S. Olympic team (2000).

COLLEGIATE RECORD

NOTES: THE SPORTING NEWS All-America first team (1994). ... Led NCAA Division I with 3.8 steals per game (1993). ... Led NCAA Division I with 9.1 assists per game (1994).

												AVERAGES		
Season Team	G	Min.	FGM	FGA	Pct.	FTM	FTA	Pct.	Reb.	Ast.	Pts.	RPG	APG	PPG
92-93—California........................	29	922	133	287	.463	88	134	.657	142	222	378	4.9	7.7	13.0
93-94—California........................	30	1053	166	352	.472	117	169	.692	207	272	500	6.9	9.1	16.7
Totals	59	1975	299	639	.468	205	303	.677	349	494	878	5.9	8.4	14.9

Three-point field goals: 1992-93, 24-for-84 (.286). 1993-94, 51-for-141 (.362). Totals, 75-for-225 (.333).

NBA REGULAR-SEASON RECORD

RECORDS: Shares single-game record for most turnovers—14 (November 17, 2000, vs. New York).
HONORS: NBA Co-Rookie of the Year (1995). ... All-NBA first team (1999, 2000, 2001, 2002, 2004). ... All-NBA second team (2003). ... NBA All-Defensive first team (1999, 2001, 2002, 2006). ... NBA All-Defensive second team (2000, 2003, 2004, 2005). ... NBA All-Rookie first team (1995).

									REBOUNDS								AVERAGES		
Season Team	G	Min.	FGM	FGA	Pct.	FTM	FTA	Pct.	Off.	Def.	Tot.	Ast.	St.	Blk.	TO	Pts.	RPG	APG	PPG
94-95—Dallas.............	79	2668	330	857	.385	192	275	.698	152	278	430	607	151	24	250	922	5.4	7.7	11.7
95-96—Dallas.............	81	3034	493	1293	.381	229	331	.692	203	350	553	783	175	26	*328	1348	6.8	9.7	16.6
96-97—Dal.-Pho.	55	1964	213	529	.403	112	165	.679	64	185	249	496	124	20	142	599	4.5	9.0	10.9

Season Team	G	Min.	FGM	FGA	Pct.	FTM	FTA	Pct.	Off.	Def.	Tot.	Ast.	St.	Blk.	TO	Pts.	RPG	APG	PPG
									REBOUNDS								**AVERAGES**		
97-98—Phoenix	82	3118	357	859	.416	167	209	.799	108	402	510	745	162	26	261	954	6.2	9.1	11.6
98-99—Phoenix	50	*2060	310	698	.444	181	239	.757	87	252	339	*539	114	19	150	846	6.8	*10.8	16.9
99-00—Phoenix	67	2616	350	855	.409	203	245	.829	96	387	483	678	134	28	226	959	7.2	*10.1	14.3
00-01—Phoenix	77	3065	451	1097	.411	328	403	.814	91	403	494	*753	166	23	286	1299	6.4	*9.8	16.9
01-02—New Jersey	82	3056	445	1138	.391	201	247	.814	130	465	595	808	*175	20	*286	1208	7.3	9.9	14.7
02-03—New Jersey	80	2989	515	1244	.414	339	403	.841	110	394	504	*711	179	25	296	1495	6.3	*8.9	18.7
03-04—New Jersey	67	2450	368	959	.384	206	249	.827	85	343	428	618	122	14	214	1036	6.4	*9.2	15.5
04-05—New Jersey	66	2435	340	855	.398	142	192	.740	94	394	488	545	123	9	167	951	7.4	8.3	14.4
05-06—New Jersey	80	2975	366	905	.404	194	244	.795	86	494	580	672	150	29	192	1065	7.3	8.4	13.3
Totals	866	32430	4538	11289	.402	2494	3202	.779	1306	4347	5653	7955	1775	263	2798	12682	6.5	9.2	14.6

Three-point field goals: 1994-95, 70-for-257 (.272). 1995-96, 133-for-396 (.336). 1996-97, 61-for-165 (.370). 1997-98, 73-for-233 (.313). 1998-99, 45-for-123 (.366). 1999-00, 56-for-166 (.337). 2000-01, 69-for-232 (.297). 2001-02, 117-for-364 (.321). 2002-03, 126-for-370 (.341). 2003-04, 94-for-293 (.321). 2004-05, 129-for-358 (.360). 2005-06, 139-for-395 (.352). Totals, 1112-for-3352 (.332).

Personal fouls/disqualifications: 1994-95, 146/0. 1995-96, 155/0. 1996-97, 114/0. 1997-98, 142/0. 1998-99, 108/1. 1999-00, 148/2. 2000-01, 171/1. 2001-02, 136/0. 2002-03, 127/0. 2003-04, 110/0. 2004-05, 110/0. 2005-06, 157/0. Totals, 1624/4.

NBA PLAYOFF RECORD

Season Team	G	Min.	FGM	FGA	Pct.	FTM	FTA	Pct.	Off.	Def.	Tot.	Ast.	St.	Blk.	TO	Pts.	RPG	APG	PPG
									REBOUNDS								**AVERAGES**		
96-97—Phoenix	5	207	21	53	.396	10	19	.526	4	26	30	49	11	2	13	60	6.0	9.8	12.0
97-98—Phoenix	4	171	22	58	.379	13	16	.813	5	18	23	31	16	2	12	57	5.8	7.8	14.3
98-99—Phoenix	3	126	18	43	.419	5	7	.714	1	6	7	31	5	1	9	45	2.3	10.3	15.0
99-00—Phoenix	6	229	22	55	.400	7	9	.778	8	32	40	53	11	1	23	59	6.7	8.8	9.8
00-01—Phoenix	4	166	22	69	.319	9	12	.750	9	15	24	53	8	0	12	57	6.0	13.3	14.3
01-02—New Jersey	20	803	147	354	.415	80	99	.808	42	122	164	182	34	8	67	391	8.2	9.1	19.6
02-03—New Jersey	20	852	137	341	.402	94	114	.825	36	118	154	163	36	4	79	402	7.7	8.2	20.1
03-04—New Jersey	11	474	43	129	.333	43	53	.811	16	57	73	99	25	6	43	139	6.6	9.0	12.6
04-05—New Jersey	4	182	26	67	.388	6	11	.545	10	26	36	29	10	0	9	69	9.0	7.3	17.3
05-06—New Jersey	11	450	49	132	.371	19	23	.826	22	62	84	106	17	2	24	132	7.6	9.6	12.0
Totals	88	3660	507	1301	.390	286	363	.788	153	482	635	796	173	26	291	1411	7.2	9.0	16.0

Three-point field goals: 1996-97, 8-for-22 (.364). 1997-98, 0-for-7. 1998-99, 4-for-16 (.250). 1999-00, 8-for-22 (.364). 2000-01, 4-for-17 (.235). 2001-02, 17-for-90 (.189). 2002-03, 34-for-104 (.327). 2003-04, 10-for-48 (.208). 2004-05, 11-for-30 (.367). 2005-06, 15-for-50 (.300). Totals, 111-for-406 (.273).

Personal fouls/disqualifications: 1996-97, 11/0. 1997-98, 13/0. 1998-99, 12/0. 1999-00, 14/0. 2000-01, 13/0. 2001-02, 40/0. 2002-03, 46/0. 2003-04, 15/0. 2004-05, 16/0. 2005-06, 31/0. Totals, 211/0.

NBA ALL-STAR GAME RECORD

NOTES: Shares NBA record for career three-point field goals made—11.

Season Team	Min.	FGM	FGA	Pct.	FTM	FTA	Pct.	Off.	Def.	Tot.	Ast.	PF	Dq.	St.	Blk.	TO	Pts.
								REBOUNDS									
1996—Dallas	22	3	4	.750	0	0	...	2	4	6	10	1	0	2	0	2	7
1998—Phoenix	19	0	1	.000	0	0	...	0	1	1	9	2	0	0	0	2	0
2000—Phoenix	31	4	9	.444	0	0	...	0	1	1	10	0	0	0	0	3	11
2001—Phoenix	30	4	6	.667	0	0	...	0	4	4	2	3	0	1	0	5	11
2002—New Jersey	18	1	2	.500	0	0	...	0	1	1	3	0	0	1	0	1	2
2003—New Jersey	33	4	9	.444	2	2	1.000	1	4	5	10	0	0	5	0	2	11
2004—New Jersey	22	4	6	.667	3	4	.750	0	3	3	10	1	0	2	0	3	14
Totals	178	20	37	.541	5	6	.833	3	22	25	58	7	0	15	0	21	56

Three-point field goals: 1996, 1-for-2 (.500). 2000, 3-for-6 (.500). 2001, 3-for-4 (.750). 2002, 0-for-1. 2003, 1-for-4 (.250). 2004, 3-for-4 (.750). Totals, 11-for-21 (.524).

KIRILENKO, ANDREI F JAZZ

PERSONAL: Born February 18, 1981, in Russia. ... 6-9/210. (2.06/95.3).
TRANSACTIONS/CAREER NOTES: Played in Russia (1996-2001). ... Selected by Utah Jazz in first round (24th pick overall) of 1999 NBA Draft.
MISCELLANEOUS: Member of Russian Olympic team (2000).

RUSSIAN LEAGUE RECORD

Season Team	G	Min.	FGM	FGA	Pct.	FTM	FTA	Pct.	Reb.	Ast.	Pts.	RPG	APG	PPG
												AVERAGES		
96-97—Spartak	3	16	2	5	.400	2	4	.500	4	1	6	1.3	0.3	2.0
97-98—Spartak	41	993	164	315	.521	143	223	.641	188	58	486	4.6	1.4	11.9
98-99—CSKA	26	495	116	178	.652	86	125	.688	110	54	323	4.2	2.1	12.4
99-00—CSKA	37	841	173	235	.736	131	185	.708	227	94	488	6.1	2.5	13.2
00-01—CSKA	26	376	128	214	.598	106	162	.654	141	59	376	5.4	2.3	14.5
Totals	133	2721	583	947	.616	468	699	.670	670	266	1679	5.0	2.0	12.6

Three-point field goals: 1996-97, 0-for-1. 1997-98, 15-for-48 (.313). 1998-99, 5-for-11 (.455). 1999-00, 11-for-24 (.458). 2000-01, 14-for-42 (.333). Totals, 45-for-126 (.357).

NBA REGULAR-SEASON RECORD

HONORS: NBA All-Defensive second team (2004, 2005). ... NBA All-Rookie first team (2002). ... NBA All-Defensive first team (2006).

Season Team	G	Min.	FGM	FGA	Pct.	FTM	FTA	Pct.	Off.	Def.	Tot.	Ast.	St.	Blk.	TO	Pts.	RPG	APG	PPG
									REBOUNDS								**AVERAGES**		
01-02—Utah	82	2151	285	633	.450	285	371	.768	149	253	402	94	116	159	108	880	4.9	1.1	10.7
02-03—Utah	80	2213	315	642	.491	296	370	.800	147	273	420	138	118	175	136	963	5.3	1.7	12.0
03-04—Utah	78	2895	412	931	.443	392	496	.790	226	403	629	244	150	215	215	1284	8.1	3.1	16.5
04-05—Utah	41	1349	207	420	.493	203	259	.784	89	166	255	132	67	136	90	640	6.2	3.2	15.6

K

Season Team	G	Min.	FGM	FGA	Pct.	FTM	FTA	Pct.	Off.	Def.	Tot.	Ast.	St.	Blk.	TO	Pts.	RPG	APG	PPG
									REBOUNDS								**AVERAGES**		
05-06—Utah...............	69	2604	336	730	.460	346	495	.699	161	391	552	299	102	*220	203	1054	8.0	4.3	15.3
Totals	350	11212	1555	3356	.463	1522	1991	.764	772	1486	2258	907	553	905	752	4821	6.5	2.6	13.8

Three-point field goals: 2001-02, 25-for-100 (.250). 2002-03, 37-for-114 (.325). 2003-04, 68-for-201 (.338). 2004-05, 23-for-77 (.299). 2005-06, 36-for-117 (.308). Totals, 189-for-609 (.310).

Personal fouls/disqualifications: 2001-02, 156/2. 2002-03, 185/0. 2003-04, 174/0. 2004-05, 101/1. 2005-06, 162/0. Totals, 778/3.

NBA PLAYOFF RECORD

Season Team	G	Min.	FGM	FGA	Pct.	FTM	FTA	Pct.	Off.	Def.	Tot.	Ast.	St.	Blk.	TO	Pts.	RPG	APG	PPG
									REBOUNDS								**AVERAGES**		
01-02—Utah...............	4	122	11	28	.393	13	16	.813	4	11	15	4	7	10	6	35	3.8	1.0	8.8
02-03—Utah...............	5	145	18	43	.419	21	24	.875	8	16	24	7	3	10	6	58	4.8	1.4	11.6
Totals	9	267	29	71	.408	34	40	.850	12	27	39	11	10	20	12	93	4.3	1.2	10.3

Three-point field goals: 2001-02, 0-for-4. 2002-03, 1-for-7 (.143). Totals, 1-for-11 (.091).

Personal fouls/disqualifications: 2001-02, 10/0. 2002-03, 6/0. Totals, 16/0.

NBA ALL-STAR GAME RECORD

Season Team	Min.	FGM	FGA	Pct.	FTM	FTA	Pct.	Off.	Def.	Tot.	Ast.	PF	Dq.	St.	Blk.	TO	Pts.
								REBOUNDS									
2004—Utah	12	1	3	.333	0	0	...	0	1	1	0	0	0	0	1	0	2

Three-point field goals: 2004, 0-for-1. Totals, 0-for-1 (.000).

KLEIZA, LINAS   F   NUGGETS

PERSONAL: Born January 3, 1985, in Kaunas, Lithuania. ... 6-8/245. (2.03/111.1).
HIGH SCHOOL: Montrose Christian (Rockville, Md.) .
COLLEGE: Missouri.
TRANSACTIONS/CAREER NOTES: Selected after sophomore season by Portland Trail Blazers in first round (27th pick overall) of 2005 NBA draft. ... Draft rights traded by Trail Blazers with draft rights to F Ricky Sanchez to Denver Nuggets for draft rights to G Jarrett Jack (June 28, 2005).

COLLEGIATE RECORD

Season Team	G	Min.	FGM	FGA	Pct.	FTM	FTA	Pct.	Reb.	Ast.	Pts.	RPG	APG	PPG
												AVERAGES		
03-04—Missouri	16	370	64	146	.438	41	66	.621	135	13	177	8.4	0.8	11.1
04-05—Missouri	33	1038	165	409	.403	169	231	.732	250	53	530	7.6	1.6	16.1
Totals	49	1408	229	555	.413	210	297	.707	385	66	707	7.9	1.3	14.4

Three-point field goals: 2003-04, 8-for-23 (.348). 2004-05, 31-for-113 (.274). Totals, 39-for-136 (.287).

NBA REGULAR-SEASON RECORD

Season Team	G	Min.	FGM	FGA	Pct.	FTM	FTA	Pct.	Off.	Def.	Tot.	Ast.	St.	Blk.	TO	Pts.	RPG	APG	PPG
									REBOUNDS								**AVERAGES**		
05-06—Denver............	61	519	77	173	.445	57	81	.704	38	78	116	15	10	13	16	213	1.9	0.2	3.5

Three-point field goals: 2005-06, 2-for-13 (.154). Totals, 2-for-13 (.154).

Personal fouls/disqualifications: 2005-06, 87/0. Totals, 87/0.

NBA PLAYOFF RECORD

Season Team	G	Min.	FGM	FGA	Pct.	FTM	FTA	Pct.	Off.	Def.	Tot.	Ast.	St.	Blk.	TO	Pts.	RPG	APG	PPG
									REBOUNDS								**AVERAGES**		
05-06—Denver............	3	14	3	8	.375	0	0	...	1	3	4	2	0	0	0	6	1.3	0.7	2.0

Three-point field goals: 2005-06, 0-for-1. Totals, 0-for-1 (.000).

Personal fouls/disqualifications: 2005-06, 3/0. Totals, 3/0.

KNIGHT, BREVIN   G   BOBCATS

PERSONAL: Born November 8, 1975, in Livingston, N.J. ... 5-10/170. (1.78/77.1).
HIGH SCHOOL: Seton Hall Prep (East Orange, N.J.).
COLLEGE: Stanford.
TRANSACTIONS/CAREER NOTES: Selected by Cleveland Cavaliers in first round (16th pick overall) of 1997 NBA Draft. ... Traded by Cavaliers to Atlanta Hawks for G Jim Jackson, G Anthony Johnson and F/G Larry Robinson (January 2, 2001). ... Traded by Hawks with F/C Lorenzen Wright and draft rights to Pau Gasol to Memphis Grizzlies for F Shareef Abdur-Rahim and draft rights to G Jamaal Tinsley (July 19, 2001). ... Traded by Grizzlies with C Cezary Trybanski and F Robert Archibald to Phoenix Suns for F Bo Outlaw and C Jake Tsakalidis (September 30, 2003). ... Traded by Suns to Washington Wizards for C Jahidi White (November 5, 2003). ... Released by Wizards (March 2, 2004). ... Signed as free agent by Milwaukee Bucks (March 5, 2004). ... Signed as free agent by Charlotte Bobcats (August 31, 2004).

COLLEGIATE RECORD

NOTES: Naismith Award winner (1997). ... THE SPORTING NEWS All-America first team (1997).

Season Team	G	Min.	FGM	FGA	Pct.	FTM	FTA	Pct.	Reb.	Ast.	Pts.	RPG	APG	PPG
												AVERAGES		
93-94—Stanford	28	916	90	254	.354	121	160	.756	108	150	312	3.9	5.4	11.1
94-95—Stanford	28	912	146	321	.455	153	204	.750	109	184	464	3.9	6.6	16.6
95-96—Stanford	29	915	140	323	.433	151	178	.848	110	212	449	3.8	7.3	15.5
96-97—Stanford	30	960	139	341	.408	166	199	.834	111	234	489	3.7	7.8	16.3
Totals	115	3703	515	1239	.416	591	741	.798	438	780	1714	3.8	6.8	14.9

Three-point field goals: 1993-94, 11-for-55 (.200). 1994-95, 19-for-51 (.373). 1995-96, 18-for-61 (.295). 1996-97, 45-for-110 (.409). Totals, 93-for-277 (.336).

NBA REGULAR-SEASON RECORD

HONORS: NBA All-Rookie first team (1998).

Season Team	G	Min.	FGM	FGA	Pct.	FTM	FTA	Pct.	REBOUNDS Off.	Def.	Tot.	Ast.	St.	Blk.	TO	Pts.	RPG	APG	PPG
97-98—Cleveland	80	2483	261	592	.441	201	251	.801	67	186	253	656	*196	18	194	723	3.2	8.2	9.0
98-99—Cleveland	39	1186	134	315	.425	105	141	.745	16	115	131	302	70	7	105	373	3.4	7.7	9.6
99-00—Cleveland	65	1754	230	558	.412	140	184	.761	38	155	193	458	107	21	157	602	3.0	7.0	9.3
00-01—Clev.-Atla.	53	1457	139	371	.375	54	66	.818	23	145	168	311	101	4	91	333	3.2	5.9	6.3
01-02—Memphis	53	1151	141	334	.422	87	115	.757	11	98	109	302	79	7	111	371	2.1	5.7	7.0
02-03—Memphis	55	928	97	228	.425	20	37	.541	15	66	81	233	69	2	94	216	1.5	4.2	3.9
03-04—Pho.-Wash.-Miami	56	1037	105	246	.427	49	65	.754	14	98	112	204	84	1	72	261	2.0	3.6	4.7
04-05—Charlotte	66	1944	248	587	.422	167	196	.852	21	149	170	591	131	5	147	666	2.6	9.0	10.1
05-06—Charlotte	69	2351	308	772	.399	252	314	.803	35	188	223	610	157	4	164	871	3.2	8.8	12.6
Totals	536	14291	1663	4003	.415	1075	1369	.785	240	1200	1440	3667	994	69	1135	4416	2.7	6.8	8.2

Three-point field goals: 1997-98, 0-for-7. 1998-99, 0-for-5. 1999-00, 2-for-10 (.200). 2000-01, 1-for-10 (.100). 2001-02, 2-for-8 (.250). 2002-03, 2-for-8 (.250). 2003-04, 2-for-8 (.250). 2004-05, 3-for-20 (.150). 2005-06, 3-for-13 (.231). Totals, 15-for-89 (.169).

Personal fouls/disqualifications: 1997-98, 271/5. 1998-99, 115/1. 1999-00, 185/2. 2000-01, 155/2. 2001-02, 1. 2002-03, 123/0. 2003-04, 107/1. 2004-05, 192/1. 2005-06, 202/3. Totals, 1485/16.

NBA PLAYOFF RECORD

Season Team	G	Min.	FGM	FGA	Pct.	FTM	FTA	Pct.	REBOUNDS Off.	Def.	Tot.	Ast.	St.	Blk.	TO	Pts.	RPG	APG	PPG
97-98—Cleveland	4	132	6	21	.286	6	10	.600	0	16	16	23	10	1	8	18	4.0	5.8	4.5
03-04—Milwaukee	5	101	6	23	.261	9	11	.818	3	8	11	17	14	1	7	21	2.2	3.4	4.2
Totals	9	233	12	44	.273	15	21	.714	3	24	27	40	24	2	15	39	3.0	4.4	4.3

Personal fouls/disqualifications: 1997-98, 16/1. 2003-04, 12/1. Totals, 28/2.

KOROLEV, YAROSLAV   F   CLIPPERS

PERSONAL: Born May 7, 1987, in Moscow, Russia. ... 6-9/203. (2.06/92.1).
HIGH SCHOOL: Did not attend.
COLLEGE: Did not attend.
TRANSACTIONS/CAREER NOTES: Played for CSKA of the Russian league. ... Selected by Los Angeles Clippers in first round (12th pick overall) of 2005 NBA Draft.

RUSSIAN LEAGUE RECORD

Season Team	G	Min.	FGM	FGA	Pct.	FTM	FTA	Pct.	Reb.	Ast.	Pts.	RPG	APG	PPG
03-04—Avtodor Saratov	22	400	34	103	.330	31	50	.620	62	19	106	2.8	0.9	4.8
04-05—CSKA	4	24	4	6	.667	3	4	.750	3	2	12	0.8	0.5	3.0
Totals	26	424	38	109	.349	34	54	.630	65	21	118	2.5	0.8	4.5

Three-point field goals: 2003-04, 7-for-25 (.280), 2004-05, 1-for-3 (.333). Totals, 8-for-28 (.286).

NBA REGULAR-SEASON RECORD

Season Team	G	Min.	FGM	FGA	Pct.	FTM	FTA	Pct.	REBOUNDS Off.	Def.	Tot.	Ast.	St.	Blk.	TO	Pts.	RPG	APG	PPG
05-06—L.A. Clippers	24	127	9	30	.300	7	10	.700	5	8	13	9	3	0	6	27	0.5	0.4	1.1

Three-point field goals: 2005-06, 2-for-7 (.286). Totals, 2-for-7 (.286).
Personal fouls/disqualifications: 2005-06, 11/0. Totals, 11/0.

KORVER, KYLE   F   76ERS

PERSONAL: Born March 17, 1981, in Lakewood, Calif. ... 6-7/210. (2.01/95.3). ... Full name: Kyle Elliot Korver.
HIGH SCHOOL: Pella (Pella, Iowa).
COLLEGE: Creighton.
TRANSACTIONS/CAREER NOTES: Selected by New Jersey Nets in second round (51st pick overall) of 2003 NBA Draft. ... Draft rights traded by Nets to Philadelphia 76ers for cash considerations (June 26, 2003).

COLLEGIATE RECORD

NOTES: The SPORTING NEWS All-America second team (2003).

Season Team	G	Min.	FGM	FGA	Pct.	FTM	FTA	Pct.	Reb.	Ast.	Pts.	RPG	APG	PPG
99-00—Creighton	33	601	97	204	.475	34	38	.895	101	32	291	3.1	1.0	8.8
00-01—Creighton	32	941	148	315	.470	72	83	.867	186	63	468	5.8	2.0	14.6
01-02—Creighton	29	916	131	274	.478	97	109	.890	160	95	438	5.5	3.3	15.1
02-03—Creighton	34	1082	183	391	.468	109	120	.908	217	104	604	6.4	3.1	17.8
Totals	128	3540	559	1184	.472	312	350	.891	664	294	1801	5.2	2.3	14.1

Three-point field goals: 1999-00, 63-for-145 (.434). 2000-01, 100-for-221 (.452). 2001-02, 79-for-184 (.429). 2002-03, 129-for-269 (.480). Totals, 371-for-819 (.453).

NBA REGULAR-SEASON RECORD

NOTES: Shared the NBA lead in three-point field goals made—226 (2004).

Season Team	G	Min.	FGM	FGA	Pct.	FTM	FTA	Pct.	REBOUNDS Off.	Def.	Tot.	Ast.	St.	Blk.	TO	Pts.	RPG	APG	PPG
03-04—Philadelphia	74	882	115	327	.352	19	24	.792	30	81	111	40	25	8	41	330	1.5	0.5	4.5
04-05—Philadelphia	82	2667	317	759	.418	82	96	.854	40	339	379	182	103	33	106	942	4.6	2.2	11.5
05-06—Philadelphia	82	2563	327	761	.430	101	119	.849	27	243	270	163	65	26	98	939	3.3	2.0	11.5
Totals	238	6112	759	1847	.411	202	239	.845	97	663	760	385	193	67	245	2211	3.2	1.6	9.3

Three-point field goals: 2003-04, 81-for-207 (.391). 2004-05, 226-for-558 (.405). 2005-06, 184-for-438 (.420). Totals, 491-for-1203 (.408).
Personal fouls/disqualifications: 2003-04, 102/2. 2004-05, 265/2. 2005-06, 224/1. Totals, 591/5.

NBA PLAYOFF RECORD

Season Team	G	Min.	FGM	FGA	Pct.	FTM	FTA	Pct.	REBOUNDS Off.	Def.	Tot.	Ast.	St.	Blk.	TO	Pts.	AVERAGES RPG	APG	PPG
04-05—Philadelphia	5	147	8	28	.286	2	2	1.000	3	10	13	8	4	1	8	25	2.6	1.6	5.0

Three-point field goals: 2004-05, 7-for-24 (.292). Totals, 7-for-24 (.292).
Personal fouls/disqualifications: 2004-05, 18/0. Totals, 18/0.

KRSTIC, NENAD   F/C   NETS

PERSONAL: Born July 25, 1983, in Kraljevo, Yugoslavia. ... 6-11/210. (2.11/95.3).
TRANSACTIONS/CAREER NOTES: Played in Yugoslavia (2000-04). ... Selected by New Jersey Nets in first round (24th pick overall) of 2002 NBA Draft.
MISCELLANEOUS: Member of Serbia-Montenegro Olympic Team (2004).

YUGOSLAVIAN LEAGUE RECORD

Season Team	G	Min.	FGM	FGA	Pct.	FTM	FTA	Pct.	Reb.	Ast.	Pts.	AVERAGES RPG	APG	PPG
00-01—Partizan	8	24	1	3	.333	6	8	.750	4	0	8	0.5	0.0	1.0
01-02—Partizan	21	396	60	110	.545	50	64	.781	120	6	170	5.7	0.3	8.1
02-03—Partizan	19	522	92	152	.605	99	123	.805	119	14	285	6.3	0.7	15.0
03-04—Partizan	10	263	55	90	.611	39	52	.750	61	10	149	6.1	1.0	14.9
Totals	58	1205	208	355	.586	194	247	.785	304	30	612	5.2	0.5	10.6

Three-point field goals: 2000-01, 0-for-1. 2001-02, 0-for-2. 2002-03, 2-for-2 (1.000). 2003-04, 0-for-3. Totals, 2-for-8 (.250).

NBA REGULAR-SEASON RECORD

HONORS: NBA All-Rookie second team (2005).

Season Team	G	Min.	FGM	FGA	Pct.	FTM	FTA	Pct.	REBOUNDS Off.	Def.	Tot.	Ast.	St.	Blk.	TO	Pts.	AVERAGES RPG	APG	PPG
04-05—New Jersey	75	1965	281	570	.493	185	255	.725	161	240	401	77	32	63	112	747	5.3	1.0	10.0
05-06—New Jersey	80	2469	447	881	.507	185	265	.698	182	331	513	88	32	63	133	1080	6.4	1.1	13.5
Totals	155	4434	728	1451	.502	370	520	.712	343	571	914	165	64	126	245	1827	5.9	1.1	11.8

Three-point field goals: 2004-05, 0-for-2. 2005-06, 1-for-4 (.250). Totals, 1-for-6 (.167).
Personal fouls/disqualifications: 2004-05, 280/7. 2005-06, 297/9. Totals, 577/16.

NBA PLAYOFF RECORD

Season Team	G	Min.	FGM	FGA	Pct.	FTM	FTA	Pct.	REBOUNDS Off.	Def.	Tot.	Ast.	St.	Blk.	TO	Pts.	AVERAGES RPG	APG	PPG
04-05—New Jersey	4	154	27	48	.563	19	24	.792	10	20	30	7	1	2	6	73	7.5	1.8	18.3
05-06—New Jersey	11	366	65	129	.504	32	45	.711	25	50	75	8	5	10	22	162	6.8	0.7	14.7
Totals	15	520	92	177	.520	51	69	.739	35	70	105	15	6	12	28	235	7.0	1.0	15.7

Personal fouls/disqualifications: 2004-05, 20/1. 2005-06, 46/1. Totals, 66/2.

KUKOC, TONI   F   BUCKS

PERSONAL: Born September 18, 1968, in Split, Croatia. ... 6-11/235. (2.11/106.6). ... Name pronounced COO-coach.
TRANSACTIONS/CAREER NOTES: Played in Yugoslavia (1989-91). ... Selected by Chicago Bulls in second round (29th pick overall) of 1990 NBA Draft. ... Played in Italy (1991-93). ... Traded by Bulls to Philadelphia 76ers for F Bruce Bowen in three-way deal in which 76ers sent G Larry Hughes and F/G Billy Owens to Golden State Warriors and Warriors sent G John Starks and future first-round draft choice to Bulls (February 16, 2000). ... Traded by 76ers with F/C Theo Ratliff, C Nazr Mohammed and G Pepe Sanchez to Atlanta Hawks for C Dikembe Mutombo and F Roshown McLeod (February 22, 2001). ... Traded by Hawks with F Leon Smith and 2003 first-round draft choice to Milwaukee Bucks for F Glenn Robinson (August 2, 2002).
MISCELLANEOUS: Member of NBA championship team (1996, 1997, 1998). ... Member of silver-medal-winning Yugoslavian Olympic team (1988). ... Member of silver-medal-winning Croatian Olympic team (1992). ... Member of Croatian Olympic team (1996).

ITALIAN LEAGUE RECORD

Season Team	G	Min.	FGM	FGA	Pct.	FTM	FTA	Pct.	Reb.	Ast.	Pts.	AVERAGES RPG	APG	PPG
91-92—Benetton Treviso	22	826	173	313	.553	59	89	.663	118	121	464	5.4	5.5	21.1
92-93—Benetton Treviso	29	1084	191	363	.526	117	150	.780	187	152	551	6.4	5.2	19.0
Totals	51	1910	364	676	.538	176	239	.736	305	273	1015	6.0	5.4	19.9

Three-point field goals: 1991-92, 59-for-130 (.454). 1992-93, 52-for-130 (.400). Totals, 111-for-260 (.427).
Personal fouls/disqualifications: 1991-92, 0/2. 1992-93, 0/1. Totals, 0/3.

NBA REGULAR-SEASON RECORD

HONORS: NBA Sixth Man Award (1996). ... NBA All-Rookie second team (1994).

Season Team	G	Min.	FGM	FGA	Pct.	FTM	FTA	Pct.	REBOUNDS Off.	Def.	Tot.	Ast.	St.	Blk.	TO	Pts.	AVERAGES RPG	APG	PPG
93-94—Chicago	75	1808	313	726	.431	156	210	.743	98	199	297	252	81	33	167	814	4.0	3.4	10.9
94-95—Chicago	81	2584	487	967	.504	235	314	.748	155	285	440	372	102	16	165	1271	5.4	4.6	15.7
95-96—Chicago	81	2103	386	787	.490	206	267	.772	115	208	323	287	64	28	114	1065	4.0	3.5	13.1
96-97—Chicago	57	1610	285	605	.471	134	174	.770	94	167	261	256	60	29	91	754	4.6	4.5	13.2
97-98—Chicago	74	2235	383	841	.455	155	219	.708	121	206	327	314	76	37	154	984	4.4	4.2	13.3
98-99—Chicago	44	1654	315	750	.420	159	215	.740	65	245	310	235	49	11	121	828	7.0	5.3	18.8
99-00—Chi.-Phil.	56	1784	297	728	.408	192	265	.725	75	198	273	265	77	28	146	830	4.9	4.7	14.8
00-01—Phila.-Atlanta ..	65	1597	275	582	.473	101	160	.631	66	193	259	199	48	11	111	721	4.0	3.1	11.1
01-02—Atlanta	59	1494	211	504	.419	109	153	.712	43	175	218	210	48	17	113	584	3.7	3.6	9.9

									REBOUNDS								AVERAGES		
Season Team	G	Min.	FGM	FGA	Pct.	FTM	FTA	Pct.	Off.	Def.	Tot.	Ast.	St.	Blk.	TO	Pts.	RPG	APG	PPG
02-03—Milwaukee	63	1704	249	577	.432	137	194	.706	67	199	266	230	81	29	122	730	4.2	3.7	11.6
03-04—Milwaukee	73	1522	211	506	.417	145	199	.729	60	211	271	200	59	21	110	616	3.7	2.7	8.4
04-05—Milwaukee	53	1099	105	256	.410	44	61	.721	31	129	160	160	39	13	64	296	3.0	3.0	5.6
05-06—Milwaukee	65	1018	116	298	.389	40	56	.714	26	124	150	139	33	17	66	317	2.3	2.1	4.9
Totals	846	22212	3633	8127	.447	1813	2487	.729	1016	2539	3555	3119	817	290	1544	9810	4.2	3.7	11.6

Three-point field goals: 1993-94, 32-for-118 (.271). 1994-95, 62-for-198 (.313). 1995-96, 87-for-215 (.403). 1996-97, 50-for-151 (.331). 1997-98, 63-for-174 (.362). 1998-99, 39-for-137 (.285). 1999-00, 44-for-168 (.262). 2000-01, 70-for-157 (.446). 2001-02, 53-for-171 (.310). 2002-03, 95-for-263 (.361). 2003-04, 49-for-168 (.292). 2004-05, 42-for-116 (.362). 2005-06, 45-for-147 (.306). Totals, 731-for-2184 (.335).

Personal fouls/disqualifications: 1993-94, 122/0. 1994-95, 163/1. 1995-96, 150/0. 1996-97, 97/1. 1997-98, 149/0. 1998-99, 82/0. 1999-00, 112/0. 2000-01, 98/0. 2001-02, 91/0. 2002-03, 134/0. 2003-04, 110/0. 2004-05, 70/0. 2005-06, 87/0. Totals, 1465/2.

NBA PLAYOFF RECORD

									REBOUNDS								AVERAGES		
Season Team	G	Min.	FGM	FGA	Pct.	FTM	FTA	Pct.	Off.	Def.	Tot.	Ast.	St.	Blk.	TO	Pts.	RPG	APG	PPG
93-94—Chicago	10	194	30	67	.448	25	34	.735	11	29	40	36	5	3	17	93	4.0	3.6	9.3
94-95—Chicago	10	372	53	111	.477	18	26	.692	20	48	68	57	10	2	19	138	6.8	5.7	13.8
95-96—Chicago	15	439	59	151	.391	31	37	.838	19	44	63	58	14	4	26	162	4.2	3.9	10.8
96-97—Chicago	19	423	45	125	.360	41	58	.707	13	41	54	54	13	4	17	150	2.8	2.8	7.9
97-98—Chicago	21	637	106	218	.486	40	62	.645	24	57	81	60	26	10	27	275	3.9	2.9	13.1
99-00—Philadelphia	10	257	36	93	.387	10	17	.588	7	30	37	17	10	3	15	93	3.7	1.7	9.3
02-03—Milwaukee	6	184	32	65	.492	14	20	.700	6	19	25	22	13	1	11	89	4.2	3.7	14.8
03-04—Milwaukee	5	105	17	34	.500	4	8	.500	4	10	14	4	3	2	6	42	2.8	0.8	8.4
05-06—Milwaukee	3	53	8	14	.571	1	2	.500	0	5	5	9	1	0	3	22	1.7	3.0	7.3
Totals	99	2664	386	878	.440	184	264	.697	104	283	387	317	95	29	141	1064	3.9	3.2	10.7

Three-point field goals: 1993-94, 8-for-19 (.421). 1994-95, 14-for-32 (.438). 1995-96, 13-for-68 (.191). 1996-97, 19-for-53 (.358). 1997-98, 23-for-61 (.377). 1999-00, 11-for-34 (.324). 2002-03, 11-for-29 (.379). 2003-04, 4-for-12 (.333). 2005-06, 5-for-8 (.625). Totals, 108-for-316 (.342).

Personal fouls/disqualifications: 1993-94, 15/0. 1994-95, 23/0. 1995-96, 33/0. 1996-97, 30/0. 1997-98, 57/1. 1999-00, 26/0. 2002-03, 12/0. 2003-04, 11/0. 2005-06, 8/0. Totals, 215/1.

LAFRENTZ, RAEF   F/C   TRAIL BLAZERS

PERSONAL: Born May 29, 1976, in Hampton, Iowa. ... 6-11/240. (2.11/108.9). ... Full name: Raef Andrew LaFrentz.
HIGH SCHOOL: Mar-Mac (Monona, Iowa).
COLLEGE: Kansas.
TRANSACTIONS/CAREER NOTES: Selected by Denver Nuggets in first round (third pick overall) of 1998 NBA Draft. ... Traded by Nuggets with G Nick Van Exel, G Avery Johnson and G/F Tariq Abdul-Wahad to Dallas Mavericks for F Juwan Howard, G Tim Hardaway, F Donnell Harvey, cash considerations and first-round draft choice (February 21, 2002). ... Traded by Mavericks with F Chris Mills, G Jiri Welsch and 2004 first-round draft choice to Boston Celtics for G Tony Delk and F Antoine Walker (October 20, 2003). ... Traded by Celtics with G Dan Dickau and a first-round pick (G Randy Foye) in 2006 draft to Portland Trail Blazers for G Sebastian Telfair, F/C Theo Ratliff and a second-round pick in 2008 draft (June 28, 2006).

COLLEGIATE RECORD

NOTES: The SPORTING NEWS All-America first team (1998). ... THE SPORTING NEWS All-America second team (1997).

												AVERAGES		
Season Team	G	Min.	FGM	FGA	Pct.	FTM	FTA	Pct.	Reb.	Ast.	Pts.	RPG	APG	PPG
94-95—Kansas........................	31	732	143	268	.534	65	102	.637	231	17	353	7.5	0.5	11.4
95-96—Kansas........................	34	917	189	348	.543	74	112	.661	278	14	454	8.2	0.4	13.4
96-97—Kansas........................	36	1041	261	447	.584	143	188	.761	335	25	666	9.3	0.7	18.5
97-98—Kansas........................	30	906	232	423	.548	121	164	.738	342	30	593	11.4	1.0	19.8
Totals	131	3596	825	1486	.555	403	566	.712	1186	86	2066	9.1	0.7	15.8

Three-point field goals: 1994-95, 2-for-5 (.400). 1995-96, 1-for-5 (.200). 1996-97, 1-for-3 (.333). 1997-98, 8-for-17 (.471). Totals, 12-for-30 (.400).

NBA REGULAR-SEASON RECORD

NOTES: Led NBA with 11 disqualifications (2002).

									REBOUNDS								AVERAGES		
Season Team	G	Min.	FGM	FGA	Pct.	FTM	FTA	Pct.	Off.	Def.	Tot.	Ast.	St.	Blk.	TO	Pts.	RPG	APG	PPG
98-99—Denver	12	387	59	129	.457	36	48	.750	33	58	91	8	9	17	9	166	7.6	0.7	13.8
99-00—Denver	81	2435	392	879	.446	162	236	.686	170	471	641	97	42	180	96	1006	7.9	1.2	12.4
00-01—Denver	78	2457	387	812	.477	183	262	.698	173	434	607	107	37	206	97	1008	7.8	1.4	12.9
01-02—Denver-Dallas ..	78	2455	421	920	.458	105	151	.695	176	403	579	89	55	213	94	1051	7.4	1.1	13.5
02-03—Dallas	69	1611	266	514	.518	60	88	.682	125	205	330	54	35	91	46	639	4.8	0.8	9.3
03-04—Boston	17	328	57	124	.460	10	13	.769	30	49	79	24	8	13	11	132	4.6	1.4	7.8
04-05—Boston	80	2196	341	688	.496	120	148	.811	154	399	553	98	42	99	70	884	6.9	1.2	11.1
05-06—Boston	82	2033	238	552	.431	51	75	.680	80	326	406	115	29	72	65	639	5.0	1.4	7.8
Totals	497	13902	2161	4618	.468	727	1021	.712	941	2345	3286	592	257	891	488	5525	6.6	1.2	11.1

Three-point field goals: 1998-99, 12-for-31 (.387). 1999-00, 60-for-183 (.328). 2000-01, 51-for-139 (.367). 2001-02, 104-for-268 (.388). 2002-03, 47-for-116 (.405). 2003-04, 8-for-40 (.200). 2004-05, 82-for-225 (.364). 2005-06, 112-for-286 (.392). Totals, 476-for-1288 (.370).

Personal fouls/disqualifications: 1998-99, 38/2. 1999-00, 292/6. 2000-01, 290/9. 2001-02, 281/11. 2002-03, 264/8. 2003-04, 47/1. 2004-05, 262/2. 2005-06, 273/6. Totals, 1747/45.

NBA PLAYOFF RECORD

									REBOUNDS								AVERAGES		
Season Team	G	Min.	FGM	FGA	Pct.	FTM	FTA	Pct.	Off.	Def.	Tot.	Ast.	St.	Blk.	TO	Pts.	RPG	APG	PPG
01-02—Dallas............	8	245	39	78	.500	6	11	.545	18	43	61	5	2	22	6	90	7.6	0.6	11.3
02-03—Dallas............	20	491	68	157	.433	16	19	.842	36	52	88	5	11	43	14	160	4.4	0.3	8.0
04-05—Boston	7	185	16	41	.390	8	10	.800	6	28	34	8	6	12	7	48	4.9	1.1	6.9
Totals	35	921	123	276	.446	30	40	.750	60	123	183	18	19	77	27	298	5.2	0.5	8.5

Three-point field goals: 2001-02, 6-for-18 (.333). 2002-03, 8-for-40 (.200). 2004-05, 8-for-16 (.500). Totals, 22-for-74 (.297).

Personal fouls/disqualifications: 2001-02, 39/2. 2002-03, 86/3. 2004-05, 27/1. Totals, 152/6.

LAMPE, MACIEJ   F

PERSONAL: Born February 5, 1985, in Lodz, Poland. ... 6-11/240. (2.11/108.9). ... Full name: Maciej Boleslaw Lampe
TRANSACTIONS/CAREER NOTES: Played in Spain (2001-02 through 2002-03). ... Selected by New York Knicks in second round (30th pick overall) of 2003 NBA Draft. ... Traded by Knicks with G Howard Eisley, F Antonio McDyess, G Charlie Ward, draft rights to G Milos Vujanic, 2004 first-round draft choice and future first-round draft choice to Phoenix Suns for G Stephon Marbury, F/G Anfernee Hardaway and C Cezary Trybanski (January 5, 2004). ... Traded by Suns with G/F Casey Jacobsen and F/C Jackson Vroman to New Orleans Hornets for G Jim Jackson and a 2005 second-round draft choice (January 21, 2005). ... Traded by Hornets to Houston Rockets for G Moochie Norris (February 13, 2006).

SPANISH LEAGUE RECORD

Season Team	G	Min.	FGM	FGA	Pct.	FTM	FTA	Pct.	Reb.	Ast.	Pts.	RPG	APG	PPG
												AVERAGES		
01-02—Real Madrid II	15	460	105	258	.407	34	47	.723	130	16	261	8.7	1.1	17.4
02-03—Universidad Complutense	22	725	159	305	.521	70	88	.795	168	26	421	7.6	1.2	19.1
Totals	37	1185	264	563	.469	104	135	.770	298	42	682	8.1	1.1	18.4

Three-point field goals: 2001-02, 17-for-88 (.193). 2002-03, 33-for-73 (.452). Totals, 50-for-161 (.311).

NBA REGULAR-SEASON RECORD

Season Team	G	Min.	FGM	FGA	Pct.	FTM	FTA	Pct.	Off.	Def.	Tot.	Ast.	St.	Blk.	TO	Pts.	RPG	APG	PPG
									REBOUNDS								AVERAGES		
03-04—Phoenix	21	224	43	88	.489	10	13	.769	9	35	44	9	3	3	15	96	2.1	0.4	4.6
04-05—Phoenix-N.O.	37	380	49	132	.371	15	22	.682	24	65	89	11	5	7	17	115	2.4	0.3	3.1
05-06—NO/Okla. City-Hous.	6	28	2	11	.182	0	2	.000	4	5	9	2	0	0	3	4	1.5	0.3	0.7
Totals	64	632	94	231	.407	25	37	.676	37	105	142	22	8	10	35	215	2.2	0.3	3.4

Three-point field goals: 2003-04, 0-for-4. 2004-05, 2-for-4 (.500). Totals, 2-for-8 (.250).
Personal fouls/disqualifications: 2003-04, 28/0. 2004-05, 51/0. 2005-06, 2/0. Totals, 81/0.

LEE, DAVID   F   KNICKS

PERSONAL: Born April 29, 1983, in St. Louis, Mo. ... 6-9/249. (2.06/112.9).
HIGH SCHOOL: Chaminade Prep (St. Louis, Mo.).
COLLEGE: Florida.
TRANSACTIONS/CAREER NOTES: Selected by New York Knicks in first round (30th pick overall) of 2005 NBA draft.

COLLEGIATE RECORD

Season Team	G	Min.	FGM	FGA	Pct.	FTM	FTA	Pct.	Reb.	Ast.	Pts.	RPG	APG	PPG
												AVERAGES		
01-02—Florida	31	557	84	145	.579	50	91	.549	145	32	218	4.7	1.0	7.0
02-03—Florida	33	866	149	230	.648	73	117	.624	224	61	371	6.8	1.8	11.2
03-04—Florida	31	851	150	255	.588	112	145	.772	212	88	412	6.8	2.8	13.3
04-05—Florida	32	897	160	305	.525	115	161	.714	288	70	435	9.0	2.2	13.6
Totals	127	3171	543	935	.581	350	514	.681	869	251	1436	6.8	2.0	11.3

Three-point field goals: 2003-04, 0-for-2. 2004-05, 0-for-4. Totals, 0-for-4 (.000).

NBA REGULAR-SEASON RECORD

Season Team	G	Min.	FGM	FGA	Pct.	FTM	FTA	Pct.	Off.	Def.	Tot.	Ast.	St.	Blk.	TO	Pts.	RPG	APG	PPG
									REBOUNDS								AVERAGES		
05-06—New York	67	1129	137	230	.596	71	123	.577	109	194	303	43	30	20	51	345	4.5	0.6	5.1

Personal fouls/disqualifications: 2005-06, 124/1. Totals, 124/1.

LENARD, VOSHON   G

PERSONAL: Born May 14, 1973, in Detroit. ... 6-4/205. (1.93/93.0). ... Full name: Voshon Kelan Lenard ... Name pronounced Va-SHON.
HIGH SCHOOL: Southwestern (Detroit).
COLLEGE: Minnesota.
TRANSACTIONS/CAREER NOTES: Selected after junior season by Milwaukee Bucks in second round (46th pick overall) of 1994 NBA Draft. ... Returned to college for senior season (1994-95). ... Waived by Bucks (October 25, 1995). ... Played in Continental Basketball Association with Oklahoma City Cavalry (1995-96). ... Signed as free agent by Miami Heat for remainder of season (December 29, 1995). ... Traded by Heat with F Mark Strickland to Denver Nuggets for F/C Chris Gatling and a 2000 second-round draft choice (June 27, 2000). ... Signed as free agent by Toronto Raptors (October 23, 2002). ... Signed as free agent by Denver Nuggets (September 12, 2003). ... Traded by Nuggets to Portland Trail Blazers as part of four-way deal (February 23, 2006).

COLLEGIATE RECORD

Season Team	G	Min.	FGM	FGA	Pct.	FTM	FTA	Pct.	Reb.	Ast.	Pts.	RPG	APG	PPG
												AVERAGES		
91-92—Minnesota	32	868	139	330	.421	82	101	.812	118	86	411	3.7	2.7	12.8
92-93—Minnesota	31	883	192	399	.481	89	111	.802	113	82	531	3.6	2.6	17.1
93-94—Minnesota	33	1029	218	462	.472	103	122	.844	123	74	625	3.7	2.2	18.9
94-95—Minnesota	31	992	174	422	.412	107	141	.759	134	80	536	4.3	2.6	17.3
Totals	127	3772	723	1613	.448	381	475	.802	488	322	2103	3.8	2.5	16.6

Three-point field goals: 1991-92, 51-for-144 (.354). 1992-93, 58-for-158 (.367). 1993-94, 86-for-209 (.411). 1994-95, 81-for-244 (.332). Totals, 276-for-755 (.366).

CBA RECORD

Season Team	G	Min.	FGM	FGA	Pct.	FTM	FTA	Pct.	Reb.	Ast.	Pts.	RPG	APG	PPG
												AVERAGES		
95-96—Oklahoma City	18	711	189	387	.488	75	100	.750	60	70	541	3.3	3.9	30.1

Three-point field goals: 1995-96, 88-for-203 (.433). Totals, 88-for-203 (.433).

Personal fouls/disqualifications: 1995-96, 66/0. Totals, 66/0.

NBA REGULAR-SEASON RECORD

Season Team	G	Min.	FGM	FGA	Pct.	FTM	FTA	Pct.	Off.	Def.	Tot.	Ast.	St.	Blk.	TO	Pts.	RPG	APG	PPG
									REBOUNDS								AVERAGES		
95-96—Miami	30	323	53	141	.376	34	43	.791	12	40	52	31	6	1	23	176	1.7	1.0	5.9
96-97—Miami	73	2111	314	684	.459	86	105	.819	38	179	217	161	50	18	109	897	3.0	2.2	12.3
97-98—Miami	81	2621	363	854	.425	141	179	.788	72	220	292	180	58	16	99	1020	3.6	2.2	12.6
98-99—Miami	12	190	31	79	.392	8	11	.727	4	12	16	10	3	1	7	82	1.3	0.8	6.8
99-00—Miami	53	1434	228	560	.407	84	106	.792	37	116	153	136	41	15	80	629	2.9	2.6	11.9
00-01—Denver	80	2331	336	846	.397	153	192	.797	47	184	231	190	65	18	102	972	2.9	2.4	12.2
01-02—Denver	71	1665	315	769	.410	94	120	.783	38	145	183	130	59	25	91	813	2.6	1.8	11.5
02-03—Toronto	63	1929	325	809	.402	156	194	.804	48	164	212	144	59	21	103	898	3.4	2.3	14.3
03-04—Denver	73	2233	394	933	.422	144	182	.791	46	154	200	151	61	12	101	1038	2.7	2.1	14.2
04-05—Denver	3	54	10	26	.385	5	8	.625	0	6	6	6	1	0	2	29	2.0	2.0	9.7
05-06—Denver-Port.	26	458	75	191	.393	16	31	.516	5	42	47	41	21	4	31	191	1.8	1.6	7.3
Totals	565	15349	2444	5892	.415	921	1171	.787	347	1262	1609	1180	424	131	748	6745	2.8	2.1	11.9

Three-point field goals: 1995-96, 36-for-101 (.356). 1996-97, 183-for-442 (.414). 1997-98, 153-for-378 (.405). 1998-99, 12-for-35 (.343). 1999-00, 89-for-228 (.390). 2000-01, 147-for-382 (.385). 2001-02, 89-for-240 (.371). 2002-03, 92-for-252 (.365). 2003-04, 106-for-289 (.367). 2004-05, 4-for-12 (.333). 2005-06, 25-for-78 (.321). Totals, 936-for-2437 (.384).
Personal fouls/disqualifications: 1995-96, 31/0. 1996-97, 168/1. 1997-98, 219/0. 1998-99, 18/0. 1999-00, 127/2. 2000-01, 170/1. 2001-02, 105/0. 2002-03, 156/1. 2003-04, 177/1. 2004-05, 2/0. 2005-06, 39/0. Totals, 1212/6.

NBA PLAYOFF RECORD

Season Team	G	Min.	FGM	FGA	Pct.	FTM	FTA	Pct.	Off.	Def.	Tot.	Ast.	St.	Blk.	TO	Pts.	RPG	APG	PPG
									REBOUNDS								AVERAGES		
96-97—Miami	17	548	63	155	.406	32	37	.865	12	38	50	36	11	3	30	194	2.9	2.1	11.4
97-98—Miami	5	186	24	52	.462	15	20	.750	1	18	19	7	1	2	11	72	3.8	1.4	14.4
98-99—Miami	4	57	12	22	.545	4	4	1.000	0	1	1	3	0	1	1	37	0.3	0.8	9.3
03-04—Denver	5	161	32	75	.427	10	14	.714	4	9	13	12	4	0	9	85	2.6	2.4	17.0
Totals	31	952	131	304	.431	61	75	.813	17	66	83	58	16	6	51	388	2.7	1.9	12.5

Three-point field goals: 1996-97, 36-for-91 (.396). 1997-98, 9-for-26 (.346). 1998-99, 9-for-14 (.643). 2003-04, 11-for-24 (.458). Totals, 65-for-155 (.419).
Personal fouls/disqualifications: 1996-97, 49/0. 1997-98, 20/0. 1998-99, 4/0. 2003-04, 13/0. Totals, 86/0.

LEWIS, RASHARD   F   SUPERSONICS

PERSONAL: Born August 8, 1979, in Pineville, La. ... 6-10/215. (2.08/97.5). ... Full name: Rashard Quovon Lewis
HIGH SCHOOL: Alief (Texas) Elsik.
COLLEGE: Did not attend college.
TRANSACTIONS/CAREER NOTES: Selected out of high school by Seattle SuperSonics in second round (32nd pick overall) of 1998 NBA Draft.

NBA REGULAR-SEASON RECORD

Season Team	G	Min.	FGM	FGA	Pct.	FTM	FTA	Pct.	Off.	Def.	Tot.	Ast.	St.	Blk.	TO	Pts.	RPG	APG	PPG
									REBOUNDS								AVERAGES		
98-99—Seattle	20	145	19	52	.365	8	14	.571	13	12	25	4	8	1	20	47	1.3	0.2	2.4
99-00—Seattle	82	1575	275	566	.486	84	123	.683	127	209	336	70	62	36	78	674	4.1	0.9	8.2
00-01—Seattle	78	2720	426	887	.480	176	213	.826	143	398	541	125	91	45	129	1151	6.9	1.6	14.8
01-02—Seattle	71	2585	455	972	.468	162	200	.810	139	359	498	123	104	40	97	1195	7.0	1.7	16.8
02-03—Seattle	77	3044	519	1149	.452	283	345	.820	152	351	503	133	99	35	143	1396	6.5	1.7	18.1
03-04—Seattle	80	2931	535	1229	.435	206	270	.763	133	385	518	175	99	54	135	1421	6.5	2.2	17.8
04-05—Seattle	71	2697	532	1151	.462	220	283	.777	110	278	388	94	75	62	123	1457	5.5	1.3	20.5
05-06—Seattle	78	2876	538	1151	.467	350	428	.818	111	279	390	182	102	50	141	1568	5.0	2.3	20.1
Totals	557	18573	3299	7157	.461	1489	1876	.794	928	2271	3199	906	640	323	866	8909	5.7	1.6	16.0

Three-point field goals: 1998-99, 1-for-6 (.167). 1999-00, 40-for-120 (.333). 2000-01, 123-for-285 (.432). 2001-02, 123-for-316 (.389). 2002-03, 75-for-217 (.346). 2003-04, 145-for-386 (.376). 2004-05, 173-for-432 (.400). 2005-06, 142-for-370 (.384). Totals, 822-for-2132 (.386).
Personal fouls/disqualifications: 1998-99, 19/0. 1999-00, 163/0. 2000-01, 191/2. 2001-02, 174/3. 2002-03, 205/1. 2003-04, 233/3. 2004-05, 158/1. 2005-06, 191/0. Totals, 1334/10.

NBA PLAYOFF RECORD

Season Team	G	Min.	FGM	FGA	Pct.	FTM	FTA	Pct.	Off.	Def.	Tot.	Ast.	St.	Blk.	TO	Pts.	RPG	APG	PPG
									REBOUNDS								AVERAGES		
99-00—Seattle	5	157	26	59	.441	16	20	.800	12	19	31	3	5	3	10	77	6.2	0.6	15.4
01-02—Seattle	3	79	12	32	.375	13	13	1.000	4	7	11	2	1	0	2	38	3.7	0.7	12.7
04-05—Seattle	8	312	43	106	.406	44	50	.880	11	32	43	13	3	3	16	135	5.4	1.6	16.9
Totals	16	548	81	197	.411	73	83	.880	27	58	85	18	9	6	28	250	5.3	1.1	15.6

Three-point field goals: 1999-00, 9-for-19 (.474). 2001-02, 1-for-6 (.167). 2004-05, 5-for-25 (.200). Totals, 15-for-50 (.300).
Personal fouls/disqualifications: 1999-00, 11/0. 2001-02, 10/0. 2004-05, 25/0. Totals, 46/0.

NBA ALL-STAR GAME RECORD

Season Team	Min.	FGM	FGA	Pct.	FTM	FTA	Pct.	Off.	Def.	Tot.	Ast.	PF	Dq.	St.	Blk.	TO	Pts.
								REBOUNDS									
2005—Seattle	14	1	7	.143	0	0	...	1	3	4	1	2	0	1	0	1	2

Three-point field goals: 2005, 0-for-2. Totals, 0-for-2 (.000).

LIVINGSTON, RANDY   G   BULLS

PERSONAL: Born April 2, 1975, in New Orleans. ... 6-4/209. (1.93/94.8). ... Full name: Randy Anthony Livingston
HIGH SCHOOL: Newman (New Orleans).
COLLEGE: Louisiana State.
TRANSACTIONS/CAREER NOTES: Selected after sophomore season by Houston Rockets in second round (42nd pick overall) of 1996 NBA Draft. ... Waived by Rockets (October 30, 1997). ... Signed by Atlanta Hawks (November 7, 1997). ...

Waived by Hawks (November 20, 1997). ... Played in Continental Basketball Association with Sioux Falls Skyforce (1997-98, 1998-99 and 2001-02), Idaho Stampede (2000-01, 2003-04) and Gary Steelheads (2001-02). ... Re-signed as free agent by Hawks (December 9, 1997). ... Waived by Hawks (December 19, 1997). ... Re-signed by Hawks to 10-day contract (January 10, 1998). ... Signed as free agent by Miami Heat (January 21, 1999). ... Waived by Heat (January 30, 1999). ... Signed as free agent by Phoenix Suns for remainder of season (May 4, 1999). ... Waived by Suns (August 31, 2000). ... Signed as free agent by Seattle SuperSonics (October 2, 2000). ... Claimed on waivers by Orlando Magic (October 13, 2000). ... Waived by Magic (October 30, 2000). ... Signed as free agent by Golden State Warriors (November 15, 2000). ... Waived by Warriors (November 21, 2000). ... Played in International Basketball League with Sioux Falls Skyforce (2000-01). ... Signed as free agent by Utah Jazz (October 2, 2001). ... Waived by Jazz (October 25, 2001). ... Signed by Seattle SuperSonics to 10-day contract (March 8, 2002). ... Signed by SuperSonics for remainder of season (March 27, 2002). ... Signed as free agent by Minnesota Timberwolves (October 1, 2002). ... Waived by Timberwolves (October 28, 2002). ... Signed by New Orleans Hornets to 10-day contract (January 27, 2003). ... Waived by Hornets (February 5, 2003). ... Signed by Los Angeles Clippers to 10-day contract (March 28, 2004). ... Signed by Utah Jazz to 10-day contract (March 2, 2005). ... Signed by Chicago Bulls to 10-day contract (March 22, 2006). ... Signed by Bulls for remainder of season (April 11, 2006).

COLLEGIATE RECORD

Season Team	G	Min.	FGM	FGA	Pct.	FTM	FTA	Pct.	Reb.	Ast.	Pts.	AVERAGES RPG	APG	PPG
93-94—Louisiana State.............						Did not play—redshirted.								
94-95—Louisiana State.............	16	550	81	185	.438	42	62	.677	64	151	224	4.0	9.4	14.0
95-96—Louisiana State.............	13	318	24	83	.289	30	38	.789	30	69	79	2.3	5.3	6.1
Totals	29	868	105	268	.392	72	100	.720	94	220	303	3.2	7.6	10.4

Three-point field goals: 1994-95, 20-for-65 (.308). 1995-96, 1-for-20 (.050). Totals, 21-for-85 (.247).

NBA REGULAR-SEASON RECORD

Season Team	G	Min.	FGM	FGA	Pct.	FTM	FTA	Pct.	REBOUNDS Off.	Def.	Tot.	Ast.	St.	Blk.	TO	Pts.	AVERAGES RPG	APG	PPG
96-97—Houston.........	64	981	100	229	.437	42	65	.646	32	62	94	155	39	12	102	251	1.5	2.4	3.9
97-98—Atlanta............	12	82	3	12	.250	4	5	.800	1	5	6	5	7	2	6	10	0.5	0.4	0.8
98-99—Phoenix	1	22	5	8	.625	2	2	1.000	0	2	2	3	2	0	1	12	2.0	3.0	12.0
99-00—Phoenix	79	1081	155	373	.416	52	62	.839	25	105	130	170	49	13	92	381	1.6	2.2	4.8
00-01—Golden State...	2	7	0	2	.000	0	0	...	0	1	1	1	0	0	0	0	0.5	0.5	0.0
01-02—Seattle	13	176	15	54	.278	10	11	.909	9	16	25	26	9	2	2	41	1.9	2.0	3.2
02-03—New Orleans ...	2	12	2	4	.500	2	2	1.000	0	0	0	1	0	0	0	6	0.0	0.5	3.0
03-04—L.A. Clippers ...	4	48	2	10	.200	4	6	.667	2	5	7	4	2	0	4	8	1.8	1.0	2.0
04-05—Utah...............	17	227	22	52	.423	15	17	.882	3	9	12	45	12	2	14	64	0.7	2.6	3.8
05-06—Chicago	5	22	0	2	.000	0	0	...	1	3	4	1	1	0	1	0	0.8	0.2	0.0
Totals	199	2658	304	746	.408	131	170	.771	73	208	281	411	121	31	222	773	1.4	2.1	3.9

Three-point field goals: 1996-97, 9-for-22 (.409). 1999-00, 19-for-55 (.345). 2000-01, 0-for-1. 2001-02, 1-for-8 (.125). 2003-04, 0-for-3. 2004-05, 5-for-8 (.625). Totals, 34-for-97 (.351).
Personal fouls/disqualifications: 1996-97, 107/0. 1997-98, 6/0. 1998-99, 1/0. 1999-00, 129/1. 2001-02, 11/0. 2003-04, 7/0. 2004-05, 28/0. 2005-06, 6/0. Totals, 295/1.

NBA PLAYOFF RECORD

Season Team	G	Min.	FGM	FGA	Pct.	FTM	FTA	Pct.	REBOUNDS Off.	Def.	Tot.	Ast.	St.	Blk.	TO	Pts.	AVERAGES RPG	APG	PPG
96-97—Houston.........	2	15	1	4	.250	0	0	...	0	0	0	4	1	0	1	3	0.0	2.0	1.5
98-99—Phoenix	3	24	6	15	.400	4	4	1.000	5	2	7	2	1	0	2	16	2.3	0.7	5.3
99-00—Phoenix	7	63	6	27	.222	0	0	...	2	5	7	4	4	1	4	14	1.0	0.6	2.0
01-02—Seattle	5	80	7	17	.412	5	5	1.000	1	5	6	10	2	0	1	20	1.2	2.0	4.0
Totals	17	182	20	63	.317	9	9	1.000	8	12	20	20	8	1	8	53	1.2	1.2	3.1

Three-point field goals: 1996-97, 1-for-1 (1.000). 1998-99, 0-for-1. 1999-00, 2-for-6 (.333). 2001-02, 1-for-3 (.333). Totals, 4-for-11 (.364).
Personal fouls/disqualifications: 1996-97, 1/0. 1998-99, 6/0. 1999-00, 6/0. 2001-02, 7/0. Totals, 20/0.

CBA RECORD

NOTES: CBA All-League second team (1999).

Season Team	G	Min.	FGM	FGA	Pct.	FTM	FTA	Pct.	Reb.	Ast.	Pts.	AVERAGES RPG	APG	PPG
97-98—Sioux Falls.....................	28	1049	160	387	.413	91	128	.711	151	187	424	5.4	6.7	15.1
98-99—Sioux Falls.....................	40	1321	196	483	.406	128	159	.805	168	259	546	4.2	6.5	13.7
00-01—Idaho	24	892	128	328	.390	56	65	.862	87	174	339	3.6	7.3	14.1
01-02—Sioux Falls.....................	36	1195	128	361	.355	101	114	.886	151	259	401	4.2	7.2	11.1
01-02—Gary-Sioux Falls.............	36	1195	128	361	.355	101	114	.886	151	259	401	4.2	7.2	11.1
02-03—Sioux Falls.....................	12	494	57	149	.383	42	48	.875	64	98	168	5.3	8.2	14.0
03-04—Idaho	32	1185	139	367	.379	96	109	.881	147	303	410	4.6	9.5	12.8
04-05—Sioux Falls.....................	40	1464	167	408	.409	156	187	.834	202	336	527	5.1	8.4	13.2
05-06—Idaho	13	508	68	166	.410	52	66	.788	72	165	201	5.5	12.7	15.5
Totals	261	9303	1171	3010	.389	823	990	.831	1193	2040	3417	4.6	7.8	13.1

Three-point field goals: 1997-98, 13-for-57 (.228). 1998-99, 26-for-101 (.257). 2000-01, 27-for-105 (.257). 2001-02, 44-for-168 (.262). 2001-02, 44-for-168 (.262). 2002-03, 12-for-34 (.353). 2003-04, 36-for-114 (.316). 2004-05, 37-for-123 (.301). 2005-06, 13-for-60 (.217). Totals, 252-for-930 (.271).
Personal fouls/disqualifications: 1998-99, 132/0. 2000-01, 77/0. 2002-03, 43/0. Totals, 252/0.

INTERNATIONAL BASKETBALL LEAGUE RECORD

Season Team	G	Min.	FGM	FGA	Pct.	FTM	FTA	Pct.	Reb.	Ast.	Pts.	AVERAGES RPG	APG	PPG
00-01—Sioux Falls.....................	26	885	138	335	.412	74	88	.841	100	164	400	3.8	6.3	15.4

Three-point field goals: 2000-01, 50-for-126 (.397). Totals, 50-for-126 (.397).

LIVINGSTON, SHAUN — G — CLIPPERS

PERSONAL: Born September 11, 1985, in Peoria, Ill. ... 6-7/175. (2.01/79.4).
HIGH SCHOOL: Peoria Richwoods (Ill.), then Peoria Central (Ill.).
COLLEGE: Did not attend college.
TRANSACTIONS/CAREER NOTES: Selected out of high school by Los Angeles Clippers in first round (fourth pick overall) of 2004 NBA Draft.

NBA REGULAR-SEASON RECORD

								REBOUNDS							AVERAGES		
Season Team	G	Min.	FGM	FGA	Pct.	FTM	FTA	Pct.	Off.	Def.	Tot.	Ast.	St.	Blk.	TO	Pts.	RPG APG PPG
04-05—L.A. Clippers...	30	814	89	215	.414	44	59	.746	22	67	89	151	32	11	75	222	3.0 5.0 7.4
05-06—L.A. Clippers...	61	1525	149	349	.427	53	77	.688	41	142	183	273	46	32	111	352	3.0 4.5 5.8
Totals	91	2339	238	564	.422	97	136	.713	63	209	272	424	78	43	186	574	3.0 4.7 6.3

Three-point field goals: 2004-05, 0-for-2. 2005-06, 1-for-8 (.125). Totals, 1-for-10 (.100).
Personal fouls/disqualifications: 2004-05, 82/1. 2005-06, 160/0. Totals, 242/1.

NBA PLAYOFF RECORD

								REBOUNDS							AVERAGES		
Season Team	G	Min.	FGM	FGA	Pct.	FTM	FTA	Pct.	Off.	Def.	Tot.	Ast.	St.	Blk.	TO	Pts.	RPG APG PPG
05-06—L.A. Clippers...	12	332	36	76	.474	17	21	.810	16	40	56	57	7	6	23	90	4.7 4.8 7.5

Three-point field goals: 2005-06, 1-for-1 (1.000). Totals, 1-for-1 (1.000).
Personal fouls/disqualifications: 2005-06, 31/1. Totals, 31/1.

LUCAS, JOHN   G   ROCKETS

PERSONAL: Born November 21, 1982, in Washington, D.C. ... 5-11/165. (1.80/74.8). ... Full name: John Lucas III. ... Son of John Lucas Jr., guard with six NBA teams (1977-1990).
HIGH SCHOOL: Bellaire (Houston).
COLLEGE: Baylor, then Oklahoma State.
TRANSACTIONS/CAREER NOTES: Not drafted by an NBA franchise ... Played in NBA Development League (2005-06). ... Signed as free agent by Houston Rockets (December 9, 2005). ... Waived by Rockets (January 4, 2006). ... Re-signed by Rockets to first of two consecutive 10-day contracts (January 8, 2006). ... Signed by Rockets for remainder of season (January 28, 2006).

COLLEGIATE RECORD

											AVERAGES		
Season Team	G	Min.	FGM	FGA	Pct.	FTM	FTA	Pct.	Reb.	Ast.	Pts.	RPG APG PPG
01-02—Baylor............................	30	1006	143	330	.433	50	63	.794	76	120	395	2.5 4.0 13.2
02-03—Baylor............................	28	982	135	310	.435	54	62	.871	66	122	371	2.4 4.4 13.3
03-04—Oklahoma St..................	35	1199	183	402	.455	86	97	.887	97	158	527	2.8 4.5 15.1
04-05—Oklahoma St..................	33	1192	204	452	.451	76	84	.905	82	135	584	2.5 4.1 17.7
Totals	126	4379	665	1494	.445	266	306	.869	321	535	1877	2.5 4.2 14.9

Three-point field goals: 2001-02, 59-for-158 (.373). 2002-03, 47-for-151 (.311). 2003-04, 75-for-192 (.391). 2004-05, 100-for-232 (.431). Totals, 281-for-733 (.383).

NBA REGULAR-SEASON RECORD

								REBOUNDS							AVERAGES		
Season Team	G	Min.	FGM	FGA	Pct.	FTM	FTA	Pct.	Off.	Def.	Tot.	Ast.	St.	Blk.	TO	Pts.	RPG APG PPG
05-06—Houston..........	13	107	14	36	.389	0	0	...	2	3	5	12	5	0	7	30	0.4 0.9 2.3

Three-point field goals: 2005-06, 2-for-9 (.222). Totals, 2-for-9 (.222).
Personal fouls/disqualifications: 2005-06, 6/0. Totals, 6/0.

NBA DEVELOPMENT LEAGUE RECORD

											AVERAGES		
Season Team	G	Min.	FGM	FGA	Pct.	FTM	FTA	Pct.	Reb.	Ast.	Pts.	RPG APG PPG
05-06—Tulsa...........................	35	1226	232	456	.509	65	81	.802	112	135	590	3.2 3.9 16.9

Three-point field goals: 2005-06, 61-for-141 (.433). Totals, 61-for-141 (.433).

LUE, TYRONN   G   HAWKS

PERSONAL: Born May 3, 1977, in Mexico, Mo. ... 6-0/178. (1.83/80.7). ... Full name: Tyronn Jamar Lue
HIGH SCHOOL: Raytown (Kansas City, Mo.).
COLLEGE: Nebraska.
TRANSACTIONS/CAREER NOTES: Selected after junior season by Denver Nuggets in first round (23rd pick overall) of 1998 NBA Draft. ... Draft rights traded by Nuggets with F Tony Battie to Los Angeles Lakers for G Nick Van Exel (June 24, 1998). ... Signed as free agent by Washington Wizards (July 18, 2001). ... Signed as free agent by Orlando Magic (July 23, 2003) ... Traded by Magic with G Tracy McGrady, F Juwan Howard and G Reece Gaines to Houston Rockets for G Steve Francis, G Cuttino Mobley and C Kelvin Cato (June 29, 2004). ... Traded by Rockets to Atlanta Hawks for G Jon Barry (December 23, 2004).
MISCELLANEOUS: Member of NBA championship team (2000, 2001).

COLLEGIATE RECORD

											AVERAGES		
Season Team	G	Min.	FGM	FGA	Pct.	FTM	FTA	Pct.	Reb.	Ast.	Pts.	RPG APG PPG
95-96—Nebraska	35	1033	105	232	.453	66	96	.688	106	144	296	3.0 4.1 8.5
96-97—Nebraska	32	1150	215	476	.452	126	155	.813	93	136	603	2.9 4.3 18.8
97-98—Nebraska	32	1149	240	547	.439	120	145	.828	137	152	678	4.3 4.8 21.2
Totals	99	3332	560	1255	.446	312	396	.788	336	432	1577	3.4 4.4 15.9

Three-point field goals: 1995-96, 20-for-61 (.328). 1996-97, 47-for-137 (.343). 1997-98, 78-for-209 (.373). Totals, 145-for-407 (.356).

NBA REGULAR-SEASON RECORD

								REBOUNDS							AVERAGES		
Season Team	G	Min.	FGM	FGA	Pct.	FTM	FTA	Pct.	Off.	Def.	Tot.	Ast.	St.	Blk.	TO	Pts.	RPG APG PPG
98-99—L.A. Lakers	15	188	28	65	.431	12	21	.571	2	4	6	25	5	0	11	75	0.4 1.7 5.0
99-00—L.A. Lakers	8	146	19	39	.487	6	8	.750	2	10	12	17	3	0	9	48	1.5 2.1 6.0
00-01—L.A. Lakers	38	468	50	117	.427	19	24	.792	5	27	32	45	19	0	27	130	0.8 1.2 3.4
01-02—Washington	71	1458	222	520	.427	48	63	.762	14	108	122	246	49	0	96	555	1.7 3.5 7.8
02-03—Washington	75	1986	248	573	.433	91	104	.875	22	127	149	263	47	1	77	647	2.0 3.5 8.6

Season Team	G	Min.	FGM	FGA	Pct.	FTM	FTA	Pct.	REBOUNDS Off.	Def.	Tot.	Ast.	St.	Blk.	TO	Pts.	AVERAGES RPG	APG	PPG
03-04—Orlando	76	2332	309	714	.433	101	131	.771	26	161	187	317	61	5	124	799	2.5	4.2	10.5
04-05—Houston-Atl.	70	2007	295	654	.451	142	165	.861	14	135	149	322	33	0	105	787	2.1	4.6	11.2
05-06—Atlanta	51	1234	192	418	.459	118	138	.855	13	69	82	157	26	3	75	560	1.6	3.1	11.0
Totals	404	9819	1363	3100	.440	537	654	.821	98	641	739	1392	243	9	524	3601	1.8	3.4	8.9

Three-point field goals: 1998-99, 7-for-16 (.438). 1999-00, 4-for-8 (.500). 2000-01, 11-for-34 (.324). 2001-02, 63-for-141 (.447). 2002-03, 60-for-176 (.341). 2003-04, 80-for-209 (.383). 2004-05, 55-for-155 (.355). 2005-06, 58-for-127 (.457). Totals, 338-for-866 (.390).

Personal fouls/disqualifications: 1998-99, 28/0. 1999-00, 17/0. 2000-01, 54/1. 2001-02, 120/2. 2002-03, 151/0. 2003-04, 185/0. 2004-05, 168/2. 2005-06, 113/2. Totals, 836/7.

NBA PLAYOFF RECORD

Season Team	G	Min.	FGM	FGA	Pct.	FTM	FTA	Pct.	REBOUNDS Off.	Def.	Tot.	Ast.	St.	Blk.	TO	Pts.	AVERAGES RPG	APG	PPG
98-99—L.A. Lakers	3	33	7	17	.412	0	0	...	0	2	2	6	2	0	4	14	0.7	2.0	4.7
00-01—L.A. Lakers	15	131	10	29	.345	4	5	.800	1	9	10	10	12	1	8	29	0.7	0.7	1.9
Totals	18	164	17	46	.370	4	5	.800	1	11	12	16	14	1	12	43	0.7	0.9	2.4

Three-point field goals: 1998-99, 0-for-2. 2000-01, 5-for-13 (.385). Totals, 5-for-15 (.333).
Personal fouls/disqualifications: 1998-99, 4/0. 2000-01, 11/0. Totals, 15/0.

MACIJAUSKAS, ARVYDAS　　　　G

PERSONAL: Born January 19, 1980 ... 6-4/214. (1.93/97.1).
TRANSACTIONS/CAREER NOTES: Not drafted by an NBA franchise. ... Played in Lithuania (1996-2003). ... Played in Spain (2003-05). ... Signed as free agent by New Orleans Hornets (August 2, 2005). ... Waived by Hornets (July 12, 2006).
MISCELLANEOUS: Member of bronze medal-winning Lithuanian Olympic team (2000). ... Member of Lithuanian Olympic team (2004).

LITHUANIAN LEAGUE RECORD

Season Team	G	Min.	FGM	FGA	Pct.	FTM	FTA	Pct.	Reb.	Ast.	Pts.	AVERAGES RPG	APG	PPG
96-97—Neptunas Klaibeda	3	9	1	4	.250	0	0	...	0	0	2	0.0	0.0	0.7
97-98—Neptunas Klaibeda	28	501	93	186	.500	65	73	.890	63	40	301	2.3	1.4	10.8
98-99—Neptunas Klaibeda	34	847	171	330	.518	118	141	.837	81	59	525	2.4	1.7	15.4
99-00—Lietuvos Rytas	31	577	108	186	.581	102	113	.903	55	24	353	1.8	0.8	11.4
00-01—Lietuvos Rytas	25	650	154	262	.588	91	103	.883	56	42	456	2.2	1.7	18.2
01-02—Lietuvos Rytas	31	639	170	307	.554	73	81	.901	88	47	488	2.8	1.5	15.7
02-03—Lietuvos Rytas	36	880	217	380	.571	147	159	.925	110	82	672	3.1	2.3	18.7
Totals	188	4103	914	1655	.552	596	670	.890	453	294	2797	2.4	1.6	14.9

Three-point field goals: 1996-97, 0-for-1. 1997-98, 50-for-107 (.467). 1998-99, 65-for-130 (.500). 1999-00, 35-for-67 (.522). 2000-01, 57-for-105 (.543). 2001-02, 75-for-156 (.481). 2002-03, 91-for-171 (.532). Totals, 373-for-737 (.506).

SPANISH LEAGUE RECORD

Season Team	G	Min.	FGM	FGA	Pct.	FTM	FTA	Pct.	Reb.	Ast.	Pts.	AVERAGES RPG	APG	PPG
03-04—Tau Ceramica	32	953	190	377	.504	161	176	.915	92	47	599	2.9	1.5	18.7
04-05—Tau Ceramica	31	775	161	312	.516	94	102	.922	57	61	503	1.8	2.0	16.2
Totals	63	1728	351	689	.509	255	278	.917	149	108	1102	2.4	1.7	17.5

Three-point field goals: 2003-04, 58-for-149 (.389). 2004-05, 87-for-146 (.596). Totals, 145-for-295 (.492).

NBA REGULAR-SEASON RECORD

Season Team	G	Min.	FGM	FGA	Pct.	FTM	FTA	Pct.	REBOUNDS Off.	Def.	Tot.	Ast.	St.	Blk.	TO	Pts.	AVERAGES RPG	APG	PPG
05-06—NO/Okla. City.	19	135	14	41	.341	13	15	.867	3	7	10	5	7	0	8	44	0.5	0.3	2.3

Three-point field goals: 2005-06, 3-for-12 (.250). Totals, 3-for-12 (.250).
Personal fouls/disqualifications: 2005-06, 10/0. Totals, 10/0.

MADSEN, MARK　　　　F　　　　TIMBERWOLVES

PERSONAL: Born January 28, 1976, in Walnut Creek, Calif. ... 6-9/236. (2.06/107.0). ... Full name: Mark Ellsworth Madsen
HIGH SCHOOL: San Ramon Valley (Danville, Calif.).
COLLEGE: Stanford.
TRANSACTIONS/CAREER NOTES: Selected by Los Angeles Lakers in first round (29th pick overall) of 2000 NBA Draft. ... Signed as free agent by Minnesota Timberwolves (July 28, 2003)
MISCELLANEOUS: Member of NBA championship team (2001, 2002).

COLLEGIATE RECORD

Season Team	G	Min.	FGM	FGA	Pct.	FTM	FTA	Pct.	Reb.	Ast.	Pts.	AVERAGES RPG	APG	PPG
96-97—Stanford	25	410	51	95	.537	45	74	.608	126	8	147	5.0	0.3	5.9
97-98—Stanford	27	706	116	197	.589	83	132	.629	220	20	315	8.1	0.7	11.7
98-99—Stanford	33	969	153	253	.605	127	218	.583	297	16	433	9.0	0.5	13.1
99-00—Stanford	23	628	108	184	.587	65	113	.575	214	25	281	9.3	1.1	12.2
Totals	108	2713	428	729	.587	320	537	.596	857	69	1176	7.9	0.6	10.9

Three-point field goals: 1997-98, 0-for-1. 1998-99, 0-for-1. Totals, 0-for-2 (.000).

M

NBA REGULAR-SEASON RECORD

Season Team	G	Min.	FGM	FGA	Pct.	FTM	FTA	Pct.	Off.	Def.	Tot.	Ast.	St.	Blk.	TO	Pts.	RPG	APG	PPG
00-01—L.A. Lakers	70	641	55	113	.487	26	37	.703	74	78	152	24	8	8	27	137	2.2	0.3	2.0
01-02—L.A. Lakers	59	650	66	146	.452	35	54	.648	89	73	162	44	16	13	22	167	2.7	0.7	2.8
02-03—L.A. Lakers	54	781	69	163	.423	36	61	.590	86	73	159	38	15	19	27	174	2.9	0.7	3.2
03-04—Minnesota.......	72	1246	101	204	.495	57	118	.483	134	138	272	28	33	18	47	259	3.8	0.4	3.6
04-05—Minnesota.......	41	601	34	66	.515	20	40	.500	63	65	128	18	7	14	24	88	3.1	0.4	2.1
05-06—Minnesota.......	62	676	27	66	.409	20	47	.426	50	91	141	11	23	17	26	74	2.3	0.2	1.2
Totals	358	4595	352	758	.464	194	357	.543	496	518	1014	163	102	89	173	899	2.8	0.5	2.5

Three-point field goals: 2000-01, 1-for-1 (1.000). 2001-02, 0-for-2. 2003-04, 0-for-6. 2005-06, 0-for-7. Totals, 1-for-16 (.063).
Personal fouls/disqualifications: 2000-01, 111/2. 2001-02, 104/0. 2002-03, 116/0. 2003-04, 175/2. 2004-05, 103/1. 2005-06, 114/2. Totals, 723/7.

NBA PLAYOFF RECORD

Season Team	G	Min.	FGM	FGA	Pct.	FTM	FTA	Pct.	Off.	Def.	Tot.	Ast.	St.	Blk.	TO	Pts.	RPG	APG	PPG
00-01—L.A. Lakers	13	48	1	13	.077	3	5	.600	6	4	10	4	0	2	2	5	0.8	0.3	0.4
01-02—L.A. Lakers	7	10	0	1	.000	0	0	...	0	2	2	0	0	0	1	0	0.3	0.0	0.0
02-03—L.A. Lakers	12	169	13	31	.419	7	16	.438	14	14	28	12	3	2	8	33	2.3	1.0	2.8
03-04—Minnesota.......	17	222	17	32	.531	13	29	.448	28	30	58	2	5	4	7	47	3.4	0.1	2.8
Totals	49	449	31	77	.403	23	50	.460	48	50	98	18	8	8	18	85	2.0	0.4	1.7

Three-point field goals: 2001-02, 0-for-1. 2002-03, 0-for-1. Totals, 0-for-2 (.000).
Personal fouls/disqualifications: 2000-01, 4/0. 2001-02, 1/0. 2002-03, 32/0. 2003-04, 43/0. Totals, 80/0.

MAGGETTE, COREY   F   CLIPPERS

PERSONAL: Born November 12, 1979, in Melrose Park, Ill. ... 6-6/228. (1.98/103.4). ... Full name: Corey Antoine Maggette.
HIGH SCHOOL: Fenwick (Oak Park, Ill.).
COLLEGE: Duke.
TRANSACTIONS/CAREER NOTES: Selected after freshman season by Seattle SuperSonics in first round (13th pick overall) of 1999 NBA Draft. ... Draft rights traded by SuperSonics with F/G Billy Owens, G/F Dale Ellis and F Don MacLean to Orlando Magic for F Horace Grant and 2001 and 2002 second-round draft choices (June 30, 1999). ... Traded by Magic with F Derek Strong and draft rights to G Keyon Dooling to Los Angeles Clippers for a future first-round draft choice (June 28, 2000).

COLLEGIATE RECORD

Season Team	G	Min.	FGM	FGA	Pct.	FTM	FTA	Pct.	Reb.	Ast.	Pts.	RPG	APG	PPG
98-99—Duke..............................	39	691	137	261	.525	111	155	.716	151	59	414	3.9	1.5	10.6

Three-point field goals: 1998-99, 29-for-84 (.345). Totals, 29-for-84 (.345).

NBA REGULAR-SEASON RECORD

Season Team	G	Min.	FGM	FGA	Pct.	FTM	FTA	Pct.	Off.	Def.	Tot.	Ast.	St.	Blk.	TO	Pts.	RPG	APG	PPG
99-00—Orlando..........	77	1370	224	469	.478	196	261	.751	123	180	303	61	24	26	138	646	3.9	0.8	8.4
00-01—L.A. Clippers...	69	1359	225	487	.462	223	288	.774	88	203	291	82	35	9	106	690	4.2	1.2	10.0
01-02—L.A. Clippers...	63	1615	235	530	.443	201	251	.801	54	177	231	112	41	19	116	717	3.7	1.8	11.4
02-03—L.A. Clippers...	64	2006	343	773	.444	325	405	.802	77	245	322	123	55	16	147	1073	5.0	1.9	16.8
03-04—L.A. Clippers...	73	2628	453	1013	.447	*526	620	.848	96	334	430	224	65	16	207	1508	5.9	3.1	20.7
04-05—L.A. Clippers...	66	2436	425	986	.431	563	657	.857	70	324	394	225	70	8	195	1464	6.0	3.4	22.2
05-06—L.A. Clippers...	32	943	167	375	.445	212	256	.828	28	141	169	66	19	4	78	570	5.3	2.1	17.8
Totals	444	12357	2072	4633	.447	2246	2738	.820	536	1604	2140	893	309	98	987	6668	4.8	2.0	15.0

Three-point field goals: 1999-00, 2-for-11 (.182). 2000-01, 17-for-56 (.304). 2001-02, 46-for-139 (.331). 2002-03, 62-for-177 (.350). 2003-04, 76-for-231 (.329). 2004-05, 51-for-168 (.304). 2005-06, 24-for-71 (.338). Totals, 278-for-853 (.326).
Personal fouls/disqualifications: 1999-00, 169/1. 2000-01, 140/1. 2001-02, 155/0. 2002-03, 194/6. 2003-04, 217/2. 2004-05, 191/1. 2005-06, 95/1. Totals, 1161/12.

NBA PLAYOFF RECORD

Season Team	G	Min.	FGM	FGA	Pct.	FTM	FTA	Pct.	Off.	Def.	Tot.	Ast.	St.	Blk.	TO	Pts.	RPG	APG	PPG
05-06—L.A. Clippers...	12	292	57	122	.467	61	67	.910	7	80	87	17	7	5	26	183	7.3	1.4	15.3

Three-point field goals: 2005-06, 8-for-24 (.333). Totals, 8-for-24 (.333).
Personal fouls/disqualifications: 2005-06, 39/0. Totals, 39/0.

MAGLOIRE, JAMAAL   F/C   TRAIL BLAZERS

PERSONAL: Born May 21, 1978, in Toronto. ... 6-11/259. (2.11/117.5). ... Full name: Jamaal Dane Magloire
HIGH SCHOOL: Eastern School of Commerce (Toronto).
COLLEGE: Kentucky.
TRANSACTIONS/CAREER NOTES: Selected by Charlotte Hornets in first round (19th pick overall) of 2000 NBA Draft. ... Hornets franchise moved to New Orleans for 2002-03 season. ... Traded by Hornets to Milwaukee Bucks for G Desmond Mason and a first-round draft pick (October 26, 2005). ... Traded by Bucks to Portland Trail Blazers for G Steve Blake, F Brian Skinner and C Ha Seung-Jin (July 31, 2006).

COLLEGIATE RECORD

NOTES: Member of NCAA Division I championship team (1998).

Season Team	G	Min.	FGM	FGA	Pct.	FTM	FTA	Pct.	Reb.	Ast.	Pts.	RPG	APG	PPG
96-97—Kentucky	40	626	75	153	.490	45	82	.549	177	15	195	4.4	0.4	4.9
97-98—Kentucky	38	526	77	158	.487	43	64	.672	161	11	197	4.2	0.3	5.2

M

Season Team	G	Min.	FGM	FGA	Pct.	FTM	FTA	Pct.	Reb.	Ast.	Pts.	AVERAGES RPG	APG	PPG
98-99—Kentucky	34	668	94	177	.531	49	85	.576	151	18	237	4.4	0.5	7.0
99-00—Kentucky	33	978	148	296	.500	139	203	.685	300	18	435	9.1	0.5	13.2
Totals	145	2798	394	784	.503	276	434	.636	789	62	1064	5.4	0.4	7.3

NBA REGULAR-SEASON RECORD

Season Team	G	Min.	FGM	FGA	Pct.	FTM	FTA	Pct.	REBOUNDS Off.	Def.	Tot.	Ast.	St.	Blk.	TO	Pts.	AVERAGES RPG	APG	PPG
00-01—Charlotte	74	1095	122	271	.450	95	145	.655	103	192	295	27	18	78	61	339	4.0	0.4	4.6
01-02—Charlotte	82	1549	228	414	.551	243	333	.730	153	308	461	31	27	86	118	699	5.6	0.4	8.5
02-03—New Orleans	82	2443	305	635	.480	231	322	.717	260	464	724	88	49	111	158	841	8.8	1.1	10.3
03-04—New Orleans	82	2777	383	809	.473	353	470	.751	268	579	847	86	43	101	201	1119	10.3	1.0	13.6
04-05—New Orleans	23	703	98	227	.432	74	123	.602	79	126	205	29	8	23	59	270	8.9	1.3	11.7
05-06—Milwaukee	82	2465	287	615	.467	178	333	.535	220	558	778	56	29	80	166	752	9.5	0.7	9.2
Totals	425	11032	1423	2971	.479	1174	1726	.680	1083	2227	3310	317	174	479	763	4020	7.8	0.7	9.5

Three-point field goals: 2000-01, 0-for-2. 2001-02, 0-for-1. 2002-03, 0-for-3. 2003-04, 0-for-1. Totals, 0-for-7 (.000).
Personal fouls/disqualifications: 2000-01, 139/0. 2001-02, 201/0. 2002-03, 276/4. 2003-04, 278/6. 2004-05, 74/0. 2005-06, 276/6. Totals, 1244/16.

NBA PLAYOFF RECORD

Season Team	G	Min.	FGM	FGA	Pct.	FTM	FTA	Pct.	REBOUNDS Off.	Def.	Tot.	Ast.	St.	Blk.	TO	Pts.	AVERAGES RPG	APG	PPG
00-01—Charlotte	10	110	16	28	.571	7	23	.304	8	20	28	3	0	6	4	39	2.8	0.3	3.9
01-02—Charlotte	8	168	22	40	.550	54	71	.761	17	28	45	5	0	15	17	98	5.6	0.6	12.3
02-03—New Orleans	6	188	22	49	.449	25	33	.758	17	33	50	2	4	6	9	69	8.3	0.3	11.5
03-04—New Orleans	7	239	28	67	.418	21	28	.750	16	48	64	5	3	7	11	77	9.1	0.7	11.0
05-06—Milwaukee	5	135	18	38	.474	9	15	.600	11	29	40	5	2	6	6	45	8.0	1.0	9.0
Totals	36	840	106	222	.477	116	170	.682	69	158	227	20	9	40	47	328	6.3	0.6	9.1

Three-point field goals: 2003-04, 0-for-1. Totals, 0-for-1 (.000).
Personal fouls/disqualifications: 2000-01, 20/0. 2001-02, 30/1. 2002-03, 15/0. 2003-04, 22/1. 2005-06, 14/0. Totals, 101/2.

NBA ALL-STAR GAME RECORD

Season Team	Min.	FGM	FGA	Pct.	FTM	FTA	Pct.	REBOUNDS Off.	Def.	Tot.	Ast.	PF	Dq.	St.	Blk.	TO	Pts.
2004—New Orleans	21	9	16	.563	1	2	.500	3	5	8	0	2	0	1	1	1	19

MARBURY, STEPHON   G   KNICKS

PERSONAL: Born February 20, 1977, in Brooklyn, N.Y. ... 6-2/180. (1.88/81.6). ... Cousin of Jamel Thomas, forward with Boston Celtics (1999-2000), Golden State Warriors (1999-2000), Portland Trail Blazers (1999-2000) and New Jersey Nets (2000-01). Cousin of Sebastian Telfair, G, Boston Celtics.
HIGH SCHOOL: Abraham Lincoln (Brooklyn, N.Y.).
COLLEGE: Georgia Tech.
TRANSACTIONS/CAREER NOTES: Selected after freshman season by Milwaukee Bucks in first round (fourth pick overall) of 1996 NBA Draft. ... Draft rights traded by Bucks to Minnesota Timberwolves for draft rights to G Ray Allen and a first-round draft choice (June 26, 1996). ... Traded by Timberwolves with F Bill Curley and G Chris Carr to New Jersey Nets in three-way deal in which Nets also received G Elliot Perry from Milwaukee Bucks, Timberwolves received F Brian Evans, 1999 first-round draft choice and an undisclosed draft choice from Nets, Bucks sent G Terrell Brandon to Timberwolves, Timberwolves sent C Paul Grant to Bucks and Nets sent G Sam Cassell and F/C Chris Gatling to Bucks (March 11, 1999). ... Traded by Nets with F Johnny Newman and C Soumaila Samake to Phoenix Suns for G Jason Kidd and C Chris Dudley (July 18, 2001). ... Traded by Suns with F/G Anfernee Hardaway and C Cezary Trybanski to New York Knicks for G Howard Eisley, F Maciej Lampe, F Antonio McDyess, G Charlie Ward, draft rights to G Milo Vujanic, 2004 first-round draft choice and future first-round draft choice (January 5, 2004).
MISCELLANEOUS: Member of bronze-medal-winning U.S. Olympic Team (2004).

M

COLLEGIATE RECORD

Season Team	G	Min.	FGM	FGA	Pct.	FTM	FTA	Pct.	Reb.	Ast.	Pts.	AVERAGES RPG	APG	PPG
95-96—Georgia Tech	36	1345	235	514	.457	121	164	.738	113	161	679	3.1	4.5	18.9

Three-point field goals: 1995-96, 88-for-238 (.370). Totals, 88-for-238 (.370).

NBA REGULAR-SEASON RECORD

HONORS: All-NBA third team (2000, 2003). ... NBA All-Rookie first team (1997).

Season Team	G	Min.	FGM	FGA	Pct.	FTM	FTA	Pct.	REBOUNDS Off.	Def.	Tot.	Ast.	St.	Blk.	TO	Pts.	AVERAGES RPG	APG	PPG
96-97—Minnesota	67	2324	355	871	.408	245	337	.727	54	130	184	522	67	19	210	1057	2.7	7.8	15.8
97-98—Minnesota	82	3112	513	1237	.415	329	450	.731	58	172	230	704	104	7	256	1450	2.8	8.6	17.7
98-99—Minn.-N.J.	49	1895	378	883	.428	222	278	.799	37	105	142	437	59	8	164	1044	2.9	8.9	21.3
99-00—New Jersey	74	2881	569	1317	.432	436	536	.813	61	179	240	622	112	15	270	1640	3.2	8.4	22.2
00-01—New Jersey	67	2557	563	1277	.441	362	458	.790	53	152	205	506	79	5	197	1598	3.1	7.6	23.9
01-02—Phoenix	82	3187	625	1413	.442	353	452	.781	75	191	266	666	77	13	284	1674	3.2	8.1	20.4
02-03—Phoenix	81	3240	671	1530	.439	375	467	.803	53	210	263	654	108	20	263	1806	3.2	8.1	22.3
03-04—Phoenix-N.Y.	81	3254	598	1386	.431	356	436	.817	58	205	263	*719	129	9	249	1639	3.2	8.9	20.2
04-05—New York	82	3281	604	1308	.462	458	549	.834	50	198	248	668	122	6	233	1781	3.0	8.1	21.7
05-06—New York	60	2193	349	774	.451	246	326	.755	25	150	175	382	63	4	157	977	2.9	6.4	16.3
Totals	725	27924	5225	11996	.436	3382	4289	.789	524	1692	2216	5880	920	106	2283	14666	3.1	8.1	20.2

Three-point field goals: 1996-97, 102-for-288 (.354). 1997-98, 95-for-304 (.313). 1998-99, 66-for-197 (.335). 1999-00, 66-for-233 (.283). 2000-01, 110-for-335 (.328). 2001-02, 71-for-248 (.286). 2002-03, 89-for-296 (.301). 2003-04, 87-for-274 (.318). 2004-05, 115-for-325 (.354). 2005-06, 33-for-104 (.317). Totals, 834-for-2604 (.320).

Personal fouls/disqualifications: 1996-97, 159/2. 1997-98, 222/0. 1998-99, 125/0. 1999-00, 195/4. 2000-01, 150/1. 2001-02, 186/0. 2002-03, 200/1. 2003-04, 172/0. 2004-05, 186/1. 2005-06, 143/0. Totals, 1738/9.

NBA PLAYOFF RECORD

Season Team	G	Min.	FGM	FGA	Pct.	FTM	FTA	Pct.	REBOUNDS Off.	Def.	Tot.	Ast.	St.	Blk.	TO	Pts.	AVERAGES RPG	APG	PPG
96-97—Minnesota......	3	117	26	65	.400	6	10	.600	2	10	12	23	2	0	9	64	4.0	7.7	21.3
97-98—Minnesota......	5	209	22	72	.306	18	23	.783	5	11	16	38	12	0	18	69	3.2	7.6	13.8
02-03—Phoenix	6	272	51	136	.375	25	33	.758	6	18	24	34	7	0	23	132	4.0	5.7	22.0
03-04—New York	4	174	31	83	.373	17	25	.680	5	12	17	26	7	0	14	85	4.3	6.5	21.3
Totals	18	772	130	356	.365	66	91	.725	18	51	69	121	28	0	64	350	3.8	6.7	19.4

Three-point field goals: 1996-97, 6-for-20 (.300). 1997-98, 7-for-25 (.280). 2002-03, 5-for-22 (.227). 2003-04, 6-for-20 (.300). Totals, 24-for-87 (.276).
Personal fouls/disqualifications: 1996-97, 9/0. 1997-98, 16/0. 2002-03, 26/1. 2003-04, 9/0. Totals, 60/1.

NBA ALL-STAR GAME RECORD

Season Team	Min.	FGM	FGA	Pct.	FTM	FTA	Pct.	REBOUNDS Off.	Def.	Tot.	Ast.	PF	Dq.	St.	Blk.	TO	Pts.
2001—New Jersey	18	5	9	.556	0	2	.000	0	0	0	4	2	0	0	0	3	12
2003—Phoenix................	15	1	3	.333	2	2	1.000	0	1	1	6	0	0	0	2	2	4
Totals..........................	33	6	12	.500	2	4	.500	0	1	1	10	2	0	0	0	5	16

Three-point field goals: 2001, 2-for-3 (.667). 2003, 0-for-2. Totals, 2-for-5 (.400).

MARION, SHAWN — F — SUNS

PERSONAL: Born May 7, 1978, in Chicago. ... 6-7/215. (2.01/97.5). ... Full name: Shawn Dwayne Marion.
HIGH SCHOOL: Clarksville (Tenn.).
JUNIOR COLLEGE: Vincennes (Ind.) University.
COLLEGE: UNLV.
TRANSACTIONS/CAREER NOTES: Selected after junior season by Phoenix Suns in first round (ninth pick overall) of 1999 NBA Draft.
MISCELLANEOUS: Member of bronze-medal-winning U.S. Olympic Team (2004).

COLLEGIATE RECORD

Season Team	G	Min.	FGM	FGA	Pct.	FTM	FTA	Pct.	Reb.	Ast.	Pts.	AVERAGES RPG	APG	PPG
96-97—Vincennes.....................	36	...	346	581	.596	124	178	.697	462	124	838	12.8	3.4	23.3
97-98—Vincennes.....................	36	...	352	605	.582	122	163	.748	471	99	847	13.1	2.8	23.5
98-99—UNLV	29	954	221	418	.529	81	111	.730	269	36	543	9.3	1.2	18.7
Junior College Totals.............	72	...	698	1186	.589	246	341	.721	933	223	1685	13.0	3.1	23.4
4-Year-College Totals.............	29	954	221	418	.529	81	111	.730	269	36	543	9.3	1.2	18.7

Three-point field goals: 1996-97, 22-for-65 (.338). 1997-98, 21-for-56 (.375). 1998-99, 20-for-67 (.299). Totals, 63-for-188 (.335).

NBA REGULAR-SEASON RECORD

HONORS: NBA All-Rookie second team (2000). ... All-NBA third team (2005, 2006).

Season Team	G	Min.	FGM	FGA	Pct.	FTM	FTA	Pct.	REBOUNDS Off.	Def.	Tot.	Ast.	St.	Blk.	TO	Pts.	AVERAGES RPG	APG	PPG
99-00—Phoenix	51	1260	222	471	.471	72	85	.847	105	227	332	69	38	53	51	520	6.5	1.4	10.2
00-01—Phoenix	79	2857	557	1160	.480	234	289	.810	220	628	848	160	132	108	129	1369	10.7	2.0	17.3
01-02—Phoenix	81	3109	654	1395	.469	191	226	.845	211	592	803	162	149	86	144	1547	9.9	2.0	19.1
02-03—Phoenix	81	3373	662	1466	.452	251	295	.851	199	574	773	198	185	95	157	1716	9.5	2.4	21.2
03-04—Phoenix	79	3217	590	1341	.440	228	268	.851	212	525	737	214	*167	104	156	1498	9.3	2.7	19.0
04-05—Phoenix	81	3146	613	1289	.476	229	275	.833	235	680	915	154	163	119	125	1569	11.3	1.9	19.4
05-06—Phoenix	81	3263	716	1365	.525	241	298	.809	249	710	959	143	160	137	125	1769	11.8	1.8	21.8
Totals	533	20225	4014	8487	.473	1446	1736	.833	1431	3936	5367	1100	994	702	887	9988	10.1	2.1	18.7

Three-point field goals: 1999-00, 4-for-22 (.182). 2000-01, 21-for-82 (.256). 2001-02, 48-for-122 (.393). 2002-03, 141-for-364 (.387). 2003-04, 90-for-265 (.340). 2004-05, 114-for-341 (.334). 2005-06, 96-for-290 (.331). Totals, 514-for-1486 (.346).
Personal fouls/disqualifications: 1999-00, 113/0. 2000-01, 211/2. 2001-02, 214/0. 2002-03, 208/0. 2003-04, 203/1. 2004-05, 199/0. 2005-06, 223/2. Totals, 1371/5.

NBA PLAYOFF RECORD

Season Team	G	Min.	FGM	FGA	Pct.	FTM	FTA	Pct.	REBOUNDS Off.	Def.	Tot.	Ast.	St.	Blk.	TO	Pts.	AVERAGES RPG	APG	PPG
99-00—Phoenix	9	281	36	86	.419	9	11	.818	21	58	79	7	6	14	7	82	8.8	0.8	9.1
00-01—Phoenix	4	139	23	62	.371	12	14	.857	10	23	33	3	6	6	6	59	8.3	0.8	14.8
02-03—Phoenix	6	282	40	107	.374	22	26	.846	21	49	70	12	11	11	13	111	11.7	2.0	18.5
04-05—Phoenix	15	635	108	223	.484	30	39	.769	46	131	177	23	21	26	21	264	11.8	1.5	17.6
05-06—Phoenix	20	849	163	333	.489	59	67	.881	57	176	233	31	37	23	22	407	11.7	1.6	20.4
Totals	54	2186	370	811	.456	132	157	.841	155	437	592	76	81	80	69	923	11.0	1.4	17.1

Three-point field goals: 1999-00, 1-for-6 (.167). 2000-01, 1-for-1 (1.000). 2002-03, 9-for-28 (.321). 2004-05, 18-for-43 (.419). 2005-06, 22-for-70 (.314). Totals, 51-for-148 (.345).
Personal fouls/disqualifications: 1999-00, 17/0. 2000-01, 13/0. 2002-03, 17/0. 2004-05, 47/0. 2005-06, 65/2. Totals, 159/2.

NBA ALL-STAR GAME RECORD

Season Team	Min.	FGM	FGA	Pct.	FTM	FTA	Pct.	REBOUNDS Off.	Def.	Tot.	Ast.	PF	Dq.	St.	Blk.	TO	Pts.
2003—Phoenix................	23	4	9	.444	0	0	...	5	2	7	4	1	0	3	1	0	8
2005—Phoenix................	16	5	7	.714	0	1	.000	3	0	3	4	0	0	0	0	1	10
2006—Phoenix................	17	5	9	.556	4	7	.571	4	4	8	0	1	0	1	1	0	14
Totals..........................	56	14	25	.560	4	8	.500	12	6	18	8	2	0	4	2	1	32

Three-point field goals: 2003, 0-for-1. Totals, 0-for-1 (.000).

MARKS, SEAN　　　　　　　　F　　　　　　　　SUNS

PERSONAL: Born August 23, 1975, in Auckland, New Zealand. ... 6-10/250. (2.08/113.4). ... Full name: Sean Andrew Marks.
HIGH SCHOOL: Rangitoto School (Auckland, New Zealand).
COLLEGE: California.
TRANSACTIONS/CAREER NOTES: Selected by New York Knicks in second round (44th pick overall) of 1998 NBA Draft. ... Draft rights traded by Knicks with F Charles Oakley and cash to Toronto Raptors for F Marcus Camby (June 24, 1998). ... Traded by Raptors with G Alvin Williams and cash considerations to Boston Celtics for F Danny Fortson and a future draft choice (February 9, 2000); trade later voided because Williams failed physical. ... Played in Poland (2000-01). ... Signed by Seattle SuperSonics to 10-day contract (January 18, 2001). ... Signed as free agent by Miami Heat (October 1, 2001). ... Signed as free agent by San Antonio Spurs (September 29, 2003). ... Waived by Spurs (October 31, 2003). ... Signed by Spurs (November 17, 2003). ... Signed as free agent by Phoenix Suns (July 27, 2006).
MISCELLANEOUS: Member of New Zealand Olympic team (2000, 2004).

COLLEGIATE RECORD

Season Team	G	Min.	FGM	FGA	Pct.	FTM	FTA	Pct.	Reb.	Ast.	Pts.	RPG	APG	PPG
93-94—California						Did not play—redshirted.								
94-95—California	19	177	22	43	.512	13	24	.542	14	5	57	0.7	0.3	3.0
95-96—California	12	92	6	22	.273	1	1	1.000	24	3	13	2.0	0.3	1.1
96-97—California	29	513	90	173	.520	43	63	.683	143	20	231	4.9	0.7	8.0
97-98—California	26	678	96	201	.478	62	90	.689	197	19	256	7.6	0.7	9.8
Totals	86	1460	214	439	.487	119	178	.669	378	47	557	4.4	0.5	6.5

Three-point field goals: 1996-97, 8-for-14 (.571). 1997-98, 2-for-11 (.182). Totals, 10-for-25 (.400).

NBA REGULAR-SEASON RECORD

Season Team	G	Min.	FGM	FGA	Pct.	FTM	FTA	Pct.	Off.	Def.	Tot.	Ast.	St.	Blk.	TO	Pts.	RPG	APG	PPG
98-99—Toronto	8	28	5	8	.625	1	2	.500	0	1	1	0	1	0	3	11	0.1	0.0	1.4
99-00—Toronto	5	12	2	6	.333	4	4	1.000	0	2	2	0	1	1	3	8	0.4	0.0	1.6
01-02—Miami	21	319	38	88	.432	20	34	.588	19	56	75	8	5	10	19	96	3.6	0.4	4.6
02-03—Miami	23	223	22	59	.373	10	15	.667	8	27	35	3	5	6	14	54	1.5	0.1	2.3
03-04—San Antonio						Did not play—Injured													
04-05—San Antonio	23	244	27	80	.338	22	28	.786	18	38	56	8	3	11	14	76	2.4	0.3	3.3
05-06—San Antonio	25	181	37	71	.521	7	12	.583	12	31	43	7	5	7	7	81	1.7	0.3	3.2
Totals	105	1007	131	312	.420	64	95	.674	57	155	212	26	20	35	60	326	2.0	0.2	3.1

Three-point field goals: 1999-00, 0-for-1. 2002-03, 0-for-1. 2004-05, 0-for-3. 2005-06, 0-for-3. Totals, 0-for-8 (.000).
Personal fouls/disqualifications: 1998-99, 3/0. 1999-00, 3/0. 2001-02, 40/0. 2002-03, 37/1. 2004-05, 29/0. 2005-06, 21/1. Totals, 133/2.

POLISH LEAGUE RECORD

Season Team	G	Min.	FGM	FGA	Pct.	FTM	FTA	Pct.	Reb.	Ast.	Pts.	RPG	APG	PPG
00-01—WSK Slask Wroclaw	8	138	21	28	.750	14	21	.667	46	4	56	5.8	0.5	7.0

M

MARSHALL, DONYELL　　　　　　　　F　　　　　　　　CAVALIERS

PERSONAL: Born May 18, 1973, in Reading, Pa. ... 6-9/230. (2.06/104.3). ... Full name: Donyell Lamar Marshall ... Name pronounced Don-YELL.
HIGH SCHOOL: Reading (Pa.).
COLLEGE: Connecticut.
TRANSACTIONS/CAREER NOTES: Selected after junior season by Minnesota Timberwolves in first round (fourth pick overall) of 1994 NBA Draft. ... Traded by Timberwolves to Golden State Warriors for F Tom Gugliotta (February 18, 1995). ... Traded by Warriors to Utah Jazz as part of four-team deal in which Boston Celtics received G Robert Pack, C John Williams and cash considerations from Dallas Mavericks and a conditional first-round draft choice from Jazz, Mavericks received G Dana Barros from Celtics, F Bill Curley from Warriors and G Howard Eisley from Jazz, Jazz received C Bruno Sundov from Mavericks and Warriors received F Danny Fortson from Celtics and F Adam Keefe from Jazz (August 16, 2000). ... Signed as free agent by Chicago Bulls (August 16, 2002). ... Traded by Bulls with F Lonny Baxter and G Jalen Rose to Toronto Raptors for F/C Antonio Davis, F Chris Jefferies and F Jerome Williams (December 1, 2003). ... Signed as free agent by Cleveland Cavaliers (August 2, 2005).

COLLEGIATE RECORD

NOTES: THE SPORTING NEWS All-America first team (1994).

Season Team	G	Min.	FGM	FGA	Pct.	FTM	FTA	Pct.	Reb.	Ast.	Pts.	RPG	APG	PPG
91-92—Connecticut	30	806	125	295	.424	69	93	.742	183	45	334	6.1	1.5	11.1
92-93—Connecticut	27	854	166	332	.500	107	129	.829	210	30	459	7.8	1.1	17.0
93-94—Connecticut	34	1157	306	599	.511	200	266	.752	302	56	853	8.9	1.6	25.1
Totals	91	2817	597	1226	.487	376	488	.770	695	131	1646	7.6	1.4	18.1

Three-point field goals: 1991-92, 15-for-62 (.242). 1992-93, 20-for-54 (.370). 1993-94, 41-for-132 (.311). Totals, 76-for-248 (.306).

NBA REGULAR-SEASON RECORD

HONORS: NBA All-Rookie second team (1995).

Season Team	G	Min.	FGM	FGA	Pct.	FTM	FTA	Pct.	Off.	Def.	Tot.	Ast.	St.	Blk.	TO	Pts.	RPG	APG	PPG
94-95—Minn.-G.S.	72	2086	345	876	.394	147	222	.662	137	268	405	105	45	88	115	906	5.6	1.5	12.6
95-96—Golden State	62	934	125	314	.398	64	83	.771	65	148	213	49	22	31	48	342	3.4	0.8	5.5
96-97—Golden State	61	1022	174	421	.413	61	98	.622	92	184	276	54	25	46	55	444	4.5	0.9	7.3
97-98—Golden State	73	2611	451	1091	.413	158	216	.731	210	418	628	159	95	73	147	1123	8.6	2.2	15.4
98-99—Golden State	48	1250	208	494	.421	88	121	.727	115	227	342	66	47	37	80	530	7.1	1.4	11.0
99-00—Golden State	64	2071	331	840	.394	199	255	.780	189	448	637	167	68	68	123	910	10.0	2.6	14.2

Season Team	G	Min.	FGM	FGA	Pct.	FTM	FTA	Pct.	Off.	Def.	Tot.	Ast.	St.	Blk.	TO	Pts.	RPG	APG	PPG
									REBOUNDS								AVERAGES		
00-01—Utah	81	2326	427	849	.503	205	273	.751	172	394	566	133	85	78	128	1100	7.0	1.6	13.6
01-02—Utah	58	1750	343	661	.519	160	226	.708	158	285	443	101	50	67	124	859	7.6	1.7	14.8
02-03—Chicago	78	2378	421	918	.459	167	221	.756	234	465	699	137	95	85	135	1042	9.0	1.8	13.4
03-04—Chicago-Tor. ...	82	2988	470	1020	.461	134	182	.736	210	598	808	122	93	124	117	1205	9.9	1.5	14.7
04-05—Toronto	65	1645	262	592	.443	72	91	.791	95	333	428	81	57	46	42	747	6.6	1.2	11.5
05-06—Cleveland	81	2077	265	671	.395	92	123	.748	105	387	492	60	59	41	90	750	6.1	0.7	9.3
Totals	825	23138	3822	8747	.437	1547	2111	.733	1782	4155	5937	1234	741	784	1204	9958	7.2	1.5	12.1

Three-point field goals: 1994-95, 69-for-243 (.284). 1995-96, 28-for-94 (.298). 1996-97, 35-for-111 (.315). 1997-98, 63-for-201 (.313). 1998-99, 26-for-72 (.361). 1999-00, 49-for-138 (.355). 2000-01, 41-for-128 (.320). 2001-02, 13-for-42 (.310). 2002-03, 33-for-87 (.379). 2003-04, 131-for-325 (.403). 2004-05, 151-for-363 (.416). 2005-06, 128-for-395 (.324). Totals, 767-for-2199 (.349).

Personal fouls/disqualifications: 1994-95, 157/1. 1995-96, 83/0. 1996-97, 96/0. 1997-98, 226/1. 1998-99, 123/1. 1999-00, 180/1. 2000-01, 196/0. 2001-02, 150/1. 2002-03, 234/3. 2003-04, 247/1. 2004-05, 136/0. 2005-06, 160/0. Totals, 1988/9.

NBA PLAYOFF RECORD

Season Team	G	Min.	FGM	FGA	Pct.	FTM	FTA	Pct.	Off.	Def.	Tot.	Ast.	St.	Blk.	TO	Pts.	RPG	APG	PPG
									REBOUNDS								AVERAGES		
00-01—Utah	5	160	22	54	.407	7	9	.778	13	25	38	8	2	5	9	52	7.6	1.6	10.4
01-02—Utah	4	124	21	50	.420	12	16	.750	14	17	31	11	3	6	5	57	7.8	2.8	14.3
05-06—Cleveland	13	345	45	104	.433	15	17	.882	24	49	73	8	7	9	13	123	5.6	0.6	9.5
Totals	22	629	88	208	.423	34	42	.810	51	91	142	27	12	20	27	232	6.5	1.2	10.5

Three-point field goals: 2000-01, 1-for-8 (.125). 2001-02, 3-for-6 (.500). 2005-06, 18-for-46 (.391). Totals, 22-for-60 (.367).
Personal fouls/disqualifications: 2000-01, 19/1. 2001-02, 5/0. 2005-06, 24/0. Totals, 48/1.

MARSHALL, RAWLE   G/F   PACERS

PERSONAL: Born February 20, 1982, in Georgetown, Guyana. ... 6-7/190. (2.01/86.2). ... Full name: Rawle Junior Kalomo Marshall
HIGH SCHOOL: Mackenzie (Detroit).
COLLEGE: Ball State, then Oakland (Mich.).
TRANSACTIONS/CAREER NOTES: Not drafted by an NBA franchise ... Played in NBA Development League (2005-06). ... Signed as free agent by Dallas Mavericks (August 5, 2005). ... Traded by Mavericks with Gs Darrell Armstrong and Josh Powell to Indiana Pacers for G Anthony Johnson (July 24, 2006).

COLLEGIATE RECORD

Season Team	G	Min.	FGM	FGA	Pct.	FTM	FTA	Pct.	Reb.	Ast.	Pts.	RPG	APG	PPG
												AVERAGES		
00-01—Ball State	13	85	10	21	.476	11	14	.786	15	3	31	1.2	0.2	2.4
01-02—Oakland					Did Not Play - Transfer Student									
02-03—Oakland	28	974	178	404	.441	124	161	.770	186	79	507	6.6	2.8	18.1
03-04—Oakland	30	1047	182	402	.453	122	180	.678	136	59	528	4.5	2.0	17.6
04-05—Oakland	32	1157	210	477	.440	177	225	.791	246	70	636	7.7	2.2	19.9
Totals	103	3263	580	1304	.445	434	597	.727	583	211	1702	5.7	2.0	16.5

Three-point field goals: 2000-01, 0-for-1. 2002-03, 27-for-106 (.255). 2003-04, 42-for-108 (.389). 2004-05, 39-for-132 (.295). Totals, 108-for-347 (.311).

NBA REGULAR-SEASON RECORD

Season Team	G	Min.	FGM	FGA	Pct.	FTM	FTA	Pct.	Off.	Def.	Tot.	Ast.	St.	Blk.	TO	Pts.	RPG	APG	PPG
									REBOUNDS								AVERAGES		
05-06—Dallas	23	241	24	60	.400	22	29	.759	8	23	31	10	8	7	15	71	1.3	0.4	3.1

Three-point field goals: 2005-06, 1-for-3 (.333). Totals, 1-for-3 (.333).
Personal fouls/disqualifications: 2005-06, 17/0. Totals, 17/0.

NBA DEVELOPMENT LEAGUE RECORD

Season Team	G	Min.	FGM	FGA	Pct.	FTM	FTA	Pct.	Reb.	Ast.	Pts.	RPG	APG	PPG
												AVERAGES		
05-06—Fort Worth	21	637	116	251	.462	123	166	.741	89	29	365	4.2	1.4	17.4

Three-point field goals: 2005-06, 10-for-26 (.385). Totals, 10-for-26 (.385).

MARTIN, DARRICK   G   RAPTORS

PERSONAL: Born March 6, 1971, in Denver. ... 5-11/170. (1.80/77.1).
HIGH SCHOOL: St. Anthony (Long Beach, Calif.).
COLLEGE: UCLA.
TRANSACTIONS/CAREER NOTES: Not drafted by an NBA franchise. ... Played with Magic Johnson All-Stars (1992-93 and 1993-94). ... Played in Continental Basketball Association with Sioux Falls Skyforce (1994-95). ... Signed by Minnesota Timberwolves to first of two consecutive 10-day contracts (February 13, 1995). ... Re-signed by Timberwolves for remainder of season (March 7, 1995). ... Signed as free agent by Vancouver Grizzlies (November 3, 1995). ... Traded by Grizzlies to Timberwolves for 1996 second-round draft choice (January 12, 1996). ... Signed as free agent by Los Angeles Clippers (September 19, 1996). ... Signed as free agent by Sacramento Kings (August 4, 1999). ... Signed as free agent by Dallas Mavericks (August 2, 2001). ... Waived by Mavericks (November 20, 2001). ... Played in American Basketball Association 2000 with Las Vegas Slam (2001-02). ... Waived by Nuggets (October 18, 2002). ... Played in Continental Basketball Association (2002-03). ... Played in Russia and Italy (2002-03). ... Signed by Minnesota Timberwolves to first of two consecutive 10-day contracts (January 30, 2004). ... Signed by Timberwolves for remainder of season (March 31, 2004). ... Signed by Los Angeles Clippers to 10-day contract (January 5, 2005). ... Signed by Toronto Raptors (November 16, 2005).

COLLEGIATE RECORD

Season Team	G	Min.	FGM	FGA	Pct.	FTM	FTA	Pct.	Reb.	Ast.	Pts.	RPG	APG	PPG
												AVERAGES		
88-89—UCLA	31	929	92	203	.453	68	91	.747	59	90	265	1.9	2.9	8.5

M

Season Team	G	Min.	FGM	FGA	Pct.	FTM	FTA	Pct.	Reb.	Ast.	Pts.	AVERAGES		
												RPG	APG	PPG
89-90—UCLA	33	1069	132	283	.466	90	126	.714	71	199	374	2.2	6.0	11.3
90-91—UCLA	32	1030	129	278	.464	90	120	.750	77	217	371	2.4	6.8	11.6
91-92—UCLA	33	642	52	120	.433	68	82	.829	43	130	185	1.3	3.9	5.6
Totals	129	3670	405	884	.458	316	419	.754	250	636	1195	1.9	4.9	9.3

Three-point field goals: 1988-89, 13-for-37 (.351). 1989-90, 20-for-63 (.317). 1990-91, 23-for-79 (.291). 1991-92, 13-for-35 (.371). Totals, 69-for-214 (.322).

CBA RECORD

NOTES: CBA All-League second team (1995).

Season Team	G	Min.	FGM	FGA	Pct.	FTM	FTA	Pct.	Reb.	Ast.	Pts.	AVERAGES		
												RPG	APG	PPG
94-95—Sioux Falls	37	1422	285	518	.550	196	226	.867	96	289	777	2.6	7.8	21.0
02-03—Yakima	20	635	118	266	.444	93	100	.930	53	138	366	2.7	6.9	18.3
03-04—Yakima-Sioux Falls	27	1028	155	371	.418	109	121	.901	82	199	470	3.0	7.4	17.4
04-05—Michigan	30	1171	163	446	.365	100	109	.917	80	214	475	2.7	7.1	15.8
Totals	114	4256	721	1601	.450	498	556	.896	311	840	2088	2.7	7.4	18.3

Three-point field goals: 1994-95, 11-for-39 (.282). 2002-03, 37-for-93 (.398). 2003-04, 51-for-137 (.372). 2004-05, 49-for-137 (.358). Totals, 148-for-406 (.365).

Personal fouls/disqualifications: 1994-95, 124/0. Totals, 124/0.

NBA REGULAR-SEASON RECORD

Season Team	G	Min.	FGM	FGA	Pct.	FTM	FTA	Pct.	REBOUNDS			Ast.	St.	Blk.	TO	Pts.	AVERAGES		
									Off.	Def.	Tot.						RPG	APG	PPG
94-95—Minnesota	34	803	95	233	.408	57	65	.877	14	50	64	133	34	0	62	254	1.9	3.9	7.5
95-96—Van.-Minn.	59	1149	147	362	.406	101	120	.842	16	66	82	217	53	3	107	415	1.4	3.7	7.0
96-97—L.A. Clippers	82	1820	292	718	.407	218	250	.872	26	87	113	339	57	2	127	893	1.4	4.1	10.9
97-98—L.A. Clippers	82	2299	275	730	.377	184	217	.848	19	145	164	331	82	10	154	841	2.0	4.0	10.3
98-99—L.A. Clippers	37	941	102	278	.367	61	76	.803	5	43	48	144	43	4	67	296	1.3	3.9	8.0
99-00—Sacramento	71	893	133	350	.380	98	119	.824	7	37	44	122	28	2	62	402	0.6	1.7	5.7
00-01—Sacramento	31	176	29	76	.382	31	35	.886	2	14	16	14	7	0	10	103	0.5	0.5	3.3
01-02—Dallas	3	22	0	10	.000	1	2	.500	0	1	1	3	2	0	1	1	0.3	1.0	0.3
03-04—Minnesota	16	172	20	67	.299	9	9	1.000	2	5	7	23	2	1	7	55	0.4	1.4	3.4
04-05—L.A. Clippers	11	190	16	50	.320	5	8	.625	3	7	10	28	6	0	6	42	0.9	2.5	3.8
05-06—Toronto	40	339	34	97	.351	18	24	.750	2	18	20	57	17	0	15	102	0.5	1.4	2.6
Totals	466	8804	1143	2971	.385	783	925	.846	96	473	569	1411	331	22	618	3404	1.2	3.0	7.3

Three-point field goals: 1994-95, 7-for-38 (.184). 1995-96, 20-for-69 (.290). 1996-97, 91-for-234 (.389). 1997-98, 107-for-293 (.365). 1998-99, 31-for-106 (.292). 1999-00, 38-for-124 (.306). 2000-01, 14-for-27 (.519). 2001-02, 0-for-2. 2003-04, 6-for-26 (.231). 2004-05, 5-for-18 (.278). 2005-06, 16-for-40 (.400). Totals, 335-for-977 (.343).

Personal fouls/disqualifications: 1994-95, 88/0. 1995-96, 123/0. 1996-97, 165/1. 1997-98, 198/2. 1998-99, 82/1. 1999-00, 89/0. 2000-01, 27/0. 2001-02, 4/0. 2003-04, 23/0. 2004-05, 19/0. 2005-06, 42/0. Totals, 860/4.

NBA PLAYOFF RECORD

Season Team	G	Min.	FGM	FGA	Pct.	FTM	FTA	Pct.	REBOUNDS			Ast.	St.	Blk.	TO	Pts.	AVERAGES		
									Off.	Def.	Tot.						RPG	APG	PPG
96-97—L.A. Clippers	3	77	11	25	.440	6	9	.667	1	1	2	13	0	0	2	33	0.7	4.3	11.0
99-00—Sacramento	2	21	3	9	.333	3	4	.750	1	2	3	2	1	0	3	10	1.5	1.0	5.0
00-01—Sacramento	2	9	0	6	.000	0	0		0	0	0	3	0	0	1	0	0.0	1.5	0.0
03-04—Minnesota	16	182	14	51	.275	16	20	.800	5	9	14	23	4	0	8	50	0.9	1.4	3.1
Totals	23	289	28	91	.308	25	33	.758	7	12	19	41	5	0	14	93	0.8	1.8	4.0

Three-point field goals: 1996-97, 5-for-9 (.556). 1999-00, 1-for-3 (.333). 2000-01, 0-for-2. 2003-04, 6-for-20 (.300). Totals, 12-for-34 (.353).
Personal fouls/disqualifications: 1996-97, 9/0. 1999-00, 4/0. 2000-01, 1/0. 2003-04, 17/0. Totals, 31/0.

AMERICAN BASKETBALL ASSOCIATION 2000 RECORD

Season Team	G	Min.	FGM	FGA	Pct.	FTM	FTA	Pct.	Reb.	Ast.	Pts.	AVERAGES		
												RPG	APG	PPG
01-02—Las Vegas	16	505	89	224	.397	46	55	.836	45	77	265	2.8	4.8	16.6

Three-point field goals: 2001-02, 41-for-108 (.380). Totals, 41-for-108 (.380).

ITALIAN LEAGUE RECORD

Season Team	G	Min.	FGM	FGA	Pct.	FTM	FTA	Pct.	Reb.	Ast.	Pts.	AVERAGES		
												RPG	APG	PPG
02-03—Rida Scafati	3	97	12	35	.343	9	12	.750	8	9	40	2.7	3.0	13.3

Three-point field goals: 2002-03, 7-for-18 (.389). Totals, 7-for-18 (.389).

RUSSIAN LEAGUE RECORD

Season Team	G	Min.	FGM	FGA	Pct.	FTM	FTA	Pct.	Reb.	Ast.	Pts.	AVERAGES		
												RPG	APG	PPG
02-03—Avtodor Saratov	4	106	17	38	.447	12	14	.857	8	11	51	2.0	2.8	12.8

Three-point field goals: 2002-03, 5-for-14 (.357). Totals, 5-for-14 (.357).

M

MARTIN, KENYON   F   NUGGETS

PERSONAL: Born December 30, 1977, in Saginaw, Mich. ... 6-9/230. (2.06/104.3). ... Full name: Kenyon Lee Martin
HIGH SCHOOL: Bryan Adams (Dallas).
COLLEGE: Cincinnati.
TRANSACTIONS/CAREER NOTES: Selected by New Jersey Nets in first round (first pick overall) of 2000 NBA Draft. ... Traded by Nets to Denver Nuggets for three future first-round draft choices (July 15, 2004).

COLLEGIATE RECORD

NOTES: The SPORTING NEWS College Player of the Year (2000). ... Wooden Award winner (2000). ... Naismith Award winner (2000). ... The SPORTING NEWS All-America first team (2000).

Season Team	G	Min.	FGM	FGA	Pct.	FTM	FTA	Pct.	Reb.	Ast.	Pts.	RPG	APG	PPG
96-97—Cincinnati	22	233	26	40	.650	10	32	.313	74	10	62	3.4	0.5	2.8
97-98—Cincinnati	30	858	124	198	.626	50	105	.476	267	41	298	8.9	1.4	9.9
98-99—Cincinnati	33	900	142	248	.573	50	89	.562	228	49	334	6.9	1.5	10.1
99-00—Cincinnati	31	909	221	389	.568	141	206	.684	300	42	585	9.7	1.4	18.9
Totals	116	2900	513	875	.586	251	432	.581	869	142	1279	7.5	1.2	11.0

Three-point field goals: 1997-98, 0-for-1. 1998-99, 0-for-1. 1999-00, 2-for-7 (.286). Totals, 2-for-9 (.222).

NBA REGULAR-SEASON RECORD

HONORS: NBA All-Rookie first team (2001).

Season Team	G	Min.	FGM	FGA	Pct.	FTM	FTA	Pct.	Off.	Def.	Tot.	Ast.	St.	Blk.	TO	Pts.	RPG	APG	PPG
00-01—New Jersey	68	2272	346	777	.445	121	192	.630	137	365	502	131	78	113	138	814	7.4	1.9	12.0
01-02—New Jersey	73	2504	445	962	.463	181	267	.678	113	275	388	192	90	121	172	1086	5.3	2.6	14.9
02-03—New Jersey	77	2628	509	1082	.470	256	392	.653	164	476	640	185	98	70	192	1283	8.3	2.4	16.7
03-04—New Jersey	65	2252	439	900	.488	201	294	.684	133	484	617	160	95	82	168	1086	9.5	2.5	16.7
04-05—Denver	70	2272	444	907	.490	199	308	.646	146	365	511	170	100	78	149	1087	7.3	2.4	15.5
05-06—Denver	56	1546	297	600	.495	121	170	.712	93	260	353	79	43	52	72	720	6.3	1.4	12.9
Totals	409	13474	2480	5228	.474	1079	1623	.665	786	2225	3011	917	504	516	891	6076	7.4	2.2	14.9

Three-point field goals: 2000-01, 1-for-11 (.091). 2001-02, 15-for-67 (.224). 2002-03, 9-for-43 (.209). 2003-04, 7-for-25 (.280). 2004-05, 0-for-12. 2005-06, 5-for-22 (.227). Totals, 37-for-180 (.206).

Personal fouls/disqualifications: 2000-01, 281/10. 2001-02, 261/8. 2002-03, 294/6. 2003-04, 230/5. 2004-05, 228/4. 2005-06, 171/1. Totals, 1465/34.

NBA PLAYOFF RECORD

Season Team	G	Min.	FGM	FGA	Pct.	FTM	FTA	Pct.	Off.	Def.	Tot.	Ast.	St.	Blk.	TO	Pts.	RPG	APG	PPG
01-02—New Jersey	20	749	129	304	.424	76	110	.691	30	86	116	57	24	25	52	336	5.8	2.9	16.8
02-03—New Jersey	20	777	149	329	.453	79	114	.693	50	137	187	57	29	31	58	378	9.4	2.9	18.9
03-04—New Jersey	11	409	81	152	.533	48	64	.750	25	96	121	12	13	14	32	210	11.0	1.1	19.1
04-05—Denver	5	164	27	58	.466	8	13	.615	7	21	28	6	5	5	7	62	5.6	1.2	12.4
05-06—Denver	2	35	4	13	.308	1	2	.500	6	3	9	1	4	2	3	9	4.5	0.5	4.5
Totals	58	2134	390	856	.456	212	303	.700	118	343	461	133	75	77	152	995	7.9	2.3	17.2

Three-point field goals: 2001-02, 2-for-9 (.222). 2002-03, 1-for-11 (.091). 2003-04, 0-for-4. 2004-05, 0-for-1. Totals, 3-for-25 (.120).

Personal fouls/disqualifications: 2001-02, 86/3. 2002-03, 92/2. 2003-04, 50/3. 2004-05, 22/1. 2005-06, 5/0. Totals, 255/9.

NBA ALL-STAR GAME RECORD

Season Team	Min.	FGM	FGA	Pct.	FTM	FTA	Pct.	Off.	Def.	Tot.	Ast.	St.	Blk.	TO	Pts.
2004—New Jersey	23	8	10	.800	1	2	.500	4	3	7	3	1	0	0	17

MARTIN, KEVIN   G   KINGS

PERSONAL: Born February 1, 1983, in Zanesville, Ohio. ... 6-7/185. (2.01/83.9). ... Full name: Kevin Dallas Martin
HIGH SCHOOL: Zanesville (Ohio).
COLLEGE: Western Carolina.
TRANSACTIONS/CAREER NOTES: Selected after junior season by Sacramento Kings in first round (26th pick overall) of 2004 NBA Draft.

COLLEGIATE RECORD

Season Team	G	Min.	FGM	FGA	Pct.	FTM	FTA	Pct.	Reb.	Ast.	Pts.	RPG	APG	PPG
01-02—Western Carolina	28	913	196	405	.484	154	186	.828	133	43	619	4.8	1.5	22.1
02-03—Western Carolina	24	759	161	380	.424	174	197	.883	91	43	546	3.8	1.8	22.8
03-04—Western Carolina	27	843	208	439	.474	206	252	.817	130	47	673	4.8	1.7	24.9
Totals	79	2515	565	1224	.462	534	635	.841	354	133	1838	4.5	1.7	23.3

Three-point field goals: 2001-02, 73-for-191 (.382). 2002-03, 50-for-160 (.313). 2003-04, 51-for-152 (.336). Totals, 174-for-503 (.346).

NBA REGULAR-SEASON RECORD

Season Team	G	Min.	FGM	FGA	Pct.	FTM	FTA	Pct.	Off.	Def.	Tot.	Ast.	St.	Blk.	TO	Pts.	RPG	APG	PPG
04-05—Sacramento	45	455	45	117	.385	36	55	.655	29	29	58	22	16	3	24	131	1.3	0.5	2.9
05-06—Sacramento	72	1913	262	546	.480	188	222	.847	58	203	261	97	55	9	81	778	3.6	1.3	10.8
Totals	117	2368	307	663	.463	224	277	.809	87	232	319	119	71	12	105	909	2.7	1.0	7.8

Three-point field goals: 2004-05, 5-for-25 (.200). 2005-06, 66-for-179 (.369). Totals, 71-for-204 (.348).

Personal fouls/disqualifications: 2004-05, 35/0. 2005-06, 138/0. Totals, 173/0.

NBA PLAYOFF RECORD

Season Team	G	Min.	FGM	FGA	Pct.	FTM	FTA	Pct.	Off.	Def.	Tot.	Ast.	St.	Blk.	TO	Pts.	RPG	APG	PPG
05-06—Sacramento	6	197	22	54	.407	29	29	1.000	10	20	30	3	3	2	2	79	5.0	0.5	13.2

Three-point field goals: 2005-06, 6-for-19 (.316). Totals, 6-for-19 (.316).

Personal fouls/disqualifications: 2005-06, 11/0. Totals, 11/0.

MASON, DESMOND   G   HORNETS

PERSONAL: Born October 11, 1977, in Waxahachie, Texas. ... 6-5/222. (1.96/100.7). ... Full name: Desmond Tremaine Mason
HIGH SCHOOL: Waxahachie (Texas).
COLLEGE: Oklahoma State.
TRANSACTIONS/CAREER NOTES: Selected by Seattle SuperSonics in first round (17th pick overall) of 2000 NBA Draft. ... Traded by SuperSonics with G Gary Payton to Milwaukee Bucks for G Ray Allen, G Kevin Ollie, G Ronald Murray and conditional first-round draft choice (February 20, 2003). ... Traded by Bucks with a first-round draft pick to New Orleans Hornets for F/C Jamaal Magloire (October 26, 2005).

COLLEGIATE RECORD

Season Team	G	Min.	FGM	FGA	Pct.	FTM	FTA	Pct.	Reb.	Ast.	Pts.	RPG	APG	PPG
96-97—Oklahoma State	32	539	52	138	.377	23	37	.622	80	22	144	2.5	0.7	4.5
97-98—Oklahoma State	29	947	157	299	.525	86	126	.683	223	45	422	7.7	1.6	14.6
98-99—Oklahoma State	34	1180	196	408	.480	106	142	.746	267	28	525	7.9	0.8	15.4
99-00—Oklahoma State	34	1202	211	423	.499	125	163	.767	225	52	611	6.6	1.5	18.0
Totals	129	3868	616	1268	.486	340	468	.726	795	147	1702	6.2	1.1	13.2

Three-point field goals: 1996-97, 17-for-52 (.327). 1997-98, 22-for-69 (.319). 1998-99, 27-for-79 (.342). 1999-00, 64-for-149 (.430). Totals, 130-for-349 (.372).

NBA REGULAR-SEASON RECORD

HONORS: Slam Dunk championship winner (2001). ... NBA All-Rookie second team (2001).

Season Team	G	Min.	FGM	FGA	Pct.	FTM	FTA	Pct.	Off.	Def.	Tot.	Ast.	St.	Blk.	TO	Pts.	RPG	APG	PPG
00-01—Seattle	78	1522	189	439	.431	67	91	.736	72	177	249	63	39	20	53	463	3.2	0.8	5.9
01-02—Seattle	75	2420	357	769	.464	201	237	.848	92	259	351	104	67	27	104	931	4.7	1.4	12.4
02-03—Seattle-Mil.	80	2763	457	1017	.449	212	283	.749	154	369	523	163	67	32	115	1147	6.5	2.0	14.3
03-04—Milwaukee	82	2534	409	867	.472	356	463	.769	93	266	359	152	60	24	148	1183	4.4	1.9	14.4
04-05—Milwaukee	80	2893	478	1079	.443	420	524	.802	85	227	312	217	58	27	164	1377	3.9	2.7	17.2
05-06—NO/Okla. City	70	2102	275	690	.399	206	302	.682	64	234	298	66	42	17	113	757	4.3	0.9	10.8
Totals	465	14234	2165	4861	.445	1462	1900	.769	560	1532	2092	765	333	147	697	5858	4.5	1.6	12.6

Three-point field goals: 2000-01, 18-for-67 (.269). 2001-02, 16-for-59 (.271). 2002-03, 21-for-72 (.292). 2003-04, 9-for-39 (.231). 2004-05, 1-for-8 (.125). 2005-06, 1-for-6 (.167). Totals, 66-for-251 (.263).
Personal fouls/disqualifications: 2000-01, 146/0. 2001-02, 170/0. 2002-03, 210/1. 2003-04, 191/2. 2004-05, 198/1. 2005-06, 136/1. Totals, 1051/5.

NBA PLAYOFF RECORD

Season Team	G	Min.	FGM	FGA	Pct.	FTM	FTA	Pct.	Off.	Def.	Tot.	Ast.	St.	Blk.	TO	Pts.	RPG	APG	PPG
01-02—Seattle	5	205	24	57	.421	10	17	.588	5	26	31	9	4	2	5	59	6.2	1.8	11.8
02-03—Milwaukee	6	204	28	55	.509	22	31	.710	6	36	42	5	6	4	7	78	7.0	0.8	13.0
03-04—Milwaukee	5	198	25	74	.338	22	26	.846	4	20	24	12	4	2	12	72	4.8	2.4	14.4
Totals	16	607	77	186	.414	54	74	.730	15	82	97	26	14	8	24	209	6.1	1.6	13.1

Three-point field goals: 2001-02, 1-for-3 (.333). 2002-03, 0-for-4. 2003-04, 0-for-2. Totals, 1-for-9 (.111).
Personal fouls/disqualifications: 2001-02, 11/0. 2002-03, 19/1. 2003-04, 16/0. Totals, 46/1.

M

MAXIELL, JASON   F   PISTONS

PERSONAL: Born February 18, 1983, in Chicago, Ill. ... 6-7/260. (2.01/117.9). ... Full name: Jason Dior Maxiell
HIGH SCHOOL: Newman Smith (Carrollton, Texas).
COLLEGE: Cincinnati.
TRANSACTIONS/CAREER NOTES: Selected by Detroit Pistons in first round (26th pick overall) of 2005 NBA Draft.

COLLEGIATE RECORD

Season Team	G	Min.	FGM	FGA	Pct.	FTM	FTA	Pct.	Reb.	Ast.	Pts.	RPG	APG	PPG
01-02—Cincinnati	35	732	117	212	.552	48	82	.585	237	3	282	6.8	0.1	8.1
02-03—Cincinnati	29	879	129	290	.445	86	128	.672	195	13	344	6.7	0.4	11.9
03-04—Cincinnati	32	915	152	304	.500	130	191	.681	222	43	434	6.9	1.3	13.6
04-05—Cincinnati	33	1037	164	302	.543	176	273	.645	254	28	506	7.7	0.8	15.3
Totals	129	3563	562	1108	.507	440	674	.653	908	87	1566	7.0	0.7	12.1

Three-point field goals: 2002-03, 0-for-1. 2003-04, 0-for-1. 2004-05, 2-for-5 (.400). Totals, 2-for-7 (.286).

NBA REGULAR-SEASON RECORD

Season Team	G	Min.	FGM	FGA	Pct.	FTM	FTA	Pct.	Off.	Def.	Tot.	Ast.	St.	Blk.	TO	Pts.	RPG	APG	PPG
05-06—Detroit	26	159	23	54	.426	14	42	.333	12	16	28	3	4	5	11	60	1.1	0.1	2.3

Personal fouls/disqualifications: 2005-06, 14/0. Totals, 14/0.

MAY, SEAN   F   BOBCATS

PERSONAL: Born April 4, 1984, in Chicago, Ill. ... 6-9/266. (2.06/120.7). ... Full name: Sean Gregory May
HIGH SCHOOL: Bloomington North (Ill.).
COLLEGE: North Carolina.
TRANSACTIONS/CAREER NOTES: Selected after junior season by Charlotte Bobcats in first round (13th pick overall) of 2005 NBA Draft.

COLLEGIATE RECORD

NOTES: Member of NCAA Division I championship team (2005). ... NCAA Division I Tournament Most Outstanding Player (2005). ... The SPORTING NEWS All-America second team (2005).

Season Team	G	Min.	FGM	FGA	Pct.	FTM	FTA	Pct.	Reb.	Ast.	Pts.	AVERAGES		
												RPG	APG	PPG
02-03—North Carolina	11	308	51	108	.472	23	40	.575	89	11	125	8.1	1.0	11.4
03-04—North Carolina	29	839	163	352	.463	115	167	.689	285	40	441	9.8	1.4	15.2
04-05—North Carolina	37	992	228	402	.567	191	252	.758	397	62	647	10.7	1.7	17.5
Totals	77	2139	442	862	.513	329	459	.717	771	113	1213	10.0	1.5	15.8

Three-point field goals: 2002-03, 0-for-4. 2003-04, 0-for-4. 2004-05, 0-for-3. Totals, 0-for-11 (.000).

NBA REGULAR-SEASON RECORD

Season Team	G	Min.	FGM	FGA	Pct.	FTM	FTA	Pct.	REBOUNDS			Ast.	St.	Blk.	TO	Pts.	AVERAGES		
									Off.	Def.	Tot.						RPG	APG	PPG
05-06—Charlotte	23	398	70	171	.409	49	64	.766	42	67	109	22	17	12	33	189	4.7	1.0	8.2

Three-point field goals: 2005-06, 0-for-5. Totals, 0-for-5 (.000).
Personal fouls/disqualifications: 2005-06, 58/0. Totals, 58/0.

MBENGA, D.J.   C   MAVERICKS

PERSONAL: Born December 30, 1980, in Kinshasa, Congo. ... 7-0/245. (2.13/111.1).
TRANSACTIONS/CAREER NOTES: Not drafted by an NBA franchise. ... Played in Belgium (2002-04). ... Signed as free agent by Dallas Mavericks (September 14, 2004).

BELGIAN LEAGUE RECORD

Season Team	G	Min.	FGM	FGA	Pct.	FTM	FTA	Pct.	Reb.	Ast.	Pts.	AVERAGES		
												RPG	APG	PPG
02-03—Spirou Charleroi	21	...	77	157	.490	16	33	.485	171	12	170	8.1	0.6	8.1
03-04—Spirou Charleroi	34	490	88	161	.547	35	50	.700	149	14	211	4.4	0.4	6.2
Totals	55	490	165	318	.519	51	83	.614	320	26	381	5.8	0.5	6.9

NBA REGULAR-SEASON RECORD

Season Team	G	Min.	FGM	FGA	Pct.	FTM	FTA	Pct.	REBOUNDS			Ast.	St.	Blk.	TO	Pts.	AVERAGES		
									Off.	Def.	Tot.						RPG	APG	PPG
04-05—Dallas	15	58	6	14	.429	3	4	.750	3	5	8	0	0	5	5	15	0.5	0.0	1.0
05-06—Dallas	43	237	32	60	.533	10	20	.500	19	37	56	2	6	25	16	74	1.3	0.0	1.7
Totals	58	295	38	74	.514	13	24	.542	22	42	64	2	6	30	21	89	1.1	0.0	1.5

Three-point field goals: 2005-06, 0-for-1. Totals, 0-for-1 (.000).
Personal fouls/disqualifications: 2004-05, 13/0. 2005-06, 47/0. Totals, 60/0.

NBA PLAYOFF RECORD

Season Team	G	Min.	FGM	FGA	Pct.	FTM	FTA	Pct.	REBOUNDS			Ast.	St.	Blk.	TO	Pts.	AVERAGES		
									Off.	Def.	Tot.						RPG	APG	PPG
05-06—Dallas	9	28	1	3	.333	2	2	1.000	1	7	8	0	0	1	3	4	1.1	0.0	0.6

Personal fouls/disqualifications: 2005-06, 9/0. Totals, 9/0.

MCCANTS, RASHAD   G   TIMBERWOLVES

PERSONAL: Born September 25, 1984, in Asheville, N.C. ... 6-4/207. (1.93/93.9). ... Full name: Rashad Dion McCants
HIGH SCHOOL: Erwin (Ashville, N.C.), then New Hampton Prep (N.H.)
COLLEGE: North Carolina.
TRANSACTIONS/CAREER NOTES: Selected after junior season by Minnesota Timberwolves in first round (14th pick overall) of 2005 NBA draft.

COLLEGIATE RECORD

NOTES: Member of NCAA Division I championship team (2005). ... The SPORTING NEWS All-America third team (2004).

Season Team	G	Min.	FGM	FGA	Pct.	FTM	FTA	Pct.	Reb.	Ast.	Pts.	AVERAGES		
												RPG	APG	PPG
02-03—North Carolina	35	1046	215	438	.491	92	132	.697	162	51	594	4.6	1.5	17.0
03-04—North Carolina	30	961	216	451	.479	89	119	.748	137	65	599	4.6	2.2	20.0
04-05—North Carolina	33	856	183	374	.489	91	126	.722	99	88	528	3.0	2.7	16.0
Totals	98	2863	614	1263	.486	272	377	.721	398	204	1721	4.1	2.1	17.6

Three-point field goals: 2002-03, 72-for-174 (.414). 2003-04, 78-for-191 (.408). 2004-05, 71-for-168 (.423). Totals, 221-for-533 (.415).

NBA REGULAR-SEASON RECORD

Season Team	G	Min.	FGM	FGA	Pct.	FTM	FTA	Pct.	REBOUNDS			Ast.	St.	Blk.	TO	Pts.	AVERAGES		
									Off.	Def.	Tot.						RPG	APG	PPG
05-06—Minnesota	79	1362	241	535	.450	78	106	.736	29	114	143	63	44	22	86	627	1.8	0.8	7.9

Three-point field goals: 2005-06, 67-for-180 (.372). Totals, 67-for-180 (.372).
Personal fouls/disqualifications: 2005-06, 176/1. Totals, 176/1.

MCCARTY, WALTER   F   CLIPPERS

PERSONAL: Born February 1, 1974, in Evansville, Ind. ... 6-10/230. (2.08/104.3). ... Full name: Walter Lee McCarty
HIGH SCHOOL: Harrison (Evansville, Ind.).
COLLEGE: Kentucky.
TRANSACTIONS/CAREER NOTES: Selected by New York Knicks in first round (19th pick overall) of 1996 NBA Draft. ... Traded by Knicks with F Dontae' Jones, F John Thomas, G Scott Brooks and two future second-round draft choices to

Boston Celtics for F Chris Mills (October 22, 1997). ... Traded by Celtics to Phoenix Suns for second-round pick in 2005 draft (February 8, 2005). ... Signed as free agent by Los Angeles Clippers (September 29, 2005).

COLLEGIATE RECORD

NOTES: Member of NCAA Division I championship team (1996).

Season Team	G	Min.	FGM	FGA	Pct.	FTM	FTA	Pct.	Reb.	Ast.	Pts.	RPG	APG	PPG
92-93—Kentucky						Did not play—ineligible.								
93-94—Kentucky	34	484	72	153	.471	31	56	.554	131	39	194	3.9	1.1	5.7
94-95—Kentucky	33	744	128	251	.510	61	84	.726	185	50	345	5.6	1.5	10.5
95-96—Kentucky	36	888	152	280	.543	75	104	.721	206	92	407	5.7	2.6	11.3
Totals	103	2116	352	684	.515	167	244	.684	522	181	946	5.1	1.8	9.2

Three-point field goals: 1993-94, 19-for-50 (.380). 1994-95, 28-for-77 (.364). 1995-96, 28-for-60 (.467). Totals, 75-for-187 (.401).

NBA REGULAR-SEASON RECORD

Season Team	G	Min.	FGM	FGA	Pct.	FTM	FTA	Pct.	Off.	Def.	Tot.	Ast.	St.	Blk.	TO	Pts.	RPG	APG	PPG
96-97—New York	35	192	26	68	.382	8	14	.571	8	15	23	13	7	9	17	64	0.7	0.4	1.8
97-98—Boston	82	2340	295	730	.404	144	194	.742	141	223	364	177	110	44	141	788	4.4	2.2	9.6
98-99—Boston	32	659	64	177	.362	40	57	.702	36	79	115	40	24	13	40	181	3.6	1.3	5.7
99-00—Boston	61	879	78	230	.339	39	54	.722	33	77	110	70	24	23	67	229	1.8	1.1	3.8
00-01—Boston	60	478	45	126	.357	22	28	.786	24	57	81	39	14	7	20	131	1.4	0.7	2.2
01-02—Boston	56	718	80	180	.444	13	19	.684	32	96	128	41	18	7	22	212	2.3	0.7	3.8
02-03—Boston	82	1949	173	418	.414	61	98	.622	64	224	288	106	78	28	67	498	3.5	1.3	6.1
03-04—Boston	77	1900	203	523	.388	62	82	.756	28	211	239	124	72	22	91	605	3.1	1.6	7.9
04-05—Bos.-Phoenix	72	906	95	235	.404	15	29	.517	29	109	138	37	25	15	36	260	1.9	0.5	3.6
05-06—L.A. Clippers	36	353	33	99	.333	12	21	.571	15	53	68	23	8	5	19	88	1.9	0.6	2.4
Totals	593	10374	1092	2786	.392	416	596	.698	410	1144	1554	670	380	173	520	3056	2.6	1.1	5.2

Three-point field goals: 1996-97, 4-for-14 (.286). 1997-98, 54-for-175 (.309). 1998-99, 13-for-50 (.260). 1999-00, 34-for-110 (.309). 2000-01, 19-for-56 (.339). 2001-02, 39-for-99 (.394). 2002-03, 91-for-248 (.367). 2003-04, 137-for-366 (.374). 2004-05, 55-for-155 (.355). 2005-06, 10-for-45 (.222). Totals, 456-for-1318 (.346).

Personal fouls/disqualifications: 1996-97, 38/0. 1997-98, 274/6. 1998-99, 88/0. 1999-00, 83/1. 2000-01, 82/0. 2001-02, 83/0. 2002-03, 188/1. 2003-04, 179/1. 2004-05, 144/1. 2005-06, 52/0. Totals, 1211/10.

NBA PLAYOFF RECORD

Season Team	G	Min.	FGM	FGA	Pct.	FTM	FTA	Pct.	Off.	Def.	Tot.	Ast.	St.	Blk.	TO	Pts.	RPG	APG	PPG
96-97—New York	2	4	2	2	1.000	0	0	...	0	0	0	0	1	0	0	4	0.0	0.0	2.0
01-02—Boston	14	194	17	38	.447	7	9	.778	8	26	34	4	4	0	4	44	2.4	0.3	3.1
02-03—Boston	10	352	36	75	.480	6	7	.857	10	33	43	22	8	5	11	99	4.3	2.2	9.9
03-04—Boston	4	127	11	23	.478	0	0	...	3	18	21	8	2	2	4	28	5.3	2.0	7.0
04-05—Phoenix	8	55	2	9	.222	0	2	.000	0	6	6	3	2	2	1	6	0.8	0.4	0.8
05-06—L.A. Clippers	8	10	1	4	.250	0	0	...	0	1	1	0	0	0	0	2	0.1	0.0	0.3
Totals	46	742	69	151	.457	13	18	.722	21	84	105	37	17	9	20	183	2.3	0.8	4.0

Three-point field goals: 2001-02, 3-for-18 (.167). 2002-03, 21-for-52 (.404). 2003-04, 6-for-15 (.400). 2004-05, 2-for-6 (.333). 2005-06, 0-for-1. Totals, 32-for-92 (.348).

Personal fouls/disqualifications: 2001-02, 19/0. 2002-03, 35/0. 2003-04, 7/0. 2004-05, 13/0. 2005-06, 2/0. Totals, 76/0.

M

MCDYESS, ANTONIO   F   PISTONS

PERSONAL: Born September 7, 1974, in Quitman, Miss. ... 6-9/245. (2.06/111.1). ... Full name: Antonio Keithflen McDyess ... Name pronounced mick-DICE.

HIGH SCHOOL: Quitman (Miss.).

COLLEGE: Alabama.

TRANSACTIONS/CAREER NOTES: Selected after sophomore season by Los Angeles Clippers in first round (second pick overall) of 1995 NBA Draft. ... Draft rights traded by Clippers with G Randy Woods to Denver Nuggets for F Rodney Rogers and draft rights to G Brent Barry (June 28, 1995). ... Traded by Nuggets to Phoenix Suns for a minimum of three first-round draft choices and two second-round draft choices (October 1, 1997). ... Signed as free agent by Nuggets (January 22, 1999). ... Traded by Nuggets with draft rights to G Frank Williams and 2003 second-round draft choice to New York Knicks for F/C Marcus Camby, G Mark Jackson and draft rights to F/C Nene Hilario (June 26, 2002). ... Traded by Knicks with G Howard Eisley, F Maciej Lampe, G Charlie Ward, draft rights to G Milos Vujanic, 2004 first-round draft choice and future first-round draft choice to Phoenix Suns for G Stephon Marbury, F/G Anfernee Hardaway and C Cezary Trybanski (January 5, 2004). ... Signed as free agent by Detroit Pistons (July 16, 2004).

MISCELLANEOUS: Member of gold-medal-winning U.S. Olympic team (2000).

COLLEGIATE RECORD

Season Team	G	Min.	FGM	FGA	Pct.	FTM	FTA	Pct.	Reb.	Ast.	Pts.	RPG	APG	PPG
93-94—Alabama	26	618	132	234	.564	32	60	.533	210	11	296	8.1	0.4	11.4
94-95—Alabama	33	861	185	361	.512	88	132	.667	337	21	458	10.2	0.6	13.9
Totals	59	1479	317	595	.533	120	192	.625	547	32	754	9.3	0.5	12.8

Three-point field goals: 1994-95, 0-for-1. Totals, 0-for-1 (.000).

NBA REGULAR-SEASON RECORD

HONORS: All-NBA Third Team (1999). ... NBA All-Rookie first team (1996).

Season Team	G	Min.	FGM	FGA	Pct.	FTM	FTA	Pct.	Off.	Def.	Tot.	Ast.	St.	Blk.	TO	Pts.	RPG	APG	PPG
95-96—Denver	76	2280	427	881	.485	166	243	.683	229	343	572	75	54	114	154	1020	7.5	1.0	13.4
96-97—Denver	74	2565	536	1157	.463	274	387	.708	155	382	537	106	62	126	199	1352	7.3	1.4	18.3
97-98—Phoenix	81	2441	497	927	.536	231	329	.702	206	407	613	106	100	135	142	1225	7.6	1.3	15.1
98-99—Denver	50	1937	415	882	.471	230	338	.680	168	369	537	82	73	115	138	1061	10.7	1.6	21.2

Season Team	G	Min.	FGM	FGA	Pct.	FTM	FTA	Pct.	Off.	Def.	Tot.	Ast.	St.	Blk.	TO	Pts.	RPG	APG	PPG
99-00—Denver	81	2698	614	1211	.507	323	516	.626	234	451	685	159	69	139	230	1551	8.5	2.0	19.1
00-01—Denver	70	2555	577	1165	.495	304	434	.700	240	605	845	146	43	102	162	1458	12.1	2.1	20.8
01-02—Denver	10	236	43	75	.573	27	33	.818	18	37	55	18	10	8	20	113	5.5	1.8	11.3
02-03—New York								Did not play—injured											
03-04—New York-Pho.	42	927	126	268	.470	38	69	.551	70	187	257	36	37	24	57	290	6.1	0.9	6.9
04-05—Detroit	77	1797	307	598	.513	126	192	.656	177	305	482	71	46	52	93	740	6.3	0.9	9.6
05-06—Detroit	82	1733	285	560	.509	68	122	.557	156	280	436	90	46	48	76	638	5.3	1.1	7.8
Totals	643	19169	3827	7724	.495	1787	2663	.671	1653	3366	5019	889	540	863	1271	9448	7.8	1.4	14.7

Three-point field goals: 1995-96, 0-for-4. 1996-97, 6-for-35 (.171). 1997-98, 0-for-2. 1998-99, 1-for-9 (.111). 1999-00, 0-for-2. 2004-05, 0-for-1. 2005-06, 0-for-1. Totals, 7-for-55 (.127).

Personal fouls/disqualifications: 1995-96, 250/4. 1996-97, 276/9. 1997-98, 292/6. 1998-99, 175/5. 1999-00, 316/12. 2000-01, 220/2. 2001-02, 20/0. 2003-04, 117/5. 2004-05, 204/3. 2005-06, 220/0. Totals, 2090/46.

NBA PLAYOFF RECORD

									REBOUNDS								AVERAGES		
Season Team	G	Min.	FGM	FGA	Pct.	FTM	FTA	Pct.	Off.	Def.	Tot.	Ast.	St.	Blk.	TO	Pts.	RPG	APG	PPG
97-98—Phoenix	4	147	31	65	.477	9	14	.643	18	35	53	4	2	6	5	71	13.3	1.0	17.8
04-05—Detroit	25	494	88	181	.486	25	36	.694	46	101	147	19	14	23	25	201	5.9	0.8	8.0
05-06—Detroit	18	370	57	102	.559	23	42	.548	39	70	109	11	8	13	14	137	6.1	0.6	7.6
Totals	47	1011	176	348	.506	57	92	.620	103	206	309	34	24	42	44	409	6.6	0.7	8.7

Three-point field goals: 2005-06, 0-for-1. Totals, 0-for-1 (.000).
Personal fouls/disqualifications: 1997-98, 12/0. 2004-05, 78/0. 2005-06, 54/0. Totals, 144/0.

NBA ALL-STAR GAME RECORD

								REBOUNDS								
Season Team	Min.	FGM	FGA	Pct.	FTM	FTA	Pct.	Off.	Def.	Tot.	Ast.	PF	Dq.	St.	Blk.	TO	Pts.
2001—Denver	15	4	9	.444	0	0	...	3	5	8	2	2	0	1	0	0	8

MCGRADY, TRACY   G   ROCKETS

PERSONAL: Born May 24, 1979, in Bartow, Fla. ... 6-8/210. (2.03/95.3). ... Full name: Tracy Lamar McGrady.
HIGH SCHOOL: Auburndale (Tampa, Fla.), then Mount Zion Christian Academy (N.C.).
COLLEGE: Did not attend college.
TRANSACTIONS/CAREER NOTES: Selected out of high school by Toronto Raptors in first round (ninth pick overall) of 1997 NBA Draft. ... Traded by Raptors to Orlando Magic for future first-round draft choice (August 3, 2000). ... Traded by Magic with F Juwan Howard, G Tyronn Lue and G Reece Gaines to Houston Rockets for G Steve Francis, G Cuttino Mobley and C Kelvin Cato (June 29, 2004).

NBA REGULAR-SEASON RECORD

HONORS: NBA Most Improved Player award (2001). ... All-NBA first team (2002, 2003). ... All-NBA second team (2001, 2004). ... All-NBA third team (2005).

									REBOUNDS								AVERAGES		
Season Team	G	Min.	FGM	FGA	Pct.	FTM	FTA	Pct.	Off.	Def.	Tot.	Ast.	St.	Blk.	TO	Pts.	RPG	APG	PPG
97-98—Toronto	64	1179	179	398	.450	79	111	.712	105	164	269	98	49	61	66	451	4.2	1.5	7.0
98-99—Toronto	49	1106	168	385	.436	114	157	.726	120	158	278	113	52	66	80	458	5.7	2.3	9.3
99-00—Toronto	79	2462	459	1018	.451	277	392	.707	188	313	501	263	90	151	160	1213	6.3	3.3	15.4
00-01—Orlando	77	3087	788	1724	.457	430	587	.733	192	388	580	352	116	118	198	2065	7.5	4.6	26.8
01-02—Orlando	76	2912	715	1586	.451	415	555	.748	150	447	597	400	119	73	189	1948	7.9	5.3	25.6
02-03—Orlando	75	2954	829	1813	.457	576	726	.793	121	367	488	411	124	59	195	2407	6.5	5.5	*32.1
03-04—Orlando	67	2675	653	1566	.417	398	500	.796	95	307	402	370	93	42	179	1878	6.0	5.5	*28.0
04-05—Houston	78	3182	715	1660	.431	431	557	.774	71	413	484	448	135	52	201	2003	6.2	5.7	25.7
05-06—Houston	47	1745	410	1011	.406	254	340	.747	46	261	307	225	59	41	120	1147	6.5	4.8	24.4
Totals	612	21302	4916	11161	.440	2974	3925	.758	1088	2818	3906	2680	837	663	1388	13570	6.4	4.4	22.2

Three-point field goals: 1997-98, 14-for-41 (.341). 1998-99, 8-for-35 (.229). 1999-00, 18-for-65 (.277). 2000-01, 59-for-166 (.355). 2001-02, 103-for-283 (.364). 2002-03, 173-for-448 (.386). 2003-04, 174-for-513 (.339). 2004-05, 142-for-435 (.326). 2005-06, 73-for-234 (.312). Totals, 764-for-2220 (.344).

Personal fouls/disqualifications: 1997-98, 86/0. 1998-99, 94/1. 1999-00, 201/2. 2000-01, 160/0. 2001-02, 139/1. 2002-03, 156/0. 2003-04, 129/1. 2004-05, 167/0. 2005-06, 88/0. Totals, 1220/5.

NBA PLAYOFF RECORD

									REBOUNDS								AVERAGES		
Season Team	G	Min.	FGM	FGA	Pct.	FTM	FTA	Pct.	Off.	Def.	Tot.	Ast.	St.	Blk.	TO	Pts.	RPG	APG	PPG
99-00—Toronto	3	111	17	44	.386	14	16	.875	10	11	21	9	3	3	10	50	7.0	3.0	16.7
00-01—Orlando	4	178	51	123	.415	31	38	.816	6	20	26	33	7	5	8	135	6.5	8.3	33.8
01-02—Orlando	4	178	42	91	.462	34	46	.739	6	19	25	22	2	7	13	123	6.3	5.5	30.8
02-03—Orlando	7	308	74	165	.448	58	75	.773	10	37	47	33	14	6	26	222	6.7	4.7	31.7
04-05—Houston	7	301	78	171	.456	42	51	.824	12	40	52	47	11	10	26	215	7.4	6.7	30.7
Totals	25	1076	262	594	.441	179	226	.792	44	127	171	144	37	31	83	745	6.8	5.8	29.8

Three-point field goals: 1999-00, 2-for-7 (.286). 2000-01, 2-for-10 (.200). 2001-02, 5-for-16 (.313). 2002-03, 16-for-47 (.340). 2004-05, 17-for-46 (.370). Totals, 42-for-126 (.333).

Personal fouls/disqualifications: 1999-00, 10/0. 2000-01, 11/0. 2001-02, 11/0. 2002-03, 16/0. 2004-05, 20/0. Totals, 68/0.

NBA ALL-STAR GAME RECORD

								REBOUNDS								
Season Team	Min.	FGM	FGA	Pct.	FTM	FTA	Pct.	Off.	Def.	Tot.	Ast.	PF	Dq.	St.	Blk.	TO	Pts.
2001—Orlando	21	1	4	.250	0	0	...	1	0	1	0	0	0	2	1	4	2
2002—Orlando	23	9	15	.600	4	4	1.000	2	1	3	4	1	0	3	0	1	24
2003—Orlando	36	10	17	.588	5	6	.833	1	4	5	2	3	0	0	0	1	29
2004—Orlando	23	5	11	.455	2	4	.500	1	3	4	3	0	0	0	0	1	13
2005—Houston	24	4	13	.308	0	0	...	1	4	5	1	0	0	3	2	3	8
2006—Houston	27	15	26	.577	2	7	.286	0	0	0	2	1	0	1	0	1	36
Totals	154	44	86	.512	13	21	.619	6	12	18	16	6	0	9	3	11	112

Three-point field goals: 2001, 0-for-1. 2002, 2-for-4 (.500). 2003, 4-for-7 (.571). 2004, 1-for-6 (.167). 2005, 0-for-4. 2006, 4-for-10 (.400). Totals, 11-for-32 (.344).

MCINNIS, JEFF G NETS

PERSONAL: Born October 22, 1974, in Charlotte. ... 6-4/190. (1.93/86.2). ... Full name: Jeff Lemans McInnis
HIGH SCHOOL: West Charlotte (Charlotte), then Oak Hill Academy (Mouth of Wilson, Va.).
COLLEGE: North Carolina.
TRANSACTIONS/CAREER NOTES: Selected after junior season by Denver Nuggets in second round (37th pick overall) of 1996 NBA Draft. ... Waived by Nuggets (December 12, 1996). ... Played in Greece (1996-97). ... Played in Continental Basketball Association with Quad City Thunder (1997-98 through 1999-2000). ... Signed as free agent by Washington Wizards (January 21, 1999). ... Traded by Wizards with F/C Terry Davis, F Ben Wallace and G Tim Legler to Orlando Magic for C Isaac Austin (August 11, 1999). ... Waived by Magic (September 16, 1999). ... Signed by Los Angeles Clippers to first of two consecutive 10-day contracts (February 26, 2000). ... Re-signed by Clippers for remainder of season (March 16, 2000). ... Signed as free agent by Portland Trail Blazers (August 12, 2002). ... Traded by Trail Blazers with C Ruben Boumtje-Boumtje to Cleveland Cavaliers for F Darius Miles (January 21, 2004). ... Signed as free agent by New Jersey Nets (August 11, 2005).

COLLEGIATE RECORD

												AVERAGES		
Season Team	G	Min.	FGM	FGA	Pct.	FTM	FTA	Pct.	Reb.	Ast.	Pts.	RPG	APG	PPG
93-94—North Carolina	35	512	70	153	.458	30	47	.638	58	85	197	1.7	2.4	5.6
94-95—North Carolina	34	981	155	316	.491	66	99	.667	138	180	420	4.1	5.3	12.4
95-96—North Carolina	31	1067	178	409	.435	88	110	.800	81	170	511	2.6	5.5	16.5
Totals	100	2560	403	878	.459	184	256	.719	277	435	1128	2.8	4.4	11.3

Three-point field goals: 1993-94, 27-for-65 (.415). 1994-95, 44-for-112 (.393). 1995-96, 67-for-171 (.392). Totals, 138-for-348 (.397).

GREEK LEAGUE RECORD

												AVERAGES		
Season Team	G	Min.	FGM	FGA	Pct.	FTM	FTA	Pct.	Reb.	Ast.	Pts.	RPG	APG	PPG
96-97—Panionios	6	227	46	121	.380	19	25	.760	19	22	123	3.2	3.7	20.5

Three-point field goals: 1996-97, 12-for-44 (.273). Totals, 12-for-44 (.273).

NBA REGULAR-SEASON RECORD

									REBOUNDS								AVERAGES		
Season Team	G	Min.	FGM	FGA	Pct.	FTM	FTA	Pct.	Off.	Def.	Tot.	Ast.	St.	Blk.	TO	Pts.	RPG	APG	PPG
96-97—Denver	13	117	23	49	.469	7	10	.700	2	4	6	18	2	1	13	65	0.5	1.4	5.0
98-99—Washington	35	427	50	134	.373	21	28	.750	9	12	21	73	19	1	30	130	0.6	2.1	3.7
99-00—L.A. Clippers	25	597	80	186	.430	13	17	.765	18	54	72	89	15	2	27	180	2.9	3.6	7.2
00-01—L.A. Clippers	81	2831	432	933	.463	130	161	.807	41	179	220	447	75	7	113	1046	2.7	5.5	12.9
01-02—L.A. Clippers	81	3030	463	1121	.413	183	219	.836	45	168	213	500	63	6	147	1184	2.6	6.2	14.6
02-03—Portland	75	1311	188	423	.444	50	67	.746	22	75	97	170	21	2	75	432	1.3	2.3	5.8
03-04—Port.-Cleve.	70	2365	334	747	.447	114	143	.797	33	143	176	430	72	6	120	828	2.5	6.1	11.8
04-05—Cleveland	76	2651	377	915	.412	130	160	.813	32	125	157	391	56	1	117	975	2.1	5.1	12.8
05-06—New Jersey	28	486	63	143	.441	20	29	.690	11	39	50	52	11	2	29	149	1.8	1.9	5.3
Totals	484	13815	2010	4651	.432	668	834	.801	213	799	1012	2170	334	28	671	4989	2.1	4.5	10.3

Three-point field goals: 1996-97, 12-for-26 (.462). 1998-99, 9-for-35 (.257). 1999-00, 7-for-21 (.333). 2000-01, 52-for-144 (.361). 2001-02, 75-for-234 (.321). 2002-03, 6-for-35 (.171). 2003-04, 46-for-127 (.362). 2004-05, 91-for-264 (.345). 2005-06, 3-for-16 (.188). Totals, 301-for-902 (.334).
Personal fouls/disqualifications: 1996-97, 16/0. 1998-99, 36/0. 1999-00, 55/0. 2000-01, 19/2. 2001-02, 202/2. 2002-03, 117/1. 2003-04, 163/4. 2004-05, 177/1. 2005-06, 37/0. Totals, 1002/10.

NBA PLAYOFF RECORD

									REBOUNDS								AVERAGES		
Season Team	G	Min.	FGM	FGA	Pct.	FTM	FTA	Pct.	Off.	Def.	Tot.	Ast.	St.	Blk.	TO	Pts.	RPG	APG	PPG
02-03—Portland	7	99	9	26	.346	3	4	.750	5	7	12	19	2	1	6	21	1.7	2.7	3.0

Three-point field goals: 2002-03, 0-for-3. Totals, 0-for-3 (.000).
Personal fouls/disqualifications: 2002-03, 11/0. Totals, 11/0.

CBA RECORD

NOTES: Member of CBA championship team (1998). ... CBA Newcomer of the Year (1998). ... CBA All-League second team (1998). ... CBA All-Defensive team (1998). ... CBA Most Valuable Player (2000). ... CBA All-League first team (2000).

												AVERAGES		
Season Team	G	Min.	FGM	FGA	Pct.	FTM	FTA	Pct.	Reb.	Ast.	Pts.	RPG	APG	PPG
97-98—Quad City	56	1734	315	705	.447	168	206	.816	135	316	834	2.4	5.6	14.9
98-99—Quad City	21	825	175	348	.503	65	88	.739	54	119	442	2.6	5.7	21.0
99-00—Quad City	41	1629	316	719	.439	123	149	.826	136	*319	807	3.3	7.8	19.7
Totals	118	4188	806	1772	.455	356	443	.804	325	754	2083	2.8	6.4	17.7

Three-point field goals: 1997-98, 36-for-119 (.303). 1998-99, 27-for-77 (.351). 1999-00, 52-for-167 (.311). Totals, 115-for-363 (.317).
Personal fouls/disqualifications: 1997-98, 121/0. 1998-99, 57/0. 1999-00, 95/0. Totals, 273/0.

MCKIE, AARON G LAKERS

PERSONAL: Born October 2, 1972, in Philadelphia. ... 6-5/209. (1.96/94.8). ... Full name: Aaron Fitzgerald McKie ... Name pronounced mik-KEY.
HIGH SCHOOL: Simon Gratz (Philadelphia).
COLLEGE: Temple.
TRANSACTIONS/CAREER NOTES: Selected by Portland Trail Blazers in first round (17th pick overall) of 1994 NBA Draft. ... Traded by Trail Blazers with G Randolph Childress and G Reggie Jordan to Detroit Pistons for F Stacey Augmon (January 24, 1997). ... Traded by Pistons with C Theo Ratliff and conditional first-round draft choice to Philadelphia 76ers for G Jerry Stackhouse and C Eric Montross (December 18, 1997). ... Signed as free agent by Los Angeles Lakers (August 26, 2005).

M

COLLEGIATE RECORD

Season Team	G	Min.	FGM	FGA	Pct.	FTM	FTA	Pct.	Reb.	Ast.	Pts.	AVERAGES RPG	APG	PPG
90-91—Temple............................						Did not play—ineligible.								
91-92—Temple............................	28	1011	130	300	.433	86	114	.754	167	94	388	6.0	3.4	13.9
92-93—Temple............................	33	1272	240	555	.432	123	156	.788	195	109	680	5.9	3.3	20.6
93-94—Temple............................	31	1214	193	481	.401	137	168	.815	224	98	582	7.2	3.2	18.8
Totals	92	3497	563	1336	.421	346	438	.790	586	301	1650	6.4	3.3	17.9

Three-point field goals: 1991-92, 42-for-131 (.321). 1992-93, 77-for-196 (.393). 1993-94, 59-for-159 (.371). Totals, 178-for-486 (.366).

HONORS: NBA Sixth Man Award (2001).

NBA REGULAR-SEASON RECORD

Season Team	G	Min.	FGM	FGA	Pct.	FTM	FTA	Pct.	REBOUNDS Off.	Def.	Tot.	Ast.	St.	Blk.	TO	Pts.	AVERAGES RPG	APG	PPG
94-95—Portland..........	45	827	116	261	.444	50	73	.685	35	94	129	89	36	16	39	293	2.9	2.0	6.5
95-96—Portland..........	81	2259	337	722	.467	152	199	.764	86	218	304	205	92	21	135	864	3.8	2.5	10.7
96-97—Port.-Detroit ...	83	1625	150	365	.411	92	110	.836	40	181	221	161	77	22	90	433	2.7	1.9	5.2
97-98—Det.-Phila...	81	1813	139	381	.365	42	55	.764	58	173	231	175	101	13	76	332	2.9	2.2	4.1
98-99—Philadelphia	50	959	95	237	.401	44	62	.710	27	113	140	100	63	3	57	240	2.8	2.0	4.8
99-00—Philadelphia	82	1952	244	593	.411	121	146	.829	47	199	246	240	108	18	113	653	3.0	2.9	8.0
00-01—Philadelphia	76	2394	338	714	.473	149	194	.768	33	278	311	377	106	8	203	878	4.1	5.0	11.6
01-02—Philadelphia	48	1471	220	490	.449	96	122	.787	26	166	192	179	56	14	93	587	4.0	3.7	12.2
02-03—Philadelphia ...	80	2374	286	666	.429	112	134	.836	61	289	350	278	131	9	109	721	4.4	3.5	9.0
03-04—Philadelphia ...	75	2112	265	577	.459	84	111	.757	45	208	253	195	85	23	103	689	3.4	2.6	9.2
04-05—Philadelphia ...	68	1118	61	142	.430	10	16	.625	20	152	172	103	48	17	31	152	2.5	1.5	2.2
05-06—L.A. Lakers	14	121	3	12	.250	1	2	.500	3	17	20	11	5	0	2	7	1.4	0.8	0.5
Totals	783	19025	2254	5160	.437	953	1224	.779	481	2088	2569	2113	908	164	1051	5849	3.3	2.7	7.5

Three-point field goals: 1994-95, 11-for-28 (.393). 1995-96, 38-for-117 (.325). 1996-97, 41-for-103 (.398). 1997-98, 12-for-63 (.190). 1998-99, 6-for-31 (.194). 1999-00, 44-for-121 (.364). 2000-01, 53-for-170 (.312). 2001-02, 51-for-128 (.398). 2002-03, 37-for-112 (.330). 2003-04, 75-for-172 (.436). 2004-05, 20-for-62 (.323). 2005-06, 0-for-2. Totals, 388-for-1109 (.350).

Personal fouls/disqualifications: 1994-95, 97/1. 1995-96, 205/5. 1996-97, 130/1. 1997-98, 164/0. 1998-99, 90/1. 1999-00, 194/3. 2000-01, 178/3. 2001-02, 74/0. 2002-03, 177/2. 2003-04, 142/1. 2004-05, 116/2. 2005-06, 7/0. Totals, 1574/19.

NBA PLAYOFF RECORD

Season Team	G	Min.	FGM	FGA	Pct.	FTM	FTA	Pct.	REBOUNDS Off.	Def.	Tot.	Ast.	St.	Blk.	TO	Pts.	AVERAGES RPG	APG	PPG
94-95—Portland..........	3	34	8	14	.571	0	0	...	0	2	2	1	3	0	0	17	0.7	0.3	5.7
95-96—Portland..........	5	134	11	30	.367	7	9	.778	4	14	18	9	6	2	9	31	3.6	1.8	6.2
96-97—Detroit	5	97	7	20	.350	0	0	...	1	9	10	10	6	2	3	15	2.0	2.0	3.0
98-99—Philadelphia	6	97	7	23	.304	6	7	.857	4	11	15	11	4	0	1	20	2.5	1.8	3.3
99-00—Philadelphia	10	331	50	103	.485	26	31	.839	4	32	36	46	4	2	16	138	3.6	4.6	13.8
00-01—Philadelphia ...	23	892	125	301	.415	59	75	.787	24	95	119	121	34	3	46	336	5.2	5.3	14.6
01-02—Philadelphia ..	5	146	20	46	.435	7	10	.700	2	16	18	12	10	0	10	53	3.6	2.4	10.6
02-03—Philadelphia ..	12	315	38	71	.535	12	14	.857	5	38	43	22	10	2	15	93	3.6	1.8	7.8
04-05—Philadelphia ..	5	85	3	7	.429	0	0	...	1	11	12	5	4	0	7	7	2.4	1.0	1.4
05-06—L.A. Lakers	1	8	0	0	...	0	0	...	0	0	0	0	0	0	0	0	0.0	0.0	0.0
Totals	75	2139	269	615	.437	117	146	.801	45	228	273	237	81	11	101	710	3.6	3.2	9.5

Three-point field goals: 1994-95, 1-for-2 (.500). 1995-96, 2-for-8 (.250). 1996-97, 1-for-5 (.200). 1998-99, 0-for-1. 1999-00, 12-for-35 (.343). 2000-01, 27-for-64 (.422). 2001-02, 6-for-16 (.375). 2002-03, 5-for-9 (.556). 2004-05, 1-for-3 (.333). Totals, 55-for-143 (.385).

Personal fouls/disqualifications: 1994-95, 4/0. 1995-96, 13/0. 1996-97, 12/0. 1998-99, 17/0. 1999-00, 26/0. 2000-01, 67/0. 2001-02, 12/0. 2002-03, 31/0. 2004-05, 9/0. Totals, 191/0.

M

MCLEOD, KEITH G WARRIORS

PERSONAL: Born November 5, 1979, in Canton, Ohio. ... 6-2/190. (1.88/86.2).
HIGH SCHOOL: Canton McKinley (Canton, Ohio).
COLLEGE: Bowling Green.
TRANSACTIONS/CAREER NOTES: Not drafted by an NBA franchise. ... Played in Italy (2002-04). ... Signed as free agent by Minnesota Timberwolves (September 30, 2003). ... Waived by Timberwolves (October 21, 2003). ... Signed by Timberwolves (October 25, 2003). ... Waived by Timberwolves (January 7, 2004). ... Signed as free agent by Utah Jazz (2004). ... Traded by Jazz with Gs Devin Brown and Andre Owens to Golden State Warriors for G Derek Fisher (July 12, 2006).

COLLEGIATE RECORD

Season Team	G	Min.	FGM	FGA	Pct.	FTM	FTA	Pct.	Reb.	Ast.	Pts.	AVERAGES RPG	APG	PPG
98-99—Bowling Green State.......	20	596	84	213	.394	55	70	.786	57	47	247	2.9	2.4	12.4
99-00—Bowling Green State.......	30	927	115	269	.428	105	144	.729	65	77	386	2.2	2.6	12.9
00-01—Bowling Green State.......	28	936	149	365	.408	174	214	.813	96	82	507	3.4	2.9	18.1
01-02—Bowling Green State.......	33	1109	224	496	.452	218	270	.807	137	90	755	4.2	2.7	22.9
Totals	111	3568	572	1343	.426	552	698	.791	355	296	1895	3.2	2.7	17.1

Three-point field goals: 1998-99, 24-for-77 (.312). 1999-00, 51-for-107 (.477). 2000-01, 35-for-99 (.354). 2001-02, 89-for-216 (.412). Totals, 199-for-499 (.399).

ITALIAN LEAGUE RECORD

Season Team	G	Min.	FGM	FGA	Pct.	FTM	FTA	Pct.	Reb.	Ast.	Pts.	AVERAGES RPG	APG	PPG
02-03—Mabo...........................	31	876	126	296	.426	99	124	.798	61	57	389	2.0	1.8	12.5
03-04—Lottomatica RM..............	11	332	56	126	.444	28	41	.683	35	35	154	3.2	3.2	14.0
Totals	42	1208	182	422	.431	127	165	.770	96	92	543	2.3	2.2	12.9

Three-point field goals: 2002-03, 38-for-113 (.336). 2003-04, 14-for-54 (.259). Totals, 52-for-167 (.311).

NBA REGULAR-SEASON RECORD

								REBOUNDS								AVERAGES		
Season Team	G	Min.	FGM	FGA	Pct.	FTM	FTA	Pct.	Off.	Def.	Tot.	Ast.	St.	Blk.	TO	Pts.	RPG	APG	PPG
03-04—Minnesota.......	33	391	27	82	.329	33	43	.767	5	29	34	59	16	1	29	88	1.0	1.8	2.7
04-05—Utah..............	53	1382	143	408	.350	112	146	.767	20	93	113	236	63	12	99	416	2.1	4.5	7.8
05-06—Utah..............	66	1232	120	340	.353	106	133	.797	11	67	78	151	42	9	76	370	1.2	2.3	5.6
Totals	152	3005	290	830	.349	251	322	.780	36	189	225	446	121	22	204	874	1.5	2.9	5.8

Three-point field goals: 2003-04, 1-for-10 (.100). 2004-05, 18-for-72 (.250). 2005-06, 24-for-82 (.293). Totals, 43-for-164 (.262).
Personal fouls/disqualifications: 2003-04, 39/0. 2004-05, 138/0. 2005-06, 131/2. Totals, 308/2.

MEDVEDENKO, SLAVA   F

PERSONAL: Born April 4, 1979, in Ukraine. ... 6-10/250. (2.08/113.4).
TRANSACTIONS/CAREER NOTES: Not drafted by an NBA franchise. ... Played in Lithuania (1998-99). ... Played in Ukraine (1999-2000). ... Signed as free agent by Los Angeles Lakers (August 15, 2000). ... Waived by Lakers (March 6, 2006).
MISCELLANEOUS: Member of NBA championship team (2001, 2002).

LITHUANIAN LEAGUE RECORD

												AVERAGES		
Season Team	G	Min.	FGM	FGA	Pct.	FTM	FTA	Pct.	Reb.	Ast.	Pts.	RPG	APG	PPG
98-99—Alytus Alita	24	698	166	300	.553	75	97	.773	180	25	410	7.5	1.0	17.1

Three-point field goals: 1998-99, 3-for-8 (.375). Totals, 3-for-8 (.375).

UKRANIAN LEAGUE RECORD

												AVERAGES		
Season Team	G	Min.	FGM	FGA	Pct.	FTM	FTA	Pct.	Reb.	Ast.	Pts.	RPG	APG	PPG
99-00—Kyiv Kiev	19	554	169	337	.501	64	95	.674	143	21	405	7.5	1.1	21.3

Three-point field goals: 1999-00, 3-for-18 (.167). Totals, 3-for-18 (.167).

NBA REGULAR-SEASON RECORD

								REBOUNDS								AVERAGES		
Season Team	G	Min.	FGM	FGA	Pct.	FTM	FTA	Pct.	Off.	Def.	Tot.	Ast.	St.	Blk.	TO	Pts.	RPG	APG	PPG
00-01—L.A. Lakers	7	39	12	25	.480	7	12	.583	1	8	9	2	1	1	3	32	1.3	0.3	4.6
01-02—L.A. Lakers	71	729	145	304	.477	41	62	.661	85	73	158	43	29	11	42	331	2.2	0.6	4.7
02-03—L.A. Lakers	58	620	112	258	.434	31	43	.721	66	75	141	18	11	8	37	255	2.4	0.3	4.4
03-04—L.A. Lakers	68	1442	237	537	.441	89	116	.767	148	195	343	57	38	18	59	563	5.0	0.8	8.3
04-05—L.A. Lakers	43	423	71	156	.455	23	28	.821	31	48	79	13	9	2	13	165	1.8	0.3	3.8
05-06—L.A. Lakers	2	6	1	2	.500	0	0	...	0	0	0	1	0	0	0	2	0.0	0.5	1.0
Totals	249	3259	578	1282	.451	191	261	.732	331	399	730	134	88	40	154	1348	2.9	0.5	5.4

Three-point field goals: 2000-01, 1-for-1 (1.000). 2001-02, 0-for-4. 2002-03, 0-for-2. 2003-04, 0-for-3. 2004-05, 0-for-1. Totals, 1-for-11 (.091).
Personal fouls/disqualifications: 2000-01, 9/0. 2001-02, 119/0. 2002-03, 118/0. 2003-04, 191/1. 2004-05, 64/0. 2005-06, 1/0. Totals, 502/1.

NBA PLAYOFF RECORD

								REBOUNDS								AVERAGES		
Season Team	G	Min.	FGM	FGA	Pct.	FTM	FTA	Pct.	Off.	Def.	Tot.	Ast.	St.	Blk.	TO	Pts.	RPG	APG	PPG
01-02—L.A. Lakers	7	21	3	5	.600	0	0	...	1	3	4	0	0	0	1	6	0.6	0.0	0.9
02-03—L.A. Lakers	9	73	15	27	.556	4	6	.667	4	14	18	1	1	1	3	34	2.0	0.1	3.8
03-04—L.A. Lakers	21	237	33	75	.440	17	21	.810	23	30	53	10	4	4	5	83	2.5	0.5	4.0
Totals	37	331	51	107	.477	21	27	.778	28	47	75	11	5	5	9	123	2.0	0.3	3.3

Personal fouls/disqualifications: 2001-02, 8/0. 2002-03, 14/0. 2003-04, 50/0. Totals, 72/0.

MIHM, CHRIS   F/C   LAKERS

PERSONAL: Born July 16, 1979, in Milwaukee. ... 7-0/265. (2.13/120.2). ... Full name: Christopher Steven Mihm
HIGH SCHOOL: Westlake (Austin, Texas).
COLLEGE: Texas.
TRANSACTIONS/CAREER NOTES: Selected after junior season by Chicago Bulls in first round (seventh pick overall) of 2000 NBA Draft. ... Draft rights traded by Bulls to Cleveland Cavaliers for draft rights to G Jamal Crawford and cash (June 28, 2000). ... Traded by Cavaliers with G Ricky Davis, C Michael Stewart and a second-round draft choice to Boston Celtics for F/C Tony Battie, F Kedrick Brown and F Eric Williams (December 15, 2003). ... Traded by Celtics with G Chucky Atkins and F Jumaine Jones to Los Angeles Lakers for G Gary Payton, F Rick Fox and a first-round draft choice (August 6, 2004).

COLLEGIATE RECORD

NOTES: The SPORTING NEWS All-America second team (2000).

												AVERAGES		
Season Team	G	Min.	FGM	FGA	Pct.	FTM	FTA	Pct.	Reb.	Ast.	Pts.	RPG	APG	PPG
97-98—Texas	31	769	148	288	.514	86	133	.647	248	14	384	8.0	0.5	12.4
98-99—Texas	32	1027	144	321	.449	149	218	.683	351	19	437	11.0	0.6	13.7
99-00—Texas	33	1014	206	394	.523	164	232	.707	346	22	583	10.5	0.7	17.7
Totals	96	2810	498	1003	.497	399	583	.684	945	55	1404	9.8	0.6	14.6

Three-point field goals: 1997-98, 2-for-11 (.182). 1998-99, 0-for-4. 1999-00, 7-for-15 (.467). Totals, 9-for-30 (.300).

HONORS: NBA All-Rookie second team (2001).

NBA REGULAR-SEASON RECORD

								REBOUNDS								AVERAGES		
Season Team	G	Min.	FGM	FGA	Pct.	FTM	FTA	Pct.	Off.	Def.	Tot.	Ast.	St.	Blk.	TO	Pts.	RPG	APG	PPG
00-01—Cleveland	59	1166	173	391	.442	100	126	.794	106	174	280	16	20	53	80	446	4.7	0.3	7.6
01-02—Cleveland	74	1659	221	526	.420	124	179	.693	133	259	392	24	18	89	97	569	5.3	0.3	7.7

M

Season Team	G	Min.	FGM	FGA	Pct.	FTM	FTA	Pct.	Off.	Def.	Tot.	Ast.	St.	Blk.	TO	Pts.	RPG	APG	PPG
									REBOUNDS								**AVERAGES**		
02-03—Cleveland	52	809	116	287	.404	76	105	.724	93	138	231	28	18	38	48	308	4.4	0.5	5.9
03-04—Cleve.-Bos.	76	1330	186	381	.488	110	166	.663	156	257	413	21	37	63	90	482	5.4	0.3	6.3
04-05—L.A. Lakers	75	1870	280	552	.507	175	258	.678	197	305	502	50	14	108	110	735	6.7	0.7	9.8
05-06—L.A. Lakers	59	1541	230	459	.501	144	201	.716	137	236	373	61	16	73	83	604	6.3	1.0	10.2
Totals	395	8375	1206	2596	.465	729	1035	.704	822	1369	2191	200	123	424	508	3144	5.5	0.5	8.0

Three-point field goals: 2000-01, 0-for-1. 2001-02, 3-for-7 (.429). 2002-03, 0-for-3. 2004-05, 0-for-2. Totals, 3-for-13 (.231).
Personal fouls/disqualifications: 2000-01, 156/2. 2001-02, 260/7. 2002-03, 124/0. 2003-04, 208/3. 2004-05, 237/1. 2005-06, 214/5. Totals, 1199/18.

NBA PLAYOFF RECORD

Season Team	G	Min.	FGM	FGA	Pct.	FTM	FTA	Pct.	Off.	Def.	Tot.	Ast.	St.	Blk.	TO	Pts.	RPG	APG	PPG
									REBOUNDS								**AVERAGES**		
03-04—Boston	4	65	7	22	.318	6	10	.600	8	10	18	0	4	4	3	20	4.5	0.0	5.0

Personal fouls/disqualifications: 2003-04, 12/1. Totals, 12/1.

MILES, AARON   G

PERSONAL: Born April 13, 1983, in Portland, Ore. ... 6-1/175. (1.85/79.4). ... Full name: Aaron Marquez Miles
HIGH SCHOOL: Thomas Jefferson (Portland, Ore.).
COLLEGE: Kansas.
TRANSACTIONS/CAREER NOTES: Not drafted by an NBA franchise ... Played in NBA Development League (2005-06). ... Signed as free agent by Golden State Warriors (September 29, 2005). ... Waived by Warriors (January 5, 2006).

COLLEGIATE RECORD

Season Team	G	Min.	FGM	FGA	Pct.	FTM	FTA	Pct.	Reb.	Ast.	Pts.	RPG	APG	PPG
												AVERAGES		
01-02—Kansas	37	1017	91	225	.404	69	87	.793	100	252	264	2.7	6.8	7.1
02-03—Kansas	38	1172	119	292	.408	78	104	.750	125	244	340	3.3	6.4	8.9
03-04—Kansas	33	1117	100	249	.402	72	103	.699	125	242	300	3.8	7.3	9.1
04-05—Kansas	30	992	86	188	.457	67	85	.788	106	216	279	3.5	7.2	9.3
Totals	138	4298	396	954	.415	286	379	.755	456	954	1183	3.3	6.9	8.6

Three-point field goals: 2001-02, 13-for-45 (.289). 2002-03, 24-for-98 (.245). 2003-04, 28-for-84 (.333). 2004-05, 40-for-80 (.500). Totals, 105-for-307 (.342).

NBA REGULAR-SEASON RECORD

Season Team	G	Min.	FGM	FGA	Pct.	FTM	FTA	Pct.	Off.	Def.	Tot.	Ast.	St.	Blk.	TO	Pts.	RPG	APG	PPG
									REBOUNDS								**AVERAGES**		
05-06—Golden State ...	19	118	6	18	.333	4	4	1.000	0	14	14	24	4	1	11	16	0.7	1.3	0.8

Personal fouls/disqualifications: 2005-06, 13/0. Totals, 13/0.

NBA DEVELOPMENT LEAGUE RECORD

Season Team	G	Min.	FGM	FGA	Pct.	FTM	FTA	Pct.	Reb.	Ast.	Pts.	RPG	APG	PPG
												AVERAGES		
05-06—Fort Worth....................	27	755	105	231	.455	59	75	.787	79	178	273	2.9	6.6	10.1

Three-point field goals: 2005-06, 4-for-11 (.364). Totals, 4-for-11 (.364).

MILES, C.J.   G   JAZZ

PERSONAL: Born March 18, 1987, in Dallas, Texas. ... 6-6/210. (1.98/95.3).
HIGH SCHOOL: Skyline (Dallas, Texas).
COLLEGE: Did not attend college.
TRANSACTIONS/CAREER NOTES: Selected out of high school by Utah Jazz in second round (34th pick overall) of 2005 NBA Draft.

NBA REGULAR-SEASON RECORD

Season Team	G	Min.	FGM	FGA	Pct.	FTM	FTA	Pct.	Off.	Def.	Tot.	Ast.	St.	Blk.	TO	Pts.	RPG	APG	PPG
									REBOUNDS								**AVERAGES**		
05-06—Utah...............	23	203	28	76	.368	18	24	.750	18	20	38	16	7	2	9	79	1.7	0.7	3.4

Three-point field goals: 2005-06, 5-for-20 (.250). Totals, 5-for-20 (.250).
Personal fouls/disqualifications: 2005-06, 20/0. Totals, 20/0.

NBA DEVELOPMENT LEAGUE RECORD

Season Team	G	Min.	FGM	FGA	Pct.	FTM	FTA	Pct.	Reb.	Ast.	Pts.	RPG	APG	PPG
												AVERAGES		
05-06—Albuquerque..................	11	309	45	108	.417	39	56	.696	38	18	140	3.5	1.6	12.7

Three-point field goals: 2005-06, 11-for-33 (.333). Totals, 11-for-33 (.333).

MILES, DARIUS   F   TRAIL BLAZERS

PERSONAL: Born October 9, 1981, in Belleville, Ill. ... 6-9/210. (2.06/95.3). ... Full name: Darius LaVar Miles
HIGH SCHOOL: East St. Louis (Ill.).
COLLEGE: Did not attend college.
TRANSACTIONS/CAREER NOTES: Selected out of high school by Los Angeles Clippers in first round (third pick overall) of 2000 NBA Draft. ... Traded by Clippers with F Harold Jamison to Cleveland Cavaliers for G Andre Miller and G Bryant Stith (July 30, 2002). ... Traded by Cavaliers to Portland Trail Blazers for G Jeff McInnis and C Ruben Boumtje-Boumtje (January 21, 2004).

M

HONORS: NBA All-Rookie first team (2001).

Season Team	G	Min.	FGM	FGA	Pct.	FTM	FTA	Pct.	Off.	Def.	Tot.	Ast.	St.	Blk.	TO	Pts.	RPG	APG	PPG
									REBOUNDS								AVERAGES		
00-01—L.A. Clippers...	81	2133	318	630	.505	124	238	.521	127	350	477	99	51	125	147	761	5.9	1.2	9.4
01-02—L.A. Clippers...	82	2227	309	642	.481	158	255	.620	109	344	453	184	71	103	160	779	5.5	2.2	9.5
02-03—Cleveland........	67	2008	263	642	.410	92	155	.594	113	250	363	176	67	69	178	618	5.4	2.6	9.2
03-04—Cleve.-Port......	79	2079	365	753	.485	124	193	.642	112	247	359	162	67	61	130	861	4.5	2.1	10.9
04-05—Portland..........	63	1699	336	697	.482	129	215	.600	71	228	299	129	75	78	157	809	4.7	2.0	12.8
05-06—Portland..........	40	1286	235	510	.461	87	163	.534	24	158	182	73	42	39	99	559	4.6	1.8	14.0
Totals..................	412	11432	1826	3874	.471	714	1219	.586	556	1577	2133	823	373	475	871	4387	5.2	2.0	10.6

Three-point field goals: 2000-01, 1-for-19 (.053). 2001-02, 3-for-19 (.158). 2002-03, 0-for-14. 2003-04, 7-for-40 (.175). 2004-05, 8-for-23 (.348). 2005-06, 2-for-10 (.200). Totals, 21-for-125 (.168).

Personal fouls/disqualifications: 2000-01, 191/1. 2001-02, 184/2. 2002-03, 159/3. 2003-04, 168/0. 2004-05, 189/0. 2005-06, 100/1. Totals, 991/7.

MILICIC, DARKO F/C MAGIC

PERSONAL: Born June 20, 1985, in Novi Sad, Montenegro. ... 7-0/245. (2.13/111.1).
HIGH SCHOOL: Hemiska (Montenegro).
TRANSACTIONS/CAREER NOTES: Played in Yugoslavia (2001-03). ... Played in North European Basketball League in 2002-03. ... Selected by Detroit Pistons in first round (second pick overall) of 2003 NBA Draft. ... Traded by Pistons with G Carlos Arroyo to Orlando Magic for C Kelvin Cato and a future first-round draft choice (February 15, 2006).
MISCELLANEOUS: Member of NBA championship team (2004).

YUGOSLAVIAN LEAGUE RECORD

Season Team	G	Min.	FGM	FGA	Pct.	FTM	FTA	Pct.	Reb.	Ast.	Pts.	RPG	APG	PPG
												AVERAGES		
01-02—Hemofarm	18	338	38	81	.469	20	31	.645	55	8	97	3.1	0.4	5.4
02-03—Hemofarm	20	395	59	124	.476	71	105	.676	92	15	190	4.6	0.8	9.5
Totals	38	733	97	205	.473	91	136	.669	147	23	287	3.9	0.6	7.6

Three-point field goals: 2001-02, 1-for-5 (.200). 2002-03, 1-for-5 (.200). Totals, 2-for-10 (.200).

NBA REGULAR-SEASON RECORD

Season Team	G	Min.	FGM	FGA	Pct.	FTM	FTA	Pct.	Off.	Def.	Tot.	Ast.	St.	Blk.	TO	Pts.	RPG	APG	PPG
									REBOUNDS								AVERAGES		
03-04—Detroit	34	159	17	65	.262	14	24	.583	11	32	43	7	7	15	13	48	1.3	0.2	1.4
04-05—Detroit	37	254	25	76	.329	17	24	.708	3	40	43	7	2	17	16	67	1.2	0.2	1.8
05-06—Detroit-Orl.	55	767	119	234	.509	28	50	.560	44	107	151	41	14	77	51	266	2.7	0.7	4.8
Totals	126	1180	161	375	.429	59	98	.602	58	179	237	55	23	109	80	381	1.9	0.4	3.0

Three-point field goals: 2003-04, 0-for-1. 2005-06, 0-for-2. Totals, 0-for-3 (.000).

Personal fouls/disqualifications: 2003-04, 33/0. 2004-05, 31/0. 2005-06, 92/1. Totals, 156/1.

NBA PLAYOFF RECORD

Season Team	G	Min.	FGM	FGA	Pct.	FTM	FTA	Pct.	Off.	Def.	Tot.	Ast.	St.	Blk.	TO	Pts.	RPG	APG	PPG
									REBOUNDS								AVERAGES		
03-04—Detroit	8	14	0	4	.000	1	4	.250	1	2	3	1	1	0	3	1	0.4	0.1	0.1
04-05—Detroit	9	21	2	7	.286	1	1	1.000	1	3	4	1	0	1	1	5	0.4	0.1	0.6
Totals	17	35	2	11	.182	2	5	.400	2	5	7	2	1	1	4	6	0.4	0.1	0.4

Personal fouls/disqualifications: 2003-04, 1/0. 2004-05, 3/0. Totals, 4/0.

MILLER, ANDRE G NUGGETS

PERSONAL: Born March 19, 1976, in Los Angeles. ... 6-2/200. (1.88/90.7). ... Full name: Andre Lloyd Miller
HIGH SCHOOL: Verbum Dei (Los Angeles).
COLLEGE: Utah.
TRANSACTIONS/CAREER NOTES: Selected by Cleveland Cavaliers in first round (eighth pick overall) of 1999 NBA Draft. ... Traded by Cavaliers with G Bryant Stith to Los Angeles Clippers for F Darius Miles and F Harold Jamison (July 30, 2002). ... Signed as free agent by Denver Nuggets (August 1, 2003).

COLLEGIATE RECORD

NOTES: The SPORTING NEWS All-America first team (1999).

Season Team	G	Min.	FGM	FGA	Pct.	FTM	FTA	Pct.	Reb.	Ast.	Pts.	RPG	APG	PPG
												AVERAGES		
94-95—Utah						Did not play—ineligible.								
95-96—Utah	34	872	104	195	.533	78	113	.690	126	157	292	3.7	4.6	8.6
96-97—Utah	33	974	121	249	.486	71	122	.582	154	201	323	4.7	6.1	9.8
97-98—Utah	34	1076	173	315	.549	117	162	.722	185	177	483	5.4	5.2	14.2
98-99—Utah	33	1092	190	387	.491	118	171	.690	178	186	520	5.4	5.6	15.8
Totals	134	4014	588	1146	.513	384	568	.676	643	721	1618	4.8	5.4	12.1

Three-point field goals: 1995-96, 6-for-19 (.316). 1996-97, 10-for-35 (.286). 1997-98, 20-for-60 (.333). 1998-99, 22-for-83 (.265). Totals, 58-for-197 (.294).

Personal fouls/disqualifications: 1995-96, 67/1. 1996-97, 62/1. 1997-98, 72/1. Totals, 201/3.

NBA REGULAR-SEASON RECORD

HONORS: NBA All-Rookie first team (2000).

Season Team	G	Min.	FGM	FGA	Pct.	FTM	FTA	Pct.	Off.	Def.	Tot.	Ast.	St.	Blk.	TO	Pts.	RPG	APG	PPG
									REBOUNDS								AVERAGES		
99-00—Cleveland........	82	2093	339	755	.449	226	292	.774	85	195	280	476	84	17	166	914	3.4	5.8	11.1

M

Season Team	G	Min.	FGM	FGA	Pct.	FTM	FTA	Pct.	Off.	Def.	Tot.	Ast.	St.	Blk.	TO	Pts.	RPG	APG	PPG
00-01—Cleveland	82	2848	452	999	.452	375	450	.833	94	266	360	657	119	28	265	1296	4.4	8.0	15.8
01-02—Cleveland	81	3023	474	1045	.454	365	447	.817	108	271	379	*882	126	34	245	1335	4.7	*10.9	16.5
02-03—L.A. Clippers...	80	2913	377	928	.406	311	391	.795	84	232	316	537	99	11	206	1088	4.0	6.7	13.6
03-04—Denver	82	2838	430	941	.457	342	411	.832	127	239	366	501	142	25	215	1214	4.5	6.1	14.8
04-05—Denver	82	2852	427	895	.477	253	302	.838	100	238	338	569	121	8	220	1113	4.1	6.9	13.6
05-06—Denver	82	2937	404	872	.463	313	424	.738	92	259	351	674	106	18	256	1126	4.3	8.2	13.7
Totals	571	19504	2903	6435	.451	2185	2717	.804	690	1700	2390	4296	797	141	1573	8086	4.2	7.5	14.2

Three-point field goals: 1999-00, 10-for-49 (.204). 2000-01, 17-for-64 (.266). 2001-02, 22-for-87 (.253). 2002-03, 23-for-108 (.213). 2003-04, 12-for-65 (.185). 2004-05, 6-for-39 (.154). 2005-06, 5-for-27 (.185). Totals, 95-for-439 (.216).

Personal fouls/disqualifications: 1999-00, 194/1. 2000-01, 229/0. 2001-02, 228/1. 2002-03, 203/3. 2003-04, 194/2. 2004-05, 204/1. 2005-06, 213/1. Totals, 1465/9.

NBA PLAYOFF RECORD

Season Team	G	Min.	FGM	FGA	Pct.	FTM	FTA	Pct.	Off.	Def.	Tot.	Ast.	St.	Blk.	TO	Pts.	RPG	APG	PPG
03-04—Denver	5	174	34	72	.472	9	11	.818	15	8	23	16	8	0	10	77	4.6	3.2	15.4
04-05—Denver	5	184	28	66	.424	23	32	.719	9	17	26	26	10	1	12	81	5.2	5.2	16.2
05-06—Denver	5	182	34	77	.442	14	17	.824	8	14	22	36	5	1	16	82	4.4	7.2	16.4
Totals	15	540	96	215	.447	46	60	.767	32	39	71	78	23	2	38	240	4.7	5.2	16.0

Three-point field goals: 2003-04, 0-for-2. 2004-05, 2-for-4 (.500). Totals, 2-for-6 (.333).

Personal fouls/disqualifications: 2003-04, 16/1. 2004-05, 22/2. 2005-06, 12/0. Totals, 50/3.

MILLER, BRAD　　　　　　C　　　　　　KINGS

PERSONAL: Born April 12, 1976, in Fort Wayne, Ind. ... 7-0/261. (2.13/118.4). ... Full name: Bradley Alan Miller

HIGH SCHOOL: East Noble (Berwick, Maine), then Maine Central Institute.

COLLEGE: Purdue.

TRANSACTIONS/CAREER NOTES: Not drafted by an NBA franchise. ... Played in Italy (1998-99). ... Signed as free agent by Charlotte Hornets (January 21, 1999). ... Signed as free agent by Chicago Bulls (September 7, 2000). ... Traded by Bulls with G Ron Mercer, G/F Ron Artest and G Kevin Ollie to Indiana Pacers for G Jalen Rose, G Travis Best, G Norman Richardson and conditional second-round draft choice (February 19, 2002). ... Traded by Pacers to Sacramento Kings in three-team deal in which Pacers also traded G Ron Mercer to San Antonio Spurs and acquired F Scot Pollard from Kings and F Danny Ferry from Spurs. Spurs also acquired F/G Hedo Turkoglu from Kings (July 24, 2003).

MISCELLANEOUS: Member of bronze-medal-winning U.S. World Championship team (1998).

COLLEGIATE RECORD

Season Team	G	Min.	FGM	FGA	Pct.	FTM	FTA	Pct.	Reb.	Ast.	Pts.	RPG	APG	PPG
94-95—Purdue	32	574	71	122	.582	66	100	.660	153	39	208	4.8	1.2	6.5
95-96—Purdue	32	682	100	193	.518	107	145	.738	158	46	308	4.9	1.4	9.6
96-97—Purdue	30	929	128	239	.536	171	220	.777	249	86	400	8.1	2.8	13.7
97-98—Purdue	33	964	186	291	.639	196	251	.781	291	84	571	8.8	2.5	17.3
Totals	127	3149	485	845	.574	540	716	.754	851	255	1517	6.7	2.0	11.9

Three-point field goals: 1995-96, 1-for-6 (.167). 1996-97, 3-for-11 (.273). 1997-98, 3-for-9 (.333). Totals, 7-for-26 (.269).

ITALIAN LEAGUE RECORD

Season Team	G	Min.	FGM	FGA	Pct.	FTM	FTA	Pct.	Reb.	Ast.	Pts.	RPG	APG	PPG
98-99—Bini Viaggi	16	484	95	170	.559	61	73	.836	140	17	253	8.8	1.1	15.8

Three-point field goals: 1998-99, 2-for-6 (.333). Totals, 2-for-6 (.333).

NBA REGULAR-SEASON RECORD

Season Team	G	Min.	FGM	FGA	Pct.	FTM	FTA	Pct.	Off.	Def.	Tot.	Ast.	St.	Blk.	TO	Pts.	RPG	APG	PPG
98-99—Charlotte	38	469	78	138	.565	81	102	.794	35	82	117	22	9	18	32	238	3.1	0.6	6.3
99-00—Charlotte	55	961	135	293	.461	153	195	.785	113	180	293	45	23	35	48	423	5.3	0.8	7.7
00-01—Chicago	57	1434	168	386	.435	168	226	.743	144	275	419	107	33	38	73	505	7.4	1.9	8.9
01-02—Chi.-Indiana	76	2263	366	733	.499	297	383	.775	252	369	621	152	76	41	115	1032	8.2	2.0	13.6
02-03—Indiana..........	73	2270	329	667	.493	292	357	.818	185	418	603	193	65	43	118	955	8.3	2.6	13.1
03-04—Sacramento ...	72	2621	373	731	.510	256	329	.778	191	552	743	312	68	86	144	1014	10.3	4.3	14.1
04-05—Sacramento ...	56	2089	319	609	.524	233	287	.812	139	382	521	220	69	68	82	876	9.3	3.9	15.6
05-06—Sacramento ...	79	2923	434	877	.495	280	338	.828	122	493	615	374	61	62	180	1182	7.8	4.7	15.0
Totals	506	15030	2202	4434	.497	1760	2217	.794	1181	2751	3932	1425	404	391	792	6225	7.8	2.8	12.3

Three-point field goals: 1998-99, 1-for-2 (.500). 1999-00, 0-for-2. 2000-01, 1-for-5 (.200). 2001-02, 3-for-7 (.429). 2002-03, 5-for-16 (.313). 2003-04, 12-for-38 (.316). 2004-05, 5-for-19 (.263). 2005-06, 34-for-88 (.386). Totals, 61-for-177 (.345).

Personal fouls/disqualifications: 1998-99, 65/0. 1999-00, 111/1. 2000-01, 176/5. 2001-02, 244/3. 2002-03, 203/0. 2003-04, 247/7. 2004-05, 181/4. 2005-06, 234/1. Totals, 1461/21.

NBA PLAYOFF RECORD

Season Team	G	Min.	FGM	FGA	Pct.	FTM	FTA	Pct.	Off.	Def.	Tot.	Ast.	St.	Blk.	TO	Pts.	RPG	APG	PPG
99-00—Charlotte	4	62	9	17	.529	12	15	.800	8	5	13	3	0	3	9	30	3.3	0.8	7.5
01-02—Indiana..........	5	180	20	44	.455	16	20	.800	17	32	49	7	4	2	7	56	9.8	1.4	11.2
02-03—Indiana..........	6	135	18	40	.450	16	22	.727	10	23	33	15	5	0	9	52	5.5	2.5	8.7
03-04—Sacramento ...	12	366	48	91	.527	29	48	.604	30	74	104	38	9	11	20	126	8.7	3.2	10.5
04-05—Sacramento ...	5	139	23	40	.575	10	14	.714	8	11	19	16	1	3	6	56	3.8	3.2	11.2
05-06—Sacramento ...	6	166	21	52	.404	12	13	.923	3	15	18	15	7	5	7	55	3.0	2.5	9.2
Totals	38	1048	139	284	.489	95	132	.720	76	160	236	94	26	24	61	375	6.2	2.5	9.9

Three-point field goals: 2003-04, 1-for-7 (.143). 2004-05, 0-for-2. 2005-06, 1-for-7 (.143). Totals, 2-for-16 (.125).

M

Personal fouls/disqualifications: 1999-00, 11/0. 2001-02, 16/0. 2002-03, 17/1. 2003-04, 46/0. 2004-05, 21/0. 2005-06, 20/0. Totals, 131/1.

NBA ALL-STAR GAME RECORD

Season Team	Min.	FGM	FGA	Pct.	FTM	FTA	Pct.	REBOUNDS Off.	Def.	Tot.	Ast.	PF	Dq.	St.	Blk.	TO	Pts.
2003—Indiana	17	2	4	.500	1	2	.500	3	3	6	3	2	0	0	0	2	5
2004—Sacramento	10	4	5	.800	0	0	...	1	2	3	0	0	0	0	0	2	8
Totals	27	6	9	.667	1	2	.500	4	5	9	3	2	0	0	0	4	13

MILLER, MIKE — F — GRIZZLIES

PERSONAL: Born February 19, 1980, in Mitchell, S.D. ... 6-9/218. (2.06/98.9). ... Full name: Michael Lloyd Miller
HIGH SCHOOL: Mitchell (S.D.).
COLLEGE: Florida.
TRANSACTIONS/CAREER NOTES: Selected after sophomore season by Orlando Magic in first round (fifth pick overall) of 2000 NBA Draft. ... Traded by Magic with F Ryan Humphrey, 2003 first-round draft choice and 2004 second-round draft choice to Memphis Grizzlies for F Drew Gooden and F Gordan Giricek (February 19, 2003).

COLLEGIATE RECORD

Season Team	G	Min.	FGM	FGA	Pct.	FTM	FTA	Pct.	Reb.	Ast.	Pts.	AVERAGES RPG	APG	PPG
98-99—Florida	28	677	115	233	.494	80	114	.702	146	58	341	5.2	2.1	12.2
99-00—Florida	37	1058	175	368	.476	124	170	.729	243	91	521	6.6	2.5	14.1
Totals	65	1735	290	601	.483	204	284	.718	389	149	862	6.0	2.3	13.3

Three-point field goals: 1998-99, 31-for-87 (.356). 1999-00, 47-for-139 (.338). Totals, 78-for-226 (.345).

NBA REGULAR-SEASON RECORD

HONORS: NBA Rookie of the Year (2001). ... NBA All-Rookie first team (2001). ... NBA Sixth Man Award winner (2006).

Season Team	G	Min.	FGM	FGA	Pct.	FTM	FTA	Pct.	REBOUNDS Off.	Def.	Tot.	Ast.	St.	Blk.	TO	Pts.	AVERAGES RPG	APG	PPG
00-01—Orlando	82	2390	368	845	.436	91	128	.711	66	261	327	140	51	19	97	975	4.0	1.7	11.9
01-02—Orlando	63	2123	351	802	.438	138	181	.762	49	224	273	198	47	23	108	956	4.3	3.1	15.2
02-03—Orl-Mem	65	2186	373	859	.434	156	186	.839	46	295	341	170	42	21	125	1011	5.2	2.6	15.6
03-04—Memphis	65	1770	270	616	.438	102	141	.723	42	174	216	232	59	14	107	722	3.3	3.6	11.1
04-05—Memphis	76	2278	387	766	.505	108	150	.720	36	264	300	220	54	23	127	1022	3.9	2.9	13.4
05-06—Memphis	74	2268	354	760	.466	168	210	.800	42	355	397	200	52	27	140	1014	5.4	2.7	13.7
Totals	425	13015	2103	4648	.452	763	996	.766	281	1573	1854	1160	305	127	704	5700	4.4	2.7	13.4

Three-point field goals: 2000-01, 148-for-364 (.407). 2001-02, 116-for-303 (.383). 2002-03, 109-for-300 (.363). 2003-04, 80-for-215 (.372). 2004-05, 140-for-323 (.433). 2005-06, 138-for-339 (.407). Totals, 731-for-1844 (.396).

Personal fouls/disqualifications: 2000-01, 200/2. 2001-02, 145/0. 2002-03, 173/2. 2003-04, 162/3. 2004-05, 197/2. 2005-06, 173/4. Totals, 1050/13.

NBA PLAYOFF RECORD

Season Team	G	Min.	FGM	FGA	Pct.	FTM	FTA	Pct.	REBOUNDS Off.	Def.	Tot.	Ast.	St.	Blk.	TO	Pts.	AVERAGES RPG	APG	PPG
00-01—Orlando	4	112	19	48	.396	3	4	.750	5	13	18	7	0	3	3	48	4.5	1.8	12.0
01-02—Orlando	4	72	7	21	.333	4	4	1.000	0	5	5	5	4	0	4	19	1.3	1.3	4.8
03-04—Memphis	4	98	12	34	.353	1	3	.333	0	12	12	3	5	0	5	30	3.0	0.8	7.5
04-05—Memphis	4	110	18	37	.486	4	4	1.000	0	10	10	11	0	3	5	48	2.5	2.8	12.0
05-06—Memphis	4	107	12	30	.400	9	9	1.000	1	14	15	7	2	2	8	34	3.8	1.8	8.5
Totals	20	499	68	170	.400	21	24	.875	6	54	60	33	11	8	25	179	3.0	1.7	9.0

Three-point field goals: 2000-01, 7-for-18 (.389). 2001-02, 1-for-8 (.125). 2003-04, 5-for-13 (.385). 2004-05, 8-for-17 (.471). 2005-06, 1-for-8 (.125). Totals, 22-for-64 (.344).

Personal fouls/disqualifications: 2000-01, 13/0. 2001-02, 8/0. 2003-04, 4/0. 2004-05, 7/0. 2005-06, 11/0. Totals, 43/0.

MOBLEY, CUTTINO — G — CLIPPERS

PERSONAL: Born September 1, 1975, in Philadelphia. ... 6-4/210. (1.93/95.3). ... Full name: Cuttino Rashawn Mobley
HIGH SCHOOL: Cardinal Dougherty (Philadelphia), then Maine Central Institute.
COLLEGE: Rhode Island.
TRANSACTIONS/CAREER NOTES: Selected by Houston Rockets in second round (41st pick overall) of 1998 NBA Draft. ... Traded by Rockets with G Steve Francis and C Kelvin Cato to Orlando Magic for G Tracy McGrady, F Juwan Howard, G Tyronn Lue and G Reece Gaines (June 29, 2004). ... Traded by Magic with F Michael Bradley to Sacramento Kings for G/F Doug Christie (January 10, 2005). ... Signed as free agent by Los Angeles Clippers (August 3, 2005).

NOTES: Granted medical redshirt (1995-96).

COLLEGIATE RECORD

Season Team	G	Min.	FGM	FGA	Pct.	FTM	FTA	Pct.	Reb.	Ast.	Pts.	AVERAGES RPG	APG	PPG
93-94—Rhode Island						Did not play—redshirted.								
94-95—Rhode Island	27	864	126	334	.377	63	81	.778	129	39	358	4.8	1.4	13.3
95-96—Rhode Island	2	35	9	14	.643	1	2	.500	0	5	24	0.0	2.5	12.0
96-97—Rhode Island	30	730	138	315	.438	61	76	.803	117	44	366	3.9	1.5	12.2
97-98—Rhode Island	34	1133	193	402	.480	131	153	.856	147	88	586	4.3	2.6	17.2
Totals	93	2762	466	1065	.438	256	312	.821	393	176	1334	4.2	1.9	14.3

Three-point field goals: 1994-95, 43-for-142 (.303). 1995-96, 5-for-7 (.714). 1996-97, 29-for-97 (.299). 1997-98, 69-for-166 (.416). Totals, 146-for-412 (.354).

NBA REGULAR-SEASON RECORD

HONORS: NBA All-Rookie second team (1999).

Season Team	G	Min.	FGM	FGA	Pct.	FTM	FTA	Pct.	Off.	Def.	Tot.	Ast.	St.	Blk.	TO	Pts.	RPG	APG	PPG
98-99—Houston	49	1456	172	405	.425	90	110	.818	22	89	111	121	44	23	79	487	2.3	2.5	9.9
99-00—Houston	81	2496	437	1016	.430	299	353	.847	59	229	288	208	87	32	186	1277	3.6	2.6	15.8
00-01—Houston	79	3002	527	1214	.434	394	474	.831	83	314	397	195	84	26	165	1538	5.0	2.5	19.5
01-02—Houston	74	3116	595	1358	.438	267	314	.850	63	237	300	187	109	37	180	1606	4.1	2.5	21.7
02-03—Houston	73	3044	463	1067	.434	242	282	.858	70	233	303	208	95	36	166	1280	4.2	2.8	17.5
03-04—Houston	80	3229	460	1081	.426	176	217	.811	40	322	362	258	107	33	180	1260	4.5	3.2	15.8
04-05—Orlando-Sac.	66	2388	408	932	.438	168	205	.820	45	184	229	188	74	30	133	1134	3.5	2.8	17.2
05-06—L.A. Clippers	79	2979	429	1008	.426	229	273	.839	50	291	341	238	93	36	145	1170	4.3	3.0	14.8
Totals	581	21710	3491	8081	.432	1865	2228	.837	432	1899	2331	1603	693	253	1234	9752	4.0	2.8	16.8

Three-point field goals: 1998-99, 53-for-148 (.358). 1999-00, 104-for-292 (.356). 2000-01, 90-for-252 (.357). 2001-02, 149-for-377 (.395). 2002-03, 112-for-318 (.352). 2003-04, 164-for-420 (.390). 2004-05, 150-for-342 (.439). 2005-06, 83-for-245 (.339). Totals, 905-for-2394 (.378).

Personal fouls/disqualifications: 1998-99, 98/0. 1999-00, 171/0. 2000-01, 169/1. 2001-02, 189/3. 2002-03, 185/0. 2003-04, 179/0. 2004-05, 152/1. 2005-06, 208/2. Totals, 1351/7.

NBA PLAYOFF RECORD

Season Team	G	Min.	FGM	FGA	Pct.	FTM	FTA	Pct.	Off.	Def.	Tot.	Ast.	St.	Blk.	TO	Pts.	RPG	APG	PPG
98-99—Houston	4	94	7	15	.467	10	11	.909	0	4	4	11	2	0	5	28	1.0	2.8	7.0
03-04—Houston	5	210	29	75	.387	8	10	.800	5	19	24	14	3	3	18	72	4.8	2.8	14.4
04-05—Sacramento	5	159	31	70	.443	5	7	.714	4	10	14	9	6	2	6	74	2.8	1.8	14.8
05-06—L.A. Clippers	12	473	61	143	.427	26	29	.897	10	47	57	24	8	3	23	159	4.8	2.0	13.3
Totals	26	936	128	303	.422	49	57	.860	19	80	99	58	19	8	52	333	3.8	2.2	12.8

Three-point field goals: 1998-99, 4-for-7 (.571). 2003-04, 6-for-21 (.286). 2004-05, 7-for-25 (.280). 2005-06, 11-for-30 (.367). Totals, 28-for-83 (.337).
Personal fouls/disqualifications: 1998-99, 11/0. 2003-04, 14/0. 2004-05, 13/0. 2005-06, 28/0. Totals, 66/0.

MOHAMMED, NAZR   C   PISTONS

PERSONAL: Born September 5, 1977, in Chicago. ... 6-10/250. (2.08/113.4). ... Full name: Nazr Tahiru Mohammed ... Name pronounced NAH-zee.
HIGH SCHOOL: Kenwood (Chicago).
COLLEGE: Kentucky.
TRANSACTIONS/CAREER NOTES: Selected after junior season by Utah Jazz in first round (29th pick overall) of 1998 NBA Draft. ... Draft rights traded by Jazz to Philadelphia 76ers for future first-round draft choice (June 24, 1998). ... Traded by 76ers with F/C Theo Ratliff, F/G Toni Kukoc and G Pepe Sanchez to Atlanta Hawks for C Dikembe Mutombo and F Roshown McLeod (February 22, 2001). ... Traded by Hawks to New York Knicks in three-team trade in which Hawks acquired C Joel Przybilla from Milwaukee Bucks and C Michael Doleac and 2005 second-round draft choice from New York Knicks. Knicks acquired F Tim Thomas from Bucks and traded F Keith Van Horn to Bucks (February 15, 2004). ... Traded by Knicks with G Jamison Brewer to San Antonio Spurs for F Malik Rose and conditional first-round picks in 2005 and 2006 NBA drafts (February 24, 2005). ... Signed as free agent by Detroit Pistons (July 18, 2006).
MISCELLANEOUS: Member of NBA championship team (2005).

COLLEGIATE RECORD

NOTES: Member of NCAA Division I championship team (1996, 1998).

Season Team	G	Min.	FGM	FGA	Pct.	FTM	FTA	Pct.	Reb.	Ast.	Pts.	RPG	APG	PPG
95-96—Kentucky	16	88	13	29	.448	11	24	.458	24	3	37	1.5	0.2	2.3
96-97—Kentucky	39	617	132	259	.510	45	89	.506	226	12	309	5.8	0.3	7.9
97-98—Kentucky	39	819	190	318	.597	88	135	.652	282	28	468	7.2	0.7	12.0
Totals	94	1524	335	606	.553	144	248	.581	532	43	814	5.7	0.5	8.7

Three-point field goals: 1996-97, 0-for-2. Totals, 0-for-2 (.000).

NBA REGULAR-SEASON RECORD

Season Team	G	Min.	FGM	FGA	Pct.	FTM	FTA	Pct.	Off.	Def.	Tot.	Ast.	St.	Blk.	TO	Pts.	RPG	APG	PPG
98-99—Philadelphia	26	121	15	42	.357	12	21	.571	18	19	37	2	5	4	12	42	1.4	0.1	1.6
99-00—Philadelphia	28	190	21	54	.389	12	22	.545	16	34	50	2	4	12	18	54	1.8	0.1	1.9
00-01—Phila.-Atlanta	58	912	176	369	.477	89	126	.706	115	192	307	19	29	35	64	441	5.3	0.3	7.6
01-02—Atlanta	82	2168	329	713	.461	137	222	.617	242	409	651	33	63	61	118	795	7.9	0.4	9.7
02-03—Atlanta	35	445	67	159	.421	26	41	.634	47	82	129	6	16	21	25	160	3.7	0.2	4.6
03-04—Atlanta-N.Y.	80	1611	246	472	.521	100	169	.592	178	296	474	36	55	52	96	592	5.9	0.5	7.4
04-05—N.Y.-S.A.	77	1933	289	602	.480	153	227	.674	247	339	586	34	58	86	108	731	7.6	0.4	9.5
05-06—San Antonio	80	1389	190	377	.504	113	144	.785	163	255	418	40	21	49	91	493	5.2	0.5	6.2
Totals	466	8769	1333	2788	.478	642	972	.660	1026	1626	2652	172	251	320	532	3308	5.7	0.4	7.1

Three-point field goals: 2000-01, 0-for-1. 2001-02, 0-for-1. 2004-05, 0-for-1. Totals, 0-for-3 (.000).
Personal fouls/disqualifications: 1998-99, 22/0. 1999-00, 29/0. 2000-01, 113/0. 2001-02, 252/2. 2002-03, 79/0. 2003-04, 195/1. 2004-05, 236/3. 2005-06, 220/2. Totals, 1146/8.

NBA PLAYOFF RECORD

Season Team	G	Min.	FGM	FGA	Pct.	FTM	FTA	Pct.	Off.	Def.	Tot.	Ast.	St.	Blk.	TO	Pts.	RPG	APG	PPG
98-99—Philadelphia	3	3	0	0	...	0	0	...	0	0	0	0	0	0	0	0	0.0	0.0	0.0
03-04—New York	4	97	15	30	.500	11	16	.688	10	13	23	1	6	3	7	41	5.8	0.3	10.3
04-05—San Antonio	23	528	66	125	.528	30	47	.638	75	79	154	8	14	23	24	163	6.7	0.3	7.1
05-06—San Antonio	8	94	11	15	.733	13	18	.722	15	16	31	1	3	6	8	36	3.9	0.1	4.5
Totals	38	722	92	170	.541	54	81	.667	100	108	208	10	23	32	39	240	5.5	0.3	6.3

Three-point field goals: 2004-05, 1-for-1 (1.000). 2005-06, 1-for-1 (1.000). Totals, 2-for-2 (1.000).
Personal fouls/disqualifications: 2003-04, 18/1. 2004-05, 65/0. 2005-06, 17/0. Totals, 100/1.

MONIA, SERGEI   F

PERSONAL: Born April 15, 1983, in Saratov, Russia. ... 6-8/220. (2.03/99.8).
TRANSACTIONS/CAREER NOTES: Played in Russia (2000-05). ... Selected by Portland Trail Blazers in first round (23rd pick overall of 2004 NBA Draft. ... Traded by Trail Blazers to Sacramento Kings in four-team deal (February 23, 2006). ... Waived by Kings (July 25, 2006).

RUSSIAN LEAGUE RECORD

Season Team	G	Min.	FGM	FGA	Pct.	FTM	FTA	Pct.	Reb.	Ast.	Pts.	RPG	APG	PPG
00-01—Avtodor Saratov	2	21	3	8	.375	0	0	...	6	0	6	3.0	0.0	3.0
01-02—Avtodor Saratov	40	785	115	284	.405	59	93	.634	182	47	309	4.6	1.2	7.7
02-03—CSKA	28	436	75	151	.497	23	32	.719	89	22	205	3.2	0.8	7.3
03-04—CSKA	32	577	77	174	.443	50	68	.735	123	35	232	3.8	1.1	7.3
04-05—CSKA	32	536	67	151	.444	27	39	.692	102	43	186	3.2	1.3	5.8
Totals	134	2355	337	768	.439	159	232	.685	502	147	938	3.7	1.1	7.0

Three-point field goals: 2000-01, 0-for-3. 2001-02, 20-for-73 (.274). 2002-03, 32-for-76 (.421). 2003-04, 28-for-81 (.346). 2004-05, 25-for-64 (.391). Totals, 105-for-297 (.354).

NBA REGULAR-SEASON RECORD

Season Team	G	Min.	FGM	FGA	Pct.	FTM	FTA	Pct.	REBOUNDS Off.	Def.	Tot.	Ast.	St.	Blk.	TO	Pts.	RPG	APG	PPG
05-06—Portland-Sac...	26	343	29	87	.333	10	14	.714	11	41	52	19	7	5	12	77	2.0	0.7	3.0

Three-point field goals: 2005-06, 9-for-34 (.265). Totals, 9-for-34 (.265).
Personal fouls/disqualifications: 2005-06, 41/0. Totals, 41/0.

NBA DEVELOPMENT LEAGUE RECORD

Season Team	G	Min.	FGM	FGA	Pct.	FTM	FTA	Pct.	Reb.	Ast.	Pts.	RPG	APG	PPG
05-06—Fort Worth	8	180	25	60	.417	13	16	.813	27	13	67	3.4	1.6	8.4

Three-point field goals: 2005-06, 4-for-14 (.286). Totals, 4-for-14 (.286).

MOORE, MIKKI   C   NETS

PERSONAL: Born November 4, 1975, in Orangeburg, S.C. ... 7-0/225. (2.13/102.1).
HIGH SCHOOL: Blackburg (Gaffney, S.C.).
COLLEGE: Nebraska.
TRANSACTIONS/CAREER NOTES: Not drafted by an NBA franchise. ... Signed as free agent by Minnesota Timberwolves (September 30, 1997). ... Waived by Timberwolves (October 28, 1997). ... Played in Continental Basketball Association with Fort Wayne Fury (1997-99). ... Played in Greece (1998-99). ... Signed as free agent by Minnesota Timberwolves (January 21, 1999). ... Waived by Timberwolves (January 27, 1999). ... Signed as free agent by Detroit Pistons (January 29, 1999). ... Waived by Pistons (February 18, 1999). ... Signed as free agent by Pistons (October 5, 1999). ... Waived by Pistons (August 5, 2002). ... Waived by Spurs (October 24, 2002). ... Played in NBA Development League with Roanoke Dazzle (2002-03, 2003-04). ... Signed by Boston Celtics to 10-day contract (January 6, 2003). ... Signed by Atlanta Hawks for remainder of season (April 14, 2003). ... Signed as free agent by Seattle SuperSonics (September 27, 2003). ... Waived by SuperSonics (October 21, 2003). ... Signed as free agent by New Jersey Nets (December 22, 2003). ... Waived by Nets (January 7, 2004). ... Signed by Utah Jazz to first of two consecutive 10-day contracts (January 28, 2004). ... Signed by Jazz for remainder of season (March 4, 2004). ... Signed as free agent by Los Angeles Clippers (August 20, 2004). ... Signed as free agent by Seattle SuperSonics (August 31, 2005). ... Traded by SuperSonics to New Jersey Nets for second-round pick in 2009 draft (July 27, 2006).

COLLEGIATE RECORD

Season Team	G	Min.	FGM	FGA	Pct.	FTM	FTA	Pct.	Reb.	Ast.	Pts.	RPG	APG	PPG
93-94—Nebraska	14	87	10	22	.455	11	18	.611	13	1	31	0.9	0.1	2.2
94-95—Nebraska	32	788	102	205	.498	49	89	.551	198	25	255	6.2	0.8	8.0
95-96—Nebraska	35	968	118	202	.584	79	115	.687	205	36	315	5.9	1.0	9.0
96-97—Nebraska	33	1011	144	247	.583	96	137	.701	245	43	385	7.4	1.3	11.7
Totals	114	2854	374	676	.553	235	359	.655	661	105	986	5.8	0.9	8.6

Three-point field goals: 1993-94, 0-for-2. 1994-95, 2-for-8 (.250). 1996-97, 1-for-2 (.500). Totals, 3-for-12 (.250).
Personal fouls/disqualifications: 1993-94, 13/0. 1994-95, 94/0. 1995-96, 112/0. 1996-97, 105/0. Totals, 324/0.

CBA RECORD

NOTES: CBA All-League first team (1999). ... CBA All-Defensive team (1999). ... CBA All-Rookie team (1998).

Season Team	G	Min.	FGM	FGA	Pct.	FTM	FTA	Pct.	Reb.	Ast.	Pts.	RPG	APG	PPG
97-98—Fort Wayne	55	1478	262	450	.582	122	174	.701	346	60	647	6.3	1.1	11.8
98-99—Fort Wayne	29	1026	156	277	*.563	143	195	.733	219	41	455	7.6	1.4	15.7
Totals	84	2504	418	727	.575	265	369	.718	565	101	1102	6.7	1.2	13.1

Three-point field goals: 1997-98, 1-for-9 (.111). Totals, 1-for-9 (.111).
Personal fouls/disqualifications: 1997-98, 190/0. 1998-99, 98/0. Totals, 288/0.

GREEK LEAGUE RECORD

Season Team	G	Min.	FGM	FGA	Pct.	FTM	FTA	Pct.	Reb.	Ast.	Pts.	RPG	APG	PPG
98-99—Papagou	9	283	39	71	.549	22	29	.759	78	8	106	8.7	0.9	11.8

Three-point field goals: 1998-99, 6-for-12 (.500). Totals, 6-for-12 (.500).

NBA REGULAR-SEASON RECORD

Season Team	G	Min.	FGM	FGA	Pct.	FTM	FTA	Pct.	REBOUNDS Off.	Def.	Tot.	Ast.	St.	Blk.	TO	Pts.	RPG	APG	PPG
98-99—Detroit	2	6	1	1	1.000	2	2	1.000	0	1	1	0	0	0	0	4	0.5	0.0	2.0
99-00—Detroit	29	488	87	140	.621	54	68	.794	44	68	112	17	9	31	23	228	3.9	0.6	7.9

Season Team	G	Min.	FGM	FGA	Pct.	FTM	FTA	Pct.	REBOUNDS Off.	Def.	Tot.	Ast.	St.	Blk.	TO	Pts.	AVERAGES RPG	APG	PPG
00-01—Detroit	81	1154	132	268	.493	95	130	.731	121	195	316	33	24	61	74	359	3.9	0.4	4.4
01-02—Detroit	30	217	29	61	.475	20	26	.769	22	31	53	11	7	9	14	79	1.8	0.4	2.6
02-03—Bos-Atl	8	43	5	13	.385	8	10	.800	6	2	8	3	0	4	2	18	1.0	0.4	2.3
03-04—N.J.-Utah	32	395	50	99	.505	30	35	.857	29	55	84	19	7	13	22	130	2.6	0.6	4.1
04-05—L.A. Clippers	74	1178	144	287	.502	107	136	.787	97	149	246	47	19	32	63	396	3.3	0.6	5.4
05-06—Seattle	47	583	54	124	.435	46	62	.742	44	86	130	27	7	15	40	154	2.8	0.6	3.3
Totals	303	4064	502	993	.506	362	469	.772	363	587	950	157	73	165	238	1368	3.1	0.5	4.5

Three-point field goals: 2000-01, 0-for-1. 2001-02, 1-for-2 (.500). 2004-05, 1-for-5 (.200). 2005-06, 0-for-2. Totals, 2-for-10 (.200).

Personal fouls/disqualifications: 1999-00, 104/5. 2000-01, 202/2. 2001-02, 35/0. 2002-03, 7/0. 2003-04, 65/1. 2004-05, 173/1. 2005-06, 92/1. Totals, 678/10.

NBA PLAYOFF RECORD

Season Team	G	Min.	FGM	FGA	Pct.	FTM	FTA	Pct.	REBOUNDS Off.	Def.	Tot.	Ast.	St.	Blk.	TO	Pts.	AVERAGES RPG	APG	PPG
99-00—Detroit	3	42	5	12	.417	8	8	1.000	7	5	12	3	1	0	4	18	4.0	1.0	6.0

Personal fouls/disqualifications: 1999-00, 9/0. Totals, 9/0.

NBA DEVELOPMENT LEAGUE RECORD

Season Team	G	Min.	FGM	FGA	Pct.	FTM	FTA	Pct.	Reb.	Ast.	Pts.	AVERAGES RPG	APG	PPG
02-03—Roanoke	42	1409	252	477	.528	164	218	.752	352	104	674	8.4	2.5	16.0
03-04—Roanoke	17	687	122	226	.540	101	132	.765	152	48	347	8.9	2.8	20.4
Totals	59	2096	374	703	.532	265	350	.757	504	152	1021	8.5	2.6	17.3

Three-point field goals: 2002-03, 6-for-24 (.250). Totals, 6-for-24 (.250).

Personal fouls/disqualifications: 2002-03, 162/0. Totals, 162/0.

MORRIS, TERENCE — F

PERSONAL: Born January 11, 1979, in Frederick, Md. ... 6-9/221. (2.06/100.2). ... Full name: Terence Darea Morris
HIGH SCHOOL: Gov. Thomas Johnson (Frederick, Md.).
COLLEGE: Maryland.
TRANSACTIONS/CAREER NOTES: Selected by Atlanta Hawks in second round (34th pick overall) of 2001 NBA Draft. ... Draft rights traded by Hawks to Houston Rockets for future first-round draft choice (June 27, 2001). ... Played in NBA Development League (2003-04). ... Played in Greece (2004-05) Signed as free agent by Los Angeles Clippers (September 30, 2004). ... Waived by Clippers (October 28, 2004). ... Signed by Orlando Magic (September 29, 2005).

COLLEGIATE RECORD

Season Team	G	Min.	FGM	FGA	Pct.	FTM	FTA	Pct.	Reb.	Ast.	Pts.	AVERAGES RPG	APG	PPG
97-98—Maryland	32	511	91	174	.523	41	59	.695	113	25	236	3.5	0.8	7.4
98-99—Maryland	34	999	195	354	.551	104	126	.825	242	56	521	7.1	1.6	15.2
99-00—Maryland	34	1103	200	406	.493	102	134	.761	293	80	537	8.6	2.4	15.8
00-01—Maryland	36	993	158	366	.432	97	122	.795	277	68	439	7.7	1.9	12.2
Totals	136	3606	644	1300	.495	344	441	.780	925	229	1733	6.8	1.7	12.7

Three-point field goals: 1997-98, 13-for-37 (.351). 1998-99, 27-for-76 (.355). 1999-00, 35-for-96 (.365). 2000-01, 26-for-90 (.289). Totals, 101-for-299 (.338).

Personal fouls/disqualifications: 1997-98, 57/0. 1998-99, 79/0. 1999-00, 89/0. 2000-01, 94/0. Totals, 319/0.

NBA REGULAR-SEASON RECORD

Season Team	G	Min.	FGM	FGA	Pct.	FTM	FTA	Pct.	REBOUNDS Off.	Def.	Tot.	Ast.	St.	Blk.	TO	Pts.	AVERAGES RPG	APG	PPG
01-02—Houston	68	1110	111	289	.384	18	28	.643	77	134	211	64	21	27	45	255	3.1	0.9	3.8
02-03—Houston	49	632	82	176	.466	11	14	.786	40	88	128	25	8	17	29	182	2.6	0.5	3.7
05-06—Orlando	22	192	16	49	.327	3	3	1.000	6	32	38	4	6	5	7	35	1.7	0.2	1.6
Totals	139	1934	209	514	.407	32	45	.711	123	254	377	93	35	49	81	472	2.7	0.7	3.4

Three-point field goals: 2001-02, 15-for-78 (.192). 2002-03, 7-for-32 (.219). 2005-06, 0-for-2. Totals, 22-for-112 (.196).

Personal fouls/disqualifications: 2001-02, 72/1. 2002-03, 35/0. 2005-06, 19/0. Totals, 126/1.

NBA DEVELOPMENT LEAGUE RECORD

Season Team	G	Min.	FGM	FGA	Pct.	FTM	FTA	Pct.	Reb.	Ast.	Pts.	AVERAGES RPG	APG	PPG
03-04—Columbus	46	1220	220	482	.456	60	83	.723	340	87	526	7.4	1.9	11.4

Three-point field goals: 2003-04, 26-for-80 (.325). Totals, 26-for-80 (.325).

GREEK LEAGUE RECORD

Season Team	G	Min.	FGM	FGA	Pct.	FTM	FTA	Pct.	Reb.	Ast.	Pts.	AVERAGES RPG	APG	PPG
04-05—Apollon Patras	16	470	79	152	.520	9	11	.818	112	11	192	7.0	0.7	12.0

Three-point field goals: 2004-05, 25-for-64 (.391). Totals, 25-for-64 (.391).

MOURNING, ALONZO — C — HEAT

PERSONAL: Born February 8, 1970, in Chesapeake, Va. ... 6-10/261. (2.08/118.4).
HIGH SCHOOL: Indian River (Chesapeake, Va.).
COLLEGE: Georgetown.
TRANSACTIONS/CAREER NOTES: Selected by Charlotte Hornets in first round (second pick overall) of 1992 NBA Draft. ... Traded by Hornets with C LeRon Ellis and G Pete Myers to Miami Heat for G/F Glen Rice, G Khalid Reeves, C Matt Geiger and 1996 first-round draft choice (November 3, 1995). ... Signed as free agent by New Jersey Nets (July 16, 2003) ... Traded by Nets with F Eric Williams and F Aaron Williams and two first-round picks in the 2005 draft to Toronto Raptors for Vince Carter (December 17, 2004). ...

Waived by Raptors (February 11, 2005). ... Signed as free agent by Miami Heat (March 1, 2005).
MISCELLANEOUS: Member of gold-medal-winning U.S. Olympic team (2000). ... Member of bronze-medal-winning U.S. World Championship team (1990) and gold-medal-winning U.S. World Championship team (1994). ... Charlotte Hornets all-time blocked shots leader with 684 (1992-93 through 1994-95). ... Miami Heat all-time blocked shots leader with 1,405 (1995-96 through 2001-02 and 2004-06). ... Member of NBA championship team (2006).

COLLEGIATE RECORD

NOTES: THE SPORTING NEWS All-America second team (1990, 1992). ... Led NCAA Division I with 4.97 blocked shots per game (1989). ... Led NCAA Division I in blocked shots with 169 (1989) and 160 (1992).

													AVERAGES		
Season Team	G	Min.	FGM	FGA	Pct.	FTM	FTA	Pct.	Reb.	Ast.	Pts.		RPG	APG	PPG
88-89—Georgetown	34	962	158	262	.603	130	195	.667	248	24	447		7.3	0.7	13.1
89-90—Georgetown	31	937	145	276	.525	220	281	.783	265	36	510		8.5	1.2	16.5
90-91—Georgetown	23	682	105	201	.522	149	188	.793	176	25	363		7.7	1.1	15.8
91-92—Georgetown	32	1051	204	343	.595	272	359	.758	343	33	681		10.7	1.7	21.3
Totals	120	3632	612	1082	.566	771	1023	.754	1032	138	2001		8.6	1.2	16.7

Three-point field goals: 1988-89, 1-for-4 (.250). 1989-90, 0-for-2. 1990-91, 4-for-13 (.308). 1991-92, 6-for-23 (.261). Totals, 11-for-42 (.262).

NBA REGULAR-SEASON RECORD

HONORS: J. Walter Kennedy Citizenship Award (2002). ... NBA Defensive Player of the Year (1999, 2000). ... All-NBA first team (1999). ... All-NBA second team (2000). ... NBA All-Defensive first team (1999, 2000). ... NBA All-Rookie first team (1993).
NOTES: Led NBA with 3.91 blocked shots per game (1999) and 3.7 blocks per game (2000).

									REBOUNDS								AVERAGES		
Season Team	G	Min.	FGM	FGA	Pct.	FTM	FTA	Pct.	Off.	Def.	Tot.	Ast.	St.	Blk.	TO	Pts.	RPG	APG	PPG
92-93—Charlotte	78	2644	572	1119	.511	495	634	.781	263	542	805	76	27	271	236	1639	10.3	1.0	21.0
93-94—Charlotte	60	2018	427	845	.505	433	568	.762	177	433	610	86	27	188	199	1287	10.2	1.4	21.5
94-95—Charlotte	77	2941	571	1101	.519	490	644	.761	200	561	761	111	49	225	241	1643	9.9	1.4	21.3
95-96—Miami	70	2671	563	1076	.523	488	712	.685	218	509	727	159	70	189	262	1623	10.4	2.3	23.2
96-97—Miami	66	2320	473	885	.534	363	565	.642	189	467	656	104	56	189	226	1310	9.9	1.6	19.8
97-98—Miami	58	1939	403	732	.551	309	465	.665	193	365	558	52	40	130	179	1115	9.6	0.9	19.2
98-99—Miami	46	1753	324	634	.511	276	423	.652	166	341	507	74	34	*180	139	924	11.0	1.6	20.1
99-00—Miami	79	2748	652	1184	.551	414	582	.711	215	538	753	123	40	*294	217	1718	9.5	1.6	21.7
00-01—Miami	13	306	73	141	.518	31	55	.564	35	66	101	12	4	31	28	177	7.8	0.9	13.6
01-02—Miami	75	2455	447	866	.516	283	431	.657	182	450	632	87	27	186	182	1178	8.4	1.2	15.7
02-03—Miami							Did not play—injured												
03-04—New Jersey	12	215	33	71	.465	30	34	.882	8	19	27	8	2	6	10	96	2.3	0.7	8.0
04-05—N.J.-Tor.-Miami	37	702	100	212	.472	82	141	.582	53	145	198	18	8	74	57	282	5.4	0.5	7.6
05-06—Miami	65	1302	188	315	.597	133	224	.594	125	234	359	11	13	173	79	509	5.5	0.2	7.8
Totals	736	24014	4826	9181	.526	3827	5478	.699	2024	4670	6694	921	397	2136	2055	13501	9.1	1.3	18.3

Three-point field goals: 1992-93, 0-for-3. 1993-94, 0-for-2. 1994-95, 11-for-34 (.324). 1995-96, 9-for-30 (.300). 1996-97, 1-for-9 (.111). 1998-99, 0-for-2. 1999-00, 0-for-4. 2000-01, 0-for-1. 2001-02, 1-for-3 (.333). 2005-06, 0-for-1. Totals, 22-for-89 (.247).
Personal fouls/disqualifications: 1992-93, 286/6. 1993-94, 207/3. 1994-95, 275/5. 1995-96, 245/5. 1996-97, 272/9. 1997-98, 208/4. 1998-99, 161/1. 1999-00, 308/8. 2000-01, 24/0. 2001-02, 258/7. 2003-04, 32/0. 2004-05, 82/1. 2005-06, 177/4. Totals, 2535/53.

NBA PLAYOFF RECORD

									REBOUNDS								AVERAGES		
Season Team	G	Min.	FGM	FGA	Pct.	FTM	FTA	Pct.	Off.	Def.	Tot.	Ast.	St.	Blk.	TO	Pts.	RPG	APG	PPG
92-93—Charlotte	9	367	71	148	.480	72	93	.774	28	61	89	13	6	31	37	214	9.9	1.4	23.8
94-95—Charlotte	4	174	24	57	.421	36	43	.837	14	39	53	11	3	13	14	88	13.3	2.8	22.0
95-96—Miami	3	92	17	35	.486	20	28	.714	3	15	18	4	2	3	16	54	6.0	1.3	18.0
96-97—Miami	17	630	107	218	.491	86	155	.555	44	129	173	18	11	46	70	303	10.2	1.1	17.8
97-98—Miami	4	138	29	56	.518	19	29	.655	10	24	34	5	3	10	8	77	8.5	1.3	19.3
98-99—Miami	5	194	38	73	.521	32	49	.653	7	34	41	4	8	14	12	108	8.2	0.8	21.6
99-00—Miami	10	376	76	157	.484	64	96	.667	31	69	100	14	2	33	24	216	10.0	1.4	21.6
00-01—Miami	3	91	12	25	.480	11	19	.579	3	13	16	3	0	5	5	35	5.3	1.0	11.7
04-05—Miami	15	254	31	44	.705	29	52	.558	21	51	72	5	5	33	22	91	4.8	0.3	6.1
05-06—Miami	21	226	26	37	.703	28	42	.667	17	44	61	3	5	24	17	80	2.9	0.1	3.8
Totals	91	2542	431	850	.507	397	606	.655	178	479	657	80	45	212	225	1266	7.2	0.9	13.9

Three-point field goals: 1992-93, 0-for-2. 1994-95, 4-for-8 (.500). 1996-97, 3-for-8 (.375). 1999-00, 0-for-1. Totals, 7-for-19 (.368).
Personal fouls/disqualifications: 1992-93, 37/1. 1994-95, 17/0. 1995-96, 13/1. 1996-97, 73/2. 1997-98, 18/0. 1998-99, 19/0. 1999-00, 40/1. 2000-01, 9/0. 2004-05, 49/2. 2005-06, 49/0. Totals, 324/7.

NBA ALL-STAR GAME RECORD

							REBOUNDS									
Season Team	Min.	FGM	FGA	Pct.	FTM	FTA	Pct.	Off.	Def.	Tot.	Ast.	PF	Dq.	St.	Blk.	TO	Pts.
1994—Charlotte						Selected, did not play—injured											
1995—Charlotte	19	4	9	.444	2	3	.667	0	8	8	1	5	0	0	1	1	10
1996—Miami	13	1	6	.167	0	0	...	0	1	1	0	2	0	0	1	2	2
1997—Miami						Selected, did not play—injured											
2000—Miami	27	7	11	.636	1	2	.500	2	5	7	1	4	0	3	4	1	15
2001—Miami						Selected, did not play—injured											
2002—Miami	16	6	7	.857	1	1	1.000	1	2	3	2	1	0	0	2	1	13
Totals	75	18	33	.545	4	6	.667	3	16	19	4	12	0	3	8	5	40

Three-point field goals: 1995, 0-for-1. Totals, 0-for-1 (.000).

MURPHY, TROY   F   WARRIORS

PERSONAL: Born May 2, 1980, in Sparta, N.J. ... 6-11/245. (2.11/111.1). ... Full name: Troy Brandon Murphy
HIGH SCHOOL: Delbarton (Morristown, N.J.).
COLLEGE: Notre Dame.
TRANSACTIONS/CAREER NOTES: Selected after junior season by Golden State Warriors in first round (14th pick overall) of 2001 NBA Draft.

NOTES: The SPORTING NEWS All-America first team (2001). ... The SPORTING NEWS All-America second team (2000).

Season Team	G	Min.	FGM	FGA	Pct.	FTM	FTA	Pct.	Reb.	Ast.	Pts.	AVERAGES RPG	APG	PPG
98-99—Notre Dame	27	890	180	340	.529	149	201	.741	267	38	519	9.9	1.4	19.2
99-00—Notre Dame	37	1318	274	557	.492	261	323	.808	380	58	839	10.3	1.6	22.7
00-01—Notre Dame	30	1090	223	473	.471	177	231	.766	277	62	653	9.2	2.1	21.8
Totals	94	3298	677	1370	.494	587	755	.777	924	158	2011	9.8	1.7	21.4

Three-point field goals: 1998-99, 4-for-13 (.308). 1999-00, 30-for-92 (.326). 2000-01, 30-for-86 (.349). Totals, 64-for-191 (.335).
Personal fouls/disqualifications: 1998-99, 77/0. 1999-00, 101/0. 2000-01, 96/0. Totals, 274/0.

NBA REGULAR-SEASON RECORD

Season Team	G	Min.	FGM	FGA	Pct.	FTM	FTA	Pct.	REBOUNDS Off.	Def.	Tot.	Ast.	St.	Blk.	TO	Pts.	AVERAGES RPG	APG	PPG
01-02—Golden State	82	1448	178	423	.421	121	156	.776	99	223	322	70	36	21	84	480	3.9	0.9	5.9
02-03—Golden State	79	2510	338	749	.451	244	290	.841	228	578	806	106	65	30	111	923	10.2	1.3	11.7
03-04—Golden State	28	610	107	243	.440	60	80	.750	48	125	173	20	12	17	34	279	6.2	0.7	10.0
04-05—Golden State	70	2375	392	947	.414	233	319	.730	251	505	756	97	53	33	108	1076	10.8	1.4	15.4
05-06—Golden State	74	2516	363	838	.433	251	319	.787	195	548	743	101	47	26	108	1035	10.0	1.4	14.0
Totals	333	9459	1378	3200	.431	909	1164	.781	821	1979	2800	394	213	127	445	3793	8.4	1.2	11.4

Three-point field goals: 2001-02, 3-for-9 (.333). 2002-03, 3-for-14 (.214). 2003-04, 5-for-17 (.294). 2004-05, 59-for-148 (.399). 2005-06, 58-for-181 (.320). Totals, 128-for-369 (.347).
Personal fouls/disqualifications: 2001-02, 217/2. 2002-03, 246/1. 2003-04, 58/1. 2004-05, 190/2. 2005-06, 191/2. Totals, 902/8.

MURRAY, LAMOND   F   NETS

PERSONAL: Born April 20, 1973, in Pasadena, Calif. ... 6-7/236. (2.01/107.0). ... Full name: Lamond Maurice Murray ... Cousin of Tracy Murray, forward with six NBA teams (1993-2004).
HIGH SCHOOL: John Kennedy (Fremont, Calif.).
COLLEGE: California.
TRANSACTIONS/CAREER NOTES: Selected after junior season by Los Angeles Clippers in first round (seventh pick overall) of 1994 NBA Draft. ... Traded by Clippers to Cleveland Cavaliers for G Derek Anderson and F Johnny Newman (August 4, 1999). ... Traded by Cavaliers with future second-round draft choice to Toronto Raptors for C Michael Stewart and future first-round draft choice (September 25, 2002). ... Waived by Raptors (September 2, 2005). ... Signed by New Jersey Nets (September 8, 2005).

COLLEGIATE RECORD

Season Team	G	Min.	FGM	FGA	Pct.	FTM	FTA	Pct.	Reb.	Ast.	Pts.	AVERAGES RPG	APG	PPG
91-92—California	28	745	152	321	.474	66	93	.710	171	56	387	6.1	2.0	13.8
92-93—California	30	897	230	445	.517	76	121	.628	189	41	572	6.3	1.4	19.1
93-94—California	30	1047	262	550	.476	159	208	.764	236	63	729	7.9	2.1	24.3
Totals	88	2689	644	1316	.489	301	422	.713	596	160	1688	6.8	1.8	19.2

Three-point field goals: 1991-92, 17-for-56 (.304). 1992-93, 36-for-99 (.364). 1993-94, 46-for-139 (.331). Totals, 99-for-294 (.337).

NBA REGULAR-SEASON RECORD

Season Team	G	Min.	FGM	FGA	Pct.	FTM	FTA	Pct.	REBOUNDS Off.	Def.	Tot.	Ast.	St.	Blk.	TO	Pts.	AVERAGES RPG	APG	PPG
94-95—L.A. Clippers	81	2556	439	1093	.402	199	264	.754	132	222	354	133	72	55	163	1142	4.4	1.6	14.1
95-96—L.A. Clippers	77	1816	257	575	.447	99	132	.750	89	157	246	84	61	25	108	650	3.2	1.1	8.4
96-97—L.A. Clippers	74	1295	181	435	.416	156	211	.739	85	148	233	57	53	29	86	549	3.1	0.8	7.4
97-98—L.A. Clippers	79	2579	473	984	.481	220	294	.748	172	312	484	142	118	54	171	1220	6.1	1.8	15.4
98-99—L.A. Clippers	50	1317	226	578	.391	126	157	.803	59	136	195	61	58	20	99	612	3.9	1.2	12.2
99-00—Cleveland	74	2365	460	1019	.451	204	268	.761	127	296	423	132	105	36	184	1175	5.7	1.8	15.9
00-01—Cleveland	78	2225	391	925	.423	155	211	.735	104	236	340	124	83	27	141	998	4.4	1.6	12.8
01-02—Cleveland	71	2312	430	986	.436	215	263	.817	81	291	372	157	70	43	141	1176	5.2	2.2	16.6
02-03—Toronto																Did not play—injured		
03-04—Toronto	33	518	76	215	.353	24	35	.686	14	76	90	28	15	7	38	197	2.7	0.8	6.0
04-05—Toronto	62	918	132	310	.426	61	80	.763	44	120	164	47	32	16	54	371	2.6	0.8	6.0
05-06—New Jersey	57	576	72	181	.398	25	40	.625	29	103	132	13	17	7	22	196	2.3	0.2	3.4
Totals	736	18477	3137	7301	.430	1484	1955	.759	936	2097	3033	978	684	319	1207	8286	4.1	1.3	11.3

Three-point field goals: 1994-95, 65-for-218 (.298). 1995-96, 37-for-116 (.319). 1996-97, 31-for-91 (.341). 1997-98, 54-for-153 (.353). 1998-99, 34-for-103 (.330). 1999-00, 51-for-139 (.367). 2000-01, 61-for-165 (.370). 2001-02, 101-for-238 (.424). 2003-04, 21-for-60 (.350). 2004-05, 46-for-105 (.438). 2005-06, 27-for-78 (.346). Totals, 528-for-1466 (.360).
Personal fouls/disqualifications: 1994-95, 180/3. 1995-96, 151/0. 1996-97, 113/3. 1997-98, 193/3. 1998-99, 107/1. 1999-00, 208/2. 2000-01, 173/0. 2001-02, 148/1. 2003-04, 47/0. 2004-05, 85/0. 2005-06, 66/0. Totals, 1471/13.

NBA PLAYOFF RECORD

Season Team	G	Min.	FGM	FGA	Pct.	FTM	FTA	Pct.	REBOUNDS Off.	Def.	Tot.	Ast.	St.	Blk.	TO	Pts.	AVERAGES RPG	APG	PPG
96-97—L.A. Clippers	3	65	6	20	.300	7	7	1.000	2	9	11	3	2	3	4	21	3.7	1.0	7.0
05-06—New Jersey	11	197	21	54	.389	9	11	.818	9	29	38	2	3	0	3	63	3.5	0.2	5.7
Totals	14	262	27	74	.365	16	18	.889	11	38	49	5	5	3	7	84	3.5	0.4	6.0

Three-point field goals: 1996-97, 2-for-8 (.250). 2005-06, 12-for-34 (.353). Totals, 14-for-42 (.333).
Personal fouls/disqualifications: 1996-97, 7/0. 2005-06, 25/0. Totals, 32/0.

MURRAY, RONALD   G   PISTONS

PERSONAL: Born July 29, 1979, in Philadelphia. ... 6-4/190. (1.93/86.2). ... Nickname: Flip
HIGH SCHOOL: Strawberry Mansion (Philadelphia).
JUNIOR COLLEGE: Meridian (Miss.) Community College, then Philadelphia C.C.
COLLEGE: Shaw (N.C.).
TRANSACTIONS/CAREER NOTES: Selected by Milwaukee Bucks in second round (42nd pick overall) of 2002 NBA Draft.

... Traded by Bucks with G Ray Allen, G Kevin Ollie and conditional first-round draft choice to Seattle SuperSonics for G Gary Payton and G Desmond Mason (February 20, 2003). ... Traded by SuperSonics to Cleveland Cavaliers for G Mike Wilks and cash (February 23, 2006). ... Signed as free agent by Detroit Pistons (July 18, 2006).

COLLEGIATE RECORD

Season Team	G	Min.	FGM	FGA	Pct.	FTM	FTA	Pct.	Reb.	Ast.	Pts.	RPG	APG	PPG
97-98—Meridian C.C.	...	...	...	...	...	...	...	...	...	...	...	3.5	2.0	17.8
98-99—Meridian C.C.	34	...	255	506	.504	123	177	.695	169	56	681	5.0	1.6	20.0
99-00—Philadelphia C.C.						Did not play.								
00-01—Shaw	23	876	173	382	.453	139	192	.724	129	109	510	5.6	4.7	22.2
01-02—Shaw	33	1202	256	526	.487	220	285	.772	209	205	777	6.3	6.2	23.5
Junior College Totals	34	...	255	506	.504	123	177	.695	169	56	681	5.0	1.6	20.0
4-Year-College Totals	56	2078	429	908	.472	359	477	.753	338	314	1287	6.0	5.6	23.0

Three-point field goals: 1998-99, 48-for-145 (.331). 2000-01, 25-for-71 (.352). 2001-02, 45-for-129 (.349). Totals, 118-for-345 (.342).

NBA REGULAR-SEASON RECORD

Season Team	G	Min.	FGM	FGA	Pct.	FTM	FTA	Pct.	Off.	Def.	Tot.	Ast.	St.	Blk.	TO	Pts.	RPG	APG	PPG
02-03—Mil.-Seattle	14	62	11	31	.355	5	8	.625	0	4	4	5	4	0	8	27	0.3	0.4	1.9
03-04—Seattle	82	2021	389	915	.425	168	235	.715	45	159	204	205	81	28	149	1013	2.5	2.5	12.4
04-05—Seattle	49	883	131	363	.361	59	80	.738	15	83	98	65	30	11	57	345	2.0	1.3	7.0
05-06—Seattle-Cleve...	76	2112	321	768	.418	172	242	.711	33	120	153	197	68	11	135	851	2.0	2.6	11.2
Totals	221	5078	852	2077	.410	404	565	.715	93	366	459	472	183	50	349	2236	2.1	2.1	10.1

Three-point field goals: 2002-03, 0-for-5. 2003-04, 67-for-229 (.293). 2004-05, 24-for-95 (.253). 2005-06, 37-for-141 (.262). Totals, 128-for-470 (.272). Personal fouls/disqualifications: 2003-04, 158/0. 2004-05, 59/0. 2005-06, 133/0. Totals, 350/0.

NBA PLAYOFF RECORD

Season Team	G	Min.	FGM	FGA	Pct.	FTM	FTA	Pct.	Off.	Def.	Tot.	Ast.	St.	Blk.	TO	Pts.	RPG	APG	PPG
04-05—Seattle	4	62	4	19	.211	4	7	.571	2	4	6	5	0	2	2	12	1.5	1.3	3.0
05-06—Cleveland	13	399	37	112	.330	26	32	.813	11	31	42	21	9	2	9	105	3.2	1.6	8.1
Totals	17	461	41	131	.313	30	39	.769	13	35	48	26	9	4	11	117	2.8	1.5	6.9

Three-point field goals: 2004-05, 0-for-2. 2005-06, 5-for-24 (.208). Totals, 5-for-26 (.192). Personal fouls/disqualifications: 2004-05, 8/0. 2005-06, 27/0. Totals, 35/0.

MUTOMBO, DIKEMBE   C   ROCKETS

PERSONAL: Born June 25, 1966, in Kinshasa, Zaire. ... 7-2/261. (2.18/118.4). ... Name pronounced di-KEM-bay moo-TUM-bow.
HIGH SCHOOL: Institute Boboto (Kinshasa, Zaire).
COLLEGE: Georgetown.
TRANSACTIONS/CAREER NOTES: Selected by Denver Nuggets in first round (fourth pick overall) of 1991 NBA Draft. ... Signed as free agent by Atlanta Hawks (July 15, 1996). ... Traded by Hawks with F Roshown McLeod to Philadelphia 76ers for F/C Theo Ratliff, F/G Toni Kukoc, C Nazr Mohammed and G Pepe Sanchez (February 22, 2001). ... Traded by 76ers to New Jersey Nets for F Keith Van Horn and C Todd MacCulloch (August 6, 2002). ... Waived by Nets (October 7, 2003). ... Signed as free agent by New York Knicks (October 9, 2003). ... Traded by Knicks with F Othella Harrington, C Cezary Trybanski and G Frank Williams to Chicago Bulls for G Jamal Crawford and F Jerome Williams (August 5, 2004). ... Traded by Bulls to Houston Rockets for G Mike Wilks, G/F Eric Piatkowski and G/F Adrian Griffin (September 8, 2004).
MISCELLANEOUS: Denver Nuggets franchise all-time blocked shots leader with 1,486 (1991-92 through 1995-96).

COLLEGIATE RECORD

NOTES: THE SPORTING NEWS All-America third team (1991).

Season Team	G	Min.	FGM	FGA	Pct.	FTM	FTA	Pct.	Reb.	Ast.	Pts.	RPG	APG	PPG
87-88—Georgetown							Did not play.							
88-89—Georgetown	33	374	53	75	.707	23	48	.479	109	5	129	3.3	0.2	3.9
89-90—Georgetown	31	797	129	182	.709	73	122	.598	325	18	331	10.5	0.6	10.7
90-91—Georgetown	32	1090	170	290	.586	147	209	.703	389	52	487	12.2	1.6	15.2
Totals	96	2261	352	547	.644	243	379	.641	823	75	947	8.6	0.8	9.9

NBA REGULAR-SEASON RECORD

RECORDS: Holds career record for most consecutive seasons leading league in blocked shots per game—3 (1993-94 through 1995-96).
HONORS: J. Walter Kennedy Citizenship Award (2001). ... NBA Defensive Player of the Year (1995, 1997, 1998, 2001). ... IBM Award, for all-around contributions to team's success (1999). ... All-NBA second team (2001). ... All-NBA Third Team (1998, 2002). ... NBA All-Defensive first team (1997, 1998, 2001). ... NBA All-Defensive second team (1995, 1999, 2002). ... NBA All-Rookie first team (1992).
NOTES: Led NBA with 4.10 blocked shots per game (1994), 3.91 blocked shots per game (1995) and 4.49 blocked shots per game (1996).

Season Team	G	Min.	FGM	FGA	Pct.	FTM	FTA	Pct.	Off.	Def.	Tot.	Ast.	St.	Blk.	TO	Pts.	RPG	APG	PPG
91-92—Denver	71	2716	428	869	.493	321	500	.642	316	554	870	156	43	210	252	1177	12.3	2.2	16.6
92-93—Denver	82	3029	398	781	.510	335	492	.681	344	726	1070	147	43	287	216	1131	13.0	1.8	13.8
93-94—Denver	82	2853	365	642	.569	256	439	.583	286	685	971	127	59	*336	206	986	11.8	1.5	12.0
94-95—Denver	82	3100	349	628	.556	248	379	.654	319	*710	1029	113	40	*321	192	946	12.5	1.4	11.5
95-96—Denver	74	2713	284	559	.499	246	354	.695	249	622	871	108	38	*332	150	814	11.8	1.5	11.0
96-97—Atlanta	80	2973	380	721	.527	306	434	.705	268	661	929	110	49	*264	186	1066	11.6	1.4	13.3
97-98—Atlanta	82	2917	399	743	.537	303	452	.670	276	656	932	82	34	*277	168	1101	11.4	1.0	13.4
98-99—Atlanta	50	1829	173	338	.512	195	285	.684	*192	*418	610	57	16	147	94	541	12.2	1.1	10.8
99-00—Atlanta	82	2984	322	573	.562	298	421	.708	*304	*853	1157	105	27	269	174	942	*14.1	1.3	11.5
00-01—Atlanta-Phila.	75	2591	269	556	.484	211	291	.725	307	708	*1015	76	29	203	144	749	*13.5	1.0	10.0
01-02—Philadelphia	80	2907	321	641	.501	278	364	.764	254	609	863	83	29	190	156	920	10.8	1.0	11.5

Season Team	G	Min.	FGM	FGA	Pct.	FTM	FTA	Pct.	Off.	Def.	Tot.	Ast.	St.	Blk.	TO	Pts.	RPG	APG	PPG
									REBOUNDS								**AVERAGES**		
02-03—New Jersey.....	24	514	49	131	.374	40	55	.727	54	99	153	19	4	37	34	138	6.4	0.8	5.8
03-04—New York.......	65	1494	141	295	.478	81	119	.681	145	292	437	25	17	123	54	363	6.7	0.4	5.6
04-05—Houston........	80	1212	108	217	.498	106	143	.741	150	276	426	10	16	101	51	322	5.3	0.1	4.0
05-06—Houston.........	64	955	50	95	.526	69	91	.758	100	206	306	4	17	57	35	169	4.8	0.1	2.6
Totals	1073	34787	4036	7799	.518	3293	4819	.683	3564	8075	11639	1222	461	3154	2112	11365	10.8	1.1	10.6

Three-point field goals: 1993-94, 0-for-1. 1995-96, 0-for-1. Totals, 0-for-2 (.000).
Personal fouls/disqualifications: 1991-92, 273/1. 1992-93, 284/5. 1993-94, 262/2. 1994-95, 284/2. 1995-96, 258/4. 1996-97, 249/3. 1997-98, 254/1. 1998-99, 145/2. 1999-00, 248/3. 2000-01, 204/2. 2001-02, 242/2. 2002-03, 54/0. 2003-04, 141/0. 2004-05, 135/1. 2005-06, 128/0. Totals, 3161/28.

NBA PLAYOFF RECORD

Season Team	G	Min.	FGM	FGA	Pct.	FTM	FTA	Pct.	Off.	Def.	Tot.	Ast.	St.	Blk.	TO	Pts.	RPG	APG	PPG
									REBOUNDS								**AVERAGES**		
93-94—Denver...........	12	511	50	108	.463	59	98	.602	40	104	144	21	8	69	30	159	12.0	1.8	13.3
94-95—Denver...........	3	84	6	10	.600	6	9	.667	4	15	19	1	0	7	7	18	6.3	0.3	6.0
96-97—Atlanta...........	10	415	54	86	.628	46	64	.719	37	86	123	13	1	26	20	154	12.3	1.3	15.4
97-98—Atlanta...........	4	136	11	24	.458	10	16	.625	13	38	51	1	1	9	8	32	12.8	0.3	8.0
98-99—Atlanta...........	9	380	40	71	.563	33	47	.702	36	89	125	11	5	23	18	113	13.9	1.2	12.6
00-01—Philadelphia....	23	981	102	208	.490	115	148	.777	113	203	316	17	15	72	36	319	13.7	0.7	13.9
01-02—Philadelphia....	5	173	14	31	.452	16	26	.615	14	39	53	3	2	9	11	44	10.6	0.6	8.8
02-03—New Jersey....	10	115	7	15	.467	4	4	1.000	8	19	27	6	3	9	8	18	2.7	0.6	1.8
03-04—New York......	3	38	2	6	.333	3	3	1.000	4	6	10	0	1	4	3	7	3.3	0.0	2.3
04-05—Houston.........	7	101	6	11	.545	10	13	.769	11	24	35	2	2	7	7	22	5.0	0.3	3.1
Totals	86	2934	292	570	.512	302	428	.706	280	623	903	75	38	235	148	886	10.5	0.9	10.3

Three-point field goals: 2000-01, 0-for-1. Totals, 0-for-1 (.000).
Personal fouls/disqualifications: 1993-94, 42/0. 1994-95, 15/1. 1996-97, 30/0. 1997-98, 10/0. 1998-99, 28/0. 2000-01, 56/1. 2001-02, 16/0. 2002-03, 21/0. 2003-04, 6/0. 2004-05, 15/0. Totals, 239/2.

NBA ALL-STAR GAME RECORD

Season Team	Min.	FGM	FGA	Pct.	FTM	FTA	Pct.	Off.	Def.	Tot.	Ast.	PF	Dq.	St.	Blk.	TO	Pts.
								REBOUNDS									
1992—Denver	10	2	4	.500	0	0	...	1	1	2	1	0	0	1	0	2	4
1995—Denver	20	6	8	.750	0	0	...	3	5	8	1	3	0	4	0	4	12
1996—Denver	11	2	4	.500	0	0	...	6	3	9	0	3	0	0	0	3	4
1997—Atlanta................	15	1	5	.200	1	2	.500	2	6	8	0	0	0	0	1	1	3
1998—Atlanta................	19	4	5	.800	1	2	.500	1	6	7	0	3	...	0	1	0	9
2000—Atlanta................	16	2	4	.500	0	0	...	2	6	8	0	0	0	0	0	2	4
2001—Atlanta................	28	2	2	1.000	2	2	1.000	3	19	22	0	5	0	2	3	2	6
2002—Philadelphia	21	3	5	.600	2	2	1.000	6	4	10	0	0	0	0	1	2	8
Totals.........................	140	22	37	.595	6	8	.750	24	50	74	2	14	0	3	10	12	50

N'DONG, BONIFACE   C   CLIPPERS

PERSONAL: Born September 3, 1977, in Mbour, Senegal. ... 7-0/205. (2.13/93.0).
TRANSACTIONS/CAREER NOTES: [illegible] ... Played in Germany (2000-2003) ... Played in France (2003-05). ... Signed as free agent by Los Angeles Clippers (October 1, 2005).

GERMAN LEAGUE RECORD

Season Team	G	Min.	FGM	FGA	Pct.	FTM	FTA	Pct.	Reb.	Ast.	Pts.	RPG	APG	PPG
												AVERAGES		
02-03—Bamberg.....................	8	121	18	38	.474	1	5	.200	33	5	37	4.1	0.6	4.6

Three-point field goals: 2002-03, 0-for-1. Totals, 0-for-1 (.000).

FRENCH LEAGUE RECORD

Season Team	G	Min.	FGM	FGA	Pct.	FTM	FTA	Pct.	Reb.	Ast.	Pts.	RPG	APG	PPG
												AVERAGES		
03-04—Dijon	9	222	42	79	.532	22	34	.647	75	6	106	8.3	0.7	11.8
04-05—Dijon	34	987	203	393	.517	90	131	.687	287	46	497	8.4	1.4	14.6
Totals	43	1209	245	472	.519	112	165	.679	362	52	603	8.4	1.2	14.0

Three-point field goals: 2003-04, 0-for-1. 2004-05, 1-for-4 (.250). Totals, 1-for-5 (.200).

NBA REGULAR-SEASON RECORD

Season Team	G	Min.	FGM	FGA	Pct.	FTM	FTA	Pct.	Off.	Def.	Tot.	Ast.	St.	Blk.	TO	Pts.	RPG	APG	PPG
									REBOUNDS								**AVERAGES**		
05-06—L.A. Clippers .	23	152	22	53	.415	6	9	.667	15	22	37	7	2	5	6	50	1.6	0.3	2.2

Three-point field goals: 2005-06, 0-for-1. Totals, 0-for-1 (.000).
Personal fouls/disqualifications: 2005-06, 23/0. Totals, 23/0.

NACHBAR, BOSTJAN   F   NETS

PERSONAL: Born July 3, 1980, in Slovenj Gradec, Slovenia. ... 6-9/221. (2.06/100.2).
TRANSACTIONS/CAREER NOTES: Played in Slovenia (1996-2000). ... Played in Italy (2000-02). ... Selected by Houston Rockets in first round (15th pick overall) of 2002 NBA Draft. ... Traded with G Jim Jackson to New Orleans Hornets for G David Wesley (December 27, 2004). ... Traded by Hornets to New Jersey Nets for F/C Marc Jackson, F Linton Johnson and cash (February 23, 2006).

SLOVENIAN LEAGUE RECORD

Season Team	G	Min.	FGM	FGA	Pct.	FTM	FTA	Pct.	Reb.	Ast.	Pts.	RPG	APG	PPG
												AVERAGES		
96-97—KK Maribor....................	8	107	18	35	.514	12	21	.571	14	3	52	1.8	0.4	6.5
97-98—Olimpija Ljubljana...........	24	475	67	123	.545	38	50	.760	58	19	178	2.4	0.8	7.4

N

Season Team	G	Min.	FGM	FGA	Pct.	FTM	FTA	Pct.	Reb.	Ast.	Pts.	RPG	APG	PPG
98-99—KK Maribor	26	633	106	217	.488	101	131	.771	84	19	321	3.2	0.7	12.3
99-00—KK Pivovarna Lasko	32	1002	95	186	.511	81	117	.692	84	37	288	2.6	1.2	9.0
Totals	90	2217	286	561	.510	232	319	.727	240	78	839	2.7	0.9	9.3

Three-point field goals: 1996-97, 4-for-11 (.364). 1997-98, 6-for-28 (.214). 1998-99, 8-for-44 (.182). 1999-00, 17-for-40 (.425). Totals, 35-for-123 (.285).

ITALIAN LEAGUE RECORD

Season Team	G	Min.	FGM	FGA	Pct.	FTM	FTA	Pct.	Reb.	Ast.	Pts.	RPG	APG	PPG
00-01—Benetton Treviso	30	329	42	109	.385	37	48	.771	51	11	128	1.7	0.4	4.3
01-02—Benetton Treviso	35	863	169	326	.518	109	139	.784	146	49	491	4.2	1.4	14.0
Totals	65	1192	211	435	.485	146	187	.781	197	60	619	3.0	0.9	9.5

Three-point field goals: 2000-01, 7-for-29 (.241). 2001-02, 44-for-119 (.370). Totals, 51-for-148 (.345).

NBA REGULAR-SEASON RECORD

Season Team	G	Min.	FGM	FGA	Pct.	FTM	FTA	Pct.	REBOUNDS Off.	Def.	Tot.	Ast.	St.	Blk.	TO	Pts.	RPG	APG	PPG
02-03—Houston	14	77	11	31	.355	5	10	.500	3	8	11	3	2	2	6	29	0.8	0.2	2.1
03-04—Houston	45	516	47	132	.356	21	29	.724	8	62	70	30	14	14	23	138	1.6	0.7	3.1
04-05—Houston-N.O.	71	1341	161	411	.392	97	117	.829	24	158	182	74	29	16	73	494	2.6	1.0	7.0
05-06—NO/Okla. City-N.J.	36	502	54	156	.346	30	44	.682	8	52	60	27	16	5	24	157	1.7	0.8	4.4
Totals	166	2436	273	730	.374	153	200	.765	43	280	323	134	61	37	126	818	1.9	0.8	4.9

Three-point field goals: 2002-03, 2-for-10 (.200). 2003-04, 23-for-63 (.365). 2004-05, 75-for-196 (.383). 2005-06, 19-for-71 (.268). Totals, 119-for-340 (.350).
Personal fouls/disqualifications: 2002-03, 13/0. 2003-04, 72/1. 2004-05, 183/1. 2005-06, 65/0. Totals, 333/2.

NBA PLAYOFF RECORD

Season Team	G	Min.	FGM	FGA	Pct.	FTM	FTA	Pct.	REBOUNDS Off.	Def.	Tot.	Ast.	St.	Blk.	TO	Pts.	RPG	APG	PPG
03-04—Houston	5	41	4	9	.444	5	5	1.000	1	5	6	2	1	0	2	14	1.2	0.4	2.8
05-06—New Jersey	1	1	0	0	...	0	0	...	0	0	0	0	0	0	0	0	0.0	0.0	0.0
Totals	6	42	4	9	.444	5	5	1.000	1	5	6	2	1	0	2	14	1.0	0.3	2.3

Three-point field goals: 2003-04, 1-for-3 (.333). Totals, 1-for-3 (.333).
Personal fouls/disqualifications: 2003-04, 9/0. Totals, 9/0.

NAILON, LEE   F

PERSONAL: Born February 22, 1975, in South Bend, Ind. ... 6-8/241. (2.03/109.3).
HIGH SCHOOL: Clay (South Bend, Ind.).
JUNIOR COLLEGE: Southeastern Community (Iowa), then Butler County (Kan.).
COLLEGE: Texas Christian.
TRANSACTIONS/CAREER NOTES: Selected by Charlotte Hornets in second round (43rd pick overall) of 1999 NBA Draft. ... Played in Italy (1999-2000). ... Waived by Hornets (October 23, 2002). ... Signed as free agent by New York Knicks (October 30, 2002). ... Signed as free agent by Atlanta Hawks (September 30, 2003). ... Waived by Hawks (December 29, 2003). ... Played in Continental Basketball Association (2003-04). ... Signed by Orlando Magic to first of two consecutive 10-day contracts (January 5, 2004). ... Signed by Cleveland Cavaliers to first of two consecutive 10-day contracts (March 3, 2004). ... Signed by Cavaliers for remainder of season (March 23, 2004). ... Signed as free agent by New Orleans Hornets (September 30, 2004). ... Signed by Philadelphia 76ers (September 22, 2005). ... Traded by 76ers with a second-round draft choice to Cavaliers for a conditional second-round draft choice (February 23, 2006). ... Waived by Cavaliers (February 24, 2006).

COLLEGIATE RECORD

Season Team	G	Min.	FGM	FGA	Pct.	FTM	FTA	Pct.	Reb.	Ast.	Pts.	RPG	APG	PPG
95-96—Southeastern C.C.	31	892	311	500	.622	112	155	.723	252	83	735	8.1	2.7	23.7
96-97—Butler County C.C.	34	887	292	443	.659	101	154	.656	250	117	686	7.4	3.4	20.2
97-98—Texas Christian	32	1066	329	594	.554	137	184	.745	285	61	796	8.9	1.9	24.9
98-99—Texas Christian	31	990	266	524	.508	171	239	.715	288	79	707	9.3	2.5	22.8
Junior College Totals	65	1779	603	943	.639	213	309	.689	502	200	1421	7.7	3.1	21.9
4-Year-College Totals	63	2056	595	1118	.532	308	423	.728	573	140	1503	9.1	2.2	23.9

Three-point field goals: 1995-96, 1-for-13 (.077). 1996-97, 0-for-1. 1997-98, 1-for-2 (.500). 1998-99, 4-for-15 (.267). Totals, 6-for-31 (.194).
Personal fouls/disqualifications: 1997-98, 110/0. Totals, 110/0.

ITALIAN LEAGUE RECORD

Season Team	G	Min.	FGM	FGA	Pct.	FTM	FTA	Pct.	Reb.	Ast.	Pts.	RPG	APG	PPG
99-00—Milano	18	584	139	260	.535	45	61	.738	79	20	327	4.4	1.1	18.2

Three-point field goals: 1999-00, 4-for-10 (.400). Totals, 4-for-10 (.400).

NBA REGULAR-SEASON RECORD

Season Team	G	Min.	FGM	FGA	Pct.	FTM	FTA	Pct.	REBOUNDS Off.	Def.	Tot.	Ast.	St.	Blk.	TO	Pts.	RPG	APG	PPG
00-01—Charlotte	42	469	66	136	.485	32	43	.744	29	63	92	24	9	5	27	164	2.2	0.6	3.9
01-02—Charlotte	79	1912	369	764	.483	112	150	.747	103	188	291	94	59	17	96	851	3.7	1.2	10.8
02-03—New York	38	405	84	190	.442	42	51	.824	32	38	70	26	6	3	32	210	1.8	0.7	5.5
03-04—Atl.-Orl.Cleve.	57	780	147	327	.450	47	58	.810	64	79	143	38	15	8	45	341	2.5	0.7	6.0
04-05—New Orleans	68	2017	415	869	.478	133	165	.806	128	170	298	109	36	16	110	963	4.4	1.6	14.2
05-06—Philadelphia	22	237	40	80	.500	13	15	.867	23	19	42	7	8	4	10	93	1.9	0.3	4.2
Totals	306	5820	1121	2366	.474	379	482	.786	379	557	936	298	133	53	320	2622	3.1	1.0	8.6

Three-point field goals: 2000-01, 0-for-1. 2001-02, 1-for-2 (.500). 2002-03, 0-for-1. 2003-04, 0-for-3. 2004-05, 0-for-2. Totals, 1-for-9 (.111).
Personal fouls/disqualifications: 2000-01, 60/0. 2001-02, 175/1. 2002-03, 46/0. 2003-04, 93/0. 2004-05, 190/1. 2005-06, 32/0. Totals, 596/2.

NBA PLAYOFF RECORD

Season Team	G	Min.	FGM	FGA	Pct.	FTM	FTA	Pct.	REBOUNDS Off.	Def.	Tot.	Ast.	St.	Blk.	TO	Pts.	AVERAGES RPG	APG	PPG
01-02—Charlotte........	9	160	27	59	.458	15	19	.789	10	14	24	6	3	0	7	69	2.7	0.7	7.7

Three-point field goals: 2001-02, 0-for-1. Totals, 0-for-1 (.000).
Personal fouls/disqualifications: 2001-02, 17/0. Totals, 17/0.

CBA RECORD

Season Team	G	Min.	FGM	FGA	Pct.	FTM	FTA	Pct.	Reb.	Ast.	Pts.	AVERAGES RPG	APG	PPG
03-04—Gary	3	81	29	58	.500	9	9	1.000	30	3	67	10.0	1.0	22.3

NAJERA, EDUARDO   F   NUGGETS

PERSONAL: Born July 11, 1976, in Meoqui, Chihuahua, Mexico. ... 6-8/240. (2.03/108.9). ... Full name: Eduardo Alonso Najera
HIGH SCHOOL: Cornerstone Christian Academy (San Antonio).
COLLEGE: Oklahoma.
TRANSACTIONS/CAREER NOTES: Selected by Houston Rockets in second round (38th pick overall) of 2000 NBA Draft. ... Draft rights traded by Rockets with a future second-round draft pick to Dallas Mavericks for draft rights to F Dan Langhi (June 28, 2000). ... Traded by Mavericks with F/C Christian Laettner, draft rights to G Luis Flores and G Mladen Sekularac, two future first-round draft choices and cash to Golden State Warriors for C Erick Dampier, G Dan Dickau and draft rights to G Steve Logan (August 24, 2004). ... Traded by Warriors with G Luis Flores and future first-round pick to Denver Nuggets for F Nikoloz Tskitishvili and F Rodney White (February 24, 2005).

COLLEGIATE RECORD

Season Team	G	Min.	FGM	FGA	Pct.	FTM	FTA	Pct.	Reb.	Ast.	Pts.	AVERAGES RPG	APG	PPG
96-97—Oklahoma	30	739	72	178	.404	64	92	.696	167	32	211	5.6	1.1	7.0
97-98—Oklahoma	30	855	119	280	.425	64	101	.634	163	42	315	5.4	1.4	10.5
98-99—Oklahoma	32	1100	187	451	.415	70	109	.642	266	69	495	8.3	2.2	15.5
99-00—Oklahoma	34	1162	234	514	.455	139	202	.688	314	72	625	9.2	2.1	18.4
Totals	126	3856	612	1423	.430	337	504	.669	910	215	1646	7.2	1.7	13.1

Three-point field goals: 1996-97, 3-for-15 (.200). 1997-98, 13-for-49 (.265). 1998-99, 51-for-149 (.342). 1999-00, 18-for-82 (.220). Totals, 85-for-295 (.288).

NBA REGULAR-SEASON RECORD

Season Team	G	Min.	FGM	FGA	Pct.	FTM	FTA	Pct.	REBOUNDS Off.	Def.	Tot.	Ast.	St.	Blk.	TO	Pts.	AVERAGES RPG	APG	PPG
00-01—Dallas..............	40	431	58	111	.523	14	33	.424	41	54	95	27	13	8	17	131	2.4	0.7	3.3
01-02—Dallas............	62	1357	150	300	.500	100	148	.676	149	193	342	38	56	30	40	400	5.5	0.6	6.5
02-03—Dallas..............	48	1103	129	231	.558	62	91	.681	90	133	223	47	40	22	23	320	4.6	1.0	6.7
03-04—Dallas..............	76	710	71	161	.441	51	90	.566	111	188	199	44	48	18	42	193	2.1	0.6	2.5
04-05—G.S.-Denver	68	1185	145	322	.450	58	91	.637	102	141	243	65	41	24	61	354	3.6	1.0	5.2
05-06—Denver	64	1449	127	301	.422	89	114	.781	128	197	325	52	53	34	54	347	5.1	0.8	5.4
Totals	340	6245	681	1427	.477	353	523	.675	577	807	1384	254	238	137	224	1728	4.1	0.7	5.1

Three-point field goals: 2000-01, 1-for-3 (.333). 2001-02, 0-for-2. 2002-03, 0-for-1. 2003-04, 2-for-4 (.500). 2004-05, 6-for-21 (.286). 2005-06, 4-for-12 (.333). Totals, 13-for-43 (.302).
Personal fouls/disqualifications: 2000-01, 48/0. 2001-02, 156/2. 2002-03, 129/1. 2003-04, 90/1. 2004-05, 148/0. 2005-06, 165/0. Totals, 736/4.

NBA PLAYOFF RECORD

Season Team	G	Min.	FGM	FGA	Pct.	FTM	FTA	Pct.	REBOUNDS Off.	Def.	Tot.	Ast.	St.	Blk.	TO	Pts.	AVERAGES RPG	APG	PPG
00-01—Dallas..............	7	44	9	17	.529	0	0	...	7	8	15	1	1	1	1	21	2.1	0.1	3.0
01-02—Dallas..............	8	122	16	23	.696	5	8	.625	3	10	13	1	3	0	2	37	1.6	0.1	4.6
02-03—Dallas..............	19	394	39	86	.453	38	48	.792	36	38	74	15	14	4	16	116	3.9	0.8	6.1
03-04—Dallas..............	5	57	5	11	.455	2	2	1.000	10	7	17	3	3	2	1	12	3.4	0.6	2.4
04-05—Denver	2	13	0	2	.000	0	0	...	1	1	2	1	0	0	1	0	1.0	0.5	0.0
05-06—Denver	4	89	3	14	.214	2	4	.500	4	11	15	2	3	0	4	8	3.8	0.5	2.0
Totals	45	719	72	153	.471	47	62	.758	61	75	136	23	24	7	26	194	3.0	0.5	4.3

Three-point field goals: 2000-01, 3-for-4 (.750). Totals, 3-for-4 (.750).
Personal fouls/disqualifications: 2000-01, 8/0. 2001-02, 22/0. 2002-03, 53/1. 2003-04, 12/0. 2005-06, 13/0. Totals, 109/1.

NASH, STEVE   G   SUNS

PERSONAL: Born February 7, 1974, in Johannesburg, South Africa. ... 6-3/195. (1.91/88.5). ... Full name: Stephen John Nash
HIGH SCHOOL: St. Michael's Victoria (British Columbia).
COLLEGE: Santa Clara.
TRANSACTIONS/CAREER NOTES: Selected by Phoenix Suns in first round (15th pick overall) of 1996 NBA Draft. ... Traded by Suns to Dallas Mavericks for F Martin Muursepp, G/F Bubba Wells, draft rights to F Pat Garrity and 1999 first-round draft choice (June 24, 1998). ... Signed as free agent by Suns (July 14, 2004).
MISCELLANEOUS: Member of Canadian Olympic team (2000).

COLLEGIATE RECORD

Season Team	G	Min.	FGM	FGA	Pct.	FTM	FTA	Pct.	Reb.	Ast.	Pts.	AVERAGES RPG	APG	PPG
92-93—Santa Clara...................	31	743	78	184	.424	47	57	.825	79	67	252	2.5	2.2	8.1
93-94—Santa Clara...................	26	778	122	295	.414	69	83	.831	65	95	380	2.5	3.7	14.6

Season Team	G	Min.	FGM	FGA	Pct.	FTM	FTA	Pct.	Reb.	Ast.	Pts.	AVERAGES		
												RPG	APG	PPG
94-95—Santa Clara..................	27	902	164	369	.444	153	174	.879	102	174	565	3.8	6.4	20.9
95-96—Santa Clara..................	29	979	164	381	.430	101	113	.894	102	174	492	3.5	6.0	17.0
Totals	113	3402	528	1229	.430	370	427	.867	348	510	1689	3.1	4.5	14.9

Three-point field goals: 1992-93, 49-for-120 (.408). 1993-94, 67-for-168 (.399). 1994-95, 84-for-185 (.454). 1995-96, 63-for-183 (.344). Totals, 263-for-656 (.401).

NBA REGULAR-SEASON RECORD

HONORS: All-NBA third team (2002, 2003). ... NBA Most Valuable Player (2005, 2006). ... All-NBA first team (2005, 2006).

Season Team	G	Min.	FGM	FGA	Pct.	FTM	FTA	Pct.	REBOUNDS			Ast.	St.	Blk.	TO	Pts.	AVERAGES		
									Off.	Def.	Tot.						RPG	APG	PPG
96-97—Phoenix	65	684	74	175	.423	42	51	.824	16	47	63	138	20	0	63	213	1.0	2.1	3.3
97-98—Phoenix	76	1664	268	584	.459	74	86	.860	32	128	160	262	63	4	98	691	2.1	3.4	9.1
98-99—Dallas.............	40	1269	114	314	.363	38	46	.826	32	82	114	219	37	2	83	315	2.9	5.5	7.9
99-00—Dallas.............	56	1532	173	363	.477	75	85	.882	34	87	121	272	37	3	102	481	2.2	4.9	8.6
00-01—Dallas.............	70	2387	386	792	.487	231	258	.895	46	177	223	509	72	5	205	1092	3.2	7.3	15.6
01-02—Dallas.............	82	2837	525	1088	.483	260	293	.887	50	204	254	634	53	4	229	1466	3.1	7.7	17.9
02-03—Dallas.............	82	2711	518	1114	.465	308	339	.909	63	171	234	598	85	6	192	1455	2.9	7.3	17.7
03-04—Dallas.............	78	2612	397	845	.470	230	251	.916	59	173	232	687	67	8	209	1128	3.0	8.8	14.5
04-05—Phoenix	75	2573	430	857	.502	211	238	.887	57	192	249	*861	74	6	245	1165	3.3	*11.5	15.5
05-06—Phoenix	79	2796	541	1056	.512	257	279	*.921	47	286	333	*826	61	12	276	1489	4.2	*10.5	18.8
Totals	703	21065	3426	7188	.477	1726	1926	.896	436	1547	1983	5006	569	50	1702	9495	2.8	7.1	13.5

Three-point field goals: 1996-97, 23-for-55 (.418). 1997-98, 81-for-195 (.415). 1998-99, 49-for-131 (.374). 1999-00, 60-for-149 (.403). 2000-01, 89-for-219 (.406). 2001-02, 156-for-343 (.455). 2002-03, 111-for-269 (.413). 2003-04, 104-for-257 (.405). 2004-05, 94-for-218 (.431). 2005-06, 150-for-342 (.439). Totals, 917-for-2178 (.421).

Personal fouls/disqualifications: 1996-97, 92/1. 1997-98, 145/1. 1998-99, 98/2. 1999-00, 122/1. 2000-01, 158/0. 2001-02, 164/0. 2002-03, 134/0. 2003-04, 139/0. 2004-05, 136/0. 2005-06, 120/1. Totals, 1308/6.

NBA PLAYOFF RECORD

Season Team	G	Min.	FGM	FGA	Pct.	FTM	FTA	Pct.	REBOUNDS			Ast.	St.	Blk.	TO	Pts.	AVERAGES		
									Off.	Def.	Tot.						RPG	APG	PPG
96-97—Phoenix	4	15	2	9	.222	0	0	...	1	0	1	1	1	1	2	5	0.3	0.3	1.3
97-98—Phoenix	4	51	8	18	.444	5	8	.625	2	8	10	7	2	0	3	22	2.5	1.8	5.5
00-01—Dallas.............	10	370	45	108	.417	30	34	.882	6	26	32	64	6	1	25	136	3.2	6.4	13.6
01-02—Dallas.............	8	323	51	118	.432	34	35	.971	7	25	32	70	4	0	30	156	4.0	8.8	19.5
02-03—Dallas.............	20	729	115	257	.447	55	63	.873	15	55	70	145	17	1	51	322	3.5	7.3	16.1
03-04—Dallas.............	5	197	27	70	.386	8	9	.889	6	20	26	45	4	0	12	68	5.2	9.0	13.6
04-05—Phoenix	15	610	140	269	.520	57	62	.919	9	63	72	170	14	3	70	358	4.8	11.3	23.9
05-06—Phoenix	20	798	146	291	.502	83	91	.912	9	64	73	204	8	5	67	407	3.7	10.2	20.4
Totals	86	3093	534	1140	.468	272	302	.901	55	261	316	706	56	11	260	1474	3.7	8.2	17.1

Three-point field goals: 1996-97, 1-for-4 (.250). 1997-98, 1-for-5 (.200). 2000-01, 16-for-39 (.410). 2001-02, 20-for-45 (.444). 2002-03, 37-for-76 (.487). 2003-04, 6-for-16 (.375). 2004-05, 21-for-54 (.389). 2005-06, 32-for-87 (.368). Totals, 134-for-326 (.411).

Personal fouls/disqualifications: 1996-97, 5/0. 1997-98, 7/0. 2000-01, 19/0. 2001-02, 20/0. 2002-03, 47/0. 2003-04, 14/0. 2004-05, 36/0. 2005-06, 38/0. Totals, 186/0.

NBA ALL-STAR GAME RECORD

NOTES: Won NBA All-Star Skills competition (2005).

Season Team	Min.	FGM	FGA	Pct.	FTM	FTA	Pct.	REBOUNDS			Ast.	PF	Dq.	St.	Blk.	TO	Pts.
								Off.	Def.	Tot.							
2002—Dallas	24	3	9	.333	0	0	...	2	1	3	9	1	0	1	0	0	8
2003—Dallas	16	1	3	.333	0	1	.000	2	3	5	3	1	0	1	0	4	2
2005—Phoenix...............	17	1	2	.500	0	0	...	0	0	0	6	0	0	0	0	3	2
2006—Phoenix...............	28	1	2	.500	0	0	...	1	4	5	6	2	0	1	0	2	2
Totals	85	6	16	.375	0	1	.000	5	8	13	24	4	0	3	0	9	14

Three-point field goals: 2002, 2-for-4 (.500). 2003, 0-for-2. 2005, 0-for-1. Totals, 2-for-7 (.286).

NELSON, JAMEER   G   MAGIC

PERSONAL: Born February 9, 1982, in Chester, Pa. ... 6-0/190. (1.83/86.2).
HIGH SCHOOL: Chester (Pa.).
COLLEGE: Saint Joseph's.
TRANSACTIONS/CAREER NOTES: Selected by Denver Nuggets in first round (20th pick overall) of 2004 NBA Draft. ... Draft rights traded by Nuggets to Orlando Magic for future first-round draft choice (June 24, 2004).

COLLEGIATE RECORD

NOTES: The SPORTING NEWS Player of the Year (2004). ... The SPORTING NEWS All-America first team (2004). ... Naismith Award winner (2004). ... Wooden Award winner (2004).

Season Team	G	Min.	FGM	FGA	Pct.	FTM	FTA	Pct.	Reb.	Ast.	Pts.	AVERAGES		
												RPG	APG	PPG
00-01—St. Joseph's...................	33	1114	131	284	.461	109	133	.820	133	213	412	4.0	6.5	12.5
01-02—St. Joseph's...................	30	1064	144	329	.438	93	122	.762	144	188	432	4.8	6.3	14.4
02-03—St. Joseph's...................	30	1048	194	444	.437	139	180	.772	154	142	591	5.1	4.7	19.7
03-04—St. Joseph's...................	32	1085	234	493	.475	118	149	.792	150	170	659	4.7	5.3	20.6
Totals	125	4311	703	1550	.454	459	584	.786	581	713	2094	4.6	5.7	16.8

Three-point field goals: 2000-01, 41-for-110 (.373). 2001-02, 51-for-142 (.359). 2002-03, 64-for-189 (.339). 2003-04, 73-for-187 (.390). Totals, 229-for-628 (.365).

NBA REGULAR-SEASON RECORD

HONORS: NBA All-Rookie second team (2005).

Season Team	G	Min.	FGM	FGA	Pct.	FTM	FTA	Pct.	REBOUNDS Off.	Def.	Tot.	Ast.	St.	Blk.	TO	Pts.	AVERAGES RPG	APG	PPG
04-05—Orlando..........	79	1612	286	628	.455	73	107	.682	52	141	193	237	78	3	117	689	2.4	3.0	8.7
05-06—Orlando..........	62	1784	347	719	.483	141	181	.779	39	141	180	302	70	9	148	905	2.9	4.9	14.6
Totals	141	3396	633	1347	.470	214	288	.743	91	282	373	539	148	12	265	1594	2.6	3.8	11.3

Three-point field goals: 2004-05, 44-for-141 (.312). 2005-06, 70-for-165 (.424). Totals, 114-for-306 (.373).
Personal fouls/disqualifications: 2004-05, 199/4. 2005-06, 174/2. Totals, 373/6.

NENE   F/C   NUGGETS

PERSONAL: Born September 13, 1982, in Sao Carlos, Brazil. ... 6-11/260. (2.11/117.9). ... Formerly known as Maybyner Rodney Hilario.
HIGH SCHOOL: Instituto Alvaro Guiao (Sao Carlos, Brazil).
TRANSACTIONS/CAREER NOTES: Played in Brazil (2000-02). ... Selected by New York Knicks in first round (seventh pick overall) of 2002 NBA Draft. ... Draft rights traded by Knicks with F/C Marcus Camby and G Mark Jackson to Denver Nuggets for F Antonio McDyess, draft rights to G Frank Williams and 2003 second-round draft choice (June 26, 2002).

BRAZILIAN LEAGUE RECORD

Season Team	G	Min.	FGM	FGA	Pct.	FTM	FTA	Pct.	Reb.	Ast.	Pts.	AVERAGES RPG	APG	PPG
00-01—Vasco da Gama	38	...	118	171	.690	68	117	.581	224	27	304	5.9	0.7	8.0
01-02—Vasco da Gama	15	450	78	117	.667	41	60	.683	151	25	198	10.1	1.7	13.2
Totals	53	450	196	288	.681	109	177	.616	375	52	502	7.1	1.0	9.5

NBA REGULAR-SEASON RECORD

HONORS: NBA All-Rookie first team (2003).

Season Team	G	Min.	FGM	FGA	Pct.	FTM	FTA	Pct.	REBOUNDS Off.	Def.	Tot.	Ast.	St.	Blk.	TO	Pts.	AVERAGES RPG	APG	PPG
02-03—Denver	80	2258	321	619	.519	197	341	.578	208	283	491	149	127	65	181	839	6.1	1.9	10.5
03-04—Denver	77	2504	334	630	.530	240	352	.682	154	349	503	168	116	41	183	908	6.5	2.2	11.8
04-05—Denver	55	1317	194	386	.503	140	212	.660	104	221	325	84	50	48	94	528	5.9	1.5	9.6
05-06—Denver	1	3	0	1	.000	0	0	...	0	0	0	0	0	0	2	0	0.0	0.0	0.0
Totals	213	6082	849	1636	.519	577	905	.638	466	853	1319	401	293	154	460	2275	6.2	1.9	10.7

Three-point field goals: 2002-03, 0-for-3. 2003-04, 0-for-2. 2004-05, 0-for-2. Totals, 0-for-7 (.000).
Personal fouls/disqualifications: 2002-03, 295/4. 2003-04, 280/3. 2004-05, 167/0. 2005-06, 1/0. Totals, 743/7.

NBA PLAYOFF RECORD

Season Team	G	Min.	FGM	FGA	Pct.	FTM	FTA	Pct.	REBOUNDS Off.	Def.	Tot.	Ast.	St.	Blk.	TO	Pts.	AVERAGES RPG	APG	PPG
03-04—Denver	5	132	16	36	.444	7	13	.538	12	13	25	15	5	3	9	39	5.0	3.0	7.8
04-05—Denver	5	101	9	21	.429	15	23	.652	9	16	25	2	2	2	5	33	5.0	0.4	6.6
Totals	10	233	25	57	.439	22	36	.611	21	29	50	17	7	5	14	72	5.0	1.7	7.2

Personal fouls/disqualifications: 2003-04, 22/0. 2004-05, 16/0. Totals, 38/0.

NESTEROVIC, RASHO   C   RAPTORS

PERSONAL: Born May 30, 1976, in Ljubljana, Slovenia. ... 7-0/250. (2.13/113.4).
HIGH SCHOOL: Gymnasium (Sremski Karlovci, Slovenia).
TRANSACTIONS/CAREER NOTES: Played in Slovenia (1996-97). ... Played in Italy (1997-99). ... Selected by Minnesota Timberwolves in first round (17th pick overall) of 1998 NBA Draft. ... Signed as free agent by San Antonio Spurs (July 16, 2003). ... Traded by Spurs to Toronto Raptors for Fs Matt Bonner and Eric Williams and a 2009 second-round draft choice (June 21, 2006).
MISCELLANEOUS: Member of NBA championship team (2005).

N

ITALIAN LEAGUE RECORD

Season Team	G	Min.	FGM	FGA	Pct.	FTM	FTA	Pct.	Reb.	Ast.	Pts.	AVERAGES RPG	APG	PPG
97-98—Virtus Kinder Bologna	26	587	84	124	.677	13	30	.433	139	3	181	5.3	0.1	7.0
98-99—Virtus Roma	26	852	152	233	.652	47	79	.595	162	11	351	6.2	0.4	13.5
Totals	52	1439	236	357	.661	60	109	.550	301	14	532	5.8	0.3	10.2

Three-point field goals: 1997-98, 0-for-1. Totals, 0-for-1 (.000).

NBA REGULAR-SEASON RECORD

Season Team	G	Min.	FGM	FGA	Pct.	FTM	FTA	Pct.	REBOUNDS Off.	Def.	Tot.	Ast.	St.	Blk.	TO	Pts.	AVERAGES RPG	APG	PPG
98-99—Minnesota.......	2	30	3	12	.250	2	2	1.000	3	5	8	1	0	0	1	8	4.0	0.5	4.0
99-00—Minnesota.......	82	1723	206	433	.476	59	103	.573	135	244	379	93	21	85	71	471	4.6	1.1	5.7
00-01—Minnesota.......	73	1233	147	319	.461	34	65	.523	99	187	286	45	25	63	55	328	3.9	0.6	4.5
01-02—Minnesota.......	82	2218	324	657	.493	39	71	.549	200	334	534	75	45	109	94	687	6.5	0.9	8.4
02-03—Minnesota.......	77	2337	400	762	.525	61	95	.642	146	358	504	114	39	116	99	861	6.5	1.5	11.2
03-04—San Antonio	82	2353	328	700	.469	54	114	.474	257	376	633	114	51	165	107	710	7.7	1.4	8.7
04-05—San Antonio	70	1785	198	430	.460	14	30	.467	184	275	459	71	31	117	73	410	6.6	1.0	5.9
05-06—San Antonio	80	1515	172	334	.515	18	30	.600	114	195	309	33	21	88	53	362	3.9	0.4	4.5
Totals	548	13194	1778	3647	.488	281	510	.551	1138	1974	3112	546	233	743	553	3837	5.7	1.0	7.0

Three-point field goals: 1999-00, 0-for-2. 2000-01, 0-for-1. 2001-02, 0-for-1. 2002-03, 0-for-2. 2005-06, 0-for-2. Totals, 0-for-8 (.000).
Personal fouls/disqualifications: 1998-99, 5/0. 1999-00, 262/9. 2000-01, 189/3. 2001-02, 262/3. 2002-03, 256/9. 2003-04, 247/5. 2004-05, 207/1. 2005-06, 209/3. Totals, 1637/33.

NBA PLAYOFF RECORD

								REBOUNDS									AVERAGES		
Season Team	G	Min.	FGM	FGA	Pct.	FTM	FTA	Pct.	Off.	Def.	Tot.	Ast.	St.	Blk.	TO	Pts.	RPG	APG	PPG
98-99—Minnesota......	3	29	4	8	.500	0	0	...	4	3	7	3	0	0	1	8	2.3	1.0	2.7
99-00—Minnesota......	4	126	11	25	.440	3	6	.500	5	8	13	6	3	7	4	25	3.3	1.5	6.3
00-01—Minnesota......	4	49	5	13	.385	0	0	...	5	7	12	3	1	3	3	10	3.0	0.8	2.5
01-02—Minnesota......	3	92	15	31	.484	4	9	.444	6	14	20	3	1	0	4	34	6.7	1.0	11.3
02-03—Minnesota......	6	169	19	38	.500	4	6	.667	9	21	30	4	1	4	5	42	5.0	0.7	7.0
03-04—San Antonio....	10	261	29	67	.433	1	6	.167	21	34	55	10	3	11	8	59	5.5	1.0	5.9
04-05—San Antonio....	15	114	5	12	.417	0	2	.000	11	15	26	2	1	5	4	10	1.7	0.1	0.7
05-06—San Antonio....	9	114	11	19	.579	2	2	1.000	7	23	30	1	2	5	2	25	3.3	0.1	2.8
Totals	54	954	99	213	.465	14	31	.452	68	125	193	32	12	35	31	213	3.6	0.6	3.9

Three-point field goals: 2003-04, 0-for-1. 2005-06, 1-for-1 (1.000). Totals, 1-for-2 (.500).
Personal fouls/disqualifications: 1998-99, 4/0. 1999-00, 20/1. 2000-01, 9/0. 2001-02, 10/0. 2002-03, 28/1. 2003-04, 38/0. 2004-05, 16/0. 2005-06, 17/0. Totals, 142/2.

NEWBLE, IRA   F   CAVALIERS

PERSONAL: Born January 20, 1975, in Detroit. ... 6-7/220. (2.01/99.8).
HIGH SCHOOL: Southfield (Mich.).
JUNIOR COLLEGE: Mississippi Gulf Coast Junior College.
COLLEGE: Miami of Ohio.
TRANSACTIONS/CAREER NOTES: Not drafted by an NBA franchise. ... Played in International Basketball Association with Wisconsin Blast (1997-98). ... Played in Continental Basketball Association with Idaho Stampede (1997-98 through 1999-2000) and Flint Fuze (2001-02). ... Signed as free agent by San Antonio Spurs (September 25, 1999). ... Waived by Spurs (October 27, 1999). ... Played in Cyprus (1999-2000). ... Re-signed by Spurs (August 12, 2000). ... Signed as free agent by Atlanta Hawks (October 1, 2001). ... Waived by Hawks (October 24, 2001). ... Re-signed by Hawks to 10-day contract (January 23, 2002). ... Signed by Hawks for remainder of season (February 12, 2002). ... Signed as free agent by Cleveland Cavaliers (July 22, 2003).

COLLEGIATE RECORD

												AVERAGES		
Season Team	G	Min.	FGM	FGA	Pct.	FTM	FTA	Pct.	Reb.	Ast.	Pts.	RPG	APG	PPG
93-94—Mississippi Gulf Coast....						Statistics unavailable.								
94-95—Mississippi Gulf Coast....						Statistics unavailable.								
95-96—Miami of Ohio	29	452	86	178	.483	14	24	.583	152	12	186	5.2	0.4	6.4
96-97—Miami of Ohio	29	756	138	231	.597	49	74	.662	218	35	329	7.5	1.2	11.3
Totals	58	1208	224	409	.548	63	98	.643	370	47	515	6.4	0.8	8.9

Three-point field goals: 1995-96, 0-for-7. 1996-97, 4-for-10 (.400). Totals, 4-for-17 (.235).
Personal fouls/disqualifications: 1995-96, 51/0. 1996-97, 93/0. Totals, 144/0.

CBA RECORD

												AVERAGES		
Season Team	G	Min.	FGM	FGA	Pct.	FTM	FTA	Pct.	Reb.	Ast.	Pts.	RPG	APG	PPG
97-98—Idaho	16	260	50	87	.575	20	29	.690	66	10	123	4.1	0.6	7.7
98-99—Idaho	31	838	148	267	.554	57	85	.671	141	37	359	4.5	1.2	11.6
99-00—Idaho	53	2026	330	622	.531	133	174	.764	369	149	818	7.0	2.8	15.4
01-02—Flint	15	584	123	249	.494	70	82	.854	108	43	321	7.2	2.9	21.4
Totals	115	3708	651	1225	.531	280	370	.757	684	239	1621	5.9	2.1	14.1

Three-point field goals: 1997-98, 3-for-6 (.500). 1998-99, 6-for-25 (.240). 1999-00, 25-for-67 (.373). 2001-02, 5-for-25 (.200). Totals, 39-for-123 (.317).
Personal fouls/disqualifications: 1997-98, 40/0. 1998-99, 74/0. 1999-00, 173/0. Totals, 287/0.

IBA RECORD

												AVERAGES		
Season Team	G	Min.	FGM	FGA	Pct.	FTM	FTA	Pct.	Reb.	Ast.	Pts.	RPG	APG	PPG
97-98—Wisconsin	13	369	92	165	.558	26	41	.634	98	20	214	7.5	1.5	16.5

Three-point field goals: 1997-98, 4-for-4 (1.000). Totals, 4-for-4 (1.000).

CYPRUS RECORD

												AVERAGES		
Season Team	G	Min.	FGM	FGA	Pct.	FTM	FTA	Pct.	Reb.	Ast.	Pts.	RPG	APG	PPG
99-00—Keravnos Keo Nicosia	44	1649	259	499	.519	108	141	.766	312	126	642	7.1	2.9	14.6

Three-point field goals: 1999-00, 16-for-46 (.348). Totals, 16-for-46 (.348).

NBA REGULAR-SEASON RECORD

								REBOUNDS									AVERAGES		
Season Team	G	Min.	FGM	FGA	Pct.	FTM	FTA	Pct.	Off.	Def.	Tot.	Ast.	St.	Blk.	TO	Pts.	RPG	APG	PPG
00-01—San Antonio	27	184	21	55	.382	8	16	.500	13	22	35	6	2	4	7	54	1.3	0.2	2.0
01-02—Atlanta	42	1273	131	263	.498	75	88	.852	80	142	222	45	38	20	49	338	5.3	1.1	8.0
02-03—Atlanta	73	1931	231	467	.495	70	90	.778	86	185	271	99	50	26	69	564	3.7	1.4	7.7
03-04—Cleveland	64	1245	108	276	.391	36	46	.783	65	90	155	72	25	19	54	254	2.4	1.1	4.0
04-05—Cleveland	74	1832	182	424	.429	55	69	.797	78	142	220	91	50	18	61	438	3.0	1.2	5.9
05-06—Cleveland	36	353	17	57	.298	11	16	.688	21	35	56	9	5	10	12	48	1.6	0.3	1.3
Totals	316	6818	690	1542	.447	255	325	.785	343	616	959	322	170	97	252	1696	3.0	1.0	5.4

Three-point field goals: 2000-01, 4-for-9 (.444). 2001-02, 1-for-7 (.143). 2002-03, 32-for-84 (.381). 2003-04, 2-for-19 (.105). 2004-05, 19-for-53 (.358). 2005-06, 3-for-13 (.231). Totals, 61-for-185 (.330).
Personal fouls/disqualifications: 2000-01, 18/0. 2001-02, 117/2. 2002-03, 174/1. 2003-04, 109/1. 2004-05, 144/1. 2005-06, 47/0. Totals, 609/5.

NBA PLAYOFF RECORD

								REBOUNDS									AVERAGES		
Season Team	G	Min.	FGM	FGA	Pct.	FTM	FTA	Pct.	Off.	Def.	Tot.	Ast.	St.	Blk.	TO	Pts.	RPG	APG	PPG
05-06—Cleveland	5	11	3	3	1.000	0	0	...	1	1	2	0	1	0	1	7	0.4	0.0	1.4

Three-point field goals: 2005-06, 1-for-1 (1.000). Totals, 1-for-1 (1.000).
Personal fouls/disqualifications: 2005-06, 1/0. Totals, 1/0.

N

NOCIONI, ANDRES　　　　　　　　F　　　　　　　　BULLS

PERSONAL: Born November 30, 1979, in Santa Fe, Argentina. ... 6-7/225. (2.01/102.1).
TRANSACTIONS/CAREER NOTES: Not drafted by an NBA franchise. ... Played in Argentina (1995-99). ... Played in Spain (1999-2004). ... Signed as free agent by Chicago Bulls (August 11, 2004).
MISCELLANEOUS: Member of gold-medal-winning Argentinian Olympic Team (2004).

ARGENTINIAN LEAGUE RECORD

Season Team	G	Min.	FGM	FGA	Pct.	FTM	FTA	Pct.	Reb.	Ast.	Pts.	RPG	APG	PPG
95-96—Racing Club Avellaneda..	31	...	76	130	.585	24	43	.558	47	10	185	1.5	0.3	6.0
96-97—Olympia Venada Tuerto ..	34	...	68	135	.504	57	84	.679	63	4	205	1.9	0.1	6.0
97-98—Independiente General Pico	50	...	168	292	.575	112	169	.663	187	14	453	3.7	0.3	9.1
98-99—Independiente General Pico	60	...	274	478	.573	145	217	.668	265	31	717	4.4	0.5	12.0
Totals	175		586	1035	.566	338	513	.659	562	59	1560	3.2	0.3	8.9

Three-point field goals: 1995-96, 9-for-16 (.563). 1996-97, 12-for-29 (.414). 1997-98, 5-for-19 (.263). 1998-99, 24-for-53 (.453). Totals, 50-for-117 (.427).

SPANISH LEAGUE RECORD

Season Team	G	Min.	FGM	FGA	Pct.	FTM	FTA	Pct.	Reb.	Ast.	Pts.	RPG	APG	PPG
99-00—Tau Ceramica..................	8	84	11	21	.524	9	15	.600	16	1	33	2.0	0.1	4.1
00-01—Tau Ceramica..................	33	768	137	292	.469	78	106	.736	176	28	395	5.3	0.8	12.0
02-03—Tau Ceramica..................	34	1036	209	451	.463	122	158	.772	232	52	590	6.8	1.5	17.4
03-04—Tau Ceramica..................	29	880	170	364	.467	79	110	.718	222	52	465	7.7	1.8	16.0
Totals	104	2768	527	1128	.467	288	389	.740	646	133	1483	6.2	1.3	14.3

Three-point field goals: 1999-00, 2 for 3 (.667). 2000-01, 43-for-127 (.339). 2002-03, 50-for-139 (.360). 2003-04, 46-for-119 (.387). Totals, 141-for-388 (.363).

NBA REGULAR-SEASON RECORD

Season Team	G	Min.	FGM	FGA	Pct.	FTM	FTA	Pct.	Off.	Def.	Tot.	Ast.	St.	Blk.	TO	Pts.	RPG	APG	PPG
04-05—Chicago	81	1892	241	601	.401	170	222	.766	69	317	386	122	37	34	135	677	4.8	1.5	8.4
05-06—Chicago	82	2239	383	831	.461	204	242	.843	89	411	500	117	40	52	120	1063	6.1	1.4	13.0
Totals	163	4131	624	1432	.436	374	464	.806	158	728	886	239	77	86	255	1740	5.4	1.5	10.7

Three-point field goals: 2004-05, 25-for-97 (.258). 2005-06, 93-for-238 (.391). Totals, 118-for-335 (.352).
Personal fouls/disqualifications: 2004-05, 208/3. 2005-06, 252/3. Totals, 460/6.

NBA PLAYOFF RECORD

Season Team	G	Min.	FGM	FGA	Pct.	FTM	FTA	Pct.	Off.	Def.	Tot.	Ast.	St.	Blk.	TO	Pts.	RPG	APG	PPG
04-05—Chicago	6	202	27	67	.403	17	23	.739	8	41	49	14	1	6	11	77	8.2	2.3	12.8
05-06—Chicago	6	230	47	84	.888	88	88	.637	5	48	53	9	5	2	14	134	8.8	1.5	22.3
Totals	12	432	74	151	.490	47	58	.810	13	89	102	23	6	8	25	211	8.5	1.9	17.6

Three-point field goals: 2004-05, 6-for-17 (.353). 2005-06, 10-for-21 (.476). Totals, 16-for-38 (.421).
Personal fouls/disqualifications: 2004-05, 20/0. 2005-06, 21/0. Totals, 41/0.

NORRIS, MOOCHIE　　　　　　　　G

PERSONAL: Born July 27, 1973, in Washington, D.C. ... 6-1/175. (1.85/79.4).
HIGH SCHOOL: Cardoza (Washington, D.C.).
JUNIOR COLLEGE: Odessa (Texas) Junior College.
COLLEGE: Auburn, then West Florida.
TRANSACTIONS/CAREER NOTES: Selected by Milwaukee Bucks in second round (33rd pick overall) of 1996 NBA Draft. ... Waived by Bucks (November 22, 1996). ... Played in Continental Basketball Association with Florida Beachdogs (1996-97) and Fort Wayne Fury (1996-97 through 1999-2000). ... Signed as free agent by Vancouver Grizzlies (December 12, 1996). ... Waived by Grizzlies (December 30, 1996). ... Played in France (1997-98). ... Signed as free agent by Seattle SuperSonics (January 21, 1999). ... Waived by SuperSonics (March 23, 1999). ... Signed by Houston Rockets to first of two consecutive 10-day contracts (February 8, 2000). ... Re-signed by Rockets for remainder of season (February 28, 2000). ... Traded by Rockets with F/C John Amaechi to New York Knicks for F Clarence Weatherspoon (December 30, 2003). ... Traded by Knicks with F Vin Baker and second-round pick in 2006 draft to Houston Rockets for F Maurice Taylor (February 24, 2005). ... Traded by Rockets to New Orleans Hornets for F Maciej Lampe (February 13, 2006). ... Waived by Hornets (July 5, 2006).

COLLEGIATE RECORD

Season Team	G	Min.	FGM	FGA	Pct.	FTM	FTA	Pct.	Reb.	Ast.	Pts.	RPG	APG	PPG
92-93—Odessa J.C.	32	...	160	290	.552	121	171	.708	91	225	459	2.8	7.0	14.3
93-94—Odessa J.C.	27	...	147	264	.557	83	120	.692	104	214	401	3.9	7.9	14.9
94-95—Auburn	29	1009	124	312	.397	58	83	.699	116	143	363	4.0	4.9	12.5
95-96—West Florida	16	615	121	265	.457	86	113	.761	92	143	378	5.8	8.9	23.6
Junior College Totals	75	615	428	819	.523	290	404	.718	287	582	1238	3.8	7.8	16.5
4-Year-College Totals	29	1009	124	312	.397	58	83	.699	116	143	363	4.0	4.9	12.5

Three-point field goals: 1992-93, 18-for-43 (.419). 1993-94, 24-for-60 (.400). 1994-95, 57-for-161 (.354). 1995-96, 50-for-118 (.424). Totals, 149-for-382 (.390).

CBA RECORD

NOTES: CBA All-League second team (1998). ... CBA All-Rookie second team (1997). ... CBA All-League first team (2000).

Season Team	G	Min.	FGM	FGA	Pct.	FTM	FTA	Pct.	Reb.	Ast.	Pts.	RPG	APG	PPG
96-97—Florida-Fort Wayne	31	745	97	226	.429	58	81	.716	82	94	273	2.6	3.0	8.8
97-98—Fort Wayne	46	1413	208	404	.515	126	167	.754	226	244	552	4.9	5.3	12.0
98-99—Fort Wayne	18	669	95	189	.503	80	97	.825	105	144	278	5.8	8.0	15.4
99-00—Fort Wayne	33	1372	239	488	.490	165	202	.817	166	200	664	5.0	6.1	20.1
Totals	128	4199	639	1307	.489	429	547	.784	579	682	1767	4.5	5.3	13.8

Three-point field goals: 1996-97, 21-for-76 (.276). 1997-98, 10-for-39 (.256). 1998-99, 8-for-16 (.500). 1999-00, 21-for-61 (.344). Totals, 60-for-192 (.313).

Personal fouls/disqualifications: 1996-97, 54/0. 1997-98, 93/0. 1998-99, 29/0. 1999-00, 76/0. Totals, 252/0.

NBA REGULAR-SEASON RECORD

Season Team	G	Min.	FGM	FGA	Pct.	FTM	FTA	Pct.	REBOUNDS Off.	Def.	Tot.	Ast.	St.	Blk.	TO	Pts.	AVERAGES RPG	APG	PPG
96-97—Vancouver	8	89	4	22	.182	2	5	.400	3	9	12	23	4	0	5	12	1.5	2.9	1.5
98-99—Seattle	12	140	13	40	.325	6	16	.375	4	16	20	24	7	0	16	38	1.7	2.0	3.2
99-00—Houston	30	502	69	159	.434	57	73	.781	16	52	68	94	23	1	30	207	2.3	3.1	6.9
00-01—Houston	82	1654	184	413	.446	151	194	.778	44	154	198	283	69	2	107	544	2.4	3.5	6.6
01-02—Houston	82	2249	251	631	.398	127	169	.751	73	173	246	403	81	4	156	665	3.0	4.9	8.1
02-03—Houston	82	1375	134	330	.406	78	114	.684	37	122	159	196	55	4	86	357	1.9	2.4	4.4
03-04—Houston-N.Y.	66	847	80	217	.369	54	71	.761	10	55	65	121	44	5	64	234	1.0	1.8	3.5
04-05—New York-Hous.	38	360	35	109	.321	20	24	.833	10	36	46	39	18	2	27	90	1.2	1.0	2.4
05-06—Hous.-NO/Okla. City	45	424	46	112	.411	29	42	.690	12	42	54	50	20	1	33	125	1.2	1.1	2.8
Totals	445	7640	816	2033	.401	524	708	.740	209	659	868	1233	321	19	524	2272	2.0	2.8	5.1

Three-point field goals: 1996-97, 2-for-10 (.200). 1998-99, 6-for-15 (.400). 1999-00, 12-for-29 (.414). 2000-01, 25-for-89 (.281). 2001-02, 36-for-134 (.269). 2002-03, 11-for-45 (.244). 2003-04, 20-for-58 (.345). 2004-05, 0-for-12. 2005-06, 4-for-14 (.286). Totals, 116-for-406 (.286).

Personal fouls/disqualifications: 1996-97, 5/0. 1998-99, 17/0. 1999-00, 32/0. 2000-01, 84/0. 2001-02, 130/0. 2002-03, 72/0. 2003-04, 51/0. 2004-05, 44/0. 2005-06, 49/0. Totals, 484/0.

NBA PLAYOFF RECORD

Season Team	G	Min.	FGM	FGA	Pct.	FTM	FTA	Pct.	REBOUNDS Off.	Def.	Tot.	Ast.	St.	Blk.	TO	Pts.	AVERAGES RPG	APG	PPG
04-05—Houston	2	7	0	1	.000	0	0	...	0	0	0	0	0	0	0	0	0.0	0.0	0.0

FRENCH LEAGUE RECORD

Season Team	G	Min.	FGM	FGA	Pct.	FTM	FTA	Pct.	Reb.	Ast.	Pts.	AVERAGES RPG	APG	PPG
97-98—Pau Orthez	8	177	26	45	.578	24	33	.727	33	21	79	4.1	2.6	9.9

VENEZUELAN LEAGUE RECORD

Season Team	G	Min.	FGM	FGA	Pct.	FTM	FTA	Pct.	Reb.	Ast.	Pts.	AVERAGES RPG	APG	PPG
99-00—Gaiteros	6	217	44	86	.512	37	64	.578	17	48	136	2.8	8.0	22.7

Three-point field goals: 1999-00, 7-for-22 (.318). Totals, 7-for-22 (.318).
Personal fouls/disqualifications: 1999-00, 18/0. Totals, 18/0.

NOWITZKI, DIRK   F   MAVERICKS

N

PERSONAL: Born June 19, 1978, in Wurzburg, Germany. ... 7-0/250. (2.13/113.4).
HIGH SCHOOL: Rontgen Gymnasium (Wurzburg, Germany).
TRANSACTIONS/CAREER NOTES: Played in Germany (1997-99). ... Selected by Milwaukee Bucks in first round (ninth pick overall) of 1998 NBA Draft. ... Draft rights traded by Bucks with draft rights to F Pat Garrity to Dallas Mavericks for draft rights to F Robert Traylor (June 24, 1998).

GERMAN LEAGUE RECORD

Season Team	G	Min.	FGM	FGA	Pct.	FTM	FTA	Pct.	Reb.	Ast.	Pts.	AVERAGES RPG	APG	PPG
97-98—DJK Wurzburg	20	699	206	367	.561	135	177	.763	198	20	565	9.9	1.0	28.3
98-99—DJK Wurzburg	16	599	123	275	.447	100	128	.781	135	50	366	8.4	3.1	22.9
Totals	36	1298	329	642	.512	235	305	.770	333	70	931	9.3	1.9	25.9

Three-point field goals: 1997-98, 18-for-54 (.333). 1998-99, 20-for-76 (.263). Totals, 38-for-130 (.292).

NBA REGULAR-SEASON RECORD

HONORS: All-NBA second team (2002, 2003). ... All-NBA third team (2001, 2004). ... All-NBA first team (2005, 2006).

Season Team	G	Min.	FGM	FGA	Pct.	FTM	FTA	Pct.	REBOUNDS Off.	Def.	Tot.	Ast.	St.	Blk.	TO	Pts.	AVERAGES RPG	APG	PPG
98-99—Dallas	47	958	136	336	.405	99	128	.773	41	121	162	47	29	27	73	385	3.4	1.0	8.2
99-00—Dallas	82	2938	515	1118	.461	289	348	.830	102	430	532	203	63	68	141	1435	6.5	2.5	17.5
00-01—Dallas	82	3125	591	1247	.474	451	538	.838	119	635	754	173	79	101	156	1784	9.2	2.1	21.8
01-02—Dallas	76	2891	600	1258	.477	440	516	.853	120	635	755	186	83	77	145	1779	9.9	2.4	23.4
02-03—Dallas	80	3117	690	1489	.463	483	548	.881	81	710	791	239	111	82	152	2011	9.9	3.0	25.1
03-04—Dallas	77	2915	605	1310	.462	371	423	.877	90	580	670	207	92	104	135	1680	8.7	2.7	21.8
04-05—Dallas	78	3020	663	1445	.459	615	708	.869	96	661	757	240	97	119	176	2032	9.7	3.1	26.1
05-06—Dallas	81	3089	751	1564	.480	539	598	.901	115	613	728	226	58	83	156	2151	9.0	2.8	26.6
Totals	603	22053	4551	9767	.466	3287	3807	.863	764	4385	5149	1521	612	661	1134	13257	8.5	2.5	22.0

Three-point field goals: 1998-99, 14-for-68 (.206). 1999-00, 116-for-306 (.379). 2000-01, 151-for-390 (.387). 2001-02, 139-for-350 (.397). 2002-03, 148-for-390 (.379). 2003-04, 99-for-290 (.341). 2004-05, 91-for-228 (.399). 2005-06, 110-for-271 (.406). Totals, 868-for-2293 (.379).

Personal fouls/disqualifications: 1998-99, 105/5. 1999-00, 256/4. 2000-01, 245/1. 2001-02, 222/2. 2002-03, 206/2. 2003-04, 216/3. 2004-05, 219/1. 2005-06, 164/1. Totals, 1633/19.

NBA PLAYOFF RECORD

Season Team	G	Min.	FGM	FGA	Pct.	FTM	FTA	Pct.	Off.	Def.	Tot.	Ast.	St.	Blk.	TO	Pts.	RPG	APG	PPG
00-01—Dallas............	10	399	69	163	.423	83	94	.883	14	67	81	14	11	8	14	234	8.1	1.4	23.4
01-02—Dallas............	8	357	73	164	.445	65	74	.878	17	88	105	18	16	6	22	227	13.1	2.3	28.4
02-03—Dallas............	17	722	150	313	.479	103	113	.912	15	181	196	37	21	16	40	430	11.5	2.2	25.3
03-04—Dallas............	5	212	45	100	.450	36	42	.857	13	46	59	7	7	13	6	133	11.8	1.4	26.6
04-05—Dallas............	13	551	103	256	.402	92	111	.829	25	106	131	43	18	21	33	308	10.1	3.3	23.7
05-06—Dallas............	23	983	196	419	.468	205	229	.895	47	221	268	67	25	14	49	620	11.7	2.9	27.0
Totals	76	3224	636	1415	.449	584	663	.881	131	709	840	186	98	78	164	1952	11.1	2.4	25.7

Three-point field goals: 2000-01, 13-for-46 (.283). 2001-02, 16-for-28 (.571). 2002-03, 27-for-61 (.443). 2003-04, 7-for-15 (.467). 2004-05, 10-for-30 (.333). 2005-06, 23-for-67 (.343). Totals, 96-for-247 (.389).

Personal fouls/disqualifications: 2000-01, 37/1. 2001-02, 27/1. 2002 03, 52/0. 2003-04, 16/0. 2004-05, 42/0. 2005-06, 64/0. Totals, 238/2.

NBA ALL-STAR GAME RECORD

NOTES: Three-point shooting champion (2006).

Season Team	Min.	FGM	FGA	Pct.	FTM	FTA	Pct.	Off.	Def.	Tot.	Ast.	PF	Dq.	St.	Blk.	TO	Pts.
2002—Dallas..................	24	5	11	.455	1	1	1.000	2	6	8	3	1	0	0	0	2	12
2003—Dallas..................	16	4	8	.500	0	0	...	0	1	1	1	1	0	0	0	2	9
2004—Dallas..................	13	1	3	.333	0	0	...	0	0	0	1	0	0	2	0	2	2
2005—Dallas..................	21	4	10	.400	1	2	.500	3	5	8	2	1	0	4	4	3	10
2006—Dallas..................	16	4	8	.500	2	3	.667	3	3	6	0	2	0	0	0	0	10
Totals	90	18	40	.450	4	6	.667	8	15	23	7	5	0	6	4	9	43

Three-point field goals: 2002, 1-for-4 (.250). 2003, 1-for-4 (.250). 2004, 0-for-1. 2005, 1-for-3 (.333). 2006, 0-for-3. Totals, 3-for-15 (.200).

O'NEAL, JERMAINE   F/C   PACERS

PERSONAL: Born October 13, 1978, in Columbia, S.C. ... 6-11/230. (2.11/104.3).
HIGH SCHOOL: Eau Claire (Columbia, S.C.).
COLLEGE: Did not attend college.
TRANSACTIONS/CAREER NOTES: Selected out of high school by Portland Trail Blazers in first round (17th pick overall) of 1996 NBA Draft. ... Traded by Trail Blazers with C Joe Kleine to Indiana Pacers for F Dale Davis (August 31, 2000).

NBA REGULAR-SEASON RECORD

HONORS: NBA Most Improved Player Award (2002). ... All-NBA second team (2004). ... All-NBA third team (2002, 2003).

Season Team	G	Min.	FGM	FGA	Pct.	FTM	FTA	Pct.	Off.	Def.	Tot.	Ast.	St.	Blk.	TO	Pts.	RPG	APG	PPG
96-97—Portland........	45	458	69	153	.451	47	78	.603	39	85	124	8	2	26	27	185	2.8	0.2	4.1
97-98—Portland........	60	808	112	231	.485	45	89	.506	80	121	201	17	15	58	55	269	3.4	0.3	4.5
98-99—Portland........	36	311	36	83	.434	18	35	.514	42	55	97	13	4	14	14	90	2.7	0.4	2.5
99-00—Portland........	70	859	108	222	.486	57	98	.582	97	132	229	18	11	55	47	273	3.3	0.3	3.9
00-01—Indiana.........	81	2641	404	868	.465	233	388	.601	249	545	794	98	44	128	161	1041	9.8	1.2	12.9
01-02—Indiana.........	72	2661	419	1108	.378	281	418	.666	100	509	737	118	45	166	174	1371	10.5	1.6	19.0
02-03—Indiana.........	77	2864	610	1260	.484	373	510	.731	202	594	796	155	66	178	180	1600	10.3	2.0	20.8
03-04—Indiana.........	78	2788	608	1400	.434	348	460	.757	193	585	778	164	59	199	181	1566	10.0	2.1	20.1
04-05—Indiana.........	44	1530	386	854	.452	295	391	.754	85	303	388	82	25	88	131	1068	8.8	1.9	24.3
05-06—Indiana.........	51	1802	380	805	.472	261	368	.709	102	374	476	133	27	117	151	1024	9.3	2.6	20.1
Totals	614	16768	3256	7009	.465	1961	2830	.693	1277	3363	4640	806	303	1129	1121	8487	7.6	1.3	13.8

Three-point field goals: 1996-97, 0-for-1. 1997-98, 0-for-2. 1998-99, 0-for-1. 1999-00, 0-for-1. 2000-01, 0-for-5. 2001-02, 1-for-14 (.071). 2002-03, 7-for-21 (.333). 2003-04, 2-for-18 (.111). 2004-05, 1-for-6 (.167). 2005-06, 3-for-10 (.300). Totals, 14-for-79 (.177).

Personal fouls/disqualifications: 1996-97, 46/0. 1997-98, 101/0. 1998-99, 41/0. 1999-00, 127/1. 2000-01, 280/5. 2001-02, 269/4. 2002-03, 277/5. 2003-04, 248/2. 2004-05, 173/4. 2005-06, 177/2. Totals, 1739/23.

NBA PLAYOFF RECORD

Season Team	G	Min.	FGM	FGA	Pct.	FTM	FTA	Pct.	Off.	Def.	Tot.	Ast.	St.	Blk.	TO	Pts.	RPG	APG	PPG
96-97—Portland........	2	4	0	2	.000	0	2	.000	0	1	1	0	0	1	0	0	0.5	0.0	0.0
97-98—Portland........	1	3	0	3	.000	0	0	...	1	0	1	0	0	2	0	0	1.0	0.0	0.0
98-99—Portland........	9	55	4	10	.400	6	12	.500	8	9	17	1	0	3	2	14	1.9	0.1	1.6
99-00—Portland........	8	38	3	11	.273	6	9	.667	2	5	7	1	0	3	0	12	0.9	0.1	1.5
00-01—Indiana.........	4	157	17	39	.436	5	10	.500	12	38	50	7	0	10	7	39	12.5	1.8	9.8
01-02—Indiana.........	5	192	34	76	.447	18	24	.750	6	32	38	5	4	8	14	86	7.6	1.0	17.2
02-03—Indiana.........	6	272	43	92	.467	51	65	.785	24	81	105	4	3	18	18	137	17.5	0.7	22.8
03-04—Indiana.........	16	604	115	272	.423	77	110	.700	29	117	146	19	8	36	29	307	9.1	1.2	19.2
04-05—Indiana.........	13	476	77	211	.365	54	72	.750	21	83	104	29	7	34	36	208	8.0	2.2	16.0
05-06—Indiana.........	6	216	44	84	.524	38	53	.717	9	36	45	10	3	14	26	126	7.5	1.7	21.0
Totals	70	2017	337	800	.421	255	357	.714	112	402	514	76	25	129	132	929	7.3	1.1	13.3

Three-point field goals: 1996-97, 0-for-1. 1997-98, 0-for-1. 2000-01, 0-for-1. 2001-02, 0-for-1. 2002-03, 0-for-3. 2003-04, 0-for-4. 2004-05, 0-for-3. 2005-06, 0-for-2. Totals, 0-for-16 (.000).

Personal fouls/disqualifications: 1997-98, 1/0. 1998-99, 11/0. 1999-00, 9/0. 2000-01, 13/0. 2001-02, 24/1. 2002-03, 22/0. 2003-04, 53/0. 2004-05, 48/1. 2005-06, 28/1. Totals, 209/3.

NBA ALL-STAR GAME RECORD

Season Team	Min.	FGM	FGA	Pct.	FTM	FTA	Pct.	Off.	Def.	Tot.	Ast.	PF	Dq.	St.	Blk.	TO	Pts.
2002—Indiana..............	17	2	5	.400	3	4	.750	0	7	7	0	1	0	0	0	1	7
2003—Indiana..............	33	3	10	.300	4	6	.667	4	6	10	0	2	0	2	4	2	10
2004—Indiana..............	28	7	13	.538	2	4	.500	2	7	9	2	0	0	1	0	2	16
2005—Indiana..............	19	6	10	.600	3	4	.750	1	4	5	1	1	0	1	1	1	15
Totals	97	18	38	.474	12	18	.667	7	24	31	3	4	0	4	5	6	48

O

O'NEAL, SHAQUILLE C HEAT

PERSONAL: Born March 6, 1972, in Newark, N.J. ... 7-1/315. (2.16/142.9). ... Full name: Shaquille Rashaun O'Neal ... Nickname: Shaq. ... Name pronounced shuh-KEEL.
HIGH SCHOOL: Cole (San Antonio).
COLLEGE: Louisiana State.
TRANSACTIONS/CAREER NOTES: Selected after junior season by Orlando Magic in first round (first pick overall) of 1992 NBA Draft. ... Signed as free agent by Los Angeles Lakers (July 18, 1996). ... Traded by Lakers to Miami Heat for F Lamar Odom, F Caron Butler, F Brian Grant, a first-round draft choice and a second-round draft choice (July 14, 2004).
CAREER HONORS: NBA 50th Anniversary All-Time Team (1996).
MISCELLANEOUS: Member of NBA championship team (2000, 2001, 2002, 2006). ... Member of gold-medal-winning U.S. Olympic team (1996). ... Member of gold-medal-winning U.S. World Championship team (1994). ... Orlando Magic all-time leading rebounder with 3,691 and all-time blocked shots leader with 824 (1992-93 through 1995-96).

COLLEGIATE RECORD

NOTES: THE SPORTING NEWS All-America first team (1991, 1992). ... Led NCAA Division I with 14.7 rebounds per game (1991). ... Led NCAA Division I with 5.2 blocked shots per game (1992).

Season Team	G	Min.	FGM	FGA	Pct.	FTM	FTA	Pct.	Reb.	Ast.	Pts.	RPG	APG	PPG
89-90—Louisiana State	32	901	180	314	.573	85	153	.556	385	61	445	12.0	1.9	13.9
90-91—Louisiana State	28	881	312	497	.628	150	235	.638	411	45	774	14.7	1.6	27.6
91-92—Louisiana State	30	959	294	478	.615	134	254	.528	421	46	722	14.0	1.5	24.1
Totals	90	2741	786	1289	.610	369	642	.575	1217	152	1941	13.5	1.7	21.6

NBA REGULAR-SEASON RECORD

RECORDS: Holds single-game record for most free throws attempted, none made—11 (December 8, 2000, vs. Seattle).
HONORS: NBA Most Valuable Player (2000). ... NBA Rookie of the Year (1993). ... IBM Award, for all-around contributions to team's success (2000, 2001). ... All-NBA first team (1998, 2000, 2001, 2002, 2003, 2004, 2005, 2006). ... All-NBA second team (1995, 1999). ... All-NBA third team (1994, 1996, 1997). ... NBA All-Defensive second team (2000, 2001, 2003). ... NBA All-Rookie first team (1993).

Season Team	G	Min.	FGM	FGA	Pct.	FTM	FTA	Pct.	Off.	Def.	Tot.	Ast.	St.	Blk.	TO	Pts.	RPG	APG	PPG
92-93—Orlando	81	3071	733	1304	.562	427	721	.592	342	780	1122	152	60	286	*307	1893	13.9	1.9	23.4
93-94—Orlando	81	3224	*953	1591	*.599	471	850	.554	384	688	1072	195	76	231	222	2377	13.2	2.4	29.3
94-95—Orlando	79	2923	*930	*1594	.583	455	*854	.533	328	573	901	214	73	192	204	*2315	11.4	2.7	*29.3
95-96—Orlando	54	1946	592	1033	.573	249	511	.487	182	414	596	155	34	115	155	1434	11.0	2.9	26.6
96-97—L.A. Lakers	51	1941	552	991	.557	232	479	.484	195	445	640	159	46	147	146	1336	12.5	3.1	26.2
97-98—L.A. Lakers	60	2175	670	1147	*.584	359	681	.527	208	473	681	142	39	144	175	1699	11.4	2.4	28.3
98-99—L.A. Lakers	49	1705	*510	885	.576	269	*498	.540	187	338	525	114	36	82	122	*1289	10.7	2.3	26.3
99-00—L.A. Lakers	79	3163	*956	*1665	*.574	*432	*824	.524	336	742	1078	299	36	239	223	*2344	13.6	3.8	*29.7
00-01—L.A. Lakers	74	2924	*813	1422	*.572	499	*972	.513	291	649	940	277	47	204	218	2125	12.7	3.7	28.7
01-02—L.A. Lakers	67	2422	712	1229	*.579	398	*717	.555	235	480	715	200	41	137	171	1822	10.7	3.0	27.2
02-03—L.A. Lakers	67	2535	695	1211	.574	451	725	.622	259	483	742	206	38	159	196	1841	11.1	3.1	27.5
03-04—L.A. Lakers	67	2464	554	948	*.584	331	*676	.490	246	523	769	196	34	146	195	1439	11.5	2.9	21.5
04-05—Miami	73	2492	658	1095	*.601	353	765	.461	253	507	760	200	36	171	203	1669	10.4	2.7	22.9
05-06—Miami	59	1806	480	800	*.600	221	471	.469	172	369	541	113	23	104	168	1181	9.2	1.9	20.0
Totals	941	34791	9808	16915	.580	5147	9744	.528	3618	7464	11082	2622	619	2377	2705	24764	11.8	2.8	26.3

Three-point field goals: 1992-93, 0-for-2. 1993-94, 0-for-2. 1994-95, 0-for-5. 1995-96, 1-for-2 (.500). 1996-97, 0-for-4. 1998-99, 0-for-1. 1999-00, 0-for-2. 2000-01, 0-for-2. 2001-02, 0-for-1. Totals, 1-for-20 (.050).
Personal fouls/disqualifications: 1992-93, 321/8. 1993-94, 281/3. 1994-95, 258/1. 1995-96, 193/1. 1996-97, 180/2. 1997-98, 193/1. 1998-99, 155/4. 1999-00, 255/2. 2000-01, 256/6. 2001-02, 199/2. 2002-03, 229/4. 2003-04, 225/3. 2004-05, 262/4. 2005-06, 230/4. Totals, 3237/45.

NBA PLAYOFF RECORD

NOTES: NBA Finals Most Valuable Player (2000, 2001). ... Holds NBA Finals records for most points in a four game series—145, most free throw attempts—68, and most free throws made—45 (2002, vs. New Jersey). ... Holds NBA Finals single-game record for most free throws attempted in one quarter—16 (June 9, 2000, vs. Indiana; June 5, 2002, vs. New Jersey); most free throws made in one half—13; and most free throws attempted in one game—39 (June 9, 2000, vs. Indiana). ... Shares NBA Finals single-game records for most free throws made in one quarter—9 (June 9, 2000, vs. Indiana); and most blocked shots—8 (June 8, 2001, vs. Philadelphia). ... Holds single-game playoff record for most free throws attempted—39 (June 9, 2000, vs. Indiana); most free throws attempted in one half—27; and most free throws attempted in one quarter—25 (May 20, 2000, vs. Portland).

Season Team	G	Min.	FGM	FGA	Pct.	FTM	FTA	Pct.	Off.	Def.	Tot.	Ast.	St.	Blk.	TO	Pts.	RPG	APG	PPG
93-94—Orlando	3	126	23	45	.511	16	34	.471	17	23	40	7	2	9	10	62	13.3	2.3	20.7
94-95—Orlando	21	805	195	338	.577	149	261	.571	95	155	250	70	18	40	73	539	11.9	3.3	25.7
95-96—Orlando	12	459	131	216	.606	48	122	.393	49	71	120	55	9	15	44	310	10.0	4.6	25.8
96-97—L.A. Lakers	9	326	89	173	.514	64	105	.610	38	57	95	29	5	17	22	242	10.6	3.2	26.9
97-98—L.A. Lakers	13	501	158	258	.612	80	159	.503	48	84	132	38	7	34	43	396	10.2	2.9	30.5
98-99—L.A. Lakers	8	315	79	155	.510	55	118	.466	44	49	93	18	7	23	18	213	11.6	2.3	26.6
99-00—L.A. Lakers	23	1000	286	505	.566	135	296	.456	119	236	355	71	13	55	56	707	15.4	3.1	30.7
00-01—L.A. Lakers	16	676	191	344	.555	105	200	.525	91	156	247	51	7	38	57	487	15.4	3.2	30.4
01-02—L.A. Lakers	19	776	203	384	.529	135	208	.649	67	172	239	54	10	48	62	541	12.6	2.8	28.5
02-03—L.A. Lakers	12	481	121	226	.535	82	132	.621	63	115	178	44	7	34	35	324	14.8	3.7	27.0
03-04—L.A. Lakers	22	917	182	307	.593	109	254	.429	91	200	291	55	7	61	55	473	13.2	2.5	21.5
04-05—Miami	13	431	101	181	.558	50	106	.472	19	83	102	25	5	19	42	252	7.8	1.9	19.4
05-06—Miami	23	759	178	291	.612	68	182	.374	75	150	225	39	11	34	85	424	9.8	1.7	18.4
Totals	194	7572	1937	3423	.566	1096	2177	.503	816	1551	2367	556	108	427	602	4970	12.2	2.9	25.6

Personal fouls/disqualifications: 1993-94, 13/0. 1994-95, 84/1. 1995-96, 40/0. 1996-97, 31/1. 1997-98, 41/1. 1998-99, 29/0. 1999-00, 67/1. 2000-01, 55/2. 2001-02, 62/1. 2002-03, 34/1. 2003-04, 90/1. 2004-05, 45/0. 2005-06, 84/0. Totals, 688/10.

NBA ALL-STAR GAME RECORD

NOTES: NBA All-Star Game Most Valuable Player (2004). ... NBA All-Star Game co-Most Valuable Player (2000).

Season Team	Min.	FGM	FGA	Pct.	FTM	FTA	Pct.	REBOUNDS Off.	Def.	Tot.	Ast.	PF	Dq.	St.	Blk.	TO	Pts.
1993—Orlando	25	4	9	.444	6	9	.667	3	4	7	0	3	0	0	0	0	14
1994—Orlando	26	2	12	.167	4	11	.364	4	6	10	0	2	0	1	4	1	8
1995—Orlando	26	9	16	.563	4	7	.571	4	3	7	1	2	0	3	2	2	22
1996—Orlando	28	10	16	.625	5	11	.455	3	7	10	1	3	0	1	2	2	25
1997—L.A. Lakers						Selected, did not play—injured											
1998—L.A. Lakers	18	5	10	.500	2	4	.500	2	2	4	1	2	...	0	0	2	12
2000—L.A. Lakers	25	11	20	.550	0	2	.000	4	5	9	3	2	0	0	3	4	22
2001—L.A. Lakers						Selected, did not play—injured											
2002—L.A. Lakers						Selected, did not play—injured											
2003—L.A. Lakers	26	8	14	.571	3	5	.600	3	10	13	1	3	0	2	1	3	19
2004—L.A. Lakers	24	12	19	.632	0	1	.000	5	6	11	1	3	0	2	2	4	24
2005—Miami	25	6	11	.545	0	3	.000	0	6	6	1	2	0	3	3	0	12
2006—Miami	23	7	9	.778	3	5	.600	3	6	9	4	5	0	1	0	2	17
Totals	246	74	136	.544	27	58	.466	31	55	86	13	27	0	13	17	20	175

Three-point field goals: 1995, 0-for-1. 2005, 0-for-1. Totals, 0-for-2 (.000).

OBERTO, FABRICIO   F   SPURS

PERSONAL: Born March 21, 1975 ... 6-10/245. (2.08/111.1).
TRANSACTIONS/CAREER NOTES: Played in Greece (1998-99). ... Played in Spain (1999-2005). ... Not drafted by an NBA franchise. ... Signed as free agent by San Antonio Spurs (August 2, 2005).
MISCELLANEOUS: Member of gold medal-winning Argentinian Olympic team (2004).

GREEK LEAGUE RECORD

Season Team	G	Min.	FGM	FGA	Pct.	FTM	FTA	Pct.	Reb.	Ast.	Pts.	AVERAGES RPG	APG	PPG
98-99—Olympiakos S.F.P.	24	436	66	107	.617	30	49	.612	132	20	163	5.5	0.8	6.8

Three-point field goals: 1998-99, 1-for-2 (.500). Totals, 1-for-2 (.500).

SPANISH LEAGUE RECORD

Season Team	G	Min.	FGM	FGA	Pct.	FTM	FTA	Pct.	Reb.	Ast.	Pts.	AVERAGES RPG	APG	PPG
99-00—Tau Ceramica	12	240	50	74	.676	9	23	.391	44	11	109	3.7	0.9	9.1
00-01—Tau Ceramica	34	802	131	193	.679	44	96	.458	209	41	306	6.1	1.2	9.0
01-02—Tau Ceramica	32	905	155	249	.622	43	88	.489	202	48	353	6.3	1.5	11.0
02-03—Pamesa Valencia	34	910	188	296	.635	58	105	.552	180	69	434	5.3	2.0	12.8
03-04—Pamesa Valencia	34	898	177	290	.610	39	90	.433	182	62	393	5.4	1.8	11.6
04-05—Pamesa Valencia	30	856	191	292	.654	43	95	.453	218	64	425	7.3	2.1	14.2
Totals	176	4611	892	1394	.640	236	497	.475	1035	295	2020	5.9	1.7	11.5

Three-point field goals: 2002-03, 0-for-3. 2003-04, 0-for-1. Totals, 0-for-4 (.000).

NBA REGULAR-SEASON RECORD

Season Team	G	Min.	FGM	FGA	Pct.	FTM	FTA	Pct.	REBOUNDS Off.	Def.	Tot.	Ast.	St.	Blk.	TO	Pts.	AVERAGES RPG	APG	PPG
05-06—San Antonio	59	490	44	93	.473	15	27	.556	57	66	123	27	9	11	28	103	2.1	0.5	1.7

Three-point field goals: 2005-06, 0-for-2. Totals, 0-for-2 (.000).
Personal fouls/disqualifications: 2005-06, 91/0. Totals, 91/0.

NBA PLAYOFF RECORD

Season Team	G	Min.	FGM	FGA	Pct.	FTM	FTA	Pct.	REBOUNDS Off.	Def.	Tot.	Ast.	St.	Blk.	TO	Pts.	AVERAGES RPG	APG	PPG
05-06—San Antonio	7	34	3	9	.333	1	4	.250	3	3	6	1	1	3	2	7	0.9	0.1	1.0

Personal fouls/disqualifications: 2005-06, 7/0. Totals, 7/0.

ODOM, LAMAR   F   LAKERS

PERSONAL: Born November 6, 1979, in Jamaica, N.Y. ... 6-10/221. (2.08/100.2). ... Full name: Lamar Joseph Odom
HIGH SCHOOL: Christian Redemption Academy (Troy, N.Y.), then Christ the King (Queens, N.Y.).
COLLEGE: UNLV, then Rhode Island.
TRANSACTIONS/CAREER NOTES: Selected after sophomore season by Los Angeles Clippers in first round (fourth pick overall) of 1999 NBA Draft. ... Signed as free agent by Miami Heat (August 26, 2003). ... Traded by Heat with F Caron Butler, F Brian Grant, a first-round draft choice and a second-round draft choice to Los Angeles Lakers for C Shaquille O'Neal (July 14, 2004).
MISCELLANEOUS: Member of bronze-medal-winning U.S. Olympic Team (2004).

COLLEGIATE RECORD

Season Team	G	Min.	FGM	FGA	Pct.	FTM	FTA	Pct.	Reb.	Ast.	Pts.	AVERAGES RPG	APG	PPG
97-98—Rhode Island							Did not play.							
98-99—Rhode Island	32	1116	203	421	.482	125	182	.687	302	122	564	9.4	3.8	17.6
Totals	32	1116	203	421	.482	125	182	.687	302	122	564	9.4	3.8	17.6

Three-point field goals: 1998-99, 33-for-100 (.330). Totals, 33-for-100 (.330).

NBA REGULAR-SEASON RECORD

HONORS: NBA All-Rookie first team (2000).
NOTES: Tied for NBA lead with 13 disqualifications (2000).

O

Season Team	G	Min.	FGM	FGA	Pct.	FTM	FTA	Pct.	Off.	Def.	Tot.	Ast.	St.	Blk.	TO	Pts.	RPG	APG	PPG
99-00—L.A. Clippers...	76	2767	449	1024	.438	302	420	.719	159	436	595	317	91	95	258	1259	7.8	4.2	16.6
00-01—L.A. Clippers....	76	2836	481	1046	.460	262	386	.679	110	482	592	392	74	122	264	1304	7.8	5.2	17.2
01-02—L.A. Clippers...	29	999	151	360	.419	61	93	.656	31	145	176	171	23	36	97	379	6.1	5.9	13.1
02-03—L.A. Clippers...	49	1679	268	611	.439	136	175	.777	59	267	326	178	42	41	140	714	6.7	3.6	14.6
03-04—Miami	80	3003	485	1127	.430	340	458	.742	160	616	776	327	85	71	236	1371	9.7	4.1	17.1
04-05—L.A. Lakers	64	2320	366	774	.473	207	298	.695	134	519	653	238	42	65	161	975	10.2	3.7	15.2
05-06—L.A. Lakers	80	3221	445	925	.481	216	313	.690	181	557	738	443	75	64	213	1186	9.2	5.5	14.8
Totals	454	16825	2645	5867	.451	1524	2143	.711	834	3022	3856	2066	432	494	1369	7188	8.5	4.6	15.8

Three-point field goals: 1999-00, 59-for-164 (.360). 2000-01, 80-for-253 (.316). 2001-02, 16-for-84 (.190). 2002-03, 42-for-129 (.326). 2003-04, 61-for-205 (.298). 2004-05, 36-for-117 (.308). 2005-06, 80-for-215 (.372). Totals, 374-for-1167 (.320).

Personal fouls/disqualifications: 1999-00, 291/13. 2000-01, 236/4. 2001-02, 91/3. 2002-03, 181/6. 2003-04, 273/5. 2004-05, 211/3. 2005-06, 256/4. Totals, 1539/38.

NBA PLAYOFF RECORD

Season Team	G	Min.	FGM	FGA	Pct.	FTM	FTA	Pct.	Off.	Def.	Tot.	Ast.	St.	Blk.	TO	Pts.	RPG	APG	PPG
03-04—Miami	13	512	81	182	.445	49	72	.681	32	76	108	37	15	10	42	219	8.3	2.8	16.8
05-06—L.A. Lakers	7	314	49	99	.495	30	45	.667	15	62	77	34	3	8	23	134	11.0	4.9	19.1
Totals	20	826	130	281	.463	79	117	.675	47	138	185	71	18	18	65	353	9.3	3.6	17.7

Three-point field goals: 2003-04, 8-for-26 (.308). 2005-06, 6-for-30 (.200). Totals, 14-for-56 (.250).
Personal fouls/disqualifications: 2003-04, 58/2. 2005-06, 23/0. Totals, 81/2.

OKAFOR, EMEKA   F/C   BOBCATS

PERSONAL: Born September 28, 1982, in Houston. ... 6-10/252. (2.08/114.3). ... Full name: Chukwuemeka Noubuisi Okafor
HIGH SCHOOL: Bellaire (Houston).
COLLEGE: Connecticut.
TRANSACTIONS/CAREER NOTES: Selected after junior season by Charlotte Bobcats in first round (second pick overall) of 2004 NBA Draft.
MISCELLANEOUS: Member of bronze-medal-winning U.S. Olympic Team (2004).

COLLEGIATE RECORD

NOTES: Member of NCAA Division I championship team (2004). ... The SPORTING NEWS All-America first team (2004). ... NCAA Tournament Division I Most Outstanding Player (2004). ... Led NCAA Division I with 4.7 blocked shots per game (2002-03).

Season Team	G	Min.	FGM	FGA	Pct.	FTM	FTA	Pct.	Reb.	Ast.	Pts.	RPG	APG	PPG
01-02—Connecticut	34	1021	105	178	.590	57	92	.620	306	27	267	9.0	0.8	7.9
02-03—Connecticut	33	1087	221	381	.580	82	137	.599	370	18	524	11.2	0.5	15.9
03-04—Connecticut	36	1166	261	436	.599	113	218	.518	415	36	635	11.5	1.0	17.6
Totals	103	3274	587	995	.590	252	447	.564	1091	81	1426	10.6	0.8	13.8

NBA REGULAR-SEASON RECORD

HONORS: NBA Rookie of the Year (2005). ... NBA All-Rookie first team (2005).

Season Team	G	Min.	FGM	FGA	Pct.	FTM	FTA	Pct.	Off.	Def.	Tot.	Ast.	St.	Blk.	TO	Pts.	RPG	APG	PPG
04-05—Charlotte	73	2600	448	1003	.447	209	343	.609	275	520	795	64	62	125	125	1105	10.9	0.9	15.1
05-06—Charlotte	26	874	131	316	.415	82	125	.656	94	167	261	31	22	50	53	344	10.0	1.2	13.2
Totals	99	3474	579	1319	.439	291	468	.622	369	687	1056	95	84	175	178	1449	10.7	1.0	14.6

Three-point field goals: 2004-05, 0-for-1. Totals, 0-for-1 (.000).
Personal fouls/disqualifications: 2004-05, 214/0. 2005-06, 88/1. Totals, 302/1.

OKUR, MEHMET   F/C   JAZZ

PERSONAL: Born May 26, 1979, in Yalova, Turkey. ... 6-11/249. (2.11/112.9).
HIGH SCHOOL: Cem Sultan (Gazcilar Bursa).
COLLEGE: Did not attend college.
TRANSACTIONS/CAREER NOTES: Played in Turkey (1997-2002). ... Selected by Detroit Pistons in second round (38th pick overall) of 2001 NBA Draft. ... Signed as free agent by Utah Jazz (July 27, 2004).
MISCELLANEOUS: Member of NBA championship team (2004).

TURKISH LEAGUE RECORD

Season Team	G	Min.	FGM	FGA	Pct.	FTM	FTA	Pct.	Reb.	Ast.	Pts.	RPG	APG	PPG
97-98—Oyak Renau	25	332	47	108	.435	17	26	.654	81	18	111	3.2	0.7	4.4
98-99—Tofas Bursa	33	440	55	112	.491	29	42	.690	142	12	155	4.3	0.4	4.7
99-00—Tofas Bursa	37	731	94	212	.443	35	50	.700	210	32	243	5.7	0.9	6.6
00-01—Efes Pilsen......................	26	477	91	163	.558	35	42	.833	161	12	231	6.2	0.5	8.9
01-02—Efes Pilsen......................	22	602	112	211	.531	62	77	.805	186	30	298	8.5	1.4	13.5
Totals	143	2582	399	806	.495	178	237	.751	780	104	1038	5.5	0.7	7.3

Three-point field goals: 1998-99, 16-for-31 (.516). 1999-00, 20-for-60 (.333). 2000-01, 14-for-27 (.519). 2001-02, 12-for-28 (.429). Totals, 62-for-146 (.425).
Personal fouls/disqualifications: 2000-01, 45/0. Totals, 45/0.

NBA REGULAR-SEASON RECORD

Season Team	G	Min.	FGM	FGA	Pct.	FTM	FTA	Pct.	Off.	Def.	Tot.	Ast.	St.	Blk.	TO	Pts.	RPG	APG	PPG
02-03—Detroit	72	1366	180	423	.426	96	131	.733	117	218	335	71	25	39	66	494	4.7	1.0	6.9
03-04—Detroit	71	1580	251	542	.463	162	209	.775	160	261	421	69	36	63	101	682	5.9	1.0	9.6

O

Season Team	G	Min.	FGM	FGA	Pct.	FTM	FTA	Pct.	Off.	Def.	Tot.	Ast.	St.	Blk.	TO	Pts.	RPG	APG	PPG
									REBOUNDS								AVERAGES		
04-05—Utah	82	2304	354	756	.468	329	387	.850	194	422	616	166	32	68	141	1054	7.5	2.0	12.9
05-06—Utah	82	2945	519	1128	.460	354	454	.780	211	535	746	194	40	73	163	1472	9.1	2.4	18.0
Totals	307	8195	1304	2849	.458	941	1181	.797	682	1436	2118	500	133	243	471	3702	6.9	1.6	12.1

Three-point field goals: 2002-03, 38-for-112 (.339). 2003-04, 18-for-48 (.375). 2004-05, 17-for-63 (.270). 2005-06, 80-for-234 (.342). Totals, 153-for-457 (.335).
Personal fouls/disqualifications: 2002-03, 167/0. 2003-04, 178/0. 2004-05, 227/2. 2005-06, 285/4. Totals, 817/6.

NBA PLAYOFF RECORD

Season Team	G	Min.	FGM	FGA	Pct.	FTM	FTA	Pct.	Off.	Def.	Tot.	Ast.	St.	Blk.	TO	Pts.	RPG	APG	PPG
									REBOUNDS								AVERAGES		
02-03—Detroit	17	323	35	80	.438	17	32	.531	24	46	70	13	12	12	14	94	4.1	0.8	5.5
03-04—Detroit	22	252	31	66	.470	18	26	.692	16	45	61	8	5	9	15	82	2.8	0.4	3.7
Totals	39	575	66	146	.452	35	58	.603	40	91	131	21	17	21	29	176	3.4	0.5	4.5

Three-point field goals: 2002-03, 7-for-13 (.538). 2003-04, 2-for-5 (.400). Totals, 9-for-18 (.500).
Personal fouls/disqualifications: 2002-03, 39/0. 2003-04, 20/0. Totals, 59/0.

OLLIE, KEVIN G 76ERS

PERSONAL: Born December 27, 1972, in Dallas. ... 6-4/195. (1.93/88.5). ... Full name: Kevin Jermaine Ollie ... Cousin of Arnaz Battle, wide receiver, San Francisco 49ers.
HIGH SCHOOL: Crenshaw (Los Angeles).
COLLEGE: Connecticut.
TRANSACTIONS/CAREER NOTES: Not drafted by an NBA franchise. ... Signed as free agent by Golden State Warriors (October 4, 1995). ... Waived by Warriors (October 11, 1995). ... Played in Continental Basketball Association with Connecticut Pride (1995-96 through 1997-98 and 1999-2000). ... Signed as free agent by Dallas Mavericks (October 7, 1997). ... Waived by Mavericks (December 17, 1997). ... Signed by Orlando Magic to first of two consecutive 10-day contracts (March 2, 1998). ... Signed by Magic for remainder of season (March 22, 1998). ... Signed as free agent by Sacramento Kings (January 21, 1999). ... Waived by Kings (February 19, 1999). ... Re-signed by Magic to 10-day contract (March 8, 1999). ... Waived by Magic (March 14, 1999). ... Signed as free agent by Mavericks (October 6, 1999). ... Waived by Mavericks (October 29, 1999). ... Signed as free agent by Philadelphia 76ers (November 24, 1999). ... Signed as free agent by New Jersey Nets (October 3, 2000). ... Waived by Nets (December 15, 2000). ... Signed as free agent by 76ers (December 22, 2000). ... Signed as free agent by Chicago Bulls (September 24, 2001). ... Traded by Bulls with C Brad Miller, G Ron Mercer and G/F Ron Artest to Indiana Pacers for G Jalen Rose, G Travis Best, G Norman Richardson and conditional second-round draft choice (February 19, 2002). ... Signed as free agent by Milwaukee Bucks (September 6, 2002). ... Traded by Bucks with G Ray Allen, G Ronald Murray and conditional first-round draft choice to Seattle SuperSonics for G Gary Payton and G Desmond Mason (February 20, 2003). ... Signed as free agent by Cleveland Cavaliers (July 17, 2003) ... Traded by Cavaliers with F Kedrick Brown to Philadelphia 76ers for G Eric Snow (July 20, 2004).

COLLEGIATE RECORD

Season Team	G	Min.	FGM	FGA	Pct.	FTM	FTA	Pct.	Reb.	Ast.	Pts.	RPG	APG	PPG
												AVERAGES		
91-92—Connecticut	29	294	17	45	.378	28	39	.718	23	40	62	0.8	1.4	2.1
92-93—Connecticut	28	864	69	176	.392	81	109	.743	64	158	220	2.3	5.6	7.9
93-94—Connecticut	34	973	73	155	.471	71	97	.732	83	209	219	2.4	6.1	6.4
94-95—Connecticut	33	1025	112	222	.505	87	108	.806	82	212	324	2.5	6.4	9.8
Totals	124	3156	271	598	.453	267	353	.756	252	619	825	2.0	5.0	6.7

Three-point field goals: 1992-93, 1-for-9 (.111). 1993-94, 2-for-10 (.200). 1994-95, 13-for-42 (.310). Totals, 16-for-61 (.262).

CBA RECORD

NOTES: Member of CBA championship team (1999).

Season Team	G	Min.	FGM	FGA	Pct.	FTM	FTA	Pct.	Reb.	Ast.	Pts.	RPG	APG	PPG
												AVERAGES		
95-96—Connecticut	56	1448	161	378	.426	134	178	.753	154	226	459	2.8	4.0	8.2
96-97—Connecticut	52	2226	277	565	.490	204	251	.813	202	300	763	3.9	5.8	14.7
97-98—Connecticut	24	886	177	379	.467	108	136	.794	77	118	474	3.2	4.9	19.8
99-00—Connecticut	2	81	12	24	.500	15	16	.938	7	15	40	3.5	7.5	20.0
Totals	134	4641	627	1346	.466	461	581	.793	440	659	1736	3.3	4.9	13.0

Three-point field goals: 1995-96, 3-for-18 (.167). 1996-97, 5-for-14 (.357). 1997-98, 12-for-34 (.353). 1999-00, 1-for-2 (.500). Totals, 21-for-68 (.309).
Personal fouls/disqualifications: 1995-96, 84/0. 1996-97, 136/0. 1997-98, 55/0. 1999-00, 6/0. Totals, 281/0.

NBA REGULAR-SEASON RECORD

Season Team	G	Min.	FGM	FGA	Pct.	FTM	FTA	Pct.	Off.	Def.	Tot.	Ast.	St.	Blk.	TO	Pts.	RPG	APG	PPG
									REBOUNDS								AVERAGES		
97-98—Dallas-Orlando	35	430	37	98	.378	49	70	.700	9	30	39	65	13	0	44	123	1.1	1.9	3.5
98-99—Sac.-Orlando	8	72	4	14	.286	5	7	.714	0	7	7	3	3	1	3	13	0.9	0.4	1.6
99-00—Philadelphia	40	290	22	49	.449	28	37	.757	4	27	31	46	10	0	10	72	0.8	1.2	1.8
00-01—N.J.-Phila.	70	925	76	192	.396	63	89	.708	16	79	95	146	30	1	49	216	1.4	2.1	3.1
01-02—Chi.-Indiana	81	1723	137	353	.388	187	227	.824	25	159	184	291	62	2	106	462	2.3	3.6	5.7
02-03—Mil.-Seattle	82	1897	199	441	.451	134	178	.753	25	157	182	291	69	5	72	534	2.2	3.5	6.5
03-04—Cleveland	82	1401	95	257	.370	147	176	.835	23	147	170	234	51	8	81	341	2.1	2.9	4.2
04-05—Philadelphia	26	158	11	31	.355	6	9	.667	3	16	19	19	5	0	6	28	0.7	0.7	1.1
05-06—Philadelphia	70	1069	75	174	.431	41	49	.837	13	85	98	101	33	3	29	192	1.4	1.4	2.7
Totals	494	7965	656	1609	.408	660	842	.784	118	707	825	1196	276	20	400	1981	1.7	2.4	4.0

Three-point field goals: 1997-98, 0-for-1. 1998-99, 5-for-7 (.714). 2000-01, 1-for-3 (.333). 2001-02, 1-for-2 (.500). 2002-03, 2-for-6 (.333). 2003-04, 4-for-9 (.444). 2005-06, 1-for-3 (.333). Totals, 14-for-31 (.452).
Personal fouls/disqualifications: 1997-98, 31/0. 1998-99, 9/0. 1999-00, 27/0. 2000-01, 84/0. 2001-02, 97/1. 2002-03, 122/0. 2003-04, 119/0. 2004-05, 16/0. 2005-06, 103/1. Totals, 608/2.

NBA PLAYOFF RECORD

Season Team	G	Min.	FGM	FGA	Pct.	FTM	FTA	Pct.	Off.	Def.	Tot.	Ast.	St.	Blk.	TO	Pts.	RPG	APG	PPG
									REBOUNDS								AVERAGES		
99-00—Philadelphia	10	65	6	12	.500	8	9	.889	0	5	5	12	2	0	3	20	0.5	1.2	2.0
00-01—Philadelphia	23	123	10	27	.370	13	14	.929	2	7	9	23	0	0	8	33	0.4	1.0	1.4
01-02—Indiana	5	118	11	26	.423	6	6	1.000	0	12	12	23	3	0	5	29	2.4	4.6	5.8
Totals	38	306	27	65	.415	27	29	.931	2	24	26	58	5	0	16	82	0.7	1.5	2.2

Three-point field goals: 2001-02, 1-for-2 (.500). Totals, 1-for-2 (.500).
Personal fouls/disqualifications: 1999-00, 5/0. 2000-01, 12/0. 2001-02, 6/0. Totals, 23/0.

OLOWOKANDI, MICHAEL　　　　C　　　　　　　CELTICS

PERSONAL: Born April 3, 1975, in Lagos, Nigeria. ... 7-0/269. (2.13/122.0).
HIGH SCHOOL: Newlands Manor School (East Sussex, England).
COLLEGE: Brunel (Middlesex, England); did not play basketball, then Pacific.
TRANSACTIONS/CAREER NOTES: Selected by Los Angeles Clippers in first round (first pick overall) of 1998 NBA Draft. ... Played in Italy (1998-99). ... Signed as free agent by Minnesota Timberwolves (July 16, 2003) ... Traded by Timberwolves with F Wally Szczerbiak, F/C Dwayne Jones and a future first-round draft choice to Boston Celtics for G Ricky Davis, C Mark Blount, G Marcus Banks, SF Justin Reed and two second-round draft choices (January 26, 2006).

COLLEGIATE RECORD

Season Team	G	Min.	FGM	FGA	Pct.	FTM	FTA	Pct.	Reb.	Ast.	Pts.	RPG	APG	PPG
95-96—Pacific	25	257	40	76	.526	20	36	.556	84	4	100	3.4	0.2	4.0
96-97—Pacific	19	433	94	165	.570	19	57	.333	126	8	207	6.6	0.4	10.9
97-98—Pacific	33	1046	309	508	.608	114	235	.485	369	26	732	11.2	0.8	22.2
Totals	77	1736	443	749	.591	153	328	.466	579	38	1039	7.5	0.5	13.5

ITALIAN LEAGUE RECORD

Season Team	G	Min.	FGM	FGA	Pct.	FTM	FTA	Pct.	Reb.	Ast.	Pts.	RPG	APG	PPG
98-99—Bologna Arimo	3	52	6	14	.429	2	4	.500	17	1	14	5.7	0.3	4.7

Personal fouls/disqualifications: 1998-99, 6/0. Totals, 6/0.

NBA REGULAR-SEASON RECORD

HONORS: NBA All-Rookie second team (1999).

Season Team	G	Min.	FGM	FGA	Pct.	FTM	FTA	Pct.	Off.	Def.	Tot.	Ast.	St.	Blk.	TO	Pts.	RPG	APG	PPG
98-99—L.A. Clippers	45	1279	172	399	.431	57	118	.483	120	237	357	25	27	55	85	401	7.9	0.6	8.9
99-00—L.A. Clippers	80	2493	330	756	.437	123	189	.651	194	462	656	38	35	140	177	783	8.2	0.5	9.8
00-01—L.A. Clippers	82	2127	308	708	.435	85	156	.545	168	357	525	46	30	108	169	701	6.4	0.6	8.5
01-02—L.A. Clippers	80	2568	384	886	.433	117	188	.622	164	547	711	90	55	145	175	885	8.9	1.1	11.1
02-03—L.A. Clippers	36	1369	186	436	.427	69	105	.657	57	271	328	47	18	79	98	441	9.1	1.3	12.3
03-04—Minnesota	43	925	121	285	.425	36	61	.590	78	167	245	24	16	68	54	278	5.7	0.6	6.5
04-05—Minnesota	62	1215	161	353	.456	46	69	.667	106	218	324	29	15	56	68	368	5.2	0.5	5.9
05-06—Minn.-Boston	48	918	107	240	.446	24	47	.511	50	170	220	23	22	33	55	238	4.6	0.5	5.0
Totals	476	12894	1769	4063	.435	557	933	.597	937	2429	3366	322	218	684	881	4095	7.1	0.7	8.6

Personal fouls/disqualifications: 1998-99, 137/2. 1999-00, 304/10. 2000-01, 250/4. 2001-02, 217/1. 2002-03, 110/5. 2003-04, 137/3. 2004-05, 193/3. 2005-06, 122/2. Totals, 1470/30.

NBA PLAYOFF RECORD

Season Team	G	Min.	FGM	FGA	Pct.	FTM	FTA	Pct.	Off.	Def.	Tot.	Ast.	St.	Blk.	TO	Pts.	RPG	APG	PPG
03-04—Minnesota	15	224	12	37	.324	7	8	.875	16	36	52	2	2	11	17	31	3.5	0.1	2.1

Three-point field goals: 2003-04, 0-for-1. Totals, 0-for-1 (.000).
Personal fouls/disqualifications: 2003-04, 50/0. Totals, 50/0.

OSTERTAG, GREG　　　　　C

PERSONAL: Born March 6, 1973, in Dallas. ... 7-2/280. (2.18/127.0). ... Full name: Gregory Donovan Ostertag ... Name pronounced OH-stir-tag.
HIGH SCHOOL: Duncanville (Texas).
COLLEGE: Kansas.
TRANSACTIONS/CAREER NOTES: Selected by Utah Jazz in first round (28th pick overall) of 1995 NBA Draft. ... Signed as free agent by Sacramento Kings (July 20, 2004). ... Traded by Kings to Utah Jazz in five-team trade (August 2, 2005).

COLLEGIATE RECORD

Season Team	G	Min.	FGM	FGA	Pct.	FTM	FTA	Pct.	Reb.	Ast.	Pts.	RPG	APG	PPG
91-92—Kansas	32	311	61	112	.473	36	54	.667	57	5	154	3.5	0.2	4.8
92-93—Kansas	29	389	61	118	.517	33	55	.600	118	11	155	4.1	0.4	5.3
93-94—Kansas	35	739	145	272	.533	70	111	.631	307	12	360	8.8	0.3	10.3
94-95—Kansas	31	603	121	203	.596	57	103	.553	233	13	299	7.5	0.4	9.6
Totals	127	2042	388	705	.550	192	318	.604	770	41	968	6.1	0.3	7.6

Three-point field goals: 1991-92, 0-for-1. 1993-94, 0-for-2. Totals, 0-for-3 (.000).

NBA REGULAR-SEASON RECORD

Season Team	G	Min.	FGM	FGA	Pct.	FTM	FTA	Pct.	Off.	Def.	Tot.	Ast.	St.	Blk.	TO	Pts.	RPG	APG	PPG
95-96—Utah	57	661	86	182	.473	36	54	.667	57	118	175	5	5	63	25	208	3.1	0.1	3.6
96-97—Utah	77	1818	210	408	.515	139	205	.678	180	385	565	27	24	152	74	559	7.3	0.4	7.3
97-98—Utah	63	1288	115	239	.481	67	140	.479	134	240	374	25	28	132	74	297	5.9	0.4	4.7
98-99—Utah	48	1340	99	208	.476	75	121	.620	105	243	348	23	12	131	45	273	7.3	0.5	5.7
99-00—Utah	81	1606	124	267	.464	119	187	.636	172	310	482	18	20	172	79	367	6.0	0.2	4.5
00-01—Utah	81	1491	139	281	.495	84	151	.556	164	251	415	22	22	142	63	363	5.1	0.3	4.5
01-02—Utah	74	1107	91	201	.453	63	130	.485	125	188	313	50	15	109	51	245	4.2	0.7	3.3
02-03—Utah	81	1926	169	326	.518	100	196	.510	180	323	503	55	20	147	104	438	6.2	0.7	5.4
03-04—Utah	78	2153	208	437	.476	113	195	.579	221	357	578	123	30	139	99	529	7.4	1.6	6.8

O

Season Team	G	Min.	FGM	FGA	Pct.	FTM	FTA	Pct.	Off.	Def.	Tot.	Ast.	St.	Blk.	TO	Pts.	RPG	APG	PPG
									REBOUNDS								AVERAGES		
04-05—Sacramento	56	556	37	84	.440	13	38	.342	55	112	167	37	7	40	24	87	3.0	0.7	1.6
05-06—Utah...............	60	807	61	124	.492	24	48	.500	82	143	225	58	6	66	46	146	3.8	1.0	2.4
Totals	756	14753	1339	2757	.486	833	1465	.569	1475	2670	4145	443	189	1293	684	3512	5.5	0.6	4.6

Three-point field goals: 1996-97, 0-for-4. 1999-00, 0-for-1. 2000-01, 1-for-2 (.500). 2003-04, 0-for-1. 2004-05, 0-for-2. Totals, 1-for-10 (.100).
Personal fouls/disqualifications: 1995-96, 91/1. 1996-97, 233/2. 1997-98, 166/1. 1998-99, 140/2. 1999-00, 196/2. 2000-01, 215/3. 2001-02, 152/1.
2002-03, 235/4. 2003-04, 228/1. 2004-05, 88/1. 2005-06, 129/2. Totals, 1873/20.

NBA PLAYOFF RECORD

Season Team	G	Min.	FGM	FGA	Pct.	FTM	FTA	Pct.	Off.	Def.	Tot.	Ast.	St.	Blk.	TO	Pts.	RPG	APG	PPG
									REBOUNDS								AVERAGES		
95-96—Utah...............	15	212	20	45	.444	13	21	.619	18	32	50	1	2	21	4	53	3.3	0.1	3.5
96-97— Utah...............	20	459	34	83	.410	26	35	.743	52	85	137	6	10	47	18	94	6.9	0.3	4.7
97-98—Utah...............	19	336	26	46	.565	12	25	.480	25	56	81	5	7	37	12	64	4.3	0.3	3.4
98-99—Utah...............	11	261	13	35	.371	18	28	.643	18	47	65	6	2	24	8	44	5.9	0.5	4.0
99-00—Utah...............	8	172	10	19	.526	10	22	.455	19	26	45	2	2	17	8	30	5.6	0.3	3.8
00-01—Utah...............	5	64	4	11	.364	0	4	.000	6	12	18	1	0	2	2	8	3.6	0.2	1.6
01-02—Utah...............	4	87	13	21	.619	1	10	.100	19	15	34	2	2	6	6	27	8.5	0.5	6.8
02-03—Utah...............	5	151	16	36	.444	14	19	.737	19	24	43	8	3	9	8	46	8.6	1.6	9.2
04-05—Sacramento ...	2	26	3	3	1.000	0	0	...	4	5	9	0	1	2	2	6	4.5	0.0	3.0
Totals	89	1768	139	299	.465	94	164	.573	180	302	482	31	29	165	68	372	5.4	0.3	4.2

Personal fouls/disqualifications: 1995-96, 28/0. 1996-97, 76/3. 1997-98, 51/0. 1998-99, 27/0. 1999-00, 20/0. 2000-01, 10/1. 2001-02, 14/1. 2002-03,
17/0. 2004-05, 4/0. Totals, 247/5.

OUTLAW, BO   F   MAGIC

PERSONAL: Born April 13, 1971, in San Antonio. ... 6-8/210. (2.03/95.3). ... Full name: Charles Outlaw.
HIGH SCHOOL: John Jay (San Antonio).
JUNIOR COLLEGE: South Plains College (Texas).
COLLEGE: Houston.
TRANSACTIONS/CAREER NOTES: Not drafted by an NBA franchise. ... Played in Spain (1993-94). ... Played in Continental
Basketball Association with Grand Rapids Hoops (1993-94). ... Signed by Los Angeles Clippers to first of two consecutive 10-day contracts
(February 14, 1994). ... Re-signed by Clippers for remainder of season (March 8, 1994). ... Signed as free agent by Orlando Magic (September
5, 1997). ... Traded by Magic to Phoenix Suns as part of three-way deal in which Suns traded G/F Jud Buechler to Magic, Suns acquired first-
round draft choice and cash considerations from Magic and Los Angeles Clippers acquired G Vinny Del Negro from Suns and cash considerations and right to swap 2005 second-round draft choice from Magic (November 16, 2001). ... Traded by Suns with C Jake Tsakalidis to
Memphis Grizzlies for G Brevin Knight, C Cezary Trybanski and F Robert Archibald (September 30, 2003). ... Released by Grizzlies (November
1, 2004). ... Signed as free agent by Phoenix Suns (November 8, 2004). ... Signed as free agent by Orlando Magic (September 29, 2005).

COLLEGIATE RECORD

NOTES: Led NCAA Division I with .684 field goal percentage (1992) and .658 field goal percentage (1993).

Season Team	G	Min.	FGM	FGA	Pct.	FTM	FTA	Pct.	Reb.	Ast.	Pts.	RPG	APG	PPG
													AVERAGES	
89-90—South Plains College	30	...	147	261	.563	69	136	.507	289	54	364	9.6	1.8	12.1
90-91—South Plains College	30	...	160	242	.661	70	122	.574	326	87	395	10.9	2.9	13.2
91-92—Houston	31	970	156	228	.684	57	129	.442	254	81	369	8.2	2.6	11.9
92-93—Houston	30	1055	196	298	.658	95	192	.495	301	99	487	10.0	3.3	16.2
Junior College Totals.............	60	...	307	503	.610	139	258	.539	615	141	759	10.3	2.4	12.7
4-Year-College Totals.............	61	2025	352	526	.669	152	321	.474	555	180	856	9.1	3.0	14.0

Three-point field goals: 1989-90, 0-for-1. 1990-91, 5-for-10 (.500). Totals, 5-for-11 (.455).

CBA RECORD

NOTES: Led CBA with 3.8 blocked shots per game (1994). ... CBA All-League second team (1994). ... CBA All-Defensive team (1994). ... CBA
All-Rookie first team (1994).

Season Team	G	Min.	FGM	FGA	Pct.	FTM	FTA	Pct.	Reb.	Ast.	Pts.	RPG	APG	PPG
													AVERAGES	
93-94—Grand Rapids	32	1211	167	243	*.687	83	160	.519	349	56	417	10.9	1.8	13.0

Three-point field goals: 1993-94, 0-for-1. Totals, 0-for-1 (.000).
Personal fouls/disqualifications: 1993-94, 114/0. Totals, 114/0.

NBA REGULAR-SEASON RECORD

Season Team	G	Min.	FGM	FGA	Pct.	FTM	FTA	Pct.	Off.	Def.	Tot.	Ast.	St.	Blk.	TO	Pts.	RPG	APG	PPG
									REBOUNDS								AVERAGES		
93-94—L.A. Clippers ...	37	871	98	167	.587	61	103	.592	81	131	212	36	36	37	31	257	5.7	1.0	6.9
94-95—L.A. Clippers ...	81	1655	170	325	.523	82	186	.441	121	192	313	84	90	151	78	422	3.9	1.0	5.2
95-96—L.A. Clippers ...	80	985	107	186	.575	72	162	.444	87	113	200	50	44	91	45	286	2.5	0.6	3.6
96-97—L.A. Clippers ...	82	2195	254	417	.609	117	232	.504	174	280	454	157	94	142	107	625	5.5	1.9	7.6
97-98—Orlando..........	82	2953	301	543	.554	180	313	.575	255	382	637	216	107	181	175	783	7.8	2.6	9.5
98-99—Orlando..........	31	851	84	154	.545	35	81	.432	54	113	167	56	40	43	58	203	5.4	1.8	6.5
99-00—Orlando..........	82	2326	204	339	.602	82	162	.506	202	323	525	245	113	148	133	490	6.4	3.0	6.0
00-01—Orlando..........	80	2534	226	368	.614	129	225	.573	211	408	619	225	105	137	141	582	7.7	2.8	7.3
01-02—Orl.-Phoenix ...	83	1928	166	299	.555	43	102	.422	147	217	364	127	70	92	96	376	4.4	1.5	4.5
02-03—Phoenix	80	1800	153	278	.550	72	116	.621	134	234	368	112	50	71	76	378	4.6	1.4	4.7
03-04—Memphis	82	1606	159	312	.510	61	116	.526	125	217	342	90	73	70	69	379	4.2	1.1	4.6
04-05—Phoenix	39	214	12	34	.353	5	9	.556	16	37	53	13	6	12	8	29	1.4	0.3	0.7
05-06—Orlando..........	32	355	35	58	.603	5	8	.625	31	46	77	14	10	12	17	75	2.4	0.4	2.3
Totals	871	20273	1969	3480	.566	944	1815	.520	1638	2693	4331	1425	838	1187	1034	4885	5.0	1.6	5.6

Three-point field goals: 1993-94, 0-for-2. 1994-95, 0-for-5. 1995-96, 0-for-3. 1996-97, 0-for-8. 1997-98, 1-for-4 (.250). 1998-99, 0-for-3. 1999-00, 0-for-
3. 2000-01, 1-for-2 (.500). 2001-02, 1-for-2 (.500). 2002-03, 0-for-2. 2003-04, 0-for-4. Totals, 3-for-38 (.079).

Personal fouls/disqualifications: 1993-94, 94/1. 1994-95, 227/4. 1995-96, 127/0. 1996-97, 227/5. 1997-98, 260/1. 1998-99, 79/1. 1999-00, 203/0. 2000-01, 241/4. 2001-02, 205/1. 2002-03, 194/1. 2003-04, 170/0. 2004-05, 29/0. 2005-06, 50/0. Totals, 2106/18.

NBA PLAYOFF RECORD

Season Team	G	Min.	FGM	FGA	Pct.	FTM	FTA	Pct.	Off.	Def.	Tot.	Ast.	St.	Blk.	TO	Pts.	RPG	APG	PPG
									REBOUNDS								AVERAGES		
96-97—L.A. Clippers ...	3	66	6	11	.545	3	10	.300	6	8	14	4	1	2	3	15	4.7	1.3	5.0
98-99—Orlando	4	83	6	10	.600	6	13	.462	3	12	15	2	1	8	6	18	3.8	0.5	4.5
00-01—Orlando	4	134	16	26	.615	2	11	.182	11	31	42	9	5	6	9	34	10.5	2.3	8.5
02-03—Phoenix	6	70	1	10	.100	2	4	.500	6	7	13	5	1	1	6	4	2.2	0.8	0.7
03-04—Memphis	4	61	0	7	.000	2	4	.500	1	3	4	6	2	2	3	2	1.0	1.5	0.5
04-05—Phoenix	1	2	0	1	.000	0	0	...	0	0	0	1	1	0	0	0	0.0	1.0	0.0
Totals	22	416	29	65	.446	15	42	.357	27	61	88	27	11	19	27	73	4.0	1.2	3.3

Three-point field goals: 1996-97, 0-for-1. Totals, 0-for-1 (.000).
Personal fouls/disqualifications: 1996-97, 5/0. 1998-99, 9/0. 2000-01, 15/0. 2002-03, 19/1. 2003-04, 9/0. Totals, 57/1.

SPANISH LEAGUE RECORD

Season Team	G	Min.	FGM	FGA	Pct.	FTM	FTA	Pct.	Reb.	Ast.	Pts.	RPG	APG	PPG
												AVERAGES		
93-94—Estudiante Caja Postal....	2	10	0	3	.000	0	2	.000	2	0	0	1.0	0.0	0.0

OUTLAW, TRAVIS   F   TRAIL BLAZERS

PERSONAL: Born September 18, 1984, in Starkville, Miss. ... 6-9/210. (2.06/95.3). ... Full name: Travis Marquez Outlaw
HIGH SCHOOL: Starkville (Starkville, Miss.).
COLLEGE: Did not attend college.
TRANSACTIONS/CAREER NOTES: Selected out of high school by Portland Trail Blazers in first round (23rd pick overall) of 2003 NBA Draft.

NBA REGULAR-SEASON RECORD

Season Team	G	Min.	FGM	FGA	Pct.	FTM	FTA	Pct.	Off.	Def.	Tot.	Ast.	St.	Blk.	TO	Pts.	RPG	APG	PPG
									REBOUNDS								AVERAGES		
03-04—Portland	8	19	3	7	.429	2	4	.500	2	2	4	1	1	0	1	8	0.5	0.1	1.0
04-05—Portland	59	793	133	267	.498	49	75	.653	40	81	121	35	30	40	39	319	2.1	0.6	5.4
05-06—Portland	69	1153	162	368	.440	62	89	.697	48	141	189	34	31	46	37	400	2.7	0.5	5.8
Totals	136	1965	298	642	.464	113	168	.673	90	224	314	70	62	86	77	727	2.3	0.5	5.3

Three-point field goals: 2004-05, 4-for-10 (.400). 2005-06, 14-for-53 (.264). Totals, 18-for-63 (.286).
Personal fouls/disqualifications: 2003-04, 1/0. 2004-05, 77/0. 2005-06, 112/0. Totals, 190/0.

OWENS, ANDRE   G   WARRIORS

PERSONAL: Born October 31, 1980, in Indianapolis. ... 6-4/200. (1.93/90.7).
HIGH SCHOOL: Perry Meridian (Indianapolis).
COLLEGE: Indiana, then Houston.
TRANSACTIONS/CAREER NOTES: Not drafted by an NBA franchise. ... Signed as free agent by Utah Jazz (October 3, 2005). ... Traded by Jazz with Gs Devin Brown and Keith McLeod to Golden State Warriors for G Derek Fisher (July 12, 2006).

COLLEGIATE RECORD

Season Team	G	Min.	FGM	FGA	Pct.	FTM	FTA	Pct.	Reb.	Ast.	Pts.	RPG	APG	PPG
												AVERAGES		
00-01—Indiana	30	424	48	106	.453	23	31	.742	42	22	140	1.4	0.7	4.7
01-02—Houston					Did Not Play - Transfer Student									
02-03—Houston	28	1003	128	360	.356	68	89	.764	144	89	389	5.1	3.2	13.9
03-04—Houston	27	998	147	395	.372	77	105	.733	145	80	433	5.4	3.0	16.0
04-05—Houston	32	1114	195	485	.402	95	132	.720	155	67	585	4.8	2.1	18.3
Totals	117	3539	518	1346	.385	263	357	.737	486	258	1547	4.2	2.2	13.2

Three-point field goals: 2000-01, 21-for-54 (.389). 2002-03, 65-for-198 (.328). 2003-04, 62-for-197 (.315). 2004-05, 100-for-280 (.357). Totals, 248-for-729 (.340).

NBA REGULAR-SEASON RECORD

Season Team	G	Min.	FGM	FGA	Pct.	FTM	FTA	Pct.	Off.	Def.	Tot.	Ast.	St.	Blk.	TO	Pts.	RPG	APG	PPG
									REBOUNDS								AVERAGES		
05-06—Utah	23	210	27	74	.365	12	18	.667	11	10	21	8	5	0	13	69	0.9	0.3	3.0

Three-point field goals: 2005-06, 3-for-16 (.188). Totals, 3-for-16 (.188).
Personal fouls/disqualifications: 2005-06, 25/0. Totals, 25/0.

PACHULIA, ZAZA   F/C   HAWKS

PERSONAL: Born February 10, 1984, in Tbilisi, Georgia. ... 6-11/240. (2.11/108.9). ... Full name: Zaur Pachulia
TRANSACTIONS/CAREER NOTES: Played in Turkey (1999-2003). ... Selected by Orlando Magic in second round (42nd pick overall) of 2003 NBA Draft. ... Selected by Charlotte Bobcats from Magic in NBA Expansion Draft (June 22, 2004). ... Traded by Bobcats to Milwaukee Bucks for 2004 second-round draft choice (June 23, 2004). ... Signed as free agent by Atlanta Hawks (August 11, 2005).

TURKISH LEAGUE RECORD

Season Team	G	Min.	FGM	FGA	Pct.	FTM	FTA	Pct.	Reb.	Ast.	Pts.	RPG	APG	PPG
												AVERAGES		
99-00—Ulker	10	...	11	22	.500	9	13	.692	24	5	31	2.4	0.5	3.1

P

Season Team	G	Min.	FGM	FGA	Pct.	FTM	FTA	Pct.	Reb.	Ast.	Pts.	RPG	APG	PPG
00-01—Ulker	17	...	25	48	.521	9	18	.500	39	6	59	2.3	0.4	3.5
01-02—Ulker	25	...	52	95	.547	41	64	.641	101	10	145	4.0	0.4	5.8
02-03—Ulker	21	...	69	120	.575	62	79	.785	115	17	200	5.5	0.8	9.5
Totals	73	...	157	285	.551	121	174	.695	279	38	435	3.8	0.5	6.0

NBA REGULAR-SEASON RECORD

Season Team	G	Min.	FGM	FGA	Pct.	FTM	FTA	Pct.	Off.	Def.	Tot.	Ast.	St.	Blk.	TO	Pts.	RPG	APG	PPG
03-04—Orlando	59	664	68	175	.389	58	90	.644	69	105	174	13	21	12	34	194	2.9	0.2	3.3
04-05—Milwaukee	74	1397	160	354	.452	138	185	.746	131	247	378	60	44	34	70	458	5.1	0.8	6.2
05-06—Atlanta	78	2452	307	681	.451	297	404	.735	264	349	613	129	89	39	180	911	7.9	1.7	11.7
Totals	211	4513	535	1210	.442	493	679	.726	464	701	1165	202	154	85	284	1563	5.5	1.0	7.4

Three-point field goals: 2004-05, 0-for-1. 2005-06, 0-for-2. Totals, 0-for-3 (.000).
Personal fouls/disqualifications: 2003-04, 87/0. 2004-05, 166/0. 2005-06, 286/6. Totals, 539/6.

PADGETT, SCOTT   F

PERSONAL: Born April 19, 1976, in Louisville, Ky. ... 6-9/240. (2.06/108.9). ... Full name: Scott Anthony Padgett
HIGH SCHOOL: St. Xavier (Louisville, Ky.).
COLLEGE: Kentucky.
TRANSACTIONS/CAREER NOTES: Selected by Utah Jazz in first round (28th pick overall) of 1999 NBA Draft. ... Signed as free agent by Houston Rockets (October 28, 2003). ... Signed as free agent by New Jersey Nets (September 8, 2005). ... Waived by Nets (June 30, 2006).

COLLEGIATE RECORD

NOTES: Member of NCAA Division I championship team (1998).

Season Team	G	Min.	FGM	FGA	Pct.	FTM	FTA	Pct.	Reb.	Ast.	Pts.	RPG	APG	PPG
94-95—Kentucky	14	57	7	27	.259	10	12	.833	17	4	28	1.2	0.3	2.0
95-96—Kentucky						Did not play—ineligible.								
96-97—Kentucky	32	759	100	244	.410	61	80	.763	162	56	308	5.1	1.8	9.6
97-98—Kentucky	39	1089	161	338	.476	87	102	.853	255	82	449	6.5	2.1	11.5
98-99—Kentucky	37	1075	156	335	.466	94	138	.681	217	96	467	5.9	2.6	12.6
Totals	122	2980	424	944	.449	252	332	.759	651	238	1252	5.3	2.0	10.3

Three-point field goals: 1994-95, 4-for-13 (.308). 1996-97, 47-for-138 (.341). 1997-98, 40-for-107 (.374). 1998-99, 61-for-160 (.381). Totals, 152-for-418 (.364).
Personal fouls/disqualifications: 1994-95, 12/0. 1996-97, 91/6. 1997-98, 93/1. Totals, 196/7.

NBA REGULAR-SEASON RECORD

Season Team	G	Min.	FGM	FGA	Pct.	FTM	FTA	Pct.	Off.	Def.	Tot.	Ast.	St.	Blk.	TO	Pts.	RPG	APG	PPG
99-00—Utah	47	432	44	140	.314	19	27	.704	24	64	88	25	14	8	22	120	1.9	0.5	2.6
00-01—Utah	27	127	18	43	.419	15	20	.750	19	20	39	5	6	3	10	56	1.4	0.2	2.1
01-02—Utah	75	1295	188	395	.476	75	102	.735	111	174	285	82	43	13	69	500	3.8	1.1	6.7
02-03—Utah	82	1321	170	423	.402	81	107	.757	83	189	272	86	41	24	70	466	3.3	1.0	5.7
03-04—Houston	58	547	74	167	.443	24	32	.750	46	93	139	23	12	13	22	200	2.4	0.4	3.4
04-05—Houston	66	942	98	233	.421	29	40	.725	47	138	185	55	33	10	30	275	2.8	0.8	4.2
05-06—New Jersey	62	718	71	201	.353	27	34	.794	56	109	165	41	28	12	21	211	2.7	0.7	3.4
Totals	417	5382	663	1602	.414	270	362	.746	386	787	1173	317	177	83	244	1828	2.8	0.8	4.4

Three-point field goals: 1999-00, 13-for-44 (.295). 2000-01, 5-for-9 (.556). 2001-02, 49-for-113 (.434). 2002-03, 45-for-133 (.338). 2003-04, 28-for-65 (.431). 2004-05, 50-for-126 (.397). 2005-06, 42-for-121 (.347). Totals, 232-for-611 (.380).
Personal fouls/disqualifications: 1999-00, 55/1. 2000-01, 21/0. 2001-02, 140/0. 2002-03, 148/1. 2003-04, 73/0. 2004-05, 119/0. 2005-06, 90/0. Totals, 646/2.

NBA PLAYOFF RECORD

Season Team	G	Min.	FGM	FGA	Pct.	FTM	FTA	Pct.	Off.	Def.	Tot.	Ast.	St.	Blk.	TO	Pts.	RPG	APG	PPG
99-00—Utah	8	59	6	16	.375	0	0	...	3	14	17	5	1	2	4	15	2.1	0.6	1.9
01-02—Utah	4	47	6	13	.462	4	5	.800	7	7	14	2	1	1	5	16	3.5	0.5	4.0
02-03—Utah	4	53	8	19	.421	1	2	.500	6	3	9	4	3	0	5	19	2.3	1.0	4.8
03-04—Houston	4	14	2	5	.400	0	0	...	1	2	3	0	1	1	1	5	0.8	0.0	1.3
04-05—Houston	7	109	9	24	.375	2	2	1.000	9	10	19	4	3	2	3	25	2.7	0.6	3.6
05-06—New Jersey	3	9	1	2	.500	1	2	.500	2	1	3	0	1	0	0	3	1.0	0.0	1.0
Totals	30	291	32	79	.405	8	11	.727	28	37	65	15	10	6	18	83	2.2	0.5	2.8

Three-point field goals: 1999-00, 3-for-9 (.333). 2001-02, 0-for-3. 2002-03, 2-for-7 (.286). 2003-04, 1-for-3 (.333). 2004-05, 5-for-12 (.417). 2005-06, 0-for-1. Totals, 11-for-35 (.314).
Personal fouls/disqualifications: 1999-00, 10/0. 2001-02, 6/0. 2002-03, 6/0. 2003-04, 1/0. 2004-05, 18/0. 2005-06, 3/0. Totals, 44/0.

PALACIO, MILT   G

PERSONAL: Born February 7, 1978, in Los Angeles. ... 6-3/195. (1.91/88.5). ... Full name: Milton S. Palacio
HIGH SCHOOL: Gardena (Los Angeles).
JUNIOR COLLEGE: Midland (Texas) College.
COLLEGE: Colorado State.
TRANSACTIONS/CAREER NOTES: Not drafted by an NBA franchise. ... Signed as free agent by Vancouver Grizzlies (September 29, 1999). ... Signed as free agent by Washington Wizards (October 2, 2000). ... Waived by Wizards (October 16, 2000). ... Signed as free agent by Boston Celtics (December 7, 2000). ... Waived by Celtics (January 5, 2001). ... Re-signed by Celtics to the first of two con-

P

secutive 10-day contracts (January 10, 2001). ... Signed by Celtics for remainder of season (January 29, 2001). ... Traded by Celtics with G/F Joe Johnson, G Randy Brown and 2002 first-round draft choice to Phoenix Suns for G Tony Delk and F Rodney Rogers (February 20, 2002). ... Traded by Suns to Cleveland Cavaliers for future second-round draft choice (September 17, 2002). ... Signed as free agent by Toronto Raptors (July 16, 2003) ... Signed as free agent by Utah Jazz (September 1, 2005).

COLLEGIATE RECORD

Season Team	G	Min.	FGM	FGA	Pct.	FTM	FTA	Pct.	Reb.	Ast.	Pts.	RPG	APG	PPG
												AVERAGES		
95-96—Midland	29	...	83	167	.497	65	84	.774	114	142	254	3.9	4.9	8.8
96-97—Colorado State	29	898	75	151	.497	62	89	.697	111	147	230	3.8	5.1	7.9
97-98—Colorado State	29	957	98	205	.478	64	97	.660	103	148	283	3.6	5.1	9.8
98-99—Colorado State	30	1073	188	418	.450	135	179	.754	154	130	552	5.1	4.3	18.4
Junior College Totals	29		83	167	.497	65	84	.774	114	142	254	3.9	4.9	8.8
4-Year-College Totals	88	2928	361	774	.466	261	365	.715	368	425	1065	4.2	4.8	12.1

Three-point field goals: 1995-96, 23-for-57 (.404). 1996-97, 18-for-47 (.383). 1997-98, 23-for-61 (.377). 1998-99, 41-for-119 (.345). Totals, 105-for-284 (.370).

Personal fouls/disqualifications: 1995-96, 69/0. 1996-97, 62/0. 1997-98, 67/0. 1998-99, 72/0. Totals, 270/0.

NBA REGULAR-SEASON RECORD

Season Team	G	Min.	FGM	FGA	Pct.	FTM	FTA	Pct.	Off.	Def.	Tot.	Ast.	St.	Blk.	TO	Pts.	RPG	APG	PPG
									REBOUNDS								AVERAGES		
99-00—Vancouver	53	394	43	98	.439	22	37	.595	17	34	51	48	20	0	44	108	1.0	0.9	2.0
00-01—Boston	58	1141	126	267	.472	78	92	.848	25	77	102	151	48	0	80	342	1.8	2.6	5.9
01-02—Bos.-Phoenix	69	790	82	214	.383	54	74	.730	11	62	73	83	30	4	40	231	1.1	1.2	3.3
02-03—Cleveland	80	1976	162	388	.418	65	87	.747	48	187	235	259	68	16	131	397	2.9	3.2	5.0
03-04—Toronto	59	1211	104	298	.349	45	68	.662	15	87	102	184	41	11	87	257	1.7	3.1	4.4
04-05—Toronto	80	1533	175	392	.446	115	155	.742	26	108	134	279	48	13	104	467	1.7	3.5	5.8
05-06—Utah	71	1376	171	403	.424	98	150	.653	17	117	134	190	47	14	110	441	1.9	2.7	6.2
Totals	470	8421	863	2060	.419	477	663	.719	159	672	831	1194	302	58	596	2243	1.8	2.5	4.8

Three-point field goals: 1999-00, 0-for-2. 2000-01, 12-for-36 (.333). 2001-02, 13-for-41 (.317). 2002-03, 8-for-37 (.216). 2003-04, 4-for-26 (.154). 2004-05, 2-for-12 (.167). 2005-06, 1-for-16 (.063). Totals, 40-for-170 (.235).

Personal fouls/disqualifications: 1999-00, 32/0. 2000-01, 83/0. 2001-02, 61/0. 2002-03, 168/2. 2003-04, 90/0. 2004-05, 126/0. 2005-06, 125/1. Totals, 685/3.

PARGO, JANNERO   G   HORNETS

PERSONAL: Born September 22, 1979, in Chicago. ... 6-2/170. (1.88/77.1).
HIGH SCHOOL: Robeson (Chicago).
JUNIOR COLLEGE: Neosho County Community College (Kan.).
COLLEGE: Arkansas.
TRANSACTIONS/CAREER NOTES: Not drafted by an NBA franchise. ... Signed as free agent by Los Angeles Lakers (July 26, 2002). ... Waived by Lakers (January 7, 2004). ... Signed by Toronto Raptors for remainder of season (February 24, 2004). ... Released by Raptors (March 5, 2004). ... Signed by Chicago Bulls to 10-day contract (March 15, 2004). ... Signed by Bulls for remainder of season (March 25, 2004). ... Signed as free agent by New Orleans/Oklahoma City Hornets (August 9, 2006).

COLLEGIATE RECORD

Season Team	G	Min.	FGM	FGA	Pct.	FTM	FTA	Pct.	Reb.	Ast.	Pts.	RPG	APG	PPG
												AVERAGES		
98-99—Neosho County C.C.	26	...	112	257	.436	64	78	.821	84	140	356	3.2	5.4	13.7
99-00—Neosho County C.C.	32	...	226	499	.453	107	131	.817	148	200	708	4.6	6.3	22.1
00-01—Arkansas	31	742	132	294	.449	43	49	.878	64	72	380	2.1	2.3	12.3
01-02—Arkansas	29	789	165	359	.460	57	73	.781	69	96	482	2.4	3.3	16.6
Junior College Totals	58	...	338	756	.447	171	209	.818	232	340	1064	4.0	5.9	18.3
4-Year-College Totals	60	1531	297	653	.455	100	122	.820	133	168	862	2.2	2.8	14.4

Three-point field goals: 1998-99, 68-for-154 (.442). 1999-00, 149-for-348 (.428). 2000-01, 73-for-175 (.417). 2001-02, 95-for-220 (.432). Totals, 385-for-897 (.429).

NBA REGULAR-SEASON RECORD

Season Team	G	Min.	FGM	FGA	Pct.	FTM	FTA	Pct.	Off.	Def.	Tot.	Ast.	St.	Blk.	TO	Pts.	RPG	APG	PPG
									REBOUNDS								AVERAGES		
02-03—L.A. Lakers	34	342	37	93	.398	4	4	1.000	9	28	37	39	13	2	23	85	1.1	1.1	2.5
04-05—Chicago	32	453	82	213	.385	17	23	.739	12	35	47	76	16	1	45	204	1.5	2.4	6.4
05-06—Chicago	57	646	109	292	.373	17	21	.810	8	53	61	94	24	2	61	274	1.1	1.6	4.8
Totals	123	1441	228	598	.381	38	48	.792	29	116	145	209	53	5	129	563	1.2	1.7	4.6

Three-point field goals: 2002-03, 7-for-24 (.292). 2004-05, 23-for-66 (.348). 2005-06, 39-for-103 (.379). Totals, 69-for-193 (.358).
Personal fouls/disqualifications: 2002-03, 45/0. 2004-05, 53/0. 2005-06, 57/1. Totals, 155/1.

NBA PLAYOFF RECORD

Season Team	G	Min.	FGM	FGA	Pct.	FTM	FTA	Pct.	Off.	Def.	Tot.	Ast.	St.	Blk.	TO	Pts.	RPG	APG	PPG
									REBOUNDS								AVERAGES		
02-03—L.A. Lakers	11	129	8	24	.333	3	4	.750	3	6	9	14	8	1	7	23	0.8	1.3	2.1
04-05—Chicago	5	76	18	51	.353	3	5	.600	1	4	5	10	3	0	8	52	1.0	2.0	10.4
05-06—Chicago	5	19	5	12	.417	4	5	.800	1	5	6	3	0	0	3	17	1.2	0.6	3.4
Totals	21	224	31	87	.356	10	14	.714	5	15	20	27	11	1	18	92	1.0	1.3	4.4

Three-point field goals: 2002-03, 4-for-15 (.267). 2004-05, 13-for-32 (.406). 2005-06, 3-for-5 (.600). Totals, 20-for-52 (.385).
Personal fouls/disqualifications: 2002-03, 22/0. 2004-05, 14/0. Totals, 36/0.

AMERICAN BASKETBALL ASSOCIATION RECORD

Season Team	G	Min.	FGM	FGA	Pct.	FTM	FTA	Pct.	Reb.	Ast.	Pts.	RPG	APG	PPG
												AVERAGES		
03-04—Long Beach	3	...	15	30	.500	3	4	.750	5	7	42	1.7	2.3	14.0

Three-point field goals: 2003-04, 9-for-19 (.474). Totals, 9-for-19 (.474).

P

PARKER, TONY   G   SPURS

PERSONAL: Born May 17, 1982, in Bruges, Belgium. ... 6-2/177. (1.88/80.3). ... Full name: William Anthony Parker
HIGH SCHOOL: INSEP (Paris, France).
COLLEGE: Did not attend college.
TRANSACTIONS/CAREER NOTES: Played in France (1997-2001). ... Selected by San Antonio Spurs in first round (28th pick overall) of 2001 NBA Draft.
MISCELLANEOUS: Member of NBA championship team (2003, 2005).

FRENCH LEAGUE RECORD

Season Team	G	Min.	FGM	FGA	Pct.	FTM	FTA	Pct.	Reb.	Ast.	Pts.	RPG	APG	PPG
97-98—Centre Federal	29	...	146	292	.500	97	145	.669	78	162	426	2.7	5.6	14.7
98-99—Centre Federal	30	...	252	488	.516	113	173	.653	120	195	663	4.0	6.5	22.1
99-00—Paris Racing	23	231	33	76	.434	13	26	.500	20	40	90	0.9	1.7	3.9
00-01—Paris Racing	30	992	163	333	.489	80	107	.748	82	168	440	2.7	5.6	14.7
Totals	112	1223	594	1189	.500	303	451	.672	300	565	1619	2.7	5.0	14.5

Three-point field goals: 1997-98, 37-for-108 (.343). 1998-99, 46-for-156 (.295). 1999-00, 11-for-34 (.324). 2000-01, 34-for-112 (.304). Totals, 128-for-410 (.312).

Personal fouls/disqualifications: 2000-01, 89/0. Totals, 89/0.

NBA REGULAR-SEASON RECORD

HONORS: NBA All-Rookie first team (2002).

Season Team	G	Min.	FGM	FGA	Pct.	FTM	FTA	Pct.	REBOUNDS Off.	Def.	Tot.	Ast.	St.	Blk.	TO	Pts.	AVERAGES RPG	APG	PPG
01-02—San Antonio	77	2267	268	639	.419	108	160	.675	33	164	197	334	89	7	151	705	2.6	4.3	9.2
02-03—San Antonio	82	2774	484	1043	.464	219	290	.755	33	183	216	432	71	4	198	1269	2.6	5.3	15.5
03-04—San Antonio	75	2577	423	946	.447	191	272	.702	43	194	237	411	61	7	179	1099	3.2	5.5	14.7
04-05—San Antonio	80	2735	539	1118	.482	210	323	.650	47	251	298	491	98	4	215	1331	3.7	6.1	16.6
05-06—San Antonio	80	2715	623	1136	.548	253	358	.707	38	223	261	460	83	4	249	1510	3.3	5.8	18.9
Totals	394	13068	2337	4882	.479	981	1403	.699	194	1015	1209	2128	402	26	992	5914	3.1	5.4	15.0

Three-point field goals: 2001-02, 61-for-189 (.323). 2002-03, 82-for-243 (.337). 2003-04, 62-for-199 (.312). 2004-05, 43-for-156 (.276). 2005-06, 11-for-36 (.306). Totals, 259-for-823 (.315).

Personal fouls/disqualifications: 2001-02, 166/1. 2002-03, 174/2. 2003-04, 148/0. 2004-05, 167/0. 2005-06, 161/1. Totals, 816/4.

NBA PLAYOFF RECORD

Season Team	G	Min.	FGM	FGA	Pct.	FTM	FTA	Pct.	REBOUNDS Off.	Def.	Tot.	Ast.	St.	Blk.	TO	Pts.	AVERAGES RPG	APG	PPG
01-02—San Antonio	10	341	62	136	.456	21	28	.750	5	24	29	40	9	1	22	155	2.9	4.0	15.5
02-03—San Antonio	24	814	135	335	.403	67	94	.713	8	58	66	85	22	3	47	352	2.8	3.5	14.7
03-04—San Antonio	10	386	72	168	.429	23	35	.657	5	16	21	70	13	1	31	184	2.1	7.0	18.4
04-05—San Antonio	23	858	166	366	.454	55	87	.632	13	53	66	100	17	2	71	396	2.9	4.3	17.2
05-06—San Antonio	13	475	104	226	.460	64	79	.810	8	39	47	50	13	1	40	274	3.6	3.8	21.1
Totals	80	2874	539	1231	.438	230	323	.712	39	190	229	345	74	8	211	1361	2.9	4.3	17.0

Three-point field goals: 2001-02, 10-for-27 (.370). 2002-03, 15-for-56 (.268). 2003-04, 17-for-43 (.395). 2004-05, 9-for-48 (.188). 2005-06, 2-for-9 (.222). Totals, 53-for-183 (.290).

Personal fouls/disqualifications: 2001-02, 22/0. 2002-03, 51/0. 2003-04, 15/0. 2004-05, 69/0. 2005-06, 31/0. Totals, 188/0.

NBA ALL-STAR GAME RECORD

Season Team	Min.	FGM	FGA	Pct.	FTM	FTA	Pct.	REBOUNDS Off.	Def.	Tot.	Ast.	PF	Dq.	St.	Blk.	TO	Pts.
2006—San Antonio	20	3	8	.375	2	2	1.000	0	0	0	4	1	0	0	0	5	8

Three-point field goals: 2006, 0-for-1. Totals, 0-for-1 (.000).

PARKER, SMUSH   G   LAKERS

PERSONAL: Born June 1, 1981, in Newark, N.J. ... 6-4/180. (1.93/81.6). ... Full name: William Parker.
HIGH SCHOOL: Newtown (N.Y.).
JUNIOR COLLEGE: College of Southern Idaho
COLLEGE: Fordham.
TRANSACTIONS/CAREER NOTES: Not drafted by an NBA franchise. ... Signed as free agent by Cleveland Cavaliers (September 26, 2002). ... Played in CBA (2003-04). ... Played in Greece (2003-04). ... Played in NBA Development League (2004-05). ... Signed as free agent by Detroit Pistons (October 1, 2004). ... Waived by Pistons (January 4, 2005). ... Signed by Phoenix Suns to 10-day contract (January 19, 2005). ... Waived by Suns (February 8, 2005). ... Signed as free agent by Los Angeles Lakers (August 2, 2005).

COLLEGIATE RECORD

Season Team	G	Min.	FGM	FGA	Pct.	FTM	FTA	Pct.	Reb.	Ast.	Pts.	RPG	APG	PPG
99-00—Southern Idaho	21	473	88	184	.478	51	63	.810	60	126	245	2.9	6.0	11.7
00-01—Fordham						Did Not Play								
01-02—Fordham	28	980	153	353	.433	100	137	.730	122	125	463	4.4	4.5	16.5
Junior College Totals	21	473	88	184	.478	51	63	.810	60	126	245	2.9	6.0	11.7
4-Year-College Totals	28	980	153	353	.433	100	137	.730	122	125	463	4.4	4.5	16.5

Three-point field goals: 1999-00, 18-for-70 (.257). 2001-02, 57-for-174 (.328). Totals, 75-for-244 (.307).

NBA REGULAR-SEASON RECORD

Season Team	G	Min.	FGM	FGA	Pct.	FTM	FTA	Pct.	REBOUNDS Off.	Def.	Tot.	Ast.	St.	Blk.	TO	Pts.	AVERAGES RPG	APG	PPG
02-03—Cleveland	66	1103	136	338	.402	98	118	.831	29	90	119	162	48	12	133	408	1.8	2.5	6.2

P

Season Team	G	Min.	FGM	FGA	Pct.	FTM	FTA	Pct.	REBOUNDS Off.	Def.	Tot.	Ast.	St.	Blk.	TO	Pts.	AVERAGES RPG	APG	PPG
04-05—Detroit-Pho.....	16	144	18	43	.419	9	13	.692	4	8	12	15	5	0	19	48	0.8	0.9	3.0
05-06—L.A. Lakers	82	2773	348	779	.447	125	180	.694	37	234	271	302	140	16	147	941	3.3	3.7	11.5
Totals	164	4020	502	1160	.433	232	311	.746	70	332	402	479	193	28	299	1397	2.5	2.9	8.5

Three-point field goals: 2002-03, 38-for-118 (.322). 2004-05, 3-for-13 (.231). 2005-06, 120-for-328 (.366). Totals, 161-for-459 (.351).

Personal fouls/disqualifications: 2002-03, 106/1. 2004-05, 16/0. 2005-06, 213/1. Totals, 335/2.

NBA PLAYOFF RECORD

Season Team	G	Min.	FGM	FGA	Pct.	FTM	FTA	Pct.	REBOUNDS Off.	Def.	Tot.	Ast.	St.	Blk.	TO	Pts.	AVERAGES RPG	APG	PPG
05-06—L.A. Lakers	7	258	24	72	.333	10	10	1.000	9	12	21	11	15	1	12	62	3.0	1.6	8.9

Three-point field goals: 2005-06, 4-for-26 (.154). Totals, 4-for-26 (.154).

Personal fouls/disqualifications: 2005-06, 24/1. Totals, 24/1.

CBA RECORD

Season Team	G	Min.	FGM	FGA	Pct.	FTM	FTA	Pct.	Reb.	Ast.	Pts.	AVERAGES RPG	APG	PPG
03-04—Idaho	9	353	61	112	.545	55	77	.714	41	44	189	4.6	4.9	21.0

Three-point field goals: 2003-04, 12-for-35 (.343). Totals, 12-for-35 (.343).

GREEK LEAGUE RECORD

Season Team	G	Min.	FGM	FGA	Pct.	FTM	FTA	Pct.	Reb.	Ast.	Pts.	AVERAGES RPG	APG	PPG
03-04—Aris...............................	15	450	69	155	.445	60	78	.769	44	83	217	2.9	5.5	14.5

Three-point field goals: 2003-04, 19-for-62 (.306). Totals, 19-for-62 (.306).

NBA DEVELOPMENT LEAGUE RECORD

Season Team	G	Min.	FGM	FGA	Pct.	FTM	FTA	Pct.	Reb.	Ast.	Pts.	AVERAGES RPG	APG	PPG
04-05—Florida	23	833	166	348	.477	94	129	.729	109	209	440	4.7	9.1	19.1

Three-point field goals: 2004-05, 14-for-32 (.438). Totals, 14-for-32 (.438).

PATTERSON, RUBEN F BUCKS

PERSONAL: Born July 31, 1975, in Cleveland. ... 6-5/224. (1.96/101.6). ... Full name: Ruben Nathaniel Patterson
HIGH SCHOOL: John Hay (Cleveland).
JUNIOR COLLEGE: Independence (Kan.) Community College.
COLLEGE: Cincinnati.
TRANSACTIONS/CAREER NOTES: Selected by Los Angeles Lakers in second round (31st pick overall) of 1998 NBA Draft. ... Played in Greece (1998-99). ... Signed as free agent by Seattle SuperSonics (August 10, 1999). ... Signed as free agent by Portland Trail Blazers (July 30, 2001). ... Traded by Trail Blazers to Denver Nuggets as part of four-team deal (February 23, 2006). ... Traded by Nuggets to Milwaukee Bucks for F Joe Smith (August 10, 2006).

COLLEGIATE RECORD

Season Team	G	Min.	FGM	FGA	Pct.	FTM	FTA	Pct.	Reb.	Ast.	Pts.	AVERAGES RPG	APG	PPG
94-95—Independence C.C.	33	...	274	417	.657	132	220	.600	210	48	690	6.4	1.5	20.9
95-96—Independence C.C.	32	...	296	464	.638	260	382	.681	298	79	868	9.3	2.5	27.1
96-97—Cincinnati	31	723	164	299	.548	87	144	.604	174	44	426	5.6	1.4	13.7
97-98—Cincinnati	19	530	109	231	.472	77	126	.611	119	41	313	6.3	2.2	16.5
Junior College Totals.............	65	...	570	881	.647	392	602	.651	508	127	1558	7.8	2.0	24.0
4-Year-College Totals.............	50	1253	273	530	.515	164	270	.607	293	85	739	5.9	1.7	14.8

Three-point field goals: 1994-95, 10-for-18 (.556). 1995-96, 16-for-39 (.410). 1996-97, 11-for-39 (.282). 1997-98, 18-for-67 (.269). Totals, 55-for-163 (.337).

Personal fouls/disqualifications: 1994-95, 76/0. Totals, 76/0.

GREEK LEAGUE RECORD

Season Team	G	Min.	FGM	FGA	Pct.	FTM	FTA	Pct.	Reb.	Ast.	Pts.	AVERAGES RPG	APG	PPG
98-99—AEK	10	275	45	93	.484	28	42	.667	34	20	124	3.4	2.0	12.4

Three-point field goals: 1998-99, 6-for-23 (.261). Totals, 6-for-23 (.261).

NBA REGULAR-SEASON RECORD

Season Team	G	Min.	FGM	FGA	Pct.	FTM	FTA	Pct.	REBOUNDS Off.	Def.	Tot.	Ast.	St.	Blk.	TO	Pts.	AVERAGES RPG	APG	PPG
98-99—L.A. Lakers	24	144	21	51	.412	22	31	.710	17	13	30	2	5	3	12	65	1.3	0.1	2.7
99-00—Seattle	81	2097	354	661	.536	222	321	.692	218	216	434	126	94	40	144	942	5.4	1.6	11.6
00-01—Seattle	76	2059	370	749	.494	246	361	.681	183	199	382	161	103	45	155	988	5.0	2.1	13.0
01-02—Portland	75	1765	319	619	.515	192	274	.701	155	143	298	107	79	37	114	839	4.0	1.4	11.2
02-03—Portland	78	1655	254	516	.492	138	220	.627	120	144	264	101	73	29	117	649	3.4	1.3	8.3
03-04—Portland	73	1651	200	395	.506	105	190	.553	129	139	268	139	84	21	105	507	3.7	1.9	6.9
04-05—Portland	70	1957	319	601	.531	169	282	.599	126	147	273	138	106	21	143	809	3.9	2.0	11.6
05-06—Portland-Den. .	71	1793	327	635	.515	203	338	.601	118	126	244	127	76	21	150	858	3.4	1.8	12.1
Totals	548	13121	2164	4227	.512	1297	2017	.643	1066	1127	2193	901	620	217	940	5657	4.0	1.6	10.3

Three-point field goals: 1998-99, 1-for-6 (.167). 1999-00, 12-for-27 (.444). 2000-01, 2-for-36 (.056). 2001-02, 9-for-36 (.250). 2002-03, 3-for-20 (.150). 2003-04, 2-for-12 (.167). 2004-05, 2-for-25 (.080). 2005-06, 1-for-13 (.077). Totals, 32-for-175 (.183).

Personal fouls/disqualifications: 1998-99, 16/0. 1999-00, 190/0. 2000-01, 176/1. 2001-02, 140/1. 2002-03, 161/0. 2003-04, 152/0. 2004-05, 164/0. 2005-06, 150/0. Totals, 1149/2.

NBA PLAYOFF RECORD

Season Team	G	Min.	FGM	FGA	Pct.	FTM	FTA	Pct.	REBOUNDS Off.	Def.	Tot.	Ast.	St.	Blk.	TO	Pts.	AVERAGES RPG	APG	PPG
98-99—L.A. Lakers	3	5	0	1	.000	0	0	...	0	0	0	0	0	0	1	0	0.0	0.0	0.0
99-00—Seattle	5	84	14	26	.538	13	15	.867	9	6	15	2	3	2	8	41	3.0	0.4	8.2
01-02—Portland.........	3	65	5	15	.333	6	8	.750	2	5	7	1	3	1	3	16	2.3	0.3	5.3
02-03—Portland.........	7	155	25	52	.481	20	29	.690	14	12	26	11	4	1	10	70	3.7	1.6	10.0
05-06—Denver..........	4	58	9	17	.529	2	5	.400	5	1	6	3	1	0	3	20	1.5	0.8	5.0
Totals	22	367	53	111	.477	41	57	.719	30	24	54	17	11	4	25	147	2.5	0.8	6.7

Three-point field goals: 1999-00, 0-for-2. 2001-02, 0-for-1. 2002-03, 0-for-4. Totals, 0-for-7 (.000).
Personal fouls/disqualifications: 1999-00, 6/0. 2001-02, 7/0. 2002-03, 10/0. 2005-06, 6/0. Totals, 29/0.

PAUL, CHRIS   G   HORNETS

PERSONAL: Born May 6, 1985, in Winston-Salem, N.C. ... 6-0/175. (1.83/79.4). ... Full name: Christopher Emmanuel Paul.
HIGH SCHOOL: West Forsyth (Winston-Salem, N.C.).
COLLEGE: Wake Forest.
TRANSACTIONS/CAREER NOTES: Selected after sophomore season by New Orleans Hornets in first round (fourth pick overall) of 2005 NBA Draft.

COLLEGIATE RECORD

NOTES: The SPORTING NEWS All-America first team (2005).

Season Team	G	Min.	FGM	FGA	Pct.	FTM	FTA	Pct.	Reb.	Ast.	Pts.	AVERAGES RPG	APG	PPG
03-04—Wake Forest	31	1041	135	272	.496	150	178	.843	101	183	460	3.3	5.9	14.8
04-05—Wake Forest	32	1069	143	317	.451	156	187	.834	144	212	488	4.5	6.6	15.3
Totals	63	2110	278	589	.472	306	365	.838	245	395	948	3.9	6.3	15.0

Three-point field goals: 2003-04, 40-for-86 (.465). 2004-05, 46-for-97 (.474). Totals, 86-for-183 (.470).

NBA REGULAR-SEASON RECORD

HONORS: NBA All-Rookie first team (2006). ... NBA Rookie of the Year (2006).

Season Team	G	Min.	FGM	FGA	Pct.	FTM	FTA	Pct.	REBOUNDS Off.	Def.	Tot.	Ast.	St.	Blk.	TO	Pts.	AVERAGES RPG	APG	PPG
05-06—NO/Okla. City ..	78	2808	407	947	.430	394	465	.847	61	339	400	611	*175	6	183	1258	5.1	7.8	16.1

Three-point field goals: 2005-06, 50-for-177 (.282). Totals, 50 for 177 (.202).
Personal fouls/disqualifications: 2005-06, 218/0. Totals, 218/0.

PAVLOVIC, SASHA   F   CAVALIERS

PERSONAL: Born November 15, 1983, in Bar, Serbia & Montenegro. ... 6-7/210. (2.01/95.3).
TRANSACTIONS/CAREER NOTES: Played in Yugoslavia (1999-00). ... Selected by Utah Jazz in first round (19th pick overall) of 2003 NBA Draft. ... Selected by Charlotte Bobcats from Jazz in NBA Expansion Draft (June 22, 2004). ... Traded by Bobcats to Cleveland Cavaliers for future first-round draft choice (June 23, 2004).
MISCELLANEOUS: Member of Serbia-Montenegro Olympic Team (2004).

YUGOSLAVIAN LEAGUE RECORD

Season Team	G	Min.	FGM	FGA	Pct.	FTM	FTA	Pct.	Reb.	Ast.	Pts.	AVERAGES RPG	APG	PPG
00-01—Buducnost.....................	14	68	7	19	.368	2	2	1.000	6	1	18	0.4	0.1	1.3
01-02—Buducnost.....................	3	45	7	10	.700	3	4	.750	1	1	20	0.3	0.3	6.7
02-03—Buducnost.....................	20	394	76	155	.490	34	48	.708	48	16	201	2.4	0.8	10.1
Totals	37	507	90	184	.489	39	54	.722	55	18	239	1.5	0.5	6.5

Three-point field goals: 2000-01, 2-for-9 (.222). 2001-02, 3-for-4 (.750). 2002-03, 15-for-54 (.278). Totals, 20-for-67 (.299).

NBA REGULAR-SEASON RECORD

Season Team	G	Min.	FGM	FGA	Pct.	FTM	FTA	Pct.	REBOUNDS Off.	Def.	Tot.	Ast.	St.	Blk.	TO	Pts.	AVERAGES RPG	APG	PPG
03-04—Utah	79	1144	149	376	.396	65	84	.774	44	115	159	60	41	16	67	382	2.0	0.8	4.8
04-05—Cleveland	65	862	120	276	.435	44	64	.688	15	56	71	49	29	4	47	314	1.1	0.8	4.8
05-06—Cleveland	53	813	87	212	.410	32	49	.653	16	64	80	25	19	6	42	241	1.5	0.5	4.5
Totals	197	2819	356	864	.412	141	197	.716	75	235	310	134	89	26	156	937	1.6	0.7	4.8

Three-point field goals: 2003-04, 19-for-70 (.271). 2004-05, 30-for-78 (.385). 2005-06, 35-for-96 (.365). Totals, 84-for-244 (.344).
Personal fouls/disqualifications: 2003-04, 187/3. 2004-05, 121/0. 2005-06, 103/3. Totals, 411/6.

NBA PLAYOFF RECORD

Season Team	G	Min.	FGM	FGA	Pct.	FTM	FTA	Pct.	REBOUNDS Off.	Def.	Tot.	Ast.	St.	Blk.	TO	Pts.	AVERAGES RPG	APG	PPG
05-06—Cleveland	3	4	0	2	.000	0	0	...	0	1	1	0	0	0	0	0	0.3	0.0	0.0

Three-point field goals: 2005-06, 0-for-1. Totals, 0-for-1 (.000).

PAYTON, GARY   G   HEAT

PERSONAL: Born July 23, 1968, in Oakland. ... 6-4/180. (1.93/81.6). ... Full name: Gary Dwayne Payton.
HIGH SCHOOL: Skyline (Oakland).
COLLEGE: Oregon State.
TRANSACTIONS/CAREER NOTES: Selected by Seattle SuperSonics in first round (second pick overall) of 1990 NBA Draft. ... Traded by SuperSonics with G Desmond Mason to Milwaukee Bucks for G Ray Allen, G Kevin Ollie, G Ronald Murray

P

and conditional first-round draft choice (February 20, 2003). ... Signed as free agent by Los Angeles Lakers (July 16, 2003) ... Traded by Lakers with F Rick Fox and a first-round draft choice to Boston Celtics for F/C Chris Mihm, G Chucky Atkins and F Jumaine Jones (August 6, 2004). ... Traded by Celtics with F Tom Gugliotta, C Michael Stewart and 2005 draft or future first-round pick to Atlanta Hawks for F Antoine Walker (February 24, 2005). ... Waived by Hawks (March 1, 2005). ... Signed by Boston Celtics (March 4, 2005). ... Signed as free agent by Miami Heat (September 22, 2005).

MISCELLANEOUS: Member of gold-medal-winning U.S. Olympic team (2000). ... Member of gold-medal-winning U.S. Olympic team (1996). ... Seattle SuperSonics franchise all-time points leader with 18,207, all-time assists leader with 7,384 and all-time steals leader with 2,107 (1990-91 through 2001-02). ... Member of NBA championship team (2006).

COLLEGIATE RECORD

NOTES: THE SPORTING NEWS All-America first team (1990).

Season Team	G	Min.	FGM	FGA	Pct.	FTM	FTA	Pct.	Reb.	Ast.	Pts.	AVERAGES RPG	APG	PPG
86-87—Oregon State	30	1115	153	333	.459	55	82	.671	120	229	374	4.0	7.6	12.5
87-88—Oregon State	31	1178	180	368	.489	58	83	.699	103	230	449	3.3	7.4	14.5
88-89—Oregon State	30	1140	208	438	.475	105	155	.677	122	244	603	4.1	8.1	20.1
89-90—Oregon State	29	1095	288	571	.504	118	171	.690	135	235	746	4.7	8.1	25.7
Totals	120	4528	829	1710	.485	336	491	.684	480	938	2172	4.0	7.8	18.1

Three-point field goals: 1986-87, 13-for-35 (.371). 1987-88, 31-for-78 (.397). 1988-89, 82-for-213 (.385). 1989-90, 52-for-156 (.333). Totals, 178-for-482 (.369).

NBA REGULAR-SEASON RECORD

HONORS: NBA Defensive Player of the Year (1996). ... All-NBA first team (1998, 2000). ... All-NBA second team (1995, 1996, 1997, 1999, 2002). ... All-NBA third team (1994, 2001). ... NBA All-Defensive first team (1994, 1995, 1996, 1997, 1998, 1999, 2000, 2001, 2002). ... NBA All-Rookie second team (1991).
NOTES: Led NBA with 2.85 steals per game (1996).

Season Team	G	Min.	FGM	FGA	Pct.	FTM	FTA	Pct.	REBOUNDS Off.	Def.	Tot.	Ast.	St.	Blk.	TO	Pts.	AVERAGES RPG	APG	PPG
90-91—Seattle	82	2244	259	575	.450	69	97	.711	108	135	243	528	165	15	180	588	3.0	6.4	7.2
91-92—Seattle	81	2549	331	734	.451	99	148	.669	123	172	295	506	147	21	174	764	3.6	6.2	9.4
92-93—Seattle	82	2548	476	963	.494	151	196	.770	95	186	281	399	177	21	148	1110	3.4	4.9	13.5
93-94—Seattle	82	2881	584	1159	.504	166	279	.595	105	164	269	494	188	19	173	1349	3.3	6.0	16.5
94-95—Seattle	82	3015	685	1345	.509	249	348	.716	108	173	281	583	204	13	201	1689	3.4	7.1	20.6
95-96—Seattle	81	3162	618	1276	.484	229	306	.748	104	235	339	608	*231	19	260	1563	4.2	7.5	19.3
96-97—Seattle	82	3213	706	1482	.476	254	355	.715	106	272	378	583	197	13	215	1785	4.6	7.1	21.8
97-98—Seattle	82	3145	579	1278	.453	279	375	.744	77	299	376	679	185	18	229	1571	4.6	8.3	19.2
98-99—Seattle	50	2008	401	923	.434	199	276	.721	62	182	244	436	109	12	154	1084	4.9	8.7	21.7
99-00—Seattle	82	3425	747	1666	.448	311	423	.735	100	429	529	*732	153	18	224	1982	6.5	8.9	24.2
00-01—Seattle	79	3244	725	1591	.456	271	354	.766	73	288	361	642	127	26	209	1823	4.6	8.1	23.1
01-02—Seattle	82	3301	737	1578	.467	267	335	.797	80	316	396	737	131	26	209	1815	4.8	9.0	22.1
02-03—Seattle-Mil.	80	3208	665	1466	.454	250	352	.710	79	255	334	663	133	20	187	1634	4.2	8.3	20.4
03-04—L.A. Lakers	82	2825	482	1024	.471	180	252	.714	72	270	342	449	96	19	151	1199	4.2	5.5	14.6
04-05—Atlanta-Boston	77	2541	339	725	.468	153	201	.761	48	188	236	469	88	12	148	873	3.1	6.1	11.3
05-06—Miami	81	2305	230	547	.420	100	126	.794	34	199	233	257	71	10	102	626	2.9	3.2	7.7
Totals	1267	45614	8564	18332	.467	3227	4423	.730	1374	3763	5137	8765	2402	282	2964	21455	4.1	6.9	16.9

Three-point field goals: 1990-91, 1-for-13 (.077). 1991-92, 3-for-23 (.130). 1992-93, 7-for-34 (.206). 1993-94, 15-for-54 (.278). 1994-95, 70-for-232 (.302). 1995-96, 98-for-299 (.328). 1996-97, 119-for-380 (.313). 1997-98, 134-for-397 (.338). 1998-99, 83-for-281 (.295). 1999-00, 177-for-520 (.340). 2000-01, 102-for-272 (.375). 2001-02, 74-for-236 (.314). 2002-03, 54-for-182 (.297). 2003-04, 55-for-165 (.333). 2004-05, 42-for-129 (.326). 2005-06, 66-for-230 (.287). Totals, 1100-for-3447 (.319).

Personal fouls/disqualifications: 1990-91, 249/3. 1991-92, 248/0. 1992-93, 250/1. 1993-94, 227/0. 1994-95, 206/1. 1995-96, 221/1. 1996-97, 208/1. 1997-98, 195/0. 1998-99, 115/0. 1999-00, 178/0. 2000-01, 184/0. 2001-02, 179/0. 2002-03, 181/0. 2003-04, 169/0. 2004-05, 121/0. 2005-06, 169/0. Totals, 3100/7.

NBA PLAYOFF RECORD

NOTES: Shares single-game playoff record for most three-point field goal attempts in one half—11 (May 4, 1996, vs. Houston).

Season Team	G	Min.	FGM	FGA	Pct.	FTM	FTA	Pct.	REBOUNDS Off.	Def.	Tot.	Ast.	St.	Blk.	TO	Pts.	AVERAGES RPG	APG	PPG
90-91—Seattle	5	135	11	27	.407	2	2	1.000	5	8	13	32	8	1	9	24	2.6	6.4	4.8
91-92—Seattle	8	221	27	58	.466	7	12	.583	6	15	21	38	8	2	10	61	2.6	4.8	7.6
92-93—Seattle	19	605	104	235	.443	25	37	.676	22	41	63	70	34	3	34	234	3.3	3.7	12.3
93-94—Seattle	5	181	34	69	.493	8	19	.421	6	11	17	28	8	2	8	79	3.4	5.6	15.8
94-95—Seattle	4	172	32	67	.478	5	12	.417	6	4	10	21	5	0	8	71	2.5	5.3	17.8
95-96—Seattle	21	911	162	334	.485	69	109	.633	19	89	108	143	37	7	62	434	5.1	6.8	20.7
96-97—Seattle	12	546	105	255	.412	50	61	.820	20	45	65	104	26	4	35	285	5.4	8.7	23.8
97-98—Seattle	10	428	87	183	.475	47	50	.940	9	25	34	70	18	1	26	240	3.4	7.0	24.0
99-00—Seattle	5	221	50	113	.442	20	26	.769	8	30	38	37	9	1	18	129	7.6	7.4	25.8
01-02—Seattle	5	207	45	106	.425	17	29	.586	10	33	43	29	3	2	13	111	8.6	5.8	22.2
02-03—Milwaukee	6	251	48	112	.429	14	20	.700	4	14	18	52	8	1	13	111	3.0	8.7	18.5
03-04—L.A. Lakers	22	772	68	186	.366	21	28	.750	19	53	72	116	23	4	28	171	3.3	5.3	7.8
04-05—Boston	7	239	33	74	.446	5	6	.833	8	21	29	32	6	1	11	72	4.1	4.6	10.3
05-06—Miami	23	560	49	116	.422	18	25	.720	6	34	40	36	23	3	18	133	1.7	1.6	5.8
Totals	152	5449	855	1935	.442	308	436	.706	148	423	571	808	216	32	293	2155	3.8	5.3	14.2

Three-point field goals: 1990-91, 0-for-1. 1991-92, 0-for-2. 1992-93, 1-for-6 (.167). 1993-94, 3-for-9 (.333). 1994-95, 2-for-10 (.200). 1995-96, 41-for-100 (.410). 1996-97, 25-for-75 (.333). 1997-98, 19-for-50 (.380). 1999-00, 9-for-23 (.391). 2001-02, 4-for-15 (.267). 2002-03, 1-for-15 (.067). 2003-04, 14-for-56 (.250). 2004-05, 1-for-14 (.071). 2005-06, 17-for-58 (.293). Totals, 137-for-434 (.316).

Personal fouls/disqualifications: 1990-91, 16/0. 1991-92, 26/1. 1992-93, 64/1. 1993-94, 15/0. 1994-95, 13/0. 1995-96, 69/0. 1996-97, 26/0. 1997-98, 31/1. 1999-00, 16/0. 2001-02, 12/0. 2002-03, 18/0. 2003-04, 60/0. 2004-05, 10/0. 2005-06, 55/0. Totals, 431/3.

NBA ALL-STAR GAME RECORD

Season Team	Min.	FGM	FGA	Pct.	FTM	FTA	Pct.	REBOUNDS Off.	Def.	Tot.	Ast.	PF	Dq.	St.	Blk.	TO	Pts.
1994—Seattle	17	3	4	.750	0	0	...	2	4	6	9	2	0	0	0	0	6
1995—Seattle	23	3	10	.300	0	0	...	3	2	5	15	1	0	3	0	3	6

P

Season Team	Min.	FGM	FGA	Pct.	FTM	FTA	Pct.	REBOUNDS Off.	Def.	Tot.	Ast.	PF	Dq.	St.	Blk.	TO	Pts.
1996—Seattle	28	6	10	.600	6	6	1.000	3	2	5	5	1	0	5	0	6	18
1997—Seattle	28	7	15	.467	2	2	1.000	0	1	1	10	2	0	2	0	4	17
1998—Seattle	24	3	7	.429	0	0	...	2	1	3	13	0	0	2	0	4	7
2000—Seattle	20	1	8	.125	3	3	1.000	0	4	4	8	1	0	2	0	2	5
2001—Seattle	18	0	5	.000	0	0	...	2	2	4	5	2	0	2	0	1	0
2002—Seattle	22	7	13	.538	0	0	...	0	1	1	6	1	0	3	0	3	18
2003—Seattle	15	4	6	.667	0	0	...	1	0	1	2	3	0	0	0	3	8
Totals	195	34	78	.436	11	11	1.000	13	17	30	73	13	0	19	0	26	85

Three-point field goals: 1995, 0-for-3. 1996, 0-for-1. 1997, 1-for-5 (.200). 1998, 1-for-3 (.333). 2000, 0-for-4. 2002, 4-for-6 (.667). 2003, 0-for-1. Totals, 6-for-23 (.261).

PERKINS, KENDRICK   C   CELTICS

PERSONAL: Born November 10, 1984, in Nederland, Texas. ... 6-10/280. (2.08/127.0).
HIGH SCHOOL: Clifton J. Ozen (Beaumont, Texas.).
COLLEGE: Did not attend college.
TRANSACTIONS/CAREER NOTES: Selected out of high school by Memphis Grizzlies in first round (27th pick overall) of 2003 NBA Draft. ... Draft rights traded by Grizzlies with draft rights to G Marcus Banks to Boston Celtics for draft rights to G Troy Bell and G/F Dahntay Jones (June 26, 2003).

NBA REGULAR-SEASON RECORD

Season Team	G	Min.	FGM	FGA	Pct.	FTM	FTA	Pct.	REBOUNDS Off.	Def.	Tot.	Ast.	St.	Blk.	TO	Pts.	AVERAGES RPG	APG	PPG
03-04—Boston	10	35	8	15	.533	6	9	.667	5	9	14	3	0	2	5	22	1.4	0.3	2.2
04-05—Boston	60	548	56	119	.471	37	58	.638	53	123	176	21	9	37	43	149	2.9	0.4	2.5
05-06—Boston	68	1332	137	266	.515	80	130	.615	140	264	404	69	21	105	107	354	5.9	1.0	5.2
Totals	138	1915	201	400	.503	123	197	.624	198	396	594	93	30	144	155	525	4.3	0.7	3.8

Three-point field goals: 2005-06, 0-for-2. Totals, 0-for-2 (.000).
Personal fouls/disqualifications: 2003-04, 6/0. 2004-05, 98/1. 2005-06, 199/3. Totals, 303/4.

NBA PLAYOFF RECORD

Season Team	G	Min.	FGM	FGA	Pct.	FTM	FTA	Pct.	REBOUNDS Off.	Def.	Tot.	Ast.	St.	Blk.	TO	Pts.	AVERAGES RPG	APG	PPG
04-05—Boston	6	28	4	5	.800	1	3	.333	3	3	6	0	0	3	3	9	1.0	0.0	1.5

Personal fouls/disqualifications: 2004-05, 7/0. Totals, 7/0.

PETERSON, MORRIS   F   RAPTORS

PERSONAL: Born August 26, 1977, in Flint, Mich. ... 6-7/215. (2.01/97.5).
HIGH SCHOOL: Northwestern (Flint, Mich.).
COLLEGE: Michigan State.
TRANSACTIONS/CAREER NOTES: Selected by Toronto Raptors in first round (21st pick overall) of 2000 NBA Draft.

NOTES: Granted medical redshirt (1995-96). ... Member of NCAA Division I championship team (2000). ... The SPORTING NEWS All-America first team (2000).

COLLEGIATE RECORD

Season Team	G	Min.	FGM	FGA	Pct.	FTM	FTA	Pct.	Reb.	Ast.	Pts.	AVERAGES RPG	APG	PPG
95-96—Michigan State	4	12	1	1	1.000	0	1	.000	3	2	2	0.8	0.5	0.5
96-97—Michigan State	29	518	72	166	.434	36	51	.706	97	18	196	3.3	0.6	6.8
97-98—Michigan State	27	503	81	182	.445	32	58	.552	94	24	217	3.5	0.9	8.0
98-99—Michigan State	38	907	190	343	.554	114	140	.814	216	36	516	5.7	0.9	13.6
99-00—Michigan State	39	1136	218	469	.465	136	176	.773	235	49	657	6.0	1.3	16.8
Totals	137	3076	562	1161	.484	318	426	.746	645	129	1588	4.7	0.9	11.6

Three-point field goals: 1996-97, 16-for-59 (.271). 1997-98, 23-for-69 (.333). 1998-99, 22-for-59 (.373). 1999-00, 85-for-200 (.425). Totals, 146-for-387 (.377).

HONORS: NBA All-Rookie first team (2001).

NBA REGULAR-SEASON RECORD

Season Team	G	Min.	FGM	FGA	Pct.	FTM	FTA	Pct.	REBOUNDS Off.	Def.	Tot.	Ast.	St.	Blk.	TO	Pts.	AVERAGES RPG	APG	PPG
00-01—Toronto	80	1809	290	673	.431	104	145	.717	112	147	259	105	63	20	78	747	3.2	1.3	9.3
01-02—Toronto	63	1988	336	768	.438	127	169	.751	91	132	223	153	73	11	86	883	3.5	2.4	14.0
02-03—Toronto	82	2949	421	1073	.392	195	247	.789	97	266	363	188	88	32	128	1153	4.4	2.3	14.1
03-04—Toronto	82	2148	238	587	.405	76	94	.809	35	226	261	113	88	14	69	678	3.2	1.4	8.3
04-05—Toronto	82	2510	356	848	.420	188	226	.832	71	269	340	169	91	18	93	1029	4.1	2.1	12.5
05-06—Toronto	82	3140	478	1096	.436	241	294	.820	65	316	381	190	104	15	126	1374	4.6	2.3	16.8
Totals	471	14544	2119	5045	.420	931	1175	.792	471	1356	1827	918	507	110	580	5864	3.9	1.9	12.5

Three-point field goals: 2000-01, 63-for-165 (.382). 2001-02, 84-for-231 (.364). 2002-03, 116-for-344 (.337). 2003-04, 126-for-340 (.371). 2004-05, 129-for-335 (.385). 2005-06, 177-for-448 (.395). Totals, 695-for-1863 (.373).
Personal fouls/disqualifications: 2000-01, 164/0. 2001-02, 174/2. 2002-03, 232/1. 2003-04, 206/0. 2004-05, 219/2. 2005-06, 223/2. Totals, 1218/7.

NBA PLAYOFF RECORD

Season Team	G	Min.	FGM	FGA	Pct.	FTM	FTA	Pct.	REBOUNDS Off.	Def.	Tot.	Ast.	St.	Blk.	TO	Pts.	AVERAGES RPG	APG	PPG
00-01—Toronto	8	110	18	35	.514	3	4	.750	2	10	12	15	6	0	6	43	1.5	1.9	5.4
01-02—Toronto	5	154	18	49	.367	8	10	.800	3	11	14	11	5	3	7	46	2.8	2.2	9.2
Totals	13	264	36	84	.429	11	14	.786	5	21	26	26	11	3	13	89	2.0	2.0	6.8

Three-point field goals: 2000-01, 4-for-9 (.444). 2001-02, 2-for-17 (.118). Totals, 6-for-26 (.231).
Personal fouls/disqualifications: 2000-01, 10/0. 2001-02, 17/0. Totals, 27/0.

P

PETRO, JOHAN   C   SUPERSONICS

PERSONAL: Born January 27, 1986, in Paris, France. ... 7-0/247. (2.13/112.0).
COLLEGE: Did not attend.
TRANSACTIONS/CAREER NOTES: Played in France (2001-05). ... Selected by Seattle SuperSonics in the first round (25th pick overall) of the 2005 NBA Draft.

FRENCH LEAGUE RECORD

Season Team	G	Min.	FGM	FGA	Pct.	FTM	FTA	Pct.	Reb.	Ast.	Pts.	RPG	APG	PPG
01-02—INSEP	22	510	76	138	.551	31	67	.463	148	11	183	6.7	0.5	8.3
02-03—INSEP	13	332	56	109	.514	24	41	.585	81	10	136	6.2	0.8	10.5
03-04—Pau Orthez	16	130	20	47	.426	6	12	.500	49	6	46	3.1	0.4	2.9
04-05—Pau Orthez	31	365	70	134	.522	31	43	.721	92	14	171	3.0	0.5	5.5
Totals	82	1337	222	428	.519	92	163	.564	370	41	536	4.5	0.5	6.5

Three-point field goals: 2002-03, 0-for-1. Totals, 0-for-1 (.000).

NBA REGULAR-SEASON RECORD

Season Team	G	Min.	FGM	FGA	Pct.	FTM	FTA	Pct.	Off.	Def.	Tot.	Ast.	St.	Blk.	TO	Pts.	RPG	APG	PPG
05-06—Seattle	68	1282	153	300	.510	47	75	.627	109	187	296	15	25	51	60	353	4.4	0.2	5.2

Personal fouls/disqualifications: 2005-06, 213/2. Totals, 213/2.

PIATKOWSKI, ERIC   G/F   SUNS

PERSONAL: Born September 30, 1970, in Steubenville, Ohio. ... 6-6/215. (1.98/97.5). ... Full name: Eric Todd Piatkowski ... Son of Walt Piatkowski, forward with Denver Rockets and Miami Floridians of American Basketball Association (1968-69 through 1971-1972). ... Name pronounced pie-it-COW-ski.
HIGH SCHOOL: Stevens (Rapid City, S.D.).
COLLEGE: Nebraska.
TRANSACTIONS/CAREER NOTES: Selected by Indiana Pacers in first round (15th pick overall) of 1994 NBA Draft. ... Draft rights traded by Pacers with F Malik Sealy and G Pooh Richardson to Los Angeles Clippers for G Mark Jackson and draft rights to G Greg Minor (June 30, 1994). ... Signed as free agent by Houston Rockets (July 26, 2003) ... Traded by Rockets with G Mike Wilks and G/F Adrian Griffin to Chicago Bulls for C Dikembe Mutombo (September 8, 2004). ... Signed as free agent by Phoenix Suns (July 13, 2006).

COLLEGIATE RECORD

Season Team	G	Min.	FGM	FGA	Pct.	FTM	FTA	Pct.	Reb.	Ast.	Pts.	RPG	APG	PPG
89-90—Nebraska						Did not play—redshirted.								
90-91—Nebraska	34	679	128	275	.465	72	86	.837	125	68	372	3.7	2.0	10.9
91-92—Nebraska	29	873	144	338	.426	79	109	.725	184	97	414	6.3	3.3	14.3
92-93—Nebraska	30	894	178	367	.485	98	129	.760	171	75	502	5.7	2.5	16.7
93-94—Nebraska	30	972	226	456	.496	131	165	.794	189	82	646	6.3	2.7	21.5
Totals	123	3418	676	1436	.471	380	489	.777	669	322	1934	5.4	2.6	15.7

Three-point field goals: 1990-91, 44-for-127 (.346). 1991-92, 47-for-136 (.346). 1992-93, 48-for-129 (.372). 1993-94, 63-for-172 (.366). Totals, 202-for-564 (.358).

NBA REGULAR-SEASON RECORD

Season Team	G	Min.	FGM	FGA	Pct.	FTM	FTA	Pct.	Off.	Def.	Tot.	Ast.	St.	Blk.	TO	Pts.	RPG	APG	PPG
94-95—L.A. Clippers	81	1208	201	456	.441	90	115	.783	63	70	133	77	37	15	63	566	1.6	1.0	7.0
95-96—L.A. Clippers	65	784	98	242	.405	67	82	.817	40	63	103	48	24	10	45	301	1.6	0.7	4.6
96-97—L.A. Clippers	65	747	134	298	.450	69	84	.821	49	56	105	52	33	10	46	388	1.6	0.8	6.0
97-98—L.A. Clippers	67	1740	257	568	.452	140	170	.824	70	166	236	85	51	12	80	760	3.5	1.3	11.3
98-99—L.A. Clippers	49	1242	180	417	.432	88	102	.863	39	101	140	53	44	6	53	513	2.9	1.1	10.5
99-00—L.A. Clippers	75	1712	238	573	.415	85	100	.850	74	148	222	81	44	13	57	654	3.0	1.1	8.7
00-01—L.A. Clippers	81	2144	291	672	.433	158	181	.873	54	187	241	96	46	19	76	860	3.0	1.2	10.6
01-02—L.A. Clippers	71	1718	207	471	.439	101	113	.894	43	141	184	112	41	12	64	626	2.6	1.6	8.8
02-03—L.A. Clippers	62	1360	210	446	.471	101	122	.828	44	112	156	70	33	9	56	601	2.5	1.1	9.7
03-04—Houston	49	703	72	191	.377	14	16	.875	10	63	73	26	16	5	29	201	1.5	0.5	4.1
04-05—Chicago	68	841	111	258	.430	45	56	.804	15	64	79	51	29	1	37	324	1.2	0.8	4.8
05-06—Chicago	29	228	24	61	.393	2	5	.400	4	19	23	13	6	1	11	59	0.8	0.4	2.0
Totals	762	14427	2023	4653	.435	960	1146	.838	505	1190	1695	764	404	113	617	5853	2.2	1.0	7.7

Three-point field goals: 1994-95, 74-for-198 (.374). 1995-96, 38-for-114 (.333). 1996-97, 51-for-120 (.425). 1997-98, 106-for-259 (.409). 1998-99, 65-for-165 (.394). 1999-00, 93-for-243 (.383). 2000-01, 120-for-297 (.404). 2001-02, 111-for-238 (.466). 2002-03, 80-for-201 (.398). 2003-04, 43-for-122 (.352). 2004-05, 57-for-134 (.425). 2005-06, 9-for-33 (.273). Totals, 847-for-2124 (.399).

Personal fouls/disqualifications: 1994-95, 150/1. 1995-96, 83/0. 1996-97, 85/0. 1997-98, 137/0. 1998-99, 86/0. 1999-00, 140/0. 2000-01, 123/0. 2001-02, 110/0. 2002-03, 92/0. 2003-04, 42/0. 2004-05, 67/0. 2005-06, 20/0. Totals, 1135/1.

NBA PLAYOFF RECORD

Season Team	G	Min.	FGM	FGA	Pct.	FTM	FTA	Pct.	Off.	Def.	Tot.	Ast.	St.	Blk.	TO	Pts.	RPG	APG	PPG
96-97—L.A. Clippers	3	38	4	11	.364	6	7	.857	1	1	2	0	1	0	0	16	0.7	0.0	5.3
03-04—Houston	1	4	0	1	.000	0	0	...	0	1	1	0	0	0	0	0	1.0	0.0	0.0
04-05—Chicago	5	66	6	19	.316	6	7	.857	1	8	9	3	4	1	1	23	1.8	0.6	4.6
05-06—Chicago	6	28	3	6	.500	2	2	1.000	1	4	5	1	0	1	0	10	0.8	0.2	1.7
Totals	15	136	13	37	.351	14	16	.875	3	14	17	4	5	2	1	49	1.1	0.3	3.3

Three-point field goals: 1996-97, 2-for-5 (.400). 2004-05, 5-for-13 (.385). 2005-06, 2-for-5 (.400). Totals, 9-for-23 (.391).
Personal fouls/disqualifications: 1996-97, 5/0. 2003-04, 1/0. 2004-05, 3/0. 2005-06, 1/0. Totals, 10/0.

P

PIERCE, PAUL   F   CELTICS

PERSONAL: Born October 13, 1977, in Oakland. ... 6-6/230. (1.98/104.3). ... Full name: Paul Anthony Pierce
HIGH SCHOOL: Inglewood (Calif.).
COLLEGE: Kansas.
TRANSACTIONS/CAREER NOTES: Selected after junior season by Boston Celtics in first round (10th pick overall) of 1998 NBA Draft.

COLLEGIATE RECORD

NOTES: The SPORTING NEWS All-America first team (1998).

Season Team	G	Min.	FGM	FGA	Pct.	FTM	FTA	Pct.	Reb.	Ast.	Pts.	RPG	APG	PPG
95-96—Kansas	34	862	143	341	.419	83	137	.606	180	61	404	5.3	1.8	11.9
96-97—Kansas	36	1013	215	441	.488	124	173	.717	243	77	587	6.8	2.1	16.3
97-98—Kansas	38	1155	287	559	.513	163	221	.738	253	98	777	6.7	2.6	20.4
Totals	108	3030	645	1341	.481	370	531	.697	676	236	1768	6.3	2.2	16.4

Three-point field goals: 1995-96, 35-for-115 (.304). 1996-97, 33-for-71 (.465). 1997-98, 40-for-116 (.345). Totals, 108-for-302 (.358).

NBA REGULAR-SEASON RECORD

HONORS: All-NBA third team (2002, 2003). ... NBA All-Rookie first team (1999).

Season Team	G	Min.	FGM	FGA	Pct.	FTM	FTA	Pct.	Off.	Def.	Tot.	Ast.	St.	Blk.	TO	Pts.	RPG	APG	PPG
98-99—Boston	48	1632	284	647	.439	139	195	.713	117	192	309	115	82	50	113	791	6.4	2.4	16.5
99-00—Boston	73	2583	486	1099	.442	359	450	.798	83	313	396	221	152	62	178	1427	5.4	3.0	19.5
00-01—Boston	82	3120	687	1513	.454	550	738	.745	94	428	522	253	138	69	262	2071	6.4	3.1	25.3
01-02—Boston	82	3302	707	1598	.442	520	643	.809	81	485	566	261	154	86	241	*2144	6.9	3.2	26.1
02-03—Boston	79	3096	663	1592	.416	*604	753	.802	106	472	578	349	139	62	288	2048	7.3	4.4	25.9
03-04—Boston	80	3099	602	1497	.402	517	631	.819	69	453	522	410	131	52	*303	1836	6.5	5.1	23.0
04-05—Boston	82	2960	556	1223	.455	549	668	.822	78	461	539	348	133	39	230	1769	6.6	4.2	21.6
05-06—Boston	79	3084	689	1462	.471	627	812	.772	77	453	530	375	107	34	273	2116	6.7	4.7	26.8
Totals	605	22876	4674	10631	.440	3865	4890	.790	705	3257	3962	2332	1036	454	1888	14202	6.5	3.9	23.5

Three-point field goals: 1998-99, 84-for-204 (.412). 1999-00, 96-for-280 (.343). 2000-01, 147-for-384 (.383). 2001-02, 210-for-520 (.404). 2002-03, 118-for-391 (.302). 2003-04, 115-for-384 (.299). 2004-05, 108-for-292 (.370). 2005-06, 111-for-314 (.354). Totals, 989-for-2769 (.357).
Personal fouls/disqualifications: 1998-99, 139/1. 1999-00, 237/5. 2000-01, 251/3. 2001-02, 237/1. 2002-03, 227/2. 2003-04, 234/3. 2004-05, 255/1. 2005-06, 223/3. Totals, 1803/19.

NBA PLAYOFF RECORD

NOTES: Holds single-game record for most free throws made, none missed—21 (April 19, 2003).

Season Team	G	Min.	FGM	FGA	Pct.	FTM	FTA	Pct.	Off.	Def.	Tot.	Ast.	St.	Blk.	TO	Pts.	RPG	APG	PPG
01-02—Boston	16	672	122	303	.403	120	157	.764	27	110	137	66	27	20	61	394	8.6	4.1	24.6
02-03—Boston	10	445	77	193	.399	101	117	.863	11	79	90	67	21	8	44	271	9.0	6.7	27.1
03-04—Boston	4	162	26	76	.342	26	31	.839	6	29	35	10	5	4	25	83	8.8	2.5	20.8
04-05—Boston	7	277	47	93	.505	59	68	.868	7	47	54	32	13	10	19	160	7.7	4.6	22.9
Totals	37	1556	272	665	.409	306	373	.820	51	265	316	175	66	42	149	908	8.5	4.7	24.5

Three-point field goals: 2001-02, 30-for-86 (.349). 2002-03, 16-for-46 (.348). 2003-04, 5-for-17 (.294). 2004-05, 7-for-27 (.259). Totals, 58-for-193 (.301).
Personal fouls/disqualifications: 2001-02, 52/0. 2002-03, 38/0. 2003-04, 12/0. 2004-05, 18/0. Totals, 120/0.

NBA ALL-STAR GAME RECORD

Season Team	Min.	FGM	FGA	Pct.	FTM	FTA	Pct.	Off.	Def.	Tot.	Ast.	PF	Dq.	St.	Blk.	TO	Pts.
2002—Boston	23	9	18	.500	0	0	...	3	4	7	3	1	0	1	0	0	19
2003—Boston	18	4	11	.364	0	0	...	0	2	2	3	1	0	4	0	2	8
2004—Boston	13	4	8	.500	0	0	...	0	1	1	2	2	0	1	0	1	8
2005—Boston	14	4	7	.571	1	1	1.000	0	3	3	3	2	0	2	0	0	9
2006—Boston	15	3	6	.500	1	2	.500	0	2	2	1	0	0	1	0	0	7
Totals	83	24	50	.480	2	3	.667	3	12	15	12	6	0	9	0	3	51

Three-point field goals: 2002, 1-for-6 (.167). 2003, 0-for-5. 2004, 0-for-1. 2005, 0 for 2. Totals, 1-for-14 (.071).

PIETRUS, MICKAEL   G/F   WARRIORS

PERSONAL: Born February 7, 1982, in Les Abymes, Guadeloupe, France. ... 6-6/200. (1.98/90.7).
TRANSACTIONS/CAREER NOTES: Played in France (1999-2003). ... Selected by Golden State Warriors in first round (11th pick overall) of 2003 NBA Draft.

FRENCH LEAGUE RECORD

Season Team	G	Min.	FGM	FGA	Pct.	FTM	FTA	Pct.	Reb.	Ast.	Pts.	RPG	APG	PPG
99-00—Pau Orthez	7	65	8	21	.381	4	8	.500	7	0	24	1.0	0.0	3.4
00-01—Pau Orthez	29	448	86	171	.503	34	47	.723	63	34	230	2.2	1.2	7.9
01-02—Pau Orthez	30	527	79	192	.411	62	92	.674	74	33	255	2.5	1.1	8.5
02-03—Pau Orthez	28	608	110	226	.487	75	100	.750	101	47	340	3.6	1.7	12.1
Totals	94	1648	283	610	.464	175	247	.709	245	114	849	2.6	1.2	9.0

Three-point field goals: 1999-00, 4-for-12 (.333). 2000-01, 24-for-62 (.387). 2001-02, 35-for-100 (.350). 2002-03, 45-for-112 (.402). Totals, 108-for-286 (.378).

NBA REGULAR-SEASON RECORD

Season Team	G	Min.	FGM	FGA	Pct.	FTM	FTA	Pct.	Off.	Def.	Tot.	Ast.	St.	Blk.	TO	Pts.	RPG	APG	PPG
03-04—Golden State	53	748	96	231	.416	52	75	.693	48	71	119	27	32	12	40	279	2.2	0.5	5.3
04-05—Golden State	67	1340	214	501	.427	141	202	.698	65	124	189	82	46	18	92	636	2.8	1.2	9.5
05-06—Golden State	52	1179	169	418	.404	87	143	.608	58	105	163	44	33	10	78	481	3.1	0.8	9.3
Totals	172	3267	479	1150	.417	280	420	.667	171	300	471	153	111	40	210	1396	2.7	0.9	8.1

Three-point field goals: 2003-04, 35-for-105 (.333). 2004-05, 67-for-195 (.344). 2005-06, 56-for-176 (.318). Totals, 158-for-476 (.332).
Personal fouls/disqualifications: 2003-04, 100/1. 2004-05, 139/2. 2005-06, 132/0. Totals, 371/3.

P

PLANINIC, ZORAN   G/F

PERSONAL: Born September 12, 1982, in Mostar, Bosnia-Herzegovina. ... 6-7/195. (2.01/88.5).
TRANSACTIONS/CAREER NOTES: Played in Croatia (1999-2003). ... Selected by New Jersey Nets in first round (22nd pick overall) of 2003 NBA Draft. ... Waived by Nets (August 11, 2006).

CROATIAN LEAGUE RECORD

Season Team	G	Min.	FGM	FGA	Pct.	FTM	FTA	Pct.	Reb.	Ast.	Pts.	RPG	APG	PPG
99-00—Benston Zagreb	22	574	72	162	.444	37	58	.638	48	37	189	2.2	1.7	8.6
00-01—Cibona	20	328	59	115	.513	19	32	.594	46	38	145	2.3	1.9	7.3
01-02—Cibona	7	196	25	56	.446	21	35	.600	18	24	75	2.6	3.4	10.7
02-03—Cibona	21	381	56	118	.475	30	54	.556	38	47	154	1.8	2.2	7.3
Totals	70	1479	212	451	.470	107	179	.598	150	146	563	2.1	2.1	8.0

Three-point field goals: 1999-00, 8-for-38 (.211). 2000-01, 8-for-30 (.267). 2001-02, 4-for-9 (.444). 2002-03, 12-for-34 (.353). Totals, 32-for-111 (.288).

NBA REGULAR-SEASON RECORD

Season Team	G	Min.	FGM	FGA	Pct.	FTM	FTA	Pct.	Off.	Def.	Tot.	Ast.	St.	Blk.	TO	Pts.	RPG	APG	PPG
										REBOUNDS								AVERAGES	
03-04—New Jersey	49	473	53	129	.411	38	60	.633	14	41	55	68	13	3	36	153	1.1	1.4	3.1
04-05—New Jersey	43	515	78	174	.448	46	66	.697	19	50	69	44	25	0	41	217	1.6	1.0	5.0
05-06—New Jersey	56	596	66	183	.361	46	66	.697	14	60	74	53	20	4	43	191	1.3	0.9	3.4
Totals	148	1584	197	486	.405	130	192	.677	47	151	198	165	58	7	120	561	1.3	1.1	3.8

Three-point field goals: 2003-04, 9-for-32 (.281). 2004-05, 15-for-40 (.375). 2005-06, 13-for-56 (.232). Totals, 37-for-128 (.289).
Personal fouls/disqualifications: 2003-04, 70/1. 2004-05, 76/2. 2005-06, 91/1. Totals, 237/4.

NBA PLAYOFF RECORD

Season Team	G	Min.	FGM	FGA	Pct.	FTM	FTA	Pct.	Off.	Def.	Tot.	Ast.	St.	Blk.	TO	Pts.	RPG	APG	PPG
										REBOUNDS								AVERAGES	
03-04—New Jersey	6	15	0	2	.000	1	2	.500	0	1	1	2	0	0	2	1	0.2	0.3	0.2
04-05—New Jersey	3	3	0	0	...	0	0	...	0	0	0	0	0	0	0	0	0.0	0.0	0.0
05-06—New Jersey	3	6	0	1	.000	0	2	.000	0	1	1	2	1	0	1	0	0.3	0.7	0.0
Totals	12	24	0	3	.000	1	4	.250	0	2	2	4	1	0	3	1	0.2	0.3	0.1

Three-point field goals: 2003-04, 0-for-1. Totals, 0-for-1 (.000).
Personal fouls/disqualifications: 2003-04, 2/0. 2005-06, 1/0. Totals, 3/0.

PODKOLZIN, PAVEL   C

PERSONAL: Born January 15, 1985, in Novosibirsk, Russia. ... 7-5/260. (2.26/117.9).
TRANSACTIONS/CAREER NOTES: Played in Italy (2001-04). ... Selected by Utah Jazz in first round (21st pick overall) of 2004 NBA Draft. ... Draft rights traded by Jazz to Dallas Mavericks for 2005 first-round draft choice (June 24, 2004). ... Waived by Mavericks (August 4, 2006).

ITALIAN LEAGUE RECORD

Season Team	G	Min.	FGM	FGA	Pct.	FTM	FTA	Pct.	Reb.	Ast.	Pts.	RPG	APG	PPG
02-03—Varese	11	62	10	16	.625	4	7	.571	20	1	24	1.8	0.1	2.2
03-04—Varese	28	248	17	37	.459	23	33	.697	50	4	57	1.8	0.1	2.0
Totals	39	310	27	53	.509	27	40	.675	70	5	81	1.8	0.1	2.1

Three-point field goals: 2003-04, 0-for-1. Totals, 0-for-1 (.000).

NBA REGULAR-SEASON RECORD

Season Team	G	Min.	FGM	FGA	Pct.	FTM	FTA	Pct.	Off.	Def.	Tot.	Ast.	St.	Blk.	TO	Pts.	RPG	APG	PPG
										REBOUNDS								AVERAGES	
04-05—Dallas	5	10	0	0	...	1	2	.500	0	2	2	0	0	0	2	1	0.4	0.0	0.2
05-06—Dallas	1	18	0	2	.000	3	6	.500	0	7	7	0	0	1	2	3	7.0	0.0	3.0
Totals	6	28	0	2	.000	4	8	.500	0	9	9	0	0	1	4	4	1.5	0.0	0.7

Personal fouls/disqualifications: 2004-05, 4/0. Totals, 4/0.

NBA DEVELOPMENT LEAGUE RECORD

Season Team	G	Min.	FGM	FGA	Pct.	FTM	FTA	Pct.	Reb.	Ast.	Pts.	RPG	APG	PPG
05-06—Fort Worth	11	207	28	55	.509	17	26	.654	64	6	73	5.8	0.5	6.6

POLLARD, SCOT   F/C   CAVALIERS

PERSONAL: Born February 12, 1975, in Murray, Utah. ... 6-11/265. (2.11/120.2).
HIGH SCHOOL: Torrey Pines (San Diego).
COLLEGE: Kansas.
TRANSACTIONS/CAREER NOTES: Selected by Detroit Pistons in first round (19th pick overall) of 1997 NBA Draft. ... Traded by Pistons with 1999 first-round draft choice to Atlanta Hawks for F/C Christian Laettner (January 22, 1999). ... Waived by Hawks (February 19, 1999). ... Signed as free agent by Sacramento Kings (February 24, 1999). ... Traded by Kings to Indiana Pacers in three-team deal in which Kings also acquired F/C Brad Miller from Pacers and traded F/G Hedo Turkoglu to San Antonio Spurs. Spurs also acquired G Ron Mercer from Pacers and traded F Danny Ferry to Pacers (July 24, 2003). ... Signed as free agent by Cleveland Cavaliers (August 18, 2006).

COLLEGIATE RECORD

Season Team	G	Min.	FGM	FGA	Pct.	FTM	FTA	Pct.	Reb.	Ast.	Pts.	RPG	APG	PPG
93-94—Kansas	35	597	95	175	.543	74	108	.685	173	13	264	4.9	0.4	7.5
94-95—Kansas	31	620	113	203	.557	89	136	.654	192	17	315	6.2	0.5	10.2

P

Season Team	G	Min.	FGM	FGA	Pct.	FTM	FTA	Pct.	Reb.	Ast.	Pts.	AVERAGES		
												RPG	APG	PPG
95-96—Kansas	34	835	123	218	.564	96	151	.636	253	10	342	7.4	0.3	10.1
96-97—Kansas	28	702	94	178	.528	99	140	.707	232	19	288	8.3	0.7	10.3
Totals	128	2754	425	774	.549	358	535	.669	850	59	1209	6.6	0.5	9.4

Three-point field goals: 1996-97, 1-for-1 (1.000). Totals, 1-for-1 (1.000).

NBA REGULAR-SEASON RECORD

Season Team	G	Min.	FGM	FGA	Pct.	FTM	FTA	Pct.	REBOUNDS			Ast.	St.	Blk.	TO	Pts.	AVERAGES		
									Off.	Def.	Tot.						RPG	APG	PPG
97-98—Detroit	33	317	35	70	.500	19	23	.826	34	40	74	9	8	10	12	89	2.2	0.3	2.7
98-99—Sacramento	16	259	33	61	.541	16	23	.696	38	44	82	4	8	18	5	82	5.1	0.3	5.1
99-00—Sacramento	76	1336	149	283	.527	114	159	.717	168	236	404	43	55	59	50	412	5.3	0.6	5.4
00-01—Sacramento	77	1658	185	395	.468	128	171	.749	173	292	465	47	48	97	66	498	6.0	0.6	6.5
01-02—Sacramento	80	1881	197	358	.550	115	166	.693	188	377	565	53	70	76	68	509	7.1	0.7	6.4
02-03—Sacramento	23	325	40	87	.460	23	38	.605	46	60	106	6	13	15	15	103	4.6	0.3	4.5
03-04—Indiana	61	678	47	114	.412	12	21	.571	67	97	164	10	23	26	22	106	2.7	0.2	1.7
04-05—Indiana	49	865	79	167	.473	33	49	.673	85	120	205	18	30	24	31	191	4.2	0.4	3.9
05-06—Indiana	45	771	70	154	.455	29	38	.763	73	145	218	24	37	20	26	169	4.8	0.5	3.8
Totals	460	8090	835	1689	.494	489	688	.711	872	1411	2283	214	292	345	295	2159	5.0	0.5	4.7

Three-point field goals: 2000-01, 0-for-2. Totals, 0-for-2 (.000).
Personal fouls/disqualifications: 1997-98, 48/0. 1998-99, 41/0. 1999-00, 213/3. 2000-01, 206/4. 2001-02, 202/1. 2002-03, 50/0. 2003-04, 110/0. 2004-05, 123/1. 2005-06, 115/1. Totals, 1108/10.

NBA PLAYOFF RECORD

Season Team	G	Min.	FGM	FGA	Pct.	FTM	FTA	Pct.	REBOUNDS			Ast.	St.	Blk.	TO	Pts.	AVERAGES		
									Off.	Def.	Tot.						RPG	APG	PPG
98-99—Sacramento	5	74	6	9	.667	3	5	.600	5	6	11	1	4	6	2	15	2.2	0.2	3.0
99-00—Sacramento	5	70	9	16	.563	2	6	.333	6	10	16	1	2	1	3	20	3.2	0.2	4.0
00-01—Sacramento	8	141	19	30	.633	10	17	.588	23	32	55	2	1	7	6	48	6.9	0.3	6.0
01-02—Sacramento	15	193	21	40	.525	8	12	.667	29	24	53	3	7	5	3	50	3.5	0.2	3.3
02-03—Sacramento	8	91	7	24	.292	10	13	.769	17	13	30	2	1	7	7	24	3.8	0.3	3.0
03-04—Indiana	3	13	0	2	.000	2	4	.500	1	3	4	0	1	0	0	2	1.3	0.0	0.7
04-05—Indiana	9	67	6	15	.400	1	2	.500	4	7	11	1	1	0	4	13	1.2	0.1	1.4
05-06—Indiana	4	15	0	1	.000	0	0	...	1	4	5	0	1	0	1	0	1.3	0.0	0.0
Totals	57	664	68	137	.496	36	59	.610	86	99	185	10	18	26	26	172	3.2	0.2	3.0

Personal fouls/disqualifications: 1998-99, 13/0. 1999-00, 18/1. 2000-01, 30/0. 2001-02, 36/1. 2002-03, 15/1. 2003-04, 2/0. 2004-05, 9/0. 2005-06, 5/0. Totals, 128/3.

POSEY, JAMES　　　　　　G/F　　　　　　HEAT

PERSONAL: Born January 13, 1977, in Cleveland. 6-8/215. (2.03/97.5). ... Full name: James Mike ....
high school. R.B. Chamberlain (Twinsburg, Ohio).
COLLEGE: Xavier.
TRANSACTIONS/CAREER NOTES: Selected by Denver Nuggets in first round (18th pick overall) of 1999 NBA Draft. ... Traded by Nuggets to Houston Rockets in three-way deal in which Rockets sent F Kenny Thomas to Philadelphia 76ers, 76ers sent F/C Mark Bryant, F Art Long and future first-round draft choice to Nuggets and Rockets sent future second-round draft choice to Nuggets (December 18, 2002). ... Signed by Memphis Grizzlies when Rockets elected not to match offer sheet (August 9, 2003) ... Traded by Grizzlies with Gs Jason Williams and Andre Emmett to Miami Heat in five-team trade (August 2, 2005).
MISCELLANEOUS: Member of NBA championship team (2006).

COLLEGIATE RECORD

Season Team	G	Min.	FGM	FGA	Pct.	FTM	FTA	Pct.	Reb.	Ast.	Pts.	AVERAGES		
												RPG	APG	PPG
95-96—Xavier						Did not play—ineligible.								
96-97—Xavier	29	780	130	232	.560	121	155	.781	226	40	387	7.8	1.4	13.3
97-98—Xavier	30	864	145	261	.556	150	182	.824	253	39	459	8.4	1.3	15.3
98-99—Xavier	36	1268	191	391	.488	179	220	.814	322	84	609	8.9	2.3	16.9
Totals	95	2912	466	884	.527	450	557	.808	801	163	1455	8.4	1.7	15.3

Three-point field goals: 1996-97, 6-for-32 (.188). 1997-98, 19-for-59 (.322). 1998-99, 48-for-131 (.366). Totals, 73-for-222 (.329).

NBA REGULAR-SEASON RECORD

HONORS: NBA All-Rookie second team (2000).

Season Team	G	Min.	FGM	FGA	Pct.	FTM	FTA	Pct.	REBOUNDS			Ast.	St.	Blk.	TO	Pts.	AVERAGES		
									Off.	Def.	Tot.						RPG	APG	PPG
99-00—Denver	81	2052	230	536	.429	120	150	.800	85	232	317	146	98	33	95	662	3.9	1.8	8.2
00-01—Denver	82	2255	243	590	.412	115	141	.816	125	306	431	163	93	40	102	666	5.3	2.0	8.1
01-02—Denver	73	2238	277	736	.376	161	203	.793	109	320	429	180	114	39	127	782	5.9	2.5	10.7
02-03—Den-Hou	83	2518	309	752	.411	205	246	.833	90	336	426	184	106	15	144	893	5.1	2.2	10.8
03-04—Memphis	82	2451	368	770	.478	278	335	.830	92	311	403	122	137	40	112	1126	4.9	1.5	13.7
04-05—Memphis	50	1382	127	356	.357	96	111	.865	45	174	219	88	48	23	69	405	4.4	1.8	8.1
05-06—Miami	67	1914	159	395	.403	48	61	.787	33	286	319	89	54	20	58	483	4.8	1.3	7.2
Totals	518	14810	1713	4135	.414	1023	1247	.820	579	1965	2544	972	650	210	707	5017	4.9	1.9	9.7

Three-point field goals: 1999-00, 82-for-220 (.373). 2000-01, 65-for-217 (.300). 2001-02, 67-for-237 (.283). 2002-03, 70-for-229 (.306). 2003-04, 112-for-290 (.386). 2004-05, 55-for-178 (.309). 2005-06, 117-for-290 (.403). Totals, 568-for-1661 (.342).
Personal fouls/disqualifications: 1999-00, 207/1. 2000-01, 226/2. 2001-02, 224/3. 2002-03, 197/1. 2003-04, 248/5. 2004-05, 134/0. 2005-06, 196/2. Totals, 1432/14.

P

NBA PLAYOFF RECORD

Season Team	G	Min.	FGM	FGA	Pct.	FTM	FTA	Pct.	REBOUNDS Off.	Def.	Tot.	Ast.	St.	Blk.	TO	Pts.	AVERAGES RPG	APG	PPG
03-04—Memphis	4	130	15	37	.405	19	21	.905	8	14	22	4	9	2	6	50	5.5	1.0	12.5
04-05—Memphis	4	100	11	25	.440	10	13	.769	1	12	13	4	2	1	5	39	3.3	1.0	9.8
05-06—Miami	22	606	49	114	.430	27	37	.730	15	110	125	20	17	2	11	160	5.7	0.9	7.3
Totals	30	836	75	176	.426	56	71	.789	24	136	160	28	28	5	22	249	5.3	0.9	8.3

Three-point field goals: 2003-04, 1-for-6 (.167). 2004-05, 7-for-15 (.467). 2005-06, 35-for-83 (.422). Totals, 43-for-104 (.413).
Personal fouls/disqualifications: 2003-04, 13/0. 2004-05, 14/0. 2005-06, 70/1. Totals, 97/1.

POTAPENKO, VITALY — F/C — KINGS

PERSONAL: Born March 21, 1975, in Kiev, Ukraine. ... 6-10/285. (2.08/129.3). ... Full name: Vitaly Nikolaevich Potapenko ... Name pronounced VEE-tal-lee poe-TAH-pen-koe.
COLLEGE: Wright State.
TRANSACTIONS/CAREER NOTES: Selected after junior season by Cleveland Cavaliers in first round (12th pick overall) of 1996 NBA Draft. ... Traded by Cavaliers to Boston Celtics for F/C Andrew DeClercq and a 1999 first-round draft choice (March 11, 1999). ... Traded by Celtics with G Kenny Anderson and G Joseph Forte to Seattle SuperSonics for F Vin Baker and G Shammond Williams (July 22, 2002). ... Traded by SuperSonics to Sacramento Kings as part of four-way deal (February 23, 2006).

COLLEGIATE RECORD

Season Team	G	Min.	FGM	FGA	Pct.	FTM	FTA	Pct.	Reb.	Ast.	Pts.	AVERAGES RPG	APG	PPG
94-95—Wright State	30	900	212	352	.602	151	206	.733	193	41	575	6.4	1.4	19.2
95-96—Wright State	25	807	197	322	.612	139	195	.713	182	36	534	7.3	1.4	21.4
Totals	55	1707	409	674	.607	290	401	.723	375	77	1109	6.8	1.4	20.2

Three-point field goals: 1995-96, 1-for-6 (.167). Totals, 1-for-6 (.167).

NBA REGULAR-SEASON RECORD

Season Team	G	Min.	FGM	FGA	Pct.	FTM	FTA	Pct.	REBOUNDS Off.	Def.	Tot.	Ast.	St.	Blk.	TO	Pts.	AVERAGES RPG	APG	PPG
96-97—Cleveland	80	1238	186	423	.440	92	125	.736	105	112	217	40	26	34	109	465	2.7	0.5	5.8
97-98—Cleveland	80	1412	234	488	.480	102	144	.708	110	203	313	57	27	28	132	570	3.9	0.7	7.1
98-99—Cleve.-Bos.	50	1394	204	412	.495	91	155	.587	114	218	332	75	35	36	100	499	6.6	1.5	10.0
99-00—Boston	79	1797	307	615	.499	109	160	.681	182	317	499	77	41	29	145	723	6.3	1.0	9.2
00-01—Boston	82	1901	248	521	.476	115	158	.728	206	289	495	64	52	23	105	611	6.0	0.8	7.5
01-02—Boston	79	1343	137	301	.455	89	120	.742	167	180	347	30	37	18	63	363	4.4	0.4	4.6
02-03—Seattle	26	403	41	93	.441	22	29	.759	25	64	89	4	9	8	25	104	3.4	0.2	4.0
03-04—Seattle	65	1419	200	409	.489	59	92	.641	101	188	289	53	22	28	77	459	4.4	0.8	7.1
04-05—Seattle	33	335	45	87	.517	27	31	.871	30	48	78	9	7	3	12	117	2.4	0.3	3.5
05-06—Seattle-Sac.	33	353	37	71	.521	10	17	.588	27	37	64	9	2	2	16	84	1.9	0.3	2.5
Totals	607	11595	1639	3420	.479	716	1031	.694	1067	1656	2723	418	258	209	784	3995	4.5	0.7	6.6

Three-point field goals: 1996-97, 1-for-2 (.500). 1997-98, 0-for-1. 1998-99, 0-for-1. 1999-00, 0-for-1. 2004-05, 0-for-1. Totals, 1-for-6 (.167).
Personal fouls/disqualifications: 1996-97, 216/3. 1997-98, 198/2. 1998-99, 169/4. 1999-00, 239/4. 2000-01, 228/2. 2001-02, 174/0. 2002-03, 46/0. 2003-04, 161/2. 2004-05, 53/0. 2005-06, 50/0. Totals, 1534/17.

NBA PLAYOFF RECORD

Season Team	G	Min.	FGM	FGA	Pct.	FTM	FTA	Pct.	REBOUNDS Off.	Def.	Tot.	Ast.	St.	Blk.	TO	Pts.	AVERAGES RPG	APG	PPG
97-98—Cleveland	4	70	6	15	.400	5	10	.500	3	8	11	3	2	0	6	17	2.8	0.8	4.3
04-05—Seattle	5	37	5	10	.500	0	0	...	3	4	7	0	0	0	0	10	1.4	0.0	2.0
05-06—Sacramento	4	9	2	4	.500	0	0	...	1	0	1	0	1	0	0	4	0.3	0.0	1.0
Totals	13	116	13	29	.448	5	10	.500	7	12	19	3	3	0	6	31	1.5	0.2	2.4

Personal fouls/disqualifications: 1997-98, 8/0. 2004-05, 8/0. 2005-06, 2/0. Totals, 18/0.

POWELL, JOSH — F — PACERS

PERSONAL: Born December 5, 1983 ... 6-9/225. (2.06/102.1).
HIGH SCHOOL: Riverdale (Ga.).
COLLEGE: North Carolina State.
TRANSACTIONS/CAREER NOTES: Not drafted by an NBA franchise. ... Played in Italy (2003-05). ... Played in Russia (2003-04). ... Signed as free agent by Dallas Mavericks (August 2, 2005). ... Traded by Mavericks with G Darrell Armstrong and G/F Rawle Marshall to Indiana Pacers for G Anthony Johnson (July 24, 2006).

COLLEGIATE RECORD

Season Team	G	Min.	FGM	FGA	Pct.	FTM	FTA	Pct.	Reb.	Ast.	Pts.	AVERAGES RPG	APG	PPG
01-02—NC State	34	662	95	180	.528	52	73	.712	131	31	244	3.9	0.9	7.2
02-03—NC State	31	838	144	252	.571	88	119	.739	163	31	385	5.3	1.0	12.4
Totals	65	1500	239	432	.553	140	192	.729	294	62	629	4.5	1.0	9.7

Three-point field goals: 2001-02, 2-for-14 (.143). 2002-03, 9-for-24 (.375). Totals, 11-for-38 (.289).

ITALIAN LEAGUE RECORD

Season Team	G	Min.	FGM	FGA	Pct.	FTM	FTA	Pct.	Reb.	Ast.	Pts.	AVERAGES RPG	APG	PPG
03-04—Euroride Scafati..............	18	564	95	162	.586	58	77	.753	163	8	248	9.1	0.4	13.8
04-05—Pepsi Caserta	30	1056	191	326	.586	113	165	.685	356	22	498	11.9	0.7	16.6
Totals	48	1620	286	488	.586	171	242	.707	519	30	746	10.8	0.6	15.5

Three-point field goals: 2003-04, 0-for-5. 2004-05, 3-for-24 (.125). Totals, 3-for-29 (.103).

P

Season Team	G	Min.	FGM	FGA	Pct.	FTM	FTA	Pct.	Reb.	Ast.	Pts.	AVERAGES RPG	APG	PPG
03-04—Lokomotiv-Rostov.........	2	11	0	2	.000	3	4	.750	2	1	3	1.0	0.5	1.5

NBA REGULAR-SEASON RECORD

Season Team	G	Min.	FGM	FGA	Pct.	FTM	FTA	Pct.	REBOUNDS Off.	Def.	Tot.	Ast.	St.	Blk.	TO	Pts.	AVERAGES RPG	APG	PPG
05-06—Dallas.............	37	429	37	81	.457	36	45	.800	28	53	81	9	7	4	22	110	2.2	0.2	3.0

Personal fouls/disqualifications: 2005-06, 52/0. Totals, 52/0.

NBA PLAYOFF RECORD

Season Team	G	Min.	FGM	FGA	Pct.	FTM	FTA	Pct.	REBOUNDS Off.	Def.	Tot.	Ast.	St.	Blk.	TO	Pts.	AVERAGES RPG	APG	PPG
05-06—Dallas.............	6	25	0	4	.000	0	0	...	2	0	2	1	0	0	1	0	0.3	0.2	0.0

Personal fouls/disqualifications: 2005-06, 5/0. Totals, 5/0.

NBA DEVELOPMENT LEAGUE RECORD

Season Team	G	Min.	FGM	FGA	Pct.	FTM	FTA	Pct.	Reb.	Ast.	Pts.	AVERAGES RPG	APG	PPG
05-06—Fort Worth.....................	3	89	22	31	.710	9	11	.818	21	1	53	7.0	0.3	17.7

PRICE, RONNIE　　　　　　　　G　　　　　　　　KINGS

PERSONAL: Born June 21, 1983, in Friendswood, Texas. ... 6-2/190. (1.88/86.2).
HIGH SCHOOL: Clear Brook (Friendswood, Texas).
COLLEGE: Nicholls State, then Utah Valley State.
TRANSACTIONS/CAREER NOTES: Not drafted by an NBA franchise. ... Signed as free agent by Sacramento Kings (August 2, 2005).

COLLEGIATE RECORD

Season Team	G	Min.	FGM	FGA	Pct.	FTM	FTA	Pct.	Reb.	Ast.	Pts.	AVERAGES RPG	APG	PPG
01-02—Nicholls State	25	746	99	267	.371	47	61	.770	58	72	282	2.3	2.9	11.3
02-03—Utah Valley State	33	893	175	423	.414	78	100	.780	119	75	505	3.6	2.3	15.3
03-04—Utah Valley State	28	876	197	454	.434	90	112	.804	108	86	565	3.9	3.1	20.2
04-05—Utah Valley State	28	1042	229	536	.427	142	180	.789	117	84	680	4.2	3.0	24.3
Junior College Totals..............	33	893	175	423	.414	78	100	.780	119	75	505	3.6	2.3	15.3
4-Year-College Totals	81	2664	525	1257	.418	279	353	.790	283	242	1527	3.5	3.0	18.9

Three-point field goals: 2001-02, 37-for-134 (.276). 2002-03, 77-for-227 (.339). 2003-04, 81-for-214 (.379). 2004-05, 80-for-223 (.359). Totals, 275-for-798 (.345).

NBA REGULAR-SEASON RECORD

Season Team	G	Min.	FGM	FGA	Pct.	FTM	FTA	Pct.	REBOUNDS Off.	Def.	Tot.	Ast.	St.	Blk.	TO	Pts.	AVERAGES RPG	APG	PPG
05-06—Sacramento	29	150	21	58	.362	12	12	1.000	5	10	15	11	6	0	10	60	0.5	0.4	2.1

Three-point field goals: 2005-06, 6-for-27 (.222). Totals, 6-for-27 (.222).
Personal fouls/disqualifications: 2005-06, 10/0. Totals, 10/0.

NBA PLAYOFF RECORD

Season Team	G	Min.	FGM	FGA	Pct.	FTM	FTA	Pct.	REBOUNDS Off.	Def.	Tot.	Ast.	St.	Blk.	TO	Pts.	AVERAGES RPG	APG	PPG
05-06—Sacramento	4	9	0	3	.000	0	0	...	0	0	0	1	0	0	0	0	0.0	0.3	0.0

Personal fouls/disqualifications: 2005-06, 1/0. Totals, 1/0.

PRINCE, TAYSHAUN　　　　　　　　F　　　　　　　　PISTONS

PERSONAL: Born February 28, 1980, in Compton, Calif. ... 6-9/215. (2.06/97.5). ... Full name: Tayshaun Durell Prince
HIGH SCHOOL: Dominguez (Compton, Calif.).
COLLEGE: Kentucky.
TRANSACTIONS/CAREER NOTES: Selected by Detroit Pistons in first round (23rd pick overall) of 2002 NBA Draft.
MISCELLANEOUS: Member of NBA championship team (2004).

COLLEGIATE RECORD

NOTES: The SPORTING NEWS All-America second team (2002).

Season Team	G	Min.	FGM	FGA	Pct.	FTM	FTA	Pct.	Reb.	Ast.	Pts.	AVERAGES RPG	APG	PPG
98-99—Kentucky	37	747	82	198	.414	21	32	.656	142	45	214	3.8	1.2	5.8
99-00—Kentucky	32	1087	153	362	.423	74	105	.705	192	58	426	6.0	1.8	13.3
00-01—Kentucky	34	1117	207	418	.495	97	115	.843	221	99	575	6.5	2.9	16.9
01-02—Kentucky	32	1067	206	441	.467	83	118	.703	202	52	560	6.3	1.6	17.5
Totals	135	4018	648	1419	.457	275	370	.743	757	254	1775	5.6	1.9	13.1

Three-point field goals: 1998-99, 29-for-101 (.287). 1999-00, 46-for-150 (.307). 2000-01, 64-for-179 (.358). 2001-02, 65-for-191 (.340). Totals, 204-for-621 (.329).

NBA REGULAR-SEASON RECORD

HONORS: NBA All-Defensive second team (2005, 2006).

P

Season Team	G	Min.	FGM	FGA	Pct.	FTM	FTA	Pct.	REBOUNDS Off.	Def.	Tot.	Ast.	St.	Blk.	TO	Pts.	AVERAGES RPG	APG	PPG
02-03—Detroit	42	435	53	118	.449	11	17	.647	5	40	45	24	10	14	21	137	1.1	0.6	3.3
03-04—Detroit	82	2701	338	723	.467	108	141	.766	93	297	390	191	63	69	119	841	4.8	2.3	10.3
04-05—Detroit	82	3039	469	963	.487	221	274	.807	133	302	435	247	56	71	135	1206	5.3	3.0	14.7
05-06—Detroit	82	2898	455	999	.455	182	238	.765	104	242	346	186	62	39	91	1156	4.2	2.3	14.1
Totals	288	9073	1315	2803	.469	522	670	.779	335	881	1216	648	191	193	366	3340	4.2	2.3	11.6

Three-point field goals: 2002-03, 20-for-47 (.426). 2003-04, 57-for-157 (.363). 2004-05, 47-for-138 (.341). 2005-06, 64-for-183 (.350). Totals, 188-for-525 (.358).

Personal fouls/disqualifications: 2002-03, 25/0. 2003-04, 149/0. 2004-05, 161/1. 2005-06, 96/1. Totals, 431/2.

NBA PLAYOFF RECORD

Season Team	G	Min.	FGM	FGA	Pct.	FTM	FTA	Pct.	REBOUNDS Off.	Def.	Tot.	Ast.	St.	Blk.	TO	Pts.	AVERAGES RPG	APG	PPG
02-03—Detroit	15	382	49	115	.426	29	38	.763	11	46	57	23	8	13	16	141	3.8	1.5	9.4
03-04—Detroit	23	795	87	212	.410	41	55	.745	41	96	137	53	25	31	19	228	6.0	2.3	9.9
04-05—Detroit	25	1023	133	307	.433	48	60	.800	56	102	158	83	26	9	37	336	6.3	3.3	13.4
05-06—Detroit	18	745	106	231	.459	63	76	.829	43	59	102	54	12	15	31	296	5.7	3.0	16.4
Totals	81	2945	375	865	.434	181	229	.790	151	303	454	213	71	68	103	1001	5.6	2.6	12.4

Three-point field goals: 2002-03, 14-for-48 (.292). 2003-04, 13-for-49 (.265). 2004-05, 22-for-60 (.367). 2005-06, 21-for-46 (.457). Totals, 70-for-203 (.345).

Personal fouls/disqualifications: 2002-03, 20/0. 2003-04, 61/1. 2004-05, 50/0. 2005-06, 23/0. Totals, 154/1.

PROFIT, LARON   G/F

PERSONAL: Born August 5, 1977, in Charleston, S.C. ... 6-5/204. (1.96/92.5). ... Full name: Bronta Laron Profit
HIGH SCHOOL: Caesar Rodney (Dover, Del.).
COLLEGE: Maryland.
TRANSACTIONS/CAREER NOTES: Selected by Orlando Magic in second round (38th pick overall) of 1999 NBA Draft. ... Draft rights traded by Magic to Washington Wizards for conditional 2001 second-round draft choice (September 22, 1999). ... Traded by Wizards with future first-round draft choice to Magic for draft rights to C Brendan Haywood (August 1, 2001). ... Played in Italy (2001-02). ... Signed as free agent by Milwaukee Bucks (September 25, 2002). ... Waived by Bucks (October 24, 2002). ... Played in China (2002-04). ... Signed as free agent by Washington Wizards (October 1, 2004). ... Traded by Wizards with C Kwame Brown to Los Angeles Lakers for F Caron Butler and G Chucky Atkins (August 2, 2005). ... Waived by Lakers (January 17, 2006).

COLLEGIATE RECORD

Season Team	G	Min.	FGM	FGA	Pct.	FTM	FTA	Pct.	Reb.	Ast.	Pts.	AVERAGES RPG	APG	PPG
95-96—Maryland	27	366	54	112	.482	34	45	.756	74	32	154	2.7	1.2	5.7
96-97—Maryland	32	1033	160	337	.475	57	91	.626	171	78	412	5.3	2.4	12.9
97-98—Maryland	32	1008	184	412	.447	104	147	.707	165	104	506	5.2	3.3	15.8
98-99—Maryland	34	982	185	368	.503	100	148	.676	162	73	494	4.8	2.1	14.5
Totals	125	3389	583	1229	.474	295	431	.684	572	287	1566	4.6	2.3	12.5

Three-point field goals: 1995-96, 12-for-33 (.364). 1996-97, 35-for-99 (.354). 1997-98, 34-for-117 (.291). 1998-99, 24-for-77 (.312). Totals, 105-for-326 (.322).

NBA REGULAR-SEASON RECORD

Season Team	G	Min.	FGM	FGA	Pct.	FTM	FTA	Pct.	REBOUNDS Off.	Def.	Tot.	Ast.	St.	Blk.	TO	Pts.	AVERAGES RPG	APG	PPG
99-00—Washington	33	225	21	59	.356	4	10	.400	2	24	26	25	7	4	19	49	0.8	0.8	1.5
00-01—Washington	35	605	56	142	.394	33	45	.733	18	46	64	89	36	11	46	152	1.8	2.5	4.3
04-05—Washington	42	428	56	128	.438	16	25	.640	24	52	76	37	16	5	27	136	1.8	0.9	3.2
05-06—L.A. Lakers	25	279	40	84	.476	21	24	.875	8	35	43	15	11	5	24	104	1.7	0.6	4.2
Totals	135	1537	173	413	.419	74	104	.712	52	157	209	166	70	25	116	441	1.5	1.2	3.3

Three-point field goals: 1999-00, 3-for-17 (.176). 2000-01, 7-for-26 (.269). 2004-05, 8-for-28 (.286). 2005-06, 3-for-18 (.167). Totals, 21-for-89 (.236).
Personal fouls/disqualifications: 1999-00, 26/0. 2000-01, 43/0. 2004-05, 44/0. 2005-06, 25/0. Totals, 138/0.

NBA PLAYOFF RECORD

Season Team	G	Min.	FGM	FGA	Pct.	FTM	FTA	Pct.	REBOUNDS Off.	Def.	Tot.	Ast.	St.	Blk.	TO	Pts.	AVERAGES RPG	APG	PPG
04-05—Washington	3	5	0	2	.000	0	0	...	0	1	1	1	0	0	0	0	0.3	0.3	0.0

ITALIAN LEAGUE RECORD

Season Team	G	Min.	FGM	FGA	Pct.	FTM	FTA	Pct.	Reb.	Ast.	Pts.	AVERAGES RPG	APG	PPG
01-02—Premiata Montegranaro..	6	151	28	77	.364	17	21	.810	17	7	82	2.8	1.2	13.7

Three-point field goals: 2001-02, 9-for-25 (.360). Totals, 9-for-25 (.360).

PRZYBILLA, JOEL   C   TRAIL BLAZERS

PERSONAL: Born October 10, 1979, in Monticello, Minn. ... 7-1/255. (2.16/115.7). ... Full name: Joel Anthony Przybilla
HIGH SCHOOL: Monticello (Minn.).
COLLEGE: Minnesota.
TRANSACTIONS/CAREER NOTES: Selected after sophomore season by Houston Rockets in first round (ninth pick overall) of 2000 NBA Draft. ... Draft rights traded by Rockets to Milwaukee Bucks for draft rights to C Jason Collier and a future first-round draft choice (June 28, 2000). ... Traded by Bucks to Atlanta Hawks as part of three-team trade in which Bucks also traded F Tim Thomas to New York Knicks. Hawks also acquired C Michael Doleac and 2005 second-round draft choice from Knicks and traded C Nazr Mohammed to Knicks. Bucks acquired F Keith Van Horn from Knicks (February 15, 2004). ... Signed as free agent by Portland Trail Blazers (August 25, 2004).

COLLEGIATE RECORD

												AVERAGES		
Season Team	G	Min.	FGM	FGA	Pct.	FTM	FTA	Pct.	Reb.	Ast.	Pts.	RPG	APG	PPG
98-99—Minnesota	28	713	79	141	.560	30	52	.577	163	41	188	5.8	1.5	6.7
99-00—Minnesota	21	638	122	199	.613	55	111	.495	176	50	299	8.4	2.4	14.2
Totals	49	1351	201	340	.591	85	163	.521	339	91	487	6.9	1.9	9.9

NBA REGULAR-SEASON RECORD

									REBOUNDS								AVERAGES		
Season Team	G	Min.	FGM	FGA	Pct.	FTM	FTA	Pct.	Off.	Def.	Tot.	Ast.	St.	Blk.	TO	Pts.	RPG	APG	PPG
00-01—Milwaukee	33	270	12	35	.343	3	11	.273	29	42	71	2	3	30	13	27	2.2	0.1	0.8
01-02—Milwaukee	71	1128	76	142	.535	38	90	.422	78	205	283	21	20	118	43	190	4.0	0.3	2.7
02-03—Milwaukee	32	546	18	46	.391	12	24	.500	48	97	145	12	10	45	19	48	4.5	0.4	1.5
03-04—Mil.-Atlanta	17	347	18	50	.360	13	31	.419	32	79	111	7	5	17	18	49	6.5	0.4	2.9
04-05—Portland	76	1858	199	333	.598	90	174	.517	178	410	588	74	24	163	98	488	7.7	1.0	6.4
05-06—Portland	56	1395	131	239	.548	82	154	.532	146	245	391	43	20	130	76	344	7.0	0.8	6.1
Totals	285	5544	454	845	.537	238	484	.492	511	1078	1589	159	82	503	267	1146	5.6	0.6	4.0

Three-point field goals: 2001-02, 0-for-1. Totals, 0-for-1 (.000).
Personal fouls/disqualifications: 2000-01, 56/0. 2001-02, 199/3. 2002-03, 85/1. 2003-04, 53/1. 2004-05, 239/1. 2005-06, 149/1. Totals, 781/7.

NBA PLAYOFF RECORD

									REBOUNDS								AVERAGES		
Season Team	G	Min.	FGM	FGA	Pct.	FTM	FTA	Pct.	Off.	Def.	Tot.	Ast.	St.	Blk.	TO	Pts.	RPG	APG	PPG
00-01—Milwaukee	1	2	0	0	...	0	0	...	0	0	0	0	0	0	0	0	0.0	0.0	0.0
02-03—Milwaukee	4	33	1	1	1.000	0	0	...	2	8	10	1	0	2	1	2	2.5	0.3	0.5
Totals	5	35	1	1	1.000	0	0	...	2	8	10	1	0	2	1	2	2.0	0.2	0.4

Personal fouls/disqualifications: 2002-03, 11/0. Totals, 11/0.

RADMANOVIC, VLADIMIR   F   LAKERS

PERSONAL: Born November 19, 1980, in Trebinje, Yugoslavia. ... 6-9/206. (2.06/93.4).
COLLEGE: Did not attend college.
TRANSACTIONS/CAREER NOTES: Played in Yugoslavia (1998-2001). ... Selected by Seattle SuperSonics in first round (12th pick overall) of 2001 NBA Draft. ... Traded by SuperSonics to Los Angeles Clippers for C Chris Wilcox (February 14, 2006). ... Signed as free agent by Los Angeles Lakers (July 13, 2006).
MISCELLANEOUS: Member of Serbia-Montenegro Olympic Team (2004).

YUGOSLAVIAN LEAGUE RECORD

												AVERAGES		
Season Team	G	Min.	FGM	FGA	Pct.	FTM	FTA	Pct.	Reb.	Ast.	Pts.	RPG	APG	PPG
98-99—Crvena Zveda Belgrade	10	150	23	35	.657	6	8	.750	28	8	59	2.8	0.8	5.9
99-00—Crvena Zveda Belgrade	21	539	54	113	.478	33	45	.733	115	31	152	5.5	1.5	7.2
00-01—FMP Zeleznik	19	623	119	216	.551	56	71	.789	139	51	327	7.3	2.7	17.2
Totals	50	1312	196	364	.538	95	124	.766	282	90	538	5.6	1.8	10.8

Three-point field goals: 1998-99, 7-for-10 (.700). 1999-00, 11-for-44 (.250). 2000-01, 33-for-85 (.388). Totals, 51-for-139 (.367).

NBA REGULAR-SEASON RECORD

HONORS: NBA All-Rookie second team (2002).

									REBOUNDS								AVERAGES		
Season Team	G	Min.	FGM	FGA	Pct.	FTM	FTA	Pct.	Off.	Def.	Tot.	Ast.	St.	Blk.	TO	Pts.	RPG	APG	PPG
01-02—Seattle	61	1230	146	354	.412	49	72	.681	45	185	230	81	56	24	72	407	3.8	1.3	6.7
02-03—Seattle	72	1910	274	668	.410	72	102	.706	76	247	323	97	64	22	100	724	4.5	1.3	10.1
03-04—Seattle	77	2321	345	812	.425	95	127	.748	104	302	406	142	80	42	109	925	5.3	1.8	12.0
04-05—Seattle	63	1856	266	650	.409	81	103	.786	52	237	289	86	57	31	80	741	4.6	1.4	11.8
05-06—Seattle-L.A.C.	77	1974	262	643	.407	93	114	.816	64	294	358	136	61	29	93	755	4.6	1.8	9.8
Totals	350	9291	1293	3127	.413	390	518	.753	341	1265	1606	542	318	148	454	3552	4.6	1.5	10.1

Three-point field goals: 2001-02, 66-for-157 (.420). 2002-03, 104-for-293 (.355). 2003-04, 140-for-377 (.371). 2004-05, 128-for-329 (.389). 2005-06, 138-for-354 (.390). Totals, 576-for-1510 (.381).
Personal fouls/disqualifications: 2001-02, 119/0. 2002-03, 136/0. 2003-04, 187/1. 2004-05, 172/2. 2005-06, 210/3. Totals, 824/6.

NBA PLAYOFF RECORD

									REBOUNDS								AVERAGES		
Season Team	G	Min.	FGM	FGA	Pct.	FTM	FTA	Pct.	Off.	Def.	Tot.	Ast.	St.	Blk.	TO	Pts.	RPG	APG	PPG
01-02—Seattle	5	113	14	32	.438	3	3	1.000	6	12	18	5	1	1	5	38	3.6	1.0	7.6
04-05—Seattle	6	122	13	35	.371	1	2	.500	1	17	18	3	4	3	6	32	3.0	0.5	5.3
05-06—L.A. Clippers	12	246	31	66	.470	16	23	.696	9	39	48	13	7	6	8	97	4.0	1.1	8.1
Totals	23	481	58	133	.436	20	28	.714	16	68	84	21	12	10	19	167	3.7	0.9	7.3

Three-point field goals: 2001-02, 7-for-13 (.538). 2004-05, 5-for-21 (.238). 2005-06, 19-for-41 (.463). Totals, 31-for-75 (.413).
Personal fouls/disqualifications: 2001-02, 11/0. 2004-05, 9/0. 2005-06, 35/0. Totals, 55/0.

RAMOS, PETER JOHN   C   WIZARDS

PERSONAL: Born May 23, 1985, in Fajardo, Puerto Rico. ... 7-3/275. (2.21/124.7).
TRANSACTIONS/CAREER NOTES: Played in Puerto Rico (2000-04). ... Selected by Washington Wizards in second round (32nd pick overall) of 2004 NBA Draft. ... Played in NBA Development League (2005-06).
MISCELLANEOUS: Member of Puerto Rican Olympic team (2004).

PUERTO RICAN RECORD

Season Team	G	Min.	FGM	FGA	Pct.	FTM	FTA	Pct.	Reb.	Ast.	Pts.	RPG	APG	PPG
00-01—Criollos de Caguas	5	40	3	13	.231	0	2	.000	9	2	6	1.8	0.4	1.2
01-02—Criollos de Caguas	23	249	26	64	.406	4	10	.400	59	8	56	2.6	0.3	2.4
02-03—Criollos de Caguas	30	924	164	309	.531	40	67	.597	257	29	368	8.6	1.0	12.3
03-04—Criollos de Caguas	24	978	218	424	.514	62	108	.574	229	75	498	9.5	3.1	20.8
Totals	82	2191	411	810	.507	106	187	.567	554	114	928	6.8	1.4	11.3

NBA REGULAR-SEASON RECORD

Season Team	G	Min.	FGM	FGA	Pct.	FTM	FTA	Pct.	Off.	Def.	Tot.	Ast.	St.	Blk.	TO	Pts.	RPG	APG	PPG
04-05—Washington	6	20	5	10	.500	1	2	.500	1	3	4	0	0	1	3	11	0.7	0.0	1.8

Personal fouls/disqualifications: 2004-05, 4/0. Totals, 4/0.

NBA DEVELOPMENT LEAGUE RECORD

Season Team	G	Min.	FGM	FGA	Pct.	FTM	FTA	Pct.	Off.	Def.	Tot.	Ast.	St.	Blk.	TO	Pts.	RPG	APG	PPG
05-06—Roanoke	43	1322	266	452	.588	109	182	.599	...	...	333	42	...	...	...	641	7.7	1.0	14.9

Three-point field goals: 2005-06, 0-for-1

RANDOLPH, SHAVLIK — F — 76ERS

PERSONAL: Born November 24, 1983, in Raleigh, N.C. ... 6-10/240. (2.08/108.9). ... Full name: Ronald Shavlik Randolph
HIGH SCHOOL: Broughton (Raleigh, N.C.).
COLLEGE: Duke.
TRANSACTIONS/CAREER NOTES: Not drafted by an NBA franchise. ... Signed as free agent by Philadelphia 76ers (August 5, 2005).

COLLEGIATE RECORD

Season Team	G	Min.	FGM	FGA	Pct.	FTM	FTA	Pct.	Reb.	Ast.	Pts.	RPG	APG	PPG
02-03—Duke	26	351	65	129	.504	56	82	.683	101	9	193	3.9	0.3	7.4
03-04—Duke	37	709	94	159	.591	70	105	.667	168	20	260	4.5	0.5	7.0
04-05—Duke	29	548	46	117	.393	32	60	.533	125	27	127	4.3	0.9	4.4
Totals	92	1608	205	405	.506	158	247	.640	394	56	580	4.3	0.6	6.3

Three-point field goals: 2002-03, 7-for-19 (.368). 2003-04, 2-for-10 (.200). 2004-05, 3-for-13 (.231). Totals, 12-for-42 (.286).

NBA REGULAR-SEASON RECORD

Season Team	G	Min.	FGM	FGA	Pct.	FTM	FTA	Pct.	Off.	Def.	Tot.	Ast.	St.	Blk.	TO	Pts.	RPG	APG	PPG
05-06—Philadelphia	57	487	44	97	.454	43	71	.606	55	78	133	19	19	12	21	131	2.3	0.3	2.3

Personal fouls/disqualifications: 2005-06, 83/0. Totals, 83/0.

RANDOLPH, ZACH — F — TRAIL BLAZERS

PERSONAL: Born July 16, 1981, in Marion, Ind. ... 6-9/270. (2.06/122.5).
HIGH SCHOOL: Marion (Ind.).
COLLEGE: Michigan State.
TRANSACTIONS/CAREER NOTES: Selected after freshman season by Portland Trail Blazers in first round (19th pick overall) of 2001 NBA Draft.

COLLEGIATE RECORD

Season Team	G	Min.	FGM	FGA	Pct.	FTM	FTA	Pct.	Reb.	Ast.	Pts.	RPG	APG	PPG
00-01—Michigan State	33	654	138	235	.587	80	126	.635	221	34	356	6.7	1.0	10.8

Three-point field goals: 2000-01, 0-for-1. Totals, 0-for-1 (.000).
Personal fouls/disqualifications: 2000-01, 60/0. Totals, 60/0.

NBA REGULAR-SEASON RECORD

HONORS: NBA Most Improved Player (2004).

Season Team	G	Min.	FGM	FGA	Pct.	FTM	FTA	Pct.	Off.	Def.	Tot.	Ast.	St.	Blk.	TO	Pts.	RPG	APG	PPG
01-02—Portland	41	238	48	107	.449	18	27	.667	31	38	69	13	7	4	15	114	1.7	0.3	2.8
02-03—Portland	77	1301	264	515	.513	122	161	.758	139	204	343	41	42	14	62	650	4.5	0.5	8.4
03-04—Portland	81	3067	663	1368	.485	299	393	.761	242	609	851	163	68	41	247	1626	10.5	2.0	20.1
04-05—Portland	46	1603	332	741	.448	207	254	.815	142	300	442	86	34	17	112	871	9.6	1.9	18.9
05-06—Portland	74	2545	536	1229	.436	245	343	.714	193	399	592	144	57	14	165	1333	8.0	1.9	18.0
Totals	319	8754	1843	3960	.465	891	1178	.756	747	1550	2297	447	208	90	601	4594	7.2	1.4	14.4

Three-point field goals: 2002-03, 0-for-5. 2003-04, 1-for-5 (.200). 2004-05, 0-for-6. 2005-06, 16-for-55 (.291). Totals, 17-for-71 (.239).
Personal fouls/disqualifications: 2001-02, 29/0. 2002-03, 141/0. 2003-04, 227/0. 2004-05, 112/3. 2005-06, 185/1. Totals, 694/4.

NBA PLAYOFF RECORD

Season Team	G	Min.	FGM	FGA	Pct.	FTM	FTA	Pct.	Off.	Def.	Tot.	Ast.	St.	Blk.	TO	Pts.	RPG	APG	PPG
01-02—Portland	1	1	0	0	...	0	0	...	0	0	0	0	0	0	0	0	0.0	0.0	0.0
02-03—Portland	7	205	32	61	.525	33	37	.892	22	39	61	11	3	2	13	97	8.7	1.6	13.9
Totals	8	206	32	61	.525	33	37	.892	22	39	61	11	3	2	13	97	7.6	1.4	12.1

Personal fouls/disqualifications: 2002-03, 17/0. Totals, 17/0.

RATLIFF, THEO   F/C   CELTICS

PERSONAL: Born April 17, 1973, in Demopolis, Ala. ... 6-10/230. (2.08/104.3). ... Full name: Theo Curtis Ratliff
HIGH SCHOOL: Demopolis (Ala.).
COLLEGE: Wyoming.
TRANSACTIONS/CAREER NOTES: Selected by Detroit Pistons in first round (18th pick overall) of 1995 NBA Draft. ... Traded by Pistons with G Aaron McKie and conditional first-round draft choice to Philadelphia 76ers for G Jerry Stackhouse and C Eric Montross (December 18, 1997). ... Traded by 76ers with F/G Toni Kukoc, C Nazr Mohammed and G Pepe Sanchez to Atlanta Hawks for C Dikembe Mutombo and F Roshown McLeod (February 22, 2001). ... Traded by Hawks with F Shareef Abdur-Rahim and G Dan Dickau to Portland Trail Blazers for F Rasheed Wallace and G Wesley Person (February 9, 2004). ... Traded by Trail Blazers with G Sebastian Telfair and a 2008 second-round draft pick to Boston Celtics for G Dan Dickau, F/C Raef LaFrentz and a first-round pick (G Randy Foye) in 2006 draft (June 28, 2006).

COLLEGIATE RECORD
NOTES: Led NCAA Division I with 4.4 blocked shots per game (1993).

Season Team	G	Min.	FGM	FGA	Pct.	FTM	FTA	Pct.	Reb.	Ast.	Pts.	RPG	APG	PPG
												AVERAGES		
91-92—Wyoming	27	298	14	32	.438	21	36	.583	54	8	49	2.0	0.3	1.8
92-93—Wyoming	28	824	99	184	.538	60	116	.517	173	8	258	6.2	0.3	9.2
93-94—Wyoming	28	892	160	281	.569	111	171	.649	217	27	431	7.8	1.0	15.4
94-95—Wyoming	28	912	148	272	.544	107	169	.633	211	31	404	7.5	1.1	14.4
Totals	111	2926	421	769	.547	299	492	.608	655	74	1142	5.9	0.7	10.3

Three-point field goals: 1992-93, 0-for-1. 1993-94, 0-for-1. 1994-95, 1-for-5 (.200). Totals, 1-for-7 (.143).

NBA REGULAR-SEASON RECORD
HONORS: NBA All-Defensive second team (1999, 2004).
NOTES: Led NBA with 3.74 blocks per game (2001) and 3.23 blocks per game (2003).

Season Team	G	Min.	FGM	FGA	Pct.	FTM	FTA	Pct.	Off.	Def.	Tot.	Ast.	St.	Blk.	TO	Pts.	RPG	APG	PPG
									REBOUNDS								AVERAGES		
95-96—Detroit	75	1305	128	230	.557	85	120	.708	110	187	297	13	16	116	56	341	4.0	0.2	4.5
96-97—Detroit	76	1292	179	337	.531	81	116	.698	109	147	256	13	29	111	56	439	3.4	0.2	5.8
97-98—Det.-Phila.	82	2447	306	597	.513	197	281	.701	221	326	547	57	50	258	116	809	6.7	0.7	9.9
98-99—Philadelphia	50	1627	197	419	.470	166	229	.725	139	268	407	30	45	149	92	560	8.1	0.6	11.2
99-00—Philadelphia	57	1795	247	491	.503	182	236	.771	140	295	435	36	32	171	108	676	7.6	0.6	11.9
00-01—Phila.-Atlanta	50	1800	228	457	.499	165	217	.760	125	288	413	58	30	187	126	621	8.3	1.2	12.4
01-02—Atlanta	3	82	10	20	.500	6	11	.545	5	11	16	1	1	8	7	26	5.3	0.3	8.7
02-03—Atlanta	81	2518	276	595	.464	154	214	.720	154	453	607	73	56	*262	137	706	7.5	0.9	8.7
03-04—Atlanta-Port.	85	2664	266	549	.485	140	217	.645	195	419	614	71	54	*307	120	672	7.2	0.0	7.9
04-05—Portland	63	1731	115	257	.447	74	107	.692	111	220	331	34	23	158	56	304	5.3	0.5	4.8
05-06—Portland	55	1301	108	189	.571	54	83	.651	89	190	279	28	18	88	47	270	5.1	0.5	4.9
Totals	677	18562	2060	4141	.497	1304	1831	.712	1398	2804	4202	414	354	1815	921	5424	6.2	0.6	8.0

Three-point field goals: 1995-96, 0-for-1. Totals, 0-for-1 (.000).
Personal fouls/disqualifications: 1995-96, 144/1. 1996-97, 181/2. 1997-98, 292/8. 1998-99, 180/8. 1999-00, 185/4. 2000-01, 165/3. 2001-02, 8/0. 2002-03, 271/3. 2003-04, 300/3. 2004-05, 183/4. 2005-06, 143/1. Totals, 2052/37.

NBA PLAYOFF RECORD

Season Team	G	Min.	FGM	FGA	Pct.	FTM	FTA	Pct.	Off.	Def.	Tot.	Ast.	St.	Blk.	TO	Pts.	RPG	APG	PPG
									REBOUNDS								AVERAGES		
95-96—Detroit	1	4	0	0	...	0	0	...	0	0	0	0	0	0	0	0	0.0	0.0	0.0
96-97—Detroit	3	18	3	4	.750	2	4	.500	2	2	4	1	1	4	3	8	1.3	0.3	2.7
98-99—Philadelphia	7	204	20	43	.465	11	19	.579	23	28	51	6	5	18	7	51	7.3	0.9	7.3
99-00—Philadelphia	10	374	48	101	.475	34	47	.723	28	51	79	9	10	30	17	130	7.9	0.9	13.0
Totals	21	600	71	148	.480	47	70	.671	53	81	134	16	16	52	27	189	6.4	0.8	9.0

Personal fouls/disqualifications: 1996-97, 5/0. 1998-99, 19/0. 1999-00, 35/1. Totals, 59/1.

NBA ALL-STAR GAME RECORD

Season Team	Min.	FGM	FGA	Pct.	FTM	FTA	Pct.	Off.	Def.	Tot.	Ast.	PF	Dq.	St.	Blk.	TO	Pts.
								REBOUNDS									
2001—Philadelphia								Selected, did not play—injured									

REBRACA, ZELJKO   F   CLIPPERS

PERSONAL: Born April 9, 1972, in Prigrevica, Yugoslavia. ... 6-11/240. (2.11/108.9). ... Name pronounced Reh-bhra-tcha.
TRANSACTIONS/CAREER NOTES: Played in Yugoslavia (1993-95). ... Selected by Seattle SuperSonics in second round (54th pick overall) of 1994 NBA Draft. ... Draft rights traded by SuperSonics to Minnesota Timberwolves for 1996 second-round draft choice (June 30, 1994). ... Played in Italy (1995-99). ... Played in Greece (1999-2001). ... Traded by Timberwolves with G Micheal Williams and 1999 or 2000 first-round draft choice to Toronto Raptors in three-way deal in which Raptors also received 1999 first-round draft choice from Denver Nuggets, Timberwolves received C Dean Garrett and G Bobby Jackson from Nuggets and Nuggets received G Chauncey Billups and draft rights to G Tyson Wheeler from Raptors (January 21, 1999). ... Traded by Raptors to Detroit Pistons for 2002 second-round draft choice (July 18, 2001). ... Traded by Pistons to Atlanta Hawks as part of three-team deal in which Hawks also received G Bob Sura and a future first-round draft choice from Pistons and F Chris Mills from Boston Celtics. Pistons received F/C Rasheed Wallace from Hawks and G Mike James from Celtics. Celtics received G Chucky Atkins, G Lindsey Hunter and a 2004 first-round draft choice from Pistons (February 19, 2004). ... Signed as free agent by Los Angeles Clippers (August 12, 2004).
MISCELLANEOUS: Member of silver-medal winning Yugoslavian Olympic team (1996). ... Member of Yugoslavian Olympic team (2000).

YUGOSLAVIAN LEAGUE RECORD

Season Team	G	Min.	FGM	FGA	Pct.	FTM	FTA	Pct.	Reb.	Ast.	Pts.	RPG	APG	PPG
												AVERAGES		
93-94—Belgrade Partizan	20	...	114	251	.454	60	82	.732	131	8	288	6.6	0.4	14.4
94-95—Belgrade Partizan	20	...	...	...	...	...	...	...	136	...	518	6.8	...	25.9
Totals	40	...	114	251	.454	60	82	.732	267	8	806	6.7	0.2	20.2

Three-point field goals: 1993-94, 0-for-1. Totals, 0-for-1 (.000).

ITALIAN LEAGUE RECORD

Season Team	G	Min.	FGM	FGA	Pct.	FTM	FTA	Pct.	Reb.	Ast.	Pts.	RPG	APG	PPG
95-96—Benetton	40	1149	241	362	.666	106	137	.774	262	15	588	6.6	0.4	14.7
96-97—Benetton	38	1057	202	335	.603	120	156	.769	255	17	526	6.7	0.4	13.8
97-98—Benetton	30	931	201	320	.628	107	136	.787	217	23	509	7.2	0.8	17.0
98-99—Benetton	34	880	145	237	.612	116	147	.789	184	26	406	5.4	0.8	11.9
Totals	142	4017	789	1254	.629	449	576	.780	918	81	2029	6.5	0.6	14.3

Three-point field goals: 1995-96, 0-for-1. 1996-97, 2-for-3 (.667). 1997-98, 0-for-1. Totals, 2-for-5 (.400).

GREEK LEAGUE RECORD

Season Team	G	Min.	FGM	FGA	Pct.	FTM	FTA	Pct.	Reb.	Ast.	Pts.	RPG	APG	PPG
99-00—Panathinaikos	24	666	116	191	.607	54	74	.730	156	20	287	6.5	0.8	12.0
00-01—Panathinaikos	21	414	79	121	.653	47	63	.746	148	19	205	7.0	0.9	9.8
Totals	45	1080	195	312	.625	101	137	.737	304	39	492	6.8	0.9	10.9

Three-point field goals: 1999-00, 1-for-1 (1.000). Totals, 1-for-1 (1.000).

NBA REGULAR-SEASON RECORD

HONORS: NBA All-Rookie second team (2002).

Season Team	G	Min.	FGM	FGA	Pct.	FTM	FTA	Pct.	Off.	Def.	Tot.	Ast.	St.	Blk.	TO	Pts.	RPG	APG	PPG
01-02—Detroit	74	1179	189	374	.505	135	175	.771	84	206	290	38	28	73	84	513	3.9	0.5	6.9
02-03—Detroit	30	488	80	145	.552	38	48	.792	27	65	92	9	6	17	29	198	3.1	0.3	6.6
03-04—Detroit-Atlanta	24	273	34	77	.442	23	30	.767	23	35	58	6	5	11	17	91	2.4	0.3	3.8
04-05—L.A. Clippers	58	928	133	234	.568	73	85	.859	49	135	184	26	13	40	49	339	3.2	0.4	5.8
05-06—L.A. Clippers	29	412	52	96	.542	31	41	.756	13	51	64	9	5	19	24	135	2.2	0.3	4.7
Totals	215	3280	488	926	.527	300	379	.792	196	492	688	88	57	160	203	1276	3.2	0.4	5.9

Personal fouls/disqualifications: 2001-02, 192/0. 2002-03, 79/1. 2003-04, 52/1. 2004-05, 130/3. 2005-06, 59/0. Totals, 512/5.

NBA PLAYOFF RECORD

Season Team	G	Min.	FGM	FGA	Pct.	FTM	FTA	Pct.	Off.	Def.	Tot.	Ast.	St.	Blk.	TO	Pts.	RPG	APG	PPG
01-02—Detroit	5	69	5	11	.455	11	14	.786	4	6	10	0	1	1	4	21	2.0	0.0	4.2
02-03—Detroit	4	29	6	17	.353	5	7	.714	2	3	5	0	0	0	1	17	1.3	0.0	4.3
05-06—L.A. Clippers	3	22	1	3	.333	0	0	...	1	3	4	0	0	1	2	2	1.3	0.0	0.7
Totals	12	120	12	31	.387	16	21	.762	7	12	19	0	1	2	7	40	1.6	0.0	3.3

Personal fouls/disqualifications: 2001-02, 14/0. 2002-03, 9/1. 2005-06, 6/0. Totals, 29/1.

REDD, MICHAEL   G   BUCKS

PERSONAL: Born August 24, 1979, in Columbus, Ohio. ... 6-6/214. (1.98/97.1). ... Full name: Michael Wesley Redd
HIGH SCHOOL: West (Columbus).
COLLEGE: Ohio State.
TRANSACTIONS/CAREER NOTES: Selected after junior season by Milwaukee Bucks in second round (43rd pick overall) of 2000 NBA Draft.

COLLEGIATE RECORD

Season Team	G	Min.	FGM	FGA	Pct.	FTM	FTA	Pct.	Reb.	Ast.	Pts.	RPG	APG	PPG
97-98—Ohio State	30	1137	241	550	.438	130	211	.616	194	91	658	6.5	3.0	21.9
98-99—Ohio State	36	1183	261	560	.466	135	220	.614	203	85	703	5.6	2.4	19.5
99-00—Ohio State	30	1004	197	452	.436	90	116	.776	196	62	518	6.5	2.1	17.3
Totals	96	3324	699	1562	.448	355	547	.649	593	238	1879	6.2	2.5	19.6

Three-point field goals: 1997-98, 46-for-152 (.303). 1998-99, 46-for-135 (.341). 1999-00, 31-for-99 (.313). Totals, 123-for-386 (.319).

NBA REGULAR-SEASON RECORD

RECORDS: Holds single-game record for most three-point field goals made in one quarter—8 (February 20, 2002, vs. Houston). ... Shares single-game record for most three-point field goals made in one half—8 (February 20, 2002, vs. Houston).
HONORS: All-NBA third team (2004).

Season Team	G	Min.	FGM	FGA	Pct.	FTM	FTA	Pct.	Off.	Def.	Tot.	Ast.	St.	Blk.	TO	Pts.	RPG	APG	PPG
00-01—Milwaukee	6	35	5	19	.263	3	6	.500	3	1	4	1	1	0	1	13	0.7	0.2	2.2
01-02—Milwaukee	67	1417	294	609	.483	91	115	.791	77	147	224	91	42	7	57	767	3.3	1.4	11.4
02-03—Milwaukee	82	2316	455	971	.469	149	185	.805	98	273	371	117	100	13	74	1241	4.5	1.4	15.1
03-04—Milwaukee	82	3021	633	1439	.440	383	441	.868	118	289	407	185	81	6	116	1776	5.0	2.3	21.7
04-05—Milwaukee	75	2848	625	1418	.441	369	432	.854	72	240	312	172	63	8	133	1723	4.2	2.3	23.0
05-06—Milwaukee	80	3130	682	1516	.450	501	571	.877	78	264	342	229	95	5	170	2028	4.3	2.9	25.4
Totals	392	12767	2694	5972	.451	1496	1750	.855	446	1214	1660	795	382	39	551	7548	4.2	2.0	19.3

Three-point field goals: 2000-01, 0-for-3. 2001-02, 88-for-198 (.444). 2002-03, 182-for-416 (.438). 2003-04, 127-for-363 (.350). 2004-05, 104-for-293 (.355). 2005-06, 163-for-413 (.395). Totals, 664-for-1686 (.394).

Personal fouls/disqualifications: 2000-01, 2/0. 2001-02, 96/0. 2002-03, 143/0. 2003-04, 152/0. 2004-05, 152/0. 2005-06, 157/1. Totals, 702/1.

NBA PLAYOFF RECORD

Season Team	G	Min.	FGM	FGA	Pct.	FTM	FTA	Pct.	Off.	Def.	Tot.	Ast.	St.	Blk.	TO	Pts.	RPG	APG	PPG
02-03—Milwaukee	6	128	21	52	.404	13	14	.929	9	12	21	11	2	1	7	58	3.5	1.8	9.7
03-04—Milwaukee	5	192	34	83	.410	16	21	.762	6	19	25	13	0	0	19	90	5.0	2.6	18.0
05-06—Milwaukee	5	185	44	84	.524	41	46	.891	16	11	27	8	4	0	10	136	5.4	1.6	27.2
Totals	16	505	99	219	.452	70	81	.864	31	42	73	32	6	1	36	284	4.6	2.0	17.8

Three-point field goals: 2002-03, 3-for-12 (.250). 2003-04, 6-for-20 (.300). 2005-06, 7-for-15 (.467). Totals, 16-for-47 (.340).
Personal fouls/disqualifications: 2002-03, 15/0. 2003-04, 16/0. 2005-06, 11/0. Totals, 42/0.

NBA ALL-STAR GAME RECORD

Season Team	Min.	FGM	FGA	Pct.	FTM	FTA	Pct.	REBOUNDS Off.	Def.	Tot.	Ast.	PF	Dq.	St.	Blk.	TO	Pts.
2004—Milwaukee	15	5	12	.417	0	0	...	2	1	3	2	0	0	3	0	1	13

Three-point field goals: 2004, 3-for-6 (.500). Totals, 3-for-6 (.500).

REED, JUSTIN   F   TIMBERWOLVES

PERSONAL: Born January 16, 1982, in Jackson, Miss. ... 6-8/240. (2.03/108.9). ... Full name: Justin Michael Reed
HIGH SCHOOL: Provine (Jackson, Miss.).
COLLEGE: Mississippi.
TRANSACTIONS/CAREER NOTES: Selected by Boston Celtics in second round (40th pick overall) of 2004 NBA Draft. ... Traded by Celtics with G Ricky Davis, C Mark Blount, G Marcus Banks and two second-round draft choices to Minnesota Timberwolves for F Wally Sczcerbiak, C Michael Olowokandi, F/C Dwayne Jones and a future first-round draft choice (January 26, 2006).

COLLEGIATE RECORD

Season Team	G	Min.	FGM	FGA	Pct.	FTM	FTA	Pct.	Reb.	Ast.	Pts.	AVERAGES RPG	APG	PPG
00-01—Mississippi	35	862	160	335	.478	62	113	.549	205	27	385	5.9	0.8	11.0
01-02—Mississippi	31	870	167	348	.480	111	141	.787	205	34	453	6.6	1.1	14.6
02-03—Mississippi	28	825	159	326	.488	92	126	.730	147	30	430	5.3	1.1	15.4
03-04—Mississippi	28	939	193	416	.464	117	160	.731	209	41	517	7.5	1.5	18.5
Totals	122	3496	679	1425	.476	382	540	.707	766	132	1785	6.3	1.1	14.6

Three-point field goals: 2000-01, 3-for-23 (.130). 2001-02, 8-for-29 (.276). 2002-03, 20-for-47 (.426). 2003-04, 14-for-59 (.237). Totals, 45-for-158 (.285).

NBA REGULAR-SEASON RECORD

Season Team	G	Min.	FGM	FGA	Pct.	FTM	FTA	Pct.	REBOUNDS Off.	Def.	Tot.	Ast.	St.	Blk.	TO	Pts.	AVERAGES RPG	APG	PPG
04-05—Boston	23	121	15	29	.517	11	15	.733	8	8	16	10	3	1	5	41	0.7	0.4	1.8
05-06—Boston-Minn...	72	997	119	295	.403	87	120	.725	53	71	124	41	23	15	52	325	1.7	0.6	4.5
Totals	95	1118	134	324	.414	98	135	.726	61	79	140	51	26	16	57	366	1.5	0.5	3.9

Three-point field goals: 2004-05, 0-for-3. 2005-06, 0-for-1. Totals, 0-for-4 (.000).
Personal fouls/disqualifications: 2004-05, 12/0. 2005-06, 163/1. Totals, 175/1.

NBA PLAYOFF RECORD

Season Team	G	Min.	FGM	FGA	Pct.	FTM	FTA	Pct.	REBOUNDS Off.	Def.	Tot.	Ast.	St.	Blk.	TO	Pts.	AVERAGES RPG	APG	PPG
04-05—Boston	6	22	2	6	.333	3	4	.750	0	1	1	0	0	0	2	7	0.2	0.0	1.2

Three-point field goals: 2004-05, 0-for-1 (.000).
Personal fouls/disqualifications: 2004-05, 2/0. Totals, 2/0.

RICHARDSON, JASON   G   WARRIORS

PERSONAL: Born January 20, 1981, in Saginaw, Mich. ... 6-6/220. (1.98/99.8). ... Full name: Jason Anthony Richardson
HIGH SCHOOL: Arthur Hill (Saginaw, Mich.).
COLLEGE: Michigan State.
TRANSACTIONS/CAREER NOTES: Selected after sophomore season by Golden State Warriors in first round (fifth pick overall) of 2001 NBA Draft.

COLLEGIATE RECORD

NOTES: The SPORTING NEWS All-America second team (2001). ... Member of NCAA Division I championship team (2000).

Season Team	G	Min.	FGM	FGA	Pct.	FTM	FTA	Pct.	Reb.	Ast.	Pts.	AVERAGES RPG	APG	PPG
99-00—Michigan State	37	582	79	157	.503	23	42	.548	153	23	189	4.1	0.6	5.1
00-01—Michigan State	33	940	182	362	.503	73	106	.689	195	73	486	5.9	2.2	14.7
Totals	70	1522	261	519	.503	96	148	.649	348	96	675	5.0	1.4	9.6

Three-point field goals: 1999-00, 8-for-27 (.296). 2000-01, 49-for-122 (.402). Totals, 57-for-149 (.383).
Personal fouls/disqualifications: 1999-00, 56/0. 2000-01, 74/0. Totals, 130/0.

NBA REGULAR-SEASON RECORD

HONORS: Slam Dunk championship winner (2002, 2003). ... NBA All-Rookie first team (2002). ... MVP of Rookie Challenge (2002).

Season Team	G	Min.	FGM	FGA	Pct.	FTM	FTA	Pct.	REBOUNDS Off.	Def.	Tot.	Ast.	St.	Blk.	TO	Pts.	AVERAGES RPG	APG	PPG
01-02—Golden State	80	2629	454	1090	.417	141	210	.671	124	216	340	236	106	31	160	1151	4.3	3.0	14.4
02-03—Golden State	82	2698	476	1161	.410	207	271	.764	111	267	378	247	90	23	179	1282	4.6	3.0	15.6
03-04—Golden State	78	2936	563	1284	.438	258	377	.684	124	400	524	226	86	41	196	1461	6.7	2.9	18.7
04-05—Golden State	72	2724	610	1368	.446	214	309	.693	125	299	424	281	105	32	169	1559	5.9	3.9	21.7
05-06—Golden State	75	2877	641	1438	.446	276	410	.673	105	333	438	232	97	37	167	1741	5.8	3.1	23.2
Totals	387	13864	2744	6341	.433	1096	1577	.695	589	1515	2104	1222	484	164	871	7194	5.4	3.2	18.6

Three-point field goals: 2001-02, 82-for-246 (.333). 2002-03, 123-for-334 (.368). 2003-04, 77-for-273 (.282). 2004-05, 125-for-370 (.338). 2005-06, 183-for-477 (.384). Totals, 590-for-1700 (.347).
Personal fouls/disqualifications: 2001-02, 195/2. 2002-03, 201/1. 2003-04, 182/1. 2004-05, 156/0. 2005-06, 206/1. Totals, 940/5.

RICHARDSON, QUENTIN   G   KNICKS

PERSONAL: Born April 13, 1980, in Chicago. ... 6-6/236. (1.98/107.0). ... Full name: Quentin L. Richardson
HIGH SCHOOL: Whitney Young (Chicago).
COLLEGE: DePaul.
TRANSACTIONS/CAREER NOTES: Selected after sophomore season by Los Angeles Clippers in first round (18th pick overall) of 2000 NBA Draft. ... Signed as free agent by Phoenix Suns (July 29, 2004). ... Traded by Suns with draft rights to F Nate Robinson and future considerations to New York Knicks for F Kurt Thomas and draft rights to F Dijon Thompson (June 28, 2005).

COLLEGIATE RECORD

NOTES: The SPORTING NEWS Freshman of the Year (1999).

| | | | | | | | | | | | | AVERAGES | | |
Season Team	G	Min.	FGM	FGA	Pct.	FTM	FTA	Pct.	Reb.	Ast.	Pts.	RPG	APG	PPG
98-99—DePaul	31	1040	203	425	.478	136	183	.743	327	32	586	10.5	1.0	18.9
99-00—DePaul	33	1150	202	468	.432	84	119	.706	325	72	561	9.8	2.2	17.0
Totals	64	2190	405	893	.454	220	302	.728	652	104	1147	10.2	1.6	17.9

Three-point field goals: 1998-99, 44-for-127 (.346). 1999-00, 73-for-190 (.384). Totals, 117-for-317 (.369).

NBA REGULAR-SEASON RECORD

NOTES: Shared the NBA lead for three-point field goals made with 226 (2004).

| | | | | | | | | | REBOUNDS | | | | | | | | AVERAGES | | |
Season Team	G	Min.	FGM	FGA	Pct.	FTM	FTA	Pct.	Off.	Def.	Tot.	Ast.	St.	Blk.	TO	Pts.	RPG	APG	PPG
00-01—L.A. Clippers	76	1358	232	525	.442	99	158	.627	105	152	257	62	42	7	64	613	3.4	0.8	8.1
01-02—L.A. Clippers	81	2152	400	926	.432	143	187	.765	113	221	334	128	78	21	102	1076	4.1	1.6	13.3
02-03—L.A. Clippers	59	1368	203	546	.372	85	124	.685	98	183	281	52	35	10	64	552	4.8	0.9	9.4
03-04—L.A. Clippers	65	2338	425	1068	.398	151	204	.740	146	268	414	139	67	19	141	1121	6.4	2.1	17.2
04-05—Phoenix	79	2839	407	1045	.389	136	184	.739	91	388	479	158	96	27	102	1176	6.1	2.0	14.9
05-06—New York	55	1442	163	459	.355	61	91	.670	65	165	230	88	39	6	56	451	4.2	1.6	8.2
Totals	415	11497	1830	4569	.401	675	948	.712	618	1377	1995	627	357	90	529	4989	4.8	1.5	12.0

Three-point field goals: 2000-01, 50-for-151 (.331). 2001-02, 133-for-349 (.381). 2002-03, 61-for-198 (.308). 2003-04, 120-for-341 (.352). 2004-05, 226-for-631 (.358). 2005-06, 64-for-188 (.340). Totals, 654-for-1858 (.352).

Personal fouls/disqualifications: 2000-01, 98/0. 2001-02, 142/2. 2002-03, 92/0. 2003-04, 130/0. 2004-05, 197/4. 2005-06, 134/0. Totals, 793/6.

NBA PLAYOFF RECORD

| | | | | | | | | | REBOUNDS | | | | | | | | AVERAGES | | |
Season Team	G	Min.	FGM	FGA	Pct.	FTM	FTA	Pct.	Off.	Def.	Tot.	Ast.	St.	Blk.	TO	Pts.	RPG	APG	PPG
04-05—Phoenix	15	564	62	154	.403	23	36	.639	24	53	77	25	19	3	15	179	5.1	1.7	11.9

Three-point field goals: 2004-05, 32-for-82 (.390). Totals, 32-for-82 (.390).
Personal fouls/disqualifications: 2004-05, 53/0. Totals, 53/0.

RIDNOUR, LUKE   G   SUPERSONICS

PERSONAL: Born February 13, 1981, in Coeur d' Alene, Idaho. ... 6-2/175. (1.88/79.4). ... Full name: Lukas Robin Ridnour
HIGH SCHOOL: Blaine (Blaine, Wash.).
COLLEGE: Oregon.
TRANSACTIONS/CAREER NOTES: Selected after junior season by Seattle SuperSonics in first round (14th pick overall) of 2003 NBA Draft.

COLLEGIATE RECORD

NOTES: The SPORTING NEWS All-America third team (2003).

| | | | | | | | | | | | | AVERAGES | | |
Season Team	G	Min.	FGM	FGA	Pct.	FTM	FTA	Pct.	Reb.	Ast.	Pts.	RPG	APG	PPG
00-01—Oregon	28	848	59	174	.339	61	77	.792	70	106	208	2.5	3.8	7.4
01-02—Oregon	35	1209	169	361	.468	111	128	.867	103	176	542	2.9	5.0	15.5
02-03—Oregon	33	1169	203	470	.432	162	184	.880	112	218	649	3.4	6.6	19.7
Totals	96	3226	431	1005	.429	334	389	.859	285	500	1399	3.0	5.2	14.6

Three-point field goals: 2000-01, 29-for-99 (.293). 2001-02, 93-for-211 (.441). 2002-03, 81-for-212 (.382). Totals, 203-for-522 (.389).

NBA REGULAR-SEASON RECORD

| | | | | | | | | | REBOUNDS | | | | | | | | AVERAGES | | |
Season Team	G	Min.	FGM	FGA	Pct.	FTM	FTA	Pct.	Off.	Def.	Tot.	Ast.	St.	Blk.	TO	Pts.	RPG	APG	PPG
03-04—Seattle	69	1114	145	350	.414	65	79	.823	35	73	108	163	52	7	80	382	1.6	2.4	5.5
04-05—Seattle	82	2571	299	739	.405	159	180	.883	55	149	204	483	94	23	149	824	2.5	5.9	10.0
05-06—Seattle	79	2625	334	799	.418	199	227	.877	47	188	235	550	123	22	162	910	3.0	7.0	11.5
Totals	230	6310	778	1888	.412	423	486	.870	137	410	547	1196	269	52	391	2116	2.4	5.2	9.2

Three-point field goals: 2003-04, 27-for-80 (.338). 2004-05, 67-for-178 (.376). 2005-06, 43-for-149 (.289). Totals, 137-for-407 (.337).
Personal fouls/disqualifications: 2003-04, 105/0. 2004-05, 185/0. 2005-06, 178/0. Totals, 468/0.

NBA PLAYOFF RECORD

| | | | | | | | | | REBOUNDS | | | | | | | | AVERAGES | | |
Season Team	G	Min.	FGM	FGA	Pct.	FTM	FTA	Pct.	Off.	Def.	Tot.	Ast.	St.	Blk.	TO	Pts.	RPG	APG	PPG
04-05—Seattle	11	378	42	107	.393	19	20	.950	10	26	36	47	13	8	18	107	3.3	4.3	9.7

Three-point field goals: 2004-05, 4-for-17 (.235). Totals, 4-for-17 (.235).
Personal fouls/disqualifications: 2004-05, 23/0. Totals, 23/0.

ROBERSON, ANTHONY   G

PERSONAL: Born February 14, 1983, in Saginaw, Mich. ... 6-2/180. (1.88/81.6).
HIGH SCHOOL: Saginaw (Mich.).
COLLEGE: Florida.
TRANSACTIONS/CAREER NOTES: Not drafted by an NBA franchise ... Played in NBA Development League (2005-06). ... Signed as free agent by Memphis Grizzlies (August 18, 2005). ... Waived by Grizzlies (July 26, 2006).

COLLEGIATE RECORD

Season Team	G	Min.	FGM	FGA	Pct.	FTM	FTA	Pct.	Reb.	Ast.	Pts.	RPG	APG	PPG
02-03—Florida	33	844	141	345	.409	50	61	.820	81	61	406	2.5	1.8	12.3
03-04—Florida	30	937	180	390	.462	79	92	.859	89	108	538	3.0	3.6	17.9
04-05—Florida	30	951	193	423	.456	81	90	.900	65	77	561	2.2	2.6	18.7
Totals	93	2732	514	1158	.444	210	243	.864	235	246	1505	2.5	2.6	16.2

Three-point field goals: 2002-03, 74-for-190 (.389). 2003-04, 99-for-233 (.425). 2004-05, 94-for-242 (.388). Totals, 267-for-665 (.402).

NBA REGULAR-SEASON RECORD

Season Team	G	Min.	FGM	FGA	Pct.	FTM	FTA	Pct.	Off.	Def.	Tot.	Ast.	St.	Blk.	TO	Pts.	RPG	APG	PPG
05-06—Memphis	16	88	14	31	.452	2	2	1.000	0	6	6	5	1	0	3	35	0.4	0.3	2.2

Three-point field goals: 2005-06, 5-for-10 (.500). Totals, 5-for-10 (.500).
Personal fouls/disqualifications: 2005-06, 6/0. Totals, 6/0.

NBA DEVELOPMENT LEAGUE RECORD

Season Team	G	Min.	FGM	FGA	Pct.	FTM	FTA	Pct.	Reb.	Ast.	Pts.	RPG	APG	PPG
05-06—Arkansas	10	271	64	141	.454	29	35	.829	30	15	179	3.0	1.5	17.9

Three-point field goals: 2005-06, 22-for-50 (.440). Totals, 22-for-50 (.440).

ROBERTS, LAWRENCE   F   GRIZZLIES

PERSONAL: Born October 20, 1982, in Houston. ... 6-9/240. (2.06/108.9). ... Full name: Lawrence Edward Roberts
HIGH SCHOOL: Lamar (Houston).
COLLEGE: Baylor, then Mississippi State.
TRANSACTIONS/CAREER NOTES: Selected by Seattle Supersonics in second round (55th pick overall) of 2005 NBA draft. ... Draft rights traded by Supersonics to Memphis Grizzlies for two future second-round picks and cash (June 28, 2005).

COLLEGIATE RECORD

NOTES: The SPORTING NEWS All-America second team (2004).

Season Team	G	Min.	FGM	FGA	Pct.	FTM	FTA	Pct.	Reb.	Ast.	Pts.	RPG	APG	PPG
01-02—Baylor	30	858	174	391	.445	124	183	.678	247	39	498	8.2	1.3	16.6
02-03—Baylor	26	888	133	316	.421	115	174	.661	271	40	396	10.4	1.5	15.2
03-04—Mississippi State	30	982	175	337	.519	144	227	.634	303	37	506	10.1	1.2	16.9
04-05—Mississippi State	32	1023	171	382	.448	188	288	.653	351	61	542	11.0	1.9	16.9
Totals	118	3701	653	1426	.458	575	872	.659	1172	177	1942	9.9	1.5	16.5

Three-point field goals: 2001-02, 26-for-79 (.329). 2002-03, 11-for-42 (.262). 2003-04, 12-for-40 (.300). 2004-05, 12-for-41 (.293). Totals, 61-for-202 (.302).

NBA REGULAR-SEASON RECORD

Season Team	G	Min.	FGM	FGA	Pct.	FTM	FTA	Pct.	Off.	Def.	Tot.	Ast.	St.	Blk.	TO	Pts.	RPG	APG	PPG
05-06—Memphis	33	181	20	44	.455	11	23	.478	26	23	49	5	8	2	5	51	1.5	0.2	1.5

Three-point field goals: 2005-06, 0-for-2. Totals, 0-for-2 (.000).
Personal fouls/disqualifications: 2005-06, 30/0. Totals, 30/0.

NBA DEVELOPMENT LEAGUE RECORD

Season Team	G	Min.	FGM	FGA	Pct.	FTM	FTA	Pct.	Reb.	Ast.	Pts.	RPG	APG	PPG
05-06—Arkansas	10	369	80	154	.519	38	58	.655	12	8	198	1.2	0.8	19.8

Three-point field goals: 2005-06, 0-for-1. Totals, 0-for-1 (.000).

ROBINSON, BERNARD   G/F   BOBCATS

PERSONAL: Born December 26, 1980, in Washington, D.C. ... 6-6/210. (1.98/95.3). ... Full name: Bernard Gregory Robinson
HIGH SCHOOL: Dunbar (Washington, D.C.).
COLLEGE: Michigan.
TRANSACTIONS/CAREER NOTES: Selected by Charlotte Bobcats in second round (45th pick overall) of 2004 NBA Draft.

COLLEGIATE RECORD

Season Team	G	Min.	FGM	FGA	Pct.	FTM	FTA	Pct.	Reb.	Ast.	Pts.	RPG	APG	PPG
00-01—Michigan	28	813	142	304	.467	93	116	.802	136	63	404	4.9	2.3	14.4
01-02—Michigan	29	825	134	328	.409	71	83	.855	132	71	351	4.6	2.4	12.1
02-03—Michigan	29	933	124	272	.456	78	92	.848	178	100	339	6.1	3.4	11.7
03-04—Michigan	34	1095	150	347	.432	94	122	.770	194	130	411	5.7	3.8	12.1
Totals	120	3666	550	1251	.440	336	413	.814	640	364	1505	5.3	3.0	12.5

Three-point field goals: 2000-01, 27-for-78 (.346). 2001-02, 12-for-49 (.245). 2002-03, 13-for-37 (.351). 2003-04, 17-for-68 (.250). Totals, 69-for-232 (.297).

NBA REGULAR-SEASON RECORD

									REBOUNDS								AVERAGES		
Season Team	G	Min.	FGM	FGA	Pct.	FTM	FTA	Pct.	Off.	Def.	Tot.	Ast.	St.	Blk.	TO	Pts.	RPG	APG	PPG
04-05—Charlotte	31	328	36	81	.444	18	26	.692	14	34	48	30	11	4	20	93	1.5	1.0	3.0
05-06—Charlotte	66	1303	157	365	.430	106	134	.791	62	157	219	77	81	10	74	422	3.3	1.2	6.4
Totals	97	1631	193	446	.433	124	160	.775	76	191	267	107	92	14	94	515	2.8	1.1	5.3

Three-point field goals: 2004-05, 3-for-8 (.375). 2005-06, 2-for-21 (.095). Totals, 5-for-29 (.172).
Personal fouls/disqualifications: 2004-05, 42/1. 2005-06, 141/1. Totals, 183/2.

ROBINSON, CLIFFORD   F   NETS

PERSONAL: Born December 16, 1966, in Buffalo. ... 6-10/225. (2.08/102.1). ... Full name: Clifford Ralph Robinson.
HIGH SCHOOL: Riverside (Buffalo).
COLLEGE: Connecticut.
TRANSACTIONS/CAREER NOTES: Selected by Portland Trail Blazers in second round (36th pick overall) of 1989 NBA Draft. ... Signed as free agent by Phoenix Suns (August 25, 1997). ... Traded by Suns to Detroit Pistons for G/F Jud Buechler and F John Wallace (July 18, 2001). ... Traded by Pistons with G Pepe Sanchez to Golden State Warriors for G Bob Sura (August 21, 2003). ... Traded by Warriors to New Jersey Nets for second-round picks in 2005 and 2007 NBA drafts.

COLLEGIATE RECORD

												AVERAGES		
Season Team	G	Min.	FGM	FGA	Pct.	FTM	FTA	Pct.	Reb.	Ast.	Pts.	RPG	APG	PPG
85-86—Connecticut	28	442	60	164	.366	36	59	.610	88	14	156	3.1	0.5	5.6
86-87—Connecticut	16	556	107	255	.420	69	121	.570	119	32	289	7.4	2.0	18.1
87-88—Connecticut	34	1079	222	463	.479	156	238	.655	233	44	600	6.9	1.3	17.6
88-89—Connecticut	31	974	235	500	.470	145	212	.684	228	46	619	7.4	1.5	20.0
Totals	109	3051	624	1382	.452	406	630	.644	668	136	1664	6.1	1.2	15.3

Three-point field goals: 1986-87, 6-for-18 (.333). 1988-89, 4-for-12 (.333). Totals, 10-for-30 (.333).

NBA REGULAR-SEASON RECORD

HONORS: NBA Sixth Man Award (1993). ... NBA All-Defensive second team (2000, 2002).

									REBOUNDS								AVERAGES		
Season Team	G	Min.	FGM	FGA	Pct.	FTM	FTA	Pct.	Off.	Def.	Tot.	Ast.	St.	Blk.	TO	Pts.	RPG	APG	PPG
89-90—Portland	82	1565	298	751	.397	138	251	.550	110	198	308	72	53	53	129	746	3.8	0.9	9.1
90-91—Portland	82	1940	373	806	.463	205	314	.653	123	226	349	151	78	76	133	957	4.3	1.8	11.7
91-92—Portland	82	2124	398	854	.466	219	330	.664	140	276	416	137	85	107	154	1016	5.1	1.7	12.4
92-93—Portland	82	2575	632	1336	.473	287	416	.690	165	377	542	182	98	163	173	1570	6.6	2.2	19.1
93-94—Portland	82	2853	641	1404	.457	352	460	.765	164	386	550	159	118	111	169	1647	6.7	1.9	20.1
94-95—Portland	75	2725	597	1320	.452	265	382	.694	152	271	423	198	79	82	158	1601	5.6	2.6	21.3
95-96—Portland	78	2980	553	1306	.423	360	542	.664	123	320	443	190	86	68	194	1644	5.7	2.4	21.1
96-97—Portland	81	3077	444	1043	.426	215	309	.696	90	231	321	261	99	66	172	1224	4.0	3.2	15.1
97-98—Portland	80	2359	429	895	.479	248	360	.689	152	258	410	170	92	90	140	1133	5.1	2.1	14.2
98-99—Phoenix	50	1740	299	629	.475	163	234	.697	69	158	227	128	75	59	88	819	4.5	2.6	16.4
99-00—Phoenix	80	2839	530	1142	.464	298	381	.782	105	254	359	224	90	61	166	1478	4.5	2.8	18.5
00-01—Phoenix	82	2751	501	1186	.422	253	357	.709	105	229	334	237	87	82	186	1345	4.1	2.9	16.4
01-02—Detroit	80	2855	454	1069	.425	143	206	.694	79	307	386	202	89	95	151	1166	4.8	2.5	14.6
02-03—Detroit	81	2825	372	935	.398	161	238	.676	81	237	318	268	87	88	158	992	3.9	3.3	12.2
03-04—Golden State	82	2846	366	945	.387	123	173	.711	54	268	322	271	68	73	173	967	3.9	3.3	11.8
04-05—G.S.-N.J.	71	1689	202	523	.386	62	97	.639	54	155	209	104	62	53	66	533	2.9	1.5	7.5
05-06—New Jersey	80	1863	219	513	.427	52	79	.658	55	212	267	89	44	40	62	550	3.3	1.1	6.9
Totals	1330	41606	7308	16657	.439	3544	5129	.691	1821	4363	6184	3043	1390	1367	2472	19388	4.6	2.3	14.6

Three-point field goals: 1989-90, 12-for-44 (.273). 1990-91, 6-for-19 (.316). 1991-92, 1-for-11 (.091). 1992-93, 19-for-77 (.247). 1993-94, 13-for-53 (.245). 1994-95, 142-for-383 (.371). 1995-96, 178-for-471 (.378). 1996-97, 121-for-350 (.346). 1997-98, 27-for-84 (.321). 1998-99, 58-for-139 (.417). 1999-00, 120-for-324 (.370). 2000-01, 90-for-249 (.361). 2001-02, 115-for-304 (.378). 2002-03, 87-for-259 (.336). 2003-04, 112-for-314 (.357). 2004-05, 67-for-193 (.347). 2005-06, 60-for-175 (.343). Totals, 1228-for-3449 (.356).
Personal fouls/disqualifications: 1989-90, 226/4. 1990-91, 263/2. 1991-92, 274/11. 1992-93, 287/8. 1993-94, 263/0. 1994-95, 240/3. 1995-96, 248/3. 1996-97, 251/6. 1997-98, 249/5. 1998-99, 153/2. 1999-00, 239/3. 2000-01, 258/6. 2001-02, 243/4. 2002-03, 259/5. 2003-04, 237/2. 2004-05, 181/3. 2005-06, 206/0. Totals, 4077/67.

NBA PLAYOFF RECORD

									REBOUNDS								AVERAGES		
Season Team	G	Min.	FGM	FGA	Pct.	FTM	FTA	Pct.	Off.	Def.	Tot.	Ast.	St.	Blk.	TO	Pts.	RPG	APG	PPG
89-90—Portland	21	391	54	151	.358	29	52	.558	32	55	87	23	19	24	25	137	4.1	1.1	6.5
90-91—Portland	16	354	63	117	.538	38	69	.551	24	39	63	18	7	16	25	165	3.9	1.1	10.3
91-92—Portland	21	522	91	197	.462	44	77	.571	25	63	88	43	22	21	28	227	4.2	2.0	10.8
92-93—Portland	4	131	16	61	.262	9	22	.409	10	7	17	6	6	7	8	41	4.3	1.5	10.3
93-94—Portland	4	149	28	68	.412	7	8	.875	11	14	25	10	3	6	11	65	6.3	2.5	16.3
94-95—Portland	3	119	17	47	.362	9	16	.563	7	12	19	8	2	1	8	47	6.3	2.7	15.7
95-96—Portland	5	181	21	61	.344	28	37	.757	4	14	18	8	7	5	16	76	3.6	1.6	15.2
96-97—Portland	4	161	17	47	.362	11	16	.688	12	15	27	12	2	4	10	48	6.8	3.0	12.0
97-98—Phoenix	4	92	9	33	.273	7	9	.778	6	6	12	3	3	2	5	25	3.0	0.8	6.3
98-99—Phoenix	3	117	19	40	.475	7	11	.636	7	9	16	8	6	1	7	47	5.3	2.7	15.7
99-00—Phoenix	9	333	56	145	.386	33	45	.733	18	36	54	19	11	7	18	158	6.0	2.1	17.6
00-01—Phoenix	4	114	21	50	.420	14	22	.636	6	10	16	4	6	2	9	60	4.0	1.0	15.0
01-02—Detroit	10	409	45	124	.363	24	30	.800	5	25	30	29	18	19	21	132	3.0	2.9	13.2
02-03—Detroit	17	525	57	159	.358	22	37	.595	14	32	46	49	16	13	28	158	2.7	2.9	9.3
04-05—New Jersey	4	71	11	27	.407	2	2	1.000	2	8	10	5	3	1	0	28	2.5	1.3	7.0
05-06—New Jersey	8	198	13	39	.333	4	5	.800	2	24	26	5	9	3	10	36	3.3	0.6	4.5
Totals	137	3867	538	1366	.394	288	458	.629	185	369	554	250	140	132	229	1450	4.0	1.8	10.6

Three-point field goals: 1989-90, 0-for-4. 1990-91, 1-for-3 (.333). 1991-92, 1-for-6 (.167). 1992-93, 0-for-1. 1993-94, 2-for-9 (.222). 1994-95, 4-for-16 (.235). 1995-96, 6-for-23 (.261). 1996-97, 3-for-16 (.188). 1997-98, 0-for-1. 1998-99, 2-for-9 (.222). 1999-00, 13-for-40 (.325). 2000-01, 4-for-16 (.250).

2001-02, 18-for-53 (.340). 2002-03, 22-for-59 (.373). 2004-05, 4-for-14 (.286). 2005-06, 6-for-19 (.316). Totals, 86-for-290 (.297).
Personal fouls/disqualifications: 1989-90, 71/1. 1990-91, 47/1. 1991-92, 84/3. 1992-93, 17/1. 1993-94, 13/0. 1994-95, 13/0. 1995-96, 19/0. 1996-97, 13/0. 1997-98, 19/1. 1998-99, 12/1. 1999-00, 35/0. 2000-01, 14/0. 2001-02, 28/0. 2002-03, 62/1. 2004-05, 20/1. 2005-06, 28/1. Totals, 495/11.

NBA ALL-STAR GAME RECORD

Season Team	Min.	FGM	FGA	Pct.	FTM	FTA	Pct.	REBOUNDS Off.	Def.	Tot.	Ast.	PF	Dq.	St.	Blk.	TO	Pts.
1994—Portland	18	5	8	.625	0	0	...	1	1	2	5	0	0	1	0	0	10

Three-point field goals: 1994, 0-for-1. Totals, 0-for-1 (.000).

ROBINSON, NATE G KNICKS

PERSONAL: Born May 31, 1984, in Seattle, Wash. ... 5-9/180. (1.75/81.6).
HIGH SCHOOL: Logan (Oakland, Calif.), then Rainier Beach (Seattle).
COLLEGE: Washington.
TRANSACTIONS/CAREER NOTES: Selected after junior season by Phoenix Suns in first round (21st pick overall) of 2005 NBA draft. ... Draft rights traded by Suns with G Quentin Richardson and cash to New York Knicks for F Kurt Thomas and draft rights to Dijon Thompson (June 28, 2005).

COLLEGIATE RECORD

NOTES: Naismith Award winner (2005).

Season Team	G	Min.	FGM	FGA	Pct.	FTM	FTA	Pct.	Reb.	Ast.	Pts.	AVERAGES RPG	APG	PPG
02-03—Washington	23	576	120	260	.462	41	57	.719	89	52	300	3.9	2.3	13.0
03-04—Washington	31	833	138	309	.447	87	102	.853	121	84	409	3.9	2.7	13.2
04-05—Washington	35	1101	188	406	.463	136	174	.782	135	159	574	3.9	4.5	16.4
Totals	89	2510	446	975	.457	264	333	.793	345	295	1283	3.9	3.3	14.4

Three-point field goals: 2002-03, 19-for-74 (.257). 2003-04, 46-for-130 (.354). 2004-05, 62-for-161 (.385). Totals, 127-for-365 (.348).

NBA REGULAR-SEASON RECORD

HONORS: Slam Dunk championship winner (2006).

Season Team	G	Min.	FGM	FGA	Pct.	FTM	FTA	Pct.	REBOUNDS Off.	Def.	Tot.	Ast.	St.	Blk.	TO	Pts.	AVERAGES RPG	APG	PPG
05-06—New York	72	1544	230	565	.407	152	202	.752	56	111	167	147	59	1	114	670	2.3	2.0	9.3

Three-point field goals: 2005-06, 58-for-146 (.397). Totals, 58-for-146 (.397).
Personal fouls/disqualifications: 2005-06, 201/5. Totals, 201/5.

ROSE, JALEN G KNICKS

PERSONAL: Born January 30, 1973, in Detroit. ... 6-8/210. (2.03/95.3). ... Son of Jimmy Walker, guard with Detroit Pistons (1967-68 through 1971-72), Houston Rockets (1972-73 and 1973-74), Kansas City/Omaha Kings (1973-74 and 1974-75) and Kansas City Kings (1975-76). ... Name pronounced JAY-lin.
HIGH SCHOOL: Southwestern (Detroit)
COLLEGE: Michigan
TRANSACTIONS/CAREER NOTES: Selected after junior season by Denver Nuggets in first round (13th pick overall) of 1994 NBA Draft. ... Traded by Nuggets with F Reggie Williams and 1996 first-round draft choice to Indiana Pacers for G Mark Jackson, G Ricky Pierce and 1996 first-round draft choice (June 13, 1996). ... Traded by Pacers with G Travis Best, G Norman Richardson and conditional second-round draft choice to Chicago Bulls for C Brad Miller, G Ron Mercer, G/F Ron Artest and G Kevin Ollie (February 19, 2002). ... Traded by Bulls with F Lonny Baxter and F Donyell Marshall to Toronto Raptors for F/C Antonio Davis, F Chris Jefferies and F Jerome Williams (December 1, 2003). ... Traded by Raptors with a first-round draft choice to New York Knicks for F/C Antonio Davis (February 3, 2006).

COLLEGIATE RECORD

NOTES: THE SPORTING NEWS All-America first team (1994).

Season Team	G	Min.	FGM	FGA	Pct.	FTM	FTA	Pct.	Reb.	Ast.	Pts.	AVERAGES RPG	APG	PPG
91-92—Michigan	34	1126	206	424	.486	149	197	.756	146	135	597	4.3	4.0	17.6
92-93—Michigan	36	1232	203	455	.446	116	161	.720	150	140	555	4.2	3.9	15.4
93-94—Michigan	32	1152	220	477	.461	141	192	.734	181	126	636	5.7	3.9	19.9
Totals	102	3510	629	1356	.464	406	550	.738	477	401	1788	4.7	3.9	17.5

Three-point field goals: 1991-92, 36-for-111 (.324). 1992-93, 33-for-103 (.320). 1993-94, 55-for-155 (.355). Totals, 124-for-369 (.336).

NBA REGULAR-SEASON RECORD

HONORS: NBA Most Improved Player (2000). ... NBA All-Rookie second team (1995).

Season Team	G	Min.	FGM	FGA	Pct.	FTM	FTA	Pct.	REBOUNDS Off.	Def.	Tot.	Ast.	St.	Blk.	TO	Pts.	AVERAGES RPG	APG	PPG
94-95—Denver	81	1798	227	500	.454	173	234	.739	57	160	217	389	65	22	160	663	2.7	4.8	8.2
95-96—Denver	80	2134	290	604	.480	191	277	.690	46	214	260	495	53	39	234	803	3.3	6.2	10.0
96-97—Indiana...........	66	1188	172	377	.456	117	156	.750	27	94	121	155	57	18	107	482	1.8	2.3	7.3
97-98—Indiana...........	82	1706	290	607	.478	166	228	.728	28	167	195	155	56	14	132	771	2.4	1.9	9.4
98-99—Indiana...........	49	1238	200	496	.403	125	158	.791	34	120	154	93	50	15	72	542	3.1	1.9	11.1
99-00—Indiana...........	80	2978	563	1196	.471	254	307	.827	42	345	387	320	84	49	188	1457	4.8	4.0	18.2
00-01—Indiana...........	72	2943	567	1242	.457	285	344	.828	37	322	359	435	65	43	211	1478	5.0	6.0	20.5
01-02—Indiana-Chi.	82	3153	663	1458	.455	281	335	.839	43	330	373	355	78	45	201	1696	4.5	4.3	20.4
02-03—Chicago..........	82	3351	642	1583	.406	399	467	.854	68	283	351	395	72	23	285	1816	4.3	4.8	22.1
03-04—Chicago-Tor. ...	66	2497	383	952	.402	187	231	.810	34	232	266	329	51	22	208	1022	4.0	5.0	15.5
04-05—Toronto	81	2710	527	1159	.455	333	390	.854	44	232	276	209	63	10	180	1495	3.4	2.6	18.5
05-06—Tor.-New York..	72	1982	290	685	.423	248	318	.780	28	183	211	181	30	13	115	887	2.9	2.5	12.3
Totals	894	27678	4814	10859	.443	2759	3445	.801	488	2682	3170	3511	724	313	2093	13112	3.5	3.9	14.7

Three-point field goals: 1994-95, 36-for-114 (.316). 1995-96, 32-for-108 (.296). 1996-97, 21-for-72 (.292). 1997-98, 25-for-73 (.342). 1998-99, 17-for-

65 (.262). 1999-00, 77-for-196 (.393). 2000-01, 59-for-174 (.339). 2001-02, 89-for-246 (.362). 2002-03, 133-for-359 (.370). 2003-04, 69-for-202 (.342). 2004-05, 108-for-274 (.394). 2005-06, 59-for-172 (.343). Totals, 725-for-2055 (.353).

Personal fouls/disqualifications: 1994-95, 206/0. 1995-96, 229/3. 1996-97, 136/1. 1997-98, 171/0. 1998-99, 128/0. 1999-00, 234/1. 2000-01, 230/2. 2001-02, 251/2. 2002-03, 271/2. 2003-04, 184/2. 2004-05, 190/0. 2005-06, 156/3. Totals, 2386/16.

NBA PLAYOFF RECORD

								REBOUNDS								AVERAGES		
Season Team	G	Min.	FGM	FGA	Pct.	FTM	FTA	Pct.	Off.	Def.	Tot.	Ast.	St.	Blk.	TO	Pts.	RPG	APG	PPG
94-95—Denver	3	99	13	28	.464	3	5	.600	4	7	11	18	3	2	9	30	3.7	6.0	10.0
97-98—Indiana	15	293	48	100	.480	20	27	.741	1	26	27	28	11	6	25	122	1.8	1.9	8.1
98-99—Indiana	13	355	61	138	.442	28	34	.824	11	20	31	32	13	5	25	158	2.4	2.5	12.2
99-00—Indiana	23	964	171	391	.437	107	133	.805	10	91	101	78	16	11	50	479	4.4	3.4	20.8
00-01—Indiana	4	164	30	79	.380	7	7	1.000	3	15	18	11	6	1	9	72	4.5	2.8	18.0
Totals	58	1875	323	736	.439	165	206	.801	29	159	188	167	49	25	118	861	3.2	2.9	14.8

Three-point field goals: 1994-95, 1-for-4 (.250). 1997-98, 6-for-16 (.375). 1998-99, 8-for-23 (.348). 1999-00, 30-for-70 (.429). 2000-01, 5-for-16 (.313). Totals, 50-for-129 (.388).

Personal fouls/disqualifications: 1994-95, 9/0. 1997-98, 37/0. 1998-99, 39/0. 1999-00, 71/0. 2000-01, 18/0. Totals, 174/0.

ROSE, MALIK   F   KNICKS

PERSONAL: Born November 23, 1974, in Philadelphia. ... 6-7/255. (2.01/115.7). ... Full name: Malik Jabari Rose ... Name pronounced Ma-leek.
HIGH SCHOOL: Overbrook (Philadelphia).
COLLEGE: Drexel.
TRANSACTIONS/CAREER NOTES: Selected by Charlotte Hornets in second round (44th pick overall) of 1996 NBA Draft. ... Signed as free agent by San Antonio Spurs (September 29, 1997). ... Traded by Spurs with conditional first-round picks in 2005 and 2006 NBA drafts to New York Knicks for F Nazr Mohammed and G Jamison Brewer (February 24, 2005).
MISCELLANEOUS: Member of NBA championship team (1999, 2003).

COLLEGIATE RECORD

												AVERAGES		
Season Team	G	Min.	FGM	FGA	Pct.	FTM	FTA	Pct.	Reb.	Ast.	Pts.	RPG	APG	PPG
92-93—Drexel	29	820	144	287	.502	107	190	.563	330	10	395	11.4	0.3	13.6
93-94—Drexel	30	875	154	296	.520	110	202	.545	371	20	418	12.4	0.7	13.9
94-95—Drexel	30	984	216	384	.563	152	213	.714	404	36	584	13.5	1.2	19.5
95-96—Drexel	31	972	219	368	.595	182	255	.714	409	53	627	13.2	1.7	20.2
Totals	120	3651	733	1335	.549	551	860	.641	1514	119	2024	12.6	1.0	16.9

Three-point field goals: 1994-95, 0-for-3. 1995-96, 7-for-21 (.333). Totals, 7-for-24 (.292).

NBA REGULAR-SEASON RECORD

								REBOUNDS								AVERAGES		
Season Team	G	Min.	FGM	FGA	Pct.	FTM	FTA	Pct.	Off.	Def.	Tot.	Ast.	St.	Blk.	TO	Pts.	RPG	APG	PPG
96-97—Charlotte	54	525	61	128	.477	38	62	.613	70	94	164	32	28	17	41	160	3.0	0.6	3.0
97-98—San Antonio	53	429	59	136	.434	39	61	.639	40	50	90	19	21	7	44	158	1.7	0.4	3.0
98-99—San Antonio	47	608	93	201	.463	98	146	.671	90	92	182	29	40	22	56	284	3.9	0.6	6.0
99-00—San Antonio	74	1341	176	385	.457	143	198	.722	133	202	335	47	35	52	99	496	4.5	0.6	6.7
00-01—San Antonio	57	1219	160	368	.435	114	160	.713	95	213	308	48	59	40	74	437	5.4	0.8	7.7
01-02—San Antonio	82	1725	293	633	.463	185	257	.720	172	320	492	61	70	42	140	772	6.0	0.7	9.4
02-03—San Antonio	79	1933	289	630	.459	242	306	.791	148	358	506	124	57	40	170	822	6.4	1.6	10.4
03-04—San Antonio	67	1256	173	404	.428	183	225	.813	110	210	320	69	36	24	112	529	4.8	1.0	7.9
04-05—S.A.-N.Y.	76	1475	198	441	.449	137	186	.737	129	212	341	59	46	16	102	534	4.5	0.8	7.0
05-06—New York	72	1119	105	281	.374	107	137	.781	84	175	259	67	43	14	80	318	3.6	0.9	4.4
Totals	661	11630	1607	3607	.446	1286	1738	.740	1071	1926	2997	555	435	274	918	4510	4.5	0.8	6.8

Three-point field goals: 1996-97, 0-for-2. 1997-98, 1-for-3 (.333). 1998-99, 0-for-1. 1999-00, 1-for-3 (.333). 2000-01, 3-for-17 (.176). 2001-02, 1-for-12 (.083). 2002-03, 2-for-5 (.400). 2003-04, 0-for-3. 2004-05, 1-for-10 (.100). 2005-06, 1-for-1 (1.000). Totals, 10-for-57 (.175).

Personal fouls/disqualifications: 1996-97, 114/3. 1997-98, 79/1. 1998-99, 120/0. 1999-00, 232/2. 2000-01, 148/1. 2001-02, 208/2. 2002-03, 206/2. 2003-04, 164/1. 2004-05, 208/2. 2005-06, 145/1. Totals, 1624/15.

NBA PLAYOFF RECORD

								REBOUNDS								AVERAGES		
Season Team	G	Min.	FGM	FGA	Pct.	FTM	FTA	Pct.	Off.	Def.	Tot.	Ast.	St.	Blk.	TO	Pts.	RPG	APG	PPG
96-97—Charlotte	2	12	2	4	.500	0	0	...	4	1	5	1	0	0	2	4	2.5	0.5	2.0
97-98—San Antonio	5	18	4	6	.667	2	4	.500	3	4	7	1	1	0	4	10	1.4	0.2	2.0
98-99—San Antonio	17	194	14	38	.368	18	26	.692	17	22	39	3	7	4	10	46	2.3	0.2	2.7
99-00—San Antonio	4	83	8	18	.444	5	9	.556	5	14	19	1	2	3	7	21	4.8	0.3	5.3
00-01—San Antonio	13	215	23	55	.418	17	20	.850	16	33	49	4	3	1	10	64	3.8	0.3	4.9
01-02—San Antonio	10	292	46	96	.479	37	50	.740	27	52	79	14	10	5	12	129	7.9	1.4	12.9
02-03—San Antonio	24	560	75	179	.419	72	94	.766	49	89	138	24	16	11	43	222	5.8	1.0	9.3
03-04—San Antonio	7	58	4	16	.250	2	4	.500	12	5	17	6	4	2	8	10	2.4	0.9	1.4
Totals	82	1432	176	412	.427	153	207	.739	133	220	353	54	43	26	96	506	4.3	0.7	6.2

Three-point field goals: 2000-01, 1-for-3 (.333). 2001-02, 0-for-1. 2002-03, 0-for-3. 2003-04, 0-for-2. Totals, 1-for-9 (.111).

Personal fouls/disqualifications: 1996-97, 2/0. 1997-98, 2/0. 1998-99, 52/0. 1999-00, 12/0. 2000-01, 38/0. 2001-02, 31/0. 2002-03, 72/0. 2003-04, 6/0. Totals, 215/0.

ROSS, QUINTON   G   CLIPPERS

PERSONAL: Born July 30, 1981 ... 6-6/193. (1.98/87.5).
HIGH SCHOOL: Justin F. Kimball (Dallas).
COLLEGE: Southern Methodist.
TRANSACTIONS/CAREER NOTES: Not drafted by an NBA franchise. ... Played in Belgium (2003-04). ... Signed as free agent by Los Angeles Clippers (August 16, 2004).

COLLEGIATE RECORD

Season Team	G	Min.	FGM	FGA	Pct.	FTM	FTA	Pct.	Reb.	Ast.	Pts.	AVERAGES		
												RPG	APG	PPG
99-00—SMU	30	585	76	175	.434	50	78	.641	120	40	224	4.0	1.3	7.5
00-01—SMU	30	970	146	307	.476	86	116	.741	152	59	426	5.1	2.0	14.2
01-02—SMU	29	1004	162	386	.420	123	160	.769	188	60	505	6.5	2.1	17.4
02-03—SMU	30	1056	191	422	.453	184	232	.793	191	63	608	6.4	2.1	20.3
Totals	119	3615	575	1290	.446	443	586	.756	651	222	1763	5.5	1.9	14.8

Three-point field goals: 1999-00, 22-for-61 (.361). 2000-01, 48-for-129 (.372). 2001-02, 58-for-182 (.319). 2002-03, 42-for-141 (.298). Totals, 170-for-513 (.331).

BELGIAN LEAGUE RECORD

Season Team	G	Min.	FGM	FGA	Pct.	FTM	FTA	Pct.	Reb.	Ast.	Pts.	AVERAGES		
												RPG	APG	PPG
03-04—Telindus Oostende	31	...	186	365	.510	77	109	.706	150	56	517	4.8	1.8	16.7

Three-point field goals: 2003-04, 68-for-153 (.444). Totals, 68-for-153 (.444).

NBA REGULAR-SEASON RECORD

Season Team	G	Min.	FGM	FGA	Pct.	FTM	FTA	Pct.	REBOUNDS			Ast.	St.	Blk.	TO	Pts.	AVERAGES		
									Off.	Def.	Tot.						RPG	APG	PPG
04-05—L.A. Clippers	78	1659	161	373	.432	74	110	.673	59	151	210	109	51	22	54	397	2.7	1.4	5.1
05-06—L.A. Clippers	67	1515	130	308	.422	57	75	.760	38	132	170	79	51	16	47	317	2.5	1.2	4.7
Totals	145	3174	291	681	.427	131	185	.708	97	283	380	188	102	38	101	714	2.6	1.3	4.9

Three-point field goals: 2004-05, 1-for-4 (.250). 2005-06, 0-for-7. Totals, 1-for-11 (.091).
Personal fouls/disqualifications: 2004-05, 165/0. 2005-06, 155/0. Totals, 320/0.

NBA PLAYOFF RECORD

Season Team	G	Min.	FGM	FGA	Pct.	FTM	FTA	Pct.	REBOUNDS			Ast.	St.	Blk.	TO	Pts.	AVERAGES		
									Off.	Def.	Tot.						RPG	APG	PPG
05-06—L.A. Clippers	12	294	39	73	.534	14	16	.875	8	24	32	9	7	8	9	92	2.7	0.8	7.7

Personal fouls/disqualifications: 2005-06, 36/0. Totals, 36/0.

RUFFIN, MICHAEL   F   WIZARDS

PERSONAL: Born January 21, 1977, in Denver. ... 6-8/248. (2.03/112.5). ... Full name: Michael David Ruffin.
HIGH SCHOOL: Cherry Creek (Englewood, Colo.).
COLLEGE: Tulsa.
TRANSACTIONS/CAREER NOTES: Selected by Chicago Bulls in second round (32nd pick overall) of 1999 NBA Draft. ... Waived by Bulls (October 25, 2001). ... Signed as free agent by Philadelphia 76ers (November 22, 2001). ... Waived by 76ers (December 28, 2001). ... Played in Spain (2001-03). ... Signed as free agent by Utah Jazz (August 6, 2003) ... Signed as free agent by Washington Wizards (August 3, 2004).

COLLEGIATE RECORD

Season Team	G	Min.	FGM	FGA	Pct.	FTM	FTA	Pct.	Reb.	Ast.	Pts.	AVERAGES		
												RPG	APG	PPG
95-96—Tulsa	30	689	78	146	.534	57	123	.463	232	22	213	7.7	0.7	7.1
96-97—Tulsa	34	965	98	174	.563	95	150	.633	341	37	291	10.0	1.1	8.6
97-98—Tulsa	31	1030	109	217	.502	104	154	.675	296	46	322	9.5	1.5	10.4
98-99—Tulsa	33	1063	117	222	.527	149	247	.603	342	45	383	10.4	1.4	11.6
Totals	128	3747	402	759	.530	405	674	.601	1211	150	1209	9.5	1.2	9.4

Three-point field goals: 1995-96, 0-for-1. 1996-97, 0-for-1. 1997-98, 0-for-4. 1998-99, 0-for-4. Totals, 0-for-10 (.000).

NBA REGULAR-SEASON RECORD

Season Team	G	Min.	FGM	FGA	Pct.	FTM	FTA	Pct.	REBOUNDS			Ast.	St.	Blk.	TO	Pts.	AVERAGES		
									Off.	Def.	Tot.						RPG	APG	PPG
99-00—Chicago	71	975	58	138	.420	43	88	.489	117	133	250	44	26	26	59	159	3.5	0.6	2.2
00-01—Chicago	45	879	40	90	.444	39	77	.506	101	161	262	39	30	38	46	119	5.8	0.9	2.6
01-02—Philadelphia	15	169	7	26	.269	2	8	.250	23	28	51	5	5	8	11	16	3.4	0.3	1.1
03-04—Utah	41	733	38	117	.325	16	38	.421	78	129	207	41	22	21	42	92	5.0	1.0	2.2
04-05—Washington	79	1262	41	99	.414	29	67	.433	157	175	332	64	43	41	44	111	4.2	0.8	1.4
05-06—Washington	76	1010	34	77	.442	37	74	.500	122	149	271	27	33	31	38	105	3.6	0.4	1.4
Totals	327	5028	218	547	.399	166	352	.472	598	775	1373	220	159	165	240	602	4.2	0.7	1.8

Three-point field goals: 2004-05, 0-for-1. 2005-06, 0-for-2. Totals, 0-for-3 (.000).
Personal fouls/disqualifications: 1999-00, 170/1. 2000-01, 131/2. 2001-02, 23/0. 2003-04, 103/1. 2004-05, 193/4. 2005-06, 179/1. Totals, 799/9.

NBA PLAYOFF RECORD

Season Team	G	Min.	FGM	FGA	Pct.	FTM	FTA	Pct.	REBOUNDS			Ast.	St.	Blk.	TO	Pts.	AVERAGES		
									Off.	Def.	Tot.						RPG	APG	PPG
04-05—Washington	9	156	7	10	.700	9	16	.563	15	22	37	9	3	3	4	23	4.1	1.0	2.6
05-06—Washington	6	70	1	2	.500	0	2	.000	6	10	16	4	1	2	2	2	2.7	0.7	0.3
Totals	15	226	8	12	.667	9	18	.500	21	32	53	13	4	5	6	25	3.5	0.9	1.7

Personal fouls/disqualifications: 2004-05, 33/2. 2005-06, 10/0. Totals, 43/2.

SPANISH LEAGUE RECORD

Season Team	G	Min.	FGM	FGA	Pct.	FTM	FTA	Pct.	Reb.	Ast.	Pts.	AVERAGES		
												RPG	APG	PPG
01-02—Caprabo Lleida	20	577	47	95	.495	24	50	.480	163	14	118	8.2	0.7	5.9
02-03—Caprabo Lleida	34	855	81	165	.491	53	116	.457	251	31	215	7.4	0.9	6.3
Totals	54	1432	128	260	.492	77	166	.464	414	45	333	7.7	0.8	6.2

Three-point field goals: 2001-02, 0-for-2. Totals, 0-for-2 (.000).
Personal fouls/disqualifications: 2002-03, 106/0. Totals, 106/0.

RUSH, KAREEM G

PERSONAL: Born October 30, 1980, in Kansas City, Mo. ... 6-6/215. (1.98/97.5). ... Full name: Kareem Lamar Rush
HIGH SCHOOL: Pembroke Hill (Kansas City, Mo.).
COLLEGE: Missouri.
TRANSACTIONS/CAREER NOTES: Selected after junior season by Toronto Raptors in first round (20th pick overall) of 2002 NBA Draft. ... Draft rights traded by Raptors with F Tracy Murray to Los Angeles Lakers for G Lindsey Hunter and draft rights to F Chris Jeffries (June 26, 2002). ... Traded by Lakers to Charlotte Bobcats for second-round draft choices in 2005 and 2008 (December 6, 2004). ... Released by Bobcats (April 1, 2006).

COLLEGIATE RECORD

Season Team	G	Min.	FGM	FGA	Pct.	FTM	FTA	Pct.	Reb.	Ast.	Pts.	RPG	APG	PPG
99-00—Missouri	22	591	109	216	.505	59	78	.756	94	34	323	4.3	1.5	14.7
00-01—Missouri	26	796	192	434	.442	96	120	.800	174	51	549	6.7	2.0	21.1
01-02—Missouri	36	1149	249	585	.426	103	134	.769	188	89	712	5.2	2.5	19.8
Totals	84	2536	550	1235	.445	258	332	.777	456	174	1584	5.4	2.1	18.9

Three-point field goals: 1999-00, 46-for-108 (.426). 2000-01, 69-for-154 (.448). 2001-02, 111-for-274 (.405). Totals, 226-for-536 (.422).

NBA REGULAR-SEASON RECORD

Season Team	G	Min.	FGM	FGA	Pct.	FTM	FTA	Pct.	Off.	Def.	Tot.	Ast.	St.	Blk.	TO	Pts.	RPG	APG	PPG
02-03—L.A. Lakers	76	872	96	244	.393	16	23	.696	26	68	94	68	10	11	63	227	1.2	0.9	3.0
03-04—L.A. Lakers	72	1244	190	432	.440	31	52	.596	20	77	97	59	33	20	48	459	1.3	0.8	6.4
04-05—L.A.L.-Char.	48	968	157	406	.387	37	48	.771	20	69	89	68	20	7	47	402	1.9	1.4	8.4
05-06—Charlotte	47	1111	181	469	.386	55	77	.714	18	85	103	50	38	13	65	474	2.2	1.1	10.1
Totals	243	4195	624	1551	.402	139	200	.695	84	299	383	245	101	51	223	1562	1.6	1.0	6.4

Three-point field goals: 2002-03, 19-for-68 (.279). 2003-04, 48-for-138 (.348). 2004-05, 51-for-137 (.372). 2005-06, 57-for-164 (.348). Totals, 175-for-507 (.345).
Personal fouls/disqualifications: 2002-03, 71/0. 2003-04, 109/0. 2004-05, 74/0. 2005-06, 79/0. Totals, 333/0.

NBA PLAYOFF RECORD

Season Team	G	Min.	FGM	FGA	Pct.	FTM	FTA	Pct.	Off.	Def.	Tot.	Ast.	St.	Blk.	TO	Pts.	RPG	APG	PPG
02-03—L.A. Lakers	9	64	11	29	.379	4	4	1.000	2	1	3	2	1	0	3	30	0.3	0.2	3.3
03-04—L.A. Lakers	22	315	30	78	.385	2	3	.667	0	16	16	17	10	3	14	82	0.7	0.8	3.7
Totals	31	379	41	107	.383	6	7	.857	2	17	19	19	11	3	17	112	0.6	0.6	3.6

Three-point field goals: 2002-03, 4-for-11 (.364). 2003-04, 20-for-50 (.400). Totals, 24-for-61 (.393).
Personal fouls/disqualifications: 2002-03, 2/0. 2003-04, 33/0. Totals, 35/0.

RUSSELL, BRYON F

PERSONAL: Born December 31, 1970, in San Bernardino, Calif. ... 6-7/225. (2.01/102.1). ... Full name: Bryon Demetrise Russell
HIGH SCHOOL: San Bernardino (Calif.).
COLLEGE: Long Beach State.
TRANSACTIONS/CAREER NOTES: Selected by Utah Jazz in second round (45th pick overall) of 1993 NBA Draft. ... Signed as free agent by Washington Wizards (September 10, 2002). ... Signed as free agent by Los Angeles Lakers (October 1, 2003). ... Signed as free agent by Denver Nuggets (October 6, 2004). ... Traded by Nuggets to Seattle SuperSonics as part of four-way deal (February 23, 2006). ... Waived by SuperSonics (March 1, 2006).

COLLEGIATE RECORD

Season Team	G	Min.	FGM	FGA	Pct.	FTM	FTA	Pct.	Reb.	Ast.	Pts.	RPG	APG	PPG
89-90—Long Beach State						Did not play—ineligible.								
90-91—Long Beach State	28	552	83	193	.430	45	69	.652	162	41	220	5.8	1.5	7.9
91-92—Long Beach State	26	776	126	227	.555	99	151	.656	192	30	362	7.4	1.2	13.9
92-93—Long Beach State	32	1006	153	285	.537	104	143	.727	213	66	421	6.7	2.1	13.2
Totals	86	2334	362	705	.513	248	363	.683	567	137	1003	6.6	1.6	11.7

Three-point field goals: 1990-91, 9-for-28 (.321). 1991-92, 11-for-28 (.393). 1992-93, 11-for-34 (.324). Totals, 31-for-90 (.344).

NBA REGULAR-SEASON RECORD

Season Team	G	Min.	FGM	FGA	Pct.	FTM	FTA	Pct.	Off.	Def.	Tot.	Ast.	St.	Blk.	TO	Pts.	RPG	APG	PPG
93-94—Utah	67	1121	135	279	.484	62	101	.614	61	120	181	54	68	19	55	334	2.7	0.8	5.0
94-95—Utah	63	860	104	238	.437	62	93	.667	44	97	141	34	48	11	42	283	2.2	0.5	4.5
95-96—Utah	59	577	56	142	.394	48	67	.716	28	62	90	29	29	8	36	174	1.5	0.5	2.9
96-97—Utah	81	2525	297	620	.479	171	244	.701	79	252	331	123	129	27	94	873	4.1	1.5	10.8
97-98—Utah	82	2219	226	525	.430	213	278	.766	78	248	326	101	90	31	81	738	4.0	1.2	9.0
98-99—Utah	50	1770	217	468	.464	136	171	.795	65	201	266	74	76	15	76	622	5.3	1.5	12.4
99-00—Utah	82	2900	408	914	.446	237	316	.750	99	328	427	158	128	23	101	1159	5.2	1.9	14.1
00-01—Utah	78	2473	308	700	.440	222	285	.779	94	236	330	160	96	20	113	933	4.2	2.1	12.0
01-02—Utah	66	1998	222	584	.380	115	140	.821	79	216	295	136	64	19	110	636	4.5	2.1	9.6
02-03—Washington	70	1388	108	306	.353	53	69	.768	43	165	208	72	70	7	55	315	3.0	1.0	4.5
03-04—L.A. Lakers	72	945	98	244	.402	50	65	.769	32	114	146	71	32	12	37	289	2.0	1.0	4.0
04-05—Denver	70	1026	95	252	.377	61	77	.792	50	122	172	72	44	11	35	307	2.5	1.0	4.4
05-06—Denver-Seattle	1	3	0	0	...	0	0	...	0	1	1	1	0	0	0	0	1.0	1.0	0.0
Totals	841	19805	2274	5272	.431	1430	1906	.750	752	2162	2914	1085	874	203	835	6663	3.5	1.3	7.9

Three-point field goals: 1993-94, 2-for-22 (.091). 1994-95, 13-for-44 (.295). 1995-96, 14-for-40 (.350). 1996-97, 108-for-264 (.409). 1997-98, 73-for-

214 (.341). 1998-99, 52-for-147 (.354). 1999-00, 106-for-268 (.396). 2000-01, 95-for-230 (.413). 2001-02, 77-for-226 (.341). 2002-03, 46-for-140 (.329). 2003-04, 43-for-112 (.384). 2004-05, 56-for-149 (.376). Totals, 685-for-1856 (.369).
Personal fouls/disqualifications: 1993-94, 138/0. 1994-95, 101/0. 1995-96, 66/0. 1996-97, 237/2. 1997-98, 229/2. 1998-99, 154/3. 1999-00, 255/3. 2000-01, 229/1. 2001-02, 205/1. 2002-03, 130/1. 2003-04, 110/0. 2004-05, 130/0. Totals, 1984/13.

NBA PLAYOFF RECORD

Season Team	G	Min.	FGM	FGA	Pct.	FTM	FTA	Pct.	REBOUNDS Off.	Def.	Tot.	Ast.	St.	Blk.	TO	Pts.	AVERAGES RPG	APG	PPG
93-94—Utah	6	36	4	10	.400	6	6	1.000	4	5	9	3	0	0	1	16	1.5	0.5	2.7
94-95—Utah	2	13	4	7	.571	1	2	.500	1	1	2	3	1	0	0	11	1.0	1.5	5.5
95-96—Utah	18	459	58	124	.468	31	38	.816	17	58	75	22	23	9	10	172	4.2	1.2	9.6
96-97—Utah	20	758	89	193	.461	31	43	.721	18	74	92	27	21	6	20	245	4.6	1.4	12.3
97-98—Utah	20	698	69	147	.469	58	81	.716	12	81	93	22	21	5	17	219	4.7	1.1	11.0
98-99—Utah	11	387	49	115	.426	26	36	.722	17	50	67	13	20	2	11	133	6.1	1.2	12.1
99-00—Utah	10	371	48	114	.421	31	41	.756	9	43	52	21	16	5	15	140	5.2	2.1	14.0
00-01—Utah	5	214	25	56	.446	11	12	.917	4	32	36	15	3	1	2	71	7.2	3.0	14.2
01-02—Utah	4	120	9	36	.250	4	4	1.000	6	11	17	7	4	0	9	28	4.3	1.8	7.0
03-04—L.A. Lakers	6	16	0	3	.000	0	0	...	1	0	1	2	1	0	0	0	0.2	0.3	0.0
04-05—Denver	3	9	0	1	.000	3	3	1.000	0	0	0	0	0	0	0	3	0.0	0.0	1.0
Totals	105	3081	355	806	.440	202	266	.759	89	355	444	135	110	28	85	1038	4.2	1.3	9.9

Three-point field goals: 1993-94, 2-for-3 (.667). 1994-95, 2-for-4 (.500). 1995-96, 25-for-53 (.472). 1996-97, 36-for-101 (.356). 1997-98, 23-for-63 (.365). 1998-99, 9-for-36 (.250). 1999-00, 13-for-45 (.289). 2000-01, 10-for-22 (.455). 2001-02, 6-for-15 (.400). 2003-04, 0-for-2. 2004-05, 0-for-1. Totals, 126-for-345 (.365).
Personal fouls/disqualifications: 1993-94, 3/0. 1994-95, 2/0. 1995-96, 42/0. 1996-97, 59/1. 1997-98, 49/0. 1998-99, 37/0. 1999-00, 27/0. 2000-01, 13/0. 2001-02, 15/1. 2003-04, 2/0. Totals, 249/2.

SALMONS, JOHN   G/F   KINGS

PERSONAL: Born December 12, 1979, in Philadelphia. ... 6-7/210. (2.01/95.3). ... Full name: John Rashall Salmons.
HIGH SCHOOL: Plymouth Whitemarsh (Plymouth Meeting, Pa.).
COLLEGE: Miami.
TRANSACTIONS/CAREER NOTES: Selected by San Antonio Spurs in first round (26th pick overall) of 2002 NBA Draft. ... Draft rights traded by Spurs with F/C Mark Bryant and draft rights to F Randy Holcomb to Philadelphia 76ers for G Craig Claxton (June 26, 2002). ... Signed as free agent by Sacramento Kings (July 24, 2006).

COLLEGIATE RECORD

Season Team	G	Min.	FGM	FGA	Pct.	FTM	FTA	Pct.	Reb.	Ast.	Pts.	AVERAGES RPG	APG	PPG
98-99—Miami (Fla.)	29	705	61	127	.480	29	40	.725	141	57	161	4.9	2.0	5.6
99-00—Miami (Fla.)	34	1104	109	240	.454	73	92	.793	182	66	320	5.4	1.9	9.4
00-01—Miami (Fla.)	29	928	137	289	.474	88	111	.793	173	115	387	6.0	4.0	13.3
01-02—Miami (Fla.)	32	1077	137	297	.461	123	146	.842	191	195	419	6.0	6.1	13.1
Totals	124	3814	444	953	.466	313	389	.805	687	433	1287	5.5	3.5	10.4

Three-point field goals: 1998-99, 10-for-41 (.244). 1999-00, 29-for-85 (.341). 2000-01, 25-for-71 (.352). 2001-02, 22-for-71 (.310). Totals, 86-for-268 (.321).

NBA REGULAR-SEASON RECORD

Season Team	G	Min.	FGM	FGA	Pct.	FTM	FTA	Pct.	REBOUNDS Off.	Def.	Tot.	Ast.	St.	Blk.	TO	Pts.	AVERAGES RPG	APG	PPG
02-03—Philadelphia	64	504	48	116	.414	26	35	.743	16	43	59	47	17	6	29	132	0.9	0.7	2.1
03-04—Philadelphia	77	1603	161	416	.387	71	92	.772	38	158	196	134	62	16	77	443	2.5	1.7	5.8
04-05—Philadelphia	58	993	85	210	.405	35	48	.729	12	109	121	114	40	13	51	236	2.1	2.0	4.1
05-06—Philadelphia	82	2059	219	521	.420	155	200	.775	48	172	220	223	73	13	125	619	2.7	2.7	7.5
Totals	281	5159	513	1263	.406	287	375	.765	114	482	596	518	192	48	282	1430	2.1	1.8	5.1

Three-point field goals: 2002-03, 10-for-31 (.323). 2003-04, 50-for-147 (.340). 2004-05, 31-for-91 (.341). 2005-06, 26-for-87 (.299). Totals, 117-for-356 (.329).
Personal fouls/disqualifications: 2002-03, 53/1. 2003-04, 122/0. 2004-05, 92/1. 2005-06, 178/0. Totals, 445/2.

NBA PLAYOFF RECORD

Season Team	G	Min.	FGM	FGA	Pct.	FTM	FTA	Pct.	REBOUNDS Off.	Def.	Tot.	Ast.	St.	Blk.	TO	Pts.	AVERAGES RPG	APG	PPG
02-03—Philadelphia	6	16	0	1	.000	0	2	.000	0	3	3	0	0	0	2	0	0.5	0.0	0.0
04-05—Philadelphia	2	4	0	0	...	0	0	...	0	0	0	1	0	0	0	0	0.0	0.5	0.0
Totals	8	20	0	1	.000	0	2	.000	0	3	3	1	0	0	2	0	0.4	0.1	0.0

Three-point field goals: 2002-03, 0-for-1. Totals, 0-for-1 (.000).

SAMPSON, JAMAL   F/C   NUGGETS

PERSONAL: Born May 15, 1983, in Inglewood, Calif. ... 6-11/235. (2.11/106.6). ... Full name: Jamal Wesley Sampson.
HIGH SCHOOL: Mater Dei (Santa Ana, Calif.).
COLLEGE: California.
TRANSACTIONS/CAREER NOTES: Selected after freshman season by Utah Jazz in second round (47th pick overall) of 2002 NBA Draft. ... Draft rights traded by Jazz with draft rights to F Ryan Humphrey to Orlando Magic for draft rights to C Curtis Borchardt (June 26, 2002). ... Draft rights traded by Magic to Milwaukee Bucks for C Rashard Griffith (June 26, 2002). ... Signed as free agent by Los Angeles Lakers (July 24, 2003). ... Selected by Charlotte Bobcats from Lakers in NBA Expansion Draft (June 22, 2004). ... Waived by Bobcats (February 8, 2005). ... Signed as free agent by Sacramento Kings (August 10, 2005). ... Signed as free agent by Denver Nuggets (July 28, 2006).

COLLEGIATE RECORD

Season Team	G	Min.	FGM	FGA	Pct.	FTM	FTA	Pct.	Reb.	Ast.	Pts.	AVERAGES RPG	APG	PPG
01-02—California	32	797	78	183	.426	50	95	.526	209	38	206	6.5	1.2	6.4

NBA REGULAR-SEASON RECORD

Season Team	G	Min.	FGM	FGA	Pct.	FTM	FTA	Pct.	REBOUNDS			Ast.	St.	Blk.	TO	Pts.	AVERAGES		
									Off.	Def.	Tot.						RPG	APG	PPG
02-03—Milwaukee	5	8	0	2	.000	0	0	...	1	1	2	1	1	0	0	0	0.4	0.2	0.0
03-04—L.A. Lakers	10	130	11	23	.478	7	12	.583	23	29	52	7	2	4	6	29	5.2	0.7	2.9
04-05—Charlotte	23	329	28	62	.452	23	39	.590	36	86	122	8	4	17	17	79	5.3	0.3	3.4
05-06—Sacramento	12	39	5	7	.714	0	2	.000	5	13	18	5	0	4	0	10	1.5	0.4	0.8
Totals	50	506	44	94	.468	30	53	.566	65	129	194	21	7	25	23	118	3.9	0.4	2.4

Personal fouls/disqualifications: 2003-04, 16/0. 2004-05, 53/0. 2005-06, 5/0. Totals, 74/0.

SANDERS, MELVIN G SPURS

PERSONAL: Born January 3, 1981, in Pine Bluff, Ark. ... 6-5/210. (1.96/95.3).
HIGH SCHOOL: Liberal (Kan.).
JUNIOR COLLEGE: Seward County (Kan.).
COLLEGE: Oklahoma State.
TRANSACTIONS/CAREER NOTES: Not drafted by an NBA franchise ... Played in CBA (2003-05) ... Played in Italy (2003-04) ... Played in Belgium (2004-05) ... Played in NBA Development League (2005-06). ...Signed as free agent by San Antonio Spurs (November 9, 2005).

COLLEGIATE RECORD

Season Team	G	Min.	FGM	FGA	Pct.	FTM	FTA	Pct.	Reb.	Ast.	Pts.	AVERAGES		
												RPG	APG	PPG
99-00—Seward County CC	32	...	168	359	.468	61	83	.735	174	61	439	5.4	1.9	13.7
00-01—Oklahoma State.............	30	872	96	226	.425	23	39	.590	132	26	239	4.4	0.9	8.0
01-02—Oklahoma State.............	32	798	100	237	.422	30	48	.625	124	41	277	3.9	1.3	8.7
02-03—Oklahoma State.............	32	1008	155	351	.442	48	71	.676	155	52	413	4.8	1.6	12.9
Junior College Totals.............	32	...	168	359	.468	61	83	.735	174	61	439	5.4	1.9	13.7
4-Year College Totals	94	2678	351	814	.431	101	158	.639	411	119	929	4.4	1.3	9.9

Three-point field goals: 1999-00, 42-for-127 (.331). 2000-01, 24-for-72 (.333). 2001-02, 47-for-132 (.356). 2002-03, 55-for-161 (.342). 4-Year Totals, 126-for-365 (.345).

CBA RECORD

Season Team	G	Min.	FGM	FGA	Pct.	FTM	FTA	Pct.	Reb.	Ast.	Pts.	AVERAGES		
												RPG	APG	PPG
03-04—Dakota.............	44	1316	264	497	.531	66	89	.742	194	102	614	4.4	2.3	14.0
04-05—Dakota.............	48	1615	349	678	.515	159	186	.855	278	145	898	5.8	3.0	18.7
Totals	92	2931	613	1175	.522	225	275	.818	472	247	1512	5.1	2.7	16.4

Three-point field goals: 2003-04, 20-for-54 (.370). 2004-05, 41-for-109 (.376). Totals, 61-for-163 (.374).

ITALIAN LEAGUE RECORD

Season Team	G	Min.	FGM	FGA	Pct.	FTM	FTA	Pct.	Reb.	Ast.	Pts.	AVERAGES		
												RPG	APG	PPG
03-04—Matis Varese	11	220	49	112	.438	13	19	.684	33	10	126	3.0	0.9	11.5

Three-point field goals: 2003-04, 15-for-44 (.341). Totals, 15-for-44 (.341).

BELGIAN LEAGUE RECORD

Season Team	G	Min.	FGM	FGA	Pct.	FTM	FTA	Pct.	Reb.	Ast.	Pts.	AVERAGES		
												RPG	APG	PPG
04-05—Oostende	5	...	12	34	.353	5	10	.500	18	7	31	3.6	1.4	6.2

Three-point field goals: 2004-05, 4-for-18 (.222). Totals, 4-for-18 (.222).

NBA REGULAR-SEASON RECORD

Season Team	G	Min.	FGM	FGA	Pct.	FTM	FTA	Pct.	REBOUNDS			Ast.	St.	Blk.	TO	Pts.	AVERAGES		
									Off.	Def.	Tot.						RPG	APG	PPG
05-06—San Antonio	16	113	16	33	.485	7	10	.700	4	19	23	3	5	0	8	41	1.4	0.2	2.6

Three-point field goals: 2005-06, 2-for-3 (.667). Totals, 2-for-3 (.667).
Personal fouls/disqualifications: 2005-06, 20/0. Totals, 20/0.

NBA DEVELOPMENT LEAGUE RECORD

Season Team	G	Min.	FGM	FGA	Pct.	FTM	FTA	Pct.	Reb.	Ast.	Pts.	AVERAGES		
												RPG	APG	PPG
05-06—Fayetteville......................	19	601	111	238	.466	49	65	.754	75	41	274	3.9	2.2	14.4

Three-point field goals: 2005-06, 3-for-23 (.130). Totals, 3-for-23 (.130).

SCALABRINE, BRIAN F CELTICS

PERSONAL: Born March 18, 1978, in Long Beach, Calif. ... 6-9/240. (2.06/108.9). ... Full name: Brian David Scalabrine.
HIGH SCHOOL: Enumclaw (Wash.).
JUNIOR COLLEGE: Highline (Wash.).
COLLEGE: Southern California.
TRANSACTIONS/CAREER NOTES: Selected by New Jersey Nets in second round (35th pick overall) of 2000 NBA Draft. ... Signed as free agent by Boston Celtics (August 2, 2005).

COLLEGIATE RECORD

Season Team	G	Min.	FGM	FGA	Pct.	FTM	FTA	Pct.	Reb.	Ast.	Pts.	AVERAGES		
												RPG	APG	PPG
96-97—Highline C.C.	32	932	207	350	.591	108	144	.750	308	94	522	9.6	2.9	16.3

Season Team	G	Min.	FGM	FGA	Pct.	FTM	FTA	Pct.	Reb.	Ast.	Pts.	RPG	APG	PPG
											AVERAGES			
97-98—Highline C.C.								Did not play—redshirted.						
98-99—Southern California	28	869	152	286	.531	103	130	.792	178	68	408	6.4	2.4	14.6
99-00—Southern California	30	1052	203	382	.531	103	144	.715	180	85	534	6.0	2.8	17.8
00-01—Southern California	34	1116	173	362	.478	133	166	.801	202	96	499	5.9	2.8	14.7
Junior College Totals............	32	932	207	350	.591	108	144	.750	308	94	522	9.6	2.9	16.3
4-Year-College Totals............	92	3037	528	1030	.513	339	440	.770	560	249	1441	6.1	2.7	15.7

Three-point field goals: 1996-97, 0-for-6. 1998-99, 1-for-6 (.167). 1999-00, 25-for-62 (.403). 2000-01, 20-for-66 (.303). Totals, 46-for-140 (.329).
Personal fouls/disqualifications: 1996-97, 83/0. 1998-99, 81/0. 1999-00, 87/0. 2000-01, 89/0. Totals, 340/0.

NBA REGULAR-SEASON RECORD

Season Team	G	Min.	FGM	FGA	Pct.	FTM	FTA	Pct.	REBOUNDS Off.	Def.	Tot.	Ast.	St.	Blk.	TO	Pts.	AVERAGES RPG	APG	PPG
01-02—New Jersey	28	290	23	67	.343	11	15	.733	12	39	51	21	9	2	24	60	1.8	0.8	2.1
02-03—New Jersey	59	724	68	169	.402	30	36	.833	40	101	141	46	16	18	46	180	2.4	0.8	3.1
03-04—New Jersey	69	928	86	218	.394	58	70	.829	42	131	173	65	21	14	42	240	2.5	0.9	3.5
04-05—New Jersey	54	1167	132	332	.398	53	69	.768	83	161	244	88	34	18	66	339	4.5	1.6	6.3
05-06—Boston	71	938	74	193	.383	26	36	.722	27	87	114	51	21	19	50	205	1.6	0.7	2.9
Totals	281	4047	383	979	.391	178	226	.788	204	519	723	271	101	71	228	1024	2.6	1.0	3.6

Three-point field goals: 2001-02, 3-for-10 (.300). 2002-03, 14-for-39 (.359). 2003-04, 10-for-41 (.244). 2004-05, 22-for-68 (.324). 2005-06, 31-for-87 (.356). Totals, 80-for-245 (.327).
Personal fouls/disqualifications: 2001-02, 39/0. 2002-03, 77/0. 2003-04, 113/0. 2004-05, 111/3. 2005-06, 127/0. Totals, 467/3.

NBA PLAYOFF RECORD

Season Team	G	Min.	FGM	FGA	Pct.	FTM	FTA	Pct.	REBOUNDS Off.	Def.	Tot.	Ast.	St.	Blk.	TO	Pts.	AVERAGES RPG	APG	PPG
01-02—New Jersey	6	14	1	3	.333	0	0	...	1	2	3	0	0	1	1	2	0.5	0.0	0.3
02-03—New Jersey	7	20	2	4	.500	0	0	...	1	3	4	0	0	0	1	4	0.6	0.0	0.6
03-04—New Jersey	9	73	11	17	.647	3	6	.500	7	5	12	1	3	0	4	30	1.3	0.1	3.3
04-05—New Jersey	4	61	2	11	.182	4	4	1.000	2	5	7	2	1	2	4	9	1.8	0.5	2.3
Totals	26	168	16	35	.457	7	10	.700	11	15	26	3	4	3	10	45	1.0	0.1	1.7

Three-point field goals: 2001-02, 0-for-1. 2002-03, 0-for-1. 2003-04, 5-for-6 (.833). 2004-05, 1-for-4 (.250). Totals, 6-for-12 (.500).
Personal fouls/disqualifications: 2002-03, 3/0. 2003-04, 15/0. 2004-05, 6/0. Totals, 24/0.

SCALES, ALEX   G

PERSONAL: Born July 3, 1978, in Racine, Wis. ... 6-4/185. (1.93/83.9).
HIGH SCHOOL: Racine Lutheran (Wis.).
JUNIOR COLLEGE: San Jacinto.
COLLEGE: Oregon.
TRANSACTIONS/CAREER NOTES: Not drafted by an NBA franchise ... Played in Italy (2000-01) ... Played in China (2001-02, 2003-04) ... Played in CBA (2002-03) ... Played in NBA Development League (2003-04, 2005-06) ... Played in Korea (2004-05) ... Played in Spain (2005-06). ... Signed as free agent by Houston Rockets (September 8, 2003). ... Waived by Rockets (October 23, 2003). ... Signed by New Jersey Nets (October 4, 2004). ... Waived by Nets (October 25, 2004). ... Signed by Seattle SuperSonics (September 30, 2005). ... Waived by SuperSonics (November 30, 2005). ... Signed by San Antonio Spurs (November 7, 2005). ... Waived by Spurs (November 28, 2005).

COLLEGIATE RECORD

Season Team	G	Min.	FGM	FGA	Pct.	FTM	FTA	Pct.	Reb.	Ast.	Pts.	AVERAGES RPG	APG	PPG
96-97—San Jacinto	35	916	137	320	.428	35	45	.778	186	89	363	5.3	2.5	10.4
97-98—San Jacinto	30	803	150	337	.445	82	104	.788	196	73	434	6.5	2.4	14.5
98-99—Oregon	32	948	164	406	.404	79	107	.738	188	101	457	5.9	3.2	14.3
99-00—Oregon	30	961	179	393	.455	78	100	.780	129	75	490	4.3	2.5	16.3
Junior College Totals............	65	1719	287	657	.437	117	149	.785	382	162	797	5.9	2.5	12.3
4-Year College Totals	62	1909	343	799	.429	157	207	.758	317	176	947	5.1	2.8	15.3

Three-point field goals: 1996-97, 54-for-164 (.329). 1997-98, 52-for-166 (.313). 1998-99, 50-for-162 (.309). 1999-00, 54-for-160 (.338). 4-Year Totals, 104-for-322 (.323).

ITALIAN LEAGUE RECORD

Season Team	G	Min.	FGM	FGA	Pct.	FTM	FTA	Pct.	Reb.	Ast.	Pts.	AVERAGES RPG	APG	PPG
00-01—Livorno	14	345	55	156	.353	24	33	.727	31	10	149	2.2	0.7	10.6

Three-point field goals: 2000-01, 15-for-61 (.246). Totals, 15-for-61 (.246).

CBA RECORD

Season Team	G	Min.	FGM	FGA	Pct.	FTM	FTA	Pct.	Reb.	Ast.	Pts.	AVERAGES RPG	APG	PPG
02-03—Grand Rapids	46	1473	333	706	.472	164	209	.785	121	130	907	2.6	2.8	19.7

Three-point field goals: 2002-03, 77-for-219 (.352). Totals, 77-for-219 (.352).

NBA DEVELOPMENT LEAGUE RECORD

Season Team	G	Min.	FGM	FGA	Pct.	FTM	FTA	Pct.	Reb.	Ast.	Pts.	AVERAGES RPG	APG	PPG
03-04—Huntsville	12	365	76	158	.481	26	34	.765	29	23	181	2.4	1.9	15.1
05-06—Austin	23	585	72	177	.407	53	65	.815	52	42	223	2.3	1.8	9.7
Totals	35	950	148	335	.442	79	99	.798	81	65	404	2.3	1.9	11.5

Three-point field goals: 2003-04, 3-for-25 (.120). 2005-06, 26-for-73 (.356). Totals, 29-for-98 (.296).

NBA REGULAR-SEASON RECORD

Season Team	G	Min.	FGM	FGA	Pct.	FTM	FTA	Pct.	REBOUNDS Off.	Def.	Tot.	Ast.	St.	Blk.	TO	Pts.	AVERAGES RPG	APG	PPG
05-06—San Antonio....	1	0	0	0	...	0	0	...	0	0	0	0	0	0	0	0	0.0	0.0	0.0

Season Team	G	Min.	FGM	FGA	Pct.	FTM	FTA	Pct.	Reb.	Ast.	Pts.	AVERAGES RPG	APG	PPG
05-06—Real Madrid	13	240	37	91	.407	19	23	.826	27	11	111	2.1	0.8	8.5

Three-point field goals: 2005-06, 18-for-46 (.391). Totals, 18-for-46 (.391).

SCHENSCHER, LUKE — C — BULLS

PERSONAL: Born December 31, 1982, in Hope Forest, South Australia. ... 7-1/265. (2.16/120.2). ... Full name: Luke Dean Schenscher
HIGH SCHOOL: Australian Institute of Sport (Canberra, Australia).
COLLEGE: Georgia Tech.
TRANSACTIONS/CAREER NOTES: Not drafted by an NBA franchise ... Played in NBA Development League (2005-06). ... Signed as free agent by Denver Nuggets (August 18, 2005). ... Signed as free agent by Chicago Bulls (March 5, 2006).

COLLEGIATE RECORD

Season Team	G	Min.	FGM	FGA	Pct.	FTM	FTA	Pct.	Reb.	Ast.	Pts.	AVERAGES RPG	APG	PPG
01-02—Georgia Tech	19	304	37	63	.587	18	35	.514	61	15	92	3.2	0.8	4.8
02-03—Georgia Tech	30	376	50	106	.472	10	19	.526	92	10	111	3.1	0.3	3.7
03-04—Georgia Tech	38	1035	140	248	.565	68	99	.687	252	30	348	6.6	0.8	9.2
04-05—Georgia Tech	32	831	132	245	.539	57	89	.640	235	40	322	7.3	1.3	10.1
Totals	119	2546	359	662	.542	153	242	.632	640	95	873	5.4	0.8	7.3

Three-point field goals: 2002-03, 1-for-1 (1.000). 2004-05, 1-for-4 (.250). Totals, 2-for-5 (.400).

NBA REGULAR-SEASON RECORD

Season Team	G	Min.	FGM	FGA	Pct.	FTM	FTA	Pct.	REBOUNDS Off.	Def.	Tot.	Ast.	St.	Blk.	TO	Pts.	AVERAGES RPG	APG	PPG
05-06—Chicago	20	149	16	26	.615	4	13	.308	8	21	29	7	1	3	5	36	1.5	0.4	1.8

Personal fouls/disqualifications: 2005-06, 21/0. Totals, 21/0.

NBA PLAYOFF RECORD

Season Team	G	Min.	FGM	FGA	Pct.	FTM	FTA	Pct.	REBOUNDS Off.	Def.	Tot.	Ast.	St.	Blk.	TO	Pts.	AVERAGES RPG	APG	PPG
05-06—Chicago	3	17	2	2	1.000	3	4	.750	3	4	7	0	0	0	1	7	2.3	0.0	2.3

Personal fouls/disqualifications: 2005-06, 2/0. Totals, 2/0.

NBA DEVELOPMENT LEAGUE RECORD

Season Team	G	Min.	FGM	FGA	Pct.	FTM	FTA	Pct.	Reb.	Ast.	Pts.	AVERAGES RPG	APG	PPG
05-06—Fort Worth	36	887	122	230	.530	51	84	.607	220	45	295	6.1	1.3	8.2

SIMIEN, WAYNE — F — HEAT

PERSONAL: Born March 9, 1983, in Leavenworth, Kan. ... 6-9/255. (2.06/115.7). ... Full name: Wayne Anthony Simien
HIGH SCHOOL: Leavenworth (Kan.).
COLLEGE: Kansas.
TRANSACTIONS/CAREER NOTES: Selected by Miami Heat in first round (29th pick overall) of 2005 NBA Draft.
MISCELLANEOUS: Member of NBA championship team (2006).

COLLEGIATE RECORD

NOTES: The SPORTING NEWS All-America first team (2005).

Season Team	G	Min.	FGM	FGA	Pct.	FTM	FTA	Pct.	Reb.	Ast.	Pts.	AVERAGES RPG	APG	PPG
01-02—Kansas	32	490	99	179	.553	62	84	.738	169	9	260	5.3	0.3	8.1
02-03—Kansas	16	390	95	147	.646	46	68	.676	131	9	236	8.2	0.6	14.8
03-04—Kansas	32	1045	200	376	.532	167	206	.811	297	39	569	9.3	1.2	17.8
04-05—Kansas	26	892	191	346	.552	142	174	.816	287	36	528	11.0	1.4	20.3
Totals	106	2817	585	1048	.558	417	532	.784	884	93	1593	8.3	0.9	15.0

Three-point field goals: 2003-04, 2-for-11 (.182). 2004-05, 4-for-14 (.286). Totals, 6-for-25 (.240).

NBA REGULAR-SEASON RECORD

Season Team	G	Min.	FGM	FGA	Pct.	FTM	FTA	Pct.	REBOUNDS Off.	Def.	Tot.	Ast.	St.	Blk.	TO	Pts.	AVERAGES RPG	APG	PPG
05-06—Miami	43	414	58	120	.483	30	34	.882	38	50	88	7	13	1	24	146	2.0	0.2	3.4

Personal fouls/disqualifications: 2005-06, 70/2. Totals, 70/2.

NBA PLAYOFF RECORD

Season Team	G	Min.	FGM	FGA	Pct.	FTM	FTA	Pct.	REBOUNDS Off.	Def.	Tot.	Ast.	St.	Blk.	TO	Pts.	AVERAGES RPG	APG	PPG
05-06—Miami	2	7	0	3	.000	0	0	...	1	0	1	0	0	0	1	0	0.5	0.0	0.0

Personal fouls/disqualifications: 2005-06, 1/0. Totals, 1/0.

SIMMONS, BOBBY — G/F — BUCKS

PERSONAL: Born June 2, 1980, in Chicago. ... 6-7/210. (2.01/95.3).
HIGH SCHOOL: Simeon (Chicago).
COLLEGE: DePaul.
TRANSACTIONS/CAREER NOTES: Selected after junior season by Seattle SuperSonics in second round (42nd pick overall) of 2001 NBA Draft. ... Draft rights traded by SuperSonics to Washington Wizards for draft rights to C Predrag Drobnjak

(June 27, 2001). ... Traded by Wizards with G/F Richard Hamilton and G Hubert Davis to Detroit Pistons for G/F Jerry Stackhouse, F Brian Cardinal and G Hubert Davis (September 11, 2002). ... Waived by Pistons (September 24, 2002). ... Signed as free agent by Wizards (October 1, 2002). ... Signed as free agent by Los Angeles Clippers (September 27, 2003). ... Signed as free agent by Milwaukee Bucks (August 8, 2005).

COLLEGIATE RECORD

Season Team	G	Min.	FGM	FGA	Pct.	FTM	FTA	Pct.	Reb.	Ast.	Pts.	RPG	APG	PPG
98-99—DePaul	31	949	112	300	.373	92	116	.793	190	82	347	6.1	2.6	11.2
99-00—DePaul	33	1009	142	308	.461	120	158	.759	262	53	433	7.9	1.6	13.1
00-01—DePaul	29	981	149	333	.447	124	155	.800	248	72	483	8.6	2.5	16.7
Totals	93	2939	403	941	.428	336	429	.783	700	207	1263	7.5	2.2	13.6

Three-point field goals: 1998-99, 31-for-112 (.277). 1999-00, 29-for-89 (.326). 2000-01, 61-for-165 (.370). Totals, 121-for-366 (.331).
Personal fouls/disqualifications: 1998-99, 77/0. 1999-00, 97/0. 2000-01, 97/0. Totals, 271/0.

NBA REGULAR-SEASON RECORD

HONORS: NBA Most Improved Player (2005).

Season Team	G	Min.	FGM	FGA	Pct.	FTM	FTA	Pct.	Off.	Def.	Tot.	Ast.	St.	Blk.	TO	Pts.	RPG	APG	PPG
01-02—Washington	30	343	43	95	.453	22	30	.733	25	27	52	17	13	5	14	112	1.7	0.6	3.7
02-03—Washington	36	378	44	112	.393	32	35	.914	33	44	77	20	10	3	8	120	2.1	0.6	3.3
03-04—L.A. Clippers...	56	1376	147	373	.394	141	169	.834	115	147	262	96	51	17	73	437	4.7	1.7	7.8
04-05—L.A. Clippers...	75	2799	474	1017	.466	231	273	.846	128	318	446	205	106	16	135	1229	5.9	2.7	16.4
05-06—Milwaukee	75	2538	366	808	.453	165	200	.825	91	242	333	172	86	21	123	1002	4.4	2.3	13.4
Totals	272	7434	1074	2405	.447	591	707	.836	392	778	1170	510	266	62	353	2900	4.3	1.9	10.7

Three-point field goals: 2001-02, 4-for-14 (.286). 2002-03, 0-for-5. 2003-04, 2-for-12 (.167). 2004-05, 50-for-115 (.435). 2005-06, 105-for-250 (.420). Totals, 161-for-396 (.407).
Personal fouls/disqualifications: 2001-02, 31/1. 2002-03, 51/0. 2003-04, 169/2. 2004-05, 227/4. 2005-06, 254/8. Totals, 732/15.

NBA PLAYOFF RECORD

Season Team	G	Min.	FGM	FGA	Pct.	FTM	FTA	Pct.	Off.	Def.	Tot.	Ast.	St.	Blk.	TO	Pts.	RPG	APG	PPG
05-06—Milwaukee	5	159	14	42	.333	0	0	...	4	14	18	10	9	1	6	33	3.6	2.0	6.6

Three-point field goals: 2005-06, 5-for-12 (.417). Totals, 5-for-12 (.417).
Personal fouls/disqualifications: 2005-06, 11/0. Totals, 11/0.

NBA DEVELOPMENT LEAGUE RECORD

Season Team	G	Min.	FGM	FGA	Pct.	FTM	FTA	Pct.	Reb.	Ast.	Pts.	RPG	APG	PPG
02-03—Mobile	14	423	76	180	.422	86	103	.835	73	22	240	5.2	1.6	17.1

Three-point field goals: 2002-03, 2-for-10 (.200). Totals, 2-for-10 (.200).
Personal fouls/disqualifications: 2002-03, 47/0. Totals, 47/0.

SINGLETON, JAMES   F   CLIPPERS

PERSONAL: Born July 20, 1981. ... 6-8/215 (2,03/97,5)
HIGH SCHOOL: Thornton Metro (Chicago).
JUNIOR COLLEGE: Pearl River (Miss.).
COLLEGE: Murray State.
TRANSACTIONS/CAREER NOTES: Played in Italy (2003-05). ... Not drafted by an NBA franchise. ... Signed as free agent by Los Angeles Clippers (August 30, 2005).

COLLEGIATE RECORD

Season Team	G	Min.	FGM	FGA	Pct.	FTM	FTA	Pct.	Reb.	Ast.	Pts.	RPG	APG	PPG
99-00—Pearl River CC							Statistics Unavailable							
00-01—Pearl River CC	27	827	146	238	.613	84	123	.683	373	30	376	13.8	1.1	13.9
01-02—Murray State	31	931	145	243	.597	85	108	.787	312	36	378	10.1	1.2	12.2
02-03—Murray State	29	953	153	283	.541	112	140	.800	320	54	433	11.0	1.9	14.9
Junior College Totals	27	827	146	238	.613	84	123	.683	373	30	376	13.8	1.1	13.9
4-Year-College Totals	60	1884	298	526	.567	197	248	.794	632	90	811	10.5	1.5	13.5

Three-point field goals: 2000-01, 0-for-2. 2001-02, 3-for-8 (.375). 2002-03, 15-for-34 (.441). Totals, 18-for-44 (.409).

ITALIAN LEAGUE RECORD

Season Team	G	Min.	FGM	FGA	Pct.	FTM	FTA	Pct.	Reb.	Ast.	Pts.	RPG	APG	PPG
03-04—Sicc Cucine Jesi-A2	32	1016	166	325	.511	62	89	.697	386	24	426	12.1	0.8	13.3
04-05—Armani Jeans Milano-A1	34	892	160	325	.492	72	98	.735	284	21	414	8.4	0.6	12.2
Totals	66	1908	326	650	.502	134	187	.717	670	45	840	10.2	0.7	12.7

Three-point field goals: 2003-04, 32-for-89 (.360). 2004-05, 22-for-74 (.297). Totals, 54-for-163 (.331).

NBA REGULAR-SEASON RECORD

Season Team	G	Min.	FGM	FGA	Pct.	FTM	FTA	Pct.	Off.	Def.	Tot.	Ast.	St.	Blk.	TO	Pts.	RPG	APG	PPG
05-06—L.A. Clippers...	59	753	77	151	.510	39	50	.780	63	134	197	29	19	21	28	203	3.3	0.5	3.4

Three-point field goals: 2005-06, 10-for-20 (.500). Totals, 10-for-20 (.500).
Personal fouls/disqualifications: 2005-06, 95/1. Totals, 95/1.

NBA PLAYOFF RECORD

Season Team	G	Min.	FGM	FGA	Pct.	FTM	FTA	Pct.	Off.	Def.	Tot.	Ast.	St.	Blk.	TO	Pts.	RPG	APG	PPG
05-06—L.A. Clippers...	7	12	1	3	.333	0	0	...	0	3	3	2	0	0	0	2	0.4	0.3	0.3

Three-point field goals: 2005-06, 0-for-2. Totals, 0-for-2 (.000).
Personal fouls/disqualifications: 2005-06, 3/0. Totals, 3/0.

PERSONAL: Born May 19, 1976, in Temple, Texas. ... 6-9/255. (2.06/115.7).
HIGH SCHOOL: Temple (Texas).
COLLEGE: Baylor.
TRANSACTIONS/CAREER NOTES: Selected by Los Angeles Clippers in first round (22nd pick overall) of 1998 NBA Draft. ... Traded by Clippers with rights to C Tyson Chandler to Chicago Bulls for F Elton Brand (June 27, 2001). ... Traded by Bulls to Toronto Raptors for F Charles Oakley and 2002 second-round draft choice (July 18, 2001). ... Traded by Raptors to Cleveland Cavaliers as part of three-way deal in which Cavaliers sent F/C Chris Gatling to Cavaliers, Heat sent G Ricky Davis to Cavaliers and Heat sent F Don MacLean and cash considerations to Raptors (October 26, 2001). ... Signed as free agent by Philadelphia 76ers (August 27, 2002). ... Signed as free agent by Milwaukee Bucks (July 17, 2003). ... Signed as free agent by 76ers (July 14, 2004). ... Traded by 76ers with Fs Kenny Thomas and Corliss Williamson to Sacramento Kings for Fs Chris Webber, Michael Bradley and Matt Barnes (February 23, 2005). ... Traded by Kings to Portland Trail Blazers as part of four-way deal (February 23, 2005). ... Traded by Trail Blazers with G Steve Blake and C Ha Seung-Jin to Milwaukee Bucks for C Jamaal Magloire (July 31, 2006).

S

COLLEGIATE RECORD

Season Team	G	Min.	FGM	FGA	Pct.	FTM	FTA	Pct.	Reb.	Ast.	Pts.	RPG	APG	PPG
												AVERAGES		
94-95—Baylor	18	501	98	164	.598	40	95	.421	147	9	236	8.2	0.5	13.1
95-96—Baylor	27	900	187	311	.601	101	163	.620	250	16	475	9.3	0.6	17.6
96-97—Baylor	30	973	196	349	.562	92	172	.535	253	26	484	8.4	0.9	16.1
97-98—Baylor	28	908	192	347	.553	123	208	.591	265	15	507	9.5	0.5	18.1
Totals	103	3282	673	1171	.575	356	628	.558	915	66	1702	8.9	0.6	16.5

NBA REGULAR-SEASON RECORD

Season Team	G	Min.	FGM	FGA	Pct.	FTM	FTA	Pct.	Off.	Def.	Tot.	Ast.	St.	Blk.	TO	Pts.	RPG	APG	PPG
									REBOUNDS								**AVERAGES**		
98-99—L.A. Clippers	21	258	33	71	.465	20	33	.606	20	33	53	1	10	13	19	86	2.5	0.0	4.1
99-00—L.A. Clippers	33	775	68	134	.507	43	65	.662	63	138	201	11	16	44	37	179	6.1	0.3	5.4
00-01—L.A. Clippers	39	584	64	161	.398	32	59	.542	55	113	168	18	14	11	32	160	4.3	0.5	4.1
01-02—Cleveland	65	1107	88	162	.543	48	79	.608	93	188	281	17	24	61	42	224	4.3	0.3	3.4
02-03—Philadelphia	77	1381	182	331	.550	97	161	.602	136	230	366	19	47	53	62	461	4.8	0.2	6.0
03-04—Milwaukee	56	1577	255	513	.497	79	138	.572	119	292	411	49	30	61	78	589	7.3	0.9	10.5
04-05—Phila.-Sac.	49	941	104	205	.507	25	70	.357	107	173	280	43	31	49	40	233	5.7	0.9	4.8
05-06—Sac.Portland	65	944	82	160	.513	27	56	.482	76	152	228	30	25	43	45	191	3.5	0.5	2.9
Totals	405	7567	876	1737	.504	371	661	.561	669	1319	1988	188	197	335	355	2123	4.9	0.5	5.2

Three-point field goals: 2004-05, 0-for-1. Totals, 0-for-1 (.000).

Personal fouls/disqualifications: 1998-99, 20/0. 1999-00, 75/0. 2000-01, 61/0. 2001-02, 130/1. 2002-03, 176/1. 2003-04, 165/3. 2004-05, 102/0. 2005-06, 119/1. Totals, 848/6.

NBA PLAYOFF RECORD

Season Team	G	Min.	FGM	FGA	Pct.	FTM	FTA	Pct.	Off.	Def.	Tot.	Ast.	St.	Blk.	TO	Pts.	RPG	APG	PPG
									REBOUNDS								**AVERAGES**		
02-03—Philadelphia	8	38	1	6	.167	4	4	1.000	3	3	6	0	0	1	2	6	0.8	0.0	0.8
03-04—Milwaukee	5	94	11	21	.524	5	12	.417	8	14	22	0	1	3	7	27	4.4	0.0	5.4
04-05—Sacramento	4	47	4	8	.500	0	0		6	5	11	2	2	4	5	8	2.8	0.5	2.0
Totals	17	179	16	35	.457	9	16	.563	17	22	39	2	3	8	14	41	2.3	0.1	2.4

Three-point field goals: 2002-03, 0-for-1. Totals, 0-for-1 (.000).

Personal fouls/disqualifications: 2002-03, 6/0. 2003-04, 8/0. 2004-05, 5/0. Totals, 19/0.

PERSONAL: Born August 22, 1975, in Fort Worth, Texas. ... 6-4/194. (1.93/88.0). ... Full name: Charles Cornelius Smith.
HIGH SCHOOL: Dunbar (Fort Worth, Texas).
COLLEGE: New Mexico.
TRANSACTIONS/CAREER NOTES: Selected by Miami Heat in first round (26th pick overall) of 1997 NBA Draft. ... Traded by Heat with C Isaac Austin and 1998 first-round draft choice to Los Angeles Clippers for G Brent Barry (February 19, 1998). ... Waived by Clippers (October 28, 1999). ... Played in Continental Basketball Association with Rockford Lightning (1999-2000) and La Crosse Bobcats (2000-01). ... Played in Greece (2003-04). ... Played in Italy (1999-2001; 2004-05). ... Signed as free agent by San Antonio Spurs (August 2, 2001). ... Traded by Spurs with G Antonio Daniels and F/C Amal McCaskill to Portland Trail Blazers for G Erick Barkley and G Steve Kerr (August 5, 2002). ... Played in Turkey (2005-06). ... Signed by Trail Blazers (August 4, 2005). ... Traded by Trail Blazers to Denver Nuggets as part of four-way deal (February 23, 2006). ... Waived by Nuggets (March 1, 2006).

COLLEGIATE RECORD

Season Team	G	Min.	FGM	FGA	Pct.	FTM	FTA	Pct.	Reb.	Ast.	Pts.	RPG	APG	PPG
												AVERAGES		
93-94—New Mexico	31	799	121	290	.417	31	51	.608	113	68	313	3.6	2.2	10.1
94-95—New Mexico	29	929	180	400	.450	70	105	.667	127	95	461	4.4	3.3	15.9
95-96—New Mexico	33	1083	233	506	.460	107	132	.811	153	102	642	4.6	3.1	19.5
96-97—New Mexico	33	972	203	444	.457	104	139	.748	181	93	577	5.5	2.8	17.5
Totals	126	3783	737	1640	.449	312	427	.731	574	358	1993	4.6	2.8	15.8

Three-point field goals: 1993-94, 40-for-119 (.336). 1994-95, 31-for-116 (.267). 1995-96, 69-for-188 (.367). 1996-97, 67-for-182 (.368). Totals, 207-for-605 (.342).

Personal fouls/disqualifications: 1993-94, 57/0. 1994-95, 58/0. 1995-96, 55/1. Totals, 170/1.

NBA REGULAR-SEASON RECORD

Season Team	G	Min.	FGM	FGA	Pct.	FTM	FTA	Pct.	Off.	Def.	Tot.	Ast.	St.	Blk.	TO	Pts.	RPG	APG	PPG
									REBOUNDS								**AVERAGES**		
97-98—Mia.-L.A.C.	34	292	49	125	.392	6	11	.545	13	14	27	21	12	6	27	119	0.8	0.6	3.5

Season Team	G	Min.	FGM	FGA	Pct.	FTM	FTA	Pct.	REBOUNDS Off.	Def.	Tot.	Ast.	St.	Blk.	TO	Pts.	AVERAGES RPG	APG	PPG
98-99—L.A. Clippers...	23	317	35	97	.361	7	16	.438	7	17	24	13	17	14	20	84	1.0	0.6	3.7
01-02—San Antonio....	60	1141	182	428	.425	42	65	.646	34	99	133	80	52	44	59	441	2.2	1.3	7.4
02-03—Portland.........	3	13	1	4	.250	3	4	.750	0	0	0	1	1	0	1	5	0.0	0.3	1.7
05-06—Portland-Denver	22	210	30	72	.417	5	8	.625	3	13	16	9	5	6	4	80	0.7	0.4	3.6
Totals...................	142	1973	297	726	.409	63	104	.606	57	143	200	124	87	70	111	729	1.4	0.9	5.1

Three-point field goals: 1997-98, 15-for-47 (.319). 1998-99, 7-for-33 (.212). 2001-02, 35-for-131 (.267). 2002-03, 0-for-1. 2005-06, 15-for-38 (.395). Totals, 72-for-250 (.288).

Personal fouls/disqualifications: 1997-98, 24/0. 1998-99, 35/0. 2001-02, 114/1. 2002-03, 3/0. 2005-06, 28/0. Totals, 204/1.

NBA PLAYOFF RECORD

Season Team	G	Min.	FGM	FGA	Pct.	FTM	FTA	Pct.	REBOUNDS Off.	Def.	Tot.	Ast.	St.	Blk.	TO	Pts.	AVERAGES RPG	APG	PPG
01-02—San Antonio....	4	19	2	3	.667	1	2	.500	2	1	3	2	2	1	3	5	0.8	0.5	1.3

Personal fouls/disqualifications: 2001-02, 5/0. Totals, 5/0.

CBA RECORD

NOTES: CBA Newcomer of the Year (2000). ... CBA All-League second team (2000).

Season Team	G	Min.	FGM	FGA	Pct.	FTM	FTA	Pct.	Reb.	Ast.	Pts.	AVERAGES RPG	APG	PPG
99-00—Rockford	56	1786	*376	804	.468	124	179	.693	202	119	936	3.6	2.1	16.7
00-01—La Crosse	5	165	32	65	.492	14	21	.667	22	44	80	4.4	8.8	16.0
Totals	61	1951	408	869	.470	138	200	.690	224	163	1016	3.7	2.7	16.7

Three-point field goals: 1999-00, 60-for-183 (.328). 2000-01, 2-for-13 (.154). Totals, 62-for-196 (.316).

Personal fouls/disqualifications: 1999-00, 161/0. 2000-01, 12/0. Totals, 173/0.

ITALIAN LEAGUE RECORD

Season Team	G	Min.	FGM	FGA	Pct.	FTM	FTA	Pct.	Reb.	Ast.	Pts.	AVERAGES RPG	APG	PPG
99-00—Snaidero UD..................	3	106	32	53	.604	1	4	.250	10	4	76	3.3	1.3	25.3
00-01—Snaidero UD..................	34	1113	303	630	.481	124	170	.729	155	25	820	4.6	0.7	24.1
04-05—Scavolini Pesaro.............	32	1047	221	504	.438	93	119	.782	120	65	626	3.8	2.0	19.6
Totals	69	2266	556	1187	.468	218	293	.744	285	94	1522	4.1	1.4	22.1

Three-point field goals: 1999-00, 11-for-20 (.550). 2000-01, 92-for-243 (.379). 2004-05, 91-for-270 (.337). Totals, 194-for-533 (.364).

GREEK LEAGUE RECORD

Season Team	G	Min.	FGM	FGA	Pct.	FTM	FTA	Pct.	Reb.	Ast.	Pts.	AVERAGES RPG	APG	PPG
03-04—Makedonikos	2	36	3	18	.167	2	2	1.000	6	2	8	3.0	1.0	4.0

TURKISH LEAGUE RECORD

Season Team	G	Min.	FGM	FGA	Pct.	FTM	FTA	Pct.	Reb.	Ast.	Pts.	AVERAGES RPG	APG	PPG
05-06—Efes Pilsen.....................	16	440	69	167	.413	21	31	.677	50	28	195	3.1	1.8	12.2

Three-point field goals: 2005-06, 36-for-104 (.346). Totals, 36-for-104 (.346).

SMITH, DONTA   G   HAWKS

PERSONAL: Born November 27, 1983, in Louisville, Ky. ... 6-7/215. (2.01/97.5). ... Full name: Donta Lamont Smith
HIGH SCHOOL: Oldham County (LaGrange, Ky.).
JUNIOR COLLEGE: Southeastern Illinois.
TRANSACTIONS/CAREER NOTES: Selected after sophomore season by Atlanta Hawks in second round (34th pick overall) of 2004 NBA Draft.

COLLEGIATE RECORD

Season Team	G	Min.	FGM	FGA	Pct.	FTM	FTA	Pct.	Reb.	Ast.	Pts.	AVERAGES RPG	APG	PPG
02-03—Southeastern Illinois College	36	...	219	376	.582	97	136	.713	199	107	582	5.5	3.0	16.2
03-04—Southeastern Illinois College	33	...	278	515	.540	231	284	.813	236	113	851	7.2	3.4	25.8
Totals	69		497	891	.558	328	420	.781	435	220	1433	6.3	3.2	20.8

Three-point field goals: 2002-03, 47-for-101 (.465). 2003-04, 64-for-165 (.388). Totals, 111-for-266 (.417).

NBA REGULAR-SEASON RECORD

Season Team	G	Min.	FGM	FGA	Pct.	FTM	FTA	Pct.	REBOUNDS Off.	Def.	Tot.	Ast.	St.	Blk.	TO	Pts.	AVERAGES RPG	APG	PPG
04-05—Atlanta	38	433	44	113	.389	33	48	.688	19	33	52	39	23	5	25	127	1.4	1.0	3.3
05-06—Atlanta	23	127	15	27	.556	6	12	.500	3	11	14	9	8	0	4	38	0.6	0.4	1.7
Totals	61	560	59	140	.421	39	60	.650	22	44	66	48	31	5	29	165	1.1	0.8	2.7

Three-point field goals: 2004-05, 6-for-22 (.273). 2005-06, 2-for-4 (.500). Totals, 8-for-26 (.308).

Personal fouls/disqualifications: 2004-05, 50/0. 2005-06, 20/0. Totals, 70/0.

NBA DEVELOPMENT LEAGUE RECORD

Season Team	G	Min.	FGM	FGA	Pct.	FTM	FTA	Pct.	Reb.	Ast.	Pts.	AVERAGES RPG	APG	PPG
05-06—Arkansas	29	965	158	278	.568	76	104	.731	124	86	402	4.3	3.0	13.9

Three-point field goals: 2005-06, 10-for-31 (.323). Totals, 10-for-31 (.323).

SMITH, J.R.　　　　　　　　G　　　　　　　　NUGGETS

PERSONAL: Born September 9, 1985, in Freehold,N.J. ... 6-6/220. (1.98/99.8). ... Full name: Earl Smith III
HIGH SCHOOL: Lakewood (N.J.), then St. Benedict's Prep (Newark, N.J.).
COLLEGE: Did not attend college.
TRANSACTIONS/CAREER NOTES: Selected out of high school by New Orleans Hornets in first round (18th pick overall) in 2004 NBA Draft. ... Traded by Hornets with F P.J. Brown to Chicago Bulls for F Tyson Chandler (July 13, 2006). ... Traded by Bulls to Denver Nuggets for G Howard Eisley and two second-round picks in 2007 draft (July 20, 2006).

NBA REGULAR-SEASON RECORD

								REBOUNDS								AVERAGES		
Season Team	G	Min.	FGM	FGA	Pct.	FTM	FTA	Pct.	Off.	Def.	Tot.	Ast.	St.	Blk.	TO	Pts.	RPG	APG	PPG
04-05—New Orleans ...	76	1859	295	748	.394	111	161	.689	39	113	152	142	55	11	109	782	2.0	1.9	10.3
05-06—NO/Okla. City ..	55	989	144	366	.393	83	101	.822	19	91	110	58	37	4	54	423	2.0	1.1	7.7
Totals	131	2848	439	1114	.394	194	262	.740	58	204	262	200	92	15	163	1205	2.0	1.5	9.2

Three-point field goals: 2004-05, 81-for-281 (.288). 2005-06, 52-for-140 (.371). Totals, 133-for-421 (.316).
Personal fouls/disqualifications: 2004-05, 135/0. 2005-06, 90/0. Totals, 225/0.

SMITH, JOE　　　　　　　　F　　　　　　　　NUGGETS

PERSONAL: Born July 26, 1975, in Norfolk, Va. ... 6-10/225. (2.08/102.1). ... Full name: Joseph Leynard Smith
HIGH SCHOOL: Maury (Norfolk, Va.).
COLLEGE: Maryland.
TRANSACTIONS/CAREER NOTES: Selected after sophomore season by Golden State Warriors in first round (first pick overall) of 1995 NBA Draft. ... Traded by Warriors with G Brian Shaw to Philadelphia 76ers for F Clarence Weatherspoon and G Jim Jackson (February 17, 1998). ... Signed as free agent by Minnesota Timberwolves (January 22, 1999). ... Contract voided by NBA (October 25, 2000). ... Signed as free agent by Detroit Pistons (November 20, 2000). ... Signed as free agent by Timberwolves (July 30, 2001). ... Traded by Timberwolves with G Anthony Peeler to Milwaukee Bucks for G Sam Cassell and C Ervin Johnson (June 27, 2003). ... Traded by Bucks to Denver Nuggets for F Ruben Patterson (August 10, 2006).

COLLEGIATE RECORD

NOTES: Naismith Award winner (1995). ... THE SPORTING NEWS All-America second team (1995).

											AVERAGES		
Season Team	G	Min.	FGM	FGA	Pct.	FTM	FTA	Pct.	Reb.	Ast.	Pts.	RPG	APG	PPG
93-94—Maryland	30	988	206	395	.522	168	229	.734	321	25	582	10.7	0.8	19.4
94-95—Maryland	34	1110	245	424	.578	209	282	.741	362	40	708	10.6	1.2	20.8
Totals	64	2098	451	819	.551	377	511	.738	683	65	1290	10.7	1.0	20.2

Three-point field goals: 1993-94, 2-for-5 (.400). 1994-95, 9-for-21 (.429). Totals, 11-for-26 (.423).

NBA REGULAR-SEASON RECORD

HONORS: NBA All-Rookie first team (1996).

								REBOUNDS								AVERAGES		
Season Team	G	Min.	FGM	FGA	Pct.	FTM	FTA	Pct.	Off.	Def.	Tot.	Ast.	St.	Blk.	TO	Pts.	RPG	APG	PPG
95-96—Golden State ...	82	2821	469	1024	.458	303	392	.773	300	417	717	79	85	134	138	1251	8.7	1.0	15.3
96-97—Golden State ...	80	3086	587	1293	.454	307	377	.814	261	418	679	125	74	86	192	1493	8.5	1.6	18.7
97-98—G.S.-Phila.	79	2344	464	1070	.434	227	293	.775	199	272	471	94	62	51	158	1155	6.0	1.2	14.6
98-99—Minnesota.......	43	1418	223	522	.427	142	188	.755	154	200	354	68	32	66	66	588	8.2	1.6	13.7
99-00—Minnesota.......	78	1975	289	623	.464	195	258	.756	186	298	484	88	45	85	119	774	6.2	1.1	9.9
00-01—Detroit	69	1941	308	765	.403	231	287	.805	160	331	491	79	47	50	88	847	7.1	1.1	12.3
01-02—Minnesota.......	72	1922	297	581	.511	171	206	.830	152	301	453	82	39	59	86	767	6.3	1.1	10.7
02-03—Minnesota.......	54	1117	151	328	.460	102	131	.779	111	159	270	38	14	55	44	404	5.0	0.7	7.5
03-04—Milwaukee	76	2254	311	708	.439	207	241	.859	230	413	643	78	47	94	82	830	8.5	1.0	10.9
04-05—Milwaukee	74	2265	319	621	.514	175	228	.768	179	362	541	67	43	38	79	813	7.3	0.9	11.0
05-06—Milwaukee	44	887	145	305	.475	89	115	.774	83	147	230	31	24	13	40	379	5.2	0.7	8.6
Totals	751	22030	3563	7840	.454	2149	2716	.791	2015	3318	5333	829	512	731	1091	9301	7.1	1.1	12.4

Three-point field goals: 1995-96, 10-for-28 (.357). 1996-97, 12-for-46 (.261). 1997-98, 0-for-8. 1998-99, 0-for-3. 1999-00, 1-for-1 (1.000). 2000-01, 0-for-5. 2001-02, 2-for-3 (.667). 2002-03, 0-for-2. 2003-04, 1-for-5 (.200). 2004-05, 0-for-1. 2005-06, 0-for-2. Totals, 26-for-104 (.250).
Personal fouls/disqualifications: 1995-96, 224/5. 1996-97, 244/3. 1997-98, 263/2. 1998-99, 147/3. 1999-00, 302/8. 2000-01, 258/6. 2001-02, 250/2. 2002-03, 171/2. 2003-04, 209/1. 2004-05, 222/5. 2005-06, 120/1. Totals, 2410/37.

NBA PLAYOFF RECORD

								REBOUNDS								AVERAGES		
Season Team	G	Min.	FGM	FGA	Pct.	FTM	FTA	Pct.	Off.	Def.	Tot.	Ast.	St.	Blk.	TO	Pts.	RPG	APG	PPG
98-99—Minnesota.......	4	120	11	37	.297	8	11	.727	10	16	26	5	2	8	5	30	6.5	1.3	7.5
99-00—Minnesota.......	4	79	8	17	.471	2	2	1.000	7	5	12	1	3	1	4	18	3.0	0.3	4.5
01-02—Minnesota.......	3	43	3	7	.429	7	8	.875	4	7	11	0	0	1	1	13	3.7	0.0	4.3
02-03—Minnesota.......	5	40	4	6	.667	6	6	1.000	0	6	6	0	1	1	3	14	1.2	0.0	2.8
03-04—Milwaukee	5	175	27	55	.491	12	13	.923	23	27	50	2	4	10	6	66	10.0	0.4	13.2
05-06—Milwaukee	5	106	16	33	.485	6	9	.667	6	21	27	3	2	2	1	38	5.4	0.6	7.6
Totals	26	563	69	155	.445	41	49	.837	50	82	132	11	12	23	20	179	5.1	0.4	6.9

Three-point field goals: 1999-00, 0-for-1. 2003-04, 0-for-1. Totals, 0-for-2 (.000).
Personal fouls/disqualifications: 1998-99, 15/0. 1999-00, 15/0. 2001-02, 8/0. 2002-03, 14/0. 2003-04, 15/0. 2005-06, 16/0. Totals, 83/0.

SMITH, JOSH　　　　　　　　F　　　　　　　　HAWKS

PERSONAL: Born December 5, 1985, in College Park, Ga. ... 6-9/210. (2.06/95.3).
HIGH SCHOOL: McEachern (Powder Springs, Ga.), then Oak Hill Academy (Mouth of Wilson, Va.).
COLLEGE: Did not attend college.
TRANSACTIONS/CAREER NOTES: Selected out of high school by Atlanta Hawks in first round (17th overall pick) of 2004 NBA Draft.

S

NBA REGULAR-SEASON RECORD

HONORS: NBA All-Rookie second team (2005).

Season Team	G	Min.	FGM	FGA	Pct.	FTM	FTA	Pct.	Off.	Def.	Tot.	Ast.	St.	Blk.	TO	Pts.	RPG	APG	PPG
04-05—Atlanta	74	2050	274	602	.455	163	237	.688	147	310	457	127	59	144	135	715	6.2	1.7	9.7
05-06—Atlanta	80	2559	329	774	.425	210	292	.719	176	355	531	191	64	208	162	902	6.6	2.4	11.3
Totals	154	4609	603	1376	.438	373	529	.705	323	665	988	318	123	352	297	1617	6.4	2.1	10.5

Three-point field goals: 2004-05, 4-for-23 (.174). 2005-06, 34-for-110 (.309). Totals, 38-for-133 (.286).
Personal fouls/disqualifications: 2004-05, 157/1. 2005-06, 260/5. Totals, 417/6.

SNOW, ERIC   G   CAVALIERS

PERSONAL: Born April 24, 1973, in Canton, Ohio. ... 6-3/204. (1.91/92.5). ... Brother of Percy Snow, linebacker with Kansas City Chiefs (1990 through 1992), Chicago Bears (1993) and Rhein Fire of World League (1996).
HIGH SCHOOL: McKinley (Canton, Ohio).
COLLEGE: Michigan State.
TRANSACTIONS/CAREER NOTES: Selected by Milwaukee Bucks in second round (43rd pick overall) of 1995 NBA Draft. ... Draft rights traded by Bucks to Seattle SuperSonics for draft rights to C Aurelijius Zukauskas and 1996 second-round draft choice (June 28, 1995). ... Traded by SuperSonics to Philadelphia 76ers for 1998 second-round draft choice (January 18, 1998). ... Traded by 76ers to Cleveland Cavaliers for F Kedrick Brown and G Kevin Ollie (July 20, 2004).

COLLEGIATE RECORD

Season Team	G	Min.	FGM	FGA	Pct.	FTM	FTA	Pct.	Reb.	Ast.	Pts.	RPG	APG	PPG
91-92—Michigan State	25	144	12	25	.480	3	15	.200	15	24	27	0.6	1.0	1.1
92-93—Michigan State	28	798	53	97	.546	15	56	.268	73	145	121	2.6	5.2	4.3
93-94—Michigan State	32	992	91	177	.514	22	49	.449	111	213	217	3.5	6.7	6.8
94-95—Michigan State	28	916	117	225	.520	62	102	.608	92	217	303	3.3	7.8	10.8
Totals	113	2850	273	524	.521	102	222	.459	291	599	668	2.6	5.3	5.9

Three-point field goals: 1991-92, 0-for-2. 1992-93, 0-for-5. 1993-94, 13-for-45 (.289). 1994-95, 7-for-24 (.292). Totals, 20-for-76 (.263).

NBA REGULAR-SEASON RECORD

HONORS: NBA Sportsmanship Award (2000). ... NBA All-Defensive second team (2003).

Season Team	G	Min.	FGM	FGA	Pct.	FTM	FTA	Pct.	Off.	Def.	Tot.	Ast.	St.	Blk.	TO	Pts.	RPG	APG	PPG
95-96—Seattle	43	389	42	100	.420	29	49	.592	9	34	43	73	28	0	38	115	1.0	1.7	2.7
96-97—Seattle	67	775	74	164	.451	47	66	.712	17	53	70	159	37	3	48	199	1.0	2.4	3.0
97-98—Seattle-Phila. ..	64	918	79	184	.429	49	71	.690	19	62	81	177	60	5	63	209	1.3	2.8	3.3
98-99—Philadelphia	48	1716	149	348	.428	110	150	.733	25	137	162	301	100	1	111	413	3.4	6.3	8.6
99-00—Philadelphia	82	2866	257	597	.430	126	177	.712	42	219	261	624	140	8	162	651	3.2	7.6	7.9
00-01—Philadelphia	50	1740	182	435	.418	122	154	.792	27	139	166	369	77	7	124	491	3.3	7.4	9.8
01-02—Philadelphia	61	2228	272	674	.441	103	117	.000	34	181	216	060	108	8	118	700	0.1	0.0	10.1
02-03—Philadelphia	82	3108	361	799	.452	325	379	.858	71	230	301	544	133	11	194	1054	3.7	6.6	12.9
03-04—Philadelphia	82	2966	295	715	.413	252	316	.797	62	219	281	563	97	6	187	844	3.4	6.9	10.3
04-05—Cleveland	81	1844	125	327	.382	59	80	.738	37	118	155	317	67	16	89	322	1.9	3.9	4.0
05-06—Cleveland	82	2351	168	399	.409	64	93	.688	38	160	198	346	76	19	116	391	2.4	4.2	4.8
Totals	742	20898	2003	4692	.427	1366	1762	.775	380	1553	1933	3873	910	85	1270	5427	2.6	5.2	7.3

Three-point field goals: 1995-96, 2-for-10 (.200). 1996-97, 4-for-15 (.267). 1997-98, 2-for-17 (.118). 1998-99, 5-for-21 (.238). 1999-00, 11-for-45 (.244). 2000-01, 5-for-19 (.263). 2001-02, 3-for-27 (.111). 2002-03, 7-for-32 (.219). 2003-04, 2-for-18 (.111). 2004-05, 13-for-45 (.289). 2005-06, 1-for-10 (.100). Totals, 55-for-259 (.212).
Personal fouls/disqualifications: 1995-96, 53/0. 1996-97, 94/0. 1997-98, 114/0. 1998-99, 149/2. 1999-00, 243/2. 2000-01, 123/1. 2001-02, 167/1. 2002-03, 235/2. 2003-04, 213/1. 2004-05, 189/0. 2005-06, 218/4. Totals, 1798/13.

NBA PLAYOFF RECORD

Season Team	G	Min.	FGM	FGA	Pct.	FTM	FTA	Pct.	Off.	Def.	Tot.	Ast.	St.	Blk.	TO	Pts.	RPG	APG	PPG
95-96—Seattle	10	24	1	7	.143	0	0	...	0	4	4	6	2	0	4	2	0.4	0.6	0.2
96-97—Seattle	8	48	5	11	.455	1	2	.500	0	2	2	12	4	0	13	13	0.3	1.5	1.6
98-99—Philadelphia	8	306	37	88	.420	22	27	.815	3	30	33	57	8	1	25	99	4.1	7.1	12.4
99-00—Philadelphia	5	138	15	31	.484	4	4	1.000	0	10	10	35	4	1	7	37	2.0	7.0	7.4
00-01—Philadelphia	23	717	87	210	.414	40	55	.727	26	60	86	104	27	2	45	214	3.7	4.5	9.3
01-02—Philadelphia	5	171	18	56	.321	17	22	.773	3	19	22	27	6	0	15	54	4.4	5.4	10.8
02-03—Philadelphia	12	415	43	102	.422	51	58	.879	9	31	40	67	18	0	30	138	3.3	5.6	11.5
05-06—Cleveland	13	408	32	76	.421	22	29	.759	10	33	43	36	11	3	21	86	3.3	2.8	6.6
Totals	84	2227	238	581	.410	157	197	.797	51	189	240	344	80	7	147	643	2.9	4.1	7.7

Three-point field goals: 1995-96, 0-for-2. 1996-97, 2-for-4 (.500). 1998-99, 3-for-13 (.231). 1999-00, 3-for-4 (.750). 2000-01, 0-for-7. 2001-02, 1-for-6 (.167). 2002-03, 1-for-10 (.100). 2005-06, 0-for-1. Totals, 10-for-47 (.213).
Personal fouls/disqualifications: 1995-96, 3/0. 1996-97, 7/0. 1998-99, 26/0. 1999-00, 14/0. 2000-01, 63/0. 2001-02, 13/0. 2002-03, 47/1. 2005-06, 36/0. Totals, 209/1.

SNYDER, KIRK   G   ROCKETS

PERSONAL: Born June 5, 1983, in Los Angeles. ... 6-6/225. (1.98/102.1). ... Full name: Kirk Patrick Snyder
HIGH SCHOOL: Upland (Calif.).
COLLEGE: Nevada.
TRANSACTIONS/CAREER NOTES: Selected after junior season by Utah Jazz in first round (16th pick overall) of 2004 NBA Draft. ... Traded by Jazz to New Orleans Hornets in five-team trade (August 2, 2005). ... Traded by Hornets to Houston Rockets for a second-round pick in 2008 draft (July 14, 2006).

COLLEGIATE RECORD

Season Team	G	Min.	FGM	FGA	Pct.	FTM	FTA	Pct.	Reb.	Ast.	Pts.	RPG	APG	PPG
												AVERAGES		
01-02—Nevada	18	494	81	215	.377	65	104	.625	83	26	246	4.6	1.4	13.7
02-03—Nevada	32	1013	187	420	.445	113	177	.638	259	81	520	8.1	2.5	16.3
03-04—Nevada	34	1079	209	485	.431	166	227	.731	195	117	638	5.7	3.4	18.8
Totals	84	2586	477	1120	.426	344	508	.677	537	224	1404	6.4	2.7	16.7

Three-point field goals: 2001-02, 19-for-64 (.297). 2002-03, 33-for-123 (.268). 2003-04, 54-for-155 (.348). Totals, 106-for-342 (.310).

NBA REGULAR-SEASON RECORD

Season Team	G	Min.	FGM	FGA	Pct.	FTM	FTA	Pct.	Off.	Def.	Tot.	Ast.	St.	Blk.	TO	Pts.	RPG	APG	PPG
									REBOUNDS								AVERAGES		
04-05—Utah................	68	906	122	328	.372	64	96	.667	50	71	121	36	26	19	58	338	1.8	0.5	5.0
05-06—NO/Okla. City..	68	1310	205	453	.453	86	117	.735	55	106	161	102	29	23	70	542	2.4	1.5	8.0
Totals	136	2216	327	781	.419	150	213	.704	105	177	282	138	55	42	128	880	2.1	1.0	6.5

Three-point field goals: 2004-05, 30-for-85 (.353). 2005-06, 46-for-129 (.357). Totals, 76-for-214 (.355).
Personal fouls/disqualifications: 2004-05, 116/0. 2005-06, 106/1. Totals, 222/1.

SONGAILA, DARIUS   F   WIZARDS

PERSONAL: Born February 14, 1978, in Marijampole, Lithuania. ... 6-9/248. (2.06/112.5).
HIGH SCHOOL: New Hampton Prep (New Hampton, N.H.).
COLLEGE: Wake Forest.
TRANSACTIONS/CAREER NOTES: Selected by Boston Celtics in second round (50th pick overall) of 2002 NBA Draft. ... Traded by Celtics to Sacramento Kings for 2003 and 2005 second-round picks. ... Played in Russia (2002-03). ... Signed by Kings (June 25, 2003). ... Signed as free agent by Chicago Bulls (September 23, 2005). ... Signed as free agent by Washington Wizards (July 19, 2006).
MISCELLANEOUS: Member of bronze-medal-winning Lithuanian Olympic team (2000). ... Member of Lithuanian Olympic Team (2004).

COLLEGIATE RECORD

Season Team	G	Min.	FGM	FGA	Pct.	FTM	FTA	Pct.	Reb.	Ast.	Pts.	RPG	APG	PPG
												AVERAGES		
98-99—Wake Forest	31	757	125	248	.504	123	153	.804	165	48	375	5.3	1.5	12.1
99-00—Wake Forest	35	842	162	317	.511	157	188	.835	191	41	481	5.5	1.2	13.7
00-01—Wake Forest	30	766	145	290	.500	102	125	.816	181	51	396	6.0	1.7	13.2
01-02—Wake Forest	34	1036	204	390	.523	193	226	.854	276	89	607	8.1	2.6	17.9
Totals	130	3401	636	1245	.511	575	692	.831	813	229	1859	6.3	1.8	14.3

Three-point field goals: 1998-99, 2-for-8 (.250). 1999-00, 0-for-2. 2000-01, 4-for-9 (.444). 2001-02, 6-for-16 (.375). Totals, 12-for-35 (.343).

RUSSIAN LEAGUE RECORD

Season Team	G	Min.	FGM	FGA	Pct.	FTM	FTA	Pct.	Reb.	Ast.	Pts.	RPG	APG	PPG
												AVERAGES		
02-03—CSKA............................	27	584	127	256	.496	128	153	.837	149	43	392	5.5	1.6	14.5

Three-point field goals: 2002-03, 10-for-22 (.455). Totals, 10-for-22 (.455).

NBA REGULAR-SEASON RECORD

Season Team	G	Min.	FGM	FGA	Pct.	FTM	FTA	Pct.	Off.	Def.	Tot.	Ast.	St.	Blk.	TO	Pts.	RPG	APG	PPG
									REBOUNDS								AVERAGES		
03-04—Sacramento	73	976	133	273	.487	71	88	.807	91	134	225	48	42	12	43	337	3.1	0.7	4.6
04-05—Sacramento	81	1668	257	488	.527	94	111	.847	125	219	344	114	51	18	70	608	4.2	1.4	7.5
05-06—Chicago	62	1329	236	491	.481	94	115	.817	76	170	246	88	35	16	85	568	4.0	1.4	9.2
Totals	216	3973	626	1252	.500	259	314	.825	292	523	815	250	128	46	198	1513	3.8	1.2	7.0

Three-point field goals: 2004-05, 0-for-3. 2005-06, 2-for-5 (.400). Totals, 2-for-8 (.250).
Personal fouls/disqualifications: 2003-04, 126/1. 2004-05, 206/2. 2005-06, 157/2. Totals, 489/5.

NBA PLAYOFF RECORD

Season Team	G	Min.	FGM	FGA	Pct.	FTM	FTA	Pct.	Off.	Def.	Tot.	Ast.	St.	Blk.	TO	Pts.	RPG	APG	PPG
									REBOUNDS								AVERAGES		
03-04—Sacramento	7	85	10	16	.625	6	6	1.000	6	7	13	2	0	1	5	26	1.9	0.3	3.7
04-05—Sacramento	5	75	8	19	.421	4	5	.800	6	8	14	3	2	1	2	20	2.8	0.6	4.0
Totals	12	160	18	35	.514	10	11	.909	12	15	27	5	2	2	7	46	2.3	0.4	3.8

Personal fouls/disqualifications: 2003-04, 14/1. 2004-05, 14/0. Totals, 28/1.

SOW, PAPE   F   RAPTORS

PERSONAL: Born November 22, 1981, in Dakar, Senegal. ... 6-10/250. (2.08/113.4).
HIGH SCHOOL: Jean Di La Fontaine (Dakar, Senegal).
JUNIOR COLLEGE: Chaffey (Rancho Cucamonga, Calif.).
COLLEGE: Cal State Fullerton.
TRANSACTIONS/CAREER NOTES: Selected by Miami Heat in second round (47th pick overall) of 2004 NBA Draft. ... Draft rights traded by Heat to Toronto Raptors for F Albert Miralles and a future second-round draft choice (June 24, 2004).

COLLEGIATE RECORD

Season Team	G	Min.	FGM	FGA	Pct.	FTM	FTA	Pct.	Reb.	Ast.	Pts.	RPG	APG	PPG
												AVERAGES		
00-01—Chaffey					Statistics unavailable									
01-02—Cal State Fullerton	26	867	139	330	.421	118	182	.648	223	18	402	8.6	0.7	15.5
02-03—Cal State Fullerton	18	566	82	160	.513	79	116	.681	159	13	249	8.8	0.7	13.8

S

Season Team	G	Min.	FGM	FGA	Pct.	FTM	FTA	Pct.	Reb.	Ast.	Pts.	AVERAGES RPG	APG	PPG
03-04—Cal State Fullerton	28	901	160	324	.494	156	231	.675	272	25	484	9.7	0.9	17.3
Totals	72	2334	381	814	.468	353	529	.667	654	56	1135	9.1	0.8	15.8

Three-point field goals: 2001-02, 6-for-32 (.188). 2002-03, 6-for-12 (.500). 2003-04, 8-for-24 (.333). Totals, 20-for-68 (.294).

NBA REGULAR-SEASON RECORD

Season Team	G	Min.	FGM	FGA	Pct.	FTM	FTA	Pct.	REBOUNDS Off.	Def.	Tot.	Ast.	St.	Blk.	TO	Pts.	AVERAGES RPG	APG	PPG
04-05—Toronto	27	255	23	58	.397	16	27	.593	18	39	57	2	12	4	10	62	2.1	0.1	2.3
05-06—Toronto	42	590	53	123	.431	41	57	.719	54	92	146	8	21	19	30	147	3.5	0.2	3.5
Totals	69	845	76	181	.420	57	84	.679	72	131	203	10	33	23	40	209	2.9	0.1	3.0

Personal fouls/disqualifications: 2004-05, 46/0. 2005-06, 118/2. Totals, 164/2.

NBA DEVELOPMENT LEAGUE RECORD

Season Team	G	Min.	FGM	FGA	Pct.	FTM	FTA	Pct.	Reb.	Ast.	Pts.	AVERAGES RPG	APG	PPG
05-06—Arkansas	18	607	117	224	.522	120	151	.795	208	12	354	11.6	0.7	19.7

S

STACKHOUSE, JERRY G/F MAVERICKS

PERSONAL: Born November 5, 1974, in Kinston, N.C. ... 6-6/218. (1.98/98.9). ... Full name: Jerry Darnell Stackhouse ... Brother of Tony Dawson, forward with Sacramento Kings (1990-91) and Boston Celtics (1994-95).
HIGH SCHOOL: Kinston (N.C.), then Oak Hill Academy (Mouth of Wilson, Va.).
COLLEGE: North Carolina.
TRANSACTIONS/CAREER NOTES: Selected after sophomore season by Philadelphia 76ers in first round (third pick overall) of 1995 NBA Draft. ... Traded by 76ers with C Eric Montross to Detroit Pistons for C Theo Ratliff, G Aaron McKie and conditional first-round draft choice (December 18, 1997). ... Traded by Pistons with F Brian Cardinal and C Ratko Varda to Washington Wizards for G/F Richard Hamilton, G/F Bobby Simmons and G Hubert Davis (September 11, 2002). ... Traded by Wizards with F/C Christian Laettner and draft rights to G Devin Harris to Dallas Mavericks for F Antawn Jamison (June 24, 2004).

COLLEGIATE RECORD

NOTES: THE SPORTING NEWS All-America second team (1995).

Season Team	G	Min.	FGM	FGA	Pct.	FTM	FTA	Pct.	Reb.	Ast.	Pts.	AVERAGES RPG	APG	PPG
93-94—North Carolina	35	734	138	296	.466	150	205	.732	176	69	428	5.0	2.0	12.2
94-95—North Carolina	34	1170	215	416	.517	185	260	.712	280	93	652	8.2	2.7	19.2
Totals	69	1904	353	712	.496	335	465	.720	456	162	1080	6.6	2.3	15.7

Three-point field goals: 1993-94, 2-for-20 (.100). 1994-95, 37-for-90 (.411). Totals, 39-for-110 (.355).

NBA REGULAR-SEASON RECORD

HONORS: NBA All-Rookie first team (1996).

Season Team	G	Min.	FGM	FGA	Pct.	FTM	FTA	Pct.	REBOUNDS Off.	Def.	Tot.	Ast.	St.	Blk.	TO	Pts.	AVERAGES RPG	APG	PPG
95-96—Philadelphia	72	2701	452	1091	.414	387	518	.747	90	175	265	278	76	79	252	1384	3.7	3.9	19.2
96-97—Philadelphia	81	3166	533	1308	.407	511	667	.766	156	182	338	253	93	63	316	1679	4.2	3.1	20.7
97-98—Phila.-Det	79	2545	424	975	.435	354	450	.787	105	161	266	241	89	59	224	1249	3.4	3.1	15.8
98-99—Detroit	42	1188	181	488	.371	210	247	.850	26	81	107	118	34	19	121	607	2.5	2.8	14.5
99-00—Detroit	82	3148	619	1447	.428	618	758	.815	118	197	315	365	103	36	*311	1939	3.8	4.5	23.6
00-01—Detroit	80	3215	774	*1927	.402	*666	810	.822	99	216	315	410	97	54	*326	*2380	3.9	5.1	29.8
01-02—Detroit	76	2685	524	1319	.397	495	577	.858	77	238	315	403	77	37	266	1629	4.1	5.3	21.4
02-03—Washington	70	2747	491	1201	.409	455	518	.878	61	197	258	316	65	28	193	1508	3.7	4.5	21.5
03-04—Washington	26	774	128	321	.399	83	103	.806	16	78	94	103	24	3	88	362	3.6	4.0	13.9
04-05—Dallas.............	56	1617	274	662	.414	253	298	.849	38	145	183	127	53	10	106	833	3.3	2.3	14.9
05-06—Dallas.............	55	1525	242	603	.401	195	221	.882	32	121	153	160	37	10	121	715	2.8	2.9	13.0
Totals	719	25311	4642	11342	.409	4227	5167	.818	818	1791	2609	2774	748	398	2324	14285	3.6	3.9	19.9

Three-point field goals: 1995-96, 93-for-292 (.318). 1996-97, 102-for-342 (.298). 1997-98, 47-for-195 (.241). 1998-99, 35-for-126 (.278). 1999-00, 83-for-288 (.288). 2000-01, 166-for-473 (.351). 2001-02, 86-for-300 (.287). 2002-03, 71-for-245 (.290). 2003-04, 23-for-65 (.354). 2004-05, 32-for-120 (.267). 2005-06, 36-for-130 (.277). Totals, 774-for-2576 (.300).
Personal fouls/disqualifications: 1995-96, 179/0. 1996-97, 219/2. 1997-98, 175/2. 1998-99, 79/0. 1999-00, 188/1. 2000-01, 160/1. 2001-02, 163/0. 2002-03, 130/1. 2003-04, 49/0. 2004-05, 104/0. 2005-06, 96/1. Totals, 1542/8.

NBA PLAYOFF RECORD

Season Team	G	Min.	FGM	FGA	Pct.	FTM	FTA	Pct.	REBOUNDS Off.	Def.	Tot.	Ast.	St.	Blk.	TO	Pts.	AVERAGES RPG	APG	PPG
98-99—Detroit	5	124	18	46	.391	12	14	.857	3	5	8	6	2	1	10	50	1.6	1.2	10.0
99-00—Detroit	3	120	24	59	.407	23	31	.742	1	11	12	10	2	0	14	74	4.0	3.3	24.7
01-02—Detroit	10	361	53	165	.321	52	63	.825	9	34	43	43	6	6	27	176	4.3	4.3	17.6
04-05—Dallas.............	13	403	68	176	.386	57	66	.864	20	33	53	30	8	3	21	209	4.1	2.3	16.1
05-06—Dallas.............	22	711	111	276	.402	58	74	.784	20	42	62	56	12	6	37	302	2.8	2.5	13.7
Totals	53	1719	274	722	.380	202	248	.815	53	125	178	145	30	16	109	811	3.4	2.7	15.3

Three-point field goals: 1998-99, 2-for-8 (.250). 1999-00, 3-for-7 (.429). 2001-02, 18-for-53 (.340). 2004-05, 16-for-40 (.400). 2005-06, 22-for-65 (.338). Totals, 61-for-173 (.353).
Personal fouls/disqualifications: 1998-99, 11/0. 1999-00, 4/0. 2001-02, 26/0. 2004-05, 22/0. 2005-06, 43/0. Totals, 106/0.

NBA ALL-STAR GAME RECORD

Season Team	Min.	FGM	FGA	Pct.	FTM	FTA	Pct.	REBOUNDS Off.	Def.	Tot.	Ast.	PF	Dq.	St.	Blk.	TO	Pts.
2000—Detroit..................	14	4	7	.571	0	0	...	0	1	1	2	2	0	0	1	8
2001—Detroit..................	15	3	8	.375	0	2	.000	2	0	2	2	1	0	0	0	7
Totals..........................	29	7	15	.467	0	2	.000	2	1	3	4	3	0	0	1	15

Three-point field goals: 2001, 1-for-1 (1.000). Totals, 1-for-1 (1.000).

STEVENSON, DESHAWN   G   WIZARDS

PERSONAL: Born April 3, 1981, in Fresno, Calif. ... 6-5/210. (1.96/95.3).
HIGH SCHOOL: Washington Union (Fresno, Calif.).
COLLEGE: Did not attend college.
TRANSACTIONS/CAREER NOTES: Selected out of high school by Utah Jazz in first round (23rd pick overall) of 2000 NBA Draft. ... Traded by Jazz with conditional second-round draft choice to Orlando Magic for F Gordan Giricek (February 19, 2004). ... Signed as free agent by Washington Wizards (August 5, 2006).

NBA REGULAR-SEASON RECORD

Season Team	G	Min.	FGM	FGA	Pct.	FTM	FTA	Pct.	Off.	Def.	Tot.	Ast.	St.	Blk.	TO	Pts.	RPG	APG	PPG
00-01—Utah	40	293	31	91	.341	26	38	.684	9	19	28	18	10	2	28	89	0.7	0.5	2.2
01-02—Utah	67	1134	143	371	.385	37	53	.698	44	87	131	116	29	24	68	325	2.0	1.7	4.9
02-03—Utah	61	760	114	284	.401	47	68	.691	22	63	85	40	22	8	49	279	1.4	0.7	4.6
03-04—Utah-Orlando	80	2444	376	871	.432	138	204	.676	79	219	298	158	52	17	120	909	3.7	2.0	11.4
04-05—Orlando	55	1089	174	426	.408	56	101	.554	38	64	102	69	16	9	57	429	1.9	1.3	7.8
05-06—Orlando	82	2648	359	781	.460	180	242	.744	59	182	241	160	58	17	123	900	2.9	2.0	11.0
Totals	385	8368	1197	2824	.424	484	706	.686	251	634	885	561	187	77	445	2931	2.3	1.5	7.6

Three-point field goals: 2000-01, 1-for-12 (.083). 2001-02, 2-for-25 (.080). 2002-03, 4-for-12 (.333). 2003-04, 19-for-71 (.268). 2004-05, 25-for-67 (.373). 2005-06, 2-for-15 (.133). Totals, 53-for-202 (.262).
Personal fouls/disqualifications: 2000-01, 29/0. 2001-02, 82/0. 2002-03, 57/0. 2003-04, 140/0. 2004-05, 73/0. 2005-06, 178/2. Totals, 559/2.

NBA PLAYOFF RECORD

Season Team	G	Min.	FGM	FGA	Pct.	FTM	FTA	Pct.	Off.	Def.	Tot.	Ast.	St.	Blk.	TO	Pts.	RPG	APG	PPG
00-01—Utah	1	8	1	2	.500	0	0	—	0	1	1	0	0	0	1	2	1.0	0.0	2.0
02-03—Utah	4	37	6	15	.400	6	6	1.000	2	5	7	4	1	0	0	18	1.8	1.0	4.5
Totals	5	45	7	17	.412	6	6	1.000	2	6	8	4	1	0	1	20	1.6	0.8	4.0

Three-point field goals: 2002-03, 0-for-2. Totals, 0-for-2 (.000).
Personal fouls/disqualifications: 2002-03, 3/0. Totals, 3/0.

STOJAKOVIC, PEJA   F   HORNETS

PERSONAL: Born June 9, 1977, in Belgrade, Yugoslavia. ... 6-9/229. (2.06/103.9).
COLLEGE: PAOK (Greece).
TRANSACTIONS/CAREER NOTES: Played in Greece (1995-98). ... Selected by Sacramento Kings in first round (14th pick overall) of 1996 NBA Draft. ... Traded by Kings to Indiana Pacers for G/F Ron Artest (January 26, 2006). ... Traded by Pacers to New Orleans/Oklahoma City Hornets for draft rights to C Andrew Betts (July 12, 2006).
MISCELLANEOUS: Member of Yugoslavia Olympic team (2000).

GREEK LEAGUE RECORD

Season Team	G	Min.	FGM	FGA	Pct.	FTM	FTA	Pct.	Reb.	Ast.	Pts.	RPG	APG	PPG
95-96—PAOK	31	...	185	343	.539	115	145	.793	159	47	523	5.1	1.5	16.9
96-97—PAOK	16	554	110	218	.505	71	82	.866	74	17	324	4.6	1.1	20.3
97-98—PAOK	24	884	187	405	.462	131	147	.891	118	59	574	4.9	2.5	23.9
Totals	71	1438	482	966	.499	317	374	.848	351	123	1421	4.9	1.7	20.0

Three-point field goals: 1995-96, 38-for-98 (.388). 1996-97, 33-for-86 (.384). 1997-98, 69-for-170 (.406). Totals, 140-for-354 (.395).

HONORS: All-NBA second team (2004).

NBA REGULAR-SEASON RECORD

Season Team	G	Min.	FGM	FGA	Pct.	FTM	FTA	Pct.	Off.	Def.	Tot.	Ast.	St.	Blk.	TO	Pts.	RPG	APG	PPG
98-99—Sacramento	48	1025	141	373	.378	63	74	.851	43	100	143	72	41	7	53	402	3.0	1.5	8.4
99-00—Sacramento	74	1749	321	717	.448	135	153	.882	74	202	276	106	52	7	88	877	3.7	1.4	11.9
00-01—Sacramento	75	2905	559	1189	.470	267	312	.856	93	341	434	164	91	13	146	1529	5.8	2.2	20.4
01-02—Sacramento	71	2649	547	1130	.484	283	323	.876	72	301	373	175	81	14	140	1506	5.3	2.5	21.2
02-03—Sacramento	72	2450	497	1034	.481	231	264	.875	61	336	397	141	72	5	101	1380	5.5	2.0	19.2
03-04—Sacramento	81	3264	665	1386	.480	394	425	.927	91	417	508	173	108	14	153	1964	6.3	2.1	24.2
04-05—Sacramento	66	2534	451	1016	.444	253	275	.920	62	223	285	138	79	12	102	1329	4.3	2.1	20.1
05-06—Sac.-Indiana	71	2601	445	1018	.437	238	260	.915	79	336	415	136	45	10	103	1290	5.8	1.9	18.2
Totals	558	19177	3626	7863	.461	1864	2086	.894	575	2256	2831	1105	569	82	886	10277	5.1	2.0	18.4

Three-point field goals: 1998-99, 57-for-178 (.320). 1999-00, 100-for-267 (.375). 2000-01, 144-for-360 (.400). 2001-02, 129-for-310 (.416). 2002-03, 155-for-406 (.382). 2003-04, 240-for-554 (.433). 2004-05, 174-for-433 (.402). 2005-06, 162-for-404 (.401). Totals, 1161-for-2912 (.399).
Personal fouls/disqualifications: 1998-99, 43/0. 1999-00, 97/0. 2000-01, 144/0. 2001-02, 120/0. 2002-03, 143/1. 2003-04, 159/0. 2004-05, 157/0. 2005-06, 171/2. Totals, 1034/3.

NBA PLAYOFF RECORD

Season Team	G	Min.	FGM	FGA	Pct.	FTM	FTA	Pct.	Off.	Def.	Tot.	Ast.	St.	Blk.	TO	Pts.	RPG	APG	PPG
98-99—Sacramento	5	108	9	26	.346	3	3	1.000	12	7	19	2	3	0	6	24	3.8	0.4	4.8
99-00—Sacramento	5	129	16	40	.400	6	9	.667	2	15	17	3	4	0	5	44	3.4	0.6	8.8
00-01—Sacramento	8	307	52	128	.406	60	62	.968	17	34	51	3	5	3	18	173	6.4	0.4	21.6
01-02—Sacramento	10	338	50	133	.376	35	39	.897	16	47	63	10	5	0	19	148	6.3	1.0	14.8
02-03—Sacramento	12	486	97	202	.480	51	60	.850	17	66	83	30	10	5	12	277	6.9	2.5	23.1
03-04—Sacramento	12	517	76	198	.384	35	39	.897	15	69	84	18	22	3	14	210	7.0	1.5	17.5
04-05—Sacramento	5	203	39	83	.470	21	22	.955	6	20	26	7	4	1	2	110	5.2	1.4	22.0
05-06—Indiana	2	51	8	18	.444	6	7	.857	0	9	9	4	1	1	1	22	4.5	2.0	11.0
Totals	59	2139	347	828	.419	217	241	.900	85	267	352	77	54	13	77	1008	6.0	1.3	17.1

Three-point field goals: 1998-99, 3-for-14 (.214). 1999-00, 6-for-13 (.462). 2000-01, 9-for-26 (.346). 2001-02, 13-for-48 (.271). 2002-03, 32-for-70 (.457). 2003-04, 23-for-73 (.315). 2004-05, 11-for-30 (.367). 2005-06, 0-for-3. Totals, 97-for-277 (.350).
Personal fouls/disqualifications: 1998-99, 7/0. 1999-00, 7/0. 2000-01, 17/0. 2001-02, 22/0. 2002-03, 34/0. 2003-04, 26/0. 2004-05, 15/0. 2005-06, 4/0. Totals, 132/0.

NBA ALL-STAR GAME RECORD

Season Team	Min.	FGM	FGA	Pct.	FTM	FTA	Pct.	Off.	Def.	Tot.	Ast.	PF	Dq.	St.	Blk.	TO	Pts.
2002—Sacramento..........	18	4	10	.400	0	0	...	2	0	2	1	0	0	0	0	0	11
2003—Sacramento..........	13	2	7	.286	0	0	...	0	3	3	1	0	0	1	0	1	5
2004—Sacramento..........	12	2	5	.400	0	0	...	0	1	1	1	0	0	0	0	2	5
Totals..........................	43	8	22	.364	0	0	...	2	4	6	3	0	0	1	0	3	21

Three-point field goals: 2002, 3-for-5 (.600). 2003, 1-for-4 (.250). 2004, 1-for-4 (.250). Totals, 5-for-13 (.385).

STOREY, AWVEE   F   WIZARDS

PERSONAL: Born April 18, 1977, in Chicago. ... 6-6/225. (1.98/102.1).
HIGH SCHOOL: Proviso West (Maywood, Ill.), then New Hampton Prep (N.H.).
COLLEGE: Illinois, then Arizona State.
TRANSACTIONS/CAREER NOTES: Not drafted by an NBA franchise. ... Played in Korea (2002-05). ... Played in Venezuela (2004-05). ... Played in CBA (2004-05). ... Signed as free agent by New Jersey Nets (October, 2004). ... Waived by Nets (December 9, 2004). ... Signed as free agent by Washington Wizards (October 3, 2005).

COLLEGIATE RECORD

Season Team	G	Min.	FGM	FGA	Pct.	FTM	FTA	Pct.	Reb.	Ast.	Pts.	RPG	APG	PPG
97-98—Illinois	27	153	24	57	.421	6	16	.375	32	6	54	1.2	0.2	2.0
98-99—Illinois						Did Not Play - Transfer Student								
99-00—Arizona St..................	32	794	115	274	.420	66	106	.623	243	110	296	7.6	3.4	9.3
00-01—Arizona St..................	29	769	163	327	.498	53	88	.602	263	81	381	9.1	2.8	13.1
01-02—Arizona St..................	24	388	76	165	.461	30	43	.698	96	59	182	4.0	2.5	7.6
Totals	112	2104	378	823	.459	155	253	.613	634	256	913	5.7	2.3	8.2

Three-point field goals: 1997-98, 0-for-1. 1999-00, 0-for-3. 2000-01, 2-for-4 (.500). 2001-02, 0-for-2. Totals, 2-for-10 (.200).

CBA RECORD

Season Team	G	Min.	FGM	FGA	Pct.	FTM	FTA	Pct.	Reb.	Ast.	Pts.	RPG	APG	PPG
04-05—Idaho	7	212	34	74	.459	16	24	.667	34	19	97	4.9	2.7	13.9

Three-point field goals: 2004-05, 13-for-25 (.520). Totals, 13-for-25 (.520).

NBA REGULAR-SEASON RECORD

Season Team	G	Min.	FGM	FGA	Pct.	FTM	FTA	Pct.	Off.	Def.	Tot.	Ast.	St.	Blk.	TO	Pts.	RPG	APG	PPG
04-05—New Jersey	9	32	3	10	.300	1	2	.500	4	1	5	1	0	0	0	8	0.6	0.1	0.9
05-06—Washington	25	116	16	41	.390	8	14	.571	8	14	22	4	3	1	5	43	0.9	0.2	1.7
Totals	34	148	19	51	.373	9	16	.563	12	15	27	5	3	1	5	51	0.8	0.1	1.5

Three-point field goals: 2004-05, 1-for-2 (.500). 2005-06, 3-for-7 (.429). Totals, 4-for-9 (.444).
Personal fouls/disqualifications: 2004-05, 3/0. 2005-06, 22/0. Totals, 25/0.

STOUDAMIRE, SALIM   G   HAWKS

PERSONAL: Born October 11, 1982, in Portland, Ore. ... 6-1/179. (1.85/81.2). ... Full name: Charles Salim Stoudamire. ... Cousin of Damon Stoudamire, G, Memphis Grizzlies.
HIGH SCHOOL: Lincoln (Portland, Ore.), then Lake Oswego (Ore.) .
COLLEGE: Arizona.
TRANSACTIONS/CAREER NOTES: Selected by Atlanta Hawks in second round (31st pick overall) of 2005 NBA Draft.

COLLEGIATE RECORD

NOTES: The SPORTING NEWS All-America second team (2005).

Season Team	G	Min.	FGM	FGA	Pct.	FTM	FTA	Pct.	Reb.	Ast.	Pts.	RPG	APG	PPG
01-02—Arizona	34	1021	129	291	.443	103	114	.904	72	38	434	2.1	1.1	12.8
02-03—Arizona	30	774	125	264	.473	70	81	.864	49	54	391	1.6	1.8	13.0
03-04—Arizona	29	927	151	334	.452	93	117	.795	79	86	473	2.7	3.0	16.3
04-05—Arizona	36	1126	210	417	.504	122	134	.910	83	78	662	2.3	2.2	18.4
Totals	129	3848	615	1306	.471	388	446	.870	283	256	1960	2.2	2.0	15.2

Three-point field goals: 2001-02, 73-for-161 (.453). 2002-03, 71-for-160 (.444). 2003-04, 78-for-188 (.415). 2004-05, 120-for-238 (.504). Totals, 342-for-747 (.458).

NBA REGULAR-SEASON RECORD

Season Team	G	Min.	FGM	FGA	Pct.	FTM	FTA	Pct.	Off.	Def.	Tot.	Ast.	St.	Blk.	TO	Pts.	RPG	APG	PPG
05-06—Atlanta	61	1236	204	492	.415	99	110	.900	12	104	116	75	27	3	82	589	1.9	1.2	9.7

Three-point field goals: 2005-06, 82-for-216 (.380). Totals, 82-for-216 (.380).
Personal fouls/disqualifications: 2005-06, 118/1. Totals, 118/1.

STOUDAMIRE, DAMON   G   GRIZZLIES

PERSONAL: Born September 3, 1973, in Portland, Ore. ... 5-10/171. (1.78/77.6). ... Full name: Damon Lamon Stoudamire ... Cousin of Salim Stoudamire, G, Atlanta Hawks. ... Name pronounced DAY-min STOD-a-mire.
HIGH SCHOOL: Woodrow Wilson (Portland, Ore.).
COLLEGE: Arizona.
TRANSACTIONS/CAREER NOTES: Selected by Toronto Raptors in first round (seventh pick overall) of 1995 NBA Draft. ...

Traded by Raptors with F Walt Williams and F Carlos Rogers to Portland Trail Blazers for G Kenny Anderson, G Alvin Williams, F Gary Trent and two first-round draft choices (February 13, 1998). ... Signed as free agent by Memphis Grizzlies (August 5, 2005).

COLLEGIATE RECORD

NOTES: THE SPORTING NEWS All-America first team (1995).

Season Team	G	Min.	FGM	FGA	Pct.	FTM	FTA	Pct.	Reb.	Ast.	Pts.	RPG	APG	PPG
												AVERAGES		
91-92—Arizona	30	540	76	167	.455	37	48	.771	65	76	217	2.2	2.5	7.2
92-93—Arizona	28	870	99	226	.438	72	91	.791	116	159	309	4.1	5.7	11.0
93-94—Arizona	35	1164	217	484	.448	112	140	.800	157	208	639	4.5	5.9	18.3
94-95—Arizona	30	1092	222	466	.476	128	155	.826	128	220	684	4.3	7.3	22.8
Totals	123	3666	614	1343	.457	349	434	.804	466	663	1849	3.8	5.4	15.0

Three-point field goals: 1991-92, 28-for-69 (.406). 1992-93, 39-for-102 (.382). 1993-94, 93-for-265 (.351). 1994-95, 112-for-241 (.465). Totals, 272-for-677 (.402).

NBA REGULAR-SEASON RECORD

HONORS: NBA Rookie of the Year (1996). ... NBA All-Rookie first team (1996).

Season Team	G	Min.	FGM	FGA	Pct.	FTM	FTA	Pct.	Off.	Def.	Tot.	Ast.	St.	Blk.	TO	Pts.	RPG	APG	PPG
									REBOUNDS								AVERAGES		
95-96—Toronto	70	2865	481	1129	.426	236	296	.797	59	222	281	653	98	19	267	1331	4.0	9.3	19.0
96-97—Toronto	81	3311	564	1407	.401	330	401	.823	86	244	330	709	123	13	288	1634	4.1	8.8	20.2
97-98—Tor.-Port.	71	2839	448	1091	.411	238	287	.829	87	211	298	580	113	7	223	1225	4.2	8.2	17.3
98-99—Portland	50	1673	249	629	.396	89	122	.730	41	126	167	312	49	4	110	631	3.3	6.2	12.6
99-00—Portland	78	2372	386	894	.432	122	145	.841	61	182	243	405	77	1	149	974	3.1	5.2	12.5
00-01—Portland	82	2655	406	935	.434	172	207	.831	69	234	303	468	106	8	191	1066	3.7	5.7	13.0
01-02—Portland	75	2796	369	918	.402	174	196	.888	78	214	292	490	67	7	149	1016	3.9	6.5	13.5
02-03—Portland	59	1315	156	415	.376	53	67	.791	40	115	155	204	39	6	82	409	2.6	3.5	6.9
03-04—Portland	82	3118	408	1018	.401	127	145	.876	52	256	308	500	99	9	180	1099	3.8	6.1	13.4
04-05—Portland	81	2762	457	1165	.392	182	199	.915	56	254	310	458	86	2	164	1277	3.8	5.7	15.8
05-06—Memphis	27	862	114	287	.397	53	62	.855	23	72	95	128	19	1	55	317	3.5	4.7	11.7
Totals	756	26568	4038	9888	.408	1776	2127	.835	652	2130	2782	4907	876	77	1858	10979	3.7	6.5	14.5

Three-point field goals: 1995-96, 133-for-337 (.395). 1996-97, 176-for-496 (.355). 1997-98, 91-for-304 (.299). 1998-99, 44-for-142 (.310). 1999-00, 80-for-212 (.377). 2000-01, 82-for-219 (.374). 2001-02, 104-for-295 (.353). 2002-03, 44-for-114 (.386). 2003-04, 156-for-427 (.365). 2004-05, 181-for-490 (.369). 2005-06, 36-for-104 (.346). Totals, 1127-for-3140 (.359).

Personal fouls/disqualifications: 1995-96, 166/0. 1996-97, 162/1. 1997-98, 150/0. 1998-99, 81/0. 1999-00, 173/0. 2000-01, 202/1. 2001-02, 153/0. 2002-03, 67/0. 2003-04, 173/2. 2004-05, 158/0. 2005-06, 49/0. Totals, 1534/4.

NBA PLAYOFF RECORD

Season Team	G	Min.	FGM	FGA	Pct.	FTM	FTA	Pct.	Off.	Def.	Tot.	Ast.	St.	Blk.	TO	Pts.	RPG	APG	PPG
									REBOUNDS								AVERAGES		
97-98—Portland	4	166	25	63	.397	13	13	1.000	6	11	17	38	5	1	16	71	4.3	9.5	17.8
98-99—Portland	13	403	49	129	.380	24	34	.706	7	34	41	73	8	1	38	132	3.2	5.6	10.2
99-00—Portland	16	447	56	135	.415	20	24	.833	8	34	42	58	8	4	19	142	2.6	3.6	8.9
00-01—Portland	3	114	19	46	.413	13	13	1.000	1	8	9	13	2	1	9	53	3.0	4.3	17.7
01-02—Portland	3	99	5	22	.227	2	3	.667	1	6	7	10	2	0	4	15	2.3	3.3	5.0
02-03—Portland	7	232	36	79	.456	20	21	.952	7	29	36	39	6	2	12	107	5.1	5.6	15.3
Totals	46	1461	190	474	.401	92	108	.852	30	122	152	231	31	9	98	520	3.3	5.0	11.3

Three-point field goals: 1997-98, 8-for-22 (.364). 1998-99, 10-for-22 (.455). 1999-00, 10-for-30 (.333). 2000-01, 2-for-13 (.154). 2001-02, 3-for-4 (.750). 2002-03, 15-for-31 (.484). Totals, 48-for-122 (.393).

Personal fouls/disqualifications: 1997-98, 13/0. 1998-99, 31/0. 1999-00, 43/1. 2000-01, 6/0. 2001-02, 5/0. 2002-03, 22/0. Totals, 120/1.

STOUDEMIRE, AMARE F/C SUNS

PERSONAL: Born November 16, 1982, in Lake Wales, Fla. ... 6-10/245. (2.08/111.1).
HIGH SCHOOL: Cypress Creek (Orlando).
COLLEGE: Did not attend college.
TRANSACTIONS/CAREER NOTES: Selected out of high school by Phoenix Suns in first round (ninth pick overall) of 2002 NBA Draft.
MISCELLANEOUS: Member of bronze-medal-winning U.S. Olympic Team (2004).

NBA REGULAR-SEASON RECORD

HONORS: NBA Rookie of the Year (2003). ... NBA All-Rookie first team (2003). ... All-NBA second team (2005).

Season Team	G	Min.	FGM	FGA	Pct.	FTM	FTA	Pct.	Off.	Def.	Tot.	Ast.	St.	Blk.	TO	Pts.	RPG	APG	PPG
									REBOUNDS								AVERAGES		
02-03—Phoenix	82	2570	392	830	.472	320	484	.661	250	471	721	78	62	87	189	1106	8.8	1.0	13.5
03-04—Phoenix	55	2025	411	865	.475	310	435	.713	157	339	496	78	64	89	177	1133	9.0	1.4	20.6
04-05—Phoenix	80	2889	747	1336	.559	583	*795	.733	219	494	713	131	77	130	189	2080	8.9	1.6	26.0
05-06—Phoenix	3	50	9	27	.333	8	9	.889	6	10	16	2	1	3	1	26	5.3	0.7	8.7
Totals	220	7534	1559	3058	.510	1221	1723	.709	632	1314	1946	289	204	309	556	4345	8.8	1.3	19.8

Three-point field goals: 2002-03, 2-for-10 (.200). 2003-04, 1-for-5 (.200). 2004-05, 3-for-16 (.188). 2005-06, 0-for-1. Totals, 6-for-32 (.188).
Personal fouls/disqualifications: 2002-03, 269/3. 2003-04, 188/5. 2004-05, 278/5. 2005-06, 4/0. Totals, 739/13.

NBA PLAYOFF RECORD

Season Team	G	Min.	FGM	FGA	Pct.	FTM	FTA	Pct.	Off.	Def.	Tot.	Ast.	St.	Blk.	TO	Pts.	RPG	APG	PPG
									REBOUNDS								AVERAGES		
02-03—Phoenix	6	203	34	65	.523	16	28	.571	16	31	47	7	10	9	19	85	7.8	1.2	14.2
04-05—Phoenix	15	601	153	284	.539	143	183	.781	60	100	160	18	10	30	47	449	10.7	1.2	29.9
Totals	21	804	187	349	.536	159	211	.754	76	131	207	25	20	39	66	534	9.9	1.2	25.4

Three-point field goals: 2002-03, 1-for-1 (1.000). 2004-05, 0-for-3. Totals, 1-for-4 (.250).
Personal fouls/disqualifications: 2002-03, 28/1. 2004-05, 59/1. Totals, 87/2.

NOTES: MVP of Rookie Challenge (2004).

Season Team	Min.	FGM	FGA	Pct.	FTM	FTA	Pct.	REBOUNDS Off.	Def.	Tot.	Ast.	PF	Dq.	St.	Blk.	TO	Pts.
2005—Phoenix	20	3	11	.273	0	2	.000	4	5	9	2	2	0	1	0	1	6

SWEETNEY, MIKE — F — BULLS

PERSONAL: Born October 25, 1982, in Washington, D.C. ... 6-8/260. (2.03/117.9). ... Full name: Michael Damien Sweetney
HIGH SCHOOL: Oxon Hill (Md.).
COLLEGE: Georgetown.
TRANSACTIONS/CAREER NOTES: Selected after junior season by New York Knicks in first round (ninth overall pick) of 2003 NBA Draft. ... Traded by Knicks with F Tim Thomas and G Jermaine Jackson and 2007 and 2009 second-round draft picks, a conditional 2006 first-round pick and a conditional right to swap 2007 first-round picks to Chicago Bulls for C Eddy Curry and F/C Antonio Davis (October 4, 2005).

COLLEGIATE RECORD

NOTES: The SPORTING NEWS All-America third team (2003).

Season Team	G	Min.	FGM	FGA	Pct.	FTM	FTA	Pct.	Reb.	Ast.	Pts.	AVERAGES RPG	APG	PPG
00-01—Georgetown	33	798	159	308	.516	104	168	.619	245	59	422	7.4	1.8	12.8
01-02—Georgetown	29	883	185	326	.567	182	231	.788	290	49	552	10.0	1.7	19.0
02-03—Georgetown	34	1100	264	483	.547	248	336	.738	352	66	776	10.4	1.9	22.8
Totals	96	2781	608	1117	.544	534	735	.727	887	174	1750	9.2	1.8	18.2

Three-point field goals: 2001-02, 0-for-1. 2002-03, 0-for-3. Totals, 0-for-4 (.000).

NBA REGULAR-SEASON RECORD

Season Team	G	Min.	FGM	FGA	Pct.	FTM	FTA	Pct.	REBOUNDS Off.	Def.	Tot.	Ast.	St.	Blk.	TO	Pts.	AVERAGES RPG	APG	PPG
03-04—New York	42	494	69	140	.493	42	58	.724	68	89	157	14	18	12	32	180	3.7	0.3	4.3
04-05—New York	77	1509	237	446	.531	176	235	.749	169	249	418	44	27	28	108	650	5.4	0.6	8.4
05-06—Chicago	66	1222	200	444	.450	133	204	.652	118	232	350	59	19	56	95	533	5.3	0.9	8.1
Totals	185	3225	506	1030	.491	351	497	.706	355	570	925	117	64	96	235	1363	5.0	0.6	7.4

Three-point field goals: 2003-04, 0-for-1. 2004-05, 0-for-1. Totals, 0-for-2 (.000).
Personal fouls/disqualifications: 2003-04, 57/0. 2004-05, 224/5. 2005-06, 209/4. Totals, 490/9.

NBA PLAYOFF RECORD

Season Team	G	Min.	FGM	FGA	Pct.	FTM	FTA	Pct.	REBOUNDS Off.	Def.	Tot.	Ast.	St.	Blk.	TO	Pts.	AVERAGES RPG	APG	PPG
03-04—New York	4	57	6	11	.545	4	6	.667	4	6	10	0	0	1	0	16	2.5	0.0	4.0
05-06—Chicago	6	120	14	34	.412	15	19	.789	16	17	33	7	3	6	7	43	5.5	1.2	7.2
Totals	10	177	20	45	.444	19	25	.760	20	23	43	7	3	7	7	59	4.3	0.7	5.9

Personal fouls/disqualifications: 2003-04, 7/0. 2005-06, 24/1. Totals, 31/1.

SWIFT, ROBERT — C — SUPERSONICS

PERSONAL: Born December 3, 1985, in Bakersfield, Calif. ... 7-0/245. (2.13/111.1).
HIGH SCHOOL: Garces Memorial (Bakersfield, Calif.), then Bakersfield (Calif.).
COLLEGE: Did not attend college.
TRANSACTIONS/CAREER NOTES: Selected out of high school by Seattle SuperSonics in first round (12th pick overall) of 2004 NBA Draft.

NBA REGULAR-SEASON RECORD

Season Team	G	Min.	FGM	FGA	Pct.	FTM	FTA	Pct.	REBOUNDS Off.	Def.	Tot.	Ast.	St.	Blk.	TO	Pts.	AVERAGES RPG	APG	PPG
04-05—Seattle	16	72	5	11	.455	5	9	.556	1	4	5	2	1	7	4	15	0.3	0.1	0.9
05-06—Seattle	47	987	124	241	.515	53	91	.582	94	170	264	8	15	56	49	301	5.6	0.2	6.4
Totals	63	1059	129	252	.512	58	100	.580	95	174	269	10	16	63	53	316	4.3	0.2	5.0

Personal fouls/disqualifications: 2004-05, 16/0. 2005-06, 142/3. Totals, 158/3.

SWIFT, STROMILE — F — GRIZZLIES

PERSONAL: Born November 21, 1979, in Shreveport, La. ... 6-10/220. (2.08/99.8).
HIGH SCHOOL: Fair Park (Shreveport, La.).
COLLEGE: Louisiana State.
TRANSACTIONS/CAREER NOTES: Selected after sophomore season by Vancouver Grizzlies in first round (second pick overall) of 2000 NBA Draft. ... Grizzlies franchise moved to Memphis for 2001-02 season. ... Signed as free agent by Houston Rockets (August 2, 2005). ... Traded by Rockets with draft rights to F Rudy Gay to Memphis Grizzlies for F Shane Battier (July 12, 2006).

COLLEGIATE RECORD

Season Team	G	Min.	FGM	FGA	Pct.	FTM	FTA	Pct.	Reb.	Ast.	Pts.	AVERAGES RPG	APG	PPG
98-99—Louisiana State	16	319	45	110	.409	30	50	.600	69	5	121	4.3	0.3	7.6
99-00—Louisiana State	34	1013	208	342	.608	127	206	.617	279	32	550	8.2	0.9	16.2
Totals	50	1332	253	452	.560	157	256	.613	348	37	671	7.0	0.7	13.4

Three-point field goals: 1998-99, 1-for-8 (.125). 1999-00, 7-for-25 (.280). Totals, 8-for-33 (.242).

NBA REGULAR-SEASON RECORD

Season Team	G	Min.	FGM	FGA	Pct.	FTM	FTA	Pct.	REBOUNDS Off.	Def.	Tot.	Ast.	St.	Blk.	TO	Pts.	AVERAGES RPG	APG	PPG
00-01—Vancouver.......	80	1312	153	339	.451	85	141	.603	109	175	284	28	62	82	64	391	3.6	0.4	4.9
01-02—Memphis	68	1805	293	611	.480	217	305	.711	161	269	430	50	53	113	122	803	6.3	0.7	11.8
02-03—Memphis	67	1478	235	489	.481	177	245	.722	114	270	384	45	55	104	99	647	5.7	0.7	9.7
03-04—Memphis	77	1528	268	571	.469	190	262	.725	141	237	378	38	56	118	88	727	4.9	0.5	9.4
04-05—Memphis	60	1279	219	488	.449	166	219	.758	92	181	273	43	41	92	90	604	4.6	0.7	10.1
05-06—Houston	66	1344	225	458	.491	136	209	.651	103	188	291	25	38	50	91	586	4.4	0.4	8.9
Totals	418	8746	1393	2956	.471	971	1381	.703	720	1320	2040	229	305	559	554	3758	4.9	0.5	9.0

Three-point field goals: 2000-01, 0-for-4. 2001-02, 0-for-3. 2002-03, 0-for-2. 2003-04, 1-for-4 (.250). 2004-05, 0-for-4. 2005-06, 0-for-2. Totals, 1-for-19 (.053).

Personal fouls/disqualifications: 2000-01, 160/0. 2001-02, 178/3. 2002-03, 152/3. 2003-04, 188/4. 2004-05, 182/0. 2005-06, 198/3. Totals, 1058/13.

NBA PLAYOFF RECORD

Season Team	G	Min.	FGM	FGA	Pct.	FTM	FTA	Pct.	REBOUNDS Off.	Def.	Tot.	Ast.	St.	Blk.	TO	Pts.	AVERAGES RPG	APG	PPG
03-04—Memphis	4	74	9	26	.346	6	8	.750	6	13	19	3	3	6	3	24	4.8	0.8	6.0
04-05—Memphis	3	48	12	20	.600	4	7	.571	7	7	14	1	1	0	2	28	4.7	0.3	9.3
Totals	7	122	21	46	.457	10	15	.667	13	20	33	4	4	6	5	52	4.7	0.6	7.4

Personal fouls/disqualifications: 2003-04, 6/0. 2004-05, 3/0. Totals, 9/0.

SZCZERBIAK, WALLY　　　　　F　　　　　CELTICS

PERSONAL: Born March 5, 1977, in Madrid, Spain. ... 6-7/244. (2.01/110.7). ... Full name: Walter Robert Szczerbiak ... Son of Walter Szczerbiak, forward with Pittsburgh Condors of American Basketball Association (1971-72) and Real Madrid of Spanish League.
HIGH SCHOOL: Cold Spring Harbor (N.Y.).
COLLEGE: Miami of Ohio.
TRANSACTIONS/CAREER NOTES: Selected by Minnesota Timberwolves in first round (sixth pick overall) of 1999 NBA Draft. ... Traded by Timberwolves with C Michael Olowokandi and F/C Dwayne Jones and a future first-round draft choice to Boston Celtics for G Ricky Davis, C Mark Blount, G Marcus Banks, SF Justin Reed and two second-round draft choices (January 26, 2006).

COLLEGIATE RECORD

NOTES: The SPORTING NEWS All-America first team (1999).

Season Team	G	Min.	FGM	FGA	Pct.	FTM	FTA	Pct.	Reb.	Ast.	Pts.	AVERAGES RPG	APG	PPG
95-96—Miami of Ohio	22	382	66	127	.520	22	28	.786	72	23	176	3.3	1.0	8.0
96-97—Miami of Ohio	30	927	150	316	.475	28	39	.718	162	63	384	5.4	2.1	12.8
97-98—Miami of Ohio	21	803	185	350	.529	79	98	.806	160	52	512	7.6	2.5	24.4
98-99—Miami of Ohio	32	1081	270	517	.522	172	207	.831	272	93	775	8.5	2.9	24.2
Totals	105	3193	671	1310	.512	301	372	.809	666	231	1847	6.3	2.2	17.6

Three-point field goals: 1995-96, 22-for-47 (.468). 1996-97, 56-for-121 (.463). 1997-98, 63-for-128 (.492). 1998-99, 63-for-177 (.356). Totals, 204-for-473 (.431).

NBA REGULAR-SEASON RECORD

HONORS: NBA All-Rookie first team (2000). ... MVP of Rookie Challenge (2001).

Season Team	G	Min.	FGM	FGA	Pct.	FTM	FTA	Pct.	REBOUNDS Off.	Def.	Tot.	Ast.	St.	Blk.	TO	Pts.	AVERAGES RPG	APG	PPG
99-00—Minnesota.......	73	2171	342	669	.511	133	161	.826	89	183	272	201	58	23	83	845	3.7	2.8	11.6
00-01—Minnesota.......	82	2856	469	920	.510	181	208	.870	133	314	447	260	59	33	138	1145	5.5	3.2	14.0
01-02—Minnesota.......	82	3117	609	1200	.508	226	272	.831	120	271	391	257	66	21	181	1531	4.8	3.1	18.7
02-03—Minnesota.......	52	1836	351	729	.481	150	173	.867	53	188	241	136	44	22	87	913	4.6	2.6	17.6
03-04—Minnesota.......	28	622	106	236	.449	53	64	.828	24	64	88	33	12	1	28	285	3.1	1.2	10.2
04-05—Minnesota.......	81	2558	465	919	.506	260	304	.855	82	221	303	191	40	16	132	1253	3.7	2.4	15.5
05-06—Minn.-Boston..	72	2729	493	1012	.487	278	310	.897	77	236	313	213	40	19	136	1366	4.3	3.0	19.0
Totals	470	15889	2835	5685	.499	1281	1492	.859	578	1477	2055	1291	319	135	785	7338	4.4	2.7	15.6

Three-point field goals: 1999-00, 28-for-78 (.359). 2000-01, 26-for-77 (.338). 2001-02, 87-for-191 (.455). 2002-03, 61-for-145 (.421). 2003-04, 20-for-46 (.435). 2004-05, 63-for-169 (.373). 2005-06, 102-for-255 (.400). Totals, 387-for-961 (.403).

Personal fouls/disqualifications: 1999-00, 175/3. 2000-01, 226/4. 2001-02, 188/1. 2002-03, 123/0. 2003-04, 42/0. 2004-05, 178/0. 2005-06, 150/0. Totals, 1082/8.

NBA PLAYOFF RECORD

Season Team	G	Min.	FGM	FGA	Pct.	FTM	FTA	Pct.	REBOUNDS Off.	Def.	Tot.	Ast.	St.	Blk.	TO	Pts.	AVERAGES RPG	APG	PPG
99-00—Minnesota.......	4	94	12	30	.400	0	0	...	2	6	8	2	3	1	1	24	2.0	0.5	6.0
00-01—Minnesota.......	4	143	18	37	.486	20	25	.800	4	14	18	10	5	3	12	56	4.5	2.5	14.0
01-02—Minnesota.......	3	131	21	44	.477	16	18	.889	9	12	21	6	2	0	8	60	7.0	2.0	20.0
02-03—Minnesota.......	6	252	29	61	.475	26	30	.867	6	24	30	13	6	1	18	87	5.0	2.2	14.5
03-04—Minnesota.......	12	298	47	112	.420	38	41	.927	9	30	39	20	6	2	24	142	3.3	1.7	11.8
Totals	29	918	127	284	.447	100	114	.877	30	86	116	51	22	7	63	369	4.0	1.8	12.7

Three-point field goals: 1999-00, 0-for-3. 2000-01, 0-for-1. 2001-02, 2-for-9 (.222). 2002-03, 3-for-14 (.214). 2003-04, 10-for-29 (.345). Totals, 15-for-56 (.268).

Personal fouls/disqualifications: 1999-00, 7/0. 2000-01, 6/0. 2001-02, 8/0. 2002-03, 19/0. 2003-04, 31/0. Totals, 71/0.

NBA ALL-STAR GAME RECORD

Season Team	Min.	FGM	FGA	Pct.	FTM	FTA	Pct.	REBOUNDS Off.	Def.	Tot.	Ast.	PF	Dq.	St.	Blk.	TO	Pts.
2002—Minnesota.............	12	4	6	.667	0	0	...	1	2	3	3	0	0	1	0	0	10

Three-point field goals: 2002, 2-for-3 (.667). Totals, 2-for-3 (.667).

TAFT, CHRIS   F   WARRIORS

PERSONAL: Born March 10, 1985, in Brooklyn, N.Y. ... 6-10/260. (2.08/117.9).
HIGH SCHOOL: Xaverian Prep (Brooklyn, N.Y.).
COLLEGE: Pittsburgh.
TRANSACTIONS/CAREER NOTES: Selected after sophomore season by Golden State Warriors in second round (42nd pick overall) of 2005 NBA Draft.

COLLEGIATE RECORD

Season Team	G	Min.	FGM	FGA	Pct.	FTM	FTA	Pct.	Reb.	Ast.	Pts.	RPG	AVERAGES APG	PPG
03-04—Pittsburgh	36	923	162	290	.559	68	125	.544	270	45	392	7.5	1.3	10.9
04-05—Pittsburgh	29	769	159	274	.580	68	116	.586	218	24	386	7.5	0.8	13.3
Totals	65	1692	321	564	.569	136	241	.564	488	69	778	7.5	1.1	12.0

NBA REGULAR-SEASON RECORD

Season Team	G	Min.	FGM	FGA	Pct.	FTM	FTA	Pct.	Off.	Def.	Tot.	Ast.	St.	Blk.	TO	Pts.	RPG	APG	PPG
05-06—Golden State	17	144	23	38	.605	1	6	.167	19	17	36	2	2	7	2	47	2.1	0.1	2.8

Personal fouls/disqualifications: 2005-06, 25/0. Totals, 25/0.

TAYLOR, DONNELL   G   WIZARDS

PERSONAL: Born July 26, 1982, in Washington, D.C. ... 6-4/180. (1.93/81.6). ... Full name: Quence Donnell Taylor
HIGH SCHOOL: Sidney Lanier (Montgomery, Ala.).
JUNIOR COLLEGE: Okaloosa-Walton (Niceville, Fla.).
COLLEGE: Alabama-Birmingham.
TRANSACTIONS/CAREER NOTES: Not drafted by an NBA franchise. ... Signed as free agent by Washington Wizards (November 10, 2005).

COLLEGIATE RECORD

Season Team	G	Min.	FGM	FGA	Pct.	FTM	FTA	Pct.	Reb.	Ast.	Pts.	RPG	AVERAGES APG	PPG
01-02—Okaloosa-Walton	27	...	121	250	.484	76	107	.710	146	144	327	5.4	5.3	12.1
02-03—Okaloosa-Walton	34	...	291	562	.518	103	162	.636	238	192	761	7.0	5.6	22.4
03-04—UAB	32	597	90	215	.419	46	73	.630	96	58	241	3.0	1.8	7.5
04-05—UAB	33	908	177	350	.506	110	140	.786	146	98	511	4.4	3.0	15.5
Junior CollegeTotals	61	...	412	812	.507	179	269	.665	384	336	1088	6.3	5.5	17.8
4-Year CollegeTotals	65	1505	267	565	.473	156	213	.732	242	156	752	3.7	2.4	11.6

Three-point field goals: 2001-02, 9-for-31 (.290). 2002-03, 76-for-196 (.388). 2003-04, 15-for-63 (.238). 2004-05, 47-for-119 (.395). 4-Year Totals, 62-for-182 (.341).

NBA REGULAR-SEASON RECORD

Season Team	G	Min.	FGM	FGA	Pct.	FTM	FTA	Pct.	Off.	Def.	Tot.	Ast.	St.	Blk.	TO	Pts.	RPG	APG	PPG
05-06—Washington	51	465	53	136	.390	30	43	.698	16	37	53	45	30	4	34	140	1.0	0.9	2.7

Three-point field goals: 2005-06, 4-for-17 (.235). Totals, 4-for-17 (.235).
Personal fouls/disqualifications: 2005-06, 47/0. Totals, 47/0.

NBA PLAYOFF RECORD

Season Team	G	Min.	FGM	FGA	Pct.	FTM	FTA	Pct.	Off.	Def.	Tot.	Ast.	St.	Blk.	TO	Pts.	RPG	APG	PPG
05-06—Washington	1	3	0	1	.000	0	0	...	0	0	0	1	1	0	0	0	0.0	1.0	0.0

Three-point field goals: 2005-06, 0-for-1. Totals, 0-for-1 (.000).

TAYLOR, MAURICE   F   KNICKS

PERSONAL: Born October 30, 1976, in Detroit. ... 6-9/260. (2.06/117.9). ... Full name: Maurice De Shawn Taylor
HIGH SCHOOL: Henry Ford (Detroit).
COLLEGE: Michigan.
TRANSACTIONS/CAREER NOTES: Selected after junior season by Los Angeles Clippers in first round (14th pick overall) of 1997 NBA Draft. ... Signed as free agent by Houston Rockets (August 25, 2000). ... Traded by Rockets to New York Knicks for G Moochie Norris, F Vin Baker and second-round pick in 2006 NBA draft (February 24, 2005).

COLLEGIATE RECORD

Season Team	G	Min.	FGM	FGA	Pct.	FTM	FTA	Pct.	Reb.	Ast.	Pts.	RPG	AVERAGES APG	PPG
94-95—Michigan	30	830	157	332	.473	59	98	.602	151	31	376	5.0	1.0	12.5
95-96—Michigan	32	908	194	380	.511	58	98	.592	223	42	447	7.0	1.3	14.0
96-97—Michigan	35	1055	173	341	.507	84	117	.718	218	40	431	6.2	1.1	12.3
Totals	97	2793	524	1053	.498	201	313	.642	592	113	1254	6.1	1.2	12.9

Three-point field goals: 1994-95, 3-for-7 (.429). 1995-96, 1-for-4 (.250). 1996-97, 1-for-5 (.200). Totals, 5-for-16 (.313).
Personal fouls/disqualifications: 1994-95, 98/5. 1995-96, 92/1. Totals, 190/6.

NBA REGULAR-SEASON RECORD

HONORS: NBA All-Rookie second team (1998).

Season Team	G	Min.	FGM	FGA	Pct.	FTM	FTA	Pct.	Off.	Def.	Tot.	Ast.	St.	Blk.	TO	Pts.	RPG	APG	PPG
97-98—L.A. Clippers	71	1513	321	675	.476	173	244	.709	118	178	296	53	34	40	107	815	4.2	0.7	11.5
98-99—L.A. Clippers	46	1505	311	675	.461	150	206	.728	100	142	242	67	16	29	120	773	5.3	1.5	16.8

Season Team	G	Min.	FGM	FGA	Pct.	FTM	FTA	Pct.	REBOUNDS Off.	Def.	Tot.	Ast.	St.	Blk.	TO	Pts.	AVERAGES RPG	APG	PPG
99-00—L.A. Clippers...	62	2227	458	988	.464	143	201	.711	96	304	400	101	51	48	169	1060	6.5	1.6	17.1
00-01—Houston	69	1972	390	797	.489	119	162	.735	109	269	378	104	28	38	125	899	5.5	1.5	13.0
01-02—Houston							Did not play—injured.												
02-03—Houston	67	1377	231	535	.432	100	138	.725	95	143	238	66	22	22	100	562	3.6	1.0	8.4
03-04—Houston	75	2081	367	765	.480	128	174	.736	131	253	384	107	43	47	149	862	5.1	1.4	11.5
04-05—Houston-N.Y.	65	1336	203	446	.455	63	103	.612	67	190	257	67	27	20	94	472	4.0	1.0	7.3
05-06—New York	67	1210	182	389	.468	58	83	.699	65	164	229	53	21	14	103	422	3.4	0.8	6.3
Totals	522	13221	2463	5270	.467	934	1311	.712	781	1643	2424	618	242	258	967	5865	4.6	1.2	11.2

Three-point field goals: 1997-98, 0-for-1. 1998-99, 1-for-6 (.167). 1999-00, 1-for-8 (.125). 2000-01, 0-for-4. 2002-03, 0-for-2. 2003-04, 0-for-2. 2004-05, 3-for-9 (.333). 2005-06, 0-for-1. Totals, 5-for-33 (.152).

Personal fouls/disqualifications: 1997-98, 222/7. 1998-99, 179/5. 1999-00, 217/4. 2000-01, 208/3. 2002-03, 151/0. 2003-04, 253/5. 2004-05, 180/3. 2005-06, 177/0. Totals, 1587/27.

NBA PLAYOFF RECORD

Season Team	G	Min.	FGM	FGA	Pct.	FTM	FTA	Pct.	REBOUNDS Off.	Def.	Tot.	Ast.	St.	Blk.	TO	Pts.	AVERAGES RPG	APG	PPG
03-04—Houston	5	115	18	38	.474	13	17	.765	5	11	16	5	0	1	7	49	3.2	1.0	9.8

Personal fouls/disqualifications: 2003-04, 20/0. Totals, 20/0.

TELFAIR, SEBASTIAN — G — CELTICS

PERSONAL: Born June 9, 1985, in Brooklyn, N.Y. ... 6-0/165. (1.83/74.8). ... Cousin of Stephon Marbury, G, New York Knicks. Brother of Jamel Thomas, forward with four NBA teams (1999-2001).
HIGH SCHOOL: Abraham Lincoln (Brooklyn, N.Y.).
COLLEGE: Did not attend college.
TRANSACTIONS/CAREER NOTES: Selected out of high school by Portland Trail Blazers in first round (13th pick overall) of 2004 NBA Draft. ... Traded by Trail Blazers with F/C Theo Ratliff and a 2008 second-round draft pick to Boston Celtics for G Dan Dickau, F/C Raef LaFrentz and a first-round pick (G Randy Foye) in 2006 draft (June 28, 2006).

NBA REGULAR-SEASON RECORD

Season Team	G	Min.	FGM	FGA	Pct.	FTM	FTA	Pct.	REBOUNDS Off.	Def.	Tot.	Ast.	St.	Blk.	TO	Pts.	AVERAGES RPG	APG	PPG
04-05—Portland	68	1330	169	430	.393	105	133	.789	10	94	104	224	35	4	125	460	1.5	3.3	6.8
05-06—Portland	68	1641	228	578	.394	130	175	.743	19	101	120	247	66	6	115	643	1.8	3.6	9.5
Totals	136	2971	397	1008	.394	235	308	.763	29	195	224	471	101	10	240	1103	1.6	3.5	8.1

Three-point field goals: 2004-05, 17-for-69 (.246). 2005-06, 57-for-162 (.352). Totals, 74-for-231 (.320).
Personal fouls/disqualifications: 2004-05, 120/0. 2005-06, 167/1. Totals, 287/1.

TERRY, JASON — G — MAVERICKS

PERSONAL: Born September 15, 1977, in Seattle. ... 6-2/180. (1.88/81.6). ... Full name: Jason Eugene Terry
HIGH SCHOOL: Franklin (Seattle).
COLLEGE: Arizona.
TRANSACTIONS/CAREER NOTES: Selected by Atlanta Hawks in first round (10th pick overall) of 1999 NBA Draft. ... Traded by Hawks with F Alan Henderson and a future first-round draft choice to Dallas Mavericks for F Antoine Walker and G Tony Delk (August 4, 2004).

COLLEGIATE RECORD

NOTES: Member of NCAA Division I championship team (1997). ... The SPORTING NEWS All-America first team (1999).

Season Team	G	Min.	FGM	FGA	Pct.	FTM	FTA	Pct.	Reb.	Ast.	Pts.	AVERAGES RPG	APG	PPG
95-96—Arizona	31	303	32	59	.542	16	27	.593	23	35	95	0.7	1.1	3.1
96-97—Arizona	34	1037	124	280	.443	72	101	.713	91	150	360	2.7	4.4	10.6
97-98—Arizona	35	797	124	294	.422	62	75	.827	84	149	371	2.4	4.3	10.6
98-99—Arizona	29	1107	209	472	.443	141	168	.839	97	159	635	3.3	5.5	21.9
Totals	129	3244	489	1105	.443	291	371	.784	295	493	1461	2.3	3.8	11.3

Three-point field goals: 1995-96, 15-for-26 (.577). 1996-97, 40-for-121 (.331). 1997-98, 61-for-176 (.347). 1998-99, 76-for-191 (.398). Totals, 192-for-514 (.374).
Personal fouls/disqualifications: 1995-96, 28/0. 1996-97, 66/1. 1997-98, 55/0. Totals, 149/1.

NBA REGULAR-SEASON RECORD

HONORS: NBA All-Rookie second team (2000).

Season Team	G	Min.	FGM	FGA	Pct.	FTM	FTA	Pct.	REBOUNDS Off.	Def.	Tot.	Ast.	St.	Blk.	TO	Pts.	AVERAGES RPG	APG	PPG
99-00—Atlanta	81	1888	249	600	.415	113	140	.807	24	142	166	346	90	10	156	657	2.0	4.3	8.1
00-01—Atlanta	82	3089	596	1367	.436	303	358	.846	42	227	269	403	104	12	239	1619	3.3	4.9	19.7
01-02—Atlanta	78	2967	524	1219	.430	284	340	.835	40	230	270	444	144	13	181	1504	3.5	5.7	19.3
02-03—Atlanta	81	3081	488	1141	.428	259	292	.887	37	242	279	600	126	14	249	1395	3.4	7.4	17.2
03-04—Atlanta	81	3018	499	1196	.417	215	260	.827	49	287	336	437	124	16	229	1359	4.1	5.4	16.8
04-05—Dallas	80	2401	372	743	.501	146	173	.844	38	150	188	429	109	15	147	993	2.4	5.4	12.4
05-06—Dallas	80	2798	516	1099	.470	168	210	.800	31	127	158	306	100	27	135	1371	2.0	3.8	17.1
Totals	563	19242	3244	7365	.440	1488	1773	.839	261	1405	1666	2965	797	107	1336	8898	3.0	5.3	15.8

Three-point field goals: 1999-00, 46-for-157 (.293). 2000-01, 124-for-314 (.395). 2001-02, 172-for-444 (.387). 2002-03, 160-for-431 (.371). 2003-04, 146-for-421 (.347). 2004-05, 103-for-245 (.420). 2005-06, 171-for-416 (.411). Totals, 922-for-2428 (.380).
Personal fouls/disqualifications: 1999-00, 133/0. 2000-01, 204/2. 2001-02, 156/0. 2002-03, 175/2. 2003-04, 192/2. 2004-05, 177/0. 2005-06, 196/1. Totals, 1233/7.

NBA PLAYOFF RECORD

									REBOUNDS								AVERAGES		
Season Team	G	Min.	FGM	FGA	Pct.	FTM	FTA	Pct.	Off.	Def.	Tot.	Ast.	St.	Blk.	TO	Pts.	RPG	APG	PPG
04-05—Dallas.............	13	501	81	160	.506	38	43	.884	9	45	54	60	17	7	30	227	4.2	4.6	17.5
05-06—Dallas.............	22	844	163	369	.442	59	71	.831	12	52	64	83	26	1	44	416	2.9	3.8	18.9
Totals	35	1345	244	529	.461	97	114	.851	21	97	118	143	43	8	74	643	3.4	4.1	18.4

Three-point field goals: 2004-05, 27-for-55 (.491). 2005-06, 31-for-101 (.307). Totals, 58-for-156 (.372).
Personal fouls/disqualifications: 2004-05, 28/0. 2005-06, 55/0. Totals, 83/0.

THOMAS, BILLY   G   WIZARDS

PERSONAL: Born December 23, 1975, In Shreveport, La. ... 6-5/218. (1.96/98.9).
HIGH SCHOOL: Loyola College Prep (Shreveport, La.).
COLLEGE: Kansas.
TRANSACTIONS/CAREER NOTES: Not drafted by an NBA franchise. ... Played in Argentina (1999-2000). ... Played in International Basketball League (2000-01). ... Played in Philippines (2001-02). ... Played in Italy (2003-04). ... Played in CBA (2004-05). ... Signed as free agent by Washington Wizards (October 1, 2004). ... Signed as free agent by New Jersey Nets (February 10, 2005). ... Signed as free agent by Washington Wizards (October 3, 2005).

COLLEGIATE RECORD

												AVERAGES		
Season Team	G	Min.	FGM	FGA	Pct.	FTM	FTA	Pct.	Reb.	Ast.	Pts.	RPG	APG	PPG
94-95—Kansas	31	472	77	177	.435	22	29	.759	67	20	225	2.2	0.6	7.3
95-96—Kansas	34	358	54	151	.358	10	14	.714	51	21	160	1.5	0.6	4.7
96-97—Kansas	36	573	97	242	.401	11	15	.733	64	27	278	1.8	0.8	7.7
97-98—Kansas	36	962	181	387	.468	22	32	.688	108	101	489	3.0	2.8	13.6
Totals	137	2365	409	957	.427	65	90	.722	290	169	1152	2.1	1.2	8.4

Three-point field goals: 1994-95, 49-for-126 (.389). 1995-96, 42-for-125 (.336). 1996-97, 73-for-178 (.410). 1997-98, 105-for-262 (.401). Totals, 269-for-691 (.389).

INTERNATIONAL BASKETBALL LEAGUE RECORD

												AVERAGES		
Season Team	G	Min.	FGM	FGA	Pct.	FTM	FTA	Pct.	Reb.	Ast.	Pts.	RPG	APG	PPG
00-01—Cincinnati	51	1799	291	678	.429	89	111	.802	195	165	833	3.8	3.2	16.3

Three-point field goals: 2000-01, 162-for-411 (.394). Totals, 162-for-411 (.394).

NBA DEVELOPMENT LEAGUE RECORD

												AVERAGES		
Season Team	G	Min.	FGM	FGA	Pct.	FTM	FTA	Pct.	Reb.	Ast.	Pts.	RPG	APG	PPG
01-02—Greenville	45	1373	220	529	416	105	121	.868	124	89	629	2.8	2.0	14.0
02-03—Greenville	49	1551	288	662	.435	125	162	.772	161	99	785	3.3	2.0	16.0
Totals	94	2924	508	1191	.427	230	283	.813	285	188	1414	3.0	2.0	15.0

Three-point field goals: 2001-02, 84-for-228 (.368). 2002-03, 84-for-241 (.349). Totals, 168-for-469 (.358).

ITALIAN LEAGUE RECORD

												AVERAGES		
Season Team	G	Min.	FGM	FGA	Pct.	FTM	FTA	Pct.	Reb.	Ast.	Pts.	RPG	APG	PPG
03-04—Coop Nordest Trieste......	26	773	126	279	.452	17	23	.739	73	32	330	2.8	1.2	12.7

Three-point field goals: 2003-04, 61-for-167 (.365). Totals, 61-for-167 (.365).

CBA RECORD

												AVERAGES		
Season Team	G	Min.	FGM	FGA	Pct.	FTM	FTA	Pct.	Reb.	Ast.	Pts.	RPG	APG	PPG
04-05—Dakota Wizards	24	1002	183	357	.513	64	79	.810	100	108	500	4.2	4.5	20.8

Three-point field goals: 2004-05, 70-for-157 (.446). Totals, 70-for-157 (.446).

NBA REGULAR-SEASON RECORD

									REBOUNDS								AVERAGES		
Season Team	G	Min.	FGM	FGA	Pct.	FTM	FTA	Pct.	Off.	Def.	Tot.	Ast.	St.	Blk.	TO	Pts.	RPG	APG	PPG
04-05—New Jersey	25	356	34	94	.362	7	9	.778	7	29	36	17	14	1	9	92	1.4	0.7	3.7
05-06—Washington	17	131	13	40	.325	2	2	1.000	5	9	14	9	10	1	6	38	0.8	0.5	2.2
Totals	42	487	47	134	.351	9	11	.818	12	38	50	26	24	2	15	130	1.2	0.6	3.1

Three-point field goals: 2004-05, 17-for-56 (.304). 2005-06, 10-for-30 (.333). Totals, 27-for-86 (.314).
Personal fouls/disqualifications: 2004-05, 29/0. 2005-06, 19/0. Totals, 48/0.

NBA PLAYOFF RECORD

									REBOUNDS								AVERAGES		
Season Team	G	Min.	FGM	FGA	Pct.	FTM	FTA	Pct.	Off.	Def.	Tot.	Ast.	St.	Blk.	TO	Pts.	RPG	APG	PPG
04-05—New Jersey	2	2	0	1	.000	0	0	...	0	0	0	0	0	0	0	0	0.0	0.0	0.0
05-06—Washington	3	14	0	7	.000	2	4	.500	0	1	1	0	0	0	0	2	0.3	0.0	0.7
Totals	5	16	0	8	.000	2	4	.500	0	1	1	0	0	0	0	2	0.2	0.0	0.4

Three-point field goals: 2005-06, 0-for-4. Totals, 0-for-4 (.000).
Personal fouls/disqualifications: 2005-06, 3/0. Totals, 3/0.

THOMAS, ETAN   F/C   WIZARDS

PERSONAL: Born April 1, 1978, in Harlem, N.Y. ... 6-9/256. (2.06/116.1). ... Full name: Dedreck Etan Thomas
HIGH SCHOOL: Booker T. Washington (Tulsa, Okla.).
COLLEGE: Syracuse.
TRANSACTIONS/CAREER NOTES: Selected by Dallas Mavericks in first round (12th pick overall) of 2000 NBA Draft. ... Traded by Mavericks with F/C Christian Laettner, G Courtney Alexander, F Loy Vaught, G Hubert Davis and cash consider-

ations to Washington Wizards for F Juwan Howard, C Calvin Booth and F Obinna Ekezie (February 22, 2001).

COLLEGIATE RECORD

Season Team	G	Min.	FGM	FGA	Pct.	FTM	FTA	Pct.	Reb.	Ast.	Pts.	RPG	APG	PPG
96-97—Syracuse	25	408	55	103	.534	33	71	.465	105	3	143	4.2	0.1	5.7
97-98—Syracuse	35	1009	144	236	.610	109	178	.612	230	15	397	6.6	0.4	11.3
98-99—Syracuse	33	913	148	240	.617	109	190	.574	243	17	405	7.4	0.5	12.3
99-00—Syracuse	29	940	148	246	.602	99	146	.678	269	16	395	9.3	0.6	13.6
Totals	122	3270	495	825	.600	350	585	.598	847	51	1340	6.9	0.4	11.0

NBA REGULAR-SEASON RECORD

Season Team	G	Min.	FGM	FGA	Pct.	FTM	FTA	Pct.	Off.	Def.	Tot.	Ast.	St.	Blk.	TO	Pts.	RPG	APG	PPG
00-01—Dallas-Washington								Did not play—injured.											
01-02—Washington	47	618	81	151	.536	41	74	.554	55	126	181	6	17	35	26	203	3.9	0.1	4.3
02-03—Washington	38	513	61	124	.492	60	94	.638	70	95	165	3	8	23	33	182	4.3	0.1	4.8
03-04—Washington	79	1901	257	526	.489	191	295	.647	183	345	528	68	36	123	113	705	6.7	0.9	8.9
04-05—Washington	47	976	128	255	.502	76	144	.528	85	159	244	20	17	51	50	332	5.2	0.4	7.1
05-06—Washington	71	1121	131	246	.533	75	125	.600	99	180	279	14	20	68	51	337	3.9	0.2	4.7
Totals	282	5129	658	1302	.505	443	732	.605	492	905	1397	111	98	300	273	1759	5.0	0.4	6.2

Personal fouls/disqualifications: 2001-02, 76/0. 2002-03, 66/0. 2003-04, 219/1. 2004-05, 133/2. 2005-06, 148/2. Totals, 642/5.

NBA PLAYOFF RECORD

Season Team	G	Min.	FGM	FGA	Pct.	FTM	FTA	Pct.	Off.	Def.	Tot.	Ast.	St.	Blk.	TO	Pts.	RPG	APG	PPG
04-05—Washington	8	126	19	29	.655	10	22	.455	12	24	36	2	0	7	9	48	4.5	0.3	6.0
05-06—Washington	3	18	2	5	.400	2	4	.500	2	4	6	0	2	2	0	6	2.0	0.0	2.0
Totals	11	144	21	34	.618	12	26	.462	14	28	42	2	2	9	9	54	3.8	0.2	4.9

Personal fouls/disqualifications: 2004-05, 23/0. 2005-06, 3/0. Totals, 26/0.

THOMAS, JAMES   F

PERSONAL: Born November 22, 1980, in Schenectady, N.Y. ... 6-8/235. (2.03/106.6).
HIGH SCHOOL: Hargrave Academy (Chatham, Va.).
COLLEGE: Texas.
TRANSACTIONS/CAREER NOTES: Not drafted by an NBA franchise. ... Played in NBA Development League (2004-05). ... Signed to 10-day contract by Portland Trail Blazers (January 9, 2005). ... Waived by Trail Blazers (January 31, 2005). ... Signed to 10-day contract by Cleveland Cavaliers (February 22, 2005). ... Signed for remainder of season by Atlanta Hawks (April 9, 2005). ... Waived by Hawks (July 5, 2005). ... Signed as free agent by Philadelphia 76ers (October 3, 2005). ... Waived by 76ers (December 8, 2005). ... Played in CBA (2005-06). ... Signed by Chicago Bulls to 10-day contract (January 27, 2006).

COLLEGIATE RECORD

Season Team	G	Min.	FGM	FGA	Pct.	FTM	FTA	Pct.	Reb.	Ast.	Pts.	RPG	APG	PPG
00-01—Texas	34	705	90	186	.484	58	127	.457	221	13	238	6.5	0.4	7.0
01-02—Texas	34	863	128	235	.545	107	169	.633	302	14	363	8.9	0.4	10.7
02-03—Texas	33	806	125	243	.514	117	178	.657	363	15	367	11.0	0.5	11.1
03-04—Texas	33	516	62	134	.463	57	88	.648	191	11	181	5.8	0.3	5.5
Totals	134	2890	405	798	.508	339	562	.603	1077	53	1149	8.0	0.4	8.6

NBA REGULAR-SEASON RECORD

Season Team	G	Min.	FGM	FGA	Pct.	FTM	FTA	Pct.	Off.	Def.	Tot.	Ast.	St.	Blk.	TO	Pts.	RPG	APG	PPG
04-05—Port.-Cleve.-Atl.	11	117	12	20	.600	2	6	.333	17	20	37	4	4	4	7	26	3.4	0.4	2.4
05-06—Phila.-Chicago	22	150	10	19	.526	8	14	.571	12	27	39	1	0	3	7	28	1.8	0.0	1.3
Totals	33	267	22	39	.564	10	20	.500	29	47	76	5	4	7	14	54	2.3	0.2	1.6

Personal fouls/disqualifications: 2004-05, 13/0. 2005-06, 35/0. Totals, 48/0.

NBA DEVELOPMENT LEAGUE RECORD

Season Team	G	Min.	FGM	FGA	Pct.	FTM	FTA	Pct.	Reb.	Ast.	Pts.	RPG	APG	PPG
04-05—Roanoke	36	1276	165	312	.529	118	172	.686	480	24	448	13.3	0.7	12.4

Three-point field goals: 2004-05, 0-for-1. Totals, 0-for-1 (.000).

CBA RECORD

Season Team	G	Min.	FGM	FGA	Pct.	FTM	FTA	Pct.	Reb.	Ast.	Pts.	RPG	APG	PPG
05-06—Albany	19	707	129	246	.524	115	160	.719	278	21	373	14.6	1.1	19.6

THOMAS, JOHN   F   NETS

PERSONAL: Born September 8, 1975, in Minneapolis, Minn. ... 6-9/265. (2.06/120.2).
HIGH SCHOOL: Roosevelt (Minneapolis).
COLLEGE: Minnesota.
TRANSACTIONS/CAREER NOTES: Selected by New York Knicks in first round (25th pick overall) of 1997 NBA Draft. ... Traded by Knicks with F Walter McCarty, F Dontae' Jones, G Scott Brooks and two future second-round draft choices to Boston Celtics for F Chris Mills (October 22, 1997). ... Traded by Celtics with G Chauncey Billups, G Dee Brown and F Roy Rogers to Toronto Raptors for G Kenny Anderson, C Zan Tabak and F Popeye Jones (February 18, 1998). ... Played in CBA (2002-03; 2004-05). ... Played in

Spain (2003-04). ... Signed as free agent by Minnesota Timberwolves (October 4, 2004). ... Waived by Timberwolves (November 1, 2004). ... Signed by Memphis Grizzlies (October 2, 2005). ... Waived by Grizzlies (November 22, 2005). ... Signed by New Jersey Nets (April 18, 2006).

COLLEGIATE RECORD

												AVERAGES		
Season Team	G	Min.	FGM	FGA	Pct.	FTM	FTA	Pct.	Reb.	Ast.	Pts.	RPG	APG	PPG
93-94—Minnesota	26	254	27	70	.386	10	23	.435	65	3	64	2.5	0.1	2.5
94-95—Minnesota	31	639	91	195	.467	45	84	.536	144	23	227	4.6	0.7	7.3
95-96—Minnesota	32	845	106	221	.480	66	127	.520	206	25	278	6.4	0.8	8.7
96-97—Minnesota	35	834	125	217	.576	66	115	.574	221	40	316	6.3	1.1	9.0
Totals	124	2572	349	703	.496	187	349	.536	636	91	885	5.1	0.7	7.1

Three-point field goals: 1996-97, 0-for-1. Totals, 0-for-1 (.000).
Personal fouls/disqualifications: 1993-94, 37/1. 1994-95, 81/3. 1995-96, 97/2. Totals, 215/6.

NBA REGULAR-SEASON RECORD

									REBOUNDS								AVERAGES		
Season Team	G	Min.	FGM	FGA	Pct.	FTM	FTA	Pct.	Off.	Def.	Tot.	Ast.	St.	Blk.	TO	Pts.	RPG	APG	PPG
97-98—Bos.-Tor.	54	535	55	113	.487	41	54	.759	48	58	106	17	22	12	46	151	2.0	0.3	2.8
98-99—Toronto	39	593	71	123	.577	27	48	.563	65	69	134	15	17	9	21	169	3.4	0.4	4.3
99-00—Toronto	55	477	49	107	.458	16	41	.390	37	38	75	9	12	14	14	114	1.4	0.2	2.1
04-05—Minnesota	44	521	42	86	.488	27	46	.587	39	58	97	17	15	13	18	111	2.2	0.4	2.5
05-06—Mem.-Atl.-N.J.	16	127	6	15	.400	3	4	.750	10	10	20	2	3	2	8	15	1.3	0.1	0.9
Totals	208	2253	223	444	.502	114	193	.591	199	233	432	60	69	50	107	560	2.1	0.3	2.7

Three-point field goals: 1998-99, 0-for-1. 1999-00, 0-for-1. Totals, 0-for-2 (.000).
Personal fouls/disqualifications: 1997-98, 97/0. 1998-99, 82/0. 1999-00, 106/1. 2004-05, 82/1. 2005-06, 17/0. Totals, 384/2.

NBA PLAYOFF RECORD

									REBOUNDS								AVERAGES		
Season Team	G	Min.	FGM	FGA	Pct.	FTM	FTA	Pct.	Off.	Def.	Tot.	Ast.	St.	Blk.	TO	Pts.	RPG	APG	PPG
99-00—Toronto	1	1	0	0	...	0	0	...	0	0	0	0	0	0	0	0	0.0	0.0	0.0
05-06—New Jersey	8	56	3	6	.500	1	2	.500	4	6	10	2	3	1	5	7	1.3	0.3	0.9
Totals	9	57	3	6	.500	1	2	.500	4	6	10	2	3	1	5	7	1.1	0.2	0.8

Personal fouls/disqualifications: 2005-06, 15/0. Totals, 15/0.

CBA RECORD

												AVERAGES		
Season Team	G	Min.	FGM	FGA	Pct.	FTM	FTA	Pct.	Reb.	Ast.	Pts.	RPG	APG	PPG
02-03—Dakota Wizards	6	130	31	49	.633	11	19	.579	43	8	73	7.2	1.3	12.2
04-05—Sioux Falls	20	707	123	220	.559	80	109	.734	201	37	326	10.1	1.9	16.3
Totals	26	837	154	269	.572	91	128	.711	244	45	399	9.4	1.7	15.3

Three-point field goals: 2004-05, 0-for-1. Totals, 0-for-1 (.000).

SPANISH LEAGUE RECORD

												AVERAGES		
Season Team	G	Min.	FGM	FGA	Pct.	FTM	FTA	Pct.	Reb.	Ast.	Pts.	RPG	APG	PPG
03-04—Casademont Girona	31	717	126	244	.516	63	87	.724	159	16	315	5.1	0.5	10.2

THOMAS, KENNY   F   KINGS

PERSONAL: Born July 25, 1977, in Atlanta. ... 6-7/245. (2.01/111.1). ... Full name: Kenneth Cornelius Thomas.
HIGH SCHOOL: El Paso (Texas), then Albuquerque (N.M.).
COLLEGE: New Mexico.
TRANSACTIONS/CAREER NOTES: Selected by Houston Rockets in first round (22nd pick overall) of 1999 NBA Draft. ... Traded by Rockets to Philadelphia 76ers in three-way deal in which 76ers sent F/C Mark Bryant, F Art Long and future first-round draft choice to Denver Nuggets, Nuggets sent G/F James Posey to Rockets and Rockets sent future second-round draft choice to Nuggets (December 18, 2002). ... Traded by 76ers with F Corliss Williamson and C Brian Skinner to Sacramento Kings for Fs Chris Webber, Michael Bradley and Matt Barnes (February 23, 2005).

COLLEGIATE RECORD

NOTES: The SPORTING NEWS All-America second team (1998).

												AVERAGES		
Season Team	G	Min.	FGM	FGA	Pct.	FTM	FTA	Pct.	Reb.	Ast.	Pts.	RPG	APG	PPG
95-96—New Mexico	33	981	170	294	.578	144	203	.709	256	53	484	7.8	1.6	14.7
96-97—New Mexico	32	1000	139	264	.527	155	206	.752	220	63	444	6.9	2.0	13.9
97-98—New Mexico	32	1047	195	385	.506	122	159	.767	297	95	539	9.3	3.0	16.8
98-99—New Mexico	26	903	162	297	.545	113	154	.734	259	51	464	10.0	2.0	17.8
Totals	123	3931	666	1240	.537	534	722	.740	1032	262	1931	8.4	2.1	15.7

Three-point field goals: 1995-96, 0-for-3. 1996-97, 11-for-36 (.306). 1997-98, 27-for-72 (.375). 1998-99, 27-for-73 (.370). Totals, 65-for-184 (.353).

NBA REGULAR-SEASON RECORD

									REBOUNDS								AVERAGES		
Season Team	G	Min.	FGM	FGA	Pct.	FTM	FTA	Pct.	Off.	Def.	Tot.	Ast.	St.	Blk.	TO	Pts.	RPG	APG	PPG
99-00—Houston	72	1797	212	531	.399	138	209	.660	147	290	437	113	54	22	112	594	6.1	1.6	8.3
00-01—Houston	74	1820	206	465	.443	91	126	.722	122	295	417	77	40	43	116	528	5.6	1.0	7.1
01-02—Houston	72	2484	396	829	.478	223	336	.664	158	358	516	137	85	66	143	1015	7.2	1.9	14.1
02-03—Hou-Phil	66	1978	260	559	.465	147	197	.746	185	344	529	112	62	28	116	667	8.0	1.7	10.1
03-04—Philadelphia	74	2699	381	813	.469	243	323	.752	261	489	750	111	82	33	172	1006	10.1	1.5	13.6
04-05—Phila.-Sac.	73	2167	367	781	.470	173	227	.762	184	351	535	152	67	17	131	908	7.3	2.1	12.4
05-06—Sacramento	82	2293	305	604	.505	138	204	.676	199	419	618	168	72	39	135	748	7.5	2.0	9.1
Totals	513	15238	2127	4582	.464	1153	1622	.711	1256	2546	3802	870	462	248	925	5466	7.4	1.7	10.7

Three-point field goals: 1999-00, 32-for-122 (.262). 2000-01, 25-for-92 (.272). 2001-02, 0-for-16. 2003-04, 1-for-5 (.200). 2004-05, 1-for-5 (.200). 2005-06, 0-for-1. Totals, 59-for-241 (.245).

Personal fouls/disqualifications: 1999-00, 167/0. 2000-01, 178/4. 2001-02, 195/5. 2002-03, 169/2. 2003-04, 219/2. 2004-05, 227/3. 2005-06, 196/1. Totals, 1351/17.

NBA PLAYOFF RECORD

Season Team	G	Min.	FGM	FGA	Pct.	FTM	FTA	Pct.	REBOUNDS Off.	Def.	Tot.	Ast.	St.	Blk.	TO	Pts.	AVERAGES RPG	APG	PPG
02-03—Philadelphia	12	389	54	101	.535	19	29	.655	42	70	112	11	8	5	19	127	9.3	0.9	10.6
04-05—Sacramento	5	153	23	45	.511	14	20	.700	17	27	44	12	4	2	8	60	8.8	2.4	12.0
05-06—Sacramento	6	148	13	24	.542	9	13	.692	12	15	27	8	5	0	9	35	4.5	1.3	5.8
Totals	23	690	90	170	.529	42	62	.677	71	112	183	31	17	7	36	222	8.0	1.3	9.7

Personal fouls/disqualifications: 2002-03, 42/1. 2004-05, 22/1. 2005-06, 22/1. Totals, 86/3.

THOMAS, KURT   F   SUNS

PERSONAL: Born October 4, 1972, in Dallas. ... 6-9/230. (2.06/104.3). ... Full name: Kurt Vincent Thomas
HIGH SCHOOL: Hillcrest (Dallas).
COLLEGE: Texas Christian.
TRANSACTIONS/CAREER NOTES: Selected by Miami Heat in first round (10th pick overall) of 1995 NBA Draft. ... Traded by Heat with G Sasha Danilovic and F Martin Muursepp to Dallas Mavericks for F Jamal Mashburn (February 14, 1997). ... Signed as free agent by New York Knicks (January 22, 1999). ... Traded by Knicks with draft rights to F Dijon Thompson to Phoenix Suns for G Quentin Richardson, draft rights to F Nate Robinson and future considerations (June 28, 2005).

COLLEGIATE RECORD

NOTES: Led NCAA Division I with 28.9 points per game and 14.6 rebounds per game (1995). ... One of only three players in NCAA history to lead nation in both scoring and rebounding in same season (1995).

Season Team	G	Min.	FGM	FGA	Pct.	FTM	FTA	Pct.	Reb.	Ast.	Pts.	AVERAGES RPG	APG	PPG
90-91—Texas Christian	28	42	8	18	.444	7	14	.500	13	2	23	0.5	0.1	0.8
91-92—Texas Christian	21	347	58	119	.487	34	51	.667	114	24	150	5.4	1.1	7.1
92-93—Texas Christian						Did not play—leg injury.								
93-94—Texas Christian	27	805	224	440	.509	98	152	.645	262	50	558	9.7	1.9	20.7
94-95—Texas Christian	27	872	288	526	.548	202	283	.714	393	32	781	14.6	1.2	28.9
Totals	103	2066	578	1103	.524	341	500	.682	782	108	1512	7.6	1.0	14.7

Three-point field goals: 1990-91, 0-for-2. 1993-94, 12-for-46 (.261). 1994-95, 3-for-12 (.250). Totals, 15-for-60 (.250).

NBA REGULAR-SEASON RECORD

NOTES: Led NBA with 341 personal fouls (2002),with 344 personal fouls (2003).

Season Team	G	Min.	FGM	FGA	Pct.	FTM	FTA	Pct.	REBOUNDS Off.	Def.	Tot.	Ast.	St.	Blk.	TO	Pts.	AVERAGES RPG	APG	PPG
95-96—Miami	74	1655	274	547	.501	118	178	.663	122	317	439	46	47	36	98	666	5.9	0.6	9.0
96-97—Miami	18	374	39	105	.371	35	46	.761	31	76	107	9	12	9	25	113	5.9	0.5	6.3
97-98—Dallas.............	5	73	17	45	.378	3	3	1.000	8	16	24	3	1	0	10	37	4.8	0.6	7.4
98-99—New York........	50	1182	170	368	.462	66	108	.611	82	204	286	55	45	17	73	406	5.7	1.1	8.1
99-00—New York........	80	1971	270	535	.505	100	128	.781	144	361	505	82	51	42	105	641	6.3	1.0	8.0
00-01—New York........	77	2125	314	614	.511	171	210	.814	172	343	515	63	61	69	99	800	6.7	0.8	10.4
01-02—New York........	82	2771	463	938	.494	216	265	.815	214	533	747	87	71	79	153	1143	9.1	1.1	13.9
02-03—New York........	81	2577	497	1028	.483	138	184	.750	160	477	637	162	81	97	138	1134	7.9	2.0	14.0
03-04—New York........	80	2548	392	829	.473	106	127	.835	145	517	662	149	56	80	132	890	8.3	1.9	11.1
04-05—New York........	80	2855	424	901	.471	66	84	.786	170	661	831	160	70	79	99	916	10.4	2.0	11.5
05-06—Phoenix	53	1411	190	391	.486	75	92	.815	102	313	415	57	23	54	57	455	7.8	1.1	8.6
Totals	680	19542	3050	6301	.484	1094	1425	.768	1350	3818	5168	873	518	562	989	7201	7.6	1.3	10.6

Three-point field goals: 1995-96, 0-for-2. 1996-97, 0-for-1. 1998-99, 0-for-1. 1999-00, 1-for-3 (.333). 2000-01, 1-for-3 (.333). 2001-02, 1-for-6 (.167). 2002-03, 2-for-3 (.667). 2003-04, 0-for-3. 2004-05, 2-for-4 (.500). Totals, 7-for-26 (.269).

Personal fouls/disqualifications: 1995-96, 271/7. 1996-97, 67/3. 1997-98, 19/1. 1998-99, 159/3. 1999-00, 278/6. 2000-01, 287/6. 2001-02, 341/8. 2002-03, 344/12. 2003-04, 298/4. 2004-05, 310/6. 2005-06, 193/5. Totals, 2567/61.

NBA PLAYOFF RECORD

Season Team	G	Min.	FGM	FGA	Pct.	FTM	FTA	Pct.	REBOUNDS Off.	Def.	Tot.	Ast.	St.	Blk.	TO	Pts.	AVERAGES RPG	APG	PPG
95-96—Miami	3	60	4	10	.400	4	4	1.000	4	12	16	3	2	1	5	12	5.3	1.0	4.0
98-99—New York........	20	419	45	118	.381	16	23	.696	38	72	110	7	15	12	19	106	5.5	0.4	5.3
99-00—New York........	16	251	31	61	.508	7	10	.700	18	32	50	5	3	6	14	69	3.1	0.3	4.3
00-01—New York........	5	186	25	47	.532	22	31	.710	17	39	56	9	2	5	9	72	11.2	1.8	14.4
03-04—New York........	4	139	21	49	.429	9	12	.750	9	37	46	6	7	3	10	51	11.5	1.5	12.8
05-06—Phoenix	1	6	0	0	...	1	2	.500	0	1	1	0	0	0	0	1	1.0	0.0	1.0
Totals	49	1061	126	285	.442	59	82	.720	86	193	279	30	29	27	57	311	5.7	0.6	6.3

Personal fouls/disqualifications: 1995-96, 13/1. 1998-99, 76/0. 1999-00, 44/1. 2000-01, 26/1. 2003-04, 17/0. 2005-06, 2/0. Totals, 178/3.

THOMAS, TIM   F   CLIPPERS

PERSONAL: Born February 26, 1977, in Paterson, N.J. ... 6-10/230. (2.08/104.3). ... Full name: Timothy Mark Thomas
HIGH SCHOOL: Paterson Catholic (Paterson, N.J.).
COLLEGE: Villanova.
TRANSACTIONS/CAREER NOTES: Selected after freshman season by New Jersey Nets in first round (seventh pick overall) of 1997 NBA Draft. ... Draft rights traded by Nets with draft rights to G Anthony Parker, G Jim Jackson and C Eric Montross to Philadelphia 76ers for C Michael Cage, G Lucious Harris, F Don MacLean and draft rights to F Keith Van Horn (June 27, 1997). ... Traded by 76ers with C/F Scott Williams to Milwaukee Bucks for F Tyrone Hill and F/G Jerald Honeycutt (March 11, 1999). ... Traded by Bucks to New

York Knicks as part of three-team trade in which Bucks also traded C Joel Przybilla to Atlanta Hawks. Knicks also acquired C Nazr Mohammed from Hawks and traded F Keith Van Horn to Bucks and C Michael Doleac and 2005 second-round draft choice to Hawks (February 15, 2004). ... Traded by Knicks with F Michael Sweetney and G Jermaine Jackson and 2007 and 2009 second-round draft picks, a conditional 2006 first-round pick and a conditional right to swap 2007 first-round picks to Chicago Bulls for C Eddy Curry and F/C Antonio Davis (October 4, 2005). ... Waived by Bulls (March 1, 2006). ... Signed by Phoenix Suns (March 3, 2006). ... Signed as free agent by Los Angeles Clippers (July 13, 2006).

COLLEGIATE RECORD

NOTES: The SPORTING NEWS Freshman of the Year (1997).

Season Team	G	Min.	FGM	FGA	Pct.	FTM	FTA	Pct.	Reb.	Ast.	Pts.	AVERAGES RPG	APG	PPG
96-97—Villanova	32	1005	187	416	.450	121	152	.796	193	66	542	6.0	2.1	16.9

Three-point field goals: 1996-97, 47-for-140 (.336). Totals, 47-for-140 (.336).

NBA REGULAR-SEASON RECORD

RECORDS: Shares single-game record for most three-point field goals made in one half—8 (January 5, 2001, vs. Portland).
HONORS: NBA All-Rookie second team (1998).

Season Team	G	Min.	FGM	FGA	Pct.	FTM	FTA	Pct.	REBOUNDS Off.	Def.	Tot.	Ast.	St.	Blk.	TO	Pts.	AVERAGES RPG	APG	PPG
97-98—Philadelphia	77	1779	306	684	.447	171	231	.740	107	181	288	90	54	17	118	845	3.7	1.2	11.0
98-99—Phila.-Mil.	50	812	132	279	.473	73	112	.652	49	77	126	46	26	12	46	358	2.5	0.9	7.2
99-00—Milwaukee	80	2093	347	753	.461	188	243	.774	100	232	332	113	59	31	129	945	4.2	1.4	11.8
00-01—Milwaukee	76	2086	326	758	.430	195	253	.771	79	234	313	138	78	45	114	954	4.1	1.8	12.6
01-02—Milwaukee	74	1987	316	753	.420	142	179	.793	64	236	300	105	65	32	127	869	4.1	1.4	11.7
02-03—Milwaukee	80	2358	412	930	.443	145	186	.780	97	292	389	102	70	49	133	1066	4.9	1.3	13.3
03-04—Milwaukee-N.Y.	66	2089	363	813	.447	146	171	.218	64	256	320	124	64	20	116	970	4.8	1.9	14.7
04-05—New York	71	1940	315	718	.439	136	173	.786	45	192	237	110	41	17	113	851	3.3	1.5	12.0
05-06—Chicago-Pho.	29	665	113	262	.431	28	42	.667	22	109	131	20	16	7	33	300	4.5	0.7	10.3
Totals	603	15809	2630	5950	.442	1249	1637	.763	627	1809	2436	848	473	230	929	7158	4.0	1.4	11.9

Three-point field goals: 1997-98, 62-for-171 (.363). 1998-99, 21-for-68 (.309). 1999-00, 63-for-182 (.346). 2000-01, 107-for-260 (.412). 2001-02, 95-for-291 (.326). 2002-03, 97-for-265 (.366). 2003-04, 73 for-194 (.376). 2004-05, 85 for-208 (.400). 2005-06, 46-for-111 (.414). Totals, 649-for-1750 (.371).

Personal fouls/disqualifications: 1997-98, 185/2. 1998-99, 107/2. 1999-00, 227/3. 2000-01, 194/5. 2001-02, 200/3. 2002-03, 257/5. 2003-04, 196/4. 2004-05, 222/3. 2005-06, 78/0. Totals, 1666/27.

NBA PLAYOFF RECORD

Season Team	G	Min.	FGM	FGA	Pct.	FTM	FTA	Pct.	REBOUNDS Off.	Def.	Tot.	Ast.	St.	Blk.	TO	Pts.	AVERAGES RPG	APG	PPG
98-99—Milwaukee	3	60	8	18	.444	7	12	.583	4	8	12	1	1	1	5	23	4.0	0.3	7.7
99-00—Milwaukee	5	142	29	59	.492	14	17	.824	6	18	24	10	1	4	1	77	4.8	2.0	15.4
00-01—Milwaukee	18	479	64	143	.448	53	65	.815	22	59	81	29	9	10	21	203	4.5	1.6	11.3
02-03—Milwaukee	6	191	36	78	.462	23	32	.719	8	21	29	8	3	6	8	107	4.8	1.3	17.8
03-04—New York	1	22	4	10	.400	4	5	.800	1	4	5	3	0	0	2	12	5.0	3.0	12.0
05-06—Phoenix	20	636	108	220	.491	38	49	.776	16	110	126	25	18	8	22	302	6.3	1.3	15.1
Totals	53	1530	249	528	.472	139	180	.772	57	220	277	76	32	29	59	724	5.2	1.4	13.7

Three-point field goals: 1998-99, 0-for-2. 1999-00, 5-for-15 (.333). 2000-01, 22-for-51 (.431). 2002-03, 12-for-21 (.571). 2003-04, 0-for-1. 2005-06, 48-for-108 (.444). Totals, 87-for-198 (.439).
Personal fouls/disqualifications: 1998-99, 11/0. 1999-00, 14/0. 2000-01, 52/1. 2002-03, 27/2. 2003-04, 5/0. 2005-06, 90/4. Totals, 199/7.

THOMPSON, DIJON   G/F   SUNS

PERSONAL: Born February 23, 1983, in Los Angeles, Calif. ... 6-7/195. (2.01/88.5). ... Full name: Dijon Lynn Thompson
HIGH SCHOOL: Redondo Union (Redondo Beach, Calif.).
COLLEGE: UCLA.
TRANSACTIONS/CAREER NOTES: Selected by New York Knicks in second round (54th pick overall) of 2005 NBA draft. ... Draft rights traded by Knicks with F Kurt Thomas to Phoenix Suns for G Quentin Richardson and draft rights to F Nate Robinson and cash (June 28, 2005).

COLLEGIATE RECORD

Season Team	G	Min.	FGM	FGA	Pct.	FTM	FTA	Pct.	Reb.	Ast.	Pts.	AVERAGES RPG	APG	PPG
01-02—UCLA	33	494	57	133	.429	20	23	.870	73	35	147	2.2	1.1	4.5
02-03—UCLA	28	828	155	312	.497	55	74	.743	131	78	393	4.7	2.8	14.0
03-04—UCLA	28	960	146	336	.435	61	78	.782	120	63	402	4.3	2.3	14.4
04-05—UCLA	28	970	183	386	.474	107	136	.787	222	63	516	7.9	2.3	18.4
Totals	117	3252	541	1167	.464	243	311	.781	546	239	1458	4.7	2.0	12.5

Three-point field goals: 2001-02, 13-for-48 (.271). 2002-03, 28-for-76 (.368). 2003-04, 49-for-128 (.383). 2004-05, 43-for-115 (.374). Totals, 133-for-367 (.362).

NBA REGULAR-SEASON RECORD

Season Team	G	Min.	FGM	FGA	Pct.	FTM	FTA	Pct.	REBOUNDS Off.	Def.	Tot.	Ast.	St.	Blk.	TO	Pts.	AVERAGES RPG	APG	PPG
05-06—Phoenix	10	43	11	25	.440	2	2	1.000	4	7	11	1	3	1	2	28	1.1	0.1	2.8

Three-point field goals: 2005-06, 4-for-11 (.364). Totals, 4-for-11 (.364).
Personal fouls/disqualifications: 2005-06, 6/0. Totals, 6/0.

NBA DEVELOPMENT LEAGUE RECORD

Season Team	G	Min.	FGM	FGA	Pct.	FTM	FTA	Pct.	Reb.	Ast.	Pts.	AVERAGES RPG	APG	PPG
05-06—Albuquerque	3	117	18	48	.375	12	16	.750	23	2	53	7.7	0.7	17.7

Three-point field goals: 2005-06, 5-for-8 (.625). Totals, 5-for-8 (.625).

TINSLEY, JAMAAL   G   PACERS

PERSONAL: Born February 28, 1978, in Brooklyn, N.Y. ... 6-3/195. (1.91/88.5).
HIGH SCHOOL: Samuel J. Tilden (Brooklyn, N.Y.), did not play basketball.
JUNIOR COLLEGE: Mount San Jacinto (Calif.).
COLLEGE: Iowa State.
TRANSACTIONS/CAREER NOTES: Selected by Vancouver Grizzlies in first round (27th pick overall) of 2001 NBA Draft. ... Draft rights traded by Grizzlies with F Shareef Abdur-Rahim to Atlanta Hawks for F/C Lorenzen Wright, G Brevin Knight and draft rights to F Pau Gasol (June 27, 2001). ... Draft rights traded by Hawks to Indiana Pacers for future first-round draft choice (July 19, 2001).

COLLEGIATE RECORD

NOTES: The SPORTING NEWS All-America second team (2001).

Season Team	G	Min.	FGM	FGA	Pct.	FTM	FTA	Pct.	Reb.	Ast.	Pts.	RPG	APG	PPG
97-98—Mount San Jacinto	36	...	194	403	.481	94	159	.591	153	341	509	4.3	9.5	14.1
98-99—Mount San Jacinto	37	...	281	502	.560	201	287	.700	160	362	814	4.3	9.8	22.0
99-00—Iowa State	37	1212	145	384	.378	102	151	.675	189	244	407	5.1	6.6	11.0
00-01—Iowa State	31	999	139	348	.399	128	185	.692	117	187	443	3.8	6.0	14.3
Junior College Totals	73		475	905	.525	295	446	.661	313	703	1323	4.3	9.6	18.1
4-Year-College Totals	68	2211	284	732	.388	230	336	.685	306	431	850	4.5	6.3	12.5

Three-point field goals: 1997-98, 27-for-100 (.270). 1998-99, 51-for-139 (.367). 1999-00, 15-for-62 (.242). 2000-01, 37-for-97 (.381). Totals, 130-for-398 (.327).

NBA REGULAR-SEASON RECORD

HONORS: NBA All-Rookie second team (2002).

Season Team	G	Min.	FGM	FGA	Pct.	FTM	FTA	Pct.	Off.	Def.	Tot.	Ast.	St.	Blk.	TO	Pts.	RPG	APG	PPG
01-02—Indiana	80	2442	289	760	.380	131	186	.704	78	220	298	647	138	40	270	751	3.7	8.1	9.4
02-03—Indiana	73	2237	220	556	.396	80	112	.714	58	202	260	548	125	18	192	566	3.6	7.5	7.8
03-04—Indiana	52	1378	153	370	.414	49	67	.731	28	108	136	303	84	17	110	432	2.6	5.8	8.3
04-05—Indiana	40	1301	218	522	.418	122	164	.744	26	134	160	257	81	12	134	616	4.0	6.4	15.4
05-06—Indiana	42	1122	158	386	.409	58	91	.637	35	98	133	211	49	6	109	390	3.2	5.0	9.3
Totals	287	8480	1038	2594	.400	440	620	.710	225	762	987	1966	477	93	815	2755	3.4	6.9	9.6

Three-point field goals: 2001-02, 42-for-175 (.240). 2002-03, 46-for-166 (.277). 2003-04, 77-for-207 (.372). 2004-05, 58-for-156 (.372). 2005-06, 16-for-70 (.229). Totals, 239-for-774 (.309).

Personal fouls/disqualifications: 2001-02, 248/9. 2002-03, 201/2. 2003-04, 132/2. 2004-05, 112/3. 2005-06, 96/2. Totals, 789/18.

NBA PLAYOFF RECORD

Season Team	G	Min.	FGM	FGA	Pct.	FTM	FTA	Pct.	Off.	Def.	Tot.	Ast.	St.	Blk.	TO	Pts.	RPG	APG	PPG
01-02—Indiana	5	88	8	19	.421	2	3	.667	2	8	10	25	2	0	12	18	2.0	5.0	3.6
02-03—Indiana	6	185	20	35	.571	3	6	.500	6	12	18	39	4	0	8	51	3.0	6.5	8.5
03-04—Indiana	16	422	49	123	.398	15	16	.938	6	40	46	80	28	3	31	129	2.9	5.0	8.1
04-05—Indiana	9	247	32	89	.360	12	21	.571	6	24	30	51	14	3	27	78	3.3	5.7	8.7
05-06—Indiana	1	7	1	3	.333	0	0	...	0	0	0	1	1	0	1	2	0.0	1.0	2.0
Totals	37	949	110	269	.409	32	46	.696	20	84	104	196	49	6	79	278	2.8	5.3	7.5

Three-point field goals: 2001-02, 0-for-1. 2002-03, 8-for-13 (.615). 2003-04, 16-for-54 (.296). 2004-05, 2-for-18 (.111). 2005-06, 0-for-2. Totals, 26-for-88 (.295).

Personal fouls/disqualifications: 2001-02, 12/0. 2002-03, 20/0. 2003-04, 56/2. 2004-05, 31/0. 2005-06, 1/0. Totals, 120/2.

TSAKALIDIS, JAKE   C   GRIZZLIES

PERSONAL: Born June 10, 1979, in Rustavi, Republic of Georgia. ... 7-2/285. (2.18/129.3).
TRANSACTIONS/CAREER NOTES: Played in Greece (1996-2000). ... Selected by Phoenix Suns in first round (25th overall) of 2000 NBA Draft. ... Traded by Suns with F Bo Outlaw to Memphis Grizzlies for G Brevin Knight, F Robert Archibald and C Cezary Trybanski (September 30, 2003).

GREEK LEAGUE RECORD

Season Team	G	Min.	FGM	FGA	Pct.	FTM	FTA	Pct.	Reb.	Ast.	Pts.	RPG	APG	PPG
96-97—AEK	1	13	1	2	.500	2	2	1.000	4	0	4	4.0	0.0	4.0
97-98—AEK	18	336	35	63	.556	24	43	.558	101	4	94	5.6	0.2	5.2
98-99—AEK	25	515	63	121	.521	35	55	.636	149	5	161	6.0	0.2	6.4
99-00—AEK	22	563	73	123	.593	57	103	.553	153	14	203	7.0	0.6	9.2
Totals	66	1427	172	309	.557	118	203	.581	407	23	462	6.2	0.3	7.0

NBA REGULAR-SEASON RECORD

Season Team	G	Min.	FGM	FGA	Pct.	FTM	FTA	Pct.	Off.	Def.	Tot.	Ast.	St.	Blk.	TO	Pts.	RPG	APG	PPG
00-01—Phoenix	57	947	101	215	.470	54	91	.593	83	159	242	19	10	55	66	256	4.2	0.3	4.5
01-02—Phoenix	67	1582	190	400	.475	111	159	.698	130	244	374	23	23	69	78	491	5.6	0.3	7.3
02-03—Phoenix	33	543	61	135	.452	39	58	.672	45	77	122	13	6	17	26	161	3.7	0.4	4.9
03-04—Memphis	40	533	67	133	.504	36	61	.590	37	91	128	18	9	22	23	170	3.2	0.5	4.3
04-05—Memphis	31	278	32	64	.500	14	18	.778	21	35	56	10	3	16	12	78	1.8	0.3	2.5
05-06—Memphis	51	732	100	165	.606	57	87	.655	78	134	212	13	14	32	39	257	4.2	0.3	5.0
Totals	279	4615	551	1112	.496	311	474	.656	394	740	1134	96	65	211	244	1413	4.1	0.3	5.1

Three-point field goals: 2001-02, 0-for-1. Totals, 0-for-1 (.000).

Personal fouls/disqualifications: 2000-01, 137/1. 2001-02, 193/4. 2002-03, 80/1. 2003-04, 79/1. 2004-05, 42/0. 2005-06, 107/1. Totals, 638/8.

NBA PLAYOFF RECORD

Season Team	G	Min.	FGM	FGA	Pct.	FTM	FTA	Pct.	REBOUNDS Off.	Def.	Tot.	Ast.	St.	Blk.	TO	Pts.	AVERAGES RPG	APG	PPG
00-01—Phoenix	4	75	6	16	.375	0	0	...	10	18	28	0	0	7	1	12	7.0	0.0	3.0
03-04—Memphis	1	3	0	0	...	2	2	1.000	0	0	0	0	0	0	3	2	0.0	0.0	2.0
05-06—Memphis	4	59	6	10	.600	1	2	.500	4	7	11	2	1	1	7	13	2.8	0.5	3.3
Totals	9	137	12	26	.462	3	4	.750	14	25	39	2	1	8	11	27	4.3	0.2	3.0

Personal fouls/disqualifications: 2000-01, 11/0. 2005-06, 13/0. Totals, 24/0.

TSKITISHVILI, NIKOLOZ   F

PERSONAL: Born April 14, 1983, in Tbilisi, U.S.S.R. ... 7-0/225. (2.13/102.1).
HIGH SCHOOL: 58 Sports School (Tbilisi, U.S.S.R.).
TRANSACTIONS/CAREER NOTES: Played in Slovenia (1999-2000 and 2000-01). ... Played in Italy (2001-02). ... Selected by Denver Nuggets in first round (fifth pick overall) of 2002 NBA Draft. ... Traded by Nuggets with F Rodney White to Golden State Warriors for F Eduardo Najera, G Luis Flores and future first-round draft pick (February 24, 2005). ... Signed as free agent by Minnesota Timberwolves (August 9, 2005). ... Traded by Timberwolves to Phoenix Suns for a second-round draft choice (January 26, 2006). ... Claimed on waivers by Portland Trail Blazers (June 30, 2006). ... Waived by Trail Blazers (July 5, 2006).

SLOVENIAN LEAGUE RECORD

Season Team	G	Min.	FGM	FGA	Pct.	FTM	FTA	Pct.	Reb.	Ast.	Pts.	AVERAGES RPG	APG	PPG
99-00—KK Slovan....................	31	253	33	68	.485	15	29	.517	49	5	81	1.6	0.2	2.6
00-01—KK Slovan....................	31	...	91	180	.506	55	80	.688	113	6	250	3.6	0.2	8.1
Totals	62	253	124	248	.500	70	109	.642	162	11	331	2.6	0.2	5.3

Three-point field goals: 1999-00, 0-for-3. 2000-01, 13-for-45 (.289). Totals, 13-for-48 (.271).

ITALIAN LEAGUE RECORD

Season Team	G	Min.	FGM	FGA	Pct.	FTM	FTA	Pct.	Reb.	Ast.	Pts.	AVERAGES RPG	APG	PPG
01-02—Benetton Treviso	11	140	30	50	.600	5	6	.833	20	4	73	1.8	0.4	6.6

Three-point field goals: 2001-02, 8-for-20 (.400). Totals, 8-for-20 (.400).

NBA REGULAR-SEASON RECORD

Season Team	G	Min.	FGM	FGA	Pct.	FTM	FTA	Pct.	REBOUNDS Off.	Def.	Tot.	Ast.	St.	Blk.	TO	Pts.	AVERAGES RPG	APG	PPG
02-03—Denver	81	1320	115	393	.293	48	65	.738	64	117	181	91	31	29	84	315	2.2	1.1	3.9
03-04—Denver	39	307	40	122	.328	23	29	.793	24	39	63	10	6	8	17	106	1.6	0.3	2.7
04-05—Denver-G.S.	35	220	22	74	.297	4	7	.571	12	29	41	10	8	11	19	50	1.2	0.3	1.4
05-06—Minnesota-Pho.	17	99	13	37	.351	9	14	.643	9	13	22	3	1	2	6	36	1.3	0.2	2.1
Totals	172	1946	190	626	.304	84	115	.730	109	198	307	114	46	50	126	507	1.8	0.7	2.9

Three-point field goals: 2002-03, 37-for-152 (.243). 2003-04, 3-for-11 (.273). 2004-05, 2-for-17 (.118). 2005-06, 1-for-3 (.333). Totals, 43-for-183 (.235).

Personal fouls/disqualifications: 2002-03, 100/1. 2003-04, 51/0. 2004-05, 30/0. 2005-06, 18/0. Totals, 199/1.

NBA PLAYOFF RECORD

Season Team	G	Min.	FGM	FGA	Pct.	FTM	FTA	Pct.	REBOUNDS Off.	Def.	Tot.	Ast.	St.	Blk.	TO	Pts.	AVERAGES RPG	APG	PPG
05-06—Phoenix	4	8	0	3	.000	1	2	.500	0	1	1	2	0	0	1	1	0.3	0.5	0.3

Three-point field goals: 2005-06, 0-for-1. Totals, 0-for-1 (.000).
Personal fouls/disqualifications: 2005-06, 1/0. Totals, 1/0.

TURIAF, RONNY   F   LAKERS

PERSONAL: Born January 13, 1983, in Le Robert, Martinique. ... 6-10/249. (2.08/112.9).
HIGH SCHOOL: Sporting Club Lamentinois (Le Robert, Martinique).
COLLEGE: Gonzaga.
TRANSACTIONS/CAREER NOTES: Selected by Los Angeles Lakers in second round (37th pick overall) of 2005 NBA draft. ... Played in CBA (2005-06). ... Signed by Lakers (January 17, 2006).

COLLEGIATE RECORD

Season Team	G	Min.	FGM	FGA	Pct.	FTM	FTA	Pct.	Reb.	Ast.	Pts.	AVERAGES RPG	APG	PPG
01-02—Gonzaga	32	624	73	139	.525	89	128	.695	161	16	235	5.0	0.5	7.3
02-03—Gonzaga	33	814	151	291	.519	212	279	.760	206	19	515	6.2	0.6	15.6
03-04—Gonzaga	31	834	157	299	.525	165	233	.708	197	47	480	6.4	1.5	15.9
04-05—Gonzaga	31	967	157	309	.508	177	259	.683	295	48	493	9.5	1.5	15.9
Totals	127	3239	538	1038	.518	643	899	.715	859	130	1723	6.8	1.0	13.6

Three-point field goals: 2001-02, 0-for-2. 2002-03, 1-for-6 (.167). 2003-04, 1-for-3 (.333). 2004-05, 2-for-7 (.286). Totals, 4-for-18 (.222).

CBA RECORD

Season Team	G	Min.	FGM	FGA	Pct.	FTM	FTA	Pct.	Reb.	Ast.	Pts.	AVERAGES RPG	APG	PPG
05-06—Yakima	9	215	44	76	.579	29	43	.674	57	19	117	6.3	2.1	13.0

Three-point field goals: 2005-06, 0-for-1. Totals, 0-for-1 (.000).

NBA REGULAR-SEASON RECORD

Season Team	G	Min.	FGM	FGA	Pct.	FTM	FTA	Pct.	REBOUNDS Off.	Def.	Tot.	Ast.	St.	Blk.	TO	Pts.	AVERAGES RPG	APG	PPG
05-06—L.A. Lakers	23	161	15	30	.500	15	27	.556	11	26	37	8	3	10	7	45	1.6	0.3	2.0

Personal fouls/disqualifications: 2005-06, 30/0. Totals, 30/0.

NBA PLAYOFF RECORD

Season Team	G	Min.	FGM	FGA	Pct.	FTM	FTA	Pct.	REBOUNDS Off.	Def.	Tot.	Ast.	St.	Blk.	TO	Pts.	RPG	APG	PPG
05-06—L.A. Lakers	3	25	3	5	.600	5	6	.833	4	3	7	0	0	1	2	11	2.3	0.0	3.7

Personal fouls/disqualifications: 2005-06, 5/0. Totals, 5/0.

TURKOGLU, HEDO   F   MAGIC

PERSONAL: Born March 19, 1979, in Istanbul, Turkey. ... 6-8/220. (2.03/99.8).
TRANSACTIONS/CAREER NOTES: Played in Turkey (1996-2000). ... Selected by Sacramento Kings in first round (16th pick overall) of 2000 NBA Draft. ... Traded by Kings to San Antonio Spurs in three-team trade in which Kings also traded F Scot Pollard to Indiana Pacers and acquired F/C Brad Miller from Pacers. Spurs also picked up G Ron Mercer from Pacers and traded F Danny Ferry to Pacers (July 24, 2003) ... Signed as free agent by Orlando Magic (July 14, 2004).

TURKISH LEAGUE RECORD

Season Team	G	Min.	FGM	FGA	Pct.	FTM	FTA	Pct.	Reb.	Ast.	Pts.	RPG	APG	PPG
96-97—Efes Pilsen......	11	...	27	38	.711	8	16	.500	30	17	83	2.7	1.5	7.5
97-98—Efes Pilsen......	29	386	45	93	.484	25	38	.658	87	35	121	3.0	1.2	4.2
98-99—Efes Pilsen......	23	575	69	146	.473	33	42	.786	95	37	192	4.1	1.6	8.3
99-00—Efes Pilsen......	24	812	110	211	.521	66	88	.750	129	53	328	5.4	2.2	13.7
Totals	87	...	251	488	.514	132	184	.717	341	142	724	3.9	1.6	8.3

Three-point field goals: 1996-97, 7-for-17 (.412). 1997-98, 6-for-22 (.273). 1998-99, 21-for-65 (.323). 1999-00, 42-for-81 (.519). Totals, 76-for-185 (.411).

HONORS: NBA All-Rookie second team (2001).

NBA REGULAR-SEASON RECORD

Season Team	G	Min.	FGM	FGA	Pct.	FTM	FTA	Pct.	REBOUNDS Off.	Def.	Tot.	Ast.	St.	Blk.	TO	Pts.	RPG	APG	PPG
00-01—Sacramento	74	1245	138	335	.412	87	112	.777	49	161	210	69	52	24	55	391	2.8	0.9	5.3
01-02—Sacramento	80	1970	290	687	.422	167	230	.726	63	300	363	163	57	31	81	810	4.5	2.0	10.1
02-03—Sacramento	67	1175	165	391	.422	88	110	.800	35	153	188	87	25	12	50	447	2.8	1.3	6.7
03-04—San Antonio ...	80	2073	262	645	.406	114	161	.708	52	306	358	154	80	32	94	739	4.5	1.9	9.2
04-05—Orlando..........	67	1757	328	782	.419	188	225	.836	62	171	233	153	41	18	119	937	3.5	2.3	14.0
05-06—Orlando..........	78	2615	398	877	.454	255	296	.861	70	263	333	216	70	21	130	1165	4.3	2.8	14.9
Totals	446	10835	1581	3717	.425	899	1134	.793	331	1354	1685	842	325	138	529	4489	3.8	1.9	10.1

Three-point field goals: 2000-01, 28-for-86 (.326). 2001-02, 63-for-171 (.368). 2002-03, 29-for-78 (.372). 2003-04, 101-for-241 (.419). 2004-05, 93-for-245 (.380). 2005-06, 114-for-283 (.403). Totals, 428-for-1104 (.388).
Personal fouls/disqualifications: 2000-01, 139/1. 2001-02, 184/0. 2002-03, 125/0. 2003-04, 165/0. 2004-05, 140/0. 2005-06, 234/5. Totals, 987/6.

NBA PLAYOFF RECORD

Season Team	G	Min.	FGM	FGA	Pct.	FTM	FTA	Pct.	REBOUNDS Off.	Def.	Tot.	Ast.	St.	Blk.	TO	Pts.	RPG	APG	PPG
00-01—Sacramento	8	141	20	46	.435	12	12	1.000	7	21	28	11	3	1	6	60	3.5	1.4	7.5
01-02—Sacramento	16	443	55	137	.401	16	31	.516	17	66	83	23	6	9	23	138	5.2	1.4	8.6
02-03—Sacramento	10	174	18	50	.360	13	18	.722	5	24	29	14	12	5	5	53	2.9	1.4	5.3
03-04—San Antonio ...	10	271	26	81	.321	11	18	.611	5	40	45	15	9	1	16	77	4.5	1.5	7.7
Totals	44	1029	119	314	.379	52	79	.658	34	151	185	63	30	16	50	328	4.2	1.4	7.5

Three-point field goals: 2000-01, 8-for-14 (.571). 2001-02, 12-for-34 (.353). 2002-03, 4-for-14 (.286). 2003-04, 14-for-42 (.333). Totals, 38-for-104 (.365).
Personal fouls/disqualifications: 2000-01, 18/0. 2001-02, 49/0. 2002-03, 19/0. 2003-04, 20/0. Totals, 106/0.

UDOKA, IME   G/F

PERSONAL: Born August 9, 1977, in Portland, Ore. ... 6-6/215. (1.98/97.5).
HIGH SCHOOL: Jefferson (Portland, Ore.).
COLLEGE: Eastern Utah, then San Francisco, then Portland St.
TRANSACTIONS/CAREER NOTES: Not drafted by an NBA franchise. ... Played in France and Spain (2004-05). ... Played in NBA Development League with Charleston Lowgators (2002-03; 2003-04; 2005-06). ... Signed by Los Angeles Lakers (August 13, 2003). ... Signed by Lakers to 10-day contract (January 14, 2004). ... Waived by 76ers (October 11, 2005). ...Signed as free agent by New York Knicks (April 6, 2006).

COLLEGIATE RECORD

Season Team	G	Min.	FGM	FGA	Pct.	FTM	FTA	Pct.	Reb.	Ast.	Pts.	RPG	APG	PPG
95-96—College of Eastern Utah	30	...	138	272	.507	41	56	.732	213	107	355	7.1	3.6	11.8
96-97—College of Eastern Utah	33	...	177	339	.522	90	120	.750	221	147	486	6.7	4.5	14.7
97-98—San Francisco..............	21	211	11	45	.244	10	17	.588	43	17	34	2.0	0.8	1.6
98-99—Portland State					Did not play—transfer student									
99-00—Portland State.............	24	703	112	281	.399	99	135	.733	174	71	347	7.3	3.0	14.5
Junior College Totals..........	63	...	315	611	.516	131	176	.744	434	254	841	6.9	4.0	13.3
4-Year-College Totals.........	45	914	123	326	.377	109	152	.717	217	88	381	4.8	2.0	8.5

Three-point field goals: 1995-96, 38-for-85 (.447). 1996-97, 42-for-105 (.400). 1997-98, 2-for-15 (.133). 1999-00, 24-for-77 (.312). Totals, 106-for-282 (.376).

IBA RECORD

Season Team	G	Min.	FGM	FGA	Pct.	FTM	FTA	Pct.	Reb.	Ast.	Pts.	RPG	APG	PPG
00-01—Fargo-Moorhead	12	344	58	133	.436	31	51	.608	77	37	148	6.4	3.1	12.3

Three-point field goals: 2000-01, 1-for-7 (.143). Totals, 1-for-7 (.143).

NBA DEVELOPMENT LEAGUE RECORD

Season Team	G	Min.	FGM	FGA	Pct.	FTM	FTA	Pct.	Reb.	Ast.	Pts.	RPG	APG	PPG
02-03—Charleston	50	1126	180	378	.476	128	173	.740	268	66	515	5.4	1.3	10.3

Season Team	G	Min.	FGM	FGA	Pct.	FTM	FTA	Pct.	Reb.	Ast.	Pts.	AVERAGES RPG	APG	PPG
03-04—Charleston	41	1274	252	548	.460	147	206	.714	295	104	694	7.2	2.5	16.9
05-06—Fort Worth	45	1542	275	637	.432	183	251	.729	210	155	326	4.7	3.4	7.2
Totals	136	3942	707	1563	.452	458	630	.727	773	325	1535	5.7	2.4	11.3

Three-point field goals: 2005-06, 37-for-121 (.306). Totals, 37-for-121 (.306).

NBA REGULAR-SEASON RECORD

Season Team	G	Min.	FGM	FGA	Pct.	FTM	FTA	Pct.	REBOUNDS Off.	Def.	Tot.	Ast.	St.	Blk.	TO	Pts.	AVERAGES RPG	APG	PPG
03-04—L.A. Lakers....	4	28	3	9	.333	2	4	.500	1	4	5	2	2	1	3	8	1.3	0.5	2.0
05-06—New York	8	114	9	24	.375	3	6	.500	3	14	17	6	1	0	2	22	2.1	0.8	2.8
Totals	12	142	12	33	.364	5	10	.500	4	18	22	8	3	1	5	30	1.8	0.7	2.5

Three-point field goals: 2003-04, 0-for-1. 2005-06, 1-for-3 (.333). Totals, 1-for-4 (.250).
Personal fouls/disqualifications: 2003-04, 3/0. 2005-06, 8/0. Totals, 11/0.

FRENCH LEAGUE RECORD

Season Team	G	Min.	FGM	FGA	Pct.	FTM	FTA	Pct.	Reb.	Ast.	Pts.	AVERAGES RPG	APG	PPG
04-05—Vichy	9	347	75	155	.484	42	67	.627	76	48	218	8.4	5.3	24.2

Three-point field goals: 2004-05, 26-for-64 (.406). Totals, 26-for-64 (.406).

SPANISH LEAGUE RECORD

Season Team	G	Min.	FGM	FGA	Pct.	FTM	FTA	Pct.	Reb.	Ast.	Pts.	AVERAGES RPG	APG	PPG
04-05—Auna Gran Canaria.......	15	299	42	103	.408	26	44	.591	60	14	122	4.0	0.9	8.1

Three-point field goals: 2004-05, 12-for-38 (.316). Totals, 12-for-38 (.316).

UDRIH, BENO   G   SPURS

PERSONAL: Born July 5, 1982, in Celje, Slovenia. ... 6-3/203. (1.91/92.1).
TRANSACTIONS/CAREER NOTES: Played in Slovenia (1999-2001). ... Played in Adriatic League (2001-03). ... Played in Israel (2002-03). ... Played in Russia and Italy (2003-04). ... Selected by San Antonio Spurs in first round (28th pick overall) of 2004 NBA Draft.
MISCELLANEOUS: Member of NBA championship team (2005).

SLOVENIAN LEAGUE RECORD

Season Team	G	Min.	FGM	FGA	Pct.	FTM	FTA	Pct.	Reb.	Ast.	Pts.	AVERAGES RPG	APG	PPG
98-99—Savinjski........................	8	17	0	2	.000	0	0	...	0	1	0	0.0	0.1	0.0
99-00—Savinjski........................	29	608	111	189	.587	64	91	.703	60	22	300	2.1	0.8	10.3
00-01—Olimpija Ljubljana..........	21	533	69	117	.590	38	51	.745	54	56	182	2.6	2.7	8.7
01-02—Olimpija Ljubljana..........	18	431	67	124	.540	21	33	.636	34	39	172	1.9	2.2	9.6
Totals	76	1589	247	432	.572	123	175	.703	148	118	654	1.9	1.6	8.6

Three-point field goals: 1999-00, 14-for-39 (.359). 2000-01, 6-for-16 (.375). 2001-02, 51-for-172 (.296). Totals, 67-for-50 (.656).

ISRAELI LEAGUE RECORD

Season Team	G	Min.	FGM	FGA	Pct.	FTM	FTA	Pct.	Reb.	Ast.	Pts.	AVERAGES RPG	APG	PPG
02-03—Maccabi Tel-Aviv	21	550	84	158	.532	42	49	.857	52	69	224	2.5	3.3	10.7
02-03—Maccabi Tel-Aviv	25	467	51	110	.464	8	13	.615	43	67	122	1.7	2.7	4.9
Totals	46	1017	135	268	.504	50	62	.806	95	136	346	2.1	3.0	7.5

Three-point field goals: 2002-03, 14-for-35 (.400). 2002-03, 12-for-37 (.324). Totals, 26-for-72 (.361).

ITALIAN LEAGUE RECORD

Season Team	G	Min.	FGM	FGA	Pct.	FTM	FTA	Pct.	Reb.	Ast.	Pts.	AVERAGES RPG	APG	PPG
03-04—Breil Milano	16	413	67	126	.532	25	27	.926	29	36	173	1.8	2.3	10.8

Three-point field goals: 2003-04, 14-for-33 (.424). Totals, 14-for-33 (.424).

RUSSIAN LEAGUE RECORD

Season Team	G	Min.	FGM	FGA	Pct.	FTM	FTA	Pct.	Reb.	Ast.	Pts.	AVERAGES RPG	APG	PPG
03-04—Avtodor Saratov	5	170	37	68	.544	21	29	.724	17	21	98	3.4	4.2	19.6

Three-point field goals: 2003-04, 3-for-8 (.375). Totals, 3-for-8 (.375).

NBA REGULAR-SEASON RECORD

Season Team	G	Min.	FGM	FGA	Pct.	FTM	FTA	Pct.	REBOUNDS Off.	Def.	Tot.	Ast.	St.	Blk.	TO	Pts.	AVERAGES RPG	APG	PPG
04-05—San Antonio....	80	1149	173	390	.444	67	89	.753	16	67	83	150	41	10	77	471	1.0	1.9	5.9
05-06—San Antonio....	54	586	106	233	.455	39	50	.780	18	34	52	92	14	2	53	275	1.0	1.7	5.1
Totals	134	1735	279	623	.448	106	139	.763	34	101	135	242	55	12	130	746	1.0	1.8	5.6

Three-point field goals: 2004-05, 58-for-142 (.408). 2005-06, 24-for-70 (.343). Totals, 82-for-212 (.387).
Personal fouls/disqualifications: 2004-05, 96/0. 2005-06, 55/0. Totals, 151/0.

NBA PLAYOFF RECORD

Season Team	G	Min.	FGM	FGA	Pct.	FTM	FTA	Pct.	REBOUNDS Off.	Def.	Tot.	Ast.	St.	Blk.	TO	Pts.	AVERAGES RPG	APG	PPG
04-05—San Antonio....	21	241	28	78	.359	12	14	.857	4	13	17	22	9	1	20	78	0.8	1.0	3.7
05-06—San Antonio....	7	47	10	30	.333	4	5	.800	1	3	4	8	0	0	3	25	0.6	1.1	3.6
Totals	28	288	38	108	.352	16	19	.842	5	16	21	30	9	1	23	103	0.8	1.1	3.7

Three-point field goals: 2004-05, 10-for-37 (.270). 2005-06, 1-for-6 (.167). Totals, 11-for-43 (.256).
Personal fouls/disqualifications: 2004-05, 20/0. 2005-06, 8/0. Totals, 28/0.

VAN EXEL, NICK   G   SPURS

PERSONAL: Born November 27, 1971, in Kenosha, Wis. ... 6-1/190. (1.85/86.2). ... Full name: Nickey Maxwell Van Exel ... Name pronounced van EX-el.
HIGH SCHOOL: St. Joseph's (Kenosha, Wis.).
JUNIOR COLLEGE: Trinity Valley Community College (Texas).
COLLEGE: Cincinnati.

TRANSACTIONS/CAREER NOTES: Selected by Los Angeles Lakers in second round (37th pick overall) of 1993 NBA Draft. ... Traded by Lakers to Denver Nuggets for F Tony Battie and draft rights to G Tyronn Lue (June 24, 1998). ... Traded by Nuggets with F/C Raef LaFrentz, G Avery Johnson and G/F Tariq Abdul-Wahad to Dallas Mavericks for F Juwan Howard, G Tim Hardaway, F Donnell Harvey, cash considerations and first-round draft choice (February 21, 2002). ... Traded by Mavericks with G Avery Johnson, F Popeye Jones, F Antoine Rigaudeau and C Evan Eschmeyer to Golden State Warriors for F Antawn Jamison, F Chris Mills, F Danny Fortson and G Jiri Welsch (August 18, 2003). ... Traded by Warriors to Portland Trail Blazers for F Dale Davis and G Dan Dickau (July 20, 2004). ... Waived by Trail Blazers (August 3, 2005). ... Signed as free agent by San Antonio Spurs (August 29, 2005).

COLLEGIATE RECORD

Season Team	G	Min.	FGM	FGA	Pct.	FTM	FTA	Pct.	Reb.	Ast.	Pts.	AVERAGES RPG	APG	PPG
89-90—Trinity Valley C.C.........	31	...	200	415	.482	88	128	.688	101	166	542	3.3	5.4	17.5
90-91—Trinity Valley C.C.........	27	...	190	441	.431	105	147	.714	110	185	551	4.1	6.9	20.4
91-92—Cincinnati	34	834	144	323	.446	68	101	.673	87	99	418	2.6	2.9	12.3
92-93—Cincinnati	31	1049	198	513	.386	87	120	.725	75	138	568	2.4	4.5	18.3
Junior College Totals..........	58	...	390	856	.456	193	275	.702	211	351	1093	3.6	6.1	18.8
4-Year-College Totals	65	1883	342	836	.409	155	221	.701	162	237	986	2.5	3.6	15.2

Three-point field goals: 1989-90, 71-for-186 (.382). 1990-91, 66-for-186 (.355). 1991-92, 62-for-163 (.380). 1992-93, 85-for-248 (.343). Totals, 284-for-783 (.363).

NBA REGULAR-SEASON RECORD

HONORS: NBA All-Rookie second team (1994).

Season Team	G	Min.	FGM	FGA	Pct.	FTM	FTA	Pct.	REBOUNDS Off.	Def.	Tot.	Ast.	St.	Blk.	TO	Pts.	AVERAGES RPG	APG	PPG
93-94—L.A. Lakers......	81	2700	413	1049	.394	150	192	.781	47	191	238	466	85	8	145	1099	2.9	5.8	13.6
94-95—L.A. Lakers......	80	2944	465	1107	.420	235	300	.783	27	196	223	660	97	6	220	1348	2.8	8.3	16.9
95-96—L.A. Lakers......	74	2513	396	950	.417	163	204	.799	29	152	181	509	70	10	156	1099	2.4	6.9	14.9
96-97—L.A. Lakers......	79	2937	432	1075	.402	165	200	.825	44	182	226	672	75	10	212	1206	2.9	8.5	15.3
97-98—L.A. Lakers......	64	2053	311	743	.419	136	172	.791	31	163	194	442	64	6	104	881	3.0	6.9	13.8
98-99—Denver	50	1802	306	769	.398	142	175	.811	14	99	113	368	40	3	121	826	2.3	7.4	16.5
99-00—Denver	79	2950	473	1213	.390	196	240	.817	34	277	311	714	68	11	221	1275	3.9	9.0	16.1
00-01—Denver	71	2688	460	1112	.414	204	249	.819	44	197	241	600	61	18	165	1259	3.4	8.5	17.7
01-02—Denver-Dallas ..	72	2496	501	1226	.409	201	251	.801	28	226	254	478	44	11	156	1322	3.5	6.6	18.4
02-03—Dallas............	73	2026	342	831	.412	110	144	.764	35	173	208	312	42	4	123	912	2.8	4.3	12.5
03-04—Golden State ..	39	1255	187	479	.390	70	99	.707	16	88	104	206	20	2	78	490	2.7	5.3	12.6
04-05—Portland	53	1619	214	561	.381	58	74	.784	20	141	161	227	44	0	92	586	3.0	4.3	11.1
05-06—San Antonio ..	65	986	136	343	.397	28	41	.683	6	85	91	123	16	3	57	355	1.4	1.9	5.5
Totals	880	28969	4636	11458	.405	1858	2341	.794	375	2170	2545	5777	726	92	1850	12658	2.9	6.6	14.4

Three-point field goals: 1993-94, 123-for-364 (.338). 1994-95, 183-for-511 (.358). 1995-96, 144-for-403 (.357). 1996-97, 177-for-468 (.378). 1997-98, 123-for-316 (.389). 1998-99, 72-for-234 (.308). 1999-00, 133-for-401 (.332). 2000-01, 135-for-358 (.377). 2001-02, 119-for-350 (.340). 2002-03, 118-for-312 (.378). 2003-04, 46-for-150 (.307). 2004-05, 100-for-257 (.389). 2005-06, 55-for-154 (.357). Totals, 1528-for-4278 (.357).
Personal fouls/disqualifications: 1993-94, 154/1. 1994-95, 157/0. 1995-96, 115/0. 1996-97, 110/0. 1997-98, 120/0. 1998-99, 90/0. 1999-00, 148/0. 2000-01, 109/1. 2001-02, 104/0. 2002-03, 86/1. 2003-04, 57/0. 2004-05, 70/0. 2005-06, 60/0. Totals, 1380/3.

NBA PLAYOFF RECORD

Season Team	G	Min.	FGM	FGA	Pct.	FTM	FTA	Pct.	REBOUNDS Off.	Def.	Tot.	Ast.	St.	Blk.	TO	Pts.	AVERAGES RPG	APG	PPG
94-95—L.A. Lakers....	10	464	67	162	.414	45	59	.763	9	29	38	73	21	3	22	200	3.8	7.3	20.0
95-96—L.A. Lakers....	4	137	16	54	.296	10	13	.769	4	12	16	27	2	0	11	47	4.0	6.8	11.8
96-97—L.A. Lakers....	9	353	45	119	.378	28	34	.824	6	25	31	58	10	0	18	130	3.4	6.4	14.4
97-98—L.A. Lakers....	13	367	50	151	.331	29	40	.725	9	23	32	54	8	1	22	151	2.5	4.2	11.6
01-02—Dallas...........	8	264	37	101	.366	8	12	.667	7	17	24	31	8	0	12	89	3.0	3.9	11.1
02-03—Dallas...........	20	672	150	326	.460	45	64	.703	18	50	68	82	12	0	39	389	3.4	4.1	19.5
05-06—San Antonio ..	12	133	7	32	.219	9	9	1.000	1	11	12	17	3	2	5	26	1.0	1.4	2.2
Totals	76	2390	372	945	.394	174	231	.753	54	167	221	342	64	6	129	1032	2.9	4.5	13.6

Three-point field goals: 1994-95, 21-for-66 (.318). 1995-96, 5-for-16 (.313). 1996-97, 12-for-44 (.273). 1997-98, 22-for-70 (.314). 2001-02, 7-for-34 (.206). 2002-03, 44-for-112 (.393). 2005-06, 3-for-10 (.300). Totals, 114-for-352 (.324).
Personal fouls/disqualifications: 1994-95, 33/0. 1995-96, 10/0. 1996-97, 19/0. 1997-98, 30/0. 2001-02, 26/0. 2002-03, 47/0. 2005-06, 14/0. Totals, 179/0.

NBA ALL-STAR GAME RECORD

Season Team	Min.	FGM	FGA	Pct.	FTM	FTA	Pct.	REBOUNDS Off.	Def.	Tot.	Ast.	PF	Dq.	St.	Blk.	TO	Pts.
1998—L.A. Lakers..........	20	5	14	.357	2	2	1.000	1	2	3	2	0	...	0	0	2	13

Three-point field goals: 1998, 1-for-6 (.167). Totals, 1-for-6 (.167).

VAN HORN, KEITH   F

PERSONAL: Born October 23, 1975, in Fullerton, Calif. ... 6-10/240. (2.08/108.9). ... Full name: Keith Adam Van Horn
HIGH SCHOOL: Diamond Bar (Calif.).
COLLEGE: Utah.
TRANSACTIONS/CAREER NOTES: Selected by Philadelphia 76ers in first round (second pick overall) of 1997 NBA Draft. ... Draft rights traded by 76ers with C Michael Cage, G Lucious Harris and F Don MacLean to New Jersey Nets for draft

V

rights to F Tim Thomas, draft rights to G Anthony Parker, G Jim Jackson and C Eric Montross (June 27, 1997). ... Traded by Nets with C Todd MacCulloch to 76ers for C Dikembe Mutombo (August 6, 2002). ... Traded by 76ers to New York Knicks in a three-team deal in which 76ers also traded F Randy Holcomb, a first-round draft pick and cash considerations to Atlanta Hawks and acquired F Glenn Robinson and a 2006 second-round pick from Hawks and F/C Marc Jackson from Minnesota Timberwolves. Knicks traded G Latrell Sprewell to Timberwolves and Timberwolves traded G Terrell Brandon to Hawks (July 23, 2003) ... Traded by Knicks to Milwaukee Bucks in a three-team deal in which Knicks also traded C Michael Doleac and 2005 second-round draft choice to Atlanta Hawks. Bucks also traded F Tim Thomas to Knicks and C Joel Przybilla to Hawks (February 15, 2004). ... Traded by Bucks to Dallas Mavericks for F Alan Henderson and C Calvin Booth (February 24, 2005).

COLLEGIATE RECORD

NOTES: THE SPORTING NEWS All-America first team (1997). ... THE SPORTING NEWS All-America second team (1996).

												AVERAGES		
Season Team	G	Min.	FGM	FGA	Pct.	FTM	FTA	Pct.	Reb.	Ast.	Pts.	RPG	APG	PPG
93-94—Utah	25	740	161	312	.516	100	129	.775	208	21	457	8.3	0.8	18.3
94-95—Utah	33	994	246	451	.545	143	167	.856	280	45	694	8.5	1.4	21.0
95-96—Utah	32	990	236	439	.538	160	188	.851	283	31	686	8.8	1.0	21.4
96-97—Utah	32	1008	248	504	.492	151	167	.904	303	45	705	9.5	1.4	22.0
Totals	122	3732	891	1706	.522	554	651	.851	1074	142	2542	8.8	1.2	20.8

Three-point field goals: 1993-94, 35-for-79 (.443). 1994-95, 59-for-153 (.386). 1995-96, 54-for-132 (.409). 1996-97, 58-for-150 (.387). Totals, 206-for-514 (.401).
Personal fouls/disqualifications: 1993-94, 60/2. 1994-95, 69/1. 1995-96, 63/1. Totals, 192/4.

NBA REGULAR-SEASON RECORD

HONORS: NBA All-Rookie first team (1998).

									REBOUNDS								AVERAGES		
Season Team	G	Min.	FGM	FGA	Pct.	FTM	FTA	Pct.	Off.	Def.	Tot.	Ast.	St.	Blk.	TO	Pts.	RPG	APG	PPG
97-98—New Jersey	62	2325	446	1047	.426	258	305	.846	142	266	408	106	64	25	164	1219	6.6	1.7	19.7
98-99—New Jersey	42	1576	322	752	.428	256	298	.859	114	244	358	65	43	53	133	916	8.5	1.5	21.8
99-00—New Jersey	80	2782	559	1257	.445	333	393	.847	200	476	676	158	64	60	245	1535	8.5	2.0	19.2
00-01—New Jersey	49	1733	308	708	.435	150	186	.806	78	269	347	82	40	20	103	831	7.1	1.7	17.0
01-02—New Jersey	81	2465	471	1089	.433	156	195	.800	137	472	609	164	63	42	146	1199	7.5	2.0	14.8
02-03—Philadelphia	74	2337	459	952	.482	193	240	.804	159	365	524	93	63	30	150	1176	7.1	1.3	15.9
03-04—New York-Mil.	72	2340	410	903	.454	249	290	.859	149	352	501	120	68	33	169	1162	7.0	1.7	16.1
04-05—Mil.-Dallas	62	1502	257	564	.456	128	157	.815	89	205	294	75	36	21	81	696	4.7	1.2	11.2
05-06—Dallas	53	1090	164	387	.424	94	113	.832	54	138	192	37	31	11	71	472	3.6	0.7	8.9
Totals	575	18150	3396	7659	.443	1817	2177	.835	1122	2787	3909	900	472	295	1262	9206	6.8	1.6	16.0

Three-point field goals: 1997-98, 69-for-224 (.308). 1998-99, 16-for-53 (.302). 1999-00, 84-for-228 (.368). 2000-01, 65-for-170 (.382). 2001-02, 101-for-293 (.345). 2002-03, 65-for-176 (.369). 2003-04, 93-for-233 (.399). 2004-05, 54-for-142 (.380). 2005-06, 50-for-136 (.368). Totals, 597-for-1655 (.361).
Personal fouls/disqualifications: 1997-98, 216/0. 1998-99, 134/2. 1999-00, 258/5. 2000-01, 150/4. 2001-02, 221/1. 2002-03, 251/7. 2003-04, 215/6. 2004-05, 170/2. 2005-06, 121/1. Totals, 1736/28.

NBA PLAYOFF RECORD

									REBOUNDS								AVERAGES		
Season Team	G	Min.	FGM	FGA	Pct.	FTM	FTA	Pct.	Off.	Def.	Tot.	Ast.	St.	Blk.	TO	Pts.	RPG	APG	PPG
97-98—New Jersey	3	77	13	29	.448	12	15	.800	2	7	9	1	0	0	2	38	3.0	0.3	12.7
01-02—New Jersey	20	643	97	241	.402	35	49	.714	32	101	133	41	19	9	35	266	6.7	2.1	13.3
02-03—Philadelphia	11	311	50	110	.000	0	00	.000	11	00	00	8	10	2	20	123	7.3	0.8	10.4
03-04—Milwaukee	5	137	16	48	.333	4	6	.667	5	18	23	7	7	3	10	40	4.6	1.4	8.0
04-05—Dallas	3	33	7	15	.467	8	9	.889	3	3	6	1	1	0	1	22	2.0	0.3	7.3
05-06—Dallas	14	172	20	59	.339	3	3	1.000	8	24	32	2	0	4	6	51	2.3	0.1	3.6
Totals	57	1464	195	502	.388	89	112	.795	74	219	293	61	37	18	80	542	5.1	1.1	9.5

Three-point field goals: 1997-98, 0-for-2. 2001-02, 37-for-84 (.440). 2002-03, 14-for-32 (.438). 2003-04, 4-for-11 (.364). 2004-05, 0-for-4. 2005-06, 8-for-28 (.286). Totals, 63-for-161 (.391).
Personal fouls/disqualifications: 1997-98, 7/0. 2001-02, 56/2. 2002-03, 41/1. 2003-04, 15/0. 2004-05, 6/0. 2005-06, 24/1. Totals, 149/4.

VAREJAO, ANDERSON   F   CAVALIERS

PERSONAL: Born September 28, 1982, in Santa Teresa, Brazil. ... 6-10/230. (2.08/104.3). ... Full name: Anderson Franca Varejao
TRANSACTIONS/CAREER NOTES: Played in Brazil (2000-01). ... Played in Spain (2001-04). ... Selected by Orlando Magic in second round (30th pick overall) of 2004 NBA Draft. ... Draft rights traded by Magic with F Drew Gooden and C Steven Hunter to Cleveland Cavaliers for F/C Tony Battie and two future second-round draft choices (July 23, 2004).

BRAZILIAN LEAGUE RECORD

												AVERAGES		
Season Team	G	Min.	FGM	FGA	Pct.	FTM	FTA	Pct.	Reb.	Ast.	Pts.	RPG	APG	PPG
00-01—Franca	37	394	51	96	.531	25	51	.490	88	11	127	2.4	0.3	3.4

SPANISH LEAGUE RECORD

												AVERAGES		
Season Team	G	Min.	FGM	FGA	Pct.	FTM	FTA	Pct.	Reb.	Ast.	Pts.	RPG	APG	PPG
01-02—FC Barcelona	2	28	3	8	.375	2	2	1.000	11	1	8	5.5	0.5	4.0
02-03—FC Barcelona	4	92	13	21	.619	6	13	.462	24	1	33	6.0	0.3	8.3
03-04—FC Barcelona	27	542	79	161	.491	37	61	.607	119	28	203	4.4	1.0	7.5
Totals	33	662	95	190	.500	45	76	.592	154	30	244	4.7	0.9	7.4

Three-point field goals: 2002-03, 1-for-3 (.333). 2003-04, 8-for-29 (.276). Totals, 9-for-32 (.281).

NBA REGULAR-SEASON RECORD

									REBOUNDS								AVERAGES		
Season Team	G	Min.	FGM	FGA	Pct.	FTM	FTA	Pct.	Off.	Def.	Tot.	Ast.	St.	Blk.	TO	Pts.	RPG	APG	PPG
04-05—Cleveland	54	863	99	193	.513	68	127	.535	109	148	257	27	41	38	26	266	4.8	0.5	4.9
05-06—Cleveland	48	760	79	150	.527	61	119	.513	77	158	235	19	31	19	27	219	4.9	0.4	4.6
Totals	102	1623	178	343	.519	129	246	.524	186	306	492	46	72	57	53	485	4.8	0.5	4.8

Three-point field goals: 2004-05, 0-for-2. 2005-06, 0-for-1. Totals, 0-for-3 (.000).
Personal fouls/disqualifications: 2004-05, 122/0. 2005-06, 118/2. Totals, 240/2.

NBA PLAYOFF RECORD

Season Team	G	Min.	FGM	FGA	Pct.	FTM	FTA	Pct.	REBOUNDS Off.	Def.	Tot.	Ast.	St.	Blk.	TO	Pts.	AVERAGES RPG	APG	PPG
05-06—Cleveland	13	238	31	50	.620	26	37	.703	18	40	58	3	9	2	6	88	4.5	0.2	6.8

Personal fouls/disqualifications: 2005-06, 50/2. Totals, 50/2.

VAUGHN, JACQUE   G   SPURS

PERSONAL: Born February 11, 1975, in Los Angeles. ... 6-1/190. (1.85/86.2).
HIGH SCHOOL: John Muir (Pasadena, Calif.).
COLLEGE: Kansas.
TRANSACTIONS/CAREER NOTES: Selected by Utah Jazz in first round (27th pick overall) of 1997 NBA Draft. ... Signed as free agent by Atlanta Hawks (July 30, 2001). ... Signed as free agent by Orlando Magic (July 17, 2002). ... Signed as free agent by Atlanta Hawks (September 4, 2003). ... Signed as free agent by New Jersey Nets (July 29, 2004). ... Signed as free agent by San Antonio Spurs (July 12, 2006).

COLLEGIATE RECORD

NOTES: THE SPORTING NEWS All-America first team (1997). ... THE SPORTING NEWS All-America second team (1996).

Season Team	G	Min.	FGM	FGA	Pct.	FTM	FTA	Pct.	Reb.	Ast.	Pts.	AVERAGES RPG	APG	PPG
93-94—Kansas	35	896	91	195	.467	63	94	.670	89	181	273	2.5	5.2	7.8
94-95—Kansas	31	1046	94	208	.452	92	134	.687	116	238	300	3.7	7.7	9.7
95-96—Kansas	34	1045	120	249	.482	91	131	.695	106	223	370	3.1	6.6	10.9
96-97—Kansas	26	820	79	185	.427	88	113	.779	62	162	264	2.4	6.2	10.2
Totals	126	3807	384	837	.459	334	472	.708	373	804	1207	3.0	6.4	9.6

Three-point field goals: 1993-94, 28-for-70 (.400). 1994-95, 20-for-58 (.345). 1995-96, 39-for-92 (.424). 1996-97, 18-for-54 (.333). Totals, 105-for-274 (.383).

NBA REGULAR-SEASON RECORD

Season Team	G	Min.	FGM	FGA	Pct.	FTM	FTA	Pct.	REBOUNDS Off.	Def.	Tot.	Ast.	St.	Blk.	TO	Pts.	AVERAGES RPG	APG	PPG
97-98—Utah	45	419	44	122	.361	48	68	.706	4	34	38	84	9	1	56	139	0.8	1.9	3.1
98-99—Utah	19	87	11	30	.367	20	24	.833	1	10	11	12	5	0	14	44	0.6	0.6	2.3
99-00—Utah	78	884	109	262	.416	57	76	.750	11	54	65	121	32	0	77	289	0.8	1.6	3.7
00-01—Utah	82	1620	170	393	.433	128	164	.780	18	132	150	323	48	3	129	498	1.8	3.9	6.1
01-02—Atlanta	82	1856	206	438	.470	104	126	.825	18	150	168	349	65	2	112	540	2.0	4.3	6.6
02-03—Orlando	80	1686	184	411	.448	97	125	.776	26	92	118	232	64	2	97	473	1.5	2.9	5.9
03-04—Atlanta	71	1271	107	277	.386	53	68	.779	12	104	116	195	44	2	84	270	1.6	2.7	3.8
04-05—New Jersey	71	1410	146	325	.449	76	91	.835	17	90	107	135	41	1	62	373	1.5	1.9	5.3
05-06—New Jersey	80	1234	107	245	.437	59	81	.728	16	75	91	123	42	1	52	274	1.1	1.5	3.4
Totals	608	10467	1084	2503	.433	642	823	.780	123	741	864	1574	350	12	683	2900	1.4	2.6	4.8

Three-point field goals: 1997-98, 3-for-8 (.375). 1998-99, 2-for-8 (.250). 1999-00, 14-for-34 (.412). 2000-01, 30-for-78 (.385). 2001-02, 24-for-54 (.444). 2002-03, 8-for-34 (.235). 2003-04, 3-for-20 (.150). 2004-05, 5-for-15 (.333). 2005-06, 1-for-6 (.167). Totals, 90-for-257 (.350).
Personal fouls/disqualifications: 1997-98, 63/1. 1998-99, 14/0. 1999-00, 92/0. 2000-01, 145/0. 2001-02, 183/0. 2002-03, 169/1. 2003-04, 126/0. 2004-05, 138/1. 2005-06, 140/0. Totals, 1070/3.

NBA PLAYOFF RECORD

Season Team	G	Min.	FGM	FGA	Pct.	FTM	FTA	Pct.	REBOUNDS Off.	Def.	Tot.	Ast.	St.	Blk.	TO	Pts.	AVERAGES RPG	APG	PPG
97-98—Utah	7	24	2	10	.200	2	2	1.000	0	3	3	4	0	0	4	7	0.4	0.6	1.0
98-99—Utah	2	6	1	2	.500	0	0	...	0	0	0	2	0	0	0	3	0.0	1.0	1.5
99-00—Utah	7	67	10	28	.357	7	8	.875	4	8	12	11	4	1	9	28	1.7	1.6	4.0
00-01—Utah	5	57	1	10	.100	0	0	...	0	2	2	8	0	1	1	3	0.4	1.6	0.6
02-03—Orlando	7	131	12	33	.364	10	13	.769	1	5	6	25	4	1	9	34	0.9	3.6	4.9
05-06—New Jersey	11	159	12	33	.364	4	7	.571	3	8	11	12	2	0	4	28	1.0	1.1	2.5
Totals	39	444	38	116	.328	23	30	.767	8	26	34	62	10	3	27	103	0.9	1.6	2.6

Three-point field goals: 1997-98, 1-for-2 (.500). 1998-99, 1-for-1 (1.000). 1999-00, 1-for-2 (.500). 2000-01, 1-for-2 (.500). 2002-03, 0-for-1 (.500). 2005-06, 0-for-1. Totals, 4-for-9 (.444).
Personal fouls/disqualifications: 1998-99, 2/0. 1999-00, 5/0. 2000-01, 13/0. 2002-03, 18/0. 2005-06, 23/0. Totals, 61/0.

VILLANUEVA, CHARLIE   F   BUCKS

PERSONAL: Born August 24, 1984, in Queens, N.Y. ... 6-11/240. (2.11/108.9).
HIGH SCHOOL: Blair Academy (Blairstown, N.J.).
COLLEGE: Connecticut.
TRANSACTIONS/CAREER NOTES: Selected after sophomore season by Toronto Raptors in first round (seventh pick overall) of 2005 NBA Draft. ... Traded by Raptors with cash to Milwaukee Bucks for G T.J. Ford (June 30, 2006).

COLLEGIATE RECORD

NOTES: Member of NCAA Division I championship team (2004).

Season Team	G	Min.	FGM	FGA	Pct.	FTM	FTA	Pct.	Reb.	Ast.	Pts.	AVERAGES RPG	APG	PPG
03-04—Connecticut	32	607	113	220	.514	42	63	.667	168	23	286	5.3	0.7	8.9
04-05—Connecticut	31	798	159	305	.521	97	141	.688	257	40	421	8.3	1.3	13.6
Totals	63	1405	272	525	.518	139	204	.681	425	63	707	6.7	1.0	11.2

Three-point field goals: 2003-04, 18-for-49 (.367). 2004-05, 6-for-12 (.500). Totals, 24-for-61 (.393).

V

NBA REGULAR-SEASON RECORD

HONORS: NBA All-Rookie first team (2006).

Season Team	G	Min.	FGM	FGA	Pct.	FTM	FTA	Pct.	REBOUNDS Off.	Def.	Tot.	Ast.	St.	Blk.	TO	Pts.	AVERAGES RPG	APG	PPG
05-06—Toronto	81	2361	435	940	.463	113	160	.706	181	340	521	88	60	63	99	1053	6.4	1.1	13.0

Three-point field goals: 2005-06, 70-for-214 (.327). Totals, 70-for-214 (.327).
Personal fouls/disqualifications: 2005-06, 247/4. Totals, 247/4.

VOSKUHL, JAKE   C   HORNETS

PERSONAL: Born November 1, 1977, in Tulsa, Okla. ... 6-11/245. (2.11/111.1). ... Full name: Robert Jake Voskuhl
HIGH SCHOOL: Strake Jesuit College Prep (Houston).
COLLEGE: Connecticut.
TRANSACTIONS/CAREER NOTES: Selected by Chicago Bulls in second round (33rd pick overall) of 2000 NBA Draft. ... Traded by Bulls to Phoenix Suns for C Soumalia Samake and 2003 second-round draft choice (October 29, 2001). ... Traded by Suns to Charlotte Bobcats for conditional 2007 second-round draft pick.

COLLEGIATE RECORD

NOTES: Member of NCAA Division I championship team (1999).

Season Team	G	Min.	FGM	FGA	Pct.	FTM	FTA	Pct.	Reb.	Ast.	Pts.	AVERAGES RPG	APG	PPG
96-97—Connecticut	33	678	48	99	.485	36	57	.632	181	20	132	5.5	0.6	4.0
97-98—Connecticut	37	877	100	177	.565	56	83	.675	262	27	256	7.1	0.7	6.9
98-99—Connecticut	34	728	66	129	.512	54	87	.621	218	38	186	6.4	1.1	5.5
99-00—Connecticut	34	778	109	191	.571	71	104	.683	219	39	289	6.4	1.1	8.5
Totals	138	3061	323	596	.542	217	331	.656	880	124	863	6.4	0.9	6.3

NBA REGULAR-SEASON RECORD

Season Team	G	Min.	FGM	FGA	Pct.	FTM	FTA	Pct.	REBOUNDS Off.	Def.	Tot.	Ast.	St.	Blk.	TO	Pts.	AVERAGES RPG	APG	PPG
00-01—Chicago	16	143	11	25	.440	8	14	.571	12	22	34	5	5	6	12	30	2.1	0.3	1.9
01-02—Phoenix	59	900	107	193	.554	82	109	.752	103	147	250	18	11	23	48	296	4.2	0.3	5.0
02-03—Phoenix	65	947	92	163	.564	64	96	.667	97	128	225	36	18	29	48	248	3.5	0.6	3.8
03-04—Phoenix	66	1606	152	300	.507	134	181	.740	123	220	343	57	42	25	77	438	5.2	0.9	6.6
04-05—Phoenix	38	360	27	59	.458	26	38	.684	30	62	92	17	4	11	20	80	2.4	0.4	2.1
05-06—Charlotte	51	818	114	261	.437	41	60	.683	62	121	183	39	26	23	33	270	3.6	0.8	5.3
Totals	295	4774	503	1001	.502	355	498	.713	427	700	1127	172	106	117	238	1362	3.8	0.6	4.6

Three-point field goals: 2005-06, 1-for-3 (.333). Totals, 1-for-3 (.333).
Personal fouls/disqualifications: 2000-01, 38/0. 2001-02, 139/1. 2002-03, 172/0. 2003-04, 258/8. 2004-05, 60/0. 2005-06, 157/2. Totals, 824/11.

NBA PLAYOFF RECORD

Season Team	G	Min.	FGM	FGA	Pct.	FTM	FTA	Pct.	REBOUNDS Off.	Def.	Tot.	Ast.	St.	Blk.	TO	Pts.	AVERAGES RPG	APG	PPG
02-03—Phoenix	6	98	12	17	.706	12	13	.923	9	13	22	2	4	4	6	36	3.7	0.3	6.0

Personal fouls/disqualifications: 2002-03, 21/0. Totals, 21/0.

V

VROMAN, JACKSON   F/C

PERSONAL: Born January 6, 1981, in Laguna, Calif. ... 6-10/220. (2.08/99.8).
HIGH SCHOOL: Viewmont (Bountiful, Utah).
JUNIOR COLLEGE: Snow (Utah).
COLLEGE: Iowa State.
TRANSACTIONS/CAREER NOTES: Selected by Chicago Bulls in second round (31st pick overall) of 2004 NBA Draft. ... Draft rights traded by Bulls with future first-round draft choice to Phoenix Suns for draft rights to F Luol Deng (June 24, 2004). ... Traded by Suns with G/F Casey Jacobsen and F Maciej Lampe to New Orleans Hornets for G Jim Jackson and a 2005 second-round draft choice (January 21, 2005). ... Waived by Hornets (March 31, 2006).

COLLEGIATE RECORD

Season Team	G	Min.	FGM	FGA	Pct.	FTM	FTA	Pct.	Reb.	Ast.	Pts.	AVERAGES RPG	APG	PPG
00-01—Snow College	32	...	132	243	.543	82	129	.636	179	58	346	5.6	1.8	10.8
01-02—Snow College	33	...	295	474	.622	194	290	.669	316	82	788	9.6	2.5	23.9
02-03—Iowa State	31	947	155	281	.552	79	153	.516	291	56	389	9.4	1.8	12.5
03-04—Iowa State	32	983	186	330	.564	72	142	.507	307	75	445	9.6	2.3	13.9
Junior College Totals	65	...	427	717	.596	276	419	.659	495	140	1134	7.6	2.2	17.4
4-Year-College Totals	63	1930	341	611	.558	151	295	.512	598	131	834	9.5	2.1	13.2

Three-point field goals: 2000-01, 0-for-6. 2001-02, 4-for-16 (.250). 2002-03, 0-for-6. 2003-04, 1-for-7 (.143). Totals, 5-for-35 (.143).

NBA REGULAR-SEASON RECORD

Season Team	G	Min.	FGM	FGA	Pct.	FTM	FTA	Pct.	REBOUNDS Off.	Def.	Tot.	Ast.	St.	Blk.	TO	Pts.	AVERAGES RPG	APG	PPG
04-05—Phoenix-N.O. ..	46	705	82	199	.412	48	75	.640	64	111	175	40	25	19	64	212	3.8	0.9	4.6
05-06—NO/Okla. City ..	41	406	26	66	.394	21	44	.477	33	53	86	11	12	11	21	73	2.1	0.3	1.8
Totals	87	1111	108	265	.408	69	119	.580	97	164	261	51	37	30	85	285	3.0	0.6	3.3

Three-point field goals: 2004-05, 0-for-3. Totals, 0-for-3 (.000).
Personal fouls/disqualifications: 2004-05, 105/3. 2005-06, 78/2. Totals, 183/5.

VUJACIC, SASHA   G   LAKERS

PERSONAL: Born March 8, 1984, in Maribor, Slovenia. ... 6-7/193. (2.01/87.5).
TRANSACTIONS/CAREER NOTES: Played in Italy (2001-04). ... Selected by Los Angeles Lakers in first round (27th pick overall) of 2004 NBA Draft.

ITALIAN LEAGUE RECORD

Season Team	G	Min.	FGM	FGA	Pct.	FTM	FTA	Pct.	Reb.	Ast.	Pts.	RPG	APG	PPG
												AVERAGES		
01-02—Snaidero UD	24	162	12	39	.308	3	4	.750	21	8	30	0.9	0.3	1.3
02-03—Snaidero UD	28	748	96	213	.451	76	93	.817	86	55	311	3.1	2.0	11.1
03-04—Snaidero UD	33	908	137	331	.414	143	173	.827	123	72	475	3.7	2.2	14.4
Totals	85	1818	245	583	.420	222	270	.822	230	135	816	2.7	1.6	9.6

Three-point field goals: 2001-02, 3-for-19 (.158). 2002-03, 43-for-123 (.350). 2003-04, 58-for-178 (.326). Totals, 104-for-320 (.325).

NBA REGULAR-SEASON RECORD

Season Team	G	Min.	FGM	FGA	Pct.	FTM	FTA	Pct.	Off.	Def.	Tot.	Ast.	St.	Blk.	TO	Pts.	RPG	APG	PPG
									REBOUNDS								AVERAGES		
04-05—L.A. Lakers	35	403	33	117	.282	18	19	.947	13	49	62	51	12	2	15	101	1.8	1.5	2.9
05-06—L.A. Lakers	82	1449	108	312	.346	46	52	.885	33	126	159	139	48	3	50	321	1.9	1.7	3.9
Totals	117	1852	141	429	.329	64	71	.901	46	175	221	190	60	5	65	422	1.9	1.6	3.6

Three-point field goals: 2004-05, 17-for-63 (.270). 2005-06, 59-for-172 (.343). Totals, 76-for-235 (.323).
Personal fouls/disqualifications: 2004-05, 41/1. 2005-06, 150/0. Totals, 191/1.

NBA PLAYOFF RECORD

Season Team	G	Min.	FGM	FGA	Pct.	FTM	FTA	Pct.	Off.	Def.	Tot.	Ast.	St.	Blk.	TO	Pts.	RPG	APG	PPG
									REBOUNDS								AVERAGES		
05-06—L.A. Lakers	7	129	11	26	.423	11	11	1.000	3	14	17	6	4	0	3	42	2.4	0.9	6.0

Three-point field goals: 2005-06, 9-for-15 (.600). Totals, 9-for-15 (.600).
Personal fouls/disqualifications: 2005-06, 14/0. Totals, 14/0.

WADE, DWYANE   G   HEAT

PERSONAL: Born January 17, 1982, in Chicago, Ill. ... 6-4/210. (1.93/95.3). ... Full name: Dwyane Tyrone Wade
HIGH SCHOOL: Richards (Oak Lawn, Ill.).
COLLEGE: Marquette.
TRANSACTIONS/CAREER NOTES: Selected after junior season by Miami Heat in first round (fifth pick overall) of 2003 NBA Draft.
MISCELLANEOUS: Member of bronze-medal-winning U.S. Olympic Team (2004). ... Member of NBA championship team (2006).

COLLEGIATE RECORD

NOTES: The SPORTING NEWS All-America first team (2003). ... The SPORTING NEWS All-America third team (2002).

Season Team	G	Min.	FGM	FGA	Pct.	FTM	FTA	Pct.	Reb.	Ast.	Pts.	RPG	APG	PPG
												AVERAGES		
00-01—Marquette						Did not play—ineligible								
01-02—Marquette	32	935	223	458	.487	107	155	.690	211	110	571	6.6	3.4	17.8
02-03—Marquette	33	1058	251	501	.501	194	249	.779	209	145	710	6.3	4.4	21.5
Totals	65	1993	474	959	.494	301	404	.745	420	255	1281	6.5	3.9	19.7

Three-point field goals: 2001-02, 18-for-52 (.346). 2002-03, 14-for-44 (.318). Totals, 32-for-96 (.333).

NBA REGULAR-SEASON RECORD

HONORS: NBA All-Rookie first team (2004). ... All-NBA second team (2005, 2006). ... NBA All-Defensive second team (2005).

Season Team	G	Min.	FGM	FGA	Pct.	FTM	FTA	Pct.	Off.	Def.	Tot.	Ast.	St.	Blk.	TO	Pts.	RPG	APG	PPG
									REBOUNDS								AVERAGES		
03-04—Miami	61	2126	371	798	.465	233	312	.747	85	162	247	275	86	34	196	991	4.0	4.5	16.2
04-05—Miami	77	2974	630	1318	.478	581	762	.762	110	287	397	520	121	82	321	1854	5.2	6.8	24.1
05-06—Miami	75	2892	699	1413	.495	629	803	.783	107	323	430	503	146	58	268	2040	5.7	6.7	27.2
Totals	213	7992	1700	3529	.482	1443	1877	.769	302	772	1074	1298	353	174	785	4885	5.0	6.1	22.9

Three-point field goals: 2003-04, 16-for-53 (.302). 2004-05, 13-for-45 (.289). 2005-06, 13-for-76 (.171). Totals, 42-for-174 (.241).
Personal fouls/disqualifications: 2003-04, 140/0. 2004-05, 230/4. 2005-06, 217/0. Totals, 587/4.

NBA PLAYOFF RECORD

NOTES: Named NBA Finals MVP (2006).

Season Team	G	Min.	FGM	FGA	Pct.	FTM	FTA	Pct.	Off.	Def.	Tot.	Ast.	St.	Blk.	TO	Pts.	RPG	APG	PPG
									REBOUNDS								AVERAGES		
03-04—Miami	13	510	86	189	.455	59	75	.787	16	36	52	73	17	4	54	234	4.0	5.6	18.0
04-05—Miami	14	571	136	281	.484	111	139	.799	23	57	80	93	22	16	62	384	5.7	6.6	27.4
05-06—Miami	23	959	219	441	.497	202	250	.808	28	107	135	132	51	26	90	654	5.9	5.7	28.4
Totals	50	2040	441	911	.484	372	464	.802	67	200	267	298	90	46	206	1272	5.3	6.0	25.4

Three-point field goals: 2003-04, 3-for-8 (.375). 2004-05, 1-for-10 (.100). 2005-06, 14-for-37 (.378). Totals, 18-for-55 (.327).
Personal fouls/disqualifications: 2003-04, 45/0. 2004-05, 43/0. 2005-06, 71/1. Totals, 159/1.

NBA ALL-STAR GAME RECORD

Season Team	Min.	FGM	FGA	Pct.	FTM	FTA	Pct.	Off.	Def.	Tot.	Ast.	PF	Dq.	St.	Blk.	TO	Pts.
								REBOUNDS									
2005—Miami	23	6	13	.462	2	2	1.000	2	1	3	1	2	0	2	1	1	14
2006—Miami	31	9	11	.818	2	2	1.000	3	1	4	3	1	0	2	1	3	20
Totals	54	15	24	.625	4	4	1.000	5	2	7	4	3	0	4	2	4	34

Three-point field goals: 2005, 0-for-1. Totals, 0-for-1 (.000).

WAFER, VON   G   LAKERS

PERSONAL: Born July 21, 1985, in Homer, La. ... 6-5/210. (1.96/95.3). ... Full name: Vakeaton Quamar Wafer
HIGH SCHOOL: Pineview (La.), then RL Paschal (Fort Worth, Texas), then Laurinburg Institute (N.C.), then Heritage Christian Academy (Cleveland, Texas) .
COLLEGE: Florida State.
TRANSACTIONS/CAREER NOTES: Selected after sophomore season by Los Angeles Lakers in second round (39th pick overall) of 2005 NBA draft.

COLLEGIATE RECORD

Season Team	G	Min.	FGM	FGA	Pct.	FTM	FTA	Pct.	Reb.	Ast.	Pts.	RPG	APG	PPG
03-04—Florida State	32	560	90	244	.369	30	50	.600	60	36	253	1.9	1.1	7.9
04-05—Florida State	29	758	124	284	.437	49	68	.721	73	48	362	2.5	1.7	12.5
Totals	61	1318	214	528	.405	79	118	.669	133	84	615	2.2	1.4	10.1

Three-point field goals: 2003-04, 43-for-132 (.326). 2004-05, 65-for-164 (.396). Totals, 108-for-296 (.365).

NBA REGULAR-SEASON RECORD

Season Team	G	Min.	FGM	FGA	Pct.	FTM	FTA	Pct.	Off.	Def.	Tot.	Ast.	St.	Blk.	TO	Pts.	RPG	APG	PPG
05-06—L.A. Lakers	16	73	6	38	.158	6	8	.750	5	3	8	4	3	0	1	20	0.5	0.3	1.3

Three-point field goals: 2005-06, 2-for-17 (.118). Totals, 2-for-17 (.118).
Personal fouls/disqualifications: 2005-06, 12/0. Totals, 12/0.

NBA DEVELOPMENT LEAGUE RECORD

Season Team	G	Min.	FGM	FGA	Pct.	FTM	FTA	Pct.	Reb.	Ast.	Pts.	RPG	APG	PPG
05-06—Fort Worth	8	148	23	69	.333	11	13	.846	20	7	64	2.5	0.9	8.0

Three-point field goals: 2005-06, 7-for-31 (.226). Totals, 7-for-31 (.226).

WALKER, ANTOINE   F   HEAT

PERSONAL: Born August 12, 1976, in Chicago. ... 6-9/245. (2.06/111.1). ... Full name: Antoine Devon Walker
HIGH SCHOOL: Mt. Carmel (Chicago).
COLLEGE: Kentucky.
TRANSACTIONS/CAREER NOTES: Selected after sophomore season by Boston Celtics in first round (sixth pick overall) of 1996 NBA Draft. ... Traded by Celtics with G Tony Delk to Dallas Mavericks for F/C Raef LaFrentz, F Chris Mills, G Jiri Welsch and 2004 first-round draft choice (October 20, 2003). ... Traded by Mavericks with G Tony Delk to Atlanta Hawks for G Jason Terry, F Alan Henderson and a future first-round draft choice (August 4, 2004). ... Traded by Hawks to Boston Celtics for G Gary Payton, F Tom Gugliotta, C Michael Stewart and 2005 draft or future first-round pick (February 24, 2005). ... Traded by Celtics to Miami Heat in five-team trade (August 2, 2005).
MISCELLANEOUS: Member of NBA championship team (2006)

COLLEGIATE RECORD

NOTES: Member of NCAA Division I championship team (1996).

Season Team	G	Min.	FGM	FGA	Pct.	FTM	FTA	Pct.	Reb.	Ast.	Pts.	RPG	APG	PPG
94-95—Kentucky	33	479	95	227	.419	52	73	.712	148	47	259	4.5	1.4	7.8
95-96—Kentucky	36	971	228	492	.463	82	130	.631	302	104	547	8.4	2.9	15.2
Totals	69	1450	323	719	.449	134	203	.660	450	151	806	6.5	2.2	11.7

Three-point field goals: 1994-95, 17-for-55 (.309). 1995-96, 9-for-48 (.188). Totals, 26-for-103 (.252).

NBA REGULAR-SEASON RECORD

RECORDS: Holds single-game record for most three-point field goals attempted, none made—11 (December 17, 2001, vs. Philadelphia).
HONORS: NBA All-Rookie first team (1997).
NOTES: Led NBA with 221 three-point field goals made and 603 three-point field goals attempted (2001).

Season Team	G	Min.	FGM	FGA	Pct.	FTM	FTA	Pct.	Off.	Def.	Tot.	Ast.	St.	Blk.	TO	Pts.	RPG	APG	PPG
96-97—Boston	82	2970	576	1354	.425	231	366	.631	288	453	741	262	105	53	230	1435	9.0	3.2	17.5
97-98—Boston	82	3268	722	1705	.423	305	473	.645	270	566	836	273	142	60	*292	1840	10.2	3.3	22.4
98-99—Boston	42	1549	303	735	.412	113	202	.559	106	253	359	130	63	28	119	784	8.5	3.1	18.7
99-00—Boston	82	3003	648	1506	.430	311	445	.699	199	453	652	305	117	32	259	1680	8.0	3.7	20.5
00-01—Boston	81	3396	711	1720	.413	249	348	.716	151	568	719	445	138	49	301	1892	8.9	5.5	23.4
01-02—Boston	81	*3406	666	1689	.394	240	324	.741	150	564	714	407	122	38	251	1794	8.8	5.0	22.1
02-03—Boston	78	3235	603	1554	.388	176	286	.615	99	464	563	373	116	31	260	1570	7.2	4.8	20.1
03-04—Dallas	82	2840	483	1129	.428	103	186	.554	198	486	684	369	65	65	202	1151	8.3	4.5	14.0
04-05—Atlanta-Boston	77	2955	581	1377	.422	201	373	.539	182	513	695	265	89	58	253	1473	9.0	3.4	19.1
05-06—Miami	82	2199	391	898	.435	81	129	.628	103	318	421	166	47	30	150	1000	5.1	2.0	12.2
Totals	769	28821	5684	13667	.416	2010	3132	.642	1746	4638	6384	2995	1004	444	2317	14619	8.3	3.9	19.0

Three-point field goals: 1996-97, 52-for-159 (.327). 1997-98, 91-for-292 (.312). 1998-99, 65-for-176 (.369). 1999-00, 73-for-285 (.256). 2000-01, 221-for-603 (.367). 2001-02, 222-for-645 (.344). 2002-03, 188-for-582 (.323). 2003-04, 82-for-305 (.269). 2004-05, 110-for-341 (.323). 2005-06, 137-for-383 (.358). Totals, 1241-for-3771 (.329).
Personal fouls/disqualifications: 1996-97, 271/1. 1997-98, 262/2. 1998-99, 142/2. 1999-00, 263/4. 2000-01, 251/2. 2001-02, 237/2. 2002-03, 221/4. 2003-04, 212/3. 2004-05, 217/0. 2005-06, 187/1. Totals, 2263/21.

NBA PLAYOFF RECORD

NOTES: Holds single-game playoff record for most three-point field goals made in one quarter—6 (April 28, 2002, at Philadelphia).

Season Team	G	Min.	FGM	FGA	Pct.	FTM	FTA	Pct.	Off.	Def.	Tot.	Ast.	St.	Blk.	TO	Pts.	RPG	APG	PPG
01-02—Boston	16	703	131	319	.411	50	64	.781	23	115	138	52	24	6	55	354	8.6	3.3	22.1

W

Season Team	G	Min.	FGM	FGA	Pct.	FTM	FTA	Pct.	REBOUNDS Off.	Def.	Tot.	Ast.	St.	Blk.	TO	Pts.	AVERAGES RPG	APG	PPG
02-03—Boston	10	440	73	176	.415	11	22	.500	20	67	87	43	17	4	37	173	8.7	4.3	17.3
03-04—Dallas	5	140	22	61	.361	4	7	.571	23	27	50	12	6	3	9	49	10.0	2.4	9.8
04-05—Boston	6	224	43	104	.413	7	11	.636	16	28	44	14	7	6	18	100	7.3	2.3	16.7
05-06—Miami	23	862	114	283	.403	31	54	.574	16	113	129	56	23	8	47	307	5.6	2.4	13.3
Totals	60	2369	383	943	.406	103	158	.652	98	350	448	177	77	27	166	983	7.5	3.0	16.4

Three-point field goals: 2001-02, 42-for-109 (.385). 2002-03, 16-for-45 (.356). 2003-04, 1-for-10 (.100). 2004-05, 7-for-19 (.368). 2005-06, 48-for-148 (.324). Totals, 114-for-331 (.344).

Personal fouls/disqualifications: 2001-02, 56/2. 2002-03, 44/3. 2003-04, 13/0. 2004-05, 19/0. 2005-06, 69/1. Totals, 201/6.

NBA ALL-STAR GAME RECORD

Season Team	Min.	FGM	FGA	Pct.	FTM	FTA	Pct.	REBOUNDS Off.	Def.	Tot.	Ast.	PF	Dq.	St.	Blk.	TO	Pts.
1998—Boston	15	2	8	.250	0	0	...	1	2	3	3	0	0	1	0	1	4
2002—Boston	16	3	8	.375	0	0	...	0	2	2	1	1	0	1	0	2	8
2003—Boston	9	2	4	.500	1	2	.500	0	1	1	0	0	0	0	0	1	6
Totals	40	7	20	.350	1	2	.500	1	5	6	4	1	0	2	0	4	18

Three-point field goals: 1998, 0-for-3. 2002, 2-for-4 (.500). 2003, 1-for-3 (.333). Totals, 3-for-10 (.300).

WALKER, SAMAKI   F

PERSONAL: Born February 25, 1976, in Columbus, Ohio. ... 6-9/260. (2.06/117.9). ... Full name: Samaki Ijuma Walker ... Name pronounced Suh-MAH-kee.
HIGH SCHOOL: Whitehall (Columbus, Ohio).
COLLEGE: Louisville.
TRANSACTIONS/CAREER NOTES: Selected after sophomore season by Dallas Mavericks in first round (ninth pick overall) of 1996 NBA Draft. ... Signed as free agent by San Antonio Spurs (August 26, 1999). ... Waived by Spurs (June 29, 2001). ... Signed as free agent by Los Angeles Lakers (July 20, 2001). ... Signed as free agent by Miami Heat (August 2, 2003) ... Signed as free agent by Washington Wizards (August 4, 2004). ... Released by Wizards (March 18, 2005). ... Played in Russia (2005-06). ... Signed by Indiana Pacers (October 3, 2005). ... Waived by Pacers (January 5, 2006).
MISCELLANEOUS: Member of NBA championship team (2002).

COLLEGIATE RECORD

Season Team	G	Min.	FGM	FGA	Pct.	FTM	FTA	Pct.	Reb.	Ast.	Pts.	AVERAGES RPG	APG	PPG
94-95—Louisville	29	841	153	279	.548	88	164	.537	210	37	396	7.2	1.3	13.7
95-96—Louisville	21	634	124	207	.599	70	114	.614	157	23	318	7.5	1.1	15.1
Totals	50	1475	277	486	.570	158	278	.568	367	60	714	7.3	1.2	14.3

Three-point field goals: 1994-95, 2-for-6 (.333). 1995-96, 0-for-1. Totals, 2-for-7 (.286).

NBA REGULAR-SEASON RECORD

Season Team	G	Min.	FGM	FGA	Pct.	FTM	FTA	Pct.	REBOUNDS Off.	Def.	Tot.	Ast.	St.	Blk.	TO	Pts.	AVERAGES RPG	APG	PPG
96-97—Dallas	43	602	83	187	.444	48	74	.649	47	100	147	17	15	22	39	214	3.4	0.4	5.0
97-98—Dallas	41	1027	156	321	.486	53	97	.546	96	206	302	24	30	40	61	365	7.4	0.6	8.9
98-99—Dallas	39	568	88	190	.463	53	98	.541	46	97	143	6	9	16	37	229	3.7	0.2	5.9
99-00—San Antonio	71	980	137	305	.449	86	126	.683	77	195	272	38	10	35	64	360	3.8	0.5	5.1
00-01—San Antonio	61	963	121	252	.480	78	124	.629	67	176	243	29	10	41	68	321	4.0	0.5	5.3
01-02—L.A. Lakers	69	1655	187	365	.512	86	129	.667	129	352	481	64	28	88	53	460	7.0	0.9	6.7
02-03—L.A. Lakers	67	1243	115	274	.420	66	101	.653	115	253	368	64	20	55	56	296	5.5	1.0	4.4
03-04—Miami	33	418	38	99	.384	29	44	.659	42	70	112	6	6	11	15	105	3.4	0.2	3.2
04-05—Washington	14	134	11	31	.355	2	3	.667	8	10	18	4	3	7	8	24	1.3	0.3	1.7
05-06—Indiana	7	22	0	2	.000	2	2	1.000	0	3	3	0	0	1	2	2	0.4	0.0	0.3
Totals	445	7612	936	2026	.462	503	798	.630	627	1462	2089	252	134	316	403	2376	4.7	0.6	5.3

Three-point field goals: 1996-97, 0-for-1. 1997-98, 0-for-1. 1998-99, 0-for-1. 2000-01, 1-for-3 (.333). 2002-03, 0-for-1. 2003-04, 0-for-2. Totals, 1-for-9 (.111).

Personal fouls/disqualifications: 1996-97, 71/0. 1997-98, 127/2. 1998-99, 87/3. 1999-00, 108/1. 2000-01, 103/0. 2001-02, 170/1. 2002-03, 143/4. 2003-04, 54/0. 2004-05, 25/2. 2005-06, 7/0. Totals, 895/13.

NBA PLAYOFF RECORD

Season Team	G	Min.	FGM	FGA	Pct.	FTM	FTA	Pct.	REBOUNDS Off.	Def.	Tot.	Ast.	St.	Blk.	TO	Pts.	AVERAGES RPG	APG	PPG
99-00—San Antonio	4	121	14	31	.452	8	12	.667	13	32	45	2	1	12	8	36	11.3	0.5	9.0
00-01—San Antonio	12	76	5	15	.333	4	8	.500	5	9	14	3	1	1	1	14	1.2	0.3	1.2
01-02—L.A. Lakers	19	240	24	52	.462	13	17	.765	32	46	78	4	2	6	12	62	4.1	0.2	3.3
02-03—L.A. Lakers	9	49	2	5	.400	0	0	...	4	9	13	2	1	2	3	4	1.4	0.2	0.4
03-04—Miami	4	11	0	2	.000	0	0	...	0	1	1	0	0	0	0	0	0.3	0.0	0.0
Totals	48	497	45	105	.429	25	37	.676	54	97	151	11	5	21	24	116	3.1	0.2	2.4

Three-point field goals: 2001-02, 1-for-1 (1.000). Totals, 1-for-1 (1.000).

Personal fouls/disqualifications: 1999-00, 13/0. 2000-01, 12/0. 2001-02, 42/0. 2002-03, 11/0. 2003-04, 2/0. Totals, 80/0.

RUSSIAN LEAGUE RECORD

Season Team	G	Min.	FGM	FGA	Pct.	FTM	FTA	Pct.	Reb.	Ast.	Pts.	AVERAGES RPG	APG	PPG
05-06—Unics Kazan	4	61	9	20	.450	10	14	.714	17	1	28	4.3	0.3	7.0

W

WALLACE, BEN   F   BULLS

PERSONAL: Born September 10, 1974, in White Hall, Ala. ... 6-9/240. (2.06/108.9).
HIGH SCHOOL: Central (Ala.).
JUNIOR COLLEGE: Cuyahoga Community College (Ohio).
COLLEGE: Virginia Union.
TRANSACTIONS/CAREER NOTES: Not drafted by an NBA franchise. ... Signed as free agent by Washington Bullets (October 2, 1996). ... Bullets franchise renamed Washington Wizards for 1997-98 season. ... Traded by Wizards with F/C Terry Davis, G Tim Legler and G Jeff McInnis to Orlando Magic for C Isaac Austin (August 11, 1999). ... Traded by Magic with G Chucky Atkins to Detroit Pistons for F Grant Hill (August 3, 2000). ... Signed as free agent by Chicago Bulls (July 13, 2006).
MISCELLANEOUS: Member of NBA championship team (2004).

COLLEGIATE RECORD

Season Team	G	Min.	FGM	FGA	Pct.	FTM	FTA	Pct.	Reb.	Ast.	Pts.	RPG	APG	PPG
92-93—Cuyahoga						Statistics unavailable.								
93-94—Cuyahoga						Statistics unavailable.								
94-95—Virginia Union	31	858	180	330	.545	85	209	.407	295	27	445	9.5	0.9	14.4
95-96—Virginia Union	31	902	159	318	.500	70	187	.374	325	18	388	10.5	0.6	12.5
Totals	62	1760	339	648	.523	155	396	.391	620	45	833	10.0	0.7	13.4

NBA REGULAR-SEASON RECORD

HONORS: NBA Defensive Player of the Year (2002, 2003, 2005, 2006). ... NBA All-Defensive first team (2002, 2003, 2004, 2005, 2006). ... All-NBA third team (2002, 2005). ... All-NBA second team (2003, 2004, 2006).
NOTES: Led NBA with 3.48 blocks per game (2002).

Season Team	G	Min.	FGM	FGA	Pct.	FTM	FTA	Pct.	Off.	Def.	Tot.	Ast.	St.	Blk.	TO	Pts.	RPG	APG	PPG
96-97—Washington	34	197	16	46	.348	6	20	.300	25	33	58	2	8	11	18	38	1.7	0.1	1.1
97-98—Washington	67	1124	85	104	.518	35	98	.357	112	212	324	18	61	72	28	205	4.8	0.3	3.1
98-99—Washington	46	1231	115	199	.578	47	132	.356	137	247	384	18	50	90	36	277	8.3	0.4	6.0
99-00—Orlando	81	1959	168	334	.503	54	114	.474	211	454	665	67	72	130	67	390	8.2	0.8	4.8
00-01—Detroit	80	2760	215	439	.490	80	238	.336	*303	*749	1052	123	107	186	117	511	13.2	1.5	6.4
01-02—Detroit	80	2921	255	480	.531	99	234	.423	318	721	1039	115	138	*278	70	609	*13.0	1.4	7.6
02-03—Detroit	73	2873	210	437	.481	85	189	.450	*293	833	*1126	120	104	230	88	506	*15.4	1.6	6.9
03-04—Detroit	81	3050	315	748	.421	142	290	.490	324	682	1006	138	143	246	123	773	12.4	1.7	9.5
04-05—Detroit	74	2671	295	651	.453	130	304	.428	292	610	902	123	106	176	82	721	12.2	1.7	9.7
05-06—Detroit	82	2890	237	465	.510	123	296	.416	*301	622	923	158	146	181	88	597	11.3	1.9	7.3
Totals	698	21676	1911	3963	.482	801	1915	.418	2316	5163	7479	882	935	1600	717	4627	10.7	1.3	6.6

Three-point field goals: 2000-01, 1-for-4 (.250). 2001-02, 0-for-3. 2002-03, 1-for-6 (.167). 2003-04, 1-for-8 (.125). 2004-05, 1-for-9 (.111). 2005-06, 0-for-4. Totals, 4-for-34 (.118).
Personal fouls/disqualifications: 1996-97, 27/0. 1997-98, 116/1. 1998-99, 111/0. 1999-00, 162/0. 2000-01, 192/0. 2001-02, 178/2. 2002-03, 179/0. 2003-04, 162/0. 2004-05, 159/0. 2005-06, 164/1. Totals, 1450/4.

NBA PLAYOFF RECORD

Season Team	G	Min.	FGM	FGA	Pct.	FTM	FTA	Pct.	Off.	Def.	Tot.	Ast.	St.	Blk.	TO	Pts.	RPG	APG	PPG
01-02—Detroit	10	408	28	59	.475	17	39	.436	48	113	161	12	19	26	19	73	16.1	1.2	7.3
02-03—Detroit	17	722	53	109	.486	45	101	.446	86	191	277	28	42	52	15	151	16.3	1.6	8.9
03-04—Detroit	23	924	93	205	.454	50	117	.427	95	233	328	44	44	56	37	236	14.3	1.9	10.3
04-05—Detroit	25	979	102	212	.481	47	102	.461	95	187	282	25	43	59	30	251	11.3	1.0	10.0
05-06—Detroit	18	642	33	71	.465	18	66	.273	60	129	189	31	24	22	15	84	10.5	1.7	4.7
Totals	93	3675	309	656	.471	177	425	.416	384	853	1237	140	172	215	116	795	13.3	1.5	8.5

Three-point field goals: 2002-03, 0-for-1. 2003-04, 0-for-3. 2004-05, 0-for-4. 2005-06, 0-for-1. Totals, 0-for-9 (.000).
Personal fouls/disqualifications: 2001-02, 24/0. 2002-03, 50/0. 2003-04, 58/1. 2004-05, 65/0. 2005-06, 41/0. Totals, 238/1.

NBA ALL-STAR GAME RECORD

Season Team	Min.	FGM	FGA	Pct.	FTM	FTA	Pct.	Off.	Def.	Tot.	Ast.	PF	Dq.	St.	Blk.	TO	Pts.
2003—Detroit	24	1	2	.500	0	2	.000	4	2	6	0	1	0	2	2	2	2
2004—Detroit	23	2	5	.400	0	0	...	2	5	7	0	0	0	3	1	0	4
2005—Detroit	15	3	7	.429	0	0	...	4	3	7	0	2	0	0	0	2	6
2006—Detroit	24	0	1	.000	0	2	.000	0	8	8	2	3	0	3	2	0	0
Totals	86	6	15	.400	0	4	.000	10	18	28	2	6	0	8	5	4	12

Three-point field goals: 2004, 0-for-1. Totals, 0-for-1 (.000).

WALLACE, GERALD   F   BOBCATS

PERSONAL: Born July 23, 1982, in Sylacauga, Ala. ... 6-7/215. (2.01/97.5). ... Full name: Gerald Jermaine Wallace
HIGH SCHOOL: Childersburg (Ala.).
COLLEGE: Alabama.
TRANSACTIONS/CAREER NOTES: Selected after freshman season by Sacramento Kings in first round (25th pick overall) of 2001 NBA Draft. ... Selected by Charlotte Bobcats from Kings in NBA Expansion Draft (June 22, 2004).

COLLEGIATE RECORD

Season Team	G	Min.	FGM	FGA	Pct.	FTM	FTA	Pct.	Reb.	Ast.	Pts.	RPG	APG	PPG
00-01—Alabama	36	824	126	288	.438	88	155	.568	216	55	351	6.0	1.5	9.8

Three-point field goals: 2000-01, 11-for-63 (.175). Totals, 11-for-63 (.175).
Personal fouls/disqualifications: 2000-01, 87/0. Totals, 87/0.

W

NBA REGULAR-SEASON RECORD

NOTES: Led NBA in steals per game—2.51 (2005-06).

Season Team	G	Min.	FGM	FGA	Pct.	FTM	FTA	Pct.	Off.	Def.	Tot.	Ast.	St.	Blk.	TO	Pts.	RPG	APG	PPG
01-02—Sacramento	54	430	75	175	.429	23	46	.500	49	40	89	27	19	6	22	173	1.6	0.5	3.2
02-03—Sacramento	47	571	90	183	.492	39	74	.527	38	90	128	23	24	15	44	220	2.7	0.5	4.7
03-04—Sacramento	37	337	32	89	.360	11	24	.458	35	39	74	19	14	14	8	75	2.0	0.5	2.0
04-05—Charlotte	70	2147	286	637	.449	191	289	.661	118	268	386	137	117	91	159	780	5.5	2.0	11.1
05-06—Charlotte	55	1895	317	589	.538	188	306	.614	123	289	412	96	138	115	99	836	7.5	1.7	15.2
Totals	263	5380	800	1673	.478	452	739	.612	363	726	1089	302	312	241	332	2084	4.1	1.1	7.9

Three-point field goals: 2001-02, 0-for-7. 2002-03, 1-for-4 (.250). 2003-04, 0-for-2. 2004-05, 17-for-62 (.274). 2005-06, 14-for-50 (.280). Totals, 32-for-125 (.256).

Personal fouls/disqualifications: 2001-02, 46/0. 2002-03, 68/0. 2003-04, 37/0. 2004-05, 182/2. 2005-06, 150/1. Totals, 483/3.

NBA PLAYOFF RECORD

Season Team	G	Min.	FGM	FGA	Pct.	FTM	FTA	Pct.	Off.	Def.	Tot.	Ast.	St.	Blk.	TO	Pts.	RPG	APG	PPG
01-02—Sacramento	5	14	0	1	.000	4	4	1.000	1	0	1	1	0	1	2	4	0.2	0.2	0.8
02-03—Sacramento	7	18	2	5	.400	2	2	1.000	0	5	5	0	0	1	2	6	0.7	0.0	0.9
03-04—Sacramento	3	20	3	6	.500	1	2	.500	0	2	2	1	1	1	3	7	0.7	0.3	2.3
Totals	15	52	5	12	.417	7	8	.875	1	7	8	2	1	3	7	17	0.5	0.1	1.1

Personal fouls/disqualifications: 2001-02, 3/0. 2002-03, 4/0. 2003-04, 4/0. Totals, 11/0.

WALLACE, RASHEED   F/C   PISTONS

PERSONAL: Born September 17, 1974, in Philadelphia. ... 6-11/230. (2.11/104.3). ... Full name: Rasheed Abdul Wallace
HIGH SCHOOL: Simon Gratz (Philadelphia).
COLLEGE: North Carolina.
TRANSACTIONS/CAREER NOTES: Selected after sophomore season by Washington Bullets in first round (fourth pick overall) of 1995 NBA Draft. ... Traded by Bullets with G Mitchell Butler to Portland Trail Blazers for G Rod Strickland and F Harvey Grant (July 15, 1996). ... Traded by Trail Blazers with G Wesley Person to Atlanta Hawks for F Shareef Abdur-Rahim, C Theo Ratliff and G Dan Dickau (February 9, 2004). ... Traded by Hawks to Detroit Pistons in three-team deal in which Pistons also received G Mike James from Boston Celtics for G Chucky Atkins, G Lindsey Hunter and 2004 first-round draft choice. Hawks received F Zeljko Rebraca, G Bob Sura and a future first-round draft choice from Pistons and F Chris Mills from Celtics (February 19, 2004).
MISCELLANEOUS: Member of NBA championship team (2004).

COLLEGIATE RECORD

NOTES: THE SPORTING NEWS All-America first team (1995).

Season Team	G	Min.	FGM	FGA	Pct.	FTM	FTA	Pct.	Reb.	Ast.	Pts.	RPG	APG	PPG
93-94—North Carolina	35	732	139	230	.604	55	91	.604	232	18	333	6.6	0.5	9.5
94-95—North Carolina	34	1030	238	364	.654	89	141	.631	279	35	566	8.2	1.0	16.6
Totals	69	1762	377	594	.635	144	232	.621	511	53	899	7.4	0.8	13.0

Three-point field goals: 1993-94, 0-for-1. 1994-95, 1-for-3 (.333). Totals, 1-for-4 (.250).

NBA REGULAR-SEASON RECORD

HONORS: NBA All-Rookie second team (1996).

Season Team	G	Min.	FGM	FGA	Pct.	FTM	FTA	Pct.	Off.	Def.	Tot.	Ast.	St.	Blk.	TO	Pts.	RPG	APG	PPG
95-96—Washington	65	1788	275	565	.487	78	120	.650	93	210	303	85	42	54	103	655	4.7	1.3	10.1
96-97—Portland	62	1892	380	681	.558	169	265	.638	122	297	419	74	48	59	114	938	6.8	1.2	15.1
97-98—Portland	77	2896	466	875	.533	184	278	.662	132	346	478	195	75	88	167	1124	6.2	2.5	14.6
98-99—Portland	49	1414	242	476	.508	131	179	.732	57	184	241	60	48	54	80	628	4.9	1.2	12.8
99-00—Portland	81	2845	542	1045	.519	233	331	.704	129	437	566	142	87	107	157	1325	7.0	1.8	16.4
00-01—Portland	77	2940	590	1178	.501	245	320	.766	147	455	602	212	90	135	158	1477	7.8	2.8	19.2
01-02—Portland	79	2963	603	1287	.469	201	274	.734	136	509	645	152	101	101	131	1521	8.2	1.9	19.3
02-03—Portland	74	2684	515	1094	.471	200	272	.735	113	435	548	153	70	77	140	1340	7.4	2.1	18.1
03-04—Port.-Atl.-Det. .	68	2390	425	974	.436	156	212	.736	102	357	459	156	61	122	119	1088	6.8	2.3	16.0
04-05—Detroit	79	2687	467	1062	.440	136	195	.697	174	470	644	142	65	115	127	1145	8.2	1.8	14.5
05-06—Detroit	80	2780	459	1067	.430	136	183	.743	90	457	547	182	82	130	85	1209	6.8	2.3	15.1
Totals	791	27279	4964	10304	.482	1869	2629	.711	1295	4157	5452	1553	769	1042	1381	12450	6.9	2.0	15.7

Three-point field goals: 1995-96, 27-for-82 (.329). 1996-97, 9-for-33 (.273). 1997-98, 8-for-39 (.205). 1998-99, 13-for-31 (.419). 1999-00, 8-for-50 (.160). 2000-01, 52-for-162 (.321). 2001-02, 114-for-317 (.360). 2002-03, 110-for-307 (.358). 2003-04, 82-for-248 (.331). 2004-05, 75-for-236 (.318). 2005-06, 155-for-434 (.357). Totals, 653-for-1939 (.337).

Personal fouls/disqualifications: 1995-96, 206/4. 1996-97, 198/1. 1997-98, 268/6. 1998-99, 175/6. 1999-00, 216/2. 2000-01, 206/2. 2001-02, 212/0. 2002-03, 223/2. 2003-04, 190/1. 2004-05, 236/1. 2005-06, 232/1. Totals, 2362/26.

NBA PLAYOFF RECORD

Season Team	G	Min.	FGM	FGA	Pct.	FTM	FTA	Pct.	Off.	Def.	Tot.	Ast.	St.	Blk.	TO	Pts.	RPG	APG	PPG
96-97—Portland	4	148	33	56	.589	11	20	.550	8	16	24	6	2	2	6	79	6.0	1.3	19.8
97-98—Portland	4	157	23	47	.489	8	16	.500	7	12	19	11	2	2	5	58	4.8	2.8	14.5
98-99—Portland	13	468	75	146	.514	42	58	.724	17	46	63	20	20	11	16	193	4.8	1.5	14.8
99-00—Portland	16	605	110	225	.489	58	75	.773	31	72	103	28	15	20	23	286	6.4	1.8	17.9
00-01—Portland	3	128	19	51	.373	8	14	.571	5	19	24	7	1	3	4	50	8.0	2.3	16.7
01-02—Portland	3	125	28	69	.406	13	16	.813	10	27	37	5	2	2	2	76	12.3	1.7	25.3
02-03—Portland	7	260	44	97	.454	20	28	.714	10	26	36	18	4	5	6	122	5.1	2.6	17.4
03-04—Detroit	23	804	118	286	.413	46	60	.767	47	132	179	37	13	45	43	299	7.8	1.6	13.0
04-05—Detroit	25	826	136	310	.439	40	54	.741	39	134	173	32	26	44	38	341	6.9	1.3	13.6
05-06—Detroit	18	628	96	223	.430	29	55	.527	17	97	114	32	10	15	25	253	6.3	1.8	14.1
Totals	116	4149	682	1510	.452	275	396	.694	191	581	772	196	95	149	168	1757	6.7	1.7	15.1

Three-point field goals: 1996-97, 2-for-5 (.400). 1997-98, 4-for-5 (.800). 1998-99, 1-for-9 (.111). 1999-00, 8-for-13 (.615). 2000-01, 4-for-11 (.364). 2001-02, 7-for-17 (.412). 2002-03, 14-for-35 (.400). 2003-04, 17-for-70 (.243). 2004-05, 29-for-86 (.337). 2005-06, 32-for-79 (.405). Totals, 118-for-330 (.358).

Personal fouls/disqualifications: 1996-97, 17/1. 1997-98, 16/0. 1998-99, 50/1. 1999-00, 52/0. 2000-01, 9/0. 2001-02, 12/0. 2002-03, 26/1. 2003-04, 78/1. 2004-05, 95/1. 2005-06, 65/2. Totals, 420/7.

NBA ALL-STAR GAME RECORD

Season Team	Min.	FGM	FGA	Pct.	FTM	FTA	Pct.	Off.	Def.	Tot.	Ast.	PF	Dq.	St.	Blk.	TO	Pts.
2000—Portland	21	3	6	.500	3	4	.750	2	2	4	0	0	0	1	1	0	9
2001—Portland	21	1	7	.143	0	0	...	1	3	4	2	0	0	1	0	2	2
2006—Detroit	17	1	6	.167	0	0	...	0	2	2	0	1	0	1	0	0	2
Totals	59	5	19	.263	3	4	.750	3	7	10	2	1	0	3	1	2	13

Three-point field goals: 2001, 0-for-1. 2006, 0-for-4. Totals, 0-for-5 (.000).

WALSH, MATT F

PERSONAL: Born December 2, 1982, in Holland, Pa. ... 6-6/200 (1,98/90,7). ... Full name: Matthew Vincent Walsh
HIGH SCHOOL: Germantown Academy (Fort Washington, Pa.).
COLLEGE: Florida.
TRANSACTIONS/CAREER NOTES: Not drafted by an NBA franchise ... Played in NBA Development League (2005-06). ... Signed as free agent by Miami Heat (August 15, 2005). ... Waived by Heat (November 18, 2005).

COLLEGIATE RECORD

Season Team	G	Min.	FGM	FGA	Pct.	FTM	FTA	Pct.	Reb.	Ast.	Pts.	RPG	APG	PPG
02-03—Florida	33	965	128	274	.467	88	119	.739	156	101	404	4.7	3.1	12.2
03-04—Florida	31	1026	152	342	.444	122	148	.824	150	86	489	4.8	2.8	15.8
04-05—Florida	28	837	126	278	.453	87	106	.821	102	85	408	3.6	3.0	14.6
Totals	92	2828	406	894	.454	297	373	.796	408	272	1301	4.4	3.0	14.1

NBA REGULAR-SEASON RECORD

Season Team	G	Min.	FGM	FGA	Pct.	FTM	FTA	Pct.	Off.	Def.	Tot.	Ast.	St.	Blk.	TO	Pts.	RPG	APG	PPG
05-06—Miami	2	3	1	1	1.000	0	2	.000	0	0	0	0	0	0	1	2	0.0	0.0	1.0

NBA DEVELOPMENT LEAGUE RECORD

Season Team	G	Min.	FGM	FGA	Pct.	FTM	FTA	Pct.	Reb.	Ast.	Pts.	RPG	APG	PPG
05-06—Arkansas	11	230	30	78	.385	16	19	.842	31	23	92	2.8	2.1	8.4

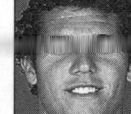

WALTON, LUKE F LAKERS

PERSONAL: Born March 28, 1980, in San Diego, Calif. ... 6-8/245. (2.03/111.1). ... Full name: Luke Theodore Walton ... Son of Bill Walton, center with Portland Trail Blazers (1974-75 through 1978-79), San Diego and Los Angeles Clippers (1979-80 through 1984-85) and Boston Celtics (1985-86 through 1987-88) and member of Naismith Memorial Basketball Hall of Fame.
HIGH SCHOOL: University (San Diego, Calif.).
COLLEGE: Arizona.
TRANSACTIONS/CAREER NOTES: Selected by Los Angeles Lakers in second round (32nd pick overall) of 2003 NBA Draft.

COLLEGIATE RECORD

NOTES: The SPORTING NEWS All-America second team (2002).

Season Team	G	Min.	FGM	FGA	Pct.	FTM	FTA	Pct.	Reb.	Ast.	Pts.	RPG	APG	PPG
98-99—Arizona						Did not play—redshirted								
99-00—Arizona	34	868	65	184	.353	52	73	.712	138	131	193	4.1	3.9	5.7
00-01—Arizona	36	736	74	176	.420	41	61	.672	140	115	198	3.9	3.2	5.5
01-02—Arizona	31	1138	174	370	.470	122	179	.682	227	194	487	7.3	6.3	15.7
02-03—Arizona	28	772	107	255	.420	59	87	.678	157	142	301	5.6	5.1	10.8
Totals	129	3514	420	985	.426	274	400	.685	662	582	1179	5.1	4.5	9.1

Three-point field goals: 1999-00, 11-for-55 (.200). 2000-01, 9-for-41 (.220). 2001-02, 17-for-60 (.283). 2002-03, 28-for-73 (.384). Totals, 65-for-229 (.284).

NBA REGULAR-SEASON RECORD

Season Team	G	Min.	FGM	FGA	Pct.	FTM	FTA	Pct.	Off.	Def.	Tot.	Ast.	St.	Blk.	TO	Pts.	RPG	APG	PPG
03-04—L.A. Lakers	72	730	65	153	.425	31	44	.705	39	88	127	113	28	8	44	174	1.8	1.6	2.4
04-05—L.A. Lakers	61	768	74	180	.411	34	48	.708	55	87	142	93	26	11	58	198	2.3	1.5	3.2
05-06—L.A. Lakers	69	1333	135	328	.412	57	76	.750	88	159	247	156	41	15	78	345	3.6	2.3	5.0
Totals	202	2831	274	661	.415	122	168	.726	182	334	516	362	95	34	180	717	2.6	1.8	3.5

Three-point field goals: 2003-04, 13-for-39 (.333). 2004-05, 16-for-61 (.262). 2005-06, 18-for-55 (.327). Totals, 47-for-155 (.303).

Personal fouls/disqualifications: 2003-04, 70/1. 2004-05, 70/0. 2005-06, 119/1. Totals, 259/2.

NBA PLAYOFF RECORD

Season Team	G	Min.	FGM	FGA	Pct.	FTM	FTA	Pct.	Off.	Def.	Tot.	Ast.	St.	Blk.	TO	Pts.	RPG	APG	PPG
03-04—L.A. Lakers	17	134	10	29	.345	7	10	.700	5	17	22	26	7	2	14	32	1.3	1.5	1.9
05-06—L.A. Lakers	7	235	38	83	.458	5	5	1.000	10	35	45	12	7	1	11	85	6.4	1.7	12.1
Totals	24	369	48	112	.429	12	15	.800	15	52	67	38	14	3	25	117	2.8	1.6	4.9

Three-point field goals: 2003-04, 5-for-13 (.385). 2005-06, 4-for-11 (.364). Totals, 9-for-24 (.375).

Personal fouls/disqualifications: 2003-04, 24/1. 2005-06, 16/0. Totals, 40/1.

WARRICK, HAKIM   F   GRIZZLIES

PERSONAL: Born July 8, 1982, in Philadelphia. ... 6-9/219. (2.06/99.3). ... Full name: Hakim Hanif Warrick
HIGH SCHOOL: Friends Central (Wynnewood, Pa.).
COLLEGE: Syracuse.
TRANSACTIONS/CAREER NOTES: Selected by Memphis Grizzlies in first round (19th pick overall) of 2005 NBA draft.

COLLEGIATE RECORD

NOTES: Member of NCAA Division I championship team (2003). ... The SPORTING NEWS All-America second team (2004, 2005).

Season Team	G	Min.	FGM	FGA	Pct.	FTM	FTA	Pct.	Reb.	Ast.	Pts.	RPG	APG	PPG
01-02—Syracuse	35	609	95	172	.552	23	60	.383	168	18	214	4.8	0.5	6.1
02-03—Syracuse	35	1146	197	364	.541	124	186	.667	297	57	518	8.5	1.6	14.8
03-04—Syracuse	31	1156	222	434	.512	171	247	.692	266	82	615	8.6	2.6	19.8
04-05—Syracuse	34	1275	253	462	.548	211	310	.681	294	50	726	8.6	1.5	21.4
Totals	135	4186	767	1432	.536	529	803	.659	1025	207	2073	7.6	1.5	15.4

Three-point field goals: 2001-02, 1-for-2 (.500). 2002-03, 0-for-1. 2003-04, 0-for-6. 2004-05, 9-for-31 (.290). Totals, 10-for-40 (.250).

NBA REGULAR-SEASON RECORD

Season Team	G	Min.	FGM	FGA	Pct.	FTM	FTA	Pct.	REBOUNDS Off.	Def.	Tot.	Ast.	St.	Blk.	TO	Pts.	RPG	APG	PPG
05-06—Memphis	68	724	101	228	.443	76	115	.661	43	101	144	30	14	21	56	278	2.1	0.4	4.1

Personal fouls/disqualifications: 2005-06, 113/0. Totals, 113/0.

NBA PLAYOFF RECORD

Season Team	G	Min.	FGM	FGA	Pct.	FTM	FTA	Pct.	REBOUNDS Off.	Def.	Tot.	Ast.	St.	Blk.	TO	Pts.	RPG	APG	PPG
05-06—Memphis	3	43	4	16	.250	12	14	.857	1	6	7	0	1	0	4	20	2.3	0.0	6.7

Three-point field goals: 2005-06, 0-for-1. Totals, 0-for-1 (.000).
Personal fouls/disqualifications: 2005-06, 7/0. Totals, 7/0.

WATSON, EARL   G   SUPERSONICS

PERSONAL: Born June 12, 1979, in Kansas City, Kan. ... 6-1/195. (1.85/88.5). ... Full name: Earl Joseph Watson
HIGH SCHOOL: Washington (Kansas City, Kan.).
COLLEGE: UCLA.
TRANSACTIONS/CAREER NOTES: Selected by Seattle SuperSonics in second round (40th pick overall) of 2001 NBA Draft. ... Signed as free agent by Memphis Grizzlies (July 20, 2002). ... Signed as free agent by Denver Nuggets (September 7, 2005). ... Traded by Nuggets to Seattle SuperSonics as part of four-way deal (February 23, 2006).

COLLEGIATE RECORD

Season Team	G	Min.	FGM	FGA	Pct.	FTM	FTA	Pct.	Reb.	Ast.	Pts.	RPG	APG	PPG
97-98—UCLA	33	1057	65	166	.392	40	66	.606	122	104	191	3.7	3.2	5.8
98-99—UCLA	31	1053	144	331	.435	90	128	.703	116	142	411	3.7	4.6	13.3
99-00—UCLA	33	1146	137	304	.451	61	94	.649	129	195	376	3.9	5.9	11.4
00-01—UCLA	32	1115	172	349	.493	89	140	.636	117	166	471	3.7	5.2	14.7
Totals	129	4371	518	1150	.450	280	428	.654	484	607	1449	3.8	4.7	11.2

Three-point field goals: 1997-98, 21-for-65 (.323). 1998-99, 33-for-103 (.320). 1999-00, 41-for-114 (.360). 2000-01, 38-for-108 (.352). Totals, 133-for-390 (.341).
Personal fouls/disqualifications: 1997-98, 84/0. 1998-99, 96/0. 1999-00, 92/0. 2000-01, 100/0. Totals, 372/0.

NBA REGULAR-SEASON RECORD

Season Team	G	Min.	FGM	FGA	Pct.	FTM	FTA	Pct.	REBOUNDS Off.	Def.	Tot.	Ast.	St.	Blk.	TO	Pts.	RPG	APG	PPG
01-02—Seattle	64	964	96	212	.453	23	36	.639	31	52	83	125	60	5	51	231	1.3	2.0	3.6
02-03—Memphis	79	1366	170	391	.435	62	86	.721	46	118	164	225	89	14	88	433	2.1	2.8	5.5
03-04—Memphis	81	1669	172	464	.371	90	138	.652	49	129	178	402	91	19	146	460	2.2	5.0	5.7
04-05—Memphis	80	1808	236	554	.426	91	138	.659	35	129	164	359	83	19	167	615	2.1	4.5	7.7
05-06—Denver-Seattle	70	1578	219	509	.430	75	111	.676	24	134	158	289	68	10	136	623	2.3	4.1	8.9
Totals	374	7385	893	2130	.419	341	509	.670	185	562	747	1400	391	67	588	2362	2.0	3.7	6.3

Three-point field goals: 2001-02, 16-for-44 (.364). 2002-03, 31-for-91 (.341). 2003-04, 26-for-106 (.245). 2004-05, 52-for-163 (.319). 2005-06, 110-for-272 (.404). Totals, 235-for-676 (.348).
Personal fouls/disqualifications: 2001-02, 93/0. 2002-03, 138/0. 2003-04, 175/3. 2004-05, 184/0. 2005-06, 159/1. Totals, 749/4.

NBA PLAYOFF RECORD

Season Team	G	Min.	FGM	FGA	Pct.	FTM	FTA	Pct.	REBOUNDS Off.	Def.	Tot.	Ast.	St.	Blk.	TO	Pts.	RPG	APG	PPG
03-04—Memphis	4	62	8	15	.533	3	3	1.000	4	5	9	7	5	0	6	19	2.3	1.8	4.8
04-05—Memphis	4	74	8	24	.333	2	2	1.000	3	7	10	15	3	1	2	19	2.5	3.8	4.8
Totals	8	136	16	39	.410	5	5	1.000	7	12	19	22	8	1	8	38	2.4	2.8	4.8

Three-point field goals: 2003-04, 0-for-3. 2004-05, 1-for-9 (.111). Totals, 1-for-12 (.083).
Personal fouls/disqualifications: 2003-04, 8/0. 2004-05, 11/0. Totals, 19/0.

W

WEBBER, CHRIS   F   76ERS

PERSONAL: Born March 1, 1973, in Detroit. ... 6-10/245. (2.08/111.1). ... Full name: Mayce Edward Christopher Webber
HIGH SCHOOL: Detroit Country Day (Beverly Hills, Mich.).
COLLEGE: Michigan.
TRANSACTIONS/CAREER NOTES: Selected after sophomore season by Orlando Magic in first round (first pick overall) of 1993 NBA Draft. ... Draft rights traded by Magic to Golden State Warriors for draft rights to G Anfernee Hardaway and 1996,

1998 and 2000 first-round draft choices (June 30, 1993). ... Traded by Warriors to Washington Bullets for F Tom Gugliotta and 1996, 1998 and 2000 first-round draft choices (November 17, 1994). ... Bullets franchise renamed Wizards for 1997-98 season. ... Traded by Wizards to Sacramento Kings for G Mitch Richmond and F Otis Thorpe (May 14, 1998). ... Traded by Kings to Philadelphia 76ers with Fs Michael Bradley and Matt Barnes for Fs Kenny Thomas and Corliss Williamson and C Brian Skinner (February 23, 2005).

COLLEGIATE RECORD

NOTES: THE SPORTING NEWS All-America first team (1993).

Season Team	G	Min.	FGM	FGA	Pct.	FTM	FTA	Pct.	Reb.	Ast.	Pts.	RPG	APG	PPG
												AVERAGES		
91-92—Michigan	34	1088	229	412	.556	56	113	.496	340	76	528	10.0	2.2	15.5
92-93—Michigan	36	1143	281	454	.619	101	183	.552	362	90	690	10.1	2.5	19.2
Totals	70	2231	510	866	.589	157	296	.530	702	166	1218	10.0	2.4	17.4

Three-point field goals: 1991-92, 14-for-54 (.259). 1992-93, 27-for-80 (.338). Totals, 41-for-134 (.306).

NBA REGULAR-SEASON RECORD

HONORS: NBA Rookie of the Year (1994). ... All-NBA first team (2001). ... All-NBA second team (1999, 2002, 2003). ... All-NBA third team (2000). ... NBA All-Rookie first team (1994).

Season Team	G	Min.	FGM	FGA	Pct.	FTM	FTA	Pct.	REBOUNDS Off.	Def.	Tot.	Ast.	St.	Blk.	TO	Pts.	AVERAGES RPG	APG	PPG
93-94—Golden State	76	2438	572	1037	.552	189	355	.532	305	389	694	272	93	164	206	1333	9.1	3.6	17.5
94-95—Washington	54	2067	464	938	.495	117	233	.502	200	318	518	256	83	85	167	1085	9.6	4.7	20.1
95-96—Washington	15	558	150	276	.543	41	69	.594	37	77	114	75	27	9	49	356	7.6	5.0	23.7
96-97—Washington	72	2806	604	1167	.518	177	313	.565	238	505	743	331	122	137	230	1445	10.3	4.6	20.1
97-98—Washington	71	2809	647	1341	.482	196	333	.589	176	498	674	273	111	124	185	1555	9.5	3.8	21.9
98-99—Sacramento	42	1719	378	778	.486	79	174	.454	149	396	545	173	60	89	148	839	*13.0	4.1	20.0
99-00—Sacramento	75	2880	748	1548	.483	311	414	.751	189	598	787	345	120	128	218	1834	10.5	4.6	24.5
00-01—Sacramento	70	2836	786	1635	.481	324	461	.703	179	598	777	294	93	118	195	1898	11.1	4.2	27.1
01-02—Sacramento	54	2071	532	1075	.495	253	338	.749	150	396	546	258	90	76	158	1322	10.1	4.8	24.5
02-03—Sacramento	67	2622	661	1433	.461	215	354	.607	160	544	704	364	106	88	215	1542	10.5	5.4	23.0
03-04—Sacramento	23	831	174	421	.413	81	114	.711	48	152	200	105	31	20	60	430	8.7	4.6	18.7
04-05—Sac.-Phila.	67	2370	555	1283	.433	181	228	.794	130	482	612	318	94	53	182	1306	9.1	4.7	19.5
05-06—Philadelphia	75	2893	617	1422	.434	263	348	.756	184	557	741	256	103	62	182	1518	9.9	3.4	20.2
Totals	761	28900	6888	14354	.480	2427	3734	.650	2145	5510	7655	3320	1133	1153	2195	16463	10.1	4.4	21.6

Three-point field goals: 1993-94, 0-for-14. 1994-95, 0-for-145 (.276). 1995-96, 15-for-34 (.441). 1996-97, 60-for-151 (.397). 1997-98, 65-for-205 (.317). 1998-99, 4-for-34 (.118). 1999-00, 27-for-95 (.284). 2000-01, 2-for-28 (.071). 2001-02, 5-for-19 (.263). 2002-03, 5-for-21 (.238). 2003-04, 1-for-5 (.200). 2004-05, 15-for-44 (.341). 2005-06, 21-for-77 (.273). Totals, 260-for-872 (.298).

Personal fouls/disqualifications: 1993-94, 247/4. 1994-95, 186/2. 1995-96, 51/1. 1996-97, 258/6. 1997-98, 269/4. 1998-99, 145/1. 1999-00, 264/7. 2000-01, 226/1. 2001-02, 181/1. 2002-03, 204/1. 2003-04, 76/1. 2004-05, 214/6. 2005-06, 219/1. Totals, 2540/36.

NBA PLAYOFF RECORD

Season Team	G	Min.	FGM	FGA	Pct.	FTM	FTA	Pct.	REBOUNDS Off.	Def.	Tot.	Ast.	St.	Blk.	TO	Pts.	AVERAGES RPG	APG	PPG
93-94—Golden State	3	109	22	40	.550	3	10	.300	13	13	26	27	3	9	9	47	8.7	9.0	15.7
96-97—Washington	3	106	19	30	.633	4	8	.500	7	17	24	10	2	7	16	47	8.0	3.3	15.7
98-99—Sacramento	5	192	31	80	.388	10	25	.400	13	34	47	22	6	3	14	78	9.4	4.4	15.6
99-00—Sacramento	5	198	47	110	.427	27	34	.794	14	34	48	27	8	10	8	122	9.6	5.4	24.4
00-01—Sacramento	8	348	76	196	.388	34	49	.694	34	58	92	25	9	8	31	186	11.5	3.1	23.3
01-02—Sacramento	16	667	160	319	.502	59	99	.596	49	124	173	75	14	25	46	379	10.8	4.7	23.7
02-03—Sacramento	7	246	67	135	.496	32	49	.653	18	40	58	25	10	8	23	166	8.3	3.6	23.7
03-04—Sacramento	12	446	90	199	.452	40	65	.615	24	75	99	44	16	10	38	221	8.3	3.7	18.4
04-05—Philadelphia	5	186	39	95	.411	12	16	.750	12	17	29	14	6	1	11	95	5.8	2.8	19.0
Totals	64	2496	551	1204	.458	221	355	.623	184	412	596	267	77	83	202	1337	9.3	4.2	20.9

Three-point field goals: 1993-94, 0-for-2. 1996-97, 5-for-11 (.455). 1998-99, 2-for-7 (.286). 1999-00, 1-for-5 (.200). 2000-01, 0-for-1. 2001-02, 0-for-4. 2002-03, 0-for-3. 2003-04, 1-for-4 (.250). 2004-05, 5-for-14 (.357). Totals, 14-for-51 (.275).

Personal fouls/disqualifications: 1993-94, 11/0. 1996-97, 18/3. 1998-99, 20/1. 1999-00, 14/1. 2000-01, 29/0. 2001-02, 64/2. 2002-03, 25/1. 2003-04, 34/0. 2004-05, 20/0. Totals, 235/8.

NBA ALL-STAR GAME RECORD

Season Team	Min.	FGM	FGA	Pct.	FTM	FTA	Pct.	REBOUNDS Off.	Def.	Tot.	Ast.	PF	Dq.	St.	Blk.	TO	Pts.
1997—Washington	14	1	4	.250	0	0	...	1	3	4	3	3	0	1	0	3	2
2000—Sacramento	13	3	10	.300	0	0	...	3	5	8	3	2	0	1	0	2	6
2001—Sacramento	29	6	14	.429	2	4	.500	4	5	9	3	2	0	1	0	1	14
2002—Sacramento	20	3	7	.429	1	4	.250	3	0	3	4	2	0	1	0	2	8
2003—Sacramento						Selected, did not play—injured											
Totals	76	13	35	.371	3	8	.375	11	13	24	13	9	0	4	0	8	30

Three-point field goals: 2001, 0-for-1. 2002, 1-for-2 (.500). Totals, 1-for-3 (.333).

WEBSTER, MARTELL   F/G   TRAIL BLAZERS

PERSONAL: Born December 4, 1986, in Edmond, Wash. ... 6-7/210. (2.01/95.3).
HIGH SCHOOL: Seattle Prep (Seattle, Wash.).
COLLEGE: Did not attend college.
TRANSACTIONS/CAREER NOTES: Selected out of high school by Portland Trail Blazers in first round (sixth pick overall) of 2005 NBA draft.

NBA REGULAR-SEASON RECORD

Season Team	G	Min.	FGM	FGA	Pct.	FTM	FTA	Pct.	REBOUNDS Off.	Def.	Tot.	Ast.	St.	Blk.	TO	Pts.	AVERAGES RPG	APG	PPG
05-06—Portland	61	1070	139	348	.399	61	71	.859	29	101	130	34	21	14	43	404	2.1	0.6	6.6

Three-point field goals: 2005-06, 65-for-182 (.357). Totals, 65-for-182 (.357).
Personal fouls/disqualifications: 2005-06, 90/0. Totals, 90/0.

W

Season Team	G	Min.	FGM	FGA	Pct.	FTM	FTA	Pct.	Reb.	Ast.	Pts.	AVERAGES RPG	APG	PPG
05-06—Fort Worth	8	203	32	85	.376	15	19	.789	27	5	86	3.4	0.6	10.8

Three-point field goals: 2005-06, 7-for-22 (.318). Totals, 7-for-22 (.318).

WELLS, BONZI G/F KINGS

PERSONAL: Born September 20, 1976, in Muncie, Ind. ... 6-5/210. (1.96/95.3). ... Full name: Gawen Deangelo Wells
HIGH SCHOOL: Central (Muncie, Ind.).
COLLEGE: Ball State.
TRANSACTIONS/CAREER NOTES: Selected by Detroit Pistons in first round (11th pick overall) of 1998 NBA Draft. ... Draft rights traded by Pistons to Portland Trail Blazers for conditional first-round draft choice (January 21, 1999); Pistons received 2000 second-round draft choice to complete deal (June 13, 2000). ... Traded by Trail Blazers to Memphis Grizzlies for F/G Wesley Person and 2004 first-round draft choice (December 3, 2003). ... Traded by Grizzlies to Sacramento Kings for C Greg Ostertag and G Bobby Jackson (August 2, 2005).

COLLEGIATE RECORD

NOTES: Led NCAA Division I with 3.6 steals per game (1998).

Season Team	G	Min.	FGM	FGA	Pct.	FTM	FTA	Pct.	Reb.	Ast.	Pts.	AVERAGES RPG	APG	PPG
94-95—Ball State	30	887	177	380	.466	87	141	.617	183	84	474	6.1	2.8	15.8
95-96—Ball State	28	910	269	544	.494	143	202	.708	246	80	712	8.8	2.9	25.4
96-97—Ball State	29	900	229	492	.465	154	223	.691	230	127	637	7.9	4.4	22.0
97-98—Ball State	29	843	238	486	.490	133	193	.689	184	95	662	6.3	3.3	22.8
Totals	116	3540	913	1902	.480	517	759	.681	843	386	2485	7.3	3.3	21.4

Three-point field goals: 1994-95, 33-for-99 (.333). 1995-96, 31-for-92 (.337). 1996-97, 25-for-104 (.240). 1997-98, 53-for-142 (.373). Totals, 142-for-437 (.325).

NBA REGULAR-SEASON RECORD

Season Team	G	Min.	FGM	FGA	Pct.	FTM	FTA	Pct.	REBOUNDS Off.	Def.	Tot.	Ast.	St.	Blk.	TO	Pts.	AVERAGES RPG	APG	PPG
98-99—Portland	7	35	11	20	.550	8	18	.444	4	5	9	3	1	1	6	31	1.3	0.4	4.4
99-00—Portland	66	1162	236	480	.492	88	129	.682	78	104	182	97	69	12	97	580	2.8	1.5	8.8
00-01—Portland	75	1995	387	726	.533	159	240	.663	120	247	367	208	94	20	169	950	4.9	2.8	12.7
01-02—Portland	74	2348	487	1039	.469	215	290	.741	121	323	444	204	113	25	191	1255	6.0	2.8	17.0
02-03—Portland	75	2396	437	990	.441	226	313	.722	98	296	394	246	123	18	215	1138	5.3	3.3	15.2
03-04—Port.-Mem.	72	1872	363	850	.427	138	183	.754	78	182	260	139	91	19	161	886	3.6	1.9	12.3
04-05—Memphis	69	1489	272	617	.441	141	188	.750	49	180	229	80	85	27	90	721	3.3	1.2	10.4
05-06—Sacramento	52	1684	284	613	.463	129	190	.679	142	259	401	144	94	25	126	707	7.7	2.8	13.6
Totals	490	12981	2477	5335	.464	1104	1551	.712	690	1596	2286	1121	670	147	1055	6268	4.7	2.3	12.8

Three-point field goals: 1998-99, 1-for-3 (.333). 1999-00, 20-for-53 (.377). 2000-01, 17-for-50 (.340). 2001-02, 66-for-172 (.384). 2002-03, 38-for-130 (.292). 2003-04, 22-for-69 (.319). 2004-05, 36-for-104 (.346). 2005-06, 10-for-45 (.222). Totals, 210-for-626 (.335).
Personal fouls/disqualifications: 1998-99, 5/0. 1999-00, 153/3. 2000-01, 203/1. 2001-02, 208/0. 2002-03, 220/2. 2003-04, 197/2. 2004-05, 165/0. 2005-06, 156/0. Totals, 1307/8.

NBA PLAYOFF RECORD

Season Team	G	Min.	FGM	FGA	Pct.	FTM	FTA	Pct.	REBOUNDS Off.	Def.	Tot.	Ast.	St.	Blk.	TO	Pts.	AVERAGES RPG	APG	PPG
99-00—Portland	14	188	37	83	.446	29	41	.707	12	23	35	13	7	0	16	105	2.5	0.9	7.5
01-02—Portland	3	106	14	38	.368	9	13	.692	4	8	12	13	6	1	11	37	4.0	4.3	12.3
02-03—Portland	7	268	49	124	.395	26	39	.667	14	34	48	26	15	3	21	133	6.9	3.7	19.0
03-04—Memphis	4	94	19	37	.514	9	14	.643	2	10	12	4	4	1	9	47	3.0	1.0	11.8
04-05—Memphis	2	25	4	9	.444	6	6	1.000	0	4	4	3	2	1	1	14	2.0	1.5	7.0
05-06—Sacramento	6	249	53	87	.609	28	43	.651	25	47	72	8	5	2	18	139	12.0	1.3	23.2
Totals	36	930	176	378	.466	107	156	.686	57	126	183	67	39	8	76	475	5.1	1.9	13.2

Three-point field goals: 1999-00, 2-for-10 (.200). 2001-02, 0-for-7. 2002-03, 9-for-30 (.300). 2003-04, 0-for-1. 2005-06, 5-for-8 (.625). Totals, 16-for-56 (.286).
Personal fouls/disqualifications: 1999-00, 33/0. 2001-02, 11/1. 2002-03, 30/1. 2003-04, 8/0. 2004-05, 1/0. 2005-06, 25/1. Totals, 108/3.

WELSCH, JIRI G

PERSONAL: Born January 27, 1980, in Pardubice, Czechoslovakia. ... 6-7/208. (2.01/94.3).
TRANSACTIONS/CAREER NOTES: Played in Czech Republic (1997-2000). ... Played in Slovenia (2000-02). ... Selected by Philadelphia 76ers in first round (16th pick overall) of 2002 NBA Draft. ... Draft rights traded by 76ers to Golden State Warriors for future first-round draft choice and future first- or second-round draft choice (June 26, 2002). ... Traded by Warriors with F Danny Fortson, F Chris Mills and F Antawn Jamison to Dallas Mavericks for G Nick Van Exel, G Avery Johnson, F Popeye Jones, F Antoine Rigaudeau and C Evan Eschmeyer (August 18, 2003). ... Traded by Mavericks with F/C Raef LaFrentz, F Chris Mills and 2004 first-round draft choice to Boston Celtics for G Tony Delk and F Antoine Walker (October 20, 2003). ... Traded by Celtics to Cleveland Cavaliers for first-round draft pick in 2007 draft (February 24, 2005). Traded by Cavaliers to Milwaukee Bucks for a 2006 second-round draft choice (June 28, 2005). ... Signed with Unicaja of Spanish League for 2006-07 season.

CZECH LEAGUE RECORD

Season Team	G	Min.	FGM	FGA	Pct.	FTM	FTA	Pct.	Reb.	Ast.	Pts.	AVERAGES RPG	APG	PPG
97-98—Pardubice	33	1073	169	384	.440	127	156	.814	90	30	482	2.7	0.9	14.6
98-99—Sparta Praha	30	679	115	227	.507	107	141	.759	75	47	354	2.5	1.6	11.8
99-00—Sparta Praha	35	1243	201	460	.437	219	276	.793	164	108	668	4.7	3.1	19.1
Totals	98	2995	485	1071	.453	453	573	.791	329	185	1504	3.4	1.9	15.3

Three-point field goals: 1997-98, 23-for-84 (.274). 1998-99, 17-for-38 (.447). 1999-00, 43-for-123 (.350). Totals, 83-for-245 (.339).

SLOVENIAN LEAGUE RECORD

Season Team	G	Min.	FGM	FGA	Pct.	FTM	FTA	Pct.	Reb.	Ast.	Pts.	AVERAGES RPG	APG	PPG
00-01—Olimpija Ljubljana	20	479	85	169	.503	33	48	.688	49	32	219	2.5	1.6	11.0
01-02—Olimpija Ljubljana	22	565	109	196	.556	95	114	.833	49	36	341	2.2	1.6	15.5
Totals	42	1044	194	365	.532	128	162	.790	98	68	560	2.3	1.6	13.3

Three-point field goals: 2000-01, 16-for-47 (.340). 2001-02, 28-for-72 (.389). Totals, 44-for-119 (.370).

NBA REGULAR-SEASON RECORD

Season Team	G	Min.	FGM	FGA	Pct.	FTM	FTA	Pct.	REBOUNDS Off.	Def.	Tot.	Ast.	St.	Blk.	TO	Pts.	AVERAGES RPG	APG	PPG
02-03—Golden State	37	234	19	75	.253	22	29	.759	12	16	28	27	8	2	19	61	0.8	0.7	1.6
03-04—Boston	81	2179	262	612	.428	153	206	.743	60	236	296	183	101	7	129	746	3.7	2.3	9.2
04-05—Boston-Cleve.	71	1317	149	371	.402	129	169	.763	26	141	167	103	44	5	73	461	2.4	1.5	6.5
05-06—Milwaukee	58	866	86	222	.387	65	87	.747	22	89	111	62	34	1	41	251	1.9	1.1	4.3
Totals	247	4596	516	1280	.403	369	491	.752	120	482	602	375	187	15	262	1519	2.4	1.5	6.1

Three-point field goals: 2002-03, 1-for-4 (.250). 2003-04, 69-for-181 (.381). 2004-05, 34-for-110 (.309). 2005-06, 14-for-49 (.286). Totals, 118-for-344 (.343).

Personal fouls/disqualifications: 2002-03, 32/1. 2003-04, 176/0. 2004-05, 121/1. 2005-06, 65/0. Totals, 394/2.

NBA PLAYOFF RECORD

Season Team	G	Min.	FGM	FGA	Pct.	FTM	FTA	Pct.	REBOUNDS Off.	Def.	Tot.	Ast.	St.	Blk.	TO	Pts.	AVERAGES RPG	APG	PPG
03-04—Boston	4	104	11	23	.478	9	9	1.000	0	12	12	9	2	0	8	32	3.0	2.3	8.0
05-06—Milwaukee	4	15	2	4	.500	3	4	.750	0	3	3	2	1	0	0	7	0.8	0.5	1.8
Totals	8	119	13	27	.481	12	13	.923	0	15	15	11	3	0	8	39	1.9	1.4	4.9

Three-point field goals: 2003-04, 1-for-4 (.250). Totals, 1-for-4 (.250).
Personal fouls/disqualifications: 2003-04, 7/0. 2005-06, 1/0. Totals, 8/0.

WESLEY, DAVID — G — ROCKETS

PERSONAL: Born November 14, 1970, in San Antonio. ... 6-1/203. (1.85/92.1). ... Full name: David Barakau Wesley
HIGH SCHOOL: Longview (Texas).
JUNIOR COLLEGE: Temple (Texas) Junior College.
COLLEGE: Baylor.
TRANSACTIONS/CAREER NOTES: Not drafted by an NBA franchise. ... Played in Continental Basketball Association with Wichita Falls Texans (1992-93). ... Signed as free agent by New Jersey Nets (July 27, 1993). ... Signed as free agent by Boston Celtics (July 20, 1994). ... Signed as free agent by Charlotte Hornets (July 1, 1997). ... Hornets franchise moved to New Orleans for 2002-03 season. ... Traded by Hornets to Houston Rockets for G Jim Jackson and F Bostjan Nachbar (December 27, 2004).

COLLEGIATE RECORD

Season Team	G	Min.	FGM	FGA	Pct.	FTM	FTA	Pct.	Reb.	Ast.	Pts.	AVERAGES RPG	APG	PPG
88-89—Temple J.C.	31	...	155	331	.468	88	125	.704	106	184	455	3.4	5.9	14.7
89-90—Baylor	18	394	61	134	.455	61	73	.836	39	37	208	2.2	2.1	11.6
90-91—Baylor	26	837	133	314	.424	125	149	.839	76	148	430	2.9	5.7	16.5
91-92—Baylor	28	1020	174	387	.450	179	219	.817	136	131	586	4.9	4.7	20.9
Junior College Totals	31	...	155	331	.468	88	125	.704	106	184	455	3.4	5.9	14.7
4-Year-College Totals	72	2251	368	835	.441	365	441	.828	251	316	1224	3.5	4.4	17.0

Three-point field goals: 1989-90, 25-for-56 (.446). 1990-91, 39-for-114 (.342). 1991-92, 59-for-156 (.378). Totals, 123-for-326 (.377).
Personal fouls/disqualifications: 1989-90, 35/1. 1990-91, 84/4. Totals, 119/5.

CBA RECORD

NOTES: CBA All-Rookie first team (1993).

Season Team	G	Min.	FGM	FGA	Pct.	FTM	FTA	Pct.	Reb.	Ast.	Pts.	AVERAGES RPG	APG	PPG
92-93—Wichita Falls	55	1830	350	759	.461	282	360	.783	218	225	948	4.0	4.1	17.2

Three-point field goals: 1992-93, 34-for-93 (.366). Totals, 34-for-93 (.366).
Personal fouls/disqualifications: 1992-93, 189/0. Totals, 189/0.

NBA REGULAR-SEASON RECORD

Season Team	G	Min.	FGM	FGA	Pct.	FTM	FTA	Pct.	REBOUNDS Off.	Def.	Tot.	Ast.	St.	Blk.	TO	Pts.	AVERAGES RPG	APG	PPG
93-94—New Jersey	60	542	64	174	.368	44	53	.830	10	34	44	123	38	4	52	183	0.7	2.1	3.1
94-95—Boston	51	1380	128	313	.409	71	94	.755	31	86	117	266	82	9	87	378	2.3	5.2	7.4
95-96—Boston	82	2104	338	736	.459	217	288	.753	68	196	264	390	100	11	159	1009	3.2	4.8	12.3
96-97—Boston	74	2991	456	974	.468	225	288	.781	67	197	264	537	162	13	211	1240	3.6	7.3	16.8
97-98—Charlotte	81	2845	383	864	.443	229	288	.795	49	164	213	529	140	30	226	1054	2.6	6.5	13.0
98-99—Charlotte	50	1848	243	545	.446	159	191	.832	23	138	161	322	100	10	142	706	3.2	6.4	14.1
99-00—Charlotte	82	2760	407	955	.426	214	275	.778	39	186	225	463	109	11	159	1116	2.7	5.6	13.6
00-01—Charlotte	82	3106	523	1239	.422	271	339	.799	64	160	224	361	128	16	171	1414	2.7	4.4	17.2
01-02—Charlotte	67	2487	364	910	.400	138	188	.734	44	99	143	236	74	15	119	951	2.1	3.5	14.2
02-03—New Orleans	73	2710	449	1037	.433	185	237	.781	38	137	175	251	109	9	132	1217	2.4	3.4	16.7
03-04—New Orleans	61	2001	311	800	.389	137	182	.753	28	106	134	175	71	14	100	851	2.2	2.9	14.0
04-05—N.O.-Houston	80	2774	334	840	.398	162	189	.857	38	190	228	265	96	9	113	948	2.9	3.3	11.9
05-06—Houston	71	2372	226	561	.403	151	187	.807	24	154	178	204	59	6	120	702	2.5	2.9	9.9
Totals	914	29920	4226	9948	.425	2203	2799	.787	523	1847	2370	4122	1268	157	1791	11769	2.6	4.5	12.9

Three-point field goals: 1993-94, 11-for-47 (.234). 1994-95, 51-for-119 (.429). 1995-96, 116-for-272 (.426). 1996-97, 103-for-286 (.360). 1997-98, 59-

W

for-170 (.347). 1998-99, 61-for-170 (.359). 1999-00, 88-for-248 (.355). 2000-01, 97-for-258 (.376). 2001-02, 85-for-256 (.332). 2002-03, 134-for-316 (.424). 2003-04, 92-for-285 (.323). 2004-05, 118-for-315 (.375). 2005-06, 99-for-271 (.365). Totals, 1114-for-3013 (.370).

Personal fouls/disqualifications: 1993-94, 47/0. 1994-95, 144/0. 1995-96, 207/0. 1996-97, 221/1. 1997-98, 229/3. 1998-99, 130/2. 1999-00, 186/2. 2000-01, 220/2. 2001-02, 147/0. 2002-03, 173/0. 2003-04, 147/1. 2004-05, 215/2. 2005-06, 212/3. Totals, 2278/16.

NBA PLAYOFF RECORD

Season Team	G	Min.	FGM	FGA	Pct.	FTM	FTA	Pct.	REBOUNDS Off.	Def.	Tot.	Ast.	St.	Blk.	TO	Pts.	RPG	APG	PPG
93-94—New Jersey.....	3	18	3	7	.429	2	2	1.000	0	0	0	3	2	0	4	9	0.0	1.0	3.0
97-98—Charlotte........	9	285	33	83	.398	15	21	.714	5	13	18	60	7	0	19	90	2.0	6.7	10.0
99-00—Charlotte........	4	152	16	48	.333	9	9	1.000	3	9	12	19	8	0	6	44	3.0	4.8	11.0
00-01—Charlotte........	10	394	63	134	.470	31	41	.756	4	26	30	39	16	1	14	170	3.0	3.9	17.0
01-02—Charlotte........	9	377	52	129	.403	21	23	.913	3	14	17	31	10	2	21	142	1.9	3.4	15.8
02-03—New Orleans ...	6	185	29	72	.403	7	7	1.000	1	6	7	13	5	1	15	79	1.2	2.2	13.2
03-04—New Orleans ...	7	243	24	74	.324	15	21	.714	1	15	16	17	5	0	16	74	2.3	2.4	10.6
04-05—Houston..........	7	280	19	54	.352	9	13	.692	4	17	21	23	9	1	9	57	3.0	3.3	8.1
Totals	55	1934	239	601	.398	109	137	.796	21	100	121	205	62	5	104	665	2.2	3.7	12.1

Three-point field goals: 1993-94, 1-for-4 (.250). 1997-98, 9-for-21 (.429). 1999-00, 3-for-10 (.300). 2000-01, 13-for-33 (.394). 2001-02, 17-for-38 (.447). 2002-03, 14-for-34 (.412). 2003-04, 11-for-30 (.367). 2004-05, 10-for-21 (.476). Totals, 78-for-191 (.408).

Personal fouls/disqualifications: 1997-98, 25/0. 1999-00, 17/0. 2000-01, 28/0. 2001-02, 30/0. 2002-03, 23/1. 2003-04, 21/0. 2004-05, 20/0. Totals, 164/1.

WEST, DAVID   F   HORNETS

PERSONAL: Born August 29, 1980, in Teaneck, N.J. ... 6-9/240. (2.06/108.9). ... Full name: David Moorer West
HIGH SCHOOL: Teaneck (N.J), then Garner Senior (N.C.), then Hargrave Military Academy (Chatham, Va.).
COLLEGE: Xavier.
TRANSACTIONS/CAREER NOTES: Selected by New Orleans Hornets in first round (18th pick overall) of 2003 NBA Draft.

COLLEGIATE RECORD

NOTES: The SPORTING NEWS All-America first team (2003). ... The SPORTING NEWS All-America third team (2002).

Season Team	G	Min.	FGM	FGA	Pct.	FTM	FTA	Pct.	Reb.	Ast.	Pts.	RPG	APG	PPG
99-00—Xavier	33	970	143	269	.532	100	150	.667	301	57	386	9.1	1.7	11.7
00-01—Xavier	29	978	174	316	.551	168	227	.740	316	58	516	10.9	2.0	17.8
01-02—Xavier	32	1094	196	366	.536	185	241	.768	313	50	586	9.8	1.6	18.3
02-03—Xavier	32	1168	213	415	.513	209	256	.816	378	102	644	11.8	3.2	20.1
Totals	126	4210	726	1366	.531	662	874	.757	1308	267	2132	10.4	2.1	16.9

Three-point field goals: 2000-01, 0-for-1. 2001-02, 9-for-28 (.321). 2002-03, 9-for-26 (.346). Totals, 18-for-55 (.327).

NBA REGULAR-SEASON RECORD

Season Team	G	Min.	FGM	FGA	Pct.	FTM	FTA	Pct.	REBOUNDS Off.	Def.	Tot.	Ast.	St.	Blk.	TO	Pts.	RPG	APG	PPG
03-04—New Orleans ...	71	930	108	228	.474	57	80	.713	117	180	297	60	27	28	48	273	4.2	0.8	3.8
04-05—New Orleans ...	30	552	75	172	.436	34	50	.680	40	89	129	23	12	16	37	186	4.3	0.8	6.2
05-06—NO/Okla. City ..	74	2526	530	1036	.512	199	236	.843	168	380	548	92	61	64	105	1262	7.4	1.2	17.1
Totals	175	4008	713	1436	.497	290	366	.792	325	649	974	175	100	108	190	1721	5.6	1.0	9.8

Three-point field goals: 2003-04, 0-for-2. 2004-05, 2-for-5 (.400). 2005-06, 3-for-11 (.273). Totals, 5-for-18 (.278).
Personal fouls/disqualifications: 2003-04, 117/0. 2004-05, 62/0. 2005-06, 214/1. Totals, 393/1.

NBA PLAYOFF RECORD

Season Team	G	Min.	FGM	FGA	Pct.	FTM	FTA	Pct.	REBOUNDS Off.	Def.	Tot.	Ast.	St.	Blk.	TO	Pts.	RPG	APG	PPG
03-04—New Orleans ...	7	111	15	28	.536	11	13	.846	8	22	30	8	2	4	7	41	4.3	1.1	5.9

Personal fouls/disqualifications: 2003-04, 10/0. Totals, 10/0.

W

WEST, DELONTE   G   CELTICS

PERSONAL: Born July 26, 1983, in Washington, D.C. ... 6-4/180. (1.93/81.6).
HIGH SCHOOL: Eleanor Roosevelt (Greenbelt, Md.).
COLLEGE: Saint Joseph's.
TRANSACTIONS/CAREER NOTES: Selected after junior season by Boston Celtics in first round (24th pick overall) of 2004 NBA Draft.

COLLEGIATE RECORD

NOTES: The SPORTING NEWS All-America third team (2004).

Season Team	G	Min.	FGM	FGA	Pct.	FTM	FTA	Pct.	Reb.	Ast.	Pts.	RPG	APG	PPG
01-02—St. Joseph's...................	31	526	76	162	.469	28	42	.667	92	36	182	3.0	1.2	5.9
02-03—St. Joseph's...................	26	785	162	342	.474	70	86	.814	113	83	449	4.3	3.2	17.3
03-04—St. Joseph's...................	32	1073	212	416	.510	124	139	.892	172	151	604	5.4	4.7	18.9
Totals	89	2384	450	920	.489	222	267	.831	377	270	1235	4.2	3.0	13.9

Three-point field goals: 2001-02, 2-for-17 (.118). 2002-03, 55-for-147 (.374). 2003-04, 56-for-136 (.412). Totals, 113-for-300 (.377).

NBA REGULAR-SEASON RECORD

Season Team	G	Min.	FGM	FGA	Pct.	FTM	FTA	Pct.	REBOUNDS Off.	Def.	Tot.	Ast.	St.	Blk.	TO	Pts.	RPG	APG	PPG
04-05—Boston	39	507	66	155	.426	19	27	.704	14	51	65	53	21	8	24	175	1.7	1.4	4.5
05-06—Boston	71	2418	333	684	.487	86	101	.851	57	232	289	329	84	46	133	836	4.1	4.6	11.8
Totals	110	2925	399	839	.476	105	128	.820	71	283	354	382	105	54	157	1011	3.2	3.5	9.2

Three-point field goals: 2004-05, 24-for-67 (.358). 2005-06, 84-for-218 (.385). Totals, 108-for-285 (.379).
Personal fouls/disqualifications: 2004-05, 69/0. 2005-06, 197/3. Totals, 266/3.

Season Team	G	Min.	FGM	FGA	Pct.	FTM	FTA	Pct.	REBOUNDS Off.	Def.	Tot.	Ast.	St.	Blk.	TO	Pts.	AVERAGES RPG	APG	PPG
04-05—Boston	7	115	11	21	.524	2	4	.500	2	7	9	4	7	1	2	29	1.3	0.6	4.1

Three-point field goals: 2004-05, 5-for-11 (.455). Totals, 5-for-11 (.455).
Personal fouls/disqualifications: 2004-05, 17/0. Totals, 17/0.

WHALEY, ROBERT   C

PERSONAL: Born April 16, 1982 ... 6-10/260. (2.08/117.9).
HIGH SCHOOL: Benton Harbor (Mich.).
JUNIOR COLLEGE: Barton County (Kan.).
COLLEGE: Cincinnati, then Walsh.
TRANSACTIONS/CAREER NOTES: Selected by Utah Jazz in second round (51st pick overall) of 2005 NBA Draft. ... Traded by Utah with F Kris Humphries to Toronto Raptors for C Rafael Araujo (June 8, 2006). ... Waived by Raptors (June 22, 2006).

COLLEGIATE RECORD

Season Team	G	Min.	FGM	FGA	Pct.	FTM	FTA	Pct.	Reb.	Ast.	Pts.	AVERAGES RPG	APG	PPG
01-02—Barton County	32	784	229	405	.565	79	138	.572	216	34	538	6.8	1.1	16.8
02-03—Barton County	29	801	203	408	.498	84	146	.575	224	30	491	7.7	1.0	16.9
03-04—Cincinnati	22	286	48	138	.348	31	47	.660	54	14	127	2.5	0.6	5.8
04-05—Walsh	35	1049	194	574	.512	105	183	.574	263	48	696	7.5	1.4	19.9
Junior College Totals	61	1585	432	813	.531	163	284	.574	440	64	1029	7.2	1.0	16.9
4-year College Totals	57	1335	342	712	.480	136	230	.591	317	62	823	5.6	1.1	14.4

Three-point field goals: 2001-02, 1-for-2 (.500). 2002-03, 1-for-4 (.250). 2003-04, 0-for-1 (.000). 2004-05, 3-for-14 (.214). Totals, 5-for-21 (.238).

NBA REGULAR-SEASON RECORD

Season Team	G	Min.	FGM	FGA	Pct.	FTM	FTA	Pct.	REBOUNDS Off.	Def.	Tot.	Ast.	St.	Blk.	TO	Pts.	AVERAGES RPG	APG	PPG
05-06—Utah	23	212	23	57	.404	3	6	.500	16	27	43	17	7	8	14	49	1.9	0.7	2.1

Personal fouls/disqualifications: 2005-06, 41/1. Totals, 41/1.

WILCOX, CHRIS   F   SUPERSONICS

PERSONAL: Born August 3, 1982, in Raleigh, N.C. ... 6-10/221. (2.08/100.2). ... Full name: Chris Ray Wilcox
HIGH SCHOOL: Whitefield (N.C.), then West Columbus (Whitefield, N.C.), then Enloe (Raleigh, N.C.).
COLLEGE: Maryland.
TRANSACTIONS/CAREER NOTES: Selected after sophomore season by Los Angeles Clippers in first round (eighth pick overall) of 2002 NBA Draft. ... Traded by Clippers to Seattle SuperSonics for F Vladimir Radmanovic (February 14, 2006).

COLLEGIATE RECORD

Season Team	G	Min.	FGM	FGA	Pct.	FTM	FTA	Pct.	Reb.	Ast.	Pts.	AVERAGES RPG	APG	PPG
00-01—Maryland	34	294	51	88	.580	20	33	.606	73	16	122	2.1	0.5	3.6
01-02—Maryland	36	866	173	343	.504	86	147	.585	257	53	432	7.1	1.5	12.0
Totals	70	1160	224	431	.520	106	180	.589	330	69	554	4.7	1.0	7.9

Three-point field goals: 2001-02, 0-for-2. Totals, 0-for-2 (.000).

NBA REGULAR-SEASON RECORD

Season Team	G	Min.	FGM	FGA	Pct.	FTM	FTA	Pct.	REBOUNDS Off.	Def.	Tot.	Ast.	St.	Blk.	TO	Pts.	AVERAGES RPG	APG	PPG
02-03—L.A. Clippers ...	46	479	73	140	.521	25	50	.500	32	72	104	21	7	12	26	171	2.3	0.5	3.7
03-04—L.A. Clippers ...	65	1340	227	436	.521	105	150	.700	125	180	305	51	29	20	80	559	4.7	0.8	8.6
04-05—L.A. Clippers ...	54	1005	169	329	.514	88	144	.611	63	165	228	38	26	24	77	426	4.2	0.7	7.9
05-06—L.A.C.-Seattle..	77	1530	257	450	.571	112	153	.732	118	292	410	52	33	34	72	626	5.3	0.7	8.1
Totals	242	4354	726	1355	.536	330	497	.664	338	709	1047	162	95	90	255	1782	4.3	0.7	7.4

Three-point field goals: 2003-04, 0-for-1. 2005-06, 0-for-2. Totals, 0-for-3 (.000).
Personal fouls/disqualifications: 2002-03, 65/2. 2003-04, 183/4. 2004-05, 129/2. 2005-06, 183/0. Totals, 560/8.

WILKINS, DAMIEN   F   SUPERSONICS

PERSONAL: Born January 11, 1980, in Washington, D.C. ... 6-6/225. (1.98/102.1). ... Full name: Damien Lamont Wilkins. ... Son of Gerald Wilkins, guard with four NBA teams (1986-99). Nephew of Dominique Wilkins, forward with five NBA teams (1982-99).
HIGH SCHOOL: Dr. Phillips (Orlando, Fla.).
COLLEGE: North Caroline State, then Georgia.
TRANSACTIONS/CAREER NOTES: Not drafted by an NBA franchise. ... Signed as free agent by Seattle SuperSonics (November 3, 2004).

COLLEGIATE RECORD

Season Team	G	Min.	FGM	FGA	Pct.	FTM	FTA	Pct.	Reb.	Ast.	Pts.	AVERAGES RPG	APG	PPG
99-00—NC State	34	1083	127	311	.408	106	159	.667	197	77	389	5.8	2.3	11.4
00-01—NC State	26	848	109	267	.408	67	94	.713	151	69	304	5.8	2.7	11.7
01-02—Georgia..........................						Did Not Play - Transfer Student								
02-03—Georgia..........................	27	569	65	158	.411	67	91	.736	79	71	203	2.9	2.6	7.5
03-04—Georgia..........................	30	1056	117	288	.406	118	150	.787	162	88	379	5.4	2.9	12.6
Totals	117	3556	418	1024	.408	358	494	.725	589	305	1275	5.0	2.6	10.9

Three-point field goals: 1999-00, 29-for-89 (.326). 2000-01, 19-for-71 (.268). 2002-03, 6-for-22 (.273). 2003-04, 27-for-84 (.321). Totals, 81-for-266 (.305).

W

NBA REGULAR-SEASON RECORD

								REBOUNDS								AVERAGES		
Season Team	G	Min.	FGM	FGA	Pct.	FTM	FTA	Pct.	Off.	Def.	Tot.	Ast.	St.	Blk.	TO	Pts.	RPG	APG	PPG
04-05—Seattle	29	520	73	168	.435	21	34	.618	29	37	66	26	22	10	16	183	2.3	0.9	6.3
05-06—Seattle	82	1525	193	435	.444	136	162	.840	79	113	192	107	72	12	85	536	2.3	1.3	6.5
Totals	111	2045	266	603	.441	157	196	.801	108	150	258	133	94	22	101	719	2.3	1.2	6.5

Three-point field goals: 2004-05, 16-for-59 (.271). 2005-06, 14-for-56 (.250). Totals, 30-for-115 (.261).
Personal fouls/disqualifications: 2004-05, 55/0. 2005-06, 144/1. Totals, 199/1.

NBA PLAYOFF RECORD

								REBOUNDS								AVERAGES		
Season Team	G	Min.	FGM	FGA	Pct.	FTM	FTA	Pct.	Off.	Def.	Tot.	Ast.	St.	Blk.	TO	Pts.	RPG	APG	PPG
04-05—Seattle	7	136	16	36	.444	4	9	.444	9	9	18	3	10	1	8	39	2.6	0.4	5.6

Three-point field goals: 2004-05, 3-for-11 (.273). Totals, 3-for-11 (.273).
Personal fouls/disqualifications: 2004-05, 17/0. Totals, 17/0.

WILKS, MIKE — G — SUPERSONICS

PERSONAL: Born May 7, 1979, in Milwaukee, Wis. ... 5-11/180. (1.80/81.6).
HIGH SCHOOL: Rufus King (Milwaukee, Wis.).
COLLEGE: Rice.
TRANSACTIONS/CAREER NOTES: Not drafted by an NBA franchise. ... Signed as a free agent by Milwaukee Bucks (August 23, 2002). ... Signed by Atlanta Hawks from NBA Development League's Huntsville franchise (December 24, 2002). ... Signed by Atlanta Hawks to first of two consecutive 10-day contract (January 9, 2003). ... Signed by Minnesota Timberwolves to 10-day contract (February 12, 2003). ... Signed by Timberwolves for remainder of season (February 22, 2003). ... Signed as free agent by Houston Rockets (September 9, 2003). ... Traded by Rockets with G/F Eric Piatkowski and G/F Adrian Griffin to Chicago Bulls for C Dikembe Mutombo (September 8, 2004). ... Waived by Bulls (October 20, 2004). ... Signed by San Antonio Spurs (October 27, 2004). ... Signed as free agent by Cleveland Cavaliers (September 27, 2005). ... Traded with cash by Cavaliers to Seattle SuperSonics for G Ronald Murray (February 23, 2006).

COLLEGIATE RECORD

											AVERAGES		
Season Team	G	Min.	FGM	FGA	Pct.	FTM	FTA	Pct.	Reb.	Ast.	Pts.	RPG	APG	PPG
97-98—Rice	28	617	46	129	.357	36	58	.621	73	72	135	2.6	2.6	4.8
98-99—Rice	28	967	68	174	.391	86	125	.688	124	116	230	4.4	4.1	8.2
99-00—Rice	21	783	112	281	.399	71	97	.732	84	70	331	4.0	3.3	15.8
00-01—Rice	30	1114	190	434	.438	168	215	.781	147	90	604	4.9	3.0	20.1
Totals	107	3481	416	1018	.409	361	495	.729	428	348	1300	4.0	3.3	12.1

Three-point field goals: 1997-98, 7-for-23 (.304). 1998-99, 8-for-29 (.276). 1999-00, 36-for-112 (.321). 2000-01, 56-for-145 (.386). Totals, 107-for-309 (.346).

NBA DEVELOPMENT LEAGUE RECORD

											AVERAGES		
Season Team	G	Min.	FGM	FGA	Pct.	FTM	FTA	Pct.	Reb.	Ast.	Pts.	RPG	APG	PPG
01-02—Huntsville	38	1136	121	292	.414	122	155	.787	143	172	387	3.8	4.5	10.2
02-03—Huntsville	16	508	60	135	.444	44	56	.786	60	58	173	3.8	3.6	10.8
Totals	54	1644	181	427	.424	166	211	.787	203	230	560	3.8	4.3	10.4

Three-point field goals: 2001-02, 23-for-60 (.383). 2002-03, 9-for-28 (.321). Totals, 32-for-88 (.364).
Personal fouls/disqualifications: 2001-02, 102/0. 2002-03, 34/0. Totals, 136/0.

NBA REGULAR-SEASON RECORD

								REBOUNDS								AVERAGES		
Season Team	G	Min.	FGM	FGA	Pct.	FTM	FTA	Pct.	Off.	Def.	Tot.	Ast.	St.	Blk.	TO	Pts.	RPG	APG	PPG
02-03—Atl.-Minn........	46	688	50	148	.338	37	47	.787	20	51	71	92	27	4	28	147	1.5	2.0	3.2
03-04—Houston..........	26	145	17	36	.472	10	12	.833	3	13	16	17	3	0	7	50	0.6	0.7	1.9
04-05—San Antonio....	48	278	32	77	.416	12	16	.750	4	21	25	33	14	1	14	81	0.5	0.7	1.7
05-06—Cleve.-Seattle..	47	347	29	90	.322	25	41	.610	9	30	39	32	14	1	24	86	0.8	0.7	1.8
Totals	167	1458	128	351	.365	84	116	.724	36	115	151	174	58	6	73	364	0.9	1.0	2.2

Three-point field goals: 2002-03, 10-for-35 (.286). 2003-04, 6-for-10 (.600). 2004-05, 5-for-16 (.313). 2005-06, 3-for-19 (.158). Totals, 24-for-80 (.300).
Personal fouls/disqualifications: 2002-03, 69/0. 2003-04, 15/0. 2004-05, 26/0. 2005-06, 34/0. Totals, 144/0.

NBA PLAYOFF RECORD

								REBOUNDS								AVERAGES		
Season Team	G	Min.	FGM	FGA	Pct.	FTM	FTA	Pct.	Off.	Def.	Tot.	Ast.	St.	Blk.	TO	Pts.	RPG	APG	PPG
02-03—Minnesota.......	4	7	1	2	.500	0	0	...	0	0	0	0	0	0	0	3	0.0	0.0	0.8
03-04—Houston.........	2	5	0	0	...	0	0	...	0	0	0	1	0	0	1	0	0.0	0.5	0.0
Totals	6	12	1	2	.500	0	0	...	0	0	0	1	0	0	1	3	0.0	0.2	0.5

Three-point field goals: 2002-03, 1-for-1 (1.000). Totals, 1-for-1 (1.000).

WILLIAMS, AARON — F — CLIPPERS

PERSONAL: Born October 2, 1971, in Evanston, Ill. ... 6-9/225. (2.06/102.1).
HIGH SCHOOL: Rolling Meadows (Ill.).
COLLEGE: Xavier.
TRANSACTIONS/CAREER NOTES: Not drafted by an NBA franchise. ... Played in Continental Basketball Association with Grand Rapids Hoops (1993-94) and Connecticut Pride (1995-96 and 1996-97). ... Played in Italy (1993-94). ... Signed as free agent by Utah Jazz (November 29, 1993). ... Waived by Jazz (December 27, 1993). ... Signed by Milwaukee Bucks (October 6, 1994). ... Waived by Bucks (November 7, 1994). ... Re-signed as free agent by Bucks (November 9, 1994). ... Waived by Bucks (March 22, 1995). ... Played in Greece (1995-96). ... Signed as free agent by Denver Nuggets (December 22, 1996). ... Waived by Nuggets (January 6, 1997). ... Signed by Vancouver Grizzlies to first of two consecutive 10-day contracts (January 29, 1997). ... Signed by Grizzlies for remainder of sea-

W

son (February 20, 1997). ... Signed as free agent by Seattle SuperSonics (August 11, 1997). ... Signed as free agent by Washington Wizards (August 17, 1999). ... Signed as free agent by New Jersey Nets (August 5, 2000). ... Traded by Nets with C Alonzo Mourning and F Eric Williams and two first round draft picks to Toronto Raptors for F Vince Carter (December 17, 2004). ... Traded by Raptors to New Orleans Hornets for a second-round draft pick in 2006 and 2009. ... Signed as free agent by Los Angeles Clippers (August 1, 2006).

COLLEGIATE RECORD

Season Team	G	Min.	FGM	FGA	Pct.	FTM	FTA	Pct.	Reb.	Ast.	Pts.	AVERAGES RPG	APG	PPG
89-90—Xavier	28	278	27	47	.574	8	20	.400	76	6	62	2.7	0.2	2.2
90-91—Xavier	32	858	237	127	.574	55	77	.714	209	33	309	6.5	1.0	9.7
91-92—Xavier	27	786	148	253	.585	79	113	.699	215	31	375	8.0	1.1	13.9
92-93—Xavier	30	843	127	247	.514	73	94	.777	213	54	327	7.1	1.8	10.9
Totals	117	2765	539	674	.800	215	304	.707	713	124	1073	6.1	1.1	9.2

CBA RECORD

NOTES: CBA All-Rookie second team (1994).

Season Team	G	Min.	FGM	FGA	Pct.	FTM	FTA	Pct.	Reb.	Ast.	Pts.	AVERAGES RPG	APG	PPG
93-94—Grand Rapids	43	863	149	267	.558	81	105	.771	242	38	379	5.6	0.9	8.8
95-96—Connecticut	13	235	51	90	.567	8	16	.500	80	4	110	6.2	0.3	8.5
96-97—Connecticut	25	968	174	316	.551	73	101	.723	247	42	421	9.9	1.7	16.8
Totals	81	2066	374	673	.556	162	222	.730	569	84	910	7.0	1.0	11.2

Three-point field goals: 1993-94, 0-for-2. 1996-97, 0-for-2. Totals, 0-for-4 (.000).
Personal fouls/disqualifications: 1993-94, 106/0. 1995-96, 104/0. 1996-97, 104/0. Totals, 251/0.

ITALIAN LEAGUE RECORD

Season Team	G	Min.	FGM	FGA	Pct.	FTM	FTA	Pct.	Reb.	Ast.	Pts.	AVERAGES RPG	APG	PPG
93-94—Teorematour Milan	6	208	30	62	.484	21	28	.750	71	2	83	11.8	0.3	13.8

Three-point field goals: 1993-94, 2-for-8 (.250). Totals, 2-for-8 (.250).

NBA REGULAR-SEASON RECORD

NOTES: Led NBA with 319 personal fouls (2001).

Season Team	G	Min.	FGM	FGA	Pct.	FTM	FTA	Pct.	REBOUNDS Off.	Def.	Tot.	Ast.	St.	Blk.	TO	Pts.	AVERAGES RPG	APG	PPG
93-94—Utah	6	12	2	8	.250	0	1	.000	1	2	3	1	0	0	1	4	0.5	0.2	0.7
94-95—Milwaukee	15	72	8	24	.333	8	12	.667	5	14	19	0	2	6	7	24	1.3	0.0	1.6
96-97—Denver-Van.	33	563	85	148	.574	33	49	.673	62	81	143	15	16	29	32	203	4.3	0.5	6.2
97-98—Seattle	65	757	115	220	.523	66	85	.776	48	99	147	14	19	38	50	296	2.3	0.2	4.6
98-99—Seattle	40	458	52	123	.423	54	74	.730	54	74	128	22	14	24	30	158	3.2	0.6	4.0
99-00—Washington	81	1545	235	450	.522	146	201	.726	159	250	409	58	41	92	80	616	5.0	0.7	7.6
00-01—New Jersey	82	2336	297	650	.457	244	310	.787	211	379	590	88	59	113	132	838	7.2	1.1	10.2
01-02—New Jersey	82	1546	231	439	.526	130	186	.699	115	224	339	77	29	76	79	592	4.1	0.9	7.2
02-03—New Jersey	81	1101	199	199	.100	182	188	.788	107	194	331	66	27	97	85	500	4.1	1.1	6.2
03-04—New Jersey	72	1337	172	342	.503	105	155	.677	101	193	294	81	34	46	89	450	4.1	1.1	6.3
04-05—N.J.-Tor.	42	315	29	63	.460	15	17	.882	17	43	60	8	5	8	17	73	1.4	0.2	1.7
05-06—Tor.-NO-Okla. City	48	791	91	176	.517	40	58	.690	64	117	181	17	17	21	30	222	3.8	0.4	4.6
Totals	647	11329	1516	3082	.492	943	1278	.738	974	1670	2644	469	263	510	632	3976	4.1	0.7	6.1

Three-point field goals: 1994-95, 0-for-1. 1996-97, 0-for-1. 1997-98, 0-for-1. 1998-99, 0-for-1. 1999-00, 0-for-3. 2000-01, 0-for-2. 2001-02, 0-for-2. 2002-03, 0-for-1. 2003-04, 1-for-3 (.333). Totals, 1-for-15 (.067).
Personal fouls/disqualifications: 1993-94, 4/0. 1994-95, 14/0. 1996-97, 72/1. 1997-98, 119/0. 1998-99, 75/1. 1999-00, 234/3. 2000-01, 319/9. 2001-02, 212/5. 2002-03, 206/5. 2003-04, 187/0. 2004-05, 70/0. 2005-06, 138/0. Totals, 1650/24.

NBA PLAYOFF RECORD

Season Team	G	Min.	FGM	FGA	Pct.	FTM	FTA	Pct.	REBOUNDS Off.	Def.	Tot.	Ast.	St.	Blk.	TO	Pts.	AVERAGES RPG	APG	PPG
97-98—Seattle	3	7	0	3	.000	2	2	1.000	1	0	1	0	0	1	1	2	0.3	0.0	0.7
01-02—New Jersey	20	416	46	96	.479	38	46	.826	24	46	70	16	8	16	23	130	3.5	0.8	6.5
02-03—New Jersey	19	340	50	106	.472	23	31	.742	33	54	87	18	6	17	13	123	4.6	0.9	6.5
03-04—New Jersey	11	149	18	33	.545	6	10	.600	7	15	22	4	0	7	15	42	2.0	0.4	3.8
Totals	53	912	114	238	.479	69	89	.775	65	115	180	38	14	41	52	297	3.4	0.7	5.6

Three-point field goals: 2001-02, 0-for-1. Totals, 0-for-1 (.000).
Personal fouls/disqualifications: 2001-02, 78/5. 2002-03, 54/0. 2003-04, 41/2. Totals, 173/7.

GREEK LEAGUE RECORD

Season Team	G	Min.	FGM	FGA	Pct.	FTM	FTA	Pct.	Reb.	Ast.	Pts.	AVERAGES RPG	APG	PPG
95-96—Ambelokipi	13	...	...	...	...	...	...	...	111	11	178	8.5	0.8	13.7

W

WILLIAMS, ALVIN   G

PERSONAL: Born August 6, 1974, in Philadelphia. ... 6-5/185. (1.96/83.9). ... Full name: Alvin Leon Williams
HIGH SCHOOL: Germantown Academy (Philadelphia).
COLLEGE: Villanova.
TRANSACTIONS/CAREER NOTES: Selected by Portland Trail Blazers in second round (48th pick overall) of 1997 NBA Draft. ... Traded by Trail Blazers with G Kenny Anderson, F Gary Trent and two first-round draft choices to Toronto Raptors for G Damon Stoudamire, F Walt Williams and F Carlos Rogers (February 13, 1998). ... Traded by Raptors with F/C Sean Marks and cash considerations to Boston Celtics for F Danny Fortson and a future draft choice (February 9, 2000); trade later voided because Williams failed physical. ... Released by Raptors (July 25, 2006).

COLLEGIATE RECORD

Season Team	G	Min.	FGM	FGA	Pct.	FTM	FTA	Pct.	Reb.	Ast.	Pts.	AVERAGES RPG	APG	PPG
93-94—Villanova	31	721	79	203	.389	67	96	.698	87	88	245	2.8	2.8	7.9
94-95—Villanova	33	963	79	195	.405	61	82	.744	116	159	234	3.5	4.8	7.1
95-96—Villanova	33	1078	129	284	.454	71	100	.710	117	177	364	3.5	5.4	11.0
96-97—Villanova	34	1163	198	412	.481	121	163	.742	169	129	580	5.0	3.8	17.1
Totals	131	3925	485	1094	.443	320	441	.726	489	553	1423	3.7	4.2	10.9

Three-point field goals: 1993-94, 20-for-51 (.392). 1994-95, 15-for-57 (.263). 1995-96, 35-for-101 (.347). 1996-97, 63-for-171 (.368). Totals, 133-for-380 (.350).

NBA REGULAR-SEASON RECORD

Season Team	G	Min.	FGM	FGA	Pct.	FTM	FTA	Pct.	REBOUNDS Off.	Def.	Tot.	Ast.	St.	Blk.	TO	Pts.	AVERAGES RPG	APG	PPG
97-98—Portland-Tor.	54	1071	125	282	.443	65	90	.722	24	57	81	103	38	3	58	324	1.5	1.9	6.0
98-99—Toronto	50	1051	95	237	.401	44	52	.846	19	63	82	130	51	12	56	248	1.6	2.6	5.0
99-00—Toronto	55	779	114	287	.397	48	65	.738	27	58	85	126	34	11	47	292	1.5	2.3	5.3
00-01—Toronto	82	2394	330	767	.430	109	145	.752	50	162	212	407	123	26	103	802	2.6	5.0	9.8
01-02—Toronto	82	2927	403	971	.415	103	140	.736	58	223	281	468	135	26	150	971	3.4	5.7	11.8
02-03—Toronto	78	2638	396	905	.438	187	239	.782	55	190	245	416	111	21	128	1027	3.1	5.3	13.2
03-04—Toronto	56	1730	201	496	.405	66	85	.776	18	132	150	224	55	10	78	494	2.7	4.0	8.8
05-06—Toronto	1	10	0	3	.000	1	2	.500	0	3	3	0	0	0	0	1	3.0	0.0	1.0
Totals	458	12600	1664	3948	.421	623	818	.762	251	888	1139	1874	547	109	620	4159	2.5	4.1	9.1

Three-point field goals: 1997-98, 9-for-28 (.321). 1998-99, 14-for-42 (.333). 1999-00, 16-for-55 (.291). 2000-01, 33-for-108 (.306). 2001-02, 62-for-193 (.321). 2002-03, 48-for-146 (.329). 2003-04, 26-for-89 (.292). 2005-06, 0-for-2. Totals, 208-for-663 (.314).
Personal fouls/disqualifications: 1997-98, 79/0. 1998-99, 94/1. 1999-00, 78/0. 2000-01, 171/1. 2001-02, 191/1. 2002-03, 170/0. 2003-04, 114/1. Totals, 897/4.

NBA PLAYOFF RECORD

Season Team	G	Min.	FGM	FGA	Pct.	FTM	FTA	Pct.	REBOUNDS Off.	Def.	Tot.	Ast.	St.	Blk.	TO	Pts.	AVERAGES RPG	APG	PPG
99-00—Toronto	1	1	0	0	...	0	0	...	0	0	0	0	0	0	0	0	0.0	0.0	0.0
00-01—Toronto	12	486	69	160	.431	17	25	.680	6	29	35	50	15	8	16	165	2.9	4.2	13.8
01-02—Toronto	5	196	24	75	.320	9	11	.818	2	22	24	28	6	2	8	60	4.8	5.6	12.0
Totals	18	683	93	235	.396	26	36	.722	8	51	59	78	21	10	24	225	3.3	4.3	12.5

Three-point field goals: 2000-01, 10-for-28 (.357). 2001-02, 3-for-14 (.214). Totals, 13-for-42 (.310).
Personal fouls/disqualifications: 2000-01, 34/0. 2001-02, 12/0. Totals, 46/0.

WILLIAMS, DERON   G   JAZZ

PERSONAL: Born July 26, 1984, in Parkersburg, W.Va. ... 6-3/210. (1.91/95.3). ... Full name: Deron Michael Williams
HIGH SCHOOL: The Colony (Texas).
COLLEGE: Illinois.
TRANSACTIONS/CAREER NOTES: Selected after junior season by Utah Jazz in first round (third pick overall) of 2005 NBA Draft.

COLLEGIATE RECORD

NOTES: The SPORTING NEWS All-America second team (2005).

Season Team	G	Min.	FGM	FGA	Pct.	FTM	FTA	Pct.	Reb.	Ast.	Pts.	AVERAGES RPG	APG	PPG
02-03—Illinois	32	868	75	176	.426	24	45	.533	95	145	202	3.0	4.5	6.3
03-04—Illinois	30	1017	147	360	.408	59	75	.787	97	185	420	3.2	6.2	14.0
04-05—Illinois	39	1315	178	411	.433	65	96	.677	142	264	489	3.6	6.8	12.5
Totals	101	3200	400	947	.422	148	216	.685	334	594	1111	3.3	5.9	11.0

Three-point field goals: 2002-03, 28-for-79 (.354). 2003-04, 67-for-170 (.394). 2004-05, 68-for-187 (.364). Totals, 163-for-436 (.374).

NBA REGULAR-SEASON RECORD

HONORS: NBA All-Rookie first team (2006).

Season Team	G	Min.	FGM	FGA	Pct.	FTM	FTA	Pct.	REBOUNDS Off.	Def.	Tot.	Ast.	St.	Blk.	TO	Pts.	AVERAGES RPG	APG	PPG
05-06—Utah	80	2307	339	805	.421	95	135	.704	35	159	194	359	60	17	145	864	2.4	4.5	10.8

Three-point field goals: 2005-06, 91-for-219 (.416). Totals, 91-for-219 (.416).
Personal fouls/disqualifications: 2005-06, 233/3. Totals, 233/3.

WILLIAMS, ERIC   F   SPURS

PERSONAL: Born July 17, 1972, in Newark, N.J. ... 6-8/220. (2.03/99.8). ... Full name: Eric C. Williams
HIGH SCHOOL: M.X. Shabazz (Newark, N.J.).
JUNIOR COLLEGE: Burlington County (N.J.) College, then Vincennes (Ind.) University.
COLLEGE: Providence.
TRANSACTIONS/CAREER NOTES: Selected by Boston Celtics in first round (14th pick overall) of 1995 NBA Draft. ... Traded by Celtics to Denver Nuggets for a second-round draft choice in 1999 and a second-round draft choice in 2001 (August 21, 1997). ... Traded by Nuggets with F Danny Fortson, G Eric Washington and first-round draft choice within the next three years to Celtics for G/F Ron Mercer, F Popeye Jones and C Dwayne Schintzius (August 3, 1999). ... Traded by Celtics with F/C Tony Battie and F Kedrick Brown to Cleveland Cavaliers for G Ricky Davis, F/C Chris Mihm, C Michael Stewart and a second-round draft choice (December 15, 2003). ... Signed as free agent by New Jersey Nets (August 6, 2004). ... Traded by Nets with C Alonzo Mourning, F Aaron Williams and two first round draft picks to Toronto Raptors for F Vince Carter (December 17, 2004). ... Traded by Raptors with F Matt Bonner and a second-round draft choice to San Antonio Spurs for C Rasho Nesterovic (June 21, 2006).

W

COLLEGIATE RECORD

Season Team	G	Min.	FGM	FGA	Pct.	FTM	FTA	Pct.	Reb.	Ast.	Pts.	AVERAGES RPG	APG	PPG
90-91—Burlington County J.C. ...								Did not play.						
91-92—Vincennes.....................	25	...	167	271	.616	103	154	.669	189	...	437	7.6	...	17.5
92-93—Vincennes.....................	35	...	273	485	.563	182	273	.667	323	96	729	9.2	2.7	20.8
93-94—Providence	30	781	166	327	.508	138	209	.660	151	37	470	5.0	1.2	15.7
94-95—Providence	30	1041	184	445	.413	134	195	.687	201	75	531	6.7	2.5	17.7
Junior College Totals.............	60	...	440	756	.582	285	427	.667	512	96	1166	8.5	1.6	19.4
4-Year-College Totals	60	1822	350	772	.453	272	404	.673	352	112	1001	5.9	1.9	16.7

Three-point field goals: 1991-92, 0-for-1. 1992-93, 1-for-2 (.500). 1993-94, 0-for-5. 1994-95, 29-for-78 (.372). Totals, 30-for-86 (.349).

NBA REGULAR-SEASON RECORD

Season Team	G	Min.	FGM	FGA	Pct.	FTM	FTA	Pct.	REBOUNDS Off.	Def.	Tot.	Ast.	St.	Blk.	TO	Pts.	AVERAGES RPG	APG	PPG
95-96—Boston	64	1470	241	546	.441	200	298	.671	92	125	217	70	56	11	88	685	3.4	1.1	10.7
96-97—Boston	72	2435	374	820	.456	328	436	.752	126	203	329	129	72	13	139	1078	4.6	1.8	15.0
97-98—Denver	4	145	24	61	.393	31	45	.689	10	11	21	12	4	0	9	79	5.3	3.0	19.8
98-99—Denver	38	780	80	219	.365	111	139	.799	34	47	81	37	27	8	49	277	2.1	1.0	7.3
99-00—Boston	68	1378	165	386	.427	134	169	.793	55	101	156	93	44	16	66	489	2.3	1.4	7.2
00-01—Boston	81	1745	162	448	.362	165	231	.714	64	143	207	112	64	13	76	535	2.6	1.4	6.6
01-02—Boston	74	1747	144	385	.374	160	219	.731	58	163	221	109	77	8	95	472	3.0	1.5	6.4
02-03—Boston	82	2350	254	575	.442	201	268	.750	143	239	382	140	86	19	97	746	4.7	1.7	9.1
03-04—Boston-Cleve..	71	1886	231	598	.386	215	283	.760	65	221	286	120	70	9	88	712	4.0	1.7	10.0
04-05—N.J.-Toronto ...	55	1322	142	330	.430	112	161	.696	44	128	172	92	38	4	60	424	3.1	1.7	7.7
05-06—Toronto	28	352	29	75	.387	28	38	.737	10	40	50	15	7	2	15	91	1.8	0.5	3.3
Totals	637	15610	1846	4443	.415	1685	2287	.737	701	1421	2122	929	545	103	782	5588	3.3	1.5	8.8

Three-point field goals: 1995-96, 3-for-10 (.300). 1996-97, 2-for-8 (.250). 1998-99, 6-for-26 (.231). 1999-00, 25-for-72 (.347). 2000-01, 46-for-139 (.331). 2001-02, 24-for-86 (.279). 2002-03, 37-for-110 (.336). 2003-04, 35-for-127 (.276). 2004-05, 28-for-73 (.384). 2005-06, 5-for-18 (.278). Totals, 211-for-669 (.315).

Personal fouls/disqualifications: 1995-96, 147/1. 1996-97, 213/0. 1997-98, 9/0. 1998-99, 76/0. 1999-00, 165/3. 2000-01, 179/1. 2001-02, 179/1. 2002-03, 234/0. 2003-04, 180/0. 2004-05, 147/2. 2005-06, 55/0. Totals, 1584/8.

NBA PLAYOFF RECORD

Season Team	G	Min.	FGM	FGA	Pct.	FTM	FTA	Pct.	REBOUNDS Off.	Def.	Tot.	Ast.	St.	Blk.	TO	Pts.	AVERAGES RPG	APG	PPG
01-02—Boston	16	487	47	94	.500	17	23	.739	18	52	70	21	25	4	11	125	4.4	1.3	7.8
02-03—Boston	10	310	33	88	.375	27	34	.794	12	20	32	17	9	0	12	96	3.2	1.7	9.6
Totals	26	797	80	182	.440	44	57	.772	30	72	102	38	34	4	23	221	3.9	1.5	8.5

Three-point field goals: 2001-02, 14-for-30 (.467). 2002-03, 3-for-15 (.200). Totals, 17-for-45 (.378).
Personal fouls/disqualifications: 2001-02, 53/1. 2002-03, 42/2. Totals, 95/3.

WILLIAMS, JASON G HEAT

PERSONAL: Born November 18, 1975, in Belle, W.Va. ... 6-1/190. (1.85/86.2). ... Full name: Jason Chandler Williams
HIGH SCHOOL: Dupont (Belle, W.Va.).
COLLEGE: Marshall (W.Va.), then Florida.
TRANSACTIONS/CAREER NOTES: Selected after junior season by Sacramento Kings in first round (seventh pick overall) of 1998 NBA Draft. ... Traded by Kings with G/F Nick Anderson to Vancouver Grizzlies for G Mike Bibby and G Brent Price (June 27, 2001). ... Grizzlies franchise moved to Memphis for 2001-02 season. ... Traded by Grizzlies with F James Posey and G Andre Emmett to Miami Heat in five-team trade (August 2, 2005).
MISCELLANEOUS: Member of NBA championship team (2006). ... Memphis Grizzlies franchise all-time assist leader—2,041 (2001-02 through 2004-05).

COLLEGIATE RECORD

Season Team	G	Min.	FGM	FGA	Pct.	FTM	FTA	Pct.	Reb.	Ast.	Pts.	AVERAGES RPG	APG	PPG
94-95—Marshall						Did not play—redshirted.								
95-96—Marshall	28	816	144	276	.522	52	70	.743	99	178	375	3.5	6.4	13.4
96-97—Florida						Did not play—transfer student.								
97-98—Florida	20	635	112	254	.441	63	75	.840	59	134	341	3.0	6.7	17.1
Totals	48	1451	256	530	.483	115	145	.793	158	312	716	3.3	6.5	14.9

Three-point field goals: 1995-96, 35-for-92 (.380). 1997-98, 54-for-134 (.403). Totals, 89-for-226 (.394).

NBA REGULAR-SEASON RECORD

HONORS: NBA All-Rookie first team (1999).

Season Team	G	Min.	FGM	FGA	Pct.	FTM	FTA	Pct.	REBOUNDS Off.	Def.	Tot.	Ast.	St.	Blk.	TO	Pts.	AVERAGES RPG	APG	PPG
98-99—Sacramento	50	1805	231	617	.374	79	105	.752	14	139	153	299	95	1	143	641	3.1	6.0	12.8
99-00—Sacramento	81	2760	363	973	.373	128	170	.753	22	208	230	589	117	8	296	999	2.8	7.3	12.3
00-01—Sacramento	77	2290	281	690	.407	60	76	.789	19	166	185	416	94	9	160	720	2.4	5.4	9.4
01-02—Memphis	65	2236	376	985	.382	80	101	.792	22	173	195	519	111	7	214	959	3.0	8.0	14.8
02-03—Memphis	76	2407	333	859	.388	110	131	.840	25	187	212	631	91	10	168	919	2.8	8.3	12.1
03-04—Memphis	72	2115	290	713	.407	82	98	.837	25	122	147	492	92	5	136	782	2.0	6.8	10.9
04-05—Memphis	71	1952	266	644	.413	80	101	.792	19	103	122	399	75	5	130	719	1.7	5.6	10.1
05-06—Miami	59	1874	268	606	.442	85	98	.867	6	133	139	287	53	5	100	728	2.4	4.9	12.3
Totals	551	17439	2408	6087	.396	704	880	.800	152	1231	1383	3632	728	50	1347	6467	2.5	6.6	11.7

Three-point field goals: 1998-99, 100-for-323 (.310). 1999-00, 145-for-505 (.287). 2000-01, 98-for-311 (.315). 2001-02, 127-for-430 (.295). 2002-03, 143-for-404 (.354). 2003-04, 120-for-364 (.330). 2004-05, 107-for-330 (.324). 2005-06, 107-for-288 (.372). Totals, 947-for-2955 (.320).

Personal fouls/disqualifications: 1998-99, 91/0. 1999-00, 140/0. 2000-01, 114/0. 2001-02, 102/0. 2002-03, 130/0. 2003-04, 97/0. 2004-05, 91/0. 2005-06, 101/0. Totals, 866/0.

NBA PLAYOFF RECORD

Season Team	G	Min.	FGM	FGA	Pct.	FTM	FTA	Pct.	REBOUNDS Off.	Def.	Tot.	Ast.	St.	Blk.	TO	Pts.	AVERAGES RPG	APG	PPG
98-99—Sacramento	5	163	16	45	.356	9	9	1.000	2	16	18	20	8	1	13	50	3.6	4.0	10.0
99-00—Sacramento	5	145	18	48	.375	8	10	.800	1	7	8	12	3	0	8	52	1.6	2.4	10.4
00-01—Sacramento	8	191	26	61	.426	7	7	1.000	0	18	18	23	8	0	21	70	2.3	2.9	8.8
03-04—Memphis	4	130	15	46	.326	7	7	1.000	1	8	9	18	2	0	7	43	2.3	4.5	10.8
04-05—Memphis	4	114	28	53	.528	2	2	1.000	1	8	9	21	6	0	8	68	2.3	5.3	17.0
05-06—Miami	23	686	75	185	.405	38	45	.844	3	43	46	90	15	0	36	214	2.0	3.9	9.3
Totals	49	1429	178	438	.406	71	80	.888	8	100	108	184	42	1	93	497	2.2	3.8	10.1

Three-point field goals: 1998-99, 9-for-29 (.310). 1999-00, 8-for-25 (.320). 2000-01, 11-for-30 (.367). 2003-04, 6-for-21 (.286). 2004-05, 10-for-21 (.476). 2005-06, 26-for-95 (.274). Totals, 70-for-221 (.317).

Personal fouls/disqualifications: 1998-99, 15/0. 1999-00, 8/0. 2000-01, 14/0. 2003-04, 10/0. 2004-05, 7/0. 2005-06, 42/0. Totals, 96/0.

WILLIAMS, LOUIS　　　　G　　　　76ERS

PERSONAL: Born October 27, 1986, in Lithonia, Ga. ... 6-2/175. (1.88/79.4).
HIGH SCHOOL: South Gwinnett (Snellville, Ga.).
COLLEGE: Did not attend college.
TRANSACTIONS/CAREER NOTES: Selected out of high school by Philadelphia 76ers in second round (45th pick overall) of 2005 NBA Draft.

NBA REGULAR-SEASON RECORD

Season Team	G	Min.	FGM	FGA	Pct.	FTM	FTA	Pct.	REBOUNDS Off.	Def.	Tot.	Ast.	St.	Blk.	TO	Pts.	AVERAGES RPG	APG	PPG
05-06—Philadelphia	30	145	23	52	.442	8	13	.615	3	16	19	10	5	0	13	56	0.6	0.3	1.9

Three-point field goals: 2005-06, 2-for-9 (.222). Totals, 2-for-9 (.222).
Personal fouls/disqualifications: 2005-06, 13/0. Totals, 13/0.

WILLIAMS, MARVIN　　　　F　　　　HAWKS

PERSONAL: Born June 19, 1986, in Bremerton, Wash. ... 6-9/230. (2.06/104.3). ... Full name: Marvin Gaye Williams
HIGH SCHOOL: Bremerton (Wash.).
COLLEGE: North Carolina.
TRANSACTIONS/CAREER NOTES: Selected after freshman season by Atlanta Hawks in first round (second pick overall) of 2005 Draft.

COLLEGIATE RECORD

NOTES: Member of NCAA Division I championship team (2005).

Season Team	G	Min.	FGM	FGA	Pct.	FTM	FTA	Pct.	Reb.	Ast.	Pts.	AVERAGES RPG	APG	PPG
04-05—North Carolina	36	800	125	247	.506	138	163	.847	236	26	407	6.6	0.7	11.3

Three-point field goals: 2004-05, 19-for-44 (.432). Totals, 19-for-44 (.432).

NBA REGULAR-SEASON RECORD

HONORS: NBA All-Rookie second team (2006).

Season Team	G	Min.	FGM	FGA	Pct.	FTM	FTA	Pct.	REBOUNDS Off.	Def.	Tot.	Ast.	St.	Blk.	TO	Pts.	AVERAGES RPG	APG	PPG
05-06—Atlanta	79	1952	235	531	.443	189	253	.747	122	261	383	63	48	24	83	672	4.8	0.8	8.5

Three-point field goals: 2005-06, 13-for-53 (.245). Totals, 13-for-53 (.245).
Personal fouls/disqualifications: 2005-06, 227/1. Totals, 227/1.

WILLIAMS, MAURICE　　　　G　　　　BUCKS

PERSONAL: Born December 19, 1982, in Jackson, Miss. ... 6-1/185. (1.85/83.9).
HIGH SCHOOL: William B.Murrah (Jackson, Miss.).
COLLEGE: Alabama.
TRANSACTIONS/CAREER NOTES: Selected after sophomore season by Utah Jazz in second round (47th pick overall) of 2003 NBA Draft. ... Signed as free agent by Milwaukee Bucks (August 21, 2004).

COLLEGIATE RECORD

NOTES: The SPORTING NEWS Freshman of the Year (2002).

Season Team	G	Min.	FGM	FGA	Pct.	FTM	FTA	Pct.	Reb.	Ast.	Pts.	AVERAGES RPG	APG	PPG
01-02—Alabama	35	1121	123	327	.376	84	98	.857	137	159	363	3.9	4.5	10.4
02-03—Alabama	29	1038	160	371	.431	98	117	.838	113	112	475	3.9	3.9	16.4
Totals	64	2159	283	698	.405	182	215	.847	250	271	838	3.9	4.2	13.1

Three-point field goals: 2001-02, 33-for-126 (.262). 2002-03, 57-for-180 (.317). Totals, 90-for-306 (.294).

NBA REGULAR-SEASON RECORD

Season Team	G	Min.	FGM	FGA	Pct.	FTM	FTA	Pct.	REBOUNDS Off.	Def.	Tot.	Ast.	St.	Blk.	TO	Pts.	AVERAGES RPG	APG	PPG
03-04—Utah	57	772	115	303	.380	44	56	.786	23	49	72	76	28	2	51	284	1.3	1.3	5.0
04-05—Milwaukee	80	2254	323	737	.438	136	160	.850	50	194	244	484	74	11	196	814	3.1	6.1	10.2
05-06—Milwaukee	58	1531	267	629	.424	96	113	.850	30	113	143	230	52	7	105	703	2.5	4.0	12.1
Totals	195	4557	705	1669	.422	276	329	.839	103	356	459	790	154	20	352	1801	2.4	4.1	9.2

Three-point field goals: 2003-04, 10-for-39 (.256). 2004-05, 32-for-99 (.323). 2005-06, 73-for-191 (.382). Totals, 115-for-329 (.350).
Personal fouls/disqualifications: 2003-04, 87/0. 2004-05, 221/3. 2005-06, 146/0. Totals, 454/3.

NBA PLAYOFF RECORD

Season Team	G	Min.	FGM	FGA	Pct.	FTM	FTA	Pct.	REBOUNDS Off.	Def.	Tot.	Ast.	St.	Blk.	TO	Pts.	AVERAGES RPG	APG	PPG
05-06—Milwaukee	5	75	17	34	.500	0	0	...	0	3	3	10	1	0	6	36	0.6	2.0	7.2

Three-point field goals: 2005-06, 2-for-11 (.182). Totals, 2-for-11 (.182).
Personal fouls/disqualifications: 2005-06, 12/0. Totals, 12/0.

WILLIAMSON, CORLISS   F   KINGS

PERSONAL: Born December 4, 1973, in Russellville, Ark. ... 6-7/245. (2.01/111.1). ... Full name: Corliss Mondari Williamson
HIGH SCHOOL: Russellville (Ark.).
COLLEGE: Arkansas.
TRANSACTIONS/CAREER NOTES: Selected after junior season by Sacramento Kings in first round (13th pick overall) of 1995 NBA Draft. ... Traded by Kings to Toronto Raptors for G/F Doug Christie (September 29, 2000). ... Traded by Raptors with F Tyrone Corbin, F Kornel David and future first-round draft choice to Detroit Pistons for F Jerome Williams and C Eric Montross (February 22, 2001). ... Traded by Pistons to Philadelphia 76ers for F Derrick Coleman and F/C Amal McCaskill (August 4, 2004). ... Traded by 76ers with F Kenny Thomas and C Brian Skinner to Sacramento Kings for Fs Chris Webber, Michael Bradley and Matt Barnes (February 23, 2005).
MISCELLANEOUS: Member of NBA championship team (2004).

COLLEGIATE RECORD

NOTES: Member of NCAA Division I championship team (1994). ... THE SPORTING NEWS All-America first team (1995). ... NCAA Division I Tournament Most Outstanding Player (1994).

Season Team	G	Min.	FGM	FGA	Pct.	FTM	FTA	Pct.	Reb.	Ast.	Pts.	AVERAGES RPG	APG	PPG
92-93—Arkansas	18	454	101	176	.574	61	98	.622	92	30	263	5.1	1.7	14.6
93-94—Arkansas	34	989	273	436	.626	149	213	.700	262	74	695	7.7	2.2	20.4
94-95—Arkansas	39	1208	283	515	.550	203	304	.668	293	89	770	7.5	2.3	19.7
Totals	91	2661	657	1127	.583	413	615	.672	647	193	1728	7.1	2.1	19.0

Three-point field goals: 1994-95, 1-for-6 (.167). Totals, 1-for-6 (.167).

NBA REGULAR-SEASON RECORD

HONORS: NBA Sixth Man Award (2002).

Season Team	G	Min.	FGM	FGA	Pct.	FTM	FTA	Pct.	REBOUNDS Off.	Def.	Tot.	Ast.	St.	Blk.	TO	Pts.	AVERAGES RPG	APG	PPG
95-96—Sacramento	53	609	125	268	.466	47	84	.560	56	58	114	23	11	9	76	297	2.2	0.4	5.6
96-97—Sacramento	79	1992	371	745	.498	173	251	.689	139	187	326	124	60	49	157	915	4.1	1.6	11.6
97-98—Sacramento	79	2819	561	1134	.495	279	443	.630	162	284	446	230	76	48	199	1401	5.6	2.9	17.7
98-99—Sacramento	50	1374	269	555	.485	120	188	.638	85	121	206	66	30	8	75	659	4.1	1.3	13.2
99-00—Sacramento	76	1707	311	622	.500	163	212	.769	122	168	290	82	38	19	110	785	3.8	1.1	10.3
00-01—Tor.-Det.	69	1686	325	647	.502	151	237	.637	110	211	321	61	50	21	110	801	4.7	0.9	11.6
01-02—Detroit	78	1701	411	806	.510	240	298	.805	117	202	319	94	49	26	137	1063	4.1	1.2	13.6
03-04—Detroit	79	1574	304	602	.505	144	197	.731	88	168	256	57	30	20	113	752	3.2	0.7	9.5
04-05—Phila.-Sac.	72	1527	273	584	.467	195	244	.799	104	155	259	78	38	15	86	741	3.6	1.1	10.3
05-06—Sacramento	37	362	43	103	.417	38	49	.776	21	46	67	14	7	4	30	126	1.8	0.4	3.4
Totals	754	17412	3367	6892	.489	1787	2503	.714	1151	1811	2962	933	433	246	1219	8527	3.9	1.2	11.3

Three-point field goals: 1995-96, 0-for-3. 1996-97, 0-for-3. 1997-98, 0-for-9. 1998-99, 1-for-5 (.200). 2000-01, 0-for-2. 2001-02, 1-for-5 (.200). 2002-03, 2-for-11 (.182). 2004-05, 0-for-0. 2005-06, 2-for-2 (1.000). Totals, 6-for-42 (.143).
Personal fouls/disqualifications: 1995-96, 115/2. 1996-97, 263/4. 1997-98, 252/4. 1998-99, 118/1. 1999-00, 192/0. 2000-01, 185/0. 2001-02, 226/1. 2002-03, 238/1. 2003-04, 204/2. 2004-05, 218/3. 2005-06, 56/0. Totals, 2067/18.

NBA PLAYOFF RECORD

Season Team	G	Min.	FGM	FGA	Pct.	FTM	FTA	Pct.	REBOUNDS Off.	Def.	Tot.	Ast.	St.	Blk.	TO	Pts.	AVERAGES RPG	APG	PPG
95-96—Sacramento	1	2	0	1	.000	1	1	1.000	0	0	0	0	0	0	0	1	0.0	0.0	1.0
98-99—Sacramento	5	130	23	40	.575	7	10	.700	7	9	16	6	2	1	6	53	3.2	1.2	10.6
99-00—Sacramento	5	87	11	16	.688	11	12	.917	4	11	15	1	1	0	5	33	3.0	0.2	6.6
01-02—Detroit	10	269	52	112	.464	29	38	.763	19	34	53	10	9	2	22	133	5.3	1.0	13.3
02-03—Detroit	15	233	37	90	.411	43	58	.741	13	20	33	15	4	3	20	117	2.2	1.0	7.8
03-04—Detroit	22	327	44	121	.364	38	47	.809	20	29	49	15	6	3	24	126	2.2	0.7	5.7
04-05—Sacramento	5	40	6	16	.375	14	18	.778	4	2	6	3	1	2	4	26	1.2	0.6	5.2
05-06—Sacramento	3	11	2	5	.400	3	3	1.000	0	1	1	0	0	0	0	7	0.3	0.0	2.3
Totals	66	1099	175	401	.436	146	187	.781	67	106	173	50	23	11	81	496	2.6	0.8	7.5

Three-point field goals: 2001-02, 0-for-1. 2003-04, 0-for-1. 2004-05, 0-for-1. Totals, 0-for-4 (.000).
Personal fouls/disqualifications: 1998-99, 13/0. 1999-00, 8/0. 2001-02, 31/0. 2002-03, 38/1. 2003-04, 59/0. 2004-05, 11/0. 2005-06, 3/0. Totals, 163/1.

WOODS, LOREN   C   KINGS

PERSONAL: Born June 21, 1978, in St. Louis. ... 7-1/245. (2.16/111.1). ... Full name: Loren Gerard Woods
HIGH SCHOOL: Cardinal Ritter (St. Louis).
COLLEGE: Wake Forest, then Arizona.
TRANSACTIONS/CAREER NOTES: Selected by Minnesota Timberwolves in second round (46th pick overall) of 2001 NBA Draft. ... Signed as free agent by Miami Heat (August 8, 2003) ... Selected by Charlotte Bobcats from Heat in NBA Expansion Draft (June 22, 2004). ... Signed as free agent by Toronto Raptors (August 18, 2004). ... Signed as free agent by Sacramento Kings (August 15, 2006).

COLLEGIATE RECORD

NOTES: Shares NCAA Division I single-game record for most blocked shots—14 (Feb. 3, 2000, vs. Oregon).

Season Team	G	Min.	FGM	FGA	Pct.	FTM	FTA	Pct.	Reb.	Ast.	Pts.	RPG	APG	PPG
96-97—Wake Forest	30	525	71	147	.483	63	93	.677	157	16	205	5.2	0.5	6.8
97-98—Wake Forest	22	554	63	157	.401	67	100	.670	157	19	194	7.1	0.9	8.8
98-99—Arizona						Did not play—transfer student.								
99-00—Arizona	26	820	154	286	.538	97	128	.758	194	38	405	7.5	1.5	15.6
00-01—Arizona	29	879	133	264	.504	117	141	.830	189	62	384	6.5	2.1	13.2
Totals	107	2778	421	854	.493	344	462	.745	697	135	1188	6.5	1.3	11.1

Three-point field goals: 1997-98, 1-for-4 (.250). 1999-00, 0-for-2. 2000-01, 1-for-3 (.333). Totals, 2-for-9 (.222).
Personal fouls/disqualifications: 1996-97, 45/0. 1997-98, 50/0. 1999-00, 50/0. 2000-01, 64/0. Totals, 209/0.

NBA REGULAR-SEASON RECORD

Season Team	G	Min.	FGM	FGA	Pct.	FTM	FTA	Pct.	REBOUNDS Off.	Def.	Tot.	Ast.	St.	Blk.	TO	Pts.	RPG	APG	PPG
01-02—Minnesota	60	516	33	96	.344	44	60	.733	46	76	122	22	17	34	36	110	2.0	0.4	1.8
02-03—Minnesota	38	353	29	76	.382	21	27	.778	27	68	95	19	10	13	23	80	2.5	0.5	2.1
03-04—Miami	38	506	44	96	.458	33	55	.600	65	69	134	10	11	19	26	121	3.5	0.3	3.2
04-05—Toronto	45	712	71	164	.433	34	59	.576	81	139	220	17	8	39	37	176	4.9	0.4	3.9
05-06—Toronto	27	324	28	59	.475	6	14	.429	44	66	110	4	9	23	16	62	4.1	0.1	2.3
Totals	208	2411	205	491	.418	138	215	.642	263	418	681	72	55	128	138	549	3.3	0.3	2.6

Three-point field goals: 2001-02, 0-for-2. 2002-03, 1-for-3 (.333). 2004-05, 0-for-1. 2005-06, 0-for-1. Totals, 1-for-7 (.143).
Personal fouls/disqualifications: 2001-02, 60/0. 2002-03, 37/0. 2003-04, 52/0. 2004-05, 78/0. 2005-06, 49/0. Totals, 276/0.

NBA PLAYOFF RECORD

Season Team	G	Min.	FGM	FGA	Pct.	FTM	FTA	Pct.	REBOUNDS Off.	Def.	Tot.	Ast.	St.	Blk.	TO	Pts.	RPG	APG	PPG
02-03—Minnesota	2	2	1	3	.333	0	0	...	1	0	1	0	0	0	0	2	0.5	0.0	1.0
03-04—Miami	1	2	0	0	...	0	0	...	0	0	0	0	0	0	0	0	0.0	0.0	0.0
Totals	3	4	1	3	.333	0	0	...	1	0	1	0	0	0	0	2	0.3	0.0	0.7

WOODS, QYNTEL   F/G   KNICKS

PERSONAL: Born February 16, 1981, in Memphis. ... 6-8/221. (2.03/100.2). ... Full name: Qyntel Deon Woods
HIGH SCHOOL: Carver (Memphis).
JUNIOR COLLEGE: Moberly (Mo.) Area Junior College, then Northeast Mississippi C.C.
TRANSACTIONS/CAREER NOTES: Selected after sophomore season by Portland Trail Blazers in first round (21st pick overall) of 2002 NBA Draft. ... Waived by Trail Blazers (January 21, 2005). ... Signed as free agent by Miami Heat (January 26, 2005). ... Traded by Heat with two second-round draft picks and draft rights to Albert Miralles to Boston Celtics in five-team deal (August 2, 2005). ... Waived by Celtics (October 4, 2005). ... Signed by New York Knicks (December 6, 2005).

COLLEGIATE RECORD

Season Team	G	Min.	FGM	FGA	Pct.	FTM	FTA	Pct.	Reb.	Ast.	Pts.	RPG	APG	PPG
99-00—Moberly Area J.C.						Did not play—redshirted.								
00-01—Moberly Area J.C.	32	867	256	534	.479	205	262	.782	264	66	749	8.3	2.1	23.4
01-02—NE Mississippi CC	23	722	239	495	.483	230	285	.807	229	42	742	10.0	1.8	32.3
Totals	55	1589	495	1029	.481	435	547	.795	493	108	1491	9.0	2.0	27.1

Three-point field goals: 2000-01, 32-for-111 (.288). 2001-02, 34-for-113 (.301). Totals, 66-for-224 (.295).

NBA REGULAR-SEASON RECORD

Season Team	G	Min.	FGM	FGA	Pct.	FTM	FTA	Pct.	REBOUNDS Off.	Def.	Tot.	Ast.	St.	Blk.	TO	Pts.	RPG	APG	PPG
02-03—Portland	53	334	59	118	.500	7	20	.350	15	38	53	12	15	1	23	128	1.0	0.2	2.4
03-04—Portland	62	673	88	237	.371	38	60	.633	46	90	136	46	20	14	52	224	2.2	0.7	3.6
04-05—Miami	3	40	5	12	.417	0	0	...	2	4	6	0	4	0	2	10	2.0	0.0	3.3
05-06—New York	49	1013	129	254	.508	49	76	.645	44	146	190	47	32	13	61	329	3.9	1.0	6.7
Totals	167	2060	281	621	.452	94	156	.603	107	278	385	105	71	28	138	691	2.3	0.6	4.1

Three-point field goals: 2002-03, 3-for-9 (.333). 2003-04, 10-for-29 (.345). 2005-06, 22-for-60 (.367). Totals, 35-for-98 (.357).
Personal fouls/disqualifications: 2002-03, 36/1. 2003-04, 88/1. 2004-05, 6/0. 2005-06, 96/1. Totals, 226/3.

NBA PLAYOFF RECORD

Season Team	G	Min.	FGM	FGA	Pct.	FTM	FTA	Pct.	REBOUNDS Off.	Def.	Tot.	Ast.	St.	Blk.	TO	Pts.	RPG	APG	PPG
02-03—Portland	4	18	3	9	.333	1	2	.500	1	1	2	0	0	0	1	7	0.5	0.0	1.8

Three-point field goals: 2002-03, 0-for-1. Totals, 0-for-1 (.000).
Personal fouls/disqualifications: 2002-03, 3/0. Totals, 3/0.

WRIGHT, ANTOINE   F/G   NETS

PERSONAL: Born February 6, 1984, in West Covina, Calif. ... 6-7/210. (2.01/95.3). ... Full name: Antoine Domonick Wright
HIGH SCHOOL: Lawrence Academy (Groton, Mass.) .
COLLEGE: Texas A&M.
TRANSACTIONS/CAREER NOTES: Selected after junior season by New Jersey Nets in first round (15th pick overall) of 2005 NBA draft.

COLLEGIATE RECORD

Season Team	G	Min.	FGM	FGA	Pct.	FTM	FTA	Pct.	Reb.	Ast.	Pts.	RPG	APG	PPG
02-03—Texas A&M	28	889	144	396	.364	55	90	.611	186	50	406	6.6	1.8	14.5

W

Season Team	G	Min.	FGM	FGA	Pct.	FTM	FTA	Pct.	Reb.	Ast.	Pts.	RPG	APG	PPG
03-04—Texas A&M	28	852	130	353	.368	72	115	.626	116	65	379	4.1	2.3	13.5
04-05—Texas A&M	31	1052	193	385	.501	96	139	.691	185	69	553	6.0	2.2	17.8
Totals	87	2793	467	1134	.412	223	344	.648	487	184	1338	5.6	2.1	15.4

Three-point field goals: 2002-03, 63-for-165 (.382). 2003-04, 47-for-158 (.297). 2004-05, 71-for-159 (.447). Totals, 181-for-482 (.376).

NBA REGULAR-SEASON RECORD

Season Team	G	Min.	FGM	FGA	Pct.	FTM	FTA	Pct.	Off.	Def.	Tot.	Ast.	St.	Blk.	TO	Pts.	RPG	APG	PPG
05-06—New Jersey	39	370	29	81	.358	11	22	.500	8	22	30	12	4	3	21	70	0.8	0.3	1.8

Three-point field goals: 2005-06, 1-for-15 (.067). Totals, 1-for-15 (.067).
Personal fouls/disqualifications: 2005-06, 42/0. Totals, 42/0.

NBA PLAYOFF RECORD

Season Team	G	Min.	FGM	FGA	Pct.	FTM	FTA	Pct.	Off.	Def.	Tot.	Ast.	St.	Blk.	TO	Pts.	RPG	APG	PPG
05-06—New Jersey	5	10	1	4	.250	2	3	.667	0	0	0	0	0	0	0	4	0.0	0.0	0.8

WRIGHT, BRACEY — G — TIMBERWOLVES

PERSONAL: Born July 1, 1984, in The Colony, Texas. ... 6-3/210. (1.91/95.3).
HIGH SCHOOL: The Colony (Texas).
COLLEGE: Indiana.
TRANSACTIONS/CAREER NOTES: Selected after junior season by Minnesota Timberwolves in second round (47th pick overall) of 2005 NBA Draft.

COLLEGIATE RECORD

Season Team	G	Min.	FGM	FGA	Pct.	FTM	FTA	Pct.	Reb.	Ast.	Pts.	RPG	APG	PPG
02-03—Indiana	30	1007	157	363	.433	106	141	.752	151	64	486	5.0	2.1	16.2
03-04—Indiana	29	1111	162	433	.374	142	180	.789	157	70	536	5.4	2.4	18.5
04-05—Indiana	26	917	150	363	.413	126	161	.783	125	70	476	4.8	2.7	18.3
Totals	85	3035	469	1159	.405	374	482	.776	433	204	1498	5.1	2.4	17.6

Three-point field goals: 2002-03, 66-for-176 (.375). 2003-04, 70-for-204 (.343). 2004-05, 50-for-152 (.329). Totals, 186-for-532 (.350).

NBA REGULAR-SEASON RECORD

Season Team	G	Min.	FGM	FGA	Pct.	FTM	FTA	Pct.	Off.	Def.	Tot.	Ast.	St.	Blk.	TO	Pts.	RPG	APG	PPG
05-06—Minnesota	7	135	21	51	.412	14	16	.875	3	15	18	5	1	0	8	62	2.6	0.7	8.9

Three-point field goals: 2005-06, 6-for-17 (.353). Totals, 6-for-17 (.353).
Personal fouls/disqualifications: 2005-06, 8/0. Totals, 8/0.

NBA DEVELOPMENT LEAGUE RECORD

Season Team	G	Min.	FGM	FGA	Pct.	FTM	FTA	Pct.	Reb.	Ast.	Pts.	RPG	APG	PPG
05-06—Florida	30	1127	218	473	.461	176	220	.800	117	124	659	3.9	4.1	22.0

Three-point field goals: 2005-06, 47-for-110 (.427). Totals, 47-for-110 (.427).

WRIGHT, DORELL — F — HEAT

PERSONAL: Born December 2, 1985, in Los Angeles. ... 6-7/210. (2.01/95.3).
HIGH SCHOOL: Leuzinger (Lawndale, Calif.), then South Kent Prep (Conn.).
COLLEGE: Did not attend college.
TRANSACTIONS/CAREER NOTES: Selected out of high school by Miami Heat in first round (19th pick overall) of 2004 NBA Draft.

NBA REGULAR-SEASON RECORD

Season Team	G	Min.	FGM	FGA	Pct.	FTM	FTA	Pct.	Off.	Def.	Tot.	Ast.	St.	Blk.	TO	Pts.	RPG	APG	PPG
04-05—Miami	3	27	3	11	.273	1	1	1.000	0	1	1	3	4	0	3	7	0.3	1.0	2.3
05-06—Miami	20	132	20	43	.465	15	17	.882	2	30	32	8	3	1	14	58	1.6	0.4	2.9
Totals	23	159	23	54	.426	16	18	.889	2	31	33	11	7	1	17	65	1.4	0.5	2.8

Three-point field goals: 2004-05, 0-for-4. 2005-06, 3-for-6 (.500). Totals, 3-for-10 (.300).
Personal fouls/disqualifications: 2004-05, 2/0. 2005-06, 12/0. Totals, 14/0.

NBA DEVELOPMENT LEAGUE RECORD

Season Team	G	Min.	FGM	FGA	Pct.	FTM	FTA	Pct.	Reb.	Ast.	Pts.	RPG	APG	PPG
05-06—Florida	6	124	33	64	.516	6	6	1.000	23	11	73	3.8	1.8	12.2

Three-point field goals: 2005-06, 1-for-3 (.333). Totals, 1-for-3 (.333).

WRIGHT, LORENZEN — F/C

PERSONAL: Born November 4, 1975, in Memphis, Tenn. ... 6-11/240. (2.11/108.9). ... Full name: Lorenzen Vern-Gagne Wright
HIGH SCHOOL: Booker T. Washington (Memphis, Tenn.).
COLLEGE: Memphis.
TRANSACTIONS/CAREER NOTES: Selected after sophomore season by Los Angeles Clippers in first round (seventh pick

W

overall) of 1996 NBA Draft. ... Traded by Clippers to Atlanta Hawks for two future first-round draft choices (August 8, 1999). ... Traded by Hawks with G Brevin Knight and draft rights to Pau Gasol to Memphis Grizzlies for F Shareef Abdur-Rahim and draft rights to G Jamaal Tinsley (July 19, 2001).

COLLEGIATE RECORD

Season Team	G	Min.	FGM	FGA	Pct.	FTM	FTA	Pct.	Reb.	Ast.	Pts.	AVERAGES		
												RPG	APG	PPG
94-95—Memphis	34	1170	198	353	.561	107	171	.626	345	50	503	10.1	1.5	14.8
95-96—Memphis	30	1058	207	382	.542	109	169	.645	313	35	523	10.4	1.2	17.4
Totals	64	2228	405	735	.551	216	340	.635	658	85	1026	10.3	1.3	16.0

Three-point field goals: 1994-95, 0-for-1. 1995-96, 0-for-1. Totals, 0-for-2 (.000).

NBA REGULAR-SEASON RECORD

Season Team	G	Min.	FGM	FGA	Pct.	FTM	FTA	Pct.	REBOUNDS			Ast.	St.	Blk.	TO	Pts.	AVERAGES		
									Off.	Def.	Tot.						RPG	APG	PPG
96-97—L.A. Clippers	77	1936	236	491	.481	88	150	.587	206	265	471	49	48	60	79	561	6.1	0.6	7.3
97-98—L.A. Clippers	69	2067	241	542	.445	141	214	.659	180	426	606	55	55	87	81	623	8.8	0.8	9.0
98-99—L.A. Clippers	48	1135	119	260	.458	81	117	.692	142	219	361	33	26	36	48	319	7.5	0.7	6.6
99-00—Atlanta	75	1205	180	361	.499	87	135	.644	117	188	305	21	29	40	66	448	4.1	0.3	6.0
00-01—Atlanta	71	1988	363	811	.448	155	216	.718	180	355	535	87	42	63	125	881	7.5	1.2	12.4
01-02—Memphis	43	1251	223	486	.459	70	123	.569	130	275	405	44	30	23	72	516	9.4	1.0	12.0
02-03—Memphis	70	1982	325	716	.454	147	223	.659	170	358	528	80	51	54	110	797	7.5	1.1	11.4
03-04—Memphis	65	1674	257	586	.439	96	131	.733	144	301	445	71	45	58	77	610	6.8	1.1	9.4
04-05—Memphis	80	2287	320	683	.469	131	198	.662	177	436	613	87	58	69	100	771	7.7	1.1	9.6
05-06—Memphis	78	1689	194	406	.478	66	117	.564	142	253	395	48	52	46	67	454	5.1	0.6	5.8
Totals	676	17214	2458	5342	.460	1062	1624	.654	1588	3076	4664	575	436	536	825	5980	6.9	0.9	8.8

Three-point field goals: 1996-97, 1-for-4 (.250). 1997-98, 0-for-2. 1998-99, 0-for-1. 1999-00, 1-for-3 (.333). 2000-01, 0-for-2. 2001-02, 0-for-2. 2002-03, 0-for-5. 2003-04, 0-for-5. 2004-05, 0-for-3. 2005-06, 0-for-2. Totals, 2-for-29 (.069).

Personal fouls/disqualifications: 1996-97, 211/2. 1997-98, 237/2. 1998-99, 162/2. 1999-00, 203/3. 2000-01, 232/2. 2001-02, 126/0. 2002-03, 209/7. 2003-04, 192/4. 2004-05, 251/1. 2005-06, 201/0. Totals, 2024/23.

NBA PLAYOFF RECORD

Season Team	G	Min.	FGM	FGA	Pct.	FTM	FTA	Pct.	REBOUNDS			Ast.	St.	Blk.	TO	Pts.	AVERAGES		
									Off.	Def.	Tot.						RPG	APG	PPG
96-97—L.A. Clippers	3	92	13	32	.406	5	5	1.000	7	15	22	2	3	2	1	31	7.3	0.7	10.3
03-04—Memphis	4	100	10	23	.435	2	6	.333	5	12	17	2	4	2	5	22	4.3	0.5	5.5
04-05—Memphis	4	85	16	28	.571	1	2	.500	6	14	20	9	1	1	2	33	5.0	2.3	8.2
05-06—Memphis	4	86	11	18	.611	7	10	.700	11	9	20	3	0	4	5	29	5.0	0.8	7.3
Totals	15	363	50	101	.495	15	23	.652	29	50	79	16	8	9	13	115	5.3	1.1	7.7

Personal fouls/disqualifications: 1996-97, 6/0. 2003-04, 15/0. 2004-05, 10/0. 2005-06, 9/0. Totals, 40/0.

YAO, MING   C   ROCKETS

PERSONAL: Born September 12, 1980, in Shanghai, China. ... 7-5/296. (2.26/134.3).
TRANSACTIONS/CAREER NOTES: Played in China (1997-2002). ... Selected by Houston Rockets in first round (first pick overall) of 2002 NBA Draft.
MISCELLANEOUS: Member of Chinese Olympic team (2000, 2004).

CHINESE LEAGUE RECORD

Season Team	G	Min.	FGM	FGA	Pct.	FTM	FTA	Pct.	Reb.	Ast.	Pts.	AVERAGES		
												RPG	APG	PPG
97-98—Shanghai	21	...	91	148	.615	32	66	.485	175	13	214	8.3	0.6	10.2
98-99—Shanghai	12	...	100	171	.585	51	73	.699	155	7	251	12.9	0.6	20.9
99-00—Shanghai	33	...	285	497	.573	127	186	.683	480	57	703	14.5	1.7	21.3
00-01—Shanghai	22	...	226	340	.665	139	174	.799	426	48	596	19.4	2.2	27.1
01-02—Shanghai	34	...	421	595	.708	255	336	.759	645	98	1107	19.0	2.9	32.6
Totals	122	...	1123	1751	.641	604	835	.723	1881	223	2871	15.4	1.8	23.5

Three-point field goals: 1999-00, 2-for-10 (.200). 2000-01, 5-for-14 (.357). 2001-02, 10-for-25 (.400). Totals, 17-for-49 (.347).

NBA REGULAR-SEASON RECORD

HONORS: All-NBA third team (2004, 2006). ... NBA All-Rookie first team (2003).

Season Team	G	Min.	FGM	FGA	Pct.	FTM	FTA	Pct.	REBOUNDS			Ast.	St.	Blk.	TO	Pts.	AVERAGES		
									Off.	Def.	Tot.						RPG	APG	PPG
02-03—Houston	82	2382	401	805	.498	301	371	.811	196	479	675	137	31	147	173	1104	8.2	1.7	13.5
03-04—Houston	82	2692	535	1025	.522	361	446	.809	197	538	735	122	22	156	204	1431	9.0	1.5	17.5
04-05—Houston	80	2447	538	975	.552	389	497	.783	208	461	669	61	34	160	196	1465	8.4	0.8	18.3
05-06—Houston	57	1949	467	900	.519	347	395	.853	148	433	581	85	30	94	147	1271	10.2	1.5	22.3
Totals	301	9470	1941	3705	.524	1388	1709	.812	749	1911	2660	405	117	557	720	5271	8.8	1.3	17.5

Three-point field goals: 2002-03, 1-for-2 (.500). 2003-04, 0-for-2. 2005-06, 0-for-1. Totals, 1-for-5 (.200).
Personal fouls/disqualifications: 2002-03, 230/1. 2003-04, 273/4. 2004-05, 298/8. 2005-06, 195/4. Totals, 996/17.

NBA PLAYOFF RECORD

Season Team	G	Min.	FGM	FGA	Pct.	FTM	FTA	Pct.	REBOUNDS			Ast.	St.	Blk.	TO	Pts.	AVERAGES		
									Off.	Def.	Tot.						RPG	APG	PPG
03-04—Houston	5	185	31	68	.456	13	17	.765	11	26	37	9	2	7	13	75	7.4	1.8	15.0
04-05—Houston	7	220	55	84	.655	40	55	.727	23	31	54	5	2	19	19	150	7.7	0.7	21.4
Totals	12	405	86	152	.566	53	72	.736	34	57	91	14	4	26	32	225	7.6	1.2	18.8

Personal fouls/disqualifications: 2003-04, 20/2. 2004-05, 31/1. Totals, 51/3.

NBA ALL-STAR GAME RECORD

Season Team	Min.	FGM	FGA	Pct.	FTM	FTA	Pct.	REBOUNDS Off.	Def.	Tot.	Ast.	PF	Dq.	St.	Blk.	TO	Pts.
2003—Houston	17	1	1	1.000	0	0	...	0	2	2	0	1	0	0	0	0	2
2004—Houston	19	8	14	.571	0	0	...	2	2	4	1	2	0	0	0	0	16
2005—Houston	22	5	9	.556	1	2	.500	3	5	8	5	1	0	0	1	1	11
2006—Houston	19	2	5	.400	1	2	.500	0	2	2	1	2	0	1	0	0	5
Totals	77	16	29	.552	2	4	.500	5	11	16	7	6	0	1	1	1	34

Three-point field goals: 2004, 0-for-2. Totals, 0-for-2 (.000).

ZIMMERMAN, DERRICK   G

PERSONAL: Born December 2, 1981, in Monroe, La. ... 6-3/195. (1.91/88.5).
HIGH SCHOOL: Wossman (Monroe, La.).
COLLEGE: Mississippi State.
TRANSACTIONS/CAREER NOTES: Selected by Golden State Warriors in second round (40th pick overall) of 2003 NBA Draft. ... Played in NBA Development League (2003-06). ... Waived by Warriors (October 7, 2003). ... Signed by Detroit Pistons (October 11, 2003). ... Waived by Pistons (October 22, 2003). ... Signed by Houston Rockets (October 4, 2004). ... Waived by Rockets (October 28, 2004). ... Signed by New Jersey Nets (October 4, 2005).

COLLEGIATE RECORD

Season Team	G	Min.	FGM	FGA	Pct.	FTM	FTA	Pct.	Reb.	Ast.	Pts.	AVERAGES RPG	APG	PPG
99-00—Mississippi State	30	495	49	124	.395	23	38	.605	62	43	130	2.1	1.4	4.3
00-01—Mississippi State	31	640	53	115	.461	32	56	.571	85	89	142	2.7	2.9	4.6
01-02—Mississippi State	35	1143	116	218	.532	80	139	.576	141	210	322	4.0	6.0	9.2
02-03—Mississippi State	31	1024	99	208	.476	63	97	.649	130	171	276	4.2	5.5	8.9
Totals	127	3302	317	665	.477	198	330	.600	418	513	870	3.3	4.0	6.9

Three-point field goals: 1999-00, 9-for-32 (.281). 2000-01, 4-for-24 (.167). 2001-02, 10-for-34 (.294). 2002-03, 15-for-52 (.288). Totals, 38-for-142 (.268).

NBA DEVELOPMENT LEAGUE RECORD

Season Team	G	Min.	FGM	FGA	Pct.	FTM	FTA	Pct.	Reb.	Ast.	Pts.	AVERAGES RPG	APG	PPG
03-04—Columbus	45	1243	127	280	.454	68	112	.607	215	238	327	4.8	5.3	7.3
04-05—Columbus	48	1442	164	350	.469	70	126	.556	207	271	401	4.3	5.6	8.4
05-06—Austin	45	1642	156	330	.473	69	128	.539	214	290	382	4.8	6.4	8.5
Totals	138	4327	447	960	.466	207	366	.566	636	799	1110	4.6	5.8	8.0

Three-point field goals: 2003-04, 5-for-20 (.250). 2004-05, 3-for-8 (.375). 2005-06, 1-for-21 (.048). Totals, 9-for-49 (.184).

NBA REGULAR-SEASON RECORD

Season Team	G	Min.	FGM	FGA	Pct.	FTM	FTA	Pct.	REBOUNDS Off.	Def.	Tot.	Ast.	PF	Dq.	St.	Blk.	TO	Pts.	AVERAGES RPG	APG	PPG
05-06—New Jersey	2	32	2	3	.667	0	0	...	1	3	4	7	0	0	4		4		2.0	3.5	2.0

Personal fouls/disqualifications: 2005-06, 4/0. Totals, 4/0.

Z

PROMISING NEWCOMERS

ADAMS, HASSAN   G   NETS

PERSONAL: Born June 20, 1984, in Inglewood, Calif. ... 6-4/220. (1.93/99.8). ... Full name: Hassan Olawale Adams
HIGH SCHOOL: Westchester (Los Angeles).
COLLEGE: Arizona.
TRANSACTIONS/CAREER NOTES: Selected by New Jersey Nets in second round (54th pick overall) of 2006 NBA Draft.

COLLEGIATE RECORD

Season Team	G	Min.	FGM	FGA	Pct.	FTM	FTA	Pct.	Reb.	Ast.	Pts.	AVERAGES RPG	APG	PPG
02-03—Arizona	32	572	118	241	.490	48	61	.787	110	18	291	3.4	0.6	9.1
03-04—Arizona	30	915	200	369	.542	77	105	.733	219	47	515	7.3	1.6	17.2
04-05—Arizona	37	1091	198	403	.491	60	84	.714	222	104	469	6.0	2.8	12.7
05-06—Arizona	31	1031	234	490	.478	58	95	.611	155	90	543	5.0	2.9	17.5
Totals	130	3609	750	1503	.499	243	345	.704	706	259	1818	5.4	2.0	14.0

Three-point field goals: 2002-03, 7-for-34 (.206). 2003-04, 38-for-99 (.384). 2004-05, 13-for-43 (.302). 2005-06, 17-for-65 (.262). Totals, 75-for-241 (.311).

AGER, MAURICE   G   MAVERICKS

PERSONAL: Born February 9, 1984, in Detroit. ... 6-5/202. (1.96/91.6). ... Full name: Maurice Darnell Ager
HIGH SCHOOL: Crocket (Detroit).
COLLEGE: Michigan State.
TRANSACTIONS/CAREER NOTES: Selected by Dallas Mavericks in first round (28th pick overall) of 2006 NBA Draft.

COLLEGIATE RECORD

Season Team	G	Min.	FGM	FGA	Pct.	FTM	FTA	Pct.	Reb.	Ast.	Pts.	AVERAGES RPG	APG	PPG
02-03—Michigan State	27	463	60	150	.400	31	40	.775	61	17	180	2.3	0.6	6.7
03-04—Michigan State	30	676	87	225	.387	43	61	.705	96	20	254	3.2	0.7	8.5
04-05—Michigan State	33	867	150	315	.476	111	135	.822	128	60	464	3.9	1.8	14.1
05-06—Michigan State	34	1170	226	495	.457	121	159	.761	139	84	656	4.1	2.5	19.3
Totals	124	3176	523	1185	.441	306	395	.775	424	181	1554	3.4	1.5	12.5

Three-point field goals: 2002-03, 29-for-73 (.397). 2003-04, 37-for-106 (.349). 2004-05, 5-for-132 (.402). 2005-06, 83-for-221 (.376). Totals, 202-for-532 (.380).

ALDRIDGE, LAMARCUS   F   TRAIL BLAZERS

PERSONAL: Born July 19, 1985, in Dallas. ... 6-11/240. (2.11/108.9). ... Full name: LaMarcus Nurae Aldridge
HIGH SCHOOL: Seagoville (Dallas).
COLLEGE: Texas.
TRANSACTIONS/CAREER NOTES: Selected after sophomore season by Chicago Bulls in first round (second pick overall) of 2006 NBA Draft. ... Draft rights traded by Bulls with conditional second-round draft pick to Portland Trail Blazers for draft rights to F Tyrus Thomas and F Viktor Khryapa (June 28, 2006).

COLLEGIATE RECORD

Season Team	G	Min.	FGM	FGA	Pct.	FTM	FTA	Pct.	Reb.	Ast.	Pts.	AVERAGES RPG	APG	PPG
04-05—Texas	16	355	57	86	.663	44	67	.657	95	14	158	5.9	0.9	9.9
05-06—Texas	37	1247	219	385	.569	117	181	.646	339	20	555	9.2	0.5	15.0
Totals	53	1602	276	471	.586	161	248	.649	434	34	713	8.2	0.6	13.5

ARMSTRONG, HILTON   F/C   HORNETS

PERSONAL: Born November 11, 1984, in Peekskill, N.Y. ... 6-11/235. (2.11/106.6). ... Full name: Hilton J. Armstrong
HIGH SCHOOL: Peekskill (N.Y.).
COLLEGE: Connecticut.
TRANSACTIONS/CAREER NOTES: Selected by New Orleans/Oklahoma City Hornets in first round (12th pick overall) of 2006 NBA Draft.

COLLEGIATE RECORD

NOTES: Member of NCAA Division I championship team (2004).

Season Team	G	Min.	FGM	FGA	Pct.	FTM	FTA	Pct.	Reb.	Ast.	Pts.	AVERAGES RPG	APG	PPG
02-03—Connecticut	32	346	36	66	.545	16	32	.500	90	22	88	2.8	0.7	2.8
03-04—Connecticut	35	318	32	64	.500	19	40	.475	98	9	83	2.8	0.3	2.4
04-05—Connecticut	30	373	41	79	.519	32	61	.525	103	17	114	3.4	0.6	3.8
05-06—Connecticut	34	943	118	194	.608	92	133	.692	226	25	329	6.6	0.7	9.7
Totals	131	1980	227	403	.563	159	266	.598	517	73	614	3.9	0.6	4.7

Three-point field goals: 2003-04, 0-for-1. 2005-06, 1-for-2 (.500). Totals, 1-for-3 (.333).

AUGUSTINE, JAMES   F   MAGIC

PERSONAL: Born February 27, 1984, in Midlothian, Ill. ... 6-10/235. (2.08/106.6). ... Full name: James Dale Augustine
HIGH SCHOOL: Lincoln-Way Central (Mokena, Ill.).
COLLEGE: Illinois.
TRANSACTIONS/CAREER NOTES: Selected by Orlando Magic in second round (41st pick overall) of 2006 NBA Draft.

COLLEGIATE RECORD

Season Team	G	Min.	FGM	FGA	Pct.	FTM	FTA	Pct.	Reb.	Ast.	Pts.	AVERAGES RPG	APG	PPG
02-03—Illinois	32	697	94	162	.580	32	45	.711	186	25	225	5.8	0.8	7.0
03-04—Illinois	33	904	125	197	.635	68	106	.642	242	21	318	7.3	0.6	9.6
04-05—Illinois	39	1037	141	227	.621	110	147	.748	295	43	392	7.6	1.1	10.1
05-06—Illinois	33	1079	174	279	.624	99	152	.651	300	59	448	9.1	1.8	13.6
Totals	137	3717	534	865	.617	309	450	.687	1023	148	1383	7.5	1.1	10.1

Three-point field goals: 2002-03, 5-for-14 (.357). 2003-04, 0-for-2. 2005-06, 1-for-2 (.500). Totals, 6-for-18 (.333).

BALKMAN, RENALDO   F   KNICKS

PERSONAL: Born July 14, 1984, in Staten Island, N.Y. ... 6-8/208. (2.03/94.3).
HIGH SCHOOL: Armwood (Seffner, Fla.), then Howard W. Blake (Tampa, Fla.), then IMG Academy (Bradenton, Fla.), then Laurinburg (N.C.) Institute.
COLLEGE: South Carolina.
TRANSACTIONS/CAREER NOTES: Selected after junior season by New York Knicks in the first round (20th pick overall) of the 2006 NBA Draft.

COLLEGIATE RECORD

Season Team	G	Min.	FGM	FGA	Pct.	FTM	FTA	Pct.	Reb.	Ast.	Pts.	AVERAGES RPG	APG	PPG
03-04—South Carolina	33	600	91	163	.558	41	79	.519	151	46	229	4.6	1.4	6.9
04-05—South Carolina	33	615	74	160	.463	24	44	.545	160	57	178	4.8	1.7	5.4
05-06—South Carolina	38	978	152	250	.608	56	104	.538	239	73	364	6.3	1.9	9.6
Totals	104	2193	317	573	.553	121	227	.533	550	176	771	5.3	1.7	7.4

Three-point field goals: 2003-04, 6-for-24 (.250). 2004-05, 6-for-18 (.333). 2005-06, 4-for-13 (.308). Totals, 16-for-55 (.291).

BARGNANI, ANDREA   F   RAPTORS

PERSONAL: Born October 26, 1985, in Rome, Italy. ... 7-0/225. (2.08/102.1).
COLLEGE: None.
TRANSACTIONS/CAREER NOTES: Played in Italy (2003-06) ... Selected by Toronto Raptors in first round (first pick overall) of 2006 NBA Draft.

ITALIAN LEAGUE RECORD

Season Team	G	Min.	FGM	FGA	Pct.	FTM	FTA	Pct.	Reb.	Ast.	Pts.	AVERAGES RPG	APG	PPG
03-04—Benetton Treviso	8	71	14	23	.609	3	8	.375	12	3	35	1.5	0.4	4.4
04-05—Benetton Treviso	20	263	40	86	.465	26	42	.619	55	11	116	2.8	0.6	5.8
05-06—Benetton Treviso	34	766	144	292	.493	72	93	.774	186	14	405	5.5	0.4	11.9
Totals	62	1100	198	401	.494	101	143	.706	253	28	556	4.1	0.5	9.0

Three-point field goals: 2003-04, 4-for-7 (.571). 2004-05, 10-for-29 (.345). 2005-06, 45-for-118 (.381). Totals, 59-for-154 (.383).

BAVCIC, EDIN   F/C   76ERS

PERSONAL: Born May 6, 1984, in Foca, Bosnia-Herzegovina. ... 6-11/220. (2.11/99.8).
TRANSACTIONS/CAREER NOTES: Played in Adriatic League (2004-06) ... Selected by Toronto Raptors in second round (56th pick overall) of 2006 NBA Draft. ... Draft rights traded by Raptors to Philadelphia 76ers for cash (June 28, 2006).

ADRIATIC LEAGUE RECORD

Season Team	G	Min.	FGM	FGA	Pct.	FTM	FTA	Pct.	Reb.	Ast.	Pts.	AVERAGES RPG	APG	PPG
04-05—Bosna	30	457	34	93	.366	23	41	.561	71	11	98	2.4	0.4	3.3
05-06—Bosna	25	376	44	92	.478	15	26	.577	48	6	116	1.9	0.2	4.6
Totals	55	833	78	185	.422	38	67	.567	119	17	214	2.2	0.3	3.9

Three-point field goals: 2004-05, 7-for-40 (.175). 2005-06, 13-for-40 (.325). Totals, 20-for-80 (.250).

BLALOCK, WILL   G   PISTONS

PERSONAL: Born September 8, 1983, in Boston. ... 6-0/205. (1.83/93.0). ... Full name: William Anthony Blalock
HIGH SCHOOL: East Boston (Mass.), then Notre Dame Prep (Fitchburg, Mass.).
COLLEGE: Iowa State.
TRANSACTIONS/CAREER NOTES: Selected after junior season by Detroit Pistons in second round (60th pick overall) of 2006 NBA Draft.

COLLEGIATE RECORD

Season Team	G	Min.	FGM	FGA	Pct.	FTM	FTA	Pct.	Reb.	Ast.	Pts.	AVERAGES RPG	APG	PPG
03-04—Iowa State	33	1014	86	216	.398	47	67	.701	91	134	249	2.8	4.1	7.5

Season Team	G	Min.	FGM	FGA	Pct.	FTM	FTA	Pct.	Reb.	Ast.	Pts.	AVERAGES		
												RPG	APG	PPG
04-05—Iowa State	30	1107	130	321	.405	85	109	.780	97	146	368	3.2	4.9	12.3
05-06—Iowa State	30	1072	177	396	.447	60	91	.659	99	184	461	3.3	6.1	15.4
Totals	93	3193	393	933	.421	192	267	.719	287	464	1078	3.1	5.0	11.6

Three-point field goals: 2003-04, 30-for-69 (.435). 2004-05, 23-for-87 (.264). 2005-06, 47-for-118 (.398). Totals, 100-for-274 (.365).

BOONE, JOSH   F/C   NETS

PERSONAL: Born November 21, 1984, in Mount Airy, Md. ... 6-10/237. (2.08/107.5). ... Full name: Oscar Joshua Boone
HIGH SCHOOL: West Nottingham Academy (Colora, Md.).
COLLEGE: Connecticut.
TRANSACTIONS/CAREER NOTES: Selected after junior season by New Jersey Nets in first round (23rd pick overall) of 2006 NBA Draft.

COLLEGIATE RECORD

NOTES: Member of NCAA Division I championship team (2004).

Season Team	G	Min.	FGM	FGA	Pct.	FTM	FTA	Pct.	Reb.	Ast.	Pts.	AVERAGES		
												RPG	APG	PPG
03-04—Connecticut	38	835	97	175	.554	32	79	.405	221	26	226	5.8	0.7	5.9
04-05—Connecticut	31	915	148	243	.609	87	131	.664	259	36	383	8.4	1.2	12.4
05-06—Connecticut	34	922	137	243	.564	76	139	.547	238	22	350	7.0	0.6	10.3
Totals	103	2672	382	661	.578	195	349	.559	718	84	959	7.0	0.8	9.3

BREWER, RONNIE   G   JAZZ

PERSONAL: Born March 20, 1985, in Portland, Ore. ... 6-7/220. (2.01/99.8).
HIGH SCHOOL: Fayetteville (Ark.).
COLLEGE: Arkansas.
TRANSACTIONS/CAREER NOTES: Selected after junior season by Utah Jazz in first round (14th pick overall) of 2006 NBA Draft.

COLLEGIATE RECORD

Season Team	G	Min.	FGM	FGA	Pct.	FTM	FTA	Pct.	Reb.	Ast.	Pts.	AVERAGES		
												RPG	APG	PPG
03-04—Arkansas	28	907	125	260	.481	74	129	.574	153	94	341	5.5	3.4	12.2
04-05—Arkansas	30	955	171	360	.475	108	165	.655	145	101	486	4.8	3.4	16.2
05-06—Arkansas	32	1112	197	447	.441	144	192	.750	154	104	589	4.8	3.3	18.4
Totals	90	2974	493	1067	.462	326	486	.671	452	299	1416	5.0	3.3	15.7

Three-point field goals: 2003-04, 17-for-64 (.266). 2004-05, 36-for-91 (.396). 2005-06, 51-for-151 (.338). Totals, 104-for-306 (.340).

BROWN, DEE   G   JAZZ

PERSONAL: Born August 17, 1984, in Jackson, Miss. ... 6-0/185. (1.83/83.9). ... Full name: Daniel Brown
HIGH SCHOOL: Proviso East (Maywood, Ill.).
COLLEGE: Illinois.
TRANSACTIONS/CAREER NOTES: Selected by Utah Jazz in second round (46th pick overall) of 2006 NBA Draft.

COLLEGIATE RECORD

NOTES: SPORTING NEWS Player of the Year (2005). ... SPORTING NEWS All-America first team (2005). ... Naismith Award winner (2006).

Season Team	G	Min.	FGM	FGA	Pct.	FTM	FTA	Pct.	Reb.	Ast.	Pts.	AVERAGES		
												RPG	APG	PPG
02-03—Illinois	32	1090	142	327	.434	49	72	.681	119	159	384	3.7	5.0	12.0
03-04—Illinois	33	1153	160	389	.411	49	73	.671	123	147	440	3.7	4.5	13.3
04-05—Illinois	39	1272	179	359	.499	61	79	.772	104	177	518	2.7	4.5	13.3
05-06—Illinois	33	1183	157	437	.359	78	103	.757	102	191	470	3.1	5.8	14.2
Totals	137	4698	638	1512	.422	237	327	.725	448	674	1812	3.3	4.9	13.2

Three-point field goals: 2002-03, 51-for-155 (.329). 2003-04, 71-for-205 (.346). 2004-05, 99-for-228 (.434). 2005-06, 78-for-243 (.321). Totals, 299-for-831 (.360).

BROWN, DENHAM   G/F   SUPERSONICS

PERSONAL: Born January 6, 1983, in Toronto, Canada. ... 6-6/220. (1.98/99.8). ... Full name: Denham W. Brown
HIGH SCHOOL: West Hill Collegiate (Toronto, Canada).
COLLEGE: Connecticut.
TRANSACTIONS/CAREER NOTES: Selected by Seattle SuperSonics in second round (40th pick overall) of 2006 NBA Draft.

COLLEGIATE RECORD

NOTES: Member of NCAA Division I championship team (2004).

Season Team	G	Min.	FGM	FGA	Pct.	FTM	FTA	Pct.	Reb.	Ast.	Pts.	AVERAGES		
												RPG	APG	PPG
02-03—Connecticut	33	712	100	221	.452	24	41	.585	112	36	254	3.4	1.1	7.7
03-04—Connecticut	39	975	130	297	.438	51	70	.729	153	48	347	3.9	1.2	8.9
04-05—Connecticut	31	815	112	263	.426	68	84	.810	124	47	323	4.0	1.5	10.4
05-06—Connecticut	32	754	117	290	.403	79	91	.868	141	44	343	4.4	1.4	10.7
Totals	135	3256	459	1071	.429	222	286	.776	530	175	1267	3.9	1.3	9.4

Three-point field goals: 2002-03, 30-for-72 (.417). 2003-04, 36-for-92 (.391). 2004-05, 31-for-103 (.301). 2005-06, 30-for-92 (.326). Totals, 127-for-359 (.354).

BROWN, SHANNON   G   CAVALIERS

PERSONAL: Born November 29, 1985, in Maywood, Ill. ... 6-4/205. (1.93/93.0).
HIGH SCHOOL: Proviso East (Maywood, Ill.).
COLLEGE: Michigan State.
TRANSACTIONS/CAREER NOTES: Selected after junior season by Cleveland Cavaliers in first round (25th pick overall) of 2006 NBA Draft.

COLLEGIATE RECORD

Season Team	G	Min.	FGM	FGA	Pct.	FTM	FTA	Pct.	Reb.	Ast.	Pts.	RPG	APG	PPG
03-04—Michigan State	30	687	88	195	.451	46	57	.807	75	38	341	2.5	1.3	11.4
04-05—Michigan State	33	829	126	282	.447	78	92	.848	104	57	486	3.2	1.7	14.7
05-06—Michigan State	34	1196	202	433	.467	117	141	.830	150	93	589	4.4	2.7	17.3
Totals	97	2712	416	910	.457	241	290	.831	329	188	1416	3.4	1.9	14.6

Three-point field goals: 2003-04, 15-for-44 (.341). 2004-05, 31-for-94 (.330). 2005-06, 64-for-164 (.390). Totals, 110-for-302 (.364).

CARNEY, RODNEY   F   76ERS

PERSONAL: Born April 15, 1984, in Memphis, Tenn. ... 6-7/205. (2.01/93.0). ... Full name: Rodney Dion Carney
HIGH SCHOOL: Northwest (Indianapolis).
COLLEGE: Memphis.
TRANSACTIONS/CAREER NOTES: Selected by Chicago Bulls in first round (16th pick overall) of 2006 NBA Draft. ... Draft rights traded by Bulls with a second-round pick in 2007 draft and cash to Philadelphia 76ers for draft rights to G Thabo Sefolosha (June 28, 2006).

COLLEGIATE RECORD

Season Team	G	Min.	FGM	FGA	Pct.	FTM	FTA	Pct.	Reb.	Ast.	Pts.	RPG	APG	PPG
02-03—Memphis	30	759	102	238	.429	43	67	.642	144	34	294	4.8	1.1	9.8
03-04—Memphis	28	753	126	325	.388	50	73	.685	159	30	364	5.7	1.1	13.0
04-05—Memphis	38	1131	211	519	.407	109	141	.773	190	44	607	5.0	1.2	16.0
05-06—Memphis	37	1027	220	505	.436	94	132	.712	168	47	636	4.3	1.3	17.2
Totals	133	3670	659	1587	.415	296	413	.717	651	155	1901	4.9	1.2	14.3

Three-point field goals: 2002-03, 47-for-130 (.362). 2003-04, 62-for-167 (.371). 2004-05, 76-for-234 (.325). 2005-06, 102-for-261 (.391). Totals, 287-for-792 (.362).

COLLINS, MARDY   G   KNICKS

PERSONAL: Born August 4, 1984, in Philadelphia. ... 6-6/220. (1.98/99.8). ... Full name: Maurice Rodney Collins
HIGH SCHOOL: Simon Gratz (Philadelphia).
COLLEGE: Temple.
TRANSACTIONS/CAREER NOTES: Selected by New York Knicks in first round (29th pick overall) of 2006 NBA Draft.

COLLEGIATE RECORD

Season Team	G	Min.	FGM	FGA	Pct.	FTM	FTA	Pct.	Reb.	Ast.	Pts.	RPG	APG	PPG
02-03—Temple	34	1205	153	414	.370	56	83	.675	99	87	407	2.9	2.6	12.0
03-04—Temple	29	1137	171	454	.377	61	102	.598	143	75	450	4.9	2.6	15.5
04-05—Temple	30	1129	192	462	.416	94	146	.644	177	109	526	5.9	3.6	17.5
05-06—Temple	32	1212	202	468	.432	90	151	.596	150	127	536	4.7	4.0	16.8
Totals	125	4683	718	1798	.399	301	482	.624	569	398	1919	4.6	3.2	15.4

Three-point field goals: 2002-03, 45-for-151 (.298). 2003-04, 47-for-162 (.290). 2004-05, 48-for-174 (.276). 2005-06, 42-for-137 (.307). Totals, 182-for-624 (.292).

DAVIS, PAUL   C   CLIPPERS

PERSONAL: Born July 21, 1984, in Detroit. ... 6-10/270. (2.08/122.5). ... Full name: Paul Russell Davis
HIGH SCHOOL: Rochester (Mich.).
COLLEGE: Michigan State.
TRANSACTIONS/CAREER NOTES: Selected by Los Angeles Clippers in second round (34th pick overall) of 2006 NBA Draft.

COLLEGIATE RECORD

Season Team	G	Min.	FGM	FGA	Pct.	FTM	FTA	Pct.	Reb.	Ast.	Pts.	RPG	APG	PPG
02-03—Michigan State	35	623	88	201	.438	97	147	.660	165	15	274	4.7	0.4	7.8
03-04—Michigan State	30	847	163	287	.568	143	179	.799	187	59	474	6.2	2.0	15.8
04-05—Michigan State	32	861	157	290	.541	77	115	.670	257	50	392	8.0	1.6	12.3
05-06—Michigan State	33	1018	206	364	.566	160	184	.870	301	54	578	9.1	1.6	17.5
Totals	130	3349	614	1142	.538	477	625	.763	910	178	1718	7.0	1.4	13.2

Three-point field goals: 2002-03, 1-for-6 (.167). 2003-04, 5-for-15 (.333). 2004-05, 1-for-8 (.125). 2005-06, 6-for-19 (.316). Totals, 13-for-48 (.271).

DIAWARA, YAKHOUBA   G   NUGGETS

PERSONAL: Born August 29, 1982, in Paris, France. ... 6-7/225. (2.01/102.1).
HIGH SCHOOL: Tremblay En France (France).
COLLEGE: Southern Idaho, then Pepperdine.
TRANSACTIONS/CAREER NOTES: Not drafted by an NBA franchise ... Played in France (2005-06) ... Signed as free agent by Denver Nuggets.

FRENCH LEAGUE RECORD

| | | | | | | | | | | | AVERAGES | | |
Season Team	G	Min.	FGM	FGA	Pct.	FTM	FTA	Pct.	Reb.	Ast.	Pts.	RPG	APG	PPG
99-00—Dijon	1	1	0	0	...	0	0	...	0	0	0	0.0	0.0	0.0
00-01—Dijon	7	23	1	9	.111	2	4	.500	2	3	4	0.3	0.4	0.6
05-06—Dijon	20	622	114	271	.421	87	117	.744	114	31	330	5.7	1.6	16.5
Totals	28	646	115	280	.411	89	121	.736	116	34	334	4.1	1.2	11.9

Three-point field goals: 2000-01, 0-for-4. 2005-06, 15-for-57 (.263). Totals, 15-for-61 (.246).

COLLEGIATE RECORD

| | | | | | | | | | | | AVERAGES | | |
Season Team	G	Min.	FGM	FGA	Pct.	FTM	FTA	Pct.	Reb.	Ast.	Pts.	RPG	APG	PPG
01-02—Southern Idaho	31	646	100	184	.543	56	87	.644	192	28	257	6.2	0.9	8.3
02-03—Southern Idaho	32	871	193	357	.541	104	186	.559	237	33	503	7.4	1.0	15.7
03-04—Pepperdine	14	476	88	173	.509	75	99	.758	92	11	264	6.6	0.8	18.9
04-05—Pepperdine	31	988	157	364	.431	98	167	.587	178	35	433	5.7	1.1	14.0
Junior College Totals	63	1517	293	541	.542	160	273	.586	429	61	760	6.8	1.0	12.1
4-Year Totals	45	1464	245	537	.456	173	266	.650	270	46	697	6.0	1.0	15.5

Three-point field goals: 2001-02, 1-for-7 (.143). 2002-03, 13-for-37 (.351). 2003-04, 13-for-27 (.481). 2004-05, 21-for-72 (.292). Four-year Totals, 34-for-99 (.343).

ITALIAN LEAGUE RECORD

| | | | | | | | | | | | AVERAGES | | |
Season Team	G	Min.	FGM	FGA	Pct.	FTM	FTA	Pct.	Reb.	Ast.	Pts.	RPG	APG	PPG
05-06—Climamio Bologna	12	238	43	63	.683	20	23	.870	51	5	124	4.3	0.4	10.3

Three-point field goals: 2005-06, 18-for-27 (.667). Totals, 18-for-27 (.667).

DIAZ, GUILLERMO   G   CLIPPERS

PERSONAL: Born March 4, 1985, in Puerto Rico. ... 6-2/185. (1.88/83.9). ... Full name: Guillermo Jose Diaz
HIGH SCHOOL: Miami Christian Academy (Fla.).
COLLEGE: Miami.
TRANSACTIONS/CAREER NOTES: Selected after junior season by Los Angeles Clippers in second round (52nd pick overall) of 2006 NBA Draft.

COLLEGIATE RECORD

| | | | | | | | | | | | AVERAGES | | |
Season Team	G	Min.	FGM	FGA	Pct.	FTM	FTA	Pct.	Reb.	Ast.	Pts.	RPG	APG	PPG
03-04—Miami (Fla.)	30	840	132	268	.493	54	77	.701	87	65	353	2.9	2.2	11.8
04-05—Miami (Fla.)	29	996	190	417	.456	97	137	.708	126	76	538	4.3	2.6	18.6
05-06—Miami (Fla.)	34	1196	194	467	.415	120	152	.789	100	97	586	2.9	2.9	17.2
Totals	93	3032	516	1152	.448	271	366	.740	313	238	1477	3.4	2.6	15.9

Three-point field goals: 2003-04, 35-for-76 (.461). 2004-05, 61-for-168 (.363). 2005-06, 78-for-214 (.364). Totals, 174-for-458 (.380).

DOUBY, QUINCY   G   KINGS

PERSONAL: Born May 16, 1984, in Brooklyn, N.Y. ... 6-3/175. (1.91/79.4).
HIGH SCHOOL: Grady (Brooklyn, N.Y.), then St. Thomas More Prep (Conn.).
COLLEGE: Rutgers.
TRANSACTIONS/CAREER NOTES: Selected after junior season by Sacramento Kings in first round (19th pick overall) of 2006 NBA Draft.

COLLEGIATE RECORD

| | | | | | | | | | | | AVERAGES | | |
Season Team	G	Min.	FGM	FGA	Pct.	FTM	FTA	Pct.	Reb.	Ast.	Pts.	RPG	APG	PPG
03-04—Rutgers	33	838	136	320	.425	71	86	.826	63	56	412	1.9	1.7	12.5
04-05—Rutgers	29	996	158	403	.392	57	76	.750	70	98	439	2.4	3.4	15.1
05-06—Rutgers	33	1211	287	621	.462	149	176	.847	141	103	839	4.3	3.1	25.4
Totals	95	3045	581	1344	.432	277	338	.820	274	257	1690	2.9	2.7	17.8

Three-point field goals: 2003-04, 69-for-162 (.426). 2004-05, 66-for-195 (.338). 2005-06, 116-for-289 (.401). Totals, 251-for-646 (.389).

ELIYAHU, LIOR   F   ROCKETS

PERSONAL: Born September 9, 1985, in Tel Aviv, Israel. ... 6-9/225. (2.06/102.1).
COLLEGE: Hapoel Galil Elyon (Israel).
TRANSACTIONS/CAREER NOTES: Played in Israel (2003-06) ... Selected by Orlando Magic in second round (44th pick overall) of 2006 NBA Draft. ... Draft rights traded by Magic to Houston Rockets for cash (June 28, 2006).

ISRAELI LEAGUE RECORD

| | | | | | | | | | | | AVERAGES | | |
Season Team	G	Min.	FGM	FGA	Pct.	FTM	FTA	Pct.	Reb.	Ast.	Pts.	RPG	APG	PPG
03-04—Hapoel Galil Elyon	22	321	41	77	.532	26	38	.684	68	14	110	3.1	0.6	5.0
04-05—Hapoel Galil Elyon	21	583	111	194	.572	63	94	.670	109	36	292	5.2	1.7	13.9

Season Team	G	Min.	FGM	FGA	Pct.	FTM	FTA	Pct.	Reb.	Ast.	Pts.	AVERAGES RPG	APG	PPG
05-06—Hapoel Galil Elyon........	29	774	173	324	.534	100	149	.671	171	89	461	5.9	3.1	15.9
Totals	72	1678	325	595	.546	189	281	.673	348	139	863	4.8	1.9	12.0

Three-point field goals: 2003-04, 2-for-4 (.500). 2004-05, 7-for-18 (.389). 2005-06, 15-for-51 (.294). Totals, 24-for-73 (.329).

FARMAR, JORDAN — G — LAKERS

PERSONAL: Born November 30, 1986, in Los Angeles. ... 6-2/180. (1.88/81.6). ... Full name: Jordan Robert Farmar
HIGH SCHOOL: Taft (Woodland Hills, Calif.).
COLLEGE: UCLA.
TRANSACTIONS/CAREER NOTES: Selected after sophomore season by Los Angeles Lakers in first round (26th pick overall) of 2006 NBA Draft.

COLLEGIATE RECORD

NOTES: SPORTING NEWS All-Freshman team (2005).

Season Team	G	Min.	FGM	FGA	Pct.	FTM	FTA	Pct.	Reb.	Ast.	Pts.	AVERAGES RPG	APG	PPG
04-05—UCLA..........................	29	997	120	292	.411	109	136	.801	101	153	383	3.5	5.3	13.2
05-06—UCLA..........................	37	1125	172	420	.410	91	127	.717	95	189	498	2.6	5.1	13.5
Totals	66	2122	292	712	.410	200	263	.760	196	342	881	3.0	5.2	13.3

Three-point field goals: 2004-05, 63-for-189 (.333). 2005-06, 34-for-102 (.333). Totals, 97-for-291 (.333).

FOYE, RANDY — G — TIMBERWOLVES

PERSONAL: Born September 9, 1983, in Newark, N.J. ... 6-4/210. (1.93/95.3).
HIGH SCHOOL: East Side (Newark, N.J.).
COLLEGE: Villanova.
TRANSACTIONS/CAREER NOTES: Selected by Boston Celtics in first round (seventh pick overall) of 2006 NBA Draft. ... Draft rights traded by Celtics with G Dan Dickau and F/C Raef LaFrentz to Portland Trail Blazers for G Sebastian Telfair, F/C Theo Ratliff and a 2008 second-round pick (June 28, 2006). ... Draft rights traded by Trail Blazers with cash to Minnesota Timberwolves for draft rights to G Brandon Roy (June 28, 2006).

COLLEGIATE RECORD

NOTES: SPORTING NEWS All-America first team (2006).

Season Team	G	Min.	FGM	FGA	Pct.	FTM	FTA	Pct.	Reb.	Ast.	Pts.	AVERAGES RPG	APG	PPG
02-03—Villanova......................	31	830	110	304	.362	69	83	.831	110	90	318	3.5	2.9	10.3
03-04—Villanova......................	35	1094	166	429	.387	99	130	.762	165	127	474	4.7	3.6	13.5
04-05—Villanova......................	32	1027	180	428	.421	85	113	.752	160	99	497	5.0	3.1	15.5
05-06—Villanova......................	33	1145	226	550	.411	136	172	.791	190	100	677	5.8	3.0	20.5
Totals	131	4096	682	1711	.399	389	498	.781	625	416	1966	4.8	3.2	15.0

Three-point field goals: 2002-03, 29-for-96 (.302). 2003-04, 43-for-144 (.299). 2004-05, 52-for-153 (.340). 2005-06, 89-for-254 (.350). Totals, 213-for-647 (.329).

FREELAND, JOEL — F — TRAIL BLAZERS

PERSONAL: Born February 7, 1987, in Aldershot, England. ... 6-10/225. (2.08/102.1). ... Full name: Joel Daniel Freeland
TRANSACTIONS/CAREER NOTES: Played in Spain (2005-06) ... Selected by Portland Trail Blazers in first round (30th pick overall) of 2006 NBA Draft.

SPANISH LEAGUE RECORD

Season Team	G	Min.	FGM	FGA	Pct.	FTM	FTA	Pct.	Reb.	Ast.	Pts.	AVERAGES RPG	APG	PPG
05-06—Gran Canaria Fadesa	29	777	189	347	.545	60	98	.612	223	19	440	7.7	0.7	15.2

Three-point field goals: 2005-06, 2-for-4 (.500). Totals, 2-for-4 (.500).

GARBAJOSA, JORGE — F — RAPTORS

PERSONAL: Born December 19, 1977, in Madrid, Spain. ... 6-9/245. (2.06/111.1).
TRANSACTIONS/CAREER NOTES: Played in Spain (1995-2000, 2004-06) ... Played in Italy (2000-04) ... Signed as free agent by Toronto Raptors (July 24, 2006).

SPANISH LEAGUE RECORD

Season Team	G	Min.	FGM	FGA	Pct.	FTM	FTA	Pct.	Reb.	Ast.	Pts.	AVERAGES RPG	APG	PPG
95-96—Taugres Vitoria	6	36	2	7	.286	0	0	...	10	0	4	1.7	0.0	0.7
96-97—Taugres Vitoria	23	236	23	46	.500	18	26	.692	47	3	64	2.0	0.1	2.8
97-98—Tau Ceramica...............	31	451	58	99	.586	59	78	.756	98	12	175	3.2	0.4	5.6
98-99—Tau Ceramica...............	15	353	44	100	.440	33	54	.611	83	8	121	5.5	0.5	8.1
99-00—Tau Ceramica...............	32	704	98	171	.573	102	138	.739	140	17	298	4.4	0.5	9.3

Season Team	G	Min.	FGM	FGA	Pct.	FTM	FTA	Pct.	Reb.	Ast.	Pts.	AVERAGES RPG	APG	PPG
04-05—Unicaja Malaga	27	814	132	270	.489	74	92	.804	180	65	389	6.7	2.4	14.4
05-06—Unicaja Malaga	31	1013	122	293	.416	99	122	.811	197	64	396	6.4	2.1	12.8
Totals	165	3607	479	986	.486	385	510	.755	755	169	1447	4.6	1.0	8.8

Three-point field goals: 1999-00, 0-for-1. 2004-05, 51-for-113 (.451). 2005-06, 53-for-168 (.315). Totals, 104-for-282 (.369).

Season Team	G	Min.	FGM	FGA	Pct.	FTM	FTA	Pct.	Reb.	Ast.	Pts.	AVERAGES		
												RPG	APG	PPG
00-01—Benetton Treviso.........	32	702	109	199	.548	94	113	.832	147	19	340	4.6	0.6	10.6
01-02—Benetton Treviso.........	31	805	127	242	.525	104	124	.839	174	26	376	5.6	0.8	12.1
02-03—Benetton Treviso.........	30	846	140	269	.520	89	112	.795	217	44	411	7.2	1.5	13.7
03-04—Benetton Treviso.........	30	892	144	280	.514	127	151	.841	181	55	447	6.0	1.8	14.9
Totals	123	3245	520	990	.525	414	500	.828	719	144	1574	5.8	1.2	12.8

Three-point field goals: 2000-01, 28-for-49 (.571). 2001-02, 56-for-121 (.463). 2002-03, 42-for-116 (.362). 2003-04, 32-for-98 (.327). Totals, 158-for-384 (.411).

GAY, RUDY   F   GRIZZLIES

PERSONAL: Born August 17, 1986, in Baltimore, Md. ... 6-9/220. (2.06/99.8). ... Full name: Rudy Carlton Gay
HIGH SCHOOL: Archbishop Spalding (Baltimore, Md.).
COLLEGE: Connecticut.
TRANSACTIONS/CAREER NOTES: Selected after sophomore season by Houston Rockets in first round (eighth pick overall) of 2006 NBA Draft. ... Draft rights traded by Rockets with F Stromile Swift to Memphis Grizzlies for F Shane Battier (July 12, 2006).

COLLEGIATE RECORD
NOTES: SPORTING NEWS All-Freshman team (2005). ... SPORTING NEWS Freshman of the Year (2005).

Season Team	G	Min.	FGM	FGA	Pct.	FTM	FTA	Pct.	Reb.	Ast.	Pts.	AVERAGES		
												RPG	APG	PPG
04-05—Connecticut	31	893	132	286	.462	75	106	.708	168	48	367	5.4	1.5	11.8
05-06—Connecticut	33	1015	187	406	.461	101	138	.732	210	68	503	6.4	2.1	15.2
Totals	64	1908	319	692	.461	176	244	.721	378	116	870	5.9	1.8	13.6

Three-point field goals: 2004-05, 28-for-60 (.467). 2005-06, 28-for-88 (.318). Totals, 56-for-148 (.378).

GELABALE, MICKAEL   F   SUPERSONICS

PERSONAL: Born May 22, 1983, in Pointe Noire, France. ... 6-7/215. (2.01/97.5).
COLLEGE: Cholet.
TRANSACTIONS/CAREER NOTES: Played in France (2001-04). ... Played in Spain (2004-06). ... Selected by Seattle SuperSonics in second round (48th pick overall) of 2005 NBA Draft.

FRENCH LEAGUE RECORD

Season Team	G	Min.	FGM	FGA	Pct.	FTM	FTA	Pct.	Reb.	Ast.	Pts.	AVERAGES		
												RPG	APG	PPG
01-02—Cholet..........................	6	24	3	5	.600	2	2	1.000	4	0	8	0.7	0.0	1.3
02-03—Cholet..........................	18	276	45	89	.506	12	19	.632	46	17	108	2.6	0.9	6.0
03-04—Cholet..........................	34	1005	128	246	.520	78	96	.813	50	75	353	1.5	2.2	10.4
Totals	58	1305	176	340	.518	92	117	.786	100	92	469	1.7	1.6	8.1

Three-point field goals: 2001-02, 0-for-1. 2002-03, 6-for-23 (.261). 2003-04, 19-for-52 (.365). Totals, 25-for-76 (.329).

SPANISH LEAGUE RECORD

Season Team	G	Min.	FGM	FGA	Pct.	FTM	FTA	Pct.	Reb.	Ast.	Pts.	AVERAGES		
												RPG	APG	PPG
04-05—Real Madrid..................	34	820	103	185	.557	52	67	.776	120	37	275	3.5	1.1	8.1
05-06—Real Madrid..................	33	720	72	175	.411	56	73	.767	112	41	216	3.4	1.2	6.5
Totals	67	1540	175	360	.486	108	140	.771	232	78	491	3.5	1.2	7.3

Three-point field goals: 2004-05, 17-for-47 (.362). 2005-06, 16-for-53 (.302). Totals, 33-for-100 (.330).

GIBSON, DANIEL   G   CAVALIERS

PERSONAL: Born February 27, 1986, in Houston. ... 6-2/190. (1.88/86.2). ... Full name: Daniel Hiram Gibson
HIGH SCHOOL: Jones (Houston).
COLLEGE: Texas.
TRANSACTIONS/CAREER NOTES: Selected after sophomore season by Cleveland Cavaliers in second round (42nd pick overall) of 2006 NBA Draft.

COLLEGIATE RECORD
NOTES: SPORTING NEWS All-Freshman team (2005).

Season Team	G	Min.	FGM	FGA	Pct.	FTM	FTA	Pct.	Reb.	Ast.	Pts.	AVERAGES		
												RPG	APG	PPG
04-05—Texas............................	31	1018	131	314	.417	103	137	.752	112	121	439	3.6	3.9	14.2
05-06—Texas............................	37	1228	163	402	.405	69	95	.726	133	116	496	3.6	3.1	13.4
Totals	68	2246	294	716	.411	172	232	.741	245	237	935	3.6	3.5	13.8

Three-point field goals: 2004-05, 74-for-186 (.398). 2005-06, 101-for-266 (.380). Totals, 175-for-452 (.387).

GREER, LYNN   G   BUCKS

PERSONAL: Born October 23, 1979, in Philadelphia, Pa. ... 6-2/175. (1.88/79.4).
TRANSACTIONS/CAREER NOTES: Not drafted by an NBA franchise ... Played in Greece (2002-03) ... Played with Greenville Groove in the NBA Development League (2002-03) ... Played in Poland (2003-04) ... Played in Russia (2004-05) ... Played in Italy (2005-06) ... Signed as free agent by Milwaukee Bucks (July 18, 2006).

PROMISING NEWCOMERS

COLLEGIATE RECORD

Season Team	G	Min.	FGM	FGA	Pct.	FTM	FTA	Pct.	Reb.	Ast.	Pts.	AVERAGES RPG	APG	PPG
97-98—Temple	30	522	69	182	.379	50	62	.806	33	33	238	1.1	1.1	7.9
98-99—Temple	6	124	19	50	.380	13	17	.765	9	8	61	1.5	1.3	10.2
99-00—Temple	33	850	135	321	.421	67	82	.817	85	64	406	2.6	1.9	12.3
00-01—Temple	37	1465	215	536	.401	164	189	.868	132	202	675	3.6	5.5	18.2
01-02—Temple	31	1232	226	560	.404	172	197	.873	97	130	719	3.1	4.2	23.2
Totals	137	4193	664	1649	.403	466	547	.852	356	437	2099	2.6	3.2	15.3

Three-point field goals: 1997-98, 50-for-106 (.472). 1998-99, 10-for-28 (.357). 1999-00, 69-for-172 (.401). 2000-01, 81-for-214 (.379). 2001-02, 95-for-246 (.386). Totals, 305-for-766 (.398).

GREEK LEAGUE RECORD

Season Team	G	Min.	FGM	FGA	Pct.	FTM	FTA	Pct.	Reb.	Ast.	Pts.	AVERAGES RPG	APG	PPG
02-03—Near East	14	468	67	172	.390	81	93	.871	35	31	234	2.5	2.2	16.7

Three-point field goals: 2002-03, 19-for-58 (.328). Totals, 19-for-58 (.328).

NBA DEVELOPMENT LEAGUE RECORD

Season Team	G	Min.	FGM	FGA	Pct.	FTM	FTA	Pct.	Reb.	Ast.	Pts.	AVERAGES RPG	APG	PPG
02-03—Greenville	13	243	44	92	.478	25	34	.735	21	27	121	1.6	2.1	9.3

Three-point field goals: 2002-03, 8-for-25 (.320). Totals, 8-for-25 (.320).

POLISH LEAGUE RECORD

Season Team	G	Min.	FGM	FGA	Pct.	FTM	FTA	Pct.	Reb.	Ast.	Pts.	AVERAGES RPG	APG	PPG
03-04—Slask Wroclaw	32	1045	218	430	.507	166	196	.847	90	148	653	2.8	4.6	20.4

Three-point field goals: 2003-04, 51-for-134 (.381). Totals, 51-for-134 (.381).

RUSSIAN LEAGUE RECORD

Season Team	G	Min.	FGM	FGA	Pct.	FTM	FTA	Pct.	Reb.	Ast.	Pts.	AVERAGES RPG	APG	PPG
04-05—Dynamo Moscow	33	688	103	265	.389	67	79	.848	64	73	302	1.9	2.2	9.2

Three-point field goals: 2004-05, 29-for-100 (.290). Totals, 29-for-100 (.290).

ITALIAN LEAGUE RECORD

Season Team	G	Min.	FGM	FGA	Pct.	FTM	FTA	Pct.	Reb.	Ast.	Pts.	AVERAGES RPG	APG	PPG
05-06—Carpisa Napoli	32	941	220	420	.524	232	254	.913	73	113	751	2.3	3.5	23.5

Three-point field goals: 2005-06, 79-for-158 (.500). Totals, 79-for-158 (.500).

HALPERIN, YOTAM   G   SUPERSONICS

PERSONAL: Born January 24, 1984, in Tel Aviv, Israel. ... 6-5/210. (1.96/95.3).
COLLEGE: None.
TRANSACTIONS/CAREER NOTES: Played in Israel (2001-05) ... Played in Adriatic League (2002-03, 2005-06) ... Selected by Seattle SuperSonics in second round (53rd pick overall) of 2006 NBA Draft.

ISRAELI LEAGUE RECORD

Season Team	G	Min.	FGM	FGA	Pct.	FTM	FTA	Pct.	Reb.	Ast.	Pts.	AVERAGES RPG	APG	PPG
01-02—Maccabi Tel-Aviv	15	136	25	39	.641	15	17	.882	9	16	77	0.6	1.1	5.1
02-03—Maccabi Tel-Aviv	22	274	33	57	.579	13	14	.929	26	29	88	1.2	1.3	4.0
03-04—Maccabi Tel-Aviv	21	319	42	80	.525	13	13	1.000	43	35	109	2.0	1.7	5.2
04-05—Maccabi Tel-Aviv	15	317	58	101	.574	24	30	.800	30	33	159	2.0	2.2	10.6
Totals	73	1046	158	277	.570	65	74	.878	108	113	433	1.5	1.5	5.9

Three-point field goals: 2001-02, 12-for-20 (.600). 2002-03, 9-for-18 (.500). 2003-04, 12-for-37 (.324). 2004-05, 19-for-40 (.475). Totals, 52-for-115 (.452).

ADRIATIC LEAGUE RECORD

Season Team	G	Min.	FGM	FGA	Pct.	FTM	FTA	Pct.	Reb.	Ast.	Pts.	AVERAGES RPG	APG	PPG
02-03—Maccabi Tel Aviv	21	312	47	88	.534	15	21	.714	29	28	121	1.4	1.3	5.8
05-06—Union Olimpija	25	844	115	212	.542	76	89	.854	68	91	355	2.7	3.6	14.2
Totals	46	1156	162	300	.540	91	110	.827	97	119	476	2.1	2.6	10.3

Three-point field goals: 2002-03, 12-for-29 (.414). 2005-06, 49-for-98 (.500). Totals, 61-for-127 (.480).

HOLLINS, RYAN   C   BOBCATS

PERSONAL: Born October 10, 1984, in Pasadena, Calif. ... 7-0/230. (2.13/104.3). ... Full name: Ryan Kenwood Hollins.
HIGH SCHOOL: John Muir (Pasadena, Calif.).
COLLEGE: UCLA.
TRANSACTIONS/CAREER NOTES: Selected by Charlotte Bobcats in second round (50th pick overall) of 2006 NBA Draft.

COLLEGIATE RECORD

Season Team	G	Min.	FGM	FGA	Pct.	FTM	FTA	Pct.	Reb.	Ast.	Pts.	AVERAGES RPG	APG	PPG
02-03—UCLA	24	401	38	64	.594	28	57	.491	85	5	104	3.5	0.2	4.3

Season Team	G	Min.	FGM	FGA	Pct.	FTM	FTA	Pct.	Reb.	Ast.	Pts.	AVERAGES RPG	APG	PPG
03-04—UCLA	28	711	64	117	.547	54	93	.581	119	15	182	4.3	0.5	6.5
04-05—UCLA	28	460	40	76	.526	44	65	.677	94	10	125	3.4	0.4	4.5
05-06—UCLA	33	710	83	134	.619	65	108	.602	157	10	231	4.8	0.3	7.0
Totals	113	2282	225	391	.575	191	323	.591	455	40	642	4.0	0.4	5.7

Three-point field goals: 2004-05, 1-for-1 (1.000). Totals, 1-for-1 (1.000).

ILIC, MILE   C   NETS

PERSONAL: Born June 2, 1984, in Tuzla, Bosnia-Herzegovina. ... 7-1/230. (2.16/104.3).
COLLEGE: Did not attend.
TRANSACTIONS/CAREER NOTES: Played in Yugoslavia (2001-03, 2005-06). ... Played in Adriatic League (2003-05). ... Selected by New Jersey Nets in the second round (43rd pick overall) of 2005 NBA Draft.

YUGOSLAVIAN LEAGUE RECORD

Season Team	G	Min.	FGM	FGA	Pct.	FTM	FTA	Pct.	Reb.	Ast.	Pts.	AVERAGES RPG	APG	PPG
01-02—FMP Zeleznik	1	2	1	3	.333	0	0	...	0	0	2	0.0	0.0	2.0
02-03—FMP Zeleznik	8	16	3	7	.429	3	4	.750	5	3	9	0.6	0.4	1.1
Totals	9	18	4	10	.400	3	4	.750	5	3	11	0.6	0.3	1.2

Three-point field goals: 2001-02, 0-for-1. 2002-03, 0-for-1. Totals, 0-for-2 (.000).

ADRIATIC LEAGUE RECORD

Season Team	G	Min.	FGM	FGA	Pct.	FTM	FTA	Pct.	Reb.	Ast.	Pts.	AVERAGES RPG	APG	PPG
03-04—KK Reflex	14	115	15	29	.517	13	17	.765	13	3	43	0.9	0.2	3.1
04-05—KK Reflex	31	486	97	143	.678	32	49	.653	106	16	226	3.4	0.5	7.3
05-06—FMP Zeleznik	29	551	98	166	.590	48	69	.696	128	17	244	4.4	0.6	8.4
Totals	74	1152	210	338	.621	93	135	.689	247	36	513	3.3	0.5	6.9

Three-point field goals: 2003-04, 0-for-1. 2004-05, 0-for-2. 2005-06, 0-for-2. Totals, 0-for-5 (.000).

ILYASOVA, ERSAN   F   BUCKS

PERSONAL: Born May 15, 1987, in Ekisehir, Turkey. ... 6-9/235. (2.06/106.6).
COLLEGE: Did not attend.
TRANSACTIONS/CAREER NOTES: Played in Turkey (2004-05). ... Selected by Milwaukee Bucks in second round (36th pick overall) of 2005 NBA Draft. ... Played in NBA Development League (2005-06).

TURKISH LEAGUE RECORD

Season Team	G	Min.	FGM	FGA	Pct.	FTM	FTA	Pct.	Reb.	Ast.	Pts.	AVERAGES RPG	APG	PPG
04-05—Ulker	15	186	21	49	.429	5	11	.455	52	8	58	3.5	0.5	3.9

Three-point field goals: 2004-05, 11-for-29 (.379). Totals, 11-for-29 (.379).

NBA DEVELOPMENT LEAGUE RECORD

Season Team	G	Min.	FGM	FGA	Pct.	FTM	FTA	Pct.	Reb.	Ast.	Pts.	AVERAGES RPG	APG	PPG
05-06—Tulsa	46	1297	218	536	.407	70	99	.707	324	46	574	7.0	1.0	12.5

Three-point field goals: 2005-06, 68-for-195 (.349). Totals, 68-for-195 (.349).

JOHNSON, ALEXANDER   F   GRIZZLIES

PERSONAL: Born February 8, 1983, in Albany, Ga. ... 6-9/240. (2.06/108.9). ... Full name: Alexander Canterell Johnson
HIGH SCHOOL: Dougherty Comprehensive (Albany, Ga.).
COLLEGE: Florida State.
TRANSACTIONS/CAREER NOTES: Selected after junior season by Indiana Pacers in second round (45th pick overall) in 2006 NBA Draft. ... Draft rights traded by Pacers with two future second-round picks to Portland Trail Blazers for G James White (June 28, 2006). ... Draft rights traded by Trail Blazers to Memphis Grizzlies for an unconditional second-round pick (June 28, 2006).

COLLEGIATE RECORD

Season Team	G	Min.	FGM	FGA	Pct.	FTM	FTA	Pct.	Reb.	Ast.	Pts.	AVERAGES RPG	APG	PPG
03-04—Florida State	33	687	103	187	.551	106	157	.675	138	27	312	4.2	0.8	9.5
04-05—Florida State	30	525	76	167	.455	50	87	.575	128	16	205	4.3	0.5	6.8
05-06—Florida State	29	723	127	235	.540	120	170	.706	216	21	383	7.4	0.7	13.2
Totals	92	1935	306	589	.520	276	414	.667	482	64	900	5.2	0.7	9.8

Three-point field goals: 2003-04, 0-for-1. 2004-05, 3-for-9 (.333). 2005-06, 9-for-29 (.310). Totals, 12-for-39 (.308).

JONES, BOBBY   F   76ERS

PERSONAL: Born January 9, 1984, in Compton, Calif. ... 6-7/215. (2.01/97.5). ... Full name: Bobby Ray Jones
HIGH SCHOOL: Dominguez (Compton, Calif.), then Long Beach Polytechnic (Calif.).
COLLEGE: Washington.
TRANSACTIONS/CAREER NOTES: Selected by Minnesota Timberwolves in second round (37th pick overall) of 2006 NBA Draft. ... Draft rights traded by Timberwolves to Philadelphia 76ers for an unconditional second-round pick and cash (June 28, 2006).

COLLEGIATE RECORD

Season Team	G	Min.	FGM	FGA	Pct.	FTM	FTA	Pct.	Reb.	Ast.	Pts.	AVERAGES RPG	APG	PPG
02-03—Washington	27	514	48	119	.403	53	69	.768	111	28	153	4.1	1.0	5.7

Season Team	G	Min.	FGM	FGA	Pct.	FTM	FTA	Pct.	Reb.	Ast.	Pts.	AVERAGES		
												RPG	APG	PPG
03-04—Washington	31	760	130	228	.570	87	131	.664	153	25	348	4.9	0.8	11.2
04-05—Washington	34	865	133	261	.510	85	125	.680	190	57	382	5.6	1.7	11.2
05-06—Washington	33	874	113	239	.473	88	118	.746	163	43	343	4.9	1.3	10.4
Totals	125	3013	424	847	.501	313	443	.707	617	153	1226	4.9	1.2	9.8

Three-point field goals: 2002-03, 4-for-20 (.200). 2003-04, 1-for-8 (.125). 2004-05, 31-for-61 (.508). 2005-06, 29-for-88 (.330). Totals, 65-for-177 (.367).

JONES, SOLOMON   F   HAWKS

PERSONAL: Born July 16, 1984, in Eustis, Fla. ... 6-10/230. (2.08/104.3).
HIGH SCHOOL: Mount Dora (Fla.).
JUNIOR COLLEGE: Daytona Beach Community College.
COLLEGE: South Florida.
TRANSACTIONS/CAREER NOTES: Selected by Atlanta Hawks in second round (33rd pick overall) of 2006 NBA Draft.

COLLEGIATE RECORD

Season Team	G	Min.	FGM	FGA	Pct.	FTM	FTA	Pct.	Reb.	Ast.	Pts.	AVERAGES		
												RPG	APG	PPG
02-03—Daytona Beach CC.........				Statistics unavailable										
03-04—Daytona Beach CC.........				Statistics unavailable										
04-05—South Florida.................	30	782	77	141	.546	44	80	.550	185	22	198	6.2	0.7	6.6
05-06—South Florida.................	29	1056	139	287	.484	105	135	.778	285	39	383	9.8	1.3	13.2
Totals	99	1838	299	572	.523	149	215	.693	734	61	926	7.4	0.6	9.4

Three-point field goals: 2005-06, 0-for-2. Totals, 0-for-2 (.000).

LOWRY, KYLE   G   GRIZZLIES

PERSONAL: Born March 25, 1986, in Philadelphia. ... 6-0/175. (1.83/79.4).
HIGH SCHOOL: Cardinal Dougherty (Philadelphia).
COLLEGE: Villanova.
TRANSACTIONS/CAREER NOTES: Selected after sophomore season by Memphis Grizzlies in first round (24th pick overall) of 2006 NBA Draft.

COLLEGIATE RECORD

Season Team	G	Min.	FGM	FGA	Pct.	FTM	FTA	Pct.	Reb.	Ast.	Pts.	AVERAGES		
												RPG	APG	PPG
04-05—Villanova....................	24	557	64	152	.421	47	74	.635	76	49	180	3.2	2.0	7.5
05-06—Villanova....................	33	967	117	251	.466	121	154	.786	143	122	363	4.3	3.7	11.0
Totals	57	1524	181	403	.449	168	228	.737	219	171	543	3.8	3.0	9.5

Three-point field goals: 2004-05, 5-for-22 (.227). 2005-06, 8-for-18 (.444). Totals, 13-for-40 (.325).

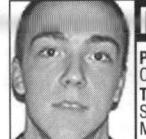

MARKOTA, DAMIR   F   BUCKS

PERSONAL: Born December 26, 1985, in Sarajevo, Bosnia. ... 6-10/225. (2.08/102.1). ... Previously known as Damir Omerhodzic.
TRANSACTIONS/CAREER NOTES: Played in Croatia (2001-03, 2004-06) ... Played in Adriatic League (2001-02, 2003-06) ... Selected by San Antonio Spurs in second round (59th pick overall) of 2006 NBA Draft. ... Draft rights traded by Spurs to Milwaukee Bucks for second-round pick in 2007 draft (June 28, 2006).

ADRIATIC LEAGUE RECORD

Season Team	G	Min.	FGM	FGA	Pct.	FTM	FTA	Pct.	Reb.	Ast.	Pts.	AVERAGES		
												RPG	APG	PPG
01-02—Zabok	3	7	0	4	.000	0	0	...	2	0	0	0.7	0.0	0.0
03-04—Cibona	4	34	6	8	.750	1	4	.250	11	2	15	2.8	0.5	3.8
04-05—Cibona	21	351	42	77	.545	16	33	.485	71	10	114	3.4	0.5	5.4
05-06—Cibona	18	392	54	113	.478	22	29	.759	79	19	149	4.4	1.1	8.3
Totals	46	784	102	202	.505	39	66	.591	163	31	278	3.5	0.7	6.0

Three-point field goals: 2001-02, 0-for-2. 2003-04, 2-for-3 (.667). 2004-05, 16-for-33 (.485). 2005-06, 19-for-51 (.373). Totals, 37-for-89 (.416).

CROATIAN LEAGUE RECORD

Season Team	G	Min.	FGM	FGA	Pct.	FTM	FTA	Pct.	Reb.	Ast.	Pts.	AVERAGES		
												RPG	APG	PPG
01-02—Zabok	4	...	1	3	.333	1	4	.250	2	0	4	0.5	0.0	1.0
02-03—Karlovac	18	...	93	222	.419	37	52	.712	113	33	256	6.3	1.8	14.2
04-05—Cibona	13	...	17	43	.395	7	12	.583	31	4	46	2.4	0.3	3.5
05-06—Cibona	18	...	40	85	.471	21	29	.724	67	13	174	3.7	0.7	9.7
Totals	53	...	151	353	.428	66	97	.680	213	50	480	4.0	0.9	9.1

Three-point field goals: 2002-03, 33-for-113 (.292). 2004-05, 5-for-17 (.294). 2005-06, 19-for-55 (.345). Totals, 57-for-185 (.308).

MAVROKEFALIDIS, LOUKAS   C   TIMBERWOLVES

PERSONAL: Born July 25, 1984, in Geseni, Czech Rep. ... 6-11/260. (2.11/117.9).
COLLEGE: None.
TRANSACTIONS/CAREER NOTES: Played in Greece (2001-06) ... Selected by Minnesota Timberwolves in second round (57th pick overall) of 2006 NBA Draft.

GREEK LEAGUE RECORD

Season Team	G	Min.	FGM	FGA	Pct.	FTM	FTA	Pct.	Reb.	Ast.	Pts.	AVERAGES		
												RPG	APG	PPG
01-02—PAOK...........................	2	8	0	2	.000	0	0	...	3	0	0	1.5	0.0	0.0

Season Team	G	Min.	FGM	FGA	Pct.	FTM	FTA	Pct.	Reb.	Ast.	Pts.	AVERAGES		
												RPG	APG	PPG
02-03—PAOK	6	27	7	11	.636	4	4	1.000	5	1	18	0.8	0.2	3.0
03-04—PAOK	19	219	31	56	.554	31	36	.861	69	8	94	3.6	0.4	4.9
04-05—PAOK	14	99	11	26	.423	9	16	.563	24	2	31	1.7	0.1	2.2
05-06—PAOK	26	832	165	298	.554	86	108	.796	212	28	429	8.2	1.1	16.5
Totals	67	1185	214	393	.545	130	164	.793	313	39	572	4.7	0.6	8.5

Three-point field goals: 2003-04, 1-for-2 (.500). 2004-05, 0-for-1. 2005-06, 13-for-47 (.277). Totals, 14-for-50 (.280).

MENSAH-BONSU, POPS — F — MAVERICKS

PERSONAL: Born September 7, 1983, in London, England. ... 6-9/240. (2.06/108.9). ... Full name: Nana Papa Yaw Mensah-Bonsu
HIGH SCHOOL: St. Augustine Prep (Richland, N.J.).
COLLEGE: George Washington.
TRANSACTIONS/CAREER NOTES: Not drafted by an NBA franchise. ... Signed as free agent by Dallas Mavericks (August 3, 2006).

COLLEGIATE RECORD

Season Team	G	Min.	FGM	FGA	Pct.	FTM	FTA	Pct.	Reb.	Ast.	Pts.	AVERAGES		
												RPG	APG	PPG
02-03—George Washington	29	716	103	176	.585	86	129	.667	164	11	292	5.7	0.4	10.1
03-04—George Washington	30	636	125	203	.616	98	143	.685	161	12	348	5.4	0.4	11.6
04-05—George Washington	30	730	141	247	.571	97	170	.571	197	24	379	6.6	0.8	12.6
05-06—George Washington	23	583	101	179	.564	87	163	.534	154	18	289	6.7	0.8	12.6
Totals	112	2665	470	805	.584	368	605	.608	676	65	1308	6.0	0.6	11.7

MILLSAP, PAUL — F — JAZZ

PERSONAL: Born February 10, 1985, in Monroe, La. ... 6-8/245. (2.03/111.1).
HIGH SCHOOL: Grambling (La.).
COLLEGE: Louisiana Tech.
TRANSACTIONS/CAREER NOTES: Selected after junior season by Utah Jazz in second round (47th pick overall) of 2006 NBA Draft.

COLLEGIATE RECORD

NOTES: Led nation in rebounds per game (2003-04, 2004-05, 2005-06).

Season Team	G	Min.	FGM	FGA	Pct.	FTM	FTA	Pct.	Reb.	Ast.	Pts.	AVERAGES		
												RPG	APG	PPG
03-04—Louisiana Tech	30	1053	175	298	.587	116	181	.641	374	22	467	12.5	0.7	15.6
04-05—Louisiana Tech	29	1061	225	391	.575	143	238	.601	360	29	593	12.4	1.0	20.4
05-06—Louisiana Tech	33	1126	258	452	.571	127	204	.623	438	36	648	13.3	1.1	19.6
Totals	92	3240	658	1141	.577	386	623	.620	1172	87	1708	12.7	0.9	18.6

Three-point field goals: 2003-04, 1-for-1 (1.000). 2004-05, 0-for-1. 2005-06, 5-for-14 (.357). Totals, 6-for-16 (.375).

MORRISON, ADAM — F — BOBCATS

PERSONAL: Born July 19, 1984, in Casper, Wyo. ... 6-8/205. (2.03/93.0).
HIGH SCHOOL: Mead (Spokane, Wash.).
COLLEGE: Gonzaga.
TRANSACTIONS/CAREER NOTES: Selected after junior season by Charlotte Bobcats in first round (third pick overall) of 2006 NBA Draft.

COLLEGIATE RECORD

NOTES: SPORTING NEWS All-America first team (2006). ... Led nation in points per game (2005-06).

Season Team	G	Min.	FGM	FGA	Pct.	FTM	FTA	Pct.	Reb.	Ast.	Pts.	AVERAGES		
												RPG	APG	PPG
03-04—Gonzaga	31	644	137	258	.531	61	84	.726	132	44	352	4.3	1.4	11.4
04-05—Gonzaga	31	1059	226	454	.498	100	132	.758	171	88	589	5.5	2.8	19.0
05-06—Gonzaga	33	1205	306	617	.496	240	311	.772	182	58	926	5.5	1.8	28.1
Totals	95	2908	669	1329	.503	401	527	.761	485	190	1867	5.1	2.0	19.7

Three-point field goals: 2003-04, 17-for-56 (.304). 2004-05, 37-for-119 (.311). 2005-06, 74-for-173 (.428). Totals, 128-for-348 (.368).

NOEL, DAVID — F — BUCKS

PERSONAL: Born February 27, 1984, in Durham, N.C. ... 6-6/230. (1.98/104.3). ... Full name: David Anthony Noel III
HIGH SCHOOL: Southern Durham (N.C.).
COLLEGE: North Carolina.
TRANSACTIONS/CAREER NOTES: Selected by Milwaukee Bucks in second round (39th pick overall) of 2006 NBA Draft.

COLLEGIATE RECORD

NOTES: Member of NCAA Division I championship team (2005).

Season Team	G	Min.	FGM	FGA	Pct.	FTM	FTA	Pct.	Reb.	Ast.	Pts.	AVERAGES		
												RPG	APG	PPG
02-03—North Carolina	35	766	84	166	.506	23	43	.535	123	49	207	3.5	1.4	5.9
03-04—North Carolina	24	510	50	89	.562	28	45	.622	117	35	130	4.9	1.5	5.4
04-05—North Carolina	37	627	57	104	.548	22	41	.537	98	56	143	2.6	1.5	3.9
05-06—North Carolina	31	1045	158	297	.532	45	72	.625	211	107	400	6.8	3.5	12.9
Totals	127	2948	349	656	.532	118	201	.587	549	247	880	4.3	1.9	6.9

Three-point field goals: 2002-03, 16-for-57 (.281). 2003-04, 2-for-12 (.167). 2004-05, 7-for-20 (.350). 2005-06, 39-for-92 (.424). Totals, 64-for-181 (.354).

NOVAK, STEVE   F   ROCKETS

PERSONAL: Born June 13, 1983, in Libertyville, Ill. ... 6-10/220. (2.08/99.8). ... Full name: Steven Michael Novak
HIGH SCHOOL: Brown Deer (Wis.).
COLLEGE: Marquette.
TRANSACTIONS/CAREER NOTES: Selected by Houston Rockets in second round (32nd pick overall) of 2006 NBA Draft.

COLLEGIATE RECORD

Season Team	G	Min.	FGM	FGA	Pct.	FTM	FTA	Pct.	Reb.	Ast.	Pts.	RPG	APG	PPG
02-03—Marquette	33	512	67	113	.593	31	33	.939	71	17	220	2.2	0.5	6.7
03-04—Marquette	31	916	118	290	.407	62	68	.912	143	39	387	4.6	1.3	12.5
04-05—Marquette	31	926	127	278	.457	76	84	.905	127	28	419	4.1	0.9	13.5
05-06—Marquette	31	1047	173	363	.477	74	76	.974	183	39	541	5.9	1.3	17.5
Totals	126	3401	485	1044	.465	243	261	.931	524	123	1567	4.2	1.0	12.4

Three-point field goals: 2002-03, 55-for-109 (.505). 2003-04, 89-for-207 (.430). 2004-05, 89-for-193 (.461). 2005-06, 121-for-259 (.467). Totals, 354-for-768 (.461).

O'BRYANT, PATRICK   C   WARRIORS

PERSONAL: Born June 20, 1986, in Oskaloosa, Iowa. ... 7-0/260. (2.13/117.9). ... Full name: Patrick Fitzgerald O'Bryant
HIGH SCHOOL: Blaine (Minn.).
COLLEGE: Bradley.
TRANSACTIONS/CAREER NOTES: Selected after sophomore season by Golden State Warriors in first round (ninth pick overall) of 2006 NBA Draft.

COLLEGIATE RECORD

Season Team	G	Min.	FGM	FGA	Pct.	FTM	FTA	Pct.	Reb.	Ast.	Pts.	RPG	APG	PPG
04-05—Bradley	27	623	108	194	.557	54	77	.701	201	17	270	7.4	0.6	10.0
05-06—Bradley	25	642	133	241	.552	69	102	.676	207	21	335	8.3	0.8	13.4
Totals	52	1265	241	435	.554	123	179	.687	408	38	605	7.8	0.7	11.6

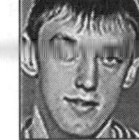

PECHEROV, OLEKSIY   C   WIZARDS

PERSONAL: Born December 8, 1985, in Donetsk, Ukraine. ... 7-0/210. (2.13/95.3).
COLLEGE: None.
TRANSACTIONS/CAREER NOTES: Played in Ukraine (2003-05) ... Played in France (2005-06). ... Selected by Washington Wizards in first round (18th pick overall) of 2006 NBA Draft.

FRENCH LEAGUE RECORD

Season Team	G	Min.	FGM	FGA	Pct.	FTM	FTA	Pct.	Reb.	Ast.	Pts.	RPG	APG	PPG
05-06—Paris Basket Racing	23	483	93	197	.472	50	60	.833	144	4	258	6.3	0.2	11.2

Three-point field goals: 2005-06, 22-for-66 (.333). Totals, 22-for-66 (.333).

PEROVIC, KOSTA   F/C   WARRIORS

PERSONAL: Born February 19, 1985, in Osijek, Croatia. ... 7-2/240. (2.18/108.9).
COLLEGE: None.
TRANSACTIONS/CAREER NOTES: Played in Yugoslavia (2000-05) ... Played in Adriatic League (2004-06) ... Selected by Golden State Warriors in second round (38th pick overall) of 2006 NBA Draft.

YUGOSLAVIAN LEAGUE RECORD

Season Team	G	Min.	FGM	FGA	Pct.	FTM	FTA	Pct.	Reb.	Ast.	Pts.	RPG	APG	PPG
00-01—KK Beopetrol	5	...	11	20	.550	3	4	.750	6	7	27	1.2	1.4	5.4
01-02—KK Beopetrol	11	...	12	33	.364	18	22	.818	34	2	43	3.1	0.2	3.9
02-03—Partizan	22	...	28	47	.596	22	29	.759	52	13	78	2.4	0.6	3.5
03-04—Partizan	30	...	112	198	.566	85	119	.714	147	23	309	4.9	0.8	10.3
04-05—Partizan	19	...	104	175	.594	73	101	.723	103	22	281	5.4	1.2	14.8
Totals	87		267	473	.564	201	275	.731	342	67	738	3.9	0.8	8.5

Three-point field goals: 2000-01, 2-for-9 (.222). 2001-02, 1-for-1 (1.000). 2003-04, 0-for-1. 2004-05, 0-for-1. Totals, 3-for-12 (.250).

ADRIATIC LEAGUE RECORD

Season Team	G	Min.	FGM	FGA	Pct.	FTM	FTA	Pct.	Reb.	Ast.	Pts.	RPG	APG	PPG
04-05—Partizan	21	514	97	185	.524	73	103	.709	49	19	267	2.3	0.9	12.7
05-06—Partizan	29	674	125	233	.536	102	157	.650	109	19	352	3.8	0.7	12.1
Totals	50	1188	222	418	.531	175	260	.673	158	38	619	3.2	0.8	12.4

Three-point field goals: 2005-06, 0-for-1. Totals, 0-for-1 (.000).

PINNOCK, J.R.   G   LAKERS

PERSONAL: Born December 11, 1983, in Fort Hood, Texas. ... 6-5/207. (1.96/93.9). ... Full name: Danilo Augustin Pinnock
HIGH SCHOOL: Eagle's Landing (McDonough, Ga.), then Coastal Christian Academy (Virginia Beach, Va).
COLLEGE: George Washington.
TRANSACTIONS/CAREER NOTES: Selected after junior season by Dallas Mavericks in second round (58th pick overall) of 2006 NBA Draft. ... Draft rights traded by Mavericks to Los Angeles Lakers for a second-round pick in 2007 draft (June 28, 2006).

COLLEGIATE RECORD

Season Team	G	Min.	FGM	FGA	Pct.	FTM	FTA	Pct.	Reb.	Ast.	Pts.	RPG	APG	PPG
03-04—George Washington	30	686	113	241	.469	48	61	.787	101	37	295	3.4	1.2	9.8
04-05—George Washington	29	851	152	308	.494	72	94	.766	147	62	390	5.1	2.1	13.4
05-06—George Washington	30	948	164	338	.485	83	117	.709	158	92	436	5.3	3.1	14.5
Totals	89	2485	429	887	.484	203	272	.746	406	191	1121	4.6	2.1	12.6

Three-point goals: 2003-04, 21-for-53 (.396). 2004-05, 14-for-51 (.275). 2005-06, 25-for-91 (.275). Totals, 60-for-195 (.308).

POWE, LEON   F   CELTICS

PERSONAL: Born January 22, 1984, in Berkeley, Calif. ... 6-8/240. (2.03/108.9). ... Full name: Leon Powe Jr.
HIGH SCHOOL: Oakland Tech (Calif.).
COLLEGE: California.
TRANSACTIONS/CAREER NOTES: Selected after sophomore season by Denver Nuggets in second round (49th pick overall) of 2006 NBA Draft. ... Draft rights traded by Nuggets to Boston Celtics for a second-round pick in 2007 draft (June 28, 2006).

COLLEGIATE RECORD

NOTES: SPORTING NEWS All-America second team (2006).

Season Team	G	Min.	FGM	FGA	Pct.	FTM	FTA	Pct.	Reb.	Ast.	Pts.	RPG	APG	PPG
03-04—California	27	804	142	291	.488	125	205	.610	256	19	409	9.5	0.7	15.1
04-05—California						Did Not Play - Redshirted								
05-06—California	27	953	178	359	.496	194	270	.719	273	38	553	10.1	1.4	20.5
Totals	54	1757	320	650	.492	319	475	.672	529	57	962	9.8	1.1	17.8

Three-point field goals: 2003-04, 0-for-1. 2005-06, 3-for-9 (.333). Totals, 3-for-10 (.300).

REDICK, J.J.   G   MAGIC

PERSONAL: Born June 24, 1984, in Cookeville, Tenn. ... 6-4/190. (1.93/86.2). ... Full name: Jonathan Clay Redick
HIGH SCHOOL: Cave Spring (Roanoke, Va.).
COLLEGE: Duke.
TRANSACTIONS/CAREER NOTES: Selected by Orlando Magic in first round (11th pick overall) of 2006 NBA Draft.

COLLEGIATE RECORD

NOTES: SPORTING NEWS player of the year (2006). ... SPORTING NEWS All-America first team (2005, 2006). ... Naismith Award winner (2006). ... Wooden Award winner (2006). ... Holds NCAA Division I record for most career three-point field goals made—457.

Season Team	G	Min.	FGM	FGA	Pct.	FTM	FTA	Pct.	Reb.	Ast.	Pts.	RPG	APG	PPG
02-03—Duke	33	1013	149	361	.413	102	111	.919	81	67	495	2.5	2.0	15.0
03-04—Duke	37	1152	172	407	.423	143	150	.953	115	58	589	3.1	1.6	15.9
04-05—Duke	33	1231	202	495	.408	196	209	.938	108	86	721	3.3	2.6	21.8
05-06—Duke	36	1336	302	643	.470	221	256	.863	71	95	964	2.0	2.6	26.8
Totals	139	4732	825	1906	.433	662	726	.912	375	306	2769	2.7	2.2	19.9

Three-point field goals: 2002-03, 95-for-238 (.399). 2003-04, 102-for-258 (.395). 2004-05, 121-for-300 (.403). 2005-06, 139-for-330 (.421). Totals, 457-for-1126 (.406).

RODRIGUEZ, SERGIO   G   TRAIL BLAZERS

PERSONAL: Born June 12, 1986, in Tenerife, Spain. ... 6-3/168. (1.91/76.2). ... Full name: Sergio Rodriguez Gomez
COLLEGE: None.
TRANSACTIONS/CAREER NOTES: Played in Spain (2004-06) ... Selected by Phoenix Suns in first round (27th pick overall) of 2006 NBA Draft. ... Draft rights traded by Suns to Portland Trail Blazers for cash (June 28, 2006).

SPANISH LEAGUE RECORD

Season Team	G	Min.	FGM	FGA	Pct.	FTM	FTA	Pct.	Reb.	Ast.	Pts.	RPG	APG	PPG
04-05—Adecco Estudiantes	34	666	122	223	.547	39	50	.780	53	98	302	1.6	2.9	8.9
05-06—Adecco Estudiantes	34	799	122	269	.454	48	71	.676	83	168	314	2.4	4.9	9.2
Totals	68	1465	244	492	.496	87	121	.719	136	266	616	2.0	3.9	9.1

Three-point field goals: 2004-05, 19-for-60 (.317). 2005-06, 22-for-72 (.306). Totals, 41-for-132 (.311).

RONDO, RAJON   G   CELTICS

PERSONAL: Born February 22, 1986, in Louisville, Ky. ... 6-1/171. (1.85/77.6).
HIGH SCHOOL: Eastern (Louisville, Ky.), then Oak Hill Academy (Mouth of Wilson, Va.).
COLLEGE: Kentucky.
TRANSACTIONS/CAREER NOTES: Selected after sophomore season by Phoenix Suns in first round (21st pick overall) of 2006 NBA Draft. ... Draft rights traded by Suns with F Brian Grant to Boston Celtics for a first-round pick in 2007 draft (June 28, 2006).

COLLEGIATE RECORD

												AVERAGES		
Season Team	G	Min.	FGM	FGA	Pct.	FTM	FTA	Pct.	Reb.	Ast.	Pts.	RPG	APG	PPG
04-05—Kentucky	34	854	102	200	.510	60	103	.583	97	118	274	2.9	3.5	8.1
05-06—Kentucky	34	1054	147	305	.482	68	119	.571	209	167	380	6.1	4.9	11.2
Totals	68	1908	249	505	.493	128	222	.577	306	285	654	4.5	4.2	9.6

Three-point field goals: 2004-05, 10-for-33 (.303). 2005-06, 18-for-66 (.273). Totals, 28-for-99 (.283).

ROY, BRANDON   G   TRAIL BLAZERS

PERSONAL: Born July 23, 1984, in Seattle. ... 6-6/215. (1.98/97.5). ... Full name: Brandon Dawayne Roy
HIGH SCHOOL: Garfield (Seattle).
COLLEGE: Washington.
TRANSACTIONS/CAREER NOTES: Selected by Minnesota Timberwolves in first round (sixth pick overall) of 2006 NBA Draft. ... Draft rights traded by Timberwolves to Portland Trail Blazers for draft rights to G Randy Foye and cash (June 28, 2006).

COLLEGIATE RECORD

NOTES: SPORTING NEWS All-America first team (2006).

												AVERAGES		
Season Team	G	Min.	FGM	FGA	Pct.	FTM	FTA	Pct.	Reb.	Ast.	Pts.	RPG	APG	PPG
02-03—Washington	13	224	30	60	.500	18	37	.486	38	13	79	2.9	1.0	6.1
03-04—Washington	31	938	144	300	.480	106	135	.785	164	102	400	5.3	3.3	12.9
04-05—Washington	26	629	131	232	.565	63	85	.741	129	58	332	5.0	2.2	12.8
05-06—Washington	33	1046	228	449	.508	171	211	.810	186	135	666	5.6	4.1	20.2
Totals	103	2837	533	1041	.512	358	468	.765	517	308	1477	5.0	3.0	14.3

Three-point field goals: 2002-03, 1-for-10 (.100). 2003-04, 6-for-27 (.222). 2004-05, 7-for-20 (.350). 2005-06, 39-for-97 (.402). Totals, 53-for-154 (.344).

SAMB, CHEICK   C   PISTONS

PERSONAL: Born October 22, 1984, in Senegal. ... 7-1/195. (2.16/88.5). ... Full name: Samb Chiekh Tidiane
COLLEGE: None.
TRANSACTIONS/CAREER NOTES: Played in Spain (2005-06) ... Selected by Los Angeles Lakers in second round (51st pick overall) of 2006 NBA Draft. ... Draft rights traded by Lakers to Detroit Pistons for G Maurice Evans (June 28, 2006).

SPANISH LEAGUE RECORD

												AVERAGES		
Season Team	G	Min.	FGM	FGA	Pct.	FTM	FTA	Pct.	Reb.	Ast.	Pts.	RPG	APG	PPG
05-06—WTC Cornella	29	756	111	221	.502	51	67	.761	223	11	277	7.7	0.4	9.6

Three-point field goals: 2005-06, 4-for-11 (.364). Totals, 4-for-11 (.364).

SEFOLOCHA, THABO   G   BULLS

PERSONAL: Born May 2, 1984, in Vevey, Sweden. ... 6-5/215. (1.96/97.5). ... Full name: Thabo Patrick Sefolosha
TRANSACTIONS/CAREER NOTES: Played in Switzerland (2001-02) ... Played in France (2002-05) ... Played in Italy (2005-06) ... Selected by Philadelphia 76ers in first round (13th pick overall) of 2006 NBA Draft. ... Draft rights traded by 76ers to Chicago Bulls for draft right to G/F Rodney Carney, a second-round pick in 2007 draft and cash (June 28, 2006).

SWISS LEAGUE RECORD

												AVERAGES		
Season Team	G	Min.	FGM	FGA	Pct.	FTM	FTA	Pct.	Reb.	Ast.	Pts.	RPG	APG	PPG
01-02—Riviera	26	...	109	201	.542	53	74	.716	83	57	360	3.2	2.2	13.8

Three-point field goals: 2001-02, 14-for-47 (.298). Totals, 14-for-47 (.298).

FRENCH LEAGUE RECORD

												AVERAGES		
Season Team	G	Min.	FGM	FGA	Pct.	FTM	FTA	Pct.	Reb.	Ast.	Pts.	RPG	APG	PPG
02-03—Chalon	1	3	0	0	...	0	0	...	0	1	0	0.0	1.0	0.0
03-04—Chalon	30	504	48	115	.417	23	38	.605	108	31	122	3.6	1.0	4.1
04-05—Chalon	34	1012	115	242	.475	57	82	.695	231	82	309	6.8	2.4	9.1
Totals	65	1519	163	357	.457	80	120	.667	339	114	431	5.2	1.8	6.6

Three-point field goals: 2003-04, 3-for-32 (.094). 2004-05, 22-for-71 (.310). Totals, 25-for-103 (.243).

ITALIAN LEAGUE RECORD

												AVERAGES		
Season Team	G	Min.	FGM	FGA	Pct.	FTM	FTA	Pct.	Reb.	Ast.	Pts.	RPG	APG	PPG
05-06—Angelico Biella	30	901	136	284	.479	56	85	.659	207	71	360	6.9	2.4	12.0

Three-point field goals: 2005-06, 32-for-78 (.410). Totals, 32-for-78 (.410).

SENE, SAER   F   SUPERSONICS

PERSONAL: Born May 12, 1986, in Thies, Senegal. ... 6-11/230. (2.11/104.3). ... Full name: Mouhamed Saer Sene
COLLEGE: None.
TRANSACTIONS/CAREER NOTES: Played in Belgium (2005-06) ... Selected by Seattle SuperSonics in first round (10th pick overall) of 2006 NBA Draft.

BELGIAN LEAGUE RECORD

												AVERAGES		
Season Team	G	Min.	FGM	FGA	Pct.	FTM	FTA	Pct.	Reb.	Ast.	Pts.	RPG	APG	PPG
05-06—Pepinster	25	307	43	60	.717	14	38	.368	131	4	100	5.2	0.2	4.0

SIMMONS, CEDRIC F HORNETS

PERSONAL: Born January 3, 1986, in Shallotte, N.C. ... 6-9/235. (2.06/106.6).
HIGH SCHOOL: West Brunswick (Shallotte, N.C.).
COLLEGE: North Carolina State.
TRANSACTIONS/CAREER NOTES: Selected after sophomore season by New Orleans/Oklahoma City Hornets in first round (15th pick overall) of 2006 NBA Draft.

COLLEGIATE RECORD

Season Team	G	Min.	FGM	FGA	Pct.	FTM	FTA	Pct.	Reb.	Ast.	Pts.	RPG	APG	PPG
04-05—NC State	31	309	42	83	.506	24	44	.545	57	14	108	1.8	0.5	3.5
05-06—NC State	32	880	128	218	.587	120	177	.678	203	54	378	6.3	1.7	11.8
Totals	63	1189	170	301	.565	144	221	.652	260	68	486	4.1	1.1	7.7

Three-point field goals: 2004-05, 0-for-2. 2005-06, 2-for-2 (1.000). Totals, 2-for-4 (.500).

SLOKAR, UROS F RAPTORS

PERSONAL: Born May 14, 1983, in Ljubljana, Slovenia. ... 6-10/238. (2.08/108.0).
COLLEGE: Did not attend.
TRANSACTIONS/CAREER NOTES: Played in Adriatic League (2001-02). ... Played in Slovenia (2002-03). ... Selected by Toronto Raptors in second round (58th pick overall) of 2005 NBA Draft. ... Played in Italy (2003-06).

ADRIATIC LEAGUE RECORD

Season Team	G	Min.	FGM	FGA	Pct.	FTM	FTA	Pct.	Reb.	Ast.	Pts.	RPG	APG	PPG
01-02—KD Slovan	15	307	46	83	.554	41	66	.621	48	9	133	3.2	0.6	8.9

Three-point field goals: 2001-02, 0-for-5. Totals, 0-for-5 (.000).

SLOVENIAN LEAGUE RECORD

Season Team	G	Min.	FGM	FGA	Pct.	FTM	FTA	Pct.	Reb.	Ast.	Pts.	RPG	APG	PPG
01-02—KD Slovan	13	...	40	65	.615	31	43	.721	36	22	113	2.8	1.7	8.7
02-03—KD Slovan	38	1206	205	369	.556	187	238	.786	239	33	627	6.3	0.9	16.5
Totals	51	...	245	434	.565	218	281	.776	275	55	740	5.4	1.1	14.5

Three-point field goals: 2001-02, 2-for-6 (.333). 2002-03, 30-for-71 (.423). Totals, 32-for-77 (.416).

ITALIAN LEAGUE RECORD

Season Team	G	Min.	FGM	FGA	Pct.	FTM	FTA	Pct.	Reb.	Ast.	Pts.	RPG	APG	PPG
03-04—Benetton Treviso	25	267	41	76	.539	24	36	.667	37	7	112	1.5	0.3	4.5
04-05—Benetton Treviso	28	426	53	92	.576	46	60	.767	121	9	159	4.3	0.3	5.7
05-06—Benetton Treviso	32	412	60	107	.561	35	51	.686	106	11	168	3.3	0.3	5.3
Totals	85	1105	154	275	.560	105	147	.714	264	27	439	3.1	0.3	5.2

Three-point field goals: 2003-04, 6-for-15 (.400). 2004-05, 7-for-17 (.412). 2005-06, 13-for-25 (.520). Totals, 26-for-57 (.456).

SMITH, CRAIG F TIMBERWOLVES

PERSONAL: Born November 10, 1983, in Inglewood, Calif. ... 6-7/250. (2.01/113.4).
HIGH SCHOOL: Fairfax (Los Angeles), then Worcester Academy (Mass.).
COLLEGE: Boston College.
TRANSACTIONS/CAREER NOTES: Selected by Minnesota Timberwolves in second round (36th pick overall) of 2006 NBA Draft.

COLLEGIATE RECORD

Season Team	G	Min.	FGM	FGA	Pct.	FTM	FTA	Pct.	Reb.	Ast.	Pts.	RPG	APG	PPG
02-03—Boston College	31	989	241	400	.603	132	194	.680	246	41	617	7.9	1.3	19.9
03-04—Boston College	34	1117	235	425	.553	99	173	.572	283	46	576	8.3	1.4	16.9
04-05—Boston College	29	1004	202	401	.504	114	170	.671	246	49	523	8.5	1.7	18.0
05-06—Boston College	36	1305	243	424	.573	146	227	.643	339	109	677	9.4	3.0	18.8
Totals	130	4415	921	1650	.558	491	764	.643	1114	245	2393	8.6	1.9	18.4

Three-point field goals: 2002-03, 3-for-15 (.200). 2003-04, 7-for-19 (.368). 2004-05, 5-for-21 (.238). 2005-06, 1-for-12 (.083). Totals, 16-for-67 (.239).

SPANOULIS, VASSILIS G ROCKETS

PERSONAL: Born July 8, 1982 ... 6-4/188. (1.93/85.3).
TRANSACTIONS/CAREER NOTES: Played in Greece (2001-06). ... Selected by Dallas Mavericks in second round (50th pick overall) of 2004 NBA Draft. ... Draft rights traded by Mavericks to Houston Rockets for draft rights to G Luis Flores and cash (June 24, 2004).
MISCELLANEOUS: Member of Greek Olympic team (2004).

GREEK LEAGUE RECORD

Season Team	G	Min.	FGM	FGA	Pct.	FTM	FTA	Pct.	Reb.	Ast.	Pts.	RPG	APG	PPG
01-02—Marousi	12	140	22	45	.489	13	20	.650	11	23	59	0.9	1.9	4.9
02-03—Marousi	26	768	86	204	.422	63	86	.733	41	91	253	1.6	3.5	9.7
03-04—Marousi	26	737	86	189	.455	88	107	.822	54	86	287	2.1	3.3	11.0
04-05—Marousi	25	759	119	275	.433	104	129	.806	51	99	392	2.0	4.0	15.7
05-06—Panathinaikos	26	692	87	189	.460	81	101	.802	41	91	286	1.6	3.5	11.0
Totals	115	3096	400	902	.443	349	443	.788	198	390	1277	1.7	3.4	11.1

Three-point field goals: 2001-02, 2-for-12 (.167). 2002-03, 18-for-69 (.261). 2003-04, 27-for-78 (.346). 2004-05, 50-for-128 (.391). 2005-06, 31-for-83 (.373). Totals, 128-for-370 (.346).

THOMAS, TYRUS   F   BULLS

PERSONAL: Born August 17, 1986, in Baton Rouge, La. ... 6-9/215. (2.06/97.5). ... Full name: Tyrus Wayne Thomas
HIGH SCHOOL: McKinley (Baton Rouge, La.).
COLLEGE: Louisiana State.
TRANSACTIONS/CAREER NOTES: Selected after freshman season by Portland Trail Blazers in first round (fourth pick overall) of 2006 NBA Draft. ... Draft rights traded by Trail Blazers with F Viktor Khryapa to Chicago Bulls for draft rights to F/C LaMarcus Aldridge and a conditional second-round pick (June 28, 2006).

COLLEGIATE RECORD

NOTES: SPORTING NEWS All-Freshman team (2006).

Season Team	G	Min.	FGM	FGA	Pct.	FTM	FTA	Pct.	Reb.	Ast.	Pts.	RPG	APG	PPG
04-05—LSU						Did Not Play - Redshirted								
05-06—LSU	32	829	152	250	.608	90	137	.657	295	42	395	9.2	1.3	12.3
Totals	32	829	152	250	.608	90	137	.657	295	42	395	9.2	1.3	12.3

Three-point field goals: 2005-06, 1-for-1 (1.000). Totals, 1-for-1 (1.000).

TUCKER, P.J.   F   RAPTORS

PERSONAL: Born May 5, 1985, in Raleigh, N.C. ... 6-5/225. (1.96/102.1). ... Full name: Anthony Leon Tucker
HIGH SCHOOL: Bonner Academy (Raleigh, N.C.), then Enloe (Raleigh, N.C.).
COLLEGE: Texas.
TRANSACTIONS/CAREER NOTES: Selected after junior season by Toronto Raptors in second round (35th pick overall) of 2006 NBA Draft.

COLLEGIATE RECORD

Season Team	G	Min.	FGM	FGA	Pct.	FTM	FTA	Pct.	Reb.	Ast.	Pts.	RPG	APG	PPG
03-04—Texas	33	742	133	243	.547	76	117	.650	225	27	342	6.8	0.8	10.4
04-05—Texas	17	500	80	152	.526	73	102	.716	136	37	233	8.0	2.2	13.7
05-06—Texas	37	1276	225	437	.515	142	190	.747	353	106	594	9.5	2.9	16.1
Totals	87	2518	438	832	.526	291	409	.711	714	170	1169	8.2	2.0	13.4

Three-point field goals: 2004-05, 0-for-1. 2005-06, 2-for-3 (.667). Totals, 2-for-4 (.500).

UGBOAJA, EJIKE   F   CAVALIERS

PERSONAL: Born May 28, 1985, in Nigeria. ... 6-9/225 (2.06/102.1).
TRANSACTIONS/CAREER NOTES: Played in Nigeria (2005-06). ... Selected by Cleveland Cavaliers in second round (55th pick overall) of 2006 NBA Draft.

VEREMEENKO, VLADIMIR   F   WIZARDS

PERSONAL: Born July 21, 1984, in Gomel, Belarus. ... 6-10/230. (2.08/104.3). ... Full name: Uladzimir Verameyenka
TRANSACTIONS/CAREER NOTES: Played in Russia (2000-06) ... Selected by Washington Wizards in second round (48th pick overall) of 2006 NBA Draft.

RUSSIAN LEAGUE RECORD

Season Team	G	Min.	FGM	FGA	Pct.	FTM	FTA	Pct.	Reb.	Ast.	Pts.	RPG	APG	PPG
02-03—Avtodor Saratov	21	539	79	174	.454	71	99	.717	121	26	234	5.8	1.2	11.1
03-04—Avtodor Saratov	26	783	144	291	.495	99	125	.792	177	51	393	6.8	2.0	15.1
04-05—Dynamo St. Petersburg	29	848	140	266	.526	110	138	.797	194	48	399	6.7	1.7	13.8
05-06—Dynamo St. Petersburg	35	946	149	260	.573	131	165	.794	221	69	444	6.3	2.0	12.7
Totals	111	3116	512	991	.517	411	527	.780	713	194	1470	6.4	1.7	13.2

Three-point field goals: 2002-03, 5-for-16 (.313). 2003-04, 6-for-20 (.300). 2004-05, 9-for-31 (.290). 2005-06, 15-for-39 (.385). Totals, 35-for-106 (.330).

VINICIUS, MARCUS   F   HORNETS

PERSONAL: Born May 31, 1984, in Sao Paulo, Brazil. ... 6-8/225. (2.03/102.1). ... Full name: Marcus Vinicius Vieira de Souza
COLLEGE: None.
TRANSACTIONS/CAREER NOTES: Played in Italy (2004-05) ... Played in Brazil (2003-04, 2005-06) ... Selected by New Orleans/Oklahoma City Hornets in second round (43rd pick overall) of 2006 NBA Draft.

BRAZILIAN LEAGUE RECORD

Season Team	G	Min.	FGM	FGA	Pct.	FTM	FTA	Pct.	Reb.	Ast.	Pts.	RPG	APG	PPG
03-04—Corinthians Sao Paulo-BNL	31	936	226	465	.486	90	112	.804	121	65	484	3.9	2.1	15.6
05-06—Objetivo Sao Carlos-Paulisa	21	720	124	310	.400	122	155	.787	140	83	410	6.7	4.0	19.5
Totals	52	1656	350	775	.452	212	267	.794	261	148	894	5.0	2.8	17.2

Three-point field goals: 2003-04, 59-for-143 (.413). 2005-06, 40-for-132 (.303). Totals, 99-for-275 (.360).

PROMISING NEWCOMERS

Season Team	G	Min.	FGM	FGA	Pct.	FTM	FTA	Pct.	Reb.	Ast.	Pts.	AVERAGES RPG	APG	PPG
04-05—Premiata Montegranaro..	30	952	156	318	.491	81	116	.698	165	21	462	5.5	0.7	15.4

Three-point field goals: 2004-05, 69-for-154 (.448). Totals, 69-for-154 (.448).

WHITE, JAMES G/F PACERS

PERSONAL: Born October 21, 1982, in Washington, D.C. ... 6-7/200. (2.01/90.7). ... Full name: James William White IV
HIGH SCHOOL: Newport (Kensignton, Md.), then Hargrave Military Academy (Chatham, Va.).
COLLEGE: Florida, then Cincinnati.
TRANSACTIONS/CAREER NOTES: Selected by Portland Trail Blazers in second round (31st pick overall) of 2006 NBA Draft. ... Draft rights traded by Trail Blazers to Indiana Pacers for draft rights to F Alexander Johnson and two future second-round picks (June 28, 2006).

COLLEGIATE RECORD

Season Team	G	Min.	FGM	FGA	Pct.	FTM	FTA	Pct.	Reb.	Ast.	Pts.	AVERAGES RPG	APG	PPG
01-02—Florida	30	615	71	169	.420	20	40	.500	86	51	182	2.9	1.7	6.1
02-03—Cincinnati						Did Not Play - Transfer Student								
03-04—Cincinnati	27	677	71	185	.384	57	71	.803	109	96	214	4.0	3.6	7.9
04-05—Cincinnati	33	940	109	246	.443	83	104	.798	158	102	337	4.8	3.1	10.2
05-06—Cincinnati	33	1104	177	363	.488	134	160	.838	167	67	537	5.1	2.0	16.3
Totals	123	3336	428	963	.444	294	375	.784	520	316	1270	4.2	2.6	10.3

Three-point field goals: 2001-02, 20-for-69 (.290). 2003-04, 15-for-63 (.238). 2004-05, 36-for-94 (.383). 2005-06, 49-for-131 (.374). Totals, 120-for-357 (.336).

WILLIAMS, MARCUS G NETS

PERSONAL: Born December 3, 1985, in Los Angeles. ... 6-3/205. (1.91/93.0). ... Full name: Marcus Darell Williams
HIGH SCHOOL: Oak Hill Academy (Mouth of Wilson, Va.).
COLLEGE: Connecticut.
TRANSACTIONS/CAREER NOTES: Selected after junior season by New Jersey Nets in first round (22nd pick overall) of 2006 NBA Draft.

COLLEGIATE RECORD

NOTES: Member of NCAA Division I championship team (2004).

Season Team	G	Min.	FGM	FGA	Pct.	FTM	FTA	Pct.	Reb.	Ast.	Pts.	AVERAGES RPG	APG	PPG
03-04—Connecticut	16	226	17	46	.370	9	13	.692	21	69	46	1.3	4.3	2.9
04-05—Connecticut	31	961	103	255	.404	64	89	.719	117	243	297	3.8	7.8	9.6
05-06—Connecticut	23	767	83	204	.407	94	109	.862	89	198	284	3.9	8.6	12.3
Totals	70	1954	203	505	.402	167	211	.791	227	510	627	3.2	7.3	9.0

Three-point field goals: 2003-04, 3-for-17 (.176). 2004-05, 26-for-67 (.388). 2005-06, 24-for-60 (.400). Totals, 53-for-144 (.368).

WILLIAMS, SHAWNE F PACERS

PERSONAL: Born February 16, 1986, in Memphis, Tenn. ... 6-9/225. (2.06/102.1). ... Full name: Shawne Brian Williams
HIGH SCHOOL: Hamilton (Memphis, Tenn.), then Laurinburg (N.C.) Institute.
COLLEGE: Memphis.
TRANSACTIONS/CAREER NOTES: Selected after freshman season by Indiana Pacers in first round (17th pick overall) of 2006 NBA Draft.

COLLEGIATE RECORD

NOTES: SPORTING NEWS All-Freshman team (2006).

Season Team	G	Min.	FGM	FGA	Pct.	FTM	FTA	Pct.	Reb.	Ast.	Pts.	AVERAGES RPG	APG	PPG
05-06—Memphis	36	1002	156	375	.416	114	145	.786	222	67	474	6.2	1.9	13.2

Three-point field goals: 2005-06, 48-for-154 (.312). Totals, 48-for-154 (.312).

WILLIAMS, SHELDEN F HAWKS

PERSONAL: Born October 21, 1983, in Oklahoma City. ... 6-9/250. (2.06/113.4). ... Full name: Shelden DeMar Williams
HIGH SCHOOL: Midwest City (Forest Park, Okla.).
COLLEGE: Duke.
TRANSACTIONS/CAREER NOTES: Selected by Atlanta Hawks in first round (fifth pick overall) of 2006 NBA Draft.

COLLEGIATE RECORD

NOTES: SPORTING NEWS All-America second team (2006).

Season Team	G	Min.	FGM	FGA	Pct.	FTM	FTA	Pct.	Reb.	Ast.	Pts.	AVERAGES RPG	APG	PPG
02-03—Duke	33	633	95	184	.516	80	128	.625	195	15	270	5.9	0.5	8.2
03-04—Duke	37	963	164	280	.586	138	200	.690	314	34	468	8.5	0.9	12.6
04-05—Duke	33	1109	191	328	.582	131	198	.662	369	31	513	11.2	0.9	15.5
05-06—Duke	36	1198	237	410	.578	201	270	.744	384	39	677	10.7	1.1	18.8
Totals	139	3903	687	1202	.572	550	796	.691	1262	119	1928	9.1	0.9	13.9

Three-point field goals: 2002-03, 0-for-1. 2003-04, 2-for-5 (.400). 2005-06, 2-for-6 (.333). Totals, 4-for-12 (.333).

PROMISING NEWCOMERS

HEAD COACHES

BICKERSTAFF, BERNIE — BOBCATS

PERSONAL: Born February 11, 1944, in Benham, Ky. ... 6-3/185. (1.91/83.9). ... Full name: Bernard Tyrone Bickerstaff
HIGH SCHOOL: East Benham (Benham, Ky.).
COLLEGE: Rio Grande (Ohio), then San Diego.

COLLEGIATE RECORD

Season Team	G	Min.	FGM	FGA	Pct.	FTM	FTA	Pct.	Reb.	Ast.	Pts.	RPG	APG	PPG
64-65—San Diego	26	...	78	211	.370	46	91	.505	135	...	202	5.2	...	7.8
65-66—San Diego	28	...	88	249	.353	82	116	.707	201	...	248	7.2	...	8.9
Totals	54	...	166	460	.361	128	207	.618	336	...	450	6.2	...	8.3

Personal fouls/disqualifications: 1964-65, 81/0. 1965-66, 92/0. Totals, 173/0.

HEAD COACHING RECORD

BACKGROUND: Assistant coach, University of San Diego (1967-68 and 1968-69). ... Assistant coach, Capital Bullets of NBA (1973-74). ... Assistant coach, Washington Bullets (1974-75 through 1984-85). ... Vice president/general manager, Denver Nuggets (July 1990 through 1995-96). ... President, Nuggets (1996-97 season). ... Named coach and general manager of St. Louis Swarm of IBA (August 31, 1999). ... General manager, Charlotte Bobcats (2004 to present).

COLLEGIATE COACHING RECORD

Season Team	W	L	Pct.	Finish
69-70—San Diego	14	12	.538	Division II Independent
70-71—San Diego	10	14	.417	Division II Independent
71-72—San Diego	12	14	.462	Division II Independent
72-73—San Diego	19	9	.679	Division II Independent
Totals	55	49	.529	

NBA COACHING RECORD

Season Team	REGULAR SEASON W	L	Pct.	Finish	PLAYOFFS W	L	Pct.
85-86—Seattle	31	51	.378	5th/Pacific Division	—	—	—
86-87—Seattle	39	43	.476	4th/Pacific Division	7	7	.500
87-88—Seattle	44	38	.537	3rd/Pacific Division	2	3	.400
88-89—Seattle	47	35	.573	3rd/Pacific Division	3	5	.375
89-90—Seattle	41	41	.500	4th/Pacific Division	—	—	—
94-95—Denver	20	12	.625	4th/Midwest Division	0	3	.000
95-96—Denver	35	47	.427	4th/Midwest Division	—	—	—
96-97—Denver	4	9	.308		—	—	—
96-97—Washington	22	13	.629	4th/Atlantic Division	0	3	.000
97-98—Washington	—	—	—		—	—	—
97-98—Washington	42	40	.510	4th/Atlantic Division	—	—	—
98-99—Washington	13	19	.406		—	—	—
04-05—Charlotte	18	64	.220	4th/ Southeast Division	—	—	—
05-06—Charlotte	26	56	.317	4th/Southeast Division	—	—	—
Totals	382	468	.449		12	21	.364

NOTES:
86-87—Defeated Dallas, 3-1, in Western Conference first round; defeated Houston, 4-2 in Western Conference semifinals; lost to Los Angeles Lakers, 4-0, in Western Conference finals.
87-88—Lost to Denver, 3-2, in Western Conference first round.
88-89—Defeated Houston, 3-1, in Western Conference first round; lost to Los Angeles Lakers, 4-0, in Western Conference semifinals.
94-95—Replaced Dan Issel (18-16) and Gene Littles (interim head coach, 3-13) as Denver head coach (February 20), with record of 21-29 and club in fourth place. Lost to San Antonio in Western Conference first round.
96-97—Replaced as Denver head coach by Dick Motta (November 26).
97-98—Replaced Jim Lynam (22-24) and Bob Staak (interim head coach, 0-1) as Washington head coach (Februrary 10) with record of 22-25 and club in fourth place. Lost to Chicago in Eastern Conference first round.

BROWN, MIKE — CAVALIERS

PERSONAL: Born March 5, 1970, in Columbus, Ohio. ... 6-3/200. (1.91/90.7).
HIGH SCHOOL: Wurzburg American (Germany).
JUNIOR COLLEGE: Mesa Community College.
COLLEGE: University of San Diego.

COLLEGIATE RECORD

Season Team	G	Min.	FGM	FGA	Pct.	FTM	FTA	Pct.	Reb.	Ast.	Pts.	RPG	APG	PPG
89-90—Mesa C.C.	35	...	156	319	.489	117	158	.741	148	113	485	4.2	3.2	13.9
90-91—San Diego	29	740	79	183	.432	64	100	.640	100	75	258	3.4	2.6	8.9
91-92—San Diego	28	695	52	135	.385	99	127	.780	86	32	212	3.1	1.1	7.6
Junior College Totals	35	...	156	319	.489	117	158	.741	148	113	485	4.2	3.2	13.9
4-Year-College Totals	57	1435	131	318	.412	163	227	.718	186	107	470	3.3	1.9	8.2

HEAD COACHING RECORD

BACKGROUND: Video coordinator/scout, Denver Nuggets (1992-97). ... Assistant coach/scout, Washington Wizards (1997-2000). ... Assistant coach, San Antonio Spurs (2000-03). ... Assistant coach, Indiana Pacers (2003-04 through June 2, 2005).

NBA COACHING RECORD

Season Team	REGULAR SEASON W	L	Pct.	Finish	PLAYOFFS W	L	Pct.
05-06—Cleveland	50	32	.610	2nd/Central Division	7	6	.538
Totals	50	32	.610		7	6	.538

NOTES:
05-06—Defeated Washington, 4-2, in Eastern Conference first round; lost to Detroit, 4-3, in Eastern Conference semifinals.

CARLISLE, RICK PACERS

PERSONAL: Born October 27, 1959, in Ogdensburg, N.Y. ... 6-5/210. (1.96/95.3). ... Full name: Richard Preston Carlisle
HIGH SCHOOL: Central.
COLLEGE: Maine, then Virginia.
TRANSACTIONS/CAREER NOTES: Selected by Boston Celtics in third round (69th pick overall) of 1984 NBA Draft. ... Waived by Celtics (November 3, 1987). ... Signed as free agent by New York Knicks (November 30, 1987). ... Played in Continental Basketball Association with Albany Patroons (1987-88). ... Signed as free agent by New Jersey Nets (October 4, 1989). ... Waived by Nets (December 1, 1989).

COLLEGIATE RECORD

| | | | | | | | | | | | | AVERAGES | | |
Season Team	G	Min.	FGM	FGA	Pct.	FTM	FTA	Pct.	Reb.	Ast.	Pts.	RPG	APG	PPG
79-80—Maine	28	...	131	236	.555	83	97	.856	96	118	345	3.4	4.2	12.3
80-81—Maine	28	...	176	322	.547	102	126	.810	118	132	454	4.2	4.7	16.2
81-82—Virginia							Did not play.							
82-83—Virginia	33	956	142	277	.513	87	104	.837	100	98	379	3.0	3.0	11.5
83-84—Virginia	33	959	149	289	.516	67	96	.698	93	95	365	2.8	2.9	11.1
Totals	122	1915	598	1124	.532	339	423	.801	407	443	1543	3.3	3.6	12.6

Three-point field goals: 1982-83, 8-for-12 (.667). Totals, 8-for-12 (.667).
Personal fouls/disqualifications: 1979-80, 66/0. 1980-81, 81/0. 1982-83, 70/0. 1983-84, 50/0. Totals, 267/0.

NBA REGULAR-SEASON RECORD

| | | | | | | | | | REBOUNDS | | | | | | | AVERAGES | | |
Season Team	G	Min.	FGM	FGA	Pct.	FTM	FTA	Pct.	Off.	Def.	Tot.	Ast.	St.	Blk.	TO	Pts.	RPG	APG	PPG
84-85—Boston	38	179	26	67	.388	15	17	.882	8	13	21	25	3	0	...	67	0.6	0.7	1.8
85-86—Boston	77	760	92	189	.487	15	23	.652	22	55	77	104	19	4	...	199	1.0	1.4	2.6
86-87—Boston	42	297	30	92	.326	15	20	.750	8	22	30	35	8	0	...	80	0.7	0.8	1.9
87-88—New York	26	204	29	67	.433	10	11	.909	6	7	13	32	11	4	...	74	0.5	1.2	2.8
89-90—New Jersey	5	21	1	7	.143	0	0	...	4	0	0	5	1	1	...	2	0.0	1.0	0.4
Totals	188	1461	178	422	.422	55	71	.775	44	97	141	201	42	9	...	422	0.8	1.1	2.2

Three-point field goals: 1984-85, 0-for-2. 1985-86, 0-for-10. 1986-87, 5-for-16 (.313). 1987-88, 6-for-17 (.353). 1989-90, 0-for-3. Totals, 11-for-48 (.229).
Personal fouls/disqualifications: 1984-85, 21/0. 1985-86, 92/1. 1986-87, 28/0. 1987-88, 39/1. 1989-90, 7/0. Totals, 187/2.

NBA PLAYOFF RECORD

| | | | | | | | | | REBOUNDS | | | | | | | AVERAGES | | |
Season Team	G	Min.	FGM	FGA	Pct.	FTM	FTA	Pct.	Off.	Def.	Tot.	Ast.	St.	Blk.	TO	Pts.	RPG	APG	PPG
85-86—Boston	10	54	8	15	.533	3	4	.750	3	2	5	8	2	0	...	19	0.5	0.8	1.9
87-88—New York	2	8	1	4	.250	0	0	...	1	1	2	0	1	0	...	2	1.0	0.0	1.0
Totals	12	62	9	19	.474	3	4	.750	4	3	7	8	3	0	...	21	0.6	0.7	1.8

Three-point field goals: 1987-88, 0-for-2. Totals, 0-for-2 (.000).
Personal fouls/disqualifications: 1985-86, 9/0. 1987-88, 1/0. Totals, 10/0.

CBA RECORD

| | | | | | | | | | | | | AVERAGES | | |
Season Team	G	Min.	FGM	FGA	Pct.	FTM	FTA	Pct.	Reb.	Ast.	Pts.	RPG	APG	PPG
87-88—Albany	6	172	38	74	.514	16	19	.842	11	14	104	1.8	2.3	17.3

Three-point field goals: 1987-88, 4-for-8 (.500). Totals, 4-for-8 (.500).

HEAD COACHING RECORD
BACKGROUND: Assistant coach, New Jersey Nets (1989-90 through 1993-94). ... Assistant coach, Portland Trail Blazers (1994-95 through 1996-97). ... Assistant coach, Indiana Pacers (1997-98 through 2000-01).

NBA COACHING RECORD

| | REGULAR SEASON | | | | PLAYOFFS | | |
Season Team	W	L	Pct.	Finish	W	L	Pct.
01-02—Detroit	50	32	.610	1st/Central Division	4	6	.400
02-03—Detroit	50	32	.610	1st/Central Division	8	9	.471
03-04—Indiana	61	21	.744	1st/Central Division	10	6	.625
04-05—Indiana	44	38	.537	3rd/Central Division	6	7	.462
05-06—Indiana	41	41	.500	T3rd/Central Conference	2	4	.333
Totals	246	164	.600		30	32	.484

NOTES:
01-02—Defeated Toronto, 3-2, in Eastern Conference first round; lost to Boston, 4-1, in Eastern Conference semifinals.
02-03—Defeated Orlando, 4-3, in Eastern Conference first round; defeated Philadelphia, 4-2, in Eastern Conference semifinals; lost to New Jersey, 4-0, in Eastern Conference finals.
03-04—Defeated Boston, 4-0, in Eastern Conference first round; defeated Miami, 4-2, in Eastern Conference semifinals; lost to Detroit, 4-2, in Eastern Conference finals.
04-05—Defeated Boston, 4-3, in Eastern Conference first round; lost to Detroit, 4-2, in Eastern Conference semifinals.
05-06—Lost to New Jersey Nets, 4-2, in Eastern Conference first round.

CASEY, DWANE TIMBERWOLVES

PERSONAL: Born April 17, 1957, in Morganfield, Ky. ... 6-2/195. (1.88/88.5).
HIGH SCHOOL: Union County (Ky.).
COLLEGE: Kentucky.

COLLEGIATE RECORD

Season Team	G	Min.	FGM	FGA	Pct.	FTM	FTA	Pct.	Reb.	Ast.	Pts.	AVERAGES RPG	APG	PPG
75-76—Kentucky	20	144	10	27	.370	5	9	.556	13	12	25	0.7	0.1	1.3
76-77—Kentucky	27	196	16	51	.314	17	25	.680	11	21	49	0.4	0.8	1.8
77-78—Kentucky	26	177	13	34	.382	6	10	.600	17	21	32	0.6	0.8	1.2
78-79—Kentucky	22	99	7	18	.389	5	7	.714	10	8	19	0.5	0.4	0.9
Totals	95	616	46	130	.354	33	51	.647	51	62	125	0.5	0.7	1.3

HEAD COACHING RECORD

BACKGROUND: Assistant coach, Western Kentucky University (1980-85). ... Assistant coach, University of Kentucky (1985-90). ... Head coach in Japan (1990-94). ... Assistant coach, Seattle SuperSonics (1994-95 through June 17, 2005).

NBA COACHING RECORD

Season Team	REGULAR SEASON W	L	Pct.	Finish	PLAYOFFS W	L	Pct.
05-06—Minnesota	33	49	.402	4th/Northwest Division	—	—	—

CHEEKS, MAURICE   76ERS

PERSONAL: Born September 8, 1956, in Chicago. ... 6-1/180. (1.85/81.6). ... Full name: Maurice Edward Cheeks
HIGH SCHOOL: Du Sable (Chicago).
COLLEGE: West Texas State.
TRANSACTIONS/CAREER NOTES: Selected by Philadelphia 76ers in second round (36th pick overall) of 1978 NBA Draft. ... Traded by 76ers with C Christian Welp and G David Wingate to San Antonio Spurs for G Johnny Dawkins and F Jay Vincent (August 28, 1989). ... Traded by Spurs to New York Knicks for G Rod Strickland (February 21, 1990). ... Traded by Knicks to Atlanta Hawks for C Tim McCormick (October 3, 1991). ... Signed as free agent by New Jersey Nets (January 7, 1993).
MISCELLANEOUS: Member of NBA championship team (1983). ... Philadelphia 76ers franchise all-time assists leader with 6,212 and all-time steals leader with 1,942 (1978-79 through 1988-89).

COLLEGIATE RECORD

Season Team	G	Min.	FGM	FGA	Pct.	FTM	FTA	Pct.	Reb.	Ast.	Pts.	AVERAGES RPG	APG	PPG
74-75—West Texas State	26	...	35	75	.467	31	53	.585	56	...	101	2.2	...	3.9
75-76—West Texas State	23	767	102	170	.600	52	84	.619	91	...	256	4.0	...	11.1
76-77—West Texas State	30	1095	149	246	.606	119	169	.704	119	212	417	4.0	7.1	13.9
77-78—West Texas State	27	941	174	319	.545	105	147	.714	152	153	453	5.6	5.7	16.8
Totals	106	2803	460	810	.568	307	453	.678	418	365	1227	3.9	3.4	11.6

NBA REGULAR-SEASON RECORD

HONORS: NBA All-Defensive first team (1983, 1984, 1985, 1986). ... NBA All-Defensive second team (1987).

Season Team	G	Min.	FGM	FGA	Pct.	FTM	FTA	Pct.	REBOUNDS Off.	Def.	Tot.	Ast.	St.	Blk.	TO	Pts.	AVERAGES RPG	APG	PPG
78-79—Philadelphia	82	2409	292	572	.510	101	140	.721	63	191	254	431	174	12	193	685	3.1	5.3	8.4
79-80—Philadelphia	79	2623	357	661	.540	180	231	.779	75	190	274	560	183	19	174	894	3.5	7.1	11.3
80-81—Philadelphia	81	2415	310	581	.534	140	178	.787	67	178	245	560	193	39	174	763	3.0	6.9	9.4
81-82—Philadelphia	79	2498	352	676	.521	171	220	.777	51	197	248	667	209	33	184	881	3.1	8.4	11.2
82-83—Philadelphia	79	2465	404	745	.542	181	240	.754	53	156	209	543	184	31	179	990	2.6	6.9	12.5
83-84—Philadelphia	75	2494	386	702	.550	170	232	.733	44	161	205	478	171	20	182	950	2.7	6.4	12.7
84-85—Philadelphia	78	2616	422	741	.570	175	199	.879	54	163	217	497	169	24	155	1025	2.8	6.4	13.1
85-86—Philadelphia	82	*3270	490	913	.537	282	335	.842	55	180	235	753	207	27	238	1266	2.9	9.2	15.4
86-87—Philadelphia	68	2624	415	788	.527	227	292	.777	47	168	215	538	180	15	173	1061	3.2	7.9	15.6
87-88—Philadelphia	79	2871	428	865	.495	227	275	.825	59	194	253	635	167	22	160	1086	3.2	8.0	13.7
88-89—Philadelphia	71	2298	336	696	.483	151	195	.774	39	144	183	554	105	17	116	824	2.6	7.8	11.6
89-90—S.A.-N.Y.	81	2519	307	609	.504	171	202	.847	50	190	240	453	124	10	121	789	3.0	5.6	9.7
90-91—New York	76	2147	241	483	.499	105	129	.814	22	151	173	435	128	10	108	592	2.3	5.7	7.8
91-92—Atlanta	56	1086	115	249	.462	26	43	.605	29	66	95	185	83	0	36	259	1.7	3.3	4.6
92-93—New Jersey	35	510	51	93	.548	24	27	.889	5	37	42	107	33	2	33	126	1.2	3.1	3.6
Totals	1101	34845	4906	9374	.523	2331	2938	.793	713	2375	3088	7392	2310	294	2268	12195	2.8	6.7	11.1

Three-point field goals: 1979-80, 4-for-9 (.444). 1980-81, 3-for-8 (.375). 1981-82, 6-for-22 (.273). 1982-83, 1-for-6 (.167). 1983-84, 8-for-20 (.400). 1984-85, 6-for-26 (.231). 1985-86, 4-for-17 (.235). 1986-87, 4-for-17 (.235). 1987-88, 3-for-22 (.136). 1988-89, 1-for-13 (.077). 1989-90, 4-for-16 (.250). 1990-91, 0-for-2 (.250). 1991-92, 3-for-6 (.500). 1992-93, 0-for-2. Totals, 52-for-204 (.255).
Personal fouls/disqualifications: 1978-79, 198/2. 1979-80, 197/1. 1980-81, 231/1. 1981-82, 247/0. 1982-83, 182/0. 1983-84, 196/1. 1984-85, 184/0. 1985-86, 160/0. 1986-87, 109/0. 1987-88, 116/0. 1988-89, 114/0. 1989-90, 78/0. 1990-91, 138/0. 1991-92, 73/0. 1992-93, 35/0. Totals, 2258/5.

NBA PLAYOFF RECORD

Season Team	G	Min.	FGM	FGA	Pct.	FTM	FTA	Pct.	REBOUNDS Off.	Def.	Tot.	Ast.	St.	Blk.	TO	Pts.	AVERAGES RPG	APG	PPG
78-79—Philadelphia	9	330	66	121	.545	37	56	.661	13	22	35	63	37	4	29	169	3.9	7.0	18.8
79-80—Philadelphia	18	675	89	174	.511	29	41	.707	22	52	74	111	45	4	45	208	4.1	6.2	11.6
80-81—Philadelphia	16	513	68	125	.544	32	42	.762	4	47	51	116	40	12	36	168	3.2	7.3	10.5
81-82—Philadelphia	21	765	125	265	.472	50	65	.769	15	47	62	172	48	6	49	301	3.0	8.2	14.3
82-83—Philadelphia	13	483	83	165	.503	45	64	.703	11	28	39	91	26	2	34	212	3.0	7.0	16.3
83-84—Philadelphia	5	171	35	67	.522	13	15	.867	2	10	12	19	13	0	10	83	2.4	3.8	16.6
84-85—Philadelphia	13	483	81	153	.529	36	42	.857	12	34	46	67	31	5	34	198	3.5	5.2	15.2
85-86—Philadelphia	12	519	94	182	.516	62	73	.849	13	43	56	85	13	3	32	250	4.7	7.1	20.8
86-87—Philadelphia	5	210	35	66	.530	18	21	.857	1	12	13	44	9	4	12	88	2.6	8.8	17.6
88-89—Philadelphia	3	128	21	41	.512	11	13	.846	3	8	11	39	7	1	3	53	3.7	13.0	17.7
89-90—New York	10	388	50	104	.481	28	31	.903	12	27	39	85	17	2	19	128	3.9	8.5	12.8
90-91—New York	3	101	14	23	.609	1	2	.500	3	6	9	16	3	1	8	30	3.0	5.3	10.0
92-93—New Jersey	5	82	11	23	.478	0	1	1.000	3	3	6	14	6	1	7	22	1.2	2.8	4.4
Totals	133	4848	772	1509	.512	362	466	.777	114	339	453	922	295	45	318	1910	3.4	6.9	14.4

Three-point field goals: 1979-80, 1-for-5 (.200). 1980-81, 0-for-3. 1981-82, 1-for-9 (.111). 1982-83, 1-for-2 (.500). 1983-84, 0-for-1. 1984-85, 0-for-5. 1985-86, 0-for-7. 1986-87, 0-for-1. 1988-89, 0-for-1. 1989-90, 4-for-12 (.333). 1990-91, 1-for-3 (.333). Totals, 4-for-41 (.098).
Personal fouls/disqualifications: 1978-79, 29/0. 1979-80, 43/0. 1980-81, 55/1. 1981-82, 58/0. 1982-83, 23/0. 1983-84, 18/0. 1984-85, 29/0. 1985-86, 18/0. 1986-87, 14/0. 1988-89, 4/0. 1989-90, 21/0. 1990-91, 9/0. 1992-93, 3/0. Totals, 324/1.

HEAD COACHES

NBA ALL-STAR GAME RECORD

Season Team	Min.	FGM	FGA	Pct.	FTM	FTA	Pct.	REBOUNDS Off.	Def.	Tot.	Ast.	PF	Dq.	St.	Blk.	TO	Pts.
1983—Philadelphia	18	3	8	.375	0	0	...	0	1	1	1	0	0	0	0	0	6
1986—Philadelphia	14	3	6	.500	0	0	...	0	0	0	2	0	0	2	0	3	6
1987—Philadelphia	8	1	2	.500	2	2	1.000	0	0	0	0	1	0	1	0	1	4
1988—Philadelphia	4	0	0	...	0	0	...	0	2	2	1	1	0	0	0	0	0
Totals...........................	44	7	16	.438	2	2	1.000	0	3	3	4	2	0	3	0	4	16

HEAD COACHING RECORD

BACKGROUND: Assistant coach, Philadelphia 76ers (1994-95 to 2000-01).

NBA COACHING RECORD

Season Team	REGULAR SEASON W	L	Pct.	Finish	PLAYOFFS W	L	Pct.
01-02—Portland	49	33	.598	3rd/Pacific Division	0	3	.000
02-03—Portland	50	32	.610	T2nd/Pacific Division	3	4	.429
03-04—Portland	41	41	.500	3rd/Pacific Division	—	—	—
04-05—Portland	22	33	.400	4th/Northwest Division	—	—	—
05-06—Philadelphia.........................	38	44	.463	2nd/Atlantic Conference	—	—	—
Totals	200	183	.522		3	7	.300

NOTES:
01-02—Lost to Los Angeles Lakers, 3-0, in Western Conference first round.
02-03—Lost to Dallas, 4-3, in Western Conference first round.
04-05—Replaced by Kevin Pritchard as head coach (March 2) with club in fourth place.

D'ANTONI, MIKE   SUNS

PERSONAL: Born May 8, 1951, in Mullens, W.Va. ... 6-3/190. (1.91/86.2). ... Full name: Michael Andrew D'Antoni
COLLEGE: Marshall.
TRANSACTIONS/CAREER NOTES: Selected by Kansas City/Omaha Kings in second round (20th pick overall) of 1973 NBA Draft. ... Waived by Kings (November 27, 1975). ... Signed by St. Louis Spirits of American Basketball Association for remainder of 1975-76 season. ... Signed as free agent by San Antonio Spurs (August 12, 1976). ... Released by Spurs (November 22, 1976). ... Played in Italy (1977-78 through 1988-89).

COLLEGIATE RECORD

Season Team	G	Min.	FGM	FGA	Pct.	FTM	FTA	Pct.	Reb.	Ast.	Pts.	AVERAGES RPG	APG	PPG
70-71—Marshall	26	...	162	341	.475	68	91	.747	106	190	392	4.1	7.3	15.1
71-72—Marshall	27	...	177	388	.456	99	125	.792	127	241	453	4.7	8.9	16.8
72-73—Marshall	27	...	152	352	.432	78	99	.788	126	228	382	4.7	8.4	14.1
Totals	80	...	491	1081	.454	245	315	.778	359	659	1227	4.5	8.2	15.3

NBA REGULAR-SEASON RECORD

Season Team	G	Min.	FGM	FGA	Pct.	FTM	FTA	Pct.	REBOUNDS Off.	Def.	Tot.	Ast.	St.	Blk.	TO	Pts.	AVERAGES RPG	APG	PPG
73-74—K.C./Omaha ..	52	989	107	266	.402	33	47	.702	24	69	93	123	75	15	...	247	1.8	2.4	4.8
74-75—K.C./Omaha ..	67	759	69	173	.399	28	36	.778	13	64	77	107	67	12	...	166	1.2	1.6	2.5
75-76—Kansas City ..	9	101	7	27	.259	2	2	1.000	4	10	14	16	10	0	...	16	1.6	1.8	1.8
76-77—San Antonio	2	9	1	3	.333	1	2	.500	0	2	2	2	0	0	...	3	1.0	1.0	1.5
Totals	130	1858	184	469	.392	64	87	.736	41	145	186	248	152	27	...	432	1.4	1.9	3.3

Personal fouls/disqualifications: 1973-74, 112/0. 1974-75, 106/0. 1975-76, 10/0. 1976-77, 3/0. Totals, 239/0.

NBA PLAYOFF RECORD

Season Team	G	Min.	FGM	FGA	Pct.	FTM	FTA	Pct.	REBOUNDS Off.	Def.	Tot.	Ast.	St.	Blk.	TO	Pts.	AVERAGES RPG	APG	PPG
74-75—K.C./Omaha ..	4	42	7	14	.500	4	4	1.000	2	5	7	1	4	1	...	18	1.8	0.3	4.5

Personal fouls/disqualifications: 1974-75, 6/0. Totals, 6/0.

ABA REGULAR-SEASON RECORD

Season Team	G	Min.	FGM	FGA	Pct.	FTM	FTA	Pct.	Reb.	Ast.	Pts.	AVERAGES RPG	APG	PPG
75-76—St. Louis.....................	50	...	77	158	.487	19	26	.731	76	115	173	1.5	2.3	3.5

Three-point field goals: 1975-76, 0-for-4. Totals, 0-for-4 (.000).

ITALIAN LEAGUE RECORD

Season Team	G	Min.	FGM	FGA	Pct.	FTM	FTA	Pct.	Reb.	Ast.	Pts.	AVERAGES RPG	APG	PPG
77-78—Milano	24	...	111	242	.459	31	45	.689	67	37	253	2.8	1.5	10.5
78-79—Milano	28	1032	114	266	.429	52	65	.800	87	33	280	3.1	1.2	10.0
79-80—Milano	31	1147	176	359	.490	60	73	.822	115	73	412	3.7	2.4	13.3
80-81—Milano	37	1438	260	545	.477	89	112	.795	109	56	609	3.0	1.5	16.5
81-82—Milano	39	1524	253	585	.432	89	107	.832	119	62	548	3.1	1.6	15.3
82-83—Milano	38	1447	221	484	.457	106	121	.876	113	100	548	3.0	2.6	14.4
83-84—Milano	31	985	159	333	.478	73	86	.849	87	73	391	2.8	2.4	12.6
84-85—Milano	36	1293	175	389	.450	86	97	.887	138	134	555	3.8	3.7	15.4
85-86—Milano	40	1525	158	393	.450	100	117	.855	115	161	524	2.9	4.0	13.1
86-87—Milano	38	1358	127	347	.366	57	66	.864	93	110	397	2.5	2.9	10.5
87-88—Milano	38	1354	127	347	.366	70	76	.921	67	117	450	1.8	3.1	11.8
88-89—Milano	42	1497	102	246	.415	68	79	.861	127	104	340	3.0	2.5	8.1
Totals	42214700		1983	4536	.437	881	1044	.844	1237	1060	5307	2.9	2.5	12.6

Three-point field goals: 1984-85, 119-for-254 (.469). 1985-86, 108-for-281 (.384). 1986-87, 86-for-231 (.372). 1987-88, 92-for-223 (.413). 1988-89, 68-for-174 (.391). Totals, 473-for-1163 (.407).

HEAD COACHING RECORD

BACKGROUND: Head coach, Philips Milan of Italian League (1990-91 through 1993-94). ... Head coach, Benetton Treviso of Italian

League (1994-95 through 1996-97). ... Director of Player Personnel, Denver Nuggets (1997-98). ... Scout, San Antonio Spurs (1999-2000) ... Assistant, Portland Trail Blazers (2000-01).

ITALIAN LEAGUE COACHING RECORD

	REGULAR SEASON				PLAYOFFS		
Season Team	W	L	Pct.	Finish	W	L	Pct.
90-91—Philips Milano	21	9	.700	1st	—	—	—
91-92—Philips Milano	22	8	.733	1st	—	—	—
92-93—Philips Milano	21	9	.700	2nd	—	—	—
93-94—Philips Milano	22	8	.733	4th	—	—	—
94-95—Benetton Treviso	20	10	.667	3rd	—	—	—
95-96—Benetton Treviso	22	8	.733	3rd	—	—	—
96-97—Benetton Treviso	22	4	.846	1st	—	—	—
01-02—Benetton Treviso	28	8	.778	1st	—	—	—
Totals	178	64	.736		...	...	...

NBA COACHING RECORD

	REGULAR SEASON				PLAYOFFS		
Season Team	W	L	Pct.	Finish	W	L	Pct.
98-99—Denver	14	36	.280	6th/Midwest Division	—	—	—
03-04—Phoenix	21	40	.344	6th/Pacific Division	—	—	—
04-05—Phoenix	62	20	.756	1st/Pacific Division	9	6	.600
05-06—Phoenix	54	28	.659	1st/Pacific Division	10	10	.500
Totals	151	124	.549		19	16	.543

NOTES:
03-04—Replaced Frank Johnson as Phoenix head coach (December 10) with 8-17 record and club in seventh place.
04-05—Defeated Memphis, 4-0, in Western Conference first round; defeated Dallas, 4-2, in Western Conference semifinals; lost to San Antonio, 4-1, in Western Conference finals.
05-06—Defeated Los Angeles Lakers, 4-3, in Western Conference first round; defeated Los Angeles Clippers, 4-3, in Western Conference semifinals; lost to Dallas Mavericks, 4-2, in Western Conference finals.

DUNLEAVY, MIKE — CLIPPERS

PERSONAL: Born March 21, 1954, in Brooklyn, N.Y. ... 6-3/180. (1.91/81.6). ... Full name: Michael Joseph Dunleavy ... Father of Mike Dunleavy, guard/forward with Golden State Warriors. ... Name pronounced DONE-lee-vee.
HIGH SCHOOL: Nazareth Regional (Brooklyn, N.Y.).
COLLEGE: South Carolina.
TRANSACTIONS/CAREER NOTES: Selected by Philadelphia 76ers in sixth round (99th pick overall) of 1976 NBA Draft. ... Waived by 76ers (November 14, 1977). ... Player/head coach with Carolina Lightning of All-America Basketball Alliance (1977-78). ... Signed as free agent by Houston Rockets (March 10, 1978). ... Signed as veteran free agent by San Antonio Spurs (October 16, 1982); Rockets waived their right of first refusal in exchange for 1983 third-round draft choice. ... Signed as veteran free agent by Milwaukee Bucks (March 8, 1984); Spurs waived their right of first refusal in exchange for 1984 fourth-round draft choice and cash. ... Waived by Bucks (October 24, 1985). ... Re-signed by Bucks to 10-day contract (February 19, 1989). ... Waived by Bucks (February 24, 1989). ... Re-signed as free agent by Bucks (December 10, 1989). ... Waived by Bucks (December 15, 1989). ... Re-signed by Bucks to 10-day contract (March 2, 1990). ... Waived by Bucks (March 9, 1990).

COLLEGIATE RECORD

												AVERAGES		
Season Team	G	Min.	FGM	FGA	Pct.	FTM	FTA	Pct.	Reb.	Ast.	Pts.	RPG	APG	PPG
72-73—South Carolina	29	803	122	236	.517	59	72	.819	60	73	303	2.1	2.5	10.4
73-74—South Carolina	27	983	167	369	.453	97	116	.836	85	95	431	3.1	3.5	16.0
74-75—South Carolina	28	1016	182	368	.495	91	119	.765	110	89	455	3.9	3.2	16.3
75-76—South Carolina	27	962	144	297	.485	109	139	.784	87	113	397	3.2	4.2	14.7
Totals	111	3764	615	1270	.484	356	446	.798	342	370	1586	3.1	3.3	14.3

NBA REGULAR-SEASON RECORD

NOTES: Led NBA with .345 three-point field goal percentage (1983).

									REBOUNDS									AVERAGES		
Season Team	G	Min.	FGM	FGA	Pct.	FTM	FTA	Pct.	Off.	Def.	Tot.	Ast.	St.	Blk.	TO	Pts.	RPG	APG	PPG
76-77—Philadelphia	32	359	60	145	.414	34	45	.756	10	24	34	56	13	2	...	154	1.1	1.8	4.8
77-78—Phila.-Hous.	15	119	20	50	.400	13	18	.722	1	9	10	28	9	1	12	53	0.7	1.9	3.5
78-79—Houston	74	1486	215	425	.506	159	184	.864	28	100	128	324	56	5	130	589	1.7	4.4	8.0
79-80—Houston	51	1036	149	319	.464	111	134	.828	26	74	100	210	40	4	110	410	2.0	4.1	8.0
80-81—Houston	74	1609	310	632	.491	156	186	.839	28	90	118	268	64	2	137	772	1.6	3.6	10.5
81-82—Houston	70	1315	206	450	.458	75	106	.708	24	80	104	227	45	3	80	520	1.5	3.2	7.4
82-83—San Antonio	79	1619	213	510	.418	120	154	.779	18	116	134	437	74	4	160	613	1.7	5.5	7.8
83-84—Milwaukee	17	404	70	127	.551	32	40	.800	6	22	28	78	12	1	36	191	1.6	4.6	11.2
84-85—Milwaukee	19	433	64	135	.474	25	29	.862	6	25	31	85	15	3	40	169	1.6	4.5	8.9
85-86—NO CLUB									Did not play.										
86-87—NO CLUB									Did not play.										
87-88—NO CLUB									Did not play.										
88-89—Milwaukee	2	5	1	2	.500	0	0	...	0	0	0	0	0	0	0	3	0.0	0.0	1.5
89-90—Milwaukee	5	43	4	14	.286	7	8	.875	0	2	2	10	1	0	8	17	0.4	2.0	3.4
Totals	438	8428	1311	2809	.467	732	904	.810	147	542	689	1723	329	25	713	3496	1.6	3.9	8.0

Three-point field goals: 1979-80, 3-for-20 (.150). 1980-81, 1-for-16 (.063). 1981-82, 33-for-86 (.384). 1982-83, 67-for-194 (.345). 1983-84, 19-for-45 (.422). 1984-85, 16-for-47 (.340). 1988-89, 1-for-2 (.500). 1989-90, 2-for-9 (.222). Totals, 142-for-419 (.339).
Personal fouls/disqualifications: 1976-77, 64/1. 1977-78, 12/0. 1978-79, 168/2. 1979-80, 120/2. 1980-81, 165/1. 1981-82, 161/0. 1982-83, 210/1. 1983-84, 51/0. 1984-85, 55/1. 1989-90, 7/0. Totals, 1013/8.

NBA PLAYOFF RECORD

									REBOUNDS									AVERAGES		
Season Team	G	Min.	FGM	FGA	Pct.	FTM	FTA	Pct.	Off.	Def.	Tot.	Ast.	St.	Blk.	TO	Pts.	RPG	APG	PPG
76-77—Philadelphia	11	68	9	25	.360	4	5	.800	1	3	4	9	3	0	...	22	0.4	0.8	2.0
78-79—Houston	1	10	0	2	.000	0	0	...	0	1	1	0	0	0	0	0	1.0	0.0	0.0
79-80—Houston	6	45	6	12	.500	5	6	.833	2	3	5	13	5	0	6	17	0.8	2.2	2.8

Season Team	G	Min.	FGM	FGA	Pct.	FTM	FTA	Pct.	REBOUNDS Off.	Def.	Tot.	Ast.	St.	Blk.	TO	Pts.	AVERAGES RPG	APG	PPG
80-81—Houston	20	472	69	152	.454	33	38	.868	9	33	42	68	15	1	30	177	2.1	3.4	8.9
81-82—Houston	3	66	9	22	.409	5	6	.833	0	3	3	9	2	0	1	23	1.0	3.0	7.7
82-83—San Antonio ..	11	174	22	65	.338	9	13	.692	3	10	13	49	9	1	14	61	1.2	4.5	5.5
83-84—Milwaukee ...	15	393	59	129	.457	33	36	.917	10	25	35	46	17	0	35	169	2.3	3.1	11.3
Totals	67	1228	174	407	.428	89	104	.856	25	78	103	194	51	2	86	469	1.5	2.9	7.0

Three-point field goals: 1979-80, 0-for-2. 1980-81, 6-for-15 (.400). 1981-82, 0-for-4. 1982-83, 8-for-30 (.267). 1983-84, 18-for-50 (.360). Totals, 32-for-101 (.317).

Personal fouls/disqualifications: 1976-77, 14/0. 1978-79, 1/0. 1979-80, 11/0. 1980-81, 59/1. 1981-82, 7/0. 1982-83, 22/0. 1983-84, 59/2. Totals, 173/3.

ALL AMERICA BASKETBALL ALLIANCE RECORD

Season Team	G	Min.	FGM	FGA	Pct.	FTM	FTA	Pct.	Reb.	Ast.	Pts.	AVERAGES RPG	APG	PPG
77-78—Carolina........................	10	332	66	123	.537	53	60	.883	52	50	191	5.2	5.0	19.1

Three-point field goals: 1977-78, 2-for-5 (.400). Totals, 2-for-5 (.400).

HEAD COACHING RECORD

BACKGROUND: Player/head coach, Carolina Lightning of All-America Basketball Alliance (1977-78). ... Assistant coach, Milwaukee Bucks (1987-88 through 1989-90).

NBA COACHING RECORD

Season Team	REGULAR SEASON W	L	Pct.	Finish	PLAYOFFS W	L	Pct.
90-91—L.A. Lakers	58	24	.707	2nd/ Pacific Division	12	7	.632
91-92—L.A. Lakers	43	39	.524	6th/Pacific Division	1	3	.250
92-93—Milwaukee	28	54	.341	7th/Central Division	—	—	—
93-94—Milwaukee	20	62	.244	T6th/Central Division	—	—	—
94-95—Milwaukee	34	48	.415	6th/Central Division	—	—	—
95-96—Milwaukee	25	57	.305	7th/Central Division	—	—	—
97-98—Portland	46	36	.561	4th/Pacific Division	1	3	.250
98-99—Portland	35	15	.700	1st/Pacific Division	7	6	.538
99-00—Portland	59	23	.720	2nd/Pacific Division	10	6	.625
00-01—Portland	50	32	.610	4th/Pacific Division	0	3	.000
03-04—L.A. Clippers	28	54	.341	7th/Pacific Division	—	—	—
04-05—L.A. Clippers	37	45	.451	3rd/Pacific Division	—	—	—
05-06—L.A. Clippers	47	35	.573	2nd/Pacific Division	7	5	.583
Totals	510	524	.493		38	33	.535

NOTES:

90-91—Defeated Houston, 3-0, in Western Conference first round; defeated Golden State, 4-1, in Western Conference semifinals; defeated Portland, 4-2, in Western Conference finals; lost to Chicago, 4-1, in NBA Finals.

91-92—Lost to Portland, 3-1, in Western Conference first round.

97-98—Lost to Los Angeles Lakers, 3-1, in Western Conference first round.

98-99—Defeated Phoenix, 3-0, in Western Conference first round; defeated Utah, 4-2, in Western Conference semifinals; lost to San Antonio, 4-0, in Western Conference finals.

99-00—Defeated Minnesota, 3-1, in Western Conference first round; defeated Utah, 4-1, in Western Conference semifinals; lost to Los Angeles Lakers, 4-3, in Western Conference finals.

00-01—Lost to Los Angeles Lakers, 3-0, in Western Conference first round.

05-06—Defeated Denver, 4-1, in Western Conference first round; lost to Phoenix, 4-3, in Western Conference semifinals.

FRANK, LAWRENCE — NETS

PERSONAL: Born August 23, 1970, in Teaneck, N.J.
HIGH SCHOOL: Teaneck (N.J.).
COLLEGE: Indiana with a Masters from Marquette.

HEAD COACHING RECORD

BACKGROUND: Staff assistant, Marquette University (1992-94). ... Assistant coach, University of Tennessee (1994-97). ... Assistant coach, Vancouver Grizzlies (1997-2000). ... Assistant coach, Nets (2000-01 through January 26, 2004).

NBA COACHING RECORD

Season Team	REGULAR SEASON W	L	Pct.	Finish	PLAYOFFS W	L	Pct.
03-04—New Jersey	25	15	.625	1st/Atlantic Division	7	4	.636
04-05—New Jersey	42	40	.512	3rd/Atlantic Division	0	4	.000
05-06—New Jersey	49	33	.598	1st/Atlantic Division	5	6	.455
Totals	116	88	.569		12	14	.462

NOTES:

03-04—Replaced Byron Scott as New Jersey head coach (January 26) with record of 22-20 and club in fifth place. Defeated New York, 4-0, in Eastern Conference first round; lost to Detroit, 4-3, in Eastern Conference semifinals.

04-05—Lost to Miami, 4-0, in Eastern Conference first round.

05-06—Defeated Indiana, 4-2, in Eastern Conference first round; lost to Miami, 4-1, in Eastern Conference semifinals.

FRATELLO, MIKE — GRIZZLIES

PERSONAL: Born February 24, 1947, in Hackensack, N.J. ... 5-7/150. (1.70/68.0). ... Full name: Michael Robert Fratello.
HIGH SCHOOL: Hackensack (N.J.).
COLLEGE: Montclair (N.J.) State College.

HEAD COACHING RECORD

BACKGROUND: Football and basketball coach, Hackensack (N.J.) High (1969-70). ... Assistant coach, Rhode Island University (1970-72). ... Assistant coach, James Madison University (1972-75). ... Assistant coach, Villanova University (1975-76 through 1977-78). ... Assistant coach, Atlanta Hawks (1978-79 through 81-82). ... Assistant coach, New York Knicks (1982-83). ... Vice president/head coach, Hawks, (1986-87 through 1989-90). ... Broadcaster, NBC television, (1990-91 through 1992-93). … Broadcaster, Turner Sports (1999-2000 through 2004).

NBA COACHING RECORD

Season Team	REGULAR SEASON				PLAYOFFS		
	W	L	Pct.	Finish	W	L	Pct.
80-81—Atlanta	0	3	.000	4th/Central Division	—	—	—
83-84—Atlanta	40	42	.488	3rd/Central Division	2	3	.400
84-85—Atlanta	34	48	.415	5th/Central Division	—	—	—
85-86—Atlanta	50	32	.610	2nd/Central Division	4	5	.444
86-87—Atlanta	57	25	.695	1st/Central Division	4	5	.444
87-88—Atlanta	50	32	.610	T2nd/Central Division	6	6	.500
88-89—Atlanta	52	30	.634	3rd/Central Division	2	3	.400
89-90—Atlanta	41	41	.500	6th/Central Division	—	—	—
93-94—Cleveland	47	35	.573	T3rd/Central Division	0	3	.000
94-95—Cleveland	43	39	.524	4th/Central Division	1	3	.250
95-96—Cleveland	47	35	.573	3rd/Central Division	0	3	.000
96-97—Cleveland	42	40	.512	5th/Central Division	—	—	—
97-98—Cleveland	47	35	.573	5th/Central Division	1	3	.250
98-99—Cleveland	28	22	.560		—	—	—
04-05—Memphis	40	26	.606	4th/Southwest Division	0	4	.000
05-06—Memphis	49	33	.598	3rd/Southwest Division	0	4	.000
Totals	667	518	.563		20	42	.323

NOTES:

80-81—Replaced Hubie Brown as Atlanta head coach (March 26), with record of 31-48 and club in fourth place. Served as interim co-head coach with Brendan Suhr for remainder of season.
83-84—Lost to Milwaukee in Eastern Conference first round.
85-86—Defeated Detroit, 3-1, in Eastern Conference first round; lost to Boston, 4-1, in Eastern Conference semifinals.
86-87—Defeated Milwaukee, 3-2, in Eastern Conference first round; lost to Detroit, 4-1, in Eastern Conference semifinals.
87-88—Defeated Milwaukee, 3-2, in Eastern Conference first round; lost to Boston, 4-3, in Eastern Conference semifinals.
93-94—Lost to Chicago, 3-0, in Eastern Conference first round.
94-95—Lost to New York, 3-1, in Eastern Conference first round.
95-96—Lost to New York, 3-0, in Eastern Conference first round.
97-98—Lost to Indiana, 3-1, in Eastern Conference first round.
04-05—Replaced Hubie Brown as Memphis head coach (December 3, 2004) with a 5-11 record. Lost to Phoenix, 4-0, in Western Conference first round.
05-06—Lost to Dallas, 4-0, in Western Conference first round.

HILL, BRIAN   MAGIC

PERSONAL: Born September 19, 1947, in East Orange, N.J. ... 5-9/175. (1.75/79.4). ... Full name: Brian Alfred Hill ... Brother of Fred Hill, head baseball coach, Rutgers University.
HIGH SCHOOL: Our Lady of the Valley (East Orange, N.J.).
COLLEGE: Kennedy (Neb.).

HEAD COACHING RECORD

BACKGROUND. Assistant coach, Piscataway (N.J.) Township High School (1969-70 and 1970-71). ... Assistant coach, Clifford J. Scott High School, N.J. (1971-72). ... Assistant coach, Montclair (N.J.) State University (1972-73 and 1973-74). ... Assistant coach, Lehigh University (1974-75). ... Assistant coach, Penn State University (1983-84 through 1985-86). ... Assistant coach, Atlanta Hawks (1986-87 through 1989-90). ... Assistant coach, Orlando Magic (1990-91 through 1992-93). ... Assistant coach, New Orleans Hornets (2001-03). ... Assistant coach, New Jersey Nets (2004-05).

NBA COACHING RECORD

Season Team	REGULAR SEASON				PLAYOFFS		
	W	L	Pct.	Finish	W	L	Pct.
93-94—Orlando	50	32	.610	2nd/Atlantic Division	0	3	.000
94-95—Orlando	57	25	.695	1st/Atlantic Division	11	10	.524
95-96—Orlando	60	22	.732	1st/Atlantic Division	7	5	.583
96-97—Orlando	24	25	.490		—	—	—
97-98—Vancouver	19	63	.232	6th/Midwest Division	—	—	—
98-99—Vancouver	8	42	.160	7th/Midwest Division	—	—	—
99-00—Vancouver	4	18	.182		—	—	—
05-06—Orlando	36	46	.439	3rd/Southeast Division	—	—	—
Totals	258	273	.486		18	18	.500

NOTES:

93-94—Lost to Indiana, 3-0, in Eastern Conference first round.
94-95—Defeated Boston, 3-1, in Eastern Conference first round; defeated Chicago, 4-2, in Eastern Conference semifinals; defeated Indiana, 4-3, in Eastern Conference finals; lost to Houston, 4-0, in NBA Finals.
95-96—Defeated Detroit, 3-0, in Eastern Conference first round; defeated Atlanta, 4-1, in Eastern Conference semifinals; lost to Chicago, 4-0, in Eastern Conference finals.
96-97—Replaced as Orlando head coach by Richie Adubato (February 18) with club in third place.
99-00—Replaced by Lionel Hollins as Vancouver coach (December 16).

HILL, BOB   SUPERSONICS

PERSONAL: Born November 24, 1948, in Columbus, Ohio. ... 6-5/200. (1.96/90.7). ... Full name: Robert W. Hill
HIGH SCHOOL: Worthington (Ohio).
COLLEGE: Bowling Green State.

COLLEGIATE RECORD

Season Team	G	Min.	FGM	FGA	Pct.	FTM	FTA	Pct.	Reb.	Ast.	Pts.	AVERAGES		
												RPG	APG	PPG
67-68—Bowling Green State	14	...	108	215	.502	41	57	.719	127	...	257	9.1	...	18.4

Season Team	G	Min.	FGM	FGA	Pct.	FTM	FTA	Pct.	Reb.	Ast.	Pts.	AVERAGES RPG	APG	PPG
68-69—Bowling Green State......	20	...	22	54	.407	12	22	.545	21	...	56	1.1	...	2.8
69-70—Bowling Green State......	16	...	5	23	.217	6	12	.500	14	...	16	0.9	...	1.0
70-71—Bowling Green State......	21	...	22	49	.449	9	16	.563	31	...	53	1.5	...	2.5
Totals	71	...	157	341	.460	68	107	.636	193	...	382	2.7	...	5.4

HEAD COACHING RECORD

BACKGROUND: Assistant coach, Bowling Green State (1971-72 through 1975). ... Assistant coach, Pittsburgh (1975 through 1977). ... Assistant coach, University of Kansas (1977-78 through 1985-86). ... Coach, Vitrus Knorr of Italian League (1988-89). ... Coach, Fordham University (1999 through 2002). ... Assistant coach, Seattle SuperSonics (August 26, 2005 through January 3, 2006).

NBA COACHING RECORD

Season Team	REGULAR SEASON W	L	Pct.	Finish	PLAYOFFS W	L	Pct.
86-87—N.Y. Knicks	20	46	.303	T-4th/Atlantic Division	—	—	—
90-91—Indiana	32	25	.561	5th/Central Division	2	3	.400
91-92—Indiana	40	42	.488	4th/Central Division	0	3	.000
92-93—Indiana	41	41	.500	5th/Central Division	1	3	.250
94-95—San Antonio	62	20	.756	1st/Midwest Division	9	6	.600
95-96—San Antonio	59	23	.720	1st/Midwest Division	5	5	.500
96-97—San Antonio	3	15	.167		—	—	—
05-06—Seattle	22	30	.423	3rd/Northwest Division	—	—	—
Totals	279	242	.536		17	20	.459

NOTES:

86-87—Replaced Hubie Brown as New York head coach (December 1) with a 4-12 record.
90-91—Replaced Dick Versace as Indiana head coach with a 9-16 record. Lost to Boston, 3-2, in Eastern Conference first round.
91-92—Lost to Boston, 3-0, in Eastern Conference first round.
92-93—Lost to New York, 3-1, in Eastern Conference first round.
94-95—Defeated Denver, 3-0, in Western Conference first round; defeated Los Angeles Lakers, 4-2, in Western Conference semifinals; lost to Houston, 4-2, in Western Conference finals.
95-96—Defeated Phoenix, 3-1, in Western Conference first round; lost to Utah, 4-2, in Western Conference semifinals.
96-97—Replaced as San Antonio head coach by Gregg Popovich (December 10).
05-06—Replaced Bob Weiss as Seattle head coach (January 3) with a record of 13-17.

JACKSON, PHIL LAKERS

PERSONAL: Born September 17, 1945, in Deer Lodge, Mont. ... 6-8/230. (2.03/104.3). ... Full name: Philip D. Jackson.
HIGH SCHOOL: Williston (N.D.).
COLLEGE: North Dakota.
TRANSACTIONS/CAREER NOTES: Selected by New York Knicks in second round (17th pick overall) of 1967 NBA Draft. ... Traded by Knicks with future draft choice to New Jersey Nets for future draft choices (June 8, 1978). ... Waived by Nets (October 11, 1978). ... Re-signed as free agent by Nets (November 10, 1978). ... Waived by Nets (October 12, 1979). ... Re-signed as free agent by Nets (February 15, 1980).
MISCELLANEOUS: Member of NBA championship team (1973).

COLLEGIATE RECORD

Season Team	G	Min.	FGM	FGA	Pct.	FTM	FTA	Pct.	Reb.	Ast.	Pts.	AVERAGES RPG	APG	PPG
63-64—North Dakota	...	...	...	...	...	...	...	...	...	...	...	...	...	...
64-65—North Dakota	31	...	129	307	.420	107	156	.686	361	...	365	11.6	...	11.8
65-66—North Dakota	29	...	238	439	.542	155	203	.764	374	...	631	12.9	...	21.8
66-67—North Dakota	26	...	252	468	.538	208	278	.748	374	...	712	14.4	...	27.4
Totals	86	...	619	1214	.510	470	637	.738	1109	...	1708	12.9	...	19.9

NBA REGULAR-SEASON RECORD

HONORS: NBA All-Rookie team (1968).
NOTES: Led NBA with 330 personal fouls (1975).

Season Team	G	Min.	FGM	FGA	Pct.	FTM	FTA	Pct.	REBOUNDS Off.	Def.	Tot.	Ast.	St.	Blk.	TO	Pts.	AVERAGES RPG	APG	PPG
67-68—New York	75	1093	182	455	.400	99	168	.589	...	...	338	55	...	...	...	463	4.5	0.7	6.2
68-69—New York	47	924	126	294	.429	80	119	.672	...	...	246	43	...	...	...	332	5.2	0.9	7.1
69-70—New York								Did not play—injured.										
70-71—New York	71	771	118	263	.449	95	133	.714	...	...	238	31	...	...	...	331	3.4	0.4	4.7
71-72—New York	80	1273	205	466	.440	167	228	.732	...	...	326	72	...	...	...	577	4.1	0.9	7.2
72-73—New York	80	1393	245	553	.443	154	195	.790	...	...	344	94	...	...	...	644	4.3	1.2	8.1
73-74—New York	82	2050	361	757	.477	191	246	.776	123	355	478	134	42	67	...	913	5.8	1.6	11.1
74-75—New York	78	2285	324	712	.455	193	253	.763	137	463	600	136	84	53	...	841	7.7	1.7	10.8
75-76—New York	80	1461	185	387	.478	110	150	.733	80	263	343	105	41	20	...	480	4.3	1.3	6.0
76-77—N.Y. Knicks	76	1033	102	232	.440	51	71	.718	75	154	229	85	33	18	...	255	3.0	1.1	3.4
77-78—New York	63	654	55	115	.478	43	56	.768	29	81	110	46	31	15	47	153	1.7	0.7	2.4
78-79—New Jersey ..	59	1070	144	303	.475	86	105	.819	59	119	178	85	45	22	78	374	3.0	1.4	6.3
79-80—New Jersey ..	16	194	29	46	.630	7	10	.700	12	12	24	12	5	4	9	65	1.5	0.8	4.1
Totals	807	14201	2076	4583	.453	1276	1734	.736	515	1447	3454	898	281	199	134	5428	4.3	1.1	6.7

Three-point field goals: 1979-80, 0-for-2. Totals, 0-for-2 (.000).
Personal fouls/disqualifications: 1967-68, 212/3. 1968-69, 168/6. 1970-71, 169/4. 1971-72, 224/4. 1972-73, 218/2. 1973-74, 277/7. 1974-75, 330/10. 1975-76, 275/3. 1976-77, 184/4. 1977-78, 106/0. 1978-79, 168/7. 1979-80, 35/1. Totals, 2366/51.

NBA PLAYOFF RECORD

Season Team	G	Min.	FGM	FGA	Pct.	FTM	FTA	Pct.	REBOUNDS Off.	Def.	Tot.	Ast.	St.	Blk.	TO	Pts.	AVERAGES RPG	APG	PPG
67-68—New York	6	90	10	35	.286	4	5	.800	...	...	25	2	...	...	...	24	4.2	0.3	4.0
68-69—New York								Did not play—injured.										
70-71—New York	5	30	4	14	.286	1	1	1.000	...	...	10	2	...	...	...	9	2.0	0.4	1.8
71-72—New York	16	320	57	120	.475	42	57	.737	...	...	82	15	...	...	...	156	5.1	0.9	9.8

Season Team	G	Min.	FGM	FGA	Pct.	FTM	FTA	Pct.	REBOUNDS Off.	Def.	Tot.	Ast.	St.	Blk.	TO	Pts.	AVERAGES RPG	APG	PPG
72-73—New York	17	338	60	120	.500	28	38	.737	...	...	72	24	...	...	...	148	4.2	1.4	8.7
73-74—New York	12	297	54	116	.466	27	30	.900	15	42	57	15	10	5	...	135	4.8	1.3	11.3
74-75—New York	3	78	10	21	.476	7	8	.875	5	20	25	2	4	3	...	27	8.3	0.7	9.0
77-78—New York	6	50	4	8	.500	4	6	.667	4	6	10	3	3	0	4	12	1.7	0.5	2.0
78-79—New Jersey ..	2	20	1	3	.333	2	2	1.000	2	1	3	0	1	0	0	4	1.5	0.0	2.0
Totals	67	1223	200	437	.458	115	147	.782	26	69	284	63	18	8	4	515	4.2	0.9	7.7

Personal fouls/disqualifications: 1967-68, 23/0. 1970-71, 8/0. 1971-72, 51/1. 1972-73, 59/3. 1973-74, 40/0. 1974-75, 15/0. 1977-78, 11/0. 1978-79, 1/0. Totals, 208/4.

HEAD COACHING RECORD

BACKGROUND: Player/assistant coach, New Jersey Nets (1978-79 and 1979-80). ... Assistant coach, Nets (1980-81). ... Broadcaster, Nets (1981-82). ... Assistant coach, Chicago Bulls (1987-88 and 1988-89).

CBA COACHING RECORD

Season Team	REGULAR SEASON W	L	Pct.	Finish	PLAYOFFS W	L	Pct.
82-83—Albany...	8	11	.421	4th/Eastern Division	—	—	—
83-84—Albany...	25	19	.568	2nd/Eastern Division	9	5	.643
84-85—Albany...	34	14	.708	1st/Eastern Division	5	5	.500
85-86—Albany...	24	24	.500	4th/Eastern Division	3	4	.429
86-87—Albany...	26	22	.542	T2nd/Eastern Division	4	4	.500
Totals..	117	90	.565		21	18	.538

NOTES:

82-83—Replaced Dean Memiger (8-15) and player/interim coach Sam Worthen (0-2) as Albany Patroons head coach (January 29), with record of 8-17.

83-84—Defeated Bay State, 3-2, in Eastern semifinals; defeated Puerto Rico, 3-1, in Eastern finals; defeated Wyoming, 3-2, in CBA Championship Series.

84-85—Defeated Toronto, 3-2, in Eastern semifinals, lost to Tampa Bay, 3-2, in Eastern finals.

85-86—Lost to Tampa Bay in Eastern semifinals.

86-87—Defeated Mississippi, 4-0, in Eastern semifinals; lost to Rapid City, 4-0, in Eastern finals.

NBA COACHING RECORD

Season Team	REGULAR SEASON W	L	Pct.	Finish	PLAYOFFS W	L	Pct.
89-90—Chicago..	55	27	.671	2nd/Central Division	10	6	.625
90-91—Chicago..	61	21	.744	1st/Central Division	15	2	.882
91-92—Chicago..	67	15	.817	1st/Central Division	15	7	.682
92-93—Chicago..	57	25	.695	1st/Central Division	15	4	.789
93-94—Chicago..	55	27	.671	2nd/Central Division	6	4	.600
94-95—Chicago..	47	35	.573	2nd/Central Division	5	5	.500
95-96—Chicago..	72	10	.878	1st/Central Division	15	3	.833
96-97—Chicago..	69	13	.841	1st/Central Division	15	4	.789
97-98—Chicago..	62	20	.756	1st/Central Division	15	6	.714
99-00—L.A. Lakers......................................	67	15	.817	1st/ Pacific Division	15	8	.652
00-01—L.A. Lakers......................................	56	26	.683	1st/Pacific Division	15	1	.938
01-02—L.A. Lakers......................................	58	24	.707	1st/Pacific Division	15	4	.789
02-03—L.A. Lakers......................................	50	32	.610	T2nd/Central Division	6	6	.500
03-04—L.A. Lakers......................................	56	26	.683	1st/Pacific Division	13	9	.591
05-06—L.A. Lakers......................................	45	37	.549	3rd/Pacific Division	3	4	.429
Totals..	877	353	.713		178	73	.709

NOTES:

89-90—Defeated Milwaukee, 3-1, in Eastern Conference first round; defeated Philadelphia, 4-1, in Eastern Conference semifinals; lost to Detroit, 4-3, in Eastern Conference finals.

90-91—Defeated New York, 3-0, in Eastern Conference first round; defeated Philadelphia, 4-1, in Eastern Conference semifinals; defeated Detroit,4-0, in Eastern Conference finals; defeated Los Angeles Lakers, 4-1, in NBA Finals.

91-92—Defeated Miami, 3,0, in Eastern Conference first round; defeated New York, 4-3 in Eastern Conference semifinals; defeated Cleveland, 4-2, in Eastern Conference finals; defeated Portland, 4-2, in NBA Finals.

92-93—Defeated Atlanta, 3-0, in Eastern Conference first round; defeated Cleveland, 4-0, in Eastern Conference semifinals; defeated New York, 4-2, in Eastern Conference finals; defeated Phoenix, 4-2, in NBA Finals.

93-94—Defeated Cleveland, 3-0, in Eastern Conference first round; lost to New York, 4-3, in Eastern Conference semifinals.

94-95—Defeated Charlotte, 3-1, in Eastern Conference first round; lost to Orlando, 4-2, in Eastern Conference semifinals.

95-96—Defeated Miami, 3-0, in Eastern Conference first round; defeated Atlanta, 4-1, in Eastern Conference semifinals; defeated Orlando, 4-0, in Eastern Conference finals; defeat Seattle, 4-2, in NBA finals.

96-97—Defeated Washington, 3-0, in Eastern Conference first round; defeated Atlanta, 4-1, in Eastern Conference semifinals; defeated Miami, 4-1, in Eastern Conference finals; defeated Utah, 4-2, in NBA finals.

97-98—Defeated New Jersey, 3-0, in Eastern Conference first round; defeated Charlotte, 4-1, in Eastern Conference semifinals; defeated Indiana, 4-3, in Eastern Conference finals; defeated Utah, 4-2, in NBA finals.

99-00—Defeated Sacramento, 3-2, in Western Conference first round;defeated Phoenix, 4-1, in Western Conference semifinals; defeated Portland, 4-3, in Western Conference finals; defeated Indiana, 4-2, in NBA Finals.

00-01—Defeated Portland, 3-0, in Western Conference first round; defeated Sacramento, 4-0, in Western Conference semifinals; defeated San Antonio, 4-0, in Western Conference finals; defeated Philadelphia, 4-1, in NBA Finals.

01-02—Defeated Portland, 3-0, in Western Conference first round; defeated San Antonio, 4-1, in Western Conference semifinals; defeated Sacramento, 4-3, in Western Conference finals; defeated New Jersey, 4-0, in NBA Finals.

02-03—Defeated Minnesota, 4-2, in Western Conference first round; lost to San Antonio, 4-2, in Western Conference semifinals.

03-04—Defeated Houston, 4-1, in Western Conference first rund; defeated San Antonio, 4-2, in Western Conference semifinals; defeated Minnesota, 4-2, in Western Conference finals; lost to Detroit, 4-1, in NBA Finals.

05-06—Lost to Phoenix, 4-3, in Western Conference first round.

JOHNSON, AVERY — MAVERICKS

PERSONAL: Born March 25, 1965, in New Orleans. ... 5-11/180. (1.80/81.6).
HIGH SCHOOL: St. Augustine (New Orleans).
JUNIOR COLLEGE: New Mexico Junior College.
COLLEGE: Cameron (Okla.), then Southern (La.).
TRANSACTIONS/CAREER NOTES: Not drafted by an NBA franchise. ... Played in United States Basketball League with Palm Beach Stingrays (1988). ... Signed as free agent by Seattle SuperSonics (August 2, 1988). ... Traded by SuperSonics to Denver Nuggets for 1997 second-round draft choice (October 24, 1990). ... Waived by Nuggets (December 24, 1990). ... Signed as free agent by San Antonio Spurs (January 17, 1991). ... Waived by Spurs (December 17, 1991). ... Signed by Houston Rockets to first of two consecutive 10-day contracts (January 10, 1992). ... Re-signed by Rockets for remainder of season (January 31, 1992). ... Signed as free agent by Spurs (November 19, 1992). ... Signed as free agent by Golden State Warriors (October 25, 1993). ... Signed as unrestricted free agent by Spurs (July 21, 1994). ... Signed as free agent by Nuggets (July 18, 2001). ... Traded by Nuggets with G Nick Van Exel, F/C Raef LaFrentz and G/F Tariq Abdul-Wahad to Dallas Mavericks for F Juwan Howard, G Tim Hardaway, F Donnell Harvey, cash considerations and first-round draft choice (February 21, 2002). ... Traded by Mavericks with G Nick Van Exel, F Popeye Jones, F Antoine Rigaudeau and C Evan Eschmeyer to Golden State Warriors for F Antawn Jamison, F Chris Mills, F Danny Fortson and G Jiri Welsch (August 18, 2003). ... Signed as free agent by Mavericks (September 30, 2004).
MISCELLANEOUS: Member of NBA championship team (1999). ... San Antonio Spurs all-time assist leader with 4,474 (1990-91 through 1992-93, and 1994-95 through 2000-01).

COLLEGIATE RECORD

NOTES: Holds NCAA Division I career record for highest assists-per-game average—12.0. ... Holds NCAA Division I single-season record for highest assists-per-game average—13.3 (1988). ... Shares NCAA Division I single-game record for most assists—22 (January 25, 1988, vs. Texas Southern). ... Led NCAA Division I with 10.74 assists per game (1987) and 13.30 assists per game (1988).

												AVERAGES		
Season Team	G	Min.	FGM	FGA	Pct.	FTM	FTA	Pct.	Reb.	Ast.	Pts.	RPG	APG	PPG
83-84—N.M. Junior College	26	583	66	102	.647	28	39	.718	30	159	160	1.2	6.1	6.2
84-85—Cameron	33	...	54	106	.509	34	55	.618	31	111	142	0.9	3.4	4.3
85-86—Southern						Did not play—transfer student.								
86-87—Southern	31	1111	86	196	.439	40	65	.615	73	333	219	2.4	10.7	7.1
87-88—Southern	30	1145	138	257	.537	44	64	.688	84	399	342	2.8	13.3	11.4
Totals	120	2839	344	661	.520	146	223	.655	218	1002	863	1.8	8.4	7.2

Three-point field goals: 1986-87, 7-for-24 (.292). 1987-88, 22-for-47 (.468). Totals, 29-for-71 (.408).

NBA REGULAR-SEASON RECORD

HONORS: NBA Sportsmanship Award (1998).

									REBOUNDS								AVERAGES		
Season Team	G	Min.	FGM	FGA	Pct.	FTM	FTA	Pct.	Off.	Def.	Tot.	Ast.	St.	Blk.	TO	Pts.	RPG	APG	PPG
88-89—Seattle	43	291	29	83	.349	9	16	.563	11	13	24	73	21	3	18	68	0.6	1.7	1.6
89-90—Seattle	53	575	55	142	.387	29	40	.725	21	22	43	162	26	1	48	140	0.8	3.1	2.6
90-91—Denver-S.A.	68	959	130	277	.469	59	87	.678	22	55	77	230	47	4	74	320	1.1	3.4	4.7
91-92—S.A.-Hou.	69	1235	158	330	.479	66	101	.653	13	67	80	266	61	9	110	386	1.2	3.9	5.6
92-93—San Antonio	75	2030	256	510	.502	144	182	.791	20	126	146	561	85	16	145	656	1.9	7.5	8.7
93-94—Golden State	82	2332	356	724	.492	178	253	.704	41	135	176	433	113	8	172	890	2.1	5.3	10.4
94-95—San Antonio	82	3011	448	863	.519	202	295	.685	49	159	208	670	114	13	207	1101	2.5	8.2	13.4
95-96—San Antonio	82	3084	438	887	.494	189	262	.721	37	169	206	789	119	21	195	1071	2.5	9.6	13.1
96-97—San Antonio	76	2472	327	685	.477	140	203	.690	32	115	147	513	96	15	146	800	1.9	6.8	10.5
97-98—San Antonio	75	2674	321	671	.478	122	168	.726	30	120	150	591	84	18	165	766	2.0	7.9	10.2
98-99—San Antonio	50	1672	218	461	.473	50	88	.568	22	96	118	369	51	11	112	487	2.4	7.4	9.7
99-00—San Antonio	82	2571	402	850	.473	114	155	.735	33	125	158	491	76	18	140	919	1.9	6.0	11.2
00-01—San Antonio	55	1290	134	300	.447	41	60	.683	21	64	85	237	33	4	60	310	1.5	4.3	5.6
01-02—Denver-Dallas	68	1352	207	432	.479	121	163	.742	14	55	69	286	40	9	76	535	1.0	4.2	7.9
02-03—Dallas	48	430	63	150	.420	30	39	.769	10	21	31	64	15	1	29	156	0.6	1.3	3.3
03-04—Golden State	46	637	80	199	.402	52	78	.667	3	30	33	111	26	3	51	212	0.7	2.4	4.6
Totals	1054	26615	3622	7564	.479	1546	2190	.706	379	1372	1751	5846	1007	154	1748	8817	1.7	5.5	8.4

Three-point field goals: 1988-89, 1-for-9 (.111). 1989-90, 1-for-4 (.250). 1990-91, 1-for-9 (.111). 1991-92, 4-for-15 (.267). 1992-93, 0-for-8. 1993-94, 0-for-12. 1994-95, 3-for-22 (.136). 1995-96, 6-for-31 (.194). 1996-97, 6-for-26 (.231). 1997-98, 2-for-13 (.154). 1998-99, 1-for-12 (.083). 1999-00, 1-for-9 (.111). 2000-01, 1-for-6 (.167). 2001-02, 0-for-2. 2003-04, 0-for-3. Totals, 27-for-186 (.145).
Personal fouls/disqualifications: 1988-89, 34/0. 1989-90, 55/0. 1990-91, 62/0. 1991-92, 89/1. 1992-93, 141/0. 1993-94, 160/0. 1994-95, 154/0. 1995-96, 179/1. 1996-97, 158/1. 1997-98, 140/0. 1998-99, 101/0. 1999-00, 150/0. 2000-01, 90/0. 2001-02, 86/0. 2002-03, 26/0. 2003-04, 34/0. Totals, 1659/3.

NBA PLAYOFF RECORD

									REBOUNDS								AVERAGES		
Season Team	G	Min.	FGM	FGA	Pct.	FTM	FTA	Pct.	Off.	Def.	Tot.	Ast.	St.	Blk.	TO	Pts.	RPG	APG	PPG
88-89—Seattle	6	31	5	12	.417	1	2	.500	2	2	4	5	4	0	0	11	0.7	0.8	1.8
90-91—San Antonio	3	19	0	5	.000	2	2	1.000	0	0	0	4	1	0	0	2	0.0	1.3	0.7
92-93—San Antonio	10	314	36	70	.514	10	14	.714	8	23	31	81	10	1	23	82	3.1	8.1	8.2
93-94—Golden State	3	41	9	17	.529	0	0		0	3	3	10	4	1	3	18	1.0	3.3	6.0
94-95—San Antonio	15	575	91	176	.517	36	58	.621	9	23	32	125	20	6	30	218	2.1	8.3	14.5
95-96—San Antonio	10	407	52	121	.430	19	27	.704	6	30	36	94	20	1	24	123	3.6	9.4	12.3
97-98—San Antonio	9	342	61	101	.604	34	51	.667	3	10	13	55	9	0	21	156	1.4	6.1	17.3
98-99—San Antonio	17	653	91	187	.487	32	47	.681	9	33	42	126	20	1	50	215	2.5	7.4	12.6
99-00—San Antonio	4	144	19	42	.452	10	14	.714	2	7	9	21	4	0	10	48	2.3	5.3	12.0
00-01—San Antonio	13	281	34	88	.386	8	15	.533	3	13	16	41	10	1	10	76	1.2	3.2	5.8
Totals	90	2807	398	819	.486	152	230	.661	42	144	186	562	102	11	171	949	2.1	6.2	10.5

Three-point field goals: 1988-89, 0-for-4. 1990-91, 0-for-1. 1992-93, 0-for-1. 1993-94, 0-for-1. 1994-95, 0-for-1. 1995-96, 0-for-2. 1997-98, 0-for-2. 1998-99, 1-for-3 (.333). 2000-01, 0-for-1. Totals, 1-for-16 (.063).
Personal fouls/disqualifications: 1988-89, 1/0. 1990-91, 3/0. 1992-93, 27/0. 1993-94, 2/0. 1994-95, 29/0. 1995-96, 21/0. 1997-98, 27/0. 1998-99, 30/0. 1999-00, 10/0. 2000-01, 24/1. Totals, 174/1.

HEAD COACHING RECORD

HONORS: NBA Coach of the Year (2006).

NBA COACHING RECORD

		REGULAR SEASON					PLAYOFFS		
Season Team	W	L	Pct.	Finish			W	L	Pct.
04-05—Dallas	16	2	.889	2nd/Southwest Division			6	7	.462
05-06—Dallas	60	22	.732	2nd/Southwest Division			14	9	.609
Totals	76	24	.760				20	16	.556

NOTES:
04-05—Replaced Don Nelson as Dallas head coach (March 19) with a 42-22 record; defeated Houston, 4-3, in Western Conference first round; lost to Phoenix, 4-2, in Western Conference semifinals.
05-06—Defeated Memphis, 4-0, in Western Conference first round; defeated San Antonio, 4-3, in Western Conference semifinals; defeated Phoenix, 4-2, in Western Conference finals; lost to Miami, 4-2, in NBA Finals.

JORDAN, EDDIE   WIZARDS

PERSONAL: Born January 29, 1955, in Washington D.C. ... 6-1/170. (1.85/77.1). ... Full name: Edward Montgomery Jordan
HIGH SCHOOL: Archbishop Carroll (Washington D.C.).
COLLEGE: Rutgers.
TRANSACTIONS/CAREER NOTES: Selected by Cleveland Cavaliers in second round (33rd pick overall) of 1977 NBA Draft. ... Claimed on waivers by New Jersey Nets (December 12, 1977). ... Traded by Nets to Los Angeles Lakers for 1982 first-round draft choice (November 20, 1980). ... Traded by Lakers with G Norm Nixon and two future second-round draft choices to San Diego Clippers for C Swen Nater and draft rights to G Byron Scott (October 10, 1983). ... Signed as free agent by Portland Trail Blazers (January 4, 1984). ... Signed as free agent by Lakers (April 11, 1984).
MISCELLANEOUS: Member of NBA championship team (1982).

COLLEGIATE RECORD

													AVERAGES		
Season Team	G	Min.	FGM	FGA	Pct.	FTM	FTA	Pct.	Reb.	Ast.		Pts.	RPG	APG	PPG
73-74—Rutgers	26		124	278	.446	40	56	.714	82	...		288	3.2	...	11.1
74-75—Rutgers	29	958	164	337	.487	57	80	.713	98	...		385	3.4	...	13.3
75-76—Rutgers	33	939	187	397	.471	90	113	.796	102	...		464	3.1	...	14.1
76-77—Rutgers	28	1025	190	413	.460	116	170	.682	124	...		496	4.4	...	17.7
Totals	116	2922	665	1425	.467	303	419	.723	406	...		1633	3.5		14.1

NBA REGULAR-SEASON RECORD

RECORDS: Shares single-game record for most steals in one half—8 (October 23, 1979, at Chicago).

									REBOUNDS								AVERAGES		
Season Team	G	Min.	FGM	FGA	Pct.	FTM	FTA	Pct.	Off.	Def.	Tot.	Ast.	St.	Blk.	TO	Pts.	RPG	APG	PPG
77-78—Clev.-N.J.	73	1213	215	538	.400	131	167	.784	35	84	119	177	126	19	106	561	1.6	2.4	7.7
78-79—New Jersey	82	2260	401	960	.418	213	274	.777	74	141	215	365	201	40	244	1015	2.6	4.5	12.4
79-80—New Jersey	82	2657	437	1017	.430	201	258	.779	62	208	270	557	223	27	258	1087	3.3	6.8	13.3
81-82—Los Angeles ..	58	608	89	208	.428	43	54	.796	4	39	43	131	62	1	66	222	0.7	2.3	3.8
82-83—Los Angeles ..	35	333	40	132	.303	11	17	.647	8	18	26	80	31	1	54	94	0.7	2.3	2.7
Totals	330	7071	1182	2855	.414	599	770	.778	183	490	673	1310	643	88	728	2979	2.0	4.0	9.0

Three-point field goals: 1981-82, 1-for-9 (.111). Totals, 1-for-9 (.111).
Personal fouls/disqualifications: 1977-78, 94/0. 1978-79, 209/0. 1979-80, 238/7. 1981-82, 98/0. 1982-83, 52/0. Totals, 691/7.

NBA PLAYOFF RECORD

									REBOUNDS								AVERAGES		
Season Team	G	Min.	FGM	FGA	Pct.	FTM	FTA	Pct.	Off.	Def.	Tot.	Ast.	St.	Blk.	TO	Pts.	RPG	APG	PPG
78-79—New Jersey	2	83	15	38	.395	8	9	.889	6	9	15	17	8	3	...	38	7.5	8.5	19.0
80-81—Los Angeles ..	2	4	0	0	...	0	0	...	0	0	0	1	0	0	...	0	0.0	0.5	0.0
81-82—Los Angeles ..	3	6	0	2	.000	0	0	...	0	0	0	5	2	0	...	0	0.0	1.7	0.0
Totals	7	93	15	40	.375	8	9	.889	6	9	15	23	10	3	...	38	2.1	3.3	5.4

Three-point field goals: 1981-82, 0-for-1. Totals, 0-for-1 (.000).
Personal fouls/disqualifications: 1978-79, 6/0. Totals, 6/0.

HEAD COACHING RECORD

BACKGROUND: Assistant coach, Rutgers University (1984-85). ... Assistant coach, Old Dominion (1985-86). ... Assistant coach, Boston College (1986-87 and 1987-88). ... Assistant coach, Rutgers University (1988-89 through 1991-92). ... Assistant coach, Sacramento Kings (1992-93 to March 10, 1997).

NBA COACHING RECORD

		REGULAR SEASON					PLAYOFFS		
Season Team	W	L	Pct.	Finish			W	L	Pct.
96-97—Sacramento	6	9	.400	6th/Pacific Division			—	—	—
97-98—Sacramento	27	55	.329	5th/Pacific Division			—	—	—
03-04—Washington	25	57	.305	6th/Atlantic Division			—	—	—
04-05—Washington	45	37	.549	2nd/Southeast Division			4	6	.400
05-06—Washington	42	40	.512	2nd/Southeast Division			2	4	.333
Totals	145	198	.423				6	10	.375

NOTES:
96-97—Replaced Garry St. Jean as Sacramento head coach (March 20), with record of 28-39 and club in fifth place.
04-05—Defeated Chicago, 4-2, in Eastern Conference first round; lost to Miami, 4-0, in Eastern Conference semifinals.
05-06—Lost to Cleveland, 4-2, in Eastern Conference first round.

KARL, GEORGE   NUGGETS

PERSONAL: Born May 12, 1951, in Penn Hills, Pa. ... 6-2/190. (1.88/86.2). ... Full name: George Matthew Karl
HIGH SCHOOL: Penn Hills (Pa.).
COLLEGE: North Carolina.
TRANSACTIONS/CAREER NOTES: Selected by New York Knicks in fourth round of 1973 NBA draft. ... Signed as free agent by San Antonio Spurs of American Basketball Association (1973). ... Spurs franchise became part of NBA for 1976-77 season.

COLLEGIATE RECORD

Season Team	G	Min.	FGM	FGA	Pct.	FTM	FTA	Pct.	Reb.	Ast.	Pts.	RPG	APG	PPG
69-70—North Carolina	6	...	56	97	.577	20	23	.870	29	...	132	4.8	...	22.0
70-71—North Carolina	32	...	150	286	.524	92	115	.800	104	78	392	3.3	2.4	12.3
71-72—North Carolina	29	...	125	241	.519	89	113	.788	72	124	339	2.5	4.3	11.7
72-73—North Carolina	33	...	219	437	.501	124	163	.761	103	192	562	3.1	5.8	17.0
Totals	100	...	550	1061	.518	325	414	.785	308	394	1425	3.1	3.9	14.3

ABA REGULAR-SEASON RECORD

Season Team	G	Min.	FGM	FGA	Pct.	FTM	FTA	Pct.	Off.	Def.	Tot.	Ast.	St.	Blk.	TO	Pts.	RPG	APG	PPG
73-74—San Antonio	74	1339	228	480	.475	94	113	.832	...	...	126	160	...	...	...	574	1.7	2.2	7.8
74-75—San Antonio	82	1629	257	511	.503	137	177	.774	...	...	155	334	...	...	...	663	1.9	4.1	8.1
75-76—San Antonio	75	1200	150	325	.462	81	106	.764	...	...	66	250	...	...	...	381	0.9	3.3	5.1
Totals	231	4168	635	1316	.483	312	396	.788	...	...	347	744	...	...	...	1618	1.5	3.2	7.0

Three-point field goals: 1973-74, 8-for-22 (.364). 1974-75, 4-for-23 (.174). 1975-76, 0-for-9. Totals, 12-for-54 (.222).

ABA PLAYOFF RECORD

Season Team	G	Min.	FGM	FGA	Pct.	FTM	FTA	Pct.	Off.	Def.	Tot.	Ast.	St.	Blk.	TO	Pts.	RPG	APG	PPG
73-74—San Antonio	7	141	13	27	.481	2	5	.400	...	...	15	23	...	...	...	28	2.1	3.3	4.0
74-75—San Antonio	4	40	1	7	.143	3	4	.750	...	...	3	5	...	...	...	5	0.8	1.3	1.3
75-76—San Antonio	6	64	10	21	.476	6	9	.667	...	...	4	17	...	...	...	26	0.7	2.8	4.3
Totals	17	245	24	55	.436	11	18	.611	...	...	22	45	...	...	...	59	1.3	2.6	3.5

Three-point field goals: 1973-74, 0-for-1 (.000), 1974-75, 0-for-1 (.000), 1976-77, 0-for-1 (.000).

NBA REGULAR-SEASON RECORD

Season Team	G	Min.	FGM	FGA	Pct.	FTM	FTA	Pct.	Off.	Def.	Tot.	Ast.	St.	Blk.	TO	Pts.	RPG	APG	PPG
76-77—San Antonio	29	251	25	73	.342	29	42	.690	4	13	17	46	10	0	...	79	0.6	1.6	2.7
77-78—San Antonio	4	30	2	6	.333	2	2	1.000	0	5	5	5	1	0	4	6	1.3	1.3	1.5
Totals	33	281	27	79	.342	31	44	.705	4	18	22	51	11	0	4	85	0.7	1.5	2.6

Personal fouls/disqualifications: 1976-77, 36/0. 1977-78, 6/0. Totals, 42/0.

NBA PLAYOFF RECORD

Season Team	G	Min.	FGM	FGA	Pct.	FTM	FTA	Pct.	Off.	Def.	Tot.	Ast.	St.	Blk.	TO	Pts.	RPG	APG	PPG
76-77—San Antonio	1	1	0	0	...	0	0	...	0	0	0	0	0	0	...	0	0.0	0.0	0.0

COMBINED NBA AND ABA REGULAR-SEASON RECORDS

	G	Min.	FGM	FGA	Pct.	FTM	FTA	Pct.	Off.	Def.	Tot.	Ast.	St.	Blk.	TO	Pts.	RPG	APG	PPG
Totals	264	4449	674	1449	.465	343	440	.780	105	264	369	795	232	20	...	1703	1.4	3.0	6.5

Three-point field goals: 12-for-54 (.222).

HEAD COACHING RECORD

BACKGROUND: Assistant coach, San Antonio Spurs (1978-79 and 1979-80). ... Director of player acquisition, Cleveland Cavaliers (1983-84). ... Head coach, Real Madrid of Spanish League (1989-90 and 1991-January 1992).
HONORS: CBA Coach of the Year (1981, 1983, 1991).

CBA COACHING RECORD

		REGULAR SEASON				PLAYOFFS		
Season Team	W	L	Pct.	Finish	W	L	Pct.
80-81—Montana	27	15	.643	1st/Western Division	5	5	.500
81-82—Montana	30	16	.652	2nd/Western Division	2	3	.400
82-83—Montana	33	11	.750	1st/Western Division	6	5	.545
88-89—Albany	36	18	.667	1st/Eastern Division	2	4	.333
90-91—Albany	50	6	.893	1st/Eastern Division	5	6	.455
Totals	176	66	.727		20	23	.465

NOTES:
80-81—Defeated Alberta, 2-0, in Western semifinals; defeated Billings, 3-1, in Western finals; lost to Rochester, 4-0, in CBA Championship Series.
81-82—Lost to Billings in Western finals.
82-83—Defeated Wyoming, 3-1, in Western finals; lost to Detroit, 4-3, in CBA Championship Series.
88-89—Lost to Wichita Falls in Eastern semifinals.
90-91—Defeated Grand Rapids, 3-2, in National Conference first round; lost to Wichita Falls, 4-2, in National Conference finals.

NBA COACHING RECORD

		REGULAR SEASON				PLAYOFFS		
Season Team	W	L	Pct.	Finish	W	L	Pct.
84-85—Cleveland	36	46	.439	4th Central Division	1	3	.250
85-86—Cleveland	25	42	.373		—	—	
86-87—Golden State	42	40	.512	3rd/Pacific Division	4	6	.400
87-88—Golden State	16	48	.250		—	—	
91-92—Seattle	27	15	.643	4th/Pacific Division	4	5	.444
92-93—Seattle	55	27	.671	2nd/Pacific Division	10	9	.526

Season Team	REGULAR SEASON				PLAYOFFS		
	W	L	Pct.	Finish	W	L	Pct.
93-94—Seattle	63	19	.768	1st/Pacific Division	2	3	.400
94-95—Seattle	57	25	.695	2nd/Pacific Division	1	3	.250
95-96—Seattle	64	18	.780	1st/Pacific Division	13	8	.619
96-97—Seattle	57	25	.695	1st/Pacific Division	6	6	.500
97-98—Seattle	61	21	.744	1st/Pacific Division	4	6	.400
98-99—Milwaukee	28	22	.560	4th/Central Division	0	3	.000
99-00—Milwaukee	42	40	.512	T-5th/Central Division	2	3	.400
00-01—Milwaukee	52	30	.634	1st/Central Division	10	8	.556
01-02—Milwaukee	41	41	.500	5th/Central Division	—	—	—
02-03—Milwaukee	42	40	.512	4th/Central Division	2	4	.333
04-05—Denver	32	8	.800	2nd/Northwest Division	1	4	.200
05-06—Denver	44	38	.537	1st/Northwest Division	1	4	.200
Totals	784	545	.590		61	75	.444

NOTES:
84-85—Lost to Boston, 3-1, in Eastern Conference first round.
85-86—Replaced as Cleveland head coach by Gene Littles (March 16).
86-87—Defeated Utah, 3-2, in Western Conference first round; lost to Los Angeles Lakers, 4-1, in Western Conference semifinals.
87-88—Resigned as Golden State head coach (March 23).
91-92—Replaced K.C. Jones and Bob Kloppenburg (2-2) as Seattle head coach (January 23), with a record of 20-20 and club in fifth place. Defeated Golden State, 3-1, in Western Conference first round; lost to Utah, 4-1, in Western Conference semifinals.
92-93—Defeated Utah, 3-2, in Western Conference first round; defeated Houston, 4-3, in Western Conference semifinals; lost to Phoenix, 4-3, in Western Conference finals.
93-94—Lost to Denver, 3-2, in Western Conference first round.
94-95—Lost to Los Angeles Lakers, 3-1, in Western Conference first round.
95-96—Defeated Sacramento, 3-1, in Western Conference first round; defeated Houston, 4-0, in Western Conference semifinals; defeated Utah, 4-3, in Western Conference finals; lost to Chicago, 4-2, in NBA Finals.
96-97—Defeated Phoenix, 3-2, in Western Conference first round; lost to Houston, 4-3, in Western Conference semifinals.
97-98—Defeated Minnesota, 3-2, in Western Conference first round; lost to Los Angeles Lakers, 4-1, in Western Conference semifinals.
98-99—Lost to Indiana, 3-0, in Eastern Conference first round.
99-00—Lost to Indiana, 3-2, in Eastern Conference first round.
00-01—Lost to Orlando, 3-1, in Eastern Conference first round; defeated Charlotte, 4-3, in Eastern Conference semifinals; lost to Philadelphia, 4-3, in Eastern Conference finals.
02-03—Lost to New Jersey, 4-2, in Eastern Conference first round.
04-05—Replaced Jeff Bzdelik (13-15) and interim coach Michael Cooper (4-10) as Denver head coach (January 27) with a record of 17-25 and the club in 11th place (Western Conference). Lost to San Antonio, 4-1, in Western Conference first round.
05-06—Lost to Los Angeles Clippers, 4-1, in Western Conference first round.

MCMILLAN, NATE — TRAIL BLAZERS

PERSONAL: Born August 3, 1964, in Raleigh, N.C. ... 6-5/200. (1.96/90.7).
HIGH SCHOOL: Enloe (Raleigh, N.C.).
JUNIOR COLLEGE: Chowan College.
COLLEGE: North Carolina State.
TRANSACTIONS/CAREER NOTES: Selected by Seattle SuperSonics in second round (30th pick overall) of 1986 NBA Draft. ... Announced retirement to become assistant coach of SuperSonics (September 29, 1998).

COLLEGIATE RECORD

Season Team	G	Min.	FGM	FGA	Pct.	FTM	FTA	Pct.	Reb.	Ast.	Pts.	AVERAGES		
												RPG	APG	PPG
82-83—Chowan College	27	...	101	174	.580	64	92	.696	134	191	266	5.0	7.1	9.9
83-84—Chowan College	35	...	180	331	.544	100	130	.769	342	411	460	9.8	11.7	13.1
84-85—North Carolina State	33	973	94	207	.454	64	95	.674	189	169	252	5.7	5.1	7.6
85-86—North Carolina State	34	1208	127	262	.485	66	90	.733	155	233	320	4.6	6.9	9.4
Junior College Totals	62	...	281	505	.556	164	222	.739	476	602	726	7.7	9.7	11.7
4-Year-College Totals	67	2181	221	469	.471	130	185	.703	344	402	572	5.1	6.0	8.5

Personal fouls/disqualifications: 1982-83, 63/0. Totals, 63/0.

NBA REGULAR-SEASON RECORD

RECORDS: Shares single-game record for most assists by a rookie—25 (February 23, 1987, vs. Los Angeles Clippers).
HONORS: NBA All-Defensive second team (1994, 1995).
NOTES: Led NBA with 2.96 steals per game (1994).

Season Team	G	Min.	FGM	FGA	Pct.	FTM	FTA	Pct.	REBOUNDS			Ast.	St.	Blk.	TO	Pts.	AVERAGES		
									Off.	Def.	Tot.						RPG	APG	PPG
86-87—Seattle	71	1972	143	301	.475	87	101	.617	101	230	331	583	125	45	155	373	4.7	8.2	5.3
87-88—Seattle	82	2453	235	496	.474	145	205	.707	117	221	338	702	169	47	189	624	4.1	8.6	7.6
88-89—Seattle	75	2341	199	485	.410	119	189	.630	143	245	388	696	156	42	211	532	5.2	9.3	7.1
89-90—Seattle	82	2338	207	438	.473	98	153	.641	127	276	403	598	140	37	187	523	4.9	7.3	6.4
90-91—Seattle	78	1434	132	305	.433	57	93	.613	71	180	251	371	104	20	122	338	3.2	4.8	4.3
91-92—Seattle	72	1652	177	405	.437	54	84	.643	92	160	252	359	129	29	112	435	3.5	5.0	6.0
92-93—Seattle	73	1977	213	459	.464	95	134	.709	84	222	306	384	173	33	139	546	4.2	5.3	7.5
93-94—Seattle	73	1887	177	396	.447	31	55	.564	50	233	283	387	*216	22	126	437	3.9	5.3	6.0
94-95—Seattle	80	2070	166	397	.418	34	58	.586	65	237	302	421	165	53	126	419	3.8	5.3	5.2
95-96—Seattle	55	1261	100	238	.420	29	41	.707	41	169	210	197	95	18	75	275	3.8	3.6	5.0
96-97—Seattle	37	798	61	149	.409	19	29	.655	15	103	118	140	58	6	32	169	3.2	3.8	4.6
97-98—Seattle	18	279	23	67	.343	1	1	1.000	13	27	40	55	14	4	12	62	2.2	3.1	3.4
Totals	796	20462	1833	4136	.443	769	1183	.650	919	2303	3222	4893	1544	356	1486	4733	4.0	6.1	5.9

Three-point field goals: 1986-87, 0-for-7. 1987-88, 9-for-24 (.375). 1988-89, 15-for-70 (.214). 1989-90, 11-for-31 (.355). 1990-91, 17-for-48 (.354). 1991-92, 27-for-98 (.276). 1992-93, 25-for-65 (.385). 1993-94, 52-for-133 (.391). 1994-95, 53-for-155 (.342). 1995-96, 46-for-121 (.380). 1996-97, 28-for-84 (.333). 1997-98, 15-for-34 (.441). Totals, 298-for-870 (.343).
Personal fouls/disqualifications: 1986-87, 238/4. 1987-88, 238/1. 1988-89, 236/3. 1989-90, 289/7. 1990-91, 211/6. 1991-92, 218/4. 1992-93, 240/6. 1993-94, 201/1. 1994-95, 275/8. 1995-96, 143/3. 1996-97, 78/0. 1997-98, 41/0. Totals, 2408/43.

NBA PLAYOFF RECORD

Season Team	G	Min.	FGM	FGA	Pct.	FTM	FTA	Pct.	REBOUNDS Off.	Def.	Tot.	Ast.	St.	Blk.	TO	Pts.	AVERAGES RPG	APG	PPG
86-87—Seattle	14	356	27	62	.435	17	24	.708	13	41	54	112	14	10	26	71	3.9	8.0	5.1
87-88—Seattle	5	127	12	35	.343	9	14	.643	6	15	21	33	2	3	8	33	4.2	6.6	6.6
88-89—Seattle	8	200	19	40	.475	16	25	.640	9	16	25	63	10	5	19	54	3.1	7.9	6.8
90-91—Seattle	5	95	6	23	.261	2	4	.500	6	12	18	22	6	1	3	14	3.6	4.4	2.8
91-92—Seattle	9	246	35	83	.422	10	14	.714	14	19	33	63	16	3	22	86	3.7	7.0	9.6
92-93—Seattle	19	415	35	103	.340	16	30	.533	21	46	67	103	40	11	25	91	3.5	5.4	4.8
93-94—Seattle	5	109	8	25	.320	1	4	.250	6	10	16	10	6	1	5	21	3.2	2.0	4.2
94-95—Seattle	4	113	8	23	.348	2	2	1.000	7	11	18	29	10	2	7	19	4.5	7.3	4.8
95-96—Seattle	19	385	28	69	.406	9	14	.643	13	57	70	52	23	5	20	84	3.7	2.7	4.4
96-97—Seattle	3	41	0	2	.000	0	...	...	1	4	5	3	1	0	2	0	1.7	1.0	0.0
97-98—Seattle	7	99	6	18	.333	2	2	1.000	2	14	16	15	3	2	2	16	2.3	2.1	2.3
Totals	98	2186	184	483	.381	84	133	.632	98	245	343	505	131	43	139	489	3.5	5.2	5.0

Three-point field goals: 1987-88, 0-for-1. 1988-89, 0-for-2. 1991-92, 6-for-26 (.231). 1992-93, 5-for-24 (.208). 1993-94, 4-for-11 (.364). 1994-95, 1-for-8 (.125). 1995-96, 19-for-40 (.475). 1996-97, 0-for-2. 1997-98, 2-for-12 (.167). Totals, 37-for-128 (.289).
Personal fouls/disqualifications: 1986-87, 42/1. 1987-88, 11/0. 1988-89, 21/0. 1990-91, 15/0. 1991-92, 35/1. 1992-93, 54/2. 1993-94, 18/1. 1994-95, 13/0. 1995-96, 34/0. 1996-97, 11/0. 1997-98, 17/0. Totals, 271/5.

HEAD COACHING RECORD

BACKGROUND: Assistant coach, Seattle SuperSonics (1998-99 through November 27, 2000).

NBA COACHING RECORD

Season Team	W	L	Pct.	Finish	PLAYOFFS W	L	Pct.
00-01—Seattle	38	29	.567	5th/Pacific Division			
01-02—Seattle	45	37	.549	4th/Pacific Division	2	3	.400
02-03—Seattle	40	42	.488	5th/Pacific Division	—	—	—
03-04—Seattle	37	45	.451	5th/Pacific Division	—	—	—
04-05—Seattle	52	30	.634	1st/Northwest Division	6	5	.545
05-06—Portland	21	61	.256	5th/Northwest Division	—	—	—
Totals	233	244	.488		8	8	.500

NOTES:
00-01—Replaced Paul Westphal as Seattle head coach (November 27), with record of 6-9 and club in fifth place.
01-02—Lost to San Antonio, 3-2, in Western Conference first round.
04-05—Defeated Sacramento, 4-1, in Western Conference first round; lost to San Antonio, 4-2, in Western Conference semifinals.

MITCHELL, SAM   RAPTORS

PERSONAL: Born September 2, 1963, in Columbus, Ga. ... 6-7/215. (2.01/97.5). ... Full name: Samuel E. Mitchell
HIGH SCHOOL: Columbus (Ga.).
COLLEGE: Mercer (Ga.).
TRANSACTIONS/CAREER NOTES: Selected by Houston Rockets in third round (54th pick overall) of 1985 NBA Draft. ... Waived by Rockets (October 22, 1985). ... Played in Continental Basketball Association with Wisconsin Flyers (1985-86 and 1986-87) and Rapid City Thrillers (1986-87). ... Played in United States Basketball League with Tampa Bay Flash (1986). ... Signed as free agent by Rockets (October 7, 1986). ... Waived by Rockets (October 28, 1986). ... Played in France (1987-88 and 1988-89). ... Signed as free agent by Minnesota Timberwolves (July 23, 1989). ... Traded by Timberwolves with G Pooh Richardson to Indiana Pacers for F Chuck Person and G Micheal Williams (September 8, 1992). ... Signed as unrestricted free agent by Timberwolves (September 29, 1995).

COLLEGIATE RECORD

Season Team	G	Min.	FGM	FGA	Pct.	FTM	FTA	Pct.	Reb.	Ast.	Pts.	AVERAGES RPG	APG	PPG
81-82—Mercer	27	...	77	155	.497	38	53	.717	100	13	192	3.7	0.5	7.1
82-83—Mercer	28	964	178	343	.519	105	134	.784	164	47	461	5.9	1.7	16.5
83-84—Mercer	26	935	219	432	.507	121	155	.781	184	46	559	7.1	1.8	21.5
84-85—Mercer	31	1157	294	570	.516	186	248	.750	255	43	774	8.2	1.4	25.0
Totals	112	3056	768	1500	.512	450	590	.763	703	149	1986	6.3	1.3	17.7

CBA RECORD

Season Team	G	Min.	FGM	FGA	Pct.	FTM	FTA	Pct.	Reb.	Ast.	Pts.	AVERAGES RPG	APG	PPG
85-86—Wisconsin	13	450	107	238	.450	55	83	.663	95	16	270	7.3	1.2	20.8
86-87—Wisconsin-Rapid City	42	1370	253	554	.457	154	210	.733	256	31	663	6.1	0.7	15.8
Totals	55	1820	360	792	.455	209	293	.713	351	47	933	6.4	0.9	17.0

Three-point field goals: 1985-86, 1-for-3 (.333). 1986-87, 3-for-12 (.250). Totals, 4-for-15 (.267).
Personal fouls/disqualifications: 1985-86, 54/0. 1986-87, 135/0. Totals, 189/0.

NBA REGULAR-SEASON RECORD

NOTES: Led NBA with 338 personal fouls (1991).

Season Team	G	Min.	FGM	FGA	Pct.	FTM	FTA	Pct.	REBOUNDS Off.	Def.	Tot.	Ast.	St.	Blk.	TO	Pts.	AVERAGES RPG	APG	PPG
89-90—Minnesota	80	2414	372	834	.446	268	349	.768	180	282	462	89	66	54	96	1012	5.8	1.1	12.7
90-91—Minnesota	82	3121	445	1010	.441	307	396	.775	188	332	520	133	66	57	104	1197	6.3	1.6	14.6
91-92—Minnesota	82	2151	307	725	.423	209	266	.786	158	315	473	94	53	39	97	825	5.8	1.1	10.1
92-93—Indiana	81	1402	215	483	.445	150	185	.811	93	155	248	76	23	10	51	584	3.1	0.9	7.2
93-94—Indiana	75	1084	140	306	.458	82	110	.745	71	119	190	65	33	9	50	362	2.5	0.9	4.8
94-95—Indiana	81	1377	201	413	.487	126	174	.724	95	148	243	61	43	20	54	529	3.0	0.8	6.5
95-96—Minnesota	78	2145	303	618	.490	237	291	.814	107	232	339	74	49	26	87	844	4.3	0.9	10.8
96-97—Minnesota	82	2044	269	603	.446	224	295	.759	112	214	326	79	51	20	93	766	4.0	1.0	9.3
97-98—Minnesota	81	2239	371	800	.464	243	292	.832	118	267	385	107	64	22	66	1000	4.8	1.3	12.3
98-99—Minnesota	50	1344	213	522	.408	126	165	.764	55	127	182	98	35	16	34	561	3.6	2.0	11.2
99-00—Minnesota	66	1227	168	376	.447	81	92	.880	28	110	138	111	27	14	44	427	2.1	1.7	6.5
00-01—Minnesota	82	983	118	289	.408	40	55	.727	28	95	123	57	26	10	36	285	1.5	0.7	3.5
Totals	920	21531	3122	6979	.447	2093	2670	.784	1233	2396	3629	1044	536	297	812	8392	3.9	1.1	9.1

Three-point field goals: 1989-90, 0-for-9. 1990-91, 0-for-9. 1991-92, 2-for-11 (.182). 1992-93, 4-for-23 (.174). 1993-94, 0-for-5. 1994-95, 1-for-10 (.100). 1995-96, 1-for-18 (.056). 1996-97, 4-for-25 (.160). 1997-98, 15-for-43 (.349). 1998-99, 9-for-38 (.237). 1999-00, 10-for-23 (.435). 2000-01, 9-for-43 (.209). Totals, 55-for-257 (.214).

Personal fouls/disqualifications: 1989-90, 301/7. 1990-91, 338/13. 1991-92, 230/3. 1992-93, 207/1. 1993-94, 152/1. 1994-95, 206/0. 1995-96, 220/3. 1996-97, 232/1. 1997-98, 200/0. 1998-99, 111/1. 1999-00, 116/0. 2000-01, 117/0. Totals, 2430/30.

NBA PLAYOFF RECORD

Season Team	G	Min.	FGM	FGA	Pct.	FTM	FTA	Pct.	Off.	Def.	Tot.	Ast.	St.	Blk.	TO	Pts.	RPG	APG	PPG
92-93—Indiana	4	25	5	8	.625	2	2	1.000	0	1	1	0	0	0	2	12	0.3	0.0	3.0
93-94—Indiana	15	99	9	26	.346	3	4	.750	5	12	17	5	2	2	4	21	1.1	0.3	1.4
94-95—Indiana	17	223	23	64	.359	22	28	.786	17	31	48	6	3	1	14	68	2.8	0.4	4.0
96-97—Minnesota	3	47	6	13	.462	5	8	.625	2	5	7	1	1	1	1	17	2.3	0.3	5.7
97-98—Minnesota	5	177	26	58	.448	17	19	.895	7	20	27	8	1	1	5	72	5.4	1.6	14.4
98-99—Minnesota	4	131	15	40	.375	9	12	.750	5	9	14	6	1	2	8	40	3.5	1.5	10.0
99-00—Minnesota	4	68	9	18	.500	3	3	1.000	2	5	7	2	0	1	4	23	1.8	0.5	5.8
00-01—Minnesota	4	50	2	10	.200	2	2	1.000	1	6	7	3	1	0	1	6	1.8	0.8	1.5
Totals	56	820	95	237	.401	63	78	.808	39	89	128	31	9	8	39	259	2.3	0.6	4.6

Three-point field goals: 1993-94, 0-for-1. 1994-95, 0-for-2. 1997-98, 3-for-14 (.214). 1998-99, 1-for-6 (.167). 1999-00, 2-for-5 (.400). 2000-01, 0-for-1. Totals, 6-for-29 (.207).

Personal fouls/disqualifications: 1992-93, 4/0. 1993-94, 22/0. 1994-95, 41/0. 1996-97, 9/0. 1997-98, 18/0. 1998-99, 13/0. 1999-00, 5/0. 2000-01, 5/0. Totals, 117/0.

HEAD COACHING RECORD

NBA COACHING RECORD

Season Team	REGULAR SEASON				PLAYOFFS		
	W	L	Pct.	Finish	W	L	Pct.
04-05—Toronto	33	49	.402	4th/Atlantic Division	—	—	—
05-06—Toronto	27	55	.329	4th/Atlantic Division	—	—	—
Totals	60	104	.366				

MUSSELMAN, ERIC — KINGS

PERSONAL: Born November 19, 1964, in Ashland, Ohio. ... 5-7. (1.70).
HIGH SCHOOL: Brecksville (Broadview Heights, Ohio).
COLLEGE: San Diego.

COLLEGIATE RECORD

Season Team	G	Min.	FGM	FGA	Pct.	FTM	FTA	Pct.	Reb.	Ast.	Pts.	RPG	APG	PPG
83-84—San Diego	11	24	7	13	.538	8	11	.727	2	7	22	0.2	0.6	2.0
84-85—San Diego	14	100	6	18	.000	0	5	.000	7	15	15	0.5	1.1	1.1
85-86—San Diego	13	51	5	18	.278	15	19	.789	7	12	25	0.5	0.9	1.9
86-87—San Diego	28	205	7	31	.226	15	26	.577	7	26	34	0.3	0.9	1.2
Totals	66	380	25	80	.313	41	61	.672	23	60	96	0.3	0.9	1.5

Three-point field goals: 1986-87, 5-for-20 (.250). Totals, 5-for-20 (.250).

HEAD COACHING RECORD

BACKGROUND: General Manager/Director of Player Personnel, Rapid City Thrillers of CBA (1988-89 and 1989-90). ... Assistant coach, Minnesota Timberwolves (1990-91). ... General Manager, Thrillers (1991-92 through 1995-96). ... Director of Operations, Florida Sharks of USBL (1995 and 1996). ... General Manager, Florida Beachdogs of CBA (1995-96 and 1996-97). ... Assistant coach/scout, Orlando Magic (1997-98). ... Assistant coach, Magic (1998-99 and 1999-2000). ... Assistant coach, Atlanta Hawks (2000-01 and 2001-02). ... Assistant coach, Memphis Grizzlies (2004-05 and 2005-06).

CBA COACHING RECORD

Season Team	REGULAR SEASON				PLAYOFFS		
	W	L	Pct.	Finish	W	L	Pct.
89-90—Rapid City	42	14	.750	1st/Midwest Division	8	8	.500
91-92—Rapid City	37	19	.661	1st/Northern Division	9	7	.563
92-93—Rapid City	44	12	.786	1st/Midwest Division	5	3	.625
93-94—Rapid City	37	19	.661	1st/Midwest Division	5	5	.500
94-95—Rapid City	31	25	.554	4th/Western Division	0	2	.000
95-96—Florida	41	15	.732	1st/Southern Division	5	3	.625
Totals	232	104	.690		32	28	.533

NOTES:
89-90—Defeated San Jose, 3-2, in National Conference semifinals; defeated Santa Barbara, 4-2, in National Conference finals; lost to La Crosse, 4-1, in CBA Finals.
91-92—Defeated Wichita Falls, 3-1, in National Conference second round; defeated Omaha, 3-2, in National Conference finals; lost to La Crosse, 4-3, in CBA Finals.
92-93—Defeated Tri-City, 3-0, in National Conference first round; lost to Omaha, 3-2, in National Conference finals.
93-94—Defeated Wichita Falls, 3-2, in National Conference first round; lost to Omaha, 3-2, in National Conference finals.
94-95—Lost to Tri-City, 0-2, in National Conference first round.
95-96—Defeated Omaha, 3-0, in National Conference first round; lost to Sioux Falls, 3-2, in National Conference finals.

NBA COACHING RECORD

Season Team	REGULAR SEASON				PLAYOFFS		
	W	L	Pct.	Finish	W	L	Pct.
02-03—Golden State	38	44	.463	6th/Pacific Division	—	—	—
Totals	38	44	.463				

NELSON, DON — WARRIORS

PERSONAL: Born May 15, 1940, in Muskegon, Mich. ... 6-6/210. (1,98/95,3). ... Full name: Don Arvid Nelson.
HIGH SCHOOL: Rock Island (Ill.).
COLLEGE: Iowa.
TRANSACTIONS: Selected by Chicago Zephyrs in third round (19th pick overall) of 1962 NBA Draft. ... Zephyrs franchise moved from Chicago to Baltimore and renamed Bullets for 1963-64 season. ... Contract sold by Bullets to Los Angeles Lakers (September 6, 1963). ... Waived by Lakers (October 21, 1965). ... Signed as free agent by Boston Celtics (October 28, 1965).
MISCELLANEOUS: Member of NBA championship team (1966, 1968, 1969, 1974, 1976). ... Head coach of gold-medal-winning 1994 USA Basketball World Championship Team.

HEAD COACHES

COLLEGIATE RECORD

Season Team	G	Min.	FGM	FGA	Pct.	FTM	FTA	Pct.	Reb.	Ast.	Pts.	RPG	APG	PPG
58-59—Iowa‡					Freshman team did not play intercollegiate schedule.									
59-60—Iowa	24	...	140	320	.438	100	155	.645	241	...	380	10.0	...	15.8
60-61—Iowa	24	...	197	377	.523	176	268	.657	258	...	570	10.8	...	23.8
61-62—Iowa	24	...	193	348	.555	186	264	.705	285	...	572	11.9	...	23.8
Varsity totals	72	...	530	1045	.507	462	687	.672	784	...	1522	10.9	...	21.1

NBA REGULAR-SEASON RECORD

Season Team	G	Min.	FGM	FGA	Pct.	FTM	FTA	Pct.	Reb.	Ast.	PF	Dq.	Pts.	RPG	APG	PPG
62-63—Chicago	62	1071	129	293	.440	161	221	.729	279	72	136	3	419	4.5	1.2	6.8
63-64—Los Angeles	80	1406	135	323	.418	149	201	.741	323	76	181	1	419	4.0	1.0	5.2
64-65—Los Angeles	39	238	36	85	.424	20	26	.769	73	24	40	1	92	1.9	0.6	2.4
65-66—Boston	75	1765	271	618	.439	223	326	.684	403	79	187	1	765	5.4	1.1	10.2
66-67—Boston	79	1202	227	509	.446	141	190	.742	295	65	143	0	595	3.7	0.8	7.5
67-68—Boston	82	1498	312	632	.494	195	268	.728	431	103	178	1	819	5.3	1.3	10.0
68-69—Boston	82	1773	374	771	.485	201	259	.776	458	92	198	2	949	5.6	1.1	11.6
69-70—Boston	82	2224	461	920	.501	337	435	.775	601	148	238	3	1259	7.3	1.8	15.4
70-71—Boston	82	2254	412	881	.468	317	426	.744	565	153	232	2	1141	6.9	1.9	13.9
71-72—Boston	82	2086	389	811	.480	356	452	.788	453	192	220	3	1134	5.5	2.3	13.8
72-73—Boston	72	1425	309	649	.476	159	188	.846	315	102	155	1	777	4.4	1.4	10.8

| | | | | | | | | | REBOUNDS | | | | | | AVERAGES | | |
Season Team	G	Min.	FGM	FGA	Pct.	FTM	FTA	Pct.	Off.	Def.	Tot.	Ast.	Stl.	Blk.	TO	Pts.	RPG	APG	PPG
73-74—Boston	82	1748	364	717	.508	215	273	.788	90	255	345	162	19	13	...	943	4.2	2.0	11.5
74-75—Boston	79	2052	423	785	*.539	263	318	.827	127	342	469	181	32	15	...	1109	5.9	2.3	14.0
75-76—Boston	75	943	175	379	.462	127	161	.789	56	126	182	77	14	7	...	477	2.4	1.0	6.4
Totals	1053	21685	4017	8373	.480	2864	3744	.765	...	...	5192	1526	65	35	...	10898	4.9	1.4	10.3

NBA PLAYOFF RECORD

Season Team	G	Min.	FGM	FGA	Pct.	FTM	FTA	Pct.	Reb.	Ast.	PF	Dq.	Pts.	RPG	APG	PPG
63-64—Los Angeles	5	56	7	13	.538	3	3	1.000	13	2	11	1	17	2.6	0.4	3.4
64-65—Los Angeles	11	212	24	53	.453	19	25	.760	59	19	31	0	67	5.4	1.7	6.1
65-66—Boston	17	316	50	118	.424	42	52	.808	85	13	50	0	142	5.0	0.8	8.4
66-67—Boston	9	142	27	59	.458	10	17	.588	42	9	12	0	64	4.7	1.0	7.1
67-68—Boston	19	468	91	175	.520	55	74	.743	143	32	49	0	237	7.5	1.7	12.5
68-69—Boston	18	348	87	168	.518	50	60	.833	83	21	51	0	224	4.6	1.2	12.4
71-72—Boston	11	308	52	99	.525	41	48	.854	61	21	30	0	145	5.5	1.9	13.2
72-73—Boston	13	303	47	101	.465	49	56	.875	38	15	29	0	143	2.9	1.2	11.0

| | | | | | | | | | REBOUNDS | | | | | | AVERAGES | | |
Season Team	G	Min.	FGM	FGA	Pct.	FTM	FTA	Pct.	Off.	Def.	Tot.	Ast.	Stl.	Blk.	TO	Pts.	RPG	APG	PPG
73-74—Boston	18	467	82	164	.500	41	53	.774	25	72	97	35	8	3	...	205	5.4	1.9	11.4
74-75—Boston	11	274	66	117	.564	37	41	.902	18	27	45	26	2	2	...	169	4.1	2.4	15.4
75-76—Boston	18	315	52	108	.481	60	69	.870	17	36	53	17	3	2	...	164	2.9	0.9	9.1
Totals	150	3209	585	1175	.498	407	498	.817	...	...	719	210	13	7	...	1577	4.8	1.4	10.5

HEAD COACHING RECORD

BACKGROUND: Assistant coach, Milwaukee Bucks (September 9-November 22, 1976). ... Head coach/director of player personnel, Bucks (November 22, 1976 through 1985). ... Head coach/vice president of basketball operations, Bucks (1985-May 27, 1987). ... Executive vice president, Golden State Warriors (1987-88). ... Head coach/general manager, Warriors (1988-89 to February 13, 1995). ... General manager, Dallas Mavericks (February 7, 1997 to August 30, 2006).
HONORS: NBA Coach of the Year (1983, 1985, 1992). ... One of the Top 10 Coaches in NBA History (1996).

NBA COACHING RECORD

| | REGULAR SEASON | | | | PLAYOFFS | | |
Season Team	W	L	Pct.	Finish	W	L	Pct.
76-77—Milwaukee	27	37	.422	6th/Midwest Division	—	—	—
77-78—Milwaukee	44	38	.537	2nd/Midwest Division	5	4	.556
78-79—Milwaukee	38	44	.463	4th/Midwest Division	—	—	—
79-80—Milwaukee	49	33	.598	1st/Midwest Division	3	4	.429
80-81—Milwaukee	60	22	.732	1st/Midwest Division	3	4	.429
81-82—Milwaukee	55	27	.671	1st/Central Division	2	4	.333
82-83—Milwaukee	51	31	.622	1st/Central Division	5	4	.556
83-84—Milwaukee	50	32	.610	1st/Central Division	8	8	.500
84-85—Milwaukee	59	23	.720	1st/Central Division	3	5	.375
85-86—Milwaukee	57	25	.695	1st/Central Division	7	7	.500
86-87—Milwaukee	50	32	.610	3rd/Central Division	6	6	.500
88-89—Golden State	43	39	.524	4th/Pacific Division	4	4	.500
89-90—Golden State	37	45	.451	5th/Pacific Division	—	—	—
90-91—Golden State	44	38	.537	4th/Pacific Division	4	5	.444
91-92—Golden State	55	27	.671	2nd/Pacific Division	1	3	.250

Season Team	REGULAR SEASON				PLAYOFFS		
	W	L	Pct.	Finish	W	L	Pct.
92-93—Golden State	34	48	.415	6th/Pacific Division	—	—	—
93-94—Golden State	50	32	.610	3rd/Pacific Division	0	3	.000
94-95—Golden State	14	31	.311		—	—	—
95-96—New York	34	25	.576		—	—	—
97-98—Dallas	16	50	.242	5th/Midwest Division	—	—	—
98-99—Dallas	19	31	.380	5th/Midwest Division	—	—	—
99-00—Dallas	40	42	.488	4th/Midwest Division	—	—	—
00-01—Dallas	53	29	.646	T2nd/Midwest Division	4	6	.400
01-02—Dallas	57	25	.695	2nd/Midwest Division	4	4	.500
02-03—Dallas	60	22	.732	2nd/Midwest Division	10	10	.500
03-04—Dallas	52	30	.634	3rd/Midwest Division	1	4	.200
04-05—Dallas	42	22	.656				
Totals (27 years)	**1190**	**880**	**.575**	**Totals (17 years)**	**70**	**85**	**.452**

WORLD CHAMPIONSHIP COACHING RECORD

Season Team	REGULAR SEASON			
	W	L	Pct.	Finish
1994—Team USA	8	0	1.000	Gold medal

NOTES:

75-76—Replaced Larry Costello as Milwaukee head coach (November 22), with record of 3-15 and club in sixth place.

77-78—Defeated Phoenix, 2-0, in Western Conference first round; lost to Denver, 4-3, in Western Conference semifinals.

79-80—Lost to Seattle in Western Conference semifinals.

80-81—Lost to Philadelphia in Eastern Conference semifinals.

81-82—Lost to Philadelphia in Eastern Conference semifinals.

82-83—Defeated Boston, 4-0, in Eastern Conference semifinals; lost to Philadelphia, 4-1, in Eastern Conference finals.

83-84—Defeated Atlanta, 3-2, in Eastern Conference first round; defeated New Jersey, 4-2, Eastern Conference semifinals; lost to Boston, 4-1, in Eastern Conference finals.

84-85—Defeated Chicago, 3-1, in Eastern Conference first round; lost to Philadelphia, 4-0, in Eastern Conference semifinals.

85-86—Defeated New Jersey, 3-0, in Eastern Conference first round; defeated Philadelphia, 4-3, in Eastern Conference semifinals; lost to Boston, 4-0, in Eastern Conference finals.

86-87—Defeated Philadelphia, 3-2, in Eastern Conference first round; lost to Boston, 4-3, in Eastern Conference semifinals.

88-89—Defeated Utah, 3-0, in Western Conference first round; lost to Phoenix, 4-1, in Western Conference semifinals.

90-91—Defeated San Antonio, 3-1, in Western Conference first round; lost to Los Angeles Lakers, 4-1, in Western Conference semifinals.

91-92—Lost to Seattle, 3-1, in Western Conference first round.

93-94—Lost to Phoenix, 3-0, in Western Conference first round.

94-95—Replaced as Golden State head coach by Bob Lanier (February 13) with club in sixth place.

95-96—Replaced as New York head coach by Jeff Van Gundy (March 8) with club in second place.

96-97—Replaced Jim Cleamons as Dallas head coach (December 4), with record of 4-12 and club in sixth place.

00-01—Defeated Utah, 3-2, in Western Conference first round; lost to San Antonio, 4-1, in Western Conference semifinals.

01-02—Defeated Minnesota, 3-0, in Western Conference first round; lost to Sacramento, 4-1, in Western Conference semifinals.

02-03—Defeated Portland, 4-3, in Western Conference first round; defeated Sacramento, 4-3, in Western Conference semifinals; lost to San Antonio, 4-2, in Western Conference finals.

03-04—Lost to Sacramento, 1-1, in Western Conference first round.

04-05—Stepped down as Dallas head coach (March 19, 2005); replaced by Avery Johnson with team in second place.

POPOVICH, GREGG   SPURS

PERSONAL: Born January 28, 1949, in East Chicago, Ind. ... 6-2/200. (1.88/90.7). ... Full name: Gregg Charles Popovich.
HIGH SCHOOL: Merrilville (Ind.)
COLLEGE: Air Force, then University of Denver.

HEAD COACHING RECORD

BACKGROUND: Assistant coach, Air Force (1972-73 through 1977-78). ... Assistant coach, San Antonio Spurs (1988-89 through 1991-92). ... Assistant coach, Golden State Warriors (1992-93 and 1993-94). ... Executive vice president of basketball operations/general manager (1994-95 through December 10, 1996).

COLLEGIATE RECORD

Season Team	G	Min.	FGM	FGA	Pct.	AVERAGES			Reb.	Ast.	Pts.	RPG	APG	PPG
						FTM	FTA	Pct.						
66-67—Air Force				Statistics unavailable										
67-68—Air Force				Statistics unavailable										
68-69—Air Force	13	51	5	18	.278	15	19	.789	7	12	25	0.5	0.9	1.9
69-70—Air Force	28	205	7	31	.226	15	26	.577	7	26	34	0.3	0.9	1.2
Totals	**66**	**380**	**25**	**80**	**.313**	**41**	**61**	**.672**	**23**	**60**	**96**	**0.3**	**0.9**	**1.5**

Three-point field goals: 1986-87, 5-for-20 (.250). Totals, 5-for-20 (.250).

COLLEGIATE COACHING RECORD

Season Team	W	L	Pct.	Finish
79-80—Pomona-Pitzer	2	22	.083	T6th/Southern California I.A.C.
80-81—Pomona-Pitzer	10	15	.400	6th/Southern California I.A.C.
81-82—Pomona-Pitzer	9	17	.346	4th/Southern California I.A.C.
82-83—Pomona-Pitzer	12	13	.480	5th/Southern California I.A.C.
83-84—Pomona-Pitzer	9	17	.346	T4th/Southern California I.A.C.
84-85—Pomona-Pitzer	11	14	.440	4th/Southern California I.A.C.
85-86—Pomona-Pitzer	16	12	.571	1st/Southern California I.A.C.
Totals	**69**	**110**	**.385**	

NBA COACHING RECORD

Season Team	REGULAR SEASON				PLAYOFFS		
	W	L	Pct.	Finish	W	L	Pct.
96-97—San Antonio	17	47	.266	6th/Midwest Division	—	—	—
97-98—San Antonio	56	26	.683	2nd/Midwest Division	4	5	.444

		REGULAR SEASON				PLAYOFFS		
Season Team	W	L	Pct.	Finish		W	L	Pct.
98-99—San Antonio	37	13	.740	T1st/Midwest Division		15	2	.882
99-00—San Antonio	53	29	.646	2nd/Midwest Division		1	3	.250
00-01—San Antonio	58	24	.707	1st/Midwest Division		7	6	.538
01-02—San Antonio	58	24	.707	1st/Midwest Division		4	6	.400
02-03—San Antonio	60	22	.732	1st/Midwest Division		16	8	.667
03-04—San Antonio	57	55	.509	2nd/Midwest Division		6	4	.600
04-05—San Antonio	59	23	.720	1st/Southwest Division		16	7	.696
05-06—San Antonio	63	19	.768	1st/Southwest Division		7	6	.538
Totals	518	282	.648			76	47	.618

NOTES:

96-97—Replaced Bob Hill as San Antonio head coach (December 10), with record of 3-15 and club in seventh place.

97-98—Defeated Phoenix, 3-1, in Western Conference first round; lost to Utah, 4-1, in Western Conference semifinals.

98-99—Defeated Minnesota, 3-1, in Western Conference first round; defeated Los Angeles Lakers, 4-0, in Western Conference semifinals; defeated Portland, 4-0, in Western Conference finals; defeated New York, 4-1, in NBA Finals.

99-00—Lost to Phoenix, 3-1, in Western Conference first round.

00-01—Defeated Seattle, 3-2, in Western Conference first round; defeated Dallas, 4-1, in Western Conference semifinals; lost to Los Angeles Lakers, 4-0, in Western Conference finals.

01-02—Defeated Seattle, 3-2, in Western Conference first round; lost to Los Angeles Lakers, 4-1, in Western Conference semifinals.

02-03—Defeated Phoenix, 4-2, in Western Conference first round; defeated Los Angeles Lakers, 4-2, in Western Conference semifinals; defeated Dallas, 4-2, in Western Conference finals; defeated New Jersey, 4-2, in NBA Finals.

03-04—Defeated Memphis, 4-0, in Western Conference first round; lost to Los Angeles Lakers, 4-2, in Western Conference semifinals.

04-05—Defeated Denver, 4-1, in Western Conference first round; defeated Seattle, 4-2, in Western Conference semifinals; defeated Phoenix, 4-1, in Western Conference finals; defeated Detroit, 4-3, in NBA Finals.

05-06—Defeated Sacramento, 4-2, in Western Conference first round; lost to Dallas, 4-3, in Western Conference semifinals.

RILEY, PAT | HEAT

PERSONAL: Born March 20, 1945, in Rome, N.Y. ... 6-4/205. (1.93/93.0). ... Full name: Patrick James Riley ... Son of Leon Riley, outfielder/catcher with Philadelphia Phillies (1944) and minor league manager; and brother of Lee Riley, defensive back with three NFL teams (1955-1960) and New York Titans of American Football League (1961 and 1962).
HIGH SCHOOL: Linton (Schenectady, N.Y.).
COLLEGE: Kentucky.
TRANSACTIONS/CAREER NOTES: Selected by San Diego Rockets in first round (seventh pick overall) of 1967 NBA Draft. ... Selected by Portland Trail Blazers from Rockets in NBA Expansion Draft (May 11, 1970). ... Contract sold by Trail Blazers to Los Angeles Lakers (October 9, 1970). ... Traded by Lakers to Phoenix Suns for draft rights to G John Roche and 1976 second-round draft choice (November 3, 1975).
MISCELLANEOUS: Member of NBA championship team (1972). ... Selected by Dallas Cowboys in 11th round of 1967 National Football League draft.

COLLEGIATE RECORD

													AVERAGES		
Season Team	G	Min.	FGM	FGA	Pct.	FTM	FTA	Pct.	Reb.	Ast.	Pts.		RPG	APG	PPG
63-64—Kentucky	16	...	120	259	.463	93	146	.637	235	...	333		14.7	...	20.8
64-65—Kentucky	25	825	160	370	.432	55	89	.618	212	27	375		8.5	1.1	15.0
65-66—Kentucky	29	1078	265	514	.516	107	153	.699	259	64	637		8.9	2.2	22.0
66-67—Kentucky	26	953	165	373	.442	122	156	.782	201	68	452		7.7	2.6	17.4
Totals	96	2856	710	1516	.468	377	544	.693	907	159	1797		9.4	1.7	18.7

NBA REGULAR-SEASON RECORD

HONORS: NBA Coach of the Year (1997).

									REBOUNDS									AVERAGES		
Season Team	G	Min.	FGM	FGA	Pct.	FTM	FTA	Pct.	Off.	Def.	Tot.	Ast.	St.	Blk.	TO	Pts.		RPG	APG	PPG
67-68—San Diego	80	1263	250	660	.379	128	202	.634	...	...	177	138	...	...	...	628		2.2	1.7	7.9
68-69—San Diego	56	1027	202	498	.406	90	134	.672	...	...	112	136	...	...	...	494		2.0	2.4	8.8
69-70—San Diego	36	474	75	180	.417	40	55	.727	...	...	57	85	...	...	...	190		1.6	2.4	5.3
70-71—Los Angeles	54	506	105	254	.413	56	87	.644	...	...	54	72	...	...	...	266		1.0	1.3	4.9
71-72—Los Angeles	67	926	197	441	.447	55	74	.743	...	...	127	75	...	...	...	449		1.9	1.1	6.7
72-73—Los Angeles	55	801	167	390	.428	65	82	.793	...	...	65	81	...	...	...	399		1.2	1.5	7.3
73-74—Los Angeles	72	1361	287	667	.430	110	144	.764	38	90	128	148	54	3	...	684		1.8	2.1	9.5
74-75—Los Angeles	46	1016	219	523	.419	69	93	.742	25	60	85	121	36	4	...	507		1.8	2.6	11.0
75-76—L.A.-Phoenix	62	813	117	301	.389	55	77	.714	16	34	50	57	22	6	...	289		0.8	0.9	4.7
Totals	528	8187	1619	3914	.414	668	948	.705	79	184	855	913	112	13	...	3906		1.6	1.7	7.4

Personal fouls/disqualifications: 1967-68, 205/1. 1968-69, 146/1. 1969-70, 68/0. 1970-71, 84/0. 1971-72, 110/0. 1972-73, 126/0. 1973-74, 173/1. 1974-75, 128/0. 1975-76, 112/0. Totals, 1152/3.

NBA PLAYOFF RECORD

									REBOUNDS									AVERAGES		
Season Team	G	Min.	FGM	FGA	Pct.	FTM	FTA	Pct.	Off.	Def.	Tot.	Ast.	St.	Blk.	TO	Pts.		RPG	APG	PPG
68-69—San Diego	5	76	16	37	.432	5	6	.833	...	...	11	2	...	...	...	37		2.2	0.4	7.4
70-71—Los Angeles	7	135	29	69	.420	8	11	.727	...	...	15	14	...	...	...	66		2.1	2.0	9.4
71-72—Los Angeles	15	244	33	99	.333	12	16	.750	...	...	29	14	...	...	...	78		1.9	0.9	5.2
72-73—Los Angeles	7	53	9	27	.333	0	0	...	...	...	5	7	...	...	...	18		0.7	1.0	2.6
73-74—Los Angeles	5	106	18	50	.360	3	4	.750	3	3	6	10	4	0	...	39		1.2	2.0	7.8
75-76—Phoenix	5	27	6	15	.400	1	1	1.000	0	0	0	5	0	0	...	13		0.0	1.0	2.6
Totals	44	641	111	297	.374	29	38	.763	3	3	66	52	4	0	...	251		1.5	1.2	5.7

Personal fouls/disqualifications: 1968-69, 13/0. 1970-71, 12/0. 1971-72, 37/0. 1972-73, 10/0. 1973-74, 11/0. 1975-76, 3/0. Totals, 86/0.

HEAD COACHING RECORD

BACKGROUND: Broadcaster, Los Angeles Lakers (1977-79). ... Assistant coach, Lakers (1979-80 to November 19, 1981). ... Broadcaster, NBC television (1990-91). ... President, Miami Heat (1995-96 to present).

NBA COACHING RECORD

		REGULAR SEASON				PLAYOFFS		
Season Team	W	L	Pct.	Finish	W	L	Pct.
81-82—L.A. Lakers	50	21	.704	1st/Pacific Division	12	2	.857
82-83—L.A. Lakers	58	24	.707	1st/Pacific Division	8	7	.533
83-84—L.A. Lakers	54	28	.659	1st/Pacific Division	14	7	.667
84-85—L.A. Lakers	62	20	.756	1st/Pacific Division	15	4	.789
85-86—L.A. Lakers	62	20	.756	1st/Pacific Division	8	6	.571
86-87—L.A. Lakers	65	17	.793	1st/Pacific Division	15	3	.833
87-88—L.A. Lakers	62	20	.756	1st/Pacific Division	15	9	.625
88-89—L.A. Lakers	57	25	.695	1st/Pacific Division	11	4	.733
89-90—L.A. Lakers	63	19	.768	1st/Pacific Division	4	5	.444
91-92—New York	51	31	.622	T1st/Atlantic Division	6	6	.500
92-93—New York	60	22	.732	1st/Atlantic Division	9	6	.600
93-94—New York	57	25	.695	1st/Atlantic Division	14	11	.560
94-95—New York	55	27	.671	2nd/Atlantic Division	6	5	.545
95-96—Miami	42	40	.512	3rd/Atlantic Division	0	3	.000
96-97—Miami	61	21	.744	1st/Atlantic Division	8	9	.471
97-98—Miami	55	27	.671	1st/Atlantic Division	2	3	.400
98-99—Miami	33	17	.660	T1st/Atlantic Division	2	3	.400
99-00—Miami	52	30	.634	1st/Atlantic Division	6	4	.600
00-01—Miami	50	32	.610	2nd/Atlantic Division	0	3	.000
01-02—Miami	36	46	.439	6th/Atlantic Division	—	—	—
02-03—Miami	25	57	.305	7th/Atlantic Division	—	—	—
05-06—Miami	41	20	.672	1st/Southeast Division	16	7	.696
Totals	1151	589	.661		171	107	.615

NOTES:

81-82—Replaced Paul Westhead as Los Angeles Lakers head coach (November 19), with a record of 7-4 and club in first place. Defeated Phoenix, 4-0, in Western Conference semifinals; defeated San Antonio, 4-0, in Western Conference finals; defeated Philadelphia, 4-2, in NBA Finals.
82-83—Defeated Portland, 4-1, in Western Conference semifinals; defeated San Antonio, 4-2, in Western Conference finals; lost to Philadelphia, 4-0, in NBA Finals.
83-84—Defeated Kansas City, 3-0, in Western Conference first round; defeated Dallas, 4-1, in Western Conference semifinals; defeated Phoenix, 4-2, in Western Conference finals; lost to Boston, 4-3, in NBA Finals.
84-85—Defeated Phoenix, 3-0, in Western Conference first round; defeated Portland, 4-1, in Western Conference semifinals; defeated Denver, 4-1, in Western Conference finals; defeated Boston, 4-2, in NBA Finals.
85-86—Defeated San Antonio, 3-0, in Western Conference first round; defeated Dallas, 4-2, in Western Conference semifinals; lost to Houston, 4-1, in Western Conference finals.
86-87—Defeated Denver, 3-0, in Western Conference first round; defeated Golden State, 4-1, in Western Conference semifinals; defeated Seattle, 4-0, in Western Conference finals; defeated Boston, 4-2, in NBA Finals.
87-88—Defeated San Antonio, 3-0, in Western Conference first round; defeated Utah, 4-3, in Western Conference semifinals; defeated Dallas, 4-3, in Western Conference finals; defeated Detroit, 4-3, in NBA Finals.
88-89—Defeated Portland, 3-0, in Western Conference first round; defeated Seattle, 4-0, in Western Conference semifinals; defeated Phoenix, 4-0, in Western Conference finals; lost to Detroit, 4-0, in NBA Finals.
89-90—Defeated Houston, 3-1, in Western Conference first round; lost to Phoenix, 4-1, in Western Conference semifinals.
91-92—Defeated Detroit, 3-2, in Eastern Conference first round; lost to Chicago, 4-3, in Eastern Conference semifinals.
92-93—Defeated Indiana, 3-1, in Eastern Conference first round; defeated Charlotte, 4-1, in Eastern Conference semifinals; lost to Chicago, 4-2, in Eastern Conference finals.
93-94—Defeated New Jersey, 3-1, in Eastern Conference first round; defeated Chicago, 4-3, in Eastern Conference semifinals; defeated Indiana, 4-3, in Eastern Conference finals; lost to Houston, 4-3, in NBA Finals.
94-95—Defeated Cleveland, 3-1, in Eastern Conference first round; lost to Indiana, 4-3, in Eastern Conference semifinals.
95-96—Lost to Chicago, 3-0, in Eastern Conference first round.
96-97—Defeated Orlando, 3-2, in Eastern Conference first round; defeated New York, 4-3, in Eastern Conference semifinals; lost to Chicago, 4-1, in Eastern Conference finals.
97-98—Lost to New York, 3-2, in Eastern Conference first round.
98-99—Lost to New York, 3-2, in Eastern Conference first round.
99-00—Defeated Detroit, 3-0, in Eastern Conference first round; lost to New York, 4-3, in Eastern Conference semifinals.
00-01—Lost to Charlotte, 3-0, in Eastern Conference first round.
05-06—Replaced Stan Van Gundy as Miami head coach (December 12) with a record of 11-10 and the club in first place. Defeated Chicago, 4-2, in Eastern Conference first round; defeated New Jersey, 4-1, in Eastern Conference semifinals; defeated Detroit, 4-2, in Eastern Conference finals; defeated Dallas, 4-2, in NBA Finals.

RIVERS, DOC   CELTICS

PERSONAL: Born October 13, 1961, in Chicago. ... 6-4/210. (1.93/95.3). ... Full name: Glenn Anton Rivers ... Nephew of Jim Brewer, forward with Cleveland Cavaliers (1973-74 through 1978-79), Detroit Pistons (1978-79), Portland Trail Blazers (1979-80) and Los Angeles Lakers (1980-81 and 1981-82); cousin of Byron Irvin, guard with Portland Trail Blazers (1989-90) and Washington Bullets (1990-91 and 1992-93); and cousin of Ken Singleton, outfielder/designated hitter with three major league baseball teams (1970 through 1984).
HIGH SCHOOL: Proviso East (Maywood, Ill.).
COLLEGE: Marquette.
TRANSACTIONS/CAREER NOTES: Selected after junior season by Atlanta Hawks in second round (31st pick overall) of 1983 NBA Draft. ... Traded by Hawks to Los Angeles Clippers for 1991 first-round draft choice and 1993 and 1994 second-round draft choices (June 26, 1991). ... Traded by Clippers with C/F Charles Smith and G Bo Kimble to New York Knicks in three-way deal in which Clippers received G Mark Jackson and 1995 second-round draft choice from Knicks and C Stanley Roberts from Orlando Magic and Magic received 1993 first-round draft choice from Knicks and 1994 first-round draft choice from Clippers (September 22, 1992). ... Waived by Knicks (December 15, 1994). ... Signed as free agent by San Antonio Spurs (December 26, 1994).
MISCELLANEOUS: Atlanta Hawks franchise all-time assists leader with 3,866 (1983-84 through 1990-91).

COLLEGIATE RECORD

												AVERAGES		
Season Team	G	Min.	FGM	FGA	Pct.	FTM	FTA	Pct.	Reb.	Ast.	Pts.	RPG	APG	PPG
80-81—Marquette	31	...	182	329	.553	70	119	.588	99	113	434	3.2	3.6	14.0
81-82—Marquette	29	...	173	382	.453	70	108	.648	99	170	416	3.4	5.9	14.3
82-83—Marquette	29	...	163	373	.437	58	95	.611	94	126	384	3.2	4.3	13.2
Totals	89	...	518	1084	.478	198	322	.615	292	409	1234	3.3	4.6	13.9

NBA REGULAR-SEASON RECORD

Season Team	G	Min.	FGM	FGA	Pct.	FTM	FTA	Pct.	Off.	Def.	Tot.	Ast.	St.	Blk.	TO	Pts.	RPG	APG	PPG
83-84—Atlanta	81	1938	250	541	.462	255	325	.785	72	148	220	314	127	30	174	757	2.7	3.9	9.3
84-85—Atlanta	69	2126	334	701	.476	291	378	.770	66	148	214	410	163	53	176	974	3.1	5.9	14.1
85-86—Atlanta	53	1571	220	464	.474	172	283	.608	49	113	162	443	120	13	141	612	3.1	8.4	11.5
86-87—Atlanta	82	2590	342	758	.451	365	441	.828	83	216	299	823	171	30	217	1053	3.6	10.0	12.8
87-88—Atlanta	80	2502	403	890	.453	319	421	.758	83	283	366	747	140	41	210	1134	4.6	9.3	14.2
88-89—Atlanta	76	2462	371	816	.455	247	287	.861	89	197	286	525	181	40	158	1032	3.8	6.9	13.6
89-90—Atlanta ..	48	1526	218	480	.454	138	170	.812	47	153	200	264	116	22	98	598	4.2	5.5	12.5
90-91—Atlanta ..	79	2586	444	1020	.435	221	262	.844	47	206	253	340	148	47	125	1197	3.2	4.3	15.2
91-92—L.A. Clippers..	59	1657	226	533	.424	163	196	.832	23	124	147	233	111	19	92	641	2.5	3.9	10.9
92-93—New York	77	1886	216	494	.437	133	162	.821	26	166	192	405	123	9	114	604	2.5	5.3	7.8
93-94—New York	19	499	55	127	.433	14	22	.636	4	35	39	100	25	5	29	143	2.1	5.3	7.5
94-95—N.Y.-S.A.	63	989	108	302	.358	60	82	.732	15	94	109	162	65	21	60	321	1.7	2.6	5.1
95-96—San Antonio ..	78	1235	108	290	.372	48	64	.750	30	108	138	123	73	21	57	311	1.8	1.6	4.0
Totals	864	23567	3295	7416	.444	2426	3093	.784	634	1991	2625	4889	1563	351	1651	9377	3.0	5.7	10.9

Three-point field goals: 1983-84, 2-for-12 (.167). 1984-85, 15-for-36 (.417). 1985-86, 0-for-16. 1986-87, 4-for-21 (.190). 1987-88, 9-for-33 (.273). 1988-89, 43-for-124 (.347). 1989-90, 24-for-66 (.364). 1990-91, 88-for-262 (.336). 1991-92, 26-for-92 (.283). 1992-93, 39-for-123 (.317). 1993-94, 19-for-52 (.365). 1994-95, 45-for-127 (.354). 1995-96, 47-for-137 (.343). Totals, 361-for-1101 (.328).

Personal fouls/disqualifications: 1983-84, 286/8. 1984-85, 250/7. 1985-86, 185/2. 1986-87, 287/5. 1987-88, 272/3. 1988-89, 263/6. 1989-90, 151/2. 1990-91, 216/2. 1991-92, 166/2. 1992-93, 215/2. 1993-94, 44/0. 1994-95, 150/2. 1995-96, 175/0. Totals, 2660/41.

NBA PLAYOFF RECORD

NOTES: Shares single-game playoff record for most assists in one half—15 (May 16, 1988, vs. Boston).

Season Team	G	Min.	FGM	FGA	Pct.	FTM	FTA	Pct.	Off.	Def.	Tot.	Ast.	St.	Blk.	TO	Pts.	RPG	APG	PPG
83-84—Atlanta	5	130	16	32	.500	36	41	.878	7	3	10	16	12	4	9	68	2.0	3.2	13.6
85-86—Atlanta	9	262	40	92	.435	31	42	.738	10	32	42	78	18	0	26	114	4.7	8.7	12.7
86-87—Atlanta	8	245	18	47	.383	26	52	.500	6	21	27	90	9	3	25	62	3.4	11.3	7.8
87-88—Atlanta	12	409	71	139	.511	39	43	.907	8	51	59	115	25	2	25	188	4.9	9.6	15.7
88-89—Atlanta ..	5	191	22	57	.386	17	24	.708	4	20	24	34	7	2	12	67	4.8	6.8	13.4
90-91—Atlanta ..	5	173	30	64	.469	17	19	.895	6	14	20	15	5	2	4	78	4.0	3.0	15.6
91-92—L.A. Clippers..	5	187	25	56	.446	22	27	.815	4	15	19	21	6	0	3	76	3.8	4.2	15.2
92-93—New York	15	458	48	106	.453	46	60	.767	6	33	39	86	29	1	30	153	2.6	5.7	10.2
94-95—San Antonio ..	15	318	37	95	.389	26	31	.839	3	26	29	24	14	9	18	117	1.9	1.6	7.8
95-96—San Antonio ..	2	20	1	3	.333	0	0	...	0	1	1	0	0	0	1	3	0.5	0.0	1.5
Totals	81	2393	308	691	.446	260	339	.767	54	270	324	479	125	23	153	926	3.3	5.9	11.4

Three-point field goals: 1983-84, 0-for-3. 1985-86, 3-for-6 (.500). 1987-88, 7-for-22 (.318). 1988-89, 6-for-19 (.316). 1990-91, 1-for-11 (.091). 1991-92, 4-for-8 (.500). 1992-93, 11-for-31 (.355). 1994-95, 17-for-46 (.370). 1995-96, 1-for-2 (.500). Totals, 50-for-148 (.338).

Personal fouls/disqualifications: 1983-84, 16/0. 1985-86, 38/2. 1986-87, 32/0. 1987-88, 40/1. 1988-89, 22/2. 1990-91, 14/0. 1991-92, 16/0. 1992-93, 44/0. 1994-95, 40/0. 1995-96, 3/0. Totals, 265/5.

NBA ALL-STAR GAME RECORD

Season Team	Min.	FGM	FGA	Pct.	FTM	FTA	Pct.	Off.	Def.	Tot.	Ast.	PF	Dq.	St.	Blk.	TO	Pts.
1988—Atlanta...................	16	2	4	.500	5	11	.455	0	3	3	6	3	0	0	0	3	9

HEAD COACHING RECORD

NBA COACHING RECORD

Season Team	W	L	Pct.	Finish	W	L	Pct.
				REGULAR SEASON		**PLAYOFFS**	
99-00—Orlando	41	41	.500	4th/Atlantic Division	—	—	—
00-01—Orlando	43	39	.524	4th/Atlantic Division	1	3	.250
01-02—Orlando	44	38	.537	3rd/Atlantic Division	1	3	.250
02-03—Orlando	42	40	.512	4th/Atlantic Division	3	4	.429
03-04—Orlando	1	10	.091		—	—	—
04-05—Boston..	45	37	.549	1st/Atlantic Division	3	4	.429
05-06—Boston..	33	49	.402	3rd/Atlantic Division	—	—	—
Totals	249	254	.495		8	14	.364

NOTES:

00-01—Lost to Milwaukee, 3-1, in Eastern Conference first round.
01-02—Lost to Charlotte, 3-1, in Eastern Conference first round.
02-03—Lost to Detroit, 4-3, in Eastern Conference first round.
03-04—Replaced as Orlando head coach by Johnny Davis (November 17) with club in seventh place.
04-05—Lost to Indiana, 4-3, in Eastern Conference first round.

SAUNDERS, FLIP   PISTONS

PERSONAL: Born February 23, 1955, in Cleveland. ... 5-11/175. (1.80/79.4). ... Full name: Phillip D. Saunders.
HIGH SCHOOL: Cuyahoga Heights (Ohio).
COLLEGE: Minnesota.

HEAD COACHING RECORD

BACKGROUND: Assistant coach, University of Minnesota (1982-83 through 1985-86). ... Assistant coach, University of Tulsa (1986-87 and 1987-88). ... General manager, Minnesota Timberwolves (1994-95 and 1995-96).
HONORS: CBA Coach of the Year (1990, 1992).

CBA COACHING RECORD

Season Team	W	L	Pct.	Finish	W	L	Pct.
				REGULAR SEASON		**PLAYOFFS**	
88-89—Rapid City	38	16	.704	1st/Western Division	6	5	.545
89-90—La Crosse	42	14	.750	1st/Central Division	11	4	.733

HEAD COACHES (vertical sidebar text)

Season Team		REGULAR SEASON					PLAYOFFS	
	W	L	Pct.	Finish		W	L	Pct.
90-91—La Crosse	32	24	.571	2nd/Central Division		2	3	.400
91-92—La Crosse	40	16	.714	2nd/Midwest Division		10	6	.625
92-93—La Crosse	32	24	.571	3rd/Mideast Division		2	3	.400
93-94—La Crosse	35	21	.625	1st/Mideast Division		3	3	.500
94-95—Sioux Falls	34	22	.607	2nd/Western Division		1	2	.333
Totals	253	137	.649			35	26	.574

NOTES:

88-89—Defeated Cedar Rapids, 4-1, in Western semifinals; lost to Rockford, 4-2, in Western finals.

89-90—Defeated Quad City, 3-0, in American semifinals; defeated Albany, 4-3, in American finals; defeated Rapid City, 4-1, in CBA Championship Series.

90-91—Lost to Quad City, 3-2, in American first round.

91-92—Defeated Grand Rapids, 3-1, in American second round; defeated Quad City, 3-2, in American finals; defeated Rapid City, 4-3, in CBA Championship Series.

92-93—Lost to Rockford, 3-2, in American first round.

93-94—Defeated Rockford, 3-0, in American first round; lost to Quad City, 3-0, in American finals.

94-95—Lost to Omaha, 2-1, in National first round.

NBA COACHING RECORD

Season Team		REGULAR SEASON					PLAYOFFS	
	W	L	Pct.	Finish		W	L	Pct.
95-96—Minnesota	20	42	.323	T5th/Midwest Division		—	—	—
96-97—Minnesota	40	42	.488	3rd/Midwest Division		0	3	.000
97-98—Minnesota	45	37	.549	3rd/Midwest Division		2	3	.400
98-99—Minnesota	25	25	.500	4th/Midwest Division		1	3	.250
99-00—Minnesota	50	32	.610	3rd/Midwest Division		1	3	.250
00-01—Minnesota	47	35	.573	4th/Midwest Division		1	3	.250
01-02—Minnesota	50	32	.610	3rd/ Midwest Division		0	3	.000
02-03—Minnesota	51	31	.622	3rd/Midwest Division		2	4	.333
03-04—Minnesota	58	24	.707	1st/Midwest Division		10	8	.556
04-05—Minnesota	25	26	.490			—	—	—
05-06—Detroit	64	18	.780	1st/Central Division		10	8	.556
Totals	475	344	.580			27	38	.415

NOTES:

95-96—Replaced Bill Blair as Minnesota head coach (December 18), with record of 6-14 and club in sixth place.

96-97—Lost to Houston, 3-0, in Western Conference first round.

97-98—Lost to Seattle, 3-2, in Western Conference first round.

98-99—Lost to San Antonio, 3-1, in Western Conference first round.

99-00—Lost to Portland, 3-1, in Western Conference first round.

00-01—Lost to San Antonio, 3-1, in Western Conference first round.

01-02—Lost to Dallas, 3-0, in Western Conference first round.

02-03—Lost to Los Angeles Lakers, 4-2, in Western Conference first round.

03-04—Defeated Denver, 4-1, in Western Conference first round; defeated Sacramento, 4-3, in Western Conference semifinals; lost to Los Angeles Lakers, 4-2, in Western Conference finals.

05-06—Defeated Milwaukee, 4-1, in Eastern Conference first round; defeated Cleveland, 4-3, in Eastern Conference semifinals; lost to Miami, 4-2, in Eastern Conference finals.

SCOTT, BYRON   HORNETS

PERSONAL: Born March 28, 1961, in Ogden, Utah. ... 6-4/200. (1.93/90.7). ... Full name: Byron Antom Scott
HIGH SCHOOL: Morningside (Inglewood, Calif.).
COLLEGE: Arizona State.
TRANSACTIONS/CAREER NOTES: Selected by San Diego Clippers in first round (fourth pick overall) of 1983 NBA Draft. ... Draft rights traded by Clippers with C Swen Nater to Los Angeles Lakers for G Norm Nixon, G Eddie Jordan and 1986 and 1987 second-round draft choices (October 10, 1983). ... Signed as free agent by Indiana Pacers (December 6, 1993). ... Selected by Vancouver Grizzlies from Pacers in NBA Expansion Draft (June 24, 1995). ... Waived by Grizzlies (July 22, 1996). ... Signed as free agent by Lakers (September 30, 1996). ... Signed to play for Panathinaikos of Greece League for 1997-98 season. ... Rights renounced by Lakers (February 28, 2000).
MISCELLANEOUS: Member of NBA championship team (1985, 1987, 1988).

COLLEGIATE RECORD

Season Team	G	Min.	FGM	FGA	Pct.	FTM	FTA	Pct.	Reb.	Ast.	Pts.	AVERAGES		
												RPG	APG	PPG
79-80—Arizona State	29	936	166	332	.500	63	86	.733	79	65	395	2.7	2.2	13.6
80-81—Arizona State	28	1003	197	390	.505	70	101	.693	106	78	464	3.8	2.8	16.6
81-82—Arizona State					Did not play—academic and pers									
82-83—Arizona State	33	1206	283	552	.513	147	188	.782	177	140	713	5.4	4.2	21.6
Totals	90	3145	646	1274	.507	280	375	.747	362	283	1572	4.0	3.1	17.5

NBA REGULAR-SEASON RECORD

HONORS: NBA All-Rookie team (1984).
NOTES: Led NBA with .433 three-point field goal percentage (1985).

Season Team	G	Min.	FGM	FGA	Pct.	FTM	FTA	Pct.	REBOUNDS			Ast.	St.	Blk.	TO	Pts.	AVERAGES		
									Off.	Def.	Tot.						RPG	APG	PPG
83-84—Los Angeles ..	74	1637	334	690	.484	112	139	.806	50	114	164	177	81	19	116	788	2.2	2.4	10.6
84-85—L.A. Lakers	81	2305	541	1003	.539	187	228	.820	57	153	210	244	100	17	138	1295	2.6	3.0	16.0
85-86—L.A. Lakers	76	2190	507	989	.513	138	176	.784	55	134	189	164	85	15	110	1174	2.5	2.2	15.4
86-87—L.A. Lakers	82	2729	554	1134	.489	224	251	.892	63	223	286	281	125	18	144	1397	3.5	3.4	17.0
87-88—L.A. Lakers	81	3048	710	1348	.527	272	317	.858	76	257	333	335	155	27	161	1754	4.1	4.1	21.7
88-89—L.A. Lakers	74	2605	588	1198	.491	195	226	.863	72	230	302	231	114	27	157	1448	4.1	3.1	19.6
89-90—L.A. Lakers	77	2593	472	1005	.470	160	209	.766	51	191	242	274	77	31	122	1197	3.1	3.6	15.5
90-91—L.A. Lakers	82	2630	501	1051	.477	118	148	.797	54	192	246	177	95	21	85	1191	3.0	2.2	14.5

Season Team	G	Min.	FGM	FGA	Pct.	FTM	FTA	Pct.	REBOUNDS Off.	Def.	Tot.	Ast.	St.	Blk.	TO	Pts.	RPG	APG	PPG
91-92—L.A. Lakers	82	2679	460	1005	.458	244	291	.838	74	236	310	226	105	28	119	1218	3.8	2.8	14.9
92-93—L.A. Lakers	58	1677	296	659	.449	156	184	.848	27	107	134	157	55	13	70	792	2.3	2.7	13.7
93-94—Indiana	67	1197	256	548	.467	157	195	.805	19	91	110	133	62	9	103	696	1.6	2.0	10.4
94-95—Indiana	80	1528	265	583	.455	193	227	.850	18	133	151	108	61	13	119	802	1.9	1.4	10.0
95-96—Vancouver......	80	1894	271	676	.401	203	243	.835	40	152	192	123	63	22	100	819	2.4	1.5	10.2
96-97—L.A. Lakers	79	1440	163	379	.430	127	151	.841	21	97	118	99	46	16	53	526	1.5	1.3	6.7
Totals	1073	30152	5918	12268	.482	2486	2985	.833	677	2310	2987	2729	1224	276	1597	15097	2.8	2.5	14.1

Three-point field goals: 1983-84, 8-for-34 (.235). 1984-85, 26-for-60 (.433). 1985-86, 22-for-61 (.361). 1986-87, 65-for-149 (.436). 1987-88, 62-for-179 (.346). 1988-89, 77-for-193 (.399). 1989-90, 93-for-220 (.423). 1990-91, 71-for-219 (.324). 1991-92, 54-for-157 (.344). 1992-93, 44-for-135 (.326). 1993-94, 27-for-74 (.365). 1994-95, 79-for-203 (.389). 1995-96, 74-for-221 (.335). 1996-97, 73-for-188 (.388). Totals, 775-for-2093 (.370).

Personal fouls/disqualifications: 1983-84, 174/0. 1984-85, 197/1. 1985-86, 167/0. 1986-87, 163/0. 1987-88, 204/2. 1988-89, 181/1. 1989-90, 180/2. 1990-91, 146/0. 1991-92, 140/0. 1992-93, 98/0. 1993-94, 80/0. 1994-95, 123/1. 1995-96, 126/0. 1996-97, 72/0. Totals, 2051/7.

NBA PLAYOFF RECORD

Season Team	G	Min.	FGM	FGA	Pct.	FTM	FTA	Pct.	REBOUNDS Off.	Def.	Tot.	Ast.	St.	Blk.	TO	Pts.	RPG	APG	PPG
83-84—Los Angeles ..	20	404	74	161	.460	21	35	.600	11	26	37	34	18	2	26	171	1.9	1.7	8.6
84-85—L.A. Lakers	19	585	138	267	.517	35	44	.795	16	36	52	50	41	4	24	321	2.7	2.6	16.9
85-86—L.A. Lakers	14	470	90	181	.497	38	42	.905	15	40	55	42	19	2	30	224	3.9	3.0	16.0
86-87—L.A. Lakers	18	608	103	210	.490	53	67	.791	20	42	62	57	19	4	25	266	3.4	3.2	14.8
87-88—L.A. Lakers	24	897	178	357	.499	90	104	.865	26	74	100	60	34	5	47	470	4.2	2.5	19.6
88-89—L.A. Lakers	11	402	79	160	.494	46	55	.836	10	35	45	25	18	2	20	219	4.1	2.3	19.9
89-90—L.A. Lakers	9	325	49	106	.462	10	13	.769	7	30	37	23	20	3	13	121	4.1	2.6	13.4
90-91—L.A. Lakers	18	678	95	186	.511	27	34	.794	13	44	57	29	23	4	17	237	3.2	1.6	13.2
91-92—L.A. Lakers	4	148	22	44	.500	24	27	.889	3	7	10	14	6	1	5	75	2.5	3.5	18.8
92-93—L.A. Lakers	5	177	21	42	.500	18	23	.783	0	11	11	9	5	0	4	68	2.2	1.8	13.6
93-94—Indiana	16	239	38	96	.396	40	51	.784	10	23	33	20	12	2	25	125	2.1	1.3	7.8
94-95—Indiana	17	298	32	94	.340	30	34	.882	5	20	25	16	10	1	22	103	1.5	0.9	6.1
96-97—L.A. Lakers	8	134	15	33	.455	17	19	.895	0	12	12	11	1	0	8	51	1.5	1.4	6.4
Totals	183	5365	934	1937	.482	449	548	.819	136	400	536	390	226	30	266	2451	2.9	2.1	13.4

Three-point field goals: 1983-84, 2-for-10 (.200). 1984-85, 10-for-21 (.476). 1985-86, 6-for-17 (.353). 1986-87, 7-for-34 (.206). 1987-88, 24-for-55 (.436). 1988-89, 15-for-39 (.385). 1989-90, 13-for-34 (.382). 1990-91, 20-for-38 (.526). 1991-92, 7-for-12 (.583). 1992-93, 8-for-15 (.533). 1993-94, 9-for-19 (.474). 1994-95, 6-for-34 (.265). 1996-97, 4-for-11 (.364). Totals, 134-for-339 (.395).

Personal fouls/disqualifications: 1983-84, 39/1. 1984-85, 47/0. 1985-86, 38/0. 1986-87, 52/0. 1987-88, 65/0. 1988-89, 31/0. 1989-90, 32/1. 1990-91, 53/0. 1991-92, 10/0. 1992-93, 11/0. 1993-94, 22/0. 1994-95, 30/0. 1996-97, 15/0. Totals, 445/2.

HEAD COACHING RECORD

BACKGROUND: Assistant coach, Sacramento Kings (1998-99 and 1999-2000).

NBA COACHING RECORD

Season Team	REGULAR SEASON W	L	Pct.	Finish	PLAYOFFS W	L	Pct.
00-01—New Jersey	26	56	.317	6th/Atlantic Division	—	—	—
01-02—New Jersey	52	30	.634	1st/Atlantic Division	11	9	.550
02-03—New Jersey	49	33	.598	1st/Atlantic Division	14	6	.700
03-04—New Jersey	22	20	.524		—	—	—
04-05—New Orleans.................................	18	64	.220	5th/Southwest Division	—	—	—
05-06—New Orleans.................................	38	44	.463	4th/Southwest Division	—	—	—
Totals	205	247	.454		25	15	.625

NOTES:
01-02—Defeated Indiana, 3-2, in Eastern Conference first round; defeated Charlotte, 4-1, in Eastern Conference semifinals; defeated Boston, 4-2, in Eastern Conference finals; lost to Los Angeles Lakers, 4-0, in NBA Finals.
02-03—Defeated Milwaukee, 4-2, in Eastern Conference first round; defeated Boston, 4-0, in Eastern Conference semifinals; defeated Detroit, 4-0, in Eastern Conference finals; lost to San Antonio, 4-2, in NBA Finals.
03-04—Replaced as New Jersey head coach by Lawrence Frank (January 26) with club in first place.

SKILES, SCOTT   BULLS

PERSONAL: Born March 5, 1964, in LaPorte, Ind. ... 6-1/180. (1.85/81.6). ... Full name: Scott Allen Skiles
HIGH SCHOOL: Plymouth (Ind.).
COLLEGE: Michigan State.
TRANSACTIONS/CAREER NOTES: Selected by Milwaukee Bucks in first round (22nd pick overall) of 1986 NBA Draft. ... Traded by Bucks to Indiana Pacers for second-round draft choice (June 22, 1987). ... Selected by Orlando Magic from Pacers in NBA Expansion Draft (June 15, 1989). ... Traded by Magic with 1996 first-round draft choice and future considerations to Washington Bullets for 1996 second-round draft choice and future considerations (July 29, 1994). ... Signed by Philadelphia 76ers for remainder of season (December 12, 1995). ... Announced retirement (January 6, 1996).
MISCELLANEOUS: Orlando Magic all-time assists leader with 2,776 (1989-90 through 1993-94).

COLLEGIATE RECORD

NOTES: THE SPORTING NEWS All-America first team (1986).

Season Team	G	Min.	FGM	FGA	Pct.	FTM	FTA	Pct.	Reb.	Ast.	Pts.	AVERAGES RPG	APG	PPG
82-83—Michigan State	30	1023	141	286	.493	69	83	.831	63	146	376	2.1	4.9	12.5
83-84—Michigan State	28	983	153	319	.480	99	119	.832	62	128	405	2.2	4.6	14.5
84-85—Michigan State	29	1107	212	420	.505	90	114	.789	93	168	514	3.2	5.8	17.7
85-86—Michigan State	31	1172	331	598	.554	188	209	.900	135	203	850	4.4	6.5	27.4
Totals	118	4285	837	1623	.516	446	525	.850	353	645	2145	3.0	5.5	18.2

Three-point field goals: 1982-83, 25-for-50 (.500). Totals, 25-for-50 (.500).

NBA REGULAR-SEASON RECORD

RECORDS: Holds single-game record for most assists—30 (December 30, 1990, vs. Denver).
HONORS: NBA Most Improved Player (1991).

Season Team	G	Min.	FGM	FGA	Pct.	FTM	FTA	Pct.	REBOUNDS Off.	Def.	Tot.	Ast.	St.	Blk.	TO	Pts.	RPG	APG	PPG
86-87—Milwaukee......	13	205	18	62	.290	10	12	.833	6	20	26	45	5	1	21	49	2.0	3.5	3.8
87-88—Indiana	51	760	86	209	.411	45	54	.833	11	55	66	180	22	3	76	223	1.3	3.5	4.4
88-89—Indiana	80	1571	198	442	.448	130	144	.903	21	128	149	390	64	2	177	546	1.9	4.9	6.8
89-90—Orlando	70	1460	190	464	.409	104	119	.874	23	136	159	334	36	4	90	536	2.3	4.8	7.7
90-91—Orlando	79	2714	462	1039	.445	340	377	.902	57	213	270	660	89	4	252	1357	3.4	8.4	17.2
91-92—Orlando	75	2377	359	868	.414	248	277	.895	36	166	202	544	74	5	233	1057	2.7	7.3	14.1
92-93—Orlando	78	3086	416	891	.467	289	324	.892	52	238	290	735	86	2	267	1201	3.7	9.4	15.4
93-94—Orlando	82	2303	276	644	.429	195	222	.878	42	147	189	503	47	2	193	815	2.3	6.1	9.9
94-95—Washington ..	62	2077	265	583	.455	179	202	.886	26	133	159	452	70	6	172	805	2.6	7.3	13.0
95-96—Philadelphia ..	10	236	20	57	.351	8	10	.800	1	15	16	38	7	0	16	63	1.6	3.8	6.3
Totals	600	16789	2290	5259	.435	1548	1741	.889	275	1251	1526	3881	500	29	1497	6652	2.5	6.5	11.1

Three-point field goals: 1986-87, 3-for-14 (.214). 1987-88, 6-for-20 (.300). 1988-89, 20 for 75 (.267). 1989-90, 52-for-132 (.394). 1990-91, 93-for-228 (.408). 1991-92, 91-for-250 (.364). 1992-93, 80-for-235 (.340). 1993-94, 68-for-165 (.412). 1994-95, 96-for-228 (.421). 1995-96, 15-for-34 (.441). Totals, 524-for-1381 (.379).

Personal fouls/disqualifications: 1986-87, 18/0. 1987-88, 97/0. 1988-89, 151/1. 1989-90, 126/0. 1990-91, 192/2. 1991-92, 188/0. 1992-93, 244/4. 1993-94, 171/1. 1994-95, 135/2. 1995-96, 21/0. Totals, 1343/10.

NBA PLAYOFF RECORD

Season Team	G	Min.	FGM	FGA	Pct.	FTM	FTA	Pct.	REBOUNDS Off.	Def.	Tot.	Ast.	St.	Blk.	TO	Pts.	RPG	APG	PPG
93-94—Orlando..........	2	23	4	8	.500	1	1	1.000	1	0	1	3	0	0	5	9	0.5	1.5	4.5

Three-point field goals: 1993-94, 0-for-2. Totals, 0-for-2 (.000).
Personal fouls/disqualifications: 1993-94, 2/0. Totals, 2/0.

HEAD COACHING RECORD

BACKGROUND: Assistant coach, Phoenix Suns (1997-98 through December 13, 1999).

NBA COACHING RECORD

	REGULAR SEASON				PLAYOFFS		
Season Team	W	L	Pct.	Finish	W	L	Pct.
99-00—Phoenix.................................	40	22	.645	3rd/Pacific Division	4	5	.444
00-01—Phoenix.................................	51	31	.622	3rd/Pacific Division	1	3	.250
01-02—Phoenix.................................	25	26	.490		—	—	—
03-04—Chicago.................................	19	47	.288	8th/Central Division	—	—	—
04-05—Chicago.................................	47	35	.573	2nd/Central Division	2	4	.333
05-06—Chicago.................................	41	41	.500	T3rd/Central Division	2	4	.333
Totals	223	202	.525		9	16	.360

NOTES:
99-00—Replaced Danny Ainge as head coach (December 13), with a record of 13-7 and club in fourth place. Defeated San Antonio, 3-1, in Western Conference first round; lost to Los Angeles Lakers, 4-1, in Western Conference semifinals.
00-01—Lost to Sacramento, 3-1, in Western Conference first round.
01-02—Replaced as Phoenix head coach by Frank Johnson (February 17) with club in sixth place.
03-04—Replaced Bill Cartwright as Chicago head coach (November 28) with 4-12 record and club in 8th place.
04-05—Lost to Washington, 4-2, in Eastern Conference first round.
05-06—Lost to Miami, 4-2, in Eastern Conference first round.

SLOAN, JERRY   JAZZ

PERSONAL: Born March 28, 1942, in McLeansboro, Ill. ... 6-5/200. (1.96/90.7). ... Full name: Gerald Eugene Sloan
HIGH SCHOOL: McLeansboro (Ill.).
COLLEGE: Illinois, then Evansville.
TRANSACTIONS/CAREER NOTES: Selected by Baltimore Bullets in third round of 1964 NBA Draft. ... Selected by Bullets in second round of 1965 NBA Draft. ... Selected by Chicago Bulls from Bullets in NBA Expansion Draft (April 30, 1966).

COLLEGIATE RECORD

NOTES: Left Illinois before 1961 basketball season. ... Outstanding Player in NCAA College Division Tournament (1964, 1965). ... THE SPORTING NEWS All-America second team (1965).

Season Team	G	Min.	FGM	FGA	Pct.	FTM	FTA	Pct.	Reb.	Ast.	Pts.	AVERAGES RPG	APG	PPG
61-62—Evansville						Did not play—transfer student.								
62-63—Evansville	27	...	152	446	.341	103	151	.682	293	...	407	10.9	...	15.1
63-64—Evansville	29	...	160	385	.416	84	114	.737	335	...	404	11.6	...	13.9
64-65—Evansville	29	...	207	458	.452	95	126	.754	425	...	509	14.7	...	17.6
Totals	85	...	519	1289	.403	282	391	.721	1053	...	1320	12.4	...	15.5

NBA REGULAR-SEASON RECORD

HONORS: NBA All-Defensive first team (1969, 1972, 1974, 1975). ... NBA All-Defensive second team (1970, 1971).

Season Team	G	Min.	FGM	FGA	Pct.	FTM	FTA	Pct.	REBOUNDS Off.	Def.	Tot.	Ast.	St.	Blk.	TO	Pts.	RPG	APG	PPG
65-66—Baltimore	59	952	120	289	.415	98	139	.705	...	...	230	110	...	...	...	338	3.9	1.9	5.7
66-67—Chicago..........	80	2942	525	1214	.432	340	427	.796	...	...	726	170	...	...	...	1390	9.1	2.1	17.4
67-68—Chicago..........	77	2454	369	959	.385	280	386	.725	...	...	591	229	...	...	...	1027	7.7	3.0	13.3
68-69—Chicago..........	78	2939	488	1179	.414	333	447	.745	...	...	619	276	...	...	...	1309	7.9	3.5	16.8
69-70—Chicago..........	53	1822	310	737	.421	207	318	.651	...	...	372	165	...	...	...	827	7.0	3.1	15.6
70-71—Chicago..........	80	3140	592	1342	.441	278	389	.715	...	...	701	281	...	...	...	1462	8.8	3.5	18.3
71-72—Chicago..........	82	3035	535	1206	.444	258	391	.660	...	...	691	211	...	...	...	1328	8.4	2.6	16.2
72-73—Chicago..........	69	2412	301	733	.411	94	133	.707	...	...	475	151	...	...	...	696	6.9	2.2	10.1
73-74—Chicago..........	77	2860	412	921	.447	194	273	.711	150	406	556	149	183	10	...	1018	7.2	1.9	13.2
74-75—Chicago..........	78	2577	380	865	.439	193	258	.748	177	361	538	161	171	17	...	953	6.9	2.1	12.2
75-76—Chicago..........	22	617	84	210	.400	55	78	.705	40	76	116	22	27	5	...	223	5.3	1.0	10.1
Totals	755	25750	4116	9655	.426	2330	3239	.719	367	843	5615	1925	381	32	...	10571	7.4	2.5	14.0

Personal fouls/disqualifications: 1965-66, 176/7. 1966-67, 293/7. 1967-68, 291/11. 1968-69, 313/6. 1969-70, 179/3. 1970-71, 289/5. 1971-72, 309/8. 1972-73, 235/5. 1973-74, 273/3. 1974-75, 265/5. 1975-76, 77/1. Totals, 2700/61.

NBA PLAYOFF RECORD

Season Team	G	Min.	FGM	FGA	Pct.	FTM	FTA	Pct.	REBOUNDS Off.	Def.	Tot.	Ast.	St.	Blk.	TO	Pts.	AVERAGES RPG	APG	PPG
65-66—Baltimore	2	34	5	12	.417	3	4	.750	...	...	16	6	...	...	...	13	8.0	3.0	6.5
66-67—Chicago.........	3	71	12	31	.387	6	9	.667	...	...	10	1	...	...	...	30	3.3	0.3	10.0
67-68—Chicago.........	5	137	12	37	.324	19	25	.760	...	...	32	12	...	...	...	43	6.4	2.4	8.6
69-70—Chicago.........	5	190	29	74	.392	16	25	.640	...	...	39	11	...	...	...	74	7.8	2.2	14.8
70-71—Chicago.........	7	284	51	117	.436	17	23	.739	...	...	63	17	...	...	...	119	9.0	2.4	17.0
71-72—Chicago.........	4	170	26	64	.406	11	19	.579	...	...	35	10	...	...	...	63	8.8	2.5	15.8
72-73—Chicago.........	7	292	45	103	.437	14	19	.737	...	...	59	14	...	...	...	104	8.4	2.0	14.9
73-74—Chicago.........	6	240	39	88	.443	22	29	.759	18	44	62	12	7	1	...	100	10.3	2.0	16.7
74-75—Chicago.........	13	470	75	163	.460	20	36	.556	24	72	96	26	20	0	...	170	7.4	2.0	13.1
Totals	52	1888	294	689	.427	128	189	.677	42	116	412	109	27	1	...	716	7.9	2.1	13.8

Personal fouls/disqualifications: 1965-66, 6/1. 1966-67, 7/0. 1967-68, 19/0. 1969-70, 18/0. 1970-71, 25/1. 1971-72, 18/1. 1972-73, 31/1. 1973-74, 17/0. 1974-75, 46/0. Totals, 187/4.

NBA ALL-STAR GAME RECORD

Season Team	Min.	FGM	FGA	Pct.	FTM	FTA	Pct.	REBOUNDS Off.	Def.	Tot.	Ast.	PF	Dq.	St.	Blk.	TO	Pts.
1967—Chicago................	22	4	9	.444	0	0	...	...	...	4	4	5	0	...	...	...	8
1969—Chicago................	18	2	8	.250	0	1	.000	...	...	3	0	5	0	...	...	...	4
Totals..........................	40	6	17	.353	0	1	.000	...	...	7	4	10	0	...	...	...	12

HEAD COACHING RECORD

BACKGROUND: Scout, Chicago Bulls (1976-77). ... Assistant coach, Bulls (1977-78 and 1978-79). ... Scout, Utah Jazz (1983-84). ... Head coach, Evansville Thunder of CBA (1984-November 19, 1984; no record). ... Assistant coach, Jazz (November 19, 1984-December 9, 1988).

NBA COACHING RECORD

Season Team	REGULAR SEASON W	L	Pct.	Finish	PLAYOFFS W	L	Pct.
79-80—Chicago	30	52	.366	4th/Midwest Division	—	—	—
80-81—Chicago	45	37	.549	2nd/Central Division	2	4	.333
81-82—Chicago	19	32	.373		—	—	—
88-89—Utah	40	25	.615	1st/Midwest Division	0	3	.000
89-90—Utah	55	27	.671	2nd/Midwest Division	2	3	.400
90-91—Utah	54	28	.659	2nd/Midwest Division	4	5	.444
91-92—Utah	55	27	.671	1st/Midwest Division	9	7	.563
92-93—Utah	47	35	.573	3rd/Midwest Division	2	3	.400
93-94—Utah	53	29	.646	3rd/Midwest Division	8	8	.500
94-95—Utah	60	22	.732	2nd/Midwest Division	2	3	.400
95-96—Utah	55	27	.671	2nd/Midwest Division	10	8	.556
96-97—Utah	64	18	.780	1st/Midwest Division	13	7	.650
97-98—Utah	62	20	.756	1st/Midwest Division	13	7	.650
98-99—Utah	37	13	.740	T1st/Midwest Division	5	6	.455
99-00—Utah	55	27	.671	1st/Midwest Division	4	6	.400
00-01—Utah	53	29	.646	2nd/Midwest Division	2	3	.400
01-02—Utah	44	38	.537	4th/Midwest Division	1	3	.250
02-03—Utah	47	35	.573	4th/Midwest Division	1	4	.200
03-04—Utah	42	40	.512	7th/Midwest Division	—	—	—
04-05—Utah	26	56	.317	5th/Northwest Division	—	—	—
05-06—Utah	41	41	.500	2nd/Northwest Division	—	—	—
Totals	984	658	.599		78	80	.494

NOTES:
80-81—Defeated New York, 2-0, in Eastern Conference first round; lost to Boston, 4-0, in Eastern Conference semifinals.
81-82—Replaced as Chicago head coach by Rod Thorn (February 17).
88-89—Replaced retiring Utah head coach Frank Layden (December 9), with record of 11-6. Lost to Golden State, 3-0, in Western Conference first round.
89-90—Lost to Phoenix, 3-2, in Western Conference first round.
90-91—Defeated Phoenix, 3-1, in Western Conference first round;lost to Portland, 4-1, in Western Conference.
91-92—Defeated Los Angeles Clippers, 3-2, in Western Conference first round; defeated Seattle, 4-1, in Western Conference semifinals; lost to Portland, 4-2, in Western Conference finals.
92-93—Lost to Seattle, 3-2, in Western Conference first round.
93-94—Defeated San Antonio, 3-1, in Western Conference first round; defeated Denver, 4-3, in Western Conference semifinals; lost to Houston, 4-1, in Western Conference finals.
94-95—Lost to Houston in Western Conference first round.
95-96—Defeated Houston, 3-2, in Western Conference first round; defeated San Antonio, 4-2, in West Conference semifinals; lost to Seattle, 4-3, in Western Conference finals.
96-97—Defeated Los Angeles Clippers, 3-0, in Western Conference first round; defeated Los Angeles Lakers, 4-1, in Western Conference semifinals; defeated Houston, 4-2, in Western Conference finals; lost to Chicago, 4-2, in NBA Finals.
97-98—Defeated Houston, 3-2, in Western Conference first round; defeated San Antonio, 4-1, in Western Conference semifinals; defeated Los Angeles Lakers, 4-0, in Western Conference finals; lost to Chicago, 4-2, in NBA Finals.
98-99—Defeated Sacramento, 3-2, in Western Conference first round; lost to Portland, 4-2, in Western Conference semifinals.
99-00—Defeated Seattle, 3-2, in Western Conference first round; lost to Portland, 4-1, in Western Conference semifinals.
00-01—Lost to Dallas, 3-2, in Western Conference first round.
01-02—Lost to Sacramento, 3-1, in Western Conference first round.
02-03—Lost to Sacramento, 4-1, in Western Conference first round.

STOTTS, TERRY   BUCKS

PERSONAL: Born November 25, 1957, in Cedar Rapids, Iowa.
COLLEGE: Oklahoma.
TRANSACTIONS/CAREER NOTES: Selected by Houston Rockets in second round (38th pick overall) of 1980 NBA Draft.

COLLEGIATE RECORD

Season Team	G	Min.	FGM	FGA	Pct.	FTM	FTA	Pct.	Reb.	Ast.	Pts.	AVERAGES RPG	APG	PPG
76-77—Oklahoma	20	...	34	104	.327	13	17	.765	59	18	81	3.0	0.9	4.1

Season Team	G	Min.	FGM	FGA	Pct.	FTM	FTA	Pct.	Reb.	Ast.	Pts.	RPG	APG	PPG
												AVERAGES		
77-78—Oklahoma	13	...	50	96	.521	20	28	.714	55	11	120	4.2	0.8	9.2
78-79—Oklahoma	31	1102	186	373	.499	76	98	.776	175	83	448	5.6	2.7	14.5
79-80—Oklahoma	27	1002	184	355	.518	87	110	.791	125	106	455	4.6	3.9	16.9
Totals	91	2104	454	928	.489	196	253	.775	414	218	1104	4.5	2.4	12.1

CBA RECORD

NOTES: All-Defensive first team (1983).

Season Team	G	Min.	FGM	FGA	Pct.	FTM	FTA	Pct.	Reb.	Ast.	Pts.	RPG	APG	PPG
												AVERAGES		
80-81—Montana	36	1088	186	440	.423	99	131	.756	172	84	475	4.8	2.3	13.2
81-82—Montana	46	1674	301	656	.459	124	162	.765	223	189	741	4.8	4.1	16.1
82-83—Montana	44	1546	227	431	.527	102	119	.857	200	150	561	4.5	3.4	12.8
90-91—Montana	11	295	37	73	.507	15	20	.750	37	43	94	3.4	3.9	8.5
Totals	137	4603	751	1600	.469	340	432	.787	632	466	1871	4.6	3.4	13.7

Three-point field goals: 1980-81, 4-for-16 (.250). 1981-82, 15-for-43 (.349). 1982-83, 5-for-17 (.294). 1990-91, 5-for-12 (.417). Totals, 29-for-88 (.330).

Personal fouls/disqualifications: 1980-81, 110/0. 1981-82, 164/0. 1982-83, 156/0. 1990-91, 43/0. Totals, 473/0.

HEAD COACHING RECORD

BACKGROUND: Assistant coach Seattle SuperSonics (1993-94 through 1997-98). ... Assistant coach Milwaukee Bucks (1998-99 through 2001-02). ... Assistant coach Atlanta Hawks (2002-03). ... Interim coach Hawks (December 26, 2002, through end of season).

NBA COACHING RECORD

	REGULAR SEASON				PLAYOFFS		
Season Team	W	L	Pct.	Finish	W	L	Pct.
03-04—Atlanta	24	31	.436	5th/Central Division	—	—	—
04-05—Atlanta	28	54	.341	7th/Central Division	—	—	—
05-06—Milwaukee	40	42	.488	5th/Central Division	1	4	.200
Totals	92	127	.420		1	4	.200

NOTES:
03-04—Replaced Lon Kruger as Atlanta interim head coach (December 26) with a record of 11-16 and club in fifth place.
05-06—Lost to Detroit, 4-1, in Eastern Conference first round.

THOMAS, ISIAH   KNICKS

PERSONAL: Born April 30, 1961, in Chicago. ... 6-1/182. (1.85/82.6). ... Full name: Isiah Lord Thomas
HIGH SCHOOL: St. Joseph's (Westchester, Ill.).
COLLEGE: Indiana.
TRANSACTIONS/CAREER NOTES: Selected after sophomore season by Detroit Pistons in first round (second pick overall) of 1981 NBA Draft. ... Announced retirement (May 11, 1994). ... Vice president, (May 24, 1994 through 1994-95 season) and part owner, Toronto Raptors. ... Executive vice president (1995-96 to 1997-98). ... Resigned as Knicks president (November 20, 1997).

CAREER HONORS: NBA 50th Anniversary All-Time Team (1996).

MISCELLANEOUS: Member of NBA championship team (1989, 1990). ... Member of U.S. Olympic team (1980). ... Detroit Pistons franchise all-time leading scorer with 18,822 points, all-time assists leader with 9,061 and all-time steals leader with 1,861 (1981-82 through 1993-94).

COLLEGIATE RECORD

NOTES: THE SPORTING NEWS All-America first team (1981). ... NCAA Division I Tournament Most Outstanding Player (1981). ... Member of NCAA Division I championship team (1981).

Season Team	G	Min.	FGM	FGA	Pct.	FTM	FTA	Pct.	Reb.	Ast.	Pts.	RPG	APG	PPG
												AVERAGES		
79-80—Indiana	29	...	154	302	.510	115	149	.772	116	159	423	4.0	5.5	14.6
80-81—Indiana	34	...	212	383	.554	121	163	.742	105	197	545	3.1	5.8	16.0
Totals	63		366	685	.534	236	312	.756	221	356	968	3.5	5.7	15.4

NBA REGULAR-SEASON RECORD

HONORS: All-NBA First Team (1984, 1985, 1986). ... All-NBA Second Team (1983, 1987). ... NBA All-Rookie team (1982).

Season Team	G	Min.	FGM	FGA	Pct.	FTM	FTA	Pct.	Off.	Def.	Tot.	Ast.	St.	Blk.	TO	Pts.	RPG	APG	PPG
									REBOUNDS								**AVERAGES**		
81-82—Detroit	72	2433	453	1068	.424	302	429	.704	57	152	209	565	150	17	†299	1225	2.9	7.8	17.0
82-83—Detroit	81	*3093	725	1537	.472	368	518	.710	105	223	328	634	199	29	*326	1854	4.0	7.8	22.9
83-84—Detroit	82	3007	669	1448	.462	388	529	.733	103	224	327	†914	204	33	307	1748	4.0	11.1	21.3
84-85—Detroit	81	3089	646	1410	.458	399	493	.809	114	247	361	*1123	187	25	302	1720	4.5	*13.9	21.2
85-86—Detroit	77	2790	609	1248	.488	365	462	.790	83	194	277	830	171	20	289	1609	3.6	10.8	20.9
86-87—Detroit	81	3013	626	1353	.463	400	521	.768	82	237	319	813	153	20	343	1671	3.9	10.0	20.6
87-88—Detroit	81	2927	621	1341	.463	305	394	.774	64	214	278	678	141	17	273	1577	3.4	8.4	19.5
88-89—Detroit	80	2924	569	1227	.464	287	351	.818	49	224	273	663	133	20	298	1458	3.4	8.3	18.2
89-90—Detroit	81	2993	579	1322	.438	292	377	.775	74	234	308	765	139	19	*322	1492	3.8	9.4	18.4
90-91—Detroit	48	1657	289	665	.435	179	229	.782	35	125	160	446	75	10	185	776	3.3	9.3	16.2
91-92—Detroit	78	2918	564	1264	.446	292	378	.772	68	179	247	560	118	15	252	1445	3.2	7.2	18.5
92-93—Detroit	79	2922	526	1258	.418	278	377	.737	71	161	232	671	123	18	284	1391	2.9	8.5	17.6
93-94—Detroit	58	1750	318	763	.417	181	258	.702	46	113	159	399	68	6	202	856	2.7	6.9	14.8
Totals	979	35516	7194	15904	.452	4036	5316	.759	951	2527	3478	9061	1861	249	3682	18822	3.6	9.3	19.2

Three-point field goals: 1981-82, 17-for-59 (.288). 1982-83, 36-for-125 (.288). 1983-84, 22-for-65 (.338). 1984-85, 29-for-113 (.257). 1985-86, 26-for-84 (.310). 1986-87, 19-for-98 (.194). 1987-88, 30-for-97 (.309). 1988-89, 33-for-121 (.273). 1989-90, 42-for-136 (.309). 1990-91, 19-for-65 (.292). 1991-92, 25-for-86 (.291). 1992-93, 61-for-198 (.308). 1993-94, 39-for-126 (.310). Totals, 398-for-1373 (.290).

Personal fouls/disqualifications: 1981-82, 253/2. 1982-83, 318/8. 1983-84, 324/8. 1984-85, 288/8. 1985-86, 245/9. 1986-87, 251/5. 1987-88, 217/0. 1988-89, 209/0. 1989-90, 206/0. 1990-91, 118/4. 1991-92, 194/2. 1992-93, 222/2. 1993-94, 126/0. Totals, 2971/48.

NBA PLAYOFF RECORD

NOTES: NBA Finals Most Valuable Player (1990). ... Holds NBA Finals single-game records for most points in one quarter—25 (June 19, 1988, vs. Los Angeles Lakers); and most field goals in one quarter—11 (June 19, 1988, vs. Los Angeles Lakers). ... Shares NBA Finals single-game record for most field goals in one half—14 (June 19, 1988, vs. Los Angeles Lakers).

Season Team	G	Min.	FGM	FGA	Pct.	FTM	FTA	Pct.	REBOUNDS Off.	Def.	Tot.	Ast.	St.	Blk.	TO	Pts.	AVERAGES RPG	APG	PPG
83-84—Detroit.........	5	198	39	83	.470	27	35	.771	7	12	19	55	13	6	23	107	3.8	11.0	21.4
84-85—Detroit.........	9	355	83	166	.500	47	62	.758	11	36	47	101	19	4	30	219	5.2	11.2	24.3
85-86—Detroit.........	4	163	41	91	.451	24	36	.667	8	14	22	48	9	3	17	106	5.5	12.0	26.5
86-87—Detroit.........	15	562	134	297	.451	83	110	.755	21	46	67	130	39	4	42	361	4.5	8.7	24.1
87-88—Detroit.........	23	911	183	419	.437	125	151	.828	26	81	107	201	66	8	85	504	4.7	8.7	21.9
88-89—Detroit.........	17	633	115	279	.412	71	96	.740	24	49	73	141	27	4	43	309	4.3	8.3	18.2
89-90—Detroit.........	20	758	148	320	.463	81	102	.794	21	88	109	163	43	7	72	409	5.5	8.2	20.5
90-91—Detroit.........	13	436	60	149	.403	50	69	.725	13	41	54	111	13	2	41	176	4.2	8.5	13.5
91-92—Detroit.........	5	200	22	65	.338	22	28	.786	3	23	26	37	5	0	16	70	5.2	7.4	14.0
Totals	111	4216	825	1869	.441	530	689	.769	134	390	524	987	234	38	369	2261	4.7	8.9	20.4

Three-point field goals: 1983-84, 2-for-6 (.333). 1984-85, 6-for-15 (.400). 1985-86, 0-for-5. 1986-87, 10-for-33 (.303). 1987-88, 13-for-44 (.295). 1988-89, 8-for-30 (.267). 1989-90, 32-for-68 (.471). 1990-91, 6-for-22 (.273). 1991-92, 4-for-11 (.364). Totals, 81-for-234 (.346).

Personal fouls/disqualifications: 1983-84, 22/1. 1984-85, 39/2. 1985-86, 17/0. 1986-87, 51/1. 1987-88, 71/2. 1988-89, 39/0. 1989-90, 65/1. 1990-91, 41/1. 1991-92, 18/0. Totals, 363/8.

NBA ALL-STAR GAME RECORD

NOTES: NBA All-Star Game Most Valuable Player (1984, 1986).

Season Team	Min.	FGM	FGA	Pct.	FTM	FTA	Pct.	REBOUNDS Off.	Def.	Tot.	Ast.	PF	Dq.	St.	Blk.	TO	Pts.
1982—Detroit...............	17	5	7	.714	2	4	.500	1	0	1	4	1	0	3	0	1	12
1983—Detroit...............	29	9	14	.643	1	1	1.000	1	3	4	7	0	0	4	0	5	19
1984—Detroit...............	39	9	17	.529	3	3	1.000	3	2	5	15	4	0	4	0	6	21
1985—Detroit...............	25	9	14	.643	1	1	1.000	1	1	2	5	2	0	2	0	1	22
1986—Detroit...............	36	11	19	.579	8	9	.889	0	1	1	10	2	0	5	0	5	30
1987—Detroit...............	24	4	6	.667	8	9	.889	2	1	3	9	3	0	0	0	5	16
1988—Detroit...............	28	4	10	.400	0	0	...	1	1	2	15	1	0	1	0	6	8
1989—Detroit...............	33	7	13	.538	4	6	.667	1	1	2	14	2	0	4	0	6	19
1990—Detroit...............	27	7	12	.583	0	0	...	1	3	4	9	0	0	3	0	1	15
1991—Detroit...............								Selected, did not play—injured									
1992—Detroit...............	28	7	14	.500	0	0	...	0	1	1	5	0	0	3	0	3	15
1993—Detroit...............	32	4	7	.571	0	2	.000	0	2	2	4	2	0	2	0	2	8
Totals	318	76	133	.571	27	35	.771	13	14	27	97	17	0	31	0	41	185

Three-point field goals: 1984, 0-for-2. 1985, 3-for-4 (.750). 1986, 0-for-1. 1989, 1-for-3 (.333). 1990, 1-for-1 (1.000). 1992, 1-for-3 (.333). 1993, 0-for-1. Totals, 6-for-15 (.400).

HEAD COACHING RECORD

BACKGROUND: Executive vice president, Toronto Raptors (1994-1999). ... NBC broadcaster (1999-July 20, 2000). ... President and general manager, New York Knicks (2003-June 22, 2006).

NBA COACHING RECORD

Season Team	REGULAR SEASON W	L	Pct.	Finish	PLAYOFFS W	L	Pct.
00-01—Indiana................	41	41	.500	4th/Central Division	1	3	.250
01-02—Indiana................	42	40	.512	T3rd/Central Division	2	3	.400
02-03—Indiana................	48	34	.585	2nd/Central Division	2	4	.333
Totals................	131	115	.533		5	10	.333

NOTES:
00-01—Lost to Philadelphia, 3-1, in Eastern Conference first round.
01-02—Lost to New Jersey, 3-2, in Eastern Conference first round.
02-03—Lost to Boston, 4-2, in Eastern Conference first round.

VAN GUNDY, JEFF   ROCKETS

PERSONAL: Born January 19, 1962, in Hemet, Calif.
COLLEGE: Nazareth (Rochester, N.Y.).

HEAD COACHING RECORD

BACKGROUND: Head coach, McQuaid Jesuit (Rochester, N.Y.) High School (1985-86). ... Graduate assistant, Providence College (1986-87). ... Assistant coach, Providence (1987-88). ... Assistant coach, Rutgers University (1988-89). ... Assistant coach, New York Knicks (1989-90 to March 8, 1996).

NBA COACHING RECORD

Season Team	REGULAR SEASON W	L	Pct.	Finish	PLAYOFFS W	L	Pct.
95-96—New York	13	10	.565	2nd/Atlantic Division	4	4	.500
96-97—New York	57	25	.695	2nd/Atlantic Division	6	4	.600
97-98—N.Y. Knicks	43	29	.597	2nd/Atlantic Division	4	6	.400
98-99—N.Y. Knicks	27	23	.540	4th/Atlantic Division	12	8	.600
99-00—N.Y. Knicks	50	32	.610	2nd/Atlantic Division	9	7	.563
00-01—N.Y. Knicks	48	34	.585	3rd/Atlantic Division	2	3	.400
01-02—N.Y. Knicks	10	9	.526		—	—	—
03-04—Houston	45	37	.549	5th/Midwest Division	1	4	.200
04-05—Houston	51	31	.622	3rd/Southwest Division	3	4	.429
05-06—Houston	34	48	.415	5th/Southwest Division	—	—	—
Totals..	378	278	.576		41	40	.506

NOTES:
95-96—Replaced Don Nelson as New York Knicks head coach (March 8), with record of 34-26 and club in second place. Defeated Cleveland, 3-0, in Eastern Conference first round; lost to Chicago, 4-1, in Eastern Conference semifinals.
96-97—Defeated Charlotte, 3-0, in Eastern Conference first round; lost to Miami, 4-3, in Eastern Conference semifinals.
97-98—Defeated Miami, 3-2, in Eastern Conference first round; lost to Indiana, 4-1, in Eastern Conference semifinals.
98-99—Defeated Miami, 3-2, in Eastern Conference first round; defeated Atlanta, 4-0, in Eastern Conference semifinals; defeated Indiana, 4-2, in Eastern Conference finals; lost to San Antonio, 4-1, in NBA Finals.
99-00—Defeated Toronto, 3-0, in Eastern Conference first round; defeated Miami, 4-3, in Eastern Conference semifinals; lost to Indiana, 4-2, in

Eastern Conference finals.
00-01—Lost to Toronto, 3-2, in Eastern Conference first round.
01-02—Replaced by Don Chaney as New York head coach (December 10) with record of 10-9 and club in third place.
03-04—Lost to Los Angeles Lakers, 4-1, in Western Conference first round.
04-05—Lost to Dallas, 4-3, in Western Conference first round.

WOODSON, MIKE   HAWKS

PERSONAL: Born March 24, 1958, in Indianapolis. ... 6-5/198. (1.96/89.8). ... Full name: Michael Dean Woodson
HIGH SCHOOL: Broad Ripple (Indianapolis).
COLLEGE: Indiana.
TRANSACTIONS/CAREER NOTES: Selected by New York Knicks in first round (12th pick overall) of 1980 NBA Draft. ... Traded by Knicks to New Jersey Nets for G Mike Newlin (June 10, 1981). ... Traded by Nets with 1982 first-round draft choice to Kansas City Kings for C Sam Lacey (November 12, 1981). ... Kings franchise moved from Kansas City to Sacramento for 1985-86 season. ... Traded by Kings with G Larry Drew, 1988 first-round draft choice and 1989 second-round draft choice to Los Angeles Clippers for G/F Junior Bridgeman, G Franklin Edwards and F Derek Smith (August 19, 1986). ... Signed as unrestricted free agent by Houston Rockets (July 19, 1988). ... Waived by Rockets (December 4, 1990). ... Signed as free agent by Cleveland Cavaliers (December 13, 1990). ... Waived by Cavaliers (December 24, 1990).

COLLEGIATE RECORD

Season Team	G	Min.	FGM	FGA	Pct.	FTM	FTA	Pct.	Reb.	Ast.	Pts.	RPG	APG	PPG
76-77—Indiana	27	...	212	407	.521	76	96	.792	182	...	500	6.7	...	18.5
77-78—Indiana	29	...	242	462	.524	93	121	.769	157	...	577	5.4	...	19.9
78-79—Indiana	34	...	265	532	.498	184	241	.763	193	...	714	5.7	...	21.0
79-80—Indiana	14	...	102	225	.453	66	79	.835	49	...	270	3.5	...	19.3
Totals	104	...	821	1626	.505	419	537	.780	581	...	2061	5.6	...	19.8

NBA REGULAR-SEASON RECORD

Season Team	G	Min.	FGM	FGA	Pct.	FTM	FTA	Pct.	Off.	Def.	Tot.	Ast.	St.	Blk.	TO	Pts.	RPG	APG	PPG
80-81—New York	81	949	165	373	.442	49	64	.766	33	64	97	75	36	12	54	380	1.2	0.9	4.7
81-82—N.J.-K.C.	83	2331	538	1069	.503	221	286	.773	102	145	247	222	142	35	153	1304	3.0	2.7	15.7
82-83—Kansas City	81	2426	584	1154	.506	298	377	.790	84	164	248	254	137	59	174	1473	3.1	3.1	18.2
83-84—Kansas City	71	1838	389	816	.477	247	302	.818	62	113	175	175	83	28	115	1027	2.5	2.5	14.5
84-85—Kansas City	78	1998	530	1068	.496	264	330	.800	69	129	198	143	117	28	139	1329	2.5	1.8	17.0
85-86—Sacramento	81	2417	510	1073	.475	242	289	.837	94	132	226	197	92	37	145	1264	2.8	2.4	15.6
86-87—L.A. Clippers	74	2126	494	1130	.437	240	290	.828	68	94	162	196	100	16	168	1262	2.2	2.6	17.1
87-88—L.A. Clippers	80	2534	562	1263	.445	296	341	.060	64	126	190	273	109	20	180	1438	2.4	3.4	18.0
88-89—Houston	81	2259	410	936	.438	195	237	.823	51	143	194	206	89	18	136	1046	2.4	2.5	12.9
89-90—Houston	61	972	160	405	.395	62	86	.721	25	63	88	66	42	11	49	394	1.4	1.1	6.5
90-91—Hous.-Cleve.	15	171	26	77	.338	11	13	.846	3	10	13	15	5	5	12	64	0.9	1.0	4.3
Totals	786	20021	4368	9364	.466	2125	2615	.813	655	1183	1838	1822	952	275	1331	10981	2.3	2.3	14.0

Three-point field goals: 1980-81, 1-for-5 (.200). 1981-82, 7-for-25 (.280). 1982-83, 7-for-33 (.212). 1983-84, 2-for-8 (.250). 1984-85, 5-for-21 (.238). 1985-86, 2-for-13 (.154). 1986-87, 34-for-123 (.276). 1987-88, 18-for-78 (.231). 1988-89, 31-for-89 (.348). 1989-90, 12-for-41 (.293). 1990-91, 1-for-7 (.143). Totals, 120-for-443 (.271).
Personal fouls/disqualifications: 1980-81, 86/0. 1981-82, 228/8. 1982-83, 238/3. 1983-84, 174/2. 1984-85, 210/1. 1985-86, 213/1. 1986-87, 201/1. 1987-88, 210/1. 1988-89, 195/1. 1989-90, 100/1. 1990-91, 18/0. Totals, 1847/11.

NBA PLAYOFF RECORD

Season Team	G	Min.	FGM	FGA	Pct.	FTM	FTA	Pct.	Off.	Def.	Tot.	Ast.	St.	Blk.	TO	Pts.	RPG	APG	PPG
80-81—New York	2	8	1	3	.333	2	2	1.000	2	0	2	0	0	0	...	4	1.0	0.0	2.0
83-84—Kansas City	3	87	18	44	.409	13	15	.867	4	4	8	9	2	0	...	49	2.7	3.0	16.3
85-86—Sacramento	3	110	22	49	.449	12	12	1.000	7	4	11	5	4	2	...	56	3.7	1.7	18.7
88-89—Houston	4	137	17	49	.347	10	12	.833	4	5	9	18	4	2	...	47	2.3	4.5	11.8
89-90—Houston	1	6	1	3	.333	0	0	...	0	0	0	2	0	0	...	2	0.0	2.0	2.0
Totals	13	348	59	148	.399	37	41	.902	17	13	30	34	10	4	...	158	2.3	2.6	12.2

Three-point field goals: 1983-84, 0-for-1. 1985-86, 0-for-2. 1988-89, 3-for-9 (.333). 1989-90, 0-for-1. Totals, 3-for-13 (.231).
Personal fouls/disqualifications: 1980-81, 3/0. 1983-84, 11/0. 1985-86, 13/0. 1988-89, 7/0. 1989-90, 1/0. Totals, 35/0.

HEAD COACHING RECORD
NBA COACHING RECORD

		REGULAR SEASON				PLAYOFFS		
Season Team	W	L	Pct.	Finish		W	L	Pct.
04-05—Atlanta	13	69	.159	5th/Southeast Division		—	—	—
05-06—Atlanta	26	56	.317	5th/Southeast Division		—	—	—
Totals	39	125	.238					

ABDUL-JABBAR, KAREEM   C

PERSONAL: Born April 16, 1947, in New York. ... 7-2/267 (2,18/121,1). ... Full name: Kareem Abdul-Jabbar. ... Formerly known as Lew Alcindor.
HIGH SCHOOL: Power Memorial (New York).
COLLEGE: UCLA.
TRANSACTIONS: Selected by Milwaukee Bucks in first round (first pick overall) of 1969 NBA Draft. ... Traded by Bucks with C Walt Wesley to Los Angeles Lakers for C Elmore Smith, G/F Brian Winters, F Dave Meyers and F/G Junior Bridgeman (June 16, 1975).
CAREER HONORS: Elected to Naismith Memorial Basketball Hall of Fame (1995). ... NBA 35th Anniversary All-Time Team (1980) and One of the 50 Greatest Players in NBA History (1996).
CAREER NOTES: Assistant coach, Los Angeles Clippers (February 18, 2000-July 1, 2000). ... Head coach, Oklahoma Storm, USBL (2002). ... Scout, New York Knicks.
MISCELLANEOUS: Member of NBA championship team (1971, 1980, 1982, 1985, 1987, 1988). ... Milwaukee Bucks all-time leading scorer with 14,211 points and all-time leading rebounder with 7,161 (1969-70 through 1974-75). ... Los Angeles Lakers franchise all-time blocked shots leader with 2,694 (1975-76 through 1988-89).

COLLEGIATE RECORD

NOTES: Member of NCAA championship team (1967, 1968, 1969). ... THE SPORTING NEWS College Player of the Year (1967, 1969). ... Naismith Award winner (1969). ... THE SPORTING NEWS All-America first team (1967, 1968, 1969). ... NCAA Tournament Most Outstanding Player (1967, 1968, 1969). ... Led NCAA Division I with .667 field goal percentage (1967) and .635 field goal percentage (1969).

| | | | | | | | | | | | | AVERAGES | | |
Season Team	G	Min.	FGM	FGA	Pct.	FTM	FTA	Pct.	Reb.	Ast.	Pts.	RPG	APG	PPG
65-66—UCLA‡	21	...	295	432	.683	106	179	.592	452	...	696	21.5	...	33.1
66-67—UCLA	30	...	346	519	.667	178	274	.650	466	...	870	15.5	...	29.0
67-68—UCLA	28	...	294	480	.613	146	237	.616	461	...	734	16.5	...	26.2
68-69—UCLA	30	...	303	477	.635	115	188	.612	440	...	721	14.7	...	24.0
Varsity totals	88	...	943	1476	.639	439	699	.628	1367	...	2325	15.5	...	26.4

NBA REGULAR-SEASON RECORD

RECORDS: Holds career records for most minutes played—57,446; most points—38,387; most field goals made—15,837; most field goals attempted—28,307. ... Holds single-season record for most defensive rebounds—1,111 (1976). ... Holds single-game record for most defensive rebounds—29 (December 14, 1975, vs. Detroit).
HONORS: NBA Most Valuable Player (1971, 1972, 1974, 1976, 1977, 1980). ... NBA Rookie of the Year (1970). ... All-NBA first team (1971, 1972, 1973, 1974, 1976, 1977, 1980, 1981, 1984, 1986). ... All-NBA second team (1970, 1978, 1979, 1983, 1985). ... NBA All-Defensive first team (1974, 1975, 1979, 1980, 1981). ... NBA All-Defensive second team (1970, 1971, 1976, 1977, 1978, 1984). ... NBA All-Rookie team (1970).
NOTES: Led NBA with 3.26 blocked shots per game (1975), 4.12 blocked shots per game (1976), 3.95 blocked shots per game (1979) and 3.41 blocked shots per game (1980).

| | | | | | | | | | | | | | | AVERAGES | | |
Season Team	G	Min.	FGM	FGA	Pct.	FTM	FTA	Pct.	Reb.	Ast.	PF	Dq.	Pts.	RPG	APG	PPG
69-70—Milwaukee	82	3534	*938	1810	.518	485	743	.653	1190	337	283	8	*2361	14.5	4.1	28.8
70-71—Milwaukee	82	3288	*1063	1843	.577	470	681	.690	1311	272	264	4	*2596	16.0	3.3	*31.7
71-72—Milwaukee	81	3583	*1159	*2019	.574	504	732	.689	1346	370	235	1	*2822	16.6	4.6	*34.8
72-73—Milwaukee	76	3254	982	1772	.554	328	460	.713	1224	379	208	0	2292	16.1	5.0	30.2

| | | | | | | | | REBOUNDS | | | | | | | | AVERAGES | | |
Season Team	G	Min.	FGM	FGA	Pct.	FTM	FTA	Pct.	Off.	Def.	Tot.	Ast.	St.	Blk.	TO	Pts.	RPG	APG	PPG
73-74—Milwaukee	81	3548	*948	1759	.539	295	420	.702	287	891	1178	386	112	283	...	2191	14.5	4.8	27.0
74-75—Milwaukee	65	2747	812	1584	.513	325	426	.763	194	718	912	264	65	212	...	1949	14.0	4.1	30.0
75-76—Los Angeles	82	*3379	914	1728	.529	447	636	.703	272	*1111	*1383	413	119	*338	...	2275	*16.9	5.0	27.7
76-77—Los Angeles	82	3016	*888	1533	*.579	376	536	.702	266	*824	*1090	319	101	*261	...	2152	13.3	3.9	26.2
77-78—Los Angeles	62	2265	663	1205	.550	274	350	.783	186	615	801	269	103	185	208	1600	12.9	4.3	25.8
78-79—Los Angeles	80	3157	777	1347	.577	349	474	.736	207	818	1025	431	76	*316	282	1903	12.8	5.4	23.8
79-80—Los Angeles	82	3143	835	1383	.604	364	476	.765	190	696	886	371	81	*280	297	2034	10.8	4.5	24.8
80-81—Los Angeles	80	2976	836	1457	.574	423	552	.766	197	624	821	272	59	228	249	2095	10.3	3.4	26.2
81-82—Los Angeles	76	2677	753	1301	.579	312	442	.706	172	487	659	225	63	207	230	1818	8.7	3.0	23.9
82-83—Los Angeles	79	2554	722	1228	.588	278	371	.749	167	425	592	200	61	170	200	1722	7.5	2.5	21.8
83-84—Los Angeles	80	2622	716	1238	.578	285	394	.723	169	418	587	211	55	143	221	1717	7.3	2.6	21.5
84-85—L.A. Lakers	79	2630	723	1207	.599	289	395	.732	162	460	622	249	63	162	197	1735	7.9	3.2	22.0
85-86—L.A. Lakers	79	2629	755	1338	.564	336	439	.765	133	345	478	280	67	130	203	1846	6.1	3.5	23.4
86-87—L.A. Lakers	78	2441	560	993	.564	245	343	.714	152	371	523	203	49	97	186	1366	6.7	2.6	17.5
87-88—L.A. Lakers	80	2308	480	903	.532	205	269	.762	118	360	478	135	48	92	159	1165	6.0	1.7	14.6
88-89—L.A. Lakers	74	1695	313	659	.475	122	165	.739	103	231	334	74	38	85	95	748	4.5	1.0	10.1
Totals	1560	57446	15837	28307	.559	6712	9304	.721	...	...	17440	5660	1160	3189	2527	38387	11.2	3.6	24.6

Three-point field goals: 1979-80, 0-for-1. 1980-81, 0-for-1. 1981-82, 0-for-3. 1982-83, 0-for-2. 1983-84, 0-for-1. 1984-85, 0-for-1. 1985-86, 0-for-2. 1986-87, 1-for-3 (.333). 1987-88, 0-for-1. 1988-89, 0-for-3. Totals, 1-for-18 (.056).
Personal fouls/disqualifications: 1973-74, 238/2. 1974-75, 205/2. 1975-76, 292/6. 1976-77, 262/4. 1977-78, 182/1. 1978-79, 230/3. 1979-80, 216/2. 1980-81, 244/4. 1981-82, 224/0. 1982-83, 220/1. 1983-84, 211/1. 1984-85, 238/3. 1985-86, 248/2. 1986-87, 245/2. 1987-88, 216/1. 1988-89, 196/1. Totals, 4657/48.

NBA PLAYOFF RECORD

NOTES: NBA Finals Most Valuable Player (1971, 1985). ... Holds career playoff records for most seasons played—18; most games played—237; most minutes played—8,851; most field goals made—2,356; most blocked shots—476; and most personal fouls—797.

| | | | | | | | | | | | | | | AVERAGES | | |
Season Team	G	Min.	FGM	FGA	Pct.	FTM	FTA	Pct.	Reb.	Ast.	PF	Dq.	Pts.	RPG	APG	PPG
69-70—Milwaukee	10	435	139	245	.567	74	101	.733	168	41	25	1	352	16.8	4.1	35.2
70-71—Milwaukee	14	577	152	295	.515	68	101	.673	238	35	45	0	372	17.0	2.5	26.6

Season Team	G	Min.	FGM	FGA	Pct.	FTM	FTA	Pct.	Reb.	Ast.	PF	Dq.	Pts.	AVERAGES RPG	APG	PPG
71-72—Milwaukee	11	510	139	318	.437	38	54	.704	200	56	35	0	316	18.2	5.1	28.7
72-73—Milwaukee	6	276	59	138	.428	19	35	.543	97	17	26	0	137	16.2	2.8	22.8

Season Team	G	Min.	FGM	FGA	Pct.	FTM	FTA	Pct.	REBOUNDS Off.	Def.	Tot.	Ast.	St.	Blk.	TO	Pts.	AVERAGES RPG	APG	PPG
73-74—Milwaukee	16	758	224	402	.557	67	91	.736	67	186	253	78	20	39	...	515	15.8	4.9	32.2
76-77—Los Angeles	11	467	147	242	.607	87	120	.725	51	144	195	45	19	38	...	381	17.7	4.1	34.6
77-78—Los Angeles	3	134	38	73	.521	5	9	.556	14	27	41	11	2	12	14	81	13.7	3.7	27.0
78-79—Los Angeles	8	367	88	152	.579	52	62	.839	18	83	101	38	8	33	29	228	12.6	4.8	28.5
79-80—Los Angeles	15	618	198	346	.572	83	105	.790	51	130	181	46	17	58	55	479	12.1	3.1	31.9
80-81—Los Angeles	3	134	30	65	.462	20	28	.714	13	37	50	12	3	8	11	80	16.7	4.0	26.7
81-82—Los Angeles	14	493	115	221	.520	55	87	.632	33	86	119	51	14	45	41	285	8.5	3.6	20.4
82-83—Los Angeles	15	588	163	287	.568	80	106	.755	25	90	115	42	17	55	50	406	7.7	2.8	27.1
83-84—Los Angeles	21	767	206	371	.555	90	120	.750	56	117	173	79	23	45	45	502	8.2	3.8	23.9
84-85—L.A. Lakers	19	610	168	300	.560	80	103	.777	50	104	154	76	23	36	52	416	8.1	4.0	21.9
85-86—L.A. Lakers	14	489	157	282	.557	48	61	.787	26	57	83	49	15	24	42	362	5.9	3.5	25.9
86-87—L.A. Lakers	18	559	124	234	.530	97	122	.795	39	84	123	36	8	35	40	345	6.8	2.0	19.2
87-88—L.A. Lakers	24	718	141	304	.464	56	71	.789	49	82	131	36	15	37	46	338	5.5	1.5	14.1
88-89—L.A. Lakers	15	351	68	147	.463	31	43	.721	13	46	59	19	5	11	22	167	3.9	1.3	11.1
Totals	237	8851	2356	4422	.533	1050	1419	.740	...	...	2481	767	189	476	447	5762	10.5	3.2	24.3

Three-point field goals: 1982-83, 0-for-1. 1986-87, 0-for-1. 1987-88, 0-for-2. 1988-89, 0-for-1. Totals, 0-for-5.

Personal fouls/disqualifications: 1973-74, 41/0. 1976-77, 42/0. 1977-78, 14/1. 1978-79, 26/0. 1979-80, 51/0. 1980-81, 14/0. 1981-82, 45/0. 1982-83, 61/1. 1983-84, 71/2. 1984-85, 67/1. 1985-86, 54/0. 1986-87, 81/1. 1987-88, 81/1. 1988-89, 43/0. Totals, 797/7.

NBA ALL-STAR GAME RECORD

NOTES: Holds career records for most games played—18; most minutes played—449; most field goals made—105; most field goals attempted—213; most points—251; most blocked shots—31; and most personal fouls—57. ... Holds single-game record for most blocked shots—6 (1980, OT).

Season Team	Min.	FGM	FGA	Pct.	FTM	FTA	Pct.	Off.	Def.	Reb/Tot.	Ast.	PF	Dq.	St.	Blk.	TO	Pts.
1970—Milwaukee	18	4	8	.500	?	2	1.000			11	4	6	1				10
1971—Milwaukee	30	8	16	.500	3	4	.750			14	1	2	0				19
1972—Milwaukee	19	5	10	.500	2	2	1.000			7	2	0	0				12
1973—Milwaukee	Selected, did not play.																
1974—Milwaukee	23	7	11	.636	0	0	...	1	7	8	6	2	0	1	1	...	14
1975—Milwaukee	19	3	10	.300	1	2	.500	5	5	10	3	2	0	0	1	...	7
1976—Los Angeles	36	9	16	.563	4	4	1.000	2	13	15	3	3	0	0	3	...	22
1977—Los Angeles	23	8	14	.571	5	6	.833	3	1	4	2	1	0	0	1	...	21
1979—Los Angeles	28	5	12	.417	1	2	.500	1	7	8	3	4	0	1	1	3	11
1980—Los Angeles	30	6	17	.353	5	6	.833	5	11	16	9	5	0	0	6	9	17
1981—Los Angeles	23	6	9	.667	3	3	1.000	2	4	6	4	3	0	0	4	3	15
1982—Los Angeles	22	1	10	.100	0	0	...	1	2	3	1	3	0	0	2	1	2
1983—Los Angeles	32	9	12	.750	2	3	.667	2	4	6	5	1	0	1	4	1	20
1984—Los Angeles	37	11	19	.579	3	4	.750	5	8	13	2	5	0	1	1	4	25
1985—L.A. Lakers	23	5	10	.500	1	2	.500	0	6	6	1	5	0	1	1	1	11
1986—L.A. Lakers	*(row partially illegible)*																21
1987—L.A. Lakers	27	4	9	.444	2	2	1.000	2	6	8	3	5	0	0	2	1	10
1988—L.A. Lakers	14	4	9	.444	2	2	1.000	2	2	4	0	3	0	0	0	0	10
1989—L.A. Lakers	13	1	6	.167	2	2	1.000	0	3	3	0	3	0	0	2	0	4
Totals	449	105	213	.493	41	50	.820	...	...	149	51	57	1	6	31	28	251

Three-point field goals: 1989, 0-for-1.

USBL COACHING RECORD

Season Team	REGULAR SEASON W	L	Pct.	Finish	PLAYOFFS W	L	Pct.
2002—Oklahoma	17	13	.567	2nd/Midwest Division	3	0	1.000

NOTES:
2002—Defeated St. Joseph in quarterfinals; defeated Brevard in semifinals; defeated Kansas in USBL Finals.

AGUIRRE, MARK   F

PERSONAL: Born December 10, 1959, in Chicago. ... 6-6/232 (1,98/105,2). ... Full name: Mark Anthony Aguirre. ... Name pronounced a-GWIRE.
HIGH SCHOOL: Austin (Chicago), then Westinghouse Vocational (Chicago).
COLLEGE: DePaul.
TRANSACTIONS: Selected after junior season by Dallas Mavericks in first round (first pick overall) of 1981 NBA Draft. ... Traded by Mavericks to Detroit Pistons for F Adrian Dantley and 1991 first-round draft choice (February 15, 1989). ... Waived by Pistons (October 7, 1993). ... Signed as free agent by Los Angeles Clippers (October 25, 1993). ... Waived by Clippers (February 1, 1994).
CAREER NOTES: Director of player development and scouting, Dallas Mavericks (1996-97). ... Special assistant, Indiana Pacers (2002-03). ... Assistant coach, New York Knicks (2003-present).
MISCELLANEOUS: Member of NBA championship team (1989, 1990). ... Member of U.S. Olympic team (1980).

COLLEGIATE RECORD

NOTES: THE SPORTING NEWS College Player of the Year (1981). ... Naismith Award winner (1980). ... THE SPORTING NEWS All-America first team (1980, 1981).

Season Team	G	Min.	FGM	FGA	Pct.	FTM	FTA	Pct.	Reb.	Ast.	Pts.	AVERAGES RPG	APG	PPG
78-79—DePaul	32	1206	302	581	.520	163	213	.765	244	86	767	7.6	2.7	24.0
79-80—DePaul	28	1049	281	520	.540	187	244	.766	213	77	749	7.6	2.8	26.8
80-81—DePaul	29	1069	280	481	.582	106	137	.774	249	131	666	8.6	4.5	23.0
Totals	89	3324	863	1582	.546	456	594	.768	706	294	2182	7.9	3.3	24.5

NBA REGULAR-SEASON RECORD

								REBOUNDS								AVERAGES		
Season Team	G	Min.	FGM	FGA	Pct.	FTM	FTA	Pct.	Off.	Def.	Tot.	Ast.	St.	Blk.	TO	Pts.	RPG	APG	PPG
81-82—Dallas..............	51	1468	381	820	.465	168	247	.680	89	160	249	164	37	22	135	955	4.9	3.2	18.7
82-83—Dallas..............	81	2784	767	1589	.483	429	589	.728	191	317	508	332	80	26	261	1979	6.3	4.1	24.4
83-84—Dallas..............	79	2900	*925	*1765	.524	465	621	.749	161	308	469	358	80	22	285	2330	5.9	4.5	29.5
84-85—Dallas..............	80	2699	794	1569	.506	440	580	.759	188	289	477	249	60	24	253	2055	6.0	3.1	25.7
85-86—Dallas..............	74	2501	668	1327	.503	318	451	.705	177	268	445	339	62	14	252	1670	6.0	4.6	22.6
86-87—Dallas..............	80	2663	787	1590	.495	429	557	.770	181	246	427	254	84	30	217	2056	5.3	3.2	25.7
87-88—Dallas..............	77	2610	746	1571	.475	388	504	.770	182	252	434	278	70	57	203	1932	5.6	3.6	25.1
88-89—Dallas-Det.......	80	2597	586	1270	.461	288	393	.733	146	240	386	278	45	36	208	1511	4.8	3.5	18.9
89-90—Detroit	78	2005	438	898	.488	192	254	.756	117	188	305	145	34	19	121	1099	3.9	1.9	14.1
90-91—Detroit	78	2006	420	909	.462	240	317	.757	134	240	374	139	47	20	128	1104	4.8	1.8	14.2
91-92—Detroit	75	1582	339	787	.431	158	230	.687	67	169	236	126	51	11	105	851	3.1	1.7	11.3
92-93—Detroit	51	1056	187	422	.443	99	129	.767	43	109	152	105	16	7	68	503	3.0	2.1	9.9
93-94—L.A. Clippers...	39	859	163	348	.468	50	72	.694	28	88	116	104	21	8	70	413	3.0	2.7	10.6
Totals	923	27730	7201	14865	.484	3664	4944	.741	1704	2874	4578	2871	687	296	2306	18458	5.0	3.1	20.0

Three-point field goals: 1981-82, 25-for-71 (.352). 1982-83, 16-for-76 (.211). 1983-84, 15-for-56 (.268). 1984-85, 27-for-85 (.318). 1985-86, 16-for-56 (.286). 1986-87, 53-for-150 (.353). 1987-88, 52-for-172 (.302). 1988-89, 51-for-174 (.293). 1989-90, 31-for-93 (.333). 1990-91, 24-for-78 (.308). 1991-92, 15-for-71 (.211). 1992-93, 30-for-83 (.361). 1993-94, 37-for-93 (.398). Totals, 392-for-1258 (.312).

Personal fouls/disqualifications: 1981-82, 152/0. 1982-83, 247/5. 1983-84, 246/5. 1984-85, 250/3. 1985-86, 229/6. 1986-87, 243/4. 1987-88, 223/1. 1988-89, 229/2. 1989-90, 201/2. 1990-91, 209/2. 1991-92, 171/0. 1992-93, 101/1. 1993-94, 98/2. Totals, 2599/33.

NBA PLAYOFF RECORD

								REBOUNDS								AVERAGES		
Season Team	G	Min.	FGM	FGA	Pct.	FTM	FTA	Pct.	Off.	Def.	Tot.	Ast.	St.	Blk.	TO	Pts.	RPG	APG	PPG
83-84—Dallas..............	10	350	88	184	.478	44	57	.772	21	55	76	32	5	5	27	220	7.6	3.2	22.0
84-85—Dallas..............	4	164	44	89	.494	27	32	.844	16	14	30	16	3	0	15	116	7.5	4.0	29.0
85-86—Dallas..............	10	345	105	214	.491	35	55	.636	21	50	71	54	9	0	23	247	7.1	5.4	24.7
86-87—Dallas..............	4	130	31	62	.500	23	30	.767	11	13	24	8	8	0	9	85	6.0	2.0	21.3
87-88—Dallas..............	17	558	147	294	.500	60	86	.698	34	66	100	56	14	9	41	367	5.9	3.3	21.6
88-89—Detroit	17	462	89	182	.489	28	38	.737	26	49	75	28	8	3	20	214	4.4	1.6	12.6
89-90—Detroit	20	439	86	184	.467	39	52	.750	31	60	91	27	10	3	30	219	4.6	1.4	11.0
90-91—Detroit	15	397	90	178	.506	42	51	.824	17	44	61	29	12	1	20	234	4.1	1.9	15.6
91-92—Detroit	5	113	16	48	.333	12	16	.750	4	5	9	12	2	1	13	45	1.8	2.4	9.0
Totals	102	2958	696	1435	.485	310	417	.743	181	356	537	262	71	22	198	1747	5.3	2.6	17.1

Three-point field goals: 1983-84, 0-for-5. 1984-85, 1-for-2 (.500). 1985-86, 2-for-6 (.333). 1986-87, 0-for-4. 1987-88, 13-for-34 (.382). 1988-89, 8-for-29 (.276). 1989-90, 8-for-24 (.333). 1990-91, 12-for-33 (.364). 1991-92, 1-for-5 (.200). Totals, 45-for-142 (.317).

Personal fouls/disqualifications: 1983-84, 34/2. 1984-85, 16/1. 1985-86, 28/1. 1986-87, 15/1. 1987-88, 49/0. 1988-89, 38/0. 1989-90, 51/0. 1990-91, 41/0. 1991-92, 9/0. Totals, 281/5.

NBA ALL-STAR GAME RECORD

							REBOUNDS								
Season Team	Min.	FGM	FGA	Pct.	FTM	FTA	Pct.	Off.	Def.	Tot.	Ast.	PF	Dq.	St.	Blk.	TO	Pts.
1984—Dallas	13	5	8	.625	3	4	.750	1	0	1	2	1	0	1	1	2	13
1987—Dallas	17	3	6	.500	2	3	.667	1	1	2	1	1	0	0	0	2	9
1988—Dallas	12	5	10	.500	3	3	1.000	0	1	1	1	3	0	1	0	3	14
Totals	42	13	24	.542	8	10	.800	2	2	4	4	5	0	2	1	7	36

Three-point field goals: 1987, 1-for-2 (.500). 1988, 1-for-3 (.333). Totals, 2-for-5 (.400).

ARCHIBALD, NATE   G

PERSONAL: Born September 2, 1948, in New York. ... 6-1/160 (1,85/72,6). ... Full name: Nathaniel Archibald. ... Nickname: Tiny.
HIGH SCHOOL: DeWitt Clinton (Bronx, N.Y.).
JUNIOR COLLEGE: Arizona Western College.
COLLEGE: Texas-El Paso.
TRANSACTIONS: Selected by Cincinnati Royals in second round (19th pick overall) of 1970 NBA Draft. ... Royals franchise moved from Cincinnati to Kansas City/Omaha and renamed Kings for 1972-73 season. ... Kings franchise moved from Kansas City/Omaha to Kansas City for 1975-76 season. ... Traded by Kings to New York Nets for G Brian Taylor, C Jim Eakins and 1977 and 1978 first-round draft choices (September 10, 1976). ... Nets franchise moved from New York to New Jersey for 1977-78 season. ... Traded by Nets to Buffalo Braves for C George Johnson and 1979 first-round draft choice (September 1, 1977). ... Braves franchise moved from Buffalo to San Diego and renamed Clippers for 1978-79 season. ... Traded by Clippers with F Marvin Barnes, F/G Billy Knight and 1981 and 1983 second-round draft choices to Boston Celtics for F Kermit Washington, C Kevin Kunnert, F Sidney Wicks and draft rights to G Freeman Williams (August 4, 1978). ... Waived by Celtics (July 22, 1983). ... Signed as free agent by Milwaukee Bucks (August 1, 1983).
CAREER HONORS: Elected to Naismith Memorial Basketball Hall of Fame (1991). ... One of the 50 Greatest Players in NBA History (1996).
CAREER NOTES: Head coach, Fayetteville Patriots, NBA Development League (January 31, 2001-January 8, 2002). ... Liaison, NBA Community Relations (2002).
MISCELLANEOUS: Member of NBA championship team (1981).

COLLEGIATE RECORD

												AVERAGES		
Season Team	G	Min.	FGM	FGA	Pct.	FTM	FTA	Pct.	Reb.	Ast.	Pts.	RPG	APG	PPG
66-67—Arizona Western College	27	...	303	...	...	190	...	...	...	...	796	...	...	29.5
67-68—Texas-El Paso	23	...	131	281	.466	102	140	.729	81	...	364	3.5	...	15.8
68-69—Texas-El Paso	25	...	199	374	.532	161	194	.830	69	...	559	2.8	...	22.4
69-70—Texas-El Paso	25	...	180	351	.513	176	225	.782	66	...	536	2.6	...	21.4
Junior college totals	27	...	303	...	...	190	...	...	...	...	796	...	...	29.5
4-year-college totals	73	...	510	1006	.507	439	559	.785	216	...	1459	3.0	...	20.0

NBA REGULAR-SEASON RECORD

HONORS: All-NBA first team (1973, 1975, 1976). ... All-NBA second team (1972, 1981).

Season Team	G	Min.	FGM	FGA	Pct.	FTM	FTA	Pct.	Reb.	Ast.	PF	Dq.	Pts.	AVERAGES RPG	APG	PPG
70-71—Cincinnati	82	2867	486	1095	.444	336	444	.757	242	450	218	2	1308	3.0	5.5	16.0
71-72—Cincinnati	76	3272	734	1511	.486	*677	*824	.822	222	701	198	3	2145	2.9	9.2	28.2
72-73—K.C./Omaha	80	*3681	*1028	*2106	.488	*663	*783	.847	223	*910	207	2	*2719	2.8	*11.4	*34.0

Season Team	G	Min.	FGM	FGA	Pct.	FTM	FTA	Pct.	REBOUNDS Off.	Def.	Tot.	Ast.	St.	Blk.	TO	Pts.	AVERAGES RPG	APG	PPG
73-74—K.C./Omaha	35	1272	222	492	.451	173	211	.820	21	64	85	266	56	7	...	617	2.4	7.6	17.6
74-75—K.C./Omaha	82	3244	759	1664	.456	*652	748	.872	48	174	222	557	119	7	...	2170	2.7	6.8	26.5
75-76—Kansas City.....	78	3184	717	1583	.453	501	625	.802	67	146	213	615	126	15	...	1935	2.7	7.9	24.8
76-77—N.Y. Nets.........	34	1277	250	560	.446	197	251	.785	22	58	80	254	59	11	...	697	2.4	7.5	20.5
77-78—Buffalo						Did not play—torn Achilles' tendon.													
78-79—Boston	69	1662	259	573	.452	242	307	.788	25	78	103	324	55	6	197	760	1.5	4.7	11.0
79-80—Boston	80	2864	383	794	.482	361	435	.830	59	138	197	671	106	10	242	1131	2.5	8.4	14.1
80-81—Boston	80	2820	382	766	.499	342	419	.816	36	140	176	618	75	18	265	1106	2.2	7.7	13.8
81-82—Boston	68	2167	308	652	.472	236	316	.747	25	91	116	541	52	3	178	858	1.7	8.0	12.6
82-83—Boston	66	1811	235	553	.425	220	296	.743	25	66	91	409	38	4	163	695	1.4	6.2	10.5
83-84—Milwaukee	46	1038	136	279	.487	64	101	.634	16	60	76	160	33	0	78	340	1.7	3.5	7.4
Totals	876	31159	5899	12628	.467	4664	5760	.810	...	...	2046	6476	719	81	1123	16481	2.3	7.4	18.8

Three-point field goals: 1979-80, 4-for-18 (.222). 1980-81, 0-for-9. 1981-82, 6-for-16 (.375). 1982-83, 5-for-24 (.208). 1983-84, 4-for-18 (.222). Totals, 19-for-85 (.224).

Personal fouls/disqualifications: 1973-74, 76/0. 1974-75, 187/0. 1975-76, 169/0. 1976-77, 77/1. 1978-79, 132/2. 1979-80, 218/2. 1980-81, 201/1. 1981-82, 131/1. 1982-83, 110/1. 1983-84, 78/0. Totals, 2002/15.

NBA PLAYOFF RECORD

Season Team	G	Min.	FGM	FGA	Pct.	FTM	FTA	Pct.	REBOUNDS Off.	Def.	Tot.	Ast.	St.	Blk.	TO	Pts.	AVERAGES RPG	APG	PPG
74-75—K.C./Omaha	6	242	43	118	.364	35	43	.814	2	9	11	32	4	0	...	121	1.8	5.3	20.2
79-80—Boston	9	332	45	89	.506	37	42	.881	3	8	11	71	10	0	38	128	1.2	7.9	14.2
80-81—Boston	17	630	95	211	.450	76	94	.809	6	22	28	107	13	0	50	266	1.6	6.3	15.6
81-82—Boston	8	277	30	70	.429	25	28	.893	1	16	17	52	5	2	23	85	2.1	6.5	10.6
82-83—Boston	7	161	22	68	.324	22	29	.759	3	7	10	44	2	0	11	67	1.4	6.3	9.6
Totals	47	1642	235	556	.423	195	236	.826	15	62	77	306	34	2	122	667	1.6	6.5	14.2

Three-point field goals: 1979-80, 1-for-2 (.500). 1980-81, 0-for-5. 1981-82, 0-for-4. 1982-83, 1-for-6 (.167). Totals, 2-for-17 (.118).

Personal fouls/disqualifications: 1974-75, 18/0. 1979-80, 28/1. 1980-81, 39/0. 1981-82, 21/0. 1982-83, 12/0. Totals, 118/1.

NBA ALL-STAR GAME RECORD

NOTES: NBA All-Star Game Most Valuable Player (1981).

Season Team	Min.	FGM	FGA	Pct.	FTM	FTA	Pct.	Reb	Ast.	PF	Dq.	Pts.
1973—Kansas City/Omaha	27	6	12	.500	5	5	1.000	1	5	1	0	17

Season Team	Min.	FGM	FGA	Pct.	FTM	FTA	Pct.	REBOUNDS Off.	Def.	Tot.	Ast.	PF	Dq.	St.	Blk.	TO	Pts.
1976—Kansas City	30	5	13	.385	3	3	1.000	2	3	5	7	0	0	2	0	...	13
1980—Boston	21	0	8	.000	2	3	.667	1	2	3	6	1	0	2	0	2	2
1981—Boston	25	4	7	.571	1	3	.333	0	5	5	9	3	0	3	0	2	9
1982—Boston	23	2	5	.400	2	2	1.000	1	1	2	7	3	0	1	0	2	6
Totals......................	162	27	60	.450	20	24	.833	...	...	18	40	10	0	11	1	6	74

NBDL COACHING RECORD

Season Team	REGULAR SEASON W	L	Pct.	Finish
01-02—Fayetteville	5	16	.238	

ARIZIN, PAUL   F

PERSONAL: Born April 9, 1928, in Philadelphia. ... 6-4/200 (1,93/90,7). ... Full name: Paul Joseph Arizin.
HIGH SCHOOL: La Salle (Philadelphia).
COLLEGE: Villanova.
TRANSACTIONS: Selected by Philadelphia Warriors in first round of 1950 NBA Draft. ... Played in Eastern Basketball League with Camden Bullets (1962-63 through 1964-65).
CAREER HONORS: Elected to Naismith Memorial Basketball Hall of Fame (1978). ... NBA 25th Anniversary All-Time Team (1970) and One of the 50 Greatest Players in NBA History (1996).
MISCELLANEOUS: Member of NBA championship team (1956).

COLLEGIATE RECORD

NOTES: THE SPORTING NEWS College Player of the Year (1950). ... THE SPORTING NEWS All-America first team (1950). ... Led NCAA Division I with 25.3 points per game (1950).

Season Team	G	Min.	FGM	FGA	Pct.	FTM	FTA	Pct.	Reb.	Ast.	Pts.	AVERAGES RPG	APG	PPG
46-47—Villanova.......................						Did not play.								
47-48—Villanova.......................	24	...	101	...	...	65	...	...	...	...	267	...	...	11.1
48-49—Villanova.......................	27	...	210	...	...	174	233	.747	...	...	594	...	...	22.0
49-50—Villanova.......................	29	...	260	527	.493	215	277	.776	...	...	735	...	...	25.3
Totals	80	...	571	...	...	454	...	...	...	...	1596	...	...	20.0

NBA REGULAR-SEASON RECORD

HONORS: All-NBA first team (1952, 1956, 1957). ... All-NBA second team (1959).

Season Team	G	Min.	FGM	FGA	Pct.	FTM	FTA	Pct.	Reb.	Ast.	PF	Dq.	Pts.	AVERAGES RPG	APG	PPG
50-51—Philadelphia	65	...	352	864	.407	417	526	.793	640	138	284	18	1121	9.8	2.1	17.2
51-52—Philadelphia	66	*2939	*548	1222	*.448	*578	*707	.818	745	170	250	5	*1674	11.3	2.6	*25.4
52-53—Philadelphia						Did not play—in military service.										
53-54—Philadelphia						Did not play—in military service.										
54-55—Philadelphia	72	*2953	*529	*1325	.399	454	585	.776	675	210	270	5	1512	9.4	2.9	21.0
55-56—Philadelphia	72	2724	617	1378	.448	507	626	.810	539	189	282	11	1741	7.5	2.6	24.2
56-57—Philadelphia	71	2767	613	1451	.422	591	*713	.829	561	150	274	13	*1817	7.9	2.1	*25.6
57-58—Philadelphia	68	2377	483	1229	.393	440	544	.809	503	135	235	7	1406	7.4	2.0	20.7
58-59—Philadelphia	70	2799	632	1466	.431	587	722	.813	637	119	264	7	1851	9.1	1.7	26.4
59-60—Philadelphia	72	2618	593	1400	.424	420	526	.798	621	165	263	6	1606	8.6	2.3	22.3
60-61—Philadelphia	79	2935	650	1529	.425	532	639	.833	681	188	*335	11	1832	8.6	2.4	23.2
61-62—Philadelphia	78	2785	611	1490	.410	484	601	.805	527	201	307	18	1706	6.8	2.6	21.9
Totals	713	...	5628	13354	.421	5010	6189	.810	6129	1665	2764	101	16266	8.6	2.3	22.8

NBA PLAYOFF RECORD

Season Team	G	Min.	FGM	FGA	Pct.	FTM	FTA	Pct.	Reb.	Ast.	PF	Dq.	Pts.	AVERAGES RPG	APG	PPG
50-51—Philadelphia	2	...	14	27	.519	13	16	.813	20	3	10	1	41	10.0	1.5	20.5
51-52—Philadelphia	3	120	24	53	.453	29	33	.879	38	8	17	2	77	12.7	2.7	25.7
55-56—Philadelphia	10	409	103	229	.450	83	99	.838	84	29	31	1	289	8.4	2.9	28.9
56-57—Philadelphia	2	22	3	8	.375	3	5	.600	8	1	3	0	9	4.0	0.5	4.5
57-58—Philadelphia	8	309	66	169	.391	56	72	.778	62	16	26	1	188	7.8	2.0	23.5
59-60—Philadelphia	9	371	84	195	.431	69	79	.873	86	33	29	0	237	9.6	3.7	26.3
60-61—Philadelphia	3	125	22	67	.328	23	33	.697	26	12	17	2	67	8.7	4.0	22.3
61-62—Philadelphia	12	459	95	253	.376	88	102	.863	80	26	44	1	278	6.7	2.2	23.2
Totals	49	...	411	1001	.411	364	439	.829	404	128	177	8	1186	8.2	2.6	24.2

NBA ALL-STAR GAME RECORD

NOTES: NBA All-Star Game Most Valuable Player (1952).

Season Team	Min.	FGM	FGA	Pct.	FTM	FTA	Pct.	Reb	Ast.	PF	Dq.	Pts.
1951—Philadelphia	...	7	12	.583	1	2	.500	7	0	2	0	15
1952—Philadelphia	32	9	13	.692	8	8	1.000	6	0	1	0	26
1955—Philadelphia	23	4	9	.444	1	2	.500	2	2	5	0	9
1956—Philadelphia	28	5	13	.385	3	5	.600	7	1	6	1	13
1957—Philadelphia	26	6	13	.462	1	2	.500	5	0	2	0	13
1958—Philadelphia	29	11	17	.647	2	2	1.000	8	2	3	0	24
1959—Philadelphia	30	4	15	.267	8	9	.889	8	0	2	0	16
1960—Philadelphia					Selected, did not play—injured.							
1961—Philadelphia	17	6	12	.500	5	6	.833	2	1	4	0	17
1962—Philadelphia	21	2	12	.167	0	0	...	2	0	4	0	4
Totals	...	54	116	.466	29	36	.806	47	6	29	1	137

EBL REGULAR-SEASON RECORD

NOTES: Eastern Basketball League Most Valuable Player (1963). ... EBL All-Star first team (1963, 1964). ... EBL All-Star second team (1965).

Season Team	G	Min.	FGM	FGA	Pct.	FTM	FTA	Pct.	Reb.	Ast.	PF	Dq.	Pts.	AVERAGES RPG	APG	PPG
62-63—Camden	28	...	264	...	...	196	249	.787	203	42	...	...	724	7.3	1.5	25.9
63-64—Camden	27	...	261	...	...	174	218	.798	226	52	...	...	696	8.4	1.9	25.8
64-65—Camden	28	...	226	...	...	196	244	.803	164	50	...	...	657	5.9	1.8	23.5
Totals	83	...	751	...	...	566	711	.796	593	144	...	...	2077	7.1	1.7	25.0

BARKLEY, CHARLES   F

PERSONAL: Born February 20, 1963, in Leeds, Ala. ... 6-6/252. (1.98 m/114 kg). ... Full Name: Charles Wade Barkley.
HIGH SCHOOL: Leeds (Ala.).
COLLEGE: Auburn.
TRANSACTIONS/CAREER NOTES: Selected after junior season by Philadelphia 76ers in first round (fifth pick overall) of 1984 NBA Draft. ... Traded by 76ers to Phoenix Suns for G Jeff Hornacek, F Tim Perry and C Andrew Lang (June 17, 1992). ... Traded by Suns with 1999 second-round draft choice to Houston Rockets for G Sam Cassell, F Chucky Brown, F Robert Horry and F Mark Bryant (August 19, 1996).
CAREER HONORS: NBA 50th Anniversary All-Time Team (1996). ... Elected to Naismith Memorial Basketball Hall of Fame (2006).
CAREER NOTES: Broadcaster, Turner Sports (2001-present).
MISCELLANEOUS: Member of gold-medal-winning U.S. Olympic teams (1992, 1996).

COLLEGIATE RECORD

Season Team	G	Min.	FGM	FGA	Pct.	FTM	FTA	Pct.	Reb.	Ast.	Pts.	AVERAGES RPG	APG	PPG
81-82—Auburn	28	746	144	242	.595	68	107	.636	275	30	356	9.8	1.1	12.7
82-83—Auburn	28	782	161	250	.644	82	130	.631	266	49	404	9.5	1.8	14.4
83-84—Auburn	28	794	162	254	.638	99	145	.683	265	58	423	9.5	2.1	15.1
Totals	84	2322	467	746	.626	249	382	.652	806	137	1183	9.6	1.6	14.1

NBA REGULAR-SEASON RECORD

RECORDS: Holds single-game records for most offensive rebounds in one quarter—11; and most offensive rebounds in one half—13 (March 4, 1987, vs. New York).
HONORS: NBA Most Valuable Player (1993). ... IBM Award, for all-around contributions to team's success (1986, 1987, 1988). ... All-NBA first team (1988, 1989, 1990, 1991, 1993). ... All-NBA second team (1986, 1987, 1992, 1994, 1995). ... All-NBA third team (1996). ... NBA All-Rookie team (1985).
NOTES: Led NBA with 333 personal fouls (1986).

Season Team	G	Min.	FGM	FGA	Pct.	FTM	FTA	Pct.	REBOUNDS Off.	Def.	Tot.	Ast.	St.	Blk.	TO	Pts.	AVERAGES RPG	APG	PPG
84-85—Philadelphia	82	2347	427	783	.545	293	400	.733	266	437	703	155	95	80	209	1148	8.6	1.9	14.0
85-86—Philadelphia	80	2952	595	1041	.572	396	578	.685	354	672	1026	312	173	125	*350	1603	12.8	3.9	20.0
86-87—Philadelphia	68	2740	557	937	.594	429	564	.761	*390	604	994	331	119	104	322	1564	*14.6	4.9	23.0
87-88—Philadelphia	80	3170	753	1283	.587	714	*951	.751	*385	566	951	254	100	103	304	2264	11.9	3.2	28.3
88-89—Philadelphia	79	3088	700	1208	.579	602	799	.753	*403	583	986	325	126	67	254	2037	12.5	4.1	25.8
89-90—Philadelphia	79	3085	706	1177	.600	557	744	.749	361	548	909	307	148	50	243	1989	11.5	3.9	25.2
90-91—Philadelphia	67	2498	665	1167	.570	475	658	.722	258	422	680	284	110	33	210	1849	10.1	4.2	27.6
91-92—Philadelphia	75	2881	622	1126	.552	454	653	.695	271	559	830	308	136	44	235	1730	11.1	4.1	23.1
92-93—Phoenix	76	2859	716	1376	.520	445	582	.765	237	691	928	385	119	74	233	1944	12.2	5.1	25.6
93-94—Phoenix	65	2298	518	1046	.495	318	452	.704	198	529	727	296	101	37	206	1402	11.2	4.6	21.6
94-95—Phoenix	68	2382	554	1141	.486	379	507	.748	203	553	756	270	110	45	150	1561	11.1	4.1	23.0
95-96—Phoenix	71	2632	580	1160	.500	440	566	.777	243	578	821	262	114	56	218	1649	11.6	3.7	23.2
96-97—Houston	53	2009	335	692	.484	288	415	.694	212	504	716	248	69	25	151	1016	13.5	4.7	19.2
97-98—Houston	68	2243	361	744	.485	296	397	.746	241	553	794	217	71	28	147	1036	11.7	3.2	15.2
98-99—Houston	42	1526	240	502	.478	192	267	.719	167	349	516	192	43	13	100	676	12.3	4.6	16.1
99-00—Houston	20	620	106	222	.477	71	110	.645	71	138	209	63	14	4	44	289	10.5	3.2	14.5
Totals	1073	39330	8435	15605	.541	6349	8643	.735	4260	8286	12546	4215	1648	888	3376	23757	11.7	3.9	22.1

Three-point field goals: 1984-85, 1-for-6 (.167). 1985-86, 17-for-75 (.227). 1986-87, 21-for-104 (.202). 1987-88, 44-for-157 (.280). 1988-89, 35-for-162 (.216). 1989-90, 20-for-92 (.217). 1990-91, 44-for-155 (.284). 1991-92, 32-for-137 (.234). 1992-93, 67-for-220 (.305). 1993-94, 48-for-178 (.270). 1994-95, 74-for-219 (.338). 1995-96, 49-for-175 (.280). 1996-97, 58-for-205 (.283). 1997-98, 18-for-84 (.214). 1998-99, 4-for-25 (.160). 1999-00, 6-for-26 (.231). Totals, 538-for-2020 (.266).

Personal fouls/disqualifications: 1984-85, 301/5. 1985-86, 333/8. 1986-87, 252/5. 1987-88, 278/6. 1988-89, 262/3. 1989-90, 250/2. 1990-91, 173/2. 1991-92, 196/2. 1992-93, 196/0. 1993-94, 160/1. 1994-95, 201/3. 1995-96, 208/3. 1996-97, 153/2. 1997-98, 187/2. 1998-99, 89/0. 1999-00, 48/0. Totals, 3287/44.

NBA PLAYOFF RECORD

NOTES: Shares single-game playoff records for most free throws made in one half—19 (June 5, 1993, vs. Seattle); and most field goals made in one half—15 (May 4, 1994, at Golden State).

Season Team	G	Min.	FGM	FGA	Pct.	FTM	FTA	Pct.	REBOUNDS Off.	Def.	Tot.	Ast.	St.	Blk.	TO	Pts.	AVERAGES RPG	APG	PPG
84-85—Philadelphia	13	408	75	139	.540	40	63	.635	52	92	144	26	23	15	35	194	11.1	2.0	14.9
85-86—Philadelphia	12	497	104	180	.578	91	131	.695	60	129	189	67	27	15	65	300	15.8	5.6	25.0
86-87—Philadelphia	5	210	43	75	.573	36	45	.800	27	36	63	12	4	8	22	123	12.6	2.4	24.6
88-89—Philadelphia	3	135	29	45	.644	22	31	.710	8	27	35	16	5	2	11	81	11.7	5.3	27.0
89-90—Philadelphia	10	419	88	162	.543	65	108	.602	66	89	155	43	8	7	30	247	15.5	4.3	24.7
90-91—Philadelphia	8	326	74	125	.592	49	75	.653	31	53	84	48	15	3	25	199	10.5	6.0	24.9
92-93—Phoenix	24	1026	230	482	.477	168	218	.771	93	233	326	102	39	25	50	638	13.6	4.3	26.6
93-94—Phoenix	10	425	110	216	.509	42	55	.764	34	96	130	48	25	9	27	276	13.0	4.8	27.6
94-95—Phoenix	10	390	91	182	.500	66	90	.733	39	95	134	32	13	11	25	257	13.4	3.2	25.7
95-96—Phoenix	4	164	31	70	.443	37	47	.787	18	36	54	15	4	4	6	102	13.5	3.8	25.5
96-97—Houston	16	605	86	198	.434	103	134	.769	64	128	192	54	19	7	43	286	12.0	3.4	17.9
97-98—Houston	4	87	12	23	.522	12	21	.571	5	16	21	4	5	0	6	36	5.3	1.0	9.0
98-99—Houston	4	157	36	68	.529	20	30	.667	10	10	55	18	8	2	9	94	13.8	3.8	23.5
Totals	123	4849	1009	1965	.513	751	1048	.717	510	1072	1582	482	193	108	353	2833	12.9	3.9	23.0

Three-point field goals: 1984-85, 4-for-6 (.667). 1985-86, 1-for-15 (.067). 1988-89, 1-for-5 (.200). 1989-90, 6-for-18 (.333). 1990-91, 2-for-20 (.100). 1992-93, 10-for-45 (.222). 1993-94, 14-for-40 (.350). 1994-95, 9-for-35 (.257). 1995-96, 3-for-12 (.250). 1996-97, 11-for-38 (.289). 1997-98, 0-for-2. 1998-99, 2-for-7 (.286). Totals, 63-for-243 (.259).

Personal fouls/disqualifications: 1984-85, 49/0. 1985-86, 52/2. 1988-89, 9/0. 1989-90, 36/0. 1990-91, 23/0. 1992-93, 73/0. 1993-94, 26/0. 1994-95, 28/0. 1995-96, 15/0. 1996-97, 52/1. 1997-98, 12/1. 1998-99, 12/0. Totals, 408/4.

NBA ALL-STAR GAME RECORD

NOTES: NBA All-Star Game Most Valuable Player (1991).

Season Team	Min.	FGM	FGA	Pct.	FTM	FTA	Pct.	REBOUNDS Off.	Def.	Tot.	Ast.	PF	Dq.	St.	Blk.	TO	Pts.
1987—Philadelphia	16	2	6	.333	3	6	.500	1	3	4	1	2	0	1	0	0	7
1988—Philadelphia	15	1	4	.250	2	2	1.000	1	2	3	0	2	0	1	1	3	4
1989—Philadelphia	20	6	11	.545	5	8	.625	3	2	5	0	0	0	2	1	1	17
1990—Philadelphia	22	7	12	.583	2	3	.667	2	2	4	0	1	0	1	1	2	17
1991—Philadelphia	35	7	15	.467	3	6	.500	8	14	22	4	5	0	1	1	3	17
1992—Philadelphia	28	6	14	.429	0	0	...	2	7	9	1	3	0	0	0	3	12
1993—Phoenix	34	5	11	.455	5	7	.714	0	4	4	7	3	0	4	0	4	16
1994—Phoenix							Selected, did not play—injured.										
1995—Phoenix	23	7	12	.583	0	0	...	5	4	9	2	1	0	2	0	2	15
1996—Phoenix	16	4	6	.667	0	0	...	0	0	0	1	1	0	0	0	2	8
1997—Houston							Selected, did not play—injured.										
Totals	209	45	91	.495	20	32	.625	22	38	60	16	18	0	12	4	20	113

Three-point field goals: 1987, 0-for-2. 1988, 0-for-1. 1990, 1-for-1. 1992, 0-for-2. 1993, 1-for-2 (.500). 1995, 1-for-4 (.250). Totals, 3-for-12 (.250)

BARRY, RICK   F

PERSONAL: Born March 28, 1944, in Elizabeth, N.J. ... 6-7/220 (2,00/99,8). ... Full name: Richard Francis Dennis Barry III. ... Father of Jon Barry, guard with Houston Rockets; father of Brent Barry, guard with San Antonio Spurs; and father of Drew Barry, guard with Atlanta Hawks (1997-98 and 1999-2000), Seattle SuperSonics (1998-99) and Golden State Warriors (1999-2000).
HIGH SCHOOL: Roselle Park (N.J.).

COLLEGE: Miami (Fla.).

TRANSACTIONS: Selected by San Francisco Warriors in first round of 1965 NBA Draft. ... Signed as free agent by Oakland Oaks of American Basketball Association (1967); court order required him to sit out option season with Warriors (1967-68). ... Oaks franchise moved to Washington and renamed Capitols for 1969-70 season. ... Capitols franchise moved from Washington to Virginia and renamed Squires for 1970-71 season. ... Traded by Squires to New York Nets for first-round draft choice and cash (August 1970). ... Returned to NBA with Golden

State Warriors for 1972-73 season. ... Signed as veteran free agent by Houston Rockets (June 17, 1978); Warriors waived their right of first refusal in exchange for G John Lucas and cash.

CAREER HONORS: Elected to Naismith Memorial Basketball Hall of Fame (1987). ... One of the 50 Greatest Players in NBA History (1996).

MISCELLANEOUS: Member of NBA championship team (1975).

COLLEGIATE RECORD

NOTES: THE SPORTING NEWS All-America second team (1965). ... Led NCAA Division I with 37.4 points per game (1965).

Season Team	G	Min.	FGM	FGA	Pct.	FTM	FTA	Pct.	Reb.	Ast.	Pts.	RPG	APG	PPG
61-62—Miami (Fla.)‡	17	...	208	...	...	73	...	...	...	...	489	...	...	28.8
62-63—Miami (Fla.)	24	...	162	341	.475	131	158	.829	351	...	455	14.6	...	19.0
63-64—Miami (Fla.)	27	...	314	572	.549	242	287	.843	448	...	870	16.6	...	32.2
64-65—Miami (Fla.)	26	...	340	651	.522	293	341	.859	475	...	973	18.3	...	37.4
Varsity totals	77	...	816	1564	.522	666	786	.847	1274	...	2298	16.5	...	29.8

NBA REGULAR-SEASON RECORD

RECORDS: Shares single-game record for most free throws made in one quarter—14 (December 6, 1966, vs. New York).

HONORS: NBA Rookie of the Year (1966). ... All-NBA first team (1966, 1967, 1974, 1975, 1976). ... All-NBA second team (1973). ... NBA All-Rookie team (1966).

NOTES: Led NBA with 2.85 steals per game (1975).

Season Team	G	Min.	FGM	FGA	Pct.	FTM	FTA	Pct.	Reb.	Ast.	PF	Dq.	Pts.	RPG	APG	PPG
65-66—San Francisco	80	2990	745	1698	.439	569	660	.862	850	173	297	2	2059	10.6	2.2	25.7
66-67—San Francisco	78	3175	*1011	*2240	.451	*753	852	.884	714	282	258	1	*2775	9.2	3.6	*35.6
72-73—Golden State	82	3075	737	1630	.452	358	397	*.902	728	399	245	2	1832	8.9	4.9	22.3

									REBOUNDS						AVERAGES		
Season Team	G	Min.	FGM	FGA	Pct.	FTM	FTA	Pct.	Off.	Def.	Tot.	Ast.	St.	Blk.	TO	Pts.	RPG APG PPG
73-74—Golden State	80	2918	796	1746	.456	417	464	.899	103	437	540	484	169	40	...	2009	6.8 6.1 25.1
74-75—Golden State	80	3235	1028	*2217	.464	394	436	*.904	92	364	456	492	*228	33	...	2450	5.7 6.2 30.6
75-76—Golden State	81	3122	707	1624	.435	287	311	*.923	74	422	496	496	202	27	...	1701	6.1 6.1 21.0
76-77—Golden State	79	2904	682	1551	.440	359	392	.916	73	349	422	475	172	58	...	1723	5.3 6.0 21.8
77-78—Golden State	82	3024	760	1686	.451	378	409	*.924	75	374	449	446	158	45	224	1898	5.5 5.4 23.1
78-79—Houston	80	2566	461	1000	.461	160	169	*.947	40	237	277	502	95	38	198	1082	3.5 6.3 13.5
79-80—Houston	72	1816	325	771	.422	143	153	*.935	53	183	236	268	80	28	152	866	3.3 3.7 12.0
Totals	794	28825	7252	16163	.449	3818	4243	.900	...	...	5168	4017	1104	269	574	18395	6.5 5.1 23.2

Three-point field goals: 1979-80, 73-for-221 (.330).

Personal fouls/disqualifications: 1973-74, 265/4. 1974-75, 225/0. 1975-76, 215/1. 1976-77, 194/2. 1977-78, 188/1. 1978-79, 195/0. 1979-80, 182/0. Totals, 2264/13.

NBA PLAYOFF RECORD

NOTES: NBA Finals Most Valuable Player (1975). ... Holds NBA Finals single-game records for most field goals attempted—48 (April 18, 1967, vs. Philadelphia); and most field goals attempted in one quarter—17 (April 14, 1967, vs. Philadelphia). ... Shares NBA Finals single-game record for most field goals made—22 (April 18, 1967, vs. Philadelphia). ... Holds single-game playoff record for most field goals attempted in one quarter—17 (April 14, 1967, vs. Philadelphia).

Season Team	G	Min.	FGM	FGA	Pct.	FTM	FTA	Pct.	Reb.	Ast.	PF	Dq.	Pts.	RPG	APG	PPG
66-67—San Francisco	15	614	197	489	.403	127	157	.809	113	58	49	0	521	7.5	3.9	34.7
72-73—Golden State	11	292	65	164	.396	50	55	.909	54	24	41	1	180	4.9	2.2	16.4

									REBOUNDS						AVERAGES		
Season Team	G	Min.	FGM	FGA	Pct.	FTM	FTA	Pct.	Off.	Def.	Tot.	Ast.	St.	Blk.	TO	Pts.	RPG APG PPG
74-75—Golden State	17	726	189	426	.444	101	110	.918	22	72	94	103	50	15	...	479	5.5 6.1 28.2
75-76—Golden State	13	532	126	289	.436	60	68	.882	20	64	84	84	38	14	...	312	6.5 6.5 24.0
76-77—Golden State	10	415	122	262	.466	40	44	.909	25	34	59	47	17	7	...	284	5.9 4.7 28.4
78-79—Houston	2	65	8	25	.320	8	8	1.000	2	6	8	9	0	2	2	24	4.0 4.5 12.0
79-80—Houston	6	79	12	33	.364	6	6	1.000	0	6	6	15	1	1	10	33	1.0 2.5 5.5
Totals	74	2723	719	1688	.426	392	448	.875	...	...	418	340	106	39	12	1833	5.6 4.6 24.8

Three-point field goals: 1979-80, 3-for-12 (.250).

Personal fouls/disqualifications: 1974-75, 51/1. 1975-76, 40/1. 1976-77, 32/0. 1978-79, 8/0. 1979-80, 11/0. Totals, 232/3.

NBA ALL-STAR GAME RECORD

NOTES: NBA All-Star Game Most Valuable Player (1967). ... Holds single-game records for most field goals attempted—27 (1967); and most steals—8 (1975).

Season Team	Min.	FGM	FGA	Pct.	FTM	FTA	Pct.	Reb	Ast.	PF	Dq.	Pts.
1966—San Francisco	17	4	10	.400	2	4	.500	2	2	6	1	10
1967—San Francisco	34	16	27	.593	6	8	.750	6	3	5	2	38
1973—Golden State					Selected, did not play—injured.							

								REBOUNDS								
Season Team	Min.	FGM	FGA	Pct.	FTM	FTA	Pct.	Off.	Def.	Tot.	Ast.	PF	Dq.	St.	Blk.	TO	Pts.
1974—Golden State	19	3	6	.500	2	2	1.000	1	3	4	3	3	0	1	0	...	8
1975—Golden State	38	11	20	.550	0	0	...	1	4	5	8	4	0	8	1	...	22
1976—Golden State	28	6	15	.400	5	5	1.000	2	2	4	2	5	0	2	0	...	17
1977—Golden State	29	7	16	.438	4	4	1.000	1	3	4	8	1	0	2	0	...	18
1978—Golden State	30	7	17	.412	1	1	1.000	2	2	4	5	6	1	3	0	5	15
Totals	195	54	111	.486	20	24	.833	...	...	29	31	30	2	16	1	5	128

ABA REGULAR-SEASON RECORD

NOTES: Member of ABA championship team (1969). ... ABA All-Star first team (1969, 1970, 1971, 1972).

Season Team	G	Min.	2-POINT FGM	FGA	Pct.	3-POINT FGM	FGA	Pct.	FTM	FTA	Pct.	Reb.	Ast.	Pts.	RPG	APG	PPG
67-68—			Did not play—sat out option year.														
68-69—Oakland	35	1361	389	757	.514	3	10	.300	403	454	*.888	329	136	*1190	9.4	3.9	*34.0
69-70—Washington	52	1849	509	907	.561	8	39	.205	400	463	.864	363	178	1442	7.0	3.4	27.7
70-71—New York	59	2502	613	1262	.486	19	86	.221	451	507	*.890	401	294	1734	6.8	5.0	29.4
71-72—New York	80	3616	829	1732	.479	73	237	.308	*641	730	*.878	602	327	2518	7.5	4.1	31.5
Totals	226	9328	2340	4658	.502	103	372	.277	1895	2154	.880	1695	935	6884	7.5	4.1	30.5

ABA PLAYOFF RECORD

Season Team	G	Min.	2-POINT FGM	FGA	Pct.	3-POINT FGM	FGA	Pct.	FTM	FTA	Pct.	Rob.	Ast.	Pts.	RPG	APG	PPG
69-70—Washington	7	302	105	194	.541	3	9	.333	62	68	.912	70	23	281	10.0	3.3	40.1
70-71—New York	6	287	46	108	.426	14	27	.519	48	59	.814	70	24	202	11.7	4.0	33.7
71-72—New York	18	749	180	368	.489	23	61	.377	125	146	.856	117	69	554	6.5	3.8	30.8
Totals	31	1338	331	670	.494	40	97	.412	235	273	.861	257	116	1037	8.3	3.7	33.5

ABA ALL-STAR GAME RECORD

Season Team	Min.	2-POINT FGM	FGA	Pct.	3-POINT FGM	FGA	Pct.	FTM	FTA	Pct.	Reb.	Ast.	Pts.
1968—Oakland	12	3	9	.333	0	0	...	4	5	.800	3	1	10
1969—Washington	27	7	12	.583	0	0	...	2	2	1.000	7	7	16
1970—New York	17	4	6	.667	0	0	...	6	6	1.000	2	2	14
1971—New York	26	2	10	.200	0	0	...	0	1	.000	12	8	4
Totals	82	16	37	.432	0	0	...	12	14	.857	24	18	44

COMBINED ABA AND NBA REGULAR-SEASON RECORDS

	G	Min.	FGM	FGA	Pct.	FTM	FTA	Pct.	REBOUNDS Off.	Def.	Tot.	Ast.	Stl.	Blk.	TO	Pts.	AVERAGES RPG	APG	PPG
Totals	1020	38153	9695	21193	.457	5713	6397	.893	...	...	6863	4952	...	...	...	25279	6.7	4.9	24.8

Three-point field goals: 176-for-593 (.297).
Personal fouls/disqualifications: 3028.

CBA COACHING RECORD

	REGULAR SEASON				PLAYOFFS		
Season Team	W	L	Pct.	Finish	W	L	Pct.
92-93—Fort Wayne	11	16	.407	4th/Eastern Division——			
93-94—Fort Wayne	14	30	.318				
Totals (2 years)	25	46	.352				

USBL COACHING RECORD

	REGULAR SEASON				PLAYOFFS		
Season Team	W	L	Pct.	Finish	W	L	Pct.
97-98—New Jersey	11	12	.888	3rd/Mid-Atlantic Division	1	1	.500
98-99—New Jersey	23	6	.793	1st/Mid-Atlantic Division	3	0	1.000
99-00—Florida	16	14	.533	3rd/Southern Division	0	1	.000
Totals (3 years)	53	32	.624	Totals (3 years)	4	2	.667

NOTES:
1998—Defeated Tampa Bay in play-in game; lost to Jacksonville in quarterfinals.
1999—Defeated Tampa Bay in quarterfinals; defeated Pennsylvania in semifinals; defeated Connecticut in USBL Finals.
2000—Lost to Kansas in quarterfinals.

BAYLOR, ELGIN   F

PERSONAL: Born September 16, 1934, in Washington, D.C. ... 6-5/225 (1,96/102,1). ... Full name: Elgin Gay Baylor.
HIGH SCHOOL: Phelps Vocational (Washington, D.C.), then Spingarn (Washington, D.C.).
COLLEGE: The College of Idaho, then Seattle.
TRANSACTIONS: Selected after junior season by Minneapolis Lakers in first round (first pick overall) of 1958 NBA Draft. ... Lakers franchise moved to Los Angeles for 1960-61 season.
CAREER HONORS: Elected to Naismith Memorial Basketball Hall of Fame (1977). ... NBA 35th Anniversary All-Time Team (1980) and One of the 50 Greatest Players in NBA History (1996).
CAREER NOTES: Vice president of basketball operations, Los Angeles Clippers (1986 to present).
MISCELLANEOUS: Los Angeles Lakers franchise all-time leading rebounder with 11,463 (1958-59 through 1971-72).

COLLEGIATE RECORD

NOTES: The Sporting News All-America first team (1958). ... NCAA University Division Tournament Most Valuable Player (1958). ... Led NCAA Division I with .235 rebound average (1957), when championship was determined by highest individual recoveries as percentage of total recoveries by both teams in all games. ... Played for Westside Ford (AAU team in Seattle) averaging 34 points per game (1955-56).

Season Team	G	Min.	FGM	FGA	Pct.	FTM	FTA	Pct.	Reb.	Ast.	Pts.	AVERAGES RPG	APG	PPG
54-55—The College of Idaho	26	...	332	651	.510	150	232	.647	492	...	814	18.9	...	31.3
55-56—Seattle			Did not play—transfer student.											
56-57—Seattle	25	...	271	555	.488	201	251	.801	508	...	743	20.3	...	29.7
57-58—Seattle	29	...	353	697	.506	237	308	.769	559	...	943	19.3	...	32.5
Totals	80	...	956	1903	.502	588	791	.743	1559	...	2500	19.5	...	31.3

NBA REGULAR-SEASON RECORD

HONORS: NBA Rookie of the Year (1959). ... All-NBA first team (1959, 1960, 1961, 1962, 1963, 1964, 1965, 1967, 1968, 1969).

Season Team	G	Min.	FGM	FGA	Pct.	FTM	FTA	Pct.	Reb.	Ast.	PF	Dq.	Pts.	AVERAGES RPG	APG	PPG
58-59—Minneapolis	70	2855	605	1482	.408	532	685	.777	1050	287	270	4	1742	15.0	4.1	24.9
59-60—Minneapolis	70	2873	755	1781	.424	564	770	.732	1150	243	234	2	2074	16.4	3.5	29.6
60-61—Los Angeles	73	3133	931	2166	.430	676	863	.783	1447	371	279	3	2538	19.8	5.1	34.8
61-62—Los Angeles	48	2129	680	1588	.428	476	631	.754	892	222	155	1	1836	18.6	4.6	38.3
62-63—Los Angeles	80	3370	1029	2273	.453	661	790	.837	1146	386	226	1	2719	14.3	4.8	34.0
63-64—Los Angeles	78	3164	756	1778	.425	471	586	.804	936	347	235	1	1983	12.0	4.4	25.4
64-65—Los Angeles	74	3056	763	1903	.401	483	610	.792	950	280	235	0	2009	12.8	3.8	27.1
65-66—Los Angeles	65	1975	415	1034	.401	249	337	.739	621	224	157	0	1079	9.6	3.4	16.6
66-67—Los Angeles	70	2706	711	1658	.429	440	541	.813	898	215	211	1	1862	12.8	3.1	26.6
67-68—Los Angeles	77	3029	757	1709	.443	488	621	.786	941	355	232	0	2002	12.2	4.6	26.0
68-69—Los Angeles	76	3064	730	1632	.447	421	567	.743	805	408	204	0	1881	10.6	5.4	24.8
69-70—Los Angeles	54	2213	511	1051	.486	276	357	.773	559	292	132	1	1298	10.4	5.4	24.0
70-71—Los Angeles	2	57	8	19	.421	4	6	.667	11	2	6	0	20	5.5	1.0	10.0
71-72—Los Angeles	9	239	42	97	.433	22	27	.815	57	18	20	0	106	6.3	2.0	11.8
Totals	846	33863	8693	20171	.431	5763	7391	.780	11463	3650	2596	14	23149	13.5	4.3	27.4

NBA PLAYOFF RECORD

RECORDS: Holds NBA Finals single-game records for most points—61; and most field goals attempted in one half—25 (April 14, 1962, vs. Boston). ... Shares NBA Finals single-game record for most field goals made—22 (April 14, 1962, vs. Boston). ... Shares single-game play-off record for most field goals attempted in one half—25 (April 14, 1962, vs. Boston).

Season Team	G	Min.	FGM	FGA	Pct.	FTM	FTA	Pct.	Reb.	Ast.	PF	Dq.	Pts.	AVERAGES RPG	APG	PPG
58-59—Minneapolis	13	556	122	303	.403	87	113	.770	156	43	52	0	331	12.0	3.3	25.5
59-60—Minneapolis	9	408	111	234	.474	79	94	.840	127	31	38	0	301	14.1	3.4	33.4
60-61—Los Angeles	12	540	170	362	.470	117	142	.824	183	55	44	1	457	15.3	4.6	38.1
61-62—Los Angeles	13	571	186	425	.438	130	168	.774	230	47	45	1	502	17.7	3.6	38.6
62-63—Los Angeles	13	562	160	362	.442	104	126	.825	177	58	48	0	424	13.6	4.5	32.6
63-64—Los Angeles	5	221	45	119	.378	31	40	.775	58	28	17	0	121	11.6	5.6	24.2
64-65—Los Angeles	1	5	0	2	.000	0	0	...	0	1	0	0	0	0.0	1.0	0.0
65-66—Los Angeles	14	586	145	328	.442	85	105	.810	197	52	38	0	375	14.1	3.7	26.8
66-67—Los Angeles	3	121	28	76	.368	15	20	.750	39	9	6	0	71	13.0	3.0	23.7
67-68—Los Angeles	15	633	176	376	.468	76	112	.679	218	60	41	0	428	14.5	4.0	28.5
68-69—Los Angeles	18	640	107	278	.385	63	97	.649	166	74	56	0	277	9.2	4.1	15.4
69-70—Los Angeles	18	667	138	296	.466	60	81	.741	173	83	50	1	336	9.6	4.6	18.7
Totals	134	5510	1388	3161	.439	847	1098	.771	1724	541	435	3	3623	12.9	4.0	27.0

NBA ALL-STAR GAME RECORD

NOTES: NBA All-Star Game co-Most Valuable Player (1959). ... Holds career record for most free throws made—78. ... Shares career record for most free throws attempted—98. ... Shares single-game record for most free throws made—12 (1962).

Season Team	Min.	FGM	FGA	Pct.	FTM	FTA	Pct.	Reb	Ast.	PF	Dq.	Pts.
1959—Minneapolis	32	10	20	.500	4	5	.800	11	1	3	0	24
1960—Minneapolis	28	10	18	.556	5	7	.714	13	3	4	0	25
1961—Los Angeles	27	3	11	.273	9	10	.900	10	4	5	0	15
1962—Los Angeles	37	10	23	.435	12	14	.857	9	4	2	0	32
1963—Los Angeles	36	4	15	.267	9	13	.692	14	7	0	0	17
1964—Los Angeles	29	5	15	.333	5	11	.455	8	5	1	0	15
1965—Los Angeles	27	5	13	.385	8	8	1.000	7	0	4	0	18
1967—Los Angeles	20	8	14	.571	4	4	1.000	5	5	2	0	20
1968—Los Angeles	27	8	13	.615	6	7	.857	6	1	5	0	22
1969—Los Angeles	32	5	13	.385	11	12	.917	9	5	2	0	21
1970—Los Angeles	26	2	9	.222	5	7	.714	7	3	3	0	9
Totals	321	70	164	.427	78	98	.796	99	38	31	0	218

NBA COACHING RECORD

BACKGROUND: Assistant coach, New Orleans Jazz (1974-75 and 1975-76).

Season Team	REGULAR SEASON W	L	Pct.	Finish	PLAYOFFS W	L	Pct.
74-75—New Orleans	0	1	.000		—	—	—
76-77—New Orleans	21	35	.375	5th/Central Division	—	—	—
77-78—New Orleans	39	43	.476	5th/Central Division	—	—	—
78-79—New Orleans	26	56	.317	6th/Central Division	—	—	—
Totals (4 years)	86	135	.389				

NOTES:
1974—Replaced Scotty Robertson as New Orleans head coach (November), with record of 1-14; replaced as New Orleans head coach by Bill van Breda Kolff (November).
1976—Replaced Bill van Breda Kolff as New Orleans head coach (December), with record of 14-12.

BELLAMY, WALT   C

PERSONAL: Born July 24, 1939, in New Bern, N.C. ... 6-11/245 (2,11/111). ... Full name: Walter Jones Bellamy. ... Nickname: Bells.
HIGH SCHOOL: J.T. Barber (New Bern, N.C.).
COLLEGE: Indiana.
TRANSACTIONS: Selected by Chicago Packers in first round (first pick overall) of 1961 NBA Draft. ... Packers franchise renamed Zephyrs for 1962-63 season. ... Zephyrs franchise moved to Baltimore and renamed Bullets for 1963-64 season. ... Traded by Bullets to New York Knicks for F John Green, G John Egan, F/C Jim Barnes and cash (November 2, 1965). ... Traded by Knicks with G Howard Komives to Detroit Pistons for F Dave DeBusschere (December 19, 1968). ... Traded by Pistons to Atlanta Hawks for future considerations

(February 1, 1970); Pistons received G John Arthurs from Milwaukee Bucks to complete deal. ... Selected by New Orleans Jazz from Hawks in NBA Expansion Draft (May 20, 1974). ... Waived by Jazz (October 18, 1974).
CAREER HONORS: Elected to Naismith Memorial Basketball Hall of Fame (1993).
MISCELLANEOUS: Member of gold-medal-winning U.S. Olympic Team (1960).

COLLEGIATE RECORD

NOTES: THE SPORTING NEWS All-America second team (1961).

Season Team	G	Min.	FGM	FGA	Pct.	FTM	FTA	Pct.	Reb.	Ast.	Pts.	RPG	APG	PPG
57-58—Indiana‡					Freshman team did not play intercollegiate schedule.									
58-59—Indiana	22	...	148	289	.512	86	141	.610	335	...	382	15.2	...	17.4
59-60—Indiana	24	...	212	396	.535	113	161	.702	324	...	537	13.5	...	22.4
60-61—Indiana	24	...	195	389	.501	132	204	.047	428	...	522	17.8	...	21.8
Varsity totals	70	...	555	1074	.517	331	506	.654	1087	...	1441	15.5	...	20.6

NBA REGULAR-SEASON RECORD

RECORDS: Holds single-season record for most games played—88 (1969).
HONORS: NBA Rookie of the Year (1962).

Season Team	G	Min.	FGM	FGA	Pct.	FTM	FTA	Pct.	Reb.	Ast.	PF	Dq.	Pts.	RPG	APG	PPG
61-62—Chicago	79	3344	973	1875	*.519	549	853	.644	1500	210	281	6	2495	19.0	2.7	31.6
62-63—Chicago	80	3306	840	1595	.527	553	821	.674	1309	233	283	7	2233	16.4	2.9	27.9
63-64—Baltimore	80	3394	811	1582	.517	537	825	.651	1361	126	300	7	2159	17.0	1.6	27.0
64-65—Baltimore	80	3301	733	1441	.509	515	752	.685	1166	191	260	2	1981	14.6	2.4	24.8
65-66—Balt.-N.Y.	80	3352	695	1373	.506	430	689	.624	1254	235	294	9	1820	15.7	2.9	22.8
66-67—New York	79	3010	565	1084	.521	369	580	.636	1064	206	275	5	1499	13.5	2.6	19.0
67-68—New York	82	2695	511	944	.541	350	529	.662	961	164	259	3	1372	11.7	2.0	16.7
68-69—N.Y.-Detroit	88	3159	563	1103	.510	401	618	.649	1101	176	320	5	1527	12.5	2.0	17.4
69-70—Detroit-Atl.	79	2028	351	671	.523	215	373	.576	707	143	260	5	917	8.9	1.8	11.6
70-71—Atlanta	82	2908	433	879	.493	336	556	.604	1060	230	271	4	1202	12.9	2.8	14.7
71-72—Atlanta	82	3187	593	1089	.545	340	581	.585	1049	262	255	2	1526	12.8	3.2	18.6
72-73—Atlanta	74	2802	455	901	.505	283	526	.538	964	179	244	1	1193	13.0	2.4	16.1

Season Team	G	Min.	FGM	FGA	Pct.	FTM	FTA	Pct.	Off.	Def.	Tot.	Ast.	St.	Blk.	TO	Pts.	RPG	APG	PPG
											REBOUNDS							AVERAGES	
73-74—Atlanta	77	2440	389	801	.486	233	383	.608	264	476	740	189	52	48	...	1011	9.6	2.5	13.1
74-75—New Orleans	1	14	2	2	1.000	2	2	1.000	0	5	5	0	0	0	...	6	5.0	0.0	6.0
Totals	1043	38940	7914	15340	.516	5113	8088	.632	...	...	14241	2544	52	48	...	20941	13.7	2.4	20.1

Personal fouls/disqualifications: 1973-74, 232/2. 1974-75, 2/0. Totals, 3536/58.

NBA PLAYOFF RECORD

Season Team	G	Min.	FGM	FGA	Pct.	FTM	FTA	Pct.	Reb.	Ast.	PF	Dq.	Pts.	RPG	APG	PPG
64-65—Baltimore	10	427	74	158	.468	61	92	.663	151	34	38	0	209	15.1	3.4	20.9
66-67—New York	4	157	28	54	.519	17	29	.586	66	12	12	0	73	16.5	3.0	18.3
67-68—New York	6	177	56	106	.528	60	70	.866	27	27	22	0	120	16.0	3.5	20.0
69-70—Atlanta	9	368	59	126	.468	33	46	.717	140	35	32	0	151	15.6	3.9	16.8
70-71—Atlanta	5	216	41	69	.594	22	29	.759	72	10	16	0	104	14.4	2.0	20.8
71-72—Atlanta	6	247	42	86	.488	27	43	.628	82	11	20	0	111	13.7	1.8	18.5
72-73—Atlanta	6	247	34	86	.395	14	31	.452	73	13	17	0	82	12.2	2.2	13.7
Totals	46	1939	323	686	.471	204	318	.642	680	136	160	0	850	14.8	3.0	18.5

NBA ALL-STAR GAME RECORD

Season Team	Min.	FGM	FGA	Pct.	FTM	FTA	Pct.	Reb	Ast.	PF	Dq.	Pts.
1962—Chicago	29	10	18	.556	3	8	.375	17	1	6	1	23
1963—Chicago	14	1	4	.250	0	2	.000	1	2	3	0	2
1964—Baltimore	23	4	11	.364	3	5	.600	7	0	3	0	11
1965—Baltimore	17	4	5	.800	4	4	1.000	5	1	3	0	12
Totals	83	19	38	.500	10	19	.526	30	4	15	1	48

BING, DAVE   G

PERSONAL: Born November 24, 1943, in Washington, D.C. ... 6-3/185 (1,90/84). ... Full name: David Bing.
HIGH SCHOOL: Spingarn (Washington, D.C.).
COLLEGE: Syracuse.
TRANSACTIONS: Selected by Detroit Pistons in first round (second pick overall) of 1966 NBA Draft. ... Traded by Pistons with 1977 first-round draft choice to Washington Bullets for G Kevin Porter (August 28, 1975). ... Waived by Bullets (September 20, 1977). ... Signed as free agent by Boston Celtics (September 28, 1977).
CAREER HONORS: Elected to Naismith Memorial Basketball Hall of Fame (1990). ... One of the 50 Greatest Players in NBA History (1996).

COLLEGIATE RECORD

NOTES: THE SPORTING NEWS All-America first team (1966).

Season Team	G	Min.	FGM	FGA	Pct.	FTM	FTA	Pct.	Reb.	Ast.	Pts.	RPG	APG	PPG
62-63—Syracuse‡	17	...	170	341	.499	97	131	.740	192	...	437	11.3	...	25.7
63-64—Syracuse	25	...	215	460	.467	126	172	.733	206	...	556	8.2	...	22.2
64-65—Syracuse	23	...	206	444	.464	121	162	.747	277	...	533	12.0	...	23.2
65-66—Syracuse	28	...	308	569	.541	178	222	.802	303	...	794	10.8	...	28.4
Varsity totals	76	...	729	1473	.495	425	556	.764	786	...	1883	10.3	...	24.8

NBA REGULAR-SEASON RECORD

HONORS: NBA Rookie of the Year (1967). ... All-NBA first team (1968, 1971). ... All-NBA second team (1974). ... NBA All-Rookie team (1967). ... J. Walter Kennedy Citizenship Award (1977).

Season Team	G	Min.	FGM	FGA	Pct.	FTM	FTA	Pct.	Reb.	Ast.	PF	Dq.	Pts.	AVERAGES		
														RPG	APG	PPG
66-67—Detroit	80	2762	664	1522	.436	273	370	.738	359	330	217	2	1601	4.5	4.1	20.0
67-68—Detroit	79	3209	*835	*1893	.441	472	668	.707	373	509	254	2	*2142	4.7	6.4	*27.1
68-69—Detroit	77	3039	678	1594	.425	444	623	.713	382	546	256	3	1800	5.0	7.1	23.4
69-70—Detroit	70	2334	575	1295	.444	454	580	.783	299	418	196	0	1604	4.3	6.0	22.9
70-71—Detroit	82	3065	799	1710	.467	*615	*772	.797	364	408	228	4	2213	4.4	5.0	27.0
71-72—Detroit	45	1936	369	891	.414	278	354	.785	186	317	138	3	1016	4.1	7.0	22.6
72-73—Detroit	82	3361	692	1545	.448	456	560	.814	298	637	229	1	1840	3.6	7.8	22.4

Season Team	G	Min.	FGM	FGA	Pct.	FTM	FTA	Pct.	REBOUNDS			Ast.	St.	Blk.	TO	Pts.	AVERAGES		
									Off.	Def.	Tot.						RPG	APG	PPG
73-74—Detroit	81	3124	582	1336	.436	356	438	.813	108	173	281	555	109	17	...	1520	3.5	6.9	18.8
74-75—Detroit	79	3222	578	1333	.434	343	424	.809	86	200	286	610	116	26	...	1499	3.6	7.7	19.0
75-76—Washington	82	2945	497	1113	.447	332	422	.787	94	143	237	492	118	23	...	1326	2.9	6.0	16.2
76-77—Washington	64	1516	271	597	.454	136	176	.773	54	89	143	275	61	5	...	678	2.2	4.3	10.6
77-78—Boston	80	2256	422	940	.449	244	296	.824	76	136	212	300	79	18	216	1088	2.7	3.8	13.6
Totals	901	32769	6962	15769	.441	4403	5683	.775	...		3420	5397	483	89	216	18327	3.8	6.0	20.3

Personal fouls/disqualifications: 1973-74, 216/1. 1974-75, 222/3. 1975-76, 262/0. 1976-77, 150/1. 1977-78, 247/2. Totals, 2615/22.

NBA PLAYOFF RECORD

Season Team	G	Min.	FGM	FGA	Pct.	FTM	FTA	Pct.	REBOUNDS			Ast.	St.	Blk.	TO	Pts.	AVERAGES		
									Off.	Def.	Tot.						RPG	APG	PPG
67-68—Detroit	6	254	68	166	.410	33	45	.733	...	...	24	29	...	...	...	169	4.0	4.8	28.2
73-74—Detroit	7	312	55	131	.420	22	30	.733	6	20	26	42	3	1	...	132	3.7	6.0	18.9
74-75—Detroit	3	134	20	47	.426	8	13	.615	3	8	11	29	5	0	...	48	3.7	9.7	16.0
75-76—Washington	7	209	34	76	.447	28	35	.800	6	12	18	28	7	2	...	96	2.6	4.0	13.7
76-77—Washington	8	55	14	32	.438	4	4	1.000	3	3	6	5	0	1	...	32	0.8	0.6	4.0
Totals	31	964	191	452	.423	95	127	.748	...		85	133	15	4	...	477	2.7	4.3	15.4

Personal fouls/disqualifications: 1967-68, 21/0. 1973-74, 20/0. 1974-75, 12/0. 1975-76, 18/0. 1976-77, 5/0. Totals, 76/0.

NBA ALL-STAR GAME RECORD

NOTES: NBA All-Star Game Most Valuable Player (1976).

Season Team	Min.	FGM	FGA	Pct.	FTM	FTA	Pct.	Reb	Ast.	PF	Dq.	Pts.
1968—Detroit	20	4	7	.571	1	1	1.000	2	4	3	0	9
1969—Detroit	13	1	3	.333	1	1	1.000	0	3	0	0	3
1971—Detroit	19	2	7	.286	0	0	...	2	2	1	0	4
1973—Detroit	19	0	4	.000	2	2	1.000	3	0	1	0	2

Season Team	Min.	FGM	FGA	Pct.	FTM	FTA	Pct.	REBOUNDS			Ast.	PF	Dq.	St.	Blk.	TO	Pts.
								Off.	Def.	Tot.							
1974—Detroit	16	2	9	.222	1	1	1.000	1	5	6	2	1	0	0	0	...	5
1975—Detroit	12	0	2	.000	2	2	1.000	0	0	0	1	0	0	0	0	...	2
1976—Washington	26	7	11	.636	2	2	1.000	1	2	3	4	1	0	0	0	...	16
Totals	125	16	43	.372	9	9	1.000			16	16	7	0	0	0	...	41

BIRD, LARRY

PERSONAL: Born December 7, 1956, in West Baden, Ind. ... 6-9/220 (2,05/99,8). ... Full name: Larry Joe Bird.

HIGH SCHOOL: Springs Valley (French Lick, Ind.).

COLLEGE: Indiana, then Northwood Institute (Ind.), then Indiana State.

TRANSACTIONS/CAREER NOTES: Selected after junior season by Boston Celtics in first round (sixth pick overall) of 1978 NBA Draft. ... Announced retirement (August 18, 1992).

CAREER NOTES: President of Basketball Operations, Indiana Pacers (July 11, 2003-present).

CAREER HONORS: Elected to Naismith Memorial Basketball Hall of Fame (1998). ... One of the 50 Greatest Players in NBA History (1996).

MISCELLANEOUS: Member of NBA championship team (1981, 1984, 1986). ... Member of gold-medal-winning U.S. Olympic team (1992). ... Boston Celtics all-time steals leader with 1,556 (1979-80 through 1991-92).

COLLEGIATE RECORD

NOTES: THE SPORTING NEWS College Player of the Year (1979). ... Naismith Award winner (1979). ... Wooden Award winner (1979). ... THE SPORTING NEWS All-America first team (1978, 1979).

Season Team	G	Min.	FGM	FGA	Pct.	FTM	FTA	Pct.	Reb.	Ast.	Pts.	AVERAGES		
												RPG	APG	PPG
74-75—Indiana						Did not play.								
75-76—Indiana State						Did not play—transfer student.								
76-77—Indiana State	28	1033	375	689	.544	168	200	.840	373	122	918	13.3	4.4	32.8
77-78—Indiana State	32	...	403	769	.524	153	193	.793	369	125	959	11.5	3.9	30.0
78-79—Indiana State	34	...	376	707	.532	221	266	.831	505	187	973	14.9	5.5	28.6
Totals	94	...	1154	2165	.533	542	659	.822	1247	434	2850	13.3	4.6	30.3

NBA REGULAR-SEASON RECORD

HONORS: NBA Most Valuable Player (1984, 1985, 1986). ... NBA Rookie of the Year (1980). ... All-NBA first team (1980, 1981, 1982, 1983, 1984, 1985, 1986, 1987, 1988). ... All-NBA second team (1990). ... NBA All-Defensive second team (1982, 1983, 1984). ... NBA All-Rookie team (1980). ... Long Distance Shootout winner (1986, 1987, 1988).

Season Team	G	Min.	FGM	FGA	Pct.	FTM	FTA	Pct.	REBOUNDS			Ast.	St.	Blk.	TO	Pts.	AVERAGES		
									Off.	Def.	Tot.						RPG	APG	PPG
79-80—Boston	82	2955	693	1463	.474	301	360	.836	216	636	852	370	143	53	263	1745	10.4	4.5	21.3
80-81—Boston	82	3239	719	1503	.478	283	328	.863	191	704	895	451	161	63	289	1741	10.9	5.5	21.2
81-82—Boston	77	2923	711	1414	.503	328	380	.863	200	637	837	447	143	66	254	1761	10.9	5.8	22.9
82-83—Boston	79	2982	747	1481	.504	351	418	.840	193	677	870	458	148	71	240	1867	11.0	5.8	23.6
83-84—Boston	79	3028	758	1542	.492	374	421	*.888	181	615	796	520	144	69	237	1908	10.1	6.6	24.2
84-85—Boston	80	3161	918	1760	.522	403	457	.882	164	678	842	531	129	98	248	2295	10.5	6.6	28.7
85-86—Boston	82	3113	796	1606	.496	441	492	*.896	190	615	805	557	166	51	266	2115	9.8	6.8	25.8
86-87—Boston	74	3005	786	1497	.525	414	455	*.910	124	558	682	566	135	70	240	2076	9.2	7.6	28.1

Season Team	G	Min.	FGM	FGA	Pct.	FTM	FTA	Pct.	Off.	Def.	Tot.	Ast.	St.	Blk.	TO	Pts.	RPG	APG	PPG
87-88—Boston	76	2965	881	1672	.527	415	453	.916	108	595	703	467	125	57	213	2275	9.3	6.1	29.9
88-89—Boston	6	189	49	104	.471	18	19	.947	1	36	37	29	6	5	11	116	6.2	4.8	19.3
89-90—Boston	75	2944	718	1517	.473	319	343	*.930	90	622	712	562	106	61	243	1820	9.5	7.5	24.3
90-91—Boston	60	2277	462	1017	.454	163	183	.891	53	456	509	431	108	58	187	1164	8.5	7.2	19.4
91-92—Boston	45	1662	353	758	.466	150	162	.926	46	388	434	306	42	33	125	908	9.6	6.8	20.2
Totals	897	34443	8591	17334	.496	3960	4471	.886	1757	7217	8974	5695	1556	755	2816	21791	10.0	6.3	24.3

Three-point field goals: 1979-80, 58-for-143 (.406). 1980-81, 20-for-74 (.270). 1981-82, 11-for-52 (.212). 1982-83, 22-for-77 (.286). 1983-84, 18-for-73 (.247). 1984-85, 56-for-131 (.427). 1985-86, 82-for-194 (.423). 1986-87, 90-for-225 (.400). 1987-88, 98-for-237 (.414). 1989-90, 65-for-195 (.333). 1990-91, 77-for-196 (.389). 1991-92, 52-for-128 (.406). Totals, 649-for-1727 (.376).

Personal fouls/disqualifications: 1979-80, 279/4. 1980-81, 239/2. 1981-82, 244/0. 1982-83, 197/0. 1983-84, 197/0. 1984-85, 208/0. 1985-86, 182/0. 1986-87, 185/3. 1987-88, 157/0. 1988-89, 18/0. 1989-90, 173/2. 1990-91, 118/0. 1991-92, 82/0. Totals, 2279/11.

NBA PLAYOFF RECORD

NOTES: NBA Finals Most Valuable Player (1984, 1986). ... Holds career playoff record for most defensive rebounds—1,323.

Season Team	G	Min.	FGM	FGA	Pct.	FTM	FTA	Pct.	Off.	Def.	Tot.	Ast.	St.	Blk.	TO	Pts.	RPG	APG	PPG
79-80—Boston	9	372	83	177	.469	22	25	.880	22	79	101	42	14	8	33	192	11.2	4.7	21.3
80-81—Boston	17	750	147	313	.470	76	85	.894	49	189	238	103	39	17	62	373	14.0	6.1	21.9
81-82—Boston	12	490	88	206	.427	37	45	.822	33	117	150	67	23	17	38	214	12.5	5.6	17.8
82-83—Boston	6	240	49	116	.422	24	29	.828	20	55	75	41	13	3	19	123	12.5	6.8	20.5
83-84—Boston	23	961	229	437	.524	167	190	.879	62	190	252	136	54	27	87	632	11.0	5.9	27.5
84-85—Boston	20	815	196	425	.461	121	136	.890	53	129	182	115	34	19	57	520	9.1	5.8	26.0
85-86—Boston	18	770	171	331	.517	101	109	.927	34	134	168	148	37	11	47	466	9.3	8.2	25.9
86-87—Boston	23	1015	216	454	.476	176	193	.912	41	190	231	165	27	19	71	622	10.0	7.2	27.0
87-88—Boston	17	763	152	338	.450	101	113	.894	29	121	150	115	36	14	49	417	8.8	6.8	24.5
89-90—Boston	5	207	44	99	.444	29	32	.906	7	39	46	44	5	5	18	122	9.2	8.8	24.4
90-91—Boston	10	396	62	152	.408	44	51	.863	8	64	72	65	13	3	19	171	7.2	6.5	17.1
91-92—Boston	4	107	21	42	.500	3	4	.750	2	16	18	21	1	2	6	45	4.5	5.3	11.3
Totals	164	6886	1458	3090	.472	901	1012	.890	360	1323	1683	1062	296	145	506	3897	10.3	6.5	23.8

Three-point field goals: 1979-80, 4-for-15 (.267). 1980-81, 3-for-8 (.375). 1981-82, 1-for-6 (.167). 1982-83, 1-for-4 (.250). 1983-84, 7-for-17 (.412). 1984-85, 7-for-25 (.280). 1985-86, 23-for-56 (.411). 1986-87, 14-for-41 (.341). 1987-88, 12-for-32 (.375). 1989-90, 5-for-19 (.263). 1990-91, 3-for-21 (.143). 1991-92, 0-for-5. Totals, 89-for-249 (.321).

Personal fouls/disqualifications: 1979-80, 30/0. 1980-81, 53/0. 1981-82, 43/0. 1982-83, 15/0. 1983-84, 71/0. 1984-85, 54/0. 1985-86, 55/0. 1986-87, 55/1. 1987-88, 45/0. 1989-90, 10/0. 1990-91, 28/0. 1991-92, 7/0. Totals, 466/1.

NBA ALL-STAR GAME RECORD

NOTES: NBA All-Star Game Most Valuable Player (1982).

Season Team	Min.	FGM	FGA	Pct.	FTM	FTA	Pct.	Off.	Def.	Tot.	Ast.	PF	Dq.	St.	Blk.	TO	Pts.
1980—Boston	23	3	6	.500	0	0	...	3	3	6	7	1	0	1	0	3	7
1981—Boston	18	1	5	.200	0	0	...	1	3	4	3	1	0	1	0	2	2
1982—Boston	28	7	12	.583	5	8	.625	0	12	12	5	3	0	1	1	4	19
1983—Boston	29	7	14	.500	0	0	...	3	10	13	7	4	0	2	0	5	14
1984—Boston	33	6	18	.333	4	4	1.000	1	6	7	2	1	0	0	0	0	16
1985—Boston	31	8	18	.000	5	5	.833	5	3	8	2	3	0	1	4	21	
1986—Boston	35	8	18	.444	5	6	.833	2	6	8	5	5	0	7	0	4	23
1987—Boston	35	7	18	.389	4	4	1.000	2	4	6	5	5	0	2	0	2	18
1988—Boston	32	2	8	.250	2	2	1.000	0	7	7	1	4	0	4	1	2	6
1990—Boston	23	3	8	.375	2	2	1.000	2	6	8	3	1	0	3	0	3	8
1991—Boston							Selected, did not play—injured.										
1992—Boston							Selected, did not play—injured.										
Totals	287	52	123	.423	27	32	.844	19	60	79	41	28	0	23	3	31	134

Three-point field goals: 1980, 1-for-2 (.500). 1983, 0-for-1. 1985, 0-for-1. 1986, 2-for-4 (.500). 1987, 0-for-3. 1988, 0-for-1. 1990, 0-for-1. Totals, 3-for-13 (.231).

HEAD COACHING RECORD

BACKGROUND: Special assistant, Boston Celtics (1992-93 through 1996-97).

NBA COACHING RECORD

HONORS: NBA Coach of the Year (1998).

Season Team	REGULAR SEASON					PLAYOFFS		
	W	L	Pct.	Finish		W	L	Pct.
97-98—Indiana	58	24	.707	2nd/Central Division		10	6	.625
98-99—Indiana	33	17	.660	1st/Central Division		9	4	.692
99-00—Indiana	56	26	.683	1st/Central Division		13	10	.565
Totals (3 years)	147	67	.687	Totals (3 years)		32	20	.615

NOTES:

1998—Defeated Cleveland, 3-1, in Eastern Conference First Round; defeated New York, 4-1, in Eastern Conference Semifinals; lost to Chicago, 4-3, in Eastern Conference Finals.

1999—Defeated Milwaukee, 3-0, in Eastern Conference First Round; defeated Philadelphia, 4-0, in Eastern Conference Semifinals; lost to New York, 4-2, in Eastern Conference Finals.

2000—Defeated Milwaukee, 3-2, in Eastern Conference First Round; defeated Philadelphia, 4-2, in Eastern Conference Semifinals; defeated New York, 4-2, in Eastern Conference Finals; lost to Los Angeles Lakers, 4-2, in NBA Finals.

BLACKMAN, ROLANDO   G

PERSONAL: Born February 26, 1959, in Panama City, Panama. ... 6-6/206 (1,98/93,4). ... Full name: Rolando Antonio Blackman. ... Name pronounced roll-ON-doe.
HIGH SCHOOL: William E. Grady Vocational Technical School (Brooklyn, N.Y.).
COLLEGE: Kansas State.
TRANSACTIONS: Selected by Dallas Mavericks in first round (ninth pick overall) of 1981 NBA Draft. ... Traded by

Mavericks to New York Knicks for 1995 first-round draft choice (June 24, 1992). ... Waived by Knicks (July 4, 1994). ... Played in Greece (1994-95). ... Played in Italy (1995-96).

CAREER NOTES: Player development, Dallas Mavericks (2000-06). ... Assistant coach, Dallas Mavericks (2006-present).

MISCELLANEOUS: Member of U.S. Olympic team (1980). ... Dallas Mavericks all-time leading scorer with 16,643 points (1981-82 through 1991-92).

COLLEGIATE RECORD

NOTES: THE SPORTING NEWS All-America first team (1981).

Season Team	G	Min.	FGM	FGA	Pct.	FTM	FTA	Pct.	Reb.	Ast.	Pts.	RPG	APG	PPG
77-78—Kansas State	29	967	127	269	.472	61	93	.656	187	45	315	6.4	1.6	10.9
78-79—Kansas State	28	1056	200	392	.510	83	113	.735	110	79	483	3.9	2.8	17.3
79-80—Kansas State	31	1103	226	419	.539	100	145	.690	145	97	552	4.7	3.1	17.8
80-81—Kansas State	33	1239	202	380	.532	90	115	.783	165	102	494	5.0	3.1	15.0
Totals	121	4365	755	1460	.517	334	466	.717	607	323	1844	5.0	2.7	15.2

NBA REGULAR-SEASON RECORD

Season Team	G	Min.	FGM	FGA	Pct.	FTM	FTA	Pct.	Off.	Def.	Tot.	Ast.	St.	Blk.	TO	Pts.	RPG	APG	PPG
81-82—Dallas	82	1979	439	855	.513	212	276	.768	97	157	254	105	46	30	113	1091	3.1	1.3	13.3
82-83—Dallas	75	2349	513	1042	.492	297	381	.780	108	185	293	185	37	29	118	1326	3.9	2.5	17.7
83-84—Dallas	81	3025	721	1320	.546	372	458	.812	124	249	373	288	56	37	169	1815	4.6	3.6	22.4
84-85—Dallas	81	2834	625	1230	.508	342	413	.828	107	193	300	289	61	16	162	1598	3.7	3.6	19.7
85-86—Dallas	82	2787	677	1318	.514	404	483	.836	88	203	291	271	79	25	189	1762	3.5	3.3	21.5
86-87—Dallas	80	2758	626	1264	.495	419	474	.884	96	182	278	266	64	21	174	1676	3.5	3.3	21.0
87-88—Dallas	71	2580	497	1050	.473	331	379	.873	82	164	246	262	64	18	144	1325	3.5	3.7	18.7
88-89—Dallas	78	2946	594	1249	.476	316	370	.854	70	203	273	288	65	20	165	1534	3.5	3.7	19.7
89-90—Dallas	80	2934	626	1256	.498	287	340	.844	88	192	280	289	77	21	174	1552	3.5	3.6	19.4
90-91—Dallas	80	2965	634	1316	.482	282	326	.865	63	193	256	301	69	19	159	1590	3.2	3.8	19.9
91-92—Dallas	75	2527	535	1161	.461	239	266	.899	78	161	239	204	50	22	153	1374	3.2	2.7	18.3
92-93—New York	60	1434	239	539	.443	71	90	.789	23	79	102	157	22	10	65	580	1.7	2.6	9.7
93-94—New York	55	969	161	369	.436	48	53	.906	23	70	93	76	25	6	44	400	1.7	1.4	7.3
Totals	980	32087	6887	13969	.493	3620	4309	.840	1047	2231	3278	2981	715	274	1829	17623	3.3	3.0	18.0

Three-point field goals: 1981-82, 1-for-4 (.250). 1982-83, 3-for-15 (.200). 1983-84, 1-for-11 (.091). 1984-85, 6-for-20 (.300). 1985-86, 4-for-29 (.138). 1986-87, 5-for-15 (.333). 1987-88, 0-for-5. 1988-89, 30-for-85 (.353). 1989-90, 13-for-43 (.302). 1990-91, 40-for-114 (.351). 1991-92, 65-for-169 (.385). 1992-93, 31-for-73 (.425). 1993-94, 30-for-84 (.357). Totals, 229-for-667 (.343).

Personal fouls/disqualifications: 1981-82, 122/0. 1982-83, 116/0. 1983-84, 127/0. 1984-85, 96/0. 1985-86, 138/0. 1986-87, 142/0. 1987-88, 112/0. 1988-89, 137/0. 1989-90, 128/0. 1990-91, 153/0. 1991-92, 134/0. 1992-93, 129/1. 1993-94, 100/0. Totals, 1634/1.

NBA PLAYOFF RECORD

Season Team	G	Min.	FGM	FGA	Pct.	FTM	FTA	Pct.	Off.	Def.	Tot.	Ast.	St.	Blk.	TO	Pts.	RPG	APG	PPG
83-84—Dallas	10	397	93	175	.531	53	63	.841	15	26	41	40	6	4	24	239	4.1	4.0	23.9
84-85—Dallas	4	169	47	92	.511	36	38	.947	11	15	26	19	2	2	14	131	6.5	4.8	32.8
85-86—Dallas	10	371	83	167	.497	42	53	.792	15	20	35	32	8	1	20	208	3.5	3.2	20.8
86-87—Dallas	4	153	36	73	.493	22	24	.917	4	10	14	17	2	0	8	94	3.5	4.3	23.5
87-88—Dallas	17	672	126	261	.483	55	62	.887	26	29	55	77	15	3	25	307	3.2	4.5	18.1
89-90—Dallas	3	127	24	54	.444	10	10	1.000	2	7	9	13	6	2	13	60	3.0	4.3	20.0
92-93—New York	15	214	22	64	.344	15	18	.833	4	13	17	16	3	2	21	63	1.1	1.1	4.2
93-94—New York	6	34	3	11	.273	0	0	...	1	2	3	3	0	0	1	8	0.5	0.5	1.3
Totals	69	2137	434	897	.484	233	268	.869	78	122	200	217	42	14	126	1110	2.9	3.1	16.1

Three-point field goals: 1984-85, 1-for-2 (.500). 1985-86, 0-for-1. 1986-87, 0-for-1. 1987-88, 0-for-3. 1989-90, 2-for-5 (.400). 1992-93, 4-for-15 (.267). 1993-94, 2-for-4 (.500). Totals, 9-for-31 (.290).

Personal fouls/disqualifications: 1983-84, 15/0. 1984-85, 8/0. 1985-86, 26/1. 1986-87, 7/0. 1987-88, 28/0. 1989-90, 7/0. 1992-93, 22/0. 1993-94, 6/0. Totals, 119/1.

NBA ALL-STAR GAME RECORD

Season Team	Min.	FGM	FGA	Pct.	FTM	FTA	Pct.	Off.	Def.	Tot.	Ast.	PF	Dq.	St.	Blk.	TO	Pts.
1985—Dallas	23	7	14	.500	1	2	.500	1	2	3	2	1	0	1	1	0	15
1986—Dallas	22	6	11	.545	0	0	...	1	3	4	8	1	0	2	1	1	12
1987—Dallas	22	9	15	.600	11	13	.846	1	3	4	1	2	0	0	0	2	29
1990—Dallas	21	7	9	.778	1	1	1.000	1	1	2	2	1	0	2	0	2	15
Totals	88	29	49	.592	13	16	.813	4	9	13	13	5	0	5	2	5	71

GREEK LEAGUE RECORD

Season Team	G	Min.	FGM	FGA	Pct.	FTM	FTA	Pct.	Reb.	Ast.	Pts.	RPG	APG	PPG
94-95—A.E.K.	14	...	69	150	.460	55	63	.873	...	19	265	...	1.4	18.9

ITALIAN LEAGUE RECORD

Season Team	G	Min.	FGM	FGA	Pct.	FTM	FTA	Pct.	Reb.	Ast.	Pts.	RPG	APG	PPG
95-96—Stefanel Milano	24	762	141	302	.467	55	64	.859	62	19	382	2.6	0.8	15.9

BLAYLOCK, MOOKIE   G

PERSONAL: Born March 20, 1967, in Garland, Texas. ... 6-1/185. (1,85/83,9). ... Full Name: Daron Oshay Blaylock.
HIGH SCHOOL: Garland (Texas).
JUNIOR COLLEGE: Midland (Texas) College.
COLLEGE: Oklahoma.
TRANSACTIONS/CAREER NOTES: Selected by New Jersey Nets in first round (12th pick overall) of 1989 NBA Draft. ... Traded by Nets with F Roy Hinson to Atlanta Hawks for G Rumeal Robinson (November 3, 1992). ... Traded by Hawks with 1999 first-round draft choice to Golden State Warriors for G Bimbo Coles, F Duane Ferrell and 1999 first-round draft choice (June 29, 1999).

MISCELLANEOUS: Atlanta Hawks franchise all-time steals leader with 1,321 (1992-93 through 1998-99).

COLLEGIATE RECORD

NOTES: THE SPORTING NEWS All-America second team (1989). ... Holds NCAA Division I career record for for most steals per game—3.8. ... Holds NCAA Division I single-season record for most steals—150 (1988). ... Holds NCAA Division I single-game record for most steals—13 (December 12, 1987, vs. Centenary; and December 17, 1988, vs. Loyola Marymount).

Season Team	G	Min.	FGM	FGA	Pct.	FTM	FTA	Pct.	Reb.	Ast.	Pts.	RPG	APG	PPG
85-86—Midland College	34	...	254	449	.566	62	84	.738	109	158	570	3.2	4.6	16.8
86-87—Midland College	33	...	258	500	.516	60	83	.723	138	161	647	4.2	4.9	19.6
87-88—Oklahoma	39	1347	241	524	.460	78	114	.684	162	232	638	4.2	5.9	16.4
88-89—Oklahoma	35	1359	272	598	.455	65	100	.650	164	233	700	4.7	6.7	20.0
Junior College Totals	67	...	512	949	.540	122	167	.731	247	319	1217	3.7	4.8	18.2
4-Year-College Totals	74	2706	513	1122	.457	143	214	.668	326	465	1338	4.4	6.3	18.1

Three-point field goals: 1987-88, 78-for-201 (.388). 1988-89, 91-for-245 (.371). Totals, 169-for-446 (.379).

NBA REGULAR-SEASON RECORD

RECORDS: Shares career record for most consecutive seasons leading league in steals—2 (1996-97 and 1997-98).
HONORS: NBA All-Defensive first team (1994, 1995). ... NBA All-Defensive second team (1996, 1997, 1998, 1999).
NOTES: Led NBA with 2.72 steals per game (1997) and 2.61 steals per game (1998).

Season Team	G	Min.	FGM	FGA	Pct.	FTM	FTA	Pct.	Off.	Def.	Tot.	Ast.	St.	Blk.	TO	Pts.	RPG	APG	PPG
89-90—New Jersey	50	1267	212	571	.371	63	81	.778	42	98	140	210	82	14	111	505	2.8	4.2	10.1
90-91—New Jersey	72	2585	432	1039	.416	139	176	.790	67	182	249	441	169	40	207	1017	3.5	6.1	14.1
91-92—New Jersey	72	2548	429	993	.432	126	177	.712	101	168	269	492	170	40	152	996	3.7	6.8	13.8
92-93—Atlanta	80	2820	414	964	.429	123	169	.728	89	191	280	671	203	23	187	1069	3.5	8.4	13.4
93-94—Atlanta	81	2915	444	1079	.411	116	159	.730	117	307	424	789	212	44	196	1118	5.2	9.7	13.8
94-95—Atlanta	80	3069	509	1198	.425	156	214	.729	117	276	393	616	200	26	242	1373	4.9	7.7	17.2
95-96—Atlanta	81	2893	455	1123	.405	127	170	.747	110	222	332	478	212	17	188	1268	4.1	5.9	15.7
96-97—Atlanta	78	3056	501	1159	.432	131	174	.753	114	299	413	463	*212	20	185	1354	5.3	5.9	17.4
97-98—Atlanta	70	2700	368	938	.392	95	134	.709	81	260	341	469	*183	21	176	921	4.9	6.7	13.2
98-99—Atlanta	48	1763	247	651	.379	69	91	.758	45	179	224	278	99	9	115	640	4.7	5.8	13.3
99-00—Golden State	73	2459	327	837	.391	67	95	.705	55	215	270	489	146	22	143	822	3.7	6.7	11.3
00-01—Golden State	69	2352	317	801	.396	53	76	.697	71	201	272	462	163	20	128	760	3.9	6.7	11.0
01-02—Golden State	35	599	50	146	.342	4	8	.500	8	44	52	114	24	4	37	119	1.5	3.3	3.4
Totals	889	31026	4705	11499	.409	1269	1724	.736	1017	2642	3659	5972	2075	300	2067	11962	4.1	6.7	13.5

Three-point field goals: 1989-90, 18-for-80 (.225). 1990-91, 14-for-91 (.154). 1991-92, 12-for-54 (.222). 1992-93, 118-for-315 (.375). 1993-94, 114-for-341 (.334). 1994-95, 199-for-555 (.359). 1995-96, 231-for-623 (.371). 1996-97, 221-for-604 (.366). 1997-98, 90-for-334 (.269). 1998-99, 77-for-251 (.307). 1999-00, 101-for-301 (.336). 2000-01, 73-for-225 (.324). 2001-02, 15-for-42 (.357). Totals, 1283-for-3816 (.336).

Personal fouls/disqualifications: 1989-90, 110/0. 1990-91, 180/0. 1991-92, 182/1. 1992-93, 156/0. 1993-94, 144/0. 1994-95, 164/3. 1995-96, 151/1. 1996-97, 141/0. 1997-98, 122/0. 1998-99, 61/0. 1999-00, 122/0. 2000-01, 134/1. 2001-02, 20/0. Totals, 1687/6.

NBA PLAYOFF RECORD

Season Team	G	Min.	FGM	FGA	Pct.	FTM	FTA	Pct.	Off.	Def.	Tot.	Ast.	St.	Blk.	TO	Pts.	RPG	APG	PPG
91-92—New Jersey	4	148	17	55	.309	3	4	.750	5	11	16	31	15	2	7	39	4.0	7.8	9.8
92-93—Atlanta	3	99	8	18	.444	3	4	.668	4	9	13	13	3	4	11	27	4.3	4.3	9.0
93-94—Atlanta	11	415	48	141	.340	25	30	.833	16	39	55	98	24	5	32	143	5.0	8.9	13.0
94-95—Atlanta	3	121	18	49	.367	7	11	.636	7	6	13	17	4	0	9	54	4.3	5.7	18.0
95-96—Atlanta	10	426	61	145	.421	16	24	.667	13	30	43	64	22	8	29	171	4.3	6.4	17.1
96-97—Atlanta	10	441	61	154	.396	14	21	.667	12	58	70	65	21	2	35	164	7.0	6.5	16.4
97-98—Atlanta	4	153	22	53	.415	7	12	.583	6	14	20	33	9	1	9	59	5.0	8.3	14.8
98-99—Atlanta	9	358	44	135	.326	7	15	.467	6	30	36	36	18	2	30	113	4.0	4.0	12.6
Totals	54	2161	280	757	.370	84	123	.683	67	199	266	357	116	24	162	769	4.9	6.6	14.2

Three-point field goals: 1991-92, 2-for-8 (.250). 1992-93, 1-for-6 (.167). 1992-93, 4-for-12 (.333). 1993-94, 22-for-64 (.344). 1994-95, 11-for-28 (.393). 1995-96, 33-for-84 (.393). 1996-97, 28-for-85 (.329). 1997-98, 8-for-27 (.296). 1998-99, 18-for-51 (.353). Totals, 125-for-357 (.350).

Personal fouls/disqualifications: 1991-92, 16/0. 1992-93, 9/0. 1993-94, 22/0. 1994-95, 6/0. 1995-96, 15/0. 1996-97, 15/0. 1997-98, 8/0. 1998-99, 11/0. Totals, 102/0.

NBA ALL-STAR GAME RECORD

Season Team	Min.	FGM	FGA	Pct.	FTM	FTA	Pct.	Off.	Def.	Tot.	Ast.	PF	Dq.	St.	Blk.	TO	Pts.
1994—Atlanta	16	2	5	.400	0	0	...	0	1	1	2	3	0	0	0	1	5

Three-point field goals: 1994, 1-for-2 (.500).

BOONE, RON   G

PERSONAL: Born September 6, 1946, in Oklahoma City. ... 6-2/200 (1,88/90,7). ... Full name: Ronald Bruce Boone.
HIGH SCHOOL: Tech (Omaha, Neb.).
JUNIOR COLLEGE: Iowa Western Community College.
COLLEGE: Idaho State.
TRANSACTIONS: Selected by Phoenix Suns in 11th round (147th pick overall) of 1968 NBA Draft. ... Selected by Dallas Chaparrals in eighth round of 1968 ABA Draft. ... Traded by Chaparrals with G Glen Combs to Utah Stars for G Donnie Freeman and C Wayne Hightower (January 8, 1971). ... Contract sold by Stars to Spirits of St. Louis (December 2, 1975). ... Selected by Kansas City Kings of NBA from Spirits in ABA dispersal draft (August 5, 1976). ... Traded by Kings with 1979 second-round draft choice to Denver Nuggets for F Darnell Hillman and draft rights to G Mike Evans (June 26, 1978). ... Traded by Nuggets with two 1979 second-round draft choices to Los Angeles Lakers for G Charlie Scott (June 26, 1978). ... Traded by Lakers to Utah Jazz for 1981 third-round draft choice (October 25, 1979). ... Waived by Jazz (January 26, 1981).

COLLEGIATE RECORD

Season Team	G	Min.	FGM	FGA	Pct.	FTM	FTA	Pct.	Reb.	Ast.	Pts.	RPG	APG	PPG
64-65—Iowa Western C.C.	9	...	...	...	...	...	...	...	...	...	227	...	...	25.2
65-66—Idaho State	10	...	46	119	.387	17	26	.654	95	...	109	9.5	...	10.9

Season Team	G	Min.	FGM	FGA	Pct.	FTM	FTA	Pct.	Reb.	Ast.	Pts.	RPG	APG	PPG
66-67—Idaho State	25	...	199	416	.478	160	215	.744	128	...	558	5.1	...	22.3
67-68—Idaho State	26	...	223	519	.430	108	159	.679	110	...	554	4.2	...	21.3
Junior college totals	9	...	...	...	...	...	...	...	...	...	227	...	...	25.2
4-year-college totals	61	...	468	1054	.444	285	400	.713	333	...	1221	5.5	...	20.0

ABA REGULAR-SEASON RECORD

NOTES: ABA All-Star first team (1975). ... ABA All-Star second team (1974). ... ABA All-Rookie team (1969). ... Member of ABA championship team (1971).

Season Team	G	Min.	2-POINT FGM	FGA	Pct.	3-POINT FGM	FGA	Pct.	FTM	FTA	Pct.	Reb.	Ast.	Pts.	RPG	APG	PPG
68-69—Dallas	78	2682	518	1182	.438	2	15	.133	436	537	.812	394	279	1478	5.1	3.6	18.9
69-70—Dallas	84	2340	406	925	.439	17	55	.309	300	382	.785	366	272	1163	4.4	3.2	13.8
70-71—Dallas-Utah	86	2476	561	1257	.446	49	138	.355	278	357	.779	564	256	1547	6.6	3.0	18.0
71-72—Utah	84	2040	391	897	.436	13	65	.200	271	341	.795	393	233	1092	4.7	2.8	13.0
72-73—Utah	84	2585	556	1096	.507	10	40	.250	415	479	.866	423	353	1557	5.0	4.2	18.5
73-74—Utah	84	3098	581	1162	.500	6	26	.231	300	343	.875	435	417	1480	5.2	5.0	17.6
74-75—Utah	84	3414	862	1743	.495	10	33	.303	363	422	.860	406	372	2117	4.8	4.4	25.2
75-76—Utah-St. Louis	78	2961	697	1424	.489	16	43	.372	277	318	.871	319	387	1719	4.1	5.0	22.0
Totals	662	21596	4572	9686	.472	123	415	.296	2640	3179	.830	3300	2569	12153	5.0	3.9	18.4

ABA PLAYOFF RECORD

Season Team	G	Min.	2-POINT FGM	FGA	Pct.	3-POINT FGM	FGA	Pct.	FTM	FTA	Pct.	Reb.	Ast.	Pts.	RPG	APG	PPG
68-69—Dallas	7	196	38	81	.469	0	4	.000	21	25	.840	22	27	97	3.1	3.9	13.9
69-70—Dallas	6	193	43	89	.483	3	8	.375	15	21	.714	27	27	110	4.5	4.5	18.3
70-71—Utah	18	569	104	229	.454	9	27	.333	74	86	.860	110	94	309	6.1	5.2	17.2
71-72—Utah	11	209	49	100	.490	1	5	.200	25	29	.862	24	26	126	2.2	2.4	11.5
72-73—Utah	10	360	68	132	.515	0	3	.000	33	34	.971	43	47	169	4.3	4.7	16.9
73-74—Utah	18	747	137	282	.486	0	7	.000	34	37	.919	108	109	308	6.0	6.1	17.1
74-75—Utah	6	219	54	127	.425	0	0	...	34	38	.895	24	41	142	4.0	6.8	23.7
Totals	76	2493	493	1040	.474	13	54	.241	236	270	.874	358	371	1261	4.7	4.9	16.6

ABA ALL-STAR GAME RECORD

Season Team	Min.	2-POINT FGM	FGA	Pct.	3-POINT FGM	FGA	Pct.	FTM	FTA	Pct.	Reb.	Ast.	Pts.
1971—Utah	4	2	4	.500	0	0	...	2	3	.667	2	0	6
1974—Utah	24	6	11	.545	1	2	.500	0	0	...	3	5	15
1975—Utah	23	4	8	.500	0	0	...	2	2	1.000	2	2	10
1976—St. Louis	16	5	11	.455	0	0	...	0	0	...	3	2	10
Totals	67	17	34	.500	1	2	.500	4	5	.800	10	9	41

NBA REGULAR-SEASON RECORD

Season Team	G	Min.	FGM	FGA	Pct.	FTM	FTA	Pct.	Off.	Def.	Tot.	Ast.	St.	Blk.	TO	Pts.	RPG	APG	PPG
76-77—Kansas City	82	3021	747	1577	.474	324	384	.844	128	193	321	338	119	19	...	1818	3.9	4.1	22.2
77-78—Kansas City	82	2653	563	1271	.443	322	377	.854	112	157	269	311	105	11	303	1448	3.3	3.8	17.7
78-79—Los Angeles	82	1583	259	569	.455	90	104	.865	53	92	145	154	66	11	147	608	1.8	1.9	7.4
79-80—L.A.-Utah	81	2392	405	915	.443	175	196	.893	54	173	227	309	97	3	197	1004	2.8	3.8	12.4
80-81—Utah	52	1146	160	371	.431	75	94	.798	17	67	84	161	33	8	111	406	1.6	3.1	7.8
Totals	379	10795	2134	4703	.454	986	1155	.854	364	682	1046	1273	420	52	758	5284	2.8	3.4	13.9

Three-point field goals: 1979-80, 19-for-50 (.380). 1980-81, 11-for-39 (.282). Totals, 30-for-89 (.337).

Personal fouls/disqualifications: 1976-77, 258/1. 1977-78, 233/3. 1978-79, 171/1. 1979-80, 232/3. 1980-81, 126/0. Totals, 1020/8.

NBA PLAYOFF RECORD

Season Team	G	Min.	FGM	FGA	Pct.	FTM	FTA	Pct.	Off.	Def.	Tot.	Ast.	St.	Blk.	TO	Pts.	RPG	APG	PPG
78-79—Los Angeles	8	226	37	77	.481	20	21	.952	7	8	15	14	9	0	14	94	1.9	1.8	11.8

Personal fouls/disqualifications: 1978-79, 28/0.

COMBINED ABA AND NBA REGULAR-SEASON RECORDS

	G	Min.	FGM	FGA	Pct.	FTM	FTA	Pct.	Off.	Def.	Tot.	Ast.	Stl.	Blk.	TO	Pts.	RPG	APG	PPG
Totals	1041	32391	6829	14804	.461	3626	4334	.837	...	...	4346	3842	...	...	...	17437	4.2	3.7	16.8

Three-point field goals: 153-for-504 (.304).

BRIAN, FRANK G

PERSONAL: Born May 1, 1923, in Zachary, La. ... 6-1/180 (1,85/81,6). ... Full name: Frank Sands Brian. ... Nickname: Flash.
HIGH SCHOOL: Zachary (La.).
COLLEGE: Louisiana State.
TRANSACTIONS: Signed by Anderson of National Basketball League (1947). ... Selected by Chicago from Anderson in NBL dispersal draft (April 25, 1950). ... Traded by Chicago to Tri-Cities (1950). ... Traded by Tri-Cities to Fort Wayne for C/F Howie Schultz, F/C/G Dick Mehen and cash (May 31, 1951).
MISCELLANEOUS: Member of NBL championship team (1949).

COLLEGIATE RECORD

Season Team	G	Min.	FGM	FGA	Pct.	FTM	FTA	Pct.	Reb.	Ast.	Pts.	RPG	APG	PPG
42-43—Louisiana State	15	...	77	...	...	56	...	...	...	...	210	...	...	14.0
43-44—Louisiana State						Did not play—in military service.								

Season Team	G	Min.	FGM	FGA	Pct.	FTM	FTA	Pct.	Reb.	Ast.	Pts.	AVERAGES RPG	APG	PPG
44-45—Louisiana State..............						Did not play—in military service.								
45-46—Louisiana State..............						Did not play—in military service.								
46-47—Louisiana State..............	21	...	127			86	...	...	...	...	340	...	...	16.2
Totals	36	...	204	...	...	142	...	...	...	...	550	...	...	15.3

NBL AND NBA REGULAR-SEASON RECORD

HONORS: All-NBA second team (1950, 1951). ... All-NBL first team (1949). ... All-NBL second team (1948).

Season Team	G	Min.	FGM	FGA	Pct.	FTM	FTA	Pct.	Reb.	Ast.	PF	Dq.	Pts.	AVERAGES RPG	APG	PPG
47-48—And. (NBL)	59	...	248	...	...	155	210	.738	...	...	148	...	651	...	...	11.0
48-49—And. (NBL)	64	...	216	...	...	201	256	.785	...	...	144	...	633	...	...	9.9
49-50—Anderson	64	...	368	1156	.318	402	488	˄.824	...	189	192	...	1138	...	3.0	17.8
50-51—Tri-Cities	68	...	363	1127	.322	418	508	.823	244	266	215	4	1144	3.6	3.9	16.8
51-52—Fort Wayne	66	2672	342	972	.352	367	433	.848	232	233	220	6	1051	3.5	3.5	15.9
52-53—Fort Wayne	68	1910	245	699	.351	236	297	.795	133	142	205	8	726	2.0	2.1	10.7
53-54—Fort Wayne	64	973	132	352	.375	137	182	.753	79	92	100	2	401	1.2	1.4	6.3
54-55—Fort Wayne	71	1381	237	623	.380	217	255	.851	127	142	133	0	691	1.8	2.0	9.7
55-56—Fort Wayne	37	680	78	263	.297	72	88	.818	88	74	62	0	228	2.4	2.0	6.2
Totals	561	...	2229	...	...	2205	2717	.812	...	...	1419	...	6663	...	...	11.9

NBL AND NBA PLAYOFF RECORD

Season Team	G	Min.	FGM	FGA	Pct.	FTM	FTA	Pct.	Reb.	Ast.	PF	Dq.	Pts.	AVERAGES RPG	APG	PPG
47-48—And. (NBL)	6	...	18	...	...	11	16	.688	...	...	...	...	47	...	...	7.8
48-49—And. (NBL)	7	...	26	...	...	27	32	.844	...	...	...	...	79	...	...	11.3
49-50—Anderson	8	...	26	96	.271	43	48	.896	...	19	24	...	95	...	2.4	11.9
51-52—Fort Wayne	2	81	6	24	.250	5	6	.833	6	9	10	0	17	3.0	4.5	8.5
52-53—Fort Wayne	8	146	13	42	.310	19	25	.760	9	11	23	I	45	1.1	1.4	5.6
53-54—Fort Wayne	4	106	15	36	.417	11	16	.688	12	10	7	0	41	3.0	2.5	10.3
54-55—Fort Wayne	11	269	48	120	.400	31	38	.816	??	27	26	0	127	2.0	2.5	11.5
55-56—Fort Wayne	10	166	26	68	.382	17	21	.810	12	17	15	0	69	1.2	1.7	6.9
Totals.................................	56	...	178	...	...	164	202	.812	...	...	...	...	520	...	...	9.3

NBA ALL-STAR GAME RECORD

Season Team	Min.	FGM	FGA	Pct.	FTM	FTA	Pct.	Reb	Ast.	PF	Dq.	Pts.
1951—Tri-Cities	...	5	14	.357	4	5	.800	6	3	2	...	14
1952—Fort Wayne	25	4	10	.400	5	6	.833	7	4	2	...	13
Totals	...	9	24	.375	9	11	.818	13	7	4	...	27

BRIDGES, BILL   F

PERSONAL: Born April 4, 1939, in Hobbs, N.M. ... 6-6/235 (1,98/106,6). ... Full name: William C. Bridges.
HIGH SCHOOL: Hobbs (N.M.)
COLLEGE: Kansas.
TRANSACTIONS: Selected by Chicago Packers in third round (32nd pick overall) of 1961 NBA Draft. ... Played in American Basketball League with Kansas City Steers (1961-62 and 1962-63). ... Draft rights traded by Packers with G Ralph Davis to St. Louis Hawks for G Al Ferrari and F Shellie McMillion (June 14, 1962). ... Hawks franchise moved to Atlanta for 1968-69 season. ... Traded by Hawks to Philadelphia 76ers for F/C Jim Washington (November 19, 1971). ... Traded by 76ers with C/F Mel Counts to Los Angeles Lakers for F/C Leroy Ellis and F John Q. Trapp (November 2, 1972). ... Waived by Lakers (December 6, 1974). ... Signed as free agent by Golden State Warriors (March 1, 1975).
MISCELLANEOUS: Member of NBA championship team (1975).

COLLEGIATE RECORD

Season Team	G	Min.	FGM	FGA	Pct.	FTM	FTA	Pct.	Reb.	Ast.	Pts.	AVERAGES RPG	APG	PPG
57-58—Kansas‡						Freshman team did not play intercollegiate schedule.								
58-59—Kansas	25	...	117	307	.381	74	129	.574	343	...	308	13.7	...	12.3
59-60—Kansas	28	...	112	293	.382	94	142	.662	385	...	318	13.8	...	11.4
60-61—Kansas	25	...	146	334	.437	110	155	.710	353	...	402	14.1	...	16.1
Varsity totals	78	...	375	934	.401	278	426	.653	1081	...	1028	13.9	...	13.2

ABL REGULAR-SEASON RECORD

ABL: ABL All-Star first team (1962). ... Holds single-game record for most points—55 (December 9, 1962, vs. Oakland).

Season Team	G	Min.	FGM	FGA	Pct.	FTM	FTA	Pct.	Reb.	Ast.	Pts.	AVERAGES RPG	APG	PPG
61-62—Kansas City	79	3259	638	1400	.456	412	587	.702	*1059	181	1697	13.4	2.3	21.5
62-63—Kansas City	29	1185	312	606	.515	225	289	.779	*437	87	*849	15.1	3.0	29.3
Totals	108	4444	950	2006	.474	637	876	.727	1496	268	2546	13.9	2.5	23.6

NBA REGULAR-SEASON RECORD

HONORS: NBA All-Defensive second team (1969, 1970).

Season Team	G	Min.	FGM	FGA	Pct.	FTM	FTA	Pct.	Reb.	Ast.	PF	Dq.	Pts.	AVERAGES RPG	APG	PPG
62-63—St. Louis	27	374	66	160	.413	32	51	.627	144	23	58	0	164	5.3	0.9	6.1
63-64—St. Louis	80	1949	268	675	.397	146	224	.652	680	181	269	6	682	8.5	2.3	8.5
64-65—St. Louis	79	2362	362	938	.386	186	275	.676	853	187	276	3	910	10.8	2.4	11.5
65-66—St. Louis	78	2677	377	927	.407	257	364	.706	951	208	333	11	1011	12.2	2.7	13.0
66-67—St. Louis	79	3130	503	1106	.455	367	523	.702	1190	222	325	12	1373	15.1	2.8	17.4
67-68—St. Louis	82	3197	466	1009	.462	347	484	.717	1102	253	*366	12	1279	13.4	3.1	15.6
68-69—Atlanta	80	2930	351	775	.453	239	353	.677	1132	298	290	3	941	14.2	3.7	11.8

Season Team	G	Min.	FGM	FGA	Pct.	FTM	FTA	Pct.	Reb.	Ast.	PF	Dq.	Pts.	RPG	APG	PPG
69-70—Atlanta	82	3269	443	932	.475	331	451	.734	1181	345	292	6	1217	14.4	4.2	14.8
70-71—Atlanta	82	3140	382	834	.458	211	330	.639	1233	240	317	7	975	15.0	2.9	11.9
71-72—Atl.-Phil.	78	2756	379	779	.487	222	316	.703	1051	198	269	6	980	13.5	2.5	12.6
72-73—Phil.-L.A.	82	2867	333	722	.461	179	255	.702	904	219	296	3	845	11.0	2.7	10.3

Season Team	G	Min.	FGM	FGA	Pct.	FTM	FTA	Pct.	REBOUNDS Off.	Def.	Tot.	Ast.	St.	Blk.	TO	Pts.	AVERAGES RPG	APG	PPG
73-74—Los Angeles	65	1812	216	513	.421	116	164	.707	193	306	499	148	58	31	...	548	7.7	2.3	8.4
74-75—L.A.-G.S.	32	415	35	93	.376	17	34	.500	64	70	134	31	11	5	...	87	4.2	1.0	2.7
Totals	926	30878	4181	9463	.442	2650	3824	.693	...	...	11054	2553	69	36	...	11012	11.9	2.8	11.9

Personal fouls/disqualifications: 1973-74, 219/3. 1974-75, 65/1. Totals, 3375/73.

NBA PLAYOFF RECORD

Season Team	G	Min.	FGM	FGA	Pct.	FTM	FTA	Pct.	Reb.	Ast.	PF	Dq.	Pts.	RPG	APG	PPG
62-63—St. Louis	11	204	41	96	.427	20	27	.741	86	9	31	0	102	7.8	0.8	9.3
63-64—St. Louis	12	240	26	83	.313	12	19	.632	84	24	40	0	64	7.0	2.0	5.3
64-65—St. Louis	4	145	21	59	.356	10	15	.667	67	9	19	1	52	16.8	2.3	13.0
65-66—St. Louis	10	421	86	170	.506	31	43	.721	149	28	47	2	203	14.9	2.8	20.3
66-67—St. Louis	9	369	48	128	.375	45	67	.672	169	22	36	2	141	18.8	2.4	15.7
67-68—St. Louis	6	216	38	75	.507	18	25	.720	77	14	23	0	94	12.8	2.3	15.7
68-69—Atlanta	11	442	69	156	.442	34	48	.708	178	37	48	2	172	16.2	3.4	15.6
69-70—Atlanta	9	381	44	110	.400	16	27	.593	154	29	37	1	104	17.1	3.2	11.6
70-71—Atlanta	5	229	23	58	.397	3	9	.333	104	5	17	0	49	20.8	1.0	9.8
72-73—Los Angeles	17	582	57	136	.419	38	49	.776	158	29	68	2	152	9.3	1.7	8.9

Season Team	G	Min.	FGM	FGA	Pct.	FTM	FTA	Pct.	REBOUNDS Off.	Def.	Tot.	Ast.	St.	Blk.	TO	Pts.	AVERAGES RPG	APG	PPG
73-74—Los Angeles	5	144	12	41	.293	6	13	.462	14	16	30	6	7	0	...	30	6.0	1.2	6.0
74-75—Golden State	14	148	10	23	.435	2	7	.286	13	36	49	7	9	4	...	22	3.5	0.5	1.6
Totals	113	3521	475	1135	.419	235	349	.673	...	...	1305	219	16	4	...	1185	11.5	1.9	10.5

Personal fouls/disqualifications: 1973-74, 19/0. 1974-75, 23/0. Totals, 408/10.

NBA ALL-STAR GAME RECORD

Season Team	Min.	FGM	FGA	Pct.	FTM	FTA	Pct.	Reb	Ast.	PF	Dq.	Pts.
1967—St. Louis	17	4	5	.800	0	2	.000	3	3	1	0	8
1968—St. Louis	21	7	9	.778	1	4	.250	7	1	4	0	15
1970—Atlanta	15	2	2	1.000	1	5	.200	4	2	1	0	5
Totals	53	13	16	.813	2	11	.182	14	6	6	0	28

CERVI, AL   G

PERSONAL: Born February 12, 1917, in Buffalo, N.Y. ... 5-11/185 (1,80/83,9). ... Full name: Alfred Nicholas Cervi. ... Nickname: Digger.
HIGH SCHOOL: East (Buffalo).
COLLEGE: Did not attend college.
TRANSACTIONS: Played with independent teams (1935-36, 1936-37 and 1938-39 through 1944-45 seasons). ... Syracuse Nationals franchise became part of NBA for 1949-50 season.
CAREER HONORS: Elected to Naismith Memorial Basketball Hall of Fame (1985).
MISCELLANEOUS: Member of NBL championship team (1946).

NBL AND NBA REGULAR-SEASON RECORD

HONORS: All-NBA second team (1950). ... All-NBL first team (1947, 1948, 1949). ... All-NBL second team (1946).

Season Team	G	Min.	FGM	FGA	Pct.	FTM	FTA	Pct.	Reb.	Ast.	PF	Dq.	Pts.	RPG	APG	PPG
37-38—Buff. (NBL)	9	...	19	...	...	6	...	...	...	...	...	...	44	...	...	4.9
45-46—Roc. (NBL)	28	...	112	...	...	76	108	.704	...	...	21	...	300	...	...	10.7
46-47—Roc. (NBL)	44	...	228	...	...	176	236	.746	...	...	127	...	*632	...	...	14.4
47-48—Roc. (NBL)	49	...	234	...	...	187	242	.773	...	...	118	...	655	...	...	13.4
48-49—Syr. (NBL)	57	...	204	...	...	287	382	.751	...	...	170	...	695	...	...	12.2
49-50—Syracuse	56	...	143	431	.332	287	346	.829	...	264	223	...	573	...	4.7	10.2
50-51—Syracuse	53	...	132	346	.382	194	237	.819	152	208	180	9	458	2.9	3.9	8.6
51-52—Syracuse	55	850	99	280	.354	219	248	.883	87	148	176	7	417	1.6	2.7	7.6
52-53—Syracuse	38	301	31	71	.437	81	100	.810	22	28	90	2	143	0.6	0.7	3.8
Totals	389	...	1202	...	...	1513	...	...	...	...	...	...	3917	...	...	10.1

NBL AND NBA PLAYOFF RECORD

Season Team	G	Min.	FGM	FGA	Pct.	FTM	FTA	Pct.	Reb.	Ast.	PF	Dq.	Pts.	RPG	APG	PPG
45-46—Roc. (NBL)	7	...	23	...	...	24	30	.800	...	...	21	...	70	...	...	10.0
46-47—Roc. (NBL)	11	...	49	...	...	50	68	.735	...	...	41	...	148	...	...	13.5
47-48—Roc. (NBL)	6	...	18	...	...	14	19	.737	13	...	...	...	50	2.2	...	8.3
48-49—Syr. (NBL)	6	...	12	...	...	22	30	.733	...	...	23	...	46	...	...	7.7
49-50—Syracuse	11	...	23	68	.338	38	46	.826	...	52	36	...	84	...	4.7	7.6
50-51—Syracuse	7	...	17	56	.304	44	50	.880	33	38	31	1	78	4.7	5.4	11.1
51-52—Syracuse	7	88	7	30	.233	22	23	.957	10	15	23	1	36	1.4	2.1	5.1
52-53—Syracuse	2	...	3	5	.600	12	15	.800	0	1	12	1	18	0.0	0.5	9.0
Totals	57	...	152	...	...	226	281	.804	...	...	...	...	530	...	...	9.3

HEAD COACHING RECORD
HONORS: NBL Coach of the Year (1949).

NBL AND NBA COACHING RECORD

Season Team	REGULAR SEASON				PLAYOFFS		
	W	L	Pct.	Finish	W	L	Pct.
48-49—Syracuse (NBL)	40	23	.635	2nd/Eastern Division	3	3	.500
49-50—Syracuse	51	13	.797	1st/Eastern Division	6	5	.545
50-51—Syracuse	32	34	.485	4th/Eastern Division	4	3	.571
51-52—Syracuse	40	26	.606	1st/Eastern Division	3	4	.429
52-53—Syracuse	47	24	.662	2nd/Eastern Division	0	2	.000
53-54—Syracuse	42	30	.583	3rd/Eastern Division	9	4	.692
54-55—Syracuse	43	29	.597	1st/Eastern Division	7	4	.636
55-56—Syracuse	35	37	.493	3rd/Eastern Division	5	4	.555
56-57—Syracuse	4	8	.333		—	—	—
58-59—Philadelphia	32	40	.444	4th/Eastern Division	—	—	—
Totals (10 years)	**366**	**264**	**.581**	**Totals (8 years)**	**37**	**29**	**.561**

NOTES:
1949—Defeated Hammond, 2-0, in Eastern Division First Round; lost to Anderson, 3-1, in Eastern Division Finals.

1950—Defeated Philadelphia, 2-0, in Eastern Division Semifinals; defeated New York, 2-1, in Eastern Division Finals; lost to Minneapolis, 4-2, in NBA Finals.

1951—Defeated Philadelphia, 2-0, in Eastern Division Semifinals; lost to New York, 3-2, in Eastern Division Finals.

1952—Defeated Philadelphia, 2-1, in Eastern Division Semifinals; lost to New York, 3-1, in Eastern Division Finals.

1953—Lost to Boston in Eastern Division Semifinals.

1954—Defeated Boston, 96-95 (OT); defeated New York, 75-68; defeated New York, 103-99; and defeated Boston, 98-85, in Eastern Division round robin; defeated Boston, 2-0, in Eastern Division Finals; lost to Minneapolis, 4-3, in World Championship Series.

1955—Defeated Boston, 3-1, in Eastern Division Finals; defeated Fort Wayne, 4-3, in World Championship Series.

1956—Defeated New York, 82-77, in Eastern Division third-place game; defeated Boston, 2-1, in Eastern Division Semifinals; lost to Philadelphia, 3-2, in Eastern Division Finals. Replaced as Syracuse head coach by Paul Seymour (November).

CHAMBERLAIN, WILT　　　　C

PERSONAL: Born August 21, 1936, in Philadelphia. ... Died October 12, 1999. ... 7-1/275 (2,16/124,7). ... Full name: Wilton Norman Chamberlain. ... Nickname: Wilt the Stilt and The Big Dipper.
HIGH SCHOOL: Overbrook (Philadelphia).
COLLEGE: Kansas.
TRANSACTIONS: Played with Harlem Globetrotters during 1958-59 season. ... Selected by Philadelphia Warriors in 1959 NBA Draft (territorial pick). ... Warriors franchise moved from Philadelphia to San Francisco for 1962-63 season. ... Traded by Warriors to Philadelphia 76ers for G Paul Neumann, C/F Connie Dierking, F Lee Shaffer and cash (January 15, 1965). ... Traded by 76ers to Los Angeles Lakers for F Jerry Chambers, G Archie Clark and C Darrall Imhoff (July 9, 1968).
CAREER HONORS: Elected to Naismith Memorial Basketball Hall of Fame (1978). ... NBA 35th Anniversary All-Time Team (1980) and One of the 50 Greatest Players in NBA History (1996).
MISCELLANEOUS: Member of NBA championship team (1967, 1972). ... Golden State Warriors franchise all-time leading scorer with 17,783 points (1959-60 through 1964-65).

COLLEGIATE RECORD
NOTES: The Sporting News All-America first team (1958).

Season Team	G	Min.	FGM	FGA	Pct.	FTM	FTA	Pct.	Reb.	Ast.	Pts.	AVERAGES		
												RPG	APG	PPG
55-56—Kansas‡					Freshman team did not play intercollegiate schedule.									
56-57—Kansas	27	...	275	588	.468	250	399	.627	510	...	800	18.9	...	29.6
57-58—Kansas	21	...	228	482	.473	177	291	.608	367	...	633	17.5	...	30.1
Varsity totals	**48**	...	**503**	**1070**	**.470**	**427**	**690**	**.619**	**877**	...	**1433**	**18.3**	...	**29.9**

NBA REGULAR-SEASON RECORD

RECORDS: Holds career records for most games with 50 or more points—118; most seasons leading league in field goal percentage—9; most free throws attempted—11,862; most rebounds—23,924; and highest rebounds-per-game average (minimum 400 games)—22.9. ... Shares career records for most consecutive seasons leading league in scoring—7 (1959-60 through 1965-66). ... Holds single-season records for most games with 50 or more points—45 (1962); most minutes played—3,882 (1962); most points—4,029 (1962); highest points-per-game average—50.4 (1962); most points by a rookie—2,707 (1960); most field goals made—1,597 (1962); most consecutive field goals made—35 (February 17 through February 28, 1967); most field goals attempted—3,159 (1962); highest field goal percentage—.727 (1973); most free throws attempted—1,363 (1962); most rebounds—2,149 (1961); most rebounds by a rookie—1,941 (1960); and highest rebounds-per-game average—27.2 (1961). ... Holds single-game records for most points—100; most points in one half—59; most field goals made—36; most field goals made in one half—22; most field goals attempted—63; most field goals attempted in one half—37; and most field goals attempted in one quarter—21 (March 2, 1962, vs. New York at Hershey, Pa.). ... Holds single-game records for most points by a rookie—58 (January 25, 1960, vs. Detroit); highest field goal percentage (minimum 15 made)—1.000 (January 20, 1967, vs. Los Angeles, 15-for-15; February 24, 1967, vs. Baltimore, 18-for-18; and March 19, 1967, vs. Baltimore, 16-for-16); most rebounds—55 (November 24, 1960, vs. Boston); and most rebounds by a rookie—45 (February 6, 1960, vs. Syracuse). ... Shares single-game record for most free throws made—28 (March 2, 1962, vs. New York at Hershey, Pa.).
HONORS: NBA Most Valuable Player (1960, 1966, 1967, 1968). ... NBA Rookie of the Year (1960). ... All-NBA first team (1960, 1961, 1962, 1964, 1966, 1967, 1968). ... All-NBA second team (1963, 1965, 1972). ... NBA All-Defensive first team (1972, 1973).

Season Team	G	Min.	FGM	FGA	Pct.	FTM	FTA	Pct.	Reb.	Ast.	PF	Dq.	Pts.	AVERAGES		
														RPG	APG	PPG
59-60—Philadelphia	72	†3338	*1065	*2311	.461	577	*991	.582	*1941	168	150	0	*2707	*27.0	2.3	*37.6
60-61—Philadelphia	79	*3773	*1251	*2457	.509	531	*1054	.504	*2149	148	130	0	*3033	*27.2	1.9	*38.4
61-62—Philadelphia	80	*3882	*1597	*3159	.506	*835	*1363	.613	*2052	192	123	0	*4029	*25.7	2.4	*50.4
62-63—San Francisco	80	*3806	*1463	*2770	.528	660	*1113	.593	*1946	275	136	0	*3586	*24.3	3.4	*44.8
63-64—San Francisco	80	*3689	*1204	*2298	.524	540	*1016	.532	1787	403	182	0	*2948	22.3	5.0	*36.9
64-65—S.F.-Phil.	73	3301	*1063	*2083	.510	408	*880	.464	1673	250	146	0	*2534	22.9	3.4	*34.7
65-66—Philadelphia	79	*3737	*1074	*1990	.540	501	976	.513	*1943	414	171	0	*2649	*24.6	5.2	*33.5
66-67—Philadelphia	81	*3682	785	1150	*.683	386	*875	.441	*1957	630	143	0	1956	*24.2	7.8	24.1
67-68—Philadelphia	82	*3836	819	1377	*.595	354	*932	.380	*1952	*702	160	0	1992	*23.8	8.6	24.3

Season Team	G	Min.	FGM	FGA	Pct.	FTM	FTA	Pct.	Reb.	Ast.	PF	Dq.	Pts.	AVERAGES RPG	APG	PPG
68-69—Los Angeles	81	3669	641	1099	*.583	382	*857	.446	*1712	366	142	0	1664	*21.1	4.5	20.5
69-70—Los Angeles	12	505	129	227	.568	70	157	.446	221	49	31	0	328	18.4	4.1	27.3
70-71—Los Angeles	82	3630	668	1226	.545	360	669	.538	*1493	352	174	0	1696	*18.2	4.3	20.7
71-72—Los Angeles	82	3469	496	764	*.649	221	524	.422	*1572	329	196	0	1213	*19.2	4.0	14.8
72-73—Los Angeles	82	3542	426	586	*.727	232	455	.510	*1526	365	191	0	1084	*18.6	4.5	13.2
Totals	1045	47859	12681	23497	.540	6057	11862	.511	23924	4643	2075	0	31419	22.9	4.4	30.1

NBA PLAYOFF RECORD

NOTES: NBA Finals Most Valuable Player (1972). ... Holds NBA Finals single-game record for most rebounds in one half—26 (April 16, 1967, vs. San Francisco). ... Holds single-series playoff record for highest rebounds-per-game average—32.0 (1967). ... Holds single-game play-off records for most rebounds—41 (April 5, 1967, vs. Boston); most rebounds in one half—26 (April 16, 1967, vs. San Francisco); and most points by a rookie—53 (March 14, 1960, vs. Syracuse). ... Shares single-game playoff records for most field goals made—24 (March 14, 1960, vs. Syracuse); most field goals attempted—48 (March 22, 1962, vs. Syracuse); and most field goals attempted in one half—25 (March 22, 1962, vs. Syracuse).

Season Team	G	Min.	FGM	FGA	Pct.	FTM	FTA	Pct.	Reb.	Ast.	PF	Dq.	Pts.	AVERAGES RPG	APG	PPG
59-60—Philadelphia	9	415	125	252	.496	49	110	.445	232	19	17	0	299	25.8	2.1	33.2
60-61—Philadelphia	3	144	45	96	.469	21	38	.553	69	6	10	0	111	23.0	2.0	37.0
61-62—Philadelphia	12	576	162	347	.467	96	151	.636	319	37	27	0	420	26.6	3.1	35.0
63-64—San Francisco	12	558	175	322	.543	66	139	.475	302	39	27	0	416	25.2	3.3	34.7
64-65—Philadelphia	11	536	123	232	.530	76	136	.559	299	48	29	0	322	27.2	4.4	29.3
65-66—Philadelphia	5	240	56	110	.509	28	68	.412	151	15	10	0	140	30.2	3.0	28.0
66-67—Philadelphia	15	718	132	228	.579	62	160	.388	437	135	37	0	326	29.1	9.0	21.7
67-68—Philadelphia	13	631	124	232	.534	60	158	.380	321	85	29	0	308	24.7	6.5	23.7
68-69—Los Angeles	18	832	96	176	.545	58	148	.392	444	46	56	0	250	24.7	2.6	13.9
69-70—Los Angeles	18	851	158	288	.549	82	202	.406	399	81	42	0	398	22.2	4.5	22.1
70-71—Los Angeles	12	554	85	187	.455	50	97	.515	242	53	33	0	220	20.2	4.4	18.3
71-72—Los Angeles	15	703	80	142	.563	60	122	.492	315	49	47	0	220	21.0	3.3	14.7
72-73—Los Angeles	17	801	64	116	.552	49	98	.500	383	60	48	0	177	22.5	3.5	10.4
Totals	160	7559	1425	2728	.522	757	1627	.465	3913	673	412	0	3607	24.5	4.2	22.5

NBA ALL-STAR GAME RECORD

NOTES: NBA All-Star Game Most Valuable Player (1960). ... Holds career record for most rebounds—197. ... Holds single-game records for most points—42 (1962); most free throws attempted—16 (1962); and most field goals made in one half—10 (1962). ... Shares single-game records for most field goals made—17 (1962); and most rebounds in one half—16 (1960).

Season Team	Min.	FGM	FGA	Pct.	FTM	FTA	Pct.	Reb	Ast.	PF	Dq.	Pts.
1960—Philadelphia	30	9	20	.450	5	7	.714	25	2	1	0	23
1961—Philadelphia	38	2	8	.250	8	15	.533	18	5	1	0	12
1962—Philadelphia	37	17	23	.739	8	16	.500	24	1	4	0	42
1963—San Francisco	35	7	11	.636	3	7	.429	19	0	2	0	17
1964—San Francisco	37	4	14	.286	11	14	.786	20	1	2	0	19
1965—San Francisco	31	9	15	.600	2	8	.250	16	1	4	0	20
1966—Philadelphia	25	8	11	.727	5	9	.556	9	3	2	0	21
1967—Philadelphia	39	6	7	.857	2	5	.400	22	4	1	0	14
1968—Philadelphia	25	3	4	.750	1	4	.250	7	6	2	0	7
1969—Los Angeles	27	2	3	.667	0	1	.000	12	2	2	0	4
1971—Los Angeles	18	1	1	1.000	0	0	...	8	5	0	0	2
1972—Los Angeles	24	3	3	1.000	2	8	.250	10	3	2	0	8
1973—Los Angeles	22	1	2	.500	0	0	...	7	3	0	0	2
Totals	388	72	122	.590	47	94	.500	197	36	23	0	191

ABA COACHING RECORD

Season Team	REGULAR SEASON W	L	Pct.	Finish	PLAYOFFS W	L	Pct.
73-74—San Diego	37	47	.440	T4th/Western Division	2	4	.333

NOTES:
1974—Lost to Utah in Western Division Semifinals.

CHAMBERS, TOM   F

PERSONAL: Born June 21, 1959, in Ogden, Utah. ... 6-10/230 (2,08/104,3). ... Full name: Thomas Doane Chambers.
HIGH SCHOOL: Fairview (Boulder, Colo.).
COLLEGE: Utah.
TRANSACTIONS: Selected by San Diego Clippers in first round (eighth pick overall) of 1981 NBA Draft. ... Traded by Clippers with F Al Wood, 1987 second-round draft choice and future third-round draft choice to Seattle SuperSonics for C James Donaldson, F Greg Kelser, G Mark Radford, 1984 first-round draft choice and 1985 second-round draft choice (August 18, 1983). ... Signed as unrestricted free agent by Phoenix Suns (July 5, 1988). ... Signed as unrestricted free agent by Utah Jazz (August 12, 1993). ... Played in Israel (1995-96). ... Signed as free agent by Charlotte Hornets (January 30, 1997). ... Waived by Hornets (April 8, 1997). ... Signed as free agent by Suns (August 22, 1997). ... Traded by Suns to Philadelphia 76ers for G/F Marko Milic (November 21, 1997). ... Announced retirement (December 11, 1997).
CAREER NOTES: Community relations representative, Phoenix Suns (1997-present).

COLLEGIATE RECORD

Season Team	G	Min.	FGM	FGA	Pct.	FTM	FTA	Pct.	Reb.	Ast.	Pts.	AVERAGES RPG	APG	PPG
77-78—Utah	28	355	69	139	.496	40	64	.625	104	7	178	3.7	0.3	6.4
78-79—Utah	30	853	206	379	.544	69	127	.543	266	28	481	8.9	0.9	16.0
79-80—Utah	28	792	195	359	.543	92	129	.713	244	23	482	8.7	0.8	17.2
80-81—Utah	30	959	221	372	.594	115	155	.742	262	24	557	8.7	0.8	18.6
Totals	116	2959	691	1249	.553	316	475	.665	876	82	1698	7.6	0.7	14.6

NBA REGULAR-SEASON RECORD

HONORS: All-NBA second team (1989, 1990).

Season Team	G	Min.	FGM	FGA	Pct.	FTM	FTA	Pct.	REBOUNDS Off.	Def.	Tot.	Ast.	St.	Blk.	TO	Pts.	RPG	APG	PPG
81-82—San Diego	81	2682	554	1056	.525	284	458	.620	211	350	561	146	58	46	220	1392	6.9	1.8	17.2
82-83—San Diego	79	2665	519	1099	.472	353	488	.723	218	301	519	192	79	57	234	1391	6.6	2.4	17.6
83-84—Seattle	82	2570	554	1110	.499	375	469	.800	219	313	532	133	47	51	192	1483	6.5	1.6	18.1
84-85—Seattle	81	2923	629	1302	.483	475	571	.832	164	415	579	209	70	57	260	1739	7.1	2.6	21.5
85-86—Seattle	66	2019	432	928	.466	346	414	.836	126	305	431	132	55	37	194	1223	6.5	2.0	18.5
86-87—Seattle	82	3018	660	1446	.456	535	630	.849	163	382	545	245	81	50	268	1909	6.6	3.0	23.3
87-88—Seattle	82	2680	611	1364	.448	419	519	.807	135	355	490	212	87	53	209	1674	6.0	2.6	20.4
88-89—Phoenix	81	3002	774	1643	.471	509	598	.851	143	541	684	231	87	55	231	2085	8.4	2.9	25.7
89-90—Phoenix	81	3046	810	1617	.501	557	647	.861	121	450	571	190	88	47	218	2201	7.0	2.3	27.2
90-91—Phoenix	76	2475	556	1271	.437	379	459	.826	104	386	490	194	65	52	177	1511	6.4	2.6	19.9
91-92—Phoenix	69	1948	426	989	.431	258	311	.830	86	315	401	142	57	37	103	1128	5.8	2.1	16.3
92-93—Phoenix	73	1723	320	716	.447	241	288	.837	96	249	345	101	43	23	92	892	4.7	1.4	12.2
93-94—Utah	80	1838	329	748	.440	221	281	.786	87	239	326	79	40	32	89	893	4.1	1.0	11.2
94-95—Utah	81	1240	195	427	.457	109	135	.807	66	147	213	73	25	30	52	503	2.6	0.9	6.2
95-96—										Played in Israel.									
96-97—Charlotte	12	83	7	31	.226	3	4	.750	3	11	14	4	1	0	9	19	1.2	0.3	1.6
97-98—Philadelphia	1	10	2	2	1.000	2	2	1.000	0	2	2	0	2	0	1	6	2.0	0.0	6.0
Totals	**1107**	**33922**	**7378**	**15749**	**.468**	**5066**	**6274**	**.807**	**1942**	**4761**	**6703**	**2283**	**885**	**627**	**2549**	**20049**	**6.1**	**2.1**	**18.1**

Three-point field goals: 1981-82, 0-for-2. 1982-83, 0-for-8. 1983-84, 0-for-12. 1984-85, 6-for-22 (.273). 1985-86, 13-for-48 (.271). 1986-87, 54-for-145 (.372). 1987-88, 33-for-109 (.303). 1988-89, 28-for-86 (.326). 1989-90, 24-for-86 (.279). 1990-91, 20-for-73 (.274). 1991-92, 18-for-49 (.367). 1992-93, 11-for-28 (.393). 1993-94, 14-for-45 (.311). 1994-95, 4-for-24 (.167). 1996-97, 2-for-3 (.667). Totals, 227-for-740 (.307).

Personal fouls/disqualifications: 1981-82, 341/17. 1982-83, 333/15. 1983-84, 309/8. 1984-85, 312/4. 1985-86, 248/6. 1986-87, 307/9. 1987-88, 297/4. 1988-89, 271/2. 1989-90, 260/1. 1990-91, 235/3. 1991-92, 196/1. 1992-93, 212/2. 1993-94, 232/2. 1994-95, 173/1. 1996-97, 14/0. 1997-98, 2/0. Totals, 3742/75.

NBA PLAYOFF RECORD

Season Team	G	Min.	FGM	FGA	Pct.	FTM	FTA	Pct.	REBOUNDS Off.	Def.	Tot.	Ast.	St.	Blk.	TO	Pts.	RPG	APG	PPG
83-84—Seattle	5	191	28	59	.475	12	18	.667	4	29	33	8	5	3	9	68	6.6	1.6	13.6
86-87—Seattle	14	498	118	263	.449	80	99	.808	32	58	90	32	12	13	34	322	6.4	2.3	23.0
87-88—Seattle	5	168	50	91	.549	29	35	.829	8	23	31	11	3	1	13	129	6.2	2.2	25.8
88-89—Phoenix	12	495	118	257	.459	67	78	.859	22	109	131	46	13	15	39	312	10.9	3.8	26.0
89-90—Phoenix	16	612	117	275	.425	116	132	.879	20	87	107	31	7	7	49	355	6.7	1.9	22.2
90-91—Phoenix	4	142	27	66	.409	14	19	.737	2	21	23	10	7	5	12	68	5.8	2.5	17.0
91-92—Phoenix	7	194	39	85	.459	27	32	.844	8	23	31	19	2	5	15	109	4.4	2.7	15.6
92-93—Phoenix	24	376	64	165	.388	44	54	.815	23	42	65	12	6	10	26	174	2.7	0.5	7.3
93-94—Utah	16	325	35	97	.361	23	29	.793	16	29	45	12	5	9	8	93	2.8	0.8	5.8
94-95—Utah	5	60	11	22	.500	9	13	.692	3	10	13	2	2	0	3	32	2.6	0.4	6.4
Totals	**108**	**3061**	**607**	**1380**	**.440**	**421**	**509**	**.827**	**138**	**431**	**569**	**183**	**62**	**68**	**208**	**1662**	**5.3**	**1.7**	**15.4**

Three-point field goals: 1983-84, 0-for-1. 1986-87, 6-for-17 (.353). 1987-88, 0-for-2. 1988-89, 9-for-22 (.409). 1989-90, 5-for-19 (.263). 1990-91, 0-for-5. 1991-92, 4-for-7 (.571). 1992-93, 2-for-5 (.400). 1993-94, 0-for-7. 1994-95, 1-for-3 (.333). Totals, 27-for-88 (.307).

Personal fouls/disqualifications. 1983-84, 23/0. 1986-87, 51/0. 1987-88, 24/1. 1988-89, 44/0. 1989-90, 54/0. 1990-91, 12/1. 1991-92, 25/1. 1992-93, 58/0. 1993-94, 50/1. 1994-95, 18/1. Totals, 359/5.

NBA ALL-STAR GAME RECORD

NOTES: NBA All-Star Game Most Valuable Player (1987).

Season Team	Min.	FGM	FGA	Pct.	FTM	FTA	Pct.	REBOUNDS Off.	Def.	Tot.	Ast.	PF	Dq.	St.	Blk.	TO	Pts.
1987—Seattle	29	13	25	.520	6	9	.667	3	1	4	2	5	0	4	0	3	34
1989—Phoenix	16	4	8	.500	6	6	1.000	2	3	5	1	3	0	0	0	2	14
1990—Phoenix	21	8	12	.667	5	7	.714	2	1	3	1	0	0	1	0	3	21
1991—Phoenix	18	4	11	.364	0	0	...	2	2	4	1	3	0	1	0	4	8
Totals	**84**	**29**	**56**	**.518**	**17**	**22**	**.773**	**9**	**7**	**16**	**5**	**11**	**0**	**6**	**0**	**12**	**77**

Three-point field goals: 1987, 2-for-3 (.667). 1990, 0-for-1. 1991, 0-for-1. Totals, 2-for-5 (.400).

ISRAELI LEAGUE RECORD

Season Team	G	Min.	FGM	FGA	Pct.	FTM	FTA	Pct.	Reb.	Ast.	Pts.	AVERAGES RPG	APG	PPG
95-96—Maccabo Tel-Aviv	16	...	117	197	.594	44	60	.733	101	36	283	6.3	2.3	17.7

CHEEKS, MAURICE — G

See Head Coaches, page 283.

COSTELLO, LARRY — G

See All-Time Great Coaches, page 451.

COUSY, BOB — G

PERSONAL: Born August 9, 1928, in New York. ... 6-1/175 (1,85/79,4). ... Full name: Robert Joseph Cousy. ... Nickname: Houdini of the Hardwood.
HIGH SCHOOL: Andrew Jackson (Queens, N.Y.).
COLLEGE: Holy Cross.
TRANSACTIONS: Selected by Tri-Cities Blackhawks in first round of 1950 NBA Draft. ... Traded by Blackhawks to Chicago Stags for F/G Gene Vance (1950). ... NBA rights drawn out of a hat by Boston Celtics in dispersal of Stags franchise (1950). ... Traded by

Celtics to Cincinnati Royals for F Bill Dinwiddie (November 18, 1969).

CAREER HONORS: Elected to Naismith Memorial Basketball Hall of Fame (1971). ... NBA 25th Anniversary All-Time Team (1970), 35th Anniversary All-Time Team (1980) and One of the 50 Greatest Players in NBA History (1996).

MISCELLANEOUS: Member of NBA championship team (1957, 1959, 1960, 1961, 1962, 1963). ... Commissioner of American Soccer League (1975 through mid-1980 season). ... Boston Celtics all-time assists leader with 6,945 (1950-51 through 1962-63).

COLLEGIATE RECORD

NOTES: Member of NCAA championship team (1947). ... THE SPORTING NEWS All-America first team (1950). ... THE SPORTING NEWS All-America second team (1949).

Season Team	G	Min.	FGM	FGA	Pct.	FTM	FTA	Pct.	Reb.	Ast.	Pts.	AVERAGES RPG	APG	PPG
46-47—Holy Cross	30	...	91	...	...	45	...	...	...	...	227	...	...	7.6
47-48—Holy Cross	30	...	207	...	...	72	108	.667	...	...	486	...	...	16.2
48-49—Holy Cross	27	...	195	...	...	90	134	.672	...	...	480	...	...	17.8
49-50—Holy Cross	30	...	216	659	.328	150	199	.754	...	...	582	...	...	19.4
Totals	117	...	709			357	...	...	...	...	1775	...	...	15.2

NBA REGULAR-SEASON RECORD

RECORDS: Holds single-game record for most assists in one half—19 (February 27, 1959, vs. Minneapolis).

HONORS: NBA Most Valuable Player (1957). ... All-NBA first team (1952, 1953, 1954, 1955, 1956, 1957, 1958, 1959, 1960, 1961). ... All-NBA second team (1962, 1963).

Season Team	G	Min.	FGM	FGA	Pct.	FTM	FTA	Pct.	Reb.	Ast.	PF	Dq.	Pts.	AVERAGES RPG	APG	PPG
50-51—Boston	69	...	401	1138	.352	276	365	.756	474	341	185	2	1078	6.9	4.9	15.6
51-52—Boston	66	2681	512	1388	.369	409	506	.808	421	441	190	5	1433	6.4	6.7	21.7
52-53—Boston	71	2945	464	*1320	.352	479	587	.816	449	*547	227	4	1407	6.3	*7.7	19.8
53-54—Boston	72	2857	486	1262	.385	411	522	.787	394	*518	201	3	1383	5.5	*7.2	19.2
54-55—Boston	71	2747	522	1316	.397	460	570	.807	424	*557	165	1	1504	6.0	*7.8	21.2
55-56—Boston	72	2767	440	1223	.360	476	564	.844	492	*642	206	2	1356	6.8	*8.9	18.8
56-57—Boston	64	2364	478	1264	.378	363	442	.821	309	*478	134	0	1319	4.8	*7.5	20.6
57-58—Boston	65	2222	445	1262	.353	277	326	.850	322	*463	136	1	1167	5.0	*7.1	18.0
58-59—Boston	65	2403	484	1260	.384	329	385	.855	359	*557	135	0	1297	5.5	*8.6	20.0
59-60—Boston	75	2588	568	1481	.384	319	403	.792	352	*715	146	2	1455	4.7	*9.5	19.4
60-61—Boston	76	2468	513	1382	.371	352	452	.779	331	587	196	0	1378	4.4	7.7	18.1
61-62—Boston	75	2114	462	1181	.391	251	333	.754	261	584	135	0	1175	3.5	7.8	15.7
62-63—Boston	76	1975	392	988	.397	219	298	.735	193	515	175	0	1003	2.5	6.8	13.2
69-70—Cincinnati	7	34	1	3	.333	3	3	1.000	5	10	11	0	5	0.7	1.4	0.7
Totals	924	...	6168	16468	.375	4624	5756	.803	4786	6955	2242	20	16960	5.2	7.5	18.4

NBA PLAYOFF RECORD

NOTES: Shares NBA Finals single-game record for most assists in one quarter—8 (April 9, 1957, vs. St. Louis). ... Holds single-game playoff record for most free throws made—30 (March 21, 1953, vs. Syracuse).

Season Team	G	Min.	FGM	FGA	Pct.	FTM	FTA	Pct.	Reb.	Ast.	PF	Dq.	Pts.	AVERAGES RPG	APG	PPG
50-51—Boston	2	...	9	42	.214	10	12	.833	15	12	8		28	7.5	6.0	14.0
51-52—Boston	3	138	26	65	.400	41	44	.932	12	19	13	1	93	4.0	6.3	31.0
52-53—Boston	6	270	46	120	.383	61	73	.836	25	37	21	0	153	4.2	6.2	25.5
53-54—Boston	6	259	33	116	.284	60	75	.800	32	38	20	0	126	5.3	6.3	21.0
54-55—Boston	7	299	53	139	.381	46	48	.958	43	65	26	0	152	6.1	9.3	21.7
55-56—Boston	3	124	28	56	.500	23	25	.920	24	26	4	0	79	8.0	8.7	26.3
56-57—Boston	10	440	67	207	.324	68	91	.747	61	93	27	0	202	6.1	9.3	20.2
57-58—Boston	11	457	67	196	.342	64	75	.853	71	82	20	0	198	6.5	7.5	18.0
58-59—Boston	11	460	72	221	.326	70	94	.745	76	119	28	0	214	6.9	10.8	19.5
59-60—Boston	13	468	80	262	.305	39	51	.765	48	116	27	0	199	3.7	8.9	15.3
60-61—Boston	10	337	50	147	.340	67	88	.761	43	91	33	1	167	4.3	9.1	16.7
61-62—Boston	14	474	86	241	.357	52	76	.684	64	123	43	0	224	4.6	8.8	16.0
62-63—Boston	13	393	72	204	.353	39	47	.830	32	116	44	2	183	2.5	8.9	14.1
Totals	109	...	689	2016	.342	640	799	.801	546	937	314	...	2018	5.0	8.6	18.5

NBA ALL-STAR GAME RECORD

NOTES: NBA All-Star Game Most Valuable Player (1954, 1957).

Season Team	Min.	FGM	FGA	Pct.	FTM	FTA	Pct.	Reb	Ast.	PF	Dq.	Pts.
1951—Boston	...	2	12	.167	4	5	.800	9	8	3	0	8
1952—Boston	33	4	14	.286	1	2	.500	4	13	3	0	9
1953—Boston	36	4	11	.364	7	7	1.000	5	3	1	0	15
1954—Boston	34	6	15	.400	8	8	1.000	11	4	1	0	20
1955—Boston	35	7	14	.500	6	7	.857	9	5	1	0	20
1956—Boston	24	2	8	.250	3	4	.750	7	2	6	1	7
1957—Boston	28	4	14	.286	2	2	1.000	5	7	0	0	10
1958—Boston	31	8	20	.400	4	6	.667	5	10	0	0	20
1959—Boston	32	4	8	.500	5	6	.833	5	4	0	0	13
1960—Boston	26	1	7	.143	0	0	...	5	8	2	0	2
1961—Boston	33	2	11	.182	0	0	...	3	8	6	1	4
1962—Boston	31	4	13	.308	3	4	.750	6	8	2	0	11
1963—Boston	25	4	11	.364	0	0	...	4	6	2	0	8
Totals	...	52	158	.329	43	51	.843	78	86	27	2	147

COLLEGIATE COACHING RECORD

Season Team	W	L	Pct.
63-64—Boston College	10	11	.476
64-65—Boston College	22	7	.759
65-66—Boston College	21	5	.808
66-67—Boston College	23	3	.885

Season Team	W	L	Pct.
67-68—Boston College	17	8	.680
68-69—Boston College	24	4	.857
Totals (6 years)	117	38	.755

NBA COACHING RECORD

	REGULAR SEASON					PLAYOFFS		
Season Team	W	L	Pct.	Finish		W	L	Pct.
69-70—Cincinnati	36	46	.439	5th/Eastern Division		—	—	—
70-71—Cincinnati	33	49	.402	3rd/Central Division		—	—	—
71-72—Cincinnati	30	52	.366	3rd/Central Division		—	—	—
72-73—Kansas City/Omaha	36	46	.439	4th/Midwest Division		—	—	—
73-74—Kansas City/Omaha	6	16	.273			—	—	—
Totals (5 years)	141	209	.403					

NOTES:
1965—Lost to St. John's, 114-92, in NIT first round.
1966—Defeated Louisville, 96-90 (3 OT), in NIT first round; lost to Villanova, 86-85, in quarterfinals.
1967—Defeated Connecticut, 48-42, in NCAA Tournament first round; defeated St. John's, 63-62, in regional semifinal; lost to North Carolina, 96-80, in regional final.
1968—Lost to St. Bonaventure, 102-93, in NCAA Tournament first round.
1969—Defeated Kansas, 78-62, in NIT first round; defeated Louisville, 88-83, in quarterfinals; defeated Army, 73-61, in semifinals; lost to Temple 89-76, in championship game.
1973—Replaced as Kansas City/Omaha head coach by Draff Young (November).

COWENS, DAVE   C

PERSONAL: Born October 25, 1948, in Newport, Ky. ... 6-9/230. (2,05/104,3). ... Full name: David William Cowens.
HIGH SCHOOL: Newport (Ky.) Central Catholic.
COLLEGE: Florida State.
TRANSACTIONS/CAREER NOTES: Selected by Boston Celtics in first round (fourth pick overall) of 1970 NBA Draft. ... Traded by Celtics to Milwaukee Bucks for G Quinn Buckner (September 9, 1982).
CAREER HONORS: Elected to Naismith Memorial Basketball Hall of Fame (1990). ... One of the 50 Greatest Players in NBA History (1996). ... Head coach, Chicago Sky of WNBA (2005-present).
MISCELLANEOUS: Member of NBA championship team (1974, 1976).

COLLEGIATE RECORD

NOTES: The Sporting News All-America second team (1970).

													AVERAGES		
Season Team	G	Min.	FGM	FGA	Pct.	FTM	FTA	Pct.	Reb.	Ast.	Pts.	RPG	APG	PPG
66-67—Florida State‡	18	...	105	208	.505	49	90	.544	357	...	259	19.8	...	14.4
67-68—Florida State	27	...	200	000	.000	00	101	700	470	...	700	10.0	...	10.0
68-69—Florida State	25	...	202	384	.526	104	164	.634	437	...	508	17.5	...	20.3
69-70—Florida State	26	...	174	355	.490	115	169	.680	447	...	463	17.2	...	17.8
Varsity totals	78	...	582	1122	.519	315	464	.679	1340	...	1479	17.2	...	19.0

NBA REGULAR-SEASON RECORD

HONORS: NBA Most Valuable Player (1973). ... NBA co-Rookie of the Year (1971). ... All-NBA second team (1973, 1975, 1976). ... NBA All-Defensive first team (1976). ... NBA All-Defensive second team (1975, 1980). ... NBA All-Rookie team (1971).

														AVERAGES		
Season Team	G	Min.	FGM	FGA	Pct.	FTM	FTA	Pct.	Reb.	Ast.	PF	Dq.	Pts.	RPG	APG	PPG
70-71—Boston	81	3076	550	1302	.422	273	373	.732	1216	228	*350	15	1373	15.0	2.8	17.0
71-72—Boston	79	3186	657	1357	.484	175	243	.720	1203	245	*314	10	1489	15.2	3.1	18.8
72-73—Boston	82	3425	740	1637	.452	204	262	.779	1329	333	311	7	1684	16.2	4.1	20.5

								REBOUNDS								AVERAGES		
Season Team	G	Min.	FGM	FGA	Pct.	FTM	FTA	Pct.	Off.	Def.	Tot.	Ast.	St.	Blk.	TO	Pts.	RPG	APG	PPG
73-74—Boston	80	3352	645	1475	.437	228	274	.832	264	993	1257	354	95	101	...	1518	15.7	4.4	19.0
74-75—Boston	65	2632	569	1199	.475	191	244	.783	229	729	958	296	87	73	...	1329	14.7	4.6	20.4
75-76—Boston	78	3101	611	1305	.468	257	340	.756	335	911	1246	325	94	71	...	1479	16.0	4.2	19.0
76-77—Boston	50	1888	328	756	.434	162	198	.818	147	550	697	248	46	49	...	818	13.9	5.0	16.4
77-78—Boston	77	3215	598	1220	.490	239	284	.842	248	830	1078	351	102	58	217	1435	14.0	4.6	18.6
78-79—Boston	68	2517	488	1010	.483	151	187	.807	152	500	652	242	76	51	174	1127	9.6	3.6	16.6
79-80—Boston	66	2159	422	932	.453	95	122	.779	126	408	534	206	69	61	108	940	8.1	3.1	14.2
80-81—						Did not play—retired.													
81-82—						Did not play—retired.													
82-83—Milwaukee	40	1014	136	306	.444	52	63	.825	73	201	274	82	30	15	44	324	6.9	2.1	8.1
Totals	766	29565	5744	12499	.460	2027	2590	.783	...	...	10444	2910	599	488	543	13516	13.6	3.8	17.6

Three-point field goals: 1979-80, 1-for-12 (.083). 1982-83, 0-for-2. Totals, 1-for-14 (.071).
Personal fouls/disqualifications: 1973-74, 294/7. 1974-75, 243/7. 1975-76, 314/10. 1976-77, 181/7. 1977-78, 297/5. 1978-79, 263/16. 1979-80, 216/2. 1982-83, 137/4. Totals, 2920/90.

NBA PLAYOFF RECORD

NOTES: Shares single-game playoff record for most defensive rebounds—20 (April 22, 1975, vs. Houston; and May 1, 1977, vs. Philadelphia).

													AVERAGES		
Season Team	G	Min.	FGM	FGA	Pct.	FTM	FTA	Pct.	Reb.	Ast.	PF	Dq.	Pts.	RPG	APG	PPG
71-72—Boston	11	441	71	156	.455	28	47	.596	152	33	50	2	170	13.8	3.0	15.5
72-73—Boston	13	598	129	273	.473	27	41	.659	216	48	54	2	285	16.6	3.7	21.9

Season Team	G	Min.	FGM	FGA	Pct.	FTM	FTA	Pct.	REBOUNDS Off.	Def.	Tot.	Ast.	St.	Blk.	TO	Pts.	AVERAGES RPG	APG	PPG
73-74—Boston	18	772	161	370	.435	47	59	.797	60	180	240	66	21	17	...	369	13.3	3.7	20.5
74-75—Boston	11	479	101	236	.428	23	26	.885	49	132	181	46	18	6	...	225	16.5	4.2	20.5
75-76—Boston	18	798	156	341	.457	66	87	.759	87	209	296	83	22	13	...	378	16.4	4.6	21.0
76-77—Boston	9	379	66	148	.446	17	22	.773	29	105	134	36	8	13	...	149	14.9	4.0	16.6
79-80—Boston	9	301	49	103	.476	10	11	.909	18	48	66	21	9	7	8	108	7.3	2.3	12.0
Totals	89	3768	733	1627	.451	218	293	.744	...	...	1285	333	78	56	8	1684	14.4	3.7	18.9

Three-point field goals: 1979-80, 0-for-2.
Personal fouls/disqualifications: 1973-74, 85/2. 1974-75, 50/2. 1975-76, 85/4. 1976-77, 37/3. 1979-80, 37/0. Totals, 398/15.

NBA ALL-STAR GAME RECORD

NOTES: NBA All-Star Game Most Valuable Player (1973).

Season Team	Min.	FGM	FGA	Pct.	FTM	FTA	Pct.	Reb	Ast.	PF	Dq.	Pts.
1972—Boston	32	5	12	.417	4	5	.800	20	1	4	0	14
1973—Boston	30	7	15	.467	1	1	1.000	13	1	2	0	15

Season Team	Min.	FGM	FGA	Pct.	FTM	FTA	Pct.	REBOUNDS Off.	Def.	Tot.	Ast.	PF	Dq.	St.	Blk.	TO	Pts.
1974—Boston	26	5	10	.500	1	3	.333	6	6	12	1	3	0	0	1	...	11
1975—Boston	15	3	7	.429	0	0	...	0	6	6	3	4	0	1	0	...	6
1976—Boston	23	6	13	.462	4	5	.800	8	8	16	1	3	0	1	0	...	16
1977—Boston							Selected, did not play—injured.										
1978—Boston	28	7	9	.778	0	0	...	6	8	14	5	5	0	2	0	2	14
Totals	154	33	66	.500	10	14	.714	...	...	81	12	21	0	4	1	2	76

HEAD COACHING RECORD

BACKGROUND: Assistant coach, San Antonio Spurs (1994-95 and 1995-96). ... Assistant coach, Golden State Warriors (January 31-April 20, 2000).

NBA COACHING RECORD

Season Team	REGULAR SEASON W	L	Pct.	Finish	PLAYOFFS W	L	Pct.
78-79—Boston................	27	41	.397	5th/Atlantic Division	—	—	—
96-97—Charlotte	54	28	.659	6th/Central Division	0	3	.000
97-98—Charlotte	51	31	.622	3rd/Central Division	4	5	.444
98-99—Charlotte	4	11	.267		—	—	—
00-01—Golden State	17	65	.207	7th/Pacific Division	—	—	—
01-02—Golden State	8	15	.348		—	—	—
Totals (6 years).............	161	191	.457	Totals (2 years).......	4	8	.333

CBA COACHING RECORD

Season Team	REGULAR SEASON W	L	Pct.	Finish	PLAYOFFS W	L	Pct.
84-85—Bay State................	20	28	.417	6th/Atlantic Division	—	—	—

NOTES:
1978—Replaced Tom Sanders as Boston head coach (November), with record of 2-12.
1997—Lost to New York in Eastern Conference First Round.
1998—Defeated New Jersey, 3-1, in Eastern Conference First Round; lost to Chicago, 4-1, in Eastern Conference Semifinals.
1999—Resigned as Charlotte head coach (March 7); replaced by Paul Silas with club in seventh place.
2001—Replaced as head coach by Brian Winters (December 15) with club in seventh place.

CUMMINGS, TERRY   F

PERSONAL: Born March 15, 1961, in Chicago. ... 6-9/250. (2.06 m/113 kg). ... Full Name: Robert Terrell Cummings.
HIGH SCHOOL: Carver (Chicago).
COLLEGE: DePaul.
TRANSACTIONS/CAREER NOTES: Selected after junior season by San Diego Clippers in first round (second pick overall) of 1982 NBA Draft. ... Clippers franchise moved from San Diego to Los Angeles for 1984-85 season. ... Traded by Clippers with G Craig Hodges and G/F Ricky Pierce to Milwaukee Bucks for F Marques Johnson, C/F Harvey Catchings, G/F Junior Bridgeman and cash (September 29, 1984). ... Traded by Bucks with future considerations to San Antonio Spurs for G Alvin Robertson, F/C Greg Anderson and future considerations (May 28, 1989). ... Signed as unrestricted free agent by Milwaukee Bucks (November 2, 1995). ... Signed as free agent by Seattle SuperSonics (January 13, 1997). ... Signed as free agent by Philadelphia 76ers (September 4, 1997). ... Traded by 76ers to New York Knicks for F Ronnie Grandison and C Herb Williams (February 19, 1998). ... Traded by Knicks with G John Starks and F Chris Mills to Golden State Warriors for G Latrell Sprewell (January 21, 1999). ... Announced retirement (October 2, 2000).

COLLEGIATE RECORD

NOTES: THE SPORTING NEWS All-America first team (1982).

Season Team	G	Min.	FGM	FGA	Pct.	FTM	FTA	Pct.	Reb.	Ast.	Pts.	AVERAGES RPG	APG	PPG
79-80—DePaul..............	28	861	154	303	.508	89	107	.832	263	40	397	9.4	1.4	14.2
80-81—DePaul..............	29	994	151	303	.498	75	100	.750	260	47	377	9.0	1.6	13.0
81-82—DePaul..............	28	1031	244	430	.567	136	180	.756	334	57	624	11.9	2.0	22.3
Totals	85	2886	549	1036	.530	300	387	.775	857	144	1398	10.1	1.7	16.4

NBA REGULAR-SEASON RECORD

HONORS: NBA Rookie of the Year (1983). ... All-NBA second team (1985). ... All-NBA third team (1989). ... NBA All-Rookie team (1983).

Season Team	G	Min.	FGM	FGA	Pct.	FTM	FTA	Pct.	REBOUNDS Off.	Def.	Tot.	Ast.	St.	Blk.	TO	Pts.	AVERAGES RPG	APG	PPG
82-83—San Diego	70	2531	684	1309	.523	292	412	.709	303	441	744	177	129	62	204	1660	10.6	2.5	23.7

Season Team	G	Min.	FGM	FGA	Pct.	FTM	FTA	Pct.	Off.	Def.	Tot.	Ast.	St.	Blk.	TO	Pts.	RPG	APG	PPG
83-84—San Diego......	81	2907	737	1491	.494	380	528	.720	323	454	777	139	92	57	218	1854	9.6	1.7	22.9
84-85—Milwaukee	79	2722	759	1532	.495	343	463	.741	244	472	716	228	117	67	190	1861	9.1	2.9	23.6
85-86—Milwaukee	82	2669	681	1438	.474	265	404	.656	222	472	694	193	121	51	191	1627	8.5	2.4	19.8
86-87—Milwaukee	82	2770	729	1426	.511	249	376	.662	214	486	700	229	129	81	172	1707	8.5	2.8	20.8
87-88—Milwaukee	76	2629	675	1392	.485	270	406	.665	184	369	553	181	78	46	170	1621	7.3	2.4	21.3
88-89—Milwaukee	80	2824	730	1563	.467	362	460	.787	281	369	650	198	106	72	201	1829	8.1	2.5	22.9
89-90—San Antonio	81	2821	728	1532	.475	343	440	.780	226	451	677	219	110	52	202	1818	8.4	2.7	22.4
90-91—San Antonio	67	2195	503	1039	.484	164	240	.683	194	327	521	157	61	30	131	1177	7.8	2.3	17.6
91-92—San Antonio	70	2149	514	1053	.488	177	249	.711	247	384	631	102	58	34	115	1210	9.0	1.5	17.3
92-93—San Antonio	8	76	11	29	.379	5	10	.500	6	13	19	4	1	1	2	27	2.4	0.5	3.4
93-94—San Antonio	59	1133	183	428	.428	63	107	.589	132	165	297	50	31	13	59	429	5.0	0.8	7.3
94-95—San Antonio	76	1273	224	464	.483	72	123	.585	138	240	378	59	36	19	95	520	5.0	0.8	6.8
95-96—Milwaukee	81	1777	270	584	.462	104	160	.650	162	283	445	89	56	30	69	645	5.5	1.1	8.0
96-97—Seattle	45	828	155	319	.486	57	82	.695	70	113	183	39	33	7	45	370	4.1	0.9	8.2
97-98—Phil.-New York	74	1185	200	428	.467	67	98	.684	97	186	283	47	38	10	51	467	3.8	0.6	6.3
98-99—Golden State ..	50	1011	186	424	.439	81	114	.711	95	160	255	58	46	10	58	454	5.1	1.2	9.1
99-00—Golden State ...	22	398	76	177	.429	32	39	.821	45	62	107	21	13	8	27	184	4.9	1.0	8.4
Totals	1183	33898	8045	16628	.484	3326	4711	.706	3183	5447	8630	2190	1255	650	2200	19460	7.3	1.9	16.4

Three-point field goals: 1982-83, 0-for-1. 1983-84, 0-for-3. 1984-85, 0-for-1. 1985-86, 0-for-2. 1986-87, 0-for-3. 1987-88, 1-for-3 (.333). 1988-89, 7-for-15 (.467). 1989-90, 19-for-59 (.322). 1990-91, 7-for-33 (.212). 1991-92, 5-for-13 (.385). 1993-94, 0-for-2. 1995-96, 1-for-7 (.143). 1996-97, 3-for-5 (.600). 1997-98, 0-for-1. 1998-99, 1-for-1. Totals, 44-for-149 (.295).

Personal fouls/disqualifications: 1982-83, 294/10. 1983-84, 298/6. 1984-85, 264/4. 1985-86, 283/4. 1986-87, 296/3. 1987-88, 274/6. 1988-89, 265/5. 1989-90, 286/1. 1990-91, 225/5. 1991-92, 210/4. 1993-94, 137/0. 1995-96, 263/2. 1996-97, 113/0. 1997-98, 181/1. 1998-99, 168/4. Totals, 3836/56.

NBA PLAYOFF RECORD

Season Team	G	Min.	FGM	FGA	Pct.	FTM	FTA	Pct.	Off.	Def.	Tot.	Ast.	St.	Blk.	TO	Pts.	RPG	APG	PPG
84-85—Milwaukee	8	311	86	149	.577	48	58	.828	21	49	70	20	12	7	26	220	8.8	2.5	27.5
85-86—Milwaukee	14	510	130	253	.514	43	62	.694	33	105	138	42	20	16	39	303	9.9	3.0	21.6
86-87—Milwaukee	12	443	105	215	.488	57	83	.687	29	66	95	28	12	13	15	267	7.9	2.3	22.3
87-88—Milwaukee	5	193	50	89	.562	29	44	.659	12	27	39	13	9	3	12	129	7.8	2.6	25.8
88-89—Milwaukee	5	124	25	69	.362	14	16	.875	19	14	33	7	3	0	4	64	6.6	1.4	12.8
89-90—San Antonio	10	375	103	195	.528	42	52	.808	31	63	94	22	7	4	19	249	9.4	2.2	24.9
90-91—San Antonio	4	124	25	49	.510	9	18	.500	14	23	37	4	3	2	9	59	9.3	1.0	14.8
91-92—San Antonio	3	122	34	66	.515	10	20	.500	15	19	34	7	4	4	7	78	11.3	2.3	26.0
92-93—San Antonio	10	138	31	70	.443	5	8	.625	17	22	39	5	3	1	8	67	3.9	0.5	6.7
93-94—San Antonio	4	72	11	22	.500	10	12	.833	10	15	25	2	5	3	4	32	6.3	0.5	8.0
94-95—San Antonio	15	135	18	48	.375	22	30	.733	12	19	31	4	5	1	7	58	2.1	0.3	3.9
96-97—Seattle	12	292	45	92	.489	16	24	.667	28	44	72	14	11	6	14	106	6.0	1.2	8.8
97-98—New York	8	120	15	34	.441	2	8	.250	11	24	35	5	4	2	7	32	4.4	0.6	4.0
Totals	110	2959	678	1351	.502	307	435	.706	252	490	742	173	98	62	171	1664	6.7	1.6	15.1

Three-point field goals: 1984-85, 0-for-1. 1988-89, 0-for-1. 1989-90, 1-for-5 (.200). 1990-91, 0-for-1. 1991-92, 0-for-1. 1992-93, 0-for-1. 1994-95, 0-for-1. Totals, 1-for-11 (.091).

~~(illegible line)~~ 353/3.

NBA ALL-STAR GAME RECORD

Season Team	Min.	FGM	FGA	Pct.	FTM	FTA	Pct.	Off.	Def.	Tot.	Ast.	PF	Dq.	St.	Blk.	TO	Pts.
1985—Milwaukee............	16	7	17	.412	3	4	.750	4	3	7	0	1	0	0	1	0	17
1989—Milwaukee............	19	4	9	.444	2	2	1.000	2	3	5	1	4	0	3	1	0	10
Totals........................	35	11	26	.423	5	6	.833	6	6	12	1	5	0	3	2	0	27

CUNNINGHAM, BILLY   F

See All-Time Great Coaches, page 453.

DANIELS, MEL   C

PERSONAL: Born July 20, 1944, in Detroit. ... 6-9/225 (2,06/102,1). ... Full name: Melvin Joe Daniels.
HIGH SCHOOL: Pershing (Detroit).
JUNIOR COLLEGE: Burlington (Iowa) Junior College.
COLLEGE: New Mexico.
TRANSACTIONS: Selected by Minnesota Muskies in first round of 1967 ABA draft. ... Traded by Muskies to Indiana Pacers for 1969 first-round draft choice, G James Dawson, F Ron Kozlicki and cash (May 1968). ... Traded by Pacers with G Freddie Lewis to Memphis Sounds for F Charlie Edge and cash (July 26, 1974). ... Memphis franchise transferred to Baltimore and renamed Claws for 1975-76 season. ... Baltimore franchise folded prior to 1975-76 season. ... Signed as free agent by New York Nets of NBA (October 19, 1976). ... Waived by Nets (December 13, 1976).
CAREER NOTES: Scout, Pacers (1984-85 to 1995-96). ... Director of player personnel (1996 to present).
MISCELLANEOUS: Indiana Pacers franchise all-time leading rebounder with 7,643 (1986-74).

COLLEGIATE RECORD

Season Team	G	Min.	FGM	FGA	Pct.	FTM	FTA	Pct.	Reb.	Ast.	Pts.	RPG	APG	PPG
63-64—Burlington County J.C.	34	...	334	...	...	100	...	...	...	...	768	...	...	22.6
64-65—New Mexico..................	27	...	178	366	.486	111	182	.610	302	...	467	11.2	...	17.3
65-66—New Mexico..................	23	...	191	394	.485	107	145	.738	238	...	489	10.3	...	21.3
66-67—New Mexico..................	27	...	225	468	.481	131	191	.686	313	...	581	11.6	...	21.5
Totals	111	...	928	...	...	449	...	...	...	...	2305	...	...	20.8

ABA REGULAR-SEASON RECORD

NOTES: ABA Most Valuable Player (1969, 1971). ... ABA Rookie of the Year (1968). ... All-ABA first team (1968, 1969, 1970, 1971). ... All-ABA second team (1973). ... ABA All-Rookie team (1968). ... Member of ABA championship team (1970, 1972, 1973).

Season Team	G	Min.	FGM	FGA	Pct.	FGM	FGA	Pct.	FTM	FTA	Pct.	Reb.	Ast.	Pts.	RPG	APG	PPG
				2-POINT			3-POINT									AVERAGES	
67-68—Minnesota	78	2938	669	1640	.408	1	5	.200	390	678	.575	1213	109	1729	*15.6	1.4	22.2
68-69—Indiana	76	2934	712	1496	.476	0	4	.000	400	662	.604	1256	116	1824	*16.5	1.5	24.0
69-70—Indiana	83	3039	613	1295	.473	0	2	.000	330	489	.675	1462	131	1556	17.6	1.6	18.7
70-71—Indiana	82	3170	698	1357	.514	1	13	.077	326	480	.679	1475	178	1723	*18.0	2.2	21.0
71-72—Indiana	79	2971	598	1184	.505	0	6	.000	317	451	.703	1297	176	1513	16.4	2.2	19.2
72-73—Indiana	81	3103	587	1217	.482	1	4	.250	322	446	.722	1247	177	1497	15.4	2.2	18.5
73-74—Indiana	78	2539	492	1117	.440	0	0	...	217	287	.756	906	120	1201	11.6	1.5	15.4
74-75—Memphis	71	1646	290	644	.450	0	0	...	116	183	.634	638	125	696	9.0	1.8	9.8
Totals	628	22340	4659	9950	.468	3	34	.088	2418	3676	.658	9494	1132	11739	15.1	1.8	18.7

ABA PLAYOFF RECORD

Season Team	G	Min.	FGM	FGA	Pct.	FGM	FGA	Pct.	FTM	FTA	Pct.	Reb.	Ast.	Pts.	RPG	APG	PPG
				2-POINT			3-POINT									AVERAGES	
67-68—Minnesota	10	409	98	226	.434	0	0	...	54	94	.574	161	19	253	16.1	1.9	25.3
68-69—Indiana	17	570	127	300	.423	0	1	.000	79	130	.608	237	22	333	13.9	1.3	19.6
69-70—Indiana	15	533	108	242	.446	0	1	.000	74	111	.667	265	15	290	17.7	1.0	19.3
70-71—Indiana	11	457	94	194	.485	0	0	...	47	63	.746	211	16	235	19.2	1.5	21.4
71-72—Indiana	20	744	121	249	.486	0	3	.000	64	85	.753	302	28	306	15.1	1.4	15.3
72-73—Indiana	18	636	112	238	.471	0	0	...	62	81	.765	248	40	286	13.8	2.2	15.9
73-74—Indiana	14	498	69	172	.401	0	0	...	33	43	.767	160	27	171	11.4	1.9	12.2
74-75—Indiana	4	54	11	22	.500	0	0	...	5	9	.556	24	1	27	6.0	0.3	6.8
Totals	109	3901	740	1643	.450	0	5	.000	418	616	.679	1608	168	1901	14.8	1.5	17.4

ABA ALL-STAR GAME RECORD

NOTES: ABA All-Star Game Most Valuable Player (1971).

Season Team	Min.	FGM	FGA	Pct.	FGM	FGA	Pct.	FTM	FTA	Pct.	Reb.	Ast.	Pts.
			2-POINT			3-POINT							
1968—Minnesota	29	9	18	.500	0	0	...	4	11	.364	15	0	22
1969—Indiana	31	5	16	.313	0	0	...	7	10	.700	10	2	17
1970—Indiana	26	6	14	.429	0	0	...	1	3	.333	12	1	13
1971—Indiana	30	12	19	.632	0	0	...	5	7	.714	13	3	29
1972—Indiana	26	8	14	.571	0	0	...	5	8	.625	9	1	21
1973—Indiana	33	8	19	.421	0	0	...	9	12	.750	11	1	25
1974—Indiana	20	2	11	.182	0	0	...	1	2	.500	7	0	5
Totals	195	50	111	.450	0	0	...	32	53	.604	77	8	132

NBA REGULAR-SEASON RECORD

Season Team	G	Min.	FGM	FGA	Pct.	FTM	FTA	Pct.	Off.	Def.	Tot.	Ast.	St.	Blk.	TO	Pts.	RPG	APG	PPG
										REBOUNDS								AVERAGES	
76-77—N.Y. Nets	11	126	13	35	.371	13	23	.565	10	24	34	6	3	11	...	39	3.1	0.5	3.5

Personal fouls/disqualifications: 1976-77, 29/0.

COMBINED ABA AND NBA REGULAR-SEASON RECORDS

	G	Min.	FGM	FGA	Pct.	FTM	FTA	Pct.	Off.	Def.	Tot.	Ast.	Stl.	Blk.	TO	Pts.	RPG	APG	PPG
										REBOUNDS								AVERAGES	
Totals	639	22466	4675	10019	.467	2431	3699	.657	...	...	9528	1138	...	...	...	11778	14.9	1.8	18.4

Three-point field goals: 3-for-34 (.088).
Personal fouls/disqualifications: 2309.

HEAD COACHING RECORD

BACKGROUND: Assistant coach, Indiana State (1978-79 through 1981-82). ... Assistant coach, Indiana Pacers (1984-85 through 1988-89 and 1991-92 and 1992-93).
HONORS: USBL Coach of the Year (1993).

NBA COACHING RECORD

Season Team	W	L	Pct.	Finish	W	L	Pct.
		REGULAR SEASON				PLAYOFFS	
88-89—Indiana	0	2	.000		—	—	—

NOTES:
1988—Replaced Jack Ramsay as Indiana head coach (November 17), with record of 0-7 and club in sixth place. Replaced as Indiana interim coach by George Irvine (November 21).

DANTLEY, ADRIAN   F/G

PERSONAL: Born February 28, 1956, in Washington, D.C. ... 6-5/210 (1,96/95,3). ... Full name: Adrian Delano Dantley.
HIGH SCHOOL: DeMatha Catholic (Hyattsville, Md.).
COLLEGE: Notre Dame.
TRANSACTIONS: Selected after junior season by Buffalo Braves in first round (sixth pick overall) of 1976 NBA Draft. ... Traded by Braves with F Mike Bantom to Indiana Pacers for G/F Billy Knight (September 1, 1977). ... Traded by Pacers with C/F Dave Robisch to Los Angeles Lakers for C James Edwards, G Earl Tatum and cash (December 13, 1977). ... Traded by Lakers to Utah Jazz for F Spencer Haywood (September 13, 1979). ... Traded by Jazz with 1987 and 1990 second-round draft choices to Detroit Pistons for F Kelly Tripucka and F/C Kent Benson (August 21, 1986). ... Traded by Pistons with 1991 first-round draft choice to Dallas Mavericks for F Mark Aguirre (February 15, 1989). ... Waived by Mavericks (April 2, 1990). ... Signed as free agent by Milwaukee Bucks (April 2, 1991). ... Played in Italy (1991-92).

MISCELLANEOUS: Member of gold-medal-winning U.S. Olympic team (1976).

COLLEGIATE RECORD

NOTES: The Sporting News All-America first team (1975, 1976).

Season Team	G	Min.	FGM	FGA	Pct.	FTM	FTA	Pct.	Reb.	Ast.	Pts.	AVERAGES		
												RPG	APG	PPG
73-74—Notre Dame	28	795	189	339	.558	133	161	.826	255	40	511	9.1	1.4	18.3
74-75—Notre Dame	29	1091	315	581	.542	253	314	.806	296	47	883	10.2	1.6	30.4
75-76—Notre Dame	29	1056	300	510	.588	229	294	.779	292	49	829	10.1	1.7	28.6
Totals	86	2942	804	1430	.562	615	769	.800	843	136	2223	9.8	1.6	25.8

NBA REGULAR-SEASON RECORD

RECORDS: Shares single-game records for most free throws made—28 (January 4, 1984, vs. Houston); and most free throws made in one quarter—14 (December 10, 1986, vs. Sacramento).
HONORS: NBA Rookie of the Year (1977). ... All-NBA second team (1981, 1984). ... NBA All-Rookie team (1977). ... NBA Comeback Player of the Year (1984).

Season Team	G	Min.	FGM	FGA	Pct.	FTM	FTA	Pct.	REBOUNDS			Ast.	St.	Blk.	TO	Pts.	AVERAGES		
									Off.	Def.	Tot.						RPG	APG	PPG
76-77—Buffalo	77	2816	544	1046	.520	476	582	.818	251	336	587	144	91	15	...	1564	7.6	1.9	20.3
77-78—Ind.-L.A.	79	2933	578	1128	.512	*541	680	.796	265	355	620	253	118	24	228	1697	7.8	3.2	21.5
78-79—Los Angeles	60	1775	374	733	.510	292	342	.854	131	211	342	138	63	12	155	1040	5.7	2.3	17.3
79-80—Utah	68	2674	730	1267	.576	443	526	.842	183	333	516	191	96	14	233	1903	7.6	2.8	28.0
80-81—Utah	80	*3417	*909	1627	.559	*632	784	.806	192	317	509	322	109	18	282	*2452	6.4	4.0	*30.7
81-82—Utah	81	3222	904	1586	.570	*648	818	.792	231	283	514	324	95	14	†299	2457	6.3	4.0	30.3
82-83—Utah	22	887	233	402	.580	210	248	.847	58	82	140	105	20	0	81	676	6.4	4.8	30.7
83-84—Utah	79	2984	802	1438	.558	*813	*946	.859	179	269	448	310	61	4	263	*2418	5.7	3.9	*30.6
84-85—Utah	55	1971	512	964	.531	438	545	.804	148	175	323	186	57	8	171	1462	5.9	3.4	26.6
85-86—Utah	76	2744	818	1453	.563	630	796	.791	178	217	395	264	64	4	231	2267	5.2	3.5	29.8
86-87—Detroit	81	2736	601	1126	.534	539	664	.812	104	228	332	162	63	7	181	1742	4.1	2.0	21.5
87-88—Detroit	69	2144	444	863	.514	492	572	.860	84	143	227	171	39	10	135	1380	3.3	2.5	20.0
88-89—Detroit-Dal.	73	2422	470	954	.493	460	568	.810	117	200	317	171	43	13	163	1400	4.3	2.3	19.2
89-90—Dallas	45	1300	231	484	.477	200	254	.787	78	94	172	80	20	7	75	662	3.8	1.8	14.7
90-91—Milwaukee	10	126	19	50	.380	18	26	.692	8	5	13	9	5	0	6	57	1.3	0.9	5.7
Totals	955	34151	8169	15121	.540	6832	8351	.818	2207	3248	5455	2830	944	150	2503	23177	5.7	3.0	24.3

Three-point field goals: 1979-80, 0-for-2. 1980-81, 2-for-7 (.286). 1981-82, 1-for-3 (.333). 1983-84, 1-for-4 (.250). 1985-86, 1-for-11 (.091). 1986-87, 1-for-6 (.167). 1987-88, 0-for-2. 1988-89, 0-for-1. 1989-90, 0-for-2. 1990-91, 1-for-3 (.333). Totals, 7-for-41 (.171).
Personal fouls/disqualifications: 1976-77, 215/2. 1977-78, 233/2. 1978-79, 162/0. 1979-80, 211/2. 1980-81, 245/1. 1981-82, 252/1. 1982-83, 62/2. 1983-84, 201/0. 1984-85, 133/0. 1985-86, 206/2. 1986-87, 193/1. 1987-88, 144/0. 1988-89, 186/1. 1989-90, 99/0. 1990-91, 8/0. Totals, 2550/14.

NBA PLAYOFF RECORD

Season Team	G	Min.	FGM	FGA	Pct.	FTM	FTA	Pct.	REBOUNDS			Ast.	St.	Blk.	TO	Pts.	AVERAGES		
									Off.	Def.	Tot.						RPG	APG	PPG
77-78—Los Angeles	3	104	20	35	.571	11	17	.647	9	16	25	11	5	3	6	51	8.3	3.7	17.0
78-79—Los Angeles	8	236	50	89	.562	41	52	.788	19	22	22	11	8	1	18	141	4.1	1.4	17.6
83-84—Utah	11	454	117	232	.504	120	139	.863	37	46	83	40	7	1	30	354	7.5	4.2	32.2
84-85—Utah	10	398	79	151	.523	95	122	.779	25	50	75	20	16	0	36	253	7.5	2.0	25.3
85-86—Utah								Did not play—injured.											
86-87—Detroit	15	500	111	206	.539	86	111	.775	29	39	68	35	13	0	33	308	4.5	2.3	20.5
87-88—Detroit	23	804	153	292	.524	140	178	.787	37	70	107	46	19	1	51	446	4.7	2.0	19.4
90-91—Milwaukee	3	19	1	7	.143	3	4	.750	2	2	4	0	0	0	2	5	1.3	0.0	1.7
Totals	73	2515	531	1012	.525	496	623	.796	149	246	395	169	69	6	185	1558	5.4	2.3	21.3

Three-point field goals: 1984-85, 0-for-1. 1987-88, 0-for-2. Totals, 0-for-3.
Personal fouls/disqualifications: 1977-78, 9/0. 1978-79, 24/0. 1983-84, 30/0. 1984-85, 39/1. 1986-87, 36/0. 1987-88, 50/0. Totals, 188/1.

NBA ALL-STAR GAME RECORD

Season Team	Min.	FGM	FGA	Pct.	FTM	FTA	Pct.	REBOUNDS			Ast.	PF	Dq.	St.	Blk.	TO	Pts.
								Off.	Def.	Tot.							
1980—Utah	30	8	15	.533	7	8	.875	4	1	5	2	1	0	2	0	2	23
1981—Utah	21	3	9	.333	2	2	1.000	2	3	5	0	1	0	1	0	0	8
1982—Utah	21	6	8	.750	0	1	.000	1	1	2	0	2	0	0	0	1	12
1984—Utah	18	1	8	.125	0	0	...	0	2	2	1	4	0	1	0	1	2
1985—Utah	23	2	6	.333	6	6	1.000	0	2	2	1	4	0	1	0	2	10
1986—Utah	17	3	8	.375	2	2	1.000	1	6	7	3	1	0	1	0	0	8
Totals	130	23	54	.426	17	19	.895	8	15	23	7	13	0	6	0	6	63

ITALIAN LEAGUE RECORD

Season Team	G	Min.	FGM	FGA	Pct.	FTM	FTA	Pct.	Reb.	Ast.	Pts.	AVERAGES		
												RPG	APG	PPG
91-92—Breeze Milan	27	906	253	427	.593	179	221	.810	152	10	721	5.6	0.4	26.7

DAVIES, BOB   G

PERSONAL: Born January 15, 1920, in Harrisburg, Pa. ... Died April 22, 1990. ... 6-1/175 (1,85/79,4). ... Full name: Robert Edris Davies. ... Nickname: The Harrisburg Houdini.
HIGH SCHOOL: John Harris (Harrisburg, Pa.).
COLLEGE: Franklin & Marshall (Pa.), then Seton Hall.
TRANSACTIONS: Played with Great Lakes (Ill.) Naval Training Station during 1942-43 season (led team in scoring—269 points, 114 field goals and 41 free throws). ... In military service during 1942-43, 1943-44 and 1944-45 seasons. ... Played in American Basketball League with Brooklyn Indians (1943-44) and New York Gothams (1944-45). ... Signed as free agent by Rochester Royals of National Basketball League (1945). ... Royals franchise transferred to Basketball Association of America for 1948-49 season.

CAREER HONORS: Elected to Naismith Memorial Basketball Hall of Fame (1970). ... NBA 25th Anniversary All-Time Team (1970).
MISCELLANEOUS: Member of NBA championship team (1951). ... Member of NBL championship team (1946).

COLLEGIATE RECORD

Season Team	G	Min.	FGM	FGA	Pct.	FTM	FTA	Pct.	Reb.	Ast.	Pts.	AVERAGES RPG	APG	PPG
37-38—Frank. & Marshall‡					Freshman team statistics unavailable.									
38-39—Seton Hall‡					Freshman team statistics unavailable.									
39-40—Seton Hall	18	...	78	...	...	56	...	...	...	...	212	...	...	11.8
40-41—Seton Hall	22	...	91	...	...	42	...	...	...	...	224	...	...	10.2
41-42—Seton Hall	19	...	81	...	...	63	...	...	...	...	225	...	...	11.8
Varsity totals	59	...	250	...	...	161	...	...	...	...	661	...	...	11.2

ABL REGULAR-SEASON RECORD

Season Team	G	Min.	FGM	FGA	Pct.	FTM	FTA	Pct.	Reb.	Ast.	Pts.	AVERAGES RPG	APG	PPG
43-44—Brooklyn	4	...	8	...	...	8	...	...	...	...	24	...	...	6.0
44-45—New York	5	...	21	...	...	21	...	...	...	...	63	...	...	12.6
Totals	9	...	29	...	...	29	...	...	...	...	87	...	...	9.7

NBL AND NBA REGULAR-SEASON RECORD

HONORS: All-NBA first team (1950, 1951, 1952). ... All-NBA second team (1953). ... All-BAA first team (1949). ... NBL Most Valuable Player (1947). ... All-NBL first team (1947). ... All-NBL second team (1948).

Season Team	G	Min.	FGM	FGA	Pct.	FTM	FTA	Pct.	Reb.	Ast.	PF	Dq.	Pts.	AVERAGES RPG	APG	PPG
45-46—Rochester (NBL)	27	...	86	...	...	70	103	.680	...	...	85	...	242	...	...	9.0
46-47—Rochester (NBL)	32	...	166	...	...	130	166	.783	...	...	90	...	462	...	...	14.4
47-48—Rochester (NBL)	48	...	176	...	...	120	160	.750	...	...	111	...	472	...	...	9.8
48-49—Rochester (BAA)	60	...	317	871	.364	270	348	.776	...	*321	197	...	904	...	*5.4	15.1
49-50—Rochester	64	...	317	887	.357	261	347	.752	...	294	187	...	895	...	4.6	14.0
50-51—Rochester	63	...	326	877	.372	303	381	.795	197	287	208	7	955	3.1	4.6	15.2
51-52—Rochester	65	2394	379	990	.383	294	379	.776	189	390	269	10	1052	2.9	6.0	16.2
52-53—Rochester	66	2216	339	880	.385	351	466	.753	195	280	261	7	1029	3.0	4.2	15.6
53-54—Rochester	72	2137	288	777	.371	311	433	.718	194	323	224	4	887	2.7	4.5	12.3
54-55—Rochester	72	1870	326	785	.415	220	293	.751	205	355	220	2	872	2.8	4.9	12.1
Totals	569	...	2720	...	...	2330	3076	.757	...	...	1852	...	7770	...	...	13.7

NBL AND NBA PLAYOFF RECORD

Season Team	G	Min.	FGM	FGA	Pct.	FTM	FTA	Pct.	Reb.	Ast.	PF	Dq.	Pts.	AVERAGES RPG	APG	PPG
45-46—Rochester (NBL)	7	...	28	...	...	30	41	.732	...	...	17	...	86	...	...	12.3
46-47—Rochester (NBL)	11	...	54	...	...	43	63	.683	...	...	30	...	151	...	...	13.7
47-48—Rochester (NBL)	11	...	56	...	...	49	64	.766	...	...	24	...	161	...	...	14.6
48-49—Rochester (BAA)	4	...	19	51	.373	10	13	.769	...	13	11	...	48	...	3.3	12.0
49-50—Rochester	2	...	4	17	.235	7	8	.875	...	9	11	...	15	...	4.5	7.5
50-51—Rochester	14	...	79	234	.338	64	80	.800	43	75	45	1	222	3.1	5.4	15.9
51-52—Rochester	6	233	37	92	.402	45	55	.818	13	28	18	0	119	2.2	4.7	19.8
52-53—Rochester	3	91	6	29	.207	14	20	.700	4	14	11	0	26	1.3	4.7	8.7
53-54—Rochester	6	172	17	52	.327	17	23	.739	12	14	16	0	51	2.0	2.3	8.5
54-55—Rochester	3	75	11	33	.333	3	4	.750	6	9	11	0	25	2.0	3.0	8.3
Totals	67	...	311	...	...	282	371	.760	...	...	194	...	904	...	...	13.5

NBA ALL-STAR GAME RECORD

Season Team	Min.	FGM	FGA	Pct.	FTM	FTA	Pct.	Reb	Ast.	PF	Dq.	Pts.
1951—Rochester	...	4	6	.667	5	5	1.000	5	5	3	0	13
1952—Rochester	27	4	11	.364	0	0	...	0	5	4	0	8
1953—Rochester	17	3	7	.429	3	6	.500	3	2	2	0	9
1954—Rochester	31	8	16	.500	2	3	.667	5	5	4	0	18
Totals	...	19	40	.475	10	14	.714	13	17	13	0	48

COLLEGIATE COACHING RECORD

Season Team	W	L	Pct.
46-47—Seton Hall	24	3	.889
55-56—Gettysburg	11	17	.393
56-57—Gettysburg	7	18	.280
Totals (3 years)	42	38	.525

DAVIS, WALTER   G

PERSONAL: Born September 9, 1954, in Pineville, N.C. ... 6-6/200 (1,98/90,7). ... Full name: Walter Paul Davis. ... Uncle of Hubert Davis, guard with Washington Wizards.
HIGH SCHOOL: South Mecklenburg (Charlotte).
COLLEGE: North Carolina.
TRANSACTIONS: Selected by Phoenix Suns in first round (fifth pick overall) of 1977 NBA Draft. ... Signed as unrestricted free agent by Denver Nuggets (July 6, 1988). ... Traded by Nuggets to Portland Trail Blazers in three-way deal in which Trail Blazers sent G Drazen Petrovic to New Jersey Nets, Nets sent F Greg Anderson to Nuggets, and Nuggets sent F Terry Mills to Nets (January 23, 1991); Nuggets also received 1992 first-round draft choice from Nets and 1993 second-round draft choice from Trail Blazers also received 1992 second-round draft choice from Nuggets. ... Waived by Trail Blazers (October 29, 1991). ... Signed as free agent by Nuggets (November 1, 1991).
MISCELLANEOUS: Member of gold-medal-winning U.S. Olympic team (1976). ... Phoenix Suns all-time leading scorer with 15,666 points (1977-78 through 1987-88).

COLLEGIATE RECORD

Season Team	G	Min.	FGM	FGA	Pct.	FTM	FTA	Pct.	Reb.	Ast.	Pts.	AVERAGES RPG	APG	PPG
73-74—North Carolina	27	...	161	322	.500	65	82	.793	126	72	387	4.7	2.7	14.3
74-75—North Carolina	31	...	200	396	.505	98	130	.754	195	137	498	6.3	4.4	16.1
75-76—North Carolina	29	...	190	351	.541	101	130	.777	166	96	481	5.7	3.3	16.6
76-77—North Carolina	32	...	203	351	.578	91	117	.778	183	104	497	5.7	3.3	15.5
Totals	119	...	754	1420	.531	355	459	.773	670	409	1863	5.6	3.4	15.7

NBA REGULAR-SEASON RECORD

HONORS: NBA Rookie of the Year (1978). ... All-NBA second team (1978, 1979). ... NBA All-Rookie team (1978).

Season Team	G	Min.	FGM	FGA	Pct.	FTM	FTA	Pct.	REBOUNDS Off.	Def.	Tot.	Ast.	St.	Blk.	TO	Pts.	AVERAGES RPG	APG	PPG
77-78—Phoenix	81	2590	786	1494	.526	387	466	.830	158	326	484	273	113	20	283	1959	6.0	3.4	24.2
78-79—Phoenix	79	2437	764	1362	.561	340	409	.831	111	262	373	339	147	26	293	1868	4.7	4.3	23.6
79-80—Phoenix	75	2309	657	1166	.563	299	365	.819	75	197	272	337	114	19	242	1613	3.6	4.5	21.5
80-81—Phoenix	78	2182	593	1101	.539	209	250	.836	63	137	200	302	97	12	222	1402	2.6	3.9	18.0
81-82—Phoenix	55	1182	350	669	.523	91	111	.820	21	82	103	162	46	3	112	794	1.9	2.9	14.4
82-83—Phoenix	80	2491	665	1289	.516	184	225	.818	63	134	197	397	117	12	188	1521	2.5	5.0	19.0
83-84—Phoenix	78	2546	652	1274	.512	233	270	.863	38	164	202	429	107	12	213	1557	2.6	5.5	20.0
84-85—Phoenix	23	570	139	309	.450	64	73	.877	6	29	35	98	18	0	50	345	1.5	4.3	15.0
85-86—Phoenix	70	2239	624	1287	.485	257	305	.843	54	149	203	361	99	3	219	1523	2.9	5.2	21.8
86-87—Phoenix	79	2646	779	1515	.514	288	334	.862	90	154	244	364	96	5	226	1867	3.1	4.6	23.6
87-88—Phoenix	68	1951	488	1031	.473	205	231	.887	32	127	159	278	86	3	126	1217	2.3	4.1	17.9
88-89—Denver	81	1857	536	1076	.498	175	199	.879	41	110	151	190	72	5	132	1267	1.9	2.3	15.6
89-90—Denver	69	1635	497	1033	.481	207	227	.912	46	133	179	155	59	9	102	1207	2.6	2.2	17.5
90-91—Den.-Port.	71	1483	403	862	.468	107	117	.915	71	110	181	125	80	3	88	924	2.5	1.8	13.0
91-92—Denver	46	741	185	403	.459	82	94	.872	20	50	70	68	29	1	45	457	1.5	1.5	9.9
Totals	1033	28859	8118	15871	.511	3128	3676	.851	889	2164	3053	3878	1280	133	2541	19521	3.0	3.8	18.9

Three-point field goals: 1979-80, 0-for-4. 1980-81, 7-for-17 (.412). 1981-82, 3-for-16 (.188). 1982-83, 7-for-23 (.304). 1983-84, 20-for-87 (.230). 1984-85, 3-for-10 (.300). 1985-86, 18-for-76 (.237). 1986-87, 21-for-81 (.259). 1987-88, 36-for-96 (.375). 1988-89, 20-for-69 (.290). 1989-90, 6-for 46 (.130). 1990-91, 11-for-36 (.306). 1991-92, 5-for-16 (.313). Totals, 157-for-577 (.272).

Personal fouls/disqualifications: 1977-78, 242/2. 1978-79, 250/5. 1979-80, 202/2. 1980-81, 192/3. 1981-82, 104/1. 1982-83, 186/2. 1983-84, 202/0. 1984-85, 42/0. 1985-86, 153/1. 1986-87, 184/1. 1987-88, 131/0. 1988-89, 187/1. 1989-90, 160/1. 1990-91, 150/2. 1991-92, 69/0. Totals, 2454/21.

NBA PLAYOFF RECORD

Season Team	G	Min.	FGM	FGA	Pct.	FTM	FTA	Pct.	REBOUNDS Off.	Def.	Tot.	Ast.	St.	Blk.	TO	Pts.	AVERAGES RPG	APG	PPG
77-78—Phoenix	2	66	19	40	.475	12	16	.750	4	13	17	8	3	0	6	50	8.5	4.0	25.0
78-79—Phoenix	15	490	127	244	.521	78	96	.813	24	45	69	79	26	5	66	332	4.6	5.3	22.1
79-80—Phoenix	8	245	69	137	.504	28	38	.737	9	14	23	35	4	1	20	166	2.9	4.4	20.8
80-81—Phoenix	7	199	51	106	.481	10	17	.588	7	12	19	22	7	1	17	112	2.7	3.1	16.0
81-82—Phoenix	7	173	52	116	.448	22	24	.917	5	17	22	30	5	1	12	127	3.1	4.3	18.1
82-83—Phoenix	3	113	30	69	.435	17	21	.810	5	10	15	13	6	5	5	78	5.0	4.3	26.0
83-84—Phoenix	17	623	175	327	.535	70	78	.897	15	31	46	109	29	3	43	423	2.7	6.4	24.9
88-89—Denver	3	81	27	55	.519	19	19	1.000	2	3	5	3	4	0	8	77	1.7	1.3	25.7
89-90—Denver	3	70	18	45	.400	6	6	1.000	4	5	9	6	1	0	5	42	3.0	2.0	14.0
90-91—Portland	13	111	19	48	.396	5	6	.833	7	8	15	6	4	0	7	43	1.2	0.5	3.3
Totals	78	2184	591	1192	.496	263	317	.830	82	158	240	312	88	16	189	1450	3.1	4.0	18.6

Three-point field goals: 1979-80, 0-for-3. 1980-81, 0-for-1. 1981-82, 1-for-3 (.333). 1982-83, 1-for-2 (.500). 1983-84, 3-for-11 (.273). 1988-89, 0-for-4. 1989-90, 0-for-1. 1990-91, 0-for-1. Totals, 5-for-26 (.192).

Personal fouls/disqualifications: 1977-78, 8/0. 1978-79, 41/0. 1979-80, 20/0. 1980-81, 17/0. 1981-82, 19/0. 1982-83, 6/0. 1983-84, 55/0. 1988-89, 11/0. 1989-90, 4/0. 1990-91, 5/0. Totals, 186/0.

NBA ALL-STAR GAME RECORD

Season Team	Min.	FGM	FGA	Pct.	FTM	FTA	Pct.	REBOUNDS Off.	Def.	Tot.	Ast.	PF	Dq.	St.	Blk.	TO	Pts.
1978—Phoenix	15	3	6	.500	4	4	1.000	0	1	1	6	1	0	1	0	0	10
1979—Phoenix	19	4	9	.444	0	0	...	1	3	4	4	0	0	1	0	2	8
1980—Phoenix	23	5	10	.500	2	2	1.000	2	2	4	2	2	0	4	0	3	12
1981—Phoenix	22	5	9	.556	2	2	1.000	1	6	7	1	2	0	0	0	1	12
1984—Phoenix	15	5	9	.556	0	0	...	0	2	2	1	0	0	1	0	0	10
1987—Phoenix	15	3	12	.250	0	0	...	2	0	2	1	0	0	0	0	0	7
Totals	109	25	55	.455	8	8	1.000	6	14	20	15	5	0	7	0	6	59

Three-point field goals: 1987, 1-for-1.

DeBUSSCHERE, DAVE   F

PERSONAL: Born October 16, 1940, in Detroit. ... Died May 14, 2003. ... 6-6/235 (1,98/106,6). ... Full name: David Albert DeBusschere.

HIGH SCHOOL: Austin Catholic (Detroit).

COLLEGE: Detroit.

TRANSACTIONS: Selected by Detroit Pistons in 1962 NBA Draft (territorial pick). ... Traded by Pistons to New York Knicks for C Walt Bellamy and G Howard Komives (December 19, 1968).

CAREER HONORS: Elected to Naismith Memorial Basketball Hall of Fame (1983). ... One of the 50 Greatest Players in NBA History (1996).

CAREER NOTES: General manager, New York Knicks (May 1982 through January 1986).

MISCELLANEOUS: Member of NBA championship team (1970, 1973).

COLLEGIATE RECORD

Season Team	G	Min.	FGM	FGA	Pct.	FTM	FTA	Pct.	Reb.	Ast.	Pts.	AVERAGES RPG	APG	PPG
58-59—Detroit‡	15	...	144	306	.471	68	101	.673	305	...	356	20.3	...	23.7
59-60—Detroit	27	...	288	665	.433	115	196	.587	540	...	691	20.0	...	25.6

Season Team	G	Min.	FGM	FGA	Pct.	FTM	FTA	Pct.	Reb.	Ast.	Pts.	RPG	APG	PPG
													AVERAGES	
60-61—Detroit	27	...	256	636	.403	86	155	.555	514	...	598	19.0	...	22.1
61-62—Detroit	26	...	267	616	.433	162	242	.669	498	...	696	19.2	...	26.8
Varsity totals	80	...	811	1917	.423	363	593	.612	1552	...	1985	19.4	...	24.8

NBA REGULAR-SEASON RECORD

HONORS: All-NBA second team (1969). ... NBA All-Defensive first team (1969, 1970, 1971, 1972, 1973, 1974). ... NBA All-Rookie team (1963).

Season Team	G	Min.	FGM	FGA	Pct.	FTM	FTA	Pct.	Reb.	Ast.	PF	Dq.	Pts.	RPG	APG	PPG
															AVERAGES	
62-63—Detroit	80	2352	406	944	.430	206	287	.718	694	207	247	2	1018	8.7	2.6	12.7
63-64—Detroit	15	304	52	133	.391	25	43	.581	105	23	32	1	129	7.0	1.5	8.6
64-65—Detroit	79	2769	508	1196	.425	306	437	.700	874	253	242	5	1322	11.1	3.2	16.7
65-66—Detroit	79	2696	524	1284	.408	249	378	.659	916	209	252	5	1297	11.6	2.6	16.4
66-67—Detroit	78	2897	531	1278	.416	361	512	.705	924	216	297	7	1423	11.8	2.8	18.2
67-68—Detroit	80	3125	573	1295	.442	289	435	.664	1081	181	304	3	1435	13.5	2.3	17.9
68-69—Detroit-N.Y.	76	2943	506	1140	.444	229	328	.698	888	191	290	6	1241	11.7	2.5	16.3
69-70—New York	79	2627	488	1082	.451	176	256	.688	790	194	244	2	1152	10.0	2.5	14.6
70-71—New York	81	2891	523	1243	.421	217	312	.696	901	220	237	2	1263	11.1	2.7	15.6
71-72—New York	80	3072	520	1218	.427	193	265	.728	901	291	219	1	1233	11.3	3.6	15.4
72-73—New York	77	2827	532	1224	.435	194	260	.746	787	259	215	1	1258	10.2	3.4	16.3

Season Team	G	Min.	FGM	FGA	Pct.	FTM	FTA	Pct.	Off.	Def.	Tot.	Ast.	St.	Blk.	TO	Pts.	RPG	APG	PPG
									REBOUNDS								AVERAGES		
73-74—New York	71	2699	559	1212	.461	164	217	.756	134	623	757	253	67	39	...	1282	10.7	3.6	18.1
Totals	875	31202	5722	13249	.432	2609	3730	.699	...	...	9618	2497	67	39	...	14053	11.0	2.9	16.1

Personal fouls/disqualifications: 1973-74, 222/2.

NBA PLAYOFF RECORD

Season Team	G	Min.	FGM	FGA	Pct.	FTM	FTA	Pct.	Reb.	Ast.	PF	Dq.	Pts.	RPG	APG	PPG
															AVERAGES	
62-63—Detroit	4	159	25	59	.424	30	44	.682	63	6	14	1	80	15.8	1.5	20.0
67-68—Detroit	6	263	45	106	.425	26	45	.578	97	13	23	0	116	16.2	2.2	19.3
68-69—New York	10	419	61	174	.351	41	50	.820	148	33	43	0	163	14.8	3.3	16.3
69-70—New York	19	701	130	309	.421	45	68	.662	220	46	63	1	305	11.6	2.4	16.1
70-71—New York	12	488	84	202	.416	29	44	.659	156	22	40	1	197	13.0	1.8	16.4
71-72—New York	16	616	109	242	.450	48	64	.750	193	37	51	2	266	12.1	2.3	16.6
72-73—New York	17	632	117	265	.442	31	40	.775	179	58	57	0	265	10.5	3.4	15.6

Season Team	G	Min.	FGM	FGA	Pct.	FTM	FTA	Pct.	Off.	Def.	Tot.	Ast.	St.	Blk.	TO	Pts.	RPG	APG	PPG
									REBOUNDS								AVERAGES		
73-74—New York	12	404	63	166	.380	18	29	.621	25	74	99	38	7	4	...	144	8.3	3.2	12.0
Totals	96	3682	634	1523	.416	268	384	.698	...	...	1155	253	...	...	...	1536	12.0	2.6	16.0

Personal fouls/disqualifications: 1973-74, 36/0.

NBA ALL-STAR GAME RECORD

NOTES: Shares single-game record for most field goals made in one quarter—8 (1967).

Season Team	Min.	FGM	FGA	Pct.	FTM	FTA	Pct.	Reb	Ast.	PF	Dq.	Pts.
1966—Detroit	22	1	14	.071	2	2	1.000	6	1	1	0	4
1967—Detroit	25	11	17	.647	0	0	...	6	0	1	0	22
1968—Detroit	12	0	3	.000	0	0	...	4	0	1	0	0
1970—New York	14	5	10	.500	0	0	...	7	2	1	0	10
1971—New York	19	4	7	.571	0	0	...	7	3	3	0	8
1972—New York	26	4	8	.500	0	0	...	11	0	2	0	8
1973—New York	25	4	8	.500	1	2	.500	7	2	1	0	9

Season Team	Min.	FGM	FGA	Pct.	FTM	FTA	Pct.	Off.	Def.	Tot.	Ast.	PF	Dq.	St.	Blk.	TO	Pts.
								REBOUNDS									
1974—New York	24	8	14	.571	0	0	...	2	1	3	3	2	0	1	0	...	16
Totals	167	37	81	.457	3	4	.750	...	...	51	11	12	0	1	0	...	77

NBA COACHING RECORD

BACKGROUND: Player/head coach, Detroit Pistons (November 1964 to March 1967).
MISCELLANEOUS: Youngest coach in NBA history.

Season Team	W	L	Pct.	Finish	W	L	Pct.
		REGULAR SEASON				PLAYOFFS	
64-65—Detroit	29	40	.420	4th/Western Division	—	—	—
65-66—Detroit	22	58	.275	5th/Western Division	—	—	—
66-67—Detroit	28	45	.384		—	—	—
Totals (3 years)	79	143	.356				

NOTES:
1964—Replaced Charles Wolf as Detroit head coach (November), with record of 2-9.
1967—Replaced as Detroit head coach by Donnis Butcher (March).

RECORD AS BASEBALL PLAYER

TRANSACTIONS: Signed by Chicago White Sox (April 1, 1962). ... On disabled list (June 4-20, 1964). ... On restricted list (September 7, 1965-December 19, 1968). ... Released by White Sox organization (December 23, 1968).

Year Team (League)	W	L	Pct.	ERA	G	GS	CG	ShO	Sv.	IP	H	R	ER	BB	SO
1962—Chicago (A.L.)	0	0	...	2.00	12	0	0	0	...	18	5	7	4	23	8
Savannah (S. Atl.)	10	1	.909	2.49	15	14	7	2	...	94	62	35	26	53	93
1963—Chicago (A.L.)	3	4	.429	3.11	24	10	1	1	...	84	80	35	29	34	53
1964—Indianapolis (PCL)	15	8	.652	3.93	32	30	10	2	...	174	173	88	76	66	126
1965—Indianapolis (PCL)	15	12	.556	3.65	35	*34	10	1	...	*244	*255	120	99	66	176
Major league totals (2 years)	3	4	.429	2.91	36	10	1	1	...	102	85	42	33	57	61

DREXLER, CLYDE G

PERSONAL: Born June 22, 1962, in New Orleans. ... 6-7/222 (2,00/100,7). ... Full name: Clyde Austin Drexler.
HIGH SCHOOL: Sterling (Houston).
COLLEGE: Houston.
TRANSACTIONS: Selected after junior season by Portland Trail Blazers in first round (14th pick overall) of 1983 NBA Draft. ... Traded by Trail Blazers with F Tracy Murray to Houston Rockets for F Otis Thorpe, rights to F Marcelo Nicola and 1995 first-round draft choice (February 14, 1995). ... Announced retirement, effective with the conclusion of 1997-98 season (March 18, 1998).
CAREER HONORS: One of the 50 Greatest Players in NBA History (1996). ... Elected to the Naismith Memorial Basketball Hall of Fame (2004).
CAREER NOTES: Head coach, University of Houston (1998-99 to 1999-2000). ... Special assistant to general manager, Denver Nuggets (September 27-December 30, 2001). ... Assistant coach, Nuggets (2002).
MISCELLANEOUS: Member of NBA championship team (1995). ... Member of gold-medal-winning U.S. Olympic team (1992). ... Portland Trail Blazers all-time leading scorer with 18,040 points, all-time leading rebounder with 5,339 and all-time steals leader with 1,795 (1983-84 through 1994-95).

COLLEGIATE RECORD

Season Team	G	Min.	FGM	FGA	Pct.	FTM	FTA	Pct.	Reb.	Ast.	Pts.	AVERAGES RPG	APG	PPG
80-81—Houston	30	992	153	303	.505	50	85	.588	314	78	356	10.5	2.6	11.9
81-82—Houston	32	1077	206	362	.569	73	120	.608	336	96	485	10.5	3.0	15.2
82-83—Houston	34	1186	236	440	.536	70	95	.737	298	129	542	8.8	3.8	15.9
Totals	96	3255	595	1105	.538	193	300	.643	948	303	1383	9.9	3.2	14.4

NBA REGULAR-SEASON RECORD

HONORS: All-NBA first team (1992). ... All-NBA second team (1988, 1991). ... All-NBA third team (1990, 1995).

Season Team	G	Min.	FGM	FGA	Pct.	FTM	FTA	Pct.	REBOUNDS Off.	Def.	Tot.	Ast.	St.	Blk.	TO	Pts.	AVERAGES RPG	APG	PPG
83-84—Portland	82	1408	252	559	.451	123	169	.728	112	123	235	153	107	29	123	628	2.9	1.9	7.7
84-85—Portland	80	2555	573	1161	.494	223	294	.759	217	259	476	441	177	68	223	1377	6.0	5.5	17.2
85-86—Portland	75	2576	542	1142	.475	293	381	.769	171	250	421	600	197	46	282	1389	5.6	8.0	18.5
86-87—Portland	82	3114	707	1408	.502	357	470	.760	227	291	518	566	204	71	253	1782	6.3	6.9	21.7
87-88—Portland	81	3060	849	1679	.506	476	587	.811	261	272	533	467	203	52	236	2185	6.6	5.8	27.0
88-89—Portland	78	3064	829	1672	.496	438	548	.799	289	326	615	450	213	54	250	2123	7.9	5.8	27.2
89-90—Portland	73	2683	670	1357	.494	333	430	.774	208	299	507	432	145	51	191	1703	6.9	5.9	23.3
90-91—Portland	82	2852	645	1338	.482	416	524	.794	212	334	546	493	144	60	232	1767	6.7	6.0	21.5
91-92—Portland	76	2751	694	1476	.470	401	505	.794	166	334	500	512	138	70	240	1903	6.6	6.7	25.0
92-93—Portland	49	1671	350	816	.429	245	292	.839	126	183	309	278	96	37	115	976	6.3	5.7	19.9
93-94—Portland	68	2334	473	1105	.428	286	368	.777	154	291	445	333	98	34	167	1303	6.5	4.9	19.2
94-95—Port.-Hou.	76	2728	571	1238	.461	364	442	.824	152	328	480	362	136	45	186	1653	6.3	4.8	21.8
95-96—Houston	52	1997	331	764	.433	265	338	.784	97	276	373	302	105	24	134	1005	7.2	5.8	19.3
96-97—Houston	62	2271	397	899	.442	201	268	.750	118	255	373	354	119	36	156	1114	6.0	5.7	18.0
97-98—Houston	70	2473	452	1059	.427	277	346	.801	105	241	346	382	126	42	189	1287	4.9	5.5	18.4
Totals	1086	37537	8335	17673	.472	4698	5962	.788	2615	4062	6677	6125	2207	719	2977	22195	6.1	5.6	20.4

Three-point field goals: 1983-84, 1-for-4 (.250). 1984-85, 8-for-27 (.316). 1985-86, 12-for-60 (.000). 1986-87, 11-for-47 (.234), 1987-88, 11-for-57 (.212). 1988-89, 27-for-104 (.260). 1989-90, 30-for-106 (.283). 1990-91, 61-for-191 (.319). 1991-92, 114-for-338 (.337). 1992-93, 31-for-133 (.233). 1993-94, 71-for-219 (.324). 1994-95, 147-for-408 (.360). 1995-96, 78-for-235 (.332). 1996-97, 119-for-335 (.355). 1997-98, 106-for-334 (.317). Totals, 827-for-2603 (.318).

Personal fouls/disqualifications: 1983-84, 209/2. 1984-85, 265/3. 1985-86, 270/8. 1986-87, 281/7. 1987-88, 250/2. 1988-89, 269/2. 1989-90, 222/1. 1990-91, 226/2. 1991-92, 229/2. 1992-93, 159/1. 1993-94, 202/2. 1994-95, 206/1. 1995-96, 153/0. 1996-97, 151/0. 1997-98, 193/0. Totals, 3285/33.

NBA PLAYOFF RECORD

NOTES: Holds single-game playoff record for most points in an overtime period—13 (April 29, 1992, vs. Los Angeles Lakers).

Season Team	G	Min.	FGM	FGA	Pct.	FTM	FTA	Pct.	REBOUNDS Off.	Def.	Tot.	Ast.	St.	Blk.	TO	Pts.	AVERAGES RPG	APG	PPG
83-84—Portland	5	85	15	35	.429	6	7	.857	7	10	17	8	5	1	7	36	3.4	1.6	7.2
84-85—Portland	9	339	55	134	.410	38	45	.844	27	28	55	83	23	9	29	150	6.1	9.2	16.7
85-86—Portland	4	145	26	57	.456	18	23	.783	9	16	25	26	6	3	10	72	6.3	6.5	18.0
86-87—Portland	4	153	36	79	.456	23	29	.793	16	14	30	15	7	3	6	96	7.5	3.8	24.0
87-88—Portland	4	170	32	83	.386	21	29	.724	12	16	28	21	12	2	12	88	7.0	5.3	22.0
88-89—Portland	3	128	35	71	.493	13	17	.765	13	7	20	25	6	2	12	83	6.7	8.3	27.7
89-90—Portland	21	853	172	390	.441	96	124	.774	63	88	151	150	53	18	67	449	7.2	7.1	21.4
90-91—Portland	16	633	128	269	.476	76	98	.776	40	89	129	129	34	16	61	347	8.1	8.1	21.7
91-92—Portland	21	847	198	425	.466	138	171	.807	60	95	155	147	31	20	58	553	7.4	7.0	26.3
92-93—Portland	3	116	18	43	.419	16	20	.800	8	11	19	14	5	3	3	57	6.3	4.7	19.0
93-94—Portland	4	157	31	73	.425	19	23	.826	10	31	41	22	8	2	9	84	10.3	5.5	21.0
94-95—Houston	22	849	155	322	.481	110	140	.786	45	109	154	111	33	15	45	450	7.0	5.0	20.5
95-96—Houston	8	292	49	118	.415	26	34	.765	15	47	62	40	21	4	20	133	7.8	5.0	16.6
96-97—Houston	16	623	105	241	.436	42	54	.778	25	64	89	77	26	7	36	290	5.6	4.8	18.1
97-98—Houston	5	182	21	68	.309	28	37	.757	9	18	27	23	8	3	13	75	5.4	4.6	15.0
Totals	145	5572	1076	2408	.447	670	851	.787	359	643	1002	891	278	108	397	2963	6.9	6.1	20.4

Three-point field goals: 1983-84, 0-for-1. 1984-85, 2-for-7 (.286). 1985-86, 2-for-5 (.400). 1986-87, 1-for-4 (.250). 1987-88, 3-for-6 (.500). 1988-89, 0-for-2. 1989-90, 9-for-41 (.220). 1990-91, 15-for-56 (.268). 1991-92, 19-for-81 (.235). 1992-93, 5-for-12 (.417). 1993-94, 3-for-13 (.231). 1994-95, 30-for-99 (.303). 1995-96, 9-for-34 (.265). 1996-97, 38-for-102 (.373). 1997-98, 5-for-26 (.192). Totals, 141-for-484 (.288).

Personal fouls/disqualifications: 1983-84, 11/0. 1984-85, 37/0. 1985-86, 19/1. 1986-87, 16/1. 1987-88, 14/0. 1988-89, 11/0. 1989-90, 72/2. 1990-91, 56/0. 1991-92, 77/2. 1992-93, 9/0. 1993-94, 7/0. 1994-95, 68/1. 1995-96, 22/0. 1996-97, 52/0. 1997-98, 15/0. Totals, 486/7.

NBA ALL-STAR GAME RECORD

NOTES: Teamed with Cynthia Cooper to win inaugural Nestlé Crunch All-Star 2ball championship (1998).

Season Team	Min.	FGM	FGA	Pct.	FTM	FTA	Pct.	REBOUNDS Off.	Def.	Tot.	Ast.	PF	Dq.	St.	Blk.	TO	Pts.
1986—Portland	15	5	7	.714	0	0	...	0	4	4	4	3	0	3	1	3	10
1988—Portland	15	3	5	.600	6	6	1.000	2	3	5	0	3	0	1	0	1	12

Season Team	Min.	FGM	FGA	Pct.	FTM	FTA	Pct.	REBOUNDS Off.	Def.	Tot.	Ast.	PF	Dq.	St.	Blk.	TO	Pts.
1989—Portland	25	7	19	.368	0	0	...	6	6	12	4	3	0	2	0	6	14
1990—Portland	19	2	6	.333	2	2	1.000	4	0	4	2	1	0	1	1	1	7
1991—Portland	19	4	9	.444	4	4	1.000	2	2	4	2	3	0	1	1	0	12
1992—Portland	28	10	15	.667	0	0	...	2	7	9	6	2	0	0	2	1	22
1993—Portland	11	1	3	.333	0	0	...	1	0	1	1	3	0	0	0	2	2
1994—Portland	15	3	7	.429	0	0	...	0	3	3	1	1	0	1	1	1	6
1996—Houston	19	5	8	.625	0	0	...	0	2	2	3	0	0	3	0	3	11
1997—Houston								Selected, did not play—injured.									
Totals	166	40	79	.506	12	12	1.000	17	27	44	23	19	0	12	6	18	96

Three-point field goals: 1986, 0-for-1. 1988, 0-for-1. 1990, 1-for-1. 1992, 2-for-4 (.500). 1993, 0-for-1. 1994, 0-for-2. 1996, 1-for-4 (.250). Totals, 4-for-14 (.286).

COLLEGIATE COACHING RECORD

Season Team	W	L	Pct.	
98-99—Houston	10	17	.370	6th/National Division/Conference USA
99-00—Houston	9	22	.290	6th/National Division/Conference USA

DUMARS, JOE   G

PERSONAL: Born May 24, 1963, in Shreveport, La. ... 6-3/195 (1,90/88,5). ... Full name: Joe Dumars III.
HIGH SCHOOL: Natchitoches (La.) Central.
COLLEGE: McNeese State.
TRANSACTIONS/CAREER NOTES: Selected by Detroit Pistons in first round (18th pick overall) of 1985 NBA Draft. ... Announced retirement (April 28, 1999).
MISCELLANEOUS: Member of NBA championship team (1989, 1990).
CAREER NOTES: Vice President of Player Personnel, Detroit Pistons (1999-2000). ... President of Basketball Operations, Detroit Pistons (June 6, 2000-present).
CAREER HONORS: Elected to Naismith Memorial Basketball Hall of Fame (2006).

COLLEGIATE RECORD

NOTES: THE SPORTING NEWS All-America second team (1985).

Season Team	G	Min.	FGM	FGA	Pct.	FTM	FTA	Pct.	Reb.	Ast.	Pts.	AVERAGES RPG	APG	PPG
81-82—McNeese State	29	...	206	464	.444	115	160	.719	64	80	527	2.2	2.8	18.2
82-83—McNeese State	29	...	212	487	.435	140	197	.711	128	64	569	4.4	2.2	19.6
83-84—McNeese State	31	...	276	586	.471	267	324	.824	164	80	819	5.3	2.6	26.4
84-85—McNeese State	27	...	248	501	.495	201	236	.852	132	106	697	4.9	3.9	25.8
Totals	116	...	942	2038	.462	723	917	.788	488	330	2612	4.2	2.8	22.5

Three-point field goals: 1982-83, 5-for-8 (.625).

NBA REGULAR-SEASON RECORD

HONORS: J. Walter Kennedy Citizenship Award (1994). ... NBA Sportsmanship Award (1996). ... All-NBA second team (1993). ... All-NBA third team (1990, 1991). ... NBA All-Defensive first team (1989, 1990, 1992, 1993). ... NBA All-Defensive second team (1991). ... NBA All-Rookie team (1986).

Season Team	G	Min.	FGM	FGA	Pct.	FTM	FTA	Pct.	REBOUNDS Off.	Def.	Tot.	Ast.	St.	Blk.	TO	Pts.	AVERAGES RPG	APG	PPG
85-86—Detroit	82	1957	287	597	.481	190	238	.798	60	59	119	390	66	11	158	769	1.5	4.8	9.4
86-87—Detroit	79	2439	369	749	.493	184	246	.748	50	117	167	352	83	5	171	931	2.1	4.5	11.8
87-88—Detroit	82	2732	453	960	.472	251	308	.815	63	137	200	387	87	15	172	1161	2.4	4.7	14.2
88-89—Detroit	69	2408	456	903	.505	260	306	.850	57	115	172	390	63	5	178	1186	2.5	5.7	17.2
89-90—Detroit	75	2578	508	1058	.480	297	330	.900	60	152	212	368	63	2	145	1335	2.8	4.9	17.8
90-91—Detroit	80	3046	622	1292	.481	371	417	.890	62	125	187	443	89	7	189	1629	2.3	5.5	20.4
91-92—Detroit	82	3192	587	1311	.448	412	475	.867	82	106	188	375	71	12	193	1635	2.3	4.6	19.9
92-93—Detroit	77	3094	677	1454	.466	343	397	.864	63	85	148	308	78	7	138	1809	1.9	4.0	23.5
93-94—Detroit	69	2591	505	1118	.452	276	330	.836	35	116	151	261	63	4	159	1410	2.2	3.8	20.4
94-95—Detroit	67	2544	417	970	.430	277	344	.805	47	111	158	368	72	7	219	1214	2.4	5.5	18.1
95-96—Detroit	67	2193	255	598	.426	162	197	.822	28	110	138	265	43	3	97	793	2.1	4.0	11.8
96-97—Detroit	79	2923	385	875	.440	222	256	.867	38	153	191	318	57	1	128	1158	2.4	4.0	14.7
97-98—Detroit	72	2326	329	791	.416	127	154	.825	14	90	104	253	44	2	84	943	1.4	3.5	13.1
98-99—Detroit	38	1116	144	350	.411	51	61	.836	12	56	68	134	23	2	53	428	1.8	3.5	11.3
Totals	1018	35139	5994	13026	.460	3423	4059	.843	671	1532	2203	4612	902	83	2084	16401	2.2	4.5	16.1

Three-point field goals: 1985-86, 5-for-16 (.313). 1986-87, 9-for-22 (.409). 1987-88, 4-for-19 (.211). 1988-89, 14-for-29 (.483). 1989-90, 22-for-55 (.400). 1990-91, 14-for-45 (.311). 1991-92, 49-for-120 (.408). 1992-93, 112-for-299 (.375). 1993-94, 124-for-320 (.388). 1994-95, 103-for-338 (.305). 1995-96, 121-for-298 (.406). 1996-97, 166-for-384 (.432). 1997-98, 158-for-426 (.371). 1998-99, 89-for-221 (.403). Totals, 990-for-2592 (.382).

Personal fouls/disqualifications: 1985-86, 200/1. 1986-87, 194/1. 1987-88, 155/1. 1988-89, 103/1. 1989-90, 129/1. 1990-91, 135/0. 1991-92, 145/0. 1992-93, 141/0. 1993-94, 118/0. 1994-95, 153/0. 1995-96, 106/0. 1996-97, 97/0. 1997-98, 99/0. 1998-99, 51/0. Totals, 1826/5.

NBA PLAYOFF RECORD

NOTES: NBA Finals Most Valuable Player (1989).

Season Team	G	Min.	FGM	FGA	Pct.	FTM	FTA	Pct.	REBOUNDS Off.	Def.	Tot.	Ast.	St.	Blk.	TO	Pts.	AVERAGES RPG	APG	PPG
85-86—Detroit	4	147	25	41	.610	10	15	.667	6	7	13	25	4	0	7	60	3.3	6.3	15.0
86-87—Detroit	15	473	78	145	.538	32	41	.780	8	11	19	72	12	1	27	190	1.3	4.8	12.7
87-88—Detroit	23	804	113	247	.457	56	63	.889	18	32	50	112	13	2	40	284	2.2	4.9	12.3
88-89—Detroit	17	620	106	233	.455	87	101	.861	11	33	44	96	12	1	31	300	2.6	5.6	17.6
89-90—Detroit	20	754	130	284	.458	99	113	.876	18	26	44	95	22	0	54	364	2.2	4.8	18.2
90-91—Detroit	15	588	105	245	.429	82	97	.845	21	29	50	62	16	1	17	309	3.3	4.1	20.6
91-92—Detroit	5	221	32	68	.471	15	19	.789	5	3	8	16	5	1	7	84	1.6	3.2	16.8
95-96—Detroit	3	123	16	35	.457	4	4	1.000	5	8	13	11	0	0	7	41	4.3	3.7	13.7
96-97—Detroit	5	214	22	61	.361	19	20	.950	2	7	9	10	5	0	6	69	1.8	2.0	13.8

Season Team	G	Min.	FGM	FGA	Pct.	FTM	FTA	Pct.	REBOUNDS Off.	Def.	Tot.	Ast.	St.	Blk.	TO	Pts.	AVERAGES RPG	APG	PPG
98-99—Detroit	5	153	19	39	.487	3	3	1.000	1	6	7	13	2	0	9	51	1.4	2.6	10.2
Totals	112	4097	646	1398	.462	407	476	.855	95	162	257	512	91	6	205	1752	2.3	4.6	15.6

Three-point field goals: 1986-87, 2-for-3 (.667). 1987-88, 2-for-6 (.333). 1988-89, 1-for-12 (.083). 1989-90, 5-for-19 (.263). 1990-91, 17-for-42 (.405). 1991-92, 5-for-10 (.500). 1995-96, 5-for-14 (.357). 1996-97, 6-for-23 (.261). 1998-99, 10-for-19 (.526). Totals, 53-for-148 (.358).

Personal fouls/disqualifications: 1985-86, 16/0. 1986-87, 26/0. 1987-88, 50/1. 1988-89, 31/0. 1989-90, 37/0. 1990-91, 33/1. 1991-92, 11/0. 1995-96, 5/0. 1996-97, 9/0. 1998-99, 9/0. Totals, 227/2.

NBA ALL-STAR GAME RECORD

Season Team	Min.	FGM	FGA	Pct.	FTM	FTA	Pct.	REBOUNDS Off.	Def.	Tot.	Ast.	PF	Dq.	St.	Blk.	TO	Pts.
1990—Detroit	18	3	4	.750	1	2	.500	0	1	1	5	0	0	0	0	3	9
1991—Detroit	15	1	4	.250	0	0	...	1	1	2	1	1	0	0	0	4	2
1992—Detroit	17	2	7	.286	0	0	...	0	1	1	3	0	0	0	0	2	4
1993—Detroit	17	2	8	.250	0	0	...	0	2	2	4	1	0	0	0	1	5
1995—Detroit	21	5	8	.625	0	0	...	0	0	0	6	1	0	1	0	1	11
1997—Detroit	10	1	4	.250	0	0	...	0	1	1	1	0	0	0	0	0	3
Totals	98	14	35	.400	1	2	.500	1	6	7	20	3	0	1	0	11	34

Three-point field goals: 1990, 2-for-2. 1991, 0-for-1. 1992, 0-for-2. 1993, 1-for-4 (.250). 1995, 1-for-2 (.500). 1997, 1-for-4 (.250). Totals, 5-for-15 (.333).

ELLIS, DALE — G/F

PERSONAL: Born August 6, 1960, in Marietta, Ga. ... 6-7/215. (2.01 m/98 kg).
HIGH SCHOOL: Marietta (Ga.).
COLLEGE: Tennessee.
TRANSACTIONS/CAREER NOTES: Selected by Dallas Mavericks in first round (ninth pick overall) of 1983 NBA Draft. ... Traded by Mavericks to Seattle SuperSonics for G/F Al Wood (July 23, 1986). ... Traded by SuperSonics to Milwaukee Bucks for G/F Ricky Pierce (February 15, 1991). ... Traded by Bucks to San Antonio Spurs for draft rights to F Tracy Murray (July 1, 1992). ... Signed as free agent by Denver Nuggets (October 4, 1994). ... Traded by Nuggets to SuperSonics for G Greg Graham, C Steve Scheffler, 1998 second-round draft choice and 1999 or 2002 conditional second-round draft choice (October 2, 1997). ... Became a free agent when SuperSonics did not exercise option for 1998-99 season (June 30, 1998). ... Re-signed as free agent by SuperSonics (January 21, 1999). ... Traded by SuperSonics with F/G Billy Owens, F Don MacLean and draft rights to F Corey Maggette to Orlando Magic for F Horace Grant and 2001 and 2002 second-round draft choices (June 30, 1999). ... Traded by Magic with F/C Danny Manning to Milwaukee Bucks for F/C Chris Gatling and F Armen Gilliam (August 19, 1999). ... Traded by Bucks to Charlotte Hornets for 2000 and 2001 second-round draft choices (January 18, 2000). ... Traded by Hornets with G Eddie Jones, F Anthony Mason and G Ricky Davis to Miami Heat for F P.J. Brown, F Jamal Mashburn, F/C Otis Thorpe, F Tim James and G/F Rodney Buford (August 1, 2000). ... Waived by Heat (October 30, 2000).

COLLEGIATE RECORD

NOTES: The Sporting News All-America first team (1983).

Season Team	G	Min.	FGM	FGA	Pct.	FTM	FTA	Pct.	Reb.	Ast.	Pts.	AVERAGES RPG	APG	PPG
79-80—Tennessee	27	573	81	182	.445	31	40	.775	96	34	193	3.6	1.3	7.1
80-81—Tennessee	29	1057	215	360	.597	83	111	.748	185	21	513	6.4	0.7	17.7
81-82—Tennessee	30	1134	257	393	.654	121	152	.796	189	22	635	6.3	0.7	21.2
82-83—Tennessee	32	1179	279	464	.601	166	221	.751	209	32	724	6.5	1.0	22.6
Totals	118	3943	832	1399	.595	401	524	.765	679	109	2065	5.8	0.9	17.5

NBA REGULAR-SEASON RECORD

RECORDS: Holds single-game record for most minutes played—69 (November 9, 1989, vs. Milwaukee, 5 OT).
HONORS: NBA Most Improved Player (1987). ... Long Distance Shootout winner (1989). ... All-NBA third team (1989).
NOTES: Led NBA with .464 three-point goal percentage (1998).

Season Team	G	Min.	FGM	FGA	Pct.	FTM	FTA	Pct.	REBOUNDS Off.	Def.	Tot.	Ast.	St.	Blk.	TO	Pts.	AVERAGES RPG	APG	PPG
83-84—Dallas	67	1059	225	493	.456	87	121	.719	106	144	250	56	41	9	78	549	3.7	0.8	8.2
84-85—Dallas	72	1314	274	603	.454	77	104	.740	100	138	238	56	46	7	58	667	3.3	0.8	9.3
85-86—Dallas	72	1086	193	470	.411	59	82	.720	86	82	168	37	40	9	38	508	2.3	0.5	7.1
86-87—Seattle	82	3073	785	1520	.516	385	489	.787	187	260	447	238	104	32	238	2041	5.5	2.9	24.9
87-88—Seattle	75	2790	764	1519	.503	303	395	.767	167	173	340	197	74	11	172	1938	4.5	2.6	25.8
88-89—Seattle	82	3190	857	1710	.501	377	462	.816	156	186	342	164	108	22	218	2253	4.2	2.0	27.5
89-90—Seattle	55	2033	502	1011	.497	193	236	.818	90	148	238	110	59	7	119	1293	4.3	2.0	23.5
90-91—Seattle-Mil.	51	1424	340	718	.474	120	166	.723	66	107	173	95	49	8	81	857	3.4	1.9	16.8
91-92—Milwaukee	81	2191	485	1034	.469	164	212	.774	92	161	253	104	57	18	119	1272	3.1	1.3	15.7
92-93—San Antonio	82	2731	545	1092	.499	157	197	.797	81	231	312	107	78	18	111	1366	3.8	1.3	16.7
93-94—San Antonio	77	2590	478	967	.494	83	107	.776	70	185	255	80	66	11	75	1100	3.3	1.0	15.2
94-95—Denver	81	1996	351	774	.453	110	127	.866	56	166	222	57	37	9	81	918	2.7	0.7	11.3
95-96—Denver	81	2626	459	959	.479	136	179	.760	88	227	315	139	57	7	98	1204	3.9	1.7	14.9
96-97—Denver	82	2940	477	1151	.414	215	263	.817	99	194	293	165	60	7	146	1362	3.6	2.0	16.6
97-98—Seattle	79	1939	348	700	.497	111	142	.782	51	133	184	89	60	5	74	934	2.3	1.1	11.8
98-99—Seattle	48	1232	174	395	.441	53	70	.757	25	90	115	38	25	3	45	495	2.4	0.8	10.3
99-00—Mil.-Charlotte.	42	564	66	159	.415	9	13	.692	13	43	56	14	13	0	20	178	1.3	0.3	4.2
Totals	1209	34778	7323	15275	.479	2639	3365	.784	1533	2668	4201	1746	974	183	1771	19004	3.5	1.4	15.7

Three-point field goals: 1983-84, 12-for-29 (.414). 1984-85, 42-for-109 (.385). 1985-86, 63-for-173 (.364). 1986-87, 86-for-240 (.358). 1987-88, 107-for-259 (.413). 1988-89, 162-for-339 (.478). 1989-90, 96-for-256 (.375). 1990-91, 57-for-157 (.363). 1991-92, 138-for-329 (.419). 1992-93, 119-for-297 (.401). 1993-94, 131-for-332 (.395). 1994-95, 106-for-263 (.403). 1995-96, 150-for-364 (.412). 1996-97, 192-for-528 (.364). 1997-98, 127-for-274 (.464). 1998-99, 94-for-217 (.433). 1999-00, 37-for-100 (.370). Totals, 1719-for-4266 (.403).

Personal fouls/disqualifications: 1983-84, 118/0. 1984-85, 131/1. 1985-86, 78/0. 1986-87, 267/2. 1987-88, 221/1. 1988-89, 197/0. 1989-90, 124/3. 1990-91, 112/1. 1991-92, 151/0. 1992-93, 179/0. 1993-94, 141/0. 1994-95, 142/0. 1995-96, 191/1. 1996-97, 178/0. 1997-98, 128/0. 1998-99, 77/1. 1999-00, 45/0. Totals, 2480/10.

NBA PLAYOFF RECORD

Season Team	G	Min.	FGM	FGA	Pct.	FTM	FTA	Pct.	REBOUNDS Off.	Def.	Tot.	Ast.	St.	Blk.	TO	Pts.	AVERAGES RPG	APG	PPG
83-84—Dallas	8	178	26	80	.325	6	8	.750	19	23	42	4	10	2	5	59	5.3	0.5	7.4
84-85—Dallas	4	68	10	23	.435	1	2	.500	4	3	7	3	4	0	4	23	1.8	0.8	5.8

Season Team	G	Min.	FGM	FGA	Pct.	FTM	FTA	Pct.	REBOUNDS Off.	Def.	Tot.	Ast.	St.	Blk.	TO	Pts.	AVERAGES RPG	APG	PPG
85-86—Dallas.............	7	67	9	22	.409	5	5	1.000	3	4	7	2	2	2	4	30	1.0	0.3	4.3
86-87—Seattle	14	530	148	304	.487	44	54	.815	37	53	90	37	10	6	33	353	6.4	2.6	25.2
87-88—Seattle	5	172	40	83	.482	21	29	.724	11	12	23	15	3	2	12	104	4.6	3.0	20.8
88-89—Seattle	8	304	72	160	.450	24	33	.727	14	18	32	10	11	1	21	183	4.0	1.3	22.9
92-93—San Antonio....	10	305	51	113	.451	13	16	.813	9	26	35	11	4	0	10	125	3.5	1.1	12.5
93-94—San Antonio....	4	114	17	43	.395	3	5	.600	3	7	10	1	3	0	4	42	2.5	0.3	10.5
94-95—Denver	3	73	10	28	.357	12	13	.923	6	8	14	3	2	1	2	36	4.7	1.0	12.0
97-98—Seattle	10	170	20	53	.377	5	6	.833	4	9	13	6	2	0	2	56	1.3	0.6	5.6
Totals	73	1981	403	909	.443	134	171	.784	110	163	273	92	51	14	97	1011	3.7	1.3	13.8

Three-point field goals: 1983-84, 1-for-12 (.083). 1984-85, 2-for-5 (.400). 1985-86, 7-for-12 (.583). 1986-87, 13-for-36 (.361). 1987-88, 3-for-12 (.250). 1988-89, 15-for-37 (.405). 1992-93, 10-for-32 (.313). 1993-94, 5-for-17 (.294). 1994-95, 4-for-13 (.308). 1997-98, 11-for-26 (.423). Totals, 71-for-202 (.351).

Personal fouls/disqualifications: 1983-84, 17/0. 1984-85, 3/0. 1985-86, 6/0. 1986-87, 54/1. 1987-88, 17/0. 1988-89, 19/1. 1992-93, 25/0. 1993-94, 6/0. 1994-95, 6/0. 1997-98, 10/0. Totals, 163/2.

NBA ALL-STAR GAME RECORD

Season Team	Min.	FGM	FGA	Pct.	FTM	FTA	Pct.	REBOUNDS Off.	Def.	Tot.	Ast.	PF	Dq.	St.	Blk.	TO	Pts.
1989—Seattle..................	26	12	16	.750	2	2	1.000	3	3	6	2	2	0	0	0	2	27
Totals..........................	26	12	16	.750	2	2	1.000	3	3	6	2	2	0	0	0	2	27

Three-point field goals: 1989, 1-for-1.

ENGLISH, ALEX   F

PERSONAL: Born January 5, 1954, in Columbia, S.C. ... 6-7/190 (2,00/86,2). ... Full name: Alexander English.
HIGH SCHOOL: Dreher (Columbia, S.C.).
COLLEGE: South Carolina.
TRANSACTIONS: Selected by Milwaukee Bucks in second round (23rd pick overall) of 1976 NBA Draft. ... Signed as veteran free agent by Indiana Pacers (June 8, 1978); Bucks waived their right of first refusal in exchange for 1979 first-round draft choice (October 3, 1978). ... Traded by Pacers with 1980 first-round draft choice to Denver Nuggets for F George McGinnis (February 1, 1980). ... Signed as unrestricted free agent by Dallas Mavericks (August 15, 1990). ... Played in Italy (1991-92).
CAREER HONORS: Elected to Naismith Memorial Basketball Hall of Fame (1997).
CAREER NOTES: Assistant coach, Philadelphia 76ers (2003-04). ... Assistant coach, Toronto Raptors (2004-present).
MISCELLANEOUS: Denver Nuggets franchise all-time leading scorer with 21,645 points and all-time assists leader with 3,679 (1979-80 through 1989-90).

COLLEGIATE RECORD

Season Team	G	Min.	FGM	FGA	Pct.	FTM	FTA	Pct.	Reb.	Ast.	Pts.	AVERAGES RPG	APG	PPG
72-73—South Carolina...............	29	1037	189	368	.514	44	70	.629	306	25	422	10.6	0.9	14.6
73-74—South Carolina...............	27	1007	209	395	.529	75	112	.670	237	28	493	8.8	1.0	18.3
74-75—South Carolina...............	28	1024	199	359	.554	49	77	.636	244	30	447	8.7	1.1	16.0
75-76—South Carolina...............	27	1045	258	468	.551	94	134	.702	277	27	610	10.3	1.0	22.6
Totals	111	4113	855	1590	.538	262	393	.667	1064	110	1972	9.6	1.0	17.8

NBA REGULAR-SEASON RECORD

HONORS: All-NBA second team (1982, 1983, 1986). ... J. Walter Kennedy Citizenship Award (1988).

Season Team	G	Min.	FGM	FGA	Pct.	FTM	FTA	Pct.	REBOUNDS Off.	Def.	Tot.	Ast.	St.	Blk.	TO	Pts.	AVERAGES RPG	APG	PPG
76-77—Milwaukee	60	648	132	277	.477	46	60	.767	68	100	168	25	17	18	...	310	2.8	0.4	5.2
77-78—Milwaukee	82	1552	343	633	.542	104	143	.727	144	251	395	129	41	55	137	790	4.8	1.6	9.6
78-79—Indiana...........	81	2696	563	1102	.511	173	230	.752	253	402	655	271	70	78	196	1299	8.1	3.3	16.0
79-80—Ind.-Denver......	78	2401	553	1113	.497	210	266	.789	269	336	605	224	73	62	214	1318	7.8	2.9	16.9
80-81—Denver...........	81	3093	768	1555	.494	390	459	.850	273	373	646	290	106	100	241	1929	8.0	3.6	23.8
81-82—Denver...........	82	3015	855	1553	.551	372	443	.840	210	348	558	433	87	120	261	2082	6.8	5.3	25.4
82-83—Denver...........	82	2988	*959	*1857	.516	406	490	.829	263	338	601	397	116	126	263	*2326	7.3	4.8	*28.4
83-84—Denver...........	82	2870	907	1714	.529	352	427	.824	216	248	464	406	83	95	222	2167	5.7	5.0	26.4
84-85—Denver...........	81	2924	*939	1812	.518	383	462	.829	203	255	458	344	101	46	251	2262	5.7	4.2	27.9
85-86—Denver...........	81	3024	*951	1888	.504	511	593	.862	192	213	405	320	73	29	249	*2414	5.0	4.0	29.8
86-87—Denver...........	82	3085	965	1920	.503	411	487	.844	146	198	344	422	73	21	214	2345	4.2	5.1	28.6
87-88—Denver...........	80	2818	843	1704	.495	314	379	.829	166	207	373	377	70	23	181	2000	4.7	4.7	25.0
88-89—Denver...........	82	2990	924	1881	.491	325	379	.858	148	178	326	383	66	12	198	2175	4.0	4.7	26.5
89-90—Denver...........	80	2211	635	1293	.491	161	183	.880	119	167	286	225	51	23	93	1433	3.6	2.8	17.9
90-91—Dallas.............	79	1748	322	734	.439	119	140	.850	108	146	254	105	40	25	101	763	3.2	1.3	9.7
Totals	1193	38063	10659	21036	.507	4277	5141	.832	2778	3760	6538	4351	1067	833	2821	25613	5.5	3.6	21.5

Three-point field goals: 1979-80, 2-for-6 (.333). 1980-81, 3-for-5 (.600). 1981-82, 0-for-8. 1982-83, 2-for-12 (.167). 1983-84, 1-for-7 (.143). 1984-85, 1-for-5 (.200). 1985-86, 1-for-5 (.200). 1986-87, 4-for-15 (.267). 1987-88, 0-for-6. 1988-89, 2-for-8 (.250). 1989-90, 2-for-5 (.400). 1990-91, 0-for-1. Totals, 18-for-83 (.217).

Personal fouls/disqualifications: 1976-77, 78/0. 1977-78, 178/1. 1978-79, 214/3. 1979-80, 206/0. 1980-81, 255/2. 1981-82, 261/2. 1982-83, 235/1. 1983-84, 252/3. 1984-85, 259/1. 1985-86, 235/1. 1986-87, 216/0. 1987-88, 193/1. 1988-89, 174/0. 1989-90, 130/0. 1990-91, 141/0. Totals, 3027/15.

NBA PLAYOFF RECORD

Season Team	G	Min.	FGM	FGA	Pct.	FTM	FTA	Pct.	REBOUNDS Off.	Def.	Tot.	Ast.	St.	Blk.	TO	Pts.	AVERAGES RPG	APG	PPG
77-78—Milwaukee	9	208	48	78	.615	25	32	.781	16	26	42	13	6	7	12	121	4.7	1.4	13.4
81-82—Denver...........	3	118	26	55	.473	6	7	.857	8	15	23	17	3	3	4	58	7.7	5.7	19.3
82-83—Denver...........	7	270	67	150	.447	47	53	.887	20	24	44	42	4	7	21	181	6.3	6.0	25.9
83-84—Denver...........	5	203	60	102	.588	25	28	.893	16	24	40	28	3	2	7	145	8.0	5.6	29.0
84-85—Denver...........	14	536	163	304	.536	97	109	.890	36	56	92	63	17	5	30	423	6.6	4.5	30.2

Season Team	G	Min.	FGM	FGA	Pct.	FTM	FTA	Pct.	REBOUNDS Off.	Def.	Tot.	Ast.	St.	Blk.	TO	Pts.	AVERAGES RPG	APG	PPG
85-86—Denver	10	394	106	229	.463	61	71	.859	18	17	35	52	4	4	28	273	3.5	5.2	27.3
86-87—Denver	3	76	25	49	.510	6	7	.857	10	4	14	10	0	0	8	56	4.7	3.3	18.7
87-88—Denver	11	438	116	255	.455	35	43	.814	31	28	59	48	7	3	16	267	5.4	4.4	24.3
88-89—Denver	3	108	32	62	.516	14	16	.875	8	5	13	11	1	0	14	78	4.3	3.7	26.0
89-90—Denver	3	76	25	44	.568	9	11	.818	3	6	9	9	2	1	2	59	3.0	3.0	19.7
Totals	68	2427	668	1328	.503	325	377	.862	166	205	371	293	47	32	142	1661	5.5	4.3	24.4

Three-point field goals: 1982-83, 0-for-2. 1983-84, 0-for-1. 1984-85, 0-for-1. 1985-86, 0-for-1. 1987-88, 0-for-3. Totals, 0-for-8.
Personal fouls/disqualifications: 1977-78, 20/0. 1981-82, 6/0. 1982-83, 21/0. 1983-84, 17/0. 1984-85, 40/1. 1985-86, 29/0. 1986-87, 9/1. 1987-88, 34/0. 1988-89, 6/0. 1989-90, 6/0. Totals, 188/2.

NBA ALL-STAR GAME RECORD

Season Team	Min.	FGM	FGA	Pct.	FTM	FTA	Pct.	REBOUNDS Off.	Def.	Tot.	Ast.	PF	Dq.	St.	Blk.	TO	Pts.
1982—Denver	12	2	6	.333	0	0	...	2	3	5	1	2	0	1	0	1	4
1983—Denver	23	7	14	.500	0	1	.000	2	2	4	0	2	0	1	2	2	14
1984—Denver	19	6	8	.750	1	1	1.000	0	0	0	2	2	0	1	1	3	13
1985—Denver	14	0	3	.000	0	0	...	1	1	2	1	1	0	0	0	2	0
1986—Denver	16	8	12	.667	0	0	...	1	0	1	2	0	0	0	1	1	16
1987—Denver	13	0	6	.000	0	0	...	0	0	0	1	1	0	0	0	2	0
1988—Denver	22	5	10	.500	0	0	...	2	1	3	4	0	0	1	0	0	10
1989—Denver	29	8	13	.615	0	0	...	1	2	3	4	0	0	2	0	3	16
Totals	148	36	72	.500	1	2	.500	9	9	18	15	8	0	6	4	14	73

ITALIAN LEAGUE RECORD

Season Team	G	Min.	FGM	FGA	Pct.	FTM	FTA	Pct.	Reb.	Ast.	Pts.	AVERAGES RPG	APG	PPG
91-92—Depi Napoli	18	566	103	214	.481	44	55	.800	86	5	251	4.8	0.3	13.9

NBDL COACHING RECORD

Season Team	REGULAR SEASON W	L	Pct.	Finish	PLAYOFFS W	L	Pct.
01-02—North Charleston	36	20	.640	1st	2	4	.200

NOTES:
01-02—Defeated Mobile in semifinals; lost to Greenville in NBDL Finals.

ERVING, JULIUS   F

PERSONAL: Born February 22, 1950, in Roosevelt, N.Y. ... 6-7/210 (2,00/95,3). ... Full name: Julius Winfield Erving II. ... Cousin of Mark Williams, linebacker with four NFL teams (1994-96). ... Nickname: Dr. J.
HIGH SCHOOL: Roosevelt (N.Y.).
COLLEGE: Massachusetts.
TRANSACTIONS: Signed as free agent after junior ~~~~~ by Virginia Squires in American Basketball Association (April 6, 1971). ... Selected by Milwaukee Bucks in first round (12th pick overall) of 1972 NBA draft. ... Traded by Squires with C Willie Sojourner to New York Nets for F George Carter, draft rights to F/C Kermit Washington and cash (August 1, 1973). ... Nets franchise became part of NBA for 1976-77 season. ... Contract sold by Nets to Philadelphia 76ers (October 20, 1976).
CAREER HONORS: Elected to Naismith Memorial Basketball Hall of Fame (1993). ... NBA 35th Anniversary All-Time Team (1980) and One of the 50 Greatest Players in NBA History (1996).
CAREER NOTES: Executive vice president, Orlando Magic (1997-98 to 2002-03).
MISCELLANEOUS: Member of NBA championship team (1983). ... Philadelphia 76ers franchise all-time blocked shots leader with 1,293 (1976-77 through 1986-87).

COLLEGIATE RECORD

Season Team	G	Min.	FGM	FGA	Pct.	FTM	FTA	Pct.	Reb.	Ast.	Pts.	AVERAGES RPG	APG	PPG
68-69—Massachusetts‡	15	...	112	216	.519	49	81	.605	214	...	273	14.3	...	18.2
69-70—Massachusetts	25	969	238	468	.509	167	230	.726	522	89	643	20.9	3.6	25.7
70-71—Massachusetts	27	1029	286	609	.470	155	206	.752	527	99	727	19.5	3.7	26.9
Varsity totals	52	1998	524	1077	.487	322	436	.739	1049	188	1370	20.2	3.6	26.3

ABA REGULAR-SEASON RECORD

NOTES: ABA Most Valuable Player (1974, 1976). ... ABA co-Most Valuable Player (1975). ... ABA All-Star first team (1973, 1974, 1975, 1976). ... ABA All-Star second team (1972). ... ABA All-Defensive team (1976). ... ABA All-Rookie team (1972). ... Member of ABA championship team (1974, 1976). ... Holds career record for highest points-per-game average (minimum 250 games)—28.7.

Season Team	G	Min.	2-POINT FGM	FGA	Pct.	3-POINT FGM	FGA	Pct.	FTM	FTA	Pct.	Reb.	Ast.	Pts.	AVERAGES RPG	APG	PPG
71-72—Virginia	84	3513	907	1810	.501	3	16	.188	467	627	.745	1319	335	2290	15.7	4.0	27.3
72-73—Virginia	71	2993	889	1780	.499	5	24	.208	475	612	.776	867	298	*2268	12.2	4.2	*31.9
73-74—New York	84	3398	897	1742	.515	17	43	.395	454	593	.766	899	434	*2299	10.7	5.2	*27.4
74-75—New York	84	3402	885	1719	.515	29	87	.333	486	608	.799	914	462	2343	10.9	5.5	27.9
75-76—New York	84	3244	915	1770	.517	34	103	.330	530	662	.801	925	423	*2462	11.0	5.0	*29.3
Totals	407	16550	4493	8821	.509	88	273	.322	2412	3102	.778	4924	1952	11662	12.1	4.8	28.7

ABA PLAYOFF RECORD

NOTES: ABA Playoff Most Valuable Player (1974, 1976).

Season Team	G	Min.	2-POINT FGM	FGA	Pct.	3-POINT FGM	FGA	Pct.	FTM	FTA	Pct.	Reb.	Ast.	Pts.	AVERAGES RPG	APG	PPG
71-72—Virginia	11	504	146	280	.521	1	4	.250	71	85	.835	224	72	366	20.4	6.5	33.3
72-73—Virginia	5	219	59	109	.541	0	3	.000	30	40	.750	45	16	148	9.0	3.2	29.6

Season Team	G	Min.	2-POINT FGM	FGA	Pct.	3-POINT FGM	FGA	Pct.	FTM	FTA	Pct.	Reb.	Ast.	Pts.	AVERAGES RPG	APG	PPG
73-74—New York	14	579	156	294	.531	5	11	.455	63	85	.741	135	67	390	9.6	4.8	27.9
74-75—New York	5	211	55	113	.487	0	8	.000	27	32	.844	49	28	137	9.8	5.6	27.4
75-76—New York	13	551	156	286	.545	4	14	.286	127	158	.804	164	64	451	12.6	4.9	34.7
Totals	48	2064	572	1082	.529	10	40	.250	318	400	.795	617	247	1492	12.9	5.1	31.1

ABA ALL-STAR GAME RECORD

Season Team	Min.	2-POINT FGM	FGA	Pct.	3-POINT FGM	FGA	Pct.	FTM	FTA	Pct.	Reb.	Ast.	Pts.
1972—Virginia	25	9	15	.600	0	0	...	2	2	1.000	6	3	20
1973—Virginia	30	8	16	.500	0	0	...	6	8	.750	5	1	22
1974—New York	27	6	15	.400	0	0	...	2	2	1.000	11	8	14
1975—New York	27	5	11	.455	1	1	1.000	8	10	.800	7	7	21
1976—New York	25	9	12	.750	0	1	.000	5	7	.714	7	5	23
Totals	134	37	69	.536	1	2	.500	23	29	.793	36	24	100

NBA REGULAR-SEASON RECORD

HONORS: NBA Most Valuable Player (1981). ... All-NBA first team (1978, 1980, 1981, 1982, 1983). ... All-NBA second team (1977, 1984). ... J. Walter Kennedy Citizenship Award (1983).

Season Team	G	Min.	FGM	FGA	Pct.	FTM	FTA	Pct.	REBOUNDS Off.	Def.	Tot.	Ast.	St.	Blk.	TO	Pts.	AVERAGES RPG	APG	PPG
76-77—Philadelphia	82	2940	685	1373	.499	400	515	.777	192	503	695	306	159	113	...	1770	8.5	3.7	21.6
77-78—Philadelphia	74	2429	611	1217	.502	306	362	.845	179	302	481	279	135	97	238	1528	6.5	3.8	20.6
78-79—Philadelphia	78	2802	715	1455	.491	373	501	.745	198	366	564	357	133	100	315	1803	7.2	4.6	23.1
79-80—Philadelphia	78	2812	838	1614	.519	420	534	.787	215	361	576	355	170	140	284	2100	7.4	4.6	26.9
80-81—Philadelphia	82	2874	794	1524	.521	422	536	.787	244	413	657	364	173	147	266	2014	8.0	4.4	24.6
81-82—Philadelphia	81	2789	780	1428	.546	411	539	.763	220	337	557	319	161	141	214	1974	6.9	3.9	24.4
82-83—Philadelphia	72	2421	605	1170	.517	330	435	.759	173	318	491	263	112	131	196	1542	6.8	3.7	21.4
83-84—Philadelphia	77	2683	678	1324	.512	364	483	.754	190	342	532	309	141	139	230	1727	6.9	4.0	22.4
84-85—Philadelphia	78	2535	610	1236	.494	338	442	.765	172	242	414	233	135	109	208	1561	5.3	3.0	20.0
85-86—Philadelphia	74	2474	521	1085	.480	289	368	.785	169	201	370	248	113	82	214	1340	5.0	3.4	18.1
86-87—Philadelphia	60	1918	400	850	.471	191	235	.813	115	149	264	191	76	94	158	1005	4.4	3.2	16.8
Totals	836	28677	7237	14276	.507	3844	4950	.777	2067	3534	5601	3224	1508	1293	2323	18364	6.7	3.9	22.0

Three-point field goals: 1979-80, 4-for-20 (.200). 1980-81, 4-for-18 (.222). 1981-82, 3-for-11 (.273). 1982-83, 2-for-7 (.286). 1983-84, 7-for-21 (.333). 1984-85, 3-for-14 (.214). 1985-86, 9-for-32 (.281). 1986-87, 14-for-53 (.264). Totals, 46-for-176 (.261).

Personal fouls/disqualifications: 1976-77, 251/1. 1977-78, 207/0. 1978-79, 207/0. 1979-80, 208/0. 1980-81, 233/0. 1981-82, 229/1. 1982-83, 202/1. 1983-84, 217/3. 1984-85, 199/0. 1985-86, 196/3. 1986-87, 137/0. Totals, 2286/9.

NBA PLAYOFF RECORD

Season Team	G	Min.	FGM	FGA	Pct.	FTM	FTA	Pct.	REBOUNDS Off.	Def.	Tot.	Ast.	St.	Blk.	TO	Pts.	AVERAGES RPG	APG	PPG
76-77—Philadelphia	19	758	204	390	.523	110	134	.821	41	81	122	85	41	23	...	518	6.4	4.5	27.3
77-78—Philadelphia	10	358	88	180	.489	42	56	.750	40	57	97	40	15	18	35	218	9.7	4.0	21.8
78-79—Philadelphia	9	372	89	172	.517	51	67	.761	29	41	70	53	18	17	38	229	7.8	5.9	25.4
79-80—Philadelphia	18	694	165	338	.488	108	136	.794	31	105	136	79	36	37	56	440	7.6	4.4	24.4
80-81—Philadelphia	16	592	143	301	.475	81	107	.757	52	62	114	54	22	41	55	367	7.1	3.4	22.9
81-82—Philadelphia	21	780	168	324	.519	124	165	.752	57	99	156	99	37	37	67	461	7.4	4.7	22.0
82-83—Philadelphia	13	493	95	211	.450	49	68	.721	32	67	99	44	15	27	39	239	7.6	3.4	18.4
83-84—Philadelphia	5	194	36	76	.474	19	22	.864	9	23	32	25	8	6	21	91	6.4	5.0	18.2
84-85—Philadelphia	13	434	84	187	.449	54	63	.857	29	44	73	48	25	11	37	222	5.6	3.7	17.1
85-86—Philadelphia	12	433	81	180	.450	48	65	.738	26	44	70	50	11	16	39	212	5.8	4.2	17.7
86-87—Philadelphia	5	180	34	82	.415	21	25	.840	14	11	25	17	7	6	9	91	5.0	3.4	18.2
Totals	141	5288	1187	2441	.486	707	908	.779	360	634	994	594	235	239	396	3088	7.0	4.2	21.9

Three-point field goals: 1979-80, 2-for-9 (.222). 1980-81, 0-for-1. 1981-82, 1-for-6 (.167). 1982-83, 0-for-1. 1983-84, 0-for-1. 1984-85, 0-for-1. 1985-86, 2-for-11 (.182). 1986-87, 2-for-6 (.333). Totals, 7-for-36 (.194).

Personal fouls/disqualifications: 1976-77, 45/0. 1977-78, 30/0. 1978-79, 22/0. 1979-80, 56/0. 1980-81, 54/0. 1981-82, 55/0. 1982-83, 42/1. 1983-84, 14/0. 1984-85, 34/0. 1985-86, 32/0. 1986-87, 19/0. Totals, 403/1.

NBA ALL-STAR GAME RECORD

NOTES: NBA All-Star Game Most Valuable Player (1977, 1983). ... Holds single-game record for most free throws attempted in one quarter—11 (1978). ... Shares single-game record for most free throws made in one quarter—9 (1978).

Season Team	Min.	FGM	FGA	Pct.	FTM	FTA	Pct.	REBOUNDS Off.	Def.	Tot.	Ast.	PF	Dq.	St.	Blk.	TO	Pts.
1977—Philadelphia	30	12	20	.600	6	6	1.000	5	7	12	3	2	0	4	1	...	30
1978—Philadelphia	27	3	14	.214	10	12	.833	2	6	8	3	1	0	0	1	2	16
1979—Philadelphia	39	10	22	.455	9	12	.750	6	2	8	5	4	0	2	0	1	29
1980—Philadelphia	20	4	12	.333	3	4	.750	2	3	5	2	5	0	2	1	2	11
1981—Philadelphia	29	6	15	.400	6	7	.857	3	0	3	2	2	0	2	1	2	18
1982—Philadelphia	32	7	16	.438	2	4	.500	3	5	8	2	4	0	1	2	4	16
1983—Philadelphia	28	11	19	.579	3	3	1.000	3	3	6	3	1	0	1	2	2	25
1984—Philadelphia	36	14	22	.636	6	8	.750	4	4	8	5	4	0	2	2	1	34
1985—Philadelphia	23	5	15	.333	2	2	1.000	2	2	4	3	3	0	1	0	1	12
1986—Philadelphia	19	4	10	.400	0	2	.000	1	3	4	2	2	0	2	0	2	8
1987—Philadelphia	33	9	13	.692	3	3	1.000	3	1	4	5	3	0	1	1	2	22
Totals	316	85	178	.478	50	63	.794	34	36	70	35	31	0	18	11	19	221

Three-point field goals: 1987, 1-for-1.

COMBINED ABA AND NBA REGULAR-SEASON RECORDS

	G	Min.	FGM	FGA	Pct.	FTM	FTA	Pct.	REBOUNDS Off.	Def.	Tot.	Ast.	Stl.	Blk.	TO	Pts.	AVERAGES RPG	APG	PPG
Totals	1243	45227	11818	23370	.506	6256	8052	.777	...	...	10525	5176	...	...	...	30026	8.5	4.2	24.2

Three-point field goals: 134-for-449 (.298).
Personal fouls/disqualifications: 3494.

EWING, PATRICK   C

PERSONAL: Born August 5, 1962, in Kingston, Jamaica. ... 7-0/255. (2,13/115,7). ... Full Name: Patrick Aloysius Ewing.
HIGH SCHOOL: Cambridge (Mass.) Rindge & Latin School.
COLLEGE: Georgetown.
TRANSACTIONS/CAREER NOTES: Selected by New York Knicks in first round (first pick overall) of 1985 NBA Draft. ... Traded by Knicks to Seattle SuperSonics as part of four-team trade in which Knicks acquired F Glen Rice, C Luc Longley, F/C Travis Knight, G Vernon Maxwell, C Vladimir Stepania, F Lazaro Borrell, two 2001 first-round draft choices and two 2001 second-round draft choices, Phoenix Suns acquired C Chris Dudley and 2001 first-round draft choice and Los Angeles Lakers acquired F Horace Grant, C Greg Foster, F Chuck Person and G Emanual Davis (September 20, 2000). ... Signed as free agent by Orlando Magic (July 18, 2001).
CAREER HONORS: NBA 50th Anniversary All-Time Team (1996).
CAREER NOTES: Assistant coach, Washington Wizards (2002-03). ... Assistant coach, Houston Rockets (2003-present).
MISCELLANEOUS: Member of gold-medal-winning U.S. Olympic teams (1984, 1992). , ... New York Knicks all-time leading scorer with 23,665 points, all-time leading rebounder with 10,759, all-time steals leader with 1,061 and all-time blocked shots leader with 2,758 (1985-86 through 1999-2000).

COLLEGIATE RECORD

NOTES: The Sporting News College Player of the Year (1985). ... Naismith Award winner (1985). ... The Sporting News All-America first team (1985). ... The Sporting News All-America second team (1983, 1984). ... NCAA Division I Tournament Most Outstanding Player (1984). ... Member of NCAA Division I championship team (1984).

Season Team	G	Min.	FGM	FGA	Pct.	FTM	FTA	Pct.	Reb.	Ast.	Pts.	RPG	APG	PPG
81-82—Georgetown	37	1064	183	290	.631	103	167	.617	279	23	469	7.5	0.6	12.7
82-83—Georgetown	32	1024	212	372	.570	141	224	.629	325	26	565	10.2	0.8	17.7
83-84—Georgetown	37	1179	242	368	.658	124	189	.656	371	31	608	10.0	0.8	16.4
84-85—Georgetown	37	1132	220	352	.625	102	160	.638	341	48	542	9.2	1.3	14.6
Totals	143	4399	857	1382	.620	470	740	.635	1316	128	2184	9.2	0.9	15.3

NBA REGULAR-SEASON RECORD

HONORS: NBA Rookie of the Year (1986). ... All-NBA first Team (1990). ... All-NBA second Team (1988, 1989, 1991, 1992, 1993, 1997). ... NBA All-Defensive second team (1988, 1989, 1992). ... NBA All-Rookie team (1986).
NOTES: Led NBA with 332 personal fouls (1988).

									REBOUNDS								AVERAGES		
Season Team	G	Min.	FGM	FGA	Pct.	FTM	FTA	Pct.	Off.	Def.	Tot.	Ast.	St.	Blk.	TO	Pts.	RPG	APG	PPG
85-86—New York	50	1771	386	814	.474	226	306	.739	124	327	451	102	54	103	172	998	9.0	2.0	20.0
86-87—New York	63	2206	530	1053	.503	296	415	.713	157	398	555	104	89	147	229	1356	8.8	1.7	21.5
87-88—New York	82	2546	656	1183	.555	341	476	.716	245	431	676	125	104	245	287	1653	8.2	1.5	20.2
88-89—New York	80	2896	727	1282	.567	361	484	.746	213	527	740	188	117	281	266	1815	9.3	2.4	22.7
89-90—New York	82	3165	922	1673	.551	502	648	.775	235	658	893	182	78	327	278	2347	10.9	2.2	28.6
90-91—New York	81	3104	845	1645	.514	464	623	.745	194	711	905	244	80	258	291	2154	11.2	3.0	26.6
91-92—New York	82	3150	796	1525	.522	377	511	.738	228	693	921	156	88	245	209	1970	11.2	1.9	24.0
92-93—New York	81	3003	779	1550	.503	400	556	.719	191	*789	980	151	74	161	265	1959	12.1	1.9	24.2
93-94—New York	79	2972	745	1503	.496	445	582	.765	219	666	885	179	90	217	260	1939	11.2	2.3	24.5
94-95—New York	79	2920	730	1452	.503	420	560	.750	157	710	867	212	68	159	256	1886	11.0	2.7	23.9
95-96—New York	76	2700	678	1456	.466	351	461	.761	157	649	806	160	68	184	221	1711	10.6	2.1	22.5
96-97—New York	78	2887	655	1342	.488	439	582	.754	175	659	834	156	69	189	269	1751	10.7	2.0	22.4
97-98—New York	26	848	203	403	.504	134	186	.720	59	206	265	28	16	58	77	540	10.2	1.1	20.8
98-99—New York	38	1300	247	568	.435	163	231	.706	74	303	377	43	30	100	99	657	9.9	1.1	17.3
99-00—New York	62	2035	361	775	.466	207	283	.731	140	464	604	58	36	84	142	929	9.7	0.9	15.0
00-01—Seattle	79	2107	294	684	.430	172	251	.685	124	461	585	92	53	91	151	760	7.4	1.2	9.6
01-02—Orlando	65	901	148	333	.444	94	134	.701	60	203	263	35	22	45	65	390	4.0	0.5	6.0
Totals	1183	40594	9702	19241	.504	5392	7289	.740	2752	8855	11607	2215	1136	2894	3537	24815	9.8	1.9	21.0

Three-point field goals: 1985-86, 0-for-5. 1986-87, 0-for-7. 1987-88, 0-for-3. 1988-89, 0-for-6. 1989-90, 1-for-4 (.250). 1990-91, 0-for-6. 1991-92, 1-for-6 (.167). 1992-93, 1-for-7 (.143). 1993-94, 4-for-14 (.286). 1994-95, 6-for-21 (.286). 1995-96, 4-for-28 (.143). 1996-97, 2-for-9 (.222). 1997-98, 0-for-2. 1998-99, 0-for-2. 1999-00, 0-for-2. 2000-01, 0-for-2. 2001-02, 0-for-1. Totals, 19-for-125 (.152).

Personal fouls/disqualifications: 1985-86, 191/7. 1986-87, 248/5. 1987-88, 332/5. 1988-89, 311/5. 1989-90, 325/7. 1990-91, 287/3. 1991-92, 277/2. 1992-93, 286/2. 1993-94, 275/3. 1994-95, 272/3. 1995-96, 247/2. 1996-97, 250/2. 1997-98, 74/0. 1998-99, 105/1. 1999-00, 196/1. 2000-01, 229/1. 2001-02, 129/0. Totals, 4034/49.

NBA PLAYOFF RECORD

NOTES: Holds NBA Finals single-series record for most blocked shots—30 (1994, vs. Houston). ... Shares NBA Finals single-game record for most blocked shots—8 (June 17, 1994, vs. Houston).

									REBOUNDS								AVERAGES		
Season Team	G	Min.	FGM	FGA	Pct.	FTM	FTA	Pct.	Off.	Def.	Tot.	Ast.	St.	Blk.	TO	Pts.	RPG	APG	PPG
87-88—New York	4	153	28	57	.491	19	22	.864	16	35	51	10	6	13	11	75	12.8	2.5	18.8
88-89—New York	9	340	70	144	.486	39	52	.750	23	67	90	20	9	18	15	179	10.0	2.2	19.9
89-90—New York	10	395	114	219	.521	65	79	.823	21	84	105	31	13	20	27	294	10.5	3.1	29.4
90-91—New York	3	110	18	45	.400	14	18	.778	2	28	30	6	1	5	11	50	10.0	2.0	16.7
91-92—New York	12	482	109	239	.456	54	73	.740	33	100	133	27	7	31	23	272	11.1	2.3	22.7
92-93—New York	15	604	165	322	.512	51	80	.638	43	121	164	36	17	31	39	382	10.9	2.4	25.5
93-94—New York	25	1032	210	481	.437	123	163	.755	88	205	293	65	32	76	83	547	11.7	2.6	21.9
94-95—New York	11	399	80	156	.513	48	70	.686	17	89	106	27	6	25	30	209	9.6	2.5	19.0
95-96—New York	8	328	65	137	.474	41	63	.651	11	74	85	15	1	25	30	172	10.6	1.9	21.5
96-97—New York	9	357	88	167	.527	27	42	.643	26	69	95	17	3	22	27	203	10.6	1.9	22.6
97-98—New York	4	132	20	56	.357	16	27	.593	9	23	32	5	3	5	10	56	8.0	1.3	14.0
98-99—New York	11	347	58	135	.430	28	36	.778	14	82	96	6	7	8	10	144	8.7	0.5	13.1
99-00—New York	14	461	71	170	.418	62	89	.697	29	104	133	6	16	20	27	204	9.5	0.4	14.6
01-02—Orlando	4	67	8	25	.320	10	17	.588	5	17	22	4	1	4	2	26	5.5	1.0	6.5
Totals	139	5207	1104	2353	.469	597	831	.718	337	1098	1435	275	122	303	345	2813	10.3	2.0	20.2

Three-point field goals: 1985-86, 0-for-1. 1989-90, 1-for-2 (.500). 1991-92, 0-for-1. 1992-93, 1-for-1. 1993-94, 4-for-11 (.364). 1994-95, 1-for-3 (.333). 1995-96, 1-for-2 (.500). 1996-97, 0-for-1. 2001-02, 0-for-1. Totals, 8-for-23 (.348).

Personal fouls/disqualifications: 1987-88, 17/0. 1988-89, 35/0. 1989-90, 41/0. 1990-91, 12/0. 1991-92, 49/1. 1992-93, 60/2. 1993-94, 94/1. 1994-95, 51/1. 1995-96, 22/0. 1996-97, 30/0. 1997-98, 16/0. 1998-99, 35/0. 1999-00, 48/0. 2001-02, 12/0. Totals, 522/5.

NBA ALL-STAR GAME RECORD

Season Team	Min.	FGM	FGA	Pct.	FTM	FTA	Pct.	REBOUNDS Off.	Def.	Tot.	Ast.	PF	Dq.	St.	Blk.	TO	Pts.
1986—New York							Selected, did not play—injured.										
1988—New York	16	4	8	.500	1	1	1.000	1	5	6	0	1	0	0	1	1	9
1989—New York	17	2	8	.250	0	4	.000	1	5	6	2	2	0	1	2	3	4
1990—New York	27	5	9	.556	2	2	1.000	1	9	10	1	5	0	1	5	5	12
1991—New York	30	8	10	.800	2	2	1.000	2	8	10	0	5	0	1	4	2	18
1992—New York	17	4	7	.571	2	5	.400	2	2	4	0	3	0	2	1	2	10
1993—New York	25	7	11	.636	1	1	1.000	3	7	10	1	4	0	2	2	4	15
1994—New York	24	7	15	.467	6	7	.857	4	4	8	1	2	0	0	0	1	20
1995—New York	22	4	7	.571	2	2	1.000	0	3	3	1	3	0	1	0	5	10
1996—New York	12	3	7	.429	2	2	1.000	1	2	3	1	2	0	3	1	0	8
1997—New York							Selected, did not play—injured.										
Totals	190	44	82	.537	18	26	.692	15	45	60	7	27	0	11	16	23	106

FLOYD, SLEEPY   G

PERSONAL: Born March 6, 1960, in Gastonia, N.C. ... 6-3/185 (1,90/83,9). ... Full name: Eric Augustus Floyd.
HIGH SCHOOL: Hunter Huss (Gastonia, N.C.).
COLLEGE: Georgetown.
TRANSACTIONS: Selected by New Jersey Nets in first round (13th pick overall) of 1982 NBA Draft. ... Traded by Nets with F Mickey Johnson to Golden State Warriors for G Micheal Ray Richardson (February 6, 1983). ... Traded by Warriors with C Joe Barry Carroll to Houston Rockets for C Ralph Sampson and G Steve Harris (December 12, 1987). ... Waived by Rockets (August 2, 1993). ... Signed as free agent by San Antonio Spurs (August 13, 1993). ... Signed as free agent by Nets (October 6, 1994).

COLLEGIATE RECORD

NOTES: THE SPORTING NEWS All-America second team (1982).

Season Team	G	Min.	FGM	FGA	Pct.	FTM	FTA	Pct.	Reb.	Ast.	Pts.	AVERAGES RPG	APG	PPG
78-79—Georgetown	29	975	177	388	.456	126	155	.813	119	78	480	4.1	2.7	16.6
79-80—Georgetown	32	1052	246	444	.554	106	140	.757	98	95	598	3.1	3.0	18.7
80-81—Georgetown	32	1115	237	508	.467	133	165	.806	133	83	607	4.2	2.6	19.0
81-82—Georgetown	37	1200	249	494	.504	121	168	.720	127	99	619	3.4	2.7	16.7
Totals	130	4342	909	1834	.496	486	628	.774	477	355	2304	3.7	2.7	17.7

NBA REGULAR-SEASON RECORD

Season Team	G	Min.	FGM	FGA	Pct.	FTM	FTA	Pct.	REBOUNDS Off.	Def.	Tot.	Ast.	St.	Blk.	TO	Pts.	AVERAGES RPG	APG	PPG
82-83—N.J.-G.S.	76	1248	226	527	.429	150	180	.833	56	81	137	138	58	17	106	612	1.8	1.8	8.1
83-84—Golden State	77	2555	484	1045	.463	315	386	.816	87	184	271	269	103	31	196	1291	3.5	3.5	16.8
84-85—Golden State	82	2873	610	1372	.445	336	415	.810	62	140	202	406	134	41	251	1598	2.5	5.0	19.5
85-86—Golden State	82	2764	510	1007	.506	351	441	.796	76	221	297	746	157	16	290	1410	3.6	9.1	17.2
86-87—Golden State	82	3064	503	1030	.488	462	537	.860	56	212	268	848	146	18	280	1541	3.3	10.3	18.8
87-88—G.S.-Hou.	77	2514	420	969	.433	301	354	.850	77	219	296	544	95	12	223	1155	3.8	7.1	15.0
88-89—Houston	82	2788	396	893	.443	261	309	.845	48	258	306	709	124	11	253	1162	3.7	8.6	14.2
89-90—Houston	82	2630	362	803	.451	187	232	.806	46	152	198	600	94	11	204	1000	2.4	7.3	12.2
90-91—Houston	82	1850	386	939	.411	185	246	.752	52	107	159	317	95	17	140	1005	1.9	3.9	12.3
91-92—Houston	82	1662	286	704	.406	135	170	.794	34	116	150	239	57	21	128	744	1.8	2.9	9.1
92-93—Houston	52	867	124	305	.407	81	102	.794	14	72	86	132	32	6	68	345	1.7	2.5	6.6
93-94—San Antonio	53	737	70	209	.335	52	78	.667	10	60	70	101	12	8	61	200	1.3	1.9	3.8
94-95—New Jersey	48	831	71	212	.335	30	43	.698	8	46	54	126	13	6	51	197	1.1	2.6	4.1
Totals	957	26383	4448	10015	.444	2846	3493	.815	626	1868	2494	5175	1120	215	2251	12260	2.6	5.4	12.8

Three-point field goals: 1982-83, 10-for-25 (.400). 1983-84, 8-for-45 (.178). 1984-85, 42-for-143 (.294). 1985-86, 39-for-119 (.328). 1986-87, 73-for-190 (.384). 1987-88, 14-for-72 (.194). 1988-89, 109-for-292 (.373). 1989-90, 89-for-234 (.380). 1990-91, 48-for-176 (.273). 1991-92, 37-for-123 (.301). 1992-93, 16-for-56 (.286). 1993-94, 8-for-36 (.222). 1994-95, 25-for-88 (.284). Totals, 518-for-1599 (.324).

Personal fouls/disqualifications: 1982-83, 134/3. 1983-84, 216/0. 1984-85, 226/1. 1985-86, 199/2. 1986-87, 199/1. 1987-88, 190/1. 1988-89, 196/1. 1989-90, 159/0. 1990-91, 122/0. 1991-92, 128/0. 1992-93, 59/0. 1993-94, 71/0. 1994-95, 73/0. Totals, 1972/9.

NBA PLAYOFF RECORD

NOTES: Holds single-game playoff records for most points in one half—39; most points in one quarter—29; and most field goals in one quarter—12 (May 10, 1987, vs. Los Angeles Lakers). ... Shares single-game playoff record for most field goals made in one half—15 (May 10, 1987, vs. Los Angeles Lakers).

Season Team	G	Min.	FGM	FGA	Pct.	FTM	FTA	Pct.	REBOUNDS Off.	Def.	Tot.	Ast.	St.	Blk.	TO	Pts.	AVERAGES RPG	APG	PPG
86-87—Golden State	10	414	77	152	.507	47	51	.922	9	21	30	102	18	2	35	214	3.0	10.2	21.4
87-88—Houston	4	154	26	61	.426	19	22	.864	3	4	7	34	8	0	12	75	1.8	8.5	18.8
88-89—Houston	4	160	22	46	.478	10	14	.714	3	15	18	26	8	1	10	62	4.5	6.5	15.5
89-90—Houston	4	172	30	64	.469	11	17	.647	7	8	15	41	5	1	15	74	3.8	10.3	18.5
90-91—Houston	3	41	8	24	.333	0	0	—	0	2	2	7	2	1	7	16	0.7	2.3	5.3
92-93—Houston	7	60	6	19	.316	7	10	.700	1	3	4	8	2	0	9	20	0.6	1.1	2.9
93-94—San Antonio	4	37	2	8	.250	2	4	.500	0	1	1	1	0	0	4	6	0.3	0.3	1.5
Totals	36	1038	171	374	.457	96	118	.814	23	54	77	219	43	5	92	467	2.1	6.1	13.0

Three-point field goals: 1986-87, 13-for-28 (.464). 1987-88, 4-for-8 (.500). 1988-89, 8-for-15 (.533). 1989-90, 3-for-12 (.250). 1990-91, 0-for-4. 1992-93, 1-for-3 (.333). Totals, 29-for-70 (.414).

Personal fouls/disqualifications: 1986-87, 24/0. 1987-88, 10/0. 1988-89, 10/0. 1989-90, 5/0. 1990-91, 4/0. 1992-93, 2/0. 1993-94, 3/0. Totals, 58/0.

NBA ALL-STAR GAME RECORD

Season Team	Min.	FGM	FGA	Pct.	FTM	FTA	Pct.	REBOUNDS Off.	Def.	Tot.	Ast.	PF	Dq.	St.	Blk.	TO	Pts.
1987—Golden State	19	4	7	.571	5	7	.714	2	3	5	1	2	0	1	0	2	14

Three-point field goals: 1987, 1-for-3 (.333).

FOUST, LARRY C/F

PERSONAL: Born June 24, 1928, in Painesville, Ohio. ... Died October 27, 1984. ... 6-9/250 (2,06/113,4). ... Full name: Lawrence Michael Foust.
HIGH SCHOOL: South Catholic (Philadelphia).
COLLEGE: La Salle.
TRANSACTIONS: Selected by Chicago Stags in first round of 1950 NBA Draft. ... Draft rights selected by Fort Wayne Pistons in dispersal of Stags franchise (1950). ... Pistons franchise moved from Fort Wayne to Detroit for 1957-58 season. ... Traded by Pistons with cash to Minneapolis Lakers for C Walt Dukes (September 12, 1957). ... Traded by Lakers to St. Louis Hawks for C Charlie Share, draft rights to G Nick Mantis, G Willie Merriweather and cash (February 1, 1960).

COLLEGIATE RECORD

NOTES: The Sporting News All-America fifth team (1950).

Season Team	G	Min.	FGM	FGA	Pct.	FTM	FTA	Pct.	Reb.	Ast.	Pts.	RPG	APG	PPG
46-47—La Salle	26	...	103	...	...	49	...	...	...	...	255	...	...	9.8
47-48—La Salle	24	...	157	...	...	87	...	...	...	...	401	...	...	16.7
48-49—La Salle	28	...	177	...	...	99	164	.604	...	...	453	...	...	16.2
49-50—La Salle	25	...	136	...	...	83	122	.680	...	...	355	...	...	14.2
Totals	103	...	573	...	...	318	...	...	...	...	1464	...	...	14.2

NBA REGULAR-SEASON RECORD

HONORS: All-NBA first team (1955). ... All-NBA second team (1952).

Season Team	G	Min.	FGM	FGA	Pct.	FTM	FTA	Pct.	Reb.	Ast.	PF	Dq.	Pts.	RPG	APG	PPG
50-51—Fort Wayne	68	...	327	944	.346	261	396	.659	681	90	247	6	915	10.0	1.3	13.5
51-52—Fort Wayne	66	2615	390	989	.394	267	394	.678	†880	200	245	10	1047	13.3	3.0	15.9
52-53—Fort Wayne	67	2303	311	865	.360	336	465	.723	769	151	267	16	958	11.5	2.3	14.3
53-54—Fort Wayne	72	2693	376	919	.409	338	475	.712	967	161	258	4	1090	13.4	2.2	15.1
54-55—Fort Wayne	70	2264	398	818	*.487	393	513	.766	700	118	264	9	1189	10.0	1.7	17.0
55-56—Fort Wayne	72	2024	367	821	.447	432	555	.778	648	127	263	7	1166	9.0	1.8	16.2
56-57—Fort Wayne	61	1533	243	617	.394	273	380	.718	555	71	221	7	759	9.1	1.2	12.4
57-58—Minneapolis	72	2200	391	982	.398	428	566	.756	876	108	299	11	1210	12.2	1.5	16.8
58-59—Minneapolis	72	1933	301	771	.390	280	366	.765	627	91	233	5	882	8.7	1.3	12.3
59-60—Minn.-St.L.	72	1964	312	766	.407	253	320	.791	621	96	241	7	877	8.6	1.3	12.2
60-61—St. Louis	68	1208	194	489	.397	164	208	.788	389	77	165	0	552	5.7	1.1	8.1
61-62—St. Louis	57	1153	204	433	.471	145	178	.815	328	78	186	2	553	5.8	1.4	9.7
Totals	817	...	3814	9414	.405	3570	4816	.741	8041	1368	2889	84	11198	9.8	1.7	13.7

NBA PLAYOFF RECORD

Season Team	G	Min.	FGM	FGA	Pct.	FTM	FTA	Pct.	Reb.	Ast.	PF	Dq.	Pts.	RPG	APG	PPG
50-51—Fort Wayne	3	...	14	45	.311	8	10	.800	37	5	5	...	36	12.3	1.7	12.0
51-52—Fort Wayne	2	77	12	23	.522	6	7	.857	29	5	9	1	30	10.0	1.8	10.0
52-53—Fort Wayne	8	332	46	121	.397	57	68	.838	111	6	34	2	153	13.9	0.8	19.1
53-54—Fort Wayne	4	129	11	41	.268	19	25	.760	38	7	21	2	41	9.5	1.8	10.3
54-55—Fort Wayne	11	331	60	152	.395	52	73	.712	107	26	43	0	172	9.7	2.4	15.6
55-56—Fort Wayne	10	289	49	130	.377	70	89	.787	127	14	38	2	168	12.7	1.4	16.8
56-57—Fort Wayne	2	64	13	23	.565	19	23	.826	25	6	10	0	45	12.5	3.0	22.5
58-59—Minneapolis	13	404	56	134	.418	41	50	.820	136	12	47	2	153	10.5	0.9	11.8
59-60—St. Louis	12	205	29	74	.392	20	25	.800	68	11	36	0	78	5.7	0.9	6.5
60-61—St. Louis	8	89	9	20	.450	8	14	.571	28	2	13	0	26	3.5	0.3	3.3
Totals	73	...	301	763	.394	300	384	.781	707	94	255	...	902	9.7	1.3	12.4

NBA ALL-STAR GAME RECORD

Season Team	Min.	FGM	FGA	Pct.	FTM	FTA	Pct.	Reb	Ast.	PF	Dq.	Pts.
1951—Fort Wayne	...	1	6	.167	0	0	...	5	2	3	0	2
1952—Fort Wayne				Selected, did not play—injured.								
1953—Fort Wayne	18	5	7	.714	0	0	...	6	0	4	0	10
1954—Fort Wayne	27	1	9	.111	1	1	1.000	15	0	1	0	3
1955—Fort Wayne	24	3	10	.300	1	1	1.000	7	1	1	0	7
1956—Fort Wayne	20	3	9	.333	3	4	.750	4	0	1	0	9
1958—Minneapolis	13	1	4	.250	8	8	1.000	3	0	3	0	10
1959—Minneapolis	16	3	9	.333	2	2	1.000	9	0	3	0	8
Totals	...	17	54	.315	15	16	.938	49	3	16	0	49

FRAZIER, WALT G

PERSONAL: Born March 29, 1945, in Atlanta. ... 6-4/205 (1,93/93,0). ... Full name: Walter Frazier Jr. ... Nickname: Clyde.
HIGH SCHOOL: David Howard (Atlanta).
COLLEGE: Southern Illinois.
TRANSACTIONS: Selected by New York Knicks in first round (fifth pick overall) of 1967 NBA Draft. ... Acquired by Cleveland Cavaliers as compensation for Knicks signing veteran free agent G Jim Cleamons (October 7, 1977). ... Waived by Cavaliers (October 19, 1979).
CAREER HONORS: Elected to Naismith Memorial Basketball Hall of Fame (1987). ... One of the 50 Greatest Players in NBA History (1996).
MISCELLANEOUS: Member of NBA championship team (1970, 1973). ... New York Knicks all-time assists leader with 4,791 (1967-68 through 1976-77).

COLLEGIATE RECORD

NOTES: The Sporting News All-America second team (1967).

ALL-TIME GREAT PLAYERS

Season Team	G	Min.	FGM	FGA	Pct.	FTM	FTA	Pct.	Reb.	Ast.	Pts.	AVERAGES		
												RPG	APG	PPG
63-64—Southern Illinois‡	14	...	133	225	.591	52	85	.612	129	...	318	9.2	...	22.7
64-65—Southern Illinois	24	...	161	353	.456	88	111	.793	221	...	410	9.2	...	17.1
65-66—Southern Illinois						Did not play—ineligible.								
66-67—Southern Illinois	26	...	192	397	.484	90	126	.714	310	...	474	11.9	...	18.2
Varsity totals	50	...	353	750	.471	178	237	.751	531	...	884	10.6	...	17.7

NBA REGULAR-SEASON RECORD

HONORS: All-NBA first team (1970, 1972, 1974, 1975). ... All-NBA second team (1971, 1973). ... NBA All-Defensive first team (1969, 1970, 1971, 1972, 1973, 1974, 1975). ... NBA All-Rookie team (1968).

Season Team	G	Min.	FGM	FGA	Pct.	FTM	FTA	Pct.	Reb.	Ast.	PF	Dq.	Pts.	AVERAGES		
														RPG	APG	PPG
67-68—New York	74	1588	256	568	.451	154	235	.655	313	305	199	2	666	4.2	4.1	9.0
68-69—New York	80	2949	531	1052	.505	341	457	.746	499	635	245	2	1403	6.2	7.9	17.5
69-70—New York	77	3040	600	1158	.518	409	547	.748	465	629	203	1	1609	6.0	8.2	20.9
70-71—New York	80	3455	651	1317	.494	434	557	.779	544	536	240	1	1736	6.8	6.7	21.7
71-72—New York	77	3126	669	1307	.512	450	557	.808	513	446	185	0	1788	6.7	5.8	23.2
72-73—New York	78	3181	681	1389	.490	286	350	.817	570	461	186	0	1648	7.3	5.9	21.1

Season Team	G	Min.	FGM	FGA	Pct.	FTM	FTA	Pct.	REBOUNDS			Ast.	St.	Blk.	TO	Pts.	AVERAGES		
									Off.	Def.	Tot.						RPG	APG	PPG
73-74—New York	80	3338	674	1429	.472	295	352	.838	120	416	536	551	161	15	...	1643	6.7	6.9	20.5
74-75—New York	78	3204	672	1391	.483	331	400	.828	90	375	465	474	190	14	...	1675	6.0	6.1	21.5
75-76—New York	59	2427	470	969	.485	186	226	.823	79	321	400	351	106	9	...	1126	6.8	5.9	19.1
76-77—N.Y. Knicks	76	2687	532	1089	.489	259	336	.771	52	241	293	403	132	9	...	1323	3.9	5.3	17.4
77-78—Cleveland	51	1664	336	714	.471	153	180	.850	54	155	209	209	77	9	113	825	4.1	4.1	16.2
78-79—Cleveland	12	279	54	122	.443	21	27	.778	7	13	20	32	13	2	22	129	1.7	2.7	10.8
79-80—Cleveland	3	27	4	11	.364	2	2	1.000	1	2	3	8	2	1	4	10	1.0	2.7	3.3
Totals	825	30965	6130	12516	.490	3321	4226	.786	...	...	4830	5040	681	59	139	15581	5.9	6.1	18.9

Three-point field goals: 1979-80, 0-for-1.

Personal fouls/disqualifications: 1973-74, 212/2. 1974-75, 205/2. 1975-76, 163/1. 1976-77, 194/0. 1977-78, 124/1. 1978-79, 22/0. 1979-80, 2/0. Totals, 2180/12.

NBA PLAYOFF RECORD

Season Team	G	Min.	FGM	FGA	Pct.	FTM	FTA	Pct.	Reb.	Ast.	PF	Dq.	Pts.	AVERAGES		
														RPG	APG	PPG
67-68—New York	4	119	12	33	.364	14	18	.778	22	25	12	0	38	5.5	6.3	9.5
68-69—New York	10	415	89	177	.503	34	57	.597	74	91	30	0	212	7.4	9.1	21.2
69-70—New York	19	834	118	247	.478	68	89	.764	149	156	53	0	304	7.8	8.2	16.0
70-71—New York	12	501	108	204	.529	55	75	.733	70	54	45	0	271	5.8	4.5	22.6
71-72—New York	16	704	148	276	.536	92	125	.736	112	98	48	0	388	7.0	6.1	24.3
72-73—New York	17	765	150	292	.514	73	94	.777	124	106	52	1	373	7.3	6.2	21.9

Season Team	G	Min.	FGM	FGA	Pct.	FTM	FTA	Pct.	REBOUNDS			Ast.	St.	Blk.	TO	Pts.	AVERAGES		
									Off.	Def.	Tot.						RPG	APG	PPG
73-74—New York	12	491	113	225	.502	44	49	.898	21	74	95	48	21	4	...	270	7.9	4.0	22.5
74-75—New York	3	124	29	46	.630	13	16	.813	3	17	20	21	11	0	...	71	6.7	7.0	23.7
Totals	93	3953	767	1500	.511	393	523	.751	...	...	666	599	32	4	...	1927	7.2	6.4	20.7

Personal fouls/disqualifications: 1973-74, 41/1. 1974-75, 4/0. Totals, 285/2.

NBA ALL-STAR GAME RECORD

NOTES: NBA All-Star Game Most Valuable Player (1975).

Season Team	Min.	FGM	FGA	Pct.	FTM	FTA	Pct.	Reb	Ast.	PF	Dq.	Pts.
1970—New York	24	3	7	.429	1	2	.500	3	4	2	0	7
1971—New York	26	3	9	.333	0	0	...	6	5	2	0	6
1972—New York	25	7	11	.636	1	2	.500	3	5	2	0	15
1973—New York	26	5	15	.333	0	0	...	6	2	1	0	10

Season Team	Min.	FGM	FGA	Pct.	FTM	FTA	Pct.	REBOUNDS			Ast.	PF	Dq.	St.	Blk.	TO	Pts.
								Off.	Def.	Tot.							
1974—New York	28	5	12	.417	2	2	1.000	1	1	2	5	1	0	3	0	...	12
1975—New York	35	10	17	.588	10	11	.909	0	5	5	2	2	0	4	0	...	30
1976—New York	19	2	7	.286	4	4	1.000	0	2	2	3	0	0	2	0	...	8
Totals	183	35	78	.449	18	21	.857	...	...	27	26	10	0	9	0	...	88

FREE, WORLD B.   G

PERSONAL: Born December 9, 1953, in Atlanta. ... 6-3/190 (1,90/86,2). ... Formerly known as Lloyd Free.
HIGH SCHOOL: Canarsie (Brooklyn, N.Y.).
COLLEGE: Guilford (N.C.).
TRANSACTIONS: Selected after junior season by Philadelphia 76ers in second round (23rd pick overall) of 1975 NBA Draft. ... Traded by 76ers to San Diego Clippers for 1984 first-round draft choice (October 12, 1978). ... Traded by Clippers to Golden State Warriors for G Phil Smith and 1984 first-round draft choice (August 28, 1980). ... Traded by Warriors to Cleveland Cavaliers for G Ron Brewer (December 15, 1982). ... Signed as veteran free agent by 76ers (December 30, 1986); Cavaliers waived their right of first refusal in exchange for 1990 second-round draft choice. ... Waived by 76ers (March 4, 1987). ... Played in United States Basketball League with Miami Tropics (1987). ... Signed as free agent by Houston Rockets (October 1, 1987).
CAREER NOTES: Named strength and conditioning coach of Philadelphia 76ers (September 28, 1994). ... Community relations player representative, Philadelphia 76ers (1996-97 to present).

COLLEGIATE RECORD

NOTES: Member of NAIA championship team (1973). ... Most Valuable Player in NAIA tournament (1973).

Season Team	G	Min.	FGM	FGA	Pct.	FTM	FTA	Pct.	Reb.	Ast.	Pts.	AVERAGES RPG	APG	PPG
72-73—Guilford (N.C.)	33	...	272	572	.476	153	217	.705	191	...	697	5.8	...	21.1
73-74—Guilford (N.C.)	24	...	216	456	.474	165	225	.733	200	...	597	8.3	...	24.9
74-75—Guilford (N.C.)	28	...	247	486	.508	218	291	.749	163	...	712	5.8	...	25.4
Totals	85	...	735	1514	.485	536	733	.731	554	...	2006	6.5	...	23.6

HONORS: All-NBA second team (1979).

NBA REGULAR-SEASON RECORD

Season Team	G	Min.	FGM	FGA	Pct.	FTM	FTA	Pct.	REBOUNDS Off.	Def.	Tot.	Ast.	St.	Blk.	TO	Pts.	AVERAGES RPG	APG	PPG
75-76—Philadelphia	71	1121	239	533	.448	112	186	.602	64	61	125	104	37	6	...	590	1.8	1.5	8.3
76-77—Philadelphia	78	2253	467	1022	.457	334	464	.720	97	140	237	200	75	25	...	1268	3.0	3.4	16.3
77-78—Philadelphia	76	2050	390	857	.455	411	562	.731	92	120	212	306	68	41	200	1191	2.8	4.0	15.7
78-79—San Diego	78	2954	795	1653	.481	*654	*865	.756	127	174	301	340	111	35	297	2244	3.9	4.4	28.8
79-80—San Diego	68	2585	737	1556	.474	*572	760	.753	129	109	238	283	81	32	228	2055	3.5	4.2	30.2
80-81—Golden State	65	2370	516	1157	.446	528	649	.814	48	111	159	361	85	11	195	1565	2.4	5.6	24.1
81-82—Golden State	78	2796	650	1452	.448	479	647	.740	118	130	248	419	71	8	208	1789	3.2	5.4	22.9
82-83—G.S.-Clev.	73	2638	649	1423	.456	430	583	.738	92	109	201	290	97	15	209	1743	2.8	4.0	23.9
83-84—Cleveland	75	2375	626	1407	.445	395	504	.784	89	128	217	226	94	8	154	1669	2.9	3.0	22.3
84-85—Cleveland	71	2249	609	1328	.459	308	411	.749	61	150	211	320	75	16	139	1597	3.0	4.5	22.5
85-86—Cleveland	75	2535	652	1433	.455	379	486	.780	72	146	218	314	91	19	172	1754	2.9	4.2	23.4
86-87—Philadelphia	20	285	39	123	.317	36	47	.766	5	14	19	30	5	4	18	116	1.0	1.5	5.8
87-88—Houston	58	682	143	350	.409	80	100	.800	14	30	44	60	20	3	49	374	0.8	1.0	6.4
Totals	886	26893	6512	14294	.456	4718	6264	.753	1008	1422	2430	3319	910	223	1869	17955	2.7	3.7	20.3

Three-point field goals: 1979-80, 9-for-25 (.360). 1980-81, 5-for-31 (.161). 1981-82, 10-for-56 (.179). 1982-83, 15-for-45 (.333). 1983-84, 22-for-69 (.319). 1984-85, 71-for-193 (.368). 1985-86, 71-for-169 (.420). 1986-87, 2-for-9 (.222). 1987-88, 8-for-35 (.229). Totals, 213-for-632 (.337).
Personal fouls/disqualifications: 1975-76, 107/0. 1976-77, 207/2. 1977-78, 199/0. 1978-79, 253/8. 1979-80, 195/0. 1980-81, 183/1. 1981-82, 222/1. 1982-83, 241/4. 1983-84, 214/2. 1984-85, 163/0. 1985-86, 186/1. 1986-87, 26/0. 1987-88, 74/2. Totals, 2270/21.

NBA PLAYOFF RECORD

Season Team	G	Min.	FGM	FGA	Pct.	FTM	FTA	Pct.	REBOUNDS Off.	Def.	Tot.	Ast.	St.	Blk.	TO	Pts.	AVERAGES RPG	APG	PPG
75-76—Philadelphia	3	62	11	28	.393	10	13	.769	1	0	1	5	3	0	...	32	0.3	1.7	10.7
76-77—Philadelphia	15	281	63	170	.371	53	77	.688	10	22	32	29	12	8	...	179	2.1	1.9	11.9
77-78—Philadelphia	10	268	51	124	.411	59	81	.728	10	21	31	37	4	6	26	161	3.1	3.7	16.1
84-85—Cleveland	4	150	41	93	.441	23	25	.920	4	6	10	31	6	0	6	105	2.5	7.8	26.3
87-88—Houston	2	12	0	2	.000	0	0	...	1	1	2	1	0	0	3	0	1.0	0.5	0.0
Totals	34	773	166	417	.398	145	196	.740	26	50	76	103	25	14	35	477	2.2	3.0	14.0

Three-point field goals: 1984-85, 0-for-4. 1987-88, 0-for-1. Totals, 0-for-5.
Personal fouls/disqualifications: 1975-76, 6/0. 1976-77, 33/0. 1977-78, 26/0. 1984-85, 12/0. 1987-88, 2/0. Totals, 79/0.

NBA ALL-STAR GAME RECORD

Season Team	Min.	FGM	FGA	Pct.	FTM	FTA	Pct.	REBOUNDS Off.	Def.	Tot.	Ast.	PF	Dq.	St.	Blk.	TO	Pts.
1980—San Diego	21	7	13	.538	0	1	.000	1	2	3	5	1	0	0	1	5	14

FULKS, JOE   F/C

PERSONAL: Born October 26, 1921, in Birmingham, Ky. ... Died March 21, 1976. ... 6-5/190 (1,96/86,2). ... Full name: Joseph Franklin Fulks. ... Nickname: Jumpin' Joe.
HIGH SCHOOL: Birmingham (Ky.), then Kuttawa (Ky.).
COLLEGE: Murray State.
TRANSACTIONS: In military service (1943-44 through 1945-46 seasons). ... Signed by Philadelphia Warriors of Basketball Association of America (1946).
CAREER HONORS: Elected to Naismith Memorial Basketball Hall of Fame (1978). ... NBA 25th Anniversary All-Time Team (1970).
MISCELLANEOUS: Member of BAA championship team (1947).

COLLEGIATE RECORD

NOTES: Elected to NAIA Basketball Hall of Fame (1952).

Season Team	G	Min.	FGM	FGA	Pct.	FTM	FTA	Pct.	Reb.	Ast.	Pts.	AVERAGES RPG	APG	PPG
41-42—Murray State	22	...	117	...	...	50	76	.658	...	...	284	...	...	12.9
42-43—Murray State	25	...	135	...	...	67	100	.670	...	...	337	...	...	13.5
Totals	47	...	252	...	...	117	176	.665	...	...	621	...	...	13.2

NBA REGULAR-SEASON RECORD

HONORS: All-NBA second team (1951). ... All-BAA first team (1947, 1948, 1949).

Season Team	G	Min.	FGM	FGA	Pct.	FTM	FTA	Pct.	Reb.	Ast.	PF	Dq.	Pts.	AVERAGES RPG	APG	PPG
46-47—Philadelphia (BAA)	60	...	*475	*1557	.305	*439	*601	.730	...	25	199	...	*1389	...	0.4	*23.2
47-48—Philadelphia (BAA)	43	...	326	*1258	.259	*297	390	.762	...	26	162	...	949	...	0.6	*22.1
48-49—Philadelphia (BAA)	60	...	529	*1689	.313	502	638	.787	...	74	262	...	1560	...	1.2	26.0
49-50—Philadelphia	68	...	336	1209	.278	293	421	.696	...	56	240	...	965	...	0.8	14.2
50-51—Philadelphia	66	...	429	1358	.316	378	442	*.855	523	117	247	8	1236	7.9	1.8	18.7
51-52—Philadelphia	61	1904	336	1078	.312	250	303	.825	368	123	255	13	922	6.0	2.0	15.1
52-53—Philadelphia	70	2085	332	960	.346	168	231	.727	387	138	319	20	832	5.5	2.0	11.9
53-54—Philadelphia	61	501	61	229	.266	28	49	.571	101	28	90	0	150	1.7	0.5	2.5
Totals	489	...	2824	9338	.302	2355	3075	.766	...	587	1774	...	8003	...	1.2	16.4

NBA PLAYOFF RECORD

														AVERAGES		
Season Team	G	Min.	FGM	FGA	Pct.	FTM	FTA	Pct.	Reb.	Ast.	PF	Dq.	Pts.	RPG	APG	PPG
46-47—Philadelphia (BAA)	10	...	74	257	.288	74	94	.787	...	3	32	...	222	...	0.3	22.2
47-48—Philadelphia (BAA)	13	...	92	380	.242	98	121	.810	...	3	55	...	282	...	0.2	21.7
48-49—Philadelphia (BAA)	1	...	0	0	...	0	0	...	...	0	1	0	0	...	0.0	0.0
49-50—Philadelphia	2	...	5	26	.192	5	10	.500	...	2	10	...	15	...	1.0	7.5
50-51—Philadelphia	2	...	16	49	.327	20	27	.741	16	1	9	0	52	8.0	0.5	26.0
51-52—Philadelphia	3	70	5	33	.152	7	9	.778	12	2	13	1	17	4.0	0.7	5.7
Totals	31	...	192	745	.258	204	261	.782	...	11	120	...	588	...	0.4	19.0

NBA ALL-STAR GAME RECORD

Season Team	Min.	FGM	FGA	Pct.	FTM	FTA	Pct.	Reb	Ast.	PF	Dq.	Pts.
1951—Philadelphia	...	6	15	.400	7	9	.778	7	3	5	0	19
1952—Philadelphia	9	3	7	.429	0	1	.000	5	2	2	0	6
Totals	...	9	22	.409	7	10	.700	12	5	7	0	25

GALLATIN, HARRY   F/C

PERSONAL: Born April 26, 1927, in Roxana, Ill. ... 6-6/215 (1,98/97,5). ... Full name: Harry Junior Gallatin. ... Nickname: The Horse.
HIGH SCHOOL: Roxana (Ill.).
COLLEGE: Northeast Missouri State Teachers College.
TRANSACTIONS: Selected by New York Knicks in first round of 1948 BAA Draft. ... Knicks franchise became part of NBA for 1949-50 season. ... Traded by Knicks with G Dick Atha and C/F Nat Clifton to Detroit Pistons for F Mel Hutchins and first-round draft choice (April 3, 1957).
CAREER HONORS: Elected to Naismith Memorial Basketball Hall of Fame (1991).

COLLEGIATE RECORD

NOTES: Elected to NAIA Basketball Hall of Fame (1957).

											AVERAGES		
Season Team	G	Min.	FGM	FGA	Pct.	FTM	FTA	Pct.	Reb.	Ast.	Pts.	RPG	APG	PPG
46-47—NE Missouri St.	31	...	149	...	...	53	89	.596	...	...	351	...	...	11.3
47-48—NE Missouri St.	31	...	178	465	.383	109	162	.673	...	...	465	...	...	15.0
Totals	62	...	327	...	...	162	251	.645	...	...	816	...	...	13.2

NBA REGULAR-SEASON RECORD

HONORS: All-NBA first team (1954). ... All-NBA second team (1955).

														AVERAGES		
Season Team	G	Min.	FGM	FGA	Pct.	FTM	FTA	Pct.	Reb.	Ast.	PF	Dq.	Pts.	RPG	APG	PPG
48-49—New York (BAA)	52	...	157	479	.328	120	169	.710	...	63	127	...	434	...	1.2	8.3
49-50—New York	68	...	263	664	.396	277	366	.757	...	56	215	...	803	...	0.8	11.8
50-51—New York	66	...	293	705	.416	259	354	.732	800	180	244	4	845	12.1	2.7	12.8
51-52—New York	66	1931	233	527	.442	275	341	.806	661	115	223	5	741	10.0	1.7	11.2
52-53—New York	70	2333	282	635	.444	301	430	.700	916	126	224	6	865	13.1	1.8	12.4
53-54—New York	72	2690	258	639	.404	433	552	.784	*1098	153	208	2	949	*15.3	2.1	13.2
54-55—New York	72	2548	330	859	.384	393	483	.814	995	176	206	5	1053	13.8	2.4	14.6
55-56—New York	72	2378	322	834	.386	358	455	.787	740	168	220	6	1002	10.3	2.3	13.9
56-57—New York	72	1943	332	817	.406	415	519	.800	725	85	202	1	1079	10.1	1.2	15.0
57-58—Detroit	72	1990	340	898	.379	392	498	.787	749	86	217	5	1072	10.4	1.2	14.9
Totals	682	...	2810	7057	.398	3223	4167	.773	...	1208	2086	...	8843	...	1.8	13.0

NBA PLAYOFF RECORD

														AVERAGES		
Season Team	G	Min.	FGM	FGA	Pct.	FTM	FTA	Pct.	Reb.	Ast.	PF	Dq.	Pts.	RPG	APG	PPG
48-49—New York (BAA)	6	...	20	56	.357	32	39	.821	...	10	31	...	72	...	1.7	12.0
49-50—New York	5	...	20	52	.385	25	32	.781	...	6	23	...	65	...	1.2	13.0
50-51—New York	14	...	49	140	.350	67	87	.770	163	26	57	3	165	11.6	1.9	11.8
51-52—New York	14	471	50	122	.410	51	66	.773	134	19	45	1	151	9.6	1.4	10.8
52-53—New York	11	303	36	86	.419	44	59	.746	120	15	29	0	116	10.9	1.4	10.5
53-54—New York	4	151	16	35	.457	22	31	.710	61	6	12	0	54	15.3	1.5	13.5
54-55—New York	3	108	19	42	.452	17	22	.773	44	7	11	0	55	14.7	2.3	18.3
57-58—Detroit	7	182	32	87	.368	26	37	.703	70	11	27	1	90	10.0	1.6	12.9
Totals	64	...	242	620	.390	284	373	.761	...	100	235	...	768	...	1.6	12.0

NBA ALL-STAR GAME RECORD

Season Team	Min.	FGM	FGA	Pct.	FTM	FTA	Pct.	Reb	Ast.	PF	Dq.	Pts.
1951—New York	...	2	4	.500	1	1	1.000	5	2	4	0	5
1952—New York	22	3	5	.600	1	4	.250	9	3	3	0	7
1953—New York	19	1	4	.250	1	2	.500	3	2	1	0	3
1954—New York	28	0	2	.000	5	6	.833	18	3	0	0	5
1955—New York	36	4	7	.571	5	5	1.000	14	3	2	0	13
1956—New York	30	5	12	.417	6	7	.857	5	2	4	0	16
1957—New York	24	4	7	.571	0	2	.000	11	1	3	0	8
Totals	...	19	41	.463	19	27	.704	65	16	17	0	57

HEAD COACHING RECORD

HONORS: NBA Coach of the Year (1963).

COLLEGIATE COACHING RECORD

Season Team	W	L	Pct.	Finish
58-59—Southern Illinois-Carbondale	17	10	.630	2nd/Interstate Intercollegiate Athletic Conference
59-60—Southern Illinois-Carbondale	20	9	.690	T1st/Interstate Intercollegiate Athletic Conference
60-61—Southern Illinois-Carbondale	21	6	.778	1st/Interstate Intercollegiate Athletic Conference
61-62—Southern Illinois-Carbondale	21	10	.677	1st/Interstate Intercollegiate Athletic Conference
67-68—Southern Ill.-Edwardsville	5	5	.500	
68-69—Southern Ill.-Edwardsville	7	10	.412	
69-70—Southern Ill.-Edwardsville	7	16	.304	
Totals (7 years)	98	66	.598	

NBA COACHING RECORD

	REGULAR SEASON				PLAYOFFS		
Season Team	W	L	Pct.	Finish	W	L	Pct.
62-63—St. Louis	48	32	.600	2nd/Western Division	6	5	.545
63-64—St. Louis	46	34	.575	2nd/Western Division	6	6	.500
64-65—St. Louis	17	16	.515		—	—	—
—New York	19	23	.452	4th/Eastern Division	—	—	—
65-66—New York	6	15	.286		—	—	—
Totals (4 years)	136	120	.531	Totals (2 years)	12	11	.522

NOTES:

1959—Defeated Wittenberg, 90-80, in NCAA College Division Tournament regional semifinal; lost to Belmont Academy, 79-70, in regional final.

1960—Defeated McKendree, 97-71, in NCAA College Division Tournament regional; lost to Oklahoma Baptist, 75-71, in semifinal.

1961—Defeated Trinity (Tex.), 96-84, in NCAA College Division Tournament regional semifinal; lost to Southeast Missouri, 87-84, in regional final.

1962—Defeated Union, 78-56, in NCAA College Division Tournament regional semifinal; defeated Evansville, 88-83, in regional final; defeated Northeastern, 73-57, in quarterfinal; lost to Mount St. Mary's, 58-57, in semifinals; defeated Nebraska Wesleyan 98-81, in third-place game.

1963—Defeated Detroit, 3-1, in Western Division Semifinals; lost to Los Angeles, 4-3, in Western Division Finals.

1964—Defeated Los Angeles, 3-2, in Western Division Semifinals; lost to San Francisco, 4-3, in Western Division Finals. Replaced as St. Louis head coach by Richie Guerin (November).

1965—Replaced Eddie Donovan as New York head coach (January), with record of 12-26. Replaced as New York head coach by Dick McGuire (November 29).

RECORD AS BASEBALL PLAYER

TRANSACTIONS: Signed by Erwin (Tenn.) of Appalachian League (January 1945). ... On military service list (July 1945-February 24, 1949). ... Placed on suspended list (July 13, 1950). ... Released (September 29, 1950).

Year Team (League)	W	L	Pct.	ERA	G	GS	CG	ShO	Sv.	IP	H	R	ER	BB	SO
1949—Decatur (Three I)	7	9	.438	4.28	32	...	10	1	...	166	171	88	79	85	78

GERVIN, GEORGE   G/F

PERSONAL: Born April 27, 1952, in Detroit. ... 6-7/185 (2,00/83,9). ... Full name: George Gervin. ... Nickname: Iceman. ... Brother of Derrick Gervin, guard with New Jersey Nets (1989-90 and 1990-91).
HIGH SCHOOL: Martin Luther King (Detroit).
COLLEGE: Long Beach State, then Eastern Michigan.
TRANSACTIONS: Selected after sophomore season by Virginia Squires in first round of 1973 ABA special circumstance draft. ... Selected by Phoenix Suns in third round (40th pick overall) of 1974 NBA Draft. ... Contract sold by Squires to San Antonio Spurs (January 30, 1974). ... Spurs franchise became part of NBA for 1976-77 season. ... Traded by Spurs to Chicago Bulls for F David Greenwood (October 24, 1985). ... Played in Italy (1986-87). ... Played with Quad City Thunder of Continental Basketball Association (1989-90).
CAREER NOTES: Assistant coach, San Antonio Spurs (1992-93 and 1993-94). ... Community relations representative, Spurs (1993-94 to 1999-2000). ... Head coach, Detroit Dogs, ABA 2000. ... Vice president of basketball operations, Detroit Dogs (2001-present).
CAREER HONORS: Elected to Naismith Memorial Basketball Hall of Fame (1996). ... One of the 50 Greatest Players in NBA History (1996).

COLLEGIATE RECORD

NOTES: Left Long Beach State before the start of 1969-70 season.

Season Team	G	Min.	FGM	FGA	Pct.	FTM	FTA	Pct.	Reb.	Ast.	Pts.	RPG	APG	PPG
70-71—Eastern Mich.	9	300	65	123	.528	28	39	.718	104	29	158	11.6	3.2	17.6
71-72—Eastern Mich.	30	1098	339	571	.594	208	265	.785	458	103	886	15.3	3.4	29.5
Totals	39	1398	404	694	.582	236	304	.776	562	132	1044	14.4	3.4	26.8

ABA REGULAR-SEASON RECORD

NOTES: ABA All-Star second team (1975, 1976). ... ABA All-Rookie team (1973).

			2-POINT			3-POINT									AVERAGES		
Season Team	G	Min.	FGM	FGA	Pct.	FGM	FGA	Pct.	FTM	FTA	Pct.	Reb.	Ast.	Pts.	RPG	APG	PPG
72-73—Virginia	30	689	155	315	.492	6	26	.231	96	118	.814	128	34	424	4.3	1.1	14.1
73-74—Virginia-San Antonio	74	2511	664	1370	.485	8	56	.143	378	464	.815	624	142	1730	8.4	1.9	23.4
74-75—San Antonio	84	3113	767	1600	.479	17	55	.309	380	458	.830	697	207	1965	8.3	2.5	23.4
75-76—San Antonio	81	2748	692	1359	.509	14	55	.255	342	399	.857	546	201	1768	6.7	2.5	21.8
Totals	269	9061	2278	4644	.491	45	192	.234	1196	1439	.831	1995	584	5887	7.4	2.2	21.9

ABA PLAYOFF RECORD

			2-POINT			3-POINT									AVERAGES		
Season Team	G	Min.	FGM	FGA	Pct.	FGM	FGA	Pct.	FTM	FTA	Pct.	Reb.	Ast.	Pts.	RPG	APG	PPG
72-73—Virginia	5	200	33	72	.458	1	5	.200	23	34	.676	38	8	93	7.6	1.6	18.6
73-74—San Antonio	7	226	56	114	.491	1	1	1.000	29	31	.935	52	19	144	7.4	2.7	20.6

Season Team	G	Min.	2-POINT			3-POINT			FTM	FTA	Pct.	Reb.	Ast.	Pts.	AVERAGES		
			FGM	FGA	Pct.	FGM	FGA	Pct.							RPG	APG	PPG
74-75—San Antonio	6	276	76	159	.478	3	12	.250	43	52	.827	84	8	204	14.0	1.3	34.0
75-76—San Antonio	7	288	67	125	.536	0	3	.000	56	69	.812	64	19	190	9.1	2.7	27.1
Totals	25	990	232	470	.494	5	21	.238	151	186	.812	238	54	631	9.5	2.2	25.2

ABA ALL-STAR GAME RECORD

Season Team	Min.	2-POINT			3-POINT			FTM	FTA	Pct.	Reb.	Ast.	Pts.
		FGM	FGA	Pct.	FGM	FGA	Pct.						
1974—Virginia	21	3	8	.375	0	1	.000	3	4	.750	5	3	9
1975—San Antonio	30	8	14	.571	0	1	.000	7	8	.875	6	3	23
1976—San Antonio	16	3	13	.231	0	0	...	1	2	.500	6	1	8
Totals	67	14	35	.400	0	2	.000	11	14	.786	17	7	40

NBA REGULAR-SEASON RECORD

RECORDS: Holds single-game record for most points in one quarter—33 (April 9, 1978, vs. New Orleans).
HONORS: All-NBA first team (1978, 1979, 1980, 1981, 1982). ... All-NBA second team (1977, 1983).

Season Team	G	Min.	FGM	FGA	Pct.	FTM	FTA	Pct.	REBOUNDS			Ast.	St.	Blk.	TO	Pts.	AVERAGES		
									Off.	Def.	Tot.						RPG	APG	PPG
76-77—San Antonio	82	2705	726	1335	.544	443	532	.833	134	320	454	238	105	104	...	1895	5.5	2.9	23.1
77-78—San Antonio	82	2857	*864	1611	.536	504	607	.830	118	302	420	302	136	110	306	*2232	5.1	3.7	*27.2
78-79—San Antonio	80	2888	*947	*1749	.541	471	570	.826	142	258	400	219	137	91	286	*2365	5.0	2.7	*29.6
79-80—San Antonio	78	2934	*1024	*1940	.528	505	593	.852	154	249	403	202	110	79	254	*2585	5.2	2.6	*33.1
80-81—San Antonio	82	2765	850	1729	.492	512	620	.826	126	293	419	260	94	56	251	2221	5.1	3.2	27.1
81-82—San Antonio	79	2817	*993	*1987	.500	555	642	.864	138	254	392	187	77	45	210	*2551	5.0	2.4	*32.3
82-83—San Antonio	78	2830	757	1553	.487	517	606	.853	111	246	357	264	88	67	247	2043	4.6	3.4	26.2
83-84—San Antonio	76	2584	765	1561	.490	427	507	.842	106	207	313	220	79	47	224	1967	4.1	2.9	25.9
84-85—San Antonio	·72	2091	600	1182	.508	324	384	.844	79	155	234	178	66	48	198	1524	3.3	2.5	21.2
85-86—Chicago	82	2065	519	1100	.472	283	322	.879	78	137	215	144	49	23	161	1325	2.6	1.8	16.2
Totals	791	26536	8045	15747	.511	4541	5383	.844	1186	2421	3607	2214	941	670	2137	20708	4.6	2.8	26.2

Three-point field goals: 1979-80, 32-for-102 (.314). 1980-81, 9-for-35 (.257). 1981-82, 10-for-36 (.278). 1982-83, 12-for-33 (.364). 1983-84, 10-for-24 (.417). 1984-85, 0-for-10. 1985-86, 4-for-19 (.211). Totals, 77-for-259 (.297).

Personal fouls/disqualifications: 1976-77, 286/12. 1977-78, 255/3. 1978-79, 275/5. 1979-80, 208/0. 1980-81, 212/4. 1981-82, 215/2. 1982-83, 243/5. 1983-84, 219/3. 1984-85, 208/2. 1985-86, 210/4. Totals, 2331/40.

NBA PLAYOFF RECORD

Season Team	G	Min.	FGM	FGA	Pct.	FTM	FTA	Pct.	REBOUNDS			Ast.	St.	Blk.	TO	Pts.	AVERAGES		
									Off.	Def.	Tot.						RPG	APG	PPG
76-77—San Antonio	2	62	19	44	.432	12	15	.800	5	6	11	3	1	2	...	50	5.5	1.5	25.0
77-78—San Antonio	6	227	78	142	.549	43	56	.768	11	23	34	19	6	16	19	199	5.7	3.2	33.2
78-79—San Antonio	14	513	158	295	.536	84	104	.808	33	49	82	35	27	14	40	400	5.9	2.5	28.6
79-80—San Antonio	3	122	37	74	.500	26	30	.867	9	11	20	12	5	3	9	100	6.7	4.0	33.3
80-81—San Antonio	7	274	77	154	.500	36	45	.800	9	26	35	24	5	5	20	190	5.0	3.4	27.1
81-82—San Antonio	9	373	103	228	.452	59	71	.831	19	47	66	41	10	4	31	265	7.3	4.6	29.4
82-83—San Antonio	11	437	108	208	.519	61	69	.884	21	53	74	37	12	4	46	277	6.7	3.4	25.2
84-85—San Antonio	5	183	42	79	.532	27	34	.794	3	15	18	14	3	3	20	111	3.6	2.8	22.2
85-86—Chicago	2	11	0	1	.000	0	0	...	0	1	1	1	0	0	2	0	0.5	0.5	0.0
Totals	59	2202	622	1225	.508	348	424	.821	110	231	341	186	69	51	187	1592	5.8	3.2	27.0

Three-point field goals: 1979-80, 0-for-2. 1980-81, 0-for-3. 1981-82, 0-for-3. 1982-83, 0-for-2. 1984-85, 0-for-3. Totals, 0-for-13.

Personal fouls/disqualifications: 1976-77, 9/1. 1977-78, 23/0. 1978-79, 51/1. 1979-80, 8/0. 1980-81, 19/1. 1981-82, 36/1. 1982-83, 39/1. 1984-85, 19/0. 1985-86, 3/0. Totals, 207/5.

NBA ALL-STAR GAME RECORD

NOTES: NBA All-Star Game Most Valuable Player (1980).

Season Team	Min.	FGM	FGA	Pct.	FTM	FTA	Pct.	REBOUNDS			Ast.	PF	Dq.	St.	Blk.	TO	Pts.
								Off.	Def.	Tot.							
1977—San Antonio	12	0	6	.000	0	0	...	0	1	1	0	1	0	0	1	...	0
1978—San Antonio	18	4	11	.364	1	3	.333	1	1	2	1	2	0	2	1	2	9
1979—San Antonio	34	8	16	.500	10	11	.909	2	4	6	2	4	0	1	1	3	26
1980—San Antonio	40	14	26	.538	6	9	.667	4	6	10	3	2	0	3	0	3	34
1981—San Antonio	24	5	9	.556	1	2	.500	1	2	3	0	3	0	2	1	2	11
1982—San Antonio	27	5	14	.357	2	2	1.000	1	5	6	1	3	0	3	3	0	12
1983—San Antonio	14	3	8	.375	2	2	1.000	0	0	0	3	3	0	0	0	0	9
1984—San Antonio	21	5	6	.833	3	3	1.000	0	2	2	1	5	0	0	1	6	13
1985—San Antonio	25	10	12	.833	3	4	.750	0	3	3	1	2	0	5	0	1	23
Totals	215	54	108	.500	28	36	.778	9	24	33	12	25	0	16	9	20	137

COMBINED ABA AND NBA REGULAR-SEASON RECORDS

	G	Min.	FGM	FGA	Pct.	FTM	FTA	Pct.	REBOUNDS			Ast.	Stl.	Blk.	TO	Pts.	AVERAGES		
									Off.	Def.	Tot.						RPG	APG	PPG
Totals	1060	35597	10368	20583	.504	5737	6822	.841	...	...	5602	2798	...	...	...	26595	5.3	2.6	25.1

Three-point field goals: 122-for-451 (.271).
Personal fouls/disqualifications: 3250.

ITALIAN LEAGUE RECORD

Season Team	G	Min.	FGM	FGA	Pct.	FTM	FTA	Pct.	Reb.	Ast.	Pts.	AVERAGES		
												RPG	APG	PPG
86-87—Banco Roma	27	893	263	525	.501	159	190	.837	134	9	704	5.0	0.3	26.1

CBA REGULAR-SEASON RECORD

Season Team	G	Min.	FGM	FGA	Pct.	FTM	FTA	Pct.	Reb.	Ast.	Pts.	AVERAGES		
												RPG	APG	PPG
89-90—Quad City	14	391	115	235	.489	54	73	.740	91	20	284	6.5	1.4	20.3

ABA 2000 COACHING RECORD

Season Team	REGULAR SEASON					PLAYOFFS		
	W	L	Pct.	Finish		W	L	Pct.
00-01—Detroit	21	20	.512	1st		3	0	1.000

NOTES:
2001—Defeated Tampa Bay in Eastern Division Semifinals; defeated Indiana in Eastern Division Finals; defeated Chicago in ABA 2000 Finals.

GILMORE, ARTIS   C

PERSONAL: Born September 21, 1949, in Chipley, Fla. ... 7-2/265 (2,18/120,2). ... Full name: Artis Gilmore.
HIGH SCHOOL: Roulhac (Chipley, Fla.), then Carver (Dothan, Ala.).
JUNIOR COLLEGE: Gardner-Webb Junior College (N.C.).
COLLEGE: Jacksonville.
TRANSACTIONS: Selected by Chicago Bulls in seventh round (117th pick overall) of 1971 NBA Draft. ... Selected by Kentucky Colonels in first round of 1971 ABA draft. ... Selected by Bulls from Colonels in ABA dispersal draft (August 5, 1976). ... Traded by Bulls to San Antonio Spurs for C Dave Corzine, F Mark Olberding and cash (July 22, 1982). ... Traded by Spurs to Bulls for 1988 second-round draft choice (June 22, 1987). ... Waived by Bulls (December 26, 1987). ... Signed as free agent by Boston Celtics (January 8, 1988). ... Played in Italy (1988-89).
MISCELLANEOUS: Chicago Bulls all-time blocked shots leader with 1,017 (1976-77 through 1981-82 and 1987-88).

COLLEGIATE RECORD

NOTES: The Sporting News All-America first team (1971). ... The Sporting News All-America second team (1970). ... Holds NCAA career record for average rebounds per game—22.7. ... Led NCAA Division I with 22.2 rebounds per game (1970) and 23.2 rebounds per game (1971).

Season Team	G	Min.	FGM	FGA	Pct.	FTM	FTA	Pct.	Reb.	Ast.	Pts.	AVERAGES		
												RPG	APG	PPG
67-68—Gardner-Webb J.C.	31	...	296	...	...	121	...	...	...	...	713	...	...	23.0
68-69—Gardner-Webb J.C.	36	...	326	...	...	140	...	...	...	...	792	...	...	22.0
69-70—Jacksonville	28	...	307	529	.580	128	202	.634	621	51	742	22.2	1.8	26.5
70-71—Jacksonville	26	...	229	405	.565	112	188	.596	603	42	570	23.2	1.6	21.9
Junior college totals	67	...	622	...	...	261	...	...	...	...	1505	...	...	22.5
4-year-college totals	54	...	536	934	.574	240	390	.615	1224	93	1312	22.7	1.7	24.3

ABA REGULAR-SEASON RECORD

NOTES: ABA Most Valuable Player (1972). ... ABA Rookie of the Year (1972). ... ABA All-Star first team (1972, 1973, 1974, 1975, 1976). ... ABA All-Defensive team (1973, 1974, 1975, 1976). ... ABA All-Rookie team (1972). ... Member of ABA championship team (1975). ... Holds single-game record for most rebounds—40 (February 3, 1974, vs. New York). ... Holds single-season record for most blocked shots—422 (1972). ... Led ABA with 341 personal fouls (1976).

Season Team	G	Min.	2-POINT			3-POINT			FTM	FTA	Pct.	Reb.	Ast.	Pts.	AVERAGES		
			FGM	FGA	Pct.	FGM	FGA	Pct.							RPG	APG	PPG
71-72—Kentucky	84	*3666	806	1348	*.598	0	0	...	561	...	...	*1491	230	2173	*17.8	2.7	23.0
72-73—Kentucky	84	3502	687	1226	.560	1	2	.500	368	572	.643	*1476	295	1743	*17.6	3.5	20.8
73-74—Kentucky	84	*3502	621	1257	.494	0	3	.000	326	489	.667	*1538	329	1568	*18.3	3.9	18.7
74-75—Kentucky	84	*3493	783	1349	.580	1	2	.500	412	592	.696	*1361	208	1981	16.2	2.5	23.6
75-76—Kentucky	84	3286	773	1401	.552	0	0	...	521	*764	.682	*1303	211	2067	*15.5	2.5	24.6
Totals	420	17449	3669	6581	.558	2	7	.286	2018	3022	.668	7169	1273	9362	17.1	3.0	22.3

ABA PLAYOFF RECORD

NOTES: ABA Playoff Most Valuable Player (1975).

Season Team	G	Min.	2-POINT			3-POINT			FTM	FTA	Pct.	Reb.	Ast.	Pts.	AVERAGES		
			FGM	FGA	Pct.	FGM	FGA	Pct.							RPG	APG	PPG
71-72—Kentucky	6	285	52	90	.578	0	1	.000	27	38	.711	106	25	131	17.7	4.2	21.8
72-73—Kentucky	19	780	142	261	.544	0	0	...	77	123	.626	260	75	361	13.7	3.9	19.0
73-74—Kentucky	8	344	71	127	.559	0	0	...	38	66	.576	149	28	180	18.6	3.5	22.5
74-75—Kentucky	15	679	132	245	.539	0	0	...	98	127	.772	264	38	362	17.6	2.5	24.1
75-76—Kentucky	10	390	93	153	.608	0	0	...	56	74	.757	152	19	242	15.2	1.9	24.2
Totals	58	2478	490	876	.559	0	1	.000	296	428	.692	931	185	1276	16.1	3.2	22.0

ABA ALL-STAR GAME RECORD

NOTES: ABA All-Star Game Most Valuable Player (1974).

Season Team	Min.	2-POINT			3-POINT			FTM	FTA	Pct.	Reb.	Ast.	Pts.
		FGM	FGA	Pct.	FGM	FGA	Pct.						
1972—Kentucky	27	4	5	.800	0	0	...	6	10	.600	10	2	14
1973—Kentucky	31	3	8	.375	0	0	...	4	8	.500	16	0	10
1974—Kentucky	27	8	12	.667	0	0	...	2	3	.667	13	1	18
1975—Kentucky	28	4	8	.500	0	0	...	3	7	.429	13	2	11
1976—Kentucky	27	5	7	.714	0	0	...	4	6	.667	7	1	14
Totals	140	24	40	.600	0	0	...	19	34	.559	59	6	67

NBA REGULAR-SEASON RECORD

RECORDS: Holds career record for highest field goal percentage (minimum 2,000 made)—.599.
HONORS: NBA All-Defensive second team (1978).

Season Team	G	Min.	FGM	FGA	Pct.	FTM	FTA	Pct.	REBOUNDS			Ast.	St.	Blk.	TO	Pts.	AVERAGES		
									Off.	Def.	Tot.						RPG	APG	PPG
76-77—Chicago	82	2877	570	1091	.522	387	586	.660	313	757	1070	199	44	203	...	1527	13.0	2.4	18.6
77-78—Chicago	82	3067	704	1260	.559	471	*669	.704	318	753	1071	263	42	181	*366	1879	13.1	3.2	22.9
78-79—Chicago	82	3265	753	1310	.575	434	587	.739	293	750	1043	274	50	156	310	1940	12.7	3.3	23.7

ALL-TIME GREAT PLAYERS

Season Team	G	Min.	FGM	FGA	Pct.	FTM	FTA	Pct.	Off.	Def.	Tot.	Ast.	St.	Blk.	TO	Pts.	RPG	APG	PPG
79-80—Chicago	48	1568	305	513	.595	245	344	.712	108	324	432	133	29	59	133	855	9.0	2.8	17.8
80-81—Chicago	82	2832	547	816	*.670	375	532	.705	220	608	828	172	47	198	236	1469	10.1	2.1	17.9
81-82—Chicago	82	2796	546	837	*.652	424	552	.768	224	611	835	136	40	220	227	1517	10.2	1.7	18.5
82-83—San Antonio	82	2797	556	888	*.626	367	496	.740	299	685	984	126	40	192	254	1479	12.0	1.5	18.0
83-84—San Antonio	64	2034	351	556	*.631	280	390	.718	213	449	662	70	36	132	149	982	10.3	1.1	15.3
84-85—San Antonio	81	2756	532	854	.623	484	646	.749	231	615	846	131	40	173	241	1548	10.4	1.6	19.1
85-86—San Antonio	71	2395	423	684	.618	338	482	.701	166	434	600	102	39	108	186	1184	8.5	1.4	16.7
86-87—San Antonio	82	2405	346	580	.597	242	356	.680	185	394	579	150	39	95	178	934	7.1	1.8	11.4
87-88—Chi.-Boston	71	893	99	181	.547	67	128	.523	69	142	211	21	15	30	67	265	3.0	0.3	3.7
Totals	909	29685	5732	9570	.599	4114	5768	.713	2639	6522	9161	1777	470	1747	2347	15579	10.1	2.0	17.1

Three-point field goals: 1981-82, 1-for-1. 1982-83, 0-for-6. 1983-84, 0-for-3. 1984-85, 0-for-2. 1985-86, 0-for-1. Totals, 1-for-13 (.077).
Personal fouls/disqualifications: 1976-77, 266/4. 1977-78, 261/4. 1978-79, 280/2. 1979-80, 167/5. 1980-81, 295/2. 1981-82, 287/4. 1982-83, 273/4. 1983-84, 229/4. 1984-85, 306/4. 1985-86, 239/3. 1986-87, 235/2. 1987-88, 148/0. Totals, 2986/38.

NBA PLAYOFF RECORD

Season Team	G	Min.	FGM	FGA	Pct.	FTM	FTA	Pct.	Off.	Def.	Tot.	Ast.	St.	Blk.	TO	Pts.	RPG	APG	PPG
76-77—Chicago	3	126	19	40	.475	18	23	.783	15	24	39	6	3	8	...	56	13.0	2.0	18.7
80-81—Chicago	6	247	35	59	.593	38	55	.691	24	43	67	12	6	17	17	108	11.2	2.0	18.0
82-83—San Antonio	11	401	76	132	.576	32	46	.696	37	105	142	18	9	34	27	184	12.9	1.6	16.7
84-85—San Antonio	5	185	29	52	.558	31	45	.689	10	40	50	7	2	7	23	89	10.0	1.4	17.8
85-86—San Antonio	3	107	16	24	.667	8	14	.571	7	11	18	3	1	10	10	40	6.0	1.0	13.3
87-88—Boston	14	86	4	8	.500	7	14	.500	4	16	20	1	0	4	4	15	1.4	0.1	1.1
Totals	42	1152	179	315	.568	134	197	.680	97	239	336	47	27	71	81	492	8.0	1.1	11.7

Personal fouls/disqualifications: 1976-77, 9/0. 1980-81, 15/0. 1982-83, 46/1. 1984-85, 18/0. 1985-86, 11/0. 1987-88, 14/0. Totals, 113/1.

NBA ALL-STAR GAME RECORD

Season Team	Min.	FGM	FGA	Pct.	FTM	FTA	Pct.	Off.	Def.	Tot.	Ast.	PF	Dq.	St.	Blk.	TO	Pts.
1978—Chicago	13	2	4	.500	6	8	.750	0	2	2	0	1	0	1	2	1	10
1979—Chicago	15	3	4	.750	2	2	1.000	1	0	1	2	1	0	0	0	1	8
1981—Chicago	22	5	7	.714	1	2	.500	1	5	6	2	4	0	0	1	0	11
1982—Chicago	16	3	6	.500	1	1	1.000	1	2	3	2	4	0	0	1	2	7
1983—San Antonio	16	2	4	.500	1	2	.500	1	4	5	1	4	0	1	0	1	5
1986—San Antonio	13	3	4	.750	4	4	1.000	1	1	2	1	1	0	2	0	0	10
Totals	95	18	29	.621	15	19	.789	5	14	19	8	18	0	4	4	5	51

COMBINED ABA AND NBA REGULAR-SEASON RECORDS

	G	Min.	FGM	FGA	Pct.	FTM	FTA	Pct.	Off.	Def.	Tot.	Ast.	Stl.	Blk.	TO	Pts.	RPG	APG	PPG
Totals	1329	33356	9403	16158	.582	6132	8790	.698	...	...	16330	3050	...	...	...	24041	12.3	2.3	18.1

Three-point field goals: 3-for-20 (.150).
Personal fouls/disqualifications: 4529.

ITALIAN LEAGUE RECORD

Season Team	G	Min.	FGM	FGA	Pct.	FTM	FTA	Pct.	Reb.	Ast.	Pts.	RPG	APG	PPG
88-89—Bologna Arimo	30	952	144	226	.637	85	131	.649	333	20	373	11.1	0.7	12.4

GOODRICH, GAIL   G

PERSONAL: Born April 23, 1943, in Los Angeles. ... 6-1/175 (1,85/79,4). ... Full name: Gail Charles Goodrich Jr.
HIGH SCHOOL: Los Angeles Polytechnic.
COLLEGE: UCLA.
TRANSACTIONS: Selected by Los Angeles Lakers in 1965 NBA Draft (territorial pick). ... Selected by Phoenix Suns from Lakers in NBA Expansion Draft (May 6, 1968). ... Traded by Suns to Lakers for F Mel Counts (May 20, 1970). ... Signed as veteran free agent by New Orleans Jazz (July 19, 1976); Lakers received 1977 and 1979 first-round draft choices and 1980 second-round draft choice as compensation; Jazz received 1977 second-round draft choice to complete transaction (October 6, 1976).
CAREER HONORS: Elected to Naismith Memorial Basketball Hall of Fame (1996).
MISCELLANEOUS: Member of NBA championship team (1972).

COLLEGIATE RECORD

NOTES: THE SPORTING NEWS All-America first team (1965). ... Member of NCAA Division I championship team (1964, 1965).

Season Team	G	Min.	FGM	FGA	Pct.	FTM	FTA	Pct.	Reb.	Ast.	Pts.	RPG	APG	PPG
61-62—UCLA‡	20	...	189	385	.491	110	155	.710	122	...	488	6.1	...	24.4
62-63—UCLA	29	...	117	280	.418	66	103	.641	101	...	300	3.5	...	10.3
63-64—UCLA	30	...	243	530	.459	160	225	.711	156	...	646	5.2	...	21.5
64-65—UCLA	30	...	277	528	.525	190	265	.717	158	...	744	5.3	...	24.8
Varsity totals	89	...	637	1338	.476	416	593	.702	415	...	1690	4.7	...	19.0

NBA REGULAR-SEASON RECORD

HONORS: All-NBA first team (1974).

Season Team	G	Min.	FGM	FGA	Pct.	FTM	FTA	Pct.	Reb.	Ast.	PF	Dq.	Pts.	RPG	APG	PPG
65-66—Los Angeles	65	1008	203	503	.404	103	149	.691	130	103	103	1	509	2.0	1.6	7.8
66-67—Los Angeles	77	1780	352	776	.454	253	337	.751	251	210	194	3	957	3.3	2.7	12.4
67-68—Los Angeles	79	2057	395	812	.486	302	392	.770	199	205	228	2	1092	2.5	2.6	13.8
68-69—Phoenix	81	3236	718	1746	.411	495	663	.747	437	518	253	3	1931	5.4	6.4	23.8

Season Team	G	Min.	FGM	FGA	Pct.	FTM	FTA	Pct.	Reb.	Ast.	PF	Dq.	Pts.	AVERAGES RPG	APG	PPG
69-70—Phoenix	81	3234	568	1251	.454	488	604	.808	340	605	251	3	1624	4.2	7.5	20.0
70-71—Los Angeles	79	2808	558	1174	.475	264	343	.770	260	380	258	3	1380	3.3	4.8	17.5
71-72—Los Angeles	82	3040	826	1695	.487	475	559	.850	295	365	210	0	2127	3.6	4.5	25.9
72-73—Los Angeles	76	2697	750	1615	.464	314	374	.840	263	332	193	1	1814	3.5	4.4	23.9

Season Team	G	Min.	FGM	FGA	Pct.	FTM	FTA	Pct.	REBOUNDS Off.	Def.	Tot.	Ast.	St.	Blk.	TO	Pts.	AVERAGES RPG	APG	PPG
73-74—Los Angeles....	82	3061	784	1773	.442	*508	*588	.864	95	155	250	427	126	12	...	2076	3.0	5.2	25.3
74-75—Los Angeles	72	2668	656	1429	.459	318	378	.841	96	123	219	420	102	6	...	1630	3.0	5.8	22.6
75-76—Los Angeles	75	2646	583	1321	.441	293	346	.847	94	120	214	421	123	17	...	1459	2.9	5.6	19.5
76-77—New Orleans	27	609	136	305	.446	68	85	.800	25	36	61	74	22	2	...	340	2.3	2.7	12.6
77-78—New Orleans	81	2553	520	1050	.495	264	332	.795	75	102	177	388	82	22	205	1304	2.2	4.8	16.1
78-79—New Orleans	74	2130	382	850	.449	174	204	.853	68	115	183	357	90	13	185	938	2.5	4.8	12.7
Totals	1031	33527	7431	16300	.456	4319	5354	.807	...	...	3279	4805	545	72	390	19181	3.2	4.7	18.6

Personal fouls/disqualifications: 1973-74, 227/3. 1974-75, 214/1. 1975-76, 238/3. 1976-77, 43/0. 1977-78, 186/0. 1978-79, 177/1. Totals, 2775/24.

NBA PLAYOFF RECORD

Season Team	G	Min.	FGM	FGA	Pct.	FTM	FTA	Pct.	Reb.	Ast.	PF	Dq.	Pts.	AVERAGES RPG	APG	PPG
65-66—Los Angeles	11	290	43	92	.467	29	43	.674	42	33	35	0	115	3.8	3.0	10.5
66-67—Los Angeles	3	81	11	31	.355	11	18	.611	9	10	5	0	33	3.0	3.3	11.0
67-68—Los Angeles	10	100	23	47	.489	14	18	.778	14	14	10	0	60	1.4	1.4	6.0
69-70—Phoenix	7	265	56	118	.475	30	35	.857	32	38	21	0	142	4.6	5.4	20.3
70-71—Los Angeles	12	518	105	247	.425	95	113	.841	38	91	38	0	305	3.2	7.6	25.4
71-72—Los Angeles	15	575	130	292	.445	97	108	.898	38	50	50	0	357	2.5	3.3	23.8
72-73—Los Angeles	17	604	139	310	.448	62	79	.785	61	67	53	1	340	3.6	3.9	20.0

Season Team	G	Min.	FGM	FGA	Pct.	FTM	FTA	Pct.	REBOUNDS Off.	Def.	Tot.	Ast.	St.	Blk.	TO	Pts.	AVERAGES RPG	APG	PPG
73-74—Los Angeles....	5	189	35	90	.389	28	33	.848	7	9	16	30	7	1	...	98	3.2	6.0	19.6
Totals	80	2622	542	1227	.442	366	447	.819	...	...	250	333	7	1	...	1450	3.1	4.2	18.1

Personal fouls/disqualifications: 1973-74, 7/0.

NBA ALL-STAR GAME RECORD

Season Team	Min.	FGM	FGA	Pct.	FTM	FTA	Pct.	Reb	Ast.	PF	Dq.	Pts.
1969—Phoenix	6	2	4	.500	1	2	.500	1	1	1	0	5
1972—Los Angeles	14	2	7	.286	0	0	...	1	2	2	0	4
1973—Los Angeles	16	1	7	.143	0	0	...	2	1	2	0	2

Season Team	Min.	FGM	FGA	Pct.	FTM	FTA	Pct.	REBOUNDS Off.	Def.	Tot.	Ast.	PF	Dq.	St.	Blk.	TO	Pts.
1974—Los Angeles	26	9	16	.563	0	0	...	1	3	4	6	2	0	1	0	...	18
1975—Los Angeles	15	2	4	.500	0	0	...	0	1	1	4	1	0	0	0	...	4
Totals	77	16	38	.421	1	2	.500	...	...	9	14	8	0	1	0	...	33

GREER, HAL   G

PERSONAL: Born June 26, 1936, in Huntington, W.Va. ... 6-2/175 (1,88/79,4). ... Full name: Harold Everett Greer.
HIGH SCHOOL: Douglass (Huntington, W.Va.).
COLLEGE: Marshall.
TRANSACTIONS: Selected by Syracuse Nationals in second round (14th pick overall) of 1958 NBA Draft. ... Nationals franchise moved from Syracuse to Philadelphia and renamed 76ers for 1963-64 season.
CAREER HONORS: Elected to Naismith Memorial Basketball Hall of Fame (1982). ... One of the 50 Greatest Players in NBA History (1996).
MISCELLANEOUS: Member of NBA championship team (1967). ... Philadelphia 76ers franchise all-time leading scorer with 21,586 points (1958-59 through 1972-73).

COLLEGIATE RECORD

Season Team	G	Min.	FGM	FGA	Pct.	FTM	FTA	Pct.	Reb.	Ast.	Pts.	AVERAGES RPG	APG	PPG
54-55—Marshall‡	...	...	...	...	...	...	...	...	...	...	...	...	...	18.0
55-56—Marshall	23	...	128	213	.601	101	145	.697	153	...	357	6.7	...	15.5
56-57—Marshall	24	...	167	329	.508	119	156	.763	332	...	453	13.8	...	18.9
57-58—Marshall	24	...	236	432	.546	95	114	.833	280	...	567	11.7	...	23.6
Varsity totals	71	...	531	974	.545	315	415	.759	765	...	1377	10.8	...	19.4

NBA REGULAR-SEASON RECORD

HONORS: All-NBA second team (1963, 1964, 1965, 1966, 1967, 1968, 1969).

Season Team	G	Min.	FGM	FGA	Pct.	FTM	FTA	Pct.	Reb.	Ast.	PF	Dq.	Pts.	AVERAGES RPG	APG	PPG
58-59—Syracuse	68	1625	308	679	.454	137	176	.778	196	101	189	1	753	2.9	1.5	11.1
59-60—Syracuse	70	1979	388	815	.476	148	189	.783	303	188	208	4	924	4.3	2.7	13.2
60-61—Syracuse	79	2763	623	1381	.451	305	394	.774	455	302	242	0	1551	5.8	3.8	19.6
61-62—Syracuse	71	2705	644	1442	.447	331	404	.819	524	313	252	2	1619	7.4	4.4	22.8
62-63—Syracuse	80	2631	600	1293	.464	362	434	.834	457	275	286	4	1562	5.7	3.4	19.5
63-64—Philadelphia	80	3157	715	1611	.444	435	525	.829	484	374	291	6	1865	6.1	4.7	23.3
64-65—Philadelphia	70	2600	539	1245	.433	335	413	.811	355	313	254	7	1413	5.1	4.5	20.2
65-66—Philadelphia	80	3326	703	1580	.445	413	514	.804	473	384	315	6	1819	5.9	4.8	22.7
66-67—Philadelphia	80	3086	699	1524	.459	367	466	.788	422	303	302	5	1765	5.3	3.8	22.1
67-68—Philadelphia	82	3263	777	1626	.478	422	549	.769	444	372	289	6	1976	5.4	4.5	24.1
68-69—Philadelphia	82	3311	732	1595	.459	432	543	.796	435	414	294	8	1896	5.3	5.0	23.1
69-70—Philadelphia	80	3024	705	1551	.455	352	432	.815	376	405	300	8	1762	4.7	5.1	22.0

Season Team	G	Min.	FGM	FGA	Pct.	FTM	FTA	Pct.	Reb.	Ast.	PF	Dq.	Pts.	RPG	APG	PPG
70-71—Philadelphia	81	3060	591	1371	.431	326	405	.805	364	369	289	4	1508	4.5	4.6	18.6
71-72—Philadelphia	81	2410	389	866	.449	181	234	.774	271	316	268	10	959	3.3	3.9	11.8
72-73—Philadelphia	38	848	91	232	.392	32	39	.821	106	111	76	1	214	2.8	2.9	5.6
Totals	1122	39788	8504	18811	.452	4578	5717	.801	5665	4540	3855	72	21586	5.0	4.0	19.2

NBA PLAYOFF RECORD

Season Team	G	Min.	FGM	FGA	Pct.	FTM	FTA	Pct.	Reb.	Ast.	PF	Dq.	Pts.	RPG	APG	PPG
58-59—Syracuse	9	277	39	93	.419	26	32	.813	47	20	35	2	104	5.2	2.2	11.6
59-60—Syracuse	3	84	22	43	.512	3	4	.750	14	10	5	0	47	4.7	3.3	15.7
60-61—Syracuse	8	232	41	106	.387	33	40	.825	33	19	32	1	115	4.1	2.4	14.4
61-62—Syracuse	1	5	0	0	...	0	0	...	0	0	1	0	0	0.0	0.0	0.0
62-63—Syracuse	5	214	44	87	.506	29	35	.829	27	21	21	1	117	5.4	4.2	23.4
63-64—Philadelphia	5	211	37	95	.389	33	39	.846	28	30	19	1	107	5.6	6.0	21.4
64-65—Philadelphia	11	505	101	222	.455	69	87	.793	81	55	45	2	271	7.4	5.0	24.6
65-66—Philadelphia	5	226	32	91	.352	18	23	.783	36	21	21	0	82	7.2	4.2	16.4
66-67—Philadelphia	15	688	161	375	.429	94	118	.797	88	79	55	1	416	5.9	5.3	27.7
67-68—Philadelphia	13	553	120	278	.432	95	111	.856	79	55	49	1	335	6.1	4.2	25.8
68-69—Philadelphia	5	204	26	81	.321	28	36	.778	30	23	23	0	80	6.0	4.6	16.0
69-70—Philadelphia	5	178	33	74	.446	11	13	.846	17	27	16	0	77	3.4	5.4	15.4
70-71—Philadelphia	7	265	49	112	.438	27	36	.750	25	33	35	4	125	3.6	4.7	17.9
Totals	92	3642	705	1657	.425	466	574	.812	505	393	357	13	1876	5.5	4.3	20.4

NBA ALL-STAR GAME RECORD

NOTES: NBA All-Star Game Most Valuable Player (1968).

Season Team	Min.	FGM	FGA	Pct.	FTM	FTA	Pct.	Reb	Ast.	PF	Dq.	Pts.
1961—Syracuse	18	7	11	.636	0	0	...	6	2	2	0	14
1962—Syracuse	24	3	14	.214	2	7	.286	10	9	3	0	8
1963—Syracuse	15	3	7	.429	0	0	...	3	2	4	0	6
1964—Philadelphia	20	5	10	.500	3	4	.750	3	4	1	0	13
1965—Philadelphia	21	5	11	.455	3	4	.750	4	1	2	0	13
1966—Philadelphia	23	4	13	.308	1	1	1.000	5	1	4	0	9
1967—Philadelphia	31	5	16	.313	7	8	.875	4	1	5	0	17
1968—Philadelphia	17	8	8	1.000	5	7	.714	3	3	2	0	21
1969—Philadelphia	17	0	1	.000	4	5	.800	3	2	2	0	4
1970—Philadelphia	21	7	11	.636	1	1	1.000	4	3	4	0	15
Totals	207	47	102	.461	26	37	.703	45	28	29	0	120

CBA COACHING RECORD

Season Team	REGULAR SEASON				PLAYOFFS		
	W	L	Pct.	Finish	W	L	Pct.
80-81—Philadelphia	17	23	.425	3rd/Eastern Division	3	3	.500

NOTES:
1981—Defeated Atlantic City, 2-1, in Eastern Division Semifinals; lost to Rochester, 2-1, in Eastern Division Finals.

GUERIN, RICHIE　　　　G

PERSONAL: Born May 29, 1932, in New York. ... 6-4/210 (1,93/95,3). ... Full name: Richard V. Guerin.
HIGH SCHOOL: Mount St. Michael Academy (Bronx, N.Y.).
COLLEGE: Iona.
TRANSACTIONS: Selected by New York Knicks in second round of 1954 NBA Draft. ... In military service during 1954-55 and 1955-56 seasons; played with Quantico Marines and Marine All-Star teams. ... Traded by Knicks to St. Louis Hawks for cash and second-round draft choice (October 18, 1963). ... Selected by Seattle SuperSonics from Hawks in NBA Expansion Draft (1967). ... Traded by SuperSonics to Atlanta Hawks for Dick Smith (November 15, 1968).

COLLEGIATE RECORD

Season Team	G	Min.	FGM	FGA	Pct.	FTM	FTA	Pct.	Reb.	Ast.	Pts.	RPG	APG	PPG
50-51—Iona‡					Freshman team statistics unavailable.									
51-52—Iona	27	...	159	...	...	146	...	...	...	...	464	...	...	17.2
52-53—Iona	21	...	139	283	.491	114	172	.663	...	...	392	...	...	18.7
53-54—Iona	21	...	171	405	.422	177	249	.711	...	...	519	...	...	24.7
Varsity totals	69	...	469	...	...	437	...	...	...	...	1375	...	...	19.9

NBA REGULAR-SEASON RECORD

HONORS: All-NBA second team (1959, 1960, 1962).

Season Team	G	Min.	FGM	FGA	Pct.	FTM	FTA	Pct.	Reb.	Ast.	PF	Dq.	Pts.	RPG	APG	PPG
56-57—New York	72	1793	257	699	.368	181	292	.620	334	182	186	3	695	4.6	2.5	9.7
57-58—New York	63	2368	344	973	.354	353	511	.691	489	317	202	3	1041	7.8	5.0	16.5
58-59—New York	71	2558	443	1046	.424	405	505	.802	518	364	255	1	1291	7.3	5.1	18.2
59-60—New York	74	2429	579	1379	.420	457	591	.773	505	468	242	3	1615	6.8	6.3	21.8
60-61—New York	79	3023	612	1545	.396	496	626	.792	628	503	310	3	1720	7.9	6.4	21.8
61-62—New York	78	3348	839	1897	.442	625	762	.820	501	539	299	3	2303	6.4	6.9	29.5
62-63—New York	79	2712	596	1380	.432	509	600	.848	331	348	228	2	1701	4.2	4.4	21.5
63-64—N.Y.-St.L.	80	2366	351	846	.415	347	424	.818	256	375	276	4	1049	3.2	4.7	13.1
64-65—St. Louis	57	1678	295	662	.446	231	301	.767	149	271	193	1	821	2.6	4.8	14.4
65-66—St. Louis	80	2363	414	998	.415	362	446	.812	314	388	256	4	1190	3.9	4.9	14.9
66-67—St. Louis	80	2275	394	904	.436	304	416	.731	192	345	247	2	1092	2.4	4.3	13.7

Season Team	G	Min.	FGM	FGA	Pct.	FTM	FTA	Pct.	Reb.	Ast.	PF	Dq.	Pts.	AVERAGES RPG	APG	PPG
67-68—						Did not play—retired.										
68-69—Atlanta	27	472	47	111	.423	57	74	.770	59	99	66	0	151	2.2	3.7	5.6
69-70—Atlanta	8	64	3	11	.273	1	1	1.000	2	12	9	0	7	0.3	1.5	0.9
Totals	848	27449	5174	12451	.416	4328	5549	.780	4278	4211	2769	29	14676	5.0	5.0	17.3

NBA PLAYOFF RECORD

Season Team	G	Min.	FGM	FGA	Pct.	FTM	FTA	Pct.	Reb.	Ast.	PF	Dq.	Pts.	AVERAGES RPG	APG	PPG
58-59—New York	2	77	9	35	.257	12	14	.857	18	15	11	1	30	9.0	7.5	15.0
63-64—St. Louis	12	428	75	169	.444	67	85	.788	50	49	54	1	217	4.2	4.1	18.1
64-65—St. Louis	4	125	25	65	.385	19	25	.760	8	21	14	0	69	2.0	5.3	17.3
65-66—St. Louis	10	399	72	159	.453	62	76	.816	37	79	41	0	206	3.7	7.9	20.6
66-67—St. Louis	9	228	36	86	.419	24	30	.800	23	39	23	0	96	2.6	4.3	10.7
68-69—Atlanta	3	32	1	4	.250	1	2	.500	5	7	8	0	3	1.7	2.3	1.0
69-70—Atlanta	2	56	13	21	.619	7	7	1.000	8	4	6	0	33	4.0	2.0	16.5
Totals	42	1345	231	539	.429	192	239	.803	149	214	157	2	654	3.5	5.1	15.6

NBA ALL-STAR GAME RECORD

Season Team	Min.	FGM	FGA	Pct.	FTM	FTA	Pct.	Reb	Ast.	PF	Dq.	Pts.
1958—New York	22	2	10	.200	3	4	.750	8	7	3	0	7
1959—New York	22	1	7	.143	3	5	.600	3	3	1	0	5
1960—New York	22	5	11	.455	2	2	1.000	4	4	4	0	12
1961—New York	15	3	8	.375	5	6	.833	0	2	1	0	11
1962—New York	27	10	17	.588	3	6	.500	3	1	6	1	23
1963—New York	14	2	3	.667	1	3	.333	1	1	2	0	5
Totals	122	23	56	.411	17	26	.654	19	18	17	1	63

NBA COACHING RECORD

HONORS: NBA Coach of the Year (1968).

	REGULAR SEASON				PLAYOFFS		
Season Team	W	L	Pct.	Finish	W	L	Pct.
64-65—St. Louis	28	19	.596	2nd/Western Division	1	3	.250
65-66—St. Louis	36	44	.450	3rd/Western Division	6	4	.600
66-67—St. Louis	39	42	.481	2nd/Western Division	5	4	.556
67-68—St. Louis	56	26	.683	1st/Western Division	2	4	.333
68-69—Atlanta	48	34	.585	2nd/Western Division	5	6	.455
69-70—Atlanta	48	34	.585	1st/Western Division	4	5	.444
70-71—Atlanta	36	46	.439	2nd/Central Division	1	4	.200
71-72—Atlanta	36	46	.439	2nd/Central Division	2	4	.333
Totals (8 years)	327	291	.529	Totals (8 years)	26	34	.433

NOTES:

1964—Replaced Harry Gallatin as St. Louis head coach (November), with record of 17-16.
1965—Lost to Baltimore in Western Division Semifinals.
1966—Defeated Baltimore, 3-0, in Western Division Semifinals; lost to Los Angeles, 4-3, in Western Division Finals.
1967—Defeated Chicago, 3-0, in Western Division Semifinals; lost to San Francisco, 4-2, in Western Division Finals.
1968—Lost to San Francisco in Western Division Semifinals. Hawks franchise moved to Atlanta for 1968-69 season.
1969—Defeated San Diego, 4-2, in Western Division Semifinals; lost to Los Angeles, 4-1, in Western Division Finals.
1970—Defeated Chicago, 4-1, in Western Division Semifinals; lost to Los Angeles, 4-0, in Western Division Finals.
1971—Lost to New York in Eastern Conference Semifinals.
1972—Lost to Boston in Eastern Conference Semifinals.

HAGAN, CLIFF   F

PERSONAL: Born December 9, 1931, in Owensboro, Ky. ... 6-4/215 (1,93/97,5). ... Full name: Clifford Oldham Hagan. ... Nickname: Li'l Abner.
HIGH SCHOOL: Owensboro (Ky.).
COLLEGE: Kentucky.
TRANSACTIONS: Selected by Boston Celtics in third round of 1953 NBA Draft. ... In military service during 1954-55 and 1955-56 seasons; played at Andrews Air Force Base. ... Draft rights traded by Celtics with C/F Ed Macauley to St. Louis Hawks for draft rights to C Bill Russell (April 29, 1956). ... Signed as player/head coach by Dallas Chaparrals of American Basketball Association (June 1967).
CAREER HONORS: Elected to Naismith Memorial Basketball Hall of Fame (1978).
MISCELLANEOUS: Member of NBA championship team (1958).

COLLEGIATE RECORD

NOTES: Member of NCAA championship team (1951).

Season Team	G	Min.	FGM	FGA	Pct.	FTM	FTA	Pct.	Reb.	Ast.	Pts.	AVERAGES RPG	APG	PPG
49-50—Kentucky‡	12	...	114	244	.467	42	58	.724	...	...	270	...	...	22.5
50-51—Kentucky	20	...	69	188	.367	45	61	.738	169	...	183	8.5	...	9.2
51-52—Kentucky	32	...	264	633	.417	164	235	.698	528	...	692	16.5	...	21.6
52-53—Kentucky					Did not play—team suspended for season.									
53-54—Kentucky	25	...	234	514	.455	132	191	.691	338	...	600	13.5	...	24.0
Varsity totals	77	...	567	1335	.425	341	487	.700	1035	...	1475	13.4	...	19.2

NBA REGULAR-SEASON RECORD

HONORS: All-NBA second team (1958, 1959).

Season Team	G	Min.	FGM	FGA	Pct.	FTM	FTA	Pct.	Reb.	Ast.	PF	Dq.	Pts.	AVERAGES		
														RPG	APG	PPG
56-57—St. Louis	67	971	134	371	.361	100	145	.690	247	86	165	3	368	3.7	1.3	5.5
57-58—St. Louis	70	2190	503	1135	.443	385	501	.768	707	175	267	9	1391	10.1	2.5	19.9
58-59—St. Louis	72	2702	646	1417	.456	415	536	.774	783	245	275	10	1707	10.9	3.4	23.7
59-60—St. Louis	75	2798	719	1549	.464	421	524	.803	803	299	270	4	1859	10.7	4.0	24.8
60-61—St. Louis	77	2701	661	1490	.444	383	467	.820	715	381	286	9	1705	9.3	4.9	22.1
61-62—St. Louis	77	2784	701	1490	.470	362	439	.825	633	370	282	8	1764	8.2	4.8	22.9
62-63—St. Louis	79	1716	491	1055	.465	244	305	.800	341	193	211	2	1226	4.3	2.4	15.5
63-64—St. Louis	77	2279	572	1280	.447	269	331	.813	377	193	273	4	1413	4.9	2.5	18.4
64-65—St. Louis	77	1739	393	901	.436	214	268	.799	276	136	182	0	1000	3.6	1.8	13.0
65-66—St. Louis	74	1851	419	942	.445	176	206	.854	234	164	177	1	1014	3.2	2.2	13.7
Totals	745	21731	5239	11630	.450	2969	3722	.798	5116	2242	2388	50	13447	6.9	3.0	18.0

NBA PLAYOFF RECORD

Season Team	G	Min.	FGM	FGA	Pct.	FTM	FTA	Pct.	Reb.	Ast.	PF	Dq.	Pts.	AVERAGES		
														RPG	APG	PPG
56-57—St. Louis	10	319	62	143	.434	46	63	.730	112	28	47	3	170	11.2	2.8	17.0
57-58—St. Louis	11	418	111	221	.502	83	99	.838	115	37	48	3	305	10.5	3.4	27.7
58-59—St. Louis	6	259	63	123	.512	45	54	.833	72	16	21	0	171	12.0	2.7	28.5
59-60—St. Louis	14	544	125	296	.422	89	109	.817	138	54	54	1	339	9.9	3.9	24.2
60-61—St. Louis	12	455	104	235	.443	56	69	.812	118	54	45	1	264	9.8	4.5	22.0
62-63—St. Louis	11	255	83	179	.464	37	53	.698	55	34	42	4	203	5.0	3.1	18.5
63-64—St. Louis	12	392	75	175	.429	45	54	.833	74	57	34	0	195	6.2	4.8	16.3
64-65—St. Louis	4	123	34	75	.453	6	12	.500	21	7	14	0	74	6.5	1.8	18.5
65-66—St. Louis	10	200	44	97	.454	25	27	.926	34	18	15	0	113	3.4	1.8	11.3
Totals	90	2965	701	1544	.454	432	540	.800	744	305	320	12	1834	8.3	3.4	20.4

NBA ALL-STAR GAME RECORD

Season Team	Min.	FGM	FGA	Pct.	FTM	FTA	Pct.	Reb	Ast.	PF	Dq.	Pts.
1958—St. Louis					Selected, did not play—injured.							
1959—St. Louis	22	6	12	.500	3	3	1.000	8	3	5	0	15
1960—St. Louis	21	1	9	.111	0	0	...	3	2	1	0	2
1961—St. Louis	13	0	2	.000	2	2	1.000	2	0	1	0	2
1962—St. Louis	9	1	3	.333	0	0	...	2	1	1	0	2
Totals	65	8	26	.308	5	5	1.000	15	6	8	0	21

ABA REGULAR-SEASON RECORD

Season Team	G	Min.	2-POINT			3-POINT			FTM	FTA	Pct.	Reb.	Ast.	Pts.	AVERAGES		
			FGM	FGA	Pct.	FGM	FGA	Pct.							RPG	APG	PPG
67-68—Dallas	56	1737	371	756	.491	0	3	.000	277	351	.789	334	276	1019	6.0	4.9	18.2
68-69—Dallas	35	579	132	258	.512	0	1	.000	123	144	.854	102	122	387	2.9	3.5	11.1
69-70—Dallas	3	27	8	12	.667	0	1	.000	1	2	.500	3	6	17	1.0	2.0	5.7
Totals	94	2343	511	1026	.498	0	5	.000	401	497	.807	439	404	1423	4.7	4.3	15.1

ABA PLAYOFF RECORD

Season Team	G	Min.	2-POINT			3-POINT			FTM	FTA	Pct.	Reb.	Ast.	Pts.	AVERAGES		
			FGM	FGA	Pct.	FGM	FGA	Pct.							RPG	APG	PPG
67-68—Dallas	3	70	14	37	.378	0	0	...	9	13	.692	13	9	37	4.3	3.0	12.3
68-69—Dallas	2	45	5	14	.357	0	0	...	8	10	.800	6	14	18	3.0	7.0	9.0
Totals	5	115	19	51	.373	0	0	...	17	23	.739	19	23	55	3.8	4.6	11.0

ABA ALL-STAR GAME RECORD

Season Team	Min.	2-POINT			3-POINT			FTM	FTA	Pct.	Reb.	Ast.	Pts.
		FGM	FGA	Pct.	FGM	FGA	Pct.						
1968—Dallas	24	4	11	.364	0	0	...	2	2	1.000	0	5	10

COMBINED ABA AND NBA REGULAR-SEASON RECORDS

	G	Min.	FGM	FGA	Pct.	FTM	FTA	Pct.	REBOUNDS			Ast.	Stl.	Blk.	TO	Pts.	AVERAGES		
									Off.	Def.	Tot.						RPG	APG	PPG
Totals	839	24074	5750	12661	.454	3370	4219	.799	...	...	5555	2646	...	...	...	14870	6.6	3.2	17.7

Three-point field goals: 0-for-5.
Personal fouls/disqualifications: 2678/58.

ABA COACHING RECORD

BACKGROUND: Player/head coach, Dallas Chaparrals of American Basketball Association (1967-68 to January 1970).

Season Team	REGULAR SEASON				PLAYOFFS		
	W	L	Pct.	Finish	W	L	Pct.
67-68—Dallas	46	32	.590	2nd/Western Division	4	4	.500
68-69—Dallas	41	37	.526	4th/Western Division	3	4	.426
69-70—Dallas	22	21	.512		—	—	—
Totals (3 years)	109	90	.548	Totals (2 years)	7	8	.467

NOTES:
1968—Defeated Houston, 3-0, in Western Division Semifinals; lost to New Orleans, 4-1, in Western Division Finals.
1969—Lost to New Orleans in Western Division Semifinals.
1970—Replaced as Dallas head coach by Max Williams (January).

HARDAWAY, TIM   G

PERSONAL: Born September 1, 1966, in Chicago ... 6-0/195. (1,83/88,5). ... Full Name: Timothy Duane Hardaway.
HIGH SCHOOL: Carver (Chicago).
COLLEGE: Texas-El Paso.
TRANSACTIONS/CAREER NOTES: Selected by Golden State Warriors in first round (14th pick overall) of 1989 NBA Draft. ... Traded by Warriors with F/C Chris Gatling to Miami Heat for F/C Kevin Willis and G Bimbo Coles (February 22, 1996). ... Traded by Heat to Dallas Mavericks for 2003 or 2004 second-round draft choice (August 22, 2001). ... Traded by Mavericks with F Juwan Howard, F Donnell Harvey, cash considerations and first-round draft choice to Denver Nuggets for G Nick Van Exel, F/C Raef LaFrentz, G Avery Johnson and G/F Tariq Abdul-Wahad (February 21, 2002). ... Waived by Nuggets (June 25, 2002). ... Signed as free agent by Indiana Pacers (March 27, 2003).
MISCELLANEOUS: Member of gold-medal-winning U.S. Olympic team (2000). ... Member of gold-medal-winning U.S. World Championship team (1994). ... Miami Heat all-time assists leader with 2,867 (1995-96 through 2000-01).

COLLEGIATE RECORD

NOTES: Frances Pomeroy Naismith Award winner (1989).

Season Team	G	Min.	FGM	FGA	Pct.	FTM	FTA	Pct.	Reb.	Ast.	Pts.	RPG	AVERAGES APG	PPG
85-86—Texas-El Paso	28	435	37	71	.521	41	63	.651	35	53	115	1.3	1.9	4.1
86-87—Texas-El Paso	31	922	120	245	.490	67	101	.663	62	148	310	2.0	4.8	10.0
87-88—Texas-El Paso	32	1036	159	354	.449	98	130	.754	93	183	434	2.9	5.7	13.6
88-89—Texas-El Paso	33	1182	255	509	.501	169	228	.741	131	179	727	4.0	5.4	22.0
Totals	124	3575	571	1179	.484	375	522	.718	321	563	1586	2.6	4.5	12.8

Three-point field goals: 1986-87, 3-for-12 (.250). 1987-88, 18-for-53 (.340). 1988-89, 48-for-131 (.366). Totals, 69-for-196 (.352).

NBA REGULAR-SEASON RECORD

RECORDS: Holds single-game record for most field goals attempted, none made—17 (December 27, 1991, OT, at San Antonio).
HONORS: All-NBA first team (1997). ... All-NBA second team (1992, 1998, 1999). ... All-NBA third team (1993). ... NBA All-Rookie first team (1990).

Season Team	G	Min.	FGM	FGA	Pct.	FTM	FTA	Pct.	Off.	REBOUNDS Def.	Tot.	Ast.	St.	Blk.	TO	Pts.	RPG	AVERAGES APG	PPG
89-90—Golden State	79	2663	464	985	.471	211	276	.764	57	253	310	689	165	12	260	1162	3.9	8.7	14.7
90-91—Golden State	82	3215	739	1551	.476	306	381	.803	87	245	332	793	214	12	270	1881	4.0	9.7	22.9
91-92—Golden State	81	3332	734	1592	.461	298	389	.766	81	229	310	807	164	13	267	1893	3.8	10.0	23.4
92-93—Golden State	66	2609	522	1168	.447	273	367	.744	60	203	263	699	116	12	220	1419	4.0	10.6	21.5
93-94—Golden State							Did not play—knee injury.												
94-95—Golden State	62	2321	430	1007	.427	219	288	.760	46	144	190	578	88	12	214	1247	3.1	9.3	20.1
95-96—G.S.-Miami	80	2534	419	992	.422	241	305	.790	35	194	229	640	132	17	235	1217	2.9	8.0	15.2
96-97—Miami	81	3136	575	1384	.415	291	364	.799	49	228	277	695	151	9	230	1644	3.4	8.6	20.3
97-98—Miami	81	3031	558	1296	.431	257	329	.781	48	251	299	672	136	16	224	1528	3.7	8.3	18.9
98-99—Miami	48	1772	301	752	.400	121	149	.812	15	137	152	352	57	6	131	835	3.2	7.3	17.4
99-00—Miami	52	1672	246	638	.386	110	133	.827	25	125	150	385	49	4	119	696	2.9	7.4	13.4
00-01—Miami	77	2613	408	1042	.392	145	181	.801	26	178	204	493	90	6	177	1108	2.6	6.4	14.4
01-02—Dallas-Denver	66	1881	226	620	.365	77	97	.794	14	110	124	278	57	10	117	652	1.8	4.1	9.6
02-03—Indiana	10	127	18	49	.367	2	4	.500	1	14	15	24	9	0	11	49	1.5	2.4	4.9
Totals	867	30626	5640	13076	.431	2551	3263	.782	544	2311	2855	7095	1428	129	2481	15373	3.3	8.2	17.7

Three-point field goals: 1989-90, 23-for-84 (.274). 1990-91, 97-for-252 (.385). 1991-92, 127-for-376 (.338). 1992-93, 102-for-309 (.330). 1994-95, 168-for-444 (.378). 1995-96, 138-for-379 (.364). 1996-97, 203-for-590 (.344). 1997-98, 155-for-442 (.351). 1998-99, 112-for-311 (.360). 1999-00, 94-for-256 (.367). 2000-01, 189-for-517 (.366). 2001-02, 123-for-354 (.347). 2002-03, 11-for-31 (.355). Totals, 1542-for-4345 (.355).

Personal fouls/disqualifications: 1989-90, 232/6. 1990-91, 228/7. 1991-92, 208/1. 1992-93, 152/0. 1994-95, 155/1. 1995-96, 201/3. 1996-97, 165/2. 1997-98, 200/2. 1998-99, 102/1. 1999-00, 112/0. 2000-01, 155/1. 2001-02, 109/0. 2002-03, 8/0. Totals, 2027/24.

NBA PLAYOFF RECORD

Season Team	G	Min.	FGM	FGA	Pct.	FTM	FTA	Pct.	Off.	REBOUNDS Def.	Tot.	Ast.	St.	Blk.	TO	Pts.	RPG	AVERAGES APG	PPG
90-91—Golden State	9	396	90	185	.486	30	38	.789	5	28	33	101	28	7	25	227	3.7	11.2	25.2
91-92—Golden State	4	176	32	80	.400	24	37	.649	6	9	15	29	13	0	14	98	3.8	7.3	24.5
95-96—Miami	3	110	20	43	.465	5	7	.714	1	4	5	17	3	0	15	53	1.7	5.7	17.7
96-97—Miami	17	701	103	287	.359	70	88	.795	13	56	69	119	27	1	53	318	4.1	7.0	18.7
97-98—Miami	5	222	42	94	.447	29	37	.784	3	14	17	33	6	0	18	130	3.4	6.6	26.0
98-99—Miami	5	182	15	56	.268	10	16	.625	3	11	14	32	5	1	18	45	2.8	6.4	9.0
99-00—Miami	7	182	20	68	.294	7	10	.700	1	14	15	33	5	0	11	54	2.1	4.7	7.7
00-01—Miami	2	36	2	9	.222	0	0	...	1	1	2	9	0	0	8	5	1.0	4.5	2.5
02-03—Indiana	4	47	5	15	.333	0	0	...	0	2	2	9	1	0	3	13	0.5	2.3	3.3
Totals	56	2052	329	837	.393	175	233	.751	33	139	172	382	88	2	165	943	3.1	6.8	16.8

Three-point field goals: 1990-91, 17-for-48 (.354). 1991-92, 10-for-29 (.345). 1995-96, 8-for-22 (.364). 1996-97, 42-for-134 (.313). 1997-98, 17-for-39 (.436). 1998-99, 5-for-25 (.200). 1999-00, 7-for-34 (.206). 2000-01, 1-for-3 (.333). 2002-03, 3-for-10 (.300). Totals, 110-for-344 (.320).

Personal fouls/disqualifications: 1990-91, 22/0. 1991-92, 14/0. 1995-96, 10/0. 1996-97, 37/0. 1997-98, 9/0. 1998-99, 14/0. 1999-00, 10/0. 2000-01, 4/0. 2002-03, 2/0. Totals, 122/0.

NBA ALL-STAR GAME RECORD

Season Team	Min.	FGM	FGA	Pct.	FTM	FTA	Pct.	Off.	REBOUNDS Def.	Tot.	Ast.	PF	Dq.	St.	Blk.	TO	Pts.
1991—Golden State	12	2	7	.286	0	0	...	2	1	3	4	1	0	2	0	0	5
1992—Golden State	20	5	10	.500	2	2	1.000	0	0	0	7	2	0	1	0	2	14
1993—Golden State	21	3	9	.333	9	12	.750	1	5	6	4	1	0	1	0	3	16
1997—Miami	14	4	10	.400	0	0	...	0	3	3	2	1	0	1	0	2	10
1998—Miami	17	3	8	.375	0	0	...	0	1	1	6	0	0	0	0	6	8
Totals	84	17	44	.386	11	14	.786	3	10	13	23	5	0	5	0	13	53

Three-point field goals: 1991, 1-for-2 (.500). 1992, 2-for-5 (.400). 1993, 1-for-3 (.333). 1997, 2-for-6 (.333). 1998, 2-for-5 (.400). Totals, 8-for-21 (.381).

HARPER, DEREK   G

PERSONAL: Born October 13, 1961, in Elberton, Ga. ... 6-4/206 (1,93/93,4). ... Full name: Derek Ricardo Harper.
HIGH SCHOOL: North Shore (West Palm Beach, Fla.).
COLLEGE: Illinois.
TRANSACTIONS/CAREER NOTES: Selected after junior season by Dallas Mavericks in first round (11th pick overall) of 1983 NBA Draft. ... Traded by Mavericks to New York Knicks for G/F Tony Campbell and 1997 first-round draft choice (January 6, 1994). ... Signed as free agent by Mavericks (July 26, 1996). ... Traded by Mavericks with F Ed O'Bannon to Orlando Magic for G Dennis Scott and cash (September 24, 1997). ... Signed as free agent by Los Angeles Lakers (January 21, 1999). ... Traded by Lakers to Detroit Pistons for draft rights to G Melvin Levett (September 21, 1999). ... Placed on suspension by Pistons (did not report) (October 5, 1999). ... Announced retirement (January 30, 2000).
CAREER NOTES: Vice president of business relations, Dallas Mavericks (February-April 2000).
MISCELLANEOUS: Dallas Mavericks all-time assists leader with 5,111 and all-time steals leader with 1,551 (1983-84 through 1993-94 and 1996-97).

COLLEGIATE RECORD

Season Team	G	Min.	FGM	FGA	Pct.	FTM	FTA	Pct.	Reb.	Ast.	Pts.	RPG	APG	PPG
80-81—Illinois	29	934	104	252	.413	33	46	.717	75	156	241	2.6	5.4	8.3
81-82—Illinois	29	1059	105	230	.457	34	45	.756	133	145	244	4.6	5.0	8.4
82-83—Illinois	32	1182	198	369	.537	83	123	.675	112	118	492	3.5	3.7	15.4
Totals	90	3175	407	851	.478	150	214	.701	320	419	977	3.6	4.7	10.9

Three-point field goals: 1982-83, 13-for-24 (.542).

HONORS: NBA All-Defensive second team (1987, 1990).

NBA REGULAR-SEASON RECORD

Season Team	G	Min.	FGM	FGA	Pct.	FTM	FTA	Pct.	Off.	Def.	Tot.	Ast.	St.	Blk.	TO	Pts.	RPG	APG	PPG
83-84—Dallas	82	1712	200	451	.443	66	98	.673	53	119	172	239	95	21	111	469	2.1	2.9	5.7
84-85—Dallas	82	2218	329	633	.520	111	154	.721	47	152	199	360	144	37	123	790	2.4	4.4	9.6
85-86—Dallas	79	2150	390	730	.534	171	229	.747	75	151	226	416	153	23	144	963	2.9	5.3	12.2
86-87—Dallas	77	2556	497	993	.501	160	234	.684	51	148	199	609	167	25	138	1230	2.6	7.9	16.0
87-88—Dallas	82	3032	536	1167	.459	261	344	.759	71	175	246	634	168	35	190	1393	3.0	7.7	17.0
88-89—Dallas	81	2968	538	1127	.477	229	284	.806	46	182	228	570	172	41	205	1404	2.8	7.0	17.3
89-90—Dallas	82	3007	567	1161	.488	250	315	.794	54	190	244	609	187	26	207	1473	3.0	7.4	18.0
90-91—Dallas	77	2879	572	1226	.467	286	391	.731	59	174	233	548	147	14	177	1519	3.0	7.1	19.7
91-92—Dallas	65	2252	448	1011	.443	198	261	.759	49	121	170	373	101	17	154	1152	2.6	5.7	17.7
92-93—Dallas	62	2108	393	939	.419	239	316	.756	42	81	123	334	80	16	136	1126	2.0	5.4	18.2
93-94—Dallas-N.Y.	82	2204	303	744	.407	112	163	.687	20	121	141	334	125	8	135	791	1.7	4.1	9.6
94-95—New York	80	2716	337	756	.446	139	192	.724	31	163	194	458	79	10	151	919	2.4	5.7	11.5
95-96—New York	82	2893	436	939	.464	156	206	.757	32	170	202	352	131	5	178	1149	2.5	4.3	14.0
96-97—Dallas	75	2210	299	674	.444	95	128	.742	30	107	137	321	92	12	132	753	1.8	4.3	10.0
97-98—Orlando	66	1761	226	542	.417	55	79	.696	23	80	103	233	72	10	101	566	1.6	3.5	8.6
98-99—L.A. Lakers	45	1120	120	291	.412	26	32	.813	13	54	67	187	44	4	52	309	1.5	4.2	6.9
Totals	1199	37786	6191	13384	.463	2554	3426	.745	696	2188	2884	6577	1957	304	2334	16006	2.4	5.5	13.3

Three-point field goals: 1983-84, 3-for-26 (.115). 1984-85, 21-for-61 (.344). 1985-86, 12-for-51 (.235). 1986-87, 76-for-212 (.358). 1987-88, 60-for-192 (.313). 1988-89, 99-for-278 (.356). 1989-90, 89-for-240 (.371). 1990-91, 89-for-246 (.362). 1991-92, 58-for-186 (.312). 1992-93, 101-for-257 (.393). 1993-94, 73-for-203 (.360). 1994-95, 106-for-292 (.363). 1995-96, 121-for-325 (.372). 1996-97, 60-for-176 (.341). 1997-98, 59-for-164 (.360). 1998-99, 43-for-117 (.368). Totals, 1070-for-3026 (.354).

Personal fouls/disqualifications: 1983-84, 143/0. 1984-85, 194/1. 1985-86, 166/1. 1986-87, 195/0. 1987-88, 164/0. 1988-89, 219/3. 1989-90, 224/1. 1990-91, 221/1. 1991-92, 150/0. 1992-93, 145/1. 1993-94, 163/0. 1994-95, 219/0. 1995-96, 201/0. 1996-97, 144/0. 1997-98, 140/0. 1998-99, 66/0. Totals, 2755/8.

NBA PLAYOFF RECORD

NOTES: Shares NBA Finals single-series record for most three-point field goals made—17 (1994, vs. Houston).

Season Team	G	Min.	FGM	FGA	Pct.	FTM	FTA	Pct.	Off.	Def.	Tot.	Ast.	St.	Blk.	TO	Pts.	RPG	APG	PPG
83-84—Dallas	10	226	21	54	.389	5	7	.714	8	12	20	28	11	2	6	50	2.0	2.8	5.0
84-85—Dallas	4	132	10	21	.476	5	7	.714	1	11	12	20	6	1	4	26	3.0	5.0	6.5
85-86—Dallas	10	348	57	107	.533	12	16	.750	13	6	19	76	23	0	23	134	1.9	7.6	13.4
86-87—Dallas	4	123	20	40	.500	24	30	.800	2	10	12	27	7	0	5	66	3.0	6.8	16.5
87-88—Dallas	17	602	89	202	.441	43	59	.729	11	32	43	121	32	5	32	230	2.5	7.1	13.5
89-90—Dallas	3	119	21	48	.438	11	16	.688	2	6	8	23	4	0	12	58	2.7	7.7	19.3
93-94—New York	23	750	99	231	.429	36	56	.643	13	41	54	103	42	1	41	263	2.3	4.5	11.4
94-95—New York	11	388	56	109	.514	18	24	.750	5	33	38	62	11	1	26	157	3.5	5.6	14.3
95-96—New York	8	293	29	82	.354	11	15	.733	0	17	17	38	10	1	14	80	2.1	4.8	10.0
98-99—L.A. Lakers	7	113	13	31	.419	3	6	.500	1	9	10	15	2	0	4	30	1.4	2.1	4.3
Totals	97	3094	415	925	.449	168	236	.712	56	177	233	513	148	11	167	1094	2.4	5.3	11.3

Three-point field goals: 1983-84, 3-for-8 (.375). 1984-85, 1-for-3 (.333). 1985-86, 8-for-14 (.571). 1986-87, 2-for-9 (.222). 1987-88, 9-for-36 (.250). 1989-90, 5-for-16 (.313). 1993-94, 29-for-85 (.341). 1994-95, 27-for-47 (.574). 1995-96, 11-for-35 (.314). 1998-99, 1-for-10 (.100). Totals, 96-for-263 (.365).

Personal fouls/disqualifications: 1983-84, 16/0. 1984-85, 12/0. 1985-86, 27/0. 1986-87, 7/0. 1987-88, 44/0. 1989-90, 13/0. 1993-94, 63/1. 1994-95, 29/0. 1995-96, 24/0. 1998-99, 2/0. Totals, 237/1.

HAVLICEK, JOHN   F/G

PERSONAL: Born April 8, 1940, in Martins Ferry, Ohio. ... 6-5/205 (1,96/93,0). ... Full name: John J. Havlicek. ... Nickname: Hondo.
HIGH SCHOOL: Bridgeport (Ohio).
COLLEGE: Ohio State.
TRANSACTIONS: Selected by Boston Celtics in first round of 1962 NBA Draft.
CAREER HONORS: Elected to Naismith Memorial Basketball Hall of Fame (1984). ... NBA 35th Anniversary All-Time Team (1980) and One of the 50 Greatest Players in NBA History (1996).

MISCELLANEOUS: Member of NBA championship team (1963, 1964, 1965, 1966, 1968, 1969, 1974, 1976). ... Selected as wide receiver by Cleveland Browns in seventh round of 1962 National Football League draft. ... Boston Celtics all-time leading scorer with 26,395 points (1962-63 through 1977-78).

COLLEGIATE RECORD

NOTES: The Sporting News All-America second team (1962). ... Member of NCAA championship team (1960).

Season Team	G	Min.	FGM	FGA	Pct.	FTM	FTA	Pct.	Reb.	Ast.	Pts.	AVERAGES RPG	APG	PPG
58-59—Ohio State‡					Freshman team did not play intercollegiate schedule.									
59-60—Ohio State	28	...	144	312	.462	53	74	.716	205	...	341	7.3	...	12.2
60-61—Ohio State	28	...	173	321	.539	61	87	.701	244	...	407	8.7	...	14.5
61-62—Ohio State	28	...	196	377	.520	83	109	.761	271	...	475	9.7	...	17.0
Varsity totals	84	...	513	1010	.508	197	270	.730	720	...	1223	8.6	...	14.6

NBA REGULAR-SEASON RECORD

HONORS: All-NBA first team (1971, 1972, 1973, 1974). ... All-NBA second team (1964, 1966, 1968, 1969, 1970, 1975, 1976). ... NBA All-Defensive first team (1972, 1973, 1974, 1975, 1976). ... NBA All-Defensive second team (1969, 1970, 1971).

Season Team	G	Min.	FGM	FGA	Pct.	FTM	FTA	Pct.	Reb.	Ast.	PF	Dq.	Pts.	RPG	APG	PPG
62-63—Boston	80	2200	483	1085	.445	174	239	.728	534	179	189	2	1140	6.7	2.2	14.3
63-64—Boston	80	2587	640	1535	.417	315	422	.746	428	238	227	1	1595	5.4	3.0	19.9
64-65—Boston	75	2169	570	1420	.401	235	316	.744	371	199	200	2	1375	4.9	2.7	18.3
65-66—Boston	71	2175	530	1328	.399	274	349	.785	423	210	158	1	1334	6.0	3.0	18.8
66-67—Boston	81	2602	684	1540	.444	365	441	.828	532	278	210	0	1733	6.6	3.4	21.4
67-68—Boston	82	2921	666	1551	.429	368	453	.812	546	384	237	2	1700	6.7	4.7	20.7
68-69—Boston	82	3174	692	1709	.405	387	496	.780	570	441	247	0	1771	7.0	5.4	21.6
69-70—Boston	81	3369	736	1585	.464	488	578	.844	635	550	211	1	1960	7.8	6.8	24.2
70-71—Boston	81	*3678	892	1982	.450	554	677	.818	730	607	200	0	2338	9.0	7.5	28.9
71-72—Boston	82	*3698	897	1957	.458	458	549	.834	672	614	183	1	2252	8.2	7.5	27.5
72-73—Boston	80	3367	766	1704	.450	370	431	.858	567	529	195	1	1902	7.1	6.6	23.8

Season Team	G	Min.	FGM	FGA	Pct.	FTM	FTA	Pct.	REBOUNDS Off.	Def.	Tot.	Ast.	St.	Blk.	TO	Pts.	AVERAGES RPG	APG	PPG
73-74—Boston	76	3091	685	1502	.456	346	416	.832	138	349	487	447	95	32	...	1716	6.4	5.9	22.6
74-75—Boston	82	3132	642	1411	.455	289	332	.870	154	330	484	432	110	16	...	1573	5.9	5.3	19.2
75-76—Boston	76	2598	504	1121	.450	281	333	.844	116	198	314	278	97	29	...	1289	4.1	3.7	17.0
76-77—Boston	79	2913	580	1283	.452	235	288	.816	109	273	382	400	84	18	...	1395	4.8	5.1	17.7
77-78—Boston	82	2797	546	1217	.449	230	269	.855	93	239	332	328	90	22	204	1322	4.0	4.0	16.1
Totals	1270	46471	10513	23930	.439	5369	6589	.815	...	...	8007	6114	476	117	204	26395	6.3	4.8	20.8

Personal fouls/disqualifications: 1973-74, 196/1. 1974-75, 231/2. 1975-76, 204/1. 1976-77, 208/4. 1977-78, 185/2. Totals, 3281/21.

NBA PLAYOFF RECORD

NOTES: NBA Finals Most Valuable Player (1974). ... Shares NBA Finals single-game record for most points in an overtime period—9 (May 10, 1974, vs. Milwaukee). ... Shares single-game playoff record for most field goals made—24 (April 1, 1973, vs. Atlanta).

Season Team	G	Min.	FGM	FGA	Pct.	FTM	FTA	Pct.	Reb.	Ast.	PF	Dq.	Pts.	RPG	APG	PPG
62-63—Boston	11	254	56	125	.448	18	27	.667	53	17	28	1	130	4.8	1.5	11.8
63-64—Boston	10	289	61	159	.384	35	44	.795	43	32	26	0	157	4.3	3.2	15.7
64-65—Boston	12	405	88	250	.352	46	55	.836	88	29	44	1	222	7.3	2.4	18.5
65-66—Boston	17	719	153	374	.409	95	113	.841	154	70	69	2	401	9.1	4.1	23.6
66-67—Boston	9	330	95	212	.448	57	71	.803	73	28	30	0	247	8.1	3.1	27.4
67-68—Boston	19	862	184	407	.452	125	151	.828	164	142	67	1	493	8.6	7.5	25.9
68-69—Boston	18	850	170	382	.445	118	138	.855	179	100	58	2	458	9.9	5.6	25.4
71-72—Boston	11	517	108	235	.460	85	99	.859	92	70	35	1	301	8.4	6.4	27.4
72-73—Boston	12	479	112	235	.477	61	74	.824	62	65	24	0	285	5.2	5.4	23.8

Season Team	G	Min.	FGM	FGA	Pct.	FTM	FTA	Pct.	REBOUNDS Off.	Def.	Tot.	Ast.	St.	Blk.	TO	Pts.	AVERAGES RPG	APG	PPG
73-74—Boston	18	811	199	411	.484	89	101	.881	28	88	116	108	24	6	...	487	6.4	6.0	27.1
74-75—Boston	11	464	83	192	.432	66	76	.868	18	39	57	51	16	1	...	232	5.2	4.6	21.1
75-76—Boston	15	505	80	180	.444	38	47	.809	18	38	56	51	12	5	...	198	3.7	3.4	13.2
76-77—Boston	9	375	62	167	.371	41	50	.820	15	34	49	62	8	4	...	165	5.4	6.9	18.3
Totals	172	6860	1451	3329	.436	874	1046	.836	...	...	1186	825	60	16	...	3776	6.9	4.8	22.0

Personal fouls/disqualifications: 1973-74, 43/0. 1974-75, 38/1. 1975-76, 22/0. 1976-77, 33/0. Totals, 517/9.

NBA ALL-STAR GAME RECORD

Season Team	Min.	FGM	FGA	Pct.	FTM	FTA	Pct.	Reb	Ast.	PF	Dq.	Pts.
1966—Boston	25	6	16	.375	6	6	1.000	6	1	2	0	18
1967—Boston	17	7	14	.500	0	0	...	2	1	1	0	14
1968—Boston	22	9	15	.600	8	11	.727	5	4	0	0	26
1969—Boston	31	6	14	.429	2	2	1.000	7	2	2	0	14
1970—Boston	29	7	15	.467	3	3	1.000	5	7	2	0	17
1971—Boston	24	6	12	.500	0	2	.000	3	2	3	0	12
1972—Boston	24	5	13	.385	5	5	1.000	3	2	2	0	15
1973—Boston	22	6	10	.600	2	5	.400	3	5	1	0	14

Season Team	Min.	FGM	FGA	Pct.	FTM	FTA	Pct.	REBOUNDS Off.	Def.	Tot.	Ast.	PF	Dq.	St.	Blk.	TO	Pts.
1974—Boston	18	5	10	.500	0	2	.000	0	0	0	2	2	0	1	0	...	10
1975—Boston	31	7	12	.583	2	2	1.000	1	5	6	1	2	0	2	0	...	16
1976—Boston	21	3	10	.300	3	3	1.000	1	1	2	2	0	0	1	0	...	9
1977—Boston	17	2	5	.400	0	0	...	0	1	1	1	1	0	0	0	...	4
1978—Boston	22	5	8	.625	0	0	...	0	3	3	1	2	0	0	0	4	10
Totals	303	74	154	.481	31	41	.756	...	...	46	31	20	0	4	0	4	179

HAWKINS, CONNIE   F/C

PERSONAL: Born July 17, 1942, in Brooklyn, N.Y. ... 6-8/215 (2,03/97,5). ... Full name: Cornelius L. Hawkins.
HIGH SCHOOL: Boys (Brooklyn, N.Y.).
COLLEGE: Iowa.
TRANSACTIONS: Signed after freshman season by Pittsburgh Rens of American Basketball League (1961). ... ABL ceased operations (December 31, 1962). ... Played with Harlem Globetrotters (1963-64 through 1966-67) ... Signed by Pittsburgh Pipers of the American Basketball Association (1967). ... Pipers franchise transferred to Minnesota (1968). ... Signed as free agent by Phoenix Suns of NBA (June 20, 1969). ... Traded by Suns to Los Angeles Lakers for Keith Erickson and second-round draft choice (October 30, 1973). ... Traded by Lakers to Atlanta Hawks for draft choices (August 8, 1975). ... Waived by Hawks (1976).
CAREER NOTES: Community relations representative, Phoenix Suns (1992-93 to present).

COLLEGIATE RECORD

Season Team	G	Min.	FGM	FGA	Pct.	FTM	FTA	Pct.	Reb.	Ast.	Pts.	RPG	APG	PPG
60-61—Iowa						Freshman team did not play intercollegiate schedule.								

ABL REGULAR-SEASON RECORD

ABL: ABL Most Valuable Player (1962). ... ABL All-Star first team (1962).

Season Team	G	Min.	FGM	FGA	Pct.	FTM	FTA	Pct.	Reb.	Ast.	Pts.	RPG	APG	PPG
61-62—Pittsburgh	78	3349	760	1490	.510	622	787	.790	1038	183	2145	13.3	2.3	*27.5
62-63—Pittsburgh	16	668	160	326	.491	127	165	.770	205	42	447	12.8	2.6	27.9
Totals	94	4017	920	1816	.507	749	952	.787	1243	225	2592	13.2	2.4	27.6

ABL PLAYOFF RECORD

Season Team	G	Min.	FGM	FGA	Pct.	FTM	FTA	Pct.	Reb.	Ast.	Pts.	RPG	APG	PPG
61-62—Pittsburgh	1	53	14	23	.609	13	14	.929	17	4	41	17.0	4.0	41.0

ABA REGULAR-SEASON RECORD

NOTES: ABA Most Valuable Player (1968). ... ABA All-Star first team (1968 and 1969). ... Member of ABA championship team (1968). ... Led ABA in scoring with 26.79 average (1968).

Season Team	G	Min.	2-POINT FGM	2-POINT FGA	2-POINT Pct.	3-POINT FGM	3-POINT FGA	3-POINT Pct.	FTM	FTA	Pct.	Reb.	Ast.	Pts.	RPG	APG	PPG
67-68—Pittsburgh	70	3146	633	1214	.521	2	9	.222	603	789	.764	945	320	1875	13.5	4.6	*26.8
68-69—Minnesota	47	1852	493	949	.520	3	22	.136	425	554	.767	534	184	1420	11.4	3.9	30.2
Totals	117	4998	1126	2163	.521	5	31	.161	1028	1343	.765	1479	504	3295	12.6	4.3	28.2

ABA PLAYOFF RECORD

Season Team	G	Min.	2-POINT FGM	2-POINT FGA	2-POINT Pct.	3-POINT FGM	3-POINT FGA	3-POINT Pct.	FTM	FTA	Pct.	Reb.	Ast.	Pts.	RPG	APG	PPG
67-68—Pittsburgh	14	616	145	244	.594	0	0	...	129	177	.729	172	64	419	12.3	4.6	29.9
68-69—Minnesota	7	320	61	164	.372	4	8	.500	40	62	.645	86	27	174	12.3	3.9	24.9
Totals	21	936	206	408	.505	...	4	...	169	239	.707	258	91	593	12.3	4.3	28.2

NBA REGULAR-SEASON RECORD

HONORS: All-NBA first team (1970).

Season Team	G	Min.	FGM	FGA	Pct.	FTM	FTA	Pct.	Reb.	Ast.	PF	Dq.	Pts.	RPG	APG	PPG
69-70—Phoenix	81	3312	709	1447	.490	577	741	.779	846	391	287	4	1995	10.4	4.8	24.6
70-71—Phoenix	71	2662	512	1181	.434	457	560	.816	643	322	197	2	1481	9.1	4.5	20.9
71-72—Phoenix	76	2798	571	1244	.459	456	565	.807	633	296	235	2	1598	8.3	3.9	21.0
72-73—Phoenix	75	2768	441	920	.479	322	404	.797	641	304	229	5	1204	8.5	4.1	16.1

Season Team	G	Min.	FGM	FGA	Pct.	FTM	FTA	Pct.	Off.	Def.	Tot.	Ast.	St.	Blk.	TO	Pts.	RPG	APG	PPG
73-74—Pho-Lakers	79	2761	404	807	.501	191	251	.761	176	389	565	407	113	81	...	999	7.2	5.2	12.6
74-75—Los Angeles	43	1026	139	324	.429	68	99	.687	54	144	198	120	51	23	...	346	4.6	2.8	8.0
75-76—Atlanta	74	1907	237	530	.447	136	191	.712	102	343	445	212	80	46	...	610	6.0	2.9	8.2
Totals	499	17234	3013	6453	.467	2207	2811	.785	...	...	3971	2052	...	...	...	8233	8.0	4.1	16.5

Personal fouls/disqualifications: 1973-74, 223/1. 1974-75, 116/1. 1975-76, 172/2. Totals, 1459/17.

NBA PLAYOFF RECORD

Season Team	G	Min.	FGM	FGA	Pct.	FTM	FTA	Pct.	Reb.	Ast.	PF	Dq.	Pts.	RPG	APG	PPG
69-70—Phoenix	7	328	62	150	.413	54	66	.818	97	41	22	0	178	13.9	5.9	25.4

Season Team	G	Min.	FGM	FGA	Pct.	FTM	FTA	Pct.	Off.	Def.	Tot.	Ast.	St.	Blk.	TO	Pts.	RPG	APG	PPG
73-74—Los Angeles	5	172	21	60	.350	12	15	.800	14	26	40	16	7	1	...	54	8.0	3.2	10.8
Totals	12	500	83	210	.395	66	81	.815	...	...	137	57	7	1	...	232	11.4	4.8	19.3

Personal fouls/disqualifications: 1973-74, 13/0.

NBA ALL-STAR GAME RECORD

Season Team	Min.	FGM	FGA	Pct.	FTM	FTA	Pct.	Reb	Ast.	PF	Dq.	Pts.
1970—Phoenix	19	2	4	.500	6	6	1.000	4	2	3	...	10
1971—Phoenix	1	0	0	...	0	0	...	0	0	0	...	0
1972—Phoenix	14	5	7	.714	3	4	.750	4	0	1	0	13
1973—Phoenix	11	1	5	.200	0	0	...	2	3	1	0	2
Totals	45	8	16	.500	9	10	.900	10	5	5	...	25

COMBINED ABA AND NBA REGULAR-SEASON RECORDS

								REBOUNDS							AVERAGES		
	G	Min.	FGM	FGA	Pct.	FTM	FTA	Pct.	Off.	Def.	Tot.	Ast.	Stl.	Blk.	TO	Pts.	RPG APG PPG
Totals	616	22232	4144	8647	.479	3235	4154	.779	...	...	5450	2556	...	...	...	11528	8.8 4.1 18.7

Three-point field goals: 5-for-31 (.161).
Personal fouls/disqualifications: 1873/22.

HAYES, ELVIN   F/C

PERSONAL: Born November 17, 1945, in Rayville, La. ... 6-9/235 (2,06/106,6). ... Full name: Elvin Ernest Hayes.
HIGH SCHOOL: Eula D. Britton (Rayville, La.).
COLLEGE: Houston.
TRANSACTIONS: Selected by San Diego Rockets in first round (first pick overall) of 1968 NBA Draft. ... Rockets franchise moved from San Diego to Houston for 1971-72 season. ... Traded by Rockets to Baltimore Bullets for F Jack Marin and future considerations (June 23, 1972). ... Bullets franchise moved from Baltimore to Washington and renamed Capital Bullets for 1973-74 season. ... Bullets franchise renamed Washington Bullets for 1974-75 season. ... Traded by Bullets to Rockets for 1981 and 1983 second-round draft choices (June 8, 1981).
CAREER HONORS: Elected to Naismith Memorial Basketball Hall of Fame (1990). ... One of the 50 Greatest Players in NBA History (1996).
MISCELLANEOUS: Member of NBA championship team (1978). ... Washington Wizards franchise all-time leading scorer with 15,551 points and all-time blocked shots leader with 1,558 (1973-74 through 1980-81).

COLLEGIATE RECORD

NOTES: The Sporting News College Player of the Year (1968). ... The Sporting News All-America first team (1967, 1968). ... The Sporting News All-America second team (1966).

												AVERAGES		
Season Team	G	Min.	FGM	FGA	Pct.	FTM	FTA	Pct.	Reb.	Ast.	Pts.	RPG	APG	PPG
64-65—Houston‡	21	...	217	478	.454	93	176	.528	500	43	527	23.8	2.0	25.1
65-66—Houston	29	946	323	570	.567	143	257	.556	490	6	789	16.9	0.2	27.2
66-67—Houston	31	1119	373	750	.497	135	227	.595	488	33	881	15.7	1.1	28.4
67-68—Houston	33	1270	519	945	.549	176	285	.618	624	59	1214	18.9	1.8	36.8
Varsity totals	93	3335	1215	2265	.536	454	769	.590	1602	98	2884	17.2	1.1	31.0

NBA REGULAR-SEASON RECORD

RECORDS: Holds single-season record for most minutes played by a rookie—3,695 (1969).
HONORS: All-NBA first team (1975, 1977, 1979). ... All-NBA second team (1973, 1974, 1976). ... NBA All-Defensive second team (1974, 1975). ... NBA All-Rookie team (1969).

													AVERAGES		
Season Team	G	Min.	FGM	FGA	Pct.	FTM	FTA	Pct.	Reb.	Ast.	PF	Dq.	Pts.	RPG	APG	PPG
68-69—San Diego	82	*3695	*930	*2082	.447	467	746	.626	1406	113	266	2	*2327	17.1	1.4	*28.4
69-70—San Diego	82	*3665	914	*2020	.452	428	622	.688	*1386	162	270	5	2256	16.9	2.0	27.5
70-71—San Diego	82	3633	948	*2215	.428	454	676	.672	1362	186	225	1	2350	16.6	2.3	28.7
71-72—Houston	82	3461	832	1918	.434	399	615	.649	1197	270	233	1	2063	14.6	3.3	25.2
72-73—Baltimore	81	3347	713	1607	.444	291	434	.671	1177	137	232	2	1717	14.5	1.6	21.0

									REBOUNDS							AVERAGES		
Season Team	G	Min.	FGM	FGA	Pct.	FTM	FTA	Pct.	Off.	Def.	Tot.	Ast.	St.	Blk.	TO	Pts.	RPG APG PPG
73-74—Capital	81	*3602	689	1627	.423	357	495	.721	*354	*1109	*1463	163	86	240	...	1735	18.1 2.0 21.4
74-75—Washington	82	3465	739	1668	.443	409	534	.766	221	783	1004	206	158	187	...	1887	12.2 2.5 23.0
75-76—Washington	80	2975	649	1381	.470	287	457	.628	210	668	878	121	104	202	...	1585	11.0 1.5 19.8
76-77—Washington	82	*3364	760	1516	.501	422	614	.687	289	740	1029	158	87	220	...	1942	12.5 1.9 23.7
77-78—Washington	81	3246	636	1409	.451	326	514	.634	335	740	1075	149	96	229	...	1598	13.3 1.8 19.7
78-79—Washington	82	3105	720	1477	.487	349	534	.654	312	682	994	143	75	190	235	1789	12.1 1.7 21.8
79-80—Washington	81	3183	761	1677	.454	334	478	.699	269	627	896	129	62	189	215	1859	11.1 1.6 23.0
80-81—Washington	81	2931	584	1296	.451	271	439	.617	235	554	789	98	68	171	189	1439	9.7 1.2 17.8
81-82—Houston	82	3032	519	1100	.472	280	422	.664	267	480	747	144	62	104	208	1318	9.1 1.8 16.1
82-83—Houston	81	2302	424	890	.476	196	287	.683	199	417	616	158	50	81	200	1046	7.6 2.0 12.9
83-84—Houston	81	994	158	389	.406	86	132	.652	87	173	260	71	16	28	82	402	3.2 0.9 5.0
Totals	1303	50000	10976	24272	.452	5356	7999	.670	...	...	16279	2398	864	1771	1358	27313	12.5 1.8 21.0

Three-point field goals: 1979-80, 3-for-13 (.231). 1980-81, 0-for-10. 1981-82, 0-for-5. 1982-83, 2-for-4 (.500). 1983-84, 0-for-2. Totals, 5-for-34 (.147).
Personal fouls/disqualifications: 1973-74, 252/1. 1974-75, 238/0. 1975-76, 293/5. 1976-77, 312/1. 1977-78, 313/7. 1978-79, 308/5. 1979-80, 309/9. 1980-81, 300/6. 1981-82, 287/4. 1982-83, 232/2. 1983-84, 123/1. Totals, 4193/53.

NBA PLAYOFF RECORD

NOTES: Shares NBA Finals single-game record for most offensive rebounds—11 (May 27, 1979, vs. Seattle).

													AVERAGES		
Season Team	G	Min.	FGM	FGA	Pct.	FTM	FTA	Pct.	Reb.	Ast.	PF	Dq.	Pts.	RPG	APG	PPG
68-69—San Diego	6	278	60	114	.526	35	53	.660	83	5	21	0	155	13.8	0.8	25.8
72-73—Baltimore	5	228	53	105	.505	23	33	.697	57	5	16	0	129	11.4	1.0	25.8

									REBOUNDS							AVERAGES		
Season Team	G	Min.	FGM	FGA	Pct.	FTM	FTA	Pct.	Off.	Def.	Tot.	Ast.	St.	Blk.	TO	Pts.	RPG APG PPG
73-74—Capital	7	323	76	143	.531	29	41	.707	31	80	111	21	5	15	...	181	15.9 3.0 25.9
74-75—Washington	17	751	174	372	.468	86	127	.677	46	140	186	37	26	39	...	434	10.9 2.2 25.5
75-76—Washington	7	305	54	122	.443	32	55	.582	16	72	88	10	5	28	...	140	12.6 1.4 20.0
76-77—Washington	9	405	74	173	.428	41	59	.695	29	93	122	17	10	21	...	189	13.6 1.9 21.0
77-78—Washington	21	868	189	385	.491	79	133	.594	103	176	279	43	32	52	58	457	13.3 2.0 21.8
78-79—Washington	19	786	170	396	.429	87	130	.669	94	172	266	38	17	52	56	427	14.0 2.0 22.5
79-80—Washington	2	92	16	41	.390	8	10	.800	10	12	22	6	0	4	4	40	11.0 3.0 20.0
81-82—Houston	3	124	17	50	.340	8	15	.533	7	23	30	3	2	10	6	42	10.0 1.0 14.0
Totals	96	4160	883	1901	.464	428	656	.652	...	...	1244	185	77	222	124	2194	13.0 1.9 22.9

Personal fouls/disqualifications: 1973-74, 23/0. 1974-75, 70/3. 1975-76, 24/0. 1976-77, 39/0. 1977-78, 86/2. 1978-79, 79/3. 1979-80, 8/0. 1981-82, 12/0. Totals, 378/8.

ALL-TIME GREAT PLAYERS

NBA ALL-STAR GAME RECORD

Season Team	Min.	FGM	FGA	Pct.	FTM	FTA	Pct.	Reb.	Ast.	PF	Dq.	Pts.
1969—San Diego	21	4	9	.444	3	3	1.000	5	0	4	0	11
1970—San Diego	35	9	21	.429	6	12	.500	15	1	1	0	24
1971—San Diego	19	4	13	.308	2	3	.667	4	2	1	0	10
1972—Houston	11	1	6	.167	2	2	1.000	2	0	2	0	4
1973—Baltimore	16	4	13	.308	2	2	1.000	12	0	0	0	10

Season Team	Min.	FGM	FGA	Pct.	FTM	FTA	Pct.	Off.	Def.	Tot.	Ast.	PF	Dq.	St.	Blk.	TO	Pts.
1974—Capital	35	5	13	.385	2	3	.667	4	11	15	6	4	0	0	1	...	12
1975—Washington	17	2	6	.333	0	0	...	0	5	5	2	1	0	1	0	...	4
1976—Washington	31	6	14	.429	0	2	.000	3	7	10	1	5	0	1	0	...	12
1977—Washington	11	6	6	1.000	0	0	...	0	2	2	1	5	0	0	0	...	12
1978—Washington	11	1	7	.143	0	0	...	3	1	4	0	4	0	1	0	1	2
1979—Washington	28	5	11	.455	3	5	.600	4	9	13	0	5	0	1	1	1	13
1980—Washington	29	5	10	.500	2	2	1.000	2	3	5	4	5	0	1	4	3	12
Totals	264	52	129	.403	22	34	.647	...	...	92	17	37	0	5	6	5	126

HAYWOOD, SPENCER   F/C

PERSONAL: Born April 22, 1949, in Silver City, Miss. ... 6-9/225 (2,05/102,1). ... Full name: Spencer Haywood.
HIGH SCHOOL: Pershing (Detroit).
JUNIOR COLLEGE: Trinidad State Junior College (Colo.).
COLLEGE: Detroit.
TRANSACTIONS: Signed as free agent after sophomore season by Denver Rockets of American Basketball Association (August 16, 1969). ... Selected by Buffalo Braves in second round (30th pick overall) of 1971 NBA Draft. ... Terminated contract with Rockets and signed by Seattle SuperSonics (1971). ... Traded by SuperSonics to New York Knicks for cash and the option of F Eugene Short or future draft choice (October 24, 1975). ... Traded by Knicks to New Orleans Jazz for C Joe C. Meriweather (January 5, 1979). ... Jazz franchise moved from New Orleans to Utah for 1979-80 season. ... Traded by Jazz to Los Angeles Lakers for F Adrian Dantley (September 13, 1979). ... Waived by Lakers (August 19, 1980). ... Played in Italy (1980-81 and 1981-82). ... Signed as free agent by Washington Bullets (October 24, 1981). ... Waived by Bullets (March 9, 1983).
MISCELLANEOUS: Member of NBA championship team (1980). ... Member of gold-medal-winning U.S. Olympic team (1968).

COLLEGIATE RECORD

NOTES: THE SPORTING NEWS All-America first team (1969). ... Led NCAA Division I with 22.1 rebounds per game (1969).

Season Team	G	Min.	FGM	FGA	Pct.	FTM	FTA	Pct.	Reb.	Ast.	Pts.	AVERAGES RPG	APG	PPG
67-68—Trinidad State J.C.	30	...	358	675	.530	129	195	.662	663	...	845	22.1	...	28.2
68-69—Detroit	24	...	288	508	.567	195	254	.768	530	...	771	22.1	...	32.1
Junior college totals	30	...	358	675	.530	129	195	.662	663	...	845	22.1	...	28.2
4-year-college totals	24	...	288	508	.567	195	254	.768	530	...	771	22.1	...	32.1

ABA REGULAR-SEASON RECORD

NOTES: ABA Most Valuable Player (1970). ... ABA Rookie of the Year (1970). ... ABA All-Star first team (1970). ... ABA All-Rookie team (1970). ... Holds single-season records for most minutes played—3,808; most field goals made—986; most rebounds—1,637; and highest rebounds-per-game average—19.5 (1970).

Season Team	G	Min.	2-POINT FGM	FGA	Pct.	3-POINT FGM	FGA	Pct.	FTM	FTA	Pct.	Reb.	Ast.	Pts.	AVERAGES RPG	APG	PPG
69-70—Denver	84	*3808	*986	1987	.496	0	11	.000	547	705	.776	*1637	190	*2519	*19.5	2.3	*30.0

ABA PLAYOFF RECORD

Season Team	G	Min.	2-POINT FGM	FGA	Pct.	3-POINT FGM	FGA	Pct.	FTM	FTA	Pct.	Reb.	Ast.	Pts.	AVERAGES RPG	APG	PPG
69-70—Denver	12	568	185	362	.511	1	5	.200	69	83	.831	237	39	440	19.8	3.3	36.7

ABA ALL-STAR GAME RECORD

NOTES: ABA All-Star Game Most Valuable Player (1970).

Season Team	Min.	2-POINT FGM	FGA	Pct.	3-POINT FGM	FGA	Pct.	FTM	FTA	Pct.	Reb.	Ast.	Pts.
1970—Denver	39	10	19	.526	0	0	...	3	4	.750	19	2	23

NBA REGULAR-SEASON RECORD

HONORS: All-NBA first team (1972, 1973). ... All-NBA second team (1974, 1975).

Season Team	G	Min.	FGM	FGA	Pct.	FTM	FTA	Pct.	Reb.	Ast.	PF	Dq.	Pts.	AVERAGES RPG	APG	PPG
70-71—Seattle	33	1162	260	579	.449	160	218	.734	396	48	84	1	680	12.0	1.5	20.6
71-72—Seattle	73	3167	717	1557	.461	480	586	.819	926	148	208	0	1914	12.7	2.0	26.2
72-73—Seattle	77	3259	889	1868	.476	473	564	.839	995	196	213	2	2251	12.9	2.5	29.2

Season Team	G	Min.	FGM	FGA	Pct.	FTM	FTA	Pct.	Off.	Def.	Tot.	Ast.	St.	Blk.	TO	Pts.	AVERAGES RPG	APG	PPG
73-74—Seattle	75	3039	694	1520	.457	373	458	.814	318	689	1007	240	65	106	...	1761	13.4	3.2	23.5
74-75—Seattle	68	2529	608	1325	.459	309	381	.811	198	432	630	137	54	108	...	1525	9.3	2.0	22.4
75-76—New York	78	2892	605	1360	.445	339	448	.757	234	644	878	92	53	80	...	1549	11.3	1.2	19.9
76-77—N.Y. Knicks	31	1021	202	449	.450	109	131	.832	77	203	280	50	14	29	...	513	9.0	1.6	16.5
77-78—New York	67	1765	412	852	.484	96	135	.711	141	301	442	126	37	72	140	920	6.6	1.9	13.7
78-79—N.Y.-N.O.	68	2361	595	1205	.494	231	292	.791	172	361	533	127	40	82	200	1421	7.8	1.9	20.9
79-80—Los Angeles	76	1544	288	591	.487	159	206	.772	132	214	346	93	35	57	134	736	4.6	1.2	9.7
81-82—Washington	76	2086	395	829	.476	219	260	.842	144	278	422	64	45	68	175	1009	5.6	0.8	13.3
82-83—Washington	38	775	125	312	.401	63	87	.724	77	106	183	30	12	27	67	313	4.8	0.8	8.2
Totals	760	25600	5790	12447	.465	3011	3766	.800	...	...	7038	1351	355	629	716	14592	9.3	1.8	19.2

Three-point field goals: 1979-80, 1-for-4 (.250). 1981-82, 0-for-3. 1982-83, 0-for-1. Totals, 1-for-8 (.125).
Personal fouls/disqualifications: 1973-74, 198/2. 1974-75, 173/1. 1975-76, 255/1. 1976-77, 72/0. 1977-78, 188/1. 1978-79, 236/8. 1979-80, 197/2. 1981-82, 249/6. 1982-83, 94/2. Totals, 2167/26.

NBA PLAYOFF RECORD

Season Team	G	Min.	FGM	FGA	Pct.	FTM	FTA	Pct.	Off.	Def.	Tot.	Ast.	St.	Blk.	TO	Pts.	RPG	APG	PPG
74-75—Seattle	9	337	47	131	.359	47	61	.771	20	61	81	18	7	11	...	141	9.0	2.0	15.7
77-78—New York	6	177	43	85	.506	11	11	1.000	19	23	42	12	2	5	10	97	7.0	2.0	16.2
79-80—Los Angeles....	11	145	25	53	.472	13	16	.813	14	12	26	4	0	6	20	63	2.4	0.4	5.7
81-82—Washington	7	231	57	115	.496	26	35	.743	16	23	39	7	4	14	15	140	5.6	1.0	20.0
Totals	33	890	172	384	.448	97	123	.789	69	119	188	41	13	36	45	441	5.7	1.2	13.4

Three-point field goals: 1979-80, 0-for-1.
Personal fouls/disqualifications: 1974-75, 29/0. 1977-78, 24/1. 1979-80, 17/0. 1981-82, 28/0. Totals, 98/1.

NBA ALL-STAR GAME RECORD

Season Team	Min.	FGM	FGA	Pct.	FTM	FTA	Pct.	Reb	Ast.	PF	Dq.	Pts.
1972—Seattle	25	4	10	.400	3	4	.750	7	1	2	0	11
1973—Seattle	22	5	10	.500	2	2	1.000	10	0	5	0	12

Season Team	Min.	FGM	FGA	Pct.	FTM	FTA	Pct.	Off.	Def.	Tot.	Ast.	PF	Dq.	St.	Blk.	TO	Pts.
1974—Seattle	33	10	17	.588	3	3	1.000	2	9	11	5	5	0	0	3	...	23
1975—Seattle	17	1	9	.111	0	0	....	1	2	3	0	1	0	0	0	...	2
Totals	97	20	46	.435	8	9	.889	...	...	31	6	13	0	0	3	...	48

COMBINED ABA AND NBA REGULAR-SEASON RECORDS

	G	Min.	FGM	FGA	Pct.	FTM	FTA	Pct.	Off.	Def.	Tot.	Ast.	Stl.	Blk.	TO	Pts.	RPG	APG	PPG
Totals	844	29408	6776	14445	.470	3558	4471	.796	...	...	8675	1541	...	...	...	17111	10.3	1.8	20.3

Three-point field goals: 1-for-19 (.053).
Personal fouls/disqualifications: 2388/27.

ITALIAN LEAGUE RECORD

Season Team	G	Min.	FGM	FGA	Pct.	FTM	FTA	Pct.	Reb.	Ast.	Pts.	RPG	APG	PPG
80-81—Venezia	34	...	334	601	.556	132	179	.737	354	...	800	10.4	...	23.5
81-82—Carrera	5	175	63	100	.630	24	32	.750	37	...	150	7.4	...	30.0
Totals	39	...	397	701	.566	156	211	.739	391	...	950	10.0	...	24.4

HEINSOHN, TOM   F

See All-Time Great Coaches, page 460.

HORNACEK, JEFF   G

PERSONAL: Born May 3, 1963, in Elmhurst, Ill. ... 6-4/190. (1.93 m/86 kg). ... Full Name: Jeffrey John Hornacek. ... Name pronounced HORN-a-sek.
HIGH SCHOOL: Lyons Township (La Grange, Ill.).
COLLEGE: Iowa State.
TRANSACTIONS/CAREER NOTES: Selected by Phoenix Suns in second round (46th pick overall) of 1986 NBA Draft. ... Traded by Suns with C Andrew Lang and F Tim Perry to Philadelphia 76ers for F Charles Barkley (June 17, 1992). ... Traded by 76ers with G Sean Green and 1995 or 1996 second-round draft choice to Utah Jazz for G Jeff Malone and 1994 conditional first-round draft choice (February 24, 1994). ... Announced retirement effective at end of 1999-2000 season.

COLLEGIATE RECORD

Season Team	G	Min.	FGM	FGA	Pct.	FTM	FTA	Pct.	Reb.	Ast.	Pts.	RPG	APG	PPG
81-82—Iowa State					Did not play—redshirted.									
82-83—Iowa State	27	583	57	135	.422	32	45	.711	62	82	146	2.3	3.0	5.4
83-84—Iowa State	29	1065	104	208	.500	83	105	.790	101	198	291	3.5	6.8	10.0
84-85—Iowa State	34	1224	172	330	.521	81	96	.844	122	166	425	3.6	4.9	12.5
85-86—Iowa State	33	1229	177	370	.478	97	125	.776	127	219	451	3.8	6.6	13.7
Totals	123	4101	510	1043	.489	293	371	.790	412	665	1313	3.3	5.4	10.7

NBA REGULAR-SEASON RECORD

RECORDS: Shares single-game record for most three-point field goals without a miss—8 (November 23, 1994, vs. Seattle).
HONORS: Long Distance Shootout winner (1998 and 2000).

Season Team	G	Min.	FGM	FGA	Pct.	FTM	FTA	Pct.	Off.	Def.	Tot.	Ast.	St.	Blk.	TO	Pts.	RPG	APG	PPG
86-87—Phoenix	80	1561	159	350	.454	94	121	.777	41	143	184	361	70	5	153	424	2.3	4.5	5.3
87-88—Phoenix	82	2243	306	605	.506	152	185	.822	71	191	262	540	107	10	156	781	3.2	6.6	9.5
88-89—Phoenix	78	2487	440	889	.495	147	178	.826	75	191	266	465	129	8	111	1054	3.4	6.0	13.5
89-90—Phoenix	67	2278	483	901	.536	173	202	.856	86	227	313	337	117	14	125	1179	4.7	5.0	17.6
90-91—Phoenix	80	2733	544	1051	.518	201	224	.897	74	247	321	409	111	16	130	1350	4.0	5.1	16.9
91-92—Phoenix	81	3078	635	1240	.512	279	315	.886	106	301	407	411	158	31	119	1632	5.0	5.1	20.1
92-93—Philadelphia	79	2860	582	1239	.470	250	289	.865	84	258	342	548	131	21	222	1511	4.3	6.9	19.1
93-94—Phil.-Utah	80	2820	472	1004	.470	260	296	.878	60	219	279	419	127	13	171	1274	3.5	5.2	15.9
94-95—Utah..............	81	2696	482	937	.514	284	322	.882	53	157	210	347	129	17	145	1337	2.6	4.3	16.5
95-96—Utah..............	82	2588	442	880	.502	259	290	.893	62	147	209	340	106	20	127	1247	2.5	4.1	15.2
96-97—Utah..............	82	2592	413	856	.482	293	326	.899	60	181	241	361	124	26	134	1191	2.9	4.4	14.5
97-98—Utah..............	80	2460	399	828	.482	285	322	.885	65	205	270	349	109	15	132	1139	3.4	4.4	14.2

Season Team	G	Min.	FGM	FGA	Pct.	FTM	FTA	Pct.	REBOUNDS Off.	Def.	Tot.	Ast.	St.	Blk.	TO	Pts.	AVERAGES RPG	APG	PPG
98-99—Utah	48	1435	214	449	.477	125	140	.893	33	127	160	192	52	14	82	587	3.3	4.0	12.2
99-00—Utah	77	2133	358	728	.492	171	180	*.950	49	133	182	202	66	16	113	953	2.4	2.6	12.4
Totals	1077	33964	5929	11957	.496	2973	3390	.877	919	2727	3646	5281	1536	226	1971	15659	3.4	4.9	14.5

Three-point field goals: 1986-87, 12-for-43 (.279). 1987-88, 17-for-58 (.293). 1988-89, 27-for-81 (.333). 1989-90, 40-for-98 (.408). 1990-91, 61-for-146 (.418). 1991-92, 83-for-189 (.439). 1992-93, 97-for-249 (.390). 1993-94, 70-for-208 (.337). 1994-95, 89-for-219 (.406). 1995-96, 104-for-223 (.466). 1996-97, 72-for-195 (.369). 1997-98, 56-for-127 (.441). 1998-99, 34-for-81 (.420). 1999-00, 66-for-138 (.478). Totals, 828-for-2055 (.403).

Personal fouls/disqualifications: 1986-87, 130/0. 1987-88, 151/0. 1988-89, 188/0. 1989-90, 144/2. 1990-91, 185/1. 1991-92, 218/1. 1992-93, 203/2. 1993-94, 186/0. 1994-95, 181/1. 1995-96, 171/1. 1996-97, 188/1. 1997-98, 175/1. 1998-99, 95/0. 1999-00, 149/1. Totals, 2364/11.

NBA PLAYOFF RECORD

Season Team	G	Min.	FGM	FGA	Pct.	FTM	FTA	Pct.	REBOUNDS Off.	Def.	Tot.	Ast.	St.	Blk.	TO	Pts.	AVERAGES RPG	APG	PPG
88-89—Phoenix	12	374	74	149	.497	21	25	.840	25	44	69	62	16	3	18	169	5.8	5.2	14.1
89-90—Phoenix	16	583	112	219	.511	68	73	.932	13	49	62	73	24	0	34	298	3.9	4.6	18.6
90-91—Phoenix	4	145	22	51	.431	26	28	.929	3	22	25	8	3	2	3	73	6.3	2.0	18.3
91-92—Phoenix	8	343	62	128	.484	31	34	.912	12	39	51	42	14	2	19	163	6.4	5.3	20.4
93-94—Utah	16	558	85	179	.475	62	68	.912	11	28	39	64	24	6	28	247	2.4	4.0	15.4
94-95—Utah	5	178	26	51	.510	11	14	.786	3	3	6	20	8	1	7	70	1.2	4.0	14.0
95-96—Utah	18	644	104	207	.502	73	82	.890	22	43	65	60	19	3	27	315	3.6	3.3	17.5
96-97—Utah	20	704	90	208	.433	92	105	.876	22	67	89	73	21	4	36	291	4.5	3.7	14.6
97-98—Utah	20	636	74	178	.416	55	65	.846	7	43	50	64	20	4	32	217	2.5	3.2	10.9
98-99—Utah	11	304	49	106	.462	29	33	.879	9	32	41	26	11	0	12	134	3.7	2.4	12.2
99-00—Utah	10	297	43	102	.422	20	24	.833	9	21	30	33	10	0	15	115	3.0	3.3	11.5
Totals	140	4766	741	1578	.470	488	551	.886	136	391	527	525	170	25	231	2092	3.8	3.8	14.9

Three-point field goals: 1988-89, 0-for-7. 1989-90, 6-for-24 (.250). 1990-91, 3-for-6 (.500). 1991-92, 8-for-17 (.471). 1993-94, 15-for-34 (.441). 1994-95, 7-for-13 (.538). 1995-96, 34-for-58 (.586). 1996-97, 19-for-53 (.358). 1997-98, 14-for-30 (.467). 1998-99, 7-for-18 (.389). 1999-00, 9-for-22 (.409). Totals, 122-for-282 (.433).

Personal fouls/disqualifications: 1988-89, 34/0. 1989-90, 43/1. 1990-91, 13/0. 1991-92, 23/0. 1993-94, 45/0. 1994-95, 19/1. 1995-96, 41/1. 1996-97, 53/1. 1997-98, 51/1. 1998-99, 34/1. 1999-00, 28/0. Totals, 384/6.

NBA ALL-STAR GAME RECORD

Season Team	Min.	FGM	FGA	Pct.	FTM	FTA	Pct.	REBOUNDS Off.	Def.	Tot.	Ast.	PF	Dq.	St.	Blk.	TO	Pts.
1992—Phoenix	24	5	7	.714	0	0	...	1	1	2	3	0	0	1	0	0	11
Totals	24	5	7	.714	0	0	...	1	1	2	3	0	0	1	0	0	11

Three-point field goals: 1992, 1-for-2 (.500). Totals, 1-for-2 (.500).

HOWELL, BAILEY   F

PERSONAL: Born January 20, 1937, in Middleton, Tenn. ... 6-7/220 (2,00/99,8). ... Full name: Bailey E. Howell.
HIGH SCHOOL: Middleton (Tenn.).
COLLEGE: Mississippi State.
TRANSACTIONS: Selected by Detroit Pistons in first round of 1959 NBA Draft. ... Traded by Pistons with C/F Bob Ferry, G Don Ohl, G Wali Jones and F Les Hunter to Baltimore Bullets for F/G Terry Dischinger, F Don Kojis and G Rod Thorn (June 18, 1964). ... Traded by Bullets to Boston Celtics for F/C Mel Counts (September 1, 1966). ... Selected by Buffalo Braves from Celtics in NBA Expansion Draft (May 11, 1970). ... Traded by Braves to Philadelphia 76ers for C Bob Kauffman and cash or future draft choice (May 11, 1970).
CAREER HONORS: Elected to Naismith Memorial Basketball Hall of Fame (1997).
MISCELLANEOUS: Member of NBA championship team (1968, 1969).

COLLEGIATE RECORD

NOTES: THE SPORTING NEWS All-America first team (1959). ... Led NCAA major college division with .568 field goal percentage (1957).

Season Team	G	Min.	FGM	FGA	Pct.	FTM	FTA	Pct.	Reb.	Ast.	Pts.	AVERAGES RPG	APG	PPG
55-56—Mississippi State‡						Freshman team statistics unavailable.								
56-57—Mississippi State	25	...	217	382	.568	213	285	.747	492	...	647	19.7	...	25.9
57-58—Mississippi State	25	...	226	439	.515	243	315	.771	406	...	695	16.2	...	27.8
58-59—Mississippi State	25	...	231	464	.498	226	292	.774	379	...	688	15.2	...	27.5
Varsity totals	75	...	674	1285	.525	682	892	.765	1277	...	2030	17.0	...	27.1

NBA REGULAR-SEASON RECORD

HONORS: All-NBA second team (1963).

Season Team	G	Min.	FGM	FGA	Pct.	FTM	FTA	Pct.	Reb.	Ast.	PF	Dq.	Pts.	AVERAGES RPG	APG	PPG
59-60—Detroit	75	2346	510	1119	.456	312	422	.739	790	63	282	13	1332	10.5	0.8	17.8
60-61—Detroit	77	2952	607	1293	.469	601	798	.753	1111	196	297	10	1815	14.4	2.5	23.6
61-62—Detroit	79	2857	553	1193	.464	470	612	.768	996	186	317	10	1576	12.6	2.4	19.9
62-63—Detroit	79	2971	637	1235	.516	519	650	.798	910	232	300	9	1793	11.5	2.9	22.7
63-64—Detroit	77	2700	598	1267	.472	470	581	.809	776	205	290	9	1666	10.1	2.7	21.6
64-65—Baltimore	80	2975	515	1040	.495	504	629	.801	869	208	*345	10	1534	10.9	2.6	19.2
65-66—Baltimore	78	2328	481	986	.488	402	551	.730	773	155	306	12	1364	9.9	2.0	17.5
66-67—Boston	81	2503	636	1242	.512	349	471	.741	677	103	296	4	1621	8.4	1.3	20.0
67-68—Boston	82	2801	643	1336	.481	335	461	.727	805	133	285	4	1621	9.8	1.6	19.8
68-69—Boston	78	2527	612	1257	.487	313	426	.735	685	137	285	3	1537	8.8	1.8	19.7
69-70—Boston	82	2078	399	931	.429	235	308	.763	550	120	261	4	1033	6.7	1.5	12.6
70-71—Philadelphia	82	1589	324	686	.472	230	315	.730	441	115	234	2	878	5.4	1.4	10.7
Totals	950	30627	6515	13585	.480	4740	6224	.762	9383	1853	3498	90	17770	9.9	2.0	18.7

NBA PLAYOFF RECORD

Season Team	G	Min.	FGM	FGA	Pct.	FTM	FTA	Pct.	Reb.	Ast.	PF	Dq.	Pts.	AVERAGES RPG	APG	PPG
59-60—Detroit	2	72	14	41	.341	6	8	.750	17	3	8	0	34	8.5	1.5	17.0
60-61—Detroit	5	144	20	57	.351	16	23	.696	46	22	22	1	56	9.2	4.4	11.2
61-62—Detroit	10	378	69	163	.423	62	75	.827	96	23	48	3	200	9.6	2.3	20.0
62-63—Detroit	4	163	24	64	.375	23	27	.852	42	11	19	1	71	10.5	2.8	17.8
64-65—Baltimore	9	350	67	130	.515	53	70	.757	105	19	38	3	187	11.7	2.1	20.8
65-66—Baltimore	3	94	23	50	.460	8	11	.727	30	2	13	1	54	10.0	0.7	18.0
66-67—Boston	9	241	59	122	.484	20	30	.667	66	5	35	2	138	7.3	0.6	15.3
67-68—Boston	19	597	135	264	.511	74	107	.692	146	22	84	6	344	7.7	1.2	18.1
68-69—Boston	18	551	112	229	.489	46	64	.719	118	19	84	3	270	6.6	1.1	15.0
70-71—Philadelphia	7	122	19	45	.422	9	18	.500	31	4	25	1	47	4.4	0.0	6.7
Totals	86	2712	542	1165	.465	317	433	.732	697	130	376	21	1401	8.1	1.5	16.3

NBA ALL-STAR GAME RECORD

Season Team	Min.	FGM	FGA	Pct.	FTM	FTA	Pct.	Reb	Ast.	PF	Dq.	Pts.
1961—Detroit	16	5	10	.500	3	4	.750	3	3	4	0	13
1962—Detroit	8	1	2	.500	0	0	...	0	1	1	0	2
1963—Detroit	11	2	3	.667	0	0	...	1	1	2	0	4
1964—Detroit	6	1	3	.333	0	0	...	2	0	0	0	2
1966—Baltimore	26	3	11	.273	1	2	.500	2	2	4	0	7
1967—Boston	14	1	4	.250	2	2	1.000	2	1	1	0	4
Totals	81	13	33	.394	6	8	.750	10	8	12	0	32

HUDSON, LOU   F/G

PERSONAL: Born July 11, 1944, in Greensboro, N.C. ... 6-5/210 (1,96/95,3). ... Full name: Louis Clyde Hudson. ... Nickname: Sweet Lou.
HIGH SCHOOL: Dudley Senior (Greensboro, N.C.).
COLLEGE: Minnesota.
TRANSACTIONS: Selected by St. Louis Hawks in first round (fourth pick overall) of 1966 NBA Draft. ... Hawks franchise moved from St. Louis to Atlanta for 1968-69 season. ... Traded by Hawks to Los Angeles Lakers for F Ollie Johnson (September 30, 1977).

COLLEGIATE RECORD

Season Team	G	Min.	FGM	FGA	Pct	FTM	FTA	Pct.	Reb.	Act.	Pts.	AVERAGES RPG	APG	PPG
62-63—Minnesota‡					Freshman team did not play intercollegiate schedule.									
63-64—Minnesota	24	...	191	435	.439	53	85	.624	191	...	435	8.0	...	18.1
64-65—Minnesota	24	...	231	463	.499	96	123	.780	247	...	558	10.3	...	23.3
65-66—Minnesota	17	...	143	303	.472	50	77	.649	138	...	336	8.1	...	19.8
Varsity totals	65	...	565	1201	.470	199	285	.698	576	...	1329	8.9	...	20.4

NBA REGULAR-SEASON RECORD

HONORS: All NBA second team (1970). ... NBA All-Rookie team (1967).

Season Team	G	Min.	FGM	FGA	Pct.	FTM	FTA	Pct.	Reb.	Ast.	PF	Dq.	Pts.	AVERAGES RPG	APG	PPG
66-67—St. Louis	80	2446	620	1328	.467	231	327	.706	435	95	277	3	1471	5.4	1.2	18.4
67-68—St. Louis	46	966	227	500	.454	120	164	.732	193	65	113	2	574	4.2	1.4	12.5
68-69—Atlanta	81	2869	716	1455	.492	338	435	.777	533	216	248	0	1770	6.6	2.7	21.9
69-70—Atlanta	80	3091	830	1564	.531	371	450	.824	373	276	225	1	2031	4.7	3.5	25.4
70-71—Atlanta	76	3113	829	1713	.484	381	502	.759	386	257	186	0	2039	5.1	3.4	26.8
71-72—Atlanta	77	3042	775	1540	.503	349	430	.812	385	309	225	0	1899	5.0	4.0	24.7
72-73—Atlanta	75	3027	816	1710	.477	397	481	.825	467	258	197	1	2029	6.2	3.4	27.1

Season Team	G	Min.	FGM	FGA	Pct.	FTM	FTA	Pct.	REBOUNDS Off.	Def.	Tot.	Ast.	St.	Blk.	TO	Pts.	AVERAGES RPG	APG	PPG
73-74—Atlanta	65	2588	678	1356	.500	295	353	.836	126	224	350	213	160	29	...	1651	5.4	3.3	25.4
74-75—Atlanta	11	380	97	225	.431	48	57	.842	14	33	47	40	13	2	...	242	4.3	3.6	22.0
75-76—Atlanta	81	2558	569	1205	.472	237	291	.814	104	196	300	214	124	17	...	1375	3.7	2.6	17.0
76-77—Atlanta	58	1745	413	905	.456	142	169	.840	48	81	129	155	67	19	...	968	2.2	2.7	16.7
77-78—Los Angeles	82	2283	493	992	.497	137	177	.774	80	108	188	193	94	14	150	1123	2.3	2.4	13.7
78-79—Los Angeles	78	1686	329	636	.517	110	124	.887	64	76	140	141	58	17	99	768	1.8	1.8	9.8
Totals	890	29794	7392	15129	.489	3156	3960	.797	...	...	3926	2432	516	98	249	17940	4.4	2.7	20.2

Personal fouls/disqualifications: 1973-74, 205/3. 1974-75, 33/1. 1975-76, 241/3. 1976-77, 160/2. 1977-78, 196/0. 1978-79, 133/1. Totals, 2439/17.

NBA PLAYOFF RECORD

Season Team	G	Min.	FGM	FGA	Pct.	FTM	FTA	Pct.	Reb.	Ast.	PF	Dq.	Pts.	AVERAGES RPG	APG	PPG
66-67—St. Louis	9	317	77	179	.430	49	68	.721	48	15	35	1	203	5.3	1.7	22.6
67-68—St. Louis	6	181	44	99	.444	42	47	.894	43	14	21	0	130	7.2	2.3	21.7
68-69—Atlanta	11	424	101	216	.468	40	52	.769	59	32	43	1	242	5.4	2.9	22.0
69-70—Atlanta	9	360	78	187	.417	41	50	.820	40	33	34	2	197	4.4	3.7	21.9
70-71—Atlanta	5	213	49	108	.454	29	39	.744	35	15	19	0	127	7.0	3.0	25.4
71-72—Atlanta	6	266	63	139	.453	24	29	.828	33	21	13	0	150	5.5	3.5	25.0
72-73—Atlanta	6	255	76	166	.458	26	29	.897	47	17	16	0	178	7.8	2.8	29.7

Season Team	G	Min.	FGM	FGA	Pct.	FTM	FTA	Pct.	REBOUNDS Off.	Def.	Tot.	Ast.	St.	Blk.	TO	Pts.	AVERAGES RPG	APG	PPG
77-78—Los Angeles	3	93	14	38	.368	7	8	.875	7	2	9	5	0	5	5	35	3.0	3.0	11.7
78-79—Los Angeles	6	90	17	32	.531	4	4	1.000	1	3	4	8	1	0	5	38	0.7	1.3	6.3
Totals	61	2199	519	1164	.446	262	326	.804	...	...	318	164	6	0	10	1300	5.2	2.7	21.3

Personal fouls/disqualifications: 1977-78, 9/0. 1978-79, 6/0. Totals, 196/4.

ALL-TIME GREAT PLAYERS

NBA ALL-STAR GAME RECORD

Season Team	Min.	FGM	FGA	Pct.	FTM	FTA	Pct.	Reb	Ast.	PF	Dq.	Pts.
1969—Atlanta	20	6	13	.462	1	1	1.000	1	1	0	0	13
1970—Atlanta	18	5	12	.417	5	5	1.000	1	0	1	0	15
1971—Atlanta	17	6	13	.462	2	3	.667	3	1	3	0	14
1972—Atlanta	18	2	7	.286	2	2	1.000	3	3	3	0	6
1973—Atlanta	9	2	8	.250	2	2	1.000	2	0	2	0	6

| | | | | | | | | REBOUNDS | | | | | | | | |
Season Team	Min.	FGM	FGA	Pct.	FTM	FTA	Pct.	Off.	Def.	Tot.	Ast.	PF	Dq.	St.	Blk.	TO	Pts.
1974—Atlanta	17	5	8	.625	2	2	1.000	1	2	3	1	2	0	0	1	...	12
Totals	99	26	61	.426	14	15	.933	...	...	13	6	11	0	0	1	...	66

ISSEL, DAN   F

PERSONAL: Born October 25, 1948, in Batavia, Ill. ... 6-9/240. (2,06/108,4). ... Full name: Daniel Paul Issel.
HIGH SCHOOL: Batavia (Ill.).
COLLEGE: Kentucky.
TRANSACTIONS: Selected by Detroit Pistons in eighth round (122nd pick overall) of 1970 NBA Draft. ... Selected by Kentucky Colonels in first round of 1970 ABA draft. ... Traded by Colonels to Baltimore Claws for C Tom Owens and cash (September 19, 1975). ... Traded by Claws to Denver Nuggets for C Dave Robisch and cash (October 8, 1975). ... Nuggets franchise became part of NBA for 1976-77 season.
CAREER HONORS: Elected to Naismith Memorial Basketball Hall of Fame (1993).
MISCELLANEOUS: Denver Nuggets franchise all-time leading rebounder with 6,630 (1976-77 through 1984-85).
CAREER NOTES: Vice president, Denver Nuggets (March 1998 to August 2001).

COLLEGIATE RECORD

NOTES: The Sporting News All-America first team (1970). ... The Sporting News All-America second team (1969).

| | | | | | | | | | | | AVERAGES | | |
Season Team	G	Min.	FGM	FGA	Pct.	FTM	FTA	Pct.	Reb.	Ast.	Pts.	RPG	APG	PPG
66-67—Kentucky‡	20	...	168	332	.506	80	111	.721	355	...	416	17.8	...	20.8
67-68—Kentucky	27	836	171	390	.438	102	154	.662	328	10	444	12.1	0.4	16.4
68-69—Kentucky	28	1063	285	534	.534	176	232	.759	381	49	746	13.6	1.8	26.6
69-70—Kentucky	28	1044	369	667	.553	210	275	.764	369	39	948	13.2	1.4	33.9
Varsity totals	83	2943	825	1591	.519	488	661	.738	1078	98	2138	13.0	1.2	25.8

ABA REGULAR-SEASON RECORD

NOTES: ABA co-Rookie of the Year (1971). ... ABA All-Star first team (1972). ... ABA All-Star second team (1971, 1973, 1974, 1976). ... ABA All-Rookie team (1971). ... Member of ABA championship team (1975). ... Holds single-season record for most points—2,538 (1972).

| | | | 2-POINT | | | 3-POINT | | | | | | | | AVERAGES | | |
Season Team	G	Min.	FGM	FGA	Pct.	FGM	FGA	Pct.	FTM	FTA	Pct.	Reb.	Ast.	Pts.	RPG	APG	PPG
70-71—Kentucky	83	3274	938	1989	.472	0	5	.000	604	748	.807	1093	162	*2480	13.2	2.0	*29.9
71-72—Kentucky	83	3570	969	1990	.487	3	11	.273	591	*753	.785	931	195	*2538	11.2	2.3	30.6
72-73—Kentucky	84	*3531	899	1742	.516	3	15	.200	485	635	.764	922	220	*2292	11.0	2.6	27.3
73-74—Kentucky	83	3347	826	1709	.483	3	17	.176	457	581	.787	847	137	2118	10.2	1.7	25.5
74-75—Kentucky	83	2864	614	1298	.473	0	5	.000	237	321	.738	710	188	1465	8.6	2.3	17.7
75-76—Denver	84	2858	751	1468	.512	1	4	.250	425	521	.816	923	201	1930	11.0	2.4	23.0
Totals	500	19444	4997	10196	.490	10	57	.175	2799	3559	.786	5426	1103	12823	10.9	2.2	25.6

ABA PLAYOFF RECORD

| | | | 2-POINT | | | 3-POINT | | | | | | | | AVERAGES | | |
Season Team	G	Min.	FGM	FGA	Pct.	FGM	FGA	Pct.	FTM	FTA	Pct.	Reb.	Ast.	Pts.	RPG	APG	PPG
70-71—Kentucky	19	670	207	408	.507	0	0	...	123	141	.872	221	28	536	11.6	1.5	28.2
71-72—Kentucky	6	269	47	113	.416	0	1	.000	38	50	.760	54	5	132	9.0	0.8	22.0
72-73—Kentucky	19	821	197	392	.503	1	6	.167	124	156	.795	225	28	521	11.8	1.5	27.4
73-74—Kentucky	8	311	60	135	.444	0	0	...	28	33	.848	87	14	148	10.9	1.8	18.5
74-75—Kentucky	15	578	122	261	.467	0	0	...	60	74	.811	119	29	304	7.9	1.9	20.3
75-76—Denver	13	470	111	226	.491	0	1	.000	44	56	.786	156	32	266	12.0	2.5	20.5
Totals	80	3119	744	1535	.485	1	8	.125	417	510	.818	862	136	1907	10.8	1.7	23.8

ABA ALL-STAR GAME RECORD

NOTES: ABA All-Star Game Most Valuable Player (1972).

| | | 2-POINT | | | 3-POINT | | | | | | | |
Season Team	Min.	FGM	FGA	Pct.	FGM	FGA	Pct.	FTM	FTA	Pct.	Reb.	Ast.	Pts.
1971—Kentucky	34	8	15	.533	0	0	...	5	8	.625	11	0	21
1972—Kentucky	23	9	13	.692	0	0	...	3	4	.750	9	5	21
1973—Kentucky	29	6	14	.429	0	0	...	2	2	1.000	7	4	14
1974—Kentucky	26	10	15	.667	0	0	...	1	1	1.000	4	1	21
1975—Kentucky	20	3	6	.500	0	0	...	1	2	.500	7	1	7
1976—Denver	31	6	16	.375	0	0	...	7	9	.778	9	5	19
Totals	163	42	79	.532	0	0	...	19	26	.731	47	16	103

NBA REGULAR-SEASON RECORD

HONORS: J. Walter Kennedy Citizenship Award (1985).

| | | | | | | | | | REBOUNDS | | | | | | | | AVERAGES | | |
Season Team	G	Min.	FGM	FGA	Pct.	FTM	FTA	Pct.	Off.	Def.	Tot.	Ast.	St.	Blk.	TO	Pts.	RPG	APG	PPG
76-77—Denver	79	2507	660	1282	.515	445	558	.798	211	485	696	177	91	29	...	1765	8.8	2.2	22.3
77-78—Denver	82	2851	659	1287	.512	428	547	.782	253	577	830	304	100	41	259	1746	10.1	3.7	21.3
78-79—Denver	81	2742	532	1030	.517	316	419	.754	240	498	738	255	61	46	171	1380	9.1	3.1	17.0
79-80—Denver	82	2938	715	1416	.505	517	667	.775	236	483	719	198	88	54	163	1951	8.8	2.4	23.8

Season Team	G	Min.	FGM	FGA	Pct.	FTM	FTA	Pct.	REBOUNDS Off.	Def.	Tot.	Ast.	St.	Blk.	TO	Pts.	AVERAGES RPG	APG	PPG
80-81—Denver	80	2641	614	1220	.503	519	684	.759	229	447	676	158	83	53	130	1749	8.5	2.0	21.9
81-82—Denver	81	2472	651	1236	.527	546	655	.834	174	434	608	179	67	55	169	1852	7.5	2.2	22.9
82-83—Denver	80	2431	661	1296	.510	400	479	.835	151	445	596	223	83	43	174	1726	7.5	2.8	21.6
83-84—Denver	76	2076	569	1153	.494	364	428	.850	112	401	513	173	60	44	122	1506	6.8	2.3	19.8
84-85—Denver	77	1684	363	791	.459	257	319	.806	80	251	331	137	65	31	93	984	4.3	1.8	12.8
Totals	718	22342	5424	10711	.506	3792	4756	.797	1686	4021	5707	1804	698	396	1281	14659	7.9	2.5	20.4

Three-point field goals: 1979-80, 4-for-12 (.333). 1980-81, 2-for-12 (.167). 1981-82, 4-for-6 (.667). 1982-83, 4-for-19 (.211). 1983-84, 4-for-19 (.211). 1984-85, 1-for-7 (.143). Totals, 19-for-75 (.253).

Personal fouls/disqualifications: 1976-77, 246/7. 1977-78, 279/5. 1978-79, 233/6. 1979-80, 190/1. 1980-81, 249/6. 1981-82, 245/4. 1982-83, 227/0. 1983-84, 182/2. 1984-85, 171/1. Totals, 2022/32.

NBA PLAYOFF RECORD

Season Team	G	Min.	FGM	FGA	Pct.	FTM	FTA	Pct.	REBOUNDS Off.	Def.	Tot.	Ast.	St.	Blk.	TO	Pts.	AVERAGES RPG	APG	PPG
76-77—Denver	6	222	49	96	.510	34	45	.756	18	40	58	17	5	4	...	132	9.7	2.8	22.0
77-78—Denver	13	460	103	212	.486	56	65	.862	41	93	134	53	7	3	39	262	10.3	4.1	20.2
78-79—Denver	3	109	24	45	.533	25	31	.806	7	21	28	10	0	0	9	73	9.3	3.3	24.3
81-82—Denver	3	103	32	60	.533	12	12	1.000	8	13	21	5	3	1	7	76	7.0	1.7	25.3
82-83—Denver	8	227	69	136	.507	25	29	.862	13	45	58	25	9	5	10	163	7.3	3.1	20.4
83-84—Denver	5	153	52	102	.510	32	39	.821	10	30	40	8	6	6	15	137	8.0	1.6	27.4
84-85—Denver	15	325	73	159	.459	39	48	.813	14	40	54	27	12	5	13	186	3.6	1.8	12.4
Totals	53	1599	402	810	.496	223	269	.829	111	282	393	145	42	24	93	1029	7.4	2.7	19.4

Three-point field goals: 1982-83, 0-for-1. 1983-84, 1-for-2 (.500). 1984-85, 1-for-1. Totals, 2-for-4 (.500).

Personal fouls/disqualifications: 1976-77, 20/0. 1977-78, 43/1. 1978-79, 15/0. 1981-82, 10/0. 1982-83, 18/0. 1983-84, 15/0. 1984-85, 36/0. Totals, 157/1.

NBA ALL-STAR GAME RECORD

Season Team	Min.	FGM	FGA	Pct.	FTM	FTA	Pct.	REBOUNDS Off.	Def.	Tot.	Ast.	PF	Dq.	St.	Blk.	TO	Pts.
1977—Denver	10	0	3	.000	0	0	...	1	0	1	0	0	0	0	0	...	0

COMBINED ABA AND NBA REGULAR-SEASON RECORDS

	G	Min.	FGM	FGA	Pct.	FTM	FTA	Pct.	REBOUNDS Off.	Def.	Tot.	Ast.	Stl.	Blk.	TO	Pts.	AVERAGES RPG	APG	PPG
Totals	1218	41786	10431	20964	.498	6591	8315	.793	...	...	11133	2907	...	...	...	27482	9.1	2.4	22.6

Three-point field goals: 29-for-132 (.220).
Personal fouls/disqualifications: 3504.

NBA COACHING RECORD

Season Team	REGULAR SEASON W	L	Pct.	Finish	PLAYOFFS W	L	Pct.
92-93—Denver	36	46	.439	4th/Midwest Division	—	—	—
93-94—Denver	42	40	.512	4th/Midwest Division	6	6	.500
94-95—Denver	18	16	.529		—	—	—
99-00—Denver	35	47	.427	5th/Midwest Division	—	—	—
00-01—Denver	40	42	.488	6th/Midwest Division	—	—	—
01-02—Denver	9	17	.346		—	—	—
Totals (6 years)	180	208	.464	Totals (1 year)	6	6	.500

NOTES:
1994—Defeated Seattle, 3-2, in Western Conference First Round; lost to Utah, 4-3, in Western Conference Semifinals.
1995—Resigned as Denver head coach (January 15); replaced by Gene Littles with club in fourth place.
2001—Resigned as head coach (December 26); replaced by Mike Evans with club in fifth place.

JACKSON, MARK   G

PERSONAL: Born April 1, 1965, in Brooklyn, N.Y. ... 6-3/205. (1,91/93,0). ... Full Name: Mark A. Jackson.
HIGH SCHOOL: Bishop Loughlin Memorial (Brooklyn, N.Y.).
COLLEGE: St. John's.
TRANSACTIONS/CAREER NOTES: Selected by New York Knicks in first round (18th pick overall) of 1987 NBA Draft. ... Traded by Knicks with 1995 second-round draft choice to Los Angeles Clippers in three-way deal in which Clippers also received C Stanley Roberts from Orlando Magic, Knicks received G Doc Rivers, F Charles Smith and G Bo Kimble from Clippers and Magic received 1993 first-round draft choice from Knicks and 1994 first-round draft choice from Clippers (September 22, 1992). ... Traded by Clippers with draft rights to G Greg Minor to Indiana Pacers for G Pooh Richardson, F Malik Sealy and draft rights to F Eric Piatkowski (June 30, 1994). ... Traded by Pacers with G Ricky Pierce and 1996 first-round draft choice to Denver Nuggets for G Jalen Rose, F Reggie Williams and 1996 first-round draft choice (June 13, 1996). ... Traded by Nuggets with F/C LaSalle Thompson to Pacers for G Vincent Askew, F Eddie Johnson and 1997 and 1998 second-round draft choices (February 20, 1997). ... Signed as free agent by Toronto Raptors (August 11, 2000). ... Traded by Raptors with G Muggsy Bogues to Knicks for G Chris Childs and 2001 first-round draft choice (February 22, 2001). ... Traded by Knicks with F/C Marcus Camby and draft rights to F/C Nene Hilario to Nuggets for F Antonio McDyess, draft rights to G Frank Williams and 2003 second-round draft choice (June 26, 2002). ... Waived by Nuggets (September 27, 2002). ... Signed as free agent by Utah Jazz (October 2, 2002). ... Signed as free agent by Houston Rockets (January 15, 2004).

COLLEGIATE RECORD

NOTES: THE SPORTING NEWS All-America second team (1987). ... Led NCAA Division I with 9.11 assists per game (1986).

Season Team	G	Min.	FGM	FGA	Pct.	FTM	FTA	Pct.	Reb.	Ast.	Pts.	AVERAGES RPG	APG	PPG
83-84—St. John's	30	855	61	106	.575	53	77	.688	59	108	175	2.0	3.6	5.8
84-85—St. John's	35	601	57	101	.564	66	91	.725	44	109	180	1.3	3.1	5.1
85-86—St. John's	36	1340	151	316	.478	105	142	.739	125	328	407	3.5	9.1	11.3
86-87—St. John's	30	1184	196	389	.504	125	155	.806	110	193	566	3.7	6.4	18.9
Totals	131	3980	465	912	.510	349	465	.751	338	738	1328	2.6	5.6	10.1

Three-point field goals: 1986-87, 49-for-117 (.419). .

NBA REGULAR-SEASON RECORD

RECORDS: Holds single-season record for most assists by a rookie—868 (1988).
HONORS: NBA Rookie of the Year (1988). … NBA All-Rookie team (1988).

Season Team	G	Min.	FGM	FGA	Pct.	FTM	FTA	Pct.	Off.	Def.	Tot.	Ast.	St.	Blk.	TO	Pts.	RPG	APG	PPG
87-88—New York	82	3249	438	1013	.432	206	266	.774	120	276	396	868	205	6	258	1114	4.8	10.6	13.6
88-89—New York	72	2477	479	1025	.467	180	258	.698	106	235	341	619	139	7	226	1219	4.7	8.6	16.9
89-90—New York	82	2428	327	749	.437	120	165	.727	106	212	318	604	109	4	211	809	3.9	7.4	9.9
90-91—New York	72	1595	250	508	.492	117	160	.731	62	135	197	452	60	9	135	630	2.7	6.3	8.8
91-92—New York	81	2461	367	747	.491	171	222	.770	95	210	305	694	112	13	211	916	3.8	8.6	11.3
92-93—L.A. Clippers	82	3117	459	945	.486	241	300	.803	129	259	388	724	136	12	220	1181	4.7	8.8	14.4
93-94—L.A. Clippers	79	2711	331	732	.452	167	211	.791	107	241	348	678	120	6	232	865	4.4	8.6	10.9
94-95—Indiana	82	2402	239	566	.422	119	153	.778	73	233	306	616	105	16	210	624	3.7	7.5	7.6
95-96—Indiana	81	2643	296	626	.473	150	191	.785	66	241	307	635	100	5	201	806	3.8	7.8	10.0
96-97—Den.-Indiana	82	3054	289	679	.426	168	213	.789	91	304	395	*935	97	12	274	812	4.8	*11.4	9.9
97-98—Indiana	82	2413	249	598	.416	137	180	.761	67	255	322	713	84	2	174	678	3.9	8.7	8.3
98-99—Indiana	49	1382	138	329	.419	65	79	.823	33	151	184	386	42	3	99	373	3.8	7.9	7.6
99-00—Indiana	81	2190	246	570	.432	79	98	.806	63	233	296	650	76	10	174	660	3.7	8.0	8.1
00-01—Toronto-N.Y.	*83	2588	244	583	.419	73	93	.785	63	242	305	661	84	7	175	631	3.7	8.0	7.6
01-02—New York	82	2367	260	592	.439	87	110	.791	56	253	309	605	74	1	150	686	3.8	7.4	8.4
02-03—Utah	82	1467	147	369	.398	61	80	.763	34	142	176	375	48	3	152	382	2.1	4.6	4.7
03-04—Houston	42	577	34	100	.340	28	39	.718	10	60	70	119	17	1	53	103	1.7	2.8	2.5
Totals	1296	39121	4793	10731	.447	2169	2818	.770	1281	3682	4963	10334	1608	117	3155	12489	3.8	8.0	9.6

Three-point field goals: 1987-88, 32-for-126 (.254). 1988-89, 81-for-240 (.338). 1989-90, 35-for-131 (.267). 1990-91, 13-for-51 (.255). 1991-92, 11-for-43 (.256). 1992-93, 22-for-82 (.268). 1993-94, 36-for-127 (.283). 1994-95, 27-for-87 (.310). 1995-96, 64-for-149 (.430). 1996-97, 66-for-178 (.371). 1997-98, 43-for-137 (.314). 1998-99, 32-for-103 (.311). 1999-00, 89-for-221 (.403). 2000-01, 70-for-207 (.338). 2001-02, 79-for-195 (.405). 2002-03, 27-for-95 (.284). 2003-04, 7-for-41 (.171). Totals, 734-for-2213 (.332).

Personal fouls/disqualifications: 1987-88, 244/2. 1988-89, 163/1. 1989-90, 121/0. 1990-91, 81/0. 1991-92, 153/0. 1992-93, 158/0. 1993-94, 115/0. 1994-95, 148/0. 1995-96, 153/0. 1996-97, 161/0. 1997-98, 132/0. 1998-99, 58/0. 1999-00, 111/0. 2000-01, 139/0. 2001-02, 162/0. 2002-03, 90/0. 2003-04, 41/0. Totals, 2230/3.

NBA PLAYOFF RECORD

Season Team	G	Min.	FGM	FGA	Pct.	FTM	FTA	Pct.	Off.	Def.	Tot.	Ast.	St.	Blk.	TO	Pts.	RPG	APG	PPG
87-88—New York	4	171	22	60	.367	8	11	.727	6	13	19	39	10	0	14	57	4.8	9.8	14.3
88-89—New York	9	336	51	100	.510	19	28	.679	7	24	31	91	10	3	28	132	3.4	10.1	14.7
89-90—New York	9	81	13	31	.419	8	11	.727	1	4	5	21	2	0	7	34	0.6	2.3	3.8
90-91—New York	3	36	1	3	.333	0	0	...	0	0	0	8	1	1	5	2	0.0	2.7	0.7
91-92—New York	12	368	37	92	.402	22	27	.815	12	15	27	86	10	0	30	100	2.3	7.2	8.3
92-93—L.A. Clippers	5	188	28	64	.438	19	22	.864	8	21	29	38	8	1	13	76	5.8	7.6	15.2
94-95—Indiana	17	553	59	130	.454	34	46	.739	27	62	89	121	15	0	41	168	5.2	7.1	9.9
95-96—Indiana	5	186	18	51	.353	13	17	.765	3	22	25	30	6	0	13	53	5.0	6.0	10.6
97-98—Indiana	16	494	53	127	.417	27	34	.794	18	55	73	133	23	0	47	147	4.6	8.3	9.2
98-99—Indiana	13	451	51	103	.495	30	42	.714	14	45	59	112	14	1	35	146	4.5	8.6	11.2
99-00—Indiana	23	634	69	176	.392	28	31	.903	12	74	86	178	19	2	43	187	3.7	7.7	8.1
00-01—New York	5	156	20	40	.500	3	5	1.000	3	23	26	26	8	0	10	45	5.2	5.2	9.0
02-03—Utah	5	83	15	30	.500	1	1	1.000	2	3	5	16	3	0	4	36	1.0	3.2	7.2
03-04—Houston	5	38	1	6	.167	0	0	...	0	3	3	5	2	0	2	2	0.6	1.0	0.4
Totals	131	3775	438	1013	.432	212	273	.777	113	364	477	904	131	8	292	1185	3.6	6.9	9.0

Three-point field goals: 1987-88, 5-for-12 (.417). 1988-89, 11-for-28 (.393). 1989-90, 0-for-2. 1991-92, 4-for-21 (.190). 1992-93, 1-for-2 (.500). 1994-95, 16-for-40 (.400). 1995-96, 4-for-18 (.222). 1997-98, 14-for-37 (.378). 1998-99, 14-for-34 (.412). 1999-00, 21-for-67 (.313). 2000-01, 2-for-8 (.250). 2002-03, 5-for-9 (.556). 2003-04, 0-for-3. Totals, 97-for-281 (.345).

Personal fouls/disqualifications: 1987-88, 13/0. 1988-89, 9/0. 1989-90, 5/0. 1990-91, 1/0. 1991-92, 26/0. 1992-93, 8/0. 1994-95, 34/0. 1997-98, 28/0. 1998-99, 32/0. 1999-00, 42/0. 2000-01, 6/0. 2002-03, 11/0. 2003-04, 1/0. Totals, 225/0.

NBA ALL-STAR GAME RECORD

Season Team	Min.	FGM	FGA	Pct.	FTM	FTA	Pct.	Off.	Def.	Tot.	Ast.	PF	Dq.	St.	Blk.	TO	Pts.
1989—New York	16	3	5	.600	2	4	.500	1	1	2	4	1	0	1	1	2	9

Three-point field goals: 1989, 1-for-1.

JEANNETTE, BUDDY   G

PERSONAL: Born September 15, 1917, in New Kensington, Pa. … Died March 11, 1998. … 5-11/175 (1,81/79,4). … Full name: Harry Edward Jeannette.
HIGH SCHOOL: New Kensington (Pa.).
COLLEGE: Washington & Jefferson (Pa.).
TRANSACTIONS: Warren Penns franchise transferred to Cleveland and renamed White Horses (February 10, 1939). … Played in New York-Penn League with Elmira in 1939 and New York State League with Saratoga in 1942.
CAREER HONORS: Elected to Naismith Memorial Basketball Basketball Hall of Fame (1994).
MISCELLANEOUS: Member of BAA championship team (1948). … Member of NBL championship team (1943, 1944, 1945).

COLLEGIATE RECORD

Season Team	G	Min.	FGM	FGA	Pct.	FTM	FTA	Pct.	Reb.	Ast.	Pts.	RPG	APG	PPG
34-35—Wash. & Jefferson	14	...	62	...	...	35	...	...	...	...	159	...	...	11.4
35-36—Wash. & Jefferson	20	...	92	...	...	42	...	...	...	...	226	...	...	11.3
36-37—Wash. & Jefferson	18	...	92	...	...	56	...	...	...	...	240	...	...	13.3
37-38—Wash. & Jefferson	20	...	...	...	...	...	...	...	...	...	240	...	...	12.0
Totals	72	...	...	...	...	...	...	...	...	...	865	...	...	12.0

NBL AND NBA REGULAR-SEASON RECORD

HONORS: All-BAA second team (1948). ... All-NBL first team (1941, 1944, 1945, 1946). ... All-NBL second team (1943).

Season Team	G	Min.	FGM	FGA	Pct.	FTM	FTA	Pct.	Reb.	Ast.	PF	Dq.	Pts.	RPG	APG	PPG
38-39—W-Cl (NBL)	26	...	54	...	...	65	...	...	...	...	57	...	173	...	...	6.7
39-40—Det. (NBL)	25	...	45	...	...	52	80	.650	...	...	62	...	142	...	...	5.7
40-41—Det. (NBL)	23	...	75	...	...	54	86	.628	...	...	56	...	204	...	...	8.9
42-43—Shb. (NBL)	4	...	24	...	...	14	17	.824	...	...	8	...	62	...	...	15.5
43-44—F.W. (NBL)	22	...	68	...	...	48	65	.738	...	...	46	...	184	...	...	8.4
44-45—F.W. (NBL)	27	...	85	...	...	82	111	*.739	...	...	67	...	252	...	...	9.3
45-46—F.W. (NBL)	34	...	99	...	...	105	136	.772	...	...	184	...	303	...	...	8.9
47-48—Baltimore (BAA)	46	...	150	430	.349	191	252	.758	...	70	147	...	491	...	1.5	10.7
48-49—Baltimore (BAA)	56	...	73	199	.367	167	213	.784	...	124	157	...	313	...	2.2	5.6
49-50—Baltimore	37	...	42	148	.284	109	133	.820	...	93	82	...	193	...	2.5	5.2
Totals	300	...	715	...	...	887	...	...	...	...	866	...	2317	...	...	7.7

NBL AND NBA PLAYOFF RECORD

Season Team	G	Min.	FGM	FGA	Pct.	FTM	FTA	Pct.	Reb.	Ast.	PF	Dq.	Pts.	RPG	APG	PPG
39-40—Det. (NBL)	3	...	6	...	...	8	...	...	...	...	...	...	20	...	...	6.7
40-41—Det. (NBL)	3	...	8	...	...	5	...	...	...	...	...	...	21	...	...	7.0
42-43—Shb. (NBL)	5	...	16	...	...	17	...	...	...	...	...	...	49	...	...	9.8
43-44—F.W. (NBL)	5	...	12	...	...	10	...	...	...	...	...	...	34	...	...	6.8
44-45—F.W. (NBL)	7	...	22	...	...	23	...	...	...	...	...	...	67	...	...	9.6
45-46—F.W. (NBL)	4	...	7	...	...	5	6	.833	...	...	...	...	19	...	...	4.8
47-48—Baltimore (BAA)	11	...	30	61	.492	37	42	.881	...	12	45	...	97	...	1.1	8.8
48-49—Baltimore (BAA)	3	...	2	13	.154	4	4	1.000	...	5	11	...	8	...	1.7	2.7
Totals	41	...	103	...	...	109	...	...	...	...	...	...	315	...	...	7.7

ABL REGULAR-SEASON RECORD

Season Team	G	Min.	FGM	FGA	Pct.	FTM	FTA	Pct.	Reb.	Ast.	Pts.	RPG	APG	PPG
46-47—Baltimore	29	...	113	...	...	118	...	...	...	...	344	...	...	11.9

HEAD COACHING RECORD

BACKGROUND: Player/head coach, Baltimore Bullets of ABL (1946-47). ... Assistant coach, Pittsburgh Condors of ABA (1970-71).

ABL COACHING RECORD

Season Team	W	L	Pct.	Finish	W	L	Pct.
		REGULAR SEASON			PLAYOFFS		
46-47—Baltimore	31	3	.912	1st/Southern Division	2	1	.667

COLLEGIATE COACHING RECORD

Season Team	W	L	Pct.
52-53—Georgetown	13	7	.650
53-54—Georgetown	11	10	.519
54-55—Georgetown	12	13	.480
55-56—Georgetown	13	11	.542
Totals (4 years)	49	49	.500

NBA COACHING RECORD

Season Team	W	L	Pct.	Finish	W	L	Pct.
	REGULAR SEASON				PLAYOFFS		
47-48—Baltimore (BAA)	28	20	.583	2nd/Western Division	9	3	.750
48-49—Baltimore (BAA)	29	31	.483	3rd/Eastern Division	1	2	.333
49-50—Baltimore	25	43	.368	5th/Eastern Division	—	—	—
50-51—Baltimore	14	23	.378		—	—	—
64-65—Baltimore	37	43	.463	3rd/Western Division	5	5	.500
66-67—Baltimore	3	13	.188		—	—	—
Totals (6 years)	136	173	.440	Totals (3 years)	15	10	.600

EBL COACHING RECORD

Season Team	W	L	Pct.	Finish	W	L	Pct.
	REGULAR SEASON				PLAYOFFS		
59-60—Baltimore	20	8	.714	2nd	2	2	.500
60-61—Baltimore	19	9	.679	1st	2	0	1.000
Totals (2 years)	39	17	.696	Totals (2 years)	4	2	.667

ABA COACHING RECORD

Season Team	W	L	Pct.	Finish	W	L	Pct.
	REGULAR SEASON				PLAYOFFS		
69-70—Pittsburgh	15	30	.333	5th/Eastern Division	—	—	—

NOTES:

1948—Defeated Chicago, 75-72, in Western Division tiebreaker; defeated New York, 2-1, in quarterfinals; defeated Chicago, 2-0, in semifinals; defeated Philadelphia, 4-2, in NBA Finals.

1949—Lost to New York in Eastern Division Semifinals.

1951—Replaced as Baltimore head coach by Walt Budko (January).

1960—Defeated Allentown, 103-89, in semifinal; lost to Easton, 2-1, in EBL Finals.

1961—Defeated Scranton, 132-107, in semifinal; defeated Allentown, 119-104, in EBL Final.

1965—Defeated St. Louis, 3-1, in Western Division Semifinals; lost to Los Angeles, 4-2, in Western Division Finals.

1966—Replaced Michael Farmer as Baltimore coach, with 1-8 record (November). Replaced as Baltimore coach by Gene Shue (December).

JOHNSON, DENNIS   G

PERSONAL: Born September 18, 1954, in San Pedro, Calif. ... 6-4/202 (1,93/91,6). ... Full name: Dennis Wayne Johnson. ... Nickname: D.J.
HIGH SCHOOL: Dominquez (Compton, Calif.).
JUNIOR COLLEGE: Los Angeles Harbor Junior College.
COLLEGE: Pepperdine.
TRANSACTIONS: Selected after junior season by Seattle SuperSonics in second round (29th pick overall) of 1976 NBA Draft. ... Traded by SuperSonics to Phoenix Suns for G Paul Westphal (June 4, 1980). ... Traded by Suns with 1983 first- and third-round draft choices to Boston Celtics for F/C Rick Robey and two 1983 second-round draft choices (June 27, 1983).
CAREER NOTES: Assistant coach, Boston Celtics (1993-94 through 1996-97). ... Head coach, La Crosse Catbirds of CBA (1999-February 3, 2000). ... Assistant coach, Los Angeles Clippers (February 4, 2000 to present). ... Replaced Alvin Gentry (March 3, 2003) as head coach of Clippers and compiled 8-16 record through end of season. ... Head coach of Florida Flame (2004-05) and Austin Toros (2005-06) of NBA Development League.
MISCELLANEOUS: Member of NBA championship team (1979, 1984, 1986).

COLLEGIATE RECORD

Season Team	G	Min.	FGM	FGA	Pct.	FTM	FTA	Pct.	Reb.	Ast.	Pts.	RPG	APG	PPG
73-74—Los Angeles Harbor J.C.	...	699	103	191	.539	45	82	.549	230	...	251	...	...	...
74-75—Los Angeles Harbor J.C.	28	967	...	...	...	...	...	...	336	...	511	12.0	...	18.3
75-76—Pepperdine	27	930	181	378	.479	63	112	.563	156	88	425	5.8	3.3	15.7
Junior college totals	...	1666							566	...	762	...	...	...
4-year-college totals	27	930	181	378	.479	63	112	.563	156	88	425	5.8	3.3	15.7

NBA REGULAR-SEASON RECORD

HONORS: All-NBA first team (1981). ... All-NBA second team (1980). ... NBA All-Defensive first team (1979, 1980, 1981, 1982, 1983, 1987). ... NBA All-Defensive second team (1984, 1985, 1986).

Season Team	G	Min.	FGM	FGA	Pct.	FTM	FTA	Pct.	Off.	Def.	Tot.	Ast.	St.	Blk.	TO	Pts.	RPG	APG	PPG
76-77—Seattle	81	1667	285	566	.504	179	287	.624	161	141	302	123	123	57	...	749	3.7	1.5	9.2
77-78—Seattle	81	2209	367	881	.417	297	406	.732	152	142	294	230	118	51	164	1031	3.6	2.8	12.7
78-79—Seattle	80	2717	482	1110	.434	306	392	.781	146	228	374	280	100	97	191	1270	4.7	3.5	15.9
79-80—Seattle	81	2937	574	1361	.422	380	487	.780	173	241	414	332	144	82	227	1540	5.1	4.1	19.0
80-81—Phoenix	79	2615	532	1220	.436	411	501	.820	160	203	363	291	136	61	208	1486	4.6	3.7	18.8
81-82—Phoenix	80	2937	577	1228	.470	399	495	.806	142	268	410	369	105	55	233	1561	5.1	4.6	19.5
82-83—Phoenix	77	2551	398	861	.462	292	369	.791	92	243	335	388	97	39	204	1093	4.4	5.0	14.2
83-84—Boston	80	2665	384	878	.437	281	330	.852	87	193	280	338	93	57	172	1053	3.5	4.2	13.2
84-85—Boston	80	2976	493	1066	.462	261	306	.853	91	226	317	543	96	39	212	1254	4.0	6.8	15.7
85-86—Boston	78	2732	482	1060	.455	243	297	.818	69	199	268	456	110	35	173	1213	3.4	5.8	15.6
86-87—Boston	79	2933	423	953	.444	209	251	.833	45	216	261	594	87	38	177	1062	3.3	7.5	13.4
87-88—Boston	77	2670	352	803	.438	255	298	.856	62	178	240	598	93	29	195	971	3.1	7.8	12.6
88-89—Boston	72	2309	277	638	.434	160	195	.821	31	159	190	472	94	21	175	721	2.6	6.6	10.0
89-90—Boston	75	2036	206	475	.434	118	140	.843	48	153	201	485	81	14	117	531	2.7	6.5	7.1
Totals	1100	35954	5832	13100	.445	3791	4754	.797	1459	2790	4249	5499	1477	675	2448	15535	3.9	5.0	14.1

Three-point field goals: 1976-77, 0-for-4. 1977-78, 12-for-58 (.207). 1980-81, 11-for-51 (.216). 1981-82, 8-for-42 (.190). 1982-83, 5-for-31 (.161). 1983-84, 4-for-32 (.125). 1984-85, 7-for-26 (.269). 1985-86, 6-for-42 (.143). 1986-87, 7-for-62 (.113). 1987-88, 12-for-46 (.261). 1988-89, 7-for-50 (.140). 1989-90, 1-for-24 (.042). Totals, 80-for-464 (.172).

Personal fouls/disqualifications: 1976-77, 221/3. 1977-78, 213/2. 1978-79, 209/2. 1979-80, 267/6. 1980-81, 244/2. 1981-82, 253/6. 1982-83, 204/1. 1983-84, 251/6. 1984-85, 224/2. 1985-86, 206/3. 1986-87, 201/0. 1987-88, 204/0. 1988-89, 211/3. 1989-90, 179/2. Totals, 3087/38.

NBA PLAYOFF RECORD

NOTES: NBA Finals Most Valuable Player (1979).

Season Team	G	Min.	FGM	FGA	Pct.	FTM	FTA	Pct.	Off.	Def.	Tot.	Ast.	St.	Blk.	TO	Pts.	RPG	APG	PPG
77-78—Seattle	22	827	121	294	.412	112	159	.704	47	54	101	72	23	23	56	354	4.6	3.3	16.1
78-79—Seattle	17	681	136	302	.450	84	109	.771	44	60	104	69	28	26	51	356	6.1	4.1	20.9
79-80—Seattle	15	582	100	244	.410	52	62	.839	25	39	64	57	27	10	43	257	4.3	3.8	17.1
80-81—Phoenix	7	267	52	110	.473	32	42	.762	7	26	33	20	9	9	19	137	4.7	2.9	19.6
81-82—Phoenix	7	271	63	132	.477	30	39	.769	13	18	31	32	15	4	25	156	4.4	4.6	22.3
82-83—Phoenix	3	108	22	48	.458	10	12	.833	6	17	23	17	5	2	8	54	7.7	5.7	18.0
83-84—Boston	22	808	129	319	.404	104	120	.867	30	49	79	97	25	7	53	365	3.6	4.4	16.6
84-85—Boston	21	848	142	319	.445	80	93	.860	24	60	84	154	31	9	72	364	4.0	7.3	17.3
85-86—Boston	18	715	109	245	.445	67	84	.798	23	53	76	107	39	5	51	291	4.2	5.9	16.2
86-87—Boston	23	964	168	361	.465	96	113	.850	24	67	91	205	16	8	44	435	4.0	8.9	18.9
87-88—Boston	17	702	91	210	.433	82	103	.796	15	62	77	139	24	8	45	270	4.5	8.2	15.9
88-89—Boston	3	59	4	15	.267	0	0	...	2	2	4	9	3	0	3	8	1.3	3.0	2.7
89-90—Boston	5	162	30	62	.484	7	7	1.000	2	12	14	28	2	2	10	69	2.8	5.6	13.8
Totals	180	6994	1167	2661	.439	756	943	.802	262	519	781	1006	247	113	480	3116	4.3	5.6	17.3

Three-point field goals: 1979-80, 5-for-15 (.333). 1980-81, 1-for-5 (.200). 1981-82, 0-for-4. 1982-83, 0-for-1. 1983-84, 3-for-7 (.429). 1984-85, 0-for-14. 1985-86, 6-for-16 (.375). 1986-87, 3-for-26 (.115). 1987-88, 6-for-16 (.375). 1989-90, 2-for-6 (.333). Totals, 26-for-110 (.236).

Personal fouls/disqualifications: 1977-78, 63/0. 1978-79, 63/0. 1979-80, 48/2. 1980-81, 18/0. 1981-82, 28/2. 1982-83, 9/0. 1983-84, 75/1. 1984-85, 66/0. 1985-86, 58/2. 1986-87, 71/0. 1987-88, 51/0. 1988-89, 8/0. 1989-90, 17/1. Totals, 575/8.

NBA ALL-STAR GAME RECORD

Season Team	Min.	FGM	FGA	Pct.	FTM	FTA	Pct.	Off.	Def.	Tot.	Ast.	PF	Dq.	St.	Blk.	TO	Pts.
1979—Seattle	27	5	7	.714	2	2	1.000	1	0	1	3	3	0	0	1	1	12
1980—Seattle	20	7	13	.538	5	6	.833	2	2	4	1	3	0	2	1	2	19
1981—Phoenix	24	5	8	.625	9	10	.900	1	1	2	1	1	0	3	1	2	19
1982—Phoenix	15	0	2	.000	1	2	.500	2	3	5	1	1	0	0	2	3	1
1985—Boston	12	3	7	.429	2	2	1.000	1	5	6	3	2	0	0	0	1	8
Totals	98	20	37	.541	19	22	.864	7	11	18	9	10	0	5	4	9	59

CBA COACHING RECORD

Season Team		REGULAR SEASON				PLAYOFFS		
	W	L	Pct.	Finish		W	L	Pct.
99-00—La Crosse	14	22	.389			—	—	—

NOTES:
2000—Named assistant coach by Los Angeles Clippers (February 4).

JOHNSON, EDDIE   G/F

PERSONAL: Born May 1, 1959, in Chicago. ... 6-7/215 (2,00/97,5). ... Full name: Edward Arnet Johnson.
HIGH SCHOOL: Westinghouse Vocational (Chicago).
COLLEGE: Illinois.
TRANSACTIONS/CAREER NOTES: Selected by Kansas City Kings in second round (29th pick overall) of 1981 NBA Draft. ... Kings franchise moved from Kansas City to Sacramento for 1985-86 season. ... Traded by Kings to Phoenix Suns for F Ed Pinckney and 1988 second-round draft choice (June 21, 1987). ... Traded by Suns with 1991 first-round draft choice and 1993 or 1994 first-round draft choice to Seattle SuperSonics for F Xavier McDaniel (December 7, 1990). ... Traded by SuperSonics with G Dana Barros and option to switch 1994 first-round draft choices to Charlotte Hornets for G Kendall Gill (September 1, 1993). ... Played in Greece (1994-95). ... Signed as free agent by Indiana Pacers (October 3, 1995). ... Traded by Pacers with G Vincent Askew and 1997 and 1998 second-round draft choices to Denver Nuggets for F/C LaSalle Thompson and G Mark Jackson (February 20, 1997). ... Waived by Nuggets (February 27, 1997). ... Signed by Houston Rockets for remainder of season (March 3, 1997).

COLLEGIATE RECORD

Season Team	G	Min.	FGM	FGA	Pct.	FTM	FTA	Pct.	Reb.	Ast.	Pts.	AVERAGES		
												RPG	APG	PPG
77-78—Illinois	27	469	100	234	.427	20	27	.741	84	16	220	3.1	0.6	8.1
78-79—Illinois	30	786	168	405	.415	26	49	.531	170	52	362	5.7	1.7	12.1
79-80—Illinois	35	1215	266	576	.462	78	119	.655	310	71	610	8.9	2.0	17.4
80-81—Illinois	29	1009	219	443	.494	62	82	.756	267	70	500	9.2	2.4	17.2
Totals	121	3479	753	1658	.454	186	277	.671	831	209	1692	6.9	1.7	14.0

HONORS: NBA Sixth Man Award (1989).

NBA REGULAR-SEASON RECORD

Season Team	G	Min.	FGM	FGA	Pct.	FTM	FTA	Pct.	REBOUNDS			Ast.	St.	Blk.	TO	Pts.	AVERAGES		
									Off.	Def.	Tot.						RPG	APG	PPG
81-82—Kansas City.....	74	1517	295	643	.459	99	149	.664	128	194	322	109	50	14	97	690	4.4	1.5	9.3
82-83—Kansas City.....	82	2933	677	1370	.494	247	317	.779	191	310	501	216	70	20	181	1621	6.1	2.6	19.8
83-84—Kansas City.....	82	2920	753	1552	.485	268	331	.810	165	290	455	296	76	21	213	1794	5.5	3.6	21.9
84-85—Kansas City.....	82	3029	769	1565	.491	325	373	.871	151	256	407	273	83	22	225	1876	5.0	3.3	22.9
85-86—Sacramento	82	2514	623	1311	.475	280	343	.816	173	246	419	214	54	17	191	1530	5.1	2.6	18.7
86-87—Sacramento	81	2457	606	1309	.463	267	322	.829	146	207	353	251	42	19	163	1516	4.4	3.1	18.7
87-88—Phoenix	73	2177	533	1110	.480	204	240	.850	121	197	318	180	33	9	139	1294	4.4	2.5	17.7
88-89—Phoenix	70	2043	608	1224	.497	217	250	.868	91	215	306	162	47	7	122	1504	4.4	2.3	21.5
89-90—Phoenix	64	1811	411	907	.453	188	205	.917	69	177	246	107	32	10	108	1080	3.8	1.7	16.9
90-91—Phx.-Seattle	81	2085	504	1127	.447	190	217	.001	107	164	271	111	60	5	122	1334	3.3	1.4	16.7
91-92—Seattle	81	2366	534	1164	.459	291	338	.861	118	174	292	161	55	11	130	1386	3.6	2.0	17.1
92-93—Seattle	82	1869	463	991	.467	234	257	.911	124	148	272	135	36	4	134	1177	3.3	1.6	14.4
93-94—Charlotte	73	1460	339	738	.459	99	127	.780	80	144	224	125	36	8	84	836	3.1	1.7	11.5
95-96—Indiana...........	62	1002	180	436	.413	70	79	.886	45	108	153	69	20	4	56	475	2.5	1.1	7.7
96-97—Ind.-Hou.........	52	913	160	362	.442	55	68	.809	27	111	138	52	15	2	47	424	2.7	1.0	8.2
97-98—Houston........	75	1490	227	544	.417	113	136	.831	50	103	153	88	32	3	62	633	2.0	1.2	8.4
98-99—Houston.........	3	18	6	13	.462	0	...	...	0	2	2	1	0	0	2	12	0.7	0.3	4.0
Totals	1199	32604	7727	16361	.472	3186	3792	.840	1786	3046	4832	2550	739	160	2076	19202	4.0	2.1	16.0

Three-point field goals: 1981-82, 1-for-11 (.091). 1982-83, 20-for-71 (.282). 1983-84, 20-for-64 (.313). 1984-85, 13-for-54 (.241). 1985-86, 4-for-20 (.200). 1986-87, 37-for-118 (.314). 1987-88, 24-for-94 (.255). 1988-89, 71-for-172 (.413). 1989-90, 70-for-184 (.380). 1990-91, 39-for-120 (.325). 1991-92, 27-for-107 (.252). 1992-93, 17-for-56 (.304). 1993-94, 59-for-150 (.393). 1995-96, 45-for-128 (.352). 1996-97, 49-for-131 (.374). 1997-98, 66-for-198 (.333). 1998-99, 0-for-1. Totals, 562-for-1679 (.335).

Personal fouls/disqualifications: 1981-82, 210/6. 1982-83, 259/3. 1983-84, 266/4. 1984-85, 237/2. 1985-86, 237/0. 1986-87, 218/4. 1987-88, 190/0. 1988-89, 198/0. 1989-90, 174/4. 1990-91, 181/0. 1991-92, 199/0. 1992-93, 173/0. 1993-94, 143/2. 1995-96, 104/1. 1996-97, 81/0. 1997-98, 89/0. 1998-99, 3/0. Totals, 2962/26.

NBA PLAYOFF RECORD

Season Team	G	Min.	FGM	FGA	Pct.	FTM	FTA	Pct.	REBOUNDS			Ast.	St.	Blk.	TO	Pts.	AVERAGES		
									Off.	Def.	Tot.						RPG	APG	PPG
83-84—Kansas City.....	3	107	21	48	.438	7	7	1.000	4	6	10	12	3	1	2	51	3.3	4.0	17.0
85-86—Sacramento	3	96	24	55	.436	8	9	.889	10	11	21	4	3	1	6	56	7.0	1.3	18.7
88-89—Phoenix	12	392	85	206	.413	30	39	.769	28	59	87	25	12	2	18	213	7.3	2.1	17.8
89-90—Phoenix	16	337	72	160	.450	37	47	.787	15	42	57	17	10	4	20	196	3.6	1.1	12.3
90-91—Seattle	5	171	46	89	.517	24	29	.828	12	9	21	7	7	1	8	120	4.2	1.4	24.0
91-92—Seattle	9	247	65	137	.474	32	34	.941	8	19	27	8	3	3	15	166	3.0	0.9	18.4
92-93—Seattle	19	382	82	210	.390	29	31	.935	17	28	45	17	3	1	19	205	2.4	0.9	10.8
95-96—Indiana...........	1	9	0	5	.000	0	0	...	0	0	0	1	0	0	0	0	0.0	1.0	0.0
96-97—Houston.........	16	284	48	117	.410	23	24	.958	15	21	36	10	5	0	7	133	2.3	0.6	8.3
97-98—Houston.........	5	89	9	27	.333	7	8	.875	4	4	8	1	0	0	3	28	1.6	0.2	5.6
Totals	89	2114	452	1054	.429	197	228	.864	113	199	312	102	46	13	98	1168	3.5	1.1	13.1

Three-point field goals: 1983-84, 2-for-5 (.400). 1985-86, 0-for-3. 1988-89, 13-for-38 (.342). 1989-90, 15-for-38 (.395). 1990-91, 4-for-15 (.267). 1991-92, 4-for-22 (.182). 1992-93, 12-for-36 (.333). 1995-96, 0-for-2. 1996-97, 14-for-47 (.298). 1997-98, 3-for-10 (.300). Totals, 67-for-216 (.310).

Personal fouls/disqualifications: 1983-84, 8/0. 1985-86, 7/0. 1988-89, 41/1. 1989-90, 40/0. 1990-91, 13/0. 1991-92, 19/0. 1992-93, 44/2. 1996-97, 17/0. 1997-98, 10/0. Totals, 199/3.

GREEK LEAGUE RECORD

Season Team	G	Min.	FGM	FGA	Pct.	FTM	FTA	Pct.	Reb.	Ast.	Pts.	AVERAGES		
												RPG	APG	PPG
94-95—Olympiakos S.F.P.	25	829	188	419	.449	92	109	.844	122	48	527	4.9	1.9	21.1

ALL-TIME GREAT PLAYERS

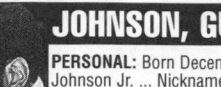

JOHNSON, GUS   F

PERSONAL: Born December 13, 1938, in Akron, Ohio. ... Died April 29, 1987. ... 6-6/235 (1,98/106,6). ... Full name: Gus Johnson Jr. ... Nickname: Honeycomb.
HIGH SCHOOL: Central Hower (Akron, Ohio).
JUNIOR COLLEGE: Boise (Idaho) Junior College.
COLLEGE: Akron, then Idaho.
TRANSACTIONS: Selected by Baltimore Bullets in second round (11th pick overall) of 1963 NBA Draft. ... Traded by Bullets to Phoenix Suns for second-round draft choice (April 10, 1972). ... Waived by Suns (December 1, 1972). ... Signed as free agent by Indiana Pacers of American Basketball Association (December 15, 1972).

COLLEGIATE RECORD

NOTES: Left Akron before start of 1959-60 basketball season.

Season Team	G	Min.	FGM	FGA	Pct.	FTM	FTA	Pct.	Reb.	Ast.	Pts.	RPG	APG	PPG
62-63—Idaho	23	...	188	438	.429	62	105	.590	466	...	438	20.3	...	19.0

NBA REGULAR-SEASON RECORD

HONORS: All-NBA second team (1965, 1966, 1970, 1971). ... NBA All-Defensive first team (1970, 1971). ... NBA All-Rookie team (1964).

Season Team	G	Min.	FGM	FGA	Pct.	FTM	FTA	Pct.	Reb.	Ast.	PF	Dq.	Pts.	RPG	APG	PPG
63-64—Baltimore	78	2847	571	1329	.430	210	319	.658	1064	169	321	†11	1352	13.6	2.2	17.3
64-65—Baltimore	76	2899	577	1379	.418	261	386	.676	988	270	258	4	1415	13.0	3.6	18.6
65-66—Baltimore	41	1284	273	661	.413	131	178	.736	546	114	136	3	677	13.3	2.8	16.5
66-67—Baltimore	73	2626	620	1377	.450	271	383	.708	855	194	281	7	1511	11.7	2.7	20.7
67-68—Baltimore	60	2271	482	1033	.467	180	270	.667	782	159	223	7	1144	13.0	2.7	19.1
68-69—Baltimore	49	1671	359	782	.459	160	223	.717	568	97	176	1	878	11.6	2.0	17.9
69-70—Baltimore	78	2919	578	1282	.451	197	272	.724	1086	264	269	6	1353	13.9	3.4	17.3
70-71—Baltimore	66	2538	494	1090	.453	214	290	.738	1128	192	227	4	1202	17.1	2.9	18.2
71-72—Baltimore	39	668	103	269	.383	43	63	.683	226	51	91	0	249	5.8	1.3	6.4
72-73—Phoenix	21	417	69	181	.381	25	36	.694	136	31	55	0	163	6.5	1.5	7.8
Totals	581	20140	4126	9383	.440	1692	2420	.699	7379	1541	2037	43	9944	12.7	2.7	17.1

NBA PLAYOFF RECORD

Season Team	G	Min.	FGM	FGA	Pct.	FTM	FTA	Pct.	Reb.	Ast.	PF	Dq.	Pts.	RPG	APG	PPG
64-65—Baltimore	10	377	62	173	.358	34	46	.739	111	34	38	1	158	11.1	3.4	15.8
65-66—Baltimore	1	8	1	4	.250	0	0	...	0	0	1	0	2	0.0	0.0	2.0
69-70—Baltimore	7	298	51	111	.459	27	34	.794	80	9	20	0	129	11.4	1.3	18.4
70-71—Baltimore	11	365	54	128	.422	35	47	.745	114	30	34	0	143	10.4	2.7	13.0
71-72—Baltimore	5	77	9	30	.300	2	2	1.000	25	3	17	0	20	5.0	0.6	4.0
Totals	34	1125	177	446	.397	98	129	.760	330	76	110	1	452	9.7	2.2	13.3

NBA ALL-STAR GAME RECORD

Season Team	Min.	FGM	FGA	Pct.	FTM	FTA	Pct.	Reb	Ast.	PF	Dq.	Pts.
1965—Baltimore	25	7	13	.538	11	13	.846	8	2	2	0	25
1968—Baltimore	16	3	9	.333	1	2	.500	6	1	2	0	7
1969—Baltimore	18	4	10	.400	5	8	.625	10	0	3	0	13
1970—Baltimore	17	5	12	.417	0	0	...	7	1	2	0	10
1971—Baltimore	23	5	12	.417	2	2	1.000	4	2	3	0	12
Totals	99	24	56	.429	19	25	.760	35	6	12	0	67

ABA REGULAR-SEASON RECORD

NOTES: Member of ABA championship team (1973).

Season Team	G	Min.	2-POINT FGM	FGA	Pct.	3-POINT FGM	FGA	Pct.	FTM	FTA	Pct.	Reb.	Ast.	Pts.	RPG	APG	PPG
72-73—Indiana	50	753	128	278	.460	4	21	.190	31	42	.738	245	62	299	4.9	1.2	6.0

ABA PLAYOFF RECORD

Season Team	G	Min.	2-POINT FGM	FGA	Pct.	3-POINT FGM	FGA	Pct.	FTM	FTA	Pct.	Reb.	Ast.	Pts.	RPG	APG	PPG
72-73—Indiana	17	184	15	56	.268	0	3	.000	12	16	.750	69	15	42	4.1	0.9	2.5

COMBINED ABA AND NBA REGULAR-SEASON RECORDS

	G	Min.	FGM	FGA	Pct.	FTM	FTA	Pct.	REBOUNDS Off.	Def.	Tot.	Ast.	Stl.	Blk.	TO	Pts.	RPG	APG	PPG
Totals	631	20893	4258	9682	.440	1723	2462	.700	...	...	7624	1603	...	...	...	10243	12.1	2.5	16.2

Three-point field goals: 4-for-21 (.190).
Personal fouls/disqualifications: 2150.

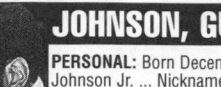

JOHNSON, KEVIN   G

PERSONAL: Born March 4, 1966, in Sacramento. ... 6-1/190. (1,85/86). ... Full Name: Kevin Maurice Johnson. ... Nickname: K.J.
HIGH SCHOOL: Sacramento.
COLLEGE: California.
TRANSACTIONS/CAREER NOTES: Selected by Cleveland Cavaliers in first round (seventh pick overall) of 1987 NBA Draft. ... Traded by Cavaliers with G/F Tyrone Corbin, F/C Mark West, 1988 first- and second-round draft choices and 1989 second-round draft choice to Phoenix Suns for F Larry Nance, F Mike Sanders and 1988 second-round draft choice (February 25, 1988). ... Announced retire-

ment (October 12, 1999). ... Activated from retirement (March 25, 2000). ... Announced retirement (August 8, 2000).
MISCELLANEOUS: Member of gold-medal winning U.S. World Championship team (1994). ... Phoenix Suns all-time assists leader with 6,518 (1987-88 through 1997-98 and 1999-2000).

COLLEGIATE RECORD

Season Team	G	Min.	FGM	FGA	Pct.	FTM	FTA	Pct.	Reb.	Ast.	Pts.	AVERAGES RPG	APG	PPG
83-84—California	28	773	98	192	.510	75	104	.721	83	65	271	3.0	2.3	9.7
84-85—California	27	902	127	282	.450	94	142	.662	104	111	348	3.9	4.1	12.9
85-86—California	29	1024	164	335	.490	123	151	.815	104	175	451	3.6	6.0	15.6
86-87—California	34	1115	212	450	.471	113	138	.819	132	170	585	3.9	5.0	17.2
Totals	118	3814	601	1259	.477	405	535	.757	423	521	1655	3.6	4.4	14.0

Three-point field goals: 1986-87, 48-for-124 (.387).

NBA REGULAR-SEASON RECORD

HONORS: NBA Most Improved Player (1989). ... All-NBA second team (1989, 1990, 1991, 1994). ... All-NBA third team (1992).

Season Team	G	Min.	FGM	FGA	Pct.	FTM	FTA	Pct.	REBOUNDS Off.	Def.	Tot.	Ast.	St.	Blk.	TO	Pts.	AVERAGES RPG	APG	PPG
87-88—Cle.-Phoenix	80	1917	275	596	.461	177	211	.839	36	155	191	437	103	24	146	732	2.4	5.5	9.2
88-89—Phoenix	81	3179	570	1128	.505	508	576	.882	46	294	340	991	135	24	&322	1650	4.2	12.2	20.4
89-90—Phoenix	74	2782	578	1159	.499	501	598	.838	42	228	270	846	95	14	263	1665	3.6	11.4	22.5
90-91—Phoenix	77	2772	591	1145	.516	519	616	.843	54	217	271	781	163	11	269	1710	3.5	10.1	22.2
91-92—Phoenix	78	2899	539	1125	.479	448	555	.807	61	231	292	836	116	23	272	1536	3.7	10.7	19.7
92-93—Phoenix	49	1643	282	565	.499	226	276	.819	30	74	104	384	85	19	151	791	2.1	7.8	16.1
93-94—Phoenix	67	2449	477	980	.487	380	464	.819	55	112	167	637	125	10	235	1340	2.5	9.5	20.0
94-95—Phoenix	47	1352	246	523	.470	234	289	.810	32	83	115	360	47	18	105	730	2.4	7.7	15.5
95-96—Phoenix	56	2007	342	674	.507	342	398	.859	42	179	221	517	82	13	170	1047	3.9	9.2	18.7
96-97—Phoenix	70	2658	441	890	.496	439	515	.852	54	199	253	653	102	12	217	1410	3.6	9.3	20.1
97-98—Phoenix	50	1290	155	347	.447	162	186	.871	35	129	164	245	27	8	101	476	3.3	4.9	9.5
99-00—Phoenix	6	113	16	28	.571	7	7	1.000	0	16	16	24	2	0	7	40	2.7	4.0	6.7
Totals	735	25061	4512	9160	.493	3943	4691	.841	487	1917	2404	6711	1082	176	2258	13127	3.3	9.1	17.9

Three-point field goals: 1987-88, 5-for-24 (.208). 1988-89, 2-for-22 (.091). 1989-90, 8-for-41 (.195). 1990-91, 9-for-44 (.205). 1991-92, 10-for-46 (.217). 1992-93, 1-for-8 (.125). 1993-94, 6-for-27 (.222). 1994-95, 4-for-26 (.154). 1995-96, 21-for-57 (.368). 1996-97, 89-for-202 (.441). 1997-98, 4-for-26 (.154). 1999-00, 1-for-1. Totals, 160-for-524 (.305).

Personal fouls/disqualifications: 1987-88, 155/1. 1988-89, 226/1. 1989-90, 143/0. 1990-91, 174/0. 1991-92, 180/1. 1992-93, 100/0. 1993-94, 127/1. 1994-95, 88/0. 1995-96, 144/0. 1996-97, 141/0. 1997-98, 57/0. 1999-00, 6/0. Totals, 1541/3.

NBA PLAYOFF RECORD

NOTES: Holds NBA Finals single-game record for most minutes played—62 (June 13, 1993, at Chicago, 3 OT).

Season Team	G	Min.	FGM	FGA	Pct.	FTM	FTA	Pct.	REBOUNDS Off.	Def.	Tot.	Ast.	St.	Blk.	TO	Pts.	AVERAGES RPG	APG	PPG
88-89—Phoenix	12	494	90	182	.495	102	110	.927	12	39	51	147	19	5	55	285	4.3	12.3	23.8
89-90—Phoenix	16	582	123	257	.479	92	112	.821	9	44	53	170	25	0	62	340	3.3	10.6	21.3
90-91—Phoenix	4	146	16	53	.302	18	30	.600	2	11	13	00	0	1	1?	?1	?	?	?
91-92—Phoenix	8	300	62	128	.484	62	72	.861	8	25	33	93	12	2	25	189	4.1	11.6	23.6
92-93—Phoenix	23	914	143	298	.480	124	156	.795	10	52	62	182	35	13	84	410	2.7	7.9	17.8
93-94—Phoenix	10	427	97	212	.458	69	81	.852	10	25	35	96	10	1	34	266	3.5	9.6	26.6
94-95—Phoenix	10	371	86	150	.573	71	84	.845	7	34	41	93	9	4	34	248	4.1	9.3	24.8
95-96—Phoenix	4	151	27	57	.474	14	17	.824	2	15	17	43	2	2	11	69	4.3	10.8	17.3
96-97—Phoenix	5	208	26	88	.295	29	33	.879	8	14	22	30	13	0	18	84	4.4	6.0	16.8
97-98—Phoenix	4	122	23	42	.548	8	12	.667	2	7	9	19	2	1	6	55	2.3	4.8	13.8
99-00—Phoenix	9	129	12	37	.324	5	6	.833	0	13	13	23	3	1	13	29	1.4	2.6	3.2
Totals	105	3879	705	1504	.469	594	713	.833	70	279	349	935	132	30	354	2026	3.3	8.9	19.3

Three-point field goals: 1988-89, 3-for-10 (.300). 1989-90, 2-for-11 (.182). 1990-91, 1-for-7 (.143). 1991-92, 3-for-6 (.500). 1992-93, 0-for-3. 1993-94, 3-for-10 (.300). 1994-95, 5-for-10 (.500). 1995-96, 1-for-4 (.250). 1996-97, 3-for-22 (.136). 1997-98, 1-for-4 (.250). 1999-00, 0-for-3. Totals, 22-for-90 (.244).

Personal fouls/disqualifications: 1988-89, 28/0. 1989-90, 28/0. 1990-91, 9/0. 1991-92, 24/1. 1992-93, 57/1. 1993-94, 23/0. 1994-95, 25/0. 1995-96, 8/0. 1996-97, 15/1. 1997-98, 6/0. 1999-00, 10/0. Totals, 233/3.

NBA ALL-STAR GAME RECORD

Season Team	Min.	FGM	FGA	Pct.	FTM	FTA	Pct.	REBOUNDS Off.	Def.	Tot.	Ast.	PF	Dq.	St.	Blk.	TO	Pts.
1990—Phoenix	14	1	1	1.000	0	0	...	0	0	0	4	2	0	0	0	3	2
1991—Phoenix	23	2	5	.400	1	2	.500	1	1	2	7	2	0	3	1	3	5
1994—Phoenix	14	3	6	.500	0	1	.000	0	1	1	2	1	0	1	0	2	6
Totals	51	6	12	.500	1	3	.333	1	2	3	13	5	0	4	1	8	13

JOHNSON, MAGIC   G

PERSONAL: Born August 14, 1959, in Lansing, Mich. ... 6-9/225 (2,05/102,1). ... Full name: Earvin Johnson Jr.
HIGH SCHOOL: Everett (Lansing, Mich.).
COLLEGE: Michigan State.
TRANSACTIONS: Selected after sophomore season by Los Angeles Lakers in first round (first pick overall) of 1979 NBA Draft. ... On voluntarily retired list (November 7, 1991-January 29, 1996). ... Activated from retirement by Lakers (January 29, 1996). ... Announced retirement (May 14, 1996). ... Rights renounced by Lakers (July 16, 1996).
CAREER NOTES: Broadcaster, NBC Sports (1992-1994). ... Vice president, Los Angeles Lakers (1994-95 to present). ... Analyst, Turner Sports.
CAREER HONORS: One of the 50 Greatest Players in NBA History (1996). ... Selected to Naismith Basketball Hall of Fame (2002).
MISCELLANEOUS: Member of NBA championship team (1980, 1982, 1985, 1987, 1988). ... Member of gold-medal-winning U.S. Olympic team (1992). ... Los Angeles Lakers franchise all-time assists leader with 10,141 and all-time steals leader with 1,724 (1979-80 through 1990-91 and 1995-96).

COLLEGIATE RECORD

NOTES: Member of NCAA championship team (1979). ... NCAA Division I Tournament Most Outstanding Player (1979). ... THE SPORTING NEWS All-America first team (1979).

Season Team	G	Min.	FGM	FGA	Pct.	FTM	FTA	Pct.	Reb.	Ast.	Pts.	AVERAGES		
												RPG	APG	PPG
77-78—Michigan State	30	...	175	382	.458	161	205	.785	237	222	511	7.9	7.4	17.0
78-79—Michigan State	32	1159	173	370	.468	202	240	.842	234	269	548	7.3	8.4	17.1
Totals	62	...	348	752	.463	363	445	.816	471	491	1059	7.6	7.9	17.1

NBA REGULAR-SEASON RECORD

RECORDS: Holds career record for highest assists-per-game average—11.2. ... Shares career record for most consecutive seasons leading league in steals—2.

HONORS: NBA Most Valuable Player (1987, 1989, 1990). ... IBM Award, for all-around contributions to team's success (1984). ... All-NBA first team (1983, 1984, 1985, 1986, 1987, 1988, 1989, 1990, 1991). ... All-NBA second team (1982). ... NBA All-Rookie team (1980). ... J. Walter Kennedy Citizenship Award (1992).

NOTES: Led NBA with 3.43 steals per game (1981) and 2.67 steals per game (1982).

Season Team	G	Min.	FGM	FGA	Pct.	FTM	FTA	Pct.	REBOUNDS			Ast.	St.	Blk.	TO	Pts.	AVERAGES		
									Off.	Def.	Tot.						RPG	APG	PPG
79-80—Los Angeles	77	2795	503	949	.530	374	462	.810	166	430	596	563	187	41	305	1387	7.7	7.3	18.0
80-81—Los Angeles	37	1371	312	587	.532	171	225	.760	101	219	320	317	127	27	143	798	8.6	8.6	21.6
81-82—Los Angeles	78	2991	556	1036	.537	329	433	.760	252	499	751	743	208	34	286	1447	9.6	9.5	18.6
82-83—Los Angeles	79	2907	511	933	.548	304	380	.800	214	469	683	*829	176	47	301	1326	8.6	*10.5	16.8
83-84—Los Angeles	67	2567	441	780	.565	290	358	.810	99	392	491	875	150	49	306	1178	7.3	*13.1	17.6
84-85—L.A. Lakers	77	2781	504	899	.561	391	464	.843	90	386	476	968	113	25	305	1406	6.2	12.6	18.3
85-86—L.A. Lakers	72	2578	483	918	.526	378	434	.871	85	341	426	*907	113	16	273	1354	5.9	*12.6	18.8
86-87—L.A. Lakers	80	2904	683	1308	.522	535	631	.848	122	382	504	*977	138	36	300	1909	6.3	*12.2	23.9
87-88—L.A. Lakers	72	2637	490	996	.492	417	489	.853	88	361	449	858	114	13	269	1408	6.2	11.9	19.6
88-89—L.A. Lakers	77	2886	579	1137	.509	513	563	*.911	111	496	607	988	138	22	312	1730	7.9	12.8	22.5
89-90—L.A. Lakers	79	2937	546	1138	.480	567	637	.890	128	394	522	907	132	34	289	1765	6.6	11.5	22.3
90-91—L.A. Lakers	79	2933	466	976	.477	519	573	.906	105	446	551	989	102	17	*314	1531	7.0	12.5	19.4
91-92—L.A. Lakers							Did not play—retired.												
92-93—L.A. Lakers							Did not play—retired.												
93-94—L.A. Lakers							Did not play—retired.												
94-95—L.A. Lakers							Did not play—retired.												
95-96—L.A. Lakers	32	958	137	294	.466	172	201	.856	40	143	183	220	26	13	103	468	5.7	6.9	14.6
Totals	906	33245	6211	11951	.520	4960	5850	.848	1601	4958	6559	10141	1724	374	3506	17707	7.2	11.2	19.5

Three-point field goals: 1979-80, 7-for-31 (.226). 1980-81, 3-for-17 (.176). 1981-82, 6-for-29 (.207). 1982-83, 0-for-21. 1983-84, 6-for-29 (.207). 1984-85, 7-for-37 (.189). 1985-86, 10-for-43 (.233). 1986-87, 8-for-39 (.205). 1987-88, 11-for-56 (.196). 1988-89, 59-for-188 (.314). 1989-90, 106-for-276 (.384). 1990-91, 80-for-250 (.320). 1995-96, 22-for-58 (.379). Totals, 325-for-1074 (.303).

Personal fouls/disqualifications: 1979-80, 218/1. 1980-81, 100/0. 1981-82, 223/1. 1982-83, 200/1. 1983-84, 169/1. 1984-85, 155/0. 1985-86, 133/0. 1986-87, 168/0. 1987-88, 147/0. 1988-89, 172/0. 1989-90, 167/1. 1990-91, 150/0. 1995-96, 48/0. Totals, 2050/5.

NBA PLAYOFF RECORD

NOTES: NBA Finals Most Valuable Player (1980, 1982, 1987). ... Holds career playoff record for most assists—2,346. ... Holds NBA Finals single-series records for highest assists-per-game average—14.0 (1985); and highest assists-per-game average by a rookie—8.7 (1980). ... Holds NBA Finals single-game records for most points by a rookie—42 (May 16, 1980, vs. Philadelphia); most assists—21 (June 3, 1984, vs. Boston); most assists by a rookie—11 (May 7, 1980, vs. Philadelphia); and most assists in one half—14 (June 19, 1988, vs. Detroit). ... Shares NBA Finals single-game record for most assists in one quarter—8 (four times). ... Holds single-series playoff record for highest assists-per-game average—17.0 (1985). ... Shares single-game playoff records for most free throws made in one half—19 (May 8, 1991, vs. Golden State); most assists—24 (May 15, 1984, vs. Phoenix); and most assists in one half—15 (May 3, 1985, vs. Portland).

Season Team	G	Min.	FGM	FGA	Pct.	FTM	FTA	Pct.	REBOUNDS			Ast.	St.	Blk.	TO	Pts.	AVERAGES		
									Off.	Def.	Tot.						RPG	APG	PPG
79-80—Los Angeles	16	658	103	199	.518	85	106	.802	52	116	168	151	49	6	65	293	10.5	9.4	18.3
80-81—Los Angeles	3	127	19	49	.388	13	20	.650	8	33	41	21	8	3	11	51	13.7	7.0	17.0
81-82—Los Angeles	14	562	83	157	.529	77	93	.828	54	104	158	130	40	3	44	243	11.3	9.3	17.4
82-83—Los Angeles	15	643	100	206	.485	68	81	.840	51	77	128	192	34	12	64	268	8.5	12.8	17.9
83-84—Los Angeles	21	837	151	274	.551	80	100	.800	26	113	139	284	42	20	79	382	6.6	13.5	18.2
84-85—L.A. Lakers	19	687	116	226	.513	100	118	.847	19	115	134	289	32	4	76	333	7.1	15.2	17.5
85-86—L.A. Lakers	14	541	110	205	.537	82	107	.766	21	79	100	211	27	1	45	302	7.1	15.1	21.6
86-87—L.A. Lakers	18	666	146	271	.539	98	118	.831	28	111	139	219	31	7	51	392	7.7	12.2	21.8
87-88—L.A. Lakers	24	965	169	329	.514	132	155	.852	32	98	130	303	34	4	83	477	5.4	12.6	19.9
88-89—L.A. Lakers	14	518	85	174	.489	78	86	.907	15	68	83	165	27	3	53	258	5.9	11.8	18.4
89-90—L.A. Lakers	9	376	76	155	.490	70	79	.886	12	45	57	115	11	1	36	227	6.3	12.8	25.2
90-91—L.A. Lakers	19	823	118	268	.440	157	178	.882	23	131	154	240	23	0	77	414	8.1	12.6	21.8
95-96—L.A. Lakers	4	135	15	39	.385	28	33	.848	8	26	34	26	0	0	12	61	8.5	6.5	15.3
Totals	190	7538	1291	2552	.506	1068	1274	.838	349	1116	1465	2346	358	64	696	3701	7.7	12.3	19.5

Three-point field goals: 1979-80, 2-for-8 (.250). 1981-82, 0-for-4. 1982-83, 0-for-11. 1983-84, 0-for-7. 1984-85, 1-for-7 (.143). 1985-86, 0-for-11. 1986-87, 2-for-10 (.200). 1987-88, 7-for-14 (.500). 1988-89, 10-for-35 (.286). 1989-90, 5-for-25 (.200). 1990-91, 21-for-71 (.296). 1995-96, 3-for-9 (.333). Totals, 51-for-212 (.241).

Personal fouls/disqualifications: 1979-80, 47/1. 1980-81, 14/1. 1981-82, 50/0. 1982-83, 49/0. 1983-84, 71/0. 1984-85, 48/0. 1985-86, 43/0. 1986-87, 37/0. 1987-88, 61/0. 1988-89, 30/1. 1989-90, 28/0. 1990-91, 43/0. 1995-96, 3/0. Totals, 524/3.

NBA ALL-STAR GAME RECORD

NOTES: NBA All-Star Game Most Valuable Player (1990, 1992). ... Holds career records for most assists—127; and most three-point field goals made—10. ... Holds single-game record for most assists—22 (1984, OT).

Season Team	Min.	FGM	FGA	Pct.	FTM	FTA	Pct.	REBOUNDS			Ast.	PF	Dq.	St.	Blk.	TO	Pts.
								Off.	Def.	Tot.							
1980—Los Angeles	24	5	8	.625	2	2	1.000	2	0	2	4	3	0	3	2	2	12
1982—Los Angeles	23	5	9	.556	6	7	.857	3	1	4	7	5	0	0	0	1	16
1983—Los Angeles	33	7	16	.438	3	4	.750	3	2	5	16	2	0	5	0	7	17
1984—Los Angeles	37	6	13	.462	2	2	1.000	4	5	9	22	3	0	3	2	4	15
1985—L.A. Lakers	31	7	14	.500	7	8	.875	2	3	5	15	2	0	1	0	3	21
1986—L.A. Lakers	28	1	3	.333	4	4	1.000	0	4	4	15	4	0	1	0	9	6

Season Team	Min.	FGM	FGA	Pct.	FTM	FTA	Pct.	REBOUNDS Off.	Def.	Tot.	Ast.	PF	Dq.	St.	Blk.	TO	Pts.
1987—L.A. Lakers...........	34	4	10	.400	1	2	.500	1	6	7	13	2	0	4	0	1	9
1988—L.A. Lakers...........	39	4	15	.267	9	9	1.000	1	5	6	19	2	0	2	2	8	17
1989—L.A. Lakers...........							Selected, did not play—injured.										
1990—L.A. Lakers...........	25	9	15	.600	0	0	...	1	5	6	4	1	0	0	1	3	22
1991—L.A. Lakers...........	28	7	16	.438	0	0	...	1	3	4	3	1	0	0	0	3	16
1992—L.A. Lakers...........	29	9	12	.750	4	4	1.000	3	2	5	9	0	0	2	0	7	25
Totals.................	331	64	131	.489	38	42	.905	21	36	57	127	25	0	21	7	48	176

Three-point field goals: 1980, 0-for-1. 1983, 0-for-1. 1984, 1-for-3 (.333). 1986, 0-for-1. 1988, 0-for-1. 1990, 4-for-6 (.667). 1991, 2-for-5 (.400). 1992, 3-for-3. Totals, 10-for-21 (.476).

NBA COACHING RECORD

		REGULAR SEASON				PLAYOFFS		
Season Team	W	L	Pct.	Finish		W	L	Pct.
93-94—L.A. Lakers..................................	5	11	.313	5th/Pacific Division		—	—	—

NOTES:
1994—Replaced Randy Pfund (27-37) and Bill Bertka (1-1) as Los Angeles Lakers head coach (March 27), with record of 28-38 and club in fifth place.

JOHNSTON, NEIL   C

PERSONAL: Born February 4, 1929, in Chillicothe, Ohio. ... Died September 27, 1978. ... 6-8/210 (2,03/95,3). ... Full name: Donald Neil Johnston. ... Nickname: Gabby.
HIGH SCHOOL: Chillicothe (Ohio).
COLLEGE: Ohio State.
TRANSACTIONS: Signed as free agent by Philadelphia Warriors (1951). ... Signed as player/head coach by Pittsburgh Rens of American Basketball League (1961).
CAREER HONORS: Elected to Naismith Memorial Basketball Hall of Fame (1990).
MISCELLANEOUS: Member of NBA championship team (1956).

COLLEGIATE RECORD

NOTES: Signed pro baseball contract in 1948 and became ineligible for his final two years at Ohio State.

Season Team	G	Min.	FGM	FGA	Pct.	FTM	FTA	Pct.	Reb.	Ast.	Pts.	AVERAGES RPG	APG	PPG
46-47—Ohio State	7	...	5	...	...	3	8	.375	...	...	13	...	...	1.9
47-48—Ohio State	20	...	67	219	.306	46	87	.529	...	...	180	...	...	9.0
Totals	27	...	72	...	...	49	95	.516	...	...	193	...	...	7.1

NBA REGULAR-SEASON RECORD

HONORS: All-NBA first team (1953, 1954, 1955, 1956). All-NBA second team (1957).

Season Team	G	Min.	FGM	FGA	Pct.	FTM	FTA	Pct.	Reb.	Ast.	PF	Dq.	Pts.	AVERAGES RPG	APG	PPG
51-52—Philadelphia	64	993	141	299	.472	100	151	.662	342	39	154	5	382	5.3	0.6	6.0
52-53—Philadelphia	70	*3166	*504	1114 *.452		*556	*794	.700	976	197	248	6	*1564	13.9	2.8	*22.3
53-54—Philadelphia	72	*3296	*591	*1317	.449	*577	*772	.747	797	203	259	7	*1759	11.1	2.8	*24.4
54-55—Philadelphia	72	2917	521	1184	.440	*589	*769	.766	*1085	215	255	4	*1631	*15.1	3.0	*22.7
55-56—Philadelphia	70	2594	499	1092 *.457		549	685	.801	872	225	251	8	1547	12.5	3.2	22.1
56-57—Philadelphia	69	2531	520	1163 *.447		535	648	.826	855	203	231	2	1575	12.4	2.9	22.8
57-58—Philadelphia	71	2408	473	1102	.429	442	540	.819	790	166	233	4	1388	11.1	2.3	19.5
58-59—Philadelphia	28	393	54	164	.329	69	88	.784	139	21	50	0	177	5.0	0.8	6.3
Totals..	516	18298	3303	7435	.444	3417	4447	.768	5856	1269	1681	36	10023	11.3	2.5	19.4

NBA PLAYOFF RECORD

Season Team	G	Min.	FGM	FGA	Pct.	FTM	FTA	Pct.	Reb.	Ast.	PF	Dq.	Pts.	AVERAGES RPG	APG	PPG
51-52—Philadelphia	3	32	5	10	.500	6	8	.750	10	1	8	0	16	3.3	0.3	5.3
55-56—Philadelphia	10	397	69	169	.408	65	92	.707	143	51	41	0	203	14.3	5.1	20.3
56-57—Philadelphia	2	84	17	53	.321	4	6	.667	35	9	9	0	38	17.5	4.5	19.0
57-58—Philadelphia	8	189	30	78	.385	27	33	.818	69	14	18	0	87	8.6	1.8	10.9
Totals..	23	702	121	310	.390	102	139	.734	257	75	76	0	344	11.2	3.3	15.0

NBA ALL-STAR GAME RECORD

Season Team	Min.	FGM	FGA	Pct.	FTM	FTA	Pct.	Reb	Ast.	PF	Dq.	Pts.
1953—Philadelphia	27	5	13	.385	1	2	.500	12	2	2	0	11
1954—Philadelphia	20	2	9	.222	2	4	.500	7	2	1	0	6
1955—Philadelphia	15	1	7	.143	1	1	1.000	6	1	0	0	3
1956—Philadelphia	25	5	9	.556	7	11	.636	10	1	3	0	17
1957—Philadelphia	23	8	12	.667	3	3	1.000	9	1	2	0	19
1958—Philadelphia	22	6	13	.462	2	2	1.000	8	1	5	0	14
Totals	132	27	63	.429	16	23	.696	52	6	13	0	70

ABL REGULAR-SEASON RECORD

Season Team	G	Min.	FGM	FGA	Pct.	FTM	FTA	Pct.	Reb.	Ast.	Pts.	AVERAGES RPG	APG	PPG
61-62—Pittsburgh	5	106	15	37	.405	24	16	1.500	18	10	49	3.6	2.0	9.8

HEAD COACHING RECORD

BACKGROUND: Player/head coach, Pittsburgh Rens of American Basketball League (1961-62).

NBA COACHING RECORD

Season Team	W	L	Pct.	Finish		W	L	Pct.
				REGULAR SEASON			PLAYOFFS	
59-60—Philadelphia	49	26	.653	2nd/Eastern Division		4	5	.444
60-61—Philadelphia	46	33	.582	2nd/Eastern Division		0	3	.000
Totals (2 years)	95	59	.617		Totals (2 years)	4	8	.333

ABL COACHING RECORD

Season Team	W	L	Pct.	Finish		W	L	Pct.
61-62—Pittsburgh	41	40	.506	2nd/Eastern Division		0	1	.000
62-63—Pittsburgh	12	10	.545	3rd		—	—	—
Totals (2 years)	53	50	.515		Totals (1 year)	0	1	.000

EBL COACHING RECORD

Season Team	W	L	Pct.	Finish		W	L	Pct.
64-65—Wilmington	12	16	.429	5th		—	—	—
65-66—Wilmington	20	8	.714	1st/Eastern Division		4	2	.667
Totals (1 year)	32	24	.571		Totals (1 year)	4	2	.667

NOTES:
1960—Defeated Syracuse, 2-1, in Eastern Division Semifinals; lost to Boston, 4-2, in Eastern Division Finals.
1961—Lost to Syracuse in Eastern Division Semifinals.
1962—ABL disbanded (December 31).
1966—Defeated Trenton, 2-1, in Eastern Finals; defeated Wilkes-Barre, 2-1, in EBL Finals.

RECORD AS BASEBALL PLAYER

TRANSACTION/CAREER NOTES: Signed by Philadelphia Phillies organization (August 1948). ... Released by Phillies organization (June 1, 1952).

Year Team (League)	G	W	L	Pct.	ERA	Sv.	IP	H	R	ER	BB	SO
1949—Terre Haute (Three I)	29	10	12	.455	3.14	...	166	159	85	58	73	129
1950—Terre Haute (Three I)	28	11	12	.478	2.89	...	168	132	78	54	102	126
1951—Wilmington (Inter-State)	27	3	9	.250	5.40	...	115	126	76	69	79	104

ALL-TIME GREAT PLAYERS

JONES, BOBBY   F

PERSONAL: Born December 18, 1951, in Charlotte, N.C. ... 6-9/210 (2,05/95,3). ... Full name: Robert Clyde Jones.
HIGH SCHOOL: South Mecklenburg (Charlotte, N.C.).
COLLEGE: North Carolina
TRANSACTIONS: Selected by Carolina Cougars in second round of 1973 ABA special circumstance draft. ... Cougars franchise moved to St. Louis and renamed Spirits of St. Louis for 1974-75 season. ... Draft rights traded by Spirits of St. Louis to Denver Nuggets for draft rights to Marvin Barnes (1974). ... Nuggets franchise became part of NBA for 1976-77 season. ... Traded by Nuggets with Ralph Simpson to Philadelphia 76ers for F George McGinnis (August 16, 1978).
MISCELLANEOUS: Member of NBA championship team (1983). ... Member of silver-medal-winning U.S. Olympic team (1972).

COLLEGIATE RECORD

Season Team	G	Min.	FGM	FGA	Pct.	FTM	FTA	Pct.	Reb.	Ast.	Pts.	RPG	APG	PPG
													AVERAGES	
70-71—North Carolina	16	...	136	237	.574	86	113	.761	236	...	358	14.8	...	22.4
71-72—North Carolina	31	...	127	190	.668	62	95	.653	195	75	316	6.3	2.4	10.2
72-73—North Carolina	33	...	206	343	.601	84	128	.656	348	130	496	10.5	3.9	15.0
73-74—North Carolina	28	...	189	326	.580	74	120	.617	274	80	452	9.8	2.9	16.1
Totals	108	...	658	1096	.600	306	456	.671	1053	...	1622	9.8	...	15.0

ABA REGULAR-SEASON RECORD

NOTES: ABA All-Star second team (1976). ... ABA All-Defensive Team (1975 and 1976). ... ABA All-Rookie team (1975). ... Holds ABA single-season record for highest field goal percentage—.605 (1975).

Season Team	G	Min.	2-POINT FGM	FGA	Pct.	3-POINT FGM	FGA	Pct.	FTM	FTA	Pct.	Reb.	Ast.	Pts.	AVERAGES RPG	APG	PPG
74-75—Denver	84	2706	529	875	*.605	0	1	.000	187	269	.695	692	303	1245	8.2	3.6	14.8
75-76—Denver	83	2845	510	878	*.581	0	0	...	215	308	.698	791	331	1235	9.5	4.0	14.9
Totals	167	5551	1039	1753	.593	0	1	.000	402	577	.697	1483	634	2480	8.9	3.8	14.9

ABA PLAYOFF RECORD

Season Team	G	Min.	2-POINT FGM	FGA	Pct.	3-POINT FGM	FGA	Pct.	FTM	FTA	Pct.	Reb.	Ast.	Pts.	AVERAGES RPG	APG	PPG
74-75—Denver	13	428	69	128	.539	0	1	.000	31	40	.775	111	38	169	8.5	2.9	13.0
75-76—Denver	13	433	74	127	.583	0	0	...	30	41	.732	112	59	178	8.6	4.5	13.7
Totals	26	861	143	255	.561	0	1	.000	61	81	.753	223	97	347	8.6	3.7	13.3

ABA ALL-STAR GAME RECORD

Season Team	Min.	2-POINT FGM	FGA	Pct.	3-POINT FGM	FGA	Pct.	FTM	FTA	Pct.	Reb.	Ast.	Pts.
1976—Denver	29	8	12	.667	0	0	...	8	11	.727	10	3	24

NBA REGULAR-SEASON RECORD

HONORS: NBA Sixth Man Award (1983). ... NBA All-Defensive first team (1977, 1978, 1979, 1980, 1981, 1982, 1983, 1984) ... NBA All-Defensive second team (1985).

Season Team	G	Min.	FGM	FGA	Pct.	FTM	FTA	Pct.	REBOUNDS Off.	Def.	Tot.	Ast.	St.	Blk.	TO	Pts.	AVERAGES RPG	APG	PPG
76-77—Denver	82	2419	501	879	.570	236	329	.717	174	504	678	264	186	162	...	1238	8.3	3.2	15.1
77-78—Denver	75	2440	440	761	*.578	208	277	.751	164	472	636	252	137	126	194	1088	8.5	3.4	14.5
78-79—Philadelphia	80	2304	378	704	.537	209	277	.755	199	332	531	201	107	96	165	965	6.6	2.5	12.1
79-80—Philadelphia	81	2125	398	748	.532	257	329	.781	152	298	450	146	102	118	146	1053	5.6	1.8	13.0
80-81—Philadelphia	81	2046	407	755	.539	282	347	.813	142	293	435	226	95	74	149	1096	5.4	2.8	13.5
81-82—Philadelphia	76	2181	416	737	.564	263	333	.790	109	284	393	189	99	112	145	1095	5.2	2.5	14.4

Season Team	G	Min.	FGM	FGA	Pct.	FTM	FTA	Pct.	REBOUNDS Off.	Def.	Tot.	Ast.	St.	Blk.	TO	Pts.	AVERAGES RPG	APG	PPG
82-83—Philadelphia....	74	1749	250	460	.543	165	208	.793	102	242	344	142	85	91	109	665	4.6	1.9	9.0
83-84—Philadelphia....	75	1761	226	432	.523	167	213	.784	92	231	323	187	107	103	101	619	4.3	2.5	8.3
84-85—Philadelphia....	80	1633	207	385	.538	186	216	.861	105	192	297	155	84	50	118	600	3.7	1.9	7.5
85-86—Philadelphia....	70	1519	189	338	.559	114	145	.786	49	120	169	126	48	50	90	492	2.4	1.8	7.0
Totals	774	20177	3412	6199	.550	2087	2674	.780	1288	2968	4256	1888	1050	982	1217	8911	5.5	2.4	11.5

Three-point field goals: 1979-80, 0-for-3. 1980-81, 0-for-3. 1981-82, 0-for-3. 1982-83, 0-for-1. 1983-84, 0-for-1. 1984-85, 0-for-4. 1985-86, 0-for-1. Totals, 0-for-16.

Personal fouls/disqualifications: 1976-77, 238/3. 1977-78, 221/2. 1978-79, 245/2. 1979-80, 223/3. 1980-81, 226/2. 1981-82, 211/3. 1982-83, 199/4. 1983-84, 199/1. 1984-85, 183/2. 1985-86, 159/0. Totals, 2104/22.

NBA PLAYOFF RECORD

Season Team	G	Min.	FGM	FGA	Pct.	FTM	FTA	Pct.	REBOUNDS Off.	Def.	Tot.	Ast.	St.	Blk.	TO	Pts.	AVERAGES RPG	APG	PPG
76-77—Denver	6	187	31	64	.484	10	17	.588	11	24	35	21	17	14	...	72	5.8	3.5	12.0
77-78—Denver	13	390	66	116	.569	34	46	.739	36	66	102	35	16	9	24	166	7.8	2.7	12.8
78-79—Philadelphia ...	9	260	48	87	.552	22	26	.846	12	31	43	19	5	4	15	118	4.8	2.1	13.1
79-80—Philadelphia ...	18	470	90	172	.523	53	62	.855	29	57	86	31	21	32	23	233	4.8	1.7	12.9
80-81—Philadelphia ...	16	443	81	160	.506	73	88	.830	35	53	88	33	18	21	32	235	5.5	2.1	14.7
81-82—Philadelphia ...	21	589	94	174	.540	68	81	.840	37	62	99	52	15	22	33	256	4.7	2.5	12.2
82-83—Philadelphia ...	12	324	43	78	.551	17	20	.850	19	39	58	34	15	18	18	103	4.8	2.8	8.6
83-84—Philadelphia ...	5	130	15	31	.484	18	19	.947	9	14	23	9	3	7	8	48	4.6	1.8	9.6
84-85—Philadelphia ...	13	309	46	78	.590	14	20	.700	22	26	48	16	12	15	19	106	3.7	1.2	8.2
85-86—Philadelphia ...	12	329	39	74	.527	38	50	.760	9	23	32	34	10	14	15	116	2.7	2.8	9.7
Totals	125	3431	553	1034	.535	347	429	.809	219	395	614	284	132	156	187	1453	4.9	2.3	11.6

Three-point field goals: 1979-80, 0-for-1. 1982-83, 0-for-1. 1985-86, 0-for-1. Totals, 0-for-3.

Personal fouls/disqualifications: 1976-77, 25/1. 1977-78, 42/1. 1978-79, 30/0. 1979-80, 56/1. 1980-81, 60/1. 1981-82, 69/0. 1982-83, 29/0. 1983-84, 12/0. 1984-85, 38/0. 1985-86, 39/0. Totals, 400/4.

NBA ALL-STAR GAME RECORD

Season Team	Min.	FGM	FGA	Pct.	FTM	FTA	Pct.	REBOUNDS Off.	Def.	Tot.	Ast.	PF	Dq.	St.	Blk.	TO	Pts.
1977—Denver	14	1	4	.250	0	0	...	0	0	0	3	0	0	0	1	...	2
1978—Denver	18	1	3	.333	0	0	...	1	5	6	2	4	0	0	1	1	2
1981—Philadelphia	16	5	11	.455	1	1	1.000	1	3	4	0	2	0	1	1	0	11
1982—Philadelphia	14	2	5	.400	1	2	.500	1	3	4	1	2	0	1	0	0	5
Totals	62	9	23	.391	2	3	.667	3	11	14	6	8	0	2	3	1	20

COMBINED ABA AND NBA REGULAR-SEASON RECORDS

	G	Min.	FGM	FGA	Pct.	FTM	FTA	Pct.	REBOUNDS Off.	Def.	Tot.	Ast.	Stl.	Blk.	TO	Pts.	AVERAGES RPG	APG	PPG
Totals	941	25728	4451	7953	.560	2489	3251	.766	1759	3980	5739	2522	1387	1319	1683	11391	6.1	2.7	12.1

Three-point field goals: 0-for-17.
Personal fouls/disqualifications: 2620.

JONES, CALDWELL   F/C

PERSONAL: Born August 4, 1950, in McGehee, Ark. ... 6-11/225 (2,10/102,1). ... Full name: Caldwell Jones. ... Brother of Charles Jones, forward/center with five NBA teams (1983-84 through 1997-98); brother of Major Jones, forward/center with Houston Rockets (1979-80 through 1983-84) and Detroit Pistons (1984-85); and brother of Wilbert Jones, forward with three ABA teams (1969-70 through 1975-76) and Indiana Pacers (1976-77) and Buffalo Braves of the NBA (1977-78).
HIGH SCHOOL: Desha Central (Rohwer, Ark.).

COLLEGE: Albany State College

TRANSACTIONS: Selected by Virginia Squires in third round of 1973 ABA draft. ... Selected by Philadelphia 76ers in second round (32nd pick overall) of 1973 NBA draft. ... Signed by San Diego Conquistadors; G Larry Miller sent by Conquistadors to Squires as compensation (October 29, 1973). ... Signed by 76ers (for future services) (February 25, 1975). ... Purchased by Kentucky Colonels from disbanded San Diego franchise (Novemeber 14, 1975). ... Traded by Kentucky Colonels to St. Louis for F Maurice Lucas (December 17, 1975). ... Traded by 76ers with 1983 first-round draft choice to Houston Rockets for C Moses Malone (September 15, 1982). ... Traded by Rockets to Chicago Bulls for G Mitchell Wiggins and 1985 second- and third-round draft choices (August 10, 1984). ... Signed by Portland Trail Blazers as veteran free agent (October 1, 1985); Bulls agreed not to exercise its right of first refusal in exchange for 1987 second-round draft choice. ... Signed by San Antonio Spurs as unrestricted free agent (July 20, 1989).

COLLEGIATE RECORD

Season Team	G	Min.	FGM	FGA	Pct.	FTM	FTA	Pct.	Reb.	Ast.	Pts.	AVERAGES RPG	APG	PPG
69-70—Albany (Ga.) State	25	...	185	367	.504	80	108	.741	440	...	450	17.6	...	18.0
70-71—Albany (Ga.) State	27	...	206	437	.471	76	137	.555	576	...	488	21.3	...	18.1
71-72—Albany (Ga.) State	28	...	288	539	.534	156	219	.712	567	...	732	20.3	...	26.1
72-73—Albany (Ga.) State	29	...	238	470	.506	91	134	.679	633	...	567	21.8	...	19.6
Totals	109	...	917	1813	.506	403	598	.674	2216	...	2237	20.3	...	20.5

ABA REGULAR-SEASON RECORD

NOTES: Shares ABA single-game record for most blocks—12 (January 6, 1974, vs. Carolina). ... Led ABA with 4.00 blocked shots per game (1974) and 3.24 blocked shots per game (1975).

Season Team	G	Min.	2-POINT FGM	FGA	Pct.	3-POINT FGM	FGA	Pct.	FTM	FTA	Pct.	Reb.	Ast.	Pts.	AVERAGES RPG	APG	PPG
73-74—San Diego	79	2929	505	1083	.466	2	8	.250	171	230	.743	1095	144	1187	13.9	1.8	15.0
74-75—San Diego	76	3004	603	1229	.491	3	11	.273	264	335	.788	1074	162	1479	14.1	2.1	19.5
75-76—SD-Kty.-St.L.	76	2674	423	893	.474	0	7	.000	140	186	.753	853	147	986	11.2	1.9	13.0
Totals	231	8607	1531	3205	.478	5	26	.192	575	751	.766	3022	453	3652	13.1	2.0	15.8

ABA PLAYOFF RECORD

			2-POINT			3-POINT									AVERAGES		
Season Team	G	Min.	FGM	FGA	Pct.	FGM	FGA	Pct.	FTM	FTA	Pct.	Reb.	Ast.	Pts.	RPG	APG	PPG
73-74—San Diego	6	277	36	88	.409	0	0	...	11	16	.688	94	15	83	15.7	2.5	13.8

ABA ALL-STAR GAME RECORD

		2-POINT			3-POINT								
Season Team	Min.	FGM	FGA	Pct.	FGM	FGA	Pct.	FTM	FTA	Pct.	Reb.	Ast.	Pts.
1975—San Diego	15	2	4	.500	0	0	...	1	1	1.000	4	0	5

NBA REGULAR-SEASON RECORD

NOTES: NBA All-Defensive first team (1981, 1982).

									REBOUNDS								AVERAGES		
Season Team	G	Min.	FGM	FGA	Pct.	FTM	FTA	Pct.	Off.	Def.	Tot.	Ast.	St.	Blk.	TO	Pts.	RPG	APG	PPG
76-77—Philadelphia	82	2023	215	424	.507	64	116	.552	190	476	666	92	43	200	...	494	8.1	1.1	6.0
77-78—Philadelphia	80	1636	169	359	.471	96	153	.627	165	405	570	92	26	127	...	434	7.1	1.2	5.4
78-79—Philadelphia	78	2171	302	637	.474	121	162	.747	177	570	747	151	39	157	...	725	9.6	1.9	9.3
79-80—Philadelphia	80	2771	232	532	.436	124	178	.697	219	731	950	164	43	162	...	588	11.9	2.1	7.4
80-81—Philadelphia	81	2639	218	485	.449	148	193	.767	200	613	813	122	53	134	168	584	10.0	1.5	7.2
81-82—Philadelphia	81	2446	231	465	.497	179	219	.817	164	544	708	100	38	146	155	641	8.7	1.2	7.9
82-83—Houston	82	2440	307	677	.453	162	206	.786	222	446	668	138	46	131	171	776	8.1	1.7	9.5
83-84—Houston	81	2506	318	633	.502	164	196	.837	168	414	582	156	46	80	158	801	7.2	1.9	9.9
84-85—Chicago	42	885	53	115	.461	36	47	.766	49	162	211	34	12	31	40	142	5.0	0.8	3.4
85-86—Portland	80	1437	126	254	.496	124	150	.827	105	250	355	74	38	61	102	376	4.4	0.9	4.7
86-87—Portland	78	1578	111	224	.496	97	124	.782	114	341	455	64	23	77	87	319	5.8	0.8	4.1
87-88—Portland	79	1778	128	263	.487	78	106	.736	105	303	408	81	29	99	82	334	5.2	1.0	4.2
88-89—Portland	72	1279	77	183	.421	48	61	.787	88	212	300	59	24	85	83	202	4.2	0.8	2.8
89-90—San Antonio	72	885	67	144	.465	38	54	.704	76	154	230	20	20	27	48	173	3.2	0.3	2.4
Totals	1068	26474	2554	5395	.473	1479	1965	.753	2042	5621	7663	1347	480	1517	...	6589	7.2	1.3	6.2

Three-point field goals: 1979-80, 0-for-2. 1981-82, 0-for-3. 1982-83, 0-for-2. 1983-84, 1-for-3 (.333). 1984-85, 0-for-2. 1985-86, 0-for-7. 1986-87, 0-for-2. 1987-88, 0-for-4. 1988-89, 0-for-1. 1989-90, 1-for-5 (.200). Totals, 2-for-31 (.065).

Personal fouls/disqualifications: 1976-77, 301/3. 1977-78, 281/4. 1978-79, 303/10. 1979-80, 298/5. 1980-81, 271/2. 1981-82, 301/3. 1982-83, 278/2. 1983-84, 335/7. 1984-85, 125/3. 1985-86, 244/2. 1986-87, 227/5. 1987-88, 251/0. 1988-89, 166/0. 1989-90, 146/2. Totals, 3527/48.

NBA PLAYOFF RECORD

									REBOUNDS								AVERAGES		
Season Team	G	Min.	FGM	FGA	Pct.	FTM	FTA	Pct.	Off.	Def.	Tot.	Ast.	St.	Blk.	TO	Pts.	RPG	APG	PPG
76-77—Philadelphia	19	513	37	73	.507	18	30	.600	38	112	150	20	9	40	...	92	7.9	1.1	4.8
77-78—Philadelphia	10	301	28	56	.500	8	10	.800	22	84	106	14	5	30	...	64	10.6	1.4	6.4
78-79—Philadelphia	9	320	43	89	.483	28	36	.778	37	84	121	21	4	22	...	114	13.4	2.3	12.7
79-80—Philadelphia	18	639	58	129	.450	42	52	.808	50	135	185	34	13	37	...	158	10.3	1.9	8.8
80-81—Philadelphia	16	580	54	95	.568	31	42	.738	37	118	155	27	7	31	...	139	9.7	1.7	8.7
81-82—Philadelphia	21	679	74	160	.463	35	41	.854	52	137	189	19	11	40	...	183	9.0	0.9	8.7
84-85—Chicago	2	18	5	6	.833	0	0	...	1	4	5	0	0	1	...	10	2.5	0.0	5.0
85-86—Portland	4	73	6	17	.353	2	4	.500	9	10	19	3	0	2	...	14	4.8	0.8	3.5
86-87—Portland	4	129	5	12	.417	5	6	.833	9	22	31	6	0	6	...	15	7.8	1.5	3.8
87-88—Portland	4	98	6	16	.375	1	2	.500	4	13	17	1	2	8	...	13	4.3	0.3	3.3
88-89—Portland	3	50	2	3	.667	0	0	...	2	6	8	0	0	3	...	4	2.7	0.0	1.3
89-90—San Antonio	9	66	4	9	.444	0	1	.000	6	7	13	2	0	3	...	8	1.4	0.2	0.9
Totals	119	3466	322	665	.484	170	224	.759	267	732	999	147	51	223	...	814	8.4	1.2	6.8

Three-point field goals: 1979-80, 0-for-3. 1984-85, 0-for-1. Totals, 0-for-4.

Personal fouls/disqualifications: 1976-77, 81/4. 1977-78, 36/2. 1978-79, 36/0. 1979-80, 75/1. 1980-81, 53/0. 1981-82, 77/1. 1984-85, 7/1. 1985-86, 13/0. 1986-87, 15/0. 1987-88, 17/0. 1988-89, 6/0. 1989-90, 10/0. Totals, 426/9.

COMBINED ABA AND NBA REGULAR-SEASON RECORDS

									REBOUNDS								AVERAGES		
	G	Min.	FGM	FGA	Pct.	FTM	FTA	Pct.	Off.	Def.	Tot.	Ast.	Stl.	Blk.	TO	Pts.	RPG	APG	PPG
Totals	1299	35081	4090	8626	.474	2054	2716	.756	2921	7764	10685	1800	685	2297	...	10241	8.2	1.4	7.9

JONES, SAM   G

PERSONAL: Born June 24, 1933, in Wilmington, N.C. ... 6-4/205 (1,93/93,0). ... Full name: Samuel Jones.
HIGH SCHOOL: Laurinburg Institute (N.C.).
COLLEGE: North Carolina Central.
TRANSACTIONS: Selected by Boston Celtics in first round (eighth pick overall) of 1957 NBA Draft.
CAREER HONORS: Elected to Naismith Memorial Basketball Hall of Fame (1984). ... NBA 25th Anniversary All-Time Team (1970) and One of the 50 Greatest Players in NBA History (1996).
MISCELLANEOUS: Member of NBA championship team (1959, 1960, 1961, 1962, 1963, 1964, 1965, 1966, 1968, 1969).

COLLEGIATE RECORD

NOTES: Elected to NAIA Basketball Hall of Fame (1962).

												AVERAGES		
Season Team	G	Min.	FGM	FGA	Pct.	FTM	FTA	Pct.	Reb.	Ast.	Pts.	RPG	APG	PPG
51-52—North Carolina Central	22	...	126	263	.479	48	78	.615	150	...	300	6.8	...	13.6
52-53—North Carolina Central	24	...	169	370	.457	115	180	.639	248	...	453	10.3	...	18.9
53-54—North Carolina Central	27	...	208	432	.481	98	137	.715	223	...	514	8.3	...	19.0
54-55—					Did not play—in military service.									
55-56—					Did not play—in military service.									
56-57—North Carolina Central	27	...	174	398	.437	155	202	.767	288	...	503	10.7	...	18.6
Totals	100	...	677	1463	.463	416	597	.697	909	...	1770	9.1	...	17.7

NBA REGULAR-SEASON RECORD

HONORS: All-NBA second team (1965, 1966, 1967).

Season Team	G	Min.	FGM	FGA	Pct.	FTM	FTA	Pct.	Reb.	Ast.	PF	Dq.	Pts.	RPG	APG	PPG
57-58—Boston	56	594	100	233	.429	60	84	.714	160	37	42	0	260	2.9	0.7	4.6
58-59—Boston	71	1466	305	703	.434	151	196	.770	428	101	102	0	761	6.0	1.4	10.7
59-60—Boston	74	1512	355	782	.454	168	220	.764	375	125	101	1	878	5.1	1.7	11.9
60-61—Boston	78	2028	480	1069	.449	211	268	.787	421	217	148	1	1171	5.4	2.8	15.0
61-62—Boston	78	2388	596	1284	.464	243	297	.818	458	232	149	0	1435	5.9	3.0	18.4
62-63—Boston	76	2323	621	1305	.476	257	324	.793	396	241	162	1	1499	5.2	3.2	19.7
63-64—Boston	76	2381	612	1359	.450	249	318	.783	349	202	192	1	1473	4.6	2.7	19.4
64-65—Boston	80	2885	821	1818	.452	428	522	.820	411	223	176	0	2070	5.1	2.8	25.9
65-66—Boston	67	2155	626	1335	.469	325	407	.799	347	216	170	0	1577	5.2	3.2	23.5
66-67—Boston	72	2325	638	1406	.454	318	371	.857	338	217	191	1	1594	4.7	3.0	22.1
67-68—Boston	73	2408	621	1348	.461	311	376	.827	357	216	181	0	1553	4.9	3.0	21.3
68-69—Boston	70	1820	496	1103	.450	148	189	.783	265	182	121	0	1140	3.8	2.6	16.3
Totals	871	24285	6271	13745	.456	2869	3572	.803	4305	2209	1735	5	15411	4.9	2.5	17.7

NBA PLAYOFF RECORD

Season Team	G	Min.	FGM	FGA	Pct.	FTM	FTA	Pct.	Reb.	Ast.	PF	Dq.	Pts.	RPG	APG	PPG
57-58—Boston	8	75	10	22	.455	11	16	.688	24	4	7	0	31	3.0	0.5	3.9
58-59—Boston	11	192	40	108	.370	33	39	.846	63	17	14	0	113	5.7	1.5	10.3
59-60—Boston	13	197	45	117	.385	17	21	.810	41	18	15	0	107	3.2	1.4	8.2
60-61—Boston	10	258	50	112	.446	31	35	.886	54	22	22	0	131	5.4	2.2	13.1
61-62—Boston	14	504	123	277	.444	42	60	.700	99	44	30	0	288	7.1	3.1	20.6
62-63—Boston	13	450	120	248	.484	69	83	.831	81	32	42	1	309	6.2	2.5	23.8
63-64—Boston	10	356	91	180	.506	50	68	.735	47	23	24	0	232	4.7	2.3	23.2
64-65—Boston	12	495	135	294	.459	73	84	.869	55	30	39	1	343	4.6	2.5	28.6
65-66—Boston	17	602	154	343	.449	114	136	.838	86	53	65	1	422	5.1	3.1	24.8
66-67—Boston	9	326	95	207	.459	50	58	.862	46	28	30	1	240	5.1	3.1	26.7
67-68—Boston	19	685	162	367	.441	66	84	.786	64	50	58	0	390	3.4	2.6	20.5
68-69—Boston	18	514	124	296	.419	55	69	.797	58	37	45	1	303	3.2	2.1	16.8
Totals	154	4654	1149	2571	.447	611	753	.811	718	358	391	5	2909	4.7	2.3	18.9

NBA ALL-STAR GAME RECORD

Season Team	Min.	FGM	FGA	Pct.	FTM	FTA	Pct.	Reb	Ast.	PF	Dq.	Pts.
1962—Boston	14	1	8	.125	0	1	.000	1	0	1	0	2
1964—Boston	27	8	20	.400	0	0	...	4	3	2	0	16
1965—Boston	24	2	12	.167	2	2	1.000	5	3	2	0	6
1966—Boston	22	5	11	.455	2	2	1.000	2	5	0	0	12
1968—Boston	15	2	5	.400	1	1	1.000	2	4	1	0	5
Totals	102	18	56	.321	5	6	.833	14	15	6	0	41

HEAD COACHING RECORD

BACKGROUND: Athletic director, Federal City College, Washington, D.C. (1969-1973). ... Assistant coach, New Orleans Jazz (1974-75).

COLLEGIATE COACHING RECORD

Season Team	W	L	Pct.	Finish
69-70—Federal City College	5	8	.385	
70-71—Federal City College	12	9	.571	
71-72—Federal City College	11	9	.550	
72-73—Federal City College	11	13	.458	
73-74—North Carolina Central	5	16	.238	7th/Mid-Eastern Athletic Conference
Totals (5 years)	44	55	.444	

JORDAN, MICHAEL G

PERSONAL: Born February 17, 1963, in Brooklyn, N.Y. ... 6-6/216. (1,98/98,0). ... Full Name: Michael Jeffrey Jordan.
HIGH SCHOOL: Emsley A. Laney (Wilmington, N.C.).
COLLEGE: North Carolina.
TRANSACTIONS/CAREER NOTES: Selected after junior season by Chicago Bulls in first round (third pick overall) of 1984 NBA Draft. ... On voluntarily retired list (October 6, 1993-March 18, 1995). ... Activated from retirement (March 18, 1995). ... Announced retirement (January 13, 1999). ... Signed as free agent by Washington Wizards (September 25, 2001).
CAREER HONORS: NBA 50th Anniversary All-Time Team (1996).
MISCELLANEOUS: Member of NBA championship team (1991, 1992, 1993, 1996, 1997, 1998). ... Member of gold-medal-winning U.S. Olympic team (1984, 1992). ... Chicago Bulls all-time leading scorer with 29,277 points, all-time leading rebounder with 5,836, all-time assists leader with 5,012 and all-time steals leader with 2,306 (1984-85 through 1992-93 and 1994-95 through 1997-98). ... President of Basketball Operations, Washington Wizards and minority owner, Washington Wizards Sports and Entertainment (January 19, 2000-September 25, 2001). ... Managing Member of Basketball Operations, Charlotte Bobcats (2006-present).

COLLEGIATE RECORD

NOTES: THE SPORTING NEWS College Player of the Year (1983, 1984). ... Naismith Award winner (1984). ... Wooden Award winner (1984). ... THE SPORTING NEWS All-America first team (1983, 1984). ... Member of NCAA Division I championship team (1982).

Season Team	G	Min.	FGM	FGA	Pct.	FTM	FTA	Pct.	Reb.	Ast.	Pts.	RPG	APG	PPG
81-82—North Carolina	34	1079	191	358	.534	78	108	.722	149	61	460	4.4	1.8	13.5
82-83—North Carolina	36	1113	282	527	.535	123	167	.737	197	56	721	5.5	1.6	20.0
83-84—North Carolina	31	915	247	448	.551	113	145	.779	163	64	607	5.3	2.1	19.6
Totals	101	3107	720	1333	.540	314	420	.748	509	181	1788	5.0	1.8	17.7

Three-point field goals: 1982-83, 34-for-76 (.447).

NBA REGULAR-SEASON RECORD

RECORDS: Holds career record for most seasons leading league in scoring—10; highest points-per-game average (minimum 400 games or 10,000 points)—30.12; most seasons leading league in field goals made—10; and most seasons leading league in field goals attempted—10. ... Shares career records for most consecutive seasons leading league in scoring—7 (1986-87 through 1992-93). ... Holds single-game records for most free throws made in one half—20 (December 30, 1992, at Miami); and most free-throws attempted in one half—23 (December 30, 1992, at Miami). ... Shares single-game records for most free throws made in one quarter—14 (November 15, 1989, vs. Utah and December 30, 1992, at Miami); and most free throws attempted in one quarter—16 (December 30, 1992, at Miami).

HONORS: NBA Most Valuable Player (1988, 1991, 1992, 1996, 1998). ... NBA Defensive Player of the Year (1988). ... NBA Rookie of the Year (1985). ... IBM Award, for all-around contribution to team's success (1985, 1989). ... Slam Dunk championship winner (1987, 1988). ... All-NBA First Team (1987, 1988, 1989, 1990, 1991, 1992, 1993, 1996, 1997, 1998). ... All-NBA Second Team (1985). ... NBA All-Defensive first team (1988, 1989, 1990, 1991, 1992, 1993, 1996, 1997, 1998). ... NBA All-Rookie team (1985).

NOTES: Led NBA with 3.16 steals per game (1988), 2.77 steals per game (1990) and 2.83 steals per game (1993).

Season Team	G	Min.	FGM	FGA	Pct.	FTM	FTA	Pct.	Off.	Def.	Tot.	Ast.	St.	Blk.	TO	Pts.	RPG	APG	PPG
84-85—Chicago	82	3144	837	1625	.515	630	746	.845	167	367	534	481	196	69	291	*2313	6.5	5.9	28.2
85-86—Chicago	18	451	150	328	.457	105	125	.840	23	41	64	53	37	21	45	408	3.6	2.9	22.7
86-87—Chicago	82	*3281	*1098	*2279	.482	*833	*972	.857	166	264	430	377	236	125	272	*3041	5.2	4.6	*37.1
87-88—Chicago	82	*3311	*1069	*1998	.535	*723	860	.841	139	310	449	485	*259	131	252	*2868	5.5	5.9	*35.0
88-89—Chicago	81	*3255	*966	*1795	.538	674	793	.850	149	503	652	650	234	65	290	*2633	8.0	8.0	*32.5
89-90—Chicago	82	3197	*1034	*1964	.526	593	699	.848	143	422	565	519	*227	54	247	*2753	6.9	6.3	*33.6
90-91—Chicago	82	3034	*990	*1837	.539	571	671	.851	118	374	492	453	223	83	202	*2580	6.0	5.5	*31.5
91-92—Chicago	80	3102	*943	*1818	.519	491	590	.832	91	420	511	489	182	75	200	*2404	6.4	6.1	*30.1
92-93—Chicago	78	3067	*992	*2003	.495	476	569	.837	135	387	522	428	*221	61	207	*2541	6.7	5.5	*32.6
93-94—Chicago						Did not play—retired.													
94-95—Chicago	17	668	166	404	.411	109	136	.801	25	92	117	90	30	13	35	457	6.9	5.3	26.9
95-96—Chicago	82	3090	*916	*1850	.495	548	657	.834	148	395	543	352	180	42	197	*2491	6.6	4.3	*30.4
96-97—Chicago	82	3106	*920	*1892	.486	480	576	.833	113	369	482	352	140	44	166	*2431	5.9	4.3	*29.6
97-98—Chicago	82	3181	*881	*1893	.465	565	721	.784	130	345	475	283	141	45	185	*2357	5.8	3.5	*28.7
98-99—						Did not play—retired.													
99-00—						Did not play—retired.													
00-01—						Did not play—retired.													
01-02—Washington	60	2093	551	1324	.416	263	333	.790	50	289	339	310	85	26	162	1375	5.7	5.2	22.9
02-03—Washington	82	3031	679	1527	.445	266	324	.821	71	426	497	311	123	39	173	1640	6.1	3.8	20.0
Totals	1072	41011	12192	24537	.497	7327	8772	.835	1668	5004	6672	5633	2514	893	2924	32292	6.2	5.3	30.1

Three-point field goals: 1984-85, 9-for-52 (.173). 1985-86, 3-for-18 (.167). 1986-87, 12-for-66 (.182). 1987-88, 7-for-53 (.132). 1988-89, 27-for-98 (.276). 1989-90, 92-for-245 (.376). 1990-91, 29-for-93 (.312). 1991-92, 27-for-100 (.270). 1992-93, 81-for-230 (.352). 1994-95, 16-for-32 (.500). 1995-96, 111-for-260 (.427). 1996-97, 111-for-297 (.374). 1997-98, 30-for-126 (.238). 2001-02, 10-for-53 (.189). 2002-03, 16-for-55 (.291). Totals, 581-for-1778 (.327).

Personal fouls/disqualifications: 1984-85, 285/4. 1985-86, 46/0. 1986-87, 237/0. 1987-88, 270/2. 1988-89, 247/2. 1989-90, 241/0. 1990-91, 229/1. 1991-92, 201/1. 1992-93, 188/0. 1994-95, 47/0. 1995-96, 195/0. 1996-97, 156/0. 1997-98, 151/0. 2001-02, 119/0. 2002-03, 171/1. Totals, 2783/11.

NBA PLAYOFF RECORD

NOTES: NBA Finals Most Valuable Player (1991, 1992, 1993, 1996, 1997, 1998). ... Holds NBA Finals career records for most three-point field goals made—42; and most consecutive games with 20 or more points—35 (June 2, 1991 through June 14, 1998). ... Holds NBA Finals single-series record for highest points-per-game average—41.0 (1993). ... Holds NBA Finals single-game record for most points in one half—35 (June 3, 1992, vs. Portland). ... Shares NBA Finals single-game records for most field goals made in one half—14; and most three-point field goals made in one half—6 (June 3, 1992, vs. Portland); most free throws made in one quarter—9 (June 11, 1997, vs. Utah); and most free throws attempted in one half—15 (June 4, 1997, vs. Utah). ... Holds career playoff record for most points—5,987; highest points-per-game average (minimum 25 games or 625 points)—33.4; most field goals attempted—4,497; most free throws made—1,463; most free throws attempted—1,766; and most steals—376. ... Holds single-game playoff records for most points—63 (April 20, 1986, at Boston); and most free throws made in one quarter—13 (May 21, 1991, vs. Detroit). ... Shares single-game playoff records for most field goals made—24 (May 1, 1988, vs. Cleveland); most field goals attempted in one half—25 (May 1, 1988, vs. Cleveland); and most three-point field goals made in one half—6 (June 3, 1992, vs. Portland).

Season Team	G	Min.	FGM	FGA	Pct.	FTM	FTA	Pct.	Off.	Def.	Tot.	Ast.	St.	Blk.	TO	Pts.	RPG	APG	PPG
84-85—Chicago	4	171	34	78	.436	48	58	.828	7	16	23	34	11	4	15	117	5.8	8.5	29.3
85-86—Chicago	3	135	48	95	.505	34	39	.872	5	14	19	17	7	4	14	131	6.3	5.7	43.7
86-87—Chicago	3	128	35	84	.417	35	39	.897	7	14	21	18	6	7	8	107	7.0	6.0	35.7
87-88—Chicago	10	427	138	260	.531	86	99	.869	23	48	71	47	24	11	39	363	7.1	4.7	36.3
88-89—Chicago	17	718	199	390	.510	183	229	.799	26	93	119	130	42	13	68	591	7.0	7.6	34.8
89-90—Chicago	16	674	219	426	.514	133	159	.836	24	91	115	109	45	14	56	587	7.2	6.8	36.7
90-91—Chicago	17	689	197	376	.524	125	148	.845	18	90	108	142	40	23	43	529	6.4	8.4	31.1
91-92—Chicago	22	920	290	581	.499	162	189	.857	37	100	137	127	44	16	81	759	6.2	5.8	34.5
92-93—Chicago	19	783	251	528	.475	136	169	.805	32	96	128	114	39	17	45	666	6.7	6.0	35.1
94-95—Chicago	10	420	120	248	.484	64	79	.810	20	45	65	45	23	14	41	315	6.5	4.5	31.5
95-96—Chicago	18	733	187	407	.459	153	187	.818	31	58	89	74	33	6	42	552	4.9	4.1	30.7
96-97—Chicago	19	804	227	498	.456	123	148	.831	42	108	150	91	30	17	49	590	7.9	4.8	31.1
97-98—Chicago	21	872	243	526	.462	181	223	.812	33	74	107	74	32	12	45	680	5.1	3.5	32.4
Totals	179	7474	2188	4497	.487	1463	1766	.828	305	847	1152	1022	376	158	546	5987	6.4	5.7	33.4

Three-point field goals: 1984-85, 1-for-8 (.125). 1985-86, 1-for-1. 1986-87, 2-for-5 (.400). 1987-88, 1-for-3 (.333). 1988-89, 10-for-35 (.286). 1989-90, 16-for-50 (.320). 1990-91, 10-for-26 (.385). 1991-92, 17-for-44 (.386). 1992-93, 28-for-72 (.389). 1994-95, 11-for-30 (.367). 1995-96, 25-for-62 (.403). 1996-97, 13-for-67 (.194). 1997-98, 13-for-43 (.302). Totals, 148-for-446 (.332).

Personal fouls/disqualifications: 1984-85, 15/0. 1985-86, 13/1. 1986-87, 11/0. 1987-88, 38/1. 1988-89, 65/1. 1989-90, 54/0. 1990-91, 53/0. 1991-92, 62/0. 1992-93, 58/0. 1994-95, 30/0. 1995-96, 49/0. 1996-97, 48/0. 1997-98, 47/0. Totals, 541/3.

NBA ALL-STAR GAME RECORD

NOTES: NBA All-Star Game Most Valuable Player (1988, 1996, 1998). ... Holds career record for field goals (110), field goal attempts (233) and steals (37). Shares record for most field goal attempts in one game—27 (2003). ... Recorded only triple-double in All-Star Game history (February 9, 1997).

Season Team	Min.	FGM	FGA	Pct.	FTM	FTA	Pct.	Off.	Def.	Tot.	Ast.	PF	Dq.	St.	Blk.	TO	Pts.
1985—Chicago	22	2	9	.222	3	4	.750	3	3	6	2	4	0	3	1	1	7
1986—Chicago						Selected, did not play—injured.											

Season Team	Min.	FGM	FGA	Pct.	FTM	FTA	Pct.	REBOUNDS Off.	Def.	Tot.	Ast.	PF	Dq.	St.	Blk.	TO	Pts.
1987—Chicago	28	5	12	.417	1	2	.500	0	0	0	0	4	2	0	2	0	5	11
1988—Chicago	29	17	23	.739	6	6	1.000	3	5	8	3	5	0	4	4	2	40
1989—Chicago	33	13	23	.565	2	4	.500	1	1	2	3	1	0	5	0	4	28
1990—Chicago	29	8	17	.471	0	0	...	1	4	5	2	1	0	5	1	5	17
1991—Chicago	36	10	25	.400	6	7	.857	3	2	5	5	2	0	2	0	10	26
1992—Chicago	31	9	17	.529	0	0	...	1	0	1	5	2	0	2	0	1	18
1993—Chicago	36	10	24	.417	9	13	.692	3	1	4	5	5	0	4	0	6	30
1996—Chicago	22	8	11	.727	4	4	1.000	1	3	4	1	1	0	1	0	0	20
1997—Chicago	26	5	14	.357	4	7	.571	3	8	11	11	4	0	2	0	3	14
1998—Chicago	32	10	18	.556	2	3	.667	1	5	6	8	0	0	3	0	2	23
2002—Washington	22	4	13	.308	0	0	...	0	4	4	3	1	0	2	0	1	8
2003—Washington	36	9	27	.333	2	2	1.000	2	3	5	2	3	0	2	0	2	20
Totals	382	110	233	.472	39	52	.750	22	39	61	54	31	0	37	6	42	262

Three-point field goals: 1985, 0-for-1. 1987, 0-for-1. 1989, 0-for-1. 1990, 1-for-1. 1991, 0-for-2. 1993, 1-for-2 (.500). 1998, 1-for-1. 2003, 0-for-2. Totals, 3-for-11 (.273).

KERR, RED   C

PERSONAL: Born July 17, 1932, in Chicago. ... 6-9/230 (2,05/104,3). ... Full name: John G. Kerr.
HIGH SCHOOL: Tilden Technical School (Chicago).
COLLEGE: Illinois.
TRANSACTIONS: Selected by Syracuse Nationals in first round (sixth pick overall) of 1954 NBA Draft. ... Nationals franchise moved from Syracuse to Philadelphia and renamed 76ers for 1963-64 season. ... Traded by 76ers to Baltimore Bullets for G Wali Jones (September 22, 1965). ... Selected by Chicago Bulls from Bullets in NBA Expansion Draft (April 30, 1966).
MISCELLANEOUS: Member of NBA championship team (1955).

COLLEGIATE RECORD

Season Team	G	Min.	FGM	FGA	Pct.	FTM	FTA	Pct.	Reb.	Ast.	Pts.	AVERAGES RPG	APG	PPG
50-51—Illinois‡					Freshman team did not play intercollegiate schedule.									
51-52—Illinois	26	...	143	365	.392	71	124	.573	...	...	357	...	...	13.7
52-53—Illinois	22	...	153	397	.385	80	123	.650	...	...	386	...	...	17.5
53-54—Illinois	22	...	210	520	.404	136	214	.636	...	...	556	...	...	25.3
Varsity totals	70	...	506	1282	.395	287	461	.623	...	...	1299	...	...	18.6

NBA REGULAR-SEASON RECORD

Season Team	G	Min.	FGM	FGA	Pct.	FTM	FTA	Pct.	Reb.	Ast.	PF	Dq.	Pts.	AVERAGES RPG	APG	PPG
54-55—Syracuse	72	1529	301	718	.419	152	223	.682	474	80	165	2	754	6.6	1.1	10.5
55-56—Syracuse	72	2114	377	935	.403	207	316	.655	607	84	168	3	961	8.4	1.2	13.3
56-57—Syracuse	72	2191	333	827	.403	225	313	.719	807	62	180	1	891	11.0	1.0	12.4
57-58—Syracuse	72	2384	407	1020	.399	280	422	.664	963	88	197	4	1094	13.4	1.2	15.2
58-59—Syracuse	72	2671	502	1139	.441	281	367	.766	1008	142	183	1	1285	14.0	2.0	17.8
59-60—Syracuse	75	2372	436	1111	.392	233	310	.752	913	167	207	4	1105	12.2	2.2	14.7
60-61—Syracuse	79	2676	419	1056	.397	218	299	.729	951	199	230	4	1056	12.0	2.5	13.4
61-62—Syracuse	80	2768	541	1220	.443	222	302	.735	1176	243	272	7	1304	14.7	3.0	16.3
62-63—Syracuse	80	2561	507	1069	.474	241	320	.753	1039	214	208	3	1255	13.0	2.7	15.7
63-64—Philadelphia	80	2898	536	1250	.429	268	357	.751	1017	275	187	2	1340	12.7	3.4	16.8
64-65—Philadelphia	80	1810	264	714	.370	126	181	.696	551	197	132	1	654	6.9	2.5	8.2
65-66—Baltimore	71	1770	286	692	.413	209	272	.768	586	225	148	0	781	8.3	3.2	11.0
Totals	905	27784	4909	11751	.418	2662	3682	.723	10092	2004	2287	34	12480	11.2	2.2	13.8

NBA PLAYOFF RECORD

Season Team	G	Min.	FGM	FGA	Pct.	FTM	FTA	Pct.	Reb.	Ast.	PF	Dq.	Pts.	AVERAGES RPG	APG	PPG
54-55—Syracuse	11	363	59	151	.391	34	61	.557	118	13	27	0	152	10.7	1.2	13.8
55-56—Syracuse	8	213	37	77	.481	15	33	.455	68	10	23	0	89	8.5	1.3	11.1
56-57—Syracuse	5	162	28	65	.431	20	29	.690	69	6	7	0	76	13.8	1.2	15.2
57-58—Syracuse	3	116	18	55	.327	14	18	.778	61	3	5	0	50	20.3	1.0	16.7
58-59—Syracuse	9	312	50	142	.352	30	33	.909	108	24	20	0	130	12.0	2.7	14.4
59-60—Syracuse	3	104	15	51	.294	11	12	.917	25	9	9	0	41	8.3	3.0	13.7
60-61—Syracuse	8	210	30	88	.341	16	23	.696	99	20	18	0	76	12.4	2.5	9.5
61-62—Syracuse	5	193	41	109	.376	6	8	.750	80	10	15	0	88	16.0	2.0	17.6
62-63—Syracuse	5	187	26	60	.433	16	21	.762	75	9	12	0	68	15.0	1.8	13.6
63-64—Philadelphia	5	185	40	83	.482	15	20	.750	69	16	12	0	95	13.8	3.2	19.0
64-65—Philadelphia	11	181	24	67	.358	15	21	.714	38	28	20	0	63	3.5	2.5	5.7
65-66—Baltimore	3	49	2	11	.182	1	2	.500	17	4	5	0	5	5.7	1.3	1.7
Totals	76	2275	370	959	.386	193	281	.687	827	152	173	0	933	10.9	2.0	12.3

NBA ALL-STAR GAME RECORD

Season Team	Min.	FGM	FGA	Pct.	FTM	FTA	Pct.	Reb	Ast.	PF	Dq.	Pts.
1956—Syracuse	16	2	4	.500	0	1	.000	8	0	2	0	4
1959—Syracuse	21	3	14	.214	1	2	.500	9	2	0	0	7
1963—Syracuse	11	0	4	.000	2	2	1.000	2	1	3	0	2
Totals	48	5	22	.227	3	5	.600	19	3	5	0	13

NBA COACHING RECORD

HONORS: NBA Coach of the Year (1967).

Season Team		REGULAR SEASON					PLAYOFFS		
	W	L	Pct.	Finish			W	L	Pct.
66-67—Chicago	33	48	.407	4th/Western Division			0	3	.000
67-68—Chicago	29	53	.354	4th/Western Division			1	4	.200
68-69—Phoenix	16	66	.195	7th/Western Division			—	—	—
69-70—Phoenix	15	23	.395				—	—	—
Totals (4 years)	93	190	.329		Totals (2 years)		1	7	.125

NOTES:
1967—Lost to St. Louis in Western Division Semifinals.
1968—Lost to Los Angeles in Western Division Semifinals.
1970—Resigned as Phoenix head coach (January 2); replaced by Jerry Colangelo.

KING, BERNARD   F

PERSONAL: Born December 4, 1956, in Brooklyn, N.Y. ... 6-7/205 (2,00/93,0). ... Brother of Albert King, guard/forward with New Jersey Nets, Philadelphia 76ers, San Antonio Spurs and Washington Bullets (1981-82 through 1988-89 and 1991-92).
HIGH SCHOOL: Fort Hamilton (Brooklyn, N.Y.).
COLLEGE: Tennessee.

TRANSACTIONS: Selected after junior season by New Jersey Nets in first round (seventh pick overall) of 1977 NBA Draft. ... Traded by Nets with C/F John Gianelli and G Jim Boylan to Utah Jazz for C Rich Kelley (October 2, 1979). ... Traded by Jazz to Golden State Warriors for C/F Wayne Cooper and 1981 second-round draft choice (September 11, 1980). ... Signed as veteran free agent by New York Knicks (September 28, 1982); Warriors matched offer and traded King to Knicks for G Micheal Ray Richardson and 1984 fifth-round draft choice (October 22, 1982). ... Signed as free agent by Washington Bullets (October 16, 1987). ... Waived by Bullets (January 22, 1993). ... Signed as free agent by New Jersey Nets (February 6, 1993).

COLLEGIATE RECORD
NOTES: The Sporting News All-America second team (1977). ... Led NCAA Division I with .622 field goal percentage (1975).

Season Team	G	Min.	FGM	FGA	Pct.	FTM	FTA	Pct.	Reb.	Ast.	Pts.	AVERAGES		
												RPG	APG	PPG
74-75—Tennessee	25	...	273	439	.622	115	147	.782	308	39	661	12.3	1.6	26.4
75-76—Tennessee	25	...	260	454	.573	109	163	.669	325	40	629	13.0	1.6	25.2
76-77—Tennessee	26	...	278	481	.578	116	163	.712	371	82	672	14.3	3.2	25.8
Totals	76	...	811	1374	.590	340	473	.719	1004	161	1962	13.2	2.1	25.8

NBA REGULAR-SEASON RECORD
HONORS: NBA Comeback Player of the Year (1981). ... All-NBA first team (1984, 1985). ... All-NBA second team (1982). ... All-NBA third team (1991). ... NBA All-Rookie team (1978).

Season Team	G	Min.	FGM	FGA	Pct.	FTM	FTA	Pct.	REBOUNDS			Ast.	St.	Blk.	TO	Pts.	AVERAGES		
									Off.	Def.	Tot.						RPG	APG	PPG
77-78—New Jersey	79	3092	798	1665	.479	313	462	.677	265	486	751	193	122	36	311	1909	9.5	2.4	24.2
78-79—New Jersey	82	2859	710	1359	.522	349	619	.564	251	418	669	295	118	39	323	1769	8.2	3.6	21.6
79-80—Utah	19	419	71	137	.518	34	63	.540	24	64	88	52	7	4	50	176	4.6	2.7	9.3
80-81—Golden State	81	2914	731	1244	.588	307	437	.703	178	373	551	287	72	34	265	1771	6.8	3.5	21.9
81-82—Golden State	79	2861	740	1307	.566	352	499	.705	140	329	469	282	78	23	267	1833	5.9	3.6	23.2
82-83—New York	68	2207	603	1142	.528	280	388	.722	99	227	326	195	90	13	197	1486	4.8	2.9	21.9
83-84—New York	77	2667	795	1391	.572	437	561	.779	123	271	394	164	75	17	197	2027	5.1	2.1	26.3
84-85—New York	55	2063	691	1303	.530	426	552	.772	114	203	317	204	71	15	204	1809	5.8	3.7	*32.9
85-86—New York								Did not play—injured.											
86-87—New York	6	214	52	105	.495	32	43	.744	13	19	32	19	2	0	15	136	5.3	3.2	22.7
87-88—Washington	69	2044	470	938	.501	247	324	.762	86	194	280	192	49	10	211	1188	4.1	2.8	17.2
88-89—Washington	81	2559	654	1371	.477	361	441	.819	133	251	384	294	64	13	227	1674	4.7	3.6	20.7
89-90—Washington	82	2687	711	1459	.487	412	513	.803	129	275	404	376	51	7	248	1837	4.9	4.6	22.4
90-91—Washington	64	2401	713	1511	.472	383	485	.790	114	205	319	292	56	16	255	1817	5.0	4.6	28.4
91-92—Washington								Did not play—injured.											
92-93—New Jersey	32	430	91	177	.514	39	57	.684	35	41	76	18	11	3	21	223	2.4	0.6	7.0
Totals	874	29417	7830	15109	.518	3972	5444	.730	1704	3356	5060	2863	866	230	2791	19655	5.8	3.3	22.5

Three-point field goals: 1980-81, 2-for-6 (.333). 1981-82, 1-for-5 (.200). 1982-83, 0-for-6. 1983-84, 1-for-4. 1984-85, 1-for-10 (.100). 1987-88, 1-for-6 (.167). 1988-89, 5-for-30 (.167). 1989-90, 3-for-23 (.130). 1990-91, 8-for-37 (.216). 1992-93, 2-for-7 (.286). Totals, 23-for-134 (.172).
Personal fouls/disqualifications: 1977-78, 302/5. 1978-79, 326/10. 1979-80, 66/3. 1980-81, 304/5. 1981-82, 285/6. 1982-83, 233/5. 1983-84, 273/2. 1984-85, 191/3. 1986-87, 14/0. 1987-88, 202/3. 1988-89, 219/1. 1989-90, 230/1. 1990-91, 187/1. 1992-93, 53/0. Totals, 2885/45.

NBA PLAYOFF RECORD

Season Team	G	Min.	FGM	FGA	Pct.	FTM	FTA	Pct.	REBOUNDS			Ast.	St.	Blk.	TO	Pts.	AVERAGES		
									Off.	Def.	Tot.						RPG	APG	PPG
78-79—New Jersey	2	81	21	42	.500	10	24	.417	5	6	11	7	4	0	6	52	5.5	3.5	26.0
82-83—New York	6	184	56	97	.577	28	35	.800	8	16	24	13	2	0	10	141	4.0	2.2	23.5
83-84—New York	12	477	162	282	.574	93	123	.756	28	46	74	36	14	6	31	417	6.2	3.0	34.8
87-88—Washington	5	168	26	53	.491	17	21	.810	3	8	11	9	3	0	14	69	2.2	1.8	13.8
92-93—New Jersey	3	24	4	7	.571	0	0	...	1	0	1	0	1	0	1	8	0.3	0.0	2.7
Totals	28	934	269	481	.559	148	203	.729	45	76	121	65	24	6	62	687	4.3	2.3	24.5

Three-point field goals: 1982-83, 1-for-3 (.333). 1983-84, 0-for-1. Totals, 1-for-4 (.250).
Personal fouls/disqualifications: 1978-79, 10/0. 1982-83, 16/0. 1983-84, 48/0. 1987-88, 17/0. 1992-93, 3/0. Totals, 94/0.

NBA ALL-STAR GAME RECORD

Season Team	Min.	FGM	FGA	Pct.	FTM	FTA	Pct.	REBOUNDS			Ast.	PF	Dq.	St.	Blk.	TO	Pts.
								Off.	Def.	Tot.							
1982—Golden State	14	2	7	.286	2	2	1.000	0	4	4	1	2	0	3	1	2	6
1984—New York	13	8	13	.615	2	5	.400	2	1	3	4	2	0	0	0	0	18
1985—New York	22	6	10	.600	1	2	.500	4	3	7	1	5	0	0	1	1	13
1991—Washington	26	2	8	.250	4	4	1.000	2	1	3	3	1	0	0	1	1	8
Totals	84	18	38	.474	9	13	.692	8	9	17	9	10	0	3	2	4	45

ALL-TIME GREAT PLAYERS

LAIMBEER, BILL   C

PERSONAL: Born May 19, 1957, in Boston. ... 6-11/260 (2,10/117,9). ... Full name: William Laimbeer Jr. ... Name pronounced lam-BEER.
HIGH SCHOOL: Palos Verdes (Calif.).
JUNIOR COLLEGE: Owens Technical (Ohio).
COLLEGE: Notre Dame.
TRANSACTIONS: Selected by Cleveland Cavaliers in third round (65th pick overall) of 1979 NBA Draft. ... Played in Italy (1979-80). ... Traded by Cavaliers with F Kenny Carr to Detroit Pistons for F Phil Hubbard, C Paul Mokeski and 1982 first- and second-round draft choices (February 16, 1982). ... Announced retirement (December 1, 1993).
CAREER NOTES: Special consultant, Detroit Shock, WNBA (April 18-June 19, 2002). ... Head coach, Detroit Shock (2002-present).
MISCELLANEOUS: Member of NBA championship team (1989, 1990). ... Detroit Pistons franchise all-time leading rebounder with 9,430 (1981-82 through 1993-94).

COLLEGIATE RECORD

Season Team	G	Min.	FGM	FGA	Pct.	FTM	FTA	Pct.	Reb.	Ast.	Pts.	RPG	APG	PPG
76-77—Owens Tech.							Did not play.							
75-76—Notre Dame	10	190	32	65	.492	18	23	.783	79	10	82	7.9	1.0	8.2
77-78—Notre Dame	29	654	97	175	.554	42	62	.677	190	31	236	6.6	1.1	8.1
78-79—Notre Dame	30	614	78	145	.538	35	50	.700	164	30	191	5.5	1.0	6.4
Totals	69	1458	207	385	.538	95	135	.704	433	71	509	6.3	1.0	7.4

ITALIAN LEAGUE RECORD

Season Team	G	Min.	FGM	FGA	Pct.	FTM	FTA	Pct.	Reb.	Ast.	Pts.	RPG	APG	PPG
79-80—Brescia	29	...	258	465	.555	97	124	.782	363	...	613	12.5	...	21.1

NBA REGULAR-SEASON RECORD

Season Team	G	Min.	FGM	FGA	Pct.	FTM	FTA	Pct.	Off.	Def.	Tot.	Ast.	St.	Blk.	TO	Pts.	RPG	APG	PPG
80-81—Cleveland	81	2460	337	670	.503	117	153	.765	266	427	693	216	56	78	132	791	8.6	2.7	9.8
81-82—Clev.-Det.	80	1829	265	536	.494	184	232	.793	234	383	617	100	39	64	121	718	7.7	1.3	9.0
82-83—Detroit	82	2871	436	877	.497	245	310	.790	282	711	993	263	51	118	176	1119	12.1	3.2	13.6
83-84—Detroit	82	2864	553	1044	.530	316	365	.866	329	674 *1003		149	49	84	151	1422	12.2	1.8	17.3
84-85—Detroit	82	2892	595	1177	.506	244	306	.797	295	718	1013	154	69	71	129	1438	12.4	1.9	17.5
85-86—Detroit	82	2891	545	1107	.492	266	319	.834	305	*770 *1075		146	59	65	133	1360	*13.1	1.8	16.6
86-87—Detroit	82	2854	506	1010	.501	245	274	.894	243	712	955	151	72	69	120	1263	11.6	1.8	15.4
87-88—Detroit	82	2897	455	923	.493	187	214	.874	165	667	832	199	66	78	136	1110	10.1	2.4	13.5
88-89—Detroit	81	2640	449	900	.499	178	212	.840	138	638	776	177	51	100	129	1106	9.6	2.2	13.7
89-90—Detroit	81	2675	380	785	.484	164	192	.854	166	614	780	171	57	84	98	981	9.6	2.1	12.1
90-91—Detroit	82	2668	372	778	.478	123	147	.837	173	564	737	157	38	56	98	904	9.0	1.9	11.0
91-92—Detroit	81	2234	342	727	.471	141	176	.801	101	411	512	160	61	61	102	783	6.3	2.0	9.7
92-93—Detroit	79	1933	292	574	.509	93	104	.894	110	309	419	127	46	40	59	687	5.3	1.6	8.7
93-94—Detroit	11	248	47	90	.522	11	13	.846	9	47	56	14	6	4	10	105	5.1	1.3	9.8
Totals	1068	33956	5574	11198	.498	2440	2916	.837	2819	7581	10400	2184	710	965	1594	13790	9.7	2.0	12.9

Three-point field goals: 1981-82, 4-for-13 (.308). 1982-83, 2-for-13 (.154). 1983-84, 0-for-11. 1984-85, 4-for-18 (.222). 1985-86, 4-for-14 (.286). 1986-87, 6-for-21 (.286). 1987-88, 13-for-39 (.333). 1988-89, 30-for-86 (.349). 1989-90, 57-for-158 (.361). 1990-91, 37-for-125 (.296). 1991-92, 32-for-85 (.376). 1992-93, 10-for-27 (.370). 1993-94, 3-for-9 (.333). Totals, 202-for-619 (.326).

Personal fouls/disqualifications: 1980-81, 332/14. 1981-82, 296/5. 1982-83, 320/9. 1983-84, 273/4. 1984-85, 308/4. 1985-86, 291/4. 1986-87, 283/4. 1987-88, 284/6. 1988-89, 259/2. 1989-90, 278/4. 1990-91, 242/3. 1991-92, 225/0. 1992-93, 212/4. 1993-94, 30/0. Totals, 3633/63.

NBA PLAYOFF RECORD

NOTES: Shares NBA Finals single-game record for most points in an overtime period—9 (June 7, 1990, vs. Portland).

Season Team	G	Min.	FGM	FGA	Pct.	FTM	FTA	Pct.	Off.	Def.	Tot.	Ast.	St.	Blk.	TO	Pts.	RPG	APG	PPG
83-84—Detroit	5	165	29	51	.569	18	20	.900	14	48	62	12	4	3	12	76	12.4	2.4	15.2
84-85—Detroit	9	325	48	107	.449	36	51	.706	36	60	96	15	7	7	16	132	10.7	1.7	14.7
85-86—Detroit	4	168	34	68	.500	21	23	.913	20	36	56	1	2	3	8	90	14.0	0.3	22.5
86-87—Detroit	15	543	84	163	.515	15	24	.625	30	126	156	37	15	12	20	184	10.4	2.5	12.3
87-88—Detroit	23	779	114	250	.456	40	45	.889	43	178	221	44	18	19	30	273	9.6	1.9	11.9
88-89—Detroit	17	497	66	142	.465	25	31	.806	26	114	140	31	6	8	19	172	8.2	1.8	10.1
89-90—Detroit	20	667	91	199	.457	25	29	.862	41	170	211	28	23	18	16	222	10.6	1.4	11.1
90-91—Detroit	15	446	66	148	.446	27	31	.871	42	80	122	19	5	12	17	164	8.1	1.3	10.9
91-92—Detroit	5	145	17	46	.370	5	5	1.000	5	28	33	8	4	1	9	41	6.6	1.6	8.2
Totals	113	3735	549	1174	.468	212	259	.819	257	840	1097	195	84	83	143	1354	9.7	1.7	12.0

Three-point field goals: 1984-85, 0-for-2. 1985-86, 1-for-1. 1986-87, 1-for-5 (.200). 1987-88, 5-for-17 (.294). 1988-89, 15-for-42 (.357). 1989-90, 15-for-43 (.349). 1990-91, 5-for-17 (.294). 1991-92, 2-for-10 (.200). Totals, 44-for-137 (.321).

Personal fouls/disqualifications: 1983-84, 23/2. 1984-85, 32/1. 1985-86, 19/1. 1986-87, 53/2. 1987-88, 77/2. 1988-89, 55/1. 1989-90, 77/3. 1990-91, 54/0. 1991-92, 18/1. Totals, 408/13.

NBA ALL-STAR GAME RECORD

Season Team	Min.	FGM	FGA	Pct.	FTM	FTA	Pct.	Off.	Def.	Tot.	Ast.	PF	Dq.	St.	Blk.	TO	Pts.
1983—Detroit	6	1	1	1.000	0	0	...	1	0	1	0	1	0	0	0	1	2
1984—Detroit	17	6	8	.750	1	1	1.000	1	4	5	0	3	0	1	2	0	13
1985—Detroit	11	2	4	.500	1	2	.500	1	2	3	1	1	0	0	0	0	5
1987—Detroit	11	4	7	.571	0	0	...	0	2	2	1	2	0	1	0	0	8
Totals	45	13	20	.650	2	3	.667	3	8	11	2	7	0	2	2	1	28

ALL-TIME GREAT PLAYERS

WNBA COACHING RECORD

Season Team	W	L	Pct.	Finish		W	L	Pct.
				REGULAR SEASON			PLAYOFFS	
2002—Detroit	9	13	.409	8th/Eastern Conference				
2003—Detroit	25	9	.735	1st/Eastern Conference		6	2	.750
Totals (2 years)	34	22	.607		Totals (1 year)	6	2	.750

LANIER, BOB   C

PERSONAL: Born September 10, 1948, in Buffalo, N.Y. ... 6-11/265 (2,10/120,2). ... Full name: Robert Jerry Lanier Jr.
HIGH SCHOOL: Bennett (Buffalo).
COLLEGE: St. Bonaventure.
TRANSACTIONS: Selected by Detroit Pistons in first round (first pick overall) of 1970 NBA Draft. ... Traded by Pistons to Milwaukee Bucks for C Kent Benson and 1980 first-round draft choice (February 4, 1980).
CAREER NOTES: Chairman, NBA Stay in School Program (1989-94).
CAREER HONORS: Elected to Naismith Memorial Basketball Hall of Fame (1992).

COLLEGIATE RECORD

NOTES: THE SPORTING NEWS All-America first team (1970).

Season Team	G	Min.	FGM	FGA	Pct.	FTM	FTA	Pct.	Reb.	Ast.	Pts.	RPG	APG	PPG
												AVERAGES		
66-67—St. Bonaventure‡	15	...	...	...	...	...	...	...	...	...	450	...	...	30.0
67-68—St. Bonaventure	25	...	272	466	.584	112	175	.640	390	...	656	15.6	...	26.2
68-69—St. Bonaventure	24	...	270	460	.587	114	181	.630	374	...	654	15.6	...	27.3
69-70—St. Bonaventure	26	...	308	549	.561	141	194	.727	416	...	757	16.0	...	29.1
Varsity totals	75	...	850	1475	.576	367	550	.667	1180	...	2067	15.7	...	27.6

NBA REGULAR-SEASON RECORD

HONORS: NBA All-Rookie team (1971). ... J. Walter Kennedy Citizenship Award (1978).

Season Team	G	Min.	FGM	FGA	Pct.	FTM	FTA	Pct.	Reb.	Ast.	PF	Dq.	Pts.	RPG	APG	PPG
														AVERAGES		
70-71—Detroit	82	2017	504	1108	.455	273	376	.726	665	146	272	4	1281	8.1	1.8	15.6
71-72—Detroit	80	3092	834	1690	.494	388	505	.768	1132	248	297	6	2056	14.2	3.1	25.7
72-73—Detroit	81	3150	810	1654	.490	307	397	.773	1205	260	278	4	1927	14.9	3.2	23.8

Season Team	G	Min.	FGM	FGA	Pct.	FTM	FTA	Pct.	Off.	Def.	Tot.	Ast.	St.	Blk.	TO	Pts.	RPG	APG	PPG
										REBOUNDS								AVERAGES	
73-74—Detroit	81	3047	748	1483	.504	326	409	.797	269	805	1074	343	110	247	...	1822	13.3	4.2	22.5
74-75—Detroit	76	2987	731	1433	.510	361	450	.802	225	689	914	350	75	172	...	1823	12.0	4.6	24.0
75-76—Detroit	64	2363	541	1017	.532	284	370	.768	217	529	746	217	79	86	...	1366	11.7	3.4	21.3
76-77—Detroit	64	2446	678	1269	.534	260	318	.818	200	545	745	214	70	126	...	1616	11.6	3.3	25.3
77-78—Detroit	63	2311	622	1159	.537	298	386	.772	197	518	715	216	82	93	225	1542	11.3	3.4	24.5
78-79—Detroit	53	1835	489	950	.515	275	367	.749	164	330	494	140	50	75	175	1253	9.3	2.6	23.6
79-80—Detroit-Mil.	63	2131	466	867	.537	277	354	.782	152	400	552	184	74	89	162	1210	8.8	2.9	19.2
80-81—Milwaukee	67	1753	376	716	.525	208	277	.751	128	285	413	179	73	81	139	961	6.2	2.7	14.3
81-82—Milwaukee	74	1986	407	729	.558	182	242	.752	92	296	388	219	72	56	166	996	5.2	3.0	13.5
82-83—Milwaukee	39	978	163	332	.491	91	133	.684	58	142	200	105	34	24	82	417	5.1	2.7	10.7
83-84—Milwaukee	72	2007	392	685	.572	194	274	.708	141	314	455	186	58	51	163	978	6.3	2.6	13.6
Totals	959	32103	7761	15092	.514	3724	4858	.767	...	9698	3007	777	1100	1112	19248	10.1	3.1	20.1

Three-point field goals: 1979-80, 1-for-6 (.167). 1980-81, 1-for-1. 1981-82, 0-for-2. 1982-83, 0-for-1. 1983-84, 0-for-3. Totals, 2-for-13 (.154).
Personal fouls/disqualifications: 1973-74, 273/7. 1974-75, 237/1. 1975-76, 203/2. 1976-77, 174/0. 1977-78, 185/2. 1978-79, 181/5. 1979-80, 200/3. 1980-81, 184/0. 1981-82, 211/3. 1982-83, 125/2. 1983-84, 228/8. Totals, 3048/47.

NBA PLAYOFF RECORD

Season Team	G	Min.	FGM	FGA	Pct.	FTM	FTA	Pct.	Off.	Def.	Tot.	Ast.	St.	Blk.	TO	Pts.	RPG	APG	PPG
										REBOUNDS								AVERAGES	
73-74—Detroit	7	303	77	152	.507	30	38	.789	26	81	107	21	4	14	...	184	15.3	3.0	26.3
74-75—Detroit	3	128	26	51	.510	9	12	.750	5	27	32	19	4	12	...	61	10.7	6.3	20.3
75-76—Detroit	9	359	95	172	.552	45	50	.900	39	75	114	30	8	21	...	235	12.7	3.3	26.1
76-77—Detroit	3	118	34	54	.630	16	19	.842	13	37	50	6	3	7	...	84	16.7	2.0	28.0
79-80—Milwaukee	7	256	52	101	.515	31	42	.738	17	48	65	31	7	8	17	135	9.3	4.4	19.3
80-81—Milwaukee	7	236	50	85	.588	23	32	.719	12	40	52	28	12	8	15	123	7.4	4.0	17.6
81-82—Milwaukee	6	212	41	80	.513	14	25	.560	18	27	45	22	8	5	14	96	7.5	3.7	16.0
82-83—Milwaukee	9	250	51	89	.573	21	35	.600	17	46	63	23	5	14	21	123	7.0	2.6	13.7
83-84—Milwaukee	16	499	82	171	.480	39	44	.886	32	85	117	55	11	10	38	203	7.3	3.4	12.7
Totals	67	2361	508	955	.532	228	297	.768	179	466	645	235	62	99	105	1244	9.6	3.5	18.6

Three-point field goals: 1981-82, 0-for-1.
Personal fouls/disqualifications: 1973-74, 28/1. 1974-75, 10/0. 1975-76, 34/1. 1976-77, 10/0. 1979-80, 23/0. 1980-81, 18/0. 1981-82, 21/2. 1982-83, 32/2. 1983-84, 57/1. Totals, 233/7.

NBA ALL-STAR GAME RECORD

NOTES: NBA All-Star Game Most Valuable Player (1974).

Season Team	Min.	FGM	FGA	Pct.	FTM	FTA	Pct.	Reb	Ast.	PF	Dq.	Pts.
1972—Detroit	5	0	2	.000	2	3	.667	3	0	0	0	2
1973—Detroit	12	5	9	.556	0	0	...	6	0	1	0	10

Season Team	Min.	FGM	FGA	Pct.	FTM	FTA	Pct.	Off.	Def.	Tot.	Ast.	PF	Dq.	St.	Blk.	TO	Pts.
									REBOUNDS								
1974—Detroit	26	11	15	.733	2	2	1.000	2	8	10	2	1	0	0	2	...	24
1975—Detroit	12	1	4	.250	0	0	...	2	5	7	2	3	0	2	0	...	2
1977—Detroit	20	7	8	.875	3	3	1.000	5	5	10	4	3	0	1	1	...	17
1978—Detroit	4	0	1		1	2	.500	2	0	2	0	0	0	0	1	...	1

Season Team	Min.	FGM	FGA	Pct.	FTM	FTA	Pct.	REBOUNDS Off.	Def.	Tot.	Ast.	PF	Dq.	St.	Blk.	TO	Pts.
1979—Detroit..................	31	5	10	.500	0	0	...	1	3	4	4	4	0	1	1	0	10
1982—Milwaukee............	11	3	7	.429	2	2	1.000	2	1	3	0	3	0	0	1	1	8
Totals...........................	121	32	55	.582	10	12	.833	...	...	45	12	15	0	4	5	2	74

NBA COACHING RECORD

BACKGROUND: Assistant coach, Golden State Warriors (beginning of 1994-95 season-February 13, 1995).

Season Team	REGULAR SEASON					PLAYOFFS		
	W	L	Pct.	Finish		W	L	Pct.
94-95—Golden State	12	25	.324	6th/Pacific Division		—	—	—

NOTES:
1995—Replaced Don Nelson as head coach (February 13), with record of 14-31 and club in sixth place.

LUCAS, JERRY   F/C

PERSONAL: Born March 30, 1940, in Middletown, Ohio. ... 6-8/235 (2,03/106,6). ... Full name: Jerry Ray Lucas. ... Nickname: Luke.
HIGH SCHOOL: Middletown (Ohio).
COLLEGE: Ohio State.
TRANSACTIONS: Selected by Cincinnati Royals in 1962 NBA Draft (territorial pick). ... Signed by Cleveland Pipers of American Basketball League (1962); Pipers dropped out of ABL prior to 1962-63 season. ... Did not play pro basketball (1962-63). ... Traded by Royals to San Francisco Warriors for G Jim King and F Bill Turner (October 25, 1969). ... Traded by Warriors to New York Knicks for F Cazzie Russell (May 7, 1971).
CAREER HONORS: Elected to Naismith Memorial Basketball Hall of Fame (1980). ... One of the 50 Greatest Players in NBA History (1996).
MISCELLANEOUS: Member of NBA championship team (1973). ... Member of gold-medal-winning U.S. Olympic team (1960).

COLLEGIATE RECORD

NOTES: The Sporting News College Player of the Year (1961, 1962). ... The Sporting News All-America first team (1960, 1961, 1962). ... Member of NCAA championship team (1960). ... Led NCAA Division I with .637 field-goal percentage (1960), .623 field-goal percentage (1961) and .611 field-goal percentage (1962). ... Led NCAA Division I with .198 rebound average (1960-61) and .211 rebound average (1961-62), when championship was determined by highest individual recoveries as percentage of total recoveries by both teams in all games.

Season Team	G	Min.	FGM	FGA	Pct.	FTM	FTA	Pct.	Reb.	Ast.	Pts.	AVERAGES RPG	APG	PPG
58-59—Ohio State‡					Freshman team did not play intercollegiate schedule.									
59-60—Ohio State	27	...	283	444	.637	144	187	.770	442	...	710	16.4	...	26.3
60-61—Ohio State	27	...	256	411	.623	159	208	.764	470	...	671	17.4	...	24.9
61-62—Ohio State	28	...	237	388	.611	135	169	.799	499	...	609	17.8	...	21.8
Varsity totals	82	...	776	1243	.624	438	564	.777	1411	...	1990	17.2	...	24.3

NBA REGULAR-SEASON RECORD

HONORS: NBA Rookie of the Year (1964). ... All-NBA first team (1965, 1966, 1968). ... All-NBA second team (1964, 1967). ... NBA All-Rookie team (1964).

Season Team	G	Min.	FGM	FGA	Pct.	FTM	FTA	Pct.	Reb.	Ast.	PF	Dq.	Pts.	AVERAGES RPG	APG	PPG
63-64—Cincinnati......................	79	3273	545	1035	*.527	310	398	.779	1375	204	300	6	1400	17.4	2.6	17.7
64-65—Cincinnati......................	66	2864	558	1121	.498	298	366	.814	1321	157	214	1	1414	20.0	2.4	21.4
65-66—Cincinnati......................	79	3517	690	1523	.453	317	403	.787	1668	213	274	5	1697	21.1	2.7	21.5
66-67—Cincinnati......................	81	3558	577	1257	.459	284	359	.791	1547	268	280	2	1438	19.1	3.3	17.8
67-68—Cincinnati......................	82	3619	707	1361	.519	346	445	.778	1560	251	243	3	1760	19.0	3.1	21.5
68-69—Cincinnati......................	74	3075	555	1007	.551	247	327	.755	1360	306	206	0	1357	18.4	4.1	18.3
69-70—Cin.-San Francisco........	67	2420	405	799	.507	200	255	.784	951	173	196	2	1010	14.2	2.6	15.1
70-71—San Francisco................	80	3251	623	1250	.498	289	367	.787	1265	239	197	0	1535	15.8	3.7	19.2
71-72—New York......................	77	2926	543	1060	.512	197	249	.791	1011	318	218	1	1283	13.1	4.1	16.7
72-73—New York......................	71	2001	312	608	.513	80	100	.800	510	317	157	0	704	7.2	4.5	9.9

Season Team	G	Min.	FGM	FGA	Pct.	FTM	FTA	Pct.	REBOUNDS Off.	Def.	Tot.	Ast.	St.	Blk.	TO	Pts.	AVERAGES RPG	APG	PPG
73-74—New York.......	73	1627	194	420	.462	67	96	.698	62	312	374	230	28	24	...	455	5.1	3.2	6.2
Totals	829	32131	5709	11441	.499	2635	3365	.783	...	...12942	2730	28	24	...	14053	15.6	3.3	17.0

Personal fouls/disqualifications: 1973-74, 134/0.

NBA PLAYOFF RECORD

Season Team	G	Min.	FGM	FGA	Pct.	FTM	FTA	Pct.	Reb.	Ast.	PF	Dq.	Pts.	AVERAGES RPG	APG	PPG
63-64—Cincinnati........................	10	370	48	123	.390	26	37	.703	125	34	37	1	122	12.5	3.4	12.2
64-65—Cincinnati........................	4	195	38	75	.507	17	22	.773	84	9	12	0	93	21.0	2.3	23.3
65-66—Cincinnati........................	5	231	40	85	.471	27	35	.771	101	14	14	0	107	20.2	2.8	21.4
66-67—Cincinnati........................	4	183	24	55	.436	2	2	1.000	77	8	15	0	50	19.3	2.0	12.5
70-71—San Francisco..................	5	171	39	77	.507	11	16	.688	50	16	14	0	89	10.0	3.2	17.8
71-72—New York........................	16	737	119	238	.500	59	71	.831	173	85	49	1	297	10.8	5.3	18.6
72-73—New York........................	17	368	54	112	.482	20	23	.870	85	39	47	0	128	5.0	2.3	7.5

Season Team	G	Min.	FGM	FGA	Pct.	FTM	FTA	Pct.	REBOUNDS Off.	Def.	Tot.	Ast.	St.	Blk.	TO	Pts.	AVERAGES RPG	APG	PPG
73-74—New York.......	11	115	5	21	.238	0	0	...	6	16	22	9	4	0	...	10	2.0	0.8	0.9
Totals	72	2370	367	786	.467	162	206	.786	...	...	717	214	4	0	...	896	10.0	3.0	12.4

Personal fouls/disqualifications: 1973-74, 9/0.

NBA ALL-STAR GAME RECORD

NOTES: NBA All-Star Game Most Valuable Player (1965).

Season Team	Min.	FGM	FGA	Pct.	FTM	FTA	Pct.	Reb.	Ast.	PF	Dq.	Pts.
1964—Cincinnati......................	36	3	6	.500	5	6	.833	8	0	5	0	11
1965—Cincinnati......................	35	12	19	.632	1	1	1.000	10	1	2	0	25

Season Team	Min.	FGM	FGA	Pct.	FTM	FTA	Pct.	Reb	Ast.	PF	Dq.	Pts.
1966—Cincinnati	23	4	11	.364	2	2	1.000	19	0	2	0	10
1967—Cincinnati	22	3	5	.600	1	1	1.000	7	2	3	0	7
1968—Cincinnati	21	6	9	.667	4	4	1.000	5	4	3	0	16
1969—Cincinnati	17	2	5	.400	4	5	.800	6	1	3	0	8
1971—San Francisco	29	5	9	.556	2	2	1.000	9	4	2	0	12
Totals	183	35	64	.547	19	21	.905	64	12	20	0	89

MACAULEY, ED   C/F

PERSONAL: Born March 22, 1928, in St. Louis. ... 6-8/190 (2,03/86,2). ... Full name: Charles Edward Macauley Jr. ... Nickname: Easy Ed.
HIGH SCHOOL: St. Louis University High School (St. Louis).
COLLEGE: St. Louis.
TRANSACTIONS: Selected by St. Louis Bombers in 1949 Basketball Association of America Draft (territorial pick). ... Selected by Boston Celtics in NBA dispersal draft (April 25, 1950). ... Traded by Celtics with draft rights to F/G Cliff Hagan to St. Louis Hawks for draft rights to C Bill Russell (April 29, 1956).
CAREER HONORS: Elected to Naismith Memorial Basketball Hall of Fame (1960).
MISCELLANEOUS: Member of NBA championship team (1958).

COLLEGIATE RECORD

NOTES: The Sporting News All-America first team (1949). ... Led NCAA Division I with .524 field-goal percentage (1949).

Season Team	G	Min.	FGM	FGA	Pct.	FTM	FTA	Pct.	Reb.	Ast.	Pts.	RPG	APG	PPG
45-46—St. Louis	23	...	94	...	...	71	...	...	...	...	259	...	...	11.3
46-47—St. Louis	28	...	141	...	...	104	...	...	...	...	386	...	...	13.8
47-48—St. Louis	27	...	132	324	.407	104	159	.654	...	...	368	...	...	13.6
48-49—St. Louis	26	...	144	275	.524	116	153	.758	...	...	404	...	...	15.5
Totals	104	...	511	...	...	395	...	...	...	...	1417	...	...	13.6

NBA REGULAR-SEASON RECORD

HONORS: All-NBA first team (1951, 1952, 1953). ... All-NBA second team (1954).

Season Team	G	Min.	FGM	FGA	Pct.	FTM	FTA	Pct.	Reb.	Ast.	PF	Dq.	Pts.	RPG	APG	PPG
49-50—St. Louis	67	...	351	882	.398	379	528	.718	...	200	221	...	1081	...	3.0	16.1
50-51—Boston	68	...	459	985	.466	466	614	.759	616	252	205	4	1384	9.1	3.7	20.4
51-52—Boston	66	2631	384	888	.432	496	621	.799	529	232	174	0	1264	8.0	3.5	19.2
52-53—Boston	69	2902	451	997	.452	500	667	.750	629	280	188	0	1402	9.1	4.1	20.3
53-54—Boston	71	2792	462	950	*.486	420	554	.758	571	271	168	1	1344	8.0	3.8	18.9
54-55—Boston	71	2706	403	951	.424	442	558	.792	600	275	171	0	1248	8.5	3.9	17.6
55-56—Boston	71	2354	420	995	.422	400	504	.794	422	211	158	2	1240	5.9	3.0	17.5
56-57—St. Louis	72	2582	414	987	.419	359	479	.749	440	202	206	2	1187	6.1	2.8	16.5
57-58—St. Louis	72	1908	376	879	.428	267	369	.724	478	143	156	2	1019	6.6	2.0	14.2
58-59—St. Louis	14	196	22	75	.293	21	35	.600	40	13	20	1	65	2.9	0.9	4.6
Totals	641	...	3742	8589	.436	3750	4929	.761	...	2079	1667	...	11234	...	3.2	17.5

NBA PLAYOFF RECORD

Season Team	G	Min.	FGM	FGA	Pct.	FTM	FTA	Pct.	Reb.	Ast.	PF	Dq.	Pts.	RPG	APG	PPG
50-51—Boston	2	...	17	36	.472	10	16	.625	18	8	4	0	44	9.0	4.0	22.0
51-52—Boston	3	129	27	49	.551	16	19	.842	33	11	11	1	70	11.0	3.7	23.3
52-53—Boston	6	278	31	71	.437	39	54	.722	58	21	23	2	101	9.7	3.5	16.8
53-54—Boston	5	127	8	22	.364	9	13	.692	21	21	14	0	25	4.2	4.2	5.0
54-55—Boston	7	283	43	93	.462	41	54	.759	52	32	21	0	127	7.4	4.6	18.1
55-56—Boston	3	73	12	30	.400	7	11	.636	15	5	6	0	31	5.0	1.7	10.3
56-57—St. Louis	10	297	44	109	.404	54	74	.730	62	22	39	3	142	6.2	2.2	14.2
57-58—St. Louis	11	227	36	89	.405	36	50	.720	62	18	23	0	108	5.6	1.6	9.8
Totals	47	...	218	499	.437	212	291	.729	321	138	141	6	648	6.8	2.9	13.8

NBA ALL-STAR GAME RECORD

NOTES: NBA All-Star Game Most Valuable Player (1951).

Season Team	Min.	FGM	FGA	Pct.	FTM	FTA	Pct.	Reb	Ast.	PF	Dq.	Pts.
1951—Boston	...	7	12	.583	6	7	.857	6	1	3	0	20
1952—Boston	28	3	7	.429	9	9	1.000	7	3	2	0	15
1953—Boston	35	5	12	.417	8	8	1.000	7	3	2	0	18
1954—Boston	25	4	11	.364	5	6	.833	1	3	2	0	13
1955—Boston	27	1	5	.200	4	5	.800	4	2	1	0	6
1956—Boston	20	1	9	.111	2	4	.500	2	3	3	0	4
1957—St. Louis	19	3	6	.500	1	2	.500	5	3	0	0	7
Totals	...	24	62	.387	35	41	.854	32	18	13	0	83

NBA COACHING RECORD

	REGULAR SEASON				PLAYOFFS		
Season Team	W	L	Pct.	Finish	W	L	Pct.
58-59—St. Louis	43	19	.694	1st/Western Division	2	4	.333
59-60—St. Louis	46	29	.613	1st/Western Division	7	7	.500
Totals (2 years)	89	48	.650	Totals (2 years)	9	11	.450

NOTES:
1958—Replaced Andy Phillip as St. Louis head coach (November), with record of 6-4.
1959—Lost to Minneapolis in Western Division Finals.
1960—Defeated Minneapolis, 4-3, in Western Division Finals; lost to Boston, 4-3, in NBA Finals.

MALONE, JEFF　　　　　　　　　　G

PERSONAL: Born June 28, 1961, in Mobile, Ala. ... 6-4/205 (1,93/93,0). ... Full name: Jeffrey Nigel Malone.
HIGH SCHOOL: Southwest (Macon, Ga.).
COLLEGE: Mississippi State.
TRANSACTIONS: Selected by Washington Bullets in first round (10th pick overall) of 1983 NBA Draft. ... Traded by Bullets to Utah Jazz in three-way deal in which Sacramento Kings sent F Pervis Ellison to Bullets and Jazz sent G Bob Hansen, F/C Eric Leckner and 1990 first- and second-round draft choices to Kings (June 25, 1990); Jazz also received 1990 second-round draft choice from Kings and Kings also received 1991 second-round draft choice from Bullets. ... Traded by Jazz with 1994 conditional first-round draft choice to Philadelphia 76ers for G Jeff Hornacek and G Sean Green (February 24, 1994). ... Waived by 76ers (January 4, 1996). ... Signed by Miami Heat to first of two consecutive 10-day contracts (February 12, 1996). ... Re-signed by Heat for remainder of season (March 3, 1996). ... Played in Greece (1996-97).
CAREER NOTES: Head coach, Columbus Riverdragons (2001-05) and Florida Flame (2005-06) of the NBA Development League.

COLLEGIATE RECORD

NOTES: The Sporting News All-America first team (1983).

Season Team	G	Min.	FGM	FGA	Pct.	FTM	FTA	Pct.	Reb.	Ast.	Pts.	RPG	APG	PPG
79-80—Mississippi State	27	781	139	303	.459	42	51	.824	90	39	320	3.3	1.4	11.9
80-81—Mississippi State	27	999	219	447	.490	105	128	.820	113	43	543	4.2	1.6	20.1
81-82—Mississippi State	27	1001	225	410	.549	52	70	.743	111	20	502	4.1	0.7	18.6
82-83—Mississippi State	29	1070	323	608	.531	131	159	.824	106	66	777	3.7	2.3	26.8
Totals	110	3851	906	1768	.512	330	408	.809	420	168	2142	3.8	1.5	19.5

NBA REGULAR-SEASON RECORD

HONORS: NBA All-Rookie team (1984).

Season Team	G	Min.	FGM	FGA	Pct.	FTM	FTA	Pct.	Off.	Def.	Tot.	Ast.	St.	Blk.	TO	Pts.	RPG	APG	PPG
83-84—Washington	81	1976	408	918	.444	142	172	.826	57	98	155	151	23	13	110	982	1.9	1.9	12.1
84-85—Washington	76	2613	605	1213	.499	211	250	.844	60	146	206	184	52	9	107	1436	2.7	2.4	18.9
85-86—Washington	80	2992	735	1522	.483	322	371	.868	66	222	288	191	70	12	108	1795	3.6	2.4	22.4
86-87—Washington	80	2763	689	1509	.457	376	425	.885	50	168	218	298	75	13	182	1758	2.7	3.7	22.0
87-88—Washington	80	2655	648	1360	.476	335	380	.882	44	162	206	237	51	13	172	1641	2.6	3.0	20.5
88-89—Washington	76	2418	677	1410	.480	296	340	.871	55	124	179	219	39	14	165	1651	2.4	2.9	21.7
89-90—Washington	75	2567	781	1592	.491	257	293	.877	54	152	206	243	48	6	125	1820	2.7	3.2	24.3
90-91—Utah	69	2466	525	1034	.508	231	252	.917	36	170	206	143	50	6	108	1282	3.0	2.1	18.6
91-92—Utah	81	2922	691	1353	.511	256	285	.898	49	184	233	180	56	5	140	1639	2.9	2.2	20.2
92-93—Utah	79	2558	595	1205	.494	236	277	.852	31	142	173	128	42	4	125	1429	2.2	1.6	18.1
93-94—Utah-Phil.	77	2560	525	1081	.486	205	247	.830	51	148	199	125	40	5	85	1262	2.6	1.6	16.4
94-95—Philadelphia	19	660	144	284	.507	51	59	.864	11	44	55	29	15	0	29	350	2.9	1.5	18.4
95-96—Phil.-Miami	32	510	76	193	.394	29	32	.906	8	32	40	26	16	0	22	186	1.3	0.8	5.8
Totals	905	29660	7099	14674	.484	2947	3383	.871	572	1792	2364	2154	577	100	1538	17231	2.6	2.4	19.0

Three-point field goals: 1983-84, 24-for-74 (.324). 1984-85, 15-for-72 (.208). 1985-86, 3-for-17 (.176). 1986-87, 4-for-26 (.154). 1987-88, 10-for-24 (.417). 1988-89, 1-for-19 (.053). 1989-90, 1-for-6 (.167). 1990-91, 1-for-6 (.167). 1991-92, 1-for-12 (.083). 1992-93, 3-for-9 (.333). 1993-94, 7-for-12 (.583). 1994-95, 11-for-28 (.393). 1995-96, 5-for-16 (.313). Totals, 86-for-321 (.268).

Personal fouls/disqualifications: 1983-84, 189/0. 1984-85, 156/0. 1985-86, 179/1. 1986-87, 188/0. 1987-88, 184/6. 1988-89, 155/0. 1989-90, 116/1. 1990-91, 128/0. 1991-92, 126/1. 1992-93, 117/0. 1993-94, 123/0. 1994-95, 35/0. 1995-96, 25/0. Totals, 1695/7.

NBA PLAYOFF RECORD

Season Team	G	Min.	FGM	FGA	Pct.	FTM	FTA	Pct.	Off.	Def.	Tot.	Ast.	St.	Blk.	TO	Pts.	RPG	APG	PPG
83-84—Washington	4	71	12	26	.462	0	0	...	2	3	5	2	1	0	3	24	1.3	0.5	6.0
84-85—Washington	4	126	27	56	.482	10	13	.769	3	3	6	8	5	0	4	65	1.5	2.0	16.3
85-86—Washington	5	197	42	103	.408	26	29	.897	4	12	16	17	7	3	11	110	3.2	3.4	22.0
86-87—Washington	3	105	17	46	.370	11	11	1.000	1	6	7	9	1	0	11	45	2.3	3.0	15.0
87-88—Washington	5	199	50	97	.515	28	37	.757	3	14	17	11	5	5	14	128	3.4	2.2	25.6
90-91—Utah	9	351	71	144	.493	44	48	.917	7	28	35	29	9	1	12	186	3.9	3.2	20.7
91-92—Utah	16	610	134	275	.487	62	72	.861	12	27	39	31	8	2	26	331	2.4	1.9	20.7
92-93—Utah	5	150	29	65	.446	9	13	.692	3	13	16	3	3	1	9	67	3.2	0.6	13.4
Totals	51	1809	382	812	.470	190	223	.852	35	106	141	110	39	12	90	956	2.8	2.2	18.7

Three-point field goals: 1983-84, 0-for-1. 1984-85, 1-for-3 (.333). 1985-86, 0-for-2. 1987-88, 0-for-1. 1990-91, 0-for-2. 1991-92, 1-for-3 (.333). Totals, 2-for-12 (.167).

Personal fouls/disqualifications: 1983-84, 6/0. 1984-85, 14/1. 1985-86, 13/0. 1986-87, 8/0. 1987-88, 16/0. 1990-91, 22/0. 1991-92, 33/0. 1992-93, 11/0. Totals, 123/1.

NBA ALL-STAR GAME RECORD

Season Team	Min.	FGM	FGA	Pct.	FTM	FTA	Pct.	Off.	Def.	Tot.	Ast.	PF	Dq.	St.	Blk.	TO	Pts.
1986—Washington	12	3	5	.600	0	0	...	0	1	1	4	0	0	1	0	0	6
1987—Washington	13	3	5	.600	0	0	...	1	1	2	2	1	0	0	0	1	6
Totals	25	6	10	.600	0	0	...	1	2	3	6	1	0	1	0	1	12

Three-point field goals: 1987, 0-for-1.

GREEK LEAGUE RECORD

Season Team	G	Min.	FGM	FGA	Pct.	FTM	FTA	Pct.	Reb.	Ast.	Pts.	RPG	APG	PPG
96-97—VAO	12	423	65	165	.394	35	46	.761	29	12	175	2.4	1.0	14.6

MALONE, KARL　　　　　　　　　　F

PERSONAL: Born July 24, 1963, in Summerfield, La. ... 6-9/256. (2,06/116,1). ... Nickname: The Mailman.
HIGH SCHOOL: Summerfield (La.).
COLLEGE: Louisiana Tech.
TRANSACTIONS/CAREER NOTES: Selected after junior season by Utah Jazz in first round (13th pick overall) of 1985 NBA Draft. ... Signed as free agent by Los Angeles Lakers (July 16, 2003)

CAREER HONORS: NBA 50th Anniversary All-Time Team (1996).

MISCELLANEOUS: Member of gold-medal-winning U.S. Olympic teams (1992, 1996). ... Utah Jazz franchise all-time leading scorer with 36,374 points and all-time leading rebounder with 14,601 (1985-86 through 2002-03).

COLLEGIATE RECORD

Season Team	G	Min.	FGM	FGA	Pct.	FTM	FTA	Pct.	Reb.	Ast.	Pts.	RPG	APG	PPG
81-82—Louisiana Tech						Did not play—redshirted.								
82-83—Louisiana Tech	28	894	217	373	.582	152	244	.623	289	10	586	10.3	0.4	20.9
83-84—Louisiana Tech	32	1011	220	382	.576	161	236	.682	282	42	601	8.8	1.3	18.8
84-85—Louisiana Tech	32	926	216	399	.541	97	170	.571	288	73	529	9.0	2.3	16.5
Totals	92	2831	653	1154	.566	410	650	.631	859	125	1716	9.3	1.4	18.7

NBA REGULAR-SEASON RECORD

RECORDS: Holds career records for most seasons with 2,000 or more points—12 (1987-88 through 1997-98 and 1999-2000); most consecutive seasons with 2,000 or more points—11 (1987-88 through 1997-98); most free throws made—9,619; most free throws attempted—12,963; most seasons leading league in free throws made—8; most consecutive seasons leading league in free throws made—5; and most turnovers—4,421.

HONORS: NBA Most Valuable Player (1997, 1999). ... IBM Award, for all-around contributions to team's success (1998). ... All-NBA first team (1989, 1990, 1991, 1992, 1993, 1994, 1995, 1996, 1997, 1998, 1999). ... All-NBA second team (1988, 2000). ... All-NBA third team (2001). ... NBA All-Defensive first team (1997, 1998, 1999). ... NBA All-Defensive second team (1988). ... NBA All-Rookie team (1986).

Season Team	G	Min.	FGM	FGA	Pct.	FTM	FTA	Pct.	REBOUNDS Off.	Def.	Tot.	Ast.	St.	Blk.	TO	Pts.	AVERAGES RPG	APG	PPG
85-86—Utah................	81	2475	504	1016	.496	195	405	.481	174	544	718	236	105	44	279	1203	8.9	2.9	14.9
86-87—Utah................	82	2857	728	1422	.512	323	540	.598	278	577	855	158	104	60	237	1779	10.4	1.9	21.7
87-88—Utah................	82	3198	858	1650	.520	552	789	.700	277	709	986	199	117	50	*325	2268	12.0	2.4	27.7
88-89—Utah................	80	3126	809	1559	.519	*703	*918	.766	259	594	853	219	144	70	285	2326	10.7	2.7	29.1
89-90—Utah................	82	3122	914	1627	.562	*696	*913	.762	232	679	911	226	121	50	304	2540	11.1	2.8	31.0
90-91—Utah................	82	3302	847	1608	.527	*684	*888	.770	236	*731	967	270	89	79	244	2382	11.8	3.3	29.0
91-92—Utah................	81	3054	798	1516	.526	*673	*865	.778	225	684	909	241	108	51	248	2272	11.2	3.0	28.0
92-93—Utah................	82	3099	797	1443	.552	*619	*836	.740	227	692	919	308	124	85	240	2217	11.2	3.8	27.0
93-94—Utah................	82	3329	772	1552	.497	511	736	.694	235	705	940	328	125	126	234	2063	11.5	4.0	25.2
94-95—Utah................	82	3126	830	1548	.536	516	695	.742	156	*715	871	285	129	85	236	2187	10.6	3.5	26.7
95-96—Utah................	82	3113	789	1520	.519	512	708	.723	175	629	804	345	138	56	199	2106	9.8	4.2	25.7
96-97—Utah................	82	2998	864	1571	.550	*521	*690	.755	193	616	809	368	113	48	233	2249	9.9	4.5	27.4
97-98—Utah................	81	3030	780	1472	.530	*628	*825	.761	189	645	834	316	96	70	247	2190	10.3	3.9	27.0
98-99—Utah................	49	1832	393	797	.493	*378	480	.788	107	356	463	201	62	28	162	1164	9.4	4.1	23.8
99-00—Utah................	82	2947	752	1476	.509	589	739	.797	169	610	779	304	79	71	231	2095	9.5	3.7	25.5
00-01—Utah................	81	2895	670	1345	.498	536	676	.793	114	555	669	361	93	62	244	1878	8.3	4.5	23.2
01-02—Utah................	80	3040	635	1399	.454	509	639	.797	142	544	686	341	152	59	263	1788	8.6	4.3	22.4
02-03—Utah................	81	2936	595	1289	.462	474	621	.763	113	515	628	379	136	31	210	1667	7.8	4.7	20.6
03-04—L.A. Lakers	42	1373	193	400	.483	168	225	.747	61	306	367	163	50	20	103	554	8.7	3.9	13.2
Totals	1476	54852	13528	26210	.516	9787	13188	.742	3562	11406	14968	5248	2085	1145	4524	36928	10.1	3.6	25.0

Three-point field goals: 1985-86, 0-for-2. 1986-87, 0-for-7. 1987-88, 0-for-5. 1988-89, 5-for-16 (.313). 1989-90, 16-for-43 (.372). 1990-91, 4-for-14 (.286). 1991-92, 3-for-17 (.176). 1992-93, 4-for-20 (.200). 1993-94, 8-for-32 (.250). 1994-95, 11-for-41 (.268). 1995-96, 16-for-40 (.400). 1996-97, 0-for-13. 1997-98, 2-for-6 (.333). 1998-99, 0-for-1. 1999-00, 2-for-8 (.250). 2000-01, 2-for-5 (.400). 2001-02, 9-for-25 (.360). 2002-03, 3-for-14 (.214). 2003-04, 0-for-1. Totals, 85-for-310 (.274).

Personal fouls/disqualifications: 1985-86, 295/2. 1986-87, 323/6. 1987-88, 296/2. 1988-89, 286/3. 1989-90, 259/1. 1990-91, 268/2. 1991-92, 226/2. 1992-93, 261/2. 1993-94, 268/2. 1994-95, 269/2. 1995-96, 245/1. 1996-97, 217/0. 1997-98, 237/0. 1998-99, 134/0. 1999-00, 229/1. 2000-01, 216/0. 2001-02, 229/1. 2002-03, 204/0. 2003-04, 116/1. Totals, 4578/28.

NBA PLAYOFF RECORD

NOTES: Holds single-game playoff record for most free throws made, none missed—18 (May 10, 1997, at L.A. Lakers). ... Shares single-game playoff record for most free throws made in one half—19 (May 9, 1991, vs. Portland).

Season Team	G	Min.	FGM	FGA	Pct.	FTM	FTA	Pct.	REBOUNDS Off.	Def.	Tot.	Ast.	St.	Blk.	TO	Pts.	AVERAGES RPG	APG	PPG
85-86—Utah................	4	144	38	72	.528	11	26	.423	6	24	30	4	8	0	6	87	7.5	1.0	21.8
86-87—Utah................	5	200	37	88	.420	26	36	.722	15	33	48	6	11	4	17	100	9.6	1.2	20.0
87-88—Utah................	11	494	123	255	.482	81	112	.723	33	97	130	17	13	7	39	327	11.8	1.5	29.7
88-89—Utah................	3	136	33	66	.500	26	32	.813	22	27	49	4	3	1	13	92	16.3	1.3	30.7
89-90—Utah................	5	203	46	105	.438	34	45	.756	16	35	51	11	11	5	12	126	10.2	2.2	25.2
90-91—Utah................	9	383	95	209	.455	77	91	.846	23	97	120	29	9	11	26	267	13.3	3.2	29.7
91-92—Utah................	16	688	148	284	.521	169	210	.805	43	138	181	42	22	19	46	465	11.3	2.6	29.1
92-93—Utah................	5	216	44	97	.454	31	38	.816	12	40	52	10	6	2	20	120	10.4	2.0	24.0
93-94—Utah................	16	703	158	338	.467	118	160	.738	52	146	198	54	23	13	34	434	12.4	3.4	27.1
94-95—Utah................	5	216	48	103	.466	54	78	.692	15	51	66	19	7	2	14	151	13.2	3.8	30.2
95-96—Utah................	18	725	188	401	.469	101	176	.574	47	139	186	79	34	10	45	477	10.3	4.4	26.5
96-97—Utah................	20	816	187	430	.435	144	200	.720	60	168	228	57	27	15	54	519	11.4	2.9	26.0
97-98—Utah................	20	795	198	420	.471	130	165	.788	47	170	217	68	22	20	60	526	10.9	3.4	26.3
98-99—Utah................	11	451	86	206	.417	68	86	.791	36	88	124	52	13	8	40	240	11.3	4.7	21.8
99-00—Utah................	10	386	103	198	.520	64	79	.810	19	70	89	31	7	7	27	272	8.9	3.1	27.2
00-01—Utah................	5	199	49	121	.405	39	49	.796	9	35	44	17	5	4	19	138	8.8	3.4	27.6
01-02—Utah................	4	163	30	73	.411	20	28	.714	3	27	30	18	5	3	11	80	7.5	4.5	20.0
02-03—Utah................	5	191	34	84	.405	30	41	.732	7	27	34	20	8	2	20	98	6.8	4.0	19.6
03-04—L.A. Lakers	21	798	96	218	.450	46	73	.630	37	148	185	72	24	2	47	242	8.8	3.4	11.5
Totals	193	7907	1743	3768	.463	1269	1725	.736	502	1560	2062	610	258	135	550	4761	10.7	3.2	24.7

Three-point field goals: 1987-88, 0-for-1. 1989-90, 0-for-1. 1990-91, 0-for-8. 1991-92, 0-for-2. 1992-93, 1-for-2 (.500). 1993-94, 0-for-4. 1994-95, 1-for-3 (.333). 1995-96, 0-for-3. 1996-97, 1-for-2 (.500). 1997-98, 0-for-3. 1998-99, 0-for-1. 1999-00, 2-for-2. 2000-01, 1-for-2 (.500). 2001-02, 0-for-1. 2002-03, 0-for-1. 2003-04, 0-for-2. Totals, 6-for-37 (.162).

Personal fouls/disqualifications: 1985-86, 18/1. 1986-87, 20/1. 1987-88, 35/0. 1988-89, 16/1. 1989-90, 22/1. 1990-91, 35/0. 1991-92, 57/0. 1992-93, 21/0. 1993-94, 59/2. 1994-95, 18/0. 1995-96, 61/0. 1996-97, 59/0. 1997-98, 69/0. 1998-99, 37/0. 1999-00, 31/0. 2000-01, 13/0. 2001-02, 11/0. 2002-03, 15/0. 2003-04, 65/0. Totals, 662/6.

NBA ALL-STAR GAME RECORD

NOTES: NBA All-Star Game Most Valuable Player (1989). ... NBA All-Star Game co-Most Valuable Player (1993).

								REBOUNDS										
Season Team	Min.	FGM	FGA	Pct.	FTM	FTA	Pct.	Off.	Def.	Tot.	Ast.	PF	Dq.	St.	Blk.	TO	Pts.
1988—Utah	33	9	19	.474	4	5	.800	4	6	10	2	4	0	2	0	3	22
1989—Utah	26	12	17	.706	4	6	.667	4	5	9	3	3	0	2	0	2	28
1990—Utah							Selected, did not play—injured.										
1991—Utah	31	6	11	.545	4	6	.667	4	7	11	4	1	0	1	1	3	16
1992—Utah	19	5	7	.714	1	2	.500	0	7	7	3	1	0	1	1	1	11
1993—Utah	34	11	17	.647	6	9	.667	3	7	10	0	3	0	1	2	3	28
1994—Utah	21	3	9	.333	0	0	...	3	4	7	2	2	0	1	0	1	6
1995—Utah	16	6	6	1.000	3	4	.750	0	3	3	1	0	0	0	0	1	15
1996—Utah	20	2	6	.333	7	8	.875	0	9	9	2	1	0	1	0	1	11
1997—Utah	20	2	8	.250	0	0	...	1	3	4	0	0	0	1	1	0	4
1998—Utah	17	2	4	.500	0	0	...	0	3	3	2	1	...	2	0	0	4
2000—Utah	3	0	1	.000	0	0	...	0	0	0	0	0	0	0	0	0	0
2001—Utah	4	0	2	.000	0	0	...	0	1	1	0	0	0	0	0	0	0
2002—Utah							Selected, did not play..										
Totals	244	58	107	.542	29	40	.725	19	55	74	19	16	0	12	5	15	145

MALONE, MOSES   C

PERSONAL: Born March 23, 1955, in Petersburg, Va. ... 6-10/260 (2,08/117,9). ... Full name: Moses Eugene Malone.
HIGH SCHOOL: Petersburg (Va.).
COLLEGE: Did not attend college.
TRANSACTIONS: Selected out of high school by Utah Stars in third round of 1974 American Basketball Association Draft. ... Contract sold by Stars to Spirits of St. Louis (December 2, 1975). ... Selected by Portland Trail Blazers of NBA from Spirits in ABA dispersal draft (August 5, 1976). ... Traded by Trail Blazers to Buffalo Braves for 1978 first-round draft choice (October 18, 1976). ... Traded by Braves to Houston Rockets for 1977 and 1978 first-round draft choices (October 24, 1976). ... Signed as veteran free agent by Philadelphia 76ers (September 2, 1982); Rockets matched offer and traded Malone to 76ers for F/C Caldwell Jones and 1983 first-round draft choice (September 15, 1982). ... Traded by 76ers with F Terry Catledge and 1986 and 1988 first-round draft choices to Washington Bullets for C/F Jeff Ruland and F Cliff Robinson (June 16, 1986). ... Signed as unrestricted free agent by Atlanta Hawks (August 16, 1988). ... Signed as unrestricted free agent by Milwaukee Bucks (July 10, 1991). ... Signed as free agent by 76ers (August 12, 1993). ... Waived by 76ers (June 17, 1994). ... Signed as free agent by San Antonio Spurs (August 10, 1994).
CAREER HONORS: Elected to the Naismith Memorial Basketball Hall of Fame (2001). ... One of the 50 Greatest Players in NBA History (1996).
MISCELLANEOUS: Member of NBA championship team (1983).

ABA REGULAR-SEASON RECORD

NOTES: ABA All-Rookie team (1975).

			2-POINT			3-POINT								AVERAGES		
Season Team	G	Min.	FGM	FGA	Pct.	FGM	FGA	Pct.	FTM	FTA	Pct.	Reb.	Ast.	Pts.	RPG	APG	PPG
74-75—Utah	83	3205	591	1034	.572	0	1	.000	375	591	.635	1209	82	1557	14.6	1.0	18.8
75-76—St. Louis	43	1168	251	488	.514	0	2	.000	112	183	.612	413	58	614	9.6	1.3	14.3
Totals	126	1979	818	1500	.000	0	0	.000	001	001	010	110	010	12.0	1.1	17.2

ABA PLAYOFF RECORD

			2-POINT			3-POINT								AVERAGES		
Season Team	G	Min.	FGM	FGA	Pct.	FGM	FGA	Pct.	FTM	FTA	Pct.	Reb.	Ast.	Pts.	RPG	APG	PPG
74-75—Utah	6	235	51	80	.638	0	0	...	34	51	.667	105	9	136	17.5	1.5	22.7

ABA ALL-STAR GAME RECORD

		2-POINT			3-POINT							
Season Team	Min.	FGM	FGA	Pct.	FGM	FGA	Pct.	FTM	FTA	Pct.	Reb.	Ast.	Pts.
1975—Utah	20	2	3	.667	0	0	...	2	5	.400	10	0	6

NBA REGULAR-SEASON RECORD

RECORDS: Holds career records for most consecutive games without a disqualification—1,212 (January 7, 1978 through 1994-95 season); and most offensive rebounds—6,731. ... Holds single-season record for most offensive rebounds—587 (1979). ... Holds single-game record for most offensive rebounds—21 (February 11, 1982, vs. Seattle).
HONORS: NBA Most Valuable Player (1979, 1982, 1983). ... All-NBA first team (1979, 1982, 1983, 1985). ... All-NBA second team (1980, 1981, 1984, 1987). ... NBA All-Defensive first team (1983). ... NBA All-Defensive second team (1979).

								REBOUNDS								AVERAGES		
Season Team	G	Min.	FGM	FGA	Pct.	FTM	FTA	Pct.	Off.	Def.	Tot.	Ast.	St.	Blk.	TO	Pts.	RPG	APG	PPG
76-77—Buff.-Houston.	82	2506	389	810	.480	305	440	.693	*437	635	1072	89	67	181		1083	13.1	1.1	13.2
77-78—Houston	59	2107	413	828	.499	318	443	.718	*380	506	886	31	48	76	220	1144	15.0	0.5	19.4
78-79—Houston	82	*3390	716	1325	.540	599	811	.739	*587	*857	*1444	147	79	119	326	2031	*17.6	1.8	24.8
79-80—Houston	82	3140	778	1549	.502	563	783	.719	*573	617	1190	147	80	107	300	2119	14.5	1.8	25.8
80-81—Houston	80	3245	806	1545	.522	609	*804	.757	*474	706	*1180	141	83	150	*308	2222	*14.8	1.8	27.8
81-82—Houston	81	*3398	945	1822	.519	630	*827	.762	*558	630	*1188	142	76	125	294	2520	*14.7	1.8	31.1
82-83—Philadelphia	78	2922	654	1305	.501	*600	*788	.761	*445	*749	*1194	101	89	157	264	1908	*15.3	1.3	24.5
83-84—Philadelphia	71	2613	532	1101	.483	545	727	.750	352	598	950	96	71	110	250	1609	*13.4	1.4	22.7
84-85—Philadelphia	79	2957	602	1284	.469	*737	*904	.815	385	646	*1031	130	67	123	286	1941	*13.1	1.6	24.6
85-86—Philadelphia	74	2706	571	1246	.458	*617	*784	.787	339	533	872	90	67	71	261	1759	11.8	1.2	23.8
86-87—Washington	73	2488	595	1311	.454	570	692	.824	340	484	824	120	59	92	202	1760	11.3	1.6	24.1
87-88—Washington	79	2692	531	1090	.487	543	689	.788	372	512	884	112	59	72	249	1607	11.2	1.4	20.3
88-89—Atlanta	81	2878	538	1096	.491	561	711	.789	386	570	956	112	79	100	245	1637	11.8	1.4	20.2
89-90—Atlanta	81	2735	517	1077	.480	493	631	.781	*364	448	812	130	47	84	232	1528	10.0	1.6	18.9
90-91—Atlanta	82	1912	280	598	.468	309	372	.831	271	396	667	68	30	74	137	869	8.1	0.8	10.6
91-92—Milwaukee	82	2511	440	929	.474	396	504	.786	320	424	744	93	74	64	150	1279	9.1	1.1	15.6
92-93—Milwaukee	11	104	13	42	.310	24	31	.774	22	24	46	7	1	8	10	50	4.2	0.6	4.5

Season Team	G	Min.	FGM	FGA	Pct.	FTM	FTA	Pct.	REBOUNDS Off.	Def.	Tot.	Ast.	St.	Blk.	TO	Pts.	AVERAGES RPG	APG	PPG
93-94—Philadelphia	55	618	102	232	.440	90	117	.769	106	120	226	34	11	17	59	294	4.1	0.6	5.3
94-95—San Antonio....	17	149	13	35	.371	22	32	.688	20	26	46	6	2	3	11	49	2.7	0.4	2.9
Totals	1329	45071	9435	19225	.491	8531	11090	.769	6731	9481	16212	1796	1089	1733	3804	27409	12.2	1.4	20.6

Three-point field goals: 1979-80, 0-for-6. 1980-81, 1-for-3 (.333). 1981-82, 0-for-6. 1982-83, 0-for-1. 1983-84, 0-for-4. 1984-85, 0-for-2. 1985-86, 0-for-1. 1986-87, 0-for-11. 1987-88, 2-for-7 (.286). 1988-89, 0-for-12. 1989-90, 1-for-9 (.111). 1990-91, 0-for-7. 1991-92, 3-for-8 (.375). 1993-94, 0-for-1. 1994-95, 1-for-2 (.500). Totals, 8-for-80 (.100).

Personal fouls/disqualifications: 1976-77, 275/3. 1977-78, 179/2. 1978-79, 223/0. 1979-80, 210/0. 1980-81, 223/0. 1981-82, 208/0. 1982-83, 206/0. 1983-84, 188/0. 1984-85, 216/0. 1985-86, 194/0. 1986-87, 139/0. 1987-88, 160/0. 1988-89, 154/0. 1989-90, 158/0. 1990-91, 134/0. 1991-92, 136/0. 1992-93, 6/0. 1993-94, 52/0. 1994-95, 15/0. Totals, 3076/5.

NBA PLAYOFF RECORD

NOTES: NBA Finals Most Valuable Player (1983). ... Holds single-game playoff record for most offensive rebounds—15 (April 21, 1977, vs. Washington).

Season Team	G	Min.	FGM	FGA	Pct.	FTM	FTA	Pct.	REBOUNDS Off.	Def.	Tot.	Ast.	St.	Blk.	TO	Pts.	AVERAGES RPG	APG	PPG
76-77—Houston.........	12	518	81	162	.500	63	91	.692	84	119	203	7	13	21	...	225	16.9	0.6	18.8
78-79—Houston.........	2	78	18	41	.439	13	18	.722	25	16	41	2	1	8	8	49	20.5	1.0	24.5
79-80—Houston.........	7	275	74	138	.536	33	43	.767	42	55	97	7	4	16	22	181	13.9	1.0	25.9
80-81—Houston.........	21	955	207	432	.479	148	208	.712	125	180	305	35	13	34	59	562	14.5	1.7	26.8
81-82—Houston.........	3	136	29	67	.433	14	15	.933	28	23	51	10	2	2	6	72	17.0	3.3	24.0
82-83—Philadelphia	13	524	126	235	.536	86	120	.717	70	136	206	20	19	25	40	338	15.8	1.5	26.0
83-84—Philadelphia	5	212	38	83	.458	31	32	.969	20	49	69	7	3	11	21	107	13.8	1.4	21.4
84-85—Philadelphia	13	505	90	212	.425	82	103	.796	36	102	138	24	17	22	23	262	10.6	1.8	20.2
86-87—Washington	3	114	21	47	.447	20	21	.952	15	23	38	5	0	3	8	62	12.7	1.7	20.7
87-88—Washington	5	198	30	65	.462	33	40	.825	22	34	56	7	3	4	15	93	11.2	1.4	18.6
88-89—Atlanta	5	197	32	64	.500	40	51	.784	27	33	60	9	7	4	11	105	12.0	1.8	21.0
90-91—Atlanta	5	84	4	20	.200	13	14	.929	16	15	31	3	2	1	2	21	6.2	0.6	4.2
Totals	94	3796	750	1566	.479	576	756	.762	510	785	1295	136	84	151	215	2077	13.8	1.4	22.1

Three-point field goals: 1979-80, 0-for-1. 1980-81, 0-for-2. 1982-83, 0-for-1. 1984-85, 0-for-1. 1987-88, 0-for-1. 1988-89, 1-for-1. Totals, 1-for-7 (.143).

Personal fouls/disqualifications: 1976-77, 42/0. 1978-79, 5/0. 1979-80, 18/0. 1980-81, 54/0. 1981-82, 8/0. 1982-83, 40/0. 1983-84, 15/0. 1984-85, 39/0. 1986-87, 5/0. 1987-88, 9/0. 1988-89, 5/0. 1990-91, 4/0. Totals, 244/0.

NBA ALL-STAR GAME RECORD

Season Team	Min.	FGM	FGA	Pct.	FTM	FTA	Pct.	REBOUNDS Off.	Def.	Tot.	Ast.	PF	Dq.	St.	Blk.	TO	Pts.
1978—Houston	14	1	1	1.000	2	4	.500	1	3	4	1	1	0	1	0	0	4
1979—Houston	17	2	2	1.000	4	5	.800	2	5	7	1	0	0	1	0	1	8
1980—Houston	31	7	12	.583	6	12	.500	6	6	12	2	4	0	1	2	5	20
1981—Houston	22	3	8	.375	2	4	.500	2	4	6	3	3	0	1	0	1	8
1982—Houston	20	5	11	.455	2	6	.333	5	6	11	0	2	0	1	1	3	12
1983—Philadelphia	24	3	8	.375	4	6	.667	2	6	8	3	1	0	0	1	1	10
1984—Philadelphia							Selected, did not play—injured.										
1985—Philadelphia	33	2	10	.200	3	6	.500	5	7	12	1	4	0	0	0	3	7
1986—Philadelphia	34	5	12	.417	6	9	.667	5	8	13	0	4	0	1	0	1	16
1987—Washington...........	35	11	19	.579	5	6	.833	7	11	18	2	4	0	2	1	1	27
1988—Washington...........	22	2	6	.333	3	6	.500	5	4	9	2	2	0	0	2	1	7
1989—Atlanta	19	3	9	.333	3	3	1.000	4	4	8	0	1	0	1	1	1	9
Totals.........................	271	44	98	.449	40	67	.597	44	64	108	15	26	0	9	6	19	128

COMBINED ABA AND NBA REGULAR-SEASON RECORDS

	G	Min.	FGM	FGA	Pct.	FTM	FTA	Pct.	REBOUNDS Off.	Def.	Tot.	Ast.	Stl.	Blk.	TO	Pts.	AVERAGES RPG	APG	PPG
Totals	1455	49444	10277	20750	.495	9018	11864	.760	7382	10452	17834	1936	1199	1889	4264	29580	12.3	1.3	20.3

Three-point field goals: 8-for-83 (.096).

MARAVICH, PETE   G

PERSONAL: Born June 22, 1947, in Aliquippa, Pa. ... Died January 5, 1988. ... 6-5/200 (1,96/90,7). ... Full name: Peter Press Maravich. ... Nickname: Pistol Pete. ... Son of Press Maravich, former college coach; and guard with Youngstown Bears of National Basketball League (1945-46) and Pittsburgh Ironmen of Basketball Association of America (1946-47).
HIGH SCHOOL: Daniel (Clemson, S.C.), then Needham Broughton (Raleigh, N.C.), then Edwards Military Institute (Salemburg, N.C.).
COLLEGE: Louisiana State.
TRANSACTIONS: Selected by Atlanta Hawks in first round (third pick overall) of 1970 NBA Draft. ... Traded by Hawks to New Orleans Jazz for G Dean Meminger, C/F Bob Kauffman, 1974 and 1975 first-round draft choices and 1975 and 1976 second-round draft choices (May 3, 1974). ... Jazz franchise moved from New Orleans to Utah for 1979-80 season. ... Waived by Jazz (January 17, 1980). ... Signed as free agent by Boston Celtics (January 22, 1980).
CAREER HONORS: Elected to Naismith Memorial Basketball Hall of Fame (1987). ... One of the 50 Greatest Players in NBA History (1996).

COLLEGIATE RECORD

NOTES: THE SPORTING NEWS College Player of the Year (1970). ... Naismith Award winner (1970). ... THE SPORTING NEWS All-America first team (1968, 1969, 1970). ... Holds NCAA career records for most points—3667; highest points-per-game average—44.2; most field goals made—1387; most field goals attempted—3166; most free throws made (three-year career)—893; most free throws attempted (three-year career)—1152; and most games scoring at least 50 points—28. ... Holds NCAA single-season records for most points—1381; highest points-per-game average—44.5; most field goals made—522; most field goals attempted—1168; and most games scoring at least 50 points—10 (1970). ... Holds NCAA single-game record for most free throws made—30 (December 22, 1969, vs. Oregon State in 31 attempts). ... Led NCAA Division I with 43.8 points per game (1968), 44.2 points per game (1969) and 44.5 points per game (1970).

Season Team	G	Min.	FGM	FGA	Pct.	FTM	FTA	Pct.	Reb.	Ast.	Pts.	AVERAGES RPG	APG	PPG
66-67—Louisiana State‡.............	17	...	273	604	.452	195	234	.833	176	124	741	10.4	7.3	43.6

Season Team	G	Min.	FGM	FGA	Pct.	FTM	FTA	Pct.	Reb.	Ast.	Pts.	AVERAGES RPG	APG	PPG
67-68—Louisiana State...............	26	...	432	1022	.423	274	338	.811	195	105	1138	7.5	4.0	43.8
68-69—Louisiana State...............	26	...	433	976	.444	282	378	.746	169	128	1148	6.5	4.9	44.2
69-70—Louisiana State.............	31	...	522	1168	.447	337	436	.773	164	192	1381	5.3	6.2	44.5
Varsity totals	83	...	1387	3166	.438	893	1152	.775	528	425	3667	6.4	5.1	44.2

NBA REGULAR-SEASON RECORD

RECORDS: Shares single-game records for most free throws made in one quarter—14 (November 28, 1973, vs. Buffalo); and most free throws attempted in one quarter—16 (January 2, 1973, vs. Chicago).

HONORS: All-NBA first team (1976, 1977). ... All-NBA second team (1973, 1978). ... NBA All-Rookie team (1971).

Season Team	G	Min.	FGM	FGA	Pct.	FTM	FTA	Pct.	Reb.	Ast.	PF	Dq.	Pts.	AVERAGES RPG	APG	PPG
70-71—Atlanta	81	2926	738	1613	.458	404	505	.800	298	355	238	1	1880	3.7	4.4	23.2
71-72—Atlanta	66	2302	460	1077	.427	355	438	.811	256	393	207	0	1275	3.9	6.0	19.3
72-73—Atlanta	79	3089	789	1788	.441	485	606	.800	346	546	245	1	2063	4.4	6.9	26.1

Season Team	G	Min.	FGM	FGA	Pct.	FTM	FTA	Pct.	REBOUNDS Off.	Def.	Tot.	Ast.	St.	Blk.	TO	Pts.	AVERAGES RPG	APG	PPG
73-74—Atlanta	76	2903	819	*1791	.457	469	568	.826	98	276	374	396	111	13	...	2107	4.9	5.2	27.7
74-75—New Orleans ...	79	2853	655	1562	.419	390	481	.811	93	329	422	488	120	18	...	1700	5.3	6.2	21.5
75-76—New Orleans ...	62	2373	604	1316	.459	396	488	.811	46	254	300	332	87	23	...	1604	4.8	5.4	25.9
76-77—New Orleans ...	73	3041	886	*2047	.433	*501	600	.835	90	284	374	392	84	22	...	*2273	5.1	5.4	*31.1
77-78—New Orleans ...	50	2041	556	1253	.444	240	276	.870	49	129	178	335	101	8	248	1352	3.6	6.7	27.0
78-79—New Orleans ...	49	1824	436	1035	.421	233	277	.841	33	88	121	243	60	18	200	1105	2.5	5.0	22.6
79-80—Utah-Boston ...	43	964	244	543	.449	91	105	.867	17	61	78	83	24	6	82	589	1.8	1.9	13.7
Totals	658	24316	6187	14025	.441	3564	4344	.820	...	...	2747	3563	587	108	530	15948	4.2	5.4	24.2

Three-point field goals: 1979-80, 10-for-15 (.667).

Personal fouls/disqualifications: 1973-74, 261/4. 1974-75, 227/4. 1975-76, 197/3. 1976-77, 191/1. 1977-78, 116/1. 1978-79, 104/2. 1979-80, 79/1. Totals, 1865/18.

NBA PLAYOFF RECORD

Season Team	G	Min.	FGM	FGA	Pct.	FTM	FTA	Pct.	Reb.	Ast.	PF	Dq.	Pts.	AVERAGES RPG	APG	PPG
70-71—Atlanta	5	199	46	122	.377	18	26	.692	26	24	14	0	110	5.2	4.8	22.0
71-72—Atlanta	6	219	54	121	.446	58	71	.817	32	28	24	0	166	5.3	4.7	27.7
72-73—Atlanta	6	234	65	155	.419	27	34	.794	29	40	24	1	157	4.8	6.7	26.2

Season Team	G	Min.	FGM	FGA	Pct.	FTM	FTA	Pct.	REBOUNDS Off.	Def.	Tot.	Ast.	St.	Blk.	TO	Pts.	AVERAGES RPG	APG	PPG
79-80—Boston	9	104	25	51	.490	2	3	.667	0	8	8	6	3	0	9	54	0.9	0.7	6.0
Totals	26	756	190	449	.423	105	134	.784	...	...	95	98	3	0	9	487	3.7	3.8	18.7

Three-point field goals: 1979-80, 2-for-6 (.333).

Personal fouls/disqualifications: 1979-80, 12/0.

NBA ALL-STAR GAME RECORD

Season Team	Min.	FGM	FGA	Pct.	FTM	FTA	Pct.	Reb	Ast.	PF	Dq.	Pts.
1973—Atlanta	22	4	8	.500	0	0	...	3	5	4	0	8

Season Team	Min.	FGM	FGA	Pct.	FTM	FTA	Pct.	REBOUNDS Off.	Def.	Tot.	Ast.	PF	Dq.	St.	Blk.	TO	Pts.
1974—Atlanta.................	22	4	15	.267	7	9	.778	1	2	3	4	2	0	0	0	...	15
1977—New Orleans......	21	5	13	.385	0	0	...	0	0	0	4	1	0	4	0	...	10
1978—New Orleans.........							Selected, did not play—injured.										
1979—New Orleans.........	14	5	8	.625	0	0	...	0	2	2	2	1	0	0	0	4	10
Totals	79	18	44	.409	7	9	.778	...	...	8	15	8	0	4	0	4	43

MARTIN, SLATER   G

PERSONAL: Born October 22, 1925, in Houston. ... 5-10/170 (1,78/77,1). ... Full name: Slater Nelson Martin Jr. ... Nickname: Dugie.

HIGH SCHOOL: Jefferson Davis (Houston).

COLLEGE: Texas.

TRANSACTIONS: Selected by Minneapolis Lakers in 1949 Basketball Association of America Draft. ... Traded by Lakers with F Jerry Bird and player to be named later to New York Knicks for C Walter Dukes and draft rights to F/C Burdette Haldorson (October 26, 1956). ... Traded by Knicks to St. Louis Hawks for F Willie Naulls (December 10, 1956).

CAREER HONORS: Elected to Naismith Memorial Basketball Hall of Fame (1982).

MISCELLANEOUS: Member of NBA championship team (1950, 1952, 1953, 1954, 1958).

COLLEGIATE RECORD

NOTES: THE SPORTING NEWS All-America fifth team (1949).

Season Team	G	Min.	FGM	FGA	Pct.	FTM	FTA	Pct.	Reb.	Ast.	Pts.	AVERAGES RPG	APG	PPG
43-44—Texas	14	...	75	...	...	34	...	...	...	...	184	...	...	13.1
44-45—						Did not play—in military service.								
45-46—						Did not play—in military service.								
46-47—Texas	27	...	109	...	...	37	...	...	...	...	255	...	...	9.4
47-48—Texas	25	...	126	...	...	65	85	.765	...	...	317	...	...	12.7
48-49—Texas	24	...	165	...	...	54	...	...	...	...	384	...	...	16.0
Totals	90	...	475	...	...	190	...	...	...	...	1140	...	...	12.7

NBA REGULAR-SEASON RECORD

HONORS: All-NBA second team (1954, 1956, 1957, 1958, 1959).

Season Team	G	Min.	FGM	FGA	Pct.	FTM	FTA	Pct.	Reb.	Ast.	PF	Dq.	Pts.	AVERAGES RPG	APG	PPG
49-50—Minneapolis	67	...	106	302	.351	59	93	.634	...	148	162	...	271	...	2.2	4.0
50-51—Minneapolis	68	...	227	627	.362	121	177	.684	246	235	199	3	575	3.6	3.5	8.5
51-52—Minneapolis	66	2480	237	632	.375	142	190	.747	228	249	226	9	616	3.5	3.8	9.3
52-53—Minneapolis	70	2556	260	634	.410	224	287	.780	186	250	246	4	744	2.7	3.6	10.6
53-54—Minneapolis	69	2472	254	654	.388	176	243	.724	166	253	198	3	684	2.4	3.7	9.9
54-55—Minneapolis	72	2784	350	919	.381	276	359	.769	260	427	221	7	976	3.6	5.9	13.6
55-56—Minneapolis	72	*2838	309	863	.358	329	395	.833	260	445	202	2	947	3.6	6.2	13.2
56-57—N.Y.-St.L.	66	2401	244	736	.332	230	291	.790	288	269	193	1	718	4.4	4.1	10.9
57-58—St. Louis	60	2098	258	768	.336	206	276	.746	228	218	187	0	722	3.8	3.6	12.0
58-59—St. Louis	71	2504	245	706	.347	197	254	.776	253	336	230	8	687	3.6	4.7	9.7
59-60—St. Louis	64	1756	142	383	.371	113	155	.729	187	330	174	2	397	2.9	5.2	6.2
Totals	745	...	2632	7224	.364	2073	2720	.762	...	3160	2238	...	7337	...	4.2	9.8

NBA PLAYOFF RECORD

Season Team	G	Min.	FGM	FGA	Pct.	FTM	FTA	Pct.	Reb.	Ast.	PF	Dq.	Pts.	AVERAGES RPG	APG	PPG
49-50—Minneapolis	12	...	21	50	.420	14	24	.583	...	25	35	...	56	...	2.1	4.7
50-51—Minneapolis	7	...	18	51	.353	14	27	.519	42	25	20	...	50	6.0	3.6	7.1
51-52—Minneapolis	13	523	38	110	.345	41	56	.732	37	56	64	4	117	2.8	4.3	9.0
52-53—Minneapolis	12	453	41	103	.398	39	51	.765	31	43	49	1	121	2.6	3.6	10.1
53-54—Minneapolis	13	533	37	112	.330	52	70	.743	29	60	52	1	126	2.2	4.6	9.7
54-55—Minneapolis	7	315	28	94	.298	40	49	.816	28	31	23	0	96	4.0	4.4	13.7
55-56—Minneapolis	3	121	17	37	.459	20	24	.833	7	15	9	0	54	2.3	5.0	18.0
56-57—St. Louis	10	439	55	155	.355	56	74	.757	42	49	39	2	166	4.2	4.9	16.6
57-58—St. Louis	11	416	44	137	.321	39	63	.619	48	40	40	1	127	4.4	3.6	11.5
58-59—St. Louis	1	18	4	5	.800	0	0	...	3	2	2	0	8	3.0	2.0	8.0
59-60—St. Louis	3	58	1	13	.077	1	4	.250	3	8	9	0	3	1.0	2.7	1.0
Totals	92	...	304	867	.351	316	442	.715	...	354	342	...	924	...	3.8	10.0

NBA ALL-STAR GAME RECORD

Season Team	Min.	FGM	FGA	Pct.	FTM	FTA	Pct.	Reb	Ast.	PF	Dq.	Pts.
1953—Minneapolis	26	2	10	.200	1	1	1.000	2	1	2	0	5
1954—Minneapolis	23	1	5	.200	0	0	...	0	3	3	0	2
1955—Minneapolis	23	2	5	.400	1	2	.500	2	5	3	0	5
1956—Minneapolis	29	3	7	.429	3	3	1.000	1	7	5	0	9
1957—St. Louis	31	4	11	.364	0	0	...	2	3	1	0	8
1958—St. Louis	26	2	9	.222	2	4	.500	2	8	3	0	6
1959—St. Louis	22	2	6	.333	1	2	.500	6	1	2	0	5
Totals	180	16	53	.302	8	12	.667	15	28	19	0	40

NBA COACHING RECORD

BACKGROUND: Player/head coach, St. Louis Hawks (1957). ... Head coach/general manager, Houston Mavericks of ABA (1967-68).

		REGULAR SEASON				PLAYOFFS		
Season Team	W	L	Pct.	Finish		W	L	Pct.
56-57—St. Louis	5	3	.625					

ABA COACHING RECORD

		REGULAR SEASON				PLAYOFFS		
Season Team	W	L	Pct.	Finish		W	L	Pct.
67-68—Houston	29	49	.372	4th/Western Division		0	3	.000
68-69—Houston	3	9	.250					
Totals (2 years)	32	58	.356		Totals (1 year)	0	3	.000>

NOTES:

1957—Replaced Red Holzman as St. Louis head coach (January), with record of 14-19; replaced as St. Louis head coach by Alex Hannum (January).

1968—Lost to Dallas in Western Division Semifinals. Replaced as Houston head coach by Jim Weaver (November).

McADOO, BOB   C/F

PERSONAL: Born September 25, 1951, in Greensboro, N.C. ... 6-9/225 (2,05/102,1). ... Full name: Robert Allen McAdoo Jr.
HIGH SCHOOL: Ben Smith (Greensboro, N.C.).
JUNIOR COLLEGE: Vincennes (Ind.).University.
COLLEGE: North Carolina.
TRANSACTIONS: Selected after junior season by Buffalo Braves in first round (second pick overall) of 1972 NBA Draft. ... Traded by Braves with C/F Tom McMillen to New York Knicks for C/F John Gianelli and cash (December 9, 1976). ... Traded by Knicks to Boston Celtics for three 1979 first-round draft choices and player to be named later (February 12, 1979); Knicks acquired C Tom Barker to complete deal (February 14, 1979). ... Acquired by Detroit Pistons for two 1980 first-round draft choices to complete compensation for Celtics signing of veteran free agent F/G M.L. Carr (September 6, 1979). ... Waived by Pistons (March 11, 1981). ... Signed as free agent by New Jersey Nets (March 13, 1981). ... Traded by Nets to Los Angeles Lakers for 1983 second-round draft choice and cash (December 24, 1981). ... Signed as veteran free agent by Philadelphia 76ers (January 31, 1986); Lakers waived their right of first refusal. ... Played in Italy (1986-87 through 1992-93).
CAREER HONORS: Elected to Naismith Memorial Basketball Hall of Fame (2000).
CAREER NOTES: Assistant coach, Miami Heat (September 20, 1995 to present).
MISCELLANEOUS: Member of NBA championship team (1982, 1985).

COLLEGIATE RECORD

NOTES: THE SPORTING NEWS All-America first team (1972).

Season Team	G	Min.	FGM	FGA	Pct.	FTM	FTA	Pct.	Reb.	Ast.	Pts.	AVERAGES		
												RPG	APG	PPG
69-70—Vincennes University	32	...	258	...	...	101	134	.754	320	...	617	10.0	...	19.3
70-71—Vincennes University	27	...	273	...	...	129	164	.787	297	...	675	11.0	...	25.0
71-72—North Carolina	31	...	243	471	.516	118	167	.707	312	72	604	10.1	2.3	19.5
Junior college totals	59	...	531	...	...	230	298	.772	617	...	1292	10.5	...	21.9
4-year-college totals	31	...	243	471	.516	118	167	.707	312	72	604	10.1	2.3	19.5

NBA REGULAR-SEASON RECORD

HONORS: NBA Most Valuable Player (1975). ... NBA Rookie of the Year (1973). ... All-NBA first team (1975). ... All-NBA second team (1974). ... NBA All-Rookie team (1973).

Season Team	G	Min.	FGM	FGA	Pct.	FTM	FTA	Pct.	Reb.	Ast.	PF	Dq.	Pts.	AVERAGES		
														RPG	APG	PPG
72-73—Buffalo	80	2562	585	1293	.452	271	350	.774	728	139	256	6	1441	9.1	1.7	18.0

Season Team	G	Min.	FGM	FGA	Pct.	FTM	FTA	Pct.	REBOUNDS			Ast.	St.	Blk.	TO	Pts.	AVERAGES		
									Off.	Def.	Tot.						RPG	APG	PPG
73-74—Buffalo	74	3185	901	1647	*.547	459	579	.793	281	836	1117	170	88	246	...	*2261	15.1	2.3	*30.6
74-75—Buffalo	82	*3539	*1095	2138	.512	641	*796	.805	307	848	*1155	179	92	174	...	*2831	14.1	2.2	*34.5
75-76—Buffalo	78	3328	*934	*1918	.487	*559	*734	.762	241	724	965	315	93	160	...	*2427	12.4	4.0	*31.1
76-77—Buff-Knicks	72	2798	740	1445	.512	381	516	.738	199	727	926	205	77	99	...	1861	12.9	2.8	25.8
77-78—New York	79	3182	814	1564	.520	469	645	.727	236	774	1010	298	105	126	346	2097	12.8	3.8	26.5
78-79—N.Y.-Boston	60	2231	596	1127	.529	295	450	.656	130	390	520	168	74	67	217	1487	8.7	2.8	24.8
79-80—Detroit	58	2097	492	1025	.480	235	322	.730	100	367	467	200	73	65	238	1222	8.1	3.4	21.1
80-81—Detroit-N.J.	16	321	68	157	.433	29	41	.707	17	50	67	30	17	13	32	165	4.2	1.9	10.3
81-82—Los Angeles	41	746	151	330	.458	90	126	.714	45	114	159	32	22	36	51	392	3.9	0.8	9.6
82-83—Los Angeles	47	1019	292	562	.520	119	163	.730	76	171	247	39	40	40	68	703	5.3	0.8	15.0
83-84—Los Angeles	70	1456	352	748	.471	212	264	.803	82	207	289	74	42	50	127	916	4.1	1.1	13.1
84-85—L.A. Lakers	66	1254	284	546	.520	122	162	.753	79	216	295	67	18	53	95	690	4.5	1.0	10.5
85-86—Philadelphia	29	609	116	251	.462	62	81	.765	25	78	103	35	10	18	49	294	3.6	1.2	10.1
Totals	852	28327	7420	14751	.503	3944	5229	.754	...	8048	1951	751	1147	1223	18787	9.4	2.3	22.1

Three-point field goals: 1979-80, 3-for-24 (.125). 1980-81, 0-for-1. 1981-82, 0-for-5. 1982-83, 0-for-1. 1983-84, 0-for-5. 1984-85, 0-for-1. Totals, 3-for-37 (.081).

Personal fouls/disqualifications: 1973-74, 252/3. 1974-75, 278/3. 1975-76, 298/5. 1976-77, 262/3. 1977-78, 297/6. 1978-79, 189/3. 1979-80, 178/3. 1980-81, 38/0. 1981-82, 109/1. 1982-83, 153/2. 1983-84, 182/0. 1984-85, 170/0. 1985-86, 64/0. Totals, 2726/35.

NBA PLAYOFF RECORD

Season Team	G	Min.	FGM	FGA	Pct.	FTM	FTA	Pct.	REBOUNDS			Ast.	St.	Blk.	TO	Pts.	AVERAGES		
									Off.	Def.	Tot.						RPG	APG	PPG
73-74—Buffalo	6	271	76	159	.478	38	47	.800	14	68	82	9	6	13	...	190	13.7	1.5	31.7
74-75—Buffalo	7	327	104	216	.481	54	73	.740	25	69	94	10	6	19	...	262	13.4	1.4	37.4
75-76—Buffalo	9	406	97	215	.451	58	82	.707	31	97	128	29	7	18	...	252	14.2	3.2	28.0
77-78—New York	6	238	61	126	.484	21	35	.600	11	47	58	23	7	12	23	143	9.7	3.8	23.8
81-82—Los Angeles	14	388	101	179	.564	32	47	.681	21	74	95	22	10	21	35	234	6.8	1.6	16.7
82-83—Los Angeles	8	166	37	84	.440	11	14	.786	15	31	46	5	11	10	14	87	5.8	0.6	10.9
83-84—Los Angeles	20	447	111	215	.516	57	81	.704	30	78	108	12	12	27	39	279	5.4	0.6	14.0
84-85—L.A. Lakers	19	398	91	193	.472	35	47	.745	25	61	86	16	9	26	20	217	4.5	0.8	11.4
85-86—Philadelphia	5	73	20	36	.556	14	16	.875	8	6	14	2	4	5	2	54	2.8	0.4	10.8
Totals	94	2714	698	1423	.491	320	442	.724	180	531	711	127	72	151	145	1718	7.6	1.4	18.3

Three-point field goals: 1982-83, 2-for-6 (.333). 1983-84, 0-for-1. 1984-85, 0-for-1. Totals, 2-for-8 (.250).

Personal fouls/disqualifications: 1973-74, 25/1. 1974-75, 29/1. 1975-76, 37/3. 1977-78, 19/0. 1981-82, 43/2. 1982-83, 23/0. 1983-84, 63/0. 1984-85, 66/2. 1985-86, 13/0. Totals, 318/9.

NBA ALL-STAR GAME RECORD

Season Team	Min.	FGM	FGA	Pct.	FTM	FTA	Pct.	REBOUNDS			Ast.	PF	Dq.	St.	Blk.	TO	Pts.
								Off.	Def.	Tot.							
1974—Buffalo	13	3	4	.750	5	8	.625	1	2	3	1	4	0	0	1	...	11
1975—Buffalo	26	4	9	.444	3	3	1.000	4	2	6	2	4	0	0	0	...	11
1976—Buffalo	29	10	14	.714	2	4	.500	2	5	7	1	5	0	0	0	...	22
1977—N.Y. Knicks	38	13	23	.565	4	4	1.000	3	7	10	2	3	0	3	1	...	30
1978—New York	20	7	14	.500	0	0	...	3	1	4	0	2	0	1	0	3	14
Totals	126	37	64	.578	14	19	.737	13	17	30	6	18	0	4	2	3	88

ITALIAN LEAGUE RECORD

Season Team	G	Min.	FGM	FGA	Pct.	FTM	FTA	Pct.	Reb.	Ast.	Pts.	AVERAGES		
												RPG	APG	PPG
86-87—Tracer Milan	38	1320	387	730	.530	205	268	.765	388	54	991	10.2	1.4	26.1
87-88—Tracer Milan	30	1064	325	561	.579	175	211	.829	260	56	838	8.7	1.9	27.9
88-89—Philips Milano	27	891	173	470	.368	132	164	.805	223	48	505	8.3	1.8	18.7
89-90—Philips Milano	28	906	296	523	.566	160	195	.821	219	37	764	7.8	1.3	27.3
90-91—Filanto Forli	23	858	278	490	.567	179	225	.796	219	28	759	9.5	1.2	33.0
91-92—Filanto Forli	20	700	199	399	.499	129	159	.811	188	20	538	9.4	1.0	26.9
92-93—Teamsystem Fabriano	2	58	14	27	.519	12	17	.706	13	2	44	6.5	1.0	22.0
Totals	168	5797	1672	3200	.523	992	1239	.801	1510	245	4439	8.7	1.4	26.6

McGINNIS, GEORGE   F

PERSONAL: Born August 12, 1950, in Indianapolis. ... 6-8/235 (2,03/106,6). ... Full name: George F. McGinnis.
HIGH SCHOOL: George Washington (Indianapolis).
COLLEGE: Indiana.
TRANSACTIONS: Signed as free agent after sophomore season by Indiana Pacers of American Basketball Association in lieu of 1972 first-round draft choice (1971). ... Selected by Philadelphia 76ers in second round (22nd pick overall) of 1973 NBA Draft. ... Invoked proviso to buy his way out of contract with Pacers. ... Signed by 76ers (July 10, 1975) after Commissioner Larry

O'Brien revoked contract McGinnis had signed with New York Knicks (May 30, 1975). ... Traded by 76ers to Denver Nuggets for F Bobby Jones and G Ralph Simpson (August 16, 1978). ... Traded by Nuggets to Pacers for F Alex English and 1980 first-round draft choice (February 1, 1980). ... Waived by Pacers (October 27, 1982).

COLLEGIATE RECORD

Season Team	G	Min.	FGM	FGA	Pct.	FTM	FTA	Pct.	Reb.	Ast.	Pts.	RPG	APG	PPG
69-70—Indiana‡						Did not play—ineligible.								
70-71—Indiana	24	...	283	615	.460	153	249	.614	352	66	719	14.7	2.8	30.0
Varsity totals	24	...	283	615	.460	153	249	.614	352	66	719	14.7	2.8	30.0

ABA REGULAR-SEASON RECORD

NOTES: ABA co-Most Valuable Player (1975). ... ABA All-Star first team (1974, 1975). ... ABA All-Star second team (1973). ... ABA All-Rookie team (1972). ... Member of ABA championship team (1972, 1973).

			2-POINT			3-POINT								AVERAGES		
Season Team	G	Min.	FGM	FGA	Pct.	FGM	FGA	Pct.	FTM	FTA	Pct.	Reb.	Ast.	Pts.	RPG	APG	PPG
71-72—Indiana	73	2179	459	961	.478	6	38	.158	298	462	.645	711	137	1234	9.7	1.9	16.9
72-73—Indiana	82	3347	860	1723	.499	8	32	.250	517	*778	.665	1022	205	2261	12.5	2.5	27.6
73-74—Indiana	80	3266	784	1652	.475	5	34	.147	488	*715	.683	1197	267	2071	15.0	3.3	25.9
74-75—Indiana	79	3193	811	1759	.461	62	175	.354	*545	*753	.724	1126	495	*2353	14.3	6.3	*29.8
Totals	314	11985	2914	6095	.478	81	279	.290	1848	2708	.682	4056	1104	7919	12.9	3.5	25.2

ABA PLAYOFF RECORD

NOTES: ABA Playoff Most Valuable Player (1973).

			2-POINT			3-POINT								AVERAGES		
Season Team	G	Min.	FGM	FGA	Pct.	FGM	FGA	Pct.	FTM	FTA	Pct.	Reb.	Ast.	Pts.	RPG	APG	PPG
71-72—Indiana	20	633	102	246	.415	4	15	.267	94	150	.627	227	52	310	11.4	2.6	15.5
72-73—Indiana	18	731	161	352	.457	0	5	.000	109	149	.732	222	39	431	12.3	2.2	23.9
73-74—Indiana	14	585	117	254	.461	2	7	.286	96	129	.744	166	47	336	11.9	3.4	24.0
74-75—Indiana	18	731	190	382	.497	23	73	.315	132	192	.688	286	148	581	15.9	8.2	32.3
Totals	70	2680	570	1234	.462	29	100	.290	431	620	.695	901	286	1658	12.9	4.1	23.7

ABA ALL-STAR GAME RECORD

		2-POINT			3-POINT								
Season Team	Min.	FGM	FGA	Pct.	FGM	FGA	Pct.	FTM	FTA	Pct.	Reb.	Ast.	Pts.
1972—Indiana	34	10	14	.714	0	1	.000	3	6	.500	15	2	23
1973—Indiana	30	7	21	.333	0	0	...	0	0	...	11	1	14
1974—Indiana	32	6	13	.462	0	1	.000	6	11	.545	12	5	18
Totals	96	23	48	.479	0	2	.000	9	17	.529	38	8	55

NBA REGULAR-SEASON RECORD

HONORS: All-NBA first team (1976). ... All-NBA second team (1977).
NOTES: Tied for NBA lead with 12 disqualifications (1980).

									REBOUNDS								AVERAGES		
Season Team	G	Min.	FGM	FGA	Pct.	FTM	FTA	Pct.	Off.	Def.	Tot.	Ast.	St.	Blk.	TO	Pts.	RPG	APG	PPG
75-76—Philadelphia	77	2946	647	1552	.417	475	642	.740	260	707	967	359	198	41	...	1769	12.6	4.7	23.0
76-77—Philadelphia	79	2769	659	1439	.458	372	546	.681	324	587	911	302	163	37	...	1690	11.5	3.8	21.4
77-78—Philadelphia	78	2533	588	1270	.463	411	574	.716	282	528	810	294	137	27	312	1587	10.4	3.8	20.3
78-79—Denver	76	2552	603	1273	.474	509	765	.665	256	608	864	283	129	52	*346	1715	11.4	3.7	22.6
79-80—Denver-Ind.	73	2208	400	886	.451	270	488	.553	222	477	699	333	101	23	281	1072	9.6	4.6	14.7
80-81—Indiana	69	1845	348	768	.453	207	385	.538	164	364	528	210	99	28	221	903	7.7	3.0	13.1
81-82—Indiana	76	1341	141	378	.373	72	159	.453	93	305	398	204	96	28	131	354	5.2	2.7	4.7
Totals	528	16194	3386	7566	.448	2316	3559	.651	1601	3576	5177	1985	923	236	1291	9090	9.8	3.8	17.2

Three-point field goals: 1979-80, 2-for-15 (.133). 1980-81, 0-for-7. 1981-82, 0-for-3. Totals, 2-for-25 (.080).
Personal fouls/disqualifications: 1975-76, 334/13. 1976-77, 299/4. 1977-78, 287/6. 1978-79, 321/16. 1979-80, 303/12. 1980-81, 242/3. 1981-82, 98/1. Totals, 1884/58.

NBA PLAYOFF RECORD

									REBOUNDS								AVERAGES		
Season Team	G	Min.	FGM	FGA	Pct.	FTM	FTA	Pct.	Off.	Def.	Tot.	Ast.	St.	Blk.	TO	Pts.	RPG	APG	PPG
75-76—Philadelphia	3	120	29	61	.475	11	18	.611	9	32	41	12	1	4	...	69	13.7	4.0	23.0
76-77—Philadelphia	19	603	102	273	.374	65	114	.570	62	136	198	69	23	6	...	269	10.4	3.6	14.2
77-78—Philadelphia	10	273	53	125	.424	41	49	.837	24	54	78	30	15	1	38	147	7.8	3.0	14.7
80-81—Indiana	2	39	3	15	.200	4	8	.500	2	8	10	7	2	0	5	10	5.0	3.5	5.0
Totals	34	1035	187	474	.395	121	189	.640	97	230	327	118	41	11	43	495	9.6	3.5	14.6

Personal fouls/disqualifications: 1975-76, 14/1. 1976-77, 83/2. 1977-78, 40/1. 1980-81, 6/0. Totals, 143/4.

NBA ALL-STAR GAME RECORD

								REBOUNDS								
Season Team	Min.	FGM	FGA	Pct.	FTM	FTA	Pct.	Off.	Def.	Tot.	Ast.	PF	Dq.	St.	Blk.	TO	Pts.
1976—Philadelphia	19	4	9	.444	2	4	.500	1	6	7	2	2	0	0	0	...	10
1977—Philadelphia	26	2	9	.222	0	2	.000	5	2	7	2	3	0	4	0	...	4
1979—Denver	25	5	12	.417	6	11	.545	2	4	6	3	4	0	5	0	0	16
Totals	70	11	30	.367	8	17	.471	8	12	20	7	9	0	9	0	0	30

COMBINED ABA AND NBA REGULAR-SEASON RECORDS

									REBOUNDS							AVERAGES		
	G	Min.	FGM	FGA	Pct.	FTM	FTA	Pct.	Off.	Def.	Tot.	Ast.	Stl.	Blk.	TO	Pts.	RPG	APG	PPG
Totals	842	28179	6381	13940	.458	4164	6267	.664	...	...	9233	3089	1448	332	...	17009	11.0	3.7	20.2

Three-point field goals: 83-for-304 (.273).
Personal fouls/disqualifications: 3220.

McGUIRE, DICK　　　　　　　　　　G

PERSONAL: Born January 25, 1926, in New York. ... 6-0/180 (1,83/81,6). ... Full name: Richard Joseph McGuire. ... Brother of Al McGuire, guard with New York Knicks (1951-52 through 1953-54) and Baltimore Bullets (1954-55); and head coach, Belmont Abbey (1957-58 through 1963-64) and Marquette University (1964-65 through 1976-77). ... Nickname: Tricky Dick.
HIGH SCHOOL: LaSalle Academy (New York).
COLLEGE: St. John's and Dartmouth.
TRANSACTIONS: Selected by New York Knicks in first round of 1949 Basketball Association of America Draft. ... Traded by Knicks to Detroit Pistons for 1958 first-round draft choice (April 3, 1957).
CAREER NOTES: Director of scouting, New York Knicks (1967-68 to present).
CAREER HONORS: Elected to Naismith Memorial Basketball Hall of Fame (1993).

COLLEGIATE RECORD

NOTES: The Sporting News All-America second team (1944).

Season Team	G	Min.	FGM	FGA	Pct.	FTM	FTA	Pct.	Reb.	Ast.	Pts.	RPG	APG	PPG
43-44—St. John's	16	...	43	...	...	20	...	...	...	...	106	...	...	6.6
44-45—						Did not play—in military service.								
45-46—						Did not play—in military service.								
46-47—St. John's	21	...	63	...	...	37	...	...	...	...	163	...	...	7.8
47-48—St. John's	22	...	75	...	...	72	115	.626	...	...	222	...	...	10.1
48-49—St. John's	25	...	121	...	...	72	125	.576	...	...	314	...	...	12.6
Totals	84	...	302	...	...	201	...	...	...	...	805	...	...	9.6

NBA REGULAR-SEASON RECORD

HONORS: All-NBA second team (1951).

Season Team	G	Min.	FGM	FGA	Pct.	FTM	FTA	Pct.	Reb.	Ast.	PF	Dq.	Pts.	RPG	APG	PPG
49-50—New York	68	...	190	563	.337	204	313	.652	...	*386	160	...	584	...	5.7	8.6
50-51—New York	64	...	179	482	.371	179	276	.649	334	400	154	2	537	5.2	†6.3	8.4
51-52—New York	64	2018	204	474	.430	183	290	.631	332	388	181	4	591	5.2	6.1	9.2
52-53—New York	61	1783	142	373	.381	153	269	.569	280	296	172	3	437	4.6	4.9	7.2
53-54—New York	68	2343	201	493	.408	220	345	.638	310	354	199	3	622	4.6	5.2	9.1
54-55—New York	71	2310	226	581	.389	195	303	.644	322	542	143	0	647	4.5	7.6	9.1
55-56—New York	62	1685	152	438	.347	121	193	.627	220	362	146	0	425	3.5	5.8	6.9
56-57—New York	72	1191	140	366	.383	105	163	.644	146	222	103	0	385	2.0	3.1	5.3
57-58　Detroit	69	2311	203	544	.373	150	225	.667	291	454	178	0	556	4.2	6.6	8.1
58-59—Detroit	71	2063	232	543	.427	191	258	.740	285	443	147	1	655	4.0	6.2	9.2
59-60—Detroit	68	1466	179	402	.445	124	201	.617	264	358	112	0	482	3.9	5.3	7.1
Totals	738	...	2048	5259	.389	1825	2836	.644	...	4205	1695	...	5921	...	5.7	8.0

NBA PLAYOFF RECORD

Season Team	G	Min.	FGM	FGA	Pct.	FTM	FTA	Pct.	Reb.	Ast.	PF	Dq.	Pts.	RPG	APG	PPG
49-50—New York	5	...	22	52	.423	19	26	.731	...	27	21	...	63	...	5.4	12.6
50-51—New York	14	...	25	80	.313	24	53	.453	83	78	50	1	74	5.9	5.6	5.3
51-52—New York	14	546	48	107	.449	49	86	.570	71	90	46	1	145	5.1	6.4	10.4
52-53—New York	11	360	24	59	.407	35	55	.636	63	70	25	0	83	5.7	6.4	7.5
53-54—New York	4	68	4	16	.250	3	5	.600	4	5	12	0	11	1.0	1.3	2.8
54-55—New York	3	75	6	19	.316	8	12	.667	9	12	7	0	20	3.0	4.0	6.7
57-58—Detroit	7	236	25	60	.417	17	24	.708	33	40	13	0	67	4.7	5.7	9.6
58-59—Detroit	3	109	20	32	.625	7	11	.636	17	19	10	0	47	5.7	6.3	15.7
59-60—Detroit	2	42	5	12	.417	1	3	.333	4	9	3	0	11	2.0	4.5	5.5
Totals	63	...	179	437	.410	163	275	.593	...	350	187	...	521	...	5.6	8.3

NBA ALL-STAR GAME RECORD

Season Team	Min.	FGM	FGA	Pct.	FTM	FTA	Pct.	Reb	Ast.	PF	Dq.	Pts.
1951—New York	...	3	4	.750	0	0	...	5	10	2	0	6
1952—New York	18	0	0	...	1	3	.333	1	4	0	0	1
1954—New York	24	2	5	.400	0	0	...	4	2	1	0	4
1955—New York	25	1	2	.500	1	2	.500	3	6	1	0	3
1956—New York	29	2	9	.222	2	5	.400	0	3	1	0	6
1958—Detroit	31	2	4	.500	0	0	...	7	10	4	0	4
1959—Detroit	24	2	7	.286	1	2	.500	3	3	2	0	5
Totals	...	12	31	.387	5	12	.417	23	38	11	0	29

NBA COACHING RECORD

BACKGROUND: Player/head coach, Detroit Pistons (December 28, 1959-remainder of season).

Season Team	REGULAR SEASON				PLAYOFFS		
	W	L	Pct.	Finish	W	L	Pct.
59-60—Detroit	17	24	.415	2nd/Western Division	0	2	.000
60-61—Detroit	34	45	.430	3rd/Western Division	2	3	.400

Season Team	REGULAR SEASON				PLAYOFFS		
	W	L	Pct.	Finish	W	L	Pct.
61-62—Detroit	37	43	.463	3rd/Western Division	5	5	.500
62-63—Detroit	34	46	.425	3rd/Western Division	1	3	.250
65-66—New York	24	35	.407	4th/Eastern Division	—	—	—
66-67—New York	36	45	.444	4th/Eastern Division	1	3	.250
67-68—New York	15	22	.405		—	—	—
Totals (7 years)	197	260	.431	Totals (5 years)	9	16	.360

NOTES:
1959—Replaced Detroit head coach Red Rocha (December 28), with record of 13-21.
1960—Lost to Minneapolis in Western Division Semifinals.
1961—Lost to Los Angeles in Western Division Semifinals.
1962—Defeated Cincinnati, 3-1, in Western Division Semifinals; lost to Los Angeles, 4-2, in Western Division Finals.
1963—Lost to St. Louis in Western Division Semifinals.
1965—Replaced Harry Gallatin as New York head coach (November 29), with record of 6-15 and in fourth place.
1967—Lost to Boston in Eastern Division Semifinals. Replaced as New York head coach by Red Holzman (December).

McHALE, KEVIN — F/C

PERSONAL: Born December 19, 1957, in Hibbing, Minn. ... 6-10/225 (2,08/102,1). ... Full name: Kevin Edward McHale.
HIGH SCHOOL: Hibbing (Minn.).
COLLEGE: Minnesota.
TRANSACTIONS: Selected by Boston Celtics in first round (third pick overall) of 1980 NBA Draft.
CAREER NOTES: Assistant general manager, Minnesota Timberwolves (1994-95). ... Vice president of basketball operations, Timberwolves (May 1995 to present).
CAREER HONORS: One of the 50 Greatest Players in NBA History (1996). ... Elected to Naismith Memorial Basketball Hall of Fame (1999).
MISCELLANEOUS: Member of NBA championship team (1981, 1984, 1986).

COLLEGIATE RECORD

Season Team	G	Min.	FGM	FGA	Pct.	FTM	FTA	Pct.	Reb.	Ast.	Pts.	RPG	APG	PPG
76-77—Minnesota	27	...	133	241	.552	58	77	.753	218	36	324	8.1	1.3	12.0
77-78—Minnesota	26	...	143	242	.591	54	77	.701	192	27	340	7.4	1.0	13.1
78-79—Minnesota	27	...	202	391	.517	79	96	.823	259	33	483	9.6	1.2	17.9
79-80—Minnesota	32	...	236	416	.567	85	107	.794	281	28	557	8.8	0.9	17.4
Totals	112	...	714	1290	.553	276	357	.773	950	124	1704	8.5	1.1	15.2

NBA REGULAR-SEASON RECORD

HONORS: NBA Sixth Man Award (1984, 1985). ... All-NBA first team (1987). ... NBA All-Defensive first team (1986, 1987, 1988). ... NBA All-Defensive second team (1983, 1989, 1990). ... NBA All-Rookie team (1981).

Season Team	G	Min.	FGM	FGA	Pct.	FTM	FTA	Pct.	Off.	Def.	Tot.	Ast.	St.	Blk.	TO	Pts.	RPG	APG	PPG
80-81—Boston	82	1645	355	666	.533	108	159	.679	155	204	359	55	27	151	110	818	4.4	0.7	10.0
81-82—Boston	82	2332	465	875	.531	187	248	.754	191	365	556	91	30	185	137	1117	6.8	1.1	13.6
82-83—Boston	82	2345	483	893	.541	193	269	.717	215	338	553	104	34	192	159	1159	6.7	1.3	14.1
83-84—Boston	82	2577	587	1055	.556	336	439	.765	208	402	610	104	23	126	150	1511	7.4	1.3	18.4
84-85—Boston	79	2653	605	1062	.570	355	467	.760	229	483	712	141	28	120	157	1565	9.0	1.8	19.8
85-86—Boston	68	2397	561	978	.574	326	420	.776	171	380	551	181	29	134	149	1448	8.1	2.7	21.3
86-87—Boston	77	3060	790	1307	*.604	428	512	.836	247	516	763	198	38	172	197	2008	9.9	2.6	26.1
87-88—Boston	64	2390	550	911	*.604	346	434	.797	159	377	536	171	27	92	141	1446	8.4	2.7	22.6
88-89—Boston	78	2876	661	1211	.546	436	533	.818	223	414	637	172	26	97	196	1758	8.2	2.2	22.5
89-90—Boston	82	2722	648	1181	.549	393	440	.893	201	476	677	172	30	157	183	1712	8.3	2.1	20.9
90-91—Boston	68	2067	504	912	.553	228	275	.829	145	335	480	126	25	146	140	1251	7.1	1.9	18.4
91-92—Boston	56	1398	323	634	.509	134	163	.822	119	211	330	82	11	59	82	780	5.9	1.5	13.9
92-93—Boston	71	1656	298	649	.459	164	195	.841	95	263	358	73	16	59	92	762	5.0	1.0	10.7
Totals	971	30118	6830	12334	.554	3634	4554	.798	2358	4764	7122	1670	344	1690	1893	17335	7.3	1.7	17.9

Three-point field goals: 1980-81, 0-for-2. 1982-83, 0-for-1. 1983-84, 1-for-3 (.333). 1984-85, 0-for-6. 1986-87, 0-for-4. 1988-89, 0-for-4. 1989-90, 23-for-69 (.333). 1990-91, 15-for-37 (.405). 1991-92, 0-for-13. 1992-93, 2-for-18 (.111). Totals, 41-for-157 (.261).
Personal fouls/disqualifications: 1980-81, 260/3. 1981-82, 264/1. 1982-83, 241/3. 1983-84, 243/5. 1984-85, 234/3. 1985-86, 192/2. 1986-87, 240/1. 1987-88, 179/1. 1988-89, 223/2. 1989-90, 250/3. 1990-91, 194/2. 1991-92, 112/1. 1992-93, 126/0. Totals, 2758/27.

NBA PLAYOFF RECORD

Season Team	G	Min.	FGM	FGA	Pct.	FTM	FTA	Pct.	Off.	Def.	Tot.	Ast.	St.	Blk.	TO	Pts.	RPG	APG	PPG
80-81—Boston	17	296	61	113	.540	23	36	.639	29	30	59	14	4	25	15	145	3.5	0.8	8.5
81-82—Boston	12	344	77	134	.575	40	53	.755	41	44	85	11	5	27	16	194	7.1	0.9	16.2
82-83—Boston	7	177	34	62	.548	10	18	.556	15	27	42	5	3	7	10	78	6.0	0.7	11.1
83-84—Boston	23	702	123	244	.504	94	121	.777	62	81	143	27	3	35	38	340	6.2	1.2	14.8
84-85—Boston	21	837	172	303	.568	121	150	.807	74	134	208	32	13	46	60	465	9.9	1.5	22.1
85-86—Boston	18	715	168	290	.579	112	141	.794	51	104	155	48	8	43	48	448	8.6	2.7	24.9
86-87—Boston	21	827	174	298	.584	96	126	.762	66	128	194	39	7	30	54	444	9.2	1.9	21.1
87-88—Boston	17	716	158	262	.603	115	137	.839	55	81	136	40	7	30	39	432	8.0	2.4	25.4
88-89—Boston	3	115	20	41	.488	17	23	.739	7	17	24	9	1	2	4	57	8.0	3.0	19.0
89-90—Boston	5	192	42	69	.609	25	29	.862	8	31	39	13	2	10	14	110	7.8	2.6	22.0
90-91—Boston	11	376	78	148	.527	18	80	.825	18	54	72	20	5	14	14	228	6.5	1.8	20.7
91-92—Boston	10	306	65	126	.516	35	44	.795	21	46	67	13	5	5	9	165	6.7	1.3	16.5
92-93—Boston	4	113	32	55	.582	12	14	.857	9	20	29	3	2	7	5	76	7.3	0.8	19.0
Totals	169	5716	1204	2145	.561	766	972	.788	456	797	1253	274	65	281	326	3182	7.4	1.6	18.8

Three-point field goals: 1982-83, 0-for-1. 1983-84, 0-for-3. 1985-86, 0-for-1. 1987-88, 1-for-1. 1989-90, 1-for-3 (.333). 1990-91, 6-for-11 (.545). 1991-92, 0-for-1. Totals, 8-for-21 (.381).
Personal fouls/disqualifications: 1980-81, 51/1. 1981-82, 44/0. 1982-83, 16/0. 1983-84, 75/1. 1984-85, 73/3. 1985-86, 64/0. 1986-87, 71/2. 1987-88, 65/1. 1988-89, 13/0. 1989-90, 17/0. 1990-91, 42/0. 1991-92, 34/0. 1992-93, 6/0. Totals, 571/8.

NBA ALL-STAR GAME RECORD

Season Team	Min.	FGM	FGA	Pct.	FTM	FTA	Pct.	Off.	Def.	Tot.	Ast.	PF	Dq.	St.	Blk.	TO	Pts.
1984—Boston	11	3	7	.429	4	6	.667	2	3	5	0	1	0	0	0	2	10
1986—Boston	20	3	8	.375	2	2	1.000	3	7	10	2	4	0	0	4	0	8

ALL-TIME GREAT PLAYERS

Season Team	Min.	FGM	FGA	Pct.	FTM	FTA	Pct.	Off.	Def.	Tot.	Ast.	PF	Dq.	St.	Blk.	TO	Pts.
1987—Boston	30	7	11	.636	2	2	1.000	4	3	7	2	5	0	0	4	0	16
1988—Boston	14	0	1	.000	2	2	1.000	0	1	1	1	2	0	0	2	2	2
1989—Boston	16	5	7	.714	0	0	...	1	2	3	0	3	0	0	2	1	10
1990—Boston	20	6	11	.545	0	0	...	2	6	8	1	4	0	0	0	0	13
1991—Boston	14	0	3	.000	2	2	1.000	1	2	3	2	2	0	1	0	0	2
Totals	125	24	48	.500	12	14	.857	13	24	37	8	21	0	1	12	5	61

Three-point field goals: 1990, 1-for-1. 1991, 0-for-1. Totals, 1-for-2 (.500).

MIKAN, GEORGE   C

PERSONAL: Born June 18, 1924, in Joliet, Ill. ...Died June 1, 2005. ... 6-10/245 (2,08/111,1). ... Full name: George Lawrence Mikan Jr. ... Brother of Ed Mikan, forward/center with Chicago Stags of Basketball Association of America (1948-49) and six NBA teams (1949-50 through 1953-54); and father of Larry Mikan, forward with Cleveland Cavaliers (1970-71).

HIGH SCHOOL: Joliet (Ill.) Catholic, then Quigley Prep (Chicago).

COLLEGE: DePaul.

TRANSACTIONS: Signed by Chicago Gears of National Basketball League (March 16, 1946). ... Gears dropped out of NBL and entered Professional Basketball League of America for 1947-48 season. ... PBLA disbanded (November 13, 1947); Chicago was refused a franchise in the NBL and Mikan was awarded to Minneapolis Lakers at NBL meeting (November 17, 1947). Mikan scored 193 points in the eight PBLA games played by Gears before the league folded and led the league in total points and scoring average. ... Signed by Minneapolis Lakers of NBL (November 1947). ... Lakers franchise transferred to Basketball Association of America for 1948-49 season. ... Lakers franchise became part of NBA upon merger of BAA and NBL for 1949-50 season.

CAREER HONORS: Elected to Naismith Memorial Basketball Hall of Fame (1959). ... NBA 25th Anniversary All-Time Team (1970), 35th Anniversary All-Time Team (1980) and One of the 50 Greatest Players in NBA History (1996).

MISCELLANEOUS: Member of NBA championship team (1950, 1952, 1953, 1954). ... Member of BAA championship team (1949). ... Member of NBL championship team (1947, 1948).

COLLEGIATE RECORD

NOTES: THE SPORTING NEWS All-America first team (1944, 1945).

Season Team	G	Min.	FGM	FGA	Pct.	FTM	FTA	Pct.	Reb.	Ast.	Pts.	RPG	APG	PPG
41-42—DePaul‡														
						Freshman team statistics unavailable.								
42-43—DePaul	24	...	97	...	...	77	111	.694	...	...	271	...	...	11.3
43-44—DePaul	26	...	188	...	...	110	169	.651	...	...	486	...	...	18.7
44-45—DePaul	24	...	218	...	...	122	199	.613	...	...	558	...	...	23.3
45-46—DePaul	24	...	206	...	...	143	186	.769	...	...	555	...	...	23.1
Varsity totals	98	...	709	...	...	452	665	.680	...	...	1870	...	...	19.1

NBL AND NBA REGULAR-SEASON RECORD

HONORS: All-NBA first team (1950, 1951, 1952, 1953, 1954). ... NBL Most Valuable Player (1948). ... All-NBL first team (1947, 1948). ... All-BAA first team (1949).

Season Team	G	Min.	FGM	FGA	Pct.	FTM	FTA	Pct.	Reb.	Ast.	PF	Dq.	Pts.	RPG	APG	PPG
46-47—Chicago (NBL)	25	...	147	...	...	119	164	.726	...	...	90	...	413	...	...	*16.5
47-48—Minneapolis. (NBL)	56	...	*406	...	...	*383	*509	.752	...	...	210	...	*1195	...	...	*21.3
48-49—Minneapolis (BAA)	60	...	*583	1403	.416	*532	*689	.772	...	218	260	...	*1698	3.6	*28.3
49-50—Minneapolis	68	...	*649	*1508	.407	*567	*728	.778	...	137	297	...	1865	...	2.0	*27.4
50-51—Minneapolis	68	...	*678	*1584	.428	*576	*717	.803	958	208	*308	14	*1932	14.1	3.1	*28.4
51-52—Minneapolis	64	2572	545	*1414	.385	433	555	.780	866	194	*286	14	*1523	*13.5	3.0	*23.8
52-53—Minneapolis	70	2651	500	1252	.399	442	567	.780	*1007	201	290	12	1442	*14.4	2.9	20.6
53-54—Minneapolis	72	2362	441	1160	.380	424	546	.777	1028	174	268	4	1306	14.3	2.4	18.1
54-55—						Did not play—retired.										
55-56—Minneapolis	37	765	148	375	.395	94	122	.771	308	53	153	6	390	8.3	1.4	10.5
Totals	520	...	4097	...	...	3570	4597	.777	...	2162	...	11764	...	...	22.6

NBL AND NBA PLAYOFF RECORD

Season Team	G	Min.	FGM	FGA	Pct.	FTM	FTA	Pct.	Reb.	Ast.	PF	Dq.	Pts.	RPG	APG	PPG
46-47—Chi. (NBL)	11	...	72	...	...	73	104	.702	...	...	48	...	217	...	...	19.7
47-48—Minn. (NBL)	10	...	88	...	...	68	97	.701	...	...	37	...	244	...	...	24.4
48-49—Minneapolis (BAA)	10	...	103	227	.454	97	121	.802	...	21	44	...	303	...	2.1	30.3
49-50—Minneapolis	12	...	121	316	.383	134	170	.788	...	36	47	...	376	...	3.0	31.3
50-51—Minneapolis	7	...	62	152	.408	44	55	.800	74	9	25	1	168	10.6	1.3	24.0
51-52—Minneapolis	13	553	99	261	.379	109	138	.790	207	36	63	3	307	15.9	2.8	23.6
52-53—Minneapolis	12	463	78	213	.366	82	112	.732	185	23	56	5	238	15.4	1.9	19.8
53-54—Minneapolis	13	424	87	190	.458	78	96	.813	171	22	56	1	252	13.2	1.9	19.4
55-56—Minneapolis	3	60	13	35	.371	10	13	.769	28	5	14	0	36	9.3	1.7	12.0
Totals	91	...	723	...	...	695	906	.767	...	...	390	...	2141	...	...	23.5

NBA ALL-STAR GAME RECORD

NOTES: NBA All-Star Game Most Valuable Player (1953).

Season Team	Min.	FGM	FGA	Pct.	FTM	FTA	Pct.	Reb	Ast.	PF	Dq.	Pts.
1951—Minneapolis	...	4	17	.235	4	6	.667	11	3	2	0	12
1952—Minneapolis	29	9	19	.474	8	9	.889	15	1	5	0	26
1953—Minneapolis	40	9	26	.346	4	4	1.000	16	2	2	0	22
1954—Minneapolis	31	6	18	.333	6	8	.750	9	1	5	0	18
Totals	...	28	80	.350	22	27	.815	51	7	14	0	78

NBA COACHING RECORD

Season Team	REGULAR SEASON			PLAYOFFS		
	W	L	Pct.	W	L	Pct.
57-58—Minneapolis	9	30	.231	—	—	—

NOTES:

1958—Resigned as Minneapolis head coach and replaced by John Kundla (January).

MIKKELSEN, VERN   F/C

PERSONAL: Born October 21, 1928, in Fresno, Calif. ... 6-7/230 (2,00/104,3). ... Full name: Arild Verner Agerskov Mikkelsen.
HIGH SCHOOL: Askov (Minn.).
COLLEGE: Hamline University (Minn.).
TRANSACTIONS: Selected by Minneapolis Lakers in first round of 1949 NBA Draft.
CAREER HONORS: Elected to Naismith Memorial Basketball Hall of Fame (1995).
MISCELLANEOUS: Member of NBA championship team (1950, 1952, 1953, 1954).

COLLEGIATE RECORD
NOTES: The Sporting News All-America fourth team (1949). ... Inducted into NAIA Basketball Hall of Fame (1956). ... Led NCAA Division II with .538 field-goal percentage (1949).

Season Team	G	Min.	FGM	FGA	Pct.	FTM	FTA	Pct.	Reb.	Ast.	Pts.	AVERAGES RPG	APG	PPG
45-46—Hamline University	17	...	49	...	...	25	...	...	...	...	123	...	...	7.2
46-47—Hamline University	26	...	102	...	...	52	...	...	...	...	256	...	...	9.8
47-48—Hamline University	31	...	199	...	...	119	...	...	...	...	517	...	...	16.7
48-49—Hamline University	30	...	203	377	.538	113	177	.638	...	...	519	...	...	17.3
Totals	104		553			309					1415	...	...	13.6

NBA REGULAR-SEASON RECORD
RECORDS: Holds career record for most disqualifications—127.
HONORS: All-NBA second team (1951, 1952, 1953, 1955).

Season Team	G	Min.	FGM	FGA	Pct.	FTM	FTA	Pct.	Reb.	Ast.	PF	Dq.	Pts.	AVERAGES RPG	APG	PPG
49-50—Minneapolis	68	...	288	722	.399	215	286	.752	...	123	222	...	791	...	1.8	11.6
50-51—Minneapolis	64	...	359	893	.402	186	275	.676	655	181	260	13	904	10.2	2.8	14.1
51-52—Minneapolis	66	2345	363	866	.419	283	372	.761	681	180	282	16	1009	10.3	2.7	15.3
52-53—Minneapolis	70	2465	378	868	.435	291	387	.752	654	148	289	14	1047	9.3	2.1	15.0
53-54—Minneapolis	72	2247	288	771	.374	221	298	.742	615	119	264	7	797	8.5	1.7	11.1
54-55—Minneapolis	71	2559	440	1043	.422	447	598	.748	722	145	*319	14	1327	10.2	2.0	18.7
55-56—Minneapolis	72	2100	317	821	.386	328	408	.804	608	173	*319	†17	962	8.4	2.4	13.4
56-57—Minneapolis	72	2198	322	854	.377	342	424	.807	630	121	*312	*18	986	8.8	1.7	13.7
57-58—Minneapolis	72	2390	439	1070	.410	370	471	.786	805	166	299	*20	1248	11.2	2.3	17.3
58-59—Minneapolis	72	2139	353	904	.390	286	355	.806	570	159	246	8	992	7.9	2.2	13.8
Totals............................	699	...	3547	8812	.403	2969	3874	.766	...	1515	2812	...	10063	...	2.2	14.4

NBA PLAYOFF RECORD

Season Team	G	Min.	FGM	FGA	Pct.	FTM	FTA	Pct.	Reb.	Ast.	PF	Dq.	Pts.	AVERAGES RPG	APG	PPG
49-50—Minneapolis	12	...	55	149	.369	46	60	.767	...	18	52	...	156	...	1.5	13.0
50-51—Minneapolis	7	...	39	96	.406	31	47	.660	67	17	35	3	109	9.6	2.4	15.6
51-52—Minneapolis	13	496	60	139	.432	53	64	.828	110	20	66	4	173	8.5	1.5	13.3
52-53—Minneapolis	12	400	44	133	.331	56	66	.848	104	24	59	3	144	8.7	2.0	12.0
53-54—Minneapolis	13	375	51	111	.459	31	36	.861	73	17	52	1	133	5.6	1.3	10.2
54-55—Minneapolis	7	209	30	85	.353	36	46	.783	78	13	36	4	96	11.1	1.9	13.7
55-56—Minneapolis	3	90	11	26	.423	18	20	.900	17	2	14	2	40	5.7	0.7	13.3
56-57—Minneapolis	5	162	33	83	.398	22	34	.647	43	17	29	4	88	8.6	3.4	17.6
58-59—Minneapolis	13	371	73	177	.412	56	73	.767	93	24	54	3	202	7.2	1.8	15.5
Totals............................	85	...	396	999	.396	349	446	.783	...	152	397	...	1141	...	1.8	13.4

NBA ALL-STAR GAME RECORD

Season Team	Min.	FGM	FGA	Pct.	FTM	FTA	Pct.	Reb	Ast.	PF	Dq.	Pts.
1951—Minneapolis	...	4	11	.364	3	4	.750	9	1	3	0	11
1952—Minneapolis	23	5	8	.625	2	2	1.000	10	0	2	0	12
1953—Minneapolis	19	3	13	.231	0	0	...	6	3	3	0	6
1955—Minneapolis	25	7	15	.467	2	3	.667	9	1	5	0	16
1956—Minneapolis	22	5	13	.385	6	7	.857	9	2	4	0	16
1957—Minneapolis	21	3	10	.300	0	4	.000	9	1	3	0	6
Totals	...	27	70	.386	13	20	.650	52	8	20	0	67

ABA COACHING RECORD
BACKGROUND: General manager, Minnesota Pipers of ABA (1968-69).

Season Team	REGULAR SEASON W	L	Pct.	Finish	PLAYOFFS W	L	Pct.
68-69—Minnesota	6	7	.462		—	—	—

NOTES:
1969—Replaced Jim Harding as Minnesota head coach (January), with record of 20-12; later replaced by Gus Young.

MILLER, REGGIE   G

PERSONAL: Born August 24, 1965, in Riverside, Calif. ... 6-7/190. (2.01/86.2). ... Full name: Reginald Wayne Miller ... Brother of Darrell Miller, outfielder/catcher with California Angels (1984-88); and brother of Cheryl Miller, member of gold-medal-winning U.S. Olympic women's basketball team (1984), and head coach and general manager, Phoenix Mercury of the WNBA (1997-2000).
HIGH SCHOOL: Riverside (Calif.) Polytechnic.

COLLEGE: UCLA.
TRANSACTIONS/CAREER NOTES: Selected by Indiana Pacers in first round (11th pick overall) of 1987 NBA Draft.
MISCELLANEOUS: Member of gold-medal-winning U.S. Olympic team (1996). ... Member of gold-medal-winning U.S. World Championship team (1994). ... Indiana Pacers franchise all-time leading scorer with 25,279 points and all-time steals leader with 1,505 (1987-88 through 2004-05).

COLLEGIATE RECORD

Season Team	G	Min.	FGM	FGA	Pct.	FTM	FTA	Pct.	Reb.	Ast.	Pts.	AVERAGES RPG	APG	PPG
83-84—UCLA	28	384	56	110	.509	18	28	.643	42	21	130	1.5	0.8	4.6
84-85—UCLA	33	1174	192	347	.553	119	148	.804	141	86	503	4.3	2.6	15.2
85-86—UCLA	29	1112	274	493	.556	202	229	.882	153	69	750	5.3	2.4	25.9
86-87—UCLA	32	1166	247	455	.543	149	179	.832	173	71	712	5.4	2.2	22.3
Totals	122	3036	769	1405	.547	488	584	.836	509	247	2095	4.2	2.0	17.2

Three-point field goals: 1986-87, 69-for-157 (.439). Totals, 69-for-157 (.439).

NBA REGULAR-SEASON RECORD

RECORDS: Holds career record for most three-point field goals made—2,560; and most three-point field goals attempted—6,486. ... Shares NBA record for most seasons leading league in three-point field goals made—2.
HONORS: J. Walter Kennedy Citizenship Award (2004). ... All-NBA Third Team (1995, 1996, 1998).
NOTES: Led NBA with 167 three-point field goals made (1993) and 229 three-point field goals made (1997).

Season Team	G	Min.	FGM	FGA	Pct.	FTM	FTA	Pct.	REBOUNDS Off.	Def.	Tot.	Ast.	St.	Blk.	TO	Pts.	AVERAGES RPG	APG	PPG
87-88—Indiana	82	1840	306	627	.488	149	186	.801	95	95	190	132	53	19	101	822	2.3	1.6	10.0
88-89—Indiana	74	2536	398	831	.479	287	340	.844	73	219	292	227	93	29	143	1181	3.9	3.1	16.0
89-90—Indiana	82	3192	661	1287	.514	544	627	.868	95	200	295	311	110	18	222	2016	3.6	3.8	24.6
90-91—Indiana	82	2972	596	1164	.512	551	600	*.918	81	200	281	331	109	13	163	1855	3.4	4.0	22.6
91-92—Indiana	82	3120	562	1121	.501	442	515	.858	82	236	318	314	105	26	157	1695	3.9	3.8	20.7
92-93—Indiana	82	2954	571	1193	.479	427	485	.880	67	191	258	262	120	26	145	1736	3.1	3.2	21.2
93-94—Indiana	79	2638	524	1042	.503	403	444	.900	30	182	212	248	119	24	175	1574	2.7	3.1	19.9
94-95—Indiana	81	2665	505	1092	.462	383	427	.897	30	180	210	242	98	16	151	1588	2.6	3.0	19.6
95-96—Indiana	76	2621	504	1066	.473	430	498	.863	38	176	214	253	77	13	189	1606	2.8	3.3	21.1
96-97—Indiana	81	2966	552	1244	.444	418	475	.880	53	233	286	273	75	25	166	1751	3.5	3.4	21.6
97-98—Indiana	81	2795	516	1081	.477	382	440	.868	46	186	232	171	78	11	128	1578	2.9	2.1	19.5
98-99—Indiana	50	1787	294	671	.438	226	247	*.915	25	110	135	112	37	9	76	920	2.7	2.2	18.4
99-00—Indiana	81	2987	466	1041	.448	373	406	.919	50	189	239	187	85	25	129	1470	3.0	2.3	18.1
00-01—Indiana	81	3181	517	1176	.440	323	348	*.928	38	247	285	260	81	15	133	1527	3.5	3.2	18.9
01-02—Indiana	79	2889	414	913	.453	296	325	*.911	23	196	219	253	88	10	120	1304	2.8	3.2	16.5
02-03—Indiana	70	2117	281	637	.441	207	230	.900	21	151	172	170	62	4	66	882	2.5	2.4	12.6
03-04—Indiana	80	2254	260	594	.438	146	165	.885	18	170	188	249	65	11	68	800	2.4	3.1	10.0
04-05—Indiana	66	2105	314	719	.437	250	268	*.933	18	138	156	146	50	5	77	974	2.4	2.2	14.8
Totals	1389	47619	8241	17499	.471	6237	7026	.888	883	3299	4182	4141	1505	299	2409	25279	3.0	3.0	18.2

Three-point field goals: 1987-88, 61-for-172 (.355). 1988-89, 98-for-244 (.402). 1989-90, 150-for-362 (.414). 1990-91, 112-for-322 (.348). 1991-92, 129-for-341 (.378). 1992-93, 167-for-419 (.399). 1993-94, 123-for-292 (.421). 1994-95, 195-for-470 (.415). 1995-96, 168-for-410 (.410). 1996-97, 229-for-536 (.427). 1997-98, 164-for-382 (.429). 1998-99, 106-for-275 (.385). 1999-00, 165-for-404 (.408). 2000-01, 170-for-464 (.366). 2001-02, 180-for-443 (.406). 2002-03, 113-for-318 (.355). 2003-04, 134-for-334 (.401). 2004-05, 96-for-298 (.322). Totals, 2560-for-6486 (.395).

Personal fouls/disqualifications: 1987-98, 157/0. 1988-89, 170/0. 1989-90, 171/1. [illegible] 1990-91, 189/0. 1991-92, 188/1. 1992-93, 173/1. 1993-94, 158/2. 1994-95, 157/0. 1995-96, 175/0. 1996-97, 172/1. 1997-98, 148/2. 1998-99, 101/1. 1999-00, 126/0. 2000-01, 162/0. 2001-02, 143/0. 2002-03, 89/0. 2003-04, 96/0. 2004-05, 109/0. Totals, 2730/11.

NBA PLAYOFF RECORD

Season Team	G	Min.	FGM	FGA	Pct.	FTM	FTA	Pct.	REBOUNDS Off.	Def.	Tot.	Ast.	St.	Blk.	TO	Pts.	AVERAGES RPG	APG	PPG
89-90—Indiana	3	125	20	35	.571	19	21	.905	1	11	12	6	3	0	3	62	4.0	2.0	20.7
90-91—Indiana	5	193	34	70	.486	32	37	.865	5	11	16	14	8	2	12	108	3.2	2.8	21.6
91-92—Indiana	3	130	25	43	.581	24	30	.800	4	3	7	14	4	0	4	81	2.3	4.7	27.0
92-93—Indiana	4	175	40	75	.533	36	38	.947	4	8	12	11	3	0	10	126	3.0	2.8	31.5
93-94—Indiana	16	576	121	270	.448	94	112	.839	11	37	48	46	21	4	32	371	3.0	2.9	23.2
94-95—Indiana	17	641	138	290	.476	104	121	.860	9	52	61	36	15	4	39	434	3.6	2.1	25.5
95-96—Indiana	1	31	7	17	.412	13	15	.867	1	0	1	1	1	0	0	29	1.0	1.0	29.0
97-98—Indiana	16	628	98	230	.426	85	94	.904	5	23	28	32	19	3	27	319	1.8	2.0	19.9
98-99—Indiana	13	481	79	199	.397	77	86	.895	13	38	51	34	9	3	21	263	3.9	2.6	20.2
99-00—Indiana	22	892	174	385	.452	121	129	.938	9	44	53	60	23	10	28	527	2.4	2.7	24.0
00-01—Indiana	4	177	41	90	.456	28	30	.933	7	18	25	12	5	1	11	125	5.0	2.5	31.3
01-02—Indiana	5	198	42	83	.506	21	24	.875	0	16	16	14	8	1	14	118	3.2	2.8	23.6
02-03—Indiana	6	176	15	53	.283	21	23	.913	1	13	14	14	1	1	7	55	2.3	2.3	9.2
03-04—Indiana	16	455	45	112	.402	47	51	.922	3	34	37	45	18	3	28	161	2.3	2.8	10.1
04-05—Indiana	13	430	62	143	.434	48	51	.941	4	36	40	20	10	1	21	193	3.1	1.5	14.8
Totals	144	5308	941	2095	.449	770	862	.893	77	339	416	357	146	34	257	2972	2.9	2.5	20.6

Three-point field goals: 1989-90, 3-for-7 (.429). 1990-91, 8-for-19 (.421). 1991-92, 7-for-11 (.636). 1992-93, 10-for-19 (.526). 1993-94, 35-for-83 (.422). 1994-95, 54-for-128 (.422). 1995-96, 2-for-6 (.333). 1997-98, 38-for-95 (.400). 1998-99, 28-for-84 (.333). 1999-00, 58-for-147 (.395). 2000-01, 15-for-35 (.429). 2001-02, 13-for-31 (.419). 2002-03, 4-for-25 (.160). 2003-04, 24-for-64 (.375). 2004-05, 21-for-66 (.318). Totals, 320-for-820 (.390).

Personal fouls/disqualifications: 1989-90, 9/0. 1990-91, 14/0. 1991-92, 12/1. 1992-93, 11/0. 1993-94, 34/0. 1994-95, 35/0. 1995-96, 1/0. 1997-98, 26/0. 1998-99, 26/0. 1999-00, 37/0. 2000-01, 3/0. 2001-02, 10/0. 2002-03, 9/0. 2003-04, 25/0. 2004-05, 28/0. Totals, 275/1.

NBA ALL-STAR GAME RECORD

Season Team	Min.	FGM	FGA	Pct.	FTM	FTA	Pct.	REBOUNDS Off.	Def.	Tot.	Ast.	PF	Dq.	St.	Blk.	TO	Pts.
1990—Indiana	14	2	3	.667	0	0	...	0	1	1	3	1	0	1	0	0	4
1995—Indiana	23	3	9	.333	0	0	...	0	0	0	2	0	0	1	1	1	9
1996—Indiana	18	4	8	.500	0	0	...	0	2	2	2	1	0	1	0	1	8
1998—Indiana	20	6	8	.750	1	2	.500	0	0	0	0	2	...	1	0	0	14
2000—Indiana	21	1	7	.143	2	2	1.000	0	2	2	3	1	0	1	0	1	5
Totals	96	16	35	.457	3	4	.750	0	3	5	10	6	0	5	1	3	40

Three-point field goals: 1990, 0-for-1. 1995, 3-for-6 (.500). 1996, 0-for-4. 1998, 1-for-2 (.500). 2000, 1-for-6 (.167). Totals, 5-for-19 (.263).

ALL-TIME GREAT PLAYERS

MONCRIEF, SIDNEY   G

PERSONAL: Born September 21, 1957, in Little Rock, Ark. ... 6-3/183 (1,90/83,0). ... Full name: Sidney A. Moncrief. ... Nickname: The Squid.
HIGH SCHOOL: Hall (Little Rock, Ark.).
COLLEGE: Arkansas.
TRANSACTIONS: Selected by Milwaukee Bucks in first round (fifth pick overall) of 1979 NBA Draft. ... Signed as unrestricted free agent by Atlanta Hawks (October 4, 1990). ... Rights renounced by Hawks (September 29, 1991).
CAREER NOTES: Head coach, University of Arkansas-Little Rock (1999-2000). ... Assistant coach, Dallas Mavericks (2000-present).

COLLEGIATE RECORD

NOTES: THE SPORTING NEWS All-America second team (1979). ... Led NCAA Division I with .665 field goal percentage (1976).

Season Team	G	Min.	FGM	FGA	Pct.	FTM	FTA	Pct.	Reb.	Ast.	Pts.	AVERAGES RPG	APG	PPG
75-76—Arkansas	28	...	149	224	.665	56	77	.727	213	59	354	7.6	2.1	12.6
76-77—Arkansas	28	997	157	242	.649	117	171	.684	235	41	431	8.4	1.5	15.4
77-78—Arkansas	36	1293	209	354	.590	203	256	.793	278	60	621	7.7	1.7	17.3
78-79—Arkansas	30	1157	224	400	.560	212	248	.855	289	80	660	9.6	2.7	22.0
Totals	122	...	739	1220	.606	588	752	.782	1015	240	2066	8.3	2.0	16.9

NBA REGULAR-SEASON RECORD

HONORS: NBA Defensive Player of the Year (1983, 1984). ... All-NBA first team (1983). ... All-NBA second team (1982, 1984, 1985, 1986). ... NBA All-Defensive first team (1983, 1984, 1985, 1986). ... NBA All-Defensive second team (1982).

Season Team	G	Min.	FGM	FGA	Pct.	FTM	FTA	Pct.	REBOUNDS Off.	Def.	Tot.	Ast.	St.	Blk.	TO	Pts.	AVERAGES RPG	APG	PPG
79-80—Milwaukee	77	1557	211	451	.468	232	292	.795	154	184	338	133	72	16	117	654	4.4	1.7	8.5
80-81—Milwaukee	80	2417	400	739	.541	320	398	.804	186	220	406	264	90	37	145	1122	5.1	3.3	14.0
81-82—Milwaukee	80	2980	556	1063	.523	468	573	.817	221	313	534	382	138	22	208	1581	6.7	4.8	19.8
82-83—Milwaukee	76	2710	606	1156	.524	499	604	.826	192	245	437	300	113	23	197	1712	5.8	3.9	22.5
83-84—Milwaukee	79	3075	560	1125	.498	529	624	.848	215	313	528	358	108	27	217	1654	6.7	4.5	20.9
84-85—Milwaukee	73	2734	561	1162	.483	454	548	.828	149	242	391	382	117	39	184	1585	5.4	5.2	21.7
85-86—Milwaukee	73	2567	470	962	.489	498	580	.859	115	219	334	357	103	18	174	1471	4.6	4.9	20.2
86-87—Milwaukee	39	992	158	324	.488	136	162	.840	57	70	127	121	27	10	63	460	3.3	3.1	11.8
87-88—Milwaukee	56	1428	217	444	.489	164	196	.837	58	122	180	204	41	12	86	603	3.2	3.6	10.8
88-89—Milwaukee	62	1594	261	532	.491	205	237	.865	46	126	172	188	65	13	94	752	2.8	3.0	12.1
89-90—								Did not play—retired.											
90-91—Atlanta	72	1096	117	240	.488	82	105	.781	31	97	128	104	50	9	66	337	1.8	1.4	4.7
Totals	767	23150	4117	8198	.502	3587	4319	.831	1424	2151	3575	2793	924	226	1551	11931	4.7	3.6	15.6

Three-point field goals: 1979-80, 0-for-1. 1980-81, 2-for-9 (.222). 1981-82, 1-for-14 (.071). 1982-83, 1-for-10 (.100). 1983-84, 5-for-18 (.278). 1984-85, 9-for-33 (.273). 1985-86, 33-for-103 (.320). 1986-87, 8-for-31 (.258). 1987-88, 5-for-31 (.161). 1988-89, 25-for-73 (.342). 1990-91, 21-for-64 (.328). Totals, 110-for-387 (.284).

Personal fouls/disqualifications: 1979-80, 106/0. 1980-81, 156/1. 1981-82, 206/3. 1982-83, 180/1. 1983-84, 204/2. 1984-85, 197/1. 1985-86, 178/1. 1986-87, 73/0. 1987-88, 109/0. 1988-89, 114/1. 1990-91, 112/0. Totals, 1635/10.

NBA PLAYOFF RECORD

Season Team	G	Min.	FGM	FGA	Pct.	FTM	FTA	Pct.	REBOUNDS Off.	Def.	Tot.	Ast.	St.	Blk.	TO	Pts.	AVERAGES RPG	APG	PPG
79-80—Milwaukee	7	182	30	51	.588	27	31	.871	17	14	31	11	5	1	14	87	4.4	1.6	12.4
80-81—Milwaukee	7	277	30	69	.435	38	51	.745	19	28	47	20	12	3	21	98	6.7	2.9	14.0
81-82—Milwaukee	6	252	31	74	.419	30	38	.789	15	15	30	24	9	2	12	92	5.0	4.0	15.3
82-83—Milwaukee	9	377	62	142	.437	46	61	.754	28	32	60	33	18	3	27	170	6.7	3.7	18.9
83-84—Milwaukee	16	618	99	191	.518	106	134	.791	44	67	111	68	28	9	61	305	6.9	4.3	19.1
84-85—Milwaukee	8	319	55	99	.556	70	75	.933	10	24	34	40	5	4	20	184	4.3	5.0	23.0
85-86—Milwaukee	9	327	52	122	.426	44	63	.698	15	26	41	44	5	5	21	152	4.6	4.9	16.9
86-87—Milwaukee	12	426	78	165	.473	73	90	.811	21	33	54	36	13	6	24	233	4.5	3.0	19.4
87-88—Milwaukee	5	173	24	50	.480	26	27	.963	6	13	19	26	3	1	11	75	3.8	5.2	15.0
88-89—Milwaukee	9	184	19	48	.396	15	16	.938	8	18	26	13	5	2	11	55	2.9	1.4	6.1
90-91—Atlanta	5	91	11	22	.500	13	16	.813	6	10	16	2	3	0	3	36	3.2	0.4	7.2
Totals	93	3226	491	1033	.475	488	602	.811	189	280	469	317	106	36	225	1487	5.0	3.4	16.0

Three-point field goals: 1981-82, 0-for-1. 1982-83, 0-for-1. 1983-84, 1-for-4 (.250). 1984-85, 4-for-10 (.400). 1985-86, 4-for-14 (.286). 1986-87, 4-for-14 (.286). 1987-88, 1-for-1. 1988-89, 2-for-7 (.286). 1990-91, 1-for-6 (.167). Totals, 17-for-58 (.293).

Personal fouls/disqualifications: 1979-80, 14/0. 1980-81, 24/0. 1981-82, 22/1. 1982-83, 25/1. 1983-84, 54/1. 1984-85, 26/0. 1985-86, 30/0. 1986-87, 43/0. 1987-88, 14/0. 1988-89, 17/0. 1990-91, 16/0. Totals, 285/3.

NBA ALL-STAR GAME RECORD

Season Team	Min.	FGM	FGA	Pct.	FTM	FTA	Pct.	REBOUNDS Off.	Def.	Tot.	Ast.	PF	Dq.	St.	Blk.	TO	Pts.
1982—Milwaukee	22	3	11	.273	0	2	.000	3	1	4	1	2	0	1	0	1	6
1983—Milwaukee	23	8	14	.571	4	5	.800	3	2	5	4	1	0	6	1	1	20
1984—Milwaukee	26	3	6	.500	2	2	1.000	1	4	5	2	3	0	5	0	4	8
1985—Milwaukee	22	1	5	.200	6	6	1.000	2	3	5	4	1	0	0	0	2	8
1986—Milwaukee	26	4	11	.364	7	7	1.000	3	0	3	1	0	0	0	1	0	16
Totals	119	19	47	.404	19	22	.864	12	10	22	12	7	0	12	2	8	58

Three-point field goals: 1986, 1-for-1.

HEAD COACHING RECORD

Season Team	REGULAR SEASON W	L	Pct.	Finish	PLAYOFFS W	L	Pct.
99-00—Arkansas-Little Rock	4	23	.148	9th/Sun Belt Conference	—	—	—

MONROE, EARL   G

PERSONAL: Born November 21, 1944, in Philadelphia. ... 6-3/190 (1,90/86,2). ... Full name: Vernon Earl Monroe. ... Nickname: The Pearl.
HIGH SCHOOL: John Bartram (Philadelphia).
COLLEGE: Winston-Salem (N.C.) State.
TRANSACTIONS: Selected by Baltimore Bullets in first round (second pick overall) of 1967 NBA Draft. ... Traded by Bullets to New York Knicks for F Dave Stallworth, G Mike Riordan and cash (November 10, 1971).
CAREER HONORS: Elected to Naismith Memorial Basketball Hall of Fame (1990). ... One of the 50 Greatest Players in NBA History (1996).
MISCELLANEOUS: Member of NBA championship team (1973).

COLLEGIATE RECORD

NOTES: THE SPORTING NEWS All-America first team (1966). ... Holds NCAA Division II single-season record for most points—1329 (1967). ... Inducted into NAIA Basketball Hall of Fame (1975). ... NCAA College Division and NAIA Leading Scorer (1967). ... Outstanding Player in NCAA College Division Tournament (1967). ... Member of NCAA College Division tournament championship team (1967). ... Led NCAA Division II with 41.5 points per game (1967).

Season Team	G	Min.	FGM	FGA	Pct.	FTM	FTA	Pct.	Reb.	Ast.	Pts.	RPG	APG	PPG
63-64—Winst.-Salem State	23	...	71	...	...	21	...	...	...	...	163	...	...	7.1
64-65—Winst.-Salem State	30	...	286	...	...	125	176	.710	211	...	697	7.0	...	23.2
65-66—Winst.-Salem State	25	...	292	519	.563	162	187	.866	167	...	746	6.7	...	29.8
66-67—Winst.-Salem State	32	...	509	839	.607	311	391	.795	218	...	1329	6.8	...	41.5
Totals	110	...	1158	...	...	619	...	...	...	...	2935	...	...	26.7

NBA REGULAR-SEASON RECORD

HONORS: NBA Rookie of the Year (1968). ... All-NBA first team (1969). ... NBA All-Rookie team (1968).

Season Team	G	Min.	FGM	FGA	Pct.	FTM	FTA	Pct.	Reb.	Ast.	PF	Dq.	Pts.	RPG	APG	PPG
67-68—Baltimore	82	3012	742	1637	.453	507	649	.781	465	349	282	3	1991	5.7	4.3	24.3
68-69—Baltimore	80	3075	809	1837	.440	447	582	.768	280	392	261	1	2065	3.5	4.9	25.8
69-70—Baltimore	82	3051	695	1557	.446	532	641	.830	257	402	258	3	1922	3.1	4.9	23.4
70-71—Baltimore	81	2843	663	1501	.442	406	506	.802	213	354	220	1	1732	2.6	4.4	21.4
71-72—Balt.-N.Y.	63	1337	287	662	.434	175	224	.781	100	142	139	1	749	1.6	2.3	11.9
72-73—New York	75	2370	496	1016	.488	171	208	.822	245	288	195	1	1163	3.3	3.8	15.5

Season Team	G	Min.	FGM	FGA	Pct.	FTM	FTA	Pct.	Off.	Def.	Tot.	Ast.	St.	Blk.	TO	Pts.	RPG	APG	PPG
73-74—New York	41	1194	240	513	.468	93	113	.823	22	99	121	110	34	19	...	573	3.0	2.7	14.0
74-75—New York	78	2814	668	1462	.457	297	359	.827	56	271	327	270	108	29	...	1633	4.2	3.5	20.9
75-76—New York	76	2889	647	1354	.478	280	356	.787	48	225	273	304	111	22	...	1574	3.6	4.0	20.7
76-77—N.Y. Knicks	77	2656	613	1185	.517	307	366	.839	45	178	223	366	91	23	...	1533	2.9	4.8	19.9
77-78—New York	76	2369	556	1123	.495	242	291	.832	47	135	182	361	60	19	179	1354	2.4	4.8	17.8
78-79—New York	64	1393	329	699	.471	129	154	.838	26	48	74	189	48	6	98	787	1.2	3.0	12.3
79-80—New York	51	633	161	352	.457	56	64	.875	16	20	36	67	21	3	28	378	0.7	1.3	7.4
Totals	926	29636	6906	14898	.464	3642	4513	.807			2796	3594	473	121	305	17454	0.0	0.0	10.0

Personal fouls/disqualifications: 1967-68, 282/3. 1968-69, 261/1. 1969-70, 258/3. 1970-71, 220/1. 1971-72, 139/1. 1972-73, 195/1. 1973-74, 189/0. 1978-79, 123/0. 1979-80, 46/0. Totals, 2416/13.

NBA PLAYOFF RECORD

Season Team	G	Min.	FGM	FGA	Pct.	FTM	FTA	Pct.	Reb.	Ast.	PF	Dq.	Pts.	RPG	APG	PPG
68-69—Baltimore	4	171	44	114	.386	25	31	.806	21	16	10	0	113	5.3	4.0	28.3
69-70—Baltimore	7	299	74	154	.481	48	60	.800	23	28	23	0	196	3.3	4.0	28.0
70-71—Baltimore	18	671	145	356	.407	107	135	.793	64	74	56	0	397	3.6	4.1	22.1
71-72—New York	16	429	76	185	.411	45	57	.789	45	47	41	0	197	2.8	2.9	12.3
72-73—New York	16	504	111	211	.526	36	48	.750	51	51	39	0	258	3.2	3.2	16.1

Season Team	G	Min.	FGM	FGA	Pct.	FTM	FTA	Pct.	Off.	Def.	Tot.	Ast.	St.	Blk.	TO	Pts.	RPG	APG	PPG
73-74—New York	12	407	81	165	.491	47	55	.855	8	40	48	25	8	9	...	209	4.0	2.1	17.4
74-75—New York	3	89	12	45	.267	18	22	.818	1	8	9	6	4	2	...	42	3.0	2.0	14.0
77-78—New York	6	145	24	62	.387	11	18	.611	1	4	5	17	6	0	6	59	0.8	2.8	9.8
Totals	82	2715	567	1292	.439	337	426	.791	...	...	266	264	18	11	6	1471	3.2	3.2	17.9

Personal fouls/disqualifications: 1973-74, 26/0. 1974-75, 6/0. 1977-78, 15/0. Totals, 216/0.

NBA ALL-STAR GAME RECORD

Season Team	Min.	FGM	FGA	Pct.	FTM	FTA	Pct.	Reb	Ast.	PF	Dq.	Pts.
1969—Baltimore	27	6	15	.400	9	12	.750	4	4	4	0	21
1971—Baltimore	18	3	9	.333	0	0	...	5	2	3	0	6

Season Team	Min.	FGM	FGA	Pct.	FTM	FTA	Pct.	Off.	Def.	Tot.	Ast.	PF	Dq.	St.	Blk.	TO	Pts.
1975—New York	25	3	8	.375	3	5	.600	0	3	3	2	2	0	1	0	...	9
1977—N.Y. Knicks	15	2	7	.286	0	0	...	0	0	0	3	1	0	0	0	...	4
Totals	85	14	39	.359	12	17	.706	...	...	12	11	10	0	1	0	...	40

MULLIN, CHRIS   F

PERSONAL: Born July 30, 1963, in New York. ... 6-7/215. (2,01/97,5). ... Full Name: Christopher Paul Mullin.
HIGH SCHOOL: Power Memorial (New York), then Xaverian (Brooklyn, N.Y.).
COLLEGE: St. John's.
TRANSACTIONS: Selected by Golden State Warriors in first round (seventh pick overall) of 1985 NBA Draft. ... Traded by Warriors to Indiana Pacers for C Erick Dampier and F Duane Ferrell (August 12, 1997). ... Waived by Pacers (September

12, 2000). ... Signed as free agent by Warriors (September 28, 2000).
CAREER NOTES: Special assistant, Warriors (2002-April 22, 2004). ... Executive vice president of basketball operations, Warriors (April 22, 2004-present).
MISCELLANEOUS: Member of gold-medal-winning U.S. Olympic team (1984, 1992). ... Golden State Warriors franchise all-time steals leader with 1,376 (1985-86 through 1996-97 and 2000-01).

COLLEGIATE RECORD

NOTES: Wooden Award winner (1985). ... THE SPORTING NEWS All-America first team (1985). ... THE SPORTING NEWS All-America second team (1984).

Season Team	G	Min.	FGM	FGA	Pct.	FTM	FTA	Pct.	Reb.	Ast.	Pts.	AVERAGES RPG	APG	PPG
81-82—St. John's	30	1061	175	328	.534	148	187	.791	97	92	498	3.2	3.1	16.6
82-83—St. John's	33	1210	228	395	.577	173	197	.878	123	101	629	3.7	3.1	19.1
83-84—St. John's	27	1070	225	394	.571	169	187	.904	120	109	619	4.4	4.0	22.9
84-85—St. John's	35	1327	251	482	.521	192	233	.824	169	151	694	4.8	4.3	19.8
Totals	125	4668	879	1599	.550	682	804	.848	509	453	2440	4.1	3.6	19.5

NBA REGULAR-SEASON RECORD

HONORS: All-NBA first team (1992). ... All-NBA second team (1989, 1991). ... All-NBA third team (1990).

Season Team	G	Min.	FGM	FGA	Pct.	FTM	FTA	Pct.	REBOUNDS Off.	Def.	Tot.	Ast.	St.	Blk.	TO	Pts.	AVERAGES RPG	APG	PPG
85-86—Golden State	55	1391	287	620	.463	189	211	.896	42	73	115	105	70	23	75	768	2.1	1.9	14.0
86-87—Golden State	82	2377	477	928	.514	269	326	.825	39	142	181	261	98	36	154	1242	2.2	3.2	15.1
87-88—Golden State	60	2033	470	926	.508	239	270	.885	58	147	205	290	113	32	156	1213	3.4	4.8	20.2
88-89—Golden State	82	3093	830	1630	.509	493	553	.892	152	331	483	415	176	39	296	2176	5.9	5.1	26.5
89-90—Golden State	78	2830	682	1272	.536	505	568	.889	130	333	463	319	123	45	239	1956	5.9	4.1	25.1
90-91—Golden State	82	*3315	777	1449	.536	513	580	.884	141	302	443	329	173	63	245	2107	5.4	4.0	25.7
91-92—Golden State	81	*3346	830	1584	.524	350	420	.833	127	323	450	286	173	62	202	2074	5.6	3.5	25.6
92-93—Golden State	46	1902	474	930	.510	183	226	.810	42	190	232	166	68	41	139	1191	5.0	3.6	25.9
93-94—Golden State	62	2324	410	869	.472	165	219	.753	64	281	345	315	107	53	178	1040	5.6	5.1	16.8
94-95—Golden State	25	890	170	348	.489	94	107	.879	25	90	115	125	38	19	93	476	4.6	5.0	19.0
95-96—Golden State	55	1617	269	539	.499	137	160	.856	44	115	159	194	75	32	122	734	2.9	3.5	13.3
96-97—Golden State	79	2733	438	792	.553	184	213	.864	75	242	317	322	130	33	192	1143	4.0	4.1	14.5
97-98—Indiana	82	2177	333	692	.481	154	164	*.939	38	211	249	186	95	39	117	927	3.0	2.3	11.3
98-99—Indiana	50	1179	177	371	.477	80	92	.870	25	135	160	81	47	13	60	507	3.2	1.6	10.1
99-00—Indiana	47	582	80	187	.428	37	41	.902	14	62	76	37	28	9	28	242	1.6	0.8	5.1
00-01—Golden State	20	374	36	106	.340	24	28	.857	10	31	41	19	16	10	19	115	2.1	1.0	5.8
Totals	986	32163	6740	13243	.509	3616	4178	.865	1026	3008	4034	3450	1530	549	2315	17911	4.1	3.5	18.2

Three-point field goals: 1985-86, 5-for-27 (.185). 1986-87, 19-for-63 (.302). 1987-88, 34-for-97 (.351). 1988-89, 23-for-100 (.230). 1989-90, 87-for-234 (.372). 1990-91, 40-for-133 (.301). 1991-92, 64-for-175 (.366). 1992-93, 60-for-133 (.451). 1993-94, 55-for-151 (.364). 1994-95, 42-for-93 (.452). 1995-96, 59-for-150 (.393). 1996-97, 83-for-202 (.411). 1997-98, 107-for-243 (.440). 1998-99, 73-for-157 (.465). 1999-00, 45-for-110 (.409). 2000-01, 19-for-52 (.365). Totals, 815-for-2120 (.384).

Personal fouls/disqualifications: 1985-86, 130/1. 1986-87, 217/1. 1987-88, 136/3. 1988-89, 178/1. 1989-90, 142/1. 1990-91, 176/2. 1991-92, 171/1. 1992-93, 76/0. 1993-94, 114/0. 1994-95, 53/0. 1995-96, 127/0. 1996-97, 155/0. 1997-98, 186/0. 1998-99, 101/0. 1999-00, 60/0. 2000-01, 28/0. Totals, 2050/10.

NBA PLAYOFF RECORD

Season Team	G	Min.	FGM	FGA	Pct.	FTM	FTA	Pct.	REBOUNDS Off.	Def.	Tot.	Ast.	St.	Blk.	TO	Pts.	AVERAGES RPG	APG	PPG
86-87—Golden State	10	262	49	98	.500	12	16	.750	2	13	15	23	9	2	16	113	1.5	2.3	11.3
88-89—Golden State	8	341	88	163	.540	58	67	.866	11	36	47	36	14	11	32	235	5.9	4.5	29.4
90-91—Golden State	8	366	69	131	.527	43	50	.860	9	49	58	23	15	12	25	190	7.3	2.9	23.8
91-92—Golden State	4	168	27	63	.429	13	14	.929	3	9	12	12	5	2	8	71	3.0	3.0	17.8
93-94—Golden State	3	135	30	51	.588	10	11	.909	4	10	14	11	0	5	7	76	4.7	3.7	25.3
97-98—Indiana	16	412	52	113	.460	18	21	.857	13	44	57	23	15	9	24	142	3.6	1.4	8.9
98-99—Indiana	13	283	41	100	.410	20	23	.870	2	18	20	15	10	3	20	124	1.5	1.2	9.5
99-00—Indiana	9	90	10	21	.476	9	11	.818	2	12	14	5	6	1	4	31	1.6	0.6	3.4
Totals	71	2057	366	740	.495	183	213	.859	46	191	237	148	74	45	136	982	3.3	2.1	13.8

Three-point field goals: 1986-87, 3-for-4 (.750). 1988-89, 1-for-8 (.125). 1990-91, 9-for-13 (.692). 1991-92, 4-for-12 (.333). 1993-94, 6-for-12 (.500). 1997-98, 20-for-52 (.385). 1998-99, 22-for-55 (.400). 1999-00, 2-for-8 (.250). Totals, 67-for-164 (.409).

Personal fouls/disqualifications: 1986-87, 31/0. 1988-89, 19/0. 1990-91, 23/0. 1991-92, 8/0. 1993-94, 4/0. 1997-98, 32/0. 1998-99, 21/0. 1999-00, 7/0. Totals, 145/0.

NBA ALL-STAR GAME RECORD

Season Team	Min.	FGM	FGA	Pct.	FTM	FTA	Pct.	REBOUNDS Off.	Def.	Tot.	Ast.	PF	Dq.	St.	Blk.	TO	Pts.
1989—Golden State	14	1	4	.250	2	2	1.000	2	0	2	2	0	0	0	0	1	4
1990—Golden State	16	1	5	.200	1	2	.500	1	2	3	1	0	0	2	1	1	3
1991—Golden State	24	4	8	.500	4	4	1.000	0	2	2	2	2	0	2	0	2	13
1992—Golden State	24	6	7	.857	0	0	...	0	1	1	3	0	0	0	0	1	13
1993—Golden State							Selected, did not play—injured.										
Totals	78	12	24	.500	7	8	.875	3	5	8	8	2	0	4	1	5	33

Three-point field goals: 1991, 1-for-1. 1992, 1-for-1. Totals, 2-for-2 (1.000).

MURPHY, CALVIN   G

PERSONAL: Born May 9, 1948, in Norwalk, Conn. ... 5-9/165 (1,76/74,8). ... Full name: Calvin Jerome Murphy.
HIGH SCHOOL: Norwalk (Conn.).
COLLEGE: Niagara.
TRANSACTIONS: Selected by San Diego Rockets in second round (18th pick overall) of 1970 NBA Draft. ... Rockets franchise moved from San Diego to Houston for 1971-72 season.
CAREER NOTES: Community services adviser, Houston Rockets (1989-90 to present).

CAREER HONORS: Elected to Naismith Memorial Basketball Hall of Fame (1993).
MISCELLANEOUS: Houston Rockets franchise all-time assists leader with 4,402 (1970-71 through 1982-83).

COLLEGIATE RECORD

NOTES: THE SPORTING NEWS All-America second team (1969, 1970).

Season Team	G	Min.	FGM	FGA	Pct.	FTM	FTA	Pct.	Reb.	Ast.	Pts.	RPG	APG	PPG
66-67—Niagara‡	19	...	364	719	.506	201	239	.841	102	...	929	5.4	...	48.9
67-68—Niagara	24	...	337	772	.437	242	288	.840	118	...	916	4.9	...	38.2
68-69—Niagara	24	...	294	700	.420	190	230	.826	87	...	778	3.6	...	32.4
69-70—Niagara	29	...	316	692	.457	222	252	.881	103	...	854	3.6	...	29.4
Varsity totals	77	...	947	2164	.438	654	770	.849	308	...	2548	4.0	...	33.1

NBA REGULAR-SEASON RECORD

RECORDS: Holds single-season record for highest free-throw percentage—.958 (1981).
HONORS: NBA All-Rookie team (1971). ... J. Walter Kennedy Citizenship Award (1979).

Season Team	G	Min.	FGM	FGA	Pct.	FTM	FTA	Pct.	Reb.	Ast.	PF	Dq.	Pts.	RPG	APG	PPG
70-71—San Diego	82	2020	471	1029	.458	356	434	.820	245	329	263	4	1298	3.0	4.0	15.8
71-72—Houston	82	2538	571	1255	.455	349	392	.890	258	393	298	6	1491	3.1	4.8	18.2
72-73—Houston	77	1697	381	820	.465	239	269	.888	149	262	211	3	1001	1.9	3.4	13.0

| | | | | | | | | | REBOUNDS | | | | | | AVERAGES | | |
Season Team	G	Min.	FGM	FGA	Pct.	FTM	FTA	Pct.	Off.	Def.	Tot.	Ast.	St.	Blk.	TO	Pts.	RPG	APG	PPG
73-74—Houston	81	2922	671	1285	.522	310	357	.868	51	137	188	603	157	4	...	1652	2.3	7.4	20.4
74-75—Houston	78	2513	557	1152	.484	341	386	.883	52	121	173	381	128	4	...	1455	2.2	4.9	18.7
75-76—Houston	82	2995	675	1369	.493	372	410	.907	52	157	209	596	151	6	...	1722	2.5	7.3	21.0
76-77—Houston	82	2764	596	1216	.490	272	307	.886	54	118	172	386	144	8	...	1464	2.1	4.7	17.9
77-78—Houston	76	2900	852	*1737	.491	245	267	.918	57	107	164	259	112	3	173	1949	2.2	3.4	25.6
78-79—Houston	82	2941	707	1424	.496	246	265	.928	78	95	173	351	117	6	187	1660	2.1	4.3	20.2
79-80—Houston	76	2676	624	1267	.493	271	302	.897	68	82	150	299	143	9	162	1520	2.0	3.9	20.0
80-81—Houston	76	2014	528	1074	.492	206	215	*.958	33	54	87	222	111	6	129	1266	1.1	2.9	16.7
81-82—Houston	64	1204	277	648	.427	100	110	.909	20	41	61	103	43	1	82	655	1.0	2.5	10.2
82-83—Houston	64	1423	337	754	.447	138	150	*.920	34	40	74	158	59	4	89	816	1.2	2.5	12.8
Totals	1002	30607	7247	15030	.482	3445	3864	.892	...	...	2103	4402	1165	51	822	17949	2.1	4.4	17.9

Three-point field goals: 1979-80, 1-for-25 (.040). 1980-81, 4-for-17 (.235). 1981-82, 1-for-16 (.063). 1982-83, 4-for-14 (.286). Totals, 10-for-72 (.139).
Personal fouls/disqualifications: 1973-74, 310/8. 1974-75, 281/8. 1975-76, 294/3. 1976-77, 281/6. 1977-78, 241/4. 1978-79, 288/5. 1979-80, 269/3. 1980-81, 209/0. 1981-82, 142/0. 1982-83, 163/3. Totals, 3250/53.

NBA PLAYOFF RECORD

| | | | | | | | | | REBOUNDS | | | | | | | | AVERAGES | | |
Season Team	G	Min.	FGM	FGA	Pct.	FTM	FTA	Pct.	Off.	Def.	Tot.	Ast.	St.	Blk.	TO	Pts.	RPG	APG	PPG
74-75—Houston	8	305	72	156	.462	51	57	.895	9	10	19	45	14	1	...	195	2.4	5.6	24.4
76-77—Houston	12	420	102	213	.479	28	30	.933	7	12	19	75	19	2	...	232	1.6	6.3	19.3
78-79—Houston	2	73	9	31	.290	8	9	.889	2	1	3	6	8	1	2	26	1.5	3.0	13.0
79-80—Houston	7	265	58	108	.537	13	13	1.000	4	6	10	26	11	0	16	131	1.4	3.7	18.7
80-81—Houston	19	540	142	287	.495	58	60	.967	7	17	24	57	20	0	45	344	1.3	3.0	18.1
81-82—Houston	3	57	5	22	.227	7	8	.875	2	1	3	4	1	0	4	17	1.0	1.3	5.7
Totals	51	1660	388	817	.475	165	177	.932	31	47	78	213	79	4	64	945	1.5	4.2	18.5

Three-point field goals: 1979-80, 2-for-4 (.500). 1980-81, 2-for-7 (.286). 1981-82, 0-for-3. Totals, 4-for-14 (.286).
Personal fouls/disqualifications: 1974-75, 36/2. 1976-77, 47/1. 1978-79, 9/0. 1979-80, 29/1. 1980-81, 69/0. 1981-82, 7/0. Totals, 197/4.

NBA ALL-STAR GAME RECORD

| | | | | | | | | REBOUNDS | | | | | | | | |
Season Team	Min.	FGM	FGA	Pct.	FTM	FTA	Pct.	Off.	Def.	Tot.	Ast.	PF	Dq.	St.	Blk.	TO	Pts.
1979—Houston	15	3	5	.600	0	0	...	0	1	1	5	4	0	2	0	4	6

NIXON, NORM — G

PERSONAL: Born October 10, 1955, in Macon, Ga. ... 6-2/175 (1,88/79,4). ... Full name: Norman Ellard Nixon.
HIGH SCHOOL: Southwest (Macon, Ga.).
COLLEGE: Duquesne.
TRANSACTIONS: Selected by Los Angeles Lakers in first round (22nd pick overall) of 1977 NBA Draft. ... Traded by Lakers with G Eddie Jordan and 1986 and 1987 second-round draft choices to San Diego Clippers for C Swen Nater and draft rights to G Byron Scott (October 10, 1983). ... Played in Italy (1988-89).
MISCELLANEOUS: Member of NBA championship team (1980, 1982).

COLLEGIATE RECORD

Season Team	G	Min.	FGM	FGA	Pct.	FTM	FTA	Pct.	Reb.	Ast.	Pts.	RPG	APG	PPG
73-74—Duquesne	24	...	113	257	.440	31	45	.689	99	144	257	4.1	6.0	10.7
74-75—Duquesne	25	...	147	282	.521	69	92	.750	88	105	363	3.5	4.2	14.5
75-76—Duquesne	25	...	214	434	.493	96	127	.756	105	150	524	4.2	6.0	21.0
76-77—Duquesne	30	1106	279	539	.518	103	138	.746	119	178	661	4.0	5.9	22.0
Totals	104	...	753	1512	.498	299	402	.744	411	577	1805	4.0	5.5	17.4

NBA REGULAR-SEASON RECORD

HONORS: NBA All-Rookie team (1978).

| | | | | | | | | | REBOUNDS | | | | | | | | AVERAGES | | |
Season Team	G	Min.	FGM	FGA	Pct.	FTM	FTA	Pct.	Off.	Def.	Tot.	Ast.	St.	Blk.	TO	Pts.	RPG	APG	PPG
77-78—Los Angeles	81	2779	496	998	.497	115	161	.714	41	198	239	553	138	7	251	1107	3.0	6.8	13.7
78-79—Los Angeles	82	3145	623	1149	.542	158	204	.775	48	183	231	737	201	17	231	1404	2.8	9.0	17.1
79-80—Los Angeles	82	*3226	624	1209	.516	197	253	.779	52	177	229	642	147	14	288	1446	2.8	7.8	17.6
80-81—Los Angeles	79	2962	576	1210	.476	196	252	.778	64	168	232	696	146	11	285	1350	2.9	8.8	17.1

Season Team	G	Min.	FGM	FGA	Pct.	FTM	FTA	Pct.	REBOUNDS Off.	Def.	Tot.	Ast.	St.	Blk.	TO	Pts.	RPG	APG	PPG
81-82—Los Angeles....	82	3024	628	1274	.493	181	224	.808	38	138	176	652	132	7	238	1440	2.1	8.0	17.6
82-83—Los Angeles....	79	2711	533	1123	.475	125	168	.744	61	144	205	566	104	4	237	1191	2.6	7.2	15.1
83-84—San Diego.......	82	3053	587	1270	.462	206	271	.760	56	147	203	914	94	4	257	1391	2.5	11.1	17.0
84-85—L.A. Clippers...	81	2894	596	1281	.465	170	218	.780	55	163	218	711	95	4	273	1395	2.7	8.8	17.2
85-86—L.A. Clippers...	67	2138	403	921	.438	121	162	.809	45	135	180	576	84	3	190	979	2.7	8.6	14.6
87-88—L.A. Clippers ...						Did not play—Achilles' tendon injury.													
88-89—L.A. Clippers	53	1318	153	370	.414	48	65	.738	13	65	78	339	46	0	118	362	1.5	6.4	6.8
Totals	768	27250	5219	10805	.483	1527	1978	.772	473	1518	1991	6386	1187	71	2368	12065	2.6	8.3	15.7

Three-point field goals: 1979-80, 1-for-8 (.125). 1980-81, 2-for-12 (.167). 1981-82, 3-for-12 (.250). 1982-83, 0-for-13. 1983-84, 11-for-46 (.239). 1984-85, 33-for-99 (.333). 1985-86, 42-for-121 (.347). 1988-89, 8-for-29 (.276). Totals, 100-for-340 (.294).

Personal fouls/disqualifications: 1977-78, 259/3. 1978-79, 250/6. 1979-80, 241/1. 1980-81, 226/2. 1981-82, 264/3. 1982-83, 176/1. 1983-84, 180/1. 1984-85, 175/2. 1985-86, 143/0. 1988-89, 69/0. Totals, 1983/19.

NBA PLAYOFF RECORD

Season Team	G	Min.	FGM	FGA	Pct.	FTM	FTA	Pct.	REBOUNDS Off.	Def.	Tot.	Ast.	St.	Blk.	TO	Pts.	RPG	APG	PPG
77-78—Los Angeles....	3	92	11	24	.458	2	3	.667	4	5	9	16	4	1	5	24	3.0	5.3	8.0
78-79—Los Angeles....	8	327	56	119	.471	11	15	.733	6	22	28	94	11	0	24	123	3.5	11.8	15.4
79-80—Los Angeles....	16	648	114	239	.477	41	51	.804	13	43	56	125	32	3	49	270	3.5	7.8	16.9
80-81—Los Angeles....	3	133	25	49	.510	8	10	.800	1	10	11	26	1	1	5	58	3.7	8.7	19.3
81-82—Los Angeles....	14	549	121	253	.478	43	57	.754	13	30	43	114	23	2	34	286	3.1	8.1	20.4
82-83—Los Angeles....	14	538	113	237	.477	37	50	.740	13	35	48	89	18	1	34	266	3.4	6.4	19.0
Totals	58	2287	440	921	.478	142	186	.763	50	145	195	464	89	8	151	1027	3.4	8.0	17.7

Three-point field goals: 1979-80, 1-for-5 (.200). 1981-82, 1-for-3 (.333). 1982-83, 3-for-7 (.429). Totals, 5-for-15 (.333).

Personal fouls/disqualifications: 1977-78, 13/0. 1978-79, 37/1. 1979-80, 59/0. 1980-81, 9/0. 1981-82, 43/0. 1982-83, 40/0. Totals, 201/1.

NBA ALL-STAR GAME RECORD

Season Team	Min.	FGM	FGA	Pct.	FTM	FTA	Pct.	REBOUNDS Off.	Def.	Tot.	Ast.	PF	Dq.	St.	Blk.	TO	Pts.
1982—Los Angeles	19	7	14	.500	0	0	...	0	0	0	2	0	0	1	0	0	14
1985—L.A. Clippers	19	5	7	.714	1	2	.500	0	2	2	8	0	0	1	0	1	11
1987—L.A. Clippers					Did not play—Achilles' tendon injury.												
Totals	38	12	21	.571	1	2	.500	0	2	2	10	0	0	2	0	1	25

ITALIAN LEAGUE RECORD

Season Team	G	Min.	FGM	FGA	Pct.	FTM	FTA	Pct.	Reb.	Ast.	Pts.	RPG	APG	PPG
88-89—Scavolini Pesaro.............	6	217	37	75	.493	4	7	.571	15	19	87	2.5	3.2	14.5

OAKLEY, CHARLES   F

PERSONAL: Born December 18, 1963, in Cleveland. ... 6-9/245. (2,06/111,1).
HIGH SCHOOL: John Hay (Cleveland).
COLLEGE: Virginia Union.
TRANSACTIONS/CAREER NOTES: Selected by Cleveland Cavaliers in first round (ninth pick overall) of 1985 NBA Draft. ... Draft rights traded by Cavaliers with draft rights to G Calvin Duncan to Chicago Bulls for G Ennis Whatley and draft rights to F Keith Lee (June 18, 1985). ... Traded by Bulls with 1988 first- and third-round draft choices to New York Knicks for C Bill Cartwright and 1988 first- and third-round draft choices (June 27, 1988). ... Traded by Knicks with draft rights to F/C Sean Marks and cash to Toronto Raptors for F Marcus Camby (June 25, 1998). ... Traded by Raptors with 2002 second-round draft choice to Bulls for F/C Brian Skinner (July 18, 2001). ... Signed as free agent by Washington Wizards (October 12, 2002). ... Signed by Houston Rockets to first of two consecutive 10-day contracts (March 18, 2004).

COLLEGIATE RECORD

NOTES: Led NCAA Division II with 17.3 rebounds per game (1985).

Season Team	G	Min.	FGM	FGA	Pct.	FTM	FTA	Pct.	Reb.	Ast.	Pts.	RPG	APG	PPG
81-82—Virginia Union	28	...	169	274	.617	106	174	.609	349	...	444	12.5	0.0	15.9
82-83—Virginia Union	28	...	220	378	.582	100	170	.588	365	28	540	13.0	1.0	19.3
83-84—Virginia Union	30	...	256	418	.612	139	224	.621	393	...	651	13.1	0.0	21.7
84-85—Virginia Union	31	...	283	453	.625	178	266	.669	535	66	744	17.3	2.1	24.0
Totals	117	...	928	1523	.609	523	834	.627	1642	...	2379	14.0	...	20.3

NBA REGULAR-SEASON RECORD

HONORS: NBA All-Defensive first team (1994). ... NBA All-Defensive second team (1998). ... NBA All-Rookie team (1986).

Season Team	G	Min.	FGM	FGA	Pct.	FTM	FTA	Pct.	REBOUNDS Off.	Def.	Tot.	Ast.	St.	Blk.	TO	Pts.	RPG	APG	PPG
85-86—Chicago	77	1772	281	541	.519	178	269	.662	255	409	664	133	68	30	175	740	8.6	1.7	9.6
86-87—Chicago	82	2980	468	1052	.445	245	357	.686	299	*775	*1074	296	85	36	299	1192	13.1	3.6	14.5
87-88—Chicago	82	2816	375	776	.483	261	359	.727	326	*740	*1066	248	68	28	241	1014	13.0	3.0	12.4
88-89—New York	82	2604	426	835	.510	197	255	.773	343	518	861	187	104	14	248	1061	10.5	2.3	12.9
89-90—New York	61	2196	336	641	.524	217	285	.761	258	469	727	146	64	16	165	889	11.9	2.4	14.6
90-91—New York	76	2739	307	595	.516	239	305	.784	305	615	920	204	62	17	215	853	12.1	2.7	11.2
91-92—New York	82	2309	210	402	.522	86	117	.735	256	444	700	133	67	15	123	506	8.5	1.6	6.2
92-93—New York	82	2230	219	431	.508	127	176	.722	288	420	708	126	85	15	124	565	8.6	1.5	6.9
93-94—New York	82	2932	363	760	.478	243	313	.776	349	616	965	218	110	18	193	969	11.8	2.7	11.8
94-95—New York	50	1567	192	393	.489	119	150	.793	155	290	445	126	60	7	103	506	8.9	2.5	10.1
95-96—New York	53	1775	211	448	.471	175	210	.833	162	298	460	137	58	14	104	604	8.7	2.6	11.4
96-97—New York	80	2873	339	694	.488	181	224	.808	246	535	781	221	111	21	171	864	9.8	2.8	10.8
97-98—New York	79	2734	307	698	.440	97	114	.851	218	506	724	201	123	22	126	711	9.2	2.5	9.0
98-99—Toronto	50	1633	140	327	.428	67	83	.807	96	278	374	168	46	21	96	348	7.5	3.4	7.0

Season Team	G	Min.	FGM	FGA	Pct.	FTM	FTA	Pct.	Off.	Def.	Tot.	Ast.	St.	Blk.	TO	Pts.	RPG	APG	PPG
99-00—Toronto	80	2431	234	560	.418	66	85	.776	117	423	540	253	102	45	154	548	6.8	3.2	6.9
00-01—Toronto	78	2767	305	786	.388	127	152	.836	142	599	741	264	76	48	139	748	9.5	3.4	9.6
01-02—Chicago	57	1383	97	263	.369	21	28	.750	72	271	343	114	49	11	87	216	6.0	2.0	3.8
02-03—Washington	42	514	23	55	.418	28	34	.824	37	70	107	40	13	6	21	74	2.5	1.0	1.8
03-04—Houston	7	25	2	6	.333	5	6	.833	0	5	5	2	0	0	1	9	0.7	0.3	1.3
Totals	1282	40280	4835	10263	.471	2679	3522	.761	3924	8281	12205	3217	1351	384	2785	12417	9.5	2.5	9.7

Three-point field goals: 1985-86, 0-for-3. 1986-87, 11-for-30 (.367). 1987-88, 3-for-12 (.250). 1988-89, 12-for-48 (.250). 1989-90, 0-for-3. 1990-91, 0-for-2. 1991-92, 0-for-3. 1992-93, 0-for-1. 1993-94, 0-for-3. 1994-95, 3-for-12 (.250). 1995-96, 7-for-26 (.269). 1996-97, 5-for-19 (.263). 1997-98, 0-for-6. 1998-99, 1-for-5 (.200). 1999-00, 14-for-41 (.341). 2000-01, 11-for-49 (.224). 2001-02, 1-for-6 (.167). Totals, 68-for-269 (.253).

Personal fouls/disqualifications: 1985-86, 250/9. 1986-87, 315/4. 1987-88, 272/2. 1988-89, 270/1. 1989-90, 220/3. 1990-91, 288/4. 1991-92, 258/2. 1992-93, 289/5. 1993-94, 293/4. 1994-95, 179/3. 1995-96, 195/6. 1996-97, 305/4. 1997-98, 280/4. 1998-99, 182/4. 1999-00, 294/6. 2000-01, 258/0. 2001-02, 175/2. 2002-03, 90/0. 2003-04, 8/0. Totals, 4421/63.

NBA PLAYOFF RECORD

Season Team	G	Min.	FGM	FGA	Pct.	FTM	FTA	Pct.	Off.	Def.	Tot.	Ast.	St.	Blk.	TO	Pts.	RPG	APG	PPG
85-86—Chicago	3	88	11	21	.524	8	13	.615	10	20	30	3	6	2	5	30	10.0	1.0	10.0
86-87—Chicago	3	129	19	50	.380	20	24	.833	17	29	46	6	4	1	8	60	15.3	2.0	20.0
87-88—Chicago	10	373	40	91	.440	21	24	.875	39	89	128	32	6	4	18	101	12.8	3.2	10.1
88-89—New York	9	299	35	73	.479	16	24	.667	43	58	101	11	12	1	22	87	11.2	1.2	9.7
89-90—New York	10	336	43	84	.512	34	52	.654	39	71	110	27	11	2	22	121	11.0	2.7	12.1
90-91—New York	3	100	10	21	.476	3	6	.500	15	16	31	3	2	1	7	23	10.3	1.0	7.7
91-92—New York	12	354	22	58	.379	20	27	.741	44	64	108	8	8	5	15	64	9.0	0.7	5.3
92-93—New York	15	507	63	131	.481	40	55	.727	71	94	165	17	16	2	36	166	11.0	1.1	11.1
93-94—New York	25	992	125	262	.477	79	102	.775	116	176	292	59	35	5	65	329	11.7	2.4	13.2
94-95—New York	11	421	49	109	.450	42	51	.824	31	62	93	41	19	6	24	144	8.5	3.7	13.1
95-96—New York	8	308	39	78	.500	25	36	.694	28	41	69	14	8	0	28	105	8.6	1.8	13.1
96-97—New York	10	358	38	86	.442	22	29	.759	23	65	88	16	22	3	18	98	8.8	1.6	9.8
97-98—New York	10	342	29	71	.408	23	25	.920	21	64	85	14	11	2	13	81	8.5	1.4	8.1
99-00—Toronto	3	110	14	29	.483	0	1	.000	2	21	23	11	6	1	5	30	7.7	3.7	10.0
00-01—Toronto	12	391	47	108	.435	14	17	.824	20	56	76	21	12	7	22	111	6.3	1.8	9.3
Totals	144	5108	584	1272	.459	367	486	.755	519	926	1445	283	178	42	308	1550	10.0	2.0	10.8

Three-point field goals: 1986-87, 2-for-4 (.500). 1987-88, 0-for-2. 1988-89, 1-for-2 (.500). 1989-90, 1-for-1. 1994-95, 4-for-10 (.400). 1995-96, 2-for-6 (.333). 1996-97, 0-for-1. 1999-00, 2-for-7 (.286). 2000-01, 3-for-8 (.375). Totals, 15-for-41 (.366).

Personal fouls/disqualifications: 1985-86, 13/0. 1986-87, 13/0. 1987-88, 33/0. 1988-89, 31/1. 1989-90, 33/1. 1990-91, 13/0. 1991-92, 36/0. 1992-93, 51/1. 1993-94, 87/1. 1994-95, 42/0. 1995-96, 33/1. 1996-97, 37/0. 1997-98, 38/1. 1999-00, 14/0. 2000-01, 29/0. Totals, 503/6.

NBA ALL-STAR GAME RECORD

Season Team	Min.	FGM	FGA	Pct.	FTM	FTA	Pct.	Off.	Def.	Tot.	Ast.	PF	Dq.	St.	Blk.	TO	Pts.
1994—New York	11	1	3	.333	0	0	...	1	2	3	3	3	0	0	0	0	2

OLAJUWON, HAKEEM   C

PERSONAL: Born January 21, 1963, in Lagos, Nigeria. ... 7-0/255. (2,13/115,7). ... Full Name: Hakeem Abdul Olajuwon. ... Known as Akeem Olajuwon until March 9, 1991. ... Nickname: The Dream. ... Name pronounced ah-KEEM a-lie-shoe-on.
HIGH SCHOOL: Muslim Teachers College (Lagos, Nigeria).
COLLEGE: Houston.
TRANSACTIONS/CAREER NOTES: Selected by Houston Rockets in first round (first pick overall) of 1984 NBA Draft. ... Traded by Rockets to Toronto Raptors for 2002 first-round draft choice and 2002 second-round draft choice (August 2, 2001).
CAREER HONORS: NBA 50th Anniversary All-Time Team (1996).
MISCELLANEOUS: Member of NBA championship team (1994, 1995). ... Member of gold-medal-winning U.S. Olympic team (1996). ... Houston Rockets franchise all-time leading scorer with 26,511 points, all-time leading rebounder with 13,382, all-time steals leader with 2,088 and all-time blocked shots leader with 3,740 (1984-85 through 2000-01).

COLLEGIATE RECORD

NOTES: The Sporting News All-America first team (1984). ... NCAA Division I Tournament Most Outstanding Player (1983). ... Led NCAA Division I with .675 field goal percentage (1984). ... Led NCAA Division I with 13.5 rebounds per game (1984). ... Led NCAA Division I with 5.6 blocked shots per game (1984).

Season Team	G	Min.	FGM	FGA	Pct.	FTM	FTA	Pct.	Reb.	Ast.	Pts.	RPG	APG	PPG
80-81—Houston							Did not play.							
81-82—Houston	29	529	91	150	.607	58	103	.563	179	11	240	6.2	0.4	8.3
82-83—Houston	34	932	192	314	.611	88	148	.595	388	29	472	11.4	0.9	13.9
83-84—Houston	37	1260	249	369	.675	122	232	.526	500	48	620	13.5	1.3	16.8
Totals	100	2721	532	833	.639	268	483	.555	1067	88	1332	10.7	0.9	13.3

NBA REGULAR-SEASON RECORD

RECORDS: Holds career record for most blocked shots—3,830.
HONORS: NBA Most Valuable Player (1994). ... NBA Defensive Player of the Year (1993, 1994). ... IBM Award, for all-around contributions to team's success (1993). ... All-NBA First Team (1987, 1988, 1989, 1993, 1994, 1997). ... All-NBA Second Team (1986, 1990, 1996). ... All-NBA Third Team (1991, 1995, 1999). ... NBA All-Defensive first team (1987, 1988, 1990, 1993, 1994). ... NBA All-Defensive second team (1985, 1991, 1996, 1997). ... NBA All-Rookie team (1985).
NOTES: Led NBA with 4.59 blocked shots per game (1990), 3.95 blocked shots per game (1991) and 4.17 blocked shots per game (1993). ... Led NBA with 344 personal fouls (1985).

Season Team	G	Min.	FGM	FGA	Pct.	FTM	FTA	Pct.	Off.	Def.	Tot.	Ast.	St.	Blk.	TO	Pts.	RPG	APG	PPG
84-85—Houston	82	2914	677	1258	.538	338	551	.613	*440	534	974	111	99	220	234	1692	11.9	1.4	20.6

Season Team	G	Min.	FGM	FGA	Pct.	FTM	FTA	Pct.	REBOUNDS			Ast.	St.	Blk.	TO	Pts.	AVERAGES		
									Off.	Def.	Tot.						RPG	APG	PPG
85-86—Houston.........	68	2467	625	1188	.526	347	538	.645	333	448	781	137	134	231	195	1597	11.5	2.0	23.5
86-87—Houston.........	75	2760	677	1332	.508	400	570	.702	315	543	858	220	140	254	228	1755	11.4	2.9	23.4
87-88—Houston.........	79	2825	712	1385	.514	381	548	.695	302	657	959	163	162	214	243	1805	12.1	2.1	22.8
88-89—Houston.........	82	3024	790	1556	.508	454	652	.696	338	*767	*1105	149	213	282	275	2034	*13.5	1.8	24.8
89-90—Houston.........	82	3124	806	1609	.501	382	536	.713	299	*850	*1149	234	174	*376	316	1995	*14.0	2.9	24.3
90-91—Houston.........	56	2062	487	959	.508	213	277	.769	219	551	770	131	121	221	174	1187	13.8	2.3	21.2
91-92—Houston.........	70	2636	591	1177	.502	328	428	.766	246	599	845	157	127	304	187	1510	12.1	2.2	21.6
92-93—Houston.........	82	3242	848	1603	.529	444	570	.779	283	785	1068	291	150	*342	262	2140	13.0	3.5	26.1
93-94—Houston.........	80	3277	894	*1694	.528	388	542	.716	229	726	955	287	128	297	271	2184	11.9	3.6	27.3
94-95—Houston.........	72	2853	798	1545	.517	406	537	.756	172	603	775	255	133	242	237	2005	10.8	3.5	27.8
95-96—Houston.........	72	2797	768	1494	.514	397	548	.724	176	608	784	257	113	207	247	1936	10.9	3.6	26.9
96-97—Houston.........	78	2852	727	1426	.510	351	446	.787	173	543	716	236	117	173	281	1810	9.2	3.0	23.2
97-98—Houston.........	47	1633	306	633	.483	160	212	.755	116	344	460	143	84	96	126	772	9.8	3.0	16.4
98-99—Houston.........	50	1784	373	725	.514	195	272	.717	106	372	478	88	82	123	139	945	9.6	1.8	18.9
99-00—Houston.........	44	1049	193	421	.458	69	112	.616	65	209	274	61	41	70	73	455	6.2	1.4	10.3
00-01—Houston.........	58	1545	283	568	.498	123	198	.621	124	307	431	72	70	88	81	689	7.4	1.2	11.9
01-02—Houston.........	61	1378	194	418	.464	47	84	.560	98	268	366	66	74	90	98	435	6.0	1.1	7.1
02-03—Toronto.........								Did not play—injured.											
Totals..................	1238	44222	10749	20991	.512	5423	7621	.712	4034	9714	13748	3058	2162	3830	3667	26946	11.1	2.5	21.8

Three-point field goals: 1986-87, 1-for-5 (.200). 1987-88, 0-for-4. 1988-89, 0-for-10. 1989-90, 1-for-6 (.167). 1990-91, 0-for-4. 1991-92, 0-for-1. 1992-93, 0-for-8. 1993-94, 8-for-19 (.421). 1994-95, 3-for-16 (.188). 1995-96, 3-for-14 (.214). 1996-97, 5-for-16 (.313). 1997-98, 0-for-3. 1998-99, 4-for-13 (.308). 1999-00, 0-for-2. 2000-01, 0-for-1. 2001-02, 0-for-2. Totals, 25-for-124 (.202).

Personal fouls/disqualifications: 1984-85, 344/10. 1985-86, 271/9. 1986-87, 294/8. 1987-88, 324/7. 1988-89, 329/10. 1989-90, 314/6. 1990-91, 221/5. 1991-92, 263/7. 1992-93, 305/5. 1993-94, 289/4. 1994-95, 250/3. 1995-96, 242/0. 1996-97, 249/3. 1997-98, 152/0. 1998-99, 160/3. 1999-00, 88/0. 2000-01, 141/0. 2001-02, 147/0. Totals, 4383/80.

NBA PLAYOFF RECORD

NOTES: NBA Finals Most Valuable Player (1994, 1995). ... Shares NBA Finals single-game record for most blocked shots—8 (June 5, 1986, vs. Boston). ... Shares single-game playoff record for most blocked shots—10 (April 29, 1990, vs. Los Angeles Lakers).

Season Team	G	Min.	FGM	FGA	Pct.	FTM	FTA	Pct.	REBOUNDS			Ast.	St.	Blk.	TO	Pts.	AVERAGES		
									Off.	Def.	Tot.						RPG	APG	PPG
84-85—Houston.........	5	187	42	88	.477	22	46	.478	33	32	65	7	7	13	11	106	13.0	1.4	21.2
85-86—Houston.........	20	766	205	387	.530	127	199	.638	101	135	236	39	40	69	43	537	11.8	2.0	26.9
86-87—Houston.........	10	389	110	179	.615	72	97	.742	39	74	113	25	13	43	36	292	11.3	2.5	29.2
87-88—Houston.........	4	162	56	98	.571	38	43	.884	20	47	67	7	9	11	9	150	16.8	1.8	37.5
88-89—Houston.........	4	162	42	81	.519	17	25	.680	14	38	52	12	10	11	10	101	13.0	3.0	25.3
89-90—Houston.........	4	161	31	70	.443	12	17	.706	15	31	46	8	10	23	11	74	11.5	2.0	18.5
90-91—Houston.........	3	129	26	45	.578	14	17	.824	12	32	44	6	4	8	8	66	14.7	2.0	22.0
92-93—Houston.........	12	518	123	238	.517	62	75	.827	52	116	168	57	21	59	45	308	14.0	4.8	25.7
93-94—Houston.........	23	989	267	514	.519	128	161	.795	55	199	254	98	40	92	83	664	11.0	4.3	28.9
94-95—Houston.........	22	929	306	576	.531	111	163	.681	44	183	227	98	26	62	69	725	10.3	4.5	33.0
95-96—Houston.........	8	329	75	147	.510	29	40	.725	17	56	73	31	15	17	29	179	9.1	3.9	22.4
96-97—Houston.........	16	629	147	249	.590	76	104	.731	46	128	174	54	33	41	46	370	10.9	3.4	23.1
97-98—Houston.........	5	190	39	99	.394	24	33	.727	9	45	54	12	5	16	13	102	10.8	2.4	20.4
98-99—Houston.........	4	123	23	54	.426	7	8	.875	5	24	29	2	5	3	5	53	7.3	0.5	13.3
01-02—Toronto.........	5	86	12	22	.545	4	6	.667	9	10	19	2	7	4	6	28	3.8	0.4	5.6
Totals..................	145	5749	1504	2847	.528	743	1034	.719	471	1150	1621	458	245	472	424	3755	11.2	3.2	25.9

Three-point field goals: 1985-86, 0-for-1. 1986-87, 0-for-1. 1987-88, 0-for-1. 1990-91, 0-for-1. 1992-93, 0-for-1. 1993-94, 2-for-4 (.500). 1994-95, 2-for-4 (.500). 1995-96, 0-for-1. 1996-97, 0-for-3. 1997-98, 0-for-1. Totals, 4-for-18 (.222).

Personal fouls/disqualifications: 1984-85, 22/0. 1985-86, 87/3. 1986-87, 44/1. 1987-88, 14/0. 1988-89, 17/0. 1989-90, 19/0. 1990-91, 11/0. 1992-93, 37/0. 1993-94, 82/0. 1994-95, 95/0. 1995-96, 28/1. 1996-97, 61/0. 1997-98, 18/0. 1998-99, 18/0. 2001-02, 9/0. Totals, 562/5.

NBA ALL-STAR GAME RECORD

NOTES: Shares single-game records for most offensive rebounds—9 (1990); and most blocked shots in one half—4 (1994).

Season Team	Min.	FGM	FGA	Pct.	FTM	FTA	Pct.	REBOUNDS			Ast.	PF	Dq.	St.	Blk.	TO	Pts.
								Off.	Def.	Tot.							
1985—Houston	15	2	2	1.000	2	6	.333	2	3	5	1	1	0	0	2	0	6
1986—Houston	15	1	8	.125	1	2	.500	1	4	5	0	3	0	1	2	1	3
1987—Houston	26	2	6	.333	6	8	.750	4	9	13	2	6	1	0	3	1	10
1988—Houston	28	8	13	.615	5	7	.714	7	2	9	2	3	0	2	2	4	21
1989—Houston	25	5	12	.417	2	3	.667	4	3	7	3	2	0	3	2	3	12
1990—Houston	31	2	14	.143	4	10	.400	9	7	16	2	1	0	1	1	4	8
1992—Houston	20	3	6	.500	1	2	.500	0	4	4	2	3	0	2	1	3	7
1993—Houston	21	1	5	.200	1	2	.500	2	5	7	1	3	0	2	2	3	3
1994—Houston	30	8	15	.533	3	6	.500	4	7	11	2	4	0	2	5	3	19
1995—Houston	25	6	13	.462	0	2	.000	4	7	11	1	2	0	2	2	3	13
1996—Houston	14	2	8	.250	0	0	....	1	2	3	0	2	0	0	0	0	4
1997—Houston	20	5	8	.625	1	2	.500	0	3	3	1	1	0	0	1	1	11
Totals........................	270	45	110	.409	26	50	.520	38	56	94	17	31	1	15	23	26	117

Three-point field goals: 1995, 1-for-1. Totals, 1-for-1 (1.000).

PARISH, ROBERT   C

PERSONAL: Born August 30, 1953, in Shreveport, La. ... 7-1/244 (2,16/110,7). ... Full name: Robert Lee Parish. ... Second cousin of Larry Robinson, forward/guard with eight NBA teams (1990-91 through 2001-02). ... Nickname: Chief.
HIGH SCHOOL: Woodlawn (Shreveport, La.).
COLLEGE: Centenary (La.).
TRANSACTIONS/CAREER NOTES: Selected by Golden State Warriors in first round (eighth pick overall) of 1976 NBA Draft. ... Traded by Warriors with 1980 first-round draft choice to Boston Celtics for two 1980 first-round draft choices (June 9, 1980). ... Signed as unrestricted free agent by Charlotte Hornets (August 4, 1994). ... Signed as free agent by Chicago Bulls (September 25, 1996). ...

Announced retirement (August 25, 1997).
CAREER HONORS: Elected to Naismith Memorial Basketball Hall of Fame (2003). ... One of the 50 Greatest Players in NBA History (1996).
MISCELLANEOUS: Member of NBA championship team (1981, 1984, 1986, 1997). ... Boston Celtics all-time blocked shots leader with 1,703 (1980-81 through 1993-94).
CAREER NOTES: Head coach, Maryland Mustangs (USBL).

COLLEGIATE RECORD

NOTES: The Sporting News All-America first team (1976).

Season Team	G	Min.	FGM	FGA	Pct.	FTM	FTA	Pct.	Reb.	Ast.	Pts.	RPG	APG	PPG
72-73—Centenary	27	885	285	492	.579	50	82	.610	505	25	620	18.7	0.9	23.0
73-74—Centenary	25	841	224	428	.523	49	78	.628	382	34	497	15.3	1.4	19.9
74-75—Centenary	29	900	237	423	.560	74	112	.661	447	43	548	15.4	1.5	18.9
75-76—Centenary	27	939	288	489	.589	93	134	.694	486	48	669	18.0	1.8	24.8
Totals	108	3565	1034	1832	.564	266	406	.655	1820	150	2334	16.9	1.4	21.6

NBA REGULAR-SEASON RECORD

RECORDS: Holds career records for most seasons played—21; most games played—1,611; and most defensive rebounds—10,117.
HONORS: All-NBA second team (1982). ... All-NBA third team (1989).

Season Team	G	Min.	FGM	FGA	Pct.	FTM	FTA	Pct.	Off.	Def.	Tot.	Ast.	St.	Blk.	TO	Pts.	RPG	APG	PPG
76-77—Golden State	77	1384	288	573	.503	121	171	.708	201	342	543	74	55	94	...	697	7.1	1.0	9.1
77-78—Golden State	82	1969	430	911	.472	165	264	.625	211	469	680	95	79	123	201	1025	8.3	1.2	12.5
78-79—Golden State	76	2411	554	1110	.499	196	281	.698	265	651	916	115	100	217	233	1304	12.1	1.5	17.2
79-80—Golden State	72	2119	510	1006	.507	203	284	.715	247	536	783	122	58	115	225	1223	10.9	1.7	17.0
80-81—Boston	82	2298	635	1166	.545	282	397	.710	245	532	777	144	81	214	191	1552	9.5	1.8	18.9
81-82—Boston	80	2534	669	1235	.542	252	355	.710	288	578	866	140	68	192	221	1590	10.8	1.8	19.9
82-83—Boston	78	2459	619	1125	.550	271	388	.698	260	567	827	141	79	148	185	1509	10.6	1.8	19.3
83-84—Boston	80	2867	623	1140	.546	274	368	.745	243	614	857	139	55	116	184	1520	10.7	1.7	19.0
84-85—Boston	79	2850	551	1016	.542	292	393	.743	263	577	840	125	56	101	186	1394	10.6	1.6	17.6
85-86—Boston	81	2567	530	966	.549	245	335	.731	246	524	770	145	65	116	187	1305	9.5	1.8	16.1
86-87—Boston	80	2995	588	1057	.556	227	309	.735	254	597	851	173	64	144	191	1403	10.6	2.2	17.5
87-88—Boston	74	2312	442	750	.589	177	241	.734	173	455	628	115	55	84	154	1061	8.5	1.6	14.3
88-89—Boston	80	2840	596	1045	.570	294	409	.719	342	654	996	175	79	116	200	1486	12.5	2.2	18.6
89-90—Boston	79	2396	505	871	.580	233	312	.747	259	537	796	103	38	69	169	1243	10.1	1.3	15.7
90-91—Boston	81	2441	485	811	.598	237	309	.767	271	585	856	66	66	103	153	1207	10.6	0.8	14.9
91-92—Boston	79	2285	468	874	.535	179	232	.772	219	486	705	70	68	97	131	1115	8.9	0.9	14.1
92-93—Boston	79	2146	416	777	.535	162	235	.689	246	494	740	61	57	107	120	994	9.4	0.8	12.6
93-94—Boston	74	1987	356	725	.491	154	208	.740	141	401	542	82	42	96	108	866	7.3	1.1	11.7
94-95—Charlotte	81	1352	159	372	.427	71	101	.703	93	257	350	44	27	36	66	389	4.3	0.5	4.8
95-96—Charlotte	74	1086	120	241	.498	50	71	.704	89	214	303	29	21	54	50	290	4.1	0.4	3.9
96-97—Chicago	43	406	70	143	.490	21	31	.677	42	47	89	22	6	19	28	161	2.1	0.5	3.7
Totals	1611	45704	9614	17914	.537	4106	5691	.721	4598	10117	14715	2180	1219	2361	3183	23334	9.1	1.4	14.5

Three-point field goals: 1979-80, 0-for-1. 1980-81, 0-for-1. 1982-83, 0-for-1. 1986-87, 0-for-1. 1987-88, 0-for-1. 1990-91, 0-for-1. Totals, 0-for-6.
Personal fouls/disqualifications: 1976-77, 224/7. 1977-78, 291/10. 1978-79, 303/10. 1979-80, 264/6. 1980-81, 310/6. 1981-82, 267/6. 1982-83, 280/6. 1983-84, 266/3. 1984-85, 272/2. 1985-86, 215/3. 1986-87, 266/5. 1987-88, 198/5. 1988-89, 209/2. 1989-90, 189/2. 1990-91, 197/1. 1991-92, 172/2. 1992-93, 201/3. 1993-94, 190/3. 1994-95, 132/0. 1995-96, 80/0. 1996-97, 40/0. Totals, 4443/86.

NBA PLAYOFF RECORD

NOTES: Holds career playoff record for most offensive rebounds—571.

Season Team	G	Min.	FGM	FGA	Pct.	FTM	FTA	Pct.	Off.	Def.	Tot.	Ast.	St.	Blk.	TO	Pts.	RPG	APG	PPG
76-77—Golden State	10	239	52	108	.481	17	26	.654	43	60	103	11	7	11	...	121	10.3	1.1	12.1
80-81—Boston	17	492	108	219	.493	39	58	.672	50	96	146	19	21	39	44	255	8.6	1.1	15.0
81-82—Boston	12	426	102	209	.488	51	75	.680	43	92	135	18	5	48	39	255	11.3	1.5	21.3
82-83—Boston	7	249	43	89	.483	17	20	.850	21	53	74	9	5	9	17	103	10.6	1.3	14.7
83-84—Boston	23	869	139	291	.478	64	99	.646	76	172	248	27	23	41	45	342	10.8	1.2	14.9
84-85—Boston	21	803	136	276	.493	87	111	.784	57	162	219	31	21	34	50	359	10.4	1.5	17.1
85-86—Boston	18	591	106	225	.471	58	89	.652	52	106	158	25	9	30	44	270	8.8	1.4	15.0
86-87—Boston	21	734	149	263	.567	79	103	.767	59	139	198	28	18	35	38	377	9.4	1.3	18.0
87-88—Boston	17	626	100	188	.532	50	61	.820	51	117	168	21	11	19	38	250	9.9	1.2	14.7
88-89—Boston	3	112	20	44	.455	7	9	.778	6	20	26	6	4	2	6	47	8.7	2.0	15.7
89-90—Boston	5	170	31	54	.574	17	18	.944	23	27	50	13	5	7	12	79	10.0	2.6	15.8
90-91—Boston	10	296	58	97	.598	42	61	.689	33	59	92	6	8	7	16	158	9.2	0.6	15.8
91-92—Boston	10	335	50	101	.495	20	28	.714	38	59	97	14	7	15	9	120	9.7	1.4	12.0
92-93—Boston	4	146	31	57	.544	6	7	.857	13	25	38	5	1	6	6	68	9.5	1.3	17.0
94-95—Charlotte	4	71	6	11	.545	2	5	.400	4	5	9	1	0	3	1	14	2.3	0.3	3.5
96-97—Chicago	2	18	1	7	.143	0	0	...	2	2	4	0	0	2	2	2	2.0	0.0	1.0
Totals	184	6177	1132	2239	.506	556	770	.722	571	1194	1765	234	145	309	365	2820	9.6	1.3	15.3

Three-point field goals: 1986-87, 0-for-1.
Personal fouls/disqualifications: 1976-77, 42/1. 1980-81, 74/2. 1981-82, 47/1. 1982-83, 18/0. 1983-84, 100/6. 1984-85, 68/0. 1985-86, 47/1. 1986-87, 79/4. 1987-88, 42/0. 1988-89, 5/0. 1989-90, 21/0. 1990-91, 34/1. 1991-92, 22/0. 1992-93, 14/0. 1994-95, 2/0. 1996-97, 2/0. Totals, 617/16.

NBA ALL-STAR GAME RECORD

Season Team	Min.	FGM	FGA	Pct.	FTM	FTA	Pct.	Off.	Def.	Tot.	Ast.	PF	Dq.	St.	Blk.	TO	Pts.
1981—Boston	25	5	18	.278	6	6	1.000	6	4	10	2	3	0	0	2	1	16
1982—Boston	20	9	12	.750	3	4	.750	0	7	7	1	2	0	2	1	1	21
1983—Boston	18	5	6	.833	3	4	.750	0	3	3	0	2	0	1	1	1	13
1984—Boston	28	5	11	.455	2	4	.500	4	11	15	2	1	0	3	0	4	12
1985—Boston	10	2	5	.400	0	0	...	3	3	6	1	0	0	0	0	0	4
1986—Boston	7	0	0	...	0	2	.000	0	1	1	0	0	0	0	1	1	0
1987—Boston	8	2	3	.667	0	0	...	0	3	3	0	1	0	0	1	0	4

Season Team	Min.	FGM	FGA	Pct.	FTM	FTA	Pct.	REBOUNDS Off.	Def.	Tot.	Ast.	PF	Dq.	St.	Blk.	TO	Pts.
1990—Boston	21	7	11	.636	0	1	.000	2	2	4	2	4	0	0	1	1	14
1991—Boston	5	1	2	.500	0	0	...	1	3	4	0	2	0	0	0	1	2
Totals	142	36	68	.529	14	21	.667	16	37	53	8	15	0	4	8	10	86

NOTES: USBL Coach of the Year (2001).

USBL COACHING RECORD

Season Team	REGULAR SEASON W	L	Pct.	Finish	PLAYOFFS W	L	Pct.
00-01—Maryland	19	11	.633	1st	0	1	.000

NOTES:
2001—Lost to Dodge City in quarterfinals.

PETTIT, BOB   F/C

PERSONAL: Born December 12, 1932, in Baton Rouge, La. ... 6-9/215 (2,05/97,5). ... Full name: Robert Lee Pettit Jr.
HIGH SCHOOL: Baton Rouge (La.).
COLLEGE: Louisiana State.
TRANSACTIONS: Selected by Milwaukee Hawks in first round of 1954 NBA Draft. ... Hawks franchise moved from Milwaukee to St. Louis for 1955-56 season.
CAREER HONORS: Elected to Naismith Memorial Basketball Hall of Fame (1970). ... NBA 25th Anniversary All-Time Team (1970), 35th Anniversary All-Time Team (1980) and One of the 50 Greatest Players in NBA History (1996).
MISCELLANEOUS: Member of NBA championship team (1958). ... Atlanta Hawks franchise all-time leading rebounder with 12,851 (1954-55 through 1964-65).

COLLEGIATE RECORD

Season Team	G	Min.	FGM	FGA	Pct.	FTM	FTA	Pct.	Reb.	Ast.	Pts.	AVERAGES RPG	APG	PPG
50-51—Louisiana State‡	10	...	...	...	...	...	...	...	...	...	270	...	...	27.0
51-52—Louisiana State	23	...	237	549	.432	115	192	.599	315	...	589	13.7	...	25.6
52-53—Louisiana State	21	...	193	394	.490	133	215	.619	263	...	519	12.5	...	24.7
53-54—Louisiana State	25	...	281	573	.490	223	308	.724	432	...	785	17.3	...	31.4
Varsity totals	69	...	711	1516	.469	471	715	.659	1010	...	1893	14.6	...	27.4

NBA REGULAR-SEASON RECORD

HONORS: NBA Most Valuable Player (1956, 1959). ... NBA Rookie of the Year (1955). ... All-NBA first team (1955, 1956, 1957, 1958, 1959, 1960, 1961, 1962, 1963, 1964). ... All-NBA second team (1965).

Season Team	G	Min.	FGM	FGA	Pct.	FTM	FTA	Pct.	Reb.	Ast.	PF	Dq.	Pts.	AVERAGES RPG	APG	PPG
54-55—Milwaukee	72	2659	520	1279	.407	426	567	.751	994	229	258	5	1466	13.8	3.2	20.4
55-56—St. Louis	72	2794	*646	*1507	.429	*557	*757	.736	*1164	189	202	1	*1849	16.2	2.6	*25.7
56-57—St. Louis	71	2491	*613	*1477	.415	529	684	.773	1037	133	181	1	1755	14.6	1.9	24.7
57-58—St. Louis	70	2528	581	1418	.410	557	744	.749	1216	157	222	6	1719	17.4	2.2	24.6
58-59—St. Louis	72	2873	*719	1640	.438	*667	*879	.759	1182	221	200	3	*2105	16.4	3.1	*29.2
59-60—St. Louis	72	2896	669	1526	.438	544	722	.753	1221	257	204	0	1882	17.0	3.6	26.1
60-61—St. Louis	76	3027	769	1720	.447	582	804	.724	1540	262	217	1	2120	20.3	3.4	27.9
61-62—St. Louis	78	3282	867	1928	.450	695	901	.771	1457	289	296	4	2429	18.7	3.7	31.1
62-63—St. Louis	79	3090	778	1746	.446	*685	885	.774	1195	245	282	8	2241	15.1	3.1	28.4
63-64—St. Louis	80	3296	791	1708	.463	608	771	.789	1224	259	300	3	2190	15.3	3.2	27.4
64-65—St. Louis	50	1754	396	923	.429	332	405	.820	621	128	167	0	1124	12.4	2.6	22.5
Totals	792	30690	7349	16872	.436	6182	8119	.761	12851	2369	2529	32	20880	16.2	3.0	26.4

NBA PLAYOFF RECORD

NOTES: Holds NBA Finals single-game record for most free throws made—19 (April 9, 1958, vs. Boston). ... Shares NBA Finals record for most free throws attempted in one quarter—11 (April 9, 1958, vs. Boston).

Season Team	G	Min.	FGM	FGA	Pct.	FTM	FTA	Pct.	Reb.	Ast.	PF	Dq.	Pts.	AVERAGES RPG	APG	PPG
55-56—St. Louis	8	274	47	128	.367	59	70	.843	84	18	20	0	153	10.5	2.3	19.1
56-57—St. Louis	10	430	98	237	.414	102	133	.767	168	25	33	0	298	16.8	2.5	29.8
57-58—St. Louis	11	430	90	230	.391	86	118	.729	181	20	31	0	266	16.5	1.8	24.2
58-59—St. Louis	6	257	58	137	.423	51	65	.785	75	14	20	0	167	12.5	2.3	27.8
59-60—St. Louis	14	576	129	292	.442	107	142	.754	221	52	43	1	365	15.8	3.7	26.1
60-61—St. Louis	12	526	117	284	.412	109	144	.757	211	38	42	0	343	17.6	3.2	28.6
62-63—St. Louis	11	463	119	259	.459	112	144	.778	166	33	34	0	350	15.1	3.0	31.8
63-64—St. Louis	12	494	93	226	.412	66	79	.835	174	33	44	0	252	14.5	2.8	21.0
64-65—St. Louis	4	95	15	41	.366	16	20	.800	24	8	10	0	46	6.0	2.0	11.5
Totals	88	3545	766	1834	.418	708	915	.774	1304	241	277	1	2240	14.8	2.7	25.5

NBA ALL-STAR GAME RECORD

NOTES: NBA All-Star Game Most Valuable Player (1956, 1958, 1962). ... NBA All-Star Game co-Most Valuable Player (1959). ... Holds single-game records for most rebounds—27; and most rebounds in one quarter—10 (1962). ... Shares single-game record for most rebounds in one half—16 (1962).

Season Team	Min.	FGM	FGA	Pct.	FTM	FTA	Pct.	Reb	Ast.	PF	Dq.	Pts.
1955—Milwaukee	27	3	14	.214	2	4	.500	9	2	0	0	8
1956—St. Louis	31	7	17	.412	6	7	.857	24	7	4	0	20
1957—St. Louis	31	8	18	.444	5	6	.833	11	2	2	0	21
1958—St. Louis	38	10	21	.476	8	10	.800	26	1	1	0	28
1959—St. Louis	34	8	21	.381	9	9	1.000	16	5	1	0	25
1960—St. Louis	28	4	15	.267	3	6	.500	14	2	2	0	11
1961—St. Louis	32	13	22	.591	3	7	.429	9	0	2	0	29

Season Team	Min.	FGM	FGA	Pct.	FTM	FTA	Pct.	Reb.	Ast.	PF	Dq.	Pts.
1962—St. Louis	37	10	20	.500	5	5	1.000	27	2	5	0	25
1963—St. Louis	32	7	16	.438	11	12	.917	13	0	1	0	25
1964—St. Louis	36	6	15	.400	7	9	.778	17	2	3	0	19
1965—St. Louis	34	5	14	.357	3	5	.600	12	0	4	0	13
Totals	360	81	193	.420	62	80	.775	178	23	25	0	224

NBA COACHING RECORD

	REGULAR SEASON					PLAYOFFS		
Season Team	W	L	Pct.	Finish		W	L	Pct.
61-62—St. Louis	4	2	.667	4th/Western Division		—	—	—

NOTES:
1962—Replaced Paul Seymour (5-9) and Andrew Levane (20-40) as St. Louis head coach (March), with record of 25-49.

PIPPEN, SCOTTIE   F

PERSONAL: Born September 25, 1965, in Hamburg, Ark. ... 6-7/228. (2,01/103,4).
HIGH SCHOOL: Hamburg (Ark.).
COLLEGE: Central Arkansas.
TRANSACTIONS/CAREER NOTES: Selected by Seattle SuperSonics in first round (fifth pick overall) of 1987 NBA Draft. ... Draft rights traded by SuperSonics to Chicago Bulls for draft rights to F/C Olden Polynice, 1988 or 1989 second-round draft choice and option to exchange 1989 first-round draft choices (June 22, 1987). ... Traded by Bulls to Houston Rockets for F Roy Rogers and 1999 or 2000 second-round draft choice (January 22, 1999). ... Traded by Rockets to Portland Trail Blazers for C Kelvin Cato, F Stacy Augmon, G/F Walt Williams, G Brian Shaw, G Ed Gray and F/C Carlos Rogers (October 2, 1999). ... Signed as free agent by Chicago Bulls (July 20, 2003).
CAREER HONORS: NBA 50th Anniversary All-Time Team (1996).
MISCELLANEOUS: Member of NBA championship team (1991, 1992, 1993, 1996, 1997, 1998). ... Member of gold-medal-winning U.S. Olympic teams (1992, 1996).

COLLEGIATE RECORD

Season Team	G	Min.	FGM	FGA	Pct.	FTM	FTA	Pct.	Reb.	Ast.	Pts.	AVERAGES		
												RPG	APG	PPG
83-84—Central Arkansas	20	...	36	79	.456	13	19	.684	59	14	85	3.0	0.7	4.3
84-85—Central Arkansas	19	...	141	250	.564	69	102	.676	175	30	351	9.2	1.6	18.5
85-86—Central Arkansas	29	...	229	412	.556	116	169	.686	266	102	574	9.2	3.5	19.8
86-87—Central Arkansas	25	...	231	390	.592	105	146	.719	249	107	590	10.0	4.3	23.6
Totals	93	...	637	1131	.563	303	436	.695	749	253	1600	8.1	2.7	17.2

Three-point field goals: 1986-87, 23-for-40 (.575). .

NBA REGULAR-SEASON RECORD

HONORS: All-NBA First Team (1994, 1995, 1996). ... All-NBA Second Team (1992, 1997). ... All-NBA Third Team (1993, 1998). ... NBA All-Defensive first team (1992, 1993, 1994, 1995, 1996, 1997, 1998, 1999). ... NBA All-Defensive second team (1991, 1999). ... Led NBA with 2.54 steals per game (1995).

Season Team	G	Min.	FGM	FGA	Pct.	FTM	FTA	Pct.	REBOUNDS			Ast.	St.	Blk.	TO	Pts.	AVERAGES		
									Off.	Def.	Tot.						RPG	APG	PPG
87-88—Chicago	79	1650	261	564	.463	99	172	.576	115	183	298	169	91	52	131	625	3.8	2.1	7.9
88-89—Chicago	73	2413	413	867	.476	201	301	.668	138	307	445	256	139	61	199	1048	6.1	3.5	14.4
89-90—Chicago	82	3148	562	1150	.489	199	295	.675	150	397	547	444	211	101	278	1351	6.7	5.4	16.5
90-91—Chicago	82	3014	600	1153	.520	240	340	.706	163	432	595	511	193	93	232	1461	7.3	6.2	17.8
91-92—Chicago	82	3164	687	1359	.506	330	434	.760	185	445	630	572	155	93	253	1720	7.7	7.0	21.0
92-93—Chicago	81	3123	628	1327	.473	232	350	.663	203	418	621	507	173	73	246	1510	7.7	6.3	18.6
93-94—Chicago	72	2759	627	1278	.491	270	409	.660	173	456	629	403	211	58	232	1587	8.7	5.6	22.0
94-95—Chicago	79	3014	634	1320	.480	315	440	.716	175	464	639	409	*232	89	271	1692	8.1	5.2	21.4
95-96—Chicago	77	2825	563	1216	.463	220	324	.679	152	344	496	452	133	57	207	1496	6.4	5.9	19.4
96-97—Chicago	82	3095	648	1366	.474	204	291	.701	160	371	531	467	154	45	214	1656	6.5	5.7	20.2
97-98—Chicago	44	1652	315	704	.447	150	193	.777	53	174	227	254	79	43	109	841	5.2	5.8	19.1
98-99—Houston	50	2011	261	604	.432	132	183	.721	63	260	323	293	98	37	159	726	6.5	5.9	14.5
99-00—Portland	82	2749	388	860	.451	160	223	.717	114	399	513	406	117	41	208	1022	6.3	5.0	12.5
00-01—Portland	64	2133	269	596	.451	119	161	.739	70	263	333	294	94	35	154	721	5.2	4.6	11.3
01-02—Portland	62	1996	246	599	.411	113	146	.774	77	244	321	363	101	35	171	659	5.2	5.9	10.6
02-03—Portland	64	1911	265	597	.444	121	148	.818	57	221	278	285	105	25	164	689	4.3	4.5	10.8
03-04—Chicago	23	412	53	140	.379	17	27	.630	20	48	68	50	21	9	29	136	3.0	2.2	5.9
Totals	1178	41069	7420	15700	.473	3122	4437	.704	2068	5426	7494	6135	2307	947	3257	18940	6.4	5.2	16.1

Three-point field goals: 1987-88, 4-for-23 (.174). 1988-89, 21-for-77 (.273). 1989-90, 28-for-117 (.250). 1990-91, 21-for-68 (.309). 1991-92, 16-for-80 (.200). 1992-93, 22-for-93 (.237). 1993-94, 63-for-197 (.320). 1994-95, 109-for-316 (.345). 1995-96, 150-for-401 (.374). 1996-97, 156-for-424 (.368). 1997-98, 61-for-192 (.318). 1998-99, 72-for-212 (.340). 1999-00, 86-for-263 (.327). 2000-01, 64-for-186 (.344). 2001-02, 54-for-177 (.305). 2002-03, 38-for-133 (.286). 2003-04, 13-for-48 (.271). Totals, 978-for-3002 (.326).

Personal fouls/disqualifications: 1987-88, 214/3. 1988-89, 261/8. 1989-90, 298/6. 1990-91, 270/3. 1991-92, 242/2. 1992-93, 219/3. 1993-94, 227/1. 1994-95, 238/4. 1995-96, 198/0. 1996-97, 213/0. 1997-98, 116/0. 1998-99, 118/0. 1999-00, 208/0. 2000-01, 158/2. 2001-02, 162/3. 2002-03, 149/0. 2003-04, 38/0. Totals, 3329/37.

NBA PLAYOFF RECORD

NOTES: Holds NBA Finals career record for most three-point field goals attempted—117. ... Shares NBA Finals single-game record for most three-point field goals made in one game—7 (June 6, 1997, vs. Utah). ... Holds career playoff record for most three-point field goals attempted—640.

Season Team	G	Min.	FGM	FGA	Pct.	FTM	FTA	Pct.	REBOUNDS			Ast.	St.	Blk.	TO	Pts.	AVERAGES		
									Off.	Def.	Tot.						RPG	APG	PPG
87-88—Chicago	10	294	46	99	.465	5	7	.714	24	28	52	24	8	8	26	100	5.2	2.4	10.0
88-89—Chicago	17	619	84	182	.462	32	50	.640	34	95	129	67	23	16	41	222	7.6	3.9	13.1

Season Team	G	Min.	FGM	FGA	Pct.	FTM	FTA	Pct.	Off.	Def.	Tot.	Ast.	St.	Blk.	TO	Pts.	RPG	APG	PPG
89-90—Chicago	15	612	104	210	.495	71	100	.710	33	75	108	83	31	19	49	289	7.2	5.5	19.3
90-91—Chicago	17	704	142	282	.504	80	101	.792	37	114	151	99	42	19	55	368	8.9	5.8	21.6
91-92—Chicago	22	899	152	325	.468	118	155	.761	59	134	193	147	41	25	70	428	8.8	6.7	19.5
92-93—Chicago	19	789	152	327	.465	74	116	.638	37	95	132	107	41	13	71	381	6.9	5.6	20.1
93-94—Chicago	10	384	85	196	.434	46	52	.885	17	66	83	46	24	7	37	228	8.3	4.6	22.8
94-95—Chicago	10	396	58	131	.443	48	71	.676	24	62	86	58	14	10	27	178	8.6	5.8	17.8
95-96—Chicago	18	742	112	287	.390	51	80	.638	62	91	153	107	47	16	41	305	8.5	5.9	16.9
96-97—Chicago	19	753	129	309	.417	68	86	.791	36	93	129	72	28	18	55	365	6.8	3.8	19.2
97-98—Chicago	21	836	122	294	.415	91	134	.679	49	101	150	110	45	20	51	353	7.1	5.2	16.8
98-99—Houston.........	4	172	23	70	.329	21	26	.808	20	27	47	22	7	3	13	73	11.8	5.5	18.3
99-00—Portland........	16	614	83	198	.419	52	70	.743	22	92	114	69	32	7	37	239	7.1	4.3	14.9
00-01—Portland........	3	117	16	38	.421	6	9	.667	2	15	17	7	8	2	12	41	5.7	2.3	13.7
01-02—Portland........	3	99	18	39	.462	7	8	.875	8	20	28	17	4	2	10	49	9.3	5.7	16.3
02-03—Portland........	4	75	9	22	.409	2	2	1.000	2	9	11	13	0	0	7	23	2.8	3.3	5.8
Totals	208	8105	1335	3009	.444	772	1067	.724	466	1117	1583	1048	395	185	602	3642	7.6	5.0	17.5

Three-point field goals: 1987-88, 3-for-6 (.500). 1988-89, 22-for-56 (.393). 1989-90, 10-for-31 (.323). 1990-91, 4-for-17 (.235). 1991-92, 6-for-24 (.250). 1992-93, 3-for-17 (.176). 1993-94, 12-for-45 (.267). 1994-95, 14-for-38 (.368). 1995-96, 30-for-105 (.286). 1996-97, 39-for-113 (.345). 1997-98, 18-for-79 (.228). 1998-99, 6-for-22 (.273). 1999-00, 21-for-70 (.300). 2000-01, 3-for-17 (.176). 2001-02, 6-for-11 (.545). 2002-03, 3-for-9 (.333). Totals, 200-for-660 (.303).

Personal fouls/disqualifications: 1987-88, 33/1. 1988-89, 63/2. 1989-90, 62/0. 1990-91, 58/1. 1991-92, 72/1. 1992-93, 62/0. 1993-94, 33/1. 1994-95, 40/1. 1995-96, 51/0. 1996-97, 49/0. 1997-98, 66/1. 1998-99, 12/0. 1999-00, 49/1. 2000-01, 14/1. 2001-02, 14/1. 2002-03, 8/0. Totals, 686/11.

NBA ALL-STAR GAME RECORD

NOTES: NBA All-Star Game Most Valuable Player (1994). ... Holds career record for most three-point field goal attempts—22. ... Holds single-game record for most three-point field goal attempts in one half—7 (1994). ... Shares single-game record for most three-point field goal attempts—9 (1994).

Season Team	Min.	FGM	FGA	Pct.	FTM	FTA	Pct.	Off.	Def.	Tot.	Ast.	PF	Dq.	St.	Blk.	TO	Pts.
1990 —Chicago	12	2	4	.500	0	0	...	0	1	1	0	1	0	1	1	1	4
1992 —Chicago	21	6	13	.462	2	3	.667	4	0	4	1	0	0	2	1	1	14
1993 —Chicago	29	4	14	.286	2	3	.667	2	3	5	4	4	0	5	2	0	10
1994 —Chicago	31	9	15	.600	6	10	.600	0	11	11	2	2	0	4	1	2	29
1995 —Chicago	30	5	15	.333	0	0	...	0	7	7	3	1	0	2	1	4	12
1996 —Chicago	25	4	7	.571	0	0	...	2	6	8	5	0	0	3	0	6	8
1997 —Chicago	25	4	9	.444	0	0	...	0	3	3	2	0	0	0	0	2	8
Totals..........................	173	34	77	.442	10	16	.625	8	31	39	17	8	0	17	6	16	85

Three-point field goals: 1990, 0-for-1. 1993, 0-for-2. 1994, 5-for-9 (.556). 1995, 2-for-6 (.333). 1996, 0-for-1. 1997, 0-for-3. Totals, 7-for-22 (.318).

POLLARD, JIM   F

PERSONAL: Born July 9, 1922, in Oakland, Calif. ... Died January 22, 1993. ... 6-5/185 (1,96/83,9). ... Full name: James Clifford Pollard. ... Nickname: The Kangaroo Kid.
HIGH SCHOOL: Oakland Technical.
COLLEGE: Stanford.
TRANSACTIONS: Signed by Minneapolis Lakers of National Basketball League (1947). ... Lakers franchise transferred to Basketball Association of America for 1948-49 season.
CAREER HONORS: Elected to Naismith Memorial Basketball Hall of Fame (1977).
MISCELLANEOUS: Member of NBA championship team (1950, 1952, 1953, 1954). ... Member of BAA championship team (1949). ... Member of NBL championship team (1948).

COLLEGIATE RECORD

NOTES: Member of NCAA Division I championship team (1942). ... In military service during 1942-43, 1943-44 and 1944-45 seasons; played with Alameda, Calif. Coast Guard team.

Season Team	G	Min.	FGM	FGA	Pct.	FTM	FTA	Pct.	Reb.	Ast.	Pts.	RPG	APG	PPG
40-41—Stanford‡						Freshman team statistics unavailable.								
41-42—Stanford	23	...	103	...	...	35	48	.729	...	...	241	...	...	10.5
Varsity totals	23	...	103	...	...	35	48	.729	...	...	241	...	...	10.5

AAU REGULAR-SEASON RECORD

Season Team	G	Min.	FGM	FGA	Pct.	FTM	FTA	Pct.	Reb.	Ast.	Pts.	RPG	APG	PPG
45-46—San Diego Dons	15	...	84	...	...	55	...	...	...	...	*223	...	...	14.9
46-47—Oakland Bittners............	20	...	113	...	...	53	...	...	...	...	*279	...	...	14.0
Totals	35	...	197	...	...	108	...	...	...	...	502	...	...	14.3

NBL AND NBA REGULAR-SEASON RECORD

HONORS: All-NBL first team (1950). ... All-NBA second team (1952, 1954). ... All-BAA first team (1949).

Season Team	G	Min.	FGM	FGA	Pct.	FTM	FTA	Pct.	Reb.	Ast.	PF	Dq.	Pts.	RPG	APG	PPG
47-48—Minneapolis (NBL)..............	59	...	310	...	...	140	207	.676	...	...	147	...	760	...	...	12.9
48-49—Minneapolis (BAA)..............	53	...	314	792	.396	156	227	.687	...	142	144	...	784	...	2.7	14.8
49-50—Minneapolis	66	...	394	1140	.346	185	242	.764	...	252	143	...	973	...	3.8	14.7
50-51—Minneapolis	54	...	256	728	.352	117	156	.750	484	184	157	4	629	9.0	3.4	11.6
51-52—Minneapolis	65	2545	411	1155	.356	183	260	.704	593	234	199	4	1005	9.1	3.6	15.5
52-53—Minneapolis	66	2403	333	933	.357	193	251	.769	452	231	194	3	859	6.8	3.5	13.0
53-54—Minneapolis	71	2483	326	882	.370	179	230	.778	500	214	161	0	831	7.0	3.0	11.7
54-55—Minneapolis	63	1960	265	749	.354	151	186	.812	458	160	147	3	681	7.3	2.5	10.8
Totals..	497	...	2609	...	...	1304	1759	.741	...	...	1292	...	6522	...	...	13.1

NBL AND NBA PLAYOFF RECORD

															AVERAGES		
Season Team	G	Min.	FGM	FGA	Pct.	FTM	FTA	Pct.	Reb.	Ast.	PF	Dq.	Pts.	RPG	APG	PPG
47-48—Minn. (NBL)	10	...	48	...	...	27	41	.659	...	...	...	...	123	...	...	12.3
48-49—Minneapolis (BAA)	10	...	43	147	.293	44	62	.710	...	39	31	...	130	...	3.9	13.0
49-50—Minneapolis	12	...	50	175	.286	44	62	.710	...	56	36	...	144	...	4.7	12.0
50-51—Minneapolis	7	...	35	108	.324	25	30	.833	62	27	27	1	95	8.9	3.9	13.6
51-52—Minneapolis	11	469	70	173	.405	37	50	.740	71	33	34	1	177	6.5	3.0	16.1
52-53—Minneapolis	12	455	62	167	.371	48	62	.774	86	49	37	2	172	7.2	4.1	14.3
53-54—Minneapolis	13	543	56	155	.361	48	60	.800	110	41	27	0	160	8.5	3.2	12.3
54-55—Minneapolis	7	257	33	104	.317	33	46	.717	78	14	13	0	99	11.1	2.0	14.1
Totals	82	...	397	...	...	306	413	.741	...	...	...	...	1100	...	...	13.4

NBA ALL-STAR GAME RECORD

Season Team	Min.	FGM	FGA	Pct.	FTM	FTA	Pct.	Reb	Ast.	PF	Dq.	Pts.
1951—Minneapolis	...	2	11	.182	0	0	...	4	5	1	0	4
1952—Minneapolis	29	2	17	.118	0	0	...	11	5	3	0	4
1954—Minneapolis	41	10	22	.455	3	5	.600	3	3	3	0	23
1955—Minneapolis	27	7	19	.368	3	3	1.000	4	0	1	0	17
Totals	...	21	69	.304	6	8	.750	22	13	8	0	48

COLLEGIATE COACHING RECORD

Season Team	W	L	Pct.
55-56—LaSalle	15	10	.600
56-57—LaSalle	17	9	.654
57-58—LaSalle	16	9	.640
Totals (3 years)	48	28	.632

NBA COACHING RECORD

	REGULAR SEASON					PLAYOFFS		
Season Team	W	L	Pct.	Finish		W	L	Pct.
59-60—Minneapolis	14	25	.359	3rd/Western Division		5	4	.556
61-62—Chicago	18	62	.225	5th/Western Division		—	—	—
Totals (2 years)	32	87	.269	Totals (1 year)		5	4	.556

ABA COACHING RECORD

	REGULAR SEASON					PLAYOFFS		
Season Team	W	L	Pct.	Finish		W	L	Pct.
67-68—Minnesota	50	28	.641	2nd/Eastern Division		4	6	.400
68-69—Miami	43	35	.551	2nd/Eastern Division		5	7	.417
69-70—Miami	5	15	.250			—	—	—
Totals (3 years)	98	78	.557	Totals (2 years)		9	13	.409

NOTES:

1959—Replaced John Castellani as Minneapolis head coach (January 2), with 11-25 record. Defeated Detroit, 2-0, in Western Division Semifinals; lost to St. Louis, 4-3, in Western Division Finals.

1968—Defeated Kentucky, 3-2, in Eastern Division Semifinals; lost to Pittsburgh, 4-1, in Eastern Division Finals. Minnesota Muskies franchise moved to Miami and renamed the Floridians for 1968-69 season.

1969—Defeated Minnesota, 4-3, in Eastern Division Semifinals; lost to Indiana, 4-1, in Eastern Division Finals. Replaced as Miami head coach by Hal Blitman (November).

PORTER, TERRY   G

PERSONAL: Born April 8, 1963, in Milwaukee. ... 6-3/205. (1,91/93,0).
HIGH SCHOOL: South Division (Milwaukee).
COLLEGE: Wisconsin-Stevens Point.
TRANSACTIONS: Selected by Portland Trail Blazers in first round (24th pick overall) of 1985 NBA Draft. ... Signed as free agent by Minnesota Timberwolves (October 14, 1995). ... Signed as free agent by Miami Heat (January 22, 1999). ... Signed as free agent by San Antonio Spurs (August 5, 1999).
CAREER NOTES: Hired as assistant coach by Sacramento Kings (July 29, 2002).
MISCELLANEOUS: Portland Trail Blazers all-time assists leader with 5,319 (1985-86 through 1994-95).

COLLEGIATE RECORD

												AVERAGES		
Season Team	G	Min.	FGM	FGA	Pct.	FTM	FTA	Pct.	Reb.	Ast.	Pts.	RPG	APG	PPG
81-82—Wis.-Stevens Point	25	273	21	57	.368	9	13	.692	13	21	51	0.5	0.8	2.0
82-83—Wis.-Stevens Point	30	949	140	229	.611	62	89	.697	117	157	342	3.9	5.2	11.4
83-84—Wis.-Stevens Point	32	1040	244	392	.622	112	135	.830	165	133	600	5.2	4.2	18.8
84-85—Wis.-Stevens Point	30	1042	233	405	.575	126	151	.834	155	129	592	5.2	4.3	19.7
Totals	117	3304	638	1083	.589	309	388	.796	450	440	1585	3.8	3.8	13.5

HONORS: J. Walter Kennedy Citizenship Award (1993).

NBA REGULAR-SEASON RECORD

									REBOUNDS								AVERAGES		
Season Team	G	Min.	FGM	FGA	Pct.	FTM	FTA	Pct.	Off.	Def.	Tot.	Ast.	St.	Blk.	TO	Pts.	RPG	APG	PPG
85-86—Portland	79	1214	212	447	.474	125	155	.806	35	82	117	198	81	1	106	562	1.5	2.5	7.1
86-87—Portland	80	2714	376	770	.488	280	334	.838	70	267	337	715	159	9	255	1045	4.2	8.9	13.1
87-88—Portland	82	2991	462	890	.519	274	324	.846	65	313	378	831	150	16	244	1222	4.6	10.1	14.9
88-89—Portland	81	3102	540	1146	.471	272	324	.840	85	282	367	770	146	8	248	1431	4.5	9.5	17.7
89-90—Portland	80	2781	448	969	.462	421	472	.892	59	213	272	726	151	4	245	1406	3.4	9.1	17.6
90-91—Portland	81	2665	486	944	.515	279	339	.823	52	230	282	649	158	12	189	1381	3.5	8.0	17.0

Season Team	G	Min.	FGM	FGA	Pct.	FTM	FTA	Pct.	REBOUNDS Off.	Def.	Tot.	Ast.	St.	Blk.	TO	Pts.	AVERAGES RPG	APG	PPG
91-92—Portland	82	2784	521	1129	.461	315	368	.856	51	204	255	477	127	12	188	1485	3.1	5.8	18.1
92-93—Portland	81	2883	503	1108	.454	327	388	.843	58	258	316	419	101	10	199	1476	3.9	5.2	18.2
93-94—Portland	77	2074	348	836	.416	204	234	.872	45	170	215	401	79	18	166	1010	2.8	5.2	13.1
94-95—Portland	35	770	105	267	.393	58	82	.707	18	63	81	133	30	2	58	312	2.3	3.8	8.9
95-96—Minnesota	82	2072	269	608	.442	164	209	.785	36	176	212	452	89	15	173	773	2.6	5.5	9.4
96-97—Minnesota	82	1568	187	449	.416	127	166	.765	31	145	176	295	54	11	128	568	2.1	3.6	6.9
97-98—Minnesota	82	1786	259	577	.449	167	195	.856	37	131	168	271	63	16	104	777	2.0	3.3	9.5
98-99—Miami	50	1365	172	370	.465	123	148	.831	13	127	140	146	48	11	74	525	2.8	2.9	10.5
99-00—San Antonio	68	1613	207	463	.447	137	170	.806	24	167	191	221	50	9	100	641	2.8	3.3	9.4
00-01—San Antonio	80	1678	197	440	.448	92	116	.793	24	177	201	251	52	11	104	573	2.5	3.1	7.2
01-02—San Antonio	72	1294	136	321	.424	68	83	.819	12	152	164	205	45	16	85	399	2.3	2.8	5.5
Totals	1274	35354	5428	11734	.463	3433	4107	.836	715	3157	3872	7160	1583	181	2666	15586	3.0	5.6	12.2

Three-point field goals: 1985-86, 13-for-42 (.310). 1986-87, 13-for-60 (.217). 1987-88, 24-for-69 (.348). 1988-89, 79-for-219 (.361). 1989-90, 89-for-238 (.374). 1990-91, 130-for-313 (.415). 1991-92, 128-for-324 (.395). 1992-93, 143-for-345 (.414). 1993-94, 110-for-282 (.390). 1994-95, 44-for-114 (.386). 1995-96, 71-for-226 (.314). 1996-97, 67-for-200 (.335). 1997-98, 92-for-233 (.395). 1998-99, 58-for-141 (.411). 1999-00, 90-for-207 (.435). 2000-01, 87-for-205 (.424). 2001-02, 59-for-142 (.415). Totals, 1297-for-3360 (.386).

Personal fouls/disqualifications: 1985-86, 136/0. 1986-87, 192/0. 1987-88, 204/1. 1988-89, 187/1. 1989-90, 150/0. 1990-91, 151/2. 1991-92, 155/1. 1992-93, 122/0. 1993-94, 132/0. 1994-95, 60/0. 1995-96, 154/0. 1996-97, 104/0. 1997-98, 103/0. 1998-99, 97/0. 1999-00, 79/0. 2000-01, 88/1. 2001-02, 89/0. Totals, 2203/6.

NBA PLAYOFF RECORD

NOTES: Holds NBA Finals single-game record for most free throws made, none missed—15 (June 7, 1990, at Detroit, OT).

Season Team	G	Min.	FGM	FGA	Pct.	FTM	FTA	Pct.	REBOUNDS Off.	Def.	Tot.	Ast.	St.	Blk.	TO	Pts.	AVERAGES RPG	APG	PPG
85-86—Portland	4	68	12	27	.444	2	4	.500	1	4	5	12	3	2	6	27	1.3	3.0	6.8
86-87—Portland	4	150	24	50	.480	18	20	.900	1	18	19	40	10	2	13	68	4.8	10.0	17.0
87-88—Portland	4	149	29	52	.558	9	13	.692	4	10	14	28	10	0	13	68	3.5	7.0	17.0
88-89—Portland	3	124	26	52	.500	10	12	.833	6	10	16	25	1	1	7	66	5.3	8.3	22.0
89-90—Portland	21	815	127	274	.464	139	165	.842	9	52	61	155	28	3	62	433	2.9	7.4	20.6
90-91—Portland	16	595	102	204	.500	68	79	.861	8	36	44	105	24	1	32	289	2.8	6.6	18.1
91-92—Portland	21	870	147	285	.516	119	143	.832	25	72	97	141	22	3	46	450	4.6	6.7	21.4
92-93—Portland	4	152	27	68	.397	9	11	.818	4	16	20	8	4	0	6	66	5.0	2.0	16.5
93-94—Portland	4	76	12	35	.343	11	14	.786	1	11	12	9	4	0	2	41	3.0	2.3	10.3
94-95—Portland	3	21	7	13	.538	3	5	.600	1	1	2	4	0	0	1	19	0.7	1.3	6.3
96-97—Minnesota	3	46	5	13	.385	3	4	.750	1	2	3	9	2	2	2	16	1.0	3.0	5.3
97-98—Minnesota	5	188	27	63	.429	15	18	.833	7	18	25	16	5	0	4	79	5.0	3.2	15.8
98-99—Miami	5	139	15	32	.469	12	15	.800	3	16	19	15	3	0	8	45	3.8	3.0	9.0
99-00—San Antonio	4	89	8	31	.258	0	0	...	0	1	1	5	6	0	7	20	0.3	1.3	5.0
00-01—San Antonio	13	326	39	86	.453	17	22	.773	1	23	24	44	11	0	22	108	1.8	3.4	8.3
01-02—San Antonio	10	131	13	35	.371	2	4	.500	1	8	9	8	4	0	5	33	0.9	0.8	3.3
Totals	124	3939	620	1320	.470	437	529	.826	73	298	371	624	137	14	236	1828	3.0	5.0	14.7

Three-point field goals: 1985-86, 1-for-6 (.167). 1986-87, 2-for-5 (.400). 1987-88, 1-for-3 (.333). 1988-89, 4-for-11 (.364). 1989-90, 40-for-102 (.392). 1990-91, 17-for-47 (.362). 1991-92, 37-for-78 (.474). 1992-93, 3-for-19 (.158). 1993-94, 6-for-14 (.429). 1994-95, 2-for-5 (.400). 1996-97, 3-for-9 (.333). 1997-98, 10-for-25 (.400). 1998-99, 3-for-12 (.250). 1999-00, 4-for-14 (.286). 2000-01, 13-for-39 (.333). 2001-02, 5-for-17 (.294). Totals, 151-for-406 (.372).

Personal fouls/disqualifications: 1985-86, 10/0. 1986-87, 14/0. 1987-88, 13/0. 1988-89, 8/0. 1989-90, 51/0. 1990-91, 32/0. 1991-92, 49/0. 1992-93, 10/0. 1993-94, 3/0. 1994-95, 6/0. 1996-97, 2/0. 1997-98, 10/0. 1998-99, 8/0. 1999-00, 4/0. 2000-01, 15/0. 2001-02, 10/0. Totals, 245/1.

NBA ALL-STAR GAME RECORD

Season Team	Min.	FGM	FGA	Pct.	FTM	FTA	Pct.	REBOUNDS Off.	Def.	Tot.	Ast.	PF	Dq.	St.	Blk.	TO	Pts.
1991—Portland	15	2	6	.333	0	0	...	1	2	3	4	2	0	2	1	3	4
1993—Portland	19	3	8	.375	0	0	...	0	0	0	3	1	0	1	0	1	7
Totals	34	5	14	.357	0	0	...	1	2	3	7	3	0	3	1	4	11

Three-point field goals: 1991, 0-for-2. 1993, 1-for-5 (.200). Totals, 1-for-7 (.143).

NBA COACHING RECORD

BACKGROUND: Assistant coach, Sacramento Kings (2002-03).

Season Team	REGULAR SEASON W	L	Pct.	Finish	PLAYOFFS W	L	Pct.
03-04—Milwaukee	41	41	.500	4th/Central Division	1	4	.200
04-05—Milwaukee	30	52	.366	5th/Central Division	—	—	—
Totals (2 years)	71	93	.433	Totals (1 year)	5	4	.556

NOTES:
2004—Lost to Detroit, 4-1, in Eastern Conference first round.

PRICE, MARK   G

PERSONAL: Born February 15, 1964, in Bartlesville, Okla. ... 6-0/180 (1,83/81,6). ... Full name: William Mark Price. ... Brother of Brent Price, guard with Sacramento Kings.
HIGH SCHOOL: Enid (Okla.).
COLLEGE: Georgia Tech.
TRANSACTIONS/CAREER NOTES: Selected by Dallas Mavericks in second round (25th pick overall) of 1986 NBA Draft. ... Draft rights traded by Mavericks to Cleveland Cavaliers for 1989 second-round draft choice and cash (June 17, 1986). ... Traded by Cavaliers to Washington Bullets for 1996 first-round draft choice (September 27, 1995). ... Signed as free agent by Golden State Warriors (July 21, 1996). ... Traded by Warriors to Orlando Magic for G Brian Shaw and F David Vaughn (October 28, 1997). ... Waived by Magic (June 30, 1998).
MISCELLANEOUS: Cleveland Cavaliers all-time assists leader with 4,206 and all-time steals leader with 734 (1986-87 through 1994-95).

COLLEGIATE RECORD

Season Team	G	Min.	FGM	FGA	Pct.	FTM	FTA	Pct.	Reb.	Ast.	Pts.	RPG	APG	PPG
82-83—Georgia Tech	28	1020	201	462	.435	93	106	.877	105	91	568	3.8	3.3	20.3
83-84—Georgia Tech	29	1078	191	375	.509	70	85	.824	61	121	452	2.1	4.2	15.6
84-85—Georgia Tech	35	1302	223	462	.483	137	163	.840	71	150	583	2.0	4.3	16.7
85-86—Georgia Tech	34	1204	233	441	.528	124	145	.855	94	148	590	2.8	4.4	17.4
Totals	126	4604	848	1740	.487	424	499	.850	331	510	2193	2.6	4.0	17.4

Three-point field goals: 1982-83, 73-for-166 (.440).

NBA REGULAR-SEASON RECORD

RECORDS: Holds career record for highest free throw percentage (minimum 1,200 made)—.904.

HONORS: Long Distance Shootout winner (1993, 1994). ... All-NBA first team (1993). ... All-NBA third team (1989, 1992, 1994).

									REBOUNDS								AVERAGES		
Season Team	G	Min.	FGM	FGA	Pct.	FTM	FTA	Pct.	Off.	Def.	Tot.	Ast.	St.	Blk.	TO	Pts.	RPG	APG	PPG
86-87—Cleveland	67	1217	173	424	.408	95	114	.833	33	84	117	202	43	4	105	464	1.7	3.0	6.9
87-88—Cleveland	80	2626	493	974	.506	221	252	.877	54	126	180	480	99	12	184	1279	2.3	6.0	16.0
88-89—Cleveland	75	2728	529	1006	.526	263	292	.901	48	178	226	631	115	7	212	1414	3.0	8.4	18.9
89-90—Cleveland	73	2706	489	1066	.459	300	338	.888	66	185	251	666	114	5	214	1430	3.4	9.1	19.6
90-91—Cleveland	16	571	97	195	.497	59	62	.952	8	37	45	166	42	2	56	271	2.8	10.4	16.9
91-92—Cleveland	72	2138	438	897	.488	270	285	*.947	38	135	173	535	94	12	159	1247	2.4	7.4	17.3
92-93—Cleveland	75	2380	477	986	.484	289	305	*.948	37	164	201	602	89	11	196	1365	2.7	8.0	18.2
93-94—Cleveland	76	2386	480	1005	.478	238	268	.888	39	189	228	589	103	11	189	1316	3.0	7.8	17.3
94-95—Cleveland	48	1375	253	612	.413	148	162	.914	25	87	112	335	35	4	142	757	2.3	7.0	15.8
95-96—Washington	7	127	18	60	.300	10	10	1.000	1	6	7	18	6	0	10	56	1.0	2.6	8.0
96-97—Golden State	70	1876	263	589	.447	155	171	*.906	36	143	179	342	67	3	161	793	2.6	4.9	11.3
97-98—Orlando	63	1430	229	531	.431	87	103	.845	24	105	129	297	53	5	162	597	2.0	4.7	9.5
Totals	722	21560	3939	8345	.472	2135	2362	.904	409	1439	1848	4863	860	76	1790	10989	2.6	6.7	15.2

Three-point field goals: 1986-87, 23-for-70 (.329). 1987-88, 72-for-148 (.486). 1988-89, 93-for-211 (.441). 1989-90, 152-for-374 (.406). 1990-91, 18-for-53 (.340). 1991-92, 101-for-261 (.387). 1992-93, 122-for-293 (.416). 1993-94, 118-for-297 (.397). 1994-95, 103-for-253 (.407). 1995-96, 10-for-30 (.333). 1996-97, 112-for-283 (.396). 1997-98, 52-for-155 (.335). Totals, 976-for-2428 (.402).

Personal fouls/disqualifications: 1986-87, 75/1. 1987-88, 119/1. 1988-89, 89/0. 1989-90, 89/0. 1990-91, 23/0. 1991-92, 113/0. 1992-93, 105/0. 1993-94, 93/0. 1994-95, 50/0. 1995-96, 7/0. 1996-97, 100/0. 1997-98, 92/0. Totals, 964/2.

NBA PLAYOFF RECORD

NOTES: Holds career playoff record for highest free throw percentage (minimum 100 made)—.944.

									REBOUNDS								AVERAGES		
Season Team	G	Min.	FGM	FGA	Pct.	FTM	FTA	Pct.	Off.	Def.	Tot.	Ast.	St.	Blk.	TO	Pts.	RPG	APG	PPG
87-88—Cleveland	5	205	38	67	.567	24	25	.960	3	15	18	38	3	0	8	105	3.6	7.6	21.0
88-89—Cleveland	4	158	22	57	.386	14	15	.933	4	9	13	22	3	0	19	64	3.3	5.5	16.0
89-90—Cleveland	5	192	32	61	.525	30	30	1.000	0	14	14	44	9	1	15	100	2.8	8.8	20.0
91-92—Cleveland	17	603	118	238	.496	66	73	.904	10	32	42	128	24	4	56	327	2.5	7.5	19.2
92-93—Cleveland	9	288	43	97	.443	23	24	.958	1	18	19	55	15	0	33	117	2.1	6.1	13.0
93-94—Cleveland	3	140	13	43	.349	13	14	.929	1	5	6	14	4	0	9	45	2.0	4.7	15.0
94-95—Cleveland	4	105	14	40	.000	00	08	.075	2	10	12	26	6	0	18	60	3.0	6.5	15.0
Totals	47	1691	280	603	.464	202	214	.944	21	103	124	327	64	5	158	818	2.6	7.0	17.4

Three-point field goals: 1987-88, 5-for-12 (.417). 1988-89, 6-for-16 (.375). 1989-90, 6-for-17 (.353). 1991-92, 25-for-69 (.362). 1992-93, 8-for-26 (.308). 1993-94, 2-for-9 (.222). 1994-95, 4-for-17 (.235). Totals, 56-for-166 (.337).

Personal fouls/disqualifications: 1987-88, 11/1. 1988-89, 3/0. 1989-90, 9/0. 1991-92, 34/0. 1992-93, 13/0. 1993-94, 6/0. 1994-95, 5/0. Totals, 81/1.

NBA ALL-STAR GAME RECORD

								REBOUNDS								
Season Team	Min.	FGM	FGA	Pct.	FTM	FTA	Pct.	Off.	Def.	Tot.	Ast.	PF	Dq.	St.	Blk.	TO	Pts.
1989—Cleveland	20	3	9	.333	2	2	1.000	1	2	3	1	2	0	2	0	2	9
1992—Cleveland	15	1	5	.200	4	4	1.000	0	0	0	3	1	0	1	0	3	6
1993—Cleveland	23	6	11	.545	1	2	.500	0	1	1	4	5	0	1	0	3	19
1994—Cleveland	22	8	10	.800	2	2	1.000	0	2	2	5	1	0	1	1	0	20
Totals	80	18	35	.514	9	10	.900	1	5	6	13	9	0	5	1	8	54

Three-point field goals: 1989, 1-for-4 (.250). 1992, 0-for-3. 1993, 6-for-9 (.667). 1994, 2-for-3 (.667). Totals, 9-for-19 (.474).

REED, WILLIS   C/F

PERSONAL: Born June 25, 1942, in Hico, La. ... 6-10/240 (2,08/108,4). ... Full name: Willis Reed Jr.

HIGH SCHOOL: West Side (Lillie, La.).

COLLEGE: Grambling State.

TRANSACTIONS: Selected by New York Knicks in second round (10th pick overall) of 1964 NBA Draft.

CAREER HONORS: Elected to Naismith Memorial Basketball Hall of Fame (1982). ... One of the 50 Greatest Players in NBA History (1996).

CAREER NOTES: General manager/vice president of basketball operations, New Jersey Nets (1988-89 to 1995-96). ... Senior vice president, Nets (1996-97 to 2003-04). ... Named vice president of basketball operations, New Orleans Hornets (June 29, 2004).

MISCELLANEOUS: Member of NBA championship team (1970, 1973).

COLLEGIATE RECORD

NOTES: Member of NAIA championship team (1961). ... Elected to NAIA Basketball Hall of Fame (1970).

												AVERAGES		
Season Team	G	Min.	FGM	FGA	Pct.	FTM	FTA	Pct.	Reb.	Ast.	Pts.	RPG	APG	PPG
60-61—Grambling State	35	...	146	239	.611	86	122	.705	312	...	378	8.9	...	10.8
61-62—Grambling State	26	...	189	323	.585	80	102	.784	380	...	458	14.6	...	17.6
62-63—Grambling State	33	...	282	489	.577	135	177	.763	563	...	699	17.1	...	21.2
63-64—Grambling State	28	...	301	486	.619	143	199	.719	596	...	745	21.3	...	26.6
Totals	122	...	918	1537	.597	444	600	.740	1851	...	2280	15.2	...	18.7

NBA REGULAR-SEASON RECORD

HONORS: NBA Most Valuable Player (1970). ... NBA Rookie of the Year (1965). ... All-NBA first team (1970). ... All-NBA second team (1967, 1968, 1969, 1971). ... NBA All-Defensive first team (1970). ... NBA All-Rookie team (1965).

Season Team	G	Min.	FGM	FGA	Pct.	FTM	FTA	Pct.	Reb.	Ast.	PF	Dq.	Pts.	AVERAGES RPG	APG	PPG
64-65—New York	80	3042	629	1457	.432	302	407	.742	1175	133	339	14	1560	14.7	1.7	19.5
65-66—New York	76	2537	438	1009	.434	302	399	.757	883	91	323	13	1178	11.6	1.2	15.5
66-67—New York	78	2824	635	1298	.489	358	487	.735	1136	126	293	9	1628	14.6	1.6	20.9
67-68—New York	81	2879	659	1346	.490	367	509	.721	1073	159	343	12	1685	13.2	2.0	20.8
68-69—New York	82	3108	704	1351	.521	325	435	.747	1191	190	314	7	1733	14.5	2.3	21.1
69-70—New York	81	3089	702	1385	.507	351	464	.756	1126	161	287	2	1755	13.9	2.0	21.7
70-71—New York	73	2855	614	1330	.462	299	381	.785	1003	148	228	1	1527	13.7	2.0	20.9
71-72—New York	11	363	60	137	.438	27	39	.692	96	22	30	0	147	8.7	2.0	13.4
72-73—New York	69	1876	334	705	.474	92	124	.742	590	126	205	0	760	8.6	1.8	11.0

Season Team	G	Min.	FGM	FGA	Pct.	FTM	FTA	Pct.	REBOUNDS Off.	Def.	Tot.	Ast.	St.	Blk.	TO	Pts.	AVERAGES RPG	APG	PPG
73-74—New York	19	500	84	184	.457	42	53	.792	47	94	141	30	12	21	...	210	7.4	1.6	11.1
Totals	650	23073	4859	10202	.476	2465	3298	.747	...	...	8414	1186	12	21	...	12183	12.9	1.8	18.7

Personal fouls/disqualifications: 1973-74, 49/0.

NBA PLAYOFF RECORD

NOTES: NBA Finals Most Valuable Player (1970, 1973).

Season Team	G	Min.	FGM	FGA	Pct.	FTM	FTA	Pct.	Reb.	Ast.	PF	Dq.	Pts.	AVERAGES RPG	APG	PPG
66-67—New York	4	148	43	80	.538	24	25	.960	55	7	19	1	110	13.8	1.8	27.5
67-68—New York	6	210	53	98	.541	22	30	.733	62	11	24	1	128	10.3	1.8	21.3
68-69—New York	10	429	101	198	.510	55	70	.786	141	19	40	1	257	14.1	1.9	25.7
69-70—New York	18	732	178	378	.471	70	95	.737	248	51	60	0	426	13.8	2.8	23.7
70-71—New York	12	504	81	196	.413	26	39	.667	144	27	41	0	188	12.0	2.3	15.7
72-73—New York	17	486	97	208	.466	18	21	.857	129	30	65	1	212	7.6	1.8	12.5

Season Team	G	Min.	FGM	FGA	Pct.	FTM	FTA	Pct.	REBOUNDS Off.	Def.	Tot.	Ast.	St.	Blk.	TO	Pts.	AVERAGES RPG	APG	PPG
73-74—New York	11	132	17	45	.378	3	5	.600	4	18	22	4	2	0	...	37	2.0	0.4	3.4
Totals	78	2641	570	1203	.474	218	285	.765	...	...	801	149	2	0	...	1358	10.3	1.9	17.4

Personal fouls/disqualifications: 1973-74, 26/0.

NBA ALL-STAR GAME RECORD

NOTES: NBA All-Star Game Most Valuable Player (1970).

Season Team	Min.	FGM	FGA	Pct.	FTM	FTA	Pct.	Reb	Ast.	PF	Dq.	Pts.
1965—New York	25	3	11	.273	1	2	.500	5	1	2	0	7
1966—New York	23	7	11	.636	2	2	1.000	8	1	3	0	16
1967—New York	17	2	6	.333	0	0	...	9	1	0	0	4
1968—New York	25	7	14	.500	2	3	.667	8	1	4	0	16
1969—New York	14	5	8	.625	0	0	...	4	2	2	0	10
1970—New York	30	9	18	.500	3	3	1.000	11	0	6	1	21
1971—New York	27	5	16	.313	4	6	.667	13	1	3	0	14
Totals	161	38	84	.452	12	16	.750	58	7	20	1	88

HEAD COACHING RECORD

BACKGROUND: Volunteer assistant, St. John's University (1980-81). ... Assistant coach, Atlanta Hawks (1985-86 and 1986-87). ... Assistant coach, Sacramento Kings (1987-88).

NBA COACHING RECORD

Season Team	REGULAR SEASON W	L	Pct.	Finish	PLAYOFFS W	L	Pct.
77-78—New York	43	39	.524	2nd/Atlantic Division	2	4	.333
78-79—New York	6	8	.429		—	—	—
87-88—New Jersey	7	21	.250	5th/Atlantic Division	—	—	—
88-89—New Jersey	26	56	.317	5th/Atlantic Division	—	—	—
Totals (4 years)	82	124	.398	Totals (1 year)	2	4	.333

COLLEGIATE COACHING RECORD

Season Team	W	L	Pct.	Finish
81-82—Creighton	7	20	.259	8th/Missouri Valley Conference
82-83—Creighton	8	19	.296	10th/Missouri Valley Conference
83-84—Creighton	17	14	.548	4th/Missouri Valley Conference
84-85—Creighton	20	11	.645	4th/Missouri Valley Conference
Totals (4 years)	52	64	.448	

NOTES:

1978—Defeated Cleveland, 2-0, in Eastern Conference First Round; lost to Philadelphia, 4-0, in Eastern Conference Semifinals. Replaced as New York head coach by Red Holzman (November).

1984—Lost to Nebraska, 56-54, in NIT first round.

1988—Replaced interim head coach Bob MacKinnon as New Jersey head coach (February 29), with record of 12-42.

RICE, GLEN   F

PERSONAL: Born May 28, 1967, in Flint, Mich. ... 6-8/220. (2,03/99,8). ... Full Name: Glen Anthony Rice.
HIGH SCHOOL: Northwestern Community (Flint, Mich.).
COLLEGE: Michigan.
TRANSACTIONS/CAREER NOTES: Selected by Miami Heat in first round (fourth pick overall) of 1989 NBA Draft. ... Traded by Heat with G Khalid Reeves, C Matt Geiger and 1996 first-round draft choice to Charlotte Hornets for C Alonzo Mourning, C LeRon Ellis and G Pete Myers (November 3, 1995). ... Traded by Hornets with F/C J.R. Reid and G B.J. Armstrong to Los Angeles Lakers

for G Eddie Jones and F/C Elden Campbell (March 10, 1999). ... Traded by Lakers to New York Knicks as part of four-team trade in which Knicks acquired C Luc Longley, F/C Travis Knight, G Vernon Maxwell, C Vladimir Stepania, F Lazaro Borrell, two 2001 first-round draft choices and two 2001 second-round draft choices, Seattle SuperSonics acquired C Patrick Ewing, Phoenix Suns acquired C Chris Dudley and 2001 first-round draft choice and Lakers acquired F Horace Grant, C Greg Foster, F Chuck Person and G Emanual Davis (September 20, 2000). ... Traded by Knicks to Houston Rockets as part of three-team trade in which Knicks acquired F Shandon Anderson from Rockets and G Howard Eisley from Mavericks, Mavericks acquired G Muggsy Bogues from Knicks and Rockets acquired draft rights to G Kyle Hill from Mavericks (August 10, 2001). ... Traded by Rockets with first-round draft choice and additional draft consideration to Utah Jazz for C John Amaechi, 2004 second-round draft choice and conditional second-round draft choice (September 30, 2003). ... Signed as free agent by Los Angeles Clippers (October 10, 2003). ... Waived by Clippers (January 16, 2004).

MISCELLANEOUS: Member of NBA championship team (2000). ... Miami Heat all-time leading scorer with 9,248 points (1989-90 through 1994-95).

COLLEGIATE RECORD

NOTES: Member of NCAA Division I championship team (1989). ... THE SPORTING NEWS All-America second team (1989). ... NCAA Division I Tournament Most Outstanding Player (1989).

												AVERAGES		
Season Team	G	Min.	FGM	FGA	Pct.	FTM	FTA	Pct.	Reb.	Ast.	Pts.	RPG	APG	PPG
85-86—Michigan	32	520	105	191	.550	15	25	.600	97	21	225	3.0	0.7	7.0
86-87—Michigan	32	1056	226	402	.562	85	108	.787	294	76	540	9.2	2.4	16.9
87-88—Michigan	33	1155	308	539	.571	79	98	.806	236	92	728	7.2	2.8	22.1
88-89—Michigan	37	1258	363	629	.577	124	149	.832	232	85	949	6.3	2.3	25.6
Totals	134	3989	1002	1761	.569	303	380	.797	859	274	2442	6.4	2.0	18.2

Three-point field goals: 1986-87, 3-for-12 (.250). 1987-88, 33-for-77 (.429). 1988-89, 99-for-192 (.516). Totals, 135-for-281 (.480).

NBA REGULAR-SEASON RECORD

HONORS: Long Distance Shootout winner (1995). ... All-NBA Second Team (1997). ... All-NBA Third Team (1998). ... NBA All-Rookie second team (1990).

NOTES: Led NBA with .470 three-point field goal percentage (1997).

									REBOUNDS								AVERAGES		
Season Team	G	Min.	FGM	FGA	Pct.	FTM	FTA	Pct.	Off.	Def.	Tot.	Ast.	St.	Blk.	TO	Pts.	RPG	APG	PPG
89-90—Miami	77	2311	470	1071	.439	91	124	.734	100	252	352	138	67	27	113	1048	4.6	1.8	13.6
90-91—Miami	77	2646	550	1193	.461	171	209	.818	85	296	381	189	101	26	166	1342	4.9	2.5	17.4
91-92—Miami	79	3007	672	1432	.469	266	318	.836	84	310	394	184	90	35	145	1765	5.0	2.3	22.3
92-93—Miami	82	3082	582	1324	.440	242	295	.820	92	332	424	180	92	25	157	1554	5.2	2.2	19.0
93-94—Miami	81	2999	663	1421	.467	250	284	.880	76	358	434	184	110	32	130	1708	5.4	2.3	21.1
94-95—Miami	82	3014	667	1403	.475	312	365	.855	99	279	378	192	112	14	153	1831	4.6	2.3	22.3
95-96—Charlotte	79	3142	610	1296	.471	319	381	.837	86	292	378	232	91	19	163	1710	4.8	2.9	21.6
96-97—Charlotte	79	*3362	722	1513	.477	464	535	.867	67	251	318	160	72	26	177	2115	4.0	2.0	26.8
97-98—Charlotte	82	3295	634	1386	.457	428	504	.849	89	264	353	182	77	22	182	1826	4.3	2.2	22.3
98-99—L.A. Lakers	27	985	171	396	.432	77	90	.856	9	90	99	71	17	6	45	472	3.7	2.6	17.5
99-00—L.A. Lakers	80	2530	421	980	.430	346	396	.874	56	271	327	176	47	12	114	1272	4.1	2.2	15.9
00-01—New York	75	2212	331	752	.440	155	182	.852	61	246	307	89	41	13	96	899	4.1	1.2	12.0
01-02—Houston	20	606	65	167	.389	24	30	.800	5	42	47	31	12	3	24	172	2.4	1.6	8.6
02-03—Houston	62	1533	196	457	.429	66	87	.759	18	131	149	89	40	10	80	550	2.4	1.4	8.9
03-04—L.A. Clippers	18	262	22	76	.289	17	17	1.000	9	32	41	24	6	0	13	66	2.3	1.3	3.7
Totals	1000	34985	6776	14867	.456	3225	3813	.846	946	3441	4387	2097	958	265	1733	18336	4.4	2.1	18.3

Three-point field goals: 1989-90, 17-for-69 (.246). 1990-91, 71-for-184 (.386). 1991-92, 155-for-396 (.391). 1992-93, 148-for-386 (.383). 1993-94, 132-for-346 (.382). 1994-95, 185-for-451 (.410). 1995-96, 171-for-403 (.424). 1996-97, 207-for-440 (.470). 1997-98, 130-for-300 (.433). 1998-99, 53-for-135 (.393). 1999-00, 84-for-229 (.367). 2000-01, 82-for-211 (.389). 2001-02, 18-for-64 (.281). 2002-03, 101-for-254 (.398). 2003-04, 5-for-28 (.179). Totals, 1559-for-3896 (.400).

Personal fouls/disqualifications: 1989-90, 198/1. 1990-91, 216/0. 1991-92, 170/0. 1992-93, 201/0. 1993-94, 186/0. 1994-95, 203/1. 1995-96, 217/1. 1996-97, 190/0. 1997-98, 200/0. 1998-99, 67/1. 1999-00, 179/0. 2000-01, 179/1. 2001-02, 34/0. 2002-03, 99/0. 2003-04, 22/0. Totals, 2361/5.

NBA PLAYOFF RECORD

									REBOUNDS								AVERAGES		
Season Team	G	Min.	FGM	FGA	Pct.	FTM	FTA	Pct.	Off.	Def.	Tot.	Ast.	St.	Blk.	TO	Pts.	RPG	APG	PPG
91-92—Miami	3	119	24	64	.375	6	7	.857	3	7	10	5	2	0	6	57	3.3	1.7	19.0
93-94—Miami	5	195	26	68	.382	6	8	.750	6	30	36	10	11	2	14	65	7.2	2.0	13.0
96-97—Charlotte	3	137	28	57	.491	21	23	.913	1	10	11	11	4	1	4	83	3.7	3.7	27.7
97-98—Charlotte	9	369	82	173	.474	30	36	.833	11	40	51	13	5	3	13	205	5.7	1.4	22.8
98-99—L.A. Lakers	7	307	45	101	.446	28	29	.966	4	23	27	11	5	1	9	128	3.9	1.6	18.3
99-00—L.A. Lakers	23	766	93	228	.408	71	89	.798	10	82	92	48	15	4	36	285	4.0	2.1	12.4
00-01—New York	5	144	24	52	.462	7	8	.875	3	19	22	3	3	1	7	61	4.4	0.6	12.2
Totals	55	2037	322	743	.433	169	200	.845	38	211	249	101	45	12	89	884	4.5	1.8	16.1

Three-point field goals: 1991-92, 3-for-12 (.250). 1993-94, 7-for-23 (.304). 1996-97, 6-for-15 (.375). 1997-98, 11-for-36 (.306). 1998-99, 10-for-28 (.357). 1999-00, 28-for-67 (.418). 2000-01, 6-for-14 (.429). Totals, 71-for-196 (.362).

Personal fouls/disqualifications: 1991-92, 7/0. 1993-94, 14/0. 1996-97, 11/0. 1997-98, 26/0. 1998-99, 15/0. 1999-00, 50/0. 2000-01, 10/0. Totals, 133/0.

NBA ALL-STAR GAME RECORD

NOTES: NBA All-Star Game Most Valuable Player (1997). ... Holds single-game records for most points in one half—24; most points in one quarter—20; most field-goal attempts in one half—17; and most three-point field goals made in one quarter—4 (1997). ... Shares single-game record for most field goals made in one quarter—8 (1997).

								REBOUNDS								
Season Team	Min.	FGM	FGA	Pct.	FTM	FTA	Pct.	Off.	Def.	Tot.	Ast.	PF	Dq.	St.	Blk.	TO	Pts.
1996—Charlotte	15	1	5	.200	4	4	1.000	0	0	0	2	2	0	0	0	2	7
1997—Charlotte	25	10	24	.417	2	2	1.000	1	1	2	1	2	0	2	0	1	26
1998—Charlotte	16	6	14	.429	0	0	...	1	0	1	0	0	0	0	1	1	16
Totals	56	17	43	.395	6	6	1.000	2	1	3	3	4	0	2	1	4	49

Three-point field goals: 1996, 1-for-2 (.500). 1997, 4-for-7 (.571). 1998, 4-for-6 (.667). Totals, 9-for-15 (.600).

ALL-TIME GREAT PLAYERS

RICHMOND, MITCH   G

PERSONAL: Born June 30, 1965, in Fort Lauderdale. ... 6-5/220. (1,96/99,8). ... Full Name: Mitchell James Richmond.
HIGH SCHOOL: Boyd Anderson (Fort Lauderdale).
JUNIOR COLLEGE: Moberly (Mo.) Area Junior College.
COLLEGE: Kansas State.
TRANSACTIONS/CAREER NOTES: Selected by Golden State Warriors in first round (fifth pick overall) of 1988 NBA Draft. ... Traded by Warriors with C Les Jepsen to Sacramento Kings for F/G Billy Owens (November 1, 1991). ... Traded by Kings with F Otis Thorpe to Washington Wizards for F Chris Webber (May 14, 1998). ... Waived by Wizards (July 2, 2001). ... Signed as free agent by Los Angeles Lakers (July 20, 2001).
MISCELLANEOUS: Member of NBA championship team (2002). ... Member of bronze-medal-winning U.S. Olympic team (1988) and gold-medal-winning U.S. Olympic team (1996).

COLLEGIATE RECORD

NOTES: The Sporting News All-America second team (1988).

Season Team	G	Min.	FGM	FGA	Pct.	FTM	FTA	Pct.	Reb.	Ast.	Pts.	RPG	APG	PPG
												AVERAGES		
84-85—Moberly Area J.C.	40	...	180	375	.480	55	85	.647	185	98	415	4.6	2.5	10.4
85-86—Moberly Area J.C.	38	...	242	506	.478	124	180	.689	251	99	608	6.6	2.6	16.0
86-87—Kansas State	30	964	201	450	.447	118	155	.761	170	80	559	5.7	2.7	18.6
87-88—Kansas State	34	1200	268	521	.514	186	240	.775	213	125	768	6.3	3.7	22.6
Junior College Totals	78	...	422	881	.479	179	265	.675	436	197	1023	5.6	2.5	13.1
4-Year-College Totals	64	2164	469	971	.483	304	395	.770	383	205	1327	6.0	3.2	20.7

Three-point field goals: 1986-87, 39-for-108 (.361). 1987-88, 46-for-98 (.469). Totals, 85-for-206 (.413).

NBA REGULAR-SEASON RECORD

HONORS: NBA Rookie of the Year (1989). ... All-NBA Second Team (1994, 1995, 1997). ... All-NBA Third Team (1996, 1998). ... NBA All-Rookie first team (1989).

Season Team	G	Min.	FGM	FGA	Pct.	FTM	FTA	Pct.	Off.	Def.	Tot.	Ast.	St.	Blk.	TO	Pts.	RPG	APG	PPG
									REBOUNDS								**AVERAGES**		
88-89—Golden State	79	2717	649	1386	.468	410	506	.810	158	310	468	334	82	13	269	1741	5.9	4.2	22.0
89-90—Golden State	78	2799	640	1287	.497	406	469	.866	98	262	360	223	98	24	201	1720	4.6	2.9	22.1
90-91—Golden State	77	3027	703	1424	.494	394	465	.847	147	305	452	238	126	34	230	1840	5.9	3.1	23.9
91-92—Sacramento	80	3095	685	1465	.468	330	406	.813	62	257	319	411	92	34	247	1803	4.0	5.1	22.5
92-93—Sacramento	45	1728	371	782	.474	197	233	.845	18	136	154	221	53	9	130	987	3.4	4.9	21.9
93-94—Sacramento	78	2897	635	1428	.445	426	511	.834	70	216	286	313	103	17	216	1823	3.7	4.0	23.4
94-95—Sacramento	82	3172	668	1497	.446	375	445	.843	69	288	357	311	91	29	234	1867	4.4	3.8	22.8
95-96—Sacramento	81	2946	611	1368	.447	425	491	.866	54	215	269	255	125	19	220	1872	3.3	3.1	23.1
96-97—Sacramento	81	3125	717	1578	.454	457	531	.861	59	260	319	338	118	24	237	2095	3.9	4.2	25.9
97-98—Sacramento	70	2569	543	1220	.445	407	471	.864	50	179	229	279	88	15	181	1623	3.3	4.0	23.2
98-99—Washington	50	1912	331	803	.412	251	293	.857	30	142	172	122	64	10	136	983	3.4	2.4	19.7
99-00—Washington	74	2397	447	1049	.426	298	340	.876	37	176	213	185	110	13	154	1285	2.9	2.5	17.4
00-01—Washington	37	1216	205	504	.407	143	160	.894	15	94	109	111	43	7	84	598	2.9	3.0	16.2
01-02—L.A. Lakers	64	709	100	247	.405	42	44	.955	14	80	94	57	18	6	40	260	1.5	0.9	4.1
Totals	976	34309	7305	16038	.455	4561	5365	.850	881	2920	3801	3398	1211	254	2579	20497	3.9	3.5	21.0

Three-point field goals: 1988-89, 33-for-90 (.367). 1989-90, 34-for-95 (.358). 1990-91, 40-for-115 (.348). 1991-92, 103-for-268 (.384). 1992-93, 48-for-130 (.369). 1993-94, 127-for-312 (.407). 1994-95, 156-for-424 (.368). 1995-96, 225-for-515 (.437). 1996-97, 204-for-477 (.428). 1997-98, 130-for-334 (.389). 1998-99, 70-for-221 (.317). 1999-00, 93-for-241 (.386). 2000-01, 45-for-133 (.338). 2001-02, 18-for-62 (.290). Totals, 1326-for-3417 (.388).
Personal fouls/disqualifications: 1988-89, 223/5. 1989-90, 210/3. 1990-91, 207/0. 1991-92, 231/1. 1992-93, 137/3. 1993-94, 211/3. 1994-95, 227/2. 1995-96, 233/6. 1996-97, 211/1. 1997-98, 154/0. 1998-99, 121/1. 1999-00, 191/2. 2000-01, 86/0. 2001-02, 61/0. Totals, 2503/27.

NBA PLAYOFF RECORD

Season Team	G	Min.	FGM	FGA	Pct.	FTM	FTA	Pct.	Off.	Def.	Tot.	Ast.	St.	Blk.	TO	Pts.	RPG	APG	PPG
									REBOUNDS								**AVERAGES**		
88-89—Golden State	8	314	62	135	.459	34	38	.895	10	48	58	35	14	1	24	161	7.3	4.4	20.1
90-91—Golden State	9	372	85	169	.503	23	24	.958	10	37	47	22	5	6	17	201	5.2	2.4	22.3
95-96—Sacramento	4	146	24	54	.444	28	35	.800	3	14	17	12	3	0	15	84	4.3	3.0	21.0
01-02—L.A. Lakers	2	4	1	1	1.000	1	2	.500	0	1	1	0	0	0	1	3	0.5	0.0	1.5
Totals	23	836	172	359	.479	86	99	.869	23	100	123	69	22	7	57	449	5.3	3.0	19.5

Three-point field goals: 1988-89, 3-for-16 (.188). 1990-91, 8-for-24 (.333). 1995-96, 8-for-23 (.348). Totals, 19-for-63 (.302).
Personal fouls/disqualifications: 1988-89, 25/0. 1990-91, 28/1. 1995-96, 11/0. Totals, 64/1.

NBA ALL-STAR GAME RECORD

NOTES: NBA All-Star Game Most Valuable Player (1995).

Season Team	Min.	FGM	FGA	Pct.	FTM	FTA	Pct.	Off.	Def.	Tot.	Ast.	PF	Dq.	St.	Blk.	TO	Pts.
								REBOUNDS									
1993—Sacramento								Selected, did not play—injured.									
1994—Sacramento	24	5	16	.313	0	0	...	0	2	2	3	0	0	0	0	0	10
1995—Sacramento	22	10	13	.769	0	0	...	3	1	4	2	0	0	0	0	0	23
1996—Sacramento	25	3	10	.300	1	2	.500	0	2	2	2	0	0	1	0	2	7
1997—Sacramento	22	3	7	.429	0	0	...	1	2	3	4	1	0	0	0	1	9
1998—Sacramento	17	4	11	.364	0	0	...	0	1	1	2	0	...	0	0	0	8
Totals	110	25	57	.439	1	2	.500	4	8	12	13	1	0	1	0	3	57

Three-point field goals: 1995, 3-for-3. 1996, 0-for-3. 1997, 3-for-4 (.750). 1998, 0-for-2. Totals, 6-for-12 (.500).

ROBERTSON, OSCAR   G

PERSONAL: Born November 24, 1938, in Charlotte, Tenn. ... 6-5/220 (1,96/99,8). ... Full name: Oscar Palmer Robertson. ... Nickname: Big O.
HIGH SCHOOL: Crispus Attucks (Indianapolis).
COLLEGE: Cincinnati.
TRANSACTIONS: Selected by Cincinnati Royals in 1960 NBA Draft (territorial pick). ... Traded by Royals to Milwaukee

Bucks for G Flynn Robinson and F Charlie Paulk (April 21, 1970).
CAREER HONORS: Elected to Naismith Memorial Basketball Hall of Fame (1980). ... NBA 35th Anniversary All-Time Team (1980) and One of the 50 Greatest Players in NBA History (1996).
MISCELLANEOUS: Member of NBA championship team (1971). ... Member of gold-medal-winning U.S. Olympic team (1960). ... Sacramento Kings franchise all-time leading scorer with 22,009 points and all-time assists leader with 7,731 (1960-61 through 1969-70).

COLLEGIATE RECORD

NOTES: The Sporting News College Player of the Year (1958, 1959, 1960). ... The Sporting News All-America first team (1958, 1959, 1960). ... Led NCAA Division I with 35.1 points per game (1958), 32.6 points per game (1959) and 33.7 points per game (1960).

Season Team	G	Min.	FGM	FGA	Pct.	FTM	FTA	Pct.	Reb.	Ast.	Pts.	AVERAGES RPG	APG	PPG
56-57—Cincinnati‡	13	...	151	...	...	127	178	.713	...	...	429	...	...	33.0
57-58—Cincinnati	28	1085	352	617	.571	280	355	.789	425	...	984	15.2	...	35.1
58-59—Cincinnati	30	1172	331	650	.509	316	398	.794	489	206	978	16.3	6.9	32.6
59-60—Cincinnati	30	1155	369	701	.526	273	361	.756	424	219	1011	14.1	7.3	33.7
Varsity totals	88	3412	1052	1968	.535	869	1114	.780	1338	...	2973	15.2	...	33.8

NBA REGULAR-SEASON RECORD

RECORDS: Shares single-game record for most free throws attempted in one quarter—16 (December 27, 1964, vs. Baltimore).
HONORS: NBA Most Valuable Player (1964). ... NBA Rookie of the Year (1961). ... All-NBA first team (1961, 1962, 1963, 1964, 1965, 1966, 1967, 1968, 1969). ... All-NBA second team (1970, 1971).

Season Team	G	Min.	FGM	FGA	Pct.	FTM	FTA	Pct.	Reb.	Ast.	PF	Dq.	Pts.	AVERAGES RPG	APG	PPG
60-61—Cincinnati	71	3012	756	1600	.473	653	794	.822	716	*690	219	3	2165	10.1	*9.7	30.5
61-62—Cincinnati	79	3503	866	1810	.478	700	872	.803	985	*899	258	1	2432	12.5	*11.4	30.8
62-63—Cincinnati	80	3521	825	1593	.518	614	758	.810	835	758	293	1	2264	10.4	9.5	28.3
63-64—Cincinnati	79	3559	840	1740	.483	*800	938	.853	783	*868	280	3	2480	9.9	*11.0	31.4
64-65—Cincinnati	75	3421	807	1681	.480	*665	793	.839	674	*861	205	2	2279	9.0	*11.5	30.4
65-66—Cincinnati	76	3493	818	1723	.475	742	881	.842	586	*847	227	1	2378	7.7	*11.1	31.3
66-67—Cincinnati	79	3468	838	1699	.493	736	843	.873	486	845	226	2	2412	6.2	*10.7	30.5
67-68—Cincinnati	65	2765	660	1321	.500	*576	660	.873	391	633	199	2	1896	6.0	*9.7	*29.2
68-69—Cincinnati	79	3461	656	1351	.486	*643	767	.838	502	*772	231	2	1955	6.4	*9.8	24.7
69-70—Cincinnati	69	2865	647	1267	.511	454	561	.809	422	558	175	1	1740	6.1	8.1	25.3
70-71—Milwaukee	81	3194	592	1193	.496	385	453	.850	462	668	203	0	1569	5.7	8.2	19.4
71-72—Milwaukee	64	2390	419	887	.472	276	330	.836	323	491	116	0	1114	5.0	7.7	17.4
72-73—Milwaukee	73	2737	446	983	.454	238	281	.847	360	551	167	0	1130	4.9	7.5	15.5

Season Team	G	Min.	FGM	FGA	Pct.	FTM	FTA	Pct.	REBOUNDS Off.	Def.	Tot.	Ast.	St.	Blk.	TO	Pts.	AVERAGES RPG	APG	PPG
73-74—Milwaukee	70	2477	338	772	.438	212	254	.835	71	208	279	446	77	4	...	888	4.0	6.4	12.7
Totals	1040	43886	9508	19620	.485	7694	9185	.838	...	...	7804	9887	77	4	...	26710	7.5	9.5	25.7

Personal fouls/disqualifications: 1973-74, 132/0.

NBA PLAYOFF RECORD

Season Team	G	Min.	FGM	FGA	Pct.	FTM	FTA	Pct.	Reb.	Ast.	PF	Dq.	Pts.	AVERAGES RPG	APG	PPG
61-62—Cincinnati	4	185	42	81	.519	31	39	.795	44	44	18	1	115	11.0	11.0	28.8
62-63—Cincinnati	12	570	124	264	.470	133	154	.864	156	108	41	0	381	13.0	9.0	31.8
63-64—Cincinnati	10	411	101	209	.483	100	127	.868	88	84	00	0	283	8.9	8.4	29.3
64-65—Cincinnati	4	195	38	89	.427	36	39	.923	19	48	14	0	112	4.8	12.0	28.0
65-66—Cincinnati	5	224	49	120	.408	61	68	.897	38	39	20	1	159	7.6	7.8	31.8
66-67—Cincinnati	4	183	33	64	.516	33	37	.892	16	45	9	0	99	4.0	11.3	24.8
70-71—Milwaukee	14	520	102	210	.486	52	69	.754	70	124	39	0	256	5.0	8.9	18.3
71-72—Milwaukee	11	380	57	140	.407	30	36	.833	64	83	29	0	144	5.8	7.5	13.1
72-73—Milwaukee	6	256	48	96	.500	31	34	.912	28	45	21	1	127	4.7	7.5	21.2

Season Team	G	Min.	FGM	FGA	Pct.	FTM	FTA	Pct.	REBOUNDS Off.	Def.	Tot.	Ast.	St.	Blk.	TO	Pts.	AVERAGES RPG	APG	PPG
73-74—Milwaukee	16	689	90	200	.450	44	52	.846	15	39	54	149	15	4	...	224	3.4	9.3	14.0
Totals	86	3673	675	1466	.460	560	655	.855	...	...	578	769	15	4	...	1910	6.7	8.9	22.2

Personal fouls/disqualifications: 1973-74, 46/0.

NBA ALL-STAR GAME RECORD

NOTES: NBA All-Star Game Most Valuable Player (1961, 1964, 1969). ... Shares career record for most free throws attempted—98. ... Shares single-game record for most free throws made—12 (1965).

Season Team	Min.	FGM	FGA	Pct.	FTM	FTA	Pct.	Reb	Ast.	PF	Dq.	Pts.
1961—Cincinnati	34	8	13	.615	7	9	.778	9	14	5	0	23
1962—Cincinnati	37	9	20	.450	8	14	.571	7	13	3	0	26
1963—Cincinnati	37	9	15	.600	3	4	.750	3	6	5	0	21
1964—Cincinnati	42	10	23	.435	6	10	.600	14	8	4	0	26
1965—Cincinnati	40	8	18	.444	12	13	.923	6	8	5	0	28
1966—Cincinnati	25	6	12	.500	5	6	.833	10	8	0	0	17
1967—Cincinnati	34	9	20	.450	8	10	.800	2	5	4	0	26
1968—Cincinnati	22	7	9	.778	4	7	.571	1	5	5	0	18
1969—Cincinnati	32	8	16	.500	8	8	1.000	6	5	3	0	24
1970—Cincinnati	29	9	11	.818	3	4	.750	6	4	3	0	21
1971—Milwaukee	24	2	6	.333	1	3	.333	2	2	3	0	5
1972—Milwaukee	24	3	9	.333	5	10	.500	3	3	4	0	11
Totals	380	88	172	.512	70	98	.714	69	81	41	0	246

ROBINSON, DAVID   C

PERSONAL: Born August 6, 1965, in Key West, Fla. ... 7-1/250. (2,16/113,4). ... Full Name: David Maurice Robinson. ... Nickname: The Admiral.
HIGH SCHOOL: Osbourn Park (Manassas, Va.).
COLLEGE: Navy.
TRANSACTIONS/CAREER NOTES: Selected by San Antonio Spurs in first round (first pick overall) of 1987 NBA Draft.

CAREER HONORS: NBA 50th Anniversary All-Time Team (1996).
MISCELLANEOUS: Member of NBA championship team (1999, 2003). ... Member of bronze-medal-winning U.S. Olympic team (1988) and gold-medal-winning U.S. Olympic teams (1992, 1996). ... Member of gold-medal winning U.S. World Championship team (1986). ... San Antonio Spurs all-time points leader with 20,790, all-time rebound leader with 10,497, all-time steals leader with 1,388 and all-time blocked shots leader with 2,954 (1989-90 through 2002-03).

COLLEGIATE RECORD

NOTES: THE SPORTING NEWS College Player of the Year (1987). ... Naismith Award winner (1987). ... Wooden Award winner (1987). ... THE SPORTING NEWS All-America first team (1986, 1987). ... Holds NCAA Division I single-season records for most blocked shots—207 (1986). ... Shares NCAA Division I single-game record for most blocked shots—14 (January 4, 1986, vs. UNC Wilmington). ... Led NCAA Division I with 13.0 rebounds per game (1986). ... Led NCAA Division I with 5.91 blocked shots per game (1986) and 4.50 blocked shots per game (1987).

Season Team	G	Min.	FGM	FGA	Pct.	FTM	FTA	Pct.	Reb.	Ast.	Pts.	RPG	APG	PPG
83-84—Navy	28	372	86	138	.623	42	73	.575	111	6	214	4.0	0.2	7.6
84-85—Navy	32	1075	302	469	.644	152	243	.626	370	19	756	11.6	0.6	23.6
85-86—Navy	35	1187	294	484	.607	208	331	.628	455	24	796	13.0	0.7	22.7
86-87—Navy	32	1107	350	592	.591	202	317	.637	378	33	903	11.8	1.0	28.2
Totals	127	3741	1032	1683	.613	604	964	.627	1314	82	2669	10.3	0.6	21.0

Three-point field goals: 1986-87, 1-for-1.

NBA REGULAR-SEASON RECORD

HONORS: NBA Most Valuable Player (1995). ... NBA Defensive Player of the Year (1992). ... NBA Rookie of the Year (1990). ... IBM Award, for all-around contributions to team's success (1990, 1991, 1994, 1995, 1996). ... NBA Sportsmanship Award (2001). ... All-NBA first team (1991, 1992, 1995, 1996). ... All-NBA second team (1994, 1998). ... All-NBA third team (1990, 1993, 2000, 2001). ... NBA All-Defensive first team (1991, 1992, 1995, 1996). ... NBA All-Defensive second team (1990, 1993, 1994, 1998). ... NBA All-Rookie first team (1990). ... J. Walter Kennedy Citizenship Award (2003).

NOTES: Led NBA with 4.49 blocked shots per game (1992).

Season Team	G	Min.	FGM	FGA	Pct.	FTM	FTA	Pct.	Off.	Def.	Tot.	Ast.	St.	Blk.	TO	Pts.	RPG	APG	PPG
87-88—San Antonio						Did not play—in military service.													
88-89—San Antonio						Did not play—in military service.													
89-90—San Antonio	82	3002	690	1300	.531	613	837	.732	303	680	983	164	138	319	257	1993	12.0	2.0	24.3
90-91—San Antonio	82	3095	754	1366	.552	592	777	.762	335	728	*1063	208	127	*320	270	2101	*13.0	2.5	25.6
91-92—San Antonio	68	2564	592	1074	.551	393	561	.701	261	568	829	181	158	*305	182	1578	12.2	2.7	23.2
92-93—San Antonio	82	3211	676	1348	.501	561	766	.732	229	727	956	301	127	264	241	1916	11.7	3.7	23.4
93-94—San Antonio	80	3241	840	1658	.507	*693	*925	.749	241	614	855	381	139	265	253	*2383	10.7	4.8	*29.8
94-95—San Antonio	81	3074	788	1487	.530	*656	847	.774	234	643	877	236	134	262	233	2238	10.8	2.9	27.6
95-96—San Antonio	82	3019	711	1378	.516	*626	*823	.761	319	*681	*1000	247	111	271	190	2051	12.2	3.0	25.0
96-97—San Antonio	6	147	36	72	.500	34	52	.654	19	32	51	8	6	6	8	106	8.5	1.3	17.7
97-98—San Antonio	73	2457	544	1065	.511	485	660	.735	239	536	775	199	64	192	202	1574	10.6	2.7	21.6
98-99—San Antonio	49	1554	268	527	.509	239	363	.658	148	344	492	103	69	119	108	775	10.0	2.1	15.8
99-00—San Antonio	80	2557	528	1031	.512	371	511	.726	193	577	770	142	97	183	164	1427	9.6	1.8	17.8
00-01—San Antonio	80	2371	400	823	.486	351	470	.747	208	483	691	116	80	197	122	1151	8.6	1.5	14.4
01-02—San Antonio	78	2303	341	672	.507	269	395	.681	191	456	647	94	86	140	104	951	8.3	1.2	12.2
02-03—San Antonio	64	1676	197	420	.469	152	214	.710	163	345	508	61	52	111	83	546	7.9	1.0	8.5
Totals	987	34271	7365	14221	.518	6035	8201	.736	3083	7414	10497	2441	1388	2954	2417	20790	10.6	2.5	21.1

Three-point field goals: 1989-90, 0-for-2. 1990-91, 1-for-7 (.143). 1991-92, 1-for-8 (.125). 1992-93, 3-for-17 (.176). 1993-94, 10-for-29 (.345). 1994-95, 6-for-20 (.300). 1995-96, 3-for-9 (.333). 1997-98, 1-for-4 (.250). 1998-99, 0-for-1. 1999-00, 0-for-2. 2000-01, 0-for-1. Totals, 25-for-100 (.250).

Personal fouls/disqualifications: 1989-90, 259/3. 1990-91, 264/5. 1991-92, 219/2. 1992-93, 239/5. 1993-94, 228/3. 1994-95, 230/2. 1995-96, 262/1. 1996-97, 9/0. 1997-98, 204/2. 1998-99, 143/0. 1999-00, 247/1. 2000-01, 212/1. 2001-02, 193/3. 2002-03, 126/1. Totals, 2835/29.

NBA PLAYOFF RECORD

Season Team	G	Min.	FGM	FGA	Pct.	FTM	FTA	Pct.	Off.	Def.	Tot.	Ast.	St.	Blk.	TO	Pts.	RPG	APG	PPG
89-90—San Antonio	10	375	89	167	.533	65	96	.677	36	84	120	23	11	40	24	243	12.0	2.3	24.3
90-91—San Antonio	4	166	35	51	.686	33	38	.868	11	43	54	8	6	15	15	103	13.5	2.0	25.8
92-93—San Antonio	10	421	79	170	.465	73	110	.664	29	97	126	40	10	36	25	231	12.6	4.0	23.1
93-94—San Antonio	4	146	30	73	.411	20	27	.741	13	27	40	14	3	10	9	80	10.0	3.5	20.0
94-95—San Antonio	15	623	129	289	.446	121	149	.812	57	125	182	47	22	39	56	380	12.1	3.1	25.3
95-96—San Antonio	10	353	83	161	.516	70	105	.667	37	64	101	24	15	25	24	236	10.1	2.4	23.6
97-98—San Antonio	9	353	57	134	.425	61	96	.635	41	86	127	23	11	30	25	175	14.1	2.6	19.4
98-99—San Antonio	17	600	87	180	.483	91	126	.722	36	132	168	43	28	40	40	265	9.9	2.5	15.6
99-00—San Antonio	4	155	31	83	.373	32	42	.762	17	38	55	10	7	12	8	94	13.8	2.5	23.5
00-01—San Antonio	13	409	75	159	.472	66	95	.695	39	114	153	22	17	31	28	216	11.8	1.7	16.6
01-02—San Antonio	4	81	9	19	.474	0	4	.000	6	17	23	5	3	3	2	18	5.8	1.3	4.5
02-03—San Antonio	23	539	64	118	.542	52	78	.667	45	107	152	21	18	31	24	180	6.6	0.9	7.8
Totals	123	4221	768	1604	.479	684	966	.708	367	934	1301	280	151	312	280	2221	10.6	2.3	18.1

Three-point field goals: 1990-91, 0-for-1. 1992-93, 0-for-1. 1993-94, 0-for-1. 1994-95, 1-for-5 (.200). 1999-00, 0-for-1. 2000-01, 0-for-1. Totals, 1-for-10 (.100).

Personal fouls/disqualifications: 1989-90, 35/1. 1990-91, 11/0. 1992-93, 39/0. 1993-94, 14/0. 1994-95, 63/1. 1995-96, 38/2. 1997-98, 28/1. 1998-99, 61/1. 1999-00, 15/0. 2000-01, 42/0. 2001-02, 14/0. 2002-03, 63/3. Totals, 423/9.

NBA ALL-STAR GAME RECORD

Season Team	Min.	FGM	FGA	Pct.	FTM	FTA	Pct.	Off.	Def.	Tot.	Ast.	PF	Dq.	St.	Blk.	TO	Pts.
1990—San Antonio	25	7	12	.583	1	2	.500	2	8	10	1	1	0	2	1	1	15
1991—San Antonio	18	6	13	.462	4	5	.800	3	3	6	0	5	0	2	3	2	16
1992—San Antonio	18	7	9	.778	5	8	.625	1	4	5	2	3	0	3	1	0	19
1993—San Antonio	26	7	10	.700	7	12	.583	2	8	10	1	4	0	0	1	1	21
1994—San Antonio	21	6	13	.462	7	10	.700	3	2	5	0	2	0	0	2	1	19
1995—San Antonio	14	3	5	.600	4	6	.667	0	3	3	2	2	0	2	1	1	10
1996—San Antonio	23	8	13	.615	2	2	1.000	6	5	11	2	4	0	2	1	1	18

Season Team	Min.	FGM	FGA	Pct.	FTM	FTA	Pct.	REBOUNDS Off.	Def.	Tot.	Ast.	PF	Dq.	St.	Blk.	TO	Pts.
1998—San Antonio	22	3	4	.750	9	10	.900	2	4	6	0	1	...	2	2	2	15
2000—San Antonio	7	0	1	.000	0	0	...	1	1	2	0	1	0	0	0	1	0
2001—San Antonio	10	3	5	.600	2	4	.500	2	2	4	0	3	0	0	0	1	8
Totals	184	50	85	.588	41	59	.695	22	40	62	8	26	0	13	13	11	141

RODGERS, GUY   G

PERSONAL: Born September 1, 1935, in Philadelphia. ... Died February 19, 2001. ... 6-0/185 (1,83/83,9). ... Full name: Guy William Rodgers Jr.
HIGH SCHOOL: Northeast (Philadelphia).
COLLEGE: Temple.
TRANSACTIONS: Selected by Philadelphia Warriors in 1958 NBA Draft (territorial pick). ... Warriors franchise moved from Philadelphia to San Francisco for 1962-63 season. ... Traded by Warriors to Chicago Bulls for draft choice, cash and two players to be named later (September 7, 1966); G Jim King and G Jeff Mullins sent to Warriors to complete deal. ... Traded by Bulls to Cincinnati Royals for G Flynn Robinson, cash and two future draft choices (October 20, 1967). ... Selected by Milwaukee Bucks from Royals in NBA Expansion Draft (May 6, 1968).
MISCELLANEOUS: Golden State Warriors franchise all-time assists leader with 4,855 (1958-59 through 1965-66).

COLLEGIATE RECORD

NOTES: The Sporting News All-America first team (1958).

Season Team	G	Min.	FGM	FGA	Pct.	FTM	FTA	Pct.	Reb.	Ast.	Pts.	AVERAGES RPG	APG	PPG
54-55—Temple‡	15	...	...	...	...	...	...	...	...	...	278	...	...	18.5
55-56—Temple	31	...	243	552	.440	87	155	.561	186	...	573	6.0	...	18.5
56-57—Temple	29	...	216	565	.382	159	224	.710	202	...	591	7.0	...	20.4
57-58—Temple	30	...	249	564	.441	105	171	.614	199	...	603	6.6	...	20.1
Varsity totals	90	...	708	1681	.421	351	550	.638	587	...	1767	6.5	...	19.6

NBA REGULAR-SEASON RECORD

Season Team	G	Min.	FGM	FGA	Pct.	FTM	FTA	Pct.	Reb.	Ast.	PF	Dq.	Pts.	AVERAGES RPG	APG	PPG
58-59—Philadelphia	45	1565	211	535	.394	61	112	.545	281	261	132	1	483	6.2	5.8	10.7
59-60—Philadelphia	68	2483	338	870	.389	111	181	.613	391	482	196	3	787	5.8	7.1	11.6
60-61—Philadelphia	78	2905	397	1029	.386	206	300	.687	509	677	262	3	1000	6.5	8.7	12.8
61-62—Philadelphia	80	2650	267	749	.356	121	182	.665	348	643	312	12	655	4.4	8.0	8.2
62-63—San Francisco	79	3240	445	1150	.387	208	286	.727	394	*825	296	7	1098	5.0	*10.4	13.9
63-64—San Francisco	79	2695	337	923	.365	198	280	.707	328	556	245	4	872	4.2	7.0	11.0
64-65—San Francisco	79	2699	465	1225	.380	223	325	.686	323	565	256	4	1153	4.1	7.2	14.6
65-66—San Francisco	79	2902	586	1571	.373	296	407	.727	421	846	241	6	1468	5.3	10.7	18.6
66-67—Chicago	81	3063	538	1377	.391	383	475	.806	346	*908	243	1	1459	4.3	*11.2	18.0
67-68—Chicago-Cincinnati	79	1546	148	426	.347	107	133	.805	150	380	167	1	403	1.9	4.8	5.1
68-69—Milwaukee	81	2157	325	862	.377	184	232	.793	226	561	207	2	834	2.8	6.9	10.3
69-70—Milwaukee	64	749	69	191	.050	67	55	.741	70	114	74	1	000	1.0	0.0	0.2
Totals	892	28663	4125	10908	.378	2165	3003	.721	3791	6917	2630	45	10415	4.3	7.8	11.7

NBA PLAYOFF RECORD

Season Team	G	Min.	FGM	FGA	Pct.	FTM	FTA	Pct.	Reb.	Ast.	PF	Dq.	Pts.	AVERAGES RPG	APG	PPG
59-60—Philadelphia	9	370	49	136	.360	20	36	.556	77	54	39	3	118	8.6	6.0	13.1
60-61—Philadelphia	3	121	21	57	.368	11	20	.550	21	15	16	2	53	7.0	5.0	17.7
61-62—Philadelphia	13	482	52	145	.359	35	55	.636	7	88	57	3	139	0.5	6.8	10.7
63-64—San Fran.	12	419	57	173	.329	33	47	.702	58	90	46	1	147	4.8	7.5	12.3
66-67—Chicago	3	97	15	40	.375	4	5	.800	6	18	11	0	34	2.0	6.0	11.3
69-70—Milwaukee	7	68	4	14	.286	9	12	.750	4	21	7	0	17	0.6	3.0	2.4
Totals	47	1557	198	565	.350	112	175	.640	173	286	176	9	508	3.7	6.1	10.8

NBA ALL-STAR GAME RECORD

Season Team	Min.	FGM	FGA	Pct.	FTM	FTA	Pct.	Reb	Ast.	PF	Dq.	Pts.
1963—San Francisco	17	3	6	.500	1	2	.500	2	4	2	0	7
1964—San Francisco	22	3	6	.500	0	0	...	2	2	4	0	6
1966—San Francisco	34	4	11	.364	0	0	...	7	11	4	0	8
1967—Chicago	28	0	4	.000	1	1	1.000	2	8	3	0	1
Totals	101	10	27	.370	2	3	.667	13	25	13	0	22

RODMAN, DENNIS   F

PERSONAL: Born May 13, 1961, in Trenton, N.J. ... 6-7/228. (2.01 m/103 kg). ... Full Name: Dennis Keith Rodman. ... Nickname: Worm.
HIGH SCHOOL: South Oak Cliff (Dallas), did not play basketball.
JUNIOR COLLEGE: Cooke County (Texas) Junior College.
COLLEGE: Southeastern Oklahoma State.
TRANSACTIONS/CAREER NOTES: Selected by Detroit Pistons in second round (27th pick overall) of 1986 NBA Draft. ... Traded by Pistons to San Antonio Spurs for F Sean Elliott and F David Wood (October 1, 1993). ... Traded by Spurs to Chicago Bulls for C Will Perdue (October 2, 1995). ... Signed as free agent by Los Angeles Lakers (February 23, 1999). ... Waived by Lakers (April 16, 1999). ... Signed as free agent by Dallas Mavericks (February 3, 2000). ... Waived by Mavericks (March 8, 2000).
MISCELLANEOUS: Member of NBA championship team (1989, 1990, 1996, 1997, 1998).

COLLEGIATE RECORD

NOTES: Led NAIA with 15.9 rebounds per game (1985) and 17.8 rebounds per game (1986).

ALL-TIME GREAT PLAYERS

Season Team	G	Min.	FGM	FGA	Pct.	FTM	FTA	Pct.	Reb.	Ast.	Pts.	RPG	APG	PPG
82-83—Cooke County J.C..........	16	...	114	185	.616	53	91	.582	212	...	281	13.3	0.0	17.6
83-84—SE Oklahoma State........	30	...	303	490	.618	173	264	.655	392	23	779	13.1	0.8	26.0
84-85—SE Oklahoma State........	32	...	353	545	.648	151	267	.566	510	12	857	15.9	0.4	26.8
85-86—SE Oklahoma State........	34	...	332	515	.645	165	252	.655	605	26	829	17.8	0.8	24.4
Junior College Totals..............	16	...	114	185	.616	53	91	.582	212	...	281	13.3	0.0	17.6
4-Year-College Totals	96	...	988	1550	.637	489	783	.625	1507	61	2465	15.7	0.6	25.7

NBA REGULAR-SEASON RECORD

RECORDS: Holds career records for most consecutive seasons leading league in rebounds—7; and most seasons leading league in defensive rebounds—3.

HONORS: NBA Defensive Player of the Year (1990, 1991). ... IBM Award, for all-around contributions to team's success (1992). ... All-NBA third team (1992, 1995). ... NBA All-Defensive first team (1989, 1990, 1991, 1992, 1993, 1995, 1996). ... NBA All-Defensive second team (1994).

Season Team	G	Min.	FGM	FGA	Pct.	FTM	FTA	Pct.	Off.	Def.	Tot.	Ast.	St.	Blk.	TO	Pts.	RPG	APG	PPG
86-87—Detroit	77	1155	213	391	.545	74	126	.587	163	169	332	56	38	48	93	500	4.3	0.7	6.5
87-88—Detroit	82	2147	398	709	.561	152	284	.535	318	397	715	110	75	45	156	953	8.7	1.3	11.6
88-89—Detroit	82	2208	316	531	*.595	97	155	.626	327	445	772	99	55	76	126	735	9.4	1.2	9.0
89-90—Detroit	82	2377	288	496	.581	142	217	.654	336	456	792	72	52	60	90	719	9.7	0.9	8.8
90-91—Detroit	82	2747	276	560	.493	111	176	.631	*361	665	1026	85	65	55	94	669	12.5	1.0	8.2
91-92—Detroit	82	3301	342	635	.539	84	140	.600	*523	*1007	*1530	191	68	70	140	800	*18.7	2.3	9.8
92-93—Detroit	62	2410	183	429	.427	87	163	.534	*367	765	*1132	102	48	45	103	468	*18.3	1.6	7.5
93-94—San Antonio	79	2989	156	292	.534	53	102	.520	*453	*914	*1367	184	52	32	138	370	*17.3	2.3	4.7
94-95—San Antonio	49	1568	137	240	.571	75	111	.676	274	549	823	97	31	23	98	349	*16.8	2.0	7.1
95-96—Chicago	64	2088	146	304	.480	56	106	.528	*356	596	952	160	36	27	138	351	*14.9	2.5	5.5
96-97—Chicago	55	1947	128	286	.448	50	88	.568	*320	563	883	170	32	19	111	311	*16.1	3.1	5.7
97-98—Chicago	80	2856	155	360	.431	61	111	.550	421	*780	*1201	230	47	18	147	375	*15.0	2.9	4.7
98-99—L.A. Lakers	23	657	16	46	.348	17	39	.436	62	196	258	30	10	12	31	49	11.2	1.3	2.1
99-00—Dallas............	12	389	12	31	.387	10	14	.714	48	123	171	14	2	1	19	34	14.3	1.2	2.8
Totals	911	28839	2766	5310	.521	1069	1832	.584	4329	7625	11954	1600	611	531	1484	6683	13.1	1.8	7.3

Three-point field goals: 1986-87, 0-for-1. 1987-88, 5-for-17 (.294). 1988-89, 6-for-26 (.231). 1989-90, 1-for-9 (.111). 1990-91, 6-for-30 (.200). 1991-92, 32-for-101 (.317). 1992-93, 15-for-73 (.205). 1993-94, 5-for-24 (.208). 1994-95, 0-for-2. 1995-96, 3-for-27 (.111). 1996-97, 5-for-19 (.263). 1997-98, 4-for-23 (.174). 1998-99, 0-for-1. 1999-00, 0-for-1. Totals, 82-for-354 (.232).

Personal fouls/disqualifications: 1986-87, 166/1. 1987-88, 273/5. 1988-89, 292/4. 1989-90, 276/2. 1990-91, 281/7. 1991-92, 248/0. 1992-93, 201/0. 1993-94, 229/0. 1994-95, 159/1. 1995-96, 196/1. 1996-97, 172/1. 1997-98, 238/2. 1998-99, 71/0. 1999-00, 41/2. Totals, 2843/26.

NBA PLAYOFF RECORD

NOTES: Shares NBA Finals single-game record for most offensive rebounds—11 (June 7, 1996, vs. Seattle; and June 16, 1996, vs. Seattle).

Season Team	G	Min.	FGM	FGA	Pct.	FTM	FTA	Pct.	Off.	Def.	Tot.	Ast.	St.	Blk.	TO	Pts.	RPG	APG	PPG
86-87—Detroit	15	245	40	74	.541	18	32	.563	32	39	71	3	6	17	17	98	4.7	0.2	6.5
87-88—Detroit	23	474	71	136	.522	22	54	.407	51	85	136	21	14	14	31	164	5.9	0.9	7.1
88-89—Detroit	17	409	37	70	.529	24	35	.686	56	114	170	16	6	12	24	98	10.0	0.9	5.8
89-90—Detroit	19	560	54	95	.568	18	35	.514	55	106	161	17	9	13	31	126	8.5	0.9	6.6
90-91—Detroit	15	495	41	91	.451	10	24	.417	67	110	177	14	11	10	13	94	11.8	0.9	6.3
91-92—Detroit	5	156	16	27	.593	4	8	.500	16	35	51	9	4	2	7	36	10.2	1.8	7.2
93-94—San Antonio	3	114	12	24	.500	1	6	.167	24	24	48	2	6	4	6	25	16.0	0.7	8.3
94-95—San Antonio	14	459	52	96	.542	20	35	.571	69	138	207	18	12	0	25	124	14.8	1.3	8.9
95-96—Chicago	18	620	50	103	.485	35	59	.593	98	149	247	37	14	8	41	135	13.7	2.1	7.5
96-97—Chicago	19	535	30	81	.370	15	26	.577	59	101	160	27	10	4	28	79	8.4	1.4	4.2
97-98—Chicago	21	722	39	105	.371	23	38	.605	99	149	248	41	14	13	35	102	11.8	2.0	4.9
Totals	169	4789	442	902	.490	190	352	.540	626	1050	1676	205	106	97	258	1081	9.9	1.2	6.4

Three-point field goals: 1987-88, 0-for-2. 1988-89, 0-for-4. 1990-91, 2-for-9 (.222). 1991-92, 0-for-2. 1993-94, 0-for-5. 1994-95, 0-for-5. 1996-97, 4-for-16 (.250). 1997-98, 1-for-4 (.250). Totals, 7-for-47 (.149).

Personal fouls/disqualifications: 1987-88, 87/1. 1988-89, 58/0. 1990-91, 55/1. 1991-92, 17/0. 1993-94, 14/0. 1994-95, 51/1. 1996-97, 74/3. 1997-98, 88/4. Totals, 630/12.

NBA ALL-STAR GAME RECORD

Season Team	Min.	FGM	FGA	Pct.	FTM	FTA	Pct.	Off.	Def.	Tot.	Ast.	PF	Dq.	St.	Blk.	TO	Pts.
1990—Detroit...................	11	2	4	.500	0	0	...	3	1	4	1	1	0	0	1	2	4
1992—Detroit...................	25	2	7	.286	0	0	...	7	6	13	0	1	0	1	0	2	4
Totals	36	4	11	.364	0	0	...	10	7	17	1	2	0	1	1	4	8

RUSSELL, BILL   C

PERSONAL: Born February 12, 1934, in Monroe, La. ... 6-10/220 (2,08/99,8). ... Full name: William Felton Russell.
HIGH SCHOOL: McClymonds (Oakland, Calif.).
COLLEGE: San Francisco.
TRANSACTIONS: Selected by St. Louis Hawks in first round (third pick overall) of 1956 NBA Draft. ... Draft rights traded by Hawks to Boston Celtics for F/C Ed Macauley and draft rights to F Cliff Hagan (April 29, 1956).
CAREER HONORS: Elected to Naismith Memorial Basketball Hall of Fame (1975). ... Declared Greatest Player in the History of the NBA by Professional Basketball Writers' Association of America (1980). ... NBA 25th Anniversary All-Time Team (1970), 35th Anniversary All-Time Team (1980) and One of the 50 Greatest Players in NBA History (1996).
CAREER NOTES: Consultant, Boston Celtics (1999-2000-present).
MISCELLANEOUS: Member of NBA championship team (1957, 1959, 1960, 1961, 1962, 1963, 1964, 1965, 1966, 1968, 1969). ... Member of gold-medal-winning U.S. Olympic team (1956). ... Boston Celtics all-time leading rebounder with 21,620 (1956-57 through 1968-69).

COLLEGIATE RECORD

NOTES: NCAA Tournament Most Outstanding Player (1955). ... Member of NCAA championship team (1955, 1956).

Season Team	G	Min.	FGM	FGA	Pct.	FTM	FTA	Pct.	Reb.	Ast.	Pts.	AVERAGES		
												RPG	APG	PPG
52-53—San Francisco‡	23	...	...	...	...	...	...	...	...	...	461	...	...	20.0
53-54—San Francisco	21	...	150	309	.485	117	212	.552	403	...	417	19.2	...	19.9
54-55—San Francisco	29	...	229	423	.541	164	278	.590	594	...	622	20.5	...	21.4
55-56—San Francisco	29	...	246	480	.513	105	212	.495	609	...	597	21.0	...	20.6
Varsity totals	79	...	625	1212	.516	386	702	.550	1606	...	1636	20.3	...	20.7

NBA REGULAR-SEASON RECORD

RECORDS: Holds single-game record for most rebounds in one half—32 (November 16, 1957, vs. Philadelphia).

HONORS: NBA Most Valuable Player (1958, 1961, 1962, 1963, 1965). ... All-NBA first team (1959, 1963, 1965). ... All-NBA second team (1958, 1960, 1961, 1962, 1964, 1966, 1967, 1968). ... NBA All-Defensive first team (1969).

Season Team	G	Min.	FGM	FGA	Pct.	FTM	FTA	Pct.	Reb.	Ast.	PF	Dq.	Pts.	AVERAGES		
														RPG	APG	PPG
56-57—Boston	48	1695	277	649	.427	152	309	.492	943	88	143	2	706	*19.6	1.8	14.7
57-58—Boston	69	2640	456	1032	.442	230	443	.519	*1564	202	181	2	1142	*22.7	2.9	16.6
58-59—Boston	70	*2979	456	997	.457	256	428	.598	*1612	222	161	3	1168	*23.0	3.2	16.7
59-60—Boston	74	3146	555	1189	.467	240	392	.612	1778	277	210	0	1350	24.0	3.7	18.2
60-61—Boston	78	3458	532	1250	.426	258	469	.550	1868	268	155	0	1322	23.9	3.4	16.9
61-62—Boston	76	3433	575	1258	.457	286	481	.595	1790	341	207	3	1436	23.6	4.5	18.9
62-63—Boston	78	3500	511	1182	.432	287	517	.555	1843	348	189	1	1309	23.6	4.5	16.8
63-64—Boston	78	3482	466	1077	.433	236	429	.550	*1930	370	190	0	1168	*24.7	4.7	15.0
64-65—Boston	78	*3466	429	980	.438	244	426	.573	*1878	410	204	1	1102	*24.1	5.3	14.1
65-66—Boston	78	3386	391	943	.415	223	405	.551	1779	371	221	4	1005	22.8	4.8	12.9
66-67—Boston	81	3297	395	870	.454	285	467	.610	1700	472	258	4	1075	21.0	5.8	13.3
67-68—Boston	78	2953	365	858	.425	247	460	.537	1451	357	242	2	977	18.6	4.6	12.5
68-69—Boston	77	3291	279	645	.433	204	388	.526	1484	374	231	2	762	19.3	4.9	9.9
Totals	963	40726	5687	12930	.440	3148	5614	.561	21620	4100	2592	24	14522	22.5	4.3	15.1

NBA PLAYOFF RECORD

NOTES: Holds career playoff record for most rebounds—4,104. ... Holds NBA Finals records for highest rebounds-per-game average—29.5 (1959); and highest rebounds-per-game average for a rookie—22.9 (1957) ... Shares NBA Finals single-game records for most rebounds—40 (March 29, 1960, vs. St. Louis and April 18, 1962, vs. Los Angeles); most rebounds by a rookie—32 (April 13, 1957, vs. St. Louis); and most rebounds in one quarter—19 (April 18, 1962, vs. Los Angeles).

Season Team	G	Min.	FGM	FGA	Pct.	FTM	FTA	Pct.	Reb.	Ast.	PF	Dq.	Pts.	AVERAGES		
														RPG	APG	PPG
56-57—Boston	10	409	54	148	.365	31	61	.508	244	32	41	1	139	24.4	3.2	13.9
57-58—Boston	9	355	48	133	.361	40	66	.606	221	24	24	0	136	24.6	2.7	15.1
58-59—Boston	11	496	65	159	.409	41	67	.612	305	40	28	1	171	27.7	3.6	15.5
59-60—Boston	13	572	94	206	.456	53	75	.707	336	38	38	1	241	25.8	2.9	18.5
60-61—Boston	10	462	73	171	.427	45	86	.523	299	48	24	0	191	29.9	4.8	19.1
61-62—Boston	14	672	116	253	.459	82	113	.726	370	70	49	0	314	26.4	5.0	22.4
62-63—Boston	13	617	96	212	.453	72	109	.661	326	66	36	0	264	25.1	5.1	20.3
63-64—Boston	10	451	47	132	.356	37	67	.552	272	44	33	0	131	27.2	4.4	13.1
64-65—Boston	12	561	79	150	.527	40	76	.526	302	76	43	2	198	25.2	6.3	16.5
65-66—Boston	17	814	124	261	.475	76	100	.010	428	83	00	0	324	18.1	4.9	19.1
66-67—Boston	9	390	31	86	.360	33	52	.635	198	50	32	1	95	22.0	5.6	10.6
67-68—Boston	19	869	99	242	.409	76	130	.585	434	99	73	1	274	22.8	5.2	14.4
68-69—Boston	18	829	77	182	.423	41	81	.506	369	98	65	1	195	20.5	5.4	10.8
Totals	165	7497	1003	2335	.430	667	1106	.603	4104	770	546	8	2673	24.9	4.7	16.2

NBA ALL-STAR GAME RECORD

NOTES: NBA All-Star Game Most Valuable Player (1963).

Season Team	Min.	FGM	FGA	Pct.	FTM	FTA	Pct.	Reb	Ast.	PF	Dq.	Pts.
1958—Boston	26	5	12	.417	1	3	.333	11	2	5	0	11
1959—Boston	27	3	10	.300	1	1	1.000	9	1	4	0	7
1960—Boston	27	3	7	.429	0	2	.000	8	3	1	0	6
1961—Boston	28	9	15	.600	6	8	.750	11	1	2	0	24
1962—Boston	27	5	12	.417	2	3	.667	12	2	2	0	12
1963—Boston	37	8	14	.571	3	4	.750	24	5	3	0	19
1964—Boston	42	6	13	.462	1	2	.500	21	2	4	0	13
1965—Boston	33	7	12	.583	3	9	.333	13	5	6	1	17
1966—Boston	23	1	6	.167	0	0	...	10	2	2	0	2
1967—Boston	22	1	2	.500	0	0	...	5	5	2	0	2
1968—Boston	23	2	4	.500	0	0	...	9	8	5	0	4
1969—Boston	28	1	4	.250	1	2	.500	6	3	1	0	3
Totals	343	51	111	.459	18	34	.529	139	39	37	1	120

NBA COACHING RECORD

BACKGROUND: Player/head coach, Boston Celtics (1966-67 through 1968-69). ... Head coach/general manager, Seattle Supersonics (1973-74 through 1976-77).

Season Team	REGULAR SEASON				PLAYOFFS		
	W	L	Pct.	Finish	W	L	Pct.
66-67—Boston	60	21	.741	2nd/Eastern Division	4	5	.444
67-68—Boston	54	28	.659	2nd/Eastern Division	12	7	.632
68-69—Boston	48	34	.585	4th/Eastern Division	12	6	.667
73-74—Seattle	36	46	.439	3rd/Pacific Division	—	—	—
74-75—Seattle	43	39	.524	2nd/Pacific Division	4	5	.444
75-76—Seattle	43	39	.524	2nd/Pacific Division	2	4	.333
76-77—Seattle	40	42	.488	4th/Pacific Division	—	—	—
87-88—Sacramento	17	41	.293		—	—	—
Totals (8 years)	341	290	.540	Totals (5 years)	34	27	.557

NOTES:

1967—Defeated New York, 3-1, in Eastern Division Semifinals; lost to Philadelphia, 4-1, in Eastern Division Finals.
1968—Defeated Detroit, 4-2, in Eastern Division Semifinals; defeated Philadelphia, 4-3, in Eastern Division Finals; defeated Los Angeles, 4-2, in NBA Finals.
1969—Defeated Philadelphia, 4-1, in Eastern Division Semifinals; defeated New York, 4-2, in Eastern Division Finals; defeated Los Angeles, 4-3, in NBA Finals.
1975—Defeated Detroit, 2-1, in Western Conference First Round; lost to Golden State, 4-2, in Western Conference Semifinals.
1976—Lost to Phoenix in Western Conference Semifinals.
1988—Replaced as Sacramento head coach by Jerry Reynolds (March 7).

SCHAYES, DOLPH   F/C

PERSONAL: Born May 19, 1928, in New York. ... 6-8/220 (2,03/99,8). ... Full name: Adolph Schayes. ... Father of Dan Schayes, center with seven NBA teams (1981-82 through 1998-99).
HIGH SCHOOL: DeWitt Clinton (Bronx, N.Y.).
COLLEGE: New York University.
TRANSACTIONS: Selected by Tri-Cities Hawks in 1948 National Basketball League Draft. ... NBL draft rights obtained from Hawks by Syracuse Nationals (1948). ... Nationals franchise became part of NBA for 1949-50 season. ... Nationals franchise moved from Syracuse to Philadelphia and renamed 76ers for 1963-64 season.
CAREER HONORS: Elected to Naismith Memorial Basketball Hall of Fame (1973). ... NBA 25th Anniversary All-Time Team (1970) and One of the 50 Greatest Players in NBA History (1996)
MISCELLANEOUS: Member of NBA championship team (1955). ... Philadelphia 76ers franchise all-time leading rebounder with 11,256 (1948-49 through 1963-64).

COLLEGIATE RECORD

Season Team	G	Min.	FGM	FGA	Pct.	FTM	FTA	Pct.	Reb.	Ast.	Pts.	RPG	APG	PPG
44-45—New York U.	11	...	46	...	...	23	...	...	...	...	115	...	...	10.5
45-46—New York U.	22	...	54	...	...	41	...	...	...	...	149	...	...	6.8
46-47—New York U.	21	...	66	...	...	63	...	...	...	...	195	...	...	9.3
47-48—New York U.	26	...	124	...	...	108	...	...	...	...	356	...	...	13.7
Totals	80	...	290	...	...	235	...	...	...	...	815	...	...	10.2

NBL AND NBA REGULAR-SEASON RECORD

HONORS: All-NBA first team (1952, 1953, 1954, 1955, 1957, 1958). ... All-NBA second team (1950, 1951, 1956, 1959, 1960, 1961). ... NBL Rookie of the Year (1949).

Season Team	G	Min.	FGM	FGA	Pct.	FTM	FTA	Pct.	Reb.	Ast.	PF	Dq.	Pts.	RPG	APG	PPG
48-49—Syr. (NBL)	63	...	271	...	...	267	370	.722	...	...	232	...	809	...	...	12.8
49-50—Syracuse	64	...	348	903	.385	376	486	.774	...	259	225	...	1072	...	4.0	16.8
50-51—Syracuse	66	...	332	930	.357	457	608	.752	*1080	251	271	9	1121	*16.4	3.8	17.0
51-52—Syracuse	63	2004	263	740	.355	342	424	.807	773	182	213	5	868	12.3	2.9	13.8
52-53—Syracuse	71	2668	375	1002	.374	512	619	.827	920	227	271	9	1262	13.0	3.2	17.8
53-54—Syracuse	72	2655	370	973	.380	488	590	.827	870	214	232	4	1228	12.1	3.0	17.1
54-55—Syracuse	72	2526	422	1103	.383	489	587	.833	887	213	247	6	1333	12.3	3.0	18.5
55-56—Syracuse	72	2517	465	1202	.387	542	632	.858	891	200	251	9	1472	12.4	2.8	20.4
56-57—Syracuse	72	*2851	496	1308	.379	*625	691	.904	1008	229	219	5	1617	14.0	3.2	22.5
57-58—Syracuse	72	*2918	581	1458	.399	629	696	*.904	1022	224	244	6	1791	14.2	3.1	24.9
58-59—Syracuse	72	2645	504	1304	.387	526	609	.864	962	178	280	9	1534	13.4	2.5	21.3
59-60—Syracuse	75	2741	578	1440	.401	533	597	*.893	959	256	263	10	1689	12.8	3.4	22.5
60-61—Syracuse	79	3007	594	1595	.372	*680	783	.868	960	296	296	9	1868	12.2	3.7	23.6
61-62—Syracuse	56	1480	268	751	.357	286	319	*.897	439	120	167	4	822	7.8	2.1	14.7
62-63—Syracuse	66	1438	223	575	.388	181	206	.879	375	175	177	2	627	5.7	2.7	9.5
63-64—Philadelphia	24	350	44	143	.308	46	57	.807	110	48	76	3	134	4.6	2.0	5.6
Totals	1059	...	6134	...	...	6979	8274	.843	...	...	3664	...	19247	...	...	18.2

NBL AND NBA PLAYOFF RECORD

Season Team	G	Min.	FGM	FGA	Pct.	FTM	FTA	Pct.	Reb.	Ast.	PF	Dq.	Pts.	RPG	APG	PPG
48-49—Syr. (NBL)	6	...	27	...	...	32	42	.762	...	...	26	...	86	...	...	14.3
49-50—Syracuse	11	...	57	148	.385	74	101	.733	...	28	43	...	188	...	2.5	17.1
50-51—Syracuse	7	...	47	105	.448	49	64	.766	102	20	28	2	143	14.6	2.9	20.4
51-52—Syracuse	7	248	41	91	.451	60	78	.769	90	15	34	2	142	12.9	2.1	20.3
52-53—Syracuse	2	58	4	16	.250	10	13	.769	17	1	7	0	18	8.5	0.5	9.0
53-54—Syracuse	13	374	64	140	.457	80	108	.741	136	24	40	1	208	10.5	1.8	16.0
54-55—Syracuse	11	363	60	167	.359	89	106	.840	141	40	48	3	209	12.8	3.6	19.0
55-56—Syracuse	8	310	52	142	.366	73	83	.880	111	27	27	0	177	13.9	3.4	22.1
56-57—Syracuse	5	215	29	95	.305	49	55	.891	90	14	18	0	107	18.0	2.8	21.4
57-58—Syracuse	3	131	25	64	.391	30	36	.833	45	6	10	0	80	15.0	2.0	26.7
58-59—Syracuse	9	351	78	195	.400	98	107	.916	117	41	36	0	254	13.0	4.6	28.2
59-60—Syracuse	3	126	30	66	.455	28	30	.933	48	8	10	0	88	16.0	2.7	29.3
60-61—Syracuse	8	308	51	152	.336	63	70	.900	91	21	32	2	165	11.4	2.6	20.6
61-62—Syracuse	5	95	24	66	.364	9	13	.692	35	5	21	0	57	7.0	1.0	11.4
62-63—Syracuse	5	108	20	44	.455	11	12	.917	28	7	17	0	51	5.6	1.4	10.2
Totals	103	...	609	...	...	755	918	.822	...	...	397	...	1973	...	...	19.2

NBA ALL-STAR GAME RECORD

Season Team	Min.	FGM	FGA	Pct.	FTM	FTA	Pct.	Reb	Ast.	PF	Dq.	Pts.
1951—Syracuse	...	7	10	.700	1	2	.500	14	3	1	0	15
1952—Syracuse					Selected, did not play—injured.							
1953—Syracuse	26	2	7	.286	4	4	1.000	13	3	3	0	8

ALL-TIME GREAT PLAYERS

Season Team	Min.	FGM	FGA	Pct.	FTM	FTA	Pct.	Reb	Ast.	PF	Dq.	Pts.
1954—Syracuse	24	1	3	.333	4	6	.667	12	1	1	0	6
1955—Syracuse	29	6	12	.500	3	3	1.000	13	1	4	0	15
1956—Syracuse	25	4	8	.500	6	10	.600	4	2	2	0	14
1957—Syracuse	25	4	6	.667	1	1	1.000	10	1	1	0	9
1958—Syracuse	39	6	15	.400	6	6	1.000	9	2	4	0	18
1959—Syracuse	22	3	14	.214	7	8	.875	13	1	6	1	13
1960—Syracuse	27	8	19	.421	3	3	1.000	10	0	3	0	19
1961—Syracuse	27	7	15	.467	7	7	1.000	6	3	4	0	21
1962—Syracuse	4	0	0	...	0	0	...	1	0	3	0	0
Totals	...	48	109	.440	42	50	.840	105	17	32	1	138

NBA COACHING RECORD

BACKGROUND: Player/head coach, Philadelphia 76ers (1963-64).
HONORS: NBA Coach of the Year (1966).

Season Team	REGULAR SEASON				PLAYOFFS		
	W	L	Pct.	Finish	W	L	Pct.
63-64—Philadelphia	34	46	.425	3rd/Eastern Division	2	3	.400
64-65—Philadelphia	40	40	.500	3rd/Eastern Division	6	5	.545
65-66—Philadelphia	55	25	.688	1st/Eastern Division	1	4	.200
70-71—Buffalo	22	60	.268	4th/Atlantic Division	—	—	—
71-72—Buffalo	0	1	.000		—	—	—
Totals (5 years)	151	172	.467	Totals (3 years)	9	12	.429

NOTES:
1964—Lost to Cincinnati in Eastern Division Semifinals.
1965—Defeated Cincinnati, 3-1, in Eastern Division Semifinals; lost to Boston, 4-3, in Eastern Division Finals.
1966—Lost to Boston in Eastern Division Finals.
1971—Replaced as Buffalo head coach by John McCarthy (October).

SHARMAN, BILL G

PERSONAL: Born May 25, 1926, in Abilene, Texas. ... 6-1/190 (1,85/86). ... Full name: William Walton Sharman.
HIGH SCHOOL: Narbonne (Lomita, Calif.), then Porterville (Calif.).
COLLEGE: Southern California.
TRANSACTIONS: Selected by Washington Capitols in second round of 1950 NBA Draft. ... Selected by Fort Wayne Pistons in 1951 NBA Dispersal Draft of Capitols franchise (did not report to Fort Wayne). ... Traded by Pistons with F Bob Brannum to Boston Celtics for NBA rights to C Charlie Share (1951). ... Signed as player/head coach by Los Angeles Jets of American Basketball League (1961).
CAREER HONORS: Elected to Naismith Memorial Basketball Hall of Fame as a player (1976) and a head coach (2004). ... NBA 25th Anniversary All-Time Team (1970) and One of the 50 Greatest Players in NBA History (1996).
CAREER NOTES: General manager, Los Angeles Lakers (1975-76 through 1981-82). ... President, Lakers (1982-83 through 1989-90). ... Consultant, Lakers (1990-91 to present).
MISCELLANEOUS: Member of NBA championship team (1957, 1959, 1960, 1961).

COLLEGIATE RECORD

NOTES: The Sporting News All-America first team (1950). ... The Sporting News All-America third team (1949). ... In military service during 1944-45 and 1945-46 seasons.

Season Team	G	Min.	FGM	FGA	Pct.	FTM	FTA	Pct.	Reb.	Ast.	Pts.	AVERAGES		
												RPG	APG	PPG
46-47—Southern Cal	10	...	16	...	...	9	12	.750	...	...	41	...	...	4.1
47-48—Southern Cal	24	...	100	...	...	38	44	.864	...	...	238	...	...	9.9
48-49—Southern Cal	24	...	142	...	...	98	125	.784	...	...	382	...	...	15.9
49-50—Southern Cal	24	...	171	421	.406	104	129	.806	...	...	446	...	...	18.6
Totals	82	...	429	...	...	249	310	.803	...	...	1107	...	...	13.5

NBA REGULAR-SEASON RECORD

HONORS: All-NBA first team (1956, 1957, 1958, 1959). ... All-NBA second team (1953, 1955, 1960).

Season Team	G	Min.	FGM	FGA	Pct.	FTM	FTA	Pct.	Reb.	Ast.	PF	Dq.	Pts.	AVERAGES		
														RPG	APG	PPG
50-51—Washington	31	...	141	361	.391	96	108	.889	96	39	86	3	378	3.1	1.3	12.2
51-52—Boston	63	1389	244	628	.389	183	213	.859	221	151	181	3	671	3.5	2.4	10.7
52-53—Boston	71	2333	403	925	.436	341	401	*.850	288	191	240	7	1147	4.1	2.7	16.2
53-54—Boston	72	2467	412	915	.450	331	392	*.844	255	229	211	4	1155	3.5	3.2	16.0
54-55—Boston	68	2453	453	1062	.427	347	387	*.897	302	280	212	2	1253	4.4	4.1	18.4
55-56—Boston	72	2698	538	1229	.438	358	413	*.867	259	339	197	1	1434	3.6	4.7	19.9
56-57—Boston	67	2403	516	1241	.416	381	421	*.905	286	236	188	1	1413	4.3	3.5	21.1
57-58—Boston	63	2214	550	1297	.424	347	387	.894	295	167	156	3	1402	4.7	2.7	22.3
58-59—Boston	72	2382	562	1377	.408	342	367	*.932	292	179	173	1	1466	4.1	2.5	20.4
59-60—Boston	71	1916	559	1225	.456	252	291	.866	262	144	154	2	1370	3.7	2.0	19.3
60-61—Boston	61	1538	383	908	.422	210	228	*.921	223	146	127	0	976	3.7	2.4	16.0
Totals	711	...	4761	11168	.426	3143	3559	.883	2779	2101	1925	27	12665	3.9	3.0	17.8

NBA PLAYOFF RECORD

Season Team	G	Min.	FGM	FGA	Pct.	FTM	FTA	Pct.	Reb.	Ast.	PF	Dq.	Pts.	AVERAGES		
														RPG	APG	PPG
51-52—Boston	1	27	7	12	.583	1	1	1.000	3	7	4	0	15	3.0	7.0	15.0
52-53—Boston	6	201	20	60	.333	30	32	.938	15	15	26	1	70	2.5	2.5	11.7
53-54—Boston	6	206	35	81	.432	43	50	.860	25	10	29	2	113	4.2	1.7	18.8
54-55—Boston	7	290	55	110	.500	35	38	.921	38	38	24	1	145	5.4	5.4	20.7

Season Team	G	Min.	FGM	FGA	Pct.	FTM	FTA	Pct.	Reb.	Ast.	PF	Dq.	Pts.	AVERAGES RPG	APG	PPG
55-56—Boston	3	119	18	46	.391	16	17	.941	7	12	7	0	52	2.3	4.0	17.3
56-57—Boston	10	377	75	197	.381	61	64	.953	35	29	23	1	211	3.5	2.9	21.1
57-58—Boston	11	406	90	221	.407	52	56	.929	54	25	28	0	232	4.9	2.3	21.1
58-59—Boston	11	322	82	193	.425	57	59	.966	36	28	35	0	221	3.3	2.5	20.1
59-60—Boston	13	364	88	209	.421	43	53	.811	45	20	22	1	219	3.5	1.5	16.8
60-61—Boston	10	261	68	133	.511	32	36	.889	27	17	22	0	168	2.7	1.7	16.8
Totals	78	2573	538	1262	.426	370	406	.911	285	201	220	6	1446	3.7	2.6	18.5

NBA ALL-STAR GAME RECORD

NOTES: NBA All-Star Game Most Valuable Player (1955). ... Holds single-game record for most field goals attempted in one quarter—12 (1960).

Season Team	Min.	FGM	FGA	Pct.	FTM	FTA	Pct.	Reb	Ast.	PF	Dq.	Pts.
1953—Boston	26	5	8	.625	1	1	1.000	4	0	2	0	11
1954—Boston	30	6	9	.667	2	4	.500	2	3	3	0	14
1955—Boston	18	5	10	.500	5	5	1.000	4	2	4	0	15
1956—Boston	22	2	8	.250	3	5	.600	3	1	2	1	7
1957—Boston	23	5	17	.294	2	2	1.000	6	5	1	0	12
1958—Boston	25	6	19	.316	3	3	1.000	4	3	2	0	15
1959—Boston	24	3	12	.250	5	6	.833	2	0	1	0	11
1960—Boston	26	8	21	.381	1	1	1.000	6	2	1	0	17
Totals	194	40	104	.385	22	27	.815	31	16	16	1	102

ABL REGULAR-SEASON RECORD

Season Team	G	Min.	FGM	FGA	Pct.	FTM	FTA	Pct.	Reb.	Ast.	Pts.	AVERAGES RPG	APG	PPG
61-62—Los Angeles	19	346	35	80	.438	37	34	1.088	43	37	107	2.3	1.9	5.6

HEAD COACHING RECORD

BACKGROUND: Player/head coach, Los Angeles Jets of American Basketball League (1961-62). ... Assistant coach, New Orleans Jazz (1974-75 and 1975-76).

HONORS: NBA Coach of the Year (1972). ... ABA co-Coach of the Year (1970).

COLLEGIATE COACHING RECORD

Season Team	W	L	Pct.	Finish
62-63—Cal State-Los Angeles	10	12	.455	4th/California Collegiate Athletic Association
63-64—Cal State-Los Angeles	17	8	.680	2nd/California Collegiate Athletic Association
Totals (2 years)	27	20	.574	

ABL COACHING RECORD

Season Team	REGULAR SEASON W	L	Pct.	Finish	PLAYOFFS W	L	Pct.
61-62—Los Angeles-Cleveland	43	26	.623		5	2	.714

NBA COACHING RECORD

Season Team	REGULAR SEASON W	L	Pct.	Finish	PLAYOFFS W	L	Pct.
66-67—San Francisco	44	37	.543	1st/Western Division	9	6	.600
67-68—San Francisco	43	39	.524	3rd/Western Division	4	6	.400
71-72—Los Angeles	69	13	.841	1st/Pacific Division	12	3	.800
72-73—Los Angeles	60	22	.732	1st/Pacific Division	9	8	.529
73-74—Los Angeles	47	35	.573	1st/Pacific Division	1	4	.200
74-75—Los Angeles	30	52	.366	5th/Pacific Division	—	—	—
75-76—Los Angeles	40	42	.488	4th/Pacific Division	—	—	—
Totals (7 years)	333	240	.581	Totals (5 years)	35	27	.565

ABA COACHING RECORD

Season Team	REGULAR SEASON W	L	Pct.	Finish	PLAYOFFS W	L	Pct.
68-69—Los Angeles	33	45	.423	5th/Western Division	—	—	—
69-70—Los Angeles	43	41	.512	4th/Western Division	10	7	.588
70-71—Utah	57	27	.679	2nd/Western Division	12	6	.667
Totals (3 years)	133	113	.541	Totals (2 years)	22	13	.629

NOTES:

1962—Los Angeles Jets had 24-15 record when they folded after first half of season (January 10); Sharman then replaced John McLendon, who resigned as Cleveland Pipers head coach (January 28), and guided Pipers to ABL Championship.

1967—Defeated Los Angeles, 3-0, in Western Division Semifinals; defeated St. Louis, 4-2, in Western Division Finals; lost to Philadelphia, 4-2, in World Championship Series.

1968—Defeated St. Louis, 4-2, in Western Division Semifinals; lost to Los Angeles, 4-0, in Western Division Finals.

1970—Defeated Dallas, 4-2, in Western Division Semifinals; defeated Denver, 4-1, in Western Division Finals; lost to Indiana, 4-2, in ABA Finals.

1971—Defeated Texas, 4-0, in Western Division Semifinals; defeated Indiana, 4-3, in Western Division Finals; defeated Kentucky, 4-3, in ABA Finals.

1972—Defeated Chicago, 4-0, in Western Conference Semifinals; defeated Milwaukee, 4-2, in Western Conference Finals; defeated New York, 4-1, in World Championship Series.

1973—Defeated Chicago, 4-3, in Western Conference Semifinals; defeated Golden State, 4-1, in Western Conference Finals; lost to New York, 4-1, in World Championship Series.

1974—Lost to Milwaukee in Western Conference First Round.

RECORD AS BASEBALL PLAYER

Year Team (League)	Pos.	G	BATTING AB	R	H	2B	3B	HR	RBI	Avg.	BB	SO	SB	FIELDING PO	A	E	Avg.
1950—Elmira (Eastern)	OF	10	38	5	11	2	0	1	11	.289	0	5	0	17	0	1	.944
—Pueblo (Western)	OF	111	427	65	123	22	8	11	70	.288	42	47	11	214	16	10	.958

Year	Team (League)	Pos.	G	AB	R	H	2B	3B	HR	RBI	Avg.	BB	SO	SB	PO	A	E	Avg.
							BATTING									FIELDING		
1951—Fort Worth (Texas).....		OF	157	570	84	163	18	5	8	53	.286	57	44	23	254	11	2	.993
1952—St. Paul (A.A.)..........		OF	137	411	63	121	16	4	16	77	.294	29	32	2	215	15	3	.987
1953—Mobile (South.)		OF	90	228	21	48	8	1	5	17	.211	30	26	0	136	6	2	.986
1954—								Out of organized baseball.										
1955—St. Paul (A.A.)..........		OF-3B	133	424	59	124	15	0	11	58	.292	34	33	3	183	100	11	.963

SIKMA, JACK   C/F

PERSONAL: Born November 14, 1955, in Kankakee, Ill. ... 7-0/250 (2,13/113,4). ... Full name: Jack Wayne Sikma.
HIGH SCHOOL: St. Anne (Ill.).
COLLEGE: Illinois Wesleyan.
TRANSACTIONS: Selected by Seattle SuperSonics in first round (eighth pick overall) of 1977 NBA Draft. ... Traded by SuperSonics with 1987 and 1989 second-round draft choices to Milwaukee Bucks for C Alton Lister and 1987 and 1989 first-round draft choices (July 1, 1986).
MISCELLANEOUS: Member of NBA championship team (1979). ... Seattle SuperSonics all-time leading rebounder with 7,729 (1977-78 through 1985-86).

COLLEGIATE RECORD

Season Team	G	Min.	FGM	FGA	Pct.	FTM	FTA	Pct.	Reb.	Ast.	Pts.	RPG	APG	PPG
													AVERAGES	
73-74—Illinois Wesleyan	21	...	148	306	.484	28	37	.757	223	...	324	10.6	...	15.4
74-75—Illinois Wesleyan	30	...	265	537	.493	80	112	.714	415	...	610	13.8	...	20.3
75-76—Illinois Wesleyan	25	...	204	385	.530	93	126	.738	290	...	501	11.6	...	20.0
76-77—Illinois Wesleyan	31	...	302	324	.932	189	235	.804	477	...	837	15.4	...	27.0
Totals	107	...	919	1552	.592	390	510	.765	1405	...	2272	13.1	...	21.2

NBA REGULAR-SEASON RECORD

HONORS: NBA All-Defensive second team (1982). ... NBA All-Rookie team (1978).
NOTES: Tied for NBA lead with 11 disqualifications (1988).

Season Team	G	Min.	FGM	FGA	Pct.	FTM	FTA	Pct.	Off.	Def.	Tot.	Ast.	St.	Blk.	TO	Pts.	RPG	APG	PPG
										REBOUNDS								AVERAGES	
77-78—Seattle	82	2238	342	752	.455	192	247	.777	196	482	678	134	68	40	186	876	8.3	1.6	10.7
78-79—Seattle	82	2958	476	1034	.460	329	404	.814	232	781	1013	261	82	67	253	1281	12.4	3.2	15.6
79-80—Seattle	82	2793	470	989	.475	235	292	.805	198	710	908	279	68	77	202	1175	11.1	3.4	14.3
80-81—Seattle	82	2920	595	1311	.454	340	413	.823	184	668	852	248	78	93	201	1530	10.4	3.0	18.7
81-82—Seattle	82	3049	581	1212	.479	447	523	.855	223	*815	1038	277	102	107	213	1611	12.7	3.4	19.6
82-83—Seattle	75	2564	484	1043	.464	400	478	.837	213	645	858	233	87	65	190	1368	11.4	3.1	18.2
83-84—Seattle	82	2993	576	1155	.499	411	480	.856	225	*686	911	327	95	92	236	1563	11.1	4.0	19.1
84-85—Seattle	68	2402	461	943	.489	335	393	.852	164	559	723	285	83	91	160	1259	10.6	4.2	18.5
85-86—Seattle	80	2790	508	1100	.462	355	411	.864	146	602	748	301	92	73	214	1371	9.4	3.8	17.1
86-87—Milwaukee	82	2536	390	842	.463	265	313	.847	208	614	822	203	88	90	160	1045	10.0	2.5	12.7
87-88—Milwaukee	82	2923	514	1058	.486	321	348	*.922	195	514	709	279	93	80	157	1352	8.6	3.4	16.5
88-89—Milwaukee	80	2507	389	885	.431	190	161	.811	118	512	611	200	65	91	175	1089	7.6	3.6	13.4
89-90—Milwaukee	71	2250	344	827	.416	230	260	.885	109	383	492	229	76	48	139	986	6.9	3.2	13.9
90-91—Milwaukee	77	1940	295	691	.427	166	197	.843	100	333	441	143	65	64	130	802	5.7	1.9	10.4
Totals	1107	36943	6396	13792	.464	4292	5053	.849	2542	8274	10816	3488	1162	1048	2586	17287	9.8	3.2	15.6

Three-point field goals: 1979-80, 0-for-1. 1980-81, 0-for-5. 1981-82, 2-for-13 (.154). 1982-83, 0-for-8. 1983-84, 0-for-2. 1984-85, 2-for-10 (.200). 1985-86, 0-for-13. 1986-87, 0-for-2. 1987-88, 3-for-14 (.214). 1988-89, 82-for-216 (.380). 1989-90, 68-for-199 (.342). 1990-91, 46-for-135 (.341). Totals, 203-for-618 (.328).
Personal fouls/disqualifications: 1977-78, 300/6. 1978-79, 295/4. 1979-80, 232/5. 1980-81, 282/5. 1981-82, 268/5. 1982-83, 263/4. 1983-84, 301/6. 1984-85, 239/1. 1985-86, 293/4. 1986-87, 328/14. 1987-88, 316/11. 1988-89, 300/6. 1989-90, 244/5. 1990-91, 218/4. Totals, 3879/80.

NBA PLAYOFF RECORD

Season Team	G	Min.	FGM	FGA	Pct.	FTM	FTA	Pct.	Off.	Def.	Tot.	Ast.	St.	Blk.	TO	Pts.	RPG	APG	PPG
										REBOUNDS								AVERAGES	
77-78—Seattle	22	701	115	247	.466	71	91	.780	50	128	178	27	18	11	35	301	8.1	1.2	13.7
78-79—Seattle	17	655	102	224	.455	48	61	.787	39	160	199	43	16	24	40	252	11.7	2.5	14.8
79-80—Seattle	15	534	65	163	.399	46	54	.852	30	96	126	55	17	5	35	176	8.4	3.7	11.7
81-82—Seattle	8	315	57	128	.445	50	58	.862	21	76	97	24	9	8	16	164	12.1	3.0	20.5
82-83—Seattle	2	75	11	31	.355	8	12	.667	6	20	26	11	2	2	5	30	13.0	5.5	15.0
83-84—Seattle	5	193	49	98	.500	12	14	.857	11	40	51	5	3	7	9	110	10.2	1.0	22.0
86-87—Milwaukee	12	426	73	150	.487	48	49	.980	33	97	130	23	15	10	18	194	10.8	1.9	16.2
87-88—Milwaukee	5	190	35	76	.461	25	30	.833	24	38	62	13	2	4	15	95	12.4	2.6	19.0
88-89—Milwaukee	9	301	37	94	.394	23	28	*.821	9	41	50	30	8	4	21	105	5.6	3.3	11.7
89-90—Milwaukee	4	117	6	23	.261	6	8	.750	0	14	14	7	2	4	12	20	3.5	1.8	5.0
90-91—Milwaukee	3	51	6	15	.400	1	2	.500	3	9	12	6	5	1	31	14	4.0	2.0	4.7
Totals	102	3558	556	1249	.445	338	407	.830	226	719	945	244	97	80	237	1461	9.3	2.4	14.3

Three-point field goals: 1979-80, 0-for-2. 1982-83, 0-for-1. 1983-84, 0-for-1. 1986-87, 0-for-1. 1987-88, 0-for-3. 1988-89, 8-for-28 (.286). 1989-90, 2-for-7 (.286). 1990-91, 1-for-2 (.500). Totals, 11-for-45 (.244).
Personal fouls/disqualifications: 1977-78, 101/7. 1978-79, 70/2. 1979-80, 55/1. 1981-82, 34/1. 1982-83, 7/0. 1983-84, 22/1. 1986-87, 56/3. 1987-88, 23/0. 1988-89, 41/2. 1989-90, 19/0. 1990-91, 4/0. Totals, 432/17.

NBA ALL-STAR GAME RECORD

Season Team	Min.	FGM	FGA	Pct.	FTM	FTA	Pct.	Off.	Def.	Tot.	Ast.	PF	Dq.	St.	Blk.	TO	Pts.
									REBOUNDS								
1979—Seattle	18	4	5	.800	0	0	...	1	3	4	0	1	0	0	0	0	8
1980—Seattle	28	4	10	.400	0	0	...	2	6	8	4	5	0	2	3	3	8
1981—Seattle	21	2	5	.400	2	2	1.000	1	3	4	4	5	0	1	1	1	6
1982—Seattle	21	5	11	.455	0	0	...	2	7	9	1	2	0	2	1	1	10
1983—Seattle	17	4	6	.667	0	0	...	1	2	3	1	2	0	1	1	1	5

Season Team	Min.	FGM	FGA	Pct.	FTM	FTA	Pct.	REBOUNDS Off.	Def.	Tot.	Ast.	PF	Dq.	St.	Blk.	TO	Pts.
1984—Seattle	30	5	12	.417	5	6	.833	5	7	12	1	4	0	3	0	0	15
1985—Seattle	12	0	2	.000	0	0	...	0	2	2	0	1	0	0	1	1	0
Totals	147	24	51	.471	7	8	.875	12	30	42	11	20	0	9	7	7	52

Three-point field goals: 1980, 0-for-1. 1981, 0-for-1. Totals, 0-for-2.

SILAS, PAUL F/C

PERSONAL: Born July 12, 1943, in Prescott, Ark. ... 6-7/230. (2,00/104,3). ... Full name: Paul Theron Silas.
HIGH SCHOOL: McClymonds (Oakland, Calif.).
COLLEGE: Creighton.
TRANSACTIONS: Selected by St. Louis Hawks in second round (12th pick overall) of 1964 NBA Draft. ... Played in Eastern Basketball League with Wilkes-Barre Barons (1965-66). ... Hawks franchise moved from St. Louis to Atlanta for 1968-69 season. ... Traded by Hawks to Phoenix Suns for F Gary Gregor (May 8, 1969). ... Traded by Suns to Boston Celtics (September 19, 1972) to complete deal in which Suns acquired draft rights to G Charlie Scott (March 14, 1972). ... Traded by Celtics to Denver Nuggets in three-way deal, in which F Curtis Rowe was traded by Detroit Pistons to Celtics, and G Ralph Simpson was traded by Nuggets to Pistons (October 20, 1976). ... Traded by Nuggets with F Willie Wise and C Marvin Webster to Seattle SuperSonics for C Tom Burleson, G/F Bob Wilkerson and 1977 second-round draft choice (May 24, 1977). ... Signed as veteran free agent by San Diego Clippers (May 21, 1980); SuperSonics received 1985 second-round draft choice as compensation.
MISCELLANEOUS: Member of NBA championship team (1974, 1976, 1979).

COLLEGIATE RECORD

NOTES: Led NCAA Division I with 20.6 rebounds per game (1963). ... Holds NCAA record for most rebounds in three-year career—1,751.

Season Team	G	Min.	FGM	FGA	Pct.	FTM	FTA	Pct.	Reb.	Ast.	Pts.	AVERAGES RPG	APG	PPG
60-61—Creighton‡	21	...	225	...	...	96	119	.807	568	...	546	27.0	...	26.0
61-62—Creighton	25	...	213	524	.406	125	215	.581	563	...	551	22.5	...	22.0
62-63—Creighton	27	...	220	531	.414	133	228	.583	557	...	573	20.6	...	21.2
63-64—Creighton	29	...	210	529	.397	117	194	.603	631	...	537	21.8	...	18.5
Varsity totals	81	...	643	1584	.406	375	637	.589	1751	...	1661	21.6	...	20.5

NBA REGULAR-SEASON RECORD

HONORS: NBA All-Defensive first team (1975, 1976). ... NBA All-Defensive second team (1971, 1972, 1973).

Season Team	G	Min.	FGM	FGA	Pct.	FTM	FTA	Pct.	Reb.	Ast.	PF	Dq.	Pts.	AVERAGES RPG	APG	PPG
64-65—St. Louis	79	1243	140	375	.373	83	164	.506	576	48	161	1	363	7.3	0.6	4.6
65-66—St. Louis	46	586	70	173	.405	35	61	.574	236	22	72	0	175	5.1	0.5	3.8
66-67—St. Louis	77	1570	207	482	.429	113	213	.531	669	74	208	4	527	8.7	1.0	6.8
67-68—St. Louis	82	2652	399	871	.458	299	424	.705	958	162	243	4	1097	11.7	2.0	13.4
68-69—Atlanta	79	1853	241	575	.419	204	333	.613	745	140	166	0	686	9.4	1.8	8.7
69-70—Phoenix	78	2836	373	804	.464	250	412	.607	916	214	266	5	996	11.7	2.7	12.8
70-71—Phoenix	81	2944	338	789	.428	285	416	.685	1015	247	227	3	961	12.5	3.0	11.9
71-72—Phoenix	80	3082	485	1031	.470	433	560	.773	955	343	201	2	1403	11.9	4.3	17.5
72-73—Boston	80	2618	400	851	.470	266	380	.700	1039	251	197	1	1066	13.0	3.1	13.3

Season Team	G	Min.	FGM	FGA	Pct.	FTM	FTA	Pct.	REBOUNDS Off.	Def.	Tot.	Ast.	St.	Blk.	TO	Pts.	AVERAGES RPG	APG	PPG
73-74—Boston	82	2599	340	772	.440	264	337	.783	334	581	915	186	63	20	...	944	11.2	2.3	11.5
74-75—Boston	82	2661	312	749	.417	244	344	.709	348	677	1025	224	60	22	...	868	12.5	2.7	10.6
75-76—Boston	81	2662	315	740	.426	236	333	.709	*365	660	1025	203	56	33	...	866	12.7	2.5	10.7
76-77—Denver	81	1959	206	572	.360	170	255	.667	236	370	606	132	58	23	...	582	7.5	1.6	7.2
77-78—Seattle	82	2172	184	464	.397	109	186	.586	289	377	666	145	65	16	152	477	8.1	1.8	5.8
78-79—Seattle	82	1957	170	402	.423	116	194	.598	259	316	575	115	31	19	98	456	7.0	1.4	5.6
79-80—Seattle	82	1595	113	299	.378	89	136	.654	204	232	436	66	25	5	83	315	5.3	0.8	3.8
Totals	1254	34989	4293	9949	.432	3196	4748	.673	...	...	12357	2572	358	138	333	11782	9.9	2.1	9.4

Personal fouls/disqualifications: 1973-74, 246/3. 1974-75, 229/3. 1975-76, 227/3. 1976-77, 183/0. 1977-78, 182/0. 1978-79, 177/3. 1979-80, 120/0. Totals, 3105/32.

NBA PLAYOFF RECORD

Season Team	G	Min.	FGM	FGA	Pct.	FTM	FTA	Pct.	Reb.	Ast.	PF	Dq.	Pts.	AVERAGES RPG	APG	PPG
64-65—St. Louis	4	42	4	10	.400	3	4	.750	18	1	6	0	11	4.5	0.3	2.8
65-66—St. Louis	7	80	5	18	.278	8	11	.727	34	2	11	0	18	4.9	0.3	2.6
66-67—St. Louis	8	122	9	36	.250	11	18	.611	52	6	17	0	29	6.5	0.8	3.6
67-68—St. Louis	6	178	22	51	.431	27	38	.711	57	21	17	0	71	9.5	3.5	11.8
68-69—Atlanta	11	258	21	58	.362	19	37	.514	92	21	32	0	61	8.4	1.9	5.5
69-70—Phoenix	7	286	46	109	.422	21	32	.656	111	30	29	1	113	15.9	4.3	16.1
72-73—Boston	13	512	47	120	.392	31	50	.620	196	39	39	0	125	15.1	3.0	9.6

Season Team	G	Min.	FGM	FGA	Pct.	FTM	FTA	Pct.	REBOUNDS Off.	Def.	Tot.	Ast.	St.	Blk.	TO	Pts.	AVERAGES RPG	APG	PPG
73-74—Boston	18	574	50	126	.397	44	53	.830	53	138	191	47	13	9	...	144	10.6	2.6	8.0
74-75—Boston	11	405	42	92	.457	16	25	.640	46	84	130	40	12	2	...	100	11.8	3.6	9.1
75-76—Boston	18	741	69	154	.448	56	69	.812	78	168	246	42	24	6	...	194	13.7	2.3	10.8
76-77—Denver	6	141	14	33	.424	13	24	.542	16	24	40	16	2	4	...	41	6.7	2.7	6.8
77-78—Seattle	22	605	33	94	.351	41	60	.683	73	114	187	36	12	6	28	107	8.5	1.6	4.9
78-79—Seattle	17	418	21	54	.389	31	46	.674	40	58	98	19	9	5	34	73	5.8	1.1	4.3
79-80—Seattle	15	257	13	43	.302	11	13	.846	33	42	75	15	9	2	9	37	5.0	1.0	2.5
Totals	163	4619	396	998	.397	332	480	.692	...	...	1527	335	81	34	71	1124	9.4	2.1	6.9

Personal fouls/disqualifications: 1973-74, 51/2. 1974-75, 45/1. 1975-76, 67/1. 1976-77, 23/1. 1977-78, 59/0. 1978-79, 44/1. 1979-80, 29/0. Totals, 469/7.

NBA ALL-STAR GAME RECORD

Season Team	Min.	FGM	FGA	Pct.	FTM	FTA	Pct.	Reb	Ast.	PF	Dq.	Pts.
1972—Phoenix	15	0	6	.000	2	3	.667	9	1	1	0	2

Season Team	Min.	FGM	FGA	Pct.	FTM	FTA	Pct.	REBOUNDS Off.	Def.	Tot.	Ast.	PF	Dq.	St.	Blk.	TO	Pts.
1975—Boston	15	2	4	.500	2	2	1.000	0	2	2	2	2	0	4	0	...	6
Totals	30	2	10	.200	4	5	.800	...	...	11	3	3	0	4	0	...	8

EBL REGULAR-SEASON RECORD

Season Team	G	Min.	FGM	FGA	Pct.	FTM	FTA	Pct.	Reb.	Ast.	PF	Dq.	Pts.	AVERAGES RPG	APG	PPG
65-66—Wil.-Barre	5	...	25			13	21	.619	85	9	...	...	63	17.0	1.8	12.6

NBA COACHING RECORD

BACKGROUND: Assistant coach, New Jersey Nets (1988-89 and 1992-93 through 1994-95). ... Assistant coach, New York Knicks (1989-90 through 1991-92). ... Assistant coach, Phoenix Suns (1995-96 and 1996-97). ... Assistant coach, Charlotte Hornets (1997-98 through March 7, 1999).

Season Team	REGULAR SEASON W	L	Pct.	Finish	PLAYOFFS W	L	Pct.
80-81—San Diego	36	46	.439	5th/Pacific Division	—	—	—
81-82—San Diego	17	65	.207	6th/Pacific Division	—	—	—
82-83—San Diego	25	57	.305	6th/Pacific Division	—	—	—
98-99—Charlotte	22	13	.629	5th/Central Division	—	—	—
99-00—Charlotte	49	33	.598	2nd/Central Division	1	3	.250
00-01—Charlotte	46	36	.561	3rd/Central Division	6	4	.600
01-02—Charlotte	44	38	.537	2nd/Central Division	4	5	.444
02-03—New Orleans	47	35	.573	3rd/Central Division	2	4	.333
03-04—Cleveland	35	47	.427	5th/Central Division	—	—	—
Totals (9 years)	321	370	.465	Totals (4 years)	13	16	.448

NOTES:
1999—Replaced Dave Cowens as head coach (March 7), with record of 4-11 and club in seventh place.
2000—Lost to Philadelphia in Eastern Conference first round.
2001—Defeated Miami, 3-0, in Eastern Conference first round; lost to Milwaukee, 4-3, in Eastern Conference finals.
2002—Defeated Orlando, 3-1, in Eastern Conference first round, lost to New Jersey, 4-1, in Eastern Conference semifinals.
2003—Lost to Philadelphia, 4-2, in Eastern Conference first round.

STOCKTON, JOHN　　　　　G

PERSONAL: Born March 26, 1962, in Spokane, Wash. ... 6-1/175. (1,85/79,4). ... Full Name: John Houston Stockton.
HIGH SCHOOL: Gonzaga Prep School (Spokane, Wash.).
COLLEGE: Gonzaga.
TRANSACTIONS/CAREER NOTES: Selected by Utah Jazz in first round (16th pick overall) of 1984 NBA Draft. ... Announced retirement (May 2, 2003).
CAREER HONORS: NBA 50th Anniversary All-Time Team (1996).
MISCELLANEOUS: Member of gold-medal-winning U.S. Olympic teams (1992, 1996). ... Utah Jazz franchise all-time assists leader with 15,806 and all-time steals leader with 3,265 (1984-85 through 2002-03).

COLLEGIATE RECORD

Season Team	G	Min.	FGM	FGA	Pct.	FTM	FTA	Pct.	Reb.	Ast.	Pts.	AVERAGES RPG	APG	PPG
80-81—Gonzaga	25	235	26	45	.578	26	35	.743	11	34	78	0.4	1.4	3.1
81-82—Gonzaga	27	1054	117	203	.576	69	102	.676	67	135	303	2.5	5.0	11.2
82-83—Gonzaga	27	1036	142	274	.518	91	115	.791	87	184	375	3.2	6.8	13.9
83-84—Gonzaga	28	1053	229	397	.577	126	182	.692	66	201	584	2.4	7.2	20.9
Totals	107	3378	514	919	.559	312	434	.719	231	554	1340	2.2	5.2	12.5

NBA REGULAR-SEASON RECORD

RECORDS: Holds career records for most seasons leading league in assists—9; most consecutive seasons leading league in assists—9 (1987-88 through 1995-96); most assists—15,806; and most steals—3,265. ... Holds single-season records for most assists—1,164 (1991); and highest assists-per-game average (minimum 70 games)—14.5 (1990).
HONORS: All-NBA First Team (1994, 1995). ... All-NBA Second Team (1988, 1989, 1990, 1992, 1993, 1996). ... All-NBA Third Team (1991, 1997, 1999). ... NBA All-Defensive second team (1989, 1991, 1992, 1995, 1997).
NOTES: Led NBA with 3.21 steals per game (1989) and 2.98 steals per game (1992).

Season Team	G	Min.	FGM	FGA	Pct.	FTM	FTA	Pct.	REBOUNDS Off.	Def.	Tot.	Ast.	St.	Blk.	TO	Pts.	AVERAGES RPG	APG	PPG
84-85—Utah	82	1490	157	333	.471	142	193	.736	26	79	105	415	109	11	150	458	1.3	5.1	5.6
85-86—Utah	82	1935	228	466	.489	172	205	.839	33	146	179	610	157	10	168	630	2.2	7.4	7.7
86-87—Utah	82	1858	231	463	.499	179	229	.782	32	119	151	670	177	14	164	648	1.8	8.2	7.9
87-88—Utah	82	2842	454	791	.574	272	324	.840	54	183	237	*1128	242	16	262	1204	2.9	*13.8	14.7
88-89—Utah	82	3171	497	923	.538	390	452	.863	83	165	248	*1118	*263	14	308	1400	3.0	*13.6	17.1
89-90—Utah	78	2915	472	918	.514	354	432	.819	57	149	206	*1134	207	18	272	1345	2.6	*14.5	17.2
90-91—Utah	82	3103	496	978	.507	363	434	.836	46	191	237	*1164	234	16	298	1413	2.9	*14.2	17.2
91-92—Utah	82	3002	453	939	.482	308	366	.842	68	202	270	*1126	*244	22	*286	1297	3.3	*13.7	15.8
92-93—Utah	82	2863	437	899	.486	293	367	.798	64	173	237	*987	199	21	266	1239	2.9	*12.0	15.1
93-94—Utah	82	2969	458	868	.528	272	338	.805	72	186	258	*1031	199	22	266	1236	3.1	*12.6	15.1
94-95—Utah	82	2867	429	791	.542	246	306	.804	57	194	251	*1011	194	22	267	1206	3.1	*12.3	14.7
95-96—Utah	82	2915	440	818	.538	234	282	.830	54	172	226	*916	140	15	246	1209	2.8	*11.2	14.7

Season Team	G	Min.	FGM	FGA	Pct.	FTM	FTA	Pct.	REBOUNDS Off.	Def.	Tot.	Ast.	St.	Blk.	TO	Pts.	AVERAGES RPG	APG	PPG
96-97—Utah	82	2896	416	759	.548	275	325	.846	45	183	228	860	166	15	248	1183	2.8	10.5	14.4
97-98—Utah	64	1858	270	511	.528	191	231	.827	35	131	166	543	89	10	161	770	2.6	8.5	12.0
98-99—Utah	50	1410	200	410	.488	137	169	.811	31	115	146	374	81	13	110	553	2.9	7.5	11.1
99-00—Utah	82	2432	363	725	.501	221	257	.860	45	170	215	703	143	15	179	990	2.6	8.6	12.1
00-01—Utah	82	2397	328	651	.504	227	278	.817	54	173	227	713	132	21	203	944	2.8	8.7	11.5
01-02—Utah	82	2566	401	775	.517	275	321	.857	59	204	263	674	152	24	208	1102	3.2	8.2	13.4
02-03—Utah	82	2275	309	640	.483	237	287	.826	51	150	201	629	137	16	182	884	2.5	7.7	10.8
Totals	1504	47764	7039	13658	.515	4788	5796	.826	966	3085	4051	15806	3265	315	4244	19711	2.7	10.5	13.1

Three-point field goals: 1984-85, 2-for-11 (.182). 1985-86, 2-for-15 (.133). 1986-87, 7-for-38 (.184). 1987-88, 24-for-67 (.358). 1988-89, 16-for-66 (.242). 1989-90, 47-for-113 (.416). 1990-91, 58-for-168 (.345). 1991-92, 83-for-204 (.407). 1992-93, 72-for-187 (.385). 1993-94, 48-for-149 (.322). 1994-95, 102-for-227 (.449). 1995-96, 95-for-225 (.422). 1996-97, 76-for-180 (.422). 1997-98, 39-for-91 (.429). 1998-99, 16-for-50 (.320). 1999-00, 43-for-121 (.355). 2000-01, 61-for-132 (.462). 2001-02, 25-for-78 (.321). 2002-03, 29-for-80 (.363). Totals, 845-for-2202 (.384).

Personal fouls/disqualifications: 1984-85, 203/3. 1985-86, 227/2. 1986-87, 224/1. 1987-88, 247/5. 1988-89, 241/3. 1989-90, 233/3. 1990-91, 233/1. 1991-92, 234/3. 1992-93, 224/2. 1993-94, 236/3. 1994-95, 215/3. 1995-96, 207/1. 1996-97, 194/2. 1997-98, 138/0. 1998-99, 107/0. 1999-00, 192/0. 2000-01, 194/1. 2001-02, 209/1. 2002-03, 184/1. Totals, 3942/35.

NBA PLAYOFF RECORD

NOTES: Shares NBA Finals single-game record for most assists in one quarter—8 (June 10, 1998, at Chicago). ... Holds single-game play-off record for most assists in one quarter—11 (May 5, 1994, vs. San Antonio). ... Shares single-game playoff record for most assists—24 (May 17, 1988, vs. Los Angeles Lakers).

Season Team	G	Min.	FGM	FGA	Pct.	FTM	FTA	Pct.	REBOUNDS Off.	Def.	Tot.	Ast.	St.	Blk.	TO	Pts.	AVERAGES RPG	APG	PPG
84-85—Utah	10	186	21	45	.467	26	35	.743	7	21	28	43	11	2	16	68	2.8	4.3	6.8
85-86—Utah	4	73	9	17	.529	8	9	.889	3	3	6	14	5	0	4	27	1.5	3.5	6.8
86-87—Utah	5	157	18	29	.621	10	13	.769	2	9	11	40	15	1	11	50	2.2	8.0	10.0
87-88—Utah	11	478	68	134	.507	75	91	.824	14	31	45	163	37	3	48	215	4.1	14.8	19.5
88-89—Utah	3	139	30	59	.508	19	21	.905	2	8	10	41	11	5	11	82	3.3	13.7	27.3
89-90—Utah	5	194	29	69	.420	16	20	.800	4	12	16	75	6	0	14	75	3.2	15.0	15.0
90-91—Utah	9	373	58	108	.537	37	44	.841	10	32	42	124	20	2	32	164	4.7	13.8	18.2
91-92—Utah	16	623	77	182	.423	65	78	.833	10	37	47	217	34	5	58	237	2.9	13.6	14.8
92-93—Utah	5	193	23	51	.451	15	18	.833	5	7	12	55	12	0	15	66	2.4	11.0	13.2
93-94—Utah	16	597	88	193	.456	51	63	.810	14	38	52	157	27	8	40	231	3.3	9.8	14.4
94-95—Utah	5	193	34	74	.459	13	17	.765	6	11	17	51	7	1	14	89	3.4	10.2	17.8
95-96—Utah	18	679	70	157	.446	48	59	.814	14	44	58	195	29	7	58	199	3.2	10.8	11.1
96-97—Utah	20	739	113	217	.521	77	90	.856	18	60	78	191	33	5	62	322	3.9	9.6	16.1
97-98—Utah	20	596	81	164	.494	51	71	.718	16	44	60	155	31	3	48	222	3.0	7.8	11.1
98-99—Utah	11	352	42	105	.400	34	46	.739	11	25	36	92	18	1	31	122	3.3	8.4	11.1
99-00—Utah	10	350	41	89	.461	23	30	.767	7	23	30	103	13	2	26	112	3.0	10.3	11.2
00-01—Utah	5	186	17	37	.459	15	21	.714	11	17	28	57	10	3	7	49	5.6	11.4	9.8
01-02—Utah	4	141	18	40	.450	12	13	.923	3	13	16	40	11	1	8	50	4.0	10.0	12.5
02-03—Utah	5	149	18	39	.462	20	20	1.000	5	11	16	26	8	1	14	56	3.2	5.2	11.2
Totals	182	6398	855	1809	.473	615	759	.810	162	446	608	1839	338	50	517	2436	3.3	10.1	13.4

Three-point field goals: 1984-85, 0-for-2. 1985-86, 1-for-1. 1986-87, 4-for-5 (.800). 1987-88, 4-for-14 (.286). 1988-89, 3-for-4 (.750). 1989-90, 1-for-13 (.077). 1990-91, 11-for-27 (.407). 1991-92, 18-for-58 (.310). 1992-93, 5-for-13 (.385). 1993-94, 4-for-24 (.167). 1994-95, 8-for-20 (.400). 1995-96, 11-for-38 (.289). 1996-97, 19-for-50 (.380). 1997-98, 9-for-26 (.346). 1998-99, 4-for-12 (.333). 1999-00, 7-for-18 (.389). 2000-01, 0-for-8. 2001-02, 2-for-7 (.286). 2002-03, 0-for-1. Totals, 119-for-341 (.349).

Personal fouls/disqualifications: 1984-85, 30/0. 1985-86, 10/0. 1986-87, 18/0. 1987-88, 36/0. 1988-89, 15/0. 1989-90, 20/0. 1990-91, 33/0. 1991-92, 38/0. 1992-93, 16/0. 1993-94, 44/0. 1994-95, 13/0. 1995-96, 50/0. 1996-97, 52/0. 1997-98, 54/0. 1998-99, 32/0. 1999-00, 30/0. 2000-01, 19/0. 2001-02, 16/1. 2002-03, 13/0. Totals, 539/1.

NBA ALL-STAR GAME RECORD

NOTES: NBA All-Star Game Co-Most Valuable Player (1993). ... Holds single-game record for most assists in one quarter—9 (1989).

Season Team	Min.	FGM	FGA	Pct.	FTM	FTA	Pct.	REBOUNDS Off.	Def.	Tot.	Ast.	PF	Dq.	St.	Blk.	TO	Pts.
1989—Utah	32	5	6	.833	0	0	...	0	2	2	17	4	0	5	0	12	11
1990—Utah	15	1	4	.250	0	0	...	0	0	0	6	1	0	1	1	3	2
1991—Utah	12	1	6	.167	2	4	.500	0	1	1	2	2	0	0	0	0	4
1992—Utah	18	5	8	.625	0	0	...	0	1	1	5	2	0	3	0	3	12
1993—Utah	31	3	6	.500	2	2	1.000	0	6	6	15	3	0	2	0	5	9
1994—Utah	26	6	10	.600	0	0	...	1	4	5	10	2	0	1	0	4	13
1995—Utah	14	2	6	.333	0	0	...	1	0	1	6	0	0	2	0	0	4
1996—Utah	18	2	9	.222	0	0	...	0	1	1	3	2	0	0	0	1	4
1997—Utah	20	5	6	.833	0	0	...	0	0	0	5	2	0	1	0	1	12
2000—Utah	11	5	5	1.000	0	0	...	0	0	0	2	2	0	1	0	0	10
Totals	197	35	66	.530	4	6	.667	2	15	17	71	20	0	16	1	29	81

Three-point field goals: 1989, 1-for-1. 1990, 0-for-1. 1992, 2-for-3 (.667). 1993, 1-for-2 (.500). 1994, 1-for-1. 1995, 0-for-3. 1996, 0-for-7. 1997, 2-for-2. Totals, 7-for-20 (.350).

STRICKLAND, ROD   G

PERSONAL: Born July 11, 1966, in Bronx, N.Y. ... 6-3/185. (1.91/83.9).
HIGH SCHOOL: Harry S. Truman (Bronx, N.Y.), then Oak Hill Academy (Mouth of Wilson, Va.).
COLLEGE: DePaul.
TRANSACTIONS/CAREER NOTES: Selected after junior season by New York Knicks in first round (19th pick overall) of 1988 NBA Draft. ... Traded by Knicks to San Antonio Spurs for G Maurice Cheeks (February 21, 1990). ... Signed as free agent by Portland Trail Blazers (July 3, 1992). ... Traded by Trail Blazers with F Harvey Grant to Washington Bullets for F Rasheed Wallace and G Mitchell Butler (July 15, 1996). ... Bullets franchise renamed Washington Wizards for 1997-98 season. ... Waived by Wizards (March 1, 2001). ... Signed as free agent by Trail Blazers (March 5, 2001). ... Signed as free agent by Miami Heat (October 22, 2001). ... Signed as free agent by Minnesota Timberwolves (October 27, 2002). ... Signed as free agent by Orlando Magic (November 25, 2003). ... Waived by Magic (March 1, 2004). ... Signed by Toronto Raptors for remainder of season (March 5, 2004). ... Signed as free agent by Houston Rockets (January 19, 2005).

COLLEGIATE RECORD

NOTES: THE SPORTING NEWS All-America first team (1988).

Season Team	G	Min.	FGM	FGA	Pct.	FTM	FTA	Pct.	Reb.	Ast.	Pts.	AVERAGES		
---	---	---	---	---	---	---	---	---	---	---	---	RPG	APG	PPG
85-86—DePaul	31	1063	176	354	.497	85	126	.675	84	159	437	2.7	5.1	14.1
86-87—DePaul	30	980	188	323	.582	106	175	.606	113	196	490	3.8	6.5	16.3
87-88—DePaul	26	837	207	392	.528	83	137	.606	98	202	521	3.8	7.8	20.0
Totals	87	2880	571	1069	.534	274	438	.626	295	557	1448	3.4	6.4	16.6

Three-point field goals: 1986-87, 8-for-15 (.533). 1987-88, 24-for-54 (.444). Totals, 32-for-69 (.464).

NBA REGULAR-SEASON RECORD

HONORS: All-NBA Second Team (1998). ... NBA All-Rookie second team (1989).

Season Team	G	Min.	FGM	FGA	Pct.	FTM	FTA	Pct.	REBOUNDS			Ast.	St.	Blk.	TO	Pts.	AVERAGES		
---	---	---	---	---	---	---	---	---	Off.	Def.	Tot.	---	---	---	---	---	RPG	APG	PPG
88-89—New York	81	1358	265	567	.467	172	231	.745	51	109	160	319	98	3	148	721	2.0	3.9	8.9
89-90—N.Y.-S.A.	82	2140	343	756	.454	174	278	.626	90	169	259	468	127	14	170	868	3.2	5.7	10.6
90-91—San Antonio	58	2076	314	651	.482	161	211	.763	57	162	219	463	117	11	156	800	3.8	8.0	13.8
91-92—San Antonio	57	2053	300	659	.455	182	265	.687	92	173	265	491	118	17	160	787	4.6	8.6	13.8
92-93—Portland	78	2474	396	816	.485	273	381	.717	120	217	337	559	131	24	199	1069	4.3	7.2	13.7
93-94—Portland	82	2889	528	1093	.483	353	471	.749	122	248	370	740	147	24	257	1411	4.5	9.0	17.2
94-95—Portland	64	2267	441	946	.466	283	380	.745	73	244	317	562	123	9	209	1211	5.0	8.8	18.9
95-96—Portland	67	2526	471	1023	.460	276	423	.652	89	208	297	640	97	16	255	1256	4.4	9.6	18.7
96-97—Washington	82	2997	515	1105	.466	367	497	.738	95	240	335	727	143	14	270	1410	4.1	8.9	17.2
97-98—Washington	76	3020	490	1130	.434	357	492	.726	112	293	405	*801	126	25	266	1349	5.3	*10.5	17.8
98-99—Washington	44	1632	251	603	.416	176	236	.746	56	156	212	434	76	5	142	690	4.8	9.9	15.7
99-00—Washington	69	2188	327	762	.429	214	305	.702	73	186	259	519	94	18	187	869	3.8	7.5	12.6
00-01—Wash.-Port.	54	1371	182	429	.424	130	173	.751	36	104	140	303	53	5	107	498	2.6	5.6	9.2
01-02—Miami	76	2294	316	714	.443	154	201	.766	49	183	232	463	82	11	159	794	3.1	6.1	10.4
02-03—Minnesota	47	956	120	278	.432	79	107	.738	20	75	95	215	46	6	76	320	2.0	4.6	6.8
03-04—Orlando-Tor.	61	1197	150	353	.425	72	98	.735	34	121	155	244	35	11	85	382	2.5	4.0	6.3
04-05—Houston	16	196	9	43	.209	9	10	.900	3	24	27	39	3	2	16	28	1.7	2.4	1.8
Totals	1094	33634	5418	11928	.454	3432	4759	.721	1172	2912	4084	7987	1616	215	2862	14463	3.7	7.3	13.2

Three-point field goals: 1988-89, 19-for-59 (.322). 1989-90, 8-for-30 (.267). 1990-91, 11-for-33 (.333). 1991-92, 5-for-15 (.333). 1992-93, 4-for-30 (.133). 1993-94, 2-for-10 (.200). 1994-95, 46-for-123 (.374). 1995-96, 38-for-111 (.342). 1996-97, 13-for-77 (.169). 1997-98, 12-for-48 (.250). 1998-99, 12-for-42 (.286). 1999-00, 1-for-21 (.048). 2000-01, 4-for-17 (.235). 2001-02, 8-for-26 (.308). 2002-03, 1-for-11 (.091). 2003-04, 10-for-36 (.278). 2004-05, 1-for-2 (.500). Totals, 195-for-691 (.282).

Personal fouls/disqualifications: 1988-89, 142/2. 1989-90, 160/3. 1990-91, 125/0. 1991-92, 122/0. 1992-93, 153/1. 1993-94, 171/0. 1994-95, 118/0. 1995-96, 135/2. 1996-97, 166/2. 1997-98, 182/2. 1998-99, 91/0. 1999-00, 147/1. 2000-01, 76/0. 2001-02, 114/0. 2002-03, 55/0. 2003-04, 76/0. 2004-05, 15/0. Totals, 2048/13.

NBA PLAYOFF RECORD

Season Team	G	Min.	FGM	FGA	Pct.	FTM	FTA	Pct.	REBOUNDS			Ast.	St.	Blk.	TO	Pts.	AVERAGES		
---	---	---	---	---	---	---	---	---	Off.	Def.	Tot.	---	---	---	---	---	RPG	APG	PPG
88-89—New York	9	111	22	49	.449	9	17	.529	6	7	13	25	4	1	13	54	1.4	2.8	6.0
89-90—N.Y.-S.A.	10	399	55	111	.495	11	17	.647	20	11	31	112	11	3	34	123	3.0	11.2	12.3
90-91—San Antonio	4	168	29	67	.433	17	21	.810	5	16	21	35	9	0	13	75	5.3	8.8	18.8
91-92—San Antonio	2	80	13	22	.591	5	8	.625	0	7	7	19	3	2	6	31	3.5	9.5	15.5
92-93—Portland	4	156	22	52	.423	10	12	.833	9	17	26	37	5	2	7	54	6.5	9.3	13.5
93-94—Portland	4	154	36	72	.500	22	27	.815	3	13	16	39	4	2	10	94	4.0	9.8	23.5
94-95—Portland	3	126	27	65	.415	14	18	.778	1	11	12	37	3	2	10	70	4.0	12.3	23.3
95-96—Portland	5	202	37	84	.440	23	36	.639	12	19	31	42	5	0	12	103	6.2	8.4	20.6
96-97—Washington	3	124	22	52	.423	14	19	.737	5	13	18	25	3	0	11	59	6.0	8.3	19.7
00-01—Portland	2	19	2	6	.333	4	6	.667	2	2	4	2	2	0	1	8	2.0	1.0	4.0
02-03—Minnesota	6	73	11	21	.524	6	6	1.000	6	6	17	4	2	8	28		1.0	2.8	4.7
Totals	52	1597	275	617	.446	139	197	.706	65	142	207	390	56	11	125	699	4.0	7.5	13.4

Three-point field goals: 1988-89, 1-for-1 (1.000). 1989-90, 0-for-7. 1990-91, 0-for-6. 1992-93, 0-for-1. 1993-94, 0-for-1. 1994-95, 2-for-5 (.400). 1995-96, 6-for-12 (.500). 1996-97, 1-for-2 (.500). Totals, 10-for-35 (.286).

Personal fouls/disqualifications: 1988-89, 21/0. 1989-90, 30/2. 1990-91, 14/0. 1991-92, 8/0. 1992-93, 10/0. 1993-94, 13/0. 1994-95, 11/0. 1995-96, 14/0. 1996-97, 8/0. 2000-01, 1/0. 2002-03, 5/0. Totals, 135/2.

THEUS, REGGIE   G

PERSONAL: Born October 13, 1957, in Inglewood, Calif. ... 6-7/213 (2,00/96,6). ... Full name: Reggie Wayne Theus. ... Name pronounced THEE-us.
HIGH SCHOOL: Inglewood (Calif.).
COLLEGE: UNLV.
TRANSACTIONS: Selected after junior season by Chicago Bulls in first round (ninth pick overall) of 1978 NBA Draft. ... Traded by Bulls to Kansas City Kings for C Steve Johnson, 1984 second-round draft choice and two 1985 second-round draft choices (February 15, 1984). ... Kings franchise moved from Kansas City to Sacramento for 1985-86 season. ... Traded by Kings with 1988 third-round draft choice and future considerations to Atlanta Hawks for G/F Randy Wittman and 1988 first-round draft choice (June 27, 1988). ... Selected by Orlando Magic from Hawks in NBA Expansion Draft (June 15, 1989). ... Traded by Magic to New Jersey Nets for 1993 and 1995 second-round draft choices (June 25, 1990). ... Waived by Nets (August 15, 1991). ... Played in Italy (1991-92).
CAREER NOTES: Broadcaster, Turner Sports (1994-2000).

COLLEGIATE RECORD

Season Team	G	Min.	FGM	FGA	Pct.	FTM	FTA	Pct.	Reb.	Ast.	Pts.	AVERAGES		
---	---	---	---	---	---	---	---	---	---	---	---	RPG	APG	PPG
75-76—UNLV	31	496	68	163	.417	48	60	.800	53	139	184	1.7	4.5	5.9
76-77—UNLV	32	814	178	358	.497	108	132	.818	145	136	464	4.5	4.3	14.5
77-78—UNLV	28	990	181	389	.465	167	207	.807	191	126	529	6.8	4.5	18.9
Totals	91	2300	427	910	.469	323	399	.810	389	401	1177	4.3	4.4	12.9

NBA REGULAR-SEASON RECORD

HONORS: NBA All-Rookie team (1979).

Season Team	G	Min.	FGM	FGA	Pct.	FTM	FTA	Pct.	REBOUNDS Off.	Def.	Tot.	Ast.	St.	Blk.	TO	Pts.	AVERAGES RPG	APG	PPG
78-79—Chicago	82	2753	537	1119	.480	264	347	.761	92	136	228	429	93	18	303	1338	2.8	5.2	16.3
79-80—Chicago	82	3029	566	1172	.483	500	597	.838	143	186	329	515	114	20	348	1660	4.0	6.3	20.2
80-81—Chicago	82	2820	543	1097	.495	445	550	.809	124	163	287	426	122	20	259	1549	3.5	5.2	18.9
81-82—Chicago	82	2838	560	1194	.469	363	449	.808	115	197	312	476	87	16	277	1508	3.8	5.8	18.4
82-83—Chicago	82	2856	749	1567	.478	434	542	.801	91	209	300	484	143	17	321	1953	3.7	5.9	23.8
83-84—Chi.-K.C.	61	1498	262	625	.419	214	281	.762	50	79	129	352	50	12	156	745	2.1	5.8	12.2
84-85—Kansas City	82	2543	501	1029	.487	334	387	.863	106	164	270	656	95	18	307	1341	3.3	8.0	16.4
85-86—Sacramento	82	2919	546	1137	.480	405	490	.827	73	231	304	788	112	20	327	1503	3.7	9.6	18.3
86-87—Sacramento	79	2872	577	1223	.472	429	495	.867	86	180	266	692	78	16	289	1600	3.4	8.8	20.3
87-88—Sacramento	73	2653	619	1318	.470	320	385	.831	72	160	232	463	59	16	234	1574	3.2	6.3	21.6
88-89—Atlanta	82	2517	497	1067	.466	285	335	.851	86	156	242	387	108	16	194	1296	3.0	4.7	15.8
89-90—Orlando	76	2350	517	1178	.439	378	443	.853	75	146	221	407	60	12	226	1438	2.9	5.4	18.9
90-91—New Jersey	81	2955	583	1247	.468	292	343	.851	69	160	229	378	85	35	252	1510	2.8	4.7	18.6
Totals	1026	34603	7057	14973	.471	4663	5644	.826	1182	2167	3349	6453	1206	236	3493	19015	3.3	6.3	18.5

Three-point field goals: 1979-80, 28-for-105 (.267). 1980-81, 18-for-90 (.200). 1981-82, 21-for-100 (.250). 1982-83, 21-for-91 (.231). 1983-84, 7-for-42 (.167). 1984-85, 5-for-38 (.132). 1985-86, 6-for-35 (.171). 1986-87, 17-for-78 (.218). 1987-88, 16-for-59 (.271). 1988-89, 17-for-58 (.293). 1989-90, 26-for-105 (.248). 1990-91, 52-for-144 (.361). Totals, 238-for-945 (.252).

Personal fouls/disqualifications: 1978-79, 270/2. 1979-80, 262/4. 1980-81, 258/1. 1981-82, 243/1. 1982-83, 281/6. 1983-84, 171/3. 1984-85, 250/0. 1985-86, 231/3. 1986-87, 208/3. 1987-88, 173/0. 1988-89, 236/0. 1989-90, 194/1. 1990-91, 231/0. Totals, 3008/24.

NBA PLAYOFF RECORD

Season Team	G	Min.	FGM	FGA	Pct.	FTM	FTA	Pct.	REBOUNDS Off.	Def.	Tot.	Ast.	St.	Blk.	TO	Pts.	AVERAGES RPG	APG	PPG
80-81—Chicago	6	232	40	90	.444	37	43	.860	7	14	21	38	9	0	15	119	3.5	6.3	19.8
83-84—Kansas City	3	81	17	43	.395	9	10	.900	4	7	11	16	5	0	9	43	3.7	5.3	14.3
85-86—Sacramento	3	102	18	46	.391	9	12	.750	3	5	8	19	3	2	14	45	2.7	6.3	15.0
88-89—Atlanta	5	127	14	38	.368	9	12	.750	3	4	7	24	1	0	10	37	1.4	4.8	7.4
Totals	17	542	89	217	.410	64	77	.831	17	30	47	97	18	2	48	244	2.8	5.7	14.4

Three-point field goals: 1980-81, 2-for-9 (.222). 1983-84, 0-for-3. 1985-86, 0-for-1. 1988-89, 0-for-2. Totals, 2-for-15 (.133).
Personal fouls/disqualifications: 1980-81, 22/0. 1983-84, 9/0. 1985-86, 9/0. 1988-89, 18/1. Totals, 58/1.

NBA ALL-STAR GAME RECORD

Season Team	Min.	FGM	FGA	Pct.	FTM	FTA	Pct.	REBOUNDS Off.	Def.	Tot.	Ast.	PF	Dq.	St.	Blk.	TO	Pts.
1981—Chicago	19	4	7	.571	0	0	...	0	1	1	3	0	0	2	0	4	8
1983—Chicago	8	0	5	.000	0	0	...	1	0	1	1	1	0	0	0	0	0
Totals	27	4	12	.333	0	0	...	1	1	2	4	1	0	2	0	4	8

ITALIAN LEAGUE RECORD

Season Team	G	Min.	FGM	FGA	Pct.	FTM	FTA	Pct.	Reb.	Ast.	Pts.	AVERAGES RPG	APG	PPG
91-92—Ranger Varese	30	1151	268	572	.469	288	340	.847	118	161	878	3.9	5.4	29.3

HEAD COACHING RECORD

BACKGROUND: Assistant coach, University of Louisville (2003-05). ... Head coach, New Mexico State University (2005-present).

THOMAS, ISIAH　　　　　　　　　　G

See Head Coaches, page 305.

THORPE, OTIS　　　　　　　　　　F/C

PERSONAL: Born August 5, 1962, in Boynton Beach, Fla. ... 6-10/248. (2,08/112,5). ... Full Name: Otis Henry Thorpe.
HIGH SCHOOL: Lake Worth (Fla.) Community.
COLLEGE: Providence.
TRANSACTIONS/CAREER NOTES: Selected by Kansas City Kings in first round (ninth pick overall) of 1984 NBA Draft. ... Kings franchise moved from Kansas City to Sacramento for 1985-86 season. ... Traded by Kings to Houston Rockets for F/G Rodney McCray and F/C Jim Petersen (October 11, 1988). ... Traded by Rockets with rights to F Marcelo Nicola and 1995 first-round draft choice to Portland Trail Blazers for G Clyde Drexler and F Tracy Murray (February 14, 1995). ... Traded by Trail Blazers to Detroit Pistons for F Bill Curley and draft rights to G Randolph Childress (September 20, 1995). ... Traded by Pistons to Vancouver Grizzlies for first-round draft choice between 1998 and 2003 (August 7, 1997). ... Traded by Grizzlies with G Chris Robinson to Sacramento Kings for G Bobby Hurley and F Michael Smith (February 18, 1998). ... Traded by Kings with G Mitch Richmond to Washington Wizards for F Chris Webber (May 14, 1998). ... Signed as free agent by Miami Heat (August 4, 1999). ... Traded by Heat with F P.J. Brown, F Jamal Mashburn, F Tim James and G/F Rodney Buford to Charlotte Hornets for G Eddie Jones, F Anthony Mason, G Ricky Davis and G/F Dale Ellis (August 1, 2000).
MISCELLANEOUS: Member of NBA championship team (1994).

COLLEGIATE RECORD

Season Team	G	Min.	FGM	FGA	Pct.	FTM	FTA	Pct.	Reb.	Ast.	Pts.	AVERAGES RPG	APG	PPG
80-81—Providence	26	668	100	194	.515	50	76	.658	137	11	250	5.3	0.4	9.6
81-82—Providence	27	942	153	283	.541	74	115	.643	216	36	380	8.0	1.3	14.1
82-83—Providence	31	1041	204	321	.636	91	138	.659	249	24	499	8.0	0.8	16.1
83-84—Providence	29	1051	167	288	.580	162	248	.653	300	36	496	10.3	1.2	17.1
Totals	113	3702	624	1086	.575	377	577	.653	902	107	1625	8.0	0.9	14.4

NBA REGULAR-SEASON RECORD

NOTES: Tied for NBA lead with 300 personal fouls (1996) and nine disqualifications (1999).

								REBOUNDS								AVERAGES		
Season Team	G	Min.	FGM	FGA	Pct.	FTM	FTA	Pct.	Off.	Def.	Tot.	Ast.	St.	Blk.	TO	Pts.	RPG	APG	PPG
84-85—Kansas City.....	82	1918	411	685	.600	230	371	.620	187	369	556	111	34	37	187	1052	6.8	1.4	12.8
85-86—Sacramento	75	1675	289	492	.587	164	248	.661	137	283	420	84	35	34	123	742	5.6	1.1	9.9
86-87—Sacramento	82	2956	567	1050	.540	413	543	.761	259	560	819	201	46	60	189	1547	10.0	2.5	18.9
87-88—Sacramento	82	3072	622	1226	.507	460	609	.755	279	558	837	266	62	56	228	1704	10.2	3.2	20.8
88-89—Houston..........	82	3135	521	961	.542	328	450	.729	272	515	787	202	82	37	225	1370	9.6	2.5	16.7
89-90—Houston..........	82	2947	547	998	.548	307	446	.688	258	476	734	261	66	24	229	1401	9.0	3.2	17.1
90-91—Houston..........	82	3039	549	988	.556	334	480	.696	287	559	846	197	73	20	217	1435	10.3	2.4	17.5
91-92—Houston..........	82	3056	558	943	.592	304	463	.657	285	577	862	250	52	37	237	1420	10.5	3.0	17.3
92-93—Houston..........	72	2357	385	690	.558	153	256	.598	219	370	589	181	43	19	151	923	0.2	2.5	12.8
93-94—Houston..........	82	2909	449	801	.561	251	382	.657	271	599	870	189	66	28	185	1149	10.6	2.3	14.0
94-95—Hou.-Port........	70	2096	385	681	.565	167	281	.594	202	356	558	112	41	28	132	937	8.0	1.6	13.4
95-96—Detroit	82	2841	452	853	.530	257	362	.710	211	477	688	158	53	39	195	1161	8.4	1.9	14.2
96-97—Detroit	79	2661	419	787	.532	198	303	.653	226	396	622	133	59	17	145	1036	7.9	1.7	13.1
97-98—Van.-Sac.	74	2197	294	624	.471	164	240	.683	151	386	537	222	48	30	152	752	7.3	3.0	10.2
98-99—Washington	49	1539	240	440	.545	74	106	.698	96	238	334	101	42	19	88	554	6.8	2.1	11.3
99-00—Miami	51	777	125	243	.514	29	48	.604	56	110	166	33	26	9	59	279	3.3	0.6	5.5
00-01—Charlotte	49	647	59	131	.450	20	24	.833	50	95	145	29	12	7	32	138	3.0	0.6	2.8
Totals	1257	39822	6872	12593	.546	3853	5612	.687	3446	6924	10370	2730	840	501	2774	17600	8.2	2.2	14.0

Three-point field goals: 1984-85, 0-for-2. 1986-87, 0-for-3. 1987-88, 0-for-6. 1988-89, 0-for-2. 1989-90, 0-for-10. 1990-91, 3-for-7 (.429). 1991-92, 0-for-7. 1992-93, 0-for-2. 1993-94, 0-for-2. 1994-95, 0-for-7. 1995-96, 0-for-4. 1996-97, 0-for-2. 1997-98, 0-for-5. 1998-99, 0-for-2. 1999-00, 0-for-3. Totals, 3-for-64 (.047).

Personal fouls/disqualifications: 1984-85, 256/2. 1985-86, 233/3. 1986-87, 292/11. 1987-88, 264/3. 1988-89, 259/6. 1989-90, 270/5. 1990-91, 278/10. 1991-92, 307/7. 1992-93, 234/3. 1993-94, 253/1. 1994-95, 224/3. 1995-96, 300/7. 1996-97, 298/7. 1997-98, 238/4. 1998-99, 196/9. 1999-00, 136/4. 2000-01, 108/0. Totals, 4146/85.

NBA PLAYOFF RECORD

								REBOUNDS								AVERAGES		
Season Team	G	Min.	FGM	FGA	Pct.	FTM	FTA	Pct.	Off.	Def.	Tot.	Ast.	St.	Blk.	TO	Pts.	RPG	APG	PPG
85-86—Sacramento	3	35	3	13	.231	6	13	.462	8	4	12	0	0	1	1	12	4.0	0.0	4.0
88-89—Houston..........	4	152	24	37	.649	16	21	.762	6	14	20	12	5	1	15	64	5.0	3.0	16.0
89-90—Houston..........	4	164	27	45	.600	26	38	.684	14	19	33	7	5	0	9	80	8.3	1.8	20.0
90-91—Houston..........	3	116	22	38	.579	3	6	.500	7	18	25	8	2	0	6	47	8.3	2.7	15.7
92-93—Houston..........	12	419	73	115	.635	28	43	.651	36	67	103	31	6	1	17	174	8.6	2.6	14.5
93-94—Houston..........	23	854	111	194	.572	38	67	.567	68	160	228	54	13	10	37	261	9.9	2.3	11.3
94-95—Portland..........	3	66	12	21	.571	7	10	.700	5	8	13	2	0	0	3	31	4.3	0.7	10.3
95-96—Detroit	3	101	13	24	.542	9	12	.750	14	21	35	7	0	0	7	35	11.7	2.3	11.7
96-97—Detroit	5	152	21	41	.512	7	9	.778	12	20	32	4	2	0	9	49	6.4	0.8	9.8
99-00—Miami	10	136	13	27	.481	7	14	.500	6	23	29	3	0	2	11	33	2.9	0.3	3.3
00-01—Charlotte	8	57	2	9	.222	0	0	...	6	11	17	0	0	0	2	4	2.1	0.0	0.5
Totals	78	2252	321	564	.569	147	233	.631	182	365	547	128	33	15	117	790	7.0	1.6	10.1

Three-point field goals: 1993-94, 1-for-3 (.500). 1999-00, 0-for-1. Totals, 1-for-2 (.000).
Personal fouls/disqualifications: 1985-86, 4/0. 1988-89, 17/1. 1989-90, 12/0. 1990-91, 8/0. 1992-93, 35/0. 1993-94, 86/2. 1994-95, 12/1. 1995-96, 9/0. 1996-97, 21/0. 1999-00, 29/0. 2000-01, 8/0. Totals, 241/4.

NBA ALL-STAR GAME RECORD

							REBOUNDS									
Season Team	Min.	FGM	FGA	Pct.	FTM	FTA	Pct.	Off.	Def.	Tot.	Ast.	PF	Dq.	St.	Blk.	TO	Pts.
1992—Houston	4	1	1	1.000	0	0	...	0	0	0	0	0	0	0	0	0	2

THURMOND, NATE   C/F

PERSONAL: Born July 25, 1941, in Akron, Ohio. ... 6-11/235 (2,10/106,6). ... Full name: Nathaniel Thurmond.
HIGH SCHOOL: Central Hower (Akron, Ohio).
COLLEGE: Bowling Green State.
TRANSACTIONS: Selected by San Francisco Warriors in first round of 1963 NBA Draft. ... Warriors franchise renamed Golden State Warriors for 1971-72 season. ... Traded by Warriors to Chicago Bulls for C Clifford Ray, cash and 1975 first-round draft choice (September 3, 1974). ... Traded by Bulls with F Rowland Garrett to Cleveland Cavaliers for C/F Steve Patterson and F Eric Fernsten (November 27, 1975).
CAREER HONORS: Elected to Naismith Memorial Basketball Hall of Fame (1985). ... One of the 50 Greatest Players in NBA History (1996).
CAREER NOTES: Community Relations Director, Golden State Warriors (1981-82 through 1994-95) ... Community Relations Ambassador, Warriors (1995-96-present).
MISCELLANEOUS: Golden State Warriors franchise all-time leading rebounder with 12,771 (1963-64 through 1973-74).

COLLEGIATE RECORD

NOTES: THE SPORTING NEWS All-America first team (1963).

												AVERAGES		
Season Team	G	Min.	FGM	FGA	Pct.	FTM	FTA	Pct.	Reb.	Ast.	Pts.	RPG	APG	PPG
59-60—Bowling Green‡.............	17	...	...	...	...	...	...	...	208	...	225	12.2	...	13.2
60-61—Bowling Green..............	24	...	170	427	.398	87	129	.674	449	...	427	18.7	...	17.8
61-62—Bowling Green..............	25	...	163	358	.455	67	113	.593	394	...	393	15.8	...	15.7
62-63—Bowling Green..............	27	...	206	466	.442	124	197	.629	452	...	536	16.7	...	19.9
Varsity totals	76	...	539	1251	.431	278	439	.633	1295	...	1356	17.0	...	17.8

NBA REGULAR-SEASON RECORD

RECORDS: Holds single-game record for most rebounds in one quarter—18 (February 28, 1965, vs. Baltimore).
HONORS: NBA All-Defensive first team (1969, 1971). ... NBA All-Defensive second team (1972, 1973, 1974). ... NBA All-Rookie team (1964).

Season Team	G	Min.	FGM	FGA	Pct.	FTM	FTA	Pct.	Reb.	Ast.	PF	Dq.	Pts.	RPG	APG	PPG
														AVERAGES		
63-64—San Francisco	76	1966	219	554	.395	95	173	.549	790	86	184	2	533	10.4	1.1	7.0
64-65—San Francisco	77	3173	519	1240	.419	235	357	.658	1395	157	232	3	1273	18.1	2.0	16.5
65-66—San Francisco	73	2891	454	1119	.406	280	428	.654	1312	111	223	7	1188	18.0	1.5	16.3
66-67—San Francisco	65	2755	467	1068	.437	280	445	.629	1382	166	183	3	1214	21.3	2.6	18.7
67-68—San Francisco	51	2222	382	929	.411	282	438	.644	1121	215	137	1	1046	22.0	4.2	20.5
68-69—San Francisco	71	3208	571	1394	.410	382	621	.615	1402	253	171	0	1524	19.7	3.6	21.5
69-70—San Francisco	43	1919	341	824	.414	261	346	.754	762	150	110	1	943	17.7	3.5	21.9
70-71—San Francisco	82	3351	623	1401	.445	395	541	.730	1128	257	192	1	1641	13.8	3.1	20.0
71-72—Golden State	78	3362	628	1454	.432	417	561	.743	1252	230	214	1	1673	16.1	2.9	21.4
72-73—Golden State	79	3419	517	1159	.446	315	439	.718	1349	280	240	2	1349	17.1	3.5	17.1

Season Team	G	Min.	FGM	FGA	Pct.	FTM	FTA	Pct.	REBOUNDS Off.	Def.	Tot.	Ast.	St.	Blk.	TO	Pts.	AVERAGES RPG	APG	PPG
73-74—Golden State	62	2463	308	694	.444	191	287	.666	249	629	878	165	41	179	...	807	14.2	2.7	13.0
74-75—Chicago	80	2756	250	686	.364	132	224	.589	259	645	904	328	46	195	...	632	11.3	4.1	7.9
75-76—Chi.-Clev.	78	1393	142	337	.421	62	123	.504	115	300	415	94	22	98	...	346	5.3	1.2	4.4
76-77—Cleveland	49	997	100	246	.407	68	106	.642	121	253	374	83	16	81	...	268	7.6	1.7	5.5
Totals	964	35875	5521	13105	.421	3395	5089	.667	...	...	14464	2575	125	553	...	14437	15.0	2.7	15.0

Personal fouls/disqualifications: 1973-74, 179/4. 1974-75, 271/6. 1975-76, 160/1. 1976-77, 128/2. Totals, 2624/34.

NBA PLAYOFF RECORD

Season Team	G	Min.	FGM	FGA	Pct.	FTM	FTA	Pct.	Reb.	Ast.	PF	Dq.	Pts.	AVERAGES RPG	APG	PPG
63-64—San Francisco	12	410	42	98	.429	36	53	.679	148	12	46	0	120	12.3	1.0	10.0
66-67—San Francisco	15	690	93	215	.433	52	91	.571	346	47	52	1	238	23.1	3.1	15.9
68-69—San Francisco	6	263	40	102	.392	20	34	.588	117	28	18	0	100	19.5	4.7	16.7
70-71—San Francisco	5	192	36	97	.371	16	20	.800	51	15	20	0	88	10.2	3.0	17.6
71-72—Golden State	5	230	53	122	.434	21	28	.750	89	26	12	0	127	17.8	5.2	25.4
72-73—Golden State	11	460	64	161	.398	32	40	.800	145	40	30	1	160	13.2	3.6	14.5

Season Team	G	Min.	FGM	FGA	Pct.	FTM	FTA	Pct.	REBOUNDS Off.	Def.	Tot.	Ast.	St.	Blk.	TO	Pts.	RPG	APG	PPG
74-75—Chicago	13	254	14	38	.368	18	37	.486	24	63	87	31	5	21	...	46	6.7	2.4	3.5
75-76—Cleveland	13	375	37	79	.468	13	32	.406	38	79	117	28	6	29	...	87	9.0	2.2	6.7
76-77—Cleveland	1	1	0	0	...	0	0	...	0	1	1	0	0	1	...	0	1.0	0.0	0.0
Totals	81	2875	379	912	.416	208	335	.621	...	...	1101	227	11	51	...	966	13.6	2.8	11.9

Personal fouls/disqualifications: 1974-75, 36/0. 1975-76, 52/2. Totals, 266/4.

NBA ALL-STAR GAME RECORD

Season Team	Min.	FGM	FGA	Pct.	FTM	FTA	Pct.	Reb	Ast.	PF	Dq.	Pts.
1965—San Francisco	10	0	2	.000	0	0	...	3	0	1	0	0
1966—San Francisco	33	3	16	.188	1	3	.333	16	1	1	0	7
1967—San Francisco	42	7	16	.438	2	4	.500	18	0	1	0	16
1968—San Francisco					Selected, did not play—injured.							
1970—San Francisco					Selected, did not play—injured.							
1973—Golden State	14	2	5	.400	0	0	...	4	1	2	0	4

Season Team	Min.	FGM	FGA	Pct.	FTM	FTA	Pct.	REBOUNDS Off.	Def.	Tot.	Ast.	PF	Dq.	St.	Blk.	TO	Pts.
1974—Golden State	5	2	4	.500	0	1	.000	1	2	3	0	0	0	0	0	...	4
Totals	104	14	43	.326	3	8	.375	...	...	44	2	5	0	0	0	...	31

TWYMAN, JACK F/G

PERSONAL: Born May 11, 1934, in Pittsburgh. ... 6-6/210 (1,98/95,3). ... Full name: John Kennedy Twyman.
HIGH SCHOOL: Pittsburgh Central Catholic.
COLLEGE: Cincinnati.
TRANSACTIONS: Selected by Rochester Royals in second round (10th pick overall) of 1955 NBA Draft. ... Royals franchise moved from Rochester to Cincinnati for 1957-58 season.
CAREER HONORS: Elected to Naismith Memorial Basketball Hall of Fame (1983).

COLLEGIATE RECORD

Season Team	G	Min.	FGM	FGA	Pct.	FTM	FTA	Pct.	Reb.	Ast.	Pts.	AVERAGES RPG	APG	PPG
51-52—Cincinnati	16	...	27	83	.325	13	27	.481	55	...	67	3.4	...	4.2
52-53—Cincinnati	24	716	136	323	.421	89	143	.622	362	...	361	15.1	...	15.0
53-54—Cincinnati	21	777	174	443	.393	110	145	.759	347	...	458	16.5	...	21.8
54-55—Cincinnati	29	1097	285	628	.454	142	192	.740	478	...	712	16.5	...	24.6
Totals	90	...	622	1477	.421	354	507	.698	1242	...	1598	13.8	...	17.8

NBA REGULAR-SEASON RECORD

HONORS: All-NBA second team (1960, 1962).

Season Team	G	Min.	FGM	FGA	Pct.	FTM	FTA	Pct.	Reb.	Ast.	PF	Dq.	Pts.	AVERAGES RPG	APG	PPG
55-56—Rochester	72	2186	417	987	.423	204	298	.685	466	171	239	4	1038	6.5	2.4	14.4
56-57—Rochester	72	2338	449	1023	.439	276	363	.760	354	123	251	4	1174	4.9	1.7	16.3
57-58—Cincinnati	72	2178	465	1028 *.452	307	396	.775	464	110	224	3	1237	6.4	1.5	17.2
58-59—Cincinnati	72	2713	710	*1691	.420	437	558	.783	653	209	277	6	1857	9.1	2.9	25.8
59-60—Cincinnati	75	3023	870	2063	.422	*598	762	.785	664	260	275	10	2338	8.9	3.5	31.2
60-61—Cincinnati	79	2920	796	1632	.488	405	554	.731	672	225	279	5	1997	8.5	2.8	25.3
61-62—Cincinnati	80	2991	739	1542	.479	353	435	.812	638	215	323	5	1831	8.0	2.7	22.9
62-63—Cincinnati	80	2623	641	1335	.480	304	375	.811	598	214	286	7	1586	7.5	2.7	19.8

Season Team	G	Min.	FGM	FGA	Pct.	FTM	FTA	Pct.	Reb.	Ast.	PF	Dq.	Pts.	RPG	APG	PPG
63-64—Cincinnati	68	1996	447	993	.450	189	228	.829	364	137	267	7	1083	5.4	2.0	15.9
64-65—Cincinnati	80	2236	479	1081	.443	198	239	.828	383	137	239	4	1156	4.8	1.7	14.5
65-66—Cincinnati	73	943	224	498	.450	95	117	.812	168	60	122	1	543	2.3	0.8	7.4
Totals	823	26147	6237	13873	.450	3366	4325	.778	5424	1861	2782	56	15840	6.6	2.3	19.2

NBA PLAYOFF RECORD

Season Team	G	Min.	FGM	FGA	Pct.	FTM	FTA	Pct.	Reb.	Ast.	PF	Dq.	Pts.	RPG	APG	PPG
57-58—Cincinnati	2	74	15	45	.333	7	12	.583	22	1	6	0	37	11.0	0.5	18.5
61-62—Cincinnati	4	149	34	78	.436	8	8	1.000	29	12	18	0	76	7.3	3.0	19.0
62-63—Cincinnati	12	410	92	205	.449	65	77	.844	98	30	47	1	249	8.2	2.5	20.8
63-64—Cincinnati	10	354	83	176	.472	29	49	.592	87	16	41	1	205	8.7	1.6	20.5
64-65—Cincinnati	4	97	19	48	.396	11	11	1.000	17	3	16	0	49	4.3	0.8	12.3
65-66—Cincinnati	2	11	2	4	.500	1	2	.500	2	0	3	0	5	1.0	0.0	2.5
Totals	34	1095	245	556	.441	121	159	.761	255	62	131	2	621	7.5	1.8	18.3

NBA ALL-STAR GAME RECORD

Season Team	Min.	FGM	FGA	Pct.	FTM	FTA	Pct.	Reb	Ast.	PF	Dq.	Pts.
1957—Rochester	17	1	8	.125	1	3	.333	0	1	1	0	3
1958—Cincinnati	25	8	13	.615	2	2	1.000	3	0	3	0	18
1959—Cincinnati	23	8	12	.667	2	4	.500	8	3	4	0	18
1960—Cincinnati	28	11	17	.647	5	8	.625	5	1	4	0	27
1962—Cincinnati	8	4	6	.667	3	3	1.000	1	2	0	0	11
1963—Cincinnati	16	6	12	.500	0	0	...	4	1	2	0	12
Totals	117	38	68	.559	13	20	.650	21	8	14	0	89

UNSELD, WES — C/F

PERSONAL: Born March 14, 1946, in Louisville, Ky. ... 6-7/245 (2,00/111,1). ... Full name: Westley Sissel Unseld.
HIGH SCHOOL: Seneca (Louisville, Ky.).
COLLEGE: Louisville.
TRANSACTIONS: Selected by Baltimore Bullets in first round (second pick overall) of 1968 NBA Draft. ... Bullets franchise moved from Baltimore to Washington and renamed Capital Bullets for 1973-74 season. ... Bullets franchise renamed Washington Bullets for 1974-75 season.
CAREER HONORS: Elected to Naismith Memorial Basketball Hall of Fame (1988). ... One of the 50 Greatest Players in NBA History (1996).
MISCELLANEOUS: Member of NBA championship team (1978). ... Washington Wizards franchise all-time leading rebounder with 13,769 and all-time assists leader with 3,822 (1968-69 through 1980-81).
CAREER NOTES: Vice president, Washington Bullets (1981-82 to 1995-96). ... Executive vice president/general manager, Washington Bullets (1996-97 season to present). ... Bullets franchise renamed Washington Wizards for 1997-98 season.

COLLEGIATE RECORD

NOTES: The Sporting News All-America second team (1967, 1968).

Season Team	G	Min.	FGM	FGA	Pct.	FTM	FTA	Pct.	Reb.	Ast.	Pts.	RPG	APG	PPG
64-65—Louisville‡	14	...	214	312	.686	73	124	.589	331	...	501	23.6	...	35.8
65-66—Louisville	26	...	195	374	.521	128	202	.634	505	...	518	19.4	...	19.9
66-67—Louisville	28	...	201	374	.537	121	177	.684	533	...	523	19.0	...	18.7
67-68—Louisville	28	...	234	382	.613	177	275	.644	513	...	645	18.3	...	23.0
Varsity totals	82	...	630	1130	.558	426	654	.651	1551	...	1686	18.9	...	20.6

NBA REGULAR-SEASON RECORD

HONORS: NBA Most Valuable Player (1969). ... NBA Rookie of the Year (1969). ... All-NBA first team (1969). ... NBA All-Rookie team (1969). ... J. Walter Kennedy Citizenship Award (1975).
NOTES: Led NBA with .561 field goal percentage (1976).

Season Team	G	Min.	FGM	FGA	Pct.	FTM	FTA	Pct.	Reb.	Ast.	PF	Dq.	Pts.	RPG	APG	PPG
68-69—Baltimore	82	2970	427	897	.476	277	458	.605	1491	213	276	4	1131	18.2	2.6	13.8
69-70—Baltimore	82	3234	526	1015	.518	273	428	.638	1370	291	250	2	1325	16.7	3.5	16.2
70-71—Baltimore	74	2904	424	846	.501	199	303	.657	1253	293	235	2	1047	16.9	4.0	14.1
71-72—Baltimore	76	3171	409	822	.498	171	272	.629	1336	278	218	1	989	17.6	3.7	13.0
72-73—Baltimore	79	3085	421	854	.493	149	212	.703	1260	347	168	0	991	15.9	4.4	12.5

Season Team	G	Min.	FGM	FGA	Pct.	FTM	FTA	Pct.	REBOUNDS Off.	Def.	Tot.	Ast.	St.	Blk.	TO	Pts.	RPG	APG	PPG
73-74—Capital	56	1727	146	333	.438	36	55	.655	152	365	517	159	56	16	...	328	9.2	2.8	5.9
74-75—Washington	73	2904	273	544	.502	126	184	.685	318	759	1077	297	115	68	...	672	*14.8	4.1	9.2
75-76—Washington	78	2922	318	567	*.561	114	195	.585	271	765	1036	404	84	59	...	750	13.3	5.2	9.6
76-77—Washington	82	2860	270	551	.490	100	166	.602	243	634	877	363	87	45	...	640	10.7	4.4	7.8
77-78—Washington	80	2644	257	491	.523	93	173	.538	286	669	955	326	98	45	173	607	11.9	4.1	7.6
78-79—Washington	77	2406	346	600	.577	151	235	.643	274	556	830	315	71	37	156	843	10.8	4.1	10.9
79-80—Washington	82	2973	327	637	.513	139	209	.665	334	760	1094	366	65	61	153	794	13.3	4.5	9.7
80-81—Washington	63	2032	225	429	.524	55	86	.640	207	466	673	170	52	36	97	507	10.7	2.7	8.0
Totals	984	35832	4369	8586	.509	1883	2976	.633	...	...	13769	3822	628	367	579	10624	14.0	3.9	10.8

Three-point field goals: 1979-80, 1-for-2 (.500). 1980-81, 2-for-4 (.500). Totals, 3-for-6 (.500).
Personal fouls/disqualifications: 1973-74, 121/1. 1974-75, 180/1. 1975-76, 203/3. 1976-77, 253/5. 1977-78, 234/2. 1978-79, 204/2. 1979-80, 249/5. 1980-81, 171/1. Totals, 2762/29.

NBA PLAYOFF RECORD

NOTES: NBA Finals Most Valuable Player (1978).

Season Team	G	Min.	FGM	FGA	Pct.	FTM	FTA	Pct.	Reb.	Ast.	PF	Dq.	Pts.	AVERAGES RPG	APG	PPG
68-69—Baltimore	4	165	30	57	.526	15	19	.789	74	5	14	0	75	18.5	1.3	18.8
69-70—Baltimore	7	289	29	70	.414	15	19	.789	165	24	25	1	73	23.6	3.4	10.4
70-71—Baltimore	18	759	96	208	.462	46	81	.568	339	69	60	0	238	18.8	3.8	13.2
71-72—Baltimore	6	266	32	65	.492	10	19	.526	75	25	22	0	74	12.5	4.2	12.3
72-73—Baltimore	5	201	20	48	.417	9	19	.474	76	17	12	0	49	15.2	3.4	9.8

Season Team	G	Min.	FGM	FGA	Pct.	FTM	FTA	Pct.	REBOUNDS Off.	Def.	Tot.	Ast.	St.	Blk.	TO	Pts.	AVERAGES RPG	APG	PPG
73-74—Capital	7	297	31	63	.492	9	15	.600	22	63	85	27	4	1	...	71	12.1	3.9	10.1
74-75—Washington	17	734	71	130	.546	40	61	.656	65	211	276	64	15	20	...	182	16.2	3.8	10.7
75-76—Washington	7	310	18	39	.462	13	24	.542	26	59	85	28	6	4	...	49	12.1	4.0	7.0
76-77—Washington	9	368	30	54	.556	7	12	.583	24	81	105	44	8	6	...	67	11.7	4.9	7.4
77-78—Washington	18	677	71	134	.530	27	46	.587	72	144	216	79	17	7	36	169	12.0	4.4	9.4
78-79—Washington	19	736	78	158	.494	39	64	.609	90	163	253	64	17	14	30	195	13.3	3.4	10.3
79-80—Washington	2	87	7	14	.500	4	6	.667	7	21	28	7	0	3	3	18	14.0	3.5	9.0
Totals	119	4889	513	1040	.493	234	385	.608	...	...	1777	453	67	55	69	1260	14.9	3.8	10.6

Three-point field goals: 1979-80, 0-for-1.
Personal fouls/disqualifications: 1973-74, 15/0. 1974-75, 39/0. 1975-76, 19/0. 1976-77, 32/0. 1977-78, 62/2. 1978-79, 66/2. 1979-80, 5/0. Totals, 371/5.

NBA ALL-STAR GAME RECORD

Season Team	Min.	FGM	FGA	Pct.	FTM	FTA	Pct.	Reb.	Ast.	PF	Dq.	Pts.
1969—Baltimore	14	5	7	.714	1	3	.333	8	1	3	0	11
1971—Baltimore	21	4	9	.444	0	0	...	10	2	2	0	8
1972—Baltimore	16	1	5	.200	0	0	...	7	1	3	0	2
1973—Baltimore	11	2	4	.500	0	0	...	5	1	0	0	4

Season Team	Min.	FGM	FGA	Pct.	FTM	FTA	Pct.	REBOUNDS Off.	Def.	Tot.	Ast.	PF	Dq.	St.	Blk.	TO	Pts.
1975—Washington	15	2	3	.667	2	2	1.000	2	4	6	1	2	0	2	0	...	6
Totals	77	14	28	.500	3	5	.600	...	...	36	6	10	0	2	0	...	31

NBA COACHING RECORD

BACKGROUND: Assistant coach, Bullets (1987-January 3, 1988).

Season Team	REGULAR SEASON W	L	Pct.	Finish	PLAYOFFS W	L	Pct.
87-88—Washington	30	25	.545	T2nd/Atlantic Division	2	3	.400
88-89—Washington	40	42	.488	4th/Atlantic Division	—	—	—
89-90—Washington	31	51	.378	4th/Atlantic Division	—	—	—
90-91—Washington	30	52	.366	4th/Atlantic Division	—	—	—
91-92—Washington	25	57	.305	6th/Atlantic Division	—	—	—
92-93—Washington	22	60	.268	7th/Atlantic Division	—	—	—
93-94—Washington	24	58	.293	7th/Atlantic Division	—	—	—
Totals (7 years)	202	345	.369	Totals (1 year)	2	3	.400

NOTES:
1988—Replaced Kevin Loughery as Washington head coach (January 3), with record of 8-19. Lost to Detroit in Eastern Conference First Round.

WALKER, CHET   F/G

PERSONAL: Born February 22, 1940, in Benton Harbor, Mich. ... 6-7/220 (2,00/99,8). ... Full name: Chester Walker. ... Nickname: The Jet.
HIGH SCHOOL: Benton Harbor (Mich.).
COLLEGE: Bradley.
TRANSACTIONS: Selected by Syracuse Nationals in second round (14th pick overall) of 1962 NBA Draft. ... Nationals franchise moved from Syracuse to Philadelphia and renamed 76ers for 1963-64 season. ... Traded by 76ers with F Shaler Halimon to Chicago Bulls for F Jim Washington and player to be named later (September 2, 1969).
MISCELLANEOUS: Member of NBA championship team (1967).

COLLEGIATE RECORD

NOTES: THE SPORTING NEWS All-America first team (1962). ... THE SPORTING NEWS All-America second team (1961).

Season Team	G	Min.	FGM	FGA	Pct.	FTM	FTA	Pct.	Reb.	Ast.	Pts.	AVERAGES RPG	APG	PPG
58-59—Bradley‡	15	...	146	264	.553	56	93	.602	246	...	348	16.4	...	23.2
59-60—Bradley	29	...	244	436	.560	144	234	.615	388	...	632	13.4	...	21.8
60-61—Bradley	26	...	238	423	.563	180	250	.720	327	...	656	12.6	...	25.2
61-62—Bradley	26	...	268	500	.536	151	236	.640	321	...	687	12.3	...	26.4
Varsity totals	81	...	750	1359	.552	475	720	.660	1036	...	1975	12.8	...	24.4

NBA REGULAR-SEASON RECORD

HONORS: NBA All-Rookie team (1963).

Season Team	G	Min.	FGM	FGA	Pct.	FTM	FTA	Pct.	Reb.	Ast.	PF	Dq.	Pts.	AVERAGES RPG	APG	PPG
62-63—Syracuse	78	1992	352	751	.469	253	362	.699	561	83	220	3	957	7.2	1.1	12.3
63-64—Philadelphia	76	2775	492	1118	.440	330	464	.711	784	124	232	3	1314	10.3	1.6	17.3
64-65—Philadelphia	79	2187	377	936	.403	288	388	.742	528	132	200	2	1042	6.7	1.7	13.2
65-66—Philadelphia	80	2603	443	982	.451	335	468	.716	636	201	238	3	1221	8.0	2.5	15.3
66-67—Philadelphia	81	2691	561	1150	.488	445	581	.766	660	188	232	4	1567	8.1	2.3	19.3
67-68—Philadelphia	82	2623	539	1172	.460	387	533	.726	607	157	252	2	1465	7.4	1.9	17.9
68-69—Philadelphia	82	2753	554	1145	.484	369	459	.804	640	144	244	0	1477	7.8	1.8	18.0
69-70—Chicago	78	2726	596	1249	.477	483	568	.850	604	192	203	1	1675	7.7	2.5	21.5
70-71—Chicago	81	2927	650	1398	.465	480	559	*.859	588	179	187	2	1780	7.3	2.2	22.0

Season Team	G	Min.	FGM	FGA	Pct.	FTM	FTA	Pct.	Reb.	Ast.	PF	Dq.	Pts.	AVERAGES RPG	APG	PPG
71-72—Chicago	78	2588	619	1225	.505	481	568	.847	473	178	171	0	1719	6.1	2.3	22.0
72-73—Chicago	79	2455	597	1248	.478	376	452	.832	395	179	166	1	1570	5.0	2.3	19.9

Season Team	G	Min.	FGM	FGA	Pct.	FTM	FTA	Pct.	REBOUNDS Off.	Def.	Tot.	Ast.	St.	Blk.	TO	Pts.	AVERAGES RPG	APG	PPG
73-74—Chicago	82	2661	572	1178	.486	439	502	.875	131	275	406	200	68	4	...	1583	5.0	2.4	19.3
74-75—Chicago	76	2452	524	1076	.487	413	480	.860	114	318	432	169	49	6	...	1461	5.7	2.2	19.2
Totals	1032	33433	6876	14628	.470	5079	6384	.796	...	...	7314	2126	117	10	...	18831	7.1	2.1	18.2

Personal fouls/disqualifications: 1973-74, 201/1. 1974-75, 181/0. Totals, 2727/23.

NBA PLAYOFF RECORD

Season Team	G	Min.	FGM	FGA	Pct.	FTM	FTA	Pct.	Reb.	Ast.	PF	Dq.	Pts.	AVERAGES RPG	APG	PPG
62-63—Syracuse	5	130	27	53	.509	22	30	.733	47	9	8	0	76	9.4	1.8	15.2
63-64—Philadelphia	5	190	30	77	.390	34	46	.739	52	13	15	0	94	10.4	2.6	18.8
64-65—Philadelphia	11	469	83	173	.480	57	75	.760	79	18	38	0	223	7.2	1.6	20.3
65-66—Philadelphia	5	181	24	64	.375	25	31	.806	37	15	18	0	73	7.4	3.0	14.6
66-67—Philadelphia	15	551	115	246	.467	96	119	.807	114	32	44	0	326	7.6	2.1	21.7
67-68—Philadelphia	13	485	86	210	.410	76	112	.679	96	24	44	1	248	7.4	1.8	19.1
68-69—Philadelphia	4	109	23	43	.535	8	12	.667	23	8	5	0	54	5.8	2.0	13.5
69-70—Chicago	5	178	35	83	.422	27	33	.818	42	11	14	0	97	8.4	2.2	19.4
70-71—Chicago	7	234	44	100	.440	17	24	.708	50	22	20	0	105	7.1	3.1	15.0
71-72—Chicago	4	97	16	38	.421	13	16	.813	14	4	7	0	45	3.5	1.0	11.3
72-73—Chicago	7	229	42	121	.347	33	37	.892	62	14	15	0	117	8.9	2.0	16.7

Season Team	G	Min.	FGM	FGA	Pct.	FTM	FTA	Pct.	REBOUNDS Off.	Def.	Tot.	Ast.	St.	Blk.	TO	Pts.	AVERAGES RPG	APG	PPG
73-74—Chicago	11	403	81	159	.509	68	79	.861	26	35	61	18	10	1	...	230	5.5	1.6	20.9
74-75—Chicago	13	432	81	164	.494	66	75	.880	10	50	60	24	13	1	...	228	4.6	1.8	17.5
Totals	105	3688	687	1531	.449	542	689	.787	...	...	737	212	23	2	...	1916	7.0	2.0	18.2

Personal fouls/disqualifications: 1973-74, 26/0. 1974-75, 32/2. Totals, 286/3.

NBA ALL-STAR GAME RECORD

Season Team	Min.	FGM	FGA	Pct.	FTM	FTA	Pct.	Reb	Ast.	PF	Dq.	Pts.
1964—Philadelphia	12	2	5	.400	0	0	...	0	0	1	0	4
1966—Philadelphia	25	3	10	.300	2	3	.667	6	4	2	0	8
1967—Philadelphia	22	6	9	.667	3	4	.750	4	1	2	0	15
1970—Chicago	17	1	3	.333	2	2	1.000	2	1	2	0	4
1971—Chicago	19	3	9	.333	4	5	.800	3	1	1	0	10
1973—Chicago	16	1	5	.200	2	2	1.000	1	0	2	0	4

Season Team	Min.	FGM	FGA	Pct.	FTM	FTA	Pct.	REBOUNDS Off.	Def.	Tot.	Ast.	PF	Dq.	St.	Blk.	TO	Pts.
1974—Chicago	14	4	5	.800	4	4	1.000	0	2	2	1	1	0	0	0	...	12
Totals	125	23	46	.495	17	20	.850			18	8	11	0	0	0	...	57

WALTON, BILL   C

PERSONAL: Born November 5, 1952, in La Mesa, Calif. ... 6-11/235 (2,10/106,6). ... Full name: William Theodore Walton III. ... Brother of Bruce Walton, offensive lineman with Dallas Cowboys (1973-75).
HIGH SCHOOL: Helix (La Mesa, Calif.).
COLLEGE: UCLA.
TRANSACTIONS: Selected by Portland Trail Blazers in first round (first pick overall) of 1974 NBA Draft. ... Signed as veteran free agent by San Diego Clippers (May 13, 1979); Trail Blazers received C Kevin Kunnert, F Kermit Washington, 1980 first-round draft choice and cash as compensation (September 18, 1979). ... Clippers franchise moved from San Diego to Los Angeles for 1984-85 season. ... Traded by Clippers to Boston Celtics for F Cedric Maxwell, 1986 first-round draft choice and cash (September 6, 1985).
CAREER HONORS: Elected to Naismith Memorial Basketball Hall of Fame (1993). ... One of the 50 Greatest Players in NBA History (1996).
CAREER NOTES: Broadcaster, NBC Sports (1992-2002). ... Analyst, ABC/ESPN (2002-03 – present).
MISCELLANEOUS: Member of NBA championship team (1977, 1986).

COLLEGIATE RECORD

NOTES: The Sporting News College Player of the Year (1972, 1973, 1974). ... Naismith Award winner (1972, 1973, 1974). ... The Sporting News All-America first team (1972, 1973, 1974). ... NCAA Division I Tournament Most Outstanding Player (1972, 1973). ... Member of NCAA Division I championship team (1972, 1973). ... Holds NCAA Tournament career record for highest field goal percentage (minimum of 60 made)—68.6 percent, 109-of-159 (1972 through 1974). ... Holds NCAA Tournament single-season record for highest field goal percentage (minimum of 40 made)—76.3 percent, 45-of-59 (1973).

Season Team	G	Min.	FGM	FGA	Pct.	FTM	FTA	Pct.	Reb.	Ast.	Pts.	AVERAGES RPG	APG	PPG
70-71—UCLA‡	20	...	155	266	.583	52	82	.634	321	74	362	16.1	3.7	18.1
71-72—UCLA	30	...	238	372	.640	157	223	.704	466	...	633	15.5	...	21.1
72-73—UCLA	30	...	277	426	.650	58	102	.569	506	168	612	16.9	5.6	20.4
73-74—UCLA	27	...	232	349	.665	58	100	.580	398	148	522	14.7	5.5	19.3
Varsity totals	87	...	747	1147	.651	273	425	.642	1370	...	1767	15.7	...	20.3

NBA REGULAR-SEASON RECORD

HONORS: NBA Most Valuable Player (1978). ... NBA Sixth Man Award (1986). ... All-NBA first team (1978). ... All-NBA second team (1977). ... NBA All-Defensive first team (1977, 1978).
NOTES: Led NBA with 3.25 blocked shots per game (1977).

Season Team	G	Min.	FGM	FGA	Pct.	FTM	FTA	Pct.	REBOUNDS Off.	Def.	Tot.	Ast.	St.	Blk.	TO	Pts.	AVERAGES RPG	APG	PPG
74-75—Portland	35	1153	177	345	.513	94	137	.686	92	349	441	167	29	94	...	448	12.6	4.8	12.8

Season Team	G	Min.	FGM	FGA	Pct.	FTM	FTA	Pct.	REBOUNDS Off.	Def.	Tot.	Ast.	St.	Blk.	TO	Pts.	AVERAGES RPG	APG	PPG
75-76—Portland........	51	1687	345	732	.471	133	228	.583	132	549	681	220	49	82	...	823	13.4	4.3	16.1
76-77—Portland.......	65	2264	491	930	.528	228	327	.697	211	723	934	245	66	211	...	1210	*14.4	3.8	18.6
77-78—Portland.......	58	1929	460	882	.522	177	246	.720	118	648	766	291	60	146	206	1097	13.2	5.0	18.9
78-79—Portland						Did not play—injured.													
79-80—San Diego	14	337	81	161	.503	32	54	.593	28	98	126	34	8	38	37	194	9.0	2.4	13.9
80-81—San Diego						Did not play—injured.													
81-82—San Diego						Did not play—injured.													
82-83—San Diego	33	1099	200	379	.528	65	117	.556	75	248	323	120	34	119	105	465	9.8	3.6	14.1
83-84—San Diego	55	1476	288	518	.556	92	154	.597	132	345	477	183	45	88	177	668	8.7	3.3	12.1
84-85—L.A. Clippers ...	67	1647	269	516	.521	138	203	.680	168	432	600	156	50	140	174	676	9.0	2.3	10.1
85-86—Boston	80	1546	231	411	.562	144	202	.713	136	408	544	165	38	106	151	606	6.8	2.1	7.6
86-87—Boston	10	112	10	26	.385	8	15	.533	11	20	31	9	1	10	15	28	3.1	0.9	2.8
87-88—Boston						Did not play—injured.													
Totals	468	13250	2552	4900	.521	1111	1683	.660	1103	3820	4923	1590	380	1034	865	6215	10.5	3.4	13.3

Three-point field goals: 1983-84, 0-for-2. 1984-85, 0-for-3. Totals, 0-for-4.

Personal fouls/disqualifications: 1974-75, 115/4. 1975-76, 144/3. 1976-77, 174/5. 1977-78, 145/3. 1979-80, 37/0. 1982-83, 113/0. 1983-84, 153/1. 1984-85, 184/0. 1985-86, 210/1. 1986-87, 23/0. Totals, 1298/17.

NBA PLAYOFF RECORD

NOTES: NBA Finals Most Valuable Player (1977). ... Holds NBA Finals single-game record for most defensive rebounds—20 (June 3, 1977, vs. Philadelphia; and June 5, 1977, vs. Philadelphia). ... Shares NBA Finals single-game record for most blocked shots—8 (June 5, 1977, vs. Philadelphia). ... Shares single-game NBA playoff record for most defensive rebounds—20 (June 3, 1977, vs. Philadelphia; and June 5, 1977, vs. Philadelphia).

Season Team	G	Min.	FGM	FGA	Pct.	FTM	FTA	Pct.	REBOUNDS Off.	Def.	Tot.	Ast.	St.	Blk.	TO	Pts.	AVERAGES RPG	APG	PPG
76-77—Portland..........	19	755	153	302	.507	39	57	.684	56	232	288	104	20	64	...	345	15.2	5.5	18.2
77-78—Portland	2	49	11	18	.611	5	7	.714	5	17	22	4	3	3	6	27	11.0	2.0	13.5
85-86—Boston	16	291	54	93	.581	19	23	.826	25	78	103	27	6	12	22	127	6.4	1.7	7.9
86-87—Boston	12	102	12	25	.480	5	14	.357	9	22	31	10	3	4	8	29	2.6	0.8	2.4
Totals	49	1197	230	438	.525	68	101	.673	95	349	444	145	32	83	36	528	9.1	3.0	10.8

Three-point field goals: 1985-86, 0-for-1.

Personal fouls/disqualifications: 1976-77, 80/3. 1977-78, 1/0. 1985-86, 45/1. 1986-87, 23/0. Totals, 149/4.

NBA ALL-STAR GAME RECORD

Season Team	Min.	FGM	FGA	Pct.	FTM	FTA	Pct.	REBOUNDS Off.	Def.	Tot.	Ast.	PF	Dq.	St.	Blk.	TO	Pts.
1977—Portland								Selected, did not play—injured.									
1978—Portland	31	6	14	.429	3	3	1.000	2	8	10	2	3	0	3	2	4	15
Totals	31	6	14	.429	3	3	1.000	2	8	10	2	3	0	3	2	4	15

WEST, JERRY   G

PERSONAL: Born May 28, 1938, in Chelyan, W.Va. ... 6-2/185 (1,88/83,9). ... Full name: Jerry Alan West.
HIGH SCHOOL: East Bank (W.Va.).
COLLEGE: West Virginia.
TRANSACTIONS: Selected by Minneapolis Lakers in first round (second pick overall) of 1960 NBA Draft. ... Lakers franchise moved from Minneapolis to Los Angeles for 1960-61 season.
CAREER HONORS: Elected to Naismith Memorial Basketball Hall of Fame (1980). ... NBA 35th Anniversary All-Time Team (1980) and One of the 50 Greatest Players in NBA History (1996).
CAREER NOTES: Consultant, Los Angeles Lakers (1979-80 through 1981-82). ... General manager, Lakers (1982-83 through 1993-94). ... Executive vice president, basketball operations, Lakers (1994-95 to 1999-2000). ... President of basketball operations, Memphis Grizzlies (2002-present).
MISCELLANEOUS: Member of NBA championship team (1972). ... Member of gold-medal-winning U.S. Olympic team (1960). ... Los Angeles Lakers franchise all-time leading scorer with 25,192 points (1960-61 through 1973-74).

COLLEGIATE RECORD

NOTES: THE SPORTING NEWS All-America first team (1959, 1960). ... NCAA Tournament Most Outstanding Player (1959).

Season Team	G	Min.	FGM	FGA	Pct.	FTM	FTA	Pct.	Reb.	Ast.	Pts.	AVERAGES RPG	APG	PPG
56-57—West Virginia‡...............	17	...	114	...	...	104	...	...	...	...	332			19.5
57-58—West Virginia...............	28	799	178	359	.496	142	194	.732	311	41	498	11.1	1.5	17.8
58-59—West Virginia...............	34	1210	340	656	.518	223	320	.697	419	86	903	12.3	2.5	26.6
59-60—West Virginia...............	31	1129	325	645	.504	258	337	.766	510	134	908	16.5	4.3	29.3
Varsity totals	93	3138	843	1660	.508	623	851	.732	1240	261	2309	13.3	2.8	24.8

NBA REGULAR-SEASON RECORD

RECORDS: Holds single-season record for most free throws made—840 (1966).

HONORS: All-NBA first team (1962, 1963, 1964, 1965, 1966, 1967, 1970, 1971, 1972, 1973). ... All-NBA second team (1968, 1969). ... NBA All-Defensive first team (1970, 1971, 1972, 1973). ... NBA All-Defensive second team (1969).

Season Team	G	Min.	FGM	FGA	Pct.	FTM	FTA	Pct.	Reb.	Ast.	PF	Dq.	Pts.	AVERAGES RPG	APG	PPG
60-61—Los Angeles......................	79	2797	529	1264	.419	331	497	.666	611	333	213	1	1389	7.7	4.2	17.6
61-62—Los Angeles......................	75	3087	799	1795	.445	712	926	.769	591	402	173	4	2310	7.9	5.4	30.8
62-63—Los Angeles......................	55	2163	559	1213	.461	371	477	.778	384	307	150	1	1489	7.0	5.6	27.1
63-64—Los Angeles......................	72	2906	740	1529	.484	584	702	.832	443	403	200	2	2064	6.2	5.6	28.7
64-65—Los Angeles......................	74	3066	822	1655	.497	648	789	.821	447	364	221	2	2292	6.0	4.9	31.0
65-66—Los Angeles......................	79	3218	818	1731	.473	*840	*977	.860	562	480	243	1	2476	7.1	6.1	31.3
66-67—Los Angeles......................	66	2670	645	1389	.464	602	686	.878	392	447	160	1	1892	5.9	6.8	28.7
67-68—Los Angeles......................	51	1919	476	926	.514	391	482	.811	294	310	152	1	1343	5.8	6.1	26.3

Season Team	G	Min.	FGM	FGA	Pct.	FTM	FTA	Pct.	Reb.	Ast.	PF	Dq.	Pts.	RPG	APG	PPG
68-69—Los Angeles	61	2394	545	1156	.471	490	597	.821	262	423	156	1	1580	4.3	6.9	25.9
69-70—Los Angeles	74	3106	831	1673	.497	*647	*785	.824	338	554	160	3	2309	4.6	7.5	*31.2
70-71—Los Angeles	69	2845	667	1351	.494	525	631	.832	320	655	180	0	1859	4.6	9.5	26.9
71-72—Los Angeles	77	2973	735	1540	.477	515	633	.814	327	747	209	0	1985	4.2	*9.7	25.8
72-73—Los Angeles	69	2460	618	1291	.479	339	421	.805	289	607	138	0	1575	4.2	8.8	22.8

Season Team	G	Min.	FGM	FGA	Pct.	FTM	FTA	Pct.	Off.	Def.	Tot.	Ast.	St.	Blk.	TO	Pts.	RPG	APG	PPG
73-74—Los Angeles	31	967	232	519	.447	165	198	.833	30	86	116	206	81	23	...	629	3.7	6.6	20.3
Totals	932	36571	9016	19032	.474	7160	8801	.814	...	...	5376	6238	81	23	...	25192	5.8	6.7	27.0

Personal fouls/disqualifications: 1973-74, 80/0.

NBA PLAYOFF RECORD

NOTES: NBA Finals Most Valuable Player (1969). ... Holds single-series playoff record for highest points-per-game average—46.3 (1965).

Season Team	G	Min.	FGM	FGA	Pct.	FTM	FTA	Pct.	Reb.	Ast.	PF	Dq.	Pts.	RPG	APG	PPG
60-61—Los Angeles	12	461	99	202	.490	77	106	.726	104	63	39	0	275	8.7	5.3	22.9
61-62—Los Angeles	13	557	144	310	.465	121	150	.807	88	57	38	0	409	6.8	4.4	31.5
62-63—Los Angeles	13	538	144	286	.504	74	100	.740	106	61	34	0	362	8.2	4.7	27.8
63-64—Los Angeles	5	206	57	115	.496	42	53	.792	36	17	20	0	156	7.2	3.4	31.2
64-65—Los Angeles	11	470	155	351	.442	137	154	.890	63	58	37	0	447	5.7	5.3	40.6
65-66—Los Angeles	14	619	185	357	.518	109	125	.872	88	79	40	0	479	6.3	5.6	34.2
66-67—Los Angeles	1	1	0	0	...	0	0	...	1	0	0	0	0	1.0	0.0	0.0
67-68—Los Angeles	15	622	165	313	.527	132	169	.781	81	82	47	0	462	5.4	5.5	30.8
68-69—Los Angeles	18	757	196	423	.463	164	204	.804	71	135	52	1	556	3.9	7.5	30.9
69-70—Los Angeles	18	830	196	418	.469	170	212	.802	66	151	55	1	562	3.7	8.4	31.2
71-72—Los Angeles	15	608	128	340	.376	88	106	.830	73	134	39	0	344	4.9	8.9	22.9
72-73—Los Angeles	17	638	151	336	.449	99	127	.780	76	132	49	1	401	4.5	7.8	23.6

Season Team	G	Min.	FGM	FGA	Pct.	FTM	FTA	Pct.	Off.	Def.	Tot.	Ast.	St.	Blk.	TO	Pts.	RPG	APG	PPG
73-74—Los Angeles	1	14	2	9	.222	0	0	...	0	2	2	1	0	0	...	4	2.0	1.0	4.0
Totals	153	6321	1622	3460	.469	1213	1506	.805	...	...	855	970	0	0	...	4457	5.6	6.3	29.1

Personal fouls/disqualifications: 1973-74, 1/0.

NBA ALL-STAR GAME RECORD

NOTES: NBA All-Star Game Most Valuable Player (1972).

Season Team	Min.	FGM	FGA	Pct.	FTM	FTA	Pct.	Reb	Ast.	PF	Dq.	Pts.
1961—Los Angeles	25	2	8	.250	5	6	.833	2	4	3	0	9
1962—Los Angeles	31	7	14	.500	4	6	.667	3	1	2	0	18
1963—Los Angeles	32	5	15	.333	3	4	.750	7	5	1	0	13
1964—Los Angeles	42	8	20	.400	1	1	1.000	4	5	3	0	17
1965—Los Angeles	40	8	16	.500	4	6	.667	5	6	2	0	20
1966—Los Angeles	11	1	5	.200	2	2	1.000	1	0	2	0	4
1967—Los Angeles	20	6	11	.545	4	4	1.000	1	6	0	0	16
1968—Los Angeles	32	7	17	.412	3	4	.750	6	6	4	0	17
1969—Los Angeles					Selected, did not play—injured.							
1970—Los Angeles	31	7	12	.583	8	12	.667	5	5	3	0	22
1971—Los Angeles	20	2	4	.500	1	3	.333	1	9	1	0	5
1972—Los Angeles	27	6	9	.667	1	2	.500	6	5	2	0	13
1973—Los Angeles	20	3	6	.500	0	0	...	4	4	3	0	6
1974—Los Angeles					Selected, did not play—injured.							
Totals	341	62	137	.453	36	50	.720	47	55	28	0	160

NBA COACHING RECORD

	REGULAR SEASON					PLAYOFFS		
Season Team	W	L	Pct.	Finish		W	L	Pct.
76-77—Los Angeles	53	29	.646	1st/Pacific Division		4	7	.364
77-78—Los Angeles	45	37	.549	4th/Pacific Division		1	2	.333
78-79—Los Angeles	47	35	.573	3rd/Pacific Division		3	5	.375
Totals (3 years)	145	101	.589		Totals (3 years)	8	14	.364

NOTES:
1977—Defeated Golden State, 4-3, in Western Conference Semifinals; lost to Portland, 4-0, in Western Conference Finals.
1978—Lost to Seattle in Western Conference First Round.
1979—Defeated Denver, 2-1, in Western Conference First Round; lost to Seattle, 4-1, in Western Conference Semifinals.

WESTPHAL, PAUL   G

PERSONAL: Born November 30, 1950, in Torrance, Calif. ... 6-4/195 (1,93/88,4). ... Full name: Paul Douglas Westphal.
HIGH SCHOOL: Aviation (Redondo Beach, Calif.).
COLLEGE: Southern California.
TRANSACTIONS: Selected by Boston Celtics in first round (10th pick overall) of 1972 NBA Draft. ... Traded by Celtics with 1975 and 1976 second-round draft choices to Phoenix Suns for G Charlie Scott (May 23, 1975). ... Traded by Suns to Seattle SuperSonics for G Dennis Johnson (June 4, 1980). ... Signed as veteran free agent by New York Knicks (March 12, 1982). ... Waived by Knicks (June 20, 1983). ... Signed by Suns (September 27, 1983). ... Waived by Suns (October 12, 1984).
MISCELLANEOUS: Member of NBA championship team (1974).

COLLEGIATE RECORD

NOTES: THE SPORTING NEWS All-America second team (1972).

Season Team	G	Min.	FGM	FGA	Pct.	FTM	FTA	Pct.	Reb.	Ast.	Pts.	AVERAGES		
												RPG	APG	PPG
68-69—Southern Cal‡	19	...	134	262	.511	87	119	.731	106	...	355	5.6	...	18.7
69-70—Southern Cal	26	...	147	277	.531	84	110	.764	68	45	378	2.6	1.7	14.5
70-71—Southern Cal	26	...	157	328	.479	109	150	.727	84	84	423	3.2	3.2	16.3
71-72—Southern Cal	14	...	106	219	.484	72	95	.758	74	71	284	5.3	5.1	20.3
Varsity totals	66	...	410	824	.498	265	355	.746	226	200	1085	3.4	3.0	16.4

NBA REGULAR-SEASON RECORD

HONORS: NBA Comeback Player of the Year (1983). ... All-NBA first team (1977, 1979, 1980). ... All-NBA second team (1978).

Season Team	G	Min.	FGM	FGA	Pct.	FTM	FTA	Pct.	REBOUNDS			Ast.	St.	Blk.	TO	Pts.	AVERAGES		
									Off.	Def.	Tot.						RPG	APG	PPG
72-73—Boston	60	482	89	212	.420	67	86	.779	...	...	67	69	...	...	...	245	1.1	1.2	4.1
73-74—Boston	82	1165	238	475	.501	112	153	.732	49	94	143	171	39	34	...	588	1.7	2.1	7.2
74-75—Boston	82	1581	342	670	.510	119	156	.763	44	119	163	235	78	33	...	803	2.0	2.9	9.8
75-76—Phoenix	82	2960	657	1329	.494	365	440	.830	74	185	259	440	210	38	...	1679	3.2	5.4	20.5
76-77—Phoenix	81	2600	682	1317	.518	362	439	.825	57	133	190	459	134	21	...	1726	2.3	5.7	21.3
77-78—Phoenix	80	2481	809	1568	.516	396	487	.813	41	123	164	437	138	31	280	2014	2.1	5.5	25.2
78-79—Phoenix	81	2641	801	1496	.535	339	405	.837	35	124	159	529	111	26	232	1941	2.0	6.5	24.0
79-80—Phoenix	82	2665	692	1317	.525	382	443	.862	46	141	187	416	119	35	207	1792	2.3	5.1	21.9
80-81—Seattle	36	1078	221	500	.442	153	184	.832	11	57	68	148	46	14	78	601	1.9	4.1	16.7
81-82—New York	18	451	86	194	.443	36	47	.766	9	13	22	100	19	8	47	210	1.2	5.6	11.7
82-83—New York	80	1978	318	693	.459	148	184	.804	19	96	115	439	87	16	196	798	1.4	5.5	10.0
83-84—Phoenix	59	865	144	313	.460	117	142	.824	8	35	43	148	41	6	77	412	0.7	2.5	7.0
Totals	823	20947	5079	10084	.504	2596	3166	.820	...	...	1580	3591	1022	262	1117	12809	1.9	4.4	15.6

Three-point field goals: 1979-80, 26-for-93 (.280). 1980-81, 6-for-25 (.240). 1981-82, 2-for-8 (.250). 1982-83, 14-for-48 (.292). 1983-84, 7-for-26 (.269). Totals, 55-for-200 (.275).

Personal fouls/disqualifications: 1972-73, 88/0. 1973-74, 173/1. 1974-75, 192/0. 1975-76, 218/3. 1976-77, 171/1. 1977-78, 162/0. 1978-79, 159/1. 1979-80, 162/0. 1980-81, 70/0. 1981-82, 61/1. 1982-83, 180/1. 1983-84, 69/0. Totals, 1705/8.

NBA PLAYOFF RECORD

Season Team	G	Min.	FGM	FGA	Pct.	FTM	FTA	Pct.	REBOUNDS			Ast.	St.	Blk.	TO	Pts.	AVERAGES		
									Off.	Def.	Tot.						RPG	APG	PPG
72-73—Boston	11	109	19	39	.487	5	7	.714	...	...	7	9	...	...	...	43	0.6	0.8	3.9
73-74—Boston	18	241	46	100	.460	11	15	.733	6	15	21	31	8	2	...	103	1.2	1.7	5.7
74-75—Boston	11	183	38	81	.469	12	18	.667	5	8	13	32	6	2	...	88	1.2	2.9	8.0
75-76—Phoenix	19	685	165	323	.511	71	93	.763	14	33	47	96	34	9	...	401	2.5	5.1	21.1
77-78—Phoenix	2	66	22	47	.468	8	9	.889	3	3	6	19	1	0	5	52	3.0	9.5	26.0
78-79—Phoenix	15	534	142	287	.495	52	66	.788	7	26	33	64	15	5	38	336	2.2	4.3	22.4
79-80—Phoenix	8	253	69	142	.486	28	32	.875	2	8	10	31	11	3	13	167	1.3	3.9	20.9
82-83—New York	6	156	22	50	.440	10	13	.769	0	8	8	34	2	2	9	57	1.3	5.7	9.5
83-84—Phoenix	17	222	30	80	.375	28	32	.875	3	5	8	37	12	0	24	90	0.5	2.2	5.3
Totals	107	2449	553	1149	.481	225	285	.789	...	...	153	353	89	23	89	1337	1.4	3.3	12.5

Three-point field goals: 1979-80, 1-for-12 (.083). 1982-83, 3-for-8 (.375). 1983-84, 2-for-9 (.222). Totals, 6-for-29 (.207).

Personal fouls/disqualifications: 1972-73, 24/1. 1973-74, 37/0. 1974-75, 21/0. 1975-76, 61/1. 1977-78, 4/0. 1978-79, 38/0. 1979-80, 20/0. 1982-83, 13/0. 1983-84, 23/0. Totals, 241/2.

NBA ALL-STAR GAME RECORD

Season Team	Min.	FGM	FGA	Pct.	FTM	FTA	Pct.	REBOUNDS			Ast.	PF	Dq.	St.	Blk.	TO	Pts.
								Off.	Def.	Tot.							
1977—Phoenix	31	10	16	.625	0	0	...	0	1	1	6	2	0	3	2	...	20
1978—Phoenix	24	9	14	.643	2	5	.400	0	0	0	5	4	0	1	1	3	20
1979—Phoenix	21	8	12	.667	1	2	.500	0	1	1	5	0	0	0	1	1	17
1980—Phoenix	27	8	14	.571	5	6	.833	1	0	1	5	5	0	2	1	3	21
1981—Seattle	25	8	12	.667	3	3	1.000	2	2	4	3	3	0	0	1	4	19
Totals	128	43	68	.632	11	16	.688	3	4	7	24	14	0	6	5	11	97

Three-point field goals: 1980, 0-for-2.

HEAD COACHING RECORD

BACKGROUND: Assistant coach, Phoenix Suns (1988-89 through 1991-92).

COLLEGIATE COACHING RECORD

	REGULAR SEASON			
Season Team	W	L	Pct.	Finish
85-86—S'western Baptist Bible Coll.	21	9	.700	
86-87—Grand Canyon College (Ariz.)	26	12	.684	NAIA Independent
87-88—Grand Canyon College (Ariz.)	37	6	.860	NAIA Independent
01-02—Pepperdine	22	9	.710	T1st/West Coast Conference
02-03—Pepperdine	15	13	.536	4th/West Coast Conference
03-04—Pepperdine	15	16	.484	T2nd/West Coast Conference
04-05—Pepperdine	17	14	.548	T5th/West Coast Conference
Totals (7 years)	131	70	.652	

NBA COACHING RECORD

	REGULAR SEASON				PLAYOFFS		
Season Team	W	L	Pct.	Finish	W	L	Pct.
92-93—Phoenix	62	20	.756	1st/Pacific Division	13	11	.542
93-94—Phoenix	56	26	.683	2nd/Pacific Division	6	4	.600
94-95—Phoenix	59	23	.720	1st/Pacific Division	6	4	.600
95-96—Phoenix	14	19	.424		—	—	—
98-99—Seattle	25	25	.500	5th/Pacific Division	—	—	—
99-00—Seattle	45	37	.549	4th/Pacific Division	2	3	.400
00-01—Seattle	6	9	.400		—	—	—
Totals (7 years)	273	168	.619	Totals (4 years)	27	22	.551

NOTES:

1987—Defeated Fort Lewis College (Colo.), 94-87, in NAIA District 7 first round; lost to Western State College (Colo.), 74-69, in NAIA District 7 championship.

1988—Defeated Southern Colorado, 68-62, in NAIA District 7 first round; defeated Colorado School of Mines, 113-79, in District 7 championship; defeated Hastings College (Neb.), 103-75, in NAIA Tournament first round; defeated Fort Hays State (Kan.), 101-95, in second round; defeated College of Idaho, 99-96 (OT), in third round; defeated Waynesburg State (Pa.), 108-106, in fourth round; defeated Auburn-Montgomery (Ala.), 88-86 (OT), in NAIA championship game.

1993—Defeated Los Angeles Lakers, 3-2, in Western Conference first round; defeated San Antonio, 4-2, in Western Conference semifinals; defeated Seattle, 4-3, in Western Conference finals; lost to Chicago, 4-2, in NBA Finals.

1994—Defeated Golden State, 3-0, in Western Conference first round; lost to Houston, 4-3, in Western Conference semifinals.

1995—Defeated Portland, 3-0, in Western Conference first round; lost to Houston, 4-3, in Western Conference semifinals.

1996—Replaced as Phoenix head coach by Cotton Fitzsimmons (January 16), with club in fifth place.

2000—Lost to Utah in Western Conference first round. Replaced as Seattle head coach by Nate McMillan (November 27) with club in fifth place.

2002—Lost to Wake Forest, 83-74, in NCAA Tournament first round.

WHITE, JO JO   G

PERSONAL: Born November 16, 1946, in St. Louis. ... 6-3/190 (1,90/86,2). ... Full name: Joseph Henry White.
HIGH SCHOOL: Vashon (St. Louis), then McKinley (St. Louis).
COLLEGE: Kansas.
TRANSACTIONS: Selected by Boston Celtics in first round (ninth pick overall) of 1969 NBA Draft. ... Traded by Celtics to Golden State Warriors for 1979 first-round draft choice (January 30, 1979). ... Contract sold by Warriors to Kansas City Kings (September 10, 1980). ... Played in Continental Basketball Association with Topeka Sizzlers (1987-88).
CAREER NOTES: Director of special projects, Boston Celtics (2000-present).
MISCELLANEOUS: Member of NBA championship team (1974, 1976). ... Member of gold-medal-winning U.S. Olympic team (1968).

COLLEGIATE RECORD

NOTES: The Sporting News All-America first team (1968, 1969).

Season Team	G	Min.	FGM	FGA	Pct.	FTM	FTA	Pct.	Reb.	Ast.	Pts.	RPG	APG	PPG
64-65—Kansas‡	2	...	11	34	.324	11	15	.733	25	...	33	12.5	...	16.5
65-66—Kansas‡	6	...	35	88	.398	18	27	.667	32	...	88	5.3	...	14.7
65-66—Kansas	9	...	44	112	.393	14	26	.538	68	...	102	7.6	...	11.3
66-67—Kansas	27	...	170	416	.409	59	72	.819	150	...	399	5.6	...	14.8
67-68—Kansas	30	...	188	462	.407	83	115	.722	107	...	459	3.6	...	15.3
68-69—Kansas	18	...	134	286	.469	58	79	.734	84	...	326	4.7	...	18.1
Varsity totals	84	...	536	1276	.420	214	292	.733	409	...	1286	4.9	...	15.3

NBA REGULAR-SEASON RECORD

HONORS: All-NBA second team (1975, 1977). ... NBA All-Rookie team (1970).

Season Team	G	Min.	FGM	FGA	Pct.	FTM	FTA	Pct.	Reb.	Ast.	PF	Dq	Pts	RPG	APG	PPG
69-70—Boston	60	1720	309	681	.453	111	135	.822	165	145	132	1	729	2.8	2.4	12.2
70-71—Boston	75	2787	693	1494	.464	215	269	.799	376	361	255	5	1601	5.0	4.8	21.3
71-72—Boston	79	3261	770	1788	.431	285	343	.831	446	416	227	1	1825	5.6	5.3	23.1
72-73—Boston	82	3250	717	1665	.431	178	228	.781	414	498	185	2	1612	5.0	6.1	19.7

Season Team	G	Min.	FGM	FGA	Pct.	FTM	FTA	Pct.	Off.	Def.	Tot.	Ast.	St.	Blk.	TO	Pts.	RPG	APG	PPG
73-74—Boston	82	3238	649	1445	.449	190	227	.837	100	251	351	448	105	25	...	1488	4.3	5.5	18.1
74-75—Boston	82	3220	658	1440	.457	186	223	.834	84	227	311	458	128	17	...	1502	3.8	5.6	18.3
75-76—Boston	82	3257	670	1492	.449	212	253	.838	61	252	313	445	107	20	...	1552	3.8	5.4	18.9
76-77—Boston	82	3333	638	1488	.429	333	383	.869	87	296	383	492	118	22	...	1609	4.7	6.0	19.6
77-78—Boston	46	1641	289	690	.419	103	120	.858	53	127	180	209	49	7	117	681	3.9	4.5	14.8
78-79—Boston-G.S.	76	2338	404	910	.444	139	158	.880	42	158	200	347	80	7	212	947	2.6	4.6	12.5
79-80—Golden State	78	2052	336	706	.476	97	114	.851	42	139	181	239	88	13	157	770	2.3	3.1	9.9
80-81—Kansas City	13	230	36	82	.439	11	18	.611	3	18	21	37	11	1	18	83	1.6	2.8	6.4
Totals	837	29941	6169	13884	.444	2060	2471	.834	...	...	3345	4095	686	112	504	14399	4.0	4.9	17.2

Three-point field goals: 1979-80, 1-for-6 (.167).
Personal fouls/disqualifications: 1973-74, 185/1. 1974-75, 207/1. 1975-76, 183/2. 1976-77, 193/5. 1977-78, 109/2. 1978-79, 173/1. 1979-80, 186/0. 1980-81, 21/0. Totals, 2056/21.

NBA PLAYOFF RECORD

NOTES: NBA Finals Most Valuable Player (1976).

Season Team	G	Min.	FGM	FGA	Pct.	FTM	FTA	Pct.	Reb.	Ast.	PF	Dq.	Pts.	RPG	APG	PPG
71-72—Boston	11	432	109	220	.495	40	48	.833	59	58	31	0	258	5.4	5.3	23.5
72-73—Boston	13	583	135	300	.450	49	54	.907	64	83	44	2	319	4.9	6.4	24.5

Season Team	G	Min.	FGM	FGA	Pct.	FTM	FTA	Pct.	Off.	Def.	Tot.	Ast.	St.	Blk.	TO	Pts.	RPG	APG	PPG
73-74—Boston	18	765	132	310	.426	34	46	.739	17	58	75	98	15	2	...	298	4.2	5.4	16.6
74-75—Boston	11	462	100	227	.441	27	33	.818	18	32	50	63	11	4	...	227	4.5	5.7	20.6
75-76—Boston	18	791	165	371	.445	78	95	.821	12	59	71	98	23	1	...	408	3.9	5.4	22.7
76-77—Boston	9	395	91	201	.453	28	33	.848	10	29	39	52	14	0	...	210	4.3	5.8	23.3
Totals	80	3428	732	1629	.449	256	309	.828	...	...	358	452	63	7	...	1720	4.5	5.7	21.5

Personal fouls/disqualifications: 1973-74, 56/1. 1974-75, 32/0. 1975-76, 51/0. 1976-77, 27/0. Totals, 241/3.

NBA ALL-STAR GAME RECORD

Season Team	Min.	FGM	FGA	Pct.	FTM	FTA	Pct.	Reb	Ast.	PF	Dq.	Pts.
1971—Boston	22	5	10	.500	0	0	...	9	2	2	0	10
1972—Boston	18	6	15	.400	0	2	.000	4	3	1	0	12
1973—Boston	18	3	7	.429	0	0	...	5	5	0	0	6

Season Team	Min.	FGM	FGA	Pct.	FTM	FTA	Pct.	REBOUNDS Off.	Def.	Tot.	Ast.	PF	Dq.	St.	Blk.	TO	Pts.
1974—Boston	22	6	12	.500	1	3	.333	2	4	6	4	1	0	2	1	...	13
1975—Boston	13	1	2	.500	5	6	.833	0	1	1	4	1	0	0	0	...	7
1976—Boston	16	3	7	.429	0	0	...	0	1	1	1	1	0	2	0	...	6
1977—Boston	15	5	7	.714	0	0	...	0	1	1	2	0	0	0	0	...	10
Totals	124	29	60	.483	6	11	.545	...	...	27	21	6	0	4	1	...	64

CBA REGULAR-SEASON RECORD

Season Team	G	Min.	FGM	FGA	Pct.	FTM	FTA	Pct.	Reb.	Ast.	Pts.	AVERAGES RPG	APG	PPG
87-88—Topeka	5	122	12	30	.400	4	6	.667	6	21	28	1.2	4.2	5.6

Three-point field goals: 1987-88, 0-for-3.

WILKENS, LENNY   G

See All-Time Great Coaches, page 475.

WILKINS, DOMINIQUE   F/G

PERSONAL: Born January 12, 1960, in Paris. ... 6-8/224 (2,03/101,6). ... Full name: Jacques Dominique Wilkins. ... Brother of Gerald Wilkins, guard/forward with New York Knicks (1985-86 through 1991-92), Cleveland Cavaliers (1992-93 through 1994-95), Vancouver Grizzlies (1995-96) and Orlando Magic (1996-97 through 1998-99).
HIGH SCHOOL: Washington (N.C.).
COLLEGE: Georgia.
TRANSACTIONS: Selected after junior season by Utah Jazz in first round (third pick overall) of 1982 NBA Draft. ... Draft rights traded by Jazz to Atlanta Hawks for F John Drew, G Freeman Williams and cash (September 2, 1982). ... Traded by Hawks with 1994 conditional first-round draft choice to Los Angeles Clippers for F Danny Manning (February 24, 1994). ... Signed as unrestricted free agent by Boston Celtics (July 25, 1994). ... Played in Greece (1995-96). ... Signed as free agent by San Antonio Spurs (October 4, 1996). ... Played in Italy (1997-98). ... Signed as free agent by Orlando Magic (February 5, 1999). ... Waived by Magic (June 14, 1999).
CAREER NOTES: Special assistant to executive vice president, Atlanta Hawks (2001-02-present).
MISCELLANEOUS: Atlanta Hawks franchise all-time leading scorer with 23,292 points (1982-83 through 1993-94).
CAREER HONORS: Elected to Naismith Memorial Basketball Hall of Fame (2006).

COLLEGIATE RECORD

NOTES: The Sporting News All-America second team (1981, 1982).

Season Team	G	Min.	FGM	FGA	Pct.	FTM	FTA	Pct.	Reb.	Ast.	Pts.	AVERAGES RPG	APG	PPG
79-80—Georgia	16	508	135	257	.525	27	37	.730	104	23	297	6.5	1.4	18.6
80-81—Georgia	31	1157	310	582	.533	112	149	.752	234	52	732	7.5	1.7	23.6
81-82—Georgia	31	1083	278	526	.529	103	160	.644	250	41	659	8.1	1.3	21.3
Totals	78	2748	723	1365	.530	242	346	.699	588	116	1688	7.5	1.5	21.6

NBA REGULAR-SEASON RECORD

RECORDS: Holds single-game record for most free throws made without a miss—23 (December 8, 1992, vs. Chicago).
HONORS: Slam Dunk championship winner (1985, 1990). ... All-NBA first team (1986). ... All-NBA second team (1987, 1988, 1991, 1993). ... All-NBA third team (1989, 1994). ... NBA All-Rookie team (1983).

Season Team	G	Min.	FGM	FGA	Pct.	FTM	FTA	Pct.	REBOUNDS Off.	Def.	Tot.	Ast.	St.	Blk.	TO	Pts.	AVERAGES RPG	APG	PPG
82-83—Atlanta	82	2697	601	1220	.493	230	337	.682	226	252	478	129	84	63	180	1434	5.8	1.6	17.5
83-84—Atlanta	81	2961	684	1429	.479	382	496	.770	254	328	582	126	117	87	215	1750	7.2	1.6	21.6
84-85—Atlanta	81	3023	853	*1891	.451	486	603	.806	226	331	557	200	135	54	225	2217	6.9	2.5	27.4
85-86—Atlanta	78	3049	888	*1897	.468	577	705	.818	261	357	618	206	138	49	251	2366	7.9	2.6	*30.3
86-87—Atlanta	79	2969	828	1787	.463	607	742	.818	210	284	494	261	117	51	215	2294	6.3	3.3	29.0
87-88—Atlanta	78	2948	909	1957	.464	541	655	.826	211	291	502	224	103	47	218	2397	6.4	2.9	30.7
88-89—Atlanta	80	2997	814	1756	.464	442	524	.844	256	297	553	211	117	52	181	2099	6.9	2.6	26.2
89-90—Atlanta	80	2888	810	1672	.484	459	569	.807	217	304	521	200	126	47	174	2138	6.5	2.5	26.7
90-91—Atlanta	81	3078	770	1640	.470	476	574	.829	261	471	732	265	123	65	201	2101	9.0	3.3	25.9
91-92—Atlanta	42	1601	424	914	.464	294	352	.835	103	192	295	158	52	24	122	1179	7.0	3.8	28.1
92-93—Atlanta	71	2647	741	1584	.468	519	627	.828	187	295	482	227	70	27	184	2121	6.8	3.2	29.9
93-94—Atl.-L.A.C.	74	2635	698	1588	.440	442	522	.847	182	299	481	169	92	30	172	1923	6.5	2.3	26.0
94-95—Boston	77	2423	496	1169	.424	266	340	.782	157	244	401	166	61	14	173	1370	5.2	2.2	17.8
96-97—San Antonio	63	1945	397	953	.417	281	350	.803	169	233	402	119	39	31	135	1145	6.4	1.9	18.2
98-99—Orlando	27	252	50	132	.379	29	42	.690	30	41	71	16	4	1	23	134	2.6	0.6	5.0
Totals	1074	38113	9963	21589	.461	6031	7438	.811	2950	4219	7169	2677	1378	642	2669	26668	6.7	2.5	24.8

Three-point field goals: 1982-83, 2-for-11 (.182). 1983-84, 0-for-11. 1984-85, 25-for-81 (.309). 1985-86, 13-for-70 (.186). 1986-87, 31-for-106 (.292). 1987-88, 38-for-129 (.295). 1988-89, 29-for-105 (.276). 1989-90, 59-for-183 (.322). 1990-91, 85-for-249 (.341). 1991-92, 37-for-128 (.289). 1992-93, 120-for-316 (.380). 1993-94, 85-for-295 (.288). 1994-95, 112-for-289 (.388). 1996-97, 70-for-239 (.293). 1998-99, 5-for-19 (.263). Totals, 711-for-2231 (.319).
Personal fouls/disqualifications: 1982-83, 210/1. 1983-84, 197/1. 1984-85, 170/0. 1985-86, 170/0. 1986-87, 149/0. 1987-88, 162/0. 1988-89, 138/0. 1989-90, 141/0. 1990-91, 156/0. 1991-92, 77/0. 1992-93, 116/0. 1993-94, 126/0. 1994-95, 100/0. 1996-97, 100/0. 1998-99, 19/0. Totals, 2061/2.

NBA PLAYOFF RECORD

Season Team	G	Min.	FGM	FGA	Pct.	FTM	FTA	Pct.	REBOUNDS Off.	Def.	Tot.	Ast.	St.	Blk.	TO	Pts.	AVERAGES RPG	APG	PPG
82-83—Atlanta	3	109	17	42	.405	12	14	.857	8	7	15	1	2	1	10	47	5.0	0.3	15.7
83-84—Atlanta	5	197	35	84	.417	26	31	.839	21	20	41	11	12	1	15	96	8.2	2.2	19.2
85-86—Atlanta	9	360	94	217	.433	68	79	.861	20	34	54	25	9	2	30	257	6.0	2.8	28.6
86-87—Atlanta	9	360	86	210	.410	66	74	.892	27	43	70	25	16	8	26	241	7.8	2.8	26.8
87-88—Atlanta	12	473	137	300	.457	96	125	.768	37	40	77	34	16	6	30	374	6.4	2.8	31.2
88-89—Atlanta	5	212	52	116	.448	27	38	.711	10	17	27	17	4	8	12	136	5.4	3.4	27.2
90-91—Atlanta	5	195	35	94	.372	32	35	.914	6	26	32	13	9	5	11	104	6.4	2.6	20.8

Season Team	G	Min.	FGM	FGA	Pct.	FTM	FTA	Pct.	REBOUNDS Off.	Def.	Tot.	Ast.	St.	Blk.	TO	Pts.	RPG	APG	PPG
92-93—Atlanta	3	113	32	75	.427	23	30	.767	12	4	16	9	3	1	10	90	5.3	3.0	30.0
94-95—Boston	4	150	26	61	.426	16	18	.889	17	26	43	8	2	3	9	76	10.8	2.0	19.0
98-99—Orlando	1	3	1	2	.500	0	0	...	0	0	0	0	0	0	0	2	0.0	0.0	2.0
Totals	56	2172	515	1201	.429	366	444	.824	158	217	375	143	73	35	153	1423	6.7	2.6	25.4

Three-point field goals: 1982-83, 1-for-1. 1983-84, 0-for-1. 1985-86, 1-for-5 (.200). 1986-87, 3-for-10 (.300). 1987-88, 4-for-18 (.222). 1988-89, 5-for-17 (.294). 1990-91, 2-for-15 (.133). 1992-93, 3-for-12 (.250). 1994-95, 8-for-17 (.471). Totals, 27-for-96 (.281).

Personal fouls/disqualifications: 1982-83, 9/0. 1983-84, 13/0. 1985-86, 24/0. 1986-87, 25/0. 1987-88, 24/0. 1988-89, 5/0. 1990-91, 8/0. 1992-93, 8/0. 1994-95, 7/0. Totals, 123/0.

NBA ALL-STAR GAME RECORD

Season Team	Min.	FGM	FGA	Pct.	FTM	FTA	Pct.	REBOUNDS Off.	Def.	Tot.	Ast.	PF	Dq.	St.	Blk.	TO	Pts.
1986—Atlanta.................	17	6	15	.400	1	2	.500	2	1	3	2	2	0	0	1	1	13
1987—Atlanta.................	24	3	9	.333	4	7	.571	3	2	5	1	2	0	0	1	2	10
1988—Atlanta.................	30	12	22	.545	5	6	.833	1	4	5	0	3	0	0	1	0	29
1989—Atlanta.................	15	3	8	.375	3	3	1.000	1	1	2	0	0	0	3	0	2	9
1990—Atlanta.................	16	5	10	.500	2	2	1.000	0	0	0	4	1	0	1	0	0	13
1991—Atlanta.................	22	3	11	.273	6	8	.750	3	1	4	3	4	2	0	1	1	12
1992—Atlanta.................								Selected, did not play—injured.									
1993—Atlanta.................	18	2	11	.182	4	4	1.000	4	3	7	0	2	0	1	0	1	9
1994—Atlanta.................	17	4	9	.444	3	6	.500	2	0	2	4	1	0	0	0	0	11
Totals...........................	159	38	95	.400	28	38	.737	16	11	27	15	13	0	6	4	8	106

Three-point field goals: 1990, 1-for-1. 1991, 0-for-2. 1993, 1-for-3 (.333). 1994, 0-for-1. Totals, 2-for-8 (.250).

GREEK LEAGUE RECORD

Season Team	G	Min.	FGM	FGA	Pct.	FTM	FTA	Pct.	Reb.	Ast.	Pts.	AVERAGES RPG	APG	PPG
95-96—Panathinaikos.................	14	...	...	...	...	...	...	...	95	19	292	6.8	1.4	20.9

ITALIAN LEAGUE RECORD

Season Team	G	Min.	FGM	FGA	Pct.	FTM	FTA	Pct.	Reb.	Ast.	Pts.	AVERAGES RPG	APG	PPG
97-98—Teamsystem Bologna	23	775	159	322	.494	111	134	.828	158	40	450	6.9	1.7	19.6

WILLIAMS, BUCK — F

PERSONAL: Born March 8, 1960, in Rocky Mount, N.C. ... 6-8/225 (2,03/102,1). ... Full name: Charles Linwood Williams.
HIGH SCHOOL: Rocky Mount (N.C.).
COLLEGE: Maryland.
TRANSACTIONS/CAREER NOTES: Selected after junior season by New Jersey Nets in first round (third pick overall) of 1981 NBA Draft. ... Traded by Nets to Portland Trail Blazers for C Sam Bowie and 1989 first-round draft choice (June 24, 1989). ... Rights renounced by Trail Blazers (July 23, 1996). ... Signed as free agent by New York Knicks (July 26, 1996). ... Announced retirement (January 27, 1999).
MISCELLANEOUS: Member of U.S. Olympic team (1980). ... New Jersey Nets franchise all-time leading scorer with 10,440 points and all-time leading rebounder with 7,576 (1981-82 through 1988-89).

COLLEGIATE RECORD

Season Team	G	Min.	FGM	FGA	Pct.	FTM	FTA	Pct.	Reb.	Ast.	Pts.	AVERAGES RPG	APG	PPG
78-79—Maryland	30	906	120	206	.583	60	109	.550	323	18	300	10.8	0.6	10.0
79-80—Maryland	24	872	143	236	.606	85	128	.664	242	27	371	10.1	1.1	15.5
80-81—Maryland	31	1080	183	283	.647	116	182	.637	363	31	482	11.7	1.0	15.5
Totals	85	2858	446	725	.615	261	419	.623	928	76	1153	10.9	0.9	13.6

NBA REGULAR-SEASON RECORD

HONORS: NBA Rookie of the Year (1982). ... All-NBA second team (1983). ... NBA All-Defensive first team (1990, 1991). ... NBA All-Defensive second team (1988, 1992). ... NBA All-Rookie team (1982).

Season Team	G	Min.	FGM	FGA	Pct.	FTM	FTA	Pct.	REBOUNDS Off.	Def.	Tot.	Ast.	St.	Blk.	TO	Pts.	RPG	APG	PPG
81-82—New Jersey	82	2825	513	881	.582	242	388	.624	347	658	1005	107	84	84	235	1268	12.3	1.3	15.5
82-83—New Jersey	82	2961	536	912	.588	324	523	.620	365	662	1027	125	91	110	246	1396	12.5	1.5	17.0
83-84—New Jersey	81	3003	495	926	.535	284	498	.570	*355	645	1000	130	63	125	237	1274	12.3	1.6	15.7
84-85—New Jersey	82	*3182	577	1089	.530	336	538	.625	323	682	1005	167	63	110	238	1491	12.3	2.0	18.2
85-86—New Jersey	82	3070	500	956	.523	301	445	.676	329	657	986	131	73	96	244	1301	12.0	1.6	15.9
86-87—New Jersey	82	2976	521	936	.557	430	588	.731	322	701	1023	129	78	91	280	1472	12.5	1.6	18.0
87-88—New Jersey	70	2637	466	832	.560	346	518	.668	298	536	834	109	68	44	189	1279	11.9	1.6	18.3
88-89—New Jersey	74	2446	373	702	.531	213	320	.666	249	447	696	78	61	36	142	959	9.4	1.1	13.0
89-90—Portland	82	2801	413	754	.548	288	408	.706	250	550	800	116	69	39	168	1114	9.8	1.4	13.6
90-91—Portland	80	2582	358	595	*.602	217	308	.705	227	524	751	97	47	47	137	933	9.4	1.2	11.7
91-92—Portland	80	2519	340	563	*.604	221	293	.754	260	444	704	108	62	41	130	901	8.8	1.4	11.3
92-93—Portland	82	2498	270	528	.511	138	214	.645	232	458	690	75	81	61	101	678	8.4	0.9	8.3
93-94—Portland	81	2636	291	524	.555	201	296	.679	315	528	843	80	58	47	111	783	10.4	1.0	9.7
94-95—Portland	82	2422	309	604	.512	138	205	.673	251	418	669	78	67	69	119	757	8.2	1.0	9.2
95-96—Portland	70	1672	192	384	.500	125	187	.668	159	245	404	42	40	47	90	511	5.8	0.6	7.3
96-97—New York	74	1496	175	326	.537	115	179	.642	166	231	397	53	40	38	79	465	5.4	0.7	6.3
97-98—New York	41	738	75	149	.503	52	71	.732	78	105	183	21	17	15	38	202	4.5	0.5	4.9
Totals	1307	42464	6404	11661	.549	3971	5979	.664	4526	8491 13017	1646	1080	1100	2784	16784	10.0	1.3	12.8

Three-point field goals: 1981-82, 0-for-1. 1982-83, 0-for-4. 1983-84, 0-for-1. 1984-85, 1-for-4 (.250). 1985-86, 0-for-2. 1986-87, 0-for-1. 1987-88, 0-for-1. 1988-89, 0-for-3. 1989-90, 0-for-1. 1991-92, 0-for-1. 1992-93, 0-for-1. 1993-94, 0-for-1. 1994-95, 1-for-2 (.500). 1995-96, 2-for-3 (.667). 1996-97, 0-for-1. Totals, 5-for-30 (.167).

Personal fouls/disqualifications: 1981-82, 285/5. 1982-83, 270/4. 1983-84, 298/3. 1984-85, 293/7. 1985-86, 294/9. 1986-87, 315/8. 1987-88, 266/5. 1988-89, 223/0. 1989-90, 285/4. 1990-91, 247/2. 1991-92, 244/4. 1992-93, 270/0. 1993-94, 239/1. 1994-95, 254/2. 1995-96, 187/1. 1996-97, 204/2. 1997-98, 93/1. Totals, 4267/58.

NBA PLAYOFF RECORD

Season Team	G	Min.	FGM	FGA	Pct.	FTM	FTA	Pct.	REBOUNDS Off.	Def.	Tot.	Ast.	St.	Blk.	TO	Pts.	AVERAGES RPG	APG	PPG
81-82—New Jersey	2	79	14	26	.538	7	15	.647	11	10	21	3	1	2	4	35	10.5	1.5	17.5
82-83—New Jersey	2	85	11	22	.500	16	20	.800	9	14	23	4	2	2	5	38	11.5	2.0	19.0
83-84—New Jersey	11	473	63	130	.485	45	81	.556	57	98	155	16	15	17	29	171	14.1	1.5	15.5
84-85—New Jersey	3	123	26	40	.650	22	30	.733	14	18	32	1	3	5	6	74	10.7	0.3	24.7
85-86—New Jersey	3	126	21	29	.724	20	26	.769	12	19	31	2	6	1	6	62	10.3	0.7	20.7
89-90—Portland	21	776	101	199	.508	71	105	.676	67	126	193	39	13	6	41	273	9.2	1.9	13.0
90-91—Portland	16	572	65	130	.500	35	58	.603	53	90	143	14	10	4	24	165	8.9	0.9	10.3
91-92—Portland	21	758	66	130	.508	69	91	.758	61	118	179	22	27	17	45	201	8.5	1.0	9.6
92-93—Portland	4	119	11	23	.478	13	19	.684	12	17	29	1	1	3	6	35	7.3	0.3	8.8
93-94—Portland	4	125	19	28	.679	13	15	.867	14	21	35	2	4	2	8	51	8.8	0.5	12.8
94-95—Portland	3	103	9	15	.600	7	11	.636	8	11	19	1	4	2	4	25	6.3	0.3	8.3
95-96—Portland	5	133	9	23	.391	5	7	.714	13	12	25	1	1	4	5	24	5.0	0.2	4.8
96-97—New York	10	193	17	35	.486	9	17	.529	13	27	40	6	3	4	4	43	4.0	0.6	4.3
97-98—New York	3	45	4	9	.444	6	8	.750	7	9	16	1	0	1	3	14	5.3	0.3	4.7
Totals	108	3710	436	839	.520	338	503	.672	351	590	941	113	90	70	190	1211	8.7	1.0	11.2

Three-point field goals: 1995-96, 1-for-2 (.500).

Personal fouls/disqualifications: 1981-82, 7/0. 1982-83, 12/2. 1983-84, 44/2. 1984-85, 12/0. 1985-86, 15/1. 1989-90, 74/1. 1990-91, 55/1. 1991-92, 73/1. 1992-93, 12/1. 1993-94, 11/0. 1994-95, 14/1. 1995-96, 18/0. 1996-97, 34/0. 1997-98, 5/0. Totals, 386/10.

NBA ALL-STAR GAME RECORD

Season Team	Min.	FGM	FGA	Pct.	FTM	FTA	Pct.	REBOUNDS Off.	Def.	Tot.	Ast.	PF	Dq.	St.	Blk.	TO	Pts.
1982—New Jersey	22	2	7	.286	0	2	.000	1	9	10	1	3	0	0	2	3	4
1983—New Jersey	19	3	4	.750	2	4	.500	3	4	7	1	0	0	1	0	0	8
1986—New Jersey	20	5	8	.625	3	5	.600	3	4	7	4	0	0	0	0	1	13
Totals	61	10	19	.526	5	11	.455	7	17	24	6	3	0	1	2	4	25

WILLIS, KEVIN   F/C

PERSONAL: Born September 6, 1962, in Los Angeles. ... 7-0/245. (2.13/111.1). ... Full name: Kevin Alvin Willis.
HIGH SCHOOL: Pershing (Detroit).
JUNIOR COLLEGE: Jackson Community College (Mich.).
COLLEGE: Michigan State.
TRANSACTIONS/CAREER NOTES: Selected by Atlanta Hawks in first round (11th pick overall) of 1984 NBA Draft. ... Traded by Hawks with conditional first-round draft choice to Miami Heat for G Steve Smith, F Grant Long and conditional second-round draft choice (November 7, 1994). ... Traded by Heat with G Bimbo Coles to Golden State Warriors for G Tim Hardaway and F/C Chris Gatling (February 22, 1996). ... Signed as free agent by Houston Rockets (August 19, 1996). ... Traded by Rockets to Toronto Raptors for F Roy Rogers and two first-round picks in 1998 draft (June 9, 1998). ... Traded by Raptors with C Aleksander Radojevic, C Garth Joseph and 2001 or 2002 second-round draft choice to Denver Nuggets for F Tracy Murray, F/C Keon Clark and C Mamadou N'diaye (January 12, 2001). ... Traded by Nuggets with C Aleksander Radojevic to Milwaukee Bucks for F/C Scott Williams and future first-round draft choice (October 22, 2001). ... Traded by Bucks to Houston Rockets for 2002 second-round draft choice (October 22, 2001). ... Signed as free agent by San Antonio Spurs (August 26, 2002). ... Signed as free agent by Atlanta Hawks (September 22, 2004).
MISCELLANEOUS: Member of NBA championship team (2003).

COLLEGIATE RECORD

Season Team	G	Min.	FGM	FGA	Pct.	FTM	FTA	Pct.	Reb.	Ast.	Pts.	AVERAGES RPG	APG	PPG
80-81—Jackson C.C.	...	...	...	...	...	...	...	...	...	...	...	...	...	...
81-82—Michigan State	27	518	73	154	.474	17	30	.567	113	2	163	4.2	0.1	6.0
82-83—Michigan State	27	865	162	272	.596	36	70	.514	258	8	360	9.6	0.3	13.3
83-84—Michigan State	25	738	118	240	.492	39	59	.661	192	7	275	7.7	0.3	11.0
Junior College Totals	...	...	...	...	...	...	...	...	...	...	...	...	...	...
4-Year-College Totals	79	2121	353	666	.530	92	159	.579	563	17	798	7.1	0.2	10.1

Three-point field goals: 1982-83, 0-for-1. Totals, 0-for-1 (.000).

NBA REGULAR-SEASON RECORD

HONORS: All-NBA Third Team (1992).

Season Team	G	Min.	FGM	FGA	Pct.	FTM	FTA	Pct.	REBOUNDS Off.	Def.	Tot.	Ast.	St.	Blk.	TO	Pts.	AVERAGES RPG	APG	PPG
84-85—Atlanta	82	1785	322	690	.467	119	181	.657	177	345	522	36	31	49	104	765	6.4	0.4	9.3
85-86—Atlanta	82	2300	419	811	.517	172	263	.654	243	461	704	45	66	44	177	1010	8.6	0.5	12.3
86-87—Atlanta	81	2626	538	1003	.536	227	320	.709	321	528	849	62	65	61	173	1304	10.5	0.8	16.1
87-88—Atlanta	75	2091	356	687	.518	159	245	.649	235	312	547	28	68	42	138	871	7.3	0.4	11.6
88-89—Atlanta							Did not play—injured.												
89-90—Atlanta	81	2273	418	805	.519	168	246	.683	253	392	645	57	63	47	144	1006	8.0	0.7	12.4
90-91—Atlanta	80	2373	444	881	.504	159	238	.668	259	445	704	99	60	43	153	1051	8.8	1.2	13.1
91-92—Atlanta	81	2962	591	1224	.483	292	363	.804	418	840	1258	173	72	54	197	1480	15.5	2.1	18.3
92-93—Atlanta	80	2878	616	1218	.506	196	300	.653	335	693	1028	165	68	41	213	1435	12.9	2.1	17.9
93-94—Atlanta	80	2867	627	1257	.499	268	376	.713	335	628	963	150	79	38	188	1531	12.0	1.9	19.1
94-95—Atlanta-Miami .	67	2390	473	1015	.466	205	297	.690	227	505	732	86	60	36	162	1154	10.9	1.3	17.2
95-96—Mia.-G.S.	75	2135	325	712	.456	143	202	.708	208	430	638	53	32	41	161	794	8.5	0.7	10.6
96-97—Houston	75	1964	350	728	.481	140	202	.693	146	415	561	71	42	32	119	842	7.5	0.9	11.2
97-98—Houston	81	2528	531	1041	.510	242	305	.793	232	447	679	78	55	38	170	1305	8.4	1.0	16.1
98-99—Toronto	42	1216	187	447	.418	130	155	.839	109	241	350	67	28	28	86	504	8.3	1.6	12.0
99-00—Toronto	79	1679	236	569	.415	131	164	.799	201	281	482	49	36	48	98	604	6.1	0.6	7.6
00-01—Toronto-Den. ..	78	1830	304	690	.441	113	147	.769	177	355	532	50	57	52	87	722	6.8	0.6	9.3
01-02—Houston	52	865	125	284	.440	65	87	.747	105	194	299	14	25	23	41	315	5.8	0.3	6.1
02-03—San Antonio	71	840	123	257	.479	51	83	.614	83	143	226	24	20	20	60	297	3.2	0.3	4.2

Season Team	G	Min.	FGM	FGA	Pct.	FTM	FTA	Pct.	Off.	Def.	Tot.	Ast.	St.	Blk.	TO	Pts.	RPG	APG	PPG
03-04—San Antonio....	48	373	70	150	.467	24	39	.615	37	61	98	11	21	9	32	164	2.0	0.2	3.4
04-05—Atlanta	29	344	35	90	.389	17	23	.739	29	47	76	9	8	7	15	87	2.6	0.3	3.0
Totals	1419	38319	7090	14559	.487	3021	4236	.713	4130	7763	11893	1327	956	750	2518	17241	8.4	0.9	12.2

Three-point field goals: 1984-85, 2-for-9 (.222). 1985-86, 0-for-6. 1986-87, 1-for-4 (.250). 1987-88, 0-for-2. 1989-90, 2-for-7 (.286). 1990-91, 4-for-10 (.400). 1991-92, 6-for-37 (.162). 1992-93, 7-for-29 (.241). 1993-94, 9-for-24 (.375). 1994-95, 3-for-15 (.200). 1995-96, 1-for-9 (.111). 1996-97, 2-for-14 (.143). 1997-98, 1-for-7 (.143). 1998-99, 0-for-2. 1999-00, 1-for-3 (.333). 2000-01, 1-for-6 (.167). 2001-02, 0-for-1. 2002-03, 0-for-2. 2003-04, 0-for-1. 2004-05, 0-for-2. Totals, 40-for-190 (.211).

Personal fouls/disqualifications: 1984-85, 226/4. 1985-86, 294/6. 1986-87, 313/4. 1987-88, 240/2. 1989-90, 259/4. 1990-91, 235/2. 1991-92, 223/0. 1992-93, 264/1. 1993-94, 250/2. 1994-95, 215/3. 1995-96, 253/4. 1996-97, 216/1. 1997-98, 235/1. 1998-99, 134/1. 1999-00, 256/0. 2000-01, 216/0. 2001-02, 98/0. 2002-03, 120/1. 2003-04, 61/0. 2004-05, 53/0. Totals, 4161/39.

NBA PLAYOFF RECORD

Season Team	G	Min.	FGM	FGA	Pct.	FTM	FTA	Pct.	Off.	Def.	Tot.	Ast.	St.	Blk.	TO	Pts.	RPG	APG	PPG
85-86—Atlanta	9	280	55	98	.561	15	23	.652	31	34	65	5	7	8	15	125	7.2	0.6	13.9
86-87—Atlanta	9	356	60	115	.522	21	31	.677	33	50	83	6	9	7	17	141	9.2	0.7	15.7
87-88—Atlanta	12	462	80	138	.580	34	50	.680	36	72	108	11	10	10	25	194	9.0	0.9	16.2
90-91—Atlanta	5	159	27	67	.403	21	30	.700	18	27	45	5	3	1	2	77	9.0	1.0	15.4
92-93—Atlanta	3	103	21	45	.467	8	14	.571	13	13	26	3	2	0	7	50	8.7	1.0	16.7
93-94—Atlanta	11	362	59	129	.457	16	21	.762	38	81	119	11	8	5	19	134	10.8	1.0	12.2
96-97—Houston	16	295	38	95	.400	26	38	.684	22	53	75	11	9	4	22	102	4.7	0.7	6.4
97-98—Houston	5	168	22	55	.400	12	16	.750	18	35	53	5	8	3	12	56	10.6	1.0	11.2
99-00—Toronto	3	76	12	33	.364	15	20	.750	6	20	26	1	2	0	2	39	8.7	0.3	13.0
02-03—San Antonio....	18	91	21	40	.525	3	3	1.000	19	12	31	2	1	1	8	46	1.7	0.1	2.6
03-04—San Antonio....	7	25	3	8	.375	0	1	.000	0	6	6	0	1	0	0	6	0.9	0.0	0.9
Totals	98	2377	398	823	.484	171	247	.692	234	403	637	60	60	39	129	970	6.5	0.6	9.9

Three-point field goals: 1987-88, 0-for-1. 1990-91, 2-for-3 (.667). 1992-93, 0-for-1. 1993-94, 0-for-5. 1996-97, 0-for-1. 1997-98, 0-for-1. 2002-03, 1-for-1 (1.000). 2003-04, 0-for-1. Totals, 3-for-14 (.214).

Personal fouls/disqualifications: 1985-86, 38/2. 1986-87, 33/0. 1987-88, 51/1. 1990-91, 22/0. 1992-93, 13/0. 1993-94, 37/0. 1996-97, 47/0. 1997-98, 21/0. 1999-00, 11/0. 2002-03, 16/0. 2003-04, 5/0. Totals, 294/3.

NBA ALL-STAR GAME RECORD

Season Team	Min.	FGM	FGA	Pct.	FTM	FTA	Pct.	Off.	Def.	Tot.	Ast.	PF	Dq.	St.	Blk.	TO	Pts.
1992—Atlanta.................	14	4	10	.400	0	0	...	4	0	4	0	1	0	0	0	0	8

WORTHY, JAMES — F

PERSONAL: Born February 27, 1961, in Gastonia, N.C. ... 6-9/225 (2,05/102,1). ... Full name: James Ager Worthy.
HIGH SCHOOL: Ashbrook (Gastonia, N.C.).
COLLEGE: North Carolina.
TRANSACTIONS: Selected after junior season by Los Angeles Lakers in first round (first pick overall) of 1982 NBA Draft. ... Announced retirement (November 10, 1994).
CAREER HONORS: Elected to Naismith Memorial Basketball Hall of Fame (2003). ... One of the 50 Greatest Players in NBA History (1996).
MISCELLANEOUS: Member of NBA championship team (1985, 1987, 1988).

COLLEGIATE RECORD

NOTES: Member of NCAA Division I championship team (1982). ... NCAA Division I Tournament Most Outstanding Player (1982). ... THE SPORTING NEWS All-America first team (1982).

Season Team	G	Min.	FGM	FGA	Pct.	FTM	FTA	Pct.	Reb.	Ast.	Pts.	RPG	APG	PPG
79-80—North Carolina...............	14	396	74	126	.587	27	45	.600	104	26	175	7.4	1.9	12.5
80-81—North Carolina...............	36	1214	208	416	.500	96	150	.640	301	100	512	8.4	2.8	14.2
81-82—North Carolina...............	34	1178	203	354	.573	126	187	.674	215	82	532	6.3	2.4	15.6
Totals	84	2788	485	896	.541	249	382	.652	620	208	1219	7.4	2.5	14.5

NBA REGULAR-SEASON RECORD

HONORS: All-NBA third team (1990, 1991). ... NBA All-Rookie team (1983).

Season Team	G	Min.	FGM	FGA	Pct.	FTM	FTA	Pct.	Off.	Def.	Tot.	Ast.	St.	Blk.	TO	Pts.	RPG	APG	PPG
82-83—Los Angeles....	77	1970	447	772	.579	138	221	.624	157	242	399	132	91	64	178	1033	5.2	1.7	13.4
83-84—Los Angeles....	82	2415	495	890	.556	195	257	.759	157	358	515	207	77	70	181	1185	6.3	2.5	14.5
84-85—L.A. Lakers	80	2696	610	1066	.572	190	245	.776	169	342	511	201	87	67	198	1410	6.4	2.5	17.6
85-86—L.A. Lakers	75	2454	629	1086	.579	242	314	.771	136	251	387	201	82	77	149	1500	5.2	2.7	20.0
86-87—L.A. Lakers	82	2819	651	1207	.539	292	389	.751	158	308	466	226	108	83	168	1594	5.7	2.8	19.4
87-88—L.A. Lakers	75	2655	617	1161	.531	242	304	.796	129	245	374	289	72	55	155	1478	5.0	3.9	19.7
88-89—L.A. Lakers	81	2960	702	1282	.548	251	321	.782	169	320	489	288	108	56	182	1657	6.0	3.6	20.5
89-90—L.A. Lakers	80	2960	711	1298	.548	248	317	.782	160	318	478	288	99	49	160	1685	6.0	3.6	21.1
90-91—L.A. Lakers	78	3008	716	1455	.492	212	266	.797	107	249	356	275	104	35	127	1670	4.6	3.5	21.4
91-92—L.A. Lakers	54	2108	450	1007	.447	166	204	.814	98	207	305	252	76	23	127	1075	5.6	4.7	19.9
92-93—L.A. Lakers	82	2359	510	1142	.447	171	211	.810	73	174	247	278	92	27	137	1221	3.0	3.4	14.9
93-94—L.A. Lakers	80	1597	340	838	.406	100	135	.741	48	133	181	154	45	18	97	812	2.3	1.9	10.2
Totals	926	30001	6878	13204	.521	2447	3184	.769	1561	3147	4708	2791	1041	624	1859	16320	5.1	3.0	17.6

Three-point field goals: 1982-83, 1-for-4 (.250). 1983-84, 0-for-6. 1984-85, 0-for-7. 1985-86, 0-for-13. 1986-87, 0-for-13. 1987-88, 2-for-16 (.125). 1988-89, 2-for-23 (.087). 1989-90, 15-for-49 (.306). 1990-91, 26-for-90 (.289). 1991-92, 9-for-43 (.209). 1992-93, 30-for-111 (.270). 1993-94, 32-for-111 (.288). Totals, 117-for-486 (.241).

Personal fouls/disqualifications: 1982-83, 221/2. 1983-84, 244/5. 1984-85, 196/0. 1985-86, 195/0. 1986-87, 206/0. 1987-88, 175/1. 1988-89, 175/0. 1989-90, 190/0. 1990-91, 117/0. 1991-92, 89/0. 1992-93, 87/0. 1993-94, 80/0. Totals, 1975/8.

NBA PLAYOFF RECORD

NOTES: NBA Finals Most Valuable Player (1988).

Season Team	G	Min.	FGM	FGA	Pct.	FTM	FTA	Pct.	Off.	Def.	Tot.	Ast.	St.	Blk.	TO	Pts.	RPG	APG	PPG
83-84—Los Angeles....	21	708	164	274	.599	42	69	.609	36	69	105	56	27	11	39	371	5.0	2.7	17.7
84-85—L.A. Lakers	19	626	166	267	.622	75	111	.676	35	61	96	41	17	13	26	408	5.1	2.2	21.5
85-86—L.A. Lakers	14	539	121	217	.558	32	47	.681	22	43	65	45	16	10	36	274	4.6	3.2	19.6
86-87—L.A. Lakers	18	681	176	298	.591	73	97	.753	31	70	101	63	28	22	40	425	5.6	3.5	23.6
87-88—L.A. Lakers	24	896	204	390	.523	97	128	.758	53	86	139	106	33	19	55	506	5.8	4.4	21.1
88-89—L.A. Lakers	15	600	153	270	.567	63	80	.788	37	64	101	42	18	16	33	372	6.7	2.8	24.8
89-90—L.A. Lakers	9	366	90	181	.497	36	43	.837	11	39	50	27	14	3	22	218	5.6	3.0	24.2
90-91—L.A. Lakers	18	733	161	346	.465	53	72	.736	25	48	73	70	19	2	40	379	4.1	3.9	21.1
92-93—L.A. Lakers	5	148	32	86	.372	3	5	.600	7	10	17	13	5	0	7	69	3.4	2.6	13.8
Totals	143	5297	1267	2329	.544	474	652	.727	257	490	747	463	177	96	298	3022	5.2	3.2	21.1

Three-point field goals: 1983-84, 1-for-2 (.500). 1984-85, 1-for-2 (.500). 1985-86, 0-for-4. 1986-87, 0-for-2. 1987-88, 1-for-9 (.111). 1988-89, 3-for-8 (.375). 1989-90, 2-for-8 (.250). 1990-91, 4-for-24 (.167). 1992-93, 2-for-8 (.250). Totals, 14-for-67 (.209).

Personal fouls/disqualifications: 1983-84, 57/0. 1984-85, 53/1. 1985-86, 43/0. 1986-87, 42/1. 1987-88, 58/0. 1988-89, 36/0. 1989-90, 18/0. 1990-91, 34/0. 1992-93, 11/0. Totals, 352/2.

NBA ALL-STAR GAME RECORD

Season Team	Min.	FGM	FGA	Pct.	FTM	FTA	Pct.	Off.	Def.	Tot.	Ast.	PF	Dq.	St.	Blk.	TO	Pts.
1986—L.A. Lakers	28	10	19	.526	0	0	...	2	1	3	2	3	0	0	2	1	20
1987—L.A. Lakers	29	10	14	.714	2	2	1.000	6	2	8	3	3	0	1	0	2	22
1988—L.A. Lakers	13	2	8	.250	0	1	.000	1	2	3	1	1	0	0	1	0	4
1989—L.A. Lakers	18	4	7	.571	0	0	...	0	2	2	2	0	0	2	0	0	8
1990—L.A. Lakers	19	1	11	.091	0	0	...	3	1	4	0	1	0	1	0	1	2
1991—L.A. Lakers	21	3	11	.273	3	4	.750	0	2	2	0	2	0	2	1	0	9
1992—L.A. Lakers	14	4	7	.571	1	2	.500	0	4	4	1	0	0	1	0	0	9
Totals	142	34	77	.442	6	9	.667	12	14	26	9	10	0	7	4	4	74

Three-point field goals: 1986, 0-for-2. 1989, 0-for-1. Totals, 0-for-3.

YARDLEY, GEORGE   F

PERSONAL: Born November 23, 1928, in Hollywood, Calif. ... 6-5/195 (1,96/88,4). ... Full name: George Harry Yardley III.
HIGH SCHOOL: Newport Harbor (Calif.).
COLLEGE: Stanford.
TRANSACTIONS: Selected by Fort Wayne Pistons in first round of 1950 NBA Draft. ... Played with the San Francisco Stewart Chevrolets in the National Industrial Basketball League, an Amateur Athletic Union League, during 1950-51 season (finished third in the league in scoring with a 13.1 point average on 104 field goals and 53 free throws for 261 points in 20 games). ... In military service during 1951-52 and 1952-53 seasons. ... Signed by Pistons (1953). ... Pistons franchise moved from Fort Wayne to Detroit for 1957-58 season. ... Traded by Pistons to Syracuse Nationals for F/G Ed Conlin (February 13, 1959). ... Played in American Basketball League with Los Angeles Jets (1961-62).
CAREER HONORS: Elected to Naismith Memorial Basketball Hall of Fame (1996).

COLLEGIATE RECORD

Season Team	G	Min.	FGM	FGA	Pct.	FTM	FTA	Pct.	Reb.	Ast.	Pts.	RPG	APG	PPG
46-47—Stanford‡						Freshman team statistics unavailable.								
47-48—Stanford	18	...	22	...	...	8	20	.400	...	...	52	...	...	2.9
48-49—Stanford	28	...	126	377	.334	93	131	.710	...	...	345	...	...	12.3
49-50—Stanford	25	...	164	452	.363	95	130	.731	...	...	423	...	...	16.9
Varsity totals	71	...	312	...	...	196	281	.698	...	...	820	...	...	11.5

NBA REGULAR-SEASON RECORD

HONORS: All-NBA first team (1958). ... All-NBA second team (1957).

Season Team	G	Min.	FGM	FGA	Pct.	FTM	FTA	Pct.	Reb.	Ast.	PF	Dq.	Pts.	RPG	APG	PPG
53-54—Fort Wayne	63	1489	209	492	.425	146	205	.712	407	99	166	3	564	6.5	1.6	9.0
54-55—Fort Wayne	60	2150	363	869	.418	310	416	.745	594	126	205	7	1036	9.9	2.1	17.3
55-56—Fort Wayne	71	2353	434	1067	.407	365	492	.742	686	159	212	2	1233	9.7	2.2	17.4
56-57—Fort Wayne	72	2691	522	1273	.410	503	639	.787	755	147	231	2	1547	10.5	2.0	21.5
57-58—Detroit	72	2843	673	*1624	.414	*655	*800	.811	768	97	226	3	*2001	10.7	1.3	*27.8
58-59—Det.-Syr..	61	1839	446	1042	.428	317	407	.779	431	65	159	2	1209	7.1	1.1	19.8
59-60—Syracuse	73	2402	546	1205	.453	381	467	.816	579	122	227	3	1473	7.9	1.7	20.2
Totals	472	15767	3193	7572	.422	2677	3434	.780	4220	815	1426	22	9063	8.9	1.7	19.2

NBA PLAYOFF RECORD

Season Team	G	Min.	FGM	FGA	Pct.	FTM	FTA	Pct.	Reb.	Ast.	PF	Dq.	Pts.	RPG	APG	PPG
53-54—Fort Wayne	4	107	16	33	.485	10	12	.833	24	3	10	0	42	6.0	0.8	10.5
54-55—Fort Wayne	11	420	57	143	.399	60	79	.760	99	36	37	2	174	9.0	3.3	15.8
55-56—Fort Wayne	10	406	77	183	.421	76	98	.776	139	26	25	0	230	13.9	2.6	23.0
56-57—Fort Wayne	2	85	24	53	.453	9	11	.818	19	8	7	0	57	9.5	4.0	28.5
57-58—Detroit	7	254	52	127	.409	60	67	.896	72	17	26	0	164	10.3	2.4	23.4
58-59—Syracuse	9	333	83	189	.439	60	70	.857	87	21	29	0	226	9.7	2.3	25.1
59-60—Syracuse	3	88	15	39	.385	10	12	.833	17	1	9	0	40	5.7	0.3	13.3
Totals	46	1693	324	767	.422	285	349	.817	457	112	143	2	933	9.9	2.4	20.3

NBA ALL-STAR GAME RECORD

Season Team	Min.	FGM	FGA	Pct.	FTM	FTA	Pct.	Reb	Ast.	PF	Dq.	Pts.
1955—Fort Wayne	22	4	11	.364	3	4	.750	4	2	2	0	11
1956—Fort Wayne	19	3	7	.429	2	3	.667	6	1	1	0	8
1957—Fort Wayne	25	4	10	.400	1	1	1.000	9	0	2	0	9

Season Team	Min.	FGM	FGA	Pct.	FTM	FTA	Pct.	Reb.	Ast.	PF	Dq.	Pts.
1958—Detroit	32	8	15	.533	3	5	.600	9	1	1	0	19
1959—Detroit	17	2	8	.250	2	2	1.000	4	0	3	0	6
1960—Syracuse	16	5	9	.556	1	2	.500	3	0	4	0	11
Totals	131	26	60	.433	12	17	.706	35	4	13	0	64

ABL REGULAR-SEASON RECORD

Season Team	G	Min.	FGM	FGA	Pct.	FTM	FTA	Pct.	Reb.	Ast.	Pts.	RPG	APG	PPG
61-62—Los Angeles	25	948	159	378	.421	148	122	1.213	172	65	482	6.9	2.6	19.3

ZASLOFSKY, MAX   G/F

PERSONAL: Born December 7, 1925, in Brooklyn, N.Y. ... Died October 15, 1985. ... 6-2/170 (1,88/77,1). ... Full name: Max Zaslofsky.
HIGH SCHOOL: Thomas Jefferson (Brooklyn, N.Y.).
COLLEGE: St. John's.
TRANSACTIONS: Signed after freshman season as free agent by Chicago Stags of Basketball Association of America (1946). ... Name drawn out of hat by New York Knicks in dispersal of Stags franchise (1950). ... Traded by Knicks to Baltimore Bullets for G/F Jim Baechtold (1953). ... Traded by Bullets to Milwaukee Hawks (November 1953). ... Traded by Hawks to Fort Wayne Pistons (December 1953).

COLLEGIATE RECORD

NOTES: In military service (1944-45 season).

Season Team	G	Min.	FGM	FGA	Pct.	FTM	FTA	Pct.	Reb.	Ast.	Pts.	RPG	APG	PPG
45-46—St. John's	18	...	59	...	...	22	38	.579	...	...	140	...	...	7.8

NBA REGULAR-SEASON RECORD

HONORS: All-NBA first team (1950). ... All-BAA first team (1947, 1948, 1949).

Season Team	G	Min.	FGM	FGA	Pct.	FTM	FTA	Pct.	Reb.	Ast.	PF	Dq.	Pts.	RPG	APG	PPG
46-47—Chicago (BAA)	61	...	336	1020	.329	205	278	.737	...	40	121	...	877	...	0.7	14.4
47-48—Chicago (BAA)	48	...	*373	1156	.323	261	333	.784	...	29	125	...	*1007	...	0.6	*21.0
48-49—Chicago (BAA)	58	...	425	1216	.350	347	413	.840	...	149	156	...	1197	...	2.6	20.6
49-50—Chicago	68	...	397	1132	.351	321	381	*.843	...	155	185	...	1115	...	2.3	16.4
50-51—New York	66	...	302	853	.354	231	298	.775	228	136	150	3	835	3.5	2.1	12.7
51-52—New York	66	...	322	958	.336	287	380	.755	194	156	183	5	931	2.9	2.4	14.1
52-53—New York	29	...	123	320	.384	98	142	.690	75	55	81	1	344	2.6	1.9	11.9
53-54—Bal-Mil-FW	65	...	278	756	.368	255	357	.714	160	154	142	1	811	2.5	2.4	12.5
54-55—Fort Wayne	70	...	269	821	.328	247	352	.702	191	203	130	0	785	2.7	2.9	11.2
55-56—Fort Wayne	9	...	29	81	.358	30	35	.857	16	16	18	1	88	1.8	1.8	9.8
Totals	540	...	2854	8313	.343	2282	2969	.769	1093	1291	...		7990	...	2.9	11.9

NBA PLAYOFF RECORD

Season Team	G	Min.	FGM	FGA	Pct.	FTM	FTA	Pct.	Reb.	Ast.	PF	Dq.	Pts.	RPG	APG	PPG
46-47—Chicago (BAA)	11	...	60	199	.302	29	44	.659	...	4	26	...	149	...	0.4	13.5
47-48—Chicago (BAA)	5	...	30	88	.341	37	47	.787	...	0	17	...	97	...	0.0	19.4
48-49—Chicago (BAA)	2	...	15	49	.306	14	18	.778	...	6	3	0	44	...	3.0	22.0
49-50—Chicago	2	...	15	32	.469	15	18	.833	...	6	7	...	45	...	3.0	22.5
50-51—New York	14	...	88	217	.406	74	100	.740	58	38	43	...	250	4.1	2.7	17.9
51-52—New York	14	...	69	185	.373	89	110	.809	44	23	51	...	227	3.1	1.6	16.2
53-54—Fort Wayne	4	...	11	36	.306	13	15	.867	3	6	7	...	35	0.8	1.5	8.8
54-55—Fort Wayne	11	...	18	44	.409	16	20	.800	16	18	20	...	52	1.5	1.6	4.7
Totals	63	...	306	850	.360	287	372	.772	...	101	174	...	899	...	1.6	14.3

NBA ALL-STAR GAME RECORD

Season Team	Min.	FGM	FGA	Pct.	FTM	FTA	Pct.	Reb	Ast.	PF	Dq.	Pts.
1952—New York	...	3	7	.429	5	5	1.000	4	2	0	0	11

ABA COACHING RECORD

Season Team	REGULAR SEASON				PLAYOFFS		
	W	L	Pct.	Finish	W	L	Pct.
67-68—New Jersey	36	42	.462	T4th/Eastern Division	—	—	—
67-68—New York	17	61	.218	5th/Eastern Division	—	—	—
Totals (2 years)	53	103	.340				

ALL-TIME GREAT PLAYERS

ADELMAN, RICK   KINGS

PERSONAL: Born June 16, 1946, in Lynwood, Calif. ... 6-2/180. (1.88/81.6). ... Full name: Richard Leonard Adelman ... Name pronounced ADD-el-mun.
HIGH SCHOOL: St. Pius X (Downey, Calif.).
COLLEGE: Loyola Marymount.
TRANSACTIONS/CAREER NOTES: Selected by San Diego Rockets in seventh round (79th pick overall) of 1968 NBA Draft. ... Selected by Portland Trail Blazers from Rockets in NBA Expansion Draft (May 11, 1970). ... Traded by Trail Blazers to Chicago Bulls for cash and 1974 second-round draft choice (September 14, 1973). ... Traded by Bulls to New Orleans Jazz for F//C John Block (November 11, 1974). ... Traded by Jazz with F Ollie Johnson to Kansas City//Omaha Kings for F Nate Williams (February 1, 1975). ... Kings franchise moved from Kansas City//Omaha to Kansas City for 1975-76 season. ... Released by Kings (October 21, 1975).

COLLEGIATE RECORD

Season Team	G	Min.	FGM	FGA	Pct.	FTM	FTA	Pct.	Reb.	Ast.	Pts.	RPG	APG	PPG
											AVERAGES			
64-65—Loyola (Calif.)................								Freshman team statistics unava						
65-66—Loyola (Calif.)................	26	...	149	376	.396	129	152	.849	113	...	427	4.3	...	16.4
66-67—Loyola (Calif.)................	25	...	151	349	.433	171	214	.799	124	...	473	5.0	...	18.9
67-68—Loyola (Calif.)................	25	...	177	420	.421	171	216	.792	127	...	525	5.1	...	21.0
Totals	76	...	477	1145	.417	471	582	.809	364	...	1425	4.8	...	18.8

NBA REGULAR-SEASON RECORD

Season Team	G	Min.	FGM	FGA	Pct.	FTM	FTA	Pct.	Off.	Def.	Tot.	Ast.	St.	Blk.	TO	Pts.	RPG	APG	PPG
									REBOUNDS								AVERAGES		
68-69—San Diego..........	77	1448	177	449	.394	131	204	.642	...	...	216	238	...	...	...	485	2.8	3.1	6.3
69-70—San Diego..........	35	717	96	247	.389	68	91	.747	...	...	81	113	...	...	...	260	2.3	3.2	7.4
70-71—Portland	81	2303	378	895	.422	267	369	.724	...	...	282	380	...	...	...	1023	3.5	4.7	12.6
71-72—Portland	80	2445	329	753	.437	151	201	.751	...	...	229	413	...	...	...	808	2.9	5.2	10.1
72-73—Portland	76	1822	214	525	.408	73	102	.716	...	...	157	294	...	...	...	591	2.1	3.9	7.8
73-74—Chicago............	55	618	64	170	.376	54	76	.711	16	53	69	56	36	1	...	182	1.3	1.0	3.3
74-75—Chi.-N.O.-K.C.//Omaha..	58	1074	123	291	.423	73	103	.709	25	70	95	112	70	8	...	319	1.6	1.9	5.5
88-89—Portland............									...	...	...	...	...	...	...				
Totals	462	10427	1381	3330	.415	817	1146	.713	41	123	1129	1606	106	9	...	3668	2.4	3.5	7.9

Personal fouls/disqualifications: 1968-69, 158/1. 1969-70, 90/0. 1970-71, 214/2. 1971-72, 209/2. 1972-73, 155/2. 1973-74, 63/0. 1974-75, 101/1. Totals, 990/8.

NBA PLAYOFF RECORD

Season Team	G	Min.	FGM	FGA	Pct.	FTM	FTA	Pct.	Off.	Def.	Tot.	Ast.	St.	Blk.	TO	Pts.	RPG	APG	PPG
									REBOUNDS								AVERAGES		
68-69—San Diego	6	187	24	53	.453	22	37	.595	...	...	15	29	...	...	...	70	2.5	4.8	11.7
73-74—Chicago............	9	108	16	34	.471	7	11	.636	1	9	10	7	7	0	...	39	1.1	0.8	4.3
74-75—K.C.//Omaha	6	34	3	9	.333	6	8	.750	1	1	2	3	1	0	...	12	0.3	0.5	2.0
Totals	21	329	43	96	.448	35	56	.625	2	10	27	39	8	0	...	121	1.3	1.9	5.7

Personal fouls/disqualifications: 1968-69, 18/0. 1973-74, 5/0. 1974-75, 9/0. Totals, 32/0.

HEAD COACHING RECORD

BACKGROUND: Head coach, Chemeketa Community College, Ore (1977-78 through 1982-83; record: 141-39, .783). ... Assistant coach, Portland Trail Blazers (1983-84 to February 18, 1989).

NBA COACHING RECORD

Season Team	W	L	Pct.	Finish	W	L	Pct.
	REGULAR SEASON				PLAYOFFS		
88-89—Portland	14	21	.400	5th/Pacific Division	0	3	.000
89-90—Portland	59	23	.720	2nd/Pacific Division	12	9	.571
90-91—Portland	63	19	.768	1st/Pacific Division	9	7	.563
91-92—Portland	57	25	.695	1st/Pacific Division	13	8	.619
92-93—Portland	51	31	.622	3rd/Pacific Division	1	3	.250
93-94—Portland	47	35	.573	4th/Pacific Division	1	3	.250
94-95—Golden State	36	46	.439	6th/Pacific Division	—	—	—
95-96—Golden State	30	52	.366	7th/Pacific Division	—	—	—
98-99—Sacramento	27	23	.540	T3rd/Pacific Division	2	3	.400
99-00—Sacramento	44	38	.537	5th/Pacific Division	2	3	.400
00-01—Sacramento	55	27	.671	2nd/Pacific Division	3	5	.375
01-02—Sacramento	61	21	.744	1st/Pacific Division	10	6	.625
02-03—Sacramento	59	23	.720	1st/Pacific Division	7	5	.583
03-04—Sacramento	55	27	.671	2nd/Pacific Division	7	5	.583
04-05—Sacramento	50	32	.610	2nd/Pacific Division	1	4	.200
05-06—Sacramento	44	38	.537	4th/Pacific Division	2	4	.333
Totals (16 years)	752	481	.610	**Totals (14 years)**	70	68	.507

NOTES:

88-89—Replaced Mike Schuler as Portland head coach (February 18), with record of 25-22. Lost to Los Angeles Lakers in Western Conference first round.
89-90—Defeated Dallas, 3-0, in Western Conference first round; defeated San Antonio, 4-3, in Western Conference semifinals; defeated Phoenix, 4-2, in Western Conference finals; lost to Detroit, 4-1, in NBA Finals.
90-91—Defeated Seattle, 3-2, in Western Conference first round; defeated Utah, 4-1, in Western Conference semifinals; lost to Los Angeles Lakers, 4-2, in Western Conference finals.
91-92—Defeated Los Angeles Lakers, 3-1, in Western Conference first round; defeated Phoenix, 4-1, in Western Conference semifinals; defeated Utah, 4-

2, in Western Conference finals; lost to Chicago, 4-2, in NBA Finals.
92-93—Lost to San Antonio in Western Conference first round.
93-94—Lost to Houston in Western Conference first round.
98-99—Lost to Utah Jazz in Western Conference first round.
99-00—Lost to Los Angeles Lakers in Western Conference first round.
00-01—Defeated Phoenix, 3-1, in Western Conference first round; lost to Los Angeles Lakers, 4-0, in Western Conference semifinals.
01-02—Defeated Utah, 3-1, in Western Conference first round; defeated Dallas, 4-1, in Western Conference semifinals; lost to Los Angeles Lakers, 4-3, in Western Conference finals.
02-03—Defeated Utah, 4-1, in Western Conference first round; lost to Dallas, 4-3, in Western Conference semifinals.
03-04—Defeated Dallas, 4-1, in Western Conference first round; lost to Minnesota, 4-3, in Western Conference semifinals.
04-05—Lost to Seattle SuperSonics in Western Conference first round.
05-06—Lost to San Antonio in Western Conference first round.

ATTLES, AL

PERSONAL: Born November 7, 1936, in Newark, N.J. ... 6-0/185 (1,83/83,9). ... Full name: Alvin A. Attles.
HIGH SCHOOL: Weequahic (Newark, N.J.).
COLLEGE: North Carolina A&T.
TRANSACTIONS: Selected by Philadelphia Warriors in fifth round (39th pick overall) of 1960 NBA Draft. ... Warriors franchise moved from Philadelphia to San Francisco for 1962-63 season.
CAREER NOTES: Vice president/assistant general manager, Golden State Warriors (1987-88 to present).

COLLEGIATE RECORD

Season Team	G	Min.	FGM	FGA	Pct.	FTM	FTA	Pct.	Reb.	Ast.	Pts.	AVERAGES		
---	---	---	---	---	---	---	---	---	---	---	---	RPG	APG	PPG
56-57—North Carolina A&T.......						Statistics unavailable.								
57-58—North Carolina A&T.......						Statistics unavailable.								
58-59—North Carolina A&T.......	29	...	105	225	.467	56	91	.615	...	...	266		...	9.2
59-60—North Carolina A&T.......	24	...	190	301	.631	47	71	.662	80	...	427	3.3	...	17.8
Totals	53	...	295	526	.561	103	162	.636	...	...	.693	...	...	13.1

NBA REGULAR-SEASON RECORD

Season Team	G	Min.	FGM	FGA	Pct.	FTM	FTA	Pct.	Reb.	Ast.	PF	Dq.	Pts.	AVERAGES		
---	---	---	---	---	---	---	---	---	---	---	---	---	---	RPG	APG	PPG
60-61—Philadelphia	77	1544	222	543	.409	97	162	.599	214	174	235	5	541	2.8	2.3	7.0
61-62—Philadelphia	75	2468	343	724	.474	158	267	.592	355	333	279	8	844	4.7	4.4	11.3
62-63—San Francisco............	71	1876	301	630	.478	133	206	.646	205	184	253	7	735	2.9	2.6	10.4
63-64—San Francisco............	70	1883	289	640	.452	185	275	.673	236	197	249	4	763	3.4	2.8	10.9
64-65—San Francisco............	73	1733	254	662	.384	171	274	.624	239	205	242	7	679	3.3	2.8	9.3
65-66—San Francisco............	79	2053	364	724	.503	154	252	.611	322	225	265	7	882	4.1	2.8	11.2
66-67—San Francisco............	70	1764	212	467	.454	88	151	.583	321	269	265	13	512	4.6	3.8	7.3
67-68—San Francisco............	67	1992	252	540	.467	150	216	.694	276	390	284	9	654	4.1	5.8	9.8
68-69—San Francisco............	51	1516	162	359	.451	95	149	.638	181	306	183	3	419	3.5	6.0	8.2
69-70—San Francisco............	16	818	78	202	.386	75	113	.664	74	142	103	0	231	1.8	3.2	5.1
70-71—San Francisco............	34	321	22	54	.407	24	41	.585	40	58	59	2	68	1.2	1.7	2.0
Totals............	712	17826	2499	5545	.451	1330	2106	.632	2463	2483	2417	65	6328	3.5	3.5	8.9

NBA PLAYOFF RECORD

Season Team	G	Min.	FGM	FGA	Pct.	FTM	FTA	Pct.	Reb.	Ast.	PF	Dq.	Pts.	RPG	APG	PPG
60-61—Philadelphia............	3	110	12	26	.462	5	14	.357	12	9	14	0	29	4.0	3.0	9.7
61-62—Philadelphia............	12	338	28	76	.368	17	31	.548	55	27	54	4	73	4.6	2.3	6.1
63-64—San Francisco............	12	386	58	144	.403	30	56	.536	37	30	54	5	146	3.1	2.5	12.2
66-67—San Francisco............	15	237	20	46	.435	6	16	.375	62	38	45	1	46	4.1	2.5	3.1
67-68—San Francisco............	10	277	25	62	.403	23	30	.767	53	70	49	2	73	5.3	7.0	7.3
68-69—San Francisco............	6	109	7	21	.333	1	4	.250	18	21	17	0	15	3.0	3.5	2.5
70-71—San Francisco............	4	47	4	7	.571	4	7	.571	8	11	13	0	12	2.0	2.8	3.0
Totals............	62	1504	154	382	.403	86	158	.544	245	206	246	12	394	4.0	3.3	6.4

HEAD COACHING RECORD

BACKGROUND: Assistant coach, Warriors (February 13, 1995-remainder of season).

NBA COACHING RECORD

	REGULAR SEASON				PLAYOFFS		
Season Team	W	L	Pct.	Finish	W	L	Pct.
69-70—San Francisco	8	22	.267	6th/Western Division	—	—	—
70-71—San Francisco	41	41	.500	2nd/Pacific Division	1	4	.200
71-72—Golden State	51	31	.622	2nd/Pacific Division	1	4	.200
72-73—Golden State	47	35	.573	2nd/Pacific Division	5	6	.455
73-74—Golden State	44	38	.537	2nd/Pacific Division	—	—	—
74-75—Golden State	48	34	.585	1st/Pacific Division	12	5	.706
75-76—Golden State	59	23	.720	1st/Pacific Division	7	6	.538
76-77—Golden State	46	36	.561	3rd/Pacific Division	5	5	.500
77-78—Golden State	43	39	.524	5th/Pacific Division	—	—	—
78-79—Golden State	38	44	.463	6th/Pacific Division	—	—	—
79-80—Golden State	18	43	.295	6th/Pacific Division	—	—	—
80-81—Golden State	39	43	.476	4th/Pacific Division	—	—	—
81-82—Golden State	45	37	.549	4th/Pacific Division	—	—	—
82-83—Golden State	30	52	.366	5th/Pacific Division	—	—	—
Totals (14 years)...	557	518	.518	Totals (6 years)	31	30	.508

ALL-TIME GREAT COACHES

NOTES:
1970—Replaced George Lee as San Francisco head coach with record of 22-30.
1971—Lost to Milwaukee in Western Conference Semifinals.
1972—Lost to Milwaukee in Western Conference Semifinals.
1973—Defeated Milwaukee, 4-2, in Western Conference Semifinals; lost to Los Angeles, 4-1, in Western Conference Finals.
1975—Defeated Seattle, 4-2, in Western Conference Semifinals; defeated Chicago, 4-3, in Western Conference Finals; defeated Washington, 4-0, in NBA Finals.
1976—Defeated Detroit, 4-2, in Western Conference Semifinals; lost to Phoenix, 4-3, in Western Conference Finals.
1977—Defeated Detroit, 2-1, in Western Conference First Round; lost to Los Angeles, 4-3, in Western Conference Semifinals.
1980—Missed final 21 games of season due to injury; replaced by assistant coach John Bach (6-15) for remainder of season.

AUERBACH, RED

PERSONAL: Born September 20, 1917, in Brooklyn, N.Y. ... 5-10/170 (1,78/77,1). ... Full name: Arnold Jacob Auerbach. ... Name pronounced HOUR-back.
HIGH SCHOOL: Eastern District (Brooklyn, N.Y.).
JUNIOR COLLEGE: Seth Low Junior College (N.Y.).
COLLEGE: George Washington.
CAREER NOTES: Vice president, Boston Celtics (1950-51 through 1963-64). ... Vice president and general manager, Celtics (1964-65). ... Executive vice president and general manager, Celtics (1965-66 through 1969-70). ... President and general manager, Celtics (1970-71 through 1983-84). ... President, Celtics (1984-85 through 1996-97, 2001-02-present). .. Vice chairman of the board, Celtics (1997-98 to present).
CAREER HONORS: Elected to Naismith Memorial Basketball Hall of Fame (1968). ... One of the Top 10 Coaches in NBA History (1996).

COLLEGIATE RECORD

Season Team	G	Min.	FGM	FGA	Pct.	FTM	FTA	Pct.	Reb.	Ast.	Pts.	RPG	APG	PPG
36-37—Seth Low J.C.						Statistics unavailable.								
37-38—George Washington	17	...	22	...	...	8	12	.667	...	...	52	...	...	3.1
38-39—George Washington	20	...	54	...	...	12	19	.632	...	...	120	...	...	6.0
39-40—George Washington	19	...	69	...	...	24	39	.615	...	...	162	...	...	8.5
4-year-college totals	56	...	145	...	...	44	70	.629	...	...	334	...	...	6.0

HEAD COACHING RECORD

BACKGROUND: Head coach, St. Alban's Prep (Washington, D.C.). ... Head coach, Roosevelt High School (Washington, D.C.). ... Assistant coach, Duke University (1949-50).
HONORS: NBA Coach of the Year (1965). ... NBA 25th Anniversary All-Time team coach (1970). ... NBA Executive of the Year (1980). ... Selected as the "Greatest Coach in the History of the NBA" by the Professional Basketball Writers' Association of America (1980).

NBA COACHING RECORD

	REGULAR SEASON				PLAYOFFS		
Season Team	W	L	Pct.	Finish	W	L	Pct.
46-47—Washington (BAA)	49	11	.817	1st/Eastern Division	2	4	.333
47-48—Washington (BAA)	28	20	.583	T2nd/Western Division	0	1	.000
48-49—Washington (BAA)	38	22	.633	1st/Eastern Division	6	5	.545
49-50—Tri-Cities	28	29	.491	3rd/Western Division	1	2	.333
50-51—Boston	39	30	.565	2nd/Eastern Division	0	2	.000
51-52—Boston	39	27	.591	2nd/Eastern Division	1	2	.333
52-53—Boston	46	25	.648	3rd/Eastern Division	3	3	.500
53-54—Boston	42	30	.583	T2nd/Eastern Division	2	4	.333
54-55—Boston	36	36	.500	3rd/Eastern Division	3	4	.429
55-56—Boston	39	33	.542	2nd/Eastern Division	1	2	.333
56-57—Boston	44	28	.611	1st/Eastern Division	7	3	.700
57-58—Boston	49	23	.681	1st/Eastern Division	6	5	.545
58-59—Boston	52	20	.722	1st/Eastern Division	8	3	.727
59-60—Boston	59	16	.787	1st/Eastern Division	8	5	.615
60-61—Boston	57	22	.722	1st/Eastern Division	8	2	.800
61-62—Boston	60	20	.750	1st/Eastern Division	8	6	.571
62-63—Boston	58	22	.725	1st/Eastern Division	8	5	.615
63-64—Boston	59	21	.738	1st/Eastern Division	8	2	.800
64-65—Boston	62	18	.775	1st/Eastern Division	8	4	.667
65-66—Boston	54	26	.675	2nd/Eastern Division	11	6	.647
Totals (20 years)	938	479	.662	Totals (20 years)	99	70	.586

NOTES:
1947—Lost to Chicago in BAA Semifinals.
1948—Lost to Chicago, 74-70, in Western Division tiebreaker.
1949—Defeated Philadelphia, 2-0, in Eastern Division Semifinals; defeated New York, 2-1, in Eastern Division Finals; lost to Minneapolis, 4-2, in NBA Finals. Replaced Roger Potter as Tri-Cities head coach with record of 1-6.
1950—Lost to Anderson in Western Division Semifinals.
1951—Lost to New York in Eastern Division Semifinals.
1952—Lost to New York in Eastern Division Semifinals.
1953—Defeated Syracuse, 2-0, in Eastern Division Semifinals; lost to New York, 3-1, in Eastern Division Finals.
1954—Defeated New York, 93-71; lost to Syracuse, 96-95 (OT); defeated New York, 79-78; lost to Syracuse, 98-85, in Eastern Division round robin; lost to Syracuse, 2-0, in Eastern Division Finals.
1955—Defeated New York, 2-1, in Eastern Division Semifinals; lost to Syracuse, 3-1, in Eastern Division Finals.
1956—Lost to Syracuse in Eastern Division Semifinals.
1957—Defeated Syracuse, 3-0, in Eastern Division Finals; defeated St. Louis, 4-3, in NBA Finals.
1958—Defeated Philadelphia, 4-1, in Eastern Division Finals; lost to St. Louis, 4-2, in NBA Finals.

1959—Defeated Syracuse, 4-3, in Eastern Division Finals; defeated Minneapolis, 4-0, in NBA Finals.
1960—Defeated Philadelphia, 4-2, in Eastern Division Finals; defeated St. Louis, 4-3, in NBA Finals.
1961—Defeated Syracuse, 4-1, in Eastern Division Finals; defeated St. Louis, 4-1, in NBA Finals.
1962—Defeated Philadelphia, 4-3, in Eastern Division Finals; defeated Los Angeles, 4-3, in NBA Finals.
1963—Defeated Cincinnati, 4-3, in Eastern Division Finals; defeated Los Angeles, 4-2, in NBA Finals.
1964—Defeated Cincinnati, 4-1, in Eastern Division Finals; defeated San Francisco, 4-1, in NBA Finals.
1965—Defeated Philadelphia, 4-3, in Eastern Division Finals; defeated Los Angeles, 4-1, in NBA Finals.
1966—Defeated Cincinnati, 3-2 in Eastern Division Semifinals; defeated Philadelphia, 4-1, in Eastern Division Finals; defeated Los Angeles, 4-3, in NBA Finals.

BROWN, HUBIE

PERSONAL: Born September 25, 1933, in Elizabeth, N.J. ... 6-0/160. (1,83/72,6). ... Full Name: Hubert Jude Brown.
HIGH SCHOOL: St. Mary's (Elizabeth, N.J.).
COLLEGE: Niagara.
TRANSACTIONS/CAREER NOTES: Played with Rochester in Eastern Basketball League (1958-59).

COLLEGIATE RECORD

Season Team	G	Min.	FGM	FGA	Pct.	FTM	FTA	Pct.	Reb.	Ast.	Pts.	RPG	APG	PPG
51-52—Niagara	8	...	3	...	...	4	5	.800	...	...	10	...	...	1.3
52-53—Niagara	21	...	15	...	...	15	...	...	...	...	45	...	...	2.1
53-54—Niagara	30	...	24	...	...	27	...	...	...	...	75	...	...	3.5
54-55—Niagara	23	...	63	...	...	66	...	...	...	...	192	...	...	8.3
Totals	82	...	105	...	...	112	...	...	...	...	322	...	...	3.9.

EBL REGULAR-SEASON RECORD

Season Team	G	Min.	FGM	FGA	Pct.	FTM	FTA	Pct.	Off.	Def.	Tot.	Ast.	St.	Blk.	TO	Pts.	RPG	APG	PPG
58-59—Rochester	8	...	49	...	...	12	...	...	...	...	...	...	...	...	...	110	...	...	13.8

BACKGROUND: Assistant coach, William & Mary (1967-68). ... Assistant coach, Duke University (1968-69 through 1971-72). ... Assistant coach, Milwaukee Bucks (1972-73 through 1973-74).
HONORS: Coach of ABA championship team (1974-75). ... NBA Coach of the Year (1978, 2004).

HEAD COACHING RECORD

ABA COACHING RECORD

	REGULAR SEASON					PLAYOFFS		
Season Team	W	L	Pct.	Finish		W	L	Pct.
74-75—Kentucky	58	26	.690	T1st/Eastern Division		12	3	.800
75-76—Kentucky	46	38	.548	4th/Eastern Division		5	5	.500
Totals (2 years)	104	64	.619	Totals (2 years)		17	8	.680

NBA COACHING RECORD

	REGULAR SEASON					PLAYOFFS		
Season Team	W	L	Pct.	Finish		W	L	Pct.
76-77—Atlanta	31	51	.378	6th/Central Division		—	—	—
77-78—Atlanta	41	41	.500	4th/Central Division		0	2	.000
78-79—Atlanta	46	36	.561	3rd/Central Division		5	4	.556
79-80—Atlanta	50	32	.610	1st/Central Division		1	4	.200
80-81—Atlanta	31	48	.392	4th/Atlantic Division		—	—	—
82-83—New York	44	38	.537	4th/Atlantic Division		2	4	.333
83-84—New York	47	35	.573	3rd/Atlantic Division		6	6	.500
84-85—New York	24	58	.293	5th/Atlantic Division		—	—	—
85-86—New York	23	59	.280	5th/Atlantic Division		—	—	—
86-87—New York	4	12	.250			—	—	—
02-03—Memphis	28	46	.378	6th/Midwest Division		—	—	—
03-04—Memphis	50	32	.610	4th/Midwest Division		0	4	.000
04-05—Memphis	5	7	.417					
Totals (13 years)	424	495	.461	Totals (6 years)		14	24	.368

NOTES:
1975—Defeated Memphis, 4-1, in Eastern Division semifinals; defeated St. Louis, 4-1, in Eastern Division finals; defeated Indiana, 4-1, in ABA Championship Series.
1976—Defeated Indiana, 2-1, in first round; lost to Denver, 4-3, in Eastern Division semifinals.
1978—Lost to Washington, 2-0, in Eastern Conference first round.
1979—Defeated Houston, 2-0, in Eastern Conference first round; lost to Washington, 4-3, in Eastern Conference semifinals.
1980—Lost to Philadelphia, 4-1, in Eastern Conference semifinals.
1983—Defeated New Jersey, 2-0, in Eastern Conference first round; lost to Philadelphia, 4-0, in Eastern Conference semifinals.
1984—Defeated Detroit, 3-2, in Eastern Conference first round; lost to Boston, 4-3, in Eastern Conference semifinals.
1986—Replaced by Bob Hill as New York head coach (December 1).
2002—Replaced Sidney Lowe as Memphis head coach (November 12) with record of 0-8 and club in seventh place.
2004—Stepped down as Memphis head coach (November 25); replaced by Mike Fratello with team in fourth place.

BROWN, LARRY

PERSONAL: Born September 14, 1940, in Brooklyn, N.Y. ... 5-9/160. (1.75/72.6). ... Full name: Lawrence Harvey Brown
HIGH SCHOOL: Long Beach (N.Y.).
COLLEGE: North Carolina.
TRANSACTIONS/CAREER NOTES: Signed by New Orleans Buccaneers of American Basketball Association (1967). ... Traded by Buccaneers with F//G Doug Moe to Oakland Oaks for F Steve Jones, F Ron Franz and G Barry Leibowitz (June

18, 1968). ... Oaks franchise moved from Oakland to Washington and renamed Capitols for 1969-70 season. ... Capitols franchise moved from Washington to Virginia and renamed Squires for 1970-71 season. ... Contract sold by Squires to Denver Rockets (January 23, 1971).

MISCELLANEOUS: Member of gold-medal-winning U.S. Olympic team (1964).

COLLEGIATE RECORD

Season Team	G	Min.	FGM	FGA	Pct.	FTM	FTA	Pct.	Reb.	Ast.	Pts.	RPG	APG	PPG
59-60—North Carolina	15	...	88	...	...	100	143	.699	...	...	276	...	...	18.4
60-61—North Carolina	18	...	28	54	.519	25	34	.735	28	...	81	1.6	...	4.5
61-62—North Carolina	17	...	90	204	.441	101	127	.795	52	...	281	3.1	...	16.5
62-63—North Carolina	21	...	102	231	.442	95	122	.779	50	...	299	2.4	...	14.2
Totals	71	...	308	489	.630	321	426	.754	130	...	937	1.8	...	13.2

AMATEUR RECORD

Season Team	G	Min.	FGM	FGA	Pct.	FTM	FTA	Pct.	Reb.	Ast.	Pts.	RPG	APG	PPG
63-64—Akron (Ohio)	33	...	149	...	...	31	...	...	...	...	329	...	...	10.0
64-65—Akron (Ohio)	32	...	144	297	.485	139	167	.832	90	...	427	2.8	...	13.3
Totals	65	...	293	297	.987	170	167	1.018	90	...	756	1.4	...	11.6

ABA REGULAR-SEASON RECORD

NOTES: ABA All-Star second team (1968). ... Member of ABA championship team (1969). ...Holds single-game record for most assists—23 (February 20, 1972, vs. Pittsburgh).

Season Team	G	Min.	FGM	FGA	Pct.	FTM	FTA	Pct.	Reb.	Ast.	Pts.	RPG	APG	PPG
67-68—New Orleans	78	2807	311	812	.383	366	450	.813	249	*506	1045	3.2	*6.5	13.4
68-69—Oakland	77	2381	300	671	.447	301	379	.794	235	*544	925	3.1	*7.1	12.0
69-70—Washington	82	2766	366	815	.449	362	439	.825	246	*580	1124	3.0	*7.1	13.7
70-71—Virginia-Denver	63	1343	121	319	.379	186	225	.827	109	330	446	1.7	5.2	7.1
71-72—Denver	76	2012	238	531	.448	198	244	.811	166	549	689	2.2	7.2	9.1
Totals	376	11309	1336	3148	.424	1413	1737	.813	1005	2509	4229	2.7	6.7	11.2

Three-point field goals: 1967-68, 19-for-89 (.213), 1968-69, 8-for-35 (.229), 1969-70, 10-for-39 (.256), 1970-71, 6-for-21 (.286), 1971-72, 5-for-25 (.200). Totals, 48-for-209 (.230).

ABA PLAYOFF RECORD

Season Team	G	Min.	FGM	FGA	Pct.	FTM	FTA	Pct.	Reb.	Ast.	Pts.	RPG	APG	PPG
67-68—New Orleans	17	696	86	194	.443	100	122	.820	59	129	284	3.5	7.6	16.7
68-69—Oakland	16	534	74	170	.435	76	90	.844	52	87	224	3.3	5.4	14.0
69-70—Washington	7	269	32	68	.471	30	34	.882	35	68	97	5.0	9.7	13.9
71-72—Denver	7	211	21	47	.447	23	24	.958	10	36	65	1.4	5.1	9.3
Totals	47	1710	213	479	.445	229	270	.848	156	320	670	3.3	6.8	14.3

Three-point field goals: 1967-68, 4-for-18 (.222), 1968-69, 0-for-3 (.000), 1969-70, 1-for-5 (.200), 1971-72, 0-for-3 (.000). Totals, 5-for-29 (.172).

ABA ALL-STAR GAME RECORD

NOTES: ABA All-Star Game Most Valuable Player (1968).

Season Team	Min.	FGM	FGA	Pct.	FTM	FTA	Pct.	Reb.	Ast.	Pts.	RPG	APG	PPG
1968—New Orleans	22	5	7	.714	1	1	1.000	3	5	17	...	...	...
1969—Oakland	25	1	6	.167	3	5	.600	0	7	5	...	...	...
1970—Washington	15	0	2	.000	3	3	1.000	3	3	3	...	...	...
Totals	34010858	1296	3064	.423	1428	1748	.817	991	2259	4170	2.9	6.6	12.3

Three-point field goals: 1967-68, 2-for-2 (1.000). 1968-69, 0-for-1. 1969-70, 0-for-0. Totals, 2-for-3 (.667).

HEAD COACHING RECORD

BACKGROUND: Assistant coach, University of North Carolina (1965-66 and 1966-67). ... Assistant coach, U.S. Olympic team (1980).

HONORS: NBA Coach of the Year (2001).

ALL AMERICA BASKETBALL ALLIANCE COACHING RECORD

Season Team	REGULAR SEASON				PLAYOFFS		
	W	L	Pct.	Finish	W	L	Pct.
72-73—Carolina	57	27	.679	1st/Eastern Division	7	5	.583
73-74—Carolina	47	37	.560	3rd/Eastern Division	0	4	.000
74-75—Denver	65	19	.774	1st/Western Division	7	6	.538
75-76—Denver	60	24	.714	1st/Western Division	6	7	.462
Totals (4 years)	229	107	.682	**Totals (4 years)**	20	22	.476

NOTES:

72-73—Defeated New York, 4-1, in Eastern Division semifinals; lost to Kentucky, 4-3, in Eastern Division finals.
73-74—Lost to Kentucky in Eastern Division semifinals.
74-75—Defeated Utah, 4-2, in Western Conference semifinals; lost to Indiana,4-3, in Western Division finals.
75-76—Defeated Kentucky, 4-3, in semifinals; lost to New York, 4-2, in ABA Finals.

COLLEGIATE COACHING RECORD

Season Team	W	L	Pct.	Finish
79-80—UCLA	22	10	.688	4th/Pacific-10 Conference
80-81—UCLA	20	7	.741	3rd/Pacific-10 Conference
83-84—Kansas	22	10	.688	2nd/Big Eight Conference
84-85—Kansas	26	8	.765	2nd/Big Eight Conference
85-86—Kansas	35	4	.897	1st/Big Eight Conference
86-87—Kansas	25	11	.694	T2nd/Big Eght Conference
87-88—Kansas	27	11	.711	3rd/Big Eight Conference
Totals (7 years)	177	61	.744	

NOTES:

79-80—Defeated Old Dominion, 87-74, in NCAA Tournament first round; defeated DePaul, 77-71, in second round; defeated Ohio State, 72-68, in regional semifinals; defeated Clemson, 85-74, in regional finals; defeated Purdue, 67-62, in semifinals; lost to Lou

80-81—Lost to Brigham Young, 78-55, in NCAA Tournament second round.

83-84—Defeated Alcorn State, 57-56, in NCAA Tournament first round; lost to Wake Forest, 69-59, in second round.

84-85—Defeated Ohio University, 49-38, in NCAA Tournament first round; lost to Auburn, 66-64, in second round.

85-86—Defeated North Carolina A&T, 71-46, in NCAA Tournament first round; defeated Temple, 65-43, in second round; defeated Michigan State, 96-86 (OT), in regional semifinals; defeated North Carolina State, 75-67, in regional finals; lost to Duke, 71-67, i

86-87—Defeated Houston, 66-55, in NCAA Tournament first round; defeated Southwest Missouri State, 67-63, in second round; lost to Georgetown, 70-57, in regional semifinals.

87-88—Defeated Xavier, 85-72, in NCAA Tournament first round; defeated Murray State, 61-58, in second round; defeated Vanderbilt, 77-64, in regional semifinals; defeated Kansas State, 71-58 in regional finals; defeated Duke, 66-59, in semifinals; defeated Oklahoma, 83-79, in championship game.

NBA COACHING RECORD

Season Team	REGULAR SEASON				PLAYOFFS		
	W	L	Pct.	Finish	W	L	Pct.
76-77—Denver	50	32	.610	1st/Midwest Division	2	4	.333
77-78—Denver	48	34	.585	1st/Midwest Division	6	7	.462
78-79—Denver	28	25	.528		—	—	—
81-82—New Jersey	44	38	.537	3rd/Atlantic Division	0	2	.000
82-83—New Jersey	47	29	.618		—	—	—
88-89—San Antonio	21	61	.256	5th/Midwest Division	—	—	—
89-90—San Antonio	56	26	.683	1st/Midwest Division	6	4	.600
90-91—San Antonio	55	27	.671	1st/Midwest Division	1	3	.250
91-92—San Antonio	21	17	.553		—	—	—
—L.A. Clippers	23	12	.657	5th/Pacific Division	2	3	.400
92-93—L.A. Clippers	41	41	.500	4th/Pacific Division	2	3	.400
93-94—Indiana	47	35	.573	T3rd/Central Division	10	6	.625
94-95—Indiana	52	30	.634	1st/Central Division	10	7	.588
95-96—Indiana	52	30	.634	2nd/Central Division	2	3	.400
96-97—Indiana	39	43	.476	6th/Central Division	—	—	—
97-98—Philadelphia	31	51	.378	7th/Atlantic Division	—	—	—
98-99—Philadelphia	28	22	.560	3rd/ Atlantic Division	3	5	.375
99-00—Philadelphia	49	33	.598	3rd/ Atlantic Division	5	5	.500
00-01—Philadelphia	56	26	.683	1st/Atlantic Division	12	11	.522
01-02—Philadelphia	43	39	.524	4th/ Atlantic Division	2	3	.400
02-03—Philadelphia	48	34	.585	2nd/Atlantic Division	6	6	.500
03-04—Detroit	54	28	.659	2nd/Central Division	16	7	.696
04-05—Detroit	54	28	.659	1st/Central Division	15	10	.600
05-06—N.Y. Knicks	23	59	.280	5th/Eastern Conference	—	—	—
Totals (23 years)	1,010	800	.558	Totals (17 years)	100	89	.529

NOTES:

76-77—Lost to Portland in Western Conference semifinals.

77-78—Defeated Milwaukee, 4-3, in Western Conference; lost to Seattle, 4-2, in Western Conference finals.

78-79—Resigned as Denver head coach (February 1); replaced by Donnie Walsh with club in second place.

81-82—Lost to Washington in Eastern Conference first round.

82-83—Resigned as New Jersey head coach (April 7); replaced by Bill Blair with club in third place.

89-90—Defeated Denver, 3-0, in Western Conference first round; lost to Portland, 4-3, in Western Conference semifinals.

90-91—Lost to Golden State in Western Conference first round.

91-92—Replaced as San Antonio head coach by Bob Bass with club in second place (January 21); replaced Mike Schuler (21-24) and Mack Calvin (interim head coach, 1-1) as Los Angeles Clippers head coach (February 6), with record of 22-25 and club in 6th place. Lost to Utah in Western Conference first round.

92-93—Lost to Houston in Western Conference first round.

93-94—Defeated Orlando, 3-0, in Eastern Conference first round; defeated Atlanta, 4-2, in Eastern Conference semifianls; lost to New York, 4-3, in Eastern Conference finals.

94-95—Defeated Atlanta, 3-0, in Eastern Conference first round; defeated New York, 4-3, Eastern Conference semifinals; lost to Orlando, 4-3, in Eastern Conference finals.

95-96—Lost to Atlanta in Eastern Conference first round.

98-99—Defeated Orlando, 3-1, in Eastern Conference first round; lost to Indiana, 4-0, in Eastern Conference semifinals.

99-00—Defeated Charlotte, 3-1, in Eastern first round; lost to Indiana, 4-2, in Eastern Conference semifianls.

00-01—Defeated Indiana, 3-1, in Eastern Conference first round; defeated Toronto, 4-3, in Eastern Conference semifinals; defeated by Milwaukee, 4-3, in Eastern Conference finals; lost to Los Angeles Lakers, 4-1, in NBA Finals.

01-02—Lost to Boston in Eastern Conference first round.

02-03—Defeated New Orleans, 4-2, in Eastern Conference first round; lost to Detroit, 4-2, in Eastern Conference semifinals.

03-04—Defeated Milwaukee, 4-1, in Eastern Conference first round; defeated New Jersey, 4-3, in Eastern Conference semifinals; defeated Indiana, 4-2, in Eastern Conference finals; defeated Los Angeles Lakers, 4-1, in NBA Finals.

04-05—Defeated Philadelphia, 4-1, in Eastern Conference first round; defeated Indiana, 4-2, in Eastern Conference semifinals; defeated Miami, 4-3, in Eastern Conference finals; lost to San Antonio, 4-3, in NBA Finals.

COSTELLO, LARRY

PERSONAL: Born July 2, 1931, in Minoa, N.Y. ... Died December 11, 2001. ... 6-1/188 (1,85/85,3). ... Full name: Lawrence Ronald Costello.
HIGH SCHOOL: Minoa (N.Y.).
COLLEGE: Niagara.
TRANSACTIONS: Selected by Philadelphia Warriors in second round of 1954 NBA Draft. ... Sold by Warriors to Syracuse Nationals (October 10, 1957). ... Nationals franchise moved from Syracuse to Philadelphia and renamed 76ers for 1963-64 season. ... Played in Eastern Basketball League with Wilkes-Barre Barons (1965-66). ... Drafted by Milwaukee Bucks from 76ers in NBA Expansion Draft (May 6, 1968).

MISCELLANEOUS: Member of NBA championship team (1967).

COLLEGIATE RECORD

Season Team	G	Min.	FGM	FGA	Pct.	FTM	FTA	Pct.	Reb.	Ast.	Pts.	RPG	APG	PPG
													AVERAGES	
50-51—Niagara‡					Freshman team statistics unavailable.									
51-52—Niagara	28	...	131	...	...	58	87	.667	...	...	320	...	...	11.4
52-53—Niagara	28	...	185	...	...	140	194	.722	...	...	510	...	...	18.2
53-54—Niagara	29	...	160	...	...	125	152	.822	...	...	445	...	...	15.3
Varsity totals	**85**	**...**	**476**	**...**	**...**	**323**	**433**	**.746**	**...**	**...**	**1275**	**...**	**...**	**15.0**

NBA REGULAR-SEASON RECORD

HONORS: All-NBA second team (1961).

Season Team	G	Min.	FGM	FGA	Pct.	FTM	FTA	Pct.	Reb.	Ast.	PF	Dq.	Pts.	RPG	APG	PPG
															AVERAGES	
54-55—Philadelphia	19	463	46	139	.331	26	32	.813	49	78	37	0	118	2.6	4.1	6.2
55-56—Philadelphia						Did not play—in military service.										
56-57—Philadelphia	72	2111	186	497	.374	175	222	.788	323	236	182	2	547	4.5	3.3	7.6
57-58—Syracuse	72	2746	378	888	.426	320	378	.847	378	317	246	3	1076	5.3	4.4	14.9
58-59—Syracuse	70	2750	414	948	.437	280	349	.802	365	379	263	7	1108	5.2	5.4	15.8
59-60—Syracuse	71	2469	372	822	.453	249	289	.862	388	449	234	4	993	5.5	6.3	14.0
60-61—Syracuse	75	2167	407	844	.482	270	338	.799	292	413	286	9	1084	3.9	5.5	14.5
61-62—Syracuse	63	1854	310	726	.427	247	295	.837	245	359	220	5	867	3.9	5.7	13.8
62-63—Syracuse	78	2066	285	660	.432	288	327	*.881	237	334	263	4	858	3.0	4.3	11.0
63-64—Philadelphia	45	1137	191	408	.468	147	170	.865	105	167	150	3	529	2.3	3.7	11.8
64-65—Philadelphia	64	1967	309	695	.445	243	277	*.877	169	275	242	10	861	2.6	4.3	13.5
66-67—Philadelphia	49	976	130	293	.444	120	133	.902	103	140	141	2	380	2.1	2.9	7.8
67-68—Philadelphia	28	492	67	148	.453	67	81	.827	51	68	62	0	201	1.8	2.4	7.2
Totals	**706**	**21198**	**3095**	**7068**	**.438**	**2432**	**2891**	**.841**	**2705**	**3215**	**2326**	**49**	**8622**	**3.8**	**4.6**	**12.2**

NBA PLAYOFF RECORD

Season Team	G	Min.	FGM	FGA	Pct.	FTM	FTA	Pct.	Reb.	Ast.	PF	Dq.	Pts.	RPG	APG	PPG
															AVERAGES	
56-57—Philadelphia	2	16	3	8	.375	0	1	.000	5	2	3	0	6	2.5	1.0	3.0
57-58—Syracuse	3	134	10	34	.294	14	14	1.000	25	12	6	0	34	8.3	4.0	11.3
58-59—Syracuse	9	361	54	121	.446	51	61	.836	53	54	40	2	159	5.9	6.0	17.7
59-60—Syracuse	3	122	20	47	.426	10	12	.833	14	20	15	1	50	4.7	6.7	16.7
60-61—Syracuse	8	269	42	103	.408	47	55	.855	35	52	39	3	131	4.4	6.5	16.4
61-62—Syracuse	5	167	22	51	.431	29	33	.879	16	28	21	0	73	3.2	5.6	14.6
62-63—Syracuse	5	134	16	37	.432	19	23	.826	4	23	27	2	51	0.8	4.6	10.2
63-64—Philadelphia	5	36	3	14	.214	10	10	1.000	3	4	14	1	16	0.6	0.8	3.2
64-65—Philadelphia	10	207	22	53	.415	11	16	.688	12	20	43	2	55	1.2	2.0	5.5
66-67—Philadelphia	2	25	6	8	.750	5	5	1.000	4	3	2	0	17	2.0	1.5	8.5
Totals	**52**	**1471**	**198**	**476**	**.416**	**196**	**230**	**.852**	**171**	**218**	**210**	**11**	**592**	**3.3**	**4.2**	**11.4**

NBA ALL-STAR GAME RECORD

Season Team	Min.	FGM	FGA	Pct.	FTM	FTA	Pct.	Reb.	Ast.	PF	Dq.	Pts.
1958—Syracuse	17	0	6	.000	1	1	1.000	1	4	2	0	1
1959—Syracuse	18	3	8	.375	1	1	1.000	3	3	1	0	7
1960—Syracuse	20	5	9	.556	0	0	...	4	2	1	0	10
1961—Syracuse	5	1	2	.500	0	0	...	0	0	2	0	2
1962—Syracuse					Selected, did not play—injured.							
1965—Philadelphia	11	2	7	.286	0	0	...	1	2	2	0	4
Totals	**71**	**11**	**32**	**.344**	**2**	**2**	**1.000**	**9**	**11**	**8**	**0**	**24**

EBL REGULAR-SEASON RECORD

Season Team	G	Min.	FGM	FGA	Pct.	FTM	FTA	Pct.	Reb.	Ast.	PF	Dq.	Pts.	RPG	APG	PPG
															AVERAGES	
65-66—Wilkes-Barre	12	...	54	...	...	53	59	.898	22	83	...	.	167	1.8	6.9	13.9

HEAD COACHING RECORD

BACKGROUND: Head coach, Minoa High School, N.Y. (1965-66). ... Head coach, Milwaukee Does of Women's Professional Basketball League (1979-80).

NBA COACHING RECORD

Season Team	REGULAR SEASON				PLAYOFFS		
	W	L	Pct.	Finish	W	L	Pct.
68-69—Milwaukee	27	55	.329	7th/Eastern Division	—	—	—
69-70—Milwaukee	56	26	.683	2nd/Eastern Division	5	5	.500
70-71—Milwaukee	66	16	.805	1st/Midwest Division	12	2	.857
71-72—Milwaukee	63	19	.768	1st/Midwest Division	6	5	.545
72-73—Milwaukee	60	22	.732	1st/Midwest Division	2	4	.333
73-74—Milwaukee	59	23	.720	1st/Midwest Division	11	5	.688
74-75—Milwaukee	38	44	.463	4th/Midwest Division	—	—	—
75-76—Milwaukee	38	44	.463	1st/Midwest Division	1	2	.333
76-77—Milwaukee	3	15	.167		—	—	—
78-79—Chicago	20	36	.357		—	—	—
Totals (10 years)	**430**	**300**	**.589**	**Totals (6 years)**	**37**	**23**	**.617**

COLLEGIATE COACHING RECORD

Season Team	W	L	Pct.	Finish
80-81—Utica	13	12	.520	Independent
81-82—Utica	4	22	.154	Independent

Season Team	W	L	Pct.	Finish
82-83—Utica	11	15	.423	Independent
83-84—Utica	11	15	.423	Independent
84-85—Utica	15	12	.556	Independent
85-86—Utica	13	14	.481	Independent
86-87—Utica	10	16	.385	Independent
Totals (7 years)	77	106	.421	

NOTE:

1970—Defeated Philadelphia, 4-1, in Eastern Division Semifinals; lost to New York, 4-1, in Eastern Division Finals.

1971—Defeated San Francisco, 4-1, in Western Conference Semifinals; defeated Los Angeles, 4-1, in Western Conference Finals; defeated Baltimore, 4-0, in NBA Finals.

1972—Defeated Golden State, 4-1, in Western Conference Semifinals; lost to Los Angeles, 4-2, in Western Conference Finals.

1973—Lost to Golden State in Western Conference Semifinals.

1974—Defeated Los Angeles, 4-1, in Western Conference Semifinals; defeated Chicago, 4-0, in Western Conference Finals; lost to Boston, 4-3, in NBA Finals.

1976—Lost to Detroit in Western Conference First Round. Resigned as Milwaukee head coach and replaced by Don Nelson (November 22).

1979—Replaced as Chicago head coach by Scotty Robertson (February 16).

CUNNINGHAM, BILLY

PERSONAL: Born June 3, 1943, in Brooklyn, N.Y. ... 6-7/210 (2,00/95,3). ... Full name: William John Cunningham.
HIGH SCHOOL: Erasmus Hall (Brooklyn, N.Y.).
COLLEGE: North Carolina.
TRANSACTIONS: Selected by Philadelphia 76ers in first round of 1965 NBA Draft. ... Signed as free agent by Carolina Cougars of American Basketball Association (August 1969). ... Signed as free agent by 76ers (1969). ... Suspended by NBA (1972). ... Restored by NBA (1974). ... Returned to 76ers (1974).
CAREER HONORS: Elected to Naismith Memorial Basketball Hall of Fame (1986). ... One of the 50 Greatest Players in NBA History (1996).
CAREER NOTES: Part owner, Miami Heat (1987-88 to 1994-95).
MISCELLANEOUS: Member of NBA championship team (1967).

COLLEGIATE RECORD

NOTES: THE SPORTING NEWS All-America second team (1965).

Season Team	G	Min.	FGM	FGA	Pct.	FTM	FTA	Pct.	Reb.	Ast.	Pts.	RPG	APG	PPG
												AVERAGES		
61-62—North Carolina‡	10	...	81	162	.500	46	78	.577	127	...	207	12.7	...	20.7
62-63—North Carolina	21	...	186	380	.489	105	170	.618	339	...	477	16.1	...	22.7
63-64—North Carolina	24	...	233	526	.443	157	249	.631	379	...	623	15.8	...	26.0
64-65—North Carolina	24	...	237	481	.493	135	213	.634	344	...	609	14.3	...	25.4
Varsity totals	69	...	656	1387	.473	397	632	.628	1062	...	1709	15.4	...	24.8

NBA REGULAR-SEASON RECORD

HONORS: All-NBA first team (1969, 1970, 1971). ... All-NBA second team (1972). ... NBA All-Rookie team (1966).

Season Team	G	Min.	FGM	FGA	Pct.	FTM	FTA	Pct.	Reb.	Ast.	PF	Dq.	Pts.	RPG	APG	PPG
														AVERAGES		
65-66—Philadelphia	80	2134	431	1011	.426	281	443	.634	599	207	301	12	1143	7.5	2.6	14.3
66-67—Philadelphia	81	2168	556	1211	.459	383	558	.686	589	205	260	2	1495	7.3	2.5	18.5
67-68—Philadelphia	74	2076	516	1178	.438	368	509	.723	562	187	260	3	1400	7.6	2.5	18.9
68-69—Philadelphia	82	3345	739	1736	.426	556	754	.737	1050	287	*329	10	2034	12.8	3.5	24.8
69-70—Philadelphia	81	3194	802	1710	.469	510	700	.729	1101	352	331	15	2114	13.6	4.3	26.1
70-71—Philadelphia	81	3090	702	1519	.462	455	620	.734	946	395	328	5	1859	11.7	4.9	23.0
71-72—Philadelphia	75	2900	658	1428	.461	428	601	.712	918	443	295	12	1744	12.2	5.9	23.3

Season Team	G	Min.	FGM	FGA	Pct.	FTM	FTA	Pct.	Off.	Def.	Tot.	Ast.	Stl.	Blk.	TO	Pts.	RPG	APG	PPG
									REBOUNDS								AVERAGES		
74-75—Philadelphia	80	2859	609	1423	.428	345	444	.777	130	596	726	442	91	35		1563	9.1	5.5	19.5
75-76—Philadelphia	20	640	103	251	.410	68	88	.773	29	118	147	107	24	10	...	274	7.4	5.4	13.7
Totals	654	22406	5116	11467	.446	3394	4717	.720	...	...	6638	2625	115	45	...	13626	10.1	4.0	20.8

Personal fouls/disqualifications: 1974-75. 270/4. 1975-76, 57/1. Totals, 2431/64.

NBA PLAYOFF RECORD

Season Team	G	Min.	FGM	FGA	Pct.	FTM	FTA	Pct.	Reb.	Ast.	PF	Dq.	Pts.	RPG	APG	PPG
														AVERAGES		
65-66—Philadelphia	4	69	5	31	.161	11	13	.846	18	10	11	0	21	4.5	2.5	5.3
66-67—Philadelphia	15	339	83	221	.376	59	90	.656	93	33	53	1	225	6.2	2.2	15.0
67-68—Philadelphia	3	86	24	43	.558	14	17	.824	22	10	16	1	62	7.3	3.3	20.7
68-69—Philadelphia	5	217	49	117	.419	24	38	.632	63	12	24	1	122	12.6	2.4	24.4
69-70—Philadelphia	5	205	61	123	.496	24	36	.667	52	20	19	0	146	10.4	4.0	29.2
70-71—Philadelphia	7	301	67	142	.472	47	67	.701	108	40	28	0	181	15.4	5.7	25.9
Totals	39	1217	289	677	.427	179	261	.686	356	125	151	3	757	9.1	3.2	19.4

NBA ALL-STAR GAME RECORD

Season Team	Min.	FGM	FGA	Pct.	FTM	FTA	Pct.	Reb.	Ast.	PF	Dq.	Pts.
1969—Philadelphia	22	5	10	.500	0	0	...	5	1	3	0	10
1970—Philadelphia	28	7	13	.538	5	5	1.000	4	2	3	0	19
1971—Philadelphia	19	2	8	.250	1	2	.500	4	3	1	0	5
1972—Philadelphia	24	4	13	.308	6	8	.750	10	3	4	0	14
Totals	93	18	44	.409	12	15	.800	23	9	11	0	48

ABA REGULAR-SEASON RECORD

NOTES: ABA Most Valuable Player (1973). ... ABA All-Star first team (1973).

Season Team	G	Min.	2-POINT FGM	FGA	Pct.	3-POINT FGM	FGA	Pct.	FTM	FTA	Pct.	Reb.	Ast.	Pts.	AVERAGES RPG	APG	PPG
72-73—Carolina	84	3248	757	1534	.493	14	49	.286	472	598	.789	1012	530	2028	12.0	6.3	24.1
73-74—Carolina	32	1190	252	529	.476	1	8	.125	149	187	.797	331	150	656	10.3	4.7	20.5
Totals	116	4438	1009	2063	.489	15	57	.263	621	785	.791	1343	680	2684	11.6	5.9	23.1

ABA PLAYOFF RECORD

Season Team	G	Min.	2-POINT FGM	FGA	Pct.	3-POINT FGM	FGA	Pct.	FTM	FTA	Pct.	Reb.	Ast.	Pts.	AVERAGES RPG	APG	PPG
72-73—Carolina	12	472	111	219	.507	1	4	.250	57	83	.687	142	61	282	11.8	5.1	23.5
73-74—Carolina	3	61	9	29	.310	0	2	.000	4	5	.800	16	6	22	5.3	2.0	7.3
Totals	15	533	120	248	.484	1	6	.167	61	88	.693	158	67	304	10.5	4.5	20.3

ABA ALL-STAR GAME RECORD

Season Team	Min.	2-POINT FGM	FGA	Pct.	3-POINT FGM	FGA	Pct.	FTM	FTA	Pct.	Reb.	Ast.	Pts.
1973—Carolina	20	9	11	.818	0	1	.000	0	0	...	6	4	18

COMBINED ABA AND NBA REGULAR-SEASON RECORDS

	G	Min.	FGM	FGA	Pct.	FTM	FTA	Pct.	REBOUNDS Off.	Def.	Tot.	Ast.	Stl.	Blk.	TO	Pts.	AVERAGES RPG	APG	PPG
Totals	770	26844	6140	13587	.452	4015	5502	.730	...	...	7981	3305	...	...	...	16310	10.4	4.3	21.2

Three-point field goals: 15-for-57 (.263).
Personal fouls: 2845.

NBA COACHING RECORD

Season Team	REGULAR SEASON W	L	Pct.	Finish	PLAYOFFS W	L	Pct.
77-78—Philadelphia	53	23	.697	1st/Atlantic Division	6	4	.600
78-79—Philadelphia	47	35	.573	2nd/Atlantic Division	5	4	.556
79-80—Philadelphia	59	23	.720	2nd/Atlantic Division	12	6	.667
80-81—Philadelphia	62	20	.756	T1st/Atlantic Division	9	7	.563
81-82—Philadelphia	58	24	.707	2nd/Atlantic Division	12	9	.571
82-83—Philadelphia	65	17	.793	1st/Atlantic Division	12	1	.923
83-84—Philadelphia	52	30	.634	2nd/Atlantic Division	2	3	.400
84-85—Philadelphia	58	24	.707	2nd/Atlantic Division	8	5	.615
Totals (8 years)	454	196	.698	Totals (8 years)	66	39	.629

NOTES:

1977—Replaced Gene Shue as Philadelphia head coach (November 4), with record of 2-4.

1978—Defeated New York, 4-0, in Eastern Conference Semifinals; lost to Washington, 4-2, in Eastern Conference Finals.

1979—Defeated New Jersey, 2-0, in Eastern Conference First Round; lost to San Antonio, 4-3, in Eastern Conference Semifinals.

1980—Defeated Washington, 2-0, in Eastern Conference First Round; defeated Atlanta, 4-1, in Eastern Conference Semifinals; defeated Boston, 4-1, in Eastern Conference Finals; lost to Los Angeles, 4-2, in NBA Finals.

1981—Defeated Indiana, 2-0, in Eastern Conference First Round; defeated Milwaukee, 4-3, in Eastern Conference Semifinals; lost to Boston, 4-3, in Eastern Conference Finals.

1982—Defeated Atlanta, 2-0, in Eastern Conference First Round; defeated Milwaukee, 4-2, in Eastern Conference Semifinals; defeated Boston, 4-3, in Eastern Conference Finals; lost to Los Angeles, 4-2, in NBA Finals.

1983—Defeated New York, 4-0, in Eastern Conference Semifinals; defeated Milwaukee, 4-1, in Eastern Conference Finals; defeated Los Angeles, 4-0, in NBA Finals.

1984—Lost to New Jersey in Eastern Conference First Round.

1985—Defeated Washington, 3-1, in Eastern Conference First Round; defeated Milwaukee, 4-0, in Eastern Conference Semifinals; lost to Boston, 4-1, in Eastern Conference Finals.

DALY, CHUCK

PERSONAL: Born July 20, 1930, in St. Mary's, Pa. ... 6-2/180 (1,88/81,6). ... Full name: Charles Jerome Daly.
HIGH SCHOOL: Kane Area (Pa.).
COLLEGE: St. Bonaventure, then Bloomsburg (Pa.) State.
CAREER NOTES: Broadcaster, 76ers (1982-83). ... Broadcaster, Turner Sports (1994-95 through 1996-97). ... Special consultant to the president, Vancouver Grizzlies (May 10, 2000-present). ... Vancouver franchise moved to Memphis for 2001-02 season.
MISCELLANEOUS: Head coach, gold-medal-winning U.S. Olympic team (1992).
CAREER HONORS: Elected to Naismith Memorial Basketball Hall of Fame (1994). ... One of the Top 10 Coaches in NBA History (1996).

COLLEGIATE RECORD

Season Team	G	Min.	FGM	FGA	Pct.	FTM	FTA	Pct.	Reb.	Ast.	Pts.	AVERAGES RPG	APG	PPG
48-49—St. Bonaventure‡						Freshman team statistics unavailable.								
49-50—Bloomsburg State						Did not play—transfer student.								
50-51—Bloomsburg State	16	...	...	...	...	...	...	...	...	...	215	...	...	13.4
51-52—Bloomsburg State	16	...	...	...	...	...	...	...	...	...	203	...	...	12.7
Varsity totals	32	...	...	...	...	...	...	...	...	...	418	...	...	13.1

HEAD COACHING RECORD

BACKGROUND: Head coach, Punxsutawney High School, Pa (1955-56 through 1962-63; record: 111-70, .613). ... Assistant coach, Duke University (1963-64 through 1968-69). ... Assistant coach, Philadelphia 76ers (1978-December 4, 1981).

COLLEGIATE COACHING RECORD

Season Team	W	L	Pct.	Finish
69-70—Boston College	11	13	.458	Independent
70-71—Boston College	15	11	.577	Independent
71-72—Pennsylvania	25	3	.893	1st/Ivy League
72-73—Pennsylvania	21	7	.750	1st/Ivy League
73-74—Pennsylvania	21	6	.778	1st/Ivy League
74-75—Pennsylvania	23	5	.821	1st/Ivy League
75-76—Pennsylvania	17	9	.654	2nd/Ivy League
76-77—Pennsylvania	18	8	.692	2nd/Ivy League
Totals (8 years)	151	62	.709	

NBA COACHING RECORD

Season Team	REGULAR SEASON				PLAYOFFS		
	W	L	Pct.	Finish	W	L	Pct.
81-82—Cleveland	9	32	.220		—	—	—
83-84—Detroit	49	33	.598	2nd/Central Division	2	3	.400
84-85—Detroit	46	36	.561	2nd/Central Division	5	4	.556
85-86—Detroit	46	36	.561	3rd/Central Division	1	3	.250
86-87—Detroit	52	30	.634	2nd/Central Division	10	5	.667
87-88—Detroit	54	28	.659	1st/Central Division	14	9	.609
88-89—Detroit	63	19	.768	1st/Central Division	15	2	.882
89-90—Detroit	59	23	.720	1st/Central Division	15	5	.750
90-91—Detroit	50	32	.610	2nd/Central Division	7	8	.467
91-92—Detroit	48	34	.585	3rd/Central Division	2	3	.400
92-93—New Jersey	43	39	.524	3rd/Atlantic Division	2	3	.400
93-94—New Jersey	45	37	.549	3rd/Atlantic Division	1	3	.250
97-98—Orlando	41	41	.500	5th/Atlantic Division	—	—	—
98-99—Orlando	33	17	.660	T1st/Atlantic Division	1	3	.250
Totals (14 years)	638	437	.593	Totals (12 years)	75	51	.595

OLYMPIC RECORD

Season Team	W	L	Pct.	Finish
1992—Team USA	8	0	1.000	Gold medal

NOTES:

1972—Defeated Providence, 76-60, in NCAA Tournament first round; defeated Villanova, 78-67, in second round; lost to North Carolina, 73-59, in regional final.

1973—Defeated St. John's, 62-61, in NCAA Tournament first round; lost to Providence, 87-65, in second round; lost to Syracuse, 69-68, in regional consolation game.

1974—Lost to Providence, 84-69, in NCAA Tournament first round.

1975—Lost to Kansas State, 69-62, in NCAA Tournament first round.

1981—Replaced Don Delaney (4-13) and Bob Kloppenburg (0-1) as Cleveland head coach (December 4), with record of 4-14.

1982—Replaced by Cleveland head coach by Bill Musselman (February), with record of 15-46.

1984—Lost to New York in Eastern Conference First Round.

1985—Defeated New Jersey, 3-0, in Eastern Conference First Round; lost to Boston, 4-2, in Eastern Conference Semifinals.

1986—Lost to Atlanta in Eastern Conference First Round.

1987—Defeated Washington, 3-0, in Eastern Conference First Round; defeated Atlanta, 4-1, in Eastern Conference Semifinals; lost to Boston, 4-3, in Eastern Conference Finals.

1988—Defeated Washington, 3-2, in Eastern Conference First Round; defeated Chicago, 4-1, in Eastern Conference Semifinals; defeated Boston, 4-2, in Eastern Conference Finals; lost to Los Angeles Lakers, 4-3, in NBA Finals.

1989—Defeated Boston, 3-0, in Eastern Conference First Round; defeated Milwaukee, 4-0, in Eastern Conference Semifinals; defeated Chicago, 4-2, in Eastern Conference Finals; defeated Los Angeles Lakers, 4-0, in NBA Finals.

1990—Defeated Indiana, 3-0, in Eastern Conference First Round; defeated New York, 4-1, in Eastern Conference Semifinals; defeated Chicago, 4-3, in Eastern Conference Finals; defeated Portland, 4-1, in NBA Finals.

1991—Defeated Atlanta, 3-2, in Eastern Conference First Round; defeated Boston, 4-2, in Eastern Conference Semifinals; lost to Chicago, 4-0, in Eastern Conference Finals.

1992—Lost to New York in Eastern Conference First Round.
Team USA defeated Angola, 116-48; Croatia, 103-70; Germany, 111-68; Brazil, 127-83; and Spain, 122-81, in preliminary round. Defeated Puerto Rico, 115-77, in medal round quarterfinals; defeated Lithuania, 127-76, in semifinals; defeated Croatia, 117-85, in gold-medal game.

1993—Lost to Cleveland in Eastern Conference First Round.

1994—Lost to New York in Eastern Conference First Round.

1999—Lost to Philadelphia in Eastern Conference First Round.

FITCH, BILL

PERSONAL: Born May 19, 1934, in Davenport, Iowa. ... 6-2/205 (1,88/93,0). ... Full name: Billy Charles Fitch.
HIGH SCHOOL: Cedar Rapids (Iowa).
COLLEGE: Coe College (Iowa).
CAREER HONORS: One of the Top 10 Coaches in NBA History (1996).

COLLEGIATE RECORD

Season Team	G	Min.	FGM	FGA	Pct.	FTM	FTA	Pct.	Reb.	Ast.	Pts.	AVERAGES		
												RPG	APG	PPG
50-51—Coe College					Freshman team statistics unavailable.									
51-52—Coe College	20	...	63	...	...	50	...	...	...	...	176	...	...	8.8

Season Team	G	Min.	FGM	FGA	Pct.	FTM	FTA	Pct.	Reb.	Ast.	Pts.	AVERAGES		
												RPG	APG	PPG
52-53—Coe College	19	...	83	...	...	72	...	...	...	...	238	...	...	12.5
53-54—Coe College	22	...	123	...	...	92	...	...	...	...	338	...	...	15.4
Totals	61	...	269	...	...	214	...	...	...	...	752	...	...	12.3

HEAD COACHING RECORD

BACKGROUND: Head baseball coach and assistant basketball coach, Creighton University (1956-57 and 1957-58).

HONORS: NBA Coach of the Year (1976, 1980).

COLLEGIATE COACHING RECORD

Season Team	W	L	Pct.	Finish
58-59—Coe College	11	9	.550	6th/Midwest Collegiate Athletic Conference
59-60—Coe College	12	9	.571	T5th/Midwest Collegiate Athletic Conference
60-61—Coe College	10	12	.455	T4th/Midwest Collegiate Athletic Conference
61-62—Coe College	11	10	.524	T6th/Midwest Collegiate Athletic Conference
62-63—North Dakota	14	13	.519	3rd/North Central Intercollegiate Athletic Conference
63-64—North Dakota	10	16	.385	T3rd/North Central Intercollegiate Athletic Conference
64-65—North Dakota	26	5	.839	1st/North Central Intercollegiate Athletic Conference
65-66—North Dakota	24	5	.828	1st/North Central Intercollegiate Athletic Conference
66-67—North Dakota	20	6	.769	1st/North Central Intercollegiate Athletic Conference
67-68—Bowling Green	18	7	.720	1st/Mid-American Conference
68-69—Minnesota	12	12	.500	T5th/Big Ten Conference
69-70—Minnesota	13	11	.542	5th/Big Ten Conference
Totals (12 years).................................	181	115	.611	

NBA COACHING RECORD

Season Team	REGULAR SEASON				PLAYOFFS		
	W	L	Pct.	Finish	W	L	Pct.
70-71—Cleveland............................	15	67	.183	4th/Central Division	—	—	—
71-72—Cleveland............................	23	59	.280	4th/Central Division	—	—	—
72-73—Cleveland............................	32	50	.390	4th/Central Division	—	—	—
73-74—Cleveland............................	29	53	.354	4th/Central Division	—	—	—
74-75—Cleveland............................	40	42	.488	3rd/Central Division	—	—	—
75-76—Cleveland............................	49	33	.598	1st/Central Division	6	7	.462
76-77—Cleveland............................	43	39	.524	4th/Central Division	1	2	.538
77-78—Cleveland............................	43	39	.524	3rd/Central Division	0	2	.000
78-79—Cleveland............................	30	52	.366	T4th/Central Division	—	—	—
79-80—Boston.................................	61	21	.744	1st/Atlantic Division	5	4	.556
80-81—Boston.................................	62	20	.756	T1st/Atlantic Division	12	5	.706
81-82—Boston.................................	63	19	.768	1st/Atlantic Division	7	5	.583
82-83—Boston.................................	56	26	.683	2nd/Atlantic Division	2	5	.286
83-84—Houston	29	53	.354	6th/Midwest Division	—	—	—
84-85—Houston	48	34	.585	2nd/Midwest Division	2	3	.400
85-86—Houston	51	31	.622	1st/Midwest Division	13	7	.650
86-87—Houston	42	40	.512	3rd/Midwest Division	5	5	.500
87-88—Houston	46	36	.561	4th/Midwest Division	1	3	.250
89-90—New Jersey	17	65	.207	6th/Atlantic Division	—	—	—
90-91—New Jersey	26	56	.317	5th/Atlantic Division	—	—	—
91-92—New Jersey	40	42	.489	3rd/Atlantic Division	1	3	.250
94-95—L.A. Clippers	17	65	.207	7th/Pacific Division	—	—	—
95-96—L.A. Clippers	29	53	.354	7th/Pacific Division	—	—	—
96-97—L.A. Clippers	36	46	.439	5th/Pacific Division	0	3	.000
97-98—L.A. Clippers	17	65	.207	7th/Pacific Division	—	—	—
Totals (25 years).................................	944	1106	.460	Totals (13 years).....	55	54	.505

NOTES:

1965—Defeated Minnesota-Duluth, 67-57, in College Division Tournament first round; defeated Moorhead (Minn.) State in second round; defeated Seattle Pacific, 97-83, in national quarterfinals; lost to Southern Illinois, 97-64, in national semifinals; defeated St. Michael's (Vt.), 94-86, in national third-place game.

1966—Defeated Northern Colorado, 84-71, in College Division Tournament regional semifinals; defeated Valparaiso, 112-82, in regional finals; defeated Abilene Christian, 63-62, in national quarterfinals; lost to Southern Illinois, 69-61, in national semifinals; lost to Akron, 76-71, in national third-place game.

1967—Lost to Louisiana Tech, 86-77, in College Division Tournament regional semifinals; defeated Parsons (Ia.), 107-56, in regional third-place game.

1968—Lost to Marquette, 72-71, in NCAA Tournament first round.

1976—Defeated Washington, 4-3, in Eastern Conference Semifinals; lost to Boston, 4-2, in Eastern Conference Finals.

1977—Lost to Washington in Eastern Conference First Round.

1978—Lost to New York in Eastern Conference First Round.

1980—Defeated Houston, 4-0, in Eastern Conference Semifinals; lost to Philadelphia, 4-1, in Eastern Conference Finals.

1981—Defeated Chicago, 4-0, in Eastern Conference Semifinals; defeated Philadelphia, 4-3, in Eastern Conference Finals; defeated Houston, 4-2, in NBA Finals.

1982—Defeated Washington, 4-1, in Eastern Conference Semifinals; lost to Philadelphia, 4-3, in Eastern Conference Finals.

1983—Defeated Atlanta, 2-1, in Eastern Conference First Round; lost to Milwaukee, 4-0, in Eastern Conference Semifinals.

1985—Lost to Utah in Western Conference First Round.

1986—Defeated Sacramento, 3-0, in Western Conference First Round; defeated Denver, 4-2, in Western Conference Semifinals; defeated Los Angeles Lakers, 4-1, in Western Conference Finals; lost to Boston, 4-2, in NBA Finals.

1987—Defeated Portland, 3-1, in Western Conference First Round; lost to Seattle, 4-2, in Western Conference Semifinals.

ALL-TIME GREAT COACHES

1988—Lost to Dallas in Western Conference First Round.
1992—Lost to Cleveland in Eastern Conference First Round.
1997—Lost to Utah in Western Conference First Round.

FITZSIMMONS, COTTON

PERSONAL: Born October 7, 1931, in Hannibal, Mo. ... Died July 24, 2004. ... 5-7/160 (1,70/72,6). ... Full name: Lowell Fitzsimmons.
HIGH SCHOOL: Bowling Green (Mo.).
COLLEGE: Hannibal (Mo.)-LaGrange, then Midwestern State (Texas).
CAREER NOTES: Director of player personnel, Golden State Warriors (1976-77). ... Director of player personnel, Phoenix Suns (1987-88). ... Head coach/director of player personnel, Suns (1988-89 through 1991-92). ... Senior executive vice president, Suns (1992-93 through January 16, 1996 and November 15, 1996 through present).

COLLEGIATE RECORD

Season Team	G	Min.	FGM	FGA	Pct.	FTM	FTA	Pct.	Reb.	Ast.	Pts.	RPG	APG	PPG
52-53—Hann.-LaGrange‡	33	...	...	...	...	...	...	...	...	...	838	...	...	25.4
53-54—Midwestern State.	27	...	53	161	.329	128	173	.740	...	...	234	...	...	8.7
54-55—Midwestern State.	27	...	118	258	.457	162	210	.771	...	...	398	...	...	14.7
55-56—Midwestern State.	28	...	148	319	.464	164	223	.735	...	...	460	...	...	16.4
Varsity totals	82	...	319	738	.432	454	606	.749	...	...	1092	...	...	13.3

HEAD COACHING RECORD

BACKGROUND: Assistant coach, Kansas State University (1967-68).
HONORS: NBA Coach of the Year (1979, 1989).

COLLEGE COACHING RECORD

Season Team	W	l	Pct.	Finish
58-59—Moberly J.C. (Mo.)	16	15	.516	
59-60—Moberly J.C. (Mo.)	19	8	.704	
60-61—Moberly J.C. (Mo.)	26	5	.839	
61-62—Moberly J.C. (Mo.)	26	9	.743	
62-63—Moberly J.C. (Mo.)	26	6	.813	
63-64—Moberly J.C. (Mo.)	24	5	.828	
64-65—Moberly J.C. (Mo.)	25	5	.833	
65-66—Moberly J.C. (Mo.)	29	5	.853	
66-67—Moberly J.C. (Mo.)	31	2	.939	
68-69—Kansas State	14	12	.538	T2nd/Big Eight Conference
69-70—Kansas State	20	8	.714	1st/Big Eight Conference
Junior college totals (9 years)	222	60	.787	
4-year college totals (2 years)	34	20	.630	

NBA COACHING RECORD

	REGULAR SEASON				PLAYOFFS		
Season Team	W	L	Pct.	Finish	W	L	Pct.
70-71—Phoenix	48	34	.585	3rd/Midwest Division	—	—	—
71-72—Phoenix	49	33	.598	3rd/Midwest Division	—	—	—
72-73—Atlanta	46	36	.561	2nd/Central Division	2	4	.333
73-74—Atlanta	35	47	.427	2nd/Central Division	—	—	—
74-75—Atlanta	31	51	.378	4th/Central Division	—	—	—
75-76—Atlanta	28	46	.378		—	—	—
77-78—Buffalo	27	55	.329	4th/Atlantic Division	—	—	—
78-79—Kansas City	48	34	.585	1st/Midwest Division	1	4	.200
79-80—Kansas City	47	35	.573	2nd/Midwest Division	1	2	.333
80-81—Kansas City	40	42	.488	T2nd/Midwest Division	7	8	.467
81-82—Kansas City	30	52	.366	4th/Midwest Division	—	—	—
82-83—Kansas City	45	37	.549	T2nd/Midwest Division	—	—	—
83-84—Kansas City	38	44	.463	T3rd/Midwest Division	0	3	.000
84-85—San Antonio	41	41	.500	T4th/Midwest Division	2	3	.400
85-86—San Antonio	35	47	.427	6th/Midwest Division	0	3	.000
88-89—Phoenix	55	27	.671	2nd/Pacific Division	7	5	.583
89-90—Phoenix	54	28	.659	3rd/Pacific Division	9	7	.563
90-91—Phoenix	55	27	.671	3rd/Pacific Division	1	3	.250
91-92—Phoenix	53	29	.646	3rd/Pacific Division	4	4	.500
95-96—Phoenix	27	22	.551	4th/Pacific Division	1	3	.250
96-97—Phoenix	0	8	.000		—	—	—
Totals (21 years)	832	775	.518	Totals (12 years)	35	49	.417

NOTES:

1966—Won National Junior College Athletic Association national tournament.
1967—Won National Junior College Athletic Association national tournament.
1970—Lost to New Mexico, 70-66, in NCAA Tournament regional semifinal.
1973—Lost to Boston in Eastern Conference Semifinals.
1976—Replaced as Atlanta head coach by Gene Tormohlen (March) with club in fifth place.
1979—Lost to Phoenix in Western Conference Semifinals.
1980—Lost to Phoenix in Western Conference First Round.
1981—Defeated Portland, 2-1, in Western Conference First Round; defeated Phoenix, 4-3, in Western Conference Semifinals; lost to Houston, 4-1, in Western Conference Finals.

ALL-TIME GREAT COACHES

1984—Lost to Los Angeles Lakers in Western Conference First Round.

1985—Lost to Denver in Western Conference First Round.

1986—Lost to Los Angeles Lakers in Western Conference First Round.

1989—Defeated Denver, 3-0, in Western Conference First Round; defeated Golden State, 4-1, in Western Conference Semifinals; lost to Los Angeles Lakers, 4-0, in Western Conference Finals.

1990—Defeated Utah, 3-2, in Western Conference First Round; defeated Los Angeles Lakers, 4-1, in Western Conference Semifinals; lost to Portland, 4-2, in Western Conference Finals.

1991—Lost to Utah in Western Conference First Round.

1992—Defeated San Antonio, 3-0, in Western Conference First Round; lost to Portland, 4-1, in Western Conference Semifinals.

1996—Replaced Paul Westphal as Phoenix head coach (January 16) with record of 14-19 and club in sixth place. Lost to San Antonio in Western Conference First Round. Replaced as Phoenix head coach by Danny Ainge with record of 0-8 and club in seventh place (November 15).

FRATELLO, MIKE

See Head Coaches, page 286.

HANNUM, ALEX

PERSONAL: Born July 19, 1923, in Los Angeles. ... Died January 18, 2002. ... 6-7/225 (2,00/102,1). ... Full name: Alexander Murray Hannum.
HIGH SCHOOL: Hamilton (Los Angeles).
COLLEGE: Southern California.
TRANSACTIONS: Played for Los Angeles Shamrocks, an Amateur Athletic Union team and averaged 9.8 points per game (1945-46). ... Signed by Oshkosh All-Stars of National Basketball League (1948). ... Sold by Oshkosh of NBL to Syracuse Nationals of NBA (1949). ... Traded by Nationals with Fred Scolari to Baltimore Bullets for Red Rocha (1951). ... Sold by Bullets to Rochester Royals during 1951-52 season. ... Sold by Royals to Milwaukee Hawks (1954). ... Hawks franchise moved from Milwaukee to St. Louis for 1955-56 season. ... Released by Hawks (1956). ... Signed by Fort Wayne Pistons (1956). ... Released by Pistons (December 12, 1956). ... Signed by Hawks (December 17, 1956).
CAREER HONORS: Elected to Naismith Memorial Basketball Hall of Fame (1998).

COLLEGIATE RECORD

NOTES: In military service (1943-44 through 1945-46).

Season Team	G	Min.	FGM	FGA	Pct.	FTM	FTA	Pct.	Reb.	Ast.	Pts.	RPG	APG	PPG
41-42—Southern California‡						Freshman team statistics unavailable.								
42-43—Southern California	15	...	23	...	...	9	20	.450	...	...	55	...	...	3.7
46-47—Southern California	24	...	...	...	...	...	...	...	...	...	251	...	...	10.5
47-48—Southern California	23	...	108	...	...	...	...	...	...	...	263	...	...	11.4
Varsity totals..........................	62	...	...	...	...	...	...	...	...	...	569	...	...	9.2

NBL AND NBA REGULAR-SEASON RECORD

Season Team	G	Min.	FGM	FGA	Pct.	FTM	FTA	Pct.	Reb.	Ast.	PF	Dq.	Pts.	RPG	APG	PPG
48-49—Oshkosh (NBL)..................	62	...	126	...	...	113	191	.592	...	...	188	...	365	...	...	5.9
49-50—Syracuse..........................	64	...	177	488	.363	128	186	.688	...	129	264	...	482	...	2.0	7.5
50-51—Syracuse..........................	63	...	182	494	.368	107	197	.543	301	119	271	16	471	4.8	1.9	7.5
51-52—Balt.-Roch........................	66	1508	170	462	.368	98	138	.710	336	133	271	16	438	5.1	2.0	6.6
52-53—Rochester	68	1288	129	360	.358	88	133	.662	279	81	258	18	346	4.1	1.2	5.1
53-54—Rochester	72	1707	175	503	.348	102	164	.622	350	105	279	11	452	4.9	1.5	6.3
54-55—Milwaukee	53	1088	126	358	.352	61	107	.570	245	105	206	9	313	4.6	2.0	5.9
55-56—St. Louis	71	1480	146	453	.322	93	154	.604	344	157	271	10	385	4.8	2.2	5.4
56-57—Fort Wayne-St. Louis..........	59	642	77	223	.345	37	56	.661	158	28	135	2	191	2.7	0.5	3.2
Totals....................................	578	...	1308	...	...	827	1326	.624	...	...	2143	...	3443	...	...	6.0

NBL AND NBA PLAYOFF RECORD

Season Team	G	Min.	FGM	FGA	Pct.	FTM	FTA	Pct.	Reb.	Ast.	PF	Dq.	Pts.	RPG	APG	PPG
48-49—Oshkosh (NBL)..................	7	...	12	...	...	16	26	.615	...	...	...	...	40	...	...	5.7
49-50—Syracuse..........................	11	...	38	86	.442	17	34	.500	...	10	50	...	93	...	0.9	8.5
50-51—Syracuse..........................	7	...	17	39	.436	8	10	.800	47	17	37	3	42	6.7	2.4	6.0
51-52—Rochester	6	146	16	42	.381	8	13	.615	26	8	30	3	40	4.3	1.3	6.7
52-53—Rochester	3	52	4	10	.400	3	8	.375	4	2	16	1	11	1.3	0.7	3.7
53-54—Rochester	6	107	12	29	.414	15	24	.625	22	5	28	3	39	3.7	0.8	6.5
55-56—St. Louis	8	159	21	66	.318	19	35	.543	29	10	36	3	61	3.6	1.3	7.6
56-57—St. Louis	2	6	0	2	.000	0	0	...	0	0	2	0	0	0.0	0.0	0.0
Totals....................................	50	...	120	...	...	86	150	.573	...	...	...	...	326	...	...	6.5

HEAD COACHING RECORD

HONORS: NBA Coach of the Year (1964). ... ABA Coach of the Year (1969).

NBA COACHING RECORD

Season Team	REGULAR SEASON				PLAYOFFS		
	W	L	Pct.	Finish	W	L	Pct.
56-57—St. Louis..	15	16	.484	T1st/Western Division	8	4	.667
57-58—St. Louis..	41	31	.569	1st/Western Division	8	3	.727
60-61—Syracuse..	38	41	.481	3rd/Eastern Division	4	4	.500
61-62—Syracuse..	41	39	.513	3rd/Eastern Division	2	3	.400
62-63—Syracuse..	48	32	.600	2nd/Eastern Division	2	3	.400
63-64—San Francisco....................................	48	32	.600	1st/Western Division	5	7	.417
64-65—San Francisco....................................	17	63	.215	5th/Western Division	—	—	—

| | | REGULAR SEASON | | | | PLAYOFFS | | |
Season Team	W	L	Pct.	Finish		W	L	Pct.
65-66—San Francisco	35	45	.438	4th/Western Division		—	—	—
66-67—Philadelphia	68	13	.840	1st/Eastern Division		11	4	.733
67-68—Philadelphia	62	20	.756	1st/Eastern Division		7	6	.538
69-70—San Diego	18	38	.321	7th/Western Division		—	—	—
70-71—San Diego	40	42	.488	3rd/Pacific Division		—	—	—
Totals (12 years)	471	412	.533	Totals (8 years)		47	34	.580

NIBL COACHING RECORD

| | | REGULAR SEASON | | |
Season Team	W	L	Pct.	Finish
58-59—Wichita	19	11	.633	2nd
59-60—Wichita	22	10	.688	2nd
Totals (2 years)	41	21	.661	

ABA COACHING RECORD

| | | REGULAR SEASON | | | | PLAYOFFS | | |
Season Team	W	L	Pct.	Finish		W	L	Pct.
68-69—Oakland	60	18	.769	1st/Western Division		12	4	.750
71-72—Denver	34	50	.405	4th/Western Division		3	4	.429
72-73—Denver	47	37	.560	3rd/Western Division		1	4	.200
73-74—Denver	37	47	.440	T4th/Western Division		—	—	—
Totals (4 years)	178	152	.539	Totals (3 years)		16	12	.571

NOTES:

1957—Replaced Red Holzman (14-19) and Slater Martin (5-3) as St. Louis head coach (January), with record of 19-22. Defeated Fort Wayne, 115-103, and Minneapolis, 114-111, in Western Division tiebreakers; defeated Minneapolis, 3-0, in Western Division Finals; lost to Boston, 4-3, in NBA Finals.

1958—Defeated Detroit, 4-1, in Western Division Finals; defeated Boston, 4-2, in NBA Finals.

1961—Defeated Philadelphia, 3-0, in Eastern Division Semifinals; lost to Boston, 4-1, in Eastern Division Finals.

1962—Lost to Philadelphia in Eastern Division Semifinals.

1963—Lost to Cincinnati in Eastern Division Semifinals.

1964—Defeated St. Louis, 4-3, in Western Division Finals; lost to Boston, 4-1, in NBA Finals.

1967—Defeated Cincinnati, 3-1, in Eastern Division Semifinals; defeated Boston, 4-1, in Eastern Division Finals; defeated San Francisco, 4-2, in NBA Finals.

1968—Defeated New York, 4-2, in Eastern Division Semifinals; lost to Boston, 4-3, in Eastern Division Finals.

1969—Defeated Denver, 4-3, in Western Division Semifinals; defeated New Orleans, 4-0, in Western Division Finals; defeated Indiana, 4-1, in ABA Finals. Replaced Jack McMahon as San Diego head coach (December), with record of 9-17.

1972—Lost to Indiana in Western Division Semifinals.

1973—Lost to Indiana in Western Division Semifinals.

HARRIS, DEL

PERSONAL: Born June 18, 1937, in Plainfield, Ind. ... 6-4/205 (1,93/93,0). ... Full name: Delmer W. Harris.
HIGH SCHOOL: Plainfield (Ind.).
COLLEGE: Milligan College (Tenn.).
CAREER NOTES: Vice president, Bucks (1987 through 1992). ... Consultant, Sacramento Kings (1993-94).

COLLEGIATE RECORD

NOTES: Field goal attempts for five games and rebounds for 13 games are unavailable.

| | | | | | | | | | | | | AVERAGES | | |
Season Team	G	Min.	FGM	FGA	Pct.	FTM	FTA	Pct.	Reb.	Ast.	Pts.	RPG	APG	PPG
55-56—Milligan College	24	...	101	232	.435	89	126	.706	122	...	291	5.1	...	12.1
56-57—Milligan College	24	...	162	375	.432	141	197	.716	165	...	465	6.9	...	19.4
57-58—Milligan College	22	...	167	378	.442	119	149	.799	240	...	453	10.9	...	20.6
58-59—Milligan College	21	...	136	306	.444	158	202	.782	338	...	430	16.1	...	20.5
Totals	91	...	566	1291	.438	507	674	.752	865	...	1639	9.5	...	18.0

HEAD COACHING RECORD

BACKGROUND: Head coach, Superior League, Puerto Rico (1969 through 1975). ... Assistant coach, Utah Stars of ABA (1975-76). ... Assistant coach, Houston Rockets (1976-77 through 1978-79). ... Scout, Milwaukee Bucks (1983 through 1986). ... Assistant coach, Bucks (1986-87). ... Assistant coach, Dallas Mavericks (2000-present).
HONORS: NBA Coach of the Year (1995).

COLLEGIATE COACHING RECORD

Season Team	W	L	Pct.	Finish
65-66—Earlham College	14	8	.636	Hoosier Collegiate Conference
66-67—Earlham College	15	9	.625	4th/Hoosier Collegiate Conference
67-68—Earlham College	25	3	.893	1st/Hoosier Collegiate Conference
68-69—Earlham College	18	8	.692	2nd/Hoosier Collegiate Conference
69-70—Earlham College	22	8	.733	1st/Hoosier Collegiate Conference
70-71—Earlham College	24	5	.828	1st/Hoosier Collegiate Conference
71-72—Earlham College	21	9	.700	1st/Hoosier Collegiate Conference
72-73—Earlham College	17	11	.607	3rd/Hoosier Collegiate Conference
73-74—Earlham College	19	9	.679	3rd/Hoosier Collegiate Conference
Totals (9 years)	175	70	.714	

Season Team	REGULAR SEASON W	L	Pct.	Finish	PLAYOFFS W	L	Pct.
79-80—Houston	41	41	.500	T2nd/Central Division	2	5	.286
80-81—Houston	40	42	.488	T2nd/Midwest Division	12	9	.571
81-82—Houston	46	36	.561	T2nd/Midwest Division	1	2	.333
82-83—Houston	14	68	.171	6th/Midwest Division	—	—	—
87-88—Milwaukee	42	40	.512	T4th/Central Division	2	3	.400
88-89—Milwaukee	49	33	.598	4th/Central Division	3	6	.333
89-90—Milwaukee	44	38	.537	3rd/Central Division	1	3	.250
90-91—Milwaukee	48	34	.585	3rd/Central Division	0	3	.000
91-92—Milwaukee	8	9	.471		—	—	—
94-95—L.A. Lakers	48	34	.585	3rd/Pacific Division	5	5	.500
95-96—L.A. Lakers	53	29	.646	2nd/Pacific Division	1	3	.250
96-97—L.A. Lakers	56	26	.683	2nd/Pacific Division	4	5	.444
97-98—L.A. Lakers	61	21	.744	T1st/Pacific Division	7	6	.538
98-99—L.A. Lakers	6	6	.500		—	—	—
Totals (14 years)	**556**	**457**	**.549**	**Totals (11 years)**	**38**	**50**	**.432**

NOTES:

1968—Posted 1-1 record in NAIA District Tournament.

1969—Posted 0-1 record in NAIA District Tournament.

1970—Posted 1-1 record in NAIA District Tournament.

1971—Posted 2-0 record in NAIA District Tournament; posted 1-1 record in NAIA National Tournament.

1972—Posted 1-1 record in NAIA District Tournament.

1973—Posted 2-1 record in NAIA District Tournament.

1980—Defeated San Antonio, 2-1, in Eastern Conference First Round; lost to Boston, 4-0, in Eastern Conference Semifinals.

1981—Defeated Los Angeles Lakers, 2-1, in Western Conference First Round; defeated San Antonio, 4-3, in Western Conference Semifinals; defeated Kansas City, 4-1, in Western Conference Finals; lost to Boston, 4-2, in NBA Finals.

1982—Lost to Seattle in Western Conference First Round.

1988—Lost to Atlanta in Eastern Conference First Round.

1989—Defeated Atlanta, 3-2, in Eastern Conference First Round; lost to Detroit, 4-0, in Eastern Conference Semifinals.

1990—Lost to Chicago in Eastern Conference First Round.

1991—Lost to Philadelphia in Eastern Conference First Round. Resigned as Milwaukee head coach (December 4) to concentrate on duties as team's head of basketball operations.

1995—Defeated Seattle, 3-1, in Western Conference First Round; lost to San Antonio, 4-2, in Western Conference Semifinals.

1996—Lost to Houston in Western Conference First Round.

1997—Defeated Portland, 3-1, in Western Conference First Round; lost to Utah, 4-1, in Western Conference Semifinals.

1998—Defeated Portland, 3-1, in Western Conference First Round; defeated Seattle, 4-1, in Western Conference Semifinals; lost to Utah, 4-0, in Western Conference Finals.

1999—Replaced as head coach on an interim basis by Kurt Rambis (February 24) with club in fourth place.

HEINSOHN, TOM

PERSONAL: Born August 26, 1934, in Jersey City, N.J. ... 6-7/218 (2,00/98,9). ... Full name: Thomas William Heinsohn.
HIGH SCHOOL: St. Michael's (Union City, N.J.).
COLLEGE: Holy Cross.
TRANSACTIONS: Selected by Boston Celtics in 1956 NBA Draft (territorial pick).
CAREER HONORS: Elected to Naismith Memorial Basketball Hall of Fame (1986).
MISCELLANEOUS: Member of NBA championship team (1957, 1959, 1960, 1961, 1962, 1963, 1964, 1965).

COLLEGIATE RECORD

Season Team	G	Min.	FGM	FGA	Pct.	FTM	FTA	Pct.	Reb.	Ast.	Pts.	AVERAGES RPG	APG	PPG
52-53—Holy Cross‡	15	...	97	...	...	70	...	...	...	...	264	...	...	17.6
53-54—Holy Cross	28	...	175	364	.481	94	142	.662	300	...	444	10.7	...	15.9
54-55—Holy Cross	26	...	232	499	.465	141	215	.656	385	...	605	14.8	...	23.3
55-56—Holy Cross	27	...	254	630	.403	232	304	.763	569	...	740	21.1	...	27.4
Varsity totals	**81**	...	**661**	**1493**	**.443**	**467**	**661**	**.707**	**1254**	...	**1789**	**15.5**	...	**22.1**

NBA REGULAR-SEASON RECORD

HONORS: NBA Rookie of the Year (1957). ... All-NBA second team (1961, 1962, 1963, 1964).

Season Team	G	Min.	FGM	FGA	Pct.	FTM	FTA	Pct.	Reb.	Ast.	PF	Dq.	Pts.	AVERAGES RPG	APG	PPG
56-57—Boston	72	2150	446	1123	.397	271	343	.790	705	117	304	12	1163	9.8	1.6	16.2
57-58—Boston	69	2206	468	1226	.382	294	394	.746	705	125	274	6	1230	10.2	1.8	17.8
58-59—Boston	66	2089	465	1192	.390	312	391	.798	638	164	271	11	1242	9.7	2.5	18.8
59-60—Boston	75	2420	673	1590	.423	283	386	.733	794	171	275	8	1629	10.6	2.3	21.7
60-61—Boston	74	2256	627	1566	.400	325	424	.767	732	141	260	7	1579	9.9	1.9	21.3
61-62—Boston	79	2383	692	1613	.429	358	437	.819	747	165	280	2	1742	9.5	2.1	22.1
62-63—Boston	76	2004	550	1300	.423	340	407	.835	569	95	279	4	1440	7.5	1.3	18.9
63-64—Boston	76	2040	487	1223	.398	283	342	.827	460	183	268	3	1257	6.1	2.4	16.5
64-65—Boston	67	1706	365	954	.383	182	229	.795	399	157	252	5	912	6.0	2.3	13.6
Totals	**654**	**19254**	**4773**	**11787**	**.405**	**2648**	**3353**	**.790**	**5749**	**1318**	**2454**	**58**	**12194**	**8.8**	**2.0**	**18.6**

NBA PLAYOFF RECORD

															AVERAGES		
Season Team	G	Min.	FGM	FGA	Pct.	FTM	FTA	Pct.	Reb.	Ast.	PF	Dq.	Pts.	RPG	APG	PPG
56–57—Boston	10	370	90	231	.390	49	69	.710	117	20	40	1	229	11.7	2.0	22.9
57–58—Boston	11	349	68	194	.351	56	72	.778	119	18	52	3	192	10.8	1.6	17.5
58–59—Boston	11	348	91	220	.414	37	56	.661	98	32	41	0	219	8.9	2.9	19.9
59–60—Boston	13	423	112	267	.419	60	80	.750	126	27	53	2	284	9.7	2.1	21.8
60–61—Boston	10	291	82	201	.408	33	43	.767	99	20	36	1	197	9.9	2.0	19.7
61–62—Boston	14	445	116	291	.399	58	76	.763	115	34	58	4	290	8.2	2.4	20.7
62–63—Boston	13	413	123	270	.456	75	98	.765	116	15	55	2	321	8.9	1.2	24.7
63–64—Boston	10	308	70	180	.389	34	42	.810	80	26	36	0	174	8.0	2.6	17.4
64–65—Boston	12	276	66	181	.365	20	32	.625	84	23	46	1	152	7.0	1.9	12.7
Totals	104	3223	818	2035	.402	422	568	.743	954	215	417	14	2058	9.2	2.1	19.8

NBA ALL-STAR GAME RECORD

Season Team	Min.	FGM	FGA	Pct.	FTM	FTA	Pct.	Reb.	Ast.	PF	Dq.	Pts.
1957—Boston	23	5	17	.294	2	2	1.000	7	0	3	0	12
1961—Boston	19	2	16	.125	0	0	...	6	1	4	0	4
1962—Boston	13	4	11	.364	2	2	1.000	2	1	4	0	10
1963—Boston	21	6	11	.545	3	4	.750	2	1	4	0	15
1964—Boston	21	5	12	.417	0	0	...	3	0	5	0	10
1965—Boston					Selected, did not play—injured.							
Totals	97	22	67	.328	7	8	.875	20	3	20	0	51

NOTES: NBA Coach of the Year (1973).

HEAD COACHING RECORD

NBA COACHING RECORD

	REGULAR SEASON					PLAYOFFS		
Season Team	W	L	Pct.	Finish		W	L	Pct.
69-70—Boston	34	48	.415	6th/Eastern Division		—	—	—
70-71—Boston	44	38	.537	3rd/Atlantic Division		—	—	—
71-72—Boston	56	26	.683	1st/Atlantic Division		5	6	.455
72-73—Boston	68	14	.829	1st/Atlantic Division		7	6	.538
73-74—Boston	56	26	.683	1st/Atlantic Division		12	6	.667
74-75—Boston	60	22	.732	1st/Atlantic Division		6	5	.545
75-76—Boston	54	28	.659	1st/Atlantic Division		12	6	.667
76-77—Boston	44	38	.537	2nd/Atlantic Division		5	4	.556
77-78—Boston	11	23	.324			—	—	—
Totals (9 years)	427	263	.619	Totals (6 years)		47	33	.588

NOTES:

1972—Defeated Atlanta, 4-2, in Eastern Conference Semifinals; lost to New York, 4-1, in Eastern Conference Finals.

1973—Defeated Atlanta, 4-2, in Eastern Conference Semifinals; lost to New York, 4-3, in Eastern Conference Finals.

1974—Defeated Buffalo, 4-2, in Eastern Conference Semifinals; defeated New York, 4-1, in Eastern Conference Finals; defeated Milwaukee, 4-3, in NBA Finals.

1975—Defeated Houston, 4-1, in Eastern Conference Semifinals; lost to Washington, 4-2, in Eastern Conference Finals.

1976—Defeated Buffalo, 4-2, in Eastern Conference Semifinals; defeated Cleveland, 4-2, in Eastern Conference Finals; defeated Phoenix, 4-2, in NBA Finals.

1977—Defeated San Antonio, 2-0, in Eastern Conference First Round; lost to Philadelphia, 4-3, in Eastern Conference Semifinals.

1978—Replaced as Boston head coach by Tom Sanders with club in third place (January 3).

HOLZMAN, RED

PERSONAL: Born August 10, 1920, in Brooklyn, N.Y. ... Died November 13, 1998. ... 5-10/175 (1,78/79,4). ... Full name: William Holzman.

HIGH SCHOOL: Franklin K. Lane (Brooklyn, N.Y.).

COLLEGE: Baltimore, then City College of New York.

TRANSACTIONS: Played in New York State League with Albany (1941-42). ... In military service during 1942-43, 1943-44 and 1944-45 seasons; played at Norfolk, Va., Naval Training Station and scored 305 points in 1942-43 and 258 points in 1943-44. ... Signed by Rochester Royals of National Basketball League (1945). ... Played in American Basketball League with New York (1945-46). ... Royals franchise transferred to Basketball Association of America for 1948-49 season. ... Royals franchise became part of NBA for 1949-50 season. ... Acquired from Royals by Milwaukee Hawks (1953).

CAREER NOTES: Basketball consultant, New York Knicks (1991 to 1998).

CAREER HONORS: Elected to Naismith Memorial Basketball Hall of Fame (1986). ... One of the Top 10 Coaches in NBA History (1996).

MISCELLANEOUS: Member of NBL championship team (1946). ... Member of NBA championship team (1951).

COLLEGIATE RECORD

												AVERAGES		
Season Team	G	Min.	FGM	FGA	Pct.	FTM	FTA	Pct.	Reb.	Ast.	Pts.	RPG	APG	PPG
38-39—Baltimore						Statistics unavailable.								
39-40—City College. (N.Y.)						Did not play—transfer student.								
40-41—City College. (N.Y.)	21	...	96	...	...	37	...	...	...	...	229	...	...	10.9
41-42—City College. (N.Y.)	18	...	87	...	...	51	...	...	...	...	225	...	...	12.5
Totals	39	...	183	...	...	88	...	...	...	...	454	...	...	11.6

ABL REGULAR-SEASON RECORD

												AVERAGES		
Season Team	G	Min.	FGM	FGA	Pct.	FTM	FTA	Pct.	Reb.	Ast.	Pts.	RPG	APG	PPG
45-46—New York	4	...	18	...	...	12	...	...	...	...	48	...	...	12.0

NBL AND NBA REGULAR-SEASON RECORD

HONORS: All-NBL first team (1946, 1948). ... All-NBL second team (1947).

														AVERAGES		
Season Team	G	Min.	FGM	FGA	Pct.	FTM	FTA	Pct.	Reb.	Ast.	PF	Dq.	Pts.	RPG	APG	PPG
45-46—Rochester (NBL)	34	...	144	...	...	77	115	.670	...	...	54	...	365	...	...	10.7
46-47—Rochester (NBL)	44	...	227	...	...	74	139	.532	...	...	68	...	528	...	...	12.0
47-48—Rochester (NBL)	60	...	246	...	...	117	182	.643	...	...	58	...	609	...	...	10.2
48-49—Rochester (BAA)	60	...	225	691	.326	96	157	.611	...	149	93	...	546	...	2.5	9.1
49-50—Rochester	68	...	206	625	.330	144	210	.686	...	200	67	...	556	...	2.9	8.2
50-51—Rochester	68	...	183	561	.326	130	179	.726	152	147	94	0	496	2.2	2.2	7.3
51-52—Rochester	65	1065	104	372	.280	61	85	.718	106	115	95	1	269	1.6	1.8	4.1
52-53—Rochester	46	392	38	149	.255	27	38	.711	40	35	56	2	103	0.9	0.8	2.2
53-54—Milwaukee	51	649	74	224	.330	48	73	.658	46	75	73	1	196	0.9	1.5	3.8
Totals	496		1447	...		774	1178	.657	...	...	658	...	3668	...	...	7.4

NBL AND NBA PLAYOFF RECORD

														AVERAGES		
Season Team	G	Min.	FGM	FGA	Pct.	FTM	FTA	Pct.	Reb.	Ast.	PF	Dq.	Pts.	RPG	APG	PPG
45-46—Rochester (NBL)	7	...	30	...	...	21	31	.677	...	...	10	...	81	...	...	11.6
46-47—Rochester (NBL)	11	...	42	...	...	22	29	.759	...	...	22	...	106	...	...	9.6
47-48—Rochester (NBL)	10	...	35	...	...	10	15	.667	...	...	6	...	80	...	...	8.0
48-49—Rochester (BAA)	4	...	18	40	.450	5	6	.833	...	13	3	...	41	...	3.3	10.3
49-50—Rochester	2	...	3	9	.333	1	2	.500	...	0	3	...	7	...	0.0	3.5
50-51—Rochester	14	...	31	76	.408	23	34	.676	19	20	14	0	85	1.4	1.4	6.1
51-52—Rochester	6	65	3	15	.200	1	6	.167	6	2	3	0	7	1.0	0.3	1.2
52-53—Rochester	2	14	1	5	.200	1	4	.250	1	1	4	0	3	0.5	0.5	1.5
Totals	56		163	...		84	127	.661	...	...	65	...	410	...	...	7.3

HEAD COACHING RECORD

BACKGROUND: Chief scout, New York Knicks (1959-60 through 1966-67).
HONORS: NBA Coach of the Year (1970).

NBA COACHING RECORD

	REGULAR SEASON				PLAYOFFS		
Season Team	W	L	Pct.	Finish	W	L	Pct.
53-54—Milwaukee	10	16	.385	4th/Western Division	—	—	—
54-55—Milwaukee	26	46	.361	4th/Western Division	—	—	—
55-56—St. Louis	33	39	.458	T2nd/Western Division	4	5	.444
56-57—St. Louis	14	19	.424		—	—	—
67-68—New York	28	17	.622	3rd/Eastern Division	2	4	.333
68-69—New York	54	28	.659	3rd/Eastern Division	6	4	.600
69-70—New York	60	22	.732	1st/Eastern Division	12	7	.632
70-71—New York	52	30	.634	1st/Atlantic Division	7	5	.583
71-72—New York	48	34	.585	2nd/Atlantic Division	9	7	.563
72-73—New York	57	25	.695	2nd/Atlantic Division	12	5	.706
73-74—New York	49	33	.598	2nd/Atlantic Division	5	7	.417
74-75—New York	40	42	.488	3rd/Atlantic Division	1	2	.333
75-76—New York	38	44	.463	4th/Atlantic Division	—	—	—
76-77—New York	40	42	.488	3rd/Atlantic Division	—	—	—
78-79—New York	25	43	.368	4th/Atlantic Division	—	—	—
79-80—New York	39	43	.476	T3rd/Atlantic Division	—	—	—
80-81—New York	50	32	.610	3rd/Atlantic Division	0	2	.000
81-82—New York	33	49	.402	5th/Atlantic Division	—	—	—
Totals (18 years)	696	604	.535	Totals (10 years)	58	48	.547

NOTES:
1954—Replaced Fuzzy Levane as Milwaukee head coach with record of 11-35.
1955—Milwaukee franchise transferred to St. Louis.
1956—Lost to Minneapolis, 103-97, in Western Division 2nd place game; defeated Minneapolis, 2-1, in Western Division Semifinals; lost to Fort Wayne, 3-2, in Western Division Finals.
1957—Replaced as St. Louis head coach by Slater Martin (January).
1967—Replaced Dick McGuire as New York head coach (December), with record of 15-22 and in fifth place.
1968—Lost to Philadelphia in Eastern Division Semifinals.
1969—Defeated Baltimore, 4-0, in Eastern Division Semifinals; lost to Boston, 4-2, in Eastern Division Finals.
1970—Defeated Baltimore, 4-3, in Eastern Division Semifinals; defeated Milwaukee, 4-1, in Eastern Division Finals; defeated Los Angeles, 4-3, in NBA Finals.
1971—Defeated Atlanta, 4-1, in Eastern Conference Semifinals; lost to Baltimore, 4-3, in Eastern Conference Finals.
1972—Defeated Baltimore, 4-2, in Eastern Conference Semifinals; defeated Boston, 4-1, in Eastern Conference Finals; lost to Los Angeles, 4-1, in NBA Finals.
1973—Defeated Baltimore, 4-1, in Eastern Conference Semifinals; defeated Boston, 4-3, in Eastern Conference Finals; defeated Los Angeles, 4-1, in NBA Finals.
1974—Defeated Capital, 4-3, in Eastern Conference Semifinals; lost to Boston, 4-1, in Eastern Conference Finals.
1975—Lost to Houston in Eastern Conference First Round.
1978—Replaced Willis Reed as New York head coach (November) with record of 6-8.
1981—Lost to Chicago in Eastern Conference First Round.

JACKSON, PHIL

See Head Coaches, page 288.

JONES, K.C.

PERSONAL: Born May 25, 1932, in Taylor, Texas. ... 6-1/200 (1,85/90,7).
HIGH SCHOOL: Commerce (San Francisco).
COLLEGE: San Francisco.
TRANSACTIONS: Selected by Boston Celtics in second round of 1956 NBA Draft. ... In military service (1956-57 and 1957-58); played at Fort Leonard Wood, Mo.; named to Amateur Athletic Union All-America team as a member of 1957-58 Fort Leonard Wood team. ... Played in Eastern Basketball League with Hartford Capitols (1967-68).
CAREER HONORS: Elected to Naismith Memorial Basketball Hall of Fame (1989).
MISCELLANEOUS: Member of NBA championship team (1959, 1960, 1961, 1962, 1963, 1964, 1965, 1966). ... Selected by Los Angeles Rams in 30th round of 1955 National Football League Draft. ... Member of gold-medal-winning U.S. Olympic team (1956).

COLLEGIATE RECORD

NOTES: Underwent appendectomy after one game of the 1953-54 season and was granted an extra year of eligibility by the University of San Francisco; however, he was ineligible for the 1955-56 NCAA Tournament because he was playing his fifth season of college basketball. ... Member of NCAA championship team (1955).

Season Team	G	Min.	FGM	FGA	Pct.	FTM	FTA	Pct.	Reb.	Ast.	Pts.	RPG	APG	PPG
51-52—San Francisco‡	24	...	44	128	.344	46	64	.719	...	...	134	...	...	5.6
52-53—San Francisco	23	...	63	159	.396	81	149	.544	...	...	207	...	...	9.0
53-54—San Francisco	1	...	3	12	.250	2	2	1.000	3	...	8	3.0	...	8.0
54-55—San Francisco	29	...	105	293	.358	97	144	.674	148	...	307	5.1	...	10.6
55-56—San Francisco	25	...	76	208	.365	93	142	.655	130	...	245	5.2	...	9.8
Totals	78	...	247	672	.368	273	437	.625	...	...	767	...	...	9.8

NBA REGULAR-SEASON RECORD

Season Team	G	Min.	FGM	FGA	Pct.	FTM	FTA	Pct.	Reb.	Ast.	PF	Dq.	Pts.	RPG	APG	PPG
58-59—Boston	49	609	65	192	.339	41	68	.603	127	70	58	0	171	2.6	1.4	3.5
59-60—Boston	74	1274	169	414	.408	128	170	.753	199	189	109	1	466	2.7	2.6	6.3
60-61—Boston	78	1607	203	601	.338	186	320	.581	279	253	200	3	592	3.6	3.2	7.6
61-62—Boston	79	2023	289	707	.409	145	231	.628	291	339	204	2	723	3.7	4.3	9.2
62-63—Boston	79	1945	230	591	.389	112	177	.633	263	317	221	3	572	3.3	4.0	7.2
63-64—Boston	80	2424	283	722	.392	88	168	.524	372	407	253	0	654	4.7	5.1	8.2
64-65—Boston	78	2434	253	639	.396	143	227	.630	318	437	263	5	649	4.1	5.6	8.3
65-66—Boston	80	2710	240	619	.388	209	303	.690	304	503	243	4	689	3.8	6.3	8.6
66-67—Boston	78	2446	182	459	.397	119	189	.630	239	389	273	7	483	3.1	5.0	6.2
Totals	675	17472	1914	4944	.387	1171	1853	.632	2392	2904	1824	25	4999	3.5	4.3	7.4

NBA PLAYOFF RECORD

Season Team	G	Min.	FGM	FGA	Pct.	FTM	FTA	Pct.	Reb.	Ast.	PF	Dq.	Pts.	RPG	APG	PPG
58-59—Boston	8	75	5	20	.250	5	5	1.000	12	10	8	0	15	1.5	1.3	1.9
59-60—Boston	13	232	27	80	.338	17	22	.773	45	14	28	0	71	3.5	1.1	5.5
60-61—Boston	9	102	9	00	.000	7	14	.000	15	13	17	0	11	1.7	1.3	1.2
61-62—Boston	14	329	44	102	.431	38	53	.717	56	55	50	1	126	4.0	3.9	9.0
62-63—Boston	13	250	19	64	.297	21	30	.700	36	37	42	1	59	2.8	2.8	4.5
63-64—Boston	10	312	25	72	.347	13	25	.520	37	68	40	0	63	3.7	6.8	6.3
64-65—Boston	12	396	43	104	.413	35	45	.778	39	74	49	1	121	3.3	6.2	10.1
65-66—Boston	17	543	45	109	.413	39	57	.684	52	75	65	0	129	3.1	4.4	7.6
66-67—Boston	9	254	24	75	.320	11	18	.611	24	48	36	1	59	2.7	5.3	6.6
Totals	105	2494	241	656	.367	186	269	.691	320	396	335	4	668	3.0	3.8	6.4

EBL REGULAR-SEASON RECORD

Season Team	G	Min.	FGM	FGA	Pct.	FTM	FTA	Pct.	Reb.	Ast.	PF	Dq.	Pts.	RPG	APG	PPG
67-68—Hartford	6	...	15	...	...	9	18	.500	24	41	...	...	39	4.0	6.8	6.5

HEAD COACHING RECORD

BACKGROUND: Assistant coach, Harvard University (1970-71). ... Assistant coach, Los Angeles Lakers (1971-72). ... Assistant coach, Milwaukee Bucks (1976-77). ... Assistant coach, Boston Celtics (1978-79 through 1982-83 and 1996-97). ... Vice president/basketball operations, Celtics (1988-89). ... Assistant coach, Seattle SuperSonics (1989-90). ... Assistant coach, Detroit Pistons (1994-95). ... Assistant coach, Celtics (1996-97).

COLLEGIATE COACHING RECORD

Season Team	W	L	Pct.
67-68—Brandeis	11	10	.524
68-69—Brandeis	12	9	.571
69-70—Brandeis	11	13	.458
Totals (3 years)	34	32	.515

ABA COACHING RECORD

Season Team	REGULAR SEASON				PLAYOFFS		
	W	L	Pct.	Finish	W	L	Pct.
72-73—San Diego	30	54	.357	4th/Western Division	0	4	.000

ABL COACHING RECORD

Season Team	REGULAR SEASON				PLAYOFFS		
	W	L	Pct.	Finish	W	L	Pct.
97-98—New England	24	20	.545	2nd/Eastern Conference	0	2	.000
98-99—New England	3	10	.231		—	—	—
Totals (2 years)	27	30	.474				

NBA COACHING RECORD

Season Team	REGULAR SEASON				PLAYOFFS		
	W	L	Pct.	Finish	W	L	Pct.
73-74—Capital	47	35	.573	1st/Central Division	3	4	.429
74-75—Washington	60	22	.732	1st/Central Division	8	9	.471
75-76—Washington	48	34	.585	2nd/Central Division	3	4	.429
83-84—Boston	62	20	.756	1st/Atlantic Division	15	8	.652
84-85—Boston	63	19	.768	1st/Atlantic Division	13	8	.619
85-86—Boston	67	15	.817	1st/Atlantic Division	15	3	.833
86-87—Boston	59	23	.720	1st/Atlantic Division	13	10	.565
87-88—Boston	57	25	.695	1st/Atlantic Division	9	8	.529
90-91—Seattle	41	41	.500	5th/Pacific Division	2	3	.400
91-92—Seattle	18	18	.500		—	—	—
Totals (10 years)	**522**	**252**	**.674**	**Totals (9 years)**	**81**	**57**	**.587**

NOTES:

1973—Lost to Utah in Western Division Semifinals.

1974—Lost to New York in Eastern Conference Semifinals.

1975—Defeated Buffalo, 4-3, in Eastern Conference Semifinals; defeated Boston, 4-2, in Eastern Conference Finals; lost to Golden State, 4-0, in NBA Finals.

1976—Lost to Cleveland in Eastern Conference Semifinals.

1984—Defeated Washington, 3-1, in Eastern Conference First Round; defeated New York, 4-3, in Eastern Conference Semifinals; defeated Milwaukee, 4-1, in Eastern Conference Finals; defeated Los Angeles, 4-3, in NBA Finals.

1985—Defeated Cleveland, 3-1, in Eastern Conference First Round; defeated Detroit, 4-2, in Eastern Conference Semifinals; defeated Philadelphia, 4-1, in Eastern Conference Finals; lost to Los Angeles Lakers, 4-2, in NBA Finals.

1986—Defeated Chicago, 3-0, in Eastern Conference First Round; defeated Atlanta, 4-1, in Eastern Conference Semifinals; defeated Milwaukee, 4-0, in Eastern Conference Finals; defeated Houston, 4-2, in NBA Finals.

1987—Defeated Chicago, 3-0, in Eastern Conference First Round; defeated Milwaukee, 4-3, in Eastern Conference Semifinals; defeated Detroit, 4-3, in Eastern Conference Finals; lost to Los Angeles Lakers, 4-2, in NBA Finals.

1988—Defeated New York, 3-1, in Eastern Conference First Round; defeated Atlanta, 4-3, in Eastern Conference Semifinals; lost to Detroit, 4-2, in Eastern Conference Finals.

1991—Lost to Portland in Western Conference First Round.

1992—Replaced as Seattle head coach by interim coach Bob Kloppenburg with club in sixth place (January 15).

KARL, GEORGE

See Head Coaches, page 292.

KUNDLA, JOHN

PERSONAL: Born July 3, 1916, in Star Junction, Pa. ... 6-2/180 (1,88/81,6). ... Full name: John Albert Kundla.
HIGH SCHOOL: Central (Minneapolis).
COLLEGE: Minnesota.
CAREER HONORS: Elected to Naismith Memorial Basketball Hall of Fame (1995). ... One of the Top 10 Coaches in NBA History (1996).

COLLEGIATE RECORD

Season Team	G	Min.	FGM	FGA	Pct.	FTM	FTA	Pct.	Reb.	Ast.	Pts.	AVERAGES		
												RPG	APG	PPG
35-36—Minnesota‡					Freshman team statistics unavailable.									
36-37—Minnesota	15	...	53	...	...	34	53	.642	...	...	140	...	...	9.3
37-38—Minnesota	20	...	62	...	...	41	77	.532	...	...	165	...	...	8.3
38-39—Minnesota	17	...	71	...	...	40	63	.635	...	...	182	...	...	10.7
Varsity totals	**52**	**...**	**186**	**...**	**...**	**115**	**193**	**.596**	**...**	**...**	**487**	**...**	**...**	**9.4**

HEAD COACHING RECORD

BACKGROUND: Head coach, De La Salle High School (Minn.).

COLLEGIATE COACHING RECORD

Season Team	W	L	Pct.	Finish
46-47—St. Thomas (Minn.)	11	11	.500	
59-60—Minnesota	12	12	.500	T3rd/Big Ten Conference
60-61—Minnesota	10	13	.435	T4th/Big Ten Conference
61-62—Minnesota	10	14	.417	7th/Big Ten Conference
62-63—Minnesota	12	12	.500	T4th/Big Ten Conference
63-64—Minnesota	17	7	.708	3rd/Big Ten Conference
64-65—Minnesota	19	5	.792	2nd/Big Ten Conference
65-66—Minnesota	14	10	.583	T5th/Big Ten Conference
66-67—Minnesota	9	15	.375	9th/Big Ten Conference
67-68—Minnesota	7	17	.292	T9th/Big Ten Conference
Totals (10 years)	**121**	**116**	**.511**	

NBL COACHING RECORD

Season Team	REGULAR SEASON				PLAYOFFS		
	W	L	Pct.	Finish	W	L	Pct.
47-48—Minneapolis	43	17	.717	1st/Western Division	8	2	.800

Season Team	REGULAR SEASON				PLAYOFFS		
	W	L	Pct.	Finish	W	L	Pct.
48-49—Minneapolis	44	16	.733	2nd/Western Division	8	2	.800
49-50—Minneapolis	51	17	.750	T1st/Central Division	10	2	.833
50-51—Minneapolis	44	24	.647	1st/Western Division	3	4	.429
51-52—Minneapolis	40	26	.606	2nd/Western Division	9	4	.692
52-53—Minneapolis	48	22	.686	1st/Western Division	9	3	.750
53-54—Minneapolis	46	26	.639	1st/Western Division	9	4	.692
54-55—Minneapolis	40	32	.556	2nd/Western Division	3	4	.429
55-56—Minneapolis	33	39	.458	T2nd/Western Division	1	2	.333
56-57—Minneapolis	34	38	.472	T1st/Western Division	2	3	.400
57-58—Minneapolis	10	23	.303	4th/Western Division	—	—	—
58-59—Minneapolis	33	39	.458	2nd/Western Division	6	7	.462
Totals (11 years)	423	302	.583	Totals (10 years)	60	35	.632

NOTES:

1948—Defeated Oshkosh, 3-1, in NBL playoffs; defeated Tri-Cities, 2-0, in NBL semifinals; defeated Rochester, 3-1, in NBL championship series.

1949—Defeated Chicago, 2-0, in Western Division Semifinals; defeated Rochester, 2-0, in Western Division Finals; defeated Washington, 4-2, in NBA Finals.

1950—Defeated Rochester, 78-76, in Central Division first-place game; defeated Chicago, 2-0, in Central Division Semifinals; defeated Fort Wayne, 2-0, in Central Division Finals; defeated Anderson, 2-0, in NBA Semifinals; defeated Syracuse, 4-2, in NBA Finals.

1951—Defeated Indianapolis, 2-1, in Western Division Semifinals; lost to Rochester, 3-1, in Western Division Finals.

1952—Defeated Indianapolis, 2-0, in Western Division Semifinals; defeated Rochester, 3-1, in Western Division Finals; defeated New York, 4-3, in NBA Finals.

1953—Defeated Indianapolis, 2-0, in Western Division Semifinals; defeated Fort Wayne, 3-2, in Western Division Finals; defeated New York, 4-1, in NBA Finals.

1954—Defeated Rochester, 109-88; Fort Wayne, 90-85; and Fort Wayne, 78-73, in Western Division round robin; defeated Rochester, 2-1, in Western Division Semifinals; defeated Syracuse, 4-3, in NBA Finals.

1955—Defeated Rochester, 2-1, in Western Division Semifinals; lost to Fort Wayne, 3-1, in Western Division Finals.

1956—Defeated St. Louis, 103-97, in Western Division second-place game; lost to St. Louis, 2-1, in Western Division Semifinals.

1957—Lost to St. Louis, 114-111, in Western Division tiebreaker; defeated Fort Wayne, 2-0, in Western Division Semifinals; lost to St. Louis, 3-0, in Western Division Finals.

1958—Replaced George Mikan as Minneapolis head coach (January 14), with record of 9-30 and in fourth place.

1959—Defeated Detroit, 2-1, in Western Division Semifinals; defeated St. Louis, 4-2, in Western Division Finals; lost to Boston, 4-0, in NBA Finals.

LAPCHICK, JOE

PERSONAL: Born April 12, 1900, in Yonkers, N.Y. ... Died August 10, 1970. ... 6-5/185 (1,96/83,9). ... Full name: Joseph Bohomiel Lapchick.

TRANSACTIONS: Played with independent teams, including the Original Celtics (1917 through 1920, 1924 through 1926, 1932 through 1936).

CAREER HONORS: Elected to Naismith Memorial Basketball Hall of Fame (1966).

MISCELLANEOUS: Did not play high school or college basketball.

PRO RECORD

Season Team	League	G	FGM	FTM	Pts.	Avg.
20-21—Holyoke	IL	11	14	40	68	6.2
Schenectady	NYSL	5	2	10	14	2.8
21-22—Schenectady-Troy	NYSL	32	12	95	119	3.7
Brooklyn	MBL	10	6	20	32	3.2
Holyoke	IL	16	13	40	66	4.1
22-23—Brooklyn	MBL	33	34	109	177	5.4
Troy	NYSL	24	13	59	85	3.5
Holyoke	IL			Statistics unavailable.		
26-27—Brooklyn	ABL	32	35	131	201	6.3
New York	NBL	17	20	66	106	6.2
27-28—New York	ABL	47	103	110	316	6.7
28-29—Cleveland	ABL	39	51	86	188	4.8
29-30—Cleveland	ABL	52	47	92	186	3.6
30-31—Cleveland-Toledo	ABL	30	22	49	93	3.1
32-33—Yonkers	MBL	1	0	0	0	0.0
33-34—Plymouth	PSL	1	1	3	5	5.0
ABL pro totals		200	258	468	984	4.9
MBL pro totals		44	40	129	209	4.8

COLLEGIATE COACHING RECORD

Season Team	W	L	Pct.	Finish
36-37—St. John's	12	7	.632	Independent
37-38—St. John's	15	4	.789	Independent
38-39—St. John's	18	4	.818	Independent
39-40—St. John's	15	5	.750	Independent
40-41—St. John's	11	6	.647	Independent
41-42—St. John's	16	5	.762	Independent
42-43—St. John's	21	3	.875	Independent
43-44—St. John's	18	5	.783	Independent
44-45—St. John's	21	3	.875	Independent
45-46—St. John's	17	6	.739	Independent
46-47—St. John's	16	7	.696	Independent
56-57—St. John's	14	9	.609	Independent

Season Team	W	L	Pct.	Finish
57-58—St. John's	18	8	.692	Independent
58-59—St. John's	20	6	.769	Independent
59-60—St. John's	17	8	.680	Independent
60-61—St. John's	20	5	.800	Independent
61-62—St. John's	21	5	.808	Independent
62-63—St. John's	9	15	.375	Independent
63-64—St. John's	14	11	.560	Independent
64-65—St. John's	21	8	.724	Independent
Totals (20 years)	334	130	.720	

ABL COACHING RECORD

		REGULAR SEASON				PLAYOFFS		
Season Team	W	L	Pct.	Finish		W	L	Pct.
61-62—Cleveland	6	6	.500			—	—	—

NBA COACHING RECORD

		REGULAR SEASON				PLAYOFFS		
Season Team	W	L	Pct.	Finish		W	L	Pct.
47-48—New York (BAA)	26	22	.542	2nd/Eastern Division		1	2	.333
48-49—New York (BAA)	32	28	.533	2nd/Eastern Division		3	3	.500
49-50—New York	40	28	.588	2nd/Eastern Division		3	2	.600
50-51—New York	36	30	.545	3rd/Eastern Division		8	6	.571
51-52—New York	37	29	.561	3rd/Eastern Division		8	6	.571
52-53—New York	47	23	.671	1st/Midwest Division		6	5	.545
53-54—New York	44	28	.611	1st/Eastern Division		0	4	.000
54-55—New York	38	34	.528	2nd/Eastern Division		1	2	.333
55-56—New York	26	25	.510			—	—	—
Totals (9 years)	326	247	.569	Totals (8 years)		30	30	.500

NOTES:
1939—Defeated Roanoke, 71-47, in NIT quarterfinals; lost to Loyola, 51-46, in semifinals; lost to Bradley, 40-35, in third-place game.
1940—Lost to Duquesne, 38-31, in NIT quarterfinals.
1943—Defeated Rice, 51-49, in NIT quarterfinals; defeated Fordham, 69-43, in semifinals; defeated Toledo, 48-27, in finals.
1944—Defeated Bowling Green, 44-40, in NIT quarterfinals; defeated Kentucky, 48-45, in semifinals; defeated DePaul, 47-39, in finals.
1945—Defeated Muhlenberg, 34-33, in NIT quarterfinals; lost to Bowling Green, 57-44, in semifinals; lost to Rhode Island, 64-57, in third-place game.
1946—Lost to West Virginia, 70-58, in NIT quarterfinals.
1947—Lost to North Carolina State, 61-55, in NIT quarterfinals.
1948—Lost to Baltimore in quarterfinals.
1949—Defeated Baltimore, 2-1, in Eastern Division Semifinals; lost to Washington, 2-1, in Eastern Division Finals.
1950—Defeated Washington, 2-0, in Eastern Division Semifinals; lost to Syracuse, 2-1, in Eastern Division Finals.
1951—Defeated Boston, 2-0, in Eastern Division Semifinals; defeated Syracuse, 3-2, in Eastern Division Finals; lost to Rochester, 4-3, in NBA Finals.
1952—Defeated Boston, 2-1, in Eastern Division Semifinals; defeated Syracuse, 3-1, in Eastern Division Finals; lost to Minneapolis, 4-3, in NBA Finals.
1953—Defeated Baltimore, 2-0, in Eastern Division Semifinals; defeated Boston, 3-1, in Eastern Division Finals; lost to Minneapolis, 4-1, in NBA Finals.
1954—Lost to Boston, 93-71; Syracuse, 75-68; Boston, 79-78; and Syracuse, 103-99, in Eastern Division round robin.
1955—Lost to Boston in Eastern Division Semifinals.
1956—Resigned as New York head coach.
1958—Defeated Butler, 76-69, in NIT first round; defeated Utah, 71-70, in quarterfinals; lost to Dayton, 80-56, in semifinals; lost to St. Bonaventure, 84-69, in third-place game.
1959—Defeated Villanova, 75-67, in NIT first round; defeated St. Bonaventure, 82-74, in quarterfinals; defeated Providence, 76-55, in semifinals; defeated Bradley, 76-71 (OT), in finals.
1960—Lost to St. Bonaventure, 106-71, in NIT quarterfinals.
1961—Lost to Wake Forest, 97-74, in NCAA Tournament first round.
1962—Defeated Holy Cross, 80-74, in NIT quarterfinals; defeated Duquesne, 76-65, in semifinals; lost to Dayton, 73-67, in finals.
1965—Defeated Boston College, 114-92, in NIT first round; defeated New Mexico, 61-54, in quarterfinals; defeated Army, 67-60, in semifinals; defeated Villanova, 55-51, in finals.

LOUGHERY, KEVIN

PERSONAL: Born March 28, 1940, in Brooklyn, N.Y. ... 6-3/190 (1,90/86,2). ... Full name: Kevin Michael Loughery.
HIGH SCHOOL: Cardinal Hayes (Bronx, N.Y.).
COLLEGE: Boston College, then St. John's.
TRANSACTIONS: Selected by Detroit Pistons in second round (13th pick overall) of 1962 NBA Draft. ... Traded by Pistons to Baltimore Bullets for Larry Staverman (October 28, 1963). ... Traded by Bullets with Fred Carter to Philadelphia 76ers for Archie Clark and future draft choice (October 18, 1971).
CAREER NOTES: Broadcaster (1988-89 and 1989-90). ... Scout, Miami Heat (1988-89 and 1989-90). ... Vice president/director of player personnel, Heat (February 1995 to 1995-96) ... Vice president/consultant, Heat (1996-97).

COLLEGIATE RECORD

													AVERAGES		
Season Team	G	Min.	FGM	FGA	Pct.	FTM	FTA	Pct.	Reb.	Ast.	Pts.	RPG	APG	PPG
57-58—Boston College‡	19	...	133	...	...	55	...	...	...	...	321	...	...	16.9
58-59—Boston College	19	...	128	...	...	65	...	...	...	...	321	...	...	16.9
59-60—St. John's						Did not play—transfer student.								
60-61—St. John's	25	...	106	252	.421	54	77	.701	116	...	266	4.6	...	10.6
61-62—St. John's	26	...	169	378	.447	65	76	.855	151	...	403	5.8	...	15.5
Varsity totals	70	...	403	...	...	184	...	...	...	...	990	...	...	14.1

NBA REGULAR-SEASON RECORD

Season Team	G	Min.	FGM	FGA	Pct.	FTM	FTA	Pct.	Reb.	Ast.	PF	Dq.	Pts.	RPG	APG	PPG
62-63—Detroit	57	845	146	397	.368	71	100	.710	109	104	135	1	363	1.9	1.8	6.4
63-64—Det.-Balt.	66	1459	236	631	.374	126	177	.712	138	182	175	2	598	2.1	2.8	9.1
64-65—Baltimore	80	2417	406	957	.424	212	281	.754	235	296	320	13	1024	2.9	3.7	12.8
65-66—Baltimore	74	2455	526	1264	.416	297	358	.830	227	356	273	8	1349	3.1	4.8	18.2
66-67—Baltimore	76	2577	520	1306	.398	340	412	.825	349	288	294	10	1380	4.6	3.8	18.2
67-68—Baltimore	77	2297	458	1127	.406	305	392	.778	247	256	301	13	1221	3.2	3.3	15.9
68-69—Baltimore	80	3135	717	1636	.438	372	463	.803	266	384	299	3	1806	3.3	4.8	22.6
69-70—Baltimore	55	2037	477	1082	.441	253	298	.849	168	292	183	3	1207	3.1	5.3	21.9
70-71—Baltimore	82	2260	481	1193	.403	275	331	.831	219	301	246	2	1237	2.7	3.7	15.1
71-72—Balt.-Phil.	76	1771	341	809	.422	263	320	.822	183	196	213	3	945	2.4	2.6	12.4
72-73—Philadelphia	32	955	169	427	.396	107	130	.823	113	148	104	0	445	3.5	4.6	13.9
Totals	755	22208	4477	10829	.413	2621	3262	.803	2254	2803	2543	58	11575	3.0	3.7	15.3

NBA PLAYOFF RECORD

Season Team	G	Min.	FGM	FGA	Pct.	FTM	FTA	Pct.	Reb.	Ast.	PF	Dq.	Pts.	RPG	APG	PPG
62-63—Detroit	2	26	1	10	.100	1	1	1.000	0	4	3	0	3	0.0	0.0	1.5
64-65—Baltimore	10	297	53	137	.387	34	38	.895	34	30	36	0	140	3.4	3.0	14.0
65-66—Baltimore	3	27	3	7	.429	3	6	.500	1	1	4	0	9	0.3	0.3	3.0
68-69—Baltimore	4	173	29	79	.367	23	35	.657	18	21	16	0	81	4.5	5.3	20.3
69-70—Baltimore	7	153	26	77	.338	15	21	.714	16	8	24	0	67	2.3	1.1	9.6
70-71—Baltimore	17	500	84	212	.396	64	85	.753	38	52	57	2	232	2.2	3.1	13.6
Totals	43	1176	196	522	.375	140	186	.753	107	116	140	2	532	2.5	2.7	12.4

HEAD COACHING RECORD

BACKGROUND: Player/head coach, Philadelphia 76ers (February 1973-remainder of 1972-73 season). ... Assistant coach, Atlanta Hawks (1990-91).

NBA COACHING RECORD

	REGULAR SEASON				PLAYOFFS		
Season Team	W	L	Pct.	Finish	W	L	Pct.
72-73—Philadelphia	5	26	.161	4th/Atlantic Division	—	—	—
76-77—New York Nets	22	60	.268	5th/Atlantic Division	—	—	—
77-78—New Jersey	24	58	.293	5th/Atlantic Division	—	—	—
78-79—New Jersey	37	45	.451	3rd/Atlantic Division	0	2	.000
79-80—New Jersey	34	48	.415	5th/Atlantic Division	—	—	—
80-81—New Jersey	12	23	.343		—	—	—
81-82—Atlanta	42	40	.512	2nd/Central Division	0	2	.000
82-83—Atlanta	43	39	.524	2nd/Central Division	1	2	.333
83-84—Chicago	27	55	.329	5th/Central Division	—	—	—
84-85—Chicago	38	44	.463	3rd/Central Division	1	3	.250
85-86—Washington	9	9	.000	4th/Atlantic Division	2	3	.400
86-87—Washington	42	40	.512	3rd/Atlantic Division	0	3	.000
87-88—Washington	8	19	.296		—	—	—
91-92—Miami	38	44	.463	4th/Atlantic Division	0	3	.000
92-93—Miami	36	46	.439	5th/Atlantic Division	—	—	—
93-94—Miami	42	40	.512	4th/Atlantic Division	2	3	.400
94-95—Miami	17	29	.370	5th/Atlantic Division	—	—	—
Totals (17 years)	474	662	.417	Totals (8 years)	6	21	.222

ABA COACHING RECORD

	REGULAR SEASON				PLAYOFFS		
Season Team	W	L	Pct.	Finish	W	L	Pct.
73-74—New York Nets	55	29	.655	1st/Eastern Division	12	2	.857
74-75—New York Nets	58	26	.690	T1st/Eastern Division	1	4	.200
75-76—New York Nets	55	29	.655	2nd	8	5	.615
Totals (3 years)	168	84	.667	Totals (3 years)	21	11	.656

NOTES:
1973—Replaced Roy Rubin as Philadelphia head coach (February), with record of 4-47.
1974—Defeated Virginia, 4-1, in Eastern Division Semifinals; defeated Kentucky, 4-0, in Eastern Division Finals; defeated Utah, 4-1, in ABA Finals.
1975—Lost to St. Louis in Eastern Division Semifinals.
1976—Defeated San Antonio, 4-3, in semifinals; defeated Denver, 4-2, in ABA Finals.
1979—Lost to Philadelphia in Eastern Conference First Round.
1980—Resigned as New Jersey head coach (December); replaced by Bob MacKinnon with club in fifth place.
1982—Lost to Philadelphia in Eastern Conference First Round.
1983—Lost to Boston in Eastern Conference First Round.
1985—Lost to Milwaukee in Eastern Conference First Round.
1986—Replaced Gene Shue as Washington head coach (March 19), with record of 32-37. Lost to Philadelphia in Eastern Conference First Round.
1987—Lost to Detroit in Eastern Conference First Round.
1988—Replaced as Washington head coach by Wes Unseld (January 3) with club in fourth place.
1992—Lost to Chicago in Eastern Conference First Round.
1994—Lost to Atlanta in Eastern Conference First Round.
1995—Replaced as Miami head coach by Alvin Gentry (February 14) with club in fifth place.

ALL-TIME GREAT COACHES

MacLEOD, JOHN

PERSONAL: Born October 3, 1937, in New Albany, Ind. ... 6-0/170 (1,83/77,1). ... Full name: John Matthew MacLeod.
HIGH SCHOOL: New Providence (Clarksville, Ind.).
COLLEGE: Bellarmine (Ky.).
CAREER NOTES: Head coach, Oklahoma (1967-68 through 1972-73). ... Head coach, Notre Dame (1991-92 to 1998-99).

COLLEGIATE RECORD

Season Team	G	Min.	FGM	FGA	Pct.	FTM	FTA	Pct.	Reb.	Ast.	Pts.	RPG	APG	PPG
55-56—Bellarmine						Freshman team statistics unavailable.								
56-57—Bellarmine	10	...	0	...	...	1	...	...	...	...	1	...	...	0.1
57-58—Bellarmine	8	...	2	...	...	3	10	.300	...	...	7	...	...	0.9
58-59—Bellarmine	5	...	2	...	...	4	...	...	...	...	8	...	...	1.6
Totals	23	...	4	...	...	8	...	...	...	...	16	...	...	0.7

HEAD COACHING RECORD

BACKGROUND: Assistant coach, DeSales High School, Ky. (1959-60 through 1961-62). ... Head coach, Smithville High School, Ind. (1963-64 and 1964-65; record: 16-24). ... Assistant coach, Cathedral High School, Ind. (1965-66). ... Assistant coach, University of Oklahoma (1966-67).

COLLEGIATE COACHING RECORD

Season Team	W	L	Pct.	Finish
67-68—Oklahoma	13	13	.500	T3rd/Big Eight Conference
68-69—Oklahoma	7	19	.269	8th/Big Eight Conference
69-70—Oklahoma	19	9	.679	3rd/Big Eight Conference
70-71—Oklahoma	19	8	.704	2nd/Big Eight Conference
71-72—Oklahoma	14	12	.538	3rd/Big Eight Conference
72-73—Oklahoma	18	8	.692	4th/Big Eight Conference
91-92—Notre Dame	18	15	.545	Independent
92-93—Notre Dame	9	18	.333	Independent
93-94—Notre Dame	12	17	.414	Independent
94-95—Notre Dame	15	12	.555	Independent
95-96—Notre Dame	9	18	.333	13th/Big East Conference
96-97—Notre Dame	16	14	.533	T4th/Big East Six Division/Big East Conference
97-98—Notre Dame	13	14	.481	5th/Big East Six Division/Big East Conference
98-99—Notre Dame	14	16	.467	4th/Big East Six Division/Big East Conference
Totals (14 years)	196	193	.504	

NBA COACHING RECORD

Season Team	REGULAR SEASON				PLAYOFFS		
	W	L	Pct.	Finish	W	L	Pct.
73-74—Phoenix	30	52	.396	4th/Pacific Division	—	—	
74-75—Phoenix	32	50	.390	4th/Pacific Division	—	—	
75-76—Phoenix	42	40	.512	3rd/Pacific Division	10	9	.526
76-77—Phoenix	34	48	.415	5th/Pacific Division	—	—	
77-78—Phoenix	49	33	.598	2nd/Pacific Division	0	2	.000
78-79—Phoenix	50	32	.610	2nd/Pacific Division	9	6	.600
79-80—Phoenix	55	27	.671	3rd/Pacific Division	3	5	.375
80-81—Phoenix	57	25	.695	1st/Pacific Division	3	4	.429
81-82—Phoenix	46	36	.561	3rd/Pacific Division	2	5	.286
82-83—Phoenix	53	29	.646	2nd/Pacific Division	1	2	.333
83-84—Phoenix	41	41	.500	4th/Pacific Division	9	8	.529
84-85—Phoenix	36	46	.439	3rd/Pacific Division	0	3	.000
85-86—Phoenix	32	50	.390	T3rd/Pacific Division	—	—	
86-87—Phoenix	22	34	.393		—	—	
87-88—Dallas	53	29	.646	2nd/Midwest Division	10	7	.588
88-89—Dallas	38	44	.463	4th/Midwest Division	—	—	
89-90—Dallas	5	6	.455		—	—	
90-91—New York	32	35	.478	3rd/Atlantic Division	0	3	.000
Totals (18 years)	707	657	.518	Totals (11 years)	47	54	.465

NOTES:
1970—Defeated Louisville, 74-73, in NIT first round; lost to Louisiana State, 97-94, in quarterfinals.
1971—Lost to Hawaii, 87-86 (2 OT), in NIT first round.
1976—Defeated Seattle, 4-2, in Western Conference Semifinals; defeated Golden State, 4-3, in Western Conference Finals; lost to Boston, 4-2, in NBA Finals.
1978—Lost to Milwaukee in Western Conference First Round.
1979—Defeated Portland, 2-1, in Western Conference First Round; defeated Kansas City, 4-1, in Western Conference Semifinals; lost to Seattle, 4-3, in Western Conference Finals.
1980—Defeated Kansas City, 2-1, in Western Conference First Round; lost to Los Angeles Lakers, 4-1, in Western Conference Semifinals.
1981—Lost to Kansas City in Western Conference Semifinals.
1982—Defeated Denver, 2-1, in Western Conference Semifinals; lost to Los Angeles Lakers, 4-0, in Western Conference Finals.
1983—Lost to Denver in Western Conference First Round.
1984—Defeated Portland, 3-2, in Western Conference First Round; defeated Utah, 4-2, in Western Conference Semifinals; lost to Los Angeles Lakers, 4-2, in Western Conference Finals.
1985—Lost to Los Angeles Lakers in Western Conference First Round.
1987—Replaced as Phoenix head coach by Dick Van Arsdale (February 26).
1988—Defeated Houston, 3-1, in Western Conference First Round; defeated Denver, 4-2, in Western Conference Semifinals; lost to Los Angeles Lakers, 4-3, in Western Conference Finals.
1989—Replaced as Dallas head coach by Richie Adubato (November 29).

1990—Replaced Stu Jackson as New York head coach (December 3) with record of 7-8.
1991—Lost to Chicago in Eastern Conference First Round.
1992—Defeated Western Michigan, 63-56, in NIT first round; defeated Kansas State, 64-47, in second round; defeated Manhattan, 74-58, in quarterfinals; defeated Utah, 58-55, in semifinals; lost to Virginia, 81-76, in final.
1997—Defeated Oral Roberts, 74-58, in NIT first round; defeated TCU, 82-72, in NIT second round; lost to Michigan, 67-66, in NIT quarter finals.

MOE, DOUG

PERSONAL: Born September 21, 1938, in Brooklyn, N.Y. ... 6-5/220 (1,96/99,8). ... Full name: Douglas Edwin Moe.
HIGH SCHOOL: Erasmus Hall (Brooklyn, N.Y.), then Bullis Prep School (Silver Springs, Md.).
COLLEGE: North Carolina, then Elon College (N.C.).
TRANSACTIONS: Selected by Chicago Packers in second round (22nd pick overall) of 1961 NBA Draft. ... Signed by Packers (1961); Packers later refused to honor contract when Moe was implicated in college point-shaving scandal; Moe was exonerated but did not play basketball from 1961-62 through 1964-65. ... Played with Padua, Italy (1965-66 and 1966-67). ... Signed by New Orleans Buccaneers of American Basketball Association (1967). ... Traded by Buccaneers with Larry Brown to Oakland Oaks for Steve Jones, Ron Franz and Barry Leibowitz (June 18, 1968). ... Traded by Oaks to Carolina Cougars in three-way deal in which Cougars sent Stew Johnson to Pittsburgh Pipers and Pipers sent Frank Card to Oaks (June 12, 1969). ... Traded by Cougars to Washington Capitols for Gary Bradds and Ira Harge (July 24, 1970). ... Capitols franchise moved from Washington to Virginia and renamed Squires for 1970-71 season.

COLLEGIATE RECORD

NOTES: The Sporting News All-America second team (1959, 1961).

Season Team	G	Min.	FGM	FGA	Pct.	FTM	FTA	Pct.	Reb.	Ast.	Pts.	AVERAGES RPG	APG	PPG
57-58—North Carolina‡						Freshman team statistics unavailable.								
58-59—North Carolina	25	...	106	265	.400	104	164	.634	179	67	316	7.2	2.7	12.6
59-60—North Carolina	12	...	60	144	.417	82	113	.726	135	...	202	11.3	...	16.8
60-61—North Carolina	23	...	163	401	.406	143	207	.691	321	...	469	14.0	...	20.4
Totals	60	...	329	810	.406	329	484	.680	635	...	987	10.6	...	16.5

ABA REGULAR-SEASON RECORD

NOTES: Member of ABA championship team (1969). ... ABA All-Star first team (1968). ... ABA All-Star second team (1969).

Season Team	G	Min.	2-POINT FGM	FGA	Pct.	3-POINT FGM	FGA	Pct.	FTM	FTA	Pct.	Reb.	Ast.	Pts.	AVERAGES RPG	APG	PPG
67-68—New Orleans	78	3113	662	1588	.417	3	22	.136	551	693	.795	795	202	1884	10.2	2.6	24.2
68-69—Oakland	75	2528	524	1213	.432	5	14	.357	360	444	.811	614	151	1423	8.2	2.0	19.0
69-70—Carolina	80	2671	527	1220	.432	8	34	.235	304	399	.762	437	425	1382	5.5	5.3	17.3
70-71—Virginia	78	2297	395	861	.459	2	10	.200	221	259	.853	473	270	1017	6.1	3.5	13.0
71-72—Virginia	67	1472	174	406	.429	1	9	.111	104	129	.806	241	149	455	3.6	2.2	6.8
Totals	378	12081	2282	5288	.432	19	89	.213	1540	1924	.800	2560	1197	6161	6.8	3.2	16.3

ABA PLAYOFF RECORD

Season Team	G	Min.	2-POINT FGM	FGA	Pct.	3-POINT FGM	FGA	Pct.	FTM	FTA	Pct.	Reb.	Ast.	Pts.	AVERAGES RPG	APG	PPG
67-68—New Orleans	17	715	140	335	.418	4	11	.364	107	149	.718	169	40	399	9.9	2.4	23.5
68-69—Oakland	16	593	115	280	.411	0	4	.000	87	111	.784	124	31	317	7.8	1.9	19.8
69-70—Carolina	4	168	25	72	.347	0	4	.000	12	16	.750	26	25	62	6.5	6.3	15.5
70-71—Virginia	12	421	89	174	.511	1	3	.333	31	41	.756	57	37	212	4.8	3.1	17.7
71-72—Virginia	11	245	37	84	.440	0	1	.000	22	25	.880	43	27	96	3.9	2.5	8.7
Totals	60	2142	406	945	.430	5	23	.217	259	342	.757	419	160	1086	7.0	2.7	18.1

ABA ALL-STAR GAME RECORD

Season Team	Min.	2-POINT FGM	FGA	Pct.	3-POINT FGM	FGA	Pct.	FTM	FTA	Pct.	Reb.	Ast.	Pts.
1968—New Orleans	29	7	12	.583	0	1	.000	3	5	.600	7	5	17
1969—Oakland	26	6	13	.462	0	0	...	5	8	.625	6	6	17
1970—Carolina	36	0	5	.000	0	0	...	2	3	.667	8	6	2
Totals	91	13	30	.433	0	1	.000	10	16	.625	21	17	36

HEAD COACHING RECORD

BACKGROUND: Assistant coach, Elon College, N.C. (1963-64 and 1964-65). ... Assistant coach/director of player personnel, Carolina Cougars of ABA (1972-73 and 1973-74). ... Assistant coach/director of player personnel, Denver Nuggets of ABA (1974-75 and 1975-76). ... Assistant coach, Nuggets (1980).
HONORS: NBA Coach of the Year (1988).

NBA COACHING RECORD

Season Team	REGULAR SEASON W	L	Pct.	Finish	PLAYOFFS W	L	Pct.
76-77—San Antonio	44	38	.537	3rd/Central Division	0	2	.000
77-78—San Antonio	52	30	.634	1st/Central Division	2	4	.333
78-79—San Antonio	48	34	.585	1st/Central Division	7	7	.500
79-80—San Antonio	33	33	.500				
80-81—Denver	26	25	.510	4th/Midwest Division	—	—	—
81-82—Denver	46	36	.561	T2nd/Midwest Division	1	2	.333
82-83—Denver	45	37	.549	T2nd/Midwest Division	3	5	.375
83-84—Denver	38	44	.463	T3rd/Midwest Division	2	3	.400
84-85—Denver	52	30	.634	1st/Midwest Division	8	7	.533
85-86—Denver	47	35	.573	2nd/Midwest Division	5	5	.500
86-87—Denver	37	45	.451	4th/Midwest Division	0	3	.000
87-88—Denver	54	28	.659	1st/Midwest Division	5	6	.455

Season Team	REGULAR SEASON				PLAYOFFS		
	W	L	Pct.	Finish	W	L	Pct.
88-89—Denver	44	38	.537	3rd/Midwest Division	0	3	.000
89-90—Denver	43	39	.524	4th/Midwest Division	0	3	.000
92-93—Philadelphia	19	37	.339		—	—	—
Totals (15 years)	628	529	.543	Totals (12 years)	33	50	.398

NOTES:

1977—Lost to Boston in Eastern Conference First Round.
1978—Lost to Washington in Eastern Conference Semifinals.
1979—Defeated Philadelphia, 4-3, in Eastern Conference Semifinals; lost to Washington, 4-3, in Eastern Conference Finals.
1980—Replaced as San Antonio head coach by Bob Bass (March 1). Replaced Donnie Walsh as Denver head coach (December), with record of 11-20.
1982—Lost to Phoenix in Western Conference First Round.
1983—Defeated Phoenix, 2-1, in Western Conference First Round; lost to San Antonio, 4-1, in Western Conference Semifinals.
1984—Lost to Utah in Western Conference First Round.
1985—Defeated San Antonio, 3-2, in Western Conference First Round; defeated Utah, 4-1, in Western Conference Semifinals; lost to Los Angeles Lakers, 4-1, in Western Conference Finals.
1986—Defeated Portland, 3-1, in Western Conference First Round; lost to Houston, 4-2, in Western Conference Semifinals.
1987—Lost to Los Angeles Lakers in Western Conference First Round.
1988—Defeated Seattle, 3-2, in Western Conference First Round; lost to Dallas, 4-2, in Western Conference Semifinals.
1989—Lost to Phoenix in Western Conference First Round.
1990—Lost to San Antonio, 3-0, in Western Conference First Round.
1993—Replaced as Philadelphia head coach by Fred Carter (March 7) with club in sixth place.

MOTTA, DICK

PERSONAL: Born September 3, 1931, in Midvale, Utah. ... 5-10/170 (1,78/77,1). ... Full name: John Richard Motta.
HIGH SCHOOL: Jordan (Utah); did not play varsity basketball.
COLLEGE: Utah State (did not play basketball).

HEAD COACHING RECORD

BACKGROUND: Head coach, Grace Junior High School (1954-55). ... Head coach, Grace High School (1955-56 through 1959-60). ... Head coach, Weber Junior College (1960-61 and 1961-62). ... Broadcaster, Detroit Pistons (1988 through January 1990). ... Consultant, Dallas Mavericks (1990). ... Assistant coach, Denver Nuggets (July 19-November 26, 1996).
HONORS: NBA Coach of the Year (1971).

COLLEGIATE COACHING RECORD

Season Team	W	L	Pct.	Finish
62-63—Weber State	22	4	.846	Independent
63-64—Weber State	17	8	.680	2nd/Big Sky Conference
64-65—Weber State	22	3	.880	1st/Big Sky Conference
65-66—Weber State	20	5	.765	2nd/Big Sky Conference
66-67—Weber State	18	7	.720	3rd/Big Sky Conference
67-68—Weber State	21	6	.778	1st/Big Sky Conference
Totals (6 years)	120	33	.784	

NBA COACHING RECORD

Season Team	REGULAR SEASON				PLAYOFFS		
	W	L	Pct.	Finish	W	L	Pct.
68-69—Chicago	33	49	.402	5th/Western Division	—	—	—
69-70—Chicago	39	43	.476	T3rd/Western Division	1	4	.250
70-71—Chicago	51	31	.622	2nd/Midwest Division	3	4	.429
71-72—Chicago	57	25	.695	2nd/Midwest Division	0	4	.000
72-73—Chicago	51	31	.622	2nd/Midwest Division	3	4	.429
73-74—Chicago	54	28	.659	2nd/Midwest Division	4	7	.364
74-75—Chicago	47	35	.573	T1st/Midwest Division	7	6	.538
75-76—Chicago	24	58	.293	4th/Midwest Division	—	—	—
76-77—Washington	48	34	.585	2nd/Central Division	4	5	.444
77-78—Washington	44	38	.537	2nd/Central Division	14	7	.666
78-79—Washington	54	28	.659	1st/Atlantic Division	9	10	.474
79-80—Washington	39	43	.476	3rd/Atlantic Division	0	2	.000
80-81—Dallas	15	67	.183	6th/Midwest Division	—	—	—
81-82—Dallas	28	54	.341	5th/Midwest Division	—	—	—
82-83—Dallas	38	44	.463	4th/Midwest Division	—	—	—
83-84—Dallas	43	39	.524	2nd/Midwest Division	4	6	.400
84-85—Dallas	44	38	.537	3rd/Midwest Division	1	3	.250
85-86—Dallas	44	38	.537	3rd/Midwest Division	5	5	.500
86-87—Dallas	55	27	.671	1st/Midwest Division	1	3	.250
89-90—Sacramento	16	38	.296	7th/Pacific Division	—	—	—
90-91—Sacramento	25	57	.305	7th/Pacific Division	—	—	—
91-92—Sacramento	7	18	.280		—	—	—
94-95—Dallas	36	46	.439	5th/Midwest Division	—	—	—
95-96—Dallas	26	56	.317	T5th/Midwest Division	—	—	—
96-97—Denver	17	52	.246	5th/Midwest Division	—	—	—
Totals (25 years)	935	1017	.479	Totals (14 years)	56	70	.444

NOTES:
1970—Lost to Atlanta in Western Division First Round.

1971—Lost to Los Angeles in Western Conference First Round.
1972—Lost to Los Angeles in Western Conference First Round.
1973—Lost to Los Angeles in Western Conference First Round.
1974—Defeated Detroit, 4-3, in Western Conference First Round; lost to Milwaukee, 4-0, in Western Conference Semifinals.
1975—Defeated Kansas City/Omaha, 4-2, in Western Conference First Round; lost to Golden State, 4-3, in Western Conference Semifinals.
1977—Defeated Cleveland, 2-1, in Eastern Conference First Round; lost to Houston, 4-2, in Eastern Conference Semifinals.
1978—Defeated Atlanta, 2-0, in Eastern Conference First Round; defeated San Antonio, 4-2, in Eastern Conference Semifinals; defeated Philadelphia, 4-2, in Eastern Conference Finals; defeated Seattle, 4-3, in NBA Finals.
1979—Defeated Atlanta, 4-3, in Eastern Conference Semifinals; defeated San Antonio, 4-3, in Eastern Conference Finals; lost to Seattle, 4-1, in NBA Finals.
1980—Lost to Philadelphia in Eastern Conference First Round.
1984—Defeated Seattle, 3-2, in Western Conference First Round; lost to Los Angeles Lakers, 4-1, in Western Conference Semifinals.
1985—Lost to Portland in Western Conference First Round.
1986—Defeated Utah, 3-1, in Western Conference First Round; lost to Los Angeles Lakers, 4-2, in Western Conference Semifinals.
1987—Lost to Seattle in Western Conference First Round.
1990—Replaced Jerry Reynolds as Sacramento head coach (January 4) with record of 7-21 and club in seventh place.
1991—Replaced as Sacramento head coach by Rex Hughes (December 24) with club in seventh place.
1996—Replaced Bernie Bickerstaff as Denver head coach (November 26) with record of 4-9 and club in fourth place.

NELSON, DON

See Head Coaches, page 296.

RAMSAY, JACK

PERSONAL: Born February 21, 1925, in Philadelphia. ... 6-1/180 (1,85/81,6). ... Full name: John T. Ramsay.
HIGH SCHOOL: Upper Darby Senior (Pa.).
COLLEGE: St. Joseph's, then Villanova, then Pennsylvania.
TRANSACTIONS: Played with San Diego Dons, an Amateur Athletic Union team (1945-46). ... Played in Eastern Basketball League with Harrisburg and Sunbury (1949-50 through 1954-55).
CAREER NOTES: Analyst, ESPN (January 1996-present).
CAREER HONORS: Elected to Naismith Memorial Basketball Hall of Fame (1992). ... One of the Top 10 Coaches in NBA History (1996).

COLLEGIATE RECORD

Season Team	G	Min.	FGM	FGA	Pct.	FTM	FTA	Pct.	Reb.	Ast.	Pts.	RPG	APG	PPG
42-43—St. Joseph's‡						Freshman team statistics unavailable.								
43-44						Did not play—in military service.								
44-45						Did not play—in military service.								
45-46						Did not play—in military service.								
46-47—St. Joseph's	21	...	72	214	.336	20	32	.625	...	...	164	...	...	7.8
47-48—St. Joseph's	14	...	60			38					158	...	...	11.0
48-49—St. Joseph's	23	...	75			52	...		...	...	202	...	...	8.8
Varsity totals	58	...	207			110					524	...	...	9.0

EBL REGULAR-SEASON RECORD

Season Team	G	Min.	FGM	FGA	Pct.	FTM	FTA	Pct.	Reb.	Ast.	PF	Dq.	Pts.	RPG	APG	PPG
49-50—Harrisburg	25	...	134	...	...	68	...	...	...	...	...	...	336	...	...	13.4
50-51—Harrisburg	20	...	96	...	...	43	...	...	...	...	...	...	235	...	...	11.8
51-52—Sunbury	26	...	159	...	...	86	...	...	...	...	...	...	404	...	...	15.5
52-53—Sunbury	21	...	116	...	...	97	...	...	...	...	...	...	329	...	...	15.7
53-54—Sunbury	28	...	112	...	...	101	...	...	...	...	...	...	325	...	...	11.6
54-55—Sunbury	30	...	164	...	...	155	...	...	...	...	...	...	483	...	...	16.1
Totals	130	...	685	...	...	507	...	...	...	...	...	...	1877	...	...	14.4

HEAD COACHING RECORD

BACKGROUND: Head coach, St. James High School (Pa.) and later head coach, Mount Pleasant High School, Del. (1949-1955). ... General manager, Philadelphia 76ers (1966-67 and 1967-68). ... Head coach/general manager, 76ers (1968-69 and 1969-70).

COLLEGIATE COACHING RECORD

Season Team	W	L	Pct.	Finish
55-56—St. Joseph's	23	6	.793	Independent
56-57—St. Joseph's	17	7	.708	Independent
57-58—St. Joseph's	18	9	.667	2nd/Middle Atlantic Conference
58-59—St. Joseph's	22	5	.815	1st/Middle Atlantic Conference
59-60—St. Joseph's	20	7	.741	1st/Middle Atlantic Conference
60-61—St. Joseph's	25	5	.833	1st/Middle Atlantic Conference
61-62—St. Joseph's	18	10	.643	1st/Middle Atlantic Conference
62-63—St. Joseph's	23	5	.821	1st/Middle Atlantic Conference
63-64—St. Joseph's	18	10	.643	T2nd/Middle Atlantic Conference
64-65—St. Joseph's	26	3	.897	1st/Middle Atlantic Conference
65-66—St. Joseph's	24	5	.828	1st/Middle Atlantic Conference
Totals (11 years)	234	72	.765	

NBA COACHING RECORD

Season Team	REGULAR SEASON				PLAYOFFS		
	W	L	Pct.	Finish	W	L	Pct.
68-69—Philadelphia	55	27	.671	2nd/Eastern Division	1	4	.200
69-70—Philadelphia	42	40	.512	4th/Eastern Division	1	4	.200

Season Team	REGULAR SEASON					PLAYOFFS		
	W	L	Pct.	Finish		W	L	Pct.
70-71—Philadelphia	47	35	.573	2nd/Atlantic Division		3	4	.429
71-72—Philadelphia	30	52	.366	3rd/Atlantic Division		—	—	—
72-73—Buffalo	21	61	.256	3rd/Atlantic Division		—	—	—
73-74—Buffalo	42	40	.512	3rd/Atlantic Division		2	4	.333
74-75—Buffalo	49	33	.598	2nd/Atlantic Division		3	4	.429
75-76—Buffalo	46	36	.561	T2nd/Atlantic Division		4	5	.444
76-77—Portland	49	33	.598	2nd/Pacific Division		14	5	.737
77-78—Portland	58	24	.707	1st/Pacific Division		2	4	.333
78-79—Portland	45	37	.549	4th/Pacific Division		1	2	.333
79-80—Portland	38	44	.463	4th/Pacific Division		1	2	.333
80-81—Portland	45	37	.549	3rd/Pacific Division		1	2	.333
81-82—Portland	42	40	.512	5th/Pacific Division		—	—	—
82-83—Portland	46	36	.561	4th/Pacific Division		3	4	.429
83-84—Portland	48	34	.585	2nd/Pacific Division		2	3	.400
84-85—Portland	42	40	.512	2nd/Pacific Division		4	5	.444
85-86—Portland	40	42	.488	2nd/Pacific Division		1	3	.250
86-87—Indiana	41	41	.500	4th/Central Division		1	3	.250
87-88—Indiana	38	44	.463	6th/Central Division		—	—	—
88-89—Indiana	0	7	.000			—	—	—
Totals (21 years)	**864**	**783**	**.525**	**Totals (16 years)**		**44**	**58**	**.431**

NOTES:

1956—Defeated Seton Hall, 74-65, in NIT quarterfinals; lost to Louisville, 89-79, in semifinals; defeated St. Francis-New York, 93-82, in third-place game.

1958—Defeated St. Peter's, 83-72, in NIT first round; lost to St. Bonaventure, 79-75, in quarterfinals.

1959—Lost to West Virginia, 95-92, in NCAA Tournament first round; lost to Navy, 70-59, in regional consolation game.

1960—Lost to Duke, 58-56, in NCAA Tournament first round; lost to West Virginia, 106-100, in regional consolation game.

1961—Defeated Princeton, 72-67, in NCAA Tournament regional semifinal; defeated Wake Forest, 96-86, in regional final; lost to Ohio State, 95-69, in national semifinal; defeated Utah, 127-120 (4 OT), in consolation game.

1962—Lost to Wake Forest, 96-85 (OT), in NCAA Tournament regional semifinal; lost to New York University, 94-85, in regional consolation game.

1963—Defeated Princeton, 82-81, in NCAA Tournament first round; defeated West Virginia, 97-88, in regional semifinal; lost to Duke, 73-59, in regional final.

1964—Defeated Miami (Fla.), 86-76, in NIT first round; lost to Bradley, 83-81, in quarterfinals.

1965—Defeated Connecticut, 67-61, in NCAA Tournament first round; lost to Providence, 81-73 (OT), in regional semifinal; lost to North Carolina State, 103-81, in regional consolation game.

1966—Defeated Providence, 65-48, in NCAA Tournament first round; lost to Duke, 76-74, in regional semifinal; defeated Davidson, 92-76, in regional consolation game.

1969—Lost to Boston in Eastern Division Semifinals.

1970—Lost to Milwaukee in Eastern Division Semifinals.

1971—Lost to Baltimore in Eastern Conference Semifinals.

1974—Lost to Boston in Eastern Conference Semifinals.

1975—Lost to Washington in Eastern Conference Semifinals.

1976—Defeated Philadelphia, 2-1, in Eastern Conference First Round; lost to Boston, 4-2, in Eastern Conference Semifinals.

1977—Defeated Chicago, 2-1, in Western Conference First Round; defeated Denver, 4-2, in Western Conference Semifinals; defeated Los Angeles Lakers, 4-0, in Western Conference Finals; defeated Philadelphia, 4-2, in NBA Finals.

1978—Lost to Seattle in Western Conference Semifinals.

1979—Lost to Phoenix in Western Conference First Round.

1980—Lost to Seattle in Western Conference First Round.

1981—Lost to Kansas City in Western Conference First Round.

1983—Defeated Seattle, 2-0, in Western Conference First Round; lost to Los Angeles Lakers, 4-1, in Western Conference Semifinals.

1984—Lost to Phoenix in Western Conference First Round.

1985—Defeated Dallas, 3-1, in Western Conference First Round; lost to Los Angeles Lakers, 4-1, in Western Conference Semifinals.

1986—Lost to Denver in Western Conference First Round.

1987—Lost to Atlanta in Eastern Conference First Round.

1988—Resigned as Indiana head coach (November 17); replaced by Mel Daniels with club in sixth place.

RILEY, PAT

See Head Coaches, page 298.

SHUE, GENE

PERSONAL: Born December 18, 1931, in Baltimore. ... 6-2/175 (1,88/79,4).
COLLEGE: Maryland.
TRANSACTIONS: Selected by Philadelphia Warriors in first round (third pick overall) of 1954 NBA Draft. ... Contract sold by Warriors to New York Knicks (November 29, 1954). ... Traded by Knicks to Fort Wayne Pistons for rights to G Ron Sobieszcyk (April 30, 1956). ... Pistons moved from Fort Wayne to Detroit for 1957-58 season. ... Traded by Pistons to Knicks for C Darrall Imhoff and cash (August 29, 1962). ... Traded by Knicks with C Paul Hogue to Baltimore Bullets for G/F Bill McGill (October 30, 1963).
CAREER NOTES: General manager, Philadelphia 76ers (1990-91 and 1991-92). ... Director of player personnel, 76ers (1992-93 through 1996-97).

COLLEGIATE RECORD

Season Team	G	Min.	FGM	FGA	Pct.	FTM	FTA	Pct.	Reb.	Ast.	Pts.	AVERAGES		
												RPG	APG	PPG
50-51—Maryland‡	14	...	...	...	...	...	...	...	...	...	181	...	...	12.9
51-52—Maryland	22	...	91	243	.374	53	75	.707	...	...	205	...	...	9.3
52-53—Maryland	23	...	176	375	.469	156	223	.700	...	...	508	...	...	22.1
53-54—Maryland	30	...	237	469	.505	180	228	.789	...	...	654	...	...	21.8
Varsity totals	75	...	504	1087	.464	389	526	.740	...	...	1367	...	...	18.2

NBA REGULAR-SEASON RECORD

HONORS: All-NBA first team (1960). ... All-NBA second team (1961).

Season Team	G	Min.	FGM	FGA	Pct.	FTM	FTA	Pct.	Reb.	Ast.	PF	Dq.	Pts.	AVERAGES RPG	APG	PPG
54-55—Phil.-N.Y.	62	947	100	289	.346	59	78	.756	154	89	64	0	259	2.5	1.4	4.2
55-56—New York	72	1750	240	625	.384	181	237	.764	212	179	111	0	661	2.9	2.5	9.2
56-57—Fort Wayne	72	2470	273	710	.385	241	316	.763	421	238	137	0	787	5.8	3.3	10.9
57-58—Detroit	63	2333	353	919	.384	276	327	.844	333	172	150	1	982	5.3	2.7	15.6
58-59—Detroit	72	2745	464	1197	.388	338	421	.803	335	231	129	1	1266	4.7	3.2	17.6
59-60—Detroit	75	†3338	620	1501	.413	472	541	.872	409	295	146	2	1712	5.5	3.9	22.8
60-61—Detroit	78	3361	650	1545	.421	465	543	.856	334	530	207	1	1765	4.3	6.8	22.6
61-62—Detroit	80	3143	580	1422	.408	362	447	.810	372	465	192	1	1522	4.7	5.8	19.0
62-63—New York	78	2288	354	894	.396	208	302	.689	191	259	171	0	916	2.4	3.3	11.7
63-64—Baltimore	47	963	81	276	.293	36	61	.590	94	150	98	2	198	2.0	3.2	4.2
Totals	699	23338	3715	9378	.396	2638	3273	.806	2855	2608	1405	8	10068	4.1	3.7	14.4

NBA PLAYOFF RECORD

Season Team	G	Min.	FGM	FGA	Pct.	FTM	FTA	Pct.	Reb.	Ast.	PF	Dq.	Pts.	AVERAGES RPG	APG	PPG
54-55—New York	3	49	8	17	.471	6	7	.857	12	4	5	0	22	4.0	1.3	7.3
56-57—Fort Wayne	2	79	14	27	.519	4	4	1.000	7	8	3	0	32	3.5	4.0	16.0
57-58—Detroit	7	281	45	123	.366	40	43	.930	46	33	15	0	130	6.6	4.7	18.6
58-59—Detroit	3	118	28	60	.467	27	33	.818	14	10	7	0	83	4.7	3.3	27.7
59-60—Detroit	2	89	15	38	.395	18	20	.900	12	6	5	0	48	6.0	3.0	24.0
60-61—Detroit	5	186	35	72	.486	23	29	.793	12	22	11	0	93	2.4	4.4	18.6
61-62—Detroit	10	369	62	151	.411	37	48	.771	30	49	29	0	161	3.0	4.9	16.1
Totals	32	1171	207	488	.424	155	184	.842	133	132	75	0	569	4.2	4.1	17.8

NBA ALL-STAR GAME RECORD

Season Team	Min.	FGM	FGA	Pct.	FTM	FTA	Pct.	Reb	Ast.	PF	Dq.	Pts.
1958—Detroit	25	8	11	.727	2	3	.667	2	0	3	0	18
1959—Detroit	31	6	12	.500	1	2	.500	4	3	4	0	13
1960—Detroit	34	6	13	.462	1	2	.500	6	6	0	0	13
1961—Detroit	23	6	10	.600	3	4	.750	3	6	1	0	15
1962—Detroit	17	3	6	.500	1	1	1.000	5	4	3	0	7
Totals	130	29	52	.558	8	12	.667	20	19	11	0	66

HEAD COACHING RECORD

HONORS: NBA Coach of the Year (1969, 1982).

NBA COACHING RECORD

Season Team	REGULAR SEASON W	L	Pct.	Finish	PLAYOFFS W	L	Pct.
66-67—Baltimore	16	40	.286	5th/Eastern Division	—	—	—
67-68—Baltimore	36	46	.439	6th/Eastern Division	—	—	—
68-69—Baltimore	57	25	.695	1st/Eastern Division	0	4	.000
69-70—Baltimore	50	32	.610	3rd/Central Division	3	4	.429
70-71—Baltimore	42	40	.512	1st/Central Division	8	10	.444
71-72—Baltimore	38	44	.463	1st/Central Division	2	4	.333
72-73—Baltimore	52	30	.634	1st/Central Division	1	4	.200
73-74—Philadelphia	25	57	.305	4th/Atlantic Division	—	—	—
74-75—Philadelphia	34	48	.415	4th/Atlantic Division	—	—	—
75-76—Philadelphia	46	36	.561	T2nd/Atlantic Division	1	2	.333
76-77—Philadelphia	50	32	.610	1st/Atlantic Division	10	9	.526
77-78—Philadelphia	2	4	.333		—	—	—
78-79—San Diego	43	39	.524	5th/Pacific Division	—	—	—
79-80—San Diego	35	47	.427	5th/Pacific Division	—	—	—
80-81—Washington	39	43	.476	4th/Atlantic Division	—	—	—
81-82—Washington	43	39	.524	4th/Atlantic Division	3	4	.429
82-83—Washington	42	40	.512	5th/Atlantic Division	—	—	—
83-84—Washington	35	47	.427	5th/Atlantic Division	1	3	.250
84-85—Washington	40	42	.488	4th/Atlantic Division	1	3	.250
85-86—Washington	32	37	.464		—	—	—
87-88—L.A. Clippers	17	65	.207	6th/Pacific Division	—	—	—
88-89—L.A. Clippers	10	28	.263		—	—	—
Totals (22 years)	784	861	.477	Totals (10 years)	30	47	.390

NOTES:
1966—Replaced Mike Farmer (1-8) and Buddy Jeannette (3-13) as Baltimore head coach (December) with record of 4-21.
1969—Lost to New York in Eastern Division Semifinals.
1970—Lost to New York in Eastern Division Semifinals.
1971—Defeated Philadelphia, 4-3, in Eastern Conference Semifinals; defeated New York, 4-3, in Eastern Conference Finals; lost to Milwaukee, 4-0, in NBA Finals.
1972—Lost to New York in Eastern Conference Semifinals.
1973—Lost to New York in Eastern Conference Semifinals.
1976—Lost to Buffalo in Eastern Conference First Round.
1977—Defeated Boston, 4-3, in Eastern Conference Semifinals; defeated Houston, 4-2, in Eastern Conference Finals; lost to Portland, 4-2, in NBA Finals. Replaced as Philadelphia head coach by Billy Cunningham (November 4).
1982—Defeated New Jersey, 2-0, in Eastern Conference First Round; lost to Boston, 4-1, in Eastern Conference Semifinals.
1984—Lost to Boston in Eastern Conference First Round.
1985—Lost to Philadelphia in Eastern Conference First Round.
1986—Replaced as Washington head coach by Kevin Loughery (March 19).
1989—Replaced as L.A. Clippers head coach by Don Casey (January 19).

TOMJANOVICH, RUDY

PERSONAL: Born November 24, 1948, in Hamtramck, Mich. ... 6-8/220. (2,03/99,8). ... Full name: Rudolph Tomjanovich. ... Name pronounced Tom-JOHN-a-vitch.
HIGH SCHOOL: Hamtramck (Mich.).
COLLEGE: Michigan.
TRANSACTIONS/CAREER NOTES: Selected by San Diego Rockets in first round (second pick overall) of 1970 NBA Draft. ... Rockets franchise moved from San Diego to Houston for 1971-72 season.
MISCELLANEOUS: Head coach of bronze-medal-winning 1998 USA Basketball World Championship Team. ... Head coach of gold-medal-winning 2000 U.S. Olympic Team.

COLLEGIATE RECORD

NOTES: THE SPORTING NEWS All-America first team (1970). ... THE SPORTING NEWS All-America second team (1969).

												AVERAGES		
Season Team	G	Min.	FGM	FGA	Pct.	FTM	FTA	Pct.	Reb.	Ast.	Pts.	RPG	APG	PPG
66-67—Michigan‡	3	...	28	...	...	6	15	.400	...	...	62	...	...	20.7
67-68—Michigan	24	...	210	446	.471	49	78	.628	323	...	469	13.5	...	19.5
68-69—Michigan	24	...	269	541	.497	79	131	.603	340	...	617	14.2	...	25.7
69-70—Michigan	24	...	286	604	.474	150	200	.750	376	...	722	15.7	...	30.1
Varsity totals	72	...	765	1591	.481	278	409	.680	1039	...	1808	14.4	...	25.1

NBA REGULAR-SEASON RECORD

														AVERAGES		
Season Team	G	Min.	FGM	FGA	Pct.	FTM	FTA	Pct.	Reb.	Ast.	PF	Dq.	Pts.	RPG	APG	PPG
70-71—San Diego	77	1062	168	439	.383	73	112	.652	381	73	124	0	409	4.9	0.9	5.3
71-72—Houston	78	2689	500	1010	.495	172	238	.723	923	117	193	2	1172	11.8	1.5	15.0
72-73—Houston	81	2972	655	1371	.478	250	335	.746	938	178	225	1	1560	11.6	2.2	19.3

									REBOUNDS								AVERAGES		
Season Team	G	Min.	FGM	FGA	Pct.	FTM	FTA	Pct.	Off.	Def.	Tot.	Ast.	St.	Blk.	TO	Pts.	RPG	APG	PPG
73-74—Houston	80	3227	788	1470	.536	385	454	.848	230	487	717	250	89	66	...	1961	9.0	3.1	24.5
74-75—Houston	81	3134	694	1323	.525	289	366	.790	184	429	613	236	76	24	...	1677	7.6	2.9	20.7
75-76—Houston	79	2912	622	1202	.517	221	288	.767	167	499	666	188	42	19	...	1465	8.4	2.4	18.5
76-77—Houston	81	3130	733	1437	.510	287	342	.839	172	512	684	172	57	27	...	1753	8.4	2.1	21.6
77-78—Houston	23	849	217	447	.485	61	81	.753	40	98	138	32	15	5	38	495	6.0	1.4	21.5
78-79—Houston	74	2641	620	1200	.517	168	221	.760	170	402	572	137	44	18	138	1408	7.7	1.9	19.0
79-80—Houston	62	1834	370	778	.476	118	147	.803	132	226	358	109	32	10	98	880	5.8	1.8	14.2
80-81—Houston	52	1264	263	563	.467	65	82	.793	78	130	208	81	19	6	58	603	4.0	1.6	11.6
Totals	768	25714	5630	11240	.501	2089	2666	.784	...	...	6198	1573	374	175	332	13383	8.1	2.0	17.4

Three-point field goals: 1979-80, 22-for-79 (.278). 1980-81, 12-for-51 (.235). Totals, 34-for-130 (.262).
Personal fouls/disqualifications: 1973-74, 230/0. 1974-75, 230/1. 1975-76, 206/1. 1976-77, 198/1. 1977-78, 63/0. 1978-79, 186/0. 1979-80, 161/2. 1980-81, 121/0. Totals, 1937/8.

NBA PLAYOFF RECORD

									REBOUNDS								AVERAGES		
Season Team	G	Min.	FGM	FGA	Pct.	FTM	FTA	Pct.	Off.	Def.	Tot.	Ast.	St.	Blk.	TO	Pts.	RPG	APG	PPG
74-75—Houston	8	304	72	128	.563	40	48	.833	22	42	64	23	1	4	...	184	8.0	2.9	23.0
76-77—Houston	12	457	107	212	.505	29	37	.784	24	41	65	24	7	3	...	243	5.4	2.0	20.3
78-79—Houston	2	64	9	23	.391	2	5	.400	7	7	14	2	1	1	1	20	7.0	1.0	10.0
79-80—Houston	7	185	24	64	.375	9	13	.692	12	28	40	10	2	0	14	58	5.7	1.4	8.3
80-81—Houston	8	31	1	9	.111	4	6	.667	2	4	6	0	0	0	2	6	0.8	0.0	0.8
Totals	37	1041	213	436	.489	84	109	.771	67	122	189	59	11	8	17	511	5.1	1.6	13.8

Three-point field goals: 1979-80, 1-for-7 (.143). 1980-81, 0-for-3. Totals, 1-for-10 (.100).
Personal fouls/disqualifications: 1974-75, 17/0. 1976-77, 34/0. 1978-79, 7/0. 1979-80, 21/1. 1980-81, 3/0. Totals, 78/1.

NBA ALL-STAR GAME RECORD

							REBOUNDS								
Season Team	Min.	FGM	FGA	Pct.	FTM	FTA	Pct.	Off.	Def.	Tot.	Ast.	PF	Dq.	St.	Blk.	TO	Pts.
1974—Houston	17	2	5	.400	0	0	...	2	3	5	0	1	0	0	0	...	4
1975—Houston	14	0	3	.000	0	0	...	1	2	3	0	3	0	0	0	...	0
1976—Houston	12	1	2	.500	0	0	...	1	2	3	0	2	0	0	0	...	2
1977—Houston	22	3	9	.333	0	0	...	2	8	10	1	1	0	1	1	...	6
1979—Houston	24	6	13	.462	0	0	...	4	2	6	1	2	0	0	0	...	12
Totals	89	12	32	.375	0	0	...	10	17	27	2	9	0	1	1	0	24

HEAD COACHING RECORD

BACKGROUND: Scout, Houston Rockets (1981-82 and 1982-83). ... Assistant coach, Rockets (1983-84 to February 18, 1992).

NBA COACHING RECORD

	REGULAR SEASON				PLAYOFFS		
Season Team	W	L	Pct.	Finish	W	L	Pct.
91-92—Houston	16	14	.533	3rd/Midwest Division	—	—	—
92-93—Houston	55	27	.671	1st/Midwest Division	6	6	.500
93-94—Houston	58	24	.707	1st/Midwest Division	15	8	.652
94-95—Houston	47	35	.573	3rd/Midwest Division	15	7	.682
95-96—Houston	48	34	.585	2nd/Midwest Division	3	5	.375

Season Team	REGULAR SEASON				PLAYOFFS		
	W	L	Pct.	Finish	W	L	Pct.
96-97—Houston	57	25	.695	2nd/Midwest Division	9	7	.563
97-98—Houston	41	41	.500	4th/Midwest Division	2	3	.400
98-99—Houston	31	19	.620	3rd/Midwest Division	1	3	.250
99-00—Houston	34	48	.415	6th/Midwest Division	—	—	—
00-01—Houston	45	37	.549	5th/Midwest Division	—	—	—
01-02—Houston	28	54	.341	5th/Midwest Division	—	—	—
02-03—Houston	43	39	.524	5th/Midwest Division	—	—	—
04-05—Los Angeles Lakers	24	19	.558				
Totals (13 years)	527	416	.559	Totals (7 years)	51	39	.567

WORLD CHAMPIONSHIP RECORD

Season Team	REGULAR SEASON			
	W	L	Pct.	Finish
1998—Team USA	7	2	.778	Bronze medal

OLYMPIC RECORD

Season Team	REGULAR SEASON			
	W	L	Pct.	Finish
2000—Team USA	8	0	1.000	Gold medal

NOTES:
1992—Replaced Don Chaney as Houston head coach (February 18), with record of 26-26 and club in third place.
1993—Defeated L.A. Clippers, 3-2, in Western Conference first round; lost to Seattle, 4-3, in Western Conference semifinals.
1994—Defeated Portland, 3-1, in Western Conference first round; defeated Phoenix, 4-3, in Western Conference semifinals; defeated Utah, 4-1, in Western Conference finals; defeated New York, 4-3, in NBA Finals.
1995—Defeated Utah, 3-2, in Western Conference first round, defeated Phoenix, 4-3, in Western Conference semifinals; defeated San Antonio, 4-2, in Western Conference finals; defeated Orlando, 4-0, in NBA Finals.
1996—Defeated Los Angeles Lakers, 3-1, in Western Conference first round; lost to Seattle, 4-0, in Western Conference semifinals.
1997—Defeated Minnesota, 3-0, in Western Conference first round; defeated Seattle, 4-3, in Western Conference semifinals; lost to Utah, 4-2, in Western Conference finals.
1998—Lost to Utah in Western Conference first round.
1999—Lost to Los Angeles Lakers in Western Conference first round.
2005—Stepped down as Los Angeles head coach (February 2); replaced by Frank Hamblen with team in third place.

WILKENS, LENNY　　　　G

PERSONAL: Born October 28, 1937, in Brooklyn, N.Y. ... 6-1/180 (1,85/81,6). ... Full name: Leonard Randolph Wilkens.
HIGH SCHOOL: Boys (Brooklyn, N.Y.).
COLLEGE: Providence.
TRANSACTIONS/CAREER NOTES: Selected by St. Louis Hawks in first round of 1960 NBA Draft. ... Hawks franchise moved from St. Louis to Atlanta for 1968-69 season. ... Traded by Hawks to Seattle SuperSonics for G Walt Hazzard (October 12, 1968). ... Player/head coach, SuperSonics (1969-70 through 1971-72). ... Traded by SuperSonics with F Barry Clemens to Cleveland Cavaliers for G Butch Beard (August 23, 1972). ... Playing rights transferred from Cavaliers to Portland Trail Blazers for cash (October 7, 1974).
CAREER NOTES: Director of player personnel, SuperSonics (May 13-November 1977). ... Vice president/general manager, SuperSonics (1985-86).
CAREER HONORS: Elected to Naismith Memorial Basketball Hall of Fame as player (1988) and head coach (1998). ... One of the 50 Greatest Players in NBA History (1996). ... One of the Top 10 Coaches in NBA History (1996).
MISCELLANEOUS: Head coach, 1996 gold medal-winning U.S. Olympic Team.

COLLEGIATE RECORD

NOTES: The Sporting News All-America second team (1960).

Season Team	G	Min.	FGM	FGA	Pct.	FTM	FTA	Pct.	Reb.	Ast.	Pts.	AVERAGES		
												RPG	APG	PPG
56-57—Providence‡	23	...	...	...	...	...	...	...	...	...	488	...	...	21.2
57-58—Providence	24	...	137	316	.434	84	130	.646	190	...	358	7.9	...	14.9
58-59—Providence	27	...	167	390	.428	89	144	.618	188	...	423	7.0	...	15.7
59-60—Providence	29	...	157	362	.434	98	140	.700	205	...	412	7.1	...	14.2
Varsity totals	80	...	461	1068	.432	271	414	.655	583	...	1193	7.3	...	14.9

NBA REGULAR-SEASON RECORD

Season Team	G	Min.	FGM	FGA	Pct.	FTM	FTA	Pct.	Reb.	Ast.	PF	Dq.	Pts.	AVERAGES		
														RPG	APG	PPG
60-61—St. Louis	75	1898	333	783	.425	214	300	.713	335	212	215	5	880	4.5	2.8	11.7
61-62—St. Louis	20	870	140	364	.385	84	110	.764	131	116	63	0	364	6.6	5.8	18.2
62-63—St. Louis	75	2569	333	834	.399	222	319	.696	403	381	256	6	888	5.4	5.1	11.8
63-64—St. Louis	78	2526	334	808	.413	270	365	.740	335	359	287	7	938	4.3	4.6	12.0
64-65—St. Louis	78	2854	434	1048	.414	416	558	.746	365	431	283	7	1284	4.7	5.5	16.5
65-66—St. Louis	69	2692	411	954	.431	422	532	.793	322	429	248	4	1244	4.7	6.2	18.0
66-67—St. Louis	78	2974	448	1036	.432	459	583	.787	412	442	280	6	1355	5.3	5.7	17.4
67-68—St. Louis	82	3169	546	1246	.438	546	711	.768	438	679	255	3	1638	5.3	8.3	20.0
68-69—Seattle	82	3463	644	1462	.441	547	710	.770	511	674	294	8	1835	6.2	8.2	22.4
69-70—Seattle	75	2802	448	1066	.420	438	556	.788	378	*683	212	5	1334	5.0	9.1	17.8
70-71—Seattle	71	2641	471	1125	.419	461	574	.803	319	654	201	3	1403	4.5	9.2	19.8
71-72—Seattle	80	2989	479	1027	.466	480	620	.774	338	*766	209	4	1438	4.2	9.6	18.0
72-73—Cleveland	75	2973	572	1275	.449	394	476	.828	346	628	221	2	1538	4.6	8.4	20.5

Season Team	G	Min.	FGM	FGA	Pct.	FTM	FTA	Pct.	REBOUNDS Off.	Def.	Tot.	Ast.	St.	Blk.	TO	Pts.	AVERAGES RPG	APG	PPG
73-74—Cleveland	74	2483	462	994	.465	289	361	.801	80	197	277	522	97	17	...	1213	3.7	7.1	16.4
74-75—Portland	65	1161	134	305	.439	152	198	.768	38	82	120	235	77	9	...	420	1.8	3.6	6.5
Totals	1077	38064	6189	14327	.432	5394	6973	.774	...		5030	7211	174	26	...	17772	4.7	6.7	16.5

Personal fouls/disqualifications: 1973-74, 165/2. 1974-75, 96/1. Totals, 3285/63.

NBA PLAYOFF RECORD

Season Team	G	Min.	FGM	FGA	Pct.	FTM	FTA	Pct.	Reb.	Ast.	PF	Dq.	Pts.	AVERAGES RPG	APG	PPG
60-61—St. Louis	12	437	63	166	.380	44	58	.759	72	42	51	4	170	6.0	3.5	14.2
62-63—St. Louis	11	400	57	154	.370	37	49	.755	69	69	51	2	151	6.3	6.3	13.7
63-64—St. Louis	12	413	64	143	.448	44	58	.759	60	64	42	0	172	5.0	5.3	14.3
64-65—St. Louis	4	147	20	57	.351	24	29	.828	12	15	14	0	64	3.0	3.8	16.0
65-66—St. Louis	10	391	57	143	.399	57	83	.687	54	70	43	0	171	5.4	7.0	17.1
66-67—St. Louis	9	378	58	145	.400	77	90	.856	68	65	34	0	193	7.6	7.2	21.4
67-68—St. Louis	6	237	40	91	.440	30	40	.750	38	47	23	1	110	6.3	7.8	18.3
Totals	64	2403	359	899	.399	313	407	.769	373	372	258	7	1031	5.8	5.8	16.1

NBA ALL-STAR GAME RECORD

NOTES: NBA All-Star Game Most Valuable Player (1971).

Season Team	Min.	FGM	FGA	Pct.	FTM	FTA	Pct.	Reb.	Ast.	PF	Dq.	Pts.
1963—St. Louis	25	2	7	.286	0	1	.000	2	3	0	0	4
1964—St. Louis	14	1	5	.200	1	1	1.000	0	0	3	0	3
1965—St. Louis	20	2	6	.333	4	4	1.000	3	3	3	0	8
1967—St. Louis	16	2	6	.333	2	3	.667	2	6	2	0	6
1968—St. Louis	22	4	10	.400	6	8	.750	3	3	1	0	14
1969—Seattle	24	3	15	.200	4	5	.800	7	5	3	0	10
1970—Seattle	17	5	7	.714	2	3	.667	2	4	1	0	12
1971—Seattle	20	8	11	.727	5	5	1.000	1	1	1	0	21
1973—Cleveland	24	3	8	.375	1	2	.500	2	1	1	0	7
Totals	182	30	75	.400	25	32	.781	22	26	15	0	85

HEAD COACHING RECORD

BACKGROUND: Player/head coach, Seattle SuperSonics (1969-70 through 1971-72). ... Player/head coach, Portland Trail Blazers (1974-75). ... Head coach/director of player personnel, SuperSonics (November 1977 through 1984-85). ... Assistant coach, U.S. Olympic team (1992).
HONORS: NBA Coach of the Year (1994). ... One of the Top 10 Coaches in NBA History (1996).
RECORDS: Holds NBA career record for most wins—1,332.

NBA COACHING RECORD

Season Team	REGULAR SEASON W	L	Pct.	Finish	PLAYOFFS W	L	Pct.
69-70—Seattle	36	46	.439	5th/Western Division	—	—	—
70-71—Seattle	38	44	.463	4th/Pacific Division	—	—	—
71-72—Seattle	47	35	.573	3rd/Pacific Division	—	—	—
74-75—Portland	38	44	.463	3rd/Pacific Division	—	—	—
75-76—Portland	37	45	.451	5th/Pacific Division	—	—	—
77-78—Seattle	42	18	.700	3rd/Pacific Division	13	9	.591
78-79—Seattle	52	30	.634	1st/Pacific Division	12	5	.706
79-80—Seattle	56	26	.683	2nd/Pacific Division	7	8	.467
80-81—Seattle	34	48	.415	6th/Pacific Division	—	—	—
81-82—Seattle	52	30	.634	2nd/Pacific Division	3	5	.375
82-83—Seattle	48	34	.585	3rd/Pacific Division	0	2	.000
83-84—Seattle	42	40	.512	3rd/Pacific Division	2	3	.400
84-85—Seattle	31	51	.378	4th/Pacific Division	—	—	—
86-87—Cleveland	31	51	.378	6th/Central Division	—	—	—
87-88—Cleveland	42	40	.512	T4th/Central Division	2	3	.400
88-89—Cleveland	57	25	.695	2nd/Central Division	2	3	.400
89-90—Cleveland	42	40	.512	T4th/Central Division	2	3	.400
90-91—Cleveland	33	49	.402	6th/Central Division	—	—	—
91-92—Cleveland	57	25	.695	2nd/Central Division	9	8	.529
92-93—Cleveland	54	28	.659	2nd/Central Division	3	6	.333
93-94—Atlanta	57	25	.695	1st/Central Division	5	6	.455
94-95—Atlanta	42	40	.512	5th/Central Division	0	3	.000
95-96—Atlanta	46	36	.561	4th/Central Division	4	6	.400
96-97—Atlanta	56	26	.683	2nd/Central Division	4	6	.400
97-98—Atlanta	50	32	.610	4th/Central Division	1	3	.250
98-99—Atlanta	31	19	.620	2nd/Central Division	3	6	.333
99-00—Atlanta	28	54	.341	7th/Central Division	—	—	—
00-01—Toronto	47	35	.573	2nd/Central Division	6	6	.500
01-02—Toronto	42	40	.512	T3rd/Central Division	2	3	.400
02-03—Toronto	24	58	.293	7th/Central Division	—	—	—
03-04—New York	23	19	.548	3rd/Atlantic Division	0	4	.000
04-05—New York	17	22	.294		—	—	—
Totals (32 years)	1332	1155	.536	Totals (20 years)	80	98	.450

OLYMPIC RECORD

Season Team	REGULAR SEASON W	L	Pct.	Finish	PLAYOFFS W	L	Pct.
1996—Team USA	8	0	1.000	Gold medal	—	—	—

NOTES:

1977—Replaced Bob Hopkins as Seattle head coach (November), with record of 5-17.

1978—Defeated Los Angeles Lakers, 2-1, in Western Conference first round; defeated Portland, 4-2, in Western Conference semifinals; defeated Denver, 4-2, in Western Conference finals; lost to Washington, 4-3, in NBA Finals.

1979—Defeated Los Angeles Lakers, 4-1, in Western Conference semifinals; defeated Phoenix, 4-3, in Western Conference finals; defeated Washington, 4-1, in NBA Finals.

1980—Defeated Portland, 2-1, in Western Conference first round; defeated Milwaukee, 4-3, in Western Conference semifinals; lost to Los Angeles Lakers, 4-1, in Western Conference finals.

1982—Defeated Houston, 2-1, in Western Conference first round; lost to San Antonio, 4-1, in Western Conference semifinals.

1983—Lost to Portland in Western Conference first round.

1984—Lost to Dallas in Western Conference first round.

1988—Lost to Chicago in Eastern Conference first round.

1989—Lost to Chicago in Eastern Conference first round.

1990—Lost to Philadelphia in Eastern Conference first round.

1992—Defeated New Jersey, 3-1, in Eastern Conference first round; defeated Boston, 4-3, in Eastern Conference semifinals; lost to Chicago, 4-2, in Eastern Conference finals.

1993—Defeated New Jersey, 3-2, in Eastern Conference first round; lost to Chicago, 4-0, in Eastern Conference semifinals.

1994—Defeated Miami, 3-2, in Eastern Conference first round; lost to Indiana, 4-2, in Eastern Conference semifinals.

1995—Lost to Indiana in Eastern Conference first round.

1996—Defeated Indiana, 3-2, in Eastern Conference first round; lost to Orlando, 4-1, in Eastern Conference semifinals.
   Team USA defeated Argentina, 96-68; Angola, 87-54; Lithuania, 104-82; China, 133-70; and Croatia, 102-71, in preliminary round. Defeated Brazil, 98-75, in medal round quarterfinals; defeated Australia, 101-73, in semifinals; defeated Yugoslavia, 95-69, in gold-medal game.

1997—Defeated Detroit, 3-2, in Eastern Conference first round; lost to Chicago, 4-1, in Eastern Conference semifinals.

1998—Lost to Charlotte in Eastern Conference first round.

1999—Defeated Detroit, 3-2, in Eastern Conference first round; lost to New York, 4-0, in Eastern Conference semifinals.

2001—Defeated New York, 3-2, in Eastern Conference first round; lost to Philadelphia, 4-3, in Eastern Conference semifinals.

2002—Lost to Detroit, 3-2, in Eastern Conference first round.

2004—Replaced Don Chaney as New York head coach (January 14) with record of 15-24 and club in fifth place. Lost to New Jersey, 4-0, in Eastern Conference first round.

2005—Stepped down as New York head coach (January 22); replaced by Herb Williams with team in third place.

SCORING
(minimum 70 games or 1,400 points)

	G	FGM	FTM	Pts.	Avg.
Bryant, LA-L	80	978	696	2832	35.4
Iverson, Phi.	72	815	675	2377	33.0
James, Cle.	79	875	601	2478	31.4
Arenas, Was.	80	746	655	2346	29.3
Wade, Mia.	75	699	629	2040	27.2
Pierce, Bos.	79	689	627	2116	26.8
Nowitzki, Dal.	81	751	539	2151	26.6
Anthony, Den.	80	756	573	2122	26.5
Redd, Mil.	80	682	501	2028	25.4
Allen, Sea.	78	681	324	1955	25.1
Brand, LA-C	79	756	440	1953	24.7
Carter, N.J.	79	653	480	1911	24.2
Richardson, G.S.	75	641	276	1741	23.2
Bosh, Tor.	70	549	474	1572	22.5
Marion, Pho.	81	716	241	1769	21.8
Garnett, Min.	76	626	396	1656	21.8
Bibby, Sac.	82	597	342	1728	21.1
Jamison, Was.	82	660	217	1684	20.5
Gasol, Mem.	80	600	425	1628	20.4
James, Tor.	79	576	283	1604	20.3

FIELD-GOAL PERCENTAGE
(minimum 300 made)

	FGM	FGA	Pct.
O'Neal, Mia.	480	800	.600
Curry, N.Y.	336	597	.563
Parker, S.A.	623	1136	.548
Wallace, Cha.	317	589	.538
Bogut, Mil.	323	606	.533
Howard, Orl.	468	881	.531
Brand, LA-C	756	1435	.527
Diaw, Pho.	449	853	.526
Garnett, Min.	626	1191	.526
Abdur-Rahim, Sac.	332	632	.525

FREE THROW PERCENTAGE
(minimum 125 made)

	FTM	FTA	Pct.
Nash, Pho.	257	279	.921
Stojakovic, Sac.-Ind	238	260	.915
Allen, Sea.	324	359	.903
Nowitzki, Dal.	539	598	.901
Szczerbiak, Min.-Bos	278	310	.897
Billups, Det.	465	520	.894
Stackhouse, Dal.	195	221	.882
Redd, Mil.	501	571	.877
Ridnour, Sea.	199	227	.877
Boykins, Den.	152	174	.874

ASSISTS
(minimum 70 games or 400 assists)

	G	No.	Avg.
Nash, Pho.	79	826	10.5
Davis, G.S.	54	480	8.9
Knight, Cha.	69	610	8.8
Billups, Det.	81	699	8.6
Kidd, N.J.	80	672	8.4
Miller, Den.	82	674	8.2
Paul, NO/Ok	78	611	7.8
Iverson, Phi.	72	532	7.4
Ridnour, Sea.	79	550	7.0
Alston, Hou.	63	425	6.7
Wade, Mia.	75	503	6.7
James, Cle.	79	521	6.6
Ford, Mil.	72	473	6.6
Johnson, Atl.	82	536	6.5
Hinrich, Chi.	81	514	6.3
Cassell, LA-C	78	491	6.3
Diaw, Pho.	81	503	6.2
Arenas, Was.	80	484	6.1
James, Tor.	79	460	5.8
Parker, S.A.	80	460	5.8

REBOUNDS
(minimum 70 games or 800 rebounds)

	G	Off.	Def.	Tot.	Avg.
Garnett, Min.	76	214	752	966	12.7
Howard, Orl.	82	288	734	1022	12.5
Marion, Pho.	81	249	710	959	11.8
B. Wallace, Det.	82	301	622	923	11.3
Duncan, S.A.	80	231	650	881	11.0
Murphy, G.S.	74	195	548	743	10.0
Brand, LA-C	79	236	554	790	10.0
Webber, Phi.	75	184	557	741	9.9
Kaman, LA-C	78	187	563	750	9.6
Magloire, Mil.	82	220	558	778	9.5
Jamison, Was.	82	167	598	765	9.3
Bosh, Tor.	70	204	443	647	9.2
Odom, LA-L	80	181	557	738	9.2
Okur, Utah	82	211	535	746	9.1
Chandler, Chi.	79	265	449	714	9.0
Nowitzki, Dal.	81	115	613	728	9.0
Gasol, Mem.	80	191	522	713	8.9
Gooden, Cle.	79	237	428	665	8.4
Randolph, Por.	74	193	399	592	8.0
Pachulia, Atl.	78	264	349	613	7.9

STEALS
(minimum 70 games or 125 steals)

	G	No.	Avg.
Wallace, Cha.	55	138	2.51
Knight, Cha.	69	157	2.28
Paul, NO/Ok	78	175	2.24
Arenas, Was.	80	161	2.01
Marion, Pho.	81	160	1.98
Wade, Mia.	75	146	1.95
Iverson, Phi.	72	140	1.94
Kidd, N.J.	80	150	1.88
Bryant, LA-L	80	147	1.84
B. Wallace, Det.	82	146	1.78

BLOCKED SHOTS
(minimum 70 games or 100 blocked shots)

	G	No.	Avg.
Camby, Den.	56	184	3.29
Kirilenko, Utah	69	220	3.19
Mourning, Mia.	65	173	2.66
J. Smith, Atl.	80	208	2.60
Brand, LA-C	79	201	2.54
Dalembert, Phi.	66	160	2.42
Przybilla, Por.	56	130	2.32
O'Neal, Ind.	51	117	2.29
B. Wallace, Det.	82	181	2.21
Griffin, Min.	70	148	2.11

3-POINT FIELD GOALS
(minimum 55 made)

	FGM	FGA	Pct.
Hamilton, Det.	55	120	.458
Lue, Atl.	58	127	.457
Barbosa, Pho.	87	196	.444
James, Tor.	169	382	.442
Bell, Pho.	197	446	.442
Nash, Pho.	150	342	.439
Gordon, Chi.	166	382	.435
Billups, Det.	184	425	.433
Bowen, S.A.	104	245	.424
Nelson, Orl.	70	165	.424

AWARD WINNERS

MAJOR AWARDS

NBA Most Valuable Player
Steve Nash, Phoenix

NBA Red Auerbach Coach of the Year
Avery Johnson, Dallas

T-Mobile NBA Rookie of the Year
Chris Paul, N.O./Okla. City

NBA Most Improved Player
Boris Diaw, Phoenix

NBA Executive of the Year
Elgin Baylor, L.A. Clippers

J. Walter Kennedy Citizenship Award
Kevin Garnett, Minnesota

NBA Sportsmanship Award
Elton Brand, L.A. Clippers

NBA Defensive Player of the Year
Ben Wallace, Detroit

NBA Sixth Man Award
Mike Miller, Memphis

NBA Finals Most Valuable Player
Dwyane Wade, Miami

All-Star Game Most Valuable Player
LeBron James, Cleveland

ALL-NBA TEAMS

FIRST
LeBron James, Cleveland
Kobe Bryant, L.A. Lakers
Steve Nash, Phoenix
Dirk Nowitzki, Dallas
Shaquille O'Neal, L.A. Lakers

SECOND
Chauncey Billups, Detroit
Dwyane Wade, Miami
Tim Duncan, San Antonio
Elton Brand, L.A. Clippers
Ben Wallace, Detroit

THIRD
Allen Iverson, Philadelphia
Gilbert Arenas, Washington
Shawn Marion, Phoenix
Carmelo Anthony, Denver
Yao Ming, Houston

T-MOBILE ALL-ROOKIE TEAMS

FIRST
Chris Paul, N.O./Okla. City
Charlie Villanueva, Toronto
Andrew Bogut, Milwaukee
Deron Williams, Utah
Channing Frye, New York

SECOND
Danny Granger, Indiana
Raymond Felton, Charlotte
Luther Head, Houston
Marvin Williams, Atlanta
Ryan Gomes, Boston

ALL-DEFENSIVE TEAMS

FIRST
Bruce Bowen, San Antonio
Ben Wallace, Detroit
Andrei Kirilenko, Utah
Ron Artest, Sacramento
Kobe Bryant, L.A. Lakers
Jason Kidd, New Jersey

SECOND
Tim Duncan, San Antonio
Chauncey Billups, Detroit
Kevin Garnett, Minnesota
Marcus Camby, Denver
Tayshaun Prince, Detroit

NBA PLAYERS OF THE WEEK

Nov. 7— T.J. Ford, Milwaukee (E)
Kobe Bryant, L.A. Lakers (W)
Nov. 14— Gilbert Arenas, Washington (E)
Marcus Camby, Denver (W)
Nov. 21— LeBron James, Cleveland (E)
Elton Brand, L.A. Clippers (W)
Nov. 28— Gerald Wallace, Charlotte (E)
Steve Nash, Phoenix (W)
Dec. 5— Dwyane Wade, Miami (E)
Baron Davis, Golden State (W)
Dec. 12— Allen Iverson, Philadelphia (E)
Elton Brand, L.A. Clippers (W)
Dec. 19— Joe Johnson, Atlanta (E)
Kobe Bryant, L.A. Lakers (W)
Dec. 26— Vince Carter, New Jersey (E)
Kobe Bryant, L.A. Lakers (W)
Jan. 2— Dwyane Wade, Miami (E)
Shawn Marion, Phoenix (W)
Jan. 9— Mike James, Toronto (E)
Steve Nash, Phoenix (W)
Jan. 16— Allen Iverson, Philadelphia (E)
Kevin Garnett, Minnesota (W)
Jan. 23— Richard Hamilton, Detroit (E)
Kobe Bryant, L.A. Lakers (W)
Jan. 30— LeBron James, Cleveland (E)
Elton Brand, L.A. Clippers (W)
Feb. 6— Chris Bosh, Toronto (E)
Chris Paul, New Orleans (W)
Feb. 13— Gilbert Arenas, Washington (E)
Tony Parker, San Antonio (W)
Feb. 20— All-Star Week (no award)
Feb. 27— Gilbert Arenas, Washington (E)
Yao Ming, Houston (W)
Mar. 6— Allen Iverson, Philadelphia (E)
Pau Gasol, Memphis (W)
Mar. 13— Paul Pierce, Boston (E)
Mike Bibby, Sacramento (W)
Mar. 20— LeBron James, Cleveland (E)
Carmelo Anthony, Denver (W)
Mar. 27— LeBron James, Cleveland (E)
Pau Gasol, Memphis (W)
Apr. 3— LeBron James, Cleveland (E)
Yao Ming, Houston (W)
Apr. 10— Jamal Crawford, New York (E)
Chris Wilcox, Seattle (W)
Apr. 17— Ben Gordon, Chicago (E)
Kobe Bryant, L.A. Lakers (W)

NBA PLAYERS OF THE MONTH

Nov.—LeBron James, Cleveland (E)
Elton Brand, L.A. Lakers (W)
Dec.—Vince Carter, New Jersey (E)
Dirk Nowitzki, Dallas (W)
Jan.—Chauncey Billups, Detroit (E)
Kobe Bryant, L.A. Lakers (W)
Feb.—Dwyane Wade, Miami (E)
Shawn Marion, Phoenix (W)
Mar.—LeBron James, Cleveland (E)
Carmelo Anthony, Denver (W)
Apr.—Dwight Howard, Orlando (E)
Kobe Bryant, L.A. Lakers (W)

T-MOBILE ROOKIES OF THE MONTH

Nov.—Channing Frye, New York (E)
Chris Paul, N.O./Okla. City (W)
Dec.— Charlie Villanueva, Toronto (E)
Chris Paul, N.O./Okla. City (W)
Jan.— Andrew Bogut, Milwaukee (E)
Chris Paul, N.O./Okla. City (W)
Feb.— Raymond Felton, Charlotte (E)
Chris Paul, N.O./Okla. City (W)
Mar.— Raymond Felton, Charlotte (E)
Chris Paul, N.O./Okla. City (W)
Apr.— Raymond Felton, Charlotte (E)
Chris Paul, N.O./Okla. City (W)

NBA COACHES OF THE MONTH

Nov.—Flip Saunders, Detroit (E)
Avery Johnson, Dallas (W)
Dec.—Flip Saunders, Detroit (E)
Gregg Popovich, San Antonio (W)
Jan.— Flip Saunders, Detroit (E)
Avery Johnson, Dallas (W)
Feb.— Pat Riley, Miami (E)
Mike D'Antoni, Phoenix (W)
Mar.—Lawrence Frank, New Jersey (E)
Avery Johnson, Dallas (W)
Apr.— Scott Skiles, Chicago (E)
Mike Fratello, Memphis (W)

COMMUNITY ASSIST AWARD

Oct.—Drew Gooden, Cleveland
Nov.—Kevin Garnett, Minnesota
Dec.—Chris Webber, Philadelphia
Jan.— Bruce Bowen, San Antonio
Feb.— Charlie Villanueva, Toronto
Mar.— Raja Bell, Phoenix
Apr.— Rasheed Wallace, Detroit
May— Theo Ratliff, Portland
Jun.— LeBron James, Cleveland